Modern Automotive Technology

James E. Duffy

Publisher
The Goodheart-Willcox Company, Inc.
Tinley Park, Illinois

Library of Congress Catalog Card Number 92-46515
International Standard Book Number 0-87006-043-0

6 7 8 9 10   94   97 96

Library of Congress Cataloging in Publication Data

Duffy, James E.
  Modern automotive technology / by James E. Duffy

    p. cm.
    Rev. ed. of: Modern automotive mechanics.
c1990.
    Includes index.
    ISBN 0-87006-043-0
    1. Automobiles. 2. Automobiles—Maintenance
and repair.
I. Duffy, James E. Modern automotive mechanics.
II. Title.
TL146.D84 1994
629.28'722--dc20   92-46515
                                     CIP

Introduction

Welcome to the exciting world of automotive technology!

Modern Automotive Technology was written to provide an easy-to-understand, up-to-date book summarizing the **operation** and **repair** of all makes and models of vehicles. The text uses a "building block" approach that starts with the simple and progresses gradually to the more complex. Short sentences, concise definitions, and thousands of color illustrations will help you learn quickly and easily. This edition offers full color throughout for better understanding of principles and service as well as greater "eye" appeal.

No longer can the untrained person hope to fix the modern automobile. Multiple on-board computers can now be used to monitor and control the engine, transmission, suspension, braking, emission control, and other systems. Electronic fuel injection, anti-lock brakes, four-wheel steering, four-valve cylinders, active suspension systems, computer self-diagnosis, scanners, front-wheel drive, and computerized analyzers are a few of the new topics discussed.

This book is organized into 12 sections and 76 chapters. Section 1 introduces basic information on safety, tools, shop manuals, electricity, ASE Certification, and vehicle maintenance. This section prepares you to more fully comprehend later chapters that provide in-depth coverage of auto technology. An appendix discusses recovery and disposal of chemicals and fluids from the auto repair shop.

Each automotive system is presented in two or more chapters. The first chapter explains the construction and operation of parts. The following chapter expands on this by summarizing the troubleshooting and repair of these same parts. This sequential study will provide a sound background for making actual repairs.

Even though computers are discussed in almost all chapters, three chapters (74 — Computer System Networking, 75 — Computer System Troubleshooting, and 76 — Computer System Service) explain electronics in detail. These chapters summarize and supplement the computer information given throughout the text.

"Learning Objectives" at the beginning of each chapter tell you what you are expected to learn. The end of each service chapter has both conventional and ASE Certification type Review Questions. New technical terms are highlighted in *italics* and defined when first used. These words and the ones in "Know These Terms" will give you the language of an auto technician. A glossary provides an extensive definition of terms. Metric equivalents are also given.

Modern Automotive Technology is a valuable reference for anyone interested in the operation, construction, and repair of automobiles. Car owners, who need a general guide to mechanics, will find the book interesting and informative. Those who are preparing for a career in automotive repair will find the text a "must." Experienced technicians can use it as a "refresher course" to prepare for ASE Certification Tests.

James E. Duffy
Automotive Writer

Contents

Section 10 *Suspension, Steering, and Brakes*

Section 11 *Heating and Air Conditioning*

Section 12 *Computers and Accessory Systems*

IMPORTANT SAFETY NOTICE

Proper service and repair methods are critical to the safe, reliable operation of automobiles. The procedures described in this textbook are designed to help you use a manufacturer's service manual. A service manual will give the how-to details and specifications needed to do competent work.

This book contains safety precautions which must be followed. Personal injury or part damage can result when basic safety rules are not followed. Safety cautions are printed in red; cautions in blue will help you avoid part damage. Also, remember that these cautions are general and do not cover some specialized hazards. Refer to a service manual when in doubt about any service operation!

Cutaway shows the many systems of a modern automobile.

A — This technician is using a self-contained charging station to service car's air conditioning system.

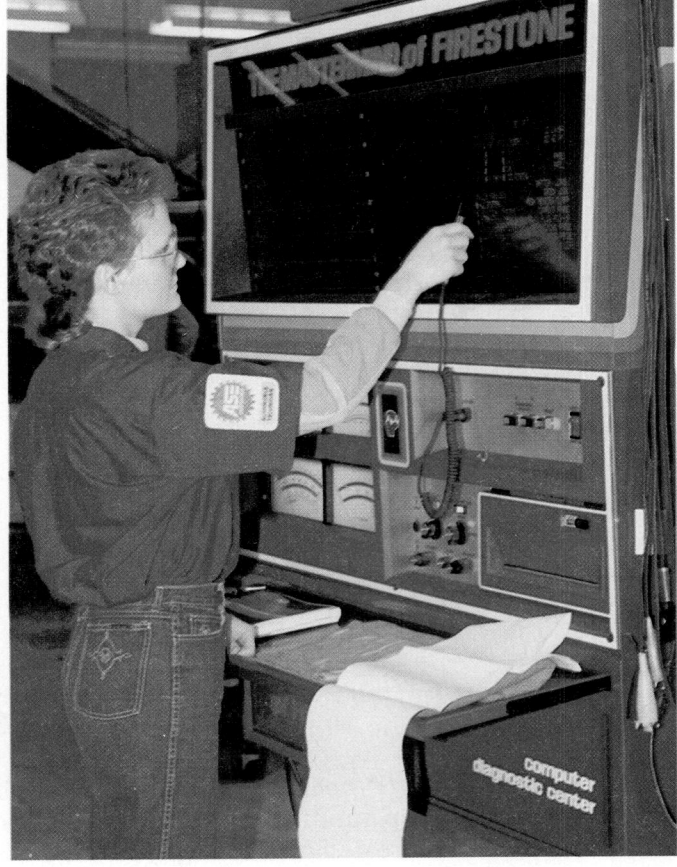

B — Automotive technician is using a computer diagnostic center to find cause of a performance problem in a car's engine.

C — Certified master auto technician is operating a digital computer alignment machine to align wheels of car.

D — Another technician is using a special analyzer to find out why a car has a ''dead battery.''

There are many job openings in auto mechanics. Note variety of interesting and challenging positions.

The Automobile

After studying this chapter, you will be able to:
□ Identify and locate the most important parts of a vehicle.
□ Describe the purpose for fundamental automotive systems.
□ Explain the interaction of automotive systems.
□ Describe major automobile design variations.
□ Comprehend the following text chapters with a minimum amount of difficulty.

This chapter begins your study of auto technology by introducing the major parts of a car. By learning about main components, you will be better prepared to study the rest of this book as it explains systems and parts in more detail. Failure of one part can affect a seemingly unrelated part. This makes a quick summary of the automobile helpful to your full understanding of auto service and repair.

Before working on vehicles, study safety rules. If you do not understand any rule, ask your instructor to explain it and, possibly, demonstrate the safe procedure. Never move a vehicle in the shop without checking that others are a safe distance away and are alerted to the vehicle's movement.

AUTOMOTIVE SYSTEMS

An *automotive system* is a group of related parts that perform a specific job. For example, a vehicle's steering wheel is part of the steering system. This system of parts allows the driver to turn the front wheels. The brake pedal is one part in the braking system. This system allows the driver to slow or stop the vehicle. Fig. 1-1 illustrates several major systems.

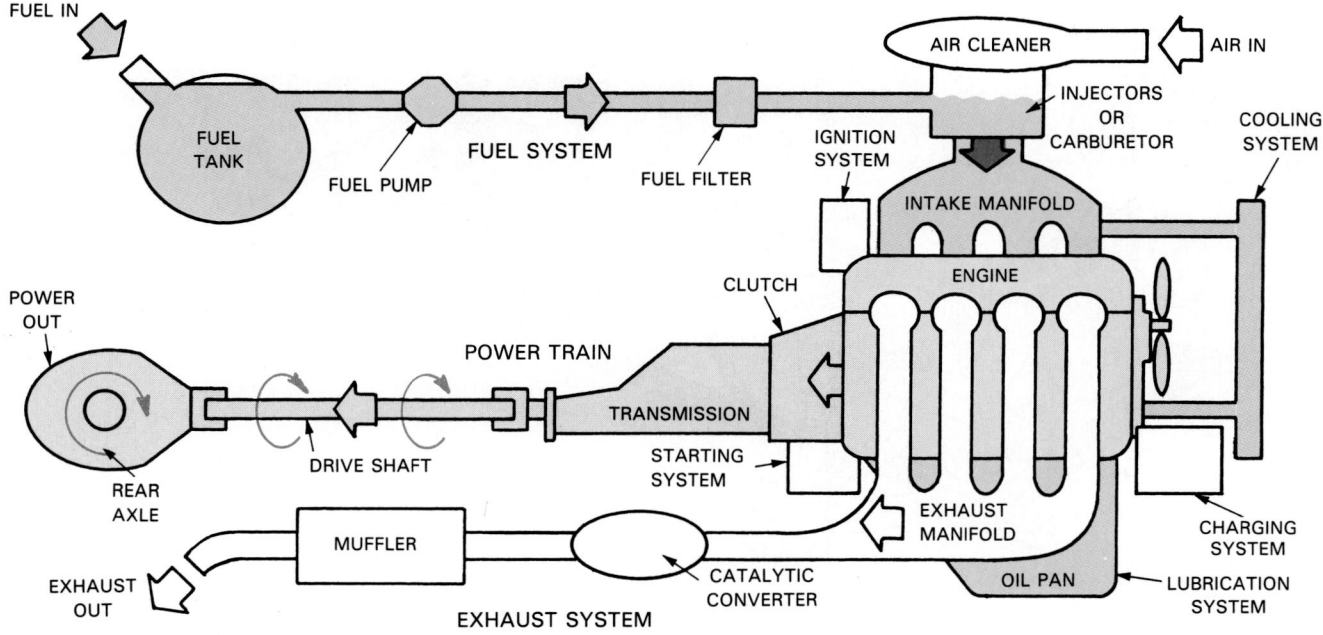

Fig. 1-1. Note location of parts. Study flow of fuel, air, exhaust, and power.

The systems of an automobile can be grouped around six major divisions:

1. BODY AND CHASSIS SYSTEMS (body, frame, suspension, steering, braking, and other systems) to support, stop, and enclose the parts.
2. ENGINE SYSTEMS (engine mechanical, fuel, cooling, lubrication systems) to provide power for the vehicle.
3. ELECTRICAL SYSTEMS (ignition, charging, starting, lighting, and computer systems) that operate the electrical devices.
4. POWER TRAIN SYSTEMS (clutch, transmission, drive shaft and rear axle assembly or transaxle and axle shafts) that use engine power for propulsion.
5. EMISSION CONTROL SYSTEMS (crankcase ventilation, catalytic converter, fuel vapor storage, air injection, and other systems) for reducing air pollution produced by the vehicle.
6. ACCESSORY SYSTEMS (air conditioning, heating, other optional systems) for increasing passenger comfort and convenience.

BODY AND CHASSIS

The body and chassis are the two largest sections of a vehicle, as illustrated in Fig. 1-2. The *body* serves

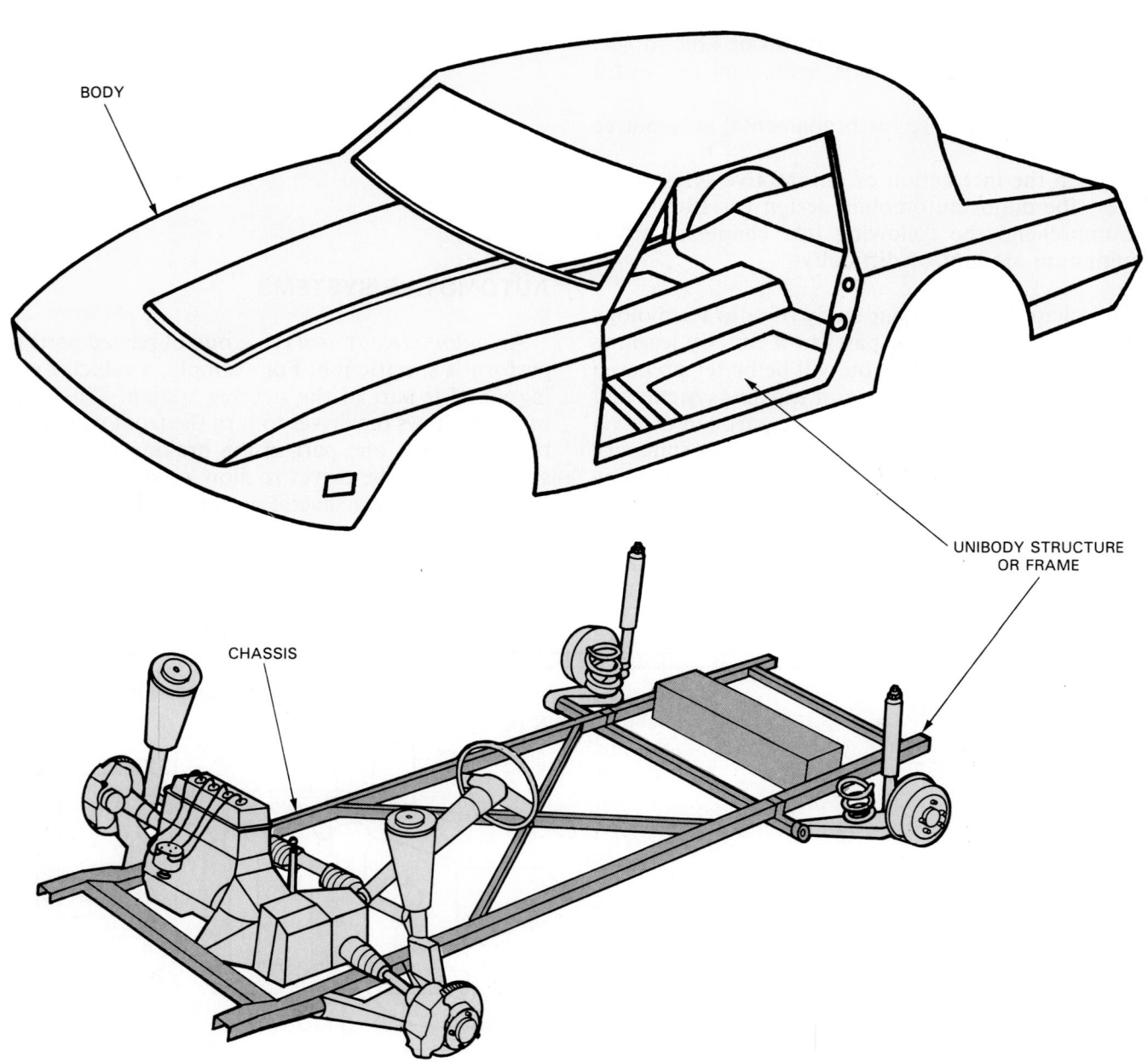

Fig. 1-2. Body is sheet metal, fiberglass, or plastic covering over chassis. Chassis includes framework and other major components.

Fig. 1-3. Suspension and steering systems mount on frame. Study part names. (Saab-Scania)

as an attractive covering for the chassis and also forms the passenger compartment. The *chassis* generally includes everything but the body.

Frame

The term, *frame,* refers to a very strong, steel structure that supports the other vehicle components. Some have a frame separate from the body. Many use the internal body structure as a frame. This is called *unitized construction, space frame,* or *unibody.* Some inner body sections are strengthened so that they can support the engine, suspension, and other major parts of the vehicle.

Suspension system

The *suspension system* lets the vehicle's wheels bounce with little or no body movement. This makes the ride smooth and safe. The suspension system must also prevent excessively leaning during turns. As you can see in Fig. 1-3, various springs, bars, swivel joints, and arms make up the suspension system.

Steering system

The *steering system* allows the driver to control vehicle direction by turning the front wheels right or left. It uses a series of gears, swivel joints, and rods. Study the names of the parts in Fig. 1-3.

Brake system

The *brake system* produces friction to reduce speed or stop the vehicle. Fig. 1-4 shows the fundamental parts of a brake system. When the driver presses the brake pedal, fluid pressure expands the brake mechanism on each wheel. The brake mechanisms then produce friction that resists wheel rotation.

ENGINE

The *engine* provides the energy to propel (move) the vehicle and operate the other systems, Fig. 1-5. Most engines consume gasoline or diesel fuel. The fuel burns in the engine to produce heat. The heat causes expan-

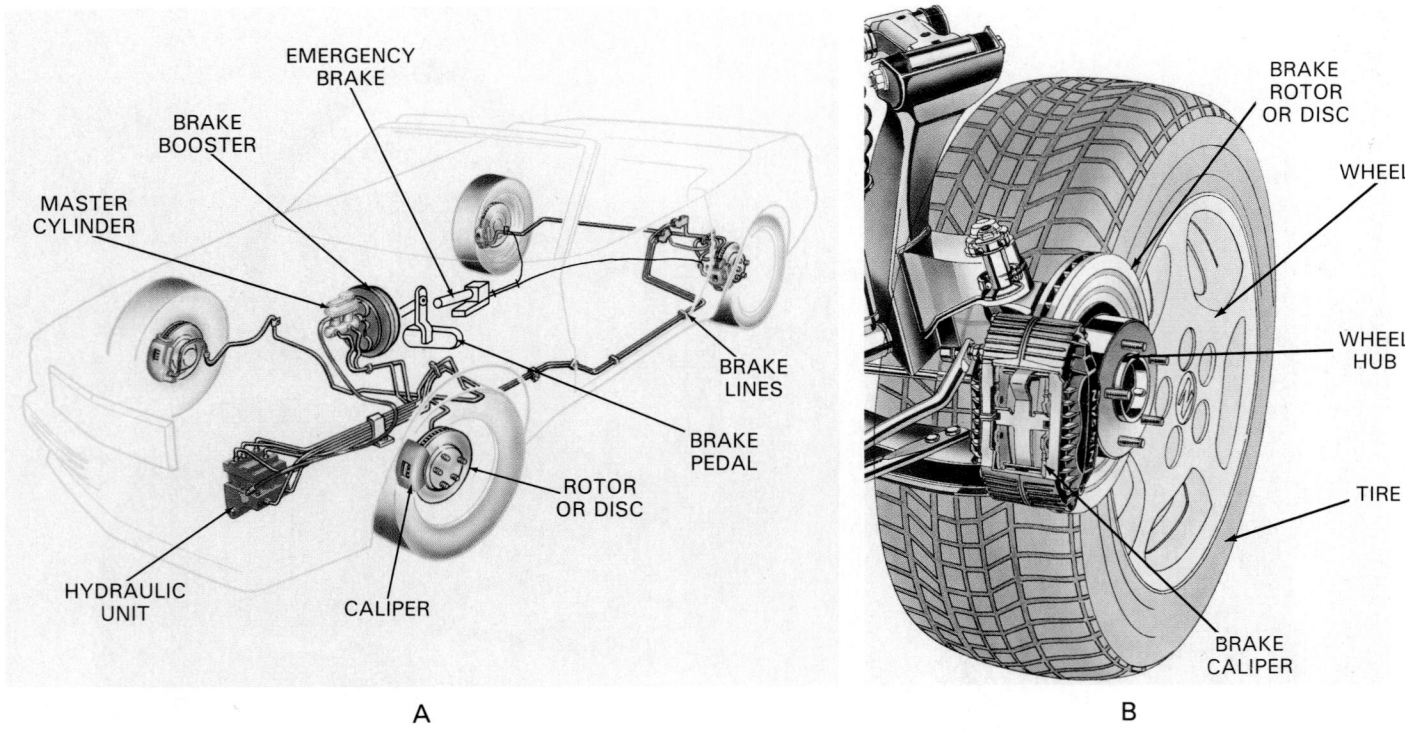

Fig. 1-4. When brake pedal is pressed, pressure is placed on a confined fluid. The fluid pressure operates brakes. Emergency brake is mechanical or cable system for applying rear wheel brakes. A—Complete system. B—Close-up. (Cadillac and Nissan)

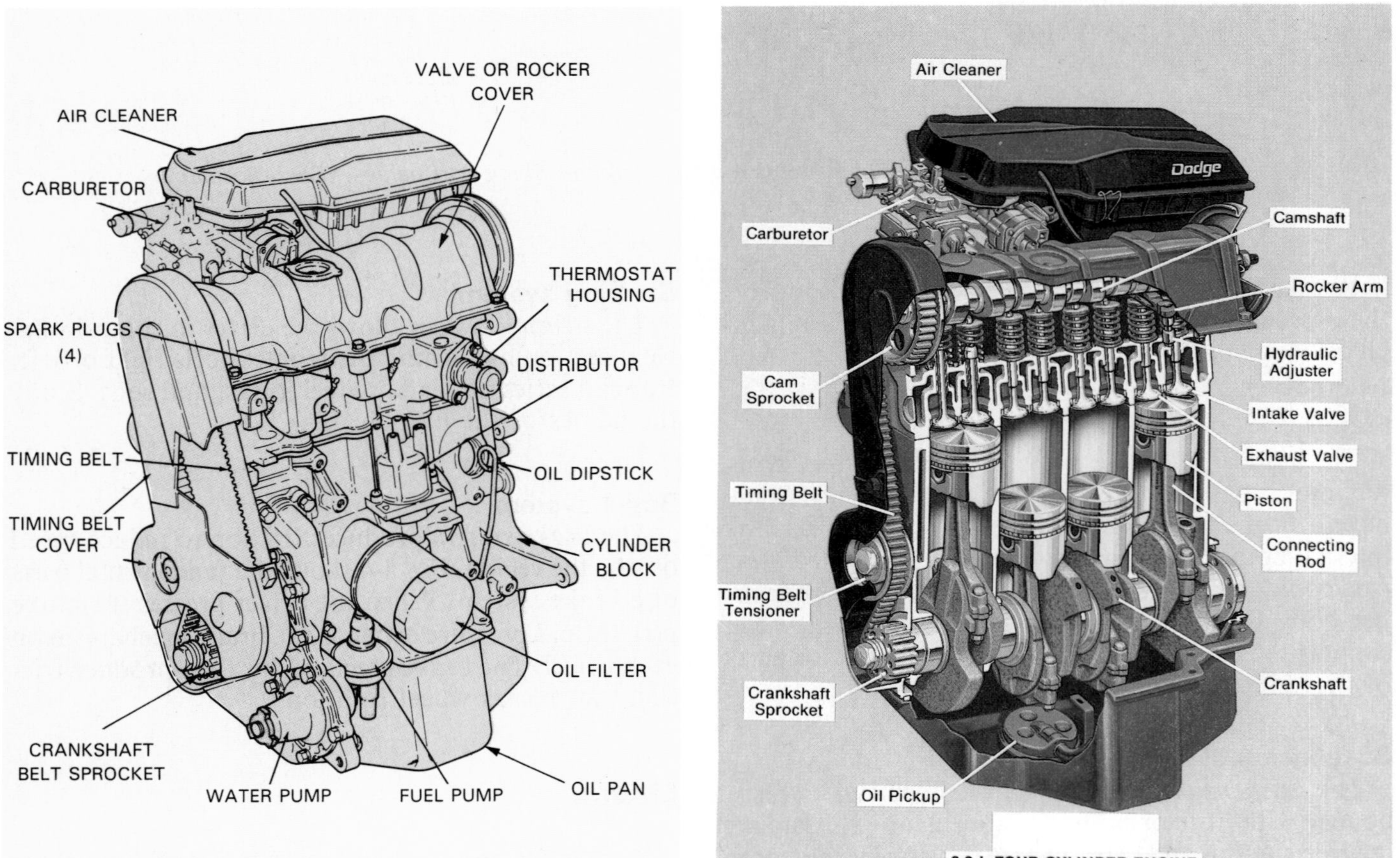

A

BRAKE BOOSTER

EMERGENCY BRAKE

MASTER CYLINDER

BRAKE LINES

BRAKE PEDAL

ROTOR OR DISC

HYDRAULIC UNIT

CALIPER

B

BRAKE ROTOR OR DISC

WHEEL

WHEEL HUB

TIRE

BRAKE CALIPER

AIR CLEANER

VALVE OR ROCKER COVER

CARBURETOR

THERMOSTAT HOUSING

SPARK PLUGS (4)

DISTRIBUTOR

OIL DIPSTICK

TIMING BELT

TIMING BELT COVER

CYLINDER BLOCK

OIL FILTER

CRANKSHAFT BELT SPROCKET

WATER PUMP

FUEL PUMP

OIL PAN

Air Cleaner

Carburetor

Cam Sprocket

Camshaft

Rocker Arm

Hydraulic Adjuster

Intake Valve

Exhaust Valve

Piston

Connecting Rod

Timing Belt

Timing Belt Tensioner

Crankshaft Sprocket

Crankshaft

Oil Pickup

2.2 L FOUR-CYLINDER ENGINE LONGITUDINAL SECTION

Fig. 1-5. An engine commonly burns gasoline or diesel oil to produce power. Note part names. (Chrysler)

sion and pressure. The pressure can then be used to move the parts of the engine and produce power.

An engine is usually located in the front of the chassis. Having the heavy engine there makes the vehicle safer in a head-on collision. A few vehicles have the engine mounted in the rear. Refer to Fig. 1-6.

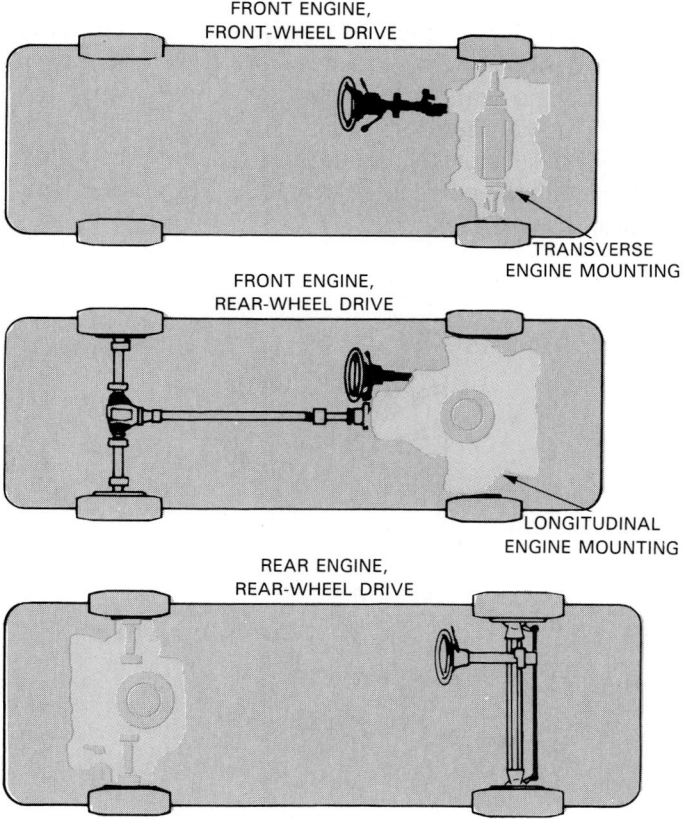

Fig. 1-6. Engine can be located in front or rear.   (Dana Corp.)

Basic engine parts

The basic parts of a one-cylinder engine are shown in Fig. 1-7. Refer to this illustration as each part is introduced.

1. The *block* holds all of the other engine parts.
2. The *cylinder* is a round hole bored (machined) in the block. It guides piston movement.
3. The *piston* transfers the energy of combustion (burning of air-fuel mixture) to the connecting rod.
4. The *rings* seal the small gap around the sides of the piston. They keep combustion pressure and oil from leaking between the piston and cylinder wall (cylinder surface).
5. The *connecting rod* links the piston to the crankshaft.
6. The *crankshaft* changes the reciprocating (up and down) motion of the piston and rod into useful rotary (spinning) motion.
7. The *cylinder head* covers and seals the top of the

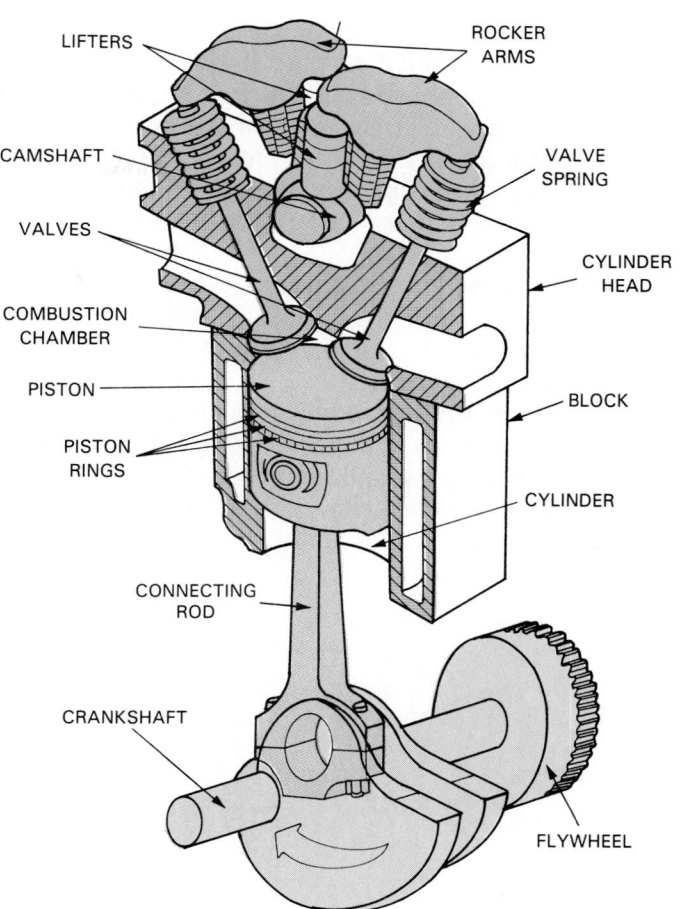

Fig. 1-7. Memorize basic parts of this one cylinder engine.

cylinder. It also holds the valves, rocker arms, and sometimes, the camshaft.

8. The *combustion chamber* is a small cavity (hollow area) between the top of the piston and the bottom of the cylinder head. The burning of the air-fuel mixture occurs in the combustion chamber of the engine.
9. The *valves* open and close to control the flow of fuel mixture into and exhaust out of the combustion chamber.
10. The *camshaft* controls the opening of the valves.
11. The *valve springs* keep the valves closed when they do not need to be open.
12. The *rocker arms* transfer camshaft action to the valves.
13. The *lifters* ride on the camshaft and transfer motion to the other parts of the valve train.
14. The *flywheel* helps keep the crankshaft turning smoothly.

Four-stroke cycle

Automobiles normally use four-stroke cycle engines. Four separate piston *strokes* (up or down movements) are needed to produce one cycle (complete series of events). The piston must slide up, down, up, and down again to make one power-producing event.

As the four strokes are described, study Fig. 1-8.

1. The *intake stroke* draws the air-fuel mixture into the engine combustion chamber. The piston slides down while the larger intake valve is open. This produces a vacuum (low pressure area) in the cylinder. Atmospheric pressure (outside air pressure) can then force air and fuel into the engine.

2. The *compression stroke* prepares the fuel mixture for combustion. With both valves closed, the piston slides up and compresses (squeezes) the trapped fuel mixture.

3. The *power stroke* produces the energy to operate the engine. With both valves still closed, the spark plug arcs (sparks) and ignites the fuel. The burning fuel expands and develops pressure in the combustion chamber and on top of the piston. This pushes the piston down with enough force to keep the crankshaft spinning until the next power stroke.

4. The *exhaust stroke* must remove the burned gases from the engine. The piston slides up while the exhaust valve is open. Since the intake valve is closed, the burned fuel mixture is pushed out of the engine.

During engine operation, these four strokes are repeated over and over. With the help of the heavy flywheel, this action produces smooth power output at the engine crankshaft.

Obviously, other devices are needed to lubricate the engine parts, operate the spark plug, cool the engine, and provide the correct fuel mixture. These topics will be discussed shortly.

1
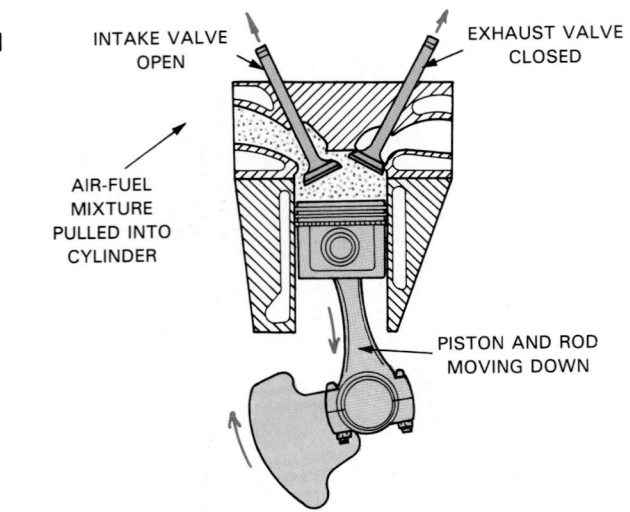

Intake stroke. Intake valve open. Exhaust valve closed. Piston slides down, forming vacuum in cylinder. Atmospheric pressure pushes air and fuel into combustion chamber.

2
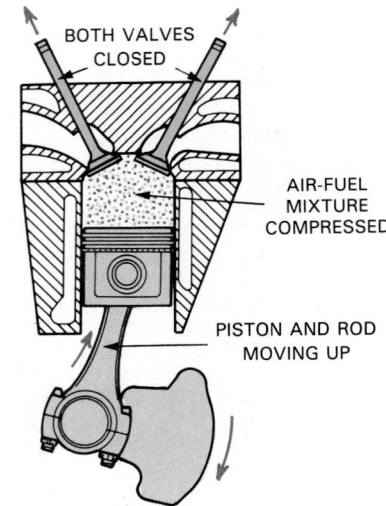

Compression stroke. Both valves are closed. Piston slides up and pressurizes air-fuel mixture. This readies mixture for combustion.

3
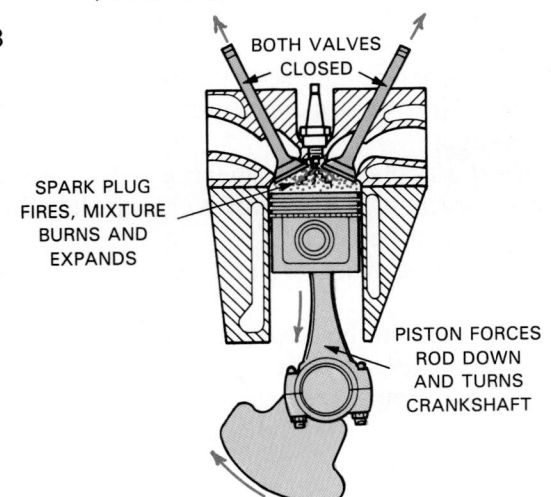

Power stroke. Spark plug sparks. Air-fuel mixture burns. High pressure forces piston down with tremendous force. Crankshaft rotates under power.

4
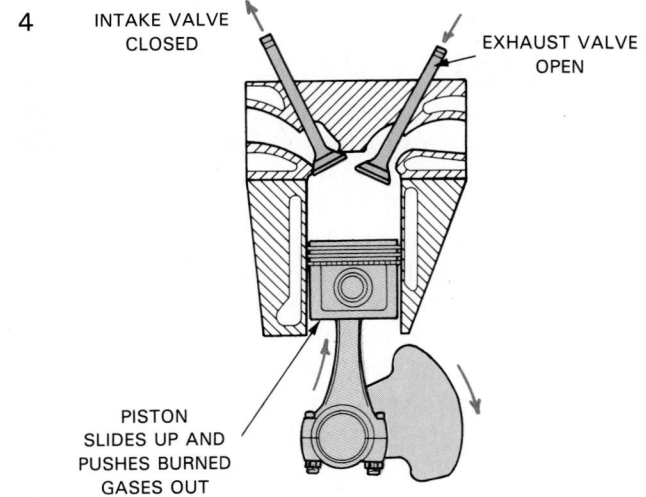

Exhaust stroke. Exhaust valve opens. Intake valve remains closed. Piston slides up, pushing burned gases out of cylinder. This prepares combustion chamber for another intake stroke.

Fig. 1-8. Gasoline engine four-stroke cycle. Study series of events.

Automotive engines

Unlike the one-cylinder engine just discussed, auto engines are multiple-cylinder engines. They have more than one piston and cylinder. Vehicles commonly have 4, 6, or 8-cylinder engines. The additional cylinders smooth engine operation because there is less time between each power stroke. This also increases power output from the engine.

Fig. 1-9 pictures an actual automotive engine. Study the shape, location, and relationship of the major parts.

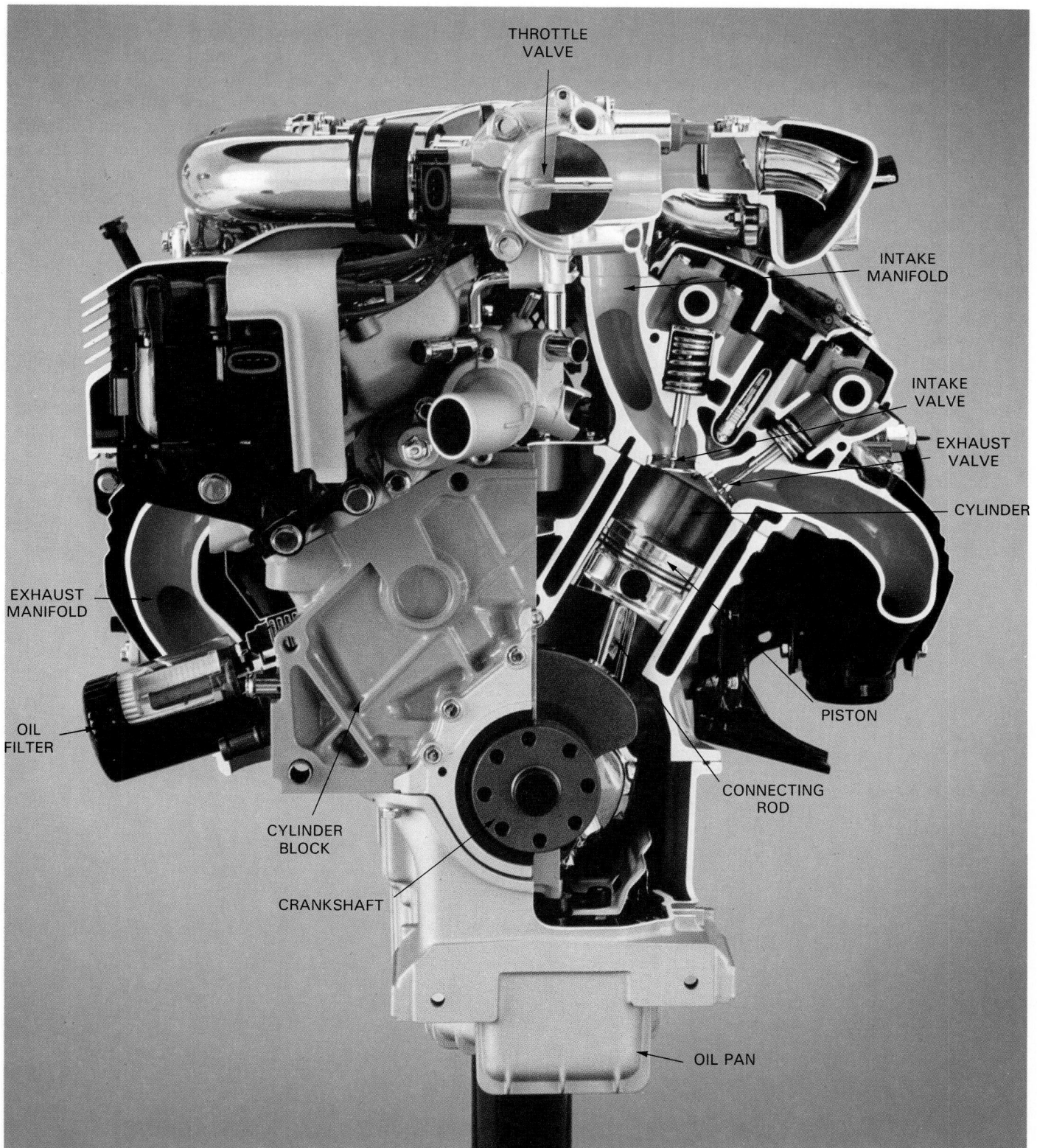

Fig. 1-9. Automotive engines are multicylinder engines. Locate major parts and visualize their operation. (Ford)

FUEL SYSTEM

The *fuel system* must provide the correct mixture of air and fuel for efficient engine operation. It must add just the right amount of fuel to the air entering or in the cylinder. This assures that a very volatile (burnable) mixture enters the combustion chambers.

The fuel system must also alter the *air-fuel ratio* (percentage of air and fuel) with changes in operating conditions (engine temperature, speed, load).

There are three basic types of automotive fuel systems: carburetor, gasoline injection, and diesel injection. Look at the three illustrations that make up Fig. 1-10.

Carburetor fuel system

The *carburetor fuel system* uses engine vacuum (suction) to draw fuel into the engine. The amount of airflow through the carburetor controls how much fuel is used. This automatically maintains the correct air-fuel ratio, Fig. 1-10A.

The fuel pump draws fuel out of the tank and delivers it to the carburetor. The engine's intake strokes form a vacuum inside the intake manifold and carburetor. This causes gasoline to be drawn from the carburetor and into the engine.

The carburetor throttle valve (air valve) is connected to the driver's gas pedal. When the pedal is pressed, the throttle valve opens. This allows more air to flow through the carburetor, pulling more fuel into the air.

The throttle can be opened or closed to control engine speed and power output.

Gasoline injection

Modern *gasoline injection systems* use a computer, engine sensors, and electrically operated injectors (fuel valves) to meter fuel into the engine. See Fig. 1-10B.

An electric fuel pump keeps a constant fuel pressure at the injectors. The computer, depending upon electrical data from the sensors, opens the injectors for the correct amount of time. Fuel sprays into and mixes with the air entering the combustion chambers.

Like a carburetor, a throttle valve is used to control airflow, engine speed, and engine power. When the throttle is open, the computer holds the injectors open longer, allowing more fuel to spray out. When the throttle is closed, the computer opens the injectors for only a short period of time.

Diesel injection

A *diesel fuel system* is a mechanical system that forces diesel oil (not gasoline) directly into the combustion chambers. A diesel does NOT use spark plugs like a gasoline engine. Instead, it uses extremely high compression stroke pressure to heat the air in the combustion chamber. The air is squeezed until hot enough to ignite the fuel. Refer to Fig. 1-10C.

When the mechanical pump sprays the diesel fuel into a combustion chamber, the hot air causes the fuel to begin to burn. The burning fuel expands and forces the piston down on the power stroke.

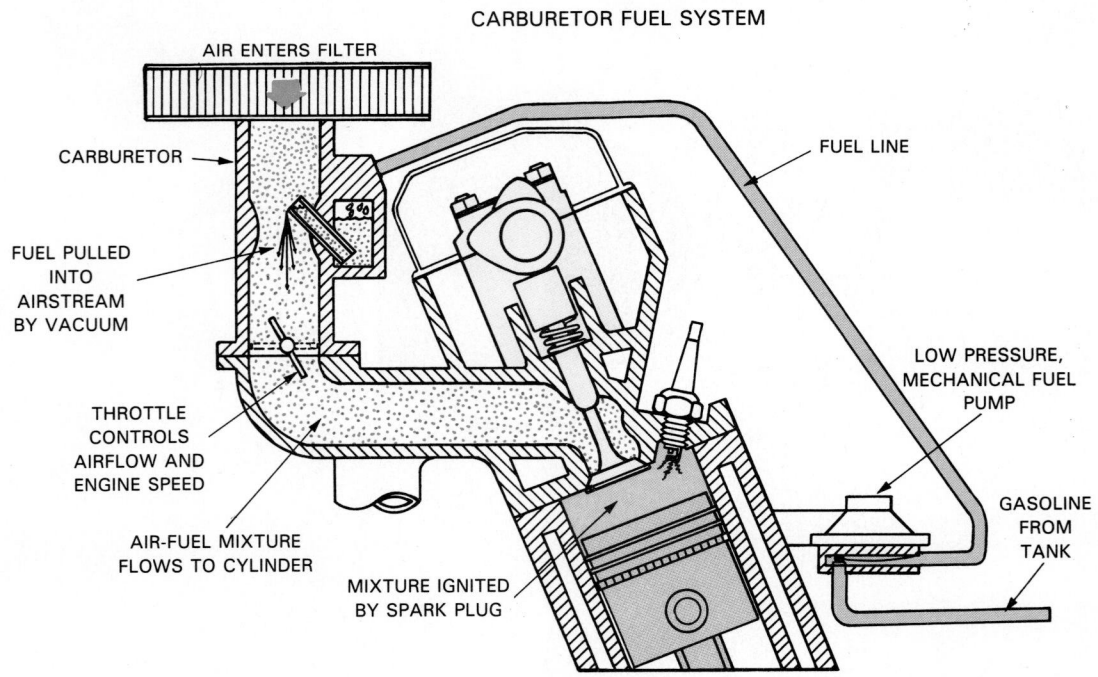

CARBURETOR FUEL SYSTEM

AIR ENTERS FILTER

CARBURETOR

FUEL PULLED INTO AIRSTREAM BY VACUUM

THROTTLE CONTROLS AIRFLOW AND ENGINE SPEED

AIR-FUEL MIXTURE FLOWS TO CYLINDER

MIXTURE IGNITED BY SPARK PLUG

FUEL LINE

LOW PRESSURE, MECHANICAL FUEL PUMP

GASOLINE FROM TANK

A — Carburetor fuel system. Fuel pump fills carburetor with fuel. When air flows through carburetor, fuel is pulled into engine in correct proportions. Throttle valve controls airflow and engine power output.

Fig. 1-10. Three basic types of fuel systems. Compare differences.

GASOLINE INJECTION SYSTEM

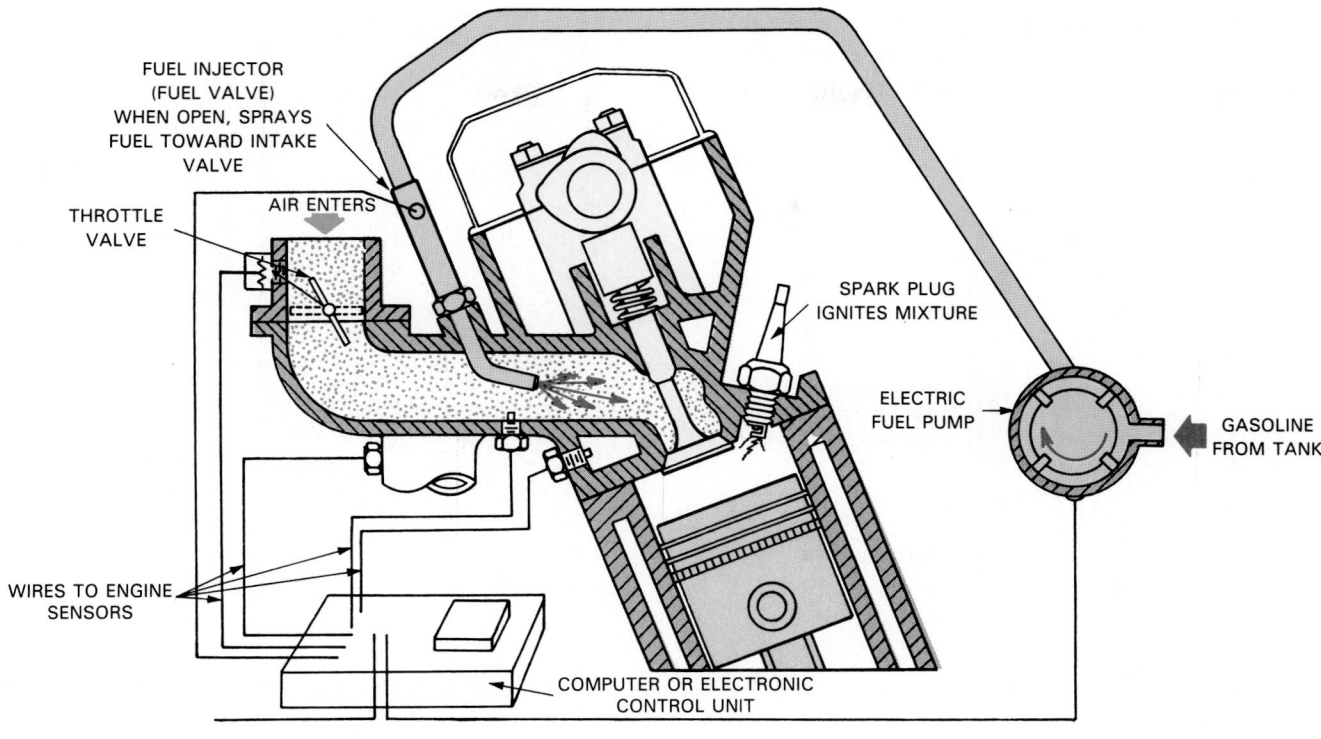

FUEL INJECTOR
(FUEL VALVE)
WHEN OPEN, SPRAYS
FUEL TOWARD INTAKE
VALVE

THROTTLE
VALVE

AIR ENTERS

SPARK PLUG
IGNITES MIXTURE

ELECTRIC
FUEL PUMP

GASOLINE
FROM TANK

WIRES TO ENGINE
SENSORS

COMPUTER OR ELECTRONIC
CONTROL UNIT

B — Gasoline injection system. Engine sensors feed information (electrical signals) to computer about engine conditions. Computer can then open injector right amount of time. This maintains correct air-fuel ratio. Spark plug ignites fuel.

DIESEL INJECTION SYSTEM

MECHANICAL INJECTION
NOZZLE SPRAYS FUEL
INTO COMBUSTION
CHAMBER

INJECTION
LINE

AIR ENTERS

HIGH PRESSURE,
MECHANICAL PUMP

FUEL IGNITES AS
IT TOUCHES HOT
AIR

NO THROTTLE
USED

DIESEL OIL
FROM TANK

ONLY AIR FLOWS
PAST INTAKE VALVE AND
INTO COMBUSTION
CHAMBER

AIR COMPRESSED
SO TIGHT, IT BECOMES
RED HOT

C — Diesel injection system. High pressure mechanical pump sprays fuel directly into combustion chamber. Piston squeezes and heats air enough to ignite diesel fuel. Fuel begins to burn as soon as it touches heated air. Note that no throttle valve nor spark plug is used. Amount of fuel injected into chamber controls diesel engine power and speed.

(Fig. 1-10 Continued)

COOLING SYSTEM

An engine *cooling system* maintains a constant engine operating temperature. It removes excess heat to prevent engine damage and also speeds engine warmup. Look at Fig. 1-11.

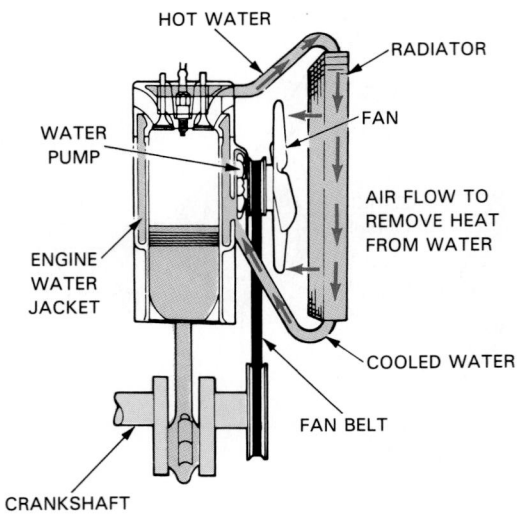

Fig. 1-11. Cooling system must protect engine from heat of combustion. Combustion heat could melt and ruin engine parts. System must also maintain constant operating temperature and speed warmup. Study part names.

The water pump forces coolant (water and antifreeze solution) through the inside of the engine. The coolant collects heat from the hot engine parts and carries it back to the radiator. The radiator allows the coolant heat to transfer into the outside air. The thermostat controls coolant flow and engine temperature.

LUBRICATION SYSTEM

The engine *lubrication system* reduces friction and wear between internal engine parts. It circulates filtered motor oil to high friction points in the engine. In Fig. 1-12, study the parts and operation of a lubrication system. Note how the oil pump pulls oil out of the pan and pushes it to the parts of the engine.

ELECTRICAL SYSTEM

The *electrical system* consists of several sub-systems: ignition system, starting system, charging system, lighting system, and other systems.

Ignition system

An *ignition system* is needed on gasoline engines to ignite the air-fuel mixture. It produces extremely high voltage that operates the spark plugs. A very hot electric arc jumps across the tip of the spark plug at the

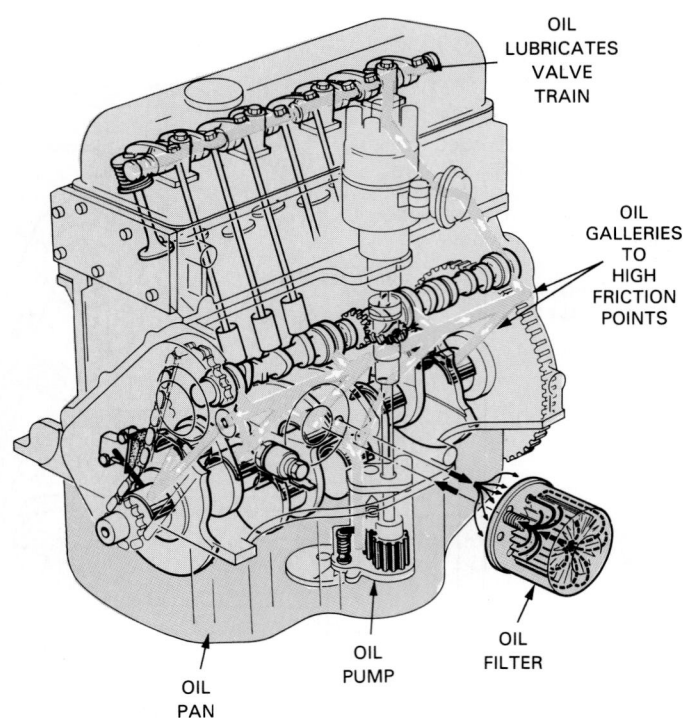

Fig. 1-12. Lubrication system uses oil to reduce friction. Pump forces oil to high friction points. (Renault)

correct time. This causes the engine's air-fuel mixture to burn and produce power. Study Fig. 1-13.

With the ignition switch ON and the engine running, the distributor produces tiny electrical signals for the amplifier or electronic control unit (electronic circuit). One signal is produced for each power stroke. The electronic control unit amplifies (increases) these pulses into on/off current signals for the ignition coil.

By turning the coil current on and off, the coil can produce a high voltage output to "fire" the spark plugs. When the ignition key is turned off, the coil stops functioning and the engine stops running.

Starting system

The *starting system* has an electric motor that rotates the engine crankshaft until the engine starts and runs on its own power. See Fig. 1-14A.

The battery provides the electricity for the starting system. When the key is turned to start, current flows to the parts of the starting system. The electric starting motor gear engages a gear on the engine flywheel. This spins the crankshaft. As soon as the engine starts, the starting system is shut off.

Charging system

The *charging system* is needed to replace electrical energy drawn from the battery during starting system operation. To reenergize the battery, the charging system forces electric current back into the battery. The fundamental parts of this system are shown in Fig. 1-14B. Study them!

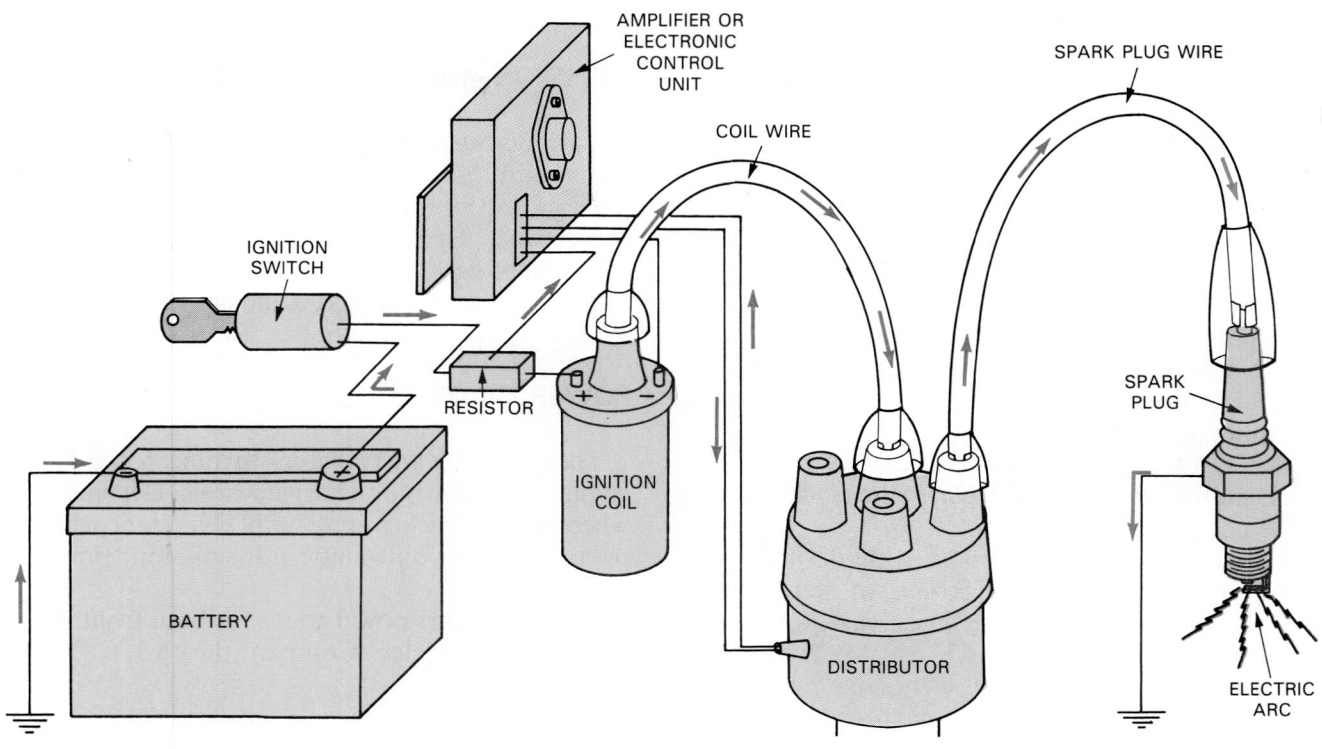

Fig. 1-13. Ignition system is used on gasoline engines to start combustion. Spark plug must fire at exactly the correct time during power stroke. Distributor operates amplifier. Amplifier operates ignition coil. Coil produces high voltage for spark plugs.

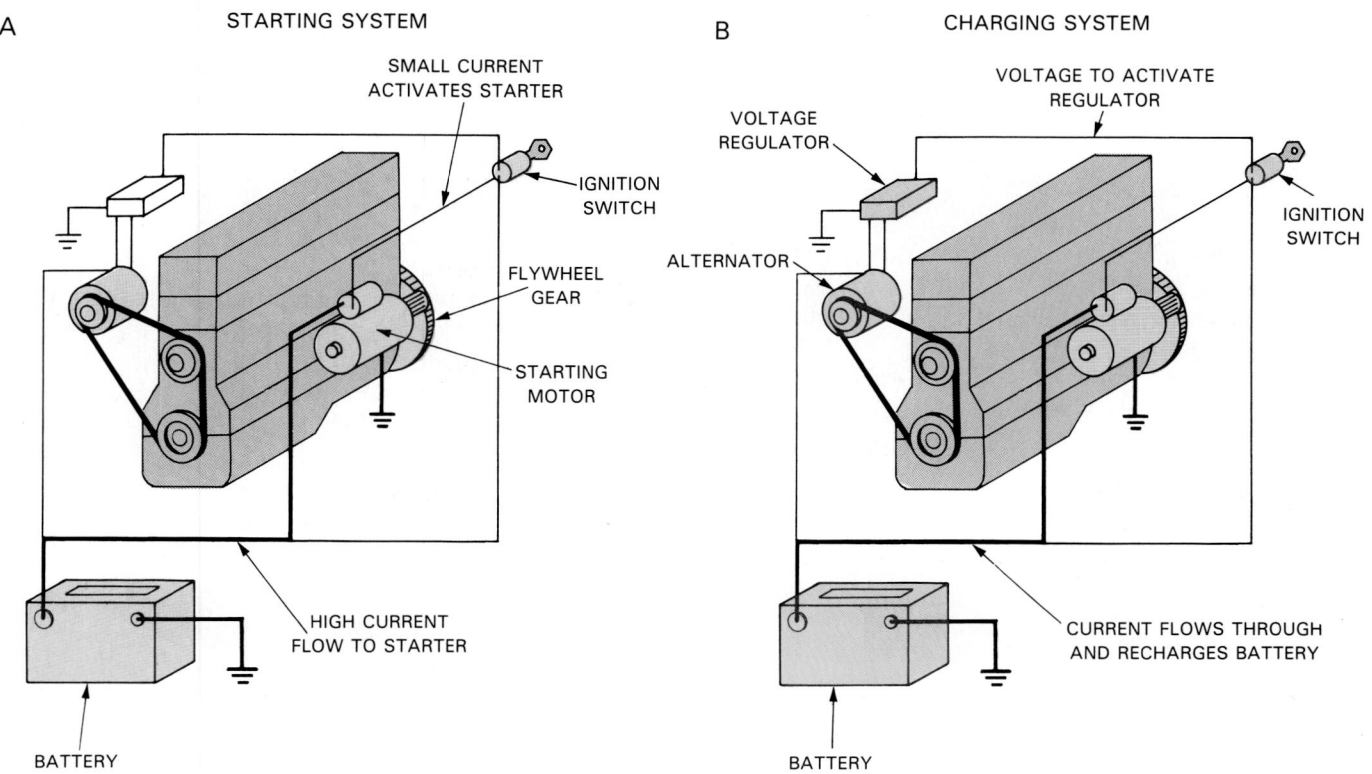

Fig. 1-14. Note basic actions and components of starting and charging systems.

When the engine is running, a fan belt spins the alternator pulley. The alternator (generator) can then produce electricity for the battery and other electrical needs of the vehicle. A voltage regulator controls the output of the alternator.

COMPUTER SYSTEM

A *computer system* uses electronic and electrical devices to improve efficiency. The three major parts of a computer system are:

1. COMPUTER (electronic circuit that uses input signals from sensors to control output devices).
2. SENSORS (input devices that can produce electrical signals with a change in a condition — motion, temperature, pressure, etc.)
3. ACTUATORS (output devices, like a small electric motor, that can move parts when energized by the computer).

Detailed throughout this book, a modern car can have several computers and dozens of sensors and actuators. The *sensors* are the "eyes, ears, and nose" of the system. The *actuators* serve as the "hands" of the computer system. The *computer* is the "brain" that makes decisions about how to control the actuators.

EXHAUST SYSTEM

The *exhaust system* quiets engine operation and routes exhaust gases to the rear of the body. Fig. 1-15

illustrates the basic parts of an exhaust system. Trace the flow of exhaust gases through the system. Learn the names of the parts.

EMISSION CONTROL SYSTEMS

Various *emission control systems* are used to reduce the amount of toxic (poisonous) substances that enter the atmosphere (air surrounding earth). Some systems prevent fuel vapors from entering the outside air. Other emission systems remove toxic chemicals from the engine exhaust. Chapters 39 and 40 cover these systems in detail.

POWER TRAIN

The *power train* transfers turning force from the engine crankshaft to the drive wheels. Depending upon whether the vehicle has rear-wheel or front-wheel drive or a manual or automatic transmission, power train designs vary.

Fig. 1-16 shows power trains for both front and rear-wheel drive vehicles. Compare the two.

Clutch

A *clutch* allows the driver to engage or disengage the engine and transmission. It is used with a manual (hand-operated) transmission or transaxle.

When the driver presses the clutch pedal, the clutch releases and the engine crankshaft no longer turns the

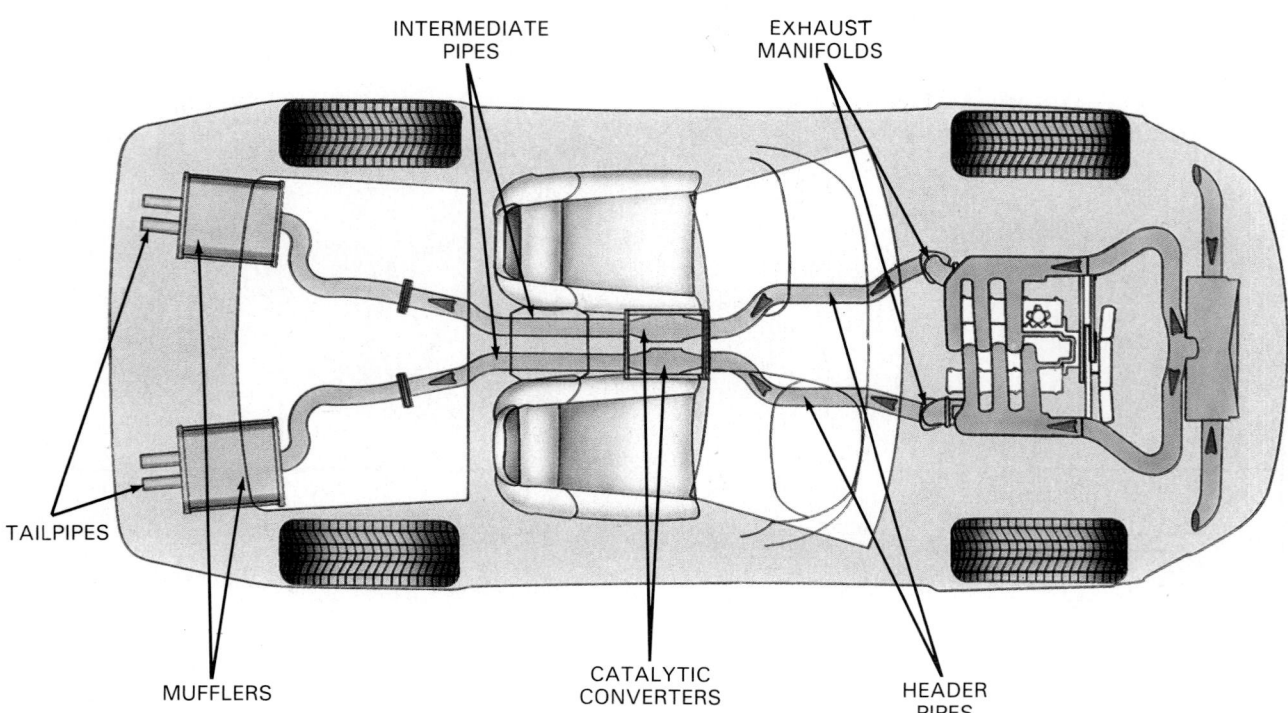

Fig. 1-15. Exhaust system carries burned gases to rear of car. It also reduces noise of engine. (Nissan)

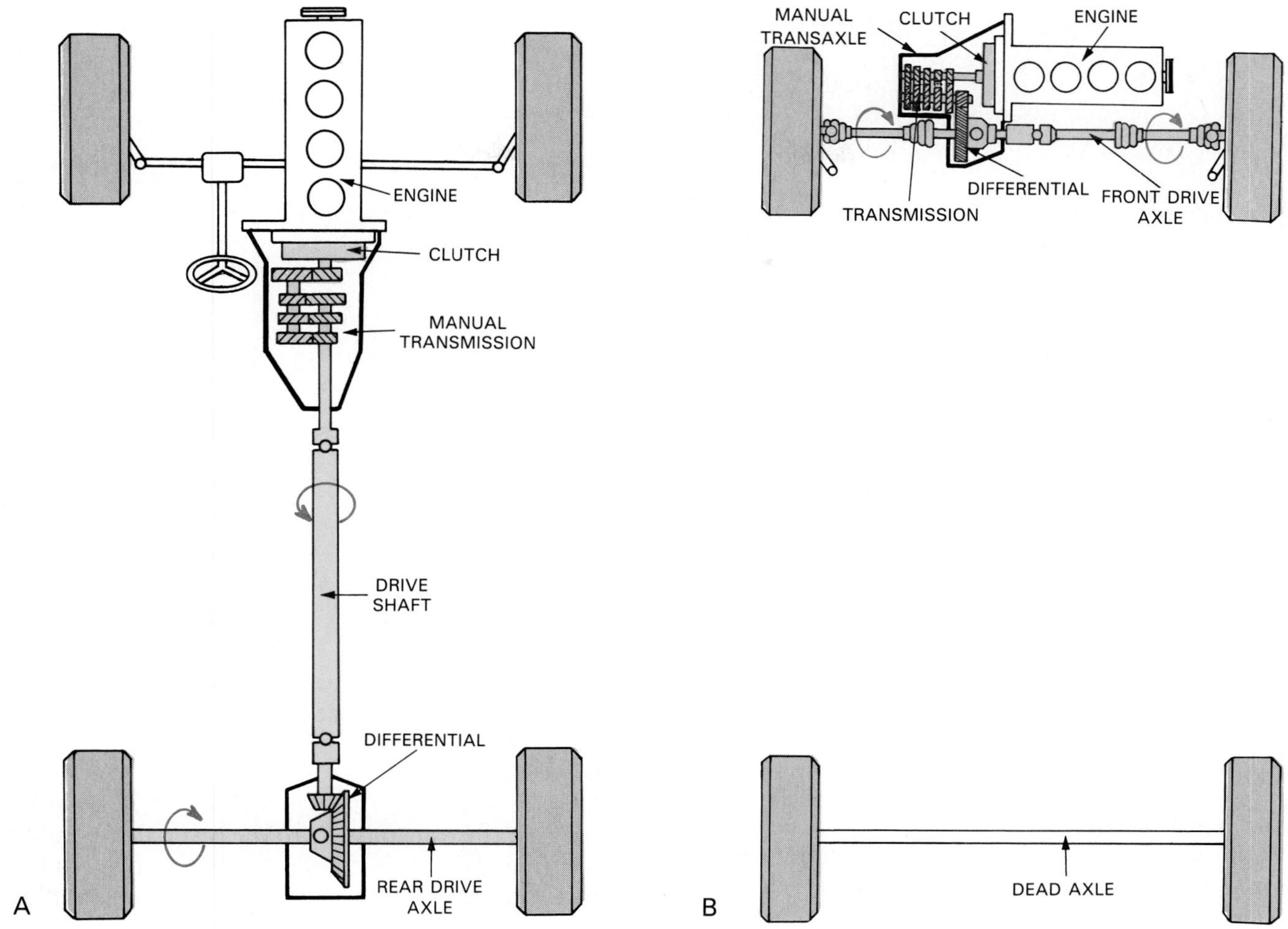

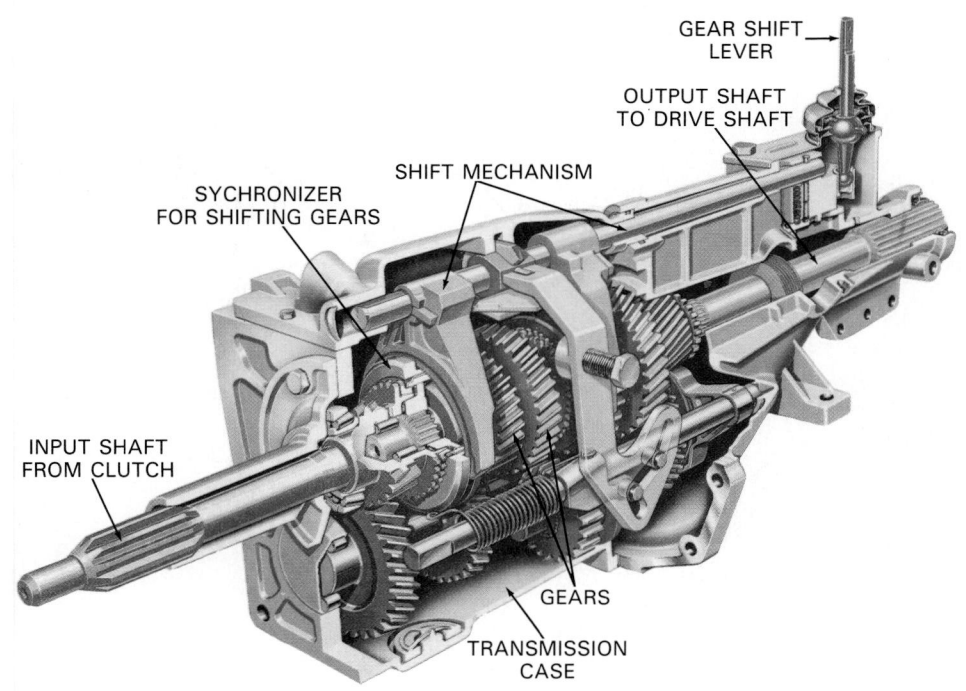

Fig. 1-16. Power train transfers engine power to drive wheels. Study differences between the two common types of systems.
A — Front engine, rear-wheel drive. B — Front engine, front-wheel drive.

Fig. 1-17. Manual transmission uses gears and shafts to allow car to accelerate quickly.
Speed of output shaft compared to speed of input shaft varies in each gear position.
This allows driver to change amount of torque going to wheels. (Ford)

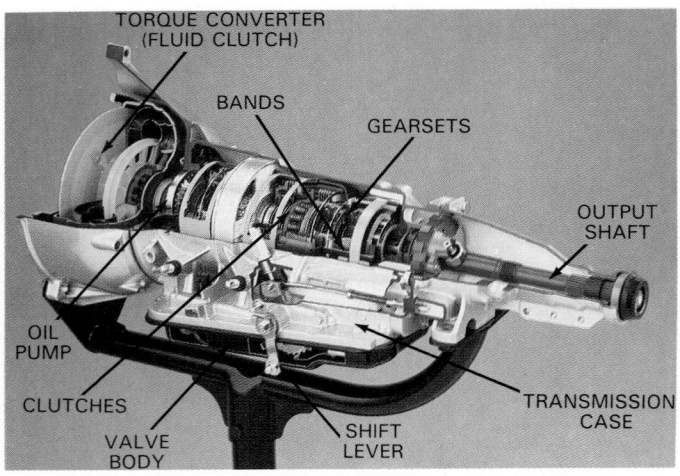

Fig. 1-18. Automatic transmission serves same function as manual transmission. However, it uses a hydraulic or oil pressure system to change gears. (Ford)

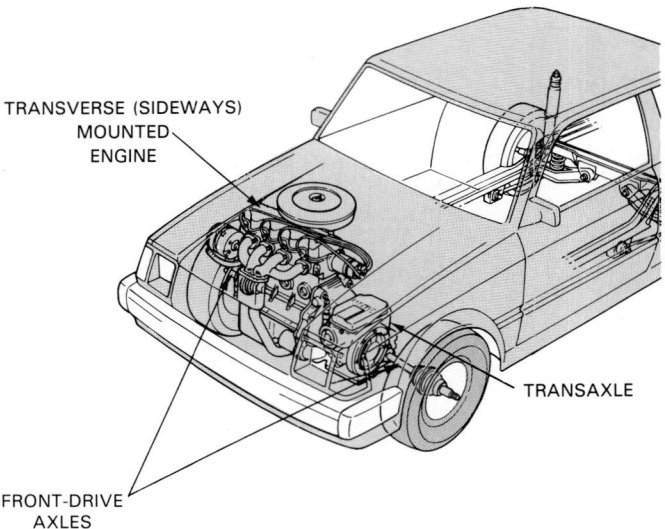

Fig. 1-20. Front-wheel drive car does not have a drive shaft and rear drive axle assembly. Complete drive line is in front. (Ford)

transmission input shaft.

When the clutch pedal is released, the clutch locks the flywheel and transmission input shaft together. This causes engine power to rotate the parts of the driveline and propel the vehicle.

Manual transmission

A *manual transmission* lets the driver change gear ratios and engine torque going to the drive wheels, Fig. 1-17. It allows the vehicle to accelerate quickly in lower transmission gears. It also provides good gas mileage in higher gears.

Automatic transmission

An *automatic transmission* does NOT have to be shifted by hand. It uses an internal hydraulic (oil

pressure) system to shift gears. Elementary parts of an automatic transmission are pictured in Fig. 1-18.

Drive shaft

The *drive shaft*, also called *propeller shaft,* transfers power from the transmission to the rear axle assembly. Look at Fig. 1-19. It is a hollow, metal tube with two or more universal (swivel) joints. The universals allow the rear suspension to move up and down without bending or breaking the drive shaft.

Rear axle assembly

The *rear axle assembly* contains a differential and two axles. The differential is a set of gears and shafts

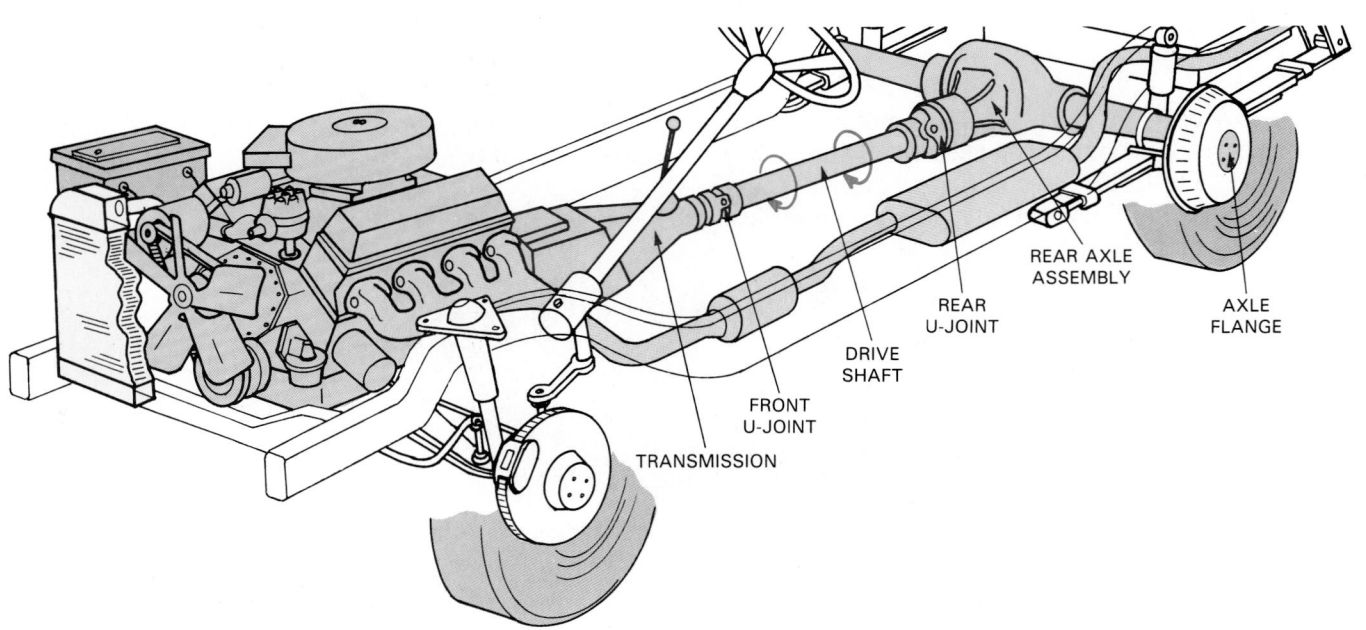

Fig. 1-19. Drive shaft sends power to rear axle assembly. Rear axle assembly contains differential and two axles that turn rear drive wheels.

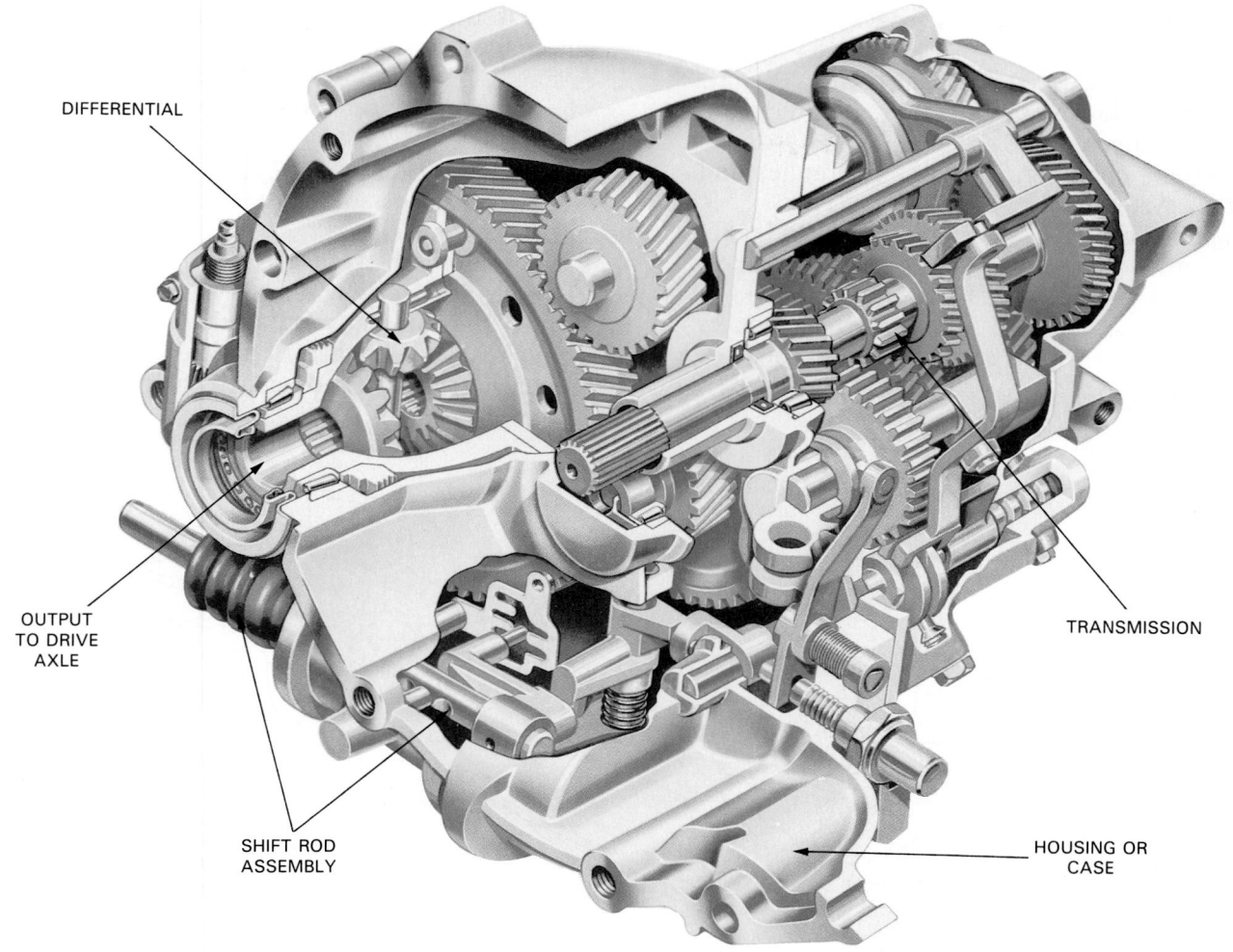

DIFFERENTIAL

OUTPUT
TO DRIVE
AXLE

SHIFT ROD
ASSEMBLY

TRANSMISSION

HOUSING OR
CASE

Fig. 1-21. Transaxle contains a transmission and a differential. (Ford)

that transmit power from the drive shaft to the axles. The axles are steel shafts that connect the differential and drive wheels, Fig. 1-19.

Transaxle

A *transaxle* contains a transmission and a differential in one case. It is commonly used with front-wheel drive vehicles, Fig. 1-20. Automatic and manual transaxles are available. They operate on the same basic principles as transmissions.

Fig. 1-21 illustrates the internal parts of a modern transaxle assembly.

ACCESSORY SYSTEMS

Accessory systems are used to increase driver and passenger comfort and convenience. Common accessory systems are the air conditioner, power seats, power windows, and rear window defogger.

KNOW THESE TERMS

System, Chassis, Frame, Unibody, Suspension system, Steering system, Brake system, Engine, Four-stroke cycle, Multi-cylinder engine, Carburetor Fuel system, Gasoline injection, Diesel injection, Cooling system, Lubrication system, Ignition system, Starting system, Charging system, Exhaust system, Emission Control system, Power train, Clutch, Manual transmission, Automatic transmission, Drive shaft, Rear axle assembly, Transaxle, Accessory systems, Computer, Sensor, Actuator.

REVIEW QUESTIONS

1. What is an automotive system?
2. List the six categories of automotive systems.
3. The suspension system mounts the car's wheels solid on the frame. True or False?
4. Which of the following is NOT part of an engine?
   a. Block.
   b. Piston.
   c. Muffler.
   d. Crankshaft.
5. Explain the engine's four-stroke cycle.
6. Most car engines are multiple-cylinder engines. True or False?
7. List and describe the three common types of fuel systems.

8. A diesel engine does NOT use spark plugs. True or False?

9. The car's electrical system consists of:
   a. Ignition, starting, lubrication, lighting, and other systems.
   b. Ignition, charging, lighting, hydraulic, and other systems.
   c. Lighting, charging, starting, ignition, and other systems.
   d. None of the above are correct.

10. The _____ _____ system reduces the amount of toxic substances entering the atmosphere.

11. What is the difference between a manual and automatic transmission?

12. A single, one-piece drive shaft rotates the drive wheels on most front-wheel drive cars. True or False?

13. A rear _____ _____ assembly contains a set of solid drive _____ and _____ .

14. Explain the term "transaxle."

15. List four accessory systems.

16. Identify the parts illustrated below. Write from 1 through 10 on your sheet of paper. Then write the correct letter and word next to each number.

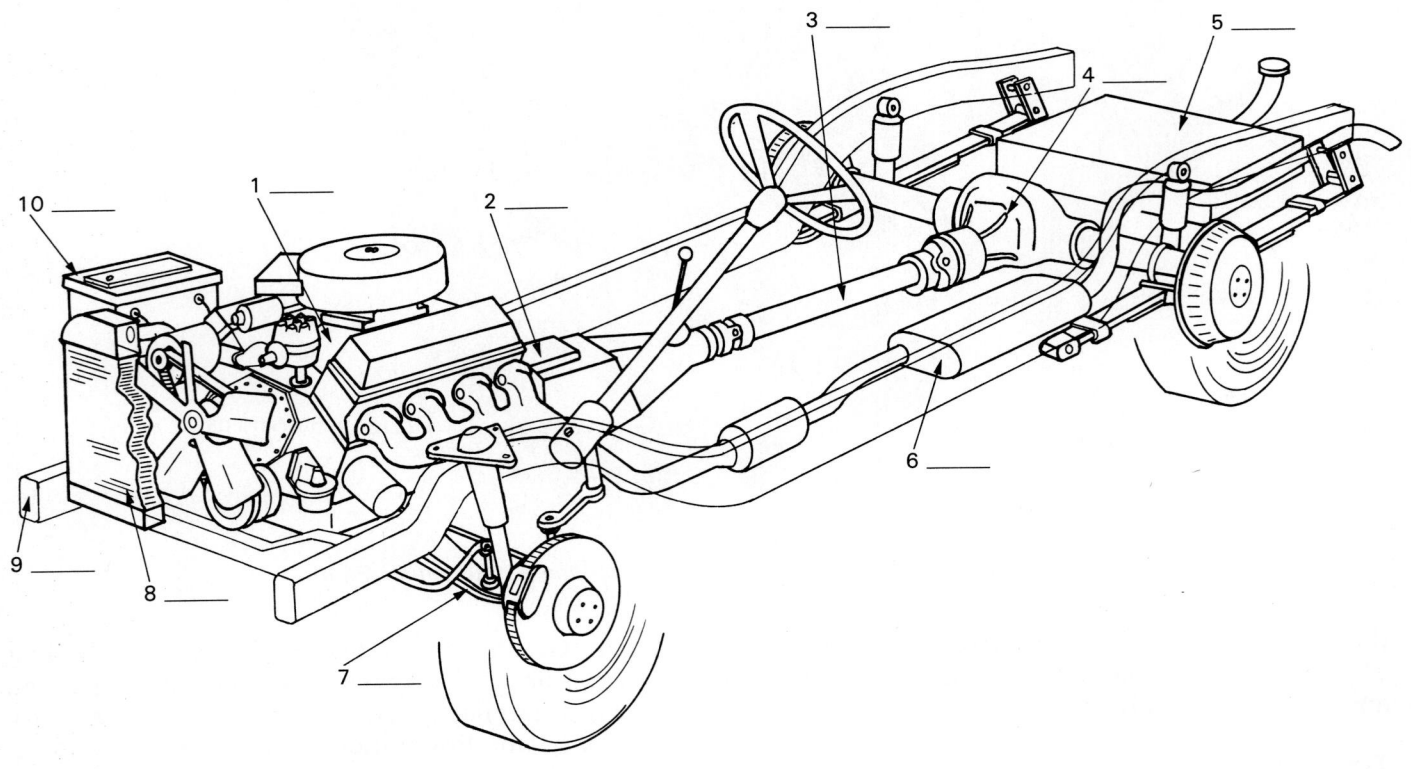

Can you identify these parts?

A. TRANSAXLE
B. FRAME
C. DRIVE LINE
D. BATTERY
E. MUFFLER

F. VAPOR SEPARATOR
G. ENGINE
H. REAR AXLE ASSEMBLY
I. TRANSMISSION

J. FUEL TANK
K. WATER PUMP
L. RADIATOR
M. SUSPENSION ARM

ACTIVITIES FOR CHAPTER 1

1. Draw a sketch of an automotive engine and drive train and label the parts. Then describe how the power is moved from the engine to the drive wheels.

2. Using illustrations from the text, produce overhead transparencies of the four-stroke cycle and demonstrate the cycle to your class.

3. Arrange a field trip to tour an automobile assembly plant, if one is nearby.

Automotive Careers, Certification

After studying this chapter, you will be able to:
- List the most common automotive careers.
- Describe the type of skills needed to be an auto technician.
- Explain the type of tasks completed by each type of auto technician.
- Summarize the NIASE (ASE) certification program.

Economists are predicting a continued demand for auto technicians for many years. Our country is, and will continue to be, a "nation on wheels."

In the last 25 years, the number of vehicles in the United States has increased 40 percent, to over one-hundred million. In one year alone, Americans spend approximately four-hundred billion dollars to own and operate their vehicles. There are about fourteen million people employed in the automotive field.

THE AUTO TECHNICIAN

An *auto technician,* also called *auto mechanic,* must be highly skilled — in a sense, a "jack of all trades." For example, an experienced master automotive technician is usually capable of performing operations common to the following trades:
1. MACHINIST (precision measurement, machining brake parts for example)
2. PLUMBER (working with fuel lines and power steering lines).
3. WELDER (gas and arc welding on exhaust systems, parts repair).
4. ELECTRICIAN (charging, starting, lighting system service).
5. METALWORKER (trim and body repair work).
6. ELECTRONIC TECHNICIAN (car has hundreds of electronic parts).
7. AIR CONDITIONING TECHNICIAN (auto air conditioning).
8. TV-RADIO TECHNICIAN (installation and repair of vehicle stereo, CBs, and radios).

9. COMPUTER TECHNICIAN (vehicles can have several on-board computers).

As this list demonstrates, an auto technician's job can be very challenging. There is normally a variety of repair tasks that prevents boredom on the job. If you like to use your mind and hands, auto service can be a rewarding and interesting profession.

Cooperative training

Many schools offer a *cooperative training* (work release) program. You can earn school credit and an hourly wage while working in a commercial repair shop. The shop owner or employer gets a tax credit while helping the student technician learn the trade.

Ask your guidance counselor or an automotive instructor about a possible cooperative training program in your school.

Service station attendant

A *service station attendant* is a very common entry job. It requires little mechanical experience, yet provides an excellent learning experience.

A "gas station" having a repair area provides better training than a station without a repair area. You could learn to make simple repairs and work your way into a position as a "light mechanic."

Apprentice mechanic

Another way to get started in automotive service is to become an *apprentice* or helper mechanic, working under an experienced technician, Fig. 2-1. This is a good way to get paid for an education. You would learn the work by "running" for parts, cleaning parts, maintaining tools, and helping with repairs.

Specialized technician

A *specialized technician* is an expert on one system of a car. This type specialist may work only on brakes, transmissions, engines, tune-ups, electrical systems, or air conditioning.

Fig. 2-1. An apprentice mechanic works under an experienced auto technician. This is an excellent way to learn the trade.

Because of the increasingly complex nature of today's vehicles, the trend is towards specialization. It is much easier to learn to repair one system than all systems. After specializing in one area, you can then expand your abilities to include other or all systems.

Following is a summary of the different kinds of specialized auto technology.

An *engine technician* must be able to troubleshoot, service, and repair automobile engines. Refer to Fig. 2-2. This requires a knowledge of all types of engines: gasoline, diesel, small 4-cylinder, 6-cylinder, large 8-cylinder. This is one of the most physically deman-

Fig. 2-2. Engine technician must be highly skilled. Late model engines are very complex. One mistake upon assembly can cause major engine damage. (Jaguar)

ding automotive jobs. It requires a fairly strong individual who can lift heavy parts and easily torque large fasteners.

A *transmission technician* usually works on automatic and manual transmissions, transaxles, clutches, and, sometimes, rear axle assemblies. Transmissions, being complex, require very specialized training and frequent retraining.

Some large garages have a *rear axle specialist* who works on nothing but differentials, axle shafts, and drive shafts.

A *front end technician* is responsible for checking, replacing, and adjusting steering and suspension components. This type of repairer will use specialized equipment, such as the wheel alignment rack, to line up the wheels. A front end technician will also take care of tire and wheel problems.

A *brake technician* specializes in brake system service and repair, Fig. 2-3. He or she is capable of rapidly diagnosing problems and making adjustments or repairs. A brake specialist is one of the easiest areas to master. Jobs are available in both small and large garages, service stations, and tire outlets.

Fig. 2-3. This brake technician is machining a brake drum. Brake repairs must be done correctly since safety of customer and passengers are dependent upon operation of brake system. (Boss)

The *electrical system technician* must be able to test and repair lighting systems, charging systems, computer control systems, starting systems, batteries, and other electrical components. Compared to other specialties, this area of repair might be desirable because it requires less physical strength than other areas, Fig. 2-4.

A *heating and air conditioning technician* must troubleshoot, service, and repair heaters, vents, and air conditioning. In large dealerships, this person must also install new air conditioning systems in vehicles. This requires considerable skill.

Fig. 2-5. *This tune-up technician is using state-of-the-art computer testing device to help find source of engine performance problem. Telephone lines are used to connect to a mainframe computer for accessing information about fixing car. (General Motors Corporation)*

Fig. 2-4. *Technician is using "computerized service manual" to look up electrical connections on a master switch. (Mitchell Manuals)*

The *tune-up technician* must test and adjust engine fuel, ignition, and emission systems. As pictured in Fig. 2-5, this involves the use of special test equipment to keep engines in top running condition. The tune-up expert must change spark plugs, as well as adjust and repair carburetors, fuel injection systems, and ignition system components.

The *lubrication specialist* changes engine oil, filters, and transmission fluid. He or she checks various fluid levels and performs "grease jobs" (lubricate pivot points on suspension and steering systems). This person relies on speed, efficiency, and amount of work completed to earn a decent wage.

General technician

A *general technician* or *master technician* is an experienced professional who has mastered ALL specialized areas and is capable of working on almost any part of a vehicle. A skilled person can service and repair engines, brakes, transmissions, rear axles, heaters, air conditioners, and electrical systems. A master technician has enough experience and ability to easily advance to a shop foreman, supervisor, or an instructor's or teacher's position.

Shop supervisor

A *shop supervisor* is in charge of other technicians in a large garage. He or she must be able to help others troubleshoot problems in all repair areas. The shop supervisor must also communicate between the service manager, parts manager, and technicians.

Service manager

The *service manager* is responsible for the complete service and repair area of a large garage or dealership. This person must use a wide range of abilities to coordinate the work of the shop supervisor, parts department, service writers, service dispatcher, and other shop personnel. The service manager must handle customer complaints, answer questions, and assure that the repairers are providing quality service for their customers.

Auto body technician

An *auto body technician,* normally working in an area separated from the main shop, fixes collision damage. This position requires specialized skills, other than those developed in auto technology.

OTHER AUTOMOTIVE CAREERS

There are numerous other automotive careers that do not require extensive mechanical ability. They do, however, require a sound knowledge of auto mechanics. A few of these careers will be discussed.

An **auto parts specialist** must have a general knowledge of the parts of a vehicle. This worker must be able to use customer requests, parts catalogs, price lists, and parts interchange sheets to quickly and accurately find needed parts.

A **service writer** prepares shop work orders on vehicles entering the garage for repair or service. Also called the **service advisor,** this person greets customers and listens to their description of the problem. Then the service writer must fill out the repair order describing what might be wrong.

A **service dispatcher** must select, organize, and assign which technician will perform each auto repair. This worker must also keep track of all the repairs taking place in the shop.

There are dozens of other job titles in automotive repair. Check with your school guidance counselor for more information. Fig. 2-6 is a chart showing automotive job opportunities. Trace the flow from manufacturer to service technician.

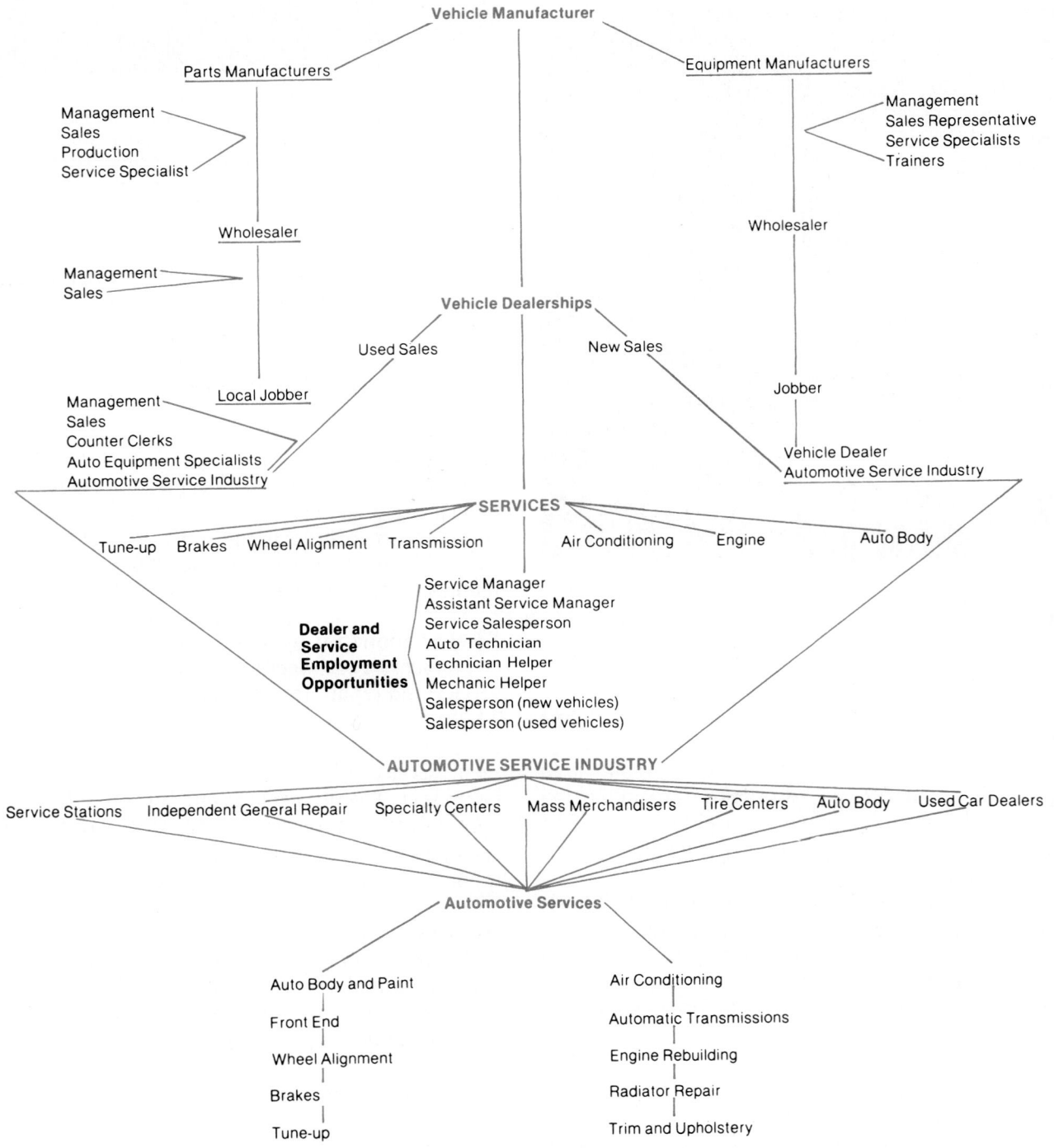

Fig. 2-6. Note many positions available in automotive field. (Florida Dept. of Voc. Ed.)

ENTREPRENEURSHIP

An *entrepreneur* is someone who starts a business. This might be a muffler shop, tune-up shop, parts house, or similar facility. To be a good entrepreneur, you must be able to organize all aspects of the business: bookkeeping, payroll, facility planning, hiring, etc. After gaining experience, you might want to consider starting your own business.

Most successful entrepreneurs have a quality known as leadership. Leaders are people who have the courage to set a course of action and get the cooperation of others in meeting goals. Leaders are willing to accept responsibility for the course of action they take. If their decisions show signs of failure, they take action to correct mistakes; if their decisions are good, they are willing to share the "glory." They readily credit the work of others who have contributed to the success of the venture.

AUTO TECHNICIAN CERTIFICATION

Auto technician certification is a program where persons voluntarily take written tests to prove their knowledge as an auto technician. These tests are administered by NIASE (National Institute for Automotive Service Excellence), also known as ASE (Automotive Service Excellence).

The ASE program lets you prove to your employer and to customers that you are a fully qualified and competent mechanic or technician.

There are eight different certification tests. There is one for each specialized area. Each of these tests is summarized in Fig. 2-7. Tests are also available in heavy-duty truck repair and auto body.

Automotive technician certification

Certified technician status is granted for each ASE or NIASE test passed.

Certified master technician status, previously called *certified general technician,* is granted when ALL of the tests areas are passed.

Sleeve or shirt patches and certificates for wall mounting are awarded for each test. This will let everyone know that you are fully capable of properly repairing their vehicle.

For more information on auto technician certification, send your name and address to:

Bulletin Of Information
ASE
13505 Dulles Technology Drive
Herndon, VA 22071-3415

ON THE JOB

Automotive technicians are valued for their job skills, but there are other values, as well. When you accept employment you take on responsibilities beyond using job skills. These include:

- Reliability. This means regular attendance and coming to work on time.
- Maintaining a cheerful positive attitude concerning other co-workers and about the job.
- Productivity. You are paid to work; use your time effectively.
- Following orders. Someone must be in charge; assume that management usually knows how the job should be done.
- Pride in your appearance as well as your work. Come to the job in clean clothes and well groomed; it instills confidence in the customer.
- Cogeniality. This means getting along with co-workers.

TEST TITLE:		TEST CONTENT:
Engine Repair (80 Questions)	TEST A1	Valve train, cylinder head, and block assemblies; lubricating, cooling, ignition, fuel and carburetion, exhaust, and battery and starting systems
Automatic Transmission/Transaxle (40 Questions)	TEST A2	Controls and linkages; hydraulic and mechanical systems.
Manual Drive Train and Axles (40 Questions)	TEST A3	Manual transmissions, clutches, front and rear drive systems
Suspension and Steering (40 Questions)	TEST A4	Manual and power steering, suspension systems, alignment, and wheels and tires
Brakes (40 Questions)	TEST A5	Drum, disc, combination, and parking brake systems; power assist and hydraulic systems
Electrical Systems (40 Questions)	TEST A6	Batteries; starting, charging, lighting, and signaling systems; electrical instruments and accessories
Heating and Air Conditioning (40 Questions)	TEST A7	Refrigeration, heating and ventilating, AC controls
Engine Performance (80 Questions)	TEST A8	Oscilloscopes and exhaust analyzers; emission control and charging systems; cooling, ignition, fuel and carburetion, exhaust, and battery and starting systems

Fig. 2-7. To become certified in a given automotive service area, you must pass one of these tests. (ASE)

TEXT ORGANIZATION AND CERTIFICATION

The material presented in this text is organized with the NIASE (ASE) certification tests in mind. The content, percent of subject coverage, amount of theory compared to service information, and review questions are designed to help you become certified.

KNOW THESE TERMS

Cooperative training, Apprentice mechanic, Specialized mechanic, Shop supervisor, Service manager, Auto mechanics certification, NIASE, ASE, Certified technician, Certified master technician.

REVIEW QUESTIONS

1. List four trade skills that may be needed when working as an auto mechanic.
2. What is a cooperative training program?
3. Which of the following is NOT a typical specialized mechanic?
   a. Engine mechanic.
   b. Front end mechanic.
   c. Brake mechanic.
   d. Drive shaft mechanic.
4. Describe some of the responsibilities of a tune-up technician.
5. A lubrication specialist may have to do "grease jobs." True or False?
6. What is a "master technician."
7. Explain the job of a service manager.
8. List the eight test categories for NIASE or ASE certification.
9. You will receive belt buckles for passing each certification exam. True or False?
10. The abbreviations _____ and _____ represent the institution that administers certification tests.

ACTIVITIES FOR CHAPTER 2

1. Research an automotive career of your choice; using a computer or a typewriter, prepare a written report covering such topics as: duties, working conditions, pay range, and opportunities for advancement.
2. Interview a manager of a parts department for a local garage. Report back on the duties performed.

Basic Hand Tools

After studying this chapter, you will be able to:
□ Identify the most common automotive hand tools.
□ List safety rules for hand tools.
□ Properly select the right tool for the job.
□ Maintain and store tools properly.
□ Use hand tools safely.

It is almost impossible to do even the simplest auto repair without using some type of tool. Tools serve as extensions to parts of our body. They increase the physical abilities of our fingers, hands, arms, legs, eyes, ears, and backs.

Professional auto technicians invest thousands of dollars in tools. A well selected set of tools will speed up repairs, improve work quality, and increase profits. Nothing is more frustrating than trying to fix a vehicle without the right tools.

Note! Specialized hand tools will be covered in later chapters. Use the index to locate these tools as needed.

TOOL RULES

There are several basic TOOL RULES that should be remembered:
1. *Purchase quality tools!* Quality tools will be lighter, stronger, easier to use, and more dependable than off-brand, bargain tools. With tools, you usually get what you pay for.
   Many tool manufacturers provide tool guarantees. Some are lifetime guarantees. If the tool fails (chrome peels, breaks, or wears), the manufacturer will replace the tool free of charge. This can save money in the long run.
2. *Keep tools organized!* There should be a place for every tool and every tool should be in its place. An auto mechanic will have hundreds of different tools. For each tool to be used quickly, the tools must be neatly arranged. If just thrown into the box, time and effort will be wasted "digging" for tools.
3. *Keep tools clean!* Wipe tools clean and dry after

each use. A greasy or oily tool is not only unprofessional—but dangerous! It is very easy for your hand to slide off a dirty wrench, cutting or even breaking a finger or hand.
4. *Use the right tool for the job!* A good mechanic will know when, where, and why a particular tool will work better than another. Even though several different tools may be used to loosen a bolt, usually one will do a better job. It may be faster, grip the bolt better, be less likely to break, or require less physical effort. Keep this in mind as you study automotive tools.

TOOL BOX

A *tool box* stores and protects a technician's tools when not in use. Shown in Fig. 3-1, there are three basic parts to a typical tool box. These include:
1. Large, bottom roll-around cabinet.
2. Upper tool box that sits on roll-around cabinet.
3. Small carrying or "tote" tray, usually placed in the upper box.

The *upper tool chest* is normally filled with commonly used tools. Being near eye level, tools can be easily seen and reached without bending. This saves time, energy, and increases production.

The lower *roll-around cabinet* holds the bulky, heavy tools. Large power tools are normally kept in this part of the box. Extra storage compartments can be bolted to the sides of the roll-around cabinet.

The small *carrying tray* is for holding commonly used tools, Fig. 3-1. For example, if a technician frequently does brake repairs, all of the special brake tools can be kept in the tray.

Tool box organization

Related tools are normally kept in the same tool box drawer. Various types of hammers may be stored in one drawer, screwdrivers in another. Small or delicate tools should NOT be kept with large heavy tools. The delicate tools could be damaged.

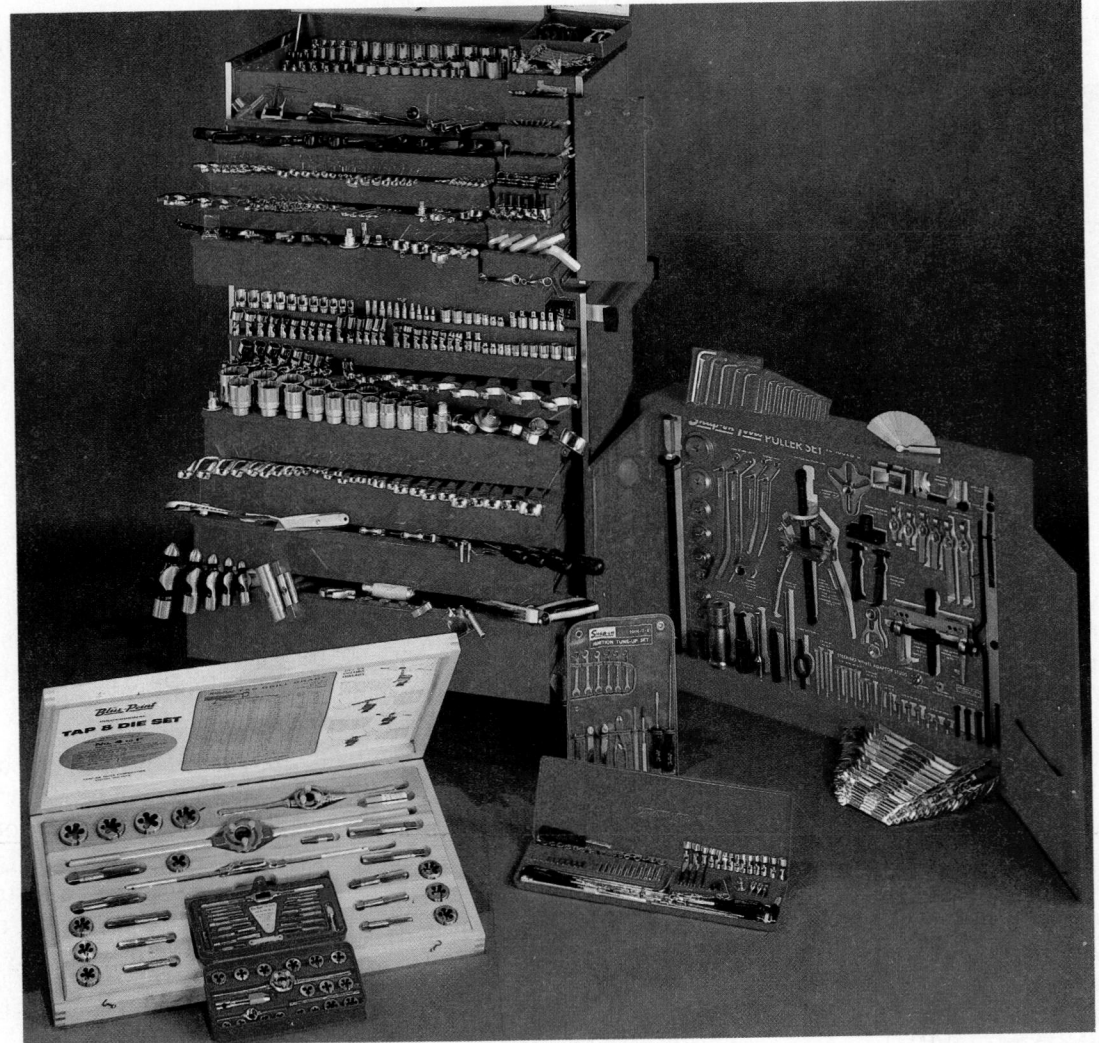

Fig. 3-1. A wide assortment of tools is essential. Note how many tools are in this set. (Snap-On)

Tool holders (small clip racks, cloth or plastic pouches, or socket trays) help organize small tools. They are often used to protect tools and to keep them organized by size. Holders also allow a full set of tools to be taken to the job.

CAUTION! Never open more than two tool box drawers at one time; the heavy tool box might FLIP OVER. Serious injury could result because a tool chest can weigh up to one-half a ton! Close each drawer before opening the next.

WRENCHES

Wrenches are used to install and remove nuts and bolts. Refer to Figs. 3-2 and 3-3.

Wrench size is determined by measuring across the wrench jaws. Wrenches come in both conventional (inch) and metric (millimeter) sizes. The size will be stamped on the side of the wrench.

Here are a few WRENCH RULES to follow:

1. Always select the right size wrench. It must fit the bolt head securely. A loose fitting wrench will round off the corners of the bolt head.

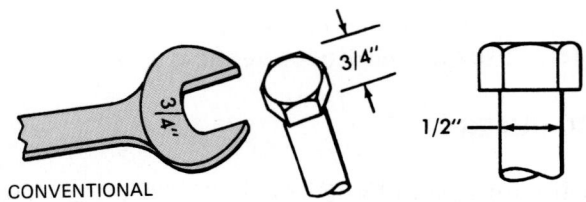

Fig. 3-2. Conventional tool sizes are given in fractions of an inch. The measurement is the width of the jaw opening. These sizes are not to be confused with bolt sizes. (Deere & Co.)

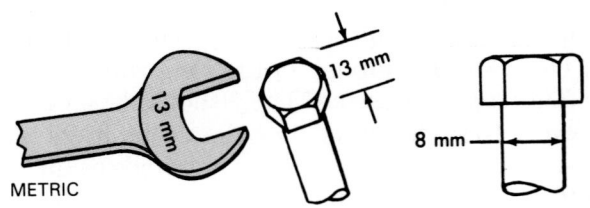

Fig. 3-3. Metric wrench sizes are marked in millimeters and also represent width of jaw opening. Note difference in bolt size and wrench size. (Deere & Co.)

2. To prevent damage to your tools, never hammer on a standard wrench to break loose a bolt. Use a longer wrench with more leverage or a special *slug wrench* (wrench designed for use with hammer).

3. When possible, PULL on the wrench. Then, if the wrench slips, you are less likely to hurt your hand. When you must push, use the palm of your hand and keep your fingers open.

4. Never use a steel bar or pipe to increase the length of a wrench for leverage. Excess force can bend or break the wrench.

To be able to select the right wrench for the job, you must learn the advantages and disadvantages of each type. Study the following material carefully.

Open end wrenches

An *open end wrench* has an open jaw on both ends. Each end will be a different size and set at an angle. Pictured in Fig. 3-4A, this angle allows the open end wrench to turn bolts and nuts with little wrench swing space. The wrench can be turned over between each swing to get a new "bite" on the bolt head.

An open end wrench has weak jaws. It should NOT be used on extremely tight nuts or bolts. Its jaws will flex outward and round off the bolt head.

Box end wrench

Box end wrenches are completely closed on both ends. They fully surround and grip the head of a bolt or nut. Look at Fig. 3-4B. A box end wrench will NOT round off bolt heads as easily as an open end wrench. Box wrenches come in 12-point and 6-point openings.

A 6-POINT is the STRONGEST wrench configuration. It should be used on extremely tight, rusted, or partially rounded bolt or nut heads.

Combination wrench

A *combination wrench* has a box end jaw on one end and an open end on the other. As in Fig. 3-4C, both ends will usually be the same size. A combination wrench provides the advantages of two wrenches for the price of one.

Line wrench

A *line wrench,* also called a *tubing wrench* or *flare nut wrench,* is a box wrench with a small opening or split in the jaw. The opening allows the wrench to be slipped over fuel lines, brake lines, power steering lines, and onto the fitting nut. Look at Fig. 3-4D. The strong box configuration will prevent damage to relatively weak, soft fittings.

Other wrench types

An *adjustable wrench* or *Crescent wrench* has jaws that can be adjusted to fit different size bolt and nut heads. It should be used only when other type wrenches will NOT fit. An adjustable wrench is a handy tool to

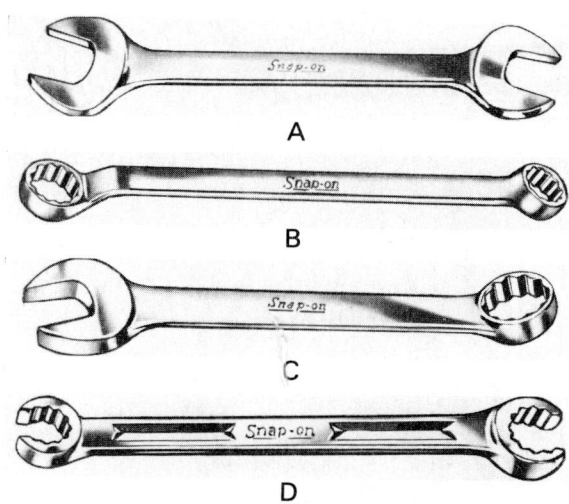

Fig. 3-4. Study four basic types of hand wrenches. A — Open end wrench. B — Box end wrench. C — Combination wrench. D — Tubing or line wrench. (Snap-On Tools)

carry for emergencies. It is like having a full set of open end wrenches. Refer to Fig. 3-5A.

A *pipe wrench* is an adjustable wrench used to grasp round objects. See Fig. 3-5B. The toothed jaws actually dig into the object. For this reason, never use it on parts that would be ruined by marrs or nicks.

An *allen wrench* is a hexagon (six sided) shaft type wrench. It is used to turn set screws on pulleys, gears, and knobs. Look at Fig. 3-5C. To prevent damage, make sure the allen wrench is fully inserted in the fastener before turning.

Fig. 3-5 shows several other wrench types.

Socket wrenches

A *socket* is a cylinder-shaped, box end tool for removing or installing bolts and nuts. See Fig. 3-6. One end fits over the fastener. The other end fits on a handle for turning.

Drive sizes and points

As pictured in Fig. 3-7, sockets come in four *drive sizes* (size of square opening for handle): 1/4, 3/8, 1/2, and 3/4 in. They also come in four different *points* (box configuration for bolt head): 4-point, 6-point, 8-point, and 12-point.

Generally, a 1/4 in. drive socket and handle should be used on bolt and nut heads 1/4 in. and smaller. A 3/8 in. socket set is adequate on bolt head sizes between 1/4 and 5/8 in. The larger 1/2 in. drive is strong enough to handle bolts or nuts heads from 5/8 in. to 1 in. The larger 3/4 in. drive is for bolts and nuts with a head size larger than 1 in.

If a small drive size (1/4 or 3/8 in.) is used on very large or tight fasteners, the socket or handle can be BROKEN. If drive size is too large, time and effort will be wasted.

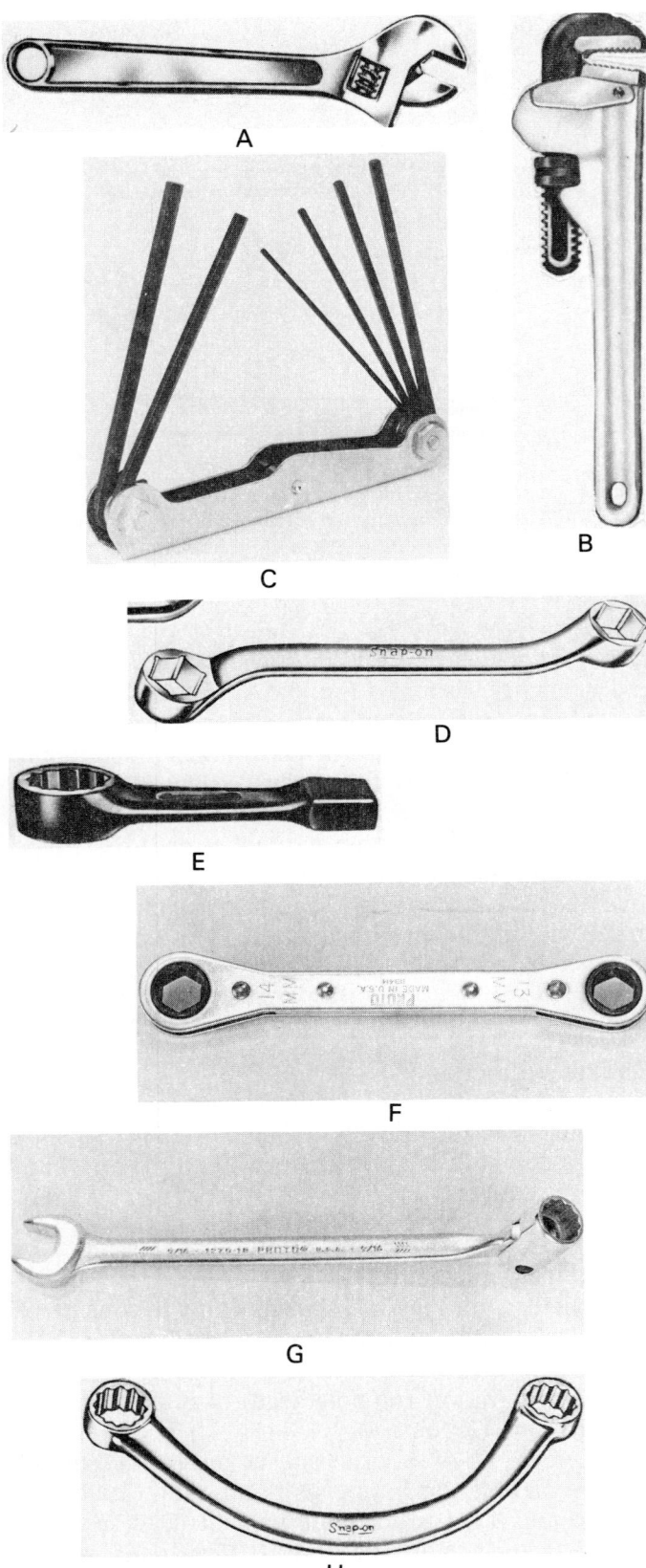

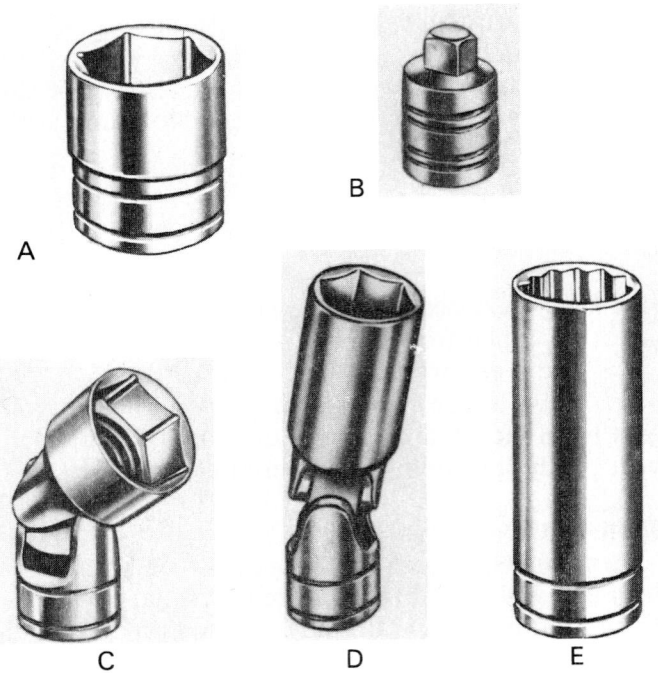

Fig. 3-6. Study socket types. A — 6-point standard socket. B — Adapter for changing drive size. C — Swivel or universal socket. D — Spark plug socket with universal. E — 12-point deep well socket. (Snap-On)

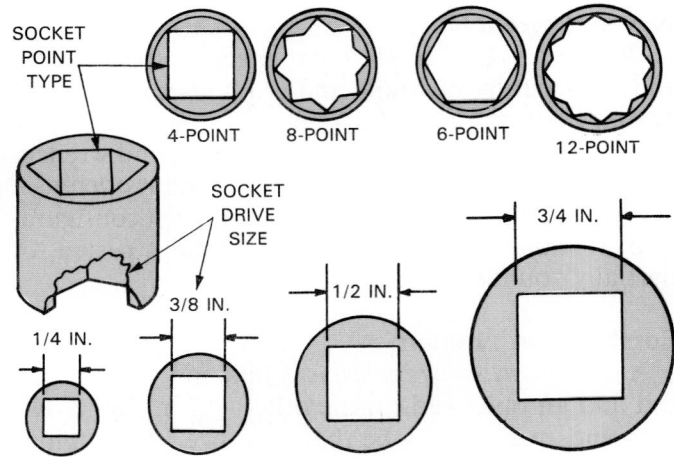

Fig. 3-7. Sockets come in four drive sizes and four point types. Most commonly used drives are 3/8 and 1/2 in. Most common points are 6 and 12-point.

Fig. 3-5. A — Adjustable or Crescent wrench. B — Pipe wrench. C — Allen or hex wrenches. D — Offset, 6-point box end wrench. E — Slug wrench can withstand hammering. F — Ratchet wrench. G — Flex-combination wrench. H — Half-moon, 12-point wrench for tight quarters. (Snap-On and Proto)

Socket handles

Socket handles fit into the square opening in the top of the socket. Several types are shown in Fig. 3-8.

A *ratchet* is the most commonly used and versatile socket handle. It has a small lever that can be moved for either loosening or tightening bolts.

A *flex bar* or *breaker bar* is the most powerful and strongest socket handle. It should be used when breaking loose large or extremely tight bolts and nuts.

A *speed handle* is the fastest hand-operated socket handle. After a bolt is loosened, a speed handle will rapidly spin out the bolt.

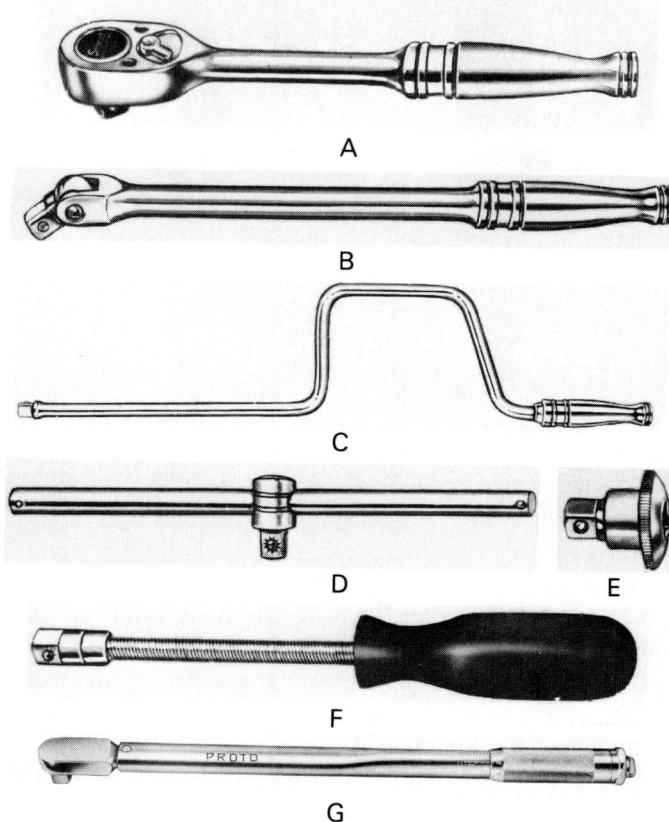

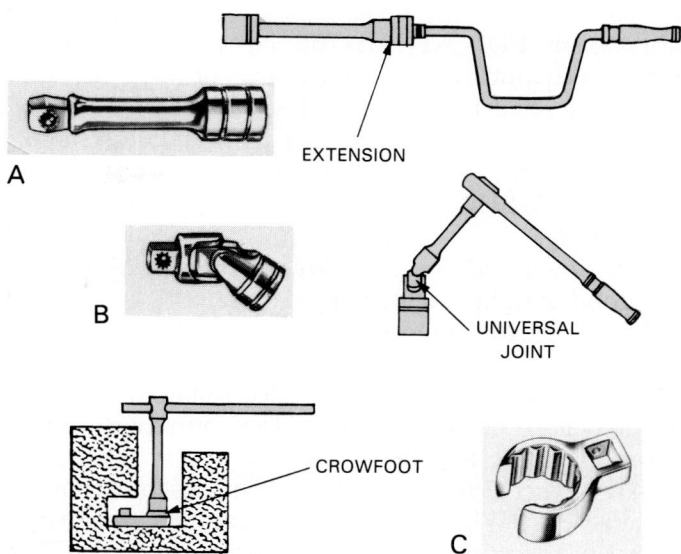

Fig. 3-9. A — Extension moves socket away from handle for more clearance. B — Universal joint allows socket to be turned from angle. C — Crowfoot is needed when obstructions surround fastener. (Snap-On)

Fig. 3-8. Various socket handles. A — Ratchet. B — Breaker bar or flex handle. C — Speed handle. D — T-handle. E — Hand spinner. F — Flexible driver. G — Torque wrench. (Snap-On and Proto)

Extensions are used between a socket and its handle. See Fig. 3-9. It allows you to reach fasteners surrounded by parts. It gives you room to swing the handle and turn the fastener.

A *universal joint* is a swivel that lets the socket wrench reach around obstructions, Fig. 3-9. It is used between the socket and drive handle, with or without an extension. Avoid putting too much bend into a universal or it may bind and break.

SCREWDRIVERS

Screwdrivers are used to remove or install screws, Fig. 3-10. They come in many shapes and sizes.

A *standard screwdriver* has a single blade that fits into a slot in the screw. See Fig. 3-10A.

A *Phillips screwdriver* has two crossing blades that fit into a star-shaped screw slot, Fig. 3-10B. A Reed and Prince screwdriver is similar to a Phillips, but it has a slightly different tip shape, Fig. 3-10E. They should NOT be interchanged or damage will result.

Torx and *clutch head* screwdrivers are shown in Fig. 3-10C and D.

When selecting a screwdriver, pick one that is wide and thick enough to COMPLETELY FILL the screw

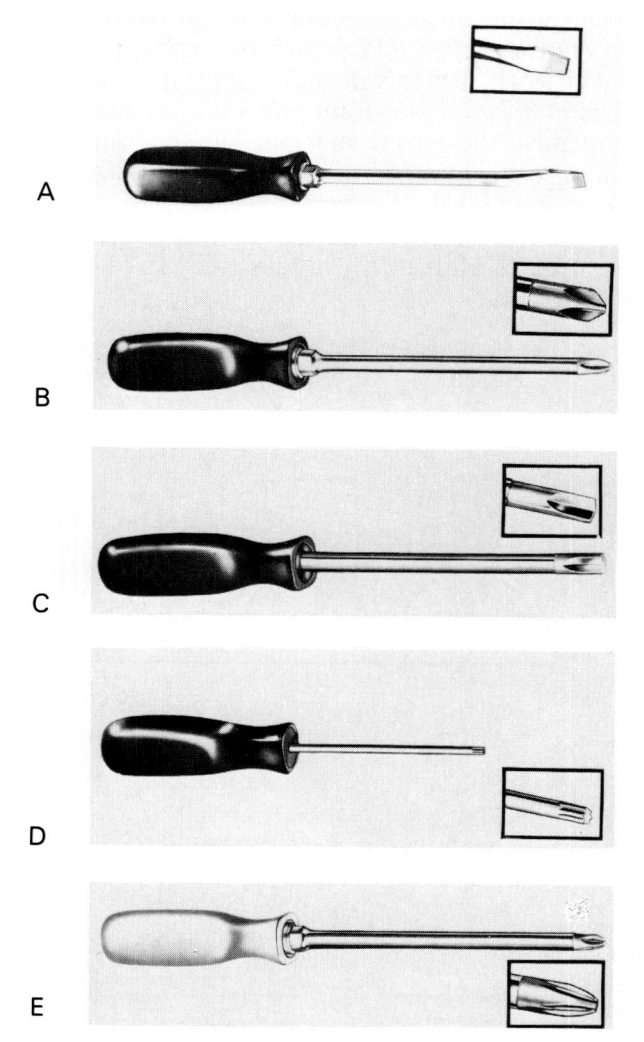

Fig. 3-10. Screwdriver types. A — Standard. B — Phillips. C — Clutch. D — Torx. E — Reed and Prince. (Snap-On)

slot, as in Fig. 3-11. If too large or too small, screwdriver and screw damage may occur.

Most screwdrivers are NOT designed to be hammered on or pryed with. Either the handle or shank will be too weak. Only special, heavy duty screwdrivers with a FULL SHANK can withstand light hammering and prying.

Offset and *stubby screwdrivers,* Fig. 3-12A and B, are good in tight places. For example, a stubby screwdriver is needed for loosening screws inside a dash glove box.

Starting screwdrivers, Fig. 3-12E, will hold the screw securely until started in its hole. They prevent the screw from dropping and being lost.

An *impact driver* can be used to loosen extremely tight screws. When struck with a hammer, the driver exerts a powerful turning and downward force. This is shown in Fig. 3-13.

PLIERS

Pliers are used to grip, cut, crimp, hold, and bend various parts. Pictured in Fig. 3-14, different pliers are helpful during different situations. Never use pliers when another type tool (wrench or socket, for example) will work. Pliers will nick and scar an object.

Combination or *slip-joint pliers* are the most common pliers of the auto technician. The slip joint allows the jaws to be adjusted to grasp different size parts. Look at Fig. 3-14I.

Rib joint, also called *channel lock* or *water pump pliers,* open extra wide for holding very large objects. See Fig. 3-14H.

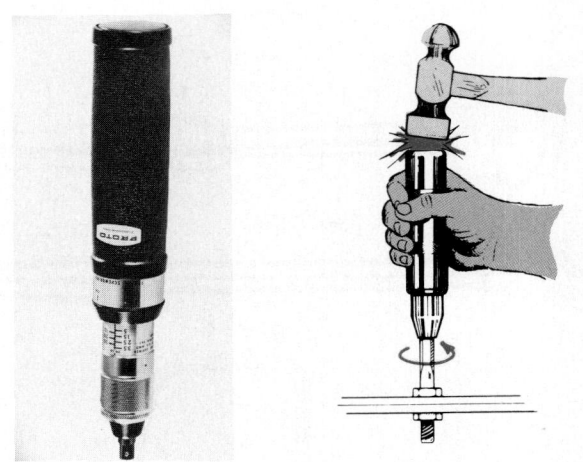

Fig. 3-13. Impact driver for loosening stubborn fasteners. Hit it with a hammer to free and turn screw. (Proto and Lisle)

Needle nose pliers are excellent for handling extremely small parts or reaching into highly restricted areas. Do NOT twist too hard on needle nose pliers or the long thin jaws can be bent. Refer to Fig. 31-14A.

Diagonal cutting pliers are the most commonly used cutting pliers. The jaw shape allows cutting flush with a surface. See Fig. 3-14D.

Vise grip or *locking pliers* will clamp onto and hold a part, Fig. 3-14C. This frees both hands to do other tasks (weld, saw, drill). Because of their clamping power, vise grips can sometimes be used to unscrew fasteners with stripped or rounded heads. NEVER use them on good nuts or bolts, however.

Snap ring pliers have sharp, pointed tips for installing and removing special, snap ring clips. Some are shown in Fig. 3-14G.

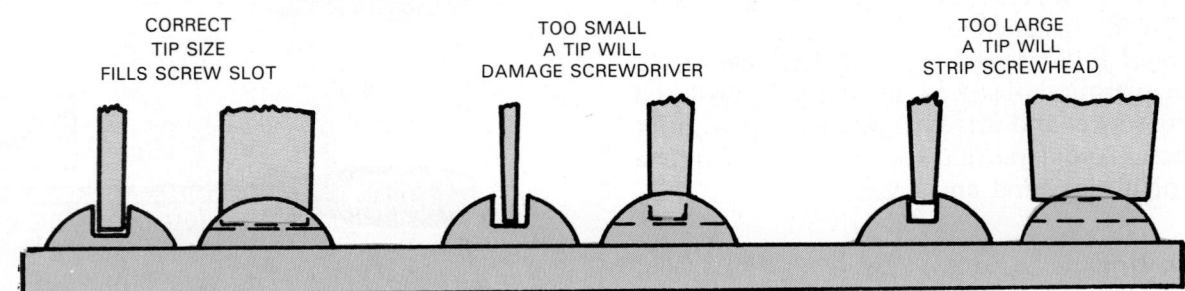

Fig. 3-11. Screwdriver tip must fit slot perfectly. If not, screwdriver and screw can be ruined.

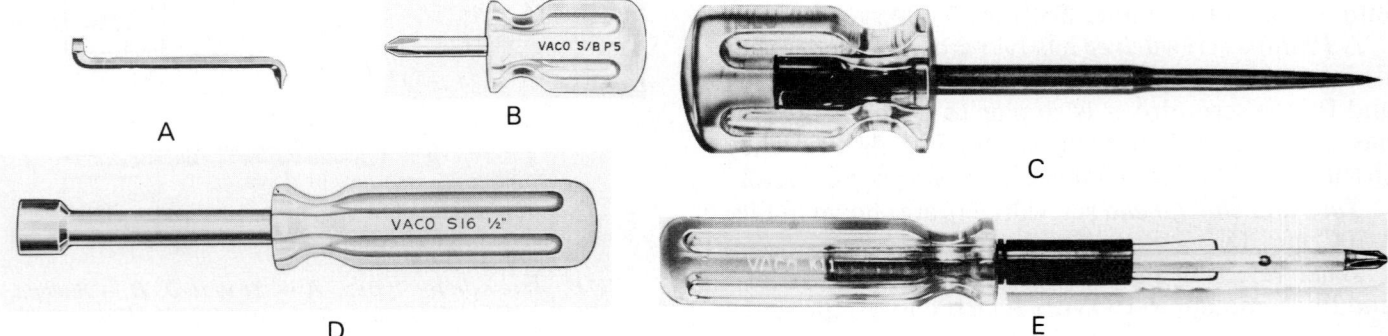

Fig. 3-12. A — Offset screwdriver. B — Stubby screwdriver. C — Scratch awl is similar to screwdriver but has pointed tip. It is for marking sheet metal and other parts. D — Socket head driver. E — Starting or clip screwdriver. (Vaco Tools)

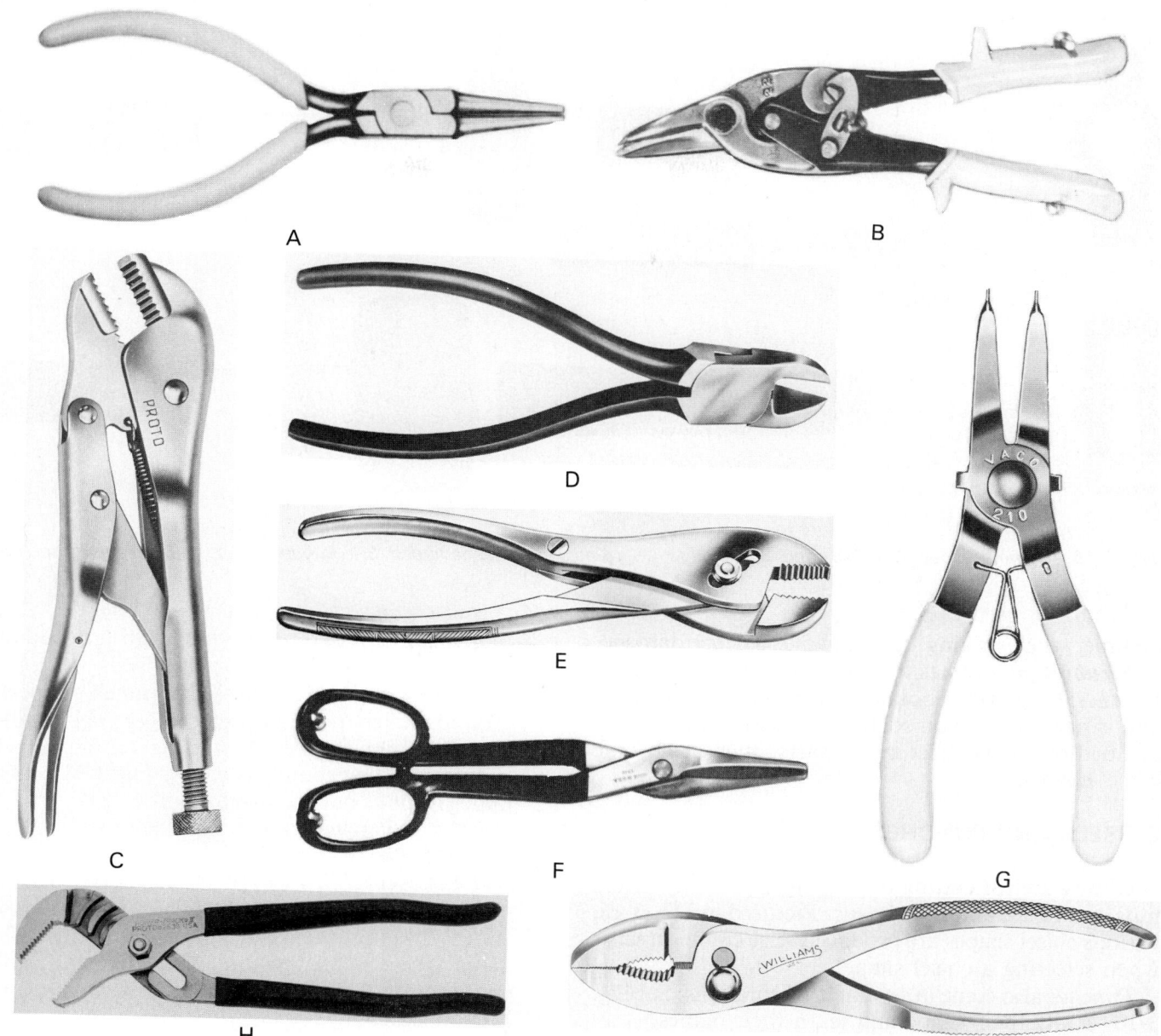

Fig. 3-14. Plier types. A — Needle nose. B — High leverage cutters. C — Vise grip. D — Diagonal cutting. E — Battery pliers. F — Tin snips. G — Snap ring. H — Rib joint. I — Slip joint. (Duro, Vaco, and Proto Tools)

HAMMERS

Various types of *hammers* are used for striking operations. It is important to use the right hammer and to use it properly. See Fig. 3-15.

1. Select the right size hammer. If a large part is struck by a small hammer, the hammer can fly backwards dangerously. If the hammer is too large, however, it may damage the part.
2. Always check that the hammer head is tight on the handle. If not, the head could fly off and cause injury or part damage.
3. Never hit a hardened part with a steel hammer. Metal chips could fly off. Use a brass or soft headed hammer.
4. Grasp the hammer near the end of the handle and strike squarely.

A *ball peen hammer* is the most commonly used type in automotive work, Fig. 3-15A. Its flat face is for general striking. Its round peen end is for shaping sheet metal or rivet heads, for example.

A *sledge hammer* has a very large head. It is usually the heaviest hammer and produces powerful blows. Look at Fig. 3-15B.

The *brass* or *lead hammer* has a soft, yet fairly heavy head, useful when part surface scarring must be avoided. The relatively soft head will deform to protect the part surface, Fig. 3-15C.

A *plastic* or *rawhide hammer* is light and has a soft head, Fig. 3-15D. It is used where light blows are needed to prevent part breakage or damage to surfaces on the smallest and most delicate parts.

A *dead blow hammer* has a heavy metal face filled with lead shot (balls). This prevents a rebound of the

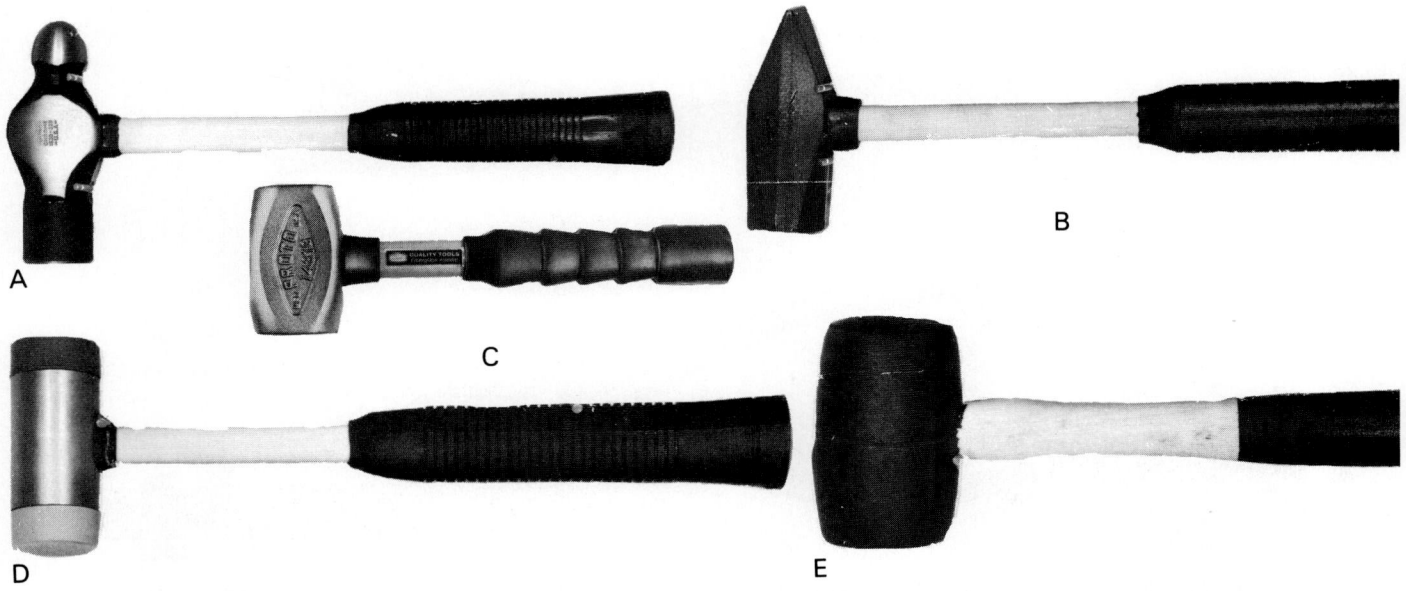

Fig. 3-15. Hammer types. A — Ball peen. B — Sledge. C — Brass. D — Plastic tipped. E — Rubber mallet.   (Duro and Proto Tools)

hammer when striking. It also avoids surface damage.

A *rubber mallet* has a head made of solid rubber, Fig. 3-15E. It will rebound or bounce upon striking and is not effective on solid metal parts. It is recommended on many sheet metal parts, such as chrome wheel covers.

CHISELS AND PUNCHES

Chisels are for cutting off damaged or badly rusted nuts and bolts, and rivet heads. Pictured in Fig. 3-16, various chisel shapes are produced. Use common sense when selecting a chisel shape.

Punches also come in several configurations. See Fig. 3-16. Study their shape and learn their names.

A *center punch* is frequently used to mark parts for reassembly and to start a drilled hole. Look at Figs. 3-16 and 3-17. The indentation made by a center punch will keep a drill bit from wandering (moving) when first starting to drill.

A *starting punch* or *drift punch* has a shank tapered all the way to the end. It is strong and can withstand moderate blows. It is used to drive pins, shafts, and metal rods partway out of holes.

A *pin punch* has a straight shank and is lighter than a starting punch. It is used AFTER a starting punch to push a shaft or rod the rest of the way out of a hole.

An *aligning punch* is long and tapered; it is handy for lining up parts during assembly. An aligning punch can be inserted into holes in parts, then wiggled or rotated to match up the holes.

Never use an aligning punch as a center punch. Its tip is too soft and would be ruined.

Remember these CHISEL and PUNCH RULES:

1. Use the largest punch or chisel that will work. If a small punch is used on a very large part, the punch can rebound and fly out with tremendous force. The same is true for chisels.

2. Keep both ends of a chisel and punch properly ground and shaped. A chisel cutting edge should be sharp and square. A starting or pin punch should also be ground flat and square. A center punch should have a sharp point.

   After prolonged hammering, the top of a chisel or punch can become "mushroomed" (deformed and enlarged). This is dangerous! Grind off the mushroom and form a chamfer, as in Fig. 3-18.

3. When grinding a chisel or punch, grind slowly to avoid overheating the tool. Excessive heat will cause the tool to turn blue, lose its temper, and become soft.

4. Make sure to wear eye protection when using or grinding a chisel or punch.

FILES

Files remove burrs, nicks, sharp edges, and perform other smoothing operations. They are useful when only a small amount of material must be removed. The basic parts of a file are shown in Fig. 3-19.

Files are classified by their length, shape, and type of cutting surface.

Generally, a *coarse file* with large cutting edges should be used on soft materials such as plastic, brass, and aluminum.

A *fine file* with small cutting edges is needed to produce a smoother surface and to cut harder materials, like cast iron or steel.

There are several FILE SAFETY RULES that should be remembered.

1. Never use a file without a handle securely attached. The pointed tang, if not covered by a handle, can

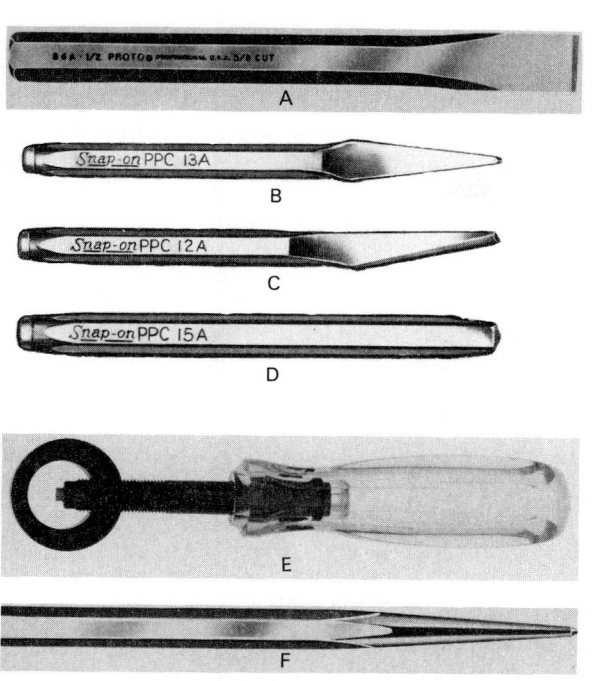

Fig. 3-16. Chisels and punches. A — Flat chisel. B — Cape chisel. C — Round nose, cape chisel. D — Diamond point chisel. E — Chisel or punch holder. F — Center punch. G — Pin punch. H — Long, taper punch. I — Starting punch. (Snap-On Tools and Proto Tools)

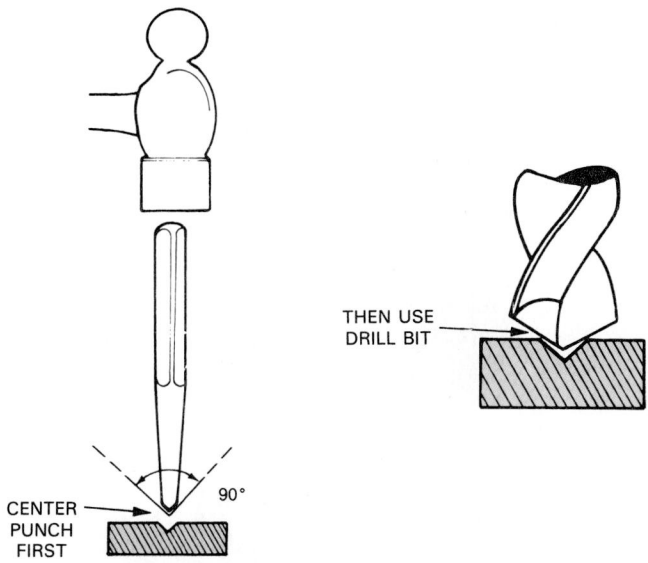

Fig. 3-17. Center punch will make a small indentation in metal parts. This can be used before drilling or for organizing parts. (Florida Dept. of Voc. Ed.)

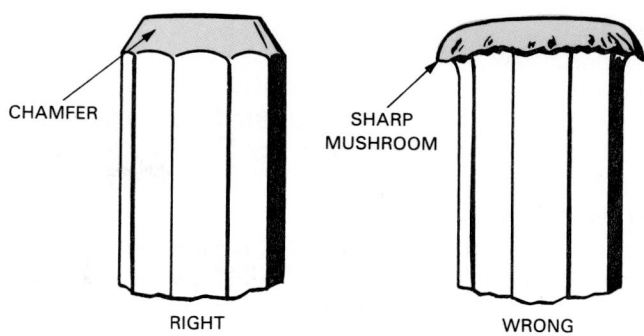

Fig. 3-18. Always keep top of a chisel or punch ground to a chamfer. Sharp, mushroomed end is dangerous. (Deere & Co.)

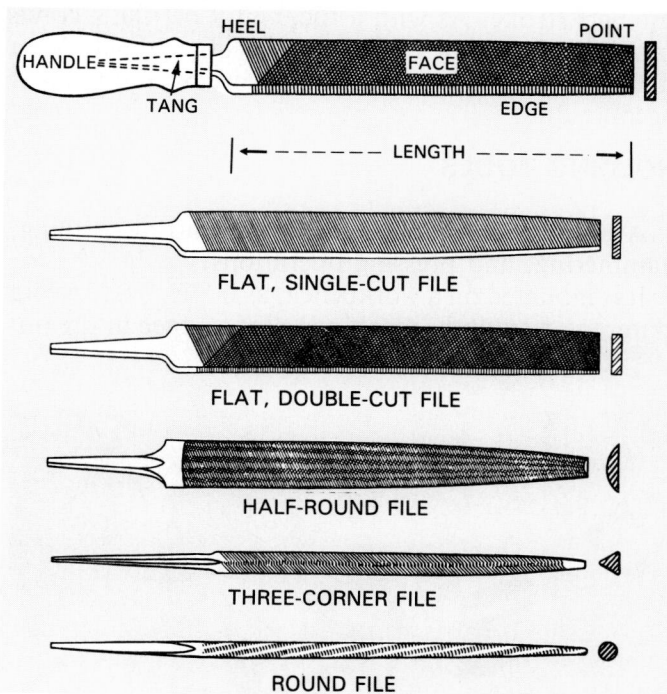

Fig. 3-19. File is used for smoothing metal. Note file parts, shapes, and cuts. (Starrett)

puncture your hand or wrist.

2. To prevent undue file wear, apply pressure only on the forward stroke. Lift the file on the backstroke.

3. When filing, place one hand on the handle and the other on the file tip. Hold the file firmly but DO NOT press too hard.

4. DO NOT file too rapidly. One file stroke every second is fast enough. Count to yourself: one thousand one, one thousand two, one thousand three, one thousand four. This will time your strokes properly to about 50 to 60 strokes per minute.

5. If a file becomes clogged, clean it with a file card or stiff wire brush.

6. Never hammer on or pry with a file. A file is very brittle and will break easily. Bits of the file can fly into your face or eyes.

SAWS

A *hacksaw* is the most frequently used saw of the mechanic. See Fig. 3-20. Various blade lengths can be mounted in its adjustable frame. The blade teeth should point AWAY from the handle. The blade should be fastened tightly in the frame.

Select the appropriate blade for the job. A "rule of thumb," at least TWO SAW TEETH should contact the material being cut. If not, the teeth can catch and be broken off on the object.

When cutting, place one hand on the hacksaw handle and the other on the end of the frame. Press down lightly on the forward stroke and release pressure on the backstroke. As with a file, count off the seconds in thousands to time each stroke. If cuts are made faster than this, the blade will quickly overheat, soften, and become dull.

HOLDING TOOLS

A *vise* is used to hold parts during cutting, drilling, hammering, and pressing operations.

It is mounted on a workbench, as in Fig. 3-21. Avoid clamping a smooth, machined part surface in the un-covered jaws of a vise. If a machined surface is scarred, the part may be ruined.

Vise caps (lead jaw covers) or *wood blocks* should be used when mounting precision parts in a vise. They will not only protect the part, but provide a more secure grip on the part.

A few VISE RULES include:
1. Never hammer on a vise handle to tighten or loosen the vise. Use the weight of your body.
2. Keep the moving parts of the vise clean and oiled.
3. Wear safety glasses when using a vise. Tremendous clamping force can be exerted. Parts can break and fly out with great force.
4. Be careful not to damage parts in the powerful jaws of a vise.
5. Use vise caps when a precision part is held in a vise. This will prevent part damage.

C-clamp

A *C-clamp* will hold parts on a work surface when drilling, filing, cutting, welding, or doing other operations. Being portable, it can be taken to the job. Refer to Fig. 3-22.

Stands, holding fixtures

Stands or *holding fixtures* can be used to help secure heavy or clumsy parts while working, Fig. 3-23. Cylinder head stands, transmission fixtures, rear axle holding stands, etc., will all make your work safe and easier. Use them when available.

HAND CLEANING TOOLS

Hand cleaning tools (scrapers and brushes) help the mechanic remove carbon, rust, dirt, grease, old gaskets, and dried oil from parts.

Fig. 3-20. Hacksaws are used to cut metal. Hold saw as shown and only push down on forward stroke. (Gould)

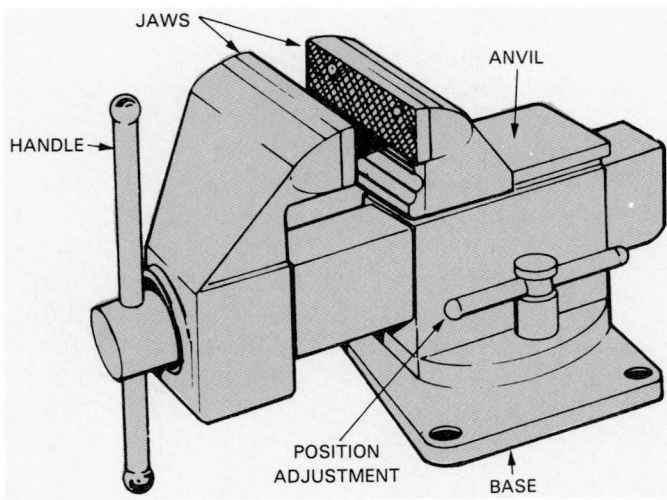

Fig. 3-21. Vise mounts on workbench. It will hold parts securely when working. (Snap-On)

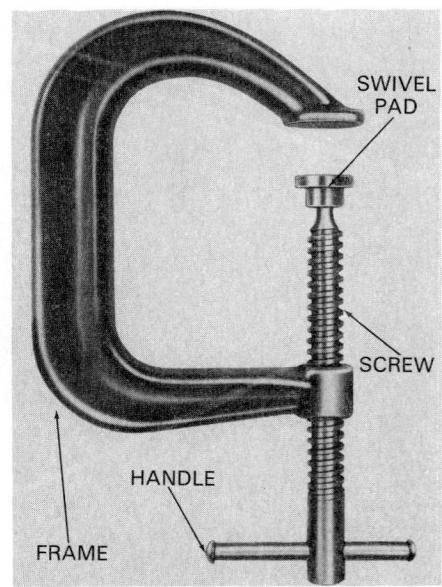

Fig. 3-22. C-clamp is a portable means of securing parts. It can also be used for light pressing operations.

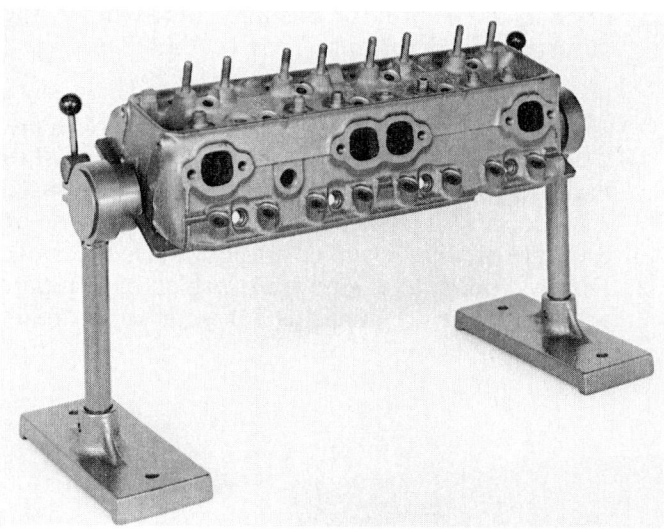

Fig. 3-23. Cylinder head stand will hold head in position during work on valves, seats, and other parts. Other specialized stands are available for transmissions, differentials, etc.

There is an old saying, "if you do the job right, you will spend most of your time cleaning parts." Dirt is a major enemy of the vehicle. One grain of sand could cause a major breakdown by clogging a passage or scarring a part.

Hand scrapers remove grease, gaskets, sludge (dried oil), and carbon on parts. They are used on flat surfaces. Never scrape towards your body; keep your other hand out of the way.

Hand brushes are used to remove light rust and dirt on parts. They are slow and only used when necessary.

PROBE AND PICKUP TOOLS

Pickup and *probing tools* are needed when small metal parts, bolts, or nuts are dropped and cannot be reached by hand. See Fig. 3-24.

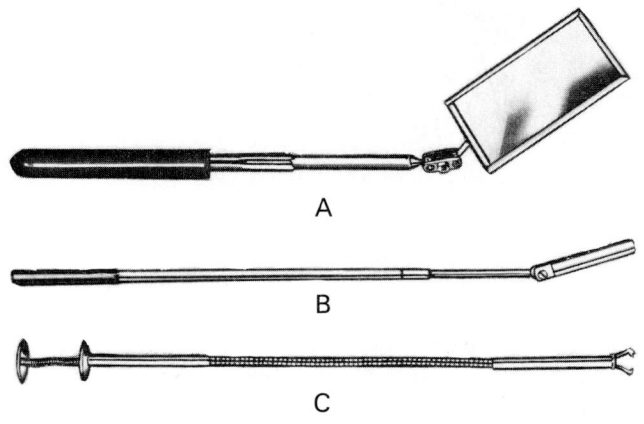

Fig. 3-24. Probe and pickup tools. A — Mirror probe. B — Magnetic pickup tool. C — Finger pickup tool.

A *magnetic pickup tool* is a magnet hinged to the end of a rod. It can usually be shortened or lengthened and swiveled to reach into any area. If a ferrous (iron) metal part is dropped, it will be attracted and stick to the magnet.

A *finger pickup tool* grasps nonmagnetic parts (aluminum, plastic, rubber) that will NOT stick to a magnet.

A *mirror probe* allows you to look around corners or behind parts. Refer to Fig. 3-24. For example, it will reflect an oil leak behind the engine.

PRY BARS

Pry bars (strong steel bars) are helpful during numerous assembly, disassembly, and adjustment operations. For example, they are commonly utilized when adjusting engine belts. They are also used to align heavy parts.

Note! When prying, always be careful NOT to damage any part of the car.

KNOW THESE TERMS

Open end, Box end, Combination wrench, 6-point, 12-point, Line wrench, Drive size, Holding tools, Probe tools.

REVIEW QUESTIONS

1. List and explain four general tool rules.
2. The most-used tools should be kept in the technician's roll-around tool cabinet. True or False?
3. Hammers, screwdrivers, and small delicate tools should be kept together for easy access. True or False?
4. A bolt head is rusted and partially rounded off. Technician A says to use an open end wrench to unscrew the damaged fastener.
   Technician B says that a 6-point box end wrench would grip the damaged bolt head better.
   Who is correct?
   a. Technician A
   b. Technician B
   c. Both A and B
   d. Neither A nor B
5. What are the four socket drive sizes? Explain when each should be used.
6. _____ or _____ screwdrivers would be useful in very tight places, inside a dash glove box for example.
7. Pliers are commonly used in place of wrenches without fastener head damage. True or False?
8. Describe four rules to follow when using hammers.
9. What is the difference between a center punch, starting punch, and aligning punch?
10. A coarse file should be used on _____ materials. A fine cut file should be used on _____ materials.

11. When should you use vise caps?
12. List and explain four vise rules.
13. Which of the following two tools are NOT cleaning tools?
    a. Hand scraper.
    b. Chisel.
    c. Probe.
    d. Hand brush.
14. A _____ _____ allows you to look around corners, as when looking for oil leaks.

15. Pry bars are helpful for assembly, disassembly, and adjustment operations. True or False?

ACTIVITIES FOR CHAPTER 3

1. Collect automotive catalogs and draw up a list of hand tools needed to equip an automotive shop. Try to find the cost of the tools and provide an estimate of what it will cost to purchase the tools.
2. Discuss tool safety with your instructor. Prepare a list of safety regulations for your shop area.

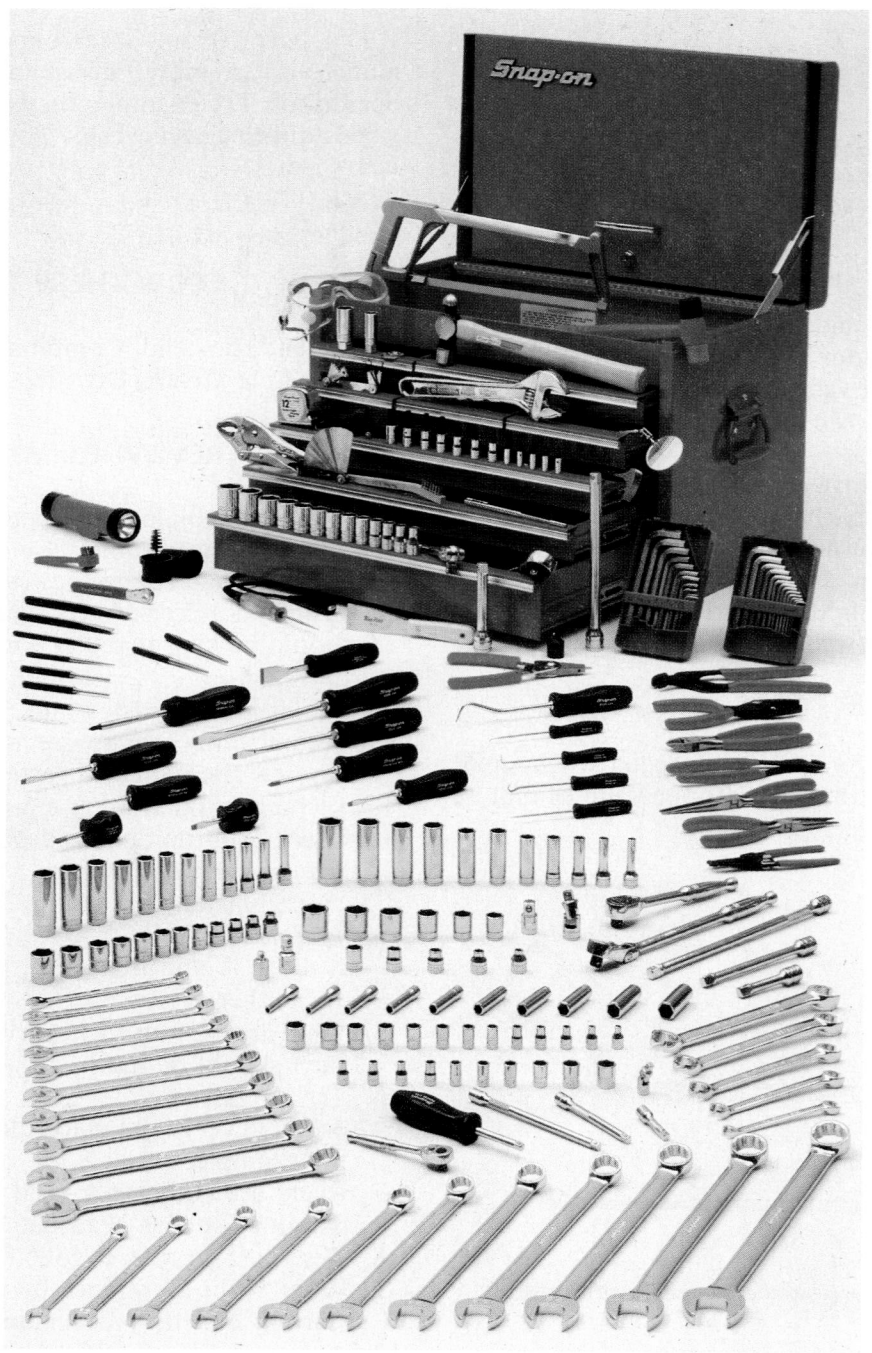

Over time, engine repair technicians build up a large assortment of hand tools and specialty tools so they will always have the right tool for the service or repair at hand. (Snap-On Tool Corp.)

Power Tools and Equipment

After studying this chapter, you will be able to:
- □ List the most commonly used power tools and equipment.
- □ Describe the uses for power tools and equipment.
- □ Compare the advantages of one type of tool over another.
- □ Explain safety rules that pertain to power tools and equipment.

To be a productive mechanic in today's auto shop, you must know when and how to use power tools and equipment. They increase the ease and speed of many repair operations.

Power tools are tools using electricity, compressed air, or hydraulics (liquid confined under pressure). Large shop tools such as floor jacks, parts cleaning tanks, and steam cleaners, are classified as *shop equipment*.

This chapter stresses the importance of properly selecting and using power tools and equipment. They can be very dangerous if misused. Always follow the operating instructions for the particular tool or piece of equipment. If in doubt, ask your instructor for a demonstration.

AIR COMPRESSOR

An *air compressor* is the source of compressed (pressurized) air for the auto shop. Look at Fig. 4-1. An air compressor normally has an electric motor that spins an air pump. The air pump forces air into a large, metal storage tank. Metal air lines feed out from the tank to several locations in the shop. The mechanic can then connect flexible air hoses to the metal lines.

An air compressor turns ON and OFF automatically to maintain a preset pressure in the system.

DANGER! Shop air pressure is usually around 100 to 150 psi (689 to 1 034 kPa). This is enough pressure to severely injure or kill. Respect shop air pressure!

Air hoses

High pressure *air hoses* are connected to the metal lines from the air compressor. Since they are flexible, they allow the mechanic to take a source of air pressure to the vehicle being repaired. Quick-disconnect type couplings are used on air hoses. To connect or disconnect an air hose, slide back the outer fitting sleeve and push or pull on the hose.

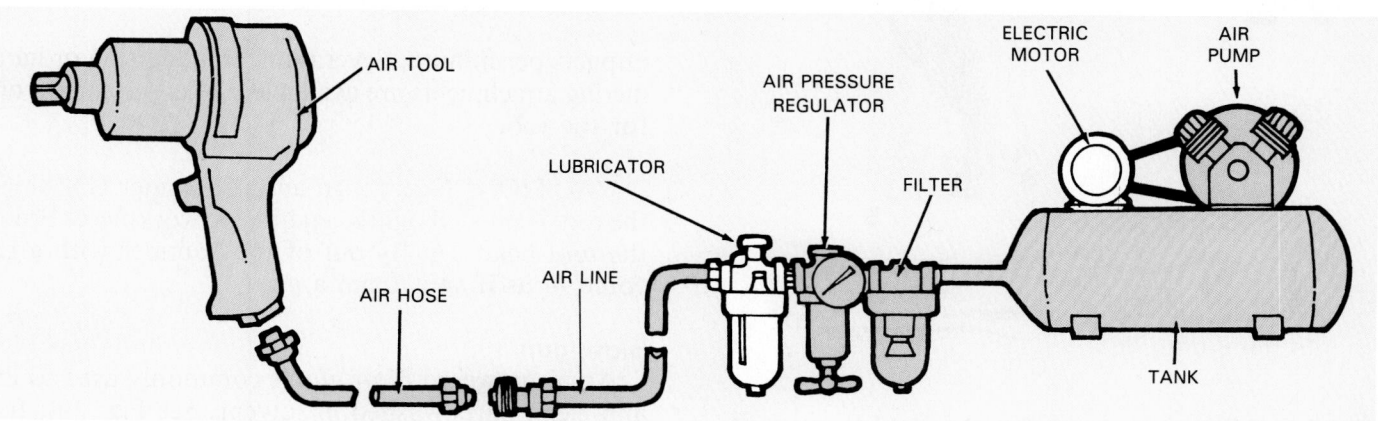

Fig. 4-1. Basic parts of a typical shop air pressure system. Air compressor develops air pressure. Filter removes moisture. Regulator allows mechanic to control system pressure. Metal line and flexible hose carry air to tool. (Florida Dept. of Voc. Ed.)

AIR TOOLS

Air tools, also called *pneumatic tools,* use air pressure for operation. They are labor-saving tools, well worth their cost.

Always lubricate an air tool before use. Squirt a few drops of air tool oil (light oil) into the air inlet fitting. This protects the internal parts of the tool, increasing service life and tool power.

Air wrenches (impact wrenches)

Air wrenches or *impact wrenches* provide a very fast means of installing or removing threaded fasteners. Look at Fig. 4-2A and B. An impact wrench uses compressed air to rotate a driving head. The driving head holds a socket which fits on the fastener head.

A button or switch on the air wrench controls the direction of rotation. In one position, the impact tightens the fastener. The impact loosens the fastener in the other direction.

Impact wrenches come in 3/8, 1/2, and 3/4 in. drive sizes. A 3/8 drive impact is ideal for smaller bolts (sockets between 1/4 and 9/16 in. for example). The 1/2 in. drive is general purpose for medium to large fasteners (head sizes between 1/2 and 1 in.). The 3/4 in. drive impact is for extremely large fasteners and is NOT commonly used in auto service.

CAUTION! Until you become familiar with the operation of an air wrench, be careful not to over-tighten bolts and nuts or leave them too loose. It is easy to strip or break fasteners with an air tool.

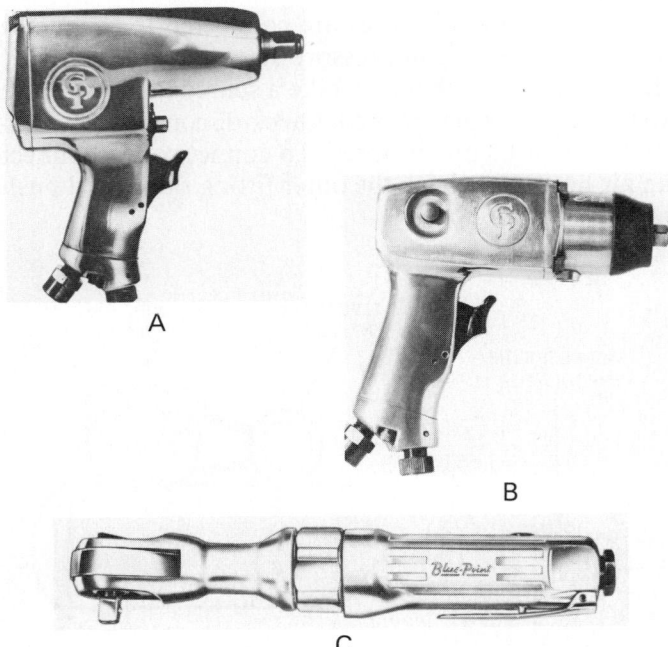

Fig. 4-2. Air wrenches. A — 1/2 in. drive impact wrench. B — 3/8 drive impact wrench. C — 3/8 in. drive air ratchet. (Hennessy Industries, Inc. and Snap-On Tools)

Air ratchet

An *air ratchet* is a special impact type wrench designed for working in tight quarters. Look at Fig. 4-2C. It is very slim and will fit into small areas. For instance, an air ratchet is commonly used when removing water pumps. It will fit between the radiator and engine easily.

An air ratchet normally has a 3/8 in. drive. It does not have very much turning power. Final tightening and initial loosening must be done by hand.

Impact sockets and extensions

Special *impact sockets* and *extensions* must be used with air wrenches. They are thicker and much stronger than conventional sockets and extensions. A conventional socket can be ruined or broken by the hammering blows of an impact wrench.

Special impact sockets and extensions are easily identified. They are usually FLAT BLACK, not chrome.

Air hammer (Chisel)

An *air hammer* or *chisel* is useful during various driving and cutting operations. Look at Fig. 4-3. The air hammer is capable of producing about 1000 to 4000

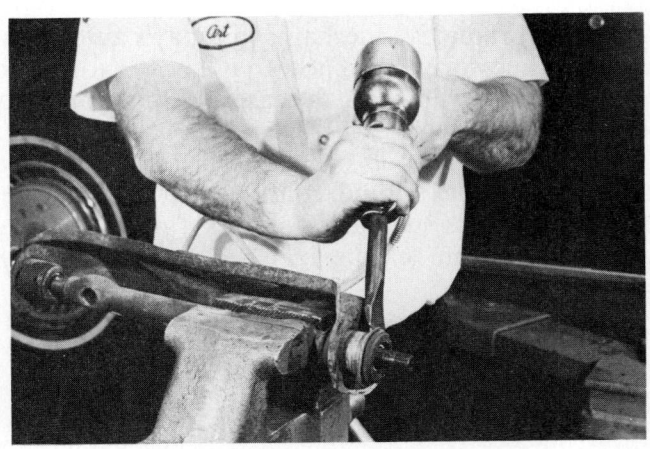

Fig. 4-3. Air hammer is being used to quickly drive bushing out of suspension arm. Wear safety glasses. (Moog)

impacts per minute. Several different cutting or hammering attachments are available. Select the correct one for the job.

CAUTION! Never turn an air hammer ON unless the tool is pressed tightly against the workpiece. If not, the tool head can fly out of the hammer with great force — as if shot from a gun!

Blow gun

An air powered *blow gun* is commonly used to dry and clean parts washed in solvent. See Fig. 4-4. It is also used to blow dust and loose dirt off a part before disassembly.

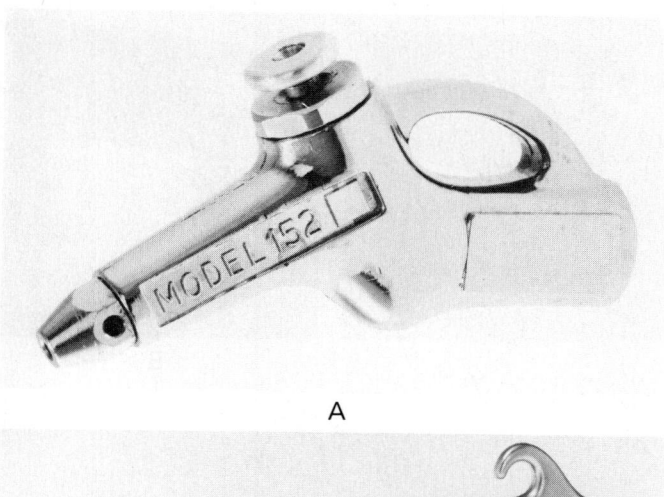

A

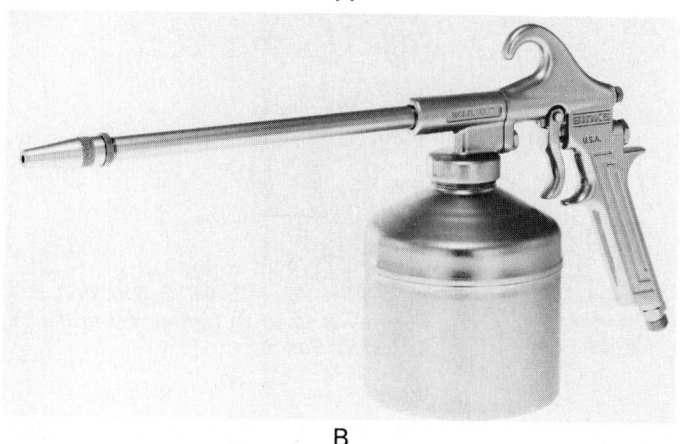

B

Fig. 4-4. A — Blow gun, commonly used to blow parts clean and dry after washing in solvent. B — Solvent gun can be used to wash parts. (Binks)

When using a blow gun, wear eye protection. Direct the blast of air away from yourself and others. Do not blow brake and clutch parts clean. These parts contain asbestos, a cancer causing substance.

Air drill

An *air drill* is excellent for many repairs because of its power output and speed adjustment capabilities. Its power and rotating speed can be set to match the job at hand. Look at Fig. 4-5. With the right attachment, air drills can drill holes, grind, polish, and clean parts.

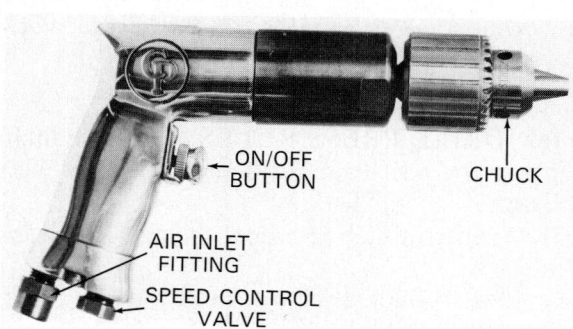

Fig. 4-5. Air drill speed can be adjusted. It is capable of very high turning force. (Hennessy Industries, Inc.)

A *rotary brush,* Fig. 4-6, is used in an air or electric drill for rapid cleaning of parts. It will quickly rub off old gasket material, carbon deposits on engine parts, and rust, with a minimum amount of effort.

CAUTION! Only use a high speed type rotary brush in an air drill. A brush designed for an electric drill may fly apart. To be safe, always adjust an air drill to the SLOWEST ACCEPTABLE SPEED.

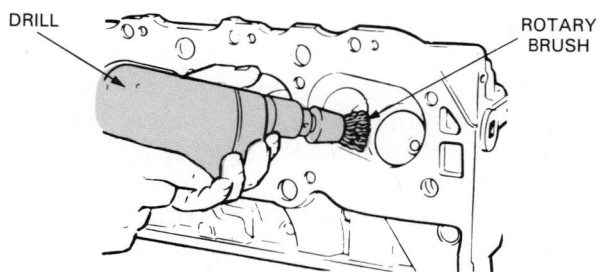

Fig. 4-6. Rotary brush is commonly used in a drill for cleaning off old gaskets or carbon. Wear eye protection!

A *rotary file* or *stone* can be used in either an air drill, electric drill, or an air (die) grinder, Fig. 4-7. It is handy for removing metal burrs and nicks.

Make sure the stone is not turned too fast by the air tool. Normally the speed specifications (maximum allowable rotating speed) will be printed on the file or stone container.

Fig. 4-7. Die grinder with a high speed stone installed. This tool is used for removing burrs and for other smoothing operations. (Robert Bosch)

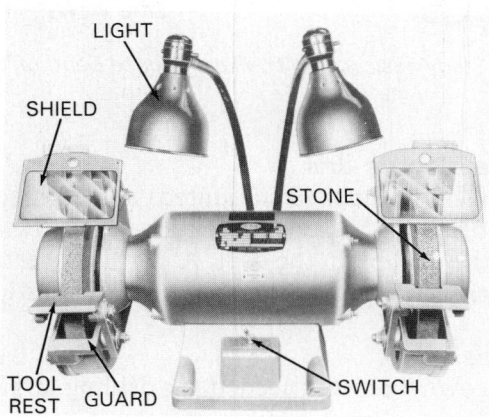

Fig. 4-8. Bench grinder stone is used to sharpen tools. Brush can be used to clean and polish small parts. Keep shields, tool rests, and guards in place. (Sioux Tools)

BENCH GRINDER

A *bench grinder,* Fig. 4-8, can be used for grinding, cleaning, or polishing operations. The hard grinding wheel is used for sharpening or deburring. The soft wire wheel is for cleaning and polishing.

A few BENCH GRINDER RULES to follow are:

1. Wear eye protection and keep your hands away from the stone and brush.
2. Keep the tool rest adjusted close to the stone and brush. If the rest is NOT up close, the part can catch in the grinder.
3. Do NOT use the wire wheel to clean soft metal parts (aluminum pistons or brass bushings, for example). The rubbing, abrasive action of the wheel can remove metal, scuff, and ruin the part. Use a solvent and a dull hand scraper on soft metal parts that could be damaged.
4. Make sure the grinder shields are in place.

DRILLS

Twist drills or *drill bits* are used to drill holes in metal and plastic parts. They fit into either an electric or air powered drill, Fig. 4-9. Drill bits are commonly made of either carbon steel or high speed steel. High speed steel is better because of its resistance to heat. It will not lose its hardness when slightly overheated.

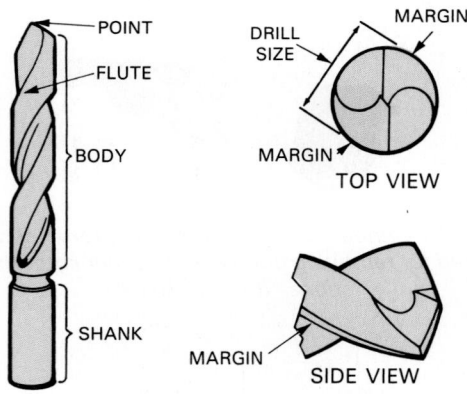

Fig. 4-9. Study basic parts of drill bit. (Florida Dept. of Voc. Ed.)

Portable electric drill

A drill bit is chucked (mounted) and rotated by an *electric drill,* Fig. 4-10. A special *key* must be used to tighten the drill bit in the drill. A portable electric drill will work fine on most small drilling operations.

Drill press

A large *drill press* is needed for drilling large holes, deep holes, or a great number of holes in several parts, Fig. 4-11. The drill press handle allows the bit to be pressed into the work with increased force. Also, the drill chuck will accept very large bits.

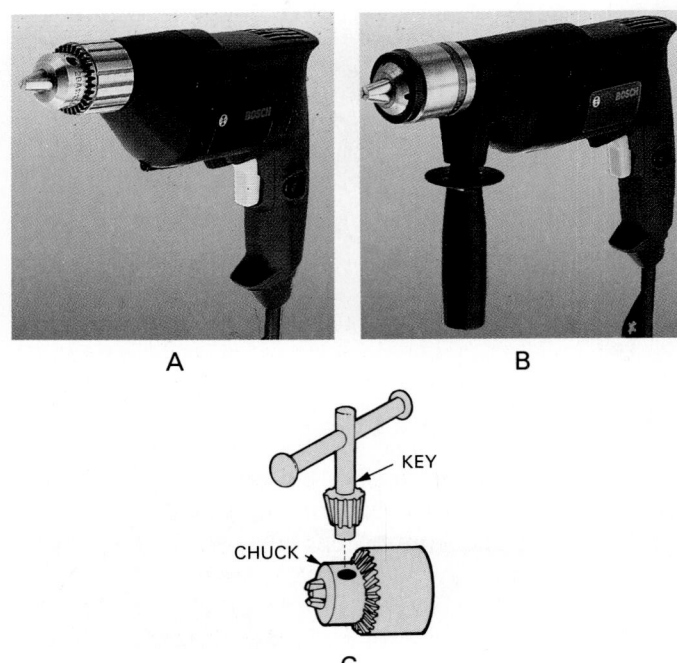

Fig. 4-10. Portable electric drills. A — Small, 3/8 in. drill. B — Larger, 1/2 in. drill. C — Key is used to tighten bit in chuck. (Robert Bosch)

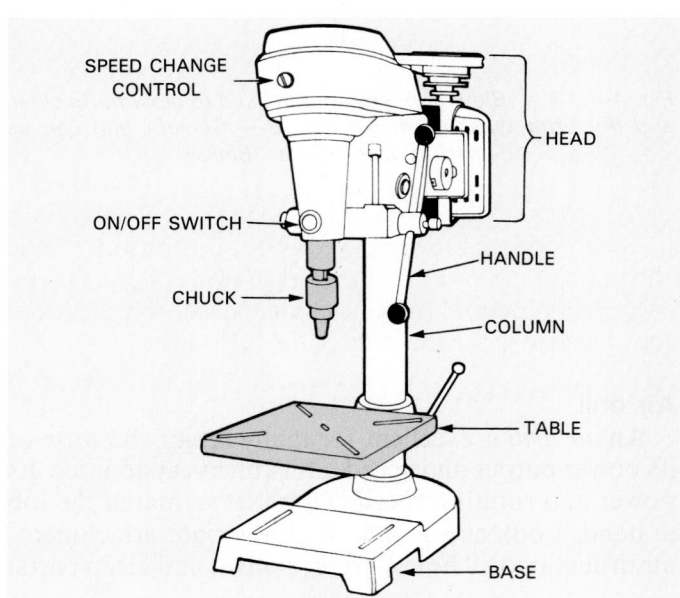

Fig. 4-11. Note parts of drill press. It is for drilling deep or large holes when part will fit on table. (Florida Dept. of Voc. Ed.)

A few DRILL PRESS RULES to follow include:

1. Secure the part to be drilled in a vise or with C-clamps.
2. Use a center punch to indent the part and start the hole.
3. Remove the key before turning on the drill.
4. To prevent possible injury, release drilling pressure right before the bit breaks through the bottom of the part. A drill bit tends to catch when breaking

through. This can cause the drill or part to rotate dangerously.

5. Oil the bit as needed.

TIRE CHANGER

A *tire changer* is a common piece of shop equipment used to remove and replace tires on wheels. Some are hand-operated and others use air pressure. Do not attempt to operate a tire changer without proper supervision. Follow the directions provided with the changer.

BUMPER LIFTS

Bumper lifts or *jacks,* either air or manually powered, are used to raise one end of a car. Lifting pads fit under the front or rear bumper. See Fig. 4-12A.

When raising the front of a car, place the transmission in neutral and release the parking brake. This will let the vehicle roll and will prevent the car from pulling off the lift.

After raising, secure on jack stands. Place in park. Apply the emergency brake and block the wheels.

FLOOR JACKS

A *floor jack* is also used to raise either the front, sides, or rear of a vehicle. Look at Fig. 4-12B.

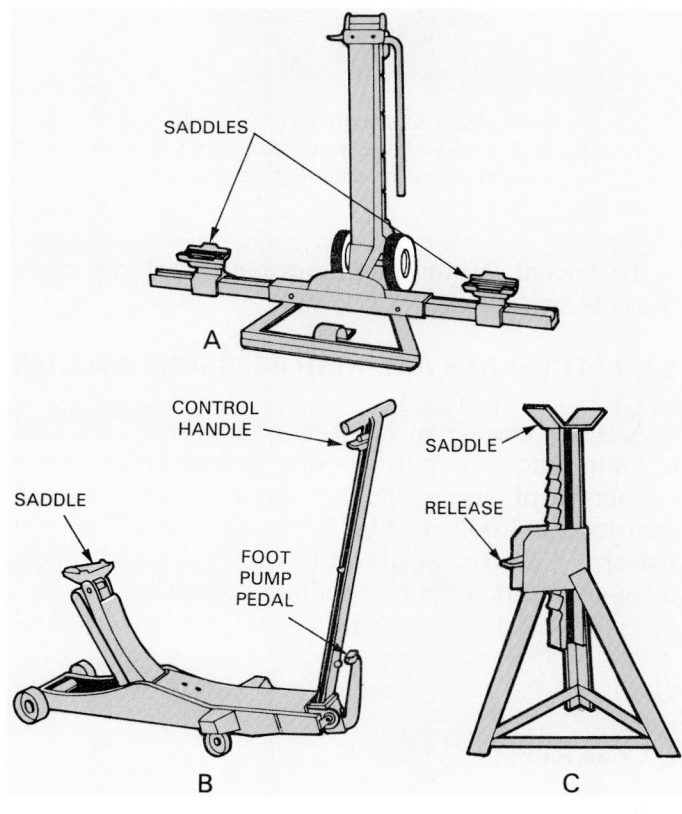

Fig. 4-12. Vehicle lifting equipment A — Bumper lift. B — Floor jack is for raising car only. C — Jack stands are needed before working under car. (Florida Dept. of Voc. Ed.)

To avoid vehicle damage, place the jack saddle under a solid part of the car (frame, suspension arm, rear axle). If you are NOT careful, it is very easy to smash an oil pan, muffler, floor pan, or other sheet metal part.

As with a bumper jack, the vehicle should be free to roll while being raised. After raising, place the vehicle on jack stands. Block wheels and place in park.

Normally, to raise the vehicle, you must turn the jack handle or knob clockwise and pump the handle. To lower, turn the pressure relief valve counterclockwise slowly.

JACK STANDS

Jack stands support a vehicle during repair. After raising it with a jack, place stands under the vehicle, Fig. 14-12C. It is NOT SAFE to work under vehicles held by a floor jack or bumper lift.

Note! The next chapter details the use of lifts, jacks, and jack stands.

TRANSMISSION JACK

Special *transmission jacks* are designed for removing and installing transmissions. One type is similar to a floor jack. However, the saddle is enlarged to fit the bottom of a transmission.

Another type of transmission jack is used when the car is raised on a vehicle lift, Fig. 4-13. It has a long post which can reach high into the air to support the transmission.

ENGINE CRANE

A portable *engine crane* is used to remove and install engines, Fig. 4-14. It has a hydraulic hand jack

Fig. 4-13. Transmission jack is designed for removing, transporting, and installing transmissions when using an overhead lift. Hydraulic lift is foot operated and raises to height of 72 in. (OTC Div. of SPX Corp.)

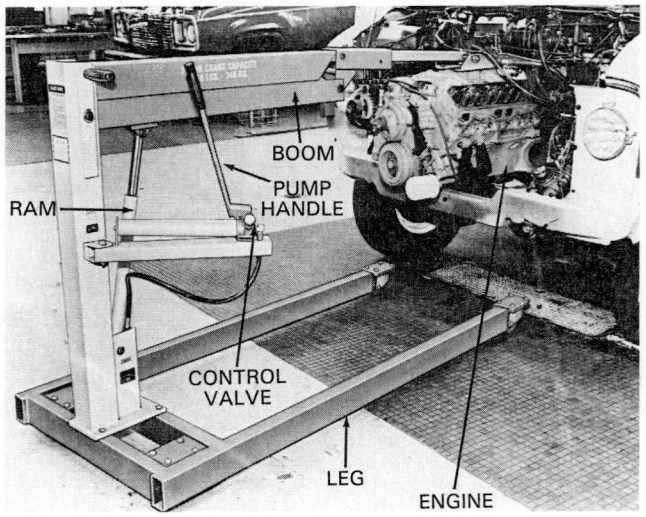

Fig. 4-14. Hydraulic engine crane can be used to lift heavy objects such as engines, transmissions, transaxles, rear axle assemblies.

for raising and a pressure release valve for lowering. An engine crane is also handy for lifting heavy engine parts (intake manifolds, cylinder heads), transmissions, and transaxles.

HYDRAULIC PRESS

A *hydraulic press* is used to install or remove gears, pulleys, bearings, seals, and other parts requiring high pushing force. One is shown in Fig. 4-15.

A hydraulic press uses a hand jack. By pumping the jack, press-fit parts can be pushed apart or together. A valve releases pressure.

NOTE! A hydraulic press can exert TONS OF FORCE. Wear face protection and use recommended procedures.

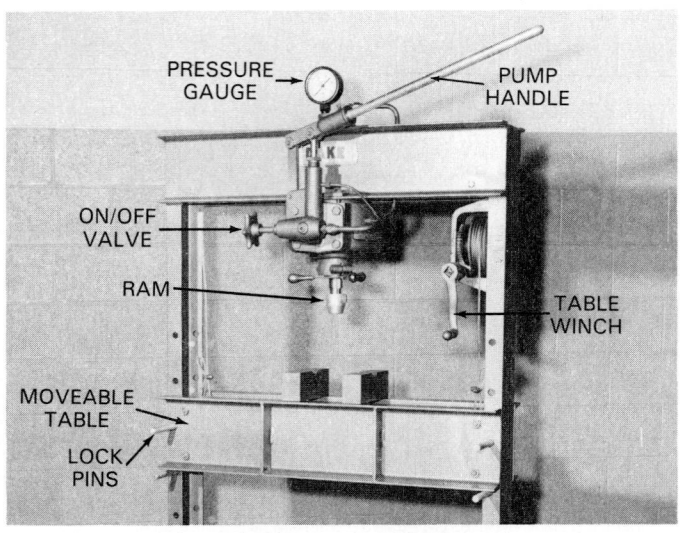

Fig. 4-15. Hydraulic press is needed for numerous pressing operations. It is commonly used to remove and install bearings, bushings, seals, and other pressed-on parts. Note! Double-check lock pins before using press. If not installed, cables in unit could snap. (Dake Corp.)

ARBOR PRESS

An *arbor press* performs the same function as a hydraulic press but at lower pressures. It is a hand-operated, mechanical press for smaller jobs.

ENGINE STAND

An *engine stand* is used to hold an engine while it is overhauled (rebuilt) or repaired. The engine bolts to the stand. For convenience, the engine can usually be rotated and held in different positions.

COLD SOLVENT TANK

A *cold solvent tank,* Fig. 4-16, removes grease and oil from parts. After removing all old gaskets and scraping off excess grease, you can scrub the parts clean

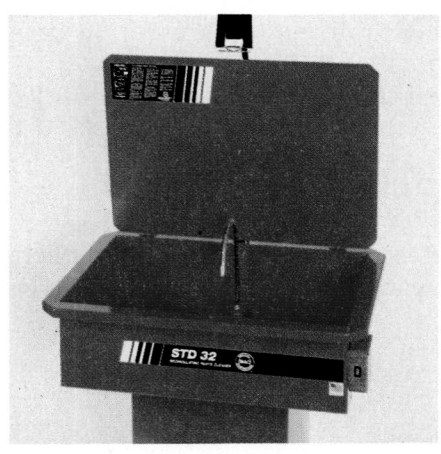

Fig. 4-16. Cold solvent tank is for removing oil and light grease from parts. Unit sprays filtered solvent on parts. Rub parts with brush for rapid cleaning. (Build-All)

in the solvent. A blow gun is normally used to remove the solvent.

STEAM CLEANER AND HIGH PRESSURE WASHER

A *steam cleaner* or *high pressure washer* are used to remove heavy deposits of dirt, grease, and oil from the outside of large assemblies (engines, transmissions, transaxles). Look at Fig. 4-17. For environmental reasons, it is often advisable to wire brush and collect oil-soaked dirt before steaming or washing.

DANGER! A steam cleaner operates at relatively high pressures and temperatures. Follow your safety rules and specific operating instructions.

OXYACETYLENE TORCH

An *oxyacetylene torch* outfit can be used to cut, bend, and weld or braze (join) metal parts, Fig. 4-18. Its rapid cutting action is extremely beneficial. For ex-

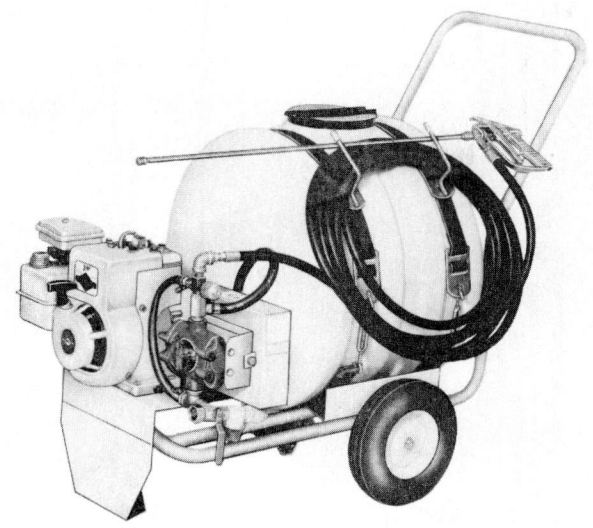

Fig. 4-17. High pressure washer will remove greasy buildup on outside of assemblies before teardown. (Sioux Tools)

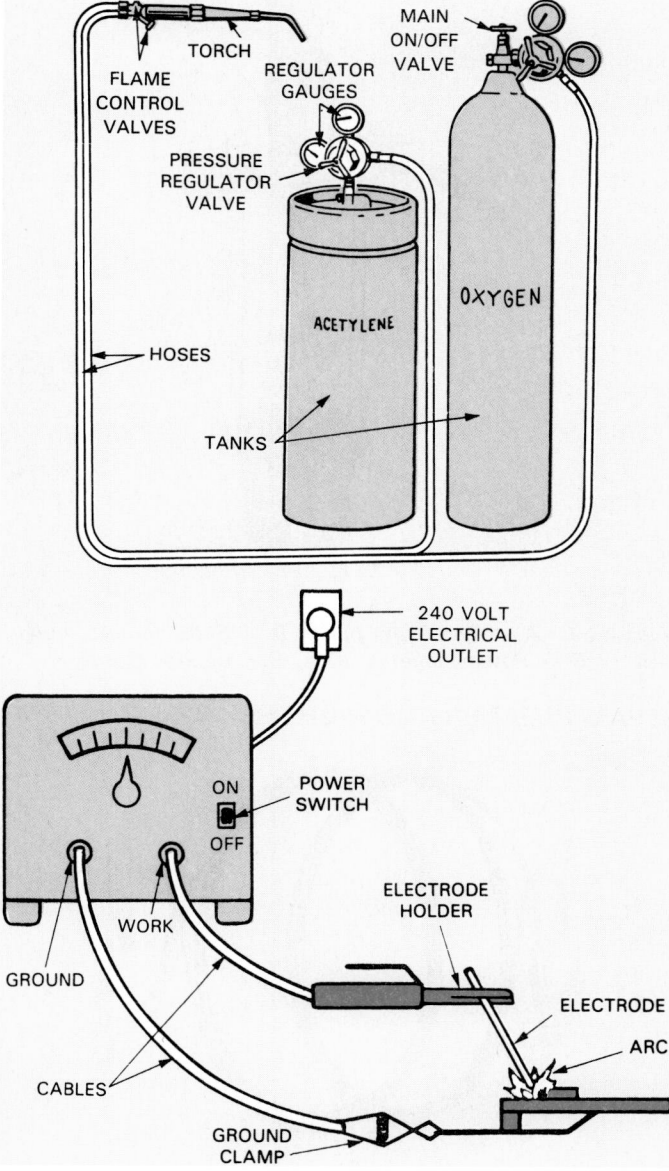

Fig. 4-18. Top. Oxyacetylene outfit can be used for cutting or welding metal. Bottom. Study basic parts of arc welder. (Sun)

ample, a cutting torch is often used to remove old, deteriorated exhaust systems. Tremendous heat is produced by burning acetylene gas and oxygen.

ARC WELDER

An *arc welder* is also used to weld metal parts together, Fig. 4-18. It uses high electric current and the resulting electric arc to produce welding heat.

If at all possible, you should take a welding course in school. This will help prepare you for auto mechanics. DO NOT attempt to weld or cut until properly trained.

SOLDERING GUN

A *soldering gun* or *iron* is normally used to solder (join) wires, Fig. 4-19. An electric current heats the tip of the gun. Then, the hot gun tip can be used to heat the wires and melt the solder. When the solder solidifies (hardens), a strong, solid connection is produced.

BATTERY CHARGER

A *battery charger* is used to recharge (energize) a discharged (de-energized) car battery. It forces current back through the battery. Normally, the red charger lead connects to the battery positive (+) terminal. The black charger lead connects to the negative (–) battery terminal.

WARNING! Always connect the battery charger leads to the battery BEFORE turning the charger ON. This will prevent sparks that could ignite any battery gas. The gases around the top of a battery can EXPLODE violently.

DROP LIGHT

A *drop light,* Fig. 4-20, provides a portable source of illumination (light). The light can be taken to the repair area under the vehicle, hood, or engine.

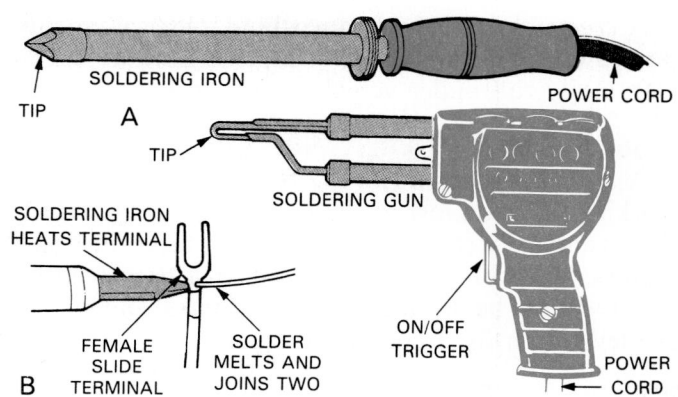

Fig. 4-19. A — Soldering iron and soldering gun. B — Soldering iron or gun produces enough heat to melt solder for joining wires and small metal terminals. (Florida Dept. of Voc. Ed.)

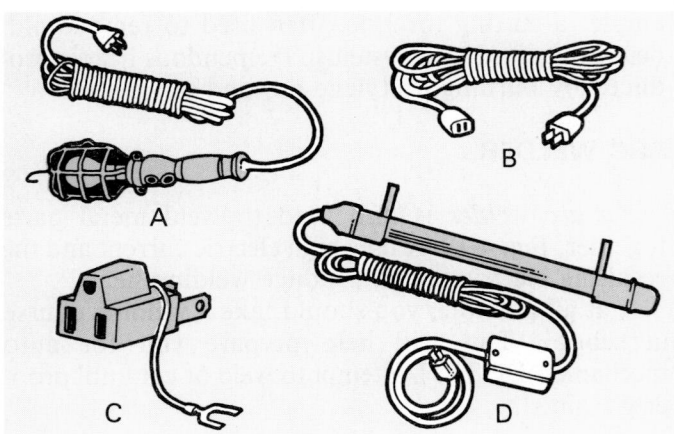

Fig. 4-20. A — Drop light. B — Drop or extension cord. C — Three-prong adapter with ground terminal and ground wire for safety. D — Fluorescent drop light. (Florida Dept. of Voc. Ed.)

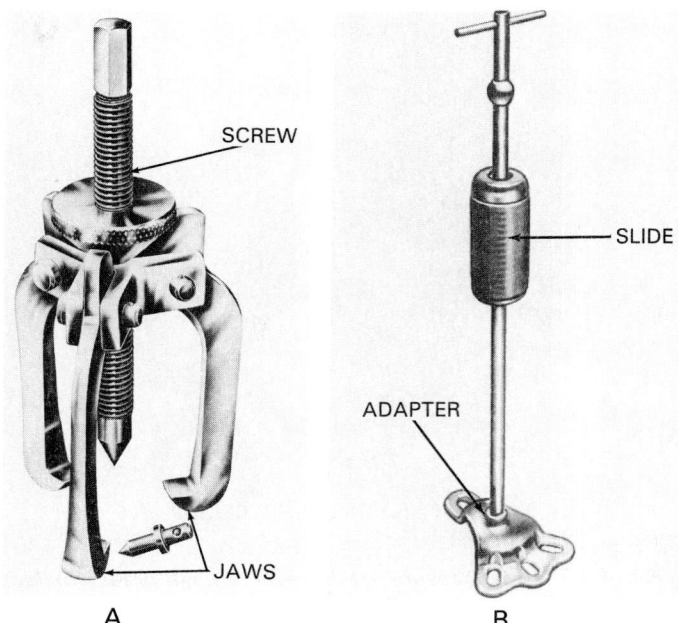

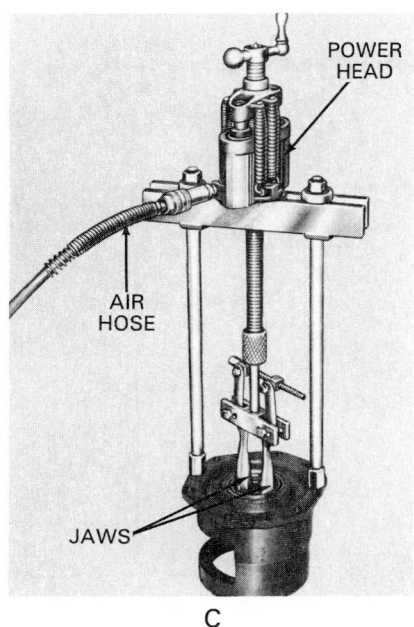

Fig. 4-21. A — Three-jaw puller. B — Slide hammer puller. C — Power puller. (OTC Div. of SPX Corp.

WHEEL PULLERS

Wheel pullers are needed to remove seals, gears, pulleys, steering wheels, axles, and other pressed-on parts. A few puller types are pictured in Fig. 4-21. Special pulling operations will be covered in later chapters.

DANGER! Pullers can exert TONS OF FORCE. They must be used properly to prevent injury or part damage. Wear eye protection!

JUMPER CABLES

Jumper cables are used to start engines with a dead (discharged) battery. The cables can be connected between the dead battery and another battery. This will let you crank and start the vehicle. See Fig. 4-22.

When connecting jumper cables, connect positive to positive and negative to negative. Also, keep sparks away from the dead battery. Connect the negative cable to the vehicle frame so that any sparks will not occur near the battery.

CREEPER

A *creeper* is useful when working under a car supported on jack stands, Fig. 4-23A. It lets the technician easily roll under vehicles without getting dirty.

Stool creeper

A *stool creeper* allows the technician to sit while working on parts low to the ground. See Fig. 4-23B. For example, a stool creeper is often used on brake repairs. The brake parts and tools can be placed on the creeper. The service technician can sit and still be eye level with the brake assembly.

ROLL-AROUND CART

A larger *roll-around cart* or table is handy for taking a number of tools to the job. One is pictured in

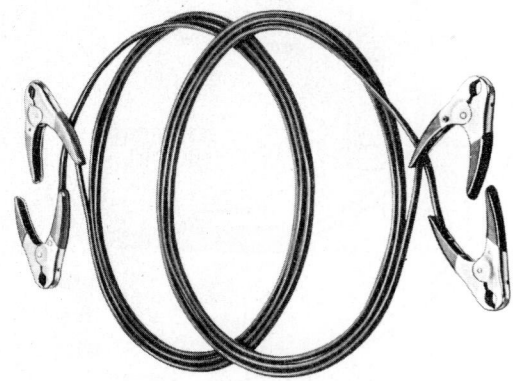

Fig. 4-22. Jumper cables are for emergency starting. Connect red lead to positive terminal of both batteries. Black is for negative and ground. (Snap-On Tools)

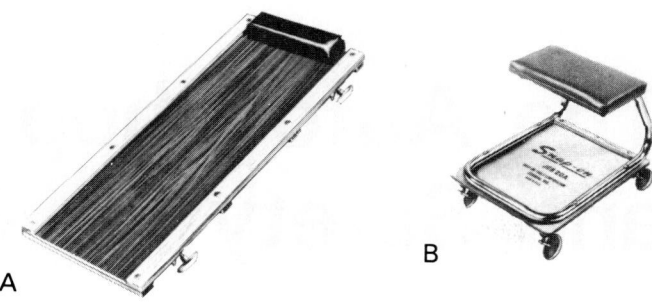

A B

Fig. 4-23. A — Creeper is for working under car. B — Stool creeper is commonly used during brake and suspension repairs. You can sit on the stool and store tools on bottom. (Snap-On Tools)

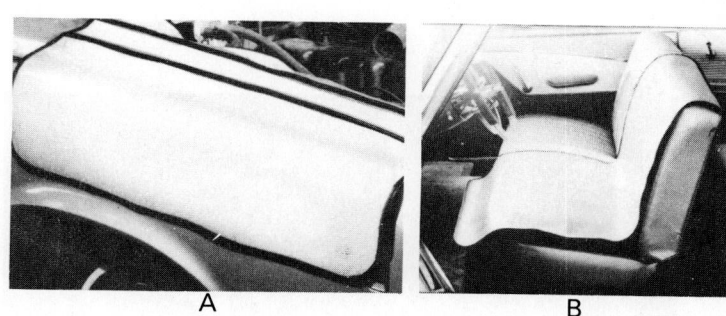

A B

Fig. 4-25. Always take good care of customer's car. A — Fender covers protect paint from nicks and dents. B — Seat cover protects upholstery from dirty work clothes. (Snap-On Tools)

Fig. 4-24. Since the technician is working on a car raised on a lift, the cart positions all of the needed tools within "hand's reach." This saves time and effort.

FENDER COVERS

Fender covers are placed over fenders, upper grille, or other body sections to protect them. They protect the finish from nicks and scratches. See Fig. 4-25A. Never lay your tools on a painted surface. Scratches could result.

Seat covers

Seat covers are placed over seats to protect them from dirt, oil, and grease that might be on your

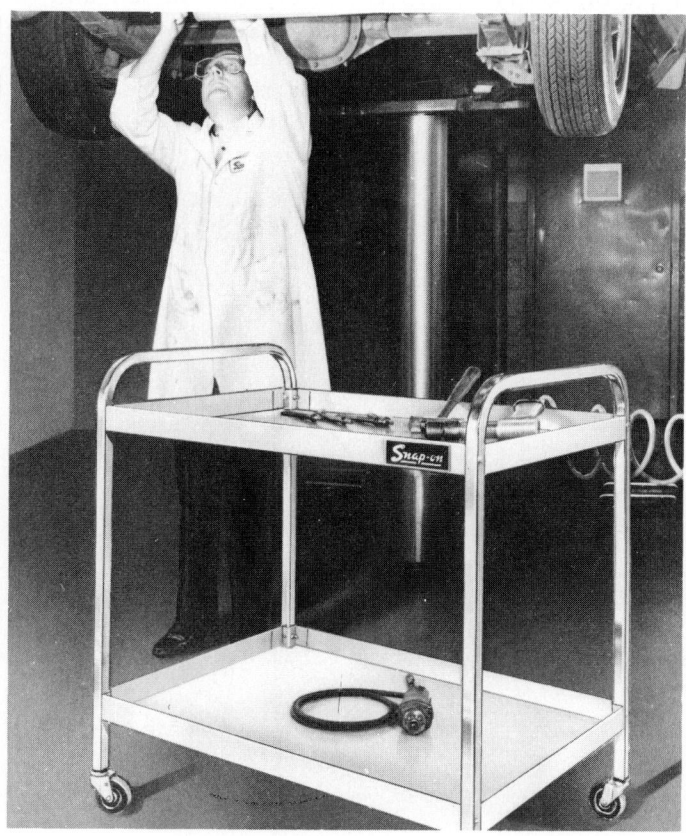

Fig. 4-24. Roll-around cart allows you to take several tools to car. This saves several trips to tool box.

workclothes. The covers are normally used while driving the vehicle in and out of the shop or while working in the passenger compartment. Look at Fig. 4-25B.

KNOW THESE TERMS

Air compressor, Air tool, Impact socket, Blow gun, Rotary brush, Engine crane, Hydraulic press, Solvent tank, Battery charger, Drop light, Wheel puller, Jumper cables, Creeper, Fender cover.

REVIEW QUESTIONS

1. Power tools use _____, _____ _____, or _____ as sources of energy.
2. Shop air pressure is only about 25 psi or 172 kPa and cannot cause injuries. True or False?
3. Which of the following is NOT a commonly used air tool?
   a. Impact wrench.   c. Air chisel.
   b. Air ratchet.   d. Air saw.
4. A _____ _____ is used to blow dirt off parts and to dry parts after cleaning.
5. A rotary brush is used in an electric or air drill for rapid cleaning of parts. True or False?
6. List four important rules for a bench grinder.
7. List five important rules for a drill press.
8. Use this tool to support the car while working under the car.
   a. Floor jack.   c. Transmission jack.
   b. Jack stands.   d. Bumper jack.
9. Explain the use of a solvent tank.
10. What are wheel pullers for?

ACTIVITIES FOR CHAPTER 4

1. Using an automotive tool catalog, develop a list of power tools needed to equip the school's automotive repair shop. Find prices and add up the cost.
2. Research safety literature on power equipment used in an automotive repair facility.
   a. Develop a bibliography of resources for safe use of power equipment.
   b. Develop a list of safety rules for their use.

The Auto Shop and Safety

After studying this chapter, you will be able to:
- Describe the typical layout and sections of an auto shop.
- List the types of accidents that can occur in an auto shop.
- Explain how to prevent auto shop accident.
- Describe general safety rules for the auto shop.

An auto shop can be a very safe and enjoyable place to work. However, if basic safety rules are NOT followed, an auto shop can be very dangerous!

Every year, thousands of technicians are injured or killed on the job. Most of these accidents resulted from a broken safety rule. The injured persons learned to respect safety rules the hard way — by experiencing a painful injury. You must learn to respect safety rules the easy way — by studying and following the safety rules given in this book.

Note! Specific safety rules on hand tools, power tools, equipment, and special operations are given elsewhere in the text. It is much easier to understand and remember these rules when they are covered fully.

While working, constantly think of safety. Look for unsafe work habits, unsafe equipment, and other potentials for accidents. See Fig. 5-1.

When working in an auto shop, you must constantly remember that you are surrounded by other students. This makes it even more important that you concentrate on safety to prevent injury to yourself and to others in the shop.

Remember! Safety is your responsibility. Only you can use correct repair methods to prevent injuries.

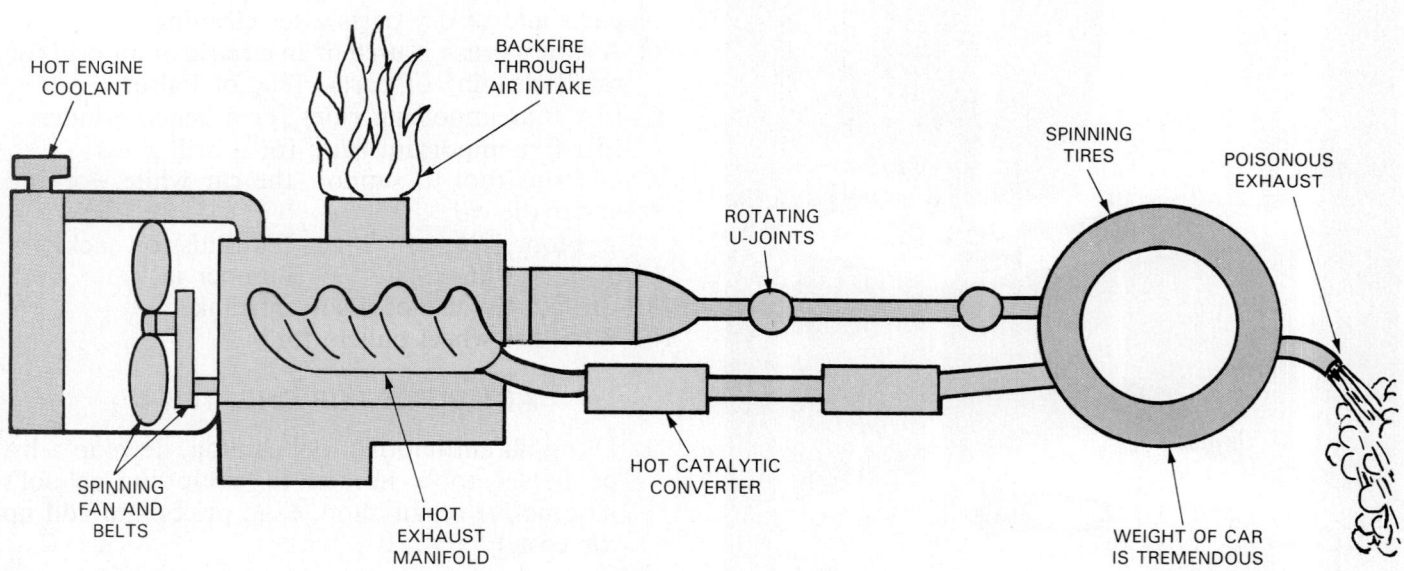

Fig. 5-1. An auto shop has the potential to be very dangerous. Note just a few of the dangers present around an automobile.

AUTO SHOP AREAS

There are several different areas in an auto shop. You must know their basic names and the rules that apply to each.

The auto shop includes the following work areas:
1. SHOP REPAIR AREA.
   a. WORK STALL.
   b. GREASE RACK (LIFT STALL).
   c. FRONT END RACK (ALIGNMENT RACK).
   d. OUTSIDE WORK AREA.
2. TOOL ROOM.
3. SHOP CLASSROOM.
4. LOCKER ROOM (DRESSING ROOM).

Shop repair area

The *shop repair area* includes any location in the shop where repair operations are performed. It normally includes every area EXCEPT the classroom, locker room, and tool room. It is important that you learn your shop layout and organization to improve work efficiency and safety.

Shop stall

A *shop stall* is a small work area where a car can be pulled into the shop for repairs. Sometimes each stall is numbered and marked off with lines painted on the floor.

Grease rack (lift)

The *grease rack* contains a lift for raising a car into the air. Refer to Fig. 5-2. It is handy for working under the car (draining oil, greasing front end parts, or repairing exhaust system).

Remember these LIFT SAFETY RULES:

1. Obtain an instructor demonstration and get permission before using the lift.
2. Center vehicle on the lift, as described in a service manual, Fig. 5-3. Raise vehicle slowly!
3. Check ceiling clearance before raising trucks and campers. Make sure the vehicle roof does not hit overhead pipes, lights, or the ceiling.
4. Make sure the lift's safety catch is engaged. Do not walk under the lift without the catch locked into position, Fig. 5-4.

Front end rack (alignment rack)

The *front end rack* or *alignment rack* is another specialized stall used to work on a car's steering and suspension systems. One is shown in Fig. 5-5. It may contain a special tool board and equipment used when replacing worn suspension parts, steering parts, and for adjusting wheel alignment.

When using an alignment rack, the car should be pulled on the rack slowly and carefully. Someone should GUIDE THE DRIVER and help keep the tires centered on the rack. As with other complicated and

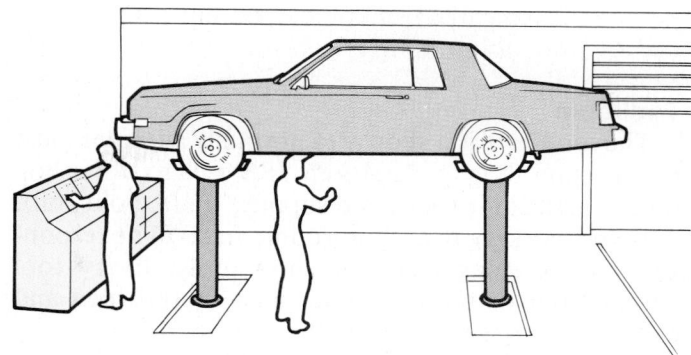

Fig. 5-2. Grease rack or lift is handy for many repairs on parts under car. It is commonly used when changing oil, greasing car, and exhaust system repairs.

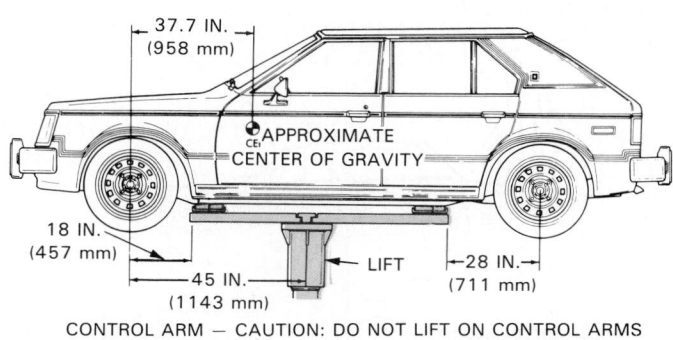

LIFT POINTS ON FRAME RAILS
■ TWIN POST LIFT POINTS
▨ FRAME CONTACT OR FLOOR JACK
▧ DRIVE ON HOIST
   SCISSORS JACK (EMERGENCY) LOCATIONS

Fig. 5-3. Follow service manual directions when raising car on lift. Note specific lifting instructions for this car. (Chrysler)

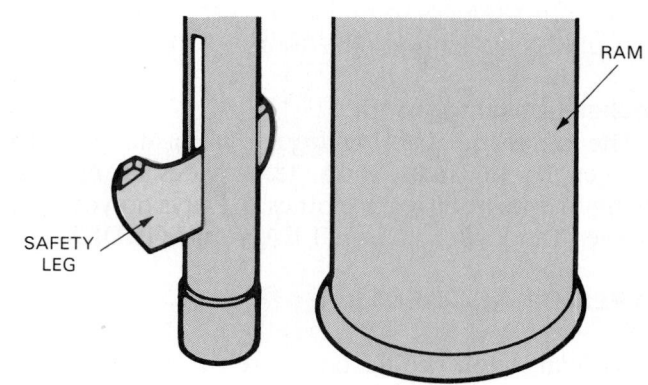

Fig. 5-4. Most lifts have a safety catch. It must be engaged before working under car. (Ford)

potentially dangerous equipment, obtain a full instructor demonstration before working.

Toolroom

The *toolroom* is a shop area normally adjacent (next to) the main shop or classroom. It is used to store shop tools, small equipment, and supplies (nuts, bolts, oil).

When working in the toolroom, you will be responsible for keeping track of shop tools. Every tool checked out of the toolroom must be recorded and called in before the end of the class period.

Normally, the tools will hang on the walls of the toolroom for easy access. Each tool will have a painted silhouette (outline) which indicates where each tool is kept, Fig. 5-6.

Your instructor will detail specific tool room policies and procedures.

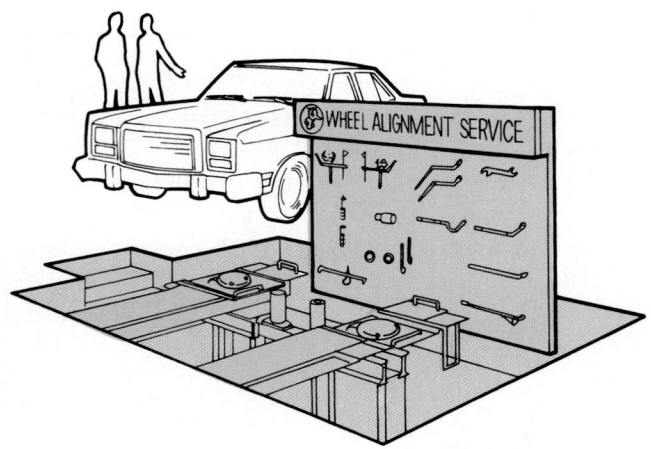

Fig. 5-5. A front end rack or wheel alignment rack is used in most garages. It is needed for steering and front end repairs.

Outside work area

Some auto shop facilities have an *outside work area* adjacent to the garage overhead doors. In good weather, this area can be used for auto repairs.

Always raise the shop doors all the way and pull cars through the doors very slowly. Check the height of trucks and campers to make sure that they will clear (top of vehicle will not hit doors).

Locker (dressing) room

The *locker room* or *dressing room* is usually located adjacent to the main shop. It provides an area for changing into your work clothes. Always do your part to keep the locker room CLEAN and ORDERLY.

TYPES OF ACCIDENTS

Basically, you should be aware of and try to prevent six kinds of accidents.
1. FIRES
2. EXPLOSIONS
3. ASPHYXIATION (airborne poisons)
4. CHEMICAL BURNS
5. ELECTRIC SHOCK
6. PHYSICAL INJURIES

ATTENTION! If an accident or injury ever occurs in the shop, notify your instructor immediately. Use common sense on deciding to get a fire extinguisher or to take other action.

Fires

Fires are terrible accidents capable of causing instant and permanent scar tissue. There are numerous combustible substances (gasoline, oily rags, paints, thinners) found in an auto shop. Any of these flammables are capable of producing a fire.

Gasoline is, by far, the most dangerous and often underestimated flammable in an auto shop. Gasoline has astonishing potential for causing a tremendous fire. Just a cup full of gasoline can instantly engulf a car in flames.

A few GASOLINE SAFETY RULES include:
1. Store gasoline and other flammables in approved, sealed containers.
2. When disconnecting a vehicle's fuel line or hose, wrap a shop rag around the fitting to keep fuel from squirting or leaking.
3. Disconnect the battery before working on a fuel system.
4. Wipe up gasoline spills immediately. Do not place quick dry (oil absorbent) on gasoline because the absorbent will become highly flammable.
5. Keep any source of heat away from the parts of a fuel system.
6. Never use gasoline as a cleaning solvent.

Oily rags can also start fires. Soiled rags should be stored in an approved *safety can* (can with lid).

Paints, thinners, and other combustible materials should be stored in a fire cabinet. Also, never set flammables near a source of sparks (grinder), flame (welder or water heater), or heat (furnace for example).

Note the location of all fire extinguishers in your shop. A few seconds time can be a "life time" during a fire!

Electrical fires can result when a "hot wire" (wire carrying current to component) touches ground (vehicle frame or body). The wire can begin to heat up, melt the insulation, and burn. Then, other wires can do the same. Dozens of wires could burn up in a matter of seconds.

To prevent electrical fires, always disconnect the battery when told to do so in a service manual.

Explosions

Several types of explosions are possible in an auto shop. You should be aware of these sources of sudden death and injury.

Car batteries can explode! Hydrogen gas can surround the top of car batteries being charged or

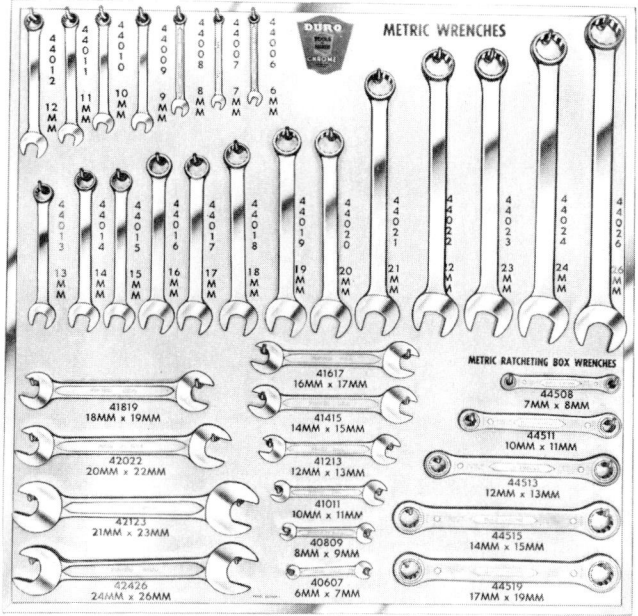

Fig. 5-6. Always keep all shop tools clean and organized. Make sure you replace every tool in its correct storage location. (Duro Tools)

discharged (used). This gas is highly explosive. The slightest spark or flame can ignite and cause the battery to explode. Chunks of battery case and acid can blow into your eyes and face. Blindness, facial cuts, acid burns, and scars can result, Fig. 5-7.

Fuel tanks can explode, even seemingly empty ones! A drained fuel tank can still contain fuel gum and varnish. When this gum is heated and melts, it can emit vapors that may ignite.

Keep sparks and heat away from fuel tanks. When a fuel tank explodes, one side will usually blow out. Then, the tank will shoot across the shop as if shot out of a cannon. You or other workers could be killed or seriously injured.

Various other sources can cause shop explosions. For example, special sodium-filled engine valves, welding tanks, and propane-filled bottles can explode if mishandled. These hazards will be discussed in later chapters.

Asphyxiation

Asphyxiation is caused by breathing toxic or poisonous substances in the air. Mild cases of asphyxiation will cause dizziness, headaches, and vomiting. Severe asphyxiation can cause death.

The most dangerous source of asphyxiation in an auto shop is an automobile engine. An engine's EXHAUST GASES ARE DEADLY POISON. As shown in Fig. 5-8, connect a shop vacuum or suction hose to the tailpipe of any vehicle being operated in the shop. Also, make sure the exhaust system is turned ON.

Discussed in related chapters, other shop substances are harmful if inhaled. A few of these harmful substances include *asbestos* (brake lining dust, clutch disc dust) and paint spray.

Respirators (filter masks) should be worn when working around any kind off airborne impurities. Refer to Fig. 5-7D.

Chemical burns

Various solvents (parts cleaners), battery acid, and other shop substances can cause *chemical burns* to the skin. Always read the directions on chemicals.

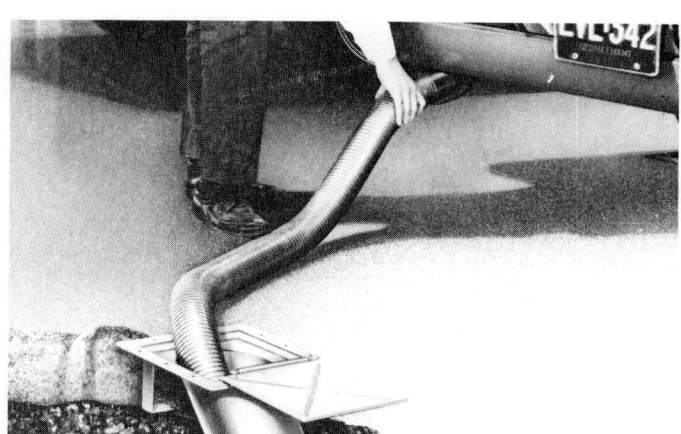

Fig. 5-8. Place an exhaust hose over tailpipe of any car running in enclosed shop. This will prevent shop from filling with poisonous fumes. (Kent-Moore)

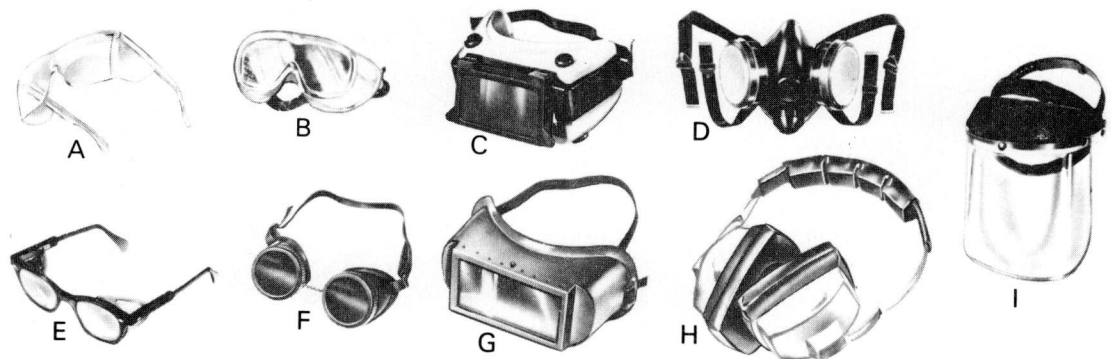

Fig. 5-7. Wear approved eye and face protection when needed. A—Safety glasses. B—Goggles. C—Welding goggles. D—Respirator. E—Safety glasses. F, G—Welding goggles. H—Noise mufflers. I—Face shield. (Snap-On Tools)

Carburetor cleaner (decarbonizing types) for example, is super powerful and can severly burn your hands in a matter of seconds. Wear rubber gloves when using carburetor cleaner. If a skin burn occurs, follow label directions.

Electric shock

Electric shock can occur when using improperly grounded electric power tools. Never use an electric tool unless it has a functional GROUND PRONG (third, round prong on plug socket). This prevents current from accidentally passing through your body. Also, never use an electric tool on a wet shop floor.

DANGER! Some late model cars have heated windshields. The alternator is designed to output over 100 volts AC to quickly warm the windshield glass. This is enough voltage to possibly cause electrocution. Work carefully around this high voltage!

Physical injury

Physical injuries (cuts, broken bones, strained backs) can result from hundreds of different accidents. As a mechanic, you must constantly think and evaluate every repair technique. Decide whether a particular operation is safe or dangerous and take action as required.

For instance, if you are pulling on a hand wrench as hard as you can and the bolt will not turn, STOP! Find another tool that is larger, has more leverage, and is safer. This mental attitude will help prevent injuries and improve your mechanical abilities as well.

GENERAL SAFETY RULES

Listed are several *general safety rules* that should be remembered and followed at all times.

1. WEAR EYE PROTECTION during any operation that could endanger your eyes. This would include operating power tools, working around a running car engine, carrying batteries, and so on.
2. A "CLOWN CAN KILL!" In other words, avoid anyone who does not take shop work seriously. Remember, a joker is "an accident just waiting to happen."
3. KEEP YOUR SHOP ORGANIZED. Return all tools and equipment to their proper storage areas. Never lay tools, creepers, or parts on the floor.
4. DRESS LIKE A TECHNICIAN, not like "Mr. or Ms. Hollywood!" Remove rings, bracelets, necklaces, watches, and other jewelry. They can get caught in engine fans, belts, driveshafts — tearing off flesh, fingers, chunks of hair, and ears. Also, roll up long sleeves and secure long hair, they too can get caught in spinning parts.
5. NEVER CARRY SHARP TOOLS or parts in your pockets. They can puncture the skin.
6. WEAR FULL FACE PROTECTION when grinding, welding, and during other operations where severe hazards are present.

7. WORK LIKE A PROFESSIONAL, not like a "crazy monkey." When learning auto repair, it is easy to get excited about your work. However, avoid working too fast. You could overlook a repair procedure or safety rule.
8. USE THE RIGHT TOOL FOR THE JOB! There is usually a "best tool" for each repair task. Always be thinking about whether a different tool will work better than another, especially when you run into difficulty.
9. KEEP GUARDS OR SHIELDS IN PLACE. If a power tool has a safety guard, use it.
10. LIFT WITH YOUR LEGS, not your back. There are many assemblies that are very heavy. When lifting, bend at your knees while keeping your back straight. On extremely heavy assemblies (transmissions, engine blocks, rear axles, transaxles) use a portable crane.
11. USE ADEQUATE LIGHTING. A portable shop light not only increases working safety, it increases working speed and precision.
12. VENTILATE WHEN NEEDED. Turn on the shop ventilation fan anytime fumes are present in the shop.
13. NEVER STIR UP ASBESTOS DUST! Asbestos dust (particles found in brake and clutch assemblies) are powerful CANCER-CAUSING AGENTS. Do NOT use compressed air to blow the dust off these parts.

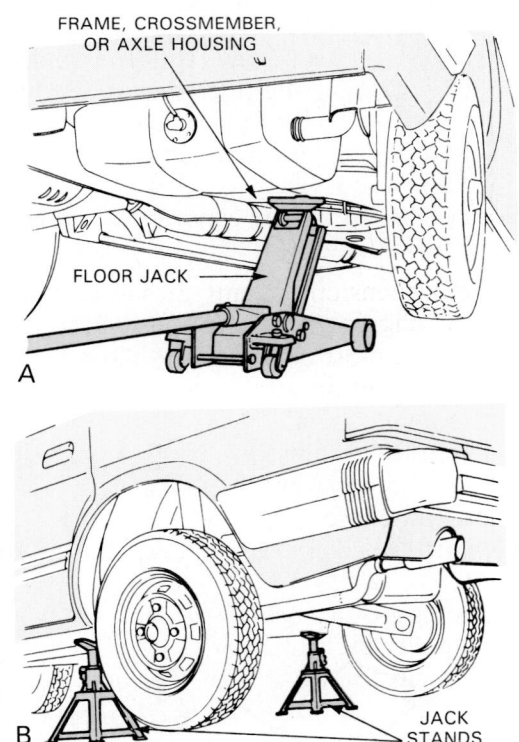

Fig. 5-9. Never work under a car only supported by a floor jack. A — Jack is only used for initial lifting. B — Jack stands are for securing car before working. Place them under recommended lift points. (Subaru)

14. JACK UP A VEHICLE SLOWLY AND SAFELY. A car can weigh between one and two tons. Never work under a vehicle not supported by jack stands. It is NOT safe to work a floor jack if it is the only support. See Fig. 5-9.

15. DRIVE SLOWLY WHEN IN THE SHOP AREA. With all of the other students and vehicles in the shop, it is very easy to have an accident.

16. REPORT UNSAFE CONDITIONS TO YOUR INSTRUCTOR. If you notice any type of hazard, let your instructor know about it.

17. STAY AWAY FROM ENGINE FANS! The fan on an engine is like a SPINNING KNIFE. It can inflict serious injuries. Also, if a part or tool is dropped into the fan, it can fly out and hit someone.

18. RESPECT RUNNING ENGINES. When an engine is running, make sure that the transmission is in park, emergency brake is set, and wheels are blocked. If the car "popped" or were knocked into gear, it could run over you or a friend.

19. NO SMOKING! No one should smoke in an auto shop. Smoking is a serious fire hazard, considering fuel lines, cleaning solvents, paints, and other flammables may be exposed.

20. OBTAIN INSTRUCTOR PERMISSION before using any new or unfamiliar power tool, lift, or other shop equipment. Your instructor will need to give a demonstration.

KNOW THESE TERMS

Stall, Grease rack, Lift, Front end rack, Electrical fire, Asphyxiation, Chemical burns, Asbestos.

REVIEW QUESTIONS

1. List four safety rules to follow when using a vehicle lift.
2. A _____ _____ _____ or _____ _____ is used when working on a car's steering and suspension systems. It has special equipment for aligning the wheels of a car.
3. Describe the most common and dangerous flammable found in an auto shop.
4. What is an electrical fire?
5. Car batteries can explode. True or False?
6. Asbestos, found in brakes and clutches, is harmful and can cause _____ .
7. Which of the following cannot cause electric shock?
   a. Missing ground prong on cord.
   b. Using electric drill on wet floor.
   c. Using electric tools with a ground prong.

8. Explain what must be done to prevent physical injuries.
9. If you are pulling on a wrench as hard as you can and the fastener does NOT turn, what should you do to prevent injury?
10. List 20 general safety rules.

ACTIVITIES FOR CHAPTER 5

1. Sketch out a floorplan of your shop and label the different areas. Study the safety cautions in this chapter and determine if there are any safety hazards. Mark their location on the floorplan.
2. On the same floorplan mark the location of fire extinguishers, exits, and water fountains.
3. Examine a fire extinguisher in the shop area; read the instructions carefully. Demonstrate its use.

Asbestos dust from brakes and clutches can cause lung cancer. Always use a vacuum system like this one to remove asbestos dust from parts. Never blow asbestos dust into the shop area. (Nilfisk)

Automotive Measurement

After studying this chapter, you will be able to:
- ☐ Compare conventional and metric measuring systems.
- ☐ Identify basic measuring tools.
- ☐ Describe the use of common measuring tools.
- ☐ Use conversion charts.
- ☐ List safety rules relating to measurement.

As a vehicle is driven, its moving parts slowly wear out. When a part wears too much, it can cause mechanical failures and performance problems. This is a major reason that a technician must be able to make accurate measurements.

Auto manufacturers give *"specs"* or *specifications* (measurements) for maximum wear limits and dimensions of specific parts. If the measurements are NOT within these specs or limits, the part must be adjusted, repaired, or replaced. As this points out, measurement is very essential to the study of auto service and repair.

This chapter introduces the most important types of measurements performed by an auto technician. It explains general measuring tools and methods using both conventional and metric systems. Study this chapter very carefully. It prepares you for other textbook chapters and for hundreds of in-shop tasks.

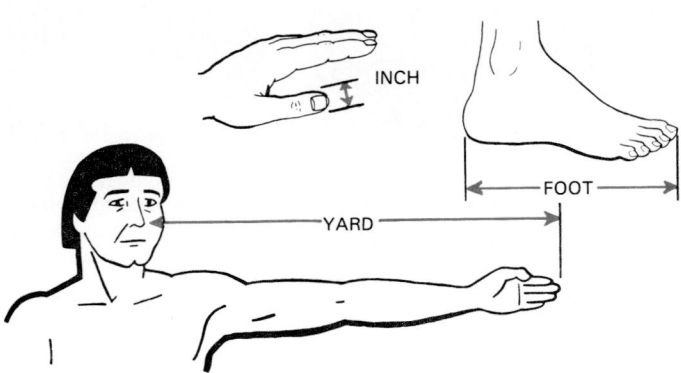

Fig. 6-1. Our conventional system is based on parts of the human body. Metric system is based on meter, a very accurate and universally accepted standard. (Starrett)

MEASURING SYSTEMS

The two *measuring systems* are the U.S. Customary Units system, also called conventional system, and the SI Metric system. Both are commonly used when working in an auto shop.

Our conventional system is mainly used in the United States. Almost all other countries use the metric system. The U.S. is slowly replacing its system with the metric system. All foreign cars and many new, American-made cars use metric bolts, nuts, and other parts. Manufacturer specifications are also given in both conventional and metric values.

Conventional measuring system

Our *conventional measuring system* originated from sizes taken from parts of the human body. For example, the width of the human thumb was used to standardize the inch, Fig. 6-1. The length of the human foot helped standardize the foot (12 inches). The distance between the tip of a finger and nose was used to set the standard for the yard (3 feet). Obviously, these are not very scientific standards.

Metric (SI) measuring system

The *metric* (SI) *measuring system* uses a power of 10 for all basic units. It is a simpler and more logical system than our conventional system. Computation often requires nothing more than adding zeros or moving a decimal point. For instance, one meter equals 10 decimeters, 100 centimeters, or 1000 millimeters.

Fig. 6-2 gives a summary and comparison of the two measuring systems.

A *measuring system conversion chart* is needed when changing from one measuring system to another: inches to centimeters, gallons to liters, liters to gallons. One is given in Fig. 6-3.

A conversion chart lets the technician quickly convert conventional values to equivalent metric values or vice versa. This is sometimes needed during brake, engine, and other repairs.

QUANTITY	USA (SYMBOL)	METRIC (SYMBOL)
Length	Inch(in)-Foot(ft)-Mile(mi)	Meter (m)
Weight (mass)	Ounce(oz)-Pound(lb)	Kilogram (kg)
Area	Square inch (sq-in)	Square Meter (m²)
Dry Volume	Cubic inch (cu-in)	Cubic Meter (m³)
Liquid Volume	Ounce(oz)-Pint(pt)-Quart(qt)-Gallon(ga)	Liter (L)
Road Speed	Miles Per Hour (mph)	Kilometer per Hour (km/h)
Torque	Foot-Pounds (ft-lb)	Newton meter (N-m)
Power	Horsepower (hp)	Kilowatt (kW)
Pressure	Pounds Per Square Inch (psi)	Kilopascal (kPa)
Temperature	Degrees Fahrenheit (°F)	Degrees Kelvin and Celsius (°C)

Fig. 6-2. Chart compares commonly used U.S. and metric values. Study them carefully.

RULER (SCALE)

A *steel ruler,* also called *scale,* is frequently used to make low precision linear (straightline) measurements. It is accurate to about 1/64 in. (0.5 mm) in most instances.

A conventional ruler has numbers that equal full inches, Fig. 6-4. The smaller, unnumbered lines or graduations represent fractions of an inch (1/2, 1/4, 1/8, 1/16). The shortest graduation lines equal the smallest fractions.

A metric ruler normally has lines or divisions representing millimeters (mm). Each numbered line usually equals 10 mm (one centimeter). This is shown in Fig. 6-4.

A *pocket rule* or *pocket scale* is extremely short (typically 6 in. long). It fits in your shirt pocket.

A *combination square* has a sliding square (frame with 90 deg. angle edge) mounted on a steel ruler. See Fig. 6-5. It is needed when the ruler must be held perfectly square (straight) against the part being measured.

APPROXIMATE CONVERSIONS

MEASUREMENT		WHEN YOU KNOW:	YOU CAN FIND:	IF YOU MULTIPLY BY:
	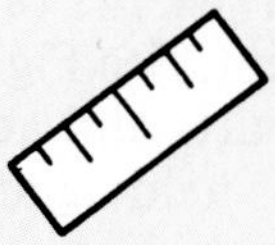 Length	inch (in) feet (ft) yard (yd) mile (mi) millimeter (mm) centimeter (cm) meter (m) kilometer (km)	millimeter (mm) meter (m) meter (m) kilometer (km) inch (in) inch (in) yard (yd) mile (mi)	25.4 .3 .9 1.6 .04 .39 1.09 .6
	 Pressure	pounds per square inch (psi) kilopascal (kPa)	kilopascal (kPa) pounds per square inch (psi)	6.89 .145
	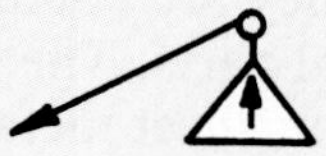 Power	horsepower (hp) kilowatt (kw)	kilowatt (kw) horsepower (hp)	.746 1.34
	 Torque	pound-feet (lb-ft) Newton-meter (N·m)	Newton-meter (N·m) pound-feet (lb-ft)	1.36 .74
	 Volume	quart (qt) liter (L) cubic inch (in³) liter (L)	liter (L) quart (qt) liter (L) cubic inch (in³)	.95 1.06 .016 61.02
	 Mass	ounce (oz) gram (g) pound (lb) kilogram (kg)	gram (g) ounce (oz) kilogram (kg) pound (lb)	28.35 .035 .45 2.20
	 Speed	miles per hour (mph) kilometers per hour (km/h)	kilometers per hour (km/h) miles per hour (mph)	1.61 .62

Fig. 6-3. To convert from one system to another, multiply known value and number in right column. This will give an approximate equal value.

Fig. 6-4. Compare inches to centimeters. Ten millimeters equals one centimeter. Twenty-five millimeters are a little more than one inch. The conventional rule is divided into 1/16 in. fractions. (Fairgate)

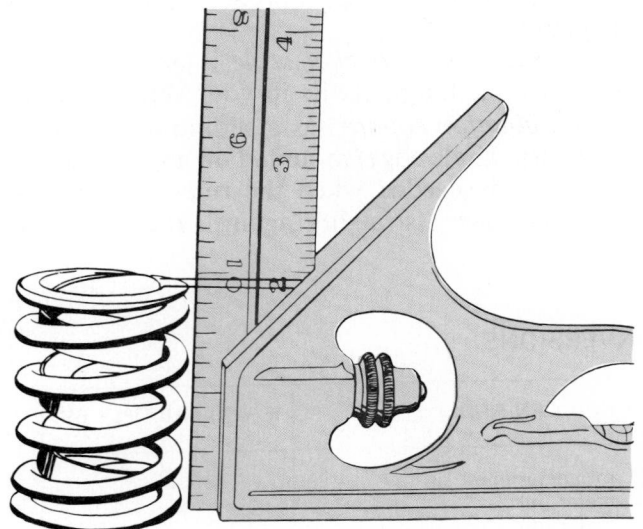

Fig. 6-5. Combination square is needed when scale must be held perfectly parallel to part. (Cadillac)

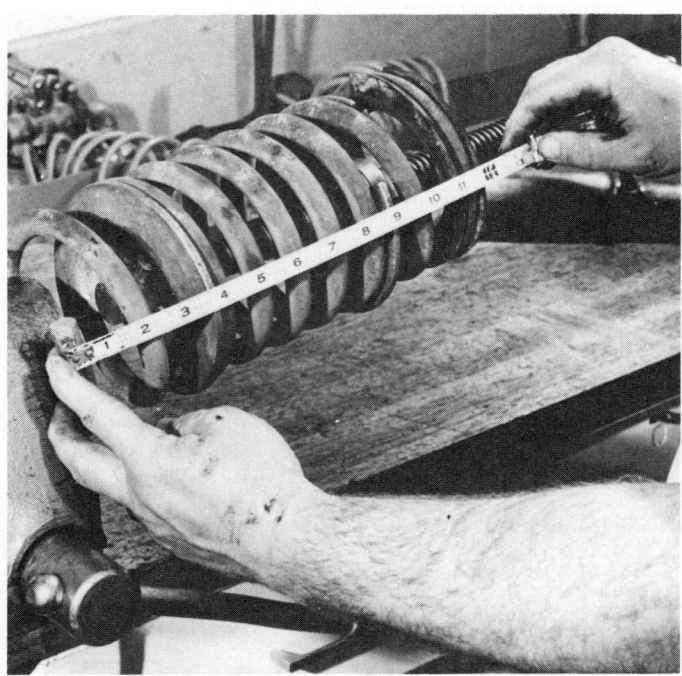

Fig. 6-6. Tape measure, as shown, or a yardstick can be used to make large straightline measurements. (Moog)

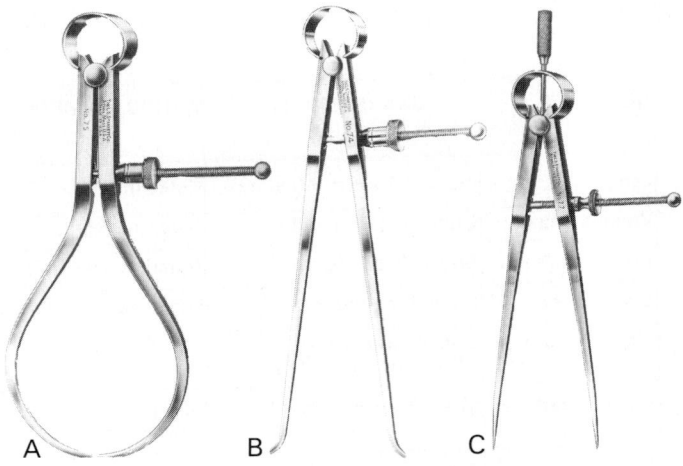

Fig. 6-7. A — Outside caliper for rough measurements on outside of part. B — Inside caliper for internal measurements. C — Dividers have sharp points for measuring or marking on metal parts. (The Starrett Co.)

A *tape measure* or *tape rule* extends to several feet or meters in length. It is sometimes needed for large distance measurements during body, suspension, and exhaust system repairs. Look at Fig. 6-6.

A *yardstick* or *meterstick* will also make large lineal measurements.

CALIPERS AND DIVIDERS

The *outside caliper* is sometimes helpful when making external measurements where 1/64 in. (approximately 0.40 mm) accuracy is sufficient. See Fig. 6-7A. It can be fitted over the outside of parts and adjusted to touch the part. Then, the caliper is held against and compared to a ruler to determine part size.

The *inside caliper* is designed for internal measurements in holes and other openings, Fig. 6-7B. It must also be compared to a ruler.

Dividers are similar to calipers but have straight, sharply pointed tips, Fig. 6-7C. They are commonly used for layout work on sheet metal parts. The sharp points will scribe circles and lines on sheet metal and plastic. Dividers will also transfer and make surface measurements, like calipers.

A *sliding caliper* can make inside, outside, and sometimes depth measurements with considerable accuracy. One is pictured in Fig. 6-8. Some sliding calipers measure as small as .001 in. (0.025 mm). A sliding caliper is a very fast and easy-to-handle tool.

A *dial caliper* is a sliding caliper with a dial gauge attached. The dial gauge makes precision measurements easier to read.

DECIMAL CONVERSION CHART

A *decimal conversion chart* is commonly used by the mechanic to interchange and find equal values for fractions, decimals, and millimeters. See Fig. 6-9. Fractions are ONLY ACCURATE TO about 1/64 of an inch. For smaller measurements, either decimals or

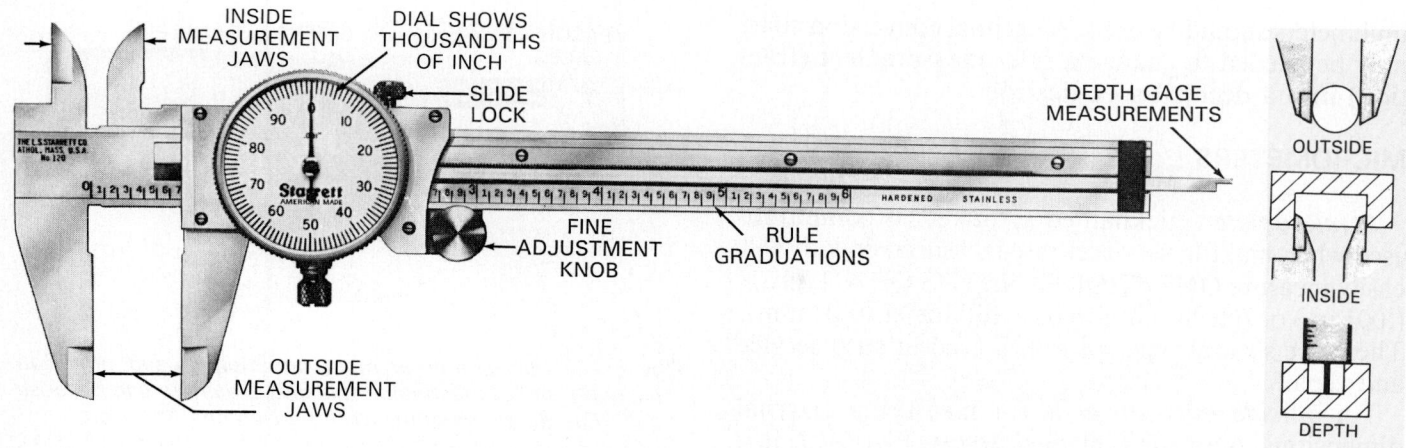

Fig. 6-8. Sliding caliper will quickly check inside, outside, and depth measurements. (Starrett and K-D Tools)

FRACTION	INCHES	M/M	FRACTION	INCHES	M/M
1/64	.01563	.397	33/64	.51563	13.097
1/32	.03125	.794	17/32	.53125	13.494
3/64	.04688	1.191	35/64	.54688	13.891
1/16	.06250	1.588	9/16	.56250	14.288
5/64	.07813	1.984	37/64	.57813	14.684
3/32	.09375	2.381	19/32	.59375	15.081
7/64	.10938	2.778	39/64	.60938	15.478
1/8	.12500	3.175	5/8	.62500	15.875
9/64	.14063	3.572	41/64	.64063	16.272
5/32	.15625	3.969	21/32	.65625	16.669
11/64	.17188	4.366	43/64	.67188	17.066
3/16	.18750	4.763	11/16	.68750	17.463
13/64	.20313	5.159	45/64	.70313	17.859
7/32	.21875	5.556	23/32	.71875	18.256
15/64	.23438	5.953	47/64	.73438	18.653
1/4	.25000	6.350	3/4	.75000	19.050
17/64	.26563	6.747	49/64	.76563	19.447
9/32	.28125	7.144	25/32	.78125	19.844
19/64	.29688	7.541	51/64	.79688	20.241
5/16	.31250	7.938	13/16	.81250	20.638
21/64	.32813	8.334	53/64	.82813	21.034
11/32	.34375	8.731	27/32	.84375	21.431
23/64	.35938	9.128	55/64	.85938	21.828
3/8	.37500	9.525	7/8	.87500	22.225
25/64	.39063	9.922	57/64	.89063	22.622
13/32	.40625	10.319	29/32	.90625	23.019
27/64	.42188	10.716	59/64	.92188	23.416
7/16	.43750	11.113	15/16	.93750	23.813
29/64	.45313	11.509	61/64	.95313	24.209
15/32	.46875	11.906	31/32	.96875	24.606
31/64	.48438	12.303	63/64	.98438	25.003
1/2	.50000	12.700	1	1.00000	25.400

Fig. 6-9. Decimal conversion chart is commonly used in auto shop. It will let you interchange fractions, decimals, and millimeters. What are equal decimal and millimeter values for 1/4 in., 15/32 in., 43/64 in., and 7/8 in.? (Parker Hannifin Corp.)

millimeters should be used. A decimal conversion chart may be needed to change a ruler measurement (fraction) into a decimal specification.

MICROMETERS

A *micrometer,* nicknamed a "mike," is commonly used when making very accurate measurements. It will easily measure ONE THOUSANDTHS OF AN INCH (.001 in.) or one hundredth of a millimeter (0.01 mm). There are several types of mikes used in auto service and repair.

An *outside micrometer* is for measuring external dimensions, diameters, or thicknesses, Fig. 6-10. It is fitted around the outside of the part. Then the thimble is turned until the part is lightly touching both the spindle and anvil, as in Fig. 6-11. Measurement is obtained by reading graduations on the hub and thimble.

Reading a conventional micrometer

To read a conventional micrometer, follow the four steps listed below:
1. Note the LARGEST NUMBER visible on the micrometer sleeve (barrel). Each number equals .100 in. (2 = .200, 3 = .300, 4 = .400). This is illustrated in Fig. 6-12.
2. Count the number of FULL GRADUATIONS to the right of the sleeve number.. Each full sleeve graduation equals .025 in. (2 full lines = .050, 3 = .075).
3. Note the THIMBLE GRADUATION aligned with the horizontal sleeve line. Each thimble graduation equals .001 in. (2 thimble graduations = .002, 3 = .003). Round off when the sleeve line is not directly aligned with a thimble graduation.
4. ADD the decimal values from steps 1, 2, and 3. Also, add any full inches. This will give you the micrometer reading, Fig. 6-12.

Reading a metric micrometer

Metric micrometers are also available. They are similar to conventional micrometers but have graduations and numbers in metric values. One revolution of the thimble equals 0.500 mm.

To read a metric micrometer, follow the four steps given below:
1. Read the SLEEVE NUMBER. Each sleeve number equals 1.00 mm (2 sleeve numbers = 2.00, 3 = 3.00). See Fig. 6-13.
2. Count and record the SLEEVE GRADUATIONS visible to the right of the sleeve number. Each sleeve line equals 0.50 mm (2 sleeve lines = 1.00, 3 = 1.50).
3. Read the THIMBLE GRADUATION lined up with the horizontal sleeve line. Each thimble graduation equals 0.01 mm (2 thimble graduations = 0.02, 3 = 0.03).
4. ADD values from the previous three steps. This

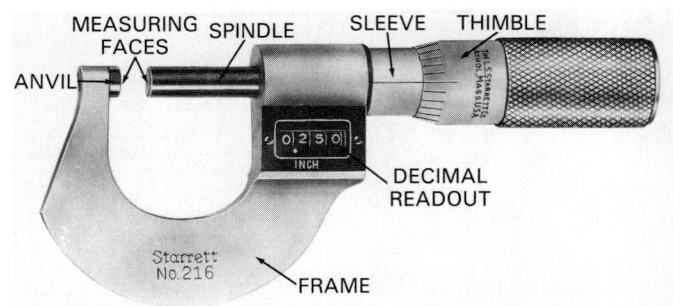

Fig. 6-10. Micrometer is most commonly used precision measuring tool of mechanic. This one is easy to use because it has digital readout. Note part names. (Starrett)

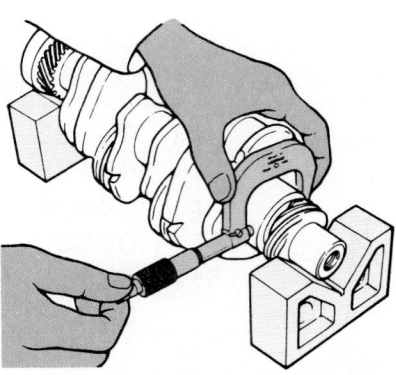

Fig. 6-11. To use a micrometer, gently rotate thimble to screw spindle into part. Move mike over part while holding it squarely. When you feel a slight drag, remove and read. (Subaru)

will give you the metric micrometer reading, as in Fig. 6-13.

Micrometer rules

A few important micrometer rules to remember include:
1. Never drop or overtighten a micrometer. It is very delicate and its accuracy can be thrown off easily.
2. Store micrometers where they cannot be damaged by large, heavy tools. Keep them in wooden or plastic storage boxes.
3. Grasp the mike frame in your palm and turn the thimble with your thumb and finger. It should just drag on the part being measured.
4. Hold the micrometer squarely with the work or false readings can result. Closely watch how the spindle is contacting the part.
5. Rock or swivel the mike as it is touched on round parts. This will assure that the most accurate diameter measurement is obtained.
6. Place a thin film of oil on the micrometer during storage. This will keep the tool from rusting.
7. Always check the accuracy of a micrometer if it is dropped, struck, or after a long period of use. Tool salespeople sometimes have standardized gauges for checking micrometer accuracy.

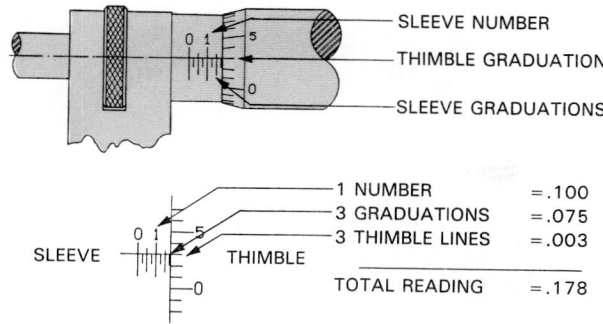

SLEEVE NUMBER
THIMBLE GRADUATION
SLEEVE GRADUATIONS

1 NUMBER	=.100
3 GRADUATIONS	=.075
3 THIMBLE LINES	=.003
TOTAL READING	=.178

Fig. 6-12. Study basic steps for reading a micrometer graduated in thousandths of an inch. Read number, then sleeve graduations, then thimble. Add these three values to obtain reading. (Starrett)

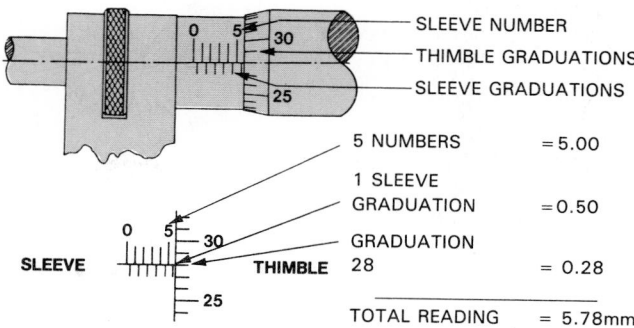

SLEEVE NUMBER
THIMBLE GRADUATIONS
SLEEVE GRADUATIONS

5 NUMBERS	=5.00
1 SLEEVE GRADUATION	=0.50
GRADUATION 28	= 0.28
TOTAL READING	= 5.78mm

Fig. 6-13. Metric micrometer is read like a conventional mike. However, note metric values for sleeve and thimble. (Starrett)

Special micrometers and gauges

Various special micrometers and gauges are used in auto mechanics. It is important for you to learn the basic types and their uses.

An *inside micrometer* is a special measuring tool used for internal measurements in large holes, cylinders, or other part openings. It is read in the same manner as an outside mike. One is pictured in Fig. 6-14A.

A *depth micrometer* is helpful when precisely measuring the depth of an opening. Look at Fig. 6-14B. The base of the mike is positioned squarely on the part. Then, the thimble is turned until the spindle contacts the bottom of the opening. The depth micrometer is read in the same way as an outside micrometer. However, the hub markings are REVERSED.

A *telescoping gauge,* like an inside mike, measures internal part bores or openings, Fig. 6-14C. The spring-loaded gauge is expanded to the size of the opening. Then, it is locked to size and measured with an outside micrometer.

A *hole gauge* is needed for measuring very small holes in parts. The hole gauge, like a telescoping gauge, is inserted and adjusted to fit the hole. Then it is removed and measured with an outside micrometer.

FEELER GAUGES

A *feeler gauge* is used to measure small clearances or gaps between parts. The two basic types of feeler gauges are shown in Fig. 6-15.

A *flat feeler gauge* has precision ground, steel blades of various thicknesses. Thickness is written on each blade in thousandths of an inch (.001, .010, .017) and/or in hundredths of a millimeter (0.01, 0.06, 0.20, 0.23). A flat feeler gauge is normally used to measure small distances between PARALLEL SURFACES.

A *wire feeler gauge* has precision sized wires which are also labeled by diameter or thickness. It is normally used to measure slightly larger spaces or gaps than a flat feeler gauge. The wire gauge's round shape also makes it more accurate for measuring UNPARALLEL or CURVED SURFACES.

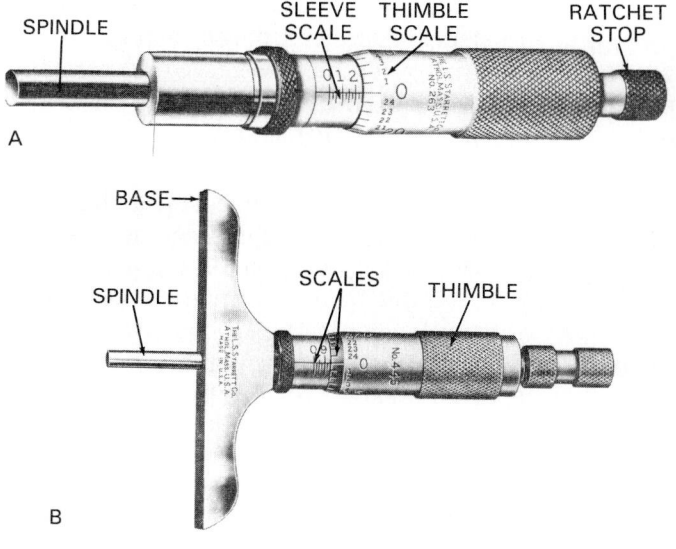

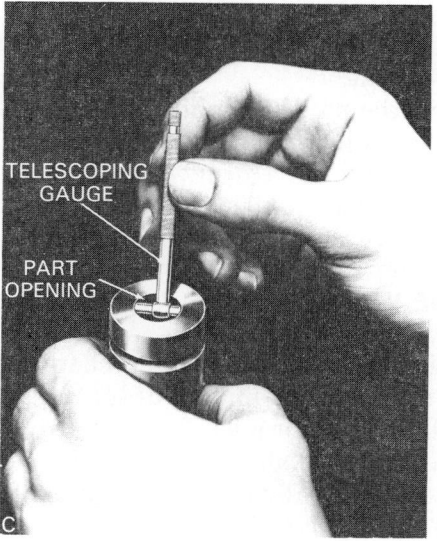

Fig. 6-14. A — Inside micrometer. B — Depth micrometer. C — Telescoping gauge.

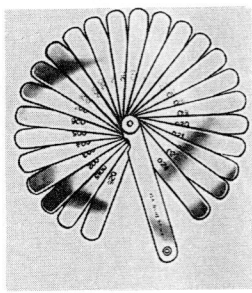

Fig. 6-15. Left — Wire feeler gauge set. Right — Flat or blade feeler gauge set.

Using a feeler gauge

To measure with either type feeler gauge, find the gauge thickness that just fits between the two parts being measured. The gauge should drag slightly when pulled between the two surfaces. The size given on the side of the gauge equals the clearance between the two components.

DIAL INDICATOR

A *dial indicator* will measure part movement in thousandths of an inch (hundredths of a millimeter). See Fig. 6-16. The needle on the indicator face registers the amount of plunger movement.

A dial indicator is frequently used to check gear teeth backlash (clearance), shaft end play, cam lobe lift, and other similar kinds of part movements. A magnetic mounting base or clamp mechanism is normally used to secure the dial indicator to or near the work.

Using a dial indicator

To measure with a dial indicator, follow these basic rules:
1. Mount the indicator securely and position the dial plunger parallel with the movement to be measured.
2. Preload or partially compress the indicator plunger before locking the indicator into place. Part movement in either direction should cause dial pointer movement.
3. Move the part back and forth or rotate the part while reading the indicator. Pointer movement equals part movement, clearance, or runout.
4. Be careful not to damage a dial indicator. It is very delicate.

TORQUE WRENCHES

Mentioned briefly in earlier chapters, a *torque wrench* measures the amount of turning force applied to a fastener (bolt or nut). Basically, a torque wrench uses the principle illustrated in Fig. 6-17. Torque wrench scales usually read in foot-pounds (ft-lb) and Newton-meters (N•m).

The three general types of torque wrenches are the flex bar, dial indicator, and sound indicating types. These are shown in Fig. 6-18.

Fig. 6-16. Dial indicator is for measurements requiring part movement. In this example, tool is set up to check height and wear of camshaft lobe. Cam is rotated. Indicator reading is compared to specs to find wear. (Central Tool Co.)

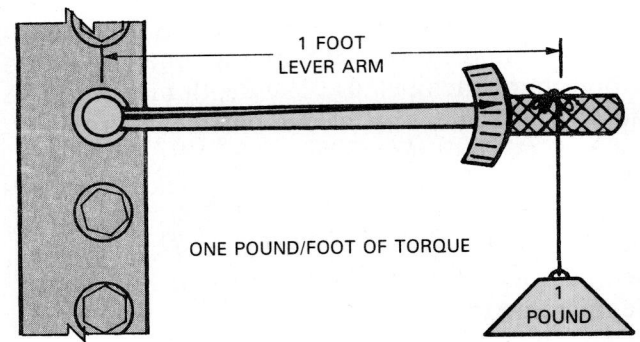

Fig. 6-17. One foot-pound equals one pound of pull on one foot long lever arm. This provides a means of measuring torque or twisting motion.

ANGLE MEASUREMENT

For measurement purposes, a circle is divided into 360 equal parts, called *degrees* (abbreviated deg. or °). As you can see in Fig. 6-19, one-half of a circle equals 180 deg., one-quarter a circle equals 90 deg., one-eighth of a circle equals 45 deg. Specifications are normally given in degrees when you are measuring rotation of a part or an angle formed by a part. Later text chapters discuss this.

PRESSURE GAUGE

A *pressure gauge* is frequently used in the auto shop to measure air and fluid pressure in various systems

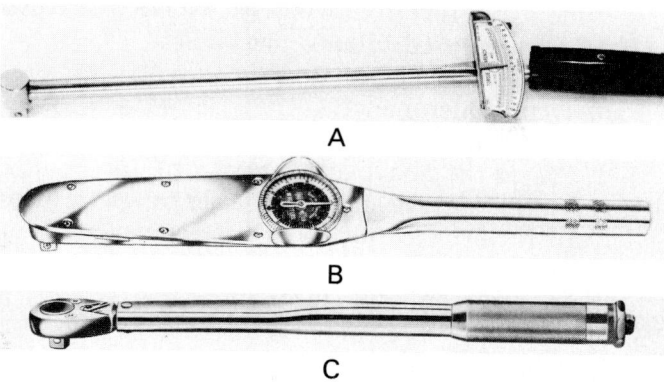

Fig. 6-18. Torque wrench types. A — Flex bar torque wrench bends metal beam to make pointer read torque on scale. B — Dial indicator torque wrench is very accurate. C — Snap or click torque wrench is fast. Set torque value by turning handle and stop when you hear click or pop sound.

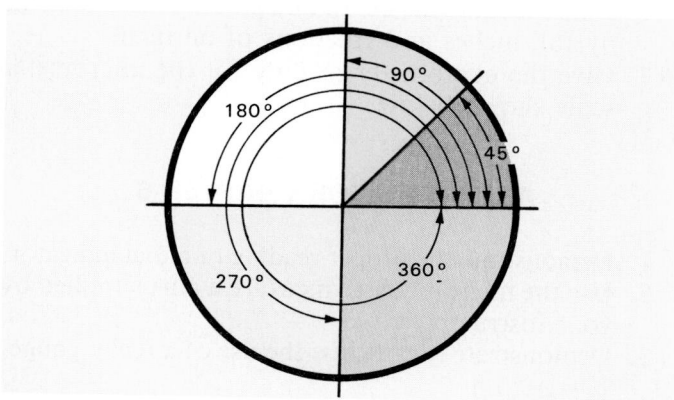

Fig. 6-19. Amount of rotation and angles are measured in degrees. Note how many degrees in a full circle and fractions of a circle.

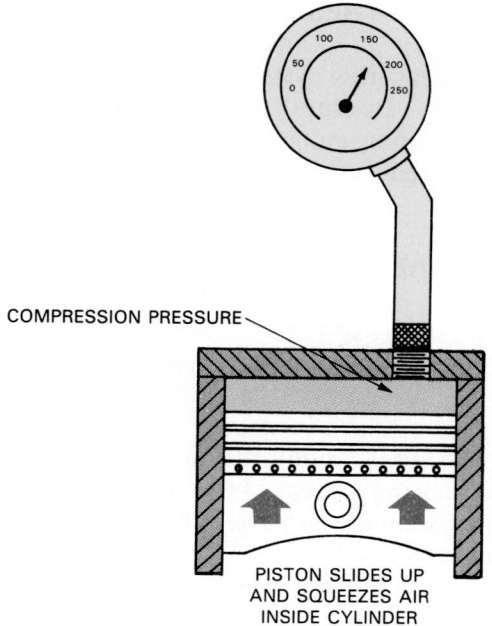

Fig. 6-20. Pressure is commonly measured in auto mechanics. This example shows pressure developed during engine compression stroke. If pressure is not high enough, engine mechanical problems are indicated.

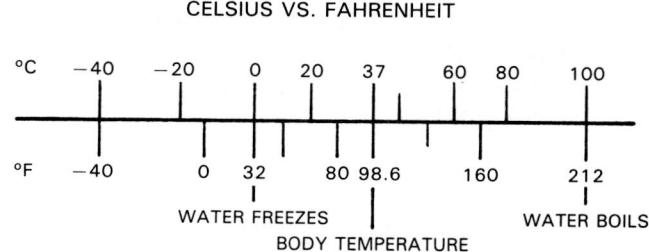

Fig. 6-21. Study relationship between conventional Fahrenheit (°F) and metric Celsius (°C) temperature values.

and components. For example, pressure gauges may be used to check tire air pressure, fuel pump pressure, air conditioning system pressure, or engine compression stroke pressure. Look at Fig. 6-20.

A pressure gauge normally reads in pounds per square inch (psi) and in kilograms per square centimeter (kg/cm²) or kilopascals (kPa). Some pressure gauges also measure vacuum.

VACUUM GAUGE

A *vacuum gauge* is commonly used to measure negative pressure or vacuum (suction). It is similar to a pressure gauge. However, the gauge reads in inches of mercury (in./hg.) and metric kilograms per square centimeter (kg/cm²). As one example, a vacuum gauge is used to measure the vacuum in an engine's intake manifold. If the reading is low or fluctuating, it may indicate an engine problem.

Note! Vacuum gauge use is detailed in Chapter 42, Engine Test Instruments.

TEMPERATURE MEASUREMENT

Special *thermometers* or *temperature gauges* are frequently used to measure the temperature of numerous components (air conditioning output temperature, and radiator temperature for example). A temperature gauge can read in either Fahrenheit (F) or Celsius (C), Fig. 6-21. The temperature obtained with the gauge can be compared to specs. Then, if the temperature is too low or too high, you would know that a repair or adjustment is needed.

OTHER MEASUREMENTS

An auto technician commonly uses many other types of measuring tools besides those just mentioned. More specialized measurements will be covered in later chapters.

KNOW THESE TERMS

Conventional measuring system, Metric measuring system, Caliper, Decimal conversion chart, Micrometer, Telescoping gauge, Feeler gauge, Dial indicator, Torque wrench.

REVIEW QUESTIONS

1. The two measuring systems are the _____ _____ _____, also called the _____ system and the _____ _____ _____ .
2. Parts of the human body are used to base the English measuring system. True or False?
3. The metric system uses a power of 16 for all basic units. True or False?
4. The following is NOT a metric value.
   a. Decimeter.
   b. Octimeter.
   c. Millimeter.
   d. Meter.
5. What is a measuring system conversion chart?
6. A decimal system conversion chart is used to _____ and find equal values for _____, _____, and _____ .
7. Describe the four steps for reading a conventional outside micrometer.
8. Describe the four steps for reading a metric outside micrometer.

9. Which of the following is NOT a special micrometer used in auto mechanics?
   a. Inside micrometer.
   b. Depth micrometer.
   c. Width micrometer.
   d. All of the above are correct.
10. A flat feeler gauge and a wire feeler gauge are identical. If not, describe their differences.
11. A dial indicator will measure part _____ in thousandths of an inch or _____ of a millimeter.
12. List the four basic rules for measuring with a dial indicator.
13. The three types of torque wrenches are the _____ _____, _____ _____, and _____ _____ .
14. For measuring purposes, the circle is divided into 720 parts, called degrees. True or False?
15. Explain the use of a vacuum gauge.
16. Note the inch rule below and give the measurement by full inches and fractions of an inch.
17. Give the micrometer reading for the micrometer scale shown below.

ACTIVITIES FOR CHAPTER 6

1. Demonstrate the proper reading of a dial indicator.
2. Use the micrometer to measure a part supplied by your instructor.
3. Demonstrate to the class the use of a feeler gauge.

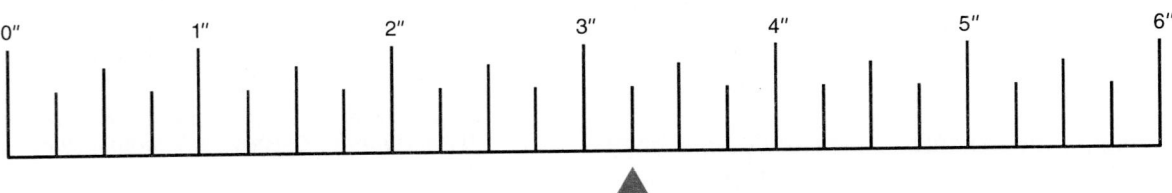

Inch rule for question 16.

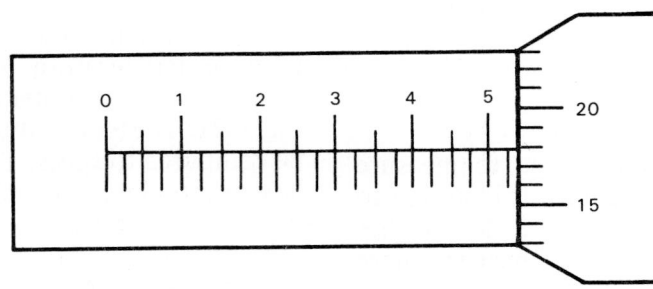

Micrometer reading for question 17.

Using Service Manuals

After studying this chapter, you will be able to:
□ Describe the different types of service manuals.
□ Find and use the service manual index and contents section.
□ Explain the different kinds of information and illustrations used in a service manual.
□ Describe the three basic types of troubleshooting charts found in service manuals.
□ Summarize the other kinds of service publications found in an auto shop.

Modern automobiles contain thousands of parts. Many of these parts are assembled to close tolerances (fits) and require precise assembly and adjustment. Sometimes a technician needs technical information to properly repair a vehicle. In these cases, he or she refers to a service manual.

SERVICE MANUALS (SHOP MANUALS)

Service manuals, also called *shop manuals,* are books with detailed information on how to repair a car. They have step-by-step procedures, specifications, diagrams, part illustrations, and other data for each car model. Every auto shop will normally have a set of service manuals. They help technicians with difficult repairs. Refer to Fig. 7-1.

Shop manuals are written in very concise, technical language. They are designed to be used by well-trained mechanics. After completing your studies in this text, you should be well prepared to understand service manuals. You will then find a service manual to be one of your MOST IMPORTANT TOOLS.

Service manual types

There are various types of service manuals: manufacturer's manuals, specialized manuals, general repair manuals. It is important for you to understand their differences.

Manufacturer's manuals are published by the various auto makers (Ford, General Motors, Chrysler, Toyota,

Nissan, Saab, and Honda). Also called *factory manuals,* each covers vehicles produced by that company, usually for a one-year period.

Specialized service manuals cover only specific repair areas. They usually come in several volumes, each covering one section of the vehicle. One may cover engines, another body components, or electrical systems. Specialized manuals are published by auto makers and also aftermarket (supplier other than major auto maker) companies.

General repair manuals are sold by companies other than the major auto makers (Mitchell Manuals, Motor Manuals, Chilton Manuals). These volumes are like manufacturer's manuals, but are NOT as detailed. They may include data on all of the American cars produced for several years. Other general repair manuals only cover foreign cars, light trucks, and large trucks.

It is often too costly for a garage to try to buy service manuals from every auto maker. Instead, a garage

Fig. 7-1. Service manuals will answer almost any repair question. The manuals are essential reference tools of automotive technicians. (Deere & Co.)

may buy two or three general repair manuals for all types of vehicles. These manuals summarize the most important and most needed information.

Service manual sections

A service manual is divided into sections such as: general information, engine, transmission, and electrical. See Fig. 7-2. You need to understand these sections and how they are organized.

The *general information section* of a shop manual helps you with a vehicle's identification, basic maintenance, lubrication, and other general subjects.

An important topic in this section is the *vehicle identification number* (VIN), which provides data about the car. It is commonly used when ordering parts. The NUMBER on the plate contains a code. The manual will explain what each part of this number code means.

Look at Fig. 7-3. The VIN number tells you engine type, transmission type, and other useful information.

The *repair sections* of a service manual cover the vehicle's major systems. These sections explain how to diagnose (recognize) problems, inspect, test, and repair each system. One page may describe how to remove the engine. Another page might say how to disassemble the engine.

Specifications (bolt tightening limits, capacities, clearances, operating temperatures) are given in the repair sections. They are commonly used during service and repair operations.

The repair sections also refer to *special tools* (tools for a limited number of repair tasks). These tools will normally be listed in the repair instructions and may be pictured at the end of the manual section. Refer to Fig. 7-4 for an example.

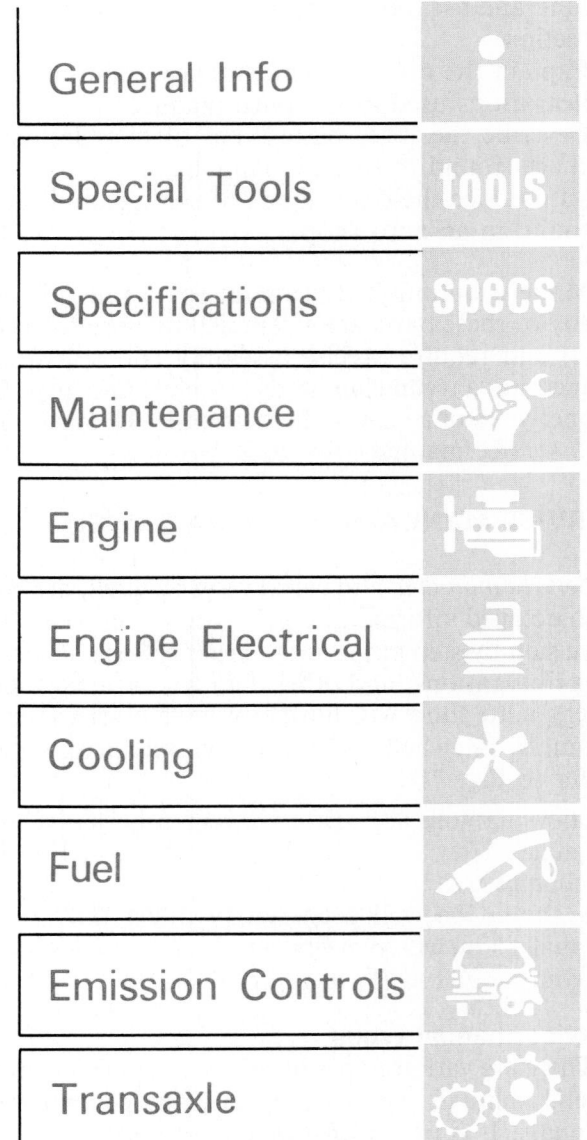

Fig. 7-2. Service manual is divided into several repair sections. This is shown by portion of a table of contents page. Read introduction and special information. It is typical of most manuals. (Honda)

Service manual illustrations

Various types of *illustrations* are used to supplement (go along with) the written information in a service manual. Some show how to measure part wear or install a part. Others show an exploded (disassembled) view of parts. Fig. 7-5 shows the most common types of service manual illustrations.

When using a service manual, you will find the illustrations essential for full understanding of the procedures and specifications. They show you what the parts look like, how they fit together, where leaks might occur, or how a part works.

Service manual diagrams

Diagrams are drawings used when working with electrical circuits, vacuum hoses, and hydraulic circuits. They represent how wires, hoses, passages, and parts connect together.

Wiring diagrams show how the wiring connects to the electrical components. See Fig. 7-5C. This subject is covered later in the text.

Vacuum diagrams, like wiring diagrams, help the technician trace and determine how vacuum hoses connect to the engine and vacuum-operated devices. Fig. 7-5 shows a vacuum hose illustration.

Hydraulic diagrams show how fluid (usually oil) flows in a circuit or part. They are helpful in understanding how a component operates or how to troubleshoot problems. They are commonly given for automatic transmissions and power steering systems.

Service manual abbreviations

Abbreviations are letters that stand for entire words. They are often used in service manuals. Sometimes,

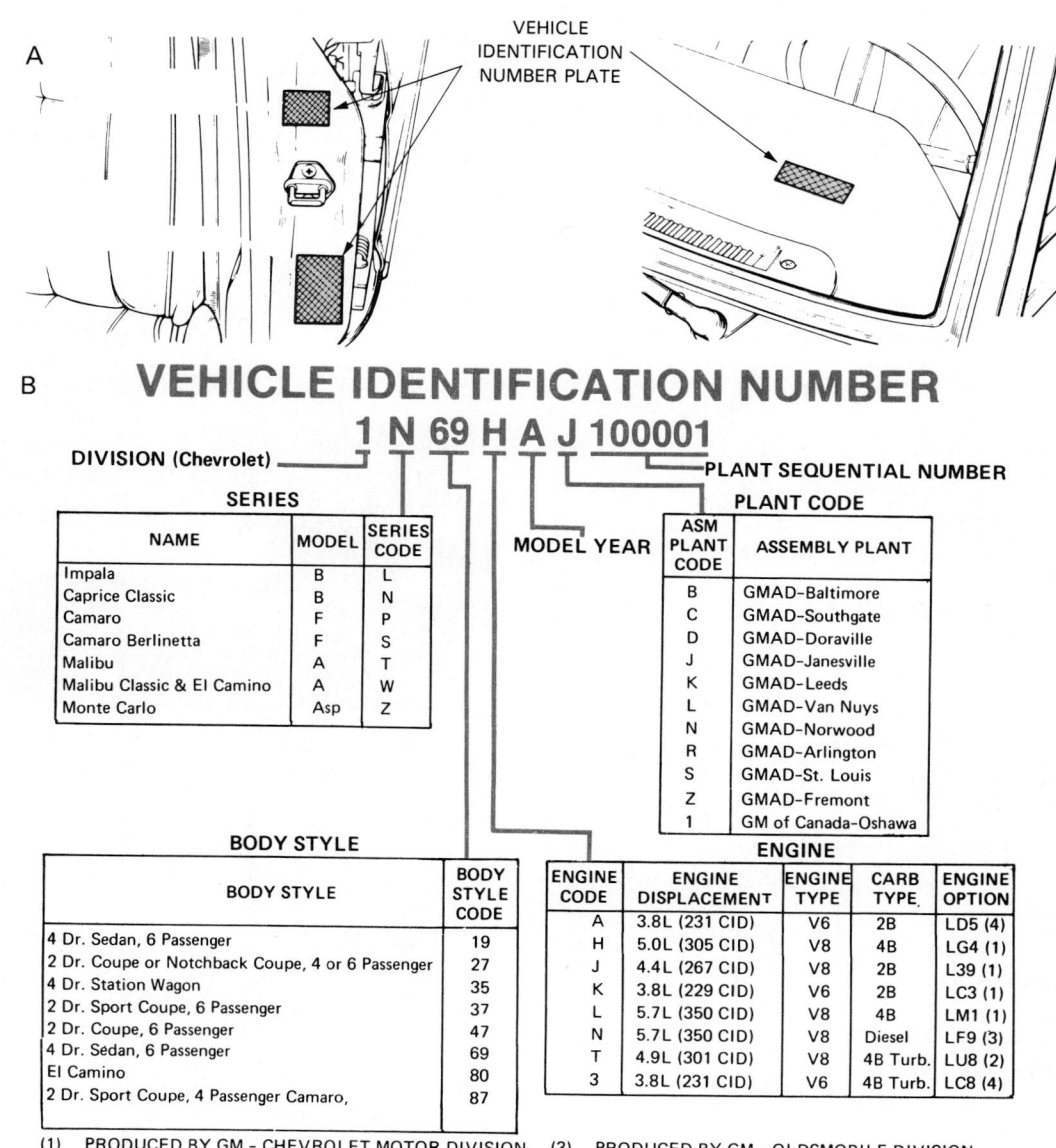

VEHICLE IDENTIFICATION NUMBER

1 N 69 H A J 100001

DIVISION (Chevrolet) ─ | ─ PLANT SEQUENTIAL NUMBER

SERIES

NAME	MODEL	SERIES CODE
Impala	B	L
Caprice Classic	B	N
Camaro	F	P
Camaro Berlinetta	F	S
Malibu	A	T
Malibu Classic & El Camino	A	W
Monte Carlo	Asp	Z

PLANT CODE

ASM PLANT CODE	ASSEMBLY PLANT
B	GMAD–Baltimore
C	GMAD–Southgate
D	GMAD–Doraville
J	GMAD–Janesville
K	GMAD–Leeds
L	GMAD–Van Nuys
N	GMAD–Norwood
R	GMAD–Arlington
S	GMAD–St. Louis
Z	GMAD–Fremont
1	GM of Canada–Oshawa

MODEL YEAR

BODY STYLE

BODY STYLE	BODY STYLE CODE
4 Dr. Sedan, 6 Passenger	19
2 Dr. Coupe or Notchback Coupe, 4 or 6 Passenger	27
4 Dr. Station Wagon	35
2 Dr. Sport Coupe, 6 Passenger	37
2 Dr. Coupe, 6 Passenger	47
4 Dr. Sedan, 6 Passenger	69
El Camino	80
2 Dr. Sport Coupe, 4 Passenger Camaro,	87

ENGINE

ENGINE CODE	ENGINE DISPLACEMENT	ENGINE TYPE	CARB TYPE	ENGINE OPTION
A	3.8L (231 CID)	V6	2B	LD5 (4)
H	5.0L (305 CID)	V8	4B	LG4 (1)
J	4.4L (267 CID)	V8	2B	L39 (1)
K	3.8L (229 CID)	V6	2B	LC3 (1)
L	5.7L (350 CID)	V8	4B	LM1 (1)
N	5.7L (350 CID)	V8	Diesel	LF9 (3)
T	4.9L (301 CID)	V8	4B Turb.	LU8 (2)
3	3.8L (231 CID)	V6	4B Turb.	LC8 (4)

(1) PRODUCED BY GM – CHEVROLET MOTOR DIVISION
(2) PRODUCED BY GM – PONTIAC MOTOR DIVISION
(3) PRODUCED BY GM – OLDSMOBILE DIVISION
(4) PRODUCED BY GM – BUICK MOTOR DIVISION

Fig. 7-3. A — Vehicle identification tag can be located on door, dashboard, in engine compartment, or other body section. B — Vehicle ID number on tag is a code. Service manual will explain code as shown. (Subaru and General Motors Corp.)

CLUTCH and TRANSMISSION SPECIAL TOOLS

TOOL NUMBER & DESCRIPTION	ILLUSTRATION
49-0813-310 CENTERING TOOL, CLUTCH DISC	
49-0500-330 INSTALLER, TRANSMISSION BEARING	
49-0259-440 TURNING HOLDER, MAINSHAFT	
49-0862-350 GUIDE, SHIFT FORK ASSEMBLY	

Fig. 7-4. Service manual explains special tool numbers. Note these special tools for clutch and transmission repairs. (Mazda)

abbreviations are explained as soon as they are used. They may also be explained at the front or rear of the manual in a chart.

Since abbreviations vary from one service manual to another, this textbook only uses universally accepted abbreviations. It does NOT use those that only apply to one auto manufacturer. Fig. 7-6 gives some abbreviations used by one manufacturer.

Troubleshooting (diagnosis) charts

Troubleshooting or *diagnosis charts* give steps (inspections, tests, measurements, and repairs) for finding and correcting problems in an automobile. If the source of the problem is hard to find, a troubleshooting chart should be used. It will guide you to the most common causes for specific problems.

There are three basic types of troubleshooting charts: Tree chart, Block chart, and Illustrated type chart.

A *tree diagnosis chart,* Fig. 7-7, provides a logical sequence for what should be inspected or tested when trying to solve a repair problem.

For instance, if a horn will not work, the top of the tree chart may tell you to check the horn's fuse. Then, if the fuse is good, it may have you measure the

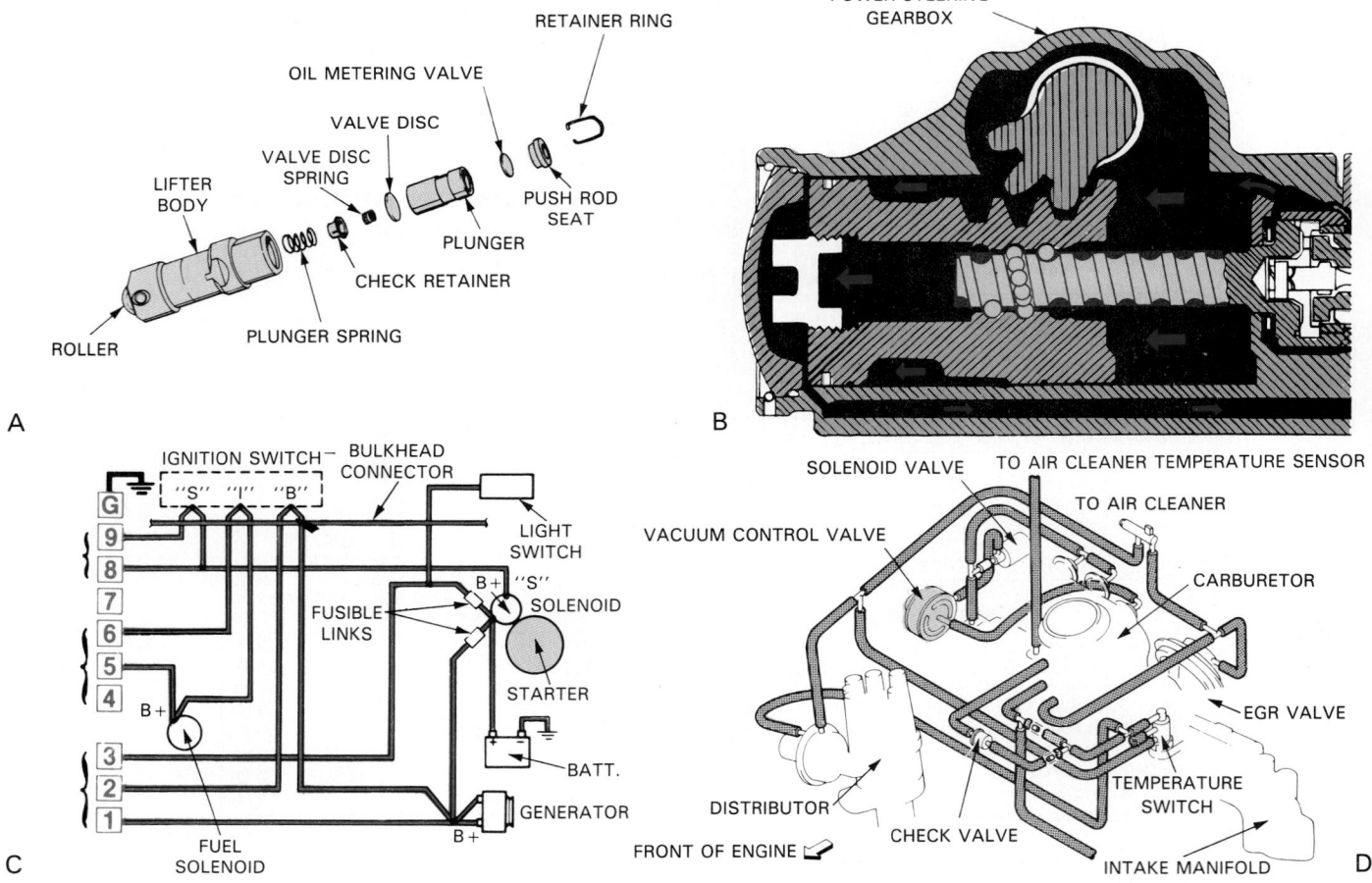

Fig. 7-5. Service manual illustrations. A — Exploded view shows how parts fit together. B — Operational illustration shows how part functions. C — Wiring diagram shows how wires connect to components. D — Vacuum diagram shows how hoses connect to components. (Oldsmobile, AMC, Buick, and Subaru)

70   Modern Automotive Technology

ABBREVIATIONS USED IN THIS MANUAL	
A/C	Air Conditioner
AI	Air Injection
A/T	Automatic Transmission
BTDC	Before Top Dead Center
EGR	Exhaust Gas Recirculation
EVAP	Evaporative (Emission Control)
EX	Exhaust (manifold, valve)
Ex.	Except
IN	Intake (manifold, valve), Inch
IG	Ignition
MC	Mixture Control
MP	Multipurpose
M/T	Manual Transmission
O/S	Oversized
PCV	Positive Crankcase Ventilation
P/S	Power Steering
SC	Spark Control
SST	Special Service Tool
STD	Standard
S/W	Switch
TDC	Top Dead Center
TP	Throttle Positioner
U/S	Undersized
W/O	Without

Fig. 7-6. These are samples of abbreviations used by one auto maker. (Toyota)

voltage going to the horn. You can work your way down the "tree" until the problem is fixed.

A *block diagnosis chart*, Fig. 7-8, lists conditions (problem symptoms), causes (problem sources) and corrections (needed repairs) in columns.

For example, if an engine overheats (runs hot), the most common cause would be the top listing (loss of

coolant in this case). You would check the coolant level and, if needed, perform the listed tasks (fill the radiator and check for leaks). If the coolant level was OK, you would go to the next listing.

An *illustrated diagnosis chart* uses pictures, symbols, and words to guide the mechanic through a sequence of tests. This type of troubleshooting chart is illustrated in Fig. 7-9.

If an engine oil pressure gauge shows low oil pressure, for example, the chart shows you exactly what to do, step by step, until the problem is corrected. This type of diagnosis chart not only tells you what to do, it shows you HOW TO DO IT.

USING A SERVICE MANUAL

To use a service manual, follow these basic steps:
1. Locate the right kind of service manual. Some manuals come in sets or volumes which cover different repair areas. Others cover all subjects and all car makes. If you are working on engines, find the manual that gives the most information for your type of engine.
2. Turn to the table of contents or the index. This will help you quickly find the needed information. NEVER thumb through a manual looking for a subject.
3. Use the page listings given at the beginning of each repair section. Most manuals have small contents tables at the beginning of each section. This will help you find a topic quickly.
4. Read the procedures carefully. A service manual

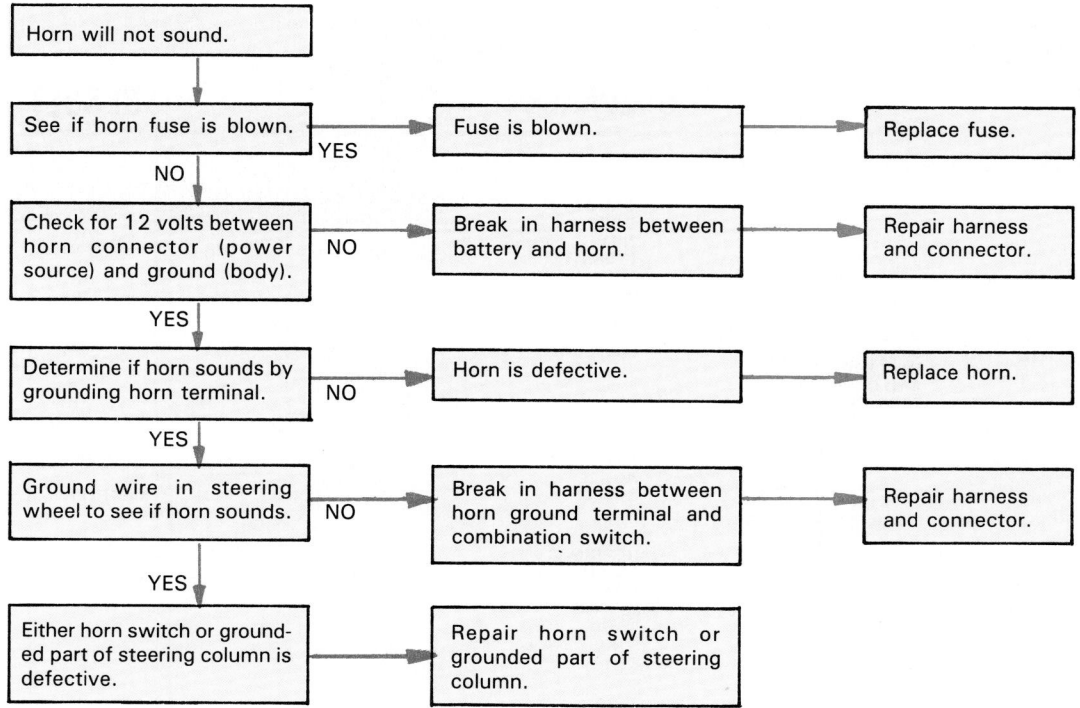

Fig. 7-7. Tree diagnosis chart starts at top and guides you through repair operations.

Condition	Possible Cause	Correction
• Loss of coolant	• Pressure cap and gasket • Exhaust leakage • Internal leakage	• Inspect, wash gasket, and test. Replace only if cap will not hold pressure test specifications. • Pressure test system. • Inspect hose, hose connections, radiator, edges of cooling system gaskets, core plugs, drain plugs, transmission oil cooler lines, water pump, heater system components. Repair or replace as required. • Check for obvious restrictions. • Check torque of head bolts. Retorque if necessary. • Disassemble engine as necessary — check for: cracked intake manifold, blown head gaskets, warped head or block gaskets surfaces, cracked cylinder head, or engine block.
• Engine overheats	• Low coolant level • Loose fan belt • Pressure cap • Radiator or A/C condenser obstruction • Closed thermostat • Fan drive clutch • Ignition • Temperature gauge or cold light • Engine • Exhaust system	• Fill as required. Check for coolant loss. • Adjust • Test. Replace if necessary. • Remove bugs and leaves. • Test, replace if necessary. • Test, replace if necessary. • Check timing and advance. Adjust as required. • Check electrical circuits and repair as required. • Check water pump and block for blockage. • Check for restrictions.
• Engine fails to reach normal operating temperature	• Thermostat stuck open. • Temperature gauge or cold light inoperative	• Test, replace if necessary. • Check electrical circuits and repair as required. Refer to electrical section.

Fig. 7-8. Block diagnosis chart lists conditions, causes, and corrections in columns. Read to right to match causes and corrections with condition. (Ford)

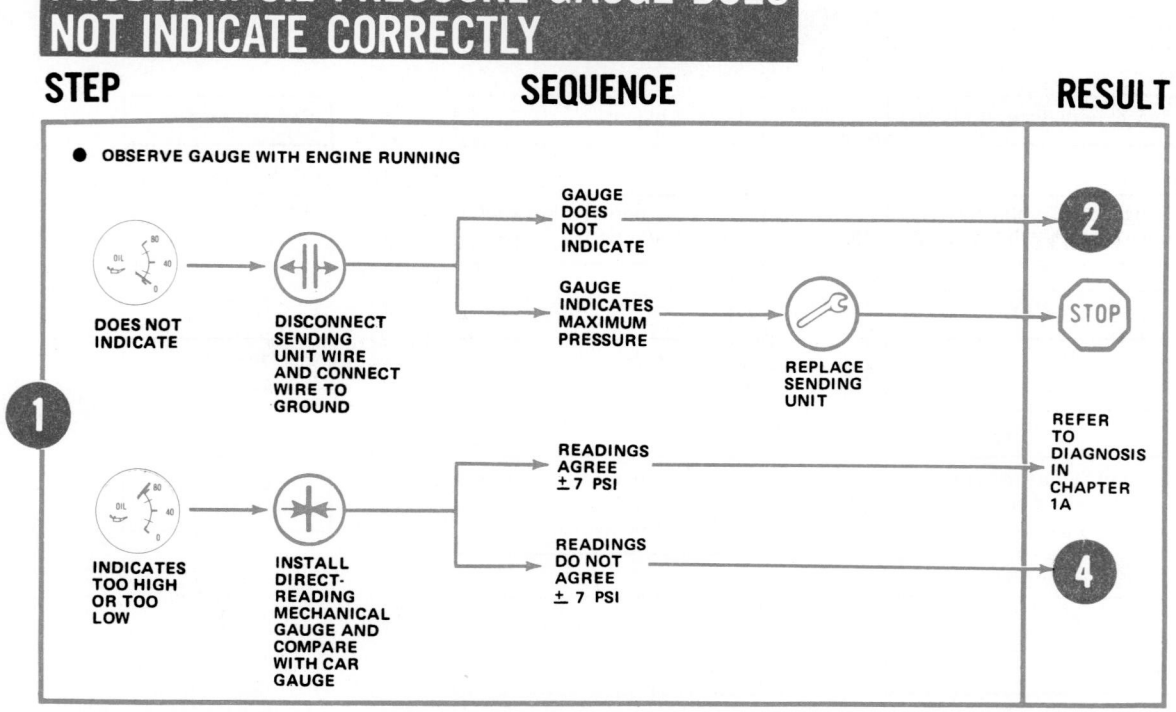

Fig. 7-9. Illustrated diagnosis chart uses small illustrations and symbols to show how to find and correct problem.

will give highly detailed instructions. You must NOT overlook any step or the repair may fail.

5. Study the manual illustrations closely. The pictures in a service manual contain essential information. They cover special tools, procedures, torque values, and other data essential to the repair.

SERVICE PUBLICATIONS

A service manual is just one kind of book which contains technical information on an automobile. Other types, called *service publications,* include: owner's manuals, technical bulletins, automotive magazines, flat rate manuals (labor estimating books), and parts books.

Owner's manual

An *owner's manual* is a small booklet given to the purchaser of a new car. It contains basic information on starting the engine, maintaining the car, and operating vehicle accessories.

Flat rate manual

A *flat rate manual* is needed to calculate how much labor to charge the customer for a repair. It contains an estimate of HOW MUCH TIME a specific repair should take. This time can then be multiplied by the shop's hourly labor rate to find the labor charge in dollars. Using the flat rate manual, you will be able to give the customer an estimate of cost before the actual repair.

Technical bulletins

Technical bulletins help the technician stay up-to-date with recent technical changes, repair problems, and other service related information. Usually, only a few pages long, they are mailed to the shop manager who passes them to the technicians. Technical bulletins are published by auto manufacturers and equipment suppliers.

KNOW THESE TERMS

Service manual, Manufacturer's manual, Specialized manual, General repair manual, Vehicle identification number, Special tools, Diagrams, Abbreviations, Troubleshooting chart, Service publications.

REVIEW QUESTIONS

1. What is a service manual?
2. Which of the following is NOT a service manual containing information on car repairs?
   a. Manufacturer's manual.
   b. Owner's manual.
   c. General repair manual.
   d. All of the above are correct.
3. The general information section of most service manuals contains an explanation about the vehicle identification number. True or False?
4. Specifications are given in all service manuals. True or False?
5. Explain the purpose of the following.
   a. Wiring diagrams.
   b. Vacuum diagrams.
   c. Hydraulic diagrams.
6. List 10 common abbreviations and explain them.
7. The following is NOT a common type of trouble-shooting chart.
   a. Track diagnosis chart.
   b. Tree diagnosis chart.
   c. Block diagnosis chart.
   d. Illustrated diagnosis chart.
8. Write the five basic steps for using a service manual.
9. A _____ _____ manual is needed to calculate how much labor to charge for a repair.
10. _____ _____ help the mechanic stay up-to-date with recent technical changes, repair problems, and other service related information.

ACTIVITIES FOR CHAPTER 7

1. Obtain a Flat Rate Manual and a parts catalog from your instructor and prepare a bill for replacement of a fuel pump on a vehicle of your choice. Check the Manual for the amount of labor involved; consult the parts catalog for the cost of the part. Add up the costs plus the state tax for your state. (Figure labor cost at $48/hour.)
2. Using a shop manual, demonstrate to your class how to find the procedure for removal and replacement of a part chosen by your instructor.
3. Fill out a repair order.

Basic Electricity
and Electronics

After studying this chapter, you will be able to:
- ☐ Explain the principles of electricity.
- ☐ Describe the action of basic electric circuits.
- ☐ Compare voltage, current, and resistance.
- ☐ Describe the principles of magnetism and magnetic fields.
- ☐ Identify basic electric and electronic terms and components.
- ☐ Explain different kinds of automotive wiring.
- ☐ Perform fundamental electrical tests.
- ☐ Overview information needed for other chapers.

Almost every system in a modern auto uses some type of electric or electronic *component* (part). Electronic ignition systems, electronic fuel injection, computerized engine systems, anti-lock brakes, and other advanced systems require technicians skilled in electricity and electronics. Even specialized technicians need this background to fix today's vehicles.

This chapter covers the most important and basic aspects of automotive electricity and electronics. It prepares you for use of this subject in later chapters.

ELECTRICITY

Everything is made of atoms, Fig. 8-1. You are made of atoms. This book is made of atoms, so is your chair,

air, our solar system, everything.

An *atom* consists of small particles called protons, neutrons, and electrons. Negatively charged electrons circle around the positively charged protons. The makeup of atoms varies in different substances.

Electricity is the movement of electrons from atom to atom. Some substances have atoms that allow electrical flow; others do not.

Conductors (wires, electrical components, and other metal objects) have atoms that allow the flow of electricity. They are substances that contain FREE ELECTRONS (extra electrons not locked to protons in orbits of atoms).

Insulators (plastic, rubber, ceramics) do NOT contain free electrons. They resist the flow of electricity. The outside of wire conductors is usually covered with plastic or rubber insulating material.

Simple circuit
A *simple circuit* consists of:
1. POWER SOURCE (battery, alternator, or generator) which supplies electricity for circuit.
2. LOAD (electrical device that uses electricity).
3. CONDUCTORS (wires or metal parts that carry current between power source and load).

Look at Fig. 8-2. The power source feeds electricity to the conductors and load. The conductors carry the electricity out to the load and back to the source. The load changes the electricity into another form of energy (light, heat, or movement).

Current, voltage, and resistance
The three basic elements of electricity are: CURRENT (amps), VOLTAGE (volts), and RESISTANCE (ohms). See Fig. 8-3.

Current (abbreviated I or A) is the FLOW of electrons through a conductor. Just as water flows through a garden hose, electrons flow through a wire in a circuit.

As an example, when current flows through a light bulb, the electrons rub against the atoms in the bulb

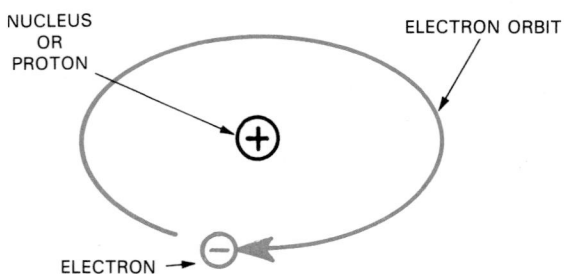

Fig. 8-1. Electricity is the flow of free electrons. Conductors contain free electrons, insulators do not. (Ford)

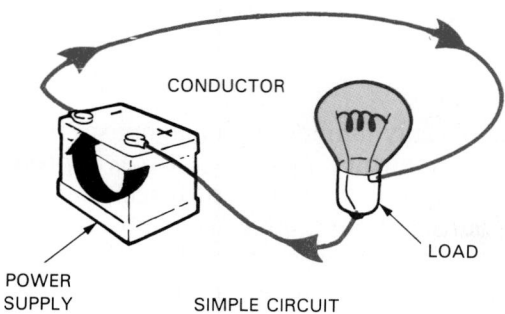

Fig. 8-2. Simple electric circuit consists of power source, load, and a conductor. Electrons will flow through circuit. (British Leyland)

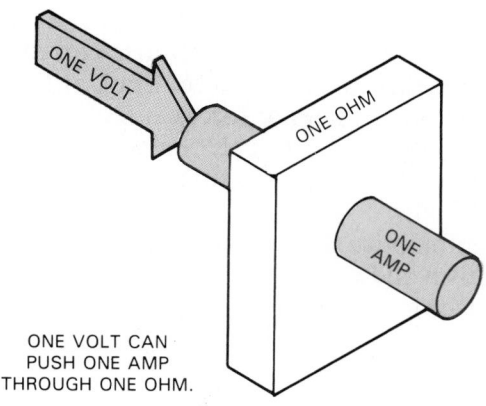

Fig. 8-3. Voltage is pressure or pushing force. Amps are flow of electrons. Ohms oppose current flow.

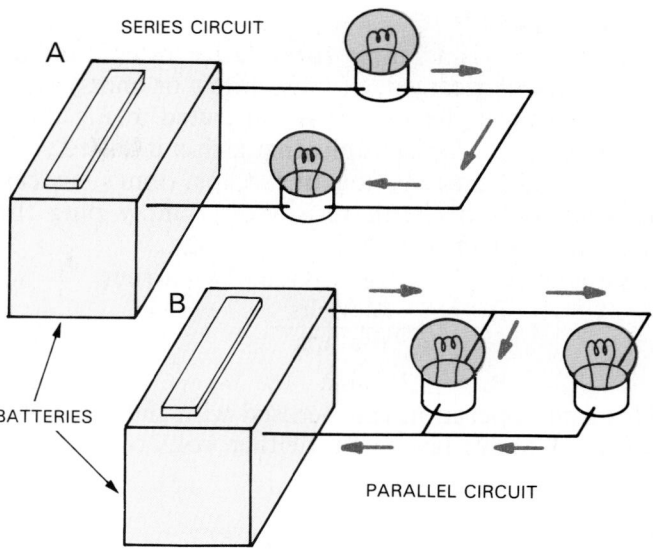

Fig. 8-4. Basic circuit types. A — Series circuit only has one path for current. B — Parallel circuit has separate path for each load.

filament (resistance wire inside bulb). This produces an "electrical friction." The friction heats the filament, making it glow "red hot."

In this text, we will use the electron theory of flow. This theory states that current flows from negative to positive.

Voltage (abbreviated V or E) is the force or ELECTRICAL PRESSURE that causes electron flow. Similarly, water pressure causes water to squirt out the end of a garden hose. An increase in voltage (pressure) causes an increase in current. A decrease in voltage causes a decrease in current. Automobiles normally use a 12V electrical system.

Resistance (abbreviated R or Ω) is the OPPOSITION to current flow. Resistance is needed to control the flow of current in a circuit. Just as the on/off valve on a garden hose can be opened or closed to control water flow, circuit resistance can be increased or decreased to control the flow of electricity. High resistance reduces current. Low resistance increases current.

Types of circuits

A *series circuit,* Fig. 8-4A, has more than one load (light bulb or other component) connected in a single electrical path. For example, inexpensive Christmas tree lights can be wired in series. With only one electrical

path, if one bulb burns out, all the bulbs stop glowing. The circuit path is broken (opened) and current stops.

A *parallel circuit,* Fig. 8-4B, has more than one electrical path or leg. Christmas tree lights wired in parallel are not prone to complete failure. One bulb can burn out without affecting the others. The other bulbs have their own leg or path to receive current.

A *series-parallel* circuit contains both a series circuit and a parallel circuit.

In a *one-wire circuit,* or frame-ground circuit, the vehicle's frame or body serves as an electrical conductor, Fig. 8-5. A cable is used to connect the negative battery terminal to the frame. Insulated wires are used to connect the frame to the load (ground wire) and the load to the positive battery terminal (hot wire). Current from the negative battery terminal travels through the vehicle's frame. From the frame, current travels through the load and into the positive battery terminal.

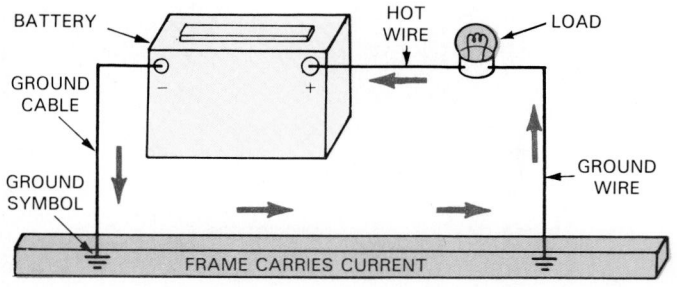

Fig. 8-5. Automobile wiring commonly uses a frame ground. Metal parts of vehicle carry current in the circuit. This reduces number of wires needed.

Ohm's Law

Ohm's Law is a simple formula for calculating an unknown electrical value (volts, amps, or ohms) when two values are given. This is illustrated in Fig. 8-6.

If you know, for example, that a circuit has 12 volts applied and a current flow of 6 amps, ohm's law can be used to find circuit resistance. Simply plug the known values into the correct formula.

Resistance = voltage divided by current

$$R = \frac{12 \text{ Volts}}{6 \text{ amps}}$$

$$R = 2 \text{ ohms}$$

This same operation can be used with the other two forms of ohm's law to find either volts or amps.

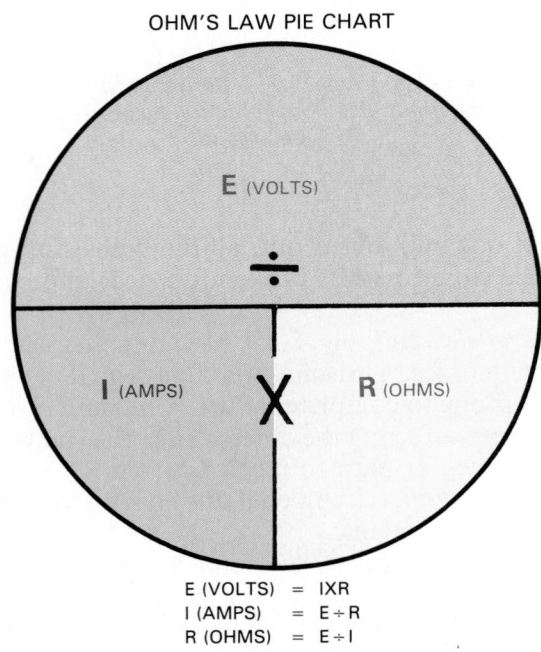

OHM'S LAW PIE CHART

E (VOLTS) = IXR
I (AMPS) = E÷R
R (OHMS) = E÷I

Fig. 8-6. Ohm's Law pie chart. Use your finger to cover one of the letters in chart. This will show you Ohm's Law formula.

Magnetic field

You are probably familiar with magnetism from using a simple permanent magnet, Fig. 8-7A. It produces an invisible *magnetic field* (lines of force) that will attract ferrous (metal containing iron) objects.

A magnetic field can also be created using electricity. A long piece of wire can be wound into a coil. The ends of the wire can be connected to a battery or other source. Then, when current passes through the wire, a magnetic field is produced.

To make the field or lines of force STRONGER, a soft iron bar or *core* can be inserted into the center of the coil. The iron core will become magnetized, making an *electromagnet* (electric magnet).

Magnetism can also create electricity. If a magnetic field is passed over a wire, an electric current is INDUCED or generated in the wire. Look at Fig. 8-7B. The wire cutting the lines of force causes a tiny amount of electricity to flow through the wire. This action called *induction* (current generated in wire by a magnetic field).

Many automotive components use the characteristics of magnetism and a magnetic field. Electronic fuel injection, electric motors, relays, ignition systems, and on-board computers are just a few examples.

Electrical terms and components

There are several electrical terms and components that auto technicians must know. The most important ones are discussed here.

A *switch* allows an electric circuit to be turned on or off manually (by hand). When the switch is CLOSED (on), the circuit is *complete* (fully connected) and will operate. When the switch is OPEN (off), the circuit is *broken* (disconnected) and does not function. See Fig. 8-8.

A *short circuit,* or "short," is an accidental low-resistance connection that results in excessive current flow. See Fig. 8-9. If a short to ground

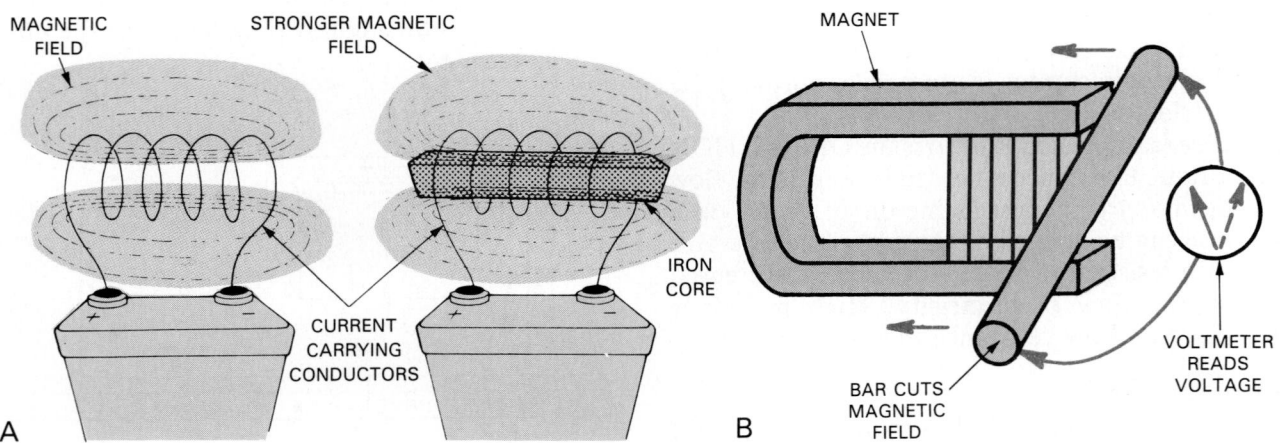

Fig. 8-7. A — When current flows through a wire, a magnetic field forms around wire. Wire can be wound into coil to strengthen field. An iron core will strengthen field even more. B — A magnetic field can be used to produce electricity. When iron bar is moved through magnet's field, current is induced in bar and wire. (British Leyland and Deere & Co.)

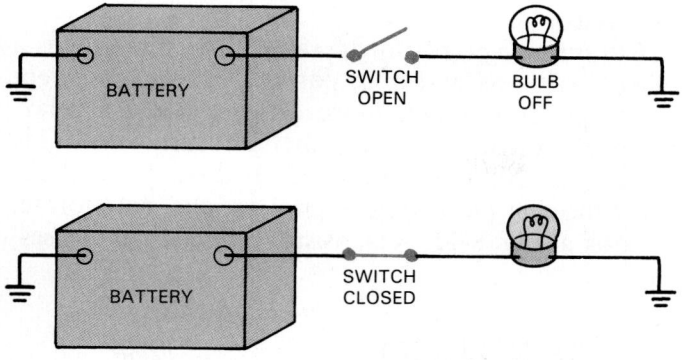

Fig. 8-8. Switch is used to break and complete circuit.

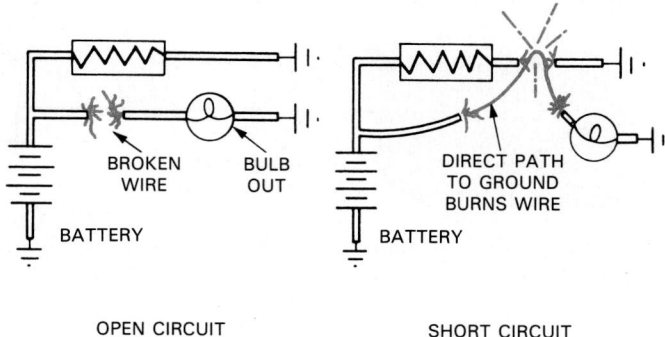

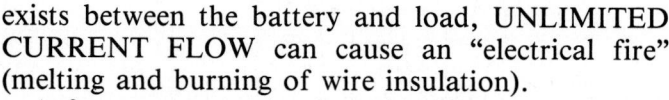

Fig. 8-9. Left. Open circuit has break in wire or electric component. Current stops flowing through circuit. Right. Short circuit has wire touching ground. High amount of current flows through short.

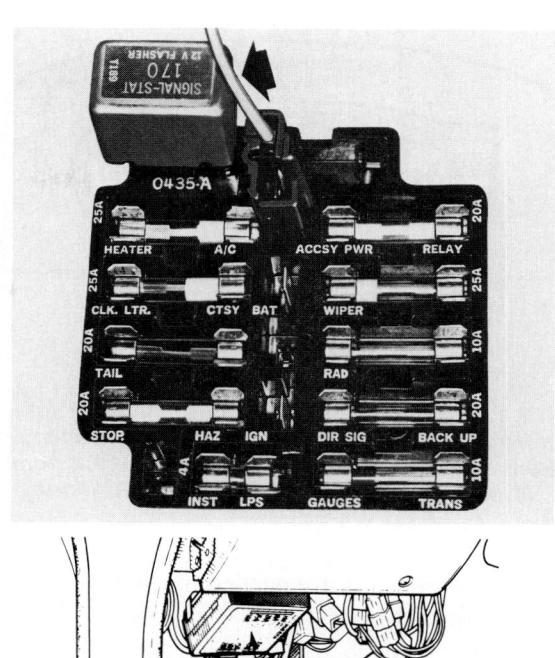

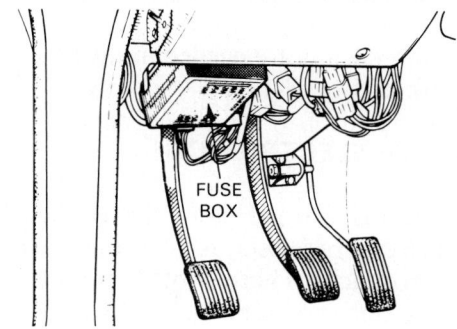

Fig. 8-11. Fuse box is normally located under dash. Fuses are normally labeled with name or circuit. Visual inspection for burning will frequently detect bad fuse. (Mazda)

exists between the battery and load, UNLIMITED CURRENT FLOW can cause an "electrical fire" (melting and burning of wire insulation).

A *fuse* protects a circuit against damage caused by a short circuit. The link in the fuse, Fig. 8-10, will melt and burn in half to stop excess current and further circuit damage. A *fuse box,* Fig. 8-11, is often located under the dashboard. It contains fuses for the various circuits.

A *circuit breaker* performs the same function as a fuse. It disconnects the power source from the circuit when current becomes too high. See Fig. 8-12. Normally, a circuit breaker will automatically reset itself when current returns to normal levels.

A *relay* is an electrically operated switch. It allows a small dash switch to control another circuit by remote control (control comes from a distant point in circuit). It also allows very small wires to be used behind the

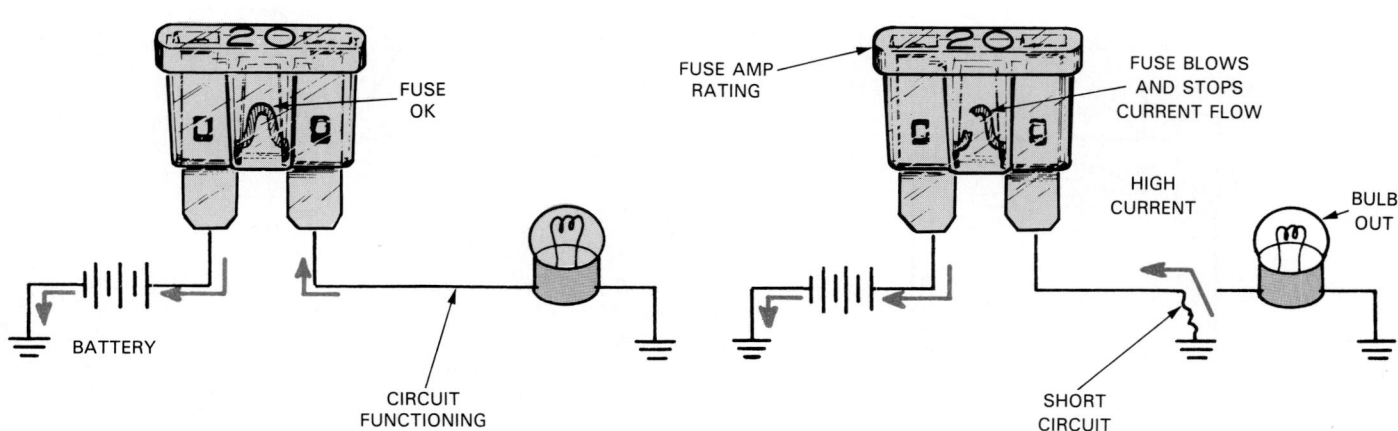

Fig. 8-10. Fuse protects against damage that would be caused by short circuit. High current heats, melts, and opens conductor in fuse. This stops current flow in circuit.

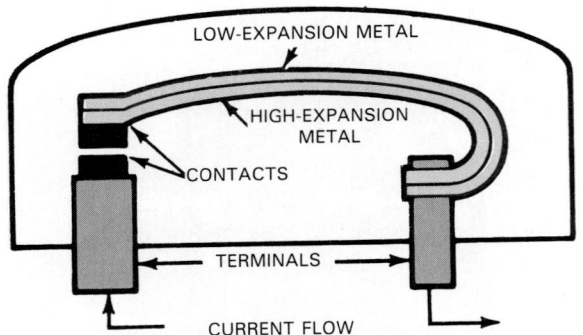

Fig. 8-12. Circuit breaker performs same function as fuse. High current heats bimetal, causing it to deform and open points. This stops current in circuit. When current drops to normal level, breaker cools and closes circuit. (Ford)

dash, while large wires are needed in the relay operated circuit. Look at Fig. 8-13.

AUTOMOTIVE ELECTRONICS

As you have just learned, some electrical components (relays and circuit breakers, for instance) use moving, mechanical contacts. These contact points can wear, burn, or pit, and are relatively slow. In electronic systems, the components are *solid state* and do NOT have moving parts.

A *semiconductor* is a special substance capable of acting as both a conductor and an insulator. This characteristic enables electronic, semiconductor devices to control current without mechanical points.

Diode

A *diode* is an "electronic check valve" that will only allow current to flow in one direction. See Fig. 8-14.

When *forward biased* (current entering in right direction), a diode acts as a CONDUCTOR and allows flow.

When *reverse biased* (current tries to enter wrong way), the diode changes into an INSULATOR. It stops current from passing through the circuit.

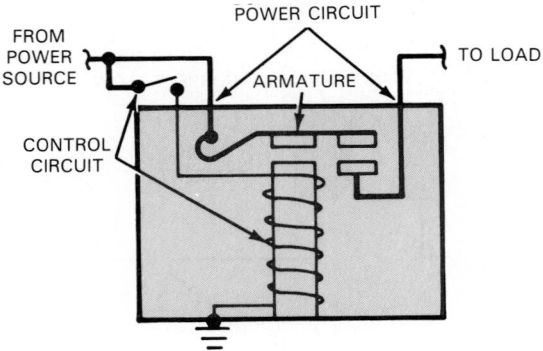

Fig. 8-13. Relay is remote control switch. Small current from dash switch can operate high current circuit elsewhere in car. When current enters control circuit, coil magnetic field pulls points closed. This completes main circuit to load. (Ford)

Transistor

A *transistor* performs the same basic function as a relay; it acts as a remote control switch or current amplifier. It is much more efficient than a relay, however. A transistor can sometimes turn on and off faster than 200 times a second. It does this without using moving parts which can wear and deteriorate.

Look at Fig. 8-15. A transistor *amplifies* (increases)

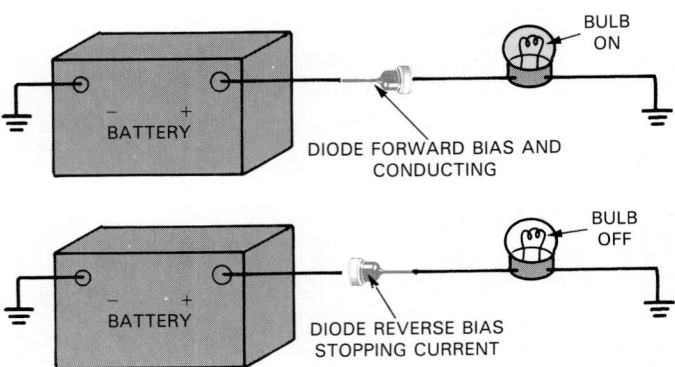

Fig. 8-14. Diode only allows current flow in one direction. Diodes are used in wide range of electric and electronic circuits.

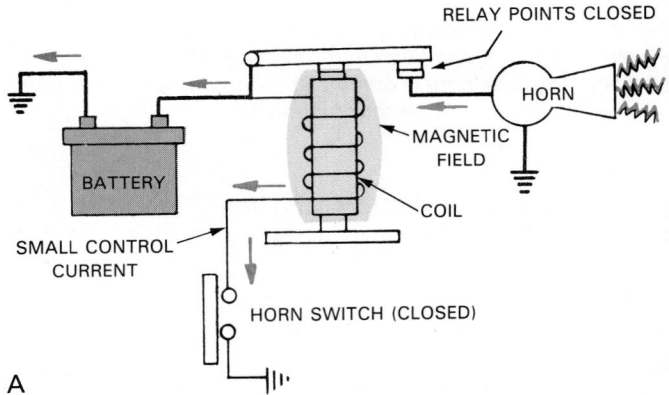

A

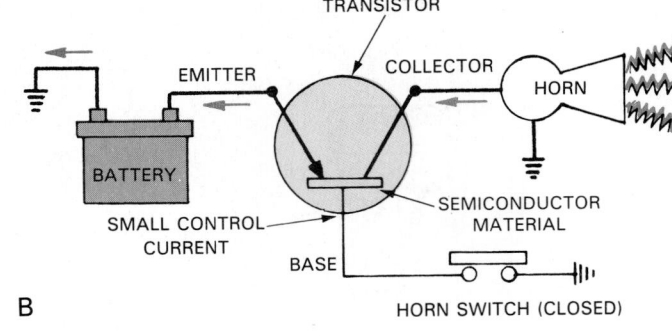

B

Fig. 8-15. Basically, relay and transistor perform same function. They allow small control current to operate larger current to load. A — When horn button is pressed, small current enters relay coil. Coil field attracts point arm. Then battery current can reach and operate horn through relay. B — When horn button pressed, small base current enters transistor. This changes semiconductor material in transistor from insulator to conductor. Then, current can flow through transistor and to horn. (Echlin)

a small control or base current. The small base current energizes the semiconductor material, changing it from an insulator to a conductor. This allows the much larger circuit current to pass through the transistor.

Other electronic devices

A *condenser* or *capacitor* is a device used to absorb unwanted electrical pulses (voltage fluctuations) in a circuit. They are used in various types of electrical and electronic circuits.

A capacitor is often connected into the supply wires going to a car radio. The capacitor absorbs any NOISE (electrical voltage pulses from alternator or ignition system) which could be heard in the radio speakers as a buzzing noise.

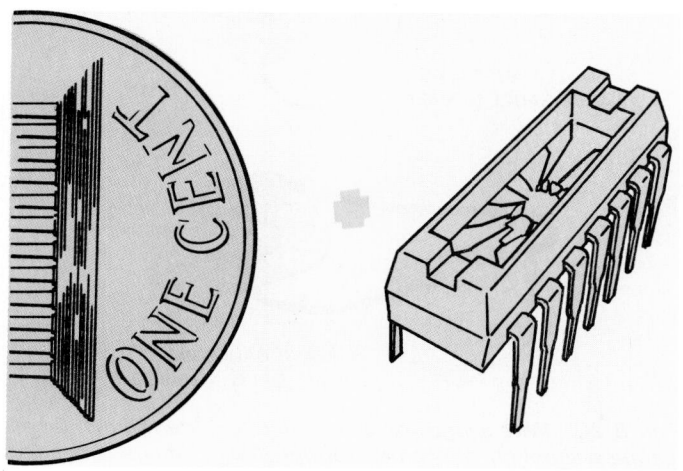

Fig. 8-16. Integrated circuit is tiny chip containing microscopic components: transistors, diodes, resistors, conductors. ICs are used in modern electronic circuits.

An *integrated circuit,* abbreviated IC, contains almost microscopic diodes, transistors, resistors, and capacitors in a wafer-like *chip* (small plastic housing with metal terminals). See Fig. 8-16. Integrated circuits are used in very complex electronic circuits.

Printed circuits do NOT use conventional, round wires; they use flat conductor strips mounted on an insulating board. This is pictured in Fig. 8-17. Printed circuits are normally used instead of wires on the back of the instrument panel. This eliminates the need for a bundle of wires going to the indicators, gauges, and instrument bulbs.

An *amplifier* is an electronic circuit designed to use a very small current to control a very large current. Its function is much the same as a transistor. However, higher output currents are possible.

A good example of an amplifier is an ignition system control unit (amplifier), introduced in Chapter one. It uses small electrical pulses from the distributor to produce strong on/off cycles to operate the ignition coil.

AUTOMOTIVE WIRING

An automobile uses various types of wiring in its many electrical systems. It is important that you learn the different types, how they are used, and how to repair them.

Wire types

Primary wire, Fig. 8-18, is small and carries battery or alternator voltage. Primary wire normally has plastic insulation to prevent shorting. The insulation is usually *color coded* (different wires are marked with different colors) for easy troubleshooting. This lets you trace (follow) wires that are partially hidden.

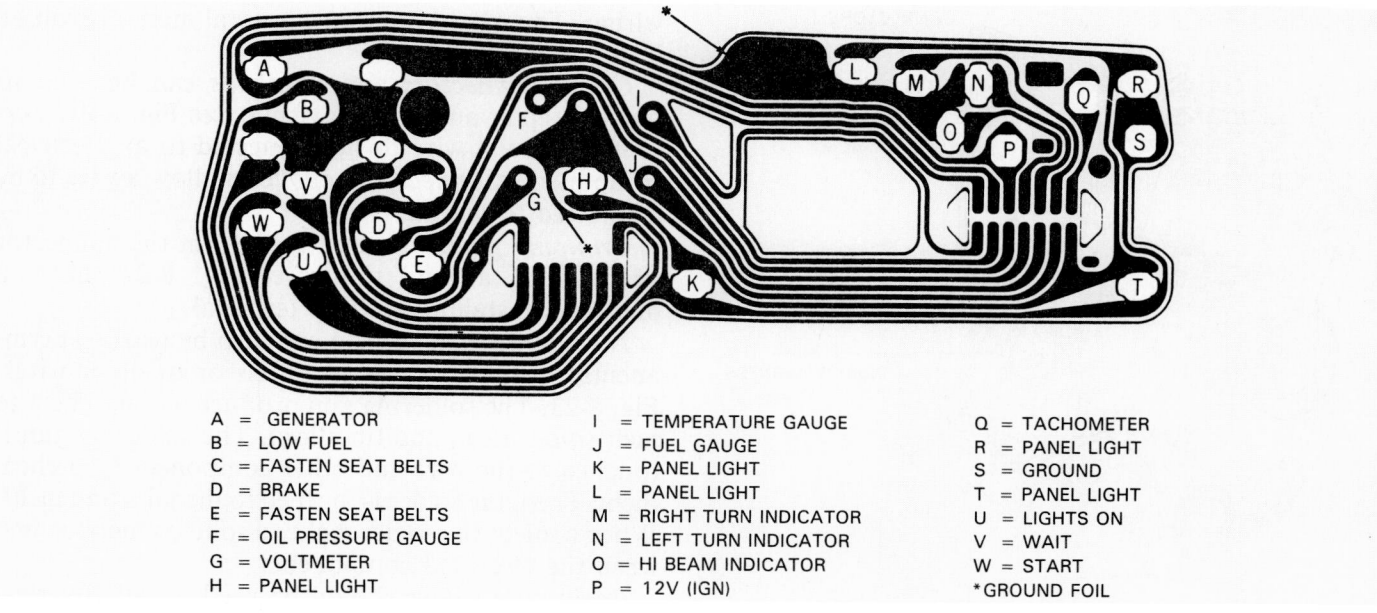

A = GENERATOR	I = TEMPERATURE GAUGE	Q = TACHOMETER
B = LOW FUEL	J = FUEL GAUGE	R = PANEL LIGHT
C = FASTEN SEAT BELTS	K = PANEL LIGHT	S = GROUND
D = BRAKE	L = PANEL LIGHT	T = PANEL LIGHT
E = FASTEN SEAT BELTS	M = RIGHT TURN INDICATOR	U = LIGHTS ON
F = OIL PRESSURE GAUGE	N = LEFT TURN INDICATOR	V = WAIT
G = VOLTMETER	O = HI BEAM INDICATOR	W = START
H = PANEL LIGHT	P = 12V (IGN)	*GROUND FOIL

Fig. 8-17. Printed circuit has flat conductor strips mounted on insulating board. Rear of this dash instrument panel is good example. (Oldsmobile)

CODE	
B	BLACK
Br	BROWN
G	GREEN
Gy	GRAY
L	BLUE
Lb	LIGHT BLUE
Lg	LIGHT GREEN
O	ORANGE
R	RED
W	WHITE
Y	YELLOW

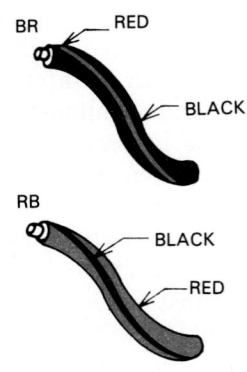

Fig. 8-18. Primary wires are color coded with different colors. This lets you trace wire through car.

As shown in Fig. 8-19, groups of primary wires are often enclosed in a wiring harness. A *wiring harness* is a plastic or tape covering that helps protect and organize the wires.

Wire size is determined by the diameter of the wire's metal conductor. The diameter is stated in *gauge size* which is a number system. The larger the gauge number is the smaller the diameter of wire conductor.

When replacing a section of wire, always use wire of equal size. If a smaller wire is used, the circuit could malfunction (not work) due to high resistance. Undersize wire could heat up and melt its protective insulation. An electrical fire could result.

Secondary wire, also called high tension cable, spark plug wire or coil wire, is only used in a car's ignition system. It has extra thick insulation for carrying high voltage from the ignition coil to the spark plugs. The conductor, however, is designed for very small currents.

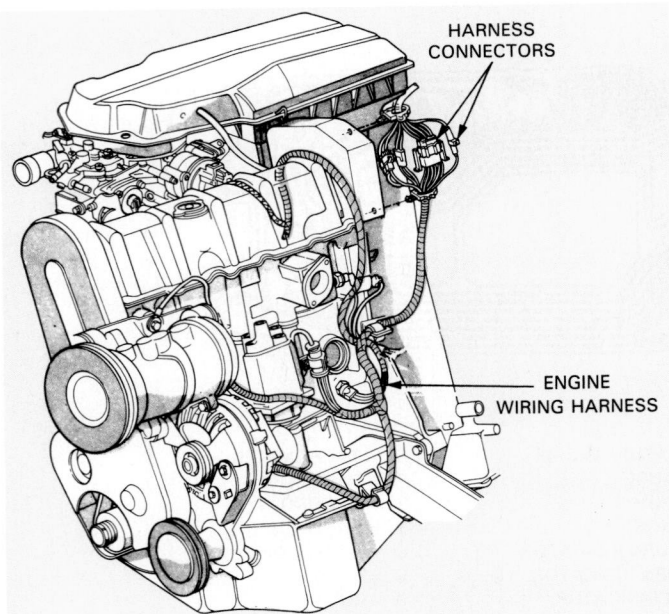

Fig. 8-19. Wiring harness is usually plastic covering around a group of primary wires. It organizes and protects wires. Also note harness connectors. (Chrysler)

Battery cable is extremely large gauge wire capable of carrying high currents from the battery to the starting motor. Look at Fig. 8-20. Usually, a starting motor draws more current than all of the other electrical components combined (normally over 100 amps). For this reason, very large conductors are required.

Ground wires or *ground straps* connect electrical components to the chassis or ground of the car. Since they connect circuits or parts to ground, insulation is NOT needed.

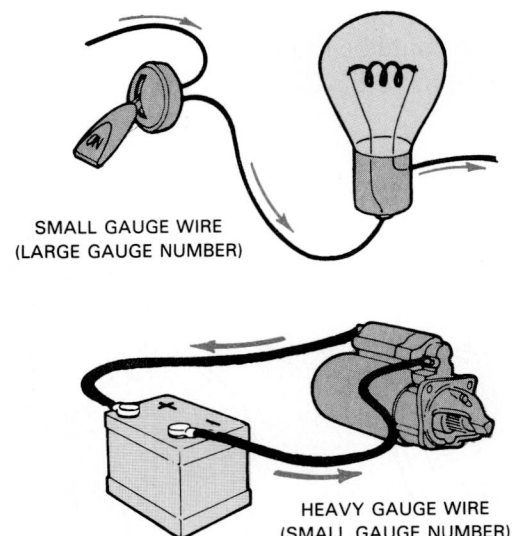

Fig. 8-20. Wire gauge size is matched to current draw. Small gauge will only handle small current. Larger gauge is needed for high current draws, starting motor for instance. (British Leyland)

Wiring repairs

Numerous methods can be used to repair automotive wiring. The most important, general methods will be introduced.

Crimp connectors and *terminals* can be used to quickly repair automotive wiring. See Fig. 8-21. *Terminals* allow a wire to be connected to an electrical component. *Connectors* or *splicers* allow a wire to be connected to another wire.

Crimping pliers are used to deform the connector or terminal around the wire. Fig. 8-22 shows a mechanic installing a crimp terminal.

A *soldering gun* or iron can also be used to permanently fasten wires to terminals or to other wires, Fig. 8-23. The soldering gun produces enough heat to melt *solder* (lead and tin alloy). The soldering gun is touched to the wire and other component to preheat them. Then, the solder is touched to the joint and melts. When cooled, the solder makes a solid connection between the electrical components.

Rosin core solder should be used on all electrical repairs. It is usually purchased in a roll form for easy use and handling.

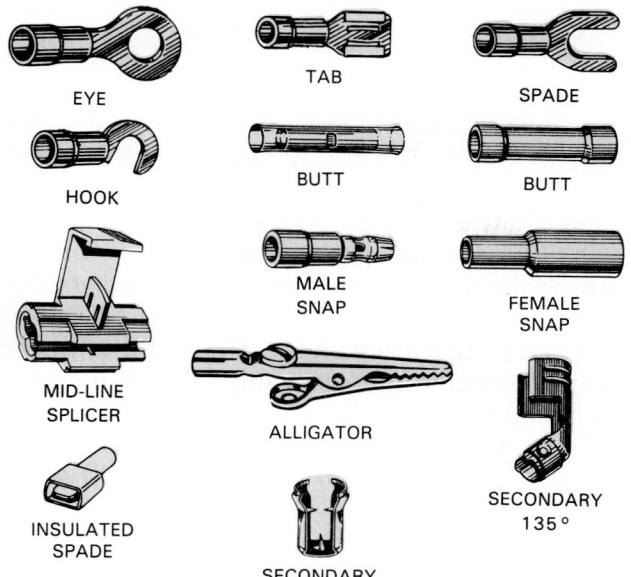

EYE TAB SPADE

HOOK BUTT BUTT

MID-LINE SPLICER MALE SNAP FEMALE SNAP

INSULATED SPADE ALLIGATOR SECONDARY 135°

SECONDARY

Fig. 8-21. Note various types of wire terminals and connectors. (Belden)

Acid core solder can cause corrosion of electrical components. It is recommended for nonelectrical repairs (radiator and heater core repairs, for example).

BASIC ELECTRICAL TESTS

Various electrical tests and testing devices are used by an auto mechanic. To be prepared for many later chapters, you should have a general understanding of these tools and how to use them.

A *jumper wire* is handy for testing switches, relays, solenoids, wires, and other components. The "jumper" can be substituted for the component, as shown in Fig. 8-24. If the circuit begins to function with the jumper in place, then the component being bypassed is defective.

A *test light* is a fast method of checking a circuit for power or voltage. It has an alligator clip that connects

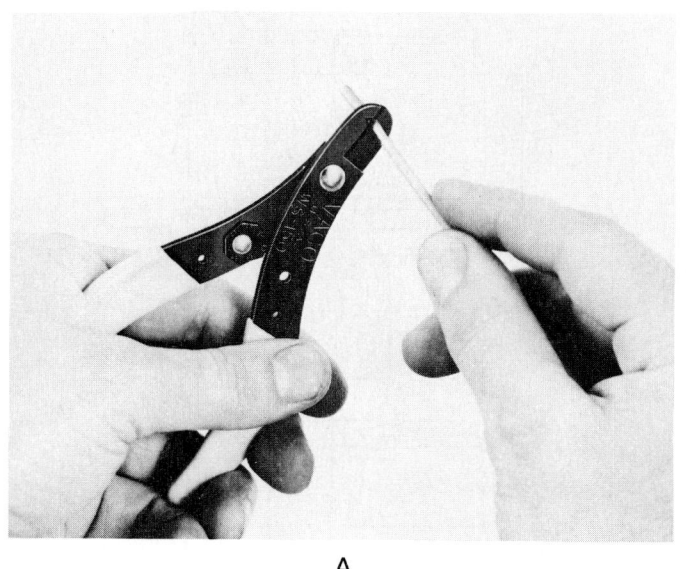

A

B

Fig. 8-22. Installing crimp type connectors and terminals. A — Strip off a short section of insulation. B — Use right size crimping jaw to form terminal or connector around wire. Tug on wire lightly to check connection. (Vaco Tool)

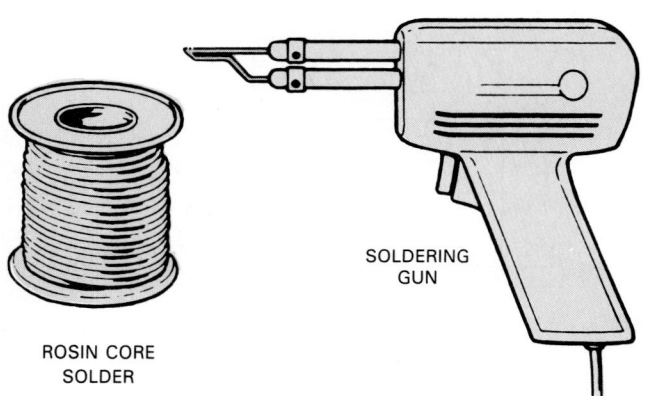

ROSIN CORE SOLDER

SOLDERING GUN

Fig. 8-23. Rosin core solder and soldering gun will make permanent connections between wires and components.

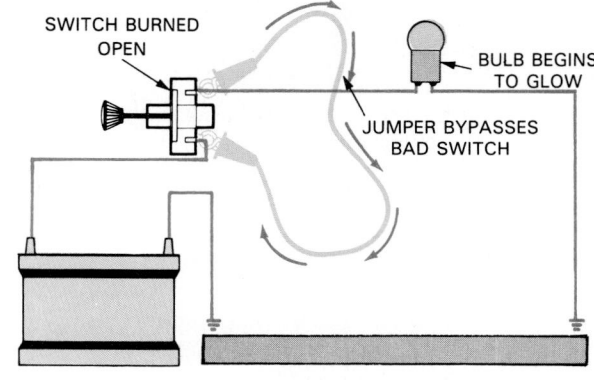

SWITCH BURNED OPEN

BULB BEGINS TO GLOW

JUMPER BYPASSES BAD SWITCH

Fig. 8-24. Jumper wire is handy for bypassing electrical components. It can also be used to supply power to section of circuit. (Ford)

to ground, Fig. 8-25. Then, the pointed tip can be touched to the circuit to check the power. If there is voltage, the light will glow. If it does not glow, there is an open or break between the power source and the test point. See Fig. 8-26.

A *self-powered test light* is similar to a flashlight with a lead attached. It contains batteries and is used to check for circuit continuity (whether circuit is complete). To use this type test light, the normal source of power (car battery or feed wire) must be disconnected. If the light glows, the circuit or part has continuity (low ohms). If it does NOT glow, there is an open or break (high ohms) between the two test points.

Voltmeter, ammeter, ohmmeter

A *voltmeter* is used to measure the amount of voltage (volts) in a circuit, Fig. 8-27A. It is normally connected across or in parallel to the circuit. The voltmeter reading can be compared to specifications to determine whether an electrical problem exists.

An *ammeter* measures the amount of current (amps) in a circuit, Fig. 8-27B. Conventional types must be connected in SERIES with the circuit. All of the current in the circuit must pass through the ammeter.

A modern *inductive* or *clip-on ammeter* is simply slipped over the outside of the wire insulation. It uses the magnetic field around the outside of the wire to

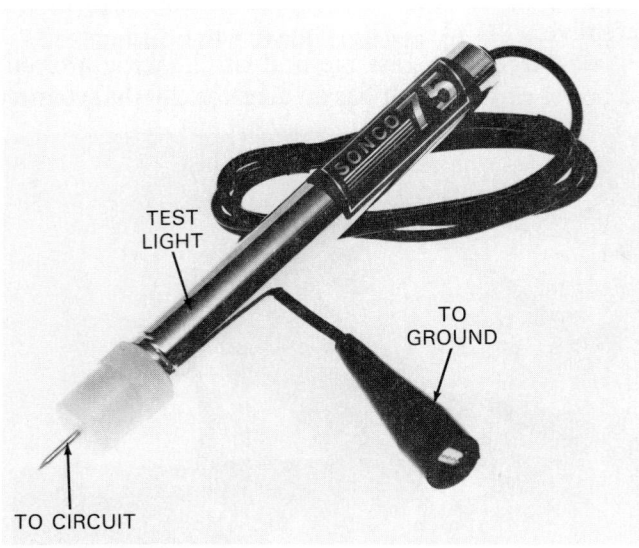

Fig. 8-25. Test light will quickly check for power in circuit. Connect alligator clip to ground and touch tip to circuit. Light will glow if there is power in circuit. (Sonco Manufacturing)

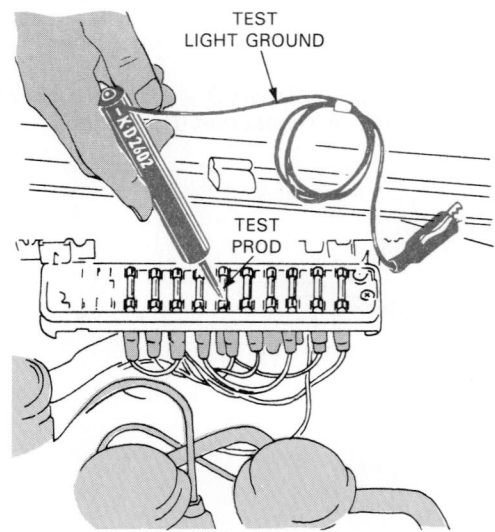

Fig. 8-26. Example of test light use is testing for a bad fuse. Blown fuse will show up when test light only glows on one side of fuse. Good fuse will cause light to glow on both sides of fuse. (K-D Tools)

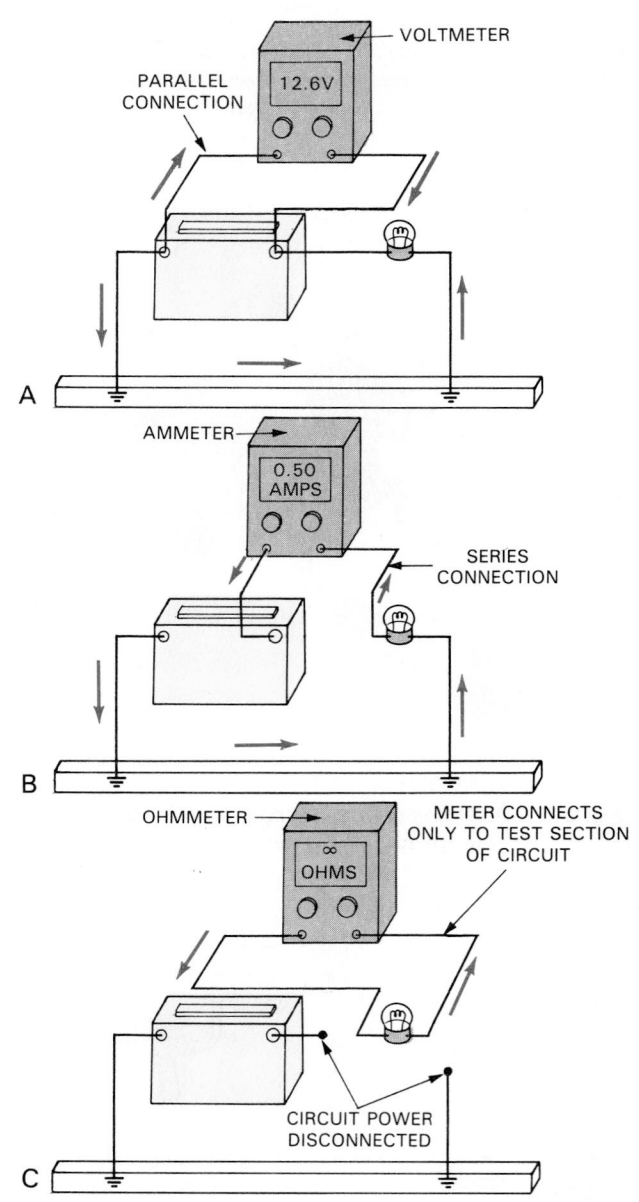

Fig. 8-27. Three basic meter connections. A — Voltmeter connects in parallel. It measures amount of electrical pressure or potential in circuit. B — Ammeter connects in series with circuit. Current flows through meter and circuit. C — Ohmmeter is connected to circuit with power disconnected. Voltage can damage some meters.

determine the amount of current in the wire. An inductive ammeter is very fast and easy to use.

An *ohmmeter* will measure the amount of resistance (ohms) in a circuit or component. To prevent damage, an ohmmeter must NEVER be connected to a source of voltage. The wire or part being tested must be disconnected from the car's battery.

As in Fig. 8-27C, the ohmmeter is connected across the wire or component being tested. Then, the ohmmeter reading can be compared to specifications. If too high or low, the part is defective.

A *multimeter,* also called a VOM, is an ohmmeter, ammeter, and voltmeter combined in one case. As pictured in Fig. 8-28, a function knob (control knob) can be turned to select the type measurement to be made (volts, amps, or ohms). It must be connected to the circuit as described for each individual meter.

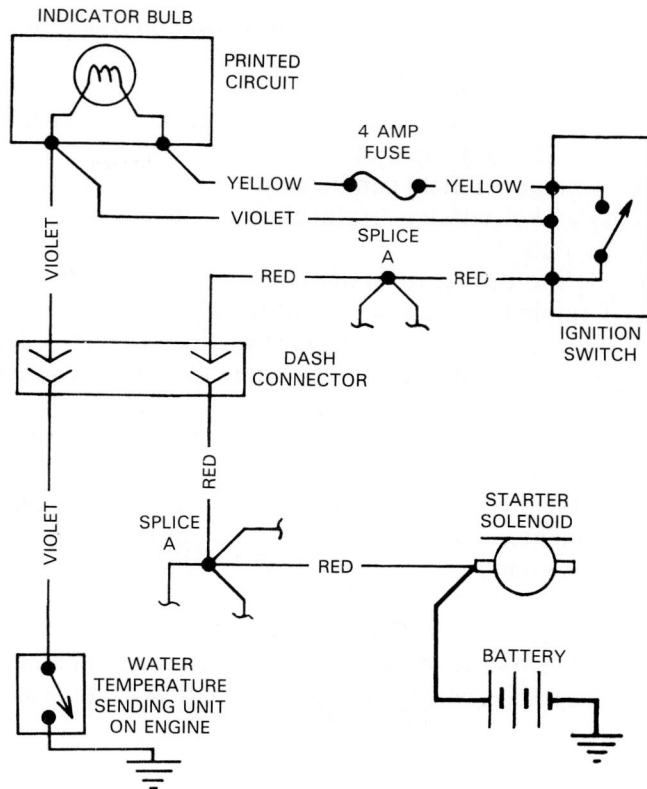

Fig. 8-29. Note how wiring diagram uses symbols to represent parts of electrical circuit.

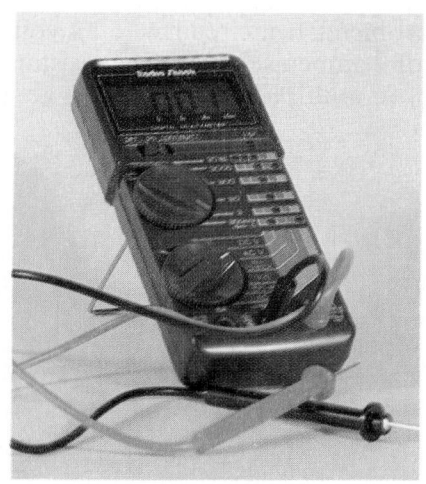

Fig. 8-28. Multimeter is voltmeter, ammeter, and ohmmeter combined. This is a digital meter because it has number display, not an indicating needle.

Wiring diagrams

A road map shows how various cities are connected by roads and highways. Similarly, a *wiring diagram* shows how electrical components are connected by wires. Look at Fig. 8-29. It serves as an "electrical map" which helps the mechanic with difficult electrical repairs.

Wiring diagrams use *symbols* to represent the electrical components in a circuit. The lines on the diagram represent the wires. In this way, you can trace each wire and see how it connects to each component.

OTHER INFORMATION

The principles of electronics are explained in numerous other chapters. The chapters on starting systems, charging systems, fuel systems, etc., all cover this topic. The new chapters (74, 75, 76) detail computers systems. Refer to the index as needed.

KNOW THESE TERMS

Conductor, Insulator, Simple circuit, Current, Voltage, Resistance, One-wire circuit, Ohm's Law, Magnetic field, Short circuit, Fuse, Circuit breaker, Relay, Semiconductor, Diode, Transistor, Integrated circuit, Printed circuit, Amplifier, Primary wire, Wiring harness, Secondary wire, Crimping pliers, Soldering gun, Rosin core solder, Jumper wire, Test light, Multimeter, Wiring Diagram.

REVIEW QUESTIONS

1. A car, this book, and people are made of atoms. True or False?
2. What is electricity?
3. Explain the difference between a conductor and an insulator.
4. Which of the following is NOT part of a simple circuit?
   a. Electric motor.
   b. Load.
   c. Power source.
   d. Conductors.
5. List and explain the three basic elements of electricity.
6. A _____ circuit has more than one load connected in a single electrical path.

7. A _____ circuit has more than one electrical path or leg.
8. What is a one-wire circuit?
9. Using Ohm's Law, find the resistance in a circuit with 12 volts and three amps.
10. A magnetic field can be used to produce electricity and electricity produces a magnetic field. True or False?
11. Define the term "short circuit."
12. Explain the functions of fuses and circuit breakers.
13. A _____ is an electrical, not electronic, device that allows a small current to control a larger current.
14. Explain the difference between an electric component and an electronic component.
15. Which of the following ARE electronic components.
    a. Diode.   c. Circuit breaker.
    b. Transistor.   d. IC.
16. An _____ is an electronic circuit that uses a very small current to control a very large current.
17. Secondary wire is used to carry battery voltage and has thick insulation. True or False?
18. Why are wires color coded?
19. Which of the following should NOT be used for electrical repairs?
    a. Acid core solder.   c. Crimp connectors.
    b. Rosin core solder.   d. Soldering gun.
20. Explain the use of a test light, voltmeter, ohmmeter, ammeter, and wiring diagrams.

ACTIVITIES FOR CHAPTER 8

1. Using sketches and principles you have learned about basic electricity, prepare a presentation showing how electricity can be created through magnetism.
2. Demonstrate the use of a continuity tester and explain what it tells you about a circuit.
3. Using the pie chart on page 76, solve the following problem: If a circuit with 12 volts has a current of 2 amperes, what is the resistance? Explain why you multiplied or divided to get the answer.

Fasteners, Gaskets, Seals, Sealants

After studying this chapter, you will be able to:
- Identify commonly used automotive fasteners.
- Select and use fasteners properly.
- Remove, select, and install gaskets, seals, and sealants correctly.
- Cite safety rules appropriate to chapter.

Fasteners, gaskets, seals, and sealants are constantly used by the auto technician. It is almost impossible to connect any two parts of a vehicle without their use. This is an important chapter. It prepares you for many repair operations and for other text chapters.

FASTENERS

Fasteners are devices that hold the parts of a car together. Thousands of fasteners are used in the construction of modern autos. Fig. 9-1 shows the most common types.

BOLTS AND NUTS

A *bolt* is a metal rod with external (outside) threads on one end and a head on the other. When a high-quality bolt is threaded into a part without a nut, it can also be called a *cap screw*.

A *nut* has internal (inside) threads and usually a hex (six sided) outer shape. When a nut is screwed onto a bolt, a powerful clamping force is produced, as shown in Fig. 9-2.

In auto technology, bolts and nuts are named after the parts they hold. For instance, the bolts holding the cylinder head on the block are termed HEAD BOLTS. The bolts on an engine connecting rod are called ROD BOLTS.

Bolt and nut terminology

Bolts and nuts come in various sizes, *grades* (strengths), and thread types. It is important to be

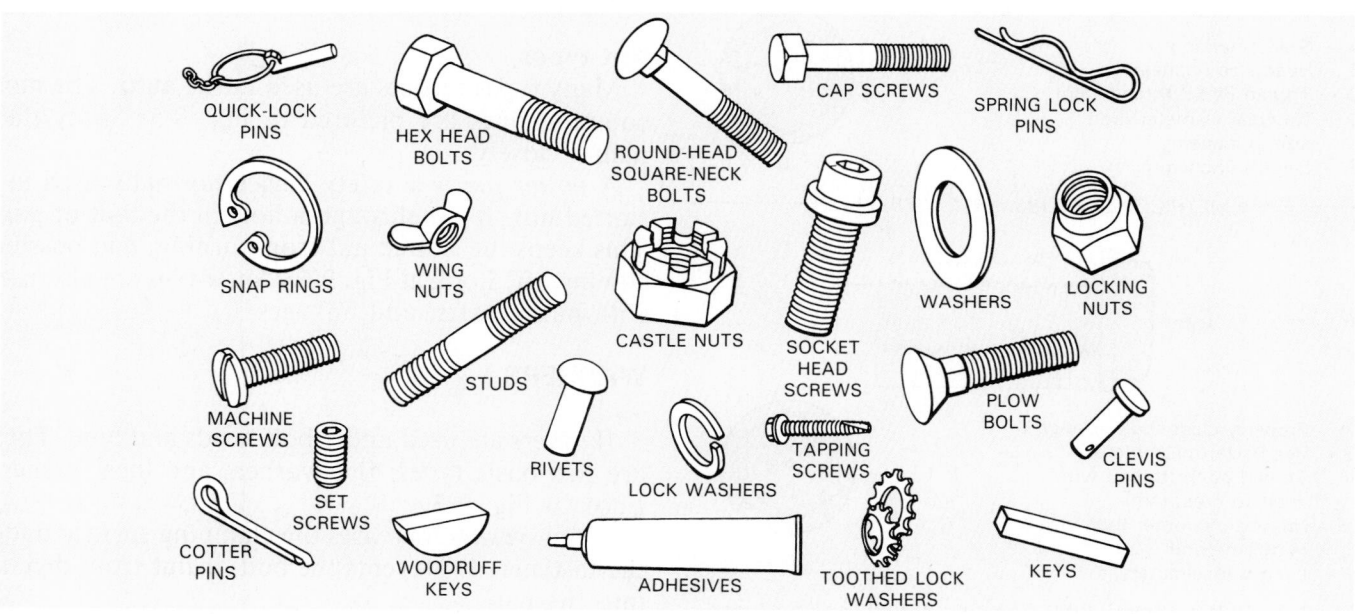

Fig. 9-1. A fastener is any device or adhesive used to hold parts of car together. Study these basic types. (Deere & Co.)

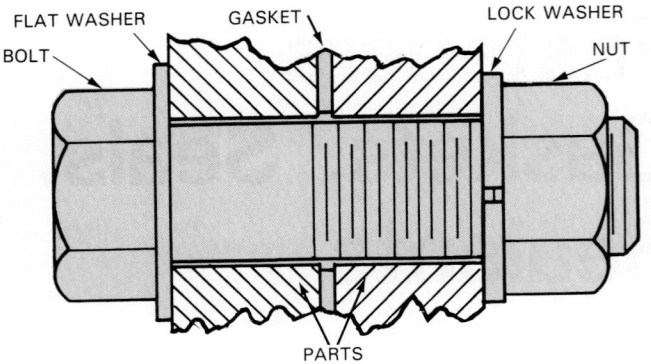

Fig. 9-2. Bolt and nut exert powerful clamping force on parts. Note washers and gasket between mating surfaces or parts.

familiar with these differences.

The most important *bolt dimensions* are:

1. *Bolt size* is a measurement of the outside diameter of the bolt threads. See Fig. 9-3.
2. *Bolt head size* is the distance across the flats or outer sides of the bolt head. It is the same as the wrench size.
3. *Bolt length* is measured from the bottom of the bolt head to the threaded end of the bolt.
4. *Thread pitch* is the same as thread coarseness. With U.S. fasteners, it is the number of threads per inch. With metric fasteners, it is the distance between each thread in millimeters. Refer again to Fig. 9-3.

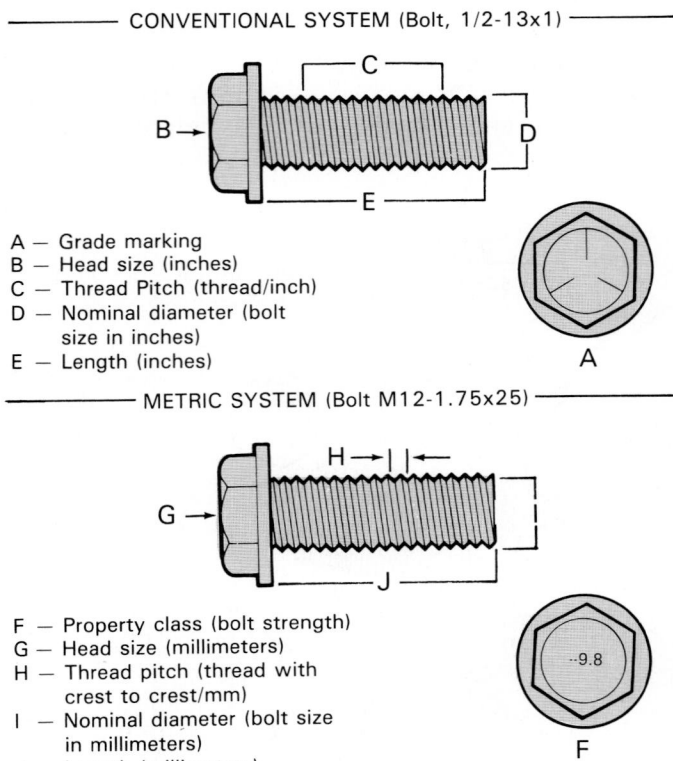

CONVENTIONAL SYSTEM (Bolt, 1/2-13x1)

A — Grade marking
B — Head size (inches)
C — Thread Pitch (thread/inch)
D — Nominal diameter (bolt size in inches)
E — Length (inches)

METRIC SYSTEM (Bolt M12-1.75x25)

F — Property class (bolt strength)
G — Head size (millimeters)
H — Thread pitch (thread with crest to crest/mm)
I — Nominal diameter (bolt size in millimeters)
J — Length (millimeters)

Fig. 9-3. Bolt nomenclature. Compare terms used with conventional and metric bolts. (Ford)

Thread types

There are three basic types of threads used on fasteners:

1. COARSE THREADS (UNC-Unified National Coarse).
2. FINE THREADS (UNF-Unified National Fine).
3. METRIC THREADS (SI).

Never interchange thread types or thread damage will result. As shown in Fig. 9-4, metric threads could be mistaken for conventional if not inspected carefully. If a metric bolt is forced into a hole with fine threads, either the bolt or part threads will be ruined.

Bolts and nuts also come in right and left-hand threads. With common *right-hand threads,* the fastener must be turned clockwise to tighten. With the less common *left-hand threads,* turn the fastener in a counterclockwise direction to tighten. The letter "L" may be stamped on fasteners with left-hand threads.

Bolt grade (head markings)

Tensile strength or *grade* refers to the amount of pull or stretch a fastener can withstand before breaking. Tensile strengths can vary. Bolts are made of different metals, some stronger than others.

Bolt head markings, also called *grade markings,* specify the tensile strength of the bolt. Conventional bolts are marked with *lines* or *slash marks.* The more lines, the stronger the bolt. A metric bolt is marked with a *numbering system.* The larger the number, the stronger the bolt. Look at Fig. 9-4.

DANGER! Never replace a high grade bolt with a lower grade bolt. The weaker bolt could easily snap, possibly causing part failure and a dangerous situation.

Bolt description

A *bolt description* is a series of numbers and letters that describe the bolt, as shown in Fig. 9-4. When purchasing new bolts, the bolt description information is needed.

Nut types

Many types of nuts are used in the auto. The most common ones are pictured in Fig. 9-5. Study their names closely.

A *cotter pin* is a safety device normally used in a slotted nut. It fits through a hole in the bolt or part. This keeps the slotted nut from turning, and possibly coming off. Look at Fig. 9-6. Cotter pins are also used with pins, shafts, and linkages.

WASHERS

Washers are used under bolt heads and nuts. There are two basic types: flat washers and lock washers. Look at Fig. 9-7.

A *flat washer* increases the clamping surface under the fastener. It prevents the bolt or nut from digging into the part.

A *lock washer* prevents the bolt or nut from becom-

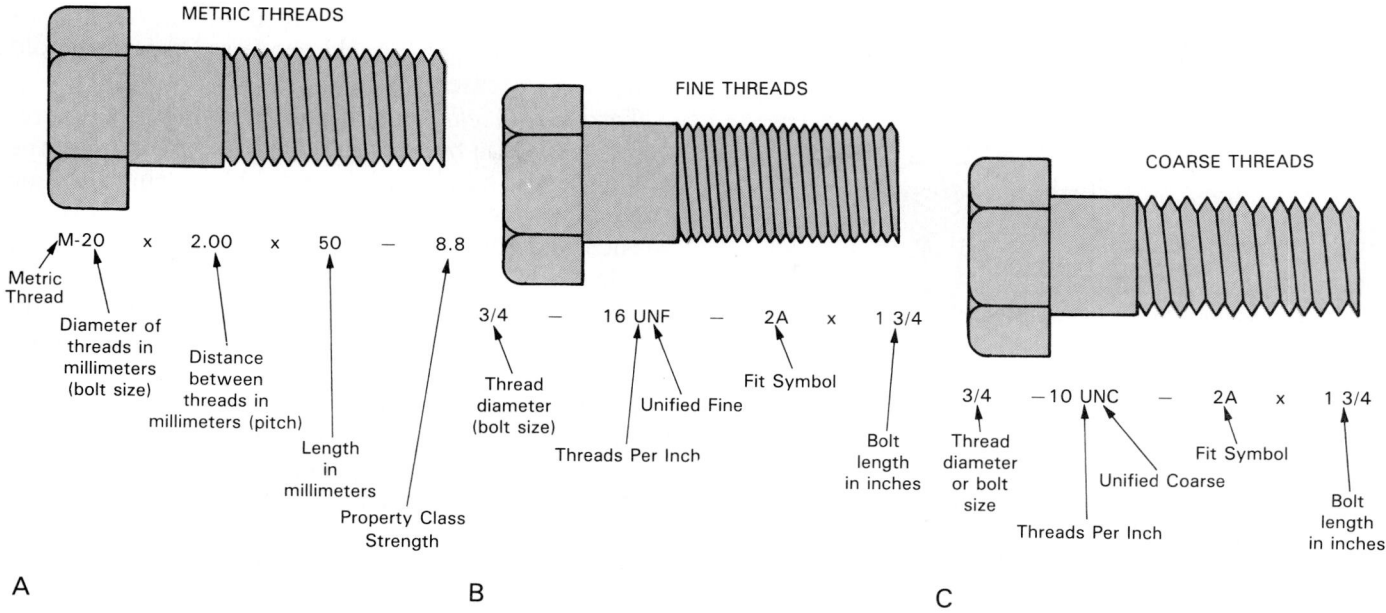

Fig. 9-4. Bolt designation number gives information about bolt. Number is commonly used when purchasing new bolts.

ing loose under stress and vibration.

Lock tabs or *plates* perform the functions of both flat and lock washers. They increase clamping surface area and secure the fastener.

TORQUING BOLTS

It is very important that bolts and nuts are *torqued* (tightened) properly. If OVERTIGHTENED, a bolt will stretch and possibly break. The threads could also fail. If UNDERTIGHTENED, a bolt could work loose and fall out. Part movement could also shear the fastener or break a gasket, causing leakage.

Torque specifications are tightening values given by the auto manufacturer. Torque specs are normally given for all precision assemblies (engines, transmission, differentials).

Fig. 9-8 shows a general *torque spec chart* that gives average bolt tightening values. It can be used when factory specs are not available. Note how bolt torque increases with bolt size and grade.

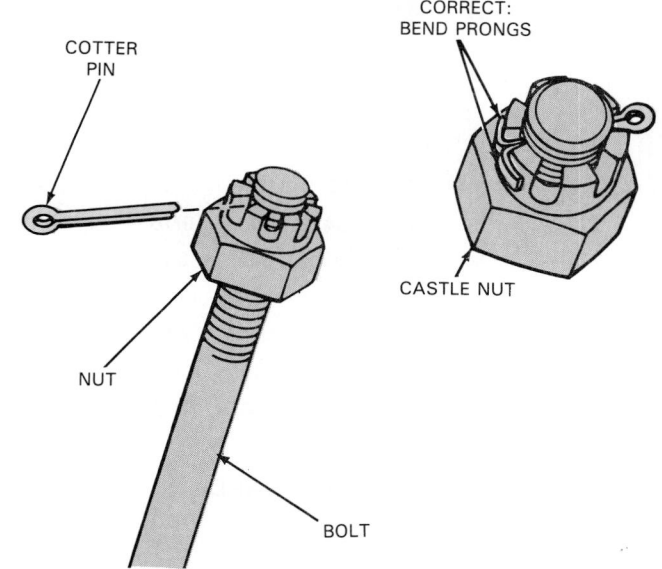

Fig. 9-6. Cotter pin slides through nut and hole in bolt. This makes sure nut cannot turn and come off. (Deere & Co.)

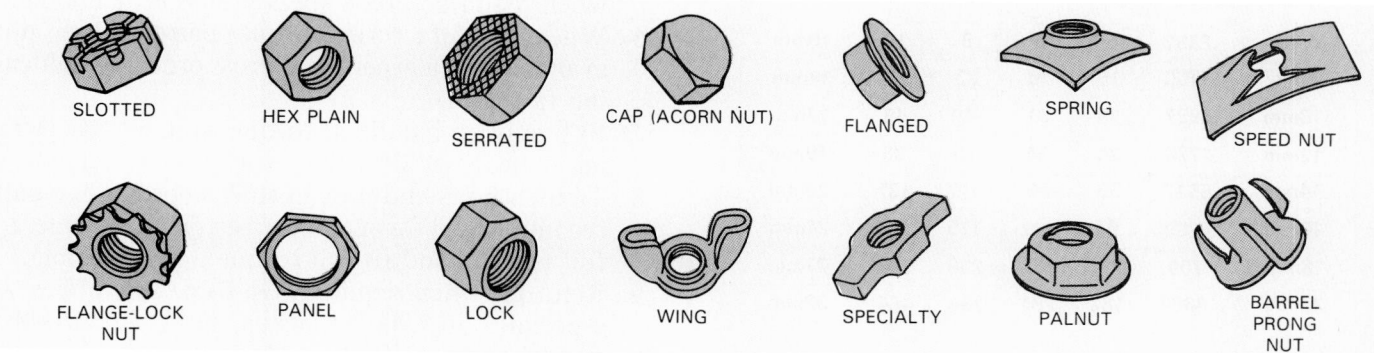

Fig. 9-5. All of these nut types are used in autos. Study them! (Deere & Co.)

Fasteners, Gaskets, Seals, Sealants 87

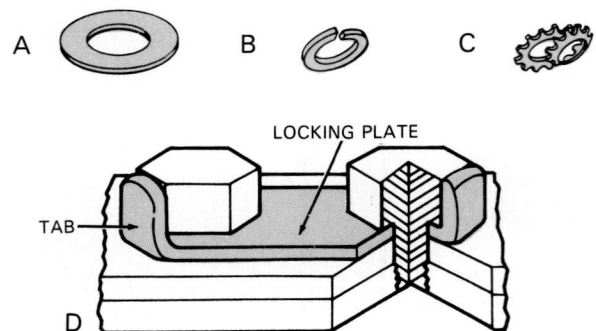

Fig. 9-7. Basic washer types. A — Plain flat washer. B — Split lock washer. C — Toothed lock washer. D — Lock plate.

CAUTION
The torque specifications listed below are approximate guidelines only and may vary depending on conditions when used such as amount and type of lubricant, type of plating on bolt, etc.

SAE STANDARD / FOOT POUNDS

GRADE OF BOLT	SAE 1 & 2	SAE 5	SAE 6	SAE 8		
MIN. TEN STRENGTH	64,000 P.S.I.	105,000 P.S.I.	133,000 P.S.I.	150,000 P.S.I.		
MARKINGS ON HEAD	⬡	⬡	⬡	⬡	SIZE OF SOCKET OR WRENCH OPENING	
U.S. STANDARD					U.S. REGULAR	
BOLT DIA.	FOOT POUNDS				BOLT HEAD	NUT
1/4	5	7	10	10.5	3/8	7/16
5/16	9	14	19	22	1/2	9/16
3/8	15	25	34	37	9/16	5/8
7/16	24	40	55	60	5/8	3/4
1/2	37	60	85	92	3/4	13/16
9/16	53	88	120	132	7/8	7/8
5/8	74	120	167	180	15/16	1.
3/4	120	200	280	296	1-1/8	1-1/8

METRIC STANDARD

GRADE OF BOLT		5D	.8G	10K	12K	
MIN. TENSILE STRENGTH		71,160 P.S.I	113,800 P.S.I	142,200 P.S.I.	170,679 P.S.I.	
GRADE MARKINGS ON HEAD		5D	8G	10K	12K	SIZE OF SOCKET OR WRENCH OPENING
METRIC						METRIC
BOLT DIA.	U.S. DEC EQUIV.	FOOT POUNDS				BOLT HEAD
6mm	.2362	5	6	8	10	10mm
8mm	.3150	10	16	22	27	14mm
10mm	.3937	19	31	40	49	17mm
12mm	.4720	34	54	70	86	19mm
14mm	.5512	55	89	117	137	22mm
16mm	.6299	83	132	175	208	24mm
18mm	.709	111	182	236	283	27mm
22mm	.8661	182	284	394	464	32mm

Fig. 9-8. General bolt torque chart. Note how torque values increase as bolt size and grade increase.

Service manuals sometimes recommend NEW bolts because of a torque-to-yield process. Discard the old bolts in such cases.

Torque-to-Yield is a bolt tightening method that requires a specific bolt torque, followed by turning the bolt a specific number of degrees. After using a torque wrench, a degree wheel adapter is placed between wrench and socket. The fastener is then turned until the degree wheel reads as specified by the manufacture. This stretches the bolt to its correct yield point and preloads the fastener for better clamping under varying conditions.

Torque stretch is determined by measuring bolt length change while torquing the bolt. For example, when building a racing engine, you could "mike" connecting rod bolts to measure length before and after tightening. Too much stretch would indicate bolt weakness. Not enough stretch might indicate thread problems, affecting torque.

Bolt tightening sequence (pattern)

A *bolt tightening sequence,* or *pattern,* is used to assure that parts are fastened evenly. An incorrect sequence or uneven tightening can cause breakage, warping, gasket leaks, and other problems.

Generally, tightening follows a *crisscross pattern* (going from one side to other). Refer to Fig. 9-9. This assures an even, gradual clamping force along the entire mating surface of the parts. Basically, you will partially tighten the middle first. Then, work your way to the other fasteners. A shop manual will illustrate the proper sequence when a torque pattern is critical.

Using a torque wrench

To use a torque wrench properly, follow these basic rules:

1. Keep a steady pull on the wrench. For accuracy, do NOT use short, jerky pull motions.
2. Clean and lightly oil the fastener threads.
3. When possible, avoid using swivel joints. They can upset torque wrench accuracy.
4. When reading a torque wrench, look straight down at the scale. Viewing from an angle can give a false reading.
5. A general torque value chart should only be used when manufacturer's specs are NOT available.
6. When manufacturer torque patterns are not available, use a general crisscross order for tightening fasteners.
7. Pull only on handle of torque wrench. DO NOT allow beam of wrench to touch anything.
8. Tighten bolts and nuts in four steps: to one-half recommended torque, to three-fourths torque, to full torque, and to full torque a second time.
9. Retorque when required. On some assemblies — especially on cylinder heads, intake manifolds, and exhaust manifolds — the bolts may have to be retightened after operation and heating.

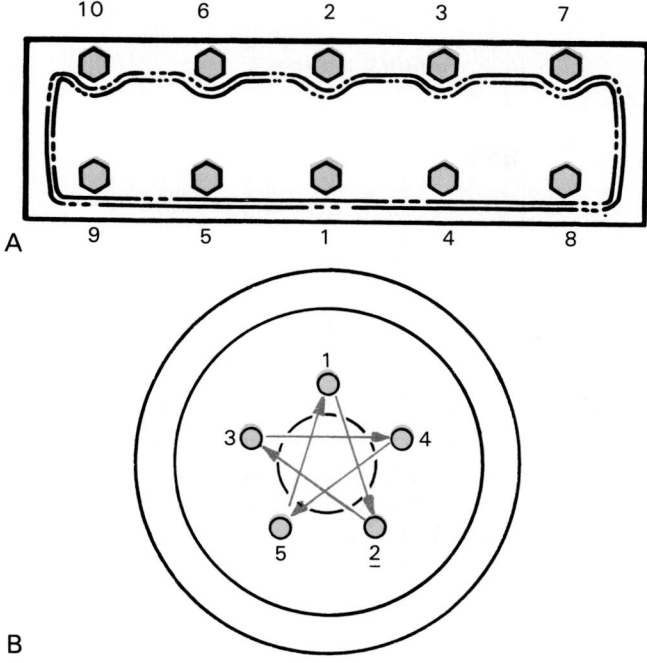

Fig. 9-9. Crisscross pattern is recommended when multiple fasteners hold part. A — Service manual pattern for engine cylinder head. B — Service manual pattern for wheel lug nuts.

Expansion and contraction, due to temperature changes, can cause the fasteners to loosen.

THREAD REPAIRS

A technician must be capable of repairing damaged threads quickly and properly. Threaded holes in parts can become damaged, requiring repairs.

Minor thread repairs

Minor thread damage includes nicks, partial flattening, and other less serious problems. Minor thread damage can usually be repaired with a thread chaser or threading tool.

A *thread chaser* "cleans up" slightly damaged internal and external threads. The chaser is run through or over the threads to restore them, Fig. 9-10.

Major thread repairs

Major thread damage generally includes badly smashed threads, stripped threads, or threads that cannot be repaired easily. Sometimes, major thread damage is repaired with either a tap or die, Fig. 9-11.

A *tap* is a threaded tool for cutting internal threads in holes. Various tap shapes are provided. Some are for starting the threads. Others are for cutting the threads all the way to the bottom of a hole, as shown in Fig. 9-11.

A *die* cuts external threads. It can be used to cut threads on metal rods, bolts, shafts, and pins.

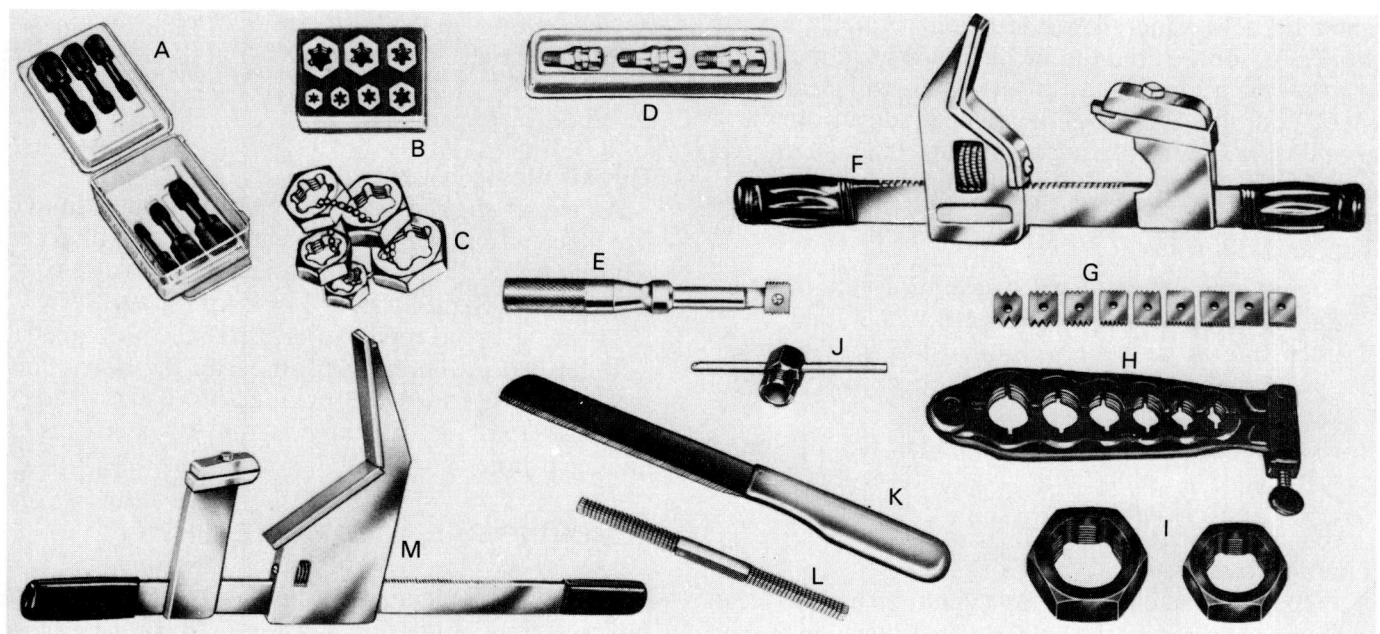

A. RETHREADING TAP
B. RETHREADING DIES
C. THREAD CHASING DIES
D. TUBE FITTING TAPS
E. INTERNAL THREAD CHASER
F. EXTERNAL RETHREADING TOOL
G. CHASERS
H. AXLE RETHREADER
I. SPINDLE DIES
J. SPECIAL THREAD CHASER
K. THREAD FILE
L. THREAD RESTORER
M. LARGE DIAMETER RETHREADING TOOL

Fig. 9-10. Thread repair tools are frequently used by auto mechanics, especially to salvage internal threads in valuable parts. Study the names of each carefully! (Snap-On Tools)

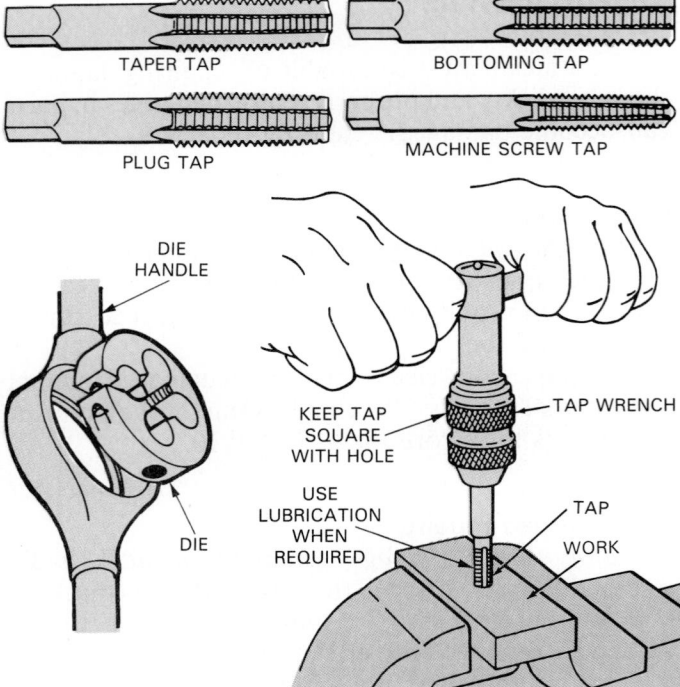

TAPER TAP BOTTOMING TAP

PLUG TAP MACHINE SCREW TAP

DIE HANDLE

KEEP TAP SQUARE WITH HOLE — TAP WRENCH

USE LUBRICATION WHEN REQUIRED

DIE

TAP

WORK

Fig. 9-11. Taps and dies fit into special handle. Handle is held square as it is turned into work. Back handle off to clean metal out of threads. Taper tap is for starting threads in hole. Then, use plug tap and bottoming tap to cut thread to bottom of hole.

Taps and dies are mounted in special handles, called tap handles and die handles. See Fig. 9-11. The tool must be held squarely while being rotated into the work. As soon as the tap or die begins to bind, back the tool off about a quarter turn. This will clear away metal cuttings. Then the cut can be made another half turn deeper. Keep rotating a half turn in and a quarter turn out until the cut is complete.

Tap and die rules

1. Never force a tap handle or the tool may break. Back off the handle to clean out metal shavings.
2. Keep the tap and die well oiled to ease cutting.
3. Always use the right size tap in a correctly sized and drilled hole.
4. Use coarse threads when threading or tapping into soft metal, like aluminum. Coarse thread will hold better than fine.

Tapping oversize

When a thread chaser or tap cannot be used to clean up damaged threads, the hole can be drilled and tapped oversize. First, drill out the hole one diameter or size larger. Then, cut new threads in the drilled hole with the correct size tap. A larger bolt can then be installed.

A *drill and tap size chart* is given in Fig. 9-12. It is useful when selecting the right size drill bit and tap. One example: the chart shows that when a 27/64 in. hole is drilled, a 1/2 in. coarse tap is required.

AMERICAN NATIONAL SCREW THREAD PITCHES

COARSE STANDARD THREAD (N. C.)				
Formerly U. S. Standard Thread				
Bolt or Tap Size	Threads Per Inch	Outside Diameter at Screw	Drill Sizes	Decimal Equivalent of Drill
1	64	.073	53	0.0595
2	56	.086	50	0.0700
3	48	.099	47	0.0785
4	40	.112	43	0.0890
5	40	.125	38	0.1015
6	32	.138	36	0.1065
8	32	.164	29	0.1360
10	24	.190	25	0.1495
12	24	.216	16	0.1770
1/4	20	.250	7	0.2010
5/16	18	.3125	F	0.2570
3/8	16	.375	5/16	0.3125
7/16	14	.4375	U	0.3680
1/2	13	.500	27/64	0.4219
9/16	12	.5625	31/64	0.4843
5/8	11	.625	17/32	0.5312
3/4	10	.750	21/32	0.6562
7/8	9	.875	49/64	0.7656
1	8	1.000	7/8	0.875
1 1/8	7	1.125	63/64	0.9843
1 1/4	7	1.250	1 7/64	1.1093

FINE STANDARD THREAD (N. F.)				
Formerly S.A.E. Thread				
Bolt or Tap Size	Threads Per Inch	Outside Diameter at Screw	Drill Sizes	Decimal Equivalent of Drill
0	80	.060	3/64	0.0469
1	72	.073	53	0.0595
2	64	.086	50	0.0700
3	56	.099	45	0.0820
4	48	.112	42	0.0935
5	44	.125	37	0.1040
6	40	.138	33	0.1130
8	36	.164	29	0.1360
10	32	.190	21	0.1590
12	28	.216	14	0.1820
1/4	28	.250	3	0.2130
5/16	24	.3125	I	0.2720
3/8	24	.375	Q	0.3320
7/16	20	.4375	25/64	0.3906
1/2	20	.500	29/64	0.4531
9/16	18	.5625	0.5062	0.5062
5/8	18	.625	0.5687	0.5687
3/4	16	.750	11/16	0.6875
7/8	14	.875	0.8020	0.8020
1	14	1.000	0.9274	0.9274
1 1/8	12	1.125	1 3/64	1.0468
1 1/4	12	1.250	1 11/64	1.1718

Fig. 9-12. Tap drill chart tells you what size hole should be drilled for different taps. Drill bit size is in two right columns. Tap and bolt size is in left column.

Thread repair insert

A *thread repair insert* should be used when an oversize hole and fastener is NOT acceptable. An insert will repair damaged internal threads and allow use of the ORIGINAL SIZE BOLT. Look at Fig. 9-13.

To use a thread repair insert, drill the hole oversize as described in the instructions. Tap the hole. Then, screw the insert into the threaded hole. The inside of the insert will act as threads the same size as the damaged hole.

REMOVING DAMAGED FASTENERS

An auto technician must be able to remove broken bolts, screws, studs, and fasteners having rusted or rounded-off heads. This is an important skill that is not covered in service manuals.

Certain tools and methods are needed for removing problem fasteners:

1. LOCKING PLIERS can sometimes be used to remove fasteners whose heads or nuts are badly rusted and rounded off. Lock the pliers tightly on the bolt or nut for removal.

2. A STUD PULLER or stud wrench will remove studs and bolts broken off above the surface of the part. It will also install studs. Position the stud puller so that it will not clamp onto and damage the threads.

3. In some cases, broken fasteners are too short to grasp with any tool. Either cut a SCREWDRIVER SLOT in the bolt with a hacksaw or weld on another BOLT HEAD. Then a screwdriver or wrench can be used to unscrew the broken bolt.

4. When the fastener is broken FLUSH with the part surface, a HAMMER and PUNCH will sometimes remove it. Angle the punch so that blows from the hammer can drive out the broken bolt.

5. A SCREW EXTRACTOR or "easy-out" can also be used to remove bolts broken flush or below the part surface. See Fig. 9-14. To use a screw extractor, drill a hole in the exact center of the broken fastener. Then, lightly tap the extractor into the hole using a hammer. Unscrew the broken bolt using a wrench.

CAUTION! Be extremely careful not to break a tap or a screw extractor. They are case hardened and cannot be easily drilled out of a hole. You will compound your problems if you overtwist and break one of these tools.

6. On some broken bolts, you may have to drill a hole almost as large as the inside diameter of the threads. Then, use a tap or punch to remove the thread shell. A *thread shell* is a thin layer of threads remaining in the hole. See Fig. 9-15.

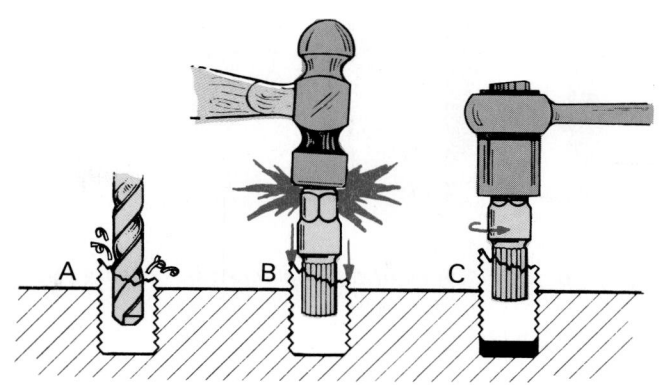

Fig. 9-14. Using a screw extractor. A — Drill hole in center of broken bolt. B — Tap extractor into hole. C — Unscrew extractor and broken bolt with wrench. (Lisle Tools)

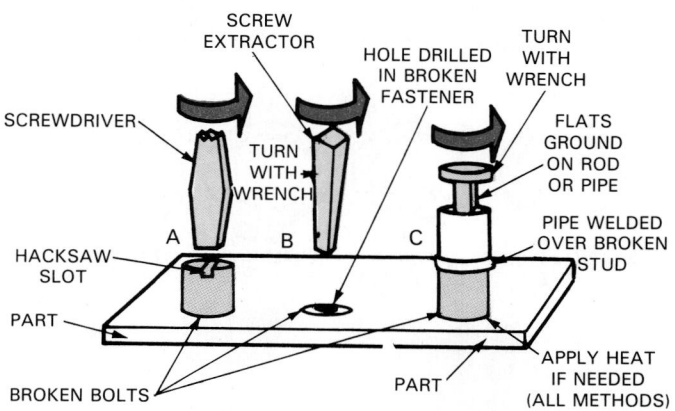

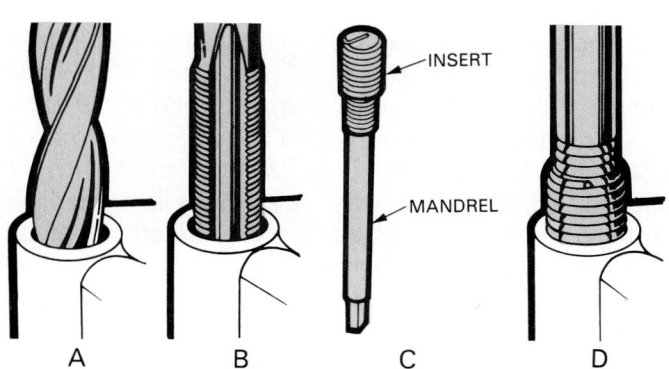

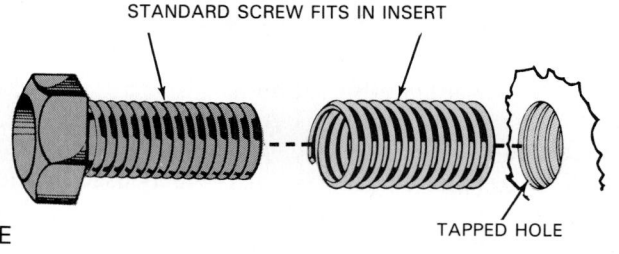

Fig. 9-13. Using an insert to repair stripped threads. A — Drill hole oversize. B — Tap hole oversize. C — Mount insert on mandrel. D — Thread into hole. E — Insert allows use of original size bolt. (Buick and Chrysler)

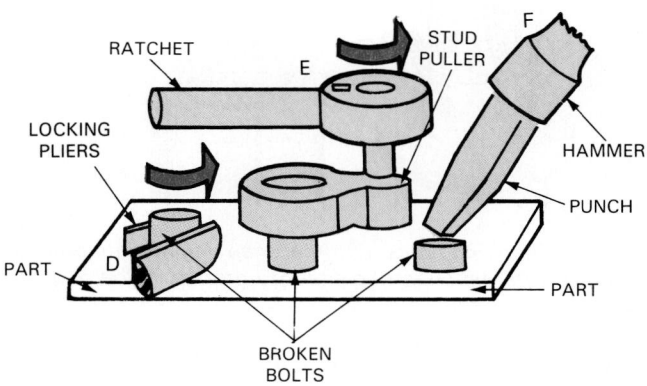

Fig. 9-15. Note various ways to remove broken bolts. A—Hacksaw a slot and use screwdriver. B—Drill hole and use easy out. C—Weld on pipe or shaft and use wrench. D—Use locking pliers. E—Use stud extractor and ratchet. F—Use hammer and punch.

MACHINE SCREWS

Machine screws are similar to bolts, but they normally have screwdriver type heads. They are threaded full length and are relatively small. Refer to Fig. 9-1. Machine screws are used to secure parts when clamping loads are light. They come in various head shapes.

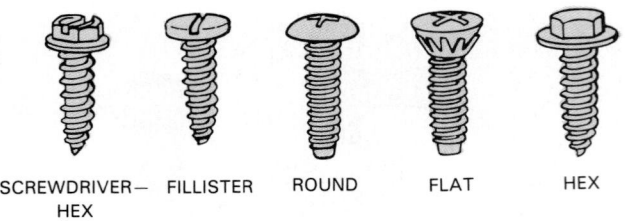

Fig. 9-16. Basic types of tapping screws. (Deere & Co.)

SCREWDRIVER— FILLISTER   ROUND   FLAT   HEX
HEX

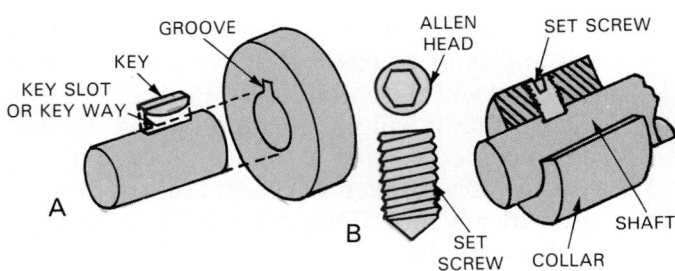

Fig. 9-18. A — Key fits into slot in shaft and part. This keeps part from turning on shaft. B — Setscrew also locks part to shaft, but with less strength. (Florida Dept. of Voc. Ed.)

SHEET METAL SCREWS

Sheet metal screws or *tapping screws* are commonly used to hold plastic and sheet metal parts (body trim, dashboard panels, and grills). Several are shown in Fig. 9-16. Study their shapes.

Sheet metal screws have tapering threads that are

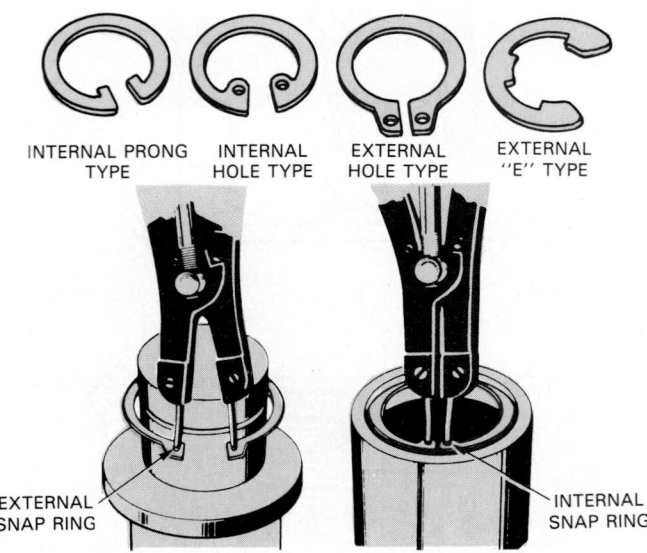

Fig. 9-17. Snap ring types. External snap ring fits into groove on shaft. Internal snap ring fits into groove inside hole.

very widely spaced. They come in a wide range of head shapes, sizes, and screwdriver head types.

NONTHREADED FASTENERS

Numerous types of *nonthreaded fasteners* are utilized in the assembly of an automobile. It is essential to learn the most common types.

Snap rings

A *snap ring* fits into a groove in a part and commonly holds shafts, bearings, gears, pins, and other similar components in place. Fig. 9-17 shows several types of snap rings.

Snap ring pliers are needed to remove and install snap rings. As pictured in Fig. 9-17, they have special

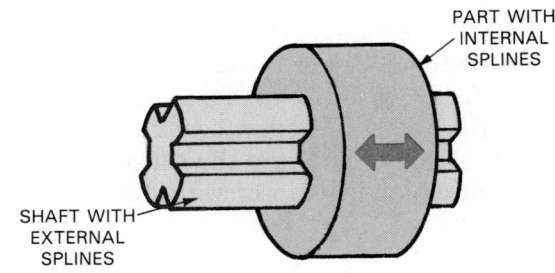

Fig. 9-19. Splines allow part to slide on shaft, but not turn on shaft.

jaws that fit and grasp the snap ring.

CAUTION! Wear eye protection when working with snap rings. When flexed, the ring can shoot into your face with considerable force.

Keys and keyways

A metal *key* fits into a *keyway* (groove) cut into a shaft and part (gear, pulley, collar). The key prevents the part from turning on its shaft. Refer to Fig. 9-18A.

Set screws are normally used to lock a part onto a shaft. See Fig. 9-18B. They may be used with or without a key and keyway. A setscrew is a headless fastener normally designed to accept an allen wrench (hex wrench) or screwdriver.

Splines

Splines are a series of slots cut into a shaft and a mating part. See Fig. 9-19. Splines have one advantage over a key. Splines allows the gear or collar to slide on the shaft but still NOT rotate. This sliding locking action is commonly used in manual transmissions, clutches, and drive shaft yokes.

Adhesives

Adhesives (special glues) are also widely used on most late model cars. They hold body moldings, rubber weatherstripping, and body emblems. See Fig. 9-20.

Some adhesives are designed to stay soft and pliable. Others dry hard. Some take hours to dry, while others dry in seconds. Observe all directions and safety precautions when using adhesives.

GASKETS AND SEALS

Gaskets and seals are used between parts to prevent leakage of engine oil, coolant, transmission oil, and other fluids. It is important to understand a few principles about gaskets and seals. If they are serviced improperly, serious customer complaints and mechanical failures can result.

GASKETS

A *gasket* is a soft, flexible material placed between parts to prevent leakage. It can be made of fiber materials, rubber, neoprene (synthetic rubber), cork, treated paper, or thin steel. See Fig. 9-21.

When the parts are fastened tightly together, the gasket is compressed and deformed. This forces the gasket material to fill small gaps, scratches, dents, or other imperfections in the part surfaces. A leakproof seal is produced. Refer back to Fig. 9-2.

Gasket rules

When working with gaskets, remember the following:

1. INSPECT FOR LEAKS BEFORE DISASSEMBLY. If the two parts are leaking, the part surfaces should be inspected closely for problems.
2. AVOID PART DAMAGE DURING DISASSEMBLY. Be careful not to nick, gouge, or dent mating surfaces while removing parts. The slightest unevenness could cause leakage.
3. CLEAN OFF OLD GASKET CAREFULLY. All of the old gasket material must be scraped or wire brushed from the parts. Use care, especially on aluminum and brass. These soft metals are easily

damaged. Use a dull scraper and wire brush lightly.

4. WASH AND DRY PARTS THOROUGHLY. After gasket removal, wash parts in solvent. Blow dry with compressed air. Then wipe mating surfaces with a clean shop rag.
5. CHECK NEW GASKET SHAPE. Compare the new gasket to the shape of the mating surface. Lay the new gasket into place and inspect. All holes and sealing surfaces must match perfectly.
6. USE SEALER IF NEEDED! Some gaskets require sealer. Sealer is normally used where two different gaskets come together. It will prevent leakage where gaskets overlap. Check a service manual for details. Use sparingly. Too much sealer could clog internal passages in the assembly.
7. HAND START ALL FASTENERS BEFORE TIGHTENING. After fitting the gasket and parts in place, screw all bolts in by hand. This will assure proper part alignment and threading of fasteners. It also lets you check bolt lengths.
8. TIGHTEN IN STEPS! When more than one bolt is used to hold a part, tighten each bolt a little at a time. Tighten one to about half of its torque spec, then the others. Tighten to three-fourths torque and to full torque. Then, RETORQUE each fastener a second time.
9. USE A CRISSCROSS TIGHTENING PATTERN. Either a basic crisscross or factory recommended torque pattern should be used when tightening parts. This will assure even gasket compression and sealing.
10. DO NOT OVERTIGHTEN FASTENERS. It is very easy to tighten the bolts enough to dent sheet metal parts and smash or break the gaskets. Apply only the specified torque.

Fig. 9-20. Always use recommended type of sealer or adhesive on gaskets. Some adhesives are oil and fuel soluble and can cause leakage. Both spray adhesive and brush-on sealer are available. They will hold gasket in place during assembly of parts. (Fel-Pro)

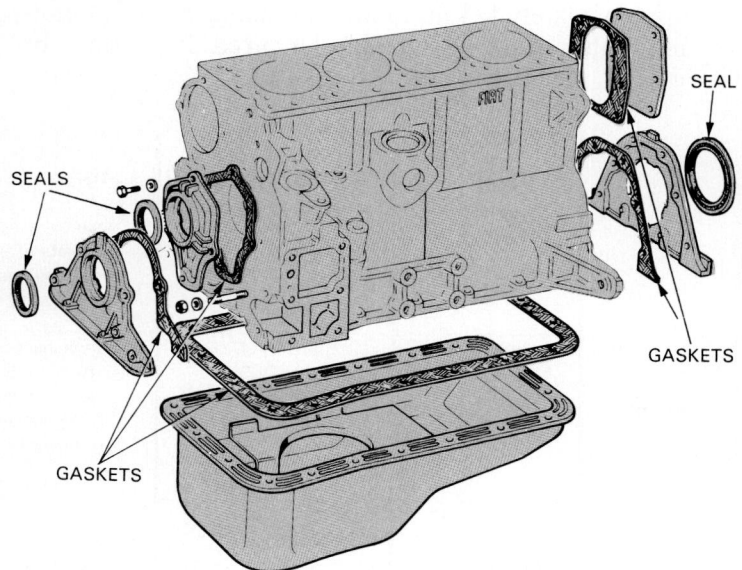

Fig. 9-21. Gasket prevents leakage between stationary parts. Seal prevents leakage between moving part and stationary part. (Fiat)

SEALERS

A *sealer* is commonly coated on a gasket to help prevent leakage, and to hold the gasket during assembly. There are numerous kinds of sealers. They have different properties and are designed for different uses. Always read the manufacturer's label and a service manual before selecting a sealer. Look at Fig. 9-22.

Hardening sealers are used on permanent assemblies such as fittings and threads, and for filling uneven surfaces. They are usually resistant to heat and most chemicals.

Nonhardening sealers are for semipermanent assemblies: cover plates, flanges, threads, hose connections, and numerous other applications. They are also resistant to most chemicals and moderate heat. *Shellac* is a nonhardening sealer. It is a gummy, sticky substance that remains pliable. It is frequently used on fiber gaskets as a sealer and to hold the gasket in place during assembly.

Form-in-place gaskets

Form-in-place gasket refers to a special sealer that is used instead of a conventional fiber or rubber gasket. Two common types of form-in-place gaskets are: RTV (room temperature vulcanizing) sealer and anaerobic sealer.

RTV sealer, also called *silicone sealer,* cures (dries) from moisture in the air. It is used to form a rubber-like gasket on thin, flexible flanges.

RTV sealer normally comes in a tube, as shown in Fig. 9-23. Depending upon the brand, it can have a shelf life from one year to two years. Always inspect the package for the expiration date before use. If too old, RTV sealer will NOT CURE (harden) and seal properly.

RTV sealer should be applied in a continuous bead approximately 1/8 in. (3 mm) in diameter. All mounting holes must be circled. Uncured RTV may be

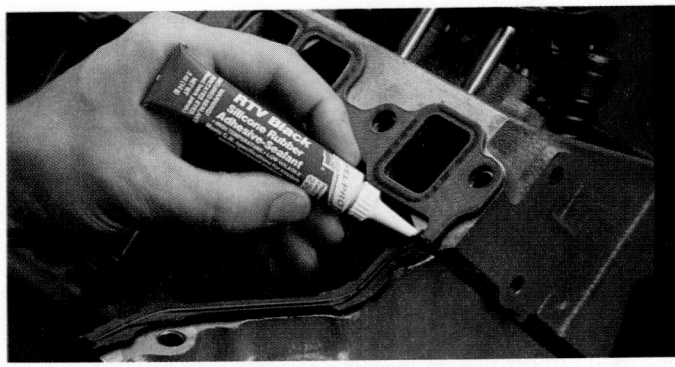

Fig. 9-23. RTV sealer is commonly recommended where two different gaskets join. Sealer prevents leakage between two gaskets.

removed with a rag.

Components should be torqued in place while the RTV is still wet to the touch (within about 10 minutes). The use of locating dowels is often recommended to prevent the sealing bead from being smeared. If the continuous bead of silicone is broken, a leak may result.

Anaerobic sealer cures to a plastic-like substance in the absence of air and is designed for tightly fitting, thick parts. It is used between two smooth, true surfaces, NOT on thin, flexible flanges.

Fig. 9-24 shows the use of both anaerobic and RTV sealer on the same part. The RTV sealed section contacts the flexible engine oil pan. The anaerobic sealed section touches the strong, machined engine block.

Anaerobic sealer should be applied sparingly. Use 1/16 to 3/32 in. (1.5 to 2 mm) diameter bead on one gasket surface. Be certain that the sealer surrounds each mounting hole. Typically, bolts should be torqued within 15 minutes.

TYPE	TEMPERATURE RANGE	USE	RESISTANT TO	CHARACTERISTICS
shellac	−65° to 350°F (−54 to 177°C)	general assembly: gaskets of paper, felt, cardboard, rubber, and metal	gasoline, kerosene, grease, water, oil, and antifreeze mixtures	dries slowly sets pliable alcohol soluble
hardening gasket sealant	−65° to 400°F (−54 to 205°C)	permanent assemblies: fittings, threaded connections, and for filling uneven surfaces	water, kerosene, steam, oil, grease, gasoline, alkali, salt solutions, mild acids, and antifreeze mixture	dries quickly sets hard alcohol soluble
nonhardening gasket sealant	−65° to 400°F (−54 to 205°C)	semi-permanent assemblies: cover plates, flanges, threaded assemblies, hose connections, and metal-to-metal assemblies	water, kerosene, steam, oil, grease, gasoline, alkali, salt solutions, mild acids, and antifreeze solutions	dries slowly nonhardening alcohol soluble

Fig. 9-22. Study use and characteristics of sealer types. (Fel-Pro)

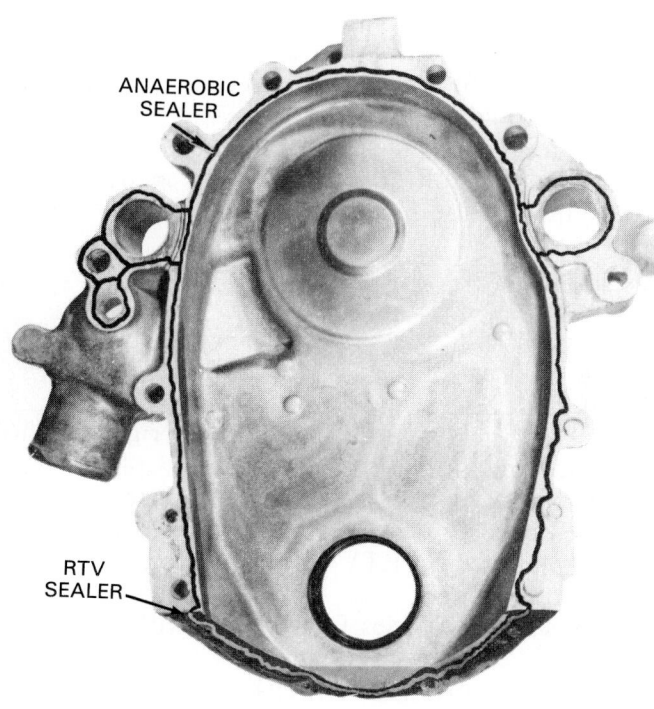

ANAEROBIC
SEALER

RTV
SEALER

Fig. 9-24. Note use of RTV and anaerobic sealers. RTV is for flexible flanges. Anaerobic is for solid, tight fitting castings. Use recommended bead size and form continuous bead to avoid leakage. (Pontiac)

When selecting a form-in-place gasket, refer to a manufacturer's service manual.

Scrape or wire brush all gasket surfaces to remove all loose material. Check that all gasket rails are flat. Using a shop rag and solvent, wipe off oil and grease. The sealing surfaces must be CLEAN and DRY before using a form-in-place gasket.

NOTE! A few gasket manufacturers sell pre-cut gaskets designed to replace form-in-place gaskets. When working on an engine installed in a vehicle, it can be difficult to properly clean the sealing surfaces. It may also be almost impossible to fit a part on the engine without hitting and breaking the bead of sealant. When this is the case, a pre-cut gasket might work better than a form-in-place gasket.

SEALS

Seals prevent leakage between a stationary part (housing, cover) and a moving part. They can be found in engines, transmissions, rear ends, power steering units, and almost any part containing fluid and moving parts. A seal allows the shaft to spin or slide inside the nonmoving part without fluid leakage. Seals are normally made of synthetic rubber molded onto a metal body, Fig. 9-25.

Seal rules

As with gaskets, there are several very important procedures to remember when working with seals.

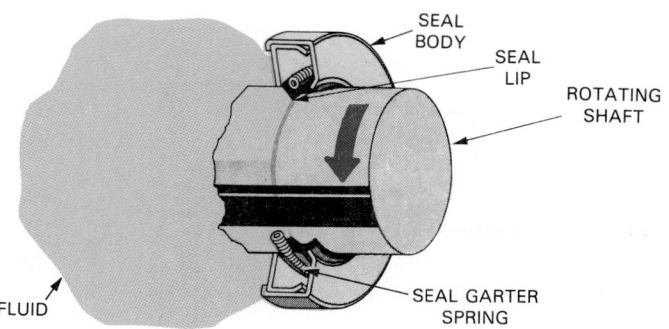

SEAL
BODY
SEAL
LIP
ROTATING
SHAFT
SEAL GARTER
SPRING
FLUID

Fig. 9-25. Seal mounted in stationary part. Shaft spins inside seal. Seal lip faces fluid and keeps fluid inside part. (Caterpillar Tractor)

1. INSPECT SEAL FOR LEAKAGE BEFORE DISASSEMBLY. If a seal is leaking, there may be other problems besides a defective seal. Look for a bent shaft, misaligned seal housing, or damaged parts. Leakage requires close inspection after disassembly.
2. REMOVE OLD SEAL CAREFULLY. Pry out the old seal without scratching the seal housing. Sometimes, a special puller is required for seal removal. This will be discussed in other chapters.
3. INSPECT SHAFT FOR WEAR AND BURRS. Look at the shaft closely where it contacts the seal. It should be smooth and flat. File off any burrs that could cut the new seal. A badly worn shaft, Fig. 9-26, will require polishing, a shaft sleeve repair kit, or replacement.
4. CHECK NEW SEAL SIZE. Compare the old seal to the new seal. Hold them next to each other. Both the inside diameter (ID) and outside diameter (OD) must be the same. To double-check inside diameter, slip the seal over the shaft. It should fit snugly to prevent leakage.
5. INSTALL NEW SEAL CORRECTLY. Coat the outside of the seal housing with approved sealer. Coat the inner lip of the seal with system fluid. Install the seal with the sealing LIP FACING THE INSIDE OF THE PART, Fig. 9-25.

If installed backwards, a tremendous leak will result. Also, check that the seal is squarely and fully seated in its bore.

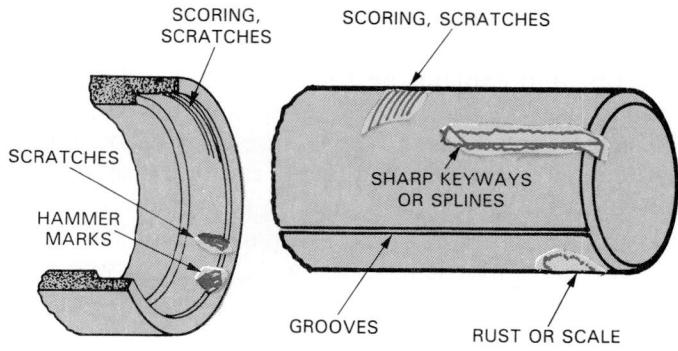

SCORING,
SCRATCHES
SCORING, SCRATCHES
SCRATCHES
HAMMER
MARKS
SHARP KEYWAYS
OR SPLINES
GROOVES
RUST OR SCALE

Fig. 9-26. Always inspect seal and shaft for damage. Slight nicks or scratches could cause leakage. (Federal Mogul)

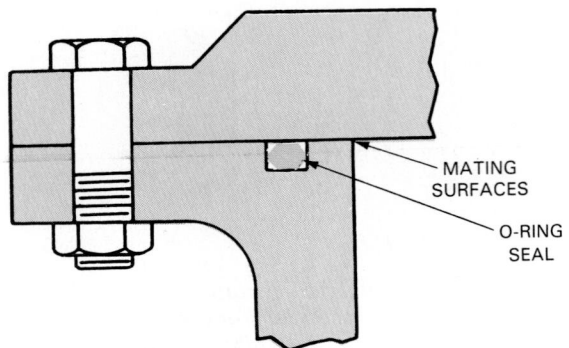

Fig. 9-27. O-ring seal prevents leakage as shown. Parts bolt together and partially compress rubber ring. (Deere & Co.)

O-ring seals

An *O-ring seal* is a stationary type seal that fits into a groove between two parts, Fig. 9-27. When the parts are assembled, the synthetic rubber seal is partially compressed and forms a leakproof joint.

Normally, O-ring seals should be coated with system fluid (engine oil, diesel fuel, transmission fluid or type fluid used in component). This will help the parts slide together without scuffing or cutting the seal.

Usually, sealants are NOT used on O-ring type seals. When in doubt about any seal installation, check in a shop manual.

OTHER INFORMATION

Special gaskets and seals sometimes require other installation techniques. These special situations will be discussed in later chapters.

KNOW THESE TERMS

Fastener, Bolt size, Thread pitch, Tensile strength, Grade markings, Torque specifications, Tightening sequence, Tap, Die, Screw extractor, Snap ring, Set screw, Key, Splines, Adhesive, Gasket, Seal, Sealant, RTV, Anaerobic sealer, O-ring seal.

REVIEW QUESTIONS

1. Define the terms "bolt" and "nut."
2. Bolts and nuts are usually named after the parts that they hold. True or False?
3. List and explain the four basic dimensions of a bolt.
4. Fine threads and metric threads can be interchanged (mixed together). True or False?
5. Conventional bolt heads are marked with _____ or _____ marks to indicate bolt strength. Metric bolts use a _____ system to indicate bolt strength.
6. A _____ _____ is a safety device commonly used with a slotted nut.
7. Describe the difference between a flat washer and a lock washer.
8. What are torque specifications?
9. What is a bolt or nut tightening sequence?
10. Which of the following is NOT used for thread repair?
    a. Tap.
    b. Die.
    c. Chaser.
    d. Chisel.
11. A _____ and _____ _____ _____ is needed to select the right size drill and tap.
12. How do you use a thread repair insert?
13. Describe six ways to remove broken fasteners.
14. Explain when RTV and anaerobic sealers are recommended.
15. Describe five rules for working with seals.

ACTIVITIES FOR CHAPTER 9

1. Demonstrate to the class the use of a thread gage.
2. Prepare a large chart for the shop showing how to read information given on a bolt.
3. Demonstrate the proper methods for repairing thread damage.

On rusted threads like this brake bleed screw, use rust penetrant or solvent to help ease turning and prevent breakage. (Fel-Pro Gaskets)

10

Vehicle Maintenance, Fluid Service

After studying this chapter, you will be able to:
☐ Check a car's fluid levels.
☐ Explain the importance of vehicle maintenance.
☐ Locate fluid leaks.
☐ Replace engine oil and filter.
☐ Change automatic transmission fluid and filter.
☐ Perform a grease job.
☐ Inspect for general problems with hoses, belts, and other components.
☐ Demonstrate safe practices while working with vehicle fluids.

All automotive technicians will, at some time, service vehicle fluids. These liquids will include engine oil, coolant, brake fluid, transmission fluid, and power steering fluid. Service station attendants, apprentice mechanics, and even experienced technicians must check, add, or replace fluids.

This chapter is extremely important. It may be your only chance to learn fluid service. Study carefully.

NOTE! EPA guidelines and state regulations affect how you handle and dispose of fluids and degreasers. Refer to the appendix for information on handling of waste and recyclables. Information on fluids is also to be found in other chapters. Check the index.

LUBRICATION SERVICE

Lubrication service typically involves:
1. Checking fluid levels and condition of the fluids.
2. Adding fluids as needed.
3. Locating fluid leaks and other obvious problems.
4. Lubricating (greasing) certain chassis parts.
5. Changing engine oil and filter.
6. Changing automatic transmission fluid.
7. Following state regulations on recycling or disposal of fluids.

VEHICLE MAINTENANCE

Vehicle maintenance includes any operation that will keep a vehicle in good running condition. Without pro-

per care, the life of an automobile can be reduced by thousands of miles. For example, fluids can become contaminated and changed chemically after prolonged use. This can cause part wear, corrosion, and mechanical failures.

As the saying goes, "You can pay now or you can pay later." This means that the customers can pay a little now for maintenance or much more later for repairs. This is very true. A poorly serviced vehicle will wear out and break down sooner than a well maintained vehicle. In the long run, vehicle maintenance saves the customer money.

CHECKING FLUID LEVELS

A service manual contains detailed information on how to check fluid levels. The manual will usually describe:
1. Location of all fluid check points, Fig. 10-1.
2. Location of fluid fill points.
3. Correct interval (time or mileage) between fluid checks or changes.
4. Correct type and quantity of fluid to be used.

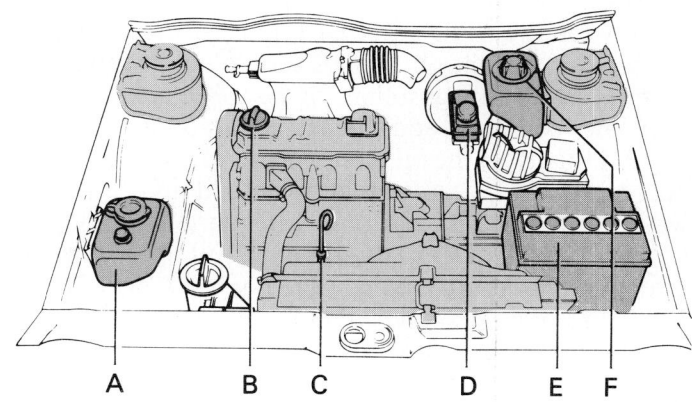

Fig. 10-1. Service manual will give locations of all fluid check points. This manual illustration shows engine compartment fluid check points. A — Engine coolant reservoir. B — Engine oil filler cap. C — Engine oil dipstick. D — Brake fluid reservoir. E — Battery. F — Windshield washer reservoir.   (VW)

This information varies from vehicle to vehicle. As one example, a diesel engine or turbocharged engine may require more frequent oil changes than a similar gasoline injected engine. Automatic transmission or transaxle fluids, differential lubricants, and other fluids can vary in chemical content.

NOTE! A car's warranty can become void if improper fluids or incorrect service procedures are used. For these reasons, refer to manufacturer's recommendations when servicing fluids.

Checking engine oil

To check engine oil, warm the engine to operating temperature. Shut off the engine and allow it to sit for a few minutes. Locate and remove the engine oil dipstick, Fig. 10-2. Wipe off the dipstick and replace it all the way into its tube. Pull the dipstick back out and hold it over your shop rag.

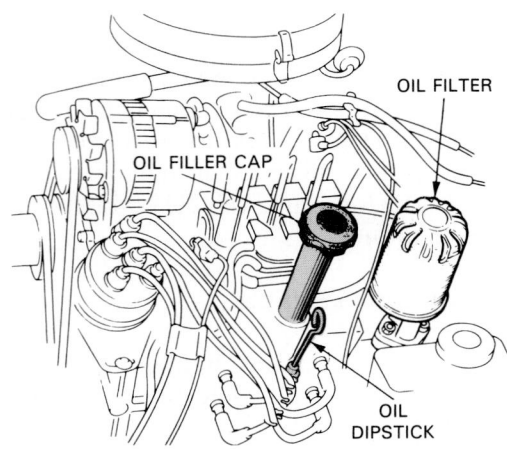

Fig. 10-2. Check amount of oil in engine with dipstick. Add oil through opening under oil filler cap or cap in valve cover. (Mazda)

As shown in Fig. 10-3, the oil level should be within the prescribed marks on the dipstick. The oil should be between the ADD and FULL marks. Also, inspect the condition of the oil. The oil should not be too thick or thin, smell like gasoline, or be too black.

If low, you must add the correct amount and type of oil. Usually, if the oil level is down to the add mark, add one quart. If halfway between add and full, you would only need to add one-half quart.

WARNING! Never add too much oil to an engine. Only pour in enough oil to reach the full mark. Overfilling can cause the oil to foam (absorb air bubbles), which reduces the oil's lubricating ability.

Adding engine oil

To add engine oil, obtain the right kind of oil. Look for a lubrication sticker in the engine compartment or on the driver's door. Use the same type of oil that was installed during the last oil change, if possible.

Install an oil filler spout into the oil can. Pour the oil into the filler opening in one of the valve covers or in the oil filler tube, Fig. 10-2.

Changing engine oil and filter

To change the engine oil, warm up the engine. Then, raise the car on a lift or place it on jack stands in a level position. Place a catch pan under the oil drain plug. See Fig. 10-4. Unscrew the plug and allow enough time for the oil to drain completely.

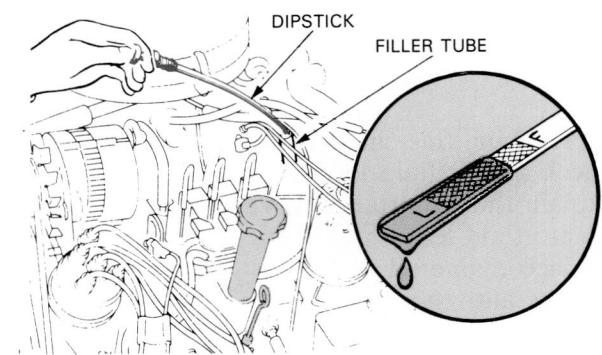

Fig. 10-3. Check oil with engine off, but warm. Oil should be between add and full marks on stick. Only add enough to bring to full mark. (Mazda)

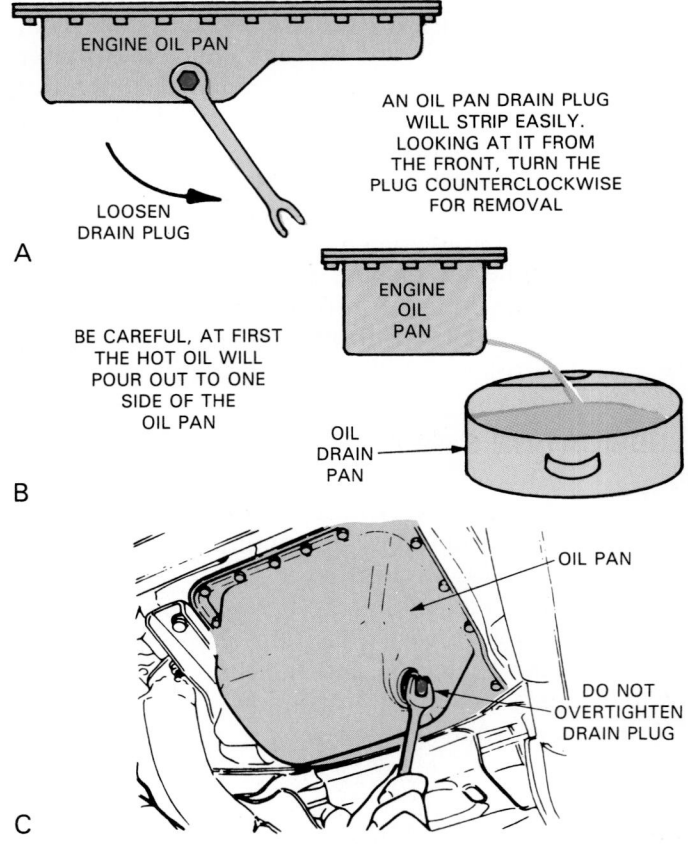

Fig. 10-4. To drain engine oil, remove oil pan drain plug. Allow oil to pour into catch pan. Be careful not to overtighten oil pan plug. Its threads will strip out easily. (Subaru)

After draining oil, reinstall the drain plug. Be careful, however; the threads in the pan and on the plug can strip easily. Apply only enough torque to draw the plug tight and prevent leakage.

To remove the engine oil filter, position your drain pan under the filter. Using an oil filter wrench, as in Fig. 10-5, unscrew the filter.

DANGER! Engine oil can be very hot. Do not let oil run down and burn your arm when draining!

Get the correct replacement filter. Compare the old and new filters. Make sure the rubber O-ring on the new filter is the same diameter as the old. Wipe some clean oil on the O-ring and install it. Tighten the filter only by hand, NOT with the filter wrench. Over-tightening will smash the O-ring and cause leakage.

Lower the car to the ground and add the correct amount and type of oil. Start the engine.

After an "oil change," make sure the oil pressure light GOES OUT. Let the engine run while checking for LEAKS under the engine.

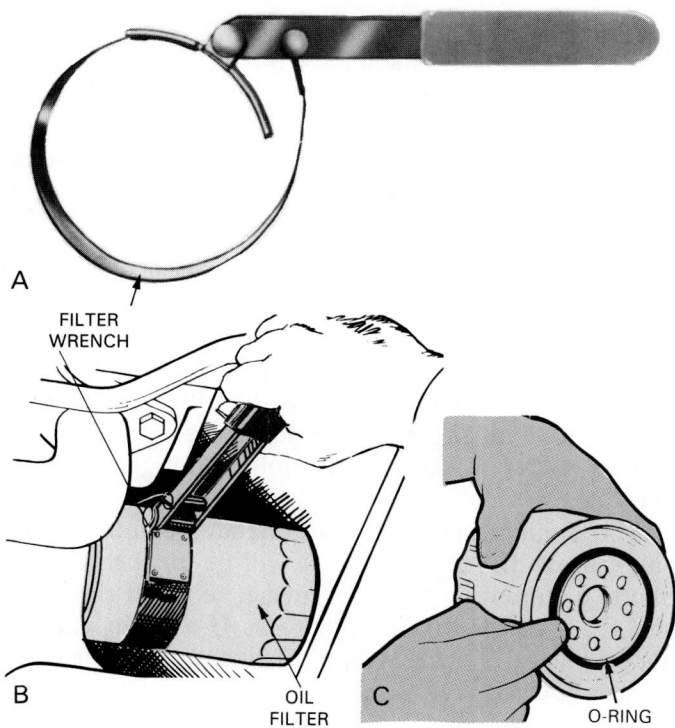

Fig. 10-5. A—Oil filter wrench is needed to unscrew oil filter. B—Turn in a counterclockwise direction. C—When installing new filter, coat O-ring seal with clean oil and hand tighten only. (Lisle)

Automatic transmission fluid service

Like engine oil, automatic transmission or transaxle fluid should be checked and changed at specified intervals. The fluid can become contaminated (filled) with metal, dirt, moisture, and friction material from internal parts. This can cause rapid part wear and premature (early) transmission failure.

To check the fluid in an automatic transmission, warm up the engine and move the gear selector through all positions. Apply the parking brake. Place the transmission in park and block the wheels.

With the engine still running, locate the transmission dipstick. See Fig. 10-6. It is normally behind the engine, near the front of the transmission.

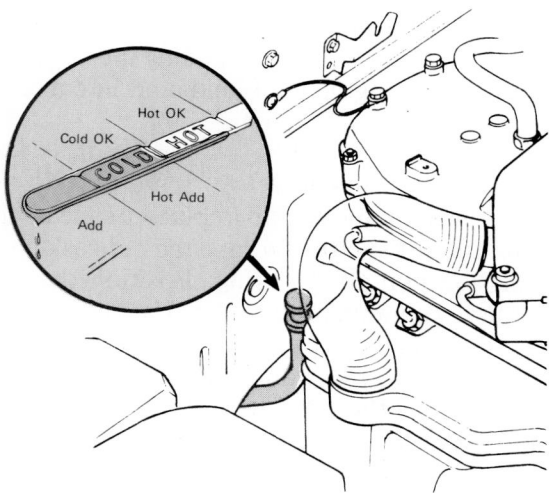

Fig. 10-6. Automatic transmission dipstick is normally behind engine, and to one side. Check it with engine running and transmission in park. If needed, add correct fluid. (Saab)

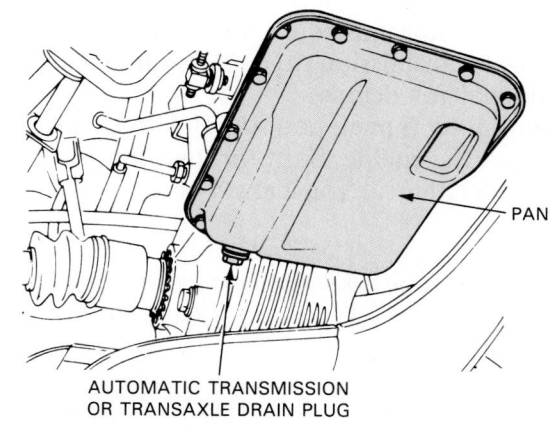

Fig. 10-7. Usually, transmission pan must be removed to drain fluid. A few pans, however, have a drain plug. Do not spill hot fluid on yourself. (Subaru)

Pull out dipstick. Wipe it off and re-insert it into tube. Remove stick again and hold it over a shop rag. The fluid should read between add and full. Also, inspect the fluid for discoloration and odor. If it smells burned, or looks dirty, the fluid should be changed.

NOTE! It is very easy to overfill an automatic transmission. Seldom do you have to add a full quart. Normally, if the dipstick reads add, only a fraction of a quart may be needed to fill the transmission. Sometimes, instructions are written on the dipstick. If in doubt, check a shop manual.

Changing automatic transmission fluid and filter

To change the fluid and filter in an automatic transmission, warm the engine and transmission. Raise the vehicle. If a drain plug is not provided, remove the bolts securing the transmission pan, Fig. 10-7. Be careful NOT to spill hot fluid.

Unscrew the last pan bolt while holding the transmission pan with a shop rag. Let the fluid pour into a catch pan.

DANGER! Be careful not to spill the hot transmission fluid. It can cause painful burns!

Next, if needed, remove and replace or clean the transmission filter, Fig. 10-8. Scrape the old gasket off the transmission pan and housing. Position the new pan gasket using an approved sealer. Use sealer sparingly because it could upset the operation of the transmission. You do not want any to squeeze out of the gasket and into the transmission housing.

Start all of the pan bolts with your fingers. Then tighten them in a crisscross pattern to their recommended torque spec. Overtightening can split the gasket or distort the transmission pan.

Some auto manufacturers recommend that the torque converter (fluid coupling in front of transmission) also be drained. A drain plug is normally located in the converter. It is usually under a rock shield on the front of the transmission housing.

Refill the transmission with the correct type and amount of transmission fluid. If required, check a service manual for details.

Using a long funnel, pour the fluid into the dipstick tube. Start the engine. Shift through the gears. Then, check under the car for leaks.

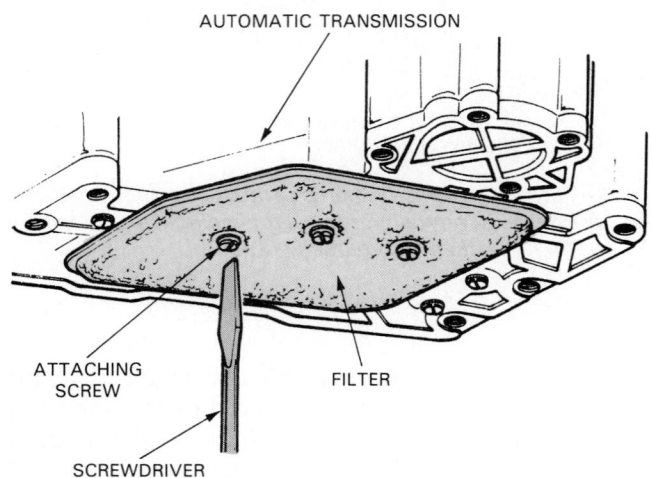

Fig. 10-8. Some manufacturers recommend periodic replacement of automatic transmission filter. It is located inside transmission pan. Tighten all fasteners to specs when assembling.

Manual transmission fluid check

To check the fluid in a manual transmission, locate the transmission filler plug, Fig. 10-9. It is normally on one side of the transmission. Generally, warm fluid should be even with the plug hole. With the transmission cold, the fluid can be slightly below the fill hole.

Some manufacturers suggest that the manual transmission fluid be changed periodically; others do not. If a fluid change is needed, remove the transmission drain plug on the bottom of the transmission. Install the right kind and quantity of fluid. Lubricate the gear shift mechanism and clutch release as described in a service manual.

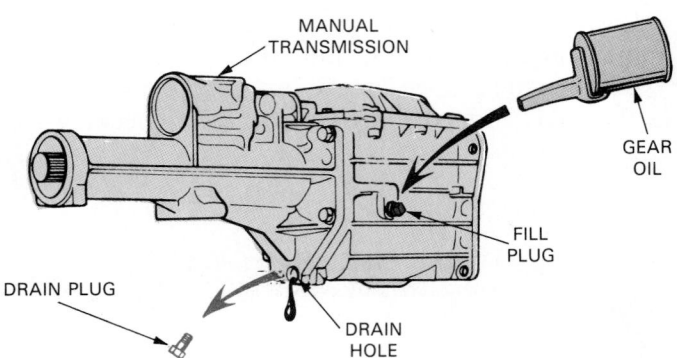

Fig. 10-9. Manual transmission will have fill plug for checking fluid level. Fluid should be almost even with hole with fluid warm. Check in service manual for details. (Chrysler)

Differential fluid check

To measure the fluid level in a differential (rear axle assembly), remove the filler plug. It will normally be on the front, back, or side of the differential. See Fig. 10-10. The lubricant should be even with the fill hole when hot. When cold, it should be slightly below the hole.

At the manufacturer's recommended change interval, remove the drain plug. It will be on the bottom of the differential. After draining, reinstall the plug and fill with the proper lubricant. If a drain plug is not provided, a special siphon (suction) gun can be used to draw out the old fluid.

NOTE! Positive traction or limited slip type differentials (both wheels pull for added traction) require a special lubricant. Refer to the vehicle identification number, a service manual, and the chapter on Rear Axle Service for details.

Engine coolant check

Engine *coolant* (mixture of water and antifreeze) is used in an engine's cooling system. Engine coolant must be changed every two years, maximum. After prolonged use, the coolant will deteriorate. It can become very corrosive and filled with rust. This may result in premature water pump, thermostat, and radiator failure.

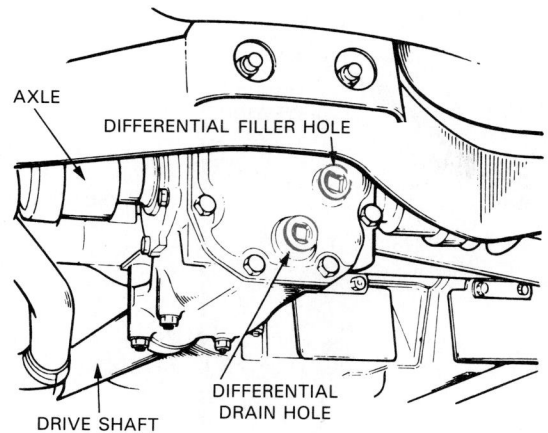

Fig. 10-10. Differential fill plug hole allows check of lubricant level. Do not accidentally remove drain plug. (Subaru)

CAUTION! Never remove a radiator cap while the engine or radiator is hot. Boiling coolant can spray out of the radiator, causing serious burns.

To check the coolant level, look at the side of the plastic overflow tank connected to the radiator. See Fig. 10-11. The coolant should be between the add and full marks. When an overflow tank is used, the radiator cap does NOT have to be removed.

Some older cars do not use an overflow tank. In this case, the radiator cap must be removed to check the coolant level. See Fig. 10-11. The coolant should be about an inch (25 mm) or so down in the radiator.

Also, inspect the condition of the coolant, Fig. 10-12. If rusty, the coolant should be drained and replaced. Watch for system leaks.

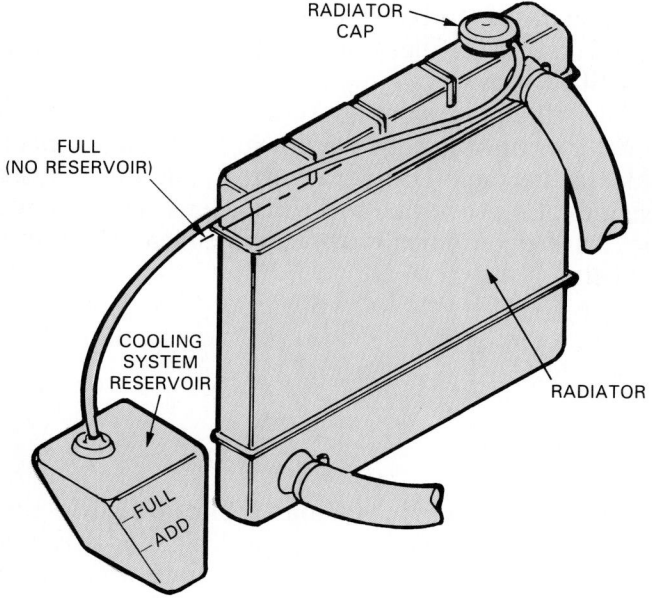

Fig. 10-11. Modern cooling systems have reservoir tank. You can check coolant level without removing radiator cap. On older systems, only remove cap after engine has cooled. Coolant should be about an inch (25 mm) down. (Florida Dept. of Ed.)

Checking power steering fluid

Power steering fluid is checked by removing the dipstick from the power steering pump, Fig. 10-13. The engine should not be running. Check the fluid level on the dipstick. If low, inspect for leaks and add the correct type and amount of fluid. Normally, a power steering system uses automatic transmission fluid.

Brake fluid check

The amount of brake fluid in a master cylinder should be inspected regularly, at least twice a year. Look at Fig. 10-14. The master cylinder is normally mounted on the firewall (body section between engine and passenger compartment).

When the master cylinder reservoir is a clear plastic, simply compare the fluid level to the markings. The fluid should be between add and full.

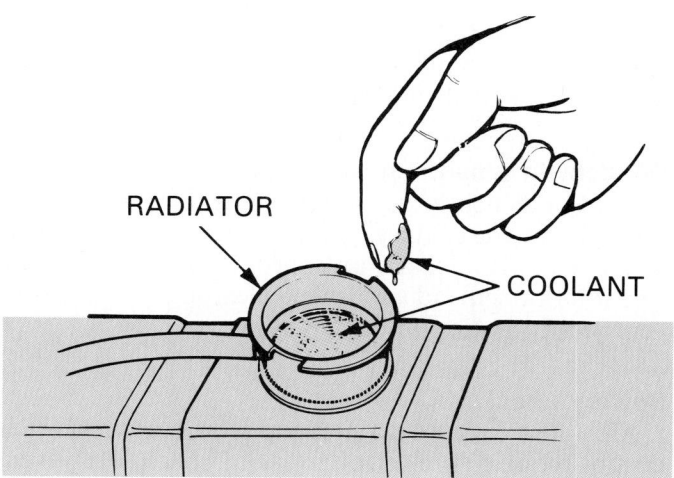

Fig. 10-12. If coolant is rusty, it should be drained and replaced. (Honda)

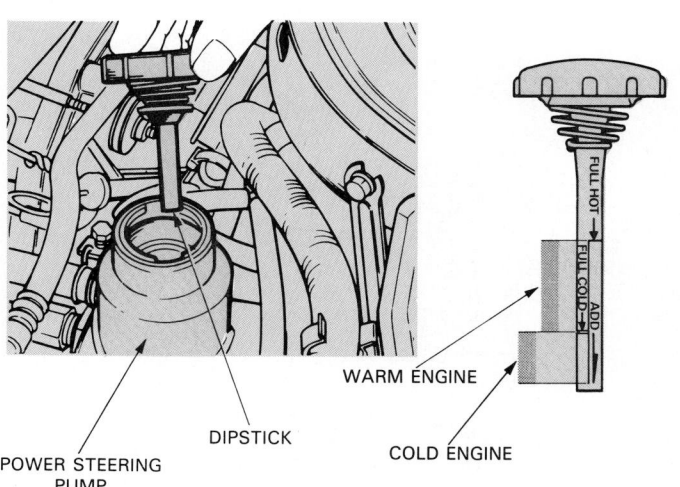

Fig. 10-13. Power steering pump normally has a cap with a dipstick. Check fluid with engine off. Compare fluid level to markings on dipstick. (Subaru)

With many master cylinders, you must remove the reservoir cover or lid to check the fluid. Generally, the fluid should be about 1/4 in. (about 6 mm) down from the top of the master cylinder. Add the recommended type brake fluid as needed.

Clutch fluid check

Some manual transmission clutches do NOT use mechanical linkage rods or cables. Instead, they use a hydraulic system to disengage the clutch. A clutch master cylinder, similar to a brake master cylinder, produces hydraulic pressure to activate the clutch release. The fluid in the clutch master cylinder should be checked. If low, add brake fluid to fill the reservoir almost full. Always watch for leaks.

Checking manual steering box fluid

Manual steering box fluid is checked by removing either a filler plug or designated bolt from the top of the box. Look at Fig. 10-15. The lubricant should be almost even with the plug or bolt opening. If not, add the recommended type fluid.

Windshield washer solvent check

The windshield washer solution is normally visible through the side of the plastic storage tank. Refer back to Fig. 10-1. If low, add an approved washer solution. The solution will aid windshield cleaning and also prevent ice formation in cold weather.

Battery check

Most new cars use maintenance-free batteries which do not require an electrolyte (acid) check. However, make sure that the battery terminals and case top are clean. A battery post and cable cleaning tool can be used on corroded connections, Fig. 10-16.

With an old style battery, remove the filler caps. Check that the acid in the battery is filled to the pro-

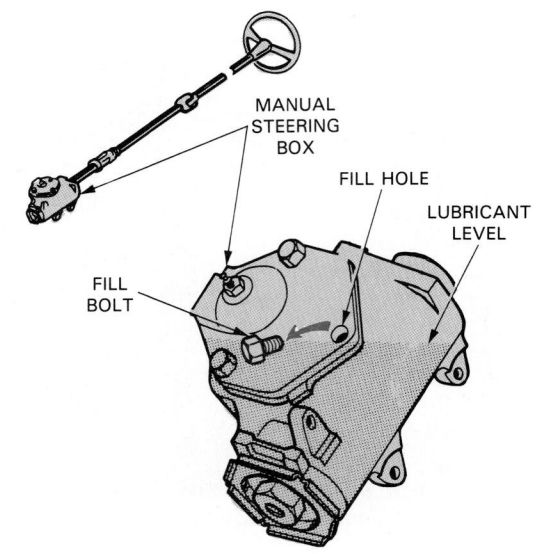

Fig. 10-15. Manual steering box will have bolt or plug for checking lubricant. If needed, fill with recommended type fluid up to fill hole. (Chrysler)

per level (slightly down from top of battery case or even with fill rings). Add distilled water to each cell as needed. Detailed battery service procedures are discussed in later chapters.

FILTER SERVICE

Quite often, various filters used in a vehicle are replaced during lubrication service. Besides the engine oil and transmission filters, the technician may also have to change or clean the air and fuel filters.

If an air filter is extremely dirty, it is normally replaced. However, some manufacturers permit light dirt and dust to be blown from the filter. Special foam or oil bath (oil filled) air filters can be cleaned as described in a service manual.

Fuel filters are commonly located inside the carburetor or throttle body inlet fitting and sometimes inside the fuel tank. Diesel, carburetor, and fuel injected engines also use in-line fuel filters. Fuel filters should be replaced periodically as recommended by the auto maker.

DANGER! Hold a shop rag around fuel line fittings when loosening. This will keep fuel from spraying or leaking out.

GREASE JOB

During a grease job, you must lubricate high-friction pivot points on the suspension, steering, and driveline systems. Most service manuals illustrate which parts must be lubricated, Fig. 10-17.

A *grease gun*, Fig. 10-18, is used to force lubricant (chassis grease) into small fittings. Inject only enough grease to fill the cavity in the part. Overgreasing can

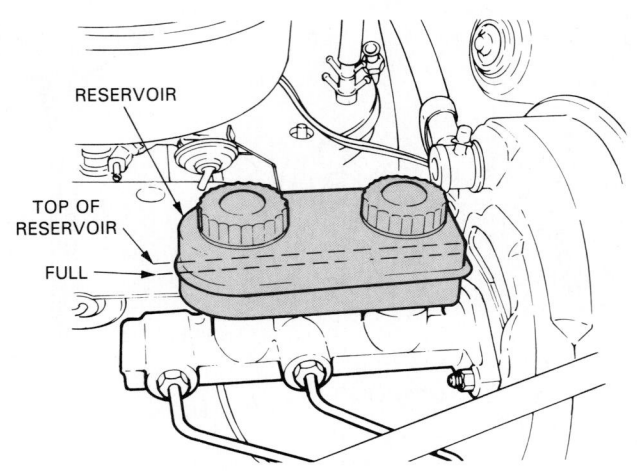

Fig. 10-14. Check brake fluid at master cylinder reservoir. Master cylinder is mounted on firewall in front of driver. Fluid should be slightly down from top of reservoir. (Chrysler)

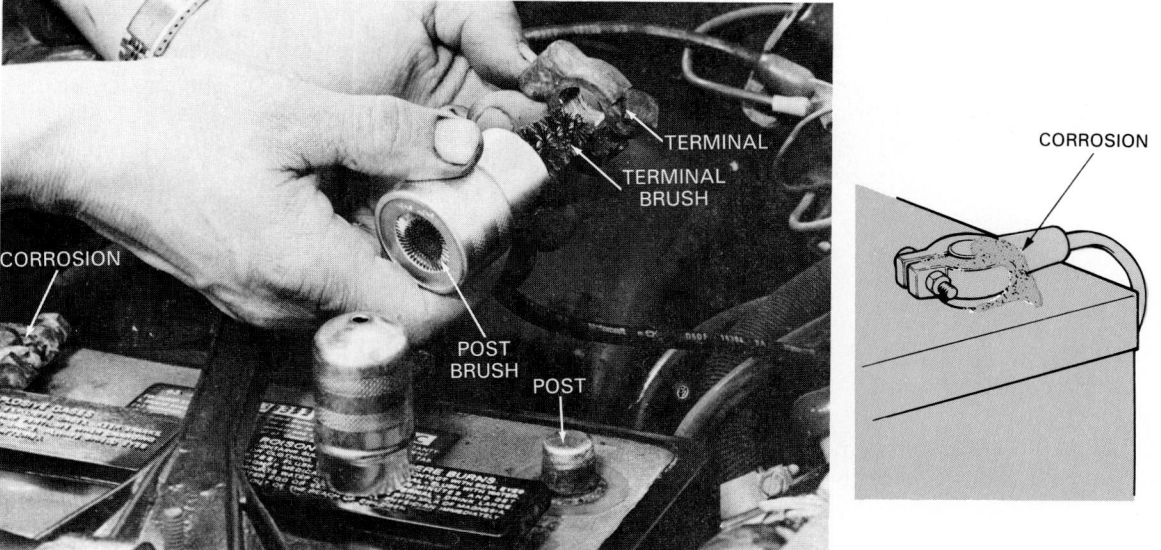

Fig. 10-16. Checking battery condition is important to vehicle maintenance. Battery problems are number one cause of engine "no start" problems. Clean battery top and terminals if needed. (Peerless)

sometimes rupture the rubber boot surrounding the joint.

BODY LUBRICATION

When performing a complete lubrication service job, you should also lubricate high friction points on body (hinges and latches on doors, hood, and trunk). Look at Fig. 10-19. This will help prevent squeaking doors, sticking hinges, and wear problems.

Be careful to always use the prescribed lubricant. Normally, rubber and plastic parts will deteriorate if exposed to petroleum-based lubricants (oils and grease). Silicone lubricant should be used on plastic and rubber components. The most common types of body lubricants are listed below:

1. ENGINE OIL may be used on hard-to-reach high friction points.
2. GRAPHITE is excellent for door and trunk locks. It will not collect dust and dirt which could upset lock operation.
3. DRY STICK (WAX) LUBRICANT is desirable on

door latches and *strikers* (post which engages door latch). See Fig. 10-19. It will not stain clothing.
4. CHASSIS GREASE is a good all-around body lubricant. It can be used on easy-to-reach hinges and latches.
5. SILICONE LUBRICANT often comes in a spray can. It is especially suited for rubber door weatherstripping and to ease window action. It is a dry lubricant that will not soil the windows and clothing.

PACKING WHEEL BEARINGS

Wheel bearings are usually *packed* (filled) with grease during lubrication service. This topic is covered in Chapters 62 and 63.

SERVICE INTERVALS

A *service interval* is the amount of time in miles (km) or months between recommended service checks or maintenance operations. The factory service manual

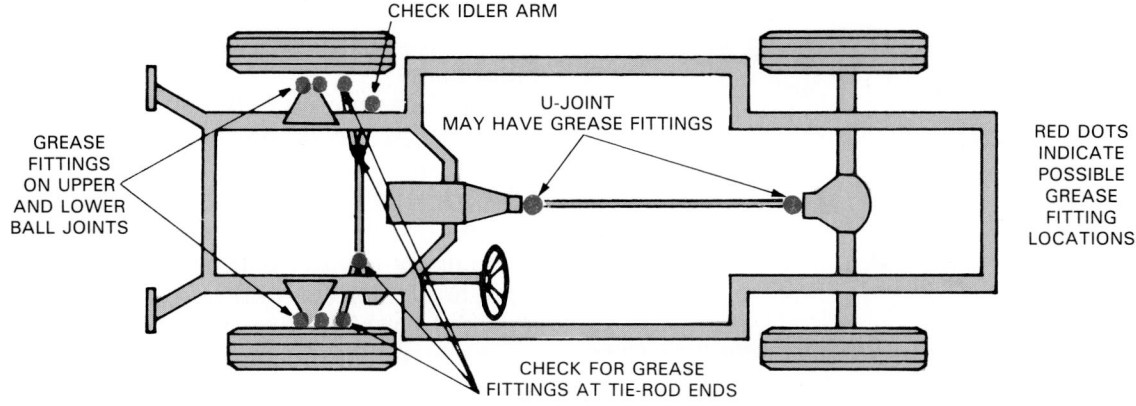

Fig. 10-17. Grease job involves lubricating pivot points shown. Some cars have more grease fittings than others. Check closely.

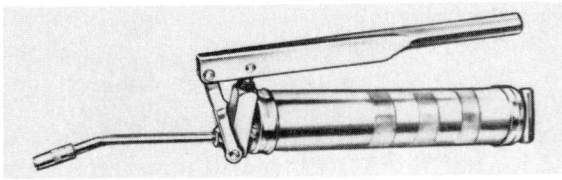

Fig. 10-18. Technician is using a power grease gun to lubricate fittings on suspension system. Also shown is a hand operated grease gun. (Texaco)

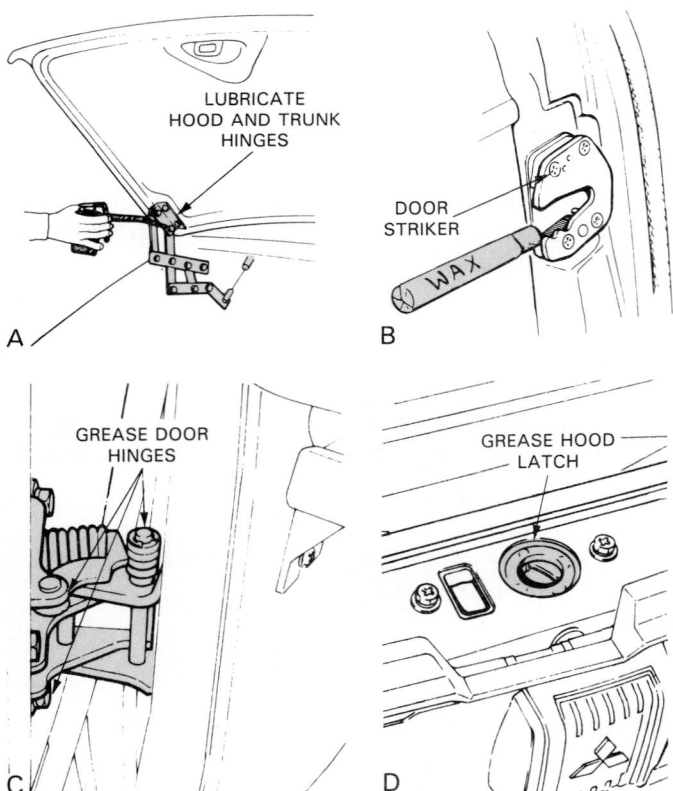

Fig. 10-19. During lubrication service, lubricate body components to prevent squeaks and wear. A — Lubricating hood and trunk hinges. B — Using non-stain wax on door strikers. C — Place a dab of grease on door hinges. D — Hood latch is common rust problem. Lubricate it as well. (Volvo)

will give exact intervals for the particular make, model, and year of vehicle.

Fig. 10-20 shows the service manual recommendations for chassis maintenance on one vehicle. Note the intervals for each service operation. They are typical.

Chapter 44, Engine Tune-up, gives general engine maintenance intervals. Refer to this chapter if needed.

GENERAL INSPECTION AND PROBLEM LOCATION

As you perform a lubrication job or any kind of auto repair, always watch for mechanical problems. Visually inspect for any signs of wear, deterioration, loose parts, or leaks. Check the condition of fan belts, water hoses, fuel hoses, vacuum hoses, and wiring. This can be done as you are working.

1. HOSES should be checked for hardening, softening, cracking, splitting, or other signs of impending failure. Look at Fig. 10-21. Feel or squeeze all of the hoses. If deteriorating, inform the customer or shop supervisor of the problem.
2. FAN BELTS should be visually inspected for splitting, tears, cuts, and wear. If worn or loose, the belt may slip and squeal. Refer to Fig. 10-22.
3. WIRING should be checked for improper routing, cracked or brittle insulation, or other obvious problem signs. Make sure wires are away from all moving or hot parts.
4. TIRES can be inspected for excessive wear, improper inflation, or physical damage.
5. The STEERING SYSTEM must not have excessive wear and play. The steering wheel should NOT move more than about an inch (25 mm) without causing front wheel movement. If it does, wear in the steering mechanism is indicated.
6. The EXHAUST SYSTEM should be inspected any time a vehicle is raised on a lift. A leaking exhaust system is very dangerous because of the poisonous exhaust fumes. Look for rust holes in the pipes, muffler, and other parts.

When working on a vehicle, be alert for these kinds of problems. This will show the shop supervisor and the customer that you are a concerned, competent technician.

Fluid leaks

Fluid leaks are very common problems that should be corrected. To become good at leak detection and correction, you should:

1. Become familiar with the COLOR and SMELL of the different fluids. Then, you will be able to quickly identify a fluid leak.
2. Fluid leaks tend to flow downward and to the rear of the vehicle. For this reason, look for leaks in front and upward from where you find fluid dripping off the vehicle.
3. If multiple leaks are indicated, fix the leak located the highest and farthest forward on the

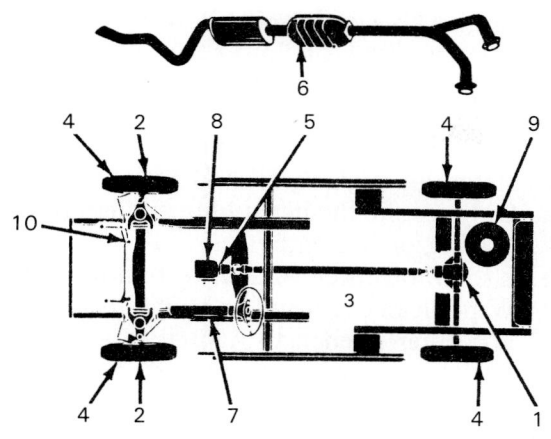

COMPONENT	SERVICE	INTERVAL
1. AXLE DIFFERENTIAL		5,000 mi (8 000 km)
		30,000 mi (48 000 km)
2. BEARINGS, FRONT WHEEL	a.	30,000 mi (48 000 km)
3. BODY LUBRICATION	b.	15,000 mi (24 000 km)
4. BRAKE INSPECTION	c.	15,000 mi (24 000 km)
5. CLUTCH LEVER AND LINKAGE		30,000 mi (48 000 km)
6. EXHAUST SYSTEM INSPECTION	d.	15,000 mi (24 000 km)
7. MANUAL STEERING GEAR	e.	5,000 mi (8 000 km)
8. MANUAL TRANSMISSION	e.	5,000 mi (8 000 km)
9. SPARE TIRE	f.	7,500 mi (12 000 km)
10. STEERING, SUSPENSION & CHASSIS	g.	15,000 mi (24 000 km)
	h.	30,000 mi (48 000 km)

Fig. 10-20. Study chassis maintenance information from a service manual. Recommendations for other parts of car are also given in manual. (Chrysler)

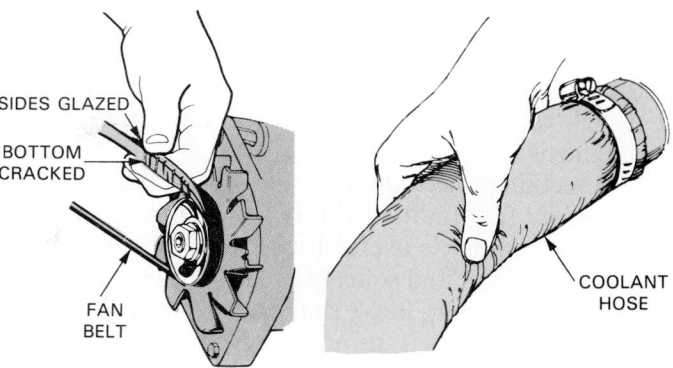

Fig. 10-21. Check condition of all hoses and belts. Feel hoses for hardening or softening. Look for leaks. Inspect belts for glazing, cracking, and fraying. (Gates Rubber Co.)

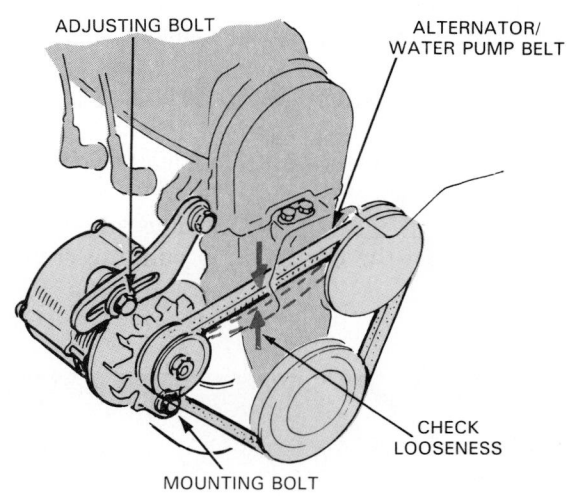

Fig. 10-22. Belts should not be too loose or too tight. To adjust, loosen correct mounting bolts and adjustment bolt. Using directions in service manual, pry component outward and tighten adjusting bolt. Then, tighten mounting bolts. Recheck belt tightness. (Honda)

vehicle. Then, repair other leaks.

4. If the leaking part is badly soiled, clean the area thoroughly. Then, you will be able to see fresh fluid leaking out of the part more easily.

5. The most frequent cause of fluid leakage is broken gaskets and worn seals. Replacement will usually correct the problem. However, you should always check the parts for warpage, cracks, or dents.

Noise detection and location

Abnormal noises are common to almost all systems of a vehicle. They indicate mechanical problems. When inspecting a vehicle, listen for *unusual sounds* (knocks, clunks, rattles, clicks, and hisses).

A *stethoscope* (device similar to that used by a doctor to listen to a patient's heart) is commonly used by an auto technician. It will pinpoint the source of internal part noises. Touch the probe on the component near the unwanted sound, Fig. 10-23. Move the stethoscope around until the sound is the loudest.

Fig. 10-23. Stethoscope will quickly find knocks and rattles inside components. Move tip around on parts. When noise becomes loudest, you have found source of problem.

NOTE! A *long screwdriver* can also be used in place of a stethoscope. Place the tip of the screwdriver on the part. Place the handle next to your ear. Sound will travel through the screwdriver and permit noise diagnosis.

A section of *vacuum hose,* Fig. 10-24, is another handy device for finding sounds not coming from inside parts. The hose is useful for locating hissing sounds, rattles, whines, and squeaks. Place one end of the hose in your ear. Then, move the other end around the area of the sound. When the noise becomes the LOUDEST, you have pinpointed the problem.

KNOW THESE TERMS

Lubrication service, Vehicle maintenance, Dipstick, Oil filler cap, Fill hose, Reservoir, Grease job, Body lubrication, Packing wheel bearings, Stethoscope.

REVIEW QUESTIONS

1. What seven steps does lubrication service typically involve?
2. _____ _____ includes any operation that will keep the car in good running condition.

Fig. 10-24. Piece of vacuum hose can be used like stethoscope to find external noises. It will find vacuum leaks, squeaks, wind noise, and other abnormal sounds. (Texaco)

3. When checking engine oil, allow the engine to cool completely. True or False?
4. Describe what can happen when too much oil is added in an engine.
5. Which of the following should NOT be done when changing an engine's oil and filter?
   a. Only torque the drain plug enough to prevent leaking or loosening.
   b. Use an oil filter wrench to remove old filter.
   c. Wipe clean engine oil on new filter O-ring seal.
   d. Use filter wrench to tighten filter.
   e. All of the above are correct.
6. The automatic transmission dipstick is normally located at the rear and side of the engine. True or False?
7. Check automatic transmission or transaxle fluid with the engine running. Check engine oil with the engine off. True or False?
8. Explain how to check the following:
   a. Radiator coolant level and condition.
   b. Power steering fluid.
   c. Brake fluid.
   d. Manual steering fluid.
   e. Battery condition.
9. A _____ _____ involves lubricating the steering, suspension, and drive line of a vehicle.
10. List and explain the use of five lubricants.
11. A _____ _____ is the amount of time in miles (km) or months between recommend service or maintenance operations.
12. Describe six general inspection points that should be done during vehicle maintenance.
13. Which of the following should be done to help with leak detection and troubleshooting skills?
   a. Become familiar with color and smell of different fluids.
   b. Trace problem to the highest point of wetness or leakage.
   c. Clean the area around the leak if the leak is difficult to isolate.
   d. All of the above.
14. A _____ is commonly used to find the source of noises inside parts.
15. A section of _____ _____ is handy for finding the source of air or vacuum leaks.

ACTIVITIES FOR CHAPTER 10

1. On a vehicle chosen by your instructor, determine the capacity of the cooling system. Then determine the amounts of water and antifreeze needed to produce a 50/50 mixture.
2. Survey the motor oils offered for sale at a local outlet. Determine the cost to change the motor oil in a vehicle names by your instructor. Add labor cost at $36/hour.
3. Change the oil and filter on a vehicle designated by your instructor.

Engine Fundamentals

After studying this chapter, you will be able to:
□ Identify the major parts of a typical automotive engine.
□ Describe the four-stroke cycle.
□ Define common engine terms.
□ Explain the basic function for the major parts of an automotive engine.
□ Cite and demonstrate safe working practices related to engines.

In the first chapter of this text, you learned a little about how an engine operates. This chapter will build upon that information by explaining each part in more detail. What you learn here will help you prepare for other coverage of engine types, engine construction, and engine service.

NOTE! If needed, quickly review the material in Chapter 1 on engines and engine systems. A sound understanding of engine theory is very important.

ENGINE OPERATION

The *engine* is the source of power for the vehicle. For this reason, it is also called a *power plant*. An energy source (usually gasoline or diesel fuel) is burned inside the engine to produce heat. The heat causes expansion (enlargement) of the fuel vapors or gases in the engine.

The burning and expansion in an enclosed space or combustion chamber produces pressure. The engine piston, connecting rod, and crankshaft converts this pressure into motion for moving the car and operating its other systems.

Fig. 11-1 shows how an engine converts fuel into a useful form of energy. Combustion pressure forces the piston down. By linking the piston to the crankshaft, an engine can produce a powerful spinning motion. The rotating crank can be used to drive gears, chains and sprockets, belts and sprockets, and other drive mechanisms.

Piston travel (TDC, BDC)

The distance the piston can travel up or down in the cylinder is limited by the crankshaft. The two points at which the piston stops and changes direction are called TDC (top dead center) and BDC (bottom dead center). See Fig. 11-2.

When the piston is at the HIGHEST POINT in the cylinder, it is at TDC. When the piston slides to its LOWEST POINT in the cylinder, it is at BDC.

Piston stroke

A *piston stroke* is the distance the piston slides up or down from TDC to BDC. This takes one-half turn

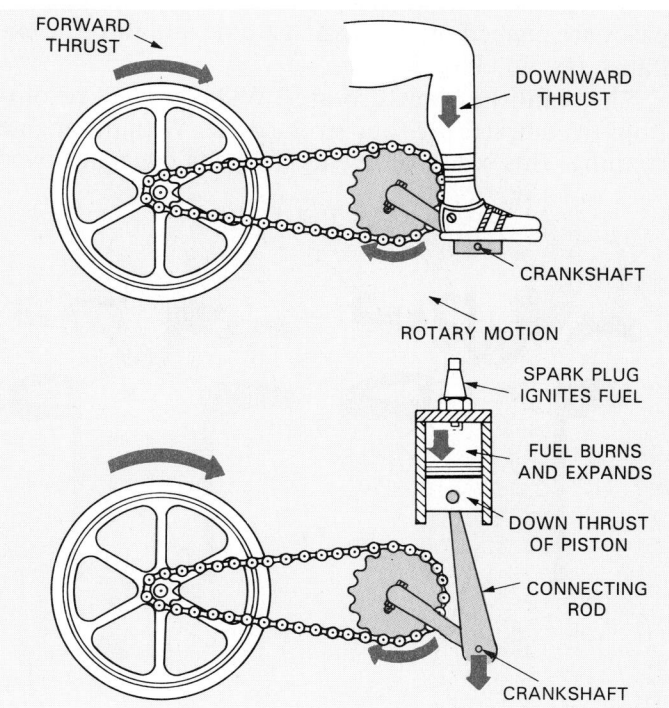

Fig. 11-1. Crank converts downward thrust of piston into useful rotating motion. Rotating motion can be used to operate drive mechanism.

of the crankshaft. The crank rotates 180 degrees during one piston stroke. Refer to Fig. 11-2.

Four-stroke cycle

The *four-stroke cycle* requires four piston strokes to complete one cycle (complete series of events). Every four strokes, the engine produces one power stroke (useful energy). Almost all automobiles use four-stroke cycle engines.

Look at Fig. 11-3 to review the four-stroke cycle.

The *intake stroke* of a gasoline engine draws fuel and air into the engine. The intake valve is open and the exhaust valve is closed. The piston slides down and forms a low pressure area or vacuum in the cylinder. Outside air pressure then pushes the air-fuel mixture into the engine, Fig. 11-3.

The *compression stroke* squeezes the air-fuel mixture to prepare it for combustion (burning). The mixture is more combustible when pressurized. During this stroke, the piston slides up with both valves closed. Look at Fig. 11-3.

The *power stroke* burns the air-fuel mixture and pushes the piston down with tremendous force. This is the only stroke that does not consume energy. It produces energy. When the spark plug fires (gasoline engine), it ignites the fuel mixture. Since both valves are still closed, pressure forms on the top of the piston. The piston is forced down, spinning the crankshaft. Refer to Fig. 11-3.

The *exhaust stroke* removes the burned gases from the engine and readies the cylinder for a fresh charge of air and fuel. The piston moves up. The intake valve is closed and the exhaust valve is open. The burned gases are pushed out the exhaust port and into the exhaust system, Fig. 11-3.

The crankshaft must rotate TWO complete revolutions to complete the four-stroke cycle. With the engine running, this series of events happens over and over very quickly.

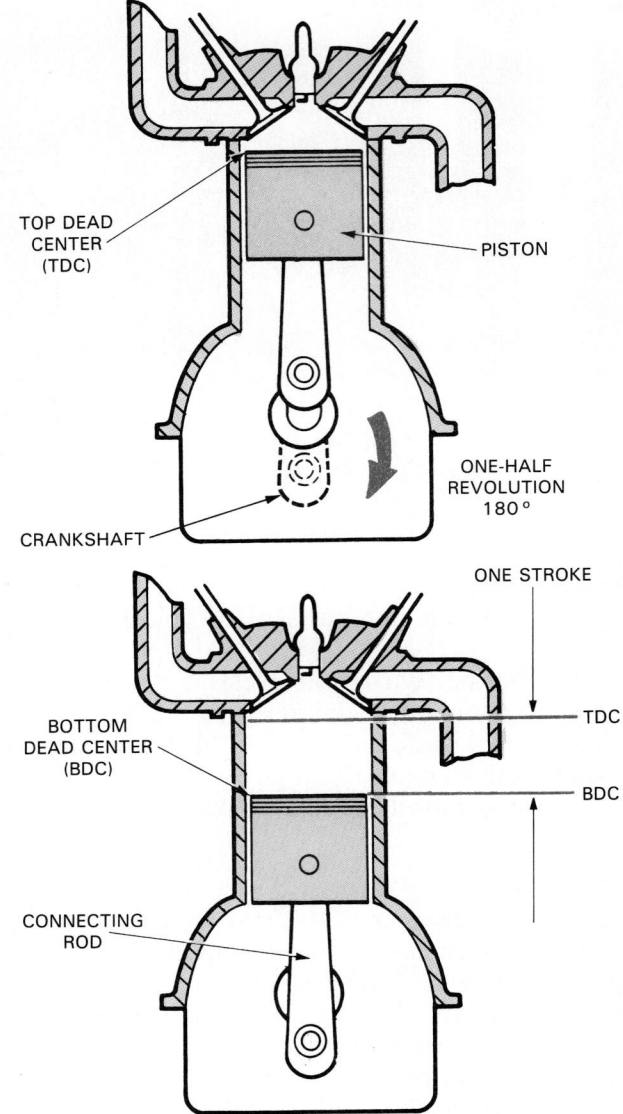

Fig. 11-2. TDC means piston is at top of stroke. BDC means piston is at bottom of stroke. Stroke is one piston movement. (Ford)

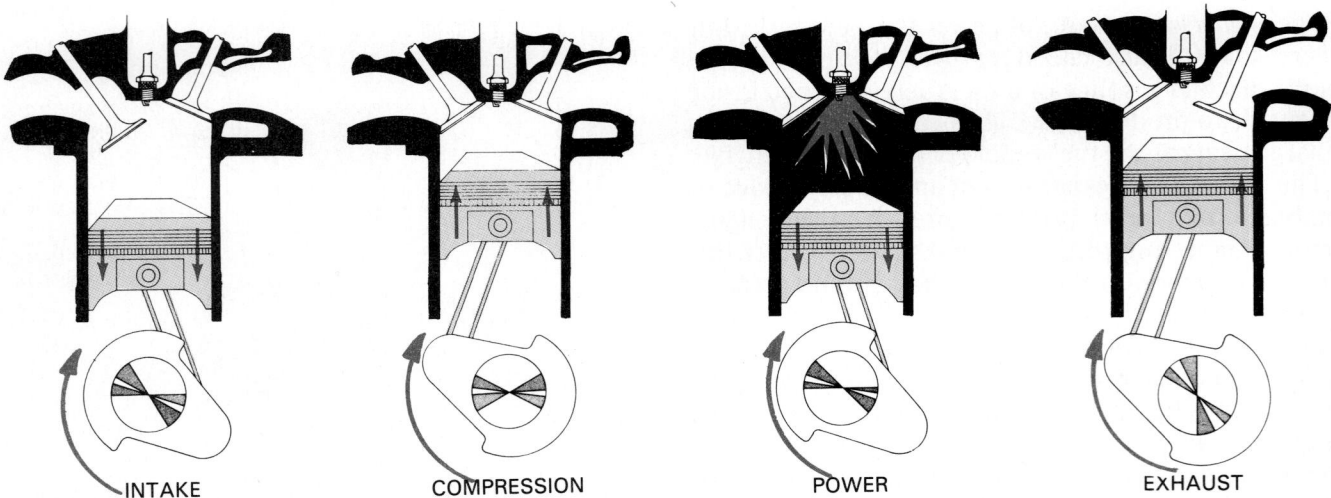

INTAKE   COMPRESSION   POWER   EXHAUST

Fig. 11-3. Restudy basic four-stroke cycle. (TRW)

ENGINE BOTTOM END

The term *engine bottom end* generally refers to the block, crankshaft, connecting rods, pistons, and related components. Another name for engine bottom end is *short block.* It is an assembled engine block with the cylinder heads, intake manifold, exhaust manifold, and other external parts REMOVED.

Engine block

The *engine block,* also called *cylinder block,* forms the main body of the engine. Other parts bolt to or fit inside the block. Fig. 11-4 shows a cutaway view of a basic block with parts installed.

The *cylinders,* also known as *cylinder bores,* are large, round holes machined through the block from top to bottom. The pistons fit into the cylinders. The cylinders are slightly larger than the pistons. This lets the pistons slide up and down freely.

The *deck* or *deck surface* is the top of the block. It is machined perfectly flat. The cylinder head bolts to the deck. Oil and coolant passages through the deck surface allow lubrication and cooling of the cylinder head parts.

Water jackets are coolant passages through the block. They allow a water and antifreeze solution to cool the cylinders.

Core plugs, nicknamed "freeze plugs," are round, metal plugs on the outside of the block. They seal holes left in the block after casting (manufacturing). The plugs prevent coolant leakage out of the water jackets. Some new engines do NOT have freeze plugs.

The *main bearing bores* are holes machined in the bottom of the block for the crankshaft. Removable

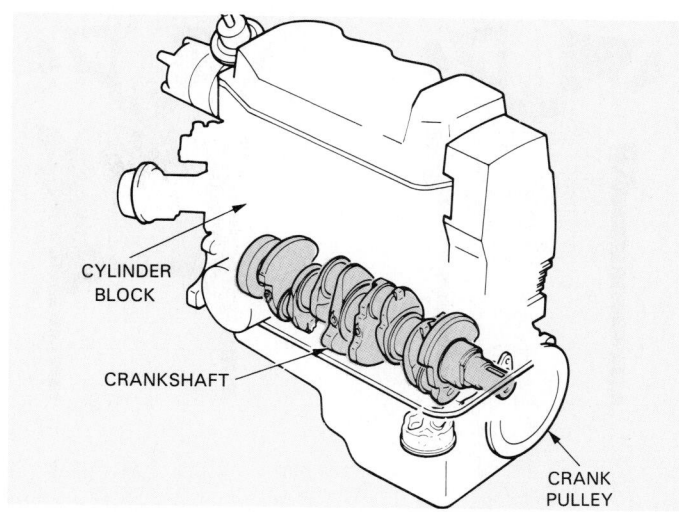

Fig. 11-5. Crankshaft fits into bottom of block.
(Ford Motor Co.)

bearings fit into these bores.

Main caps bolt to the bottom of the block and hold the crankshaft in place. Two or four large bolts normally secure each cap to the block. The caps and the block together form the main bearing bore.

The *crankcase* is the lowest portion of the block. The crankshaft rotates inside the crankcase.

Crankshaft

The *crankshaft* harnesses the tremendous force produced by the downward thrust of the pistons. It changes the up and down motion of the pistons into a rotating motion. The crankshaft fits into the bottom of the engine block, as shown in Fig. 11-5. Fig. 11-6 pictures an engine crankshaft. Refer to this illustration as it is explained.

The crankshaft *main journals* are surfaces that are precisely machined and polished. They fit into the block main bearings.

The crankshaft *rod journals* are also machined and polished surfaces, but they are offset from the main journals. The connecting rods bolt to the rod journals. With the engine running, the rod journals circle around the centerline of the crank.

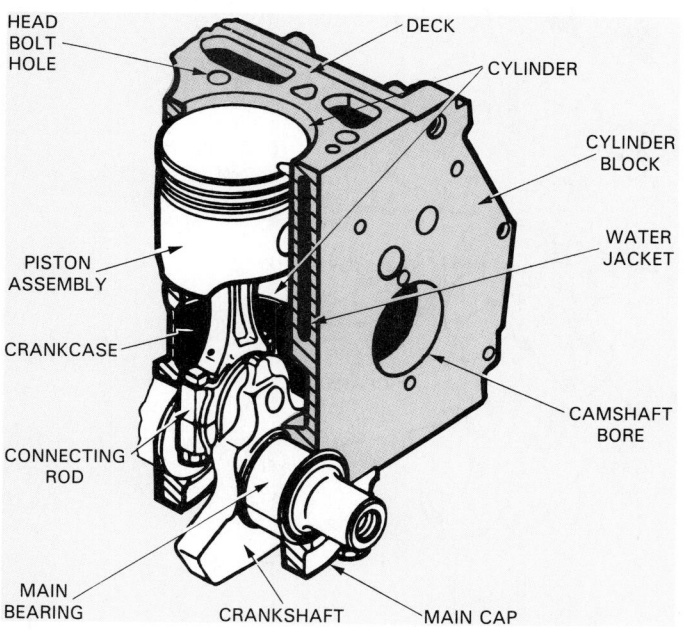

Fig. 11-4. Block is main supporting member of engine. Note how other parts fit into block. (Ford)

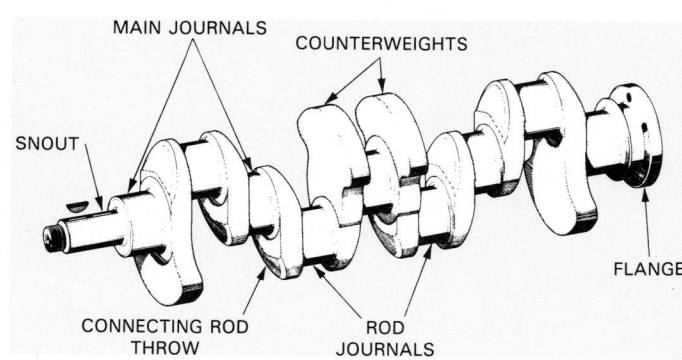

Fig. 11-6. Study basic parts of a crankshaft. Journals are very smooth surfaces for bearings. (Peugeot)

Fig. 11-7. As engine runs, connecting rod journal spins around main journal. Counterweight offsets weight of piston and rod to prevent vibration. (TRW)

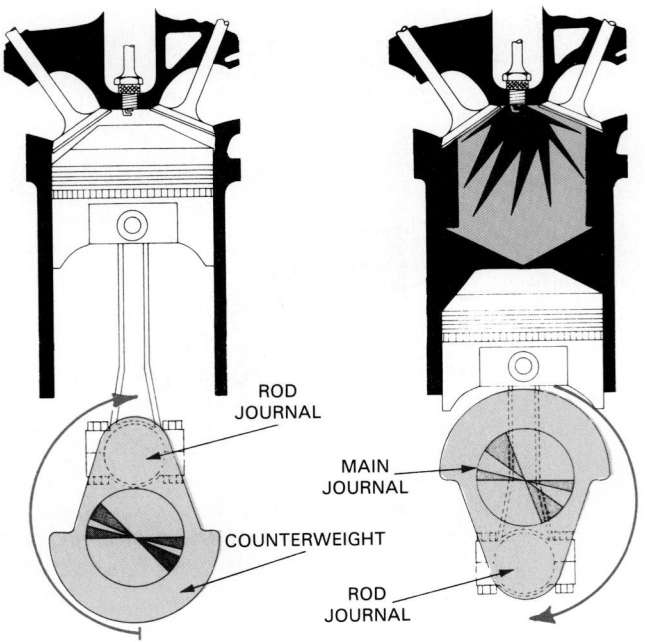

Counterweights are formed on the crankshaft to prevent vibration. The weights counteract the weight of the connecting rods, pistons, rings, and rod journal offset. See Fig. 11-7.

The crankshaft ***snout*** sticks through the front of the block. It provides a mounting place for the camshaft drive mechanism, front damper, and fan belt pulleys.

A ***flange*** for holding the flywheel is on the back of the crankshaft. The flywheel bolts to this flange. The center of the flange has a pilot hole or bushing for the tranmission torque converter or input shaft.

Automobile engines normally have 4, 6, or 8 cylinders. The crankshaft rod journals are arranged so that there is always at least one cylinder on a power stroke. Then, force is always being transmitted to the crankshaft to smooth engine operation.

Engine main bearings

The *engine main bearings* are removable inserts that fit between the block main bore and crankshaft main journals. One-half of each insert fits into the block. The other half fits into the block main caps. Refer to Fig. 11-8 and study the parts.

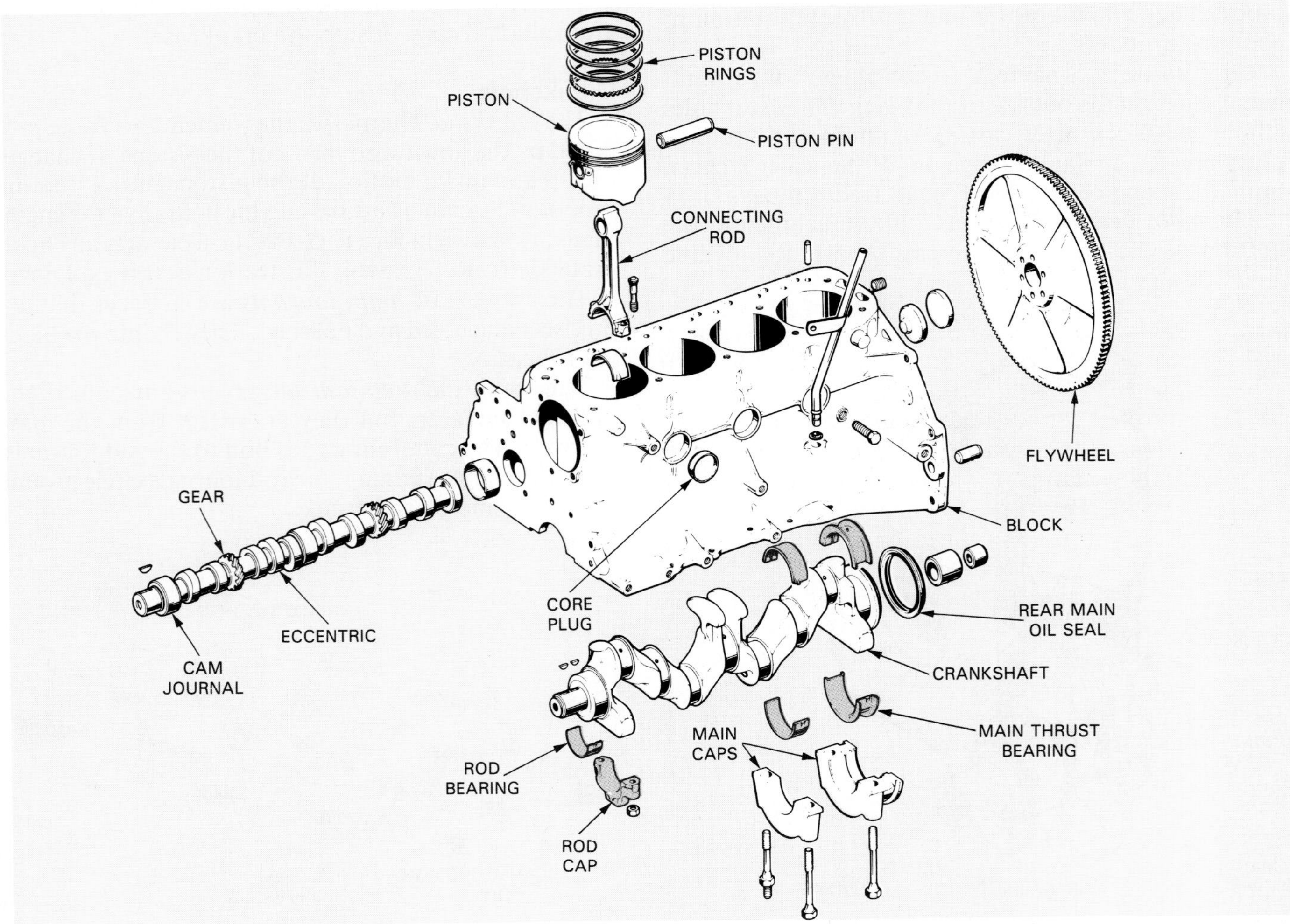

Fig. 11-8. Engine bottom end consists of these basic parts. Note crankshaft bearings and block main caps. (AMC)

Oil holes in the upper insert line up with oil holes in the block. This allows oil to flow through the block, main bearings, and into the crankshaft. The oil flows through the crank to lubricate the main bearings and the connecting rod bearings. This prevents metal-on-metal contact.

A *main thrust bearing* limits how far the crankshaft can slide forward or rearward in the block. Flanges are formed on the main bearing. The flanges almost touch the side, thrust surfaces on the crankshaft. This limits *crankshaft endplay* (front-to-rear movement). See Fig. 11-9. Normally, only one of the main bearings serves as a thrust bearing.

Main bearing clearance is the space between the crankshaft main journal and the main bearing insert. The clearance allows lubricating oil to enter and separate the journal and bearing. This allows the two to rotate without rubbing on each other and wearing.

Crankshaft oil seals

Crankshaft oil seals keep oil from leaking out the front and rear of the engine. The oil pump forces oil into the main and rod bearings. This causes oil to spray out of the bearings. Seals are placed around the front and rear of the crank to contain this oil.

The *rear main oil seal* fits around the rear of the crankshaft to prevent oil leakage, as pictured in Fig. 11-8. It can be a one-piece or a two-piece seal. The seal lip rides on a smooth, machined and polished surface on the crank. The front seal is covered later.

Flywheel

A *flywheel* is a large wheel mounted on the rear of the crankshaft. Look at Fig. 11-8. A flywheel can have several functions:
1. A flywheel for a car with a manual transmission is very heavy and can help smooth engine operation.
2. The flywheel connects the engine crankshaft to the transmission or transaxle. Either the manual clutch or the automatic transmission torque converter bolts to the flywheel.
3. A large *ring gear,* usually on the flywheel, is used to start the engine. A small gear on the starting motor engages the flywheel ring gear and turns it.

Connecting rod

The *connecting rod* fastens the piston to the crankshaft. It transfers piston movement and combustion pressure to the crankshaft rod journals. The connecting rod also causes piston movement during the nonpower-producing strokes (intake, compression, and exhaust). Refer to Fig. 11-10 as the connecting rod is discussed.

The connecting *rod small end* fits around the piston pin. Also called the *upper end,* it contains a one-piece bushing. The bushing is pressed into the rod small end.

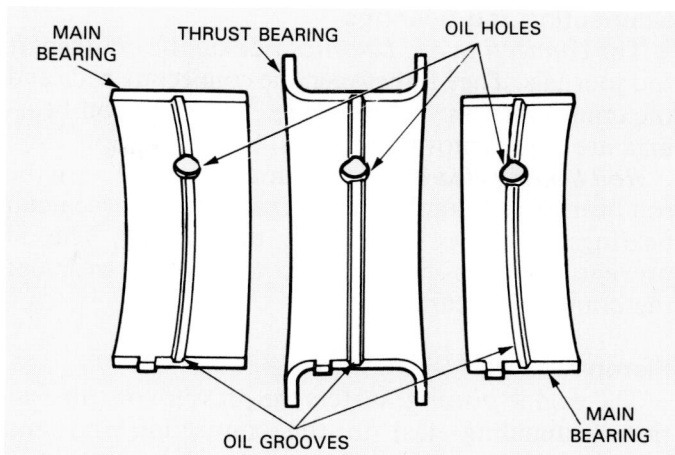

Fig. 11-9. Main bearing inserts fit between crank main journals and block. One bearing has thrust surfaces to control crankshaft end play. Oil holes and grooves allow oil to lubricate bearings. (Federal Mogul)

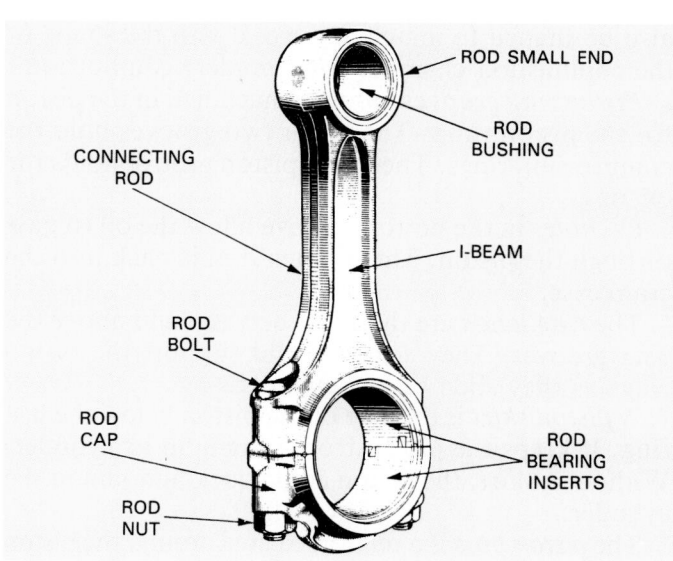

Fig. 11-10. Connecting rod is link between piston and crankshaft. (Peugeot)

The connecting *rod I-beam* is the center section of the rod. The I-beam shape has a very high strength-to-weight ratio. It prevents the rod from bending, twisting, and breaking.

The connecting *rod cap* bolts to the bottom of the connecting rod body. It can be removed for disassembly of the engine.

The connecting *rod big end* or *lower end* is a hole machined in the rod body and cap. The connecting rod bearing fits into the big end.

Connecting *rod bolts* and *nuts* clamp the rod cap and rod together. They are special high tensile strength fasteners. Some rods use cap screws without a nut. The cap screw threads into the rod itself. This design reduces rod weight.

Connecting rod bearings

The *connecting rod bearings* ride on the crankshaft rod journals. They fit between the connecting rods and the crankshaft, as shown in Fig. 11-8. The rod bearings are also removable inserts.

Rod bearing clearance is the small space between the rod bearing and crankshaft journals. As with the main bearings, it allows oil to enter the bearing. The oil prevents metal-to-metal contact that would wear out the crank and bearings.

Piston

The engine *piston* transfers the pressure of combustion (expanding gas) to the connecting rod and crankshaft. It must also hold the piston rings and piston pin while operating in the cylinder.

Fig. 11-11 shows a cutaway view of a piston. Study this illustration as the piston is described.

The *piston head* is the top of the piston, and is exposed to the heat and pressure of combustion. This area must be thick enough to withstand these forces. It must also be shaped to match and work with the shape of the combustion chamber for complete combustion.

Piston ring grooves are slots machined in the piston for the piston rings. The upper two grooves hold the compression rings. The lower piston groove holds the oil ring.

Oil holes in the bottom groove allow the oil to pass through the piston. The oil then drains back into the crankcase.

The *ring lands* are the areas between and above the ring grooves. They separate and support the piston rings as they slide on the cylinder.

A *piston skirt* is the side of the piston below the last ring. It keeps the piston from tipping in its cylinder. Without a skirt, the piston could cock and jam in the cylinder.

The *piston boss* is a reinforced area around the piston pin hole. It must be strong enough to support piston pin under severe loads.

A *pin hole* is machined through the pin boss for the piston pin. It is slightly larger than the piston pin.

Piston pin

The *piston pin,* also called *wrist pin,* allows the piston to swing on the connecting rod. The pin fits through the hole in the piston and the connecting rod small end. This is pictured in Fig. 11-12.

Piston clearance

Piston clearance is the amount of space between the sides of the piston and the cylinder wall. Clearance is needed for a lubricating film of oil and to allow for expansion when the piston heats up. The piston must always be free to slide up and down in the cylinder block.

Piston rings

The *piston rings* seal the clearance between the outside of the piston and the cylinder wall. They must keep combustion pressure from entering the crankcase. They must also keep oil from entering the combustion chambers.

Most pistons use three rings: two upper compression rings and one lower oil ring. This is shown in Fig. 11-13. Note ring locations.

The *compression rings* prevent *blow-by* (combustion pressure leaking into engine crankcase). Fig. 11-14 shows how rings install in engine.

On the compression stroke, pressure is trapped between the cylinder and piston grooves by the compression rings. Combustion pressure pushes the compression rings down in their grooves and out against the cylinder wall. This produces an almost leakproof seal.

The main job of an *oil ring* is to prevent engine oil from entering the combustion chamber. It scrapes excess oil off the cylinder wall, as in Fig. 11-15. If too

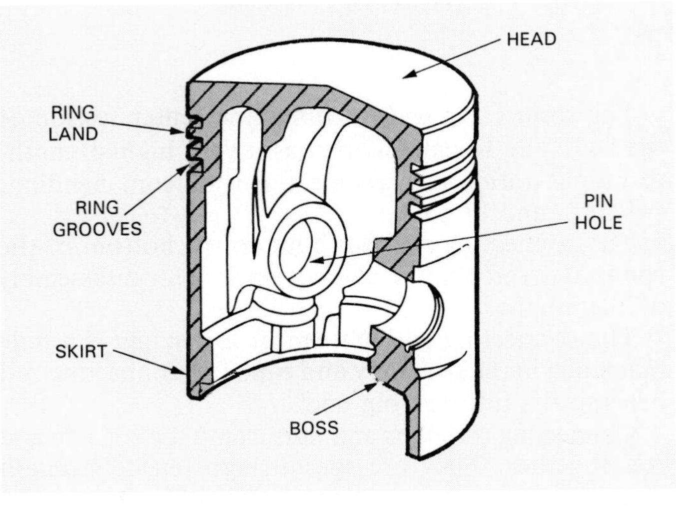

Fig. 11-11. Piston rides in cylinder and is exposed to combustion flame. It must be light, yet strong. (Deere & Co.)

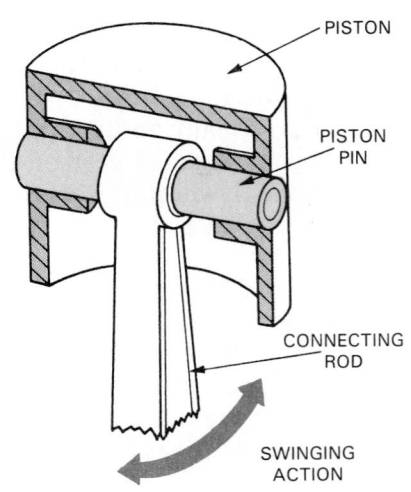

Fig. 11-12. Piston pin allows connecting rod to swing in piston. This allows crank and rod bottom end movement.

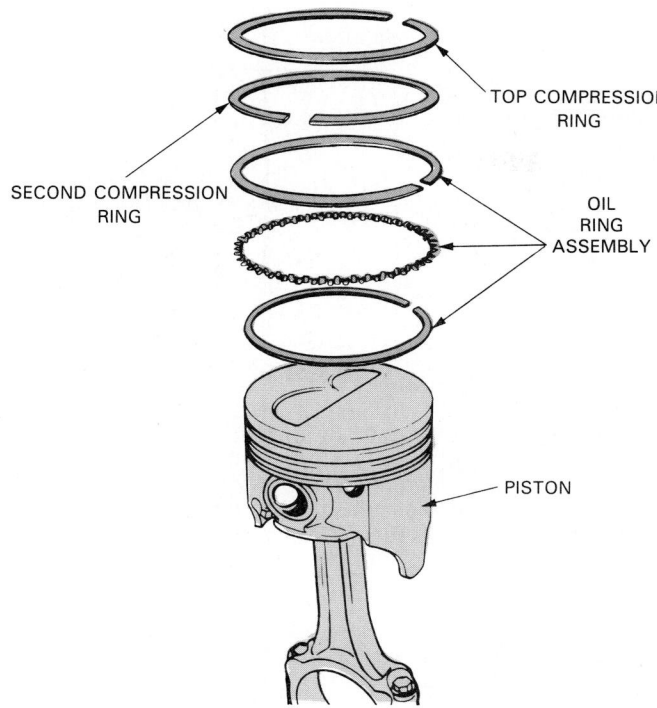

Fig. 11-13. Two top piston rings are compression rings. Bottom ring is oil ring. They fit into grooves cut in piston. (Oldsmobile)

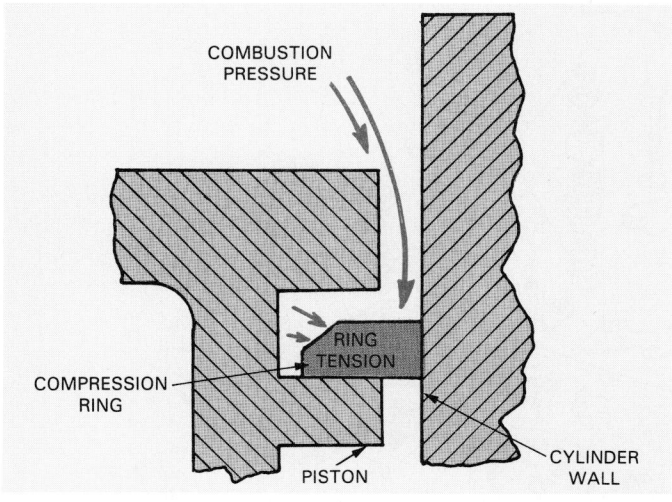

Fig. 11-14. Compression ring must prevent combustion pressure from leaking between piston and cylinder wall. Pressure actually helps push ring against cylinder to aid sealing.

much oil got into the combustion chamber and was burned, blue smoke would come out of the vehicle's exhaust pipe.

Ring gap is the split or space between the ends of a piston ring. The ring gap allows the ring to be spread open and installed on the piston. It also allows the ring to be made slightly larger in diameter than the cylinder. When squeezed together and installed in the cylinder, the ring spreads outward and presses on the cylinder wall. This aids ring sealing.

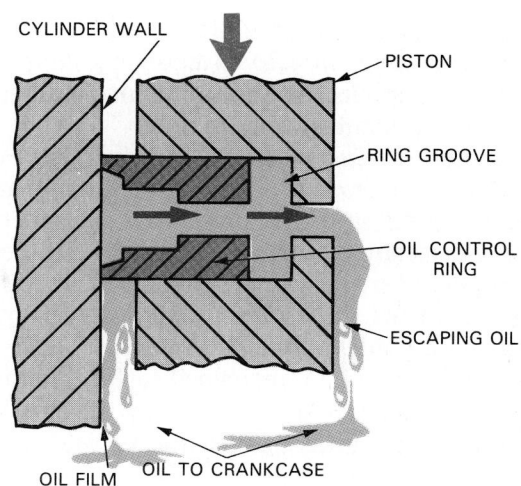

Fig. 11-15. Oil ring scrapes excess oil off cylinder wall. If oil entered combustion chamber, engine would emit blue smoke.

ENGINE TOP END

The term *engine top end* generally refers to the cylinder heads, valves, camshaft, and other related components. These parts work together to control the flow of air and fuel into the engine cylinders. They also control the flow of exhaust out of the engine. See Fig. 11-16. It shows fuel charge entering engine.

Cylinder head

The *cylinder head* bolts to the deck of the cylinder block. It covers and encloses the top of the cylinders. Refer to Fig. 11-17.

Combustion chambers are small pockets formed in the cylinder heads. The combustion chambers are located directly over the pistons. Combustion occurs

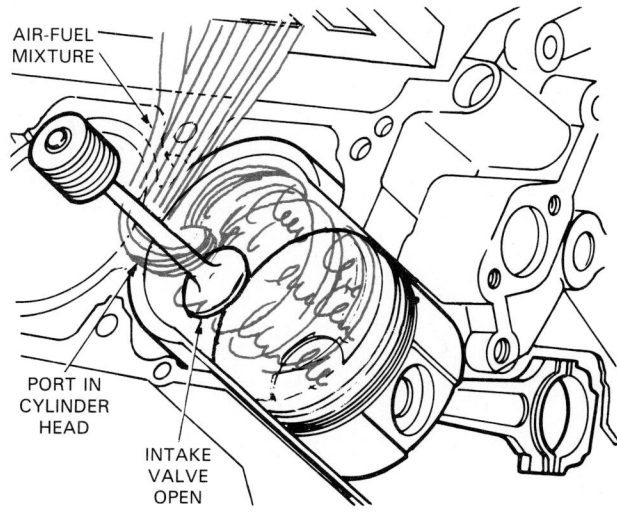

Fig. 11-16. Engine top end controls flow of mixture into cylinder. It also controls flow of exhaust out of cylinder. (Ford)

in these areas of the cylinder head. Spark plugs (gasoline engine) or injectors (diesel engine) protrude through holes and into the combustion chambers. Fig. 11-18 shows a combustion chamber.

Intake and *exhaust ports* are cast into the cylinder head. The *intake port* routes air (diesel engine) and fuel (gasoline engine) into the combustion chambers. The *exhaust port* routes burned gases out of the engine.

Valve guides are small holes machined through the cylinder head for the valves. The valves fit into and slide in these guides.

Valve seats are round, machined surfaces in the combustion chamber port openings, Fig. 11-19. When a valve is closed, it seals against the valve seat.

Valve train

The engine *valve train* consists of the parts that

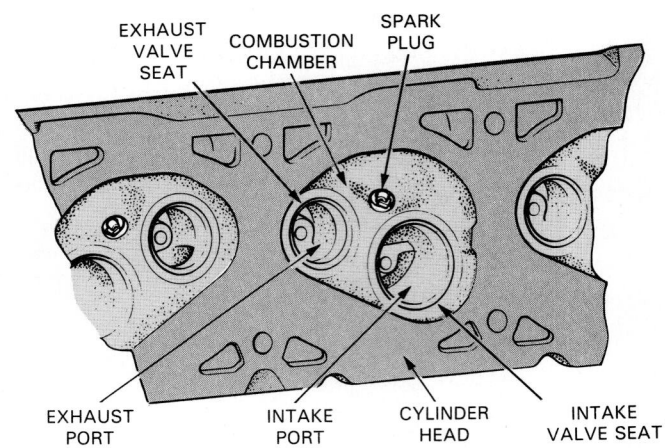

Fig. 11-18. Combustion chamber is formed in cylinder head. Valve ports enter chamber. Also, note spark plug tip and valve seats. (Cadillac)

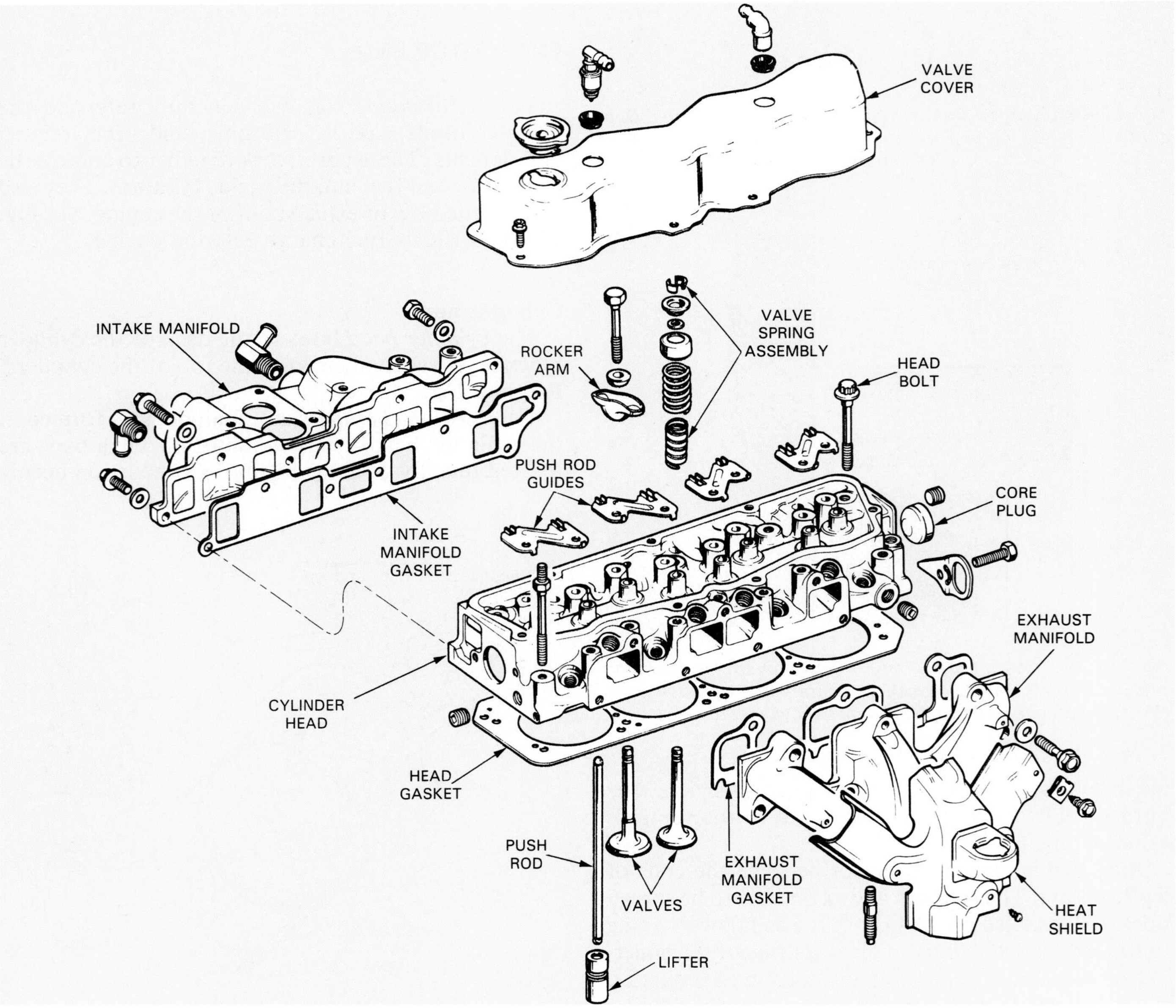

Fig. 11-17. Study basic engine top end components. Cylinder head is foundation for these parts. (Chrysler)

operate the engine valves, Fig. 11-20. These include the camshaft, lifters, push rods, rocker arms, valves, and valve spring assemblies. The valve train must open and close the engine valves at the correct time.

Note! The specific parts of a valve train vary with engine design. This is discussed in following chapters. Fig. 11-21 illustrates basic valve train action.

Camshaft

The *camshaft* has lobes that open each valve. It can be located in the engine block or in the cylinder head. Fig. 11-22 illustrates a camshaft. Study this illustration as the camshaft is explained.

The **cam lobes** are egg-shaped protrusions (bumps) machined on the camshaft. One cam lobe is provided for each engine valve. A 4-cylinder engine camshaft would have eight cam lobes, a 6-cylinder twelve lobes.

The camshaft sometimes has a **drive gear** for operating the distributor and oil pump. A gear on the ignition system distributor may mesh with this gear.

An *eccentric* (oval) may be machined on the camshaft for a mechanical (engine driven) fuel pump. It is similar to a cam lobe but is more round. As the cam turns, eccentric moves fuel pump arm up and down.

Camshaft journals are precisely machined and polished surfaces for the cam bearings. Like the crankshaft, the camshaft rotates on its journals. Oil separates the cam bearings and cam journals.

Valve lifters

A *valve lifter,* also called *tappet,* usually rides on the cam lobes and transfers motion to the rest of the valve

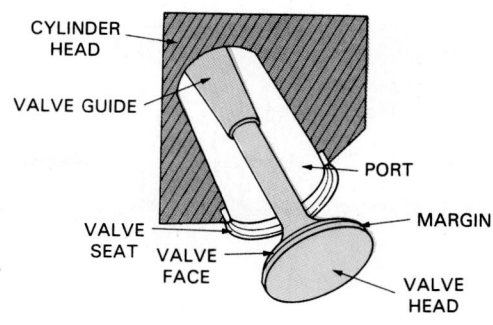

Fig. 11-19. Valve slides up and down in guide during operation. When closed, it seals against valve seat to close off port.

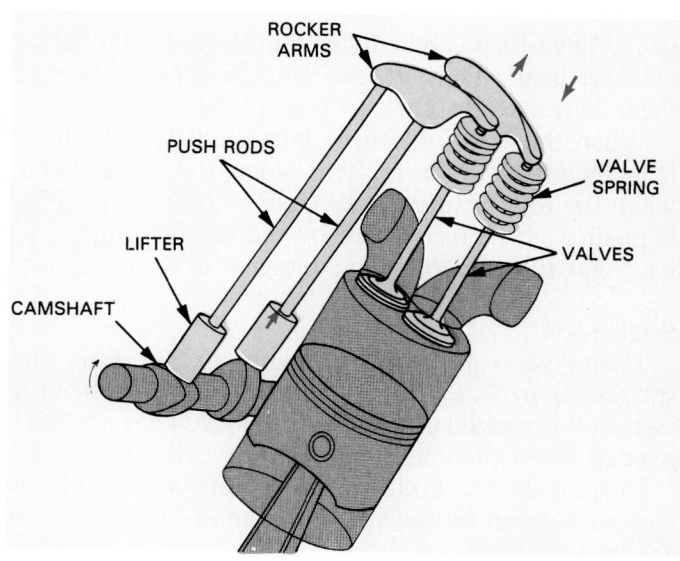

Fig. 11-20. Valve train operates engine valves. Study parts.

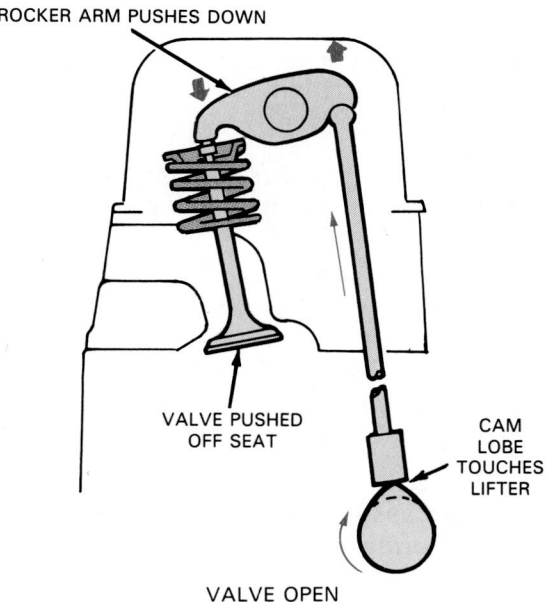

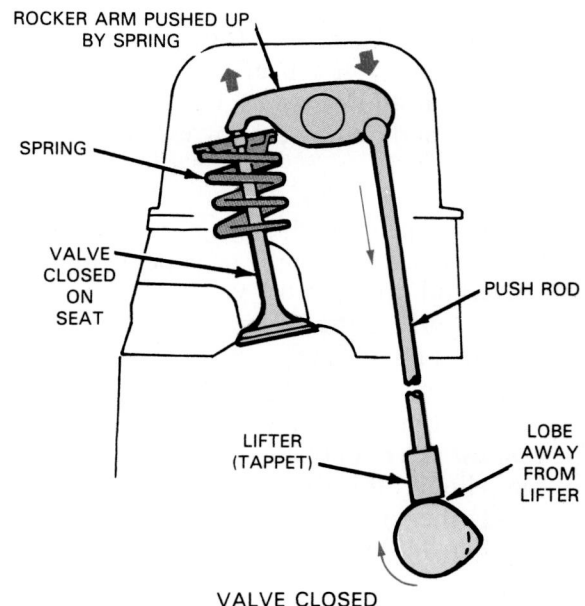

Fig. 11-21. When camshaft lobe turns into lifter, valve is pushed open. When lobe rotates away from lifter, valve spring pushes valve closed. (Ford Motor Co.)

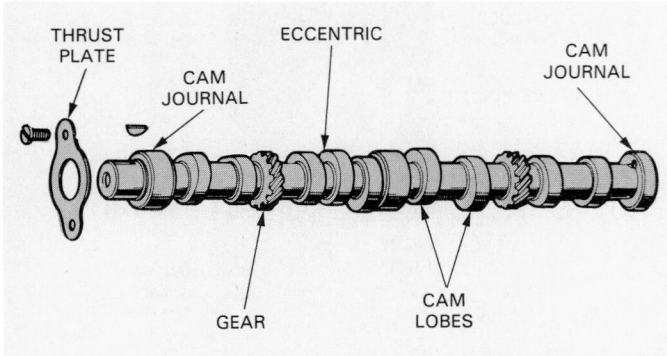

Fig. 11-22. Camshaft is long metal shaft with lobes, journals, and sometimes an eccentric and gears.

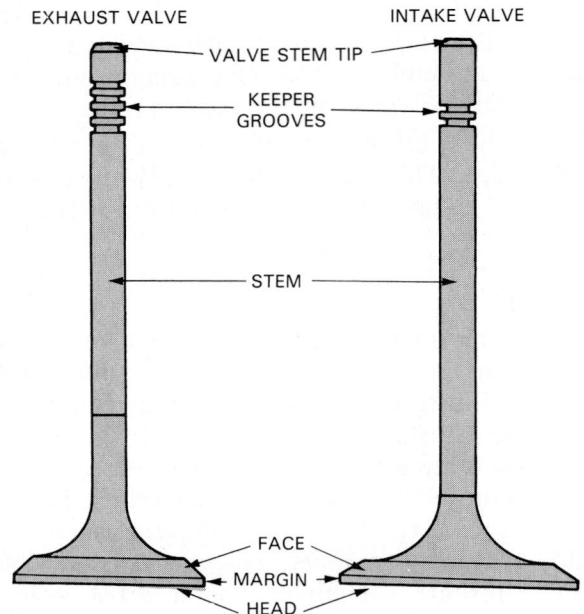

Fig. 11-23. Intake valve is larger than exhaust valve. Note parts of valve.

train. The lifters can be located in the engine block or cylinder head. They fit into machined holes, termed *lifter bores*. Refer back to Fig. 11-20.

When the cam lobe turns into the lifter, the lifter is pushed up in its bore. This opens the valve. Then, when the lobe rotates away from the lifter, the lifter is pushed down in its bore by the valve spring. This keeps the lifter in constant contact with the camshaft.

Push rods

Push rods transfer motion between the lifters and the rocker arms, Fig. 11-21. They are needed when the camshaft is located in the cylinder block. They are NOT needed when the camshaft is in the cylinder head.

Push rods are hollow metal tubes with balls or sockets formed on the ends. One end of the push rod fits into the lifter. The other end fits against the rocker arm. In this way, when the lifter slides up, the push rod moves the rocker arm.

Rocker arms

Rocker arms can be used to transfer motion to the valves. They mount on top of the cylinder head. A pivot mechanism allows the rockers to rock up and down, opening and closing the valves. See Fig. 11-21.

Valves

Engine *valves* open and close the ports in the cylinder head. Two valves are normally used per cylinder: one intake valve and one exhaust valve.

The **intake valve** is the larger valve. It controls the flow of the fuel mixture (gasoline) or air (diesel) into the combustion chamber. The intake valve fits into the port leading from the intake manifold.

The **exhaust valve** controls the flow of exhaust gases out of the cylinder. It is the smaller valve. The exhaust valve fits into the port leading to the exhaust manifold.

Look at Fig. 11-23 as the basic parts of a valve are introduced.

The *valve head* is the large, disc shaped surface exposed to the combustion chamber. Its outside diameter determines the size of the valve.

The **valve face** is a machined surface on the back of the valve head. It touches and seals against the seat in the cylinder head, Fig. 11-23.

The **valve margin** is the flat surface on the outer edge of the valve head. It is located between the valve head and face. The margin is needed to allow the valve to withstand the high temperatures of combustion. Without a margin, the valve head would melt and burn.

The **valve stem** is a long shaft extending out of the valve head. The stem is machined and polished. It fits into the guide machined through the cylinder head. Look at Fig. 11-23.

Keeper grooves or **lock grooves** are machined into the top of the valve stem. They accept small keepers or locks that hold the spring on the valve.

Valve seals

Valve seals prevent oil from entering the combustion chambers through the valve guides. This is illustrated in Fig. 11-24.

The valve seals fit over the valve stems and keep oil from entering through the clearance between the stems and guides.

Without valve seals, oil could be drawn into the engine cylinders and burned during combustion. Oil consumption and engine smoking could result.

Valve spring assembly

The *valve spring assembly* is used to close the valve. It basically consists of a valve spring, retainer, and two keepers. The keepers fit into the grooves cut in the valve stem. This locks the retainer and spring on the valve. See Fig. 11-25.

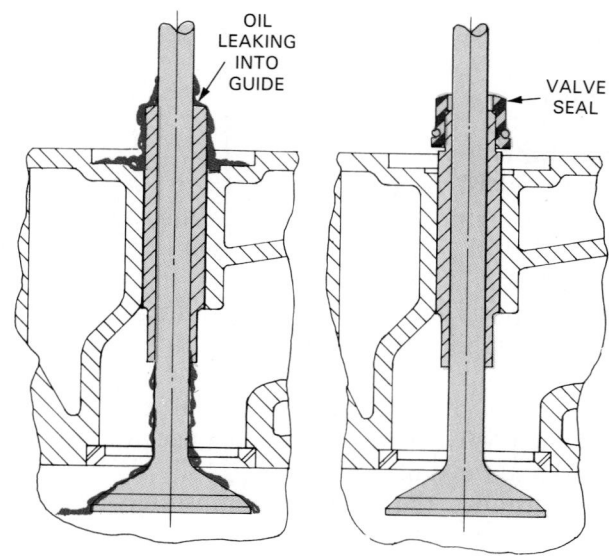

Fig. 11-24. Valve seal keeps oil from entering valve guide and combustion chamber. (American Hammered Piston Rings)

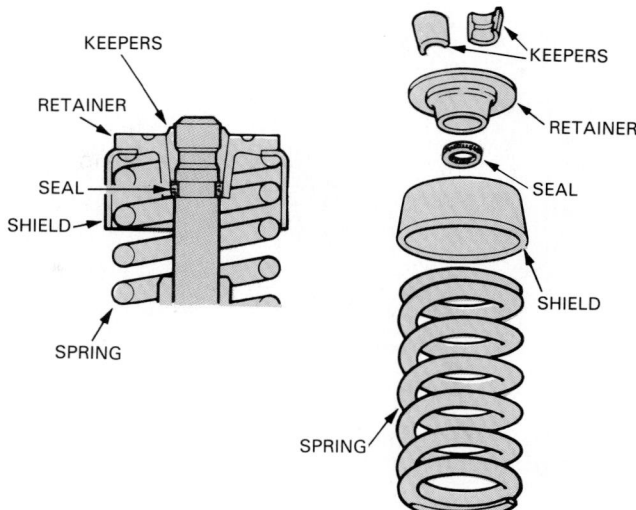

Fig. 11-25. Valve spring assembly basically consists of spring, retainer, keepers, and sometimes a shield. Note how this type seal fits on valve stem. (Buick)

Intake manifold

The engine *intake manifold* bolts to the side of the cylinder head or heads. The carburetor or fuel injectors (gasoline engine) mount on the intake manifold. It contains *runners* (passages) going to each cylinder head port. Air (diesel engine) and fuel (gasoline engine) are routed through these runners, Fig. 11-26.

Exhaust manifold

The *exhaust manifold* also bolts to the cylinder head; however, it fastens over the exhaust ports. During the exhaust strokes, hot gases blow into this manifold before entering the rest of the exhaust system. An engine exhaust manifold can be made of heavy cast iron or lightweight steel tubing.

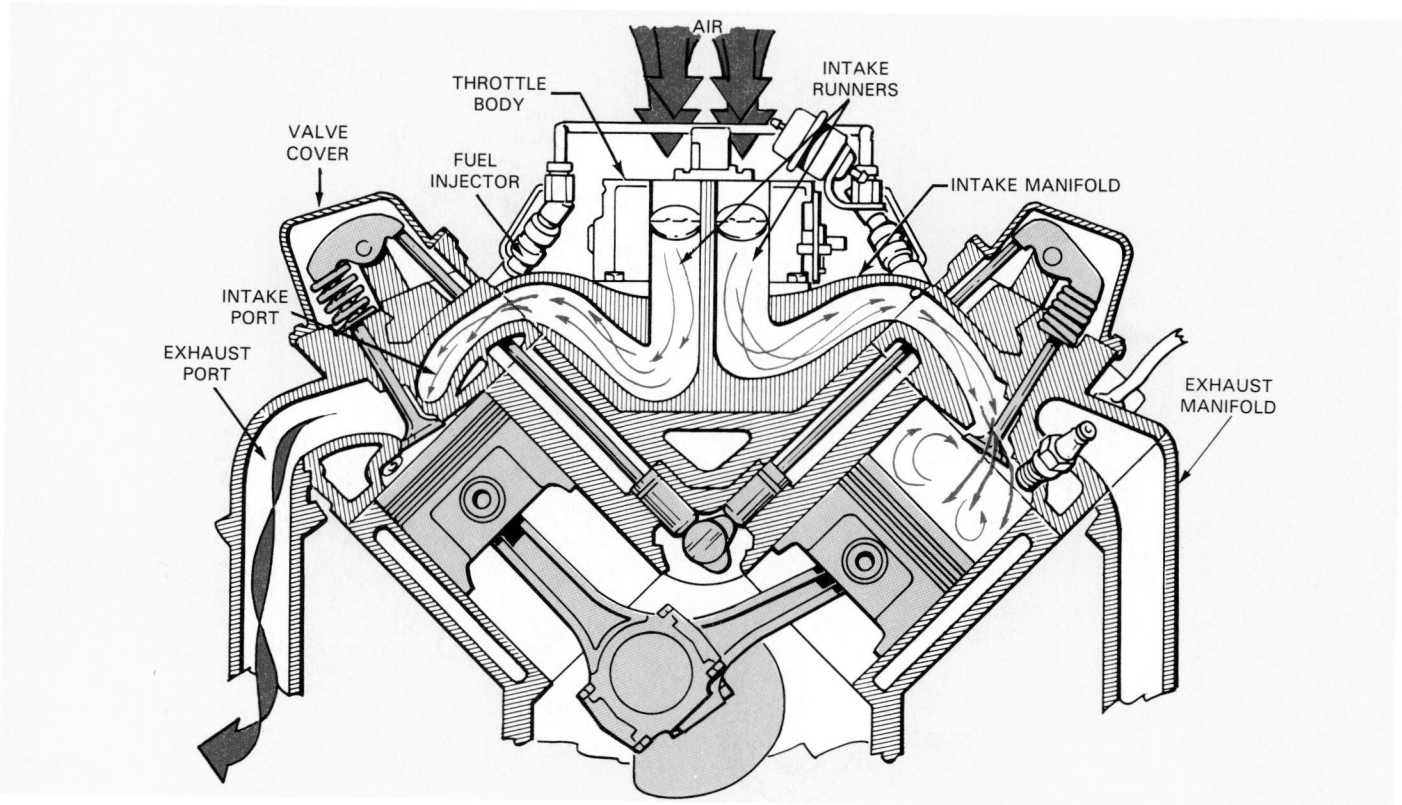

Fig. 11-26. Intake and exhaust manifolds bolt to cylinder head. Intake manifold contains runners that route fuel mixture into cylinder heads. Exhaust manifold routes burned gases into exhaust system.

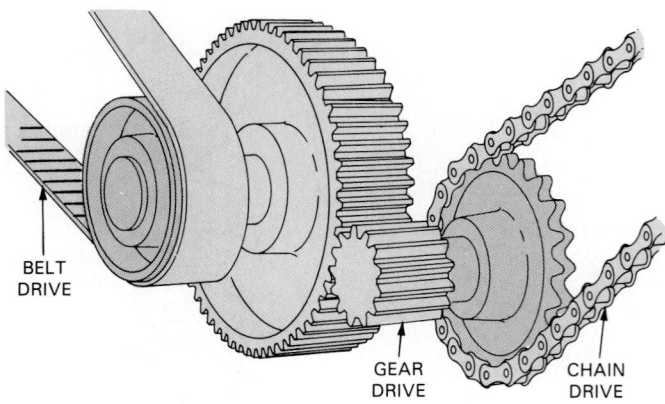

BELT DRIVE

GEAR DRIVE

CHAIN DRIVE

Fig. 11-27. Three types of drive mechanisms are used to turn engine camshaft: cogged belt, gears, or chain.

Valve cover

The *valve cover* is a thin metal or plastic cover over the top of the cylinder head. It may also be called a *rocker cover*. It simply keeps valve train oil spray from leaking out of the engine. Look at Fig. 11-26.

ENGINE FRONT END

The *engine front end* operates the engine camshaft, and sometimes the oil pump, distributor, and diesel injection pump. Basically, the engine front end con-

sists of a drive mechanism for the camshaft and other devices, a front cover, an oil seal, and crankshaft damper.

Camshaft drive

A *camshaft drive* is needed to turn the camshaft at one-half engine speed. Gears, a chain and sprockets, or a belt and sprockets can be used to turn the camshaft. Look at Fig. 11-27.

These parts can also be called timing gears, timing chain, or timing belt because they time the camshaft with the crankshaft. See Figs. 11-28, 11-29, and 11-30.

The camshaft must turn at one-half engine speed so that each valve will only open once for every two crankshaft revolutions.

For instance, the intake valve must only open on the intake stroke, not the compression, power, or exhaust strokes. To do this, the camshaft gear or sprocket is twice as big as the gear or sprocket on the crankshaft.

Front cover

The *front cover* bolts over the crankshaft snout. It holds an oil seal that seals the front of the crankshaft.

When the engine uses a gear or chain type camshaft drive, the front cover can also be called the *timing cover*, Fig. 11-28.

With a belt drive, this cover does not enclose the cam drive or timing mechanism. A second cover is installed over the belt, Fig. 11-29.

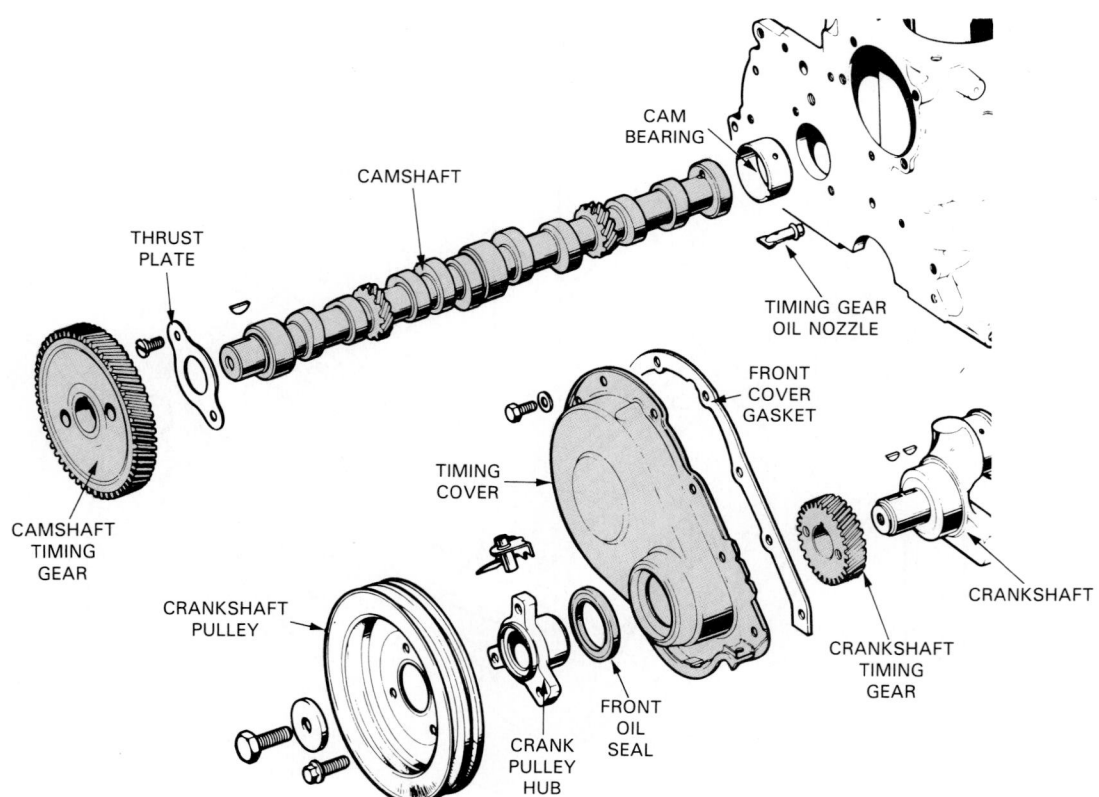

CAMSHAFT

CAM BEARING

THRUST PLATE

TIMING GEAR OIL NOZZLE

FRONT COVER GASKET

TIMING COVER

CAMSHAFT TIMING GEAR

CRANKSHAFT PULLEY

CRANKSHAFT

CRANKSHAFT TIMING GEAR

CRANK PULLEY HUB

FRONT OIL SEAL

Fig. 11-28. Engine front end components primarily operate engine camshaft. This engine uses timing gears to drive camshaft at one-half engine speed. Front cover enclose gears. Front seal prevents leakage around crankshaft snout. (Chrysler)

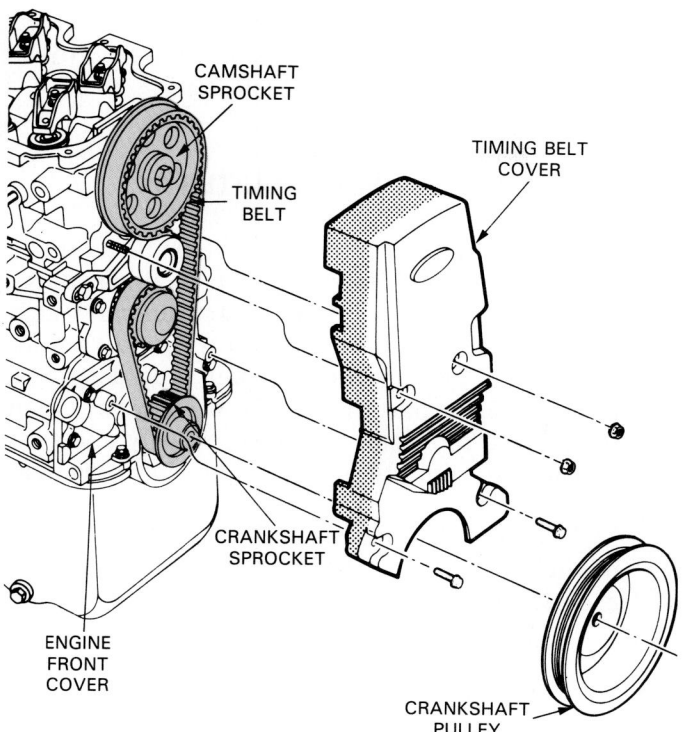

Fig. 11-29. Crankshaft sprocket turns timing belt. Timing belt turns camshaft sprocket and camshaft. Front cover simply houses front oil seal. Timing cover fits over belt. (Ford)

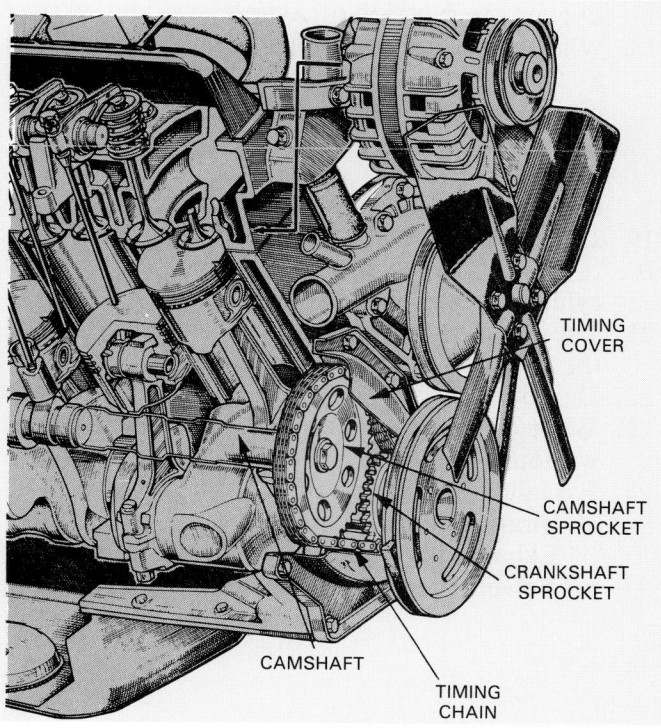

Fig. 11-30. Timing chain and sprockets operate camshaft in this engine. (Chrysler Corp.)

Crank damper

A *crank damper* is a heavy wheel on the crankshaft snout. It is mounted in rubber and helps prevent crankshaft vibration and damage. This damper is also called the *harmonic balancer* or *vibration damper*.

KNOW THESE TERMS

Intake stroke, Compression stroke, Power stroke, Exhaust stroke, TDC, BDC, Engine bottom end, Short block, Cylinder block, Cylinder bore, Main bearing bores, Main caps, Crankcase, Crankshaft, Main journals, Rod journals, Thrust bearing, Crankshaft end play, Bearing clearance, Rear main oil seal, Flywheel, Connecting rod, Piston, Piston pin, Piston clearance, Compression ring, Oil ring, Ring gap, Engine top end, Cylinder head, Combustion chamber, Intake and exhaust port, Valve guide, Valve seat, Valve, Valve train, Camshaft, Valve lifter, Push rod, Rocker arm, Valve seal, Valve spring, Engine front end, Camshaft drive, Intake manifold, Exhaust manifold, Valve cover.

REVIEW QUESTIONS

1. Usually, _____ or _____ _____ is burned inside the engine to produce heat, expansion, and resulting pressure.
2. What do TDC and BDC mean?
3. Every four strokes, the engine produces two power or energy producing strokes. True or False?
4. Explain the intake stroke.
5. Explain the compression stroke.
6. Explain the power stroke.
7. Explain the exhaust stroke.
8. _____ _____ bolt to the bottom of the block and hold the crankshaft in place.
9. The crankcase is the highest portion in the block. True or False?
10. The crankshaft changes the up and down motion of the piston into a useful _____ motion.
11. What is the function of crankshaft counterweights?
12. Describe the function of the main thrust bearing.
13. The _____ _____ transfers piston movement to the crankshaft.
14. The distance from the centerline of the crankshaft to the centerline of a rod journal is 3 in. (76 mm). What is the *total* vertical distance that the piston will travel in the cylinder (from TDC to BDC)?
15. Which of the following is NOT part of a connecting rod?
    a. I-beam.
    b. Lobe.
    c. Cap.
    d. Bushing.
16. Why is rod bearing clearance needed?

17. Explain the function of compression and oil rings.
18. Which of the following is part of the cylinder head?
    a. Combustion chambers.
    b. Intake and exhaust ports.
    c. Valve guides.
    d. Valve seats.
    e. All of the above are correct.
19. List and explain the basic parts of a camshaft.
20. _____ open and close the ports through the cylinder head.
21. The intake valves have larger diameter heads than the exhaust valves. True or False?
22. Describe the five basic parts of an engine valve.
23. What do valve seals do and what would happen without valve seals?
24. Explain the function of the following parts.
    a. Intake manifold.
    b. Exhaust manifold.
    c. Valve or rocker cover.
25. Identify the engine parts in the illustration below. Write A through N on your paper. Then write the name of the part next to each letter.

ACTIVITIES FOR CHAPTER 11

1. A camshaft changes rotary motion to up-and-down motion. Find and describe or sketch at least three other examples of ways that a mechanical system changes the type, direction, or force of a motion.
2. If possible, obtain from a repair shop a bearing or other engine part that shows severe wear. Clean the part so the wear can be seen easily and pass it around to your classmates. Discuss how the wear was caused.
3. Make a table showing the position (open or closed) of the intake valve and the exhaust valve during each stroke of the four-stroke cycle.

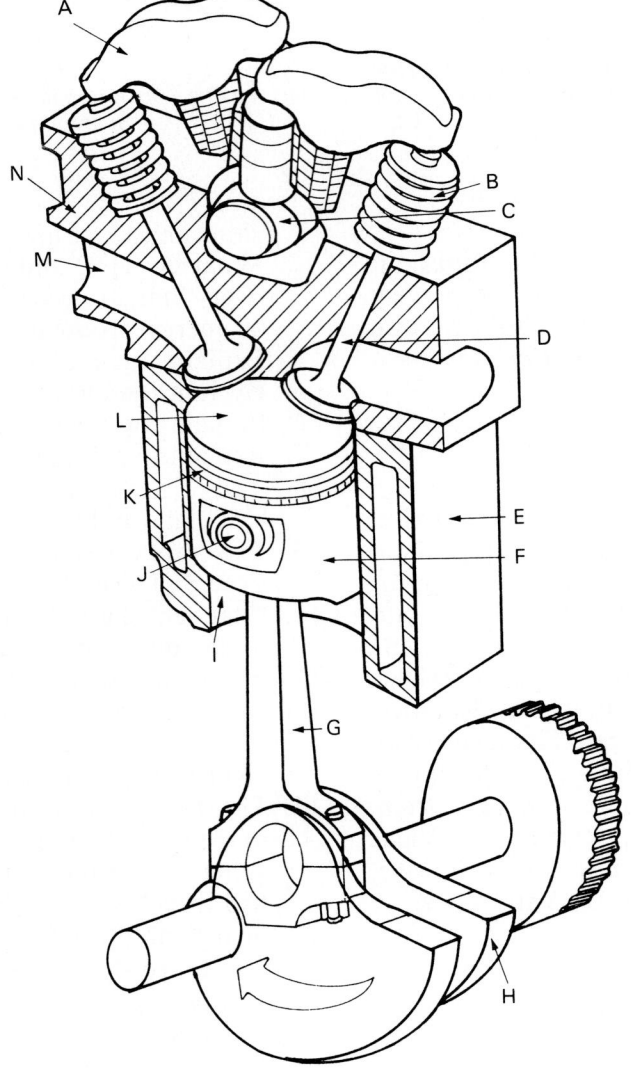

Can you identify the parts of the engine without looking at other illustrations?

Engine Classifications

After studying this chapter, you will be able to:
□ Describe basic automotive engine classifications.
□ Compare gasoline and diesel engines.
□ Compare two and four-stroke cycle engines.
□ Contrast combustion chamber designs.
□ Discuss alternate engine types.
□ Describe safety practices when working with engines.

Now that you have learned about the basic parts of an engine, you should become familiar with the various engine types used in automobiles. An experienced engine technician can glance into an engine compartment and "rattle off" dozens of engine facts.

For example, you might hear a technician say, "This is an in-line, 4-cylinder, overhead camshaft, hemi-head engine." You must understand these kinds of terms when troubleshooting and repairing vehicle engines. Study this chapter carefully. It will help you learn the "shop talk" of an engine technician.

ENGINE CLASSIFICATIONS

Even though basic parts are the same, design differences can change how engines operate and how they are repaired. For this reason, you should be able to classify engines.

Vehicle engines are commonly classified by:
1. Cylinder arrangement.
2. Number of cylinders.
3. Cooling system type.
4. Valve location.
5. Camshaft location.
6. Combustion chamber design.
7. Type of fuel burned.
8. Type of ignition.
9. Number of strokes per cycle.

Cylinder arrangement

Cylinder arrangement refers to the position of the cylinders in relation to the crankshaft. There are four basic cylinder arrangements: in-line, V-type, slant, and opposed. These are shown in Fig. 12-1.

An *in-line engine's* cylinders are lined up in a single row. Each cylinder is located in a straight line parallel to the crankshaft. Four, five, and six-cylinder engines are commonly in-line.

Viewed from either end, a *V-type engine* looks like the letter "V", Fig. 12-1. The two banks of cylinders

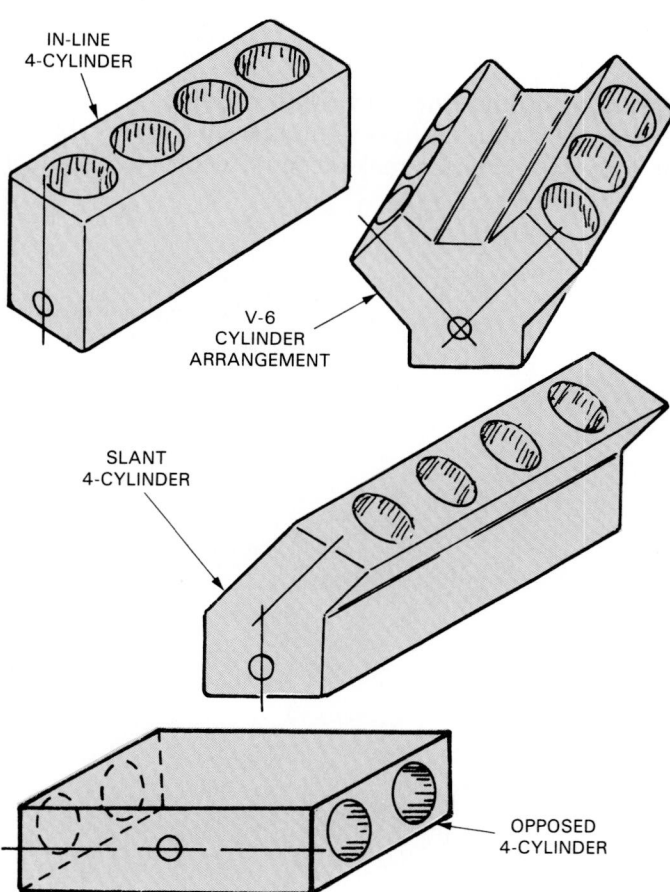

Fig. 12-1. Organization of cylinders in block determine one engine classification. These represent four basic types used in automobiles.

lie at an angle to each other. This arrangement reduces the length and the height of the engine.

A *slant engine* has only one bank of cylinders angled or leaning to one side.

As with V-type engines, this saves space, Fig. 12-1. It allows the body and hood of the vehicle to be much lower. A relatively large engine can be fitted into a small engine compartment.

Cylinders of an *opposed engine* lie flat on either side of the crankshaft, Fig. 12-1. Because of its appearance, this type is sometimes called a "pancake engine." An opposed engine may be found in older Volkswagens and a few late-model foreign sports cars (Porsche and Subaru, for example).

Number of cylinders

Normally, car and truck engines have either 4, 6, or 8 cylinders. A few engines have 3, 5, 10, 12, or 16 cylinders.

A greater number of cylinders generally increases engine smoothness and power. For instance, an 8-cylinder engine produces twice as many power strokes per crank revolution as a 4-cylinder engine. This reduces power pulsations and roughness (vibrations) at idle. Four-cylinder engines are usually in-line or slant, and sometimes opposed. Six-cylinder engines can be in-line, slant, or a V-type. Five-cylinder engines are normally in-line. Eight, 10 and 12-cylinder engines are commonly V-types.

Cylinder numbering and firing order

Engine manufacturers number each engine cylinder to help the technician make repairs. The service manual will provide an illustration of the engine, as shown in Fig. 12-2.

Cylinder numbers are normally stamped on the connecting rods. Sometimes, they are cast into the intake manifold. Cylinder numbering varies with different auto manufacturers. You should keep this in mind when referring to engine classifications. Two V-6 engines, for example, could have completely different cylinder numbering systems.

Firing order refers to the sequence in which combustion occurs in each engine cylinder. The position of the crankshaft rod journals in relation to each other determines engine firing order.

The service manual will have a drawing showing the firing order for the engine. This information may also be given on the engine intake manifold.

Two similar engines can have completely different firing orders. For example, a 4-cylinder, in-line engine may fire 1-3-4-2 or 1-2-4-3. Firing orders for 6- and 8-cylinder engines also vary.

You need to know firing order when working on the engine's ignition system. It can be used when installing spark plug wires, a distributor, or when doing other tune-up related operations, Fig. 12-2.

Cooling system type

There are two types of *cooling systems:* liquid and air. The liquid cooling system is the most common. See Fig. 12-3.

The *liquid cooling system* surrounds the cylinder with *coolant* (water and antifreeze solution). The coolant carries combustion heat out of the cylinder head and

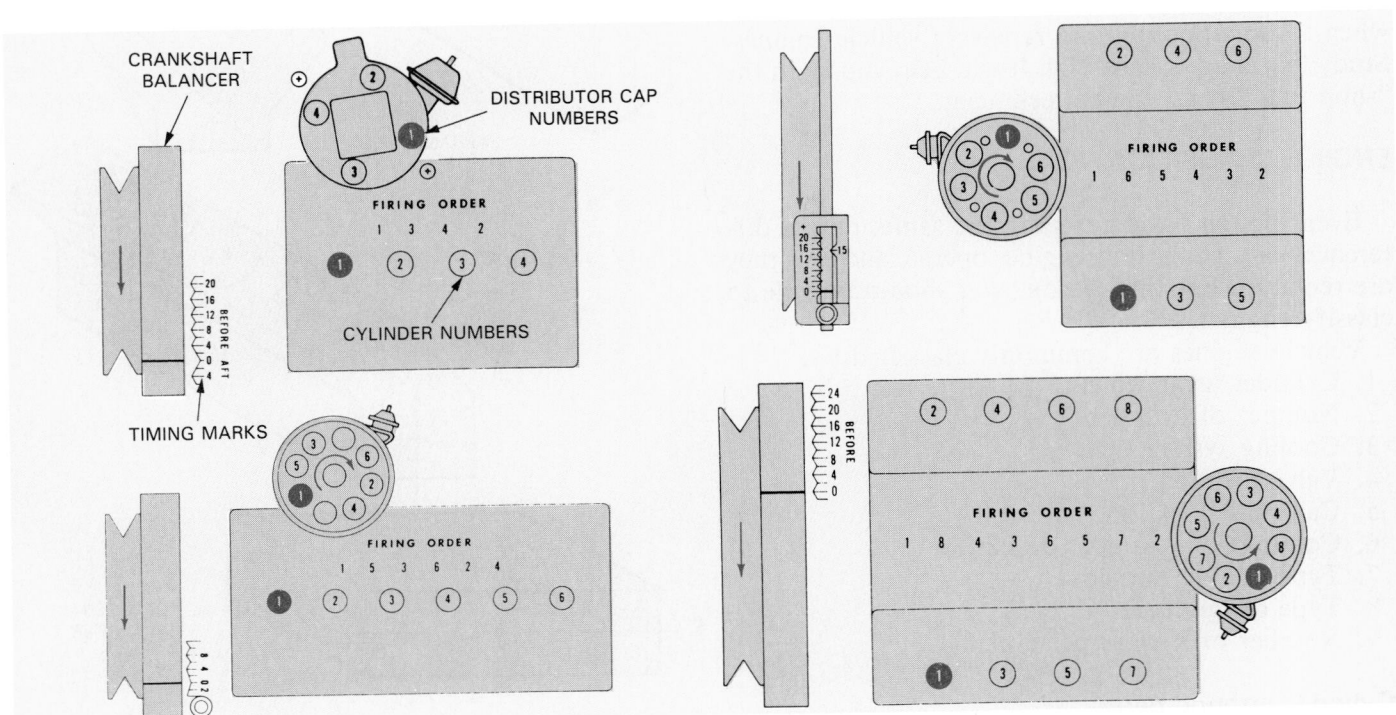

Fig. 12-2. Engine cylinder numbers, distributor cap numbers, and firing order numbers. Cylinder numbers are usually stamped on connecting rods and may be cast into intake manifold. Numbers vary from engine to engine. (Mitchell Manuals)

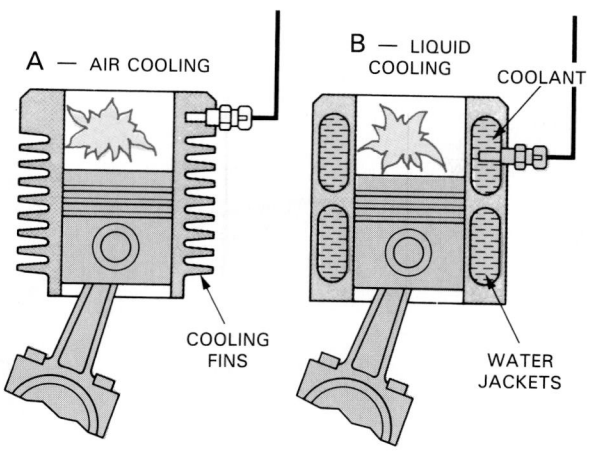

A — AIR COOLING

B — LIQUID COOLING

COOLANT

COOLING FINS

WATER JACKETS

Fig. 12-3. A — Air cooling systems uses large fins around cylinder to remove heat. B — Liquid cooling system surrounds cylinder with coolant. Liquid cooling system is commonly used in automobiles. Motorcycles and lawnmowers use air cooling system.

engine block to prevent engine damage.

An **air cooling system** circulates air over cooling fins on the cylinders. This removes heat from the cylinders to prevent overheating damage.

Air-cooled or air-oil cooled engines are seldom used in passenger cars. They can be found on motorcycles, lawnmowers, and a few high performance cars. With strict exhaust emission regulations, manufacturers have partially phased out air-cooled engines. They cannot maintain as constant a temperature as a liquid-type cooling system.

Fuel type

An engine is also classified by the type of fuel it burns. A gasoline engine burns gasoline. A diesel engine burns diesel oil. These are the most common types of fuel for vehicles.

LP-gas (liquified petroleum gas), gasohol (10% alcohol, 90% gasoline), and pure alcohol can also be used to power an auto engine. These fuels are used in limited quantities. Vehicle fuels are detailed in Chapter 17.

Ignition type

Two basic methods are used to ignite the fuel in an engine combustion chamber: an electric arc (spark plug) and hot air (compressed air). Look at Fig. 12-4.

A **spark ignition engine** uses an electric arc at the spark plug to ignite the fuel. The arc produces enough heat to start the fuel burning. *Gasoline engines* use spark ignition, Fig. 12-4.

A **compression ignition engine** squeezes the air in the combustion chamber until it is hot enough to ignite the fuel. A *diesel engine* is a compression ignition engine. No spark plugs are used, Fig. 12-4.

Valve location

Another engine classification can be made by comparing the location of the valves.

An **L-head engine** has both the intake and exhaust valves in the block, Fig. 12-5A. Also called a *flat head* engine, its cylinder head simply forms a cover over the cylinders and valves. The camshaft is in the block and pushes upward to open the valves. Most four-stroke

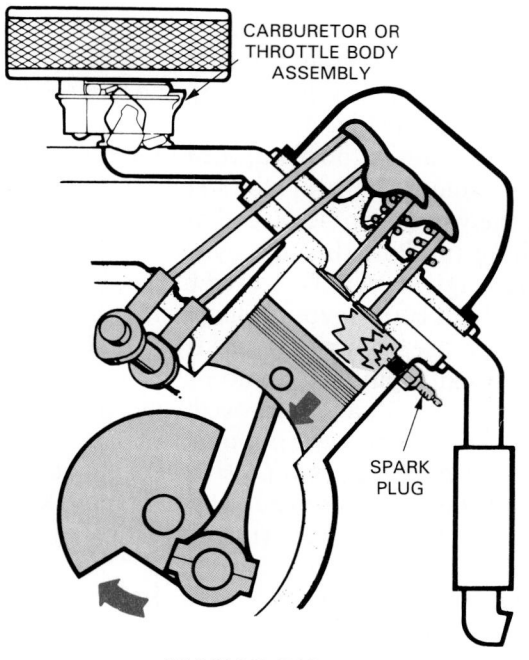

CARBURETOR OR THROTTLE BODY ASSEMBLY

SPARK PLUG

GASOLINE ENGINE

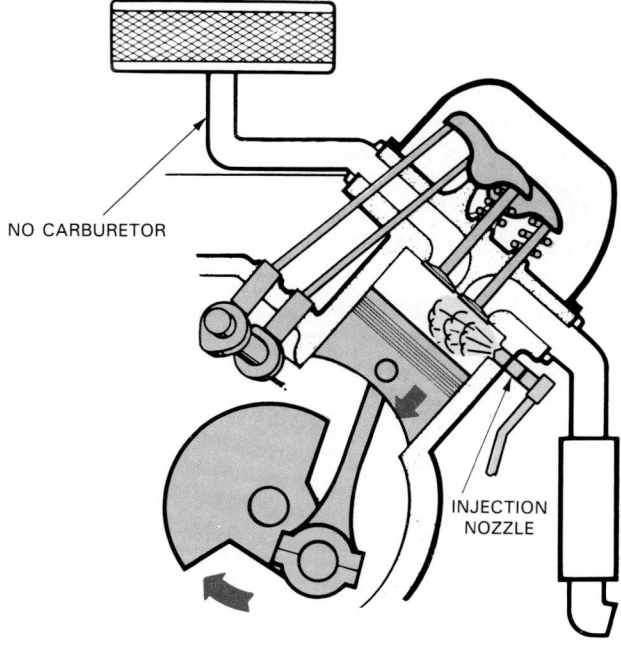

NO CARBURETOR

INJECTION NOZZLE

DIESEL ENGINE

Fig. 12-4. Gasoline and diesel engines use different means to ignite fuel. Gasoline engine uses spark plug to start power stroke. Diesel engine compresses air in cylinder until hot. When fuel is injected into cylinder, hot air makes fuel burn.

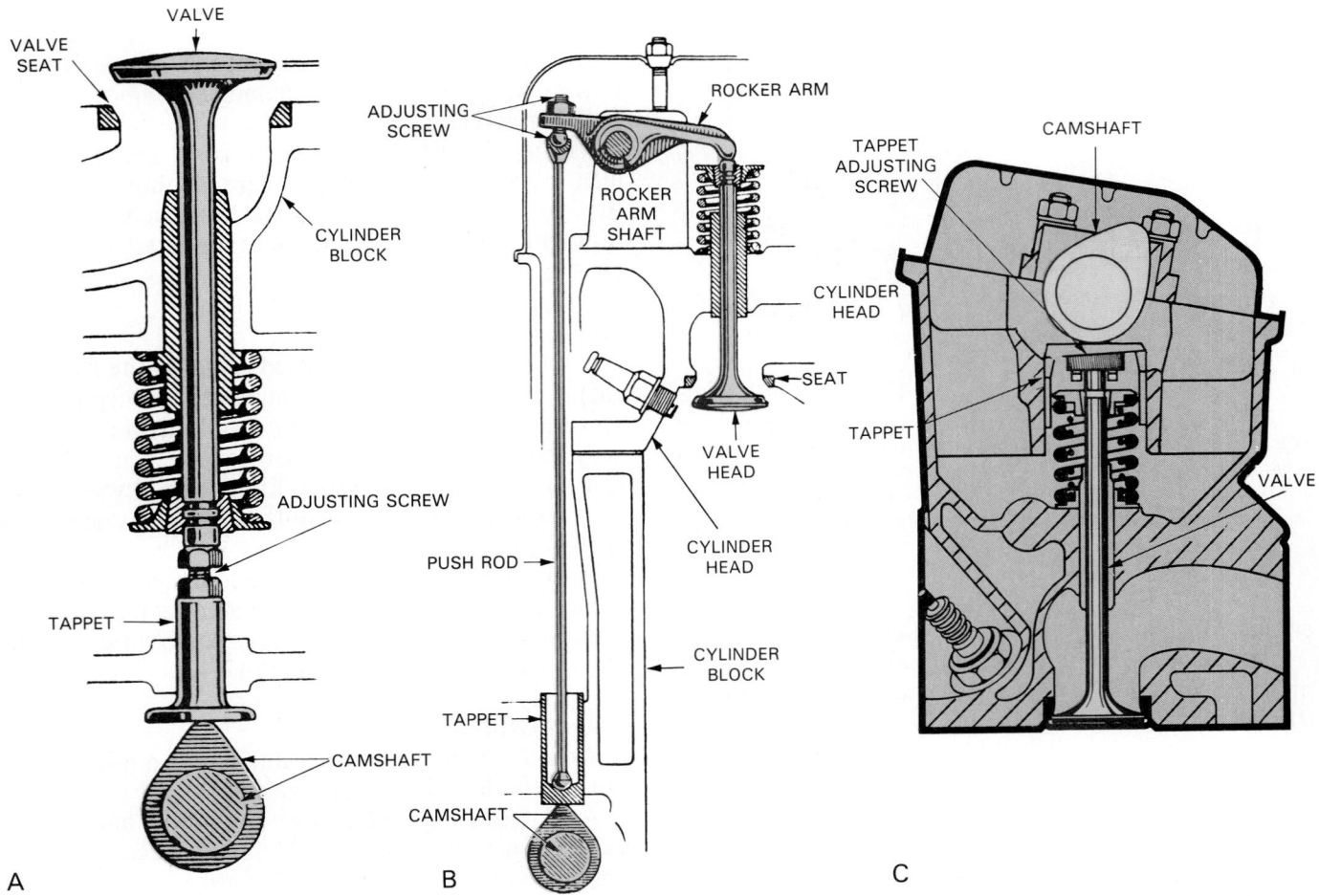

Fig. 12-5. Three common valve-camshaft locations: A — Valve in block or L-head engine is no longer used in automobiles. Small gas engines for lawnmowers, for example, use this arrangement. B — Cam-in-block, overhead valve or I-head engine is common. C — Overhead cam engine is another form of I-head engine. It is also very common in today's vehicles. (Black & Decker, Chrysler)

cycle lawnmower engines are L-head types. Vehicle engines are no longer L-head types.

In an **I-head engine,** both valves are in the cylinder head. Another name for this design is *overhead valve (OHV) engine,* Fig. 12-5B.

The OHV engine has replaced the flat head engine in vehicles. Numerous variations of the overhead valve engine are now in use.

Other valve configurations have been used in the past. However, they are so rare that their mention is not important.

Camshaft location

There are two basic locations for the engine camshaft: in the block and in the cylinder head. Both locations are common.

A **cam-in-block engine** uses push rods to transfer motion to the rocker arms and valves, Fig. 12-5B. The term overhead valve (OHV) is sometimes used instead of cam-in-block.

In an **overhead cam (OHC) engine,** the camshaft is located in the top of the cylinder head. Push rods are

NOT needed to operate the rockers and valves. This type engine is a refinement of the overhead valve engine. Refer to Fig. 12-5C.

With the cam in the head, the number of valve train parts is reduced. This cuts the weight of the valve train. Also, the valves can be placed at an angle to improve breathing (airflow through cylinder head ports).

OHC engines were first used in racing cars because of their high rpm (revolutions per minute) efficiency. Now they are commonly used in small, high rpm, economy car engines. With no push rods to flex, lower valve train weight, and improved valve positioning, the OHC is becoming very popular.

A **single overhead cam (SOHC) engine** has only one camshaft per cylinder head. The cam may act directly on the valves, or rocker arms may transfer motion to the valves.

A **dual overhead cam (DOHC) engine** has two camshafts per cylinder head. One cam operates the intake valves, the other operates the exhaust valves. Engines of this type are used only in exotic sports car and racing car engines. A DOHC engine will be shown later in the chapter.

Combustion chamber shape

The shape of the combustion chamber provides still another method of classifying an engine. The three basic combustion chamber shapes for gasoline engines are: pancake, wedge, and hemispherical. These are pictured in Fig. 12-6.

The *pancake combustion chamber,* also called the "bath tub" chamber, has valve heads almost parallel with the top of the piston. The chamber forms a flat pocket over the piston head, Fig. 12-6A.

A *wedge combustion chamber,* called a *wedge head,* is shaped like a triangle or a wedge when viewed as in Fig. 12-6B. Valves are placed side-by-side with the spark plug next to the valves.

A *squish area* is commonly formed inside a wedge type cylinder head. When the piston reaches TDC, the piston comes very close to the bottom of the cylinder head. This squeezes the air-fuel mixture in that area and causes it to squirt or squish out into the main part of the chamber. Squish can be used to improve air-fuel mixing at low engine speeds.

A *hemispherical combustion chamber,* nicknamed *hemi-head,* is shaped like a dome. The valves are canted (tilted) on each side of the chamger. The spark plug is located near the center. A hemi is shown in Fig. 12-6C. Compare it to the others.

A hemi combustion chamber is extremely efficient. There are no hidden pockets for incomplete combustion. The surface area is very small, reducing heat loss from the chamber. The centrally located spark plug produces a very short flame path for combustion. The canted valves help increase breathing ability.

The hemi-head was first used in high horsepower, racing engines. It is now used in many OHC passenger car engines. It allows the engine to operate at high rpms and makes it very fuel efficient. It also produces complete burning of the fuel to reduce emissions.

Combustion chamber types

Besides the three shapes just covered, there are several other combustion chamber classifications. Each type is designed to increase combustion efficiency, gas mileage, and power while reducing exhaust pollution.

A *swirl combustion chamber* causes the air-fuel mixture to twirl or spin as it enters from the intake port. Look at Fig. 12-7. This causes the air and fuel to mix into a finer mist that burns better.

A *four-valve combustion chamber* uses two exhaust valves and two intake valves per cylinder. This is illustrated in Fig. 12-8. The extra valves increase flow in and out of the combustion chamber. This setup is used in a few exotic high performance engines.

A *three-valve chamber* typically has two intake valves and one exhaust valve.

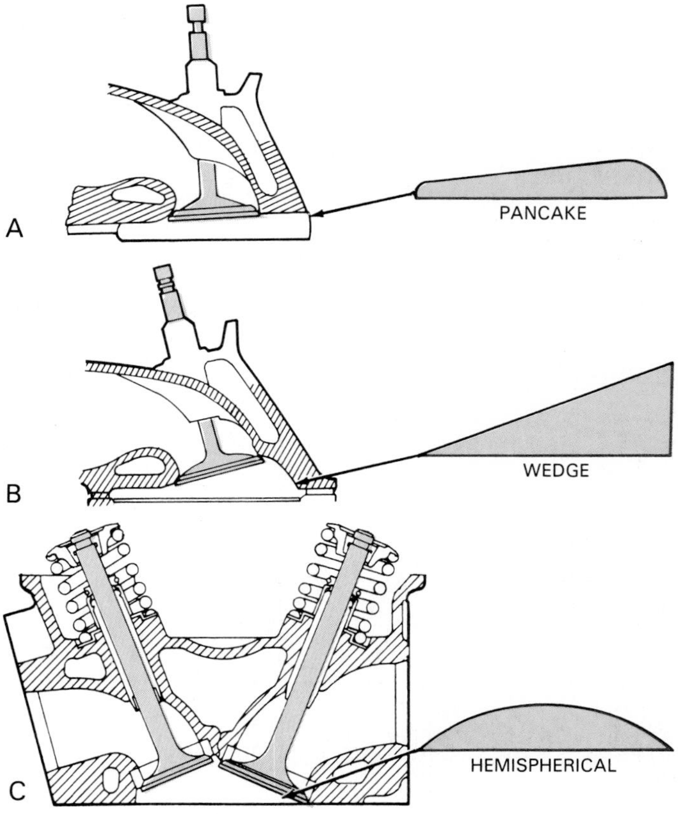

Fig. 12-6. Three basic combustion chamber shapes: A — Valve almost parallel with piston top forms pancake or bath tub shape. B — Valve at angle forms wedge-shaped combustion chamber. C — Valves at angle to each other produce hemispherical or domed chamber. (Chrysler Corp.)

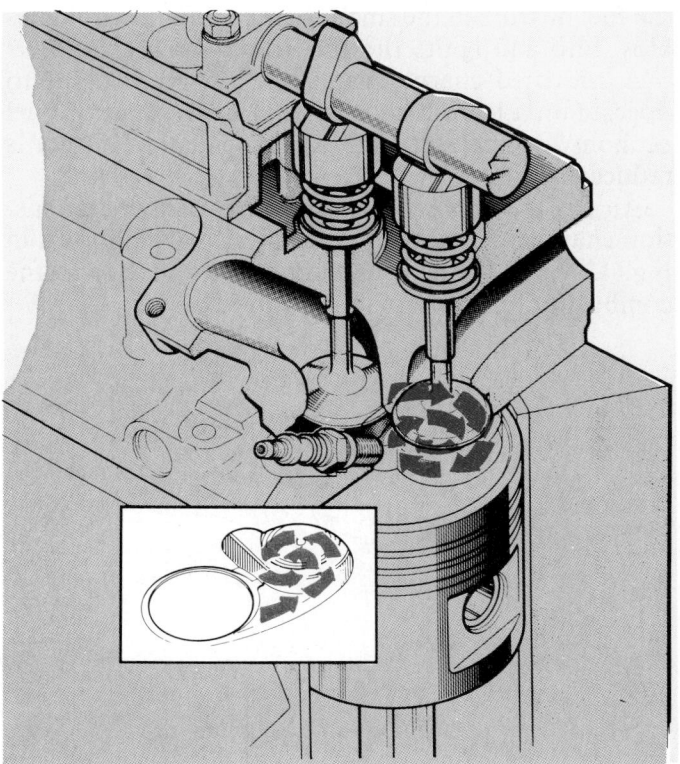

Fig. 12-7. Swirl combustion chamber has port entry designed to cause air-fuel mixture swirling. This helps stir air and fuel into finer mist for improved combustion. Many chambers use this principle. (Jaguar)

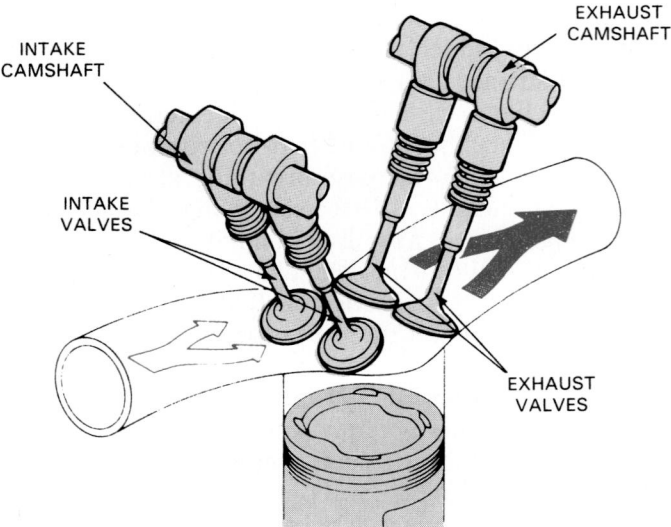

Fig. 12-8. Four-valve combustion chamber is used in exotic sports cars and racing car engines. Extra valves increase flow and engine power. (Toyota)

A *stratified charge combustion chamber* uses a small combustion chamber flame to ignite and burn the fuel in the main, large combustion chamber.

A very *lean mixture* (high ratio of air to fuel) is admitted into the main combustion chamber. The mixture is so lean that it will not ignite and burn easily.

A *richer mixture* (higher ratio of fuel to air) is admitted into the small chamber by an extra valve. When the fuel mixture in the small chamber is ignited, flames blow into and ignite the fuel in the main chamber.

A stratified charge chamber allows the engine to operate on a lean, high efficiency air-fuel ratio. Fuel economy is increased and exhaust emission output is reduced.

An *air jet combustion chamber* has a single combustion chamber fitted with an extra air valve. Shown in Fig. 12-9, a passage runs from the carburetor to the combustion chamber and jet valve.

During the intake stroke, the engine camshaft opens both the conventional intake valve and the air jet valve. This allows fuel mixture to flow into the cylinder past the conventional intake valve. At the same time, a stream of air flows into the cylinder through the jet valve.

The jet valve action causes the fuel mixture in the cylinder to swirl and mix. This increases combustion efficiency by causing more of the fuel to burn during the power stroke. The jet valve only works at idle and low engine speeds. At higher rpm, normal air-fuel mixing is adequate for efficient combustion.

A *precombustion chamber* is commonly used in automotive diesel engines. It is similar in shape to a stratified charge chamber for a gasoline engine. Also called a DIESEL PRECHAMBER, it is used to quiet engine operation and to allow the use of a *glow plug* (heating element) to aid cold weather starting. Fig. 12-10 shows a cutaway view of a diesel prechamber.

During combustion, diesel oil is injected into the prechamber. If the engine is cold, the glow plug heats the air in the prechamber. This heat, along with the heat produced by compression, causes the fuel to ignite and burn. As it burns, it expands and moves into the main chamber.

ALTERNATE ENGINES

As you have learned, vehicles generally use internal combustion, 4-stroke cycle, piston engines.

Alternate engines include all other engine types that may be used to power a vehicle. Various engine types have been developed, but few have been placed into production.

Wankel (rotary) engine

A *Wankel engine,* also known as a *rotary engine,* uses a triangular rotor instead of conventional pistons. The rotor turns inside a specially shaped housing, as shown in Fig. 12-11.

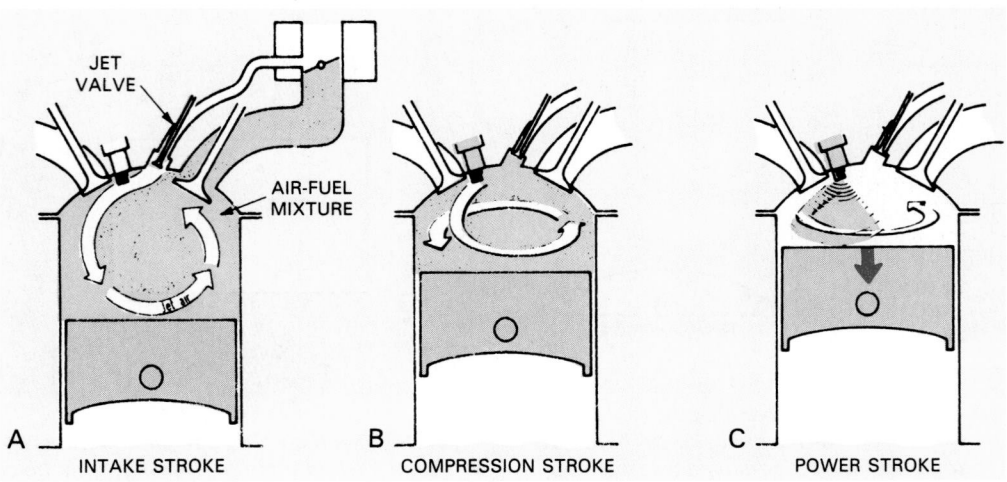

Fig. 12-9. Air jet injects stream of air into chamber at idle to improve fuel mixing and combustion. (Chrysler)

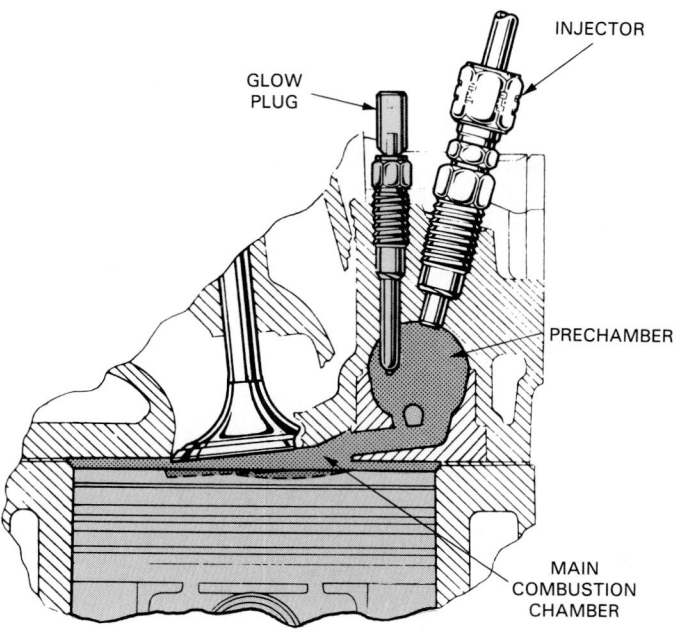

INJECTOR

GLOW PLUG

PRECHAMBER

MAIN COMBUSTION CHAMBER

Fig. 12-10. Diesel engine prechamber should not be confused with gasoline engine stratified charge chamber. Diesel prechamber quiets engine operation and allows use of glow plug. Glow plug is heating element that improves cold weather starting. (Oldsmobile)

While spinning on its own axis, the rotor orbits around a mainshaft. This eliminates the normal reciprocating (up and down) motion found in piston engines.

One complete cycle (all four strokes) takes place every time the rotor turns once. Three rotor faces produce three power strokes per revolution. Fig. 12-12 illustrates the basic operation of a rotary engine.

A rotary engine is very powerful for its size. Also, because it spins—rather than moves up and down—engine operation is very smooth and vibration-free.

A complicated emission control system is needed to make the rotary engine pass emission standards. This has limited its use. A Wankel engine is one of the few alternate engines to be mass-produced and installed in production vehicles.

Steam engine

A *steam engine* heats water to produce steam (hot water vapor). The steam pressure operates the engine pistons. Look at Fig. 12-13.

A steam engine is an *external combustion engine* since its fuel is burned outside the engine. Car engines are *internal combustion engines* because they burn fuel inside the engine.

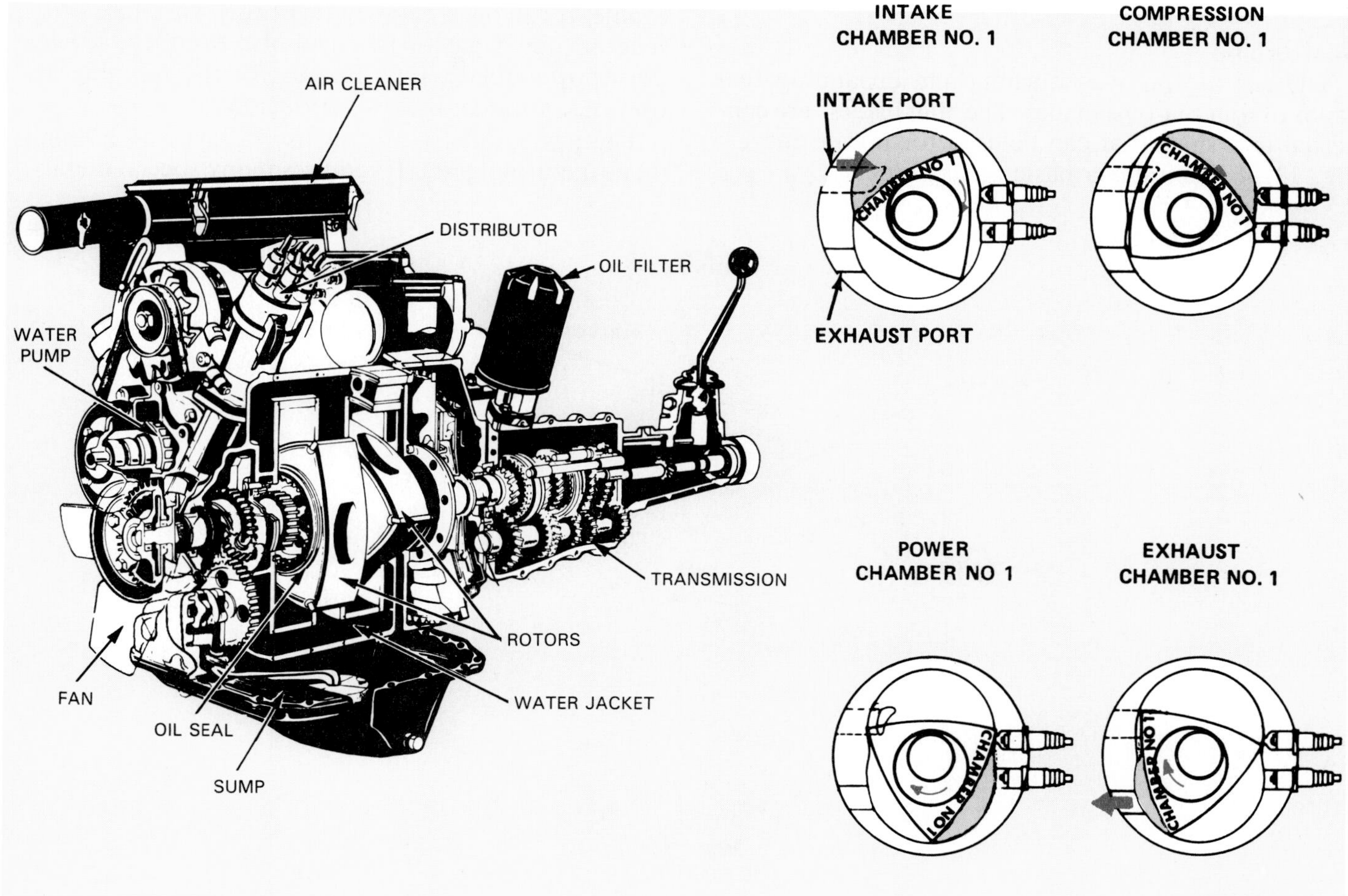

AIR CLEANER

DISTRIBUTOR

OIL FILTER

WATER PUMP

TRANSMISSION

FAN

OIL SEAL

ROTORS

WATER JACKET

SUMP

INTAKE CHAMBER NO. 1

INTAKE PORT

EXHAUST PORT

COMPRESSION CHAMBER NO. 1

POWER CHAMBER NO 1

EXHAUST CHAMBER NO. 1

Fig. 12-11. Wankel rotary engine does not use conventional pistons that move up and down in cylinder. Rotor spins in circular motion. Note engine parts. (Mazda)

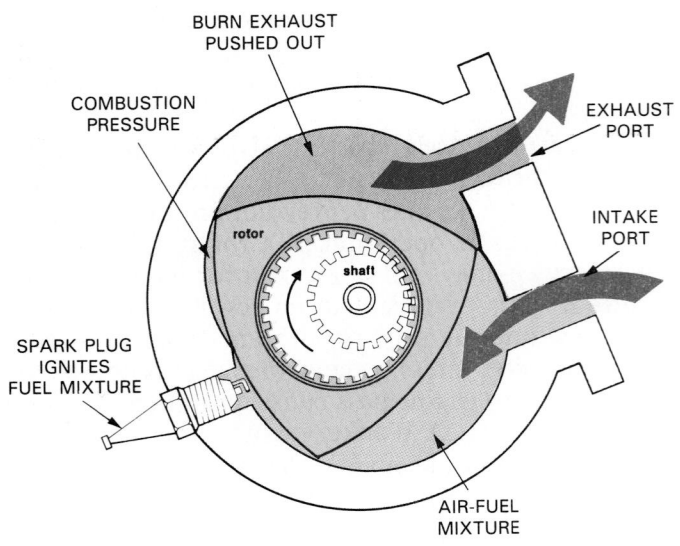

Fig. 12-12. In rotary engine, rotor movement produces low pressure area, pulling air-fuel mixture into engine. As rotor turns, mixture is compressed and ignited. As fuel burns, it expands and pushes on rotor. Rotor turns and burned gases are pushed out of engine.

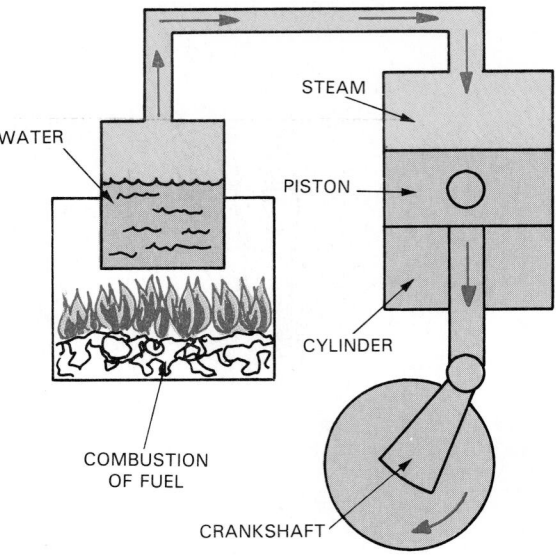

Fig. 12-13. Steam engine is an external combustion engine. It burns fuel outside of engine. Pressure is piped into cylinder to move piston.

Steam engines were used on some of the first cars. They are not used today mostly because of their low efficiency.

Gas turbine

The *gas turbine* uses burning and expanding fuel vapor to spin fan-type blades. The "fan blades" are connected to a shaft that can be used for power output. Fig. 12-14 illustrates a basic gas turbine.

A gas turbine is a very promising alternate type of engine. The turbine is capable of extremely high efficiency — much higher than a conventional piston engine. It can burn many types of fuel: gasoline, kerosene, or oil. A gas turbine can also produce tremendous power for its size. Because of the spinning action, its power output is very smooth.

The gas turbine is not in use because of its high manufacturing costs. It requires many special metals,

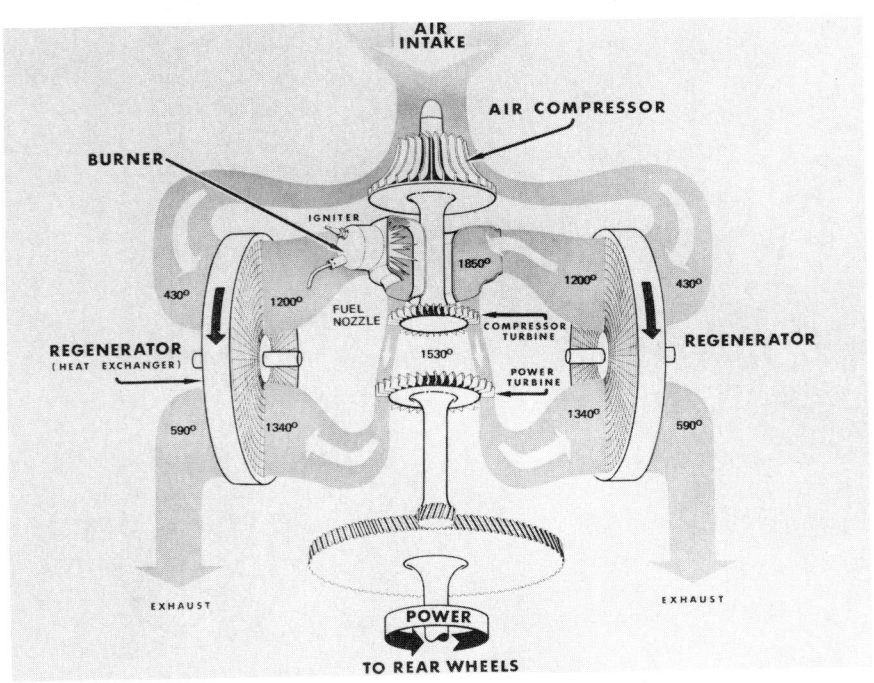

Fig. 12-14. Gas turbine uses pressure from burning fuel to spin fan-like blades. This motion is used to rotate shaft and gears for power output.

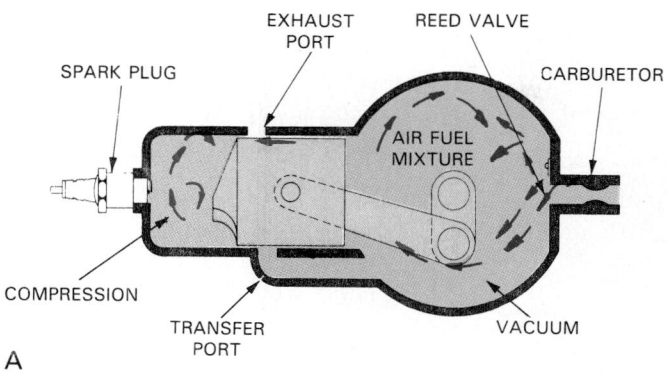

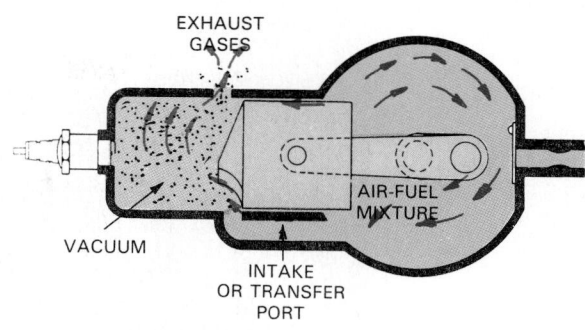

A

B

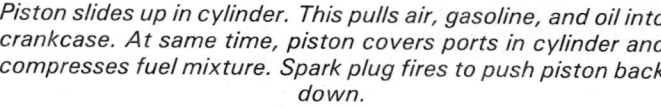

Piston slides up in cylinder. This pulls air, gasoline, and oil into crankcase. At same time, piston covers ports in cylinder and compresses fuel mixture. Spark plug fires to push piston back down.

As piston slides down, it forms pressure in engine crankcase. This closes reed valve. When piston slides down far enough, cylinder ports open. Exhaust exits one port. Crankcase pressure pushes mixture into cylinder through other port. This prepares for another power stroke.

Fig. 12-15. Two-stroke cycle engine completes all four events in two piston movements. (Ethyl Corporation)

ceramic parts, and precision machining and balancing. Some day the gas turbine may be a very common automotive engine.

Electric motor

An *electric motor* and large *storage batteries* can be used to power an automobile. Electric cars have been produced in limited numbers. They have seen some success as a means of transportation for short trips. Speed and driving distance are limited, but are improving with new technology.

Hybrid power source

A *hybrid power source* uses two different methods to power a vehicle. For example, a small gasoline engine and an electric motor and storage batteries may both be used to propel a vehicle.

The batteries and electric motor supply power when the car first accelerates. This provides enough energy to accelerate the car quickly. Once cruising speeds are reached, the gasoline engine takes over. It is a very small engine that can supply adequate power to keep the car moving. The gasoline engine also provides enough energy to recharge the batteries.

Two-stroke cycle engine

A *two-stroke cycle engine* is similar to a four-stroke cycle engine, but it requires only one revolution of the crankshaft for a complete power-producing cycle. Two piston strokes (one upward and one downward) complete the intake, compression, power and exhaust events. Fig. 12-15 illustrates the basic operation of a two-stroke cycle engine.

As the piston moves up, it compresses the air-fuel mixture in the combustion chamber. At the same time, the vacuum created in the crankcase by the piston movement draws fuel and oil into the crankcase. Either a reed valve (flexible metal flap valve) or a rotary valve

(spinning disc-shaped valve) can be used to control flow into the crankcase.

When the piston reaches the top of the cylinder, ignition occurs and the burning gases force the piston to move downward. The reed valve or rotary valve closes, compressing and pressurizing the fuel mixture in the crankcase.

As the piston moves far enough down in the cylinder, it uncovers an exhaust port in the cylinder wall. Burned gases leave the engine through the exhaust port.

As the piston continues downward, it uncovers the transfer port. Pressure in the crankcase causes a fresh fuel charge to flow into the cylinder. Upward movement of the piston again covers the transfer and exhaust ports, compression begins and the cycle is repeated.

Since the crankcase is used as a storage chamber for each successive fuel charge, the fuel and lubricating oil are premixed and introduced into the engine through the carburetor.

Inside the crankcase, some of the oil separates from the gasoline. The oil mist lubricates and protects the moving parts inside the engine.

Generally speaking, two-stroke cycle engines are NOT used in vehicles because they:

1. Produce too much exhaust pollution.
2. Have poor power output at low speeds.
3. Require more service than a four-stroke.
4. Must have motor oil mixed into the fuel.
5. Are not as fuel efficient as a four-stroke engine.

TYPICAL AUTOMOTIVE ENGINES

Figs. 12-16 through 12-26 illustrate typical automotive engines. Study each of these carefully. Note the design variations between each type. Also, study the names of all of the parts. This will help you in later chapters.

Fig. 12-16. *Porsche still uses air-oil cooled engines in some of its cars. Note how compact this engine is to fit in rear of car. It uses dual ignition systems, two oil pumps, etc. to improve high speed dependability.* (Porsche)

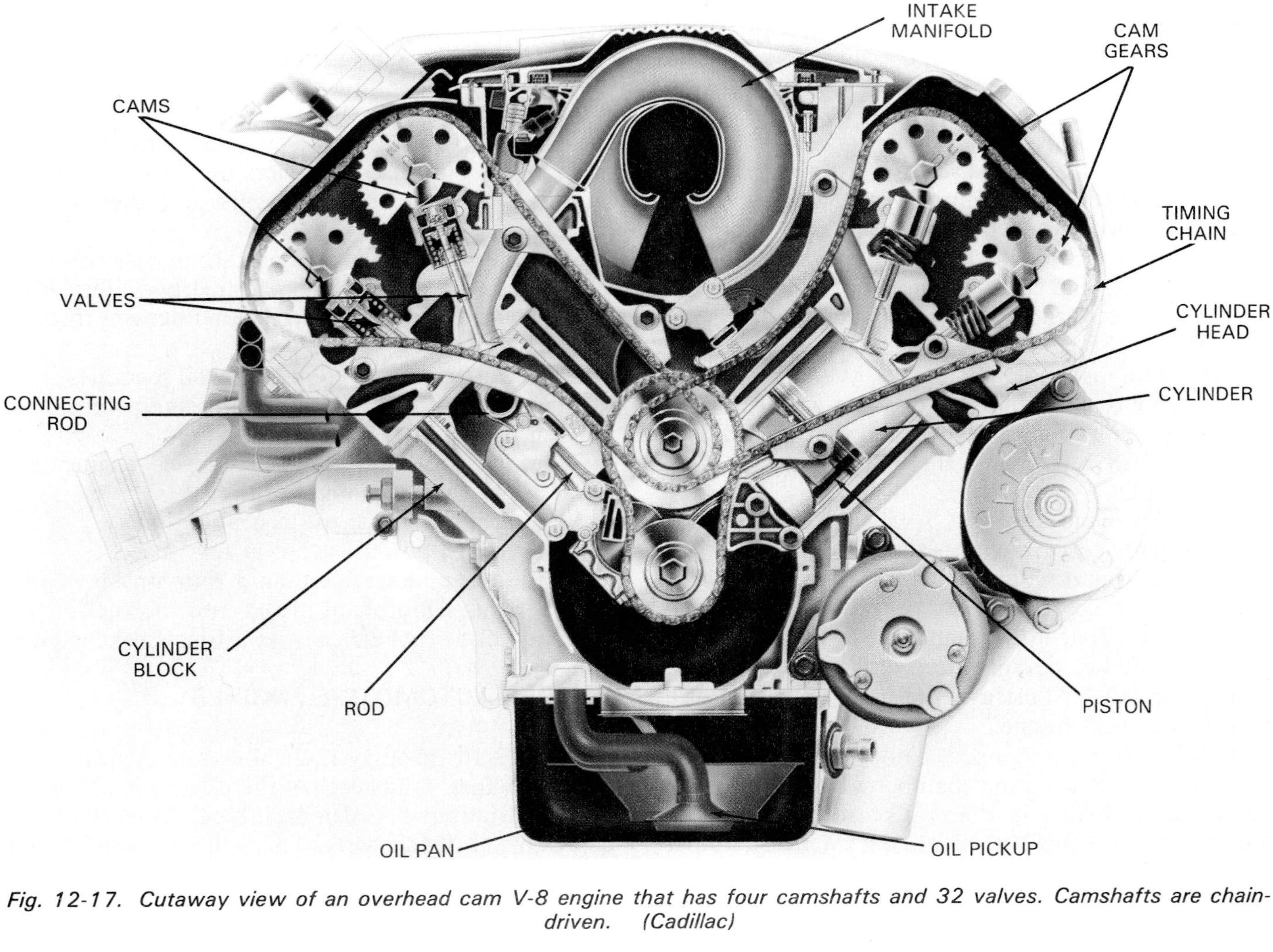

INTAKE MANIFOLD

CAM GEARS

CAMS

TIMING CHAIN

VALVES

CYLINDER HEAD

CONNECTING ROD

CYLINDER

CYLINDER BLOCK

ROD

PISTON

OIL PAN

OIL PICKUP

Fig. 12-17. *Cutaway view of an overhead cam V-8 engine that has four camshafts and 32 valves. Camshafts are chain-driven.* (Cadillac)

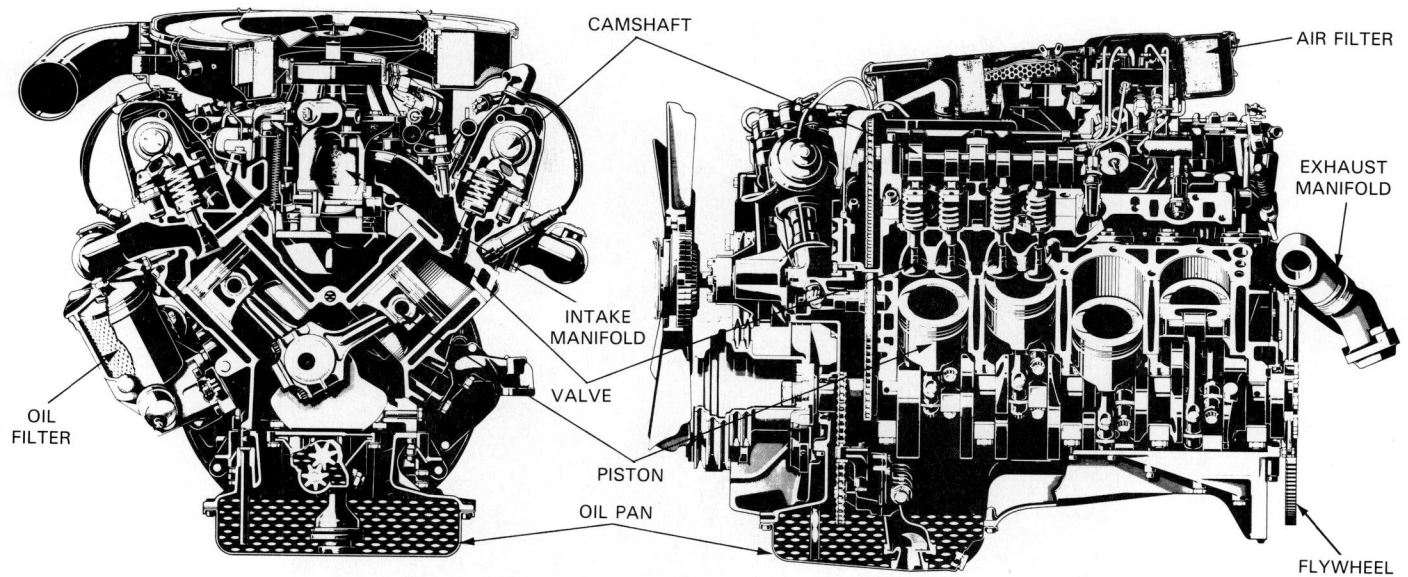

CAMSHAFT

AIR FILTER

EXHAUST MANIFOLD

INTAKE MANIFOLD

VALVE

OIL FILTER

PISTON

OIL PAN

FLYWHEEL

Fig. 12-18. Front and side views of modern SOHC V-8 engine. Note one cam in top of each cylinder head and chain type camshaft drive. (Mercedes Benz)

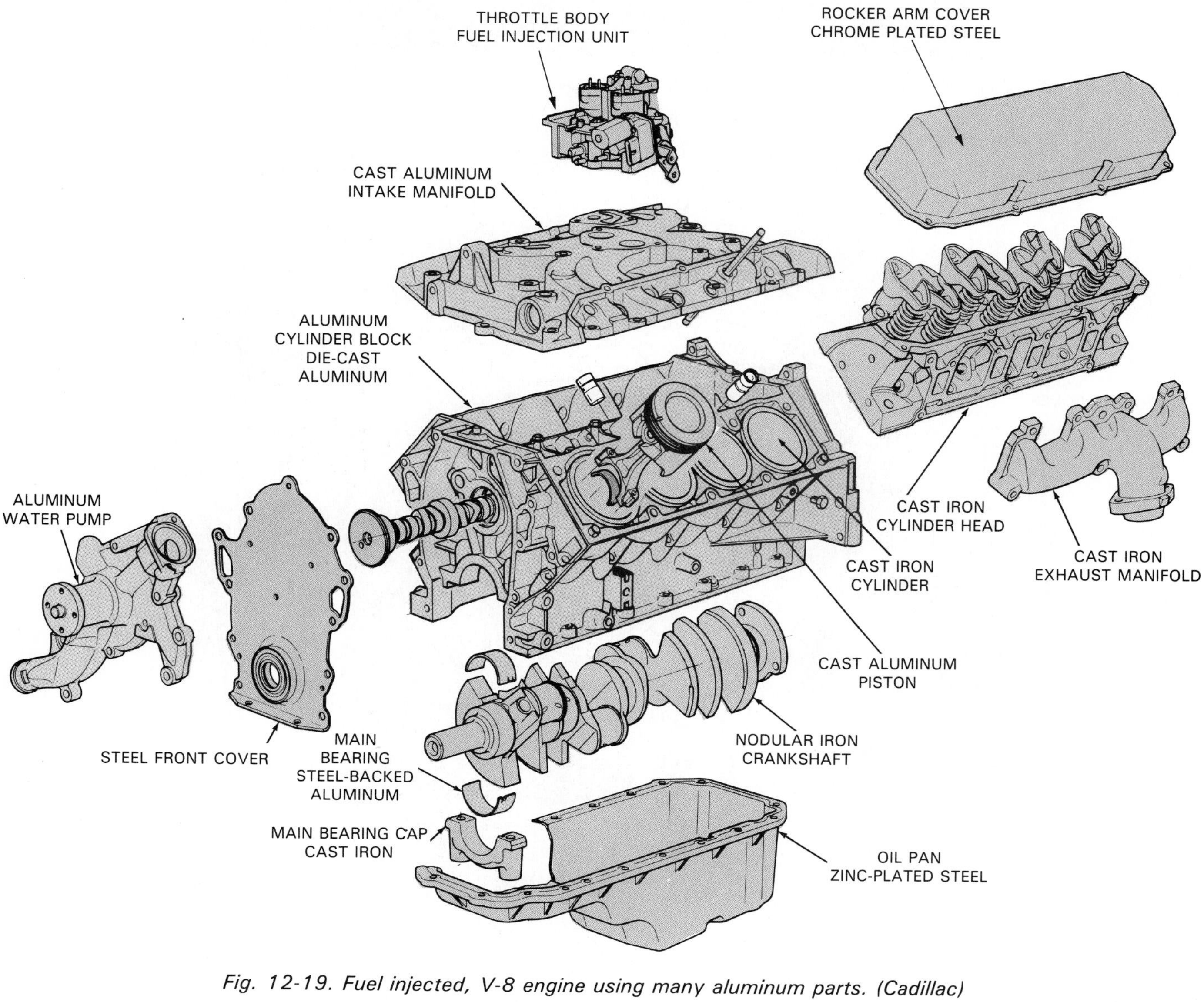

THROTTLE BODY FUEL INJECTION UNIT

ROCKER ARM COVER CHROME PLATED STEEL

CAST ALUMINUM INTAKE MANIFOLD

ALUMINUM CYLINDER BLOCK DIE-CAST ALUMINUM

CAST IRON CYLINDER HEAD

CAST IRON CYLINDER

CAST IRON EXHAUST MANIFOLD

ALUMINUM WATER PUMP

CAST ALUMINUM PISTON

STEEL FRONT COVER

MAIN BEARING STEEL-BACKED ALUMINUM

NODULAR IRON CRANKSHAFT

MAIN BEARING CAP CAST IRON

OIL PAN ZINC-PLATED STEEL

Fig. 12-19. Fuel injected, V-8 engine using many aluminum parts. (Cadillac)

Fig. 12-20. *Buick Quad-OHC engine. This high tech engine developes tremendous power for its small size.* (Buick)

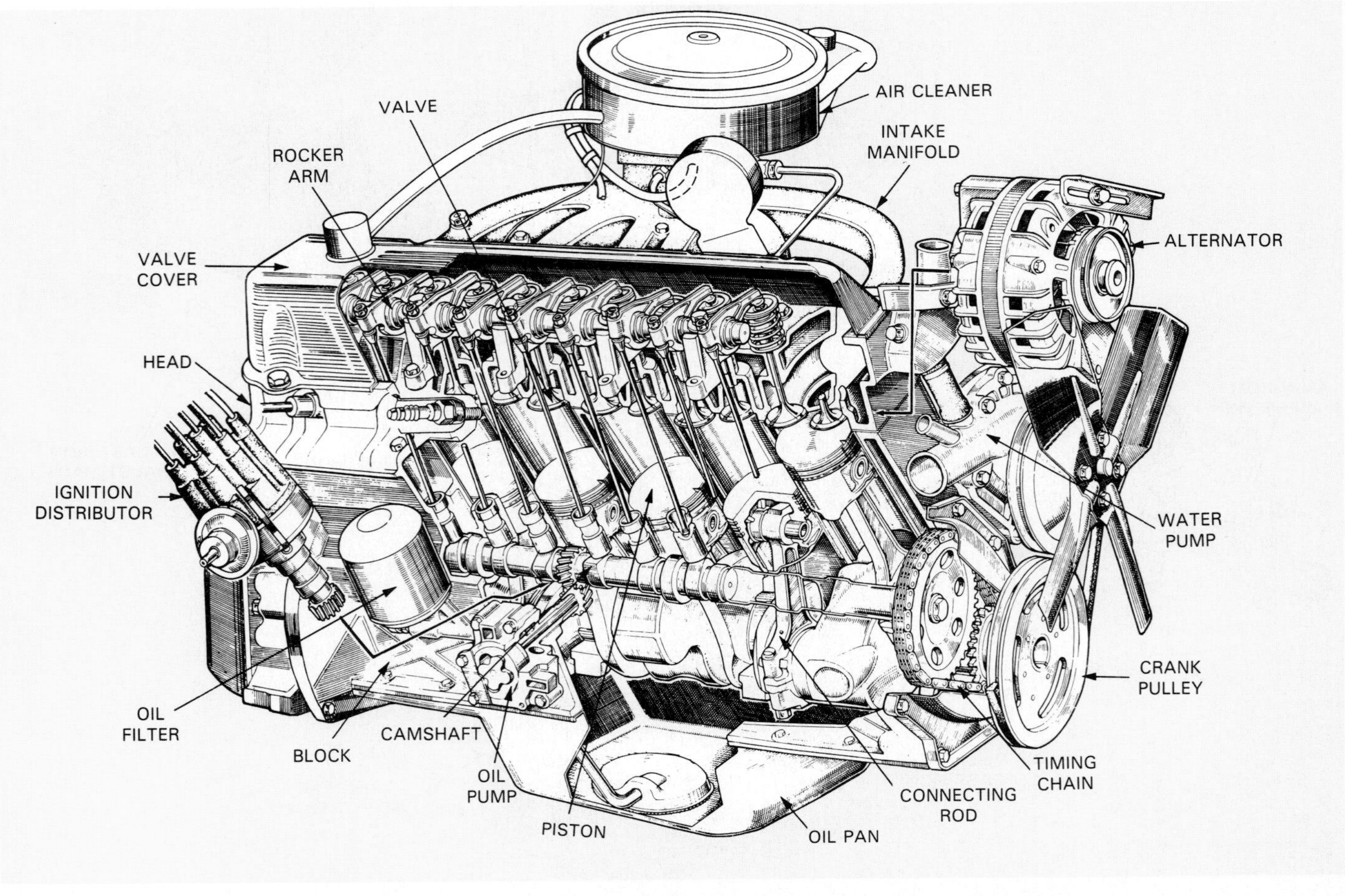

VALVE

ROCKER
ARM

VALVE
COVER

AIR CLEANER

INTAKE
MANIFOLD

ALTERNATOR

HEAD

IGNITION
DISTRIBUTOR

WATER
PUMP

CRANK
PULLEY

OIL
FILTER

BLOCK

CAMSHAFT

OIL
PUMP

PISTON

CONNECTING
ROD

OIL PAN

TIMING
CHAIN

Fig. 12-21. *Slant six, in-line engine. Study parts carefully.* (Chrysler)

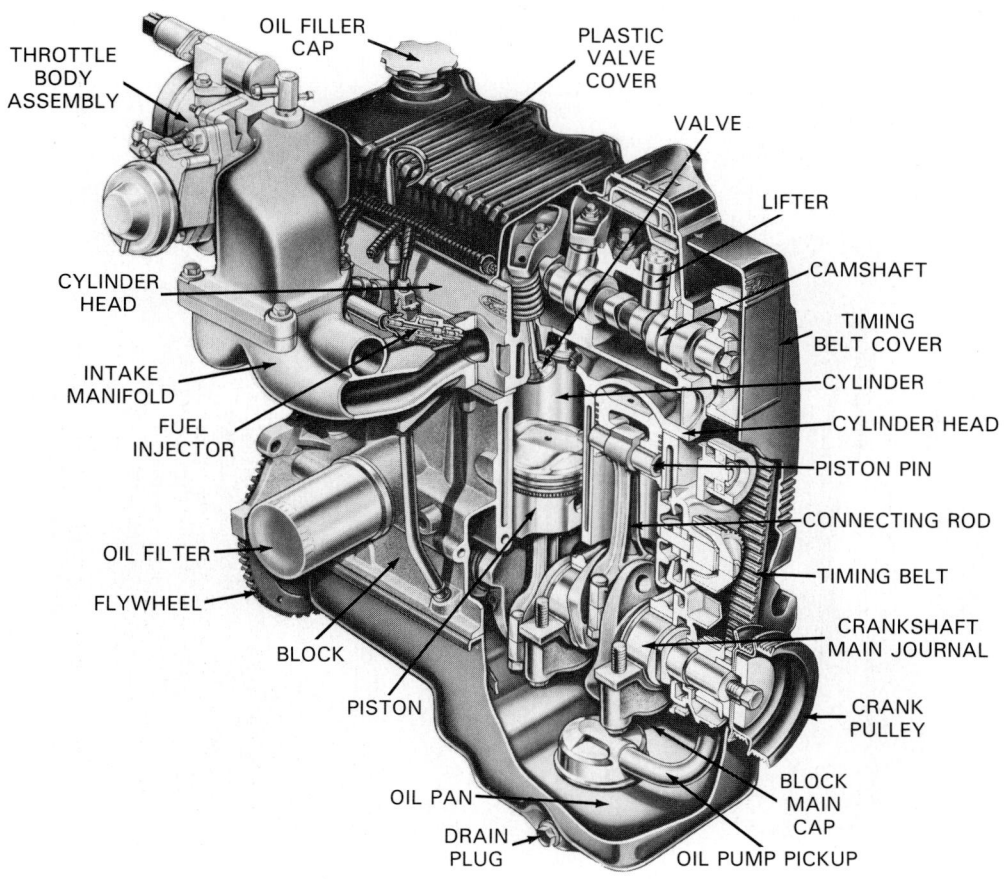

THROTTLE BODY ASSEMBLY

OIL FILLER CAP

PLASTIC VALVE COVER

VALVE

LIFTER

CAMSHAFT

TIMING BELT COVER

CYLINDER HEAD

CYLINDER

CYLINDER HEAD

PISTON PIN

CONNECTING ROD

TIMING BELT

CRANKSHAFT MAIN JOURNAL

CRANK PULLEY

BLOCK MAIN CAP

OIL PUMP PICKUP

INTAKE MANIFOLD

FUEL INJECTOR

OIL FILTER

FLYWHEEL

BLOCK

PISTON

OIL PAN

DRAIN PLUG

Fig. 12-22. Fuel injected, SOHC, hemi head, in-line, 4-cylinder engine. Note use of plastic valve cover. (Ford)

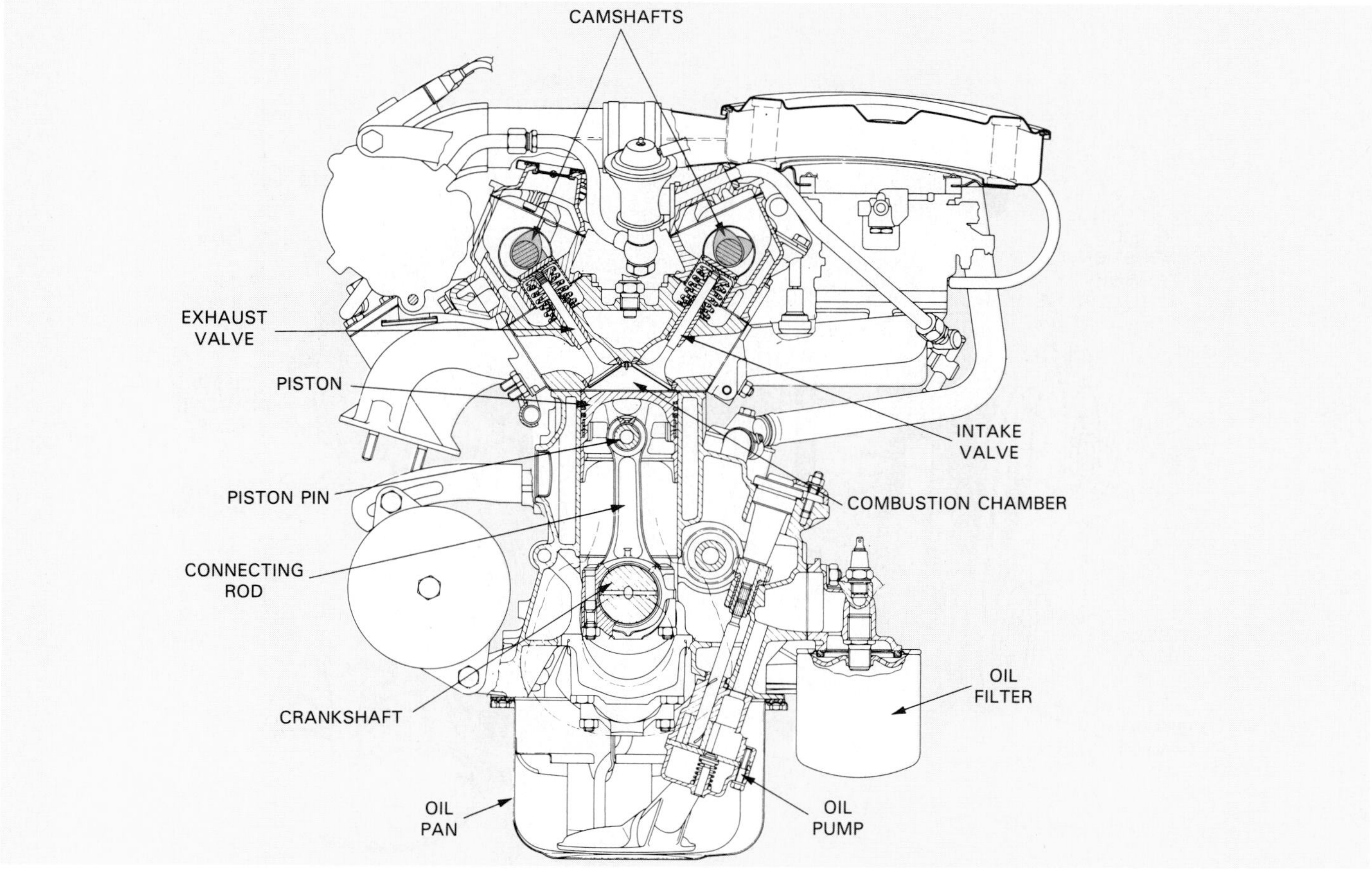

CAMSHAFTS

EXHAUST VALVE

PISTON

PISTON PIN

CONNECTING ROD

CRANKSHAFT

OIL PAN

OIL PUMP

INTAKE VALVE

COMBUSTION CHAMBER

OIL FILTER

Fig. 12-23. DOHC, in-line engine. Two camshafts are located in one cylinder head. One cam operates all of the intake valves. Other operates exhaust valves. (Fiat)

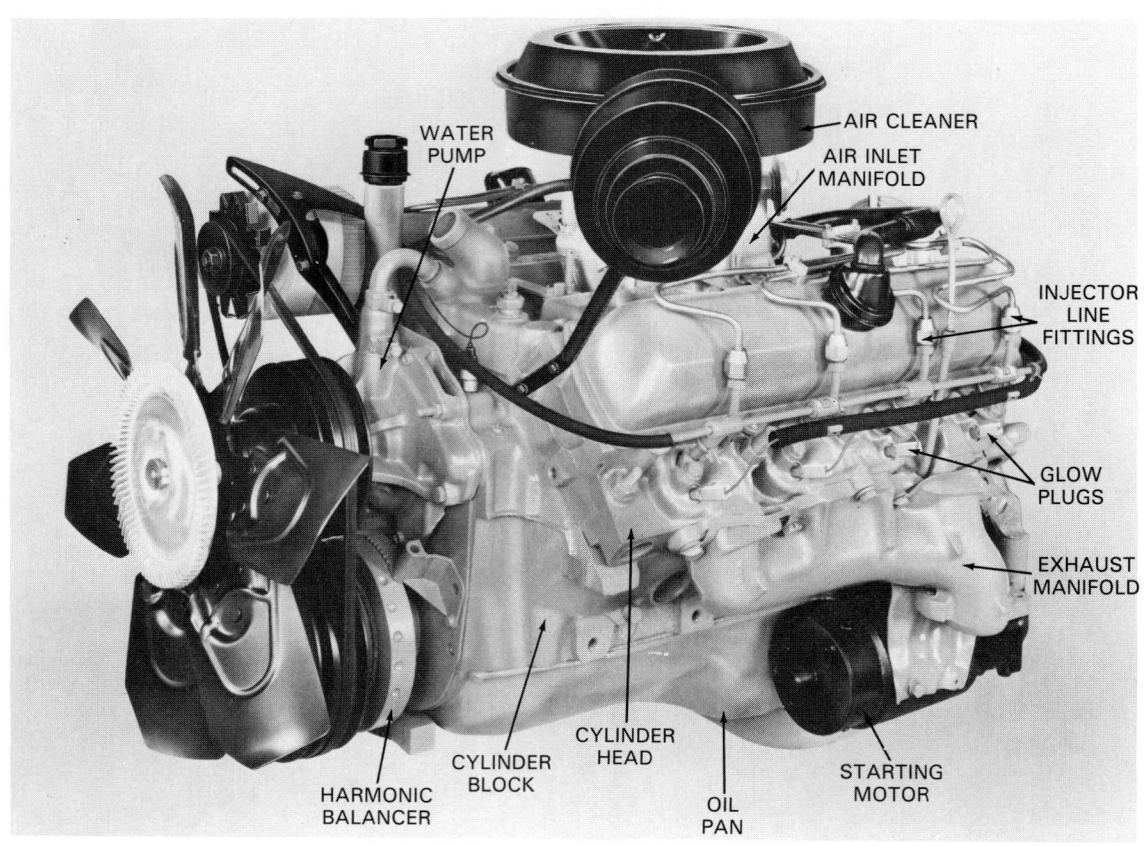

Fig. 12-24. External view of V-8, diesel engine. (Oldsmobile)

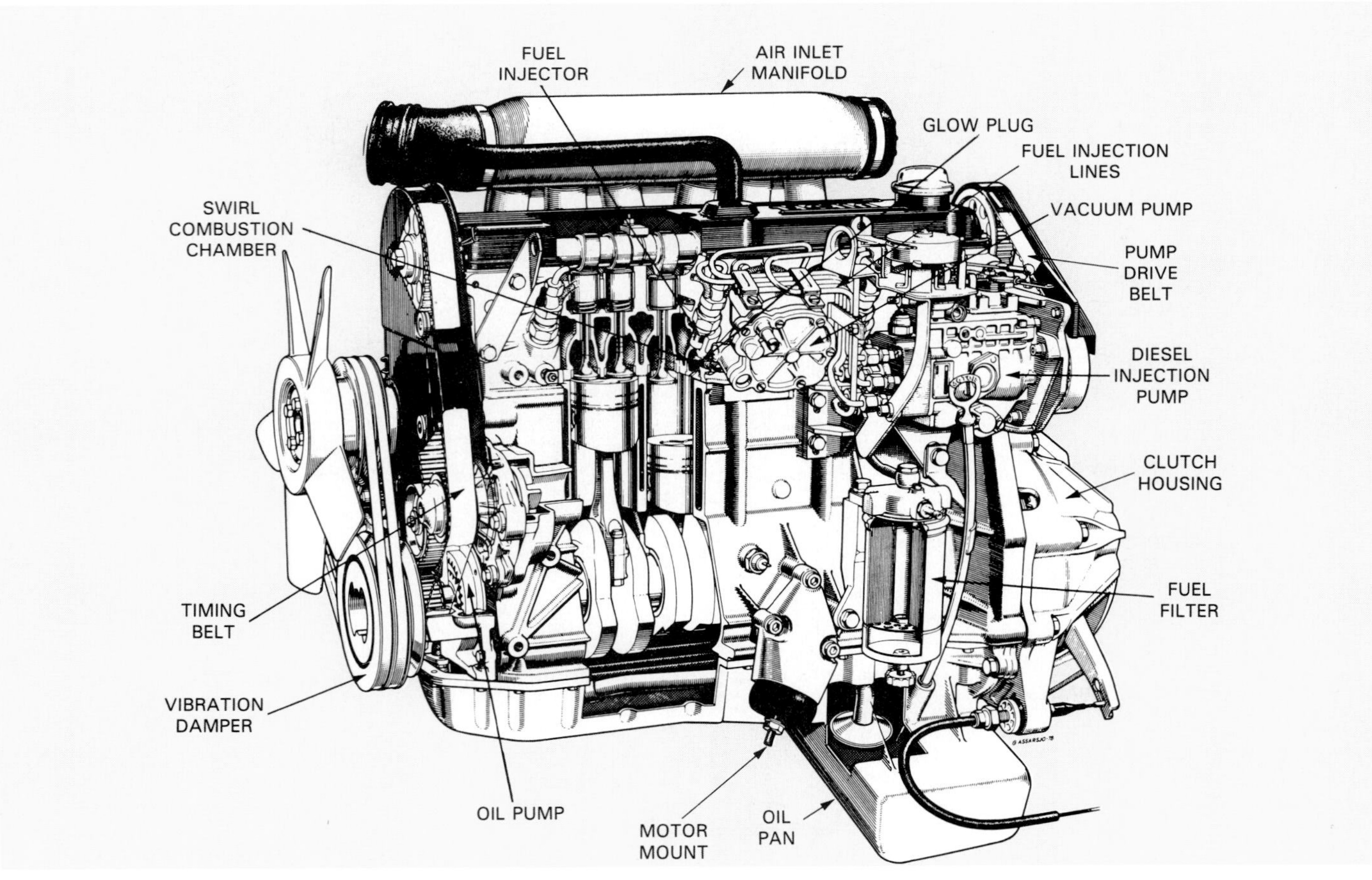

Fig. 12-25. In-line, six cylinder diesel engine. Note names of parts. Also, note rear drive belt for injection pump. (Volvo)

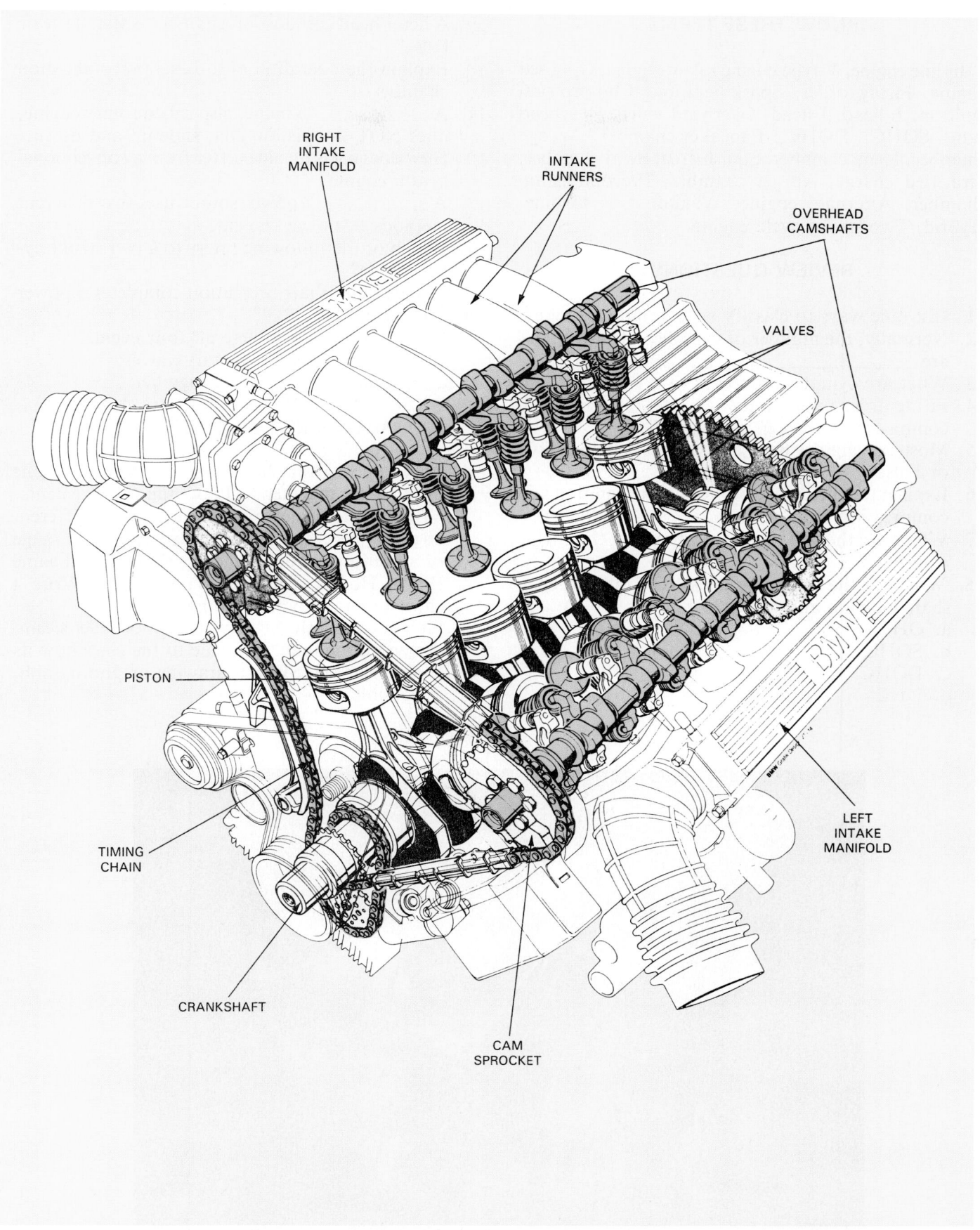

RIGHT
INTAKE
MANIFOLD

INTAKE
RUNNERS

OVERHEAD
CAMSHAFTS

VALVES

PISTON

TIMING
CHAIN

CRANKSHAFT

CAM
SPROCKET

LEFT
INTAKE
MANIFOLD

Fig. 12-26. Study the construction of this high performance V-12 cylinder engine. Two roller chains are used to drive overhead camshafts. Twelve cylinders make this a very smooth running engine because of the frequent power strokes per crankshaft revolution. (BMW)

KNOW THESE TERMS

In-line engine, V-type engine, Slant engine, Opposed engine, Firing order, Spark ignition, Compression ignition, L-head, I-head, Overhead valve, Overhead cam, SOHC, DOHC, Pancake chamber, Wedge chamber, Hemi chamber, Squish area, Swirl chamber, Stratified charge, Air jet chamber, Precombustion chamber, Alternate engine, Wankel, Gas turbine, Hybrid, Two-stroke cycle engine.

REVIEW QUESTIONS

1. List nine ways to classify an automotive engine.
2. Normally, the number of cylinders in car engines are _____, _____, or _____ .
3. What are cylinder numbers?
4. Firing order refers to the _____ in which combustion occurs in each cylinder.
5. Most car engines have air cooling systems. True or False?
6. Explain the difference between spark ignition and compression ignition.
7. Where are the two typical locations for the engine camshaft?
8. Which of the following does NOT refer to camshaft location and design?
   a. OHC
   b. SOHC
   c. DOHC
   d. UHC
9. A hemi-head combustion chamber is flat. True or False?
10. Explain the operation of a diesel precombustion chamber.
11. A _____ engine, also called rotary engine, does NOT use pistons that slide up and down.
12. How does a gas turbine differ from a conventional piston engine?
13. A _____ power source uses two different methods to power the car.
14. Which of the following refers to a two-stroke cycle engine?
    a. One crankshaft revolution completes a power stroke.
    b. Two strokes complete all four events.
    c. Uses reed valves or rotary valves.
    d. Fuel and oil are mixed together.

ACTIVITIES FOR CHAPTER 12

1. Make a poster that shows the four types of engine cylinder arrangements. Label the arrangements.
2. Visit an auto dealership and identify the different engine types offered as standard across the range of automobile models under a single brand name (Ford, Honda, Chrysler, Volvo, etc.). Write a short report on your findings.
3. Find out about the Stanley Steamer or other steam-driven automobile. Describe to the class how its engine worked. Show a drawing or photograph, if possible.

This fuel-injected V-6 engine has a distributorless ignition system. Each of the three coil packs (on top of engine, next to the alternator) serves two cylinders. (Buick)

Engine Top End Construction

After studying this chapter, you will be able to:
- Describe the construction of an engine cylinder head.
- Compare umbrella and O-ring type oil seals.
- Explain the purpose of valve spring shims, rotators, stem caps, and spring shields.
- Describe the construction and operation of a camshaft.
- Compare hydraulic and mechanical lifters.
- Describe different types of rocker arm assemblies.
- Summarize the construction and design of intake and exhaust manifolds.
- Describe safety practices used when working on engine top end components.

In previous chapters, you studied basic engine parts and engine types. This chapter builds upon what you have already learned by explaining engine top end parts in more detail.

An *engine top end* basically includes the cylinder head, valve train, valve cover, and the intake and exhaust manifolds. This is illustrated in Fig. 13-1. Understanding the construction of an engine top end will help you better understand later chapters that cover troubleshooting and repair operations on automotive engines.

CYLINDER HEAD CONSTRUCTION

A *bare cylinder head* is a head with all of its parts (valves, keepers, retainers, springs, seals, and rocker arms) removed. It is commonly made of cast iron or aluminum. The parts that fit into or on a bare cylinder head are pictured in Fig. 13-2.

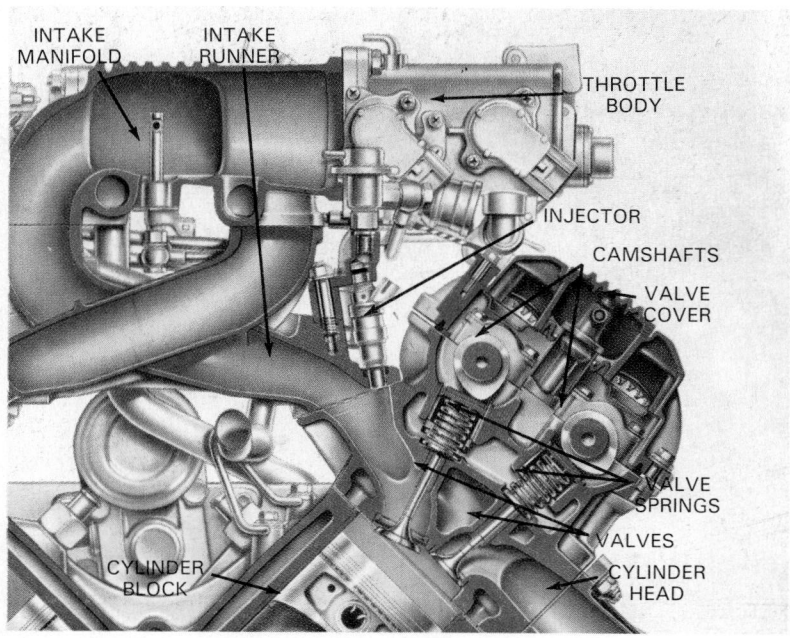

Fig. 13-1. Generally, an engine top end includes parts that fasten to top of cylinder block: head, valve train, intake manifold, exhaust manifold, valve cover. (Honda)

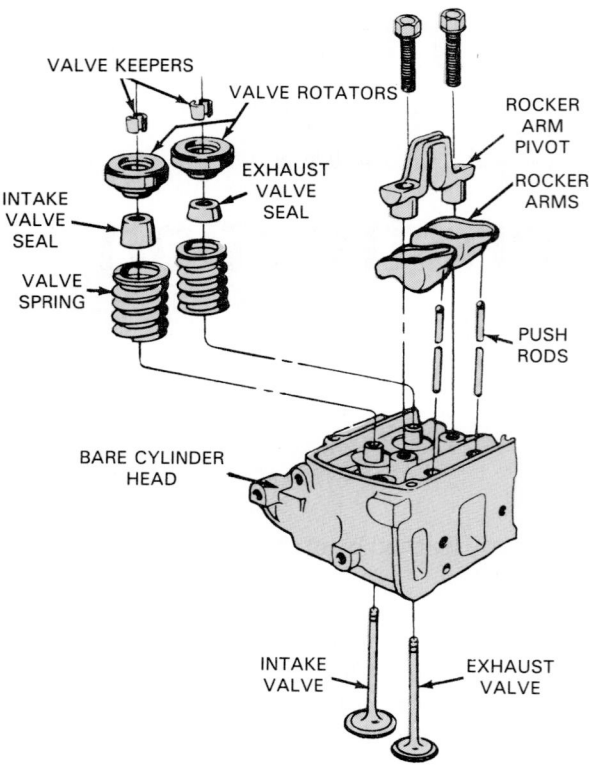

Fig. 13-2. Bare cylinder head is head casting with components removed. Note location and names of parts. (GM Trucks)

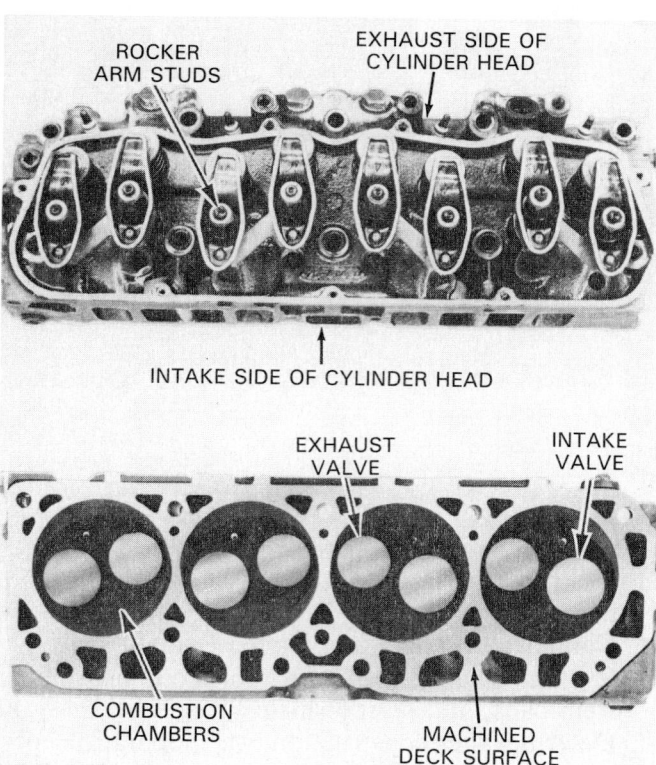

Fig. 13-4. Study top and bottom views of this V-8 engine cylinder head. (Chevrolet)

If a cylinder head becomes badly damaged in service, the technician may need to install a new, bare head. All of the old, reusable parts would be removed and installed in the new head.

The construction of a cylinder head will vary with engine design and type. It is critical that you understand the most important cylinder head variations. See Figs. 13-3 and 13-4.

Valve guide construction

There are two basic types of valve guides: integral and pressed-in. Both are used in modern engines.

An *integral valve guide* is part of the cylinder head casting. One is shown in Fig. 13-5. An integral guide is simply a hole machined through the cylinder head. This is a very common type because of its low production cost.

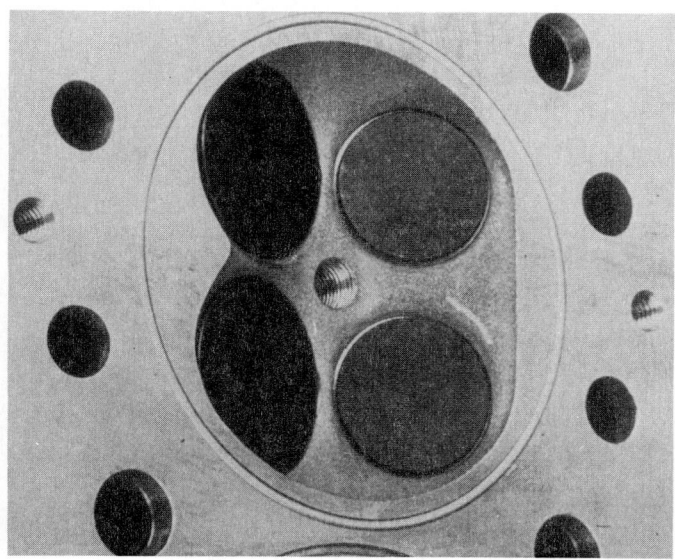

Fig. 13-3. Cylinder head can be cast from iron or more lightweight aluminum. A—Bare head with parts removed. B—Close-up of four-valve combustion chamber. (Oldsmobile)

A *pressed-in valve guide* is a separate sleeve forced into an oversize hole machined in the head. It can be made of cast iron or bronze. Look at Fig. 13-5. Friction from the press fit holds the valve guide in the cylinder head.

A pressed-in valve guide simplifies guide repair. A worn guide can be pressed out and a new guide quickly pressed in. This eliminates some of the machining needed to replace a badly worn integral guide.

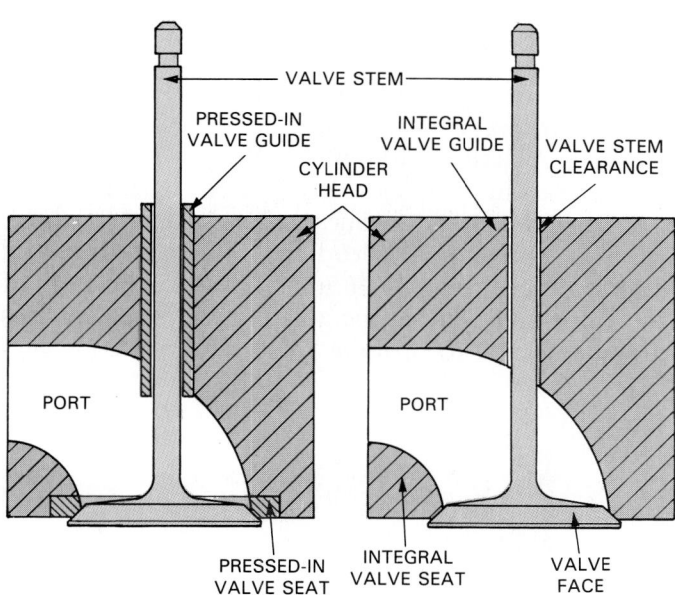

Fig. 13-5. Valve guides and seats can be made as separate inserts or as part of head.

Valve seat construction

Like valve guides, valve seats may be an integral part of the head or inserts pressed into the head. Both are commonly used.

An *integral valve seat* is simply a machined portion of the cylinder head casting. Different cutters are used to machine a precise face on the port opening into the combustion chamber.

A *pressed-in valve seat,* also called a seat insert, is a separate part forced into a recess cut in the head. Valve seat inserts are commonly used in aluminum cylinder heads. Steel inserts are needed to withstand the extreme heat. One is shown in Fig. 13-5.

The *valve seat angle* is the angle formed by the face of the seat. A 45° angle is commonly used on passenger car engines. However, some seat angles are 30°. These are found on high performance engines, especially on the intake seat. Look at Fig. 13-6.

An *interference angle* is a 1/2° to 1° difference between the valve seat face angle and the angle of the valve face, see Fig. 13-6. The interference angle reduces the contact area between the seat and valve. This increases pressure between the two and speeds valve *seating* (sealing) during engine operation.

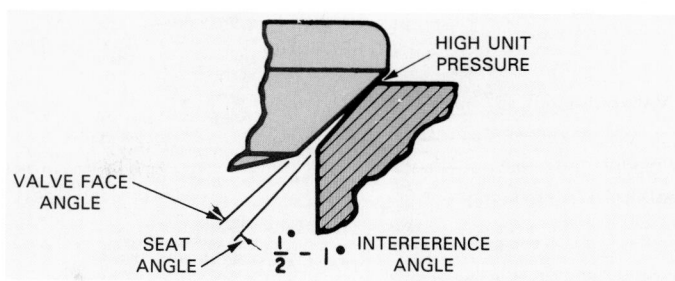

Fig. 13-6. Common valve and seat angles are 30° and 45°. Interference angle is 1° difference between valve and seat angles to increase sealing pressure and to speed seating or break-in. (TRW)

Diesel prechamber cup

A *prechamber cup* is pressed into the cylinder head of some diesel engines. Refer to Fig. 13-7. Holes are precisely machined into the cylinder head deck surface. The prechambers force-fit into these holes. Each prechamber forms an enclosure around the tip of an injector and glow plug. This area is heated by the glow plug for better cold starting.

Stratified charge chamber

A *stratified charge chamber* also fits into the cylinder head casting. It is found in gasoline engines designed to use a rich fuel mixture in the auxiliary chamber to ignite a lean mixture in the main combustion chamber. Fig. 13-8 shows how the stratified charge chamber and related components are assembled into the cylinder head. Study it closely.

VALVE TRAIN CONSTRUCTION

As you learned earlier, the *valve train* controls the opening and closing of the cylinder head ports. Although the basic function of these parts is the same, their construction can vary. To be able to work on any type of valve train, you must understand these differences.

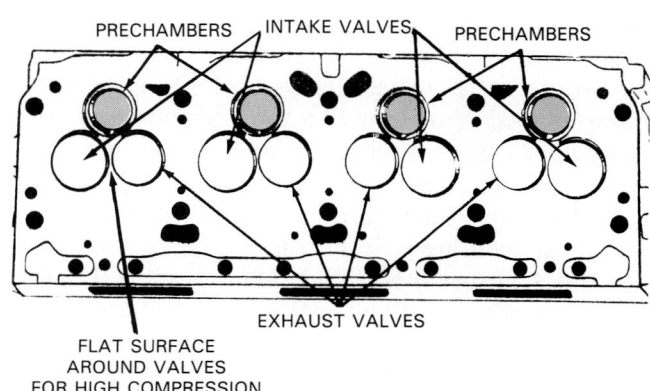

Fig. 13-7. Diesel cylinder head normally has pressed-in prechamber cups. They form the precombustion chambers for tips of glow plugs and injectors. (Oldsmobile)

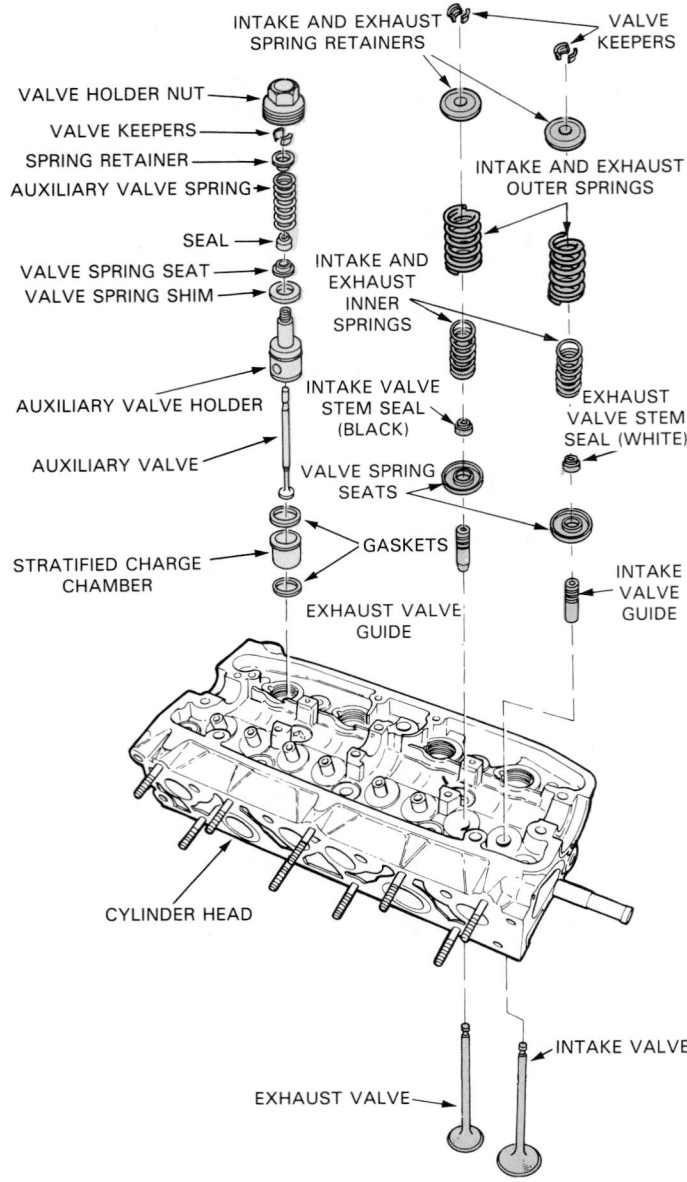

Fig. 13-8. Gasoline engine cylinder head with stratified charge auxiliary chambers. Note how chamber and extra intake valve are assembled. (Honda)

Labels in figure:
INTAKE AND EXHAUST SPRING RETAINERS
VALVE KEEPERS
VALVE HOLDER NUT
VALVE KEEPERS
SPRING RETAINER
AUXILIARY VALVE SPRING
SEAL
VALVE SPRING SEAT
VALVE SPRING SHIM
INTAKE AND EXHAUST OUTER SPRINGS
INTAKE AND EXHAUST INNER SPRINGS
AUXILIARY VALVE HOLDER
AUXILIARY VALVE
INTAKE VALVE STEM SEAL (BLACK)
EXHAUST VALVE STEM SEAL (WHITE)
VALVE SPRING SEATS
STRATIFIED CHARGE CHAMBER
GASKETS
EXHAUST VALVE GUIDE
INTAKE VALVE GUIDE
CYLINDER HEAD
INTAKE VALVE
EXHAUST VALVE

Valve construction

Automotive engines commonly use *poppet* or *mushroom valves*. These terms come from the valve's shape (shaped something like a mushroom) and action (pops open). Several engine valves are shown in Fig. 13-9. Study their differences.

Almost every surface of a valve is machined. The stem must accurately fit the guide. The face must contact the seat perfectly. The margin must be thick enough to prevent valve burning. Grooves are cut into the valve stem for the keepers.

The *valve face angle* is the angle formed between the valve face and valve head. Normal valve face angles are 45° and 30°. This is illustrated in Fig. 13-6.

The exhaust valve is exposed to higher temperatures than the intake valve. The intake valve has cooler out-

side air flowing over it. Hot combustion gases blow over the exhaust valve. If the exhaust valve does not transfer heat into the cylinder head, it will burn.

A *sodium filled valve* is used when extra valve cooling action is needed. Refer to Fig. 13-9. During engine operation, the sodium inside the hollow valve melts. When the valve opens, the sodium splashes down into the valve head and collects heat. Then, when the valve closes, the sodium splashes up into the valve stem. Heat transfers out of the sodium, into the stem, valve guide, and engine coolant. In this way, the valve is cooled.

Sodium filled valves are used in a few high performance engines. They are very light and allow high engine rpm for prolonged periods.

A *stellite valve* has a special hard metal coating on its face. A stellite coating is often used in engines designed to burn unleaded fuel. Look at Fig. 13-10.

Lead additives in gasoline, besides increasing octane, act as a lubricant. The lead coats the valve face and seat to reduce wear. With unleaded fuel, the wear of the valve and seat can be accelerated. Stellite valves may be needed to prolong valve service life.

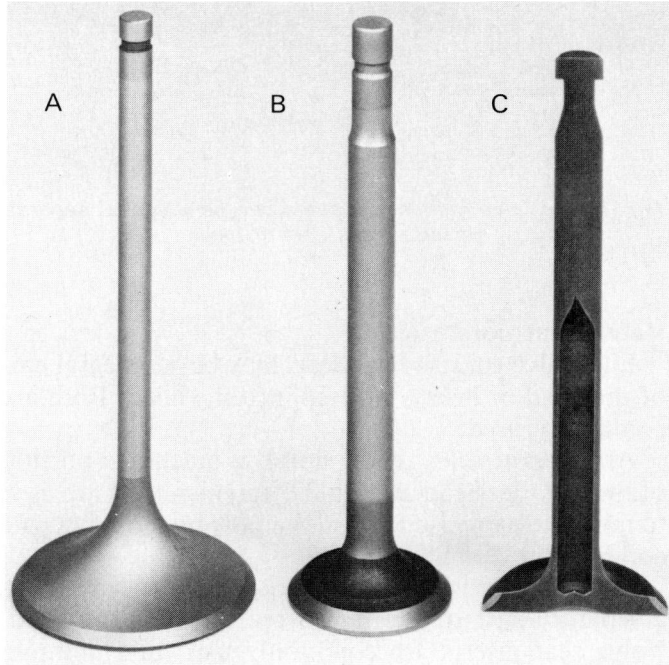

Fig. 13-9. Three typical engine valves. A — Polished intake valve. B — Stock exhaust valve. C — Hollow exhaust valve designed to hold sodium for cooling. (Dana Corp.)

Valve seal construction

Valve seals come in two basic types: umbrella and O-ring. Both are common on modern engines.

An *umbrella valve seal* is shaped like a cup and can be made of neoprene rubber or plastic. Three are shown in Fig. 13-11. An umbrella valve seal slides down over the valve stem before the spring and retainer, Fig. 13-8. It covers the small clearance between the valve stem

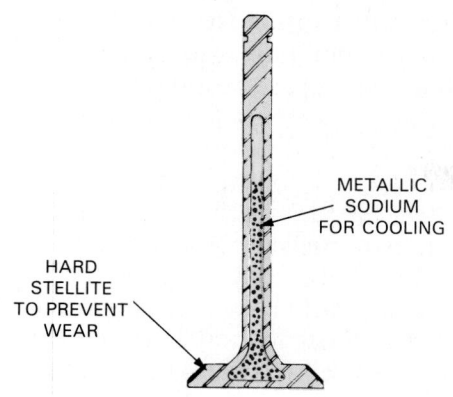

Fig. 13-10. Stellite coating on valve face retards wear and allows use of unleaded fuel.

Fig. 13-11. Umbrella valve seals form covering over opening at top of valve guides. A — Synthetic rubber seal with plastic shedder insert. B — All synthetic rubber seal. C — Plastic valve seal.

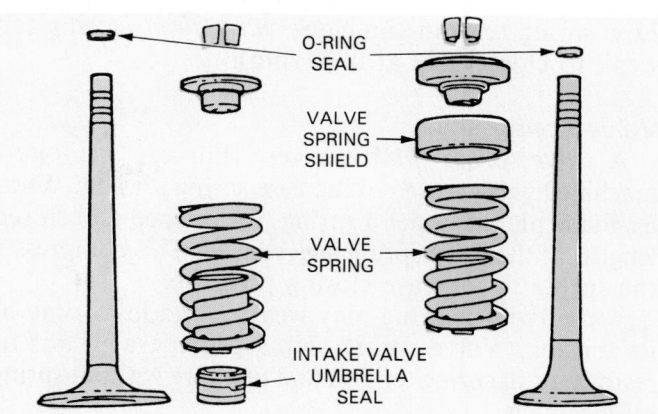

Fig. 13-12. O-ring valve seal fits into extra groove cut in valve stem. To prevent seal damage, spring and retainer must be installed before seal. This valve spring assembly uses both an O-ring seal and an umbrella seal on intake valve. (Buick)

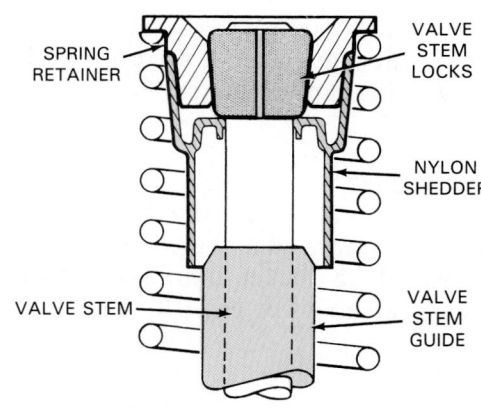

Fig. 13-13. Nylon shedder can be used as an O-ring seal and a shield to keep oil out of valve guide. (Cadillac)

and guide. This keeps oil from being drawn into the cylinder head port and combustion chamber.

An *O-ring valve seal* is a small round seal that fits into an extra groove cut in the valve stem. Look at Fig. 13-12. Unlike the umbrella type, it seals the gap between the retainer and valve stem, not the guide and stem. It stops oil from flowing through the retainer, down the stem, and into the guide.

An O-ring valve seal fits onto the valve stem AFTER the spring and retainer. It is made of soft synthetic rubber that allows it to be stretched over the valve stem and into its groove.

A *valve spring shield* is normally used with an O-ring type oil seal. The shield surrounds the top and upper sides of the spring and helps keep oil off the valve stem. See Fig. 13-12.

A *nylon shedder* also can be used to limit the amount of oil that splashes on the valve stem and guide opening. One is illustrated in Fig. 13-13. The shedder is a cross between a conventional oil seal and a valve spring shield. It seals against the valve stem like a seal and encircles the upper spring like a shield.

Valve spring construction

Valve spring construction is basically the same for all engines. However, the number and types of coils can vary. Fig. 13-13 shows single coil valve springs. Fig. 13-14 shows a valve spring with an inner and outer coil. The second coil increases the amount of pressure holding the valve closed.

Spring tension refers to the stiffness of a valve spring. Spring tension is usually stated for both opened and closed valve positions. The service manual will give the tension in pounds or kilograms for specific compressed lengths.

Free length is the length of the valve spring when removed from the engine.

Open length is its length when installed on the engine with the valve fully open. It is measured from the bottom of the spring to the bottom of the spring retainer.

Closed length is the length of the valve spring when installed on the engine with the valve closed. Measurement is the same as for open length.

As you will learn in later chapters, these spring specifications are important. They affect valve action.

Low spring tension can cause *valve float* (spring too weak to close valve at high rpm).

Valve spring shim

A *valve spring shim* is a very thin and accurately machined washer used to increase spring tension. When a shim is placed under a spring, the opened and closed lengths of the valve spring are reduced. This compresses the spring to increase closing pressure.

A used valve spring may weaken and lose some of its tension. Valve spring shims provide a means of restoring full spring tension and pressure without spring replacement.

Selection and installation of valve spring shims are covered in Chapter 48, Engine Top End Service.

Valve retainers and keepers

Valve retainers and *keepers* lock the valve spring on the valve. The retainer is a specially shaped washer that fits over the top of the valve spring. The keepers or locks fit into the valve stem grooves. This holds the retainer and spring in place. Refer to and compare Figs. 13-14 and 13-15.

Valve spring seat

A *valve spring seat* is a cup-shaped washer installed between the cylinder head and the bottom of the valve spring. It provides a pocket to hold the bottom of the valve spring, as shown in Fig. 13-15.

Valve rotators

A *valve rotator* turns the valve to prevent carbon buildup and hot spots on the valve face. One is pictured in Fig. 13-16. A valve rotator may be located under the valve spring (seat type rotator) or it may be on top of the valve spring (retainer type rotator).

Rotators are commonly used on engine exhaust valves. Exhaust valves are exposed to more heat than intake valves.

Valve stem cap

A *valve stem cap* may be placed over the end of the valve stem. It helps prevent stem and rocker arm wear.

A valve stem cap is free to turn on the valve stem. This serves as a bearing that reduces friction. Some valve stem caps are used to adjust the clearance in the valve train. Cap thickness varies and can be changed to alter rocker-to-valve stem clearance.

CAMSHAFT CONSTRUCTION

Discussed earlier, a *camshaft* controls when the valves open and close. It can be driven by gears, by a chain, or by a belt and sprockets. The camshaft will have a varying number of lobes, depending upon how many valves are used in the combustion chambers. Many engines only use one camshaft. However, others use two or more, Fig. 13-17.

There are two types of camshafts — intake camshaft and exhaust camshaft. The *intake camshaft* operates all of the intake valves in the cylinder head. The *exhaust camshaft* operates all of the exhaust valves.

Cam lobes

The *cam lobes* are precision-machined and polished surfaces on the camshaft. Each cam lobe consists of a nose, flank, heel, and base diameter, as shown in Fig. 13-18. Variations in lobe shape control:
1. When each valve opens in relation to piston position.

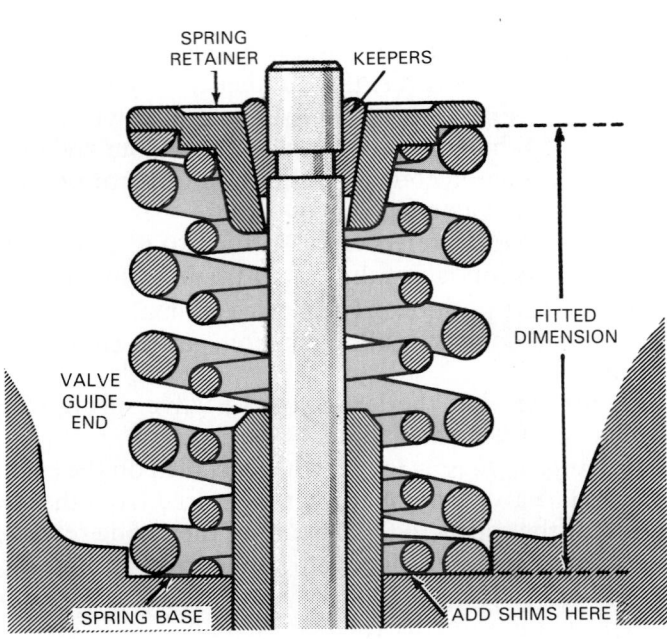

Fig. 13-14. Dual coil valve spring increases valve closing pressure. Note other parts. (Ford)

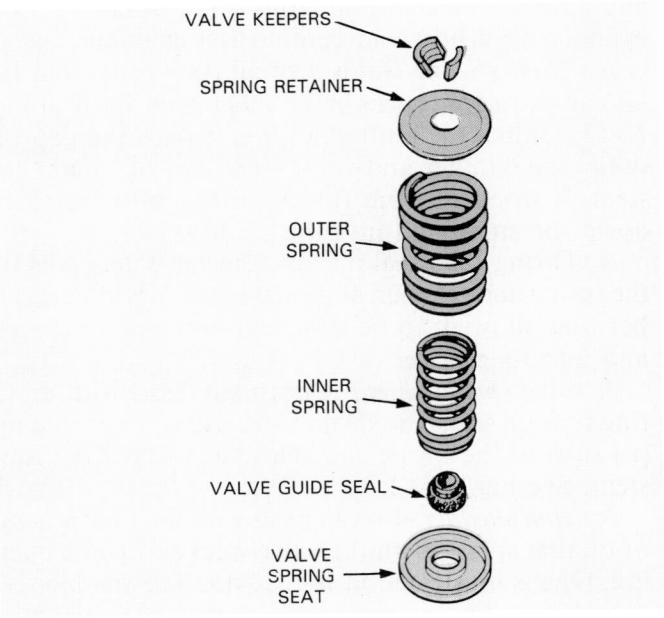

Fig. 13-15. Valve spring assembly using a spring seat. Seat keeps bottom of spring in alignment with stem. (Honda)

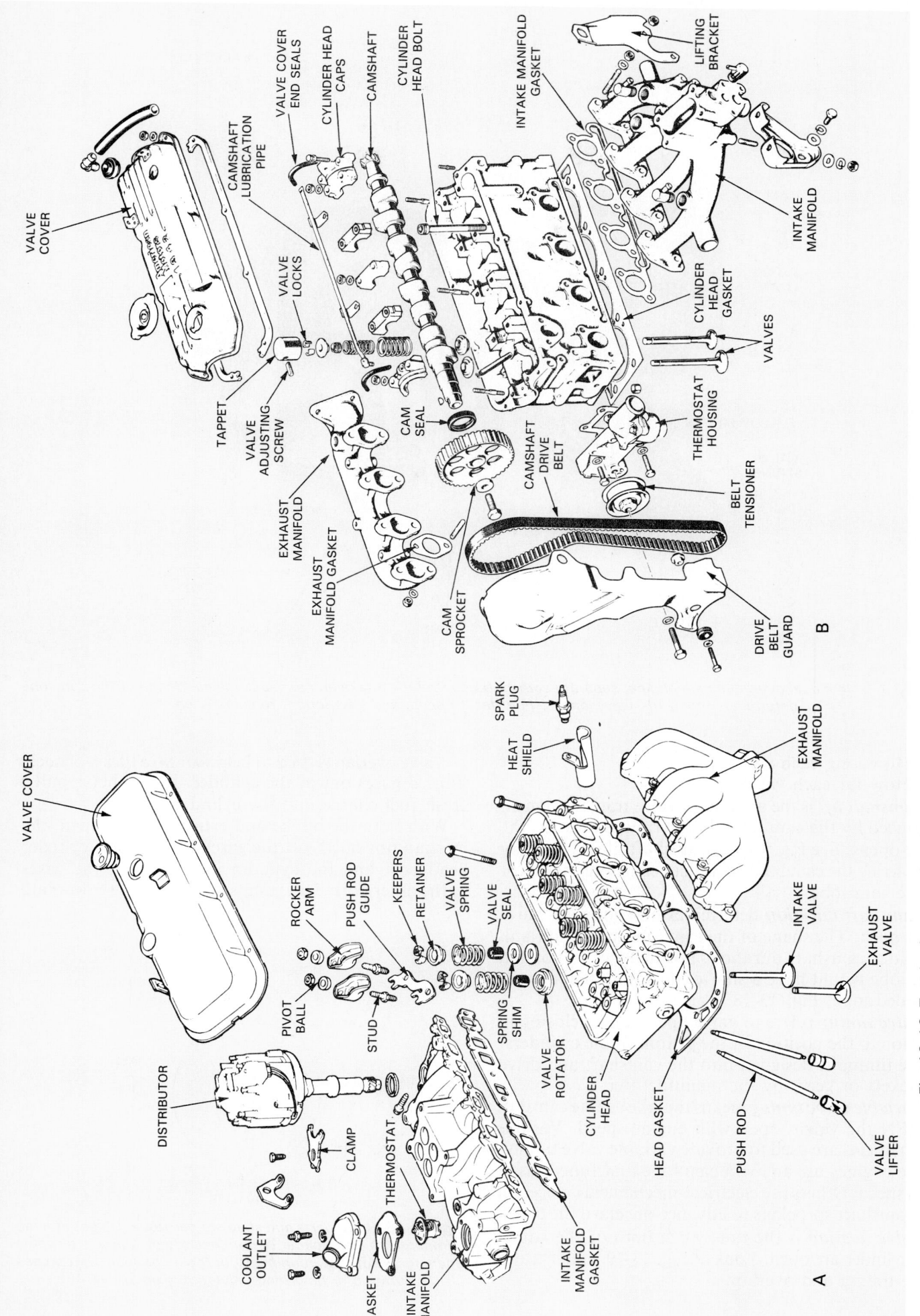

VALVE COVER

CAMSHAFT LUBRICATION PIPE

VALVE COVER END SEALS

CYLINDER HEAD CAPS

CAMSHAFT

CYLINDER HEAD BOLT

INTAKE MANIFOLD GASKET

LIFTING BRACKET

INTAKE MANIFOLD

VALVE LOCKS

TAPPET

VALVE ADJUSTING SCREW

CAM SEAL

EXHAUST MANIFOLD

EXHAUST MANIFOLD GASKET

CAM SPROCKET

CAMSHAFT DRIVE BELT

CYLINDER HEAD GASKET

VALVES

THERMOSTAT HOUSING

BELT TENSIONER

DRIVE BELT GUARD

B

VALVE COVER

SPARK PLUG

HEAT SHIELD

ROCKER ARM

PUSH ROD GUIDE

KEEPERS

RETAINER

VALVE SPRING

VALVE SEAL

EXHAUST MANIFOLD

DISTRIBUTOR

PIVOT BALL

STUD

SPRING SHIM

VALVE ROTATOR

CYLINDER HEAD

HEAD GASKET

PUSH ROD

INTAKE VALVE

EXHAUST VALVE

COOLANT OUTLET

CLAMP

GASKET

THERMOSTAT

INTAKE MANIFOLD

INTAKE MANIFOLD GASKET

VALVE LIFTER

A

Fig. 13-16. Two basic types of engine top end assemblies. A — Cam in-block V-type engine using push rods. B — OHC engine. Compare these top ends and learn part names. (GMC, AMC)

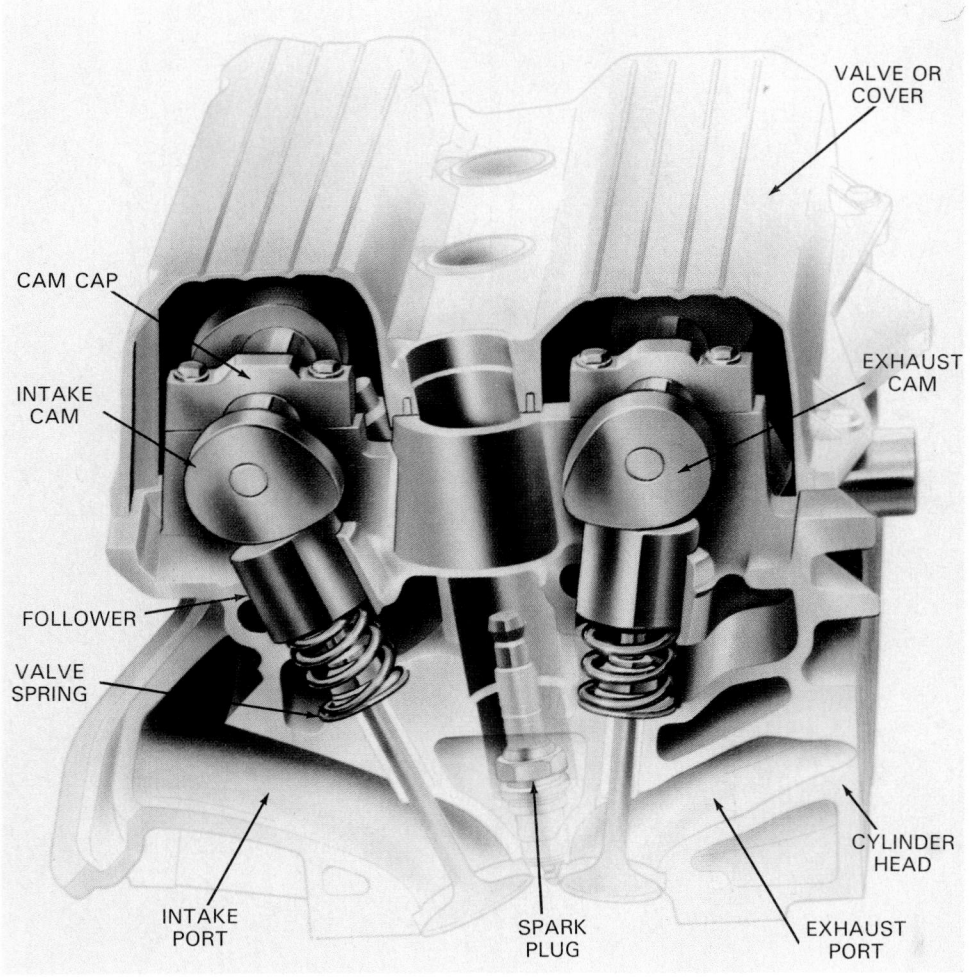

Fig. 13-17. *In a dual overhead cam engine, separate camshafts control the intake and exhaust valves. Shape of the cam lobe determines when the valve opens, how far it opens, and how long it remains open.*

2. How long each valve stays open.
3. How far each valve opens.

Camshaft lift is the amount of valve train movement produced by the cam lobe. It determines how far the valve opens. See Fig. 13-18. Camshaft lift is found by subtracting the cam base circle diameter from the height of the cam lobe.

Camshaft duration determines how long the valve stays open. The shape of the cam lobe nose and flank regulates camshaft duration. For instance, a pointed cam lobe would have a shorter duration than a more rounded lobe, Fig. 13-18.

Valve timing refers to valve opening and closing in relation to the position of the pistons in the cylinders. Valve timing is designed into the camshaft and drive sprockets or gears by the manufacturer.

Variable valve timing means that the engine can alter WHEN the valves open with engine speed. Various mechanisms are used to provide variable valve timing. Some engines use an extra cam lobe that functions at high speed. Others use electrical-mechanical devices on the camshaft sprockets to advance or retard the cams.

Valve overlap is the time when both of the valves in a cylinder are open. Look at Fig. 13-19. It illustrates valve timing and overlap.

Valve overlap is used to help *scavenge* (draw or suck) burned gases out of the cylinder. It also helps pull a fresh fuel charge into the cylinder.

With both the intake and exhaust valves open, the inertia (movement) of the gases through one cylinder head port and the cylinder itself acts on the gases in the other port. This results in slightly more flow into

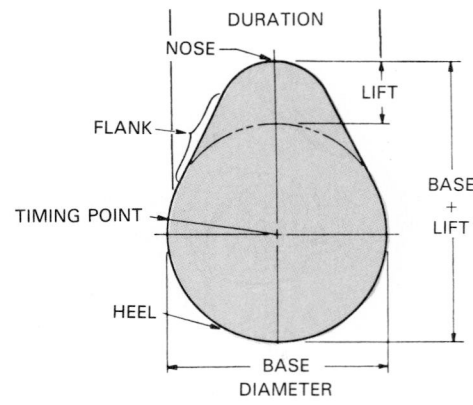

Fig. 13-18. *Basic parts and shape of cam lobe. Height of nose compared to base circle determines lift or amount of valve opening. Width or roundness of nose or lobe determines duration or how long valve stays open. (TRW)*

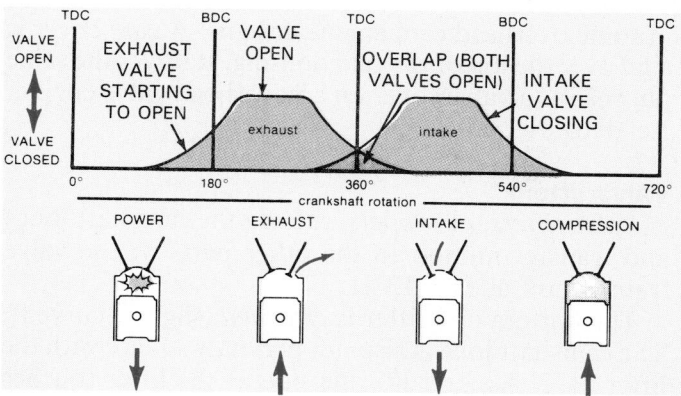

Fig. 13-19. Valve timing is measurement of when valves open in relation to piston position in cylinder. Valve overlap is period where both intake and exhaust valves in same cylinder are open. (VW)

and out of the cylinder. Valve overlap helps engine breathing, especially at higher engine speeds.

Camshaft thrust plate

A *camshaft thrust plate* is used to limit camshaft end play (front to rear movement). The thrust plate bolts to the front of the block or cylinder head. When the drive gear or sprocket is bolted in place, the thrust plate sets up a predetermined camshaft end play.

Cam bearings

Cam bearings are usually one-piece inserts pressed into the block or cylinder head. See Fig. 13-20. They can also be two-piece inserts, if mounted in the head.

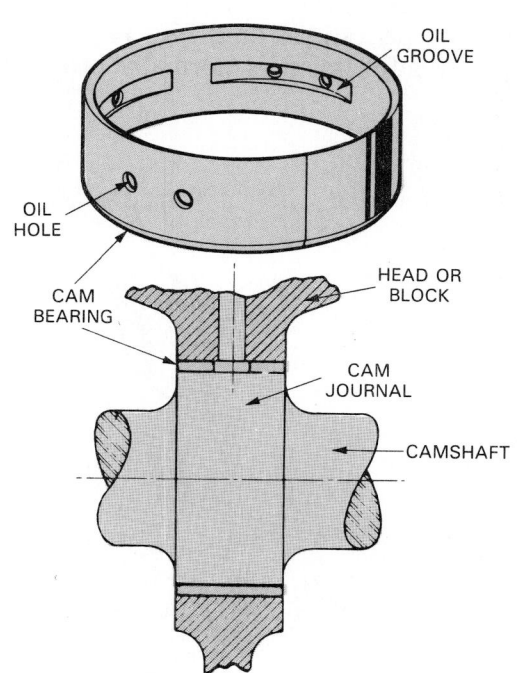

Fig. 13-20. Camshaft journals ride in cam bearings. Cam bearings may be pressed into block or cylinder head bore. When in head, bearings may also be two-piece. (Federal Mogul)

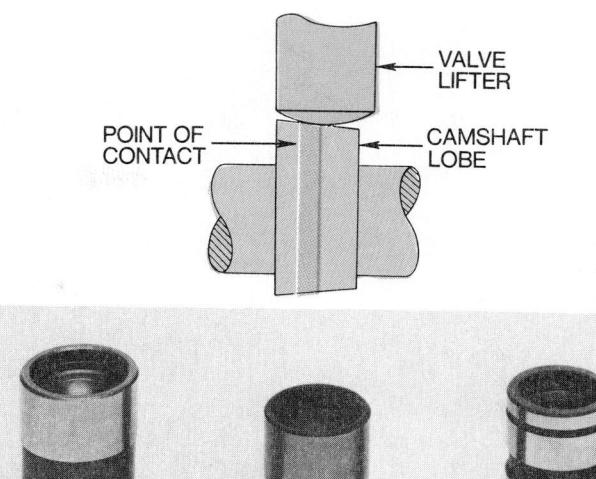

Fig. 13-21. Top. Bottom of lifter is crowned. Cam lobe is tapered. This causes rotating cam lobe to turn lifter in its bore to reduce wear. Bottom. Three styles of lifters. (Ford and Dana)

The camshaft journals ride in the cam bearings.

Cam bearings are usually constructed like engine main and connecting rod bearings. For more information on this subject, refer to Chapter 14, Engine Bottom End Construction.

Cam housing and cam cover

A *cam housing* is a casting that bolts to the top of the cylinder head to hold the engine camshaft. It is used

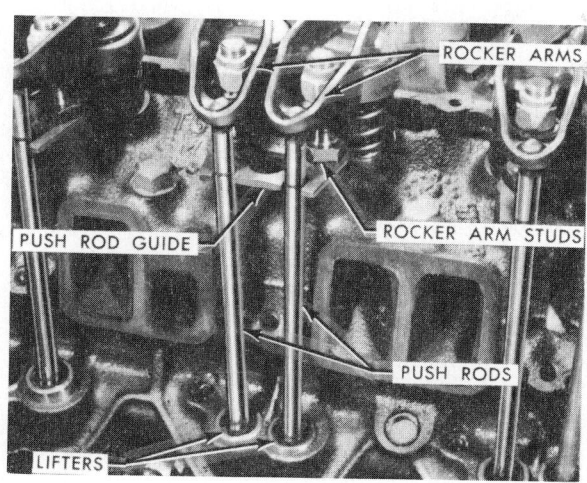

Fig. 13-22. In push rod engine, lifter bores are in block. Push rods run up to rocker arms. Rocker arms change upward movement into downward movement to open valves. (Chevrolet)

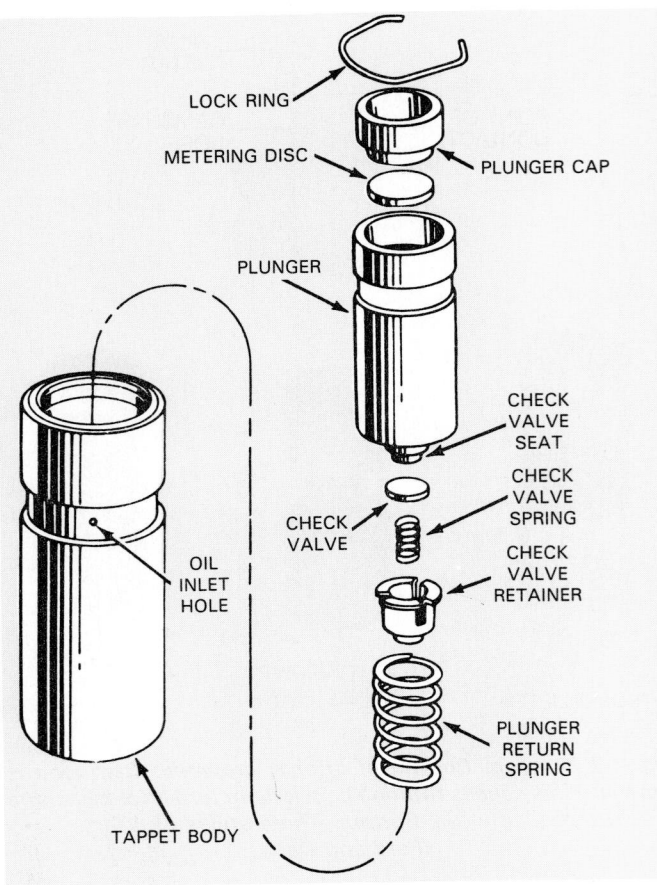

Fig. 13-23. Study parts of a hydraulic lifter. (Chrysler)

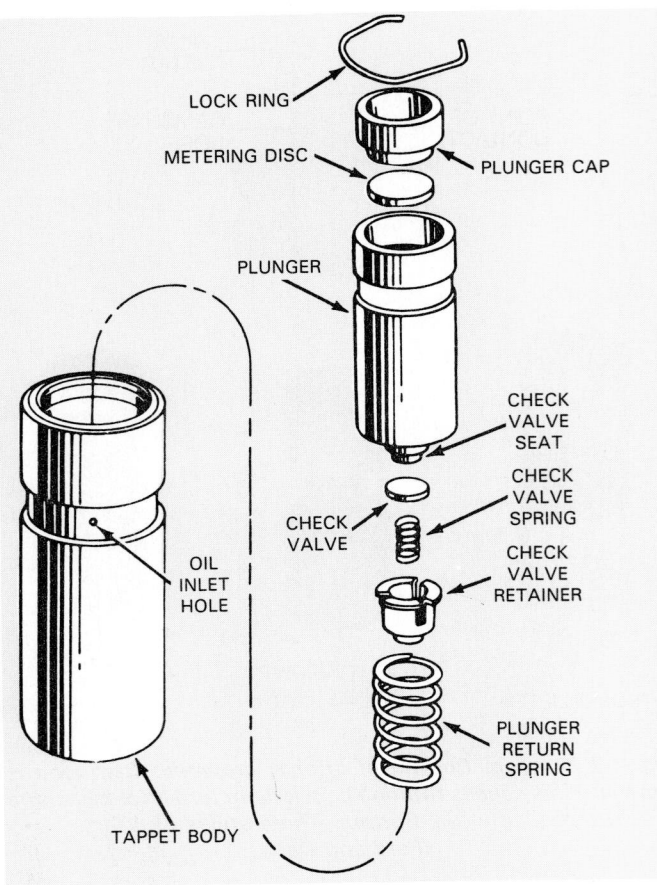

Fig. 13-24. A — When valve closes, oil rushes into lifter to push up on disc or plunger to maintain zero clearance. B — When cam acts on lifter, oil is trapped in lifter by check valve. Lifter acts as solid unit to push valve open. (Chrysler)

in some overhead cam engine designs. A *cam cover* is a lid over the top of the cam housing. It serves the same purpose as a valve cover on an overhead valve engine. Refer to Fig. 13-17B.

Valve lifters

Valve lifters, or *tappets,* ride on the camshaft lobes and transfer motion to the other parts of the valve train. Look at Fig. 13-21.

The bottom of a lifter is *crowned* (slightly curved). The camshaft lobe is also not perfectly square with the lifter base. As a result, one side of the lifter touches the cam lobe. This tends to rotate the lifter in its bore to reduce wear.

There are four basic types of lifters: hydraulic, mechanical, roller, and OHC follower.

Hydraulic valve lifters are common because they operate QUIETLY by maintaining *zero valve clearance* (no space between valve train parts). With zero clearance, the valve train does not clatter with the engine running. The oil-filled hydraulic lifter adjusts automatically with any change in temperature and wear of parts. Look at Figs. 13-22 and 13-23.

During engine operation, oil pressure fills the inside of the hydraulic lifter with motor oil, Fig. 13-24. The pressure pushes the lifter plunger up in its bore until all of the play is out of the valve train.

As the camshaft pushes on the lifter, the lifter check valve closes to seal oil inside the lifter. Since oil is NOT compressible, the lifter acts as a solid unit to open the valve.

Mechanical lifters, also called *solid lifters,* do not contain oil. They simply transfer cam lobe action to the push rod. Mechanical lifters are NOT self-adjusting and require periodic setting, Fig. 13-21.

A screw adjustment is normally provided at the

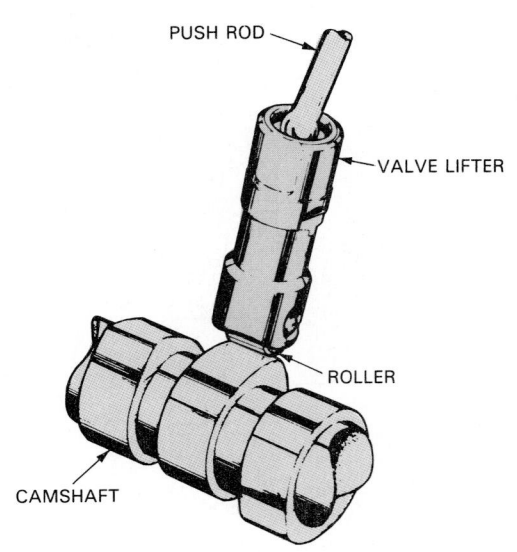

Fig. 13-25. Roller lifter is commonly used in diesel engines to reduce friction. Roller spins as camshaft rotates. (Oldsmobile)

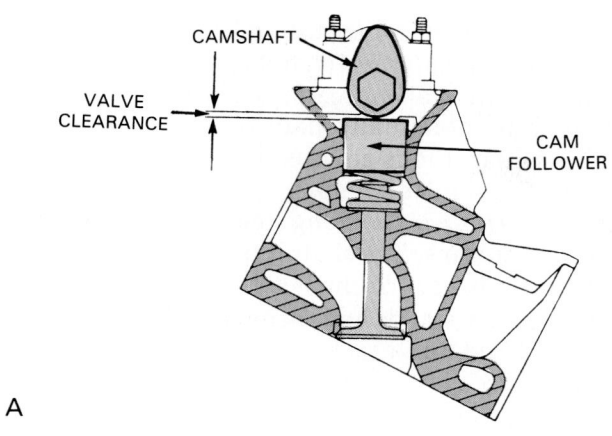

A

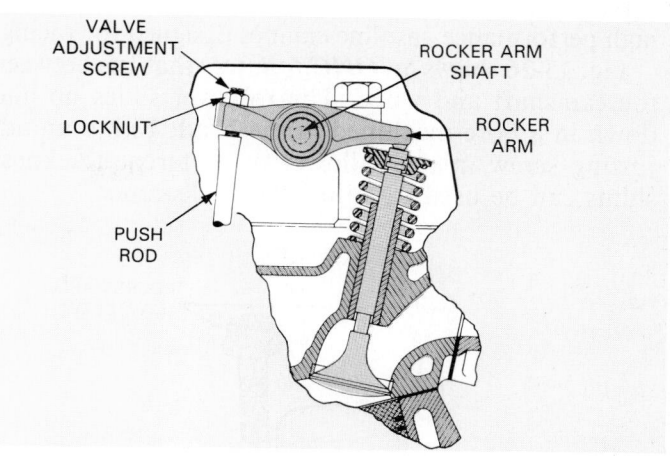

Fig. 13-28. Rocker arm shaft holding rocker arms in position. This rocker arm has adjustment screw and locknut for changing valve clearance. Rocker is cast iron. (Federal Mogul)

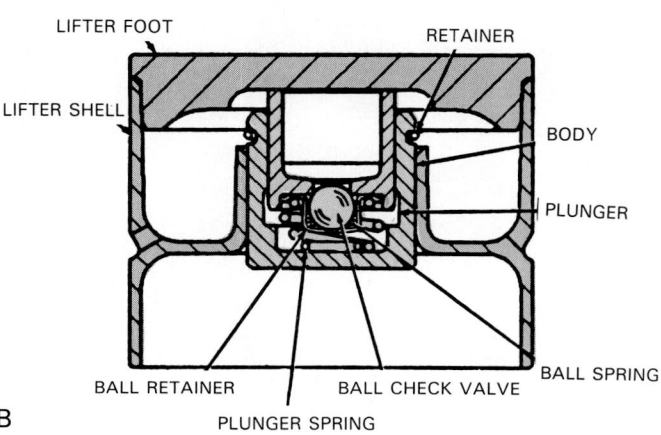

B

Fig. 13-26. A—OHC follower fits directly between camshaft and valve stem. Follower slides up and down in bore machined in head. Either spacer washer or a screw will be provided for adjusting valve clearance. B—Cutaway of cam follower. (GM)

rocker arm when solid lifters are used. Turning the adjustment screw down will reduce valve clearance (play in valve train). Unscrewing or backing off the rocker arm adjustment will increase clearance.

The small clearance needed with solid lifters causes valve train noise. A clattering or clicking noise is produced as the valves open and close. This is the main reason hydraulic lifters are more common.

A *roller lifter,* either mechanical or hydraulic, has a small roller that rides on the camshaft lobe, Fig. 13-25. The roller reduces friction and wear between the lifter and camshaft, one of the highest friction points in the engine.

A roller lifter is sometimes used in diesel engines and

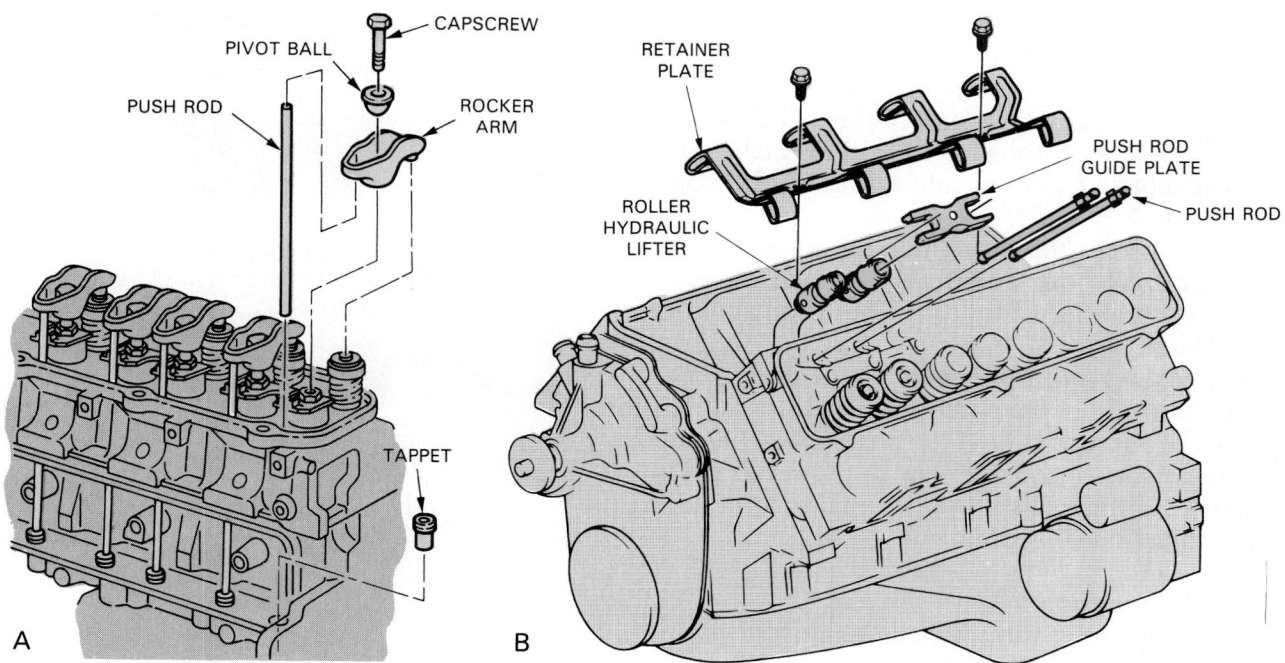

Fig. 13-27. Push rod rocker arrangements. A — In-line engine using pivot ball to hold rocker arm. B — V-type engine using pushrod guide plates. Note location of lifters in both engines. (Chrysler, Oldsmobile)

high performance gasoline engines designed for racing.

Fig. 13-26 shows an *OHC follower* that fits between the camshaft and valve. The follower slides up and down in a bore machined in the head. Either an adjusting screw in the follower or different thickness shims can be used to adjust valve clearance.

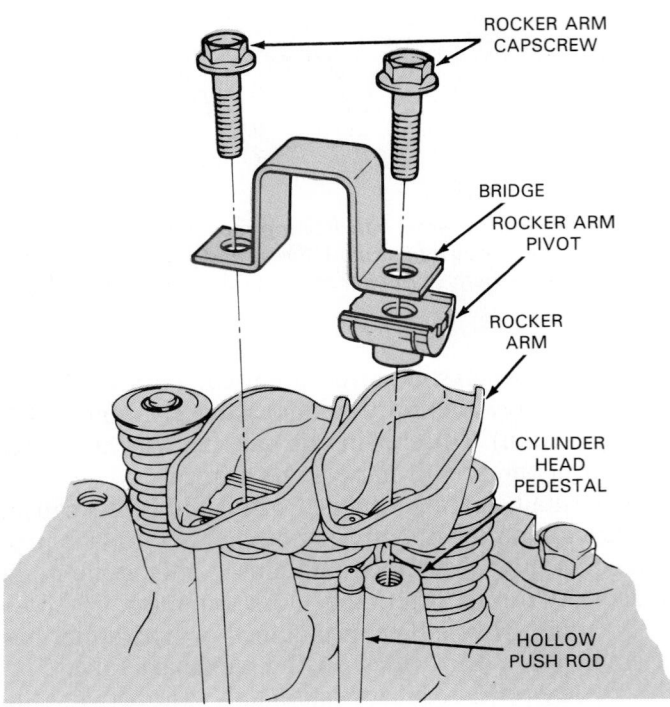

Fig. 13-29. *This engine uses rectangular rocker arm pivots. Bridge helps hold rockers in position over valve stems. These rockers are made of stamped steel. (Chrysler)*

Push rod construction

Push rods are hollow metal tubes with specially formed ends. They are used in cam-in-block engines to transfer motion from the lifters to the rocker arms, Fig. 13-27. Some push rods have a ball on each end. Others have a ball on one end and a female socket on the other end.

Hollow push rods that have holes in the ends can be used to feed oil from the lifter to the rocker arms. This prevents wear on the tip of the push rod and on the rocker arm.

In some engines, *push rod guide plates* are used to limit side movement of the push rods. Some are shown in Fig. 13-27. The guides hold the push rods in alignment with the rocker arms. When the push rods pass through holes in the cylinder head or intake manifold, guide plates are NOT needed.

Rocker arm construction

Rocker arms transfer valve train motion to the valve stem tips. In OHC engines, the camshaft may act directly on the rocker arm. Then, the rocker can act upon the valve.

In a push rod engine, the push rod acts on the rocker. Then, the rocker can transfer and reverse the direction of motion to the valve. See Fig. 13-28.

Rocker arms are usually made of either cast iron or steel. Various methods are used to support the rocker arms on the cylinder head.

A *rocker arm shaft* is a long steel bar used to secure a set of rocker arms. The shaft is held by *stands* bolted to or formed as part of the head. Oil under pressure rises through the stands and then into the shaft. Holes in the shaft feed oil to each rocker arm. Look at Fig. 13-28 again.

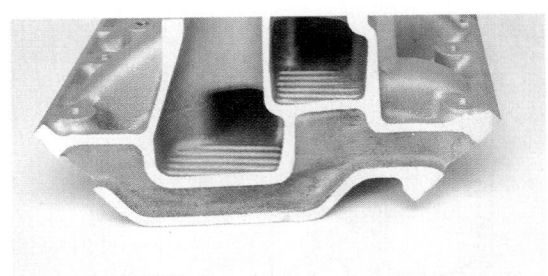

Fig. 13-30. *Cutaway of an engine intake manifold. Note intake runners for fuel and exhaust passage. This intake is made of aluminum to reduce weight. (Edelbrock)*

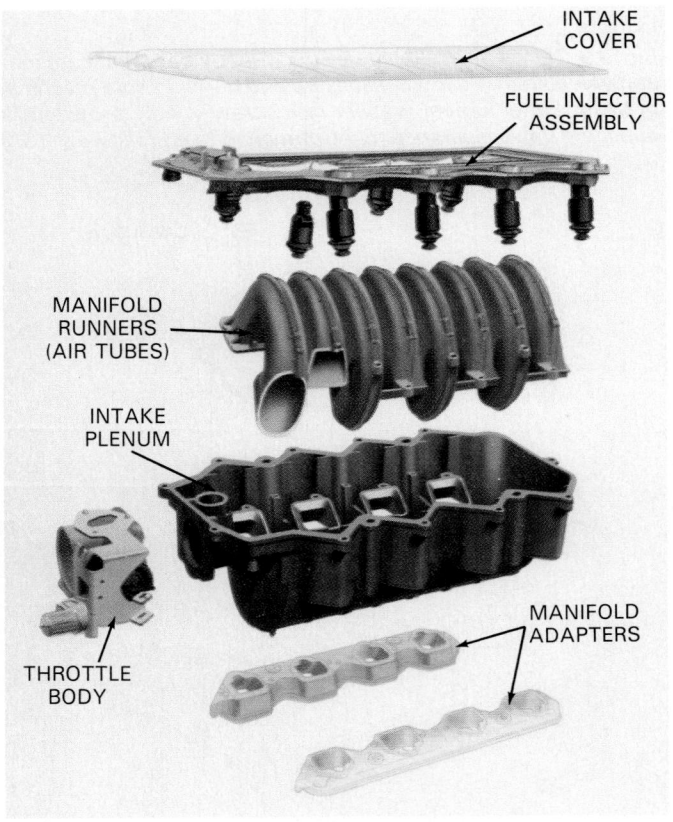

Fig. 13-31. *In Cadillac's new Northstar V-8 engine, the traditional intake manifold is replaced by this "fluid induction" assembly. Individual tubes supply air to each cylinder. (Cadillac)*

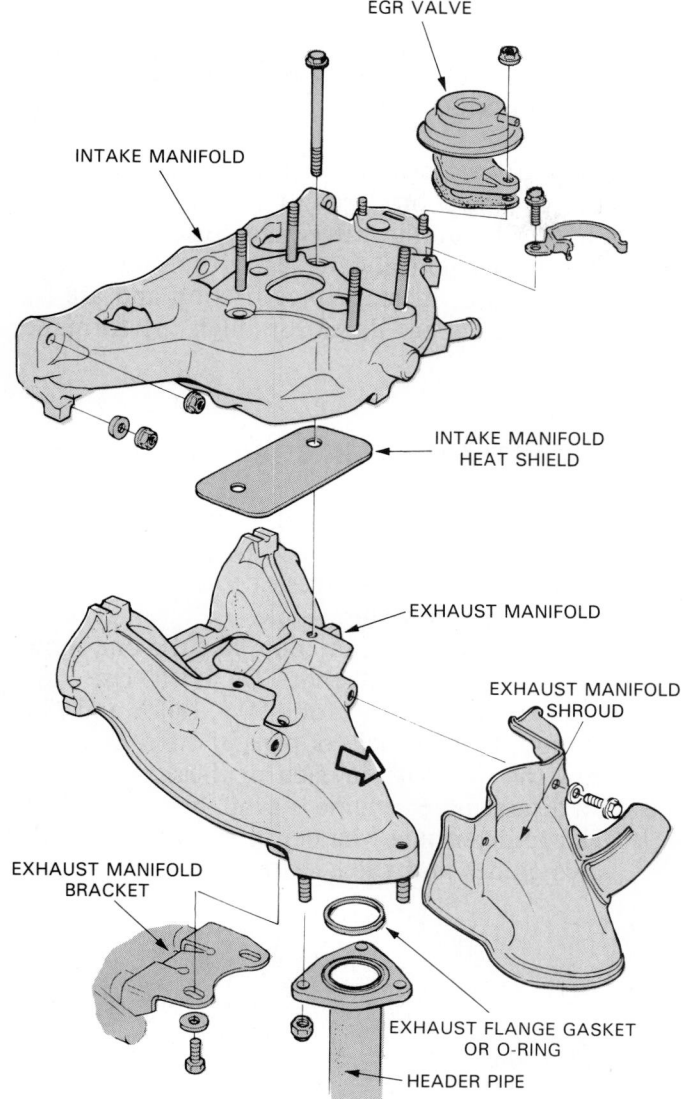

EGR VALVE

INTAKE MANIFOLD

INTAKE MANIFOLD HEAT SHIELD

EXHAUST MANIFOLD

EXHAUST MANIFOLD SHROUD

EXHAUST MANIFOLD BRACKET

EXHAUST FLANGE GASKET OR O-RING

HEADER PIPE

Fig. 13-32. Intake and exhaust manifolds with related components. (Honda)

Individual **pivot balls** or **stands** can also be used to hold the rocker arm in place over the valve. Fig. 13-29 shows one such arrangement.

A **solenoid-operated rocker arm** mechanism is used for a variable displacement (size) engine. The solenoid can be turned on or off to deactivate or activate the engine valve. In this way, cylinders can be deactivated (shut down) to reduce the effective number of engine cylinders. A V-8 engine, for example, can be converted to a 6- or 4-cylinder.

Adjustable rocker arms have a means of changing the valve train clearance. Either a screw is provided on the rocker arm or the rocker arm pivot point can be changed. Adjustable rocker arms MUST be used with mechanical lifters. Adjustable rockers are sometimes used with hydraulic lifter so that an initial setting can be made.

Nonadjustable rocker arms have no means of changing the valve clearance. They are used only with some hydraulic lifters. The rocker arm assembly is tightened to a specific torque. This presets the lifter plunger

halfway in its travel. Then, during engine operation, the hydraulic lifter automatically maintains zero clearance.

Push rod length can be changed to adjust nonadjustable rocker arms.

INTAKE AND EXHAUST MANIFOLD CONSTRUCTION

An *intake manifold* is made somewhat like a cylinder head. The intake usually contains water jackets for cooling. It can be cast of iron, aluminum, or plastic.

Runners (internal passages) formed in the intake manifold carry the air-fuel mixture (gasoline engine) or air (diesel engine) to the cylinder head ports.

Fig. 13-30 is a cutaway of an engine intake manifold. Note the exhaust passage for warming the manifold and for an exhaust gas recirculation (EGR) system. Also see Fig. 13-31.

An *exhaust manifold* routes burned exhaust gases from the cylinder head exhaust port to the car's header pipe. Because of the high operating temperatures, the exhaust manifold is usually made of cast iron.

A few high performance or sports car engines use lightweight, free-flowing steel tubing type exhaust manifolds, also called **headers.**

Fig. 13-32 shows both intake and exhaust manifolds for one particular engine. Note the related parts.

KNOW THESE TERMS

Bare cylinder head, Integral valve guide, Pressed-in valve guide, Integral valve seat, Valve seat insert, Valve seat angle, Interference angle, Prechamber cup, Valve face angle, Sodium filled valve, Stellite face, Umbrella valve seal, O-ring valve seal, Spring tension, Spring free length, Valve spring shim, Valve spring seat, Valve rotator, Valve stem cap, Camshaft lift, Camshaft duration, Valve timing, Valve overlap, Cam thrust plate, Roller lifter, Adjustable rocker arm, Non-adjustable rocker arm.

REVIEW QUESTIONS

1. What is a bare cylinder head?
2. An _____ type valve guide is part of the cylinder head.
3. A _____ valve guide is a separate sleeve forced into an oversize hole in the cylinder head.
4. All modern cylinder heads use pressed-in valve seats; integral seats are no longer used. True or False?
5. What is the function of an interference angle on the valve face and seat?
6. This part is pressed into the cylinder head on most automotive diesel engines.
   a. Stratified charge chamber.

b. Glow plug.
c. Injector nozzle.
d. Prechamber cup.

7. Car engines use mushroom or poppet valves. True or False?
8. Define the term "valve face angle."
9. Why are some valves filled with sodium?
10. Stellite valves are used in engines designed to burn _____ _____ .
11. Describe the two basic types of valve seals.
12. Which of the following does NOT pertain to valve springs?
   a. Free length.   c. Tensile strength.
   b. Tension.   d. Closed length.
13. What is the function of a valve spring shim?
14. Valve retainers and keepers lock the valve spring on the valve. True or False?
15. A _____ _____ can be used to turn the valve and prevent hot spots on the valve face.
16. Variations in camshaft lobe shape control:
   a. When each valve opens.
   b. How long each valve opens.
   c. How far or wide each valve opens.
   d. All of the above are correct.
   e. None of the above are correct.

17. Explain the following terms: Camshaft lift, Camshaft duration, Valve timing, Valve overlap, Scavenge.
18. Camshaft bearings can be either one-piece or two-piece construction. True or False?
19. Why are hydraulic valve lifters used more than solid or mechanical lifters?
20. _____ lifters reduce friction and are frequently used in diesel or high performance applications.

ACTIVITIES FOR CHAPTER 13

1. The rocker arm is a form of lever. Do research to find out what *class* of lever it is. Construct simple models of the three classes of levers and describe for the class how they work.
2. Make a sketch of a cam lobe, like the one shown in Fig. 13-18. Assume that TDC is 0°. Use a protractor to mark points for a 90°, 180°, and 270° rotation. Using pencils or pens of different colors, draw the cam lobe in each of these positions.
3. If a disassembled engine is available, examine the head to determine whether integral or pressed-in valve guides and valve seats are used.

Study the top end components of this cutaway V-6 engine. (Chevrolet)

Engine Bottom End Construction

14

After studying this chapter, you will be able to:
☐ Compare the construction of different types of cylinder blocks.
☐ Explain how piston construction affects engine operation.
☐ Describe piston ring variations.
☐ Summarize the construction of engine bearings.
☐ Compare design variations of other engine bottom end components.
☐ Discuss safe practices when working with engine bottom end components.

This chapter continues your study of engines by detailing construction techniques commonly used in an engine bottom end assembly. This information is needed before learning to repair these engine parts.

The basic parts of an *engine bottom end* are the block, crankshaft, connecting rods, and piston assemblies. These components are given in Fig. 14-1. Review each carefully.

CYLINDER BLOCK CONSTRUCTION

Engine cylinder blocks are normally made of cast iron or aluminum, Fig. 14-2.

An iron cylinder block is very heavy and strong. Nickel is sometimes added to the iron to improve strength and wear resistance.

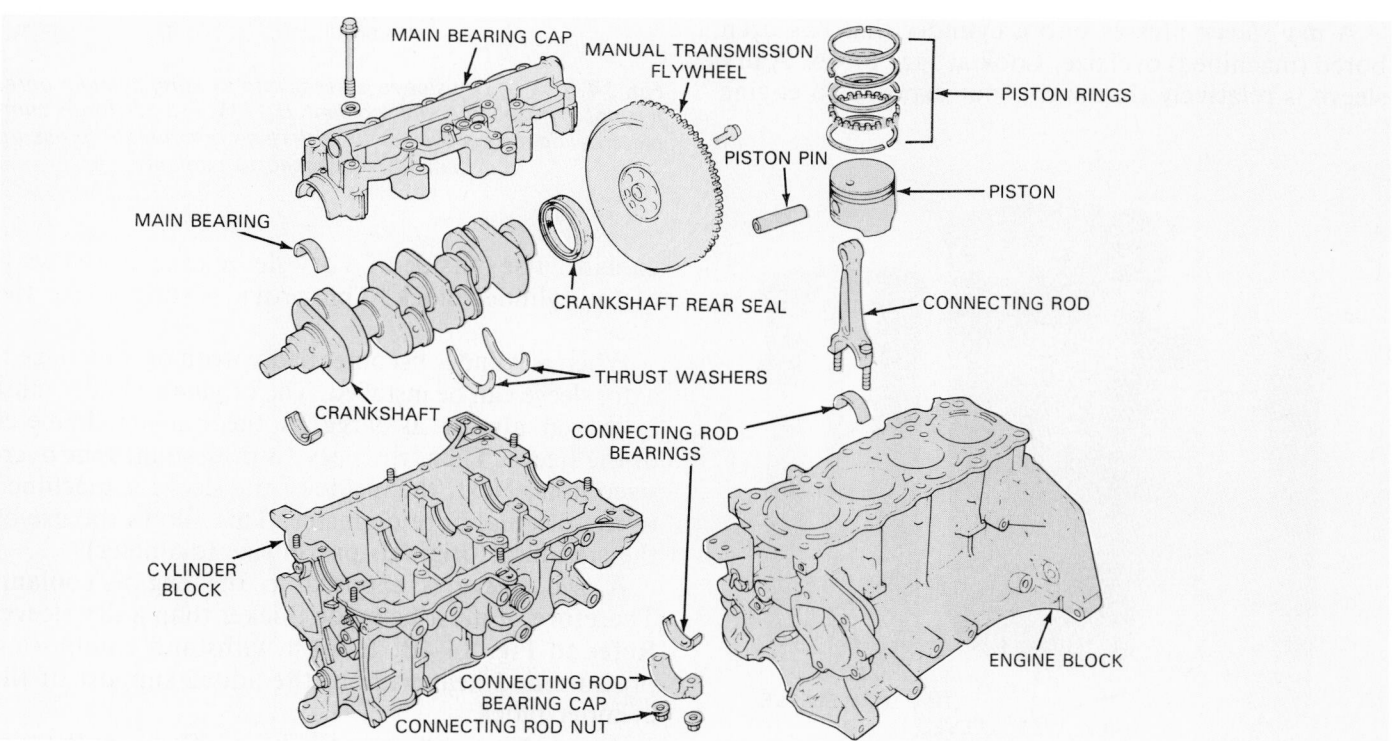

Fig. 14-1. Engine bottom end assembly consists of block, crank, rods, pistons, and rings. Understanding of their construction is very important to service and repair operations. (Honda)

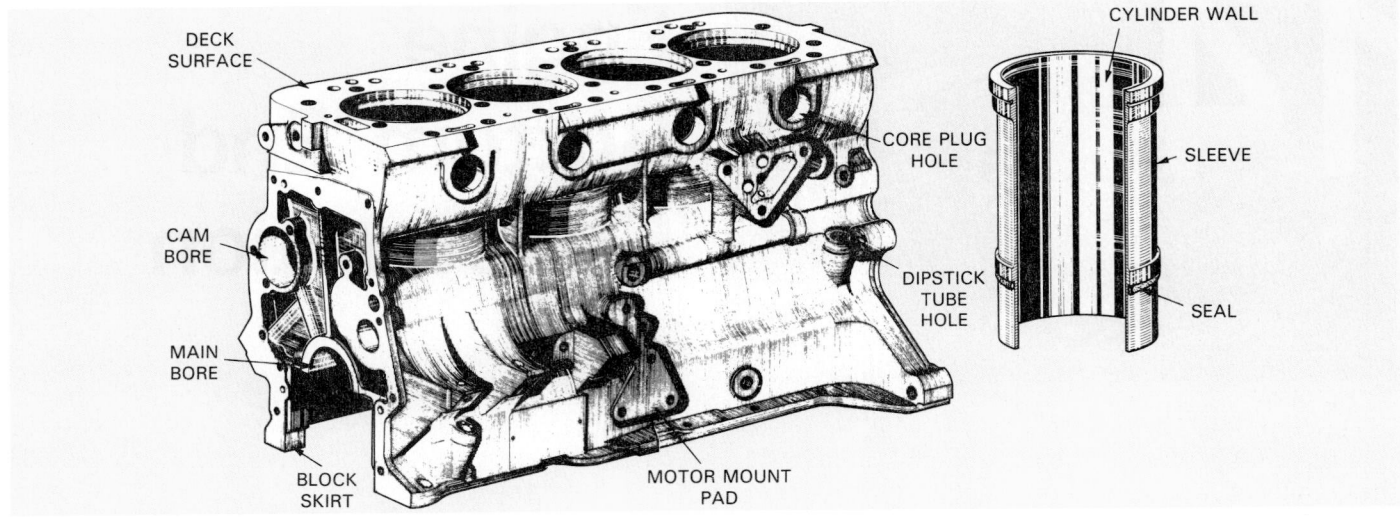

Fig. 14-2. Cylinder block may be cast from iron or aluminum. Cylinder may be integral part of block or pressed-in liners. (Peugeot)

An aluminum block is used to reduce weight. An aluminum block also dissipates heat better than iron.

Cylinder sleeves

Cylinder sleeves or *liners* are metal pipe-shaped inserts that fit into the cylinder block. They act as removable cylinder walls, Fig. 14-2. The piston slides up and down in them.

Cast iron sleeves are commonly used in aluminum cylinder blocks. They can also be installed to repair badly damaged cylinder walls.

There are two basic types of cylinder sleeves: the dry sleeve and the wet sleeve. These are shown in Fig. 14-3.

A *dry sleeve* presses into a cylinder that has been bored (machined) oversize. Look at Fig. 14-4A. A dry sleeve is relatively thin and is not exposed to engine

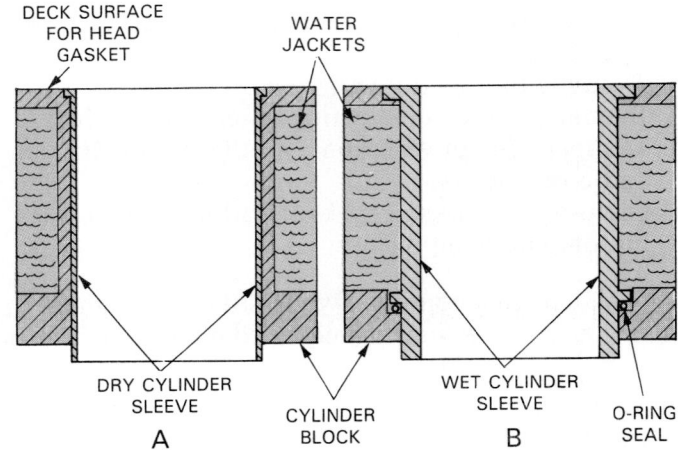

Fig. 14-4. A — Dry sleeve presses into existing cylinder bore. It is not exposed to engine coolant. B — Wet sleeve forms complete cylinder. It is thicker to withstand combustion pressure and heat. It is exposed to coolant.

coolant. The outside of a dry sleeve touches the walls of the cylinder block. This provides support for the sleeve.

When a cylinder becomes badly worn or is damaged, a dry sleeve can be installed. The original cylinder must be bored almost as large as the outside diameter of the sleeve. Then, the sleeve is pressed into the oversized hole. Next, the inside of the sleeve is machined to the original bore diameter. This allows the use of the standard (original) piston size (diameter).

A *wet sleeve* is exposed to the engine coolant. Therefore, it must be made thicker than a dry sleeve. Refer to Fig. 14-4B. It must withstand combustion pressure and heat without the added support of the cylinder block.

A wet sleeve will generally have a flange at the top. When the head is installed, the clamping action pushes down on the sleeve and holds it in position. The

Fig. 14-3. Two left sleeves are thick, wet sleeves. Sleeve on right is thinner dry sleeve. (Dana Corp.)

cylinder head gasket keeps the top of the sleeve from leaking.

A rubber or copper O-ring is used at the bottom of a wet sleeve to prevent coolant leakage into the crankcase. The O-ring seal is pinched between the block and the liner to form a leakproof joint.

Today's trend is towards aluminum cylinder blocks with cast iron, wet sleeves. The light aluminum block reduces weight for increased fuel economy. The cast iron sleeves also wear very well, increasing engine service life. Refer to Fig. 14-5.

Line boring

The term *line boring* refers to a machining operation that cuts a series of holes through the block for the crankshaft bearings. It may also be line bored for the camshaft bearings. The holes must be in perfect alignment for the crank or cam to turn freely. This can also be done to an OHC cylinder head.

Two and four-bolt mains

A *two-bolt main block* only uses two bolts (cap screws) to secure each main bearing cap to the cylinder block. A *four-bolt main block* has four bolts holding each main cap. They are used on high performance engines. A few engines use six-bolt main caps. With extra bolts, the block can withstand more crankshaft downward pressure without part failure.

PISTON CONSTRUCTION

An engine piston is normally cast from aluminum. However, forged aluminum pistons may be found in turbocharged, fuel-injected, diesel-fueled, or other engines that expose the pistons to severe stress.

Since aluminum is very light and relatively strong, it is an excellent material for engine pistons. When an engine is running at highway speeds, the piston must withstand tremendous loads. The piston may accelerate from zero to 60 mph, then back to zero in about four inches of travel. A heavy piston could break the connecting rod. A weak piston could disintegrate (fall apart) under these loads.

The design of a piston must provide maximum strength and minimum weight. Fig. 14-6 shows a cutaway view of an engine piston. Note how the piston is reinforced at stress points. The top of the piston is exposed to combustion and tremendous heat. It can reach operating temperatures as high as 650°F (345°C).

Several design methods are used to provide dependable, quiet piston operation.

Piston dimensions

Fig. 14-7 illustrates several piston dimensions. These include:

1. PISTON DIAMETER (distance measured across sides of piston).
2. PIN HOLE DIAMETER (distance measured across inside of hole for piston pin).
3. RING GROOVE WIDTH (distance measured from top to bottom of ring groove).
4. RING GROOVE DEPTH (distance measured from ring land to back of ring groove).
5. SKIRT LENGTH (distance from bottom of skirt to centerline of pin hole).
6. COMPRESSION DISTANCE (distance from centerline of pin hole to top of piston).

As you will learn, these dimensions affect how the piston functions in the cylinder. Many are also important when working on an engine.

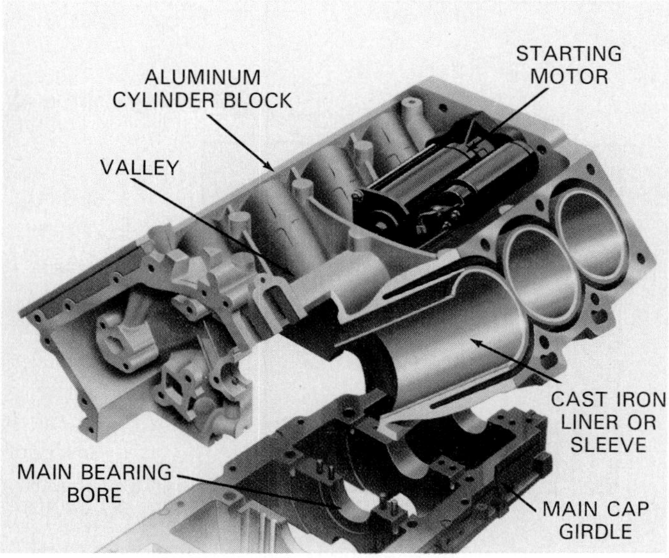

Fig. 14-5. Modern cylinder blocks are frequently made of aluminum with pressed-in, cast iron, wet sleeves. Note the unusual positioning of the starter motor. (Cadillac)

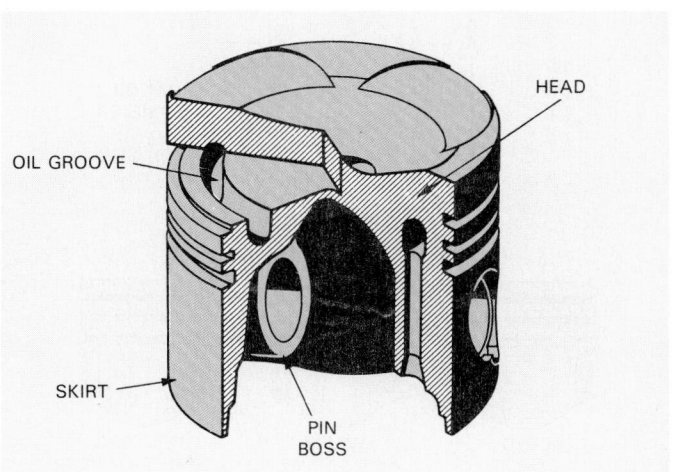

Fig. 14-6. Piston construction is critical because of extreme loads. This piston is for diesel engine and has a groove that allows oil spray to help cool piston. Diesel pistons must be made much thicker and heavier than pistons for gasoline engines. Pressure and temperatures in a diesel are higher. (Mercedes Benz)

Engine Bottom End Construction   153

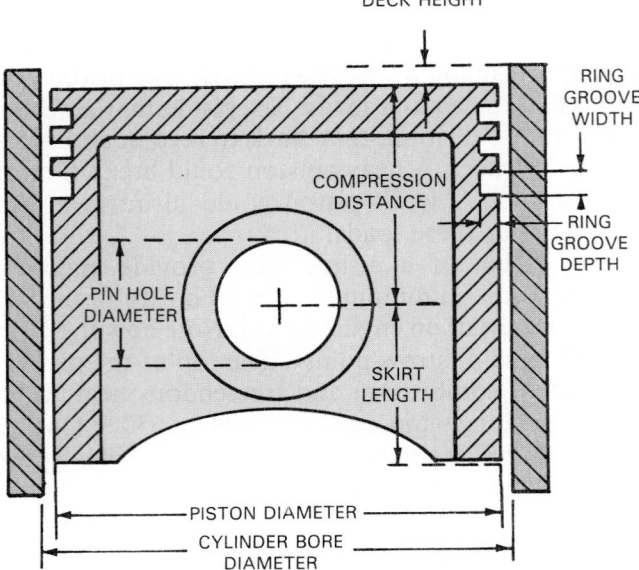

Fig. 14-7. Note basic dimensions of a piston. Cylinder bore diameter minus piston diameter equals piston clearance.

Cam ground piston

A *cam ground piston* is machined slightly out-of-round when viewed from the top. The piston is a few thousandths of an inch (hundredths of a millimeter) larger in diameter perpendicular (opposite) to the piston pin centerline. See Fig. 14-8.

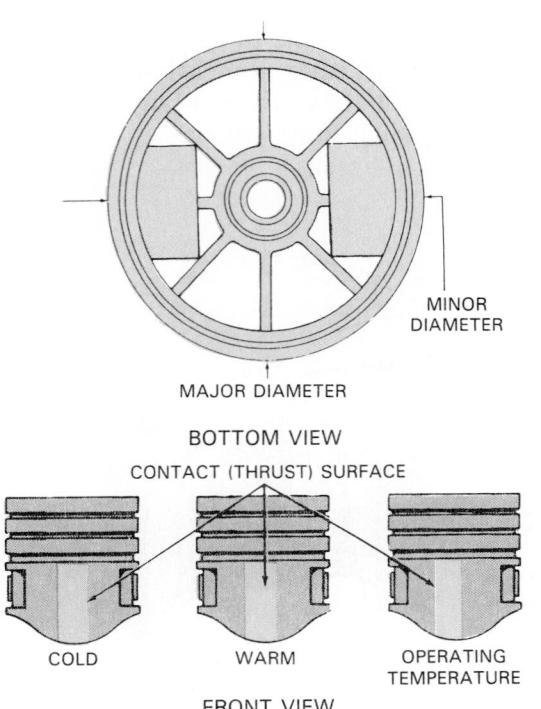

Fig. 14-8. Cam ground piston compensates for different rates of expansion. Piston is larger across major diameter. Piston expands more across minor diameter when heated. This causes piston to become round when at full operating temperature. (Ford)

Cam grinding is done to compensate for different rates of piston expansion (enlargement) due to differences in thickness. As the piston is heated by combustion, the thicker area around the pin boss causes the piston to expand more parallel to the piston pin. The cam ground (oval-shaped) piston then becomes ROUND WHEN HOT.

With cam grinding, a cold piston will have the correct piston-to-cylinder clearance. The unexpanded piston will NOT slap, flop sideways, and knock in the cylinder because of too much clearance. Yet, the cam ground piston will not become too tight in the cylinder when heated to full operating temperature.

Piston taper

Like cam grinding, *piston taper* is normally used to maintain the correct piston-to-cylinder clearance. The top of the piston is machined slightly smaller than the bottom, Fig. 14-9.

Since the piston head gets hotter than the skirt and expands more, piston taper makes the piston almost equal in size at the top and bottom when in operation.

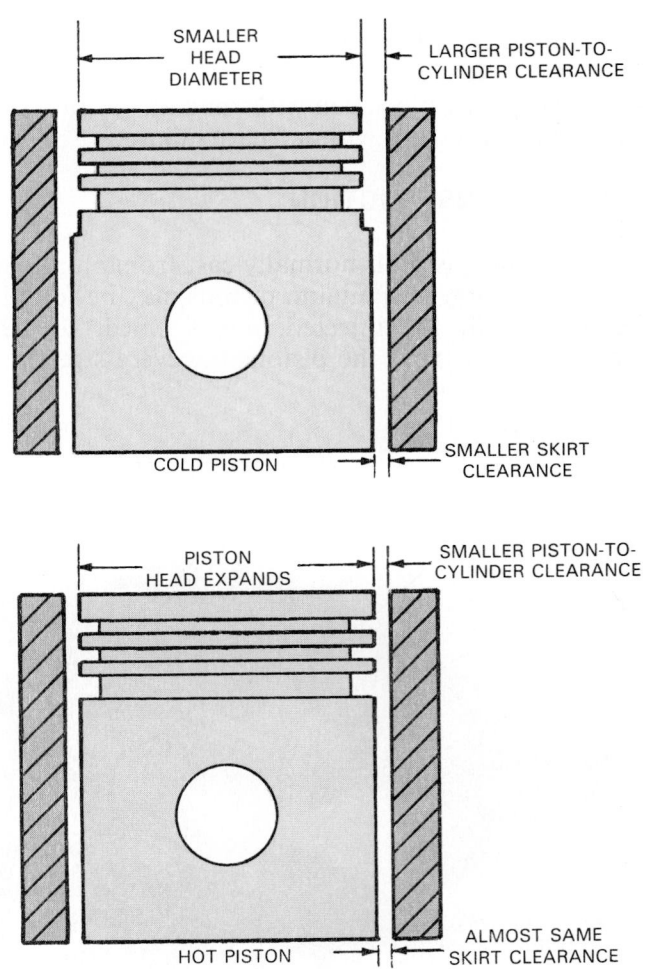

Fig. 14-9. Piston taper compensates for more expansion around piston head. Head becomes hotter than skirt and expands more. By machining head smaller, piston diameter will become almost equal at top and bottom when piston is hot.

Piston shape

Piston shape generally refers to the shape of the piston head. Usually, a piston head is shaped to match and work with the shape of the cylinder head combustion chamber. See Fig. 14-10.

Fig. 14-10. Piston head shape is designed to work with shape of cylinder head combustion chamber. This is a piston for a diesel engine having a direct injection nozzle. (Dana Corp.)

The crown of a *flat top piston* is almost flat and parallel with the block's deck surface. A flat top piston is commonly used with a wedge or pancake type cylinder head. Refer to Fig. 14-11.

A *domed* or *pop-up piston* has a head that is curved upward. This type is normally used with a hemi-type cylinder head. The piston crown must be enlarged to fill the domed combustion chamber and produce enough compression pressure.

Valve reliefs are small identations either cast or machined into the piston crown to provide ample piston-to-valve clearance. Without valve reliefs, the valves' heads could strike the pistons. Valve reliefs are shown in Fig. 14-11.

Slipper skirt

A *slipper skirt* is produced when the portions of the piston skirt below the piston pin ends are removed, as in Fig. 14-11. A slipper skirt provides clearance between the piston and the crankshaft counterweights. The piston can slide farther down in the cylinder without hitting the crankshaft.

PISTON RING CONSTRUCTION

As you learned earlier, automotive pistons normally use three rings—two compression rings and one oil

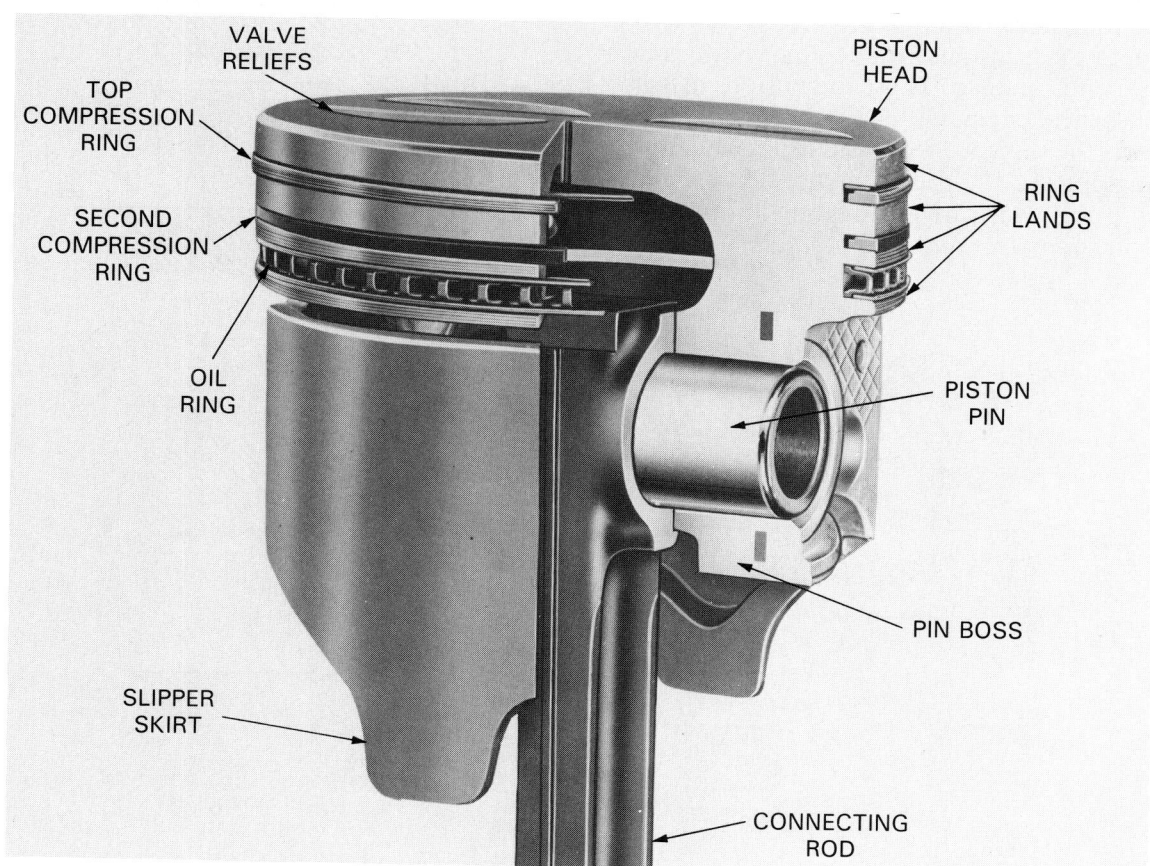

Fig. 14-11. Study basic parts of typical piston and rod assembly. Piston pin is press-fitted in rod. (Deere & Co.)

ring. It is important for you to understand how variations in ring construction provide different operating characteristics. Refer to Fig. 14-11.

The *compression rings* prevent pressure leakage into the crankcase and wipe some of the oil from the cylinder walls. To accomplish these functions, ring shapes vary, as shown in Fig. 14-12. These shapes help the ring seal and remove oil from the cylinder.

Compression rings are usually made of cast iron. An outer layer of chrome or other metal may be coated on the face of the ring to increase wear resistance.

The face of the compression rings may also be GROOVED to speed *ring seating* (initial ring wear that makes ring perfectly match surface of cylinder).

Oil rings are available in two basic designs: rail-spacer type and one-piece type. An oil ring consisting of two rails and a spacer is the most common. Fig. 14-13 shows these types of oil rings. The primary function of oil rings is to keep crankcase oil out of the combustion chambers.

A *ring expander-spacer* is part of a three-piece oil ring. It holds the two steel oil ring scrapers apart and helps push them outward. One is shown in Fig. 14-13.

A *ring expander* can be placed behind a one-piece oil ring to increase ring tension. It can also be used behind the second compression ring. The expander helps push the ring out against the cylinder wall, increasing the ring's sealing action.

Piston ring dimensions

Basic piston ring dimensions include: ring width, ring wall thickness, and ring gap. These dimensions affect the operation of the engine.

Ring width is the distance from the top to the bottom of the ring, Fig. 14-14. The difference between the ring width and the width of the piston ring groove determines *ring side clearance.*

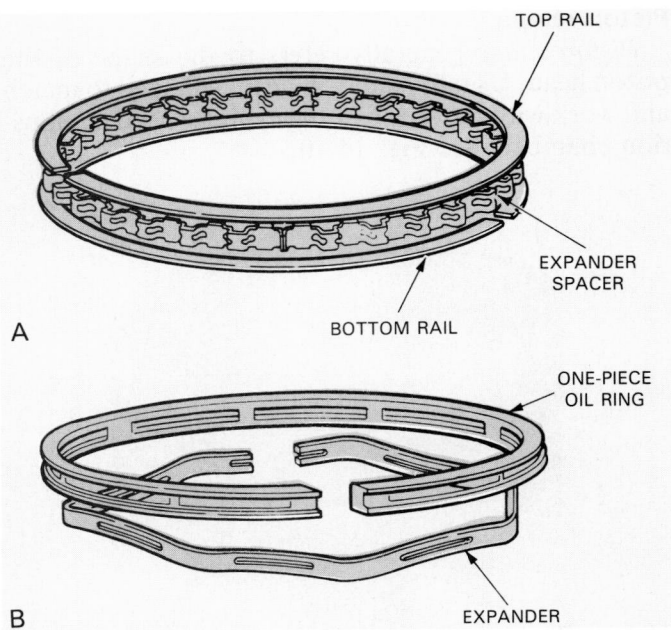

Fig. 14-13. Oil ring must wipe excess oil off cylinder wall. A — Three-piece oil ring is most common. An expander-spacer is used to hold rails apart and out against cylinder. B — One-piece oil ring is made from cast iron. Slots in ring allow oil to flow through holes in piston groove and back into oil pan. Expander pushes ring outward to aid ring scraping action. (Ford)

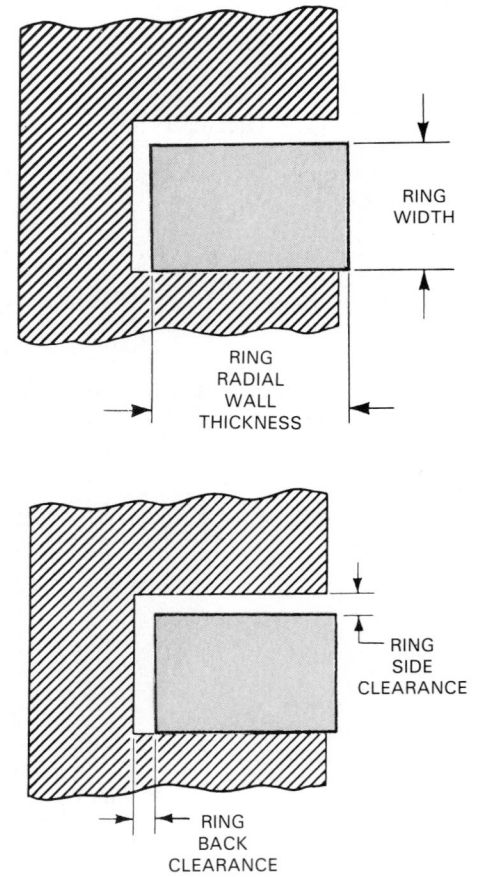

Fig. 14-14. Ring width, ring groove depth, ring radial wall thickness, and ring groove height determine ring back and side clearances. (Perfect Circle)

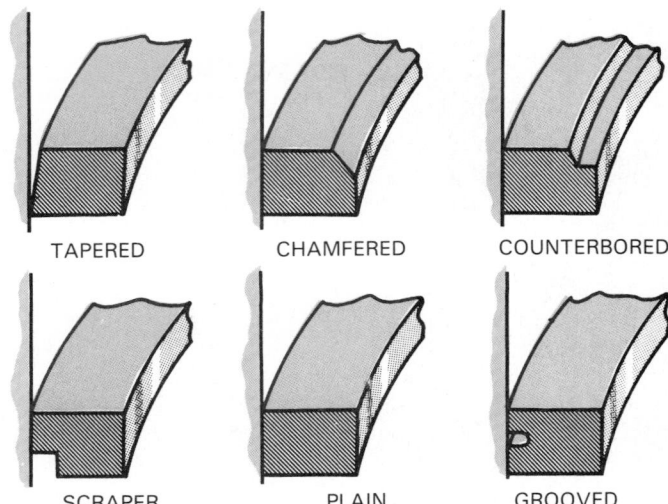

Fig. 14-12. Various compression ring shapes are available. Each type is designed to help ring prevent combustion pressure leakage into crankcase. (Ford)

Ring radial wall thickness is the distance from the face of the ring to its inner wall. See Fig. 14-14. The difference between the ring wall thickness and ring groove depth determines *ring back clearance*.

Ring gap is the distance between the ends of the ring when installed in the cylinder. This is pictured in Fig. 14-15. The ring gap allows the ring to be installed on the piston and to spring outward in its cylinder. The gap also allows the ring to conform to any variation in cylinder diameter due to wear.

As you will learn in later chapters, ring side, back, and gap clearances are very important. They must be within factory specifications or poor engine performance could result.

Piston ring coatings

Mentioned earlier, the faces of piston rings can be coated with chrome or other metals.

Soft ring coatings of porous metal (usually iron) help the ring wear in quickly, forming a good seal. The soft outer surface will wear away rapidly so the ring conforms to the shape of the cylinder. Also called *quick seal rings,* they are commonly recommended for USED CYLINDERS that are slightly worn.

Hard ring coatings, such as chrome, are used to increase ring life and reduce friction. They are used in new or freshly machined cylinders that are perfectly round and NOT worn. To aid break-in, chrome-plated rings usually have ribbed faces. The ribs hold oil and wear quickly to produce a good seal.

PISTON PIN CONSTRUCTION

Piston pins are normally made of casehardened steel. The hollow piston pin is also machined and polished to a very precise finish.

Casehardening is a heating and cooling process that increases the wear resistance of the piston pin. It hardens the outer layer of metal on the pin. The inner metal remains unhardened so the pin is not too brittle.

Piston pins in modern engines are normally held in the piston by one of two means: snap rings or a press-fit. Both are common.

A *full floating piston pin* is secured by snap rings and is free to rotate in both the rod and piston. Look at Fig. 14-16. The pin is free to "float" in both the piston pin bore and the connecting rod small end.

A bronze bushing is usually used in the connecting rod. The piston pin hole serves as the other bearing surface for the pin. The snap rings fit into grooves machined inside the piston pin hole.

A *press-fit piston pin* is forced tightly into the connecting rod's small end. It can rotate freely in the piston pin hole. The pin is NOT free, however, to move in the connecting rod, Fig. 14-16. This holds the pin inside the piston and prevents it from sliding out and rubbing on the cylinder wall.

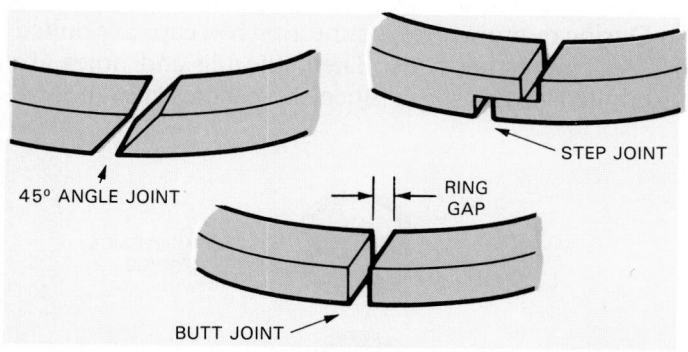

Fig. 14-15. Ring gap is small space between ends of ring when installed in cylinder. Most modern piston rings use a butt joint. (Ford)

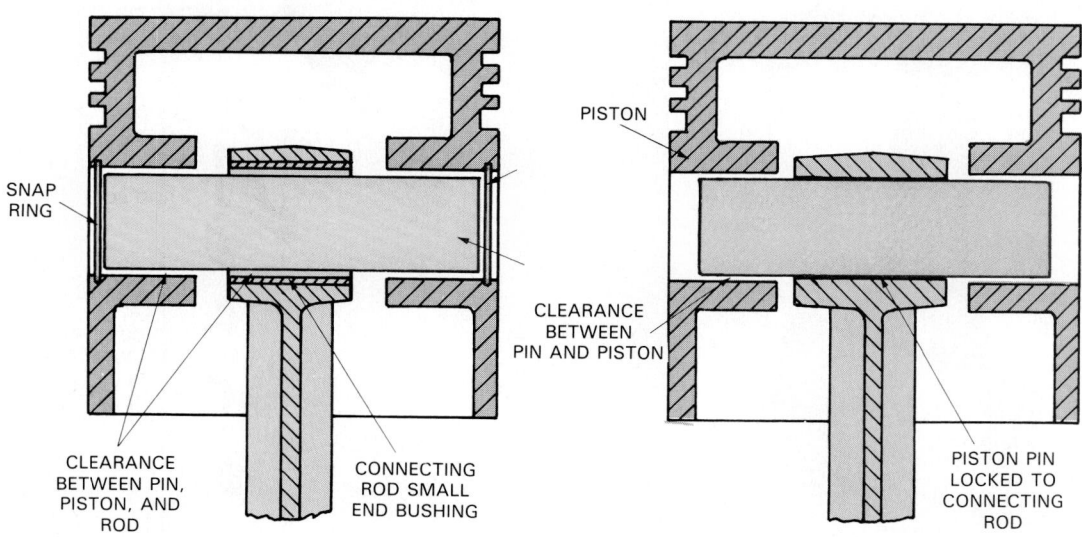

Fig. 14-16. Two modern methods of securing piston pin in piston. Full-floating piston pin has snap rings in grooves on piston. This holds pin in place. Press-fit piston pin is locked in connecting rod small end. Side of rod hits piston boss before pin can protrude out of piston to strike cylinder wall.

The press-fit is a very dependable piston pin design. It is also inexpensive to manufacture. The trend is towards the press-fit piston pin in today's engines.

Piston pin offset

Piston pin offset locates the piston pin hole slightly to one side of the piston centerline to quiet piston operation. The pin hole is moved toward the piston's major thrust surface (piston surface pushed tightly against cylinder during power stroke).

If the pin hole is centered in the piston, the piston could *slap* (knock) in the cylinder. As the piston moves up in the cylinder, it could be positioned opposite the major thrust surface. Then, during combustion, the piston could be rapidly pushed to the opposite side of the cylinder, producing a KNOCK SOUND.

With the pin offset, the piston tends to be pushed against its major thrust surface. This reduces its tendency to slap sideways in the cylinder.

A *piston notch* on the head of the piston is frequently used to indicate piston pin offset and the front of the piston. Look at Fig. 14-17.

The piston may also have the word "front" or an arrow stamped on it. This information lets you know how to position the piston in the block for correct location of piston pin offset.

Fig. 14-18 shows an exploded view of a piston and connecting rod assembly. Note how the parts are assembled.

CONNECTING ROD CONSTRUCTION

Most connecting rods are made of steel. The rod must withstand tons of force as the piston moves up and down in the cylinder. Connecting rods normally have an I-beam shape because of its high strength-to-weight ratio. Refer to Fig. 14-19.

Some connecting rods have an *oil spurt hole* that provides added lubrication for the cylinder walls, piston pin, and other surrounding parts. See Fig. 14-19. Oil under pressure from inside the crankshaft will spray out when holes align in the crank journal, bearing, and spurt hole.

A *drilled connecting rod* has a machined hole its entire length. Its purpose is to supply oil to the piston pin.

Connecting rod numbers are used to assure proper location of each connecting rod in the engine. They also assure that the rod cap is installed on the rod body correctly. Look at Fig. 14-20.

During manufacture, connecting rod caps are bolted to the connecting rods. Then, the big end holes are machined in the rods. Since these holes may not be

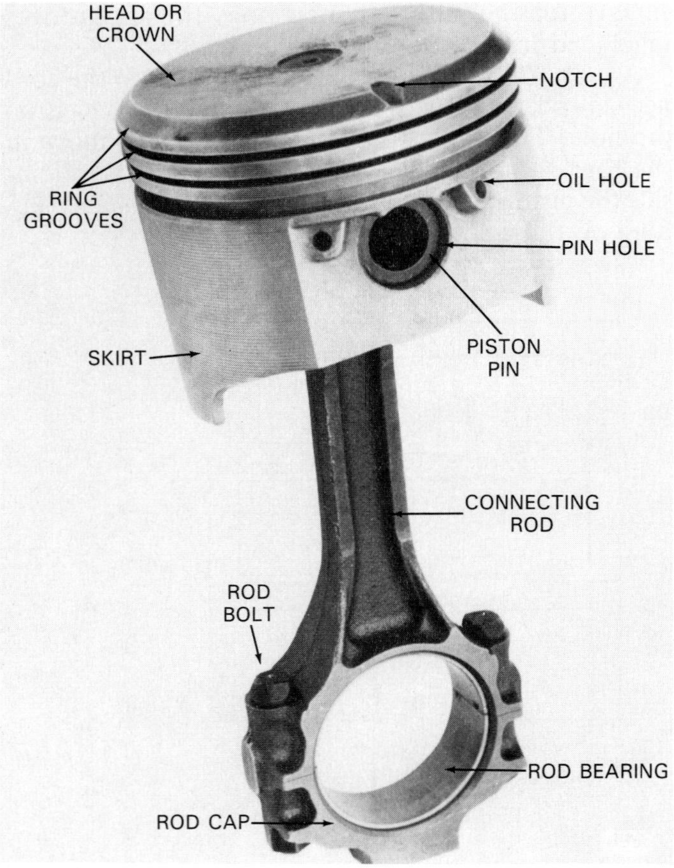

Fig. 14-17. Photo of actual piston assembly with rings removed from piston. Note part names. (Chevrolet)

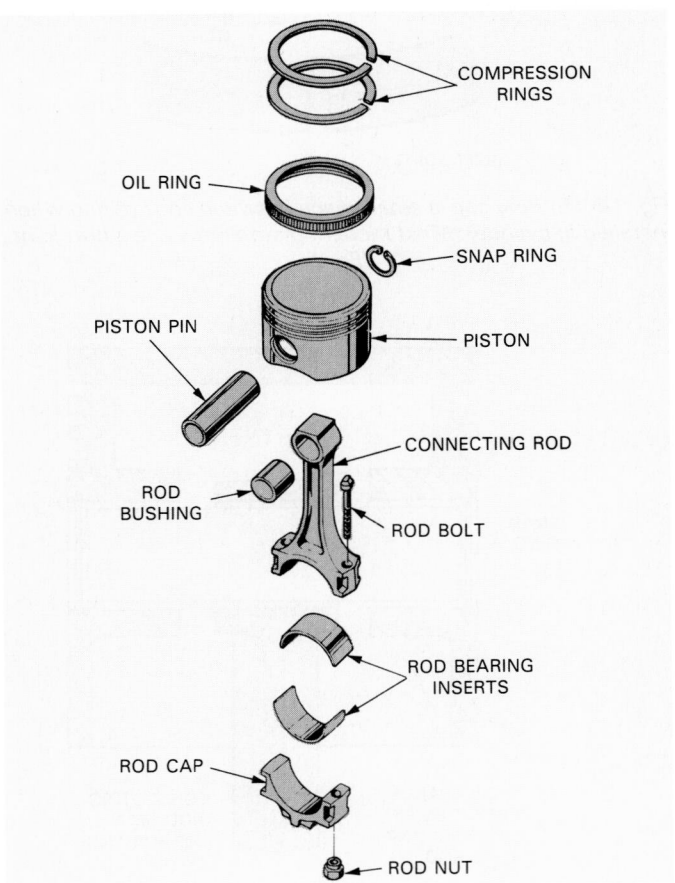

Fig. 14-18. Exploded view of piston and rod assembly. This piston has a full-floating piston pin.

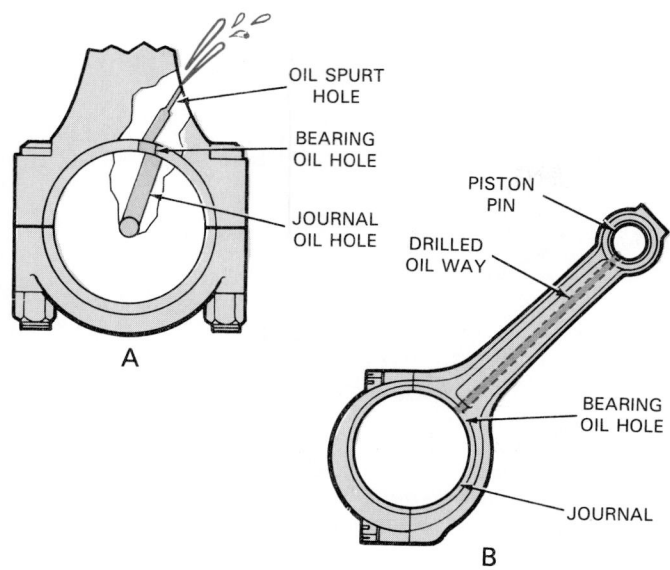

Fig. 14-19. A — Oil spurt hole provides added lubrication for piston pin, cam lobes, cylinder walls, and other surrounding parts. B — Drilled rod allows oil to enter clearance between pin and bushing. (Federal Mogul)

perfectly centered, rod caps must NOT be mixed up or turned around.

If the cap is installed without the rod numbers in alignment, the bore will NOT be perfectly round. Severe rod, crankshaft, and bearing damage will result. A *broken surface rod* is scribed and broken off when manufactured to produce a rough, irregular mating surface between the rod body and cap. This is done to help lock the rod and cap into alignment. The broken, irregular surfaces match perfectly to prevent the rod and cap from shifting during engine operation. This type of rod cannot be rebuilt. However, oversize rod bearings can still be installed during an engine rebuild.

CRANKSHAFT CONSTRUCTION

Engine crankshafts are usually made of cast iron or forged steel. Forged steel crankshafts are needed for heavy duty applications, such as turbocharged or diesel engines. A steel crankshaft is stiffer and stronger than a cast iron crankshaft. It will withstand greater forces without flexing, twisting, or breaking.

Oil passages leading to rod and main bearings are either cast or drilled in the crankshaft, Fig. 14-21. Oil enters the crankshaft at the main bearings, and passes through holes in the main bearing journals. It then flows through passages in the crank and out to the connecting rod bearings.

With an in-line engine, only ONE connecting rod fastens to each rod journal. With a V-type engine, TWO connecting rods bolt to each crankshaft journal.

The amount of *rod journal offset* controls the stroke of the piston. The journal surfaces are precision machined and polished to very accurate tolerances.

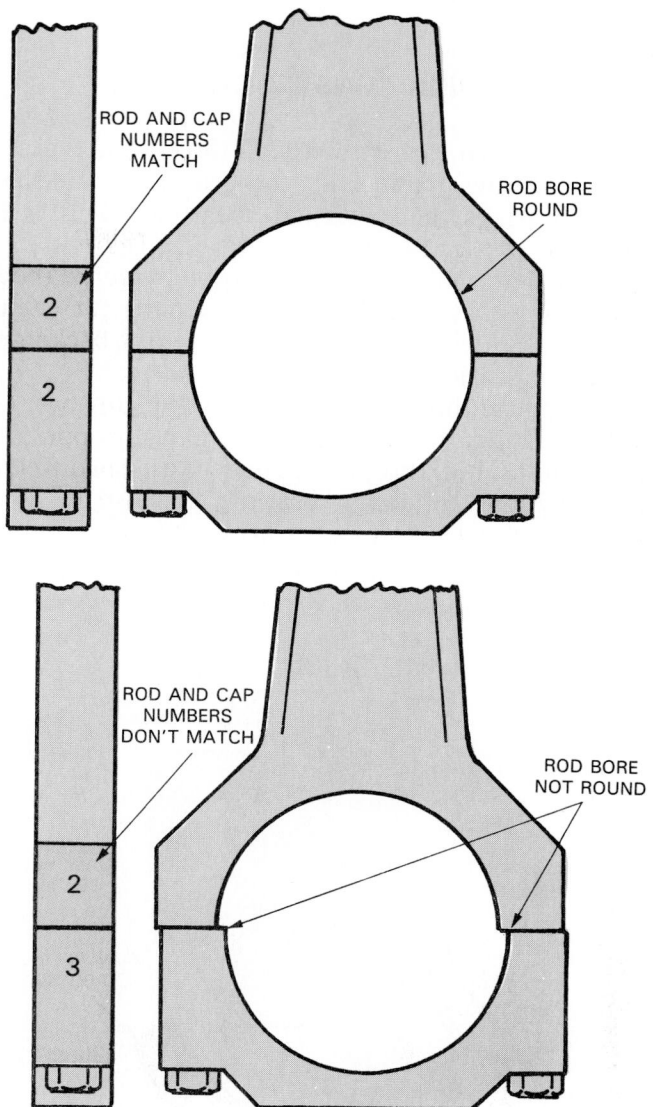

Fig. 14-20. Rod cap must be installed on rod correctly. If rod caps are mixed up or turned, bore for bearing may not be round. Bearing could be crushed into crankshaft journal, damaging both.

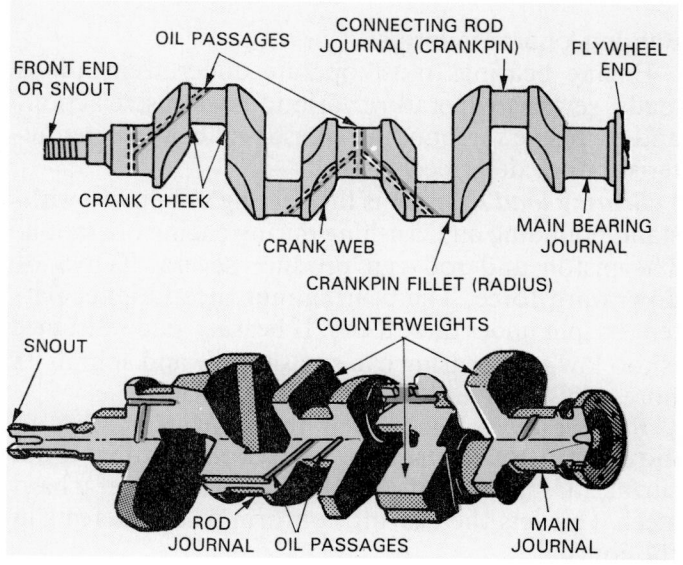

Fig. 14-21. Crankshaft has internal passages to supply oil to connecting rod bearings. Note construction. (Ford)

ENGINE BEARING CONSTRUCTION

As discussed earlier, there are three basic types of engine bearings: connecting rod bearings, crankshaft main bearings, and camshaft bearings. This is illustrated in Fig. 14-22.

Steel is normally the main *backing material* (body of bearing that contacts stationary part) for engine bearings. Softer alloys are bonded over the backing to form the bearing surface.

Any one of three metal alloys can be plated over the steel backing: babbitt (lead-tin alloy), copper, or aluminum. These three metals may be used in different combinations to design bearings for use in light, medium, heavy duty, or extra-heavy duty applications. See Fig. 14-23.

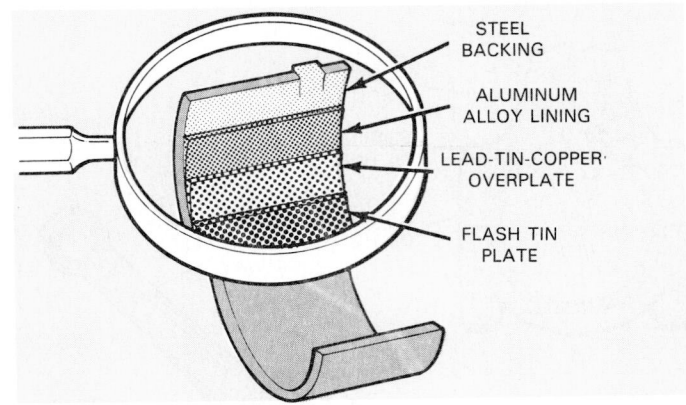

Fig. 14-23. Typical construction of an engine bearing. Steel backing forms body of bearing. Other alloys are plated over backing to provide better operating characteristics. (Federal Mogul)

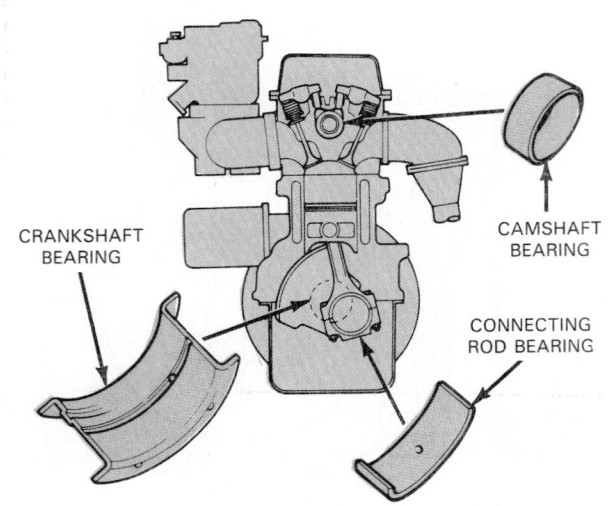

Fig. 14-22. Three basic types of engine bearings are crankshaft main bearings, connecting rod bearings, and camshaft bearings. (Federal Mogul)

Bearing characteristics

Engine bearings must operate under tremendous loads, severe temperature variations, abrasive action, and corrosive surroundings. Essential bearing characteristics are described below.

Bearing load strength is the bearing's ability to withstand pounding and crushing during engine operation. The piston and rod can produce several TONS of downward force. The bearing must not fatigue, flatten, or split under these loads. If bearing load resistance is too low, the bearing can smash, fail, and spin in its bore. This can ruin the bore or journal.

Bearing conformability is the bearing's ability to move, shift, or adjust to imperfections in the journal surface. Usually, a soft metal will be plated over a hard steel. This lets the bearing conform to any defects in the journal.

Bearing embedability refers to the bearing's ability to absorb dirt, metal, or other hard particles. Dirt or

metal are sometimes carried into the bearings. The bearing should allow the particles to sink beneath the surface into the bearing material. This will prevent the particles from scratching, wearing, and damaging the surface of the crankshaft or camshaft journal.

Bearing corrosion resistance is the bearing's ability to withstand being eaten away by acids, water, and other impurities in the engine oil. Combustion blow-by gases cause oil contamination that could also corrode the engine bearings. Aluminum-lead and other alloys are now commonly used because of their excellent corrosion resistance.

Bearing crush

Bearing crush is used to help prevent the bearing from spinning inside its bore during engine operation. Pictured in Fig. 14-24, the bearing is made slightly

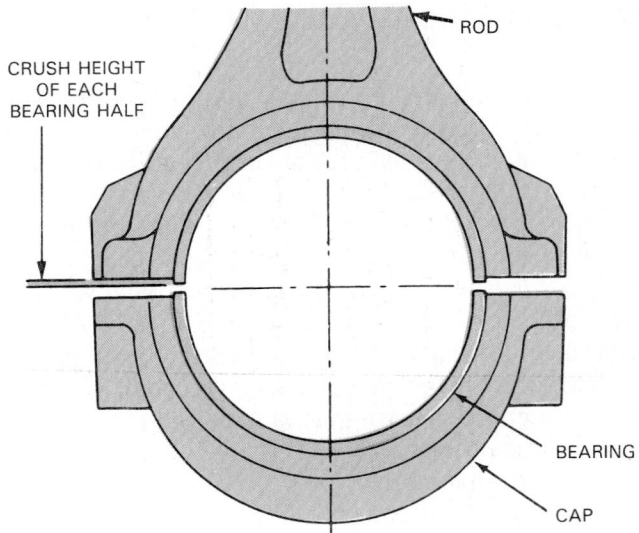

Fig. 14-24. Bearing crush is produced when bearings are made slightly larger than bearing bore. When cap is bolted down, bearing is forced into bore. This keeps bearing from turning with the crankshaft. (Deere & Co.)

larger in diameter than the bearing bore. The end of the bearing is slightly above the bore.

When the rod or main cap is tightened, the bearing ends press against each other. This jams the back sides of the bearing inserts tightly against the bore, locking them in place.

Bearing spread

Bearing spread is used on split type engine bearings to hold the bearing in place during assembly. The distance across the parting line of the bearing is slightly wider than the bearing bore. This causes the bearing insert to stick in its bore when pushed into place with your fingers. Tension from bearing spread keeps the bearing from falling out of its bore as you assemble the engine.

Standard and undersize bearings

A *standard bearing* has the original dimensions specified by the engine manufacturer for a new, unworn, or unmachined crankshaft. A standard bearing may have the abbreviation "STD" stamped on the back.

An *undersize bearing* is designed to be used on a crankshaft journal that has been machined to a smaller diameter. If the crank has been worn or damaged, it can be ground undersize by a machine shop. Then, undersize bearings would be needed.

Connecting rod and main bearings are available in undersizes of .010, .020, .030, and sometimes .040 in. The undersize will normally be stamped on the back of the bearing, as in Fig. 14-25. The crankshaft may also have an undersize number stamped on it by the machine shop.

Bearing locating lugs and dowels

Locating lugs or *dowels* position the split bearings in their bores. Look at Fig. 14-26. The bearing usually has a lug that fits into a recess machined in the bearing bore or cap. Sometimes however, a dowel in the

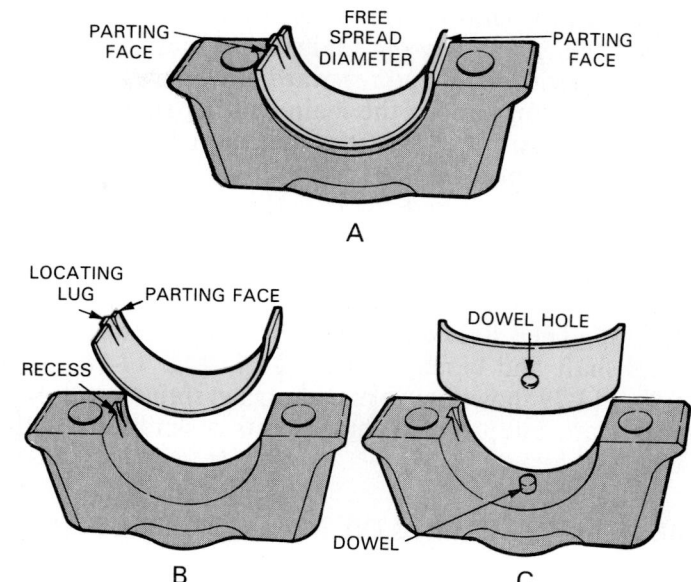

Fig. 14-26. Bearing locating lugs or dowels can be used to position engine bearings in their bore. A—Spread. B—Lug. C—Dowel. (Federal Mogul)

cap or bore fits in a hole in the bearing insert. Either method helps keep the insert from shifting or turning during crankshaft rotation.

Bearing oil holes and grooves

Oil holes and *grooves* in the engine bearings permit bearing lubrication. The holes allow oil to flow through the block and into the clearance between the bearing and crankshaft journal. The grooves provide a channel so oil can completely encircle the bearing before flowing over and out of it. See Fig. 14-27.

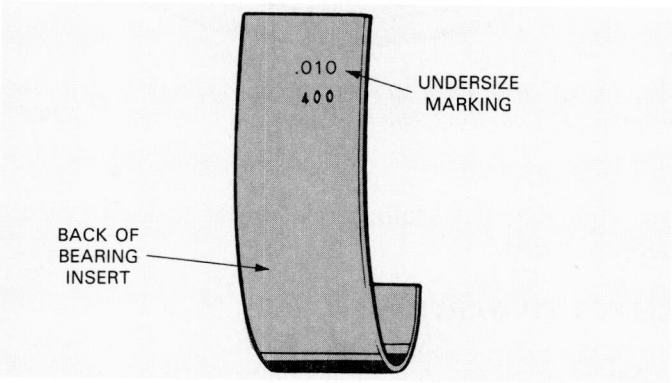

Fig. 14-25. Bearing undersize will be stamped on back of bearing. An undersize marking of .010 in., for example, means that crankshaft journal has been ground .010 smaller in diameter. Undersize bearings are needed to maintain correct bearing clearance. (Buick)

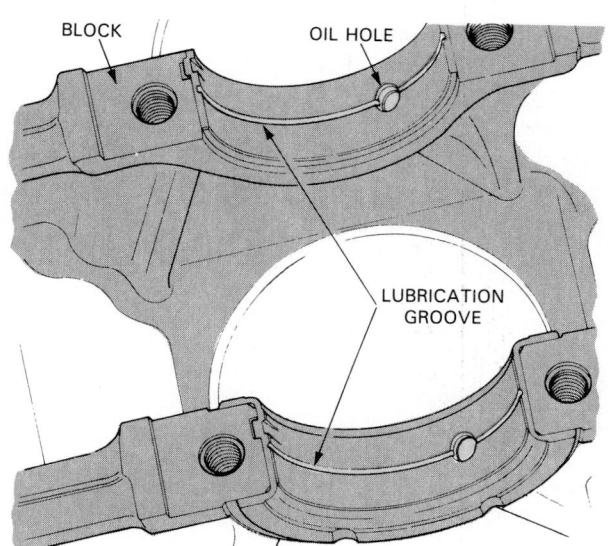

Fig. 14-27. Main bearings have holes that let oil enter bearing clearance. Grooves allow oil to circle bearing to evenly distribute lubricating oil. (Chrysler)

Main thrust bearing, thrust washers

A *main thrust bearing* limits crankshaft end play (crankshaft forward and rearward movement). Thrust flanges are formed on the main bearing sides. These flanges almost touch thrust surfaces machined on the crankshaft. Shown in Fig. 14-28, this keeps the crank from sliding back and forth in the block.

Thrust washers are sometimes used, instead of one-piece thrust bearing inserts, to limit crank end play. The thrust washers are separate parts from the main bearing. They slide down into the space between the crankshaft and block, as pictured in Fig. 14-28.

Fig. 14-29 shows how a main bearing, thrust washers, main cap, and related components assemble to the block.

REAR MAIN BEARING OIL SEAL CONSTRUCTION

The engine *rear main bearing oil seal* prevents oil leakage around the back of the crankshaft. There are several types in present use: two-piece neoprene (rubber) rear oil seal, wick or rope rear oil seal, and one-piece neoprene rear oil seal.

A *two-piece neoprene rear oil seal* usually fits into a groove cut into the block and rear main cap. Look at Figs. 14-30 and 14-31.

The seal has a lip that traps oil and another lip that keeps dust and dirt out of the engine. The sealing lips ride on a machined surface of the crankshaft. Spiral grooves may be used on this crank surface to help throw oil inward to prevent leakage.

A *rope* or *wick rear oil seal* is simply a woven rope impregnated (filled) with graphite. One piece of the rope seal fits into a groove in the block. Another piece fits in a groove in the main cap. This type seal is being replaced by one and two-piece neoprene seals.

A *one-piece neoprene rear oil seal* fits around the rear flange on the crankshaft. Fig. 14-32 shows how a retainer may be used to hold the seal on the rear of

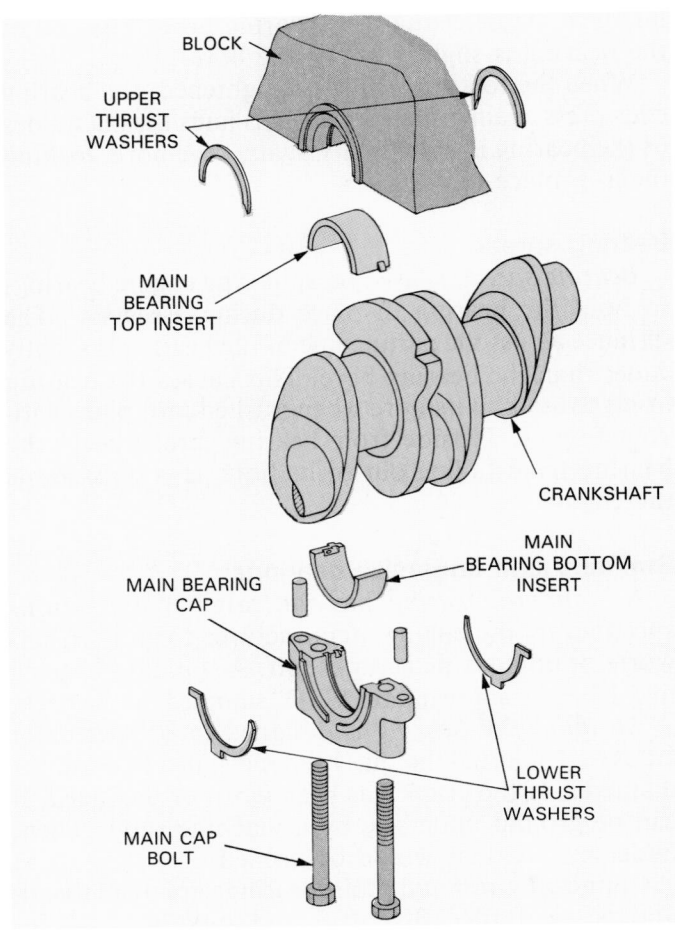

Fig. 14-29. Note how main bearing, thrust washers, crankshaft, and cap fit together. (Mercedes Benz)

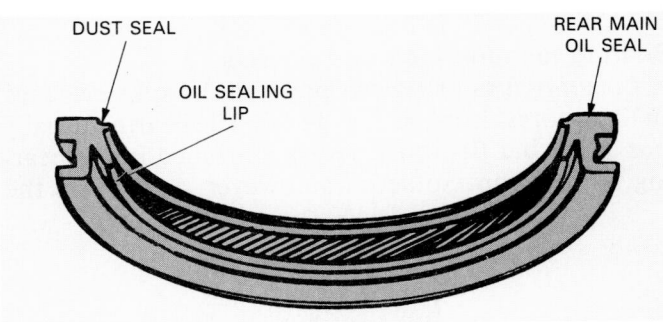

Fig. 14-30. Rear main oil seal has sealing lip that must face inside of engine. Dust seal faces outside of engine. (GMC)

the engine. It has sealing lips similar to a two-piece neoprene seal.

SELECT FIT PARTS

Select fit means that some engine parts are selected and installed in a certain position to improve the fit or clearance between parts. For example, pistons are commonly select fit into their cylinders. The engine manufacturer will measure the diameter of the cylinders. If one cylinder is machined slightly larger

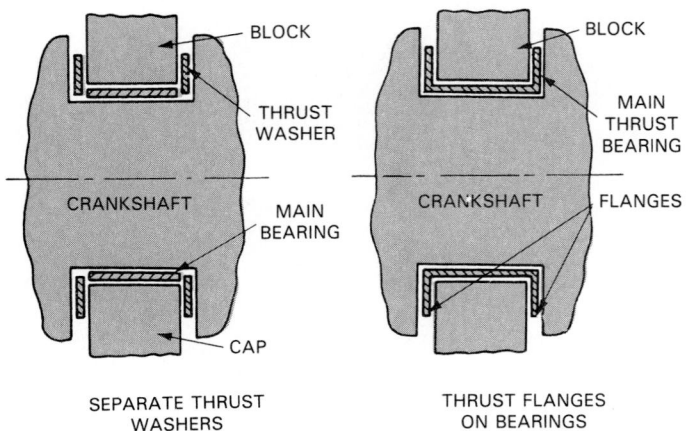

Fig. 14-28. Thrust bearing or washers limit crankshaft end play. Washers are used with conventional main bearing insert. Main thrust bearing has thrust flanges formed as part of main bearing. (Deere & Co.)

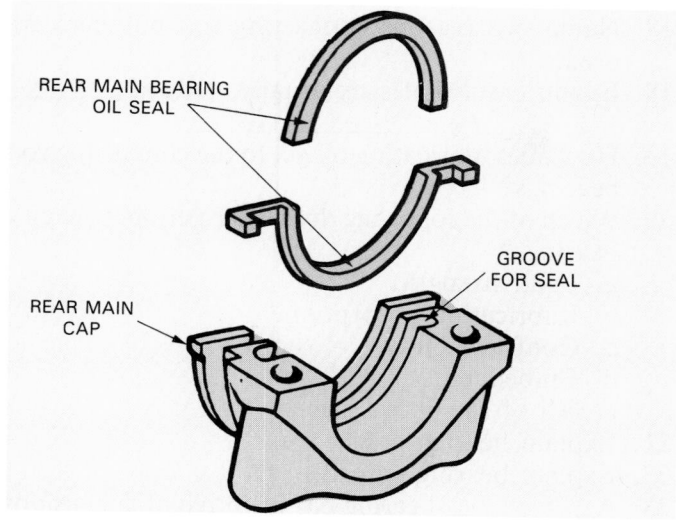

Fig. 14-31. *Two-piece seal fits into groove machined in block and rear main cap.*

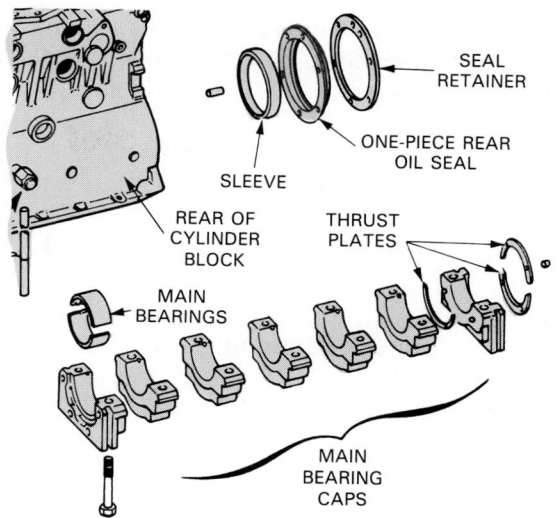

Fig. 14-32. *Some late model rear oil seals are one-piece. They assemble into rear of block around crankshaft flange. (Chrysler Corp.)*

than another, a slightly larger piston will be installed (select fit) in that cylinder. Because of select fit parts, it is important that you reinstall parts in their original locations whenever possible.

BALANCER SHAFTS

Balancer shafts are used in some engines to cancel the vibrating forces produced by crankshaft, piston, and rod movement. Fig. 14-33 shows the balancer shafts used in one particular engine.

The balancer shafts, also called *silencer shafts,* are installed in the right and left sides of the cylinder block.

Usually, a chain is used to spin the shafts at twice crankshaft rpm. The shafts are supported on bearings fitted in a bore machined in the block. Oil is pressure-fed to these bearings.

KNOW THESE TERMS

Wet sleeve, Dry sleeve, Line bore, Cam ground piston, Piston taper, Valve reliefs, Slipper skirt, Ring expander, Expander-spacer, Ring gap, Full floating piston pin, Press-fit piston pin, Piston pin offset, Oil spurt hole, Drilled rod, Rod cap numbers, Bearing

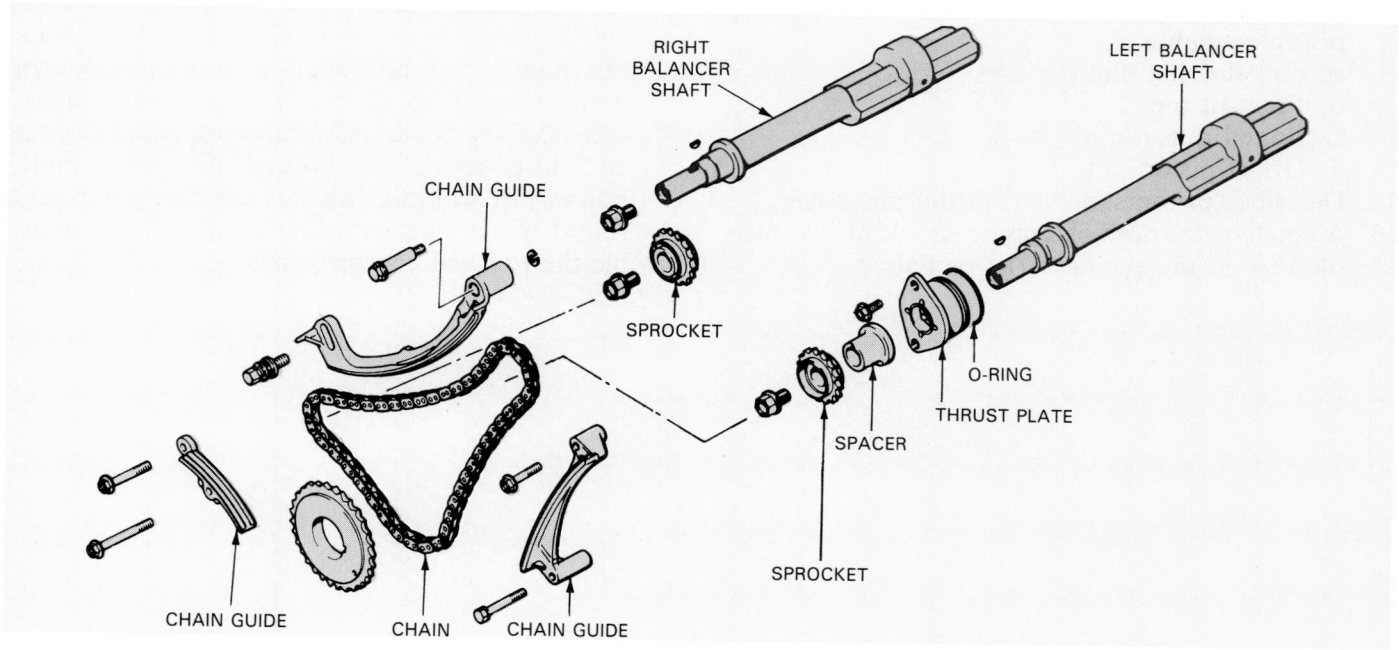

Fig. 14-33. *Balancer shafts are turned by chain, sprockets, and engine crankshaft. They counteract any vibration produced by crankshaft, pistons, and rods.*

crush, Bearing spread, Undersize bearing, Main thrust bearing, Thrust washers, Select fit parts, Balancer shaft.

REVIEW QUESTIONS

1. Cylinder blocks can be made of cast iron or aluminum. True or False?
2. Explain the difference between wet sleeves and dry sleeves.
3. Aluminum blocks commonly use _____ _____ , _____ sleeves.
4. List and define six piston dimensions.
5. A _____ _____ piston is machined slightly out-of-round when viewed from the top to compensate for different rates of piston _____ .
6. When the top of the piston outside diameter is machined slightly smaller than the bottom, it is called:
   a. A pop-up piston.
   b. A dished piston.
   c. A cam ground piston.
   d. A piston taper.
7. Valve reliefs are small identations either cast or machined in the piston skirts. True or False?
8. What is a ring expander-spacer?
9. The difference between the ring width and the width of the piston ring groove determines _____ _____ _____ .
10. The difference between the ring wall thickness and ring groove depth determines _____ _____ _____ .
11. Define the term "ring gap."
12. When should you use soft piston ring coatings?
13. Explain why some parts are casehardened.
14. Which of the following does NOT relate to modern piston assemblies:
    a. Full floating pin.
    b. Press-fit pin.
    c. Bolted piston pin.
    d. Offset piston pin.
15. Describe "piston slap" and piston pin offset.
16. A notch on the head of a piston should always face the rear of the engine. True or False?
17. Name two reasons connecting rod numbers are used.
18. Engine crankshafts are usually made of _____ _____ or _____ _____ .
19. How does lubricating oil get to the connecting rod bearings?
20. Which of the following does NOT pertain to engine bearings?
    a. Load strength.
    b. Lubrication absorption.
    c. Conformability.
    d. Embedability.
    e. All of the above are correct.
21. Explain bearing crush.
22. Explain bearing spread.
23. A _____ bearing has the original dimensions specified by the manufacturer for a new, unworn, or unmachined crankshaft.
24. A _____ bearing is designed to be used on a crankshaft journal that has been machined to a smaller diameter.
25. Describe three rear main oil seal variations.

ACTIVITIES FOR CHAPTER 14

1. Use inside and outside micrometers to measure the diameter of a piston and the engine cylinder bore. Then, find the amount of piston clearance by subtracting the piston diameter from the bore measurement.
2. If a number of pistons are available, determine whether any are *cam-ground*. Do this by measuring the diameter parallel to the piston pin, then measuring the diameter perpendicular (at a 90° angle) to the piston pin. If the piston is cam-ground, the measurement perpendicular to the pin will be larger by a few thousandths of an inch.
3. Dissamble a rod cap from its connecting rod, turn it end-for-end (so the numbers no longer align), then bolt it back into place. Can you visually detect an "out-of-round" rod bore? If not, try to think of a way to determine whether the bore is perfectly round. When finished with this activity, reassemble the rod and cap properly.

Engine Front End Construction

After studying this chapter, you will be able to:
☐ Explain the function and construction of a harmonic balancer.
☐ Compare the three types of camshaft drives.
☐ Explain the construction of a timing gear, timing chain, and timing belt assembly.
☐ Summarize the construction of engine front covers, oil slingers, and other related components.
☐ Describe safety practices related to working on engine front end components.

The typical *engine front end* assembly consists of the parts that attach to the front of the engine. These parts have changed in the past few years. Besides timing gears and chains, modern engines use timing belts, front cover-mounted oil pumps, auxiliary shafts, and other new designs.

This important chapter explains the construction of engine front end assemblies. Study it carefully. Then you will more fully understand later chapters on service and repair.

HARMONIC BALANCER (VIBRATION DAMPER) CONSTRUCTION

Harmonic vibration is a high frequency movement resulting from twisting and untwisting of the crankshaft. Each piston and rod assembly can exert over a ton of downward force on its journal. This can actually flex (bend) the crank throws in relation to each other.

If harmonic vibration is not controlled, the crankshaft could vibrate like a musician's tuning fork or a string-type musical instrument. Serious engine damage (usually crankshaft breakage) could result.

A *harmonic balancer,* also called a *vibration damper,* is a heavy wheel mounted in rubber to control harmonic vibration. Look at Fig. 15-1. The balancer is keyed to the crankshaft snout. This makes the damper spin with the crankshaft.

Fig. 15-2 illustrates the basic construction of a typical harmonic balancer. Note how a rubber ring separates

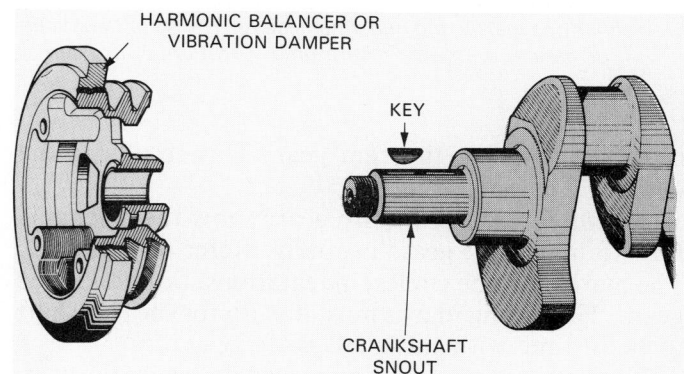

Fig. 15-1. Vibration damper or harmonic balancer installs on front of crank. Key locks damper to snout. Large bolt is commonly used to hold damper in place. (Peugeot)

the outer inertia ring and the inner sleeve. The inertia and rubber rings set up a damping action on the crankshaft as it tries to twist and untwist. This DEADENS vibrating action.

Crankshaft pulley

The *crankshaft pulley* operates belts for the alternator, water pump, and other units. As in Fig. 15-2, it is often part of the harmonic balancer, but may simply be bolted to the front of the balancer. The pulley has either V or ribbed grooves for the belts.

CAMSHAFT DRIVE CONSTRUCTION

A *camshaft drive* must turn the camshaft at one-half crankshaft speed. It must do this smoothly and dependably. There are three basic types of camshaft drives: gear drive, chain drive, and belt drive.

Timing gears

Timing gears are the two gears that operate the engine camshaft. A *crank gear* is keyed to the crankshaft snout, as shown in Fig. 15-3. It turns a *camshaft gear* on the end of the camshaft. The crank gear

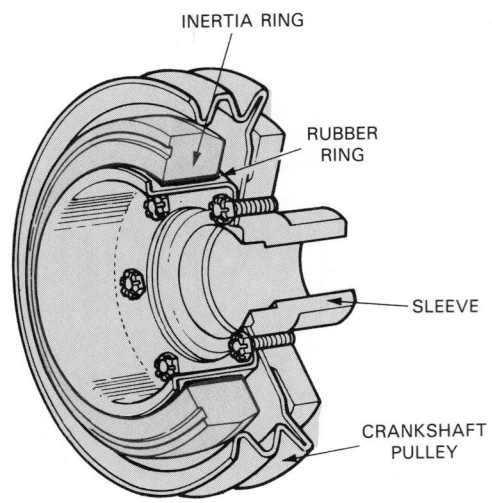

Fig. 15-2. Study construction of vibration damper. Rubber ring separates inertia ring and inner sleeve. This acts to deaden or cancel crankshaft harmonic vibration. (Chrysler)

is half as large as the cam gear. This results in the desired 2:1 reduction.

Timing marks on the two gears show the mechanic how to install the gears properly. Refer to Fig. 15-3. The marks may be circles, indentations, or lines on the gears. The timing marks must line up for the camshaft to be in time with the crankshaft.

Timing gears are commonly used on heavy-duty applications (taxi cabs or trucks). They are very dependable and long-lasting. However, they are noisier than

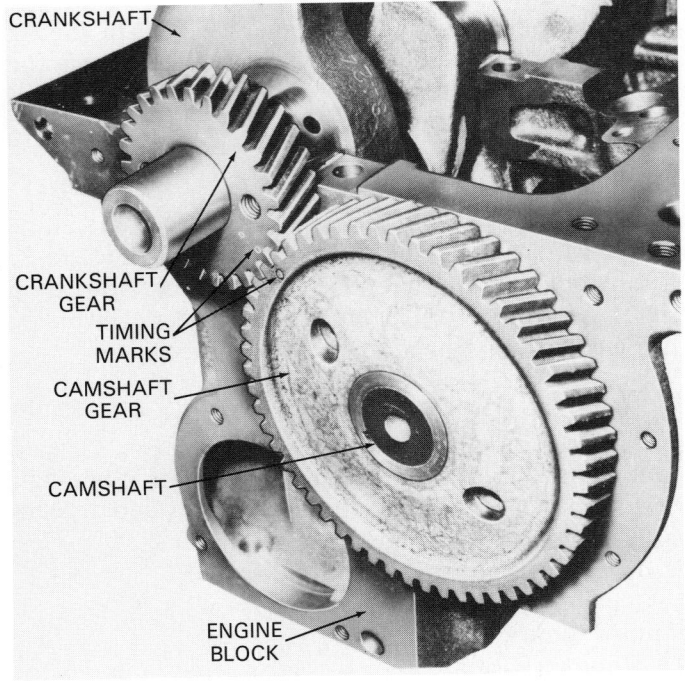

Fig. 15-3. Timing gear setup is very dependable. Crank gear turns cam gear at one-half crank speed. Timing marks allow proper assembly of gears. (Chevrolet)

a chain or belt drive. Gears are primarily used in cam-in-block engines where the crank is close to the cam.

Timing chain and sprockets

A *timing chain* and *sprockets* can also be used to turn the camshaft. See Fig. 15-4. This is the most common type of cam drive on cam-in-block engines. It may also be used in OHC engines.

A *crank sprocket* is keyed to the crank snout. A larger *cam sprocket,* with either metal or plastic teeth, bolts to the camshaft. The *timing chain* transfers power from the crank sprocket to the cam sprocket.

Like timing gears, the chain sprockets have timing marks. The marks must line up to place the camshaft in time with the crankshaft.

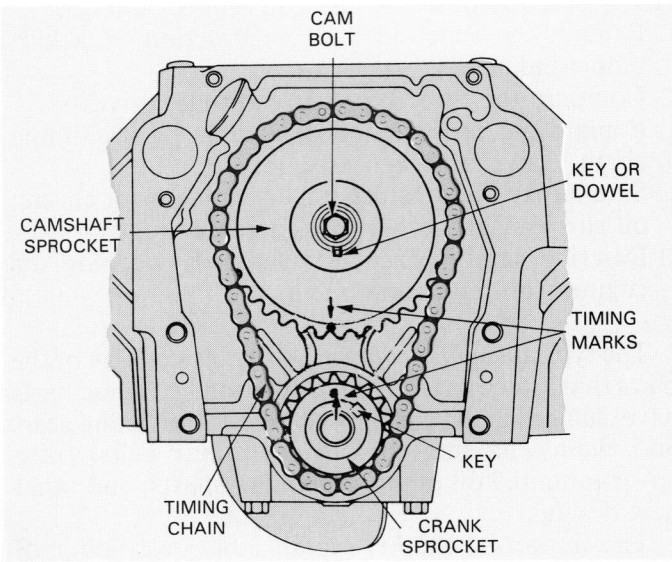

Fig. 15-4. Timing chain setup is very common. Study part names. (Buick)

A *chain guide* may be needed to prevent *chain slap* (slack lets chain flap back and forth). Fig. 15-5 shows a timing chain using chain guides. The guides have a metal body with either a plastic or Teflon® face. This allows the chain to slide on the guide with minimum friction and wear.

A *chain tensioner* may be used to take up slack (play) as the chain and sprockets wear. One is shown in Fig. 15-5. It is usually a spring-loaded plastic or fiber block. The spring pushes the block outward, keeping a constant tension on the chain.

A chain type cam drive for an OHC engine commonly uses guides and sometimes a tensioner. Refer to Fig. 15-6 for a front view of this setup.

Auxiliary chain

An *auxiliary chain* may be used to drive the engine oil pump, balancer shafts, and other units on the engine. Figs. 15-6 and 15-7 show two examples.

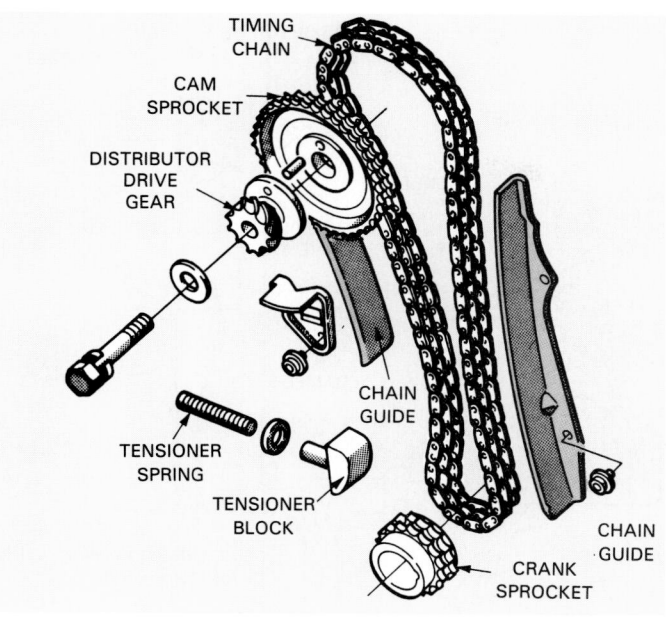

Fig. 15-5. OHC timing chain assembly normally uses chain guides and sometimes a tensioner. (Chrysler)

An auxiliary chain is driven by an extra sprocket, usually placed in front of the crankshaft timing chain sprocket. Do NOT confuse an auxiliary chain with a timing chain.

Engine front cover construction

An *engine front cover,* also called *timing cover,* encloses the timing chain or gear mechanism. As pictured in Fig. 15-8, it bolts to the front of the engine block. The cover holds the crankshaft oil seal, timing pointer, or probe holder (discussed in Chapter 32), and other parts.

The purpose of the front cover is to prevent oil leakage out the front of the engine. A gasket seals the mating surfaces between the cover and block.

A *front oil seal* prevents oil leakage between the crankshaft and cover. The seal is press-fit in the cover.

An engine front cover is commonly made of thin, stamped steel or cast aluminum. Sometimes, the water pump bolts on the front cover. The oil pump may also be housed in the cover, Fig. 15-9.

Fig. 15-6. Note dual timing chains and auxiliary chain. Chain guides are used on timing chains, and a tensioner on the auxiliary chain. (Cadillac)

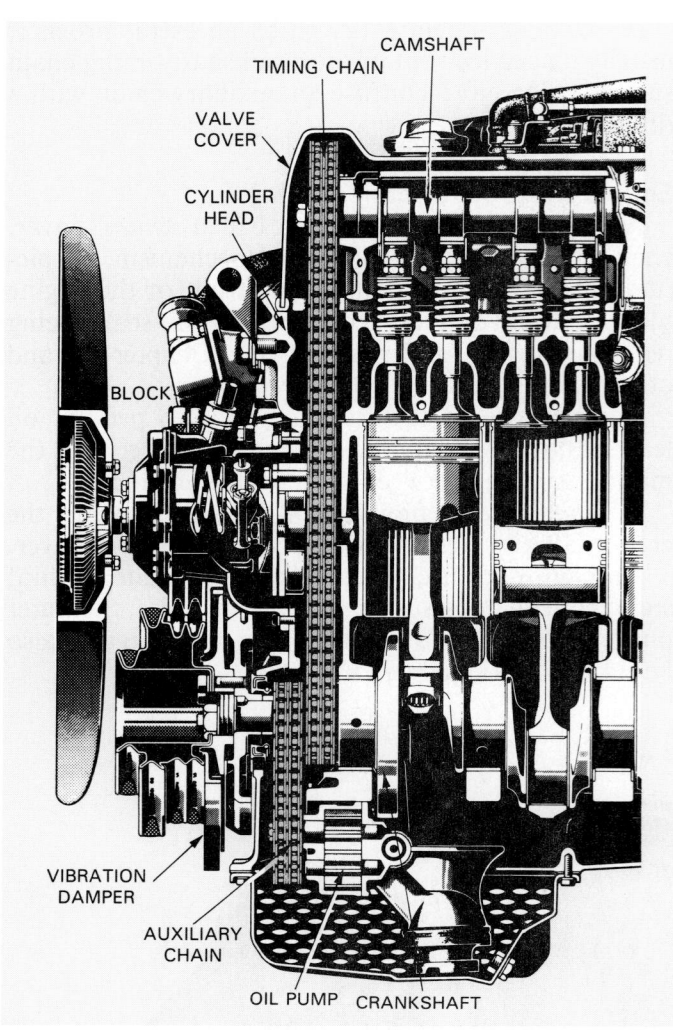

Fig. 15-7. Side view of a diesel engine using both a timing chain and an auxiliary drive chain. (Mercedes Benz)

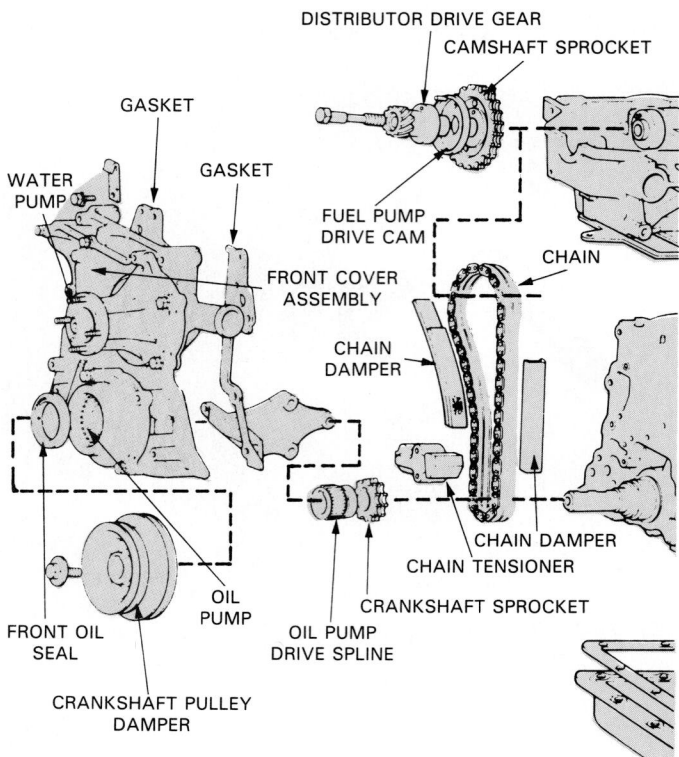

Fig. 15-9. This front cover houses engine oil pump and water pump. Drive spline in front of crank sprocket powers oil pump. Conventional V-belt drives water pump. (Honda)

Oil slinger

An *oil slinger* is a washer-shaped part that fits in front of the crankshaft sprocket. Its job is to spray oil on the timing chain to prevent wear. It also helps prevent

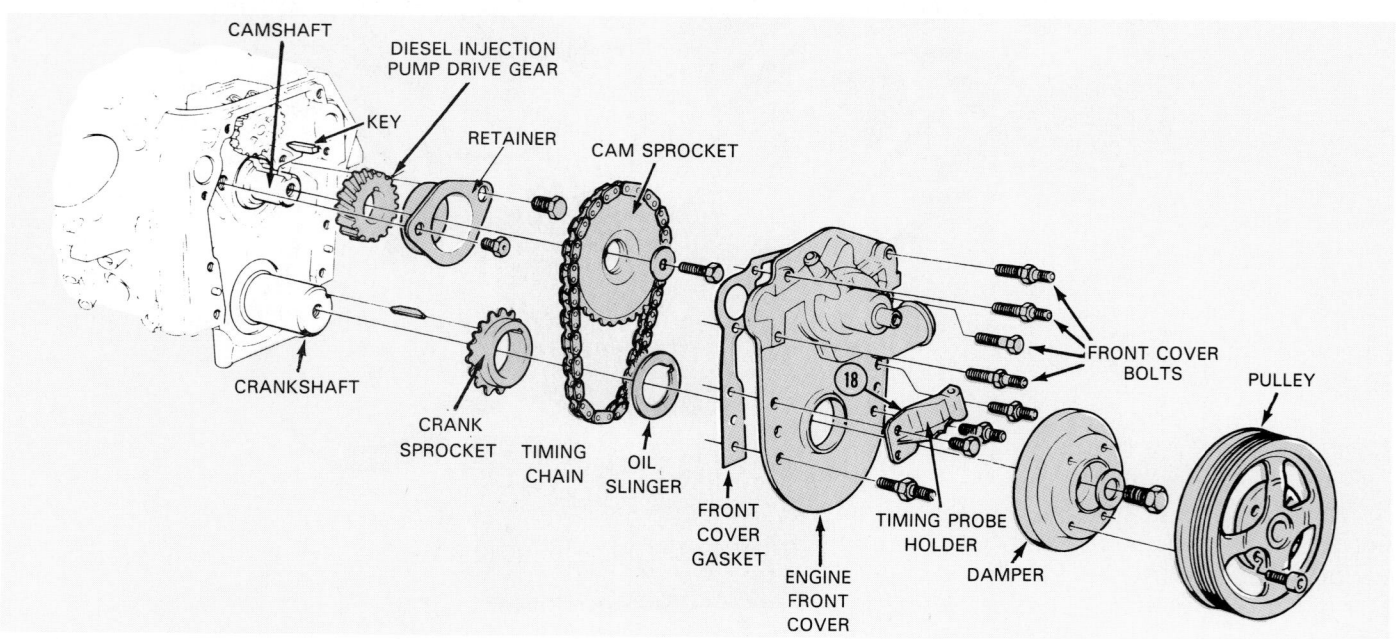

Fig. 15-8. Study construction of front cover and related parts. In particular, note oil slinger that installs in front of crank sprocket and diesel injection pump drive gear. (Buick)

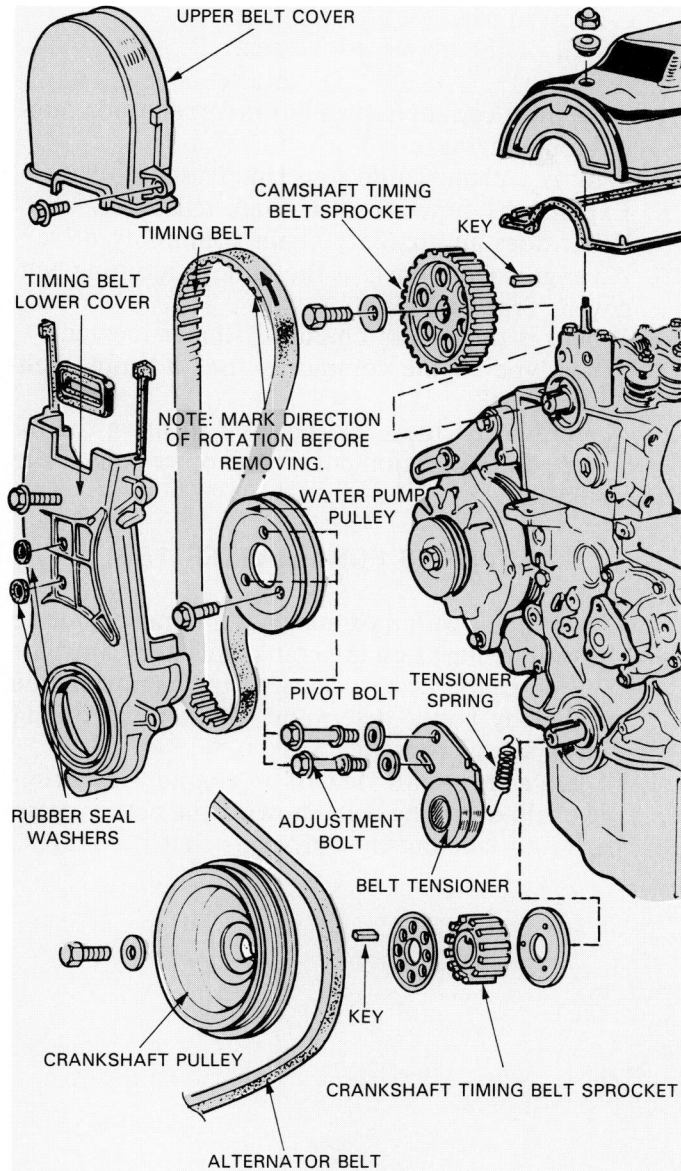

Fig. 15-10. Study parts that install on front of this OHC engine. Cogged sprockets are used with cam timing belt. V-belt operates in crank pulley. Belt cover surrounds timing belt and sprockets. (Honda)

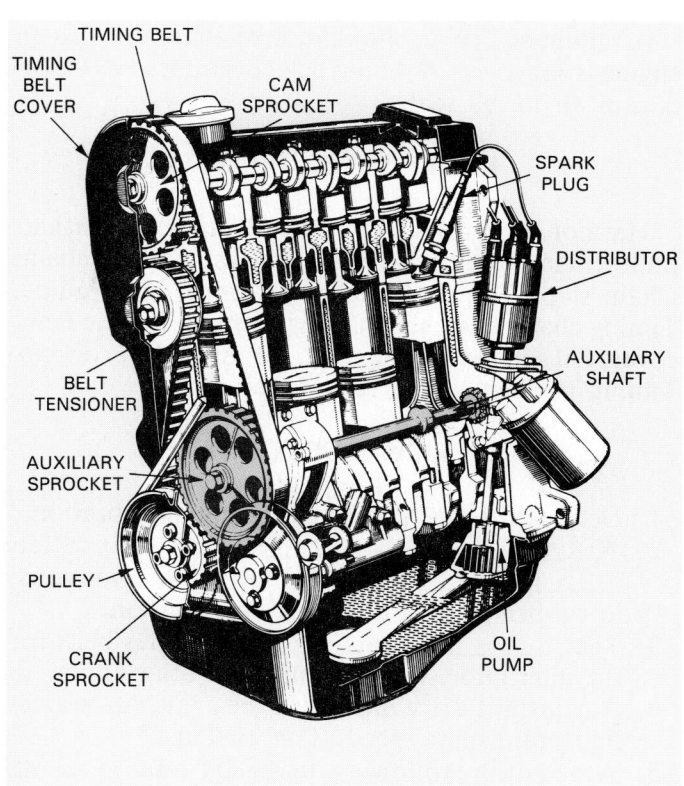

Fig. 15-11. Cutaway view of OHC engine using an auxiliary drive shaft. Auxiliary sprocket turns shaft. Shaft has small gear for operating ignition distributor and oil pump. (Chrysler)

oil from leaking out the front seal.

When the engine is running, oil squirts out of the front main bearing. Centrifugal force on the spinning slinger throws oil outward, lubricating the timing chain or gears. See Fig. 15-8.

Timing belt mechanism

A *timing belt mechanism* basically consists of a crank sprocket, cam sprocket, timing belt, and a belt tensioner. It is used to drive the camshaft on modern OHC engines. Look at Fig. 15-10.

A *timing belt* provides a very smooth and accurate method of turning the camshaft. The timing belt and the sprockets have COGGED (square) teeth that prevent belt slippage.

The *timing belt sprockets* are usually made of cast iron or aluminum, Fig. 15-10. A crank sprocket is keyed to the crankshaft snout, like a chain sprocket. The cam sprocket normally bolts to the front of the camshaft. A dowel pin may be used to position the cam sprocket correctly.

Belt sprockets have timing marks, just like timing gears and chain sprockets. The marks must be aligned with specific points on the engine. This will properly time the opening of the engine valves.

A *belt tensioner* is a spring-loaded wheel that keeps the timing belt tight on its sprockets. Illustrated in Fig. 15-11, the tensioner pushes inward on the back of the belt. This prevents the belt teeth from slipping on the sprocket teeth. It also keeps the belt firmly seated on the sprockets.

The tensioner wheel is mounted on an antifriction bearing. The bearing is *permanently sealed* (filled with grease and sealed at factory).

The timing belt may also be used to drive the oil pump, diesel injection pump, and ignition distributor. Fig. 15-11 shows an engine in which the timing belt drives an auxiliary shaft. The shaft is then used to operate the distributor and oil pump.

A *timing belt cover* simply protects the belt from damage and the technician from injury. It is made from sheet metal or plastic. See Figs. 15-10 and 15-11.

A timing belt cover should not be confused with an engine front cover. A timing belt cover does NOT contain oil or an oil seal.

KNOW THESE TERMS

Harmonic vibration, Vibration damper, Crankshaft pulley, Timing gears, Timing marks, Timing chain, Chain slap, Timing sprockets, Timing chain guide, Timing chain tensioner, Auxiliary chain, Engine front cover, Oil slinger, Timing belt, Timing belt sprockets, Timing belt tensioner, Timing belt cover.

REVIEW QUESTIONS

1. Define the term "crankshaft harmonic vibration."
2. A _____ _____ , also called _____ _____ is a heavy wheel mounted in rubber to control harmonic vibration.
3. The _____ _____ operates belts for the alternator, water pump, and other units.
4. A camshaft drive must turn the camshaft at one-half crankshaft speed. True or False?
5. Which of the following does NOT refer to timing gears?
   a. Used on heavy-duty applications.
   b. Dependable and long lasting.
   c. Very quiet.
   d. All of the above are correct.
6. A _____ _____ and set of _____ is the most common camshaft drive setup for cam-in-block engines.
7. Why is a chain guide sometimes used?
8. Explain the function of a chain tensioner.
9. What does an auxiliary chain commonly drive?
10. An engine front cover is the same as a timing belt cover. True or False?
11. Where is the timing chain oil slinger located?
12. What type engine commonly uses a timing belt mechanism?
13. A timing belt may also be used to drive the oil pump, diesel injection pump, and other units. True or False?

ACTIVITIES FOR CHAPTER 15

1. On an engine with the timing cover removed, locate the timing marks on the crankshaft and camshaft pulleys, gears, or sprockets. If the engine can be rotated by hand, determine whether the timing marks align properly.
2. Sketch a front-end view of an engine with a timing chain or timing belt, showing the belt or chain path and labeling the sprockets that it engages.

How many parts can you identify and explain on this engine? (Infiniti)

Engine Size and Performance Measurements

After studying this chapter, you will be able to:
- ☐ Describe engine size measurements based on bore, stroke, displacement, and number of cylinders.
- ☐ Explain engine compression ratio and how it affects engine performance.
- ☐ Explain engine torque and horsepower ratings.
- ☐ Describe the different methods used to measure and rate engine performance.
- ☐ Explain volumetric efficiency, thermal efficiency, mechanical efficiency, and total engine efficiency.
- ☐ Follow safe practices when making engine performance measurements.

Engine size and performance measurements are important to the technician. A shop manual will list many engine size and performance values for specific engines. You must be able to understand this information.

ENGINE SIZE MEASUREMENT

Engine size is determined by cylinder diameter, amount of piston travel on each stroke, and number of cylinders. Any of these variables can be changed to alter engine size. Engine size information is commonly used when ordering parts or when measuring wear during major engine repairs.

Bore and stroke

Cylinder bore is the diameter of the engine cylinder. See Fig. 16-1. It is measured across the cylinder, parallel with the top of the block. Cylinder bores vary in size from about 3 to 4 in. (76 to 102 mm).

Piston stroke is the distance the piston moves from TDC to BDC, Fig. 16-1. The amount of offset built into the crank journal or throw controls piston stroke. The stroke also varies from about 3 to 4 in. (76 to 102 mm).

A shop manual normally gives bore and stroke specs together. For instance, suppose a spec for bore and

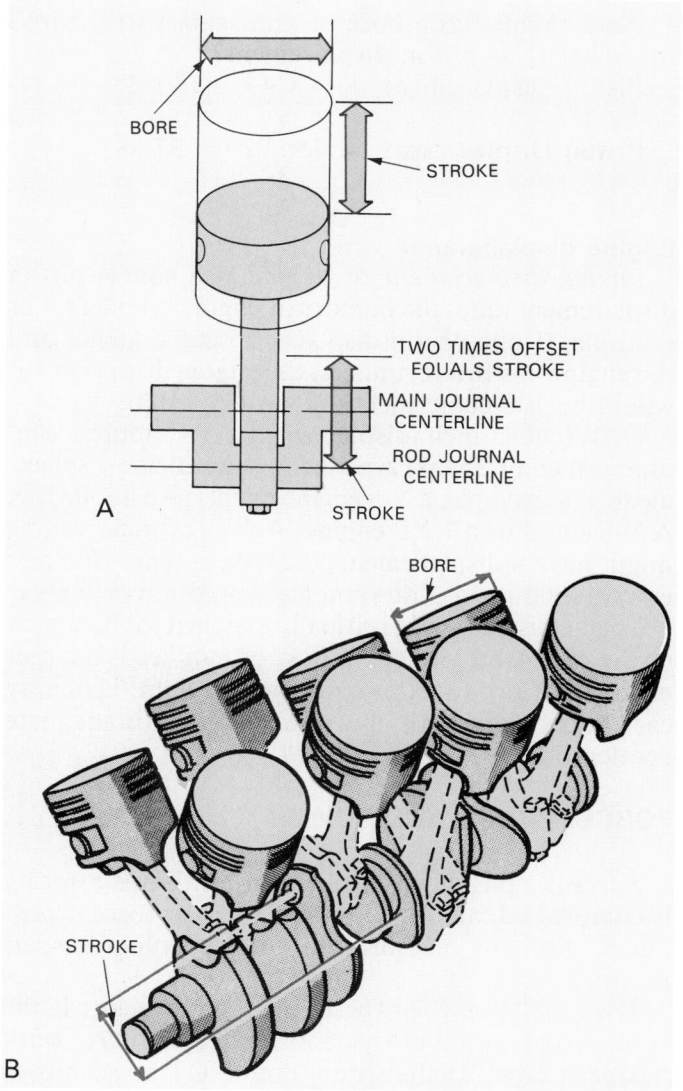

Fig. 16-1. A — Cylinder bore is measured across cylinder parallel with deck of block. Stroke is distance piston moves from BDC to TDC. Piston displacement is amount of volume piston would move in one upward stroke. B — Engine displacement is displacement for all pistons. (Ford)

stroke is given as 4.00 in. x 3.00 in. This means that the engine cylinder is 4 inches in diameter and the piston stroke is 3 inches. Bore is always the FIRST VALUE GIVEN and stroke the second.

Generally, a larger bore and stroke make an engine more powerful. It can pull in more fuel and air on each intake stroke. Then, more pressure is exerted on the head of the piston during the power stroke.

Piston displacement

Piston displacement is the volume the piston displaces (moves) from BDC to TDC. It is found by comparing cylinder diameter and piston stroke. A large cylinder diameter and large piston stroke would produce a larger piston displacement.

The formula for finding piston displacement is:

Piston Displacement =

$$\frac{\text{Bore squared x 3.14 x Stroke}}{4}$$

If an engine has a bore of 4 in. and a stroke of 3 in., what is its piston displacement?

$$\text{Piston Displacement} = \frac{4 \times 4 \times 3.14 \times 3}{4}$$

$$\text{Piston Displacement} = \frac{150.72}{4} = 37.68$$

Engine displacement

Engine displacement or *engine size* equals piston displacement times the number of engine cylinders. For example, if one piston displaces 25 cubic inches and the engine has four cylinders, the engine displacement would be 100 cubic inches (25 x 4 = 100).

CID (cubic inch displacement), CC (cubic centimeters) and L (liters) are used to state engine displacement. For example, a V-8 engine might have a 350 CID. A V-6 could be a 3.3 L engine. A four cylinder engine might have a displacement of 2300 cc. Since one liter equals 1000 cc, a 2 liter engine would have 2000 cc.

Engine displacement is usually matched to the weight of the car. A heavier car, truck, or van needs a larger engine that produces more power. A light, economy car only needs a small, low power engine for adequate acceleration.

FORCE, WORK, AND POWER

Force is a pushing or pulling action. When a spring is compressed, an outward movement or force is produced. Force is measured in pounds, kilograms, or newtons.

Work is done when force causes movement. If the compressed spring moves another engine part, work has been done. If the spring does NOT cause movement, no work has been done. Work is measured in foot-pounds, watts, or joules.

The formula for work is:

Work = distance moved x force applied.

If you use a hoist to lift a 400 lb. engine 3 ft. in the air, how much work has been done?

Work = 3 ft. x 400 lb.

= 1200 foot-pounds (ft.-lb.) of work.

Power is the rate or speed at which work is done. It is measured in foot-pounds per second or per minute. The metric unit for power is the watt or kilowatt.

High power output can do a large amount of work. Lower power can only do a small amount of work. The formula for power is:

$$\text{Power} = \frac{\text{Distance x Force}}{\text{Time in minutes}}$$

If an engine moves a 3000 lb. car 1000 feet in one minute, how much power is needed?

$$\text{Power} = \frac{1000 \times 3000}{1}$$

= 3,000,000 foot-pounds per minute.

COMPRESSION RATIO

Engine *compression ratio* compares cylinder volumes with the piston at TDC and BDC. Look at Fig. 16-2. An engine's compression ratio controls how tight the air-fuel mixture is squeezed on the compression stroke.

A compression ratio is given as two numbers. For example, an engine may have a compression ratio of 9:1 (9 to 1). This means the maximum cylinder volume

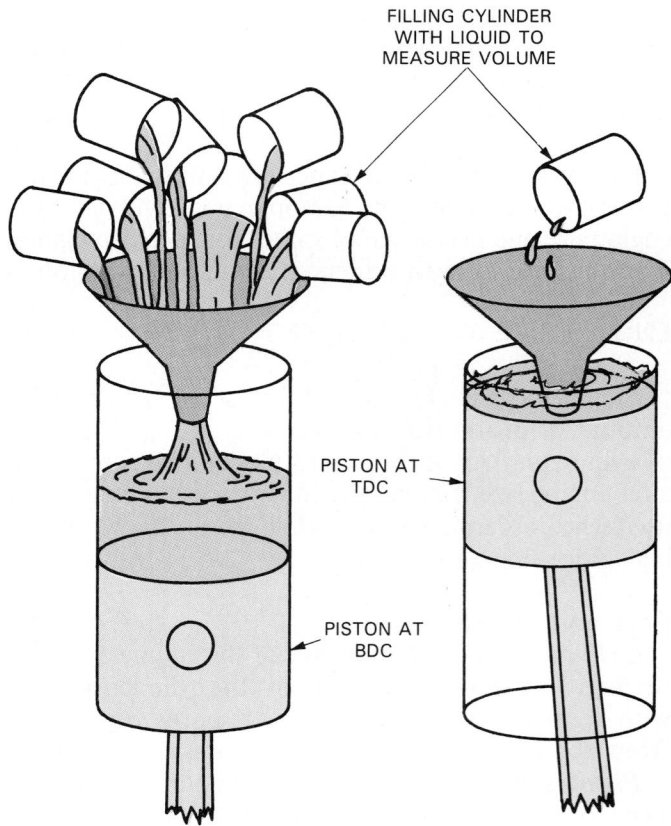

FILLING CYLINDER WITH LIQUID TO MEASURE VOLUME

PISTON AT TDC

PISTON AT BDC

Fig. 16-2. Compression ratio is comparison of cylinder volumes with piston at TDC and BDC. This engine has eight times the volume at BDC, producing 8:1 compression ratio.

is nine times as large as the minimum cylinder volume. At BDC a cylinder has maximum volume. Minimum cylinder volume occurs at TDC.

Fig. 16-3 illustrates two examples of compression ratio ratings. When the gasoline engine piston is at BDC, the cylinder volume is 40 cubic inches (0.65 L). When the piston slides to TDC, the volume reduces to five cubic inches (0.08 L). Dividing 40 by 5 (0.65 by 0.08), the compression ratio for this engine would be 8:1.

With the diesel (compression ignition) engine, BDC cylinder volume is 17 times as large as TDC cylinder volume. The compression ratio would then be 17:1.

Older engines designed for leaded gasoline had higher compression ratios. Up to a point, a high compression ratio increases engine fuel efficiency and power. However, it also causes higher exhaust emission levels.

Today's gasoline engines use a lower compression ratio (about 8 or 9 to 1). This allows the use of cleaner burning unleaded fuel. There is a slight reduction in engine power and efficiency, however.

Diesel engines have a very high compression ratio (17 to 25:1 typical). The diesel compresses the air in the cylinder hard enough for it to heat up and ignite the fuel.

Note! Automotive fuels and combustion will be explained in detail in the next chapter.

Compression pressure

Compression pressure is the amount of pressure produced in the engine cylinder on the compression stroke. Compression pressure is normally measured in pounds per square inch (psi) or kilopascals (kPa).

A gasoline engine may have compression pressure from 130 to 180 psi (896 to 1 240 kPa). A diesel engine has a much HIGHER compression pressure of about

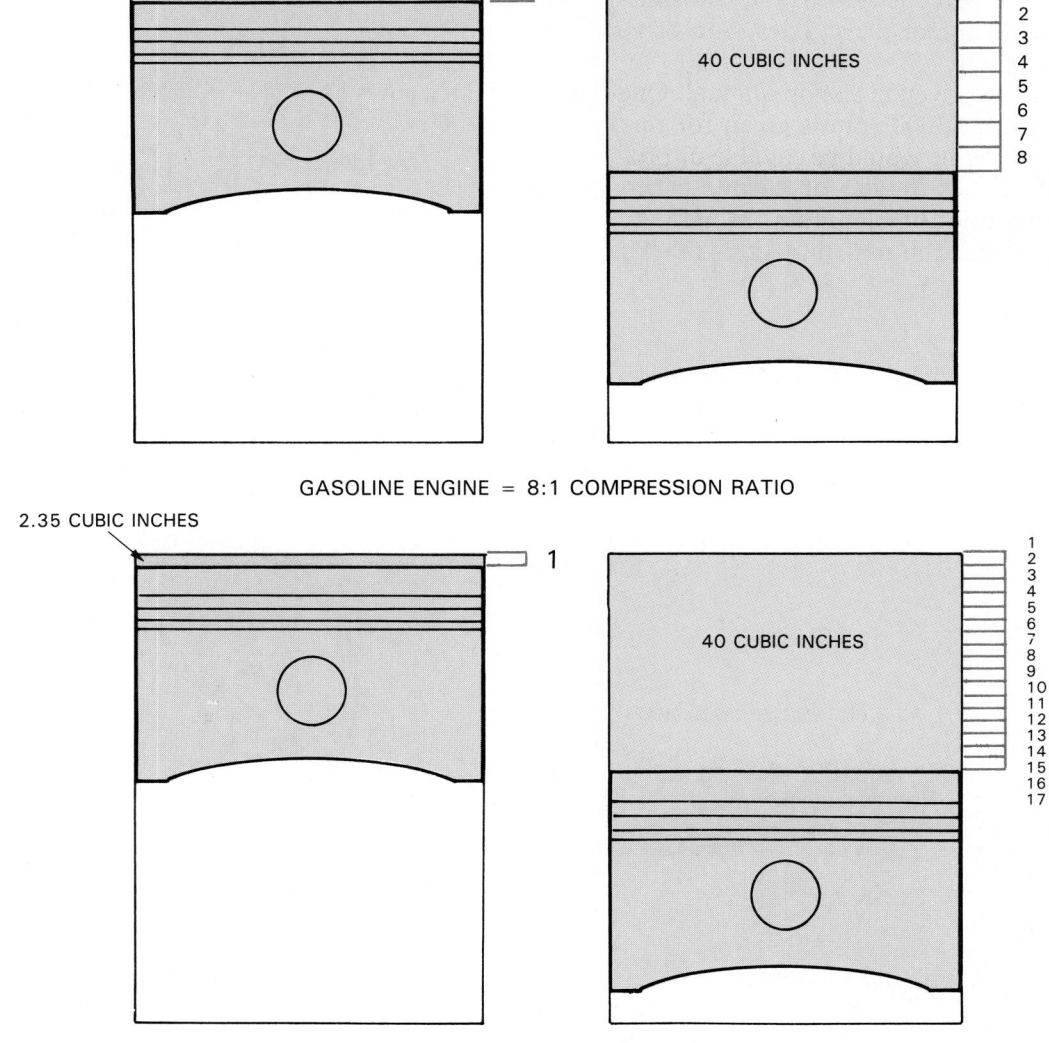

GASOLINE ENGINE = 8:1 COMPRESSION RATIO

DIESEL ENGINE = 17:1 COMPRESSION RATIO

Fig. 16-3. A diesel engine has a much higher compression ratio than a gasoline engine. A diesel must squeeze the fuel mixture very tight to cause combustion.

250 to 400 psi (1 723 to 2 756 kPa).

A *compression gauge* is used to measure compression stroke pressure. It is screwed into the spark plug, injector nozzle, or glow plug hole. The ignition or injection system is disabled. Then, the engine is cranked over with the starting motor. The gauge will read compression stroke pressure.

Discussed in later chapters, compression stroke pressure is an indicator of engine condition. If it is low, something is allowing air to leak out of the cylinder. The engine might have bad rings, burned valves, or a blown head gasket.

ENGINE TORQUE

Torque is a turning or twisting force. When you turn the car's steering wheel, you have applied torque to the steering wheel.

Engine torque is a rating of the turning force at the engine crankshaft. When combustion pressure pushes the piston down, a strong rotating force is applied to the crank. This turning force is sent to the transmission or transaxle, drive line or drive axles, and drive wheels, propelling the car.

Engine torque specs are given in a shop manual. One example, 78 ft.-lb. @ (at) 3000 rpm is given for one particular engine. This engine would be capable of producing a maximum of 78 ft.-lb. of torque when operating at 3000 revolutions per minute. In metrics, engine torque is often stated in newton-meters (N·m).

HORSEPOWER

Horsepower, abbreviated hp, is a measure of an engine's ability to perform work. At one time, one horsepower was the average strength of a horse, Fig. 16-4. A 300 hp engine could, theoretically, do the work of 300 horses.

In metric, horsepower is measured in kilowatts. Kilowatts is abbreviated kW.

One horsepower equals 33,000 ft.-lb. of work per minute. To find engine hp, use the following formula:

$$hp = \frac{Distance\ (ft.)\ x\ Weight\ (lb.)}{33,000} \text{ or } \frac{Work\ (ft.\text{-}lb.)}{33,000}$$

For a small engine to lift 500 pounds a distance of 700 feet in one minute, about how much horsepower would be needed? To calculate, apply these values to the formula:

$$hp = \frac{500\ Pounds\ x\ 700\ Feet}{33,000} = 10.6\ Horsepower$$

Factory horsepower ratings

Automobile makers rate engine hp output at a specific engine rpm. For instance, a high performance turbocharged engine might be rated at 300 hp at 5000 rpm. This engine power rating is normally stated in a service manual. There are several different methods of calculating engine horsepower.

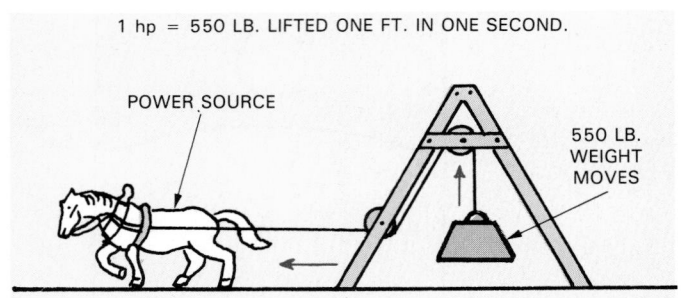

Fig. 16-4. *This represents production of one hp. In automotive work, one hp equals 33,000 lbs. lifted one ft. in one minute.*

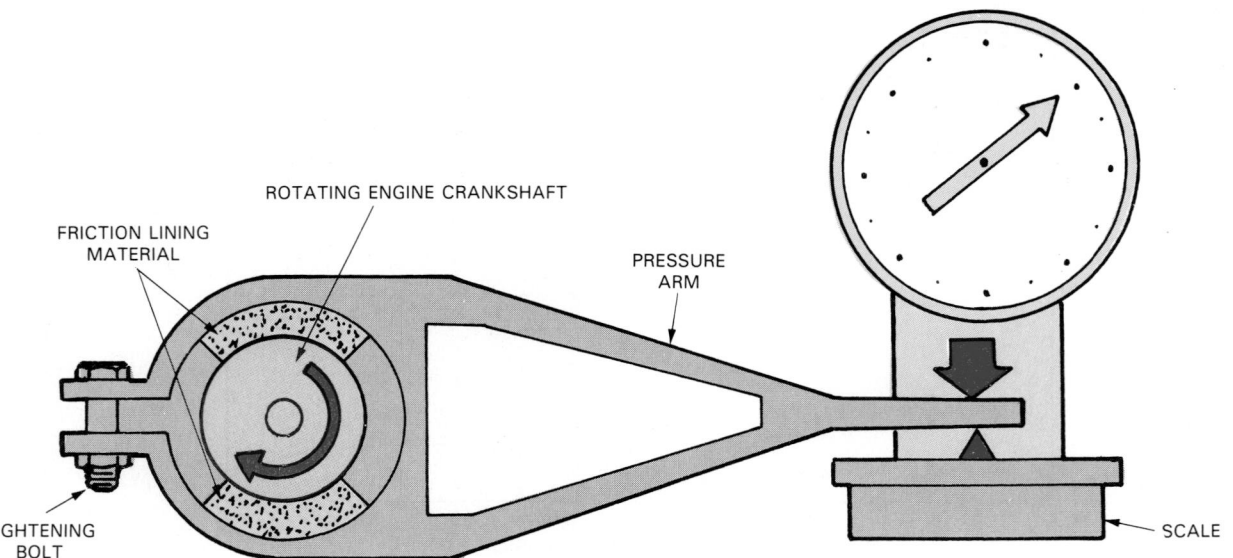

Fig. 16-5. *Prony brake will measure engine brake horsepower. Brake is applied to engine crankshaft. Amount of needle deflection can be used to find horsepower.*

Brake horsepower (bhp) measures the usable hp at the engine crankshaft. Shown in Fig. 16-5, a prony brake was first used to measure bhp. The engine spun the prony brake while the braking mechanism was applied. The resulting amount of pointer deflection could then be used to find brake horsepower.

An **engine dynamometer** (dyno) is used to measure the brake hp of modern car engines. Refer to Fig. 16-6. It functions in much the same way as a prony brake. Either an electric motor or fluid coupling is used to place a drag on the engine crankshaft. Then, power output can be determined.

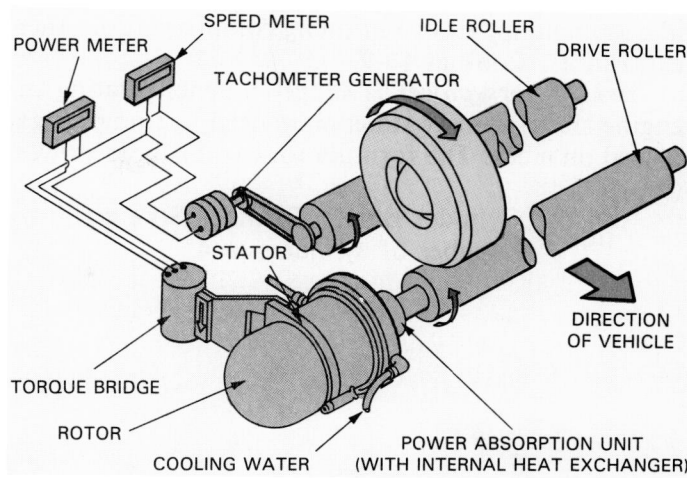

Fig. 16-7. Chassis dynamometer measures turning power at car's drive wheels. This accounts for any power consumed by driveline. (Clayton)

Fig. 16-6. Technician is using engine dynamometer and elaborate computer system to monitor engine performance. Dyno loads engine to simulate driving conditions while monitoring hp output and numerous other engine functions. (AC Spark Plug)

A **chassis dynamometer** measures the horsepower delivered to the car's drive wheels. See Fig. 16-7. It indicates the amount of horsepower available to propel the car.

Indicated horsepower (ihp) refers to the amount of power or pressure formed in the engine combustion chambers. A special pressure-sensing device is placed in the cylinder. The pressure readings are used to find indicated hp.

Frictional horsepower (fhp) is the power needed to overcome engine friction. It is a measure of the resistance to movement between engine parts.

Frictional hp is POWER LOST to friction. It reduces the amount of power left to propel the car.

Net horsepower is the maximum power developed when an engine is loaded down with all accessories (alternator, water pump, fuel pump, air injection pump, air conditioning, power steering pump). It is the amount of useful power with the engine installed in the vehicle. Net hp indicates the amount of power available to move the car. See Fig. 16-8.

Gross horsepower (ghp) is similar to net hp, but it is the engine power available with only basic accessories installed (alternator, water pump). Gross hp does NOT include the power lost to the power steering pump, air

Fig. 16-8. Net horsepower is available hp with engine operating all accessories such as air conditioning compressor, power steering pump, alternator, and water pump. (Chevrolet)

injection pump, air conditioning compressor, or other extra units. Look at 16-9.

Taxable horsepower is simply a general rating of engine size. In many states, it is used to find the tax placed on a car. The formula for taxable horsepower (thp) is:

$$\text{thp} = \frac{\text{Cylinder Bore x Cylinder Bore x}}{\text{Number of cylinders x .4}}$$

Fig. 16-9. Gross horsepower is similar to net hp rating. It does not include power lost to unneeded accessories. (Chevrolet)

ENGINE EFFICIENCY

Engine efficiency is the ratio of power produced by the engine (brake horsepower) and the power supplied to the engine (heat content of fuel). By comparing fuel consumption to engine power output, you can find engine efficiency.

If all of the heat energy in the fuel were converted into useful work, the engine would be 100 percent efficient. This much efficiency is not possible with a piston engine. Modern piston engines are only about 20 percent efficient.

Fig. 16-10 illustrates how the heat energy of the fuel is used by a piston engine. About 70 percent of the fuel's heat energy enters the cooling and exhaust systems. This leaves very LITTLE HEAT ENERGY to produce pressure on the engine pistons.

Volumetric efficiency

Volumetric efficiency is the ratio of actual air drawn into the cylinder and the maximum possible amount of air that could enter the cylinder. It refers to how well an engine can breathe on its intake stroke.

If volumetric efficiency were 100 percent, the cylinder would completely fill with air on the intake

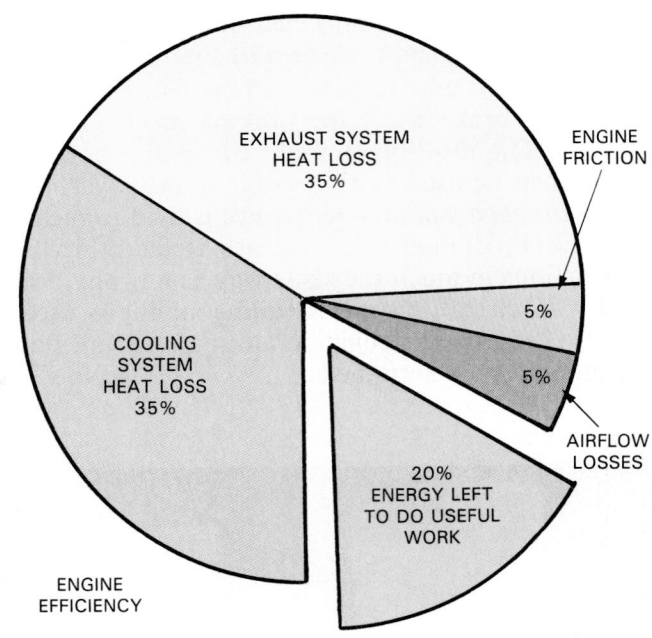

Fig. 16-10. Pie chart shows how fuel's heat energy is used by piston engine. Note that most of the heat energy is wasted.

stroke. Engines are only capable of about 80 to 90 percent volumetric efficiency. Restrictions in the ports and around the valves limit airflow.

High volumetric efficiency INCREASES ENGINE POWER because more fuel and air can be burned in the combustion chambers.

The formula for volumetric efficiency is:

Volumetric Efficiency =

$$\frac{\text{Actual volume of air taken into cylinder}}{\text{Maximum possible volume in engine cylinder}}$$

Mechanical efficiency

Mechanical efficiency compares brake hp and indicated hp. It is a measurement of mechanical friction. Remember that ihp equals the theoretical power produced by combustion. Brake hp is the actual power at the engine crankshaft. The difference between the two is due to frictional losses.

Mechanical efficiency of around 70 to 80 percent is normal. This means that about 20 to 30 percent of the engine's power is lost to friction (frictional hp loss). The friction between the piston rings and cylinder walls accounts for most of this loss.

Thermal efficiency

Thermal efficiency is heat efficiency found by comparing fuel burned and horsepower output. It indicates how well an engine can use the fuel's heat energy. Thermal efficiency measures the amount of heat energy converted into crankshaft rotation.

A gallon of gasoline, for example, has about 19,000 Btu (British thermal units) of heat energy. One horsepower equals about 42.4 Btu of heat energy per minute. With this information, you can find engine thermal efficiency.

Thermal efficiency =

$$\frac{\text{Brake hp} \times 42.2 \text{ Btu minute}}{19,000 \text{ Btu/gallon} \times \text{gallons per minute}}$$

Generally, engine thermal efficiency is around 20 to 30 percent. The rest of the heat energy is absorbed by the metal parts of the engine or blown out the exhaust.

KNOW THESE TERMS

Cylinder bore, Piston stroke, Displacement, CID, Force, Work, Power, Compression ratio, Compression pressure, Engine torque, Horsepower, bhp, Dyno, ihp, fhp, Net hp, Gross hp, Taxable hp, Engine efficiency, Volumetric efficiency, Mechanical efficiency, Thermal efficiency.

REVIEW QUESTIONS

1. Engine size is determined by cylinder _____ , amount of _____ _____ on each stroke, and _____ of _____ .
2. Cylinder bore is measured across the cylinder, parallel with the top of the block. True or False?
3. Piston stroke is the distance the piston moves during a complete four-stroke cycle. True or False?
4. _____ _____ is the volume the piston moves from BDC to TDC.
5. If an engine has a bore of 3.5 in. and a stroke of 3 in., what is the piston displacement?
6. Define the term "engine displacement."

7. Explain the difference between force, work, and power.
8. Which of the following would NOT be a compression ratio for a car engine?
   a. 2:1
   b. 8:1
   c. 17:1
   d. All of the above are correct.
9. A gasoline engine may produce a compression pressure of approximately _____ to _____ psi (_____ to _____ kPa).
10. A diesel engine can produce a compression pressure of about _____ to _____ psi (_____ to _____ kPa).
11. What is engine torque?
12. Explain the term "horsepower."
13. The ratio of actual air drawn into an engine to the maximum possible air that could enter the engine is called _____ _____ .

ACTIVITIES FOR CHAPTER 16

1. Use a compression gauge to measure the compression of each cylinder of an engine. Check your findings against the specifications for that engine. Are all the readings "in spec," or do one or more cylinders read high or low?
2. Convert your compression readings from pounds per square inch to kilopascals, or vice versa. Multiply psi readings by 6.895 to find kPa; divide kPa readings by 6.895 to find psi.

Aerodynamic body designs increase vehicle fuel economy. The vehicle must pass through air, which is actually a fluid by nature. The aerodynamic design reduces drag. (Buick)

Automotive Fuels, Gasoline and Diesel Combustion

After studying this chapter, you will be able to:
☐ Summarize how crude oil is converted into gasoline, diesel fuel, LP-gas, and other products.
☐ Describe properties of gasoline and diesel fuel.
☐ Explain octane and cetane ratings.
☐ Describe normal and abnormal combustion of gasoline and diesel fuel.
☐ Summarize the properties of alternate fuels.

A car engine burns a fuel as a source of energy. Various types of fuel will burn in an engine: gasoline, diesel oil, gasohol, alcohol, LP-gas, and other alternate fuels. As an automotive technician, you must understand how fuel burns inside an engine. Combustion (burning) is a primary factor controlling gas mileage, power, emissions, and the service life of an engine.

PETROLEUM (CRUDE OIL)

Petroleum, also called *crude oil,* is oil taken directly out of the ground. It is used to make gasoline, diesel oil, liquified petroleum gas, and many other nonfuel materials. Fig. 17-1 shows some of the products made out of petroleum.

Natural crude oil is a mixture of semisolids (neither solid nor liquid), liquids, and gases. Chemically, crude oil consists of highly flammable hydrocarbons.

Hydrocarbons are chemical mixtures of about 12 percent hydrogen (light gas vapor) and 82 percent carbon (heavy black solid). Crude oil also contains sulfur, nitrogen, metals, and salt water that must be removed.

Processing crude oil

Oil deposits are hidden inside the earth. Oil companies perform *exploration tests* (siesmic studies, surface mapping, test drilling), to find oil.

After finding where oil might be located, a drill crew bores a hole thousands of feet into the ground. A huge steel derrick is used for the drilling operation. It has a cutting bit capable of passing through dirt, sand, and rock. See Fig. 17-2.

Once the oil deposit has been reached, the oil is pumped to the surface.

Next, oil is sent to the refinery. The *refinery* converts the crude oil into more useful substances.

Distillation is the first process. It uses a *fractionating tower* to break the crude oil down into different parts or fractions (LP-gas, gasoline, kerosene, fuel oil, lubricating oils). Look at Fig. 17-3. After distillation, other processes purify these products.

GASOLINE

Gasoline is the most common type of automotive fuel. It is an abundant and highly flammable part of crude oil. Extra chemicals, called *additives* (lead, detergents, antioxidants, etc.), are mixed into gasoline to improve its operating characteristics.

Antiknock additives, usually tetraethyl lead (TEL) or tetramethyl lead (TML), slow down the ignition and burning of gasoline. This helps prevent engine *ping* or *knock* (knocking sound produced by abnormal and excessively rapid combustion).

Leaded and unleaded gasoline

Gasoline with lead antiknock additives is called "leaded." The lead allows a higher engine compression ratio without the fuel igniting prematurely.

Leaded gasoline is designed for older cars with few or no emission controls. They were not required to pass strict air pollution standards.

Note! The lead additives in gasoline also act as a LUBRICANT. The lead coats the face of the valves and seats in the engine, helping to prevent wear.

Unleaded gasoline, also called *no-lead* or *lead-free,* does NOT contain lead antiknock additives. Congress passed laws making cars meet strict emission levels. As

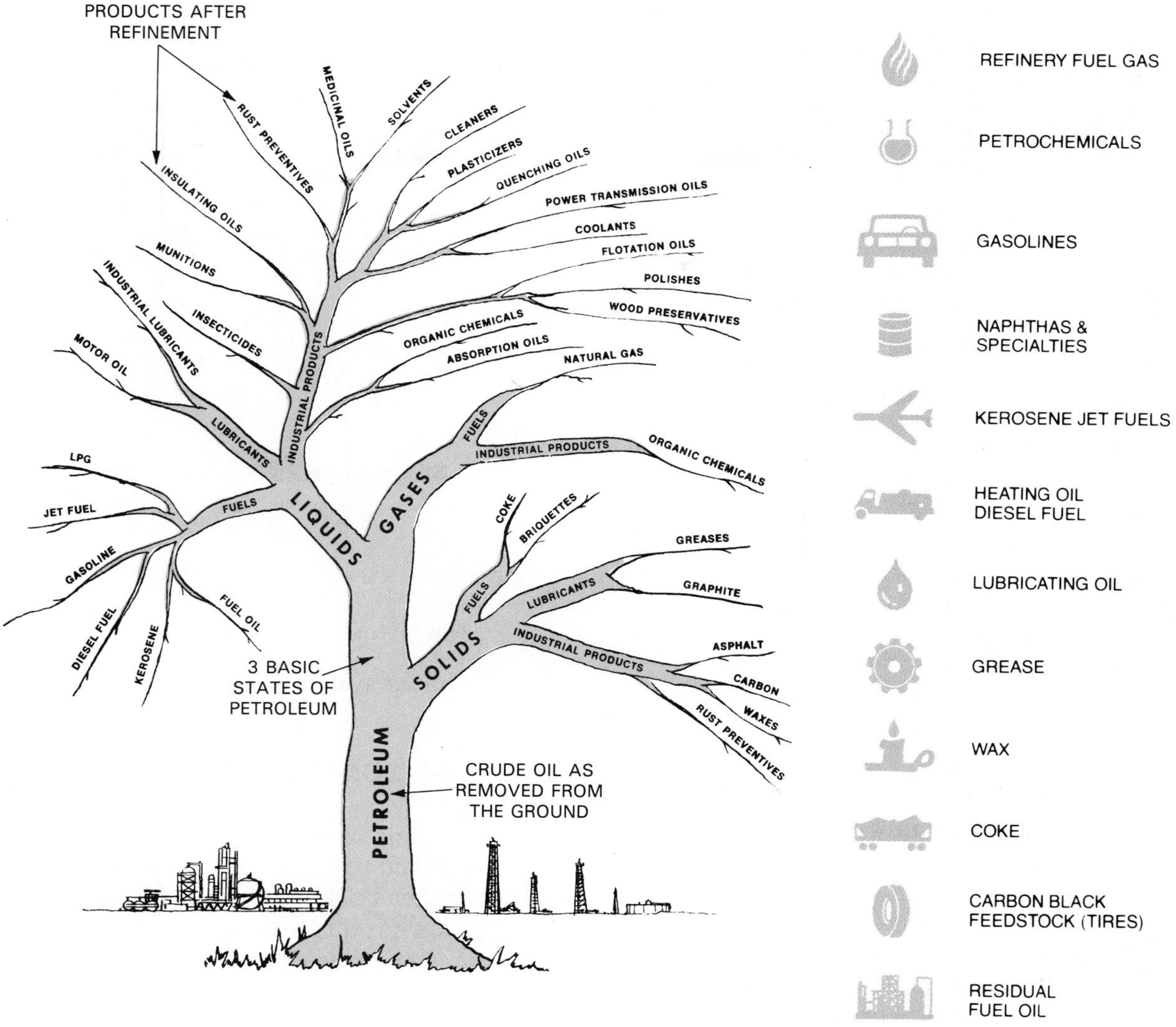

PRODUCTS AFTER
REFINEMENT

RUST PREVENTIVES

MEDICINAL OILS

SOLVENTS

CLEANERS

PLASTICIZERS

QUENCHING OILS

POWER TRANSMISSION OILS

INSULATING OILS

COOLANTS

FLOTATION OILS

POLISHES

MUNITIONS

WOOD PRESERVATIVES

INDUSTRIAL LUBRICANTS

INSECTICIDES

ORGANIC CHEMICALS

ABSORPTION OILS

MOTOR OIL

NATURAL GAS

INDUSTRIAL PRODUCTS

INDUSTRIAL PRODUCTS

ORGANIC CHEMICALS

LUBRICANTS

LPG

FUELS

COKE

BRIQUETTES

GREASES

JET FUEL

GRAPHITE

FUELS

FUELS

LUBRICANTS

GASOLINE

ASPHALT

FUEL OIL

INDUSTRIAL PRODUCTS

CARBON

DIESEL FUEL

WAXES

KEROSENE

RUST PREVENTIVES

LIQUIDS

GASES

SOLIDS

3 BASIC
STATES OF
PETROLEUM

PETROLEUM

CRUDE OIL AS
REMOVED FROM
THE GROUND

REFINERY FUEL GAS

PETROCHEMICALS

GASOLINES

NAPHTHAS &
SPECIALTIES

KEROSENE JET FUELS

HEATING OIL
DIESEL FUEL

LUBRICATING OIL

GREASE

WAX

COKE

CARBON BLACK
FEEDSTOCK (TIRES)

RESIDUAL
FUEL OIL

Fig. 17-1. Petroleum is used to make many products besides gasoline and diesel fuel. (Gulf Oil Corp. and Ethyl Corp.)

Fig. 17-2. Large cutter can penetrate dirt and rock to drill hole deep into ground. When found, oil can be pumped to surface. (Texaco)

a result, auto makers began using catalytic converters (device in exhaust system for treating exhaust emissions) and unleaded fuel.

Lead additives, gradually being discontinued, cannot be used in a car with a catalytic converter. The lead will coat the inside of the converter and prevent it from working.

If unleaded fuel is used in a car designed for leaded fuel, it can increase valve and seat wear. Use only the type of fuel recommended by the auto maker.

Gasoline octane ratings

The *octane rating* of gasoline is a measurement of the fuel's ability to resist knock or ping. A high octane rating indicates the fuel will NOT knock or ping easily. It should be used in a high compression or turbocharged engine. A low octane gasoline is suitable for a low compression engine.

Octane numbers give the antiknock value of gasoline. A high octane number (91, for example) will resist ping better than gasoline with a low octane number (87, for

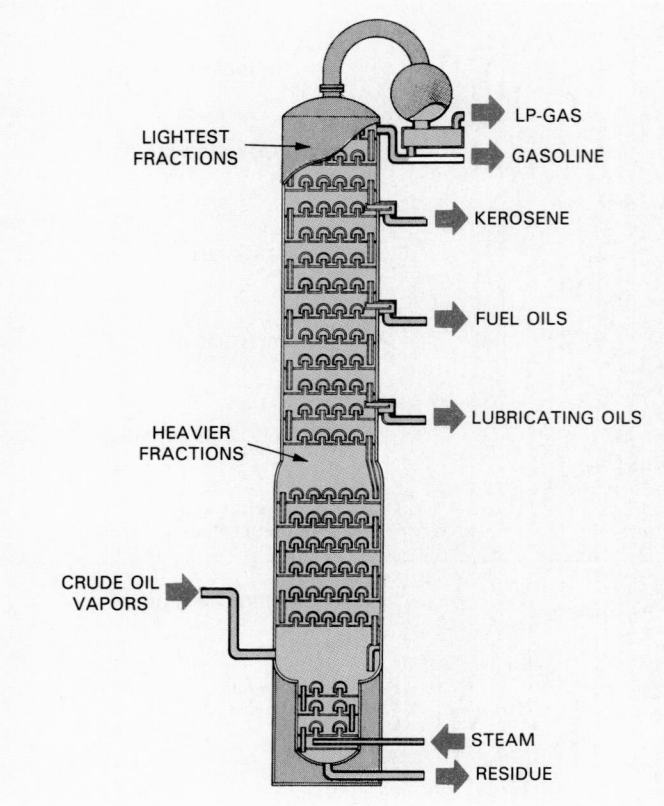

Fig. 17-3. Fractionating tower allows crude oil vapors to condense and separate into trays. (Ford Motor Co.)

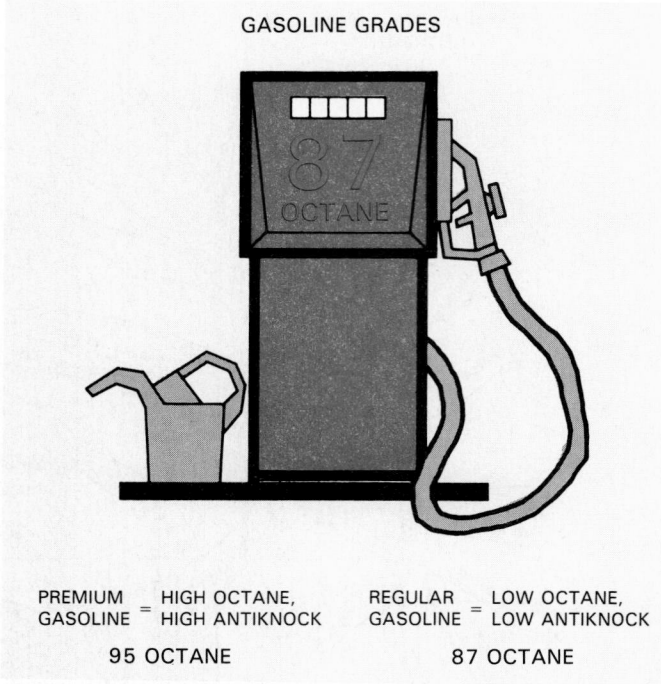

Fig. 17-4. Gasoline grade indicates antiknock value of gasoline.

example). Auto makers recommend an octane number rating for their engines.

Octane numbers are given on the side of the gas station pump. The owner's manual will give the octane number recommended for the car's engine. Use an octane rating as high or higher than the auto maker's recommendations. Look at Fig. 17-4.

Fig. 17-5 summarizes several factors that control engine octane requirements.

GASOLINE COMBUSTION

For gasoline or any other fuel to burn properly, it must be mixed with the right amount of air. The mixture must then be compressed and ignited. The resulting combustion produces heat, expansion of gases, and pressure. The pressure pushes down on the piston to turn the crankshaft. Refer to Fig. 17-6.

Normal gasoline combustion

Normal gasoline combustion occurs when the spark plug ignites the fuel and burning progresses smoothly through the fuel mixture. Maximum cylinder pressure should be produced a few degrees of crank rotation after piston TDC on the power stroke.

OCTANE REQUIREMENT FACTORS	
Octane number requirement tends to go UP when: 1. Ignition timing is advanced. 2. Air density rises due to supercharging, a larger throttle opening, or higher barometric pressures. 3. Humidity or moisture content of air decreases. 4. Inlet air temperature goes up. 5. Lean fuel-air ratios. 6. Compression ratio is increased. 7. Coolant temperature is raised. 8. Antifreeze (glycol) engine coolant is used. 9. Combustion chamber design provides little or no quench area. 10. Vehicle weight is increased. 11. Engine loading is increased such as climbing a grade, pulling a trailer or increasing wind resistance with a car-top carrier.	Octane number requirement tends to go DOWN when: 1. Car is operated at higher altitudes (lower barometric pressure). 2. Fuel-air ratio is richer or leaner than that producing maximum knock. 3. Spark plug location in combustion chamber provides shortest path of flame travel. 4. Combustion chamber design gives maximum turbulence of fuel-air charge. 5. Compression ratio is lowered. 6. Exhaust gas recycle system operates at part-throttle. 7. Ignition timing retard devices are used. 8. Humidity of the air increases. 9. Ignition timing is retarded. 10. Inlet air temperature is decreased. 11. Reduced engine loads are employed.

Fig. 17-5. Note various factors controlling octane requirements. (Ethyl Corp.)

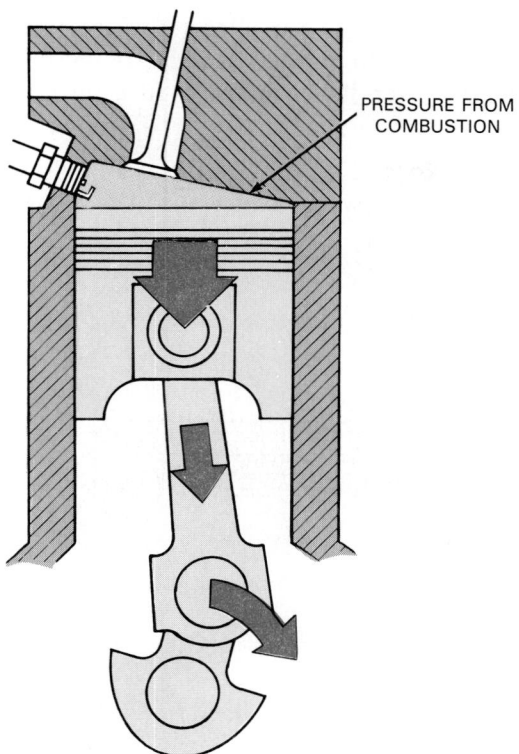

Fig. 17-6. Combustion produces heat. Heat causes gases to expand. Expansion causes pressure. Pressure pushes piston down on power stroke. (Ford)

Fig. 17-7 illustrates normal gasoline combustion.

In A, a spark at the spark plug starts the fuel burning. A small ball of flame forms around the tip of the plug. The piston is moving up in the cylinder, compressing the fuel mixture.

In B, the flame spreads faster and moves about halfway through the mixture. Generally, the flame is moving evenly through the fuel mixture. The piston is nearing TDC, causing increased pressure.

In C, the piston reaches TDC. The flame picks up more speed.

In D, the flame shoots out to consume the rest of the fuel in the chamber. Combustion is complete with the piston only a short distance down in the cylinder.

Normal combustion only takes about 3/1000 of a second. This is much slower than an explosion. Dynamite explodes in about 1/50,000 of a second.

Under some undesirable conditions, however, gasoline can be made to burn too quickly, making part of combustion like an explosion. This is detailed later.

AIR-FUEL MIXTURE RATIO

For proper combustion and engine performance, the right amounts of air and fuel must be mixed. If too much fuel or too much air is used, engine power, fuel economy, and efficiency will suffer.

A *stoichiometric fuel mixture* is a chemically correct or perfect air-fuel mixture or ratio. For gasoline,

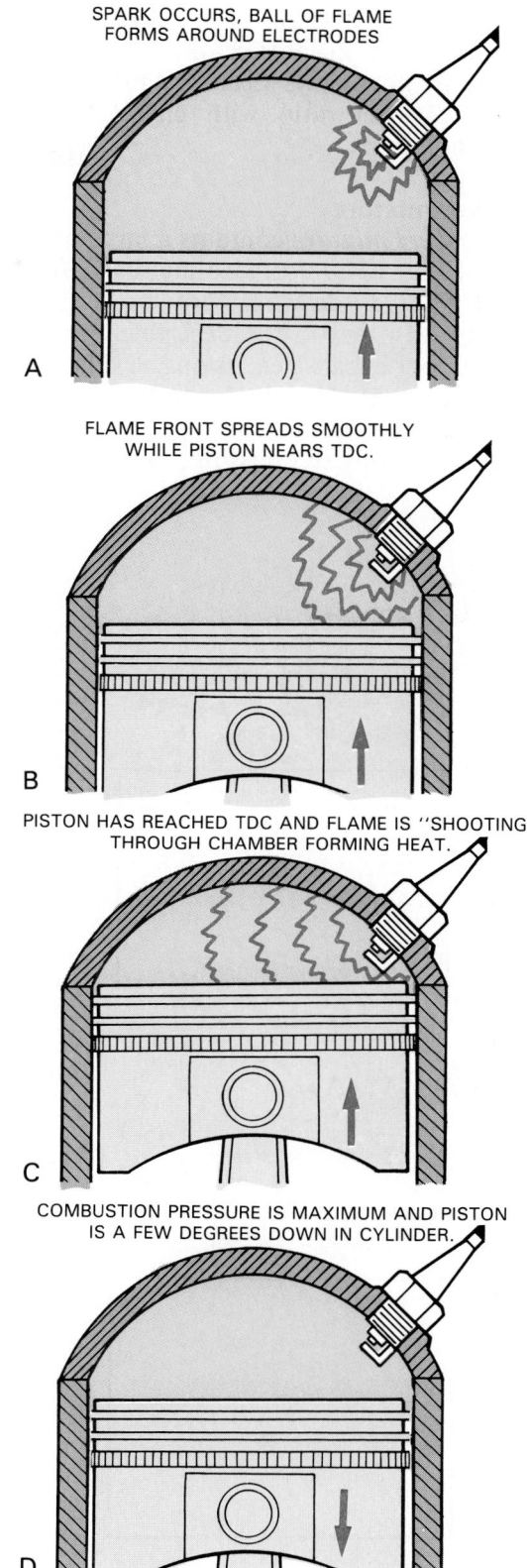

SPARK OCCURS, BALL OF FLAME FORMS AROUND ELECTRODES

A

FLAME FRONT SPREADS SMOOTHLY WHILE PISTON NEARS TDC.

B

PISTON HAS REACHED TDC AND FLAME IS "SHOOTING" THROUGH CHAMBER FORMING HEAT.

C

COMBUSTION PRESSURE IS MAXIMUM AND PISTON IS A FEW DEGREES DOWN IN CYLINDER.

D

Fig. 17-7. Study action of normal combustion. Single flame moves smoothly through air-fuel mixture.

it is a mixture ratio of about 14.7:1 (14.7 parts air to 1 part fuel by weight). Under constant engine conditions, this ratio can help assure that all of the fuel is burned during combustion.

As you will learn in later chapters, the conditions in an engine are not always ideal. The fuel system must change the air-fuel ratio with changes in engine operating conditions.

Lean air-fuel mixture

A *lean air-fuel mixture* contains a large amount of air. Look at Fig. 17-8. For gasoline, 20:1, for example, would be a very lean mixture.

A slightly lean mixture is desirable for high gas mileage and low exhaust emissions. Extra air in the cylinder assures that all of the fuel is burned. Too lean of a mixture, however, can cause poor engine performance (lack of power, missing, and even engine damage).

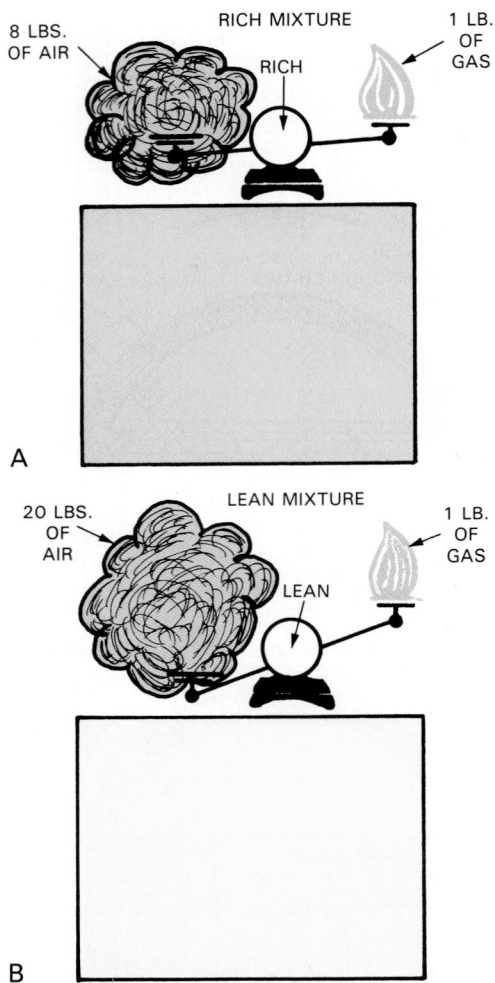

Fig. 17-8. A—Rich fuel mixture has more fuel mixed into air. B—Lean fuel mixture has less fuel mixed with air.

Rich air-fuel mixture

A *rich air-fuel mixture* is the opposite of a lean mixture; a little more fuel is mixed with the air. For gasoline, 8:1 (8 parts air to one part fuel) would be

a very rich fuel mixture. Refer to Fig. 17-8.

A slightly rich mixture tends to increase engine power. However, it also increases fuel consumption and

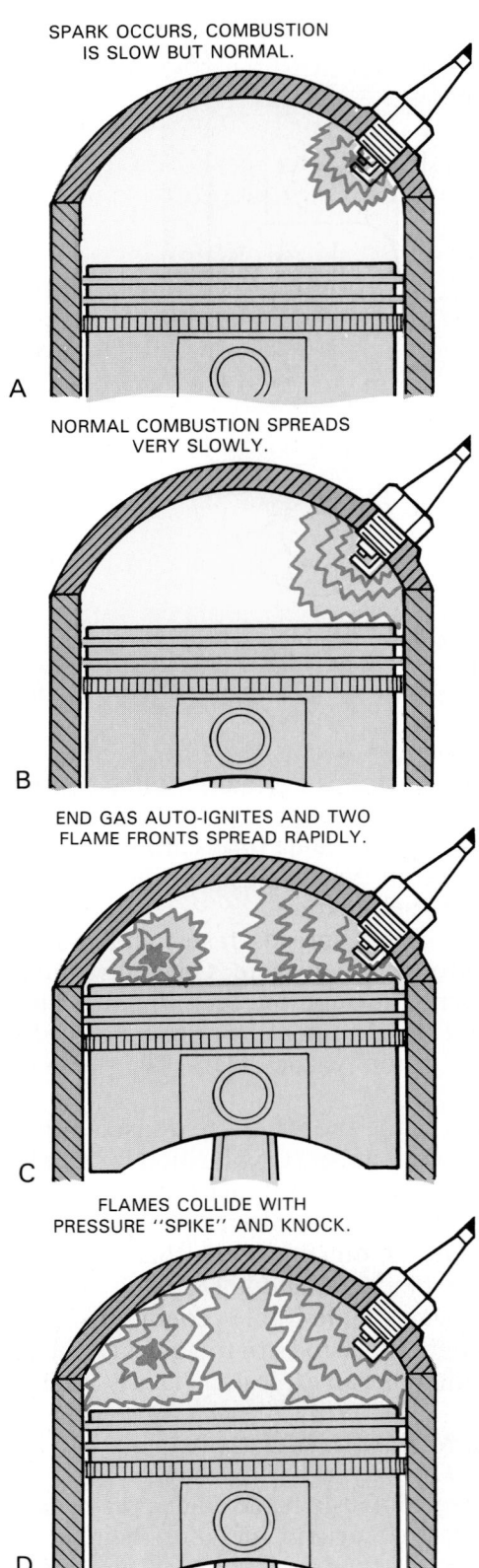

Fig. 17-9. Detonation is caused by normal combustion being too slow. End gas or unburned fuel mixture ignites and two flame fronts collide with a loud knock.

exhaust emissions. An over-rich mixture will reduce engine power, foul spark plugs, and cause incomplete burning (black smoke at engine exhaust).

ABNORMAL COMBUSTION

Abnormal combustion occurs when the flame does NOT spread evenly and smoothly through the combustion chamber. The lean air-fuel mixtures, high operating temperatures, and low octane, unleaded fuels of today make abnormal combustion a major problem.

Detonation

Detonation results when part of the unburned fuel mixture explodes violently. This is the most severe and engine-damaging type of abnormal combustion.

Engine knock is a symptom of detonation. The pressure rises so quickly that parts of the engine vibrate. Detonation sounds like a hammer hitting the side of the engine.

Fig. 17-9 shows what happens during detonation. Study the four phases.

As you can see, the *end gas* (unburned portion of mixture) is heated and pressurized for an extended period. Normal combustion is too slow because of a fuel mixture problem, lack of turbulence, or fuel distribution problem. This causes the end gas to explode with a "bang" (knock).

Detonation can greatly increase the pressure and heat in the engine combustion chamber. It can crack cylinder heads, blow head gaskets, burn pistons, and shatter spark plugs. See Figs. 17-10 and 17-11.

Preignition

Preignition results when an overheated surface in the combustion chamber ignites the fuel mixture. Termed

Fig. 17-11. Detonation has blown a hole in head of piston. (Champion Spark Plugs)

surface ignition, a "hot spot" (overheated bit of carbon, sharp edge, hot exhaust valve) causes the mixture to burn prematurely.

A *ping* or a mild knock is a light tapping noise that can be heard during preignition. It is NOT as loud nor as harmful as detonation knock.

Study Fig. 17-12. Preignition is similar to detonation, but the actions are reversed. Detonation begins AFTER the start of normal combustion. Preignition begins BEFORE the start of normal combustion.

Preignition, ping, or mild knock is very common to the modern automobile. Some auto makers say that some preignition is normal, especially when accelerating under a load.

NOTE! Prolonged preignition can produce harmful detonation. If an engine pings or knocks excessively, serious engine damage can result. Correct the problem right away.

Dieseling

Dieseling, also called *after-running* or *run-on,* is a problem where the engine keeps running after the key is turned OFF. A knocking, coughing, or fluttering noise may be heard as the fuel ignites and the crankshaft spins.

When dieseling, the gasoline engine ignites the fuel from heat and pressure, somewhat like a diesel engine. With the ignition key off, the engine runs without

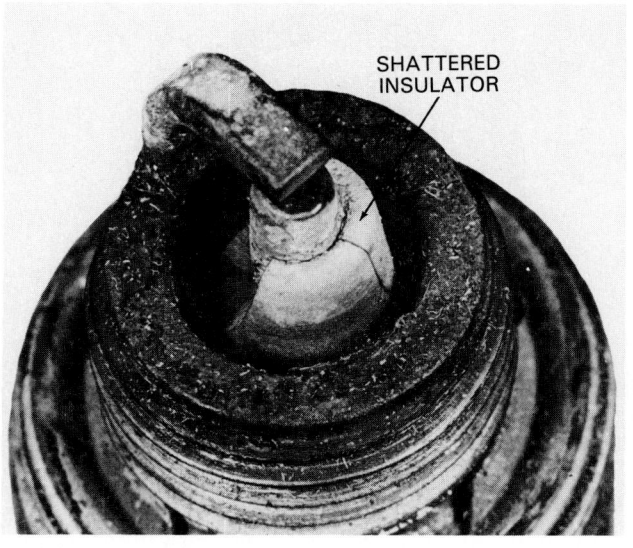

Fig. 17-10. Detonation has shattered insulator on this spark plug. (Champion Spark Plugs)

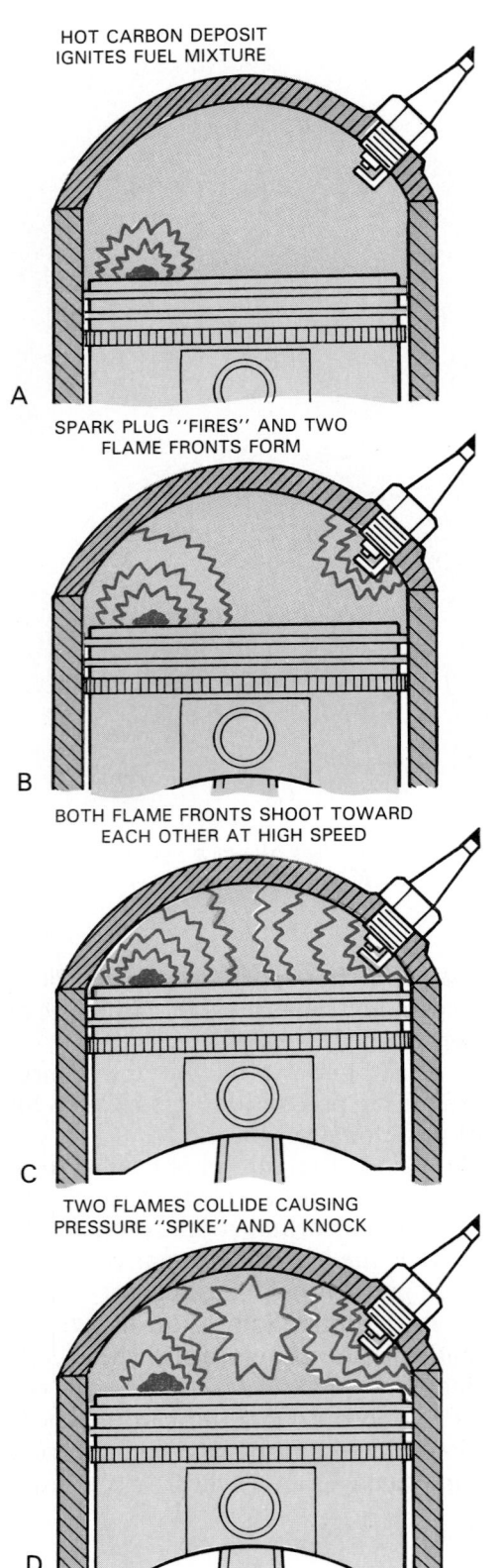

HOT CARBON DEPOSIT
IGNITES FUEL MIXTURE

A

SPARK PLUG "FIRES" AND TWO
FLAME FRONTS FORM

B

BOTH FLAME FRONTS SHOOT TOWARD
EACH OTHER AT HIGH SPEED

C

TWO FLAMES COLLIDE CAUSING
PRESSURE "SPIKE" AND A KNOCK

D

Fig. 17-12. Preignition is caused by early, abnormal ignition
of fuel mixture. Abnormal and normal flames collide, producing a pinging noise.

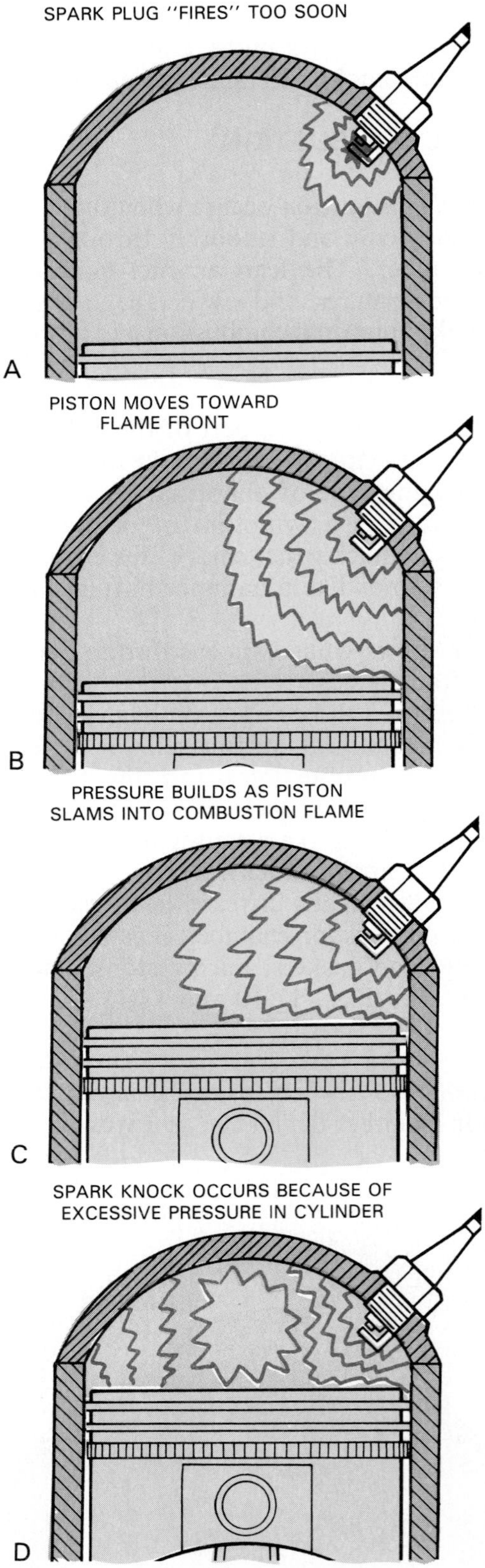

SPARK PLUG "FIRES" TOO SOON

A

PISTON MOVES TOWARD
FLAME FRONT

B

PRESSURE BUILDS AS PISTON
SLAMS INTO COMBUSTION FLAME

C

SPARK KNOCK OCCURS BECAUSE OF
EXCESSIVE PRESSURE IN CYLINDER

D

Fig. 17-13. Spark knock is generally understood to mean ping
or knock caused by an ignition timing problem.

voltage to the spark plugs.

The most common causes of dieseling are a high idle
speed, carbon deposits in combustion chambers, low

octane fuel, overheated engine, or spark plugs that have
too high a heat range. This problem will be discussed
later in the text.

Spark knock

Spark knock is another engine combustion problem caused by the spark plug firing too soon in relation to the position of the piston. The spark timing is advanced too far and is causing combustion to slam into the upward moving piston. This causes maximum cylinder pressure to form before TDC, not after TDC as it should.

Fig. 17-13 shows what happens during spark knock. Spark knock can also lead to preignition and more damaging detonation.

Spark knock and preignition produce about the same symptoms—pinging under load. To find its cause, first check the ignition timing. If timing is correct, check other possible causes.

DIESEL FUEL

Diesel fuel or *diesel oil* is the second most popular type of automotive fuel. Diesels are becoming more common because of their high fuel economy.

A gallon of diesel fuel contains more heat energy than a gallon of gasoline. It is a thicker fraction (part) of crude oil. Diesel fuel can produce more cylinder pressure and vehicle movement than an equal amount of gasoline.

Since it is thicker and has different burning characteristics, a high pressure injection system must be used to spray the fuel directly into the combustion chambers. A carburetor or low pressure injection system would not meter the thicker diesel fuel properly. Look at Fig. 17-14.

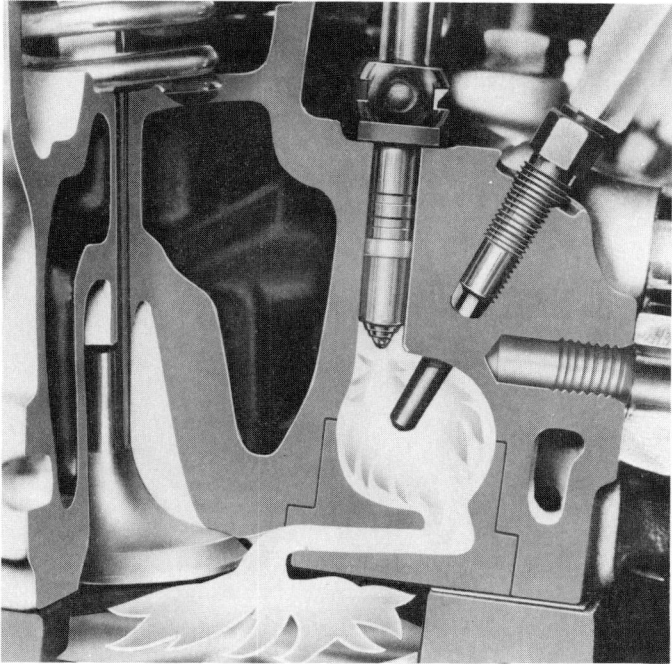

Fig. 17-14. Diesel engine is a compression ignition engine. High compression pressure heats air in cylinder. When fuel is sprayed into hot air, combustion begins.

Diesel fuel will NOT vaporize (change from a liquid to a gas) as easily as gasoline. If diesel fuel entered the intake manifold of an engine, it would collect on the inner walls of the manifold. This would upset engine operation.

Combustion requires fuel to be in a vapor state. Diesel engines inject the diesel oil directly into the combustion chamber. The compressed, hot air vaporizes and burns the fuel.

Diesel fuel grade

Diesel fuel grade assures that diesel fuel sold all over the country has uniform standards of service. Diesel engine makers are then able to select a diesel fuel grade that meets the needs of their engines.

There are three diesel fuel grades: Number 1 Diesel, Number 2 Diesel, and Number 4 Diesel.

No. 2 Diesel is normally recommended for use in automotive diesel engines. It is also the only grade of fuel available at many service stations. No. 2 has a medium viscosity (thickness or weight) which provides proper operating traits for the widest range of conditions.

Since No. 1 diesel fuel is thinner and more runny than No. 2 diesel, it is sometimes recommended as a WINTER FUEL. It is often sold at gas stations in very cold weather. Low temperatures tend to thicken diesel fuel and cause performance problems (hard starting, poor fuel delivery).

Some auto manufacturers only allow the use of No. 2 diesel fuel with special cold weather additives. In some engines, the thin No. 1 diesel fuel will NOT provide adequate lubrication protection. Metal-to-metal contact may occur, causing serious engine damage. When in doubt, refer to the vehicle's service manual.

WARNING! Diesel fuel or diesel oil should NOT be confused with FUEL OIL or HOME HEATING OIL. Diesel fuel has less impurities in it than fuel oil. Fuel oil should never be used in a diesel engine or damage will result.

Diesel fuel cloud point

One of the substances in diesel fuel is paraffin (wax). At very cold temperatures, this wax can separate from the other parts of the fuel. When this happens, the fuel will turn cloudy or milky.

Cloud point is the temperature at which wax separates out of the fuel. At cloud point, the wax can clog fuel filters and prevent diesel engine operation.

Diesel fuel water contamination

Water contamination is a common problem with diesel engines. Water, when mixed with diesel oil, can clog filters and corrode components. The parts in diesel injection pumps and nozzles are very precise. They can be easily damaged by water.

Many late model diesel injection systems have water separators to prevent water damage. These will be covered in later chapters.

Diesel fuel cetane rating

A *cetane rating* indicates the cold starting ability of diesel fuel. A numbering system is used. The higher the cetane number, the easier the engine will start and run in cold weather.

Most auto makers recommend a cetane rating of about 45. This is the average cetane value of No. 2 diesel fuel.

A *cetane number,* in some ways, is the opposite of a gasoline octane number. This is shown in Fig. 17-15. A high cetane number means that the fuel will ignite easily from heat and pressure. In a diesel, fuel should ignite and burn as soon as it touches the hot air in the combustion chamber.

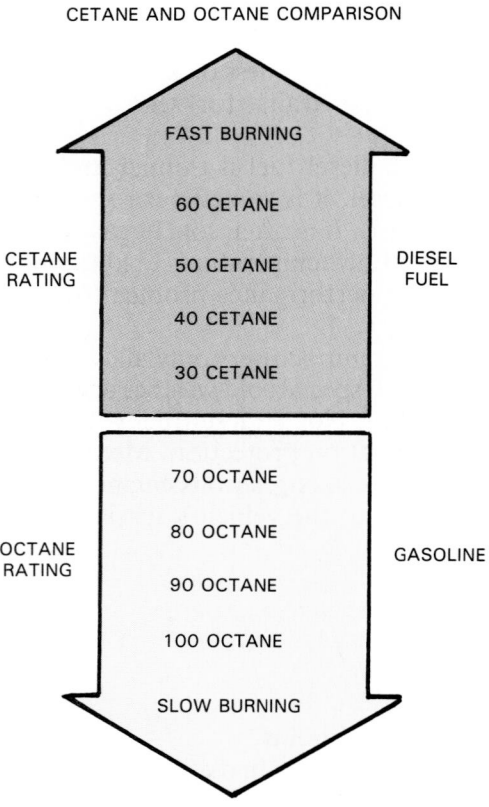

Fig. 17-15. Diesel oil cetane rating is opposite of gasoline octane rating.

DIESEL COMBUSTION

A diesel engine is a *compression ignition engine.* It compresses air until the air is hot enough to ignite the fuel. A spark plug would NOT ignite diesel fuel properly. If gasoline were used in a diesel, it would detonate on the compression stroke and not produce useful energy.

Since diesel fuel is thick and hard to ignite, a high pressure, mechanical pump and nozzles force the fuel

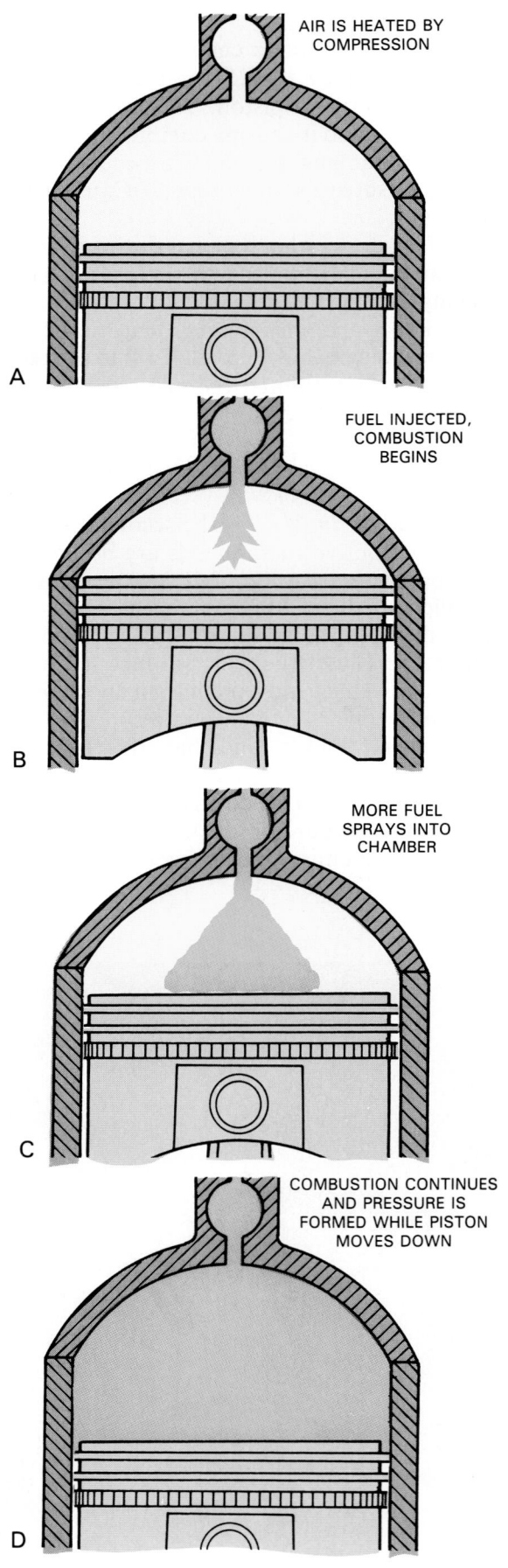

Fig. 17-16. Study action during normal diesel combustion.

into the engine combustion chambers. An extremely high compression ratio heats the air in the cylinder. Then, when fuel is sprayed into the hot air, it begins to burn.

Fig. 17-16 shows the phases of normal diesel combustion. Study this illustration closely.

In A, the piston moves up to compress and heat the air in the cylinder. Note that this is different than a gasoline engine that compresses both fuel and air.

In B, diesel oil is injected directly into the combustion chamber. The hot air makes the fuel begin to burn and expand.

In C, more fuel is sprayed into the chamber. More pressure is developed and the piston begins to move down in the cylinder.

In D, the rest of the fuel is injected into the chamber. Pressure continues to form, pushing the piston down on the power stroke.

Note that fuel was injected into the engine for several degrees of crankshaft rotation. This caused a smooth, steady build up of pressure for quiet diesel engine operation.

Diesel combustion knock

Diesel engines, when compared to gasoline engines, knock almost all of the time. You have probably heard a diesel engine running. It *clatters* or *rattles* as the diesel fuel ignites in the combustion chambers.

Diesel knock occurs when too much fuel ignites at one time, producing a louder than normal knocking noise. Excessive diesel knock can reduce engine power, fuel economy, and engine life.

Ignition lag is the time it takes diesel oil to heat up, vaporize, and begin to burn. It is the time lapse between initial fuel injection and actual ignition (burning).

Ignition lag is a major controlling factor of diesel knock. If lag time is too long, a large amount of fuel can ignite, producing a louder than normal knock. A high cetane fuel, with a short lag time, reduces the chances of diesel knock.

Fig. 17-17 shows the basic phases of diesel knock. Study this illustration.

As you can see, diesel knock is caused by too much fuel burning at one time. This can be due to a cold engine, low cetane fuel, improper fuel spray pattern,

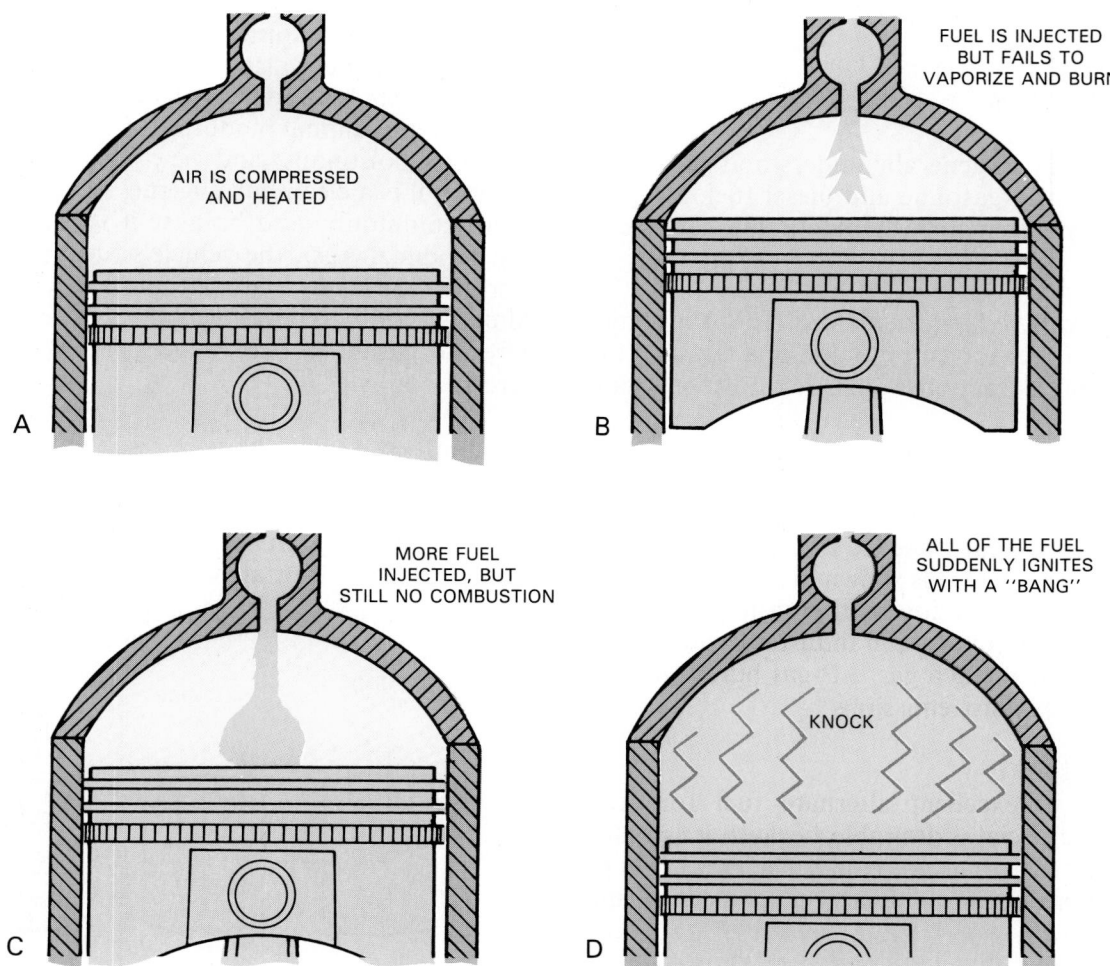

Fig. 17-17. Basically, diesel knock is caused by too much fuel igniting at one time. Fuel does not ignite quick enough when injection begins.

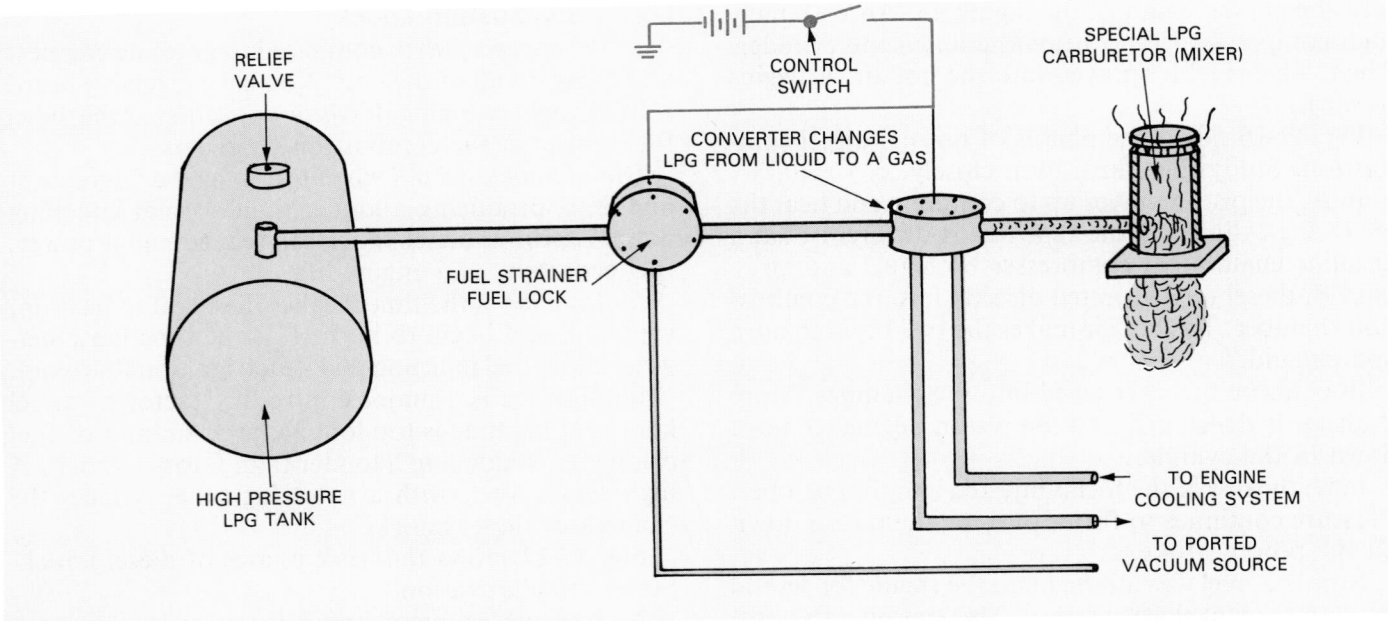

Fig. 17-18. LP-gas fuel system uses a high pressure storage tank. Fuel strainer-fuel lock cleans fuel and prevents leakage when engine is not running. Converter uses engine coolant heat to change liquid LPG into a gas. Special carburetor meters LP-gas into engine.

or incorrect injection timing. This will be discussed in later chapters.

ALTERNATE FUELS

Alternate fuels are generally understood to include any fuel other than gasoline and diesel fuel. LP-gas, alcohol, and hydrogen are examples of alternate fuels.

LP-gas

LP-gas or *liquefied petroleum gas* (LPG) is sometimes used as a fuel for automobiles and trucks. It is one of the lightest fractions of crude oil. Refer again to Fig. 17-3.

Chemically, LP-gas is similar to gasoline. However, at room temperature and pressure, LP-gas is a vapor, NOT a liquid.

A special fuel system is needed to meter the gaseous LPG into the engine. One is shown in Fig. 17-18. Note the names and construction of the basic parts.

LP-gas is commonly used in industrial equipment, such as fork lifts. Being a gas, LP-gas burns cleanly, producing few exhaust emissions.

Alcohol

Alcohol is an excellent alternate fuel for auto engines. It is especially desirable because it is made from sources other than crude oil. The two types of alcohol used in automobiles are ethyl alcohol and methyl alcohol.

Ethyl alcohol, also called *grain alcohol* or *ethanol,* is made from farm crops. Grain, wheat, sugar cane, potatoes, fruit, oats, soy beans, and other crops rich in carbohydrates can be made into ethyl alcohol. This type alcohol is a colorless, harsh tasting, toxic, and highly flammable liquid.

Methyl alcohol, also termed *"wood alcohol"* or *methanol,* can be made out of wood chips, petroleum, garbage, and animal manure. It has a strong odor, is colorless, poisonous, and very flammable.

Alcohol is a clean burning fuel for automobiles. It is not commonly used because it is expensive to use and produce. Also, the vehicle's fuel system requires modification before it can burn straight alcohol. Almost TWICE as much alcohol must be burned, compared to gasoline. This reduces fuel economy by 50 percent.

Gasohol

Gasohol, as the name implies, is a mixture of gasoline (usually 87 octane unleaded gasoline) and alcohol (usually grain alcohol). The mixture can range from 2 to 20 percent alcohol. In most cases, gasohol

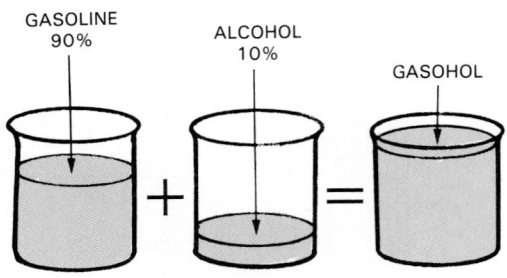

Fig. 17-19. Gasohol is usually a mixture of 10 percent alcohol and 90 percent gasoline. (Ethyl Corp.)

is a blend of 10 percent alcohol and 90 percent gasoline. See Fig. 17-19.

Gasohol is commonly used as an alternate fuel in motor vehicles because fuel system and engine modifications are NOT needed. Many gas stations sell gasohol as a high octane fuel. The alcohol tends to reduce the knocking tendencies of the gasoline. It acts like an antiknock additive.

For example, 10 percent alcohol can increase 87 octane gasoline to around 91 octane. Gasohol can be burned in a high compression, high horsepower engine without detonating and knocking.

Synthetic fuels

Synthetic fuels are fuels made from coal, shale oil (rock filled with petroleum), and tar sand (sand filled with petroleum). See Fig. 17-20.

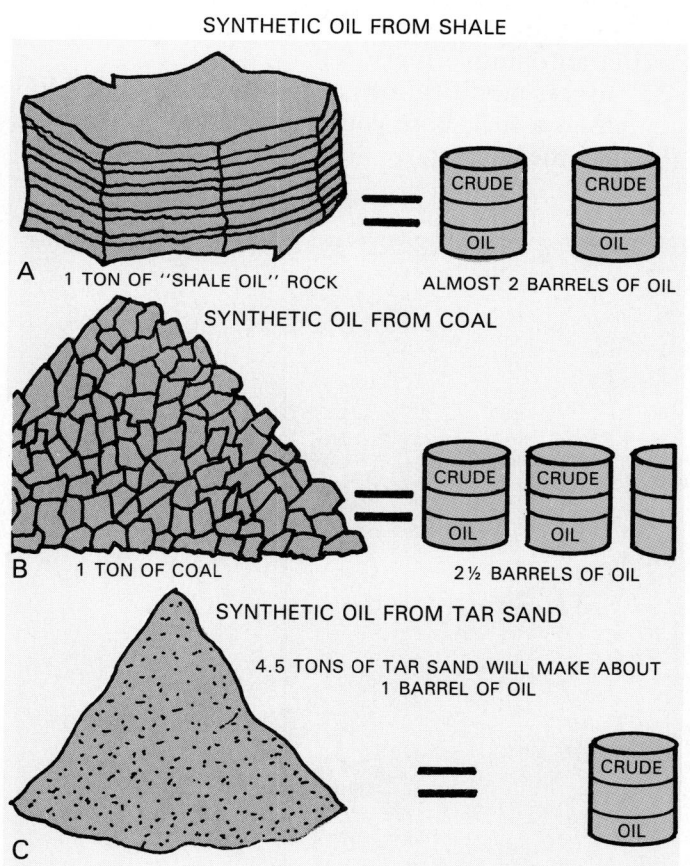

SYNTHETIC OIL FROM SHALE

A — 1 TON OF "SHALE OIL" ROCK — ALMOST 2 BARRELS OF OIL

SYNTHETIC OIL FROM COAL

B — 1 TON OF COAL — 2½ BARRELS OF OIL

SYNTHETIC OIL FROM TAR SAND

4.5 TONS OF TAR SAND WILL MAKE ABOUT 1 BARREL OF OIL

C

Fig. 17-20. Synthetic sources of oil. A — Shale rock can be converted into oil. B — Coal can produce about two and one-half barrels of oil per ton. C — Four and one-half tons of tar sand can be changed into about one barrel of oil.

Synthetic fuels are synthesized (changed) from a solid hydrocarbon (petroleum) state into a liquid or a gaseous state. Synthetic fuels are now being experimented with as a means of supplementing crude oil. As crude oil-based fuels become more expensive, synthetic fuels will become more practical.

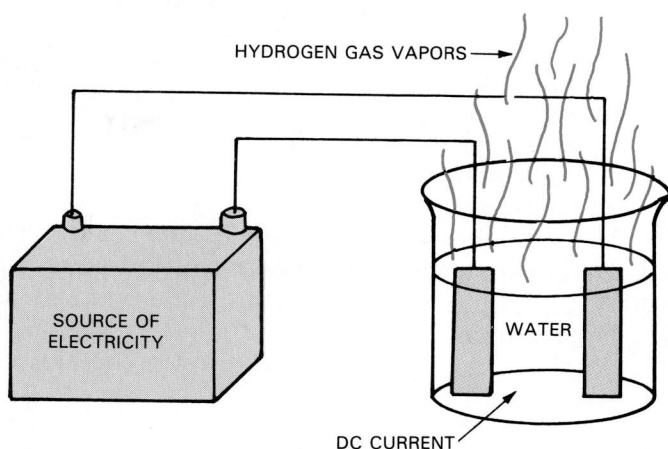

HYDROGEN PRODUCTION BY ELECTROLYSIS

HYDROGEN GAS VAPORS →

SOURCE OF ELECTRICITY

WATER

DC CURRENT

Fig. 17-21. Hydrogen gas can be made through electrolysis of water. Solar cells, wind energy, or ocean thermal energy may make production feasible some day.

Hydrogen

Hydrogen is a highly flammable gas that is a promising alternate fuel of the future. Hydrogen is one of the most abundant elements on our planet. It can be produced through the *electrolysis* of water (sending electric current through salt water to produce hydrogen gas). This is illustrated in Fig. 17-21.

Hydrogen is an ideal fuel. The sun is burning hydrogen. Hydrogen burns almost perfectly, leaving only water and harmless carbon dioxide as by-products.

Presently, hydrogen is too expensive to make and store. However, as we use up our supply of crude oil, we may someday make hydrogen a major source of automotive fuel.

KNOW THESE TERMS

Petroleum, Hydrocarbon, Leaded gasoline, Unleaded gasoline, Octane number, Stoichiometric fuel mixture, Lean air-fuel ratio, Rich air-fuel ratio, Detonation, Preignition, Knock, Ping, Spark knock, Dieseling, Diesel fuel grade, Cloud point, Cetane number, Compression ignition, Ignition lag, Alternate fuel, LPG, Ethyl alcohol, Methyl alcohol, Gasohol, Synthetic fuels.

REVIEW QUESTIONS

1. _____ , also called _____ _____ , is oil taken directly out of the ground.
2. What are hydrocarbons?
3. Explain the difference between leaded and unleaded gasoline.
4. The lead in leaded gasoline acts as a lubricant for the engine valves and valve seats. True or False?
5. The _____ _____ of gasoline is a measurement of the fuel's ability to resist knock or ping.

6. If an auto maker recommends an octane number of 91, it is ok to use 87. True or False?
7. Which of the following is NOT needed for proper combustion?
   a. air.
   b. compression.
   c. condensation.
   d. ignition.
8. Describe normal gasoline combustion.
9. Define the term "stoichiometric fuel mixture."
10. A _____ air-fuel mixture ratio contains a large amount of air.
11. A _____ air-fuel mixture ratio contains a large amount of fuel.
12. What are the results of lean and rich air-fuel mixtures?
13. Explain detonation, preignition, spark knock, and dieseling in a gasoline engine.
14. How does diesel fuel differ from gasoline?
15. Explain how ignition lag affects diesel combustion.
16. _____ _____ is made from farm crops and _____ _____ can be made out of wood chips, petroleum, garbage, and animal manure.
17. What is gasohol?
18. Gasohol can normally be used without major engine or fuel system modifications. True or False?
19. Which of the following does NOT pertain to hydrogen as an alternate fuel?
   a. Made from most abundant element.
   b. Produced through electrolysis.
   c. Burns without toxic emissions.
   d. Economical or inexpensive to make.
20. Hydrogen burns almost perfectly, leaving only _____ and harmless _____ as byproducts.

ACTIVITIES FOR CHAPTER 17

1. Write away for literature on automotive fuels and prepare a written report on additives and their properties.
2. Research magazines and newspapers for information about the manufacture of alcohol for use as an automotive fuel.
3. Discuss modifications of engines for use of LPG gas as a fuel. Base your information on research into the subject.

Note safety equipment inside the trunk of this Indy 500 pace car. Racing type fuel cell is designed to survive impact. Dual fuel pumps feed fuel to the modified engine. Trunk also holds fire extinguisher system. (Oldsmobile)

Fuel Tanks, Pumps, Lines, Filters

After studying this chapter, you will be able to:
□ List the components of a fuel supply system.
□ Describe the operation of mechanical and electric fuel pumps.
□ Describe the construction and action of air filters.
□ Explain the tests used to diagnose problems with fuel pumps, fuel filters, and fuel lines.
□ Repair a fuel line or replace a fuel hose.
□ Locate and replace fuel filters in both gasoline and diesel fuel systems.
□ State safety rules for working on fuel supply systems.

A *fuel system* provides a combustible air-fuel mixture to power the engine. First introduced in Chapter 1, there are several types of fuel systems. Today's cars commonly use carburetors, gasoline injection systems, and diesel injection systems.

A modern fuel system has three subsystems:
1. A *fuel supply system* which provides filtered fuel to carburetor, injection pump, or injectors.
2. An *air supply system* to provide clean combustion air.
3. A *fuel metering system* that controls amount of fuel that mixes with air.

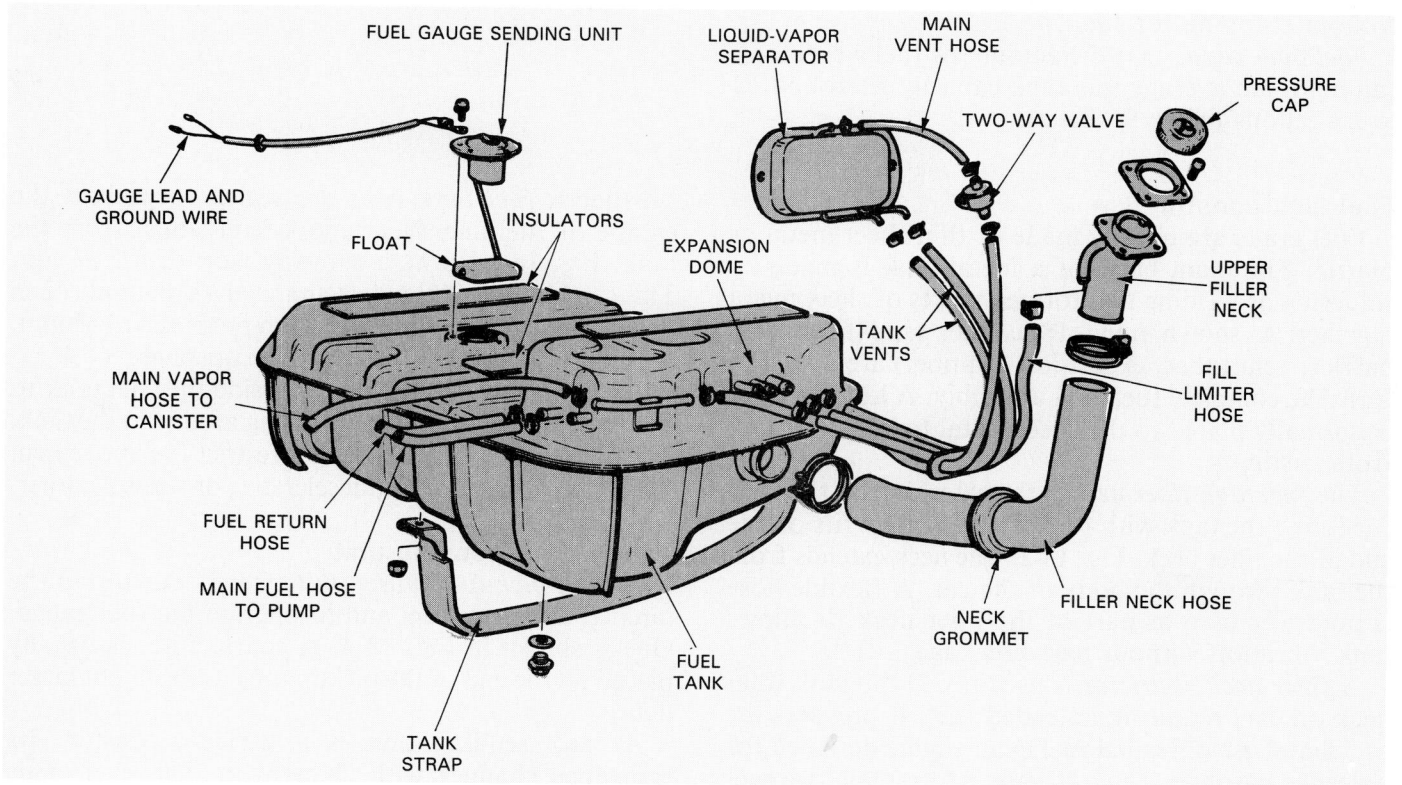

Fig. 18-1. Note basic parts of fuel tank assembly. (Chrysler)

This chapter explains the construction, operation, and service of fuel tanks, fuel lines, fuel filters, air filters, and fuel pumps. These parts make up the fuel and air supply systems. This information will prepare you for later chapters on fuel metering systems. Study carefully!

FUEL SUPPLY SYSTEM

A *fuel supply system* draws fuel from the fuel tank and forces it into the *fuel metering device* (carburetor, gasoline injectors, or diesel injection pump). One type uses a mechanical (engine driven) fuel pump. Another type uses an electric fuel pump. A few use both types.

The basic parts of a fuel supply system include:
1. FUEL TANK (stores gasoline, diesel oil, gasohol, or LP-gas).
2. FUEL LINES (carry fuel between tank, pump, and other parts).
3. FUEL PUMP (draws fuel from tank and forces it to engine or fuel metering device).
4. FUEL FILTERS (removes contaminants in fuel).

FUEL TANKS

An automotive *fuel tank* must safely hold an adequate supply of fuel for prolonged engine operation. It is normally mounted in the rear of the car, under the trunk or rear seat. See Fig. 18-1.

The size of a fuel tank determines, in part, a car's *driving range* (greatest distance car can be driven without stopping for fuel).

Fuel tank capacity is the amount of fuel a fuel tank can hold. An average fuel tank capacity is around 12 to 25 gallons (45 to 95 liters).

Fuel tank construction

Fuel tanks are usually made of thin sheet metal or plastic. The main body of a metal tank is made by soldering or welding two formed pieces of sheet metal together. As shown in Fig. 18-1, other parts (filler neck, baffles, vent tubes, expansion chamber) are added to form the complete fuel tank assembly. A lead-tin alloy is normally plated to the sheet metal to keep the tank from rusting.

The *fuel tank filler neck* is the extension on the tank for filling the tank with fuel. The *filler cap* fits on the end of the filler neck, Fig. 18-2. The neck extends from the tank through the body of the car. A flexible hose is normally used as part of the filler neck. It allows tank vibration without part breakage.

A *filler neck restrictor* is used inside the tank filler neck on cars requiring unleaded fuel. It prevents the accidental use of leaded fuel in an engine designed for unleaded gasoline. The restrictor is too small to accept the larger leaded fuel type gas station pump nozzle. Look at Fig. 18-2.

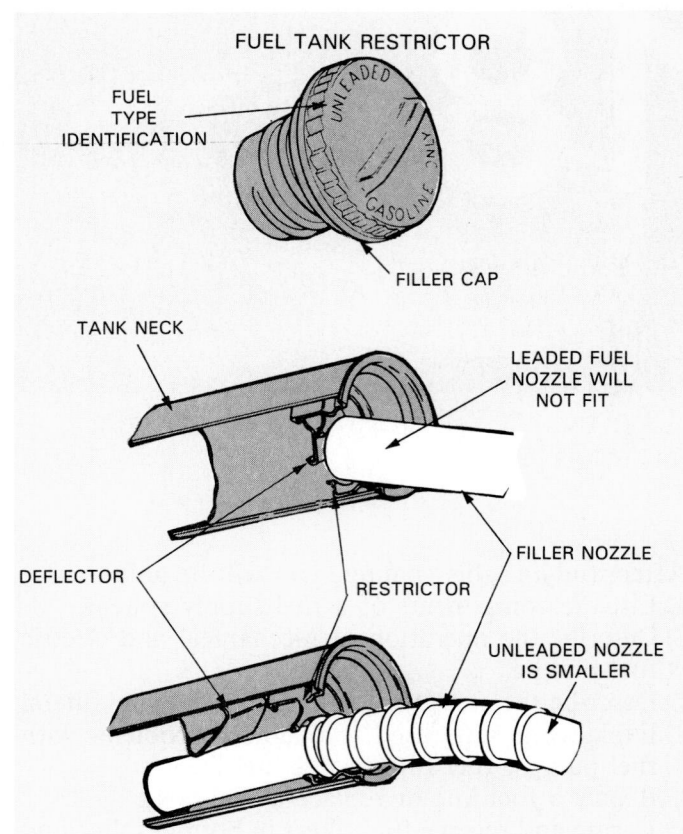

Fig. 18-2. Neck restrictor prevents leaded fuel from being used in a car designed for unleaded fuel. Never remove restrictor for customer. (Oldsmobile)

WARNING! If the neck restrictor is removed and leaded fuel is used in a car designed for unleaded fuel, the catalytic converter will be damaged. This is also a violation of federal law. NEVER remove a neck restrictor!

Modern *fuel tank caps* are sealed to prevent the escape of fuel and fuel vapors (emissions) from the tank. Fig. 18-3 shows a cutaway view of a fuel cap. This cap has pressure and vacuum valves that only open under abnormal conditions of high pressure or vacuum. Normally, it is NOT vented to atmosphere.

Fuel tank baffles are placed inside the fuel tank to keep fuel from sloshing or splashing around in the tank. The baffles are metal plates that restrict fuel movement when the car accelerates, decelerates, or turns a corner.

Tank pickup-sending unit

A *tank pickup-sending unit* extends down into the tank to draw out fuel and to operate the fuel gauge. One is shown in Fig. 18-4. A coarse filter is usually placed on the end of the pickup tube to strain out larger debris.

A tank sending unit is a variable resistor. Its resistance changes with changes in fuel level. This causes it to control the amount of current reaching the fuel gauge in the instrument panel. Fig. 18-5 shows the

SEMI-SEALED FUEL CAP
SEALING SPRING AND DISC
VACUUM VALVE
PRESSURE VALVE

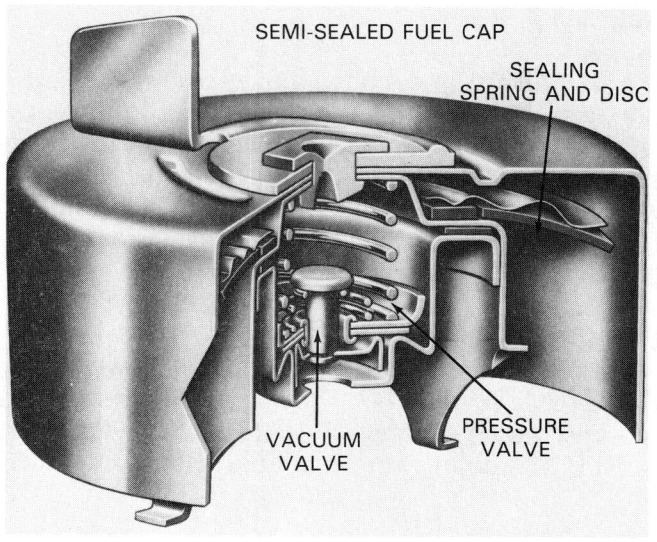

Fig. 18-3. Modern fuel tank caps prevent fuel vapors from escaping into and polluting atmosphere. Valves only release under extreme conditions. (Gates Rubber Co.)

FUEL SUPPLY TUBE
LOCATING TANG
FILTER
TERMINAL
LOCK RING
RUBBER SEAL
FUEL GAUGE (TANK UNIT)
FLOAT

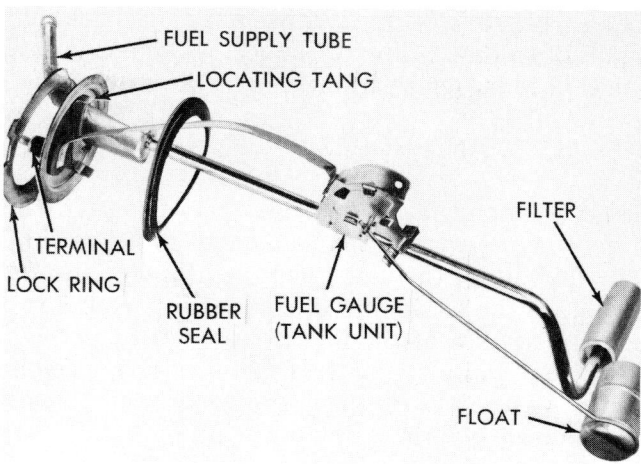

Fig. 18-4. Typical fuel tank pickup-sending unit. "Sock" filter on end of pickup strains out debris in tank. Tank sending unit operates instrument panel fuel gauge. (Chrysler)

basic action of a fuel tank sending unit.

When the fuel level in the tank is low (float down), the tank unit has a high resistance. Only a small amount of current flows to the gauge. The gauge shows a low fuel level.

When the tank is full, the float moves up, moving

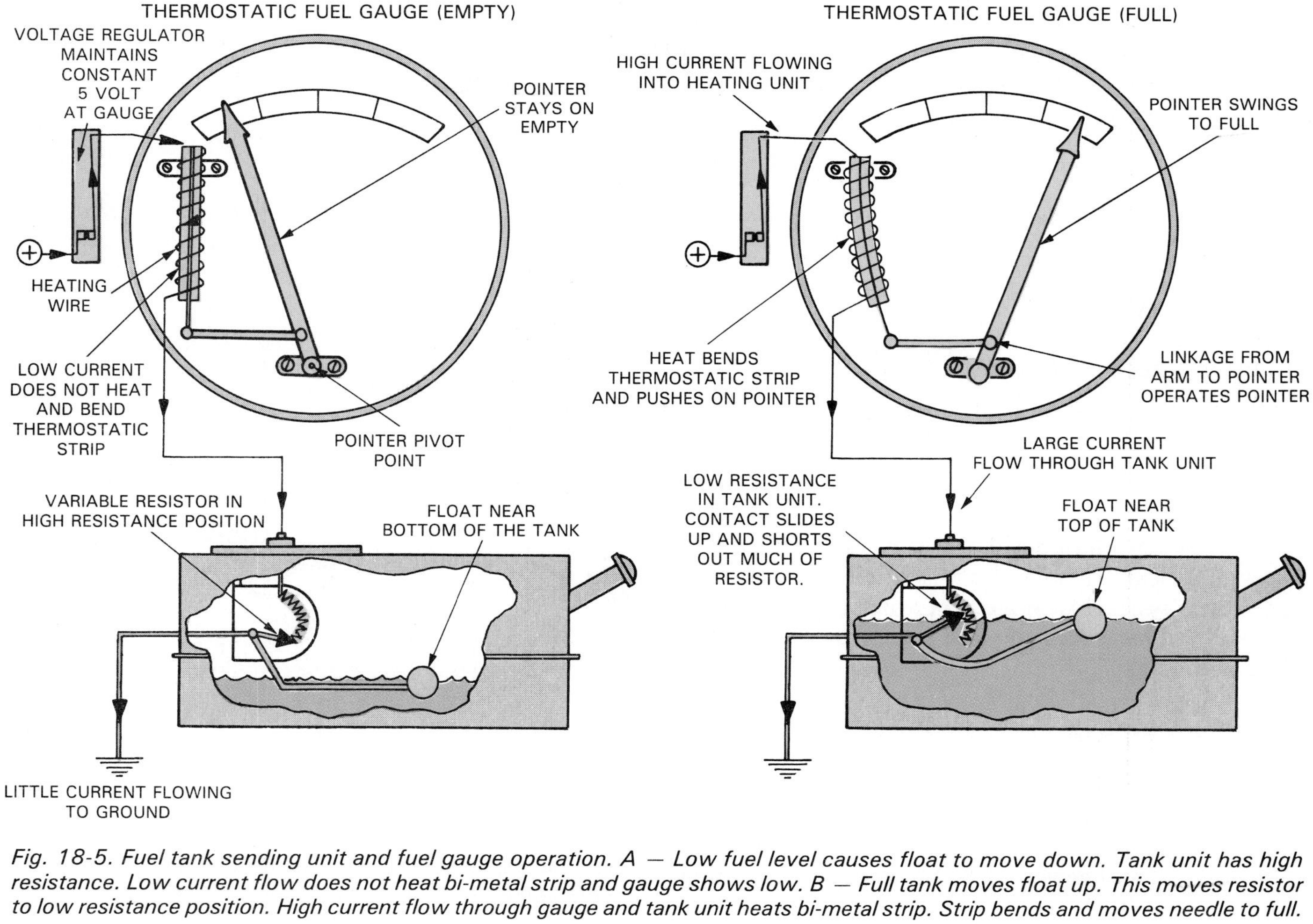

THERMOSTATIC FUEL GAUGE (EMPTY)
VOLTAGE REGULATOR MAINTAINS CONSTANT 5 VOLT AT GAUGE
POINTER STAYS ON EMPTY
HEATING WIRE
LOW CURRENT DOES NOT HEAT AND BEND THERMOSTATIC STRIP
POINTER PIVOT POINT
VARIABLE RESISTOR IN HIGH RESISTANCE POSITION
FLOAT NEAR BOTTOM OF THE TANK
LITTLE CURRENT FLOWING TO GROUND
THERMOSTATIC FUEL GAUGE (FULL)
HIGH CURRENT FLOWING INTO HEATING UNIT
POINTER SWINGS TO FULL
HEAT BENDS THERMOSTATIC STRIP AND PUSHES ON POINTER
LINKAGE FROM ARM TO POINTER OPERATES POINTER
LARGE CURRENT FLOW THROUGH TANK UNIT
LOW RESISTANCE IN TANK UNIT. CONTACT SLIDES UP AND SHORTS OUT MUCH OF RESISTOR.
FLOAT NEAR TOP OF TANK

Fig. 18-5. Fuel tank sending unit and fuel gauge operation. A — Low fuel level causes float to move down. Tank unit has high resistance. Low current flow does not heat bi-metal strip and gauge shows low. B — Full tank moves float up. This moves resistor to low resistance position. High current flow through gauge and tank unit heats bi-metal strip. Strip bends and moves needle to full.

the variable resistor in the tank unit. This causes the tank unit to have a low resistance. More current can then flow to the gauge. The gauge needle moves to full.

FUEL LINES AND HOSES

Fuel lines and *fuel hoses* carry fuel from the tank to the engine. A main fuel line allows a fuel pump to draw fuel out of the tank. The fuel is pulled through this line to the pump and then into the carburetor or metering section of the injection system.

Fig. 18-6 shows a complete set of fuel lines, including the fuel vapor lines for the evaporation control (emission control) system. Study the routing of lines. Note how they connect to the fuel system components.

FUEL FILTERS

Fuel filters stop contaminants (rust, water, corrosion, dirt) from entering the carburetor, throttle body, injectors, injection pump, and any other part that could be damaged by foreign matter. A fuel filter is normally located on the fuel tank pickup tube. A second fuel filter is located in the main fuel line or inside the carburetor or fuel pump. See Fig. 18-9.

Fuel filter construction

Some fuel filters use *pleated paper elements* to trap dirt in the fuel, Fig. 18-9. Others use a *sintered bronze* (porous metal) element, Fig. 18-9. Both types are capable of stopping very small particles. Some filters

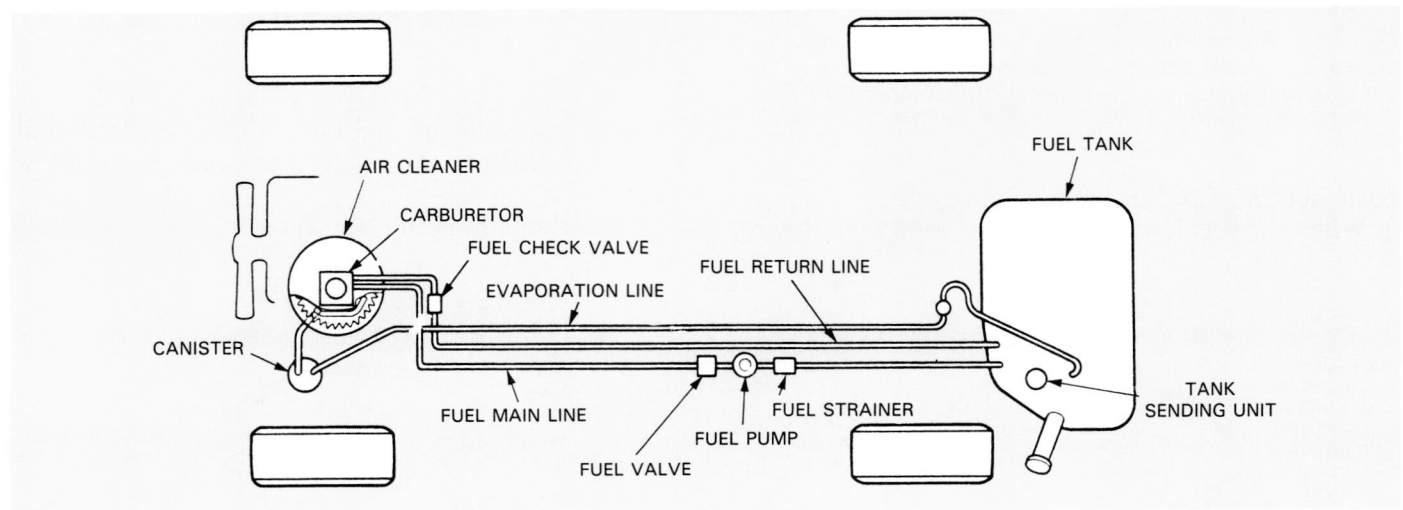

Fig. 18-6. Study fuel and emission control lines. Note location of fuel pump, filters, and other devices. (Mazda)

Fuel lines are normally made of strong, double-wall steel tubing. For fire safety reasons, a fuel line must be able to withstand the constant and severe vibration produced by the engine and road surface.

Fuel hoses made of synthetic rubber are needed where severe movement occurs between parts. For example, a fuel hose is used between the main fuel line and the engine. The engine is mounted on rubber motor mounts. The soft mounts allow the engine some movement in the car frame or body, Fig. 18-7. A flexible hose can absorb this movement without breakage.

Hose clamps secure the fuel hoses to the fuel line or to metal fittings.

Fuel return system

A *fuel return system* helps cool the fuel and prevents *vapor lock* (bubbles form in overheated fuel and stop fuel flow). Fig. 18-8 shows a fuel return system. A second return fuel line is used to carry excess fuel back to the tank. This keeps cool fuel constantly circulating through the system.

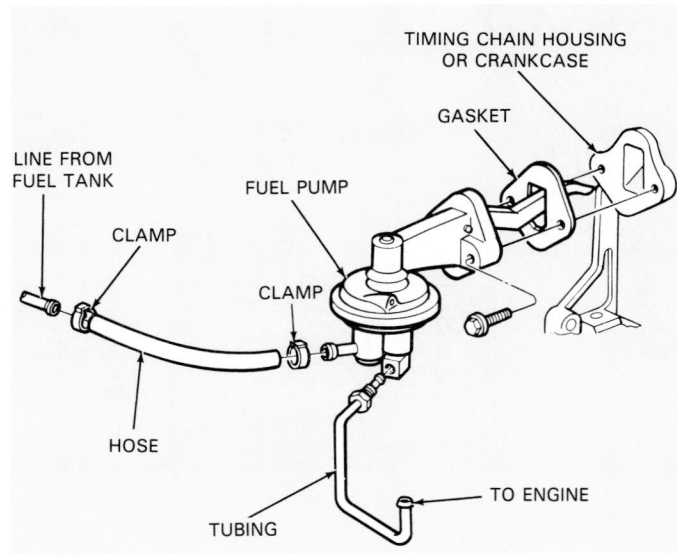

Fig. 18-7. Hose is used between pump and main fuel line to allow for engine movement on mounts. Metal tubing is used where there is no movement between two connections. (Chrysler)

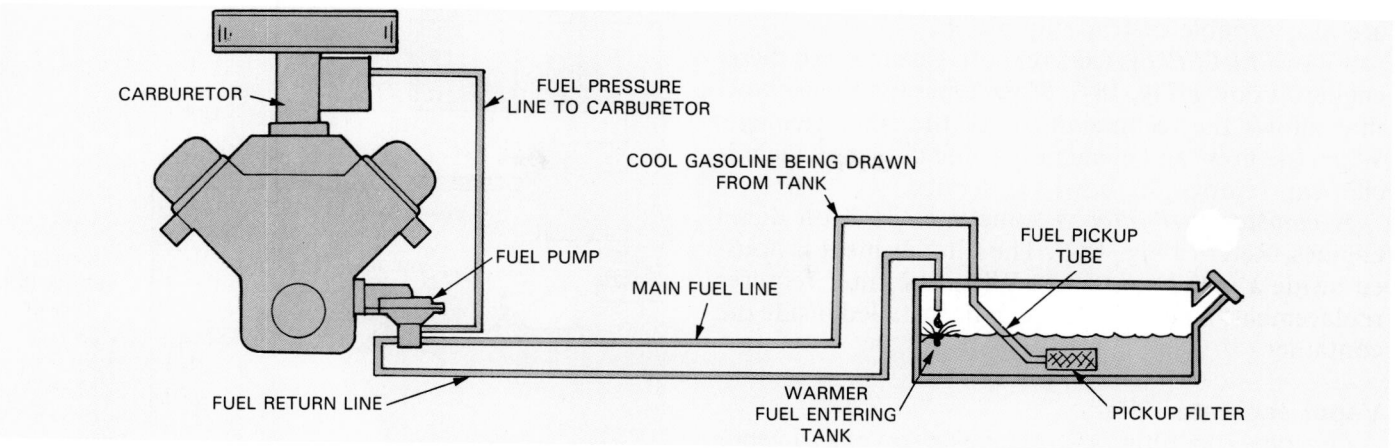

Fig. 18-8. Basic action of a fuel return system. Constant flow of fuel to and from tank cools fuel to help prevent vapor lock and other similar problems.

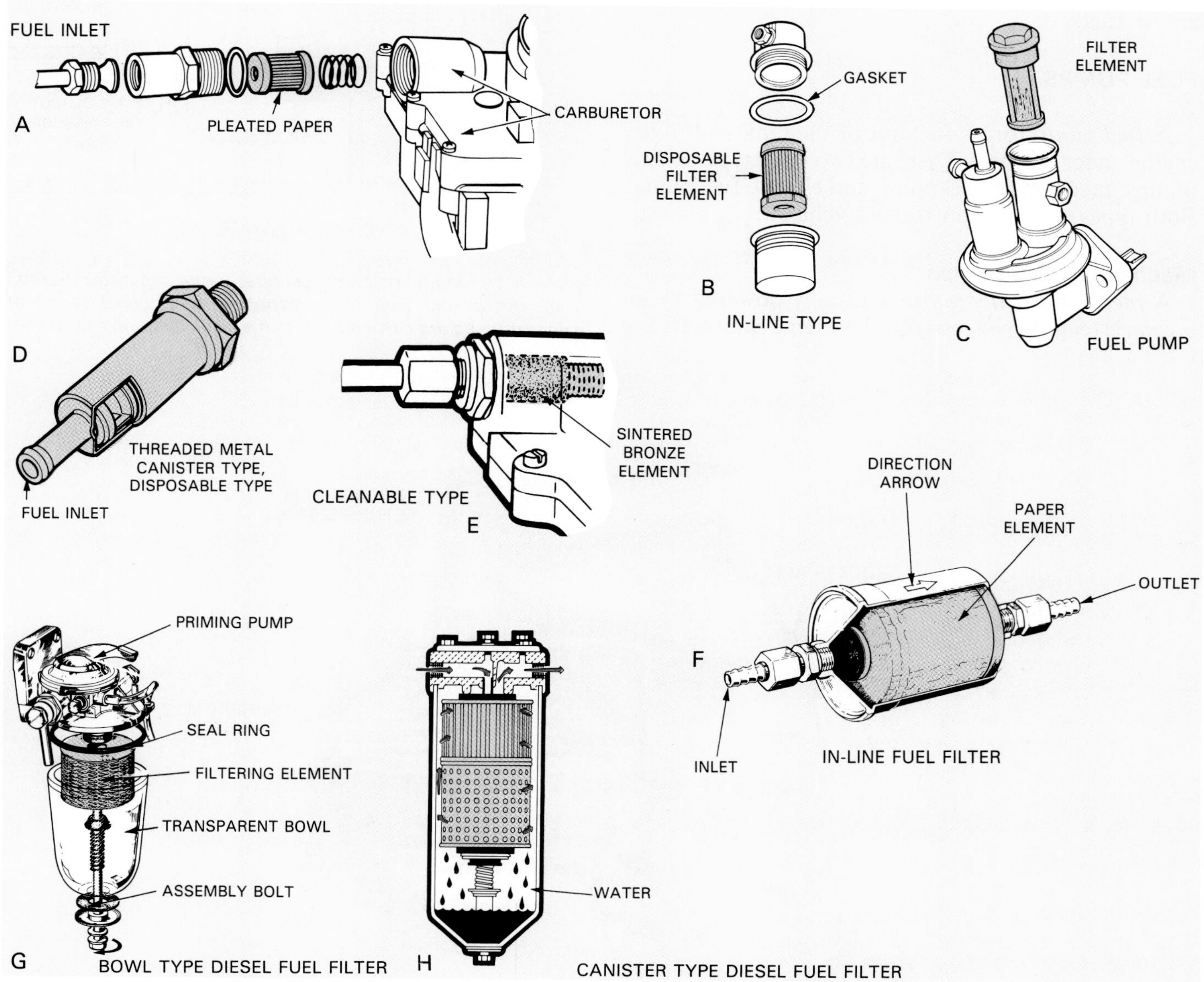

FUEL INLET

A   PLEATED PAPER

CARBURETOR

GASKET

DISPOSABLE
FILTER
ELEMENT

B   IN-LINE TYPE

FILTER
ELEMENT

C   FUEL PUMP

D   THREADED METAL
CANISTER TYPE,
DISPOSABLE TYPE

FUEL INLET

CLEANABLE TYPE

E

SINTERED
BRONZE
ELEMENT

DIRECTION
ARROW

PAPER
ELEMENT

OUTLET

F

INLET

IN-LINE FUEL FILTER

PRIMING PUMP

SEAL RING

FILTERING ELEMENT

TRANSPARENT BOWL

ASSEMBLY BOLT

G   BOWL TYPE DIESEL FUEL FILTER

WATER

H   CANISTER TYPE DIESEL FUEL FILTER

Fig. 18-9. Variations of automotive fuel filters. A — Pleated paper fuel filter in carburetor. B — In-line canister fuel filter. C — Filter element in fuel pump. D — Threaded metal canister fuel filter. E — Sintered bronze fuel filter. F — In-line paper fuel filter. G — Bowl type fuel filter for diesel system. Bowl types are also used on some gasoline fuel systems. H — Large, in-line canister fuel filter for diesel systems. (Peugeot, Fram, Saab, Ford, Chrysler)

Fuel Tanks, Pumps, Lines, Filters   195

are also capable of trapping water.

A *bowl fuel filter* is used on both gasoline and diesel engines. Look at Fig. 18-9. Many types use a glass bowl that allows the technician to see the filter element. When the bowl and element become dirty, the technician can remove the bowl for service.

A *canister fuel filter* is sometimes used on diesel engines. Refer to Fig. 18-9. The filter element is housed inside a metal container. When the filter requires replacement, a new element can be installed inside the container.

Vapor separator-filter

One type fuel filter or strainer also serves as a vapor separator, as in Fig. 18-10. If too much engine heat transfers into the fuel, bubbles can form in the fuel. The bubbles collect at the top of the vapor separator-filter. They are then carried back to the fuel tank with excess fuel.

FUEL PUMPS

A *fuel pump* forces fuel out of the tank and to the engine under pressure. There are two basic types of fuel pumps: mechanical fuel pump and electric fuel pump. Both types are used on today's vehicles.

Mechanical fuel pumps

A *mechanical fuel pump* is usually powered by an eccentric (egg shaped lobe) on the engine camshaft. See

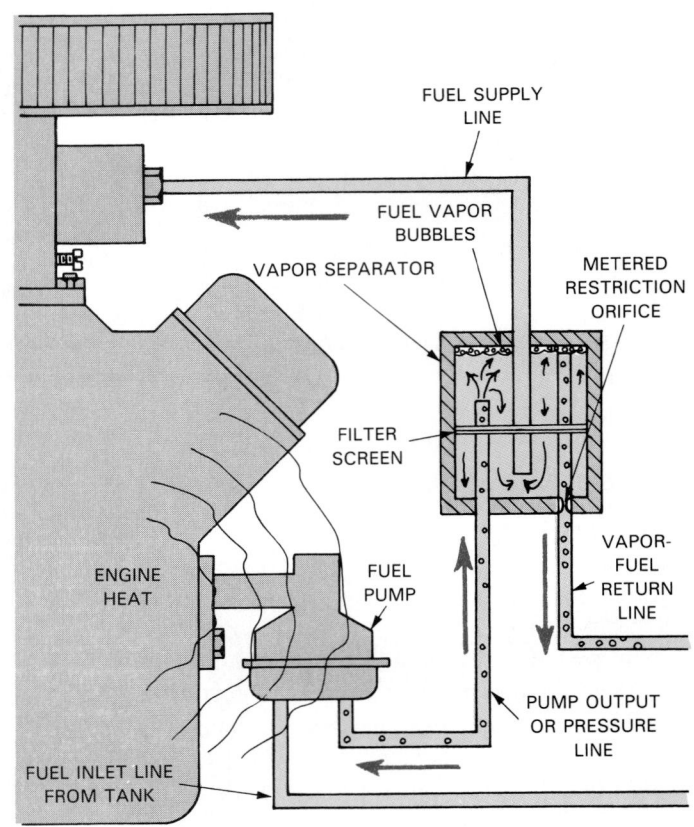

VAPOR SEPARATOR-FILTER

Fig. 18-10. Study action of fuel filter-vapor separator. Screen traps dirt in fuel. Bubbles or vapors in fuel collect at top of separator and are carried back to fuel tank through return line.

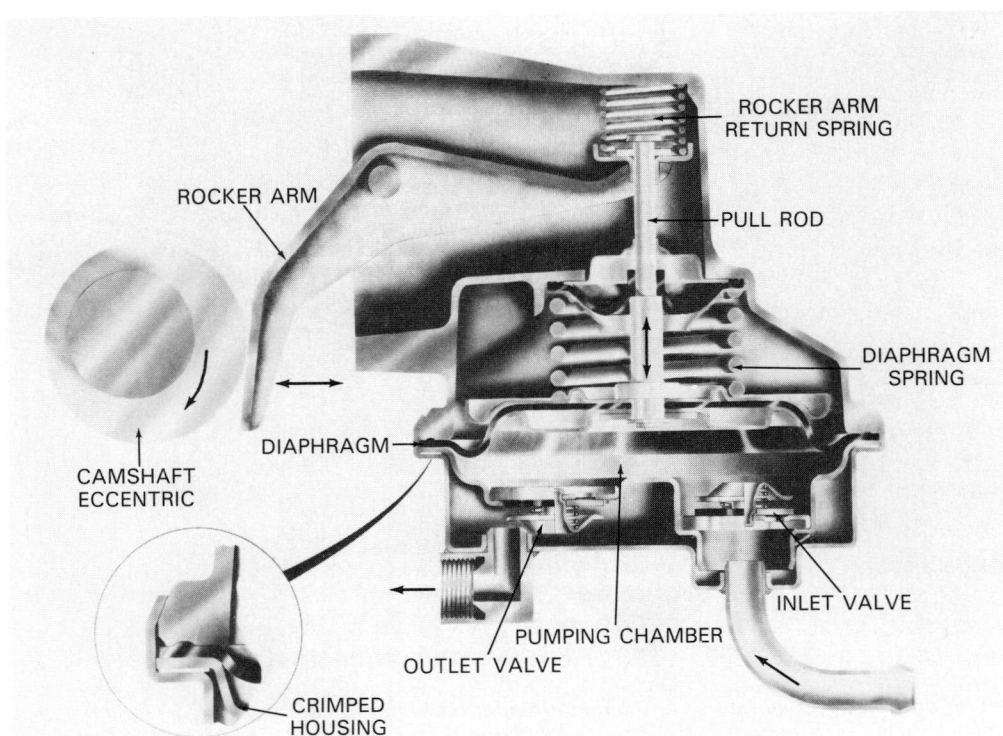

Fig. 18-11. Cutaway view of a typical mechanical fuel pump. Note part names and locations. (AC-Delco)

Fig. 18-7. The mechanical fuel pump bolts to the side of the engine block. A gasket prevents oil leakage between the pump and engine block.

Mechanical fuel pumps are commonly used with carburetor type fuel systems. They are the oldest type of fuel pump, but they are still found on many vehicles. Since the mechanical pump uses a back and forth motion, it is a RECIPROCATING type pump.

The parts of a basic mechanical fuel pump are shown in Fig. 18-11. Note how the rocker arm, diaphragm, springs, and check valves are positioned in the pump body.

Mechanical fuel pump construction

The *rocker arm,* also called an actuating lever, is a metal arm hinged in the middle. A small pin passes through the arm and fuel pump body. The outer end of the rocker arm rides on the camshaft eccentric. The inner end operates the diaphragm.

Sometimes, a push rod fits between the pump rocker arm and the eccentric. In any case, the rocker arm moves up and down as the eccentric turns.

The fuel pump *return spring* keeps the rocker arm pressed against the eccentric. Without a return spring, the rocker arm would make a loud CLATTERING SOUND as the eccentric lobe hit the rocker arm.

The *diaphragm* is a synthetic rubber disc clamped between the halves of the pump body. Refer to Fig. 18-11 once more. The core of the diaphragm is usually cloth which adds strength and durability. A metal pull rod is mounted on the diaphragm to connect the diaphragm with the rocker arm.

The *diaphragm spring,* when compressed, pushes on the diaphragm to produce fuel pressure and flow. This spring fits against the back of the diaphragm and against the pump body.

Two *check valves* are used in a mechanical fuel pump to make the fuel flow through the pump. Fig. 18-12 illustrates the basic action of a check valve. Fuel flows easily through the valve in one direction but cannot flow through in the other direction.

In a fuel pump, the two check valves are reversed. This causes the fuel to enter one valve and exit through the other.

Mechanical fuel pump operation

During the *intake stroke,* the eccentric lobe pushes on the rocker arm. See Fig. 18-13A. This pulls the diaphragm down and compresses the diaphragm spring. Since the area in the pumping chamber increases, a vacuum pulls fuel through the inlet check valve. This fills the pump with fuel.

On the *output stroke,* the eccentric lobe rotates away from the pump rocker arm. This releases the diaphragm, as in Fig. 18-13B. The diaphragm spring then pushes on the diaphragm and pressurizes the fuel in the pumping chamber. The amount of spring tension controls fuel pressure. The fuel flows out the outlet

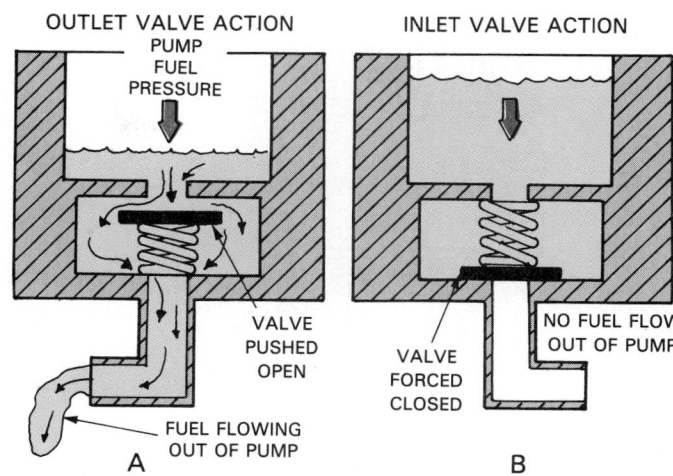

Fig. 18-12. Check valves only allow fuel flow in one direction. A — Check valve is positioned to allow fuel flow out of pressure chamber. Pressure acts on valve, compresses spring, and fuel moves through. B — Check valve is positioned to stop flow. Pressure helps close valve to seal pressure chamber.

check valve.

When the engine is running slowly, the fuel pump would produce more fuel than the engine consumes. For this reason, the fuel pump is made to *idle* when fuel is not needed. See 18-13C. The diaphragm pull rod is free to slide through the rocker arm. This lets the rocker arm move up and down while the diaphragm remains stationary. Diaphragm spring tension maintains fuel pressure.

Fig. 18-14 shows a cutaway view of another mechanical fuel pump. Study the names of the parts.

Vapor lock

Vapor lock is a problem created when bubbles in overheated fuel reduce or stop fuel flow. Fig. 18-15 shows vapor lock in a mechanical fuel pump.

During vapor lock, engine heat transfers through the metal parts of the pump and into the fuel. The fuel "boils," forming bubbles that displace fuel. This can reduce fuel pump output and cause engine performance problems.

ELECTRIC FUEL PUMPS

An *electric fuel pump,* like a mechanical pump, produces fuel pressure and flow for the fuel metering section of a fuel system. Electric fuel pumps are commonly used in gasoline fuel systems.

An electric fuel pump can be located inside the fuel tank as part of the fuel pickup-sending unit. It can also be located in the fuel line between the tank and engine. See Fig. 18-16.

An electric fuel pump has some possible advantages over a mechanical fuel pump. An electric pump can produce almost instant fuel pressure. A mechanical pump slowly builds pressure as the engine is cranked

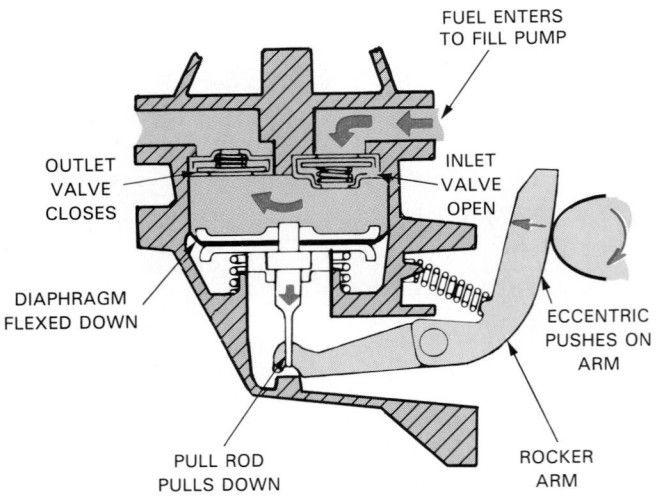

A — During intake stroke, eccentric pushes on rocker arm. Rocker arm pulls down on link and diaphragm. This pulls fuel into pump and compresses diaphragm spring.

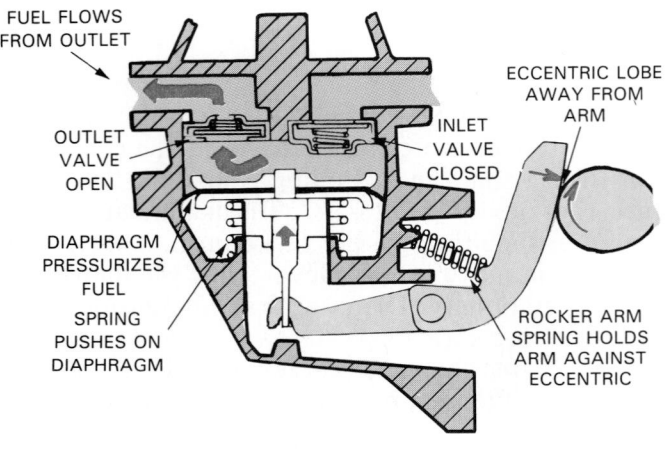

B — During output stroke, eccentric releases rocker arm. Spring then pushes on diaphragm to pressurize fuel in pump chamber. Fuel then flows out pump and to engine.

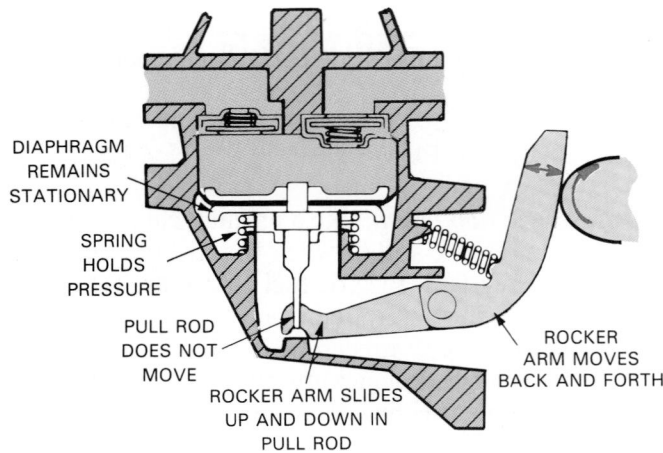

C — When idling, rocker slides in link. Diaphragm is stationary. Spring maintains pressure.

Fig. 18-13. Mechanical fuel pump operation.

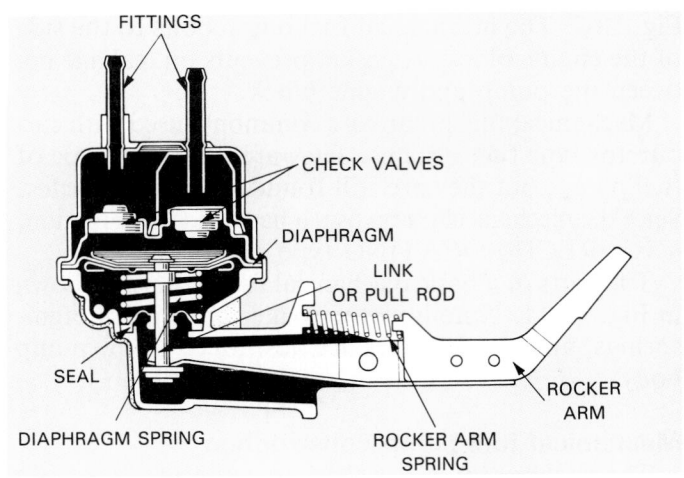

Fig. 18-14. Cutaway view of another mechanical fuel pump. (Toyota)

for starting. Also, most electric fuel pumps are a rotary type. They produce a smoother flow of fuel (less pressure pulsations) than a reciprocating, mechanical pump.

Since most electric fuel pumps are located away from the engine, they help prevent vapor lock. An electric fuel pump pressurizes all of the fuel lines that are near engine heat. This helps avoid vapor lock because pressure makes it more difficult for bubbles to form.

Rotary fuel pumps

Rotary fuel pumps include the impeller, roller vane, and sliding vane types. They use a circular or spinning motion to produce pressure.

An ***impeller electric fuel pump*** is a centrifugal type pump. Normally, it is located inside the fuel tank. See Fig. 18-17. This pump uses a small DC motor to spin the impeller (fan blade). The impeller blades cause the

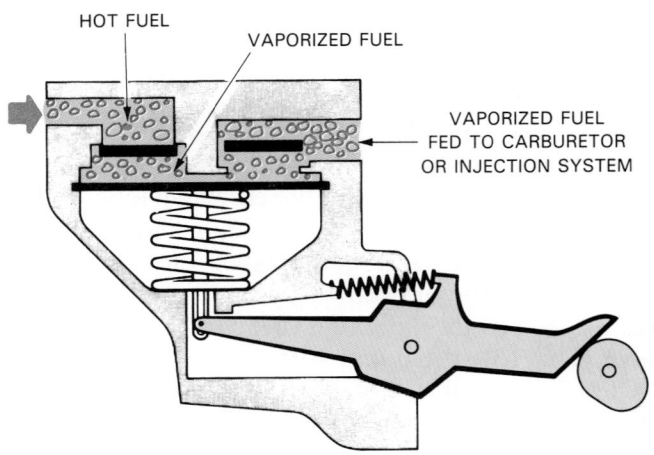

Fig. 18-15. Vapor lock is caused by too much engine heat transferring into fuel. Bubbles form and displace fuel. This can prevent fuel from flowing through system. (Ford)

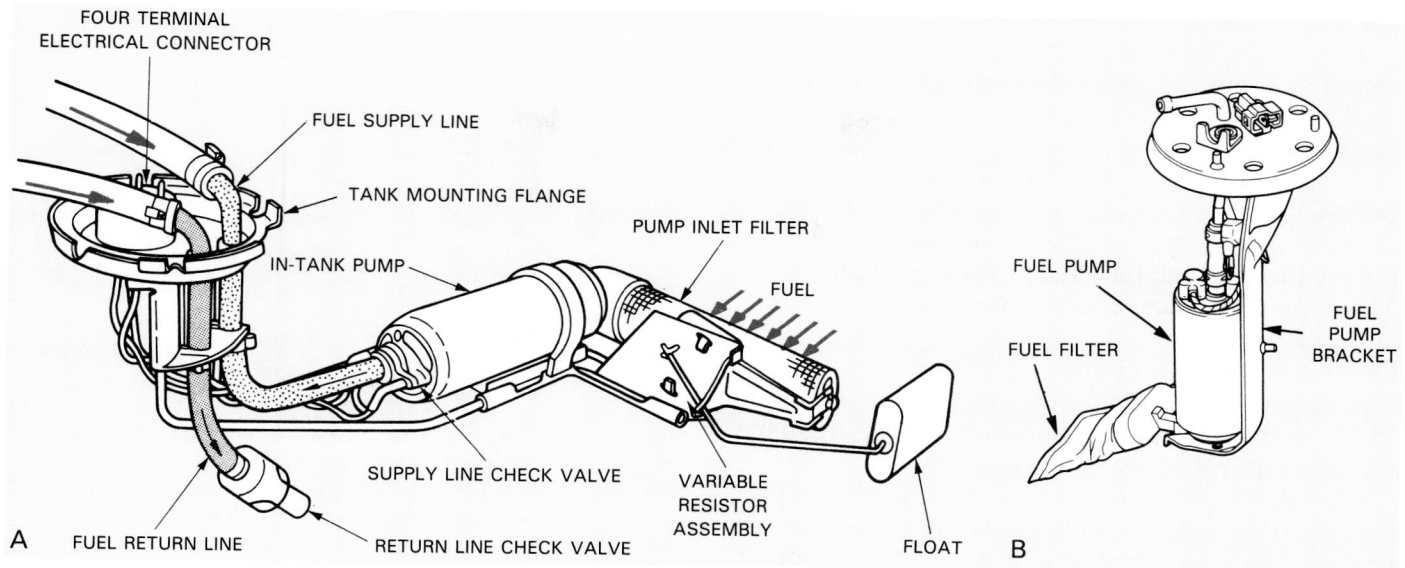

Fig. 18-16. A—This in-tank electric fuel pump has sending unit to operate fuel gauge in dash. B—This fuel pump requires a separate sending unit for fuel gauge. (Chrysler and Honda)

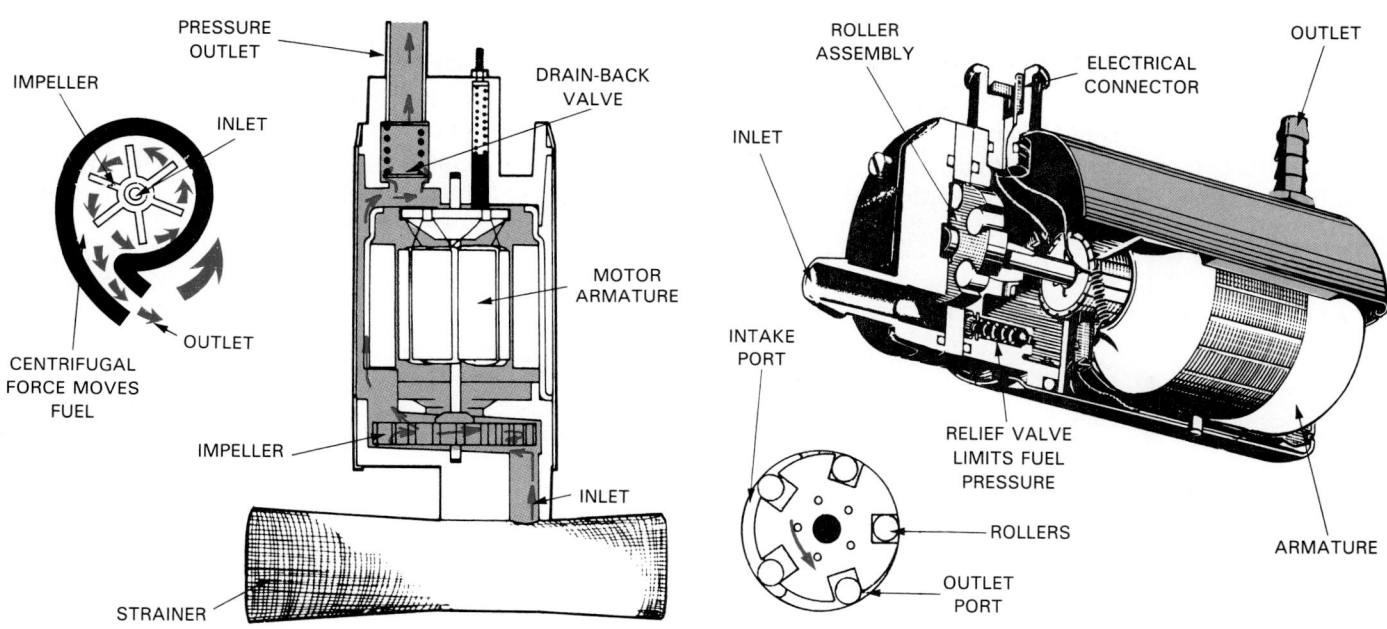

Fig. 18-17. In-tank, impeller type electric fuel pump. Impeller produces very smooth flow of fuel through system. Check valve prevents fuel from draining out of lines and back into tank when pump is not running. (Volvo, Ford)

Fig. 18-18. Roller vane electric fuel pump. This type pump is usually capable of producing higher pressure and more volume than an impeller type pump. Relief valve limits fuel pressure. (Volvo)

fuel to fly outward due to centrifugal force (spinning matter flys outward). This produces enough pressure to move the fuel through the fuel lines.

A *roller vane electric fuel pump* is a positive displacement pump (each pump rotation moves a specific amount of fuel). It is normally located in the main fuel line. Look at Fig. 18-18. Small rollers and an offset mounted rotor disc produce fuel pressure.

When the rotor disc and rollers spin, they pull fuel in on one side. Then, the fuel is trapped and pushed

to a smaller area on the opposite side of the pump housing. This squeezes the fuel between the rollers and the fuel flows out under pressure.

A *sliding vane electric fuel pump* is similar to a roller vane pump. Vanes (blades) are used instead of rollers.

As shown in Figs. 18-17 and 18-18, most rotary electric fuel pumps also have check valves and relief valves.

The electric fuel pump *check valves* keep fuel from draining out of the fuel line when the pump is not running. A *relief valve* limits the maximum output

Fuel Tanks, Pumps, Lines, Filters 199

pressure of the pump.

A *reciprocating electric fuel pump* has the same basic action as a mechanical fuel pump. However, it uses a solenoid instead of a rocker arm to produce a pumping motion.

A reciprocating pump commonly uses either a bellows or a plunger. The solenoid turns on and off to force the bellows or plunger up and down. This pushes fuel through the check valves and fuel system. This type pump is not very common.

Electric fuel pump circuit

A circuit for an electric fuel pump is shown in Fig. 18-19. Study the electrical connections. This circuit has a switch controlled by oil pressure.

The **oil pressure switch** is a safety feature that protects the engine from damage. If oil pressure drops below a safe level, the switch turns off the fuel pump, stopping the engine.

Many modern electric fuel pumps are controlled by an ON-BOARD COMPUTER. This is covered in later chapters.

AIR FILTERS

An *air filter,* or *air cleaner,* removes foreign matter (dirt and dust) from the air entering the engine intake manifold. See Fig. 18-20. Most air filters use a paper

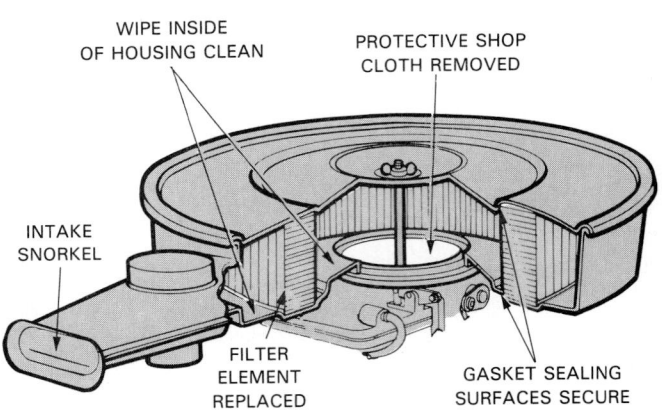

Fig. 18-20. Typical automotive air filter. Most air filters are made of pleated paper. Metal housing encloses paper element. Housing seals against top of carburetor, throttle body, or air inlet on diesel engines. (Chrysler)

element (filter material). The element fits inside a metal or plastic housing. For details of air cleaner systems, refer to Chapters 39 and 40.

FUEL SUPPLY SYSTEM SERVICE

Now that you have a basic understanding of how a fuel supply system functions, you are ready to learn about problems, tests, and repairs common to the fuel pump, lines, filters, and tank.

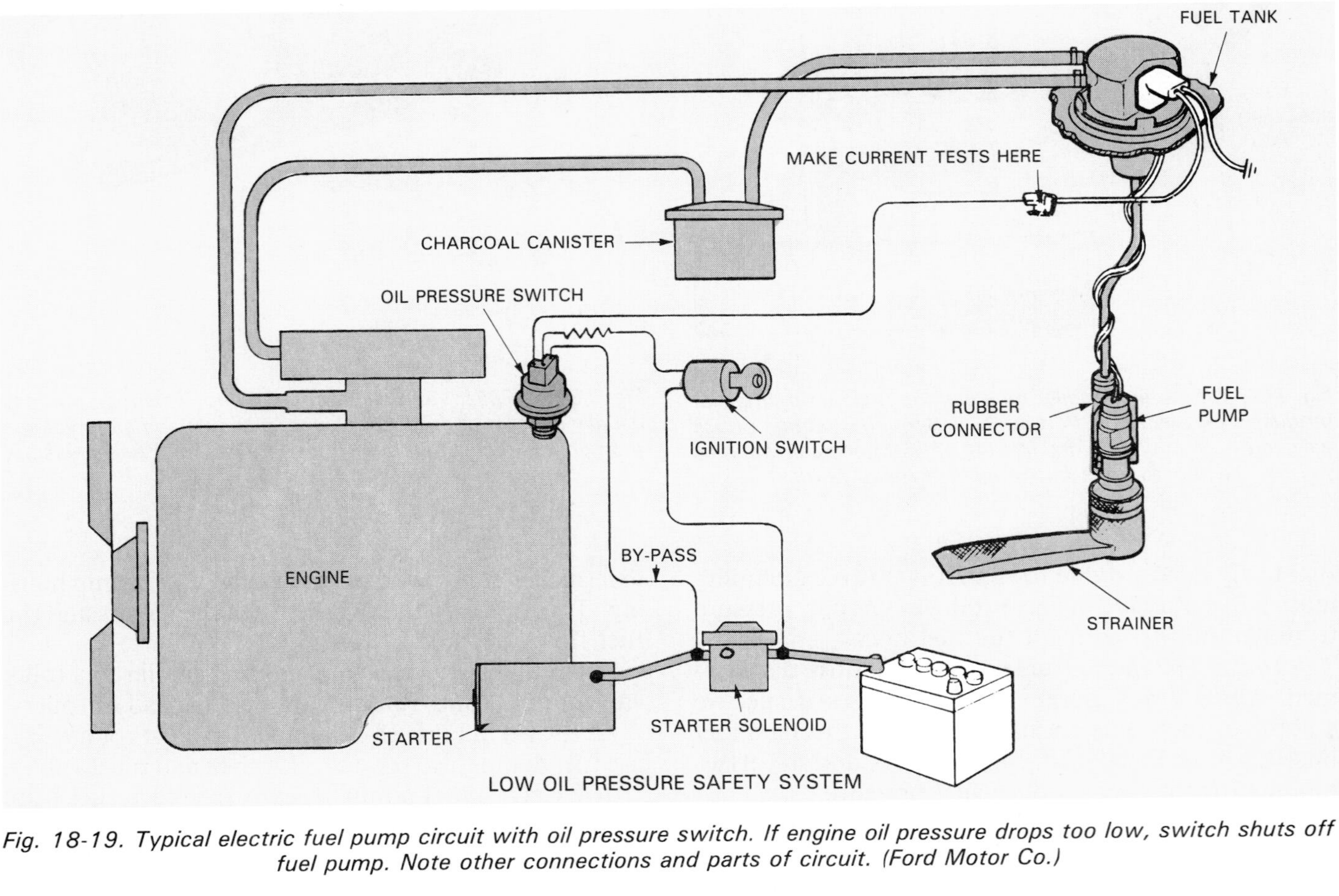

Fig. 18-19. Typical electric fuel pump circuit with oil pressure switch. If engine oil pressure drops too low, switch shuts off fuel pump. Note other connections and parts of circuit. (Ford Motor Co.)

IMPORTANT! Always keep a fire extinguisher handy when working on a car's fuel system. During a fire, a few minutes time can be a LIFETIME!

FUEL TANK SERVICE

Typical *fuel tank problems* include fuel leakage, physical damage (auto accidents), and contamination by foreign matter (rust, dirt, and water). Vibration or rusting can cause a fuel tank to develop pinhole leaks. Rocks can fly up and puncture the tank. Foreign matter can get in the fuel tank from the gas station pump, or from internal deterioration of the tank.

DANGER! Do NOT weld or solder a fuel tank. Send the leaking tank, if not badly rusted, to a well trained specialist. Even an empty tank can EXPLODE when fuel gum melts, vaporizes, and ignites from the heat of soldering or welding.

Fuel tank removal and replacement

A fuel tank can be located under the trunk, in a body panel, or under the rear seat. It may be held in the vehicle by large metal straps or by bolts passing through the tank flange.

CAUTION! Before servicing a fuel tank, empty the tank. A full tank is very heavy and can rupture if dropped. Fire could result!

To remove fuel from the tank, unscrew the drain plug and drain the fuel into an approved safety can. If a drain is NOT provided, use an approved pumping method to draw the fuel out of the tank. Fig. 18-21

Fig. 18-21. Hand-operated pump and safety container for removing fuel from tank. It will draw out and store fuel during repair. (Chrysler)

shows a special hand pump and tank designed for fuel tank service. After the tank is empty, you can remove it from the car.

DANGER! Wipe up fuel spills immediately with a shop towel or rag. Do NOT spread oil dry on fuel spills because the oil dry will become extremely flammable.

When installing a fuel tank, make sure you replace rubber insulators. Check that all fuel lines are properly secured. Replace the fuel in the tank and check for leaks. If needed, a service manual for the vehicle will detail exact tank installation procedures.

FUEL TANK SENDING UNIT SERVICE

A *faulty fuel tank sending unit* can make the fuel gauge reading inaccurate. Usually, the variable resistor in the sending unit fails. However, you should remember that the fuel gauge or the gauge circuit may be at fault.

First, test the action of the fuel gauge. Fig. 18-22 shows a fuel gauge tester. It is connected to the wire going to the fuel tank sending unit.

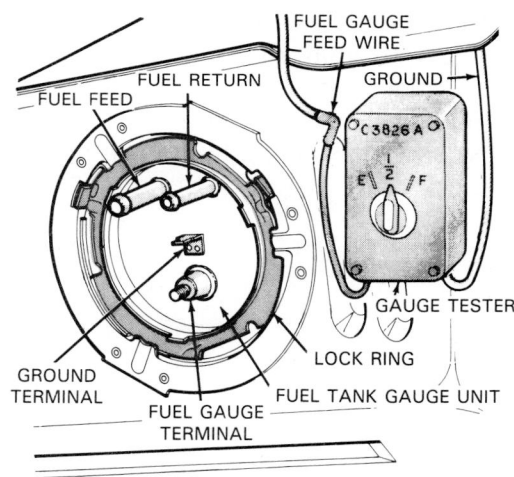

Fig. 18-22. Special tester will quickly check condition of fuel gauge and circuit. If circuit and gauge are working well, problem may be in tank sending unit. Note how sending unit is held in fuel tank by lock ring. (Chrysler)

When the tester is set on full, for example, the fuel gauge should read full.

If the gauge does NOT function, either the gauge or the gauge circuit is faulty. If the fuel gauge begins to work with the tester in place, the tank sending unit is probably bad.

If your tests indicate an inoperative fuel tank sending unit, remove the unit after draining the tank. Unscrew the cam lock holding the sending unit in the fuel tank, Fig. 18-23. Lift the unit out of the tank.

With the sending unit removed, measure its resistance with an ohmmeter, Fig. 18-24. If the resistance is not

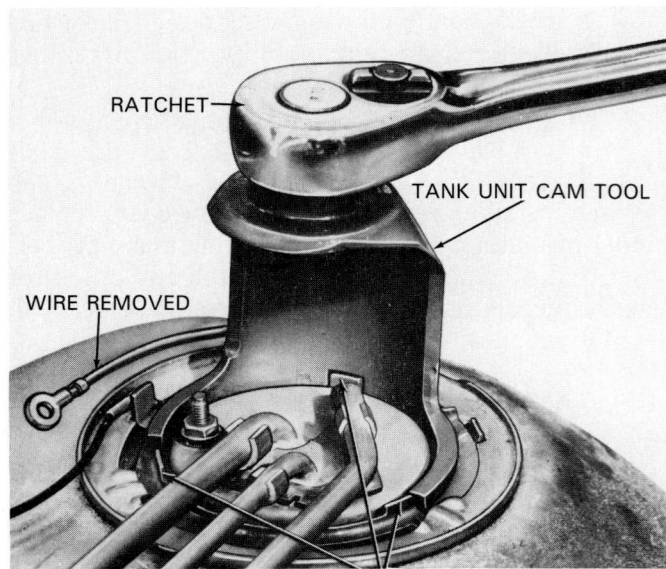

Fig. 18-23. To remove tank sending unit, turn cam lock ring. Special tool makes this easy. Light taps with a hammer on a full shank screwdriver will also work. (Cadillac)

within factory specs, install a new sending unit.

Also check the sending unit float for leakage. Shake the float next to your ear. If you can hear liquid splashing, replace the float.

If the tank unit resistance is good, check the tank ground. A poor ground could prevent operation.

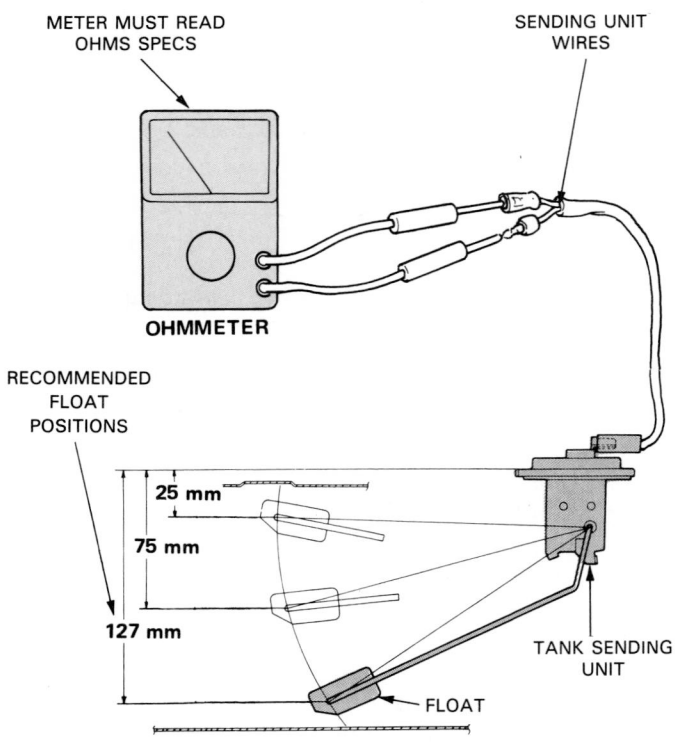

Fig. 18-24. Ohmmeter can be used to check condition of tank sending unit. Ohms should be within specs with float in prescribed positions. (Honda)

FUEL LINE AND HOSE SERVICE

Faulty fuel lines and *hoses* are a common source of fuel leaks. See Fig. 18-25. Fuel hoses can become hard and brittle after being exposed to engine heat and the elements. Engine oil can soften and swell them. Always inspect hoses closely and replace any in poor condition.

Metal fuel lines seldom cause problems. However, they should be replaced when smashed, kinked, rusted, or leaking.

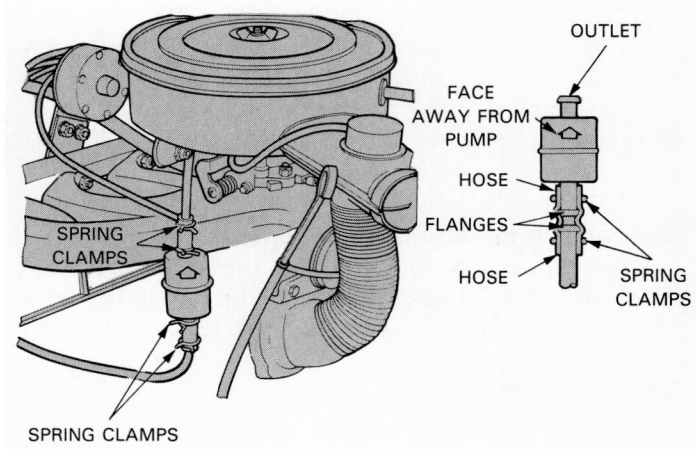

Fig. 18-25. Always check all fuel hoses for signs of deterioration. When replacing a hose, make sure it is pushed fully over fittings. (Chrysler)

Fuel line and hose service rules

Remember these rules when working with fuel lines and hoses:

1. Place a shop rag around the fuel line fitting during removal. This will keep fuel from spraying on you or on the hot engine. Use a flare nut or tubing wrench on fuel system fittings.
2. Only use approved double-wall steel tubing for fuel lines. Never use copper or plastic tubing.
3. Make smooth bends when forming a new fuel line. Use a bending spring or bending tool.
4. Form double-lap flares on the ends of the fuel line. A single lap flare is not approved for fuel lines. Refer to Fig. 18-26.
5. Reinstall fuel line hold-down clamps and brackets. If not properly supported, the fuel line can vibrate and fail.
6. Route all fuel lines and hoses away from hot or moving parts. Double-check clearance after installation.
7. Only use approved synthetic rubber hoses in a fuel system. If vacuum type rubber hose is accidentally used, the fuel can chemically attack and rapidly ruin the hose. A dangerous leak could result.
8. Make sure a fuel hose fully covers its fitting or line before installing the clamps. Pressure in the fuel

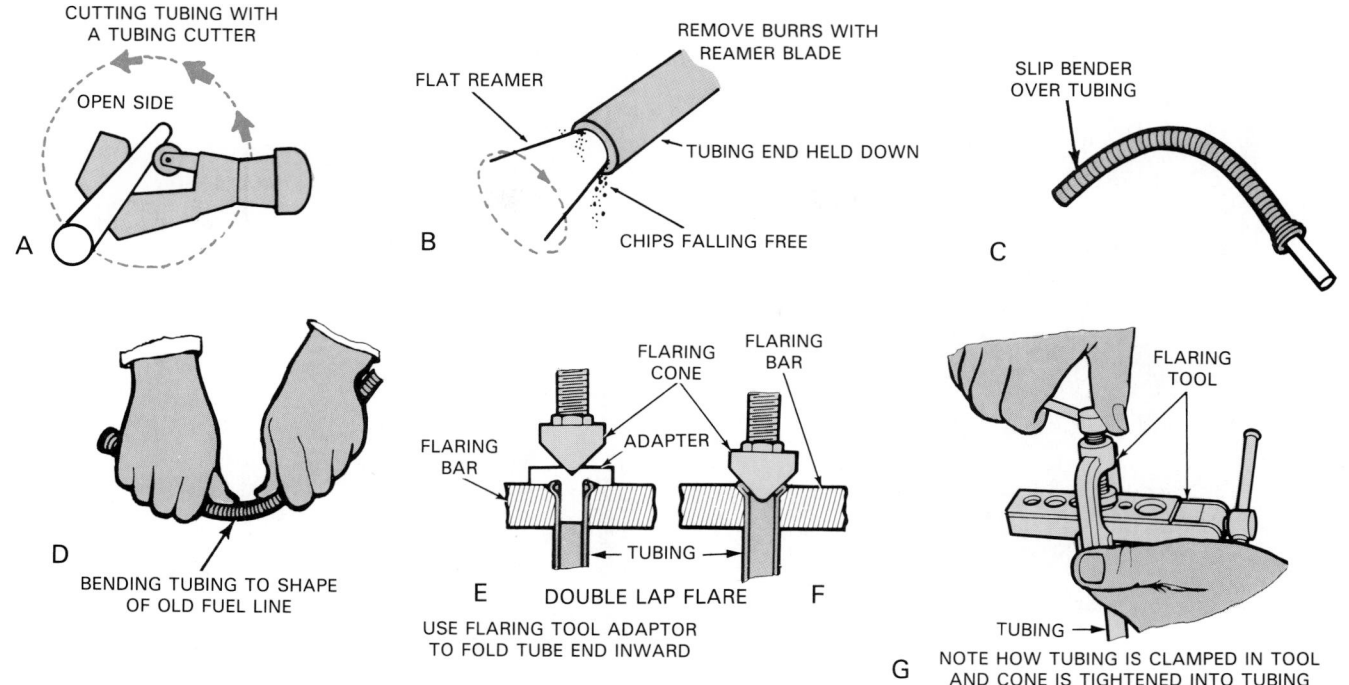

Fig. 18-26. Fuel lines need double-lap flares. Study basic steps for making a new fuel line. This procedure also applies to other lines (brake lines, steel vacuum lines, etc.). (Florida Dept. of Voc. Ed. and Chrysler)

system could force the hose off if it is not installed properly.

9. Double-check all fittings for leaks. Start the engine and inspect the connections closely.

DANGER! Most fuel injection systems have very high fuel pressure. Follow recommended procedures for bleeding or releasing pressure before disconnecting a fuel line or fitting. This will prevent fuel spray from possibly causing injury or a fire!

FUEL FILTER SERVICE

Fuel filter service involves periodic replacement or cleaning of system filters. It may also include locating clogged fuel filters that are upsetting fuel system operation. Replace paper-element filters when clogged or after prolonged service. Sintered bronze fuel filters can usually be cleaned and reinstalled.

A *clogged fuel filter* can restrict the flow of fuel to the carburetor, gasoline injectors, or diesel injection pump. Engine performance problems will usually show up at higher cruising speeds.

For example, the engine may temporarily loose power or stall when a specific engine speed is reached.

A partially clogged filter may pass enough fuel at low engine speeds. However, when engine speed and fuel flow increase, the engine may "starve" for fuel.

On older vehicles, a *clogged in-tank strainer* is a common and hard to diagnose problem. The in-tank filter, when clogged, can collapse and stop all fuel flow. Then, after the engine stalls, the strainer can open again leaving no trace of a restriction.

Some fuel filters have a check valve that opens when the filter becomes clogged. This will allow fuel contaminants to flow into the system. When contaminants are found in the filters and system, the tank, pump, and lines should be flushed with clean fuel.

Fuel filter locations

Fuel filters may be found in the following locations:

1. In the fuel line before the carburetor, fuel injectors, or diesel injection pump.
2. Inside the fuel pump.
3. In the fuel line right after the electric fuel pump.
4. Under the fuel line fitting in the carburetor.
5. A fuel strainer is also located in the fuel tank on the end of the fuel pickup tube.

When in doubt about fuel filter locations, refer to a service manual. It will give information about service intervals, cleaning, and replacement of all system filters.

If a fitting must be loosened when changing a fuel filter, use a flare nut wrench, as in Fig. 18-27. Do not overtighten and strip the fitting when replacing. Double-check that the fuel hose, if used, is fully installed over the fitting barbs.

FUEL PUMP SERVICE

Fuel pump problems usually show up as low fuel pressure, inadequate fuel flow, abnormal pump noise, or fuel leakage from the pump. Both mechanical and electric fuel pumps can fail after prolonged operation.

Low fuel pump pressure can be caused by a weak diaphragm spring, ruptured diaphragm, leaking check valves, or physical wear of moving parts. Low fuel

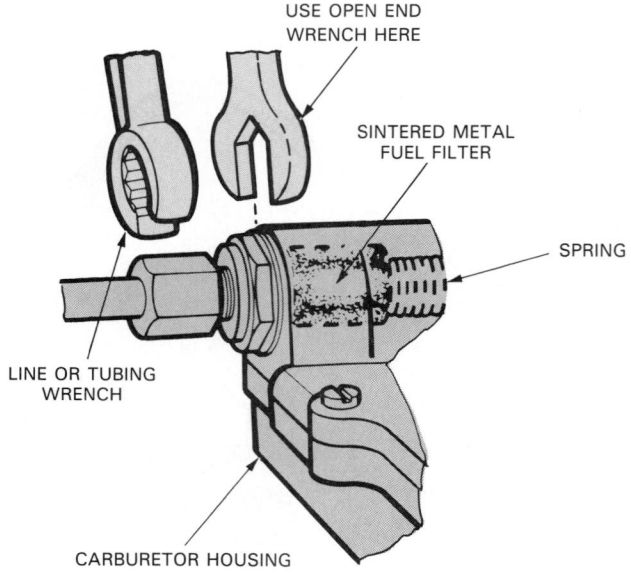

Fig. 18-27. When loosening or tightening a fuel line fitting, use a line wrench. This will help prevent rounding off soft fitting nut. Do not overtighten fittings. Their threads will strip easily. (Chrysler)

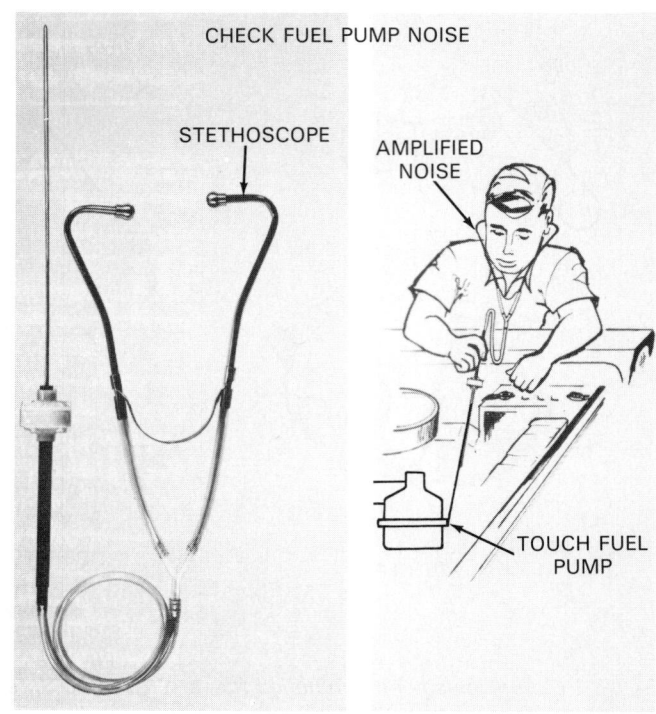

Fig. 18-28. A stethoscope will quickly locate a noisy mechanical or electric fuel pump. A clattering mechanical pump will sound like a faulty engine lifter. (Lyle Tools)

pump pressure can make the engine starve for fuel at higher engine speeds.

High fuel pump pressure, more frequent with electric pumps, indicates an inoperative pressure relief valve. If the relief valve fails to open, both pressure and volume can be above normal. High fuel pressure can produce a rich fuel mixture or even flood the engine.

Mechanical fuel pump noise (clacking sound from inside pump) is commonly caused by a weak or broken rocker arm return spring or by wear of the rocker arm pin or arm itself. Mechanical fuel pump noise can be easily confused with valve or tappet clatter. They sound very similar. To verify mechanical fuel pump noise, use a stethoscope, Fig. 18-28.

NOTE! Most electric fuel pumps make some noise (buzz or whirr sound) when running. Only when the pump noise is abnormally loud should an electric fuel pump be considered faulty.

A clogged tank strainer can cause excessive pump noise. Pump speed can increase because fuel is not entering the pump properly.

Fuel pump leaks are caused by physical damage to the pump body or deterioration of the diaphragm or gaskets. Most mechanical fuel pumps have a small vent hole in the pump body. When the diaphragm is ruptured, fuel will leak out of this hole.

It is possible for a ruptured mechanical fuel pump diaphragm to contaminate the engine oil with gasoline. Fuel can leak through the diaphragm, through the pump, into the side of the block, and down into the oil pan. When a gasoline smell is noticed in the oil, correct the pump problem; then change the oil and filter.

Fuel pump tests

Fuel pump testing commonly involves measuring fuel pump pressure and volume. Since exact procedures vary, depending upon fuel system type, refer to a manual for exact testing methods. Sometimes, fuel pump vacuum is measured as another means of determining pump and supply line condition.

WARNING! Most fuel injection systems operate on very high fuel pressure. Make sure you tighten all test connections and follow prescribed procedures when testing fuel pump output.

Always remember that there are several other problems that can produce symptoms like those caused by a bad fuel pump. Before testing a fuel pump, check for:

1. Restricted fuel filters.
2. Smashed or kinked fuel lines or hoses.
3. Air leak into vacuum side of pump or line.
4. Carburetor or injection system troubles.
5. Ignition system problems.
6. Low engine compression.

Measuring fuel pump pressure

To measure fuel pump pressure, connect a pressure gauge to the output line of the fuel pump. This is illustrated in Fig. 18-29.

Typically, you would start and idle the engine at spec rpm to test a mechanical fuel pump. To test an electric fuel pump, you may only need to activate (supply voltage to) the pump motor. Compare your pressure readings to specifications.

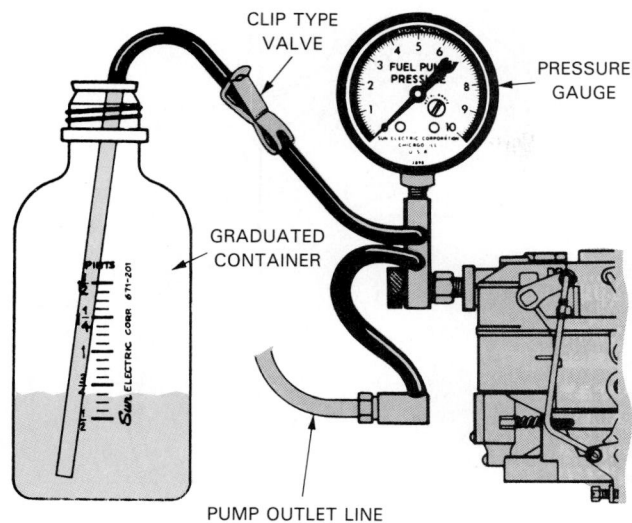

CLIP TYPE VALVE

PRESSURE GAUGE

GRADUATED CONTAINER

PUMP OUTLET LINE

FUEL PUMP SPECIFICATIONS				
	Volume (30 seconds)	Pressure (PSI) (kPa)	Vacuum (Hg)	
			Direct	Indirect
Four Cylinder	0.6 pint (0.28 liters)	4 to 6 (27.58 to 41.36)	7 23.64 kPa	3 10.13 kPa
Six Cylinder	1 pint (0.47 liters)	4 to 5 (27.58 to 34.47)	10 33.77 kPa	3 10.13 kPa
Eight Cylinder	1 pint (0.47 liters)	5 to 6.5 (34.47 to 44.81)	10 33.77 kPa	3 10.13 kPa

Fig. 18-29. To test fuel pump pressure and volume, connect test equipment as shown. Connect gauge to line before carburetor, fuel manifold, or throttle body. Close clip and start engine to measure pressure. Open clip to measure volume over prescribed time span. Chart shows fuel pump specs for one make and model car. (Sun Electric, Chrysler)

Fuel pressure for a *carburetor* type fuel system should be about 4 to 6 psi (28 to 41 kPa) pressure. A *gasoline injection* system will usually have a higher pressure output. Fuel pressure can run from 15 to almost 40 psi (103 to 276 kPa). A *diesel* supply pump should produce around 6-10 psi (41-69 kPa). It feeds fuel to the very high pressure injection pump.

Always remember to use factory values when determining fuel pump condition. Pressures vary from system to system.

If fuel pump pressure is NOT within specs, check pump volume and the lines and filters before replacing the fuel pump.

Measuring fuel pump volume

Fuel pump volume, also called *capacity,* is the amount of fuel the pump can deliver in a specific amount of time. It is measured by allowing fuel to pour into a graduated (marked) container for a certain time period.

To check fuel pump volume, use a setup similar to that in Fig. 18-29. Route the output line from the fuel pump into a special container. For safety, a valve or clip should be used to control fuel flow into the container.

With the engine idling at a set speed, allow fuel to pour into the container for the prescribed amount of time (normally 30 seconds). Close off the clip or valve. Compare volume output to specs.

Fuel pump volume output should be a minimum of about ONE PINT (0.47 liters) in 30 seconds for carburetor systems. Fuel injection systems typically have a slightly higher volume output from the supply pump. Refer to factory service manual values for the particular fuel pump and automobile.

Measuring fuel pump vacuum

Fuel pump vacuum should be checked when a fuel pump fails pressure and volume tests. A vacuum test will eliminate possible problems in the fuel lines, hoses, filters, and pickup screen in the tank.

For example, a clogged fuel pickup screen could make the fuel pump fail the volume test. If the same pump passes a vacuum test, you need to check the lines and filters for problems.

To measure fuel pump vacuum, connect a vacuum gauge to the inlet side of the pump. Leave the fuel hose in your graduated container from the volume test. Open the valve and activate the pump (start engine and allow to run on fuel in carburetor or connect voltage to electric pump). Compare your reading to specs.

Typically, *fuel pump vacuum* should be about 7 to 10 in./hg. A good vacuum reading indicates a good fuel pump. If the pump failed the pressure or volume test but passed the vacuum test, the fuel supply lines and filter may be at fault.

Electric fuel pump circuit tests

Many electric fuel pump problems are caused by circuit problems. Broken wires, bad relays, shorts, blown fuses, computer malfunctions, and other troubles can affect electric fuel pump operation.

If an electric fuel pump does NOT pass its pressure or volume tests, measure the amount of voltage being fed to the pump motor. Look at Fig. 18-30. If supply voltage is low, there is a problem in the electrical circuit to the pump.

When circuit problems must be found, use your knowledge of basic testing and a service manual. Generally, test at various points until the source of the trouble is found. Fig. 18-31 shows a wiring diagram for one electric fuel pump circuit. Note that there are only a few components and electrical connections that could upset pump operation.

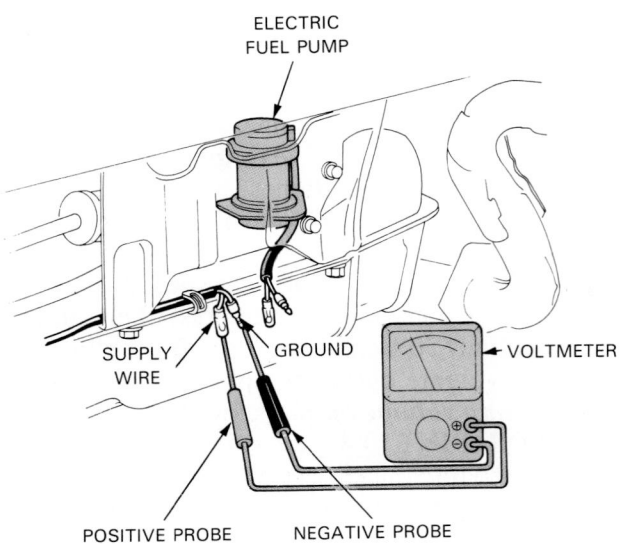

Fig. 18-30. Before condemning an electric fuel pump, make sure circuit is in good condition. Measure amount of voltage being supplied to pump and compare to specs. If voltage is low, repair circuit. (Honda)

FUEL PUMP SHUTOFF CIRCUITS

An *inertia switch* can be used to block current flow to the electrical fuel pump after a severe impact or collision. It is a safety device that can prevent a serious fire after an auto accident. The inertia switch is usually located in the trunk or near the electric fuel pump. After a collision, you must press a button on the inertia switch before the electric pump will function again.

A *low-oil pressure switch* can be used to shut off the electric fuel pump if engine oil pressure drops too low. Its circuit is designed to protect the engine from major mechanical damage.

FUEL PUMP REMOVAL AND REPLACEMENT

When a fuel pump does NOT pass its performance

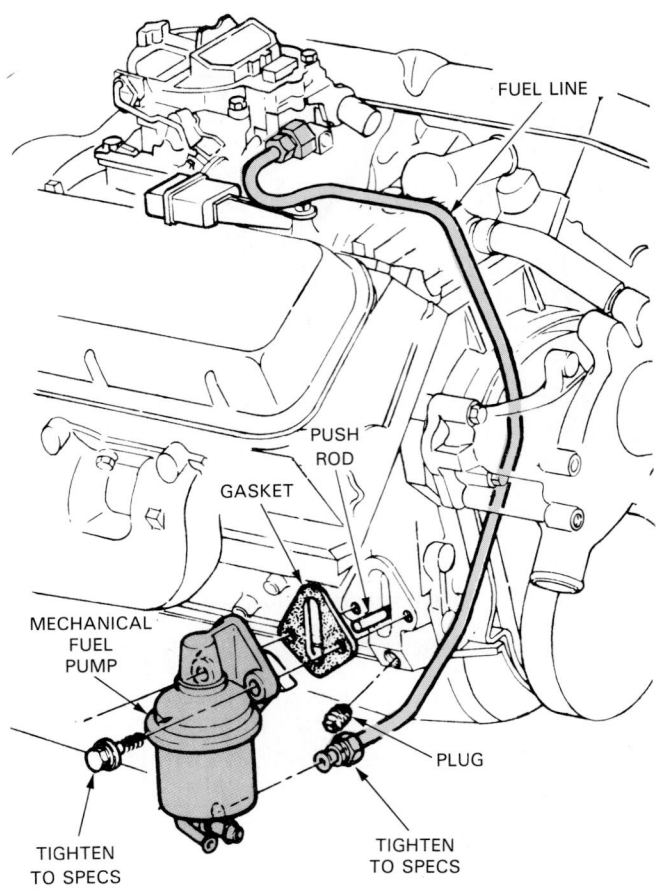

Fig. 18-32. To service mechanical fuel pump, remove lines and hoses. Then remove pump-to-block fasteners. Use new gasket when installing. Torque fasteners to specs. (Chevrolet)

tests, it must be removed for replacement or rebuilding.

To remove a mechanical fuel pump, simply disconnect the fuel lines and unbolt the pump from the engine, Fig. 18-32. If needed, tap the side of the pump with a plastic hammer to free the gasket.

An electric fuel pump may be located in the main fuel line or in the fuel tank. With an in-line pump,

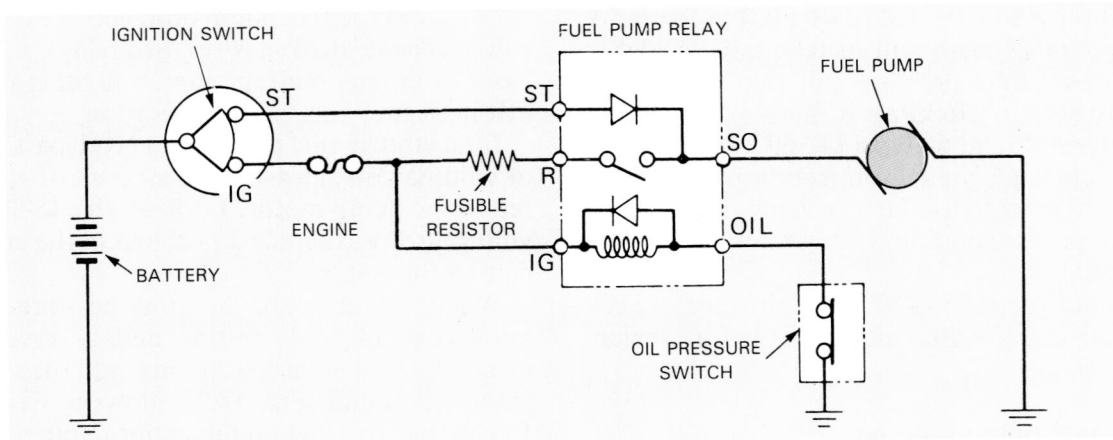

Fig. 18-31. Typical fuel pump control circuit. Note fusible resistor, relay, oil pressure switch, and pump. Any defective part could upset pump operation. (Toyota)

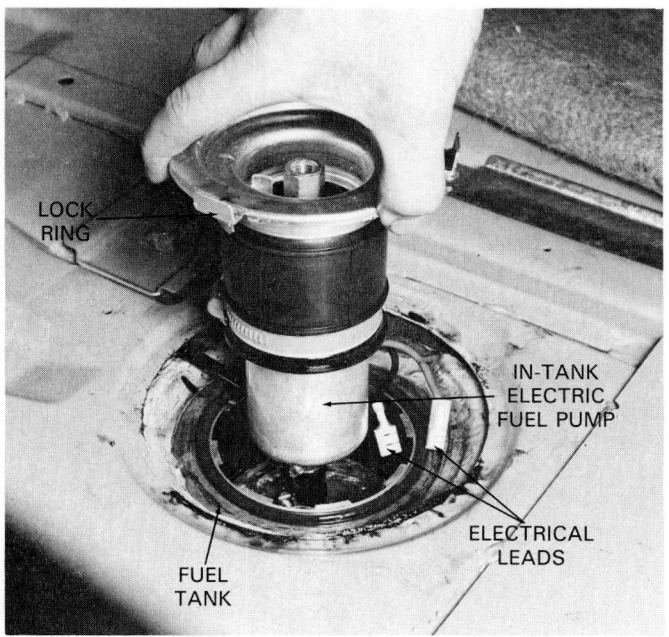

Fig. 18-33. In-tank electric fuel pump is removed like a tank pickup-sending unit. Unscrew lock and pull out. Use new O-ring seal when installing pump. (Saab)

simply disconnect the fuel fittings and remove the pump. An in-tank pump usually must be removed as part of the tank sending unit, Fig. 18-33. This procedure was described earlier in the chapter.

Fuel pump rebuilding

Modern mechanical fuel pumps and almost all elec-

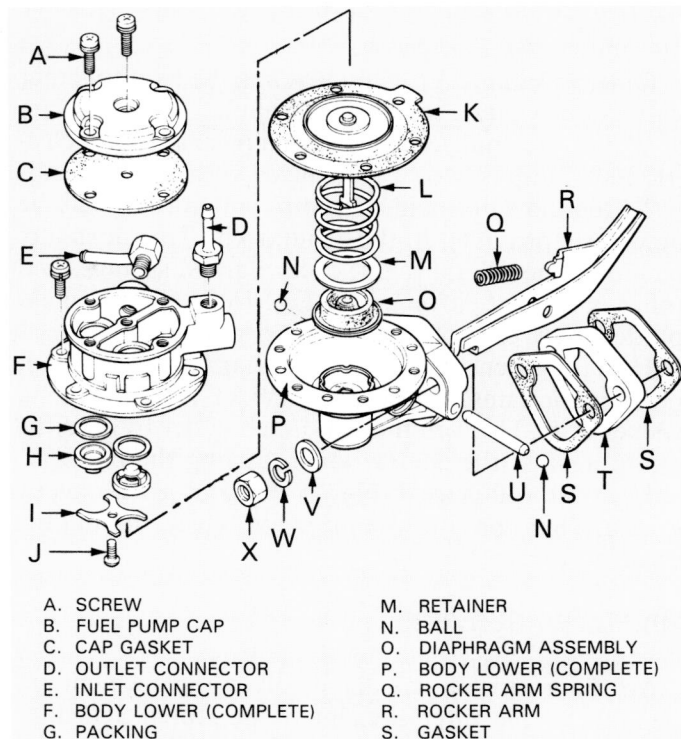

A. SCREW	M. RETAINER
B. FUEL PUMP CAP	N. BALL
C. CAP GASKET	O. DIAPHRAGM ASSEMBLY
D. OUTLET CONNECTOR	P. BODY LOWER (COMPLETE)
E. INLET CONNECTOR	Q. ROCKER ARM SPRING
F. BODY LOWER (COMPLETE)	R. ROCKER ARM
G. PACKING	S. GASKET
H. VALVE ASSEMBLY	T. SPACER
I. RETAINER	U. ROCKER PIN
J. SCREW	V. PLAIN WASHER
K. DIAPHRAGM ASSEMBLY	W. SPRING WASHER
L. DIAPHRAGM SPRING	X. NUT

Fig. 18-35. Exploded view of a mechanical pump. Rebuilding involves replacing parts suffering wear or deterioration: diaphragm, check valves, gaskets, springs, and any other part in poor condition. These parts usually come in a rebuild kit. (Nissan)

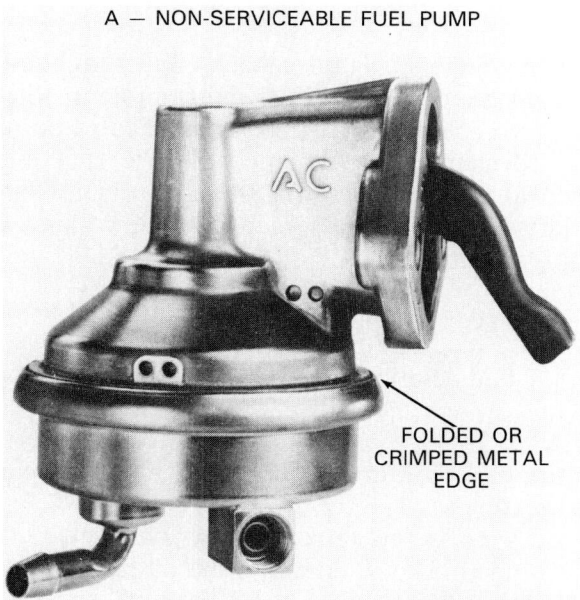

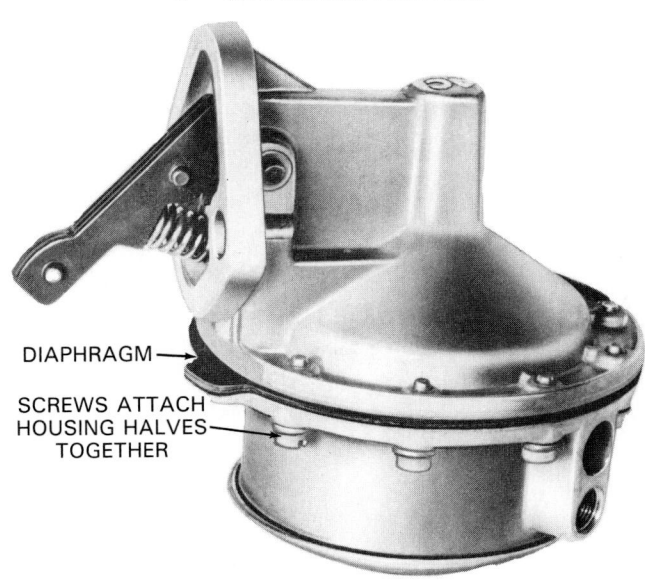

Fig. 18-34. Most mechanical fuel pumps are not serviceable. They must be replaced when bad. A — Nonserviceable pump cannot be taken apart. B — Serviceable pump is held together by screws. Check for parts availability before doing too much work on old pump. (AC-Delco)

tric fuel pumps are sealed at the factory and CANNOT be rebuilt. See Fig. 18-34.

Older mechanical fuel pumps may be held together with screws and can be overhauled if parts are available. Normally, when either a mechanical or electric fuel pump is bad, it is replaced with a new pump.

To rebuild a mechanical pump, you must install the new parts provided in the rebuild kit. This normally includes a new diaphragm, check valves, springs, and other parts that suffer wear. Fig. 18-35 shows an exploded view of a mechanical fuel pump.

HINT! When installing a mechanical fuel pump, position the camshaft eccentric AWAY from the pump rocker arm. This will make it much easier to hold the pump against the engine while starting the bolts.

If a push rod is used, Fig. 18-36, coat it with heavy grease. Then, push it up into place. This will hold the pushrod out of the way.

AIR FILTER SERVICE

Air filter service usually involves replacement or cleaning of the filter element. Paper filter elements, the most common, are usually replaced with a new unit. Look at Fig. 18-37.

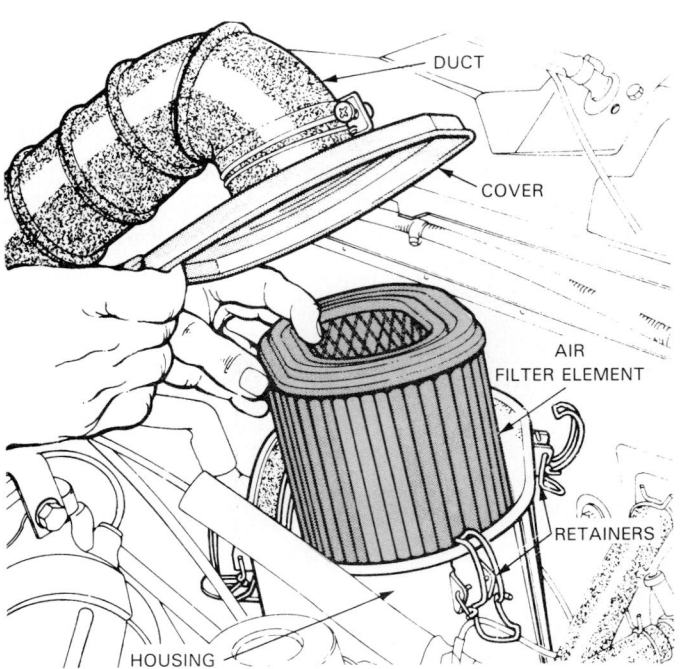

Fig. 18-37. Paper filter elements are normally replaced when dirty. Some auto makers allow using compressed air to blow dirt out of element in reverse direction. Make sure housing is secure and not leaking. (Chrysler)

When replacing a filter element, you should also wipe out the filter housing. Dirt can collect in the bottom of the housing.

CAUTION! Be careful not to drop anything into the air inlet opening in the carburetor or fuel injection system. As a precaution, place a clean shop rag over the engine's air inlet.

KNOW THESE TERMS

Driving range, Fuel tank capacity, Filler neck restrictor, Tank sending unit, Fuel return system, Pleated paper filter, Sintered bronze filter, Vapor separator-filter, Mechanical fuel pump, Electric fuel pump, Check valve, Vapor lock, Oil pressure switch, Double-lap flare, Fuel pump pressure, Fuel pump volume, Fuel pump vacuum.

REVIEW QUESTIONS

1. List and describe the three subsystems of a modern fuel system.
2. A _____ _____ system draws fuel from the fuel tank and forces it to the fuel metering device.
3. An average fuel tank capacity is around 12 to 25 gallons (45 to 95 liters). True or False?
4. What is the purpose of a filler neck restrictor in a fuel tank assembly?
5. Explain what can happen if leaded fuel is used in a car designed for unleaded fuel.

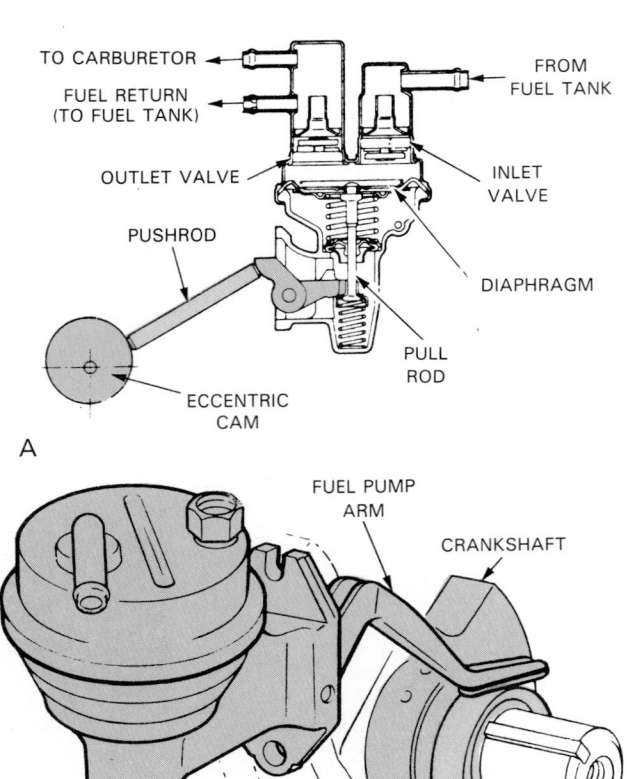

Fig. 18-36. A — This mechanical fuel pump uses a push rod between eccentric cam and rocker arm. When installing pump, use heavy grease, hacksaw blade, or special tool to hold push rod up in block. B — This supply pump works off of eccentric on diesel engine crankshaft. (Chrysler and GMC)

6. Which of the following is NOT part of a fuel tank pickup-sending unit?
   a. Vapor separator.
   b. In-tank fuel strainer or filter.
   c. Variable resistor.
   d. Pickup tube.
7. Fuel lines are normally made of single-wall steel tubing. True or False?
8. When are fuel hoses needed?
9. Explain the operation of a fuel return system.
10. The following could NOT be a fuel filter.
    a. Pleated paper filter.
    b. Sintered bronze filter.
    c. Bowl filter.
    d. Canister filter.
    e. All of the above are correct.
11. The two basic types of fuel pumps are the _____ and _____ types.
12. Explain the difference between the two types of fuel pumps in Question 11.
13. The _____ _____ controls fuel pressure in a mechanical fuel pump.
14. During the intake stroke of a mechanical fuel pump, the camshaft's eccentric pushes on the pump rocker arm. True or False?
15. Can a mechanical fuel pump idle? Explain.
16. Define the term "vapor lock."
17. Where can electric fuel pumps be located?
18. Which of the following is an advantage of an electric fuel pump?
    a. Instant fuel pressure.
    b. Very little pressure pulsations.
    c. Helps prevent vapor lock.
    d. All of the above are correct.
19. Rotary type electric fuel pumps include the _____, _____ _____, and _____ _____ types.
20. A _____ _____ limits the maximum output pressure of an electric fuel pump.
21. Why is an oil pressure switch sometimes used in an electric fuel pump circuit?
22. List nine service rules for fuel lines and hoses.
23. A car engine repeatedly stalls or quits running when driven at a constant speed higher than approximately 30 mph (48 km/h).
    Technician A says that the electric fuel pump may not be running due to a blown fuse.
    Technician B says that a fuel filter may be clogged and limiting fuel flow at higher engine speeds.
    Who is correct?
    a. Technician A
    b. Technician B
    c. Both A and B
    d. Neither A nor B
24. Name five typical fuel filter locations.
25. An engine is producing a clacking sound from the lower left side of the engine. It is a constant rapping noise that speeds up as engine speed increases.
    Technician A says that a stethoscope should be used to check for mechanical fuel pump noise. There may be a weak or broken rocker arm spring.
    Technician B says that it may be a faulty hydraulic lifter because the speed of the noise changes with engine speed. The problem could NOT be fuel system related.
    Who is correct?
    a. Technician A
    b. Technician B
    c. Both A and B
    d. Neither A nor B
26. Fuel pump pressure for a carburetor type fuel system should be approximately _____ to _____ psi or _____ to _____ kPa.
27. A gasoline injection system can have fuel pressure much higher than a carburetor type fuel system. True or False?
28. What is a fuel pump volume test?
29. An engine fuel pump has failed the pressure and volume tests.
    Technician A says that the fuel pump is bad and should be replaced or rebuilt.
    Technician B says that a fuel pump vacuum test should be done to make sure the lines and filters before the pump are in good condition.
    Who is correct?
    a. Technician A
    b. Technician B
    c. Both A and B
    d. Neither A nor B
30. If an electric fuel pump fails all performance tests, check the supply voltage to the pump before pump replacement. True or False?

ACTIVITIES FOR CHAPTER 18

1. Referring to Chapter 7, Fig. 7-7, prepare a "tree diagnosis chart" for a fuel pump problem assigned by your instructor. Your resource will be a shop manual for the specific vehicle and your instructor. If your instructor requests it, review the procedure to the class using an overhead projector and sketches.
2. Review electrical principles on resistance in a circuit and explain with sketches how a thermostatic fuel gauge works.

Carburetor Fundamentals

After studying this chapter, you will be able to:
☐ Describe and identify the basic parts of a carburetor.
☐ Compare carburetor design differences.
☐ List and explain the fundamental carburetor systems.
☐ Explain special carburetor devices.
☐ Describe the operation of computer controlled carburetors.

The principles of supplying an engine with the right amounts of fuel and air have not changed over the years. However, stricter exhaust emission laws and the need for improved fuel economy have changed carburetor requirements. Today's carburetors use numerous devices, including computers, to alter the air-fuel ratio with changes in engine speed, temperature, and load.

This chapter introduces the fundamental principles of carburetion. It discusses carburetor systems, design differences, auxiliary control devices, and closed-loop control systems. It will prepare you to study the service and repair of carburetors in the next chapter.

BASIC CARBURETOR

A *carburetor* is basically a device for mixing air and fuel in the correct proportions (amounts) for efficient combustion. The carburetor bolts to the engine intake manifold. The air cleaner fits over the top of the carburetor to trap dust and dirt. See Fig. 19-1.

When the engine is running, downward moving pistons on their intake strokes produce a suction in the intake manifold. Air rushes through the carburetor and into the engine to fill this low-pressure area. The airflow through the carburetor is used to meter fuel and mix it with the air.

Atmospheric pressure

Atmospheric pressure is the pressure formed by the air surrounding the earth. At sea level, the atmosphere exerts 14.7 psi (103 kPa) of pressure on everything. This

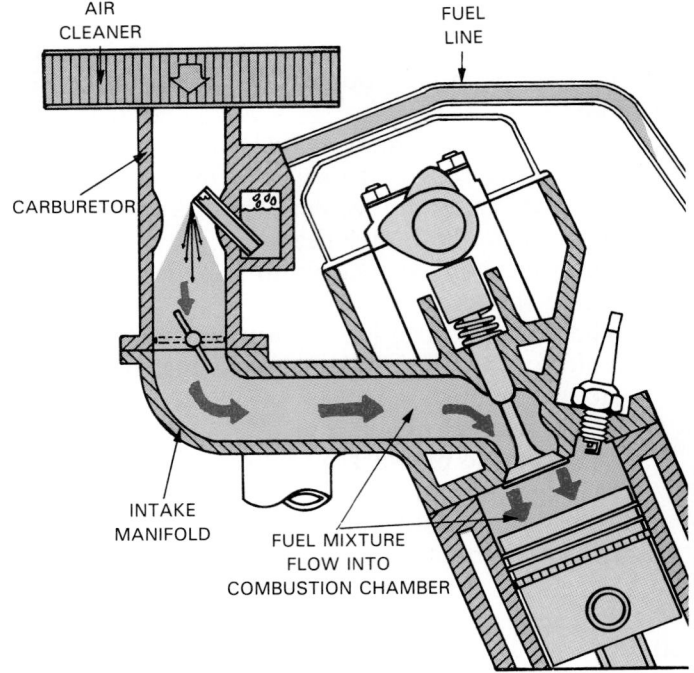

Fig. 19-1. Carburetor bolts to engine intake manifold. It meters and mixes fuel with incoming air.

pressure is caused by the weight of the air, as shown in Fig. 19-2.

Vacuum

A *vacuum* is lower than atmospheric pressure in an enclosed area. Suction is another word for vacuum. Any space with less than 14.7 psi (103 kPa) of pressure at sea level has a vacuum.

Differences in pressure cause flow

A difference in pressure between two areas can be used to cause flow. For instance, when you suck on a straw, atmospheric pressure pushes down on the liquid in the glass. This causes the liquid to flow through the straw and into the vacuum in your mouth.

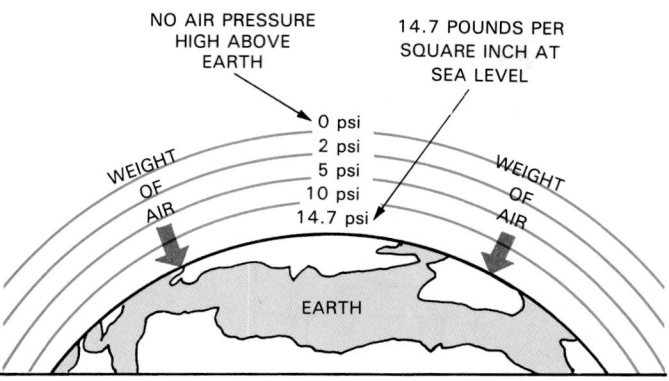

Fig. 19-2. Atmospheric pressure is produced by weight of air above earth. Pressure changes with altitude above sea level. This affects carburetion, as you will learn.

A carburetor uses differences in pressure to force fuel into the engine. The engine acts as a vacuum pump, producing a low-pressure area (vacuum) in the intake manifold. The carburetor, itself, also produces a vacuum, as you will learn shortly.

Basic carburetor parts

Fig. 19-3 shows the basic parts of a carburetor. Refer to this illustration as these parts are introduced. A basic carburetor consists of:

1. CARBURETOR BODY (main carburetor housing).
2. AIR HORN (air passage containing venturi, throttle valve, and end of main discharge tube).
3. THROTTLE VALVE (airflow control valve in air horn).
4. VENTURI (restriction or narrowed area formed in air horn).
5. MAIN DISCHARGE TUBE (fuel passage between fuel bowl and air horn).
6. FUEL BOWL (fuel storage area in body).

Carburetor body

The *carburetor body* is a cast metal housing for the other carburetor components, Fig. 19-3. It contains cast and drilled passages for air and fuel. The main discharge tube, venturi, and fuel bowl are normally made as part of the carburetor body. A flange on the bottom of the body allows the carburetor to be bolted to the engine.

Air horn

The carburetor *air horn,* also called *throat* or *barrel,* routes outside air into the engine intake manifold, Fig. 19-3. It contains the throttle valve, venturi, and outlet end of the main discharge tube.

Throttle valve

The carburetor *throttle valve* is the disc-shaped valve that controls airflow through the air horn. Look at Fig. 19-3. It is mounted on a shaft in the lower part of the air horn.

When closed, the throttle valve restricts the flow of air and fuel into the engine. When the throttle is opened, airflow, fuel flow, and engine power increase.

Fig. 19-4 shows how a car's gas pedal and throttle cable control the throttle valve. When the driver presses on the gas pedal, the throttle cable slides inside its hous-

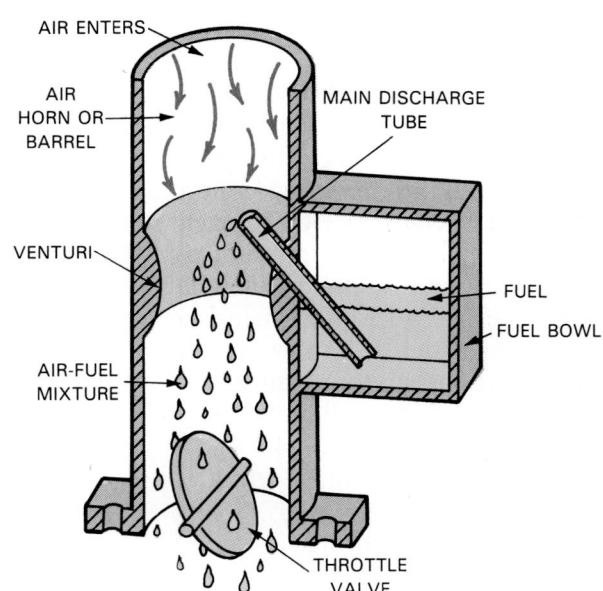

Fig. 19-3. A carburetor controls amount of air and fuel entering engine. Study basic parts.

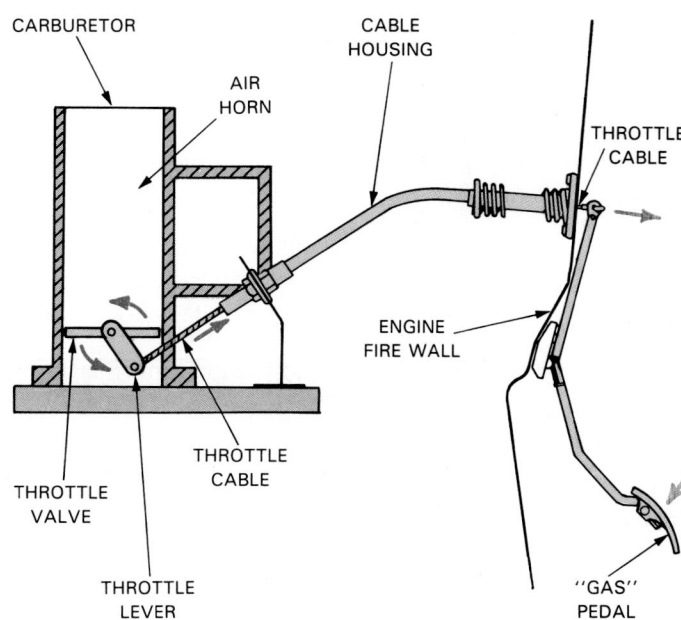

Fig. 19-4. Driver's gas pedal is connected to carburetor throttle valve. Valve controls airflow and engine power output.

Carburetor Fundamentals   211

ing. This swings the throttle open to increase engine power and speed. When the gas pedal is released, a throttle return spring pulls the throttle valve closed. This returns the engine to a slow idle speed. Look at Fig. 19-5.

fuel into the air horn and engine. Also called MAIN FUEL NOZZLE, it is a passage in the carburetor body that connects the fuel bowl to the center of the venturi. Refer to Fig. 19-3. Note how main discharge tube is located in carburetor body.

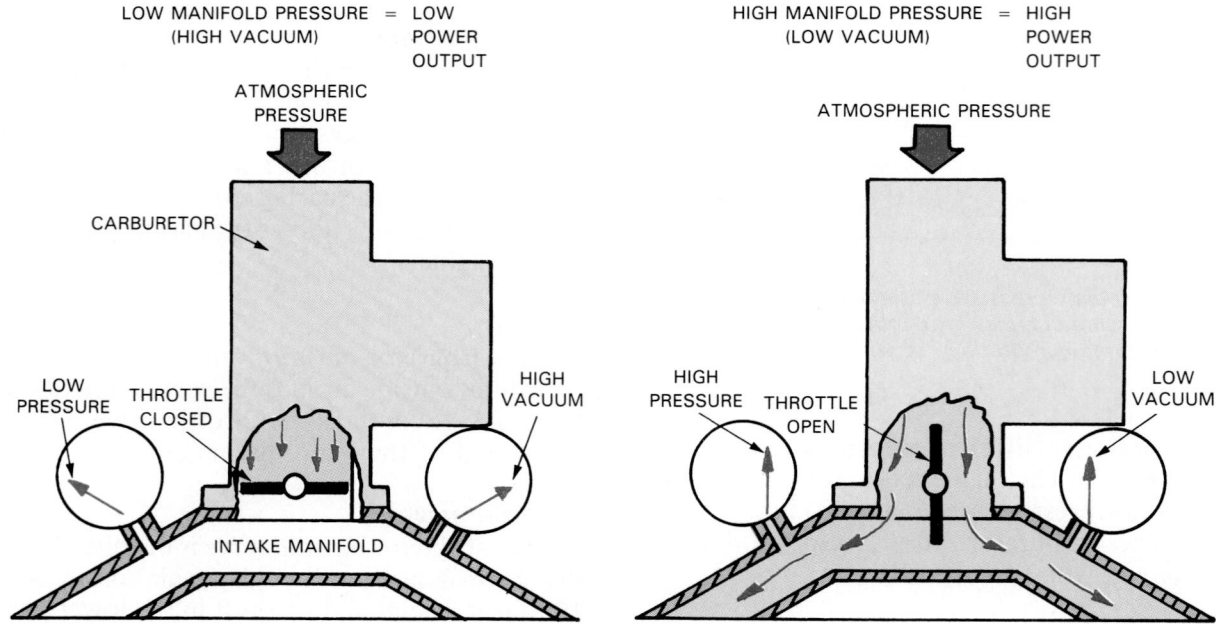

Fig. 19-5. Throttle valve position controls airflow and amount of vacuum in intake manifold. Left. Closed throttle valve produces high vacuum in manifold. Engine tries to draw air through carburetor, but cannot. Right. Open throttle allows airflow, reducing vacuum in intake manifold.

Venturi

A *venturi* produces sufficient suction to pull fuel out of the main discharge tube. Venturi action is illustrated in Fig. 19-6. Vacuum is highest inside the venturi. The narrowed airway increases air velocity, forming a low pressure area in the air horn.

Main discharge tube

The *main discharge tube* uses venturi vacuum to feed

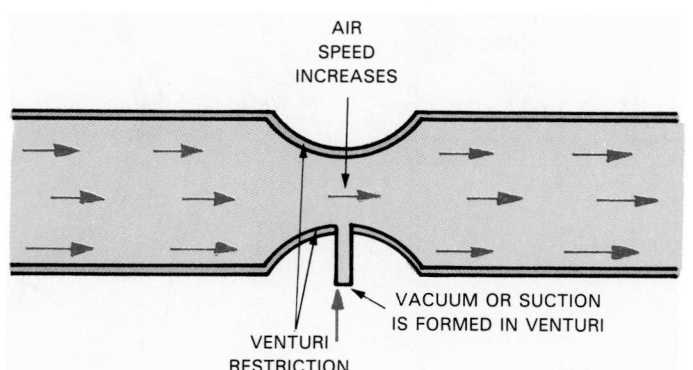

Fig. 19-6. Venturi is used to produce vacuum from airflow. Note how vacuum is highest inside venturi. (Ford)

Fuel bowl

The carburetor *fuel bowl* holds a supply of fuel that is NOT under fuel pump pressure. Several additional carburetor parts are mounted in the fuel bowl. These will be discussed later.

BASIC CARBURETOR SYSTEMS

A *carburetor system* is a network of passages and related parts that help control the air-fuel ratio under a specific engine operating condition. Also called a CARBURETOR CIRCUIT, each system applies a predetermined air-fuel mixture as the temperature, speed, and load of the engine change.

For example, a gasoline engine's air-fuel mixture may vary from a rich 8:1 ratio to a lean 18:1 ratio. An automotive carburetor, using its various systems, must be capable of providing varying air-fuel ratios of approximately:

1. 8:1 for cold engine starting.
2. 16:1 for idling.
3. 15:1 for part throttle.
4. 13:1 for full acceleration.
5. 18:1 for normal cruising at highway speeds.

Note! Older cars, not subject to strict emission control regulations, have a slightly richer air-fuel ratio.

Late model cars have leaner carburetor settings that reduce exhaust pollution.

The seven basic carburetor systems are the:
1. FLOAT SYSTEM (maintains supply of fuel in carburetor bowl).
2. IDLE SYSTEM (provides a small amount of fuel for low speed engine operation).
3. OFF-IDLE SYSTEM (provides correct air-fuel mixture slightly above idle speeds).
4. ACCELERATION SYSTEM (squirts fuel into air horn when throttle valve opens and engine speed increases).
5. HIGH SPEED SYSTEM (supplies lean air-fuel mixture at cruising speeds).
6. FULL POWER SYSTEM (enriches fuel mixture slightly when engine power demands are high).
7. CHOKE SYSTEM (provides extremely rich air-fuel mixture for cold engine starting).

It is very important that you fully understand each of these systems. As each system is discussed, try to draw a "mental picture" of how a carburetor operates under the conditions described. This will help you when diagnosing and repairing carburetor problems.

FLOAT SYSTEM

The *float system* must maintain the correct level of fuel in the carburetor bowl. Since the carburetor uses differences in pressure to force fuel into the air horn, the fuel in the bowl must be kept at atmospheric pressure. The float system keeps the fuel pump from forcing too much gasoline into the carburetor bowl.

Float system parts

Look at Fig. 19-7. A carburetor float system has a fuel bowl, float, needle valve, needle seat, bowl vent, and hinge assembly. Study the relationship of each part to the system.

The *carburetor float* rides on top of the fuel in the bowl to open and close the needle valve. It is normally made of thin brass or plastic. One end of the float is hinged to the side of the carburetor body. The other end is free to swing up and down, Fig. 19-7.

The *needle valve* in the top of the fuel bowl regulates the amount of fuel passing through the fuel inlet and needle seat. See Fig. 19-7. The needle valve is usually made of brass. Sometimes, the end of the needle valve will have a soft viton (synthetic rubber) tip. The soft tip seals better than a metal tip, especially if dirt gets caught in the needle seat.

The carburetor float *needle seat* works with the needle valve and float to control fuel flow into the bowl. It is a brass fitting that threads into the carburetor body, Fig. 19-7.

A *bowl vent* prevents a pressure or vacuum buildup in the carburetor fuel bowl. Refer to Fig. 19-7 again. Without venting, pressure could form in the bowl as the fuel pump fills the carburetor. This could also cause

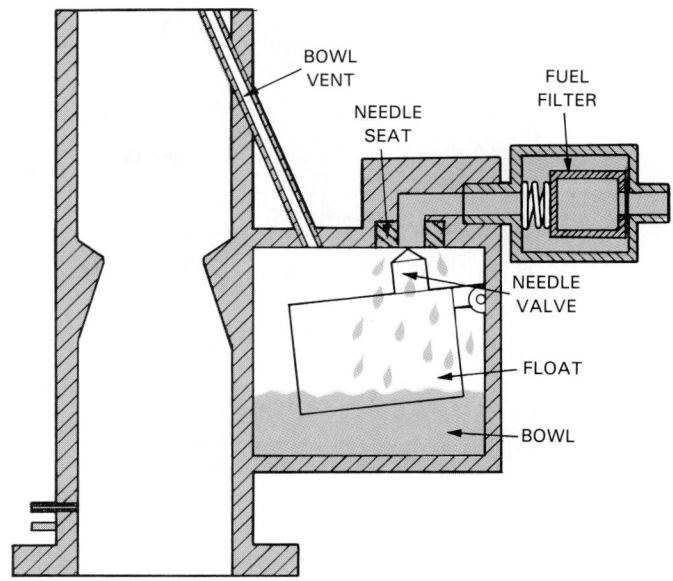

Fig. 19-7. Basic parts of a float system. Float opens and closes needle valve as fuel level falls and rises. Study part names.

vacuum to form in the bowl as fuel is drawn out of the carburetor and into the engine.

Fig. 19-8 shows a bowl vent mechanism on a car equipped with an evaporation control type emission system. Instead of venting the fuel bowl into the outside air, it is vented through a hose to a charcoal canister. Detailed in Chapter 39, the canister stores toxic fuel vapors and prevents them from entering and polluting the atmosphere.

Float system operation

When engine speed or load increases, fuel is rapidly pulled out of the fuel bowl and into the venturi.

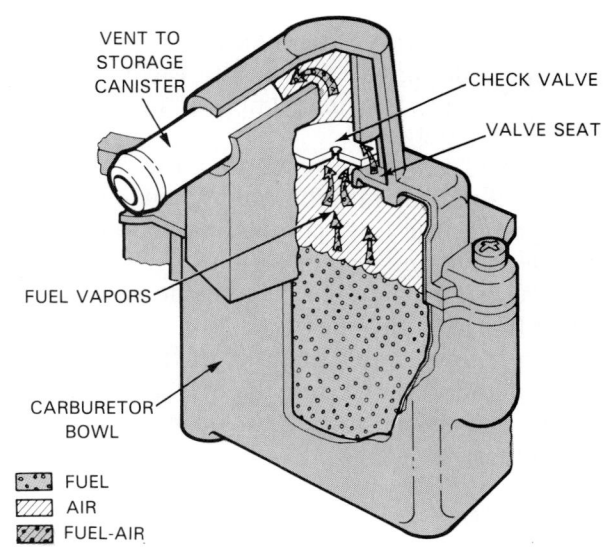

Fig. 19-8. This fuel bowl is vented to emission controlling charcoal canister. Canister stores fuel vapors until engine is started. (Ford)

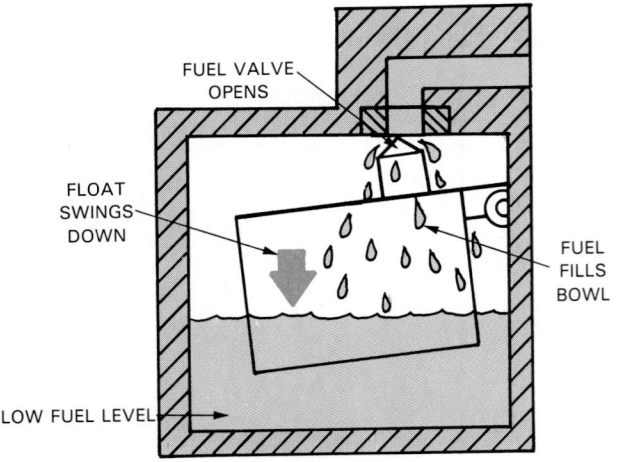

Fuel level low. Float drops and opens needle valve. Fuel flows through needle seat to refill bowl.

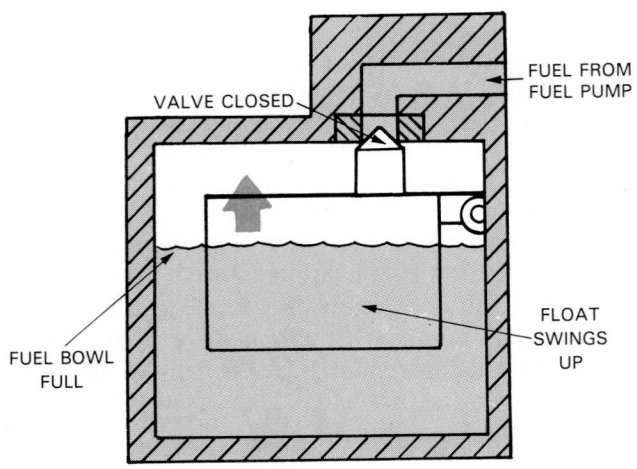

Fuel level up to specs. Float rises and pushes needle valve into needle seat. This blocks fuel entry from pump.

Fig. 19-9. Basic float operation.

Illustrated in Fig. 19-9, this makes the fuel level and float drop in the bowl. The needle valve also drops away from its seat. The fuel pump can then force more fuel into the bowl.

As the fuel level in the bowl rises, the float pushes the needle valve back into the seat. When the fuel level is high enough, the float closes the opening between the needle valve and seat.

With the engine running, the needle valve usually lets some fuel leak into the bowl. As a result, the float system maintains a stable quantity of fuel in the bowl. This is very important because the fuel level in the bowl can affect the air-fuel ratio, as you will learn in the next chapter.

IDLE SYSTEM

A carburetor *idle system* provides the engine's air-fuel mixture at speeds below approximately 800 rpm or 20 mph (32 km/h).

When an engine is idling, the throttle valve is almost closed. Airflow through the air horn is too restricted to produce enough vacuum in the venturi. Venturi vacuum cannot pull fuel out of the main discharge tube. Instead, the high intake manifold vacuum BELOW the throttle plate and a separate idle circuit are used to feed fuel into the air horn.

Idle system parts

The fundamental parts of a carburetor idle system include a section of the main discharge tube, a low speed jet, idle air bleed, bypass, idle passage, economizer, idle port, and an idle mixture screw. These parts are illustrated in Fig. 19-10.

The *low speed jet* is a restriction in the idle passage that limits maximum fuel flow in the idle circuit. It is placed in the fuel passage before the idle air bleed and economizer.

The *idle air bleed* works with the *economizer* and *bypass* to add air bubbles to the fuel flowing to the idle port. As shown in Fig. 19-10, the air bubbles help break up or atomize the fuel. This makes the air-fuel mixture burn more efficiently once in the engine.

The *idle passage* carries the air-fuel *slurry* (mixture of liquid fuel and air bubbles) to the idle screw port.

The *idle screw port* is an opening into the air horn below the throttle valve.

The *idle mixture screw* allows adjustment of the size of the opening in the idle screw port, Fig. 19-10. Turning the idle screw IN reduces the size of the idle port and amount of fuel entering the air horn. Turning the

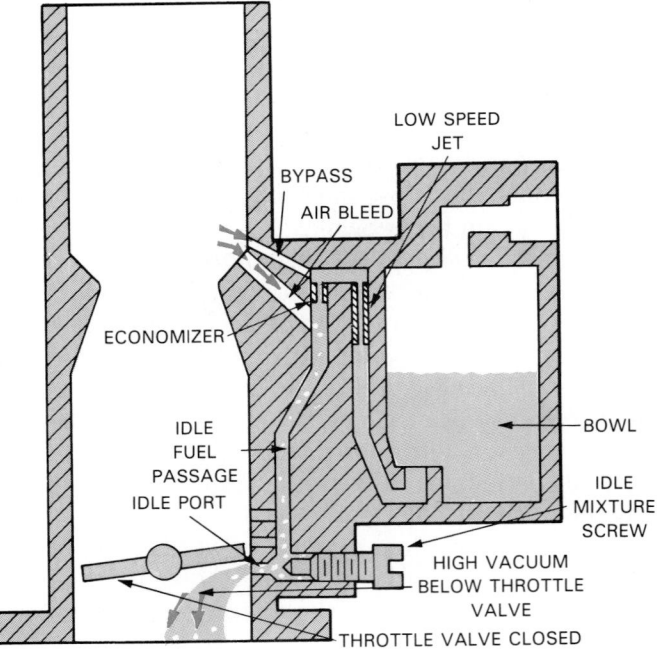

Fig. 19-10. Idle system feeds fuel when throttle is closed for low engine speed operation. High vacuum below throttle pulls fuel out idle port. Mixture screw allows adjustment of mixture at idle. Air bleed helps premix air and fuel.

idle screw OUT usually increases fuel flow, enriching the fuel mixture at idle.

Most modern carburetors have *sealed idle mixture screws* that are NOT normally adjusted. The idle mixture screws are covered with metal plugs, as pictured in Fig. 9-11. This prevents tampering with the factory setting of the idle mixture.

Sometimes, plastic *limiter caps* are pressed over the heads of the idle mixture screws. They restrict how far the screws can be turned toward either rich or lean settings. The idle screw adjustment of today's carburetors is very critical to exhaust emissions.

Idle system operation

For the idle system to function, the throttle plate must be closed. Then, high intake manifold vacuum can pull fuel out of the idle circuit. Refer to Fig. 19-10.

At idle, fuel flows out of the fuel bowl, through the main discharge, and into the low speed jet. The low speed jet restricts fuel flow.

At the bypass, outside air is pulled into the idle system. This partially atomizes the fuel into a slurry. As the fuel and air bubbles pass through the economizer, the air bubbles are reduced in size to further improve mixing.

The fuel and air slurry then enters the idle screw port. The setting of the idle screw controls how much fuel enters the air horn at idle.

OFF-IDLE SYSTEM

The *off-idle system,* often termed the PART THROTTLE CIRCUIT, feeds more fuel into the air horn when the throttle plates are partially open. Look at Fig. 19-12. It is an extension of the idle system. It functions ABOVE approximately 800 rpm or 20 mph (32 km/h).

Without the off-idle system, the fuel mixture would become too lean slightly above idle. The idle circuit alone is not capable of supplying enough fuel to the airstream passing through the carburetor. The off-idle circuit helps supply fuel during transition (change) from idle to high speed. Refer to Fig. 19-12.

Off-idle system operation

The off-idle system begins to functions when the driver presses lightly on the gas pedal and cracks open the throttle plates. As the throttle plates swing open, they expose the off-idle ports to intake manifold vacuum. Vacuum then begins to pull fuel out of the

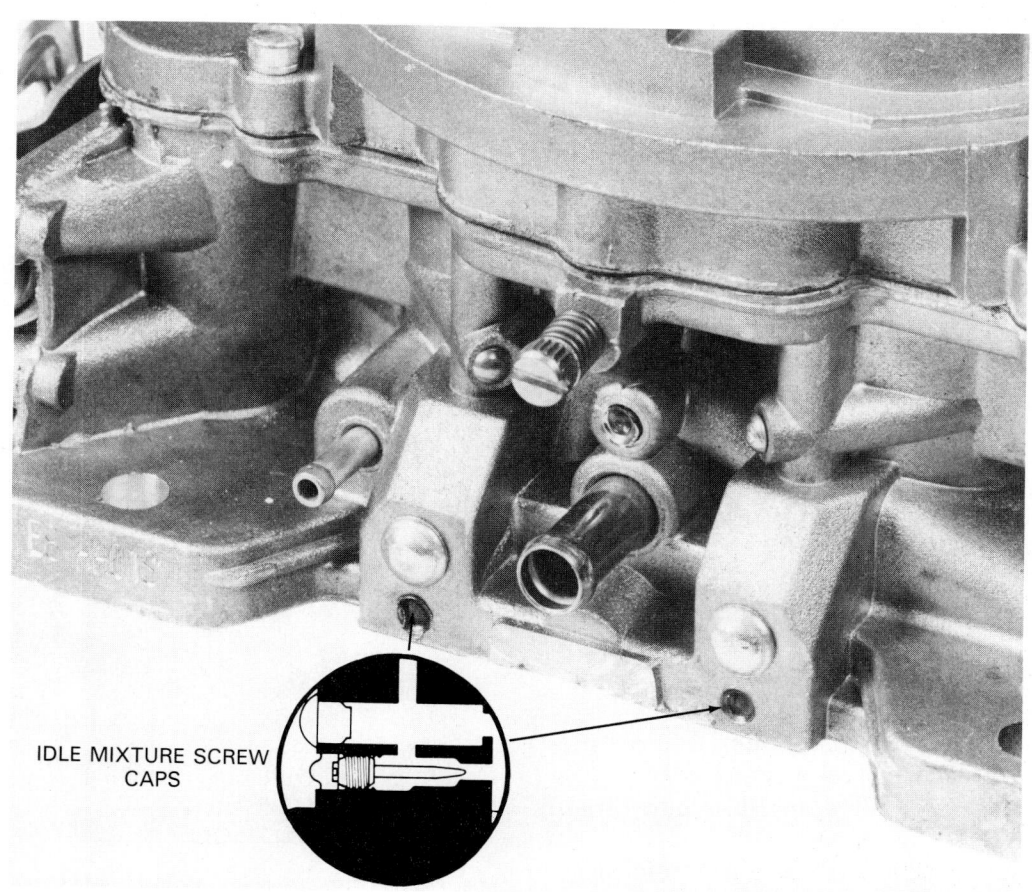

IDLE MIXTURE SCREW CAPS

Fig. 19-11. Modern idle mixture screws are covered with metal plugs. This prevents tampering which would upset mixture and increase exhaust emissions. (Carter Carburetor Div.)

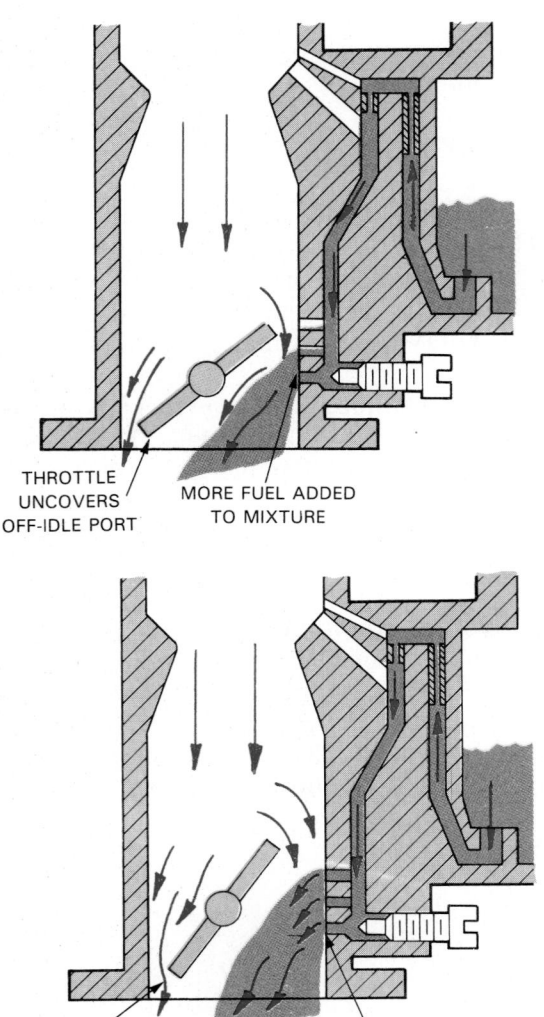

THROTTLE UNCOVERS OFF-IDLE PORT

MORE FUEL ADDED TO MIXTURE

THROTTLE SWING EVEN WIDER, NEXT OFF-IDLE PORT UNCOVERED

ENOUGH FUEL ADDED FOR INCREASED AIRFLOW

Fig. 19-12. Off-idle system feeds fuel to engine when throttle is opened slightly. It adds a little extra fuel to the extra air flowing around throttle valve.

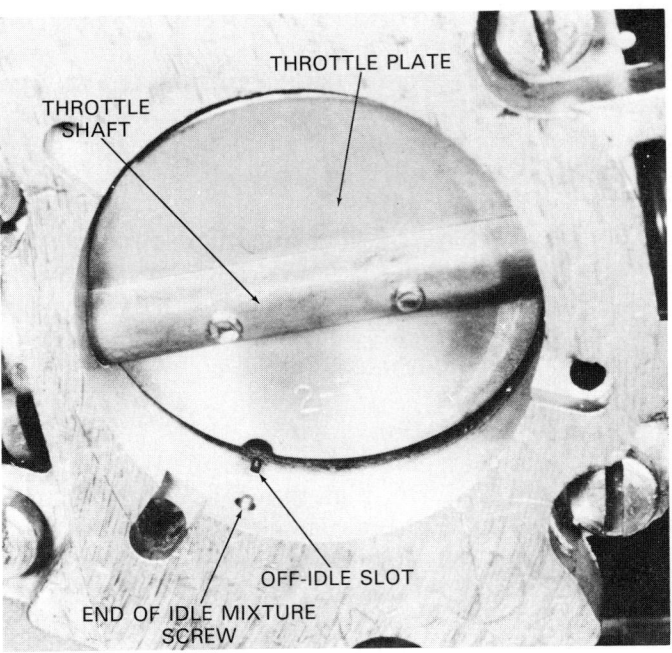

THROTTLE SHAFT

THROTTLE PLATE

OFF-IDLE SLOT

END OF IDLE MIXTURE SCREW

Fig. 19-13. Bottom view of actual carburetor shows idle mixture screw tip, idle port opening, and off-idle slot. (Carter Carburetor Div.)

idle screw port and the off-idle ports. This provides enough extra fuel to mix with the additional air flowing around the throttle plates.

Fig. 19-13 pictures the bottom of a carburetor air horn. Notice the idle screw port, idle screw tip, and off-idle ports. Study how the throttle plate exposes all of the ports to vacuum when partially opened.

ACCELERATION SYSTEM

The carburetor's *acceleration system,* like the off-idle system, provides extra fuel when changing from the idle circuit to the high speed circuit (main discharge).

The acceleration system SQUIRTS a stream of extra fuel into the air horn whenever the gas pedal is pressed (throttle valves swing open). This is illustrated in Fig. 19-14.

Without the acceleration system, too much air would rush into the engine as the throttle quickly opened. The mixture would become too lean for combustion and the engine would HESITATE or STALL. The accelera-

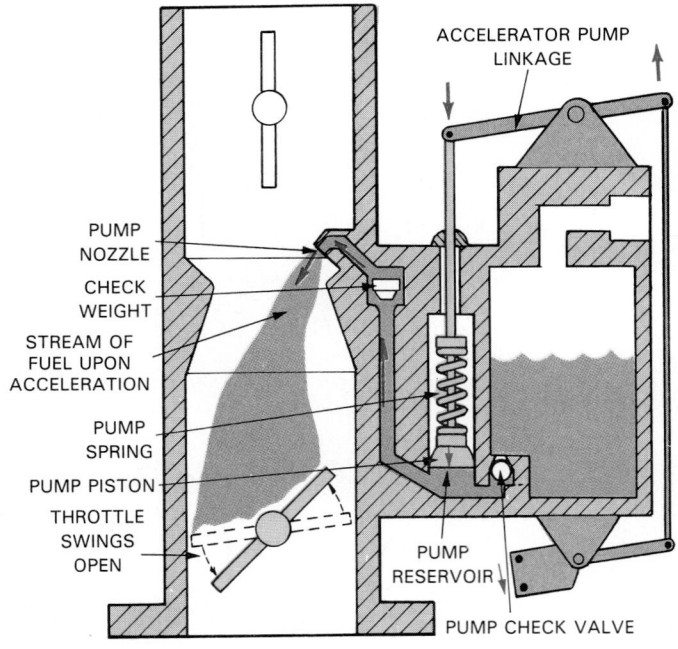

ACCELERATOR PUMP LINKAGE

PUMP NOZZLE

CHECK WEIGHT

STREAM OF FUEL UPON ACCELERATION

PUMP SPRING

PUMP PISTON

THROTTLE SWINGS OPEN

PUMP RESERVOIR

PUMP CHECK VALVE

Fig. 19-14. Accelerator pump system squirts fuel into air horn every time throttle is opened. This adds fuel to rush of air entering engine and prevents temporary lean condition. Study part names.

tion system prevents a lean air-fuel mixture from upsetting a smooth increase in engine speed.

Acceleration system parts

The basic parts of a carburetor acceleration system are the pump linkage, accelerator pump, pump check ball, pump reservoir, pump check weight, and pump nozzle. These parts are given in Fig. 19-14.

The *accelerator pump* develops the pressure to force fuel out of the pump nozzle and into the air horn. There are two types of accelerator pumps: piston and diaphragm. See Figs. 19-15 and 19-16.

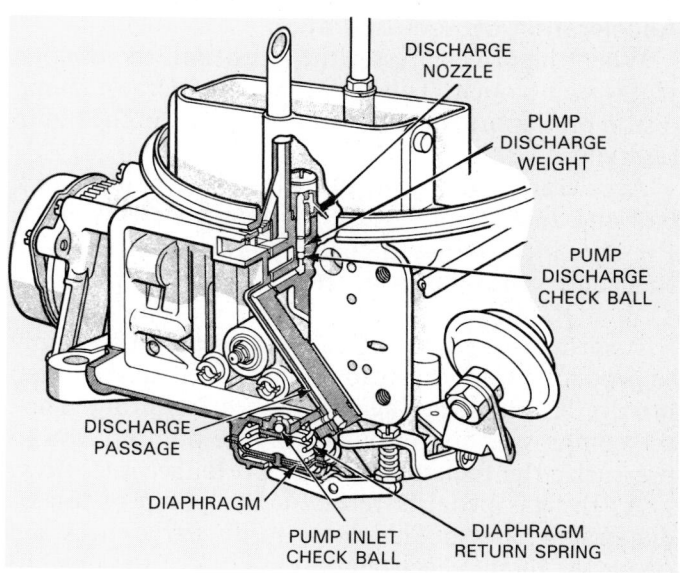

Fig. 19-16. Cutaway view of carburetor using a diaphragm type accelerator pump. (Holley Carburetors)

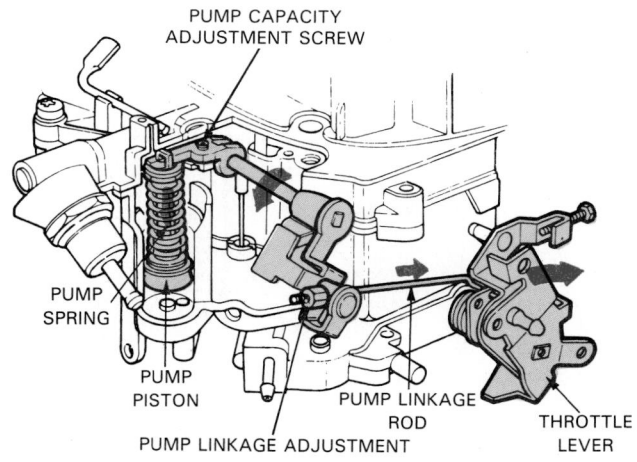

Fig. 19-15. Most accelerator pump systems use mechanical linkage from throttle lever. When driver presses gas pedal for acceleration, both the throttle valve and pump are actuated. (Ford Motor Co.)

The *pump check ball* only allows fuel to flow into the pump reservoir. It stops fuel from flowing back into the fuel bowl when the pump is actuated.

The *pump check weight* prevents fuel from being pulled into the air horn by venturi vacuum. Its weight seals the passage to the pump nozzle and prevents fuel siphoning.

The *pump nozzle,* also termed PUMP JET, has a fixed orifice (opening) that helps control fuel flow out of the pump circuit. It also guides the fuel stream into the center of the air horn, Fig. 19-14.

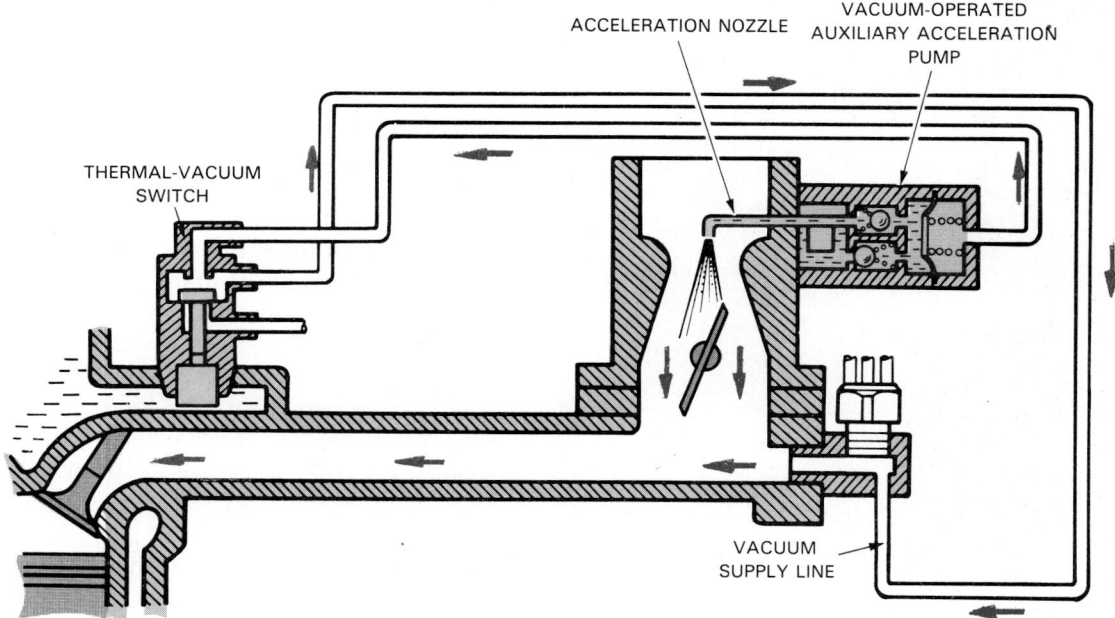

Fig. 19-17. Auxiliary accelerator pump system is sometimes used to aid conventional mechanical pump system. Thermal-vacuum valve is open when engine is cold. This allows engine vacuum to operate vacuum-operated accelerator pump.

Acceleration system operation

When the driver presses the gas pedal, the throttle plates swing open. This causes the accelerator pump piston or diaphragm to compress the fuel in the pump reservoir.

Accelerator pump pressure closes the pump check ball and fuel flows toward the pump check weight. Pressure lifts the pump check weight off its seat and fuel squirts into the carburetor air horn, as if from a TOY SQUIRT GUN.

A spring is used on the accelerator pump assembly to produce a smooth, steady flow of fuel out the pump nozzle. Throttle opening compresses the spring. Then the compressed spring pushes on the pump piston to pressurize the fuel and produce prolonged fuel flow.

As the gas pedal is released, the pump piston or diaphragm retracts. This closes the discharge check and opens the pump check. Fuel flows out of the bowl to refill the accelerator pump reservoir. The system is then ready to spray another stream of fuel into the air horn when the car accelerates.

Fig. 19-17 shows an auxiliary acceleration system. It supplements the main acceleration system when the engine is cold.

HIGH SPEED SYSTEM

The carburetor's *high speed system,* also called MAIN METERING SYSTEM, supplies the engine's air-fuel mixture at normal cruising speeds, Fig. 19-18. This circuit begins to function when the throttle plates

are open wide enough for venturi action. Airflow through the carburetor must be relatively high for venturi vacuum to draw fuel out of the main discharge tube.

The high speed system provides the leanest, most fuel efficient air-fuel ratio. It functions from about 20 to 55 mph (32 to 89 km/h) or 2000 to 3000 rpm.

High speed system parts

The high speed system is the simplest carburetor circuit. It consists of a high speed jet, main discharge passage, emulsion tube, air bleed, and venturi.

The **high speed jet** is a fitting with a precision hole drilled in the center. This jet screws into a threaded hole in the fuel bowl, Fig. 19-19. One jet is used for each air horn.

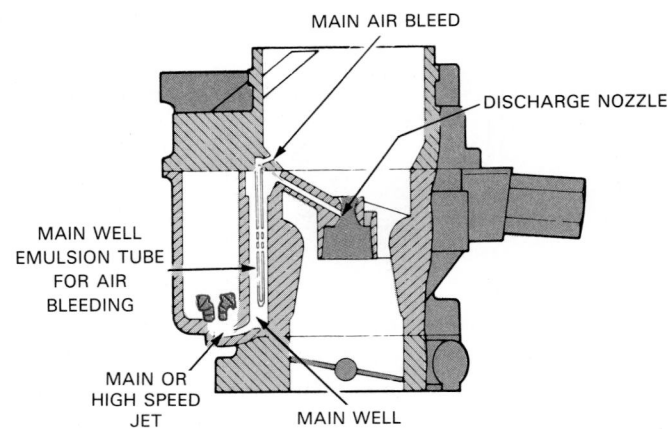

Fig. 19-19. Emulsion tube is commonly used to premix air and fuel before entry into air horn. Note screw-in main jet. (Holley)

The hole size in the main jet determines how much fuel flows through the circuit. A number is usually stamped on a high speed jet to denote the diameter of the hole in the jet. Since jet numbering systems vary, refer to the carburetor manufacturer's manual for information on jet size.

The **emulsion tube** and the **air bleed** add air to the fuel flowing through the main discharge tube. See Fig. 19-19. The premixing of air with fuel helps the fuel atomize as it discharges into the air horn.

The **primary venturi** is the venturi formed in the side of the carburetor air horn.

One or two **booster venturis** can be added inside the primary venturi to increase vacuum at lower engine speeds. This is illustrated in Fig. 19-20.

High speed system operation

When engine speed is high enough, airflow through the carburetor forms a high vacuum in the venturi. The vacuum pulls fuel through the main metering system.

Fuel flows through the main jet which meters the

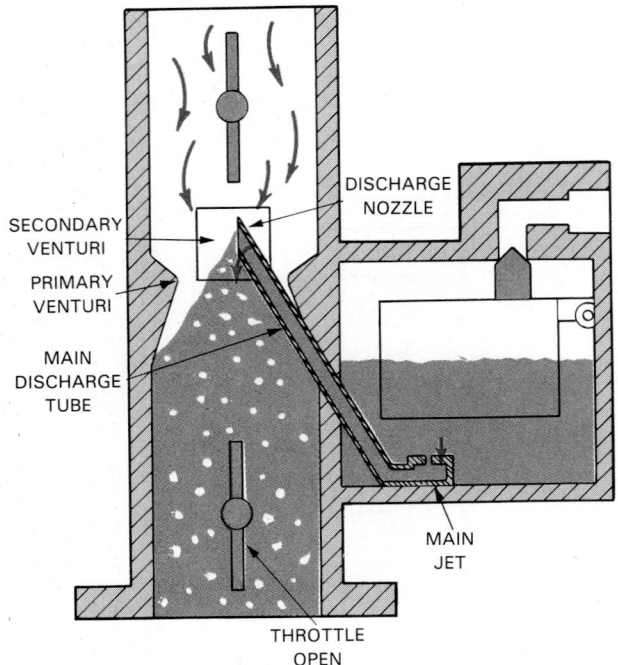

Fig. 19-18. High speed system is simple. Main jet controls fuel flow and mixture. At higher engine speeds, there is enough airflow through venturi to produce vacuum. This pulls fuel through main discharge. Study part names.

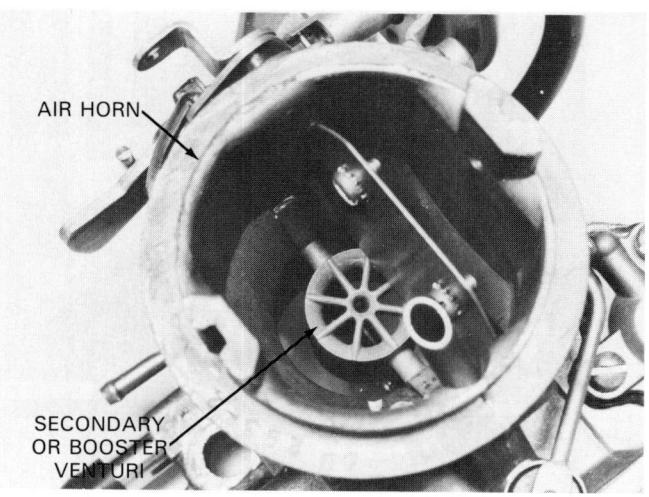

Fig. 19-20. Secondary venturi, also termed booster venturi, is placed inside primary venturi. It helps produce venturi vacuum at lower engine speeds. (Holley Carburetors)

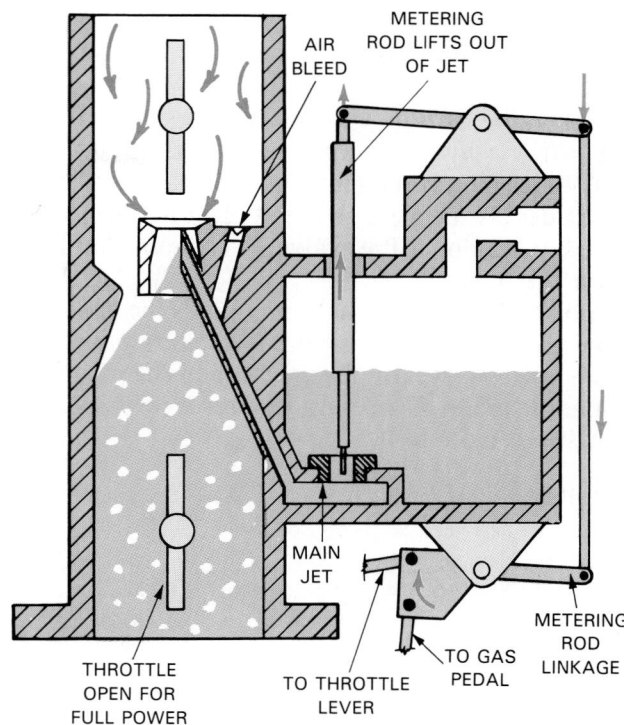

Fig. 19-21. High speed-full power system enriches high speed circuit when needed. When gas pedal is pushed down for full power, throttle linkage acts on metering rod linkage. Metering rod is lifted out of main jet to add more fuel to the mixture.

amount of gasoline entering the circuit. Then, the fuel flows into the main discharge tube and emulsion tube.

The emulsion tube causes air from the air bleed to mix with the fuel. The air-fuel mixture is finally pulled out of the main nozzle and into the engine.

FULL POWER SYSTEM

The carburetor *full power system* provides a means of enriching the fuel mixture for high speed, high power conditions. This circuit operates, for example, when the driver presses the gas pedal to pass another vehicle or to climb a steep hill. A simplified illustration of a full power system is given in Fig. 19-21.

The full power system is usually an addition to the main metering system. Either a metering rod or a power valve (jet) can be used to provide a variable, high speed air-fuel ratio.

Metering rod action

A *metering rod* is a stepped rod that moves in and out of the main jet to alter fuel flow.

As shown in Fig. 19-22, when the metering rod is down inside the jet, flow is restricted and a leaner fuel mixture results. When the metering rod is pulled out of the jet, more fuel can flow through the system to enrich the mixture for more power output.

Either mechanical linkage, engine vacuum, or an electric solenoid and computer (modified type metering rod or valve assembly) can be used to operate a metering rod.

The metering rod can be linked to the throttle lever. Then, whenever the throttle is opened wide, the linkage lifts the metering rod out of the jet.

A metering rod controlled by engine vacuum is connected to a diaphragm. At steady speeds, power demands are low and engine vacuum is high. The opposite is true under heavy power demands (wide open throttle); intake manifold vacuum drops. This vacuum-load relationship is ideal for controlling a metering rod or power valve.

NOTE! An electrically operated metering rod is

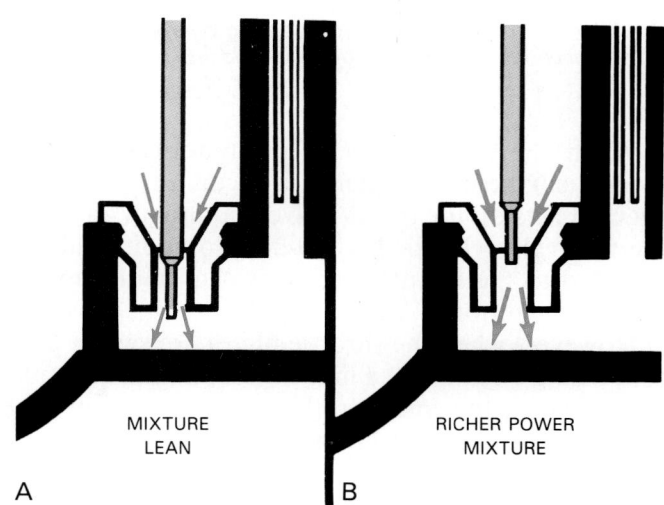

Fig. 19-22. Metering rod action. A — Metering rod lowered into jet. Less fuel can flow through jet, leaning mixture. B — Metering rod pulled out of jet. This allows more fuel flow through jet, enriching mixture.

described later in the chapter, as computer controlled carburetors are discussed.

Power valve action

A *power valve,* also known as an ECONOMIZER VALVE, performs the same function as a metering rod; it provides a variable high speed fuel mixture. A power valve consists of a fuel valve, a vacuum diaphragm, and a spring.

Look at Fig. 19-23. The spring holds the power valve in the normally open position. A vacuum passage runs to the power valve diaphragm. When the power valve is open, it serves as an extra jet that feeds fuel into the high speed circuit.

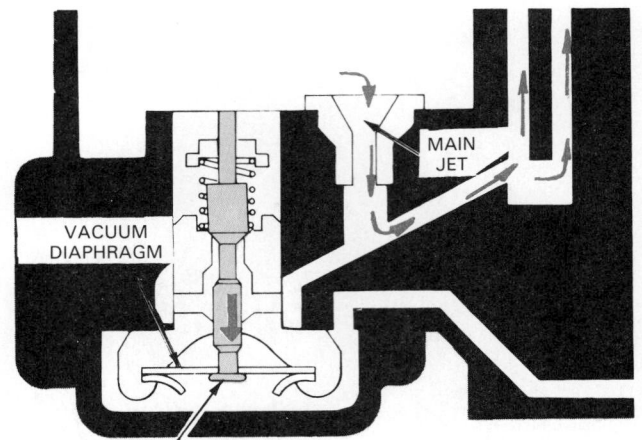

A

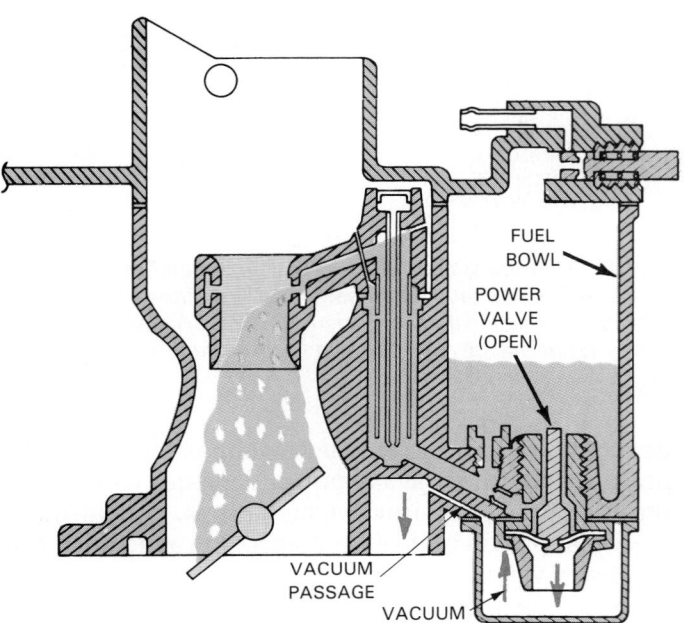

Fig. 19-23. Power valve serves same function as metering rod. It enriches mixture under high load, low intake manifold vacuum conditions. When vacuum is low, spring opens power valve. Extra fuel can then flow through valve and into main discharge.

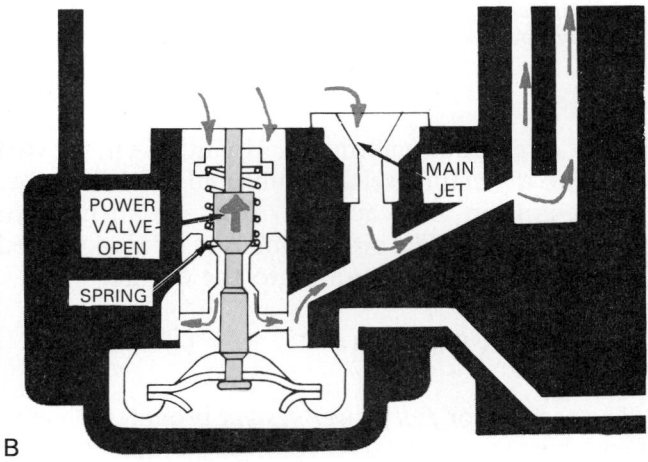

B

Fig. 19-24. Power valve action. A — High vacuum, low power output closes power valve by pulling on diaphragm. No extra fuel enters main system. B — Engine power output is high, causing intake manifold vacuum to drop. This allows spring to open power valve for more fuel.

When the engine is cruising at normal highway speeds, engine intake manifold vacuum is high. This vacuum acts on the power valve diaphragm and pulls the fuel valve closed, Fig. 19-24. No additional fuel is added to the main metering system under normal driving conditions.

However, when the throttle plates are swung open for passing or climbing a hill, engine manifold vacuum drops. Then, the spring in the power valve can push the fuel valve open. Fuel flows through the power valve and into the main metering system. This adds more fuel for more engine power.

CHOKE SYSTEM

The *choke system* is designed to supply an extremely rich air-fuel ratio to aid cold engine starting.

For the fuel mixture to burn properly, the fuel entering the intake must atomize and vaporize. When the engine is cold, the fuel entering the intake tends to condense into a liquid. As a result, not enough fuel vapors enter the combustion chambers and the engine could miss or stall when cold. A choke is used to prevent this lean condition.

Choke system parts

A choke system has a choke plate (valve), thermostatic spring, and other parts depending upon choke design. See Fig. 19-25.

The *choke plate* is a butterfly (disc) type valve located near the top of the carburetor air horn.

When the choke plate is closed, it blocks normal airflow through the carburetor. This causes high intake manifold vacuum to form below the choke plate. Vacuum pulls on the main discharge tube, even though air is not flowing through the venturi. Fuel is pulled

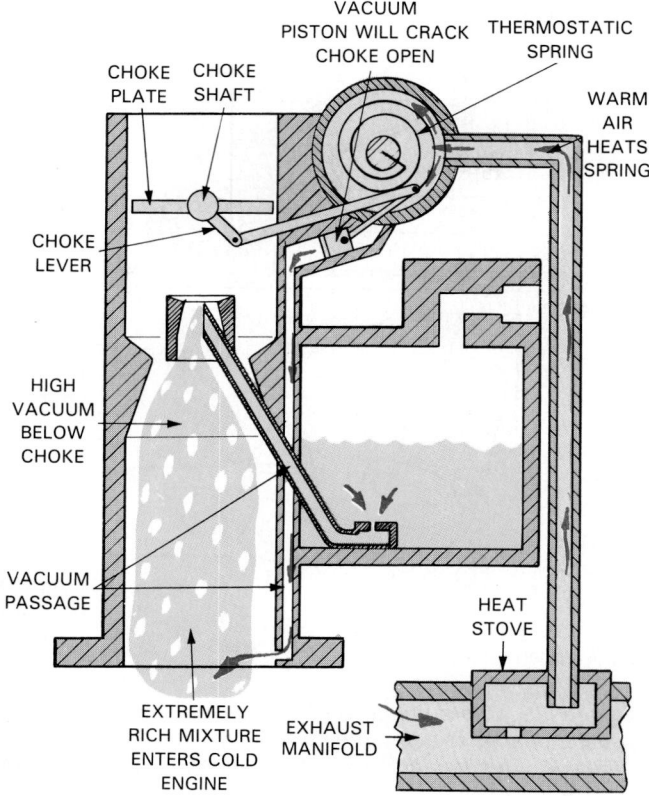

Fig. 19-25. Basic choke system parts. Thermostatic spring is main control of choke operation. When engine is cold, spring closes choke. High vacuum below choke pulls large amount of fuel out main discharge. When engine warms, hot air causes spring to open choke. Vacuum piston cracks choke upon engine starting to prevent flooding.

out to prime the engine with extra fuel.

A *thermostatic spring* may be used to open and close the choke. Refer to Fig. 19-26.

The thermostatic spring is a *bimetal spring* (spring made of two disimilar metals). The two metals have different rates of expansion that make the spring coil tighter when cold. It uncoils when heated. This coiling-uncoiling action is used to operate the choke.

Basic choke action

Before the engine starts, the cold thermostatic spring holds the choke closed. When the engine is started, the closed choke causes high vacuum in the carburetor air horn. This pulls a large amount of fuel out the main discharge. The rich mixture helps keep the cold engine running.

As the engine and thermostatic spring warm, the spring uncoils and opens the choke. This produces a leaner mixture. A warm engine would not run properly if the choke were to remain closed.

Manual choke

A *manual choke* simply uses a cable mechanism that allows the driver to open or close the choke plate. Normally, when the driver pulls on the choke knob, a cable pulls the choke plate closed for cold engine starting. The driver must open the choke plate after the engine starts and warms slightly.

Automatic chokes

Various methods are used to control the warming of a choke thermostatic spring. Hot air, engine coolant, or an electric heating element can operate the thermostatic spring.

An *integral hot air choke* is mounted on the side of the carburetor. It uses WARM AIR from the engine to heat the thermostatic spring. One is shown in Fig. 19-25. An integral choke may also use engine coolant instead of warm air, Fig. 19-26.

A *nonintegral choke* mounts the thermostatic spring in the top of the intake manifold. Then, as the engine and manifold warm, the thermostatic spring uncoils to open the choke plate. See Fig. 19-27.

An *electric assist choke* uses both hot air and an electric heating element to operate the thermostatic spring. Look at Fig. 19-27. The electric assist choke system uses a temperature sensitive switch to operate a choke

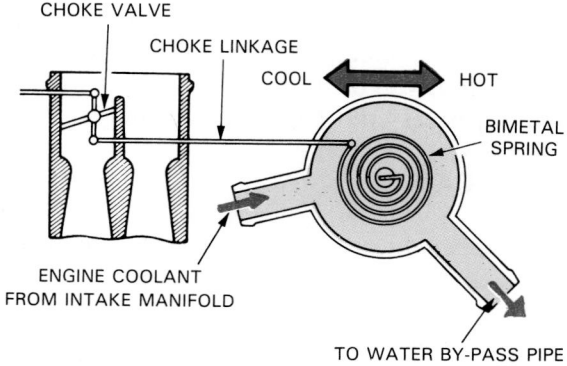

Fig. 19-26. Instead of hot air, this thermostatic choke spring is warmed by engine coolant. (Toyota)

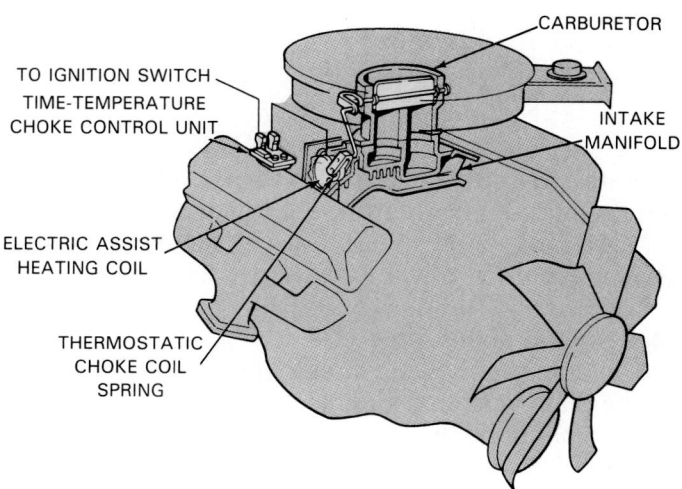

Fig. 19-27. Electric assist choke uses engine heat and an electric heating element to warm choke. (Chrysler)

heating element.

When the engine is started cold, the choke switch is open and current does not flow to the heating element. The choke thermostatic spring is only warmed by hot air and the choke remains partially closed to aid cold engine operation.

When the engine warms, the temperature sensing switch closes and current flows to the heating element. This speeds thermostatic spring action and the choke opens more quickly. As a result, the control of choke opening is more precise, reducing fuel consumption and exhaust emissions.

An **all electric choke** uses neither hot air nor coolant to aid thermostatic spring action. Instead, a two-stage heating element provides full control of choke operation. See Fig. 19-28.

When the engine is cold, only the first stage of the heating element is activated. The thermostatic spring warms slowly to keep the choke partially closed. When the engine warms, both stages of the heating element

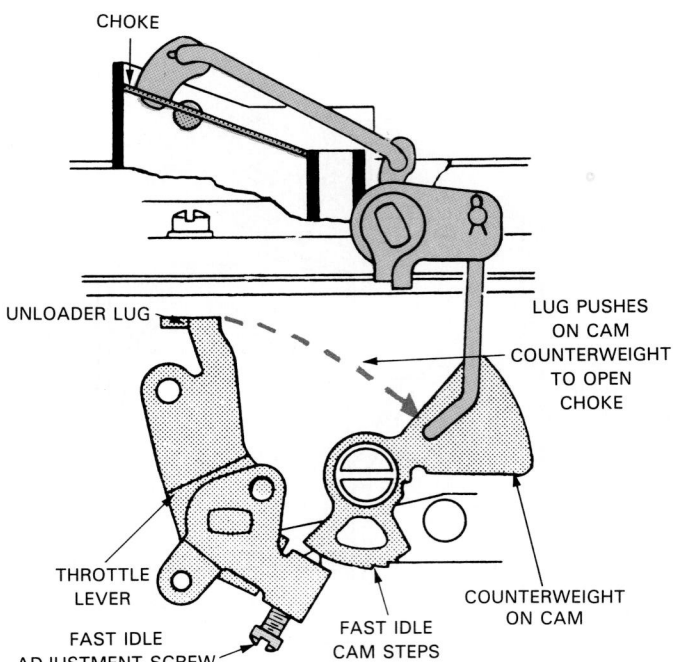

Fig. 19-29. Choke unloader physically opens choke when gas pedal is pushed to floor. The throttle lever lug moves the choke linkage. This lets driver clean out flooded engine (Carter)

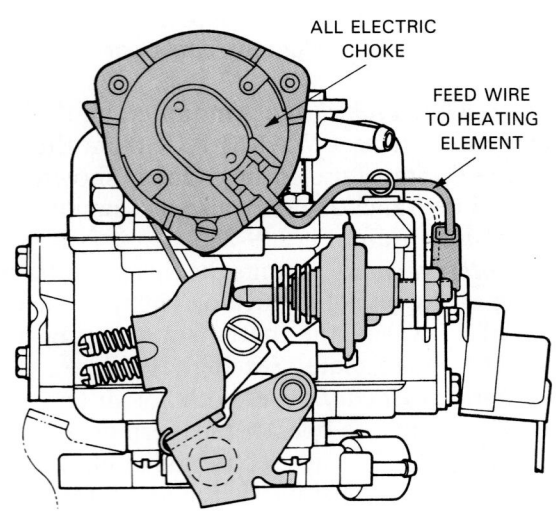

Fig. 19-28. All electric choke has two-stage heating element. One stage warms thermostatic spring when engine is cold. When engine is partially warm, both heating stages function. (Ford)

operate. The element heats up very quickly to make the thermostatic spring open the choke.

Most choke systems use other components to aid choke action. You will learn about them next.

Mechanical choke unloader

A *mechanical choke unloader* physically opens the choke plate whenever the throttle swings fully open. Look at Fig. 19-29.

A mechanical choke unloader uses a metal lug on the throttle lever. When the throttle lever moves to the fully open position, the lug pushes on the choke linkage (fast idle linkage). This gives the driver a means of

opening the choke. Air can then enter the air horn to help clear a *flooded engine* (engine with too much liquid fuel in cylinders and intake manifold).

Vacuum choke unloader

A *vacuum choke unloader,* also called CHOKE BREAK, uses engine vacuum to crack open the choke plate as soon as the engine starts. It automatically prevents the engine from flooding with too much fuel.

A vacuum choke unloader consists of a manifold vacuum fitting, vacuum hose, vacuum diaphragm (choke break), and linkage connected to the choke lever. These parts are shown in Fig. 19-30.

Before the engine starts, the choke spring holds the choke plate almost completely closed. This primes the engine with enough fuel for starting.

Then, as the engine starts, intake manifold vacuum acts on the choke break diaphragm. The diaphragm pulls on the choke linkage and lever to swing the choke plate open slightly. This helps avoid an overrich mixture and improves cold engine driveability.

FAST IDLE CAM

A *fast idle cam* increases engine idle speed when the choke is closed. It is a stepped cam fastened to the choke linkage, Fig. 19-31.

When the choke closes, the fast idle cam swings around in front of a fast idle screw. The fast idle screw is mounted on a throttle lever. As a result, the fast idle cam and fast idle screw prevent the throttle plates from

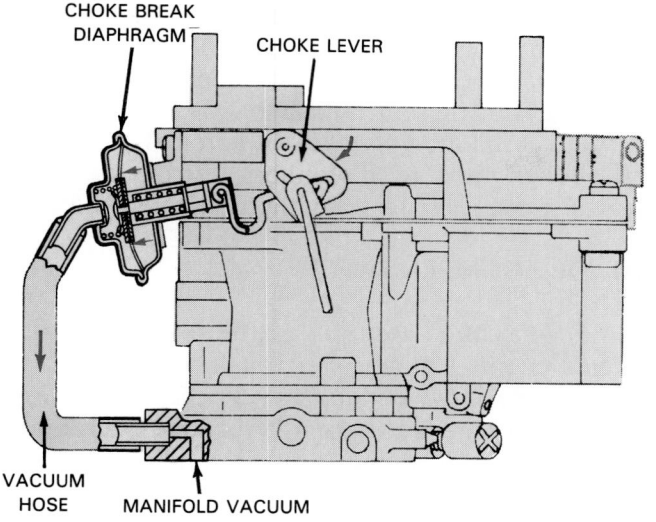

Fig. 19-30. Vacuum choke break or unloader cracks choke open as soon as engine is started. Engine vacuum pulls on diaphragm. Diaphragm pulls on choke linkage. (Chrysler)

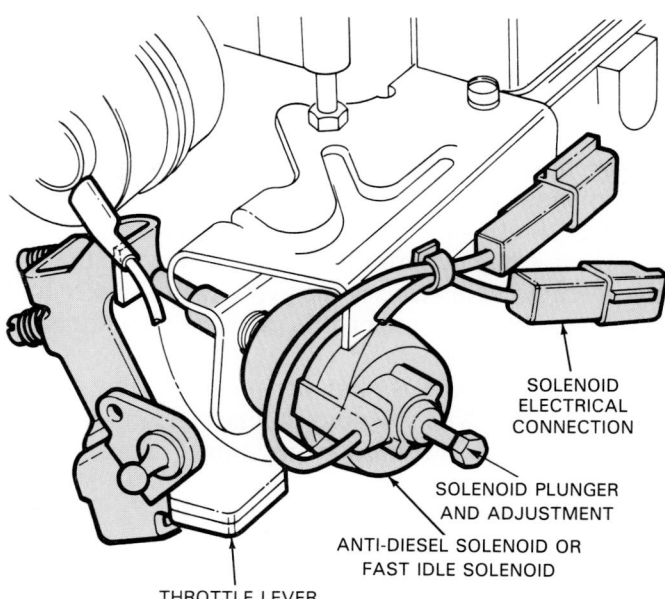

Fig. 19-32. Fast idle solenoid holds throttle open when engine is running. When ignition key is turned off, solenoid allows throttle to close more. This keeps engine from dieseling or after-running. (Ford)

closing. Engine idle speed is increased to smooth cold engine operation and prevent stalling.

As soon as the engine warms and the choke opens, the fast idle cam is deactivated. When the throttle is opened, the choke linkage swings the cam away from the fast idle screw and the engine returns to curb idle (normal, hot idle speed).

FAST IDLE SOLENOID

A *fast idle solenoid* opens the carburetor throttle plates during engine operation but allows the throttle

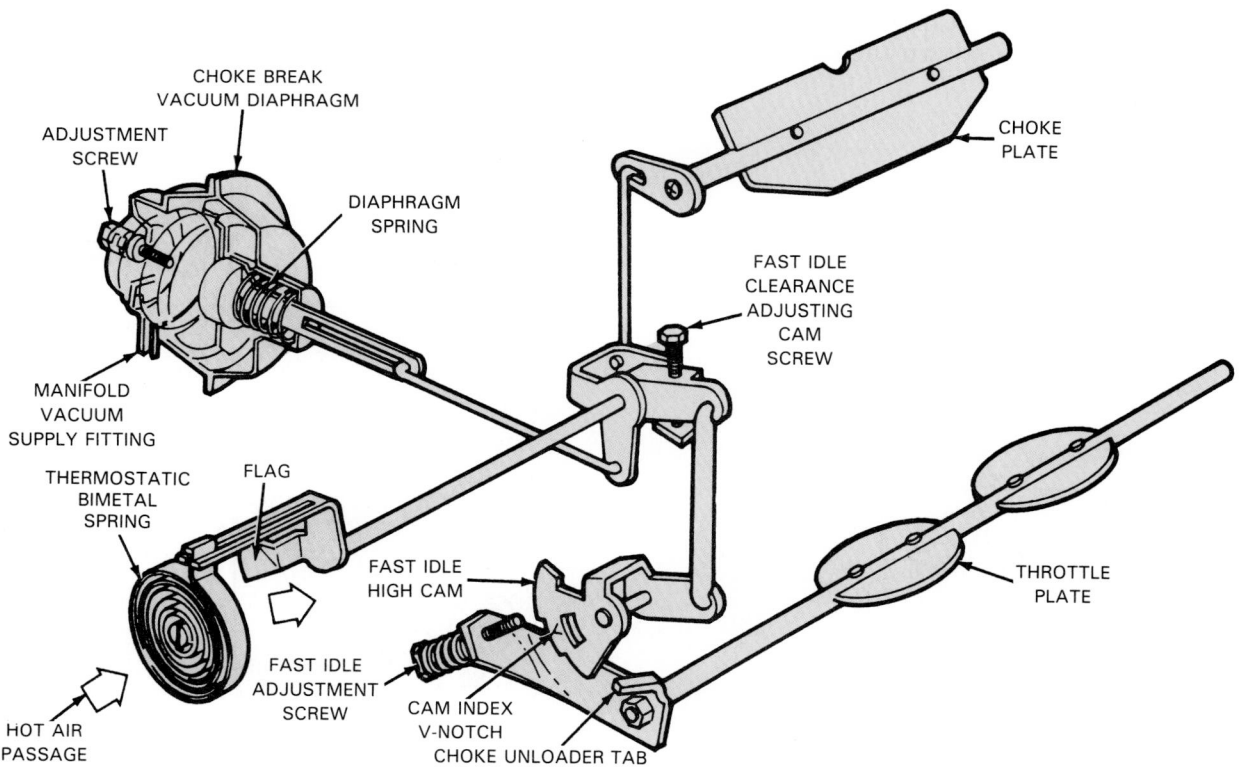

Fig. 19-31. Note relationship of these parts. They work together to provide smooth engine operation when engine is cold. (Ford Motor Co.)

plates to close as soon as the engine shuts off.

In this way, a faster idle speed can be used while still avoiding *dieseling* (engine keeps running even though ignition key is turned off).

Sometimes termed an **anti-dieseling solenoid,** the fast idle solenoid is mounted on the carburetor so that it contacts the throttle lever, as in Fig. 19-32.

When the engine is running, current flows to the fast idle solenoid. This causes the plunger in the solenoid to move outward. The throttle plates are held open to increase engine speed.

When the engine is shut off, current flow to the solenoid stops. The solenoid plunger retracts and the throttle plates are free to swing almost closed.

THROTTLE RETURN DASHPOT

A *throttle return dashpot* causes the carburetor throttle plates to close slowly, Fig. 19-33. Often called an ANTI-STALL DASHPOT, it is commonly used on carburetors for cars equipped with automatic transmission.

Without a throttle return dashpot, the engine could stall when the engine returns too quickly to an idle. The drag of the automatic transmission could "kill" the engine.

The throttle return dashpot works something like a shock absorber. It uses a spring-loaded diaphragm mounted in a sealed housing. A small hole is drilled in the diaphragm housing. The small air hole prevents rapid movement of the dashpot plunger and diaphragm. Air must bleed out the small hole slowly.

When the car is traveling down the road (throttle plates open), the spring pushes the dashpot plunger outward. Then, when the engine returns to idle, the throttle lever strikes the extended dashpot plunger. As air leaks out of the throttle return dashpot, the engine slowly returns to curb idle. This gives the automatic transmission enough time to disconnect (torque converter releases) from the engine, without engine stalling.

HOT IDLE COMPENSATOR

A *hot idle compensator* is a carburetor device that prevents engine stalling or a rough idle under high engine temperature conditions. As pictured in Fig. 19-34, it is a temperature-sensitive valve that admits extra air into the engine to increase idle speed and smoothness.

With normal engine temperatures, the hot idle compensating valve remains closed. The engine idles normally.

When temperatures are high (prolonged idling periods for example), fuel vapors can enter the air horn and enrich the air-fuel mixture. At this time, the hot idle compensator opens to allow extra air to enter the intake manifold. This compensates for the extra fuel vapors and the correct fuel mixture is maintained.

ALTITUDE COMPENSATOR

An *altitude compensator* can be used to change the carburetor's air-fuel mixture with changes in the car's height above or below sea level. An altitude compensator normally has an *aneroid* (bellows device that ex-

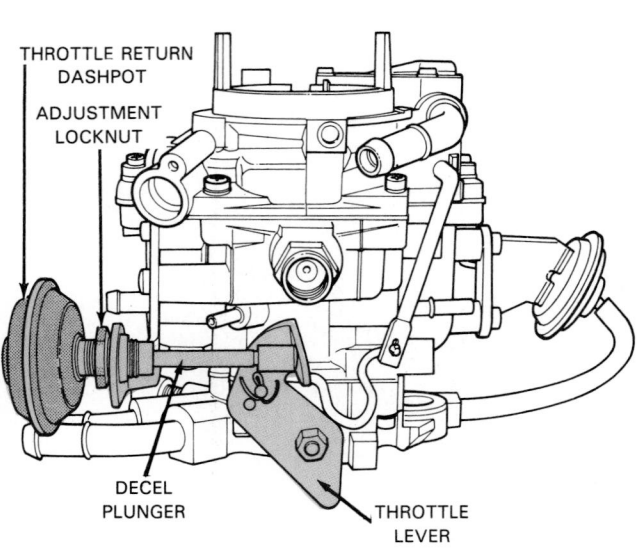

Fig. 19-33. Throttle return dashpot keeps engine from stalling when quickly returned to an idle. It is normally used on cars with automatic transmission. Dashpot makes throttle plates close slowly. (Chrysler)

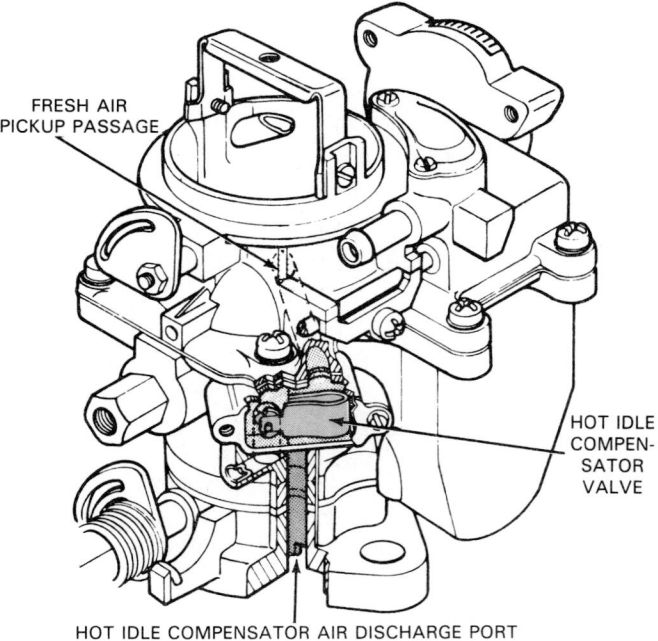

Fig. 19-34. Hot idle compensator adds extra air during high temperature conditions. More air is needed to offset extra fuel vapors caused by heat. (Ford)

pands and contracts with changes in atmospheric pressure), Fig. 19-35.

When a car is driven up a mountain, for example, the density of the air around the car decreases. This tends to make the air-fuel mixture richer. The reduced air pressure causes the aneroid to expand, opening an air valve. Extra air flows into the air horn and the air-fuel mixture becomes leaner as needed.

The opposite occurs when the car's height above sea level decreases. The greater air density and pressure tends to make the carburetor mixture too lean. The increased air pressure collapses the aneroid and the air valve closes. This enriches the mixture enough to compensate for the lower altitude.

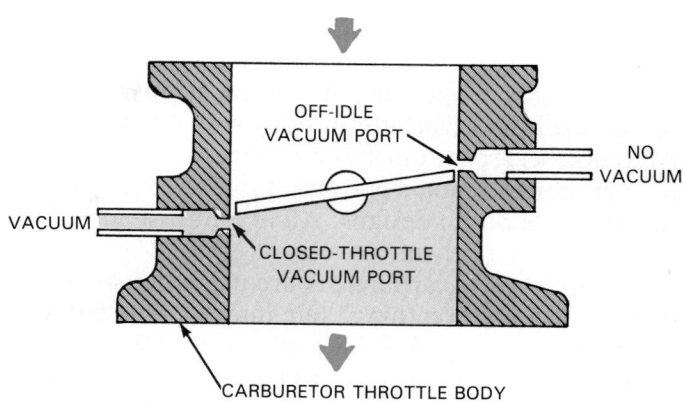

Fig. 19-36. Position of vacuum port in carburetor controls when vacuum is present. When below throttle valve, vacuum is present at idle. When above throttle, vacuum is present above idle. (Ethyl Corp.)

3. CHARCOAL CANISTER (emission control container for storing fuel vapors).
4. CHOKE BREAK (diaphragm for partially opening choke when engine is running).

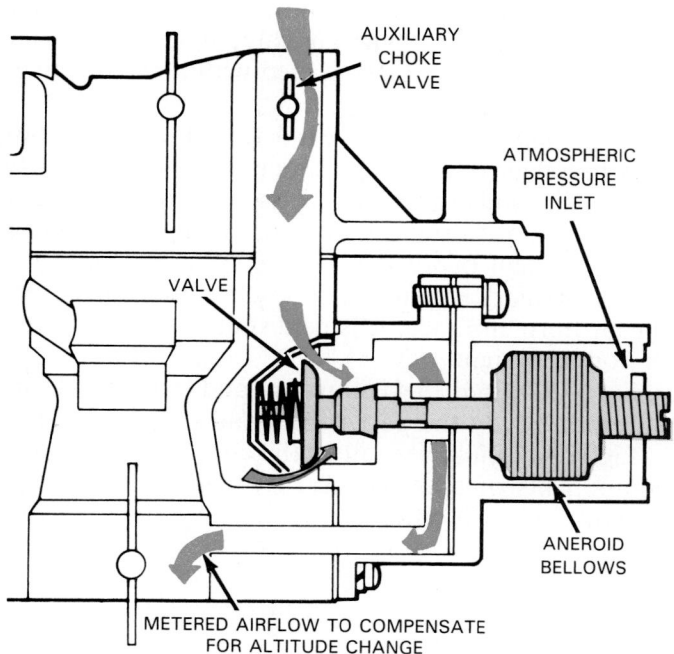

Fig. 19-35. Altitude compensation circuit uses aneroid bellows. Bellows expands and contracts with changes in altitude and atmospheric pressure. This increases or decreases airflow through circuit, maintaining correct air-fuel ratio.

CARBURETOR VACUUM CONNECTIONS

A modern carburetor has numerous vacuum connections. Look at Fig. 19-36. When the vacuum connection or port is BELOW the carburetor throttle plate, the port ALWAYS receives full intake manifold vacuum. However, when the vacuum port is ABOVE the throttle plate, vacuum is only present at the port when the THROTTLE IS OPENED.

Typical components operated off carburetor vacuum connections are:

1. EGR VALVE (exhaust emission control device).
2. DISTRIBUTOR VACUUM ADVANCE (diaphragm for advancing ignition timing).

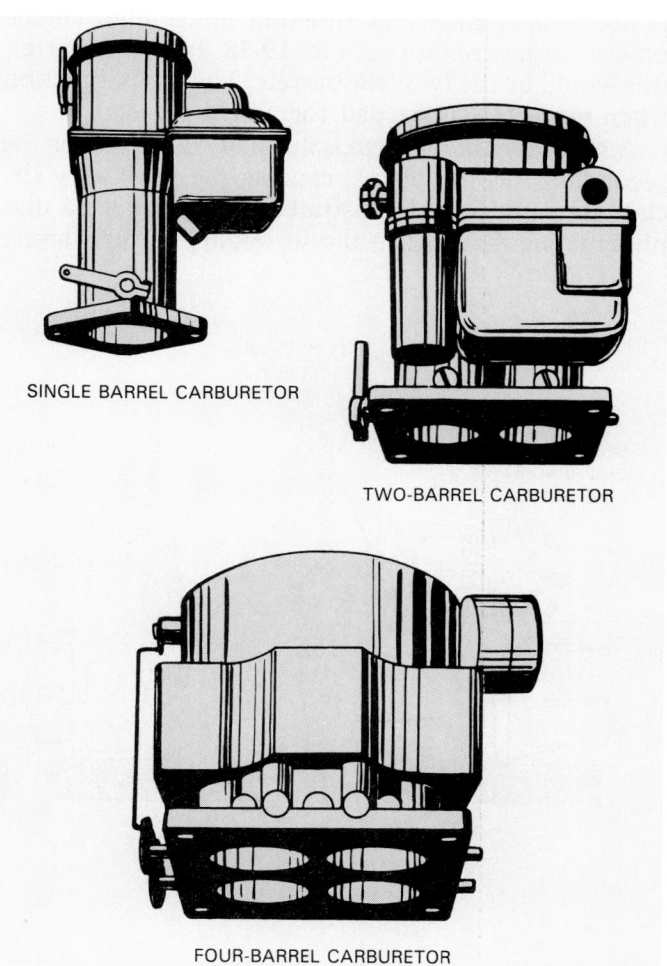

Fig. 19-37. One, two, and four-barrel carburetors are common. More barrels or air horns are used with larger engines.

TWO- AND FOUR-BARREL CARBURETORS

So far, this chapter has discussed mainly the *one-barrel carburetor* (carburetor body with one air horn). Automotive carburetors also are available in *two-barrel* (two air horns in single body) and *four-barrel* (four air horns in one body) designs. All are illustrated in Fig. 19-37. Compare them.

Multiple barrel carburetors are used to provide increased "engine breathing" (air intake). The amount of fuel and air that enter the engine is a factor limiting engine horsepower output. Extra carburetor barrels allow more air and fuel into the engine at wide open throttle. This allows the engine to develop more power.

Carburetor primary and secondary

In-line, two-barrel and all four-barrel carburetors are divided into two sections: the primary and the secondary.

The *primary* of a carburetor includes the components that operate under normal driving conditions. In a four-barrel carburetor for example, it consists of the two front throttle plates and related components. Refer to Fig. 19-38.

The *secondary* of a carburetor consists of the components or circuits that function under high engine power output conditions, Fig. 19-38. In a four-barrel, this would be the two rear barrels. They only function when more fuel is needed for added power.

A *secondary diaphragm* is normally used to open the secondary throttle plates, causing the secondary circuits to function. As illustrated in Fig. 19-38, a diaphragm is connected to the secondary throttle lever.

A vacuum passage runs from this diaphragm to the venturi in the primary throttle bore.

Under normal driving conditions, vacuum in the primary is NOT high enough to actuate the secondary diaphragm and throttles. The engine will run using only the primary of the carburetor.

If the driver passes another vehicle, for example, increased airflow in the primary produces enough vacuum to operate the secondary diaphragm. Vacuum pulls on the diaphragm and compresses the diaphragm spring. This opens the secondary throttle plates for increased engine horsepower.

AUXILIARY AIR VALVE

Some four-barrel and a few two-barrel carburetors use an auxiliary butterfly valve over the secondary throttle valves. One type air valve is shown in Fig. 19-39. It should not be confused with a choke valve. They look very similar.

An *auxiliary throttle valve* is designed to keep secondary barrel air velocity high enough to assure complete fuel mixing and atomization. It stops secondary throat operation until primary air speed is high enough to allow efficient operation.

The auxiliary air valve is normally closed and covers the air horn entrance. It is held shut by a light spring or counterweight.

Figs. 19-40 and 19-41 show two and four-barrel carburetors. Study the part names and their locations.

Fig. 19-42 illustrates all of the circuits and internal components of a carburetor. Do you remember the function of each part?

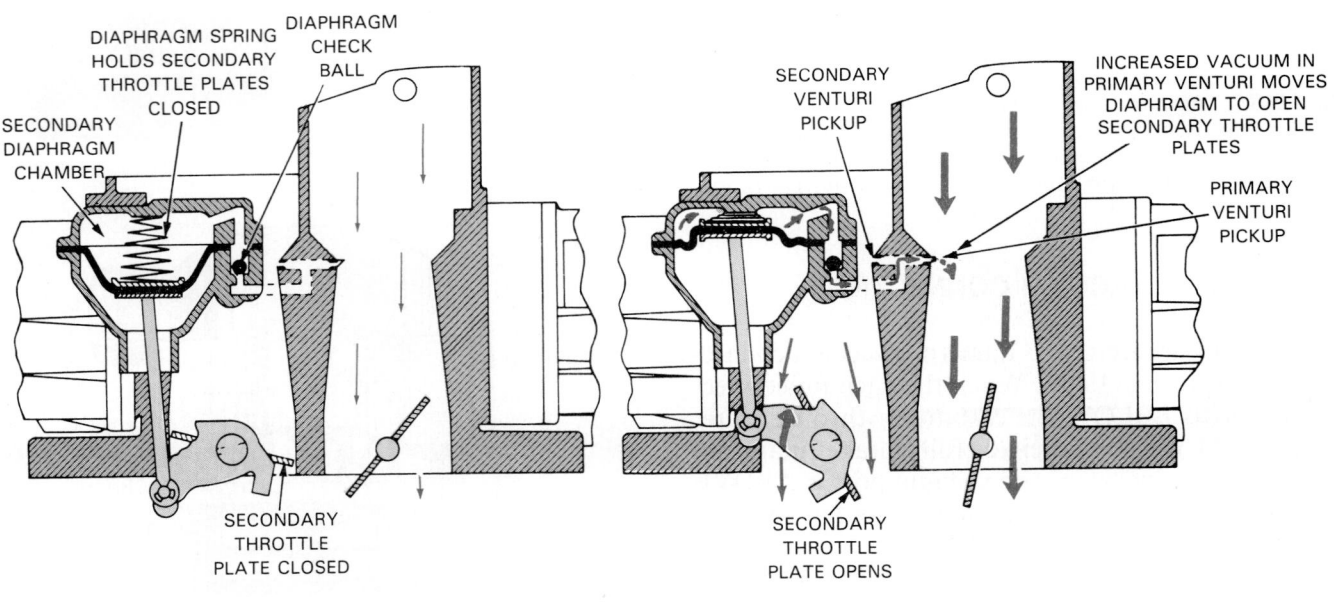

Fig. 19-38. Primary is front barrel or barrels of carburetor. Secondary is rear barrels of carburetor. Note how secondary diaphragm opens rear throttle plates when engine power output is high. (Holley Carburetors)

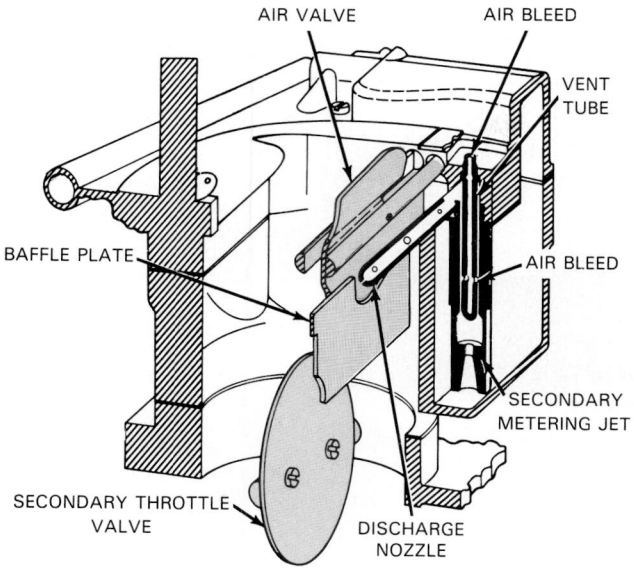

Fig. 19-39. Air valve over secondary throttles only opens if airflow is high enough for proper secondary operation. (Chrysler)

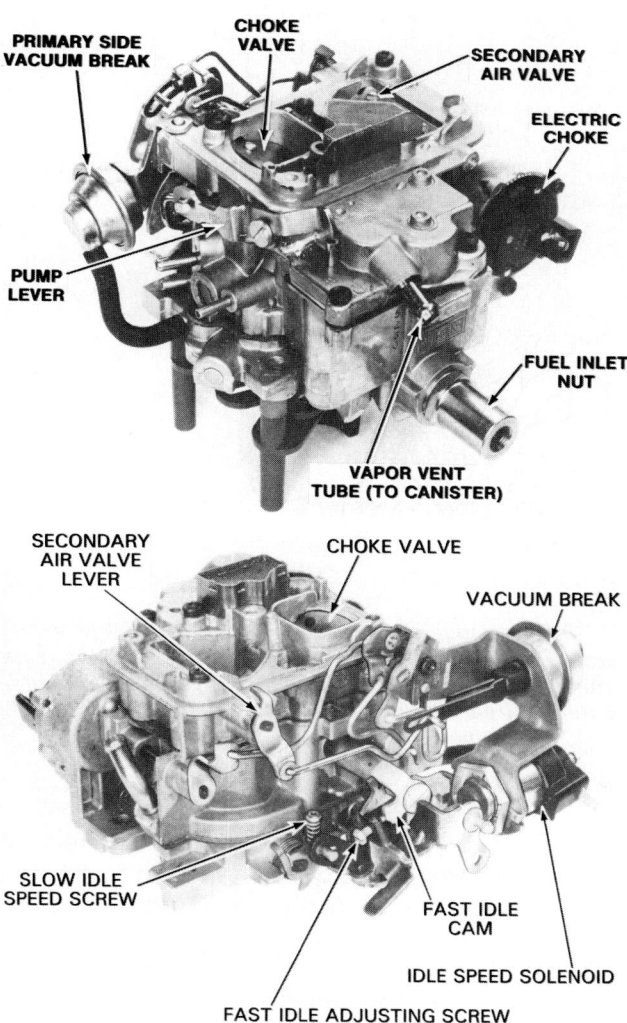

Fig. 19-40. Modern two-barrel carburetor. Note parts. (Oldsmobile)

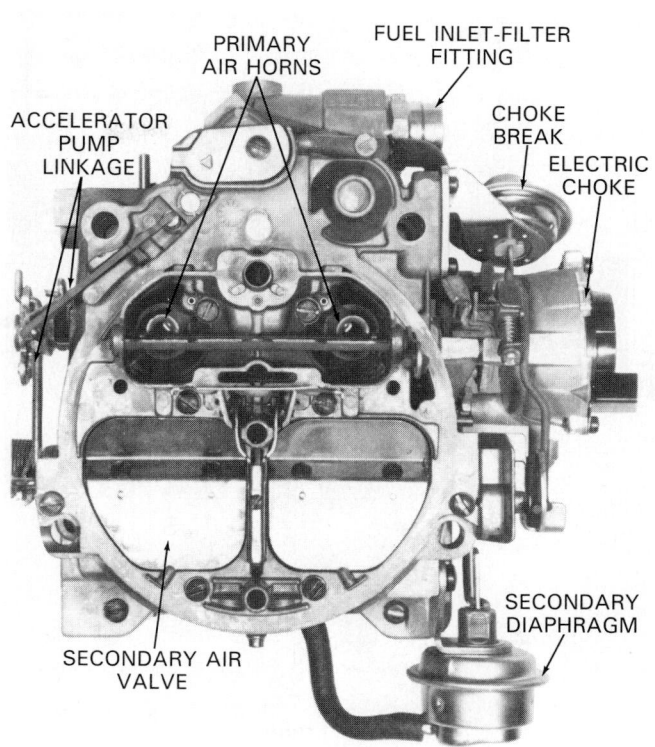

Fig. 19-41. Top view of a four-barrel carburetor. (Cadillac)

CARBURETOR SIZE

Generally, *carburetor size* is stated in CFM (cubic feet of air per minute). This is the amount of air that can flow through the carburetor at wide open throttle. CFM is an indication of maximum airflow capacity.

Usually, small CFM carburetors are more fuel efficient than larger carburetors. Air velocity, fuel mixing, and atomization is better with small throttle bores. A larger CFM rating would be desirable for high engine power output.

VARIABLE VENTURI CARBURETOR

A *variable venturi carburetor* adjusts the diameter of the venturi to maintain a relatively constant air speed in the carburetor. Many foreign cars and a few American made cars use this type.

Fig. 19-43 shows a variable venturi, slide type carburetor. A piston slides in and out to regulate the size of the venturi. This type is commonly used on motorcycles and some foreign cars.

Fig. 19-44 illustrates another type of variable venturi carburetor used by one U.S. auto maker. Note that it uses a large diaphragm to operate the movable venturi. Needle valves are mounted on the venturis so that increased fuel metering occurs as the venturis swing open for added power.

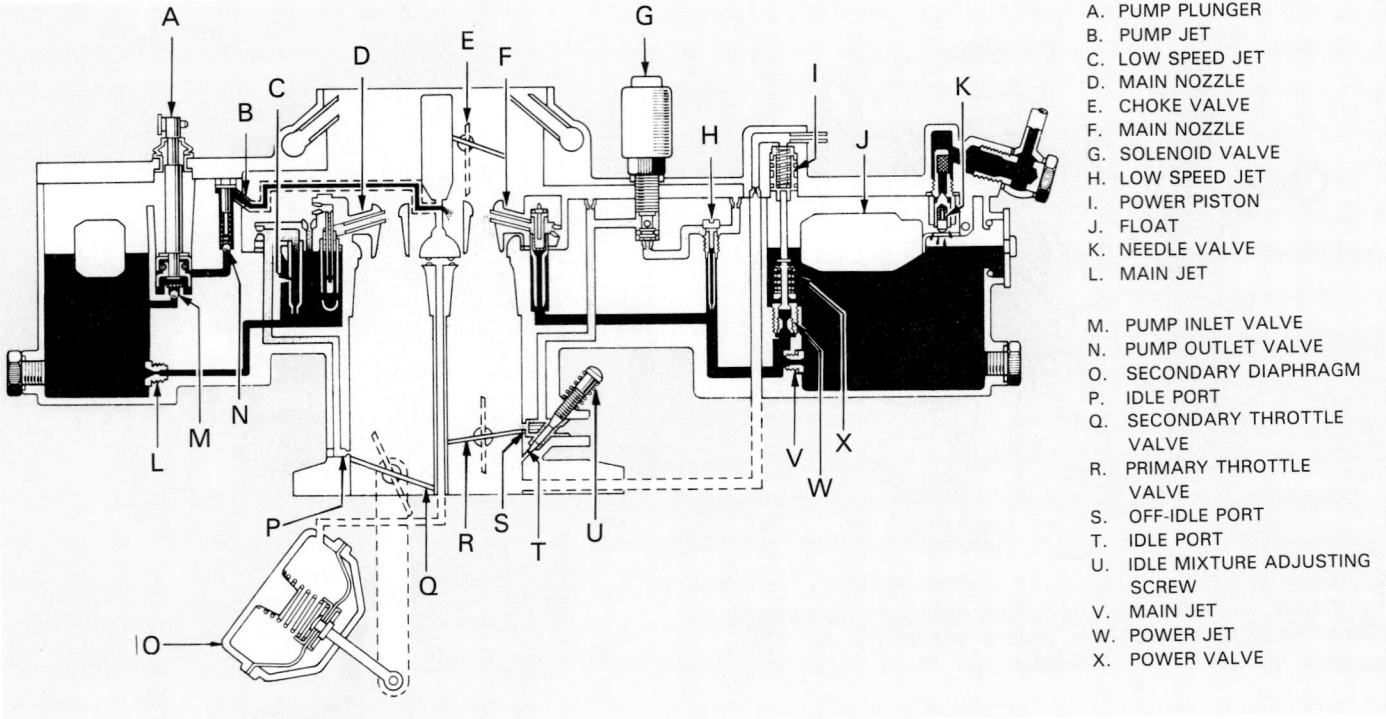

A.	PUMP PLUNGER
B.	PUMP JET
C.	LOW SPEED JET
D.	MAIN NOZZLE
E.	CHOKE VALVE
F.	MAIN NOZZLE
G.	SOLENOID VALVE
H.	LOW SPEED JET
I.	POWER PISTON
J.	FLOAT
K.	NEEDLE VALVE
L.	MAIN JET
M.	PUMP INLET VALVE
N.	PUMP OUTLET VALVE
O.	SECONDARY DIAPHRAGM
P.	IDLE PORT
Q.	SECONDARY THROTTLE VALVE
R.	PRIMARY THROTTLE VALVE
S.	OFF-IDLE PORT
T.	IDLE PORT
U.	IDLE MIXTURE ADJUSTING SCREW
V.	MAIN JET
W.	POWER JET
X.	POWER VALVE

Fig. 19-42. Try to identify and explain carburetor parts before looking at listed names. (Toyota)

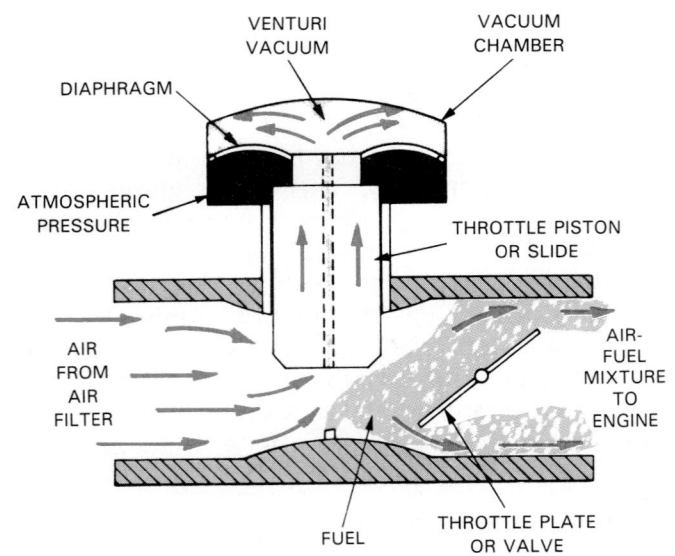

Fig. 19-43. A slide type, variable venturi carburetor. A cylinder-shaped slide moves in and out of air horn to help control fuel and airflow. Conventional throttle valve is connected to driver's gas pedal.

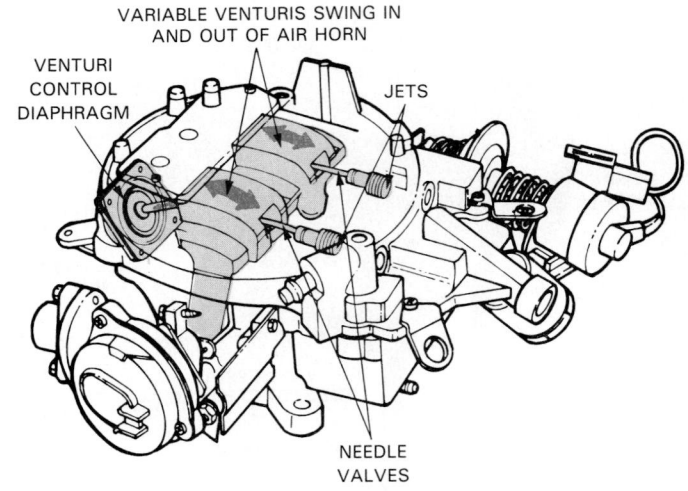

Fig. 19-44. Variable venturi carburetor has large venturis operated by diaphragm. As engine power output increases, venturis swing out of air horns. This allows more air and fuel to enter airstream. Constant velocity means that speed of air in air horns is held more constant. (Ford)

COMPUTER CONTROLLED CARBURETORS

A *computer controlled carburetor* normally uses a solenoid operated valve to respond to commands from a microcomputer (electronic control unit). A typical system is shown in Fig. 19-45.

The system uses various sensors to send information to the computer. Then, the computer calculates how

rich or lean to set the carburetor's air-fuel mixture.

A computer-controlled carburetor system, sometimes termed a computer-controlled emission system, consists of:

An *oxygen sensor* or *exhaust gas sensor* monitors the oxygen content in the engine exhaust. See Figs. 19-45 and 19-46. The amount of oxygen in the exhaust indicates the richness (low oxygen content), or leanness (high oxygen content) of the air-fuel mixture. The

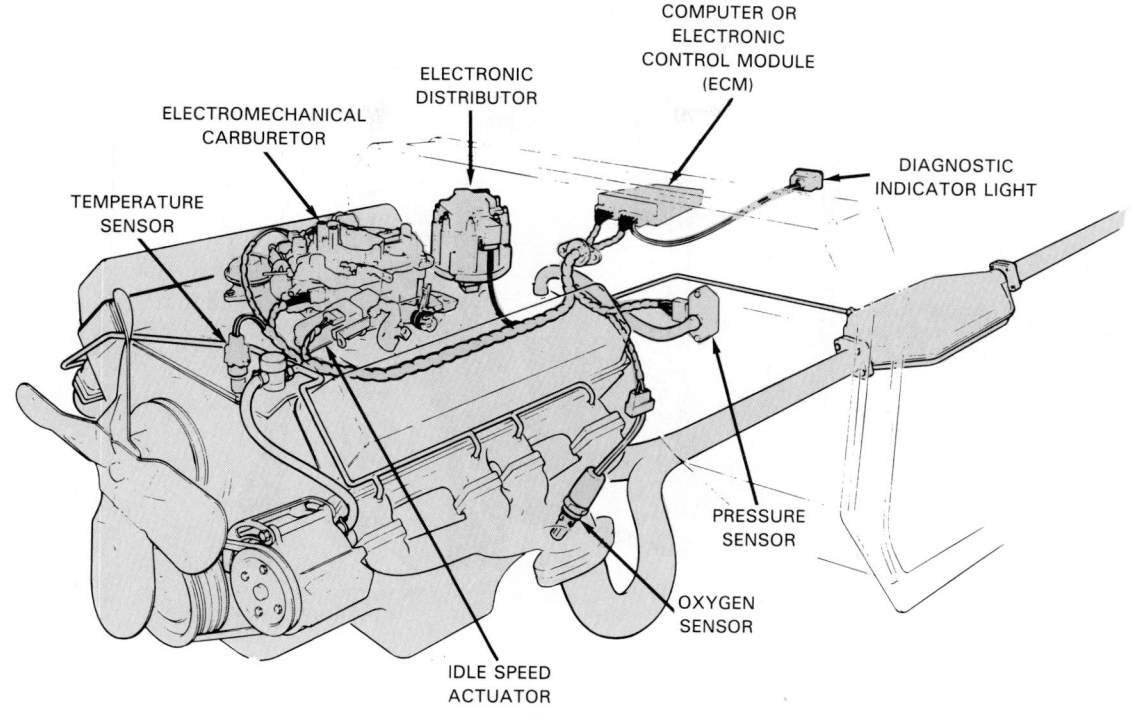

Fig. 19-45. Typical computer controlled carburetor system. Study part names and locations. (AC-Delco)

sensor's (voltage output) changes with any change in oxygen content in the exhaust gases.

The **temperature sensor** detects the operating temperature of the engine, Fig. 19-45. Its resistance

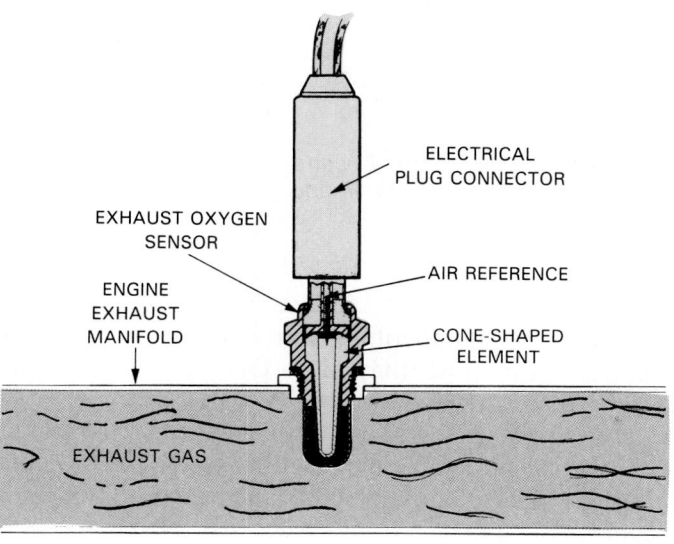

Fig. 19-46. Oxygen sensor in exhaust is main controlling sensor in system. It detects amount of oxygen in exhaust by comparing sample to outside air. A high oxygen content indicates a lean mixture. Low oxygen content in exhaust points to a richer mixture. Computer can then correct mixture for maximum efficiency. (AC)

changes with the temperature of the engine. This allows the computer to enrich the fuel mixture during cold engine operation.

A **pressure sensor** measures intake manifold vacuum and engine load. See Fig. 19-45.

High engine load or power output causes intake manifold vacuum to drop. The pressure sensor, in this way, can signal the computer with a change in resistance and current flow.

When manifold pressure drops, the computer increases the air-fuel mixture for added power. If intake manifold vacuum increases, the computer makes the carburetor setting leaner for improved economy.

An **electromechanical carburetor** is one having both electrical and mechanical control devices. This type is shown in Fig. 19-47. It is commonly used with a computer control system.

A **mixture control solenoid** in the computer controlled carburetor alters the air-fuel ratio. Electrical signals from the computer activate the solenoid to open and close air and fuel passages in the carburetor.

Fig. 19-48 and 19-49 show two other types of mixture control solenoids.

The system **computer,** also called the *electronic control unit* (ECU), uses sensor information to operate the carburetor's mixture control solenoid. One is shown in Fig. 19-50.

An **idle speed actuator** may also be used to allow the computer to change engine idle speed. It is usually

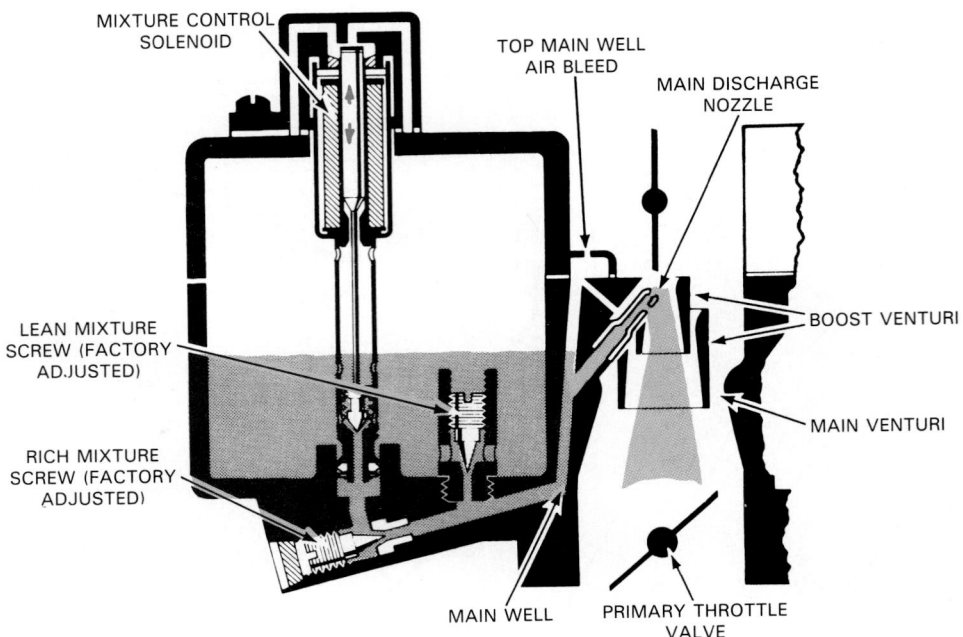

Fig. 19-47. Mixture control solenoid can quickly open or close valve to change carburetor's air-fuel ratio. Computer sends electrical pulses to solenoid. Solenoid magnetic field acts on metal plunger, operating mixture valve. (Pontiac)

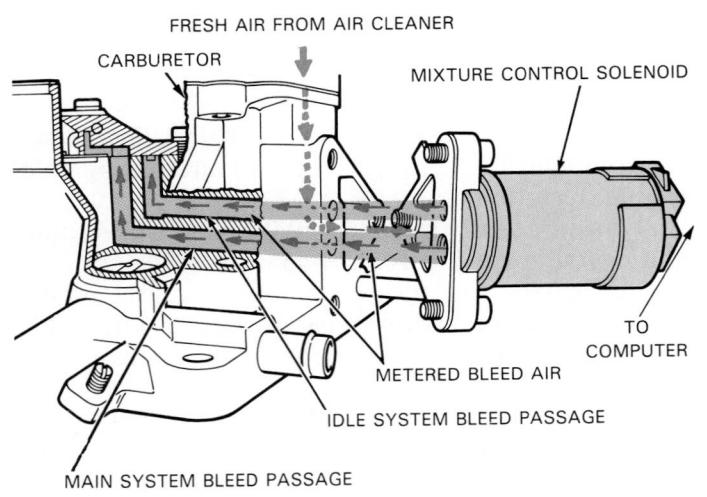

Fig. 19-48. Another design for a mixture control solenoid. This solenoid valve opens and closes air passage to control mixture ratio. This also allows computer to control carburetor. (Ford Motor Co.)

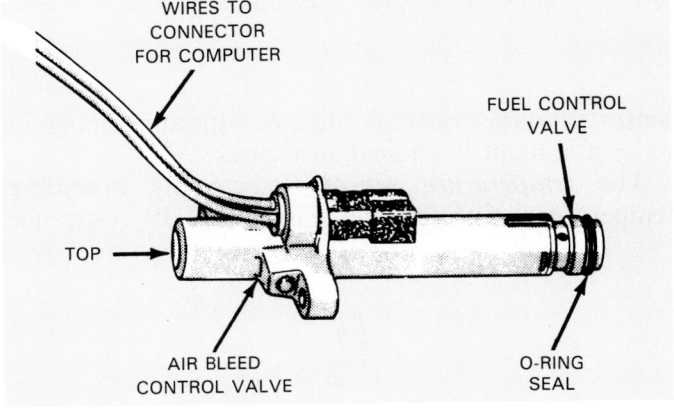

Fig. 19-49. This computer-controlled carburetor mixture solenoid regulates both air and fuel flow. (Chrysler)

a tiny electric motor and gear mechanism that holds the carburetor throttle lever in the desired position.

Computer-controlled carburetor operation

In a computer-controlled carburetor, the air-fuel ratio is maintained by *cycling* the mixture solenoid ON and OFF several times a second.

Fig. 19-51 shows how the control signals from the computer can be used to meter different amounts of fuel out of the carburetor.

When the computer sends a rich command to the solenoid, the signal voltage to the mixture solenoid is usually OFF more than it is ON. This causes the solenoid to stay open more.

During a lean signal from the computer, the signal usually has more ON time. This causes less fuel to pass through the solenoid valve. The mixture becomes leaner.

Open and closed loop operation

The term *open loop* means that the system is operating on preset values in the computer. For example, right after cold engine starting, the computer will operate open loop. The sensors, especially the oxygen sensor, CANNOT provide accurate information.

Closed loop means that the computer is using information from the oxygen sensor and other sensors. The information forms an imaginary loop (circle) from the computer, through the engine fuel system, into the exhaust, and back to the computer through the oxygen sensor information.

A computer controlled carburetor system normally operates in the closed loop mode. Using "info" from the engine sensors, a very precise air-fuel ratio can be maintained. The mixture can be changed with the slightest change in engine operating conditions.

ELECTRONIC CONTROL UNIT
CARBURETOR CONTROLLER
P/N
S/N

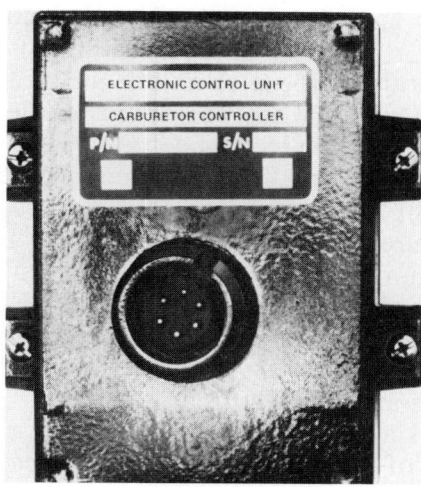

Fig. 19-50. Computer or electronic control unit is complex electronic circuit. It usually mounts under car dash, away from moisture, vibration, and engine heat. (Oldsmobile)

More information

Note! Computerized carburetor systems vary. For exact details of a particular system, refer to a factory service manual. The manual will explain how the specific system functions.

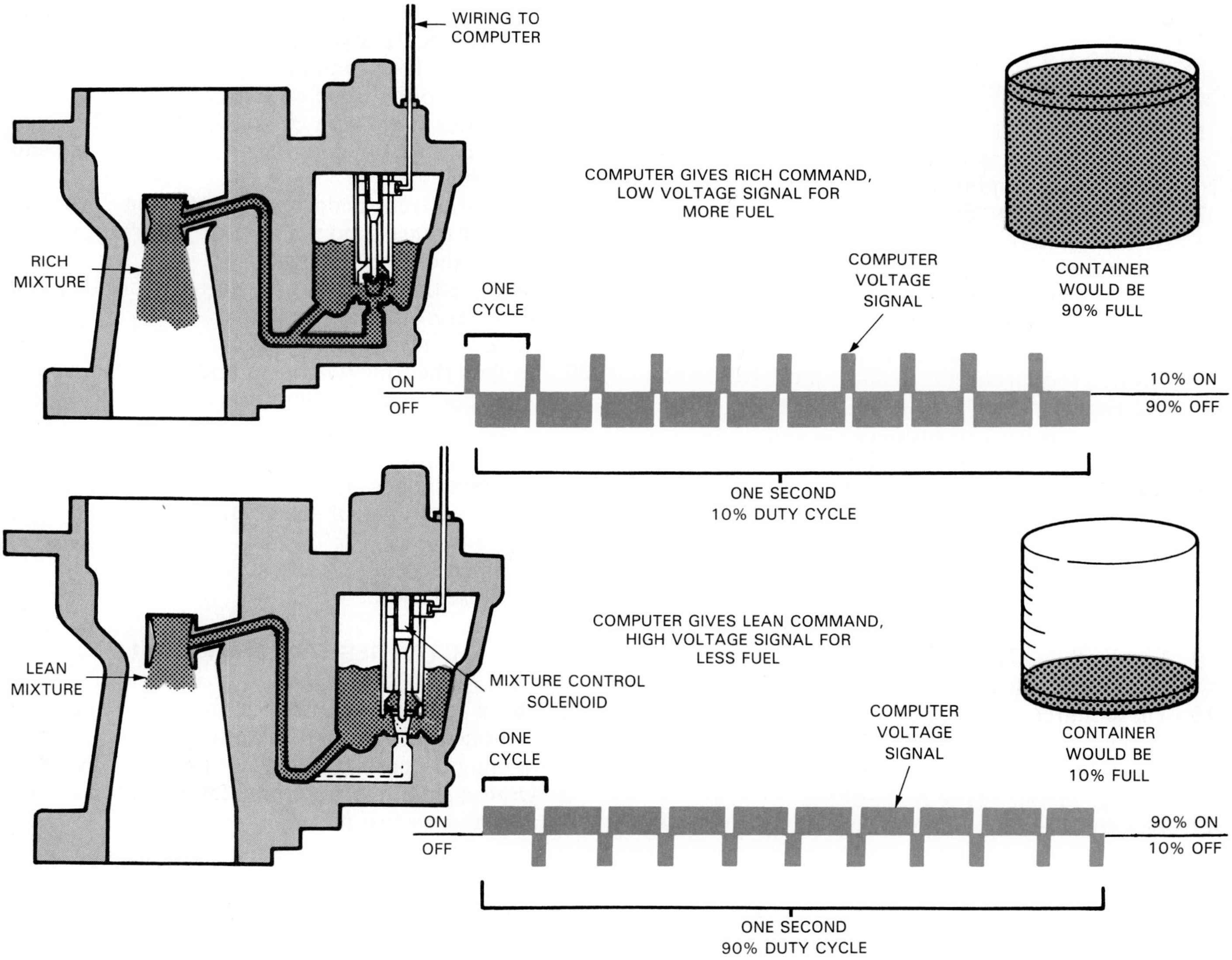

WIRING TO COMPUTER
COMPUTER GIVES RICH COMMAND, LOW VOLTAGE SIGNAL FOR MORE FUEL
RICH MIXTURE
ONE CYCLE
COMPUTER VOLTAGE SIGNAL
CONTAINER WOULD BE 90% FULL
ON
OFF
10% ON
90% OFF
ONE SECOND
10% DUTY CYCLE
COMPUTER GIVES LEAN COMMAND, HIGH VOLTAGE SIGNAL FOR LESS FUEL
LEAN MIXTURE
MIXTURE CONTROL SOLENOID
ONE CYCLE
COMPUTER VOLTAGE SIGNAL
CONTAINER WOULD BE 10% FULL
ON
OFF
90% ON
10% OFF
ONE SECOND
90% DUTY CYCLE

Fig. 19-51. Computer rapidly pulses mixture control solenoid ON and OFF to control air-fuel ratio. With this carburetor, note how longer OFF time enriches mixture. Shorter OFF time makes mixture lean. (Chrysler Corp.)

As you will learn in later chapters, a computer controlled carburetor system is very similar to ELECTRONIC FUEL INJECTION. Both systems use engine sensors, a computer, and solenoid action to control the amount of fuel entering the engine. Electronic fuel injection is detailed in Chapter 21.

KNOW THESE TERMS

Carburetor, Atmospheric pressure, Vacuum, Carburetor body, Air horn, Throttle valve, Venturi, Main discharge tube, Carburetor system, Float system, Needle valve, Bowl vent, Idle mixture screw, Accelerator pump, Main jet, Metering rod, Power valve, Thermostatic spring, Mechanical choke unloader, Vacuum choke break, Fast idle cam, Fast idle solenoid, Throttle return dashpot, Hot idle compensator, Altitude compensator, Primary, Secondary, CFM, Variable venturi carburetor, Computer-controlled carburetor, Mixture control solenoid, Engine sensors, Oxygen sensor, Electronic control unit, Open loop, Closed loop.

REVIEW QUESTIONS

1. A carburetor is basically a device for _____ air and fuel in the correct _____ (amounts) for efficient combustion.
2. Define the term "atmospheric pressure."
3. Define the term "vacuum."
4. List and explain the six major parts of a carburetor.
5. The air horn is the main fuel passage in the carburetor. True or False?
6. The _____ _____ control airflow through the carburetor to allow the driver to control engine power.
7. A venturi is used to produce vacuum in the carburetor air horn. True or False?
8. Which of the following is NOT a typical air-fuel ratio for a gasoline engine?
   a. 8:1
   b. 16:1
   c. 3:1
   d. 18:1
9. List and explain the seven major carburetor systems or circuits.
10. The carburetor _____ rides on top of the fuel to open and close the needle valve as needed.
11. A bowl vent is used to allow fuel vapors to enter the outside air. True or False?
12. The carburetor _____ system provides the

engine's air-fuel mixture at speeds below about _____ rpm or 20 mph (32 km/h).
13. What is the purpose of an idle air bleed?
14. What happens when you turn the idle mixture screw in and out?
15. Why are modern idle mixture screws covered with a metal plug?
16. A carburetor accelerator pump works like a toy squirt gun to squirt fuel into the air horn when the throttle is opened for acceleration. True or False?
17. The _____ _____ carburetor system provides the leanest, most fuel efficient air-fuel mixture at normal cruising speeds.
18. What is a high speed jet?
19. Which of the following could NOT be included in the full power system?
   a. Power valve.
   b. Metering rod.
   c. Economizer valve.
   d. Choke plate.
20. What is the function of a carburetor choke?
21. List and explain four types of automatic choke.
22. A mechanical choke unloaded uses a metal lug on the throttle lever to physically open the choke plate at full throttle. True or False?
23. How does a vacuum choke break work?
24. What carburetor component is used to prevent dieseling?
25. A throttle return dashpot is used on cars with manual transmissions. True or False?
26. Define the term "aneroid."
27. Describe the difference between the primary and secondary of a carburetor.
28. How do you measure carburetor size?
29. Explain the following parts and terms for a computer controlled carburetor system.
   a. Oxygen sensor.
   b. Temperature sensor.
   c. Pressure sensor.
   d. Mixture control solenoid.
   e. Computer.
   f. Open loop.
   g. Closed loop.

ACTIVITIES FOR CHAPTER 19

1. On a carburetor of your instructor's choice, demonstrate your understanding of its systems by naming its parts and explaining their purpose.
2. Draw a simple carburetor cutaway and show how fuel and air are mixed.

20

Carburetor Diagnosis, Service, Repair

After studying this chapter, you will be able to:
□ Diagnose common carburetor problems.
□ Describe the troubles that frequently occur in each carburetor system.
□ Properly remove and replace a carburetor.
□ Disassemble and reassemble a carburetor while following the procedures in a service manual.
□ Perform basic carburetor adjustments.
□ Describe the safety rules relating to carburetor service.
□ Observe all safety rules and cautions for carburetor service.

As you learned in Chapter 19, a carburetor is a device for metering fuel into the engine. It must adjust the air-fuel ratio as engine speed, load, and temperature change. The carburetor is very important to the efficiency and reliability of an engine. If a carburetor passage becomes clogged with dirt or if a gasket or seal deteriorates, engine performance can suffer.

CARBURETOR PROBLEM DIAGNOSIS

The first step in diagnosis is to determine whether the carburetor or another system is at fault. Troubles in the ignition system, emission control systems, and engine can produce the same general symptoms (missing, poor fuel economy, engine not starting) as carburetor problems. Chapter 41, Engine Performance Problem Diagnosis, covers information on this topic.

Visually inspect carburetor

A visual inspection of the carburetor may provide clues to the carburetor problem, Fig. 20-1. Remove the air cleaner. Look for fuel leakage, sticking choke, binding linkage, and missing or disconnected vacuum hoses.

A heavy covering of road dirt usually indicates the carburetor has been in service for a long time. Adjustments or repairs may be needed.

While inspecting the carburetor, also check the rest of the engine compartment. Look for disconnected wires and hoses. Listen for the hissing sound of a vacuum leak. Make sure the distributor cap is not cracked. Try to locate anything that could upset normal engine operation.

Incorrect air-fuel mixture

Many internal carburetor problems show up as an air-fuel mixture that is too rich or too lean.

A *lean air-fuel mixture* is caused by any condition that allows too much air and too little fuel to enter the engine. A lean mixture will cause the engine to MISS ERRATICALLY (every once in a while). The cause may be a vacuum leak, incorrect mixture screw adjustment, clogged fuel passage, low float level, or other problems.

A *rich air-fuel mixture* results from too much fuel and not enough air entering the engine. A very rich mixture will make the engine roll, lope, and emit black smoke. A clogged air bleed, restricted air filter, high float level, incorrect choke setting, or other carburetor troubles can produce a rich mixture.

Exhaust gas analyzer

An *exhaust gas analyzer* is a testing device that measures the chemical content of the engine exhaust gases. It can be used to determine the air-fuel mixture of a carburetor or fuel injection system.

The exhaust gas analyzer draws a sample of the exhaust gas out of the car's tailpipe. Modern types measure the amount of carbon monoxide (CO), hydrocarbons (HC), carbon dioxide (CO_2), and oxygen (O_2) in the exhaust. This information indicates the air-fuel ratio entering the engine.

Chapter 40, Emission Control System Diagnosis and Repair, details the use of a modern four-gas exhaust analyzer. You may want to refer to this chapter for added information.

Carburetor problems

When diagnosing carburetor problems, try to determine which carburetor system is at fault. For example,

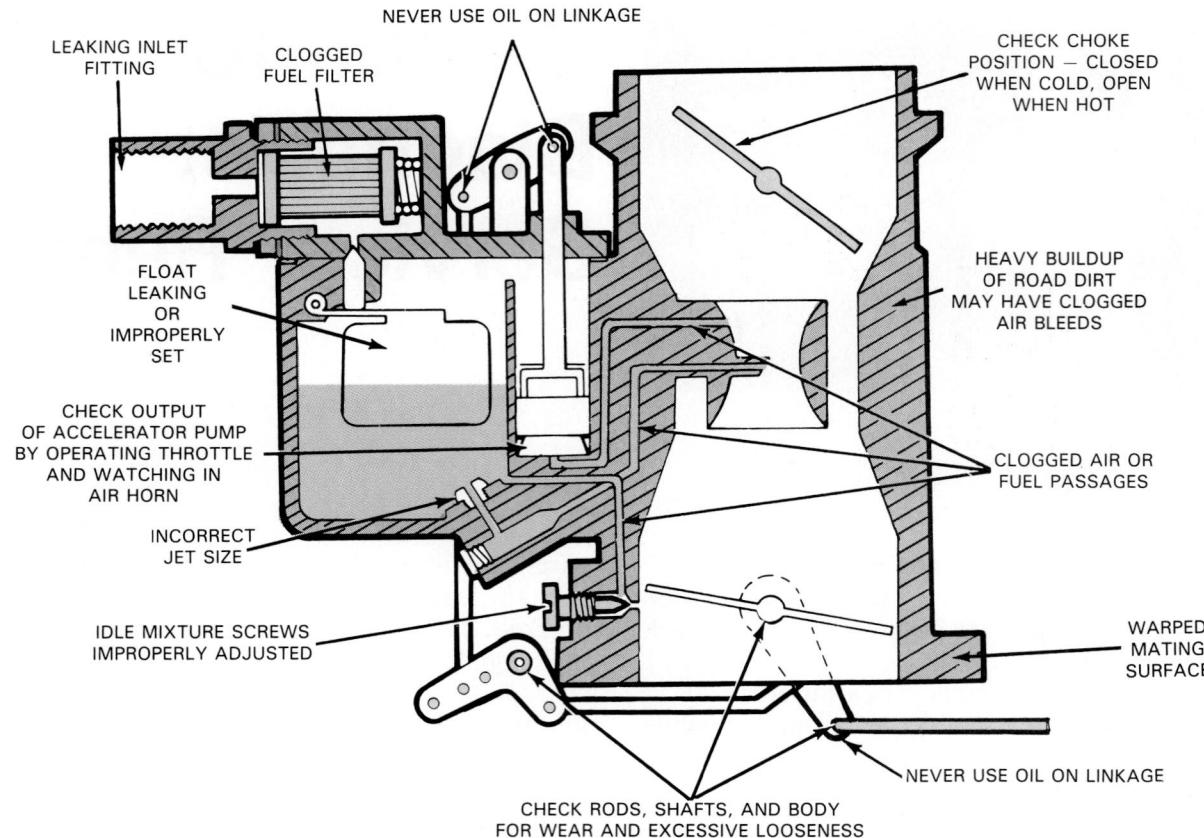

LEAKING INLET FITTING

CLOGGED FUEL FILTER

NEVER USE OIL ON LINKAGE

CHECK CHOKE POSITION — CLOSED WHEN COLD, OPEN WHEN HOT

FLOAT LEAKING OR IMPROPERLY SET

HEAVY BUILDUP OF ROAD DIRT MAY HAVE CLOGGED AIR BLEEDS

CHECK OUTPUT OF ACCELERATOR PUMP BY OPERATING THROTTLE AND WATCHING IN AIR HORN

INCORRECT JET SIZE

CLOGGED AIR OR FUEL PASSAGES

IDLE MIXTURE SCREWS IMPROPERLY ADJUSTED

WARPED MATING SURFACE

NEVER USE OIL ON LINKAGE

CHECK RODS, SHAFTS, AND BODY FOR WEAR AND EXCESSIVE LOOSENESS

Fig. 20-1. External check of carburetor can sometimes find source of problem. A few are pointed out in illustration. (Chrysler Corp.)

if the engine only runs poorly when cold, check the choke and fast idle systems. These systems are designed to aid cold engine operation.

If the engine only misses at idle, suspect the idle or low speed carburetor systems and check them first. Use this type of logic to narrow down the possible sources of carburetor problems.

Float system problems

Carburetor *float system troubles* can cause a wide range of performance problems: flooding, rich fuel mixture, lean fuel mixture, fuel starvation (no fuel), stalling, low speed engine miss, high speed engine miss. See Fig. 20-2. Improper float operation can affect the operation of the engine at ALL SPEEDS. The float system provides fuel for all of the other carburetor circuits.

Carburetor flooding

Carburetor flooding occurs when fuel pours out the top of the carburetor (vent, air bleed, or main discharge) or leaks around the bowl gasket. This problem arises when the float needle valve does NOT stop fuel flow from the fuel pump. The carburetor bowl fills too much and overflows.

DANGER! If a carburetor floods, shut the engine off immediately. Gasoline leaking onto the intake

manifold could be ignited by a spark or the hot exhaust manifold.

To correct carburetor flooding, disassemble the carburetor. Check the needle valve and seat for wear. They may need replacement. If fuel has leaked into the float, the float must be replaced. A carburetor bowl full of debris can also cause the needle valve to stick open. A complete carburetor overhaul is usually necessary.

Engine flooding

Carburetor flooding should not be confused with engine flooding.

Engine flooding is a problem resulting from too much fuel in the intake manifold and combustion chambers. Excess fuel could foul the spark plugs (fuel keeps sparks from jumping gaps) keeping the engine from running.

Engine flooding may be due to any number of reasons besides a float system problem. For example, if the driver pumps the gas pedal repeatedly, operating the accelerator pump, the engine could flood. A weak spark, stuck choke, or bad choke break diaphragm could also lead to engine flooding.

High float level

A *high float level* richens the air-fuel mixture. It can cause high fuel consumption, rough idling, and, possibly, black engine exhaust. Refer to Fig. 20-2 for typical flooding/starvation problems.

To check for float setting, start the engine and let it idle. While wearing safety glasses, check for fuel dripping from the main discharge tube (venturi). If fuel leaks out the main nozzle at idle, the float setting may be too high.

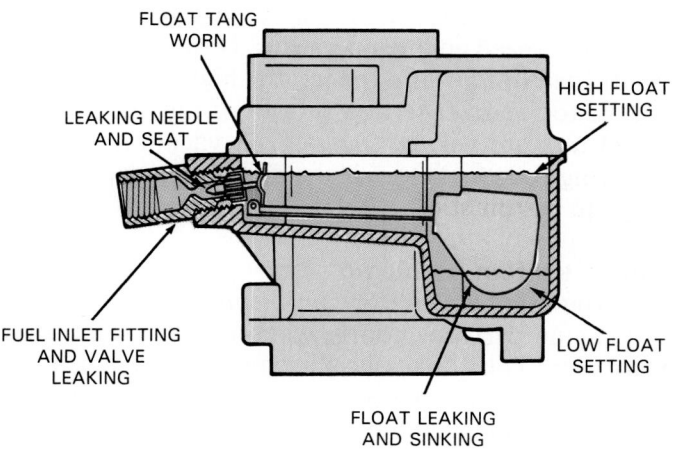

Fig. 20-2. Float system problems can cause flooding, fuel starvation, and poor performance at all engine speeds.

Low float level

A *low float level* can produce a lean air-fuel mixture. It can cause a high speed miss, stalling when cornering, and other symptoms common to fuel starvation.

Usually, you need to remove the air horn or bowl cover to check for a low fuel level. A few carburetors, however, have a glass inspection window or a fuel level screw on the side of the fuel bowl.

A high or low float level can usually be corrected by adjusting the float mechanism. This adjustment will be discussed later in the chapter.

Idle system problems

Carburetor *idle system problems* normally show up as a rough idle, stalling at low speeds, or incorrect idle speed. The engine may run fine at higher speeds, but poorly at idle. Fig. 20-3 points out common idle circuit problems.

A *clogged idle passage* can restrict fuel flow to the idle port. This causess a very lean mixture and poor idle. The jets in the idle circuit are very small. A tiny bit of dirt can easily upset idle circuit operation.

A *clogged idle air bleed,* by obstructing the premixing of air, can enrich the mixture, upsetting engine operation at idle. Since most of the air bleed jets are at the top of the carburetor, visually inspect and clean the air bleeds if needed.

To check for idle system problems on older cars, adjust the idle mixture screws. If turning the screws has

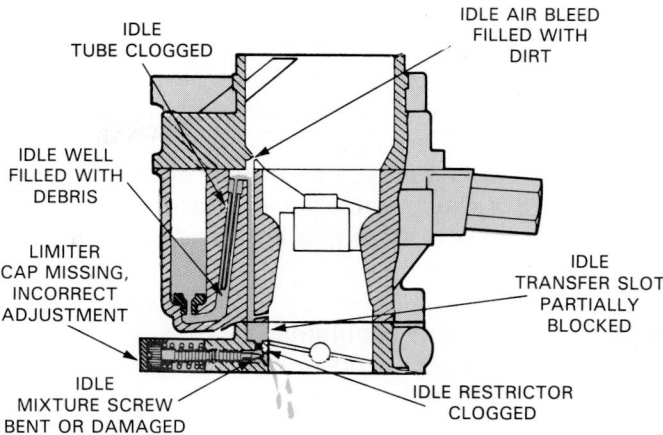

Fig. 20-3. Idle circuit problems show up at very low engine speeds. Jets and passages are so small they can be clogged by tiny dirt particles. Improper adjustment of mixture screw is another common trouble. (Chrysler Corp.)

little or no effect on idle speed and smoothness, the idle circuit is NOT functioning properly. The carburetor probably needs an overhaul.

WARNING! Late model carburetors have sealed idle mixture screws. To abide by federal law, do NOT adjust these screws unless following manufacturer's instructions.

Acceleration system problems

Carburetor *acceleration system problems* usually cause the engine to hesitate, stall, pop, backfire, or stumble when the car first moves from a standstill. If the accelerator pump does NOT squirt a strong stream of fuel into the air horn as the throttles open, the mixture will be TOO LEAN for proper engine acceleration. Look at Fig. 20-4.

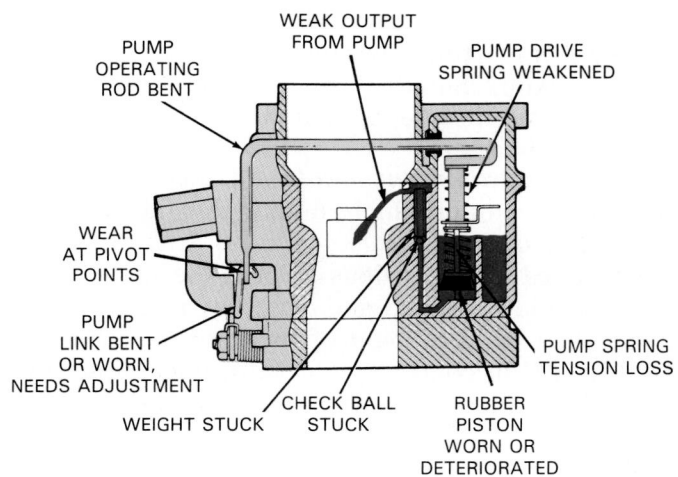

Fig. 20-4. Bad accelerator pump will make engine stumble or hesitate upon acceleration. Worn or misadjusted linkage, deteriorated pump or diaphragm, or other problems may keep fuel from squirting out nozzle when throttle opens. (Chrysler Corp.)

To check accelerator pump operation, shut the engine OFF and remove the air cleaner. Open and close the throttle while looking inside the carburetor air horn.

Each time the throttle is opened, a strong stream of fuel should spray into the air horn. The stream should start as soon as you move the throttle open. It should continue for a short time after full throttle opening.

If the stream is weak, either adjust or repair the accelerator pump.

High speed system problems

High speed system problems normally show up as a lean air-fuel mixture (miss at cruising speeds) or a rich mixture (poor fuel economy). Refer to Fig. 20-5. The high speed system is the simplest and most dependable carburetor circuit.

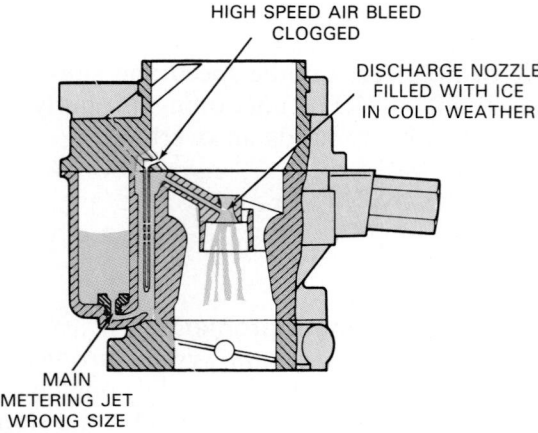

Fig. 20-5. Main metering system is very simple and dependable.

Engine surge is a condition in which engine power, at cruising speeds, seems to alternately increase and decrease. It is frequently caused by an extremely lean air-fuel mixture. Surge is a common problem stemming from the extremely lean, high efficiency mixtures of today's carburetors.

A *faulty mixture control solenoid* or *computer control circuit* can upset high, midrange, and low speed carburetor operation.

Discussed in the previous chapter, the mixture control solenoid is opened and closed by a computer to meter the correct amount of fuel into the engine. If the solenoid or control system fails, it can upset fuel system operation. This will be discussed shortly.

Full power system problems

Full power system problems can reduce fuel economy or limit engine power, as when passing another car for example. Depending upon the type of carburetor (power valve, mechanical metering rod, vacuum metering rod, solenoid metering valve), you need to use

various techniques to locate and correct a carburetor full power problem.

A *bad power valve* can leak fuel into the vacuum passage. A common problem, it causes a rough idle and poor gas mileage. When the power valve diaphragm ruptures, fuel may be pulled through the diaphragm and into the air horn by vacuum. This richens the mixture. The ruptured diaphragm can also affect high speed engine performance.

A *faulty metering rod* mechanism will generally upset only high speed engine operation. If the metering rod is adjusted too far into the jet, the high speed mixture will be too lean. If set too far out of the jet, the high speed mixture will be too rich. A vacuum operated metering rod can act up if the diaphragm ruptures or vacuum piston sticks.

Choke system problems

Carburetor *choke system problems* will usually make the engine perform poorly when cold or right after warm up. The choke should operate only when the engine is cold. Problems usually occur during or right after starting. Fig. 20-6 shows some choke-related problems. Study them!

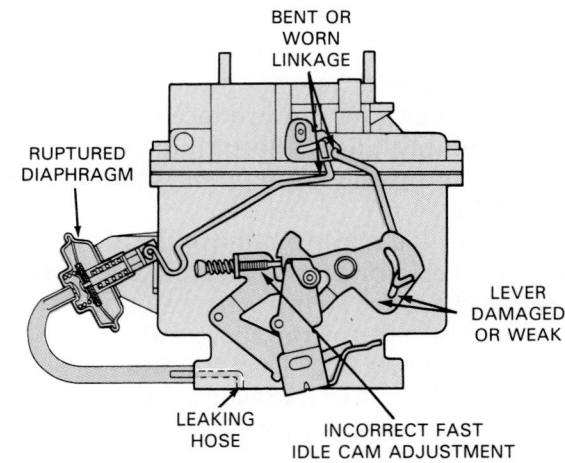

Fig. 20-6. Choke malfunctions cause problems when the engine is started cold. Engine may stall, not start easily, or may run roughly. (Chrysler Corp.)

If the *choke sticks closed,* a super-rich air-fuel mixture will pour into the engine. The engine will run extremely rough and BLACK SMOKE will blow out the car's tailpipe. The engine will lack power and may soon stall as it warms.

If the *choke sticks open,* the engine may not start when cold. Pumping the gas pedal several times will help. However, the engine will accelerate poorly and may stall several times after cold starting.

A slightly *rich choke setting* can cause the engine to run poorly after reaching operating temperature. By remaining partially closed, the choke pulls too much fuel into the engine. A slight engine miss or roll and a small amount of black exhaust smoke may result.

A *lean choke setting,* as with a choke stuck open, will make the engine hard to start in cold weather. No problems may be noticed in warm weather. A lean choke adjustment can cause the engine to stall when trying to accelerate with the engine cold.

Fast idle cam problems can make the engine idle too fast or too slow, usually when cold.

If the fast idle is too high, a cold engine may race for extended periods.

If the fast idle is too slow, a cold engine will stall or die right after start up. Fast idle cam problems may stem from choke problems or an incorrect linkage adjustment.

FACTORY DIAGNOSIS CHARTS

Use a factory or service manual diagnosis chart when you have difficulty locating a carburetor problem. Such charts are designed for each type of carburetor.

CARBURETOR REMOVAL

When carburetor diagnosis points to internal problems (dirt clogged passages, leaking gaskets or seals, worn parts), carburetor removal is usually necessary. Begin by removing the air cleaner and all wires, hoses, and linkages that would prevent removal of the carburetor.

DANGER! Wrap a shop rag around the fitting when removing a fuel line. This will keep fuel from leaking on the engine, creating a fire hazard.

Label wires and hoses

You may want to label the vacuum hoses and wires that connect to the carburetor. See Fig. 20-7. Late model cars have a large number of hoses and wires.

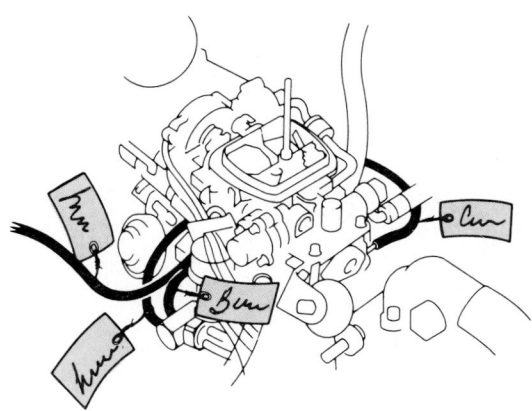

Fig. 20-7. Always mark or tag wires and hoses when servicing a carburetor. This can save time and avoid confusion when reconnecting everything. (Toyota)

If not labeled before carburetor removal, they can be confusing during reassembly.

Lifting carburetor off engine

Remove the four nuts or bolts that secure the carburetor to the engine intake manifold. Carefully lift the carburetor off the engine while holding it in a level position. Do not splash the fuel in the bowl around. This would stir up any dirt in the bottom of the bowl.

To prevent damage to the throttle plates, mount the carburetor on a stand, as in Fig. 20-8. You are now ready for carburetor disassembly.

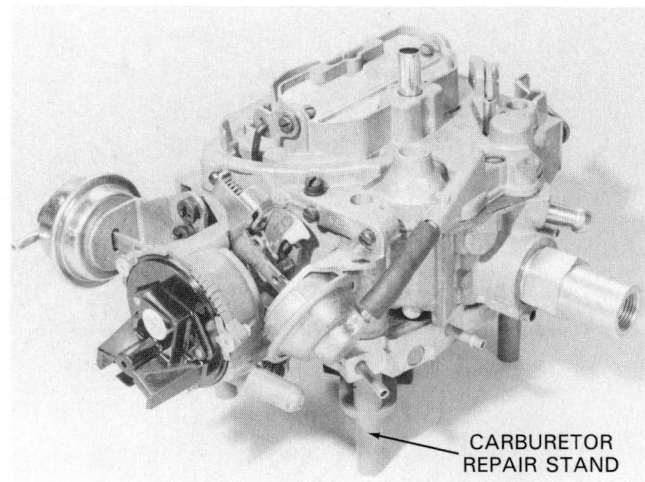

Fig. 20-8. After removing carburetor from engine, mount it on repair legs. They will hold the carburetor off work surface and protect throttle plates. (Rochester)

CARBURETOR BODY SECTIONS

Automotive carburetors are usually constructed in three sections: air horn body, main body, and throttle body. This is shown in Fig. 20-9. Sometimes however, the main body and throttle body are combined into a single casting.

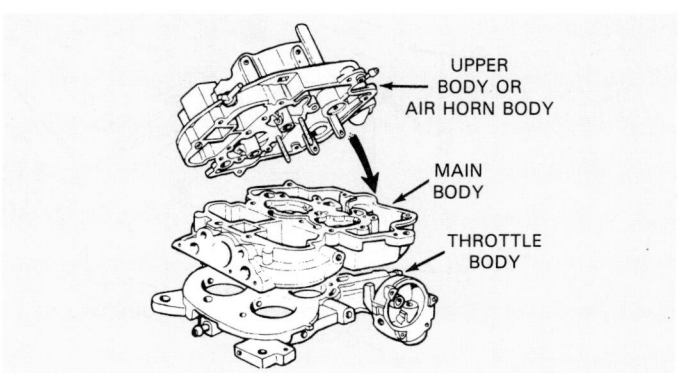

Fig. 20-9. Most carburetors have three body sections: air horn body, main body, and throttle body. (Ford Motor Co.)

When disassembling and reassembling a carburetor, you must understand these three sections.

Air horn body

The *air horn body* or *upper body* fits on the top of the main body and serves as a lid for the fuel bowl. Shown in Fig. 20-10, it is held on the main body with screws. A gasket fits between the main body and the air horn body.

The parts that often fasten to the air horn body are: the choke, hot idle compensator, fast idle linkage rod, choke vacuum break, and, sometimes, the float and pump mechanisms.

Main body

The *main body* of the carburetor is the largest sec-

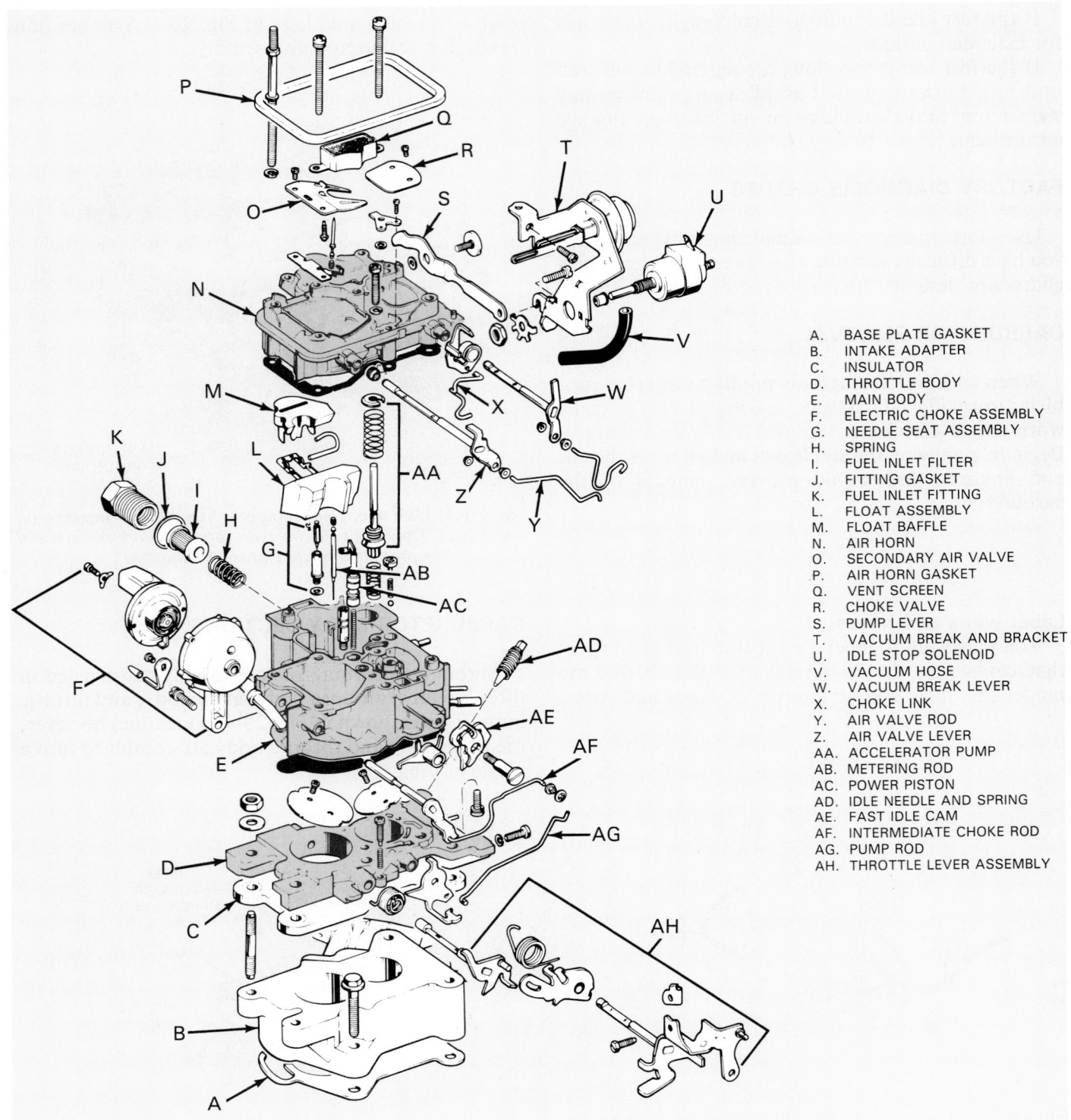

A.	BASE PLATE GASKET
B.	INTAKE ADAPTER
C.	INSULATOR
D.	THROTTLE BODY
E.	MAIN BODY
F.	ELECTRIC CHOKE ASSEMBLY
G.	NEEDLE SEAT ASSEMBLY
H.	SPRING
I.	FUEL INLET FILTER
J.	FITTING GASKET
K.	FUEL INLET FITTING
L.	FLOAT ASSEMBLY
M.	FLOAT BAFFLE
N.	AIR HORN
O.	SECONDARY AIR VALVE
P.	AIR HORN GASKET
Q.	VENT SCREEN
R.	CHOKE VALVE
S.	PUMP LEVER
T.	VACUUM BREAK AND BRACKET
U.	IDLE STOP SOLENOID
V.	VACUUM HOSE
W.	VACUUM BREAK LEVER
X.	CHOKE LINK
Y.	AIR VALVE ROD
Z.	AIR VALVE LEVER
AA.	ACCELERATOR PUMP
AB.	METERING ROD
AC.	POWER PISTON
AD.	IDLE NEEDLE AND SPRING
AE.	FAST IDLE CAM
AF.	INTERMEDIATE CHOKE ROD
AG.	PUMP ROD
AH.	THROTTLE LEVER ASSEMBLY

Fig. 20-10. Exploded view of modern carburetor shows body sections and how each part fits into place. (Chrysler Corp.)

tion. It forms the air horn and fuel bowl. See Fig. 20-10. Small passages are cast or drilled in it to carry fuel and air to the air horn or other carburetor sections.

Usually, the main body houses the fuel bowl, main jets, air bleeds, power valve, pump checks, diaphragm type accelerator pump, venturis, circuit passages, and, the float mechanism.

Throttle body

The *throttle body* is the lower section of the carburetor that contains the throttle valves. It fastens to the bottom of the main body with screws. Look at Fig. 20-10 again.

A throttle shaft passes through the sides of the throttle body to provide a hinge for the throttle valves. A gasket between the throttle and main bodies makes the joint leakproof.

Main parts found on a throttle body, besides the throttle butterflies and throttle shaft, are the throttle levers, idle mixture screws, idle speed screw, fast idle cam, dashpot, and fast idle solenoid.

Linkage rods for the choke, fast idle cam, metering rod, accelerator pump, temperature compensator, etc. run from the throttle shaft levers to the various parts.

CARBURETOR REBUILD

A carburetor rebuild or overhaul is needed when carburetor passages become clogged, gaskets or seals leak, rubber parts deteriorate, or components wear and fail.

A *carburetor rebuild* generally involves:

1. Disassembly and cleaning of major parts.
2. Inspection for wear or damage.
3. Installation of a CARBURETOR REBUILD KIT (new gaskets, seals, needle valve and seat, pump diaphragm or cup, and other nonmetal parts). A kit is shown in Fig. 20-11.
4. Reassembly of the carburetor.
5. Major adjustments.

Carburetor disassembly

When disassembling a carburetor, follow the detailed directions in a service manual. Generally, you must remove ALL PLASTIC and RUBBER parts. Also, remove any part that will prevent thorough cleaning of the carburetor passages. If not worn or damaged, the throttle plates and shaft can be left in place.

To prevent part damage, always use proper diassembly technnniques. When unscrewing jets, use a special jet tool or the correct size screwdriver. The screwdriver must be large enough to fill the slot in the jet. Refer to Fig. 20-12.

During disassembly, keep parts organized and note the location of each part. Jet sizes are sometimes different and must be reinstalled in the same location.

Cleaning carburetor parts

Carburetor cleaner, also known as decarbonizing cleaner, removes deposits from a carburetor. A very powerful cleaning agent, it will remove gum, carbon, oil, grease, and other deposits from inside air and fuel passages and on external parts. Look at Fig. 20-13.

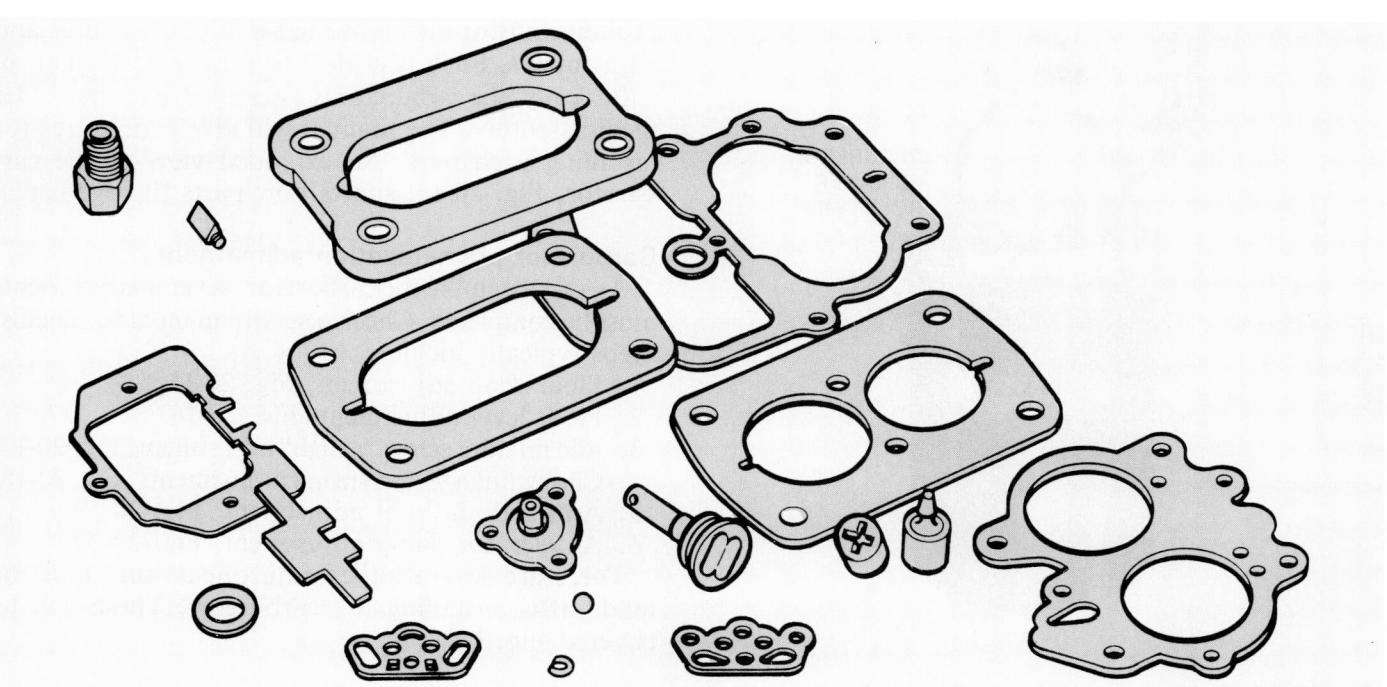

Fig. 20-11. Carburetor rebuild kit includes gaskets, seals, power valve, check balls, needle valve and seat, and any other part that commonly requires replacement. (Chrysler Corp.)

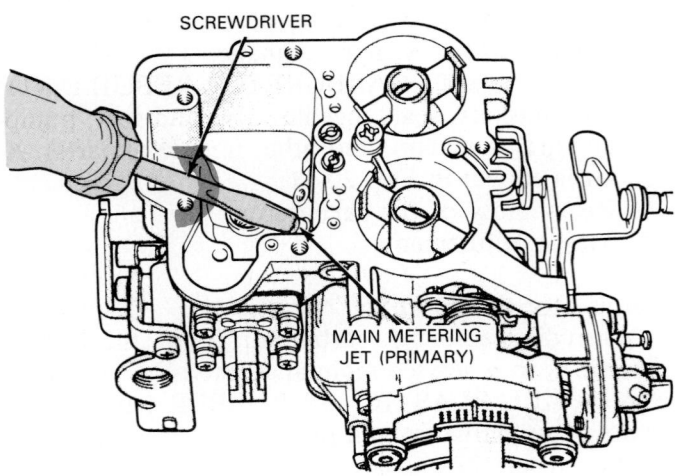

Fig. 20-12. When removing or installing jets, use a special jet tool or a screwdriver of the correct size. Be careful not to damage jet. (Chrysler)

Do not allow carburetor cleaner to contact plastic and rubber parts. Carburetor cleaner will dissolve and ruin nonmetal parts. Place metal components in a tray and lower them into the cleaner. Allow the carburetor parts to soak for the recommended amount of time.

Fig. 20-13. Carburetor cleaner is very powerful. Remove all rubber and plastic parts before soaking carburetor. Also, wear safety glasses and rubber gloves to protect against chemical burns. (BAC)

WARNING! Carburetor cleaner can cause serious chemical burns to the skin and eyes. Wear rubber gloves and eye protection when working with carburetor type cleaning solution.

After soaking them, rinse all carburetor parts with water, clean kerosene, or clean cold soak cleaning solution. Dry the parts with compressed air. FORCE air through all passages to make sure they are clear.

NOTE! Do NOT use wire or a drill to clean out carburetor passages. This could scratch and enlarge the passages, upsetting carburetor operation.

Inspecting carburetor parts

Inspect each cleaned carburetor part closely. Check for:
1. Wear and excessive play between the throttle shaft and throttle body.
2. Binding of the choke plate and linkage.
3. Warpage, cracks, and other problems with carburetor bodies.
4. Float leakage or bent hinge arm.
5. Nicks, burrs, and dirt on gasket mating surfaces.
6. Damaged or weakened springs and stripped fasteners.
7. Damage to tips of idle mixture screws.

Replace parts that show wear or damage. Also, discard all of the old parts replaced by your carburetor rebuild kit.

Carburetor reassembly

If not an experienced mechanic, follow the detailed directions in a service manual to reassemble a modern carburetor. Some car makers have as many as 20 different carburetors for just one model year. This results in thousands of different reassembly procedures and adjustments. Each is critical to proper performance.

Basically, the carburetor is assembled in reverse order of disassembly. The manual will give procedures for installing each part. An exploded view of the carburetor, Fig. 20-14, shows how parts fit together.

Carburetor preinstallation adjustments

As you assemble the carburetor, several adjustments must be completed. Check a service manual for details. Steps typically include:
1. Float drop adjustment, Fig. 20-15.
2. Float level adjustment, Fig. 20-16.
3. Idle mixture screw "rough" adjustment, Fig. 20-17.
4. Choke linkage and spring adjustments, Fig. 20-18.
5. Anti-stall dashpot adjustment, Fig. 20-19.
6. Accelerator pump adjustment, Fig. 20-20.

There are several other adjustments that must be made after installing the carburetor. These will be covered shortly.

CARBURETOR INSTALLATION

To install a carburetor, place a new base plate gasket

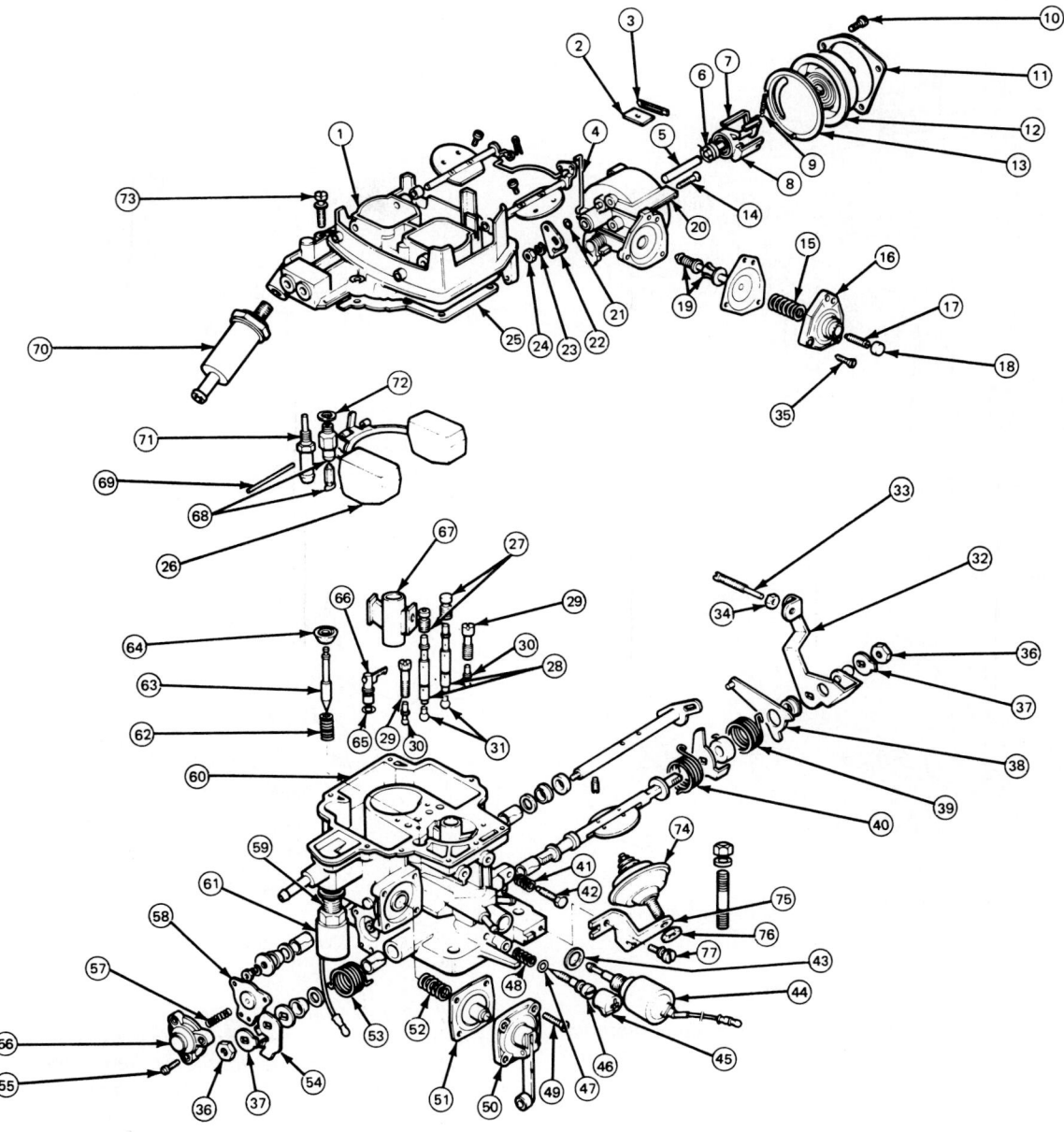

1. UPPER BODY
2. PRIMARY CHOKE LINK DIRT SEAL
3. DIRT SEAL RETAINER
4. PRIMARY CHOKE LINK
5. CHOKE BIMETAL SHAFT BUSHING
6. FAST IDLE CAM SPRING
7. CHOKE BIMETAL LEVER
8. CHOKE BIMETAL SHAFT
9. CHOKE ASSIST SPRING
10. ELECTRIC CHOKE RETAINING RIVETS (2)
11. ELECTRIC CHOKE RETAINING RING
12. ELECTRIC CHOKE UNIT
13. CHOKE HOUSING INDEX SHIELD
14. CHOKE HOUSING SCREWS
15. CHOKE PULL-DOWN SPRING
16. COVER
17. CHOKE PULL-DOWN ADJUSTING SCREW
18. CHOKE PULL-DOWN ADJUSTING SEAL
19. CHOKE PULL-DOWN DIAPHRAGM ASSEMBLY
20. CHOKE HOUSING ASSEMBLY

21. CHOKE HOUSING VACUUM SEAL (O-RING)
22. CHOKE LEVER
23. CHOKE BIMETAL SHAFT LOCK WASHER
24. CHOKE BIMETAL SHAFT NUT
25. COVER GASKET
26. FUEL BOWL FLOAT
27. HIGH SPEED AIR BLEEDS
28. WELL TUBES
29. IDLE JET HOLDER
30. IDLE JET
31. MAIN JET
32. THROTTLE LEVER
33. FAST IDLE SPEED ADJUSTING SCREW
34. FAST IDLE SPEED ADJUSTING SCREW LOCKNUT
35. CHOKE PULLDOWN DIAPHRAGM COVER RIVET
35. CHOKE PULLDOWN DIAPHRAGM COVER RIVET
36. PRIMARY THROTTLE SHAFT NUT
37. PRIMARY THROTTLE SHAFT NUT LOCKING TAB
38. SECONDARY THROTTLE OPERATING LEVER

39. SECONDARY THROTTLE RETURN SPRING
40. PRIMARY THROTTLE RETURN SPRING
41. IDLE SPEED SCREW SPRING
42. IDLE SPEED SCREW
43. IDLE FUEL SHUTOFF SOLENOID WASHER
44. IDLE FUEL SHUTOFF SOLENOID
45. IDLE MIXTURE SCREW PLUG
46. IDLE MIXTURE SCREW
47. IDLE MIXTURE SCREW O-RING
48. IDLE MIXTURE SCREW SPRING
49. ACCELERATOR PUMP COVER SCREW
50. ACCELERATOR PUMP COVER ASSEMBLY
51. ACCELERATOR PUMP DIAPHRAGM
52. ACCELERATOR PUMP SPRING
53. PRIMARY THROTTLE RETURN SPRING
54. ACCELERATOR PUMP CAM
55. POWER VALVE COVER SCREW
56. POWER VALVE COVER
57. POWER VALVE SPRING

58. POWER VALVE DIAPHRAGM WASHER
59. FUEL BOWL VENT SOLENOID WASHER
60. MAIN BODY ASSEMBLY
61. FUEL BOWL VENT SOLENOID
62. BOWL VENT SPRING
63. BOWL VENT ARM
64. VITON BOWL VENT SEAL
65. O-RING SEAL FOR PUMP NOZZLE
66. PUMP SHOOTER
67. FUEL DISCHARGE NOZZLES
68. FUEL INLET SEAT AND NEEDLE
69. FLOAT HINGE PIN
70. FUEL FILTER
71. FUEL RETURN LINE CHECK VALVE AND FITTING
72. FUEL INLET SEAT GASKET
73. COVER HOLDDOWN SCREWS
74. DASHPOT
75. DASHPOT MOUNTING BRACKET
76. DASHPOT ADJUSTING LOCKNUT
77. DASHPOT MOUNTING BRACKET SCREW

Fig. 20-14. Exploded view of carburetor shows how all parts fit together. (Ford)

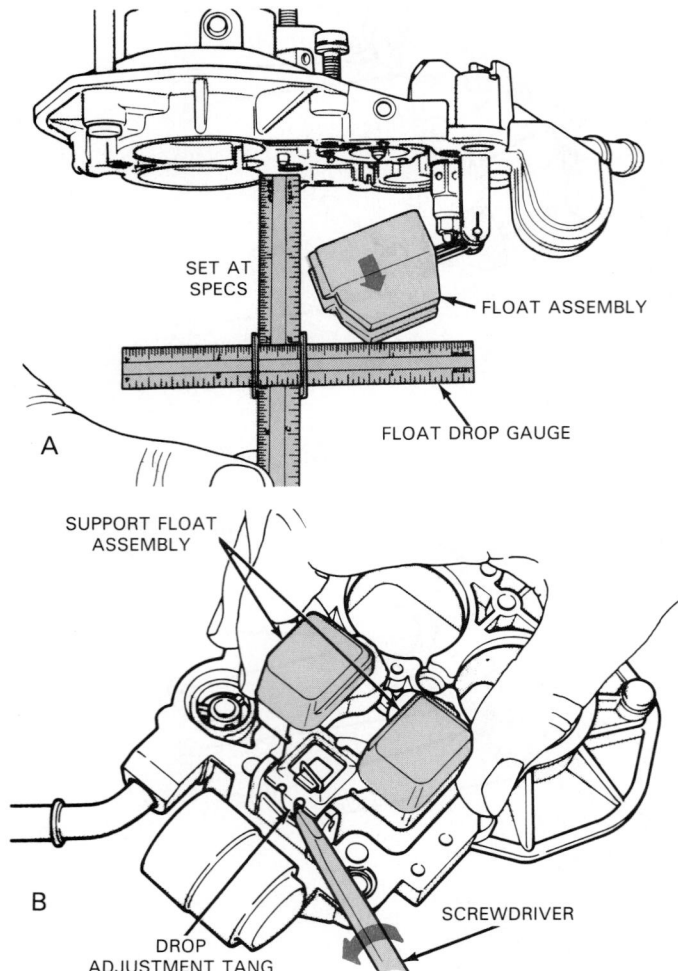

Fig. 20-15. Adjusting float drop. A — Float drop is distance float can move down in bowl. It keeps float from hitting and possibly sticking on bottom. B — Float drop is usually set by bending tang on float. (Chrysler Corp.)

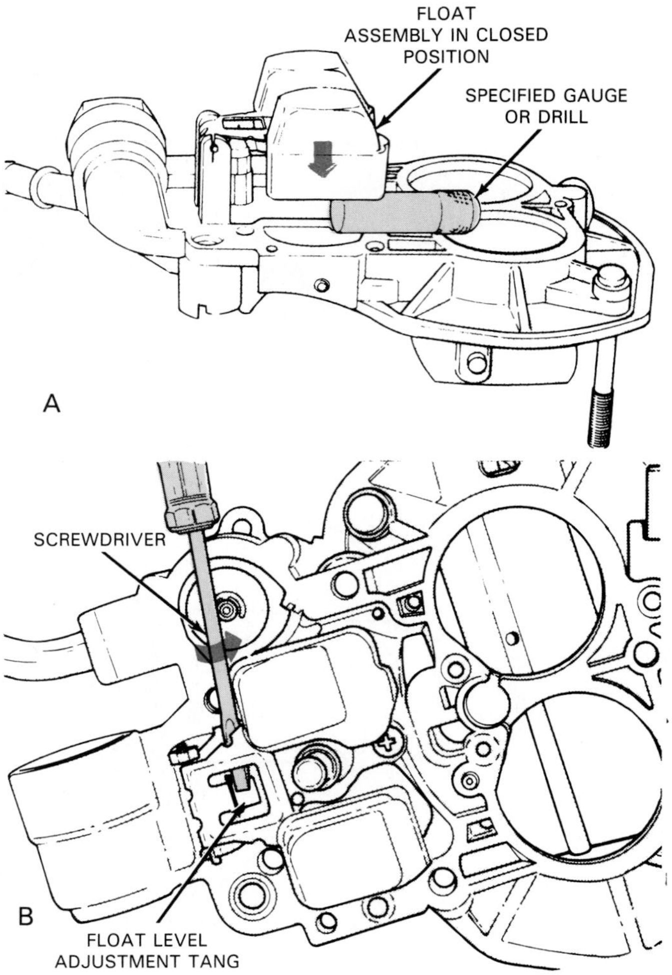

Fig. 20-16. Dry float level adjustment. A — Float level is usually set by measuring distance from float to air horn cover or top of bowl. B — To change float level, bend other metal tang on float. Wet float level is set by checking how much fuel enters bowl before needle valve closes.

on the intake manifold. Then, fit the carburetor over the mounting studs, if used. Install the fasteners that secure the carburetor to the intake manifold. Torque them to specification.

Warning! Do NOT overtighten the carburetor hold-down nuts or bolts. Overtightening can easily snap off the carburetor base flange, ruining the throttle body or main body of the carburetor.

Reinstall all of the hoses, lines, wires, and linkage rods or cables, Fig. 20-21. Double-check that all of the vacuum hoses have been installed in their correct positions. Hand operate the throttle to make sure the throttle plates are not binding or hitting on the base plate gasket.

You are ready to make the final idle speed and idle mixture adjustments on the carburetor.

Cold idle speed (fast idle cam) adjustment

To set the cold fast idle or fast idle cam, connect a tachometer to the engine. Warm the engine to

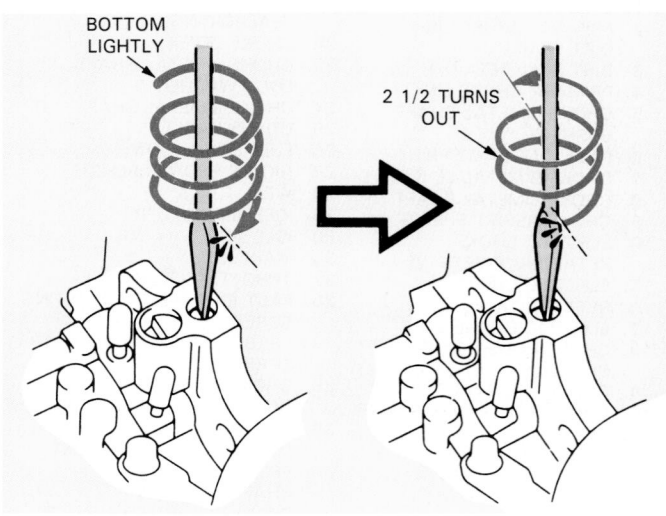

Fig. 20-17. Rough bench adjustment of idle mixture screws typically involves bottoming screw lightly. Then, back out about 2 1/2 turns. Final adjustment is done with engine running. (Toyota)

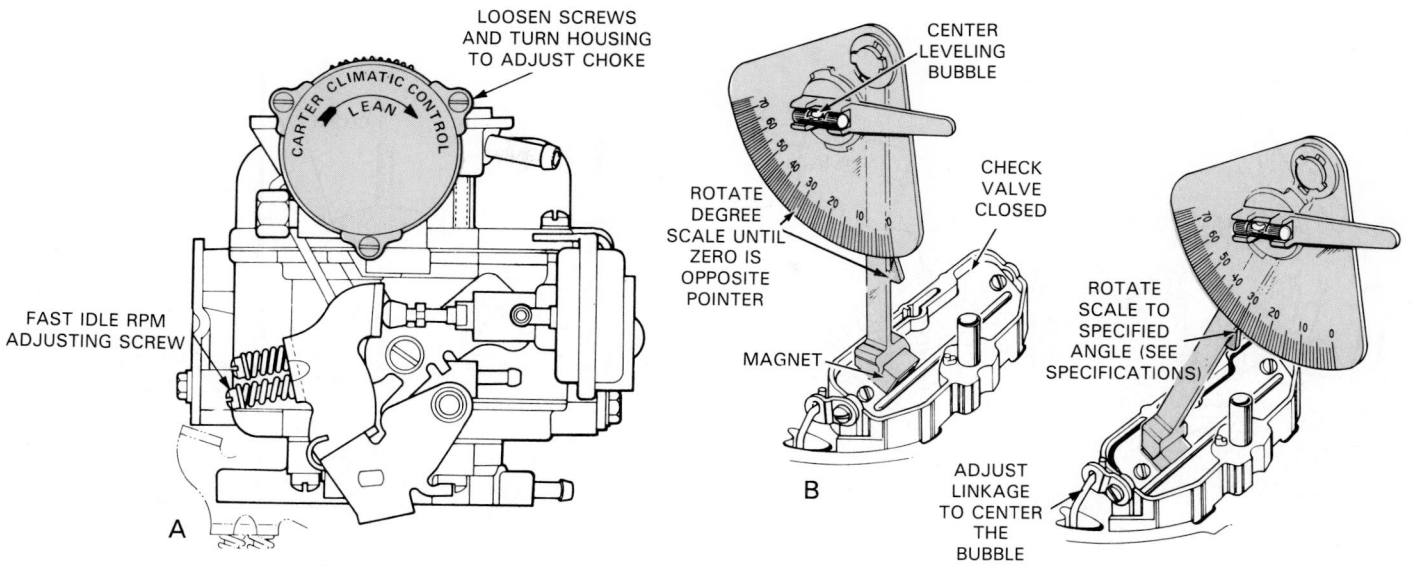

Fig. 20-18. Choke adjustments. A — Thermostatic spring and choke setting can be changed on some carburetors by rotating spring housing. B — This carburetor requires a special gauge for choke linkage adjustment. (Ford, Buick)

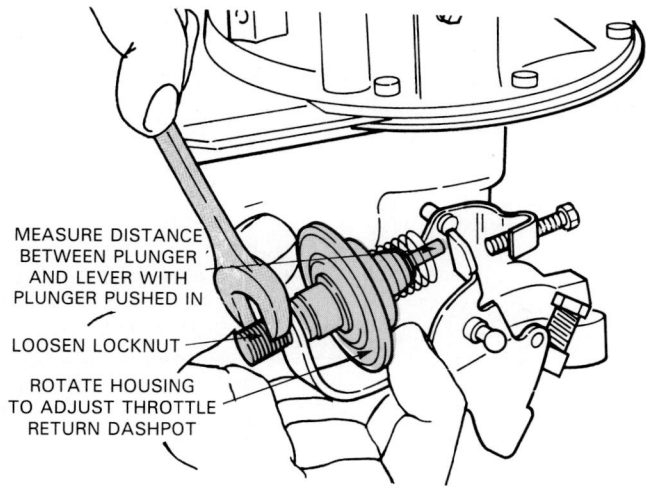

Fig. 20-19. Throttle return dashpot is adjusted by moving unit closer or farther from throttle lever. To check adjustment, depress plunger and measure distance between plunger and throttle lever with a feeler gauge. (Ford Motor Co.)

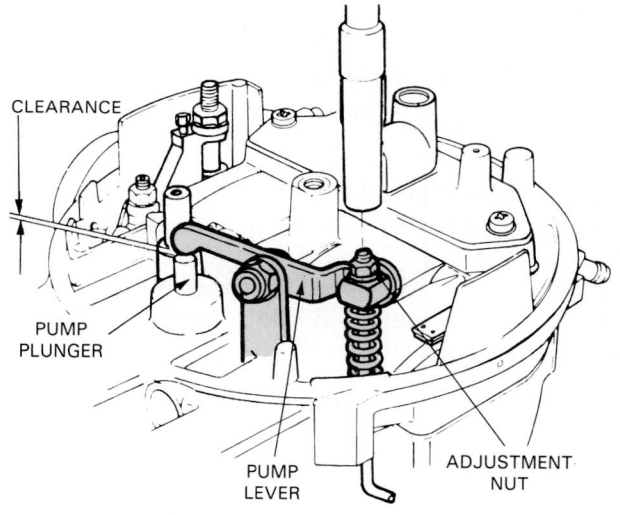

Fig. 20-20. Accelerator pump may be adjusted by turning adjustment nut or screw, by bending linkage, changing hole positions in linkage, or moving retainer clip on pump plunger. Refer to service manual for details.

operating temperature. Set the emergency brake and block the wheels of the car.

While following service manual instructions, set the fast idle cam to hold the throttle open for a fast idle. The fast idle screw must contact a specified step on the fast idle cam, Fig. 20-22.

Turn the fast idle screw until the tachometer reads within specifications. Cold fast idle speeds vary from approximately 750 to 950 rpm. Some specs are given with the automatic transmission in drive. This will reduce the cold fast idle value.

Hot idle speed adjustment

Many carburetors use a solenoid to control the hot idle speed of the engine. When the engine is running, the solenoid acts on the throttle lever to hold the throttle open for the correct idle speed.

Sometimes, a solenoid is used to maintain idle speed when the air conditioner is turned on. In any case, you must use factory recommendations to adjust the solenoid.

Look at Fig. 20-23. To set hot idle speed, turn the solenoid adjusting screw until the tachometer reads

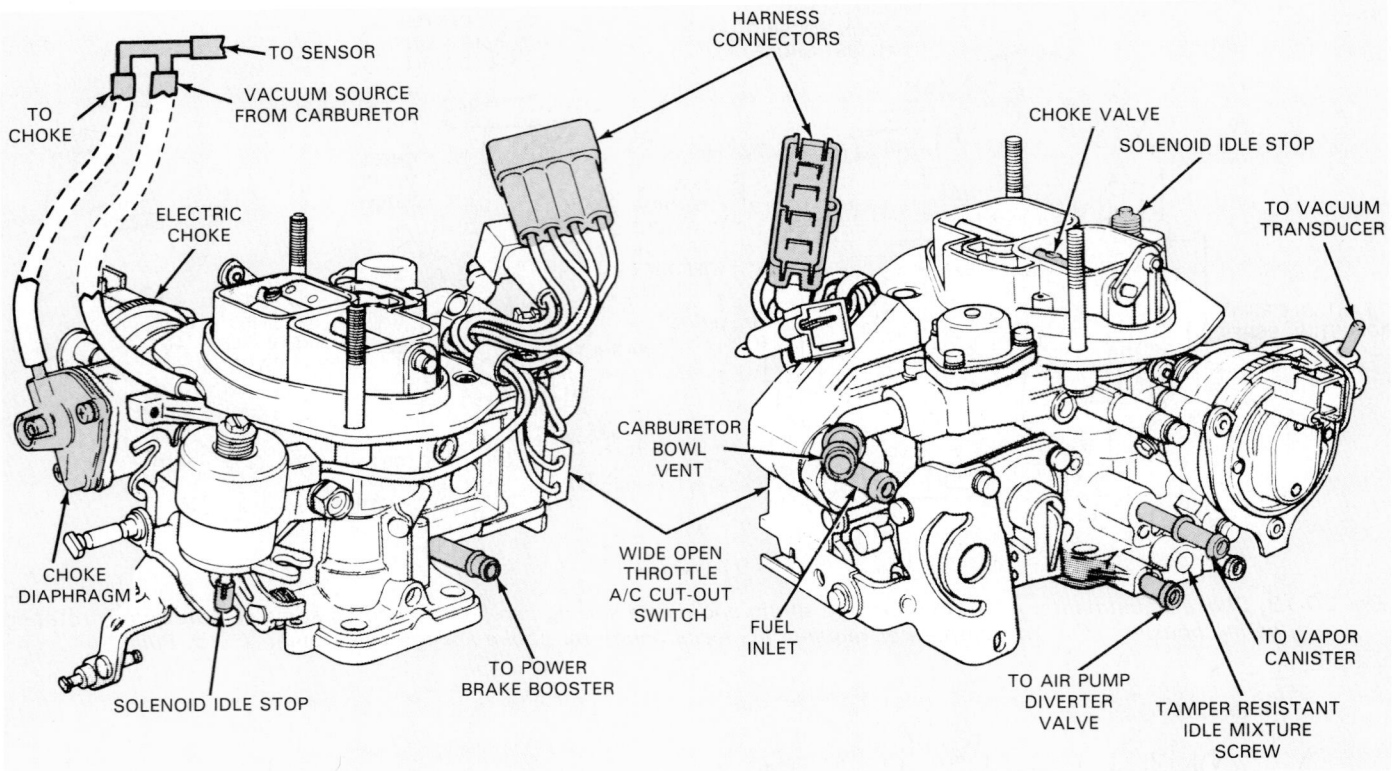

Fig. 20-21. Double-check connections of all wires and vacuum hoses. It is very easy to mix wires and hoses, causing hard-to-find troubles. (Chrysler)

correctly. Sometimes the adjustment is on the solenoid mounting bracket or it may also be on the solenoid plunger itself.

Typically, hot idle speed is from about 650 to 850 rpm. It is lower than cold idle speed but higher than curb idle speed.

CAUTION! When adjusting an idle speed solenoid, make sure it is NOT an air conditioning solenoid.

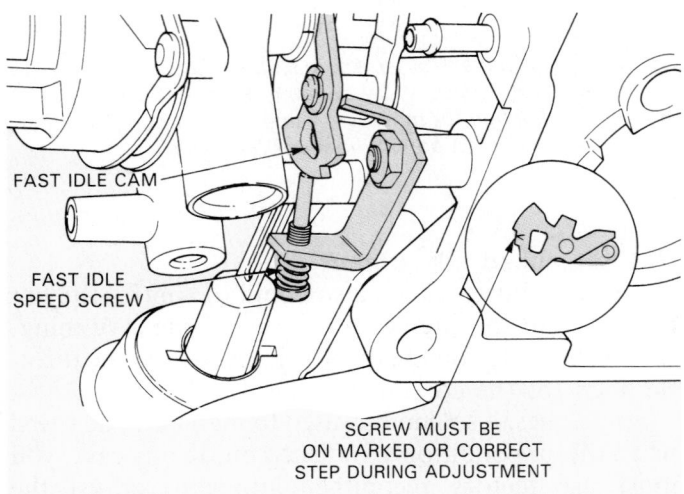

Fig. 20-22. Fast idle speed adjustment involves turning fast idle screw when screw is contacting correct step on cam. Tachometer is used to measure engine speed.

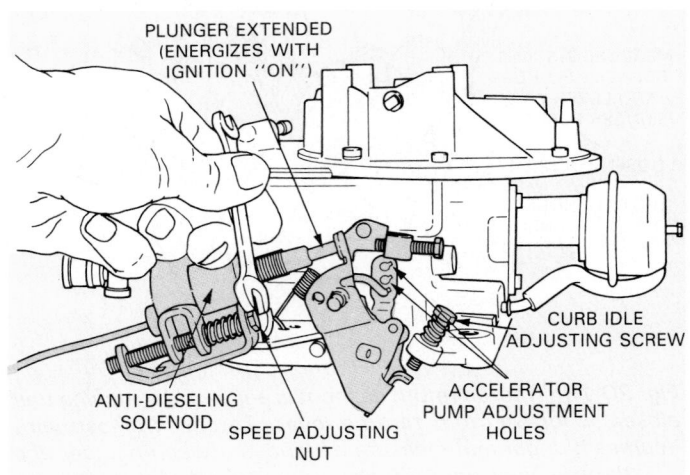

Fig. 20-23. When idle solenoid is used, energize solenoid and adjust engine rpm to specs by moving solenoid or solenoid plunger. Also note curb idle screw for lowest speed setting. (Ford)

Curb idle speed adjustment

Curb idle speed is the lowest idle speed setting. On older carburetors, it is the idle speed setting that controls engine speed under normal, warm engine conditions.

However, on late model carburetors using a fast idle solenoid, curb idle can also be termed *idle drop* or *low idle speed adjustment*. In this case, it is a very low idle speed that only occurs as the ignition is turned off. When the solenoid is de-energized, the throttle plates drop to the curb idle setting to keep the engine from dieseling (engine running with ignition key off).

To adjust curb idle, disconnect the wires going to the idle speed solenoid. Then, turn the curb idle speed screw until the tachometer reads within specifications. See Fig. 20-24.

Curb idle speed is usually very low, approximately 500 to 750 rpm.

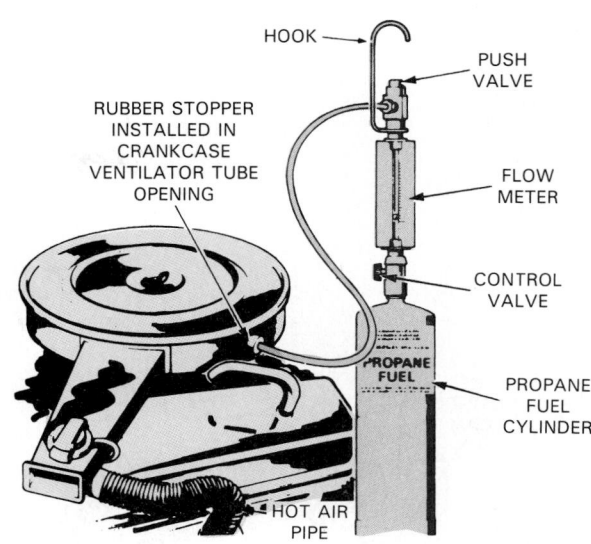

Fig. 20-25. Some modern carburetors require propane to assist in accurate idle mixture adjustment. Propane is added to mixture to richen mixture and smooth engine operation as mixture screws are set for lean, clean burning setting. Follow manual directions since procedures vary. (Sun Electric Corp.)

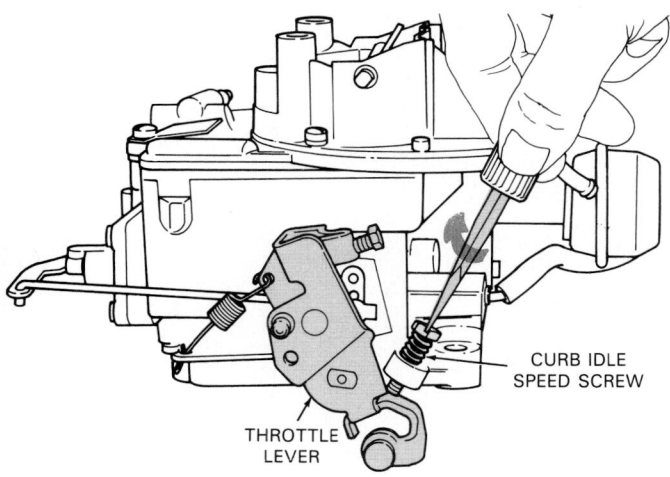

Fig. 20-24. Curb idle speed simply moves throttles open or closed when turned. Adjust to specs using a tach. (Ford Motor Co.)

Idle mixture adjustment

After setting idle speed, you may also need to adjust the carburetor idle mixture. There are several methods for doing this.

With older, pre-emission carburetors, the idle mixture screw is turned in and out until the smoothest idle mixture is obtained.

Basically, the mixture screw is turned in until the engine misses (lean miss). Then, it is turned out until the engine rolls (rich miss). The mixture screw is then set halfway between the lean miss and rich roll settings. This is done to both mixture screws if needed (two or four-barrel carburetor).

After setting the mixture, check and adjust the idle speed as needed. If you must reset the idle speed, then readjust the idle mixture again.

Propane idle mixture adjustment is required on some later model carburetors. As shown in Fig. 20-25, a bottle of propane is connected to the engine (air cleaner or intake manifold). The propane enriches the fuel mixture during carburetor adjustment. Following service manual procedures, you must meter a certain amount of propane into the engine while adjusting the mixture screws. This will provide a leaner (less exhaust emissions) setting.

WARNING! Most carburetors on late model vehicles have *sealed idle mixture screws* preset at the factory. Unless major carburetor repairs have been made, do NOT remove and tamper with these screws. To avoid a violation of federal law, follow manufacturer's prescribed procedures for carburetor adjustments.

An *exhaust gas analyzer* may be used to adjust the idle mixture on late model cars. The mixture screws are adjusted until the exhaust sampling is within specified limits. For information on this subject, refer to Chapter 40.

Figs. 20-26 through 20-28 show views of different carburetors. Study each and compare them.

COMPUTER CONTROLLED CARBURETOR SERVICE

A computer controlled carburetor system requires specialized service techniques. Most systems have a self-diagnostic mode that allows easy location of system problems. One computer system flashes a light on and off in a Morse (number) type code. The mechanic can use the code chart in the service manual to pinpoint the system trouble.

Testing computer output

Fig. 20-29 shows testing methods used on one computer controlled carburetor system. A tachometer and a dwell meter are connected to the system.

The tach measures engine speed. The dwell meter measures the length (duration) of the computer's electrical signal going to the mixture control solenoid in

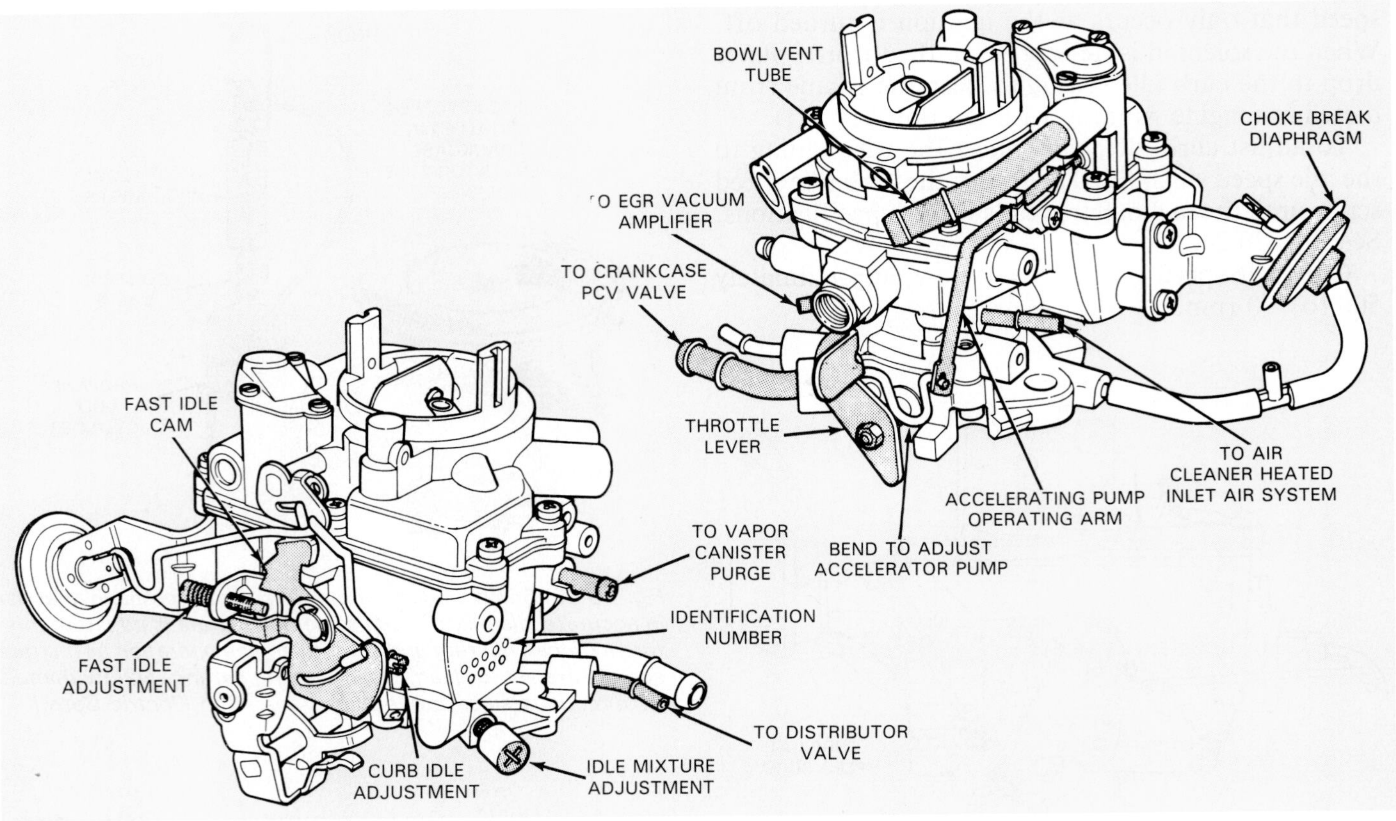

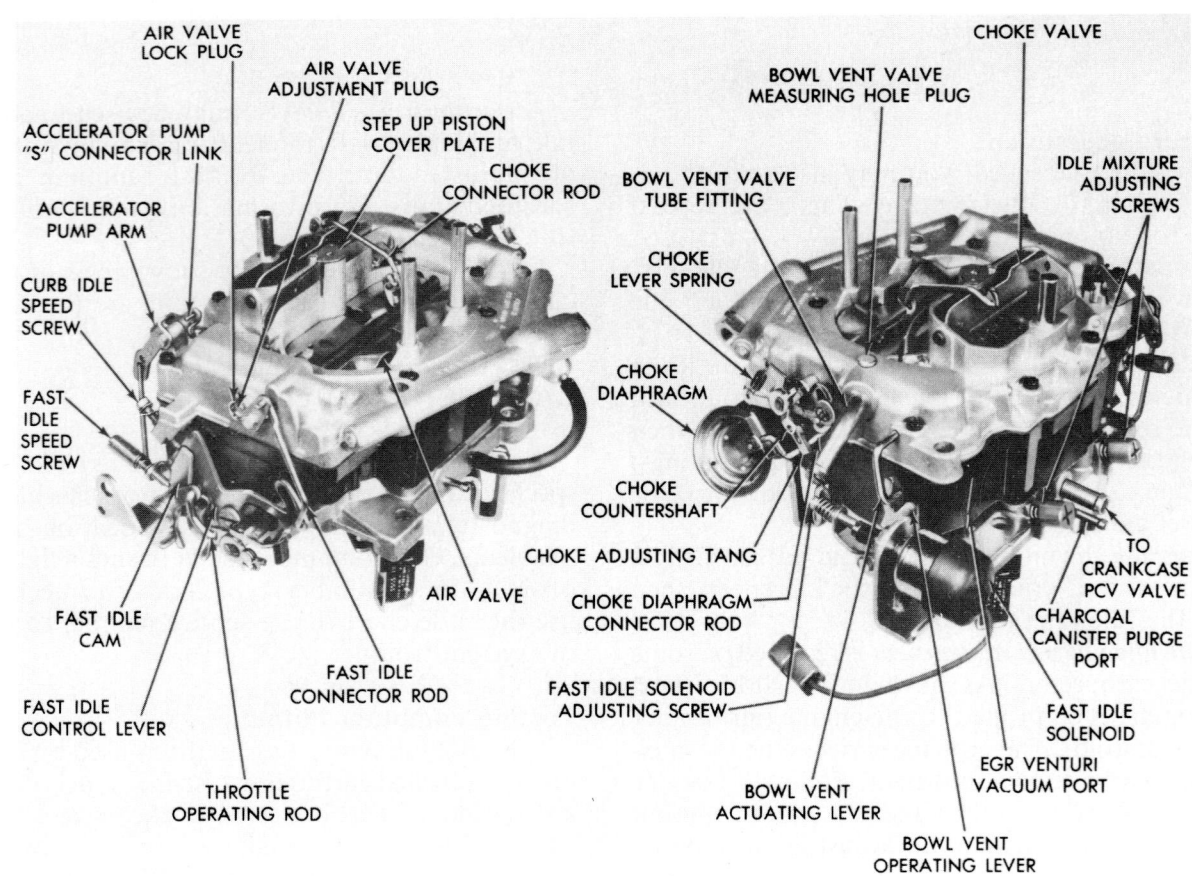

Fig. 20-26. Two views show important carburetor parts and connections. Study them. This is a one-barrel carburetor.

BOWL VENT TUBE

CHOKE BREAK DIAPHRAGM

TO EGR VACUUM AMPLIFIER

TO CRANKCASE PCV VALVE

THROTTLE LEVER

ACCELERATING PUMP OPERATING ARM

BEND TO ADJUST ACCELERATOR PUMP

TO AIR CLEANER HEATED INLET AIR SYSTEM

FAST IDLE CAM

TO VAPOR CANISTER PURGE

IDENTIFICATION NUMBER

FAST IDLE ADJUSTMENT

TO DISTRIBUTOR VALVE

CURB IDLE ADJUSTMENT

IDLE MIXTURE ADJUSTMENT

AIR VALVE LOCK PLUG

AIR VALVE ADJUSTMENT PLUG

STEP UP PISTON COVER PLATE

CHOKE CONNECTOR ROD

CHOKE VALVE

BOWL VENT VALVE MEASURING HOLE PLUG

IDLE MIXTURE ADJUSTING SCREWS

ACCELERATOR PUMP "S" CONNECTOR LINK

ACCELERATOR PUMP ARM

CURB IDLE SPEED SCREW

FAST IDLE SPEED SCREW

FAST IDLE CAM

AIR VALVE

FAST IDLE CONTROL LEVER

THROTTLE OPERATING ROD

FAST IDLE CONNECTOR ROD

BOWL VENT VALVE TUBE FITTING

CHOKE LEVER SPRING

CHOKE DIAPHRAGM

CHOKE COUNTERSHAFT

CHOKE ADJUSTING TANG

CHOKE DIAPHRAGM CONNECTOR ROD

FAST IDLE SOLENOID ADJUSTING SCREW

BOWL VENT ACTUATING LEVER

BOWL VENT OPERATING LEVER

EGR VENTURI VACUUM PORT

TO CRANKCASE PCV VALVE

CHARCOAL CANISTER PURGE PORT

FAST IDLE SOLENOID

Fig. 20-27. Four-barrel carburetor uses fiber main body to help keep fuel in bowl cool. Note part names. (Carter Carburetor Div.)

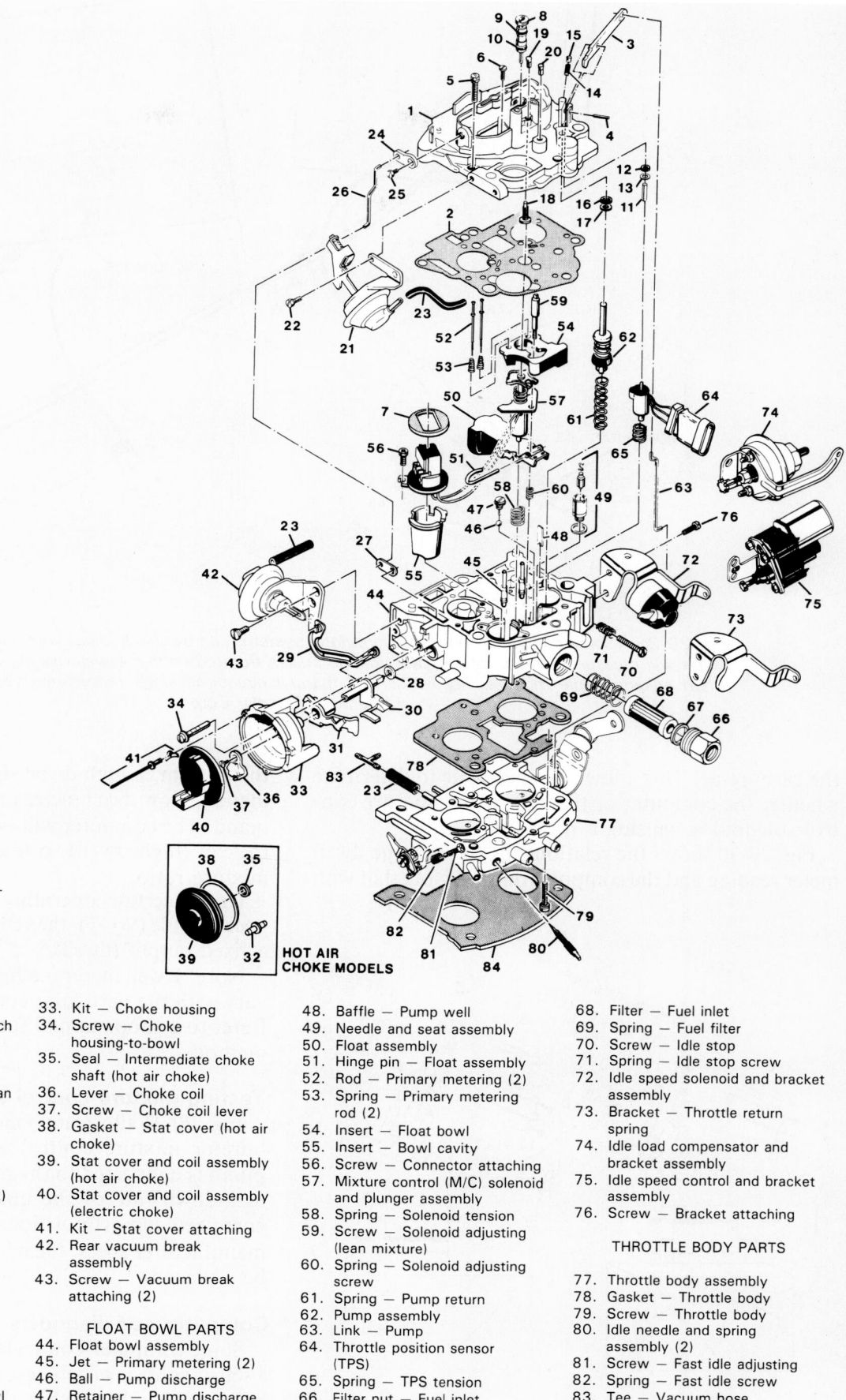

AIR HORN PARTS

1. Air horn assembly
2. Air horn gasket
3. Pump actuating lever
4. Pump lever hinge roll pin
5. Air horn short screw
6. Air horn countersunk screw
7. Gasket — solenoid connector to air horn
8. Valve — Idle air bleed
9. O-ring (thick) — Idle air bleed valve
10. O-ring (thin) — Idle air bleed valve
11. Plunger — (TPS) throttle position switch actuator
12. Seal — TPS plunger
13. Retainer — TPS seal
14. Screw — TPS adjusting
15. Plug — TPS screw
16. Seal — Plump plunger
17. Retainer — Pump seal
18. Screw — Solenoid plunger (rich stop)
19. Plug — Plunger stop screw (rich stop)
20. Plug — Solenoid adjusting (lean mixture)

CHOKE PARTS

21. Vacuum break control and bracket — front
22. Screw — Control attaching (2)
23. Hose — Vacuum
24. Lever — Choke rod (upper)
25. Screw — Choke lever
26. Rod — Choke
27. Lever — Choke rod (lower)
28. Seal — Intermediate choke shaft
29. Link — Rear (aux.) vacuum break
30. Choke shaft and lever
31. Cam — Fast idle
32. Seal — Choke housing-to-bowl (hot air choke)

33. Kit — Choke housing
34. Screw — Choke housing-to-bowl
35. Seal — Intermediate choke shaft (hot air choke)
36. Lever — Choke coil
37. Screw — Choke coil lever
38. Gasket — Stat cover (hot air choke)
39. Stat cover and coil assembly (hot air choke)
40. Stat cover and coil assembly (electric choke)
41. Kit — Stat cover attaching
42. Rear vacuum break assembly
43. Screw — Vacuum break attaching (2)

FLOAT BOWL PARTS

44. Float bowl assembly
45. Jet — Primary metering (2)
46. Ball — Pump discharge
47. Retainer — Pump discharge ball

48. Baffle — Pump well
49. Needle and seat assembly
50. Float assembly
51. Hinge pin — Float assembly
52. Rod — Primary metering (2)
53. Spring — Primary metering rod (2)
54. Insert — Float bowl
55. Insert — Bowl cavity
56. Screw — Connector attaching
57. Mixture control (M/C) solenoid and plunger assembly
58. Spring — Solenoid tension
59. Screw — Solenoid adjusting (lean mixture)
60. Spring — Solenoid adjusting screw
61. Spring — Pump return
62. Pump assembly
63. Link — Pump
64. Throttle position sensor (TPS)
65. Spring — TPS tension
66. Filter nut — Fuel inlet
67. Gasket — Filter nut

68. Filter — Fuel inlet
69. Spring — Fuel filter
70. Screw — Idle stop
71. Spring — Idle stop screw
72. Idle speed solenoid and bracket assembly
73. Bracket — Throttle return spring
74. Idle load compensator and bracket assembly
75. Idle speed control and bracket assembly
76. Screw — Bracket attaching

THROTTLE BODY PARTS

77. Throttle body assembly
78. Gasket — Throttle body
79. Screw — Throttle body
80. Idle needle and spring assembly (2)
81. Screw — Fast idle adjusting
82. Spring — Fast idle screw
83. Tee — Vacuum hose
84. Gasket — Flange

Fig. 20-28. Computer controlled carburetor exploded view. Note mixture control solenoid and idle speed control motor. (Buick)

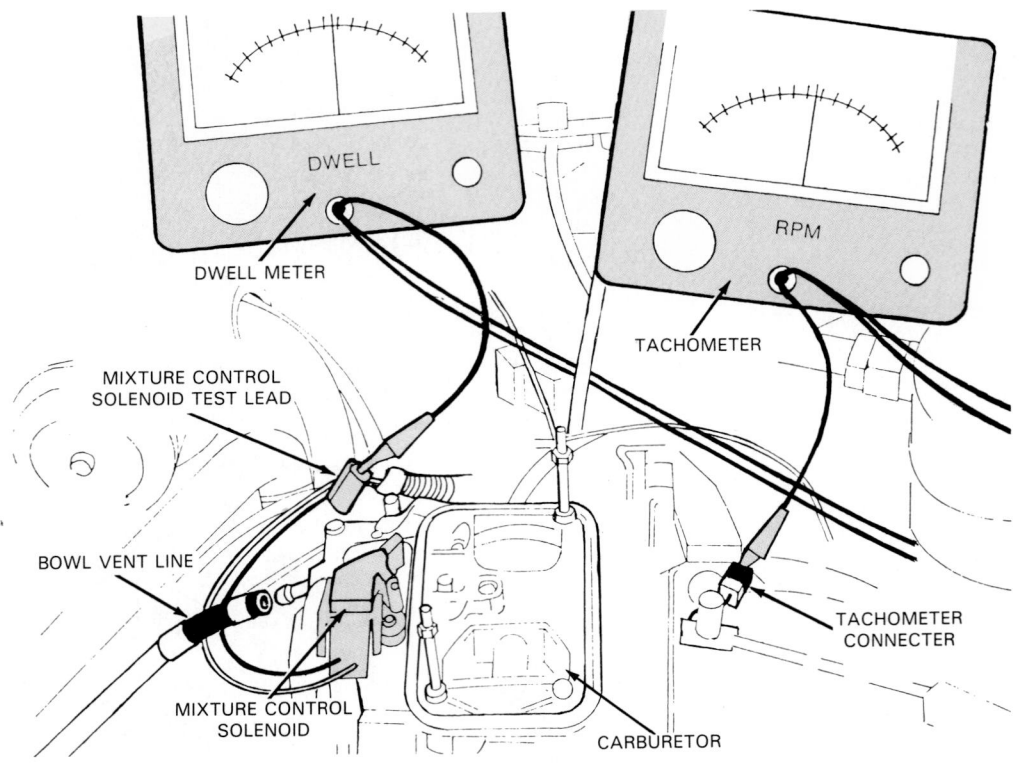

Fig. 20-29. Some computer-controlled carburetor systems can be checked out with a dwell meter. Dwell meter will measure duration of ON-OFF voltage pulses from computer. Dwell reading may also be used when adjusting idle mixture. Follow service manual directions since procedures vary with particular system.   (Chrysler Corp.)

the carburetor. This allows the mechanic to determine whether the computer or the carburetor mixture control solenoid is causing a problem.

Fig. 20-30 shows the relationship between the dwell meter reading and the computer output. Note that with

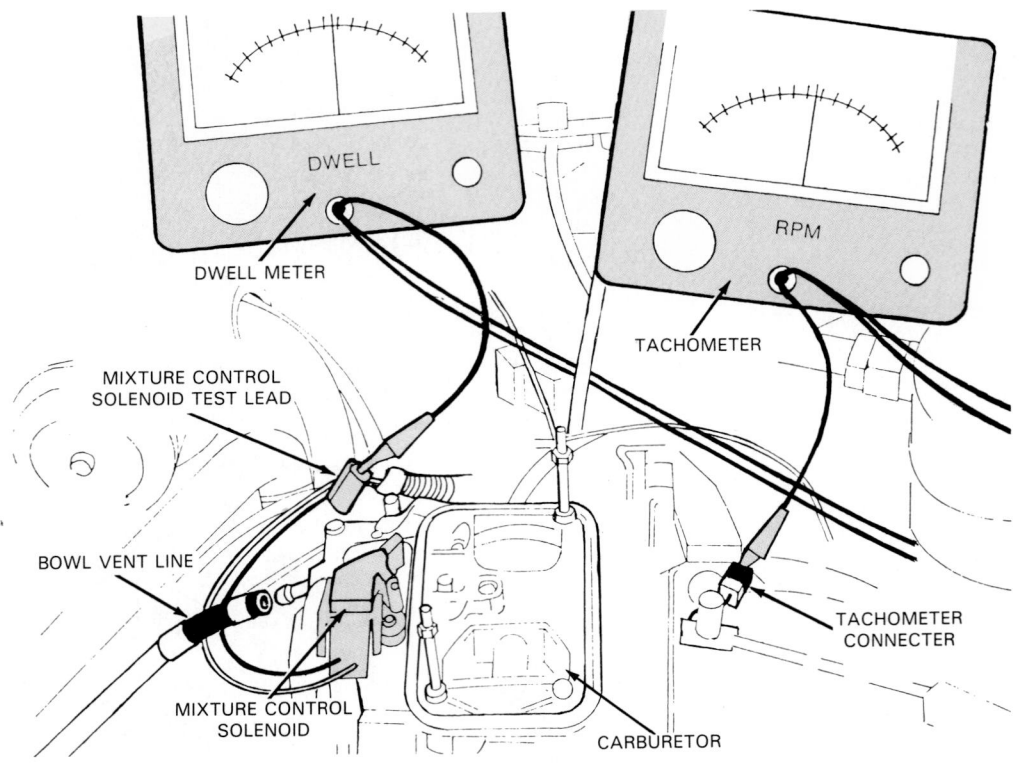

Fig. 20-30. Dwell meter reading shows computer output to carburetor mixture control solenoid. Study connections and values. (General Motors Corp.)

this system, a high dwell signal indicates a lean command. A low dwell meter reading indicates a rich command. The computer will switch from rich (low dwell) to lean (high dwell) to maintain the correct air-fuel mixture ratio.

Under certain operating conditions, such as wide open throttle (WOT), the vehicle's computer may produce a fixed output (dwell).

Note! Dwell meter readings and test procedures will vary with the particular computer-carburetor system. Refer to a shop manual for exact dwell specs and test methods.

Testing mixture control solenoid

Fig. 20-31 illustrates one method of testing a carburetor mixture control solenoid. A hand vacuum pump is connected to the mixture solenoid. Then, the leak-down rate of the unit is measured in both the energized and off positions. If leakage is NOT within manufacturer specs, the mixture control solenoid must be replaced.

Computer self-diagnosis

Some computer-controlled carburetor systems have a self-diagnosis or self-test feature. The computer will produce a code number that represents the possible problem source. This topic is discussed in several places in this textbook, especially in Chapter 75.

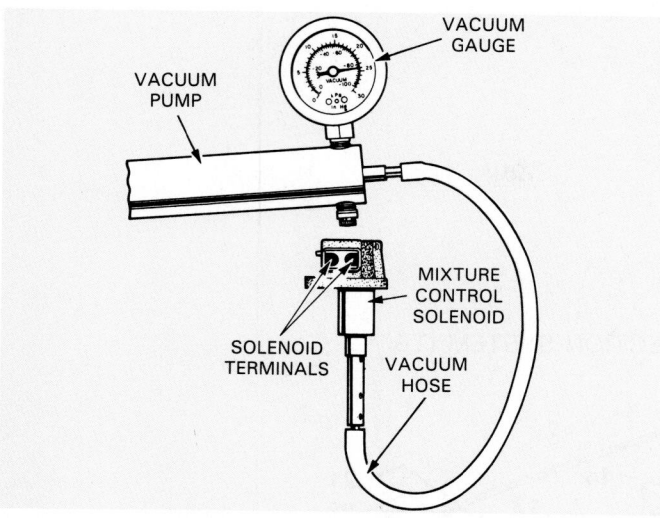

Fig. 20-31. Vacuum pump can be used to check some mixture control solenoids. Compare unit leakage to specs. Check in both the energized and unenergized positions. Most mixture solenoids must be replaced when not within specs. Adjustment is usually not permitted. (Oldsmobile)

KNOW THESE TERMS

Exhaust gas analyzer, Carburetor flooding, Engine flooding, Engine surge, Air horn body, Main body, Throttle body, Carburetor rebuild, Carburetor kit, Carburetor cleaner, Self-diagnosis, Dwell signal.

REVIEW QUESTIONS

1. The first step in diagnosis is to determine whether the _____ or _____ _____ is at fault.
2. What should you look for when inspecting a carburetor?
3. Describe the symptoms of a lean air-fuel mixture.
4. Describe the symptoms of a rich air-fuel mixture.
5. List some causes for lean and rich air-fuel mixtures.
6. How can an exhaust gas analyzer be used when troubleshooting carburetor problems?
7. When diagnosing carburetor problems, try to determine which carburetor _____ is at fault.
8. Carburetor float system problems can cause flooding, a rich fuel mixture, a lean fuel mixture, stalling, missing, and other performance problems. True or False?
9. Define the terms "carburetor flooding" and "engine flooding."
10. A clogged idle air bleed usually tends to richen the air-fuel mixture. True or False?
11. A car tends to hesitate or lose power when ac-

celerating from a dead stop with the engine both cold and warm.
Technician A says that the choke is set too rich and that a choke adjustment may be needed.
Technician B says that the accelerator pump may need adjustment or replacement because a lean mixture is indicated.
Who is correct?
   a. Technician A
   b. Technician B
   c. Both A and B
   d. Neither A nor B
12. What is engine surge?
13. A faulty mixture control solenoid can upset high, midrange, and low speed carburetor operation. True or False?
14. What happens if a power valve leaks?
15. Black smoke blowing out the car's exhaust pipe indicates a _____ air-fuel mixture that could be caused by the _____ being stuck closed.
16. Fast _____ _____ problems can make the engine idle too fast or too slow, usually when cold.
17. List and explain the three major body sections of a carburetor.
18. Describe the five major steps for a carburetor rebuild.
19. List six adjustments commonly made after a carburetor rebuild.
20. What is propane idle mixture adjustment?
21. Do not adjust sealed idle mixture screws unless absolutely necessary and follow service manual directions. True or False?
22. Many computer controlled carburetor systems have a _____ mode that can be used to quickly locate troubles.
23. Some service manuals direct the use of a dwell meter to check the computer signal going to the mixture control solenoid. True or False?
24. During carburetor adjustments, a _____ is commonly used to measure engine speed.
25. Explain a method for testing a mixture control solenoid in a computer controlled carburetor system.

ACTIVITIES FOR CHAPTER 20

1. Diagnose carburetor problem from symptoms given you by your instructor or by a customer of the automotive shop.
2. Disassemble and clean a carburetor in preparation for overhaul.
3. Determine specs for a selected carburetor and set the float drop accurately using the appropriate measuring tool.

THROTTLE BODY FUEL INJECTION SYSTEM (TBI)

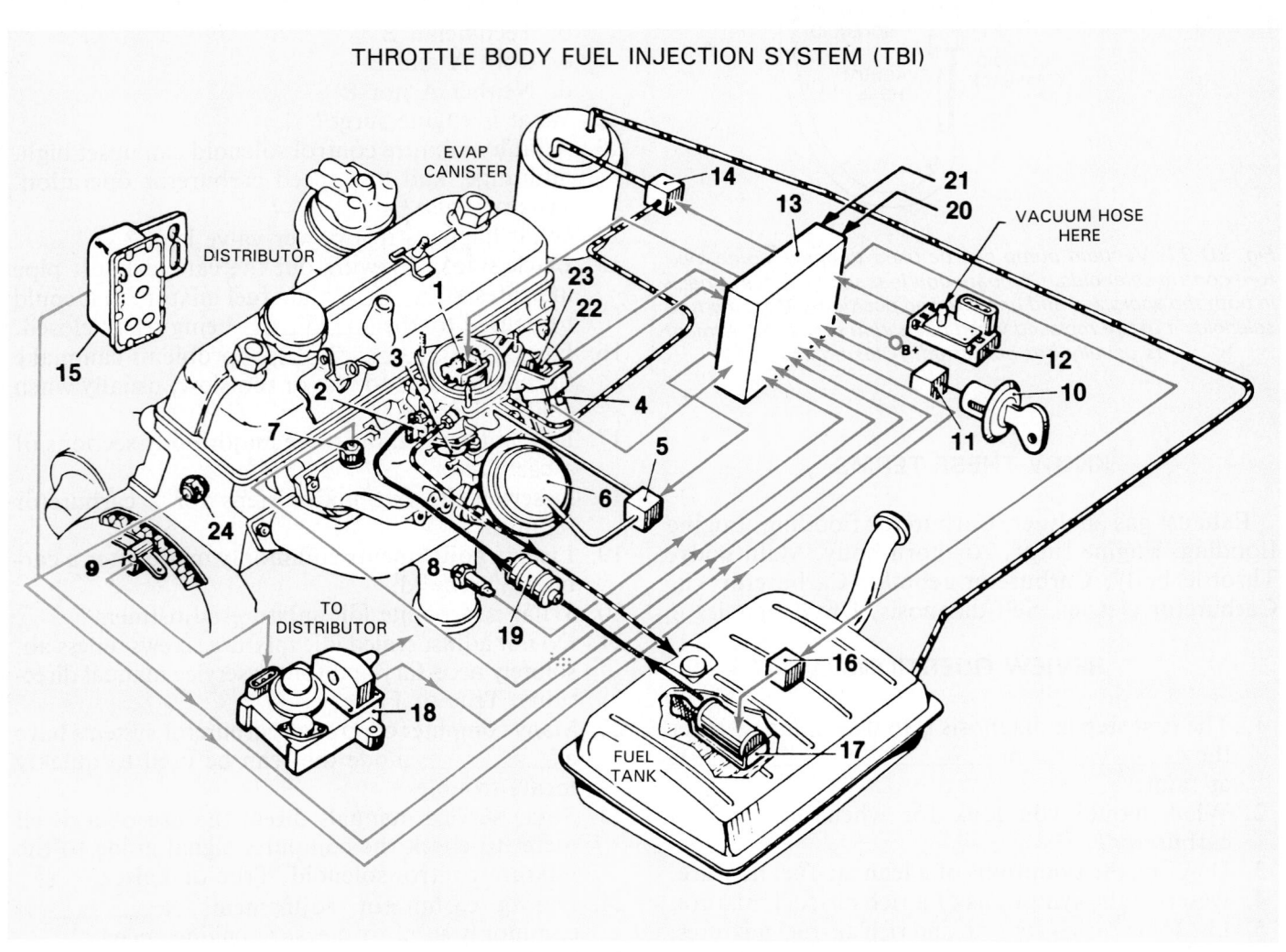

BASIC COMPONENT LOCATIONS

1. Injector
2. Throttle position sensor
3. Pressure regulator
4. Idle speed control motor
5. Solenoid-to-EGR valve
6. EGR valve

7. Manifold air-fuel temperature sensor
8. O₂-sensor
9. Speed sensor
10. Ignition switch
11. Power relay
12. Manifold pressure sensor

13. Electronic control unit
14. Solenoid-to-EVAP canister control
15. Starter motor relay
16. Fuel pump relay
17. Fuel pump
18. Ignition control module

19. In-line fuel filter
20. Air conditioner on
21. Transaxle neutral/park switch
22. Closed throttle (idle) switch
23. Wide open throttle (WOT) switch
24. Temperature sensor (coolant)

Fig. 21-1. Note general location of electronic fuel injection parts. This will help you grasp details of each component. Can you locate the fuel pump, computer, and sensors?   (Chrysler Corp.)

21

Gasoline Injection Fundamentals

After studying this chapter, you will be able to:
☐ List some of the possible advantages of gasoline injection.
☐ Describe the classifications of gasoline injection.
☐ Explain the operation of electronic single-point (throttle body) gasoline injection.
☐ Explain the operation of electronic multi-point (port) gasoline injection.
☐ Summarize the operation of electronic airflow sensing, hydraulic-mechanical (continuous), and manifold pressure sensing gasoline injection systems.
☐ Compare the various types of gasoline injection systems.

This chapter introduces the operating principles of modern gasoline injection systems. Specific systems vary, but many of the parts (sensors, fuel injectors, computer) are very similar. This chapter offers you a broad background in the many gasoline injection systems found on today's cars.

GASOLINE INJECTION FUNDAMENTALS

A modern *gasoline injection system* uses pressure from an electric fuel pump to spray fuel into the engine intake manifold. See Fig. 21-1. Like a carburetor, it must provide the engine with the correct air-fuel mixture for specific operating conditions. Unlike a carburetor however, PRESSURE, not engine vacuum (suction), is used to feed fuel into the engine. This makes a gasoline injection system very efficient.

Gasoline injection advantages

A gasoline injection system has several possible advantages over a carburetor type fuel system. A few of these include:
1. Improved atomization (fuel is forced into intake manifold under pressure which helps break fuel droplets into a fine mist).
2. Better fuel distribution (more equal flow of fuel vapors into each cylinder).
3. Smoother idle (lean fuel mixture can be used

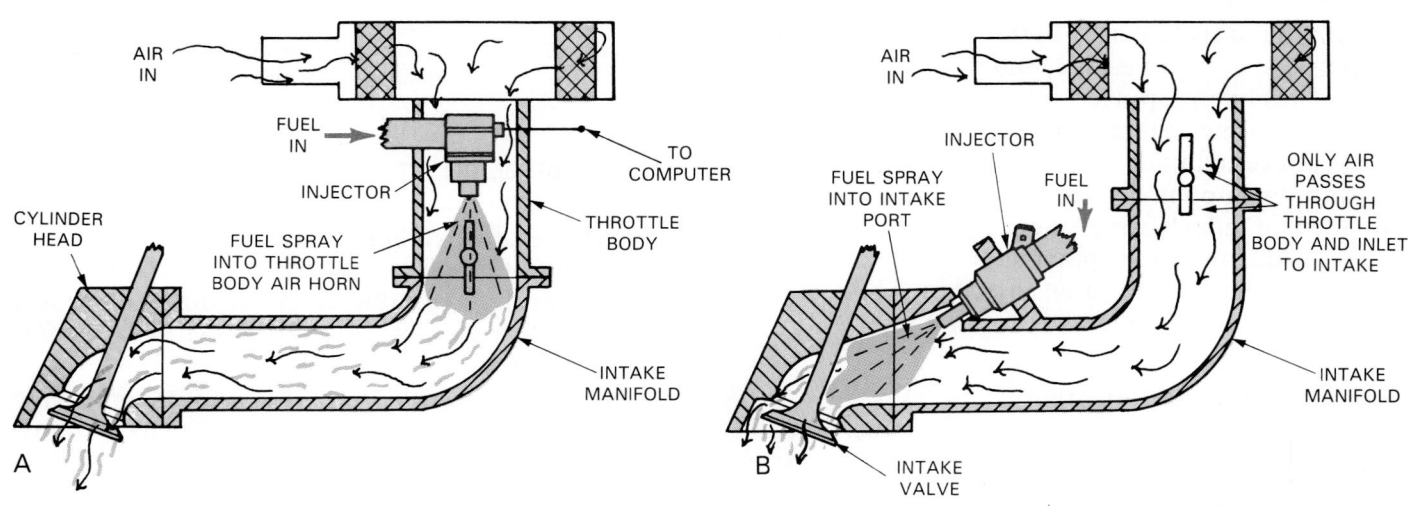

Fig. 21-2. A — Throttle body injection has injector inside throttle body. Like a carburetor, fuel enters airstream in air horn.
B — Port injection has one injector for each engine cylinder. Fuel sprays toward engine intake valve.

without rough idle because of better fuel distribution and low-speed atomization).

4. Improved fuel economy (high efficiency because of more precise fuel metering, atomization, and distribution).
5. Lower emissions (lean, efficient air-fuel mixture reduces exhaust pollution).
6. Better cold weather driveability (injection provides better control of mixture enrichment than a carburetor choke).
7. Increased engine power (precise metering of fuel to each cylinder and increased airflow can result in more horsepower output).
8. Simpler (late model, electronic fuel injection systems have fewer parts than modern computer controlled carburetor systems).

GASOLINE INJECTION CLASSIFICATIONS

There are many types of gasoline injection systems. Before studying the most common ones, you should have a basic knowledge of the different classifications of gasoline injection. This will help you relate the similarities and differences between systems.

A gasoline injection system is commonly called a *fuel injection system.* To avoid confusion, remember that a diesel injection system is also a fuel injection system. The two are quite different, however.

Single and multi-point injection

The *point* (location) of fuel injection is one way to classify a gasoline injection system.

A *single-point injection system,* also called *throttle body injection* (TBI), has the injector nozzles in a throttle body assembly on top of the engine. Fuel is sprayed into the top, center of the intake manifold. Single-point (one location) injection is illustrated in Fig. 21-2A.

A *multi-point injection system,* also called *port injection,* has a fuel injector in the port (air-fuel runner or passage) going to each cylinder. See part B in Fig. 21-2. Gasoline is sprayed into each intake port and toward each engine intake valve. Hence, the term multi-point (more than one location) fuel injection is used.

Both single-point and multi-point injection systems are used on today's cars. American made cars use both single-point and multi-point injection. Foreign cars commonly have multi-point injection. Multi-point is a more commonly used system.

Indirect and direct injection

An *indirect* injection system sprays fuel into the engine intake manifold. Most gasoline injection systems are this type.

A *direct* injection system forces fuel into the engine combustion chambers. All diesel injection systems are a direct type. Indirect and direct injection systems are shown in Fig. 21-3.

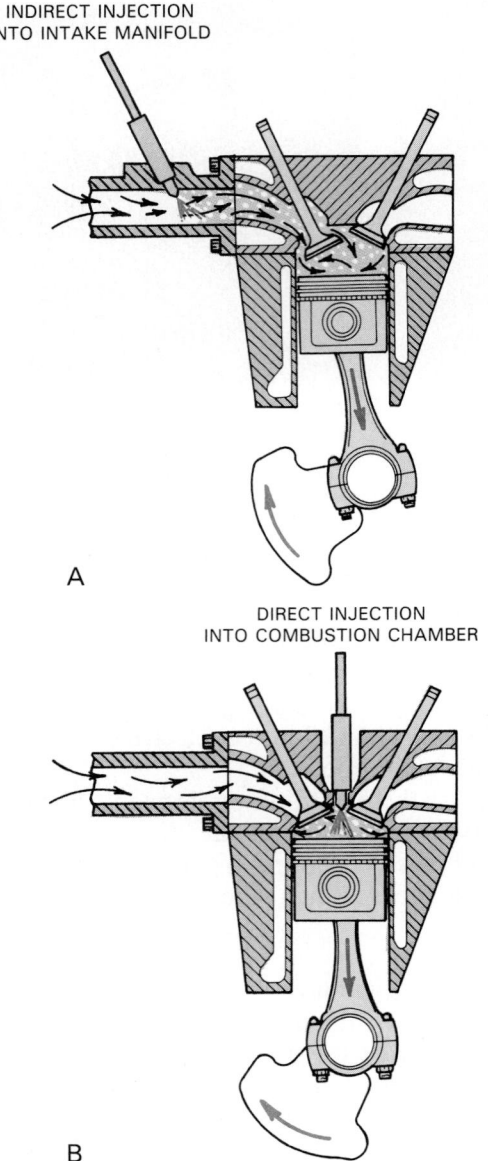

Fig. 21-3. A — Indirect injection sprays fuel into intake manifold. B — Direct injection sprays fuel into combustion chambers. Gasoline injection systems are usually indirect type. Diesels are direct type.

GASOLINE INJECTION CONTROLS

There are three common methods used to control the amount of gasoline injected into the engine: electronic controls, hydraulic controls, and mechanical controls. Older gasoline injection systems use a combination of each.

Electronic fuel injection control uses various engine sensors and a computer to control the opening and closing of the injection valves. Look at Fig. 21-4. This is the most modern and common type of gasoline injection system. It will be covered in detail.

Hydraulic fuel injection control refers to hydraulically (air or fuel pressure) moved control devices. Hydraulic control uses an airflow sensor and a fuel

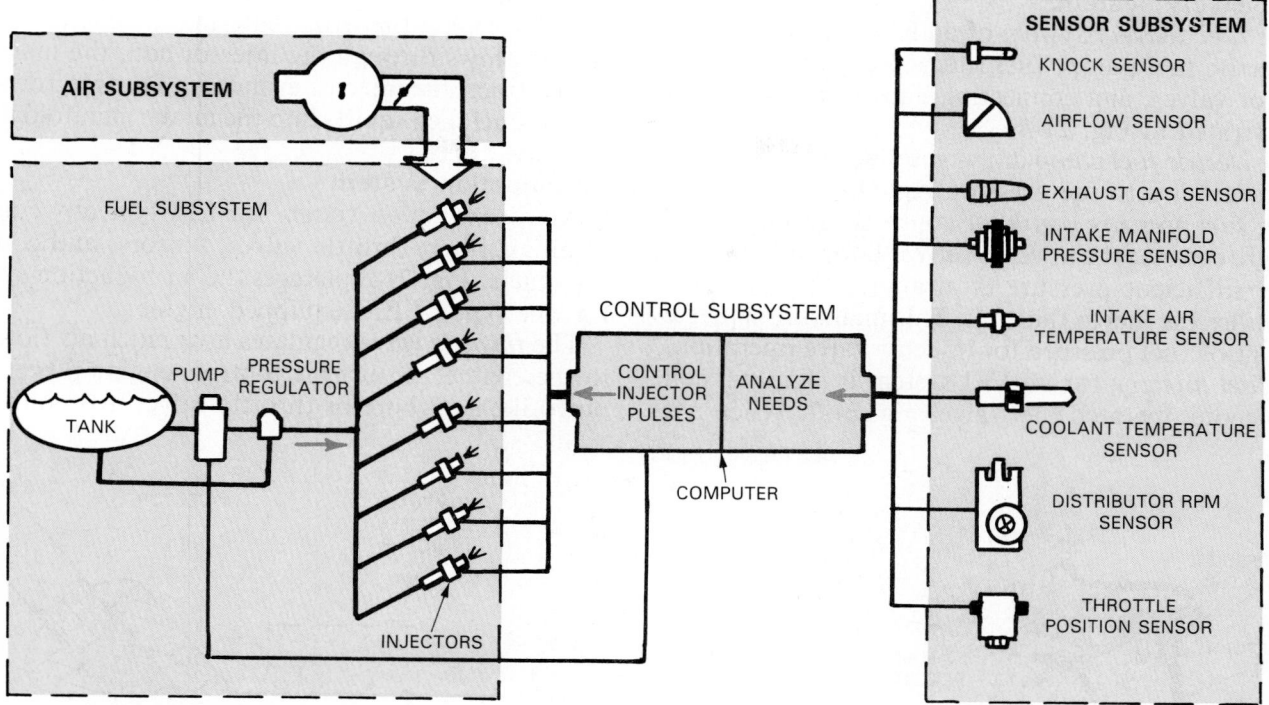

Fig. 21-4. Note four subsystems of an electronic gasoline injection system (dashed line boxes). Sensor systems feeds data to computer. Computer uses this data to operate fuel delivery system. Parts of air system can also be controlled by computer.

distributor (hydraulic valve mechanism) to meter gasoline into the engine. To be covered later, hydraulic fuel injection is used on several foreign cars.

Mechanical fuel injection controls use throttle linkage, a mechanical pump, and a governor speed device to control injection volume. This is a very old, seldom-used type injection system for high performance or racing engines. Diesel injection systems are mechanical types. Diesel systems are covered in Chapter 23, page 288.

Gasoline injection timing

The *timing* of a gasoline injection system links engine valve action to the time when fuel is sprayed into the engine intake manifold. There are three basic classifications of gasoline injection timing: intermittent, timed, and continuous.

An *intermittent* gasoline injection system opens and closes the injection valves independently of the engine intake valves. This type of injection system may spray fuel into the engine when the valves are open or when they are closed.

Another name for an intermittent injection system is MODULATED injection system. This is one of the most common types of gasoline injection.

A *timed* injection system squirts fuel into the engine right before or as the intake valves open. It is timed to the opening of the engine intake valves. The best example of timed injection is a diesel injection system.

A *continuous* gasoline injection system sprays fuel into the intake manifold all of the time. Anytime the

engine is running, some fuel is forced out of the injector nozzles and into the engine.

The air-fuel ratio is controlled by increasing or decreasing fuel pressure at the injectors. This increases or decreases fuel flow out of the injectors. A continuous type injection system is frequently used on several foreign cars and on a few American cars. This type is discussed near the end of the chapter.

Injector opening relationship

Simultaneous injection means all of the injectors open at the same time. The injectors are pulsed ON and OFF together.

Sequential injection has the injectors open one after the other. One opens and then another.

Group injection has several, but not all injectors opening at the same time. For example, a V-8 engine might have four injectors open at once and then the other four open next. A six cylinder engine would have two groups (three injectors in each group) open at different times.

ELECTRONIC FUEL INJECTION (EFI)

An *electronic fuel injection system,* abbreviated EFI, can be divided into four subsystems:
1. Fuel delivery system.
2. Air induction system.
3. Sensor system.
4. Computer control system.
These four subsystems are illustrated in Fig. 21-4.

Fuel delivery system

The *fuel delivery system* of an EFI system includes an electric fuel pump, fuel filter, pressure regulator, injector valves, and connecting lines and hoses. This is illustrated in Fig. 21-5.

The *electric fuel pump* draws gasoline out of the tank and forces it into the pressure regulator.

The *fuel pressure regulator* controls the amount of pressure entering the injector valves. Look at Fig. 21-6. When sufficient pressure is attained, the regulator returns excess fuel to the tank. This maintains a preset amount of fuel pressure for injector valve operation.

A *fuel injector* for an EFI system is simply a coil or solenoid operated fuel valve, Fig. 21-7. When not energized, spring pressure makes the injector remain closed, keeping fuel from entering the engine. When current flows through the injector coil, the magnetic field attracts the injector armature. The injector valve opens. Fuel then squirts into the intake manifold under pressure.

Air induction system

An *air induction system* for EFI typically consists of an air filter, throttle valves, sensors, and connecting ducts. Fig. 21-8 pictures the air induction system for one type of EFI equipped engine.

The *throttle valve* regulates how much air flows into the engine. In turn, it controls engine power output. Like a carburetor throttle valve, it is connected

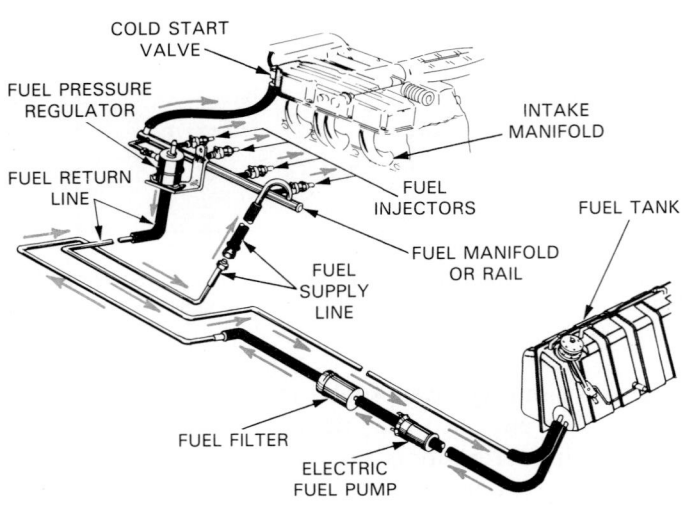

Fig. 21-5. Fuel delivery system typically consists of these parts. Pressure regulator maintains constant fuel pressure for injectors. Injectors are fuel valves that spray fuel into engine intake manifold. (Fiat)

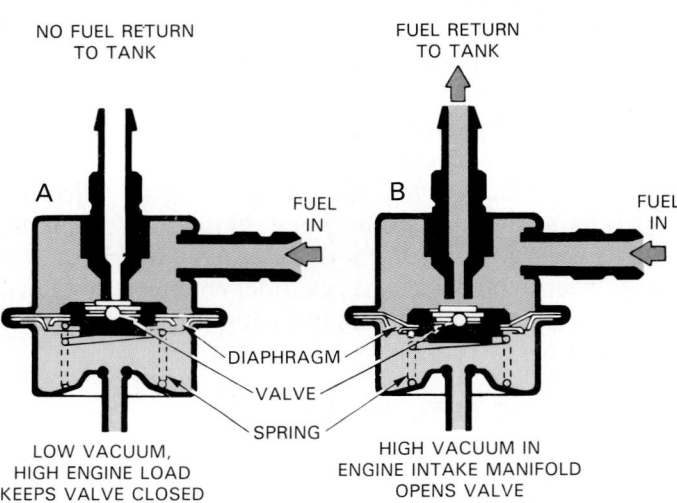

Fig. 21-6. Study pressure regulator action. A — Low engine vacuum would indicate high engine load. Spring could then hold regulator return closed to increase fuel pressure for more power. B — High engine vacuum would indicate low load. Vacuum would act on diaphragm, opening regulator return to tank. This would reduce or limit fuel pressure (Lancia)

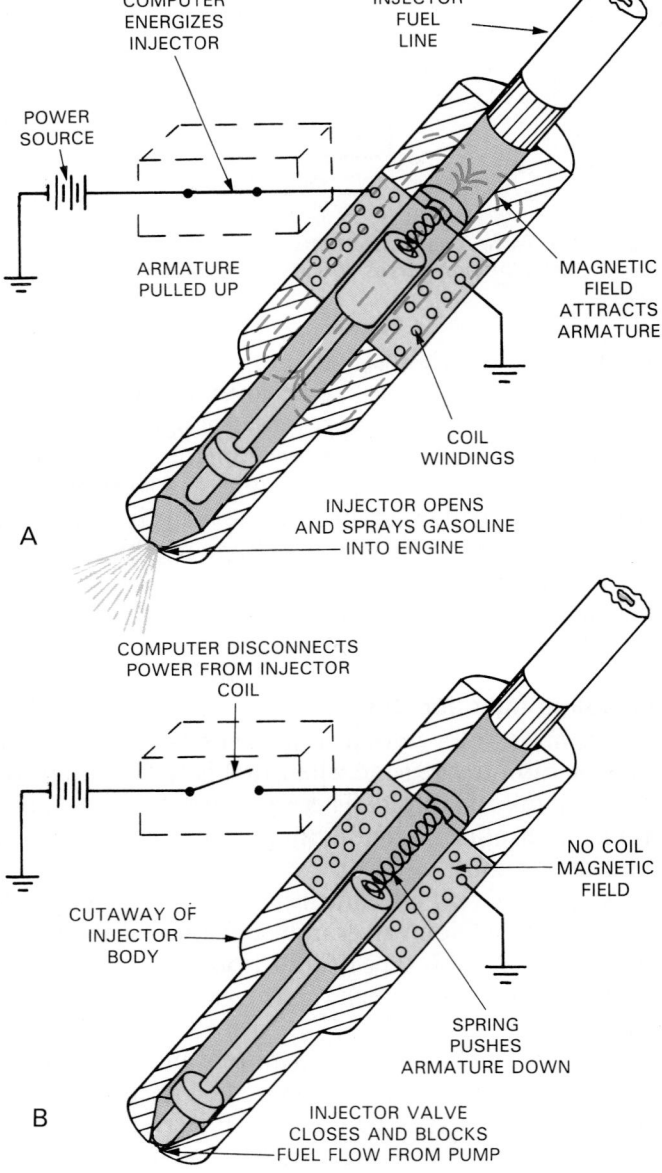

Fig. 21-7. EFI injector operation. A — Current flow through injector coil builds magnetic field. Field attracts and pulls up on armature to open injector. Fuel then sprays out injector. B — When computer breaks circuit, spring can push injector valve closed to stop fuel spray.

to the driver's gas pedal. When the pedal is depressed, the throttle valve swings open to allow more air to rush into the engine.

Sensor system

The EFI *sensor system* monitors engine operating conditions and reports this information to the computer. See Fig. 21-9. A typical EFI sensor system consists of an oxygen (exhaust gas) sensor, engine coolant temperature sensor, air inlet temperature sensor, throttle position sensor, intake manifold pressure (vacuum) sensor, engine speed sensor, and other sensors.

An *engine sensor* is an electrical device that changes circuit resistance or voltage with a change in a condition (temperature, pressure, position of parts, etc.). For example, a temperature sensor's resistance may decrease as temperature increases. The computer can use the increased current flow through the sensor to calculate any needed change in injector valve opening.

Computer control system

The *computer control system* uses electrical data from the sensors to control the operation of the fuel injectors. Refer to Fig. 21-10. A wiring harness connects the engine sensors to the input of the computer. Another wiring harness connects the output of the computer to the fuel injectors.

The *computer,* also called an ELECTRONIC CONTROL UNIT (ECU), is the "brain" of the electronic fuel injection system. Refer to Fig. 21-11. It is a *preprogrammed microcomputer* (preset, miniature electronic circuit). The ECU uses sensor output to calculate when and how long to open the fuel injectors.

To open an injector, the computer connects the injector coil to battery voltage. To close the injector, the computer opens the circuit between the battery and the injector coil.

ENGINE SENSORS

Typical sensors for an EFI system include:
1. An exhaust gas or oxygen sensor.
2. A manifold pressure sensor.
3. A throttle position sensor.
4. An engine temperature sensor.
5. An airflow sensor.
6. An inlet air temperature sensor.
7. A crankshaft position sensor.

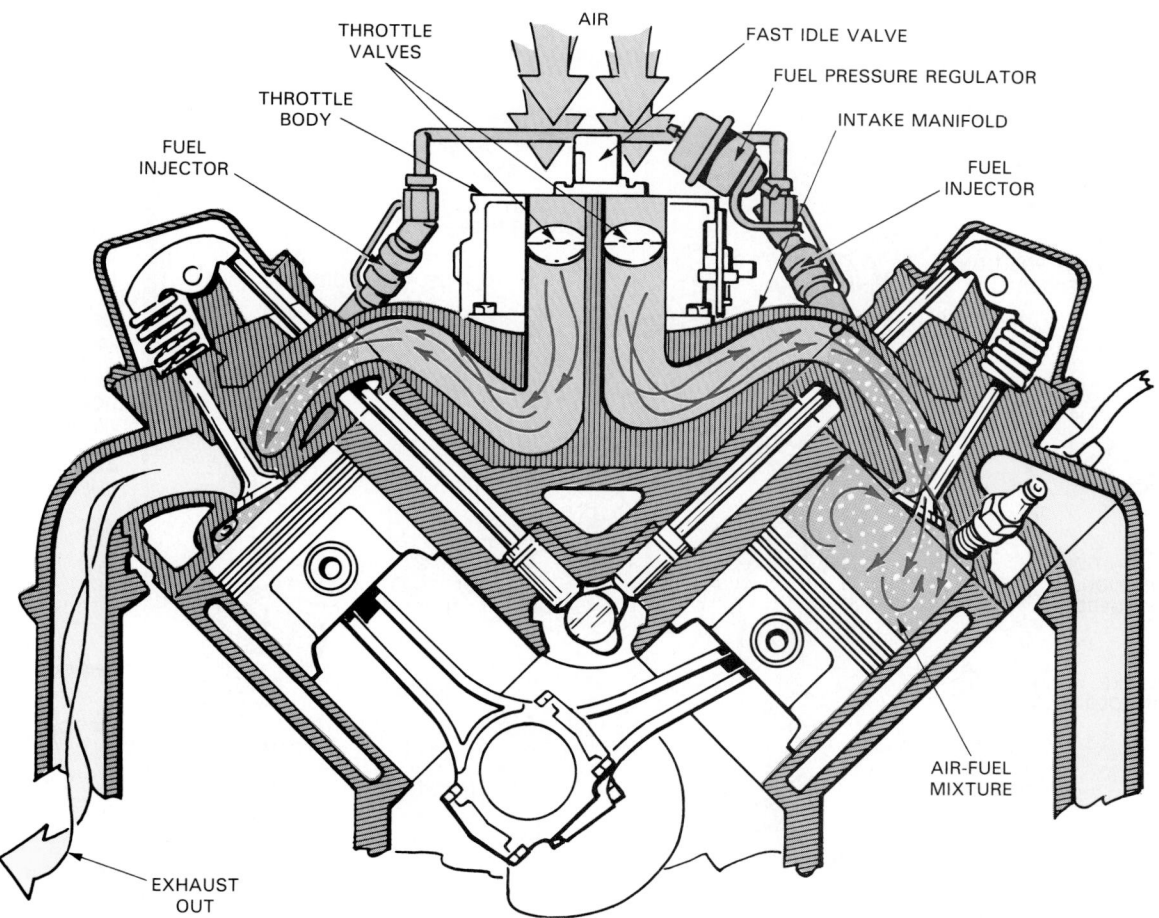

Fig. 21-8. Air induction system consists mainly of throttle body. It contains throttle plates that control airflow into engine. Also, note location of injectors in this V-type engine. (Cadillac)

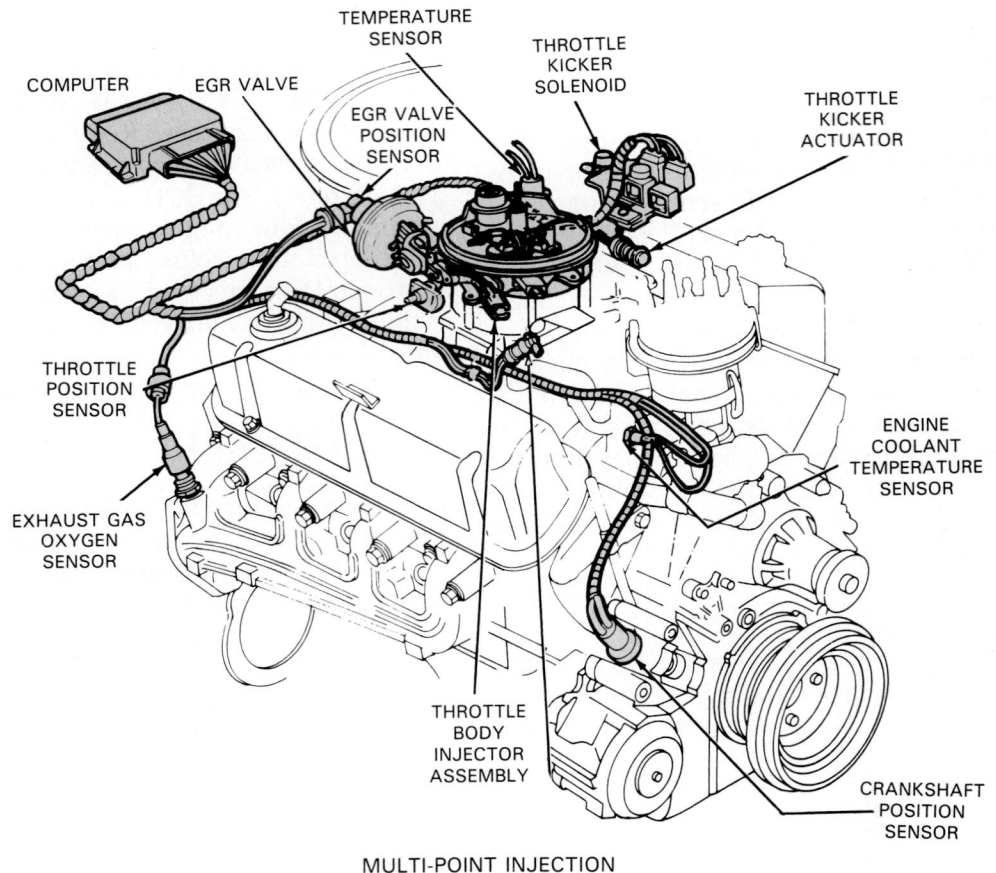

THROTTLE BODY INJECTION

COMPUTER

EGR VALVE

TEMPERATURE SENSOR

EGR VALVE POSITION SENSOR

THROTTLE KICKER SOLENOID

THROTTLE KICKER ACTUATOR

THROTTLE POSITION SENSOR

EXHAUST GAS OXYGEN SENSOR

ENGINE COOLANT TEMPERATURE SENSOR

THROTTLE BODY INJECTOR ASSEMBLY

CRANKSHAFT POSITION SENSOR

MULTI-POINT INJECTION

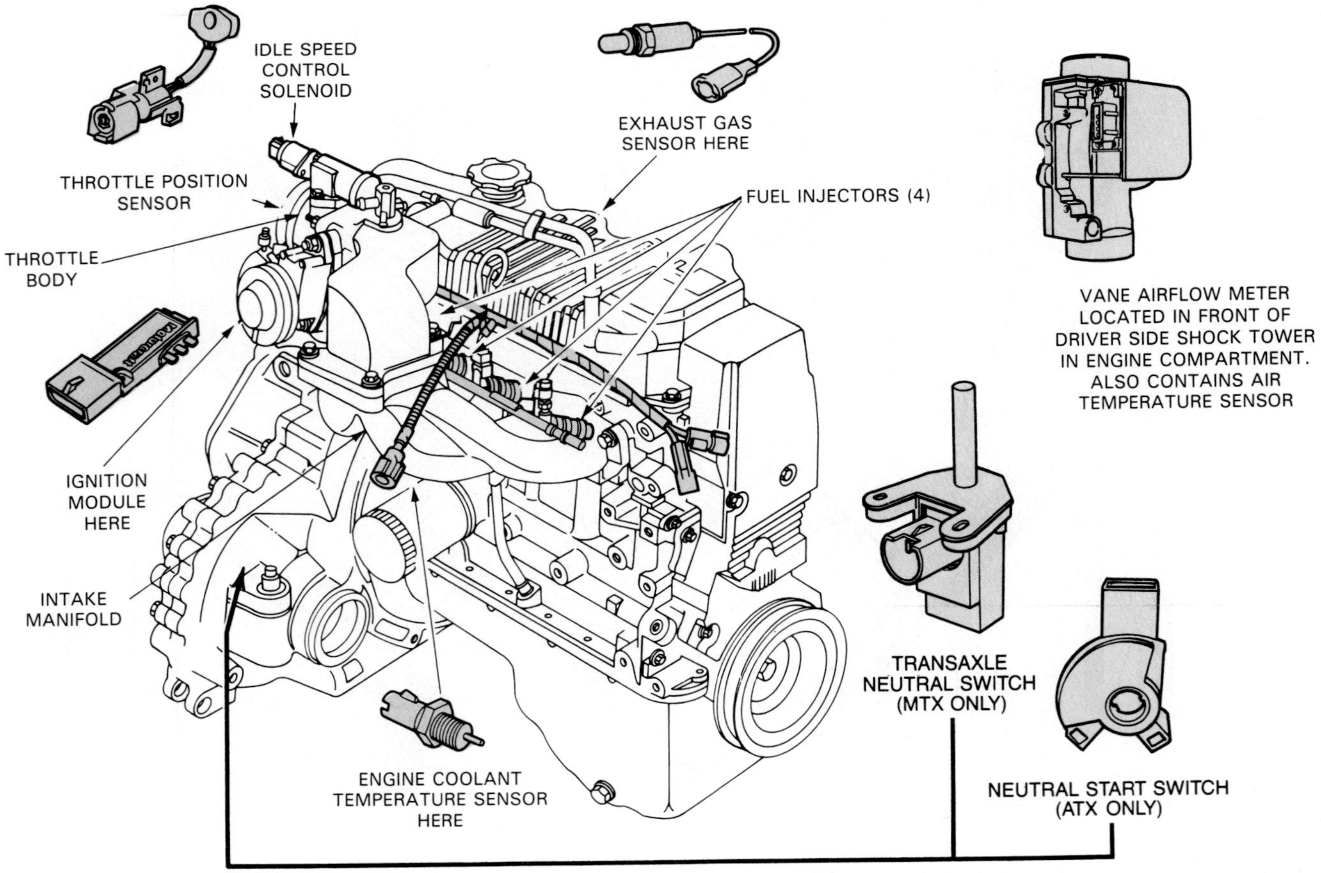

IDLE SPEED CONTROL SOLENOID

EXHAUST GAS SENSOR HERE

FUEL INJECTORS (4)

THROTTLE POSITION SENSOR

THROTTLE BODY

IGNITION MODULE HERE

INTAKE MANIFOLD

ENGINE COOLANT TEMPERATURE SENSOR HERE

VANE AIRFLOW METER LOCATED IN FRONT OF DRIVER SIDE SHOCK TOWER IN ENGINE COMPARTMENT. ALSO CONTAINS AIR TEMPERATURE SENSOR

TRANSAXLE NEUTRAL SWITCH (MTX ONLY)

NEUTRAL START SWITCH (ATX ONLY)

Fig. 21-9. Study sensors for single-point throttle body and multi-point or port injection systems. These are typical. (Ford)

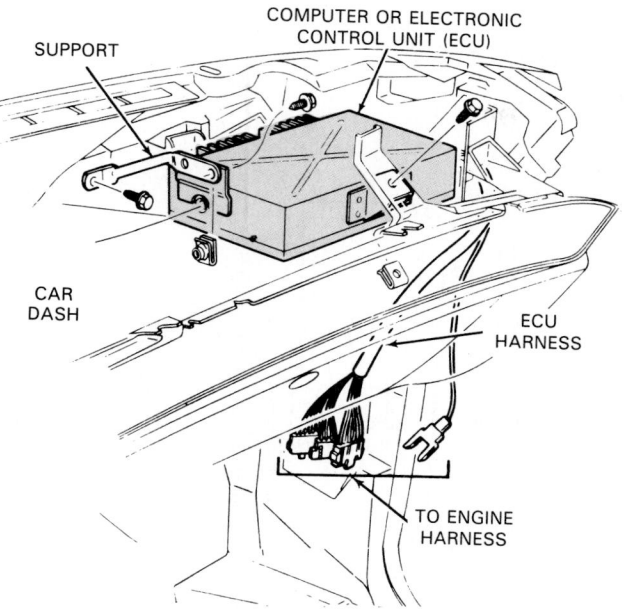

Fig. 21-10. Computer or electronic control unit is commonly mounted behind car instrument panel (dash). This keeps it away from damaging engine heat and vibration. Some systems, however, mount control unit on air cleaner or elsewhere in engine compartment. (Cadillac)

An *exhaust gas sensor,* also called an *oxygen sensor,* measures the oxygen content in the engine's exhaust system as a means of checking combustion efficiency. It fits into the exhaust manifold or pipe at a point before the catalytic converter. Look at Figs. 21-12 and 21-13.

The oxygen sensor voltage output changes with any change in the content of the exhaust. For example, an increase in oxygen (lean mixture) might make the sensor output voltage decrease. A decrease in oxygen (rich mixture) might cause the sensor output to increase.

In this way, the sensor supplies data (different current levels) to the computer. The computer can then alter the opening and closing of the injectors to maintain a correct air-fuel ratio for maximum efficiency.

A *manifold pressure sensor* (abbreviated MAP for manifold absolute pressure) measures the pressure (vacuum) inside the engine intake manifold. Discussed in earlier chapters, engine manifold pressure is an excellent indicator of engine load.

High pressure (low intake vacuum) indicates a high load, requiring a rich mixture. Low manifold pressure (high intake vacuum) indicates very little load, requiring a leaner mixture.

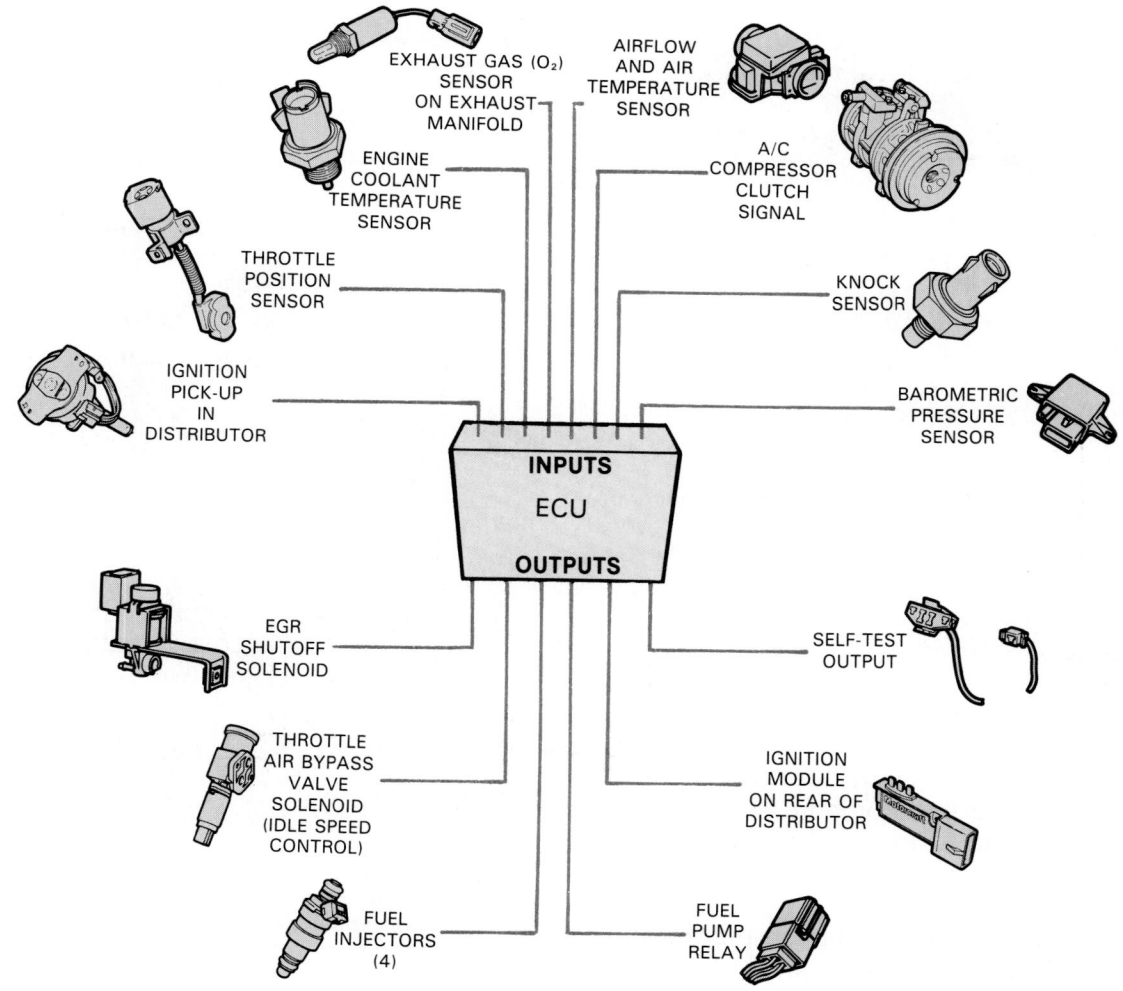

Fig. 21-11. Sensors feed information to computer. Computer uses this data to operate other components of system. (Ford)

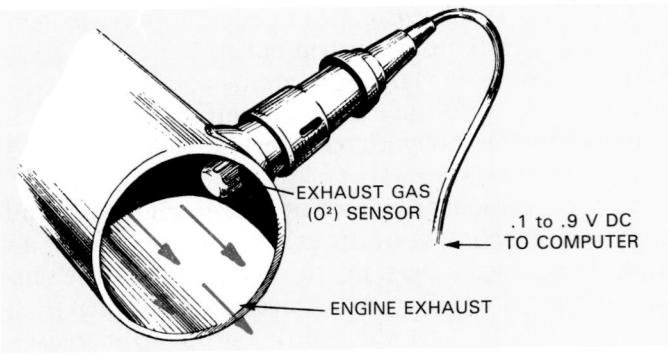

Fig. 21-12. Exhaust gas oxygen (EGO) sensor is very important sensor commonly used in EFI systems. It allows system to self-test air-fuel mixture setting by measuring oxygen in engine exhaust.

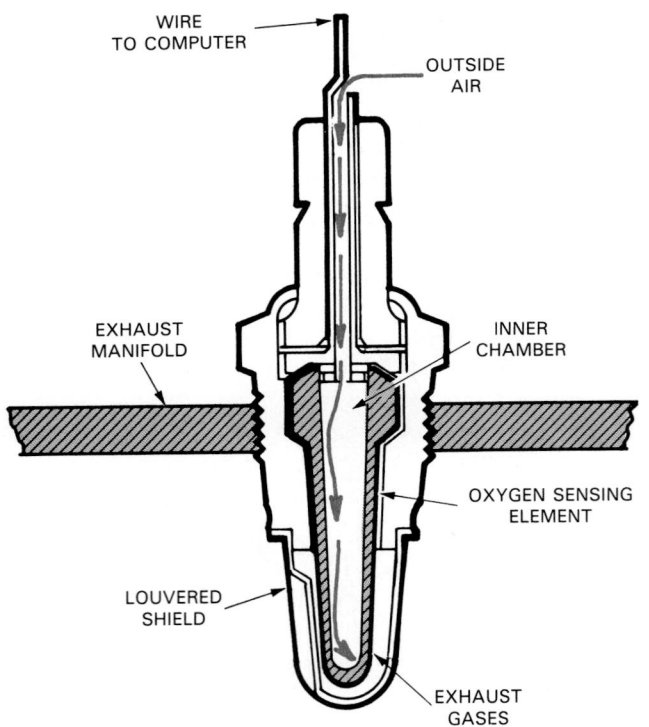

Fig. 21-13. Exhaust gas oxygen sensor compares amount of oxygen in engine exhaust with oxygen in outside air. Note passage to outside air. (GMC)

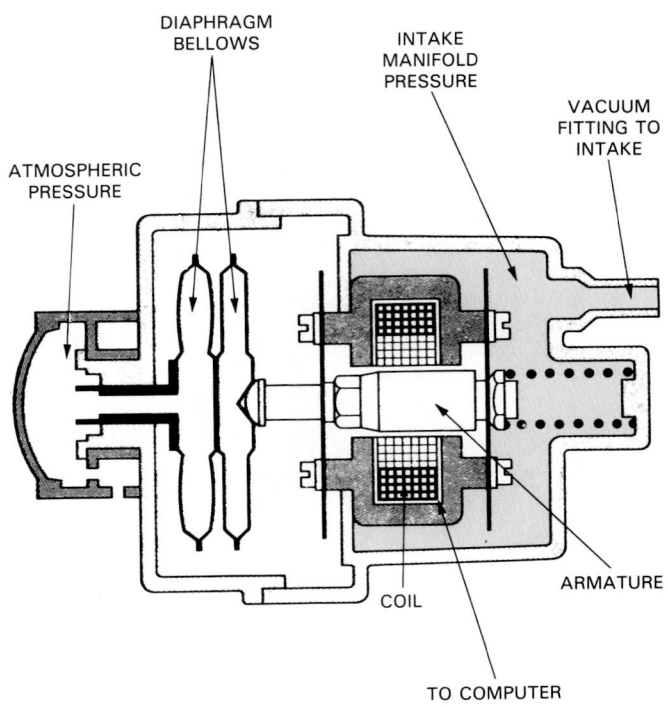

Fig. 21-14. Engine intake manifold pressure sensor changes resistance with changes in vacuum (pressure). High engine intake vacuum indicates a low-load condition. Low engine intake manifold vacuum indicates a high-load or power-output condition. Pressure sensor reports this information to computer as a change in current flow. (Robert Bosch)

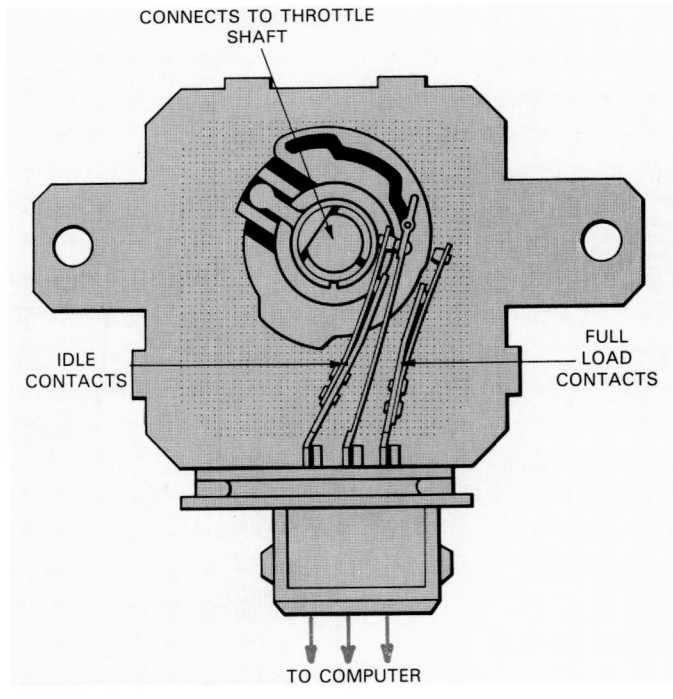

Fig. 21-15. Throttle position sensor uses contacts to report amount of throttle opening to computer. Throttle shaft rotation causes different contacts to close. Each set of contacts is connected to circuit resistor of different value. In this way, different current levels are produced for different throttle positions. Computer can then alter fuel mixture for idle and wide open throttle positions. (Robert Bosch)

The manifold pressure sensor changes resistance with changes in engine load, Fig. 21-14. This data is used by the computer to alter the fuel mixture.

A *throttle position sensor* is a variable resistor connected to the throttle plate shaft. Look at Fig. 21-15. When the throttle swings open for more power or closes for less power, the sensor changes resistance and signals the computer. The computer can then richen or lean the mixture as needed.

An *engine temperature sensor* monitors the operating temperature of the engine. It is mounted so that it is exposed to the engine coolant.

When the engine is cold, the sensor might provide

a high current flow (low resistance). The computer would then richen the air-fuel mixture for cold engine operation. When the engine warms, the sensor would supply information (high resistance for example) so that the computer could make the mixture more lean.

An *airflow sensor* is used in many EFI systems to measure the amount of outside air entering the engine. This helps the computer determine how much fuel is needed. Refer to Fig. 21-16.

Pictured in Fig. 21-17, the airflow sensor is usually an air flap or door that operates a variable resistor. Increased airflow opens the flap more to change the position of the variable resistor. Information is then sent to the computer indicating air inlet volume.

Note! An airflow sensor will be covered in more detail later in this chapter.

An *inlet air temperature sensor* measures the temperature of the air entering the engine. Look at Fig. 21-16 again.

Cold air is more dense than warm air, requiring a little more fuel. Warm air is NOT as dense as cold air, requiring a little less fuel. The air temperature sensor helps the computer compensate for changes in outside air temperature and maintain an almost perfect air-fuel mixture ratio.

A *crankshaft position sensor* is used to detect engine speed. Refer back to A in Fig. 21-9. It allows the computer to change injector opening with changes in engine rpm. Higher engine speeds generally require more fuel.

Other sensors include an A/C compressor sensor, transmission sensor, EGR sensor, and engine knock sensor. They provide additional data about operating conditions effecting engine fuel needs. Many of these are covered in the chapter on emission control systems.

Analog and digital signals

The signal from the engine sensors can be either a digital or analog type output.

Sensor *digital signals* are on-off signals. An example of a sensor providing a digital signal is the crankshaft position sensor which shows engine rpm. Voltage output or resistance goes from maximum to minimum, like a switch.

An *analog signal* changes in strength to let the computer know about a change in a condition. Sensor internal resistance may smoothly increase or decrease with temperature, pressure, or part position. The sensor acts as a variable resistor.

Open loop and closed loop

When in *open loop,* the electronic injection system does NOT use engine exhaust gas content as a main

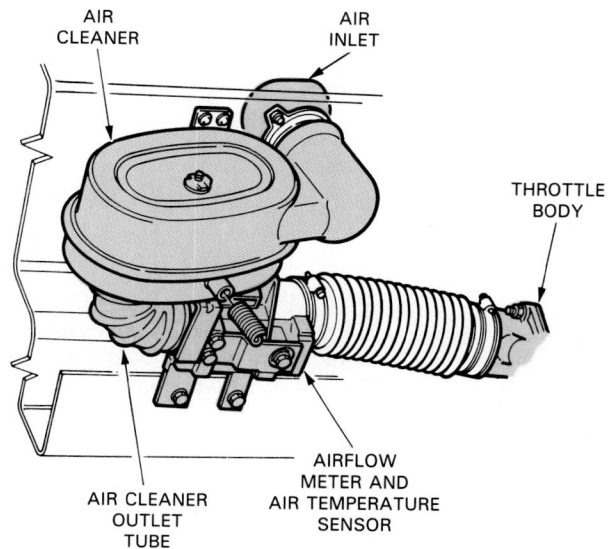

Fig. 21-16. Airflow meter and air inlet temperature sensor are housed under air cleaner on this engine. (Ford)

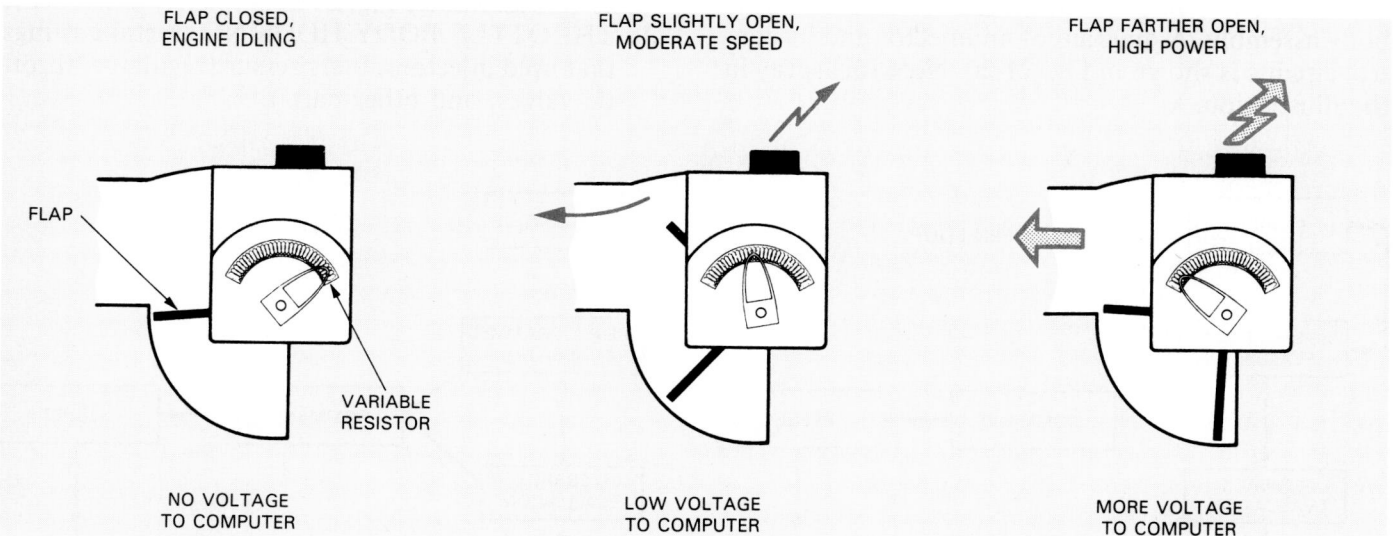

Fig. 21-17. Airflow sensor operates variable resistor. Low airflow at idle would not open sensor flap and resistance might stay high. As airflow increases, flap swings open, decreases sensor resistance and increases current flow to computer. (VW)

control of the air-fuel mixture. Illustrated in Fig. 21-18A, the system operates on information stored in the computer.

With the engine cold, the exhaust gas sensor cannot accurately provide data for the computer. The computer is set to ignore this data when the engine is cold. The system will then function in an open loop mode.

When in a *closed loop* mode, the EFI system uses information from the exhaust gas sensor and other sensors to control the air-fuel mixture. Shown in Fig. 21-18B, a complete loop (circle) is formed in theory as data flows from the sensor to the computer, and back through the system.

Under most operating conditions, an electronic gasoline injection system functions in closed loop. This lets the computer double-check the fuel mixture it is providing to the engine.

INJECTOR PULSE WIDTH

The *injector pulse width* indicates the amount of time each injector is energized and kept open. The computer controls the injector pulse width.

As an example, under full acceleration, the computer will sense a wide-open throttle, high intake manifold pressure, and high inlet airflow. The computer would then increase injector pulse width to richen the mixture for more power.

Under low load conditions, the computer will shorten the injector pulse width. With the injectors being closed a larger percentage of time, the air-fuel mixture will be leaner for better fuel economy.

Fig. 21-19 shows how pulse width controls injector output. Study the drawing carefully!

THROTTLE BODY INJECTION (TBI)

A *throttle body injection* system, abbreviated TBI, uses one or two injector valves mounted in a throttle body assembly. A diagram of an injector and its control circuits is shown in Fig. 21-20. Note fuel spray in the illustration.

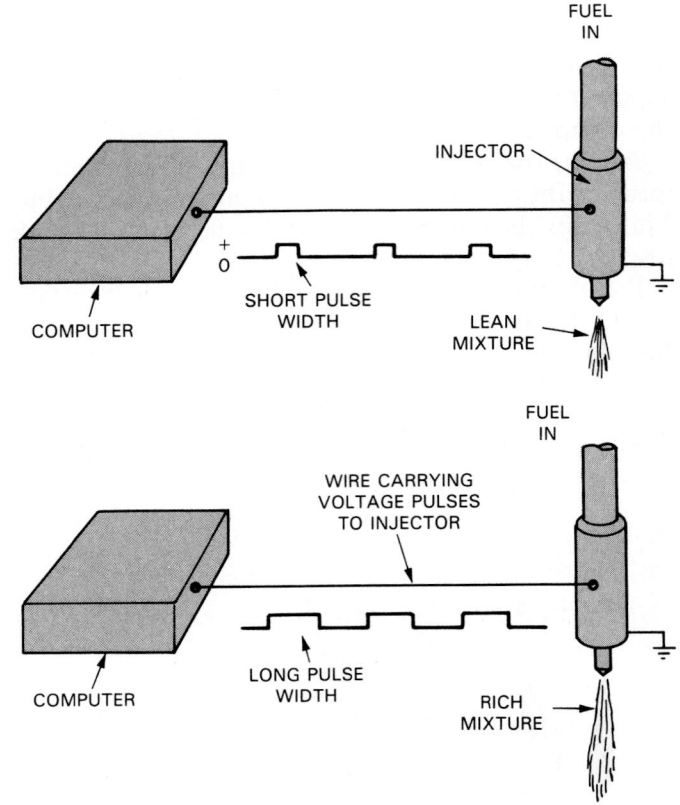

Fig. 21-19. Pulse width is used to control amount of fuel injected into engine. A longer pulse width would richen mixture. A shorter pulse width would lean mixture.

The injectors spray fuel into the top of the throttle body air horn, Fig. 21-21. The TBI fuel spray mixes with the air flowing through the air horn. The mixture is then pulled into the engine by intake manifold vacuum.

TBI assembly

The TBI *assembly,* Fig. 21-22, typically consists of:
1. THROTTLE BODY HOUSING (metal castings that hold injectors, fuel pressure regulator, throttle valves, and other parts).

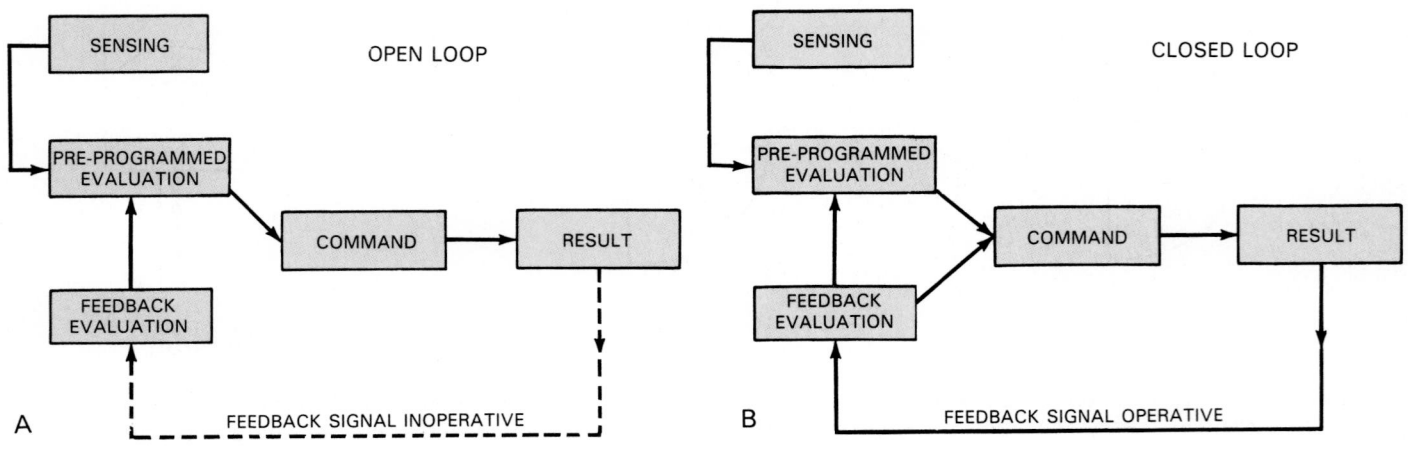

Fig. 21-18. Note basic flow of information with EFI system in open loop (A) and closed loop (B). (Chrysler)

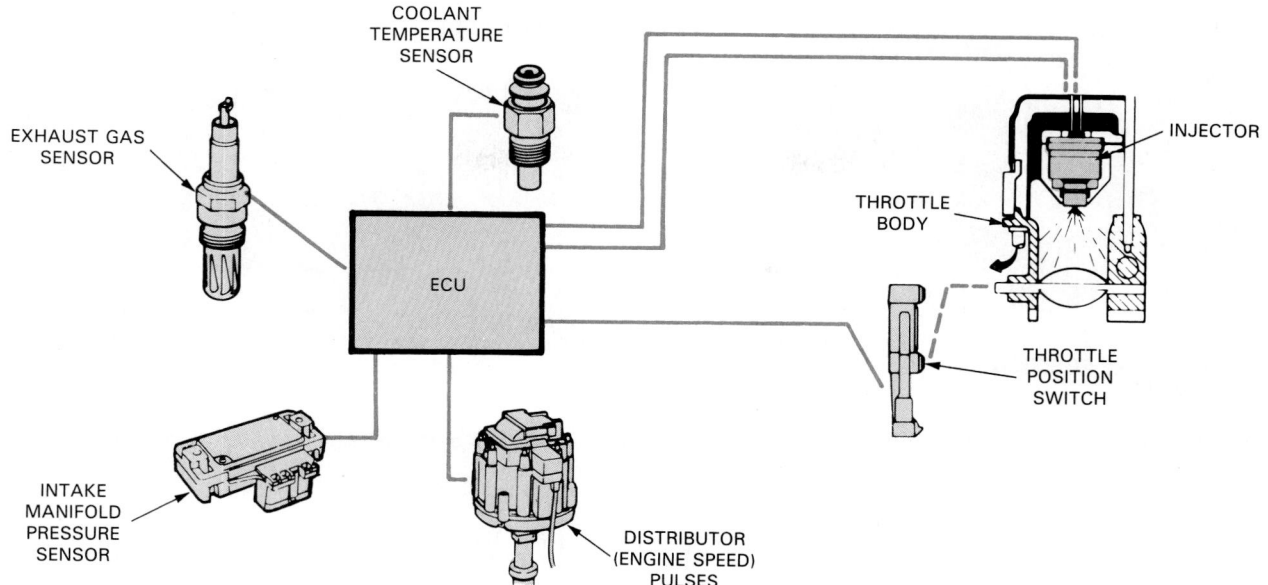

Fig. 21-20. *Throttle body injection has sensors and computer-operated injector mounted inside throttle body. It uses many of the basic components already introduced.* (Buick)

2. FUEL INJECTORS (solenoid operated fuel valves mounted in upper section of throttle body assembly).
3. FUEL PRESSURE REGULATOR (spring-loaded bypass valve that maintains constant pressure at injectors).
4. THROTTLE POSITIONER (motor assembly that open or closes throttle plates to control engine idle speed).

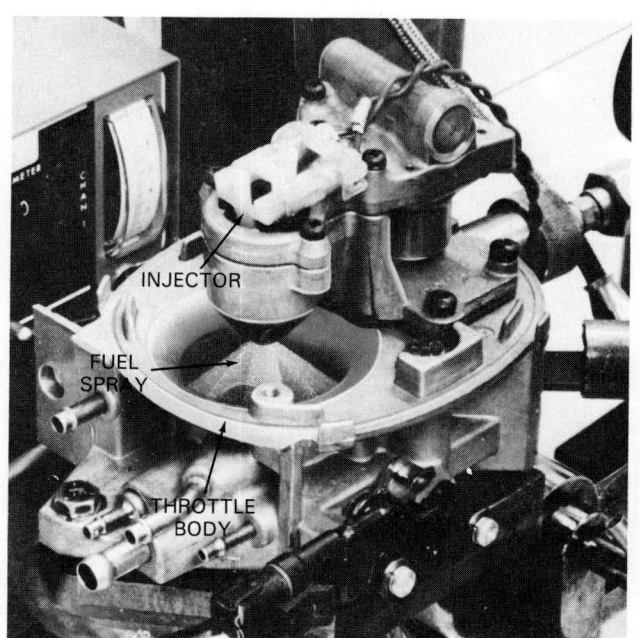

Fig. 21-21. *One or two injectors may be mounted in TBI unit. Fuel sprays into air horn, just as fuel is pulled into air horn of carburetor by vacuum. Pressure, not vacuum, forces fuel out of injector.* (Pontiac)

5. THROTTLE POSITION SENSOR (variable resistor that senses opening or closing of throttle plates).
6. THROTTLE PLATES (butterfly valves that control airflow through throttle body).

TBI throttle body

The TBI *throttle body,* like a carburetor body, bolts to the pad on the intake manifold, Fig. 21-23. Throttle plates are mounted in the lower section of the throttle body. A linkage mechanism or cable connects the throttle plates with the driver's gas pedal. An inlet fuel line connects to one fitting on the throttle body. An outlet return line to the tank connects to another fitting on the throttle body.

Throttle body injector

A *throttle body injector* consists of an electric solenoid coil, armature or plunger, ball or needle valve, ball or needle seat, and injector spring. These parts are pictured in Fig. 21-24 and on the right in Fig. 21-25.

Wires from the computer (electronic control unit) connect to the terminals on the injectors. When the computer energizes the injectors, a magnetic field is produced in the injector coil. The magnetic field pulls the plunger and valve up to open the injector. Fuel can then squirt through the injector nozzle and into the engine.

Throttle body pressure regulator

The *throttle body pressure regulator* consists of a fuel valve, diaphragm, and spring. When fuel pressure is low (initial engine starting), the spring holds the fuel valve closed. This causes pressure to build as fuel flows

Fig. 21-22. External views of actual TBI assembly show important parts. Study carefully. (Cadillac)

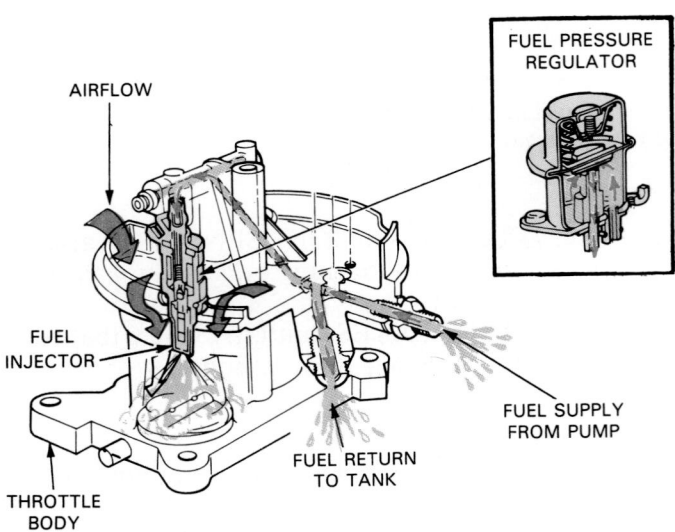

Fig. 21-23. Fuel enters throttle body from pump. It then enters pressure regulator before passing into injector. Fuel spray out of injector mixes with air entering air horn. (Ford)

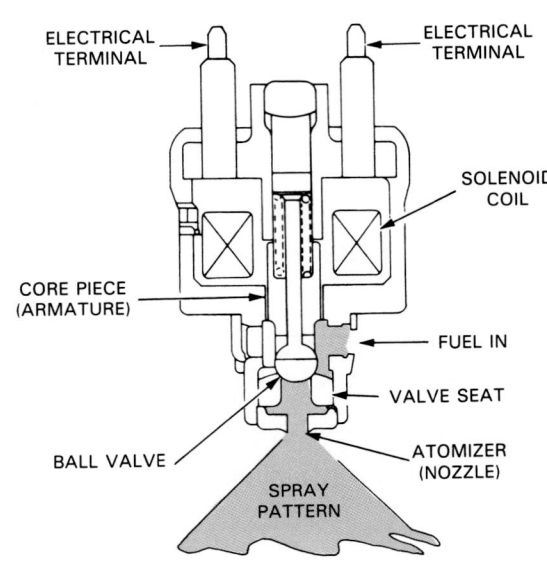

Fig. 21-24. This TBI injector uses a ball type valve, instead of a pointed needle valve. Note part names.

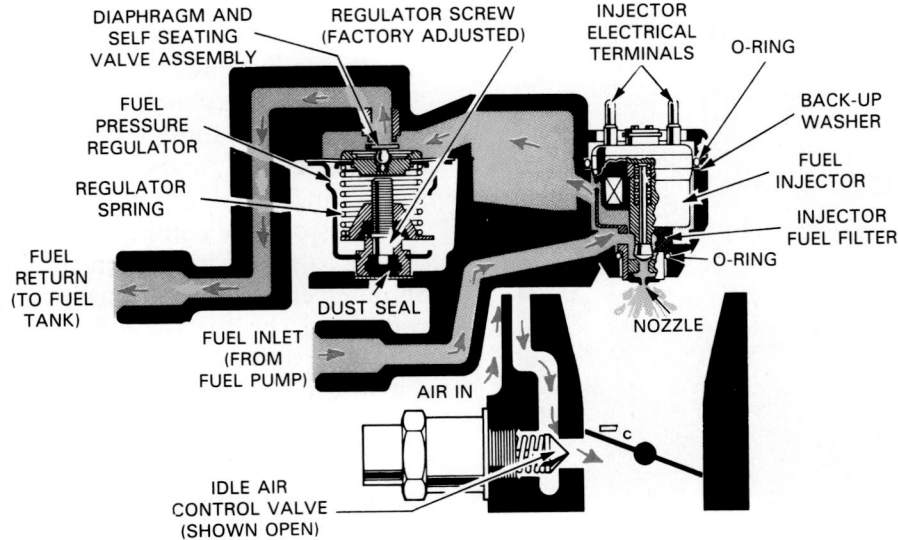

Fig. 21-25. Cutaway illustration shows basic action inside a typical throttle body assembly. Regulator limits maximum pressure inside injector to preset level. Then, pulse width will accurately control air-fuel ratio. Idle air control valve is used to increase or decrease idle speed as needed. (Pontiac)

into the regulator from the electric fuel pump. Refer to Fig. 21-23.

When a preset pressure is reached, pressure acts on the diaphragm. The diaphragm compresses the spring and opens the fuel valve. Fuel can then flow back to the fuel tank. This limits the maximum fuel pressure at the injectors.

Fig. 21-25 shows how the pressure regulator functions in one type throttle body assembly.

Idle air control valve

An *idle air control valve* may be used in a TBI throttle body to help control engine idle speed. One is shown in Fig. 21-25. It is a solenoid operated air bypass valve. The system computer or a built-in thermostat normally opens and closes the idle air control valve.

When open, the idle air control valve allows more air to enter the intake manifold. This tends to increase idle rpm. When closed, the valve decreases bypass air and idle speed. The valve can be used to control both slow and fast idle speeds. It is comparable to a carburetor's fast idle cam.

Throttle positioner

A *throttle positioner* (in addition to an idle air control valve) is often used on throttle body assemblies to control engine idle speed. The computer actuates the positioner to open or close the throttle plates.

In this way, the computer can maintain a precise idle speed with changes in engine temperature, load (air conditioning ON for example), and other conditions.

Look at Fig. 21-26. It pictures a twin throttle body injection setup. Two throttle bodies, with one injector in each, are mounted on the intake manifold. This increases engine performance.

CONTINUOUS THROTTLE BODY INJECTION

A *continuous throttle body injection* (CTBI) system sprays a solid stream of fuel into the air horn. Unlike the more common modulated system just discussed, it does NOT pulse the injectors ON and OFF to control the air-fuel mixture.

To increase or decrease fuel flow, the CTBI system alters the pressure applied to the nozzles in the throttle body. Some parts of a CTBI system are illustrated in Fig. 21-27.

Fig. 21-28 shows a diagram of how data is transferred in a continuous electronic throttle body injection system. The system measures fuel flow, airflow, and other engine conditions. The computer then increases or decreases the speed of the *control pump* (fuel pump) to meet engine needs.

The air cleaner and throttle body assembly of this type injection system contain the computer, airflow sensor, fuel control motor (pump), *spray bar* (injector nozzles), and other components. This is not a commonly used system.

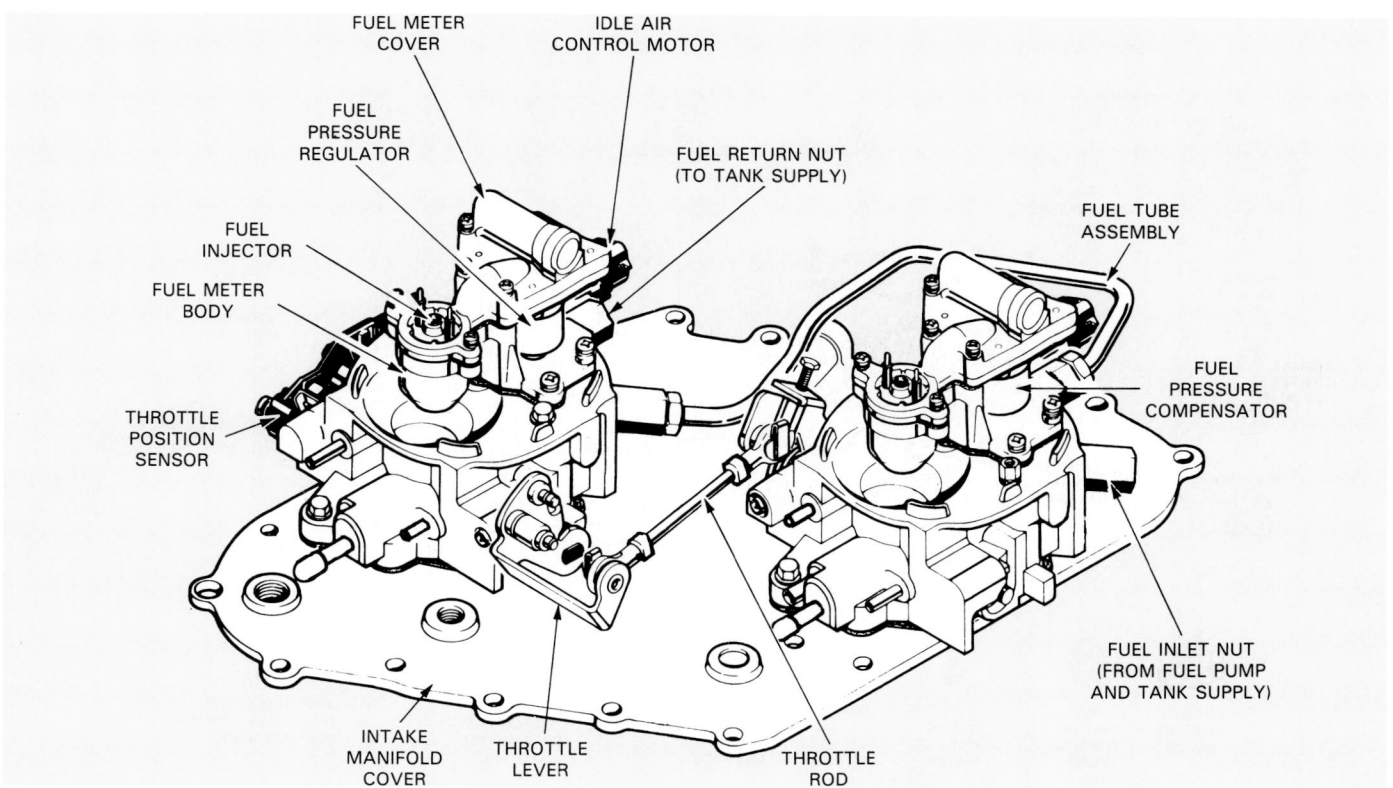

Fig. 21-26. Manifold uses two throttle body injector assemblies for high performance. Study throttle linkage and other parts. (Corvette)

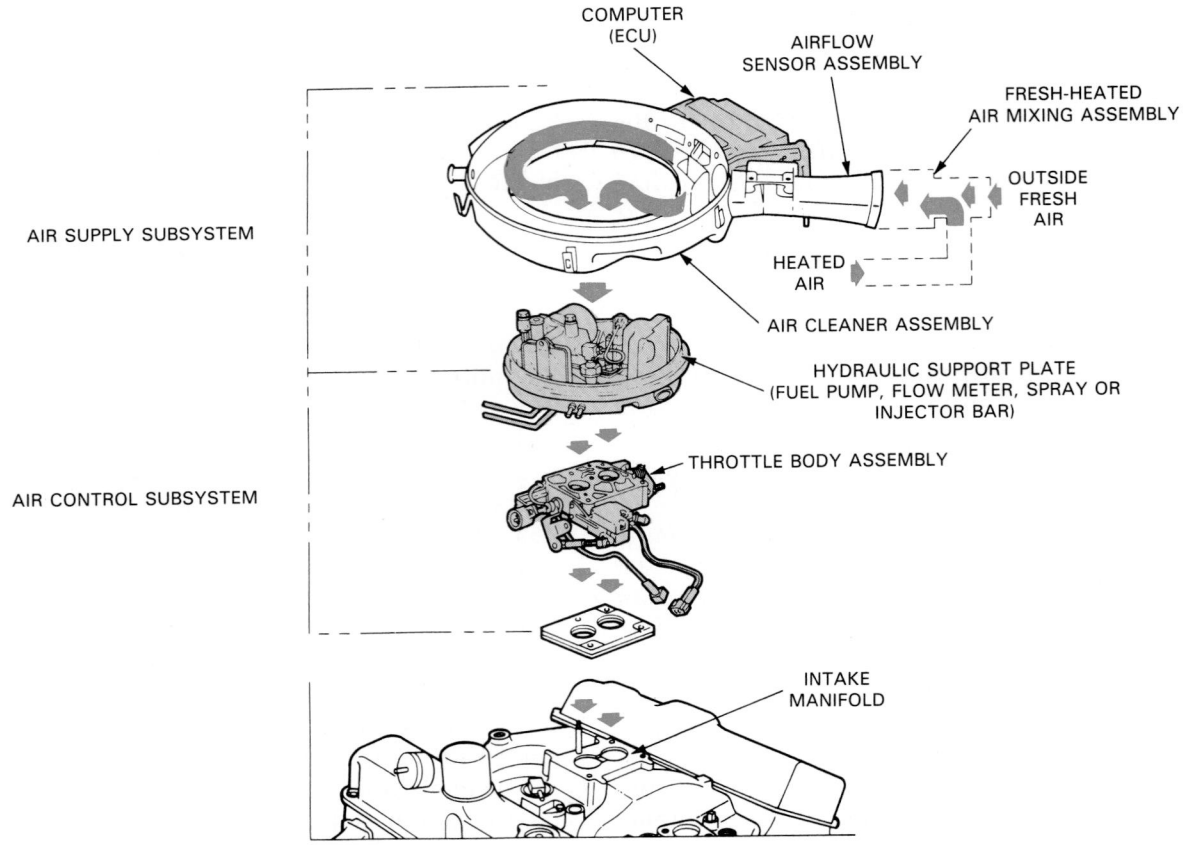

COMPUTER
(ECU)

AIRFLOW
SENSOR ASSEMBLY

FRESH-HEATED
AIR MIXING ASSEMBLY

OUTSIDE
FRESH
AIR

AIR SUPPLY SUBSYSTEM

HEATED
AIR

AIR CLEANER ASSEMBLY

HYDRAULIC SUPPORT PLATE
(FUEL PUMP, FLOW METER, SPRAY OR
INJECTOR BAR)

THROTTLE BODY ASSEMBLY

AIR CONTROL SUBSYSTEM

INTAKE
MANIFOLD

Fig. 21-27. Continuous throttle body injector is quite different from more common modulated TBI. With this particular system, computer, fuel pump, injector bar, and throttle body are all housed together. (Chrysler)

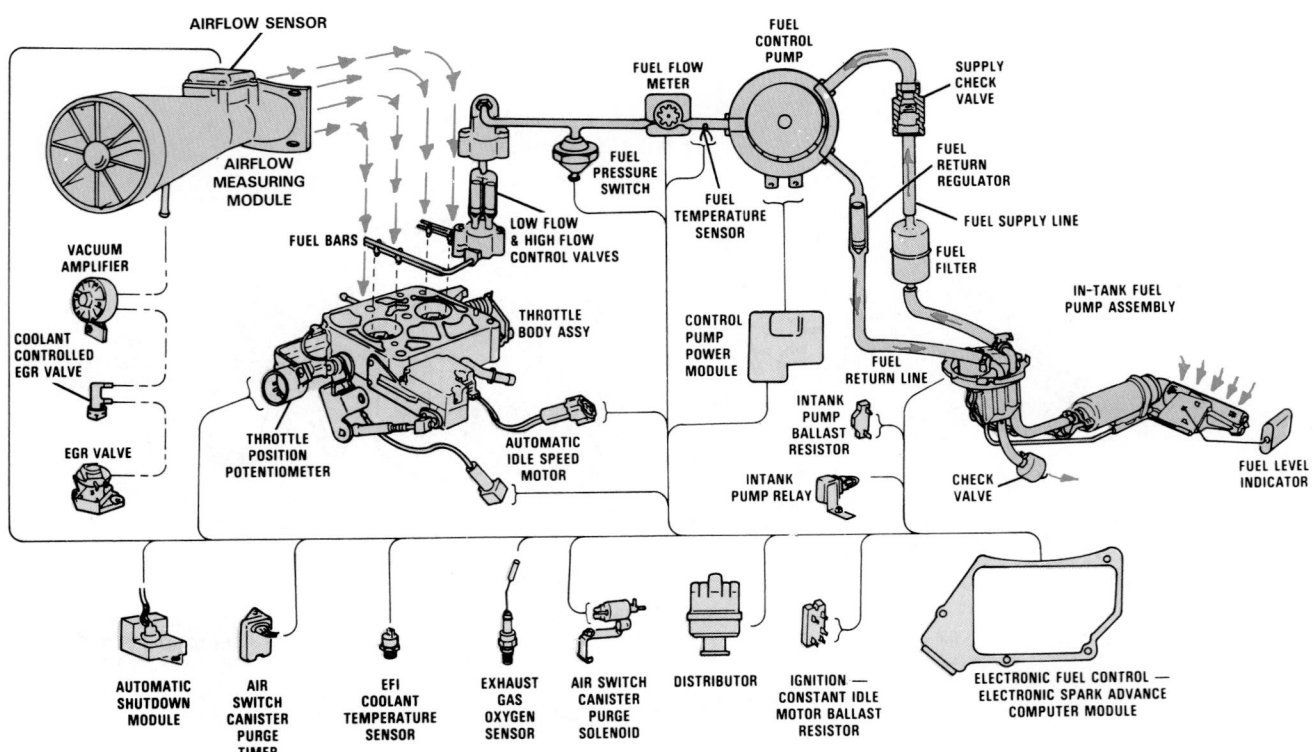

AIRFLOW SENSOR

FUEL
CONTROL
PUMP

FUEL FLOW
METER

SUPPLY CHECK
VALVE

AIRFLOW
MEASURING
MODULE

FUEL
PRESSURE
SWITCH

FUEL
TEMPERATURE
SENSOR

FUEL
RETURN
REGULATOR

FUEL SUPPLY LINE

VACUUM
AMPLIFIER

FUEL BARS

LOW FLOW
& HIGH FLOW
CONTROL VALVES

FUEL
FILTER

IN-TANK FUEL
PUMP ASSEMBLY

COOLANT
CONTROLLED
EGR VALVE

THROTTLE
BODY ASSY

CONTROL
PUMP
POWER
MODULE

FUEL
RETURN LINE

EGR VALVE

THROTTLE
POSITION
POTENTIOMETER

AUTOMATIC
IDLE SPEED
MOTOR

INTANK
PUMP
BALLAST
RESISTOR

INTANK
PUMP RELAY

CHECK
VALVE

FUEL LEVEL
INDICATOR

AUTOMATIC
SHUTDOWN
MODULE

AIR
SWITCH
CANISTER
PURGE
TIMER

EFI
COOLANT
TEMPERATURE
SENSOR

EXHAUST
GAS
OXYGEN
SENSOR

AIR SWITCH
CANISTER
PURGE
SOLENOID

DISTRIBUTOR

IGNITION —
CONSTANT IDLE
MOTOR BALLAST
RESISTOR

ELECTRONIC FUEL CONTROL —
ELECTRONIC SPARK ADVANCE
COMPUTER MODULE

Fig. 21-28. Diagram shows typical continuous throttle body injection parts and relationships. Fuel pump's speed and pressure are changed to alter air-fuel ratio. Increased pump speeds and pressure richens mixture and vice versa. (Chrysler)

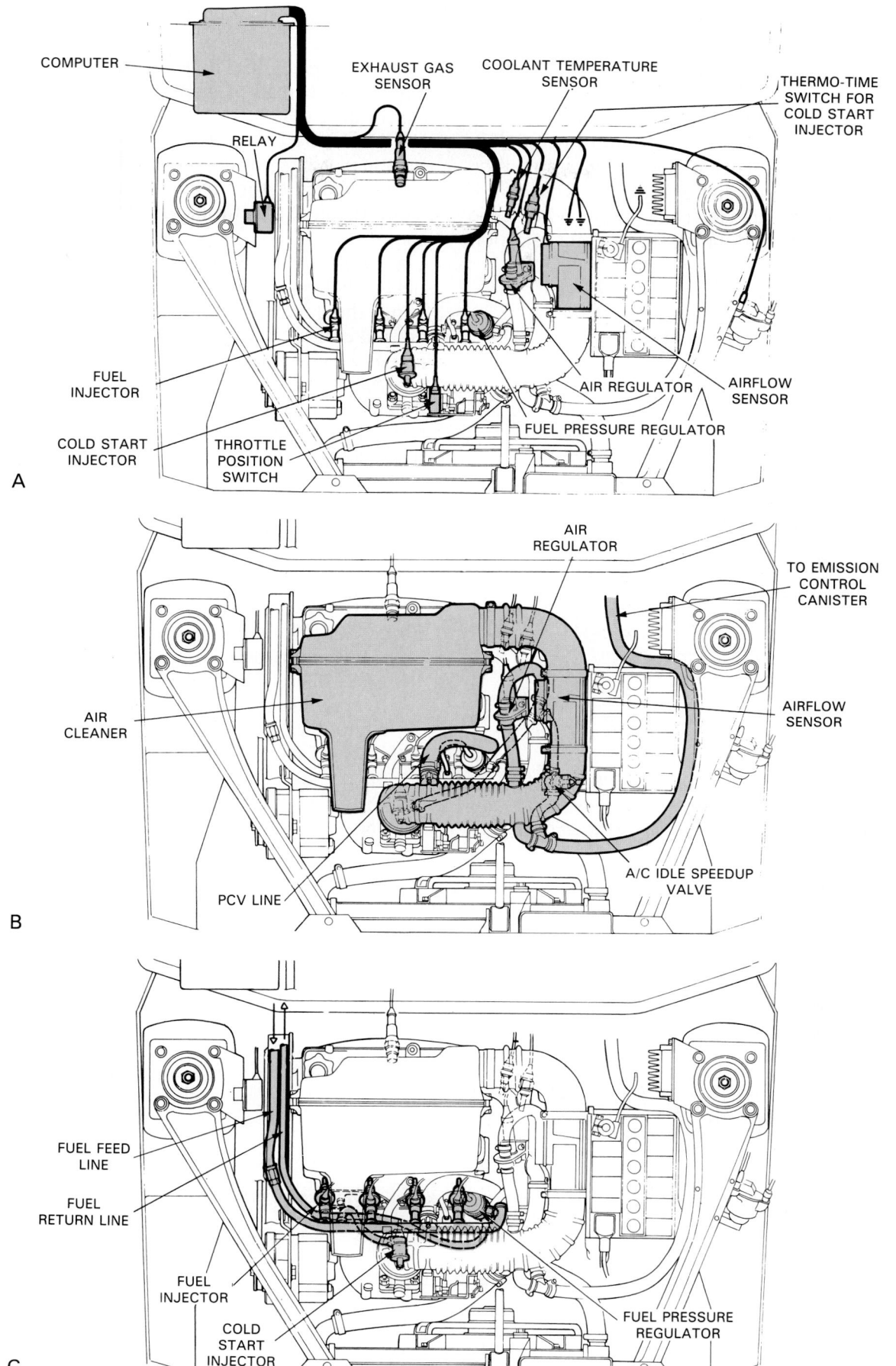

Fig. 21-29. Note systems of multi-point electronic fuel injection system. A — Sensor and control systems of EFI multi-point system. Sensors feed data to computer. Computer can then operate injectors and other components for maximum efficiency. B — Air delivery system parts. Note airflow sensor that monitors air volume entering engine. C — Fuel delivery system basically includes injectors, pressure regulator, lines, and hoses. Some systems use a cold start injector. (Lancia)

ELECTRONIC MULTI-POINT INJECTION

Electronic multi-point injection systems use a computer, engine sensors, and one solenoid injector for each engine cylinder. This is a very common type system on late model cars. Look at Fig. 21-29.

The operation of an electronic multi-point type system is similar to a modulated, single-point injection system covered earlier; however, fuel is injected at each intake port instead of at the top center of the intake manifold.

A *multi-point throttle body* assembly contains the throttle plates, throttle position sensor, but does NOT contain the injector valves. See upper right in Fig. 21-30. Its main function is to control airflow into the engine.

A *multi-point pressure regulator* is mounted in the fuel line before or after the injectors, Fig. 21-31. It performs the same function as the pressure regulator covered earlier. It maintains a constant pressure at the inlet to the injector valves by acting as a bypass branch.

A *fuel rail* feeds fuel to several of the injectors. It is a tubing assembly that connects the main fuel line to the inlet of each injector. Look at Figs. 21-30 and 21-31. Locate the fuel rail.

EFI multi-point injector

An EFI *multi-point injector valve* is usually press-fitted into the runner (port) in the intake manifold. Each injector is aimed to spray towards an engine intake valve. It is constructed something like an intermittent throttle body injector.

An EFI multi-point injector typically consists of:
1. ELECTRIC TERMINALS (electrical connection for completing circuit between injector coil and computer).
2. INJECTOR SOLENOID (armature and coil that opens and closes valve).
3. INJECTOR SCREEN (screen filter for trapping debris before it can enter injector nozzle).

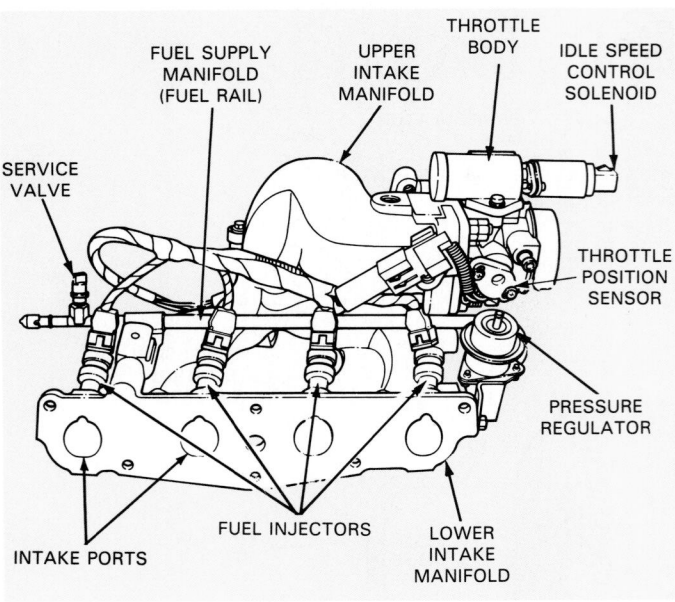

Fig. 21-30. A throttle body assembly is part of this multi-point injection system. Note how multi-point injectors install in intake runners or ports. Also note other parts. (Ford)

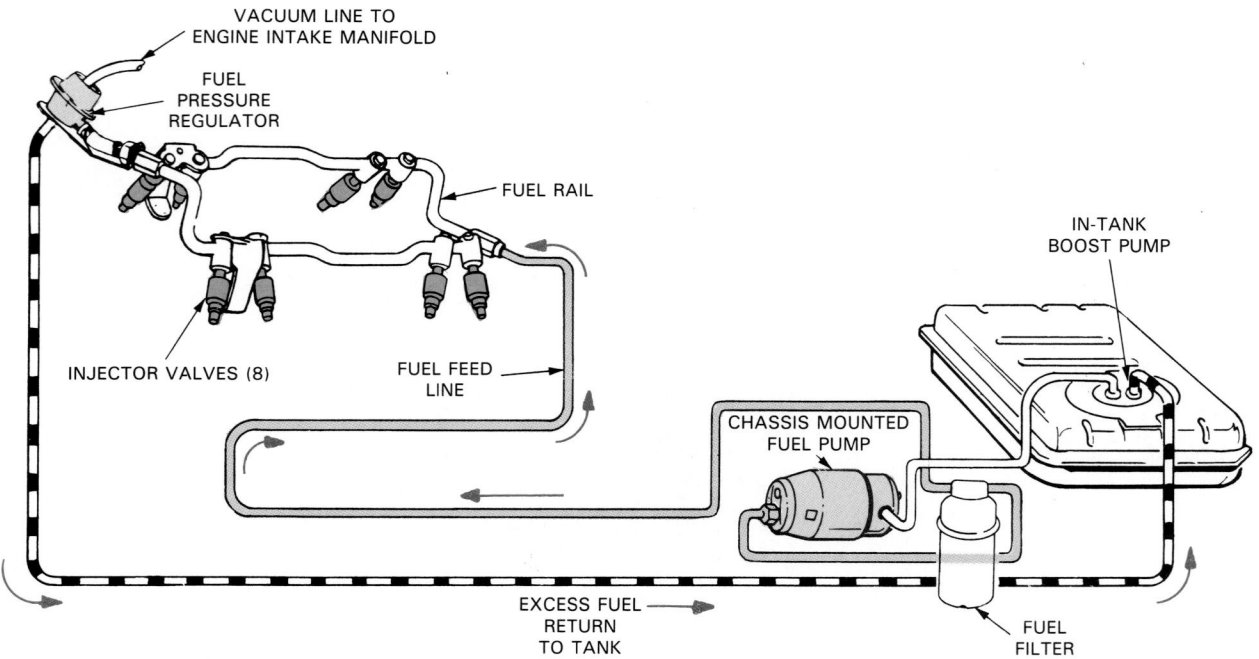

Fig. 21-31. Pressure regulator action. Fuel pump forces fuel into fuel rail, injectors, and regulator. Regulator allow excess fuel to flow back to fuel tank. Vacuum line to regulator causes fuel pressure to increase and decrease with changes in engine vacuum and load. (Cadillac)

4. NEEDLE VALVE (end of armature that seals on needle seat).
5. NEEDLE SEAT (round hole in end of injector that seals against needle valve tip).
6. INJECTOR SPRING (small spring that returns needle valve to closed position).
7. O-RING SEAL (rubber seal that fits around outside of injector body and seals in intake manifold).
8. INJECTOR NOZZLE (outlet of injector that produces fuel spray pattern).

Fig. 21-32 shows an EFI multi-point injector. Study this illustration carefully.

There are several variations of electronic multi-point injection. It is important that you understand the primary differences between each type system.

EFI (airflow sensing, multi-point)

An *airflow sensing multi-point EFI* uses an airflow sensor as a main control of the system. As shown in Fig. 21-33, an airflow sensor is placed at the inlet to the intake manifold. It and other engine sensors provide electrical data to the computer.

The **airflow sensor** is a flap-operated variable resistor, Fig. 21-34. Airflow through the sensor causes an air door (flap) to swing to one side. Since the air door is connected to a variable resistor, the amount of airflow into the engine is converted into an electrical signal for the computer.

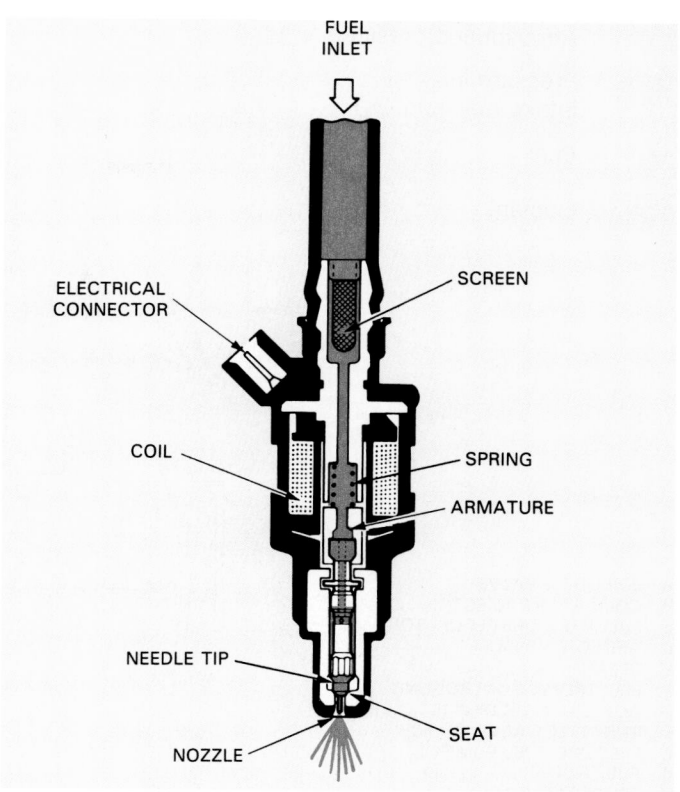

Fig. 21-32. Note basic parts of this electronic multi-point or port fuel injector. Solenoid opens injector when current flow through coil builds magnetic field and acts on armature. (Lancia)

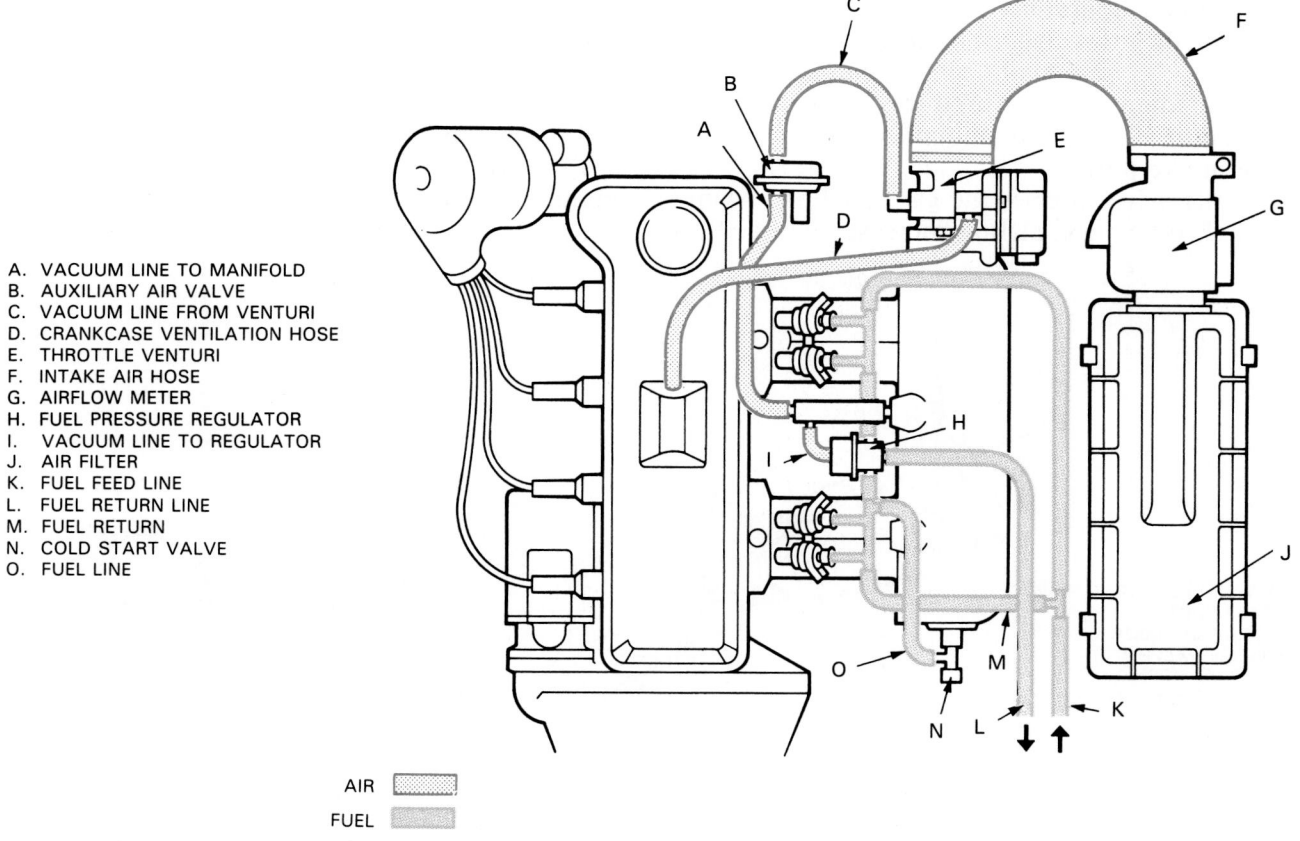

A. VACUUM LINE TO MANIFOLD
B. AUXILIARY AIR VALVE
C. VACUUM LINE FROM VENTURI
D. CRANKCASE VENTILATION HOSE
E. THROTTLE VENTURI
F. INTAKE AIR HOSE
G. AIRFLOW METER
H. FUEL PRESSURE REGULATOR
I. VACUUM LINE TO REGULATOR
J. AIR FILTER
K. FUEL FEED LINE
L. FUEL RETURN LINE
M. FUEL RETURN
N. COLD START VALVE
O. FUEL LINE

AIR
FUEL

Fig. 21-33. Top view of an airflow sensing multi-point gasoline injection system. Study location of basic parts. (Robert Bosch)

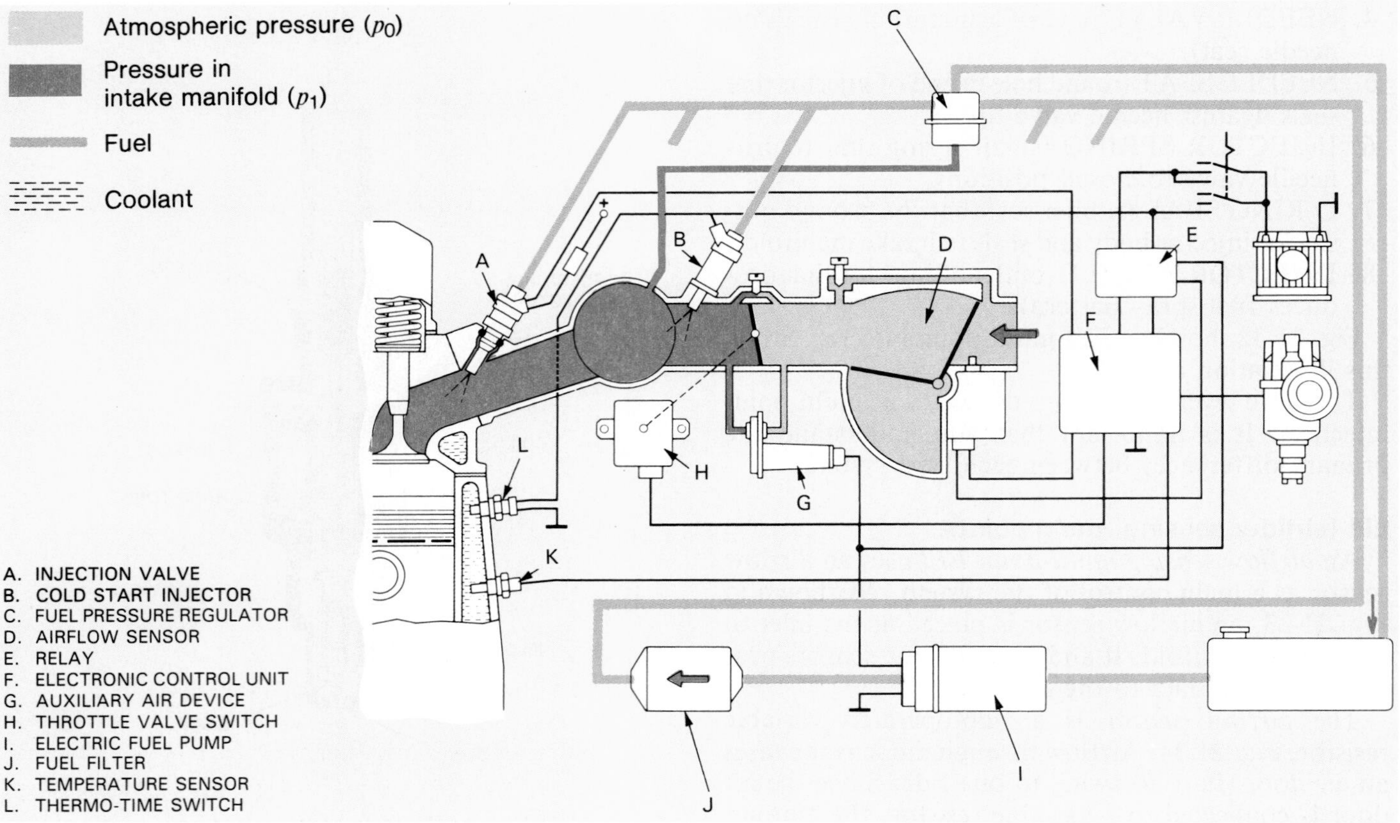

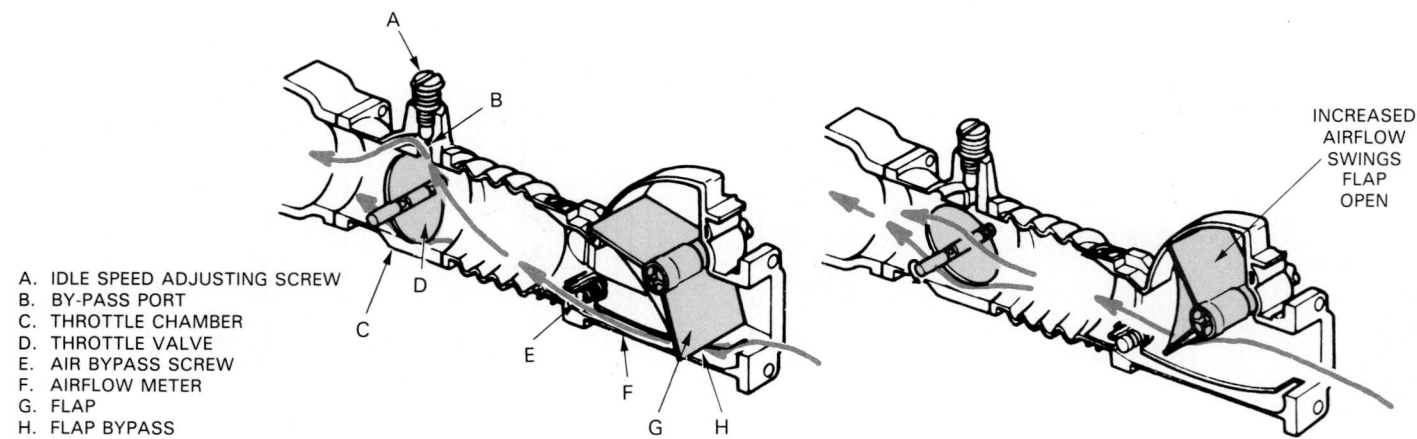

Legend (top left of figure):

- Atmospheric pressure (p_0)
- Pressure in intake manifold (p_1)
- Fuel
- Coolant

A. INJECTION VALVE
B. COLD START INJECTOR
C. FUEL PRESSURE REGULATOR
D. AIRFLOW SENSOR
E. RELAY
F. ELECTRONIC CONTROL UNIT
G. AUXILIARY AIR DEVICE
H. THROTTLE VALVE SWITCH
I. ELECTRIC FUEL PUMP
J. FUEL FILTER
K. TEMPERATURE SENSOR
L. THERMO-TIME SWITCH

Fig. 21-34. Diagram shows how each part is connected in airflow sensing EFI system. Airflow sensor is primary sensor. Also note use of cold start injector. (Robert Bosch)

Airflow sensor operation

When the throttle valve is closed (engine idling), the airflow meter door remains almost closed. See Fig. 21-35. The computer then produces a short injector pulse width. Only a small amount of fuel is injected into the intake ports.

When the driver presses the gas pedal and swings open the throttle plate, airflow increases. The airflow door is pushed out of the way, changing sensor resistance. The computer then increases injector pulse width for a richer mixture.

EFI (pressure sensing, multi-point)

Pressure sensing multi-point injection uses intake manifold pressure (vacuum) as a primary control of the system. Look at Fig. 21-36. A pressure sensor is

A. IDLE SPEED ADJUSTING SCREW
B. BY-PASS PORT
C. THROTTLE CHAMBER
D. THROTTLE VALVE
E. AIR BYPASS SCREW
F. AIRFLOW METER
G. FLAP
H. FLAP BYPASS

INCREASED AIRFLOW SWINGS FLAP OPEN

Fig. 21-35. Throttle valve controls engine speed and power output. Left — Throttle almost closed. Engine running slowly. Airflow sensor would detect little airflow. Computer would produce short injection pulse width for small injection quantity. Right — Throttle moved open for more power. Increased flow pushes sensor flap open. Computer would know to increase pulse width for richer mixture. (Nissan)

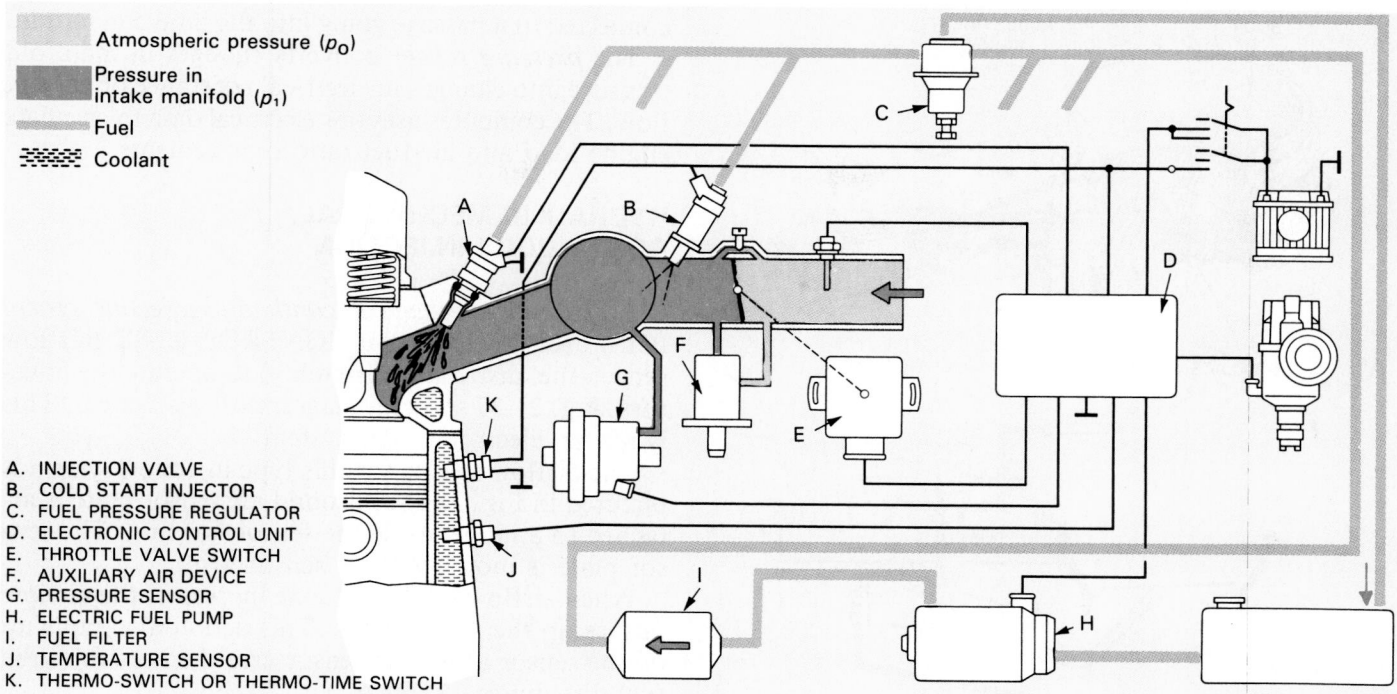

Atmospheric pressure (p_O)

Pressure in intake manifold (p_1)

Fuel

Coolant

A. INJECTION VALVE
B. COLD START INJECTOR
C. FUEL PRESSURE REGULATOR
D. ELECTRONIC CONTROL UNIT
E. THROTTLE VALVE SWITCH
F. AUXILIARY AIR DEVICE
G. PRESSURE SENSOR
H. ELECTRIC FUEL PUMP
I. FUEL FILTER
J. TEMPERATURE SENSOR
K. THERMO-SWITCH OR THERMO-TIME SWITCH

Fig. 21-36. Pressure sensing gasoline injection system uses intake manifold vacuum as main source of computer information. High intake manifold vacuum indicates a low load condition, needing a lean air-fuel mixture. Low intake vacuum would indicate a high load condition, requiring a richer mixture. Compare this system to the one in Fig. 21-34.

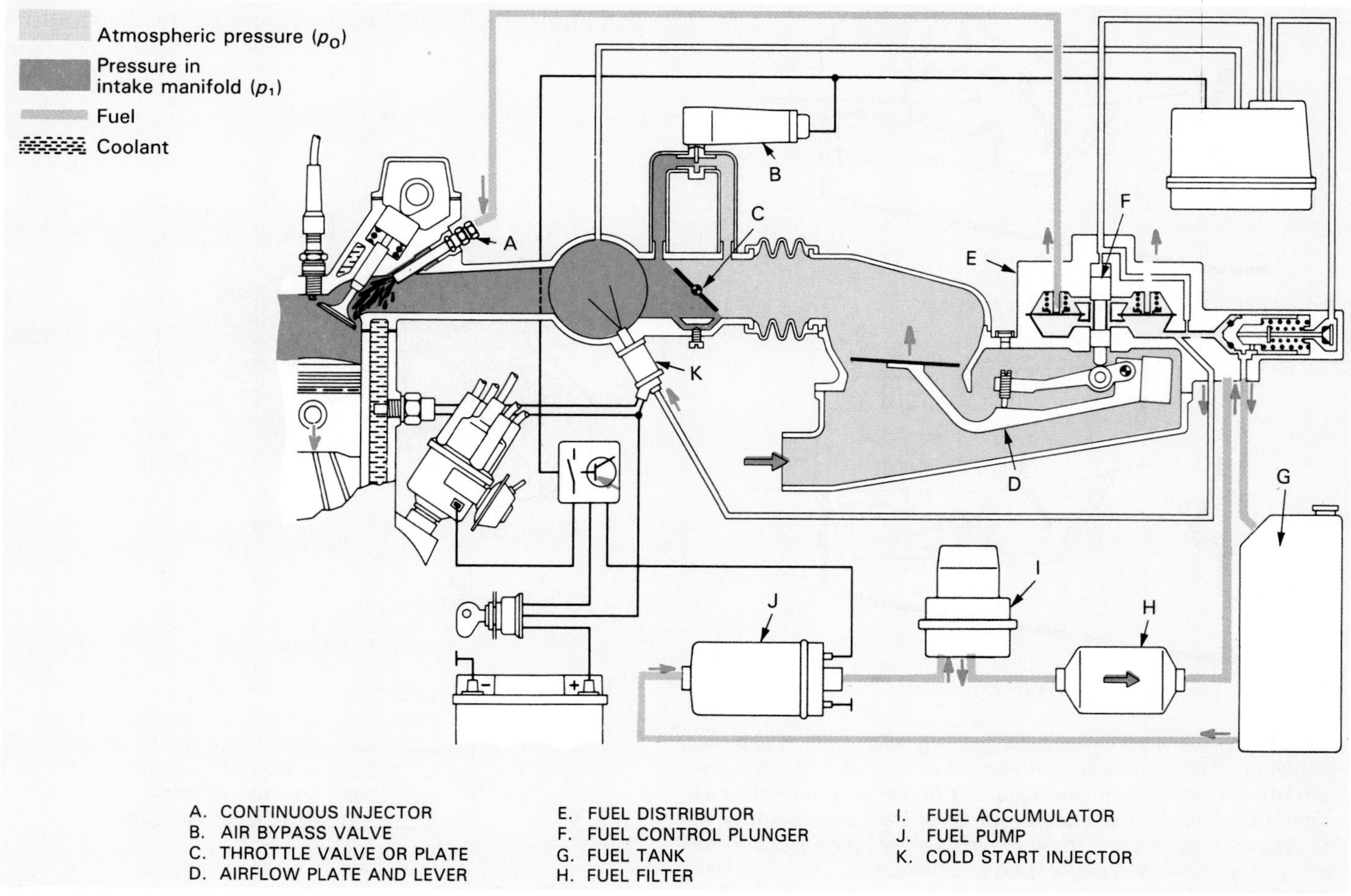

Atmospheric pressure (p_O)

Pressure in intake manifold (p_1)

Fuel

Coolant

A. CONTINUOUS INJECTOR
B. AIR BYPASS VALVE
C. THROTTLE VALVE OR PLATE
D. AIRFLOW PLATE AND LEVER
E. FUEL DISTRIBUTOR
F. FUEL CONTROL PLUNGER
G. FUEL TANK
H. FUEL FILTER
I. FUEL ACCUMULATOR
J. FUEL PUMP
K. COLD START INJECTOR

Fig. 21-37. Hydraulic-mechanical injection system uses mechanical airflow sensor to operate hydraulic fuel distributor assembly. Note that continuous injector is used to spray fuel into engine any time the engine is running. (Robert Bosch)

Gasoline Injection Fundamentals   269

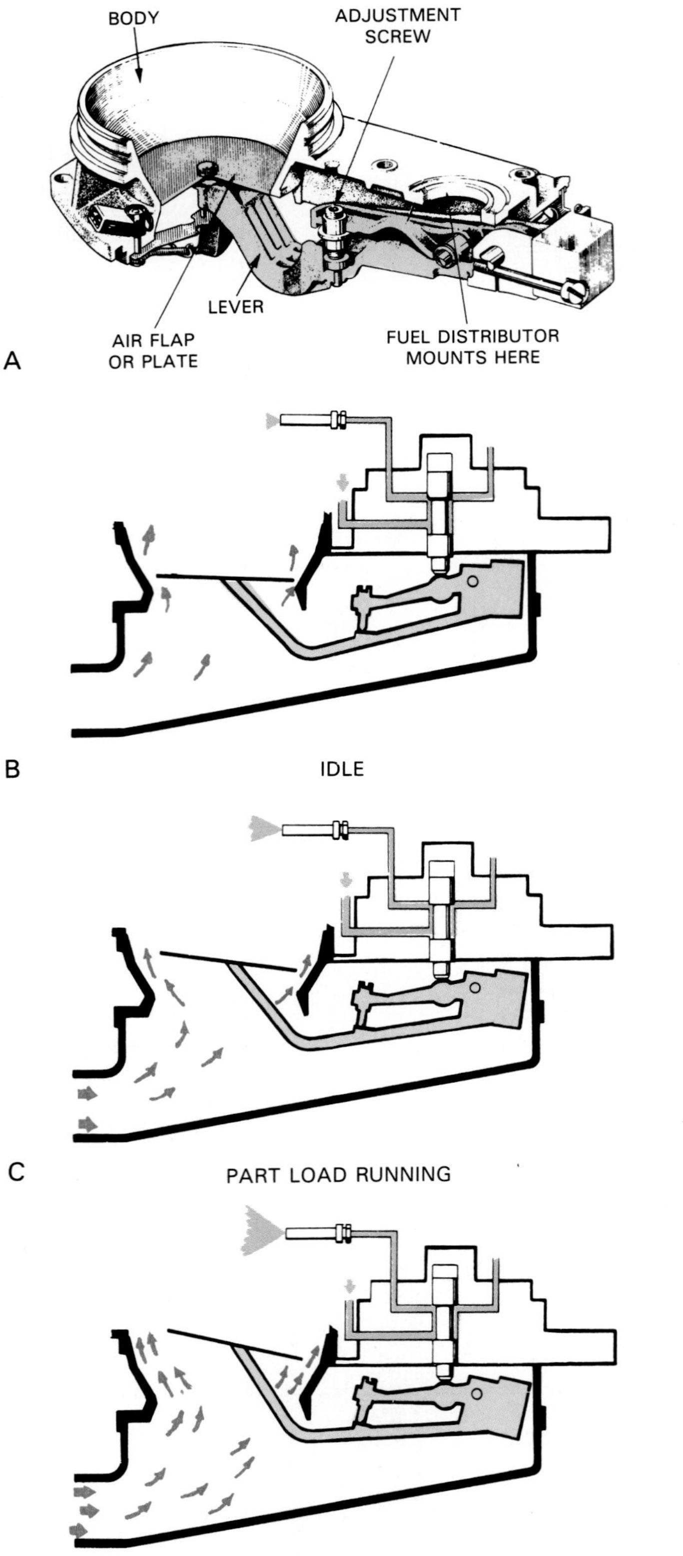

A

BODY • ADJUSTMENT SCREW • LEVER • AIR FLAP OR PLATE • FUEL DISTRIBUTOR MOUNTS HERE

B

IDLE

C

PART LOAD RUNNING

D

FULL LOAD RUNNING

Fig. 21-38. A — Airflow sensor has large disc-shaped flap that is hinged in airhorn. Disc operates lever arm. B — At idle, low airflow only moves sensor plate a little. Lever arm pushes up lightly on fuel control plunger for small injection quantity. C — At part load, more airflow moves sensor place and control plunger up more. More fuel sprays out injectors. D — Full load condition and high airflow pushes sensor plate up high. This opens fuel control plunger fully for maximum injection pressure and volume. (Robert Bosch)

connected to a passage going into the intake manifold.

The *pressure sensor* converts changes in manifold pressure into changes in electrical resistance or current flow. The computer uses this electrical data to calculate engine load and air-fuel ratio requirements.

HYDRAULIC-MECHANICAL, CONTINUOUS INJECTION

A *hydraulic-mechanical, continuous injection system* (CIS) uses a MIXTURE CONTROL UNIT (airflow sensor-fuel distributor assembly) to operate the injectors. Fig. 21-37 shows a diagram of this system. This is not an electronic type system.

The airflow sensor for this type injection system is pictured in Fig. 21-38. A round air sensor plate is attached to a hinge inside the sensor housing. The sensor plate is mounted on a sensor arm.

When airflow into the engine increases, the airflow pushes up the sensor plate. This action also pulls up on the sensor arm. The sensor arm then operates the fuel distributor. Refer to Fig. 21-39.

CIS fuel distributor

A *fuel distributor* is a hydraulically operated valve mechanism that controls fuel flow (pressure) to each CIS injector. See Figs. 21-38 and 21-39. The fuel control plunger is located in the center of the distributor.

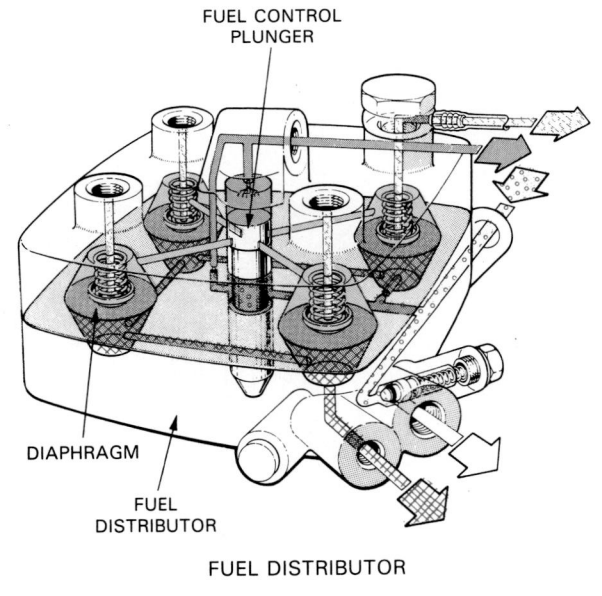

FUEL CONTROL PLUNGER • DIAPHRAGM • FUEL DISTRIBUTOR

FUEL DISTRIBUTOR

▭	LINE PRESSURE
▭	UPPER CHAMBER PRESSURE
▩	LOWER CHAMBER PRESSURE
▭	INJECTION PRESSURE
▬	CONTROL PRESSURE
▭	RETURN, NO PRESSURE

Fig. 21-39. Fuel distributor is complex set of pressure differentiating diaphragm valves. They assure that the same amount of fuel is sent to each injector. (Saab)

Fuel is fed from the plunger to spring-loaded diaphragms. The diaphragms compensate for pressure differences in each injection line. They help assure that the same amount of fuel is sent to each injector.

Note! A fuel distributor is only used in one type of CIS system. However, this is a common system found on many foreign cars.

Continuous fuel injector

A *continuous fuel injector* is simply a spring-loaded valve. It injects fuel ALL the TIME when the engine is running. See Fig. 21-40.

A spring holds the valve in a normally closed position. A filter in the injector traps dirt. The injector is usually push-fitted into plastic bushings in the cylinder head or intake manifold.

With the engine off, the injector spring holds the injector valve closed. This prevents fuel from dripping into the engine.

When the engine is cranked for starting, fuel pressure builds and pushes the injector valve open. A steady stream of gasoline then sprays toward each engine intake valve. The fuel is pulled into the engine when the intake valves open.

With CIS injectors, injection quantity (air-fuel ratio) is controlled by increasing or decreasing fuel pressure to the injectors.

Cold start injector

A *cold start injector* is an additional fuel injector valve used to supply extra gasoline for cold engine starting. Refer back to Figs. 21-36 and 21-37. Either a thermo-time switch or the system computer is used to operate the cold start injector.

A cold start injector can be used in electronic airflow sensing, electronic pressure sensing, and hydraulic-mechanical type multi-point systems. It is constructed like a conventional, solenoid type injector. One is pictured in Fig. 21-41.

Cold start injector operation

Fig. 21-42 shows a basic cold start injector-thermo-time switch circuit. It traces cold start valve action.

When the sensor detects a cold engine, the switch closes to energize the cold start injector. The cold start injector and the other injectors all spray fuel into the intake manifold. Like a carburetor choke, this provides a very rich mixture to sustain cold engine operation.

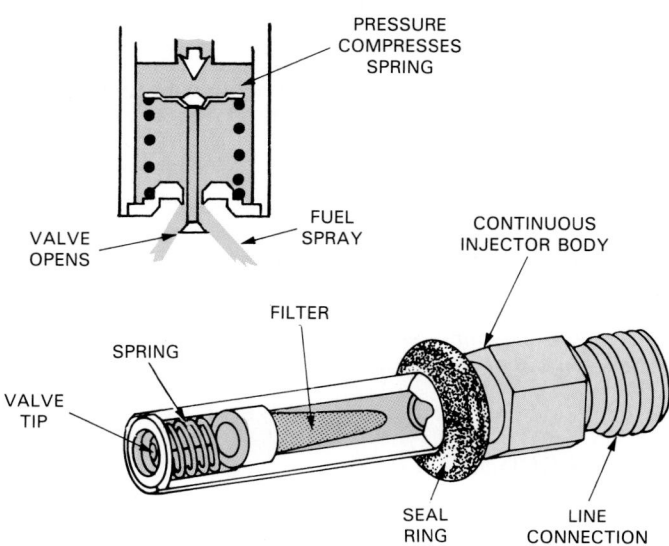

Fig. 21-40. Continuous type injector is simply spring-loaded valve. With enough fuel pressure, injector valve opens and fuel sprays into intake port of engine.

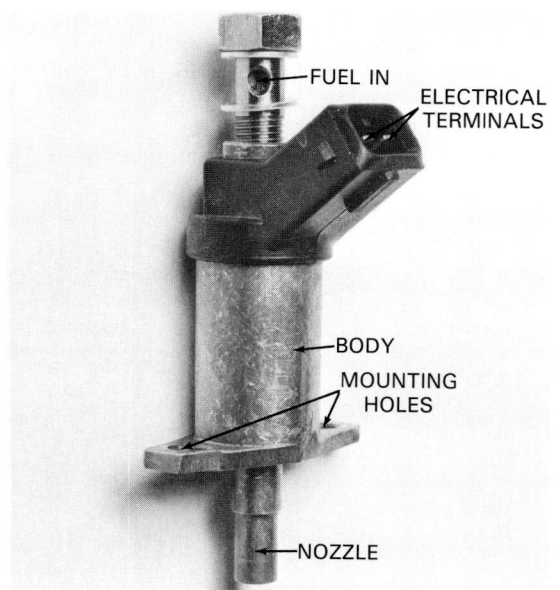

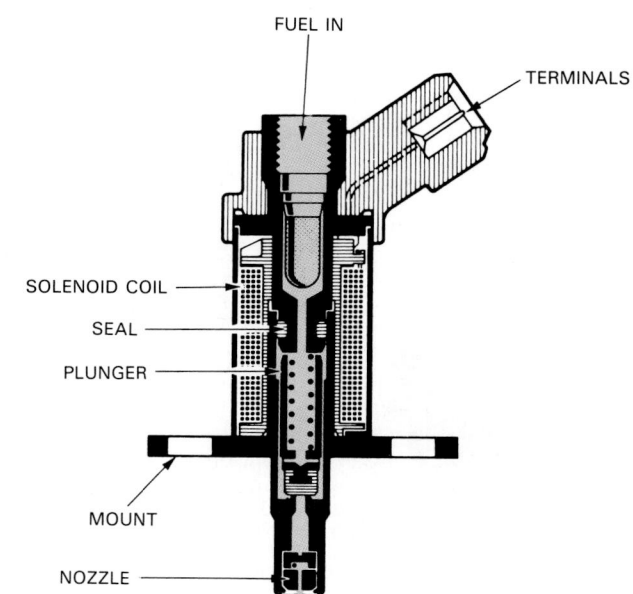

Fig. 21-41. Cold start injector is like injector for EFI system. It is a solenoid type injector valve. Note parts and construction. (Saab)

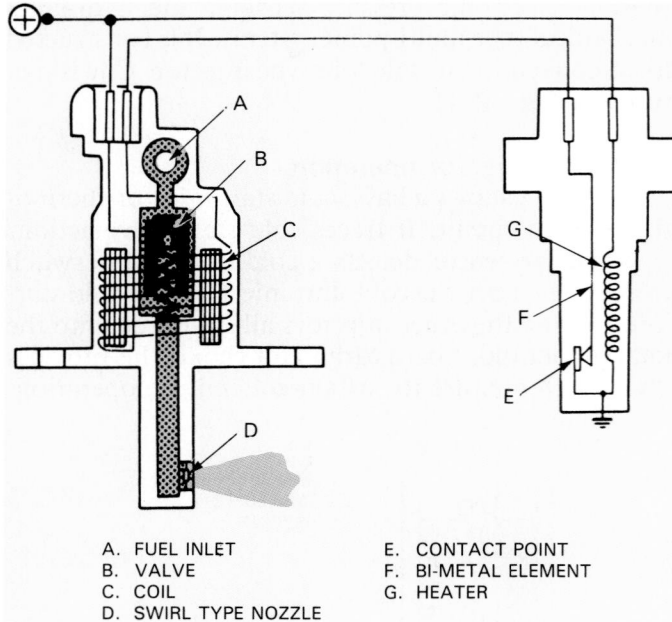

A. FUEL INLET
B. VALVE
C. COIL
D. SWIRL TYPE NOZZLE

E. CONTACT POINT
F. BI-METAL ELEMENT
G. HEATER

Fig. 21-42. Basic cold start injector, thermo-time switch circuit. Thermo-time switch energizes injector when engine temperature is low enough. Cold start injector then sprays extra fuel into engine to help keep the cold engine running smoothly. When engine warms enough, thermo-time switch opens to shut off injector. Heating element in switch assures that injector stays on a short period of time, even if engine is very cold.

FUEL ACCUMULATOR

A *fuel accumulator* can be used in an injection system to dampen pressure pulses. One is shown in Fig. 21-43. The accumulator may also maintain pressure when the system is shut down. This aids engine restarting.

OTHER INJECTION SYSTEMS

There are other fuel injection systems besides those discussed in this chapter. They use the same basic prin-ciples that have already been explained.

For complete details of a particular gasoline injection system, refer to a factory service manual. It will detail the operation of the specific system. Fuel injection systems vary.

Note! Refer to Chapters 74, 75, and 76 for more information on computers.

KNOW THESE TERMS

Gasoline injection system, Fuel injection system, Single-point, TBI, Multi-point, Port injection, EFI, Timed injection, Modulated injection, Continuous injection, Group injection, Fuel pressure regulator, Fuel injector, Throttle valve, Computer, ECU, Exhaust gas or oxygen sensor, Manifold pressure sensor, Throttle position sensor, Engine temperature sensor, Airflow sensor, Inlet air temperature sensor, Crankshaft position sensor, Digital signal, Analog signal, Open loop, Closed loop, Pulse width, Idle air control valve, Throttle positioner, Fuel rail, Fuel distributor, Cold start injector, Thermo-time switch, Fuel accumulator.

REVIEW QUESTIONS

1. A gasoline injection system uses pressure from an _____ _____ _____ to spray fuel into the engine _____ _____ .
2. List seven possible advantages of a gasoline injection system over a carburetor system.
3. Explain the difference between single-point (throttle body) and multi-point (port) injection systems.
4. Gasoline injection systems use direct injection; diesels use indirect injection. True or False?
5. This is the most common and modern type of gasoline injection system.
   a. Mechanical fuel injection.
   b. Hydraulic fuel injection.
   c. Electronic fuel injection.
   d. Pneumatic fuel injection.

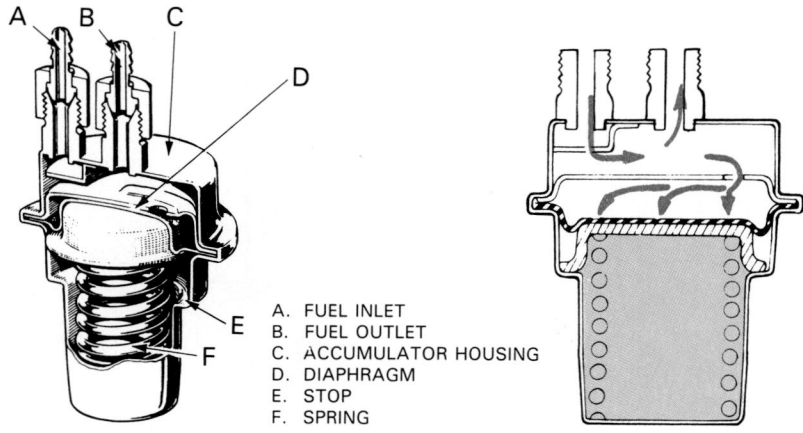
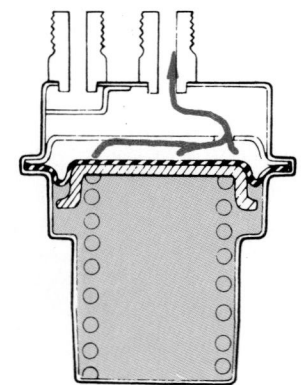

A. FUEL INLET
B. FUEL OUTLET
C. ACCUMULATOR HOUSING
D. DIAPHRAGM
E. STOP
F. SPRING

Fig. 21-43. Fuel accumulator is simply a spring-loaded diaphragm. It dampens pressure pulsations in system. It also maintains fuel pressure when engine is shut off. Left — Note basic parts of fuel accumulator. Center — With engine running, fuel pressure compresses diaphragm spring. Right — When engine is shut off, spring pushes up on diaphragm to hold pressure in system. (Volvo)

6. This type of gasoline injection pulses the injectors open and closed independently of the engine valve action.
   a. Timed injection.
   b. Intermittent injection.
   c. Continuous injection.
   d. Bank injection.
7. List the parts typically included in an EFI fuel delivery system.
8. How does an EFI injector open and close?
9. Explain the action of an EFI system throttle valve.
10. An engine _____ is an electrical device that changes circuit resistance or voltage with a change in a condition (temperature, pressure, position of part, etc.).
11. Define the term "EFI computer."
12. An _____ _____ _____ , also called _____ _____ measures the oxygen content in the engine's exhaust system as a means of checking _____ _____ .
13. When the intake manifold pressure sensor detects high pressure (low vacuum), the computer would know that a _____ mixture is needed for load conditions.
14. A throttle position sensor is a _____ _____ connected to the _____ _____ _____ .
15. Which of these is NOT a typical EFI system sensor?
   a. Exhaust back pressure sensor.
   b. Throttle position sensor.
   c. Engine temperature sensor.
   d. Air inlet temperature sensor.
16. Explain the difference between sensor analog and digital signals.
17. When an EFI system is in open loop, the computer uses stored information to operate the system. True or False?
18. When an EFI system is in closed loop, the computer uses engine sensor information to control the system. True or False?
19. Define the term "injector pulse width."
20. List and explain the six major parts of a TBI unit.
21. What are the main differences between the throttle body for multi-point injection and single-point injection?
22. An EFI multi-point injector fits into the _____ or _____ in the _____ manifold.
23. List and explain the eight major parts of an EFI multi-point injector.
24. Describe the mixture control unit in a hydraulic-mechanical, CIS.
25. A continuous fuel injector is a spring-loaded fuel valve that does NOT use an electric coil. True or False?

ACTIVITIES FOR CHAPTER 21

1. Using a shop manual on any modern fuel-injected vehicle secured from your instructor, study the section on fuel injector operation and be prepared to demonstrate to your instructor your understanding of how the injectors are controlled.
2. Develop a drawing of the fuel injection system for a gasoline engine and produce an overhead transparency from it. Using the transparency or handouts, explain to the class how the system works.
3. Prepare simple sketches to show the basic difference between a carbureted fuel system and a throttle body injection fuel system.

Gasoline Injection Diagnosis and Repair

After studying this chapter, you will be able to:
- ☐ Diagnose typical gasoline injection system problems.
- ☐ Measure fuel pressure regulator output.
- ☐ Test both electronic and continuous types of fuel injectors.
- ☐ Interpret fuel injector spray patterns.
- ☐ Describe the use of specialized EFI system analyzers.
- ☐ Explain the self-diagnostic mode found on many EFI systems.
- ☐ Use a service manual when making basic adjustments on gasoline injection systems.
- ☐ Cite safety rules for injection system service and use safe procedures.

As you have learned, several types of gasoline injection systems are used by auto makers. Most types have similar parts (injectors, computer, sensors).

This chapter describes the most common symptoms, tests, and adjustments for the major parts of gasoline injection systems.

GASOLINE INJECTION PROBLEM DIAGNOSIS

To diagnose problems in a gasoline injection system, you must use:
1. Your knowledge of system operation.
2. Basic troubleshooting skills.

CARBURETOR	GASOLINE INJECTION SYSTEM
1. Choke	1. Engine temperature sensor, manifold temperature sensor, or cold start injector
2. Float	2. Fuel pressure regulator, electric fuel pump
3. Idle circuit	3. Air bypass valve, idle control motor, engine speed sensor
4. Accelerator pump	4. Throttle position switch, manifold pressure sensor
5. Fast idle cam	5. Throttle positioner or air bypass valve
6. Power valve or metering rod	6. Manifold pressure sensor, throttle position switch, oxygen sensor
7. Fuel metering jets or mixture control solenoid	7. Injector valves, fuel pressure regulator
8. Throttle valves	8. Throttle valves
9. Carburetor body	9. Throttle body
10. Venturi and main discharge	10. Airflow sensor
11. System computer (if used)	11. System computer
12. System sensors (if used)	12. System sensors

Fig. 22-1. Study similar functions between parts of a carburetor and gasoline injection system. This will help you when trying to troubleshoot injection system problems.

3. A service manual.

As you try to locate problems, visualize the operation of the four subsystems (air, fuel, sensor, control). Relate the function of each subsystem component to the problem. This will let you eliminate several possible problem sources and concentrate on others.

It is possible to compare a carburetor fuel system with a gasoline injection system. Several parts in each system perform the same function. Fig. 22-1 gives a chart comparing the two.

Verify the problem

Before you test the system, verify the problem or complaint. Make sure that the customer or service writer has accurately described the symptoms.

Never repair a gasoline injection system until after you have checked all possible problem sources. The ignition system, for example, normally causes more problems than an injection system.

Inspecting injection system

A general inspection of the engine and related components will sometimes locate gasoline injection troubles. Look at Fig. 22-2. Check the condition of all hoses, wires, and other parts. Look for fuel leaks, vacuum leaks, kinked lines, loose electrical connections, and other troubles. Spend more time checking the components most likely to cause the particular symptoms. See Fig. 22-3.

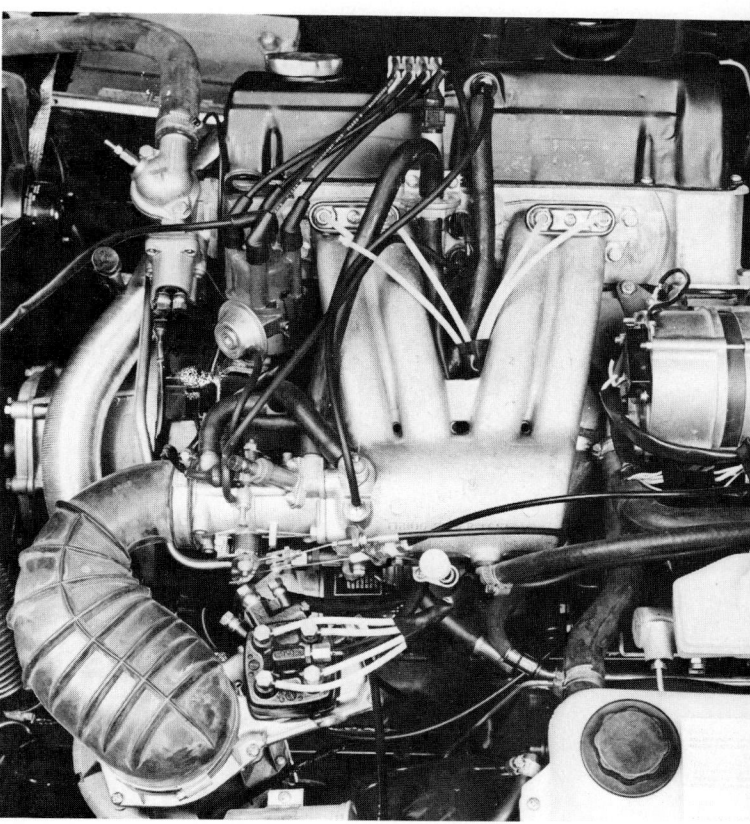

Fig. 22-2. Close inspection of engine compartment is important. Look for loose wires, leaking hoses, and other obvious troubles. (Saab)

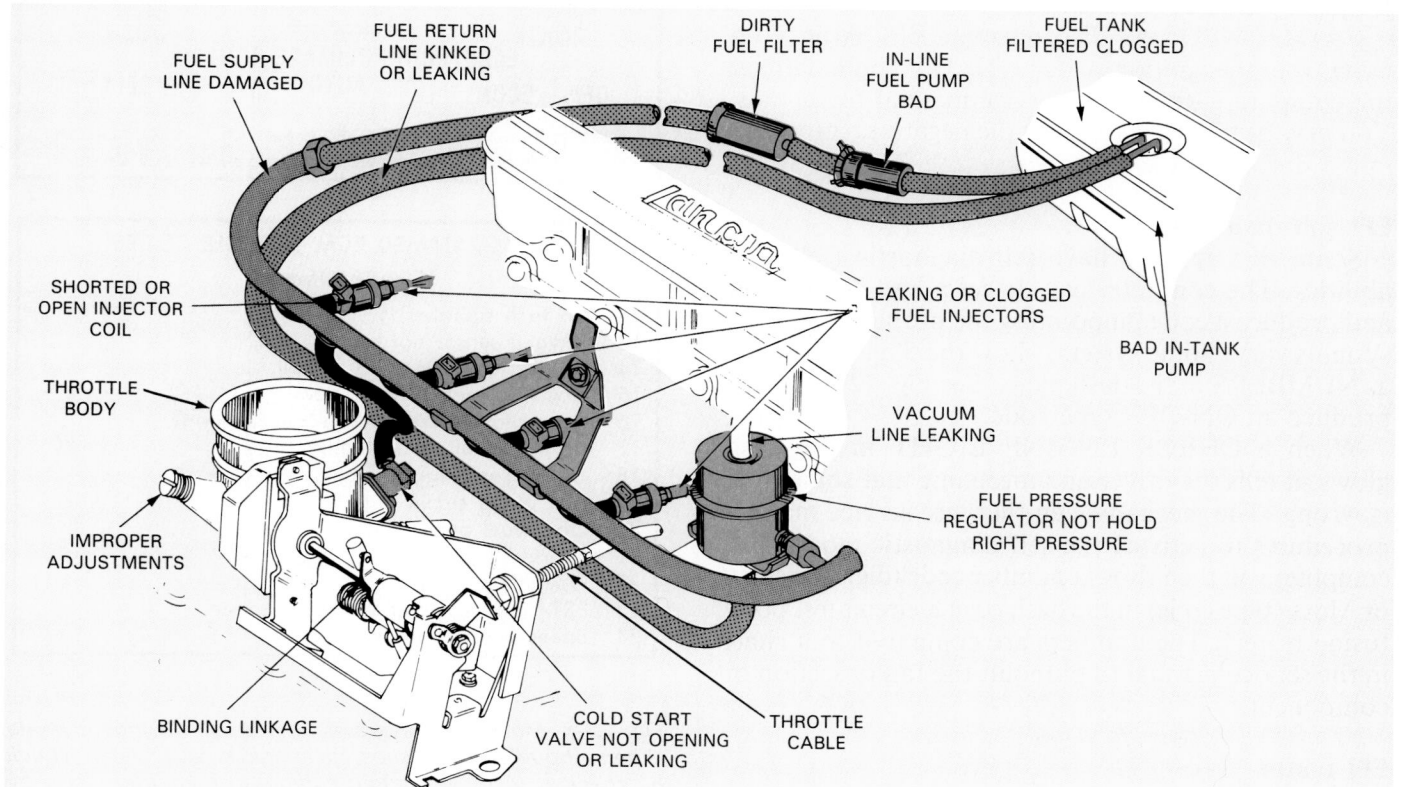

Fig. 22-3. After evaluating symptoms, try to narrow the list of components that could be at fault. Visualize operation of each part and do not overlook common problems: clogged fuel filter, for example. (Fiat)

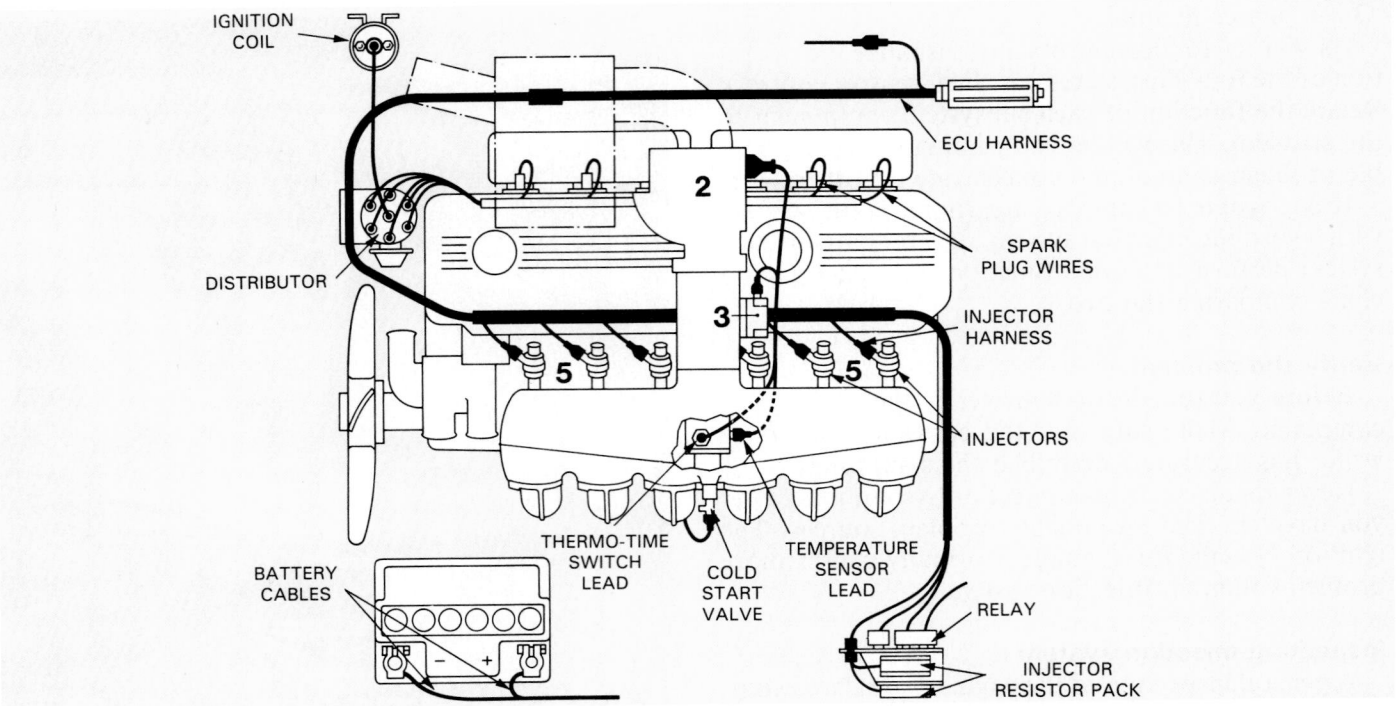

Fig. 22-4. When diagnosing problems in EFI systems, check electrical connections closely. One loose or disconnected wire could upset system operation.

With an EFI system, you may need to disconnect and check the terminals of the wiring harness. Look at Fig. 22-4. Inspect them for rust, corrosion, or burning. High resistance at terminal connections is a frequent cause of problems.

CAUTION! Do not disconnect an EFI harness terminal with the ignition switch ON. This could damage the computer. Refer to a service manual for details. You may be told to disconnect the negative battery terminal during EFI service.

EFI self-diagnosis

Some EFI systems have self-diagnostic (self-test) abilities. The computer can detect a bad component and produce a code pinpointing the problem. Specific systems vary. Some systems show the diagnostic code as NUMBERS in the dash panel. See Fig. 22-5. Others produce an ON-OFF type code.

When a CHECK ENGINE LIGHT in the dash glows, it tells the driver and mechanic that something is wrong. The mechanic can then use service manual procedures to activate the self-diagnostic mode. The computer will then show a number code (digital display or Morse type code) in the dash or at a circuit test point (using meter). The numbers are compared to a chart in the service manual to pinpoint the faulty section or component.

EFI tester

When the electronic fuel injection system does not have a self-diagnostic function, an EFI TESTER can be used to locate system troubles. Look at Fig. 22-6.

PROGRAMMED ECM TROUBLE CODES	
Code	Circuit Affected
12	No tach signal.
13	Oxygen sensor not ready.
14	Shorted coolant sensor circuit.
15	Open coolant sensor circuit.
16	Generator output voltage out of range.
17	Crank signal circuit high.
18	Open crank signal circuit.
19	Fuel pump circuit high.
20	Open fuel pump circuit.
21	Shorted TPS circuit.
22	Open TPS circuit.
23	EST/By-pass circuit shorted or open.
24	Speed sensor failure.

Fig. 22-5. Modern EFI systems have a self-diagnostic mode. When a trouble light flashes, mechanic knows system should be checked. After activating computer, computer will show a number code in dash. A — Dash number indicates trouble. B — Partial list of trouble code from one service manual. (Cadillac)

The tester, also called an EFI analyzer, is connected to the wiring harness of the system.

An EFI tester uses indicator lights and sometimes a digital meter (volt-ohmmeter-milliammeter) to check system operation. The technician refers to the instructions with the tester and uses indicator light action to make various tests. The digital meter readings must be compared to specifications. If a voltage, resistance, or current level is NOT within specs, the technician must know what repairs are needed.

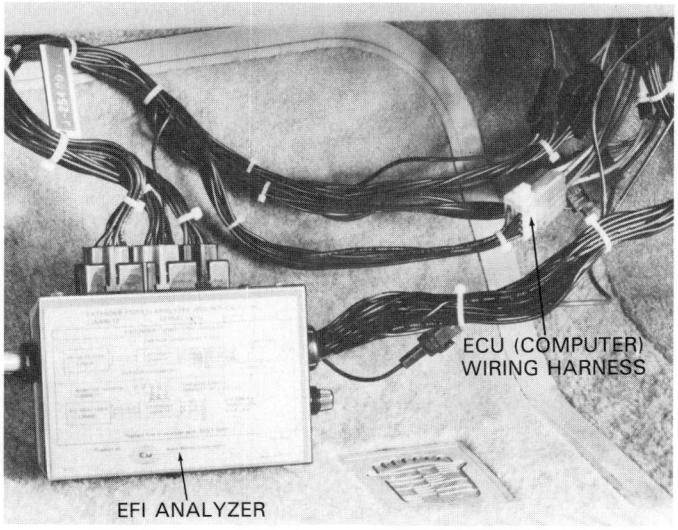

Fig. 22-6. EFI analyzer connects to main wiring harness for injection system. Special instructions with tester are used to find problem source. (Kent-Moore Tools)

Oscilloscope tests

An *oscilloscope* can sometimes be used to test or view the electrical waveforms (voltage values) at the EFI injectors. This provides a quick and easy way of diagnosing injector, wiring harness, and computer problems. For information on oscilloscopes, see Chapter 43.

FUEL PRESSURE REGULATOR SERVICE

A faulty *fuel pressure regulator* can cause an extremely rich or lean mixture. If the output pressure is high, too much fuel will spray out of the injectors, causing a rich mixture. If the regulator bypasses too much fuel to the tank (low pressure), not enough fuel will spray out each injector. This causes a lean mixture.

RELIEVING EFI SYSTEM PRESSURE

DANGER! Always relieve fuel pressure before disconnecting any EFI fuel line. Many gasoline injection systems maintain fuel pressure (as high as 50 psi or 345 kPa), even when the engine is NOT running. At this pressure, fuel could spray out with great force, causing eye injury or a fire!

Some EFI systems have a special *relief valve* for bleeding pressure back to the fuel tank; or the pressure regulator may allow pressure relief. Look at Fig. 22-7.

When a relief valve or a pressure regulator relief are NOT provided, remove the fuse for the fuel pump or disconnect its wires. Start and idle the engine. When the engine stalls from lack of fuel, the pressure has been removed from the system. It is then safe to work.

Testing fuel pressure regulator

Although exact procedures vary, you can test a fuel pressure regulator with a pressure gauge, Fig. 22-8.

Connect the gauge into the line to the pressure regulator. Start the engine and note the pressure gauge reading. If higher or lower than specs, the pressure regulator may be bad.

With low fuel pressure, check the fuel pump and fuel filters BEFORE replacing the regulator. A bad electric fuel pump or partially clogged filter could be lowering fuel pressure.

High pressure is commonly due to a bad pressure regulator.

For more information on testing fuel pumps, filters, and other fuel supply system parts, refer back to Chapter 18.

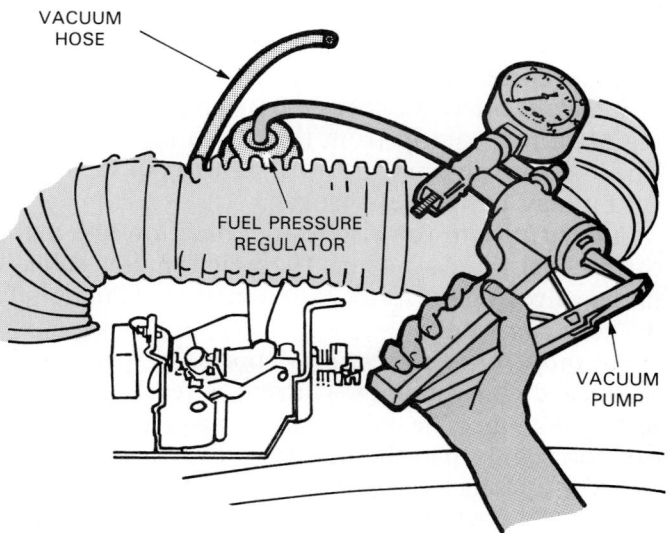

Fig. 22-7. Bleed off system pressure before working on system. When vacuum-operated pressure regulator is used, applying vacuum to regulator will relieve fuel pressure. Fuel flows back to fuel tank.   (Fiat)

Fuel pressure regulator replacement

With single-point injection, the fuel pressure regulator is normally located on the throttle body assembly. With multi-point injection, the pressure regulator is normally located on a branch connected to the fuel manifold (rail) or injectors. Look at Fig. 22-9. Replace a fuel pressure regulator according to service manual directions.

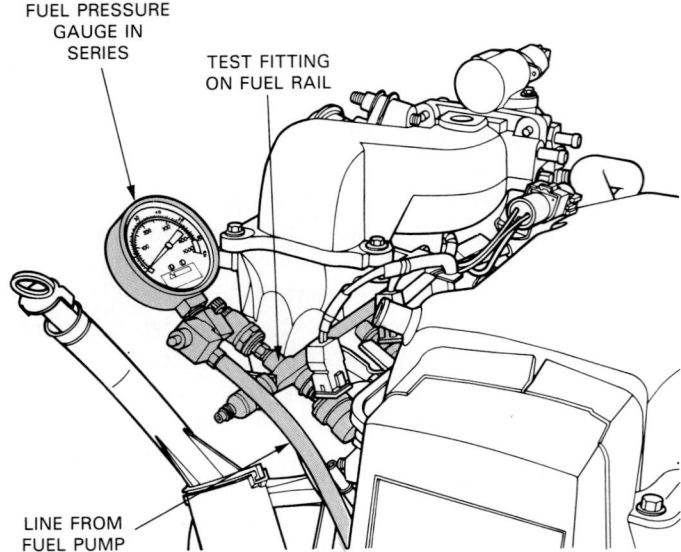

Fig. 22-8. To check pressure regulator, fuel pump, and filters, connect pressure gauge before injectors. Pressure should be within specs. If not, check filters and pump before replacing regulator. (Ford)

INJECTOR PROBLEMS

A *bad injector* can cause a wide range of problems: rough idle, hard starting, poor fuel economy, engine miss. It is very important that each fuel injector provide the correct fuel spray pattern.

A *leaking injector* richens the fuel mixture by allowing extra fuel to drip from the closed injector valve. The injector valve may be worn or dirty, or the return spring may be weak or broken.

A *dirty injector* can also restrict fuel flow and make the air-fuel ratio too lean. If foreign matter collects in the valve, a poor spray pattern and inadequate fuel delivery can result.

An *inoperative EFI injector* normally has shorted or opened coil windings. Current is reaching the injector, but since the coil is bad, a magnetic field cannot form and open the injector valve.

A continuous injector that does not use a solenoid will usually operate, but may have other problems. It may have a poor spray pattern or weak spring (incorrect opening pressure).

SINGLE-POINT INJECTOR SERVICE

You can quickly check the operation of a single-point (throttle body) injection system by WATCHING the fuel spray pattern in the throttle body. Remove the air cleaner. With the engine cranking (no-start problem) or running, each injector should form a rapidly pulsing spray of fuel.

Testing TBI injectors

If the TBI injector does not spray fuel (already

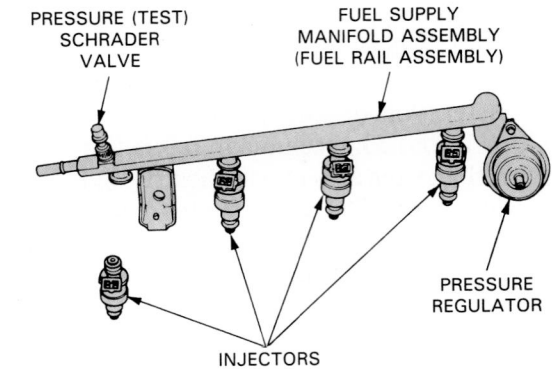

Fig. 22-9. Note location of pressure regulator and service valve on this multi-point injection fuel rail.

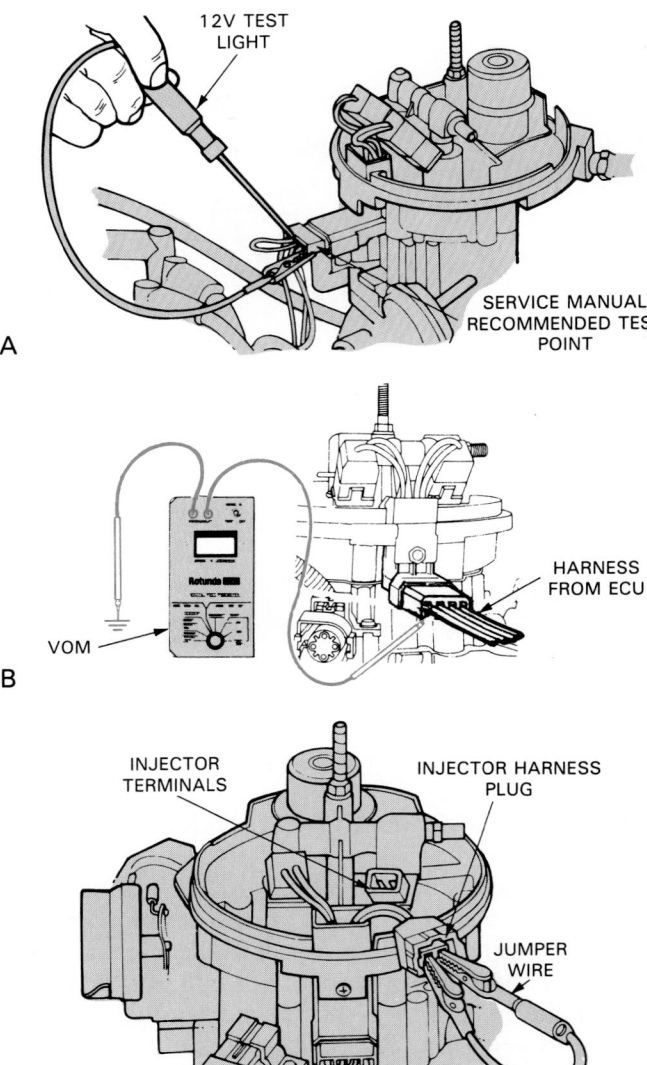

Fig. 22-10. Follow service manual directions when checking EFI system voltages and resistance. An incorrect connection or meter setting could damage parts. A — Checking for supply voltage to injector from computer. B — Measuring exact supply voltage with digital VOM. C — Jumper wire allows a check of circuit resistance. Ohmmeter can be used at other end of harness. (Ford Motor Co.)

checked system pressure), follow service manual procedures to test for power to the injector solenoid. Fig. 22-10 illustrates some simple tests recommended by one auto maker.

NO POWER (current) to the injector would indicate a problem with the wiring harness or computer (ECU).

If you have power, but NO FUEL SPRAY PATTERN, then the injector may be bad. Make sure you have adequate fuel pressure before condemning a fuel injector.

Replacing TBI injectors

Although exact procedures vary with throttle body design, there are a few rules to follow when replacing a TBI injector. These rules include:

1. Relieve system fuel pressure before removing any throttle body component.
2. Disconnect the negative battery cable.
3. Label hoses and wires before removal, Fig. 22-11.
4. Avoid damage to the throttle body housing when pulling or prying out the injector, Fig. 22-12.
5. Install new rubber O-rings. You may need to lubricate the O-ring with approved lubricant to aid new injector installation.
6. Double-check that you have installed all injector washers and O-rings correctly.
7. Push injector into the throttle body by hand. Avoid

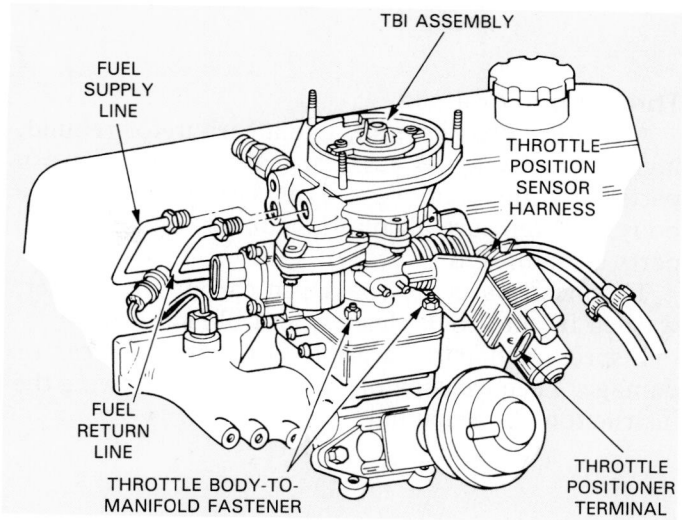

Fig. 22-11. When removing throttle body, label wires and hoses. Unscrew four fasteners and lift off unit. When installing, double-check connection of wires and hoses. Torque the fasteners properly using a crisscross pattern. (Renault)

using a hammer or pliers. You may damage the new injector. Look at Fig. 22-12.
8. Make sure the injector is fully seated in the throttle body. Normally, a tab must fit into a notch, assuring correct alignment.
9. Check for fuel leaks after TBI injector installation. Test drive the car.

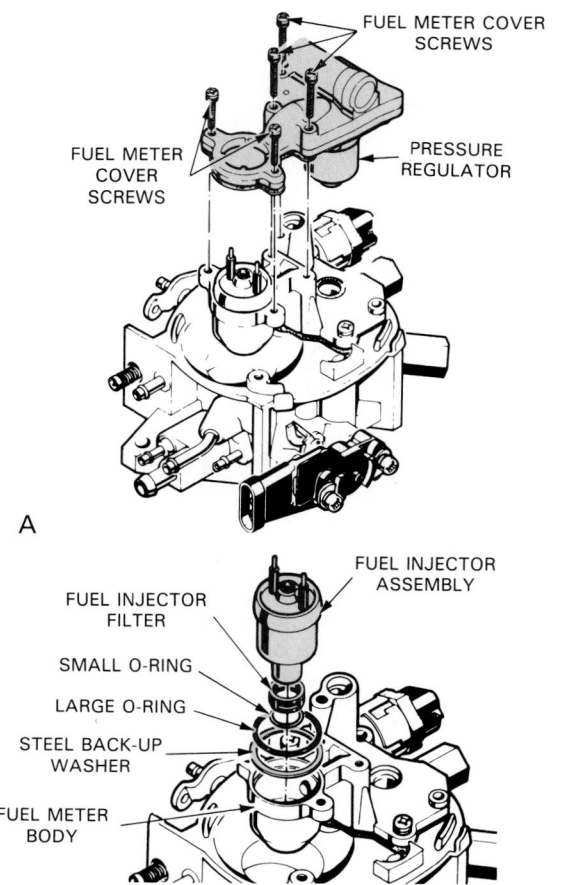

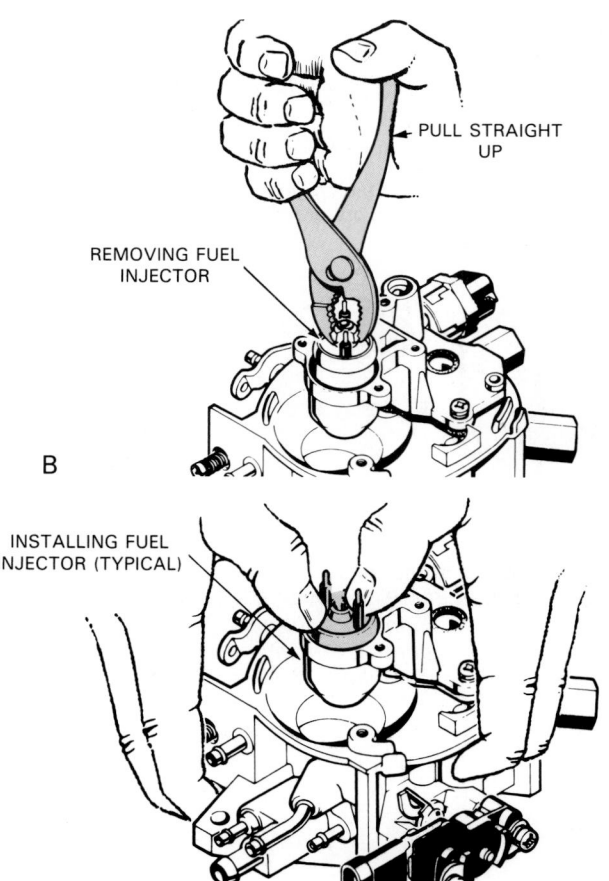

Fig. 22-12. Basic procedure for removal of TBI injector. A — Unscrew fasteners holding fuel metering body. Lift off while keeping screw lengths organized. B — Use pliers to pull out old injector. C — If needed, use new O-rings and washers. D — Carefully align and push injector into throttle body with your thumbs. (General Motors Corp.)

Throttle body rebuild

A *throttle body rebuild,* like a carburetor rebuild, involves replacing all gaskets, seals, and other worn parts. You must remove and disassemble the throttle body, making sure all plastic, rubber, and electrical parts are removed.

The metal parts are soaked in carburetor cleaner, washed in cold soak cleaner, and blown dry.

Inspect each part carefully for signs of wear or damage. Then, reassemble the TBI unit following the instructions in a manual.

DANGER! Carburetor cleaner is a very powerful solvent. Wear eye protection and rubber gloves when working this type of cleaner. Follow the directions on the solvent label in case of an accident.

Chapter 20, Carburetor Diagnosis, Service, Repair, covers subjects related to rebuilding a throttle body assembly. It covers solvent use, mounting the unit on a holding fixture, and other procedures.

Install the throttle body on the engine as you would a carburetor. Use a new base plate gasket. Tighten the hold-down fasteners equally and to the proper torque.

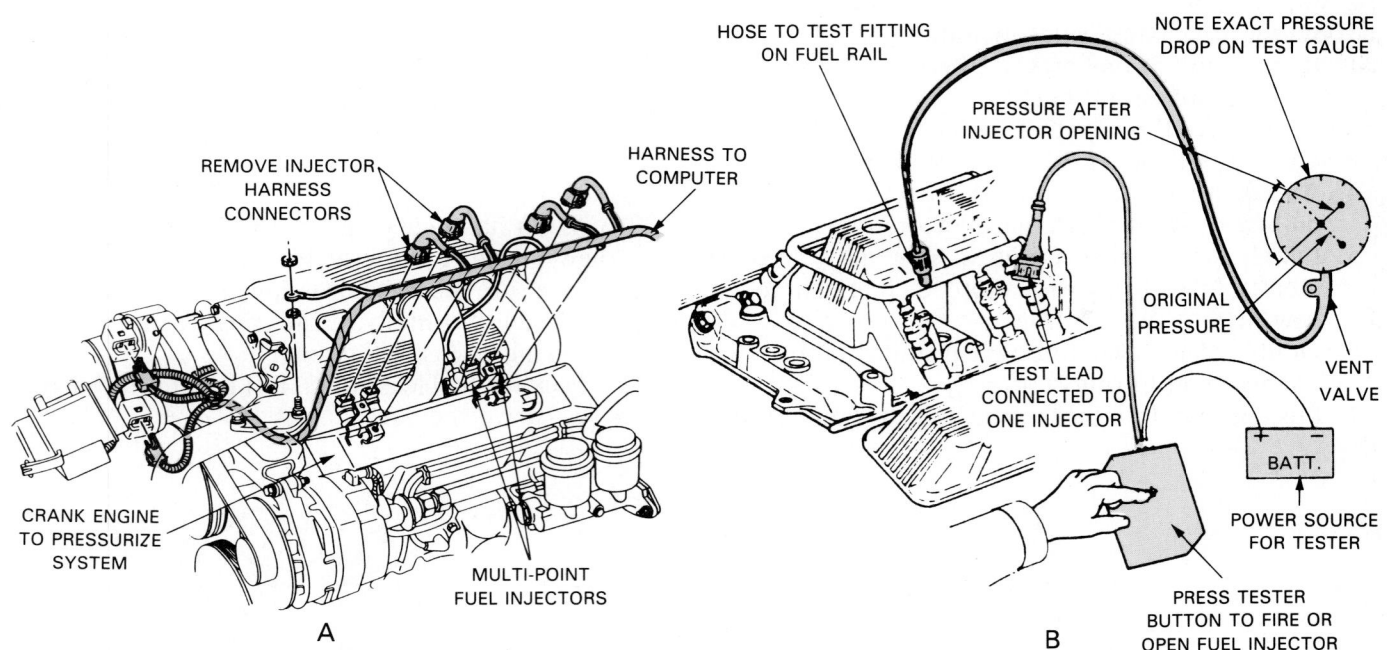

Retest injectors that appear faulty. Replace any injectors that have a 10 kPa difference either (more or less) in pressure drop.

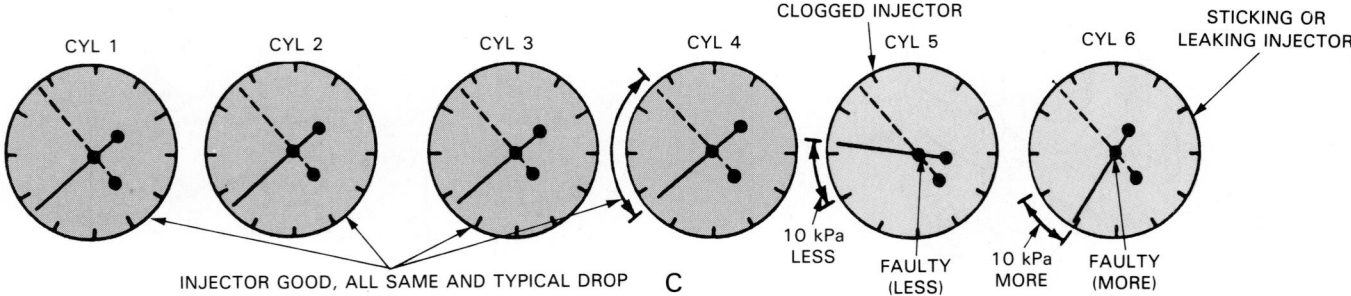

Fig. 22-13. *Basic steps for doing balance test on multi-point injectors. A—Disconnect all wires from injectors. Do not damage plastic connectors during removal. B—Connect test harness to an injector and connect pressure gauge to test fitting on fuel rail. Tester normally connects to battery. Press tester button and note pressure gauge reading. C—Pressure drop at gauge should be same for each injector. Turn key on or activate fuel pump between each test so pressure is same at each injector. If one injector has less pressure drop when fired, it might be clogged. If pressure drop is excessive, injector might be worn or sticking. If pressure does not hold, injector is leaking.   (Chevrolet)*

Make sure all vacuum hoses are connected to the correct vacuum port on the throttle body. Start the engine. Check for leaks and smooth system operation.

SERVICING EFI MULTI-POINT INJECTORS

The service of an injector for a multi-point EFI system is like the service procedures for a TBI system. However, multi-point injectors are located in the intake manifold runners, instead of the throttle body assembly. Refer to Fig. 22-14.

Checking EFI multi-point injector operation

To quickly make sure each EFI injector is opening and closing, place a STETHOSCOPE (listening device) against each injector. A clicking sound means the injector is opening and closing. If you do NOT hear a clicking sound, the injector is not working. The injector solenoid, wiring harness, or computer control circuit may be bad.

With the engine off, you can check the condition of the coils on the inoperative injector. Use an ohmmeter. Measure the resistance across the injector coil and check for shorts to ground. If the coil is open (infinite resistance) or shorted (zero resistance to ground), you must replace the injector.

If the injector tests good, you may need to check the wiring going to that injector. Following the service

manual, check supply voltage to the inoperative injector. You may also need to measure the resistance in the circuit between the injector solenoid and the computer. A high resistance would indicate a frayed wire, broken wire, or poor electrical connection.

Refer to a wiring diagram when solving complex fuel injection electrical problems. The diagram will show all electrical connections and components that can upset the function of the injection system.

CAUTION! Some EFI multi-point systems use dropping resistors before the injectors. The resistors lower the supply voltage to the injectors. Do NOT connect direct battery voltage to this type of injector or coil damage may occur.

Replacing EFI multi-point injectors

An EFI multi-point injector is easy to replace. After bleeding off fuel pressure, simply remove the hose from the injector and fuel manifold, Fig. 22-15. Unplug the electrical connection and remove any fasteners holding the injector. Pull the injector out of the engine.

Inspect the boot and other rubber parts closely. Some manufacturers suggest that you replace the boot, seals, and hose if the injector is removed for service. Refer to Fig. 22-16.

Install the new or serviced injector in reverse order. Use the directions in the shop manual for details. Exact procedures can vary.

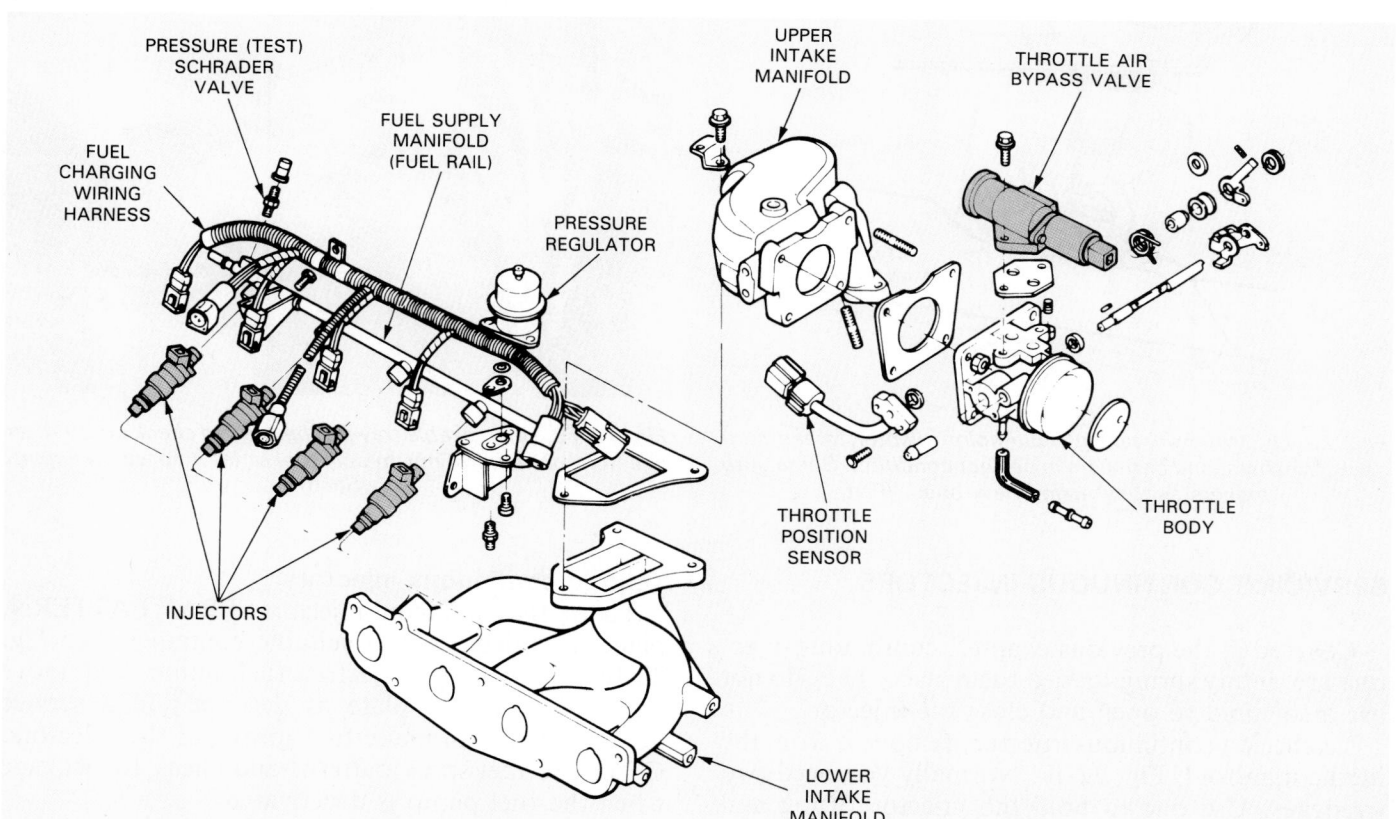

Fig. 22-14. Exploded view shows multi-point injectors, fuel rail, pressure regulator, air bypass valve, throttle body, throttle position sensor, and intake manifold assembly. Study part locations. (Ford)

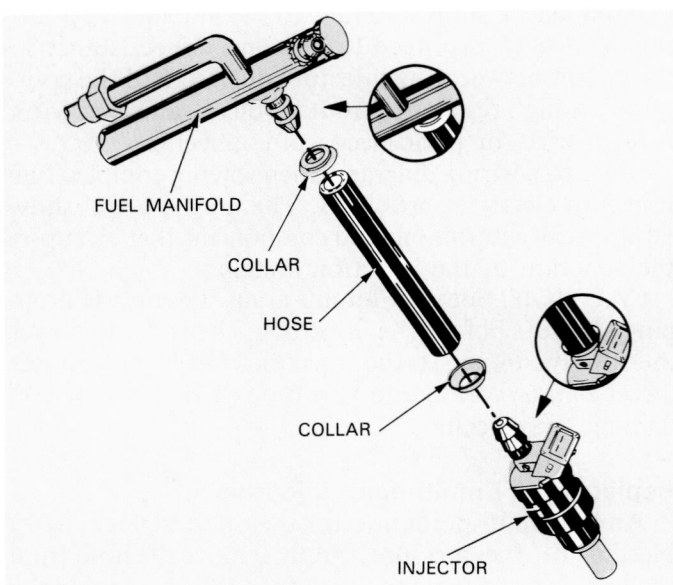

Fig. 22-15. Multi-point injector removal is simple. Remove fuel hose and electrical plug. Bolts may hold injector into manifold or injector may use a press-fit with boot. (Fiat)

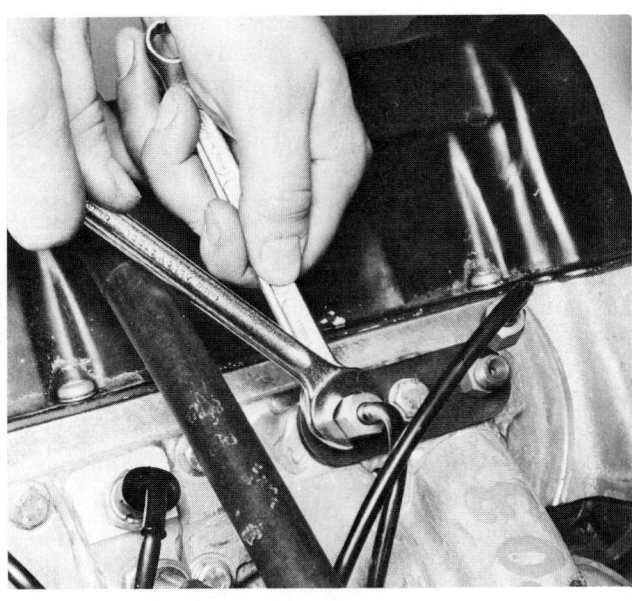

Fig. 22-17. This injector requires two wrenches for disconnecting fuel line. One wrench holds fitting. Other turns nut. Note plate that fastens injector to intake manifold. (Saab)

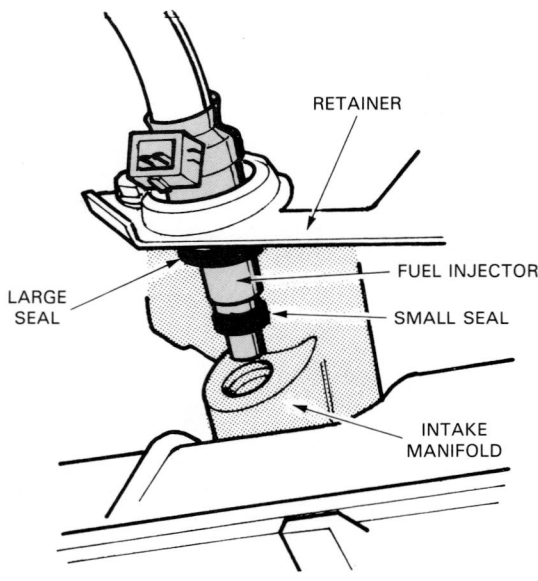

Fig. 22-16. When installing multi-point injector, make sure seals, washers, and boots are in perfect condition. Some auto makers suggest using new ones. (Fiat)

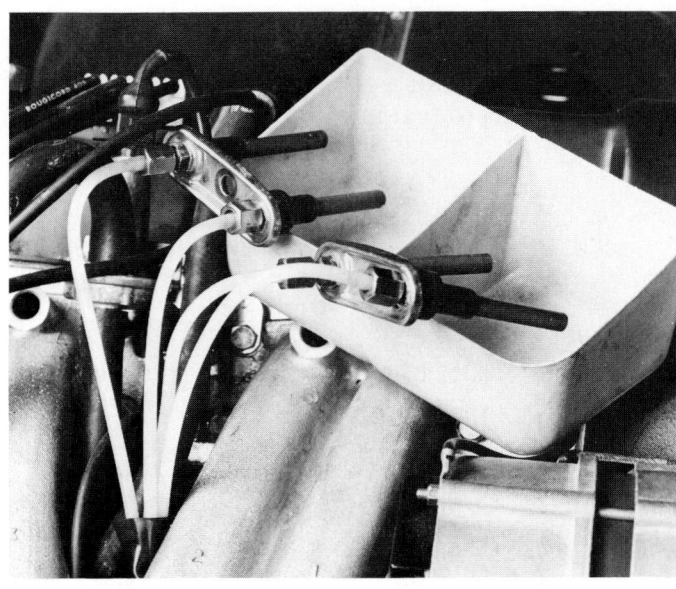

Fig. 22-18. Unbreakable tray can be used to check output from injectors. Be careful not to spill fuel or let it spray on engine. (Saab)

SERVICING CONTINUOUS INJECTORS

Covered in the previous chapter, continuous injectors are simply spring-loaded fuel valves. They do not use a solenoid to open and close the injector.

To check a continuous injector, remove it from the intake manifold, Fig. 22-17. Normally you need two wrenches. Use one to hold the injector fitting and another to loosen the injector line.

Pull the injector out of the engine. Note which runner it installs into for later reference.

Testing continuous injectors

To test the continuous injectors SPRAY PATTERN, place the injectors in a suitable container. See Fig. 22-18. Activate the electric fuel pump and move the airflow sensor plate as described in a service manual. This will make fuel spray out the injectors. Check the fuel spray patterns and check for leakage when the fuel pump is deactivated.

DANGER! Injectors can spray out enough fuel to start a tremendous fire. Make sure the fuel container and injectors are held safely in place during testing.

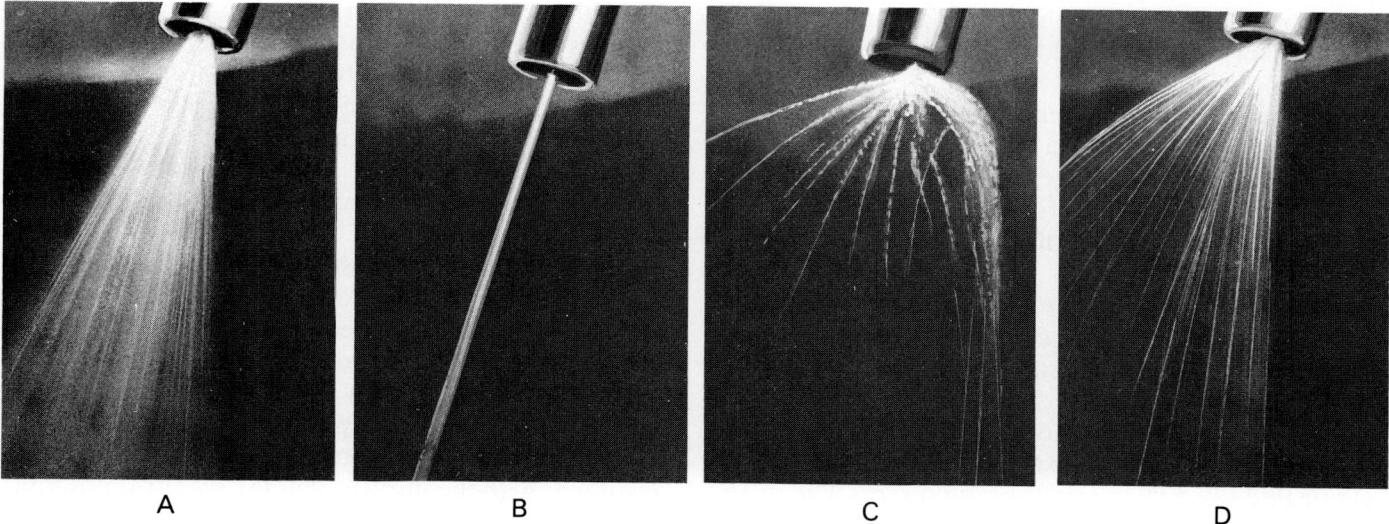

Fig. 22-19. Gasoline injector spray patterns. A — Good, even, partially atomized pattern. B — Solid stream, poor spray pattern. C — Dirty nozzle causing poor spray pattern. D — Uneven spray pattern is also unacceptable. (Saab)

If the spray pattern is bad or an injector leaks, try cleaning the injector. If cleaning does not correct the problem, install a new injector. Fig. 22-19 shows injector spray patterns.

Testing fuel volume

One CIS manufacturer suggests that you measure the INJECTOR FUEL VOLUME OUTPUT (amount of fuel output for specific time period). For efficient engine operation, it is important that each engine cylinder receive the same amount of fuel. For this test, place the injectors in graduated containers. Look at Fig. 22-20. Activate the fuel system and measure the amount of fuel spraying out each injector.

If the volume of fuel coming out of the injectors is NOT equal, there are injector or fuel distributor problems.

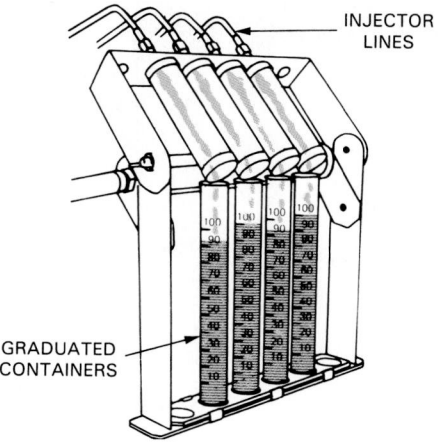

Fig. 22-20. CIS system output can be measured by allowing injectors to spray into graduated containers. Injector output should be equal. If not, injector or fuel distributor may be at fault. (VW)

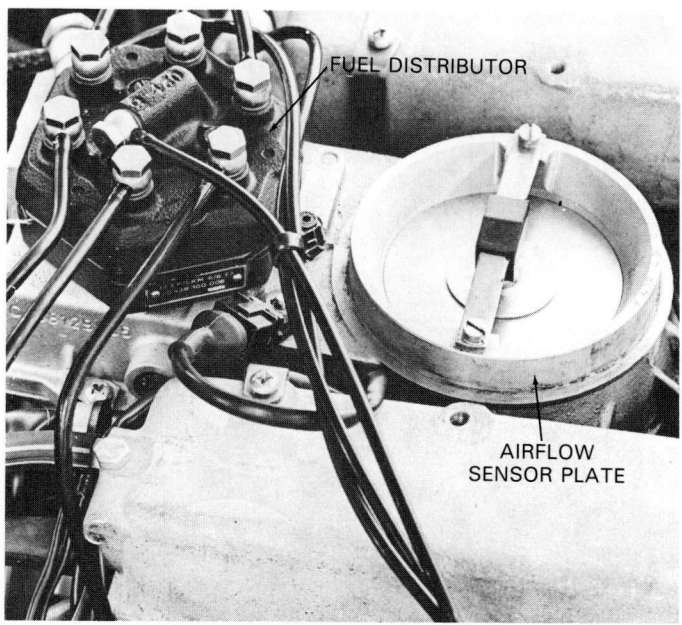

Fig. 22-21. With CIS system, check air sensor plate and lever arm for wear or damage. If fuel distributor fails test, install a new one. (Saab)

To pinpoint the trouble, switch the problem injector (injector with incorrect output) to another fuel line. If the same injector has an incorrect output, THAT INJECTOR is faulty. If the same fuel line produces an improper output, the injector is good, but the fuel line or FUEL DISTRIBUTOR is defective.

FUEL DISTRIBUTOR SERVICE

If your continuous injector tests found the fuel distributor to be bad, you would need to replace the unit. Fig. 22-21 shows a fuel distributor. If the valves in the unit do not supply the same amount of fuel to each injector, the unit should be removed from the flow sensor and a new one installed.

Refer to a shop manual when servicing a fuel distributor assembly. It is a very precise fuel metering device. The slightest change could upset its operation.

TESTING COLD START INJECTOR

If the fuel injected engine is hard to start when cold, check the operation of the cold start injector. Studied earlier, it is a solenoid operated fuel valve that richens the mixture for starting.

To test the injector, remove it from the engine, Fig. 22-22. Aim the injector into a container. Crank the cold engine and observe the fuel spray pattern. The injector should spray fuel anytime the engine temperature sensor is below a set temperature.

If the cold start injector does NOT function, test the thermo-time switch, circuit, and the injector.

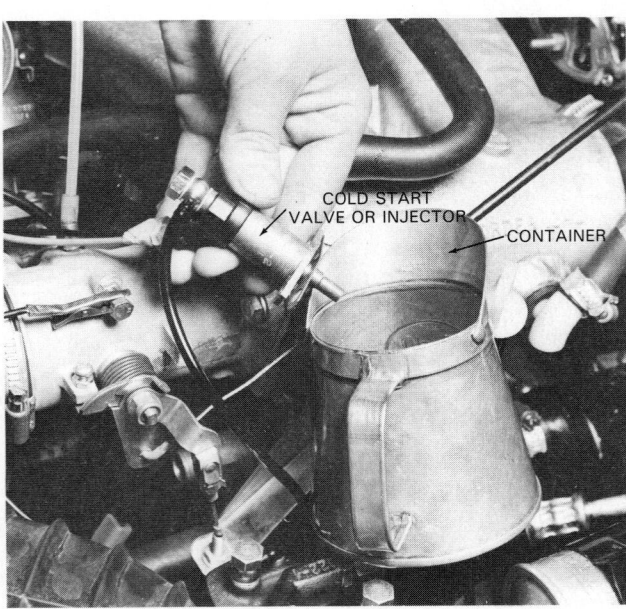

Fig. 22-22. With engine or temperature sensor below specified temperature, cold start injector should operate. Photo suggests a test. If fuel does not flow, check injector solenoid, supply voltage, circuit, and sensor. (Saab)

ENGINE SENSOR SERVICE

Most EFI engine sensors can be tested with a special tester (analyzer), as covered earlier in the chapter. However, an engine sensor can often be checked with a digital meter or a test light.

CAUTION! When a service manual directs you to measure voltage or resistance in an EFI sensor use a high impedence meter or a digital meter. An inexpensive, conventional needle type meter could damage some sensors.

Throttle position sensor service

A throttle position sensor should produce a given amount of resistance for different throttle openings. For example, the sensor might have high resistance with the throttle plates closed and a lower resistance when the throttles are open. Compare your ohmmeter readings to specs to determine the condition of a throttle position sensor.

To replace a throttle position sensor, you must usually unstake the attaching screws. They may be soldered in place to prevent tampering. Use a file to grind off the stake and remove the sensor, Fig. 22-23.

After installing the new throttle position sensor, adjust the sensor. Refer to your manual for details. For most systems, the sensors should read a prescribed resistance with the throttle plates in specified positions. Restake the sensor after adjustment.

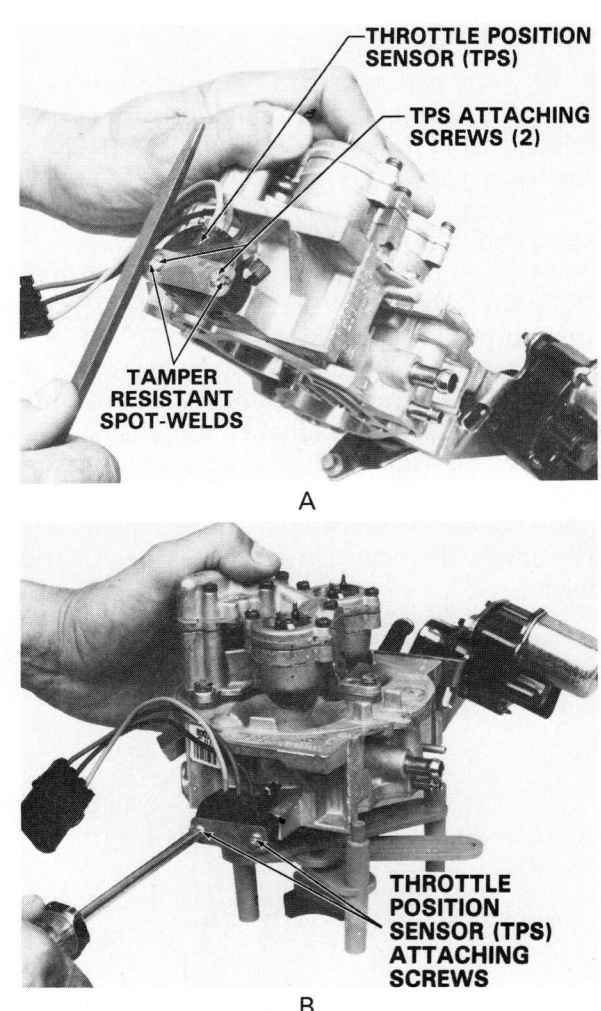

Fig. 22-23. Removing a throttle position sensor. A — Most TPS sensors are staked in place to prevent tampering. Use a file to remove stake or spot weld. B — After installing new sensor, adjust it following manual directions. Ohmmeter is used to measure sensor resistance while twisting sensor on its mount. Ohms value should be within specs with throttle in prescribed position.

Exhaust gas (oxygen) sensor service

Most auto manufacturers recommend that you test the oxygen sensor with a specialized system tester or by the self-diagnosis mode. If a VOM is recommended, use a digital type. Typically, oxygen sensor output should be about .5 volts.

To replace an oxygen sensor, unplug the wire connection at the sensor. Unscrew the old sensor. Coat the threads of the new sensor with anti-seize compound. Start the sensor by hand. Then screw in and tighten the sensor with a wrench. Do not over-tighten or the sensor may be damaged. Check fuel injection system operation after sensor installation.

Temperature sensor service

Most EFI systems use both a coolant temperature sensor and an inlet air temperature sensor. If these sensors are bad, they will make the engine run either rich or lean. The internal resistance of these sensors changes with temperature.

A digital ohmmeter is often recommended for testing a temperature sensor. As shown in Fig. 22-24, the service manual will give resistance values for various temperatures. If the ohmmeter test readings are not within specs for each temperature value, the sensor is bad and must be replaced.

Servicing other EFI sensors

The other sensors in an electronic fuel injection system are tested using the same general procedures just discussed. You would use the self-diagnosis mode, a special analyzer, or a digital meter to check each sensor. Refer to a service manual for exact procedures.

COMPUTER SERVICE

If your system tests find a bad EFI computer, you may need to replace the complete unit or a section of

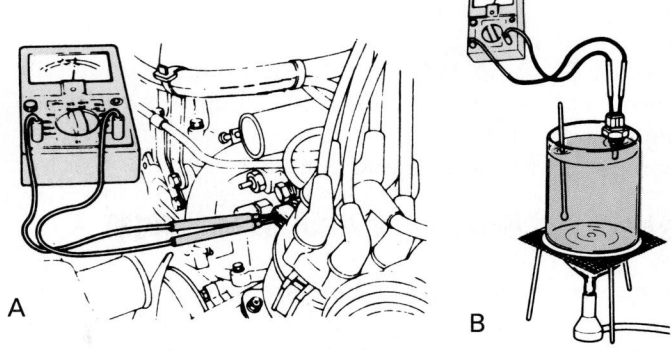

TYPICAL TEMPERATURE-TO-RESISTANCE VALUES (APPROXIMATE)		
°F	°C	OHMS
210	100	185
160	70	450
100	38	1,600
70	20	3,400
40	-4	7,500
20	-7	13,500
0	-18	25,000
-40	-40	100,700

Fig. 22-24. Ohmmeter can be used to test most engine temperature sensors. A — Connect ohmmeter across temperature sensor terminals. Ohms should be within specs for specific engine temperature. B — More accurate testing can be done with sensor out of engine. Resistance should be correct for different temperatures. Compare thermometer readings and ohmmeter readings to specs. C — Ohms-temperature spec chart for one particular sensor. (Buick and Nissan)

the unit. Again, because of system variations, follow manufacturer procedures.

A PROM (programmable read only memory) is a computer chip used in some on-board computers. It is a computer chip calibrated for the particular engine. When a computer tests faulty, you must normally reuse the old PROM in the new computer. As shown in Fig. 22-25, the PROM is lifted out of the old computer and pressed into the new computer.

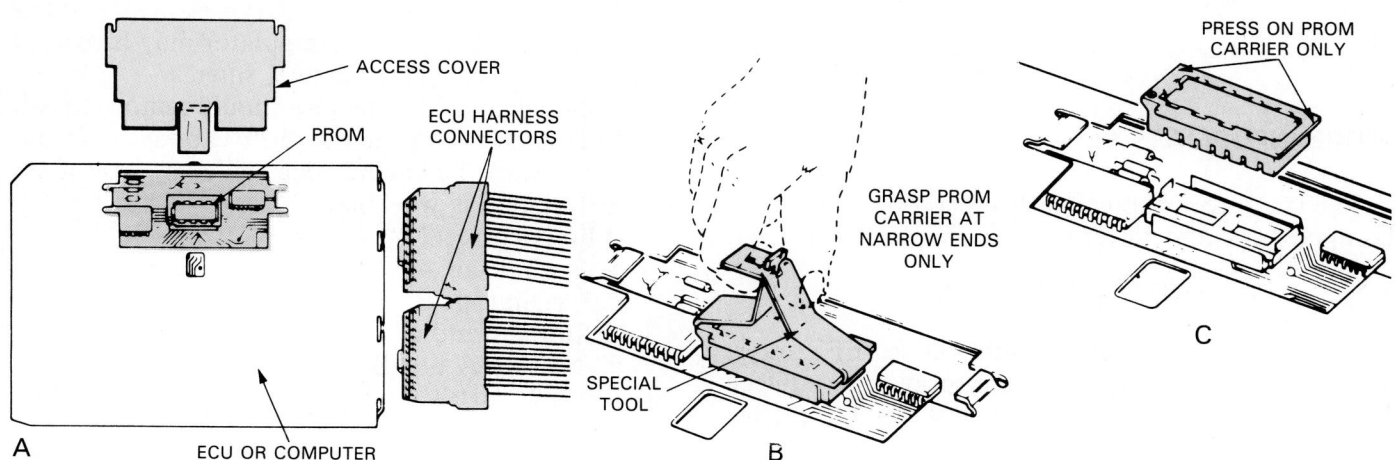

Fig. 22-25. When tests find faulty computer, you may need to replace whole computer. Sometimes however, a PROM (computer chip calibrated for exact engine) must be reused. A — Unplug computer and remove access cover. B — Pull PROM out using special tool. C — When installing new PROM, keep your fingers off the chip itself. Only press on the outer carrier. (GM)

An EFI computer is normally mounted under the dash. This keeps the electronic circuits away from engine heat and vibration. In a few cars, however, the computer is in the engine compartment.

GASOLINE INJECTION ADJUSTMENTS

As with a carburetor, there are several tune-up adjustments needed on a gasoline injection system. These include:

1. Engine idle speed adjustment, Fig. 22-26.
2. Throttle plate stop adjustment, Fig. 22-26.
3. Idle air-fuel mixture adjustment, Fig. 22-26.
4. Throttle cable adjustment.

Since there are so many types of systems, refer to a service manual for exact procedures.

NOTE! Many auto makers warn against making some adjustments on a gasoline injection system. For example, only make mixture adjustments when major problems exist or an exhaust analyzer shows high emission levels. If you must make large adjustments, there are usually other problems in the system.

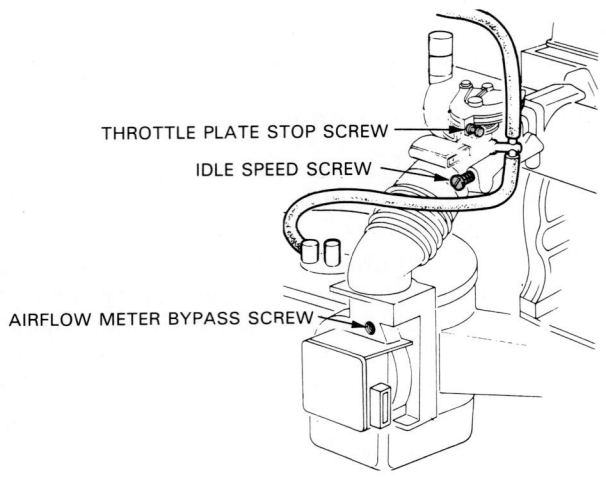

THROTTLE PLATE STOP SCREW

IDLE SPEED SCREW

AIRFLOW METER BYPASS SCREW

Fig. 22-26. Adjustments and their access locations will vary with particular model and type of gasoline injection. These are typical of one system. (Renault)

MORE INFORMATION

The last three chapters in this textbook summarize computer systems. Refer to these chapters as needed.

KNOW THESE TERMS

EFI self-diagnosis, EFI trouble code, EFI tester, leaking injector, Improper injector spray pattern, Open injector coil, Shorted injector coil, TBI rebuild, Injector output volume, PROM.

REVIEW QUESTIONS

1. What three things must be used when diagnosing problems in a gasoline injection system?
2. Explain the EFI self-diagnosis mode found on many late model cars.
3. How does an EFI tester work?
4. An oscilloscope can sometimes be used to view the electrical waveforms at the injectors for checking the computer, wiring, and injector coil. True or False?
5. Many EFI systems can retain a fuel pressure as high as _____ psi or _____ kPa. Always _____ fuel pressure before disconnecting a fuel line.
6. Which of the following does NOT pertain to a fuel pressure regulator?
   a. Can cause a rich fuel mixture.
   b. Can cause a lean fuel mixture.
   c. Tested with a dwell meter.
   d. Tested with a pressure gauge.
7. Where are the locations of the fuel pressure regulators with single-point and multi-point injection?
8. An engine with electronic multi-point injection has a rough idle, as if one cylinder is dead (not firing). The ignition system and engine are in good condition.
   Technician A says that a stethoscope should be used to listen to each injector. One of the injectors may not be operating (making a clicking sound).
   Technician B says that all of the injectors should be removed and checked for a proper spray pattern.
   Who is correct?
   a. Technician A
   b. Technician B
   c. Both A and B
   d. Neither A nor B
9. An engine with electronic throttle body injection will not run. The ignition is producing adequate spark and the engine is in good condition.
   Technician A says that the fuel pressure should be measured. The pressure regulator may be bad or there may be a clogged fuel filter.
   Technician B says that you should remove the air filter and look inside the throttle body while trying to start the engine. This will show you if the EFI system is working.
   Who is correct?
   a. Technician A
   b. Technician B
   c. Both A and B
   d. Neither A nor B
10. List nine rules to follow when replacing a throttle body injector.
11. An ohmmeter can be used to check an EFI injector coil for shorts or opens. True or False?
12. Why is injector fuel volume output important?
13. Describe how you check the fuel spray pattern of

a CIS injector.

14. A digital meter is better than a conventional needle type meter when testing EFI sensors, because it draws less current. True or False?

15. A throttle position sensor should produce a given amount of _____ for different throttle _____ .

16. An oxygen sensor is very sensitive and can be damaged if tested improperly with a VOM. True or False?

17. A _____ _____ is often recommended for testing an EFI temperature sensor.

18. What is an EFI system PROM?

19. Where is the EFI system computer normally mounted?

20. List and explain four gasoline injection system adjustments.

21. Many auto makers warn against making some gasoline injection system adjustments unless absolutely necessary. True or False?

ACTIVITIES FOR CHAPTER 22

1. Study the fuel injection section of any shop manual given you by your instructor. Develop a "diagnosis tree" for an injector that is not working.

2. Develop an overhead transparency showing various injector spray patterns. Using the transparency, explain the patterns to the class.

3. Demonstrate the proper procedure for replacement of a multi-point injector.

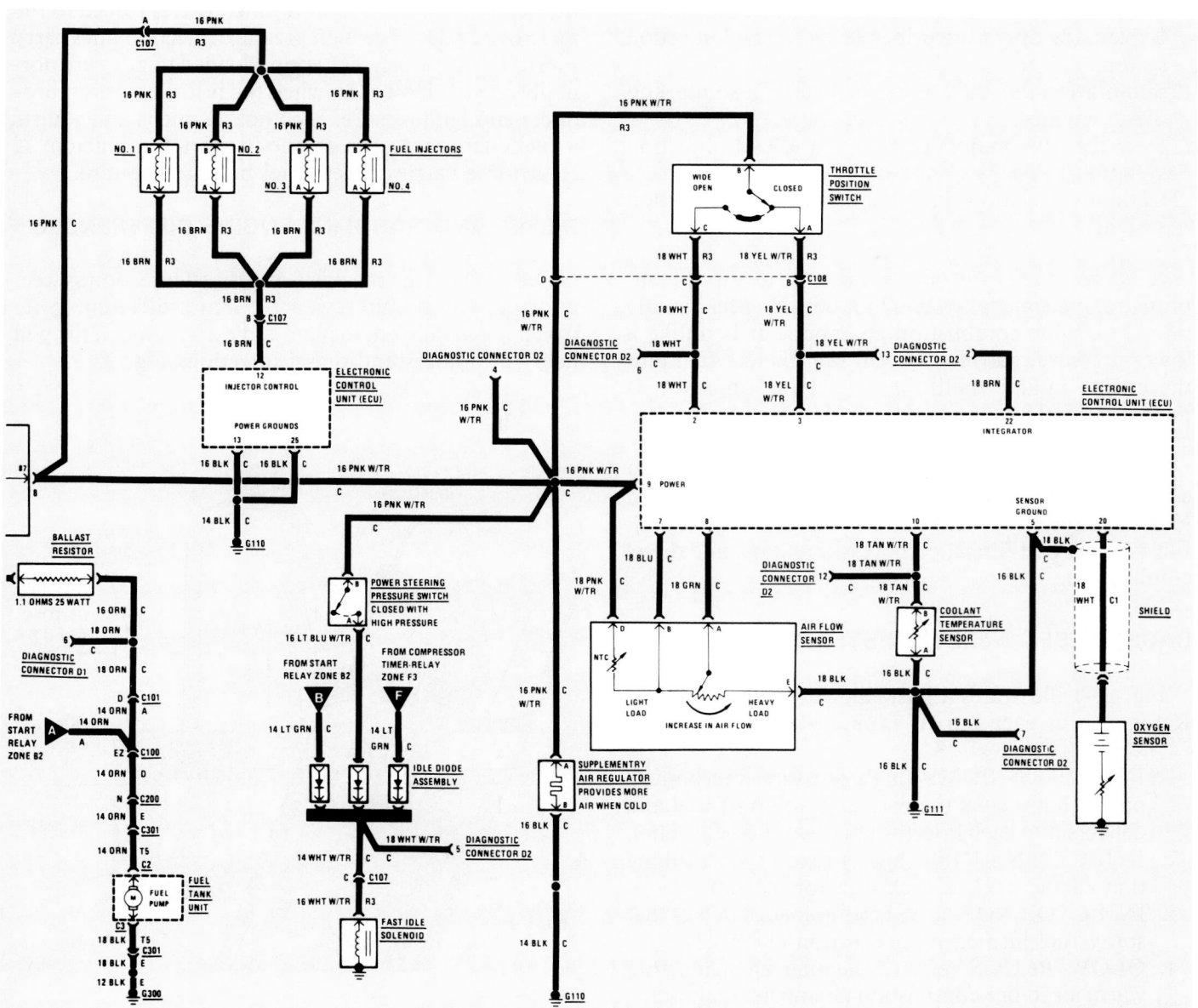

Study this partial wiring diagram for EFI multi-point injection system. Note diagnostic (troubleshooting) connectors and how injectors, oxygen sensor, airflow sensor, throttle position switch, and other components connect to ECU (computer). (Renault)

Diesel Injection Fundamentals

23

After studying this chapter, you will be able to:
- Explain the operating principles of a diesel injection system.
- Summarize the differences between gasoline and diesel engines.
- Describe the major parts of a diesel injection system.
- Compare variations in the design of diesel injection systems.

A *diesel fuel injection system* is a super-high-pressure, mechanical system that delivers fuel directly into the engine combustion chambers. It is unlike a lower pressure, gasoline system that meters fuel into the engine intake manifold. Diesel fuel injection is relatively simple. It uses a mechanical pump as the main control of the engine's air-fuel mixture.

Note! Several earlier chapters discuss information essential to this chapter. If needed, use the index to locate and review coverage of diesel engines, diesel fuel, fuel pumps, fuel filters, compression ratios, and diesel combustion.

BASIC DIESEL INJECTION SYSTEM

Fig. 23-1 illustrates a basic diesel injection system. Refer to it as each part is explained.

1. INJECTION PUMP (high pressure, mechanical pump that meters the correct amount of fuel and delivers it to each injector nozzle at the right time).
2. INJECTION LINES (high strength, steel tubing that carries fuel to each injector nozzle).
3. INJECTOR NOZZLES (spring-loaded valves that spray fuel into each combustion chamber).
4. GLOW PLUGS (electric heating elements that warm air in pre-combustion chambers to aid starting of cold engine).

The fuel supply system feeds fuel to the injection pump, Fig. 23-2. The engine-driven injection pump

then controls when and how much fuel is forced to the injector nozzles. The high pressure injection lines carry fuel to the injectors. The spring-loaded nozzles are normally closed. However, when the injection pump produces enough pressure, each nozzle opens and squirts a fuel charge into the engine to start combustion. A return line carries excess fuel back to the tank.

DIESEL AND GASOLINE ENGINE DIFFERENCES

Before covering the parts of a diesel injection system in detail, you should review the major differences between a gasoline engine and a diesel engine. This will help you understand diesel injection, Fig. 23-3.

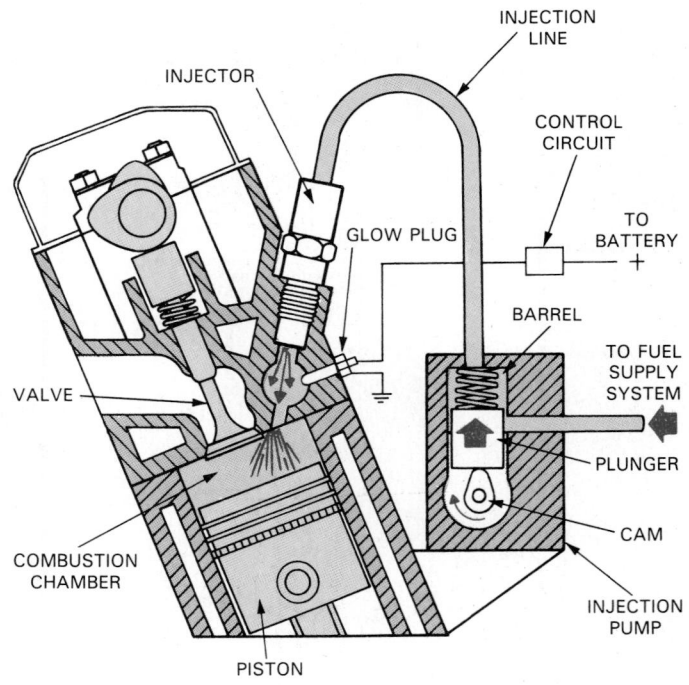

Fig. 23-1. Basic parts of simplified diesel injection system. Injection pump plunger produces very high pressure to open injector valve. Glow plug warms air in precombustion chamber when engine is cold.

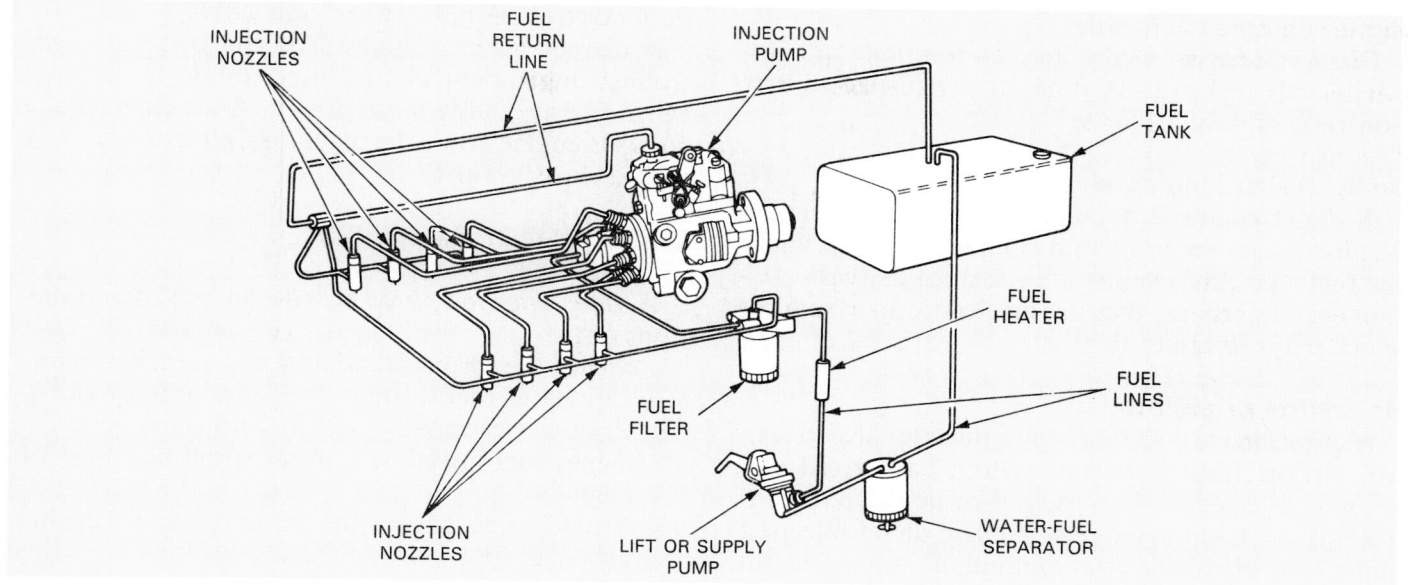

Fig. 23-2. Schematic of complete fuel injection system. Lift pump feeds fuel into injection pump. Injection pump produces high pressure for injection into combustion chambers. (Ford)

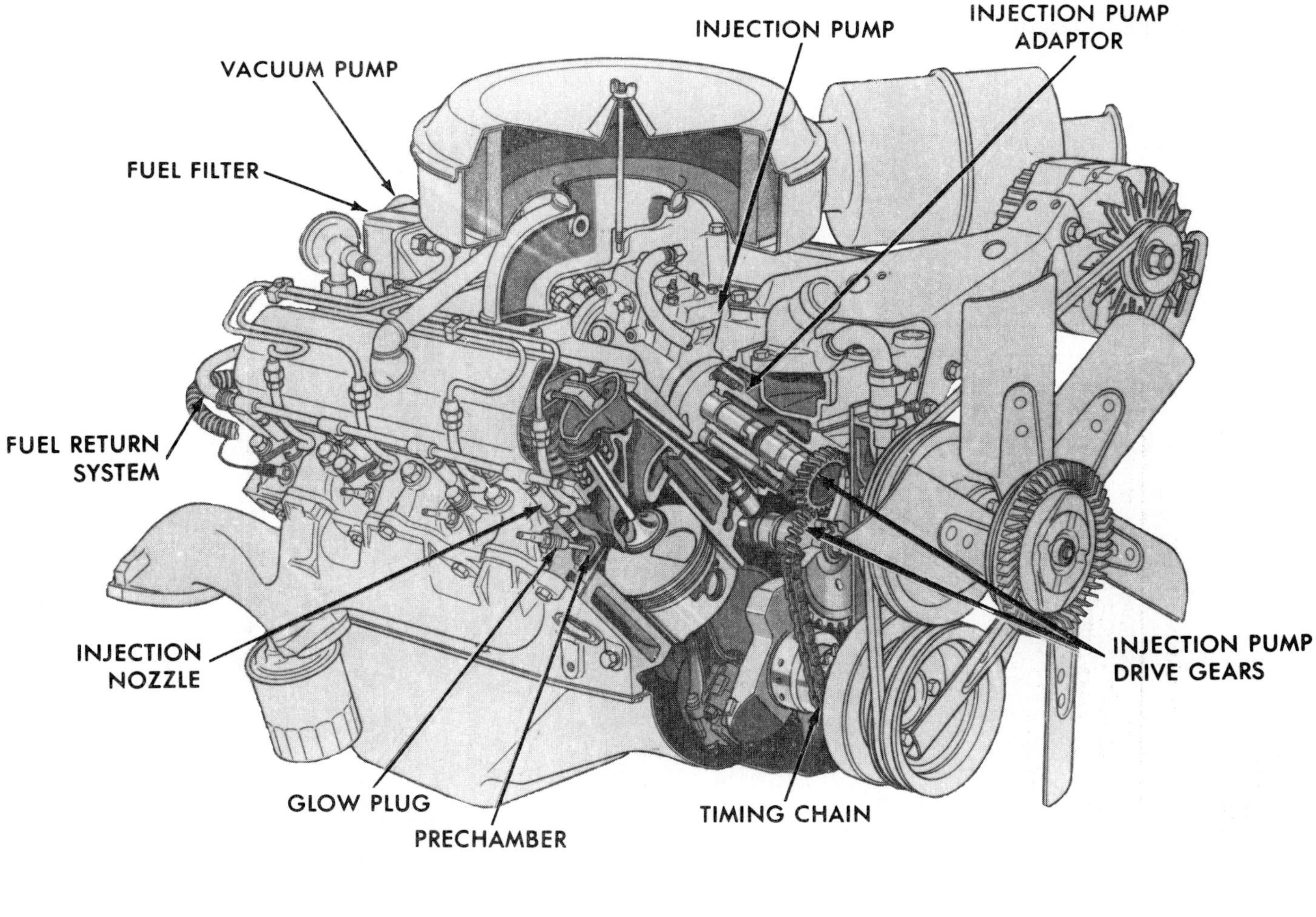

VACUUM PUMP

FUEL FILTER

INJECTION PUMP

INJECTION PUMP ADAPTOR

FUEL RETURN SYSTEM

INJECTION NOZZLE

INJECTION PUMP DRIVE GEARS

GLOW PLUG

PRECHAMBER

TIMING CHAIN

Fig. 23-3. This V-8 diesel has injection pump on top of engine. Study other parts. (Cadillac)

Diesel Injection Fundamentals   289

Higher compression ratio

Diesel engines use a very high compression ratio (approximately 17:1 to 23:1). A gasoline engine's compression ratio is only 8:1 or 9:1.

Compression ignition engine

A diesel engine is a *compression ignition* engine because it uses the heat from compressed air to ignite the fuel. Gasoline engines are classified as *spark ignition engines* because they use an electric arc (from the spark plug) to ignite the fuel.

No control of airflow

A diesel engine does NOT use a throttle valve to control airflow into the engine. (Both carbureted and gasoline injected engines use a throttle valve to control airflow and engine power.) The diesel injection pump controls engine power output, as you will learn.

Compresses only air

A diesel engine compresses only air on its compression stroke. A gasoline engine compresses a mixture of air and fuel.

Injects fuel into combustion chambers

A diesel engine forces fuel directly into the combustion chambers. A gasoline engine meters fuel into the intake manifold.

Fuel controls engine speed and power

A diesel controls engine speed and power by controlling the amount of fuel injected into the engine. More fuel produces more power. A gasoline engine controls engine power by regulating air and fuel flow with a throttle valve.

DIESEL INJECTION PUMPS

A *diesel injection pump* has several important functions. It:

1. Meters the correct amount of fuel to each injector.
2. Circulates fuel through fuel lines and nozzles.
3. Produces extremely high fuel pressure.
4. Times fuel injection to meet speed and load of engine.
5. Provides a means for the driver to control engine power output.
6. Controls engine idle speed and maximum engine speed.
7. Helps close injector nozzles after injection.
8. Provides a means of shutting off engine.

The diesel injection pump is normally bolted to the side or top of the engine. See Fig. 23-3. The fuel supply system (fuel tank, lines, filters, conventional fuel pump) pushes clean, filtered fuel, under low pressure, to the injection pump. The injection pump uses the principle pictured in Fig. 23-1. A camshaft acts on a plunger.

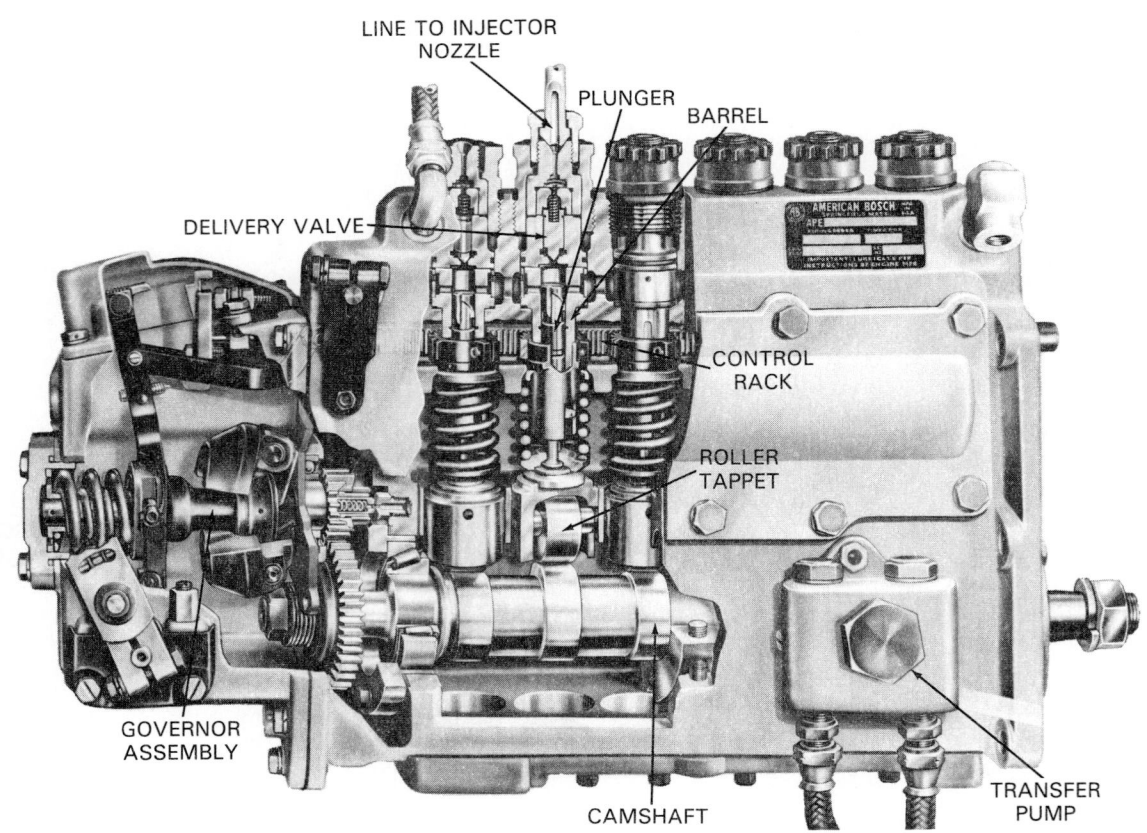

Fig. 23-4. Cutaway shows basic parts of an in-line diesel injection pump. (American Bosch)

The plunger slides up in its barrel (cylinder), compressing and pressurizing the fuel. The fuel then flows through the injection line and out the injector nozzle.

A diesel injection pump is powered by the engine. Power may be transferred by a set of gears, a chain, or toothed belt. There are two common types of automotive diesel injection pumps: in-line type and distributor type.

IN-LINE DIESEL INJECTION PUMPS

An *in-line diesel injection pump* has one pumping plunger (piston) for each engine cylinder. The pumping plungers are lined up in a row, like pistons of an in-line engine.

The major parts of an in-line injection pump are shown in Figs. 23-4 and 23-5. Refer to these illustrations as the parts are introduced.

The in-line injection pump *camshaft* operates the pumping plungers. It has lobes like an engine camshaft. When the engine turns the pump camshaft, the lobes push on the roller tappets to move them up and down.

The injection pump *roller tappets* transfer camshaft action to the pumping plungers. Like roller lifters in an engine, the rollers reduce friction and wear on the cam lobes.

In-line pump *plungers* are small pistons that push on and pressurize the diesel fuel. When the cam lobe

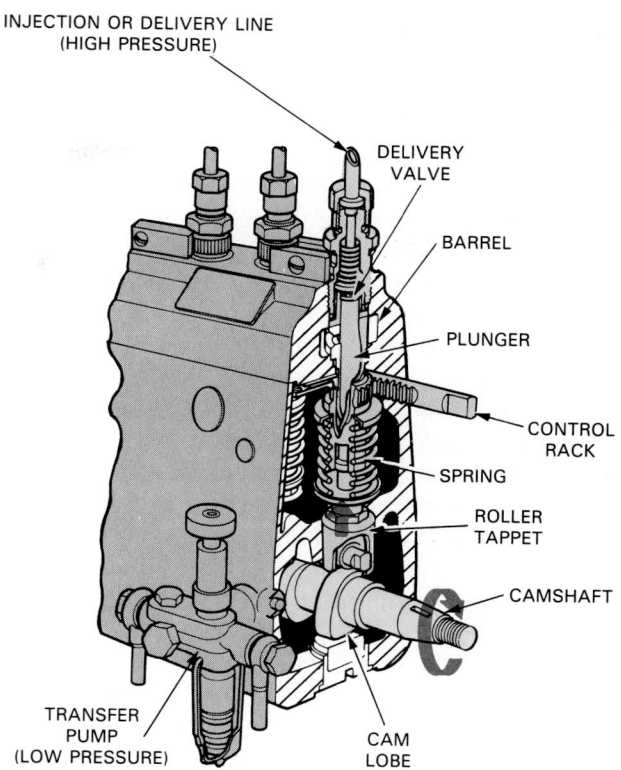

Fig. 23-5. Camshaft acts on roller tappet. Tappet pushes up on plunger to push fuel out delivery valve and into injection line. Control rack can be used to change injection quantity. (Chrysler)

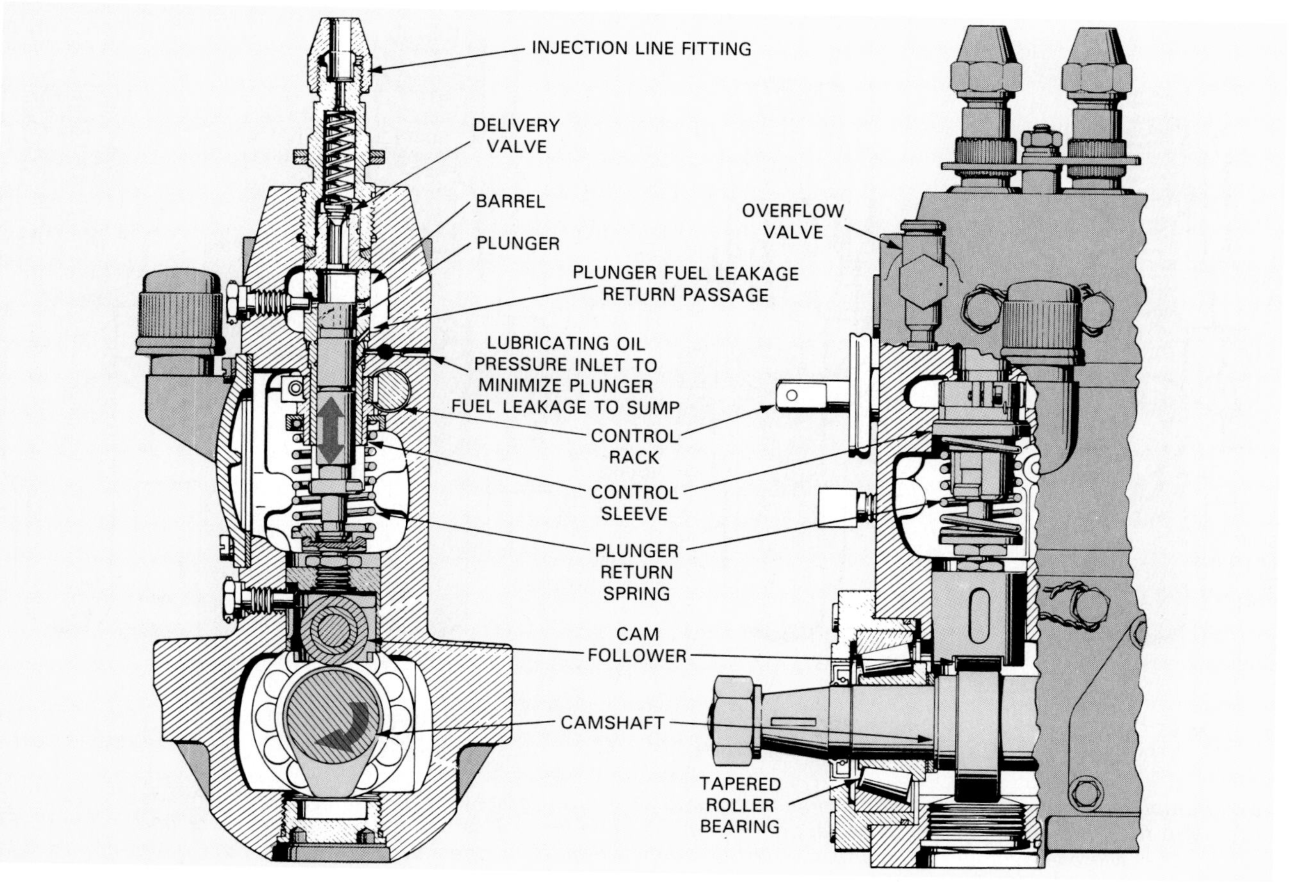

Fig. 23-6. Another view of an in-line diesel injection pump. Compare this illustration to previous ones. (Waukesha)

acts on the roller tappet, both the tappet and the plunger are pushed upward.

The *barrels* are small cylinders that hold the pumping plungers. When the plunger slides upward in its barrel, extremely high fuel pressure is formed.

The *plunger return springs* keep a downward pressure on the pumping plungers and roller tappets. This action holds the tappets against the camshaft when the lobes rotate away from the rollers.

Control sleeves turn on the pumping plungers to alter how much fuel is pushed to each injector nozzle. See Fig. 23-6 and locate the control sleeve.

A *control rod* or *rack* is a toothed shaft that acts as a throttle to control diesel engine speed and power. It rotates the control sleeves to increase or decrease injection pump output and engine power.

Delivery valves are spring-loaded valves in the outlet fittings to the injection lines. They help assure quick, leak-free closing of the injector nozzles.

In-line injection pump operation

When the engine is running, the injection pump camshaft rotates at one-half engine speed. While the cam lobe is not pushing on the roller tappet, the lift pump (supply pump) fills the barrel with fuel. Then, as the cam lobe puts pressure on the roller tappet, the plunger is forced upward in its barrel. This forces fuel through the delivery valve, through the injection line, out the nozzle, and into the engine. See Fig. 23-7.

As the plunger reaches the end of its stroke, pressure drops and the delivery valve closes. The delivery valve action helps reduce injection line pressure rapidly, keeping fuel from dripping out of the injector nozzle.

When the cam lobe moves away from the roller tappet, the plunger return spring pushes the plunger down. Fuel can again flow into and fill the barrel. This readies the plunger to supply fuel for another power stroke.

In-line injection pump fuel metering

To control the amount of fuel injected into the engine, the control rod or rack slides across the control sleeves to rotate them. Look at Fig. 23-8.

A *helix* (spiral) shaped groove and a slot are cut into the side of the plunger. When the helix is aligned with the port (hole) in the side of the barrel, the plunger CANNOT develop pressure. Fuel will flow down the slot, through the helix groove, and out the port.

The *effective plunger stroke* is the amount of plunger movement that pressurizes fuel. It controls the amount of fuel delivered to the injectors.

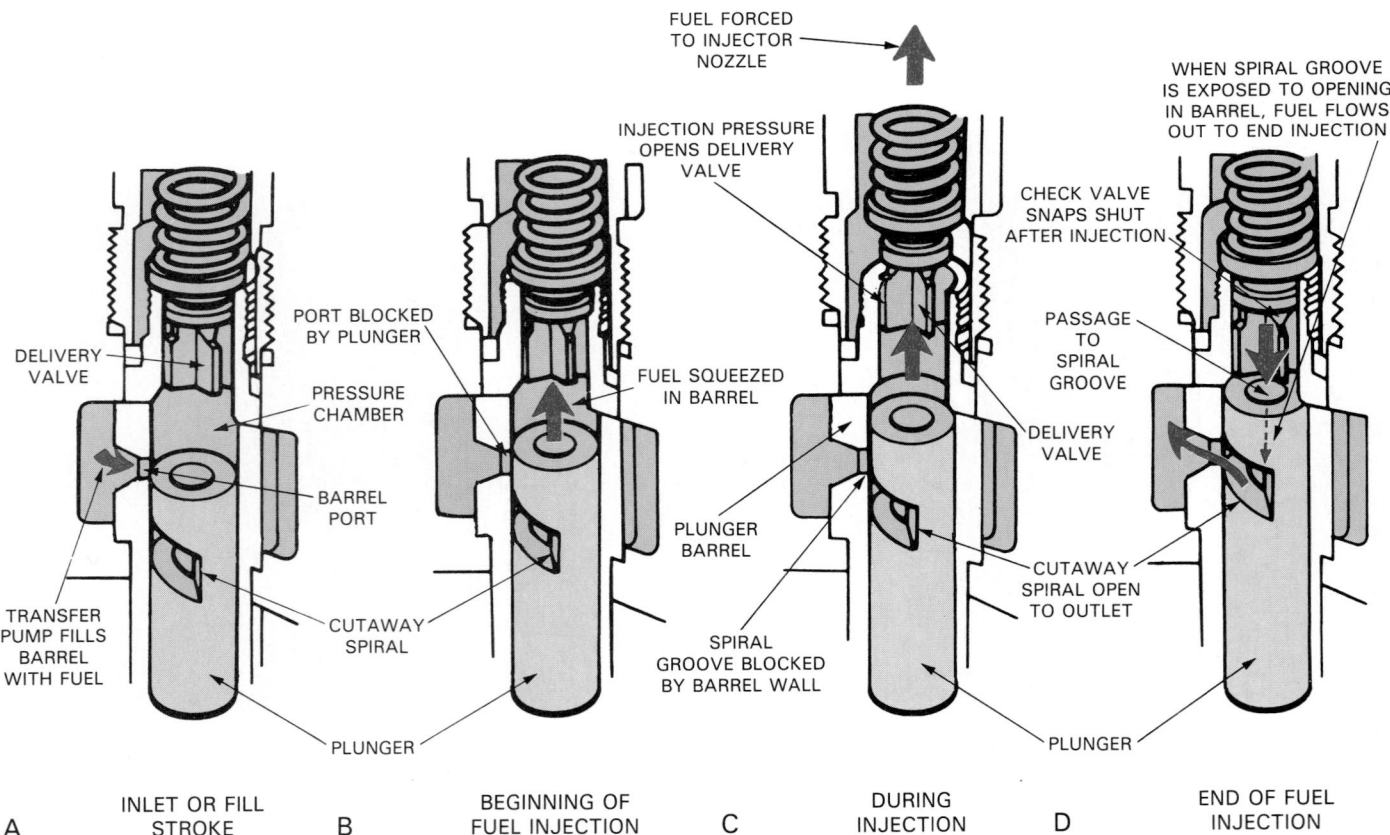

Fig. 23-7. Pumping plunger action in an in-line injection pump. A — Cam lobe away from tappet. Plunger is down. Supply pump fills barrel with fuel. B — Cam lobe acts on tappet. Plunger is moved up. This causes plunger to cover port in barrel. Fuel is pressurized. C — More movement of plunger builds enough pressure to open delivery valve. Fuel flows out to injector. D — Even more movement of plunger has exposed spiral groove in plunger. This allows fuel to pass through plunger and out port, ending fuel injection. (Chrysler)

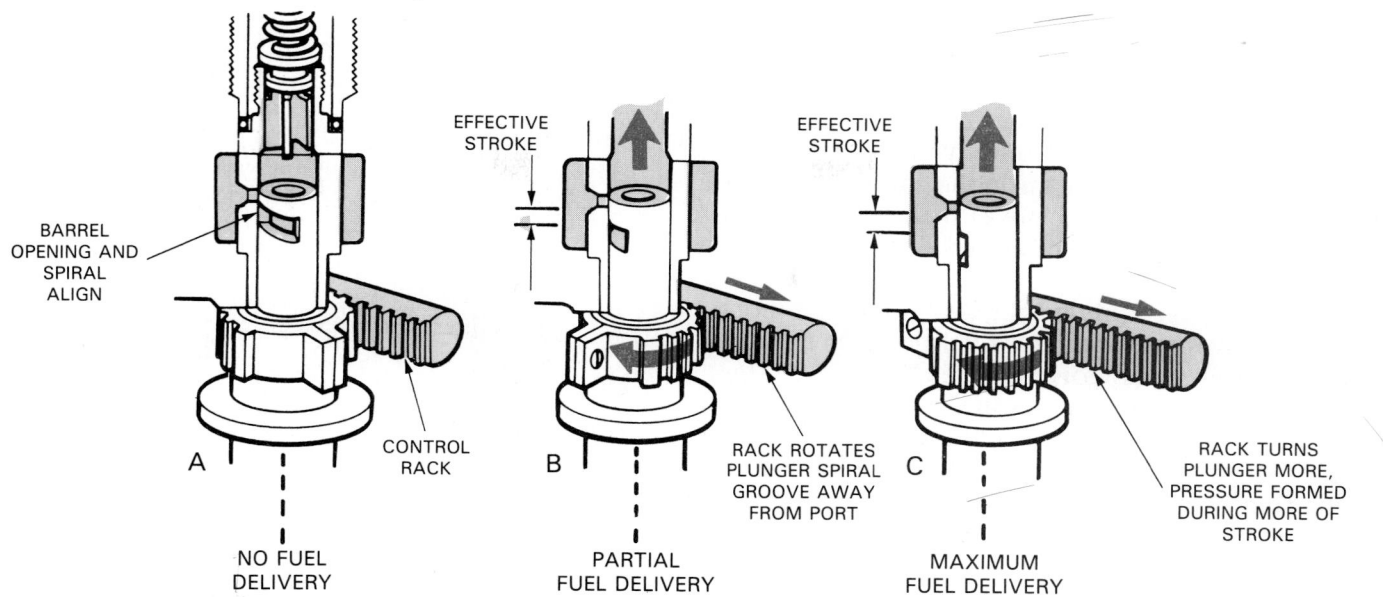

Fig. 23-8. Control rack is linked to driver's gas pedal and governor. Two forces work together to control rack position and amount of fuel injection. A — Control rack moved so that spiral groove is always open to port. This would prevent injection. B — Movement of control rack has turned plunger spiral groove away from port. This causes fuel delivery. C — More movement of rack and plunger increase plunger effective stroke. Plunger can move farther before spiral groove is open to port. (Chrysler)

When the plunger moves up and the helix is NOT aligned with the barrel port, fuel is trapped and pressurized. In this way, rotation of the sleeve can be used to regulate how much fuel is injected into the engine's combustion chambers.

In-line injection pump governor

A *governor* is used on an in-line injection pump to control engine idle speed and also to limit maximum engine speed. Look at Fig. 23-9. A diesel engine can be DAMAGED if allowed to run too fast.

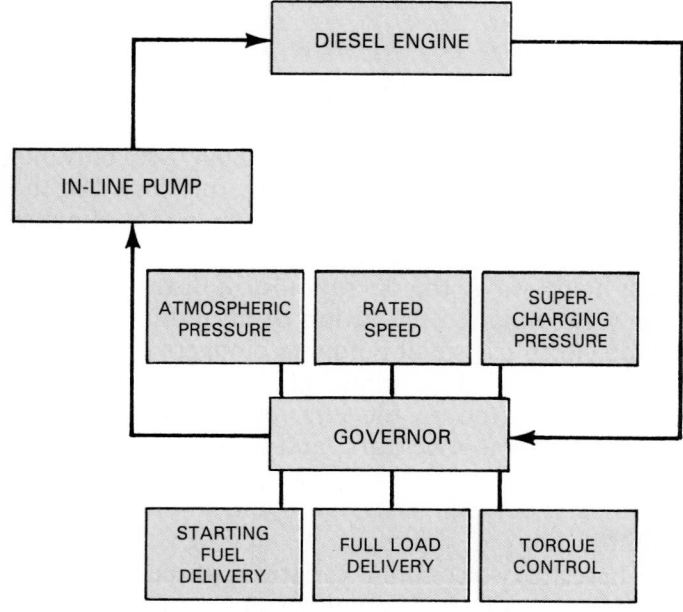

Fig. 23-9. Diagram illustrates governor operation.

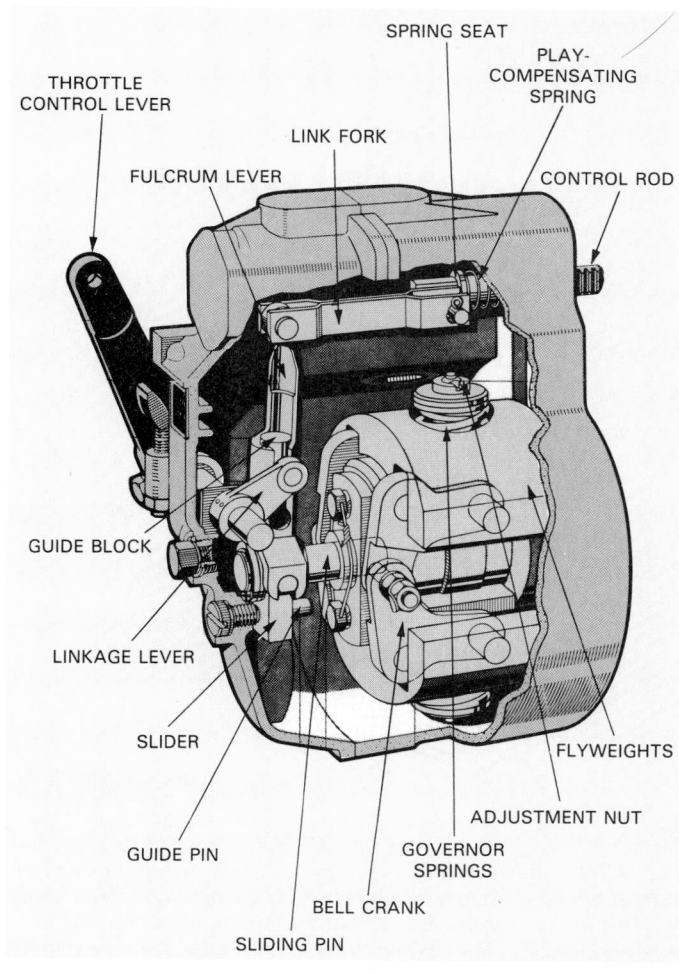

Fig. 23-10. Governor for an in-line injection pump. Note that throttle control lever and governor are both connected to control rack. (Robert Bosch)

Diesel Injection Fundamentals   293

Fig. 23-10 shows a cutaway view of an in-line injection pump governor.

Notice how the governor uses centrifugal (spinning) weights, springs, and levers, Figs. 23-10 and 23-11. The levers are connected to the control rack or rod. If engine speed increases too much, the governor weights are thrown outward. This moves the levers and control rack to reduce the effective stroke of the plungers. Engine speed and driver output are limited.

When the driver presses the gas pedal for more power, it moves a control or throttle lever on the side of the injection pump governor. See Fig. 23-12. This causes throttle lever spring pressure to overcome governor spring pressure. The control rack is moved to increase fuel delivery and engine power. Only when engine rpm reaches a preset level does the governor overcome the full-throttle lever position.

Injection timing

Injection timing refers to when fuel is injected into the combustion chambers in relation to the engine's piston position. It is similar to spark timing in a gasoline engine.

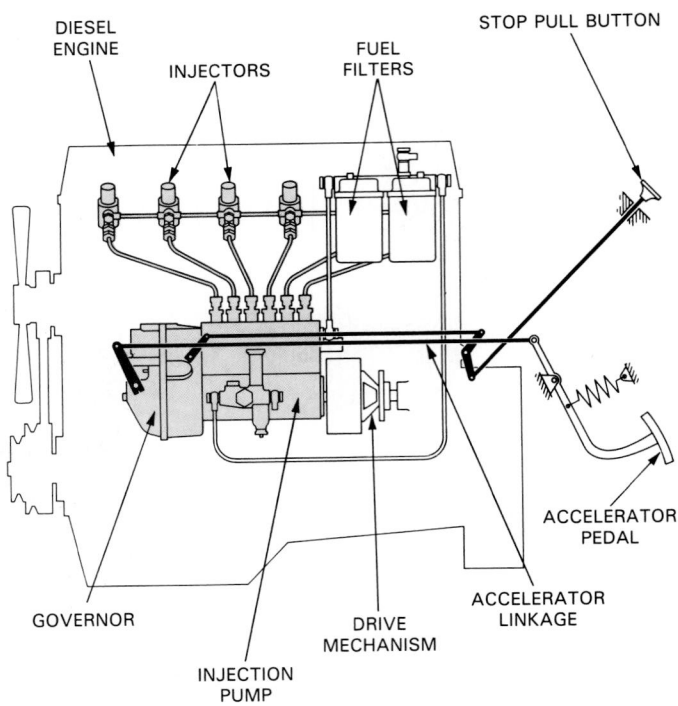

Fig. 23-12. Basic accelerator pedal-to-injection pump linkage arrangement. (Robert Bosch)

Injection timing in an in-line injection pump is usually controlled by spring-loaded weights. As engine speed increases, the weights fly outward to advance injection timing. This gives the diesel fuel more time to ignite and burn properly.

In-line injection pump fuel flow

Look at Fig. 23-13. It illustrates the flow of fuel through a diesel injection system using an in-line type pump. Note how fuel lines are provided that return to the fuel tank. This allows a steady flow of excess fuel through the system to help cool and lubricate moving parts.

DISTRIBUTOR INJECTION PUMPS

A *distributor injection pump* normally uses only one or two pumping plungers to supply fuel for all of the engine's cylinders. It is the most common type of pump used on passenger cars, Fig. 23-14.

In many ways, the operation of a distributor type pump is similar to the action of an in-line injection pump. Both use small pumping plungers to trap and pressurize fuel. Both align and misalign fuel ports to control fuel flow to the injector nozzles. Both use delivery valves, governors, and other similar parts.

It is important, however, that you understand the difference between distributor and in-line injection pumps.

There are two common variations of the distributor injection pump: single-plunger and two-plunger. Both will be discussed.

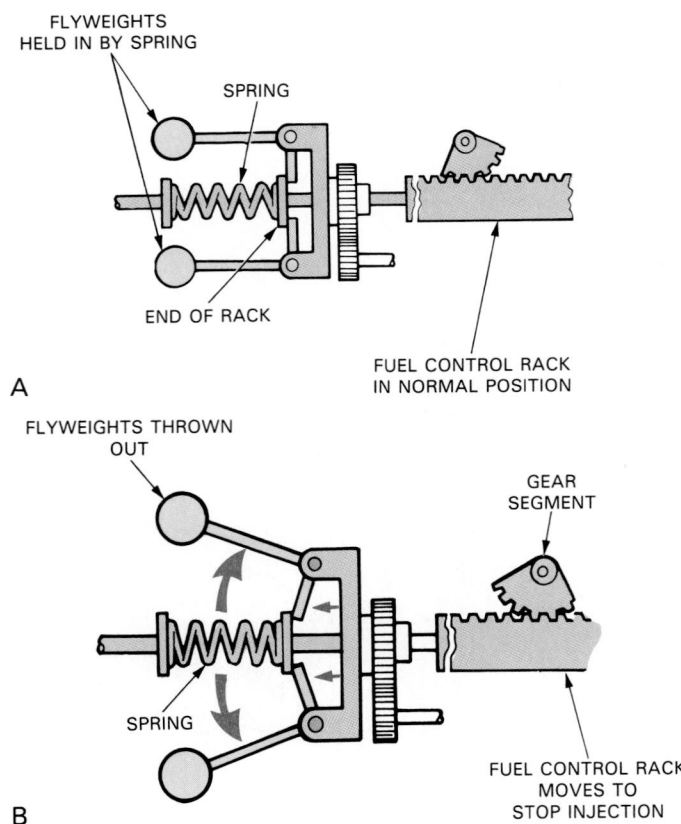

Fig. 23-11. Basic diesel injection pump centrifugal governor operation. A — At low engine speeds, spring holds flyweights in. This keeps control rack in normal position for that throttle lever position. B — When maximum speed is reached, flyweights are spinning fast enough for centrifugal force to compress spring. This causes lever action to move control rack into no injection position. This shuts off diesel engine power until rpm drops. (Chrysler)

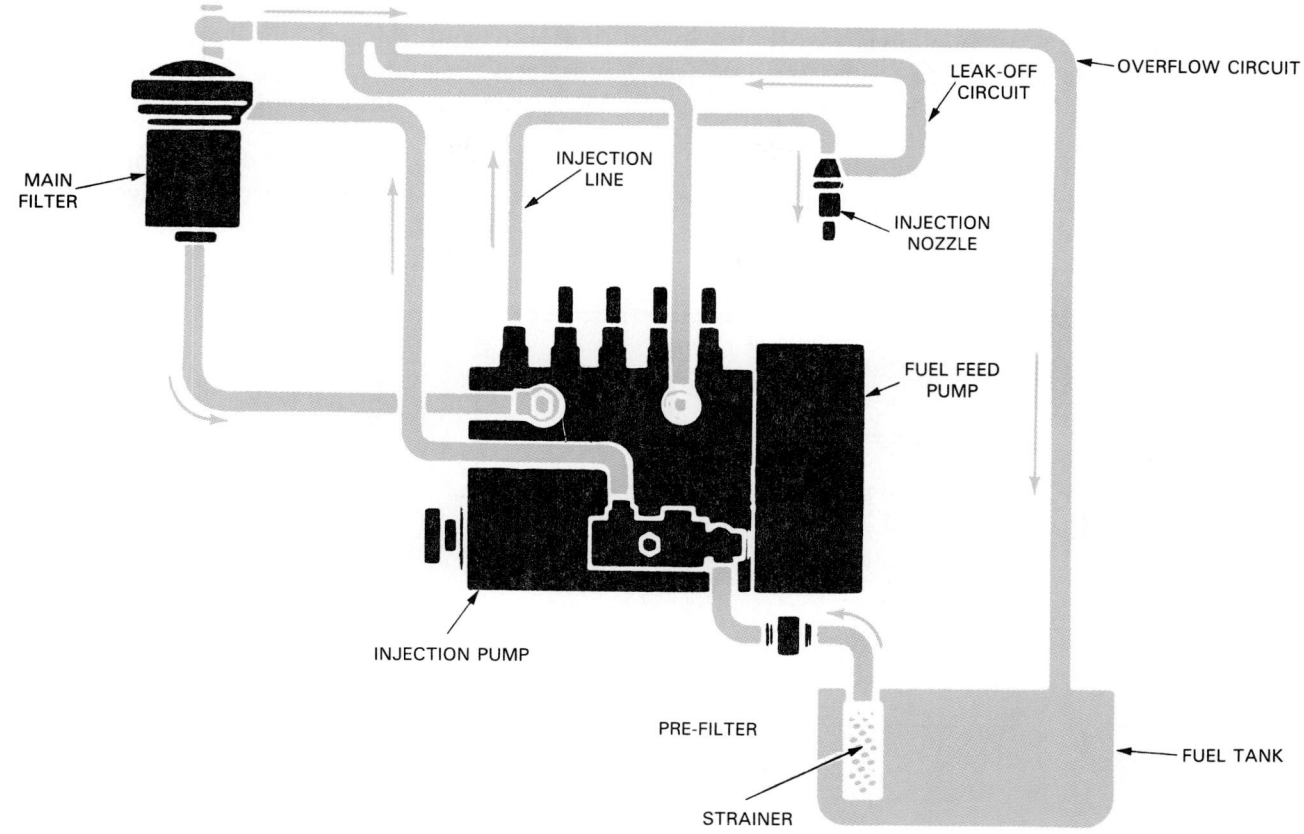

Fig. 23-13. Trace flow of fuel through injection pump and lines. (Mercedes Benz)

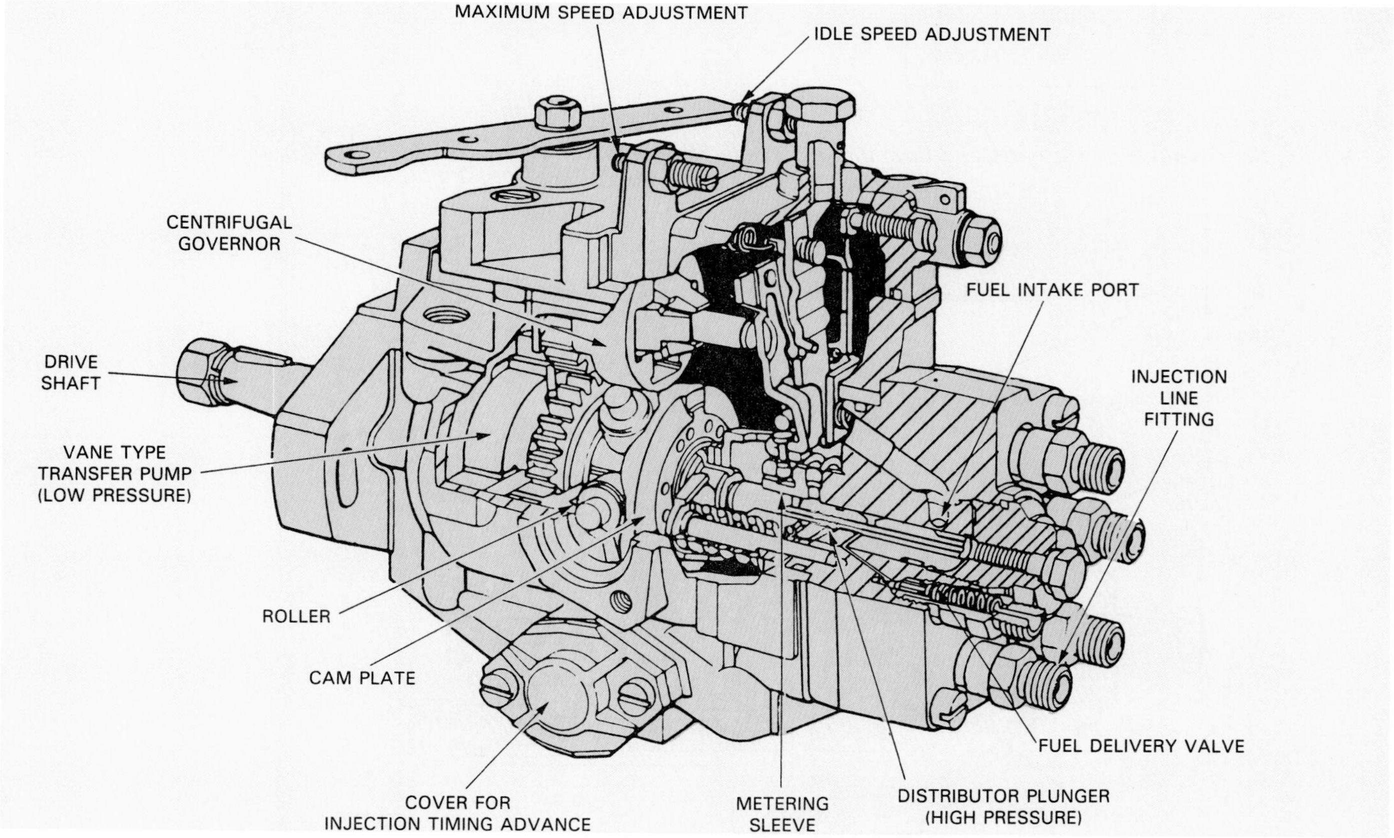

Fig. 23-14. Single-plunger distributor diesel injection pump. Study part names. (Chrysler)

Single-plunger distributor injection pump

The major parts of a single-plunger distributor injection pump are shown in Figs. 23-15 and 23-16. Refer to these illustrations as the parts are discussed.

The **drive shaft** uses engine power to operate the parts in the injection pump. The outer end of the shaft holds either a gear, chain sprocket, or a belt sprocket. This provides a drive mechanism for the pump.

A **transfer pump** is a small pump that forces diesel fuel into and through the injection pump. This lubricates the pump and fills the pumping chambers. Most transfer pumps for distributor pumps are a VANE TYPE.

A **pumping plunger** for a distributor type injection pump is a small piston that produces high fuel pressure. It is comparable to an in-line plunger.

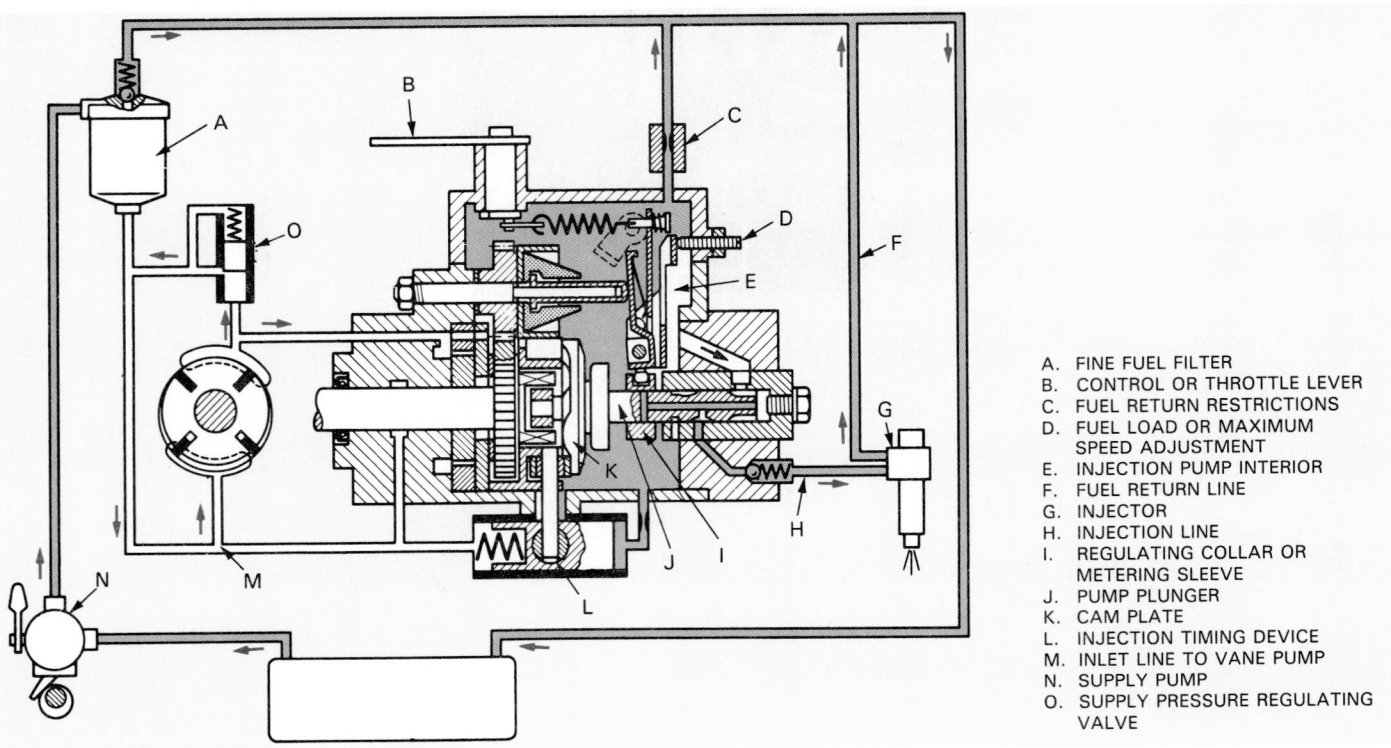

A. FINE FUEL FILTER
B. CONTROL OR THROTTLE LEVER
C. FUEL RETURN RESTRICTIONS
D. FUEL LOAD OR MAXIMUM SPEED ADJUSTMENT
E. INJECTION PUMP INTERIOR
F. FUEL RETURN LINE
G. INJECTOR
H. INJECTION LINE
I. REGULATING COLLAR OR METERING SLEEVE
J. PUMP PLUNGER
K. CAM PLATE
L. INJECTION TIMING DEVICE
M. INLET LINE TO VANE PUMP
N. SUPPLY PUMP
O. SUPPLY PRESSURE REGULATING VALVE

Fig. 23-15. Schematic showing parts and flow through single-plunger distributor pump. Trace flow from tank, through lines, pump, injector, and back to tank.

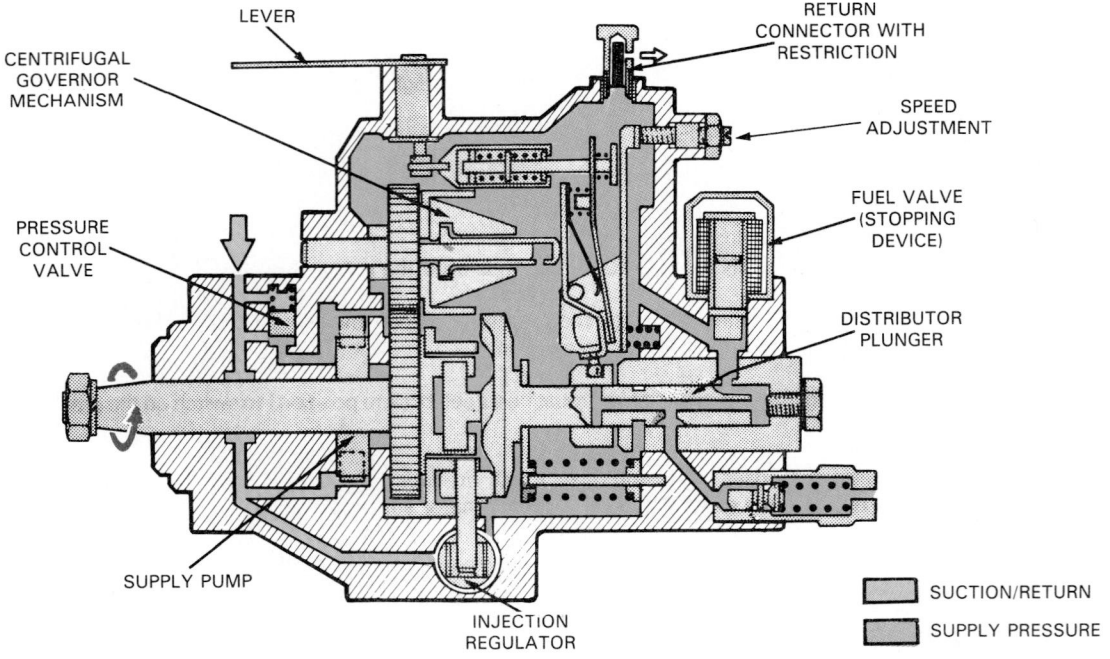

Fig. 23-16. Main parts of single plunger distributor pump. Note arrows. They show fuel flow. (Volvo)

A *cam plate* is a rotating lobed disc that operates the pumping plunger. Like an in-line pump camshaft, it forces the pumping plunger to move and develop injection pressure.

A *fuel metering sleeve* can be slid sideways on the pumping plunger to change the effective plunger stroke (plunger movement that causes fuel pressure). It surrounds the pumping plunger. The fuel metering sleeve performs the same function as the sleeves and controls rack in an in-line pump. The sleeve controls injection quantity, engine speed, and power output.

The *hydraulic head* is the housing around the pumping plunger. It contains passages for filling the plunger barrel with fuel and for allowing fuel to be injected into the delivery valves.

A *centrifugal governor* helps control the amount of fuel injected and engine speed. Flyweight action moves the metering sleeve to limit top rpm.

Single-plunger distributor pump operation

As the injection pump shaft rotates, the fill port in the hydraulic head lines up with the port in the plunger. At this point, transfer pump can force fuel into the high pressure chamber in front of the plunger. Refer to Fig. 23-17.

With more shaft and plunger rotation, the fill port moves out of alignment and an injection port lines up. At this instant, the cam plate lobe pushes the plunger sideways. Fuel is forced out the injection port to the correct injector nozzle.

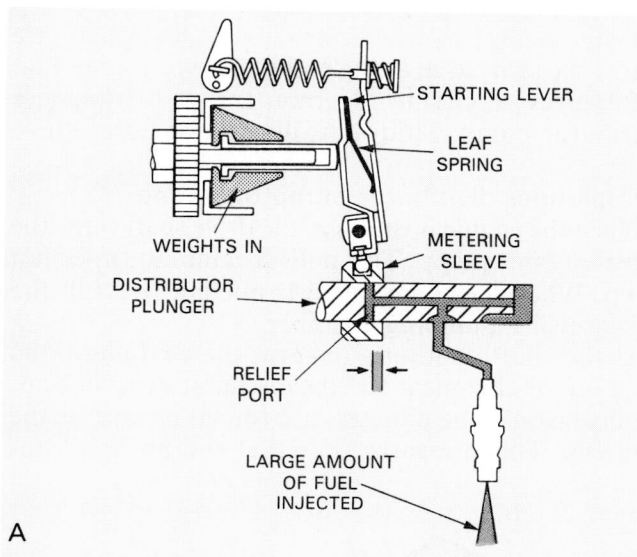

A

Starting — Leaf spring presses starting lever to left so metering sleeve moves to right. Distributor plunger moves further before relief port is exposed. Injection lasts longer.

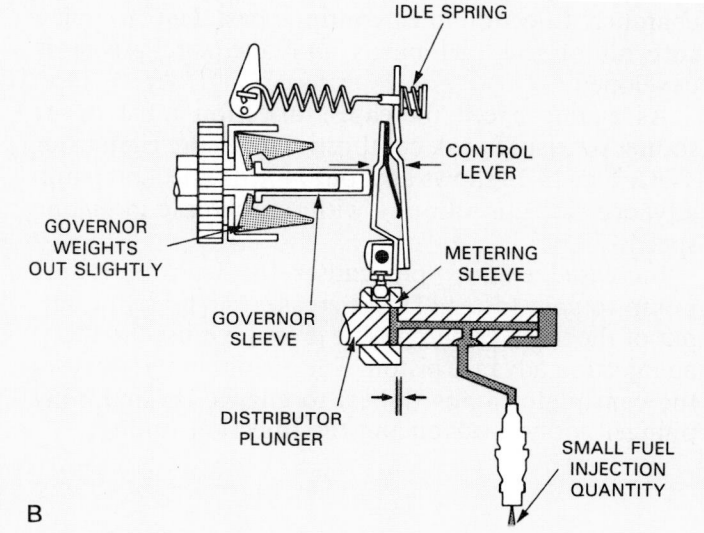

B

Idle — Weights in centrifugal governor are partly expanded so governor sleeve moves to right. Metering sleeve moves to left. Distributor plunger now moves a short distance before relief port is uncovered.

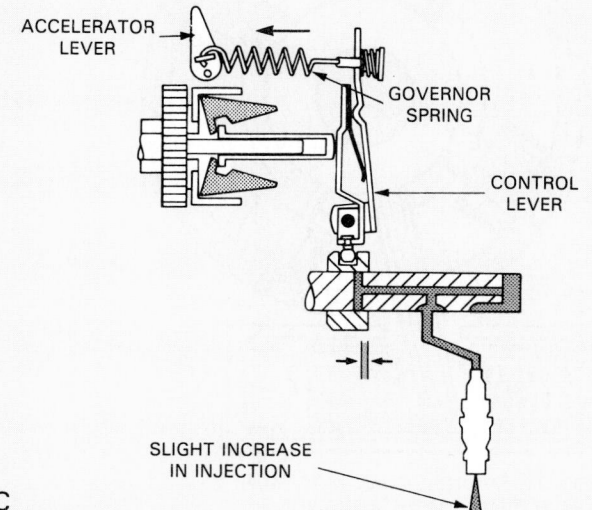

C

Acceleration — Control lever is pulled to left by linkage from accelerator pedal. Metering sleeve is moved to right. Engine speed increases until governor "neutralizes" effect of pedal linkage.

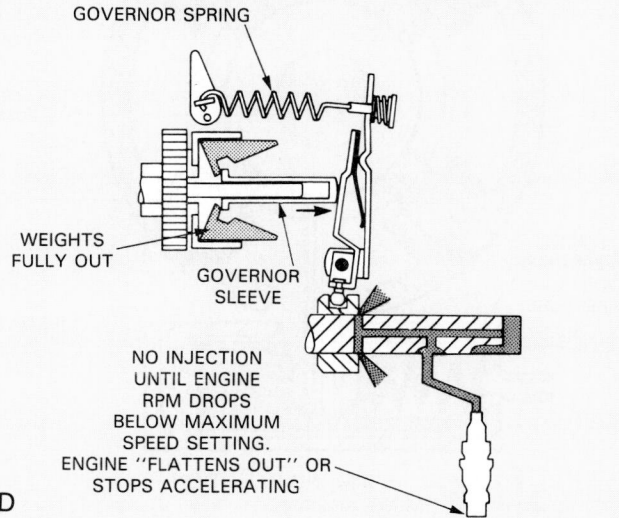

D

Maximum Speed — Governor is spinning with enough centrifugal force for governor sleeve to stretch governor spring. Metering sleeve uncovers relief port at beginning of distributor plunger stroke.

Fig. 23-17. These illustrations show the basic operation of a single-plunger distributor diesel injection pump.

This process is repeated several times during each rotation of the injection pump drive shaft. Fuel injection must be timed to occur at each nozzle as that engine piston nears TDC on its compression stroke.

Single-plunger distributor pump fuel metering

In a single-plunger distributor injection pump, the amount of fuel injected is controlled by movement of the sleeve on the pumping plunger. This is illustrated in Fig. 23-17. The sleeve slides one way to increase fuel delivery by covering the spill port. The sleeve moves the other way to reduce delivery by uncovering the spill port.

Single-plunger distributor pump injection timing

At the end of the engine compression stroke, diesel fuel must be injected directly into the precombustion chamber. Injection must continue past TDC to make sure all of the fuel burns and adequate power is developed.

As engine speed increases, injection must occur sooner to ensure peak combustion pressure right after TDC. Fig. 23-18 shows how one type of injection pump advances injection timing with an increase in engine speed.

Increased engine rpm causes the transfer (vane) pump to spin faster. This increases the pressure output of the transfer pump. The pressure is used to move an injection advance piston. The piston, in turn, causes the cam plate ramps (lobes) to engage the pumping plunger sooner, advancing the injection timing.

Two-plunger distributor pump

A two-plunger distributor injection pump is pictured in Fig. 23-19. Besides many of the basic parts already covered, this injection pump consists of:

1. TWO PUMPING PLUNGERS (two small pistons that move in and out to force fuel to each injector nozzle).
2. DISTRIBUTOR ROTOR (slotted shaft that controls fuel flow to each injector nozzle).
3. INTERNAL CAM RING (lobed collar that acts as a cam to force plungers inward for injection of more fuel).
4. FUEL METERING VALVE (rotary valve that regulates fuel injection quantity by controlling how far two pumping plungers move apart on the pump's fill stroke).

The other parts of a two-plunger distributor pump (transfer pump, hydraulic head, delivery valve) are almost the same as in a single-plunger type pump. Fig. 23-20 gives a circuit diagram for a two-plunger distributor pump. Study this illustration carefully.

Two-plunger distributor pump operation

When the engine is running, the drive shaft turns the transfer (vane) pump. This pulls fuel into the injection pump. When the charging ports line up, fuel fills the high-pressure pumping chamber.

As the shaft continues to turn, the charging ports move out of alignment and the discharge ports line up. At this instant, the plungers are forced inward by the cam ring. This pressurizes the fuel and pushes it out

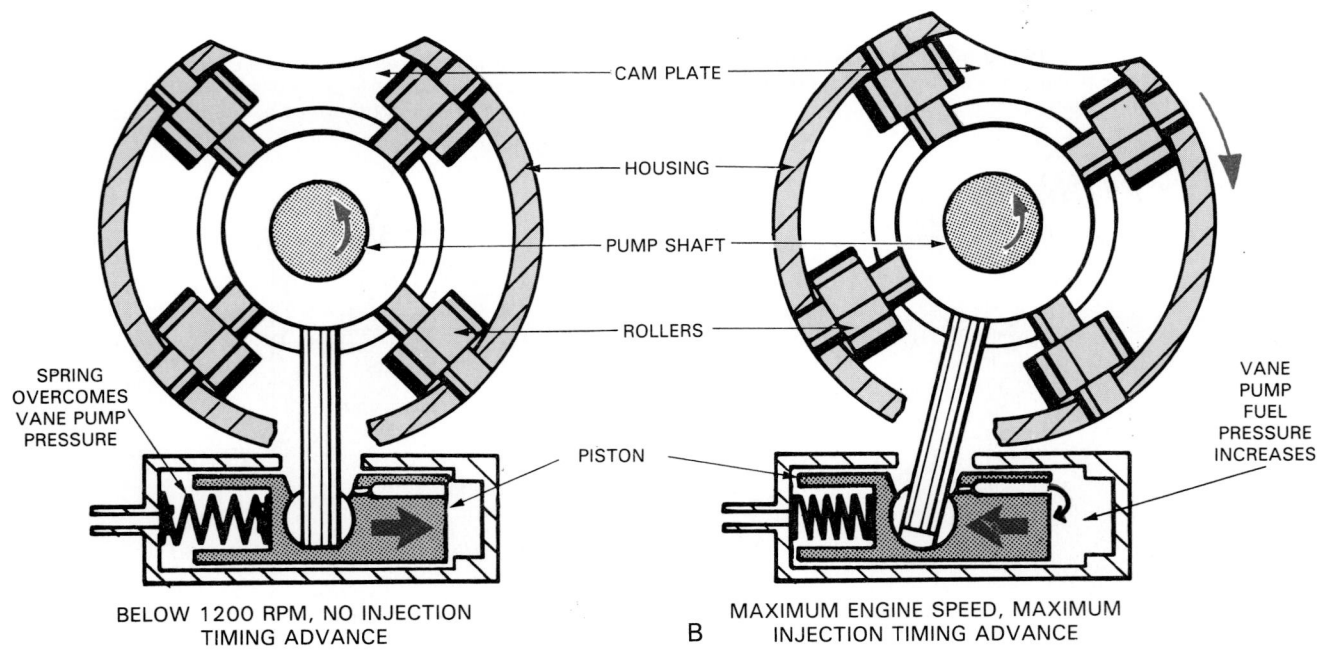

Fig. 23-18. Vane pump pressure can be used to control injection timing. A — At low engine speeds, lower vane pump pressure cannot compress spring. Injection timing remains retarded. B — At higher engine speeds, vane pump spins faster and develops more pressure. This causes piston to compress spring and rotate roller housing. Since cam plate motion is opposite piston movement, plate ramps or lobes engage rollers sooner to cause injection advance. This gives more time for fuel to burn at higher engine rpm. (VW)

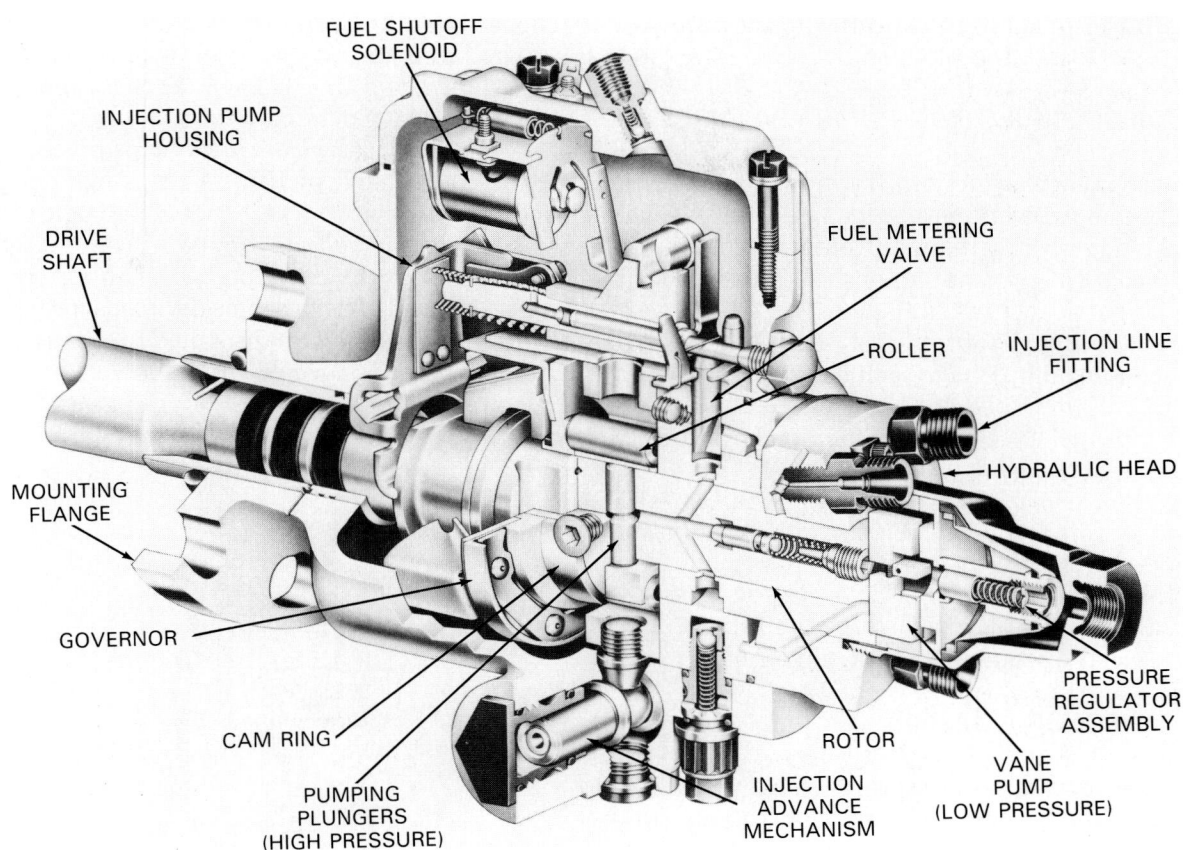

Fig. 23-19. Two-plunger distributor pump. It is similar to single-plunger type pump. Can you find the major differences and similarities? (Oldsmobile)

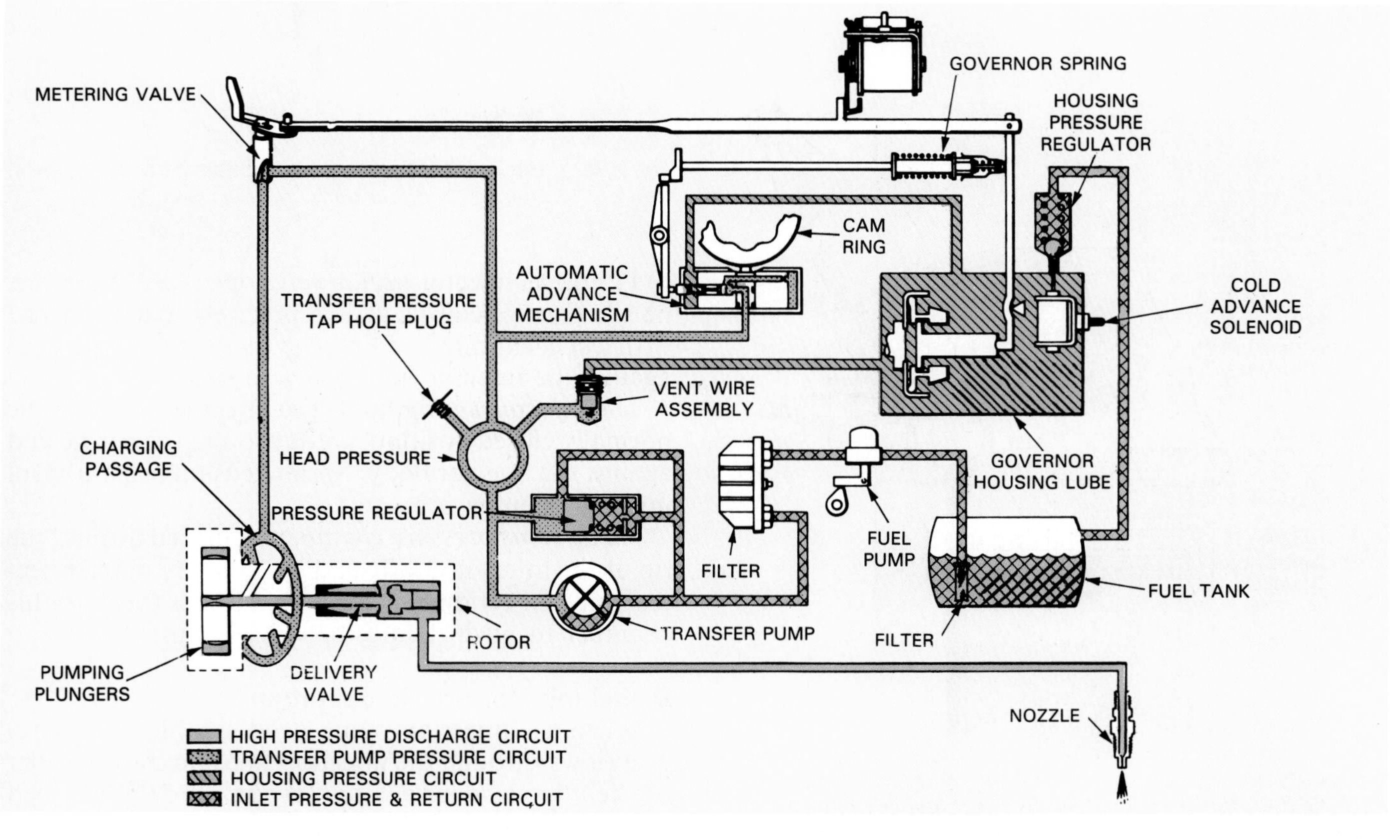

Fig. 23-20. Fuel circuit diagram for a two-plunger distributor injection pump. Can you trace fuel through system? (Oldsmobile)

of the hydraulic head to the injector nozzles. Look at Fig. 23-19 to locate the plungers.

OTHER DIESEL INJECTION PUMP FEATURES

There are numerous design variations of the injection pumps that were just described. For details of each pump design, refer to the pump manufacturer's service manual. It will explain the construction and operation of the particular pump.

A few additional features that many automotive diesel injection pumps have include:
1. An ELECTRIC FUEL SHUT-OFF is a solenoid that stops fuel injection when ignition key is turned off. See Fig. 23-19.
2. A VISCOSITY COMPENSATING VALVE allows for different fuel weights or thicknesses and temperatures.
3. An INJECTION PUMP VENT is a small passage that allows fuel to return to the fuel tank. This helps bleed air out of system, Fig. 23-20.

DIESEL INJECTOR NOZZLES

Diesel injector nozzles are spring-loaded valves that spray fuel directly into the engine precombustion chambers. See Fig. 23-21.

The injector nozzles are threaded into the cylinder head. One injector is provided for each engine cylinder. The inner tip of the injector nozzle is exposed to the heat of combustion, like a spark plug in a gasoline engine.

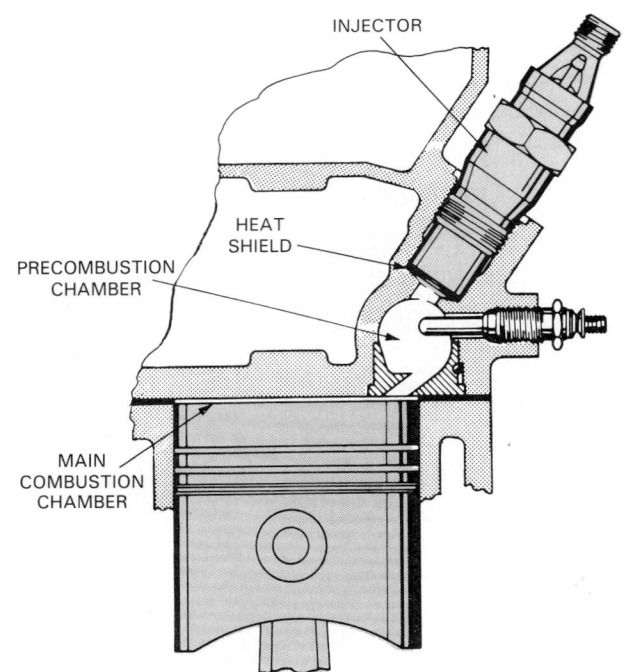

Fig. 23-21. Diesel injector screws into cylinder head. Heat shield fits between injector body and head. Fuel is injected into precombustion chamber. (VW)

Diesel injector parts

The basic parts of a diesel injector are pictured in Figs. 23-22 and 23-23. Look at these illustrations as the parts are explained.

A diesel injector *heat shield* helps protect the injector from engine heat. It also helps make a good seal between the injector and the cylinder head.

The *injector body* is the main section of the injector that holds the other parts. The body threads into the heat shield. The heat shield threads into the cylinder head. Fuel passages are provided in the injector body. A needle seat is formed by the lower opening in the injector body.

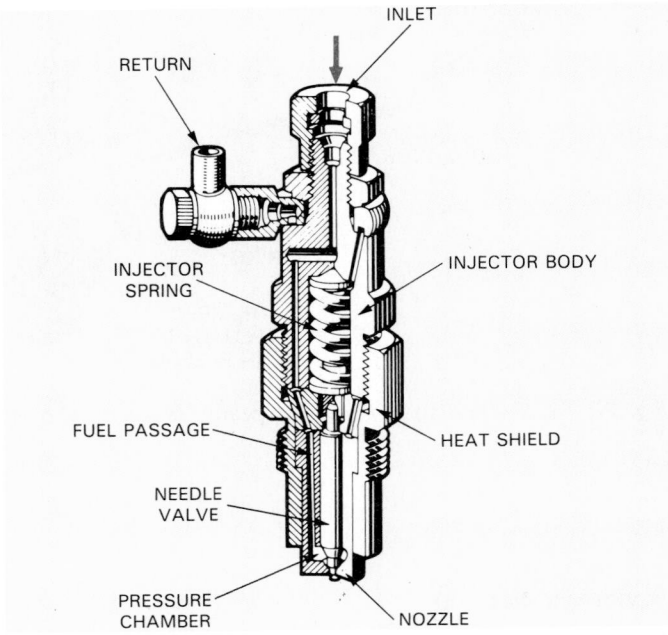

Fig. 23-22. Basic diesel injector construction. Note part names, shapes, and locations. (Robert Bosch)

The diesel injector *needle valve* opens and closes the nozzle (fuel opening). It is a precisely machined rod with a specially shaped tip. The tip of the needle seals against the injector body when closed.

The *injector spring* holds the injector needle in the normally closed position. It fits around the needle and against the injector body. Spring tension helps control injector opening pressure.

An *injector pressure chamber* is formed around the tip of the injector needle and inner cavity in the injector body. Injection pump pressure forces fuel into this chamber to push the needle valve open.

Diesel injector nozzle operation

When the injection pump produces high pressure, fuel flows through the injection line and into the inlet of the injector nozzle. Look at Fig. 23-23. Fuel then flows down through the fuel passage in the injector body and into the pressure chamber.

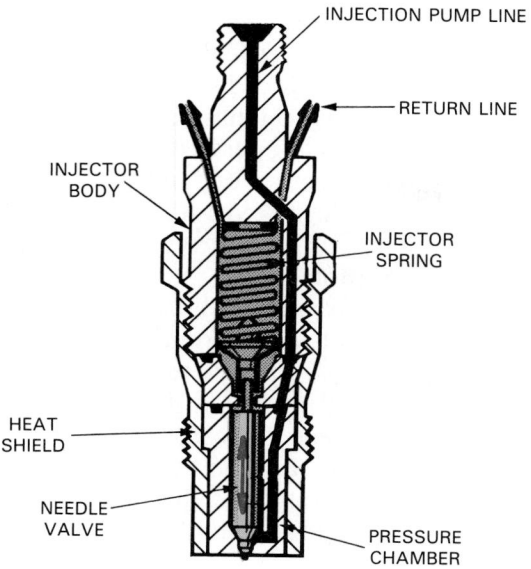

Fig. 23-23. High pressure from injection pump enters top of injector valve. Fuel flows through body passage to pressure chamber. With enough injection pressure, needle valve is pushed up and fuel sprays into precombustion chamber. (VW)

The high fuel pressure in the pressure chamber forces the needle upward, compressing the injector spring. This allows diesel fuel to spray out forming a CONE-SHAPED spray pattern. Some fuel leaks past the injector needle and returns to the fuel tank through the return lines.

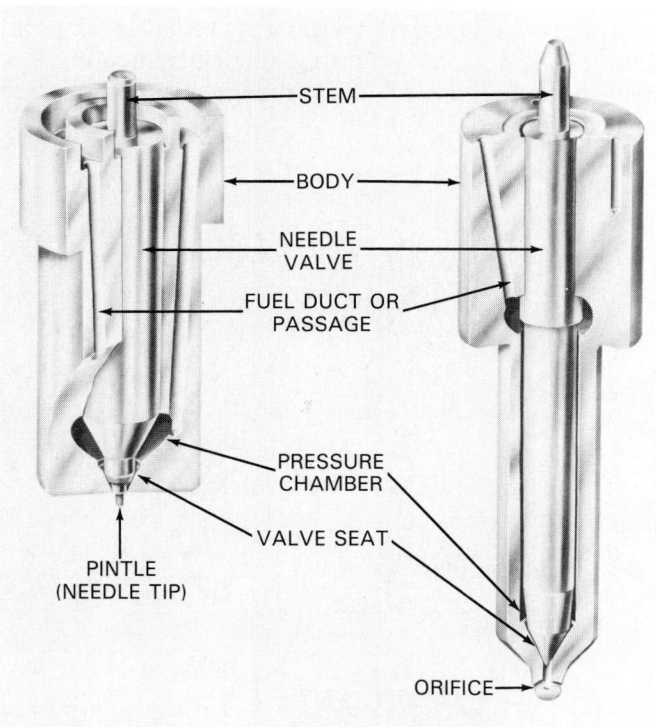

Fig. 23-24. Inward opening injector nozzles. Left — Pintle type injector is very common in automotive diesel engine. Right — Hole type injector is less common. (American Bosch)

Diesel injector nozzle types

Several types of injector nozzles are used in diesel engines. The most common of these are the:

1. Inward opening injector nozzle, Fig. 23-24.
2. Outward opening injector nozzle, Fig. 23-25.
3. Pintle injector nozzle, Fig. 23-24.
4. Hole injector nozzle, Fig. 23-24.

Most automotive diesels use an inward opening, pintle type injector nozzle. Fig. 23-25 shows some typical spray patterns.

GLOW PLUGS

Glow plugs are heating elements that warm the air in precombustion chambers to help start a cold diesel engine. Refer to Figs. 23-26 and 23-27.

The glow plugs are threaded into holes in the cylinder head. The inner tip of the glow plug extends into the precombustion chamber.

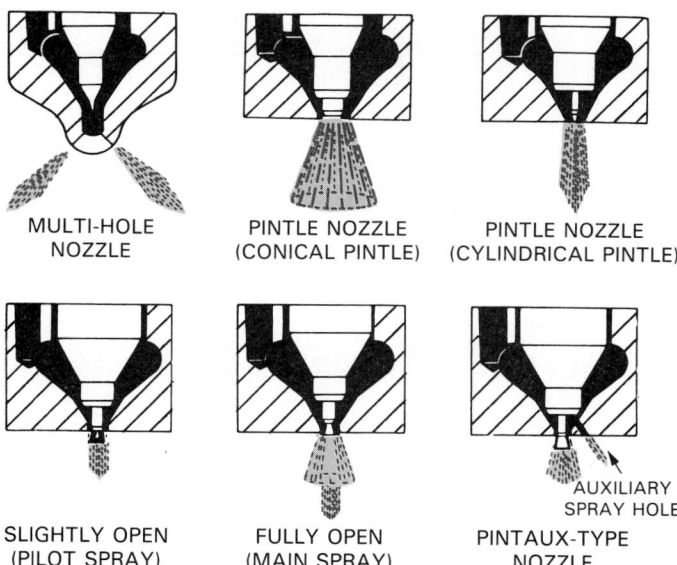

Fig. 23-25. Study spray patterns for different types of injectors. (Chrysler)

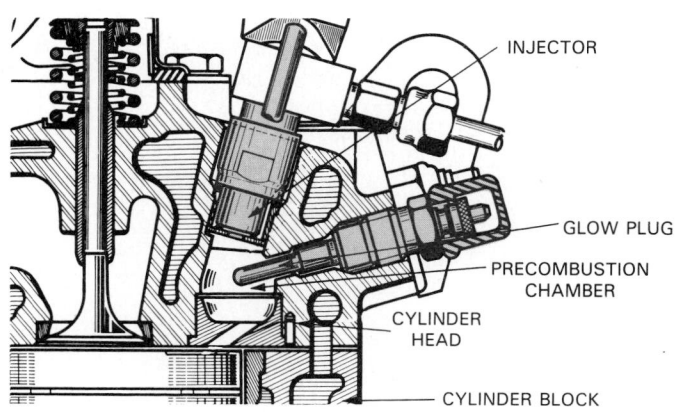

Fig. 23-26. Glow plug screws into cylinder head next to injector. Its tip protrudes into precombustion chamber. (Peugeot)

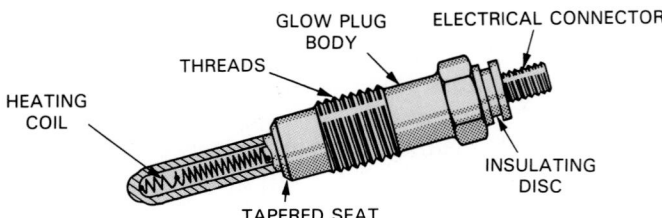

Fig. 23-27. Glow plug is simply an electric heating element. Current flow through plug heats element to warm air in precombustion chamber. This aids starting of cold engine. (Mercedes Benz)

Glow plug control circuit

A *glow plug control circuit* automatically turns the glow plugs OFF after a few seconds of operation. Fig. 23-28 shows a typical glow plug circuit.

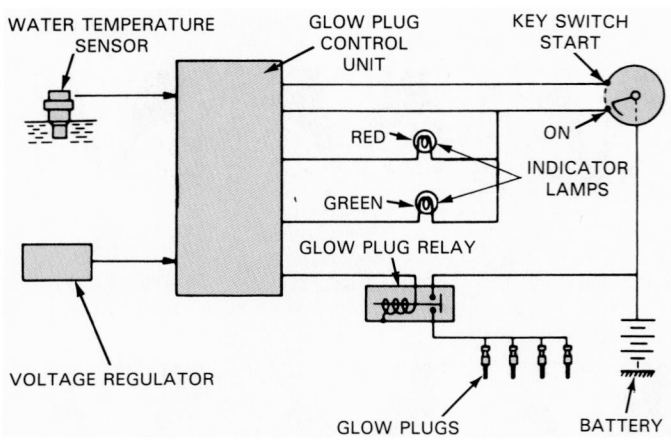

Fig. 23-28. Basic circuit for glow plugs. Control unit monitors engine temperature and informs driver whether glow plugs have been on long enough for engine starting. (Chrysler)

A sensor checks the temperature of the engine coolant. It feeds this electrical data to a control unit. Thus, if the engine is already warm, the control unit will not turn on the glow plugs.

Indicator lights, also operated by the control unit, inform the driver whether or not the engine is ready to start. The glow plugs need a few seconds to heat up.

Glow plug operation

When the engine is cold and the driver turns the ignition switch to run, a large current flows from the battery to the glow plugs. In a few seconds, the glow plug tips, Fig. 23-27, will heat to a dull red glow.

When the glow plug indicator light goes out, the driver can start the engine. The compression stroke pressure and heat, along with the heat from the glow plugs, helps the engine to start easier.

WATER DETECTOR

A *water detector* may be used to warn the driver of water in the diesel fuel. Such contamination is very harmful to a diesel fuel system. The water mixes with the fuel and can cause corrosion of the precision parts in the injection pump and injectors. Fig. 23-29 shows a circuit using an in-tank water detector.

FUEL HEATER

A *fuel heater* is sometimes used to warm the diesel fuel, preventing the fuel from *jelling* (turning into a semisolid). An optional device, it is needed in very cold climates. The heater is simply an electric heating element in the fuel line ahead of the injection pump. See Figs. 23-29 and 23-30.

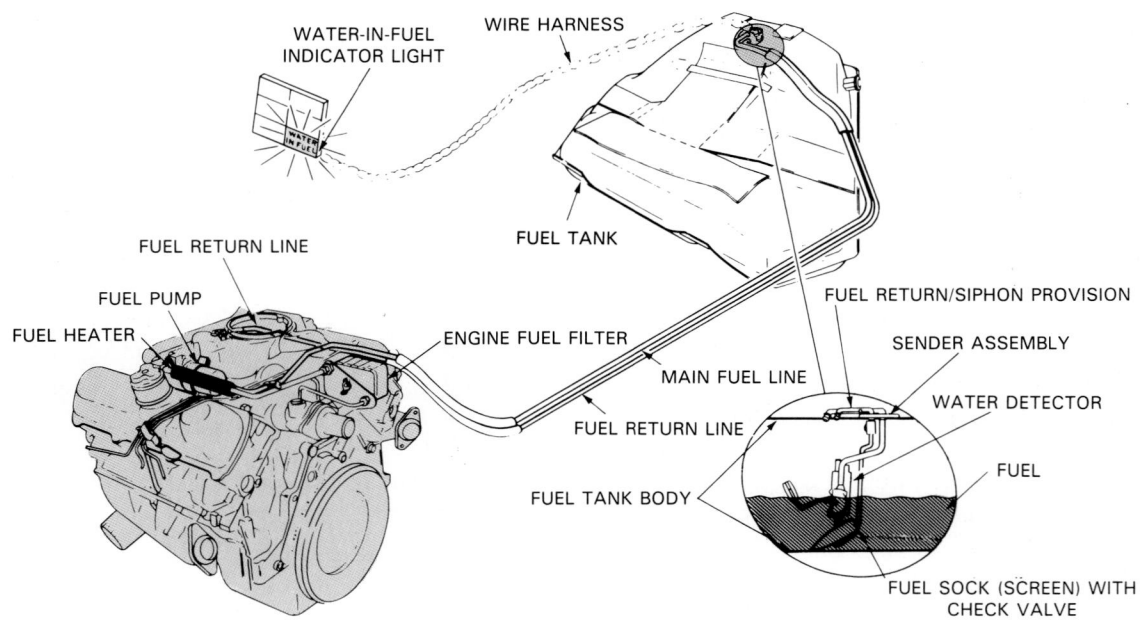

Fig. 23-29. This diesel injection system has a water detector-warning light system and a fuel heater. Indicator light glows if there is an excessive amount of water in tank. Fuel heater warms fuel in line before fuel enters injection pump. Heat is only needed in cold weather. (Oldsmobile)

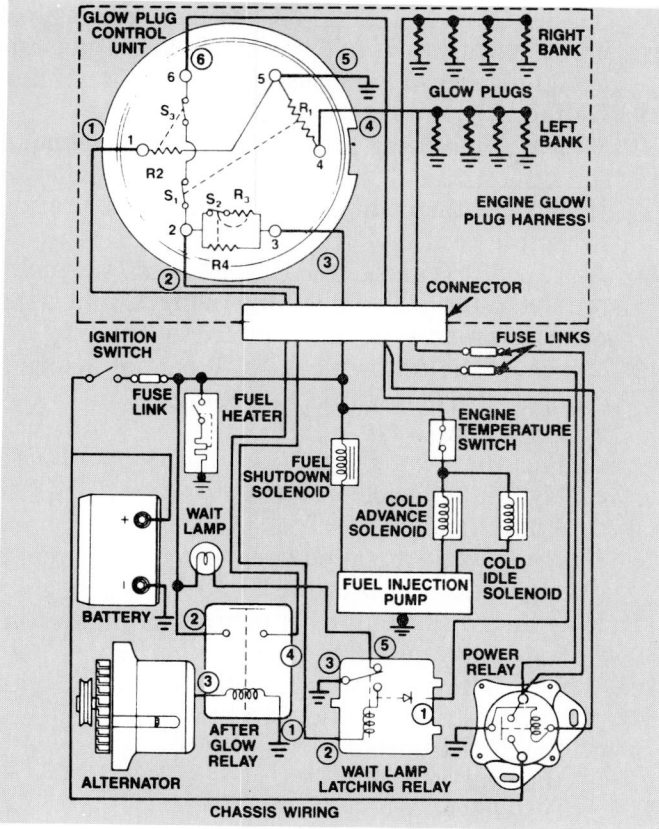

Fig. 23-30. Complete electrical circuit for a typical diesel injection system. Note parts and electrical connections. (Ford)

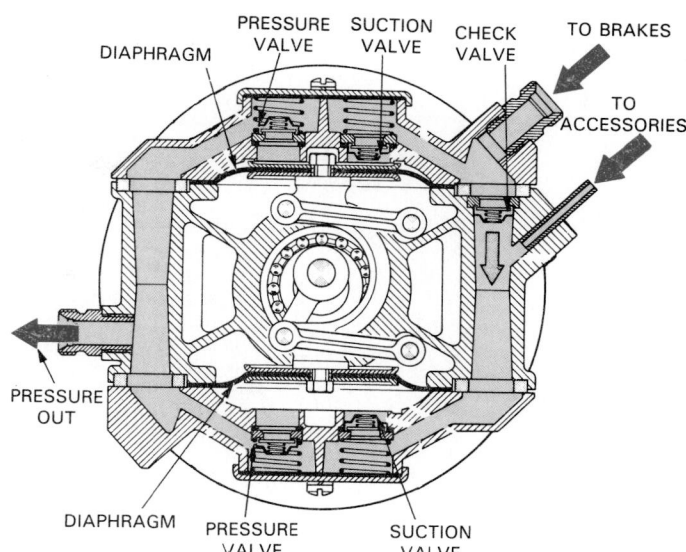

Fig. 23-31. Construction of a diaphragm vacuum pump. (Mercedes Benz)

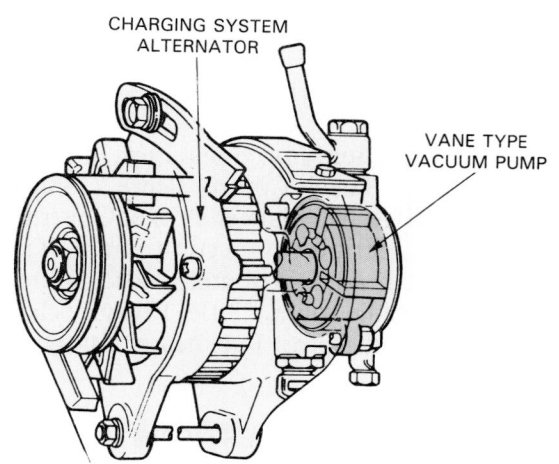

Fig. 23-32. Vane type vacuum pump is mounted in back of charging system alternator. It produces vacuum for power brakes and other vacuum operated devices. (Chrysler)

BLOCK HEATER

A *block heater* may be used to warm the engine block in cold weather. It is a heating device that plugs into a home wall electric outlet. It keeps the engine warm overnight to make the diesel engine easier to start on cold mornings.

VACUUM PUMP

A *vacuum pump* is frequently used on a diesel engine to provide a source of vacuum (suction) for the vehicle. Vacuum is needed for the power brakes, A/C-ventilation system, and emission control devices.

A gasoline engine has a natural source of vacuum in the intake manifold. A diesel engine, because it does NOT have a throttle valve restriction, has very little vacuum in the intake manifold. For this reason, a vacuum pump is needed.

A vacuum pump on a diesel engine may be a reciprocating diaphragm type bolted to the front or rear of the engine, Fig. 23-31. It may also be a rotary type pump at the rear of the alternator, Fig. 23-32.

A vacuum pump uses the same principle as a fuel pump (see Chapter 18). However, it pumps air, not liquid fuel, out of an enclosed area to reduce pressure and form a vacuum. The diesel engine provides power for the vacuum pump, usually through a belt.

COMPUTER-CONTROLLED DIESEL SYSTEM

A *computer-controlled diesel system* uses a computer, sensors, and actuators to increase the efficiency of mechanical diesel injection. A simplified illustration is given in Fig. 23-33.

In the past, diesel injection was mechanical. All of the controls for the system were mechanical: linkages, levers, rods, gears, etc. Mechanical controls were heavy and slow to react. Electronic components have been designed to replace many mechanical devices.

Injection pump solenoids can be used to control injection timing and injection quantity. They react to signals from the computer.

Diesel injection sensors are used to monitor engine temperature, speed, and other variables that affect fuel needs. The sensor feeds signals to the computer.

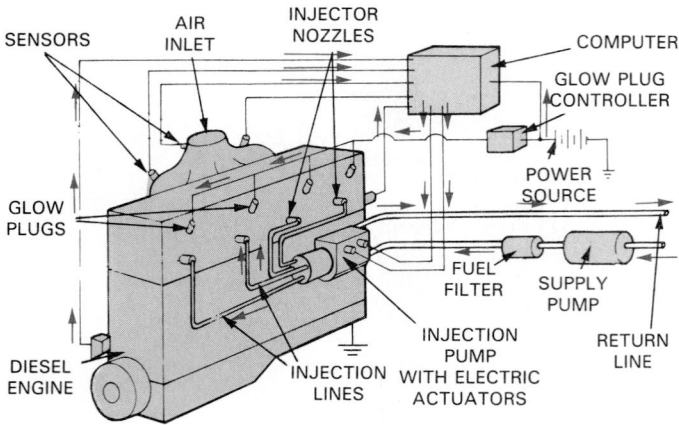

Fig. 23-33. *Study basic parts used in electronic diesel injection system.*

The *diesel injection computer* monitors sensor inputs and calculates the outputs for the actuators. In this way, the computer can more precisely control the mechanical high pressure pumping plungers inside the diesel injection pump.

KNOW THESE TERMS

Compression ignition, Injection pump, In-line pump, Pumping plunger, Barrel, Control sleeve, Control rod, Delivery valve, Effective plunger stroke, Governor, Injection timing, Distributor injection pump, Transfer pump, Hydraulic head, Distributor rotor, Internal cam ring, Injector, Needle valve, Pintle, Pressure chamber, Glow plug, Water detector, Fuel heater, Block heater, Vacuum pump.

REVIEW QUESTIONS

1. A diesel fuel injection system is a super-high pressure, mechanical system that delivers fuel directly to the engine combustion chambers. True or False?
2. List and explain the four major components of a diesel injection system.
3. Which of the following is NOT related to a diesel engine?
   a. Compression ignition.
   b. No throttle valves for air control.
   c. Fuel quantity controls engine speed.
   d. All of the above are correct.
4. There are two common types of diesel injection pumps: _____ and _____ types.
5. What is the function of a pumping plunger in an injection pump?
6. Roller tappets are commonly used in an in-line injection pump. True or False?
7. Explain how an in-line injection pump alters the amount of fuel forced to the injector nozzles.

8. _____ _____ are spring-loaded valves in the outlet fittings to the injection lines for assuring quick, leak-free closing of the injector nozzles.
9. Define the term "effective plunger stroke."
10. Why is a governor needed on a diesel engine?
11. _____ _____ refers to when fuel is injected into the combustion chambers in relation to piston position.
12. A _____ _____ _____ normally uses only one or two pumping plungers and is the most common type diesel injection pump.
13. Which of the following is NOT part of a single-plunger distributor injection pump?
   a. Drive shaft.
   b. Fuel metering sleeve.
   c. Hydraulic head.
   d. Roller tappet.
14. How does a single-plunger distributor pump develop injection pressure?
15. How does a single-plunger distributor pump control injection quantity?
16. Which of the following is NOT part of a two-plunger distributor injection pump?
   a. External camshaft.
   b. Internal cam ring.
   c. Distributor rotor.
   d. Fuel metering valve.
17. A vane type transfer pump is commonly used to pull fuel into the two-plunger distributor injection pump. True or False?
18. An electric fuel shut-off is only used on in-line type injection pumps. True or False?
19. A diesel _____ _____ is a spring-loaded valve that sprays fuel into the engine precombustion chamber.
20. List and explain the five major parts of a diesel injector.
21. Why are glow plugs needed in a diesel engine?
22. Explain the purpose of a water detector.
23. A _____ _____ can be used to help keep the diesel fuel from jelling in cold weather.
24. A block heater is a heating device operated by the car battery. True or False?
25. Explain why a diesel engine, unlike a gasoline engine, needs a vacuum pump.

ACTIVITIES FOR CHAPTER 23

1. Prepare an overhead transparency showing how the various parts of a diesel injection system are interrelated.
2. Show in a sketch the relationship of a compression ratio of 17:1.
3. Research centrifugal force as a scientific principle; relate this principle to the operation of a governor; devise a way of demonstrating the principle to the shop class.

24

Diesel Injection Diagnosis, Service, Repair

After studying this chapter, you will be able to:
- [ ] Diagnose typical diesel injection problems.
- [ ] List safety precautions pertaining to diesel injection service.
- [ ] Test, rebuild, and replace diesel injectors.
- [ ] Test and replace glow plugs.
- [ ] Perform basic maintenance operations on a diesel injection system.
- [ ] Describe the basic adjustments common to diesel injection systems.
- [ ] Demonstrate safe work habits in diesel injection service.

Since almost all auto manufacturers now offer a diesel engine, it is important for you to understand how to work on a diesel injection system. While diesel injection service procedures are different from those for a gasoline engine, they are still relatively simple.

DIESEL INJECTION DIAGNOSIS

Diesel injection diagnosis requires you to use your knowledge of engine and injection system operation, and your basic troubleshooting skills. Begin diagnosis by checking the operation of the engine. Check for:
1. Abnormal exhaust smoke.
2. Excessive knock.
3. Engine miss.
4. Engine "no start" condition.
5. Lack of engine power.
6. Poor fuel economy.

Refer to the troubleshooting chart in the vehicle's service manual. It will list the possible causes for these and other conditions. The service manual chart will be accurate because it is designed for one type of diesel injection system.

Diesel exhaust smoke

Excessive *diesel exhaust smoke* is normally due to incomplete combustion caused by injection system or engine troubles. A small amount of exhaust smoke is normal during initial start-up, cold engine operation, or during rapid acceleration.

Abnormal exhaust smoke may be black, white, or blue. See Fig. 24-1.

The main cause of excessive *black smoke* from a diesel engine is too much fuel. A rich air-fuel mixture is allowing carbon (ash) to blow out the exhaust system. Black diesel smoke may be due to problems with the injection pump, injection timing, air cleaner, injectors, fuel, or engine itself.

White smoke occurs mainly during cold starts. The smoke usually consists of condensed fuel particles. The cold engine parts cause the fuel to condense into a liquid that will not burn. The most common reasons for white exhaust smoke are: inoperative glow plugs, low engine compression, thermostat stuck open, bad injector spray pattern, late injection timing, or cold start (injection pump) problems.

Note! White smoke can also be caused by coolant leakage into the combustion chambers. The engine may have a leaking head gasket, cracked cylinder head, or cracked block.

Excessive *blue smoke* in a diesel engine's exhaust may be due to oil consumption from worn piston rings, scored cylinder walls, or leaking valve stem seals. White-blue smoke, however, is normally caused by incomplete combustion and injection system problems.

Smoke meter

A *smoke meter* is a testing device for measuring the amount of smoke (ash or soot) in diesel exhaust. See Fig. 24-2. The smoke meter measures the amount of light that can shine through an exhaust sample. If the exhaust smoke blocks too much light, engine or injection system repairs or adjustments are needed. A smoke meter is illustrated and discussed further in Chapter 42, Engine Test Instruments.

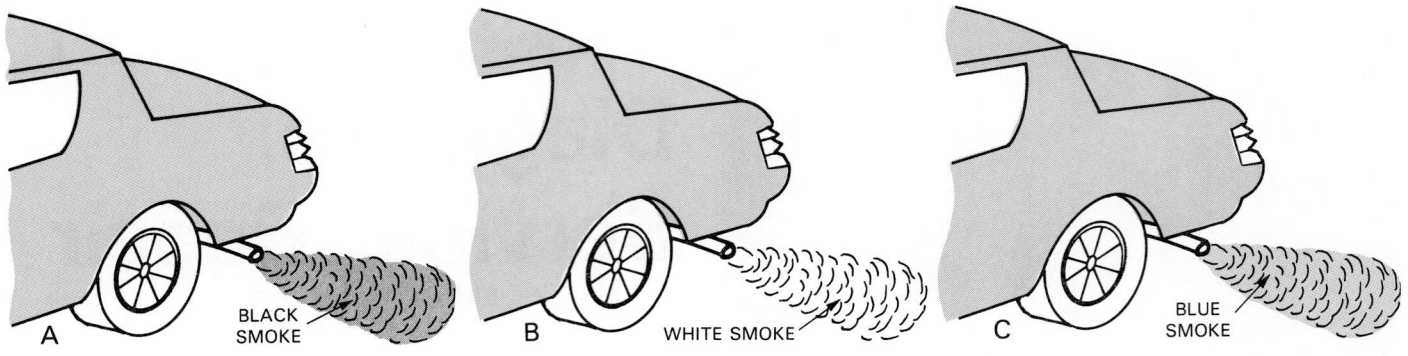

Fig. 24-1. Exhaust smoke will tell you much about diesel engine operation. A — Black exhaust smoke indicates rich fuel mixture. B — White exhaust smoke indicates partially burned fuel, as when starting cold engine. C — Blue smoke indicates engine oil is entering combustion chamber.

Excessive diesel knock

All diesels produce a knocking sound when running. This occurs because the fuel ignites spontaneously and burns very rapidly. Very high pressures produce a rumble or dull clattering sound.

Ignition lag is the time span between the injection of the diesel fuel and the ignition (burning) of the fuel.

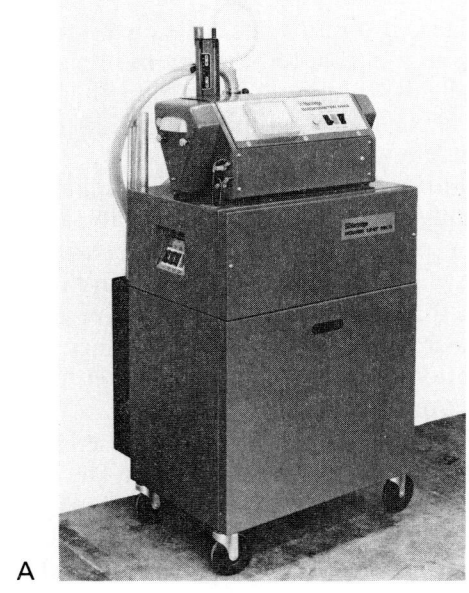

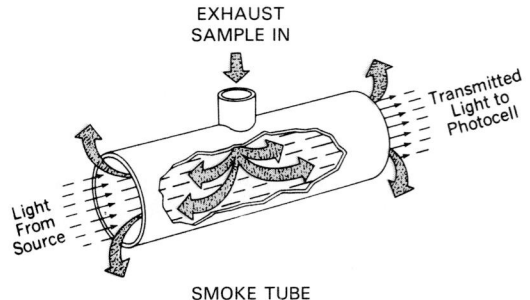

Fig. 24-2. Smoke meter can be used to check amount of smoke in diesel exhaust. A — Smoke meter. B — Principle of smoke meter operation. (Hartridge)

It is a controlling factor affecting diesel knock. If ignition lag time is TOO LONG, too much fuel will ignite at once and a mild explosion (loud knock) will result.

Abnormally loud *diesel knock* can be due to: low engine operating temperature (thermostat stuck open), early injection timing, low engine compression, fuel contamination, and oil consumption.

Diesel engine miss

A *diesel engine miss* results from one or more cylinders not firing (burning fuel) properly. Just as a gasoline engine will miss if a spark plug does not produce a spark, a diesel engine can also run roughly because of injection system problems.

A miss in a diesel engine can be due to: faulty injectors, clogged fuel filters, incorrect injection timing, low cylinder compression, injection system leak, air leak, or faulty injection pump.

Diesel engine will not start

When a diesel engine *does not start,* it may be due to inoperative glow plugs, restricted air or fuel flow, bad fuel shut-off solenoid, contaminated fuel, or injection pump problems.

Note! A slow cranking speed is a common cause of a diesel no-start condition. Being a compression ignition engine, a diesel must crank fast enough to produce sufficient heat for combustion.

Lack of engine power

When a diesel engine *lacks power,* check the throttle cable adjustment, governor setting, fuel filters, air filter, engine compression, and other factors affecting combustion. Keep in mind, however, a diesel engine does NOT produce as much power as a gasoline engine of equal size.

Poor fuel economy

Poor fuel economy may be due to a fuel leak, clogged air filter, incorrect injection timing, or leaking injectors. Normally, a diesel engine will get better fuel economy than a gasoline engine.

A check of EPA fuel economy values for the vehicle should be made before measuring actual fuel economy. If fuel mileage is much lower than these values, adjustments or repairs should be made.

More diesel diagnosis information

As each diesel injection component is discussed in this chapter, possible symptoms, problems, and corrections for that component will be explained. Refer also to Chapters 41 and 42 for more information on diagnosing diesel injection troubles. These chapters cover engine performance problems and engine test instruments.

DIESEL INJECTION SERVICE SAFETY

1. Even though diesel fuel is not as flammable as gasoline, it still poses a serious FIRE HAZARD. Follow all safety precautions that apply to gasoline.
2. NEVER attempt to remove an injection system component with the engine running. With 6000 to 8000 psi (42 000 to 56 000 kPa) fuel pressure, fuel could squirt out and puncture your skin. BLOOD POISONING or DEATH could result.
3. Always double-check that all fittings have been torqued before starting the engine.
4. Wear safety glasses when working around a diesel injection system. A leak could spray fuel into your eyes and cause BLINDNESS or DEATH.
5. Never attempt to stop a diesel engine by covering the air inlet opening. Since there is no throttle valve, there is enough suction to cause HAND INJURY or to suck rags and other objects into the engine intake manifold.

DIESEL INJECTION MAINTENANCE

Refer to a service manual for details on periodic maintenance of a diesel injection system. You will need to change or clean filters periodically. Maintenance also involves inspecting the system for signs of trouble.

If you detect signs of fuel leakage, use a piece of cardboard to find the leak. See Fig. 24-3. Move the cardboard around each fitting. If there is a serious leak, it will strike the cardboard and not your hand. Replace any injection line or return hose that is not in perfect condition, Fig. 24-4.

Fuel filters are normally located in the fuel tank (sock filter), in the fuel line (main filter), and sometimes in

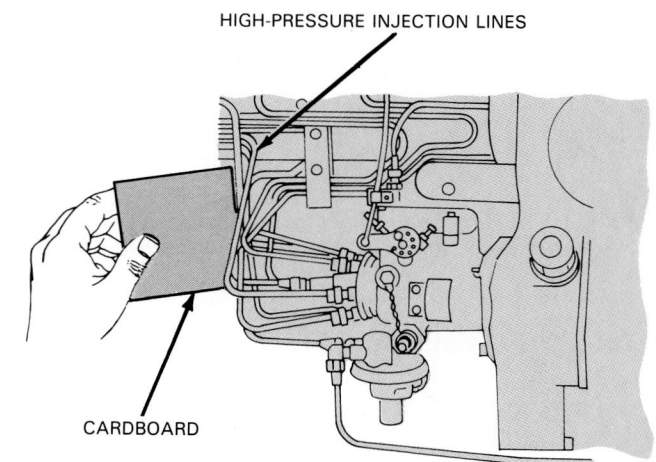

Fig. 24-3. Use a piece of cardboard to locate injection system leaks. Remember that injection pressure is high enough to make fuel spray puncture skin. (Chrysler)

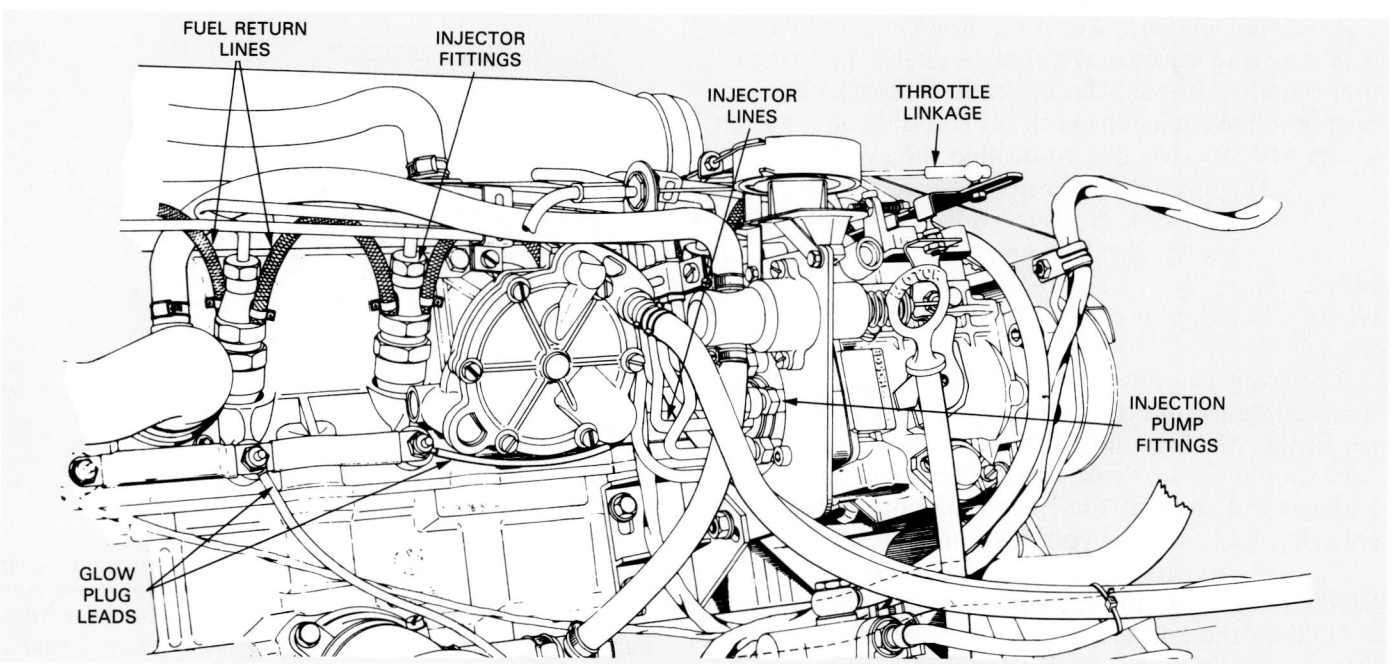

Fig. 24-4. Visual check of hoses, lines, filters, and linkages will sometimes reveal source of problem. (Volvo)

the injector assemblies (final filter screens), Fig. 24-5. For good performance, it is very important that these filters be kept clean.

The main fuel filter may have a drain. The drain can be used to bleed off trapped water. When mixed with diesel oil, WATER causes rapid corrosion and pitting of injection system components.

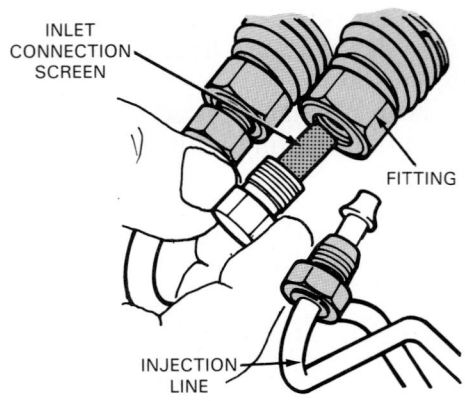

Fig. 24-5. Inlet screen at injectors are frequently used. Check them if problems point to injection system. (Chrysler)

TESTING DIESEL INJECTION OPERATION

There are several ways to check the operation of a diesel injection system. We will briefly explain the most common testing methods. Always refer to your service manual for exact instructions. Recommended testing procedures vary with the design of the injection pump, return lines, and injection nozzles.

Cylinder balance test

A *cylinder balance test* on a diesel engine involves disabling one injector at a time to check the firing of that cylinder. Just as you can remove a spark plug wire on a gasoline engine to check for combustion, you can loosen the injector line to disable the cylinder.

DANGER! When loosening an injection line, only unscrew the fitting enough to allow fuel to drip from the connection. Wear safety glasses, leather gloves, and obtain instructor approval before completing this test. Also, refer to the service manual because it may describe a safer testing method.

To perform a cylinder balance test on a diesel engine, wrap a rag around the injector and loosen one injector fitting. See Fig. 24-6. When the fitting is loosened, fuel should slowly leak out of the connection. Fuel leakage will prevent the injector from opening and spraying fuel into the combustion chamber.

As the injector line is cracked, engine RPM SHOULD DROP and the engine should idle roughly. If "killing" the cylinder does NOT affect engine operation, that cylinder has NOT been firing. There may be a bad injector, low compression, or injection pump

problem. Further tests will be needed. Check all injectors.

Diesel engine compression test

A diesel engine compression test is similar to a compression test for a gasoline engine. However, do not use a compression gauge intended for a gasoline engine. It can be damaged by the high pressures.

A *diesel compression gauge* must read up to approximately 600 psi (4 134 kPa).

Remember! A diesel engine relies on the heat produced by extreme compression to ignite the fuel. If compression is low, the fuel cannot ignite.

To perform a diesel compression test, remove either the injectors or the glow plugs. Refer to a service manual for instructions. Install the compression gauge in the recommended hole. Usually, a heat shield must be used to seal the gauge when installed in place of the injector. Disconnect the fuel shut-off solenoid to disable the injection pump. Crank the engine and note the highest reading on the gauge.

Compare your compression gauge readings to specifications. Typical compression pressure for an automotive diesel engine is 400 to 500 psi (2 756 to 3 445 kPa). Readings should be within about 50 to 75 psi (345 to 517 kPa) of each other. If not within this range, engine repairs are needed.

Note! Some auto makers warn against performing a wet compression test on a diesel. If too much oil is squirted into the cylinder, hydraulic lock and part damage could result because the oil will not compress.

For more information on compression testing, refer to the text index. Compression testing is covered in several other textbook locations.

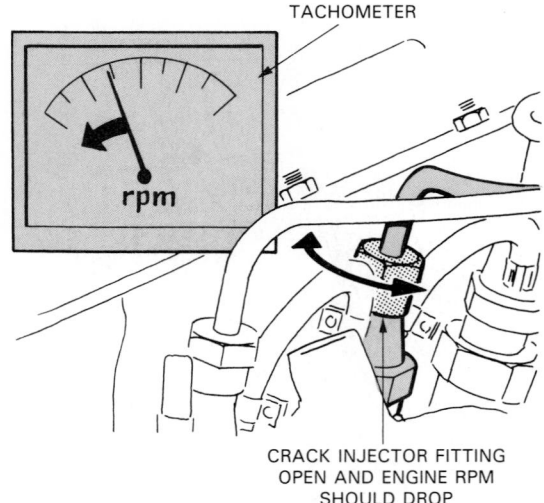

Fig. 24-6. To check for a dead cylinder or cylinder not firing, crack open each injector line one at a time. Let fuel drip from fitting with engine running. This will keep injector from opening. If rpm drops, that injector and cylinder are functioning. If rpm does not drop with injector disabled, that cylinder is not firing. (Volvo)

Glow plug resistance-balance test

A *glow plug resistance-balance test* provides a safe way of finding out if each cylinder is firing. When combustion is occuring in a cylinder, it will raise the temperature and internal resistance of the glow plug in that cylinder.

To do this test, unplug the wires to all of the glow plugs. Connect a digital ohmmeter across each glow plug and ground. Write down the ohms reading of each glow plug. Then, start the engine and let it run for a few minutes. Shut the engine off and recheck glow plug resistance.

If a cylinder is NOT firing, the resistance (ohms value) of its glow plug will NOT increase as much as the others.

Digital pyrometer balance test

A *digital pyrometer* is an electronic device for making very accurate temperature measurements. It can sometimes be used to check the operation of a diesel engine.

Touch the digital pyrometer on the exhaust manifold at each exhaust port. The temperature of the exhaust manifold with the engine running should be almost equal. If the manifold reading is cooler next to one exhaust port, that cylinder is NOT FIRING.

Injection pressure test.

An *injection pressure tester* uses special valves and a high pressure gauge to measure the amount of pressure in the injection lines. See Fig. 24-7.

Connect the injection pressure tester between the injection pump and the injectors. Follow the instructions provided with the particular tester.

Some on-car injection pressure testers allow you to check the following.
1. Injector opening pressure.
2. Injector nozzle leakage.
3. Injection line pressure balance.
4. Injection pump condition.

An injection pressure tester is a very informative test instrument. It enables you to pinpoint problems without removing major parts from the engine. For example, you can quickly locate a bad injector nozzle, clogged injector filter, or bad injection pump.

DIESEL INJECTION CLEANLINESS

When servicing a diesel engine, *cleanliness* is very important. The smallest bit of foreign material can damage or upset the operation of the injection pump or injectors. These parts are machined to precision tolerances measured in MICRONS (millionths of an inch). Keep this in mind during service.

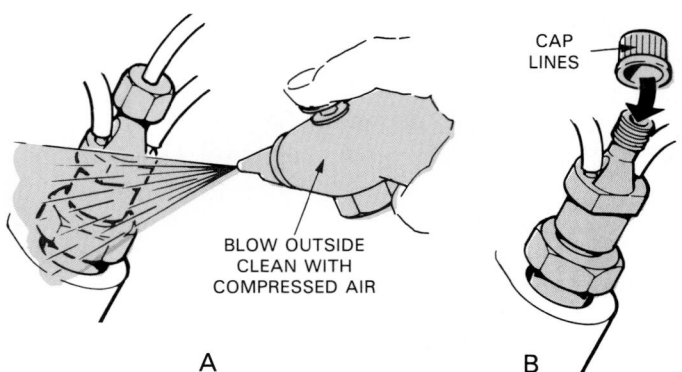

Fig. 24-8. A — Before removing injection line, blow away dirt with compressed air. B — After line removal, cap line. Smallest amount of dirt can upset injector operation.

A few rules of cleanliness to remember are:
1. Always cap and seal any injection system fitting that is disconnected. This will prevent dust from entering the system.
2. Use clean, lint-free shop rags when wiping off components. Even a piece of lint could upset the operation of the injection system.
3. Use compressed air and clean shop rags to remove dirt from around fittings before disassembly. Look at Fig. 24-8.
4. Do not spray water on a hot diesel engine. This could crack or warp the injection pump enough to cause serious problems.

DIESEL INJECTOR NOZZLE SERVICE

A *bad injector* in a diesel usually causes the engine to miss. It may also reduce engine power or cause smoking and knocking.

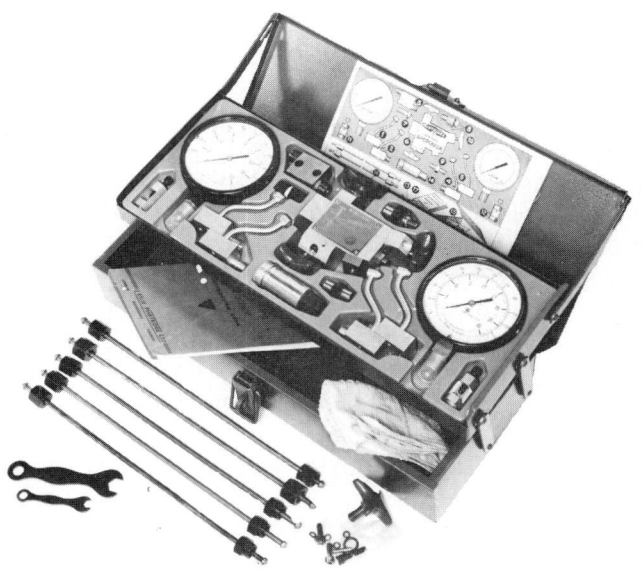

Fig. 24-7. Test setup for checking injection system operation while still on engine. This tester makes diagnosis quick and easy. (Hartridge)

The injector nozzles are exposed to the direct heat and by-products of combustion. They can wear, become clogged with carbon, or be damaged. This can result in an incorrect opening pressure, incorrect spray pattern, fuel leakage, and other problems.

Injector substitution

An easy way to verify an injector problem is to SUBSTITUTE an injector known to be good for the one being tested. If the cylinder fires with the good injector, then the old injector is faulty. If the cylinder still misses with the good injector, then other engine or injection problems exist.

Injector removal

If your tests indicate a faulty injector, you should remove the injector for service. Following the directions in the shop manual, disconnect the battery to prevent engine cranking. Using the appropriate tools, remove the injection line. Be careful not to bend or kink the high pressure line.

Normally, the injectors are threaded into the cylinder head, Fig. 24-9. They may also be held into

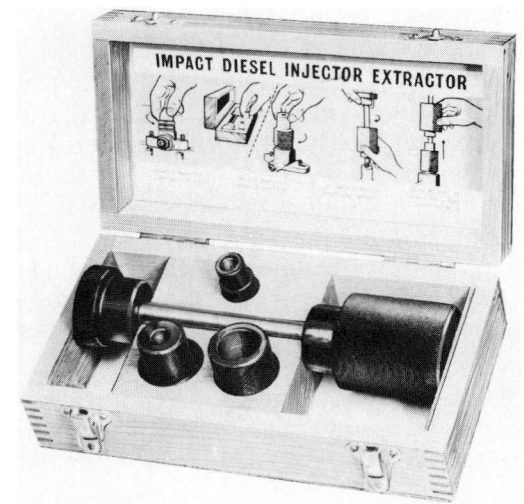

Fig. 24-10. Impact or slide hammer puller may be needed to remove press-fit type injectors. (Hartridge)

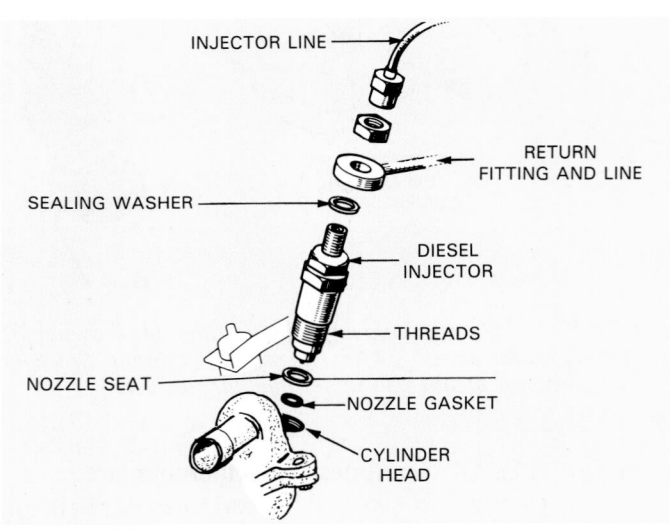

Fig. 24-9. When removing injector, note position of all parts. This injector screws into cylinder head. Some are clamped and press-fitted into head. (Toyota)

the head with bolts and a press fit. With press fitted injectors, you may need to use a special impact tool to force them out of the head. See Fig. 24-10.

Pop testing diesel injector nozzles

A *pop tester* is a device for checking a diesel injection nozzle while it is out of the engine. One type tester is pictured in Fig. 24-11.

To use a pop tester, fill the tester reservoir with the correct *calibration fluid* (test liquid). Do NOT use diesel oil because it is too flammable and test results may not be reliable.

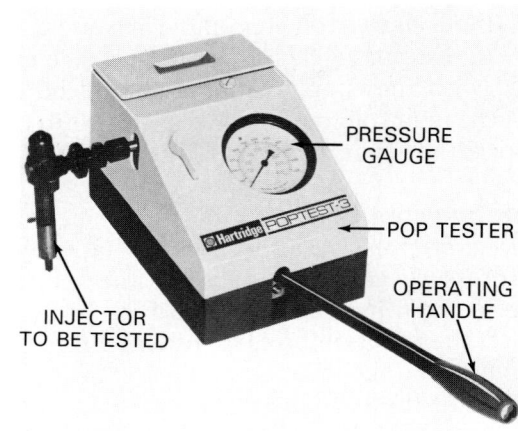

Fig. 24-11. Pop tester checks diesel injector operation. It will test injector spray pattern, opening pressure, and leakage. (Hartridge)

Open the tester valve and pump the tester handle. As soon as solid fluid (no air bubbles) sprays out the tester, close the valve. Connect the injection nozzle to the tester, as shown in Fig. 24-12.

DANGER! Extremely high pressures are developed when pop testing a diesel injector nozzle. Wear eye protection and keep your hands away from the fuel spraying out of the nozzle. It can puncture the skin.

To check *injector opening pressure,* purge any remaining air from the nozzle by pumping the tester lever up and down. Then, pump the handle slowly while watching the pressure gauge. Note the pressure reading when the injection nozzle opens. Repeat the test until you are sure you have an accurate reading.

Typical diesel injector opening pressure is approximately 1700 to 2200 psi (11 713 to 15 158 kPa). If opening pressure is NOT within service manual specs, rebuild or replace the injector.

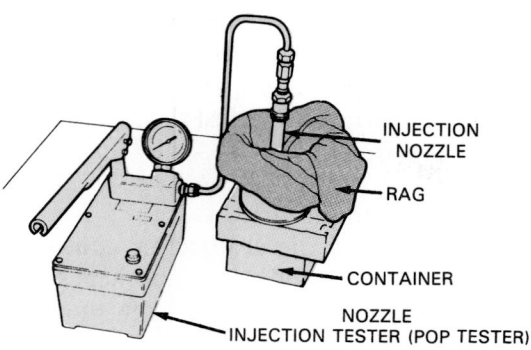

Fig. 24-12. To use a pop tester, mount injector on tester. Point injector into approved catch container. Surround the container with rags to prevent splashing. Pump tester handle while observing spray pattern, opening pressure, and leakage. Follow directions for specific tester. (Ford)

To check the *injector's spray pattern,* operate the pop tester handle while watching the fluid spray out of the nozzle. As shown in Fig. 24-13, there should be a narrow, cone-shaped mist of fluid. A solid stream of fuel, uneven spray, excessively wide spray, or spray filled with liquid droplets indicates that injector requires service or replacement.

To check *injector leakage,* slowly operate the tester handle to maintain a pressure lower than the nozzle opening pressure. Many auto manufacturers recommend a pressure of about 300 psi (2 067 kPa) below opening pressure. With this pressure, the diesel injector should NOT leak or drip for 10 seconds. Leakage would point to a dirty injector nozzle or worn components.

Note! Some diesel injectors make a chattering sound during operation. Others do not. All nozzles, however, should make a SWISHING or PINGING SOUND when spraying fuel.

Diesel injector nozzle rebuild

An *injector nozzle rebuild* involves disassembly, cleaning, inspecting, replacing bad parts, reassembly, and testing the injector.

Since injector designs vary, always follow the detailed directions in a service manual. It will give specific assembly methods, torque values, and other critical information.

To disassemble the injector, unscrew the body. Use a six-point wrench or socket. As illustrated in Fig. 24-14, remove and inspect the injector needle and nozzle opening.

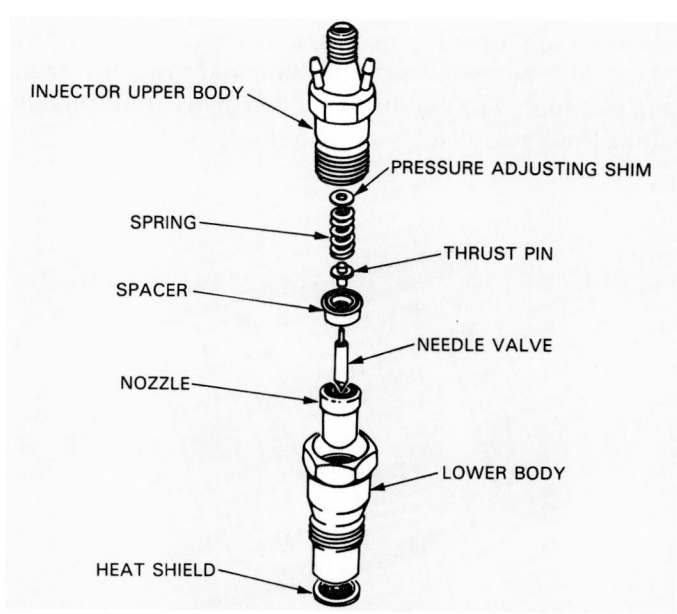

Fig. 24-14. When rebuilding a diesel injector, be careful not to damage it. Keep all parts from each injector together. Clamp injector lightly in vise to unscrew body. Inspect each part closely for carbon buildup, wear, or damage. (VW)

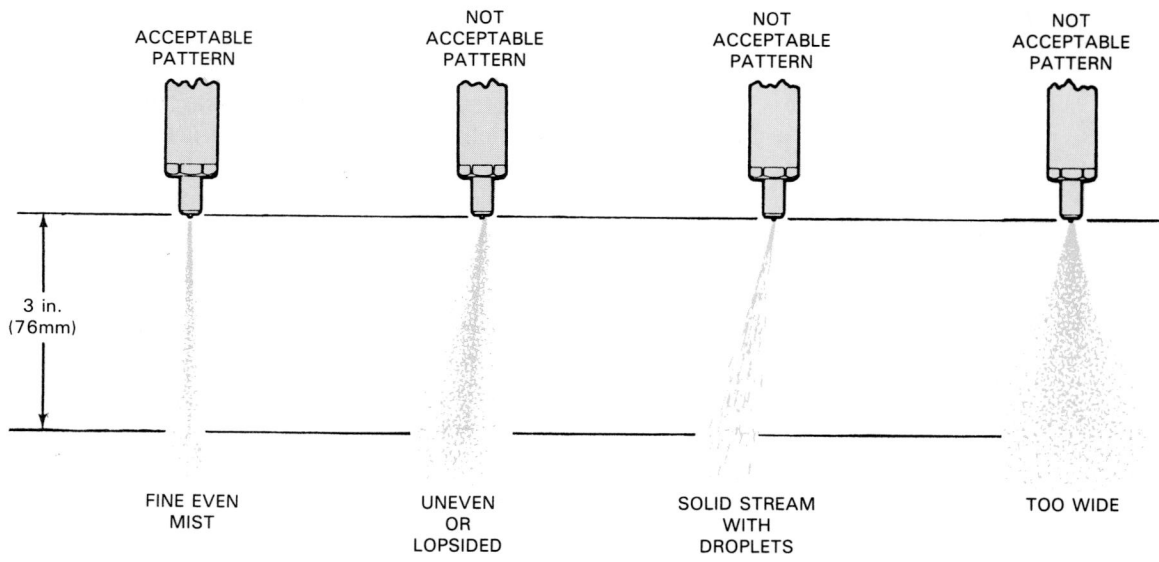

Fig. 24-13. Typical diesel injector spray patterns. Acceptable pattern produced even, uniform mist of fuel. Unacceptable patterns are uneven and do not have proper mist density. (Chrysler)

Clean the nozzle parts in solvent. Special cleaning tools (brass scrapers, brass brushes) may be needed to remove hard carbon deposits, Fig. 24-15. Use extreme care not to scratch the needle and nozzle. The smallest scratch can upset injector operation. Replace any component that shows signs of wear or damage.

If more than one injector is disassembled at the same time, make sure you do NOT MIX PARTS. Use an organizing tray to keep the parts from each injector together, Fig. 24-16. The components in each injector may be select fitted at the factory and must NOT be interchanged.

An *injector shim* is frequently used to adjust spring tension and valve opening pressure. If the pop test shows a low opening pressure, use a thicker injector shim. This increases spring tension and raises the opening pressure. The manufacture will give details on how shim thickness affects pressure.

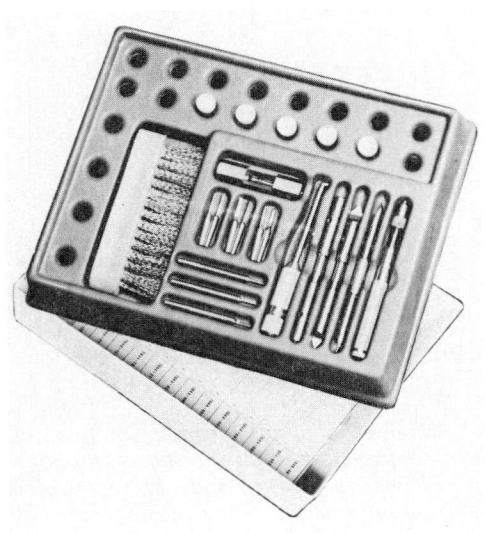

Fig. 24-15. Special tool kit for servicing diesel injectors. It contains soft brush, gauges, and other devices for rebuilding injectors. (Hartridge)

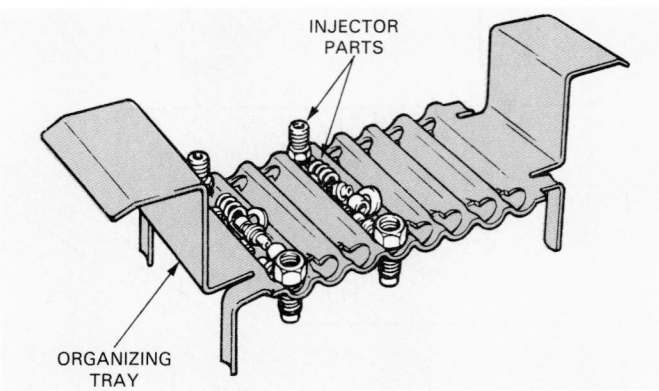

Fig. 24-16. An organizing tray is handy when servicing injectors. It will help prevent a mixup of parts. If even one part is installed in wrong injector, injector may not operate properly. (Buick)

Reassemble the injector as described in a service manual. Lubricate all parts with diesel oil. Make sure all parts are positioned properly. Torque the injector body to specifications. Pop test the injector to double-check the repair.

Installing diesel injectors

When installing a diesel injector, coat the threads with anti-sieze compound. Use a new heat shield or seal to prevent compression leakage. Screw the injector into the cylinder head by hand. Then, torque it to recommended specs. Look at Fig. 24-17. Without bending it, reconnect the injector line. Tighten the connection properly.

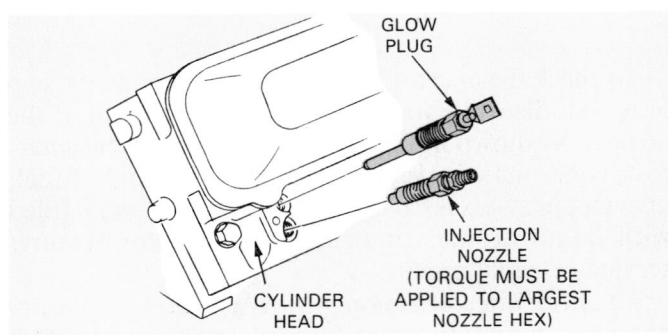

Fig. 24-17. When installing injectors or glow plugs, coat threads with anti-seize compound. Torque to specifications. (Oldsmobile)

Reconnect the wire on the fuel shut-off solenoid and start the engine. Check system for leaks and proper operation. A few systems may require you to BLEED AIR out of the system. Refer to a manual for exact details.

GLOW PLUG SERVICE

Inoperative glow plugs will make a diesel engine hard to start when cold. There will not be enough heat from compression alone to ignite the fuel. If only one or two glow plugs are inoperative, the engine may miss while the engine is still cold.

If glow plug problems are indicated, use a test light to check for voltage to the glow plugs. Touch the test light on the feed wires to the glow plugs. A clip-on ammeter can also be used to check current flow to the glow plugs. An incorrect current to the glow plugs can be caused by the supply circuit or the glow plugs themselves.

WARNING! Refer to a service manual when testing a glow plug circuit. It is possible to damage some glow plugs (6 volt type) by connecting them to direct battery voltage.

An ohmmeter can be used to determine the condition of each glow plug. Connect the ohmmeter across each glow plug terminal and ground. The resistance should be within specs. If the ohms value is too high or low, replace the glow plug. See Fig. 24-18.

Glow plug replacement

To remove glow plugs, disconnect the wires going to them. Then, use a deep well socket and ratchet to unscrew the glow plugs.

DANGER! A glow plug can reach temperatures above 1000°F (538°C). This can cause serious burns to your hand. Use extreme caution when removing glow plugs from the engine.

When the glow plugs are removed, inspect each one closely. Look for damage or a heavy coating of carbon. A carbon buildup can insulate the plug and make the engine hard to start. Clean any plugs that are to be reused. Replace all that are faulty.

When installing the glow plugs, coat the threads with anti-sieze compound. Start the plugs by hand and then tighten to specs. Overtightening can easily damage a glow plug.

Some glow plugs are 12-volt and some are 6-volt. Make sure you have the type recommended for the vehicle. Reconnect the wires and check glow plug operation.

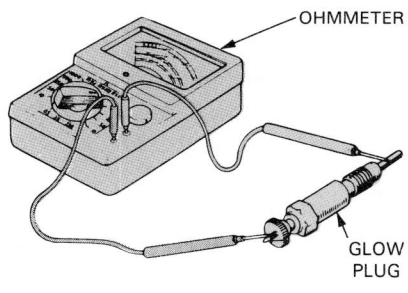

Fig. 24-18. Glow plug condition can be checked with a common ohmmeter. Plug resistance must be within specs. (Toyota)

INJECTION PUMP SERVICE

A *bad injection pump* can keep the engine from running, or cause engine missing, smoking, and other problems. The injection pump is usually a very trouble-free unit. However, water contamination, prolonged service, leaking seals, and physical damage from accidents may require replacement, repairs, or adjustment.

Most garages remove and install a NEW or FACTORY REBUILT INJECTION PUMP when internal parts are faulty. The diesel injection pump is a very precise mechanism. Specialized tools and equipment are needed for repair work.

Fig. 24-19 shows an *injection pump test stand* that checks pump performance. Its use is normally limited to specialized shops, not automotive shops.

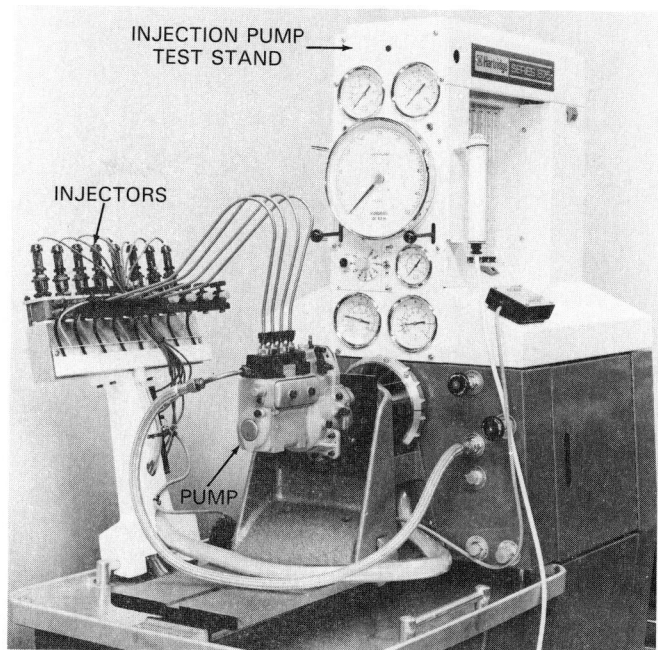

Fig. 24-19. Injection pump test stand is needed to check operation of injection pump. It is found in shops specializing in injection pump service. (Hartridge)

It is sometimes possible to replace leaking external gaskets and seals without major pump diassembly. On most pumps, other external parts (idle stop solenoid, vacuum valve, cold advance solenoid, fuel shut-off solenoid) can also be replaced in the shop. Refer to your service manual for details. See Fig. 24-20.

Injection pump replacement

To replace a diesel injection pump, crank the engine until the No. 1 piston is at TDC. Study the timing marks on the pump and engine. This will make reinstallation easier. Disconnect the battery cable to prevent accidental cranking and fuel injection.

As shown in Fig. 24-21, remove the injection lines, wires, linkages, and fasteners to allow pump removal. Cap all lines to keep out dust and dirt. Lift off the old pump carefully.

Transfer parts (solenoids, vacuum valves, drive sprocket) from the old pump to the new pump. See Fig. 24-22. Then, install the pump on the engine. Align the timing marks noted during disassembly. Torque all fasteners and lines properly. Before starting the engine, adjust injection timing.

WARNING! Never hammer or pry on a diesel injection pump housing. Also, be careful not to drop an injection pump. It can be damaged easily and is very expensive to replace.

Injection pump timing

Diesel *injection pump timing* is adjusted by rotating the injection pump on its mounting.

To advance injection pump timing, turn the pump

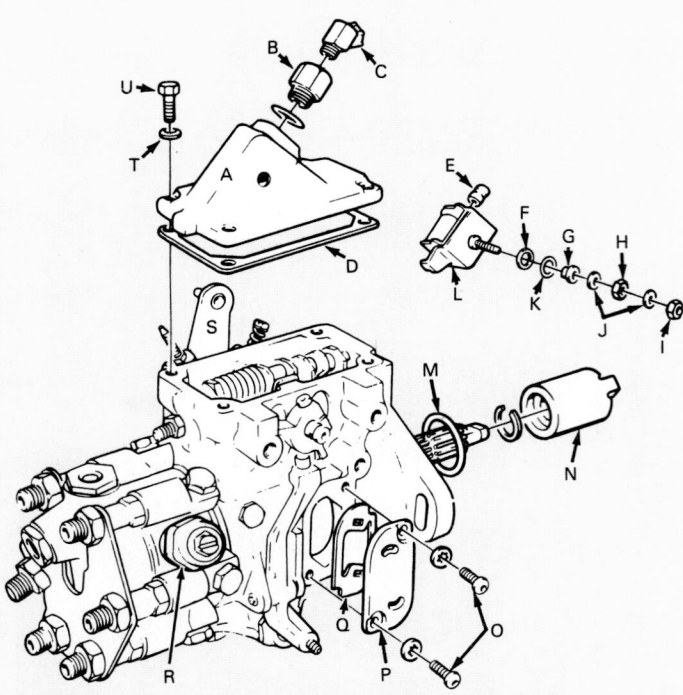

A. GOVERNOR CONTROL COVER
B. BLACK LEAKAGE CONNECTION
C. ELBOW CONNECTION
D. JOINT (GASKET)
E. SPRING FILTER
F. BACKING WASHER
G. INSULATING WASHER
H. NUT
I. LOCKNUT
J. PLAIN WASHER
K. RUBBER O-RING
L. COLD ADVANCE SOLENOID
M. RUBBER O-RING
N. TANG DRIVE HUB
O. SCREW-DOME HEADED
P. INSPECTION COVER
Q. RUBBER SEALING JOINT (GASKET)
R. STOP SOLENOID
S. THROTTLE LEVER
T. SHAKEPROOF WASHER
U. HEXAGON SOCKET SCREW

Fig. 24-20. External repairs can sometimes be made on injection pumps. Leaking seals or gaskets, bad fittings, bad solenoids, etc. can be replaced without pump teardown. Internal repairs cannot be done in average garage. (Buick)

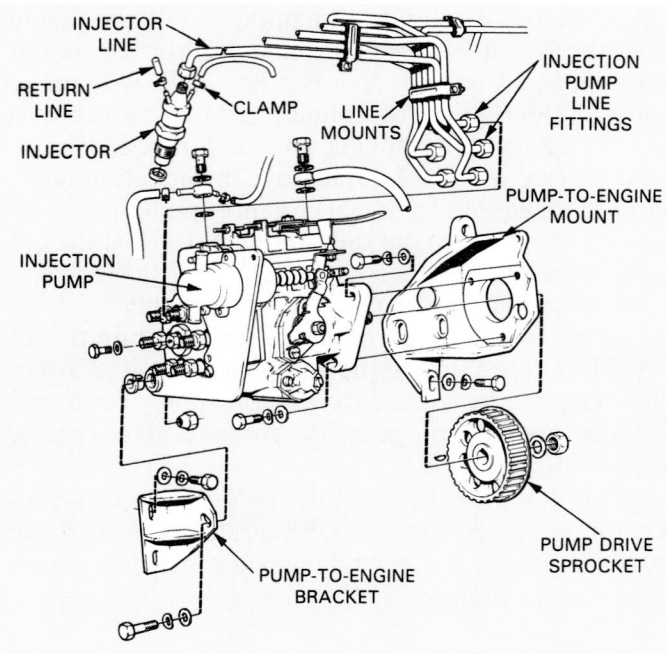

Fig. 24-21. Note parts that must be disconnected to remove injection pump. When installing, torque all fasteners and fittings to specs. Make sure dirt does not enter system. (Volvo)

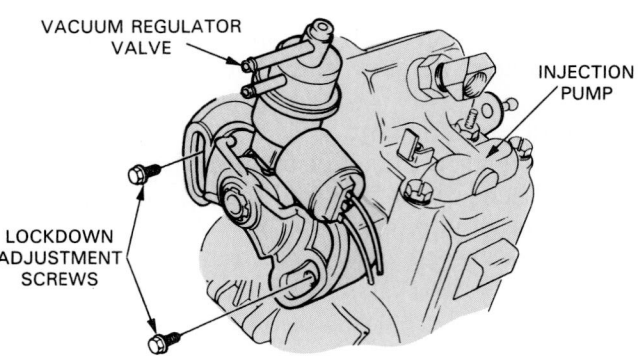

Fig. 24-22. Vacuum regulator valve must normally be reused when installing new or rebuilt injection pump. Adjustment involves check of vacuum action while rotating valve on its mount. (Oldsmobile)

opposite the pump drive shaft rotation. To retard injection pump timing, turn the pump housing WITH pump drive shaft rotation.

Injection pump timing must be set whenever the pump is removed from the engine or when an incorrect adjustment is discovered.

There are several methods for adjusting injection pump timing. Procedures vary with the particular type of engine and injection system. A diesel does not have an electrically operated ignition system for triggering a timing light. For this reason, other methods are needed to determine when the No. 1 cylinder fires.

Basically, injection pump timing can be adjusted by:
1. Aligning timing marks on engine and injection pump with No. 1 piston at TDC (rough adjustment), Fig. 24-23.
2. Using a dial indicator to measure injection pump stroke in relation to engine piston position. See Fig. 24-24. It shows this method.
3. Using a luminosity (light) device to detect combus-

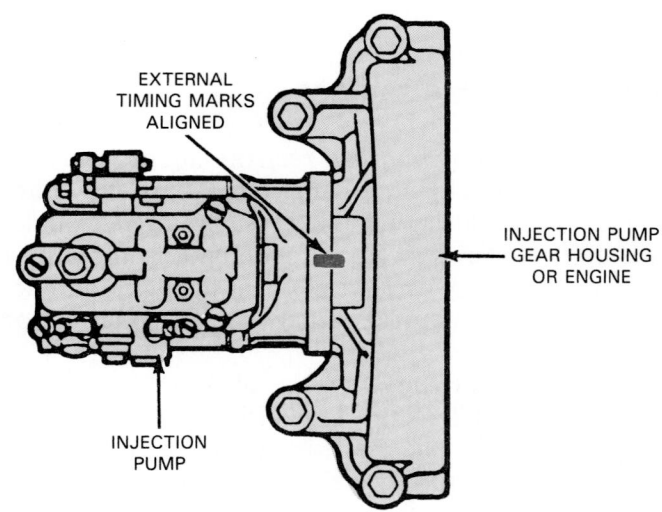

Fig. 24-23. Simple method of setting injection timing involves aligning marks on pump and engine. When two marks align, pump should be timed properly. (Ford)

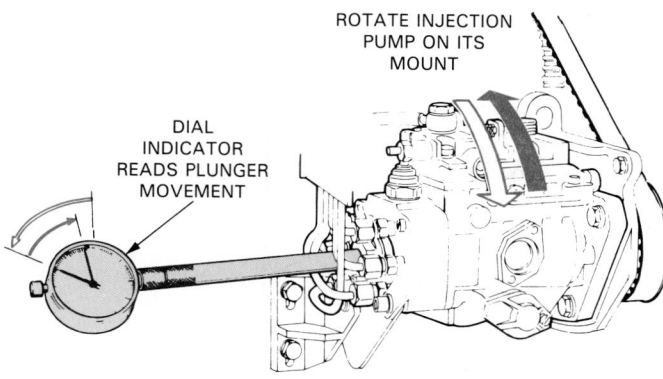

Fig. 24-24. Some auto makers recommend using a dial indicator when setting injection timing. After removing a plug in end of pump, dial indicator stem is positioned against pumping plunger. Indicator will then register plunger movement or injection. To change injection timing, rotate injection pump on engine. Tighten pump mounting fasteners to lock timing in place. (Volvo)

tion flame in No. 1 cylinder. Look at Fig. 24-25.

4. Using a fuel pressure (injection) detector.

Refer to a factory shop manual for details. The manual will describe which adjustment method should be used. Also, follow the operating instructions for the specific type of timing device. Injection timing is very critical to diesel engine performance.

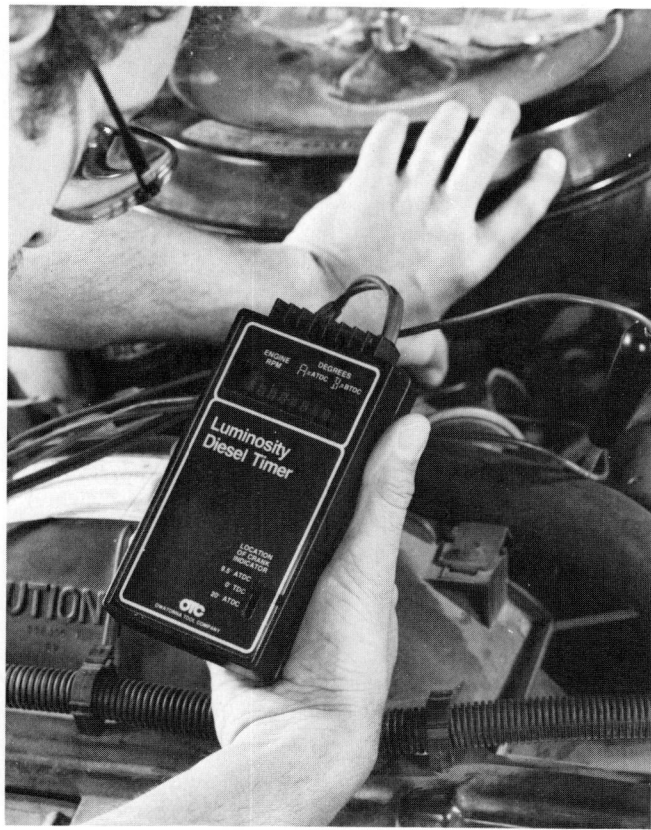

Fig. 24-25. Mechanic is using luminosity meter to detect combustion timing for adjustment of injection timing. (OTC Tools)

Injection pump throttle cable/linkage adjustment

Basically, injection pump *throttle cable* or *linkage adjustment* involves making sure the pump's throttle lever opens and closes freely. As parts wear, the cable or linkage may need to be reset. During adjustment, check for binding. Lubricate if needed. Look at Fig. 24-26. It shows basic adjustments.

A service manual will give exact directions for injection pump cable or linkage adjustment. Typically, by loosening a locknut, you can lengthen or shorten the cable housing or linkage as needed.

Fig. 24-27 shows how a carburetor angle gauge is used to adjust a transmission vacuum regulator valve. Gauge position and valve operation must correspond to specs.

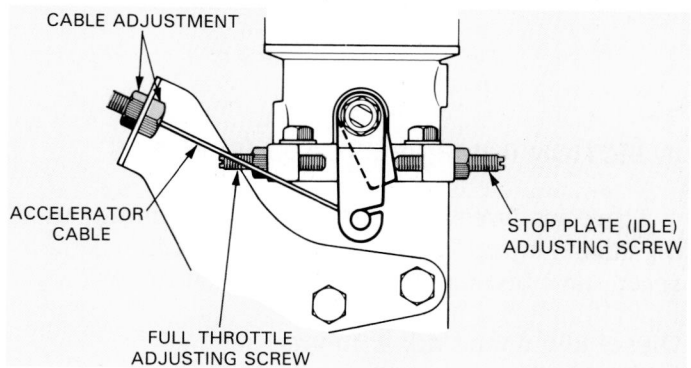

Fig. 24-26. Note basic injection pump adjustments: throttle cable, idle speed, and maximum speed. (Toyota)

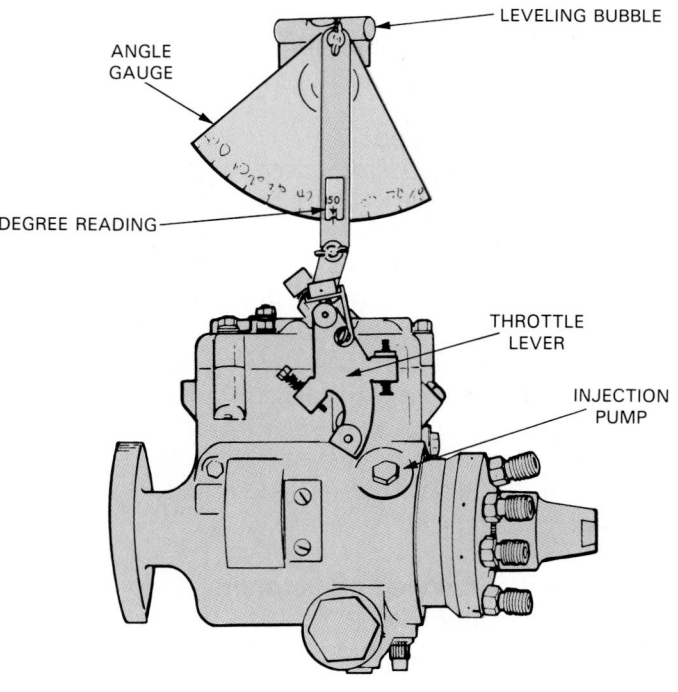

Fig. 24-27. Carburetor angle gauge is needed to set vacuum valve on this particular injection pump. Follow service manual directions for details. (GM)

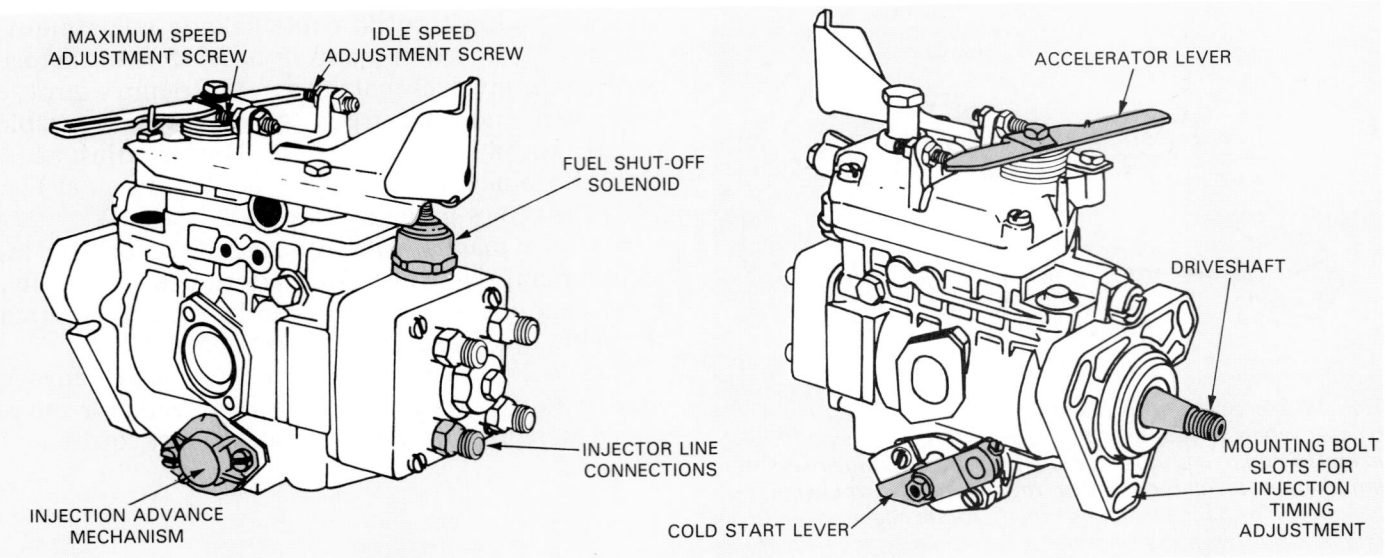

Fig. 24-28. Two views of injection pump show external adjustments and other parts. (VW)

INJECTION PUMP SPEED ADJUSTMENTS

There are three speed adjustments commonly used on a diesel injection pump: curb idle speed, maximum speed, and fast (cold) idle speed. See Fig. 24-28.

Diesel idle speed adjustments

Diesel idle speed is usually set while using a special diesel tachometer. An idle stop screw on the injection pump is turned to vary engine speed.

A *diesel tachometer* may be similar to or part of the injection timing device. It may also be an instrument like the one shown in Fig. 24-29. With all designs, the diesel tach will read engine speed in rpm (revolutions per minute).

Diesel curb idle speed

To adjust diesel *curb idle speed,* place the transmission in neutral or park. Start the engine. Allow the engine to run until it reaches full operating temperature. Connect the tachometer to the engine.

Compare the tach reading with specifications. Curb idle speed will be given on the engine compartment emission control decal or in the service manual.

If needed, turn the curb idle speed adjusting screw on the injection pump to raise or lower idle rpm. You must usually loosen a locknut before the screw will turn. Hold the screw and retighten the locknut when the tach reads correctly.

Diesel cold idle speed adjustment

To set the *cold idle speed* of a diesel, connect a jumper wire from the battery positive terminal and the fast idle solenoid terminal. This will activate the fast idle, even when the engine is warm.

Raise the engine speed momentarily to release the solenoid plunger. Again, compare your tachometer

Fig. 24-29. Since diesel does not have electrical ignition system, special tachometer is needed. Diesel tach senses crankshaft damper position, rather than gasoline engine ignition system operation. (Kent-Moore Corp.)

readings and specs. Adjust the solenoid if needed. Refer to Fig. 24-30.

Sometimes a cold start lever replaces a cold idle solenoid. Refer to manufacturer manuals for details of adjustment.

Diesel maximum speed adjustment

A *maximum speed adjustment* is used to limit the highest attainable diesel engine rpm. If maximum governor rpm is set too high, it may damage internal engine components. If diesel maximum rpm is too low, the engine will not produce enough power.

To adjust the maximum speed of a diesel, position your tachometer so that it can be read from within the driver's compartment. With the transmission in neutral or park, hold your left foot on the brake. Press the accelerator pedal slowly to the floor.

CAUTION! When performing a maximum speed test, be ready to release the accelerator pedal at any time. If the engine rpm goes above specs, engine damage could result.

Once the tachometer reads the maximum speed specs, engine speed should NO LONGER INCREASE. If the maximum speed is not within specs, turn the maximum speed adjusting screw on the injection pump, Fig. 24-31. Tighten the locknut on the screw after adjustment. Recheck maximum rpm.

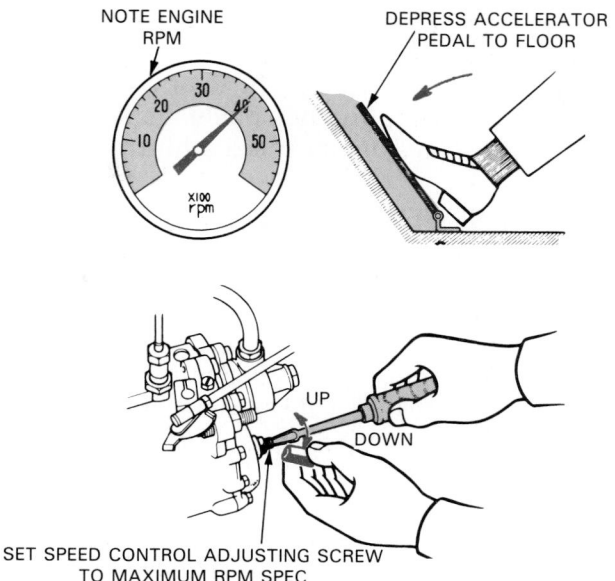

Fig. 24-31. To set diesel engine maximum speed, press gas pedal to floor while watching tach. If maximum rpm is too high or too low, turn maximum speed adjusting screw on pump. Be careful not to let engine speed go above maximum spec. (Toyota)

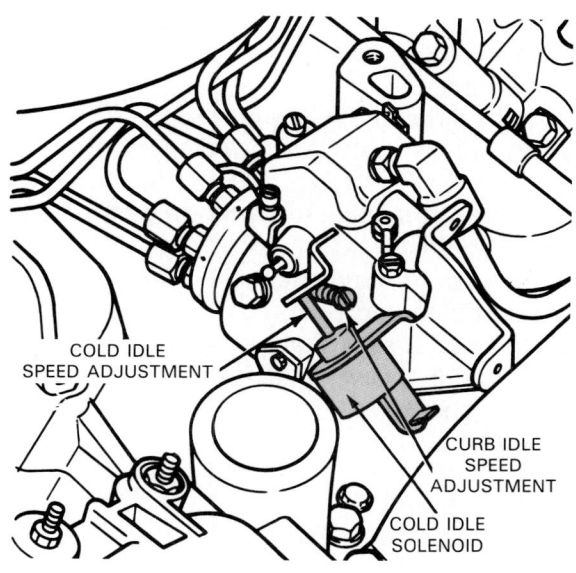

Fig. 24-30. Cold idle speed solenoid is adjusted something like a carburetor cold idle speed solenoid. Also note location of curb idle speed adjustment on injection pump. (Ford)

COMPUTERIZED DIESEL INJECTION SERVICE

Diagnosing and repairing a diesel system controlled by a computer is similar to working on other computer systems. Some systems have self-diagnosis that will help indicate the location of problems. You can use a digital meter to check for opens and shorts in wiring or to test the sensors and actuators.

For more information on servicing computer systems, refer to Chapters 74, 75, and 76 in the back of this textbook.

DIESEL INJECTION SERVICE RULES

When servicing a diesel injection system, remember these basic rules:

1. Always cap lines and fittings to prevent the entry of foreign matter.
2. Never drop or pry on a diesel injector or injection pump. They can be damaged.
3. Remember that high pressure inside a diesel injection system can cause serious injury.
4. Some diesel injection systems must be bled (air removed) after repairs.
5. Clean around fittings before they are disconnected.
6. Adhere to all torque specifications. This is extremely important on a diesel engine.
7. Never use a bent, frayed, or kinked injection line.
8. Place a piece of screen mesh over the air inlet when the engine is to be operated without the air cleaner. Rags and other objects can be sucked into the engine. Also, do not cover the air inlet with your hand with the engine running or injury may result.
9. Check fuel filters and water separators periodically. Water can cause expensive corrosion of injection system parts.
10. Follow all safety rules concerning ventilation and fire hazards.
11. Wear safety glasses when working on a diesel injection system.
12. When in doubt, refer to a service manual for the make of vehicle being serviced. The slightest mistake could upset engine performance or cause engine damage.

KNOW THESE TERMS

Smoke meter, Ignition lag, Water corrosion, Diesel cylinder balance test, Glow plug resistance-balance test,

Digital pyrometer, Injection pressure tester, Pop tester, Calibration fluid, Injector opening pressure, Injector spray pattern, Injector leakage, Injector rebuild, Injection pump test stand, Injection pump timing, Diesel tachometer, Diesel maximum speed adjustment.

REVIEW QUESTIONS

1. What is the main cause of black smoke from a diesel engine?
2. Explain the most common reasons for excessive white smoke from a diesel engine.
3. Excessive _____ smoke from a diesel may be due to oil consumption from worn _____ _____ , scored _____ _____ , or leaking _____ _____ _____ .
4. A smoke meter is for measuring the amount of smoke in diesel exhaust. True or False?
5. Which of the following is NOT a normal cause of excessive diesel knock?
   a. Long ignition lag time.
   b. Low engine operating temperature.
   c. Early injection timing.
   d. Low engine compression.
   e. All off the above are correct.
6. List five safety rules for diesel injection service.
7. The main fuel filter will often have a water drain that must be serviced periodically. True or False?
8. Explain a diesel cylinder balance test.
9. A compression gauge reading up to 250 psi (1 723 kPa) can be used to measure compression pressure in a diesel engine. True or False?
10. What are typical compression test readings with a diesel engine in good condition?
11. Why do many service manuals warn against doing a wet compression test on a diesel?
12. A glow plug _____ test relies on the fact that glow plug electrical resistance increases with temperature.
13. How can a digital pyrometer be used to check the operation of a diesel engine?
14. What four values do some on-car injection pressure testers allow you to measure?
15. The parts in a diesel injection pump can be machined so precise that they are measured in millionths of an inch. True or False?
16. Injector nozzles are exposed to combustion and can become clogged with carbon. True or False?
17. Which of the following should NOT be done when removing a diesel injector?
   a. Disconnect battery.
   b. Bend injection line out of the way.
   c. Use impact tool if needed.
   d. All of the above are correct.

18. A diesel engine has a dead miss (one cylinder not firing). Engine analyzer cranking tests indicate good engine compression.
   Technician A says that all of the injectors should be removed and rebuilt. They must be at fault.
   Technician B says that you should perform a cylinder balance test or on-car pressure tests.
   Who is correct?
   a. Technician A
   b. Technician B
   c. Both A and B
   d. Neither A nor B
19. Explain the use of a pop tester.
20. Injector nozzle parts can be interchanged. True or False?
21. Inoperative _____ _____ will make a diesel engine hard to start when cold.
22. Which of the following can be used to test diesel glow plug system operation?
   a. Test light.
   b. Ammeter.
   c. Ohmmeter.
   d. All of the above are correct.
23. Glow plugs can reach temperatures above _____ °F or _____ °C.
24. Tests show that a diesel injection pump has an internal problem.
   Technician A says that the pump should be disassembled and repaired.
   Technician B says that the pump should be replaced with a new or factory rebuilt unit.
   Who is correct?
   a. Technician A
   b. Technician B
   c. Both A and B
   d. Neither A nor B
25. What is an injection pump test stand?
26. Explain four methods of adjusting diesel injection timing.
27. List and describe three speed adjustments common to a diesel injection system.
28. List eleven diesel injection service rules.

ACTIVITIES FOR CHAPTER 24

1. Prepare an overhead transparency on the steps for troubleshooting the injectors in a vehicle that has abnormal exhaust smoke. Use it to demonstrate the steps to your class.
2. Perform a cylinder balance test on the engine's injectors.
3. Using an ohmmeter, demonstrate the proper method for checking the condition of a glow plug.

Exhaust Systems, Turbocharging

After studying this chapter, you will be able to:
- ☐ Describe the basic parts of an exhaust system.
- ☐ Compare exhaust system design differences.
- ☐ Perform exhaust system repairs.
- ☐ Explain the fundamental parts of a turbocharging system.
- ☐ Describe the construction and operation of a turbocharger and wastegate.
- ☐ Remove and replace a turbocharger and wastegate.
- ☐ Demonstrate an understanding of safety procedures for working on exhaust systems and turbochargers.

This chapter begins by covering the basic parts of an exhaust system. It then explains how to repair the system by replacing rusted or damaged components. The second part of the chapter covers turbocharging.

BASIC EXHAUST SYSTEMS

An *exhaust system* quiets engine operation and carries exhaust fumes to the rear of the vehicle. The parts of a typical exhaust system are shown in Fig. 25-1. They include:

1. EXHAUST MANIFOLD (connects cylinder head exhaust ports to header pipe).
2. HEADER PIPE (steel tubing that carries exhaust gases from exhaust manifold to catalytic converter or muffler).
3. CATALYTIC CONVERTER (device for removing pollutants from engine exhaust).
4. INTERMEDIATE PIPE (tubing sometimes used between header pipe and muffler or catalytic converter and muffler).

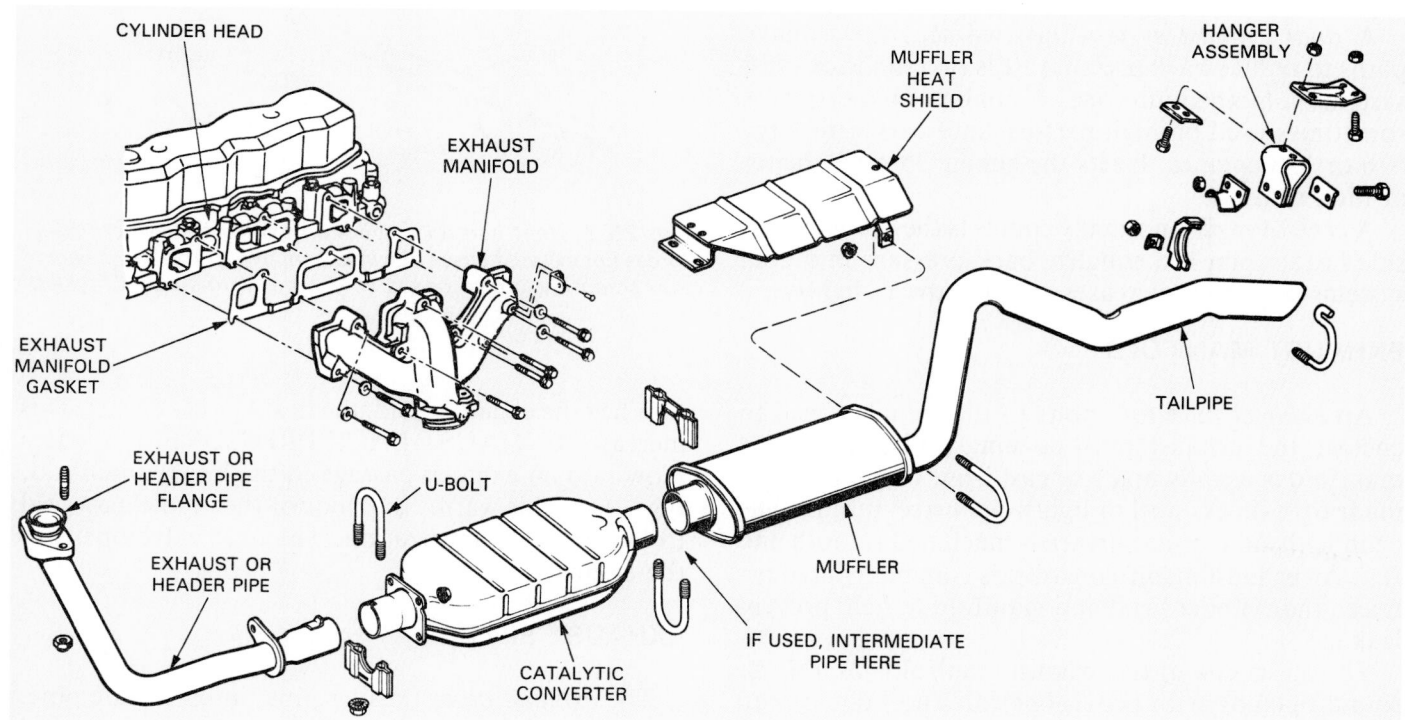

Fig. 25-1. Note parts of typical exhaust system. Exhaust comes out of cylinder head, into manifold, and then through system. (Chrysler Corp.)

5. MUFFLER (metal chamber for damping pressure pulsations to reduce exhaust noise).
6. TAILPIPE (tubing that carries exhaust from muffler to rear of car body).
7. HANGERS (devices for securing exhaust system to underside of car body).
8. HEAT SHIELDS (metal plates that prevent exhaust heat from transferring into another object).
9. MUFFLER CLAMPS (U-bolts for connecting parts of exhaust system together).

When an engine is running, extremely hot gases blow out of the cylinder head exhaust ports. The gases enter the exhaust manifold. They flow through the header pipe, catalytic converter, intermediate pipe, muffler, and out the tailpipe.

Exhaust back pressure

Exhaust back pressure is the amount of pressure developed in the exhaust system when the engine is running. High back pressure reduces engine power. A well designed exhaust system should have LOW back pressure.

The restriction of the exhaust pipes, catalytic converter, and muffler contribute to exhaust back pressure. Larger pipes and a free-flowing muffler, for example, would reduce back pressure.

Single and dual exhaust systems

A *single exhaust system* has one path for exhaust flow through the system. Typically, it has only one header pipe, main catalytic converter, muffler, and tailpipe. The most common type, it is used from the smallest four-cylinder engines, on up to large V-8 engines.

A *dual exhaust system* has two separate exhaust paths to reduce back pressure. It is two single exhaust systems combined into one. A dual exhaust system is sometimes used on high performance cars with large V-6 or V-8 engines. It lets the engine "breath" better at high rpm.

A *crossover pipe* normally connects the right and left side header pipes to equalize back pressure in a dual system. This also increases engine power slightly.

EXHAUST MANIFOLD

An *exhaust manifold* bolts to the cylinder head to enclose the exhaust port openings, Fig. 25-2. The manifold is usually made of cast iron. It is sometimes made of stainless steel or lightweight steel tubing. The cylinder head mating surface is machined smooth and flat. An exhaust manifold gasket is commonly used between the cylinder head and manifold to help prevent leakage.

The outlet end of the exhaust manifold has a single round opening with provisions for stud bolts or cap screws. A gasket or O-ring (doughnut) seals the connection between the exhaust manifold outlet and header pipe to prevent leakage.

Fig. 25-2. Lower right shows exhaust manifold which bolts over exhaust ports on side of cylinder head. Note oxygen sensor at end of manifold. (Chrysler Corp.)

Exhaust manifold heat valve

An *exhaust manifold heat valve* forces hot exhaust gases to flow into the intake manifold to aid cold weather starting. Look at Fig. 25-3.

A butterfly valve may be located in the outlet of the exhaust manifold. A heat sensitive spring or a vacuum diaphragm and temperature sensing vacuum switch may operate the valve.

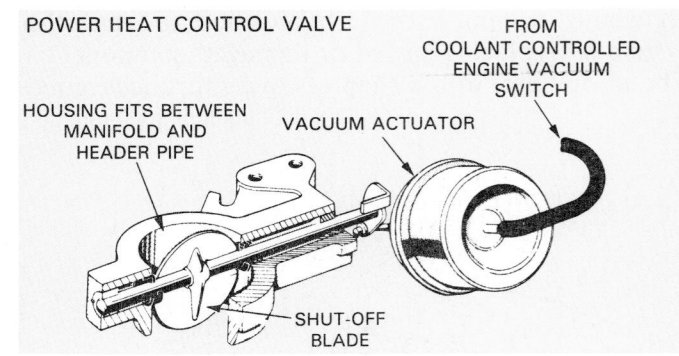

Fig. 25-3. Heat control valve, sometimes called heat riser, forces hot exhaust gases into intake manifold. This helps engine run smoothly. Valve opens as engine warms up. (Chrysler)

When the engine is cold, the heat valve is closed. This increases EXHAUST BACK PRESSURE. Hot gases blow into an exhaust passage in the intake manifold, Fig. 25-4. This warms the floor of the intake manifold to hasten fuel vaporization. The heat valve opens as the engine warms up.

EXHAUST PIPES

The *exhaust pipes* (header pipe, intermediate pipe, and tailpipe) are usually made of rust resistant steel tubing. The inlet end of the header pipe has a flange for securing the pipe to the exhaust manifold studs,

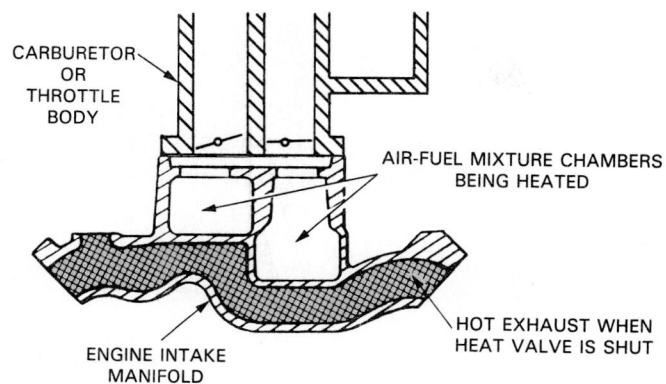

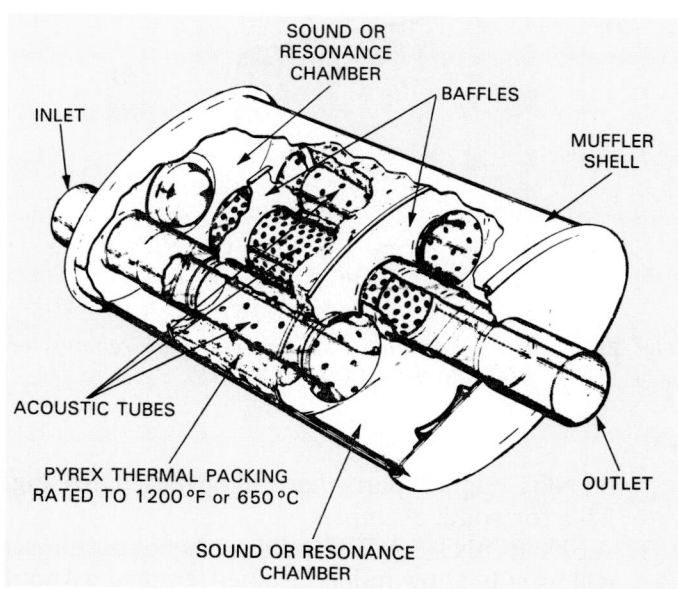

Fig. 25-4. Heat control valve causes back pressure in exhaust system. This directs a large amount of hot exhaust into chamber in bottom of intake manifold. This actions warms and helps vaporize fuel. (Pontiac)

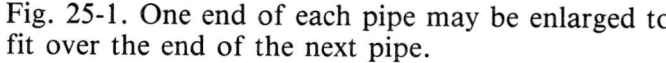

Fig. 25-1. One end of each pipe may be enlarged to fit over the end of the next pipe.

Fig. 25-5. Basic muffler contains baffles, resonance chambers, and acoustic tubes to reduce exhaust noise. (American Exhaust Industries)

HEAT SHIELDS

Heat shields are located where the exhaust system (especially catalytic converter and muffler) are close to the car body. The shields prevent too much heat from transferring into the car body or ground. Refer to Fig. 25-1.

DANGER! Always reinstall all exhaust system heat shields. Without a heat shield, car undercoating, carpeting, dry leaves on the ground, and other flammable materials could catch on fire!

CATALYTIC CONVERTER

A *catalytic converter* is used to reduce the amount of exhaust pollutants entering the atmosphere. One or more catalytic converters can be located in the exhaust system, Fig. 25-1.

For details of catalytic converters, refer to Chapters 39 and 40 which cover emission control systems.

MUFFLERS

A *muffler* reduces the pressure pulses and resulting noise produced by the engine exhaust. When an engine is running, the exhaust valves are rapidly opening and closing. Each time an exhaust valve opens, a blast of hot gas shoots out of the engine. Without a muffler, these exhaust gas pulsations are very loud.

Fig. 25-5 shows the inside of a muffler. Note how chambers, tubes, holes, and baffles are arranged to cancel out the pressure pulsations in the exhaust.

EXHAUST SYSTEM SERVICE

Exhaust system service is usually needed when a com-

ponent in the system rusts and begins to leak. Because engine combustion produces water and acids, an exhaust system can fail in a relatively short time.

DANGER! A leaking exhaust system could harm the passengers of a car. Since engine exhaust is poisonous, a leaky exhaust can allow toxic gases to flow through any opening in the body and into the passenger compartment.

Exhaust system inspection

To inspect an exhaust system, raise the car on a lift. Using a drop light, closely inspect the system for problems (rusting, loose connections, leaks). In particular, check around the muffler, all pipe connections, gaskets, and pipe bends.

DANGER! Parts of the exhaust system, especially the catalytic converter, can be VERY HOT. Remember not to touch any component until after it has cooled.

Exhaust system repairs

Faulty exhaust system parts must be removed and replaced. If only the muffler is rusted, a new muffler can be installed in the existing system. After prolonged service, several parts or ALL of the exhaust system may require replacement.

When repairing an exhaust system, remember the following:

1. Use RUST PENETRANT on all threaded fasteners that will be reused, Fig. 25-6. This is especially important on the exhaust manifold flange nuts or bolts.
2. Use an air chisel, cut-off tool, cutting torch, or hacksaw to remove faulty parts. Make sure you

Fig. 25-6. Rust penetrant or solvent will ease removal of badly rusted fasteners. (AP)

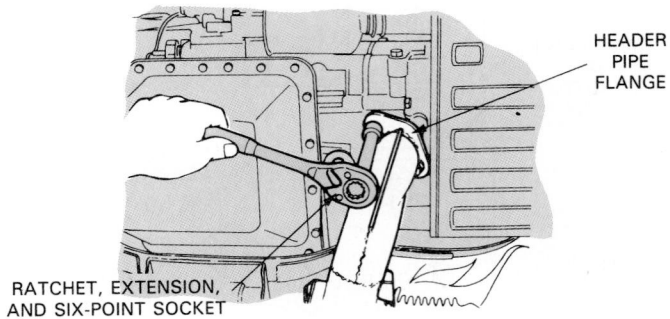

Fig. 25-8. Header pipe fasteners can be difficult to remove. Use rust penetrant, six-point socket, extension, and ratchet. This will usually remove fasteners. (Subaru)

do NOT damage parts that will be reused. See Fig. 25-7 for some examples.

3. A SIX-POINT SOCKET and ratchet or air impact will usually allow quick fastener removal without rounding off the fastener heads. Refer to Fig. 25-8.
4. Wear SAFETY GLASSES or goggles to keep rust and dirt from entering your eyes.
5. Obtain the correct replacement parts.
6. A *pipe expander* should be used to enlarge pipe ends as needed, Fig. 25-9. A *pipe shaper* can be used to straighten dented pipe ends, Fig. 25-10.
7. Make sure all pipes are fully inserted. Position all clamps properly, as in Fig. 25-11.
8. Double-check the routing of the exhaust system. Keep adequate clearance between it, the car body,

and chassis. See Fig. 25-12.
9. Tighten all clamps and hangers evenly. Torque the fasteners only enough to hold the parts. Over-tightening will smash and deform the pipes, possibly causing leakage.
10. When replacing an exhaust manifold, use a gasket and check sealing surface flatness. If the manifold is warped, it must be machined flat. Torque the exhaust manifold bolts to specs, Fig. 25-13.
11. Always use new gaskets and O-rings.
12. Check heat riser operation using the information in a service manual.
13. Install all heat shields.
14. Check the system for leaks and rattles after repairs.

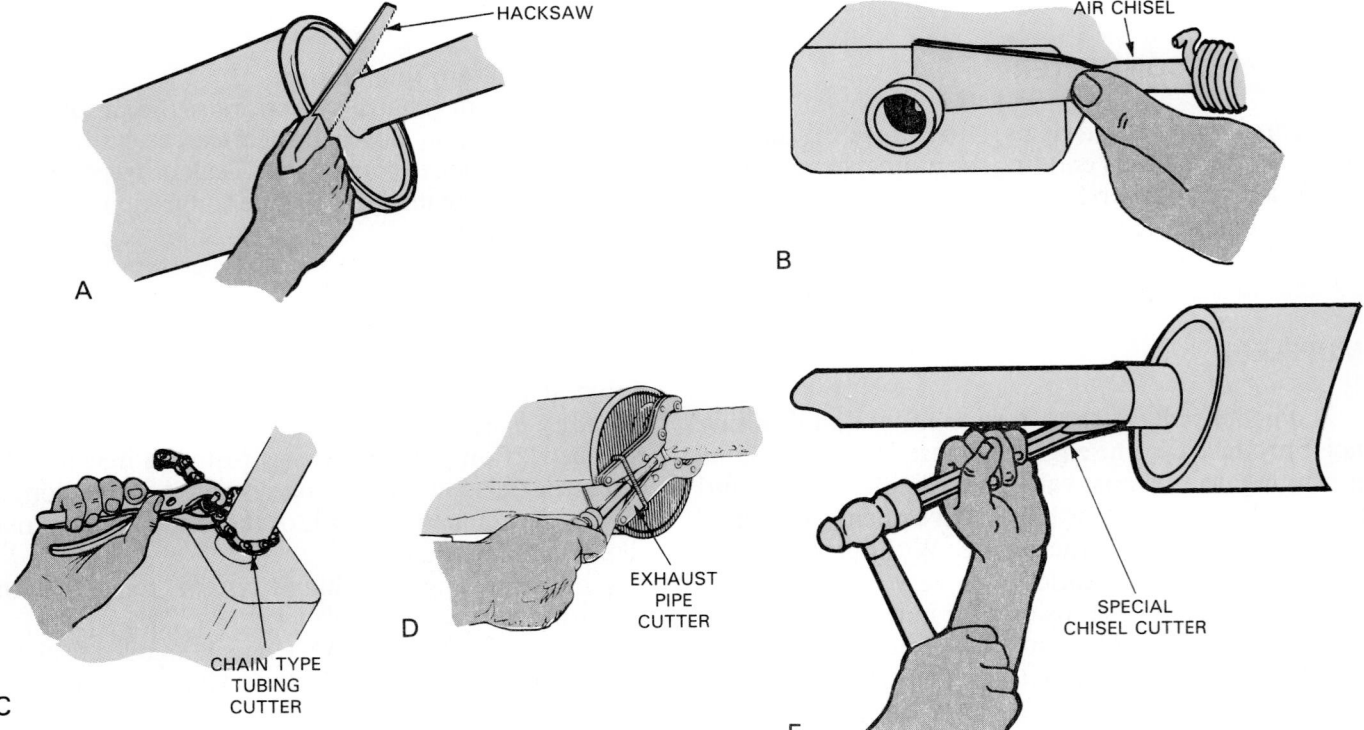

Fig. 25-7. Several methods of removing old exhaust system parts. A — Hacksaw. B — Air chisel. C — Chain type cutting tool. D — Exhaust pipe cutter. E — Specially shaped, hand type cutter or chisel. (AP Parts, Lisle, and Florida Dept. of Voc. Ed.)

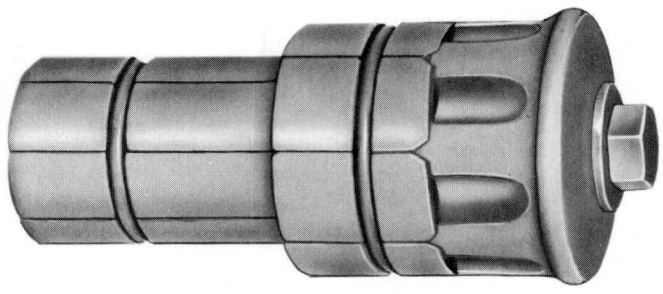

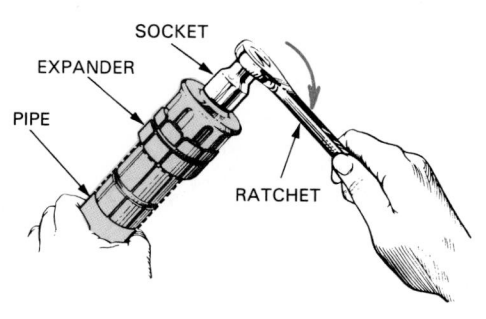

Fig. 25-9. Pipe expander will enlarge ID (inside diameter) of pipes. Then one pipe will fit over another. (Lisle)

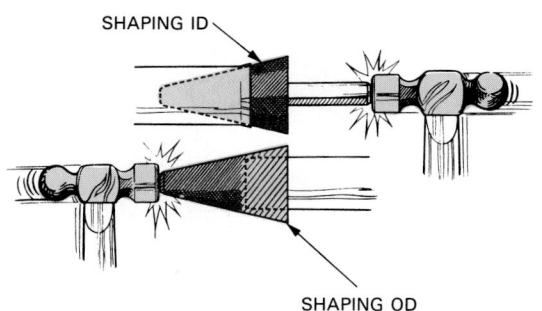

Fig. 25-10. Pipe shaper will round dented pipe ends. (Lisle)

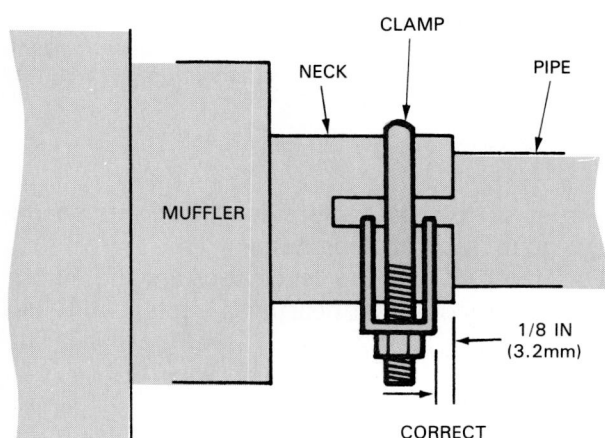

Fig. 25-11. Make sure muffler clamps are installed correctly. Clamp must be positioned around both pipes. If not, one pipe can pull out of other. (Florida Dept. of Voc. Ed.)

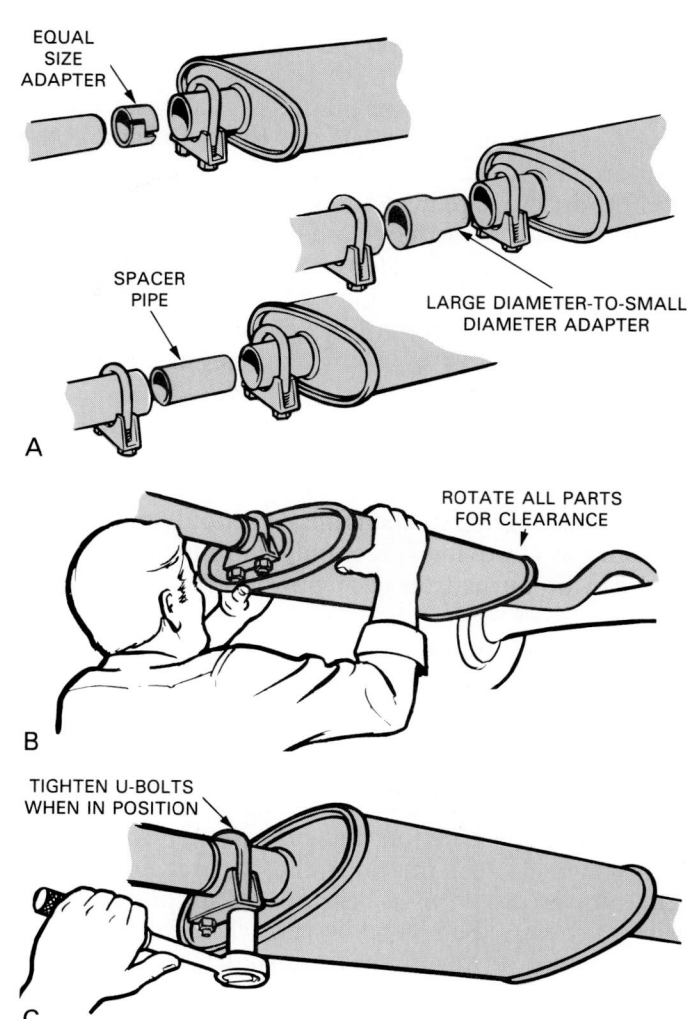

Fig. 25-12. A — Adapters are sometimes needed to make muffler work on existing system. B — Double-check exhaust system-to-car clearance carefully. C — After checking clearance, tighten all clamps evenly and properly. (AP Parts)

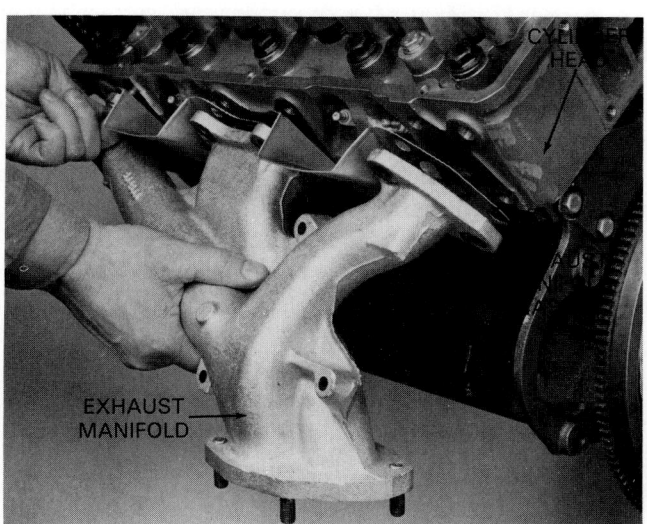

Fig. 25-13. Exhaust gasket is normally recommended. Gasket is held in position as all fasteners are started by hand. Torque fasteners to recommended value in a crisscross pattern. (Saab)

SUPERCHARGERS AND TURBOCHARGERS

A *supercharger* is an air pump that increases engine power by pushing a denser air-fuel charge into the combustion chambers. With more fuel and air, combustion produces more heat energy and pressure to push the piston down in the cylinder.

Sometimes termed a **blower,** the supercharger raises the air pressure in the engine intake manifold. Then, when the intake valves open, more air-fuel mixture (gasoline engine) or air (diesel engine) can flow into the cylinders.

A **normally aspirated engine,** nicknamed *atmospheric engine,* uses atmospheric pressure (14.7 psi or 100 kPa at sea level) to push air into the engine. It is a nonsupercharged engine. With only outside air pressure as a moving force, only a limited amount of fuel can be burned on each power stroke.

Supercharger types

There are three basic types of superchargers:
1. Centrifugal supercharger.
2. Rotor (Rootes) supercharger.
3. Vane supercharger.

These types are shown in Fig. 25-14. Note the differences in construction and operation.

In the field, the term "supercharger" generally refers to a blower driven by a belt, gears, or chain. Superchargers are used on large diesel truck engines and racing engines. However, they are sometimes found on high performance passenger cars.

The term **turbocharger** or *"turbo"* refers to a blower driven by engine exhaust gases. Turbochargers are commonly used on passenger cars, trucks, and competiton engines.

TURBOCHARGERS

A *turbocharger* is an exhaust driven supercharger (fan or blower) that forces air into the engine under pressure. Turbochargers are frequently used on small gasoline and diesel engines to increase power output. By harnessing engine exhaust energy, a turbocharger can also improve engine efficiency (fuel economy and emission levels). This is especially true with a diesel engine.

As shown in Fig. 25-15, the basic parts of a turbocharger are:
1. TURBINE WHEEL (exhaust driven fan that turns turbo shaft and compressor wheel).
2. TURBINE HOUSING (outer enclosure that routes exhaust gases around turbine wheel).
3. TURBO SHAFT (steel shaft that connects turbine and compressor wheels. It passes through center of turbo housing).
4. COMPRESSOR WHEEL (driven fan that forces air into engine intake manifold under pressure).
5. COMPRESSOR HOUSING (part of turbo hous-

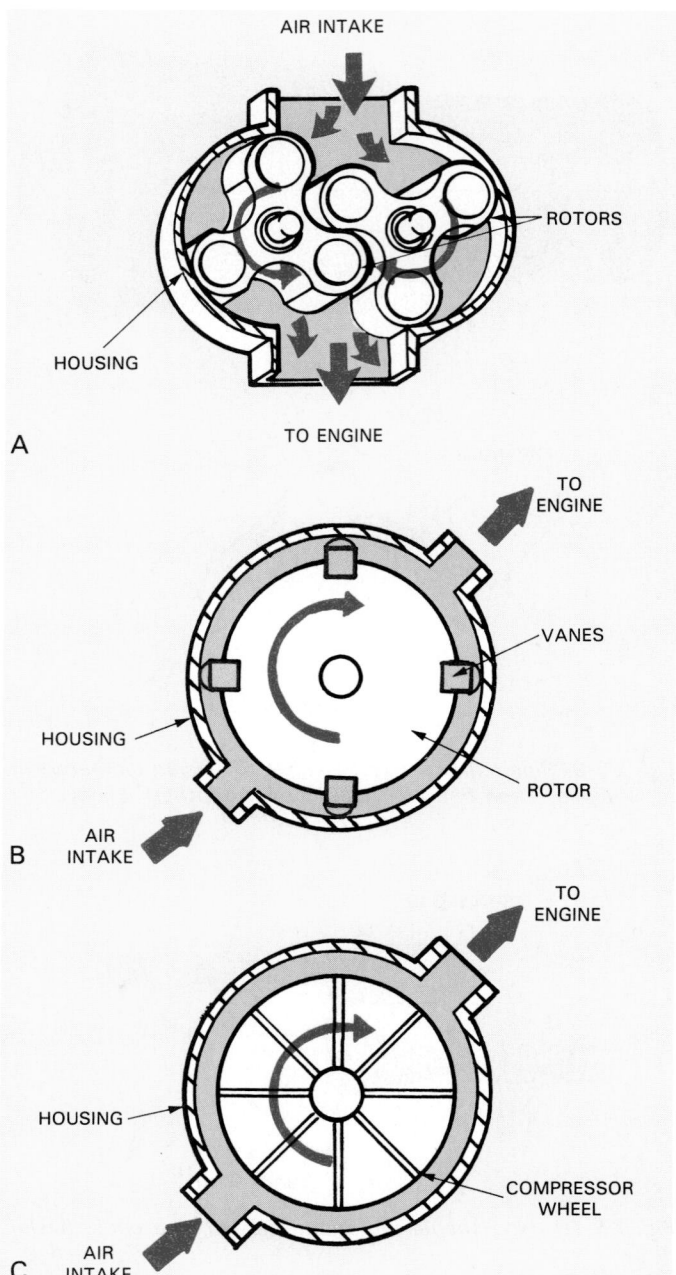

Fig. 25-14. Three basic types of superchargers. A — Rotor or Rootes type supercharger. B — Vane type supercharger. C — Centrifugal supercharger, more commonly called a turbocharger. (Chrysler)

ing that surrounds compressor wheel. Its shape helps pump air into engine).
6. BEARING HOUSING (enclosure around turbo shaft that contains bearings, seals, and oil passages).

Turbocharger operation

When the engine is running, hot exhaust gases blow out the open exhaust valves and into the exhaust manifold. The exhaust manifold and connecting tubing route these gases into the turbine housing. Refer

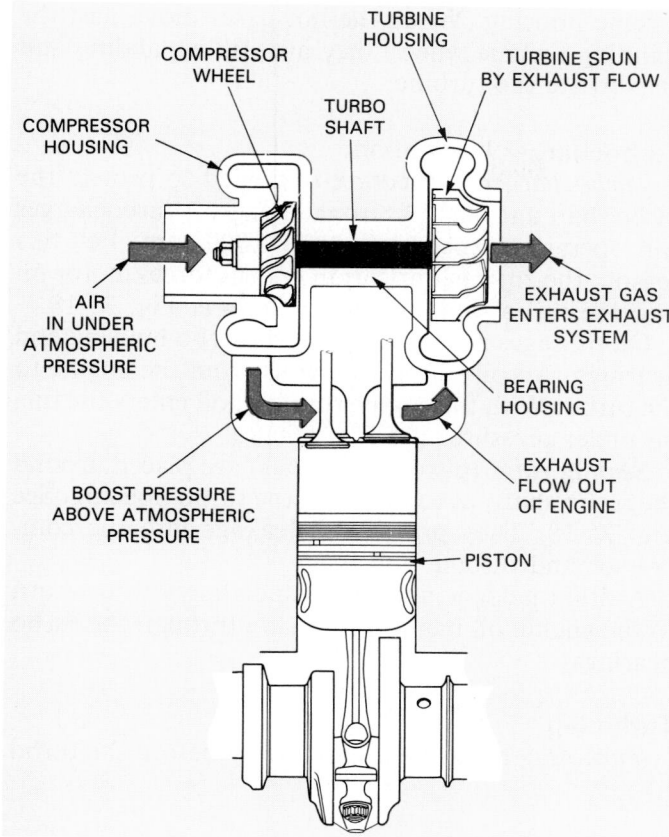

Fig. 25-15. Turbocharger uses exhaust gas flow to spin turbine wheel. Turbine wheel spins shaft and compressor wheel. Compressor wheel then pressurizes air entering engine for more power output. (Mercedes Benz)

to Fig. 25-16.

As the gases pass through the turbine housing, they strike the fins or blades on the turbine wheel. When engine load is high enough, there is enough exhaust gas flow to rapidly spin the turbine wheel, Fig. 25-16.

Since the turbine wheel is connected to the compressor wheel by the turbo shaft, the compressor wheel rotates with the turbine. Compressor wheel rotation pulls air into the compressor housing. Centrifugal force throws the spinning air outward. This causes air to flow out of the turbocharger and into the engine cylinder under pressure.

Turbocharger location

A turbocharger is usually located on one side of the engine. See Fig. 25-17. An exhaust pipe connects the engine exhaust manifold to the turbine housing. The exhaust system header pipe connects to the outlet of the turbine housing.

A *blow-through turbo system* has the turbocharger located before the carburetor or throttle body. The turbo compressor wheel only pressurizes air. Fuel is mixed with the air after air leaves the compressor.

A *draw-through turbo system* locates the turbocharger after the carburetor or throttle body assembly. As a result, both air and fuel (gasoline engine) pass through the compressor housing.

Theoretically, the turbocharger should be located as close to the engine exhaust manifold as possible. Then, a maximum amount of exhaust heat will enter the

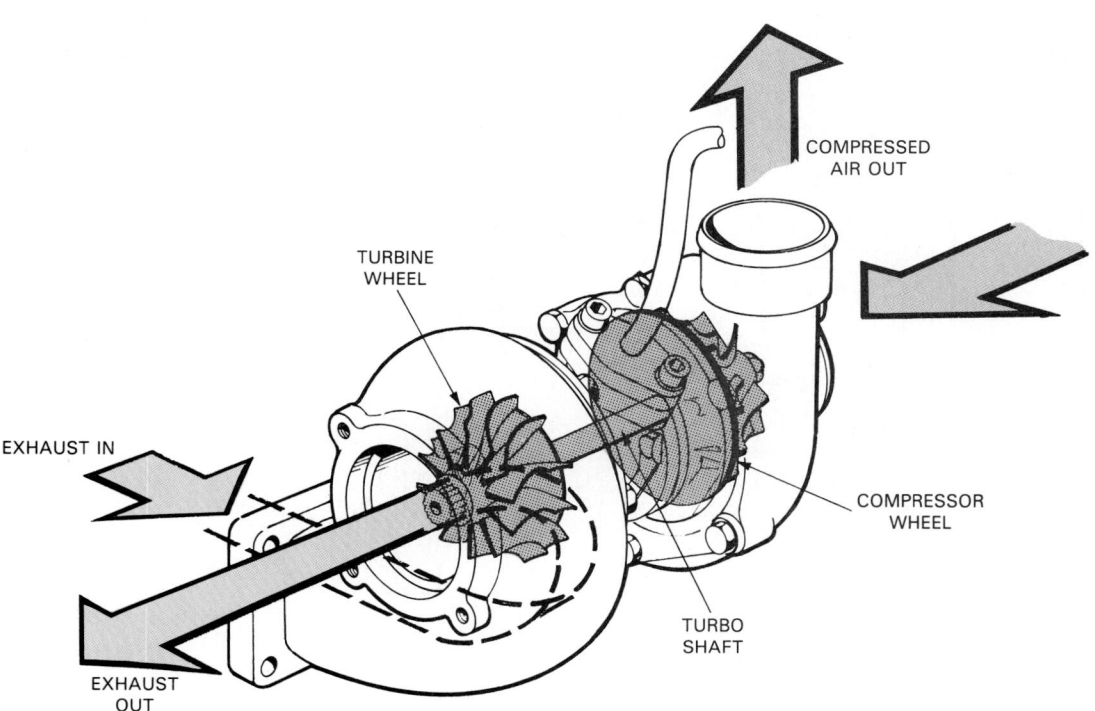

Fig. 25-16. Exhaust flow spins turbine wheel, shaft, and compressor wheel. Normally wasted energy in exhaust is used to increase compression stroke pressure in cylinders for more violent combustion. (Saab)

Fig. 25-17. Turbocharger normally bolts to one side of engine. Pipes route exhaust through turbine housing. Compressed air leaves turbo and enters intake tract and engine. (Ford)

turbine housing. When the hot gases move past the spinning turbine wheel, they are still expanding and help rotate the turbine.

Turbocharger lubrication

Turbocharger lubrication is needed to protect the turbo shaft and bearings from damage. A turbocharger can operate at speeds up to 100,000 rpm. For this reason, the engine lubrication system forces motor oil into the turbo shaft bearings. Look at Fig. 25-18.

Oil passages are provided in the turbo housing and bearings. An oil supply line runs from the engine to the turbo. With the engine running, oil enters the turbo under pressure. See Fig. 25-19.

Sealing rings (piston type rings) are placed around the turbo shaft, at each end of the turbo housing. See Fig. 25-18. They prevent oil leakage into the compressor and turbine housings.

A drain passage and drain line allow oil to return to the engine oil pan after passing through the turbo bearings.

Turbo lag

Turbo lag refers to a short delay before the turbo

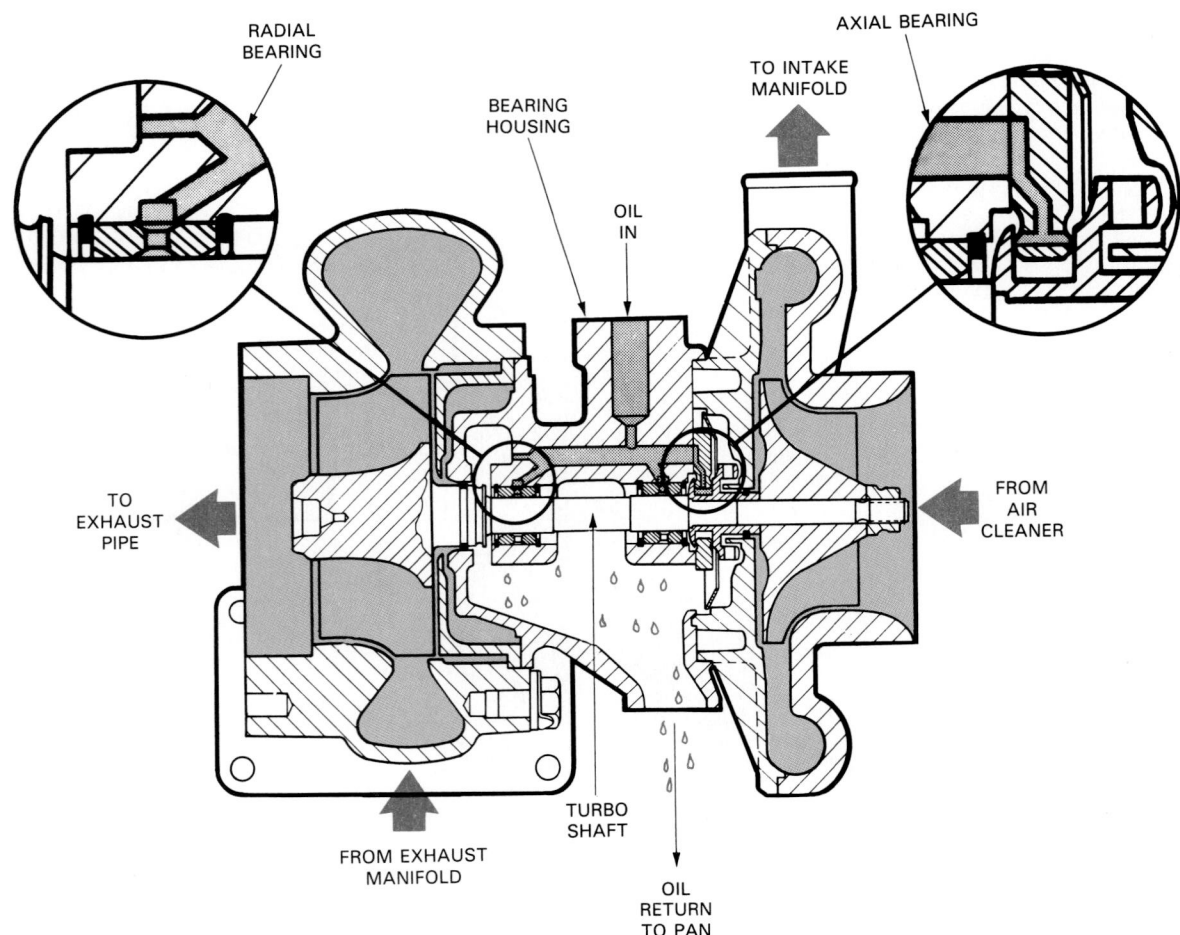

Fig. 25-18. High turbo speeds requires pressure lubrication. Engine oil is fed to turbo through oil line. Oil flows through bearings and then drains into oil pan through drain line. (Saab)

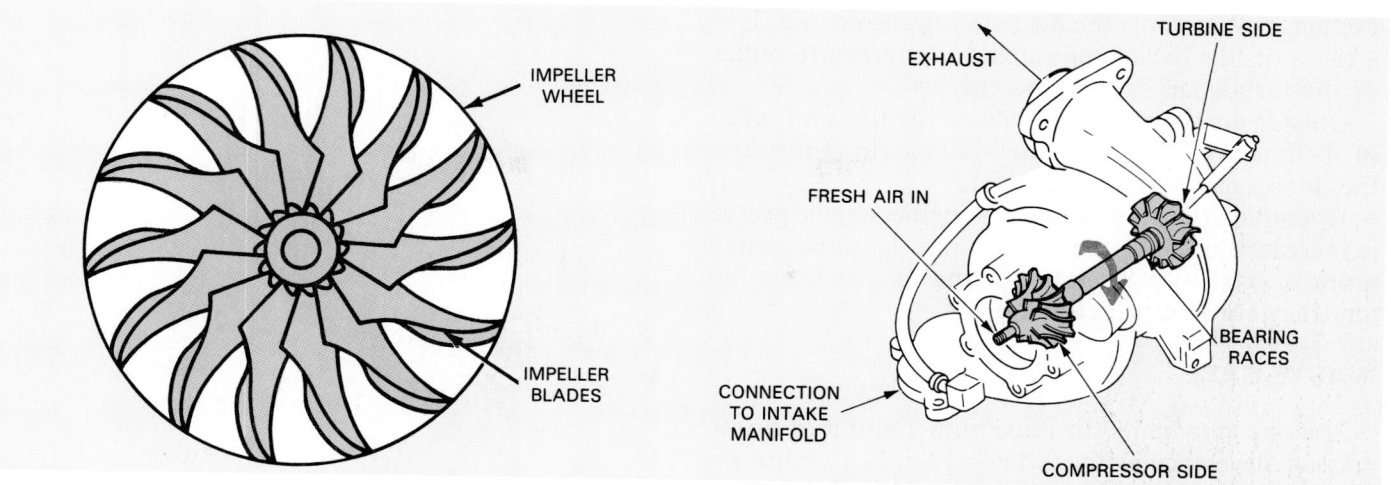

Fig. 25-19. Turbine and compressor wheels have specially shaped fins or blades that act as fans. Exhaust flow spins turbine fan. Spinning compressor fan blows air into engine under pressure. (Chrysler)

develops sufficient *boost* (pressure above atmospheric pressure).

When the car's accelerator pedal is pressed down for rapid acceleration, the engine may lack power for a few seconds. This is caused by the compressor and turbine wheels not spinning fast enough. It takes time for the exhaust gases to bring the turbo up to operating speed.

Modern turbo systems suffer very little from turbo lag. Their turbine and compressor wheels are very light so that they can accelerate up to rpm quickly.

Turbocharger intercooler

A *turbocharger intercooler* is an air-to-air heat

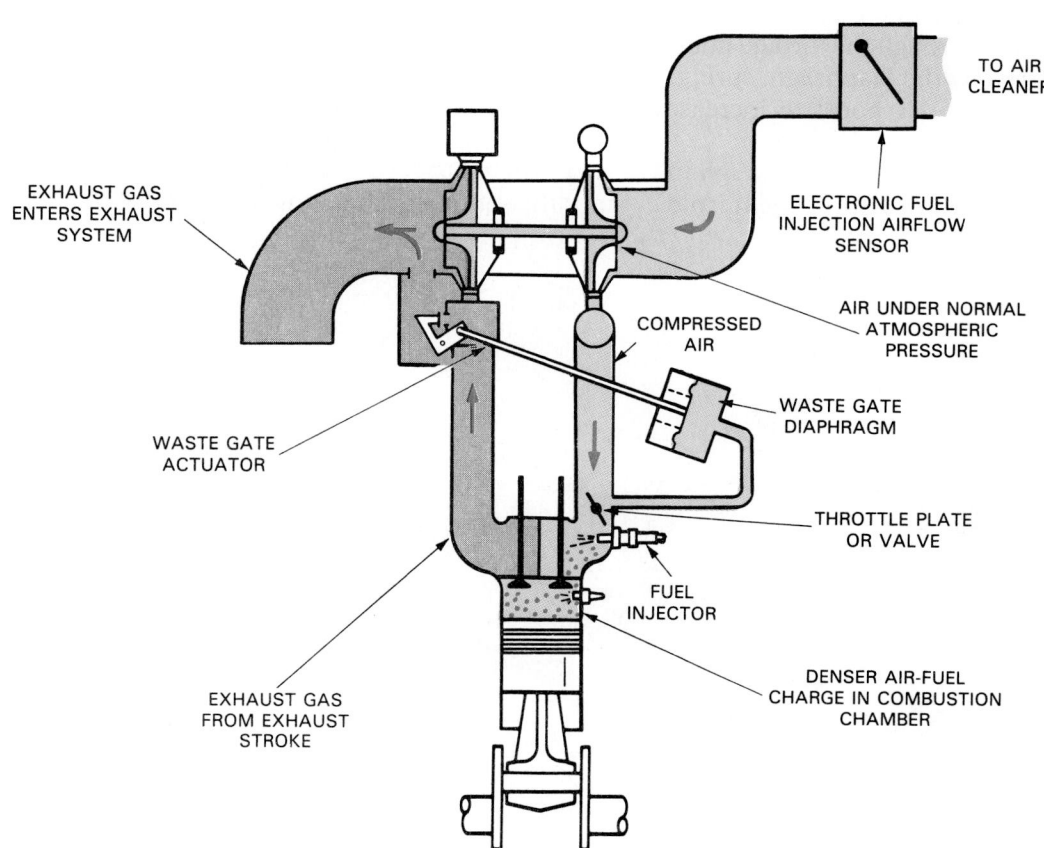

Fig. 25-20. Study basic exhaust and inlet airflow through complete turbo system. (Ford)

exchanger that cools the air entering the engine. It is a radiator-like device mounted at the pressure outlet of the turbocharger (or supercharger).

Outside air flows over and cools the fins and tubes of the intercooler. Then, when the air flows through the intercooler, heat is removed.

By cooling the air entering the engine, engine power is increased because the air is more dense (contains more oxygen by volume). Cooling also reduces the tendency for engine detonation.

WASTE GATE

A *waste gate* limits the maximum amount of boost pressure developed by the turbocharger. It is a butterfly or poppet type valve that allows exhaust to bypass the turbine wheel. See Fig. 25-20.

Without a waste gate, the turbo could produce too much pressure in the combustion chambers. This could lead to detonation (spontaneous combustion) and engine damage.

Basically, a waste gate is a valve operated by a diaphragm assembly, Fig. 25-21. Intake manifold pressure acts on the diaphragm to control waste gate valve action. The valve controls the opening and closing of a passage around the turbine housing, Fig. 25-22.

Waste gate operation

Fig. 25-23 illustrates the basic operation of a turbocharger waste gate. Under partial load, the system routes all of the exhaust gases through the turbine housing. The waste gate is closed by the diaphragm spring. This assures that there is adequate boost to increase engine power.

Under full load, boost may become high enough to overcome diaphragm spring pressure. Manifold

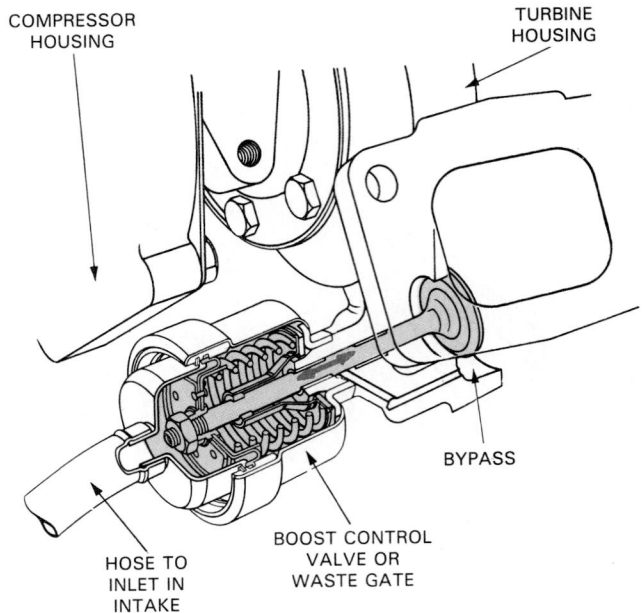

Fig. 25-22. Note hose that connects waste gate with compressor housing. When boost pressure is too high, pressure acts on waste gate diaphragm to open valve and reduce boost. (Garrett)

pressure compresses the spring and opens the waste gate valve. This permits some of the exhaust gases to flow through the waste gate passage and into the exhaust system. Less exhaust is left to spin the turbine. Boost pressure is limited to a preset value.

TURBOCHARGED ENGINE MODIFICATIONS

A turbocharged engine normally has several modifications to make it withstand the increased

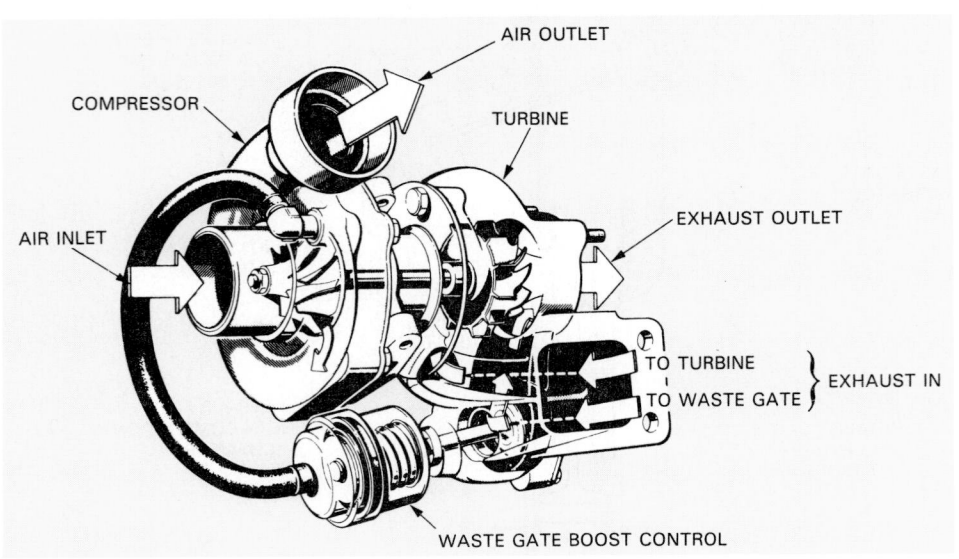

Fig. 25-21. Waste gate or boost control is a valve in turbine housing. When needed, it can open to limit boost pressure by reducing amount of exhaust acting on turbine wheel. (Mercedes Benz)

NORMAL BOOST IN SENSOR LINE
DIAPHRAGM NOT FLEXED
EXHAUST GAS
WASTE GATE CLOSED
A
DIAPHRAGM FLEXED BY EXCESS INTAKE PRESSURE
ACTUATING ROD
WASTE GATE VALVE OPEN
EXHAUST GASES BYPASS TURBO
B

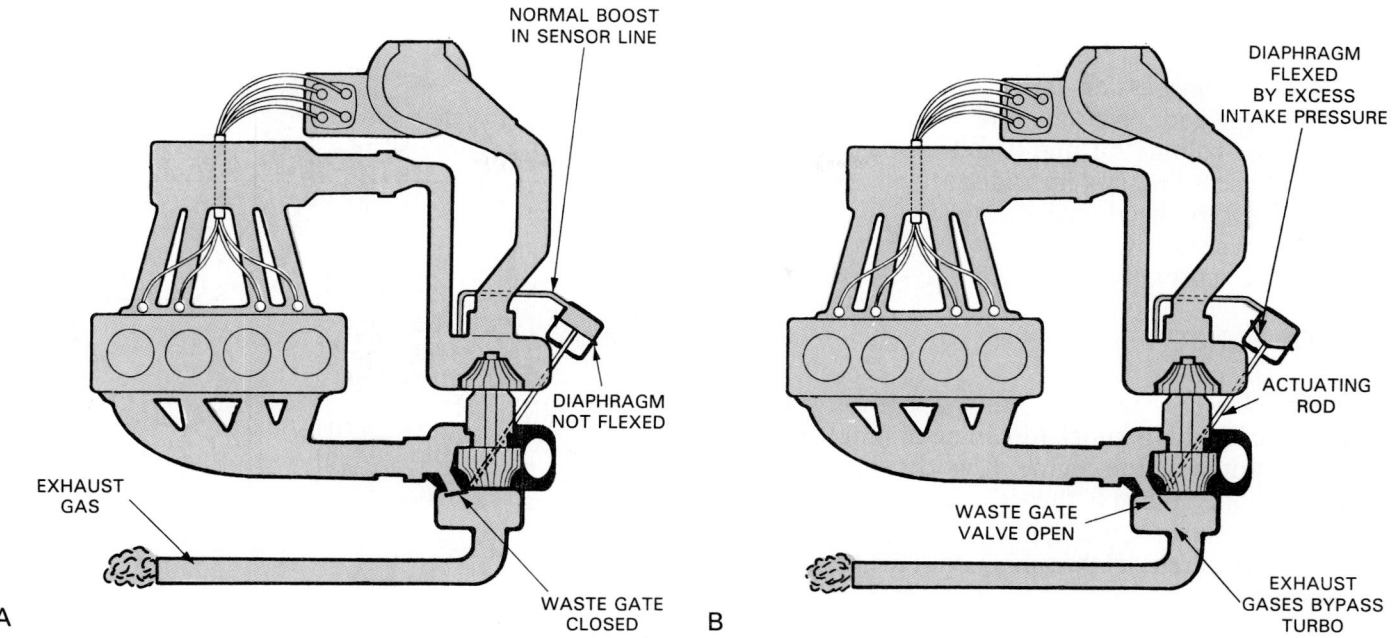

Fig. 25-23. Study operation of complete turbo system. A — Under part throttle, normal boost conditions, waste gate remains closed. All exhaust flow is directed over turbine wheel. B — Under full load, boost pressure may increase too much. High intake pressure deflects waste gate diaphragm to open waste gate valve. This allows some of the exhaust to bypass turbine wheel. Turbine wheel slows down and reduces boost pressure. (Saab)

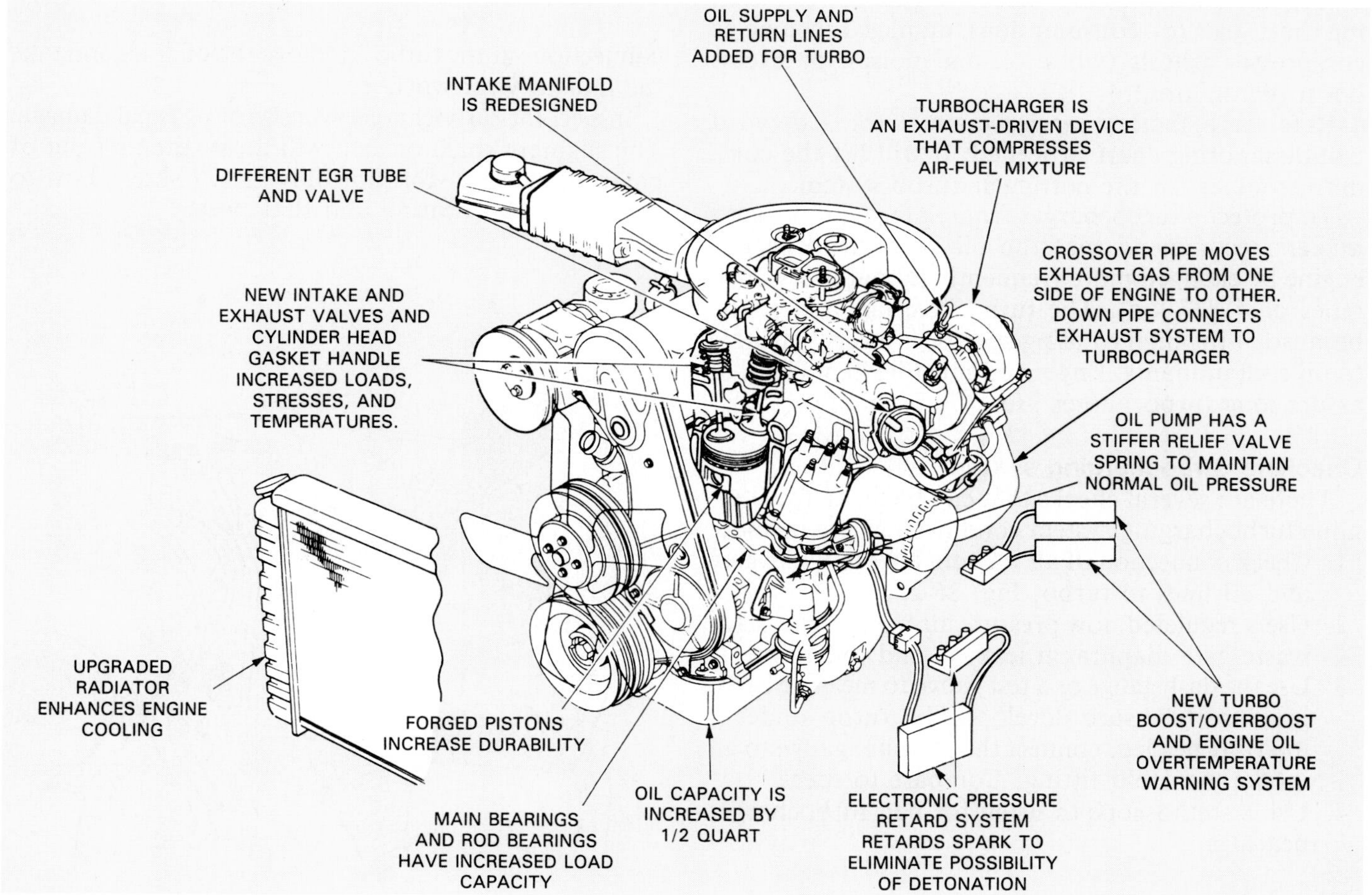

OIL SUPPLY AND RETURN LINES ADDED FOR TURBO
INTAKE MANIFOLD IS REDESIGNED
TURBOCHARGER IS AN EXHAUST-DRIVEN DEVICE THAT COMPRESSES AIR-FUEL MIXTURE
DIFFERENT EGR TUBE AND VALVE
CROSSOVER PIPE MOVES EXHAUST GAS FROM ONE SIDE OF ENGINE TO OTHER. DOWN PIPE CONNECTS EXHAUST SYSTEM TO TURBOCHARGER
NEW INTAKE AND EXHAUST VALVES AND CYLINDER HEAD GASKET HANDLE INCREASED LOADS, STRESSES, AND TEMPERATURES.
OIL PUMP HAS A STIFFER RELIEF VALVE SPRING TO MAINTAIN NORMAL OIL PRESSURE
UPGRADED RADIATOR ENHANCES ENGINE COOLING
FORGED PISTONS INCREASE DURABILITY
NEW TURBO BOOST/OVERBOOST AND ENGINE OIL OVERTEMPERATURE WARNING SYSTEM
OIL CAPACITY IS INCREASED BY 1/2 QUART
ELECTRONIC PRESSURE RETARD SYSTEM RETARDS SPARK TO ELIMINATE POSSIBILITY OF DETONATION
MAIN BEARINGS AND ROD BEARINGS HAVE INCREASED LOAD CAPACITY

Fig. 25-24. Note many engine modifications commonly used with turbocharging. Turbocharging increases demands on engine. (Ford)

horsepower. A few of these are shown in Fig. 25-24 and include:

1. Lower compression ratio.
2. Stronger rods, pistons, and crankshaft.
3. Higher volume oil pump and an oil cooler.
4. Larger cooling system radiator.
5. O-ring type head gasket.
6. Heat resistant valves.
7. Knock sensor (ignition retard system).

KNOCK SENSOR

A *knock sensor* is used to retard ignition timing if the engine begins to knock (detonate or ping). The sensor is mounted on the engine. It works something like a microphone. When it "hears" a knocking sound, an electrical signal is sent to the on-board computer. The computer then retards the timing until the knock stops.

A knock sensor helps the computer keep the ignition timing advanced as much as possible. This improves engine power and gas mileage. It also protects the engine from detonation damage.

TURBOCHARGING SYSTEM SERVICE

Turbocharging system problems usually show up as inadequate boost pressure (lack of engine power), leaking shaft seals (oil consumption), damaged turbine or compressor wheels (vibration and noise), or excess boost (detonation).

Refer to a factory service manual for a detailed troubleshooting chart if needed. It will list the common troubles for the particular turbo system.

To protect a turbocharger from damage, most auto makers recommend that the oil in a turbocharged engine be changed more frequently (about every 3000 miles or 4 827 km). The turbo bearings and shaft, because of the high rotating speeds, are very sensitive to oil contaminants. Engine oil must be kept clean to assure long turbocharger life.

Checking turbocharging system

There are several checks that can be made to determine turbocharging system condition. These include:

1. Check connection of all vacuum lines to waste gate and oil lines to turbo, Fig. 25-25.
2. Use a regulated, low pressure air hose to check for waste gate diaphragm leakage and operation.
3. Use the dash gauge or a test gauge to measure boost pressure (pressure developed by turbo under a load). If needed, connect the pressure gauge to an intake manifold fitting. Compare to specs.
4. Use a stethoscope to listen for bad turbocharger bearings.

Checking turbocharger

To check the internal condition of a turbo, remove the unit from the engine, as in Fig. 25-26. Unbolt the

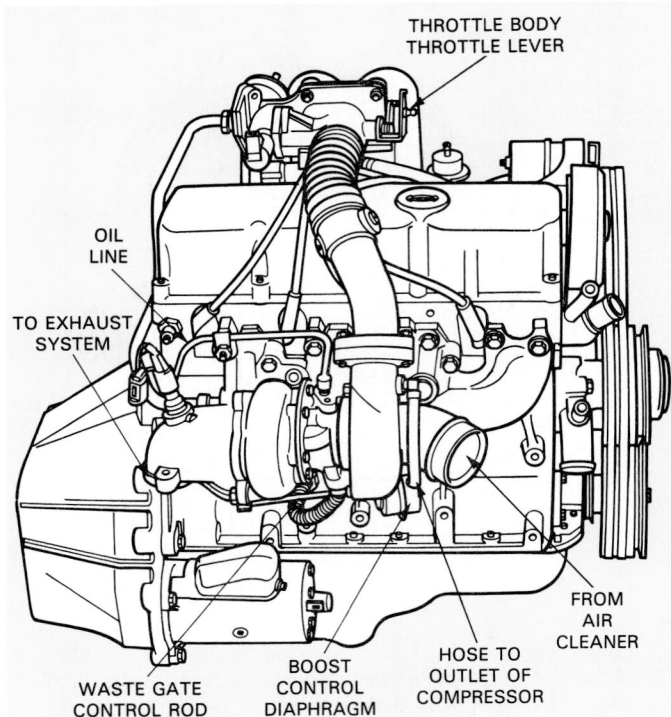

Fig. 25-25. Side view of engine shows location and mounting of turbocharger. (Ford)

connections at the turbo. Remove the oil lines and take the unit to your workbench.

Inspect the turbocharger wheels for physical damage. The slightest knick or dent will throw the unit out of balance, causing vibration. Fig. 25-27 shows how to measure turbo bearing and shaft wear.

WARNING! Never use a hard metal object or sandpaper to remove carbon deposits from the turbine

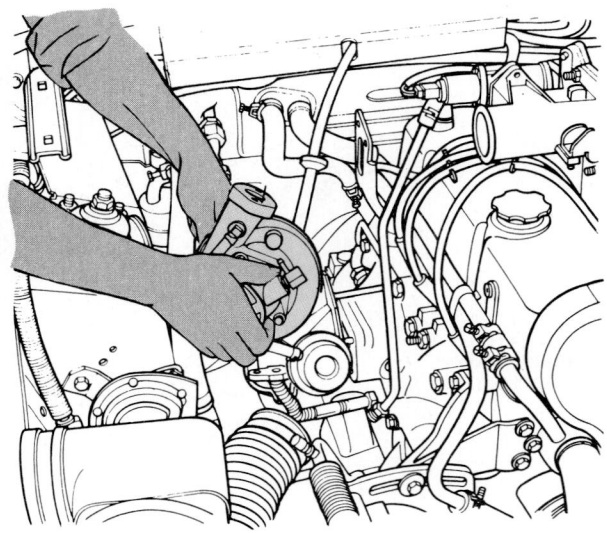

Fig. 25-26. After removing mounting fasteners and any other parts, turbo can be lifted off for replacement. A turbo cannot be repaired in-shop. A new unit is normally installed. (Ford)

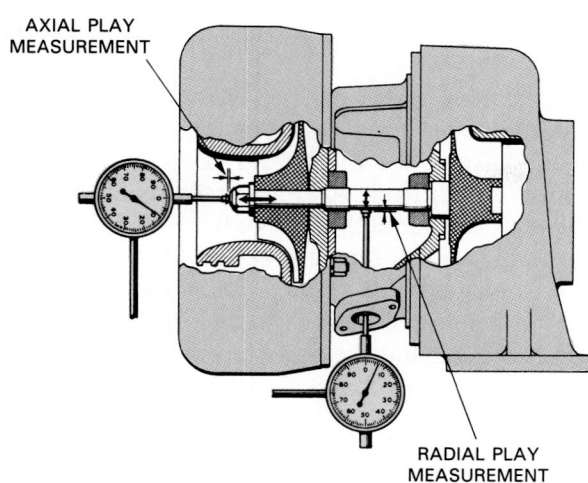

AXIAL PLAY
MEASUREMENT

RADIAL PLAY
MEASUREMENT

Fig. 25-27. Dial indicator can be used to check radial and axial play of turbo shaft. If not within specs, replace unit. (Waukesha)

wheel. If you gouge or remove metal, the wheel can vibrate and destroy the turbo. Only use a soft wire brush and solvent to clean the turbo wheels.

Installing new turbocharger

Many turbocharger problems are NOT repaired in the field, Fig. 25-28. Most mechanics install a new or rebuilt unit. When installing a turbo, you should:

1. Make sure the new turbo is the correct type. Compare part numbers.
2. Use new gaskets and seals.
3. Torque all fasteners to specs.
4. If needed, change engine oil and flush oil lines before starting engine.
5. If the failure was oil related, check oil supply pressure in feed line to turbo.

Waste gate service

An *inoperative waste gate* can either cause too much or too little boost pressure. If stuck open, the turbo will not produce boost pressure and the engine will lack power. If stuck closed, detonation and engine damage can result from excessive boost.

Before condemning the waste gate, always check other parts. Check the knock sensor (spark retard system if used) and the ignition timing. Make sure the vacuum-pressure lines are all connected properly.

Follow service manual instructions when testing or replacing a waste gate. As shown in Fig. 25-29, waste gate removal is simple. Unbolt the fasteners. Remove the lines and lift the unit off of the engine. Many manuals recommend waste gate replacement, rather than in-shop repairs.

Figs. 25-30 and 25-31 show turbocharged engines. Can you identify all of the parts. Trace flow of fuel charge into and exhaust out of engine.

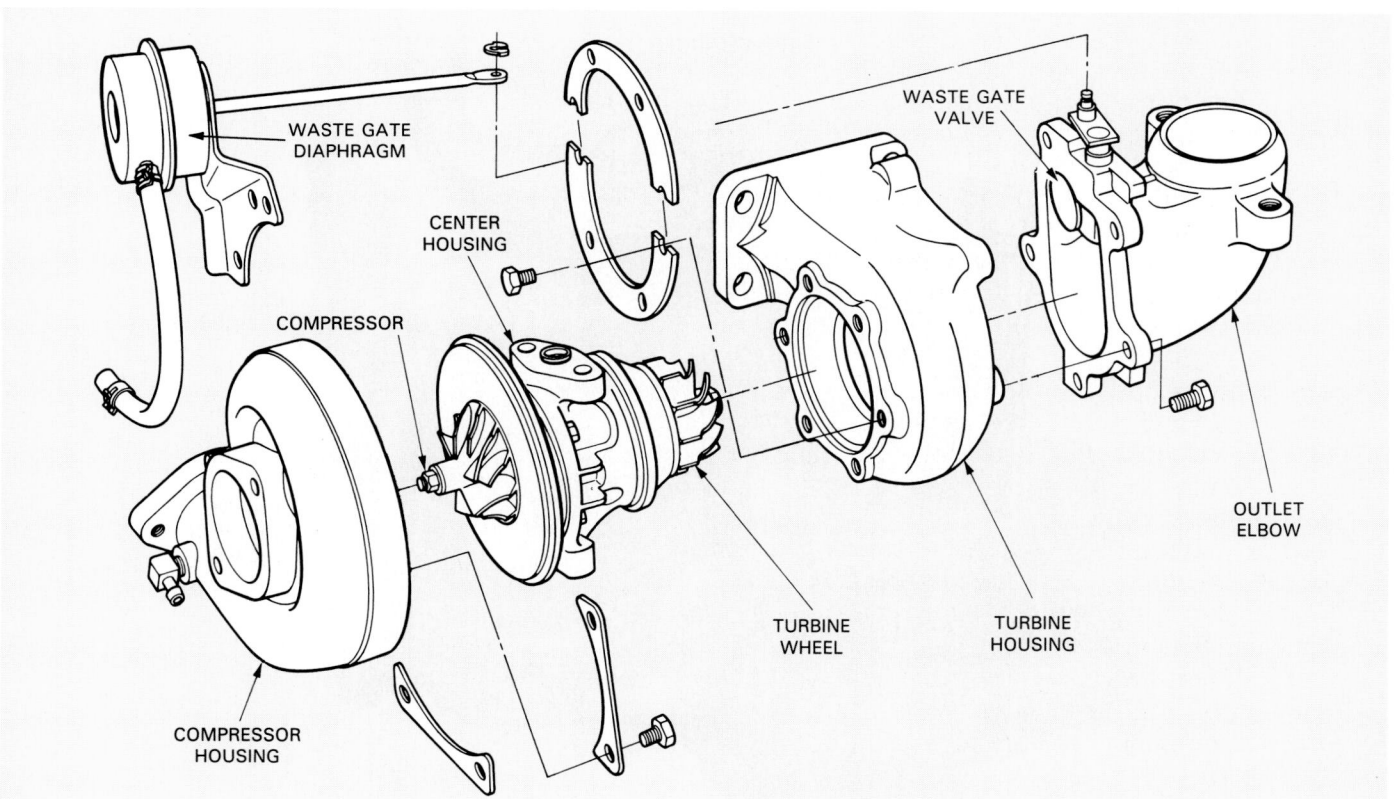

WASTE GATE
DIAPHRAGM

WASTE GATE
VALVE

CENTER
HOUSING

COMPRESSOR

OUTLET
ELBOW

COMPRESSOR
HOUSING

TURBINE
WHEEL

TURBINE
HOUSING

Fig. 25-28. Exploded view of modern turbocharger. Only external parts are servicable. Turbine-compressor wheel is very precise, balanced assembly. Slightest nick or chip on blade can cause unit to explode in service. (Ford)

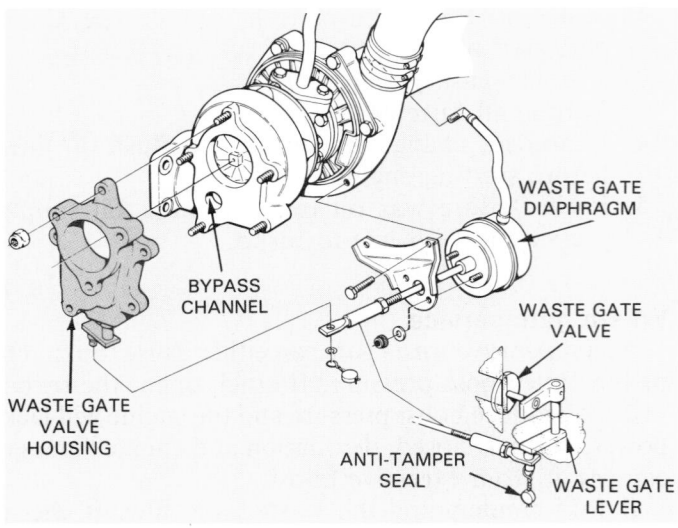

Fig. 25-29. Waste gate normally bolts to side of turbo housing. Linkage rod connects diaphragm with valve mechanism. Also note seal that prevents tampering with boost setting. Although overboost will increase power, it can also cause engine damage. (Saab)

SUPERCHARGERS

A supercharger is a compressor or blower driven by a belt, chain, or gears. Unlike a turbocharger, it is NOT driven by engine exhaust gases. Most passenger car superchargers are driven by a belt on the front of the engine. See Fig. 25-32.

The belt drives the rotors inside the supercharger. As the rotors turn, they compress the air inside the housing and force the air, under pressure, into the engine intake manifold. An intercooler is commonly used between the supercharger outlet and the engine to cool the air and to increase power (cool charge of air carries more oxygen needed for combustion).

Superchargers have the advantage of NOT suffering from turbo lag and the delay in power as the turbo gains speed. A supercharger will instantly produce boost pressure at low engine speeds because it is mechanically linked to the engine crankshaft. This low-speed power and instant throttle response is desirable in a passenger car for passing, entering high-speed interstate highways, etc.

Fig. 25-33 shows the major parts included in a supercharger system.

KNOW THESE TERMS

Exhaust manifold, Header pipe, Catalytic converter, Muffler, Tailpipe, Hangers, Heat shields, Muffler clamps, Back pressure, Crossover pipe, Exhaust manifold heat valve, Rust penetrant, Air chisel, Pipe expander, Pipe shaper, Supercharger, Turbocharger,

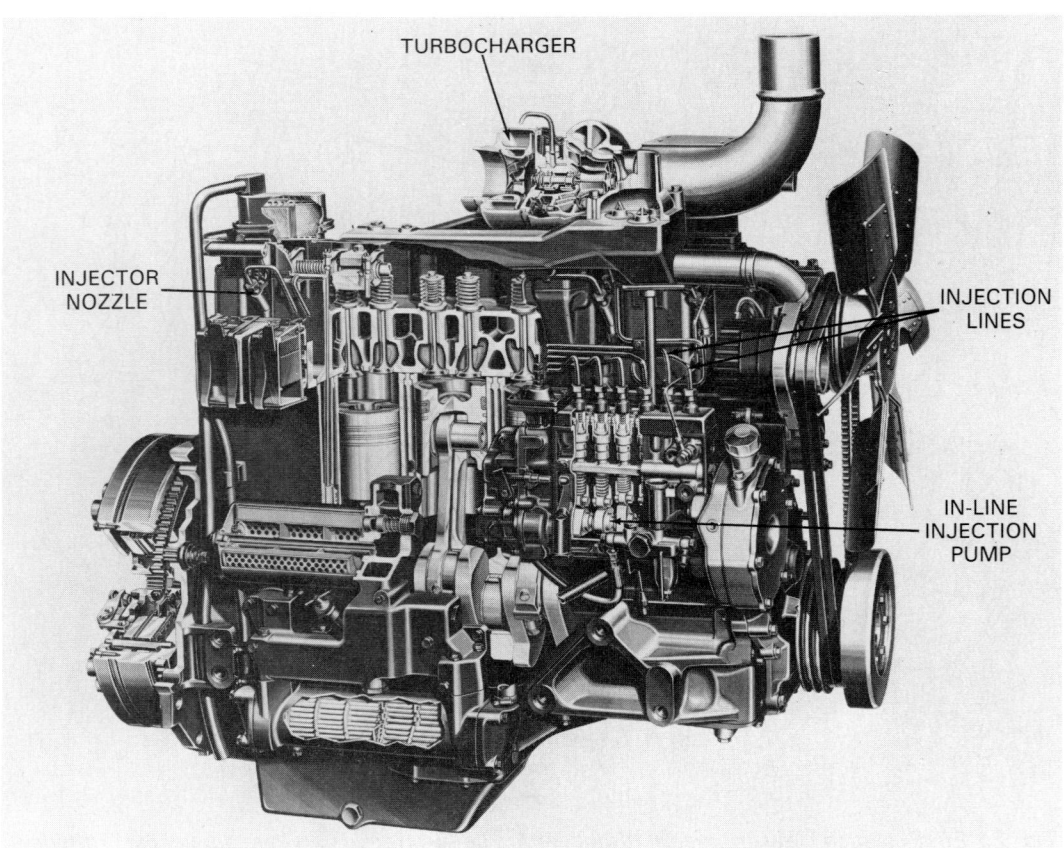

Fig. 25-30. How many parts of this turbocharged diesel engine can you identify? (Deere & Co.)

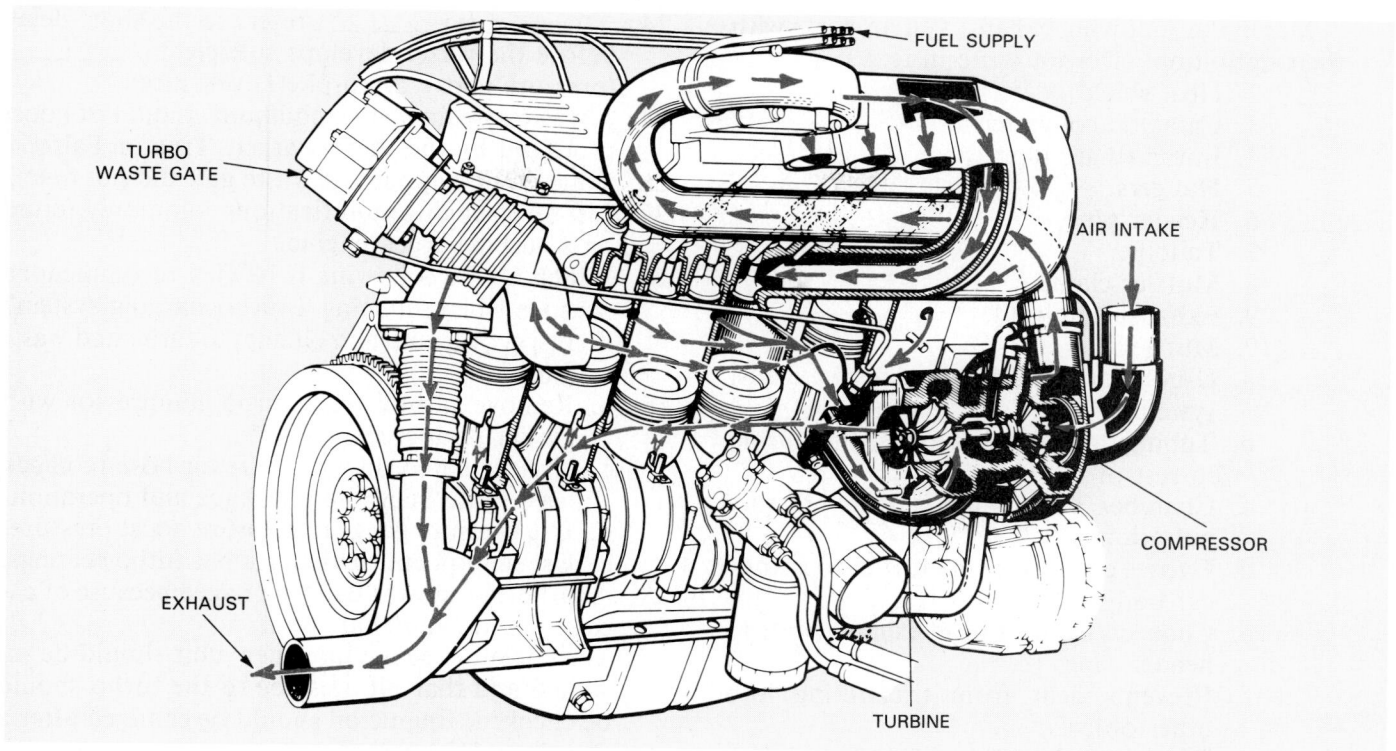

Fig. 25-31. This is a turbocharged, in-line, six-cylinder engine. (Audi)

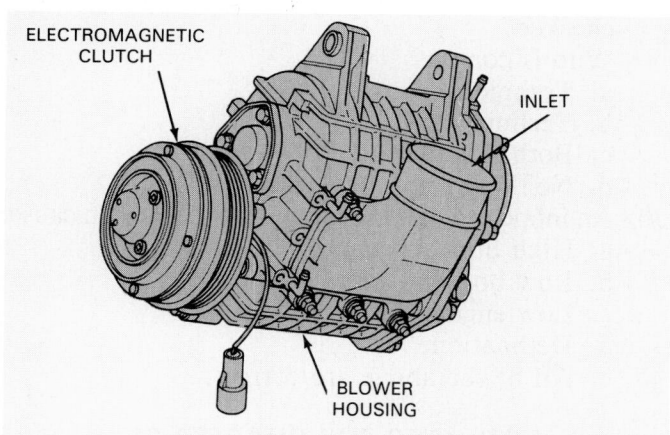

Fig. 25-32. Supercharger is normally driven by belt running up from engine crankshaft. Electric clutch can be used to turn blower on and off as needed. For example, blower might only kick on at full throttle when there is demand for more engine power. (Toyota)

Normal aspiration, Turbine wheel, Turbine housing, Turbo shaft, Compressor wheel, Compressor housing, Bearing housing, Turbo bearing, Blow-through turbo, Draw-through turbo, Sealing rings, Turbo lag, Waste gate, Knock sensor, Boost pressure.

REVIEW QUESTIONS

1. An exhaust system _____ engine operation and carries _____ _____ to the rear of the car.

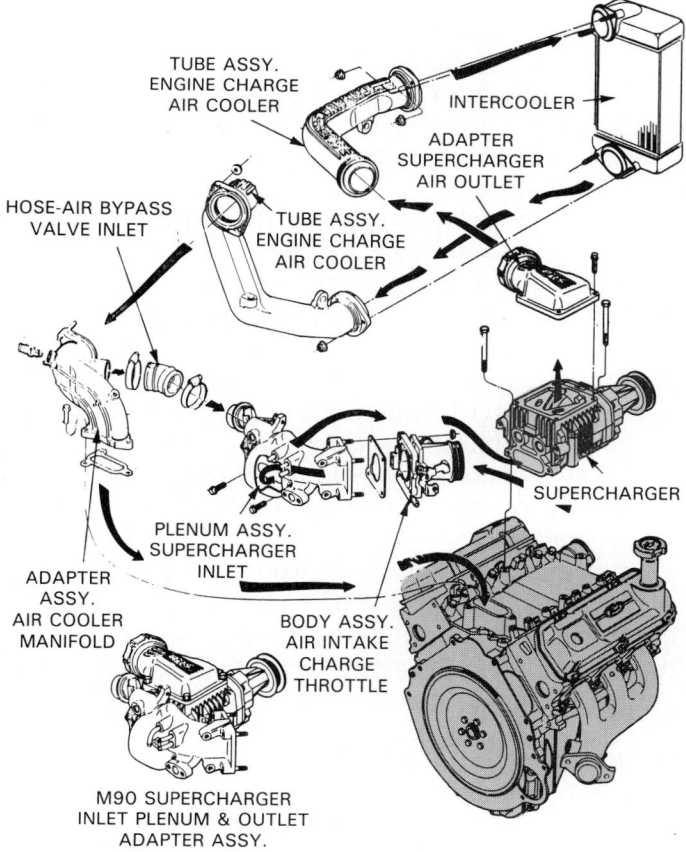

Fig. 25-33. Note basic components in a supercharging system. This supercharger bolts to top of engine. Trace flow of air through components. (Ford Motor Co.)

Match the following exhaust system parts with their definition. (Do not write in text.)

____ 2. Heat shield.
____ 3. Catalytic converter.
____ 4. Intermediate pipe.
____ 5. Hangers.
____ 6. Header pipe.
____ 7. Tailpipe.
____ 8. Muffler clamp.
____ 9. Exhaust manifold.
____ 10. Muffler.
　　a. U-bolt for connecting parts of exhaust system.
　　b. Tubing that connects exhaust manifold to rest of system.
　　c. Chamber for damping out pressure pulsations.
　　d. Carries exhaust from muffler to rear of car body.
　　e. Connects cylinder head exhaust ports to header pipe.
　　f. Prevents heat from transfering into other objects.
　　g. Connects exhaust manifold to tailpipe.
　　h. Device for removing pollutants from exhaust.
　　i. Pipe between catalytic converter and muffler.
　　j. Connects exhaust system to underside of car body.

11. Define the term "exhaust back pressure."
12. A dual exhaust system is commonly used on small, high fuel economy engines. True or False?
13. An exhaust _____ _____ _____ forces hot exhaust gases to flow into the intake manifold to aid cold weather starting.
14. When is exhaust system service commonly needed?
15. List fourteen rules to remember when servicing an exhaust system.
16. A _____ is an air pump that increases engine power by pushing a denser air-fuel charge into the combustion chambers.
17. What is a normally aspirated engine?
18. Which of the following is NOT a type of supercharger?
　　a. Vane.　　　c. Rotor.
　　b. Gear.　　　d. Centrifugal.
19. Explain the term "Turbocharger."
20. In the field, the term "supercharger" generally refers to a blower driven by a _____, _____ or _____ .
21. List and explain the six basic parts of a turbocharger.
22. A _____ turbocharger has the turbo located before the carburetor or throttle body.
23. A turbocharger can operate at speeds up to _____ rpm.

24. _____ _____ refers to the short delay before the turbo develops sufficient _____ (pressure above atmospheric pressure).
25. A waste gate limits the minimum amount of boost produced by the turbocharger. True or False?
26. What could happen if a waste gate did not open?
27. List seven engine modifications commonly found on a turbocharged engine.
28. Which of the following is NOT a recommended practice when servicing a turbocharging system?
　　a. Inspect vacuum and oil lines to turbo and waste gate.
　　b. Remove carbon from turbo compressor with gasket scraper.
　　c. Use regulated, low pressure air hose to check waste gate diaphragm leakage and operation.
　　d. Use pressure gauge to measure boost pressure.
　　e. Use stethoscope to listen for bad turbo bearings.
29. A turbocharger was badly damaged because of excess bearing and shaft wear.
　　Technician A says that a new unit should be installed and that oil pressure to the turbo should be checked. Engine oil should be changed after a short break-in period.
　　Technician B says that the oil should be drained and all lines should be flushed before installing the new turbo. Oil pressure to the unit should also be checked.
　　Who is correct?
　　a. Technician A
　　b. Technician B
　　c. Both A and B
　　d. Neither A nor B
30. An inoperative turbocharger waste gate can cause:
　　a. High boost pressure.
　　b. Low boost pressure.
　　c. Low engine power.
　　d. Detonation.
　　e. All of the above are correct.

ACTIVITIES FOR CHAPTER 25

1. Research the internal combustion process and produce a cutaway sketch of an exhaust system. Use it to explain why high backpressure will reduce engine power.
2. Using knowledge of atmospheric pressure, demonstrate to the shop class why a turbocharger or a supercharger will increase engine power.
3. Collect literature from dealerships on turbocharged and nonturbocharged engines. Develop a table of horsepower-to-displacement ratios. (This can be done by dividing the rated horsepower by the number of cubic inches or liters of displacement for each engine.) Draw up a report of your findings and present them to the class as an outside assignment.

Automotive Batteries

After studying this chapter, you will be able to:
- □ Explain the operating principles of a lead-acid battery.
- □ Describe the basic parts of an automotive battery.
- □ Compare conventional and maintenance-free batteries.
- □ Explain how temperature and other factors affect battery performance.
- □ Describe safety practices to follow when working with batteries.

Earlier textbook chapters briefly introduced battery operation and electrical fundamentals. This chapter will build upon this knowledge by discussing automotive batteries in more detail.

This chapter will prepare you for the next chapter on battery service. It will also help you with the chapters on charging and starting systems.

BATTERY PRINCIPLES

An *automotive battery* is an electrochemical device for producing and storing electricity. A cutaway of such a battery is shown in Fig. 26-1. A battery produces DC (direct current) electricity that flows in only one direction.

When *discharging* (current flowing out of battery), the battery changes chemical energy into electrical energy. In this way, it releases stored energy.

During *charging* (current flowing into battery from charging system), electrical energy is converted into chemical energy. The battery can then store energy until needed.

Basic battery cell

A simple *battery cell* consists of a negative plate, positive plate, container, and electrolyte (battery acid). Look at Fig. 26-2.

The battery plates are made of lead and lead oxide. These act as dissimilar (unlike) metals. The container is usually plastic to resist corrosion. The electrolyte is a mixture of sulfuric acid and water.

If a *load* (current-using device) is connected to our simple battery cell, current will flow through the load.

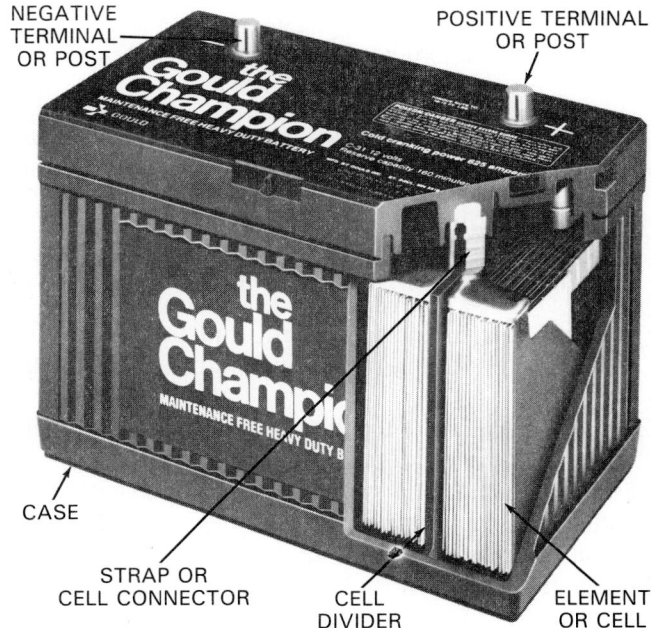

Fig. 26-1. Before learning how a battery works, study in detail its basic parts. Note part names and locations. (Gould)

If the load is a light bulb, as in Fig. 26-2, the bulb will glow because of electron movement.

Battery cell action

Fig. 26-3 shows the basic chemical-electrical action inside a battery cell. When being charged, the alternator causes free electrons (negative charges) to be deposited on the negative (−) plate. This causes the plates to have a difference in *potential* (electrical pressure or voltage).

When a load is connected across the terminals, there is a current (flow of electrons) to equalize the difference in charges on the plates. The excess electrons move from the negative to the positively charged plate.

FUNCTIONS OF A BATTERY

A vehicle battery has several important functions. It must:
1. Operate the starting motor, ignition system, elec-

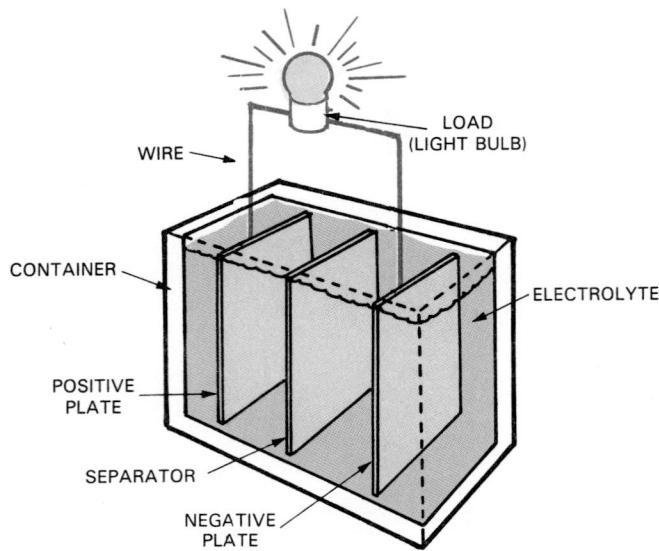

Fig. 26-2. Simple lead-acid battery cell. Positive plate and negative plate are kept apart by separator. Electrolyte causes chemical reaction between plates, producing current flow through circuit. One cell like this would produce 2.1 volts.

tronic fuel injection system, and other electrical devices for the engine during engine cranking and starting.

2. Supply ALL of the electrical power for the vehicle whenever the engine is NOT running.
3. Help the charging system provide electricity when current demands are above the output limit of the charging system.
4. Act as a capacitor (voltage stabilizer) that smooths current flow through the electrical system.

5. Store energy (electricity) for extended periods.

To illustrate these functions, imagine the following sequence of events: You are sitting in your car with the radio ON, but the engine is NOT running. The battery is supplying the electricity to operate the radio and any indicator lights. It is slowly discharging.

When you start the engine, the battery provides a tremendous amount of current. This energy operates starting motor and essential engine systems. This, too, drains current out of the battery.

As soon as the engine starts, the charging system takes over. It then recharges the battery while feeding current to the electrical units in the car.

If the load becomes too much for the charging system (engine idling slowly and all accessories on, for example), the battery may also feed current into the electrical system.

BATTERY CONSTRUCTION

An automobile battery is built to withstand severe vibration, cold weather, engine heat, corrosive chemicals, high current discharge, and prolonged periods without use. To properly test and service batteries, you must understand battery construction.

Battery element

A *battery element* is made up of positive plates, negative plates, straps, and separators. The element fits into a cell compartment in the battery case. Refer to Fig. 26-4.

The *battery plates* are made of a GRID (stiff mesh framework) coated with porous LEAD. Shown in Fig. 26-4, several battery plates are needed in each cell to

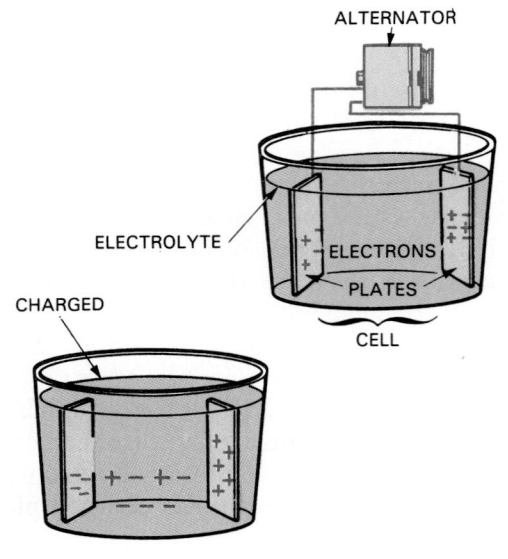

A

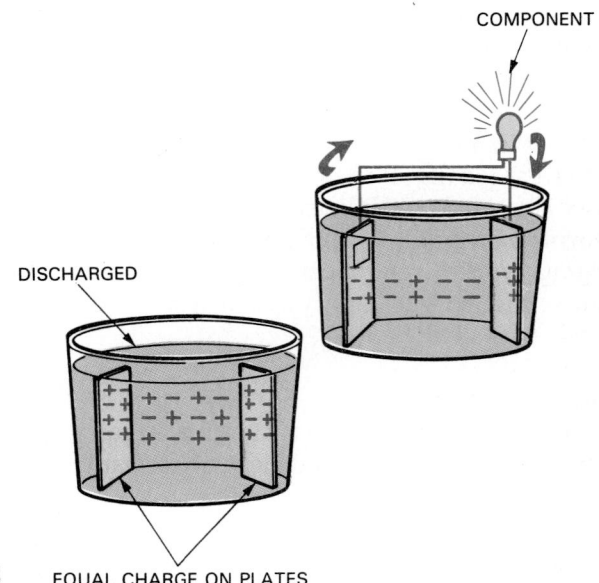

B

Fig. 26-3. Basic battery action. A — During charging cycle, alternator forces current through cell in reverse direction. This deposits negative charge on one plate and positive charge on other. B — During discharge cycle, current flow through circuit, allows charges to equalize. Movement of electrons produces current flow. (Chrysler)

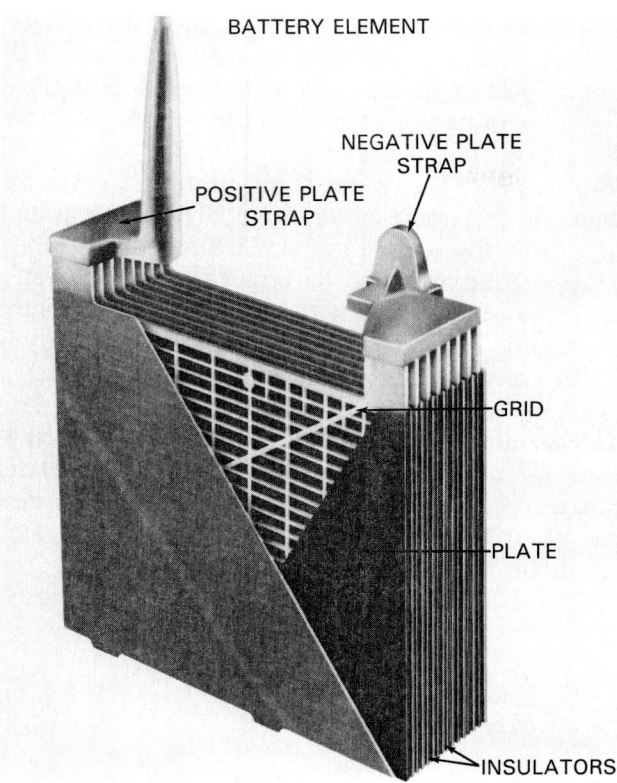

Fig. 26-4. Battery element is made up of positive plate group, negative plate group, separators, and straps. Most auto batteries have six elements. The elements fit into the battery case. (Gould)

provide enough battery power.

A lead strap connects several negative plates to form a *negative plate group*. Look at Fig. 26-4. Another lead strap connects the positive plates for the *positive plate group*.

The chemically active material in the *negative plates* is sponge (porous) lead, Fig. 26-4. The active material on the *positive plates* is lead peroxide. Calcium or antimony is normally added to the lead to increase battery performance and to decrease *gassing* (acid fumes forming during chemical reaction).

Since the lead on the plates is porous, like a sponge, the battery acid easily penetrates into the material. This aids the chemical reaction and the production of electricity.

Lead *battery straps* or connectors run along the upper portion of the case to connect the plates. The battery terminals (posts or side terminals) are constructed as part of one end of each strap.

Separators fit between the battery plates to keep them from touching against each other and shorting. The separators are made of insulating material. They have openings that allow free circulation of the electrolyte around the battery plates.

Battery case, cover, caps

The *battery case,* usually made of high quality

plastic, holds the elements and electrolyte, Fig. 26-5. The case must withstand extreme vibration, temperature change, and the corrosive action of the battery acid. Dividers in the case form individual containers for each element. A container, with its element, is one cell.

The *battery cover* is bonded to the top of the battery case. It seals the top of the case. There is an opening above each battery cell for battery caps or a cell cover. Refer to Fig. 26-5.

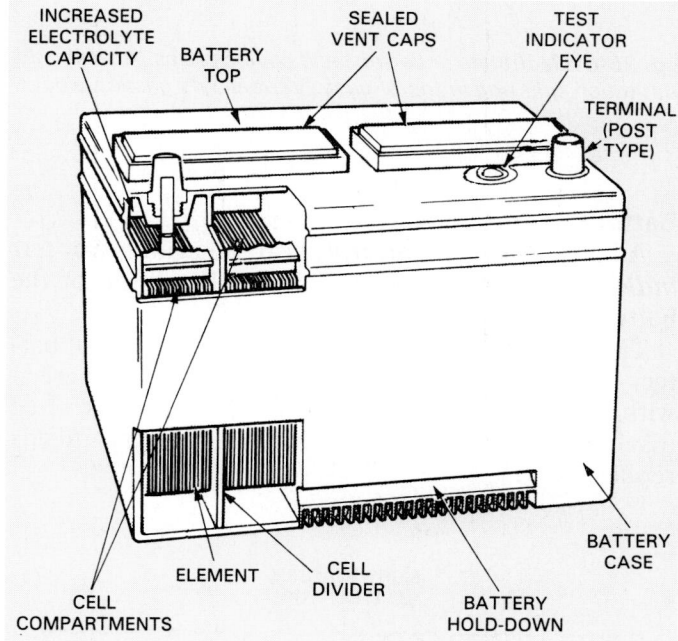

Fig. 26-5. Battery case holds elements and electrolyte. Note part names. (Chrysler Corp.)

Battery caps snap into the holes in the battery cover. They keep electrolyte from splashing out of the battery. The caps also serve as *spark arrestors* (keep sparks or flames from igniting gases inside battery). Maintenance-free batteries have a large cover that is not removed during normal service.

DANGER: Hydrogen gas can collect at the top of a battery. If this gas is exposed to a flame or spark, it can explode.

Discussed in the next chapter are several safety precautions to follow when servicing batteries.

Electrolyte (battery acid)

Electrolyte, often called battery acid, is a mixture of sulfuric acid and distilled water, Fig. 26-6. Battery acid is poured into each cell until plates are covered.

DANGER! Avoid having electrolyte come in contact with your skin or eyes. The sulfuric acid in the electrolyte can cause serious skin burns or even blindness.

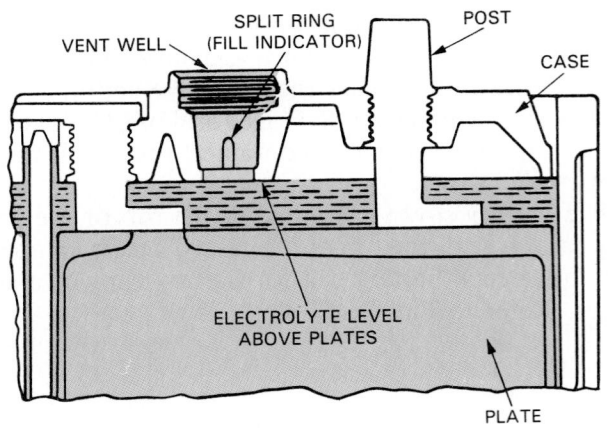

Fig. 26-6. Electrolyte or battery acid covers plates. Acid should just touch split ring in top of case. Vent allows gases to leave case. (GMC)

Battery charge indicator

A battery *charge indicator,* also called an *eye* or *test indicator,* shows the general charge condition of the battery. One is pictured in Fig. 26-7.

The charge indicator changes color with levels of battery charge. For example, the indicator may be green with the battery fully charged. It may turn black when discharged or yellow when the battery needs replacement.

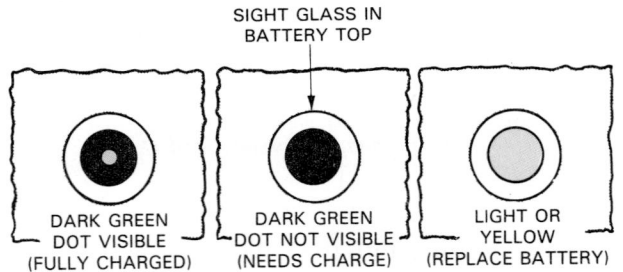

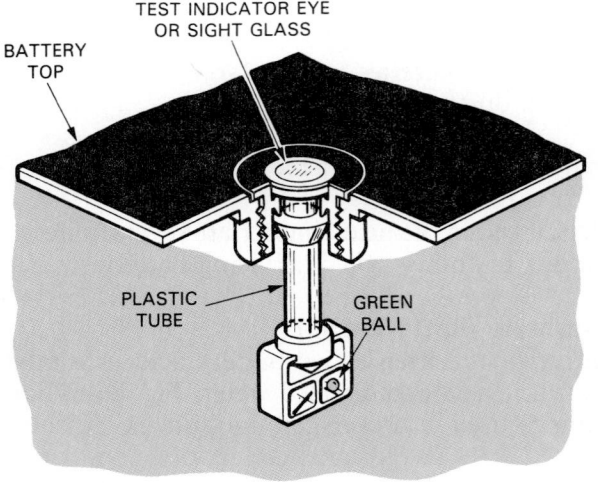

Fig. 26-7. Charge indicator provides easy way of checking battery condition. (Chrysler)

Battery terminals

Battery terminals provide a means of connecting the battery plates to the car's electrical system. Either two round posts or two side terminals can be used, as shown in Fig. 26-8.

Battery posts are round metal terminals extending through the top of the battery cover. They serve as male connections for female battery cable ends.

The *positive post* will be larger than the negative post. It may be marked with red paint and a positive (+) symbol. The *negative post* is smaller and may be black or green in color. It normally has a negative (−) symbol on or near it.

Side terminals are electrical connections located on the side of the battery. They have female threads that accept a special bolt on the battery cable end. Side terminal polarity is identified by positive and negative symbols on the case.

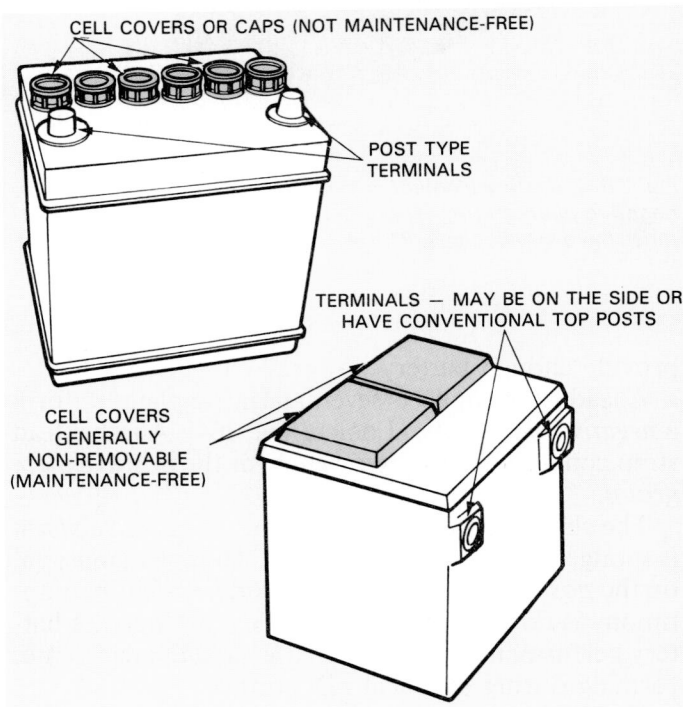

Fig. 26-8. Study differences between batteries. Maintenance-free battery does not have vent caps. Post or side terminals may be used on conventional or maintenance-free batteries. (Chrysler)

Battery voltage

Battery open circuit (no load) *cell voltage* is 2.1 volts, often rounded off to 2.0 volts. Since the cells in a battery are connected in series, battery voltage depends upon the number of cells. Refer to Fig. 26-9.

A *12-volt battery* has 6 cells that produce an open circuit voltage of 12.6 volts. Modern vehicles use a 12 V battery and 12 V electrical system.

A *6-volt battery* only has 3 cells, with an open cir-

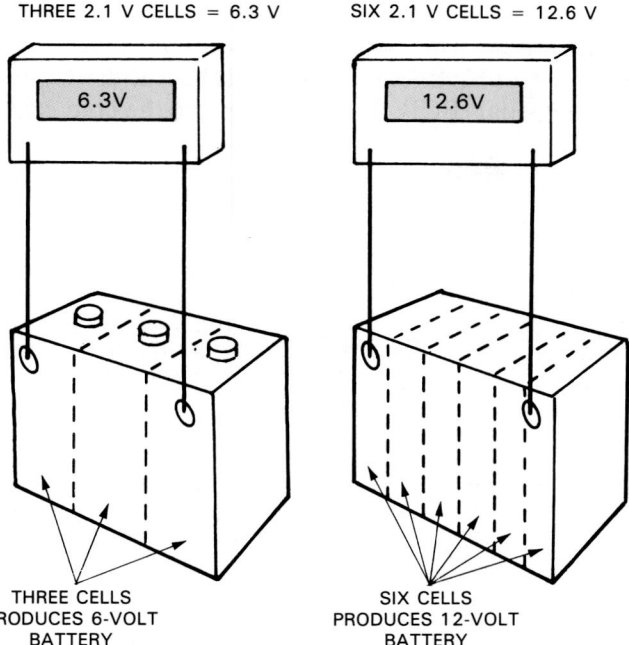

THREE 2.1 V CELLS = 6.3 V   SIX 2.1 V CELLS = 12.6 V

6.3V   12.6V

THREE CELLS PRODUCES 6-VOLT BATTERY

SIX CELLS PRODUCES 12-VOLT BATTERY

Fig. 26-9. Three cells connected in series produces 6.3 volts. The three cells are rated at, or called, a 6-volt battery. More common unit of six cells produces 12.6 volts, or a 12-volt battery.

cuit voltage of 6.3 V. See Fig. 26-9. Older vehicles are designed to use 6 V batteries.

Some cars with diesel engines use TWO 12 V batteries connected in parallel. When two batteries are in

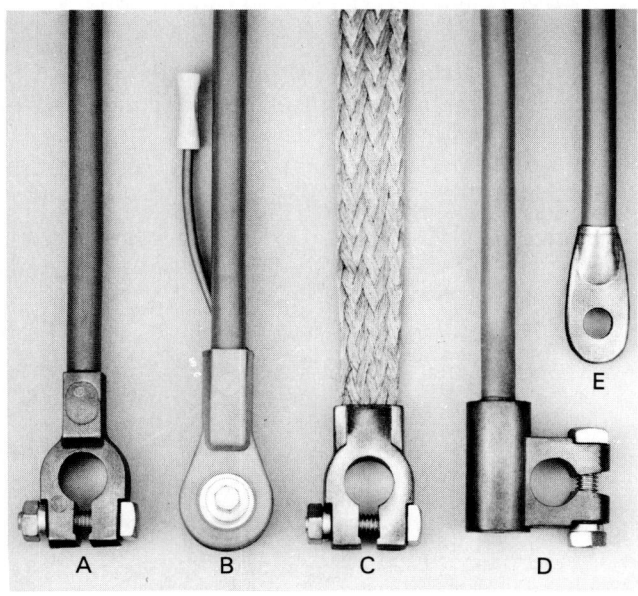

Fig. 26-10. Battery cable types: A—Post type battery cable. B—Side terminal battery cable with pigtail for ground or accessory connection. C—Braided ground cable. D—Jumper type battery cable. E—Solenoid-to-starter cable. Note large conductor size for carrying large amount of current to starter. (Belden)

parallel, their output voltage stays the same, but current output increases. Dual batteries may be needed to crank and start a compression-ignition diesel engine.

When two batteries are connected in series, their output voltage DOUBLES. Keep this in mind when working with batteries. Two 12 V batteries in series produces 24 V, which could damage electrical devices.

BATTERY CABLES

Battery cables are large wires that connect the battery terminals to the electrical system of the vehicle.

The *positive cable* is normally red and fastens to the starter solenoid (introduced in Chapter 1). The *negative battery cable* is usually black and connects to ground on the engine block.

Various types of battery cables are pictured in Fig. 26-10. Note that ground cables do not always use insulation.

Sometimes, the negative battery cable will have a **body ground wire** which assures that the vehicle body is grounded. One is shown in Fig. 26-11. If this wire does not make a good connection, a component grounded to the car body may NOT operate properly.

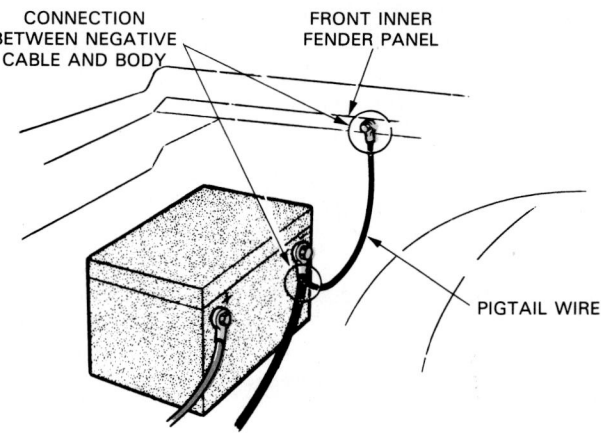

CONNECTION BETWEEN NEGATIVE CABLE AND BODY

FRONT INNER FENDER PANEL

PIGTAIL WIRE

Fig. 26-11. Note cable connections to battery. Negative cable grounds on engine block. Positive cable connects to electrical system. Pigtail grounds car body to battery negative. (Sun)

BATTERY TRAY AND RETAINER

A *battery tray* and *retainer* hold the battery securely in place. They keep battery from bouncing around during vehicle movement. Look at Fig. 26-12. It is important that the tray and retainer be in good condition and tight to prevent battery damage.

WET AND DRY CHARGED BATTERIES

There is no difference in the materials used in wet

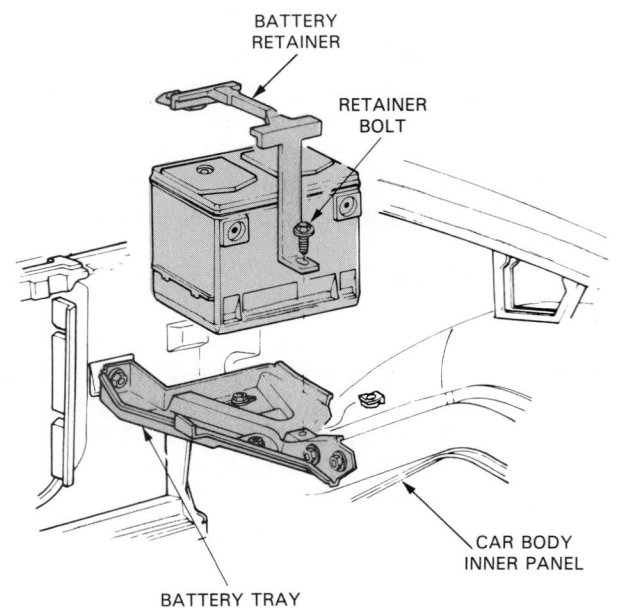

Fig. 26-12. Battery tray and retainer hold battery securely in place. Tray usually mounts on inner body panel. (Cadillac)

and dry charged batteries. The difference is in how the batteries are prepared for service.

With a **wet charged battery,** the battery is filled with electrolyte and charged at the factory. The battery is then tested and placed in stock, ready for service.

A **dry charged battery** contains fully charged elements but does not contain electrolyte. It leaves the factory in a dry state. Before use, the battery is filled with electrolyte. A dry charged battery is commonly used because it has a much longer shelf life than a wet charged battery.

Activation of a dry charged battery is covered in the next chapter.

MAINTENANCE-FREE BATTERY

A *maintenance-free battery* is easily identified because if does NOT use removable filler caps. The tops of the battery cells are covered with a large, snap-in cover. Since calcium is used to make the battery plates, water does not have to be periodically added to the electrolyte.

The calcium in the plates reduces the production of battery gases. As a result, battery gas does not carry as much of the chemicals out of the battery. This increases battery service life and decreases service requirements.

BATTERY RATINGS

Battery ratings are set according to national test standards for battery performance. They let the mechanic and consumer compare the cranking power of one battery to another.

Two methods of rating lead-acid storage batteries are common. They were developed by the Society of Automotive Engineers (SAE) and the Battery Council International (BCI). These ratings are the cold cranking rating and reserve capacity rating.

Battery cold cranking rating

The *cold cranking rating* determines how much current (in amperes) the battery can deliver for 30 seconds at 0 °F (-17.7 °C) while maintaining terminal voltage of 7.2 V or 1.2 V per cell. This rating indicates the battery's ability to crank a specific engine (based on starter current draw) at a specified temperature.

For example, one auto manufacturer recommends a battery with 305 cold cranking amps for a small 4-cylinder engine but a 450 cold-cranking-amp battery for a larger V-8 engine. A more powerful battery is needed to handle the heavier starter current draw of the larger engine.

Battery reserve capacity rating

The *reserve capacity rating* is the time needed to lower battery terminal voltage below 10.2 V (1.7 V per cell) at a discharge rate of 25 amps. This is with the battery fully charged and at 80 °F (26.7 °C).

Reserve capacity will appear on the battery as a time interval in minutes. For example, if a battery is rated at 90 minutes and the charging system fails, the driver has approximately 90 minutes (1 1/2 hours) of driving time under minimum electrical load before the battery goes completely dead.

A **watt rating** is another battery rating. It is the equivalent of the cold cranking rating.

BATTERY TEMPERATURE AND EFFICIENCY

As battery temperature drops, battery power is reduced. At low temperatures, the chemical action

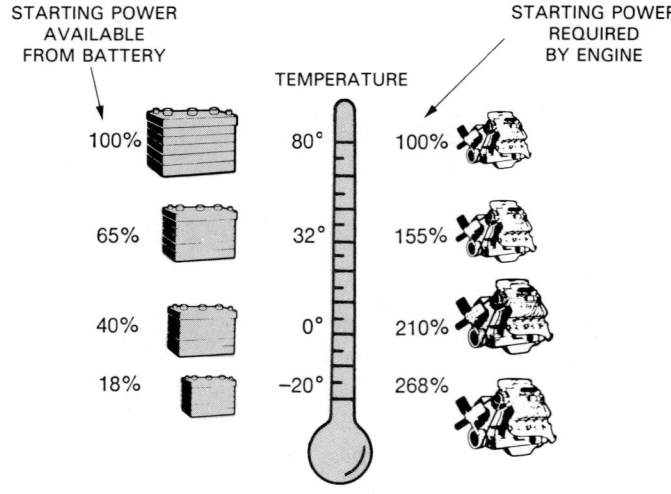

Fig. 26-13. Study how temperature affects battery power and starter current draw. This is why engines crank slowly in very cold weather. (Champion Spark Plugs)

inside the battery is slowed down. It will not produce as much current as when warm. This affects its ability to start an engine in extremely cold weather.

Also, when an engine is cold, the motor oil is very thick. This increases the amount of current needed to crank the engine with the starting motor.

Fig. 26-13 shows a chart comparing battery efficiency and required starting power. Note that at 0 °F (-18 °C), a battery may only have 40 percent of its normal cranking power. In addition, starter current draw will be up approximately 200 percent. The engine could be very difficult to start on a cold morning. The battery, starter, and electrical connections must be in almost perfect condition.

KNOW THESE TERMS

Discharging, Charging, Cell, Element, Plate, Separator, Strap, Case, Caps, Electrolyte, Charge indicator, Battery voltage, Terminals, Battery cable, Wet charged, Dry charged, Maintenance-free battery, Cold cranking rating, Reserve capacity rating.

REVIEW QUESTIONS

1. An _____ _____ is an electrochemical device for producing and storing electricity.
2. Define the terms battery "discharging" and "charging."
3. Which of the following is NOT part of a basic battery cell?
   a. Positive plate.
   b. Negative plate.
   c. Electrolyte.
   d. Spark Arrestors.
4. List five functions of a car battery.
5. Explain the function of a spark arrestor in an automotive battery.
6. _____ gas can collect around the top of batteries. If this gas is exposed to a flame or spark, it can _____ !

7. Electrolyte, also called battery acid, is a mixture of sulfuric acid and distilled water. True or False?
8. What is the purpose of a charge indicator or eye?
9. Describe the difference between battery posts and side terminals.
10. A 12-volt battery has _____ cells that produce an open circuit voltage of _____ volts.
11. Most modern vehicle batteries are 6-volt. True or False?
12. The battery positive cable normally connects to the _____ _____ and the negative cable connects to _____ on the engine _____ .
13. Explain the difference between a wet and a dry charged battery.
14. A _____ battery is easily identified because it usually does NOT have removable filler caps or covers.
15. Which of the following is NOT a conventional battery rating?
   a. Hot cranking amps.
   b. Reserve capacity rating.
   c. Watt rating.
   d. Cold cranking amps.

ACTIVITIES FOR CHAPTER 26

1. Survey the service managers of at least three businesses that sell and install vehicle batteries. Find out how they dispose of batteries that they remove from vehicles.
2. Find the best battery value. Gather information from catalogs or advertisements, or visit stores that sell automotive batteries. Find the cold cranking ratings and prices of comparable-size batteries from different stores, and make a chart of your findings. Which will give you the most for your money?
3. Construct a model of a vehicle battery element (cell) for classroom display. Clearly label all components. (See Fig. 26-4.)

Battery Testing and Service

After studying this chapter, you will be able to:
□ Visually inspect a battery for obvious problems.
□ Perform common battery tests.
□ Clean a battery case and terminals.
□ Charge a battery.
□ Jump start a car using a second battery.
□ Replace a defective battery.
□ Describe safety practices to follow when testing and servicing batteries.

A *"dead battery"* (discharged battery) is a very common problem. The engine will usually fail to crank and start. Even though the lights and horn may work, there is not enough "juice" (current) in the battery to operate the starting motor.

Since this is a common trouble, it is important for you to know how to inspect, test, and service vehicle batteries. This chapter covers the most common tasks relating to battery service. Study it carefully and you will be prepared for later chapters on starting and charging systems.

BATTERY MAINTENANCE

If a battery is not maintained properly, its service life will be reduced. Battery maintenance should be done periodically — during tune-ups, grease jobs, or anytime symptoms indicate battery problems.

Battery maintenance typically includes:
1. Checking electrolyte level or indicator eye.
2. Cleaning battery terminal connections.
3. Cleaning battery top.
4. Checking battery hold-down and tray.
5. Inspecting for physical damage to case and terminals.

Inspecting battery condition
Inspect the battery anytime the hood is opened. Check for the types of problems shown in Fig. 27-1. Look for a dirt buildup on the battery top. Look for case damage, loose or corroded connections, or any other trouble that could upset battery operation. If a problem is found, correct it before it gets worse.
DANGER! Wear eye protection when working

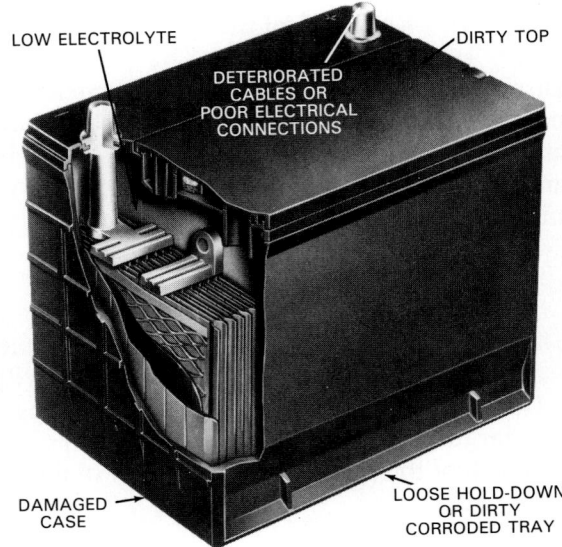

Fig. 27-1. Visually inspect batteries for these kinds of problems. If any are found, correct them. (GMC)

around batteries. Batteries contain acid that could cause blindness. Even the film buildup on a battery can contain acid.

Battery leakage test.
A *battery leakage test* will find out if current is discharging across the top of the battery case. A dirty battery can run down (discharge) when not in use. This can shorten battery life and cause starting problems.

To do a battery leakage test, set a voltmeter on a low setting. Touch the acid resistant probes on the battery as shown in Fig. 27-2. If the meter registers voltage, current is leaking out of the battery cells. You need to clean the battery top.

Cleaning battery case
If the top of the battery is dirty, wash it down with baking soda and water. See Fig. 27-3. This will neutralize and remove the acid-dirt mixture. If not a maintenance-free battery, be careful not to let debris enter the filler openings.

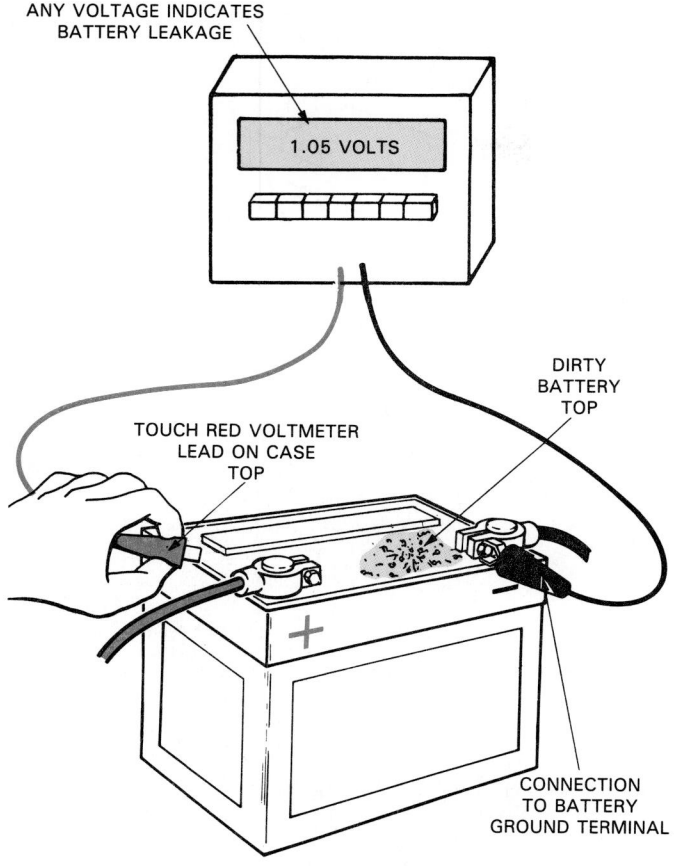

Fig. 27-2. Leak test will quickly show electrical leakage across top of battery. If voltmeter registers, clean battery. (Sun Electric)

Battery terminal test

A *battery terminal test* quickly checks for a poor electrical connection between the battery cables and terminals. A voltmeter is used to measure voltage drop across the cables and terminals, as in Fig. 27-4.

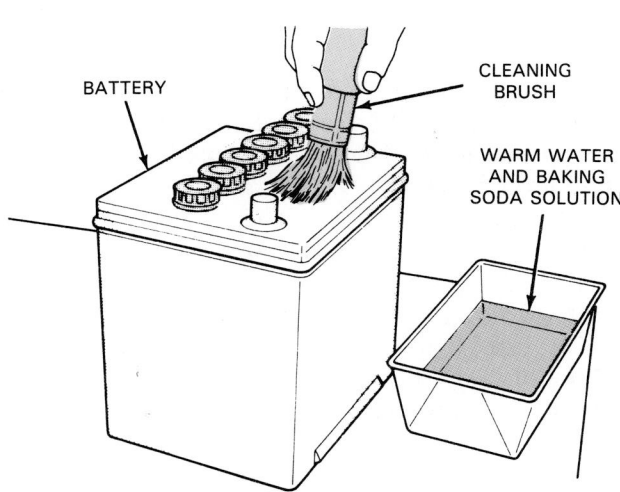

Fig. 27-3. Clean battery with baking soda-water solution and brush. Keep dirt out of filler openings. (Chrysler)

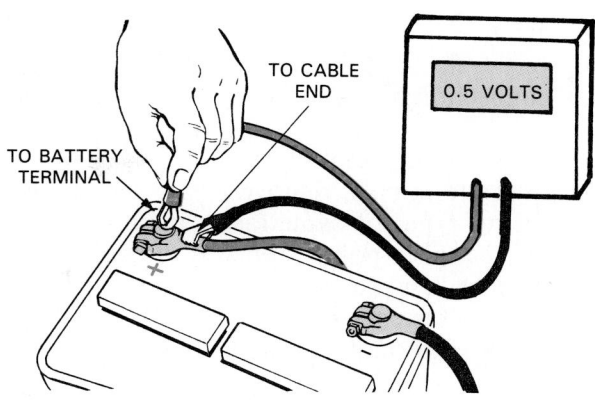

Fig. 27-4. To quickly find out if battery terminal needs cleaning, measure voltage drop across cable-to-terminal connection. Crank engine with ignition disabled. A reading of over .5 volt would require terminal and cable end cleaning. (NAPA)

Connect the negative meter lead to the cable end. Touch the positive meter lead on the battery terminal. Disable the ignition or injection system so the engine will not start. Then, crank the engine while watching the voltmeter reading.

If the voltmeter shows over about .5 volt, there is

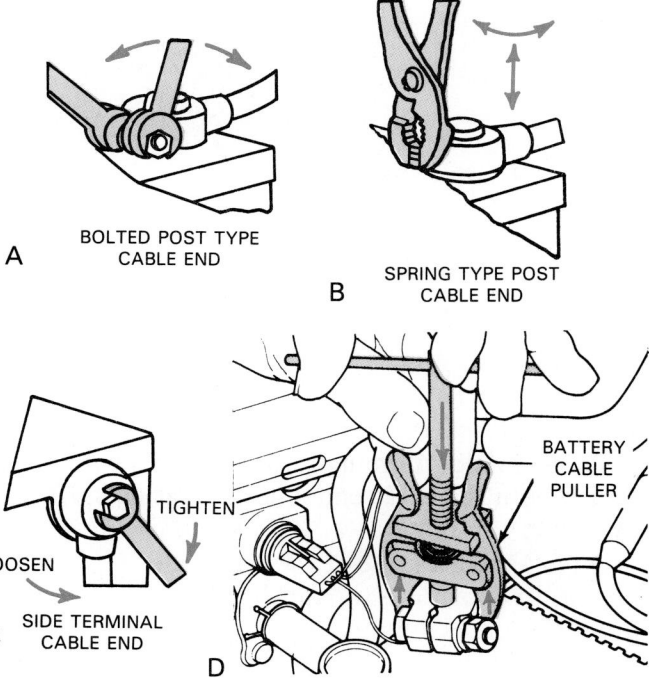

Fig. 27-5. Note methods of removing battery cable from battery terminal. Be careful not to damage post or side terminal. A — Use two wrenches if cable bolt begins to turn in cable end. A six-point wrench may be needed if fastener head is partially rounded. Use pliers only on badly damaged fasteners. B — Pliers are used to open spring-type battery cable ends. C — Loosen side terminal bolt with a wrench, not pliers. D — A battery cable puller may be needed if cable end is stuck on post. This will prevent loosening of post in case. (Chrysler)

a high resistance at the cable connection. This would tell you to clean the battery connections. A clean, good electrical connection would have less than .5 volt drop.

Cleaning battery terminals

To clean the terminals, remove the battery cables. There are three types of cable fasteners, as pictured in Fig. 27-5. Use a six-point wrench if the bolt or nut is extremely tight. Use pliers only on a spring type cable end or when the fastener head is badly corroded and rounded off. Be careful not to damage the post or side terminal with excess side force.

To clean post type terminals, use a cleaning tool like the one in Fig. 27-6. Use the female end to clean the post. Use the male end on the terminal. Twist the tool to remove the oxidized outer surface on the connections.

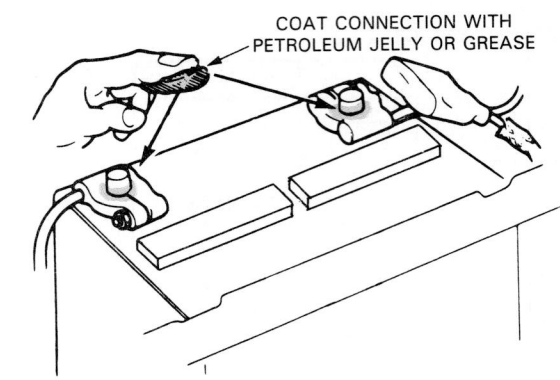

Fig. 27-7. Before reconnecting battery cables, coat connection with petroleum jelly or white grease. This will help prevent corrosion from battery gases. Do not overtighten cable fasteners or damage may result. Most terminals are made of very soft lead. (Honda)

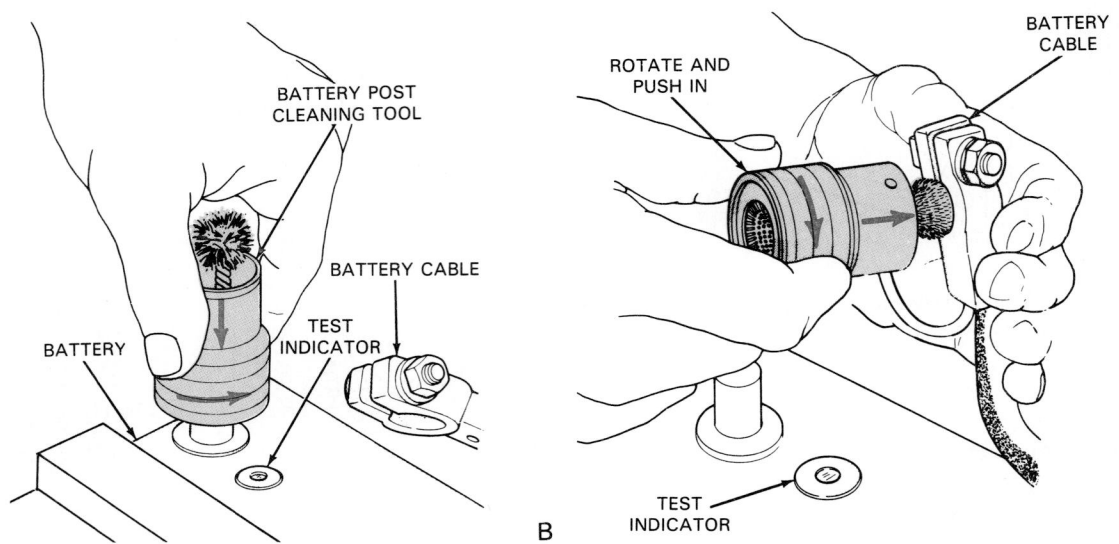

Fig. 27-6. Cleaning battery posts and cable ends. A — Use female end of cleaner on post. Rotate tool on post. B — Use male end of cleaner on cable end. Turn it until all corrosion is gone. (Chrysler)

To clean side terminals, use a small wire brush. Polish both the cable end and the mating surface on the battery terminal.

Do NOT use a knife or scraper to clean battery terminals. This removes too much metal and can ruin the terminal connection.

When reinstalling the cables, coat the terminals with petroleum jelly or white grease, Fig. 27-7. This will keep acid fumes off the connections and keep them from corroding again. Tighten the fasteners just enough to secure the connection. Overtightening can strip the cable bolt threads.

Checking battery electrolyte level

Unlike an older style battery, a maintenance-free battery does NOT need periodic electrolyte service under normal conditions. It is designed to operate for long periods without loss of electrolyte. Older batteries with removable vent caps, however, must have their electrolyte level checked.

DANGER! The invisible HYDROGEN GAS produced by the chemical reaction in a battery is very FLAMMABLE. Keep all sparks and flames away from the top of a battery. Batteries can EXPLODE if the gas is ignited!

Many old style batteries must have their vent caps removed when checking the electrolyte. The electrolyte should just cover the top of the battery plates and separators. Most batteries have a *fill ring* (electrolyte level indicator) inside the filler cap opening. The electrolyte should be even with the fill ring.

If the electrolyte is low, fill the cells to the correct

level with DISTILLED WATER (purified water). Distilled water should be used because it does not contain many of the impurities found in tap water. Water taken directly out of a water faucet can contain chemicals that reduce battery life. The chemicals can contaminate the electrolyte and collect in the bottom of the battery case. If enough contaminants collect in the battery, the cell plates can SHORT OUT, ruining the battery.

Battery overcharging.

If water must be added at frequent intervals, the charging system may be overcharging the battery. A faulty charging system can force excessive current into the battery. Battery gassing can then remove water from the battery.

Refer to the chapter on charging system service for more information on this subject.

CHECKING BATTERY CHARGE

When you measure *battery charge,* you check the condition of the battery electrolyte and battery plates. For example, if lights are left on without the engine running, the battery will run down (discharge). Current flow out of the battery will steadily reduce available battery power. There are several ways to measure battery charge.

Some modern batteries use a *charge indicator eye* that shows battery charge. You simply look at the eye in the battery cover to determine battery charge. This was covered in the previous chapter.

Hydrometer check

A *hydrometer* measures the specific gravity (weight or density) of a liquid. A *battery hydrometer* measures the specific gravity or the state of the charge for battery electrolyte. Look at Fig. 27-8.

Water has a specific gravity standard of ONE (1.000). Fully charged electrolyte has a specific gravity of between 1.265 and 1.299. The larger number denotes that electrolyte is more dense or heavier than water.

As a battery becomes discharged, its electrolyte has a larger percentage of water. Thus, a discharged battery's electrolyte will have a lower specific gravity number than a fully charged battery. This rise and drop in specific gravity can be used to check the charge in a battery.

There are several types of hand held hydrometers. Three of these are the float type, ball type, and the needle type.

To use a *float type hydrometer,* squeeze the hydrometer bulb. Immerse the end of the hydrometer in the electrolyte. Then release the bulb, Fig. 27-9. This will fill the hydrometer with electrolyte.

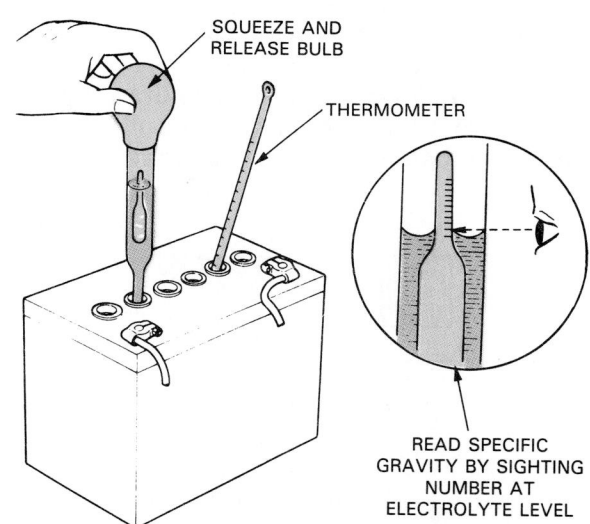

Fig. 27-9. To check battery charge, draw electrolyte into hydrometer by squeezing and releasing bulb. Read specific gravity on float at top level of electrolyte. Temperature of electrolyte will affect reading. (Mazda)

Shown in Fig. 27-9, compare the numbers on the hydrometer float with the top of the electrolyte. Hold the hydrometer even with your line of sight. Wear safety glasses and do not drip electrolyte on anything.

Most float type hydrometers are NOT temperature-correcting. However, the better models will have a built-in thermometer and a conversion chart, Fig. 27-10. This will let you compensate for battery temperature.

The *ball type battery hydrometer* is gaining popularity because you do not have to use a temperature

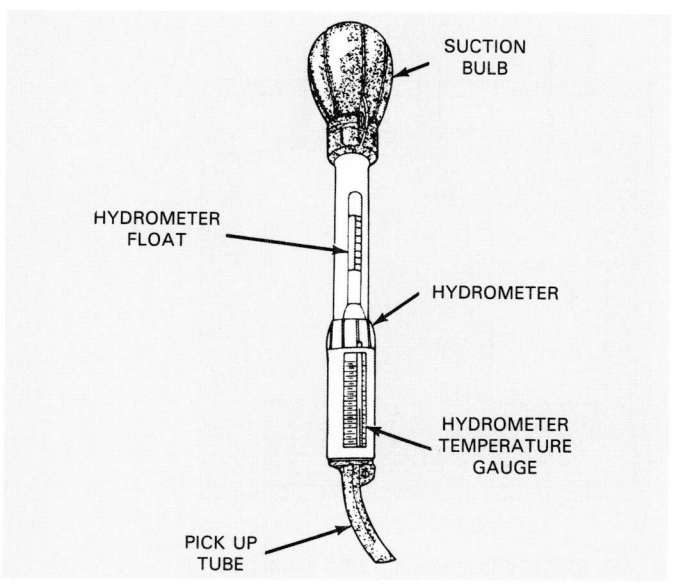

Fig. 27-8. Note basic parts of battery hydrometer. It can be used to check the state of the charge in batteries with vent caps. (Chrysler)

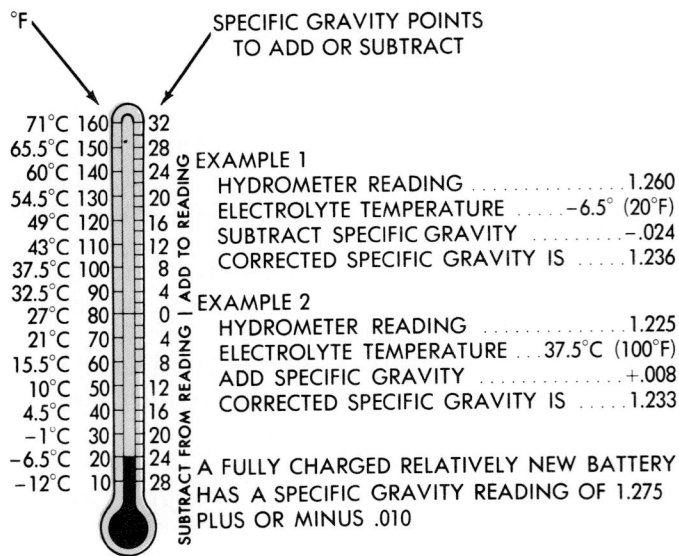

°F

SPECIFIC GRAVITY POINTS
TO ADD OR SUBTRACT

71°C	160	32
65.5°C	150	28
60°C	140	24
54.5°C	130	20
49°C	120	16
43°C	110	12
37.5°C	100	8
32.5°C	90	4
27°C	80	0
21°C	70	4
15.5°C	60	8
10°C	50	12
4.5°C	40	16
−1°C	30	20
−6.5°C	20	24
−12°C	10	28

SUBTRACT FROM READING | ADD TO READING

EXAMPLE 1
HYDROMETER READING 1.260
ELECTROLYTE TEMPERATURE . . . . . −6.5° (20°F)
SUBTRACT SPECIFIC GRAVITY . . . . −.024
CORRECTED SPECIFIC GRAVITY IS 1.236

EXAMPLE 2
HYDROMETER READING 1.225
ELECTROLYTE TEMPERATURE . . . 37.5°C (100°F)
ADD SPECIFIC GRAVITY . . . .+.008
CORRECTED SPECIFIC GRAVITY IS 1.233

A FULLY CHARGED RELATIVELY NEW BATTERY
HAS A SPECIFIC GRAVITY READING OF 1.275
PLUS OR MINUS .010

Fig. 27-10. Study examples of using a hydrometer correction chart. (Chrysler)

correction chart. The balls change temperature when submersed in the electrolyte. This allows for any temperature offset.

To use the ball type hydrometer, draw electrolyte into the hydrometer with the rubber bulb. Then note the number of balls floating in the electrolyte. Instruc-

tions on the hydrometer will tell you whether the battery is fully charged or discharged.

A *needle type hydrometer* uses the same principle as the ball type. When electrolyte is sucked into the hydrometer, it causes the plastic needle to register specific gravity.

Hydrometer readings

A *fully charged battery* should have a hydrometer reading of at least 1.265 or higher. If below 1.265, the battery needs *recharging* or it may be defective. Look at Fig. 27-11.

A *discharged battery* could be caused by:
1. Defective battery.
2. Charging system problem (loose alternator belt, for example).
3. Starting system problem.
4. Poor cable connections.
5. Engine performance problem requiring excessive cranking time.
6. Electrical problem drawing current out of battery with ignition key OFF.

A *defective battery* can be found with a hydrometer by checking the electrolyte in every cell. If the specific gravity in any cell VARIES EXCESSIVELY from other cells (25 to 50 points), the battery is usually ruined. Cells with low readings may be shorted.

When all of the cells have an equal gravity, even if all of them are low, the battery can usually be

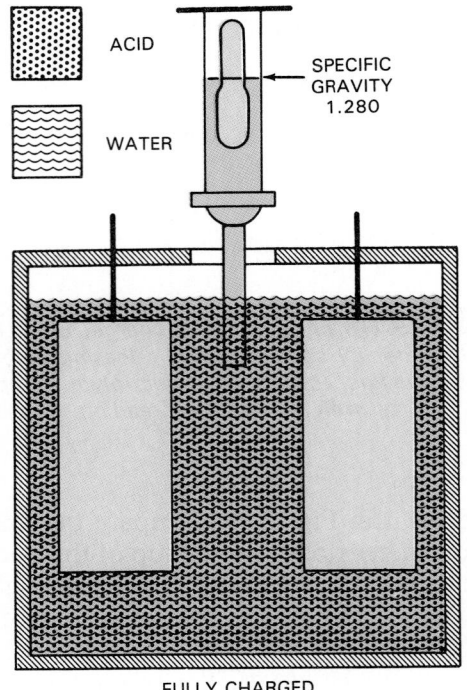

FULLY CHARGED

ACID IN WATER GIVES ELECTROLYTE
SPECIFIC GRAVITY OF 1.280

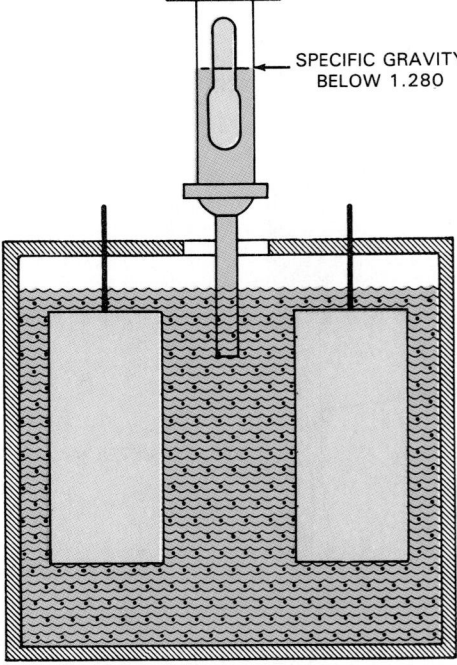

GOING DOWN

AS BATTERY DISCHARGES, ACID BEGINS TO
LODGE IN PLATES. SPECIFIC GRAVITY DROPS.

Fig. 27-11. A fully charged battery will have a hydrometer reading of 1.280. If below 1.270 specific gravity, battery needs recharging. (Sun)

regenerated by recharging.

With maintenance-free batteries, the hydrometer is not commonly used. A voltmeter and ammeter or a load tester (covered later in the chapter) can be used to quickly determine battery condition.

Battery voltage test

A *battery voltage test* is done by measuring total battery voltage with an accurate voltmeter or special tester. It will determine general state of charge and battery condition quickly. Look at Fig. 27-12.

LOAD ON BATTERY	1.265 FULL CHARGE	1.250 95% CHARGE	1.230 ¾ CHARGE	1.200 ½ CHARGE	1.175 ¼ CHARGE
BATTERY STATE OF CHARGE SPECIFIC GRAVITY AND VOLTAGE					
NO LOAD	12.7 VOLTS	12.6 VOLTS	12.5 VOLTS	12.4 VOLTS	12.2 VOLTS
5 AMPERES	12.5 VOLTS	12.4 VOLTS	12.3 VOLTS	12.1 VOLTS	11.8 VOLTS
15 AMPERES	12.3 VOLTS	12.2 VOLTS	12.0 VOLTS	11.7 VOLTS	11.3 VOLTS
25 AMPERES	12.1 VOLTS	11.9 VOLTS	11.6 VOLTS	11.2 VOLTS	10.7 VOLTS

THIS IS THE RANGE IN WHICH
MOST VEHICLE BATTERIES NORMALLY
OPERATE IN CUSTOMER SERVICE.

AT 1.180 AND BELOW, STARTING
WILL BE UNRELIABLE AND FUNCTION
OF OTHER CIRCUITS MAY BE ERRATIC.

Fig. 27-13. Chart shows how battery voltage depends on specific gravity or hydrometer readings. Voltage test is needed on maintenance-free batteries that do not have removable filler caps. (Chrysler)

Fig. 27-12. Digital voltmeter or special tester as shown will check general charge on battery. Turn on headlights for a light load. Then read meter. Generally, voltage below 11.5 indicates discharged battery. (K-D Tools)

Connect the meter across the battery terminals. Turn on the car's headlights or heater blower to provide a light load. Read the meter.

A well charged battery should have over 12 volts. If the meter reads about 11.5 volts, the battery may not be charged adequately or it may be defective.

A battery voltage test is used on maintenance-free batteries. These batteries do not have filler caps that can be easily removed for testing with a hydrometer.

Other tests are needed to find the actual problem when a battery fails a voltage test. The chart in Fig. 27-13 compares specific gravity (hydrometer readings) and battery voltage. Note the relationship.

Cell voltage test

A *cell voltage test* will let you know if the battery is defective or just discharged. Just like a hydrometer cell test, if the voltage reading on one or more cells is .2 volts or more lower than the others, the battery must be replaced.

To do a cell voltage test, insert the special cadmium (acid resistant metal) tips of a low voltage reading

voltmeter into each cell. This is pictured in Fig. 27-14. Start at one end of the battery. Work your way down, testing each cell carefully.

Note! Some manufacturers recommend battery fast charging during this test. Refer to a service manual for

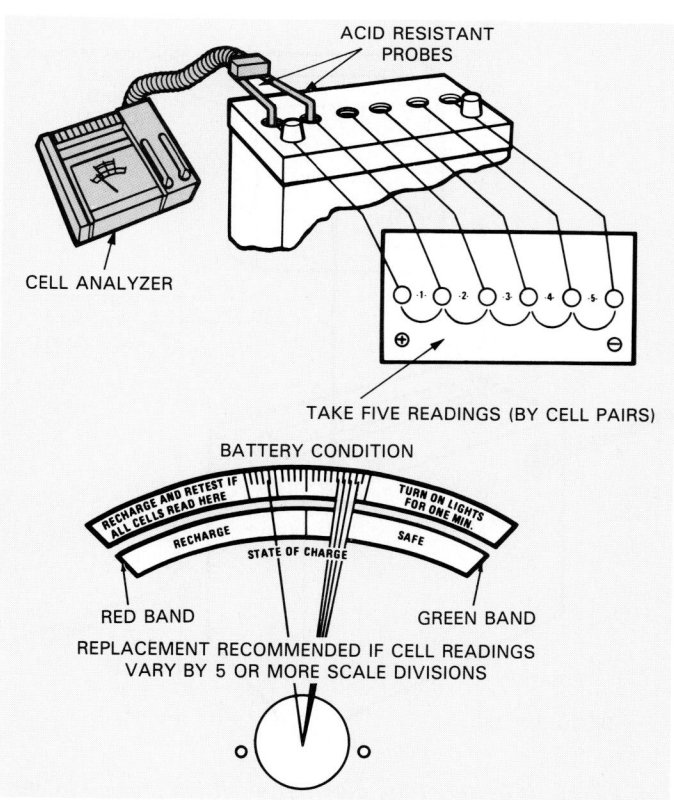

Fig. 27-14. To check battery condition, measure voltage in each cell as shown. Unequal readings indicate a faulty battery. (Chrysler)

details.

If cell voltages are low, but equal, recharging will usually restore the battery. If cell voltage readings vary more than .2 volts, the battery is BAD.

DANGER! Make sure you do not drip electrolyte on the vehicle or your skin when using a hydrometer or cell voltage tester. The acid in the electrolyte will eat the paint or burn your skin.

Battery drain test

A *battery drain test* will check for an abnormal current draw with the ignition key off. When a battery goes dead without being used, you may need to check for a current drain. It is possible that there is a short or other problem constantly discharging the battery.

A battery can be discharged if an electrical accessory remains ON when the ignition switch is shut OFF. For example, a short in a switch could cause a glove box light to always stay on. This could slowly drain the battery and cause a no-crank problem.

To perform a battery current drain test, make the ammeter connections shown in Fig. 27-15. Pull the fuse for the dash clock. Close the doors and trunk. Then read the ammeter. If everything is OFF (good condition), the ammeter should read zero. However, an ammeter reading would point to a drain and a problem.

To help pinpoint a drain, pull fuses one at a time. When the ammeter reads zero, the problem is in the circuit on that fuse.

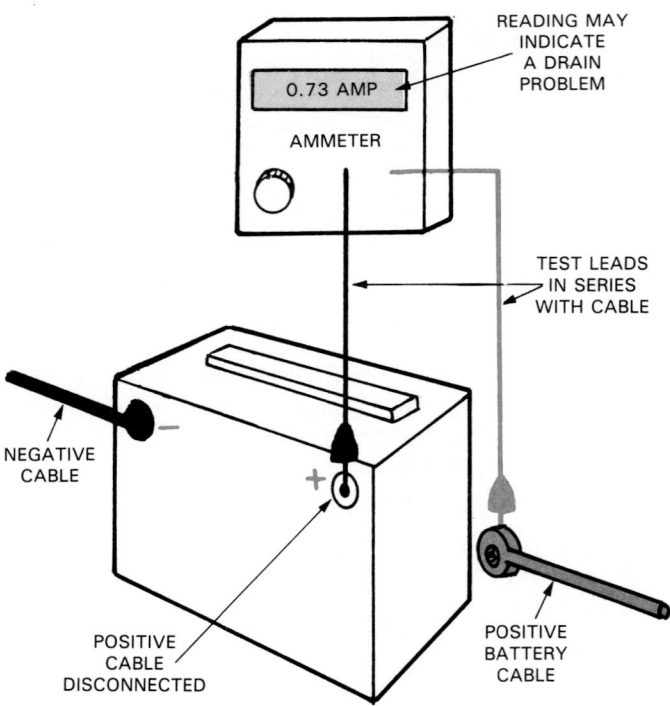

Fig. 27-15. If battery runs down after sitting unused in car, perform a battery drain test. Connect ammeter in series with positive cable. If current is flowing out of battery with everything turned off, an electrical problem is discharging battery.

BATTERY CHARGERS

When tests show that a battery is discharged, a battery charger may be used to re-energize it. The *battery charger* will force current back into the battery to restore the charge on the plates and in the electrolyte. It contains a step-down transformer that changes wall outlet voltage (around 120 volts) to slightly above battery voltage (14 to 15 volts). Refer to Fig. 27-16. It shows a battery charger.

There are two basic types of battery chargers: the slow charger and the fast charger.

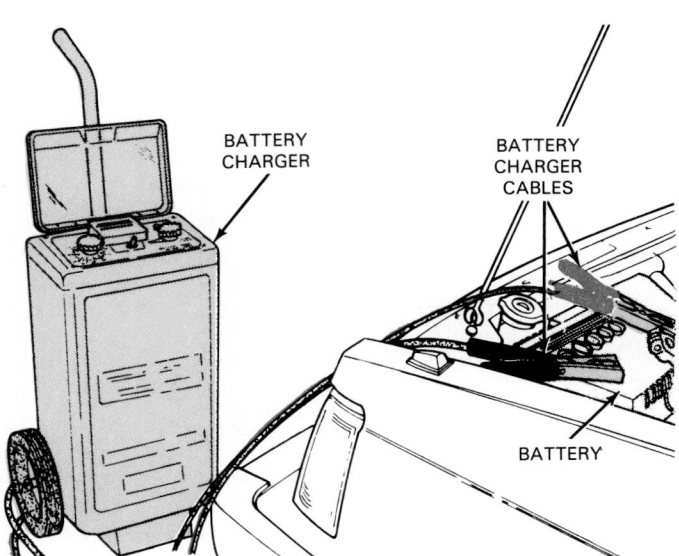

Fig. 27-16. Battery charger forces current through battery to restore charge on plates. (Chrysler)

Slow (trickle) charger

A *slow charger*, also called a *trickle charger*, feeds a small amount of current into the battery. Charging time is longer (about 12 hours at 10 amps). However, the chemical action inside the battery is improved. The active materials are plated back on the battery plates better. When time allows, use a slow charger. Look at Fig. 27-17A.

Fast (quick) charger

A *fast charger*, also called a *quick* or *boost charger*, forces a high current flow into the battery for rapid recharging. A fast charger is shown in Fig. 27-17B. It is commonly used in auto shops. When the customer needs the car, time may not allow the use of a slow charger.

Fast charging will usually allow engine starting in a matter of minutes. If possible, slow charging is usually recommended after fast charging.

Charging a battery

DANGER! Before connecting a battery charger to

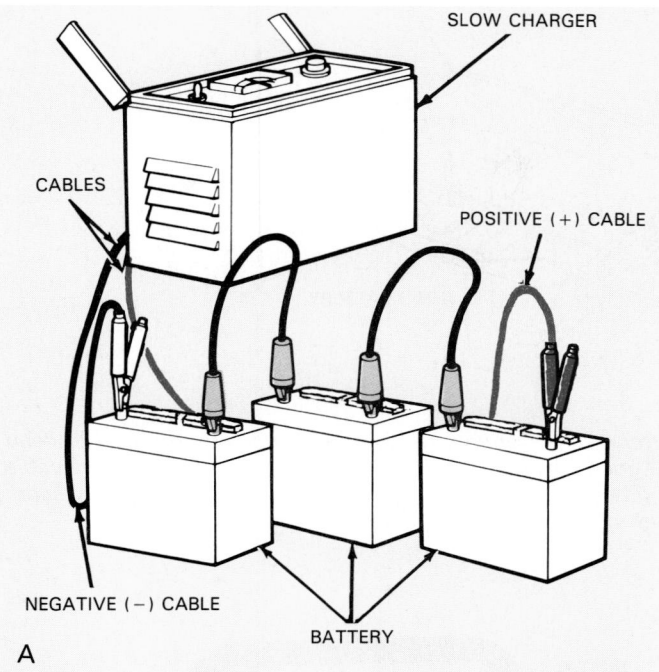

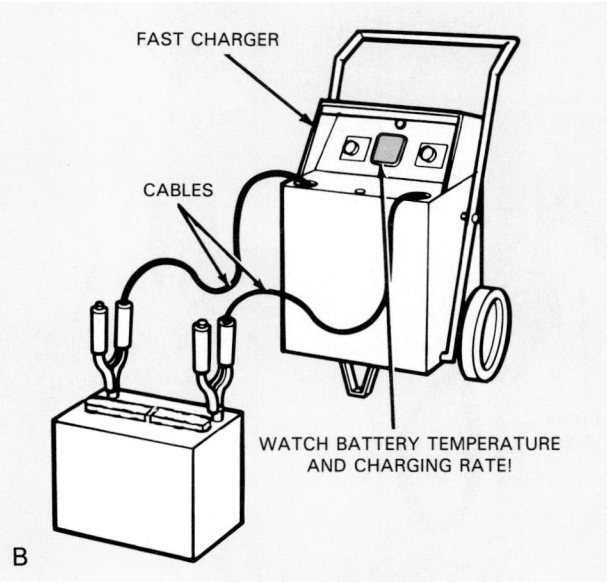

Fig. 27-17. A — Slow charger only forces small amount of current through battery. Since slow charging requires several hours, several batteries may be connected to get more done. B — Fast charging is ok in an emergency. Slow charging should follow fast charging to restore battery properly. Do not let battery temperature go above about 125°F (52°C) or battery damage may occur.

a battery, make sure the charger is turned OFF. Also, check that the work area is well ventilated. If a spark ignites any battery gas, the battery could EXPLODE. Wear eye protection!

To use a battery charger, connect the RED charger lead to the positive terminal of the battery. Connect the BLACK charger lead to the negative terminal of the battery. With side terminal batteries, use adapters like those shown in Fig. 27-18.

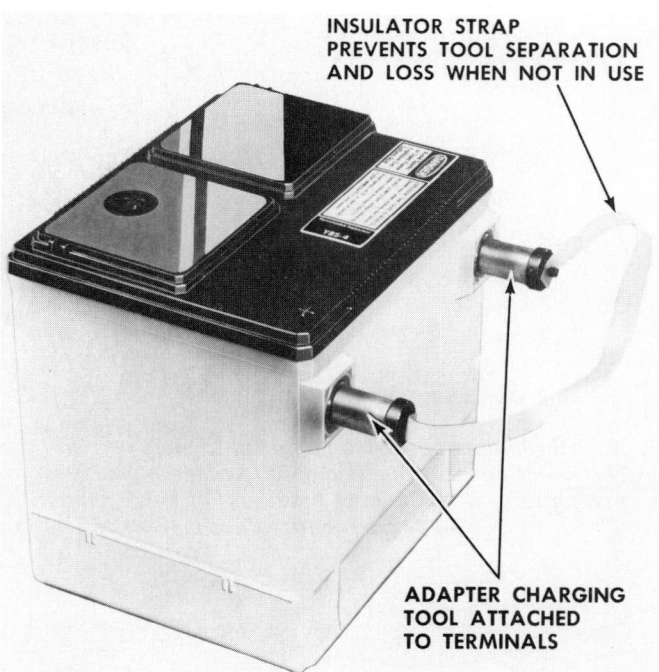

Fig. 27-18. When charging a side terminal battery, use adapters. They will let you connect charger clamps to terminals. (Chevrolet)

Make sure you do NOT reverse the charger connections or the charging system in the car could be damaged. Set the charger controls and turn on the power.

When fast charging, do NOT exceed a charge rate of about 35 amps. Also, battery temperature must NOT exceed 125°F (52°C). Exceeding either charge rate or temperature could damage the battery.

JUMP STARTING

In emergency situations, it may be necessary to *jump* start a vehicle by connecting another battery to the discharged battery. Look at Fig. 27-19. The two batteries are connected POSITIVE TO POSITIVE and NEGATIVE TO NEGATIVE.

Connect the red jumper cable to the positive terminal of both batteries. Then, connect the black jumper cable to any ground on both vehicles. See Fig. 27-20.

WARNING! Do not short jumper cables together or connect them backwards. This could cause serious damage to the charging or computer system.

BATTERY LOAD TEST

A *battery load test,* also termed a *battery capacity test,* is one of the BEST methods of checking battery condition. It tests the battery under full current load.

The hydrometer and voltage tests were general indicators of battery condition. The battery load test, however, actually measures the current output and performance of the battery. It is one of the most com-

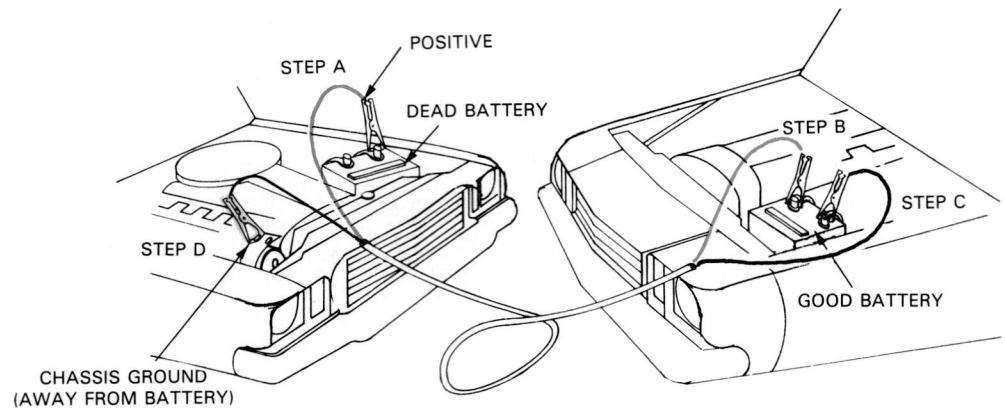

Fig. 27-19. Jumper cables can be used to start car with dead battery. A — Connect red jumper to positive terminal of dead battery. B — Connect other end of red jumper to positive terminal of good battery. C — Connect black jumper to negative cable of good battery. D — Connect other end of black jumper to good ground, away from dead battery. This will keep any spark away from battery gases. Run engine in car with good battery while starting. (Belden)

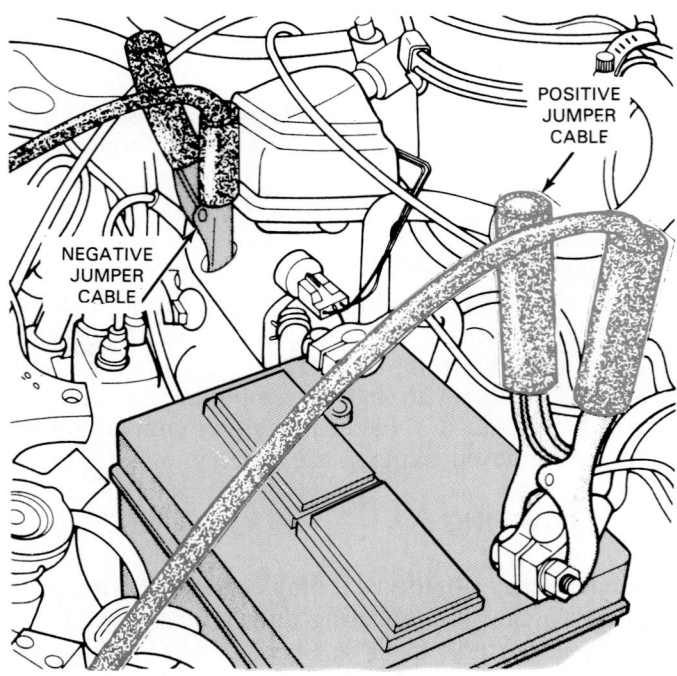

Fig. 27-20. Close up of jumper connections shows connection of negative or black jumper to chassis ground. A spark near dead battery could make battery gases explode. (Chrysler)

mon and informative battery tests used in modern automotive garages. Refer to Fig. 27-21.

Connecting load tester

Connect the load tester to the battery terminals. If the tester is an *inductive type* (clip-on ammeter lead senses field around outside of cables), use the connections shown in Fig. 27-22. If the tester is NOT inductive, you must connect the ammeter in series.

Control settings and exact procedures vary. Follow the directions provided with the testing equipment.

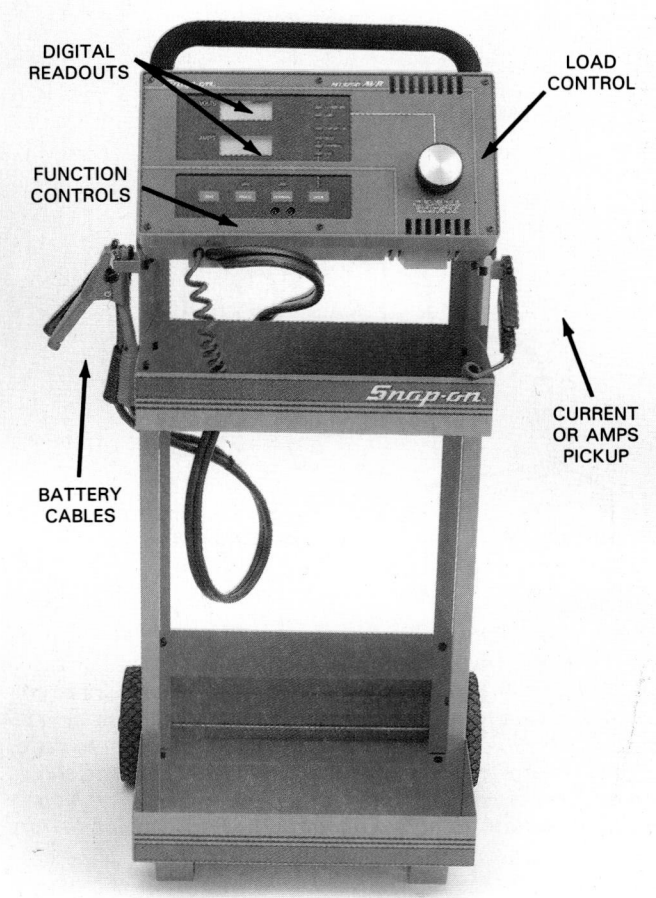

Fig. 27-21. Battery load tester is most accurate method of determining battery condition. It is a commonly used testing device that measures actual battery performance. (Snap-On Tools)

Double-check battery charge

Before load testing, make sure the battery is adequately charged. Use a hydrometer or digital voltmeter covered earlier. The load tester, itself, can be used to

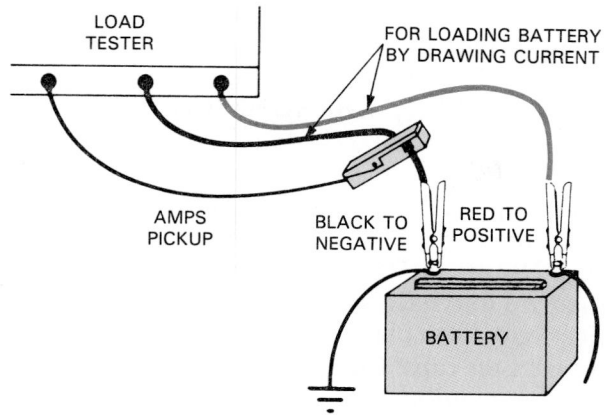

Fig. 27-22. Modern load testers are connected as shown. Clamp large cables to battery. Clip inductive amps pickup around negative tester cable. Large cables load battery by drawing current through tester. Inductive pickup operates ammeter in tester. (Marquette)

BATTERY RATINGS			LOAD TEST AMPS
Cold Cranking Current	Amp-Hour (Approx.)	Watts	
200	35-40	1800	100 amps
250	41-48	2100	125 amps
300	49-62	2500	150 amps
350	63-70	2900	175 amps
400	71-76	3250	200 amps
450	77-86	3600	225 amps
500	87-92	3900	250 amps
550	93-110	4200	275 amps

Fig. 27-23. Chart shows different battery ratings and calculated current values for load testing. (Marquette)

check battery charge. Adjust the load control to draw 50 amps for 10 seconds. This will remove any surface charge. Then, check no-load battery voltage, also called open circuit voltage (OCV), by reading the voltmeter.

A FULLY CHARGED BATTERY should have an OCV of 12.4 volts or higher. If battery voltage is BELOW 12.4 volts, charge the battery before load testing. The battery is probably bad if it fails a second test after charging.

Determine battery load

Before load testing a battery, you must calculate how much current draw should be applied to the battery.

If the *amp-hour rating* is given, load the battery to THREE TIMES its amp-hour rating. For example, if the battery is rated at 60 amp-hours, test the battery at 180 amps (60 X 3 = 180).

Many batteries are now rated in SAE *cold cranking amps,* instead of amp-hours. To determine the load test for these batteries, DIVIDE the cold crank rating BY TWO. For instance, a battery with 400 cold cranking amps rating should be loaded to 200 amps (400 ÷ 2 = 200).

The *watt* is another battery performance rating. Fig. 27-23 gives a chart which compares battery ratings.

A load conversion chart will normally be provided with the load testing equipment. Refer to this material when in doubt.

Loading the battery

After checking battery charge and finding the amp load value, you are ready to test battery output. Double-check that the tester is connected properly. Then, turn the load control knob until the ammeter reads the correct load for your battery, Fig. 27-24.

Hold the load for 15 seconds. Next, read the VOLTMETER while the load is applied. Then, turn

the load control completely OFF so the battery will not be discharged.

Load test results

If the voltmeter reads 9.5 volts or MORE at room

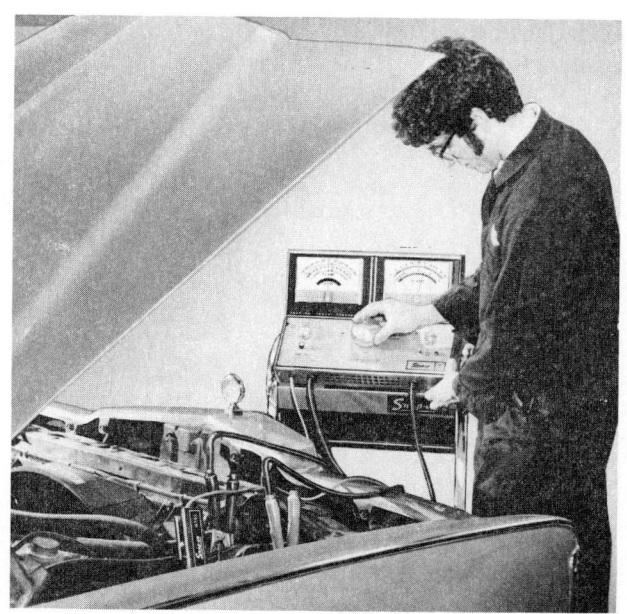

APPROXIMATE ELECTROLYTE TEMPERATURE		MINIMUM ACCEPTABLE VOLTAGE UNDER LOAD FOR GOOD BATTERY
60°F	(16°C)	9.5
50°F	(10°C)	9.4
40°F	(4°C)	9.3
30°F	(−1°C)	9.1
20°F	(−7°C)	8.9
10°F	(−12°C)	8.7
0°F	(−18°C)	8.5

Fig. 27-24. To load test battery, turn load control knob until ammeter reads calculated test current (Fig. 27-23). Hold load or current for 15 seconds and read voltmeter. If reading is below voltages in chart for specific temperature, battery is probably bad. (Snap-On Tools)

temperature, the battery is good. Six-volt batteries should maintain 4.8 volts. These voltages are based on a battery temperature above 70°F (21°C).

A cold battery may show a lower voltage. You will need a temperature compensation chart, like the one in Fig. 27-24. It allows for any reduced battery performance caused by a low temperature.

If the voltmeter reads below 9.5 volts at room temperature, battery performance is POOR. This would show that the battery is not producing enough current to properly run the starting motor. Before replacing the battery, however, a quick charge test should be completed.

Quick (3 minute) charge test

A *quick charge test,* also termed *3 minute charge test,* will determine if the battery is sulfated (plates ruined). If the battery load test results are poor, fast charge the battery. Charge for 3 minutes at 30 to 40 amps. Test the voltage while charging, as shown in Fig. 27-25. If the voltage goes ABOVE 15.5 volts (12-volt battery) or 7.8 volts (6-volt battery), the battery plates are sulfated and ruined. A new battery should be installed in the vehicle.

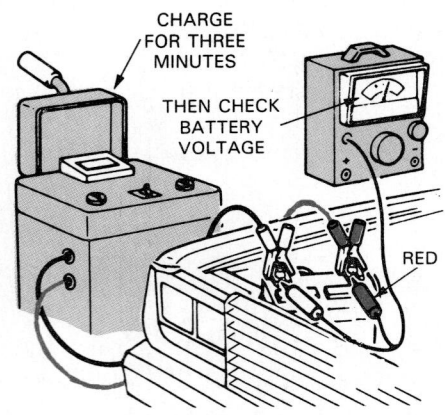

Fig. 27-25. Three minute charge test will double-check load test. Charge battery at about 40 amps while measuring battery voltage for three minutes. If voltage increases above 15.5 volts, replace battery. (GMC)

Other battery-related problems

If the battery passes all of its tests, but does not perform properly (starting motor does not crank, for example), the following are some likely problems to check out.

1. Defective charging system.
2. Battery drain (light or other accessory ON).
3. Loose alternator belt.
4. Corroded, loose, or defective battery cables.
5. Defective starting system.

Later textbook chapters cover the starting and charg-

ing systems. They will give you more information relating to battery service.

ACTIVATING DRY CHARGED BATTERY

A new, dry-charged battery must be *activated* (readied for service) before installing. Put on safety glasses and rubber gloves. Remove the cell caps or covers. Using a plastic funnel, not a metal funnel, pour electrolyte into each cell. Pour in enough electrolyte to just cover the plates and separators.

Replace the caps. Charge the battery as recommended by the manufacturer. After charging, recheck the electrolyte level. Install the battery.

REMOVING AND REPLACING BATTERY

To remove a battery, first disconnect the cables. Then loosen the battery hold-down. Using a battery strap or lifting tool, Fig. 27-26, lift the battery carefully out of the vehicle.

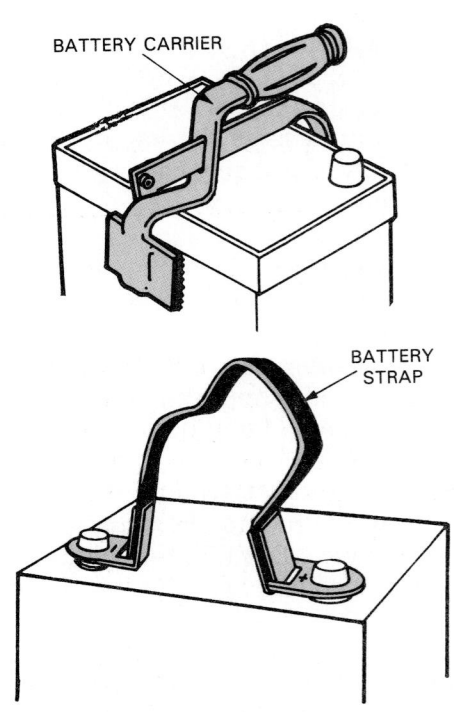

Fig. 27-26. Should you lose your grip and drop a battery, acid could splash out causing eye or skin injury. Always use a battery strap or carrier for safety. (Florida Dept. of Voc. Ed.)

DANGER! Always wear safety glasses when carrying a battery. If you were to drop a battery, electrolyte (acid) could squirt out of the vent caps or broken case and into your face and eyes.

To install a battery, gently place the battery into its clean tray or box. Check that the battery fits properly. The tray edge must not cut through and rupture the plastic case. Bolt on the hold-down and install the cables.

The replacement battery should have a power rating EQUAL to factory recommendations. If an undersize battery (lower watt rating) is installed, starting motor performance and battery service life will be reduced.

KNOW THESE TERMS

"Dead battery," Battery leakage test, Battery terminal test, Fill ring, Distilled water, Battery charge condition, Hydrometer, Specific gravity, Battery voltage test, Cell voltage test, Battery drain test, Battery charger, Slow charger, Fast charger, Jump starting, Battery load test, Quick charge test, Battery activation.

REVIEW QUESTIONS

1. What five tasks does battery maintenance typically include?
2. A _____ _____ _____ will find out if current is discharging across the top of the battery case.
3. If a voltmeter shows over .7 volt drop across the battery post-to-cable connection, what should be done?
4. A knife or scraper is a good method of cleaning corroded battery terminals. True or False?
5. When you measure _____ _____ , you check the condition of the battery electrolyte and plates.
6. List six reasons for a discharged battery.
7. A battery _____ _____ is done by measuring total battery voltage with an accurate voltmeter. A ____ _____ battery should have over 12 volts. ·
8. A customer complains that her battery goes dead when the car is not driven for an extended period. A new battery has been installed and tested by another shop.
   Technician A says that starting motor current draw should be measured. A shorted starting motor could be draining the battery.
   Technician B says that a battery drain test should be done. An electrical short could be discharging the battery, even with the ignition key off.
   Who is correct?
   a. Technician A
   b. Technician B
   c. Both A and B
   d. Neither A nor B
9. When using a battery charger, connect the red lead to positive and the black lead to negative. True or False?
10. Explain how an excessive fast charging rate can ruin a battery.
11. How do you connect jumper cables safely?

12. A _____ _____ _____ , also termed a _____ _____ _____ , is one of the best methods of checking battery condition.
13. What is an inductive type ammeter lead?
14. Explain how to do a battery load test.
15. If a 12-volt battery shows below _____ volts during a load test at 70 °F (21 °C), the battery is bad.
    a. 9.9 volts.
    b. 9.5 volts.
    c. 9.7 volts.
    d. 10.0 volts.

ACTIVITIES FOR CHAPTER 27

1. Get permission from several classmates to conduct a battery maintenance inspection on their vehicles. Check for the points listed on page 342. Make and complete a simple checklist, or write a short report, for each vehicle inspected. Give the form or report to the vehicle owner.
2. Demonstrate to the class the proper way to make a hydrometer reading of a battery that has removable cell caps. Observe all safety precautions, and note them for the class during your demonstration.
3. Show the effects of splashed electrolyte on clothing. Obtain small pieces of different clothing fabrics, attach them to a thick sheet of cardboard and label them. Wearing gloves and eye protection, carefully apply two drops of electrolyte from a battery to each sample. Ask class members to note the effect of the electrolyte on each fabric.

Batteries are usually positioned at the front of the engine compartment to allow easy access for testing and service. (GMC)

Starting System Fundamentals

After studying this chapter, you will be able to:
☐ Explain the principles of an electric motor.
☐ Describe the construction and operation of a starting motor.
☐ Sketch a simple starting system circuit.
☐ Explain the operation of solenoids.
☐ List the functions of the main starter drive parts.
☐ Describe starter drive operation.
☐ Compare different types of starting motors.
☐ Describe starting system safety features.

The starting system has helped make the modern automobile a reliable and convenient means of transportation. It provides an easy method of starting the engine. Early "model-Ts" had to be cranked by hand to get the engine running. This took considerable strength and patience.

Few car owners would be physically capable of starting a modern, multicylinder engine using a hand crank. The electric starting motor is designed to crank the engine with the simple turn of a key.

Note! If any of the principles in this chapter are unclear, use the index to locate and review earlier text material, especially Chapter 8, Electricity and Electronics.

STARTING SYSTEM PRINCIPLES

The *starting system* uses battery power and an electric motor to turn the engine crankshaft for engine starting. Fig. 28-1 shows the basic parts and action of a starting system.

The major parts of a starting system include:
1. BATTERY (source of energy for starting system).
2. IGNITION SWITCH (allows driver to control starting system operation).
3. SOLENOID (high current relay [switch] for connecting battery to starting motor).
4. STARTING MOTOR (high torque electric motor for turning gear on engine flywheel).

Starting system action

When you turn the ignition key to start, current flows through the solenoid coil. This closes the solenoid contacts, connecting battery current to the starting motor. The motor turns the flywheel ring gear until the engine starts and runs on its own power.

When the engine starts, you release the ignition key. This breaks the current flow to the solenoid and starter. The starter stops turning and the starter gear moves away from the flywheel gear.

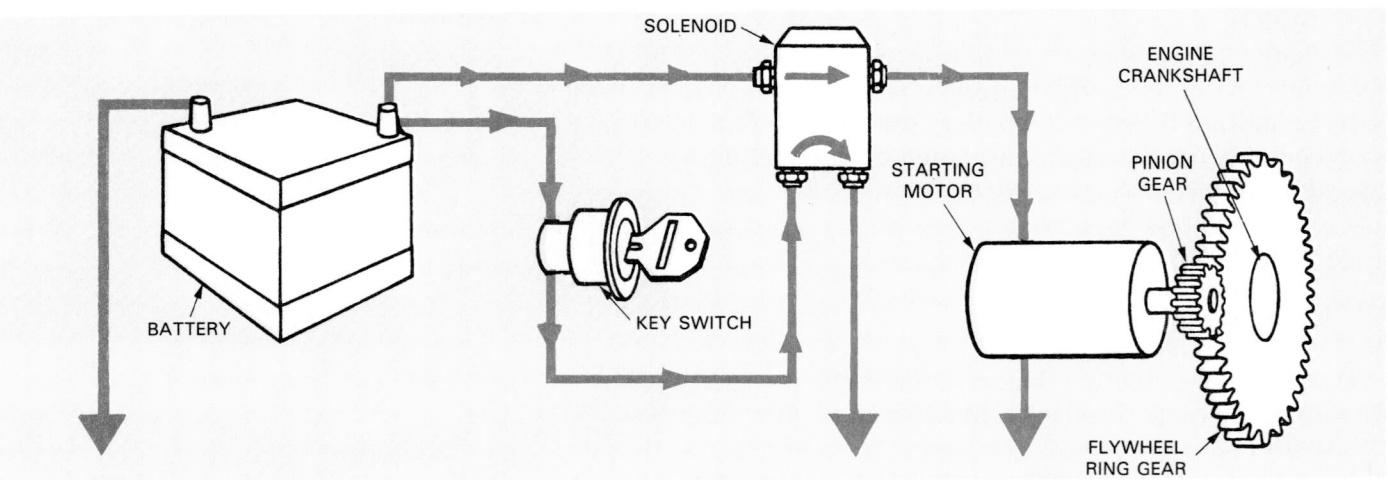

Fig. 28-1. Basic starting system operation. Ignition switch energizes solenoid. Solenoid then energizes starting motor. Motor turns flywheel gear for engine starting. (GMC)

Starting motor fundamentals

The *starting motor* converts electrical energy from the battery into mechanical or rotating energy to crank the engine. It is similar to other electric motors.

All electric motors (wiper motors, fan motors, electric fuel pump motors) produce a turning force through the interaction of magnetic fields inside the motor.

Magnetic field action

As explained in earlier text chapters, a *magnetic field* is made up of invisible magnetic lines of force. The lines of force flow between the poles of a permanent magnet. They also flow around the outside of a wire that is carrying current.

Since like charges (fields) REPEL each other and unlike charges ATTRACT, magnetic fields can be used to produce motion.

Look at Fig. 28-2. Note how the lines of force in the magnet and lines of force around the conductor act upon each other. This principle is used in electric motors.

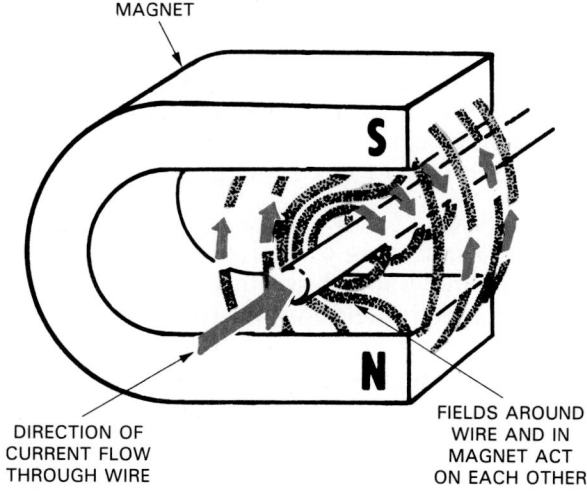

Fig. 28-2. Magnetic field in magnet and field around current carrying conductor can be used to produce motion. Note how fields interact. (GMC)

Simple electric motor

To build a basic electric motor, you would start by bending a piece of wire into a loop. When current is passed through the wire loop or *winding,* a magnetic field forms around the wire. Refer to Fig. 28-3A.

A magnet or *pole piece* would be needed to make the loop of wire move. See Fig. 28-3B. A magnetic field is set up between the pole pieces, also called pole shoes.

Changing electricity into motion

Electric current can be changed into a strong rotating motion by placing the loop of wire (winding) inside the pole pieces. When current passes through the loop, the magnetic field around the loop and the field between

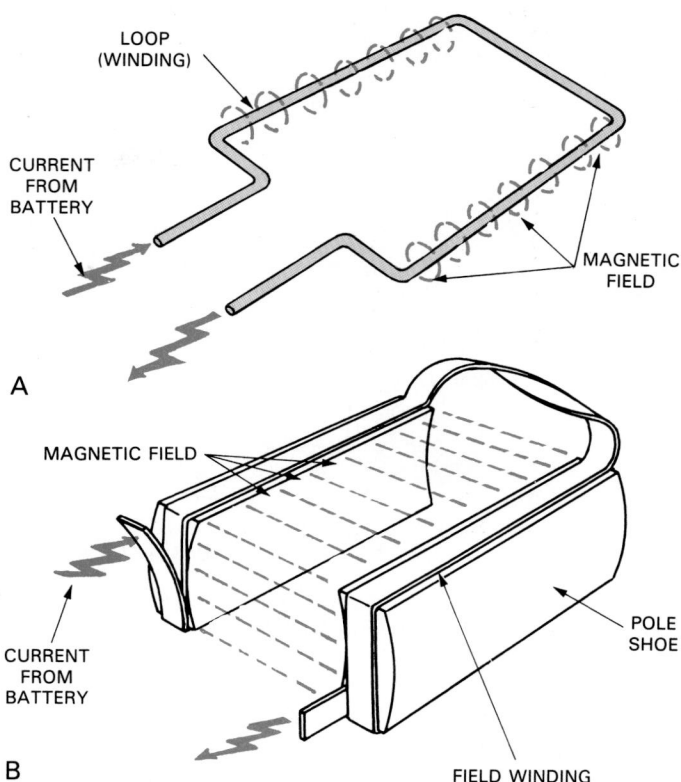

Fig. 28-3. A — Wire bent into a loop forms winding. When battery current flows through winding, field develops around wire. B — Wires wrapped around pole shoes form strong magnetic field. (Deere & Co.)

the pole shoes act upon each other. The loop of wire is pushed and pulled away from the pole shoes, towards a vertical position. This is illustrated in Fig. 28-4.

Commutator and brushes

A commutator and several brushes are used to keep the electric motor spinning by controlling the current path through the windings (wire loops). Look at Fig. 28-5. It shows a simplified motor.

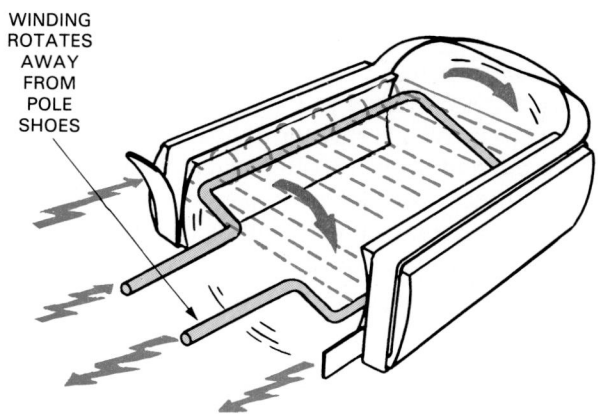

Fig. 28-4. If winding is placed inside field, winding rotates away from pole shoes. (Deere & Co.)

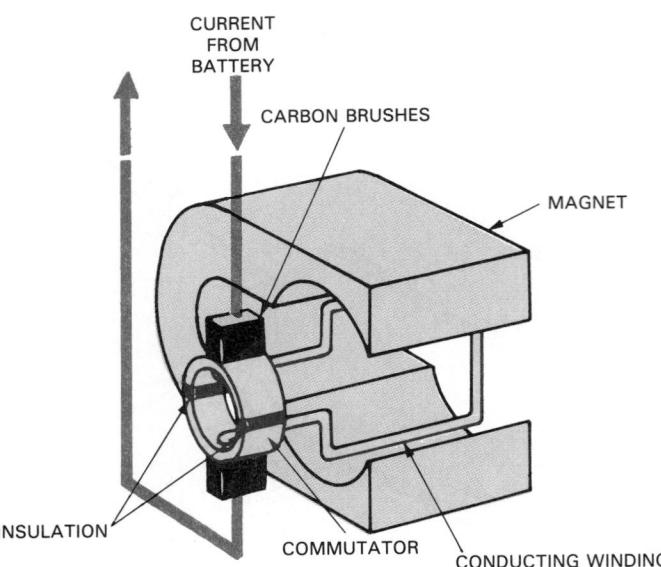

Fig. 28-5. Brushes and commutator are used to keep windings spinning. Note how commutator reverses electrical connection when loop rotates around. (Robert Bosch)

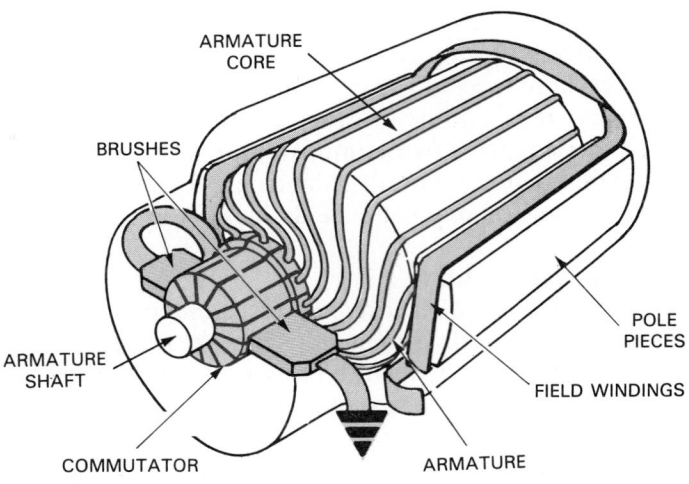

Fig. 28-6. Actual starting motor has multiple (several) commutator segments and windings to increase motor power and smoothness. (Deere & Co.)

The *commutator* serves as a sliding electrical connection between the motor windings and the brushes. The commutator has many segments (parts) insulated from each other.

The motor *brushes* ride on top of the commutator. They slide on the commutator to carry battery current to the spinning windings.

Fig. 28-5 illustrates commutator and brush action. As the winding rotates away from the pole piece, the commutator segments change the electrical connection between the brushes and winding. This reverses the magnetic field around the winding. Then the winding is again pulled around and passes the other pole piece.

The constantly changing electrical connection at the windings keeps the motor spinning. A push-pull action is set up as each loop moves around inside the pole piece area.

Increasing motor power

Several loops of wire and a commutator with many segments are normally used to increase motor power and smoothness. Shown in Fig. 28-6, each winding is connected to its own segment on the commutator. This provides current flow through each winding as the brushes contact each segment.

As the motor spins, many windings contribute to the motion. This produces a constant or smooth turning force.

Armature

A starting motor, unlike our simple motor, must produce very high torque (turning power) and relatively high speed. A system to support the windings and increase each winding's magnetic field strength is needed.

A *starter armature* consists of an armature shaft, armature core, commutator, and armature windings. Look at Fig. 28-6.

The shaft supports the armature as it spins inside the starter housing. The armature core holds the windings or wire loops in place. The commutator is mounted on one end of the armature shaft.

The armature core is made of iron. The iron increases the magnetic field strength of the windings.

Field windings

A *field winding* is a stationary set of windings (insulated wire wrapped in circular shape). It creates a strong magnetic field around the motor armature. Fig. 28-6 shows a basic set of field windings.

When current flows through the winding, the magnetic field between the pole pieces becomes very large. It can be 5 or 10 times that of a permanent magnet. Acting against the field developed by the armature, this spins the motor with extra power.

Discussed later, some later model starters do NOT have field windings. Instead, they have special permanent magnets that are strong enough to turn the armature for engine starting.

STARTER PINION GEAR

A *starter pinion gear* is a small gear on the armature shaft that engages a large gear on the engine flywheel. It moves into and meshes with the flywheel ring gear anytime the starter is energized. This is shown in Fig. 28-7. Note relationship of gears.

Most starter pinion gears are made as part of a pinion drive mechanism. The pinion drive unit slides over one end of the armature shaft, Fig. 28-8.

Overrunning clutch

The starter *overrunning clutch* locks the pinion gear in one direction and releases it in the other. This allows

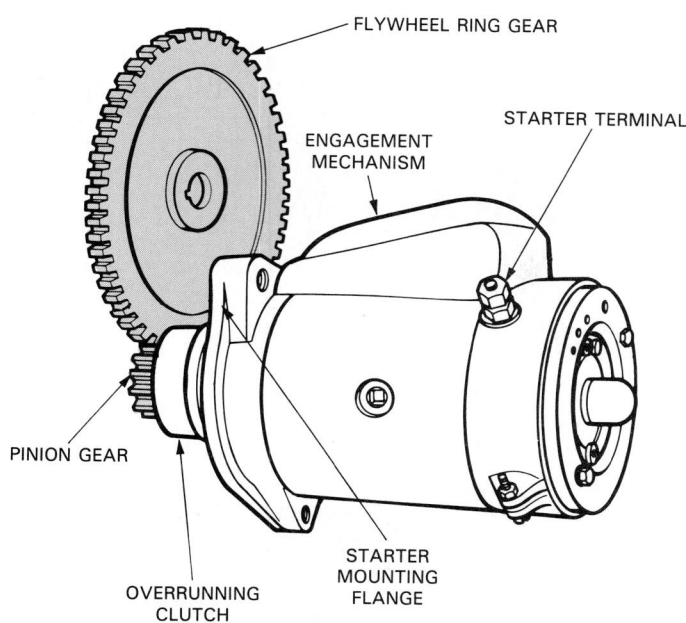

Fig. 28-7. Starter pinion gear meshes with large ring gear on engine flywheel.

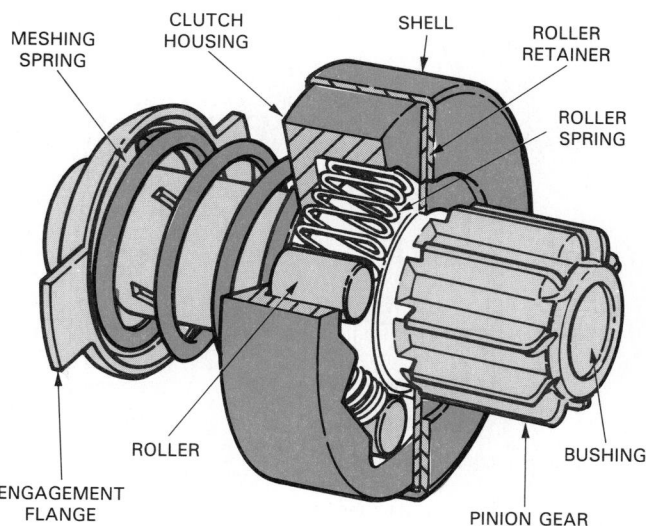

Fig. 28-9. Study construction of starting motor overrunning clutch. It is simply one-way clutch. It locks flange to pinion gear in one direction and releases in other direction. (Ford)

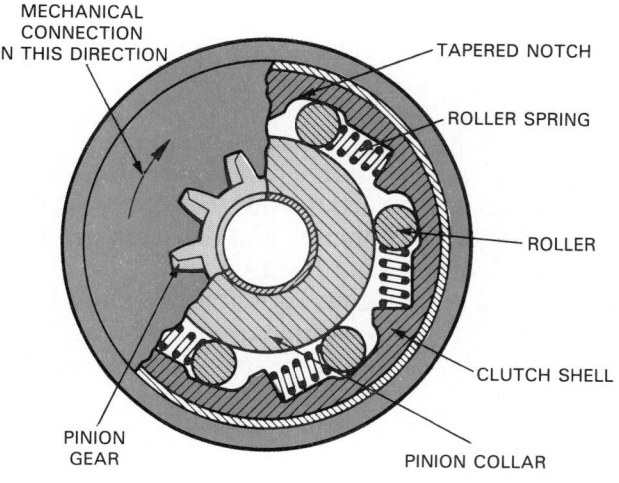

Fig. 28-10. Cutaway shows how rollers fit between pinion gear and collar. Rollers jam and lock units together one way. Going other way, they release, allowing pinion to freewheel. (Robert Bosch)

the pinion gear to turn the flywheel ring gear for starting. It also lets the pinion gear freewheel when the engine begins to run.

Fig. 28-9 shows a cutaway view of a pinion gear overrunning clutch assembly. Without the overrunning clutch, the starter could be driven by the engine flywheel. The flywheel gear could spin the starter too fast and cause armature damage.

Overrunning clutch operation

Fig. 28-10 shows the basic operation of a starter overrunning clutch. Small spring-loaded rollers are located between the pinion gear collar and the clutch shell.

The rollers wedge into the notches in the shell in one direction (driving direction). They slide back and release when driven in the other direction (freewheeling direction).

There are spiral grooves on the armature shaft and

the inside diameter of the clutch. The grooves force the shaft and pinion gear assembly to turn together. They also let the gear assembly slide on the armature shaft, Fig. 28-11.

STARTER SOLENOID

The *starter solenoid* is a high current relay. It makes an electrical connection between the battery and starting motor. The starter solenoid is an electromagnetic switch (switch using electricity and magnetism for operation). It is similar to other relays but is capable of handling much higher current levels.

A cutaway view of a starter solenoid is given in Fig. 28-12. Note the solenoid windings, contact disc, terminals, plunger, and other parts.

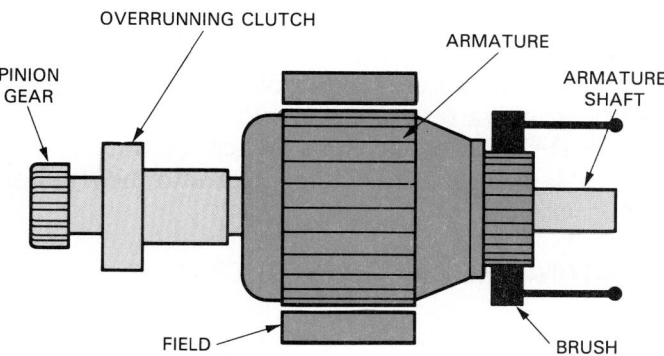

Fig. 28-8. Pinion gear clutch assembly slides onto one end of armature shaft. Note other parts. (Robert Bosch)

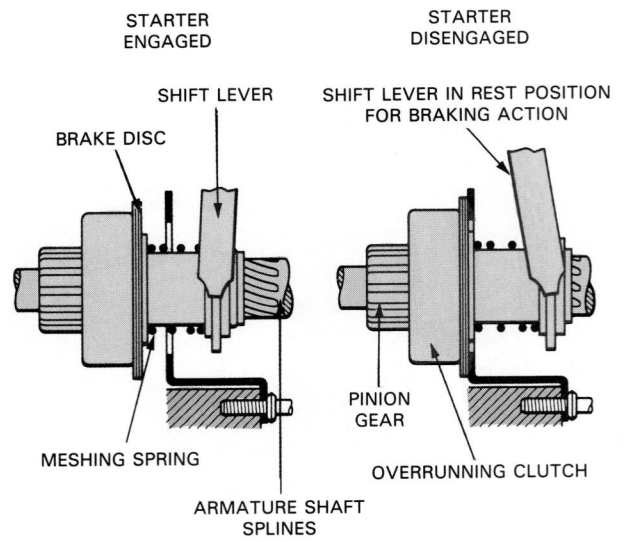

Fig. 28-11. Pinion gear assembly is splined to armature shaft. This makes pinion gear assembly turn with shaft. It also lets pinion gear slide on shaft for engagement with flywheel gear. Note how this unit also has disc brake for stopping pinion after disengagement. (Robert Bosch)

Starter solenoid operation

With the ignition key in start position, a small amount of current flows through the solenoid windings. This produces a magnetic field that pulls on the solenoid plunger. The plunger and disc are pulled into the coil windings, Fig. 28-13A.

The solenoid disc touches both of the terminals and completes the battery-to-starter circuit. About 150 to 200 amps then flows through the solenoid to the starter.

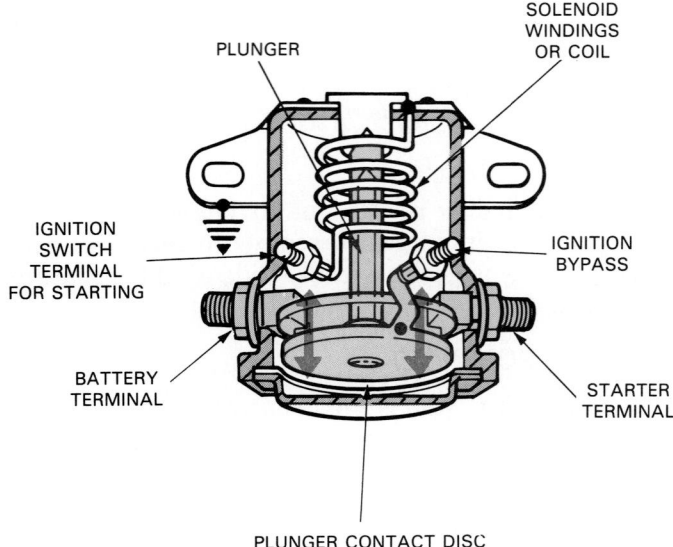

Fig. 28-12. Study construction of starter solenoid. One small terminal connects to ignition switch. Larger terminals connect to battery and starting motor. Plunger movement pulls disc into contact with two battery terminals to activate starter. (Ford)

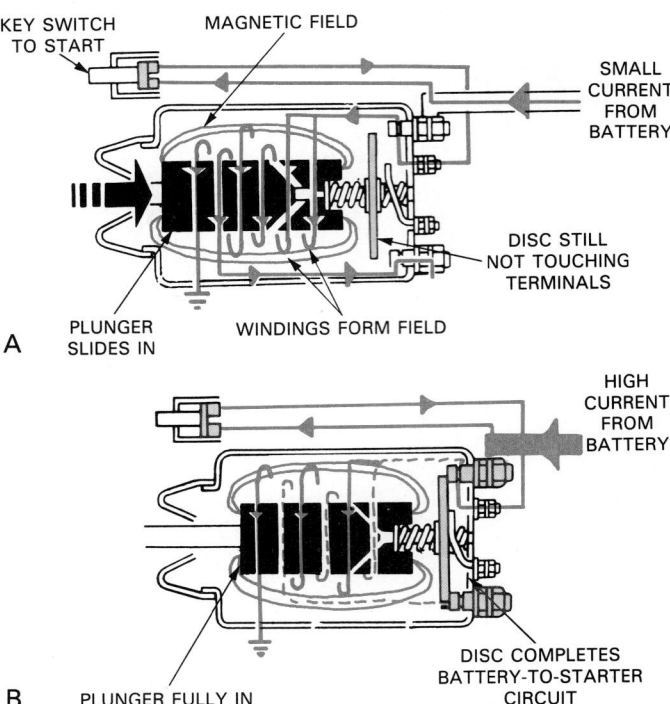

Fig. 28-13. Solenoid operation. A — With ignition key turned to start, current flows through solenoid coil. This produces field that pulls plunger inward. B — As soon as disc touches terminals, large amount of current flows to starter.

Look at Fig. 28-13B.

When the ignition key is released, current is disconnected from the solenoid windings. The magnetic field collapses and the plunger is free to slide out of the windings. This opens the disc-to-terminal connection. The open connection stops current to the starter, and the starter motor shuts off.

Starter solenoid functions

A starter solenoid, depending on starter design, may have three functions:
1. Close battery-to-starter circuit.
2. Push starter pinion gear into mesh with flywheel gear.
3. Bypass resistance wire in ignition circuit (See Chapter 32).

The starter solenoid may be located away from or on the starting motor. When mounted on a body panel (away from starter), the solenoid simply makes and breaks electrical connections. When mounted on the starter, it also slides the pinion gear into the flywheel ring gear.

STARTING MOTOR CONSTRUCTION

The construction of all starting motors is very similar. There are slight variations in design, however, that you should understand. As pictured in Fig. 28-14, the main parts of a starting motor are:

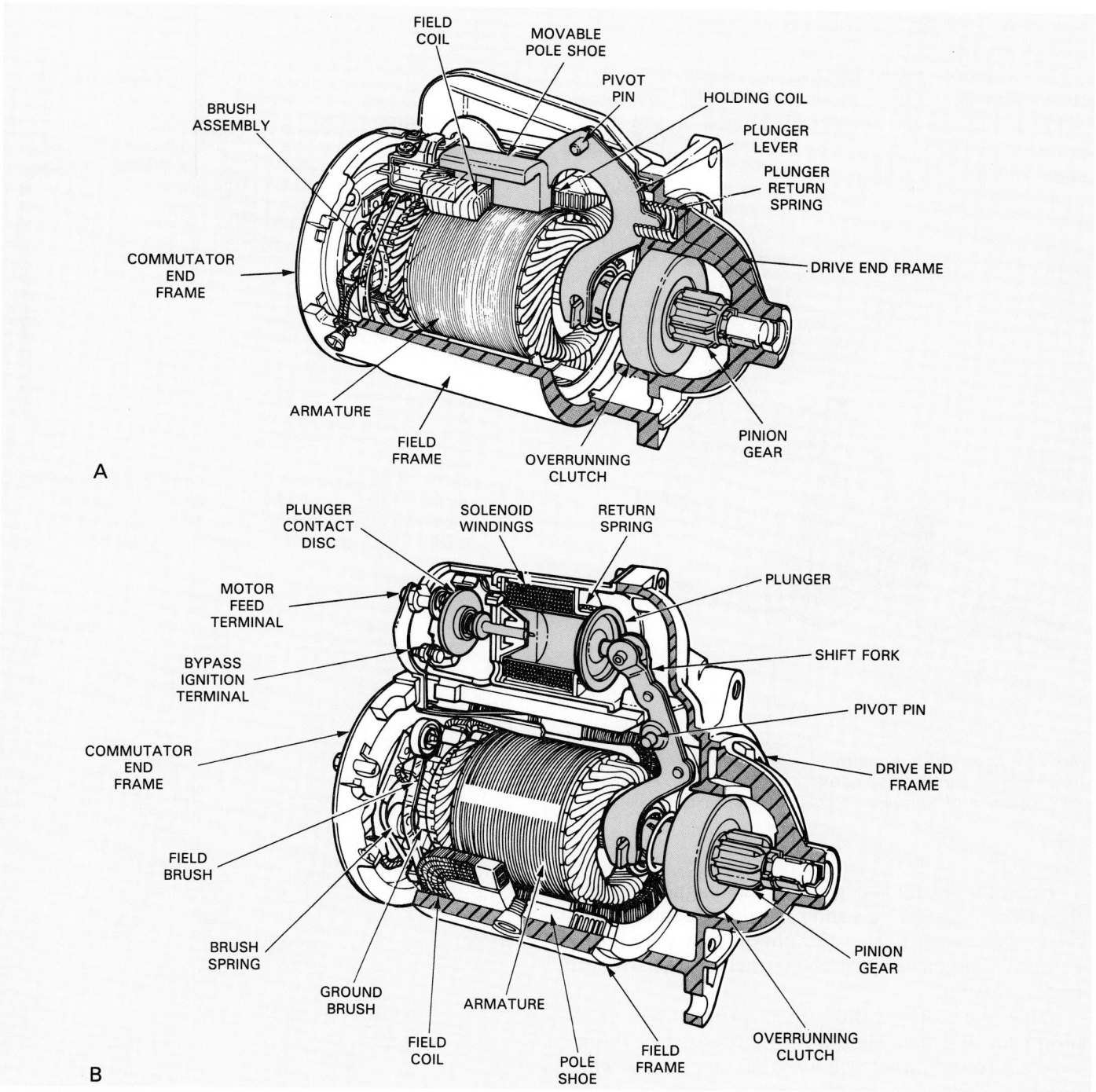

Fig. 28-14. Two common types of starting motors. A — Starter with movable pole shoe that engages pinion gear. B — Starter with solenoid to engage pinion gear, also called positive engagement starter. Study construction and compare starters. (Ford)

1. ARMATURE (windings, core, starter shaft, and commutator assembly that spins inside stationary field).
2. PINION DRIVE ASSEMBLY (pinion gear, overrunning clutch, and sometimes a shift lever and solenoid).
3. COMMUTATOR END FRAME (end housing for brushes, brush springs, and shaft bushing).
4. FIELD FRAME (center housing that holds field coils and shoes).
5. DRIVE END FRAME (end housing around pinion gear; has bushing for armature shaft).

Fig. 28-14 shows views of actual starting motors. Study their construction.

Starting motor types

There are two main starter classifications. These are grouped by type of pinion gear engagement: moveable pole shoe type and solenoid type. They are pictured in Fig. 28-14.

The *movable pole shoe* uses a yoke lever to move the pinion gear into contact with the flywheel gear. Look at Fig. 28-15. The shoe is hinged on the starter frame with a drive yoke. The drive yoke links the pole shoe and pinion gear.

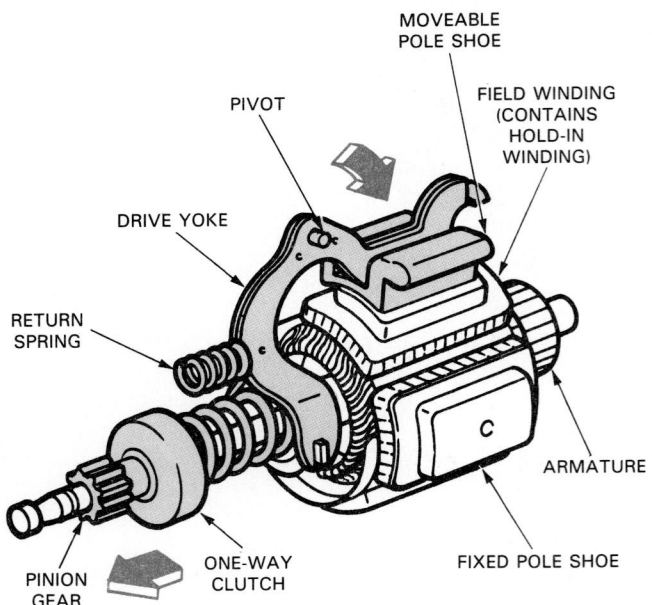

Fig. 28-15. When starter is powered, magnetic field pulls movable shoe toward armature. Yoke then slides pinion into mesh with ring gear. When starter is deactivated, small spring pushes pinion away from flywheel. (Chrysler)

When the starter is activated, the magnetic field of the motor pulls the pole shoe downward. Lever action of the yoke then pushes the pinion gear outward on its shaft. This causes gear engagement as the armature begins to spin.

When the motor is shut off, a spring moves the pinion gear and pole shoe into the released position.

A *starter-mounted solenoid* has a plunger which moves a shift lever to engage the pinion gear. The solenoid is mounted on the side of the starter field frame, as in Fig. 28-16. With this starter design, the solenoid completes the battery-to-starter circuit and it also operates the pinion gear.

Look at Fig. 28-17. It shows the basic operation of a starter-mounted solenoid. When the key is first turned to start, battery current operates the solenoid. The solenoid plunger moves and, through lever action, slides the pinion gear into mesh with the ring gear. See Fig. 28-17A.

At the end of solenoid plunger travel, the contact disc touches the two terminals to activate the motor. The motor begins to spin and crank the engine. Look at Fig. 28-17B.

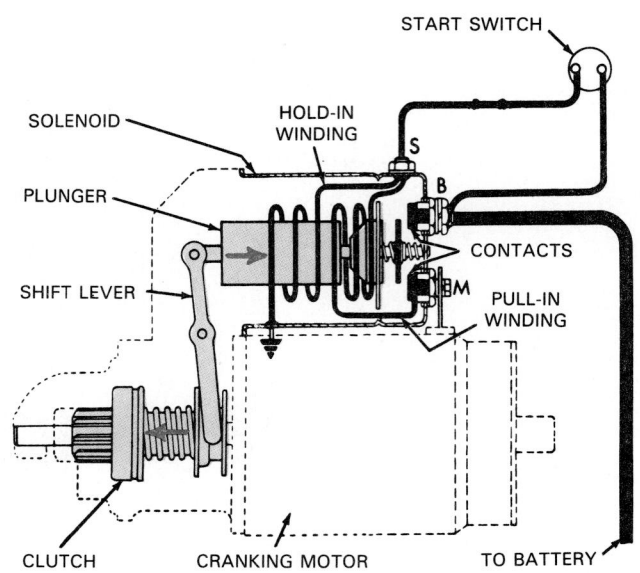

Fig. 28-16. With starter-mounted solenoid, lever is connected to solenoid plunger. When plunger moves into windings, lever slides pinion into mesh. Spring action moves pinion away from ring gear when engine starts. (GM Trucks)

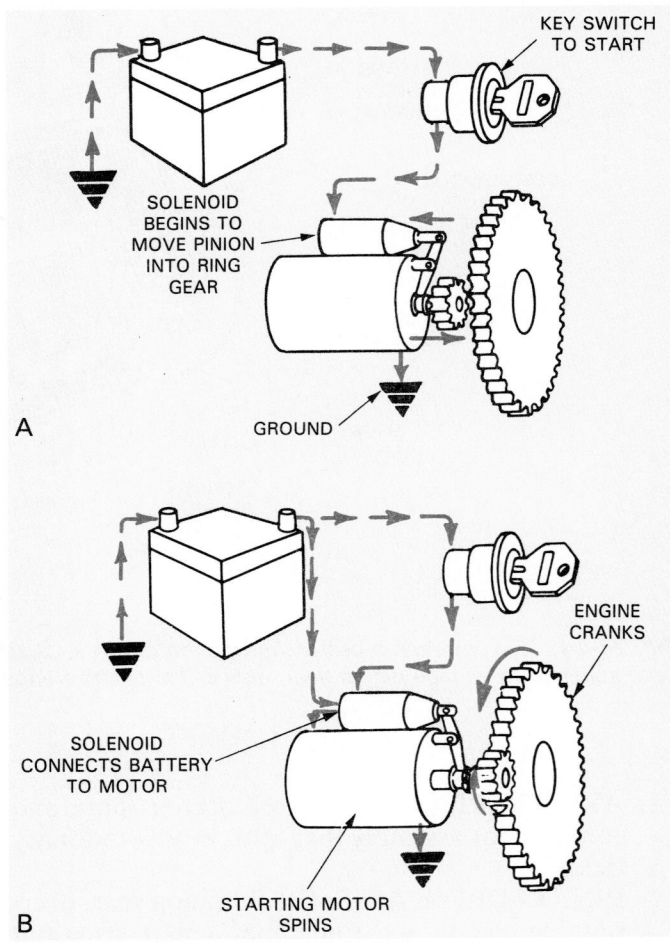

Fig. 28-17. A — Ignition switch turned to start. Current activates solenoid, which begins to slide pinion to flywheel gear. B — At end of solenoid plunger travel, disc closes starter-to-battery circuit and motor turns. (Deere & Co.)

Permanent magnet starter

A *permanent magnet starter* uses special, high-strength magnets in place of conventional field windings. The new magnets produce a strong magnetic field capable of rotating the armature with enough torque to crank the engine.

A permanent magnet starting motor is shown in Fig. 28-18. Can you find the field magnets?

Starting motor torque

A starting motor must produce high torque to start an engine. Since the pinion gear is much smaller than the flywheel ring gear, the starting motor armature turns at a relatively high speed. This helps prevent stalling of the motor. The difference in gear size also increases turning force applied to the crankshaft.

A *reduction starter* is sometimes used to further increase the rotating force applied to the engine flywheel. It uses an extra set of gears to improve the gear reduction, as in Fig. 28-19.

The starter pinion gear drives an idler gear. The idler gear drives a larger gear on the overrunning clutch assembly. This allows higher armature RPM and high torque output to the flywheel. More constant engine cranking speeds are produced by a reduction type starting motor.

INTERNAL MOTOR CIRCUITS

Direct current electric motors have three common types of internal connections. These include the series, shunt, and compound. Refer to Fig. 28-20.

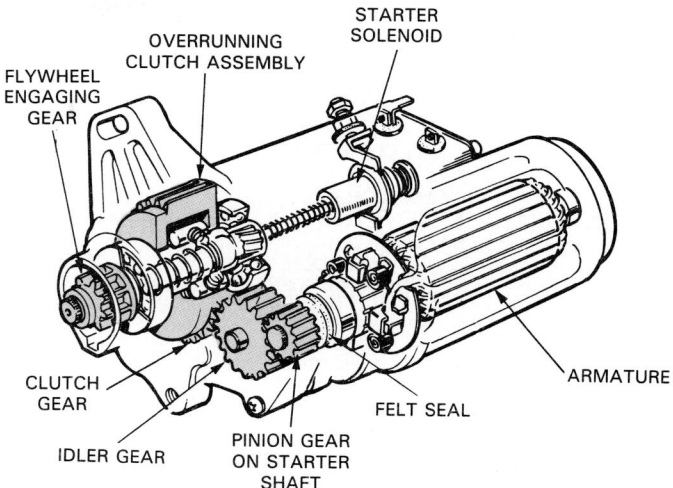

Fig. 28-19. *Reduction starter uses extra gears to increase motor torque. Gear on armature shaft turns idler gear. Idler turns larger gear on clutch for gear reduction. Exposed gear turns flywheel gear in conventional manner.* (Honda)

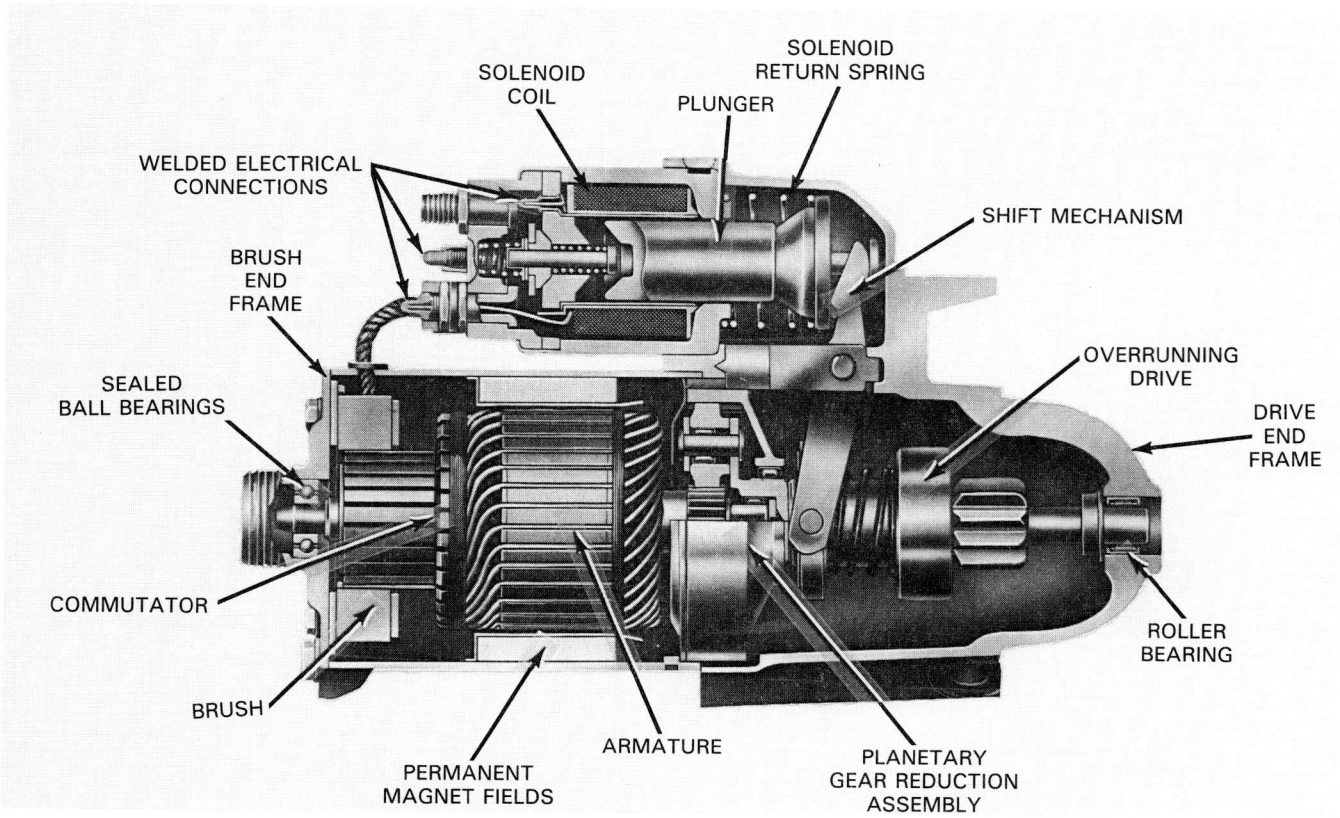

Fig. 32-18. *This is a permanent magnet starting motor. Instead of coils of wire, it uses special magnets to produce stationary magnetic field to act against armature.* (General Motors)

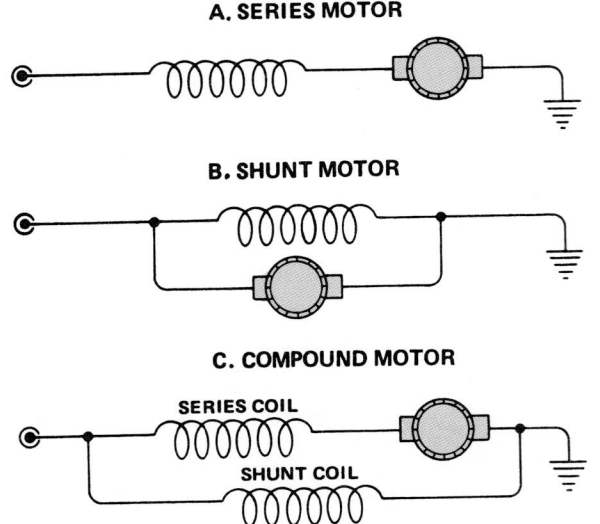

Fig. 28-20. Three types of DC motor circuits. (Sun Electric)

Generally, *series wound* starting motors develop maximum torque at initial start-up. Torque decreases as motor speed increases.

Shunt wound motors have less starting torque but more constant torque at varying speeds.

The *compound wound* motor has both series and shunt windings. It has good starting power with fairly constant operating speed.

NEUTRAL SAFETY SWITCH

A *neutral safety switch* prevents the engine from cranking unless the shift selector is in neutral or park. It keeps the starting system from working when the transmission is in gear. See Fig. 28-21. The switch provides a safety feature since injury could result if the engine were to crank and start in gear.

Cars with automatic transmissions commonly have a neutral safety switch. The switch may be mounted on the shift lever mechanism or on the transmission.

Neutral safety switch operation.

The neutral safety, Fig. 28-22, is wired into the circuit going to the starter solenoid. When the transmission is in drive or reverse, the neutral safety switch is open (disconnected). This keeps current from activating the solenoid and starter when the ignition switch is turned to start.

With the transmission in neutral, the neutral safety

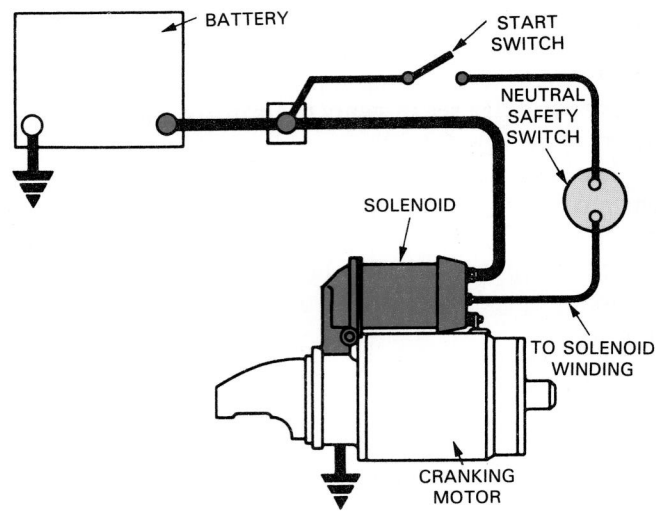

Fig. 28-21. Neutral safety switch is in series with starter solenoid. If it is open, starter will not work. Shift mechanism on automatic transmission operates neutral safety switch. (GMC)

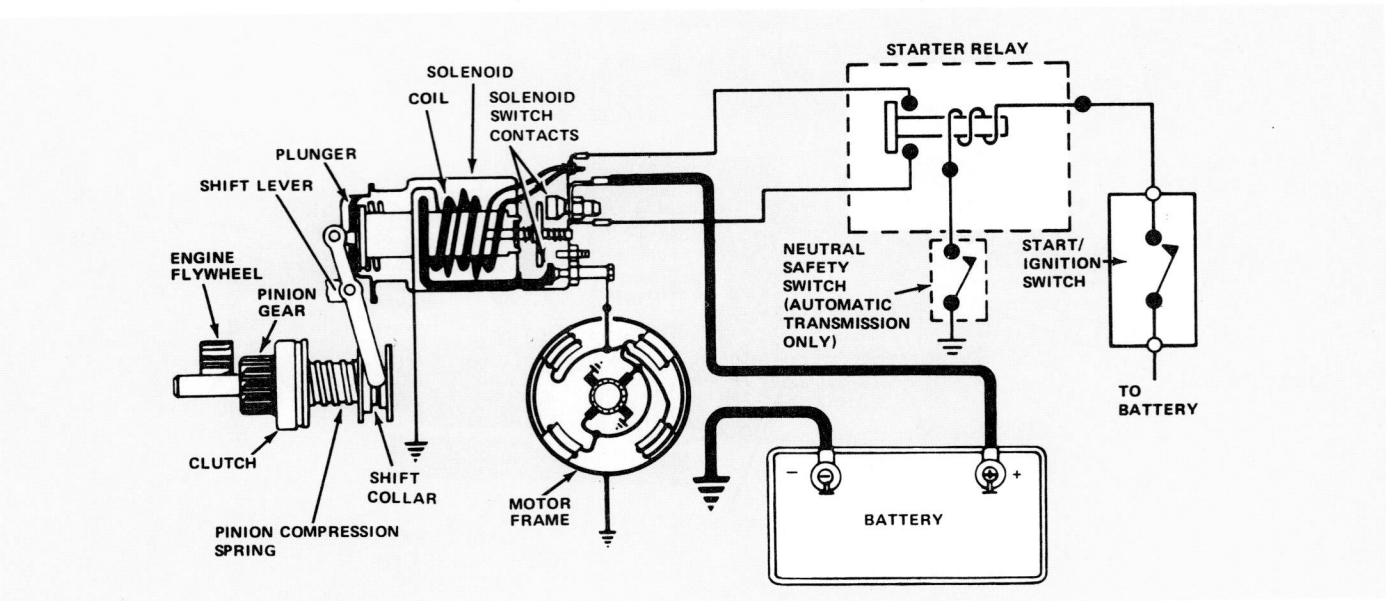

Fig. 28-22. Complete starting system circuit. This circuit has a starter relay. The relay further decreases amount of current flowing through ignition switch. Also note how relay winding is wired to neutral safety switch. (AMC)

switch is closed (connected). Current can flow to the starter when the ignition switch is turned.

STARTER RELAY

As you learned in the chapter on electricity and electronics, a *relay* is a device that opens or closes one circuit by responding to an electrical signal from another circuit. Some starting systems use a relay between the ignition switch and the starter solenoid.

A *starter relay* uses a small current flow from the ignition switch to control a slightly larger current flow to the starter solenoid. This further reduces the load on the ignition key switch.

Starter relay operation

A starter relay circuit is shown in Fig. 28-21. When the ignition switch is turned to start, current flows into the relay. This closes the relay contacts. The contacts complete the circuit to the solenoid windings and the starting system operates.

When the key is released, the relay opens. This stops the solenoid current to disengage the starting motor.

KNOW THESE TERMS

Magnetic field, Winding, Pole piece, Commutator, Brushes, Armature, Field windings, Pinion gear, Overrunning clutch, Starter solenoid, Commutator end frame, Field frame, Drive housing, Movable pole shoe, Starter mounted solenoid, Reduction starter, Neutral safety switch, Starter relay.

REVIEW QUESTIONS

1. List and describe the four major parts of a starting system.
2. The _____ _____ converts electrical energy from the battery into mechanical or rotating energy to crank the engine.
3. Like charges (fields) attract each other and unlike charges (fields) repel each other. True or False?
4. The _____ serves as a sliding electrical connection between the motor windings and the brushes.
5. Which of the following is NOT part of a starting motor?
   a. Armature.
   b. Field winding.
   c. Commutator.
   d. Slip ring.
6. What is the function of the starter pinion gear?
7. What would happen if the starting motor did NOT have an overrunning clutch (gear locked to armature shaft)?
8. The _____ _____ is a high current relay that completes the circuit between the battery and the starting motor.
9. List three functions of a starter solenoid.
10. List and explain the five major parts of a starting motor.
11. Describe the two main types of starting motors.
12. Why is a reduction starting motor sometimes used?
13. Which of the following is NOT a type of internal starting motor circuit?
    a. Parallel wound.
    b. Series wound.
    c. Shunt wound.
    d. Compound wound.
14. The _____ _____ _____ keeps the engine from cranking unless the shift selector is in neutral or park.

ACTIVITIES FOR CHAPTER 28

1. If possible, obtain an unserviceable starter motor from a shop or junk yard. Carefully disassemble and clean the components. Mount and label them for a classroom display.
2. Find out the advantages and disadvantages of installing a rebuilt starter (rather than a new one) in a vehicle. Report to the class.

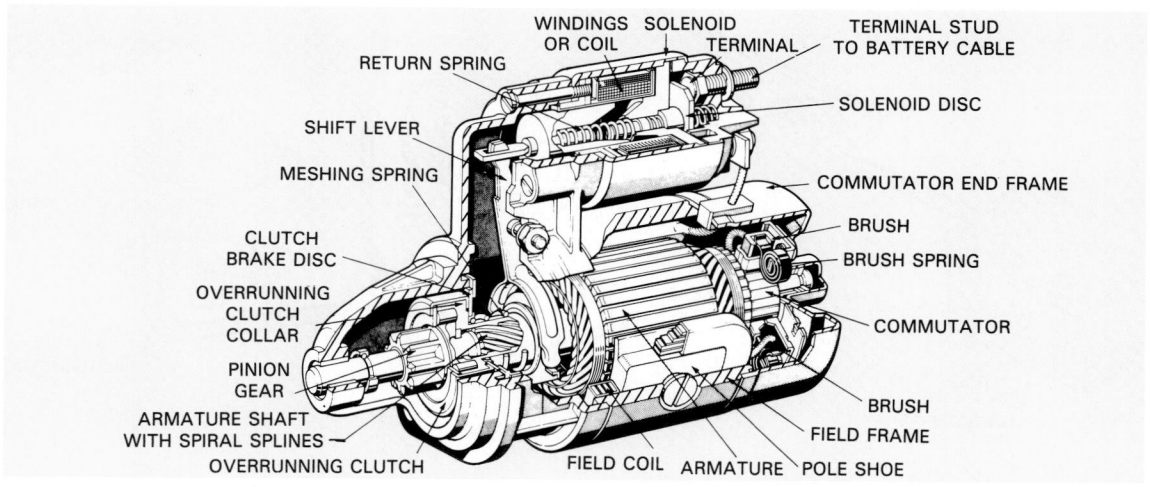

Cutaway view of modern starting motor. Can you explain the function of each part? (Robert Bosch)

Starting System Testing and Repair

After studying this chapter, you will be able to:
- [ ] Diagnose common starting system troubles.
- [ ] Make orderly starting system tests.
- [ ] Remove and replace a starting motor.
- [ ] Explain typical procedures for a starting motor rebuild.
- [ ] Adjust a neutral safety switch.
- [ ] Describe safety practices to follow when testing or repairing a starting system.

This chapter introduces the steps for testing and repairing common starting system problems. It begins by explaining on-car diagnosis and testing. Then, the service of each component is detailed. You will learn about the symptoms a faulty starting component will produce before learning how to check each component. Finally, procedures for part removal, repair, and replacement are summarized.

STARTING SYSTEM DIAGNOSIS

A starting system is easier to work on than the car's other electrical systems. It only has about five major components that cause problems.

Fig. 29-1 shows the most common starting system troubles. If any of these parts have high resistance, lower than normal resistance, damage, or wear, the engine may not crank normally.

Common starting system problems

In a *no-crank problem,* the engine crankshaft does NOT rotate properly with the ignition key at start. The most common causes are a dead battery, poor electrical connection, or faulty system component.

A *slow cranking condition* occurs when the engine crankshaft rotates at lower than normal speed. It is usually caused by the same kind of faults producing

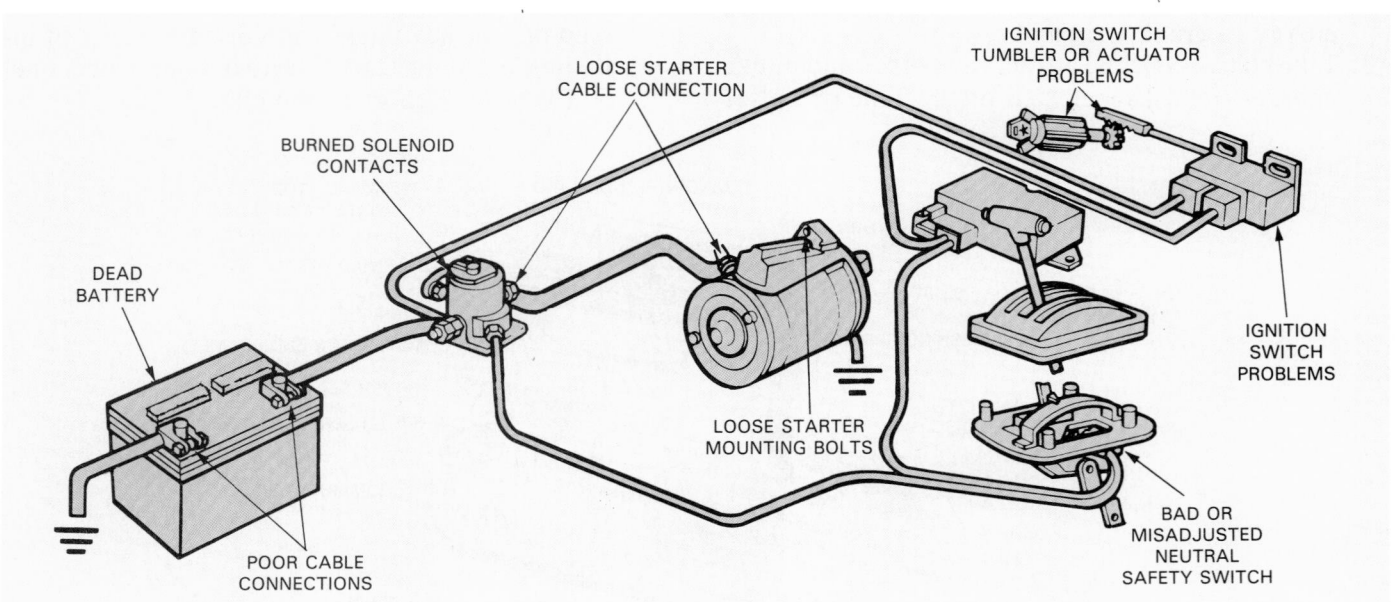

Fig. 29-1. During initial inspection, check for these kinds of starting system troubles. A loose connection, discharged battery, or any number of other problems could keep engine from cranking.

a no-crank problem.

A *buzzing* or *clicking sound* from the solenoid, without cranking, is commonly due to a discharged battery or poor battery cable connections. Low current flow is causing the solenoid plunger to rapidly kick in and out, making a clattering sound.

A *single click sound,* without cranking, may point to a bad starting motor, burned solenoid contacts, dead battery, or engine mechanical problems. The click is usually the solenoid closing or the pinion gear contacting the flywheel gear.

A *humming sound,* after momentary engine cranking, may be due to a bad starter overrunning clutch or worn pinion gear unit. Pinion gear wear can make the gear disengage from the flywheel gear too soon. This can let the motor armature spin rapidly, with a humming sound.

A *metallic grinding noise* may be caused by broken flywheel teeth or pinion gear teeth wear. The grinding may be the gears clashing against each other.

Normal *cranking, without starting,* is usually NOT caused by the starting system. There may be trouble in the fuel or ignition systems. With a diesel engine, check engine cranking speed. If cranking rpm is low, the diesel may not start.

Sometimes the starting solenoid feeds current to the ignition system after engine starting. If the engine *starts and then dies* (stops running) as the ignition key is released, check voltage from the solenoid to the ignition system. You could have an open wire or connection in the solenoid circuit. A defective ignition switch or wiring problem are other possible causes.

Starting headlight test

A *starting headlight test* will quickly indicate the causes of trouble in a starting system. Turn the headlights ON and try to start the engine. Note any sounds and watch the brightness of the headlights.

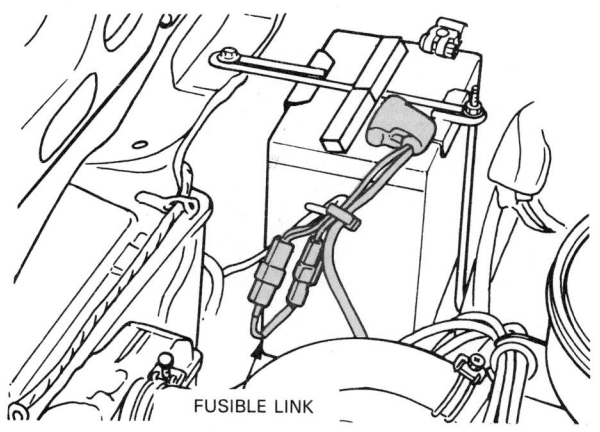

Fig. 29-2. *The battery and its cables are most common cause of improper cranking. Note fusible link attached to positive battery cable. It can burn in half during a short to protect electrical system. If major components (lights, horn, starting system) are dead, check fusible link. (Mazda)*

No cranking with *no headlights* points to a dead battery or open in the electrical system. The battery connections may be bad. The fusible link may be blown, Fig. 29-2. A main feed wire to the fuse box could also be broken or disconnected.

If the *lights go out* when cranking, the battery may be weak. The starting motor may be shorted. The engine could also be dragging from mechanical problems. Dimming headlights indicate heavy current draw or poor current supply from the battery.

If the *lights stay bright* without proper cranking, a high resistance or open in the starting circuit is likely. The problem could be in the ignition switch, wiring, solenoid, starter cable connections, or relay.

Depending upon what the headlights and starter do when testing, you can decide what further tests are needed.

Use service manual troubleshooting charts

Service manual troubleshooting charts should be used when causes are hard to find. Manual charts are designed for the exact circuit and will often reduce the list of causes.

CHECK THE BATTERY FIRST

A *dead* or *discharged battery* is one of the most common reasons the starting system fails to crank the engine properly. A starting motor draws several times the amount of current (over 200 amps) of any other electrical component. A discharged or poorly connected battery can operate the lights, but may NOT have enough power to operate the starting motor.

If needed, load-test the battery as described in the chapter on battery service. Make sure the battery is good and fully charged. A starting motor will NOT function without a fully charged and well-connected battery.

STARTER CURRENT DRAW TEST

A *starter current draw test* measures the number of amps used by the starting system. It will quickly tell you about the condition of the starting motor and other system parts. If current draw is higher or lower than specs, there is a problem.

To do a starter current draw test, connect meters to measure battery voltage and current flow out of the battery. Two testing methods are shown in Figs. 29-3 and 29-4. A load tester may also be used.

To keep the engine from starting during the test, disconnect the coil supply wire or ground the coil wire. Look at Fig. 29-5. With a diesel engine, disable the injection system. You may have to unhook the fuel shut-off solenoid. Check a shop manual for details.

WARNING! Do NOT crank the engine for more than 15-30 seconds or starter damage may result. If cranked too long, the starter could overheat. Allow the

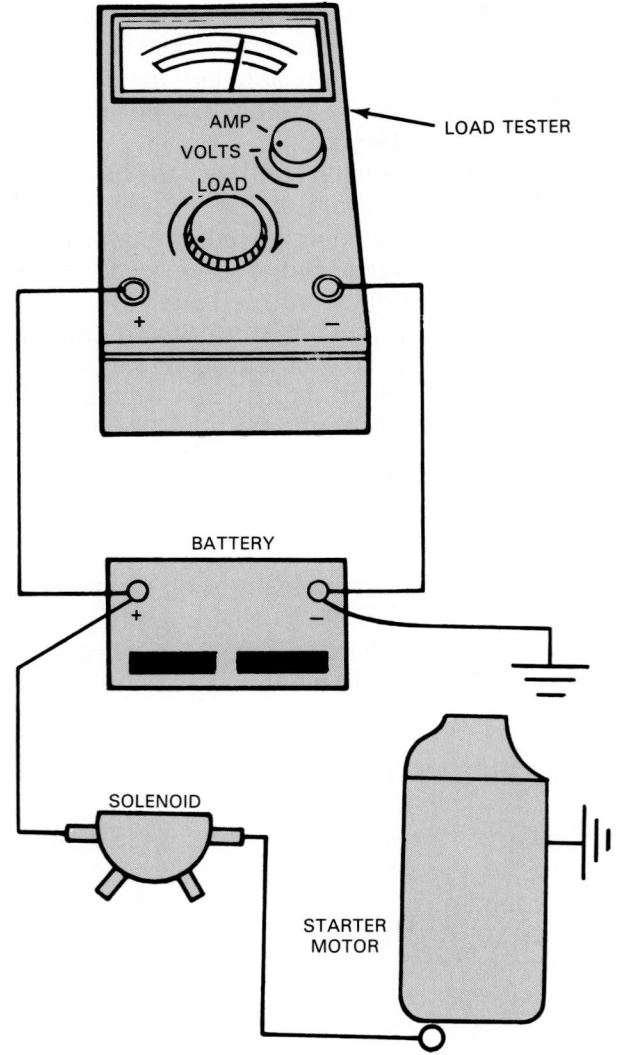

Fig. 29-3. Battery load tester can be used to check starter current draw. Crank engine and note voltage reading. Then, load battery to obtain same voltage. This will equal current draw by starting motor. (AMC)

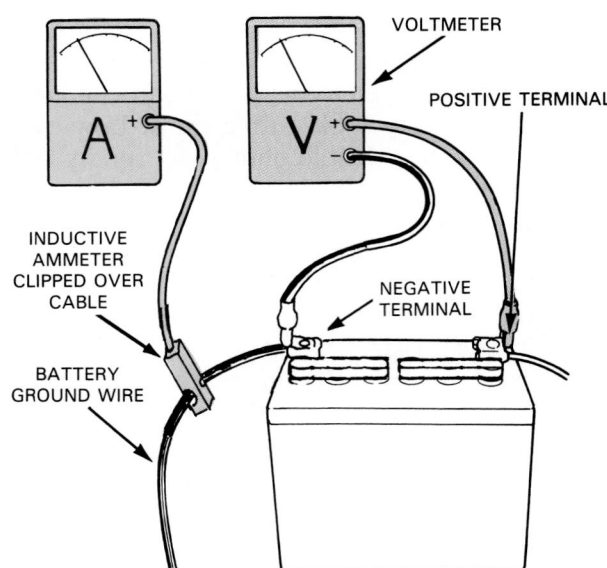

Fig. 29-4. A voltmeter and an ammeter can also be used to measure starter current draw. Voltmeter reading is needed to compare different battery conditions. If current draw is not within specs, there are starting system troubles. (Honda)

starter to cool for a few minutes if more cranking time is needed.

Crank the engine and note the voltage and current readings. If they are not within specs, something is wrong in the starting system or engine. Further tests would be needed. Fig. 29-6 gives the average current draw values for various engine sizes.

STARTING SYSTEM VOLTAGE DROP TESTS

Voltage drop tests will quickly locate a part with higher than normal resistance. They provide an easy way of checking circuit condition. You do NOT have to disconnect wires and components to check internal resistances (voltage drops).

Insulated circuit resistance test

An *insulated circuit resistance test* checks all parts

between the battery positive and the starting motor for excess resistance. Fig. 29-7A shows the basic connections for this test. Touch your voltmeter probes on the battery positive terminal and the starting motor input terminal.

Disable the ignition or injection system. Then crank the engine. The voltmeter should not read over about .2 to .5 volts. If voltage drop is greater, something has excessive resistance. There may be a loose electrical connection, burned or pitted solenoid contact, or other problem. Test each part individually.

Starter ground circuit test

A *starter ground circuit test* checks the circuit between the starting motor ground and the negative bat-

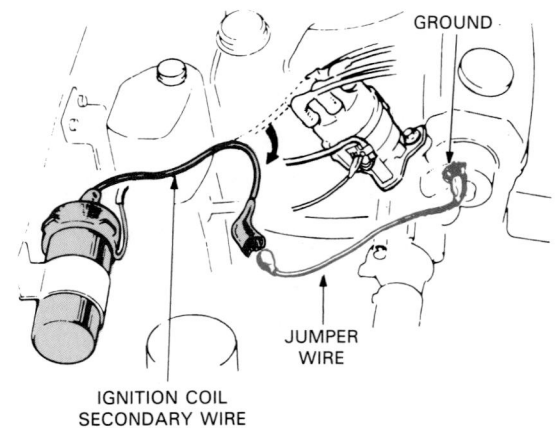

Fig. 29-5. To keep engine from running during starter current draw test, disable the ignition system. Ground coil wire as shown. You need to disconnect feed wire to coil if coil is part of distributor. With a diesel, disable injection system. (Honda)

ENGINE DISPLACEMENT	12-VOLT SYSTEM MAX. CURRENT
Most 4-6 Cylinders	125-175 Amps Max.
Under 300 C.I.D.	150-200 Amps Max.
300 C.I.D. or Over	175-250 Amps Max.

CRANKING CIRCUIT TROUBLESHOOTING CHART

Cranking Voltage	Cranking Amps	Possible Problem
Voltage Within Specs	Current Within Specs	System OK
Voltage OK	Current Low Engine Cranks Slowly	Starter Circuit Connections Faulty
Voltage Low	Current Low Engine Cranks Slowly	Battery Low
Voltage Low	Current High	Starter Motor Faulty

Fig. 29-6. Chart shows typical current draw values for different engine sizes. Ignore initial readings until engine has cranked for a few seconds. Then current draw will stabilize. Study meter readings and trouble chart. (Marquette)

tery terminal. Look at Fig. 29-7B.

Touch the voltmeter prods to the battery negative terminal and the starter end frame. Crank the engine and note the meter reading.

If higher than around .2 to .5 volt, check the voltage drop across the negative battery cable. The engine may not be grounded properly. Clean, tighten, or replace the cable if needed.

BATTERY CABLE PROBLEMS

A *battery cable problem* can produce symptoms similar to a dead battery, bad solenoid, or weak star-

ting motor. If the cables do NOT allow enough current flow, the starter will turn slowly or not at all.

Testing battery cables

To test the battery or starter cables, connect a voltmeter to each cable and perform a voltage drop test. See Fig. 29-8A. If any cable shows a high voltage drop during cranking, clean and tighten its connections. Then retest the cable. If still high (above .2 to .3 volts), replace the cable.

Replacing battery cables

When replacing battery cables, make sure the new cables are the same as the old ones. Compare cable length and diameter. Cables with lead terminals are better than ones with steel ends. The soft lead will conform to the shape of the battery terminal easier.

CAUTION! NEVER remove starting system parts without disconnecting the battery. The engine could be cranked over or an electrical fire could result if wires are shorted.

When tightening the connections on the ends of battery or starter cables, only snug down the fasteners. Many of the threaded studs, bolts, and nuts are made of soft lead or brass. They can strip and break easily.

STARTER SOLENOID SERVICE

A *bad starter solenoid* can cause a range of symptoms: click with no cranking, no cranking with no click, or slow cranking. It can also keep the engine or starting motor from shutting off.

Usually, the large disc-shaped contact will burn and pit. The disc can develop high resistance that blocks current flow to the starter.

An open or shorted solenoid winding can keep the contact disc from closing. No click will occur and the engine will not crank.

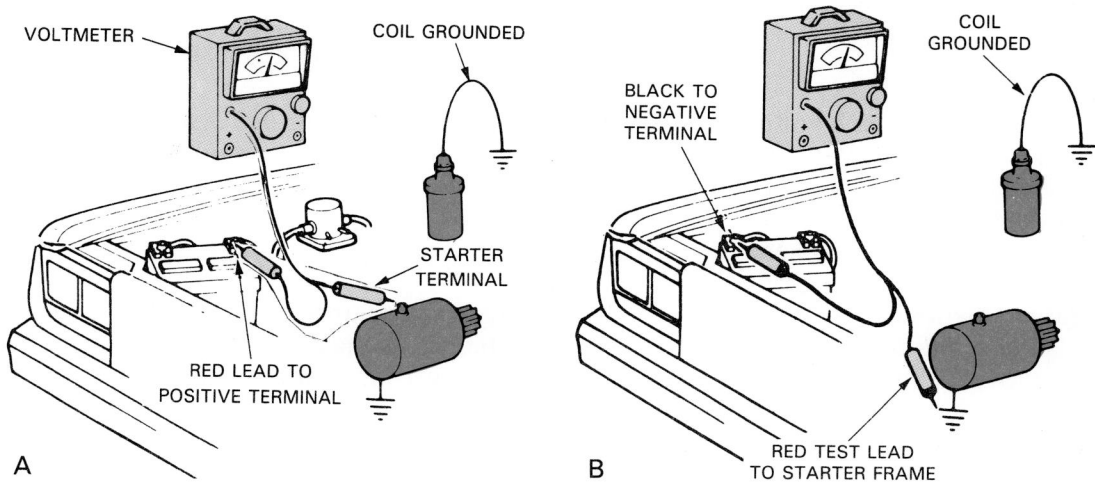

Fig. 29-7. Voltage drop tests are quick way of checking circuit resistance without disconnecting wires. A — This voltmeter connection would test the group of parts between battery and starting motor. B — This test connection would check starter ground circuit. (AMC)

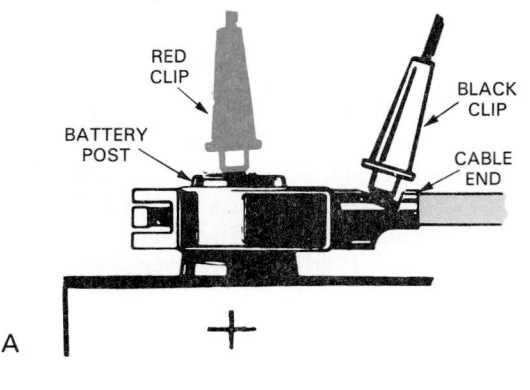

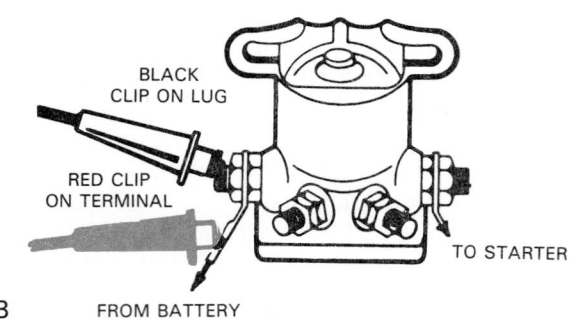

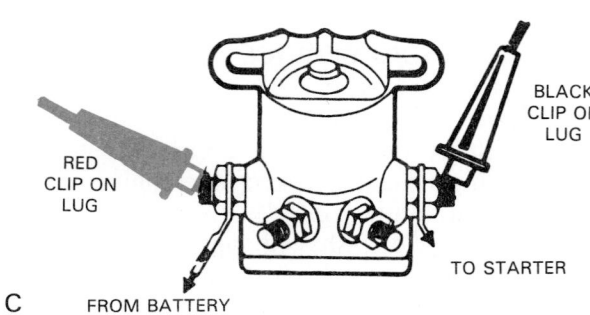

Fig. 29-8. Voltage drop measurements will also check individual components. A — Checking battery terminals for corrosion and high resistance. B — Check solenoid lug-to-cable connection for high resistance. C — Checking condition of disc contact and terminals in solenoid. (Marquette)

Testing starter solenoid

To test the solenoid, connect a voltmeter as shown in Fig. 29-8B and C. This will measure the voltage drop and resistance of the solenoid lugs and contacts. Crank the engine and note the voltmeter reading. If above .2-.3 volts, repair or replace the solenoid.

Replacing starter solenoid

To replace a solenoid mounted away from the starter, simply remove the cables and wires. Unbolt the solenoid from the fenderwell and install the new one.

If the solenoid is starter-mounted, the starter must be removed from the engine. Then, the solenoid is unscrewed from the starting motor and replaced.

The procedures for removing, assembling, and installing a starter are covered later.

IGNITION SWITCH SERVICE

A *bad ignition switch* (starter feed section of switch) can keep the starter solenoid from working. It can also keep the solenoid from releasing. The contacts in the ignition switch can wear or burn, causing either an open (no cranking problem) or short (engine cranks all the time).

Testing ignition switch

To test ignition switch with a no crank problem, touch a test light to the starter solenoid START (S) terminal. If the ignition switch is good, the test light will glow when the key is turned to start the engine. The test light should go out when the key is released.

If the test light on the solenoid does NOT glow, either a wire in the ignition switch circuit is open or the ignition switch is defective. Test the wires coming out of the ignition switch to eliminate the possibility of a bad wire.

If the test light touched to the start terminal on the solenoid glows in both the start and run position, the ignition switch is probably shorted. The engine would crank all the time.

More ignition switch service information

Again, these are simplified tests. You will need to use your own judgement and a service manual to perform more detailed and involved tests.

For more information on ignition switch service, refer to Chapter 33.

STARTER RELAY SERVICE

A *bad starter relay* will keep power from the starter solenoid. This will prevent engine cranking. The winding or the contact points in the relay could be faulty.

To test a starter relay, use a test light to check for voltage going into and coming out of the relay terminals. Refer to a wiring diagram for test points. Replace the relay if needed.

NEUTRAL SAFETY SWITCH SERVICE

A *misadjusted* or *bad neutral safety switch* can also keep the engine from cranking when the key is turned to start. If the neutral safety switch is open, current cannot flow from the ignition switch to the starter solenoid.

Checking neutral safety switch action

Before testing the switch, move the transmission gear shift lever into various positions while trying to start the engine. The switch may close, letting the starter operate. If the starter begins to work, the neutral safety switch may only need adjustment.

Adjusting neutral safety switch

To adjust a neutral safety switch, loosen the fasteners

holding the switch. The switch may be located on the steering column, shift lever, or on the transmission.

With the switch loosened, place the shift selector into park (P). Then, while holding the ignition switch to START, slide the neutral switch on its mount until the engine cranks. Without moving the switch, tighten its hold-down screws. This should make the engine start only with the shift lever in park or neutral. Check operation after adjustment.

Testing neutral safety switch

To test a neutral safety switch, touch a 12-volt test light to the switch output wire connection while moving the transmission shift lever. The light should glow as the shift lever is slid into PARK and NEUTRAL. The test light should NOT glow when the transmission is in all other positions.

If not working properly, check the mechanism that operates the neutral safety switch. There should be a prong or other device that actuates the neutral safety switch. If the problem is in the switch, remove, replace, and adjust it.

STARTER SERVICE

A *faulty starting motor* can cause a wide range of symptoms: slow cranking, no cranking, overheating of starter cables, and abnormal noises while cranking. If the battery, cables, solenoid, and other starting system parts are good but the engine does not crank properly, the starter may be bad.

A current draw test and other tests will suggest when the starter motor should be removed for further inspection and testing.

Fig. 29-9 shows an exploded view of a typical starter. Study the types of problems that can occur and require a motor rebuild.

Starting motor rebuild

A *starting motor rebuild* typically involves:
1. Removal and disassembly of starting motor.
2. Cleaning and inspection for part wear or damage.
3. Replacement of brushes, bushings, and any other worn or damaged parts.
4. Polishing or turning of commutator.

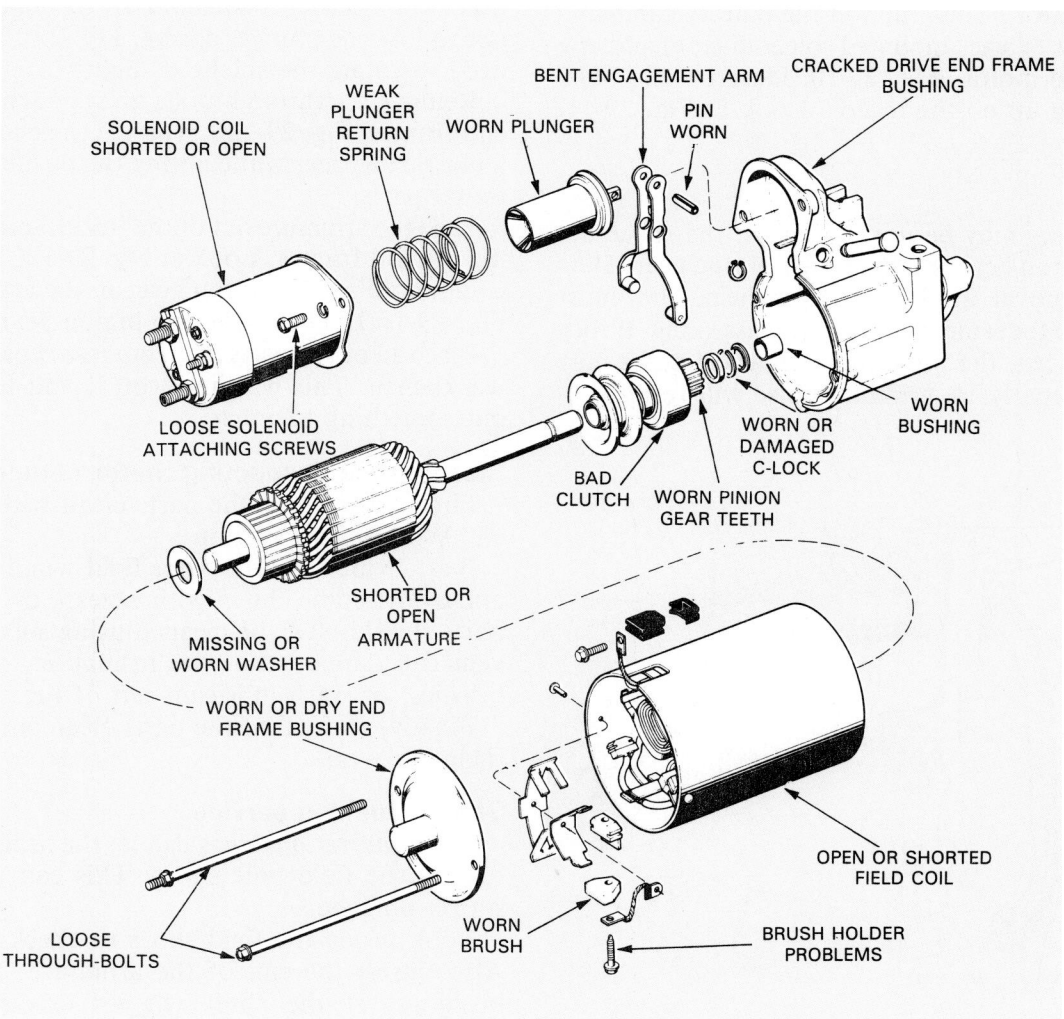

Fig. 29-9. Study types of problems requiring starting motor repairs.

5. Lubrication, reassembly, testing, and installation of starting motor.

Many shops do NOT rebuild starting motors. They purchase and install a new or factory rebuilt unit. The cost of labor may be too high to make in-shop rebuilding economical. Also, the factory rebuilt unit will have a limited warranty.

Note! When the starter must be repaired, you may only need to disassemble a section of the starter.

For example, a worn pinion gear assembly can make the gear retract. The clutch will freewheel without proper engine cranking. The pinion gear assembly can be replaced by removing only the drive end frame and a C-lock. The brushes and other end of the motor can be left together.

Starting motor removal

Before deciding to remove the starting motor, inspect it closely for problems. Check that the starter-to-engine bolts are tight. Loose starter bolts can upset motor operation by causing a poor ground or incorrect pinion gear meshing. Make sure all wires on the motor and solenoid are tight.

To remove the starting motor, first DISCONNECT THE BATTERY. Then, unbolt the battery cable and solenoid wires (starter-mounted solenoid type) and any braces on the motor, Fig. 29-10. Unscrew the bolts while holding up on the motor. Look at Fig. 29-11.

CAUTION! Be careful not to drop the starting motor during removal. It is heavy enough to cause injury if it falls.

Starter shims may be used to adjust the space between the pinion gear and the flywheel ring gear. During starter removal, always check for them. They must be returned to the same place during reassembly. If they are not replaced, the pinion and flywheel gears may not mesh properly. A grinding noise will result.

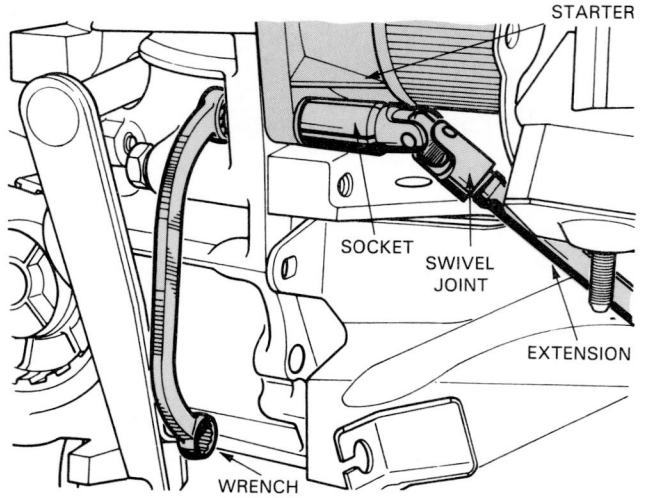

Fig. 29-10. When starting motor fasteners are hard to reach, a swivel, extension, and ratchet may help. (Renault)

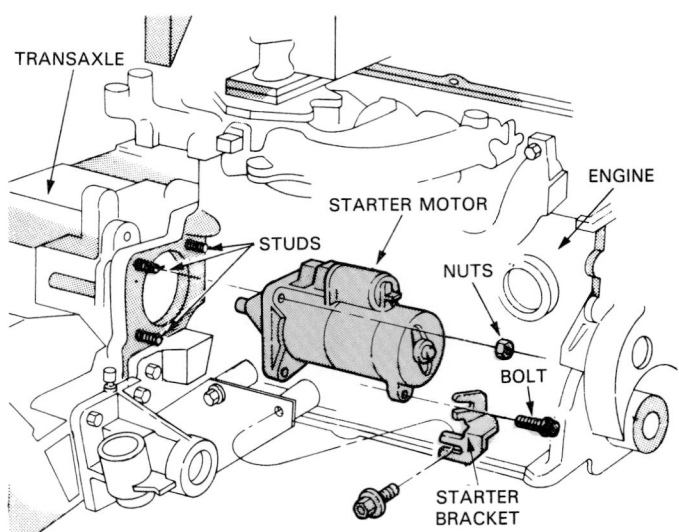

Fig. 29-11. To repair starter, remove fasteners, wires, and any brackets or heat shields. Hold starter firmly because it is fairly heavy. (Chrysler)

Starter disassembly

If the starter has a solenoid, remove the fasteners that hold it. Pull the solenoid off the motor using care not to lose the plunger spring, Fig. 29-12A. You may need to rotate the solenoid slightly.

Remove the through-bolts after punch-marking the end frames, Fig. 29-12B. Tap off the end frames with a plastic hammer while noting the positions of the internal parts.

Slide the armature out of the field frame after removing the end frames. Look at Fig. 29-12C. Remove the C-clip holding the pinion gear on the armature shaft, Fig. 29-12D. Then slide the pinion gear off.

Place all of the parts in an organized pattern on your workbench. This will help you if you forget how to put something together.

Cleaning and inspecting motor components

First, blow all of the parts clean with compressed air. Wear eye protection.

Next, wipe the armature, field windings, brushes, and overrunning clutch with a clean, dry cloth. These parts should NOT be cleaned using solvent. The solvent can damage the wire insulation, soak into the brushes, or wash lubricant out of the clutch.

Finally, with all of the parts clean and dry, inspect them for wear.

Starter bushing service

Worn starter bushings can let the armature drag or rub on the field pole shoes. This can cause serious starter damage.

Look inside the field shoes to check for rubbing. Also, insert the end of the armature shaft into the bushings. If the shaft wiggles excessively in the bushings, replace them. Press out the old bushings and press in new ones.

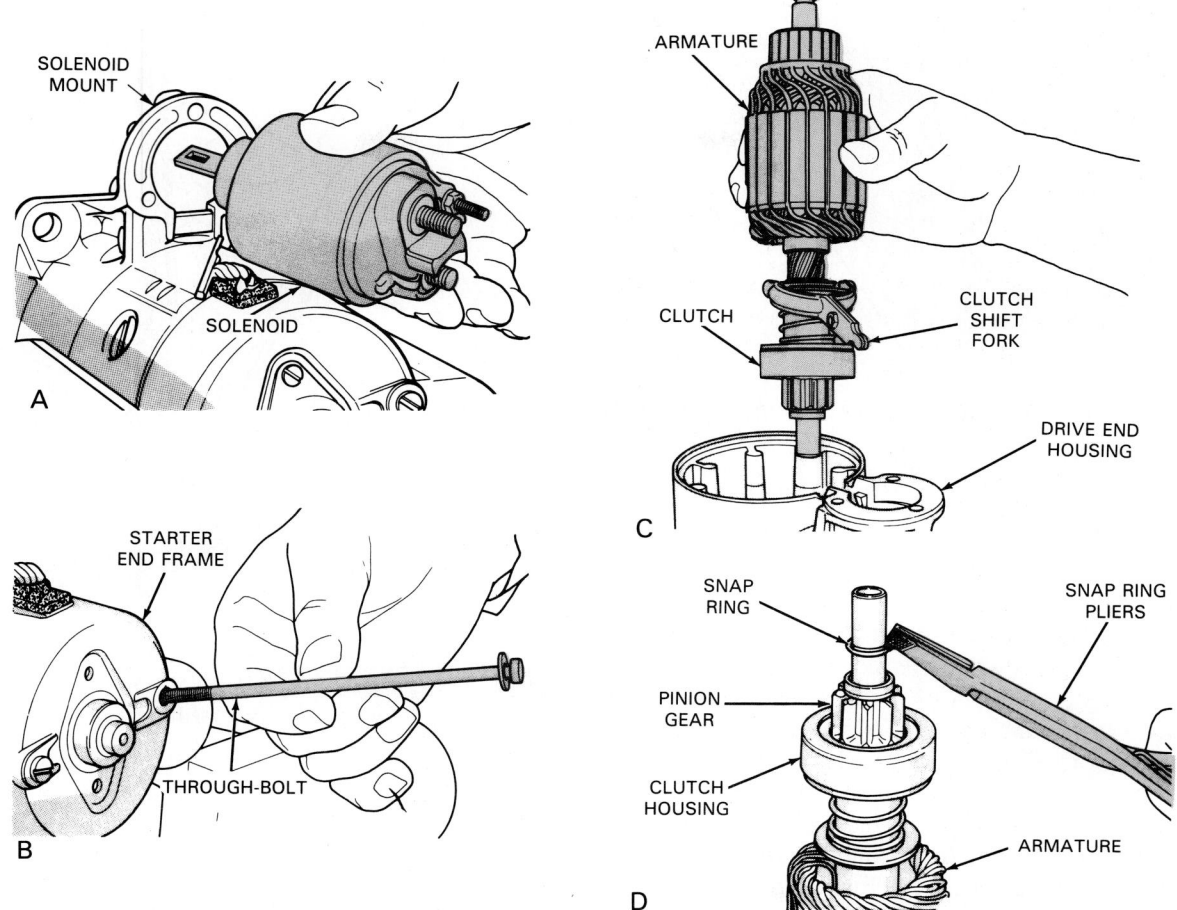

Fig. 29-12. Basic steps for starter disassembly. A — If necessary, remove solenoid. B — Unscrew and remove through-bolts. Mark end housing for alignment. C — Remove end frames and armature. D — To remove pinion gear, use snap ring pliers to open and slide off clip on shaft. (Chrysler)

Starter brush service

Check for *worn starter brushes* which can reduce starter torque or cause excessive starter current draw. As shown in Fig. 29-13A, some manufacturers recommend a minimum height for the brushes. If worn shorter than specs, the brushes must be replaced.

The brush wire leads are usually soldered in place. If so, a soldering gun and rosin core (not acid core) solder must be used to replace the brushes. Also, check the brush holder for shorts to ground, Fig. 29-13B.

Armature service

Inspect the armature for wear or damage. Look for signs of burning or overheating on the windings and commutator. If the armature has been rubbing on a field pole shoe, the shaft may be bent. Also, check the ends of the shaft for wear or burrs.

To check for an *armature short circuit,* mount the armature on a *growler* (armature tester). This is shown in Fig. 29-14.

After reading the instructions for the growler, turn on the power. Hold a thin strip of metal or hacksaw

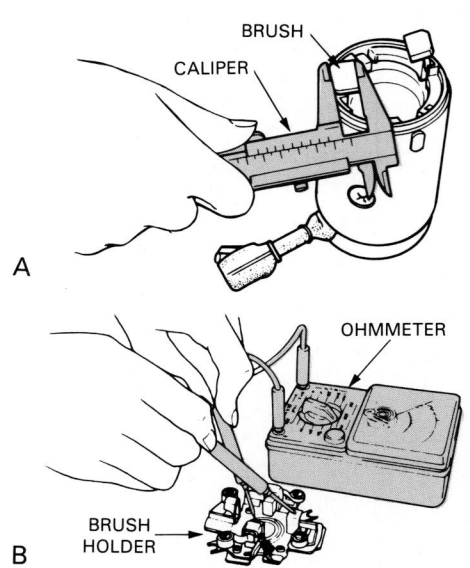

Fig. 29-13. A — Brushes must not be worn. Measure brush length and compare to specs. Replace them if needed. B — Ohmmeter can be used to check for brush holder shorts. Holder must be insulated. Check in service manual for exact directions. (Subaru)

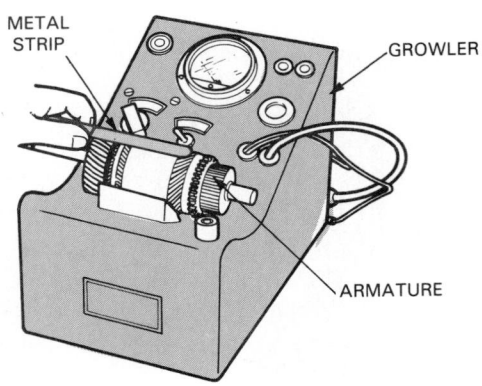

Fig. 29-14. Growler will quickly check for armature shorts. Metal strip will vibrate when moved over shorted winding. (Mazda)

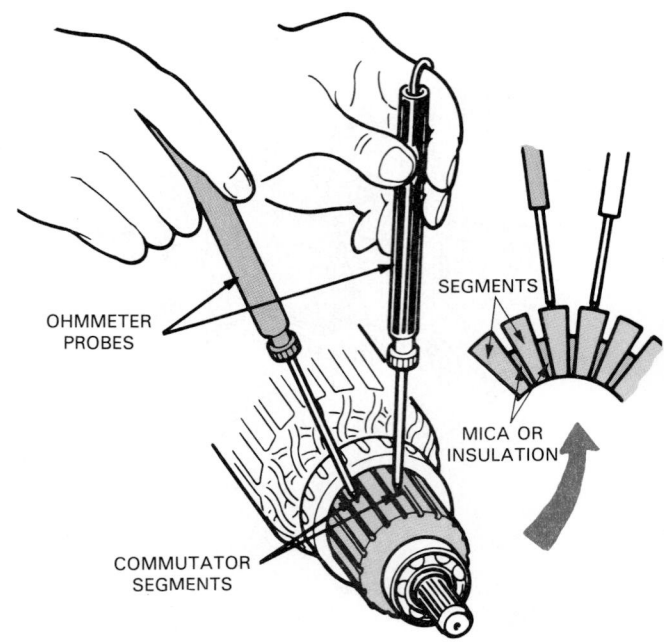

Fig. 29-15. An ohmmeter is used to check armature continuity. If open or infinite resistance exists between any commutator segment, replace armature. (Honda)

blade next to the armature while rotating the armature in the growler.

With a shorted armature, the metal strip or hacksaw blade will VIBRATE when passed over the shorted leg of the windings.

To check *armature continuity,* do an *open circuit test.* You can sometimes use a growler (type with meter) or an ohmmeter. Follow the directions provided with the growler.

When using an ohmmeter, touch the meter prods to each commutator segment, as in Fig. 29-15. If the meter reads infinite resistance on any segment, that segment winding is open. The armature must be replaced.

You should also check for an *armature ground* (short from winding to shaft or core). This test is illustrated in Fig. 29-16.

Touch the ohmmeter prods on the armature coil core and the commutator segments. Repeat this test on the commutator segments and armature shaft. If there is

continuity (low resistance), then the armature is grounded and must be replaced.

If the windings are in good condition, the commutator should be cleaned using very fine sandpaper, not emery cloth. Sand it as shown in Fig. 29-17C.

If the commutator is badly worn, it should be turned (machined) on a lathe. See Fig. 29-17. Then, the mica (insulation) between each commutator segment must usually be undercut. A special tool or a hacksaw blade can be used to cut the mica lower than the surface of the segments.

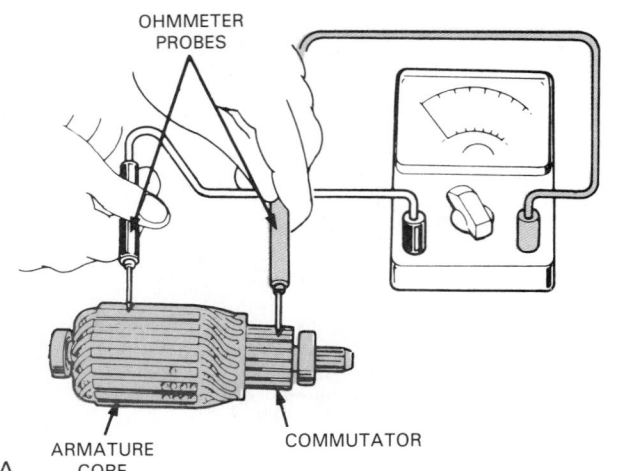

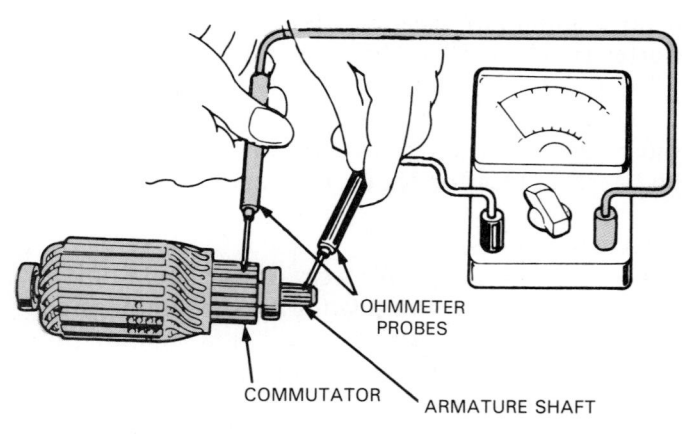

Fig. 29-16. Checking for armature shorts with an ohmmeter. A — Meter connection for checking core-to-armature shorts. B — Meter connection for checking shaft-to-commutator shorts. Low ohms reading indicates a short. If shorted, replace armature. (Honda)

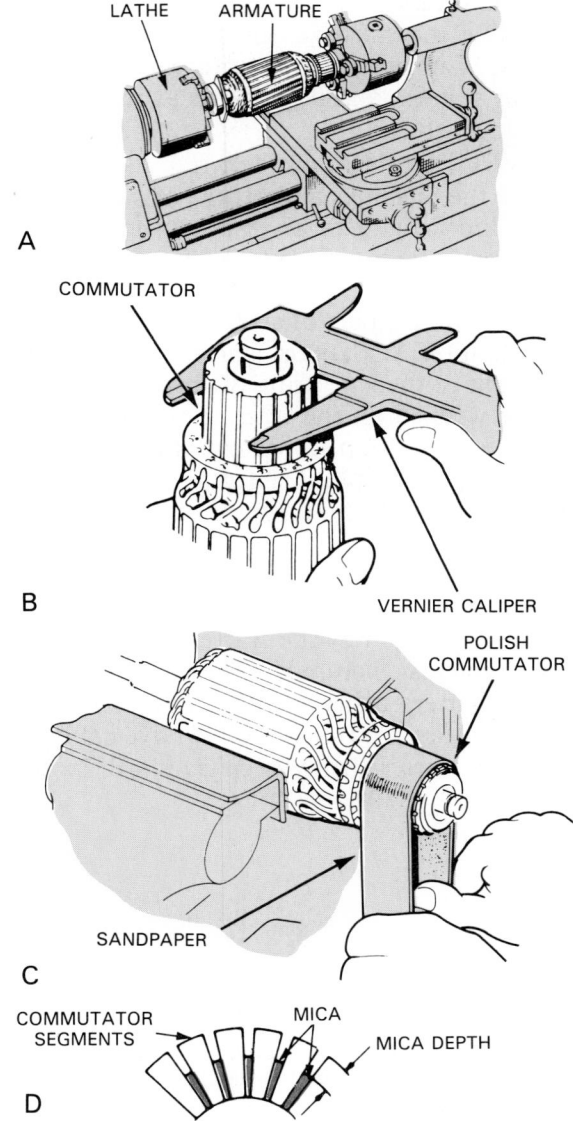

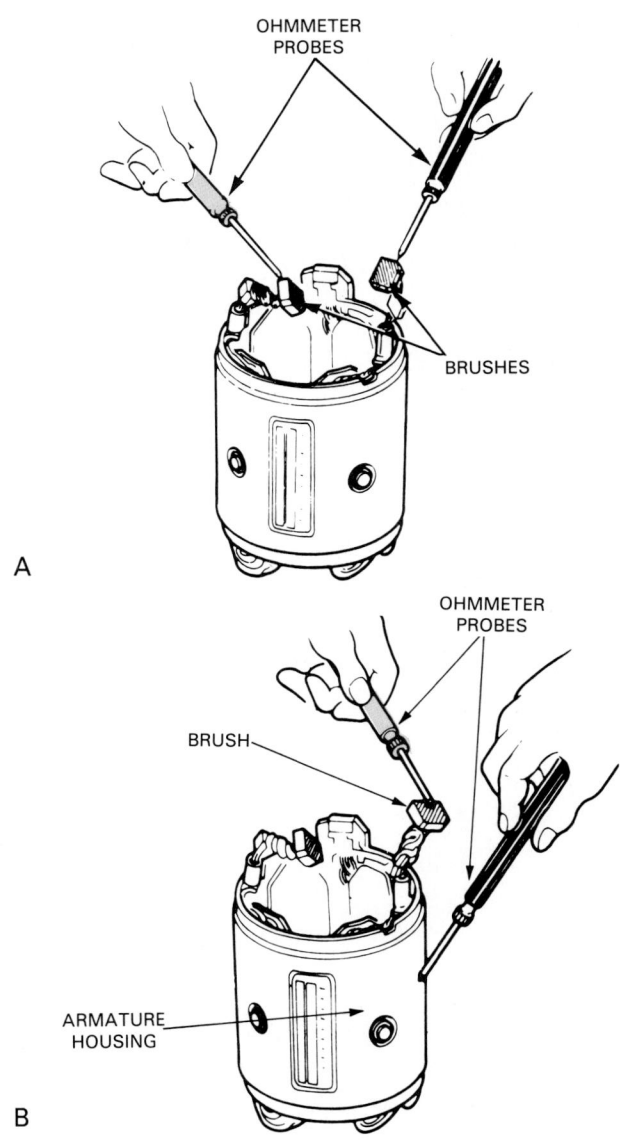

does not glow, or the meter reads infinite (maximum) resistance, the field windings are open (broken) and must be replaced.

To test for *grounded field coils* (winding shorted to frame or other starter component), touch the test light or ohmmeter prods across the field coil and ground. Look at Fig. 29-18.

The light should NOT glow or the meter should read infinite resistance. If the starter has a shunt winding, disconnect it before making the test. If a winding is grounded, it must be replaced.

Overrunning clutch (pinion gear) service

Normally, the overrunning clutch or pinion gear assembly is replaced anytime the starting motor is

Fig. 29-17. Armature service. A — If badly scored, turn commutator on a lathe. B — Make sure commutator diameter is within minimum specs. C — Smooth and clean commutator before starter reassembly. D — If recommended, undercut mica with a hacksaw blade or special cutting tool. Mica may need to be cut until slightly below commutator surface. Check a service manual for details. (Honda)

Also check the armature shaft. If there are any burrs at the lock ring groove, file them off.

Field coil service

Inspect the field windings inside the starter frame. Look for signs of physical damage or burning.

To test for *open field coils,* use a test light (battery powered type) or an ohmmeter. Look at Fig. 29-18.

Touch the test prods to wires or brushes that connect to the field windings. This connection may vary, with some starters, so check in a manual.

If the test light *glows,* or the ohmmeter reads zero, the field windings are NOT open. When the test light

Fig. 29-18. Ohmmeter being used to check for field problems. A — There should be continuity between these brushes. Meter should read low ohms. B — There should be no continuity between field coil and frame. If meter reads low ohms, replace field coil. (Honda)

disassembled. The pinion gear is subjected to extreme wear and tear when engaged and disengaged from the engine flywheel. It is usually wise to replace the pinion gear during starter service.

If the pinion gear is to be used over, check the ends of the gear teeth for wear. See Fig. 29-19. Also, check the action of the overrunning clutch. It should let the gear turn freely in one direction but lock the gear in the other direction.

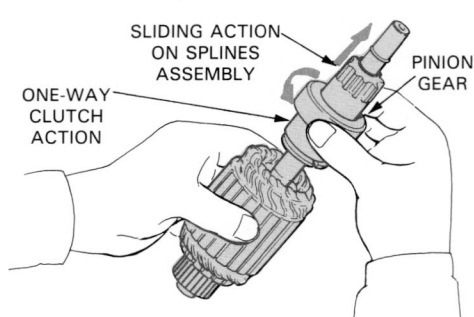

Fig. 29-19. Checking starter pinion gear action. Overrunning clutch should turn freely in one direction. It should lock in other direction. Unit should also slide freely on armature shaft splines. Most mechanics install new pinion gear during starter service. (Honda)

Starter reassembly

Reassemble the starter using the reverse order of disassembly. Lubricate the armature shaft bushings, pinion gear splines, and other parts as recommended by the manufacturer.

WARNING! Do NOT use too much oil or grease to lubricate the bushings and other parts of a starting motor. If lubricant gets on the brushes and commutator, starter service life and starter power will be reduced.

The only difficult part of starter reassembly can be brush installation. With many starters, the brushes can be locked out of the way using the brush springs. The springs are wedged on the sides of the brushes. This will hold the brushes up so you can slide the armature and commutator into place. Then, the brushes may be pushed down and snapped into place on the commutator.

Study Figs. 29-20 and 29-21. They show exploded views of modern starting motors.

After reassembly, test the starter before mounting it on the engine. As pictured in Fig. 29-22, connect the starter to a battery using jumper cables. Connect the positive cable first and then the negative cable. Hold or clamp the starter firmly because it will lurch and rotate when energized.

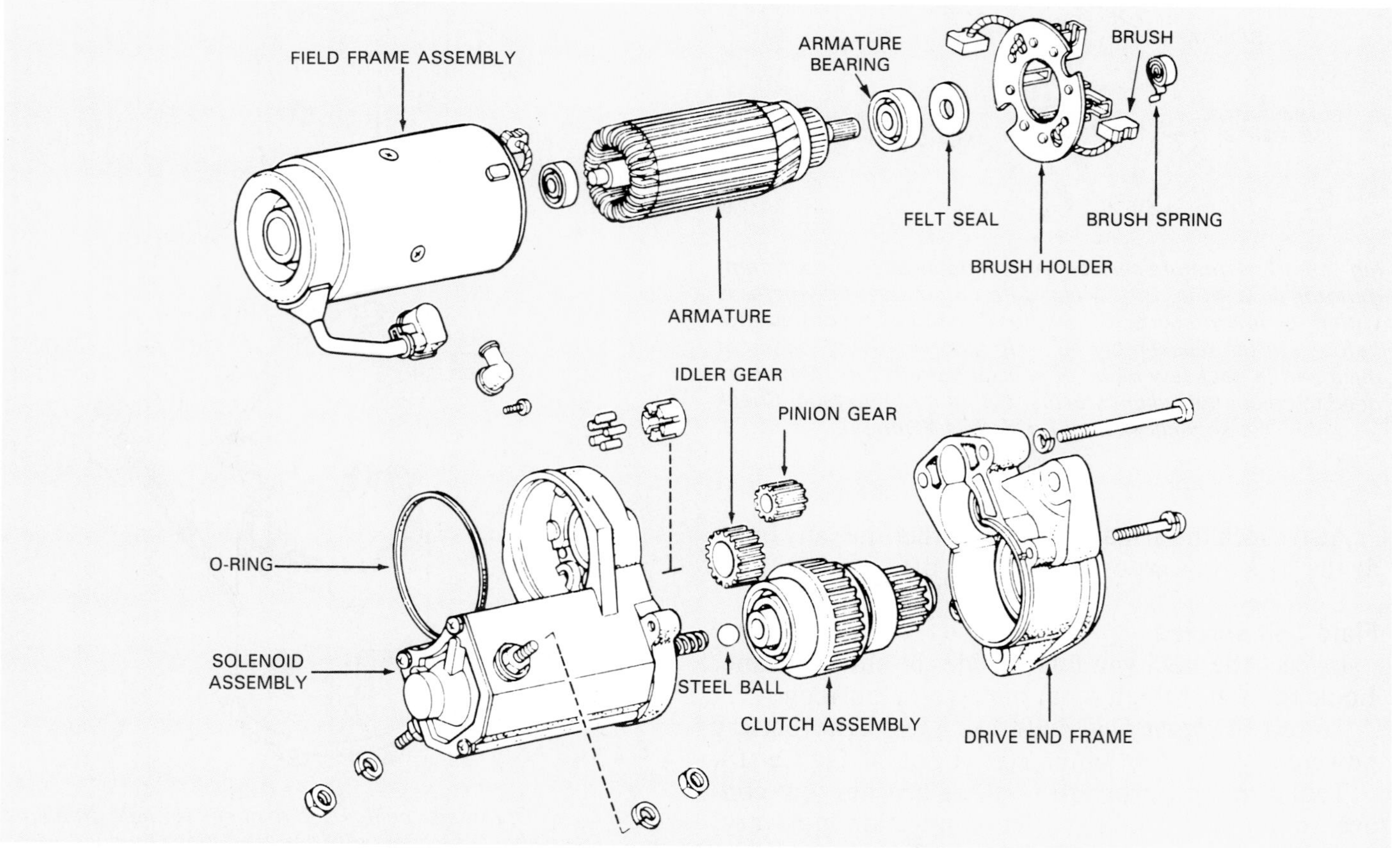

Fig. 29-20. Exploded view of a reduction type starting motor. A service manual will give similar illustration for exact starter you are servicing. It can help during reassembly. (Toyota)

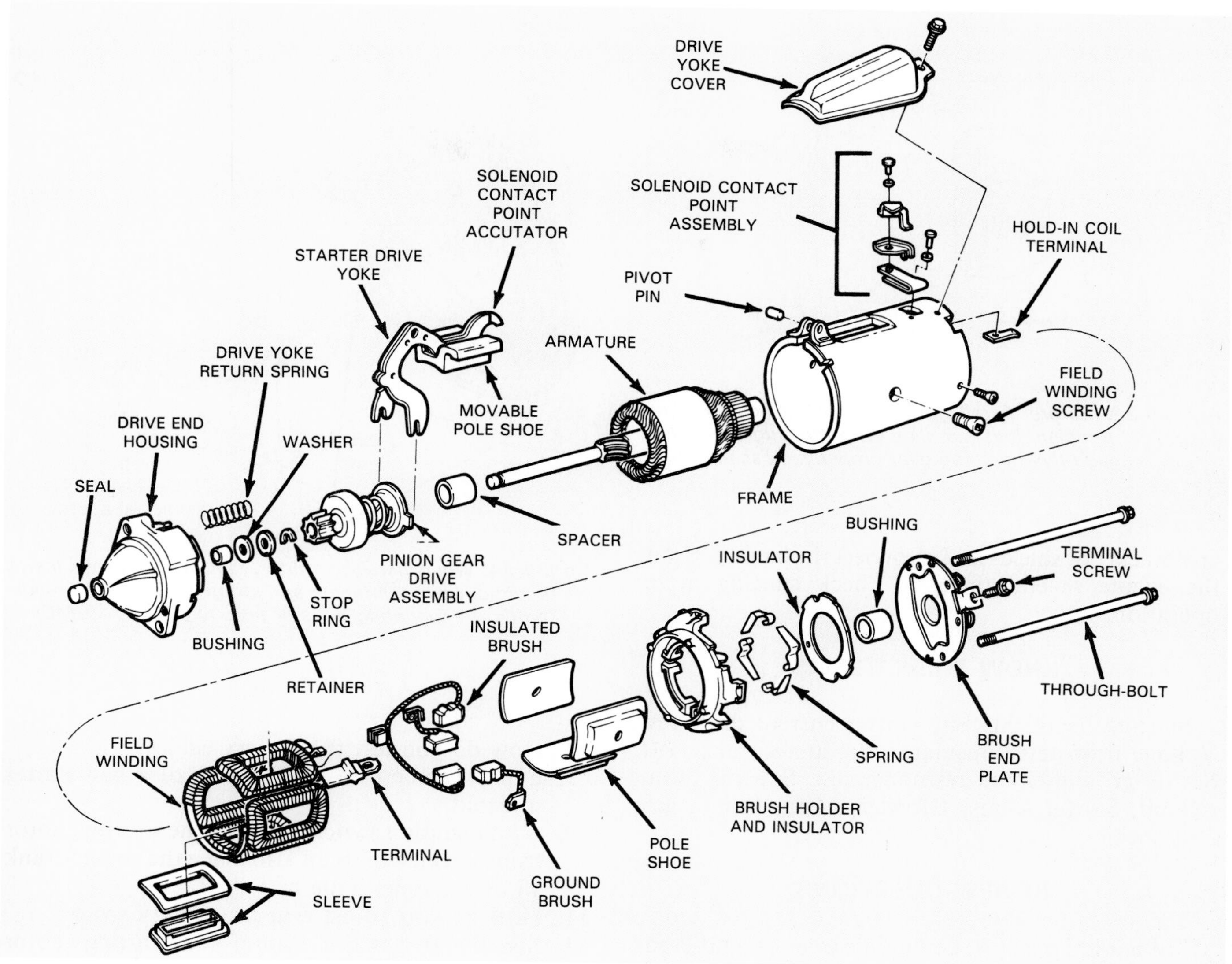

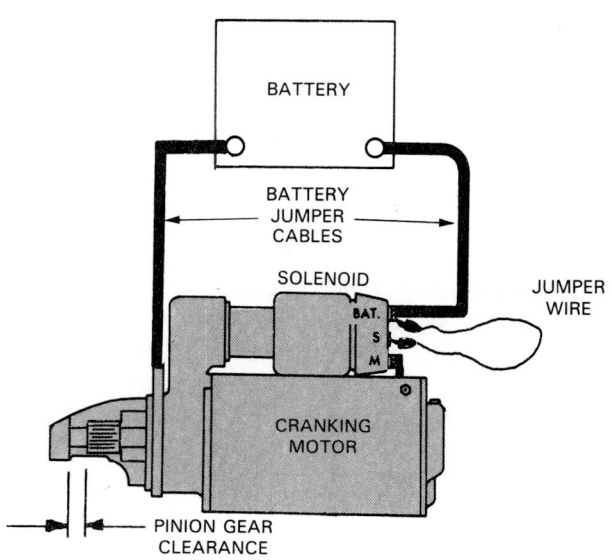

Fig. 29-21. Exploded view of another typical starting motor. Study part relationship. (AMC)

Fig. 29-22. After starter repairs, bench test the motor. Connect a battery to starter and check operation. Secure starter because it can lurch when engaged. (Buick)

Make sure the motor spins at the correct speed and that the pinion gear moves into the correct position.

Starter *pinion gear clearance* is the distance between the pinion and the drive end frame with the pinion engaged. Always check pinion gear clearance during a starter bench test. With the starter energized, check the clearance, as in Fig. 29-23.

If pinion gear clearance is NOT within specs, bend the shift lever or replace worn parts. Check in a service manual for exact specs and procedures.

Installing starting motor

Install the starter in the reverse order of removal. Make sure that any spacer shims are replaced between the motor and the engine block. If these shims are left out, the pinion gear may not mesh with the flywheel gear properly. Refer to Fig. 29-24.

If the starter has a solenoid on it, connect the wires on the solenoid before bolting the starter to the engine. Tighten the starter bolts to the torque specs. Replace

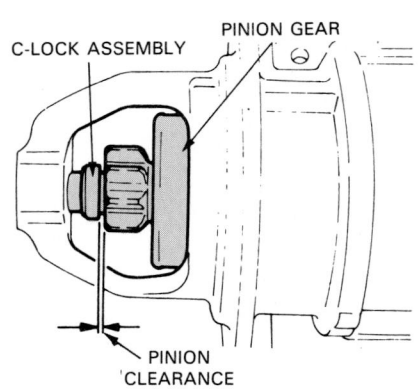

Fig. 29-23. Before installing starter, always check pinion clearance. If pinion does not slide out far enough, it will not engage flywheel ring gear properly. (Nissan)

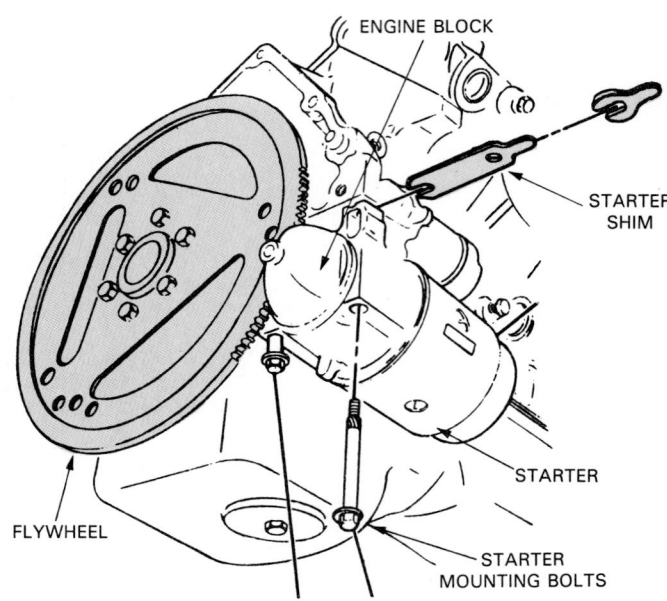

Fig. 29-24. When installing starter, replace any shims. Install wires without overtightening and stripping terminal threads. Torque the mounting bolts or nuts to specs. (GMC)

any bracket or shields and reconnect the battery. Crank the engine several times to check starting motor operation.

KNOW THESE TERMS

Starting headlight test, Starter current draw test, Voltage drop tests, Insulated circuit resistance test, Starter ground circuit resistance test, Starting motor rebuild, Starter shims, Growler, Mica, Pinion gear clearance.

REVIEW QUESTIONS

1. What are the most common causes of a no-crank problem?
2. A buzz or a click sound from the starter solenoid is normally due to a _____ _____ or poor _____ _____ connections.
3. A humming sound, after momentary engine crank-ing, may be due to a bad _____ _____ _____ or a bad _____ _____ unit.
4. What commonly causes a metallic grinding noise during starting?
5. Summarize how a starting headlight test is performed.
6. Why is a starter current draw test commonly used?
7. A high voltage drop in the starting system could indicate:
   a. High resistance.
   b. Loose electrical connection.
   c. Corroded or burned terminal.
   d. All of the above are correct.
8. How do you test the battery cables?
9. Explain some of the symptoms of a bad starter solenoid.
10. A bad ignition switch can keep the starting motor from working and can also make the engine crank all of the time. True or False?
11. How do you adjust a neutral safety switch?
12. List the five major steps for a starting motor rebuild.
13. _____ _____ may be used to adjust the space between the pinion gear and the flywheel ring gear.
14. Define the term "armature growler."
15. Always keep oil and grease away from start-ing motor brushes and commutator. True or False?

ACTIVITIES FOR CHAPTER 29

1. Demonstrate the use of a voltmeter in making voltage drop tests to detect excessive resistance in starting system components.
2. If you can obtain use of a camcorder, make a videotape to show a procedure that would be hard to demonstrate for a class, such as starting motor removal and re-installation. Narrate the finished tape and play it for the class.

Charging System Fundamentals

After studying this chapter, you will be able to:
□ List the basic parts of a charging system.
□ Explain charging system operation.
□ Describe the construction of major charging system components.
□ Compare alternator and voltage regulator design differences.
□ Explain charging system indicators.
□ Describe safety practices to follow when working with charging systems.

In the two previous chapters, you learned how the starting motor uses battery power to crank the engine. The starter consumed electricity and discharged the battery as the motor was drawing current.

In this chapter, you will learn how the charging system recharges the battery and supplies electricity for all of the car's electrical units. This chapter will give

you a background in charging system terminology and prepare you for the next chapter on testing and repair.

BASIC CHARGING SYSTEM PARTS

Fig. 30-1 pictures the major parts of a typical charging system. Study this illustration as each is introduced.

1. ALTERNATOR (generator that uses mechanical [engine] power to produce electricity).
2. VOLTAGE REGULATOR (electrical device for controlling the output voltage and current of the alternator).
3. ALTERNATOR BELT (links engine crankshaft pulley with alternator pulley to drive alternator).
4. CHARGE INDICATOR (ammeter, voltmeter, or warning light to inform driver of charging system condition).
5. CHARGING SYSTEM HARNESS (wiring that

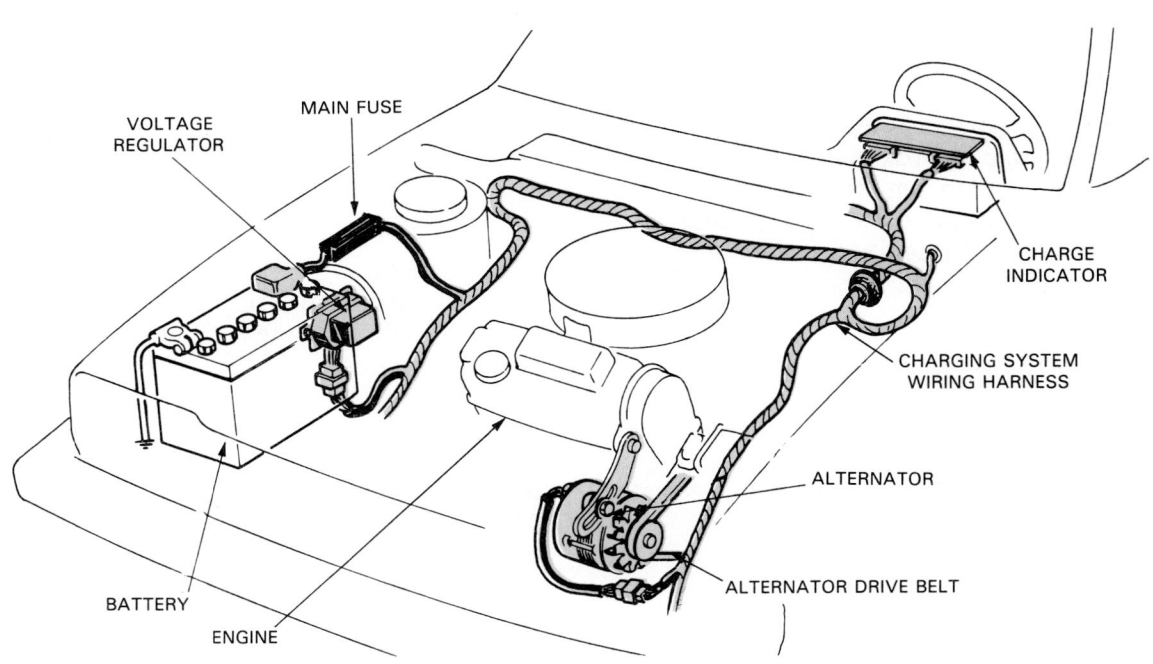

Fig. 30-1. Review names and locations for basic parts of charging system. (Honda)

connects parts of system).

6. BATTERY (provides current to initially energize or excite alternator and also helps stabilize alternator output).

During engine cranking, the battery supplies all electricity. Then, when the engine starts running, the charging system takes over to provide current to the vehicle's electrical systems.

The engine crankshaft pulley and alternator belt spins the alternator pulley. This powers the alternator and causes it to produce electricity, Fig. 30-2.

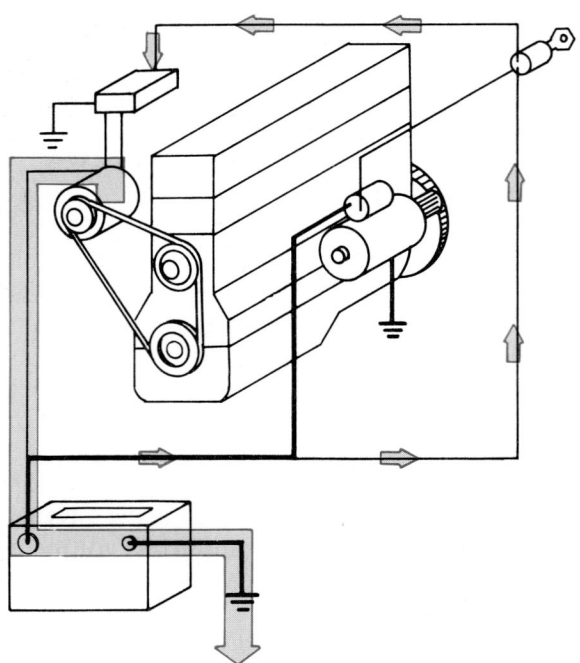

Fig. 30-2. Charging system recharges battery as well as supplies electricity when engine is running.

The voltage regulator keeps alternator output at a preset *charging voltage* (approximately 13 to 15 volts). Since this is HIGHER than battery voltage (12.6 volts), current flows back into the battery and recharges it.

Current also flows to the ignition system, electronic fuel injection system, on-board computer, radio, or any other device using electricity.

JOBS OF THE CHARGING SYSTEM

The *charging system* performs several functions:
1. It recharges the battery after engine cranking or after the use of electrical accessories with the engine shut off.
2. It supplies all of the car's electricity when the engine is running.
3. It provides a voltage output that is slightly higher than battery voltage.
4. It must change output to meet different electrical loads.

TYPES OF CHARGING SYSTEMS

There are two basic charging systems: AC generator (alternator) and DC generator types. The alternator type charging system has replaced the older DC generator. Keep in mind, however, that an alternator is sometimes called a *generator,* meaning AC generator.

Fig. 30-3 shows the fundamental differences between an alternator and a DC generator.

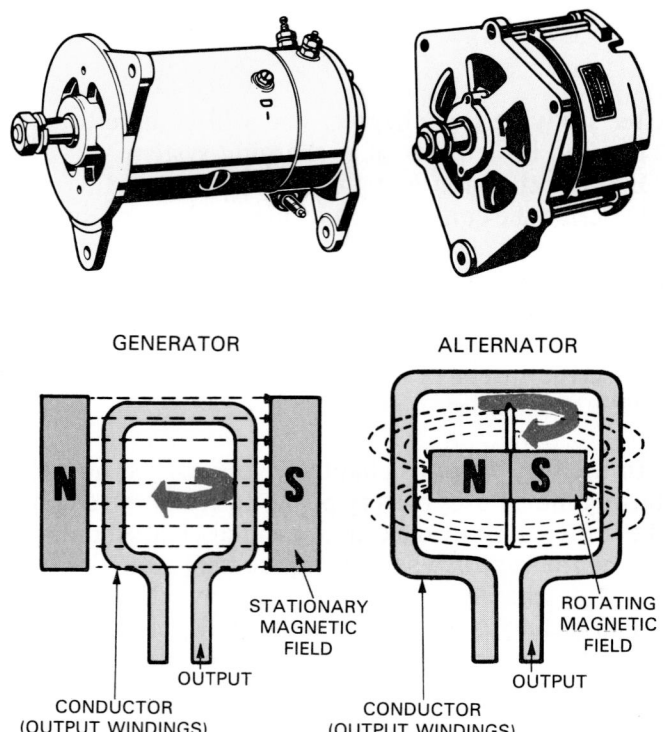

Fig. 30-3. Comparison of old DC generator and modern AC generator or alternator. Top — Typical models. Bottom — Note how fields and output conductors or windings are in opposite locations. (Ford and Bosch)

DC generator
The *DC generator* is made like an electric motor. It has a stationary magnetic field. The output conductor unit (armature) spins inside this field. This induces current output from within the armature.

The DC generator was fine for producing electricity on early model cars. However, today's cars have more electrical components, requiring high current output. A DC generator would NOT be able to supply enough current for a modern car at low idle speeds. DC generator efficiency is poor at low engine rpm.

AC generator (alternator)
The *AC generator* (alternator) has replaced the DC generator because of its improved efficiency. It is

smaller, lighter, and more dependable than a generator. The alternator will also produce more output at idle. This makes it ideal for late model cars.

The alternator has a spinning magnetic field, as illustrated in Fig. 30-3. The output conductors (windings) are stationary. As the field rotates, it induces current in the output windings. In a way, DC generator and alternator construction are reversed.

ALTERNATOR OPERATION

The two main parts of a simplified alternator are the rotor and stator, Fig. 30-4.

The *rotor* is a rotating magnetic field. It fits in the center of the alternator housing. The fan belt turns the rotor, making the field spin.

The *stator* is a stationary set of windings in the alternator. The stator surrounds the rotor. It is the output winding in the alternator. Again, refer to Fig. 30-4.

When the rotor spins, its strong magnetic field cuts across the stator windings. This induces current in the stator windings. If the stator windings are connected to a load (light bulb, for example), the load would operate (glow).

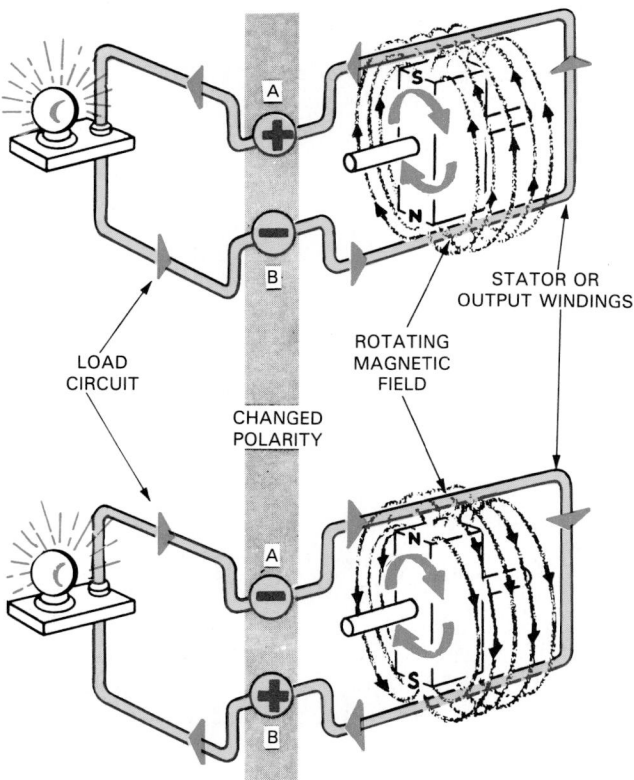

Fig. 30-4. Alternator action. Top — Rotating magnetic field moves across stationary windings. Current is induced into windings and out to load. Bottom — When rotating field turns one-half turn, polarity of field cutting output windings reverses. This causes current to flow out to load in opposite direction. AC current is produced. (Deere & Co.)

AC output

AC (alternating current) flows one way and then the other. The simple alternator in Fig. 30-4 has an AC output. As the rotor turns into one stator winding, current is induced in one direction. Then, when the same rotor pole moves into the other stator winding, current reverses and flows out in the other direction.

Rectified AC current

An automobile electrical system is designed to use DC (direct current) that only flows in one direction. It could NOT use alternating current as it comes out of the stator of the alternator. Alternator current must be *rectified* (changed) into DC current before entering the electrical system.

A *diode,* covered in Chapter 8, is an electronic device that allows current flow in only one direction. It serves as an "electrical check valve." Look at Fig. 30-5.

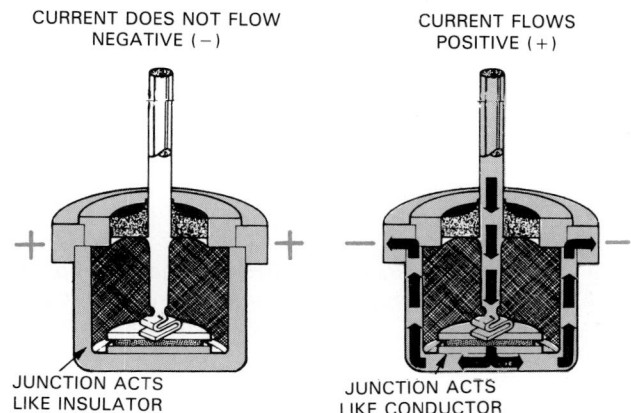

CURRENT DOES NOT FLOW
NEGATIVE (−)

CURRENT FLOWS
POSITIVE (+)

JUNCTION ACTS LIKE INSULATOR

JUNCTION ACTS LIKE CONDUCTOR

Fig. 30-5. Diode is a one-way valve. When polarity is connected one way, current flows. When polarity is reversed, current is blocked. (Motorola)

When a diode receives *forward bias,* this means the diode is connected to a voltage source so that current will pass through the diode. A forward biased diode acts as a CONDUCTOR.

With *reverse bias,* the diode is connected to a voltage source so that current does NOT pass through. A reverse biased diode acts like an INSULATOR.

If a diode were placed on the stator output of our simple alternator, current would only flow out through the circuit in one direction. This is illustrated in Fig. 30-6. Study diode action.

A single diode would NOT use all of the alternator's output, however. Also, it would result in pulsing DC, not smooth current flow. A real alternator uses several diodes connected into a rectifier circuit. This produces more efficient alternator output.

ALTERNATOR CONSTRUCTION

It is very important that you understand alternator

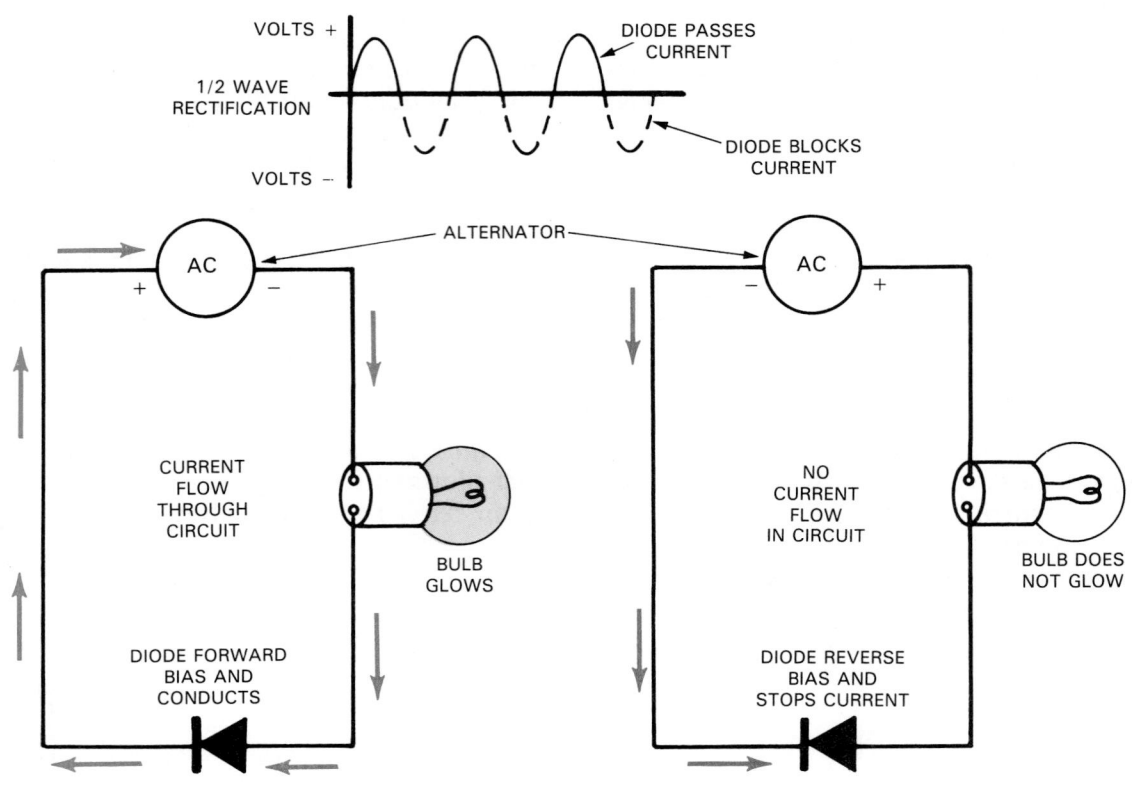

Fig. 30-6. Simple circuit shows action of diode. When alternator output places forward bias on diode, current passes through circuit. With reverse bias, diode prevents current flow. Bulb would only glow on positive output wave from alternator.

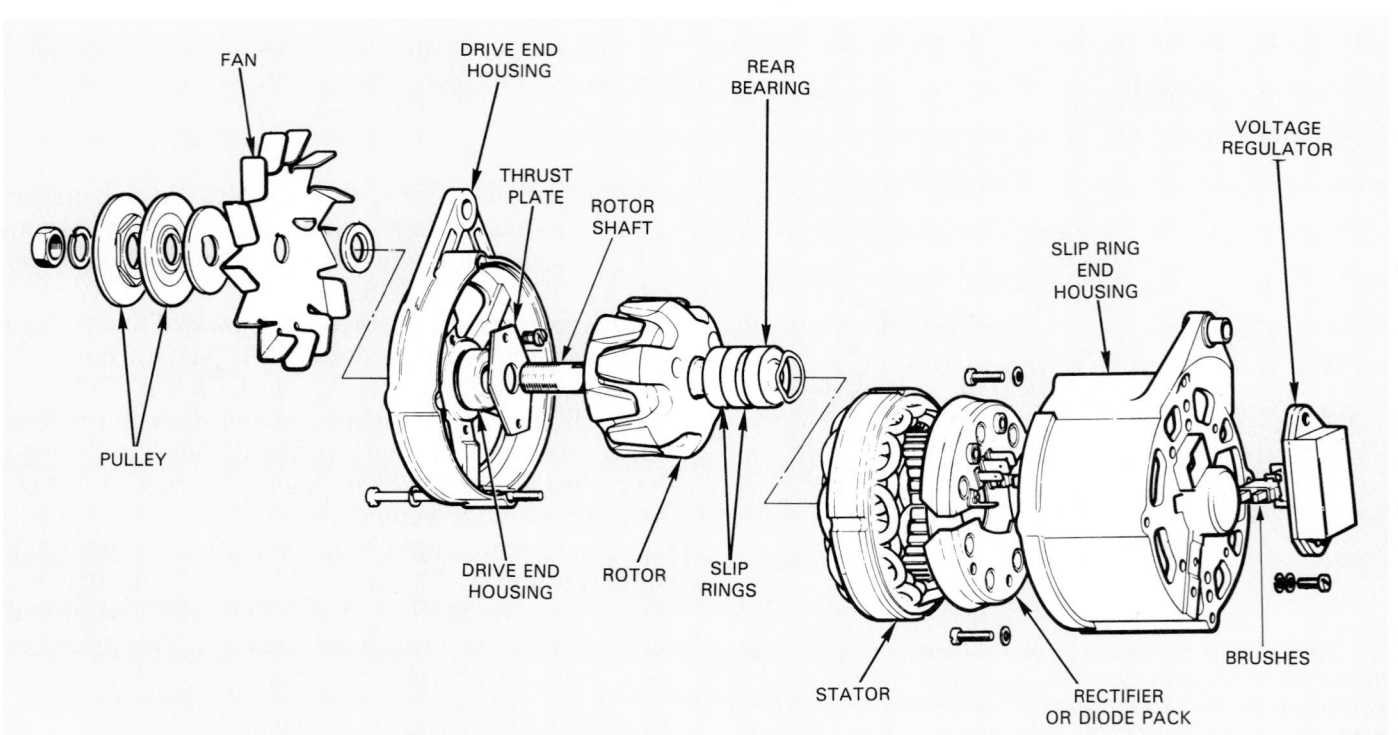

Fig. 30-7. Exposed view shows major parts of alternator. Study names of parts and general construction. (Ford)

construction. This information is essential before you can properly test and repair alternators.

Pictured in Fig. 30-7, the main components of a typical alternator are:

1. ROTOR ASSEMBLY (field windings, claw poles, rotor shaft, and slip rings).
2. STATOR ASSEMBLY (three stator windings or coils, stator core, and output wires).
3. BRUSH ASSEMBLY (brush housing, brushes, brush springs, and brush wires).
4. RECTIFIER ASSEMBLY (diodes, heat sink or diode plate, and electrical terminals).
5. HOUSING (drive end frame, slip ring end frame, end frame bolts).
6. FAN AND PULLEY ASSEMBLY (fan, spacer, pulley, lock washer, and pulley nut).
7. INTEGRAL REGULATOR (electronic voltage regulator mounted in or on rear of modern alternators).

Alternator rotor construction

An *alternator rotor* consists of field coil windings mounted on a shaft. Two claw-shaped pole pieces surround the field windings to increase magnetic field strength. This is illustrated in Fig. 30-8.

The fingers on one of the pole pieces produces S (south) poles. The fingers on the other pole piece form N (north) poles. As the rotor spins inside the alternator, an alternating N-S-N-S polarity and AC current is produced.

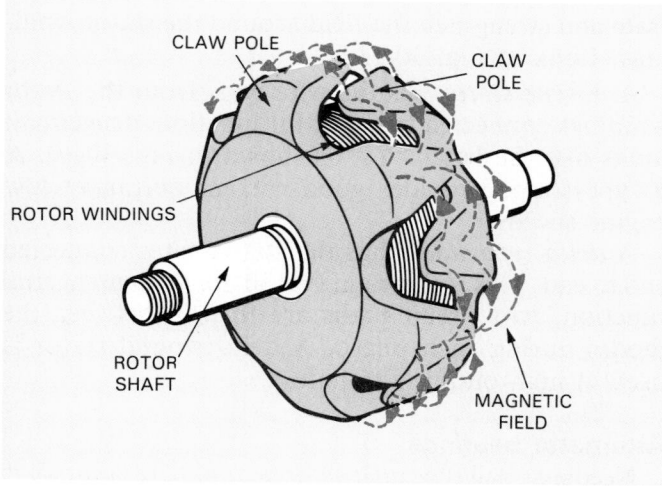

Fig. 30-8. Rotor consists of winding surrounded by claw shaped poles. Poles strengthen magnetic field around windings. Shaft supports poles and windings. (Bosch)

Alternator slip rings

Alternator slip rings are mounted on the rotor shaft to provide current to the rotor windings. Each end of the field coil connects to one of the slip rings. An ex-

ternal source of electricity is needed to excite the field. See Fig. 30-9.

Alternator brushes

Alternator brushes ride on the slip rings to make a sliding electrical connection. The brushes feed current into the slip rings and rotor windings from the battery.

Small springs hold the brushes in contact with the slip rings. Since current flow into the rotor windings is low, the brushes are small compared to motor brushes. Look at Fig. 30-9 again.

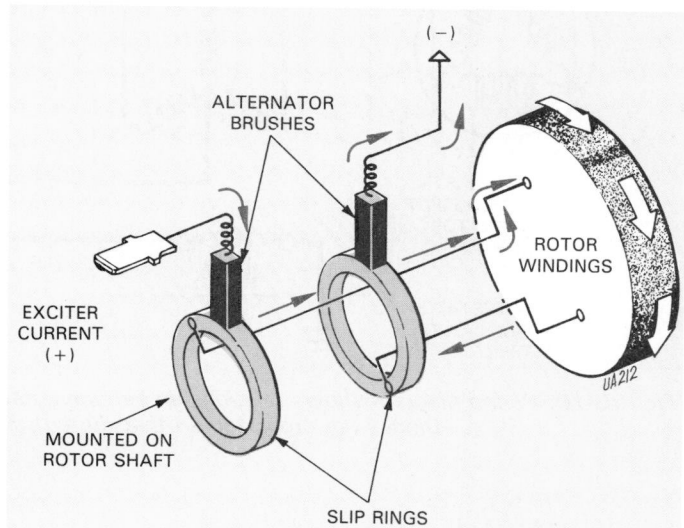

Fig. 30-9. Brushes and slip rings allow current to be fed into rotor windings. This excites windings to produce rotating magnetic field. (Motorola)

Alternator rectifier construction

An alternator *rectifier assembly,* also called a diode assembly, commonly uses six diodes to convert stator AC output into DC current. The diodes are usually wired as shown in Fig. 30-10.

The rectifier provides full wave rectification (change both + and − outputs into DC) as the different polarity rotor claws pass the stator windings.

A *diode trio* may be used to supply current to the rotor field windings. The three diodes are connected to the field through a connection in the voltage regulator. The stator output feeds the diode trio.

Fig. 30-11 shows how the rectifier assembly is connected to the stator assembly.

The rectifier diodes are mounted in a diode frame or **heat sink** (metal mount for removing excess heat from electronic parts). Three positive diodes are press-fit in an insulated frame. Three negative diodes are mounted into an uninsulated or grounded frame.

Alternator stator construction

The *alternator stator* consists of three groups of

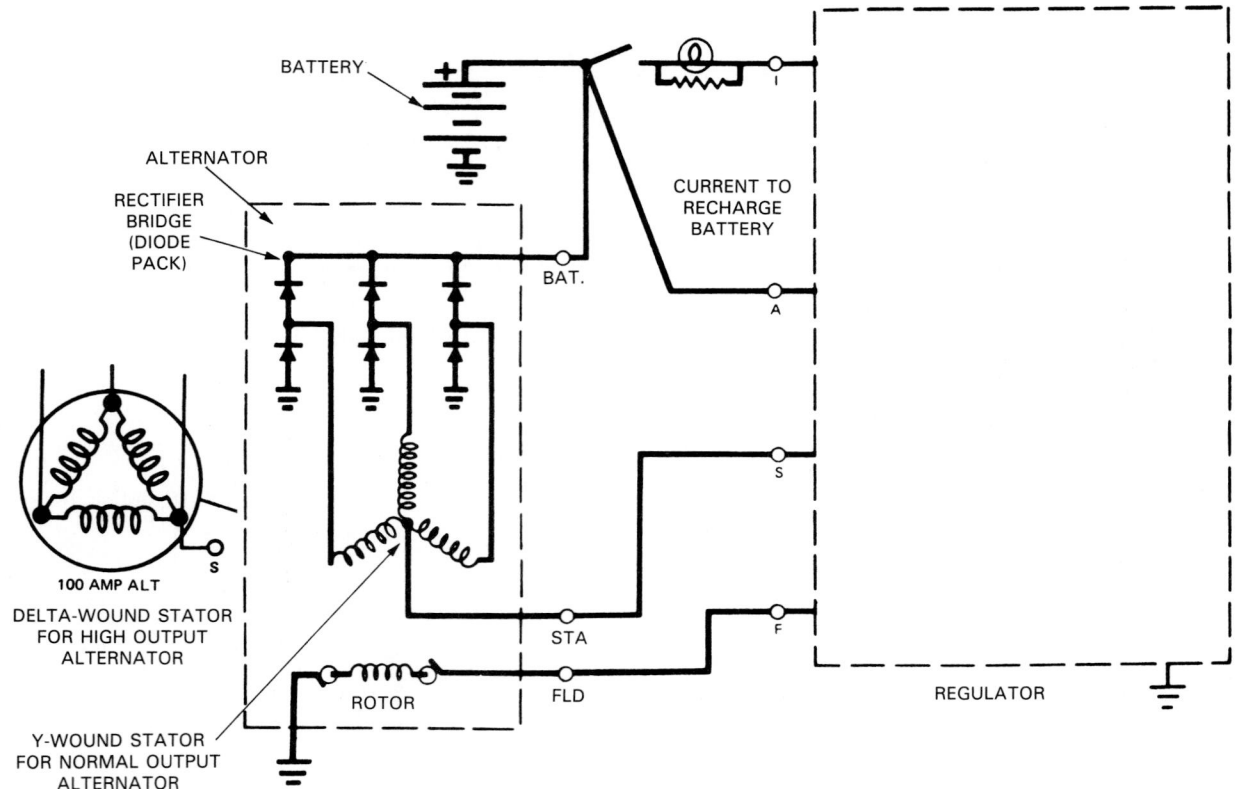

Fig. 30-10. Wiring diagram shows relationship between stator windings, rotor windings, diodes, and electrical connections. Diodes are organized so that current only flows to battery in one direction. (Ford)

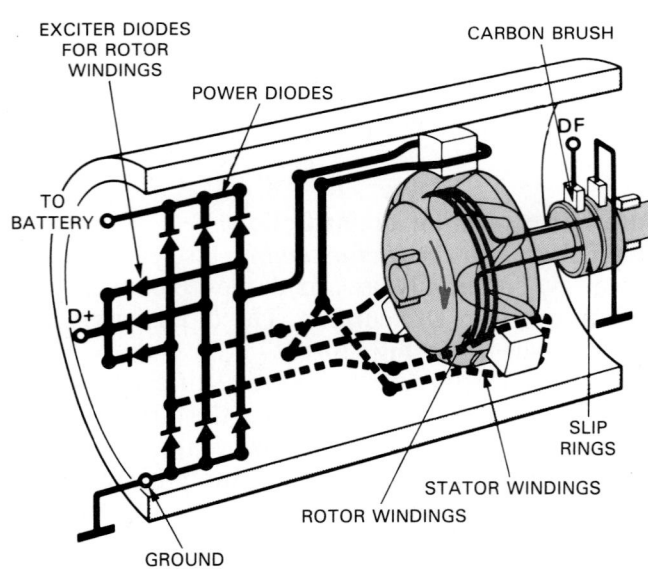

Fig. 30-11. Stator windings surround rotor windings. Rotor field cuts stator windings to produce current output. Diodes change stator AC output into DC output before current leaves alternator. Also note slip rings and brushes. (Robert Bosch)

windings or coils. The coils are wrapped around a soft, laminated iron core or ring. A stator with attached diodes is shown in Fig. 30-12.

The stator produces the electrical output of the alternator. As you can see, the stator windings connect to the diode assembly. The iron core is used to concentrate and strengthen the field around the stator windings. Look at Fig. 30-13.

A *Y-type stator* has the wire ends from the stator windings connected to a neutral junction. The circuit looks like the letter "Y," as shown in Fig. 30-10. A Y-type stator provides good current output at low engine speeds.

A *delta type stator* has the stator wires connected end to end. This is shown in Fig. 30-10. With no neutral junction, two circuit paths are formed between the diodes during each phase. A delta wound stator is used in high output alternators.

Alternator bearings

Needle or ball type *alternator bearings* are commonly used to produce a low friction surface for the rotor shaft. Refer to Fig. 30-13. These bearings support the rotor and shaft as they spin inside the stator.

The alternator bearings are normally packed with grease. The front bearing is frequently held in place with a small plate and screws. The rear bearing is usually press-fit into place.

Alternator fan

To provide cooling for the alternator, an *alternator*

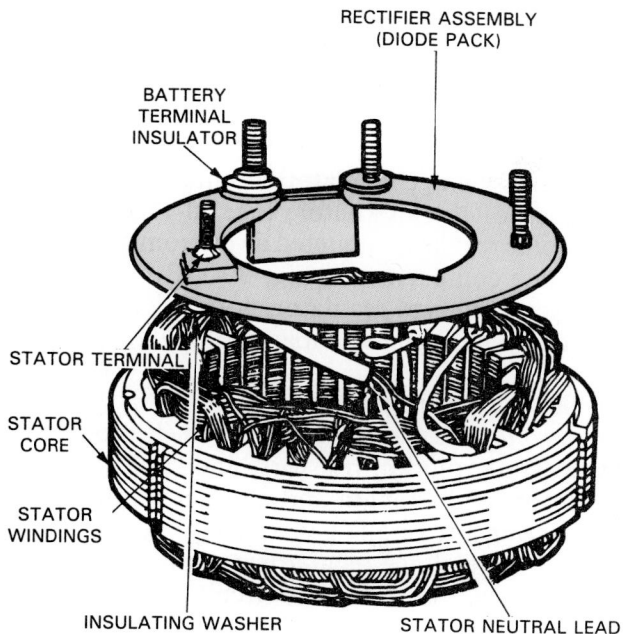

Fig. 30-12. Rectifier assembly consists of six diodes in heat sink. Wires from stator windings connect to rectifier. Iron core around stator windings increases induction into stator. (Mercury)

draw air through and over the alternator. This cools the windings and diodes to prevent overheating and damage.

Alternator pulley and belt

An *alternator pulley* is secured to the front of the rotor shaft by a large nut. It provides a means of spinning the rotor through the use of a belt. See Fig. 30-14.

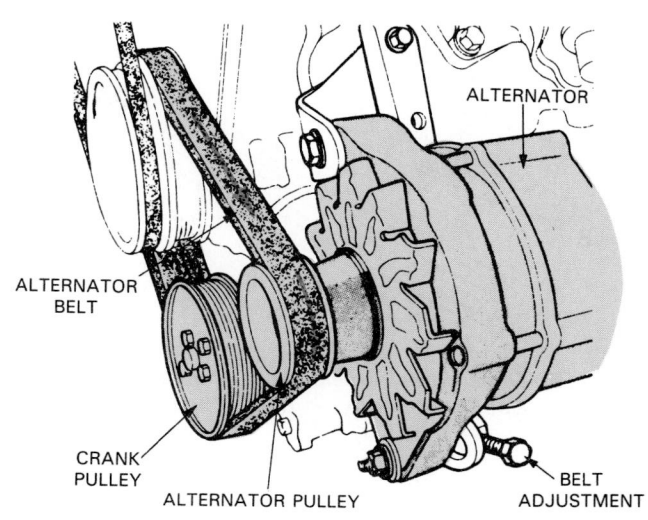

Fig. 30-14. Crankshaft pulley turns alternator belt. Belt powers alternator. This is a modern ribbed belt. (Sun Electric)

fan is mounted on the front of the rotor shaft. It is normally between the pulley and the front bearing. Look at Fig. 30-13.

As the rotor and shaft spin, the whirling fan helps

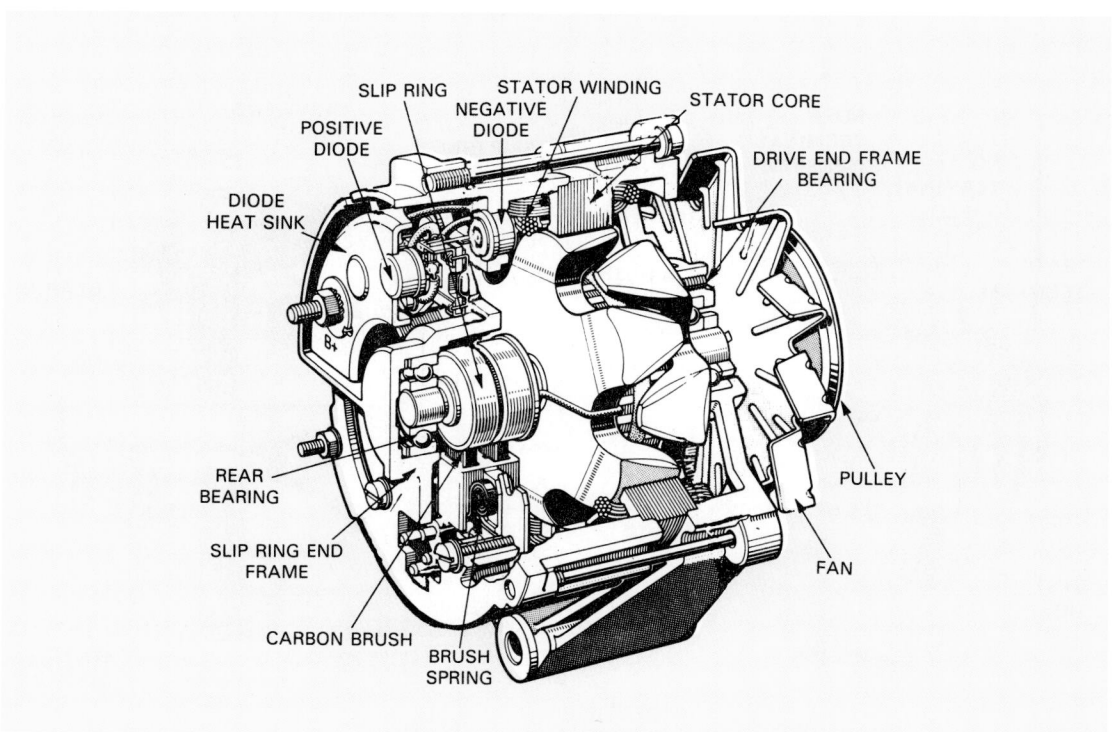

Fig. 30-13. Cutaway view shows many of the parts already discussed. Note construction. (Bosch)

An *alternator belt,* running off of the crank pulley, turns the alternator pulley and rotor. One of three types of belts may be used: V-belt, cogged V-belt, and ribbed belt. These are pictured in Fig. 30-15.

Covered in other chapters, these kinds of belts are also used to drive the power steering pump, air conditioning compressor, water pump, and other units.

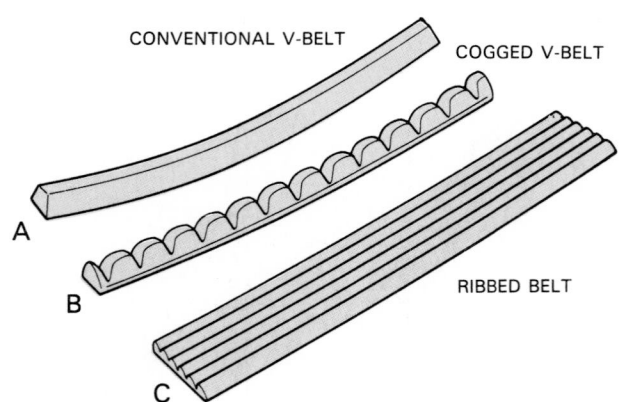

Fig. 30-15. Three types of belts. A — Conventional V-belt. B — Cogged V-belt. C — Ribbed belt. (Ford)

VOLTAGE REGULATORS

A *voltage regulator* controls alternator output by changing the amount of current flowing through the rotor windings. Any change in rotor winding current changes the field strength acting on the stator (output) windings. In this way, the voltage regulator can maintain a preset charging voltage.

Fig. 30-16 shows a common location for a voltage regulator and its terminals. There are three basic types of voltage regulators:

1. Electronic voltage regulator mounted inside or on the back of the alternator, Fig. 30-17A.
2. Electronic regulator mounted away from alternator in engine compartment, Fig. 30-17B.
3. Contact point type regulator mounted away from alternator in engine compartment, Fig. 30-17C.

Electronic voltage regulators

An *electronic voltage regulator* uses an electronic circuit (transistors, diodes, resistors, and capacitors) to control rotor field strength and alternator output. A circuit diagram for one is given in Fig. 30-18.

An electronic voltage regulator is a sealed unit and is not repairable. The electronic circuit must be sealed because it can be damaged by moisture, excessive heat, and vibration. Usually the circuit is surrounded by a rubber-like gel for protection.

An *integral voltage regulator* is an electronic regulator mounted inside or on the rear of the alternator. This is the most common type used on today's vehicles. It is very small, efficient, and dependable. Its circuit uses ICs (integrated circuits).

Electronic voltage regulator operation

To increase alternator output, the electronic voltage regulator allows more current into the rotor windings. This strengthens the magnetic field around the rotor. More current is then induced into the stator windings

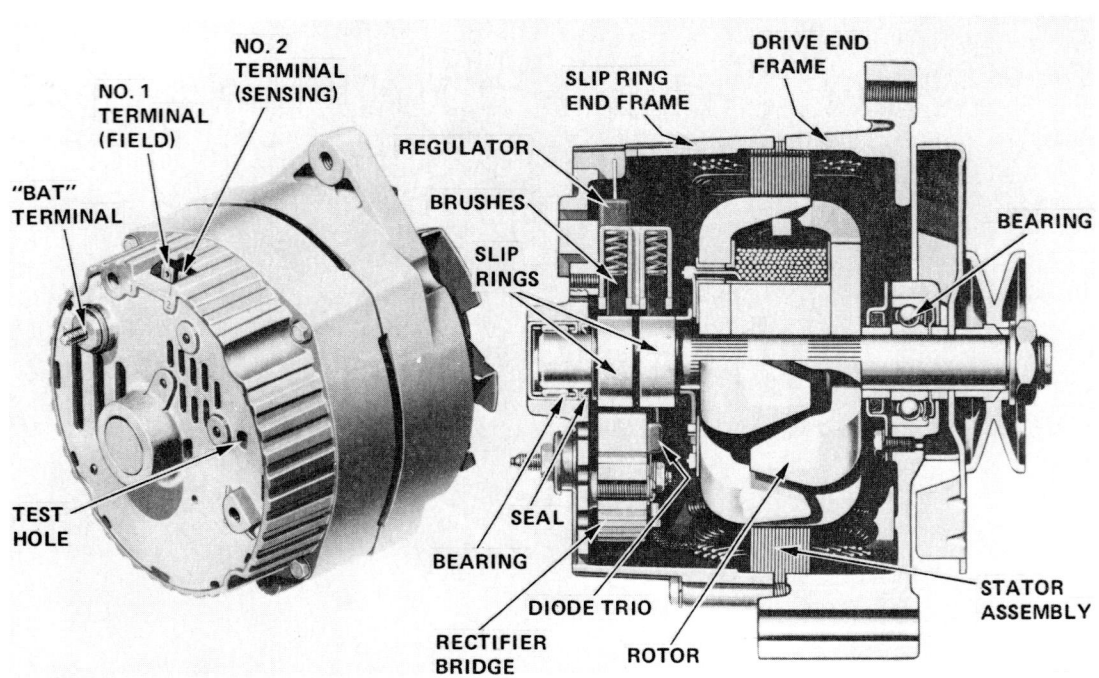

Fig. 30-16. Another type of modern alternator. Study part locations and terminal connections on rear of alternator. (Chevrolet)

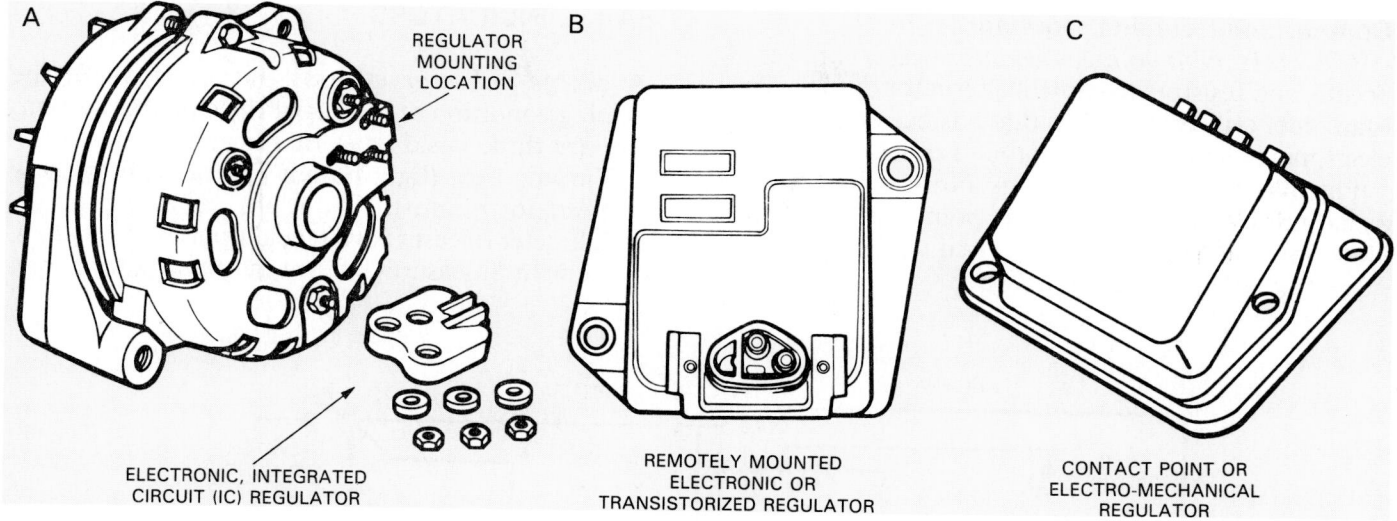

A — REGULATOR MOUNTING LOCATION

ELECTRONIC, INTEGRATED CIRCUIT (IC) REGULATOR

B — REMOTELY MOUNTED ELECTRONIC OR TRANSISTORIZED REGULATOR

C — CONTACT POINT OR ELECTRO-MECHANICAL REGULATOR

Fig. 30-17. A — Integral electronic voltage regulator on or in alternator. B — Electronic voltage regulator mounted away from alternator. C — Contact point type regulator mounted away from alternator. (Plymouth)

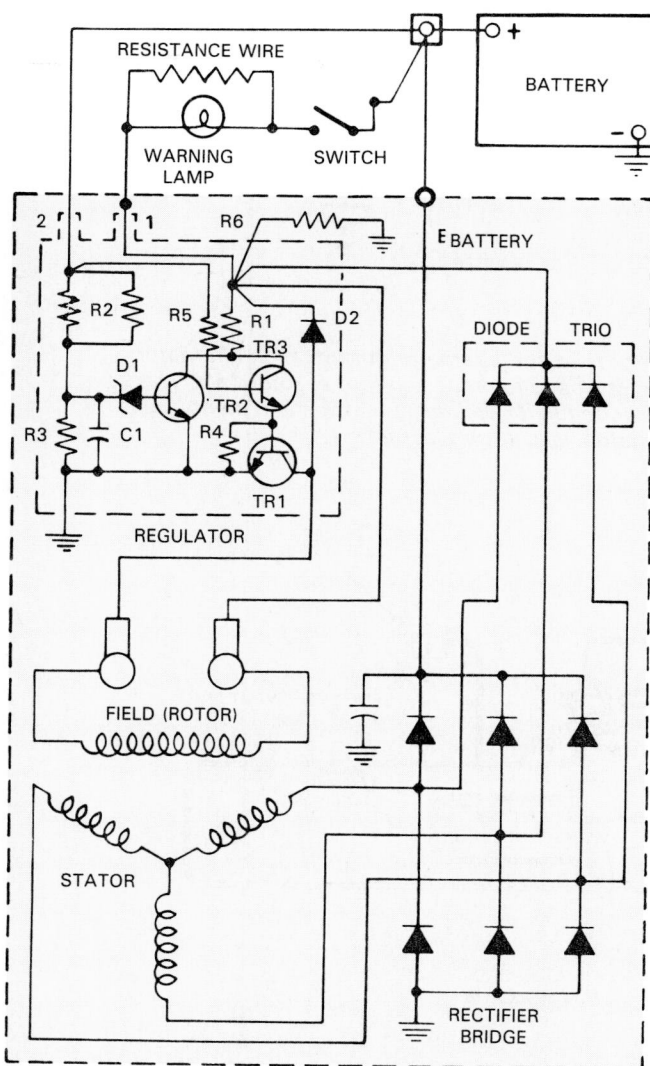

Fig. 30-18. Charging system schematic diagram. Voltage regulator is a miniature electronic circuit that is not serviceable.

and out of the alternator. Look at Fig. 30-18.

To reduce alternator output, the electronic regulator places more resistance between the battery and rotor windings. Field strength drops and less current is induced into the stator windings.

Alternator rpm and electrical load determines whether the regulator increases or decreases charging output. If load is high or rotor speed is low (engine idling), the regulator will sense a drop in system voltage. The regulator then increases rotor field current until a preset output voltage is obtained. If load drops or rotor speed increases, the opposite occurs.

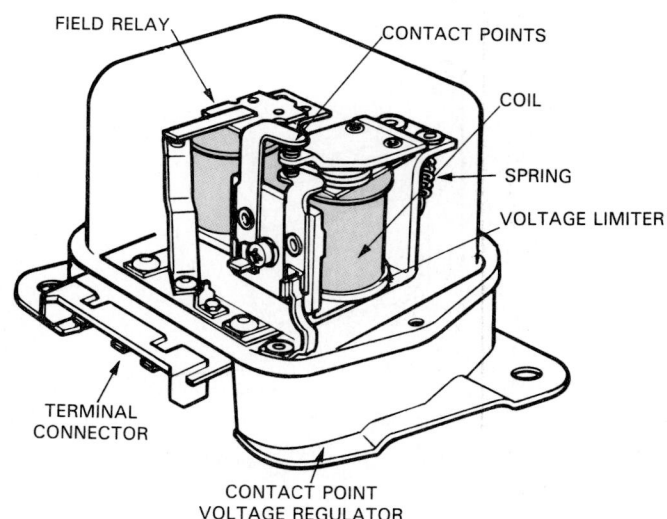

Fig. 30-19. Older contact point type voltage regulator. It used small coils and contact points to control current entering alternator rotor windings. Coil senses system voltage and causes points to open and close to control rotor field strength and alternator output. (Dodge)

Charging System Fundamentals 385

Contact point voltage regulator

A *contact point voltage regulator* uses a coil, set of points, and resistors to control alternator output. This is an older type of regulator that has been replaced by electronic or solid state regulators. Look at Fig. 30-19.

Fig. 30-20 shows and explains a wiring diagram for a charging system with a contact point type regulator. Note how the regulator coil is wired to the alternator output through the ignition switch.

CHARGE INDICATORS

A *charge indicator* informs the driver about the operating condition or output of the charging system. There are three basic types of charging indicators:
1. Warning light (light bulb is ON or OFF to show alternator output).
2. Voltmeter (measures voltage output of alternator).
3. Ammeter (measures current output of alternator).

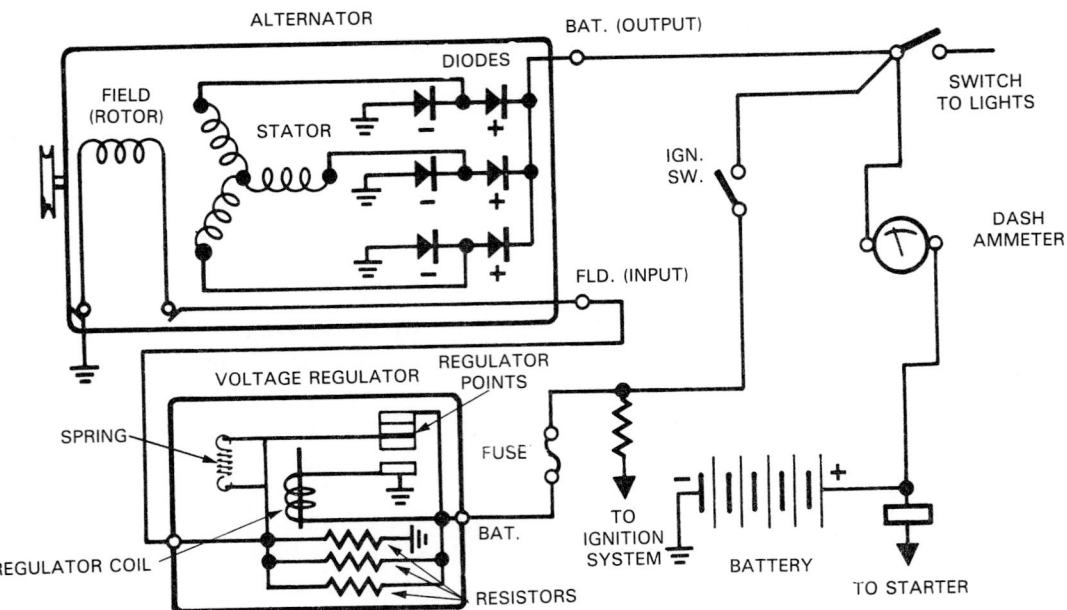

Fig. 30-20. Note how regulator coil is wired to alternator field and alternator output. High alternator output causes coil to act on regulator points and points are closed to reduce current to rotor field. This reduces alternator output. When load increases as shown, regulator coil field weakens and points can move to increase current to alternator field. (Sun Electric)

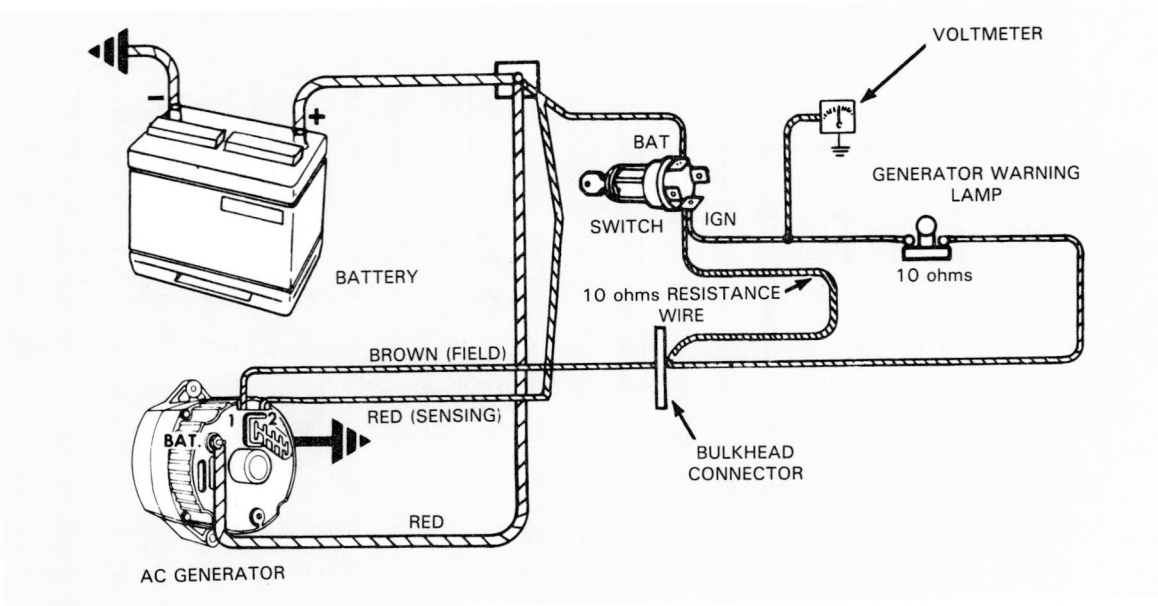

Fig. 30-21. Charging circuit shows connections for generator warning lamp and voltmeter. (Oldsmobile)

These indicators are mounted in the dash of the car. Normally, all cars have an indicator light. A voltmeter or ammeter may be added for more precise measurement of charging system action.

Alternator warning light

An *alternator warning light* is wired into the charging system so that it will glow when alternator output drops to a specified level. Fig. 30-21 shows one circuit using an alternator warning light.

If problems develop in the charging system, then the field current, trying to increase alternator output, will increase enough to light the indicator bulb. If the charging system is in good operating condition, current flow through the field will be low enough for the light not to glow.

Voltmeter indicator

A *voltmeter indicator* can also be used to warn the driver of charging system problems. Refer to Fig. 30-21. The voltmeter reads system voltage when the engine is running.

A battery actually has 12.6 volts when fully charged. To recharge the battery, alternator output must be HIGHER than battery voltage (between 13 and 15 volts).

The voltmeter type indicator simply shows voltage, which is an indicator of current output and charging system condition. If the voltmeter were to drop to battery voltage or below, then the charging system has problems.

Ammeter indicator

An *ammeter* type charging system indicator simply shows the current output of the alternator in amps. A simplified circuit showing an ammeter is given in Fig. 30-22. Study it carefully.

Basically, if the ammeter reads to the right side (positive dial mark), the battery is being charged. If the ammeter reads to the left (negative dial mark), the charging system is NOT working.

WARNING! Some late model cars are equipped with a heated windshield. During operation, the alternator is full-fielded and made to produce 110 volts AC. This is enough voltage to possibly cause electrocution and death. To prevent a painful "jolt," keep this in mind when working on this type system.

KNOW THESE TERMS

Charging voltage, DC, AC, AC generator, DC generator, alternator, Rotor, Stator, Rectified, Diode, Forward bias, Reverse bias, Slip rings, Brushes, Alternator bearings, Voltage regulator, Electronic regulator, Integral regulator, Contact point regulator, Charge indicators.

REVIEW QUESTIONS

1. List and explain the six major parts of a charging system.
2. The voltage regulator keeps alternator output at a preset _____ _____ of approximately _____ to _____ volts.
3. What are four functions of a charging system?
4. The DC generator is the most common type of automotive charging system. True or False?
5. The AC generator, normally called alternator, has replaced the DC generator. True or False?
6. The alternator is a device for changing _____ energy into _____ energy.
7. Explain the alternator's rotor and stator.
8. Define the term "rectified current."
9. This alternator device can be used to change AC current into DC current.
   a. Transistor.
   b. Capacitor.
   c. Stator.
   d. Diode.
10. What do the terms forward and reverse bias mean?
11. List and explain the seven major parts of an alternator.
12. An alternator _____ consists of field coil windings mounted on a shaft.

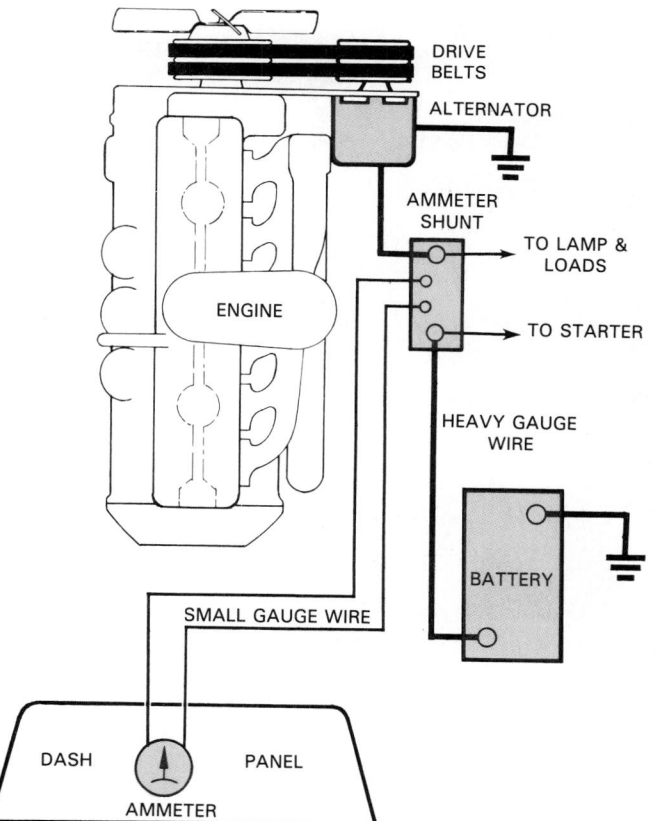

Fig. 30-22. Circuit showing basic connections for ammeter charge indicator. (Motorola)

13. Alternator brushes ride on _____ _____ to feed current to the rotor windings.
14. An alternator rectifier assembly provides full wave rectification. True or False?
15. An alternator _____ consists of three groups of windings or coils that surround the spinning _____ .
16. A voltage regulator controls alternator _____ by changing the amount of _____ flowing through the _____ _____ .
17. Which of the following is NOT a typical type of voltage regulator?
    a. Contact point type mounted away from alternator.
    b. Electronic type mounted away from alternator.
    c. Integral electronic type.
    d. Integral contact point type.

18. An _____ voltage regulator is an electronic unit mounted inside or on rear of alternator.
19. Alternator _____ and electrical _____ determine whether the regulator increases or decreases charging output.
20. List and explain three types of charging system indicators.

ACTIVITIES FOR CHAPTER 30

1. Vehicles from different manufacturers use various belt arrangements to drive the alternator. Identify at least three different belt arrangements and sketch them. Label each sketch with vehicle make and engine type.
2. A diode is sometimes called "an electrical check valve." Make sketches to show why it received that name.

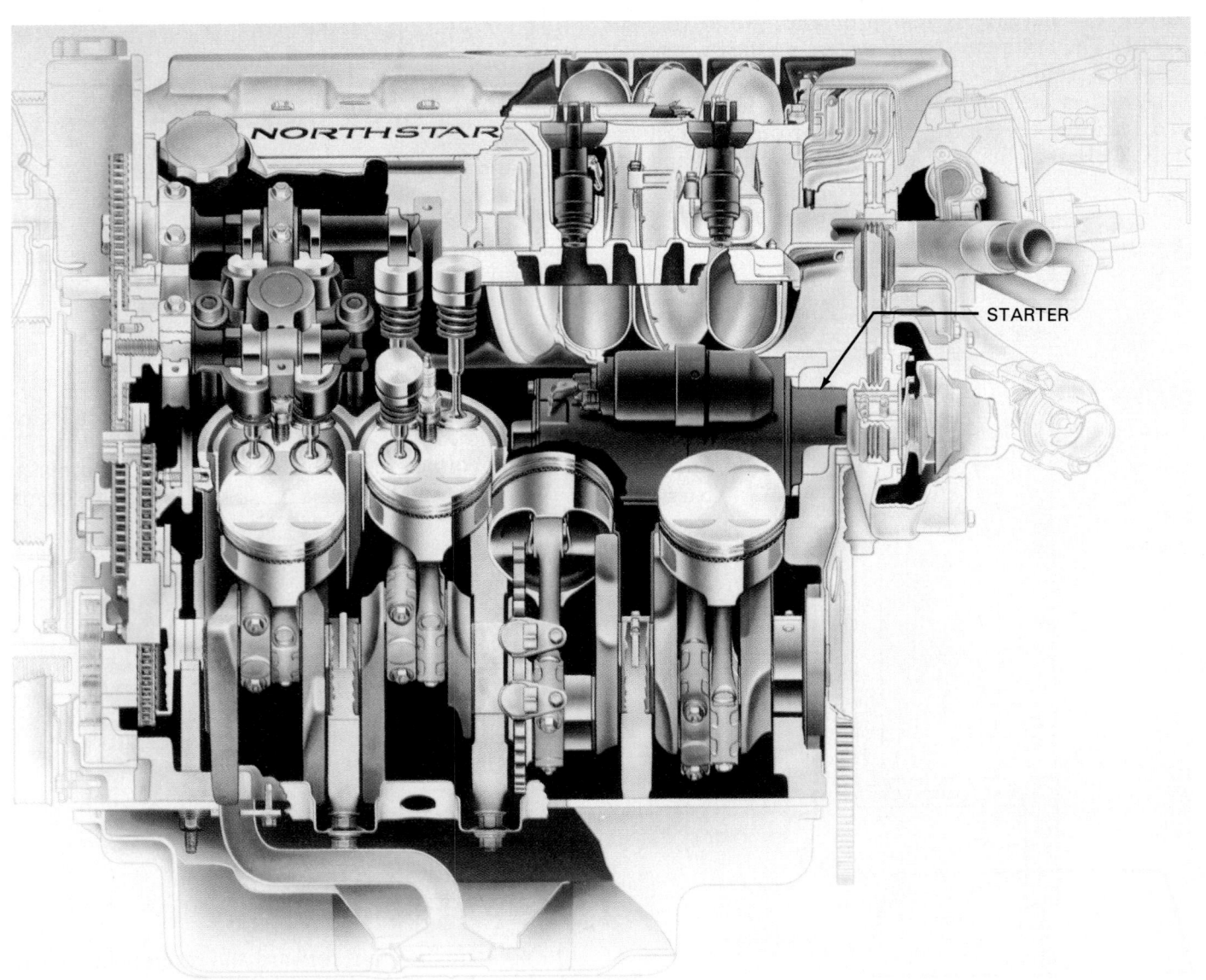

STARTER

Today's engines require a starting system in good working condition. It takes a lot of torque to rotate an engine crankshaft for starting. Note the unusual positioning of the starter. (Cadillac)

31

Charging System Diagnosis, Testing, Repair

After studying this chapter, you will be able to:
- ☐ Diagnose charging system troubles.
- ☐ Inspect a charging system and adjust an alternator belt.
- ☐ Test charging system output with a voltmeter or a load tester.
- ☐ Remove, test, repair, and replace an alternator.
- ☐ Remove and replace a voltage regulator.
- ☐ Describe safety practices to follow when testing or repairing a charging system.

The chapter begins by summarizing the types of troubles that occur in a charging system. You will learn how to do charging system tests that help locate problems. Then, the chapter covers parts removal, disassembly, repair, and reassembly. This should give you a sound background in the most common types of charging system service and repair jobs.

CHARGING SYSTEM DIAGNOSIS

Even though a charging system has only two major parts (alternator and regulator), be careful when troubleshooting problems. Sometimes, another system fault (bad starting motor, battery, or wiring) will appear to be caused by problems in the charging system.

There are four common types of symptoms caused by charging system problems:
1. Dead battery (slow or no cranking).
2. Overcharged battery (water must be added to battery frequently).
3. Abnormal noises (grinding, squealing, buzzing).
4. Indicator shows problem (light glows all the time or there is an incorrect indicator reading).

Verify these problems by starting or trying to start the engine. It is possible that the symptoms have been mistaken by the service writer or customer. For exam-

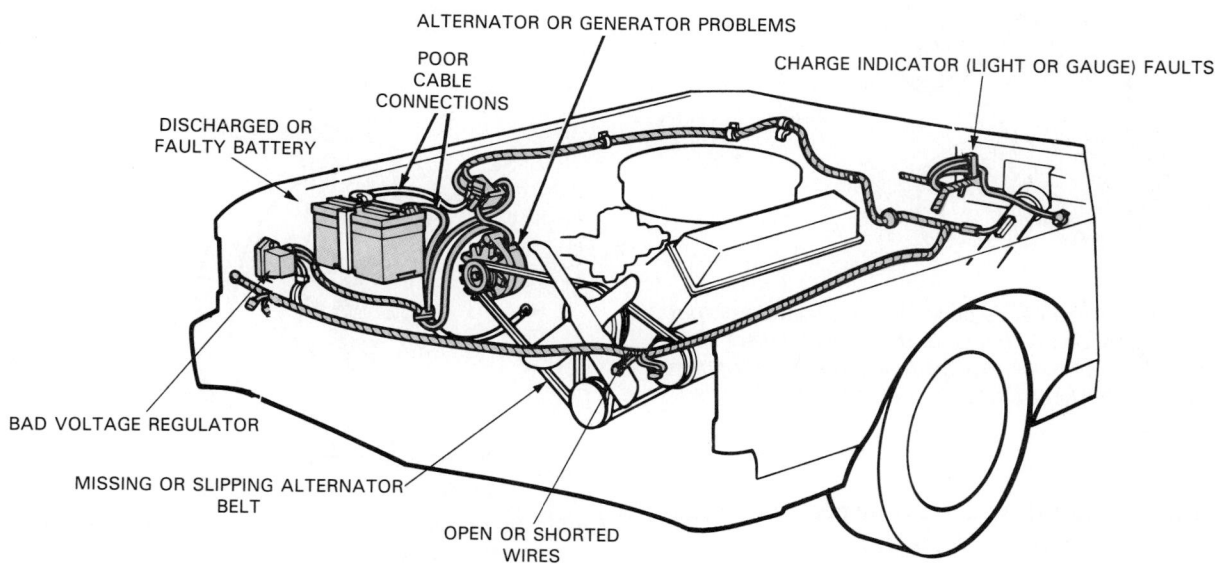

Fig. 31-1. Note types of common problems in charging system. Some of these could be found during inspection. (Mopar)

ple, a problem described as a no-charge condition may really be a shorted starting motor, battery drain, or other trouble.

Visual inspection

Open the hood and visually inspect the parts of the charging system. Check for obvious troubles, like the ones given in Fig. 31-1.

Check for *battery problems:* loose battery cables, discharged battery, corroded terminals, low water level, or case damage.

Check for *alternator belt problems,* Fig. 31-2. Make sure the belt is adjusted properly. A loose belt may

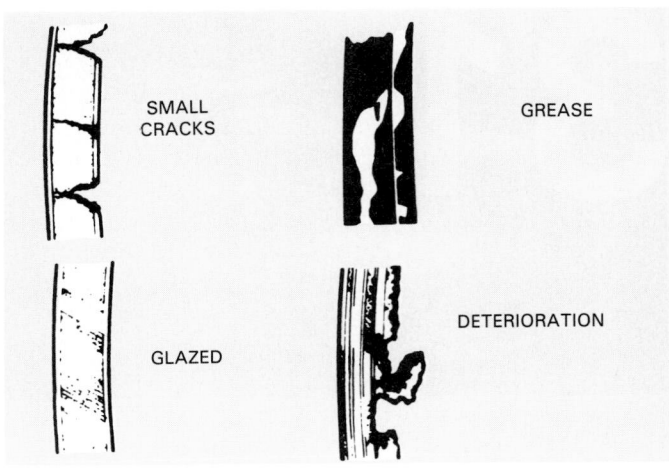

Fig. 31-3. Inspect belts closely for these kinds of problems. Replace belt if needed. (Sun Electric)

If needed, adjust alternator belt tension, Fig. 31-4. Loosen the alternator mounting and adjusting bolts. Then pry on a strong surface of the end frame. Pull hard enough to produce proper tension. Tighten the adjusting bolt while holding the pry bar. Tighten the other mounting bolt or bolts. Recheck tension.

Warning! Tighten an alternator belt only enough to prevent belt slippage or flap. Overtightening is a COM-

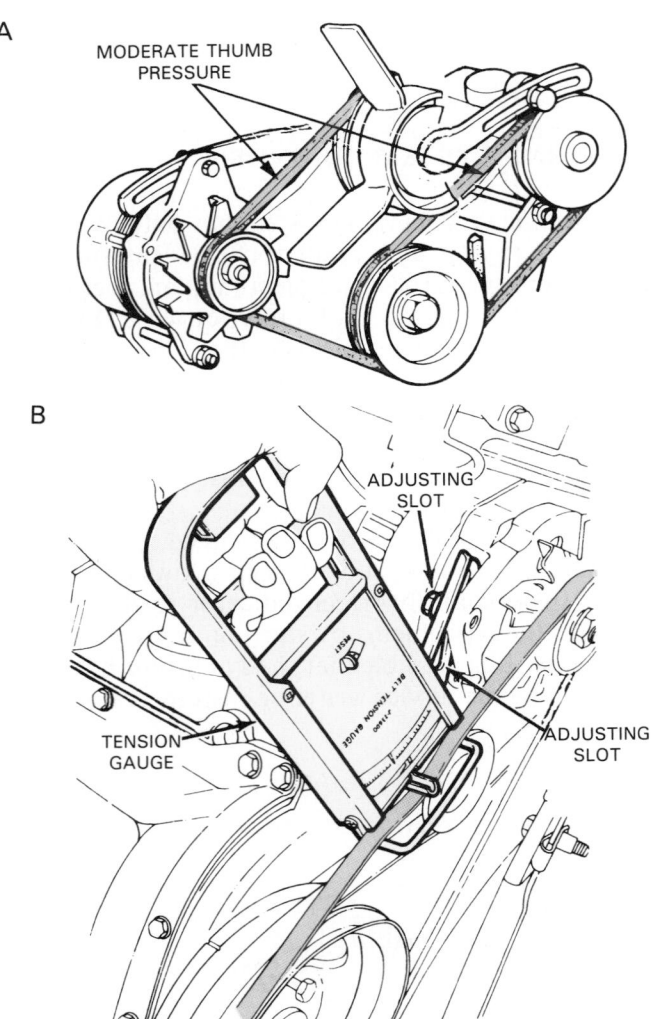

Fig. 31-2. Loose belt can cause poor charging system output. A — Press on center of belt with thumb. Belt should deflect about 1/2 in. (13mm). B — Belt tension gauge provides slower but more accurate way of checking tension.   (Mazda and Chrysler)

squeal or flap up and down. Also inspect the condition of the alternator belt. Check for cracks, glazing (hard, shiny surface), grease or oil contamination, and deterioration. These conditions are shown in Fig. 31-3.

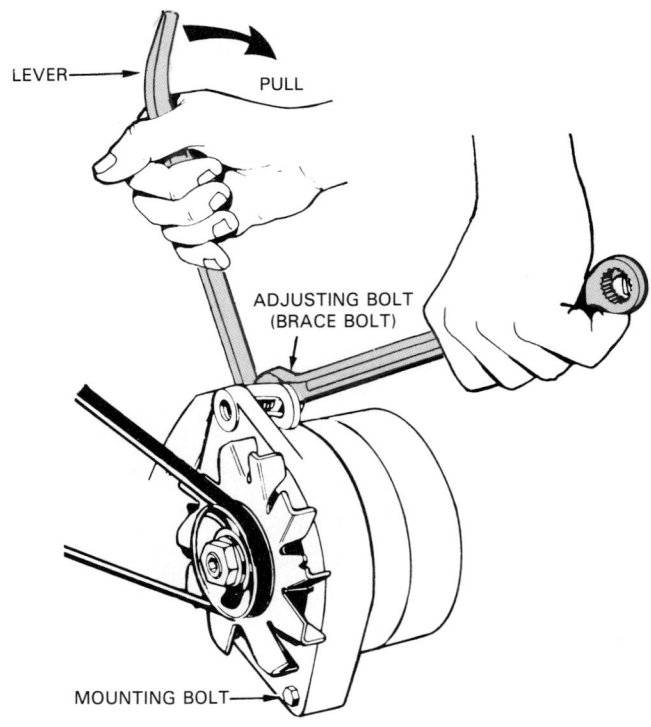

Fig. 31-4. To adjust belt, loosen mounting and adjusting bolts. Pry on thick area of end frame. Hold tension while tightening adjustment bolt. Check tension and tighten other bolt. (Florida Dept. of Voc. Ed.)

MON MISTAKE that quickly ruins alternator bearings.

Check for *wiring problems* in the charging system, Fig. 31-1. Check for loose electrical connections, corroded connections, shorted wires (missing insulation), and other problems.

In particular, check the connections on the back of the alternator and regulator (type mounted away from alternator). WIGGLE THE WIRES while running the engine. If the indicator light goes out or dash gauge begins to read properly when a wire is moved, the problem is in that area of the wiring.

Listen closely for *abnormal noises* in the alternator or regulator (contact point type). Use a stethoscope to listen to the alternator if necessary. Try to detect internal grinding (worn, dry bearings), whining (leaking diodes or overcharging), or any other unusual sounds.

CHARGING SYSTEM PRECAUTIONS

Observe the following rules when working on a charging system. They will help prevent possible damage to the charging and other electrical systems.

1. DISCONNECT THE BATTERY before removing any charging system component. If a "*hot wire*" (current carrying wire) touches ground, parts could be ruined.

   Disconnect the battery before connecting a battery charger to the battery. A voltage surge or high charge voltage can damage electronic components in the alternator, regulator, computerized ignition, fuel injection, or emission control systems.

2. NEVER REVERSE POLARITY. If battery or jumper cables are connected backwards, serious electrical damage could occur. Reversing polarity can blow the diodes in the alternator, ruin the circuit in the regulator or burn electronic components in other systems.

3. DO NOT OPERATE ALTERNATOR WITH OUTPUT DISCONNECTED. If the alternator is operated with the output wire off, alternator voltage can increase to above normal levels. Alternator or other circuit damage could result.

4. NEVER SHORT OR GROUND ANY CHARGING SYSTEM TERMINAL unless instructed to do so by a shop manual. Some circuits can be grounded or shorted without damage, others will be seriously damaged. Check in a service manual when in doubt.

5. DO NOT ATTEMPT TO POLARIZE AN ALTERNATOR. Older DC generator systems had to be polarized (voltage connected to generator field) after repairs. This must NOT be done with an alternator.

TEST THE BATTERY FIRST

When testing the charging system, it is common practice to check the condition of the battery. Even though charging system problems often show up as a dead battery, you must NOT forget that the battery itself may be bad.

Measure the battery state-of-charge and perform a battery load test (see chapter on battery service). Then, you will be sure that the battery is not affecting your charging system tests.

CHARGING SYSTEM TESTS

Charging system tests should be done when symptoms point to low alternator voltage and current. These tests will quickly determine the operating condition of the charging system.

There are four common charging system tests:
1. CHARGING SYSTEM OUTPUT TEST (measure current and voltage output of charging system under a load).
2. REGULATOR VOLTAGE TEST (measure charging system voltage under low output, low load conditions).
3. REGULATOR BYPASS TEST (connect full battery voltage to alternator field, leaving regulator out of circuit).
4. CIRCUIT RESISTANCE TESTS (measure resistance in insulated and ground circuits of system).

Charging system tests are frequently performed in two ways: using a LOAD TESTER (same tester used to check battery and starting system in earlier chapters) or a common VOM (volt-ohm-milliammeter).

A load tester provides the most accurate method of checking a charging system. See Fig. 31-5. It will measure both system current and voltage.

There are several different makes of charging system testers. The operating steps for each may vary. With any type tester, it is important to understand general test procedures. Then you can relate general test methods to any make or model of equipment.

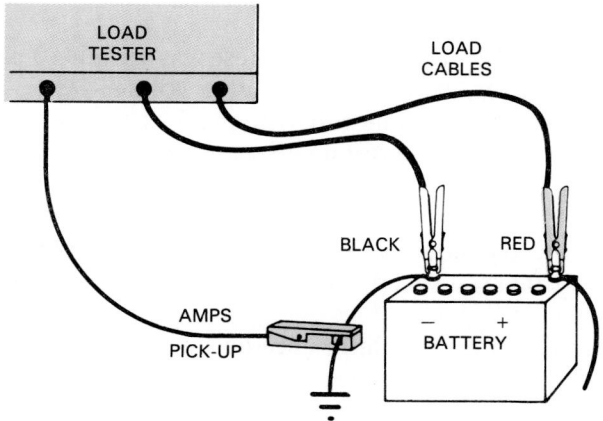

Fig. 31-5. Load testers, as used during battery and starting system tests, will also check charging output. Modern testers have an inductive, clip-on current clamp. Older testers must have ammeter connected in series. (Marquette)

Charging system output test

A *charging system output test* measures system current and voltage under maximum load (current output). To check output with a load tester, connect the tester leads as described by the manufacturer.

With modern testers, two leads fasten to the battery terminals. The inductive (clip-on) amps pickup fits around the insulation on the negative battery cable. See Fig. 31-5.

Procedures differ with non-inductive testers. Check the operating directions when in doubt.

1. With the load tester controls set properly, turn the ignition key switch to RUN. Note this ammeter reading.
2. Start the engine. Adjust the idle speed to the test specs (about 2000 rpm).
3. Adjust the load control on the tester until the ammeter reads specified current output but do NOT let voltage drop below specs (about 12 volts). Note (write down) this ammeter reading.
4. Rotate load control to OFF. Evaluate readings.

Charging output test results

To calculate charging system output, add your two ammeter readings (current with ignition switch at run plus current with engine running). This will give you total charging system output in amps. Compare this figure to specs.

Current output specs for charging systems will depend on the size (rating) of the alternator. For instance, a car with few electrical accessories may have an alternator rated at only 35 amps. A larger luxury car, with many accessories (air conditioning, speed control, power windows), might have an alternator with a much higher rating — 40 to 80 amps. Always check in a service manual to obtain exact values.

If the charging system output current tested low, complete regulator voltage and regulator bypass tests. They will let you determine whether the alternator, regulator, or circuit wiring is at fault.

Regulator voltage test

Even if the previous output test was within 10 percent of specs, perform a regulator voltage test.

A regulator voltage test will check the calibration of the voltage regulator and detect a high or low voltage setting.

Set the meter selector to the correct test position. With the load control OFF, run the engine at 2000 rpm or specified test speed. Note the voltmeter reading and compare to specs.

Most voltage regulators are designed to operate in the 13.5 to 14.5 volt range. This range is stated for normal temperatures with the battery fully charged.

If the meter reading is steady and within recommended values, then the regulator setting is OK.

If the volt reading is steady, but too high or too low, then the regulator may need adjustment or

replacement.

If the reading is not steady, then there may be a bad wiring connection, an alternator problem, or a defective regulator.

Regulator bypass test

If a charging system fails either the output or the regulator test, a regulator bypass test should be done.

A regulator bypass test is a quick and easy way of finding if the alternator, regulator, or circuit is faulty.

Procedures for a regulator bypass test are similar to the output test already explained. However, the regulator is taken out of the circuit.

Direct battery voltage (unregulated voltage) is used to excite the rotor field. This should make the alternator produce maximum output.

Depending upon system design, there are several ways to bypass the voltage regulator. One involves shorting a test tab to ground on the rear of the alternator. See Fig. 31-6. Another requires a jumper wire to connect battery voltage to the field, Fig. 31-7.

Follow manufacturer's directions to avoid damage. You must NOT short or connect voltage to the wrong

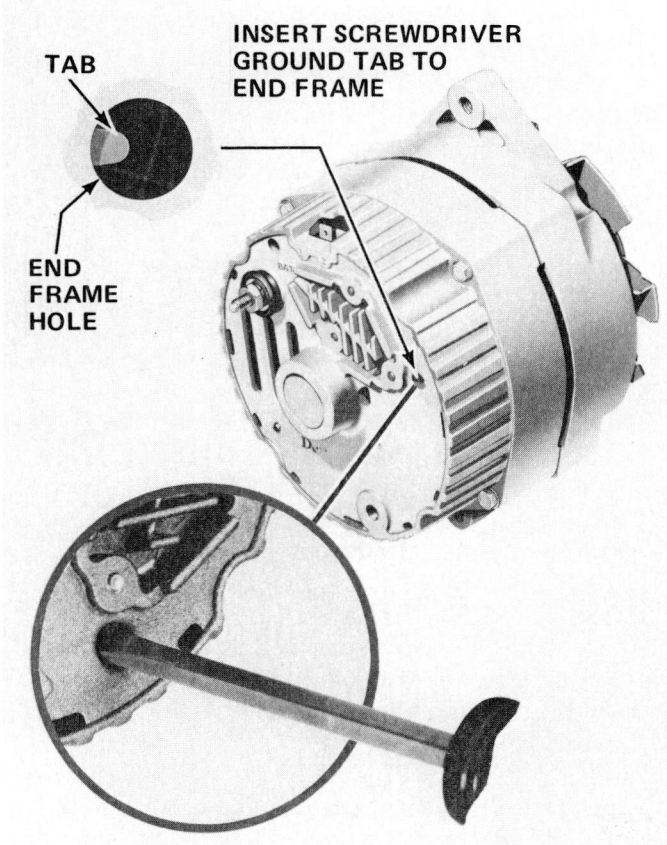

Fig. 31-6. *If charging system fails current output test, bypass the regulator to pinpoint problems. Shorting tab on this alternator should make alternator produce maximum output. If it does, regulator is bad. If it does not, then alternator may be bad. (Pontiac)*

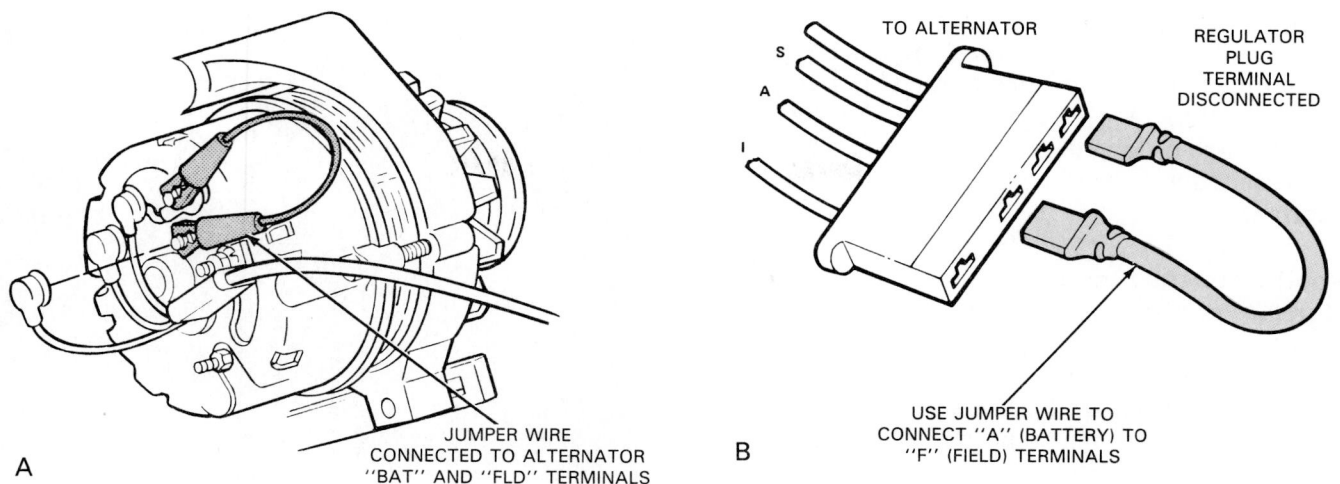

A

B

JUMPER WIRE
CONNECTED TO ALTERNATOR
"BAT" AND "FLD" TERMINALS

TO ALTERNATOR

REGULATOR
PLUG
TERMINAL
DISCONNECTED

USE JUMPER WIRE TO
CONNECT "A" (BATTERY) TO
"F" (FIELD) TERMINALS

Fig. 31-7. Other methods of bypassing regulator to find out if alternator or regulator is faulty. A — Jumper wire across battery and field terminals will fully excite rotor field. B — With remote regulator, unplug wires from regulator. Place jumper across battery and field terminals in wires to alternator. (Mercury)

wire or the diodes or regulator may be ruined.

Regulator bypass test results

If charging voltage and current INCREASE to normal levels when the regulator is bypassed, you usually have a *bad regulator.*

If system output REMAINS THE SAME when the regulator is bypassed, then you normally have a *bad alternator.*

Some late model alternators do not provide a method for full fielding. This makes it more difficult to isolate a low charging problem to the alternator or the voltage regulator. You must use a scope or load tester with a diode test function to check for abnormal voltage ripple (indicating bad alternator diodes) to isolate the trouble.

The vehicle's computer can also be used to control the charging system alternator by replacing the voltage

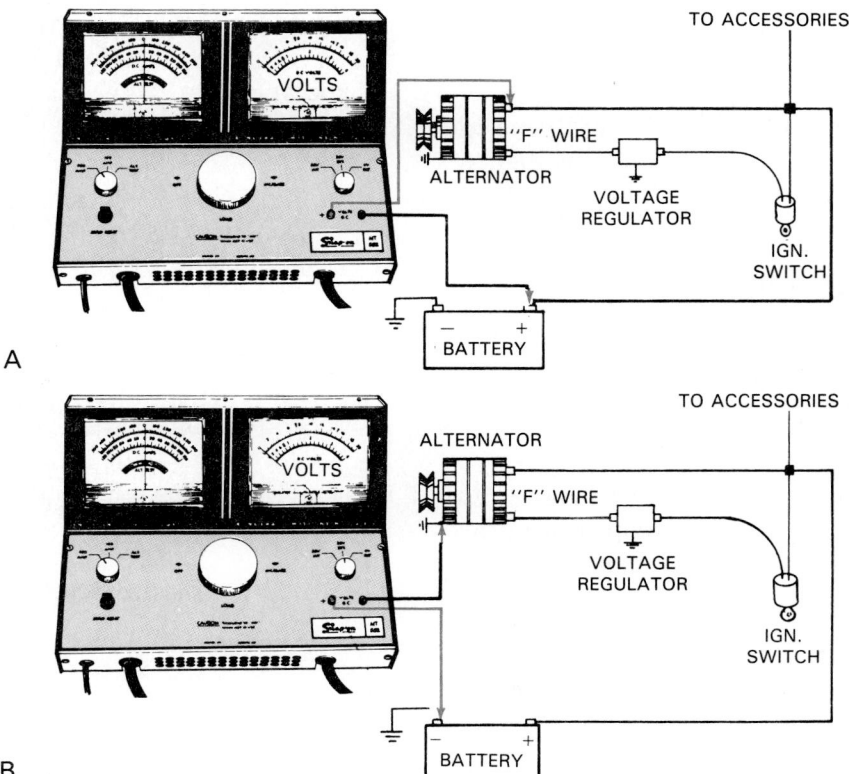

Fig. 31-8. Voltage drop or resistance tests will find problems in wiring. A — Connections for insulated circuit resistance test. B — Connections for ground circuit resistance test. Voltage reading above .1V per connection indicates resistance problems. (Snap-On Tools)

regulator. Basically, the computer controls the duty cycle of the alternator's field. *Duty cycle* is the percentage of time that current is fed to the alternator's field windings. With high electrical load, the duty cycle would be high or long to make the alternator produce high output, and vice versa. A duty cycle of about 50% is normal.

Circuit resistance tests

Circuit resistance tests are used to locate wiring problems in a charging system: loose connection, corroded terminal, partially burned wire, or other similar types of troubles. Resistance tests should be performed when symptoms point to problems other than the alternator or regulator.

There are two common circuit resistance tests: insulated resistance test and ground circuit resistance test.

To do an *insulated circuit resistance test* on a charging system, connect the tester as described by the manufacturer. One type of connection for a particular tester is shown in Fig. 31-8A. Note how the voltmeter is connected across the alternator output terminal and positive battery terminal.

With the vehicle running at a fast idle, turn the load control to obtain a 20 amp current flow at 15 volts or less. All lights and accessories should be OFF. Read the voltmeter.

If the circuit is in good condition, the voltmeter should NOT read over about .7 volt (.1 volt per electrical connection).

If the voltage drop is higher than .7V, circuit resistance is high. A poor connection exists in that section of the circuit.

A *ground circuit resistance test* is similar. However, the voltmeter is placed across the negative battery terminal and alternator housing. See Fig. 31-8B.

The voltmeter should NOT read over .1 volt per electrical connection. If the voltmeter reading is higher, look for loose connections, burned plug socket, or similar problems.

OTHER TESTER FUNCTIONS

Charging system testers, depending on make and model, may have other test modes (positions). They may be switched to check the alternator stator, diodes, or regulator for example. Read the tester instructions closely to learn about these tests.

Fig. 31-9 shows a special charging system tester using indicator lights. Fig. 31-10 shows scope waveforms for alternator diodes. For more information on these tests, refer to Chapters 42 and 43.

VOLTMETER TEST OF CHARGING SYSTEM

A voltmeter can also be used to test the output of a charging system when a load tester is not available. It will measure charging system voltage with an accessory load. The voltage reading will be an indicator

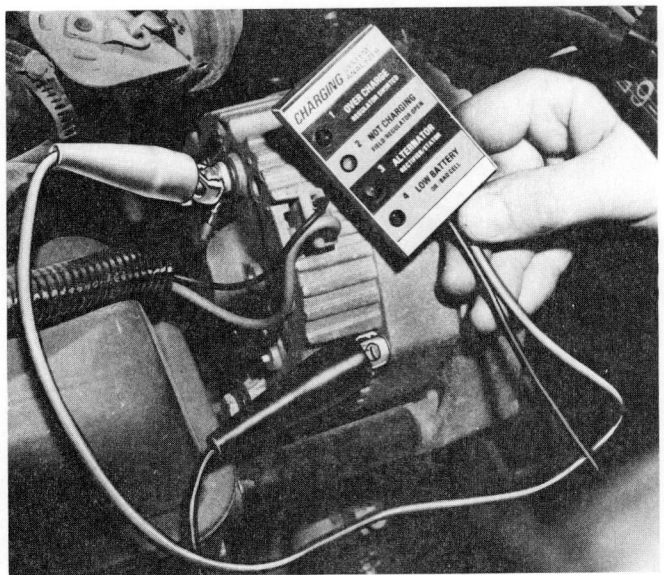

Fig. 31-9. Special charging system tester. It uses indicator lights to show specific problems. (Belden)

of current output and charging system condition. If charging system output voltage is NOT above battery voltage, the battery cannot be recharged and a problem exists.

The four basic steps are:
1. BASE VOLTAGE (measure battery voltage with engine OFF).
2. NO-LOAD VOLTAGE (measure voltage at battery with engine running, electrical accessories OFF).
3. LOAD VOLTAGE (measure voltage at battery with engine running, all electrical accessories ON).
4. CALCULATE CHARGE VOLTAGE (load voltage must be higher than base voltage for battery charging, no-load voltage must be within specs).

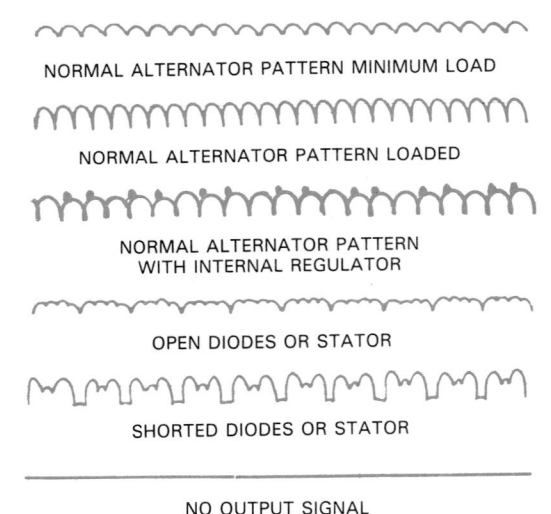

NORMAL ALTERNATOR PATTERN MINIMUM LOAD

NORMAL ALTERNATOR PATTERN LOADED

NORMAL ALTERNATOR PATTERN WITH INTERNAL REGULATOR

OPEN DIODES OR STATOR

SHORTED DIODES OR STATOR

NO OUTPUT SIGNAL AT RED VOLTMETER CLIP

Fig. 31-10. Oscilloscope will show diode problems before altnerator removal and teardown. (Marquette)

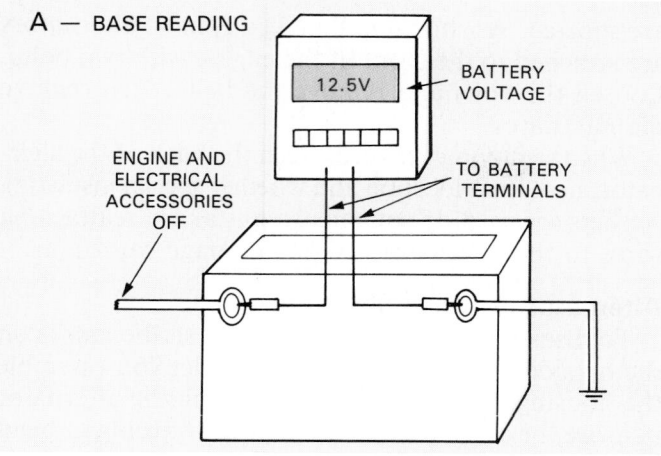

A — BASE READING

12.5V ← BATTERY VOLTAGE

ENGINE AND ELECTRICAL ACCESSORIES OFF

TO BATTERY TERMINALS

A — Measure battery voltage. This base reading should be noted. Battery voltage can vary with state of charge, electrical connections, and with different meters. Reading should be about 12.4 to 12.6 volts.

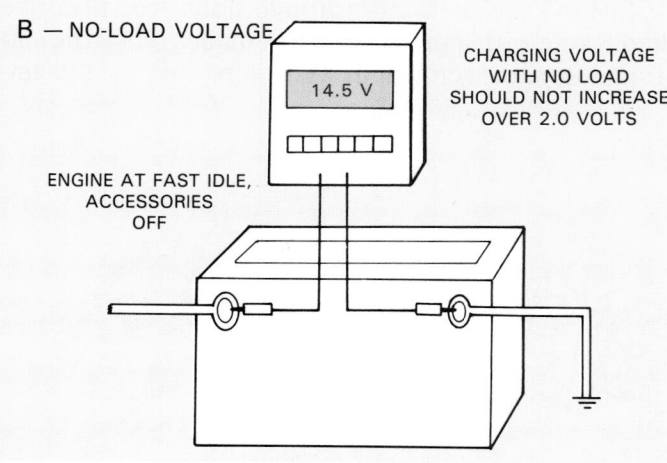

B — NO-LOAD VOLTAGE

14.5 V

CHARGING VOLTAGE WITH NO LOAD SHOULD NOT INCREASE OVER 2.0 VOLTS

ENGINE AT FAST IDLE, ACCESSORIES OFF

B — Start engine with all electrical accessories OFF. This is a no-load reading that checks voltage regulator adjustment. Meter reading should increase about two volts, but no more.

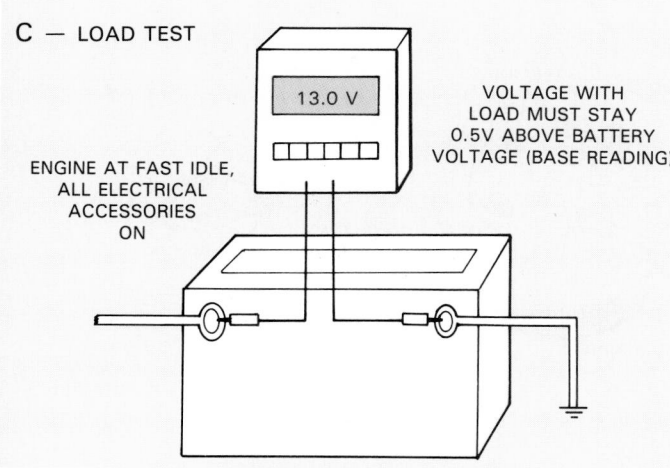

C — LOAD TEST

13.0 V

VOLTAGE WITH LOAD MUST STAY 0.5V ABOVE BATTERY VOLTAGE (BASE READING)

ENGINE AT FAST IDLE, ALL ELECTRICAL ACCESSORIES ON

C — Turn on all electrical accessories and check meter reading. Voltage must stay above base reading by at least .5 volt. If not, battery will be discharged. Repairs would be needed.

Fig. 31-11. If load tester is not available, common voltmeter can be used to test charging system output.

Voltmeter base reading

To test the charging system with a voltmeter, connect the meter probes across the terminals of the battery, Fig. 31-11A. Called the *base reading* (battery voltage with engine off), it will compensate for any variation in the condition of the battery and accuracy of your meter. The base reading should be around 12.6 volts with a good, fully charged battery.

Voltmeter no-load reading

Next, start and run the engine at about 1500 rpm with all electrical accessories OFF. This is called the *no-load test* because it measures charging system voltage without a current draw. The voltmeter reading should increase over the base reading, but NOT by more than about two volts.

For example, if your base reading is 12.5 volts, then your no-load reading should be approximately 13.0 to 14.5 volts. Look at Fig. 31-11B.

If the no-load voltage increases MORE THAN 2-3 volts, then the alternator is overcharging the battery. Either the voltage regulator or wiring is bad.

If the no-load reading is BETWEEN .5 and 2 volts higher than the base reading, then this part of the test is GOOD.

If the no-load voltage does NOT INCREASE above your base reading, then the charging system is NOT working. Either the alternator, regulator, or wiring may be bad. Bypass the regulator or perform resistance tests to isolate the problem.

Voltmeter load test

If the system passed the no-load test, you should also complete a load test. Start the engine and run it at about 2000 rpm.

Turn ON ALL ELECTRICAL ACCESSORIES (headlights, wipers, blower motor, air conditioning) to load the charging system. This will check the charging system output under high current draw conditions.

The voltmeter should read at least .5 volts HIGHER than your base battery reading, Fig. 36-11C.

The LOAD TEST shows that the charging system is providing current for all of the electrical units and still has enough current to recharge the battery.

If the load voltage is NOT .5 volts above battery voltage, bypass the regulator to determine which component (alternator or regulator) is faulty.

ALTERNATOR SERVICE

A *bad alternator* will show up during your tests as a low voltage and current output problem. Even when the regulator is bypassed and full voltage is applied to the alternator field, charging voltage and current will NOT be up to specs.

Alternator removal

Before unbolting the alternator, first DISCONNECT THE BATTERY to prevent damage to parts if wires

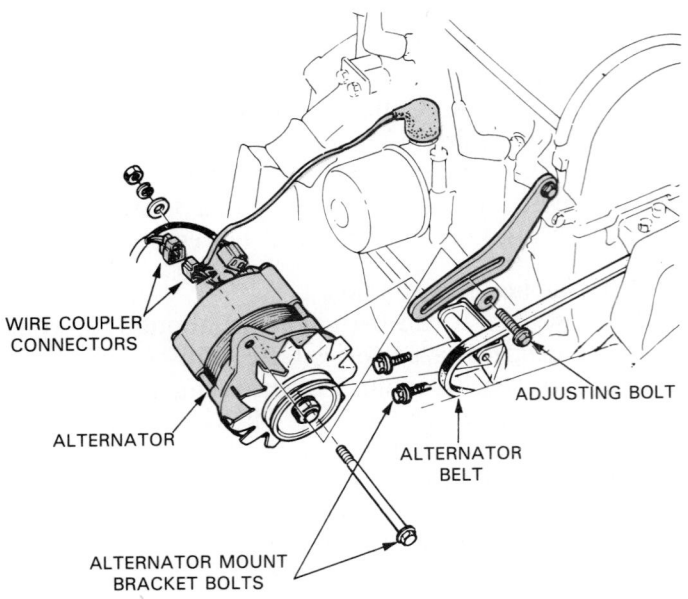

are shorted. As shown in Fig. 31-12, most alternators are attached to the front of the engine with two bolts. Loosen the bolts and remove the belt. Then remove the alternator.

When removing the wires from the back of the alternator, note their location and whether special insulating washers are used. If you make a mistake in reattaching wires to the alternator, system damage can occur.

Alternator disassembly

To disassemble an alternator, first scribe marks on the outside of the housing. This will let you assemble the housing correctly. When clamping the alternator in a vise, be careful not to damage the housing or bend the fan.

Use the directions in a shop manual to disassemble an alternator. Fig. 31-13 illustrates the basic steps. An Allen wrench may be needed to hold the shaft. Use a puller, if needed, to remove the pulley.

Remove the alternator through-bolts. Tap the drive end frame with a plastic or brass mallet. Slide the end frame from the rotor shaft. As you remove the remain-

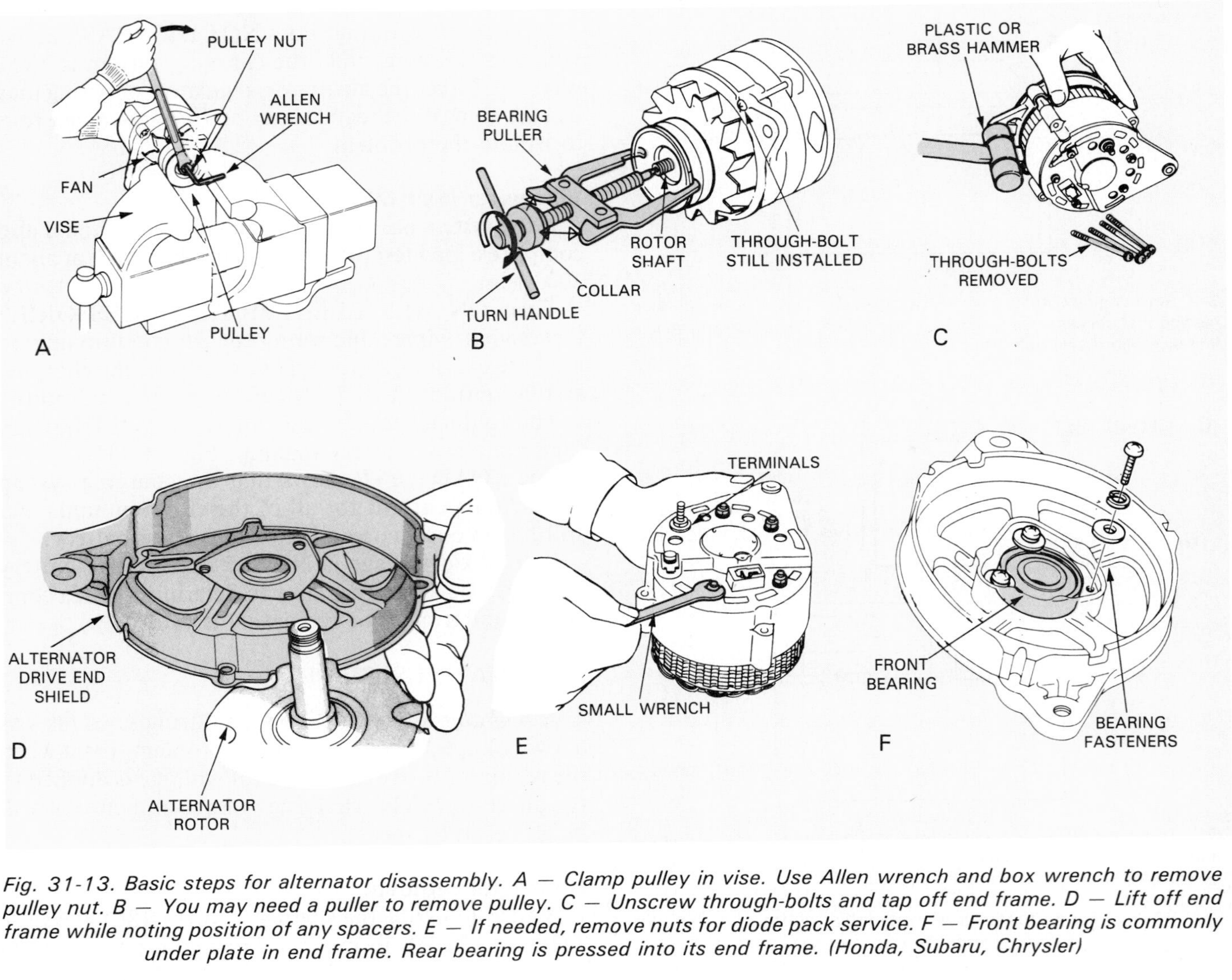

Fig. 31-12. To remove alternator, loosen bolts and slide belt off pulley. Disconnect wires and remove bolts. Take alternator to workbench. (Honda)

Fig. 31-13. Basic steps for alternator disassembly. A — Clamp pulley in vise. Use Allen wrench and box wrench to remove pulley nut. B — You may need a puller to remove pulley. C — Unscrew through-bolts and tap off end frame. D — Lift off end frame while noting position of any spacers. E — If needed, remove nuts for diode pack service. F — Front bearing is commonly under plate in end frame. Rear bearing is pressed into its end frame. (Honda, Subaru, Chrysler)

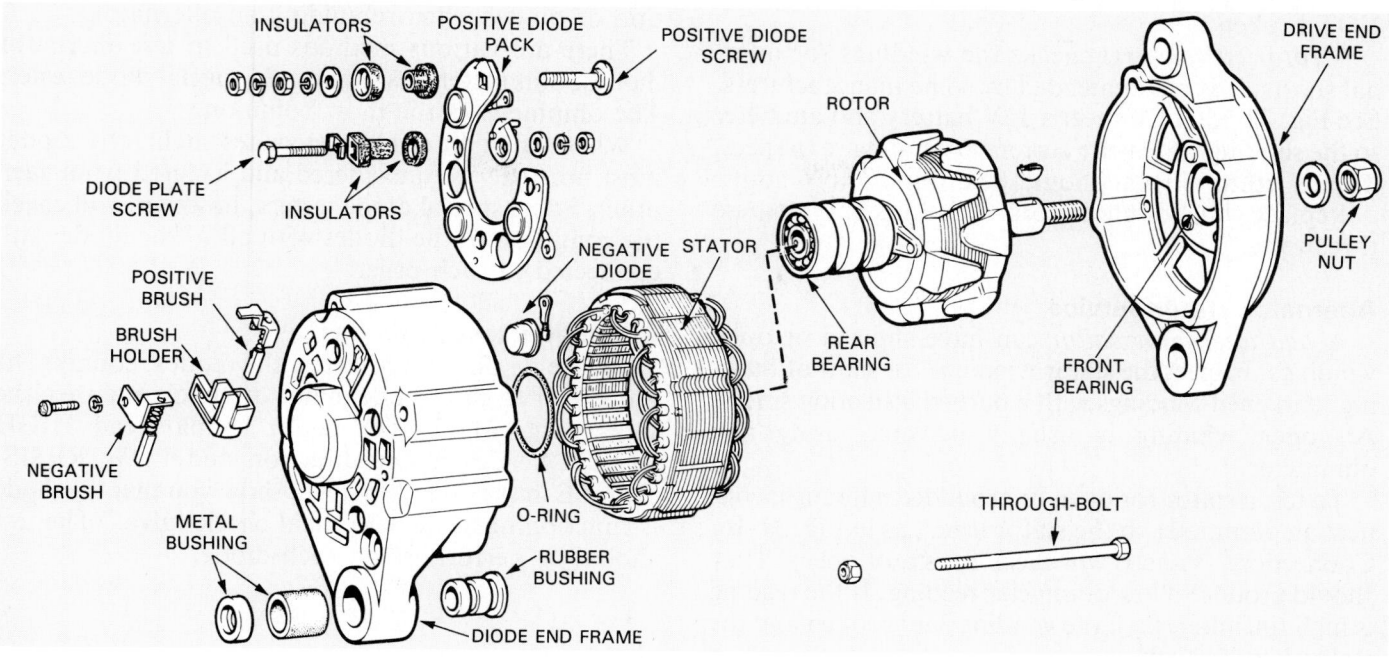

Fig. 31-14. Keep all parts organized on workbench during disassembly. Do not clean electrical parts in solvent. (Fiat)

ing alternator parts, watch how everything fits together.

Depending upon the type of repair, you may have to either completely or partially disassemble the alternator. To simply replace worn alternator bearings, you do NOT have to remove the diodes, built-in regulator, or other unrelated parts. However, if alternator output is low, you may need to completely disassemble the alternator for a major rebuild.

Keep all of your parts organized and clean, Fig. 31-14. If you get grease on the brushes, replace them. Grease or oil will ruin the brushes.

Do NOT soak the rotor, stator, diode pack, regulator, or other electrical components in solvent. Solvent could ruin these components.

Alternator rotor service

A *bad alternator rotor* can have a bent shaft, scored slip rings, open windings or shorted windings. Visually inspect the rotor closely. Make sure the rotor is in good condition before assembling the alternator. There are several tests designed to check an alternator rotor.

A *rotor winding short-to-ground test* measures resistance between the rotor shaft and windings. Look at Fig. 31-15A. The ohmmeter should read infinite (maximum) resistance to show no short to ground.

A *rotor winding open circuit test* measures the resistance between the two slip rings. Refer to Fig. 31-15B. The meter should read low resistance (about 2 to 4 ohms). This would show that the windings are

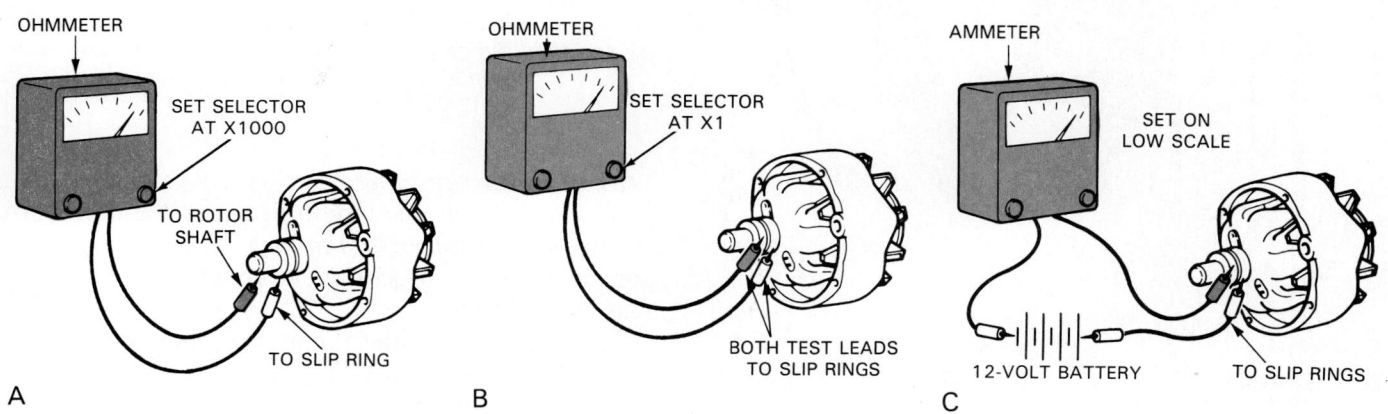

Fig. 31-15. Alternator rotor tests. A — Rotor winding short-to-ground test. Meter should read infinite ohms. B — Rotor winding open test. Meter should read low ohms. C — Rotor internal short test. Meter should show normal current draw.   (Chrysler)

NOT broken.

A *rotor current test* checks the windings for internal shorts. It is recommended by some manufacturers. See Fig. 31-15C. Connect a 12V battery and ammeter to the slip rings. Measure current and compare to specs. Typical rotor current should be around 3 to 6 amps.

Replace the alternator rotor if it fails any of these three tests.

Alternator stator service

A *bad alternator stator* can have shorted or open windings. Inspect the stator windings for signs of burning (darkened windings with a burned insulation smell). An open winding is usually detected using any ohmmeter.

To test a stator for open or grounded windings, connect an ohmmeter to the stator leads, as in Fig. 31-16. Connections A and B will check for stator opens. They should produce a low ohmmeter reading. If the reading is high (infinite), then the windings are broken and the stator is defective.

Connection C tests for a grounded winding. A high or infinite reading is desirable. If the reading is low, then the stator is grounded and should be replaced.

Alternator diode service

Bad alternator diodes reduce alternator output current and voltage. They are a very frequent cause for alternator failure. It is important to check the condition of diodes when rebuilding an alternator.

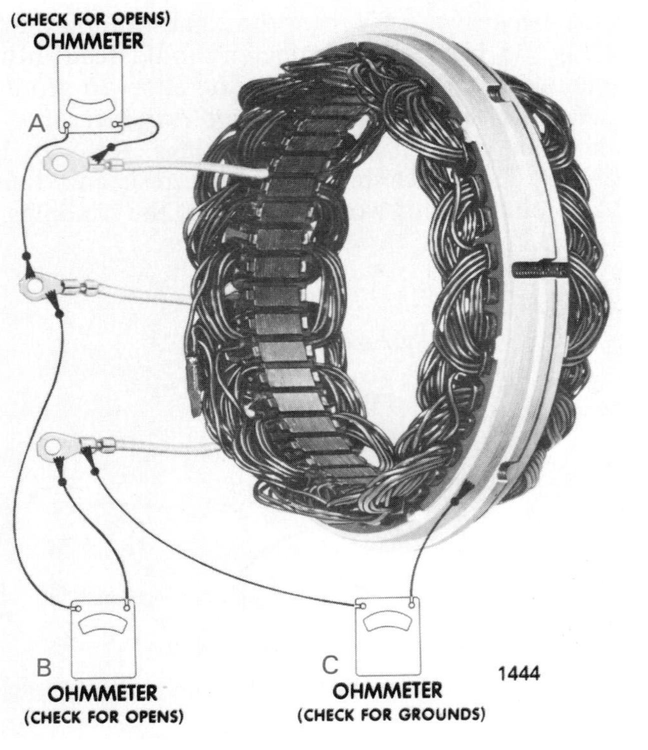

There are various methods used to test alternator diodes: ohmmeter, test light, and special diode tester. The ohmmeter is the most common.

When using an ohmmeter or test light, the diodes must normally be unsoldered and isolated from each other. Some special diode testers, however, will check the condition of the diodes with all of the diodes still connected to each other.

Ohmmeter test of diodes

To use an ohmmeter to test the diodes, connect the ohmmeter to each diode in one direction and then the other, Fig. 31-17. The meter should read HIGH RESISTANCE in one direction and LOW RESISTANCE in the other. This will show you that the diode is functioning as an "electrical check valve." The test should be performed on each diode.

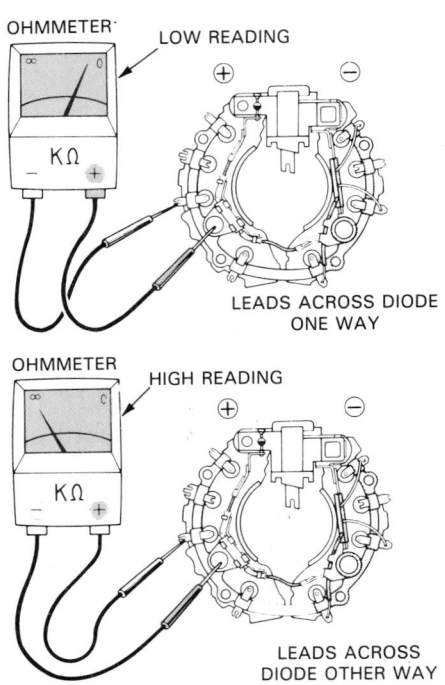

Fig. 31-17. To test diodes with ohmmeter, connect leads one way and then the other. Meter should read high ohms in one direction and low in other. (Toyota)

A *bad diode* can either be shorted or opened. An *open diode* will have a high (infinite) resistance in both directions. A *shorted diode* will have a low (zero) resistance in both directions. In either case, the diode must be replaced.

If you had to unsolder the diodes, they will have to be resoldered during installation. After pressing in the new diode or obtaining a new diode pack, use a soldering gun and rosin core solder to attach the diode leads, Fig. 31-18. Heat the wires quickly to avoid overheating the diodes. Excess heat can ruin a diode.

Fig. 31-16. Stator tests. Connect ohmmeter for three tests as shown to check windings. (Chevrolet)

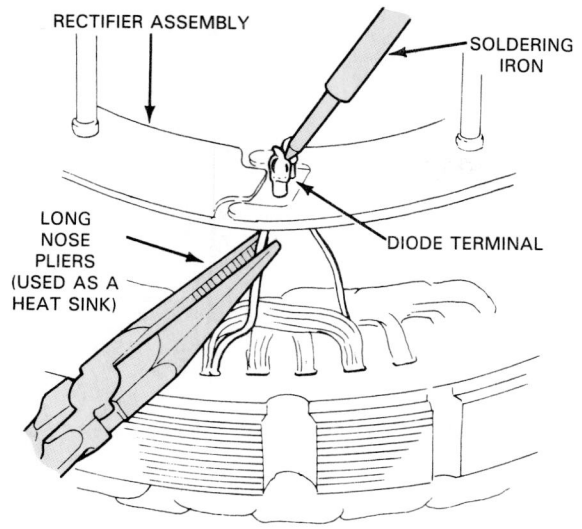

Fig. 31-18. Use rosin core solder to join stator-to-rectifier wires.

Alternator bearing service

Worn or *dry alternator bearings* produce a rumbling or grinding noise during operation. They can become loose enough to upset alternator output by allowing too much rotor shaft movement. When rebuilding an alternator, it is common practice to replace the bearings.

The front alternator bearing, also called the drive end bearing, is usually held in place with a cover plate and small screws. To replace the bearing, remove the screws and plate and lift out the old bearing.

The rear alternator bearing, also referred to as the diode or slip ring end bearing, is normally pressed into the rear end housing. It may be pressed or carefully driven out of the alternator housing for replacement.

If the bearings are relatively new and you do not replace them, make sure you put a moderate amount of grease into the rear bearing. The front bearing is usually sealed and cannot be greased.

To check the action of the front bearing, rotate it with your finger while feeling for roughness or dryness. Replace the bearing if there is any sign of failure.

Alternator brush service

Worn brushes can affect the output voltage and current of an alternator. As the brushes wear, spring tension and brush pressure on the slip rings will be reduced.

Inspect the brushes and measure their length. When the brushes are worn beyond specs or soaked in oil or grease, replace them.

Alternator assembly

After you have inspected and tested the components of an alternator, you are ready for reassembly. Since alternator construction varies, refer to a service manual describing the particular style unit. In general, assemble the alternator in reverse order of disassembly. Study Fig. 31-19.

Install all of the components in the rear or slip ring end frame: electronic regulator, diode pack, rear bearing, terminals, and nuts.

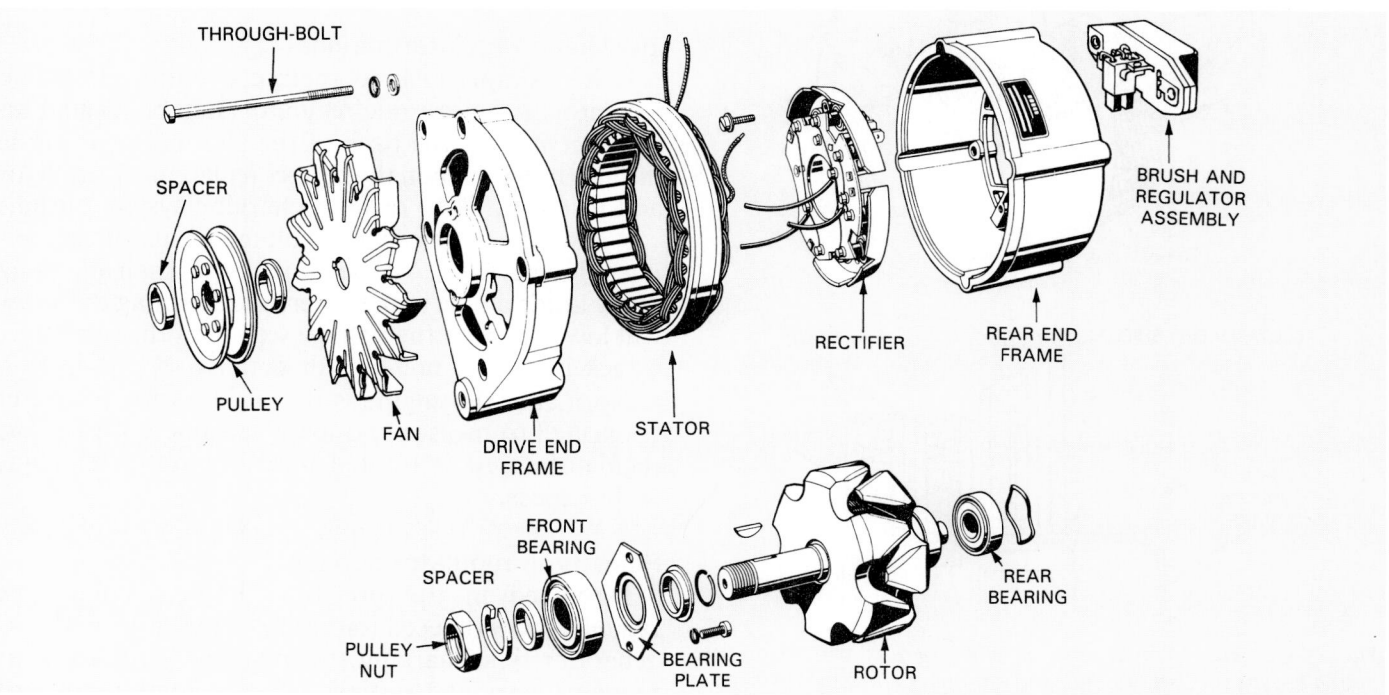

Fig. 31-19. Refer to a service manual for an illustration like this one during assembly. Exploded view shows how parts fit together. (Bosch)

When the brushes are NOT mounted on the outside rear of the end frame, you sometimes need to use a piece of stiff wire or small Allen wrench to install the brushes. Push the brush spring and brush up into place, Fig. 31-20. Then, slide your wire or Allen wrench into a hole in the rear end frame. Push the next spring and brush into place. Slide the wire the rest of the way through the hole.

The wire or Allen wrench will hold the brushes out of the way as you slide the rotor into the housing.

Fit the front end frame into position and check the alignment pins or marks. Install and tighten the through-bolts.

Pull out the piece of wire or Allen wrench. You should hear the brushes CLICK into place on the slip rings.

Finally, install any spacer, the fan, front pulley, lock washer, and nut. Torque the pulley nut to specs, Fig. 31-21. Then, spin the rotor shaft and pulley to check for free movement. The rotor should spin freely without making unusual noises.

Test alternator output on a *bench tester* (unit for off-car output test of alternator) if one is available.

Alternator installation

With the battery still disconnected, fit the alternator onto the front of the engine. If needed, install the wires on the back of the alternator first. Hand start the bolts and screw them in without tightening.

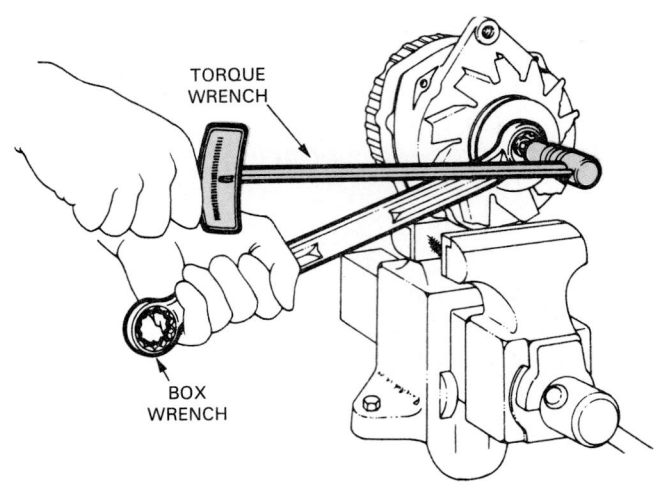

Fig. 31-21. *Use a torque wrench to properly tighten pulley nut. Be careful not to damage alternator housing or fan in vise. (Chrysler)*

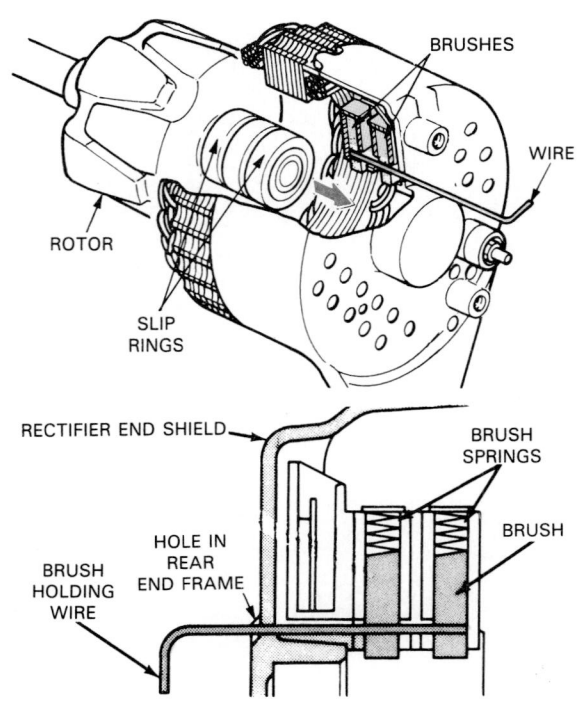

Fig. 31-20. *Top. With internal brushes, wire is often used to install brushes. Push brushes and springs up into place. Then slide wire through hole in back of alternator. Bottom. Wire will hold brushes as you fit rotor into position. Slide wire out and brushes will snap into contact with slip rings.*

Check the condition of the alternator belt. Replace it if needed. Slip the belt over the engine and alternator pulley. Make sure the belt is aligned properly on each pulley. Adjust belt tension and tighten bolts. Reconnect the battery.

REGULATOR SERVICE

When a regulator fails a voltage test, either adjustment or replacement is required. A regulator cannot be repaired. However, if the regulator setting is only slightly high or low, you can sometimes adjust it.

Electronic regulator service

It is a simple task to replace a faulty electronic regulator. An electronic regulator may be located on a fenderwell, on the back of the alternator, or inside the alternator. Obtain the correct replacement regulator and install it. Then recheck charging system output.

A few types of electronic voltage regulators are adjustable, Fig. 31-22A. They can have a small adjusting screw inside a hole in the outer case. Turning the screw will lower or raise the voltage setting of the regulator. Check in a shop manual for details.

Normally, the engine is run at idle with voltmeter connected to measure no-load charging voltage. The regulator screw is rotated until the voltmeter reads within specs.

Point type regulator service

Discussed in the previous chapter, point type regulators were used on early alternator and DC generator type charging systems. The regulator, due to point wear and pitting, was a common cause of problems.

If you should work on a car equipped with a point

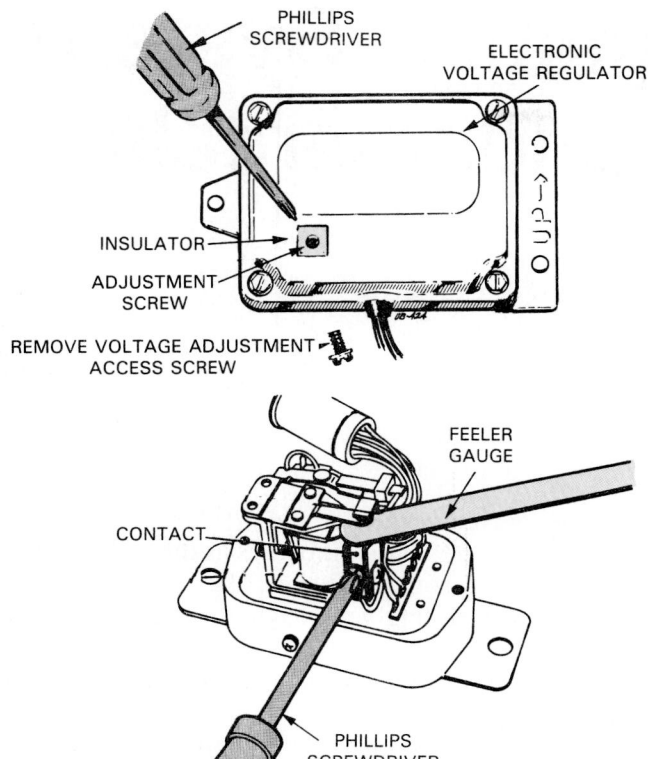

PHILLIPS SCREWDRIVER

ELECTRONIC VOLTAGE REGULATOR

INSULATOR

ADJUSTMENT SCREW

REMOVE VOLTAGE ADJUSTMENT ACCESS SCREW

FEELER GAUGE

CONTACT

PHILLIPS SCREWDRIVER

Fig. 31-22. A — A few electronic regulators are adjustable, most are not. B — Older contact point regulators are usually adjustable. Turn screw or bend spring tab to change settings. Most technicians replace regulator when adjustment is incorrect. (Motorola and Subaru)

regulator, refer to an early service manual. Circuits and regulator operation vary. You will need a manual covering the exact type regulator circuit. It will tell you how to file, test, and adjust the regulator points.

Basically, a point type regulator is adjusted as in Fig. 31-22B. Idle the engine while measuring no-load voltage. You must either turn an adjusting screw or bend an adjusting tab to obtain the correct output.

If the regulator cannot be adjusted to obtain the proper voltage, replace it.

KNOW THESE TERMS

Charging system output test, Regulator voltage test, Regulator bypass test, Circuit resistance tests, Rotor winding short, Rotor winding open, Rotor current test, Stator test, Diode test.

REVIEW QUESTIONS

1. Name four common symptoms caused by charging system problems.
2. Overtightening an alternator belt is a common mistake that ruins the alternator bearings. True or False?
3. List and explain five charging system service precautions.
4. List and explain four common charging system tests.
5. A _____ _____ is an instrument that provides the most accurate method of checking the condition of a charging system.
6. A charging system output test measures system _____ and _____ under maximum _____ conditions.
7. Depending upon alternator rating, charging system output can range from approximately 35 amps up to 80 amps. True or False?
8. Most voltage regulators are designed to maintain between 11 and 12 volts. True or False?
9. Explain the regulator bypass test.
10. A charging system has failed the output and regulator voltage tests. Voltage and current were too low. All belts, electrical connections, and other visible checks were ok.
    Technician A says that a regulator bypass test should be done next to help isolate the problem to the alternator, regulator, or circuit wiring.
    Technician B says that the alternator should be removed and tested on a bench. This will eliminate any wiring or circuit troubles.
    Who is correct?
    a. Technician A
    b. Technician B
    c. Both A and B
    d. Neither A nor B
11. What is the purpose of charging system circuit resistance tests?
12. Charging system testers and an oscilloscope can be used to help diagnose charging system troubles. True or False?
13. A bad alternator will show up as low voltage and current outputs, even when the regulator is bypassed. True or False?
14. A bad alternator rotor can have a:
    a. Bent shaft.
    b. Scored slip rings.
    c. Open windings.
    d. Shorted windings.
    e. All of the above are correct.
15. Explain three rotor tests.
16. How do you test a stator?
17. What symptoms are produced with bad alternator bearings?

ACTIVITIES FOR CHAPTER 31

1. Make a poster for classroom display, showing the steps involved in checking a charging system with a voltmeter.
2. Demonstrate use of a stiff wire to hold brushes in place when reassembling an alternator.

32  Ignition System Fundamentals

After studying this chapter, you will be able to:
- Explain the operating principles of an automotive ignition system.
- Compare contact point, electronic, and computer-controlled ignition systems.
- Describe the function of major ignition system components.
- Explain vacuum, centrifugal, and electronic ignition timing advance.
- Sketch the primary and secondary sections of an ignition system.
- Compare ignition coil, spark plug, and distributor design variations.
- Describe the safety practices to follow when working with ignition systems.

The vehicle's ignition system produces the high voltage needed to ignite the fuel charges in the cylinders of a gasoline engine. The system must create an electric arc across the gaps at the spark plugs. These events must be timed so they happen exactly as each piston nears the top of its compression stroke. The heat of the spark starts combustion and produces the engine's power stroke.

In recent years, different types of ignition systems have been developed to improve engine performance, fuel economy, and dependability, Fig. 32-1. This chapter compares the older contact point type with more modern electronic and computer-coil (distributorless) ignitions. This should give you a sound knowledge of all automotive ignition systems.

FUNCTIONS OF AN IGNITION SYSTEM

An ignition system must peform these functions:
1. Provide a method of turning a spark ignition or gasoline engine ON and OFF.
2. Be capable of operating on various supply voltages (battery or alternator voltage).
3. Produce a high voltage arc at the spark plug electrodes to start combustion.
4. Distribute high voltage pulses to each spark plug in the correct sequence.
5. Time the spark so that it occurs as the piston nears TDC on the compression stroke.
6. Vary spark timing with engine speed, load, and other conditions.

Various ignition system parts and designs are used to achieve these functions.

BASIC IGNITION SYSTEM

An *ignition system* must change low battery voltage into very high voltage and then send the high voltage to the spark plugs. The parts needed to do this are shown in Fig. 32-2.
1. BATTERY (provides power for system).
2. IGNITION SWITCH (allows driver to turn ignition and engine on and off).
3. IGNITION COIL (changes battery voltage into 30,000 volts or more).
4. SWITCHING DEVICE (contact points or electronic circuit that operates ignition coil).
5. SPARK PLUG (air gap in combustion chamber for electric arc).
6. IGNITION SYSTEM WIRES (conductors that connect components).

With the ignition switch ON, current flows to the parts of the ignition system. When the switching device is closed (conducting current), current flows through and energizes the ignition coil.

When the piston is nearing TDC on the compression stroke, the switching device opens. This causes high voltage to shoot out of the ignition coil and to the spark plug.

The electric arc at the plug ignites the fuel mixture. The mixture begins to burn, forming pressure in the cylinder for the engine's power stroke.

When the ignition key is turned to OFF, the battery-to-coil circuit is broken. Without current to the ignition coil, sparks are NOT produced at the spark plugs and the engine stops running.

An actual ignition system is much more complex than the one just discussed. Vehicles have multiple cylinder

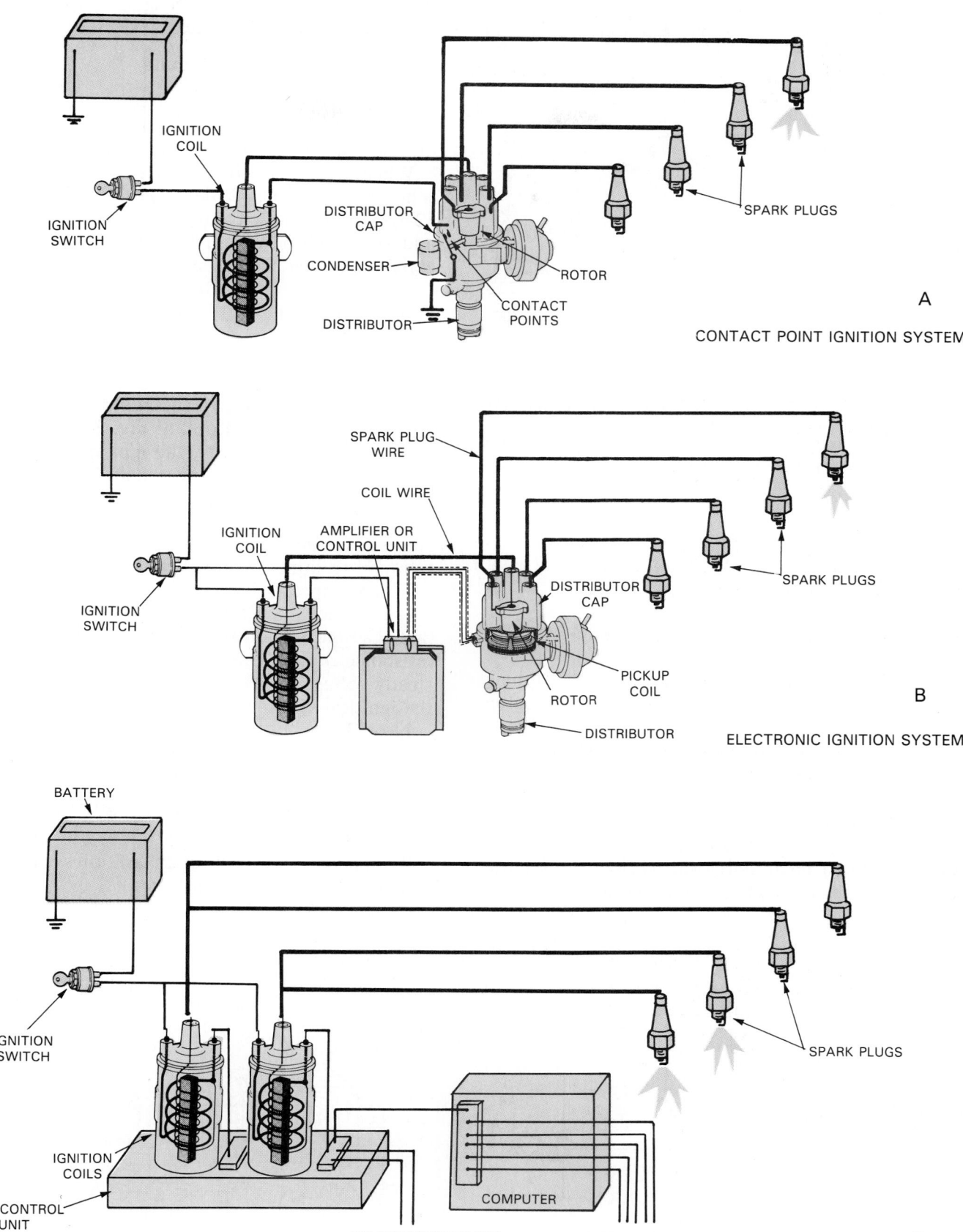

IGNITION COIL

IGNITION SWITCH

DISTRIBUTOR CAP

CONDENSER

DISTRIBUTOR

ROTOR

CONTACT POINTS

SPARK PLUGS

A

CONTACT POINT IGNITION SYSTEM

SPARK PLUG WIRE

COIL WIRE

IGNITION COIL

AMPLIFIER OR CONTROL UNIT

IGNITION SWITCH

DISTRIBUTOR CAP

SPARK PLUGS

PICKUP COIL

ROTOR

DISTRIBUTOR

B

ELECTRONIC IGNITION SYSTEM

BATTERY

IGNITION SWITCH

IGNITION COILS

COIL CONTROL UNIT

COMPUTER

TO CRANKSHAFT AND CAMSHAFT SENSORS

TO OTHER ENGINE SENSORS

SPARK PLUGS

C

DISTRIBUTORLESS IGNITION SYSTEM

Fig. 32-1. There are three basic types of automotive ignition systems. A — Older contact point. B — Modern electronic type with distributor. C — Latest computer-coil ignition does not use a distributor. (Saab)

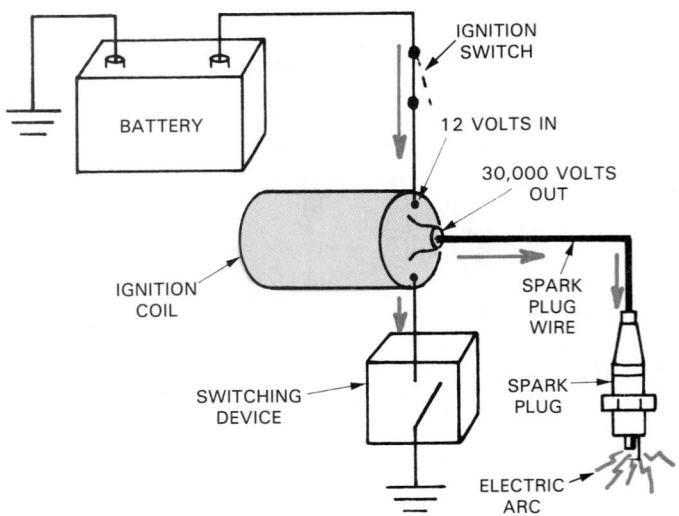

Fig. 32-2. Basic ignition system for one-cylinder engine. Battery voltage is stepped up to about 30,000 volts by the coil before it is sent to the spark plug. Switching device times voltage to coil. It can be set of mechanical breaker points or electronic switching circuit.

engines and the timing of the sparks must vary with operating conditions.

IGNITION SYSTEM SUPPLY VOLTAGE

The *ignition system supply voltage* is fed to the ignition system by the battery or alternator. The battery provides electricity when starting the engine. After the engine is running, the alternator supplies a slightly higher voltage to the battery and ignition system.

Ignition switch

The *ignition switch* is a key-operated switch in the driver's compartment. A hot wire (voltage supply wire) connects the switch to the battery. Other terminals on the switch are connected to the ignition system, starter solenoid, and other electrical devices.

Bypass and resistance circuits

An ignition system *bypass circuit* is sometimes used to supply direct battery voltage to the ignition system during starting motor operation.

When the engine is being started, the ignition switch is in the start or fully clockwise position. Shown in Fig. 32-3A, this connects the battery to the starting motor and to the ignition system. The electric motor spins the engine until the engine begins to run.

The starting motor draws high current and causes battery voltage to drop below 12.6 volts. The bypass circuit assures that there is still enough voltage and current for ignition operation and easy engine starting.

A *resistor circuit* may be used in the ignition system to limit supply voltage to the ignition system during alternator operation. Look at Fig. 32-3B.

After the engine starts, the ignition key switch is released. A spring inside the switch causes it to return to the RUN POSITION.

To protect the ignition from damage, a resistor circuit is sometimes placed between the switch and ignition coil to limit current flow.

Either a special *resistance wire* (wire having internal resistance) or a *ballast resistor* (heat sensitive resistor that can regulate voltage to ignition coil) is used in the resistance circuit. This circuit assures that a relatively steady voltage of about 9.5 to 10.5 volts is applied to the ignition system.

Note! Many electronic ignition systems do not use bypass or resistance circuits.

PRIMARY AND SECONDARY CIRCUITS

The two main sections of an ignition system are the primary and secondary circuits.

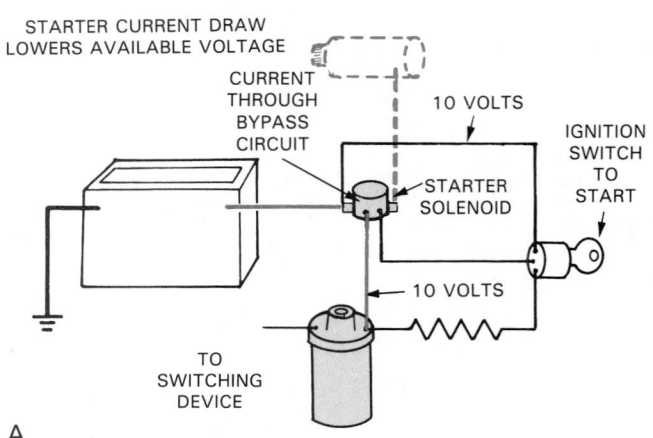

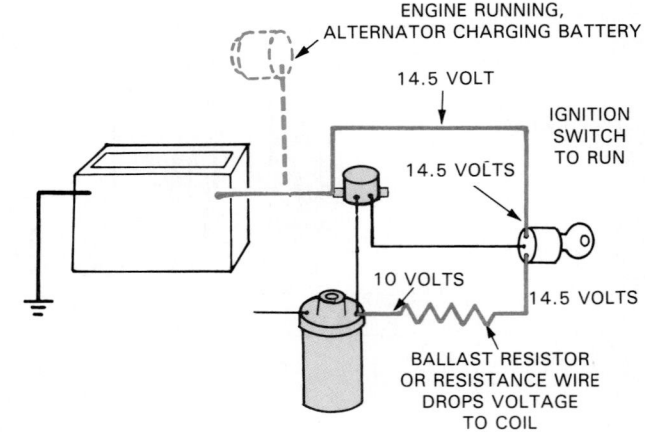

Fig. 32-3. Some ignition systems use resistance and bypass circuits to feed current to the ignition coil. A — When cranking, bypass feeds direct battery voltage to coil. B — After starting, resistance circuit feeds controlled voltage to coil. (Echlin)

The *primary circuit* of the ignition system includes all of the components and wires operating on low voltage (battery or alternator voltage). See Fig. 32-4A.

The *secondary circuit* of the ignition system is the high voltage (30,000 volt) section. It consists of the wires and parts between the coil output and the spark plug ground, Fig. 32-4B.

The primary circuit of the ignition system uses conventional wire, similar to the wire used in the other electrical systems of the car. The secondary wiring, however, must have much THICKER INSULATION to prevent *leakage* (arcing) of the high voltage.

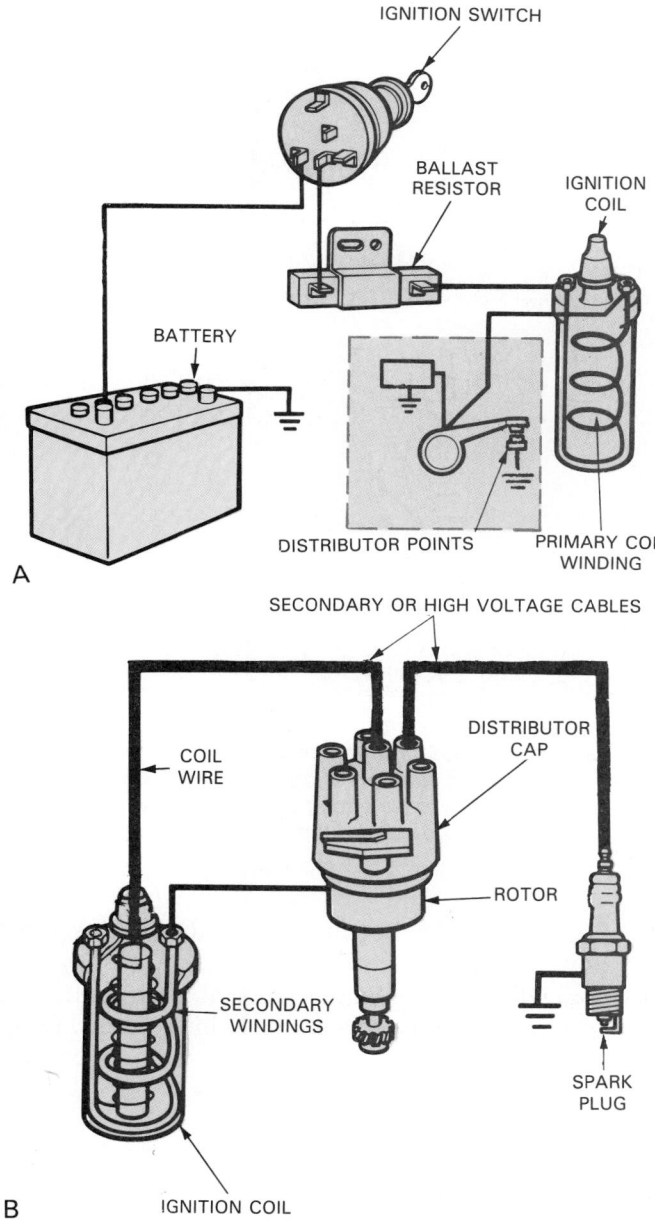

A

B

Fig. 32-4. Two major sections of an ignition system. A — Primary circuit includes all parts working on battery voltage. B — Secondary circuit consists of parts carrying high coil output voltage. (Mopar)

IGNITION COIL

An *ignition coil* produces the high voltage (30,000 volts or more) needed to make current jump the gap at the spark plugs. It is a pulse type transformer capable of producing a short burst of high voltage for starting combustion.

As in Fig. 32-4B, coil output voltage usually passes through the coil wire, distributor, plug wire, and spark plug before starting the burning process in the engine.

Ignition coil construction

Shown in Fig. 32-5, the ignition coil consists of two sets of *windings* (insulated wire wrapped in circular pattern). The coil has two primary terminals (low voltage connections), an *iron core* (long piece of iron inside windings), and a high voltage terminal (output or coil wire connection).

The *primary windings* of the coil are several hundred turns of heavy wire, wrapped around or near the secondary windings.

The *secondary windings* are several thousand turns of very fine wire located inside or near the primary windings.

Both windings are wrapped around an iron core and are housed inside the coil case.

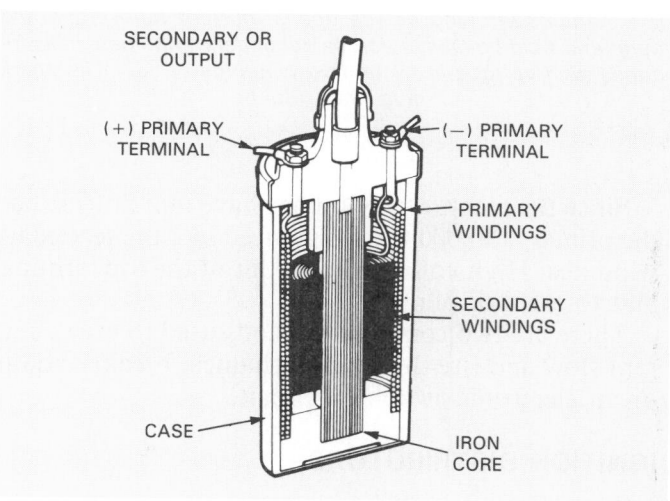

Fig. 32-5. Cutaway of ignition coil shows basic parts. Primary windings surround secondary windings. Iron core is mounted in center of windings. (Dodge)

Ignition coil operation

When battery current flows through the ignition coil primary windings, a strong magnetic field is produced. Look at Fig. 32-6A. The action of the iron core helps concentrate and strengthen the field.

When the current flowing through the coil is broken, the magnetic field COLLAPSES across the secondary windings. See Fig. 32-6B.

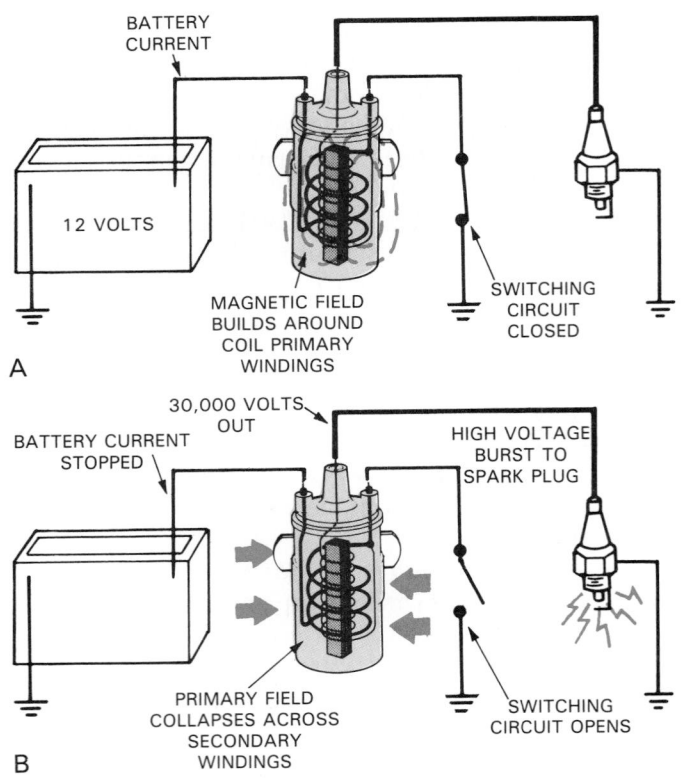

Fig. 32-6. Ignition coil operation. A — With switching device (points or electronic circuit) closed, current flows through ignition coil primary windings. Strong magnetic field builds in coil. B — When switching device opens, current flow stops and magnetic field collapses across secondary windings. This induces high voltage in secondary windings of coil. The spark plug fires. (Saab)

Since the secondary windings have more turns than the primary, 30,000 volts is induced into the secondary windings. High voltage shoots out of the top terminal and to a spark plug.

There are two common methods used to break current flow and fire the coil: mechanical breaker points or an electronic switching circuit.

IGNITION DISTRIBUTORS

Typically, an *ignition distributor,* Fig. 32-7, has several functions:

1. It actuates the ON/OFF cycles of current flow through the ignition coil primary windings.
2. It distributes the coil's high voltage pulses to each spark plug wire.
3. It must cause the spark to occur at each plug earlier in the compression stroke as engine speed increases and vice versa.
4. It changes spark timing with changes in engine load. As more load is placed on the engine, the spark timing must occur later in the compression stroke to prevent spark knock (abnormal combustion).

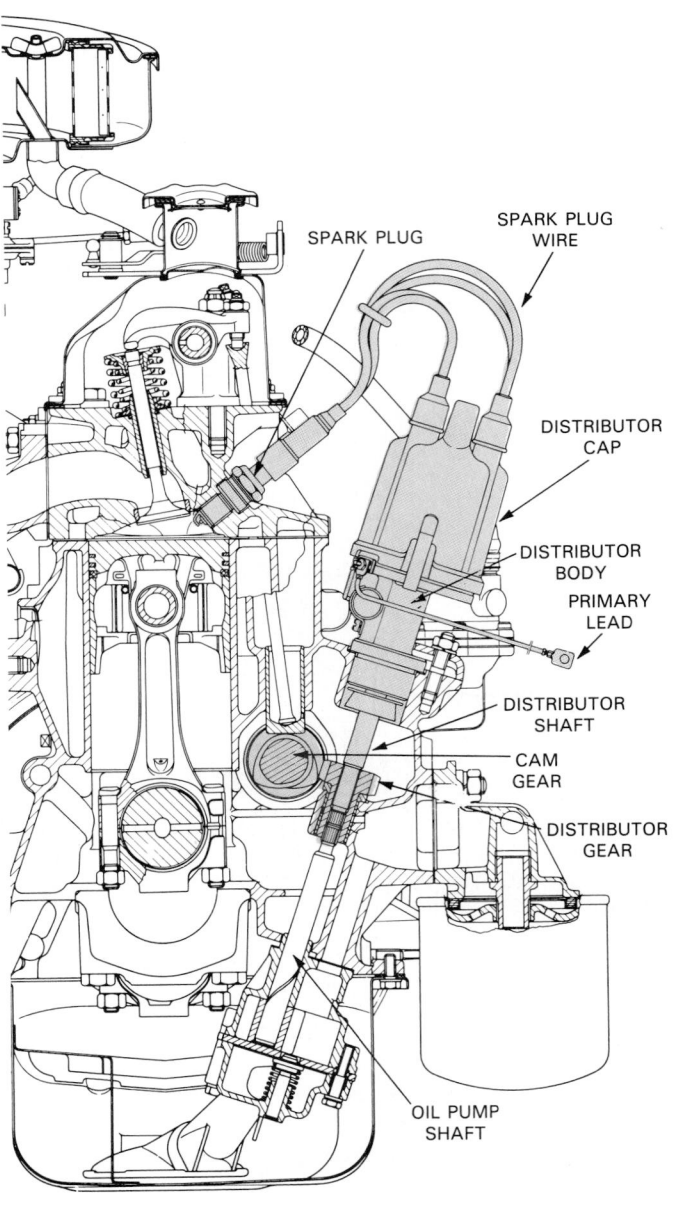

Fig. 32-7. Ignition distributor is usually driven by engine camshaft. Small gear on cam drives gear on distributor at one-half engine rpm. Main purpose of distributor is to feed coil voltage to spark plugs. (Fiat)

5. Sometimes, the bottom of the distributor shaft powers the engine oil pump.
6. Some distributors (unitized distributors) house the ignition coil and electronic switching circuit. Refer to Fig. 32-8.

Distributor types

An ignition distributor can be a contact point (mechanical) or pickup coil (used with electronic switching circuit) type. A contact point distributor is commonly used on older cars. The pickup coil type distributor is used on many modern automobiles. Note the basic differences between the two in Fig. 32-9.

A contact point distributor uses mechanical breaker

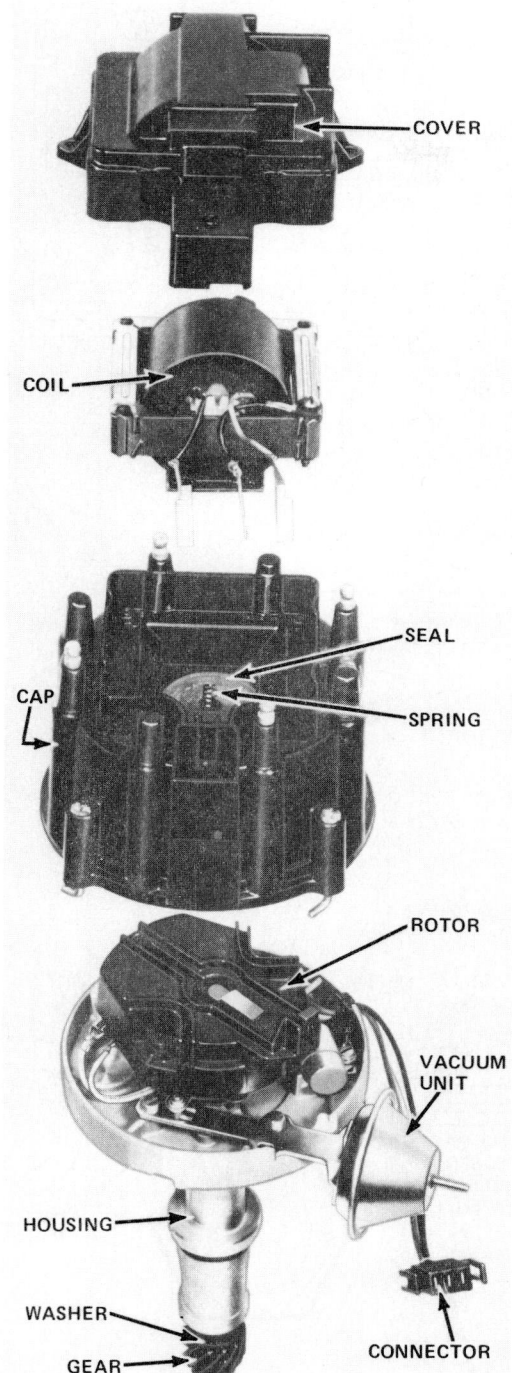

Fig. 32-8. Modern unitized distributor has ignition coil and amplifier (electronic switching circuit) mounted inside. Note part names and locations. (Chevrolet)

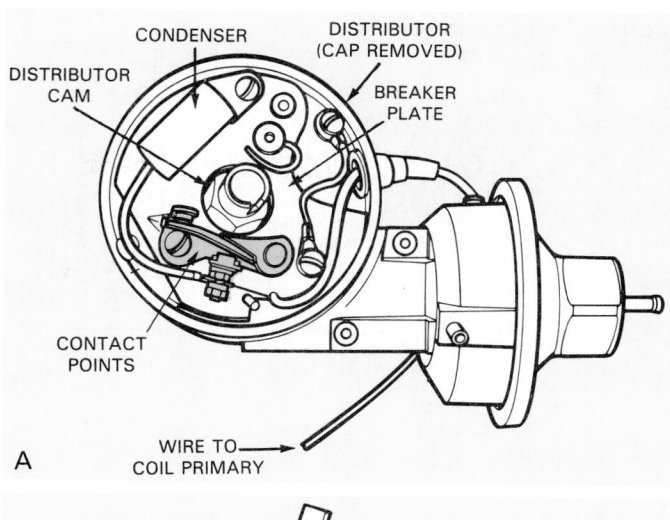

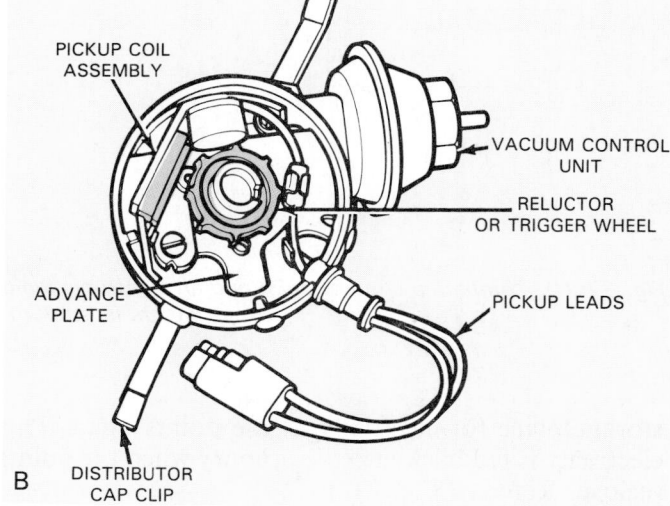

Fig. 32-9. Compare distributors. Trigger wheel and pickup coil replace points in modern electronic ignition. A — Contact point distributor. B — Pickup coil distributor for electronic ignition. (Mopar)

CONTACT POINT IGNITION SYSTEM

Before going on to study today's electronic ignition systems, you should have a basic understanding of contact point systems. The two systems are similar in many ways, Fig. 32-10.

The distributor for a contact point ignition consists of the following:

The **distributor cam** is the lobed part on the distributor shaft that opens the contact points. The cam turns with the shaft at one-half engine speed. One lobe is normally provided for each spark plug. See Fig. 21-9.

The **contact points,** also called *breaker points,* act like spring-loaded electrical switches in the distributor. Small screws hold the contact points on the distributor advance plate. A rubbing block of fiber material rides on the distributor cam. Wires from the condenser and ignition coil primary connect to the points.

The **condenser** or capacitor prevents the contact points from arcing and burning. It also provides a

points to interrupt the flow of primary current through the ignition coil. See Fig. 32-10.

A pickup coil distributor has a trigger wheel and a pickup coil instead of contact points. Wires from the pickup coil are connected to an ECU (electronic control unit). Refer to Fig. 32-9 and 32-10. The trigger wheel, pickup coil, and ECU perform the same function as contact points.

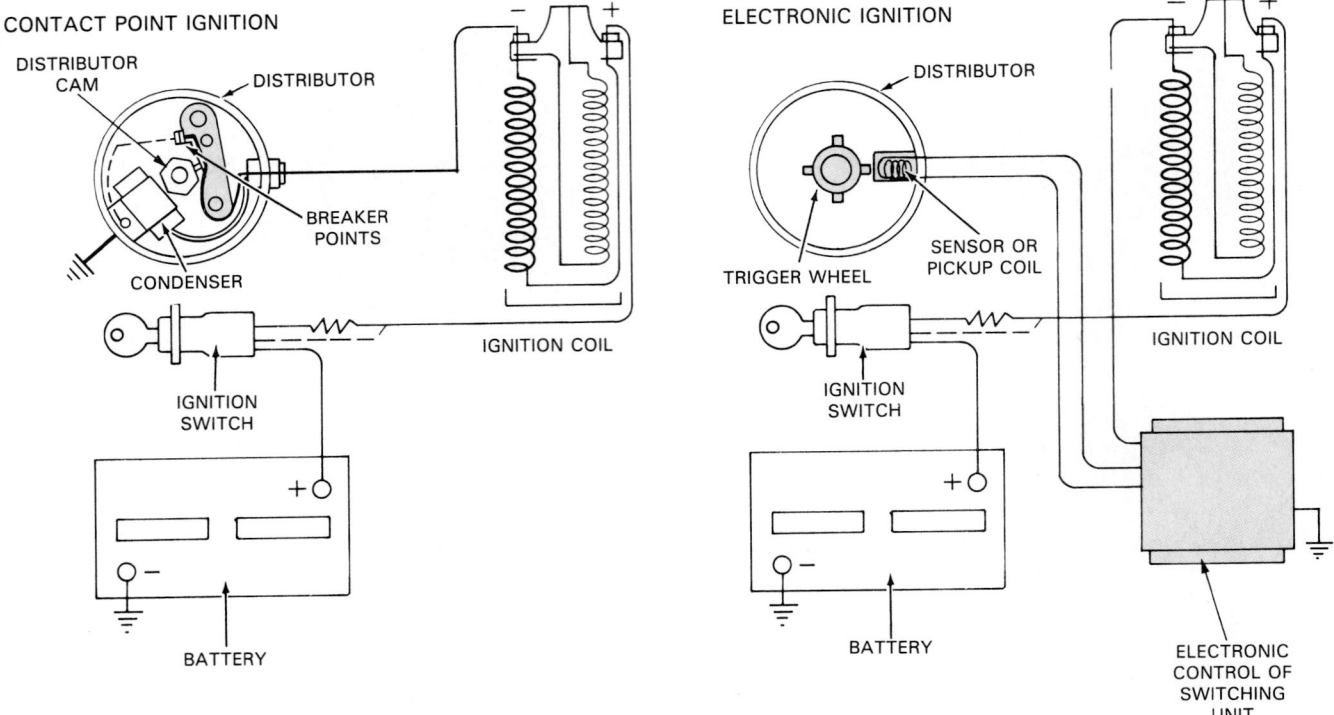

Fig. 32-10. Compare a contact point and an electronic ignition system. Note that pickup coil and control unit replace contact points in modern system. (Deere & Co.)

storage place for electricity as the points open. This electricity is fed back into the primary when the points reclose. Refer to Fig. 21-10.

Contact point ignition system operation

With the engine running, the distributor shaft and distributor cam rotate. This causes the cam to open and close the points.

Since the points are wired to the primary windings of the ignition coil, the points make and break the ignition coil primary circuit. When the points are closed, a magnetic field builds in the coil. When the points open, the field collapses and voltage is sent to one of the spark plugs.

With the distributor rotating at one-half engine rpm and with one cam lobe per engine cylinder, each spark plug fires once during a complete revolution of the distributor cam.

As you will learn, other distributor and electronic devices are used to alter when the spark plugs fire.

Point dwell (cam angle)

Dwell or *cam angle* is the amount of time, given in degrees of distributor rotation, that the points remain closed between each opening. Look at Fig. 32-11.

A dwell period is needed to assure that the coil has enough time to build up a strong magnetic field.

Without enough point dwell, a weak spark would be produced. With too much dwell, the *point gap*

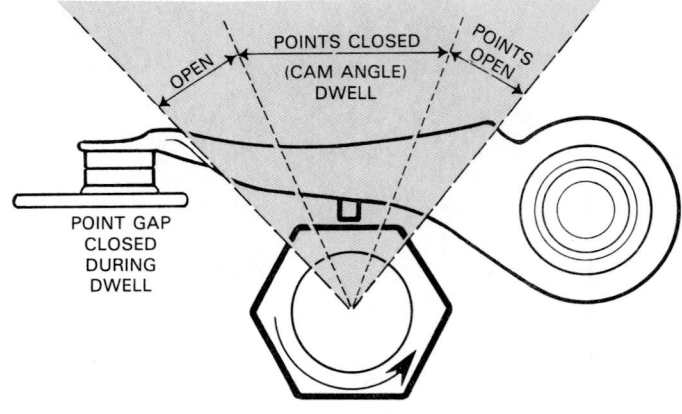

Fig. 32-11. Dwell is time points remain closed in degrees of distributor rotation. Point gap is distance between two points in fully open position. Dwell affects point gap and vice versa. (Echlin)

(distance between fully open points) would be too narrow. Point arcing and burning could result.

ELECTRONIC IGNITION SYSTEM

An *electronic ignition system,* also called a *solid state* or *transistor ignition system,* uses an electronic control circuit and a distributor pickup coil to operate the ignition coil. Refer to Fig. 32-12.

An electronic ignition is more dependable than a con-

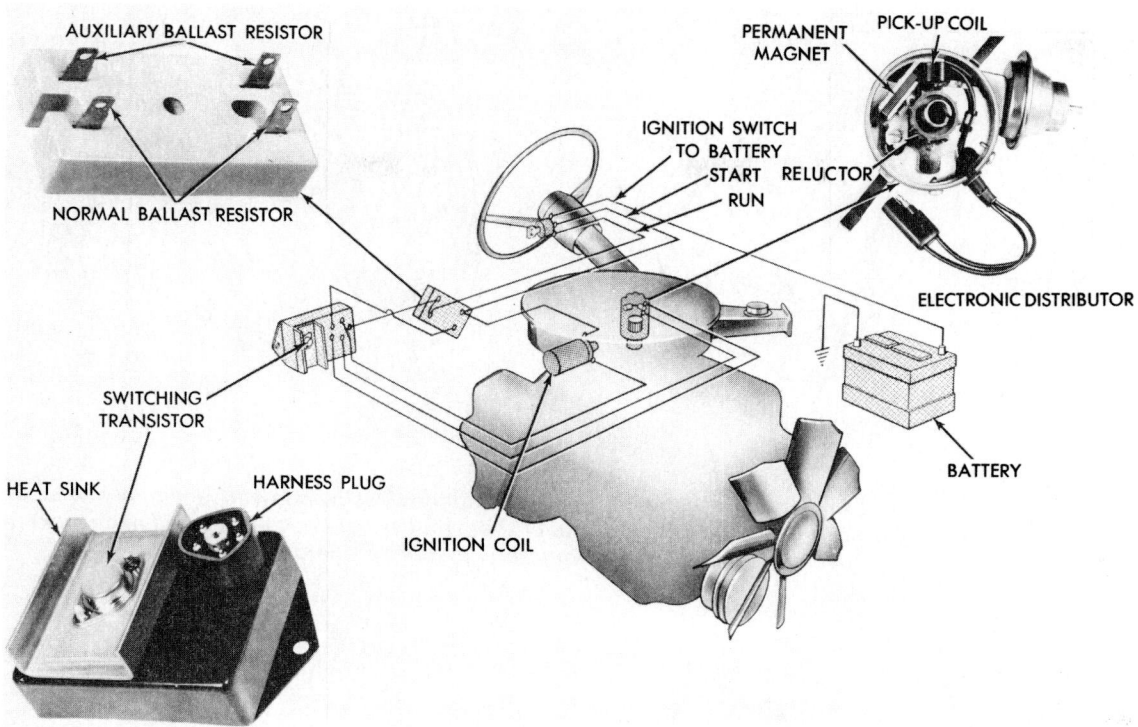

Fig. 32-12. Amplifier or control unit contains switching circuit or transistor that operates ignition coil. Note relationship of parts. (Chrysler)

tact point type. There are no mechanical breakers to wear or burn. This helps avoid trouble with ignition timing and dwell.

An electronic ignition is also capable of producing much higher secondary voltages. This is an advantage because wider spark plug gaps and higher voltages are needed to ignite lean air-fuel mixtures. Lean mixtures are now used for reduced exhaust emissions and fuel consumption.

Trigger wheel

The *trigger wheel,* also called *reluctor* or *pole piece,* is fastened to the upper end of the distributor shaft. See Fig. 32-12. The trigger wheel replaces the distributor cam used in a contact point distributor. One tooth is normally provided on the wheel for each engine cylinder.

Pickup coil

The *pickup coil,* also termed *sensor assembly* or *sensor coil,* produces tiny voltage pulses for the ignition system's electronic control unit. Look at Fig. 32-13. The sensor assembly is a small set of windings forming a coil.

As a trigger wheel tooth passes the pickup coil, it strengthens the magnetic field around the coil. This causes a change in the current flow through the coil. As a result, an electrical pulse (voltage or current change) is sent to the electronic control unit as the trigger wheel teeth pass the pickup unit.

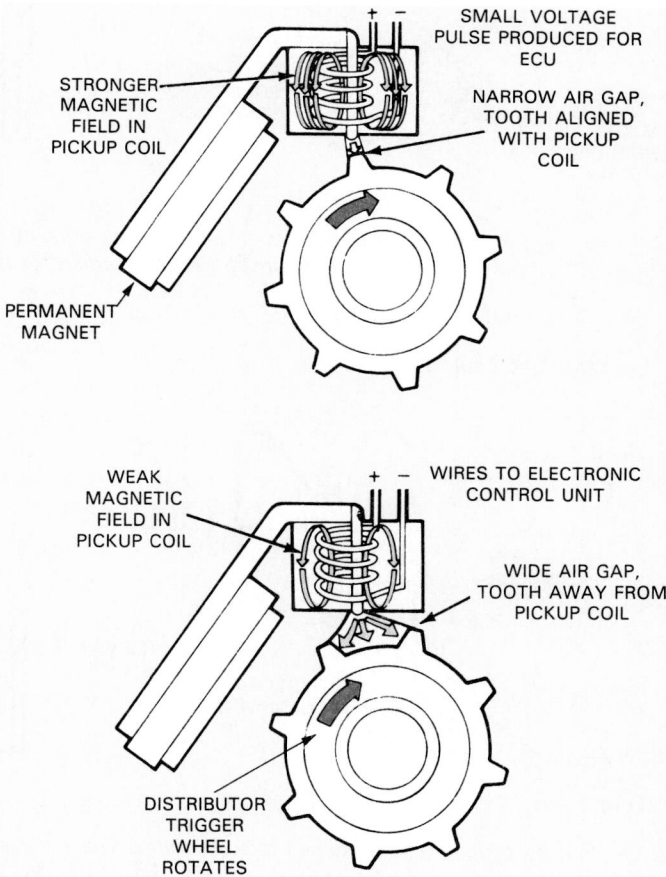

Fig. 32-13. Distributor magnetic pickup coil operation. (Chrysler)

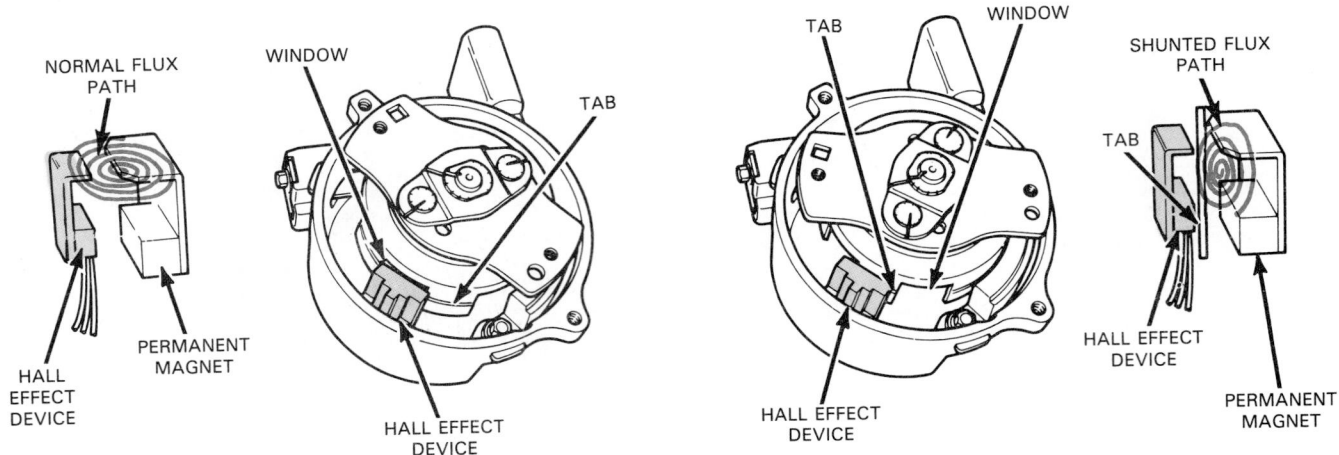

Fig. 32-14. Hall effect pickup chip is similar to magnetic pickup. A — Trigger wheel window (opening) allows strong magnetic field to develop around pickup. B — As trigger wheel rotates, tab or tooth moves between pickup and permanent magnet. This decreases pickup field strength and voltage. (Ford)

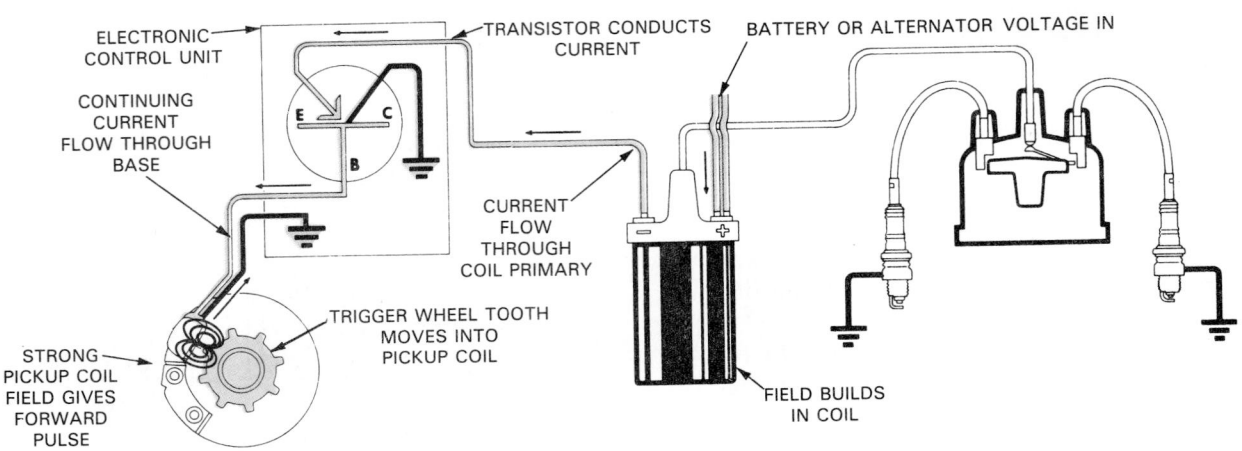

A — As trigger wheel tooth aligns with pickup coil, current flow through base of transistor turns transistor on. Current flows through ignition coil primary and through emitter-collector of transistor. Strong field builds in ignition coil primary windings.

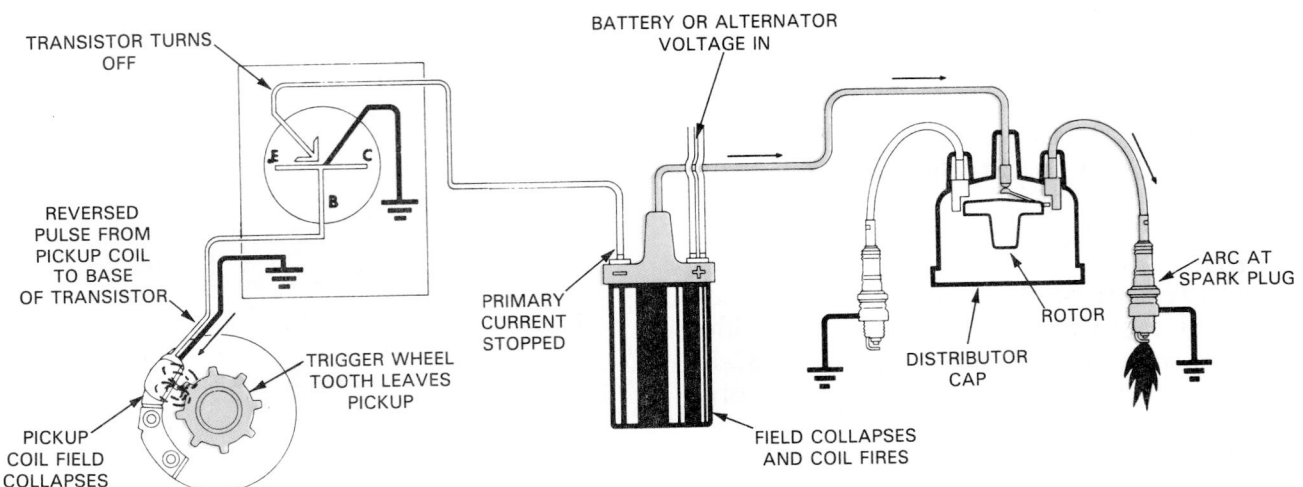

B — Just as trigger wheel passes pickup coil, current pulse flows out of pickup and to base of transistor. Electrical pulse is opposite the polarity of emitter-base voltage. This turns transistor off. Without current flow through emitter and collector, field collapses in ignition coil and 30,000 volts are induced into coil secondary windings. Spark plug fires.

Fig. 32-15. Pickup coil and amplifier switching action. (Echlin)

Hall effect pickup

Fig. 32-14 shows the action of a similar *Hall effect* pickup. This pickup is a solid state chip or module. A constant amount of current is sent through the device. A permanent magnet is located next to the Hall effect chip.

When the trigger wheel passes between the permanent magnet and the Hall effect chip, the magnetic field is blocked, decreasing the chip's output voltage (sensor or switch OFF). When the trigger wheel tooth moves out from between the magnet and chip, magnetic field action on the chip increases its voltage output (sensor or switch ON). This ON/OFF action operates the electronic control unit (ECU).

Ignition system ECU

The ignition system *electronic control unit amplifier* or *control module,* is an "electronic switch" that turns the ignition coil primary current on and off. See Fig. 32-15. The ECU does the same thing as contact points.

An ignition ECU is a network of transistors, resistors, capacitors, and other electronic components. A typical module and related wiring is shown in Fig. 32-16. The circuit is sealed in a plastic or metal housing.

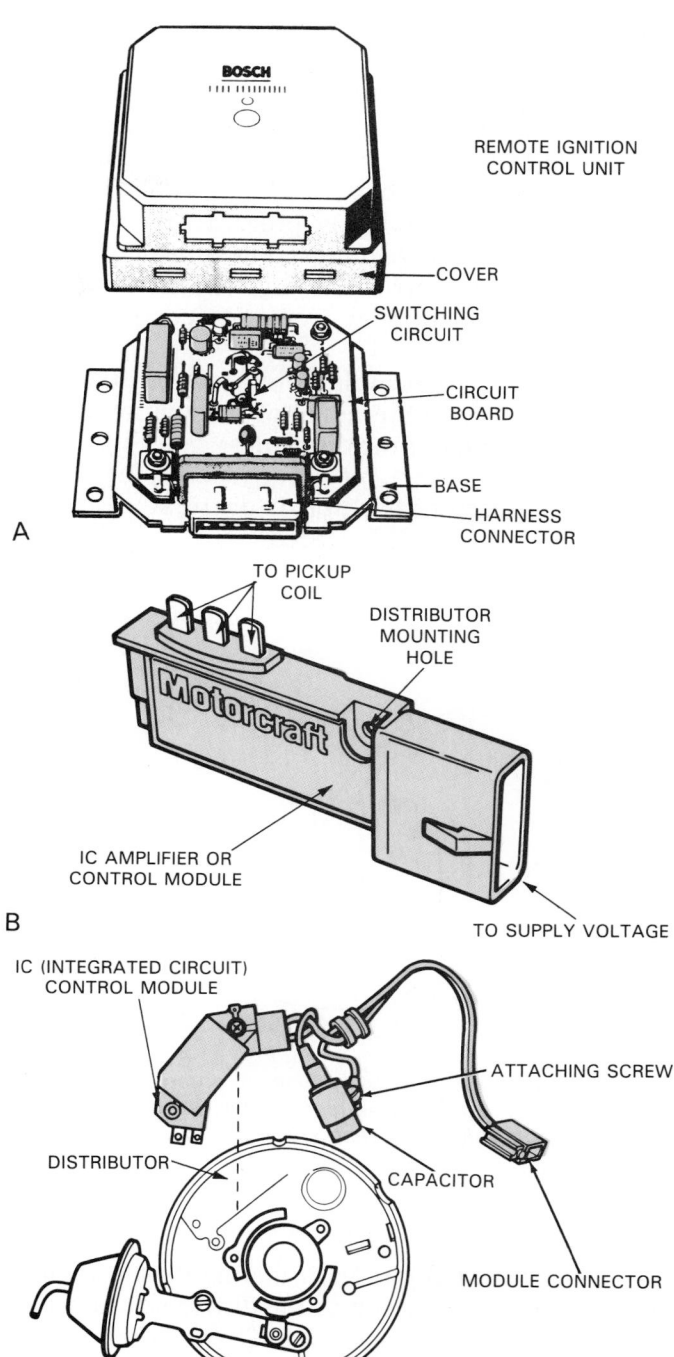

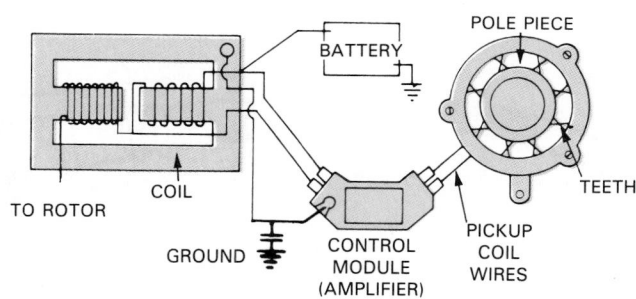

Fig. 32-16. Note electrical connections to typical amplifier. Amplifier contains electronic circuit with several transistors. (Echlin)

The ECU can be located:
1. In the engine compartment, Fig. 32-17A.
2. On the side of the distributor, Fig. 32-17B.
3. Inside the distributor, Fig. 32-17C.
4. Under the vehicle dash.

Electronic ignition system operation

With the engine running, the trigger wheel spins inside the distributor. As the teeth pass the pickup, a change in the magnetic field causes a change in output voltage or current. This results in engine rpm electrical signals entering the ECU, Fig. 32-16.

The ECU increases these tiny pulses into ON/OFF current cycles for the ignition coil. When the ECU is

Fig. 32-17. Ignition control unit variations. A — Remote mounted ignition amplifier. B — Amplifier mounted on outside of distributor body. C — Amplifier mounted inside distributor. (Bosch, Ford, Mopar)

ON, current flows through the primary windings of the ignition coil, developing a magnetic field. Then, when the trigger wheel and pickup turn OFF the ECU, the ignition coil field collapses and fires a spark plug.

ECU dwell time (number of degrees circuit conducts current to ignition coil) is designed into the ECU's electronic circuit. It is not adjustable.

SECONDARY (HIGH VOLTAGE) COMPONENTS

The *secondary components* of the ignition system operate on the high voltage from the ignition coil. Most of these parts are the same in both contact point and electronic ignition systems.

Since electronic ignitions produce much higher voltages, their parts are designed to withstand higher voltages without *electrical leakage* (electricity sparking through insulation or from one component to another).

The **coil wire** carries high voltage from the high voltage (high tension) terminal of the ignition coil to the center terminal of the distributor cap, Fig. 32-18. It is constructed like a very short spark plug wire.

With a unitized distributor or distributorless ignition, a coil wire is NOT needed.

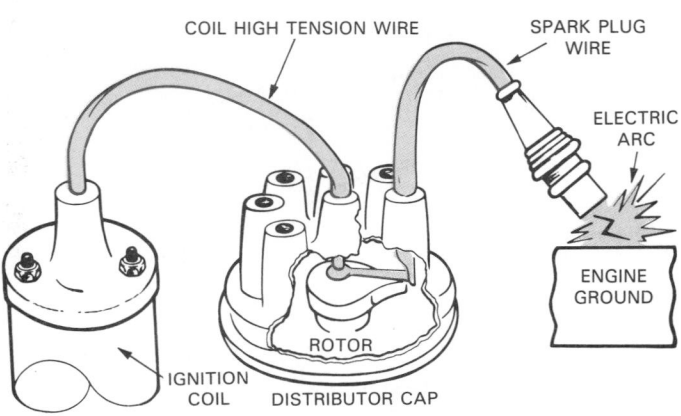

Fig. 32-18. With a distributor, ignition coil output is fed through coil wire to distributor cap center terminal. Spinning rotor then feeds high voltage to each spark plug wire. (Echlin)

Distributor cap and rotor

The *distributor cap* is an insulating plastic component that fits over the top of the distributor housing. Its center terminal transfers voltage from the coil wire to the rotor, Fig. 32-18.

The distributor cap also has outer or side terminals that send electric arcs to the spark plug wires. Metal terminals are molded into the plastic cap to make the electrical connections.

The *distributor rotor* transfers voltage from the coil wire (distributor cap center terminal) to the spark plug wires (distributor cap outer terminals). Look at Fig. 32-18 again.

The rotor is mounted on top of the distributor shaft. It is a spinning electrical switch that feeds voltage to each spark plug wire in turn.

A metal terminal on the rotor touches the distributor cap center terminal. The outer end of the rotor terminal ALMOST touches the outer cap terminals, Fig. 32-18.

Voltage is high enough that it can jump the air space between the rotor and cap. About 4000 volts is needed for the spark to jump this rotor-to-cap gap.

Spark plug wires

Spark plug wires carry coil voltage from the distributor cap side terminals to each spark plug. See Fig. 32-18. In more modern computer-coil (distributorless) ignitions, the spark plug wires carry coil voltage directly to the plugs.

Spark plug wire **boots** protect the metal connectors from corrosion, oil, and moisture. Boots usually fit over both ends of the secondary wires.

Solid wire spark plug wires are used on racing engines and very old automobiles. The wire conductor is simply a stranded metal wire. Solid wires are no longer used because they cause *radio interference* (noise or static in speakers).

Resistance spark plug wires are now used because they contain internal resistance that prevents radio noise. They consist of carbon-impregnated strands of rayon braid. Look at Fig. 32-19.

Also called *radio suppresion wires,* they have about 10,000 ohms per foot. This avoids high-voltage-induced popping or cracking in the radio speakers.

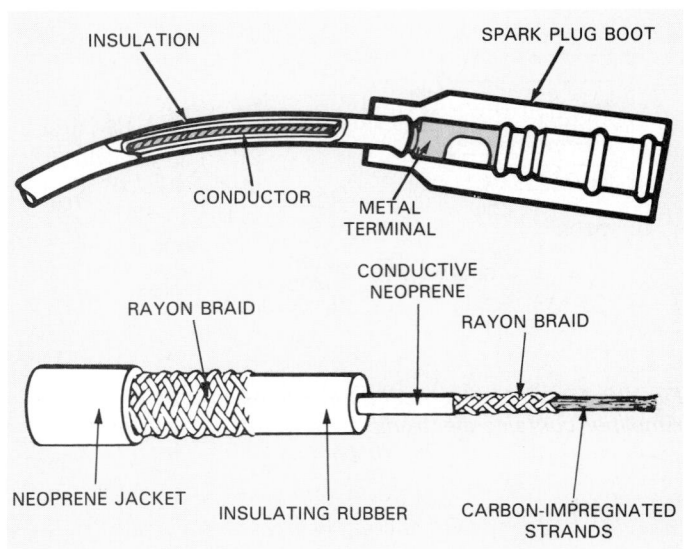

Fig. 32-19. Secondary wire has very thick insulation. Modern types contain carbon-impregnated strands that provide resistance to prevent radio interference. (Champion Spark Plugs)

SPARK PLUGS

The *spark plugs* use ignition coil high voltage to ignite the fuel mixture. Somewhere between 4000 and 10,000 volts is needed to make current jump the gap at the plug electrodes. This is much lower than the coil's output potential.

Fig. 32-20 shows the basic parts of a spark plug.

The **center terminal** conducts electricity into the combustion chamber.

The grounded **side electrode** causes the electricity to jump the gap and return to the battery through frame ground.

The ceramic **insulator** keeps the high voltage at the plug wire from shorting to ground before producing a spark in the engine cylinder.

The steel **shell** supports the other parts of the plug and has threads for screwing the plug into the engine cylinder head.

Spark plug reach

Spark plug reach is the distance between the end of the plug threads and the seat or sealing surface on the plug. Refer to Fig. 32-20. Plug reach determines how far the plug extends through the cylinder head.

If spark plug reach is too long, the plug electrode may be struck by the piston at TDC. If reach is too short, the plug electrodes may not extend far enough into the chamber and combustion efficiency may be reduced.

Resistor and non-resistor spark plugs

A **resistor spark plug,** like a resistor plug wire, has internal resistance (around 10,000 ohms) designed to reduce static in radios and television sets. Most newer vehicles require resistor plugs.

A **non-resistor spark plug** has a solid metal rod forming the center electrode. This type is NOT commonly used, except for racing or off-road applications.

Fig. 32-21 illustrates resistor and non-resistor spark plug types.

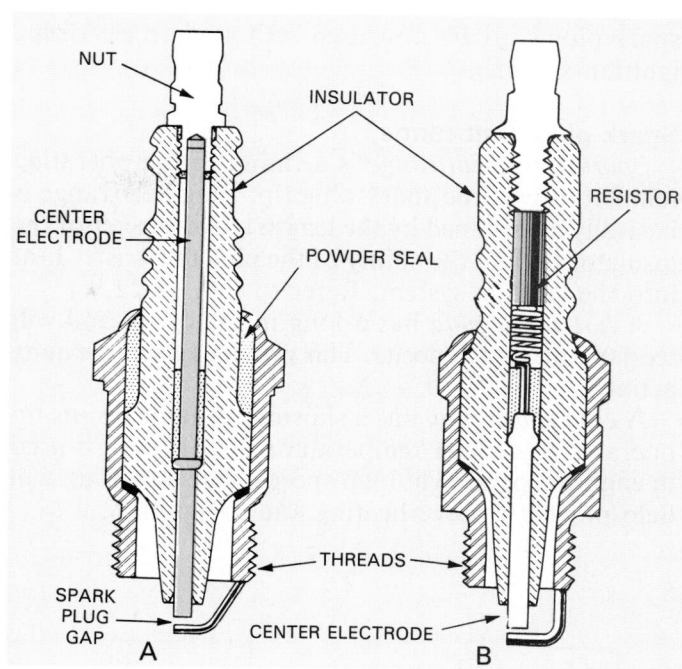

Fig. 32-21. Cutaway shows internal parts of plug. A — Non-resistor plug has solid metal center electrode. B — Resistor plug has small resistor between two-piece center electrode. Plug gap is space between side and center electrodes. (Ethyl Corp.)

Spark plug gap

Spark plug gap is the distance between the center and side electrodes, Fig. 32-21. Normal gap specs range from .030 to .060 inch (0.76 mm to 1.52 mm).

Smaller spark plug gaps are used on older cars equipped with contact point ignition systems. Larger

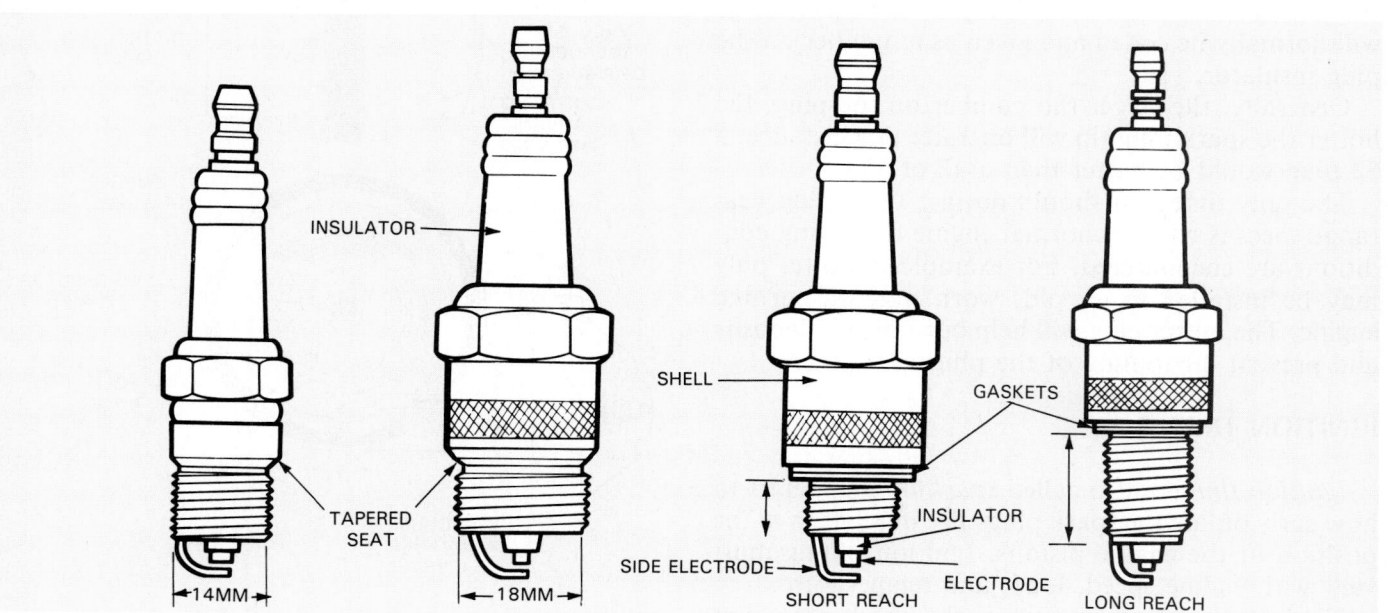

Fig. 32-20. Note spark plug variations. Small 14mm plug is commonly used in today's engines. Larger 18mm are for older engines. Reach is length of plug threads. (Mopar)

spark plug gaps are now used with modern electronic ignition systems.

Spark plug heat range

Spark plug heat range is a rating of the operating temperature of the spark plug tip. Plug heat range is basically determined by the length and diameter of the insulator tip and the ability of the plug to transfer heat into the cooling system. Refer to Fig. 32-22.

A *hot spark plug* has a long insulator tip and will tend to burn off deposits. This provides a self-cleaning action.

A *cold spark plug* has a shorter insulator tip; its tip operates at a cooler temperature. A cold plug is used in engines operated at high speeds. The cooler tip will help prevent tip overheating and preignition.

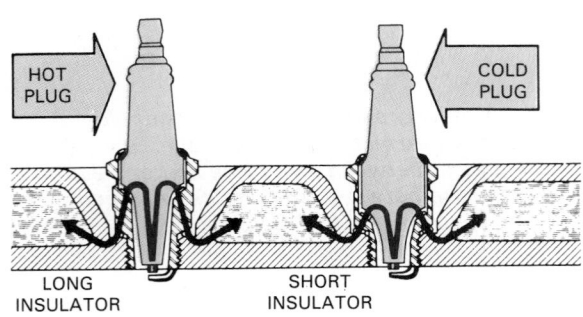

Fig. 32-22. Hot plug has long insulator that prevents heat transfer into water jackets. It will burn off oil deposits. Cold plug has shorter insulator. (Ethyl Corp.)

Heat range ratings

Auto manufacturers normally recommend a specific spark plug heat range for their engines. The heat range will normally be coded and given as a number on the plug insulator.

Generally, the larger the number on the plug, the hotter the spark plug tip will operate. For instance, a 52 plug would be hotter than a 42 or 32.

The only time you should deviate from plug heat range specs is when abnormal engine or driving conditions are encountered. For example, a hotter plug may be installed in an old, worn out, oil-burning engine. The hotter plug will help burn off oil deposits and prevent oil fouling of the plug.

IGNITION TIMING

Ignition timing, also called *spark timing,* refers to how early or late the spark plugs fire in relation to the position of the engine pistons. Ignition timing must vary with engine speed, load, and temperature.

Timing advance occurs when the spark plugs fire sooner on the engine's compression strokes. The timing is set several degrees before TDC. More timing ad-

vance is needed at higher engine speeds to give combustion enough time to develop pressure on the power stroke.

Timing retard occurs when the spark plugs fire later on the compression strokes. It is the opposite of timing advance. Spark retard is needed at lower engine speeds and under high load conditions. Timing retard prevents the fuel from burning too much on the compression stroke, causing a spark knock or ping (abnormal combustion).

There are three basic methods used to control ignition system spark timing:

1. DISTRIBUTOR CENTRIFUGAL ADVANCE (controlled by engine speed), Fig. 32-23.
2. DISTRIBUTOR VACUUM ADVANCE (controlled by engine intake manifold vacuum and engine load), Fig. 32-23.
3. ELECTRONIC (COMPUTER) ADVANCE (controlled by various engine sensors: engine rpm, temperature, intake manifold vacuum, throttle position, etc.).

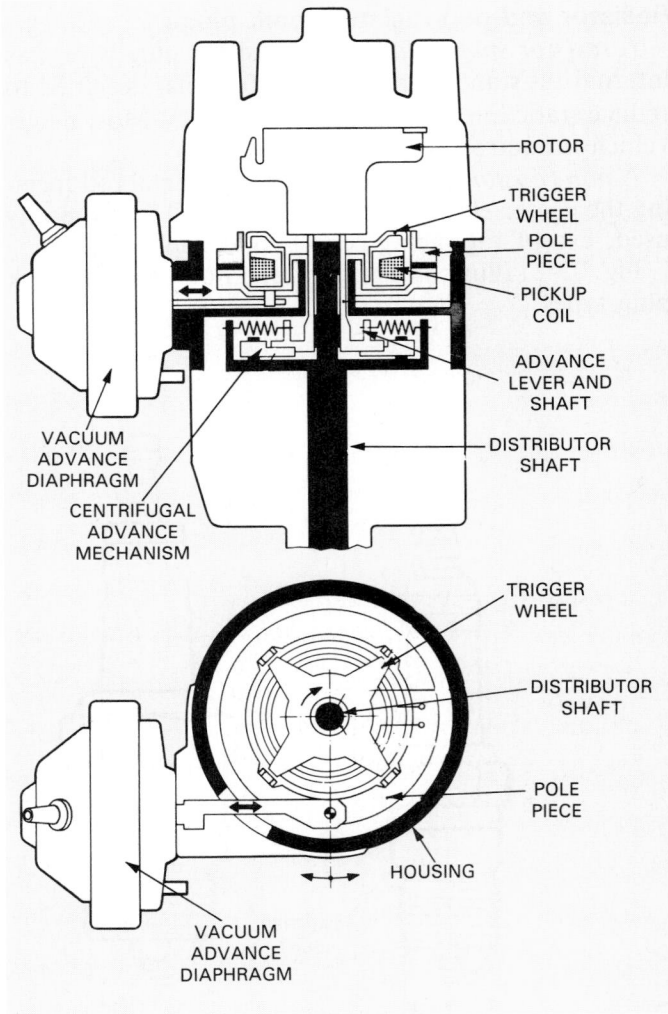

Fig. 32-23. Study parts of vacuum and centrifugal advance mechanisms. (Robert Bosch)

DISTRIBUTOR CENTRIFUGAL ADVANCE

The *distributor centrifugal advance* makes the ignition coil and spark plugs fire sooner as engine speed increases. See Fig. 32-23. It uses spring-loaded weights, centrifugal force, and lever action to rotate the distributor cam, or trigger wheel on the distributor shaft. By rotating the cam or trigger wheel against distributor shaft rotation, spark timing is advanced.

Fig. 32-24 illustrates how ignition timing must be advanced with engine speed. It helps maintain correct ignition timing for maximum ENGINE POWER.

A distributor centrifugal advance mechanism basically consists of two advance weights, two springs, and an advance lever.

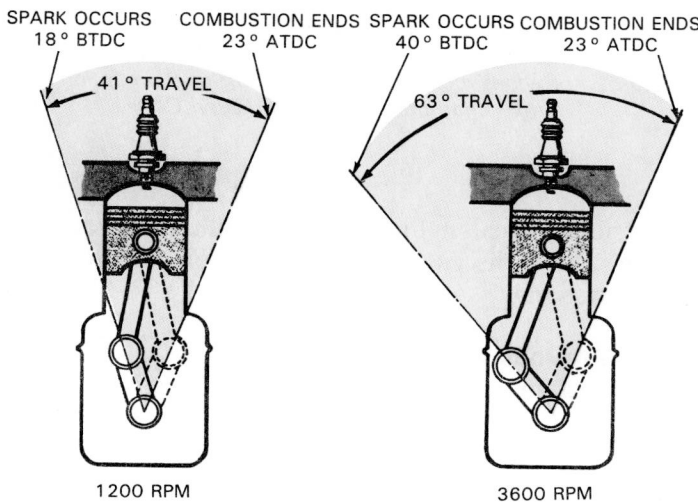

1200 RPM   3600 RPM

Fig. 32-24. Since each combustion period takes about same amount of time, spark must start combustion sooner as engine speed increases. This will assure that all of the fuel is burned on the power stroke and that sufficient pressure acts on the piston. (Sun Electric Corp.)

Centrifugal advance operation

At low engine speeds, small springs hold the advance weights inward. Look at Fig. 32-25. There is not enough centrifugal force to push the weights outward. The timing stays at its normal initial setting (as long as vacuum advance is not functioning).

As engine speed increases, centrifugal force overcomes spring tension. The weights are thrown outward. The edges of the weights act on the cam or trigger wheel lever. The lever is rotated on the distributor shaft. This also rotates the distributor cam or trigger wheel.

Since the cam or trigger wheel is turned with distributor shaft rotation, the points open sooner, or the trigger wheel and pickup coil turn off the ECU sooner. This causes the ignition coil to fire with the engine pistons not as far up in their cylinders.

As engine speed keeps increasing, the weights fly out

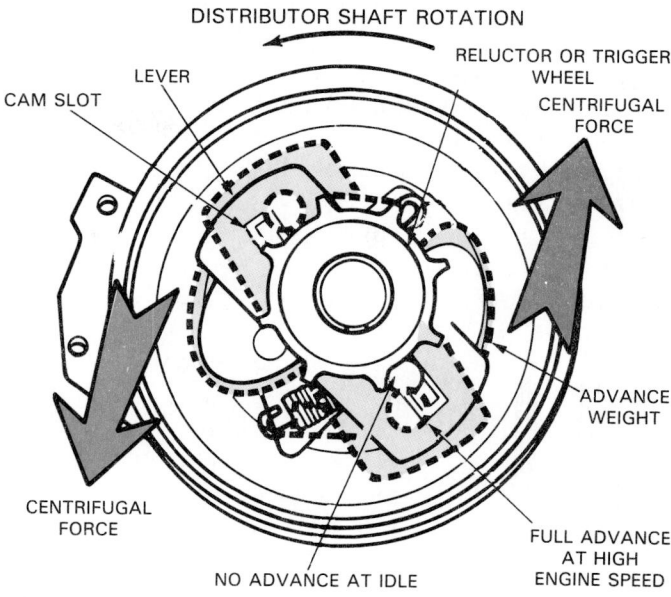

Fig. 32-25. Springs hold weights in at low engine speeds, producing no centrifugal advance. When engine speed increases, weights swing outward. Weights push on and rotate cam or trigger wheel lever. This advances ignition timing. (Dodge)

more and timing is advanced a greater amount. At a preset engine rpm, the lever strikes a stop and centrifugal advance reaches maximum.

DISTRIBUTOR VACUUM ADVANCE

The *distributor vacuum advance* provides additional spark advance when engine load is low at part (medium) throttle positions. Refer to Fig. 32-26. It is

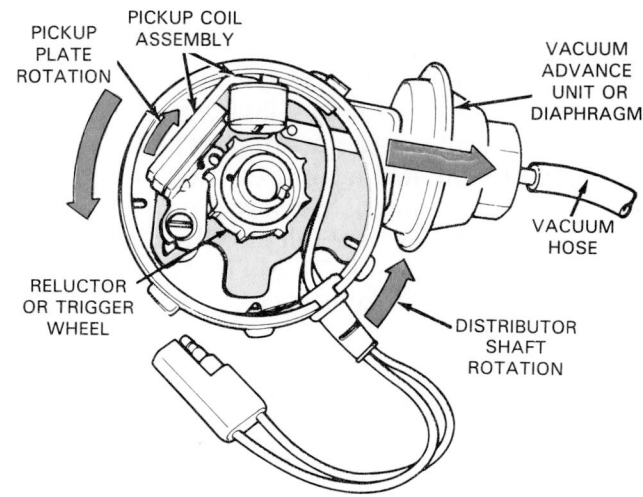

Fig. 32-26. Vacuum advance uses vacuum advance diaphragm to rotate pickup coil or contact points against direction of distributor shaft rotation. (Plymouth)

a method of matching ignition timing with engine load.

The vacuum advance mechanism increases FUEL ECONOMY because it helps maintain ideal spark advance at all times.

A distributor vacuum advance mechanism consists of a vacuum diaphragm, link, movable distributor plate, and a vacuum supply hose. These parts are shown in Fig. 32-27.

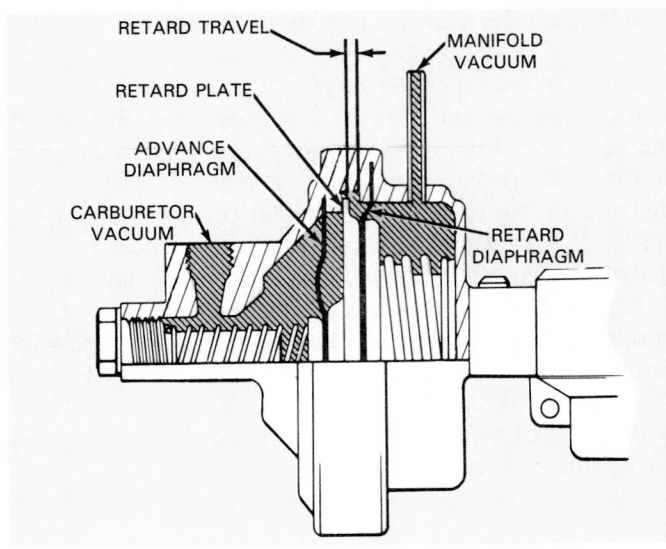

Fig. 32-28. Dual-diaphragm distributor diaphragm has two vacuum chambers. One provides vacuum advance, the other retard. It provides more positive control of ignition timing than single chamber diaphragm. (Ethyl Corp.)

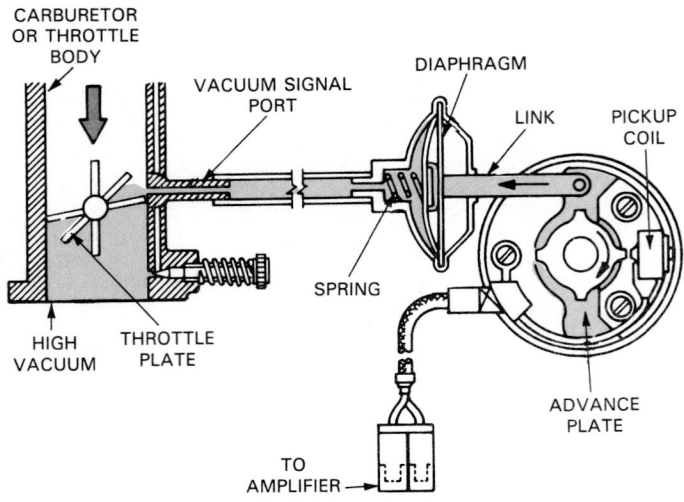

Fig. 32-27. In most units, distributor vacuum advance diaphragm is connected to ported vacuum source on carburetor or throttle body. When throttle plate swings open, vacuum is applied to diaphragm. Diaphragm flexes toward vacuum and pulls on advance plate. Pickup coil or points are rotated against distributor shaft rotation for timing advance. (Fiat)

Vacuum advance operation

At idle, the vacuum port to the distributor advance is covered. Look at Fig. 32-27. Vacuum (suction) is NOT applied to the vacuum diaphragm. Spark timing is NOT advanced.

At part throttle, the throttle valve uncovers the vacuum port and the port is exposed to engine vacuum. This causes the distributor diaphragm to be pulled toward the vacuum. The distributor plate (points or pickup coil) is rotated against distributor shaft rotation and spark timing is advanced.

During acceleration and full throttle, engine vacuum drops. Thus, vacuum is NOT applied to the distributor diaphragm and the vacuum advance does NOT operate. See Fig. 32-27.

DUAL-DIAPHRAGM DISTRIBUTOR

A *dual-diaphragm vacuum advance* mechanism, used on some distributors, contains two separate vacuum chambers: an advance chamber and a retard chamber. See Fig. 32-28.

Sometimes, a vacuum control switch is used in the

distributor vacuum line to alter vacuum diaphragm action. This is discussed in the chapter on emission control systems.

Vacuum delay valve

A *vacuum delay valve* restricts the flow of air to slow down the vacuum action on a vacuum device. Fig. 32-29 shows one in the line to the distributor vacuum advance diaphragm.

Note how the delay valve has a small orifice (opening) for vacuum. It also has a check valve that allows flow in only one direction.

The vacuum delay valve keeps the vacuum advance from working too quickly, preventing possible knock or ping. The check valve allows free release of vacuum from the diaphragm when returning to the retard position.

ELECTRONIC SPARK ADVANCE

An *electronic spark advance* system uses engine sensors and a computer to control ignition timing. A distributor may be used but it does NOT contain centrifugal or vacuum advance mechanisms. Refer to Fig. 32-30 for an example.

The *engine sensors* check various operating conditions and send electrical data to the computer. The computer can then change ignition timing for maximum engine efficiency.

Ignition system engine sensors typically include:
1. ENGINE SPEED SENSOR (reports engine rpm to computer).
2. CRANKSHAFT POSITION SENSOR (reports piston position).

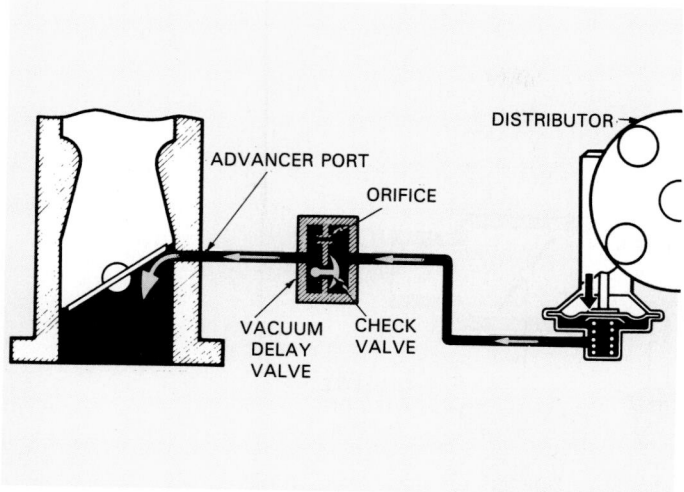

Fig. 32-29. Vacuum delay valve has small orifice that restricts access of vacuum to diaphragm. Check valve allows free flow of air out of diaphragm for quick timing retard. (Toyota)

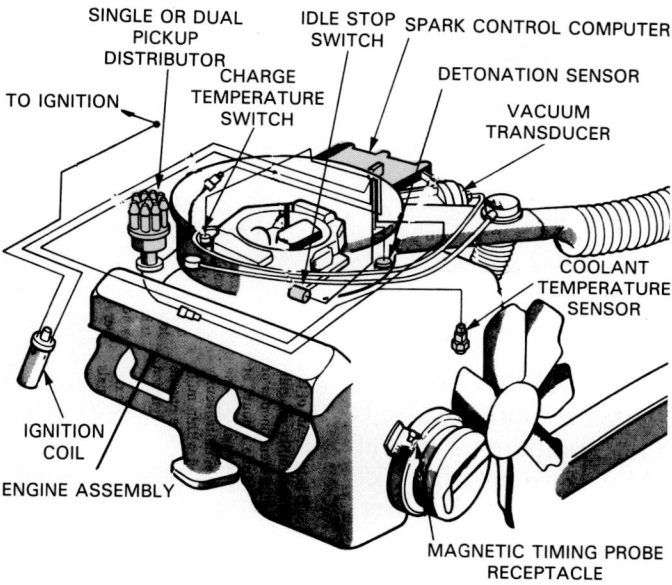

Fig. 32-30. This engine has electronic spark timing system. Computer and engine sensors replace centrifugal and vacuum advance mechanisms in distributor. Note part names and locations. (Plymouth)

3. INTAKE VACUUM SENSOR (measures engine vacuum, an indicator of load).
4. INLET AIR TEMPERATURE SENSOR (check temperature of air entering engine).
5. ENGINE COOLANT TEMPERATURE SENSOR (measures operating temperature of engine).
6. DETONATION SENSOR (allows computer to retard timing when engine pings or knocks).
7. THROTTLE POSITION SWITCH (notes position of throttle).

The *spark control computer* receives input signals (different current or voltage levels) from these sensors.

It is programmed (preset) to adjust ignition timing to meet different engine conditions. The computer may be mounted on the air cleaner, fender inner panel, under the car dash, or under a seat.

Electronic spark advance operation.

For an example of electronic spark advance, imagine a car traveling down the highway at 55 mph (88 km/h). The speed sensor would detect moderate engine rpm. The throttle position sensor would detect part throttle. The air inlet and coolant temperature sensors would report normal operating temperatures. The intake manifold pressure sensor would send high vacuum signals to the computer.

The computer could then calculate that the engine would need maximum spark advance. The timing would occur several degrees before TDC on the compression stroke. This would assure that the engine attained high fuel economy on the highway.

If the driver began to pass a car, engine intake manifold vacuum would drop to a very low level. The vacuum sensor signal would be fed to the computer. The throttle position sensor would detect WOT (wide open throttle). Other sensor outputs would stay about the same. The computer could then retard ignition timing to prevent spark knock or ping.

Since computer systems vary, refer to a service manual for more information. The manual will detail the operation of the specific system.

Base timing

Most new cars use the computer to control ignition timing. To check timing, you may have to trigger the computer to go to base timing. *Base timing* is the ignition timing without computer controlled advance.

To make the engine run on base timing, you might have to disconnect a wire near the distributor or use a scanner to trigger computer retard. This procedure can vary considerably, so refer to the factory service manuals for directions.

CRANKSHAFT TRIGGERED IGNITION

A *crankshaft triggered ignition* system places the pickup coil and trigger wheel (pulse ring) unit on the front of the engine. These parts are NOT located inside the distributor. Fig. 32-31 shows a simplified illustration of a crankshaft-triggered ignition.

A *pulse ring* is mounted on the crankshaft damper to provide engine speed information to the pickup unit. It performs the same function as the trigger wheel in a distributor for an electronic ignition. The teeth on the pulse ring correspond to the number of engine cylinders, Fig. 32-32.

The *crankshaft position sensor* is mounted next to the crank pulse ring and sends electrical pulses to the system computer. It does the same thing as a distributor

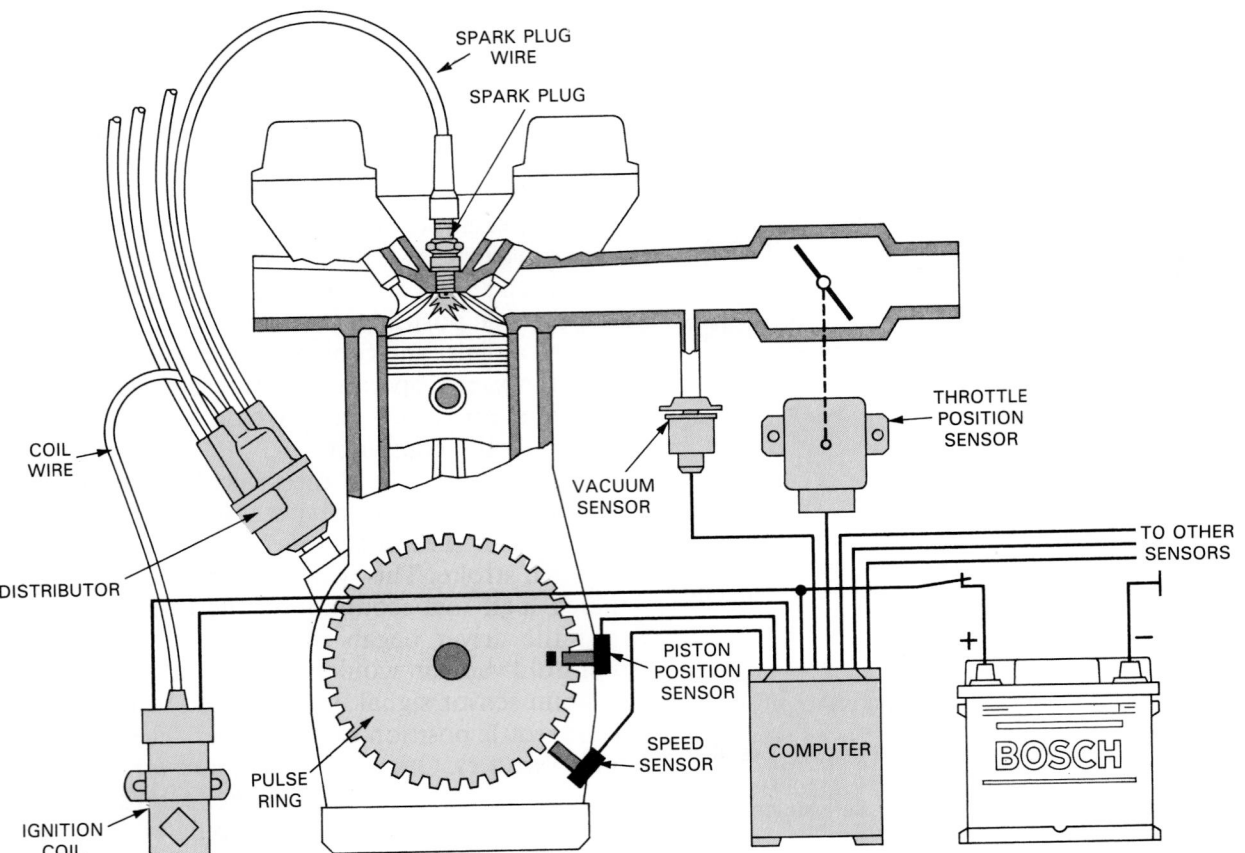

Fig. 32-31. Simplified crankshaft-triggered ignition system places pickup coil or coils next to engine crankshaft damper. Teeth on damper act as trigger wheel to send electrical pulses to computer. Computer can then operate ignition coil and control spark advance or retard. Study parts and wiring. (Robert Bosch)

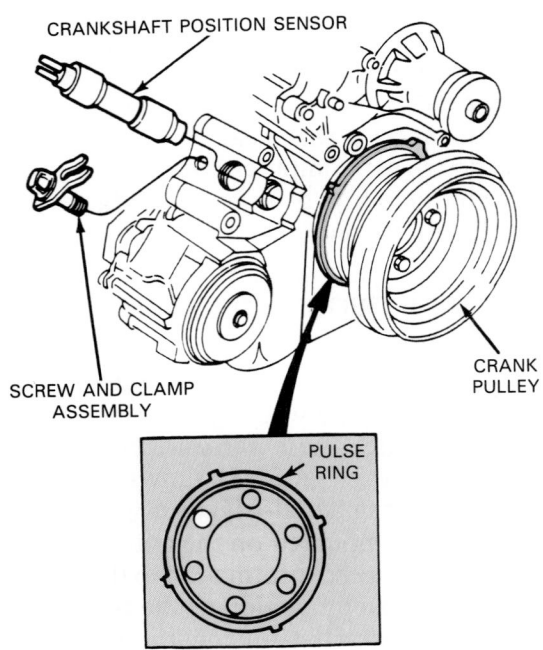

Fig. 32-32. Pulse ring for this crankshaft-triggered ignition mounts behind crank pulley. Crank position sensor fits in hole in front cover. Wires from sensor connect to on-board computer. Teeth on pulse ring change magnetic field around sensor to produce electric pulse. (Ford Motor Co.)

pickup. See Fig. 32-32.

Other sensors are also commonly used to feed data to the computer. Look at Fig. 32-33.

The distributor for a crankshaft-triggered ignition is simply used to transfer high voltage to each spark plug wire.

Crankshaft-triggered ignition operation

The operation of a crankshaft-triggered ignition is similar to the other electronic systems already covered. Refer to Fig. 32-31.

A crank-triggered ignition can maintain more precise ignition timing than a system with a distributor-mounted pickup coil. There is no backlash or play in the distributor drive gear, timing chain, or gears to upset ignition timing. Crank and piston position is "read" right off the crankshaft.

COMPUTER-COIL (DISTRIBUTORLESS) IGNITION

A *computer-coil ignition*, also called a *distributorless* (no distributor) *ignition*, uses multiple ignition coils, a coil control unit, engine sensors, and a computer to operate the spark plugs. A distributor is NOT needed. See Fig. 32-34.

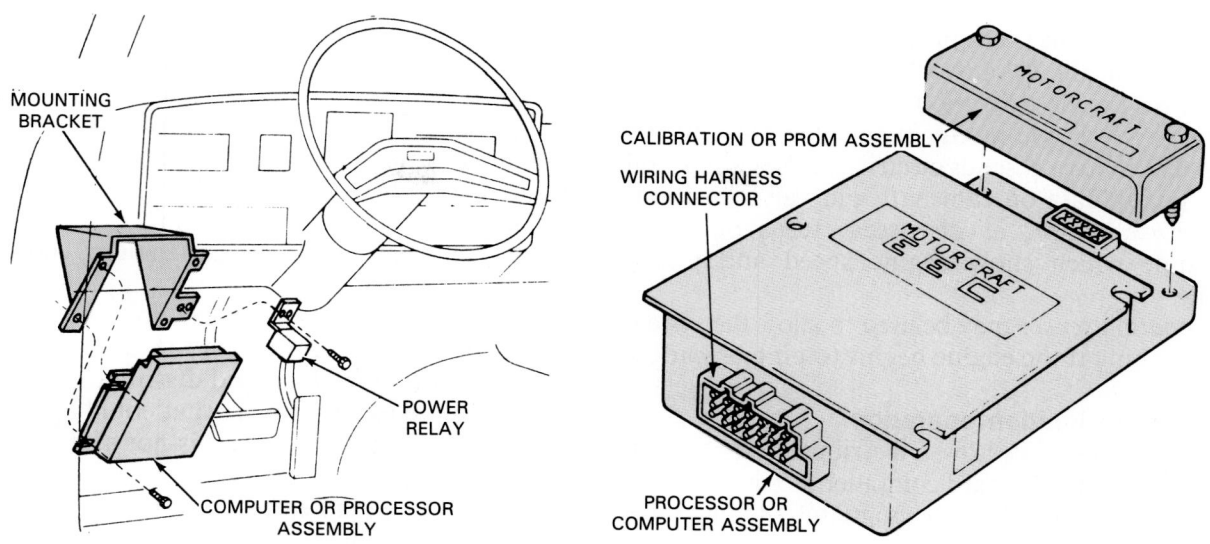

Fig. 32-33. Computer may control ignition system operation as well as fuel injection, emission control systems, and other critical functions. It is usually located in safe place under car dash. It may also be located in engine compartment or on air cleaner. (Ford)

An *electronic coil module* consists of several ignition coils and an electronic circuit for operating the coils. The module's electronic circuit performs about the same function as the ECU in an electronic ignition. It is more complex, however, because it must analyze data from engine sensors and the system computer.

A four-cylinder engine would need an electronic coil module with two ignition coils. A six-cylinder engine would need a module with three ignition coils.

The coils are wired so that they fire TWO SPARK

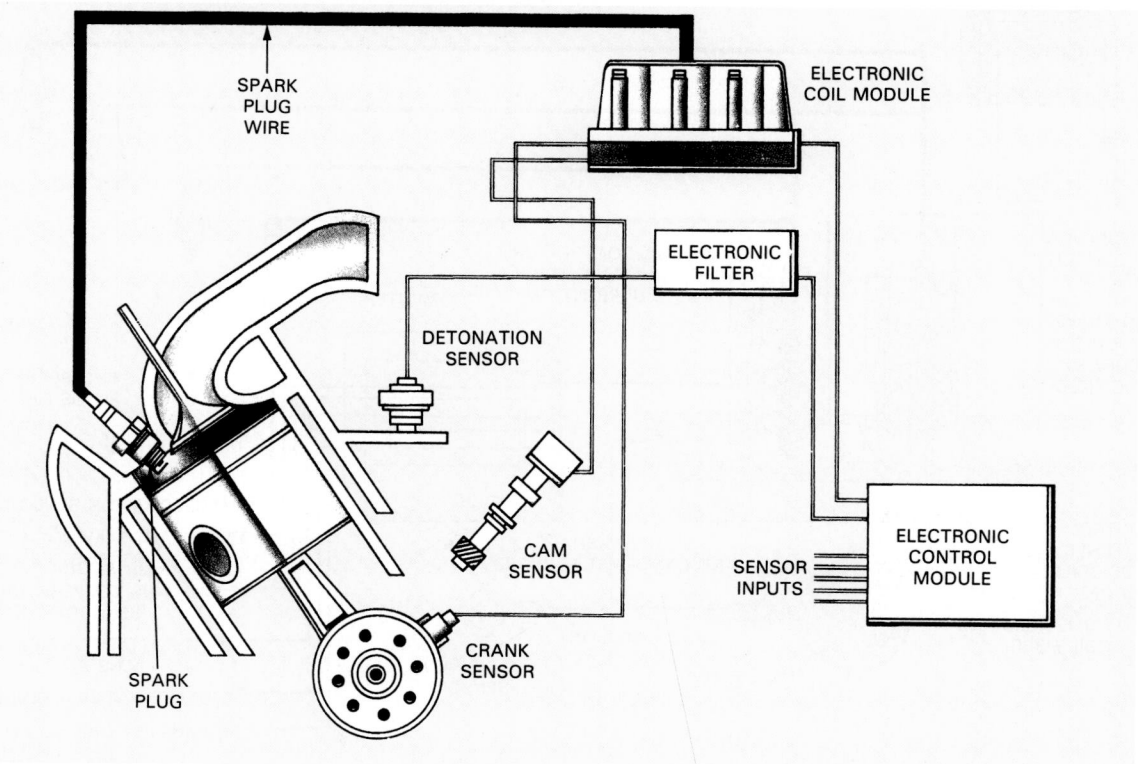

Fig. 32-34. Newest ignition system design does not use a distributor. The on-board computer and an electronic coil control module operate multiple ignition coils. Crank sensor and cam sensor send electrical signals to help control the time when coils fire. (Buick)

PLUGS at once. One spark plug is on the power stroke. The other is on the exhaust stroke, so the spark has no effect on engine operation.

A *cam sensor* is commonly installed in place of the ignition distributor. It sends electrical pulses to the coil module giving data on camshaft and valve position.

The *crank sensor,* as discussed, feeds pulses to the module which show engine speed and piston position.

A *detonation sensor* may be used to allow the system to retard timing if the engine begins to ping or knock.

Distributorless ignition operation

Fig. 32-35 illustrates how a distributorless ignition system works. The on-board computer monitors engine operating conditions and controls ignition timing. Some sensor data is also fed to the electronic coil module.

When the computer and sensors send correct electrical pulses to the coil module, the module fires one of the ignition coils.

Since each coil secondary output is wired to two spark plugs, both spark plugs fire. One produces the power stroke. The other spark plug arc does nothing because that cylinder is on the exhaust stroke. Burned gases are simply being pushed out of the cylinder.

When the next pulse ring tooth aligns with the crank sensor, the next ignition coil fires. Another two spark

plugs arc for one more power stroke. This process is repeated over and over as the engine runs.

Advantages of a distributorless ignition

A distributorless ignition system has several possible advantages over other ignition types. Some of these include:

1. No rotor nor distributor cap to burn, crack, or fail.
2. Computer-controlled advance. No mechanical weights to stick or wear. No vacuum advance diaphragm to rupture and leak.
3. Play in timing chain and distributor drive gear is eliminated as a problem that could upset ignition timing. The crank sensor is not affected by slack in timing chain or gears.
4. More dependable, because there are fewer moving parts to wear and malfunction.
5. Requires less maintenance. Ignition timing is usually NOT adjustable.

DIRECT IGNITION SYSTEM

A *direct ignition system* has an ignition coil mounted over the top of each spark plug. This is different from a distributorless ignition. *Direct* means the coils are mounted directly on the spark plugs. There is no conductor strip or plug wire to connect the coil and the

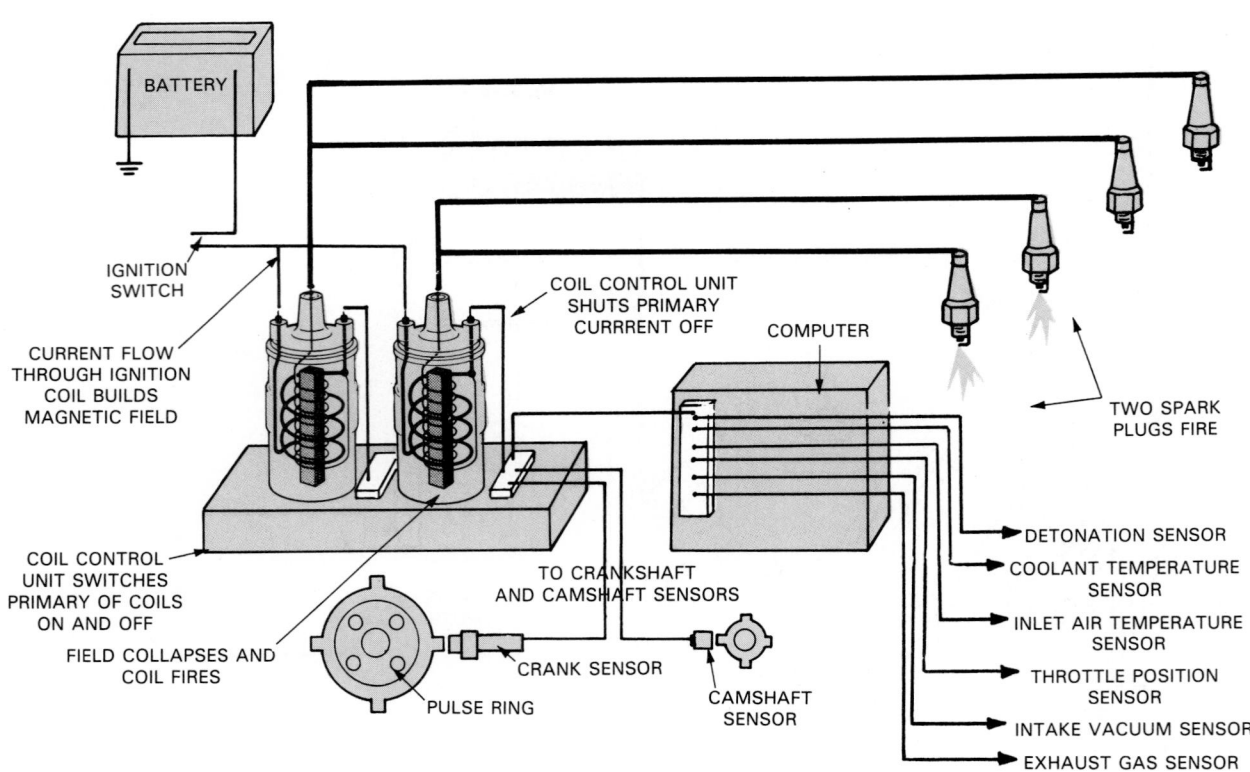

Fig. 32-35. Simplified illustration shows operation of ignition system using no distributor. Input to coil module includes signals from crank sensor, cam sensor, and computer. With correct input, coil module fires one of the ignition coils and its two spark plugs. One plug produces power stroke. Other plug sparks as burned exhaust leaves cylinder. Two coils would operate ignition for a four-cylinder engine. Three coils would be needed for a six-cylinder engine.

spark plug, Fig. 32-36.

The other components (computer, sensors, etc.) are the same in a direct ignition system. The direct ignition coils only fire on the power stroke. They do NOT fire on the exhaust strokes, like many distributorless ignition systems.

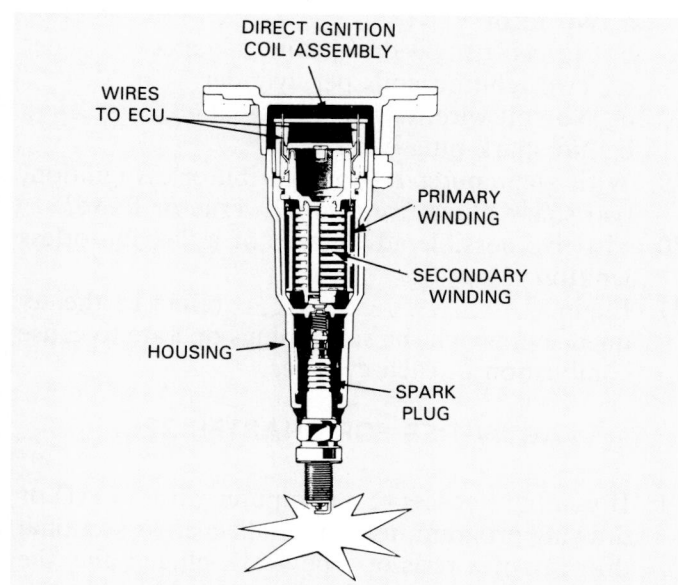

Fig. 32-36. Cutaway of an ignition coil for a direct ignition system. (Saab)

ENGINE FIRING ORDER

Engine firing order refers to the sequence in which the spark plugs fire to cause combustion in each cylinder. A four-cylinder engine may have one of two firing orders: 1-3-4-2 or 1-2-4-3. See Fig. 32-37. The cylinders are numbered 1-2-3-4 starting at the front of the engine. In this way, you can tell which cylinders will fire in sequence. Firing orders and cylinder numbers for V-6 and V-8 engines vary.

The engine firing order is sometimes cast into the top of the intake manifold. When not on the manifold, the firing order can be found in a service manual.

Discussed in later chapters, the engine firing order is commonly used when installing spark plug wires and when doing other tune-up tasks.

KNOW THESE TERMS

Primary circuit, Secondary circuit, Ignition coil, Ignition distributor, Contact points, Condenser, Dwell, Electronic ignition system, Trigger wheel, Pickup coil, Hall effect, ECU, Coil wire, Distributor cap, Rotor, Resistance plug wire, Spark plug, Plug reach, Plug heat range, Plug gap, Hot plug, Cold plug, Ignition timing, Timing advance, Timing retard, Centrifugal advance, Vacuum advance, Electronic advance, Vacuum

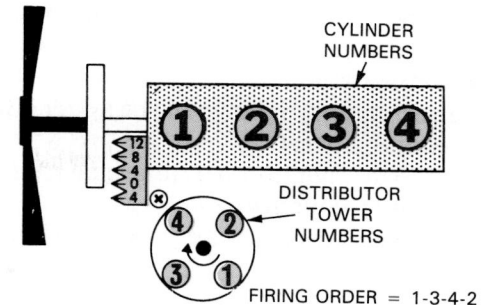

FIRING ORDER = 1-3-4-2

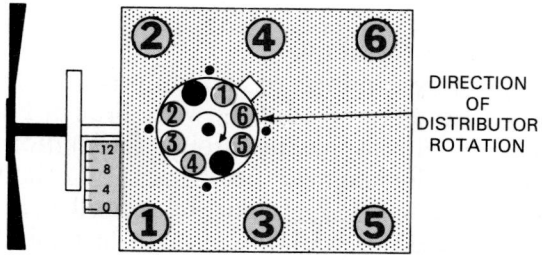

FIRING ORDER = 1-6-5-4-3-2

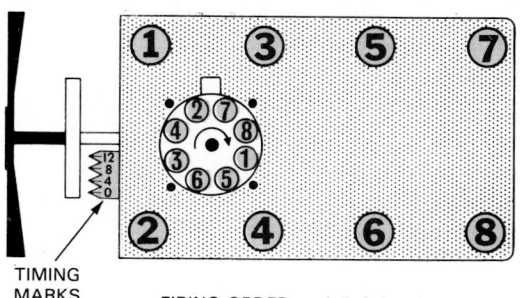

FIRING ORDER = 1-5-6-3-4-2-7-8

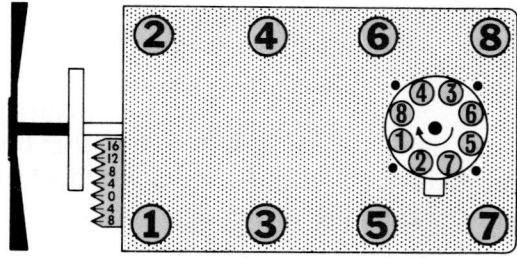

FIRING ORDER = 1-8-4-3-6-5-7-2

Fig. 32-37. Firing order is sequence that spark plugs fire in each cylinder. Firing order information is used when installing plug wires, installing distributor, setting ignition timing, and other operations covered in next chapter. (Mitchell Manuals and Echlin)

delay valve, Crankshaft triggered ignition, Pulse ring, Crank position sensor, Computer-coil ignition, Electronic coil module, Engine firing order.

REVIEW QUESTIONS

1. What are the five basic functions of an ignition system?

2. List and explain the six major parts of an ignition system.
3. An ignition system _____ circuit is used to supply direct battery voltage to the system during starting motor operation.
4. Define the terms "ignition system primary" and "ignition system secondary."
5. An ignition coil is capable of producing this voltage output.
   a. 10kv.
   b. 20kv.
   c. 30kv.
   d. None of the above.
6. The primary windings of an ignition coil are several hundred turns of heavy wire. True or False?
7. When the current flowing through the ignition coil is broken, the magnetic field _____ and induces high _____ into the secondary.
8. Explain the differences between a contact point and a pickup coil (electronic) distributor.
9. What is dwell?
10. An electronic ignition system uses an _____ circuit and a distributor _____ _____ to operate the ignition coil.
11. The trigger wheel or reluctor causes a tiny voltage pulse in the pickup coil to operate the ECU and ignition coil. True or False?
12. How does the pickup coil produce signals for the electronic control unit?
13. The ignition system _____ or _____ _____ is the "electronic switch" that turns the ignition coil primary on and off.
14. The ignition system ECU is NOT normally located in the distributor. True or False?
15. Define the term "ECU dwell time."
16. What is electrical leakage?
17. The _____ _____ is an insulating plastic component that fits over the distributor housing and sends voltage to each spark plug wire.
18. Explain the function of the distributor rotor.
19. Why do spark plug wires need internal resistance?
20. It normally takes about _____ to _____ volts to operate a spark plug.
21. Spark plug gap is the distance between the center electrode and side electrode. True or False?
22. A colder spark plug might be beneficial in an older engine that burns some oil. True or False and Why?
23. Describe the difference between timing advance and timing retard.
24. List and explain the three methods of controlling ignition timing.
25. The distributor centrifugal advance depends upon engine _____ and the vacuum advance depends upon intake manifold pressure (vacuum), an indicator of engine _____ .
26. Electronic spark advance uses engine _____ and a _____ to control ignition timing.
27. How does a crankshaft triggered electronic ignition system work?
28. Which of the following does NOT relate to a computer-coil or distributorless ignition system?
   a. No rotor.
   b. No centrifugal or vacuum advance.
   c. Two ignition coils per cylinder.
   d. No coil wire.
   e. No spark plug wires.
29. With a computer-coil or distributorless ignition, two spark plugs fire at once. True or False?
30. List five possible advantages of a distributorless ignition.
31. Engine _____ _____ refers to the sequence in which the spark plugs operate to cause combustion in each cylinder.

ACTIVITIES FOR CHAPTER 32

1. If you have access to a computer with a CAD or drawing program, use it to make a cross-sectional drawing of a resistor-type spark plug. Label the components, then output the drawing to a printer, if available.
2. Make a list of the various engine sensors used with an electronic spark advance system. Describe the purpose of each sensor.
3. Using shop manuals, identify the firing order of the spark plugs for two different makes of 4-, 6-, and 8-cylinder engines.

Central location of spark plug in center of four valves makes combustion flame spread evenly through the chamber for better burning. (Subaru)

33

Ignition System Problems, Testing, Repair

After studying this chapter, you will be able to:
- ☐ Diagnose typical ignition system problems.
- ☐ List the symptoms produced by faulty ignition system components.
- ☐ Describe common tests used to find ignition system troubles.
- ☐ Explain how to replace or repair ignition system parts.
- ☐ Summarize contact point and pickup coil adjustments.
- ☐ Adjust ignition timing.
- ☐ Describe safety practices to follow when testing or repairing an ignition system.

An ignition system is one of the most important systems on a vehicle. If a problem exists in the ignition, engine performance will suffer. As a service technician, you must be able to quickly and accurately correct ignition system troubles.

The previous chapter covered operating principles. This chapter will let you use this information when learning how to test and repair modern ignition systems. Study carefully!

IGNITION SYSTEM PROBLEM DIAGNOSIS

Diagnosis of ignition system problems can be very challenging. The ignition system and several other systems (fuel, emission, electrical systems) all work together. A problem in one system may affect, or appear to affect, the operation of another system.

For example, an inoperative gasoline injector can cause an engine miss or rough idle. An oil fouled spark plug will also cause an engine miss. The symptoms for each will be almost identical. Only proper testing methods will find the faulty component.

PRELIMINARY CHECKS OF IGNITION SYSTEM

Visually inspect the condition of the ignition system with and without the engine running. See Fig. 33-1.

Look for obvious problems: loose primary connections, spark plug wire pulled off, deteriorated secondary wire insulation, cracked distributor cap, or other trouble.

At the same time, look over other engine systems. Try to find anything that could upset engine operation.

Check for dead cylinder

A *dead cylinder* is a cylinder (combustion chamber) that is NOT burning fuel on the power stroke. There may be ignition system troubles or problems in the engine, fuel system, or another system. A very rough idle and a puffing noise in the engine exhaust may indicate a dead cylinder.

To check for a dead cylinder, pull off one spark plug wire at a time. On a "live" or firing cylinder, pulling the wire off will cause engine rpm to drop and idle to become rougher.

If idle smoothness and rpm DO NOT CHANGE with the plug wire off, that cylinder is DEAD. It is not producing power. You need to check for spark at the wire, spark plug condition, and, possibly low cylinder compression.

Evaluating the symptoms

After checking the system, you must evaluate the symptoms and narrow down the possible causes. Use your knowledge of system operation, a service manual troubleshooting chart, basic testing methods, and common sense to locate the trouble.

More diagnosis information

Chapters 41, 42, 43, and 44 cover engine problem diagnosis and tune-up. Refer to these chapters for more details.

SPARK INTENSITY TEST

A *spark intensity test,* also called a *spark test,* measures the brightness and length of the electric arc

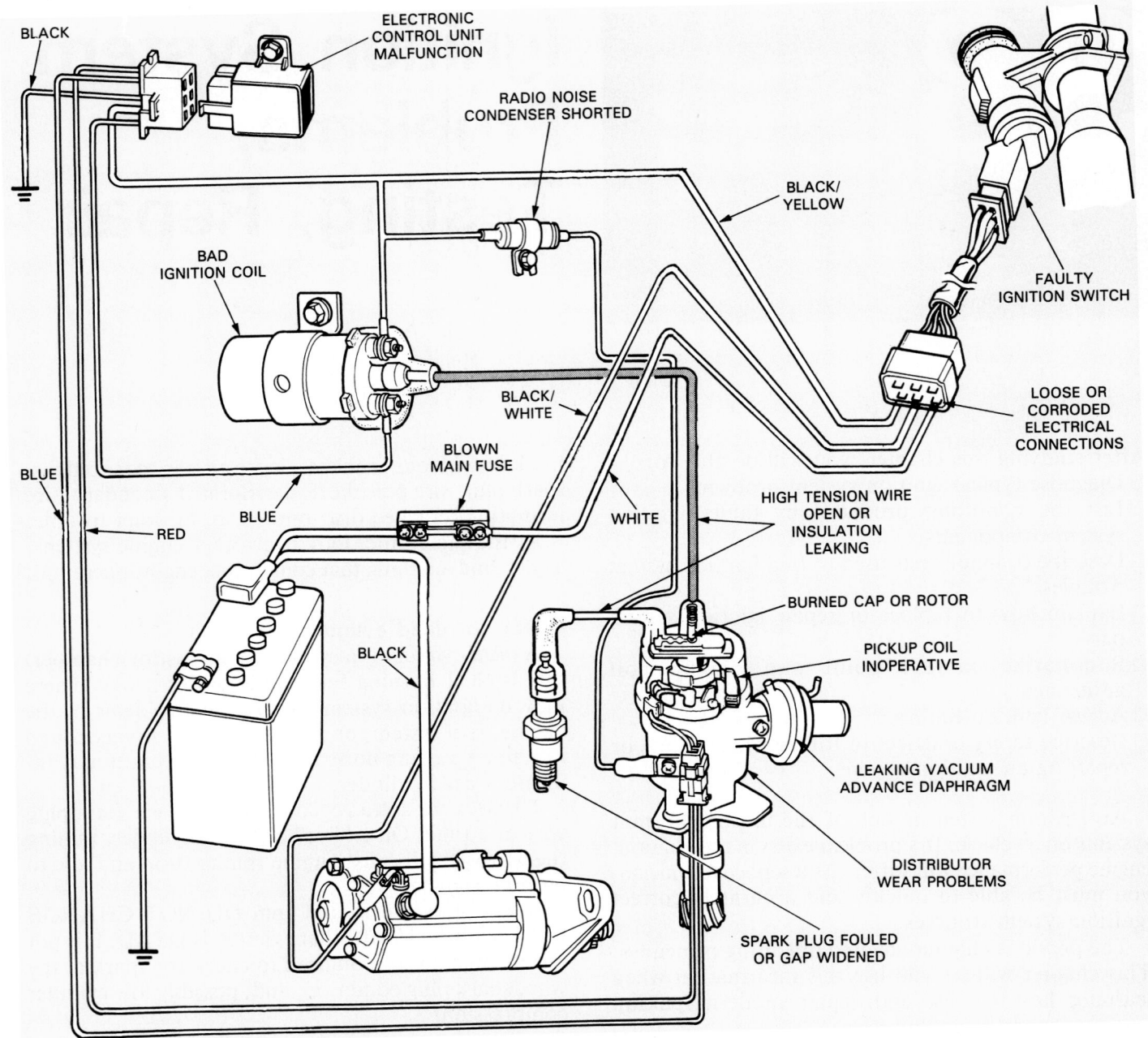

BLACK

ELECTRONIC
CONTROL UNIT
MALFUNCTION

RADIO NOISE
CONDENSER SHORTED

BLACK/
YELLOW

FAULTY
IGNITION SWITCH

BAD
IGNITION COIL

BLACK/
WHITE

LOOSE OR
CORRODED
ELECTRICAL
CONNECTIONS

BLUE

BLOWN
MAIN FUSE

BLUE

RED

WHITE

HIGH TENSION WIRE
OPEN OR
INSULATION
LEAKING

BURNED CAP OR ROTOR

BLACK

PICKUP COIL
INOPERATIVE

LEAKING VACUUM
ADVANCE DIAPHRAGM

DISTRIBUTOR
WEAR PROBLEMS

SPARK PLUG FOULED
OR GAP WIDENED

Fig. 33-1. These are some of the problems common to a modern ignition system. (Honda)

(spark) produced by the ignition system. It is a quick, easy way of checking the general condition of the ignition system.

The spark test is often used when an engine cranks, but will NOT start. The test will help tell you whether the trouble is in the fuel system ("no fuel" problem) or in the ignition system ("no spark" problem). It may also be used to check the spark plug wires, distributor cap, and other secondary components.

Spark test procedures

A *spark tester* is a device with a very large air gap for checking ignition system output voltage. It is like a spark plug with a wide gap and a ground wire. Look at Fig. 33-2.

Remove one of the secondary wires from a spark plug. Insert the spark tester into the wire. Ground it on the engine. Crank or start the engine. Observe the spark at the tester air gap, Fig. 33-2.

WARNING! Only run the engine for a short period of time with a spark plug wire off. Unburned fuel from the dead cylinder could foul and ruin the catalytic converter.

Spark test results

A *strong spark* (wide, bright, snapping electric arc) shows that ignition system voltage is good. The engine "no-start" problem might be due to fouled spark plugs, fuel system problem, or engine trouble. A strong spark indicates that the ignition coil, pickup coil, electronic

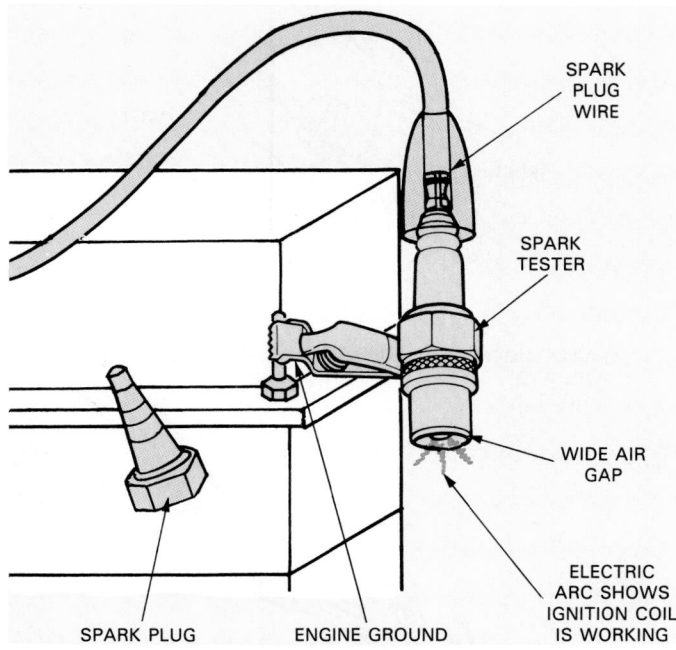

Fig. 33-2. Connect spark tester to spark plug wire. Ground tester on engine. Crank engine while watching arc in tester. No spark or weak spark indicates ignition system troubles.

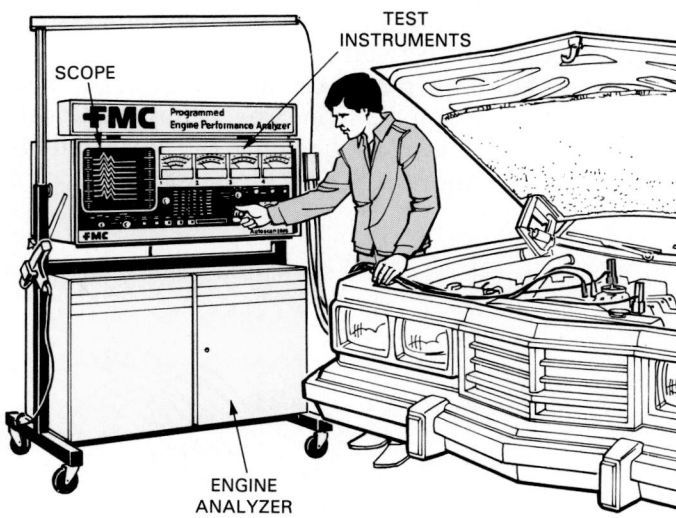

Fig. 33-3. Engine analyzer is commonly used to diagnose and locate ignition system problems. Oscilloscope shows ignition system voltages.

control unit, and other ignition system parts are functioning.

With a **weak spark** or **no spark,** something is wrong in the ignition system.

If spark is weak at all spark plug wires, the problem is common to all of the cylinders (bad ignition coil, rotor, coil wire). Other tests (to be covered shortly) are needed to pinpoint the trouble.

ENGINE ANALYZER

An *engine analyzer* contains several types of test equipment (oscilloscope, dwell meter, tachometer, VOM). They are housed in one large, roll-around cabinet. The analyzer is often used to check the operation of an ignition system. One type of analyzer is shown in Fig. 33-3.

An **oscilloscope,** usually called just *"scope,"* will precisely measure the operating voltages of an ignition system. It uses a television type picture tube to show voltage changes in relation to degrees of distributor or crankshaft rotation. To determine the condition of the system, the mechanic can compare the scope test patterns with known good patterns.

For details on using an engine analyzer and scope, refer to Chapter 43.

ELECTRONIC IGNITION TESTER

An *electronic ignition tester* is a handy instrument which speeds ignition system diagnosis by indicating specific problems. See Fig. 33-4. The ignition tester is connected to the ignition circuit or to a special test plug

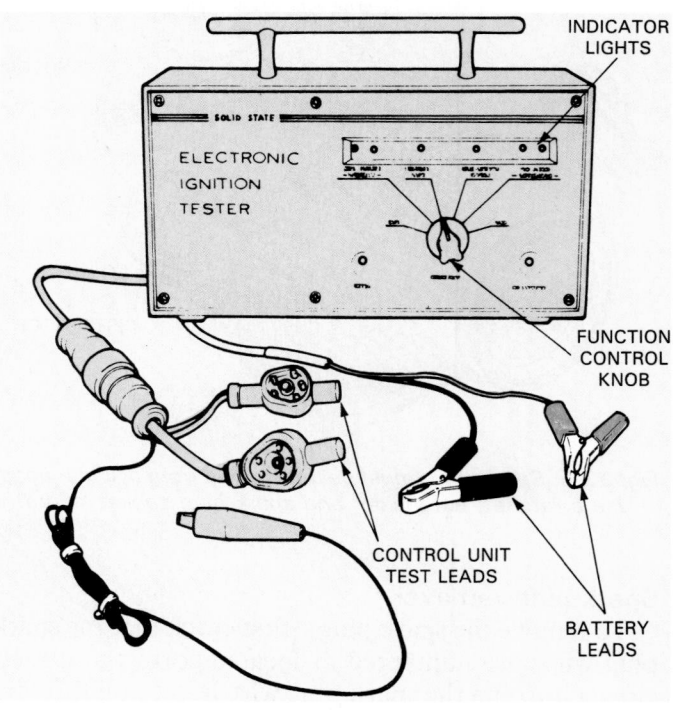

Fig. 33-4. Electronic ignition testers are made by auto makers and after-market companies. They will quickly locate problems if used properly. (Chrysler)

provided on the side of the engine compartment. Indicator lights then show whether problems exist.

SPARK PLUG SERVICE

Bad spark plugs can cause a wide range of problems: misfiring, lack of power, poor fuel economy, and hard starting. After prolonged use, the spark plug tip can become coated with ash, oil, and other substances. Also, the plug electrodes can burn and widen the gap.

This can make it more difficult for the ignition system to produce an arc between the electrodes.

To test the spark plugs, use an oscilloscope. Bad plugs will show up on the scope waveforms (patterns). If a scope is NOT available, remove the plugs and inspect their condition. Refer to Fig. 33-5.

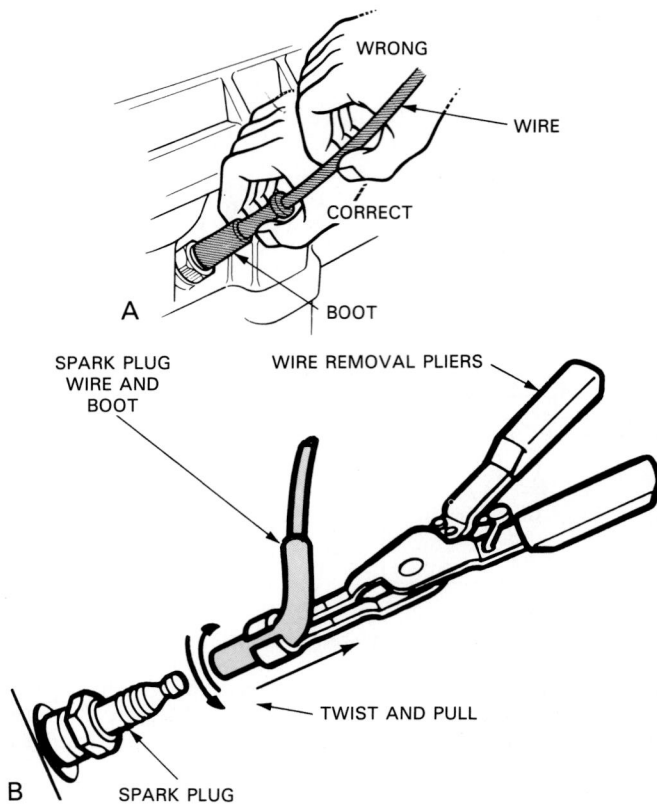

Fig. 33-6. When removing spark plug wire, pull on boot, never the wire. A — Using hands to remove wire. B — Using special pliers to grasp and pull on boot. (Toyota and Mopar)

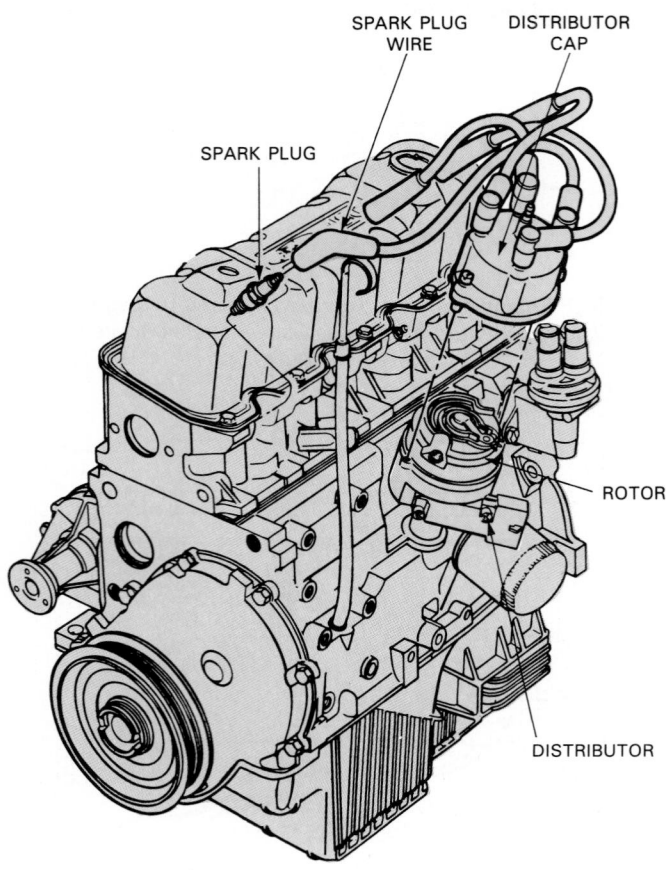

Fig. 33-5. Spark plugs must be unscrewed from cylinder head. Use a ratchet, extension, and spark plug socket. (Ford)

Spark plug removal

To remove the spark plugs, first check that the spark plug wires are numbered or located correctly in their clips. Grasping the spark plug wire boot, pull the wire off, Fig. 33-6. Twist the boot back and forth if it sticks.

WARNING! NEVER remove a spark plug wire by pulling on the wire. Always grasp and pull on the boot. If you pull on the wire, you can break the conductor in the wire.

Blow debris away from the spark plug holes with compressed air. This will prevent particles from falling into the engine cylinders when the plugs are removed.

Using a spark plug socket, extension, and ratchet, as needed, unscrew each spark plug. As you remove each plug, lay it in order on the fender cover or workbench. Do not mix up the plugs. After all of the plugs are out, inspect them to diagnose the condition of the engine.

Reading spark plugs

To *read spark plugs,* closely inspect and analyze the condition of each spark plug tip and insulator. This will give you information on the condition of the engine, fuel system, and ignition system.

For example, a properly burning plug should have a *brown* to *greyish-tan* color.

A *black* or *wet plug* indicates that the plug is NOT firing or that there is an engine problem (worn piston rings and cylinders, leaking valve stem seals, low engine compression, or rich fuel mixture) in that cylinder.

Study the spark plugs in Fig. 33-7 very carefully. Learn to read the condition of used spark plugs. They can provide valuable information when troubleshooting problems.

Cleaning spark plugs

Spark plugs may be cleaned using a *spark plug cleaner* (air powered device that blasts plug tip with abrasive). Look at Fig. 33-8.

Some manufacturers do NOT recommend spark plug cleaning. Blasting can roughen the insulator and lead to fouling, misfiring, and loss of performance.

Be very careful that abrasive (sand) does not wedge up inside the insulator. The sand could fall into the cylinder and cause cylinder scoring. Most shops install new plugs rather than taking the time to clean used spark plugs.

Fig. 33-7. Read spark plugs by inspecting condition of insulator and electrodes. Study typical examples. A — Normal burning, used plug (engine and ignition in good condition). B — Oil fouled plug (worn rings, scored cylinder, leaking valve seals). C — Ash fouled plug (poor fuel quality, some oil entering cylinder). D — Carbon fouled plug (slow speed driving, plug heat range too cold, weak ignition, or rich mixture). E — Preignition damage (timing too advanced, low octane fuel, or heat range of plug too high. F — Normal electrode erosion (old plug with high mileage). (Champion Spark Plugs)

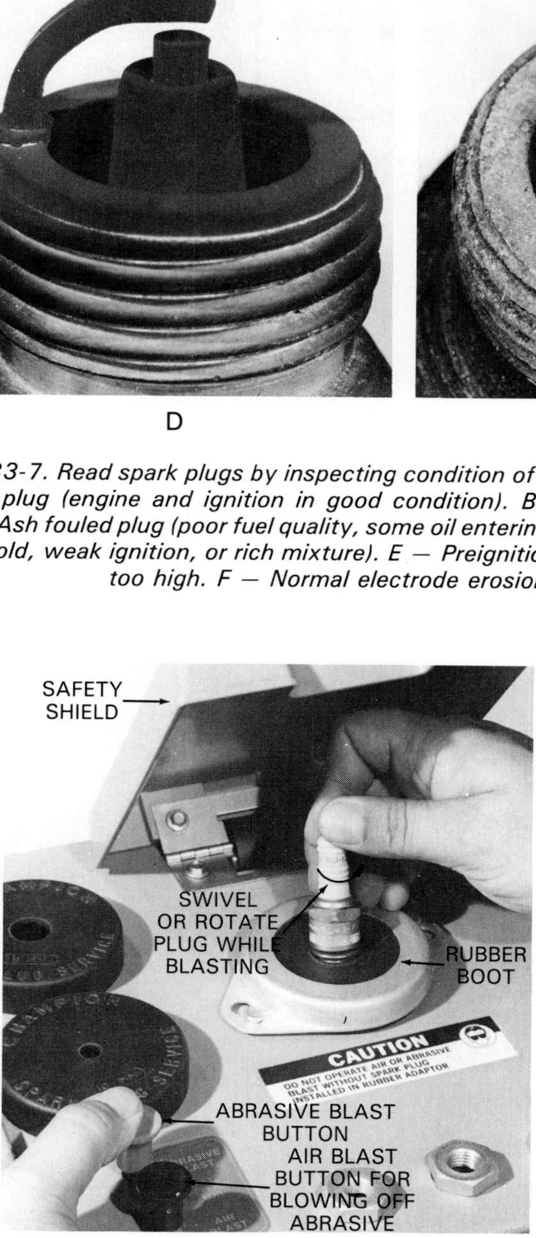

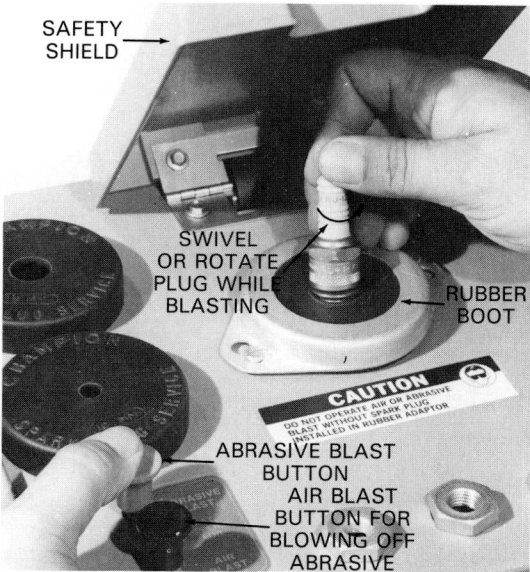

Fig. 33-8. When blast cleaning used plugs, wear safety glasses. Replace plug if electrodes are badly burned. File electrodes square and gap them after cleaning. (Champion)

Gapping spark plugs

Obtain the correct replacement plug (heat range and reach) recommended by the manufacturer. Then, set *spark plug gap* by spacing the side electrode the correct distance from the center electrode. If the new spark plugs have been dropped or mishandled, the gap may not be within specs.

A *wire feeler gauge* should be used to measure spark plug gap. As in Fig. 33-9, top, slide the feeler gauge between the electrodes. If needed, bend the side electrode until the feeler gauge fits snugly, Fig. 33-9, bottom. The gauge should drag lightly as it is pulled in and out of the gap. Spark plug gaps vary from approximately .030 inch (0.76 mm) on contact point ignitions to over .060 inch (1.52 mm) on electronic systems.

Installing spark plugs

Spark plugs set to the correct gap are ready for installation. Use your fingers, a spark plug socket, or a short piece of vacuum hose to START the plugs in their holes. Do NOT use the ratchet because the plug

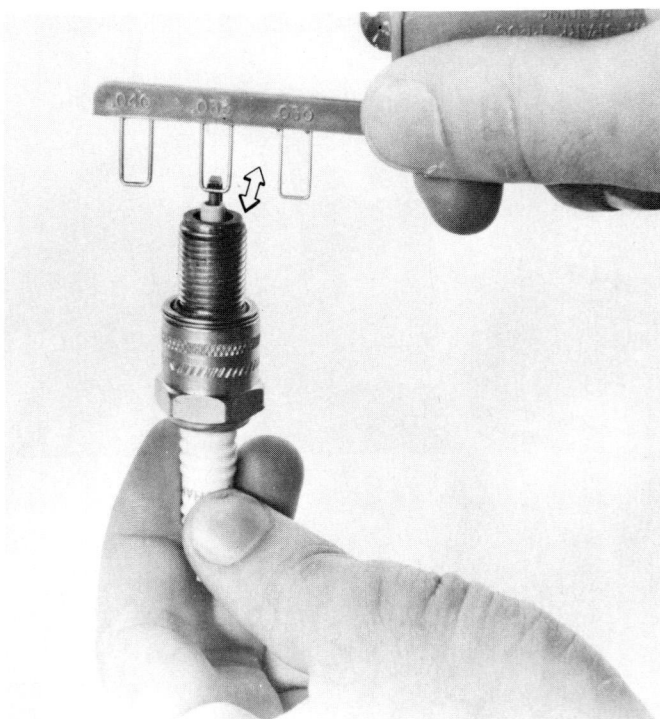

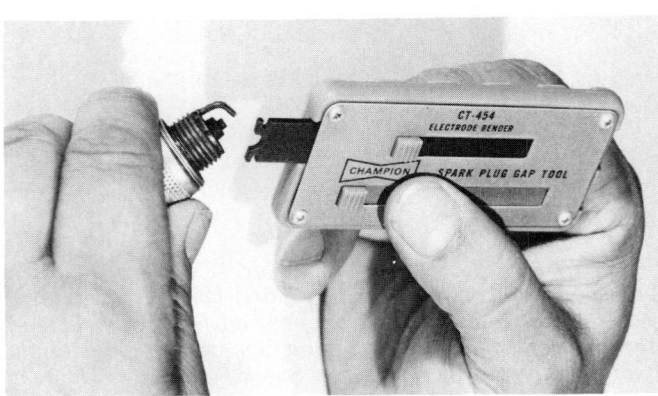

Fig. 33-9. Gapping a spark plug. Top. Use wire feeler gauge to measure gap. Both electrodes should just touch gauge. Bottom. If needed, bend side electrode with gapping tool to achieve correct electrode spacing.
(Champion Spark Plugs and Chrysler)

Most spark plug wires have a resistance conductor that is easily separated. If the conductor is broken, voltage and current cannot reach the spark plug.

If the spark plug insulation is faulty, sparks may leak through the insulation to ground or to another wire, instead of reaching the spark plugs.

Spark plug wire removal

Before removing spark plug wires, make sure they are numbered. This will simplify installation.

Remove each wire from its plug and the distributor cap or coil module. Fig. 33-10 shows several ways spark plug wires are removed from a distributor cap.

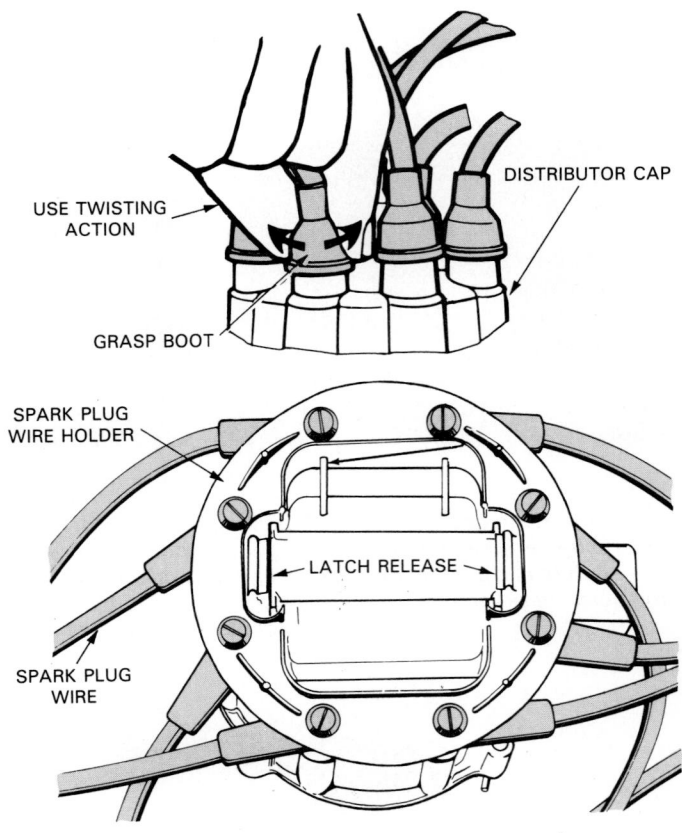

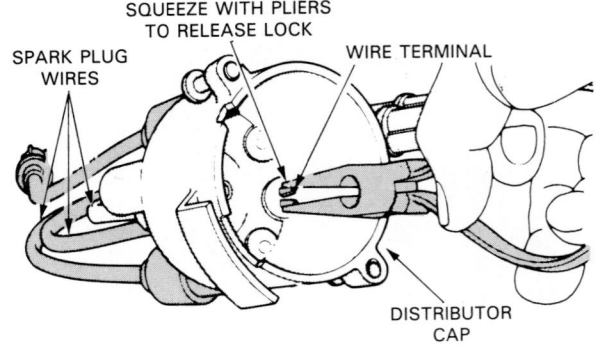

Fig. 33-10. Three typical methods of securing spark plug wires in distributor cap. Top. Press fit. Just twist and pull on boot to remove wire. Middle. Large ring holds all wires into cap. Release latches and lift off ring to release plug wires. Bottom. Snap locks hold wire terminals in cap. Use pliers to free locks before pulling on wire boots. (Mopar, Oldsmobile, Chrysler)

and cylinder head threads could be crossthreaded and damaged.

With the spark plugs threaded into the head a few turns by hand, spin them in the rest of the way with your ratchet.

Tighten the spark plugs to specs. Some auto makers give a spark plug torque. Others recommend bottoming the plugs on the seat and then turning an additional one-quarter to one-half turn. Refer to a service manual for exact procedures.

SECONDARY WIRE SERVICE

A *faulty spark plug wire* can either have a burned or broken conductor or it could have deteriorated insulation.

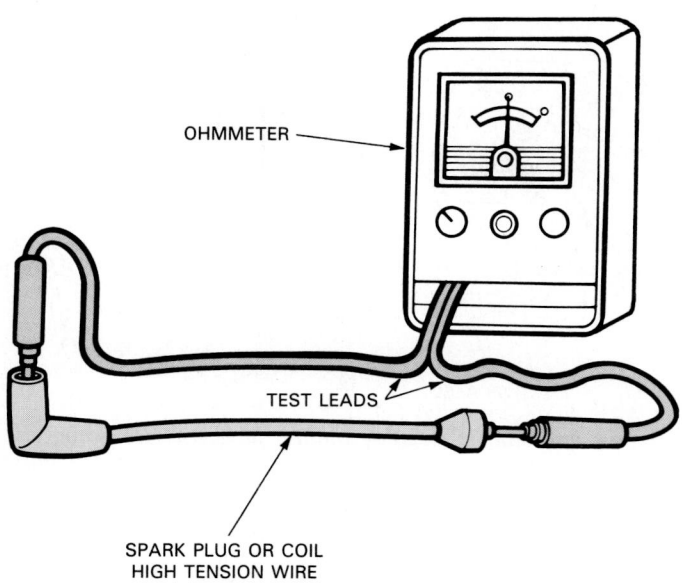

Fig. 33-11. To check conductor in spark plug or coil wire, measure wire resistance with ohmmeter. If too high, replace wire because conductor or terminal is broken. (Mopar)

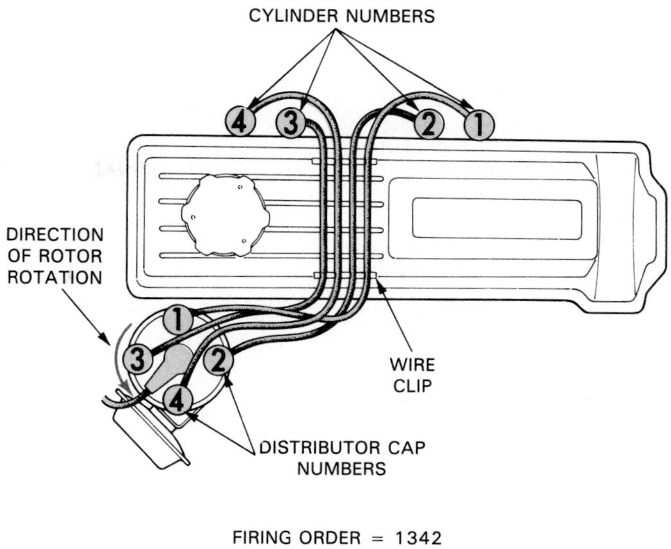

FIRING ORDER = 1342

Fig. 33-12. When installing all spark plug wires, locate service manual illustration like this one for your engine. Then, trace and install wires from correct distributor cap tower to correct spark plug. (Saab)

Secondary wire resistance test

A *secondary wire resistance test* will check the condition of a spark plug or coil wire conductor. It should be used to check for a bad wire when an oscilloscope (Chapter 43) is NOT available.

To do a wire resistance test, connect an ohmmeter across each end of the spark plug or coil wire, as in Fig. 33-11. The meter will read wire internal resistance in ohms. Compare your reading to specs.

Typically, spark plug wire resistance should NOT be over approximately 5000 ohms per inch or 100k (100,000) ohms total. Since specs vary, always check in a service manual for an exact value. A bad spark plug wire will often have almost infinite (maximum) resistance.

Secondary wire insulation test

A *secondary wire insulation test* checks for sparks arcing through the insulation to ground. An ohmmeter test will NOT detect bad insulation.

To check spark plug and coil wire insulation, place fender covers over the side of the car hood to block out light. Start the engine. Inspect each wire.

A special test light or grounded screwdriver can be moved next to the wire insulation. If sparks jump through the insulation and onto the tool, the wire is bad.

Spark plug wire leakage is a condition in which electric arcs pass through the wire insulation. This problem requires wire replacement.

Replacing spark plug wires

Installing new spark plug wires is simple, especially if one wire at a time is replaced. Compare old wire length with the length of the new wire. Replace each

wire with one of equal length. Make sure the wire is fully attached on the plug and in the distributor or coil module.

Spark plug wire replacement is more complicated if all of the wires are removed at once. Then, you must use the engine firing order and cylinder numbers to route each wire correctly.

Fig. 33-12 is similar to illustrations found in a service manual. It can be used to trace the wires from each distributor cap tower to the correct spark plug or cylinder.

DISTRIBUTOR SERVICE

A distributor is very critical to the proper operation of an ignition system. It senses engine speed, alters ignition timing, and distributes high voltage to each spark plug wire. If any part of the distributor is faulty, engine performance suffers.

DISTRIBUTOR CAP AND ROTOR SERVICE

A *bad distributor cap* or *rotor* can cause engine missing, BACKFIRING (popping noise from the throttle body or carburetor), and other engine performance problems.

A common trouble arises when a ***carbon trace*** (small line of carbon-like substance that conducts electricity) forms on the distributor cap or rotor. The carbon trace will short coil voltage to ground or to a wrong terminal lug in the distributor cap. See Fig. 33-13. A carbon trace can cause the spark plugs to fire poorly, out of sequence, or not at all.

When problems point to possible distributor cap or rotor troubles, remove and inspect them. Look at Fig.

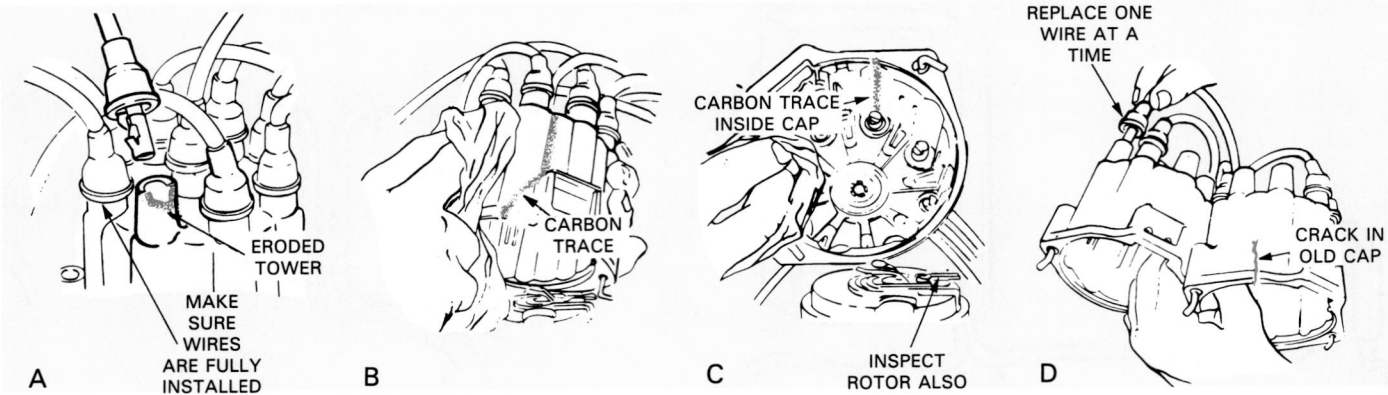

Fig. 33-13. Inspect distributor cap and rotor for burning, carbon traces, and cracks. Replace them if problems are detected. A — Burned, eroded cap tower. B — Carbon trace on outside of cap. C — Carbon trace in cap and on rotor. D — Crack in cap. Replace wires one at a time. Install in same tower. (GMC)

33-13. Using a drop light, check the inside of the cap for cracks and carbon traces. A carbon trace is black, making it difficult to see on a black colored distributor cap or rotor.

If a crack or carbon trace is found, replace the cap or rotor. Also check the rotor tip for excessive burning, damage, or looseness. Make sure the rotor fits snugly on the distributor shaft.

Distributor cap and rotor replacement

Distributor caps may be secured by either screws or spring type metal clips. Normally, turn the screws counterclockwise for removal. With clips, pry on the top of the spring clips, being careful not to crack the cap. The clip should pop free. Wiggle and pull upward to remove the cap from the distributor body.

Rotors may be held by screws or they may be force-fitted around the distributor shaft. Refer to Fig. 33-14. Pulling by hand will usually free a press-fit rotor.

However, if stuck, carefully pry under the rotor.

With some ignition systems, the ignition coil is housed inside the distributor cap. In this case, the coil must be taken out of the old cap and installed in the new one.

To install a rotor, line up the rotor on the distributor shaft properly. With a press-fit rotor, a tab inside the rotor fits into a groove or slot in the shaft. With a screw-held rotor, the rotor may have round and/or square dowels that fit into holes in the distributor.

When installing a distributor cap, a notch or tab on the cap must line up with a tab or notch on the distributor housing. This assures that the cap is correctly aligned with the rotor. Before securing the spring clips or screws, push down and twist the cap. Make sure it will NOT wobble on the distributor.

WARNING! If a distributor cap is NOT installed correctly, rotor and distributor damage can result. The whirling rotor can strike the sides of the distributor cap.

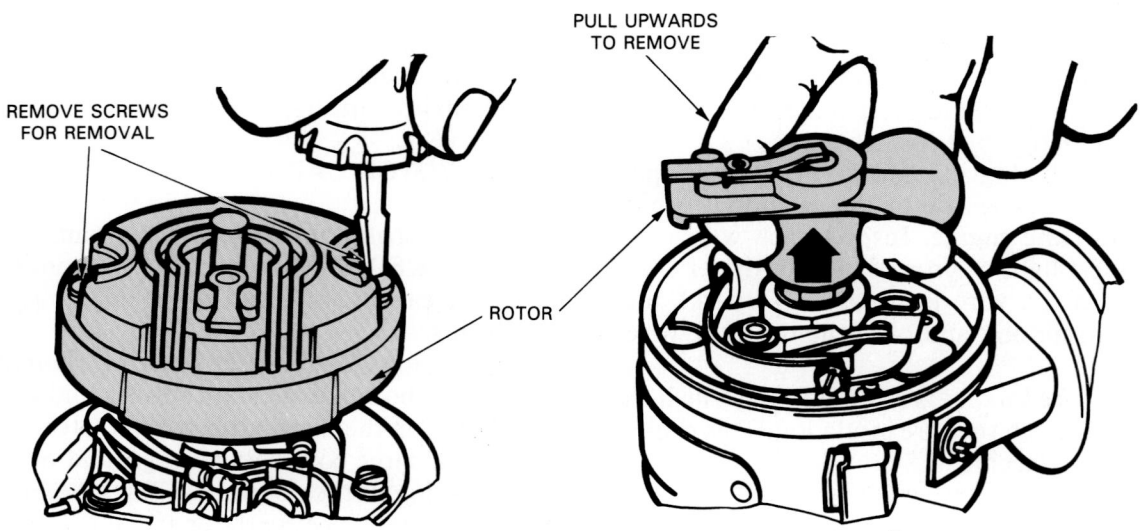

Fig. 33-14. Two types of rotor mounting. Left. Screws hold rotor onto distributor. Rotor has dowels that must line up in distributor. Right. Press-fit rotor is pulled off and pushed on distributor shaft. It has a lug that must align and fit into notch in distributor shaft. (Mopar)

ELECTRONIC IGNITION DISTRIBUTOR SERVICE

Most electronic ignition type distributors use a pickup coil to sense trigger wheel (distributor shaft) rotation and engine speed. The pickup coil sends small electrical impulses to the electronic control unit.

If the distributor fails to produce these tiny electrical signals properly, the complete ignition system can stop functioning. It is important to know how to make several basic tests on electronic ignition distributors.

PICKUP COIL SERVICE

A *bad pickup coil* can produce a wide range of engine problems: stalling, missing, no-start troubles, and loss of power at specific speeds. If the tiny windings in the pickup coil break, they can cause intermittent problems that only occur under certain conditions.

Also, because of vacuum advance movement, the thin wire leads going to the pickup coil can break. Though the insulation may look fine, the conductor could be separated inside the insulation.

Pickup coil testing

A *pickup coil ohmmeter test* compares actual pickup coil resistance with specs. If resistance is too high or low, the unit is bad. Perform this test as in Fig. 33-15.

Connect an ohmmeter across the pickup coil output leads. Observe the meter reading. WIGGLE THE WIRES to the pickup coil while watching the meter. This will help locate a break in the leads to the pickup. Also, lightly tap on the coil with the handle of a screwdriver. This could uncover any break in the coil windings.

Pickup coil resistance will usually vary between 250 and 1500 ohms. Check a service manual for exact specs. If the meter reading changes when the wire leads are moved or when the coil is tapped, replace the pickup coil.

A low-reading AC *voltmeter* can also be used to test a pickup coil. With the engine cranking, a small AC voltage should be produced by the pickup coil. Refer to specs for exact voltage values and procedures.

Pickup coil replacement

A distributor pickup coil can usually be replaced simply by removing the distributor cap, rotor, and the screws on the advance plate. Sometimes the pickup coil is mounted around the distributor shaft. Since procedures vary, find detailed directions for the particular distributor in a service manual. See Fig. 33-16.

The *pickup coil air gap* is the space between the pickup coil and a trigger wheel tooth. With some designs, it must be set after installing the pickup coil.

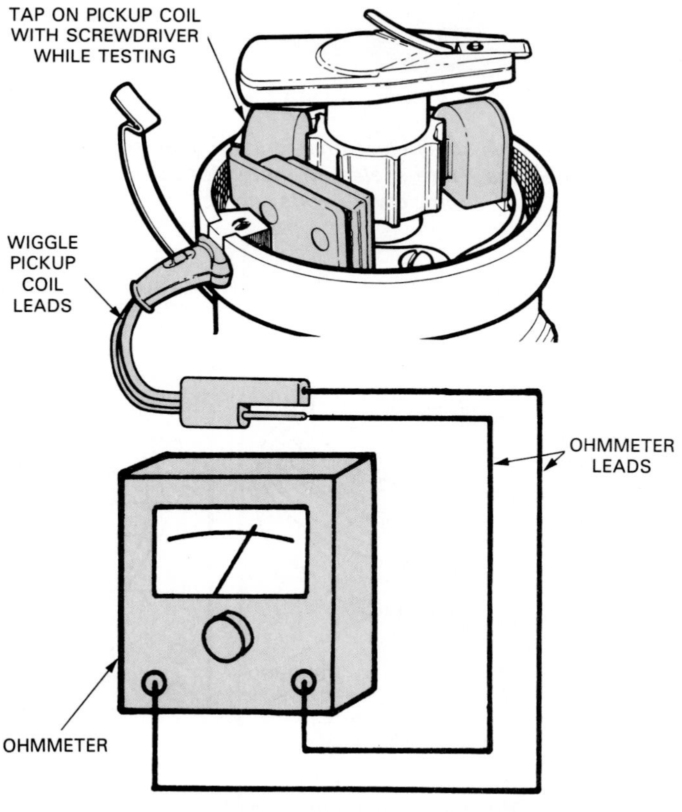

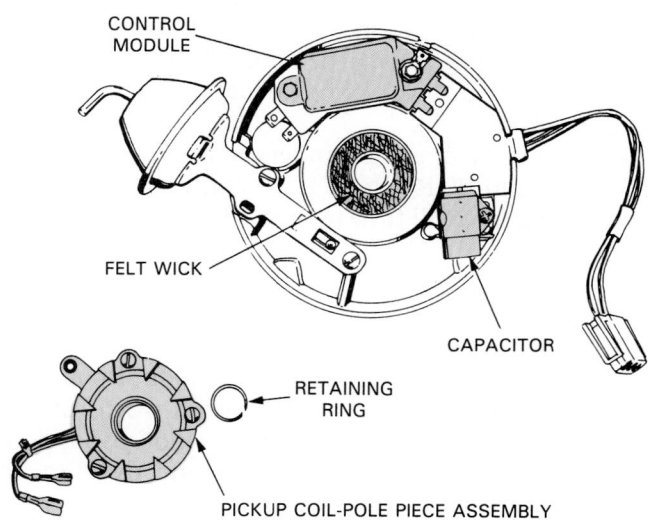

Fig. 33-16. To remove this pickup coil, you must remove distributor shaft and snap ring retainer. Many other pickup coils are simply removed like contact points, by removing two screws. (Buick)

Fig. 33-15. Connect ohmmeter to leads from pickup coil. Wiggle wires and tap on coil with screwdriver. If ohmmeter reading does not remain steady and within specs, replace pickup coil. (Chrysler)

To obtain an accurate reading, slide a NON-MAGNETIC FEELER GAUGE (plastic or brass gauge) between the pickup coil and trigger wheel. Look at Fig. 33-17. One of the trigger wheel teeth must point at the pickup coil. Move the pickup coil in or out until the correct size gauge fits in the gap. Tighten the pickup screws and double-check the air gap setting.

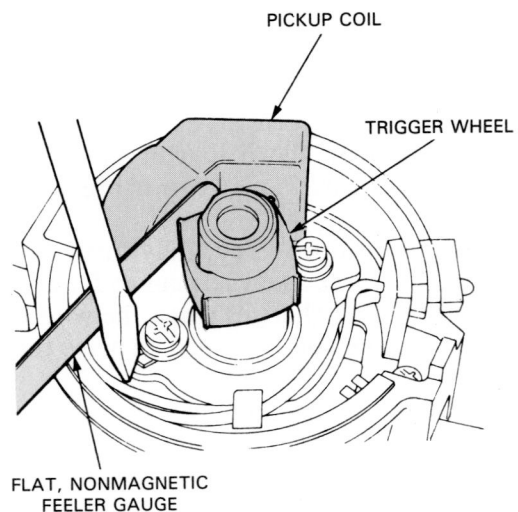

Fig. 33-17. Pickup coil air gap may need to be measured and adjusted with some distributors. With trigger wheel tooth pointing at pickup, slide correct thickness nonmagnetic feeler gauge into air gap. Adjust pickup until gauge just fits in gap.

CONTACT POINT TYPE DISTRIBUTOR SERVICE

Bad contact points (points having burned, pitted, mis-aligned contacts, or worn rubbing block) cause a wide range of engine performance problems. These problems include high speed missing, no-start problem, and many other ignition related troubles.

A *faulty condenser* may leak (allow some DC current to flow to ground), be shorted (direct electrical connection to ground), or be opened (broken lead wire to condenser foils).

If leaking or open, a condenser will cause POINT ARCING and BURNING. If the condenser is shorted, primary current will flow to ground and the engine will NOT start.

Testing distributor points

Many technicians visually inspect the surfaces of the contact points to determine their condition. Points with burned and pitted contacts, or with a worn rubbing block, must be replaced. If the points look good, point resistance should be measured. Many dwell-tachometers, Fig. 33-18, have a scale for measuring point resistance.

Crank the engine until the points are closed. Connect the meter to the primary point lead and to ground. If the resistance is too high (out of scale markings for condenser test), the points are burned and must be replaced.

Testing distributor condenser

Most technicians simply replace a condenser any time symptoms point to a condenser problem. However, an ohmmeter can be used to test a condenser.

The ohmmeter is connected to the condenser (capacitor), as in Fig. 33-19. The meter should register

slightly and then return to infinity (maximum resistance). Any continuous reading other than infinity means that the condenser is leaking and must be replaced.

Covered in Chapter 43, an oscilloscope will also detect condenser and contact point problems.

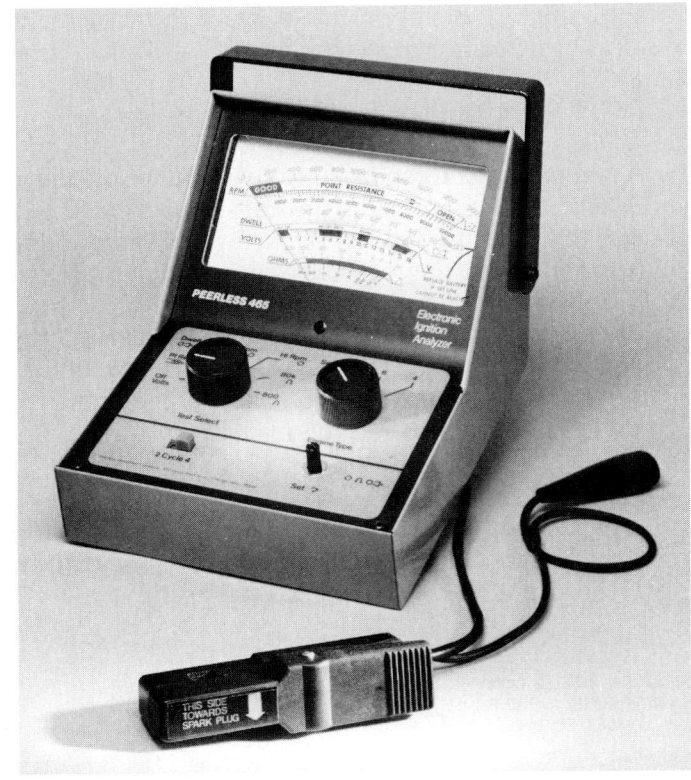

Fig. 33-18. This small electronic ignition analyzer can make several readings. Note scales on meter for point resistance, rpm, dwell, volts, ohms.

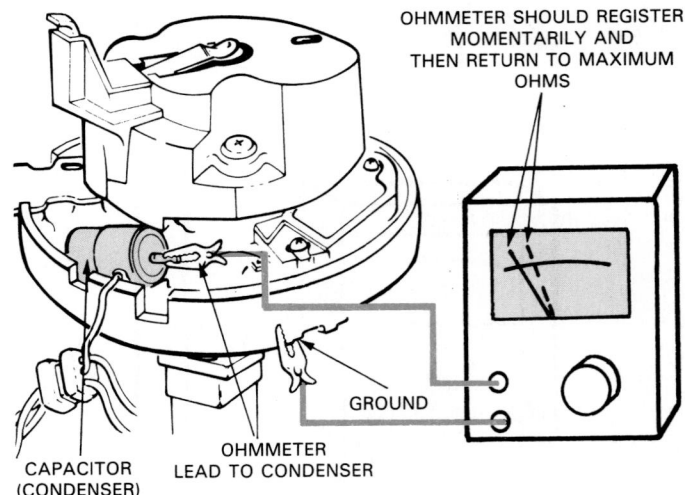

Fig. 33-19. Ohmmeter can be used to check capacitor or condenser for shorts. When meter is connected, it should register momentarily. Then, as capacitor charges from meter current, reading should return to infinity. Continuous reading shows shorted capacitor. (Echlin)

Removing points and condenser

Normally, the distributor points and condenser are held in place by small screws. See Fig. 33-20.

To prevent dropping the screws, use a magnetic or clip-type screwdriver that firmly holds the screws. If you drop one of the screws into the distributor (under advance plate), the distributor may have to be removed from the engine. Use a small wrench to disconnect the primary wires from the points.

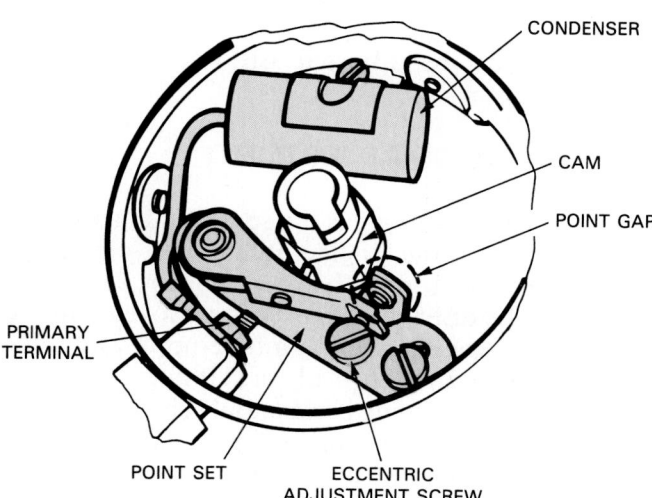

Fig. 33-20. Points and condenser are held on advance plate by small screws. Eccentric adjustment screw does not have to be removed for point removal.

Lubricating distributor and rubbing block

Wipe the distributor cam and breaker plate clean before installing the new parts. If recommended, apply a small amount of oil to lubrication points on the distributor (wick in center of shaft, cam wick, or oil hole in side of distributor housing). Do NOT apply too much oil because it could get on the points.

To prolong service life, place a small amount of grease on the side of the breaker arm rubbing block. This will reduce friction between the distributor cam and fiber block.

Installing points and condenser

Fit the points into the distributor. Install the point screws, condenser, and primary wires.

If the distributor has a window (square metal plate) in the distributor cap, fully tighten the point hold-down screws. If the distributor does NOT have a window, only partially tighten the screws so the points can be adjusted.

Adjusting distributor points

Distributor points can be adjusted using either a *feeler gauge* (metal blade ground to precise thickness) or a *dwell meter* (meter that electrically measures point setting in degrees of distributor rotation).

Gapping distributor points

To use a feeler gauge to gap (set) distributor points, crank the engine until the points are FULLY OPEN. The point rubbing block should be on top of a distributor cam lobe. This is illustrated in Fig. 33-21.

Distributor point gap is the recommended distance between the contacts in the fully open position. Look up this spec in the service manual. It may also be given on the emission sticker in the engine compartment.

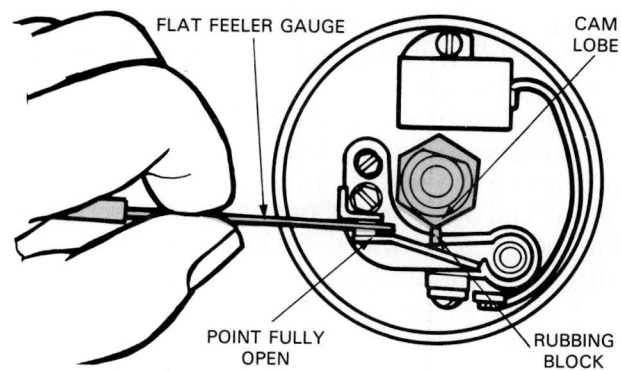

Fig. 33-21. To set points, "bump" engine until cam lobe is pushing on point rubbing block. Points must be in fully open position. Slide correct thickness feeler gauge between points. Open or close until gauge just touches both contacts. (Mopar)

Typical point gap settings average around .015 in. (0.38 mm) for eight-cylinder engines to .025 in. (0.53 mm) for six and four-cylinder engines.

With the distributor points open, slide the specified thickness feeler gauge between the points. See Fig. 33-21. Adjust the points so that there is a slight drag on the blade. Use a screwdriver or allen wrench, depending upon point design, to open or close the points, Fig. 33-22. If needed, tighten the hold-down screws and recheck point gap.

CAUTION! Make sure your feeler gauge is clean before inserting it in the points. Oil or grease will reduce the service life of the points.

Fig. 33-22. To open or close points, either turn eccentric screw or pry on stationary contact base, as shown. Tighten hold-down screws fully after adjustment. (Saab)

Using a dwell meter

To use a dwell meter for adjusting distributor points, follow the directions provided with the meter. See Fig. 33-23 for a typical example.

Typically, connect the red lead to the distributor side of the coil (wire going to contact points). Connect the black lead to ground (any metal part on engine).

If an opening is provided in the distributor cap, the points should be set with the engine running. Install the distributor cap and rotor. Start the engine. With the meter controls set properly, adjust the points using an Allen wrench or special screwdriver type tool. Turn the point adjustment screw until the dwell meter reads within specs.

If the distributor cap does NOT have an adjustment window, set the points with the cap removed. Instead of starting the engine, ground the coil wire (connect output end on engine). Crank the engine with the starting motor. This will simulate engine operation and allow point adjustment with the dwell meter.

Dwell specifications

Dwell specifications (recommended point settings in degrees) vary with the number of cylinders in the engine. An 8-cylinder engine will usually require 30 degrees of dwell. An engine with fewer cylinders will normally require more dwell time. Always obtain exact dwell values from a tune-up chart or shop manual.

Dwell variation (change in dwell meter reading) indicates distributor wear problems. Dwell should remain constant as engine speed is increased or decreased.

Generally, if dwell varies more than about three degrees, the distributor should be rebuilt or replaced. The distributor shaft, bushings, or advance plate could be worn and loose, allowing a change in dwell.

As dwell increases, point gap decreases. As dwell decreases, point gap increases. This is illustrated in Fig. 33-23. Also, any change in point gap or dwell will change ignition timing. For this reason, the points should always be adjusted BEFORE the ignition timing.

IGNITION TIMING ADJUSTMENT

Initial ignition timing is the spark timing set by the mechanic with the engine idling (no centrifugal, vacuum, or electronic advance). It must be adjusted whenever the distributor has been removed and reinstalled in an engine. During a tune-up, initial timing must be checked and then adjusted if not within specs.

Initial ignition timing is commonly changed by turning the distributor housing in the engine. This makes the pickup coil and electronic control unit or breaker points fire the ignition coil sooner or later.

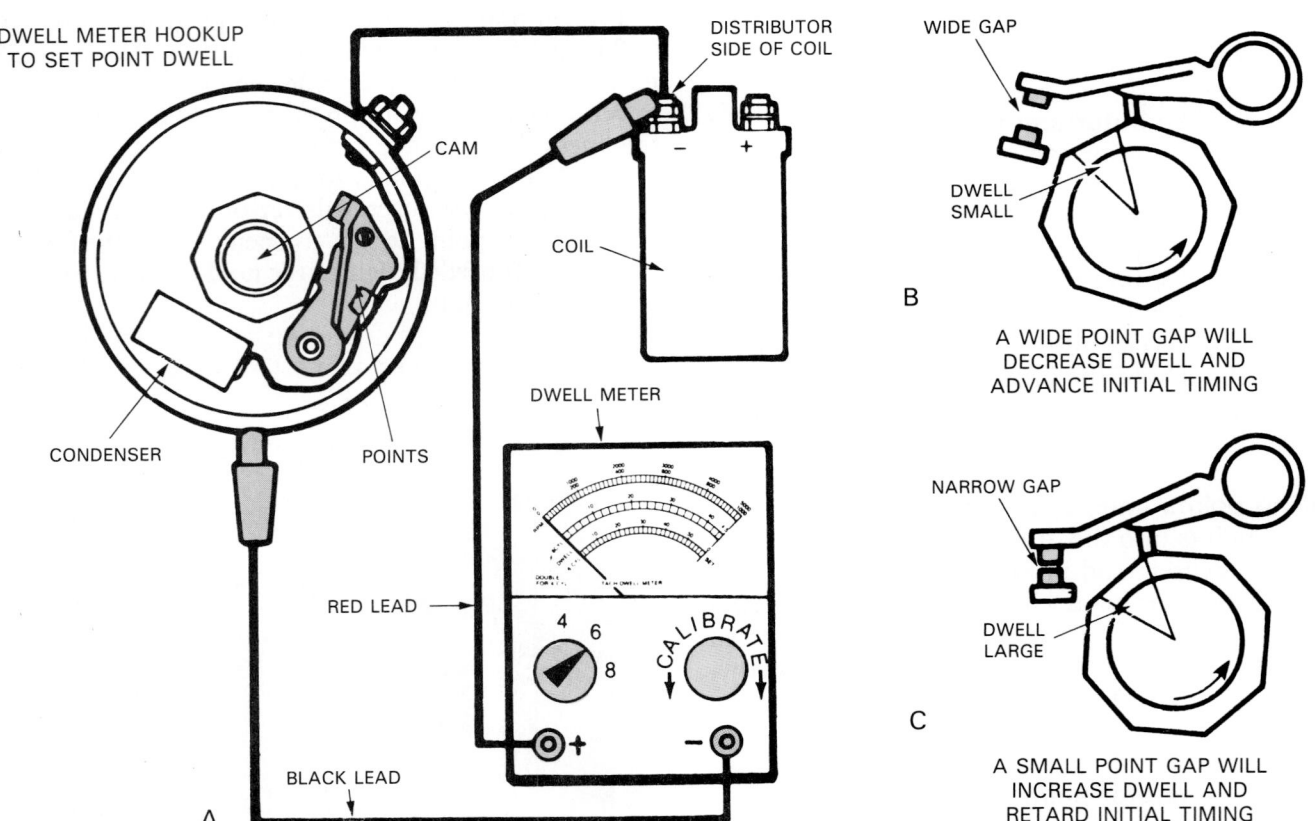

Fig. 33-23. Using dwell meter to adjust points. A — Connect meter as shown. Crank or start engine. Adjust point gap until dwell meter reads correctly. B — Wide gap decreases dwell time when coil builds magnetic field. C — Narrow gap increases dwell time but can cause point arcing and burning. (Florida Dept. of Voc. Ed.)

Turning the distributor housing against distributor shaft rotation ADVANCES THE TIMING. Turning the housing with shaft rotation RETARDS THE TIMING. Refer to Fig. 33-24.

Some computer controlled ignition systems have no provision for timing adjustment. A few, however, have a tiny screw or lever on the computer for small ignition timing changes.

When the ignition timing is *too advanced,* the engine may suffer from spark knock or ping. A light, tapping sound may result when the engine accelerates or is under a load. The *ping* (abnormal combustion) will sound like a small hammer tapping on the engine.

When ignition timing is *too retarded,* the engine will have poor fuel economy and power, and will be very sluggish during acceleration. If extremely retarded, combustion flames blowing out of the opened exhaust valve can overheat the engine and crack the exhaust manifolds.

Measuring ignition timing

A *timing light* is used to measure ignition timing. As shown in Fig. 33-25, a timing light normally has three leads. The two small leads connect to the battery. The larger lead generally connects to the NUMBER ONE spark plug wire, Fig. 33-26.

Depending upon the type of timing light, the large lead may clip around the plug wire (inductive type). It may also need to be connected directly to the metal terminal of the plug wire (conventional type).

When the engine is running, the timing light will flash ON and OFF like a strobe light. This action can be

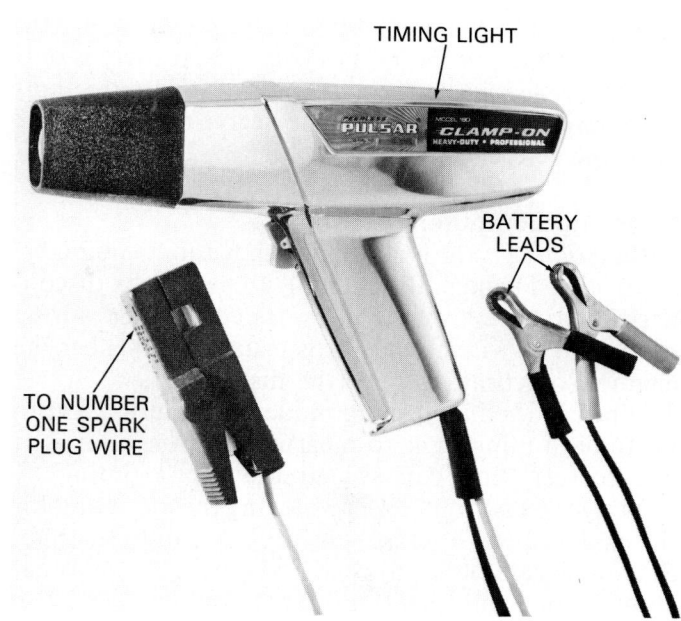

Fig. 33-25. Timing light is used to adjust ignition timing. Note lead connections. (Peerless)

used to make a moving object appear stationary (stand still) so it can be viewed.

Before measuring engine timing, disconnect and plug the vacuum advance hose going to the distributor. This will prevent the vacuum advance from functioning and upsetting your readings.

Start the engine and aim the timing light on the timing marks, as in Fig. 33-26. The timing marks may be on the front cover and harmonic balancer of the engine. The timing marks may also be on the engine flywheel. Fig. 33-27 shows engine ignition timing marks.

The flashing timing light will make the mark or marks on the harmonic balancer or flywheel appear

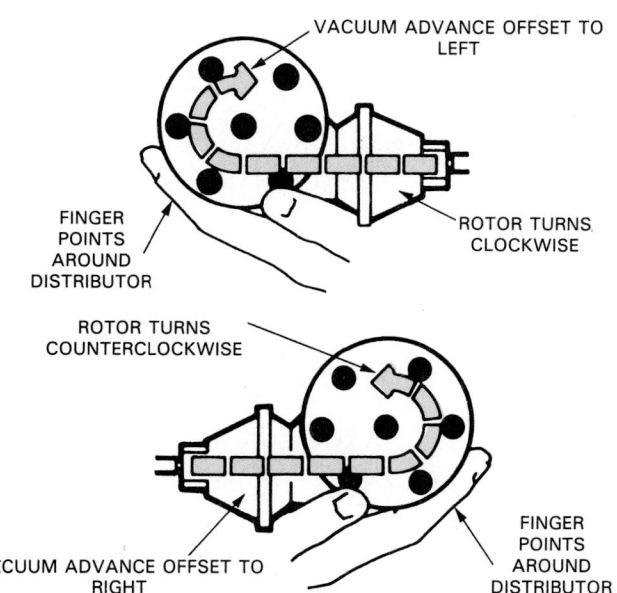

Fig. 33-24. Use finger rule to determine direction of rotor rotation. Point around distributor as shown. This will tell you how rotor turns without removing cap and watching rotor. Direction of distributor rotation is needed when installing spark plug wires and setting ignition timing. (Florida Dept. of Voc. Ed.)

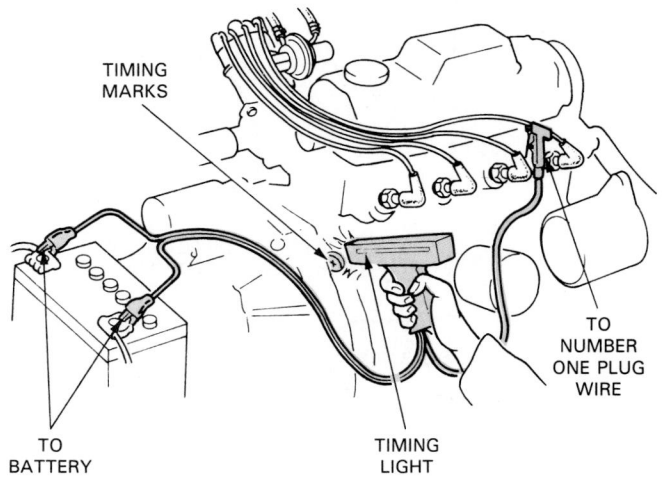

Fig. 33-26. Timing light is connected to system as shown. Large lead connects to number one plug wire. Small leads connect to battery. Light is aimed at timing marks on flywheel or front engine cover and damper. (Honda)

to stand still. This will let you determine whether the engine is timed properly. For example, if there is only one reference line on the harmonic balancer, simply read initial timing by noting the degree marks lined up with the reference line, as in Fig. 33-28.

Checking computer base timing

Base timing is the ignition timing without computer-controlled advance. Base timing is checked by disconnecting a wire connector in the computer wiring harness. The wire connector is usually on or near the engine, sometimes next to the distributor.

When in the base timing mode, you can use a conventional timing light to measure ignition timing. If not correct, you can sometimes adjust timing by rotating the distributor or by moving the mounting for the engine speed or crank position sensor. Sometimes the timing cannot be adjusted and the ECU or another component would have to be replaced.

Ignition timing specs

Ignition timing is very critical to the performance of an engine. If the ignition timing is off even 2 or 3 degrees, engine fuel economy and power can drop considerably. Always obtain the exact timing specs from the engine emission control sticker or a service manual.

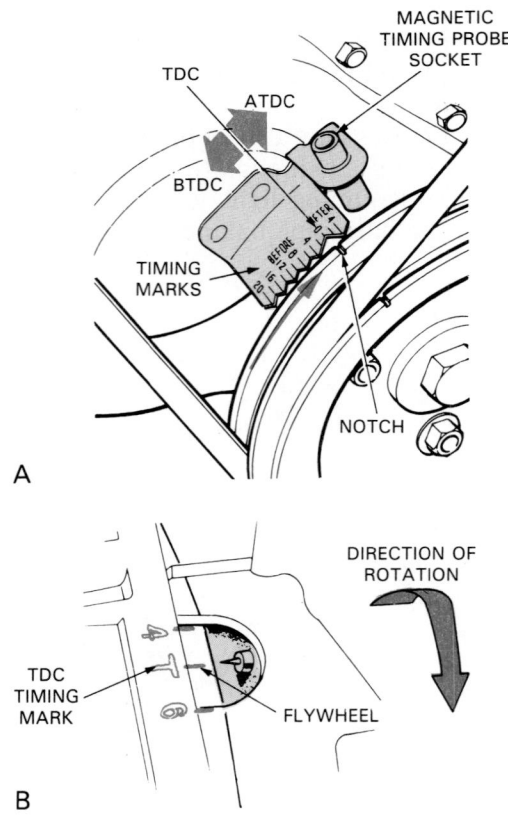

Fig. 33-27. A — Timing marks on front of engine. B — Timing marks on engine flywheel and clutch housing. *(Chrysler and Honda)*

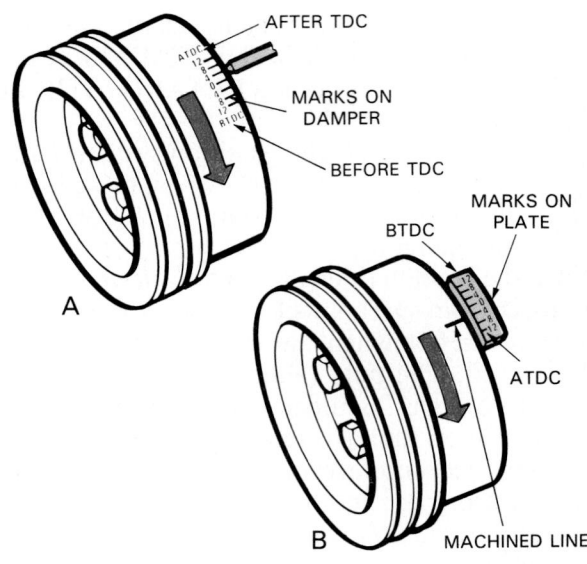

Fig. 33-28. A — When degree markings are on moving damper, read degree lined up with pointer. B — With stationary degree markings, read degree lined up next to groove in damper. When timing light is aimed on markings, rotating marks will appear to be stationary. *(Chrysler)*

Changing ignition timing

Adjust the ignition timing if the timing marks are not lined up correctly. Loosen the distributor hold-down bolt.

A *distributor wrench* (long, special shaped wrench for reaching under distributor housing) is handy. See Fig. 33-29. Only loosen the distributor bolt enough to allow distributor rotation. Do NOT remove the bolt.

With the distributor hold-down loosened, again shine the timing light on the engine timing marks. Turn the distributor one way or the other until the correct timing marks line up, Fig. 33-30. Tighten the hold-down

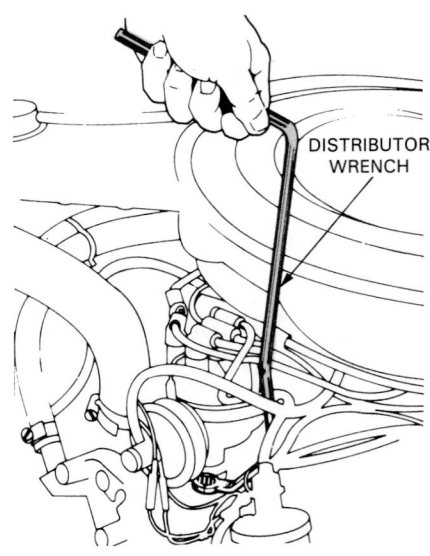

Fig. 33-29. Distributor wrench may be needed to loosen hold-down bolt on distributor. Bolt can be hard to reach. *(K-D Tools)*

Fig. 33-30. To change ignition timing, turn distributor housing in engine. Turning distributor in same direction as rotor rotation will retard timing. Turning against rotor rotation will advance timing. (Peerless)

and double-check the timing. Reconnect the distributor vacuum hose and disconnect the timing light.

DANGER! Keep your hands and the timing light leads away from the engine fan and belts. The spinning fan and belts can damage the light or cause serious injury!

DISTRIBUTOR ADVANCE SERVICE

Both electronic and contact point type distributors can use similar advance mechanisms. A faulty advance mechanism will reduce engine performance and fuel economy.

Testing centrifugal advance (in-car)

A timing light can be used to test the general operation of a distributor centrifugal advance. Connect the timing light. Remove the vacuum hose going to the distributor. Start and idle the engine.

While shining the timing light on the engine timing marks, slowly increase engine speed to approximately 3500 rpm. Note the movement of the timing mark.

If the centrifugal advance is working, the mark should steadily move to a more advanced position with the increase in speed. See Fig. 33-31A and B.

If the timing mark jumps around or DOES NOT MOVE, the centrifugal advance is faulty. It may be worn, rusted, have weak springs, or other mechanical problems.

Testing vacuum advance (in-car)

To test the distributor vacuum advance, connect a timing light. Remove the vacuum advance hose from the distributor. Start the engine and increase engine speed to approximately 1500 rpm. Note the location of the timing marks. Then, reconnect the vacuum hose on the distributor diaphragm.

As soon as vacuum is reconnected, engine speed should increase and the timing mark should advance. See Fig. 33-31C.

If the vacuum advance is NOT working, check the vacuum advance diaphragm and the supply vacuum to the distributor.

Testing vacuum advance diaphragm

To check the vacuum advance diaphragm, apply a vacuum to the unit using a vacuum pump, Fig. 33-32, or your mouth. When suction is applied to the diaphragm, the advance plate in the distributor should swing around. When vacuum is released, the advance plate should snap back into its normal position.

If the ADVANCE DIAPHRAGM LEAKS and will not hold vacuum, it must be replaced. If the advance mechanism is stuck, check components for binding, rust, or other problems.

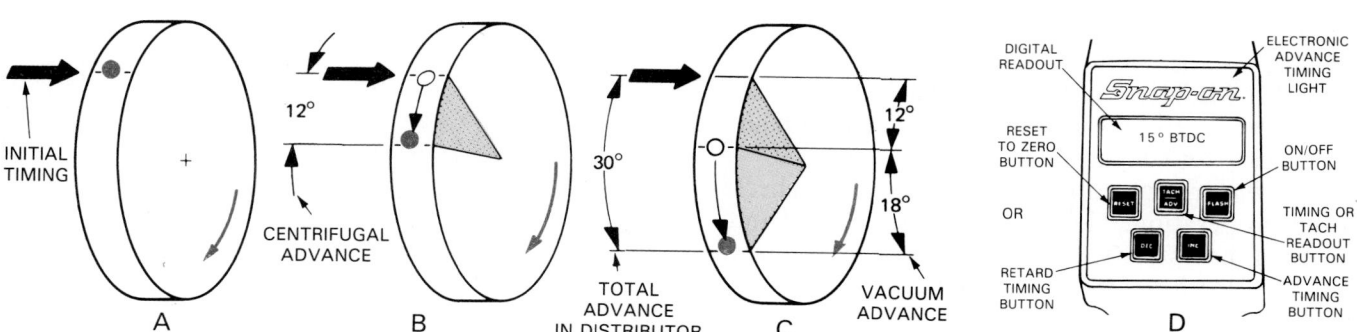

Fig. 33-31. Checking timing advance action with timing light. A — With engine idling and vacuum advance hose disconnected, initial timing marks should line up. B — When you increase engine speed, timing marks should move to advanced position. C — With vacuum applied to distributor advance diaphragm, timing should advance more and be within specs. D — Face of electronic timing light. (Snap-On Tools)

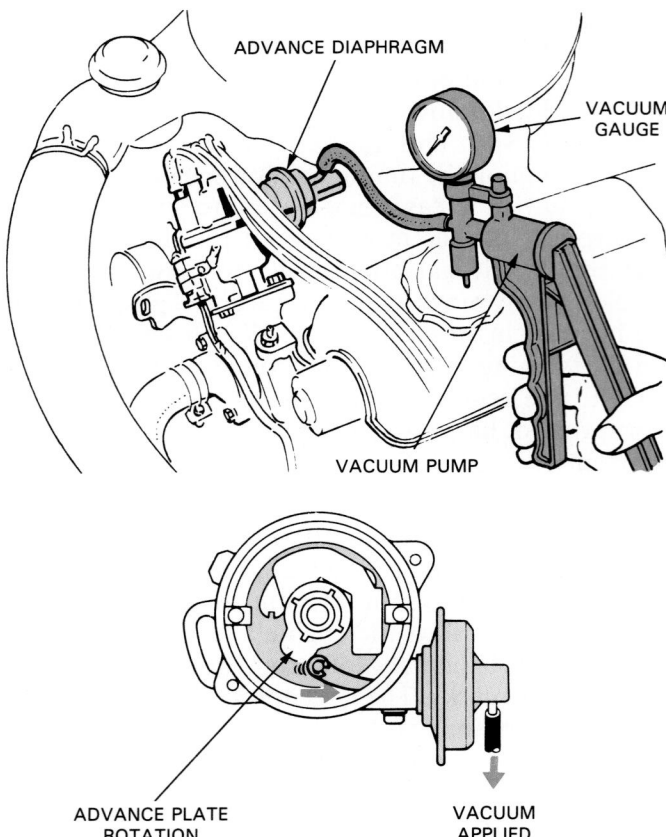

Fig. 33-32. Leaking vacuum advance diaphragm is common problem that will greatly reduce fuel economy. Use vacuum pump or mouth to check for leakage. Gauge can also be used to measure supply vacuum to distributor. (Honda)

Checking advance supply vacuum

To check the supply vacuum going to the distributor, disconnect the diaphragm vacuum hose. Connect it to a vacuum gauge. Measure the amount of vacuum with the engine running at a specified rpm. If the vacuum is not sufficient, check any part controlling vacuum to the distributor (carburetor, thermal vacuum switch, delay valve, vacuum hose).

Measuring distributor advance (in-car)

Special timing lights are available that are capable of measuring exact distributor advance with the distributor installed in the engine. The timing light has a DEGREE METER built into the back of its case. The meter will register exact centrifugal or vacuum advance quickly and accurately.

A *distributor tester* may also be used to check distributor operation. The distributor is removed and mounted in the tester. The tester will check all primary distributor functions (pickup coil output, point dwell, centrifugal and vacuum advance).

Refer to Chapter 42, Test Equipment, for more information on timing lights and distributor testers.

Removing ignition distributor

Before removing a distributor, carefully mark the

position of the rotor and distributor housing. Place marks on the engine and housing with a scribe or marking pen. Look at Fig. 33-33. Then, if the engine crankshaft is NOT rotated, you will be able to install the distributor by simply lining up your marks.

To remove the distributor, take off the distributor cap, rotor, primary wires, and distributor hold-down bolt, Fig. 33-33. Pull the distributor upward while rotating it back and forth. If stuck, use a slide hammer puller with a two-prong fork.

Rebuilding a distributor

A *distributor rebuild* involves disassembly, cleaning, inspection, worn part replacement, and reassembly. Depending upon distributor type, exact procedures vary. Always refer to a shop manual for detailed directions and specifications. The major steps for a distributor rebuild are illustrated in Fig. 33-34.

Assemble the distributor in reverse order of disassembly. See Fig. 33-35.

Installing a distributor

If you made reference marks and the engine crankshaft was NOT turned, install the distributor as it was removed. Align the rotor and housing with the marks on the engine.

Double-check the position of the rotor after installation because the rotor will turn as the distributor gear meshes with its drive gear.

To install a distributor when the engine crankshaft has been rotated, remove the number one spark plug. Bump (crank) the engine until you can feel air blowing out of the spark plug hole. As soon as air blows out, slowly turn the crankshaft until the engine timing marks are on TDC.

With the crankshaft in this position, the distributor rotor should point at the NUMBER ONE SPARK PLUG WIRE. Fit the distributor into the engine so that the rotor points at number one distributor cap tower.

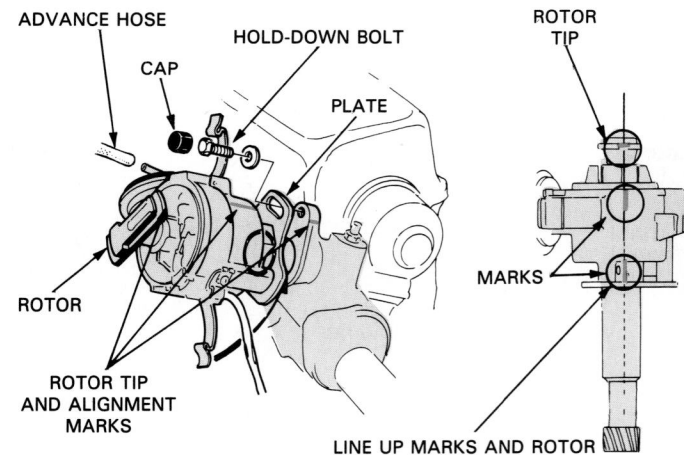

Fig. 33-33. Before removing distributor, mark distributor housing and engine below rotor tip. This will let you quickly reinstall distributor. (Honda)

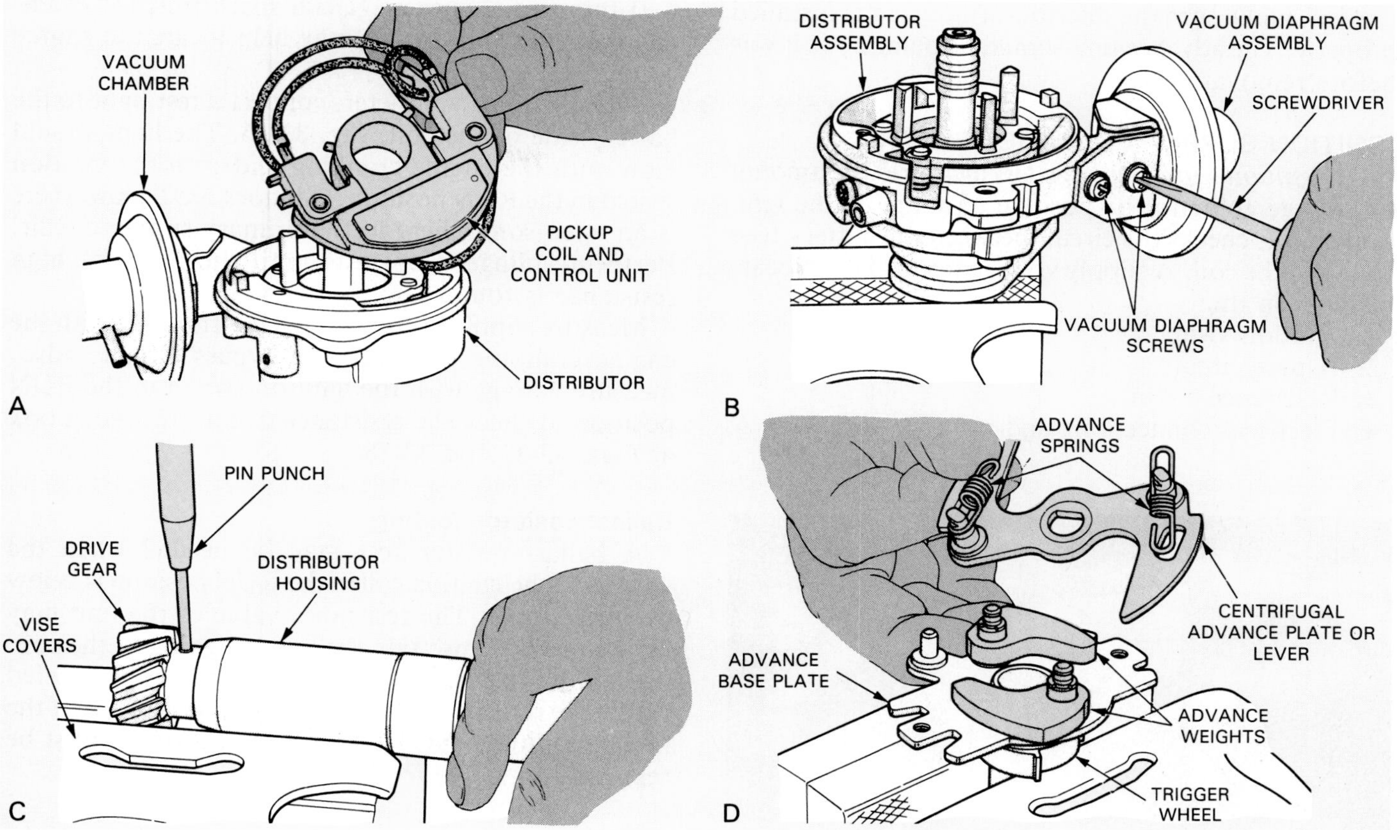

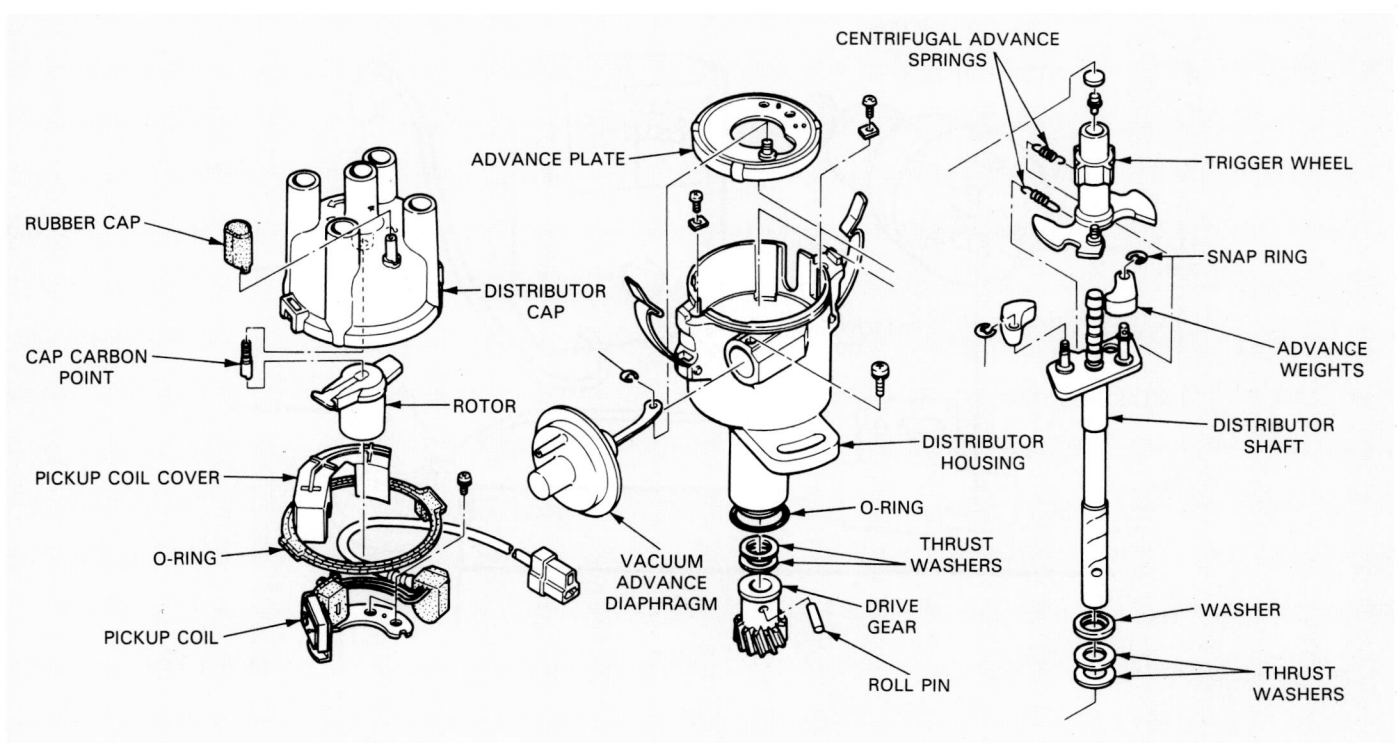

Fig. 33-34. Major steps for distributor disassembly. A — Remove cap, pickup coil, and electronic control unit, if used. B — Remove vacuum diaphragm. Small snap ring may hold advance lever on advance plate. C — Drive roll pin out of shaft to free drive gear. Slide gear off shaft and shaft out of housing. D — Disassemble centrifugal advance mechanism. Check for wear, rusting, and other problems. (Chrysler)

Fig. 33-35. Exploded view shows how distributor fits together. Service manual illustration may help with specific distributor assembly troubles. (Subaru)

Also, make sure the distributor housing is installed properly. The advance unit should be pointing as it was before removal.

IGNITION SUPPLY VOLTAGE TEST

An *ignition supply voltage test* measures the amount of voltage going to the positive terminal of the ignition coil. It checks the circuit between the battery feed wire and the coil. A supply voltage test will help locate troubles in the:

1. Ignition switch.
2. Bypass circuit.
3. Resistance circuit.
4. Electrical connections and primary wires.

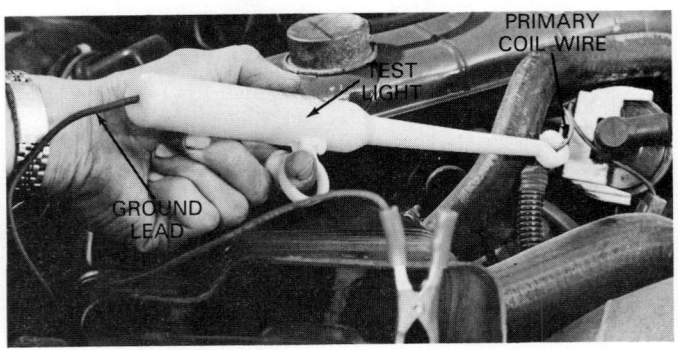

Fig. 33-36. With no-spark problem, check for voltage to ignition coil. Test light should glow with ignition switch at run and start positions. (Peerless)

If the ignition system fails a spark test, for example, a supply voltage test may help locate the source of the problem.

Before using a voltmeter, connect a test light to the battery side of the coil, Fig. 33-36. The light should glow with the engine cranking and with the ignition switch in the RUN position. If it does NOT glow, there is an open somewhere in the primary supply circuit. Perform voltage drop tests until the point of high resistance is found.

Measure supply voltage to the ignition coil with the engine cranking to check the bypass circuit. Also, measure voltage with the ignition switch in the RUN position to check the resistance circuit, if used. Look at Figs. 33-37 and 33-38.

Ballast resistor testing

A ballast resistor test may be needed when the voltage to the ignition coil in the RUN position is below or above specs. The resistance value of the unit may have changed, upsetting the voltage going to the coil.

Pictured in Fig. 33-39, an ohmmeter is connected across the resistor to measure internal resistance. If the meter reading is NOT within specs, resistor must be replaced.

Resistance wire testing

A resistance wire performs the same basic function as a ballast resistor. It limits the voltage going to the coil to prevent coil overheating and possible damage.

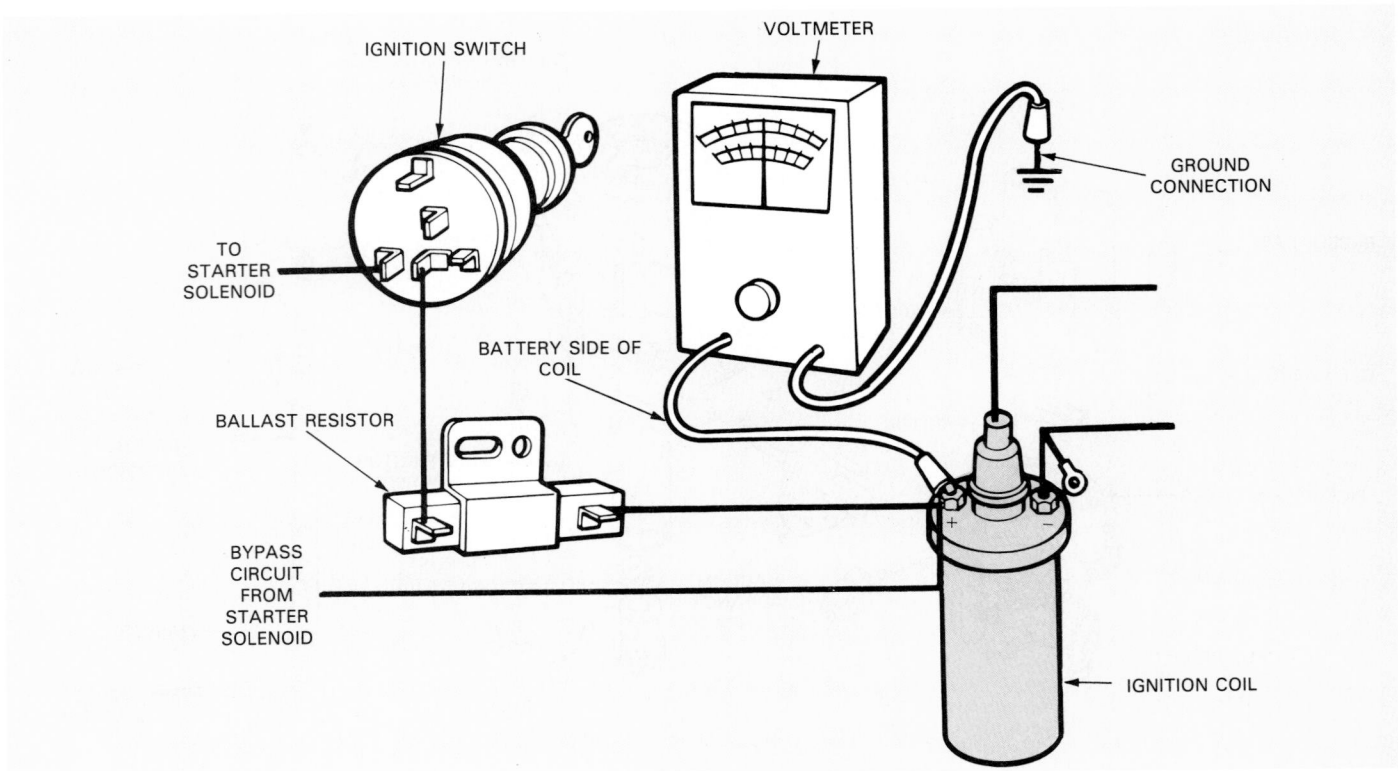

Fig. 33-37. Measure exact voltage to coil to check bypass and resistance circuits. If voltage is too high or low, repair circuit as needed. (Mopar)

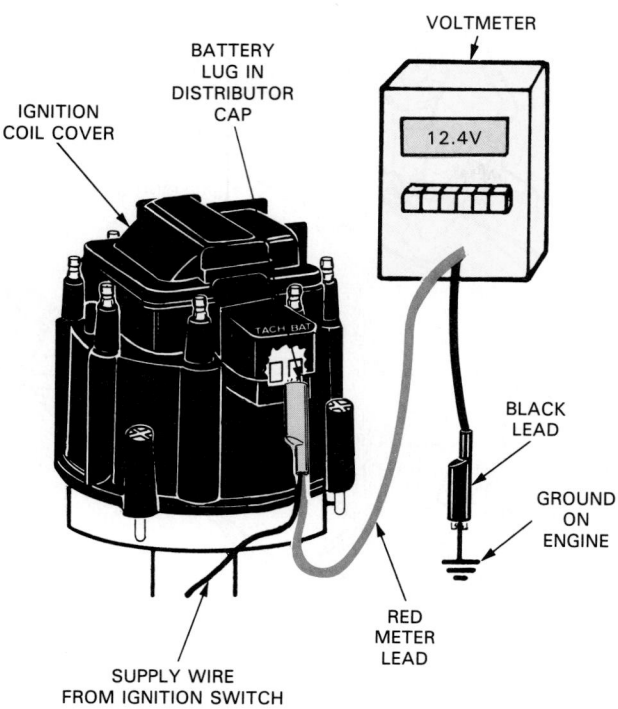

Fig. 33-38. When coil is in distributor, measure supply voltage at battery connection on cap. If voltage is below specs, check wiring and ignition switch.

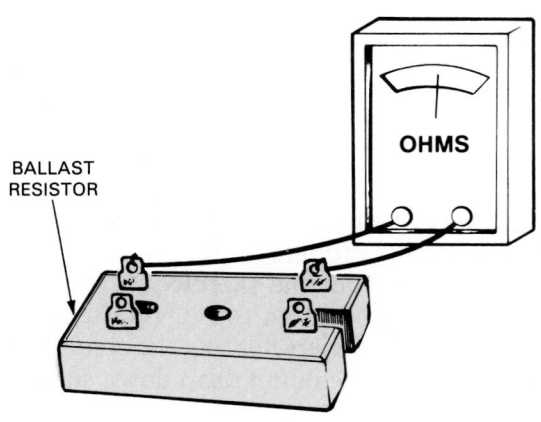

Fig. 33-39. Check ballast resistor by measuring its resistance. Ohmmeter must read within specs. (Echlin)

If the voltage going to the ignition coil is low or high, measure the resistance of the resistance wire. Compare the ohmmeter reading to specs. Replace the wire if needed.

IGNITION COIL SERVICE

A *faulty ignition coil* may result in a weak spark, intermittent spark, or no spark at all. The engine may miss, stop running when the coil heats up, or refuse to start at all. The windings inside the coil can break and produce a resistance or open in the coil circuit.

A coil may only act up when hot, after being exposed

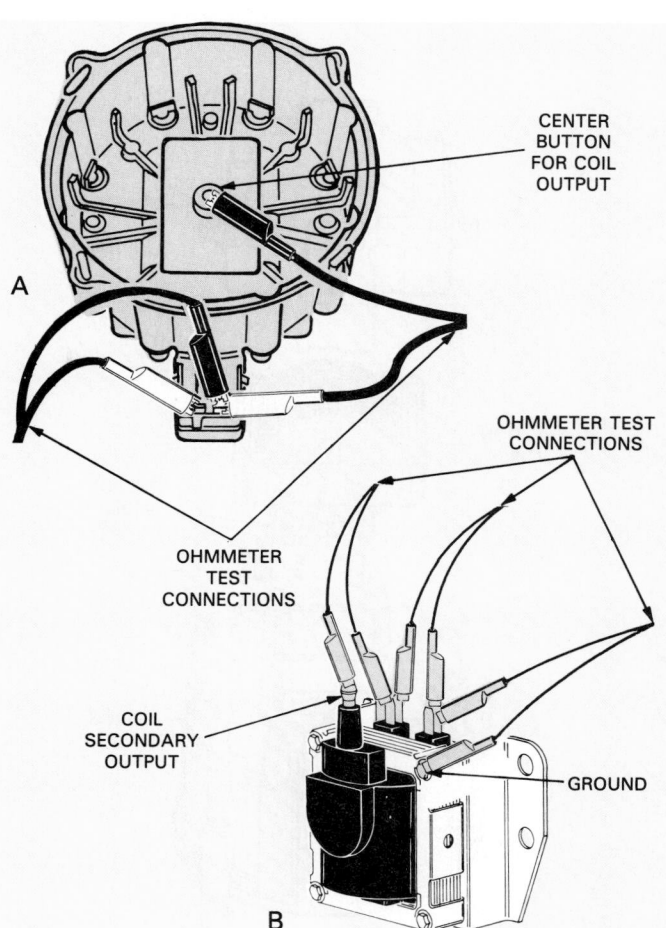

Fig. 33-40. With weak spark, you may need to test ignition coil. Follow service manual directions to measure resistance of windings. A — Checking coil mounted in distributor cap. B — Checking externally mounted ignition coil. (Peerless and Echlin)

to engine heat. The heat can make the coil windings expand and open, with a resulting loss of high voltage output.

Testing an ignition coil

A coil test may be needed when the ignition system fails the spark test but proper supply voltage is found. Since coil designs are different, testing procedures vary.

Generally, an ohmmeter is used to measure the internal resistance of the coil windings. As shown in Fig. 33-40, the meter is connected to the terminals of the coil. An infinite or out-of-specs reading would indicate a faulty ignition coil.

Replacing an ignition coil

When the ignition coil is mounted on the engine, coil replacement involves removing the wires and bolts securing the old coil. Then, bolt on the new coil.

Be careful not to connect the coil in *reverse polarity* (primary wires accidentally connected backwards). This would reduce secondary voltage output.

When the coil is mounted inside the distributor cap (unitized type ignition), the distributor cap must be disassembled to install the new coil. Refer to Fig. 33-41.

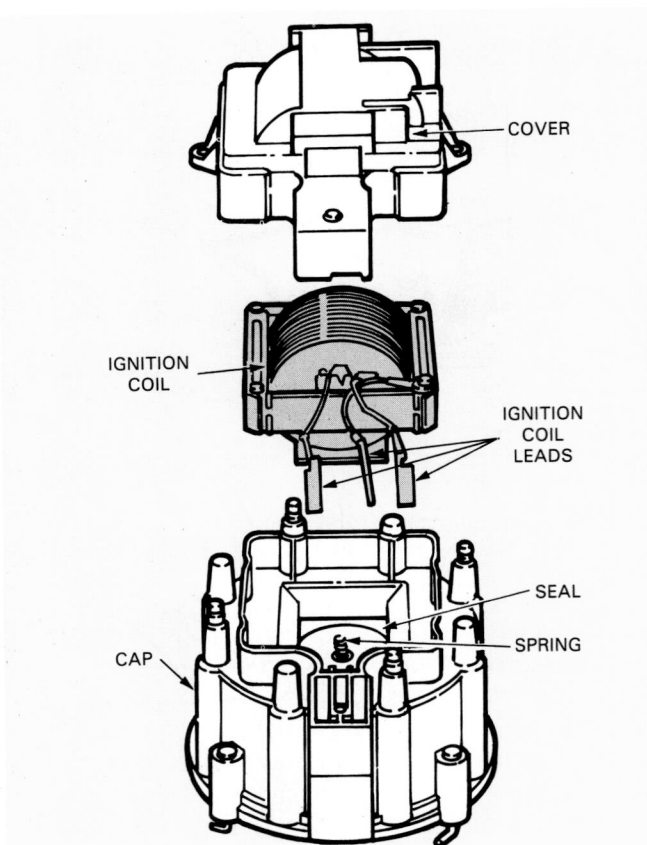

Fig. 33-41. When coil is in cap, remove screws, cap, and primary wires. Then, new coil can be installed in cap. Make sure wires are connected properly.

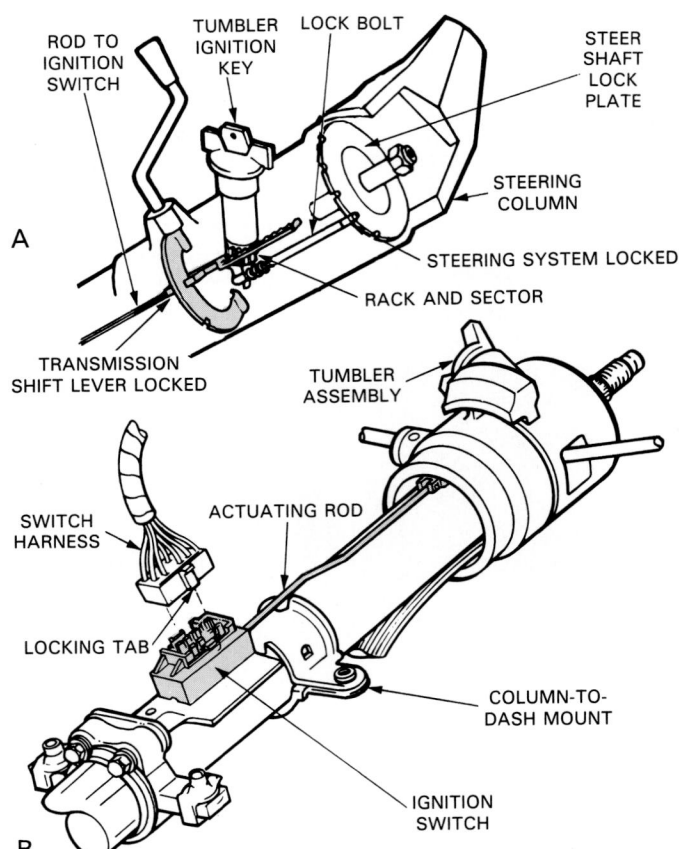

Fig. 33-42. Modern cars have ignition switch and key tumbler in steering column. A — Construction of typical steering lock mechanism. B — Small rod runs down column and to ignition switch. To remove switch, drop column by removing column-to-dash fasteners. Then, remove small nuts holding switch to top of column. (Florida Dept. of Voc. Ed. and Ford Motor Co.)

Ignition switch service

A *bad ignition switch,* Fig. 33-42, can cause several problems. The engine may NOT crank or start. The engine may NOT shut off when the ignition key is turned off. The starter may not disengage when the ignition key is returned to RUN. These types of problems point to a defective ignition switch.

Testing an ignition switch

A test light is an easy way to check the action of an ignition switch. When a test light is touched to the START terminal on the back of the switch, the light should glow only when the key has been turned to START. It should NOT glow when the key is released to the RUN position.

In the RUN position, the test light should glow when touched on the RUN terminal of the switch.

With the ignition key in the OFF position, neither switch terminal (start or run) should make the test light glow.

Replacing ignition switch

The ignition switch may be located in the dash or on the steering column.

If dash mounted, the *tumbler* (lock mechanism) must be removed from the switch. Normally, a small piece of wire is inserted into a hole in the front of the switch

and the key is turned. This will release the tumbler from the switch so the tumbler can be pulled free. Then, unplug the wires and remove the old switch.

If steering column mounted, Fig. 33-42, the ignition switch is separate from the tumbler. It is normally about halfway down and on top of the steering column. Remove the fasteners holding the column to the dash. This will let the column drop down so you can replace the ignition switch.

IGNITION CONTROL UNIT SERVICE

A *faulty ignition control unit* will produce a wide range of problems: engine stalls when hot, engine cranks but fails to start, engine misses at high or low speeds.

Quite often, an ignition control unit problem will show up after a period of engine operation. Engine heat will soak into the module, raising its temperature. The heat will upset the operation of the electronic components in the unit.

Ignition control unit testing

Many shop manuals list the ignition control unit as one of the last components to test. If all of the other components are in good working order, then the problem might be in the electronic control module.

If a specialized tester is available, it may be used to quickly determine the condition of the control module. One type of tester is shown in Fig. 33-43. The wires going to the electronic control module are unplugged. The tester is plugged into the circuit. The tester will then indicate whether an ECU fault exists.

Heating ignition control unit

The microscopic components (transistors, diodes, capacitors, resistors) inside the electronic control unit are very sensitive to high temperatures.

When testing the control unit, many technicians use a heat gun or light bulb to warm the control unit. Refer to Fig. 33-44. This will simulate the temperature in the engine compartment after the engine has been running. The heat may make the control unit act up and allow you to find an erratic problem.

WARNING! Do not apply too much heat to an electronic control unit or it may be ruined. Only heat the unit to a temperature equal to its normal operating temperature.

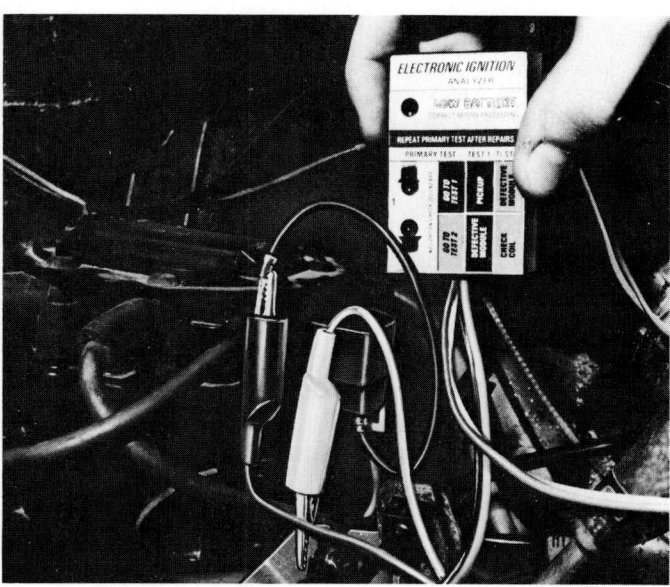

Fig. 33-43. Small electronic ignition tester will check condition of electronic control unit, pickup coil, and other components. Indicator lights show condition. (Belden)

Replacing an ignition control unit

Replacement of an ignition system control unit is a simple task. If the unit is mounted in the engine compartment or under the dash, carefully unplug the wiring harness. Unbolt the old unit and install the new unit.

If the ignition control unit is mounted inside the distributor, remove the distributor cap and screws. Before installing the new unit, check in a service manual for specific instructions.

In many cases, the bottom of the control unit must be coated with a SPECIAL GREASE (silicon grease,

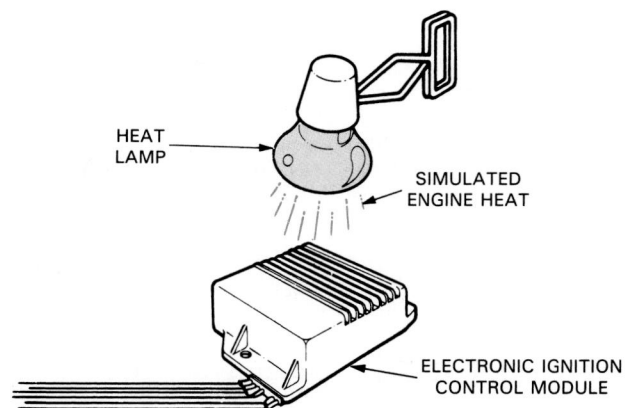

Fig. 33-44. When testing ignition control unit, heat may cause unit to act up, helping to locate erratic problem. Do not overheat unit or it could be damaged. (Ford)

dielectric heat transfer compound, or heat sink compound). The grease helps heat transfer into the distributor, protecting the electronic control unit from overheating and circuit damage. See Fig. 33-45.

Always make sure you have the correct ignition control unit. A new control unit may look identical to the old one but may have internal circuit differences. Even the same year and make car can require different ignition control units.

COMPUTERIZED IGNITION SYSTEM SERVICE

Many of the components of a computer controlled ignition system are similar to those of electronic or contact point ignition systems. See Fig. 33-46. This makes testing about the same for many parts (spark plugs,

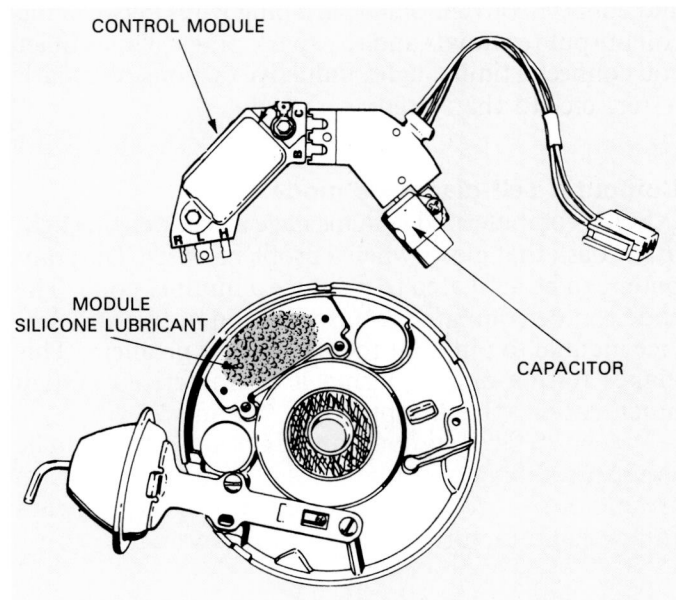

Fig. 33-45. When ignition control unit is in distributor, you may need to apply silicone lubricant to bottom of unit. Lubricant will help transfer heat out of unit, assuring proper operation. (Oldsmobile)

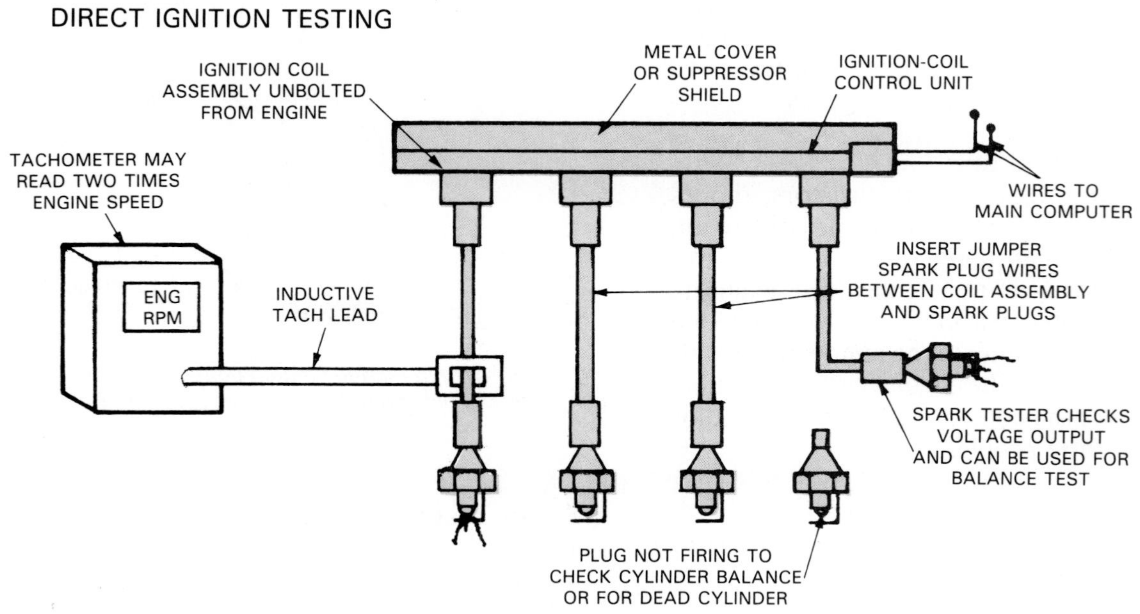

DIRECT IGNITION TESTING

Fig. 33-46. Study how to perform tests on direct ignition system. Coil-module assembly can be unbolted and removed from engine. Then, spark plug wires can be used to jump from coil assembly to spark plugs. This will let you connect inductive tachometer to engine; it may read two times actual engine speed if two plugs fire at once. You can also use spark tester to check high voltage output and to short out each plug to make sure each cylinder is firing and lowering engine rpm. Scope or timing light can also be connected to engine with this setup.

secondary wires, ignition coil). However, the computerized ignition has engine sensors and a computer, which add to the complexity of the system.

Fig. 33-46 shows some tricks for working on a distributorless ignition system. Remove the coil cover and connect conventional spark plug wires between the coil output terminals and the spark plugs. This will let you connect a timing light, inductive tachometer, spark tester, etc. to the system.

Computer self-diagnosis mode

Some computerized systems have a check engine light in the dash that glows when a problem exists. The computer can be activated to produce a number code. The code can be compared to information in the car's service manual to pinpoint the source of a problem. This makes testing and repairing a computerized system much easier. (See Chapters 73, 74, and 75.)

WARNING! A computerized ignition system can be seriously damaged if the wrong wire is shorted to ground or if a meter is connected improperly. Always follow manufacturer's testing procedures.

Computer ignition testers

Most auto makers provide specialized testing equipment for their computerized ignition systems. Like an ignition control unit tester, the computer system tester

plugs into the wiring harness. It will then measure internal resistances and voltages in the system to determine where a problem is located.

Refer to Chapters 20 and 22 for more information on problem diagnosis with computer systems. Normally, the computer system sensors (oxygen sensor, throttle position sensor, intake vacuum sensor) are common to both fuel and ignition systems.

KNOW THESE TERMS

Engine miss, Dead cylinder, Spark test, Oscilloscope, Electronic ignition tester, Reading spark plugs, Spark plug gap, Secondary wire resistance, Backfiring, Carbon trace, Pickup coil air gap, Shorted condenser, Dwell meter, Distributor point gap, Dwell variation, Initial ignition timing, Timing light, Distributor wrench, Reverse polarity, Tumbler.

REVIEW QUESTIONS

1. Define the term "dead cylinder."
2. How do you find a dead cylinder without special equipment?
3. A _____ _____ _____ , also called a _____ _____ , measures the brightness and length of the electric arc produced by the ig-

nition system. It provides a _____ and _____ way of checking the condition of the ignition system.

4. Which of the following is commonly used to check the secondary output of an ignition system?
   a. Voltmeter.
   b. Ohmmeter.
   c. Spark tester.
   d. Ammeter.
5. What kinds of test equipment is usually found in an engine analyzer?
6. What is an oscilloscope?
7. An electronic ignition tester is connected to the ignition circuit or special test plug to check system condition. True or False?
8. Explain the correct way of removing a spark plug wire from a spark plug.
9. How can "reading" spark plugs help you?
10. Which of the following does NOT pertain to setting spark plug gap?
    a. Wire feeler gauge.
    b. Bend side electrode.
    c. Space between center and side electrode.
    d. All of the above are correct.
11. When screwing a spark plug into the cylinder head, use the socket, an extension, and ratchet to start the plug threads. True or False?
12. A faulty spark plug wire can have either a burned or broken _____ or deteriorated _____ .
13. Explain both a resistance test and insulation test of a secondary wire.
14. Define the term "carbon trace."
15. Describe how either an ohmmeter or voltmeter can be used to test most distributor pickup coils.
16. Why is a nonmagnetic feeler gauge needed to set a pickup coil air gap?
17. Which of the following does NOT relate to the adjustment of new distributor contact points?
    a. Distributor cam lobe touches rubbing block.
    b. Lubricate point rubbing block.
    c. Use flat feeler gauge or dwell meter.
    d. All of the above are correct.
    e. None of the above are correct.
18. An older car with contact points is being tuned up. The dwell meter, during point adjustment, fluctuates up and down about five degrees as engine speed is increased and decreased.
    Technician A says that the distributor bushings and shaft could be worn, causing amount of point opening and dwell to vary. A distributor repair is needed.
    Technician B says that the distributor advance plate could be worn or loose, causing amount of point opening and dwell to vary. The distributor should be repaired.

Who is correct?
a. Technician A
b. Technician B
c. Both A and B
d. Neither A nor B
19. With an ignition system using a pickup coil in the distributor, how do you advance and retard ignition timing?
20. How do you check distributor centrifugal and vacuum advance?
21. Why is moderate heat sometimes applied to an ignition system electronic control unit?
22. Many of the components in a computer controlled ignition system are similar to those in an electronic or contact point ignition system. True or False?
23. Explain the computer self-diagnosis mode and how it affects troubleshooting.

ACTIVITIES FOR CHAPTER 33

1. Arrange to observe a technician at a tune-up shop or an auto dealership who is using an engine analyzer to diagnose ignition system condition. Ask the technician to explain what is being shown on the oscilloscope and other displays.
2. Demonstrate the use of a wire feeler gauge to measure the gap of a spark plug, then demonstrate the method used to set the gap to specifications.
3. Using a timing light to check the timing marks on two or three engines. Check your findings with the appropriate service manual to determine whether timing is "within spec."

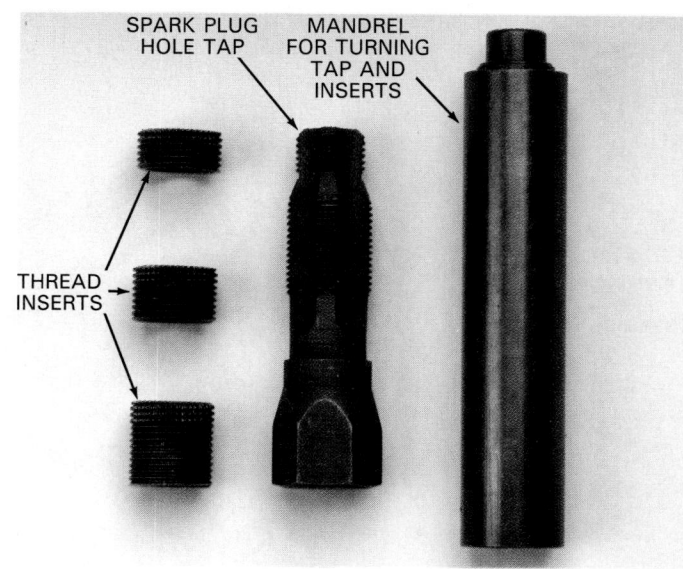

Damaged spark plug hole threads can be repaired by using a spark plug thread repair kit to install steel insert in oversize hole in head. (HeliCoil)

34 Lights, Wipers, Horn Fundamentals

After studying this chapter, you will be able to:
□ Explain the operating principles of automotive light, wiper, and horn systems.
□ Diagnose problems in light, wiper, and horn systems.
□ Replace burned-out bulbs.
□ Explain how to aim headlights.
□ Describe the safety practices to follow when working with light, wiper, and horn systems.

This chapter covers the most important parts of vehicle light, wiper-washer, and horn systems, Fig. 34-1. These are systems of the vehicle that perform essential safety functions. Although they are usually troublefree, they do require occasional repair. If you understand how each of these systems functions and you follow basic testing techniques, the systems are relatively simple to repair. Study this chapter carefully!

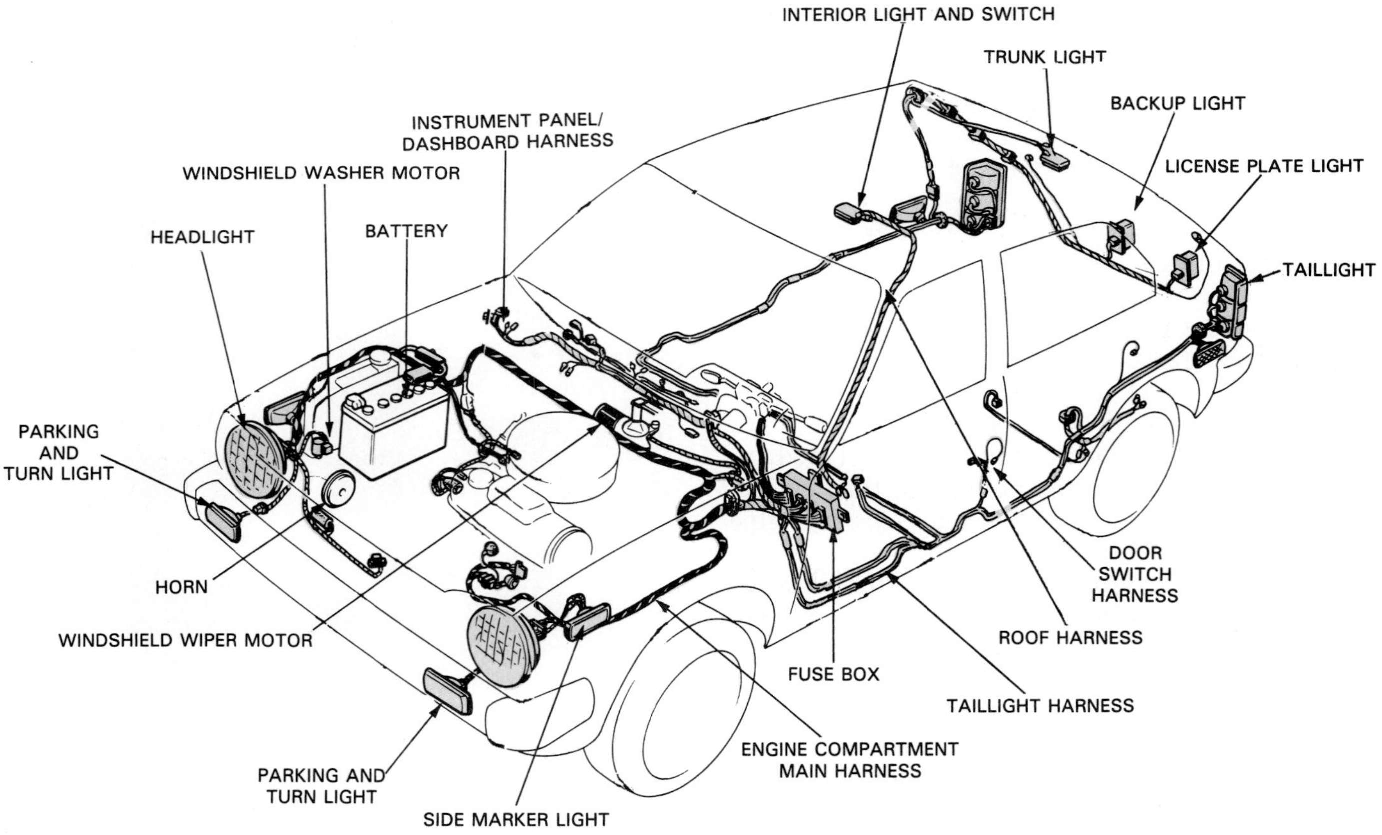

Fig. 34-1. Light, wiper, and horn systems are simple when studied separately. Note location of major components. (Honda)

LIGHTING SYSTEM

The *lighting system* consists of the components (fuses, wires, switches, relays) that operate the interior and exterior lights on a car. See Fig. 34-1.

The ***exterior lights*** typically include the headlights, turn signal lights, stoplights, parking lights, backup lights, and side marker lights.

The ***interior lights*** normally include the dome light, instrument lights in the dash, trunk light, and other courtesy lights.

Headlamp system

The *headlamp system* generally includes the battery, headlamp-related wiring, fuse panel, light switch, dimmer switch, headlamps, taillights, marker lights, and instrument lights. Look at Fig. 34-2. If the headlamps are concealed, the system also has either a vacuum or electric motor mechanism to operate the doors (flaps) over the headlamps.

The ***headlamp switch*** is an on/off switch and rheostat (variable resistor) in the dash panel or on the steering column. See Fig. 34-3. It controls current flow

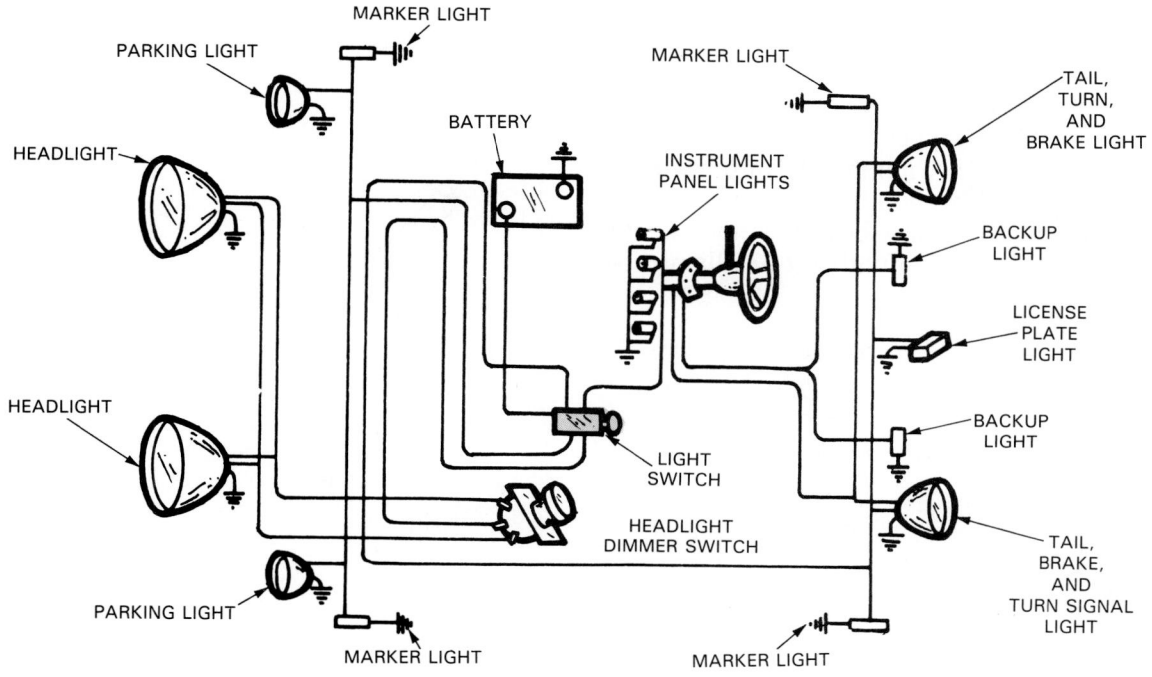

Fig. 34-2. Light switch is ''heart'' of car lighting system. It feeds current to circuits. (Florida Dept. of Voc. Ed.)

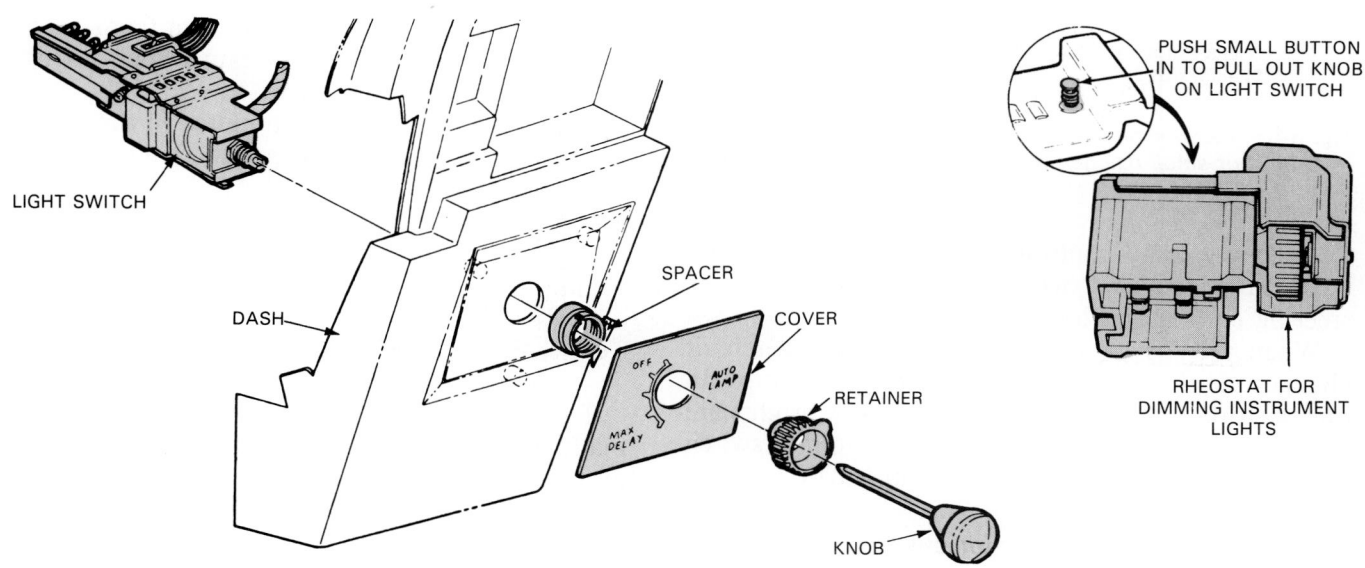

Fig. 34-3. Light switch normally mounts in dash as shown. Small button on switch is commonly provided to release knob from switch. Press button and pull out knob. Then, retainer can be removed. (Ford)

to the bulbs in the headlamp system. It also may contain a rheostat for adjusting the brightness of the instrument panel lights. A vacuum switch is added to the headlamp switch when vacuum doors are used over the headlamps.

The *headlamp bulbs* are sealed beam bulbs that illuminate the road during night driving. Headlight bulbs can have one or two elements. When current flows through the element, the element gets white hot and glows. The reflector and lens direct this light forward.

Many late model cars use halogen headlamps. See Fig. 34-4. A *halogen headlamp* contains a small, inner halogen bulb surrounded by a conventional sealed housing. A halogen headlamp increases light output by about 25 percent with no increase in current draw. The halogen bulb is also whiter than a conventional bulb, which also increases lighting ability.

There are two different types of sealed beam bulbs: number 1 and number 2. A number 1 lamp has only one lighting element. The number 2 lamp has two lighting elements (high and low beam). Vehicles with only two headlamps use two number 2 headlamps to provide high and low beams.

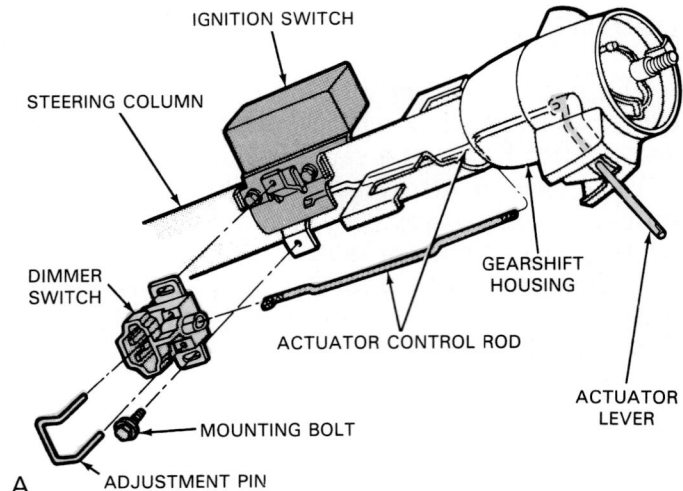

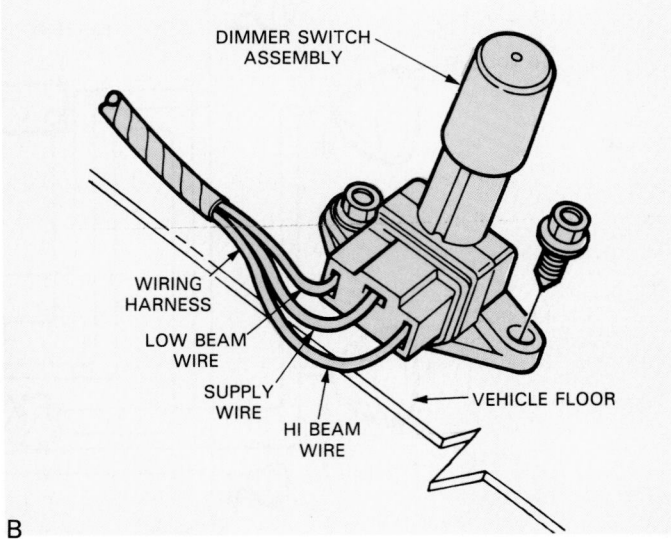

Fig. 34-5. Headlight dimmer switch. A — Dimmer switch on steering column. B — Dimmer switch on floor of car. (Chrysler and Ford)

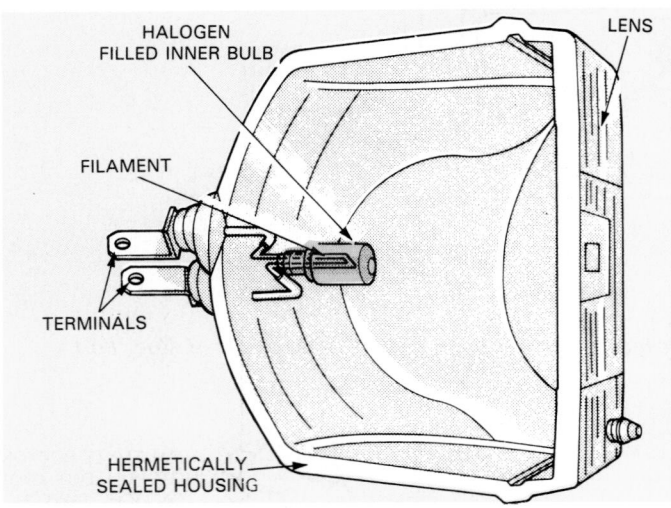

Fig. 34-4. Halogen headlamp is like conventional sealed beam lamp, but small halogen inner bulb is added. (Chrysler)

A *dimmer switch* controls the high and low headlamp beam function. This switch may be mounted on the steering column or floorboard. Refer to Fig. 34-5.

When the driver activates the dimmer switch, it changes the electrical connection to the headlamps. In one position, the headlamp high beams or brights are turned on. In the other position, the dimmer switch changes to low beams for driving in traffic.

Automatic headlamp dimmer system

An optional equipment *automatic headlight dimmer system* uses a light sensor, amplifier, and relay to control the high and low beams. The system automatically dims the lights when detecting light from oncoming traffic. It switches to high beams when no light is detected from oncoming traffic.

The light sensor may be mounted in the grille area or on the dash. The sensor produces a small amount of electric current when exposed to light. The amplifier uses this current to operate a dimmer relay. The relay changes the electrical connection from high to low beam.

TURN, EMERGENCY, STOPLIGHT SYSTEMS

The turn, emergency, and stoplight systems are normally considered separate circuits. However, they commonly use some of the same wiring, electrical connections, and light bulbs. This is illustrated in Fig. 34-6.

The lights in these systems are small incandescent bulbs. They can contain either one or two elements. Fig. 34-7 shows two common types of bulbs for turn, emergency, stop, and backup lights.

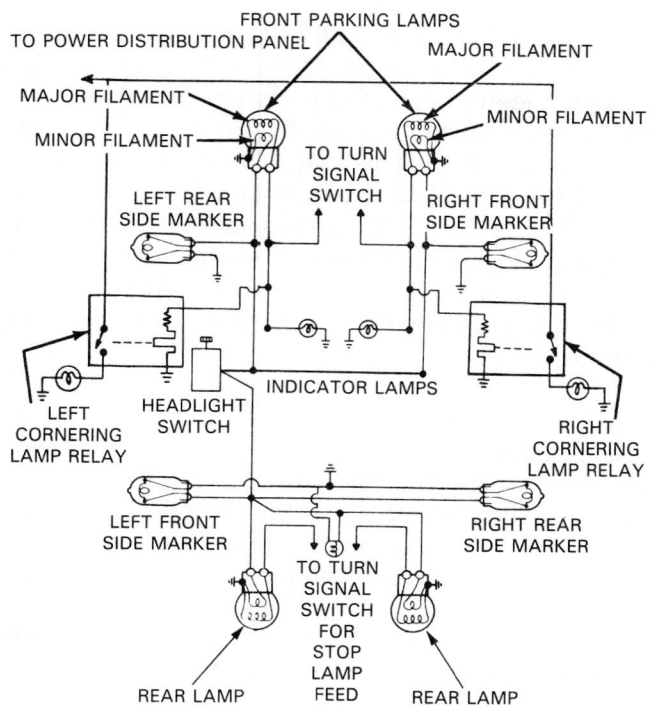

Fig. 34-6. Study basic circuit for turn signals and marker lights.

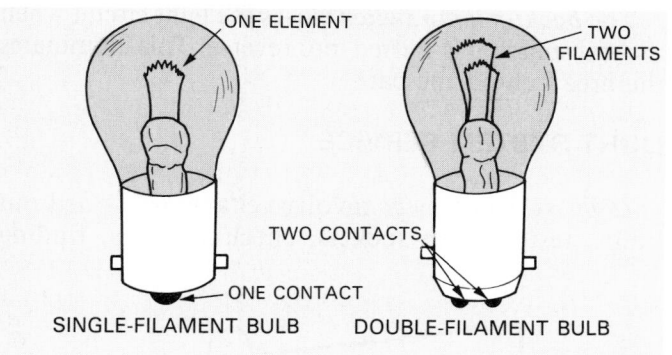

Fig. 34-7. Single-filament bulb is commonly used as backup or marker light. Double-filament bulb is needed to serve as both parking light and turn or braking light.

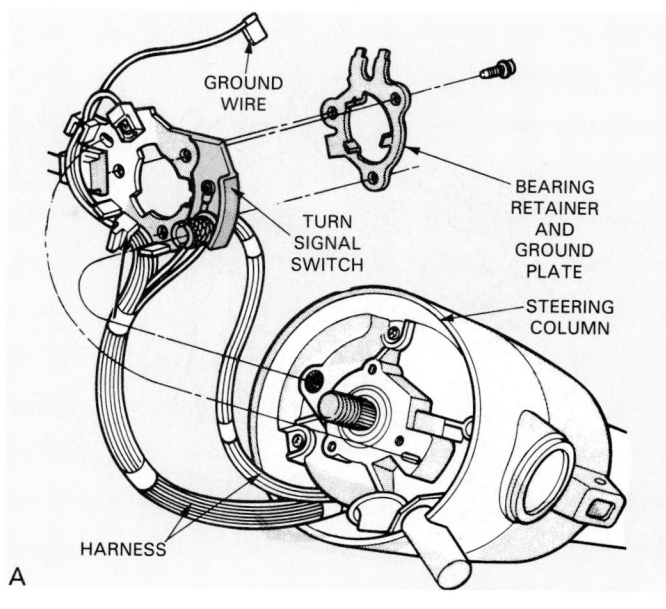

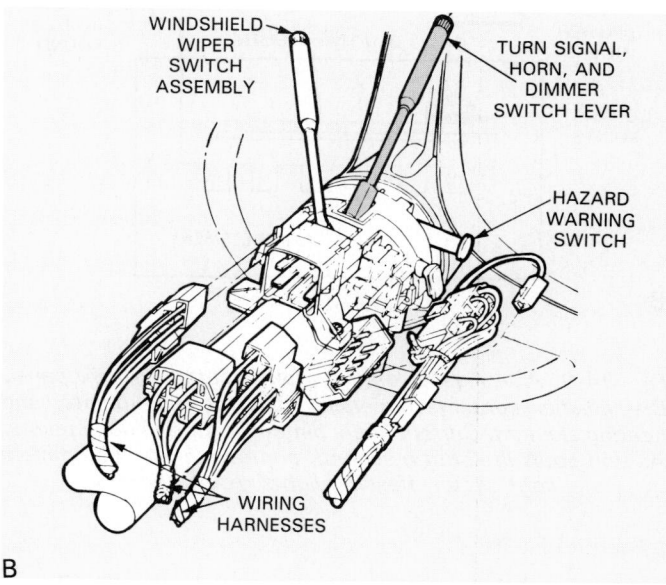

Fig. 34-8. A — Turn signal switch mounted in top of steering column, around steering shaft. B — Turn signal switch mounted on side of steering column. It also serves as horn and dimmer switch. (Chrysler and Ford)

Turnlight system

The *turnlight system* basically consists of a fuse, turnlight switch, flasher unit, turnlight bulbs, indicator bulbs, and related wiring. When the steering column mounted switch is activated, it causes the right or left side turnlamps to flash. Turn indicator lights in the instrument panel or fenders also flash.

Some turn signal light switches look like the one shown in Fig. 34-8A. This type switch mounts in the center of the steering column, under the steering wheel. Another type termed a multi-function switch, is shown in Fig. 34-8B. This switch also functions as a horn and dimmer switch.

The *turn signal flasher* automatically opens and closes the turn signal circuit, causing the bulbs to flash

ON and OFF. Look at Fig. 34-9. The flasher unit contains a temperature sensitive bimetallic strip and a heating element. The bimetal strip is connected to a set of contact points and to the fuse panel.

When current flows through the turn signal flasher, the bimetallic strip is heated and bends. This opens the contact points and breaks the circuit. As the bimetal strip rapidly cools, it closes the points and again completes the circuit. This heating and cooling cycle takes place in about a second. As a result, the turnlights flash as the points open and close.

The turn signal flasher is frequently mounted on the fuse panel, Fig. 34-9. However, on a few cars, it may be located somewhere else under the dash. A shop manual will give flasher locations.

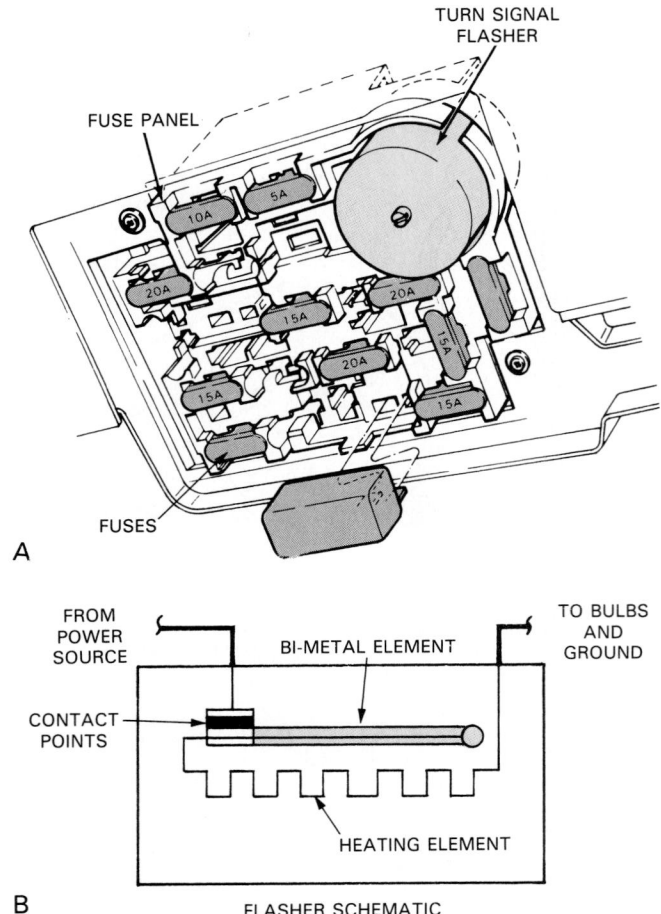

Fig. 34-9. A — Flasher unit is often located on fuse panel. B — Flasher contains bimetallic strip, contact points, and heating element. Current heats bimetallic strip to open points. As unit cools in about a second, contacts close to complete light circuit, flashing lights result. (Ford)

Emergency light system

The *emergency light system,* also termed *hazard warning system,* consists of a switch, flasher unit, four turn signal lamps, and related wiring. The emergency light switch is normally mounted on the steering column, Fig. 34-8B. It is usually a push-pull switch.

When the switch is closed, current flows through the emergency flasher. Like a turn signal flasher, the emergency flasher opens and closes the circuit to the lights. This causes all four turn signals to flash. Oncoming traffic is warned of a possible emergency or hazard.

Stoplight system

The *stoplight system* is commonly made up of a fuse, brake light switch, two rear lamps, and related wiring. The brake light switch is normally mounted on the brake pedal, as in Fig. 34-10. When the brake pedal is pressed, it closes the switch and turns on the rear brake lights.

For more information on brake light systems, refer to Chapter 69, Brake System Fundamentals.

Backup light system

A *backup light system* typically has a fuse, gear shift or transmission mounted switch, two backup lamps, and wiring to connect these components.

The *backup lamp switch* closes the light circuit when the transmission is shifted into reverse. This illuminates the area behind the car.

LIGHT SYSTEM SERVICE

Light system service involves changing burned-out bulbs, testing bulb sockets, checking fuses, finding

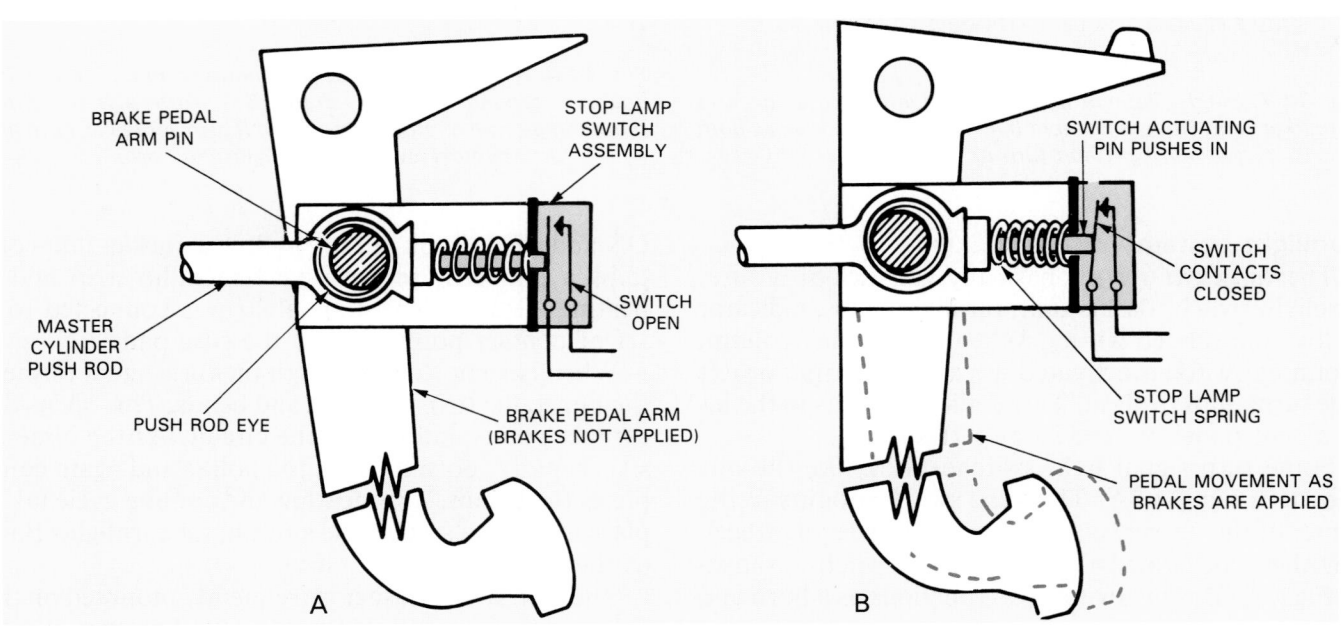

Fig. 34-10. Brake light switch action. A — Brake pedal released, contacts open, brake lights off. B — Pedal depressed, contacts close, brake lights function. Note part names. (Ford)

shorted and open circuits, aiming headlights, and other similar types of tasks. This section of the chapter will summarize the most important types of electrical tests and repairs performed on a car's lighting system.

Lamp replacement

Lamps or bulbs must be replaced when *burned out* (element burned in half). Headlamps are usually held in place with small screws and a retaining ring. See Fig. 34-11. Other bulbs are inside a lens. They are normally held in the socket by a spring and small dowels or a pressfit, Figs. 34-11 and 34-12.

Fig. 34-13 shows how to check for current in a bulb socket. With the light turned ON, there is a socket or circuit problem if the test light does NOT glow.

Flickering lights

Flickering lights (lights go on and off) point to a loose electrical connection or a circuit breaker that is kicking out because of a short.

If all or several of the lights flicker, the problem is in a section of the circuit common to those lights. Check to see if the lights flicker only with the light switch in one position.

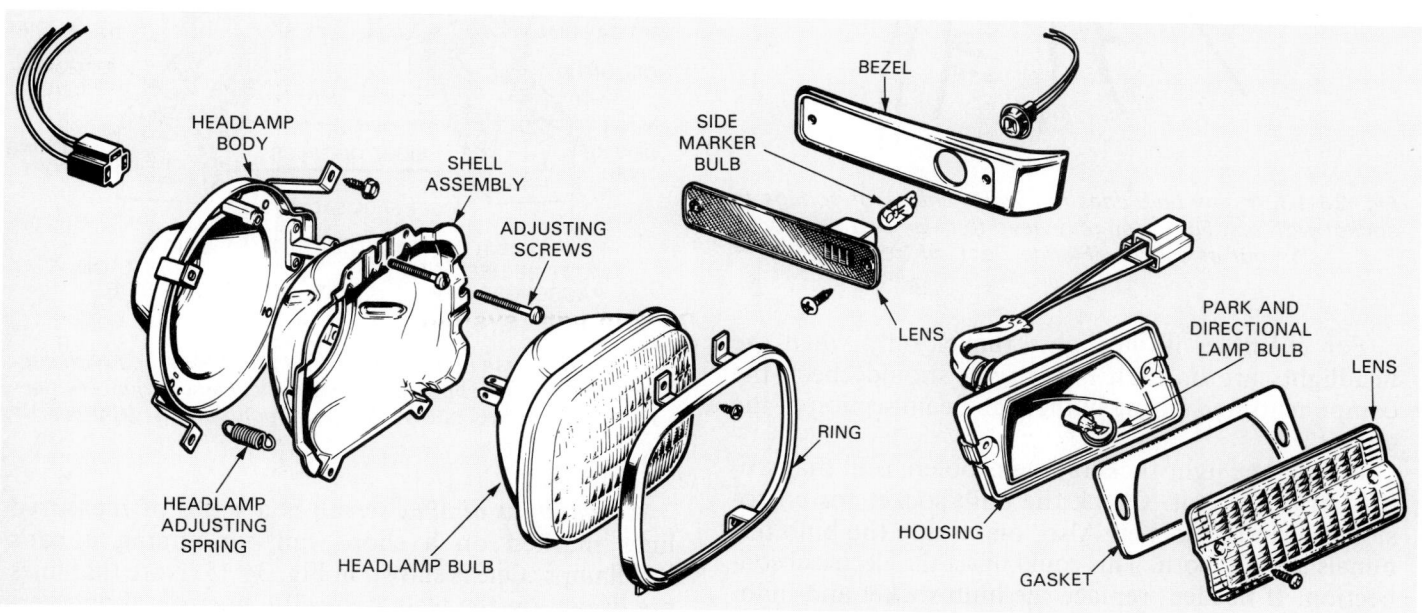

Fig. 34-11. Headlamp, parking-turn signal, and side marker or light assemblies. (Chrysler)

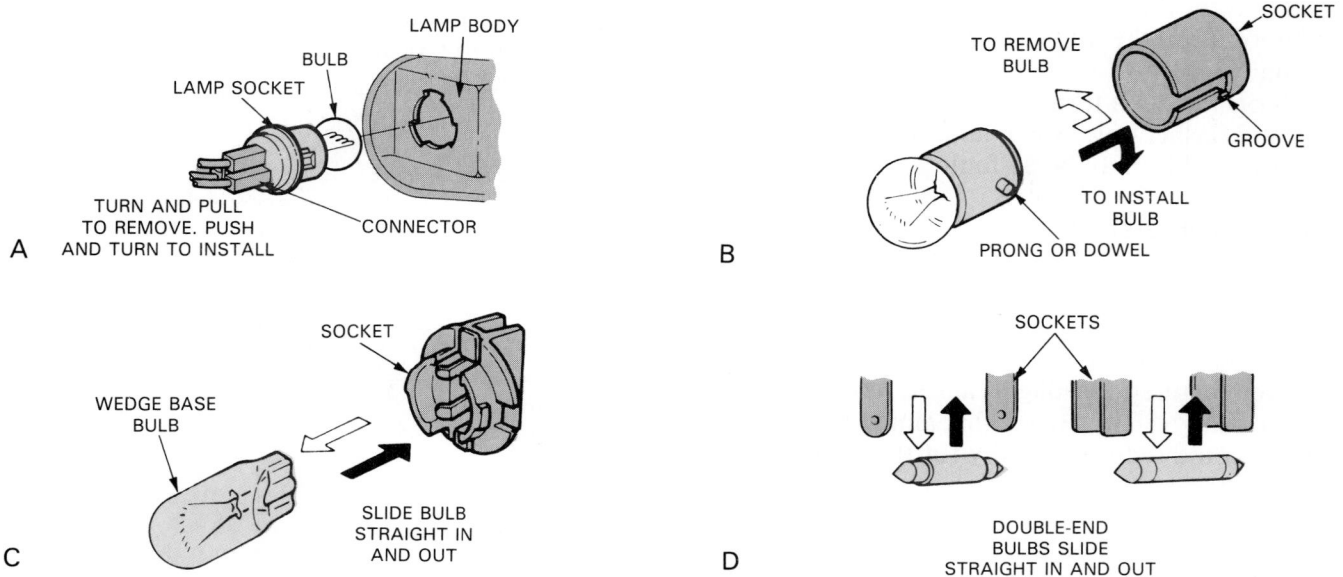

Fig. 34-12. Bulb configurations. A — Socket has lugs that lock into lamp body. Partial turn will free socket. B — Push in and turn to install or remove bulb with prongs. C — Just pull in or out on wedge base bulb. D — Double-end bulbs are snapped in and out as shown. (Nissan)

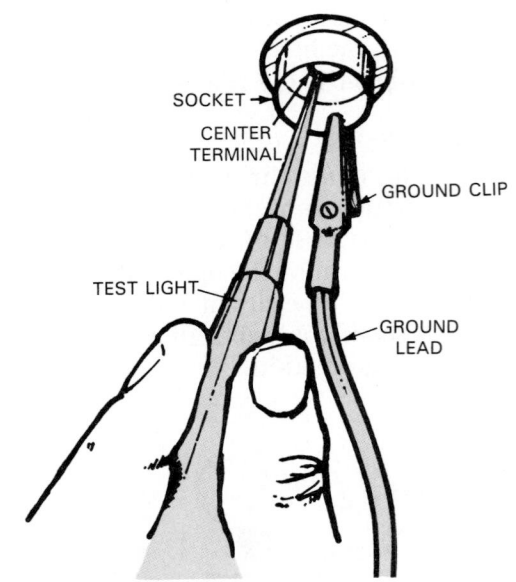

Fig. 34-13. If new bulb does not work, check for voltage to socket with test light. You may need to clean rust and corrosion out of socket. (Florida Dept. of Voc. Ed.)

For example, if the lights flicker only when the headlights are on high beam, you should check the components and wiring in the high beam section of the circuit.

If only one light flickers, the problem is in that section of the circuit. Check the bulb socket for corrosion. Clean the socket. Also, make sure the bulb terminals are not worn. This could upset the electrical connection. If needed, replace the bulb socket and bulb.

Turn signals inoperative

Check for a burned-out bulb when the turn signals fail to flash. Even one burned bulb will reduce current and prevent the flasher unit from functioning. A burned out bulb is the MOST COMMON CAUSE of turn signal problems.

If both right and left turn signals do not work, check the fuse and flasher unit. Something common to both sides of the circuit may be at fault.

AIMING HEADLIGHTS

Headlights can be aimed using mechanical aimers or a wall screen. Either method assures that the headlight beams point in the direction specified by the vehicle manufacturer. Headlights aimed too high could blind oncoming traffic. Headlights aimed too low or to one side could reduce visibility for the car's driver.

Typically, the car should have a half tank of gas and the correct tire inflation pressure. Only the normal spare tire and jack should be in the trunk. Some manufacturers recommend that someone sit in the driver and passenger seat while aiming the lights.

Headlight aimers are devices for pointing the car's headlamps in a specified position. To use aimers,

follow the instructions for the specific type of equipment. Some require a level floor. Others have internally leveling mechanisms to allow for an uneven shop floor.

Fig. 34-14 shows headlight aimers that mount on the bulbs with suction cups. This type uses leveling bubbles to indicate the vertical adjustment of the headlights. An indicator operated by reflecting mirrors shows the horizontal adjustment.

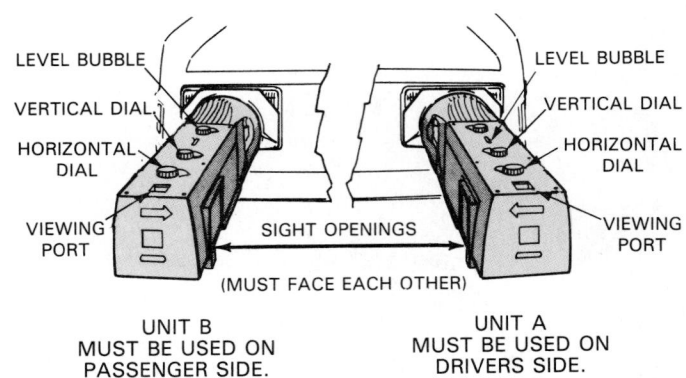

Fig. 34-14. These headlight aimers mount on lamps with suction cups. Leveling bubbles show vertical adjustment. Reflection from mirrors show horizontal adjustment. (Chrysler)

A *headlight aiming screen* is a series of measured lines marked on a shop wall for aiming a car's headlamps. One is shown in Fig. 34-15. Note that lines are drawn on the wall at specific horizontal and vertical locations.

The car is normally located 25 feet (7.6 meters) from the screen on a level floor. When the headlights are turned on, the highest points of light intensity (brightness) should be as shown in Fig. 34-15. Check both high and low beams. Refer to a service manual for added details.

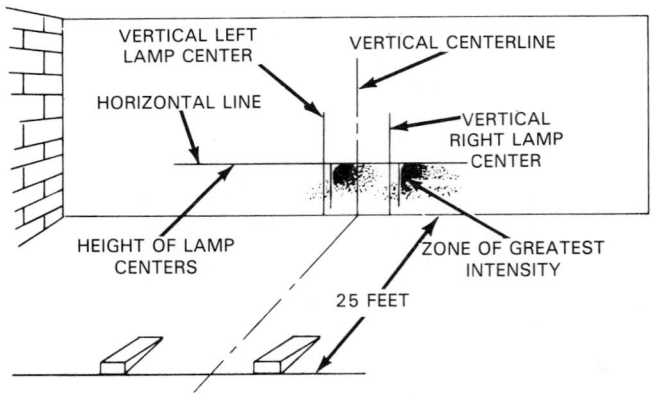

Fig. 34-15. Lines can be marked on shop wall as shown to aim headlights. Car must be located prescribed distance from wall. Adjust headlamps until they shine in designated areas on wall. (Chrysler)

Headlight adjusting screws are provided to alter the direction of the headlamp beams. See Fig. 34-16. One screw provides vertical (up and down) adjustment. Another provides horizontal (right or left) adjustment. Turn the screws until the aimer or screen show correct beam alignment.

WINDSHIELD WIPERS

A typical *windshield wiper system* is made up of a switch, wiper motor assembly, wiper linkage, wiper arms, wiper blades, and usually a windshield washer system. Either a fuse or circuit breaker protects the system. See Fig. 34-17.

The *windshield wiper switch* is a multi-position switch that sometimes contains a rheostat. Each switch position provides a different wiping speed. The rheostat operates the delay mode for a slow wiping action. A relay is frequently used to complete the circuit between battery voltage and the wiper motor.

The *wiper motor assembly* consists of a permanent magnet motor and a transmission. The *wiper motor transmission* is normally a set of plastic gears, end housing, and crank that change rotary motion into a back and forth wiping motion. Fig. 34-18 shows the parts of a typical wiper motor assembly. The drive crank on the transmission connects to the wiper linkage.

The *wiper linkage* is a set of arms that transfers motion from the wiper motor transmission to the wiper

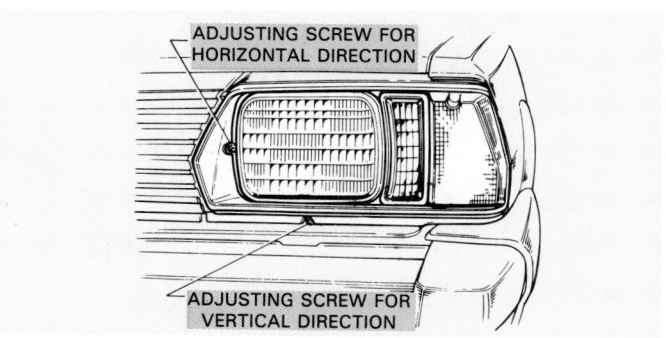

Fig. 34-16. Note location of headlight adjustment screws. They can normally be adjusted without removing trim. (Subaru)

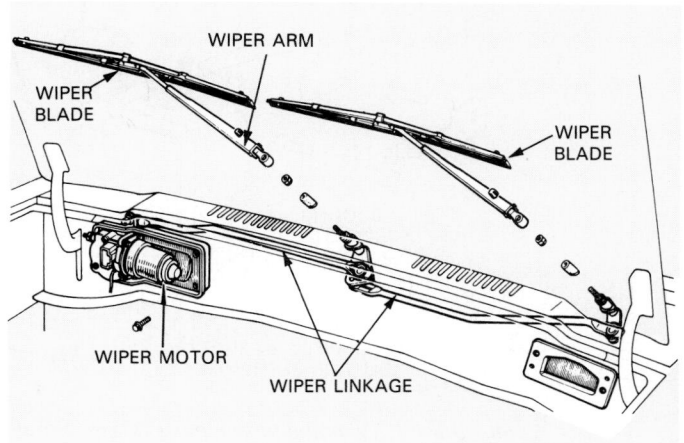

Fig. 34-17. Study basic parts of typical windshield wiper system. (Toyota)

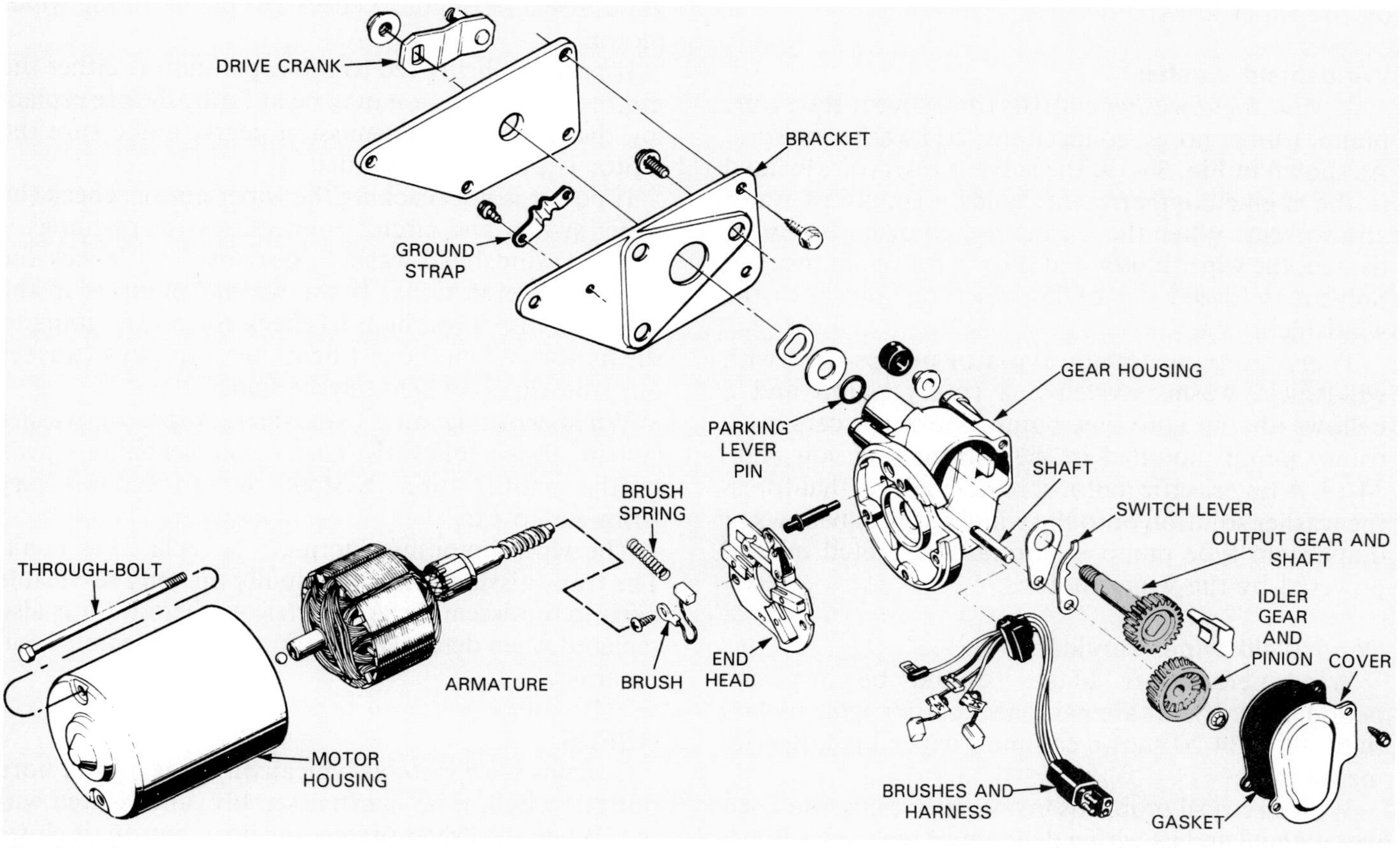

Fig. 34-18. Exploded view of wiper motor assembly. Two plastic gears are most common reason for problems. Gears are replaced when stripped or broken. (AMC)

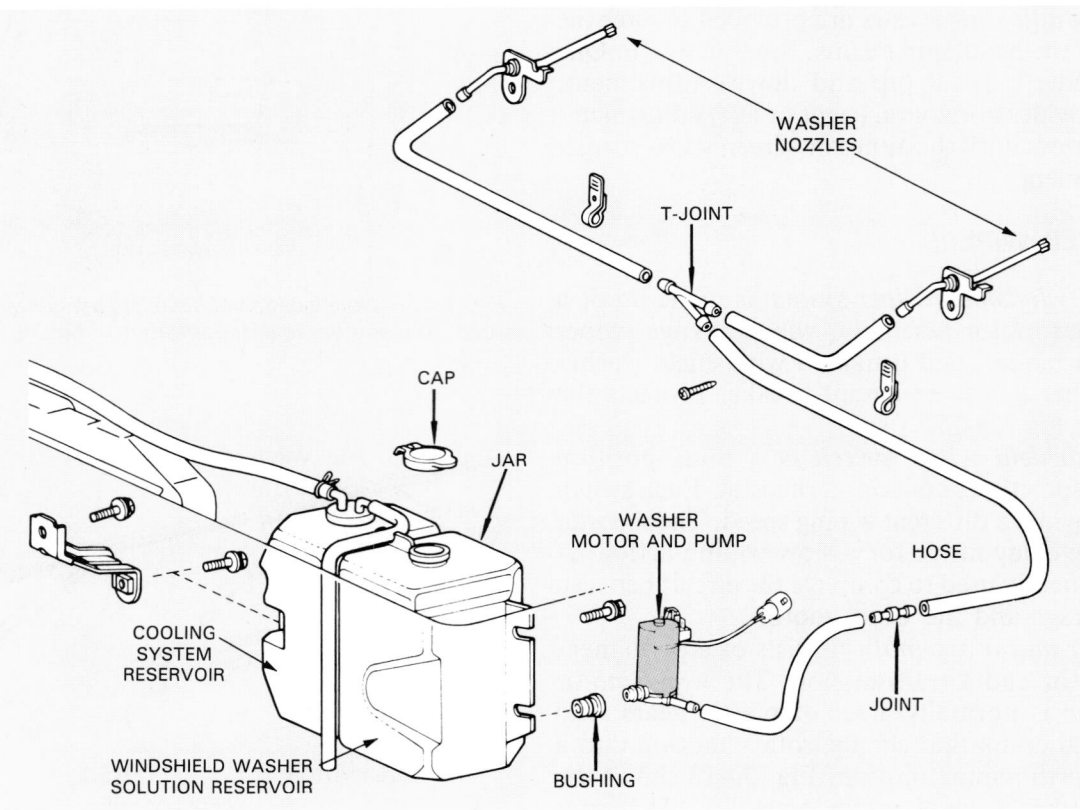

Fig. 34-19. Windshield washer system. Small electric motor and pump force solution out of reservoir, through hoses, and out nozzles. Check for debris in reservoir strainer, hoses, and nozzle when not working. Then, check pump operation.

arms. Refer to Fig. 34-17. The rubber wiper blades fit on the wiper arms.

Windshield washer

A *windshield washer* consists of a solvent reservoir, pump, rubber hoses, connections, and washer nozzles. As shown in Fig. 34-19, the solvent reservoir, located in the engine compartment, holds a supply of water and solvent. When the washer switch or button is activated, the wiper motor and the washer pump turn on. Solvent is forced out of the reservoir and onto the windshield.

There are two common types of pumps used with windshield washer systems: a rotary pump and a bellows (diaphragm) type pump. Most new cars use a rotary pump mounted in the solvent reservoir, Fig. 34-19. A tiny electric motor spins an impeller that forces the washer solution onto the windshield. A bellows or diaphragm type pump is normally mounted on and powered by the wiper motor.

Windshield wiper service

Windshield wiper blades should be inspected periodically. If they are hardened, cut, or split, replace them. Fig. 34-20 shows common wiper blade service methods.

With electrical problems in a wiper system, use a service manual and its wiring diagram of the circuit. First,

check the fuses and electrical connections. If they are good, use a test light to check for power to the wiper motor.

If power is being fed to the wiper motor, either the motor or transmission may be at fault. Before replacing the motor or transmission gears, make sure the motor is properly grounded.

If power is not reaching the wiper motor, check the wiper switch and circuit connections for openings.

If the windshield washer does not work, check the fuse and connections. If the washer pump is in the reservoir, use a test light to check for power going to the motor. When the test light does not glow (washer on), the wiper switch may be bad.

When working on a windshield wiper or washer system, always follow the exact recommendations given by the manufacturer. Systems and procedures vary from car to car.

The wiper motor must normally be replaced as a unit. The transmission gears are usually the only servicable parts in the assembly. An electric washer motor is also replaced when defective. It cannot be disassembled and repaired.

HORNS

Today's *horn systems* typically include a fuse, horn button switch, relay, horn assembly, and related wiring. When the driver presses the horn button, it closes

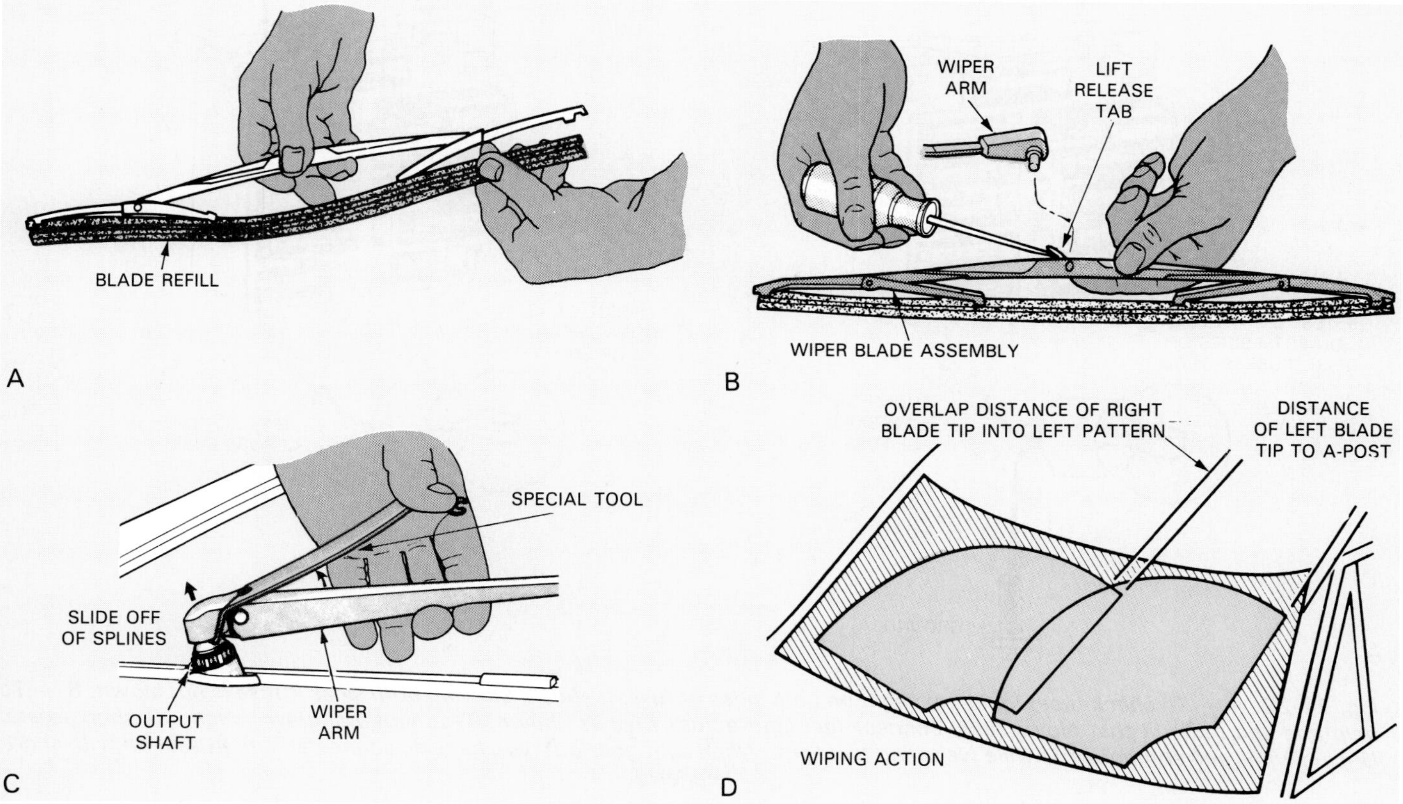

Fig. 34-20. Basic wiper service. A — New rubber wiper refill can be purchased and slid into place. B — To replace complete wiper blade assembly, free it from wiper arm. C — Arm can sometimes be removed by prying up on arm as shown. D — Typical pattern for positioning arms on output shafts. Refer to a service manual for exact procedures. (Chrysler)

the horn switch and activates the horn relay. This completes the circuit. Current then flows through the relay circuit, and to the horn.

Most horns have a diaphragm that vibrates by means of an electromagnet. When energized, the electromagnet pulls on the horn diaphragm, Fig. 34-21. This movement opens a set of contact points inside the horn. This allows the diaphragm to flex back towards its normal position. Again, the points close and the diaphragm is pulled into the electromagnet. As a result, a rapid vibrating action is produced. A honking sound is transmitted out of the horn.

When a horn will not sound, check the fuse, connections, and test for voltage at the horn terminal. If a horn blows continuously, the horn switch may be bad. A relay is another cause of horn problems. The contacts in the relay could be burned or stuck together.

Refer to a shop manual when diagnosing and repairing a horn system. Although many horns are adjustable, they are not serviceable. Use your knowledge of the system and basic testing methods to locate troubles.

COMMON ELECTRICAL PROBLEMS

There are several classifications of electrical problems. These are briefly covered in Chapter 8, Basic Electricity and Electronics. Problems include a short

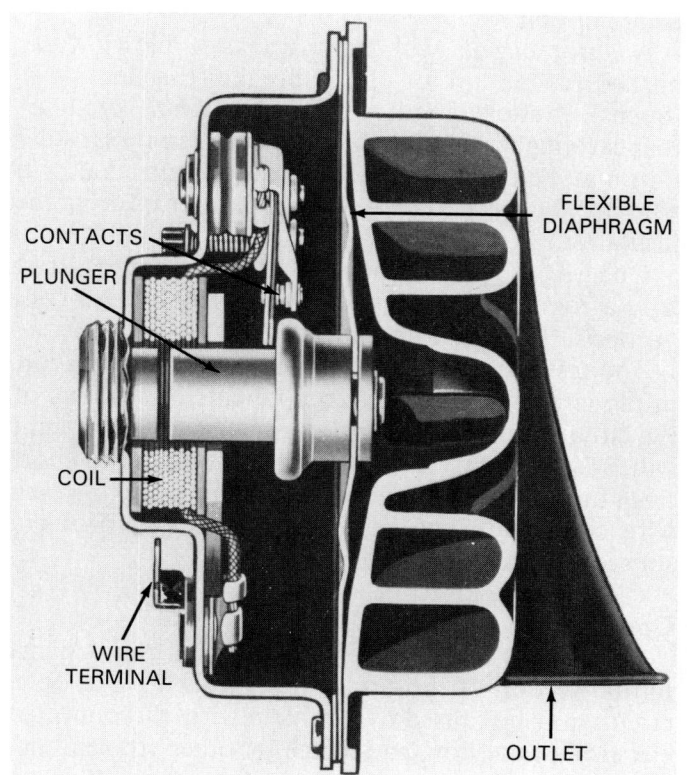

Fig. 34-21. Horn contains a coil, points, and flexible diaphragm. Coil and point actions makes plunger slide in and out of coil. Plunger moves diaphragm to produce horn sound. (Deere & Co.)

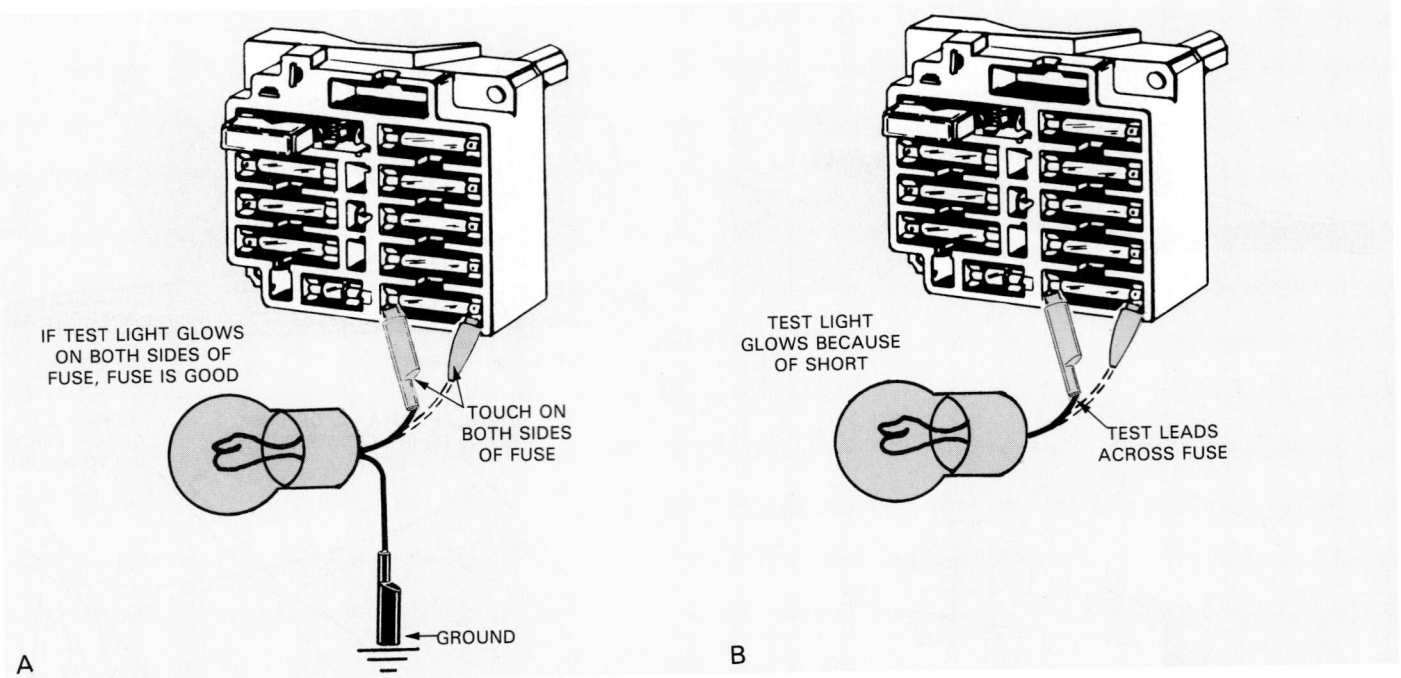

Fig. 34-22. A — To check fuse, touch test light on both sides of fuse. It should glow on both sides if fuse is not blown. B — To help find short circuit that blows fuse, connect test light across fuse as shown. Test light will glow as long as short exists. Unplug wires and components while watching test light. When light goes out, you have disconnected circuit section with short. (Peerless)

circuit, open circuit, and high circuit resistance. It is important for you to be able to quickly diagnose and locate these troubles.

Short circuit

A *short circuit* will show up as a blown fuse, burned fusible link or circuit breaker that kicks out (opens). A short circuit results when a *hot wire* (current carrying wire) is touching ground. A wire's insulation may be cut and touching body sheet metal or a wire may be pinched between two parts, rupturing the insulation.

One way to locate a short circuit is to connect a test light across the blown fuse or open circuit breaker connections. This is shown in Fig. 34-22.

The test light will glow as long as there is a short in the circuit. Disconnect components or sections of the circuit while watching the test light. The test light will STOP GLOWING when you remove the short from the circuit. Keep tracing the circuit (checking each wire connection and part) until the exact problem source is located.

Open circuit

An *open circuit* will keep the electrical components in that section of the circuit from working. An open circuit may be caused by a broken wire, disconnected electrical connection, bad switch, or other problem that prevents current flow.

An open circuit is easily located using a test light, Fig. 34-23. Start at each end of the circuit. Check for power at the supply (fuse panel). Then, go to the other

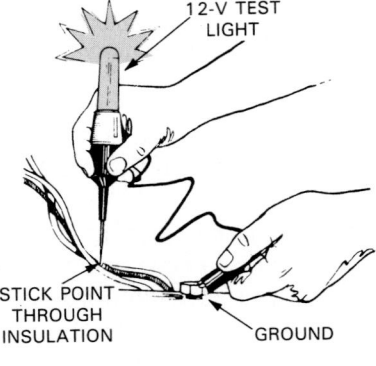

Fig. 34-23. Test light will also help you find circuit opens quickly. Push pointed tip through wire insulation and ground other lead. This will let you check for voltage in different sections of circuit quickly. If test light does not glow, that section of circuit is open. (Lisle Tools)

end of the circuit (a light socket, for example) and check for power. If you have power at the fuse but no power at the load (socket), the open is between the fuse and the load. Trace the open by testing for power at the switch and each electrical connection between the fuse panel and load.

When there is no power at the fuse panel, the fusible link may be burned. If power is being fed to a switch, but power does not come out the switch, the switch or electrical connector is bad.

Use your understanding of system operation, a wiring diagram, and this type of testing technique to find an open circuit.

High circuit resistance

High resistance in a light circuit, for example, can cause the lamps to be dimmer than normal. The high resistance reduces the amount of current flowing through the circuit. To find a high resistance, measure the voltage drop across possible problem components.

For example, if you suspect that a switch might be partially burned, measure the voltage drop across the switch. A high resistance (burned or corroded switch) will show up as a HIGH VOLTAGE DROP.

This technique can also be used to check the internal resistance of other electrical components (electrical plug connectors, wires, relays).

Typically, the voltage drop across an electrical conductor should NOT exceed about .5 volts. Remember that this applies to wires, switches, connectors, but NOT to electric motors, light bulbs, or other loads.

Using wiring diagrams

Wiring diagrams are drawings that show the relationship of the electrical components and wires in a circuit. They are useful when an electrical problem is difficult to locate and correct.

Wiring diagrams, as in Fig. 34-24, normally show:
1. WIRE COLOR CODING (special color markings on wire insulation for tracing wires through car).
2. COMPONENT LOCATION (number-letter sequence around border of diagram for quickly finding parts in circuit).
3. WIRE SPLICES AND CONNECTIONS (where

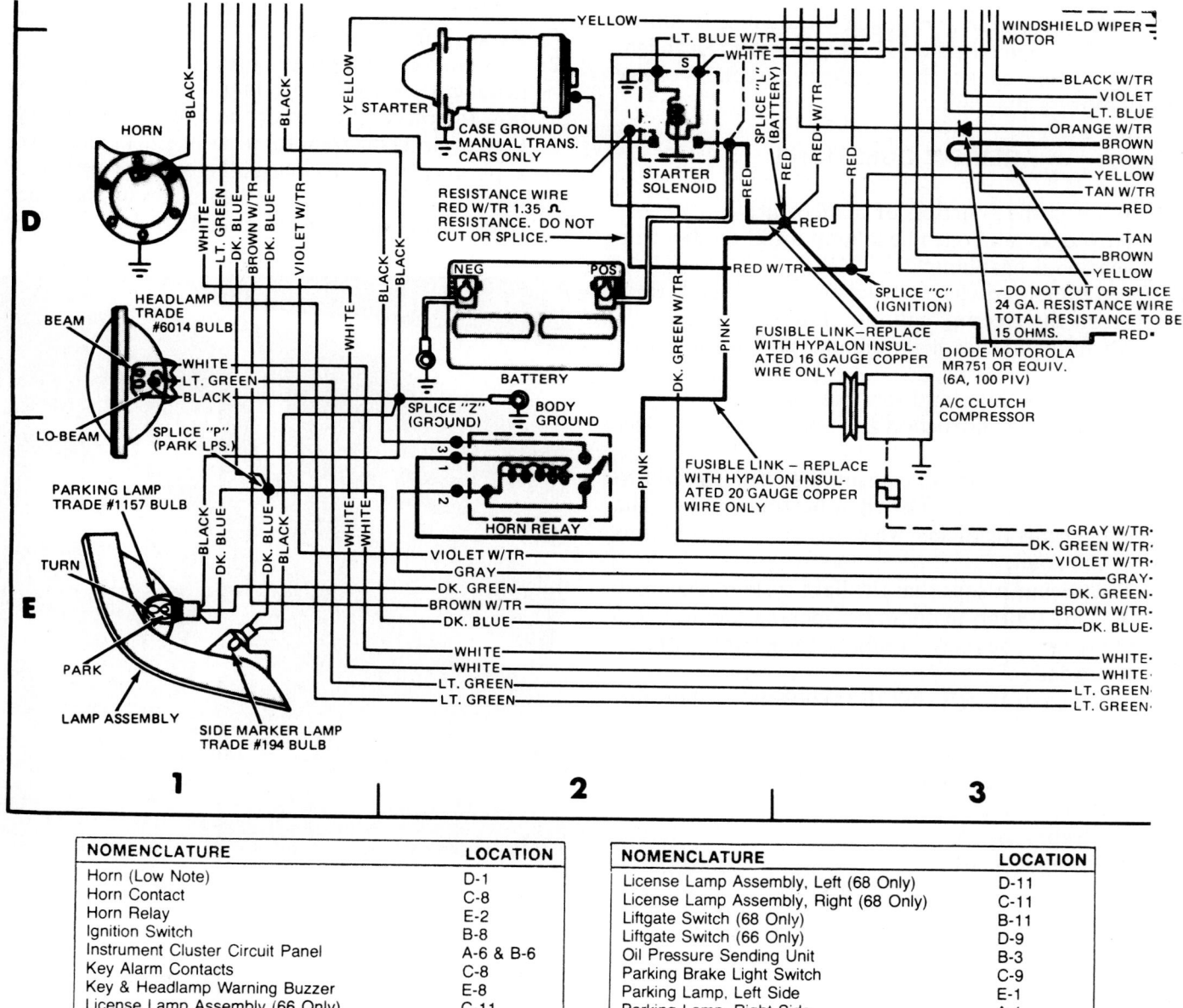

NOMENCLATURE	LOCATION
Horn (Low Note)	D-1
Horn Contact	C-8
Horn Relay	E-2
Ignition Switch	B-8
Instrument Cluster Circuit Panel	A-6 & B-6
Key Alarm Contacts	C-8
Key & Headlamp Warning Buzzer	E-8
License Lamp Assembly (66 Only)	C-11

NOMENCLATURE	LOCATION
License Lamp Assembly, Left (68 Only)	D-11
License Lamp Assembly, Right (68 Only)	C-11
Liftgate Switch (68 Only)	B-11
Liftgate Switch (66 Only)	D-9
Oil Pressure Sending Unit	B-3
Parking Brake Light Switch	C-9
Parking Lamp, Left Side	E-1
Parking Lamp, Right Side	A-1

Fig. 34-24. Study typical wiring diagram. Use nomenclature and location listing to quickly find components on diagram. For example, horn is listed as being within section D-1. Can you find it? (Ford)

and how wires are joined together).

4. ELECTRICAL SYMBOLS (simple drawings showing minor components in circuit).
5. COMPONENT DRAWINGS (simplified illustrations of major circuit components for easy location on diagram).

To use a wiring diagram, locate the parts being tested. Then, follow the lines that show where the wires go to the next component in the circuit.

For example, say you are having trouble with a horn circuit. Find the horn circuit diagram in a service manual. It will be like the one in Fig. 34-24. Trace the horn wires. You would then find a relay in the circuit between the horn and horn switch. It may be at fault.

KNOW THESE TERMS

Headlamp system, Halogen headlamp, Dimmer switch, Turn signal flasher, Headlight aimer, Headlight aiming screen, Short circuit, Open circuit, Voltage drop, Wiring diagram.

REVIEW QUESTIONS

1. What is the function of a rheostat?
2. How does a halogen headlamp differ from a conventional headlamp?
3. A dimmer switch can be located on the car's floor or on the steering column. True or False?
4. An automatic headlight dimmer system consists of a _____ sensor, _____ ,and _____ to control the high and low beams.
5. Explain the construction and operation of a flasher unit.
6. A car has a problem causing the left headlight to flicker on and off. The right headlight is ok. The light seems to flicker when the car strikes bumps in the road.
   Technician A says that the light system relay may be bad. Vibration could be opening the points in the relay. The relay should be tested and replaced if needed.
   Technician B says that the problem involves just the left headlight section of the circuit. This mechanic suggests checking the headlamp socket and electrical connections to that bulb.
   Who is correct?
   a. Technician A
   b. Technician B
   c. Both A and B
   d. Neither A nor B

7. One burned-out bulb cannot keep the turn signals from flashing on and off. True or False?
8. The two methods of aiming a cars headlights are _____ _____ or a _____ _____ .
9. List and explain the major parts of a windshield wiper system.
10. Explain the operation of a horn circuit.

ACTIVITIES FOR CHAPTER 34

1. Select a specific vehicle make and model that is at least two years old. Go to the automotive department of a discount or department store, and find the store's replacement lamp identifier system (it may be a book or large card or even a computer screen). Use it to identify the proper replacements for headlights, taillights, turn signals, brake lights, backup lights, and side marker lights (if used). List all the part numbers.
2. Demonstrate the proper procedure for checking headlight aiming, using marks on a wall. Show how to correct the aim of the lights, if necessary.
3. Find a wiring diagram for a car or truck, and make a photocopy. Use a brightly colored pencil or marker to trace the wiring that makes up the windshield wiper and washer circuit.

Horn, lights, and wiper controls are conveniently clustered for use by the driver.

35

Cooling System Fundamentals

After studying this chapter, you will be able to:
□ List the basic parts of a cooling system.
□ Describe the functions of a cooling system.
□ Explain the operation and construction of major cooling system components.
□ Compare cooling system design variations.
□ Explain the importance of antifreeze.
□ Discuss safety procedures to follow when working with cooling systems.

This chapter explains the design, construction, and operation of cooling systems. You must fully understand such systems before learning service and repair.

BASIC COOLING SYSTEM

The basic parts of a cooling system are shown in Fig. 35-1. Refer to this illustration as each part is introduced.
1. WATER PUMP (forces coolant through engine and other system parts).
2. RADIATOR HOSES (connect engine to radiator).
3. RADIATOR (transfers engine coolant heat to outside air).
4. FAN (draws air through radiator).
5. THERMOSTAT (controls coolant flow and engine operating temperature).

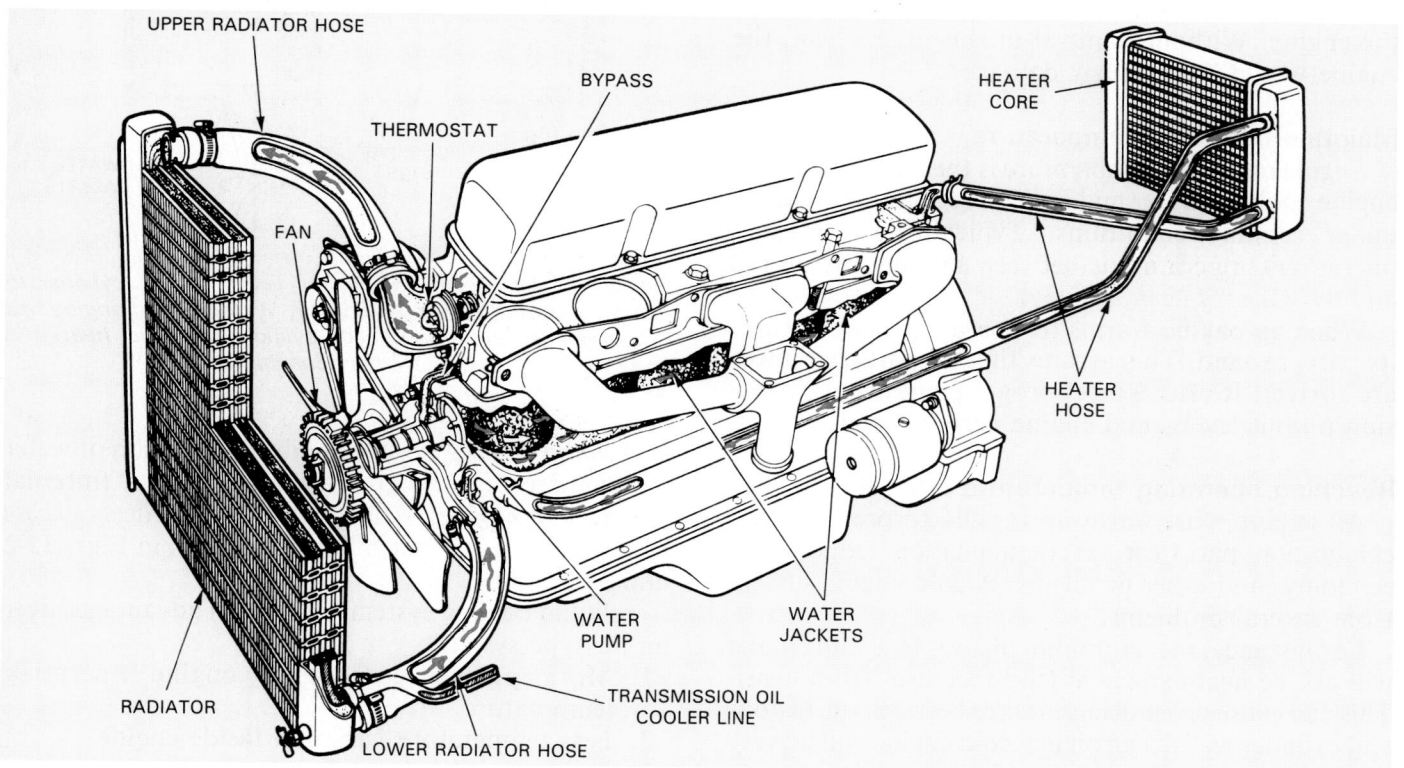

Fig. 35-1. Study basic names and location for parts of a cooling system. This will help you as each part is explained in detail. (Ford Motor Co.)

Cooling system operation

When the engine is running, a fan belt powers the water pump. The water pump forces coolant to circulate through the engine water jackets.

While the engine is cold, the thermostat remains closed, so coolant circulates inside the engine. This helps warm the engine quickly.

When the engine reaches operating temperature, the thermostat opens. Heated coolant then flows through the radiator. Excess coolant heat is transferred to the air flowing through the radiator.

Typically, coolant flows from the head of the engine to the radiator, then back into the block. *Reverse flow* cooling, used on some vehicles, follows the opposite course: coolant enters the head and exits the block.

FUNCTIONS OF A COOLING SYSTEM

A *cooling system* has several functions. It must remove excess heat from the engine, maintain a constant engine operating temperature, increase the temperature of a cold engine quickly, and provide a means for warming passenger compartment.

Removing engine heat

The burning air-fuel mixture produces a tremendous amount of heat. Combustion flame temperatures can reach 4500 °F (2484 °C). This is enough heat to melt metal parts.

Some combustion heat is used to produce expansion and pressure for piston movement. Most combustion heat flows out the exhaust and into the metal parts of the engine. Without removal of this excess heat, the engine would be seriously damaged.

Maintain operating temperature

Engine operating temperature is the temperature the engine coolant (water and antifreeze solution) reaches under running conditions. Typically, an engine's operating temperature is between 180 and 210 °F (82 and 99 °C).

When an engine warms to operating temperature, its parts expand. This assures that all part clearances are correct. It also assures proper combustion, emission output levels, and engine performance.

Reaching operating temperature quickly

An engine must warm up rapidly to prevent poor combustion, part wear, oil contamination, reduced fuel economy, and other problems. A cold engine suffers from several problems.

For instance, the aluminum pistons in a cold engine will not be heat-expanded (size increases from heat). This can cause too much clearance between the pistons and cylinder walls. The oil in a cold engine will be very thick. This can reduce lubrication and increase engine wear. The fuel mixture will also not vaporize and burn as efficiently in a cold engine.

Heater operation

A cooling system commonly circulates coolant to the vehicle's heater. Since the engine coolant is warm, its heat can be used to warm the passenger compartment. See Fig. 35-1.

Refer to Chapter 71, Heating and Air Conditioning Systems, for more information on heaters.

COOLING SYSTEM TYPES

There are two major types of automotive cooling systems: liquid and air.

An *air cooling system* uses large cylinder cooling fins and outside air to remove excess heat from the engine. Look at Fig. 35-2.

The *cooling fins* increase the surface area of the metal around the cylinder. This allows enough heat to transfer from the cylinder.

An air cooling system commonly uses plastic or sheet metal ducts and shrouds (enclosures) to route air over the cylinder fins. Thermostatically controlled flaps regulate airflow and engine operating temperature.

Note! Most air cooled automotive engines have been replaced by liquid (water) cooled engines.

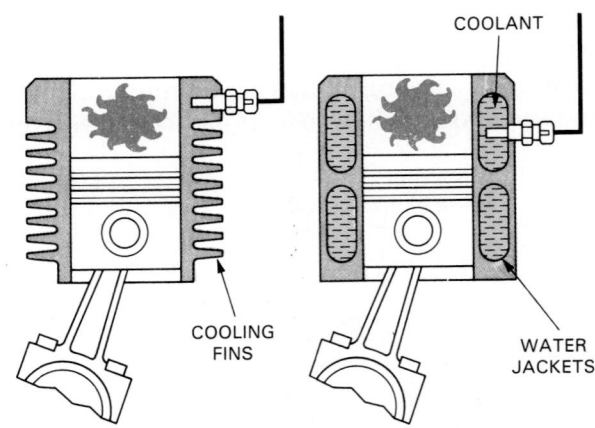

Fig. 35-2. Air-cooled engine has large fins on cylinder to dissipate heat into surrounding air. Water-cooled engine has water jackets around each cylinder to collect heat. (Robert Bosch)

A *liquid cooling system* circulates a solution of water and antifreeze through the water jackets (internal passages in engine). The coolant then collects excess heat and carries it out of the engine, as in Figs. 35-2 and 35-3.

A liquid cooling system has several advantages over an air type system:
1. More precise control of engine operating temperature.
2. Less temperature variation inside engine.
3. Reduced exhaust emissions because of better temperature control.
4. Improved heater operation to warm passengers.

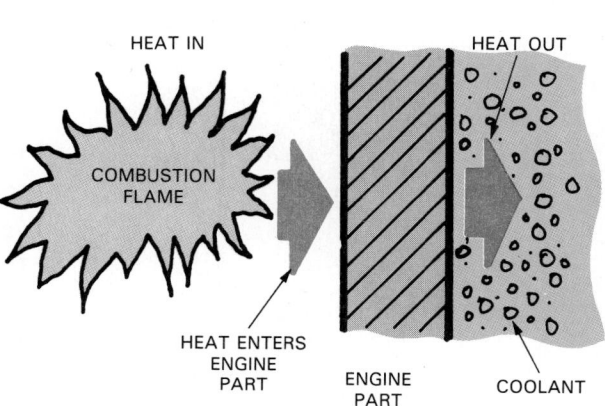

Fig. 35-3. Combustion heat transfers into cylinder wall and then into coolant. Coolant carries heat away from engine.

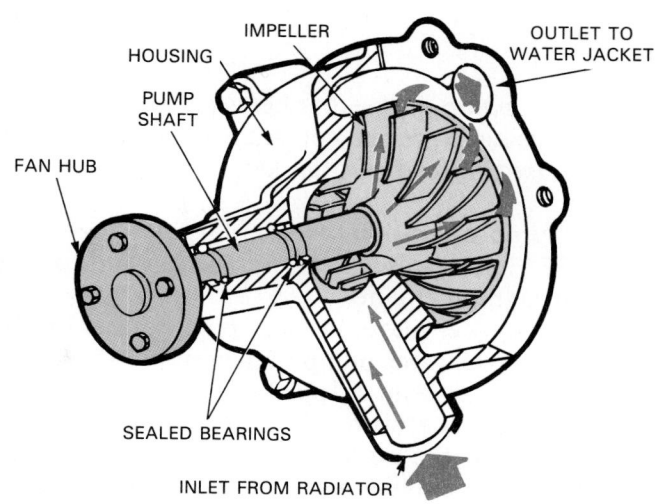

Fig. 35-5. Cutaway of simplified water pump. Note how spinning impeller throws coolant outward to produce pressure and flow. (Mopar)

WATER PUMP CONSTRUCTION

The *water pump* is an impeller or centrifugal pump that forces coolant through the engine block, cylinder head, intake manifold, hoses, and radiator. It is driven by a fan belt running off the crankshaft pulley. Look at Fig. 35-4.

The major parts of a typical water pump include:
1. WATER PUMP IMPELLER (disc with fan-like blades that spins and produces pressure and flow), Fig. 35-5.
2. WATER PUMP SHAFT (steel shaft that transfers turning force from hub to impeller).
3. WATER PUMP SEAL (prevents coolant leakage between pump shaft and pump housing), Fig. 35-6.
4. WATER PUMP BEARINGS (plain or ball bearings that allow pump shaft to spin freely in housing).
5. WATER PUMP HUB (provides mounting place for belt pulley and fan).
6. WATER PUMP HOUSING (iron or aluminum casting that forms main body of pump).

The water pump normally mounts on the front of the engine. With some transverse (sideways) mounted engines, it may bolt to the side of the engine and extend towards the front.

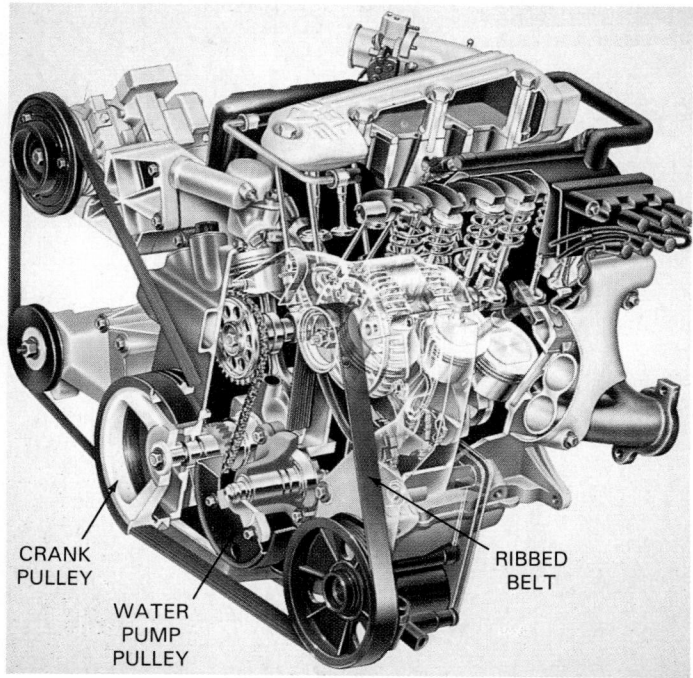

Fig. 35-4. Fan belt turns water pump pulley to operate pump. This is a modern ribbed belt that powers all accessory units. (Ford)

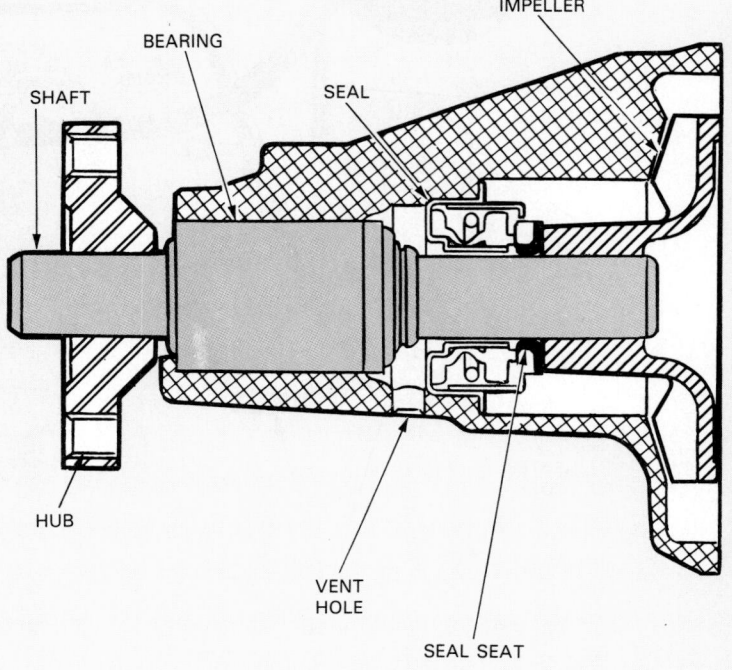

Fig. 35-6. Side view of water pump shows how seal keeps coolant from leaking out vent hole. (Chevrolet)

A *water pump gasket* fits between the engine and pump housing to prevent coolant leakage. RTV sealer may be used instead of a gasket.

Water pump operation

Fig. 35-7 illustrates water pump action and coolant flow through an engine.

The spinning engine crankshaft pulley causes the fan belt to turn the water pump pulley, pump shaft, and impeller. The coolant trapped between the impeller blades is thrown outward. This produces suction in the central area of the pump housing. It also produces pressure in the outer area of the housing.

Since the pump inlet opening is near the center, coolant is pulled out of the radiator, through the lower hose, and into the engine. After being thrown outward and pressurized, the coolant flows into the engine. It circulates through the block, around the cylinders, up through the cylinder heads, and back into the radiator.

RADIATOR AND HEATER HOSES

Radiator hoses carry coolant between the engine water jackets and the radiator. Look at Fig. 35-8. Being flexible, hoses can withstand the vibrating and rocking of the engine without breakage.

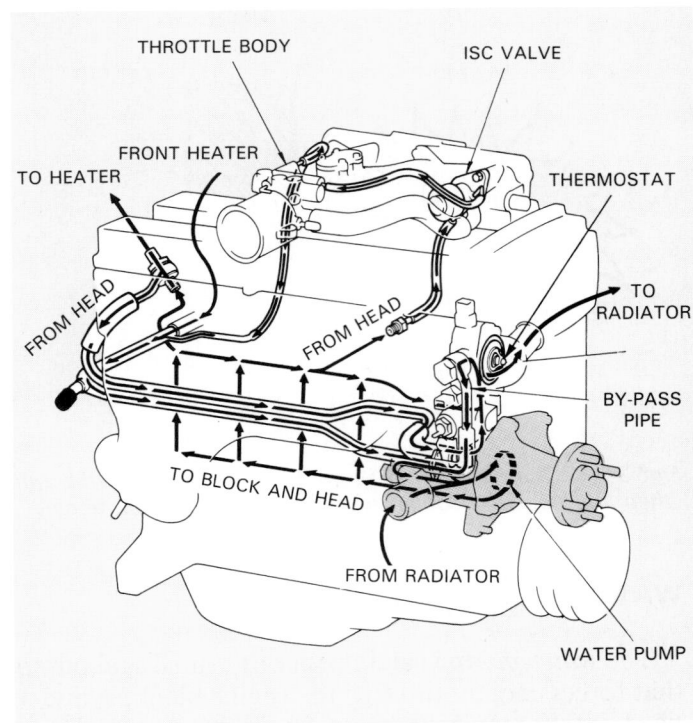

Fig. 35-7. Water pump pulls coolant out of bottom of radiator and through engine block, heads, and intake manifold. Hot coolant then re-enters radiator for cooling. (Ford)

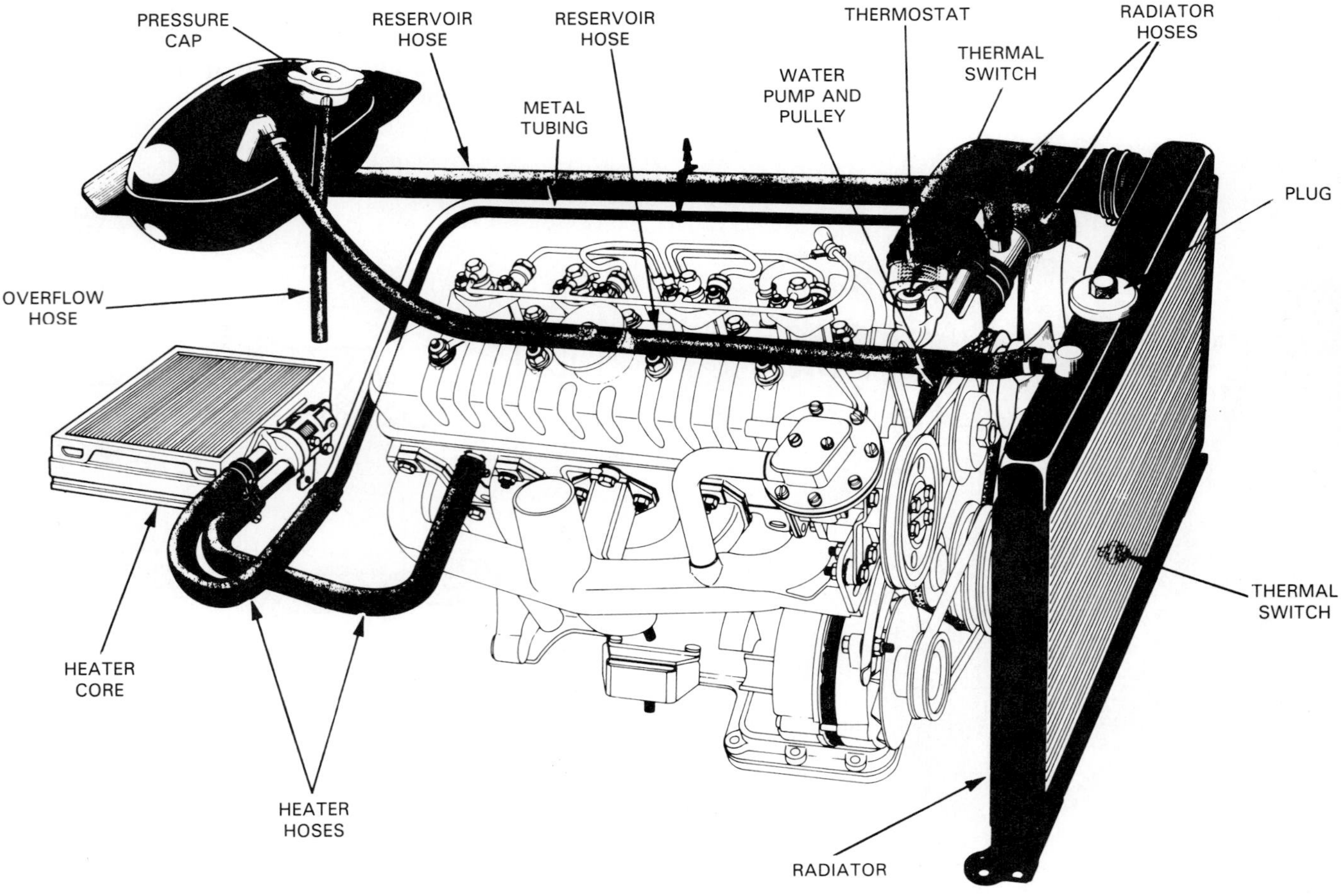

Fig. 35-8. Radiator hoses carry coolant between engine and radiator. Other hoses also contain engine coolant. (Peugeot)

The upper radiator hose normally connects to the thermostat housing on the engine intake manifold or cylinder head. Its other end fits on the radiator. The lower hose connects the water pump inlet and the radiator.

A *molded hose* is manufactured into a special shape with bends to clear parts, especially the cooling fan. It must be purchased to fit the exact year and make of car. See Fig. 35-9.

A *flexible hose* has an accordian shape and can be bent to different angles. The pleated construction allows the hose to bend without collapsing and blocking flow. It is also called a "universal" type radiator hose.

A *hose spring* is frequently used in the lower radiator hose to prevent its collapse. The lower hose is exposed to suction from the water pump. The spring assures that the inner lining of the hose does NOT tear away, close up, and stop circulation.

Heater hoses are small diameter hoses that carry coolant to the heater core (small radiator-like device under car dash). Refer to Fig. 35-8. Heaters are covered in Chapter 71.

Hose clamps hold the radiator and heater hoses on their fittings. Three types of hose clamps are pictured in Fig. 35-10.

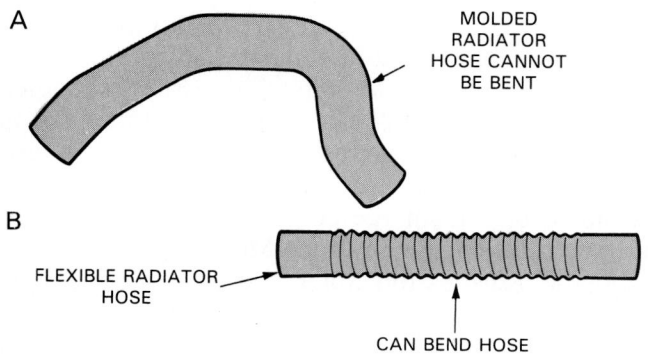

Fig. 35-9. Two basic types of radiator hoses: A — Molded hose only fits specific applications. B — Flexible hose can be used on several makes of cars if ends are correct diameter. (Chrysler)

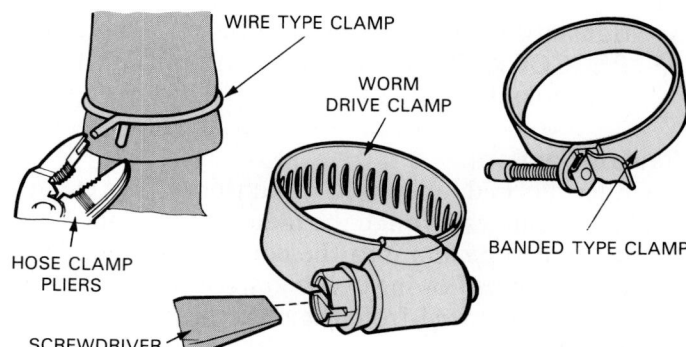

Fig. 35-10. Three basic types of hose clamps. Worm drive clamp is most common. Spring type requires hose clamp pliers with groove cut in jaws. (Mopar)

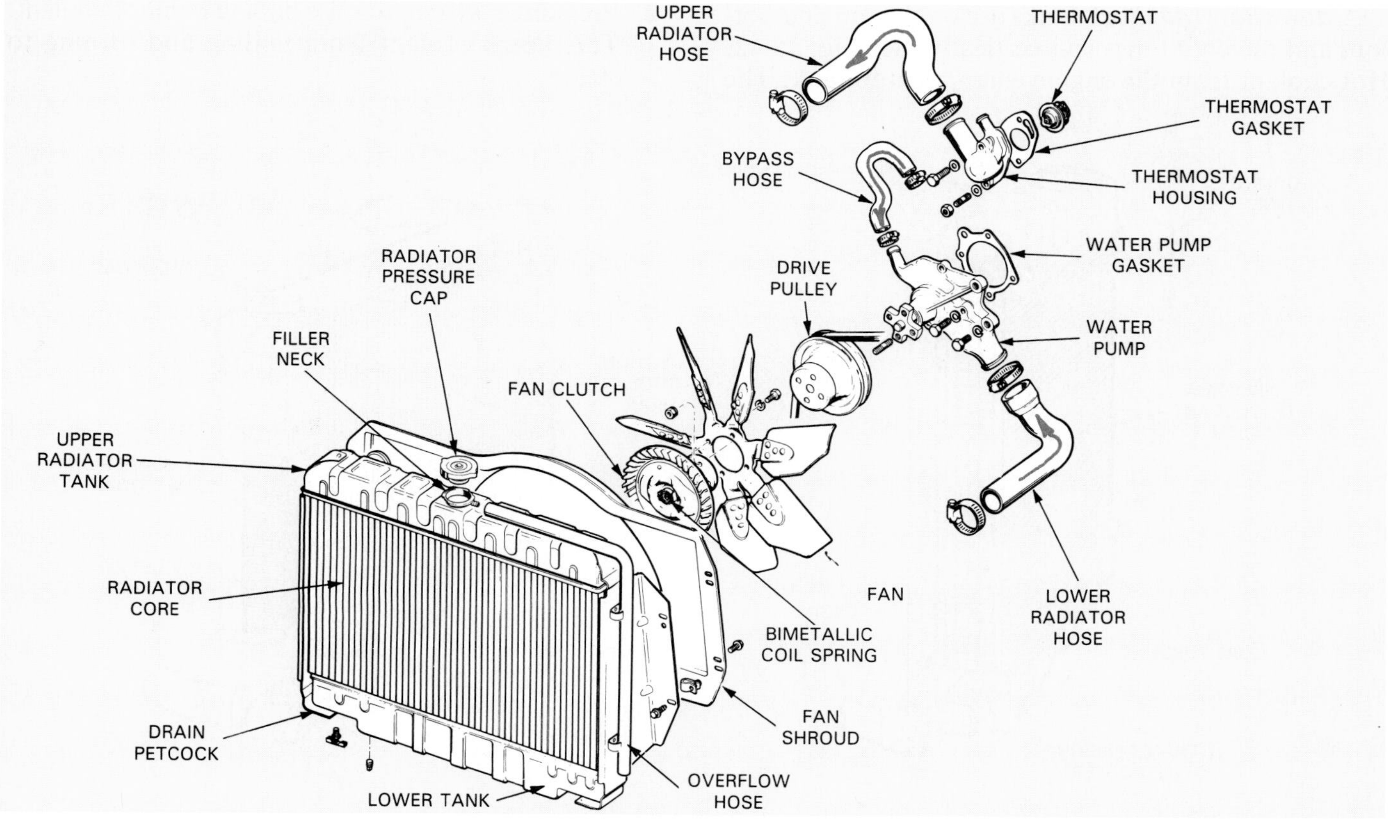

Fig. 35-11. Exploded view of major parts of cooling system. Study each component carefully! (Chrysler)

RADIATOR CONSTRUCTION

The *radiator* transfers coolant heat to the outside air. See Fig. 35-11. The radiator is normally mounted in front of the engine. Cool outside air can flow freely through it.

A radiator typically consists of:
1. CORE (center section of radiator made up of tubes and cooling fins).
2. TANKS (metal or plastic ends that fit over core tube ends to provide storage for coolant and fittings for hoses).
3. FILLER NECK (opening for adding coolant, also holds radiator cap and overflow tube).
4. OIL COOLER (inner tank for cooling automatic transmission or transaxle fluid).
5. PETCOCK (fitting on bottom of tank for draining coolant).

Radiator action

Under normal operating conditions, hot engine coolant circulates through the radiator tanks and core tubes. Heat transfers into the core's tubes and fins. Since cooler air is flowing over and through the radiator fins, heat is removed from the radiator. This reduces the temperature of the coolant before it flows back into the engine.

Radiator types

The two types of radiators are the crossflow and downflow. Both are shown in Fig. 35-12.

A *downflow radiator's* tanks are on the top and bottom and the core tubes run vertically. See Fig. 35-12. Hot coolant from the engine enters the top tank. The coolant flows downward through the core tubes. After cooling, coolant flows out the bottom tank and back into the engine.

A *crossflow radiator* is a more modern design that has its tanks on the sides of the core. The core tubes are arranged for horizontal coolant flow. Look at Fig. 35-12. The tank with the radiator cap is normally the outlet tank. A crossflow radiator can be shorter, allowing for a lower car hood.

Transmission oil cooler

A *transmission oil cooler* is often placed in the radiator on cars with automatic transmissions. It is a small tank enclosed in one of the main radiator tanks, Fig. 35-13. Since the transmission fluid is hotter than the engine coolant, heat is removed from the fluid as it passes through the radiator and cooler.

In downflow radiators, the transmission oil cooler is located in the lower tank. In crossflow radiators, it is in the tank having the radiator cap. Both tanks are cooler outlet tanks.

Line fittings from the cooler extend through the radiator tank to the outside. Metal lines from the automatic transmission connect to these fittings, Fig. 35-14. The transmission oil pump forces the fluid through the lines and cooler.

RADIATOR CAP

The *radiator cap* performs several functions:
1. Seals top of radiator filler neck to prevent leakage.
2. Pressurizes system to raise boiling point of coolant. This keeps coolant from boiling and turning to steam.

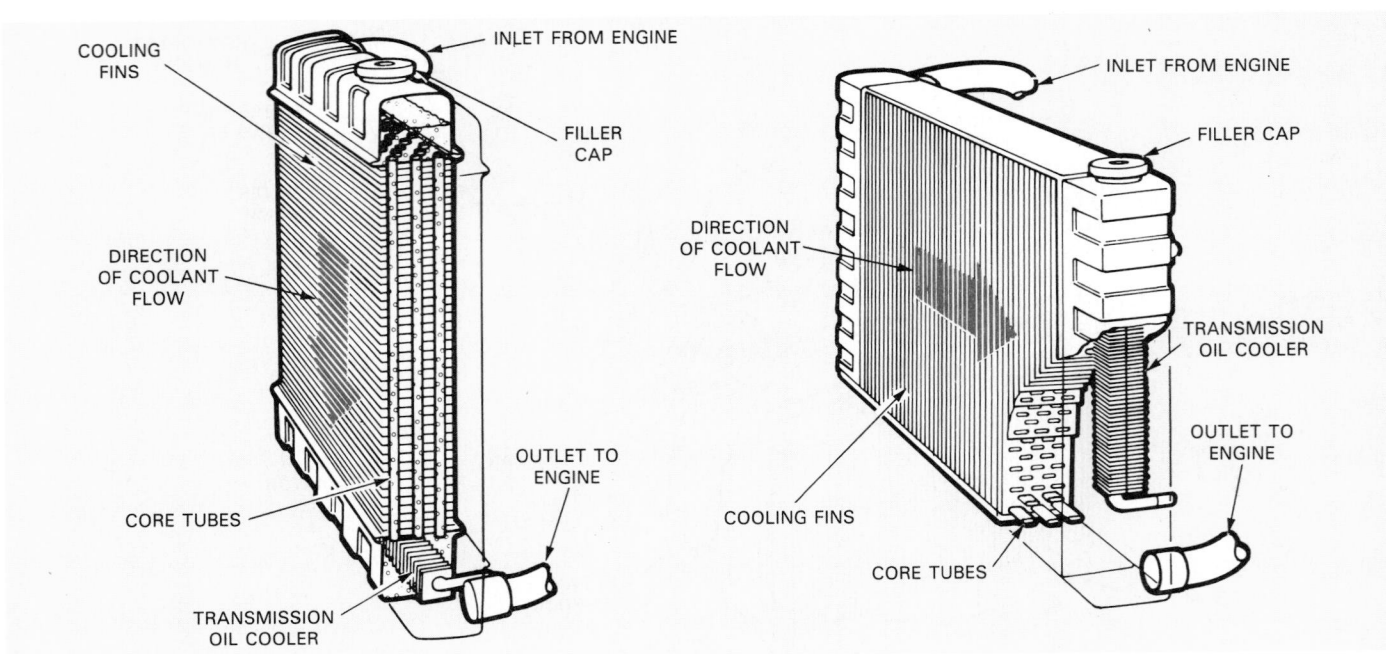

Fig. 35-12. Two types of radiators. Left. Downflow radiator has core tubes running up and down. Right. Crossflow radiator has cooling tubes running horizontally. Crossflow is more common on late model cars. (Chrysler Corp.)

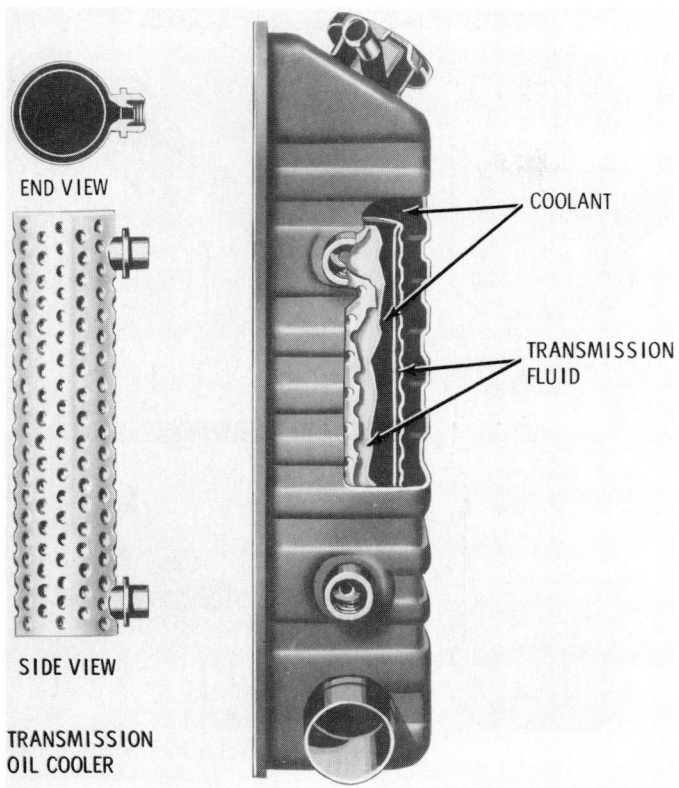

END VIEW

SIDE VIEW

TRANSMISSION
OIL COOLER

COOLANT

TRANSMISSION
FLUID

Fig. 35-13. Transmission oil cooler prevents overheating of automatic transmission fluid. It is small tank inside radiator tank. Note transmission line fittings. (Oldsmobile)

3. Relieves excess pressure to protect against system damage.
4. In a closed system, it allows coolant flow into and from coolant reservoir.

The radiator cap locks onto the radiator tank filler neck. Rubber or metal seals make the cap-to-neck joint airtight.

Radiator cap pressure valve

The *radiator cap pressure valve*, Fig. 35-15, consists of a spring-loaded disc that contacts the filler neck. The spring pushes the valve into the neck to form a seal.

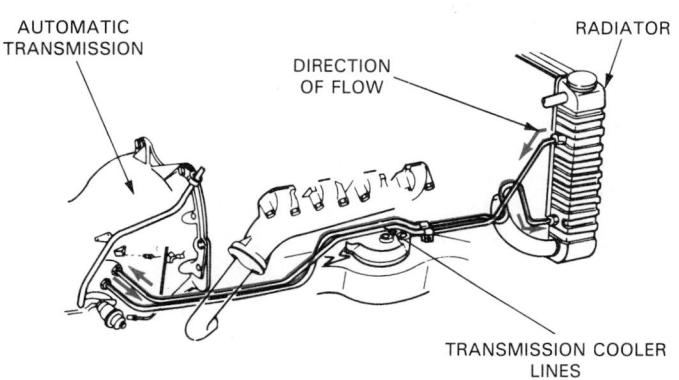

AUTOMATIC
TRANSMISSION

DIRECTION
OF FLOW

RADIATOR

TRANSMISSION COOLER
LINES

Fig. 35-14. Automatic transmission lines run from transmission to radiator oil cooler fittings. (Cadillac)

Under pressure, water's boiling point increases. Normally, water boils at 212°F (100°C). However, for every pound of pressure increase, the boiling point goes up about 3°F. The radiator cap works on this principle.

Typical *radiator cap pressure* is 12 to 16 psi (83 to 110 kPa). This raises the boiling point of the engine coolant to about 250 to 260°F (121 to 127°C). Many surfaces inside the water jackets can be above 212°F (100°C).

If the engine overheats and pressure exceeds the cap rating, the pressure valve opens. Excess pressure forces coolant out the overflow tube and into the reservoir or onto the ground. This prevents high pressure from rupturing the radiator, gaskets, seals, or hoses.

Radiator cap vacuum valve

The *radiator cap vacuum valve* opens to allow reverse flow back into the radiator when the coolant temperature drops after engine operation. Look at Fig. 35-16. It is a smaller valve located in the center, bottom of the cap.

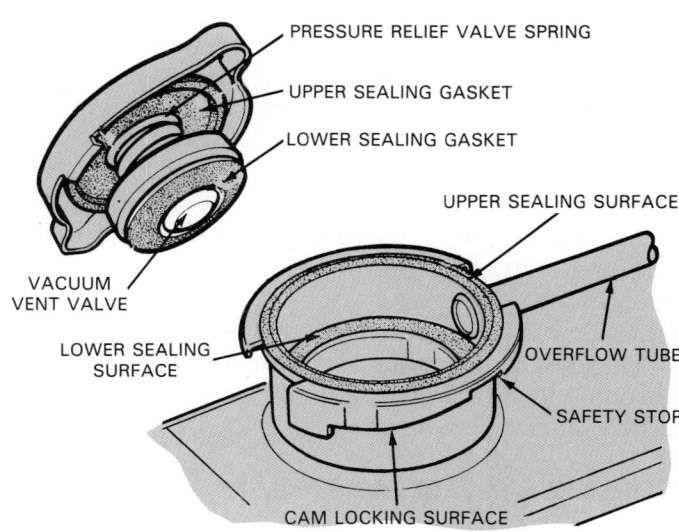

PRESSURE RELIEF VALVE SPRING

UPPER SEALING GASKET

LOWER SEALING GASKET

UPPER SEALING SURFACE

VACUUM
VENT VALVE

LOWER SEALING
SURFACE

OVERFLOW TUBE

SAFETY STOP

CAM LOCKING SURFACE

Fig. 35-15. Radiator pressure cap screws onto radiator filler neck. Rubber or metal seals prevent leakage. (Mopar)

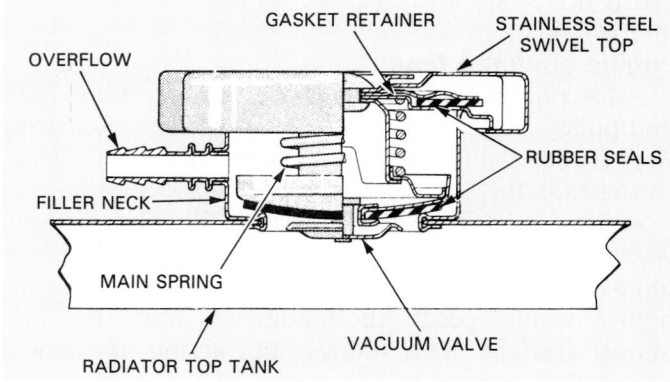

GASKET RETAINER

STAINLESS STEEL
SWIVEL TOP

OVERFLOW

RUBBER SEALS

FILLER NECK

MAIN SPRING

VACUUM VALVE

RADIATOR TOP TANK

Fig. 35-16. Cutaway view shows how pressure cap installs and seals on radiator filler neck. (Chrysler)

Cooling System Fundamentals **465**

The cooling and contraction of the coolant and air in the system could decrease coolant volume and pressure. Outside atmospheric pressure could then crush inward on the hoses and radiator. Without a cap vacuum or vent valve, the radiator hoses and radiator tanks could collapse.

CLOSED COOLING SYSTEM

A *closed cooling system* uses an expansion tank or reservoir and a special closed system radiator cap. The overflow tube is routed into the bottom of the reservoir tank. Pressure and vacuum valve action pull coolant in and out of the reservoir tank as needed. This keeps the cooling system correctly filled at all times.

Fig. 35-17 shows the operation of a closed cooling system. In A, the engine is heating up. The coolant has expanded and opened the cap pressure valve. Instead of leaking onto the ground, the coolant flows into the reservoir.

In B, the engine has been shut off. As the coolant temperature drops, its volume decreases. This causes the vacuum valve to open. Atmospheric pressure (system suction) can then force coolant back into the radiator. This will compensate for any small system leak, keeping the system properly filled.

OPEN COOLING SYSTEM

An *open cooling system* does NOT use a coolant reservoir. The overflow tube allows excess coolant to leak onto the ground. Also, it does not provide a means of adding fluid automatically as needed.

The open cooling system is no longer used on modern automobiles. It has been replaced by the closed system which requires less maintenance.

COOLING SYSTEM FANS

A *cooling system fan* pulls air through the core of the radiator and over the engine to help remove heat. It increases the volume of air flowing through the radiator, especially when the car is standing still. The fan is driven by a fan belt or an electric motor.

Engine powered fans

An *engine powered fan* bolts to the water pump hub and pulley. Refer to Fig. 35-18. Sometimes, a spacer fits between the fan and pulley to move the fan closer to the radiator.

A *flex fan* has thin, flexible blades that alter airflow with engine speed. At low speeds, the fan blades remain curved and pull air through the radiator. At higher engine speeds, the blades flex until they are almost straight. This reduces fan action and saves engine power, Fig. 35-18.

A *fluid coupling fan clutch* is designed to slip at higher engine speeds. It performs the same function

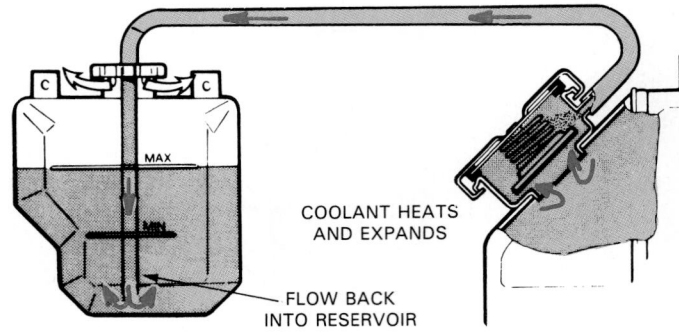

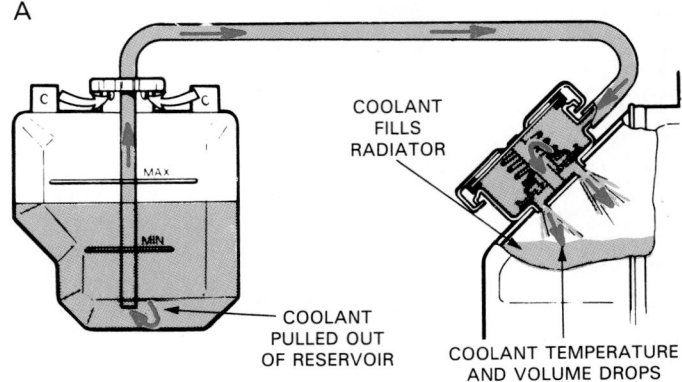

Fig. 35-17. Pressure cap operation: A — When engine heats up, coolant expands. Excess fluid opens cap pressure valve and coolant enters reservoir. B — When engine is shut off, coolant temperature drops. This causes coolant to reduce in volume. Cap vent valve opens to let coolant flow back into radiator. (Ford)

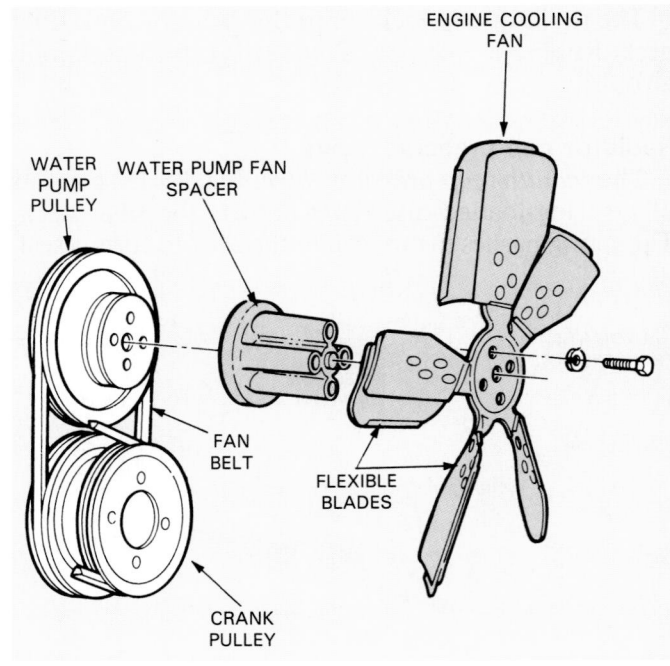

Fig. 35-18. Flex type radiator fan. High rpm causes fan blades to flex or bend and reduce blowing action. Note how spacer is used to move fan closer to radiator. (Ford)

as a flexible fan. The clutch is filled with silicone-based oil, Fig. 35-19. At a specific fan speed, there is enough load to make the clutch slip.

A *thermostatic fan clutch* has a temperature sensitive, bimetallic spring that controls fan action. See Fig. 35-20. The spring controls oil flow in the fan clutch. When cold, the spring causes the clutch to slip, speeding engine warmup. After reaching operating temperature, it locks the clutch, providing forced air circulation.

Electric engine fans

An *electric engine fan* uses an electric motor and a thermostatic switch to provide cooling action. Look at Fig. 35-21. An electric fan is needed on front-wheel drive cars having transverse (sideways) mounted

Fig. 35-21. Electric cooling fan uses battery or alternator current for power. DC motor spins metal or plastic fan blade. (Plymouth)

engines. The water pump is normally located away from the radiator.

The *fan motor* is a small, DC (direct current) motor. It mounts on a bracket secured to the radiator. A metal or plastic fan blade mounts on the end of the motor shaft.

The *fan switch* or *thermo switch* is a temperature sensitive switch that controls fan motor operation. When the engine is cold, the switch is open. This keeps the fan from spinning and speeds engine warmup. After warmup, the switch closes to operate the fan and provide cooling. This is illustrated in Fig. 35-22.

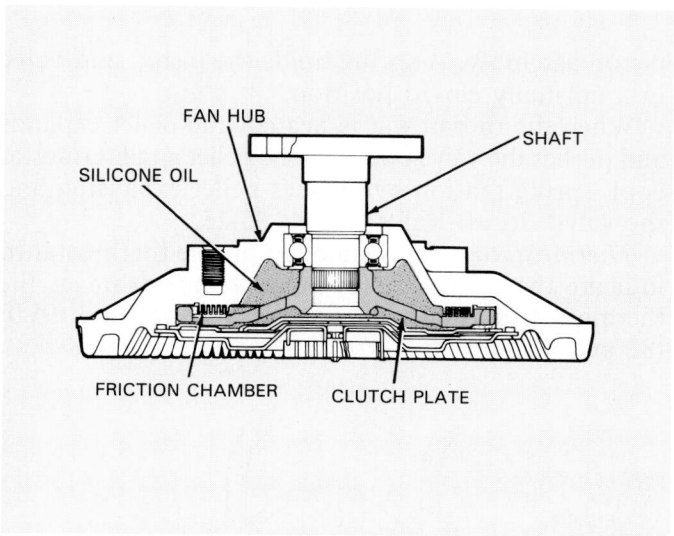

Fig. 35-19. Fluid coupling type fan clutch. Clutch plate operating in silicone-based oil causes enough friction at low speeds to turn fan. Load at high speeds overcomes friction and fan slips to save energy. (Chrysler)

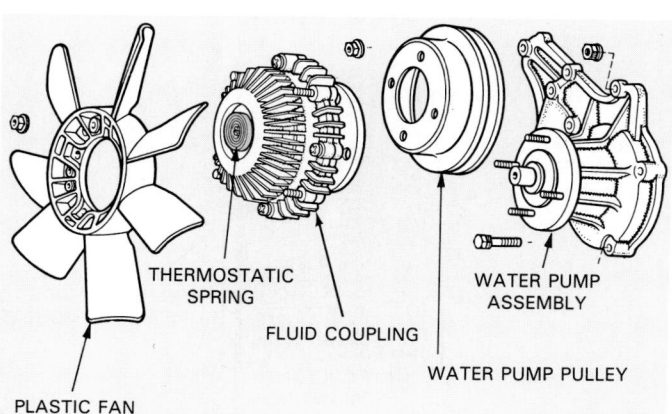

Fig. 35-20. Thermostatic fan clutch is similar to fluid coupling type clutch. Bimetal spring is used to control clutching action. Fan only operates when engine is hot and when spring activates clutch mechanism. (Toyota)

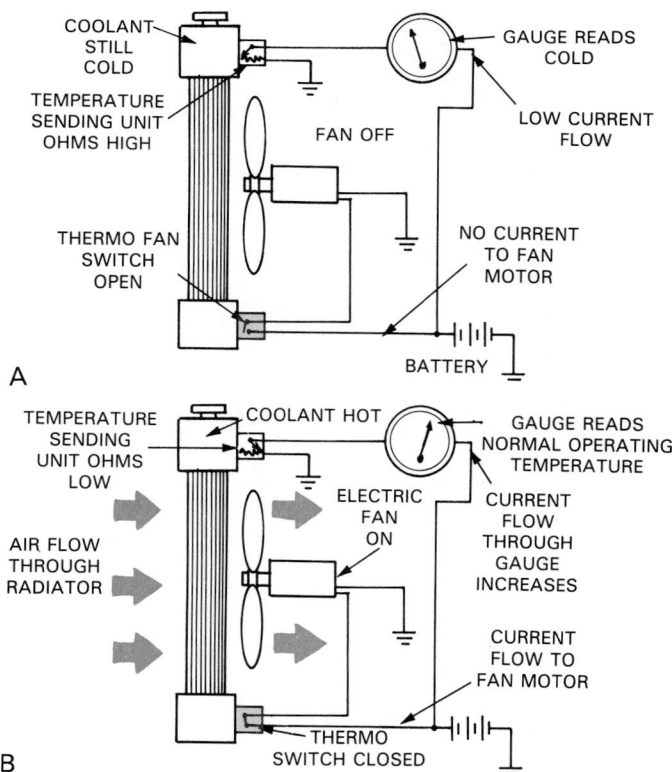

Fig. 35-22. Electric cooling fan operation. A — Engine is cold. Thermo-switch is open to prevent electric fan operation. This speeds engine warmup. B — Engine at full operating temperature. Thermo-switch closes. Current then flows to fan motor.

An electric engine fan saves energy and increases cooling system efficiency. It only functions when needed. By speeding engine warmup, it reduces emissions and fuel consumption. In cold weather, the electric fan may shut off at highway speeds. There may be enough cool air rushing through the car's grille to provide adequate cooling.

RADIATOR SHROUD

The *radiator shroud* helps assure that the fan pulls air through the radiator. See Fig. 35-23. It fastens to the rear of the radiator and surrounds the area around the fan.

When the fan is spinning, the plastic shroud keeps air from circulating between the back of the radiator and the front of the fan. As a result, a huge volume of air flows through the radiator core. Without a fan shroud, the engine could overheat.

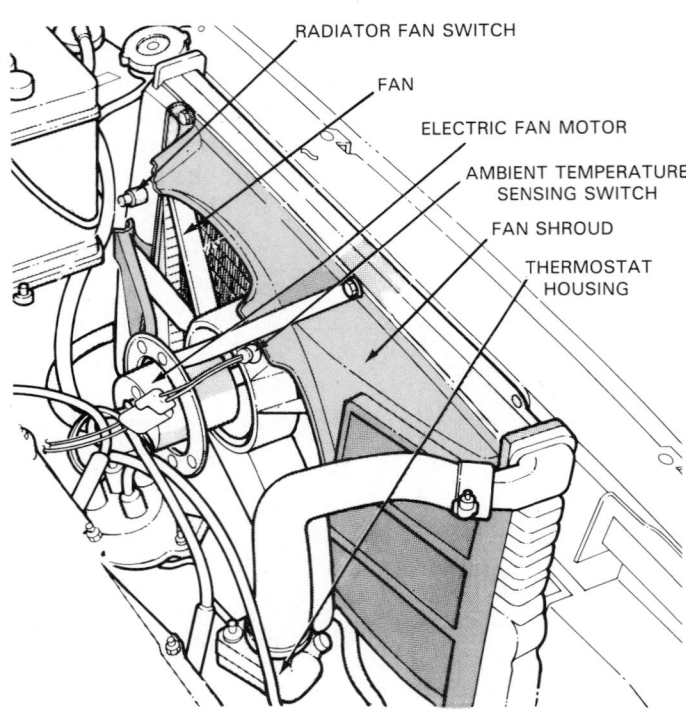

Fig. 35-23. Fan shroud assures that fan pulls air through radiator core. Without shroud, air could circulate between fan and back of radiator. Engine overheating could result. (Chrysler)

THERMOSTAT

The *thermostat* senses engine temperature and controls coolant flow through the radiator. It reduces coolant flow when the engine is cold and increases flow when the engine is hot. The thermostat normally fits under a thermostat housing between the engine and the end of the upper radiator hose.

The thermostat has a wax-filled pellet, as shown in Fig. 35-24. The pellet is contained in a cylinder and

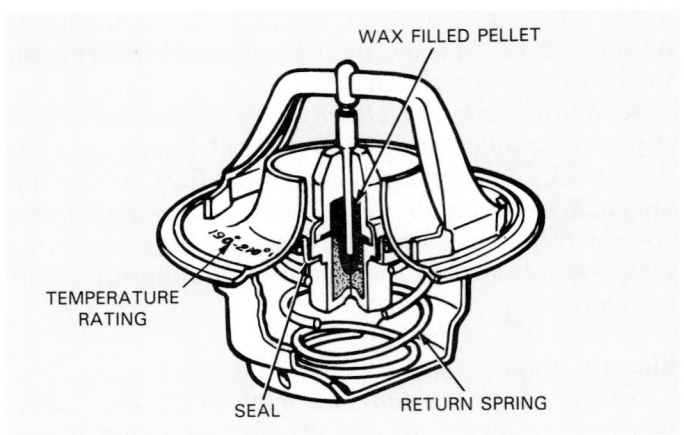

Fig. 35-24. Thermostat is temperature sensitive valve. Note pellet of wax enclosed in cylinder-piston chamber. When heated, pellet expands and pushes against spring tension. (Mopar)

piston assembly. A spring holds the piston and valve in a normally closed position.

When the thermostat is heated, the pellet expands and pushes the valve open. As the pellet and thermostat cool, spring tension overcomes pellet expansion and the valve closes. Refer to Fig. 35-25.

Thermostat rating is stamped on the thermostat to indicate the operating (opening) temperature of the thermostat. Normal ratings are between 180 and 195°F (82 and 91°C).

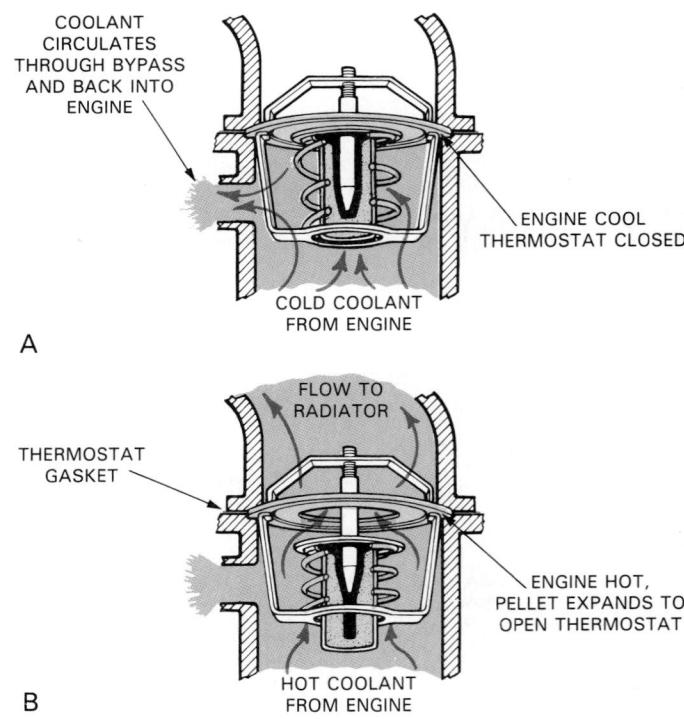

Fig. 35-25. Thermostat action. A — When coolant is cold, thermostat remains closed. Water pump forces coolant to circulate in engine, but not through radiator. B — When coolant is hot, thermostat opens. Pump can then push coolant through engine and radiator. (Chrysler)

High thermostat heat ranges are used in modern automobiles because they reduce exhaust emissions and increase combustion efficiency.

Thermostat operation

As thermostat operation is discussed, refer to Fig. 35-26. It shows thermostat action.

When the engine is cold, the thermostat will be closed and coolant cannot circulate through the radiator. Instead, the coolant circulates around inside the engine block, cylinder head, and intake manifold until the engine is warm.

As the heat range of the thermostat is reached, the hot engine coolant causes the pellet inside the thermostat to expand. The thermostat gradually opens and allows coolant to flow through the system.

Since the amount of thermostat opening is dependent upon engine temperature, the exact operating temperature of the engine can be precisely controlled.

A *bypass valve,* Fig. 35-27, or a *bypass hose* permits coolant circulation through the engine when the thermostat is closed. If the coolant could NOT circulate, hot spots could develop inside the engine.

TEMPERATURE WARNING LIGHT

A *temperature warning light* informs the driver when the engine is overheating, Fig. 35-28. When the

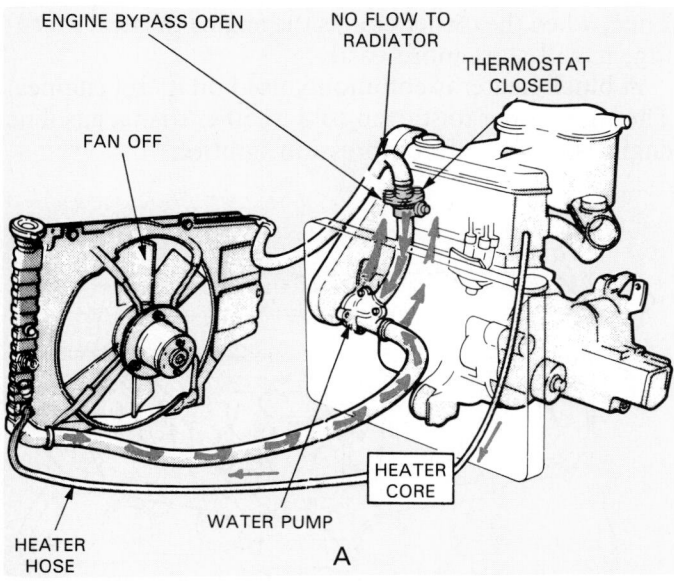

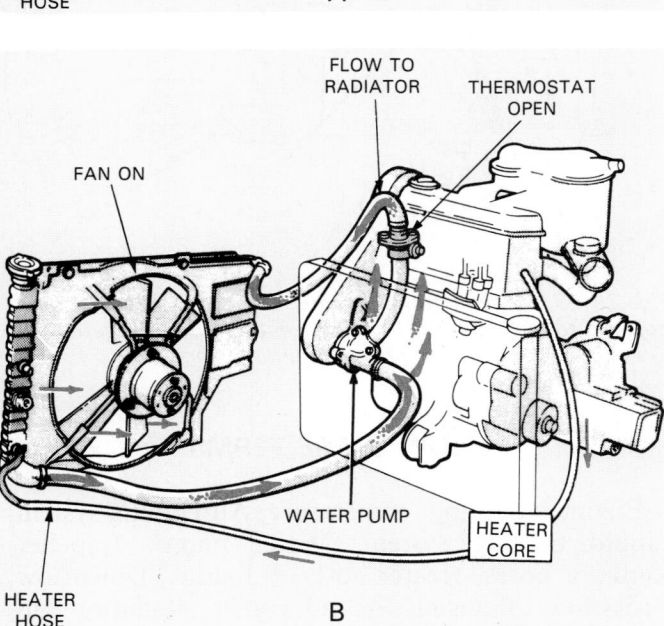

Fig. 35-26. A — Thermostat does not allow coolant to enter radiator when engine is below operating temperature. B — When at operating temperature, thermostat opens and allows flow into radiator. Thermostat moves open and closed different amounts to maintain correct temperature. (Dodge)

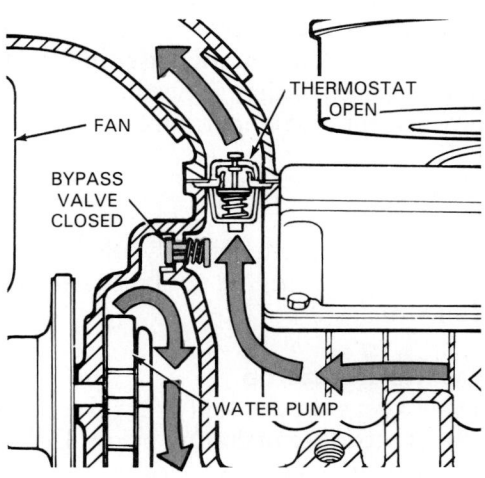

Fig. 35-27. Bypass valve is sometimes used to allow circulation in the engine. It only opens when thermostat is closed and when pressure is stronger than bypass valve spring.

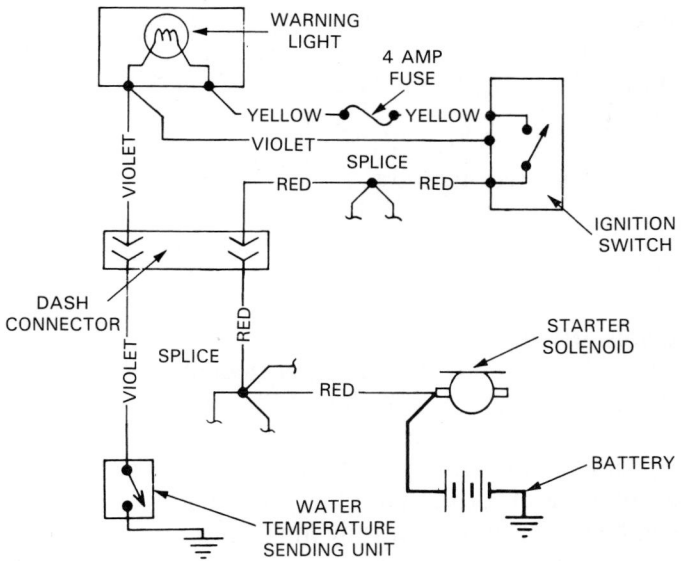

Fig. 35-28. Circuit diagram for an engine temperature warning light. Sending unit screws into engine water jacket. It closes when engine overheats to light indicator bulb. Ignition switch lights bulb when turned to start. This lets driver know bulb is not burned out. (Chrysler)

engine coolant becomes too hot, a temperature sending unit (switch) in the engine block closes. This completes the circuit and the dash indicating light glows.

When the engine is cold or at normal operating temperature, the sending unit circuit is open and the light remains OFF.

ENGINE TEMPERATURE GAUGE

An *engine temperature gauge* shows the exact operating temperature of the engine coolant. It is similar to the circuit in Fig. 35-28. However, a variable resistance sending unit and gauge are used in the circuit.

When the engine is cold, the gauge sending unit has high resistance and current does NOT flow to the gauge. The temperature gauge reads cold.

As engine temperature increases, the resistance in the sending unit drops. Current increases in the gauge circuit. Current causes the gauge needle to deflect to the right, showing engine temperature.

ANTIFREEZE

Antifreeze, usually ethylene glycol, is mixed with water to produce the engine coolant. Antifreeze has several functions.

Prevent winter freeze up

Antifreeze keeps the coolant from freezing in very cold weather (outside temperature below 32°F or 0°C).

Coolant freezing can cause serious cooling system or engine damage. As ice forms, it expands. This expansion can produce tons of force. The water pump housing, cylinder head, engine block, radiator, or other parts could be cracked and ruined.

Prevent rust and corrosion

Antifreeze also prevents rust and corrosion inside the cooling system. It provides a protective film on part surfaces.

Lubricates water pump

Antifreeze acts as a lubricant for the water pump. It increases the service life of the water pump bearings and seals.

Cools the engine

Antifreeze conducts heat better than plain water and, therefore, cools the engine better. It is normally recommended in hot weather.

For example, air conditioning increases the temperature of the air flowing through the radiator. Antifreeze can help prevent overheating in very hot weather when the air conditioning is on.

Antifreeze/water mixture

For ideal cooling and winter protection from freeze up, a 50/50 mixture of water and antifreeze is usually recommended. It will provide protection from ice formation to about -34°F (-36.7°C). Higher ratios of antifreeze may produce even lower freezing temperatures but this much protection is not normally needed.

NOTE! Plain water should NEVER be used in a cooling system or the four antifreeze functions just discussed will NOT be provided.

ENGINE BLOCK HEATER

A *block heater* may be used on an engine to aid engine starting in cold weather. It is simply a 120V heating element mounted in the block water jacket. Look at Fig. 35-29.

The heater power cord is plugged into a home wall outlet at night. This keeps the engine warm overnight. Then, when the owner cranks the engine the next morning, it will start more easily.

A block heater is commonly used on diesel engines. They are harder to start in cold weather than a gasoline engine because of compression ignition.

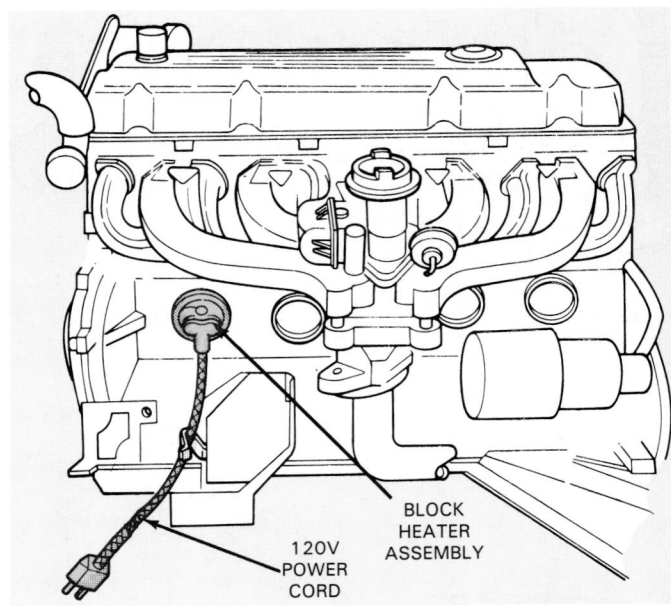

Fig. 35-29. Block heater plugs into home wall outlet. It heats coolant to aid starting in cold weather. Block heaters are common on diesel engines. (Chrysler)

KNOW THESE TERMS

Engine operating temperature, Air cooling system, Liquid cooling system, Water pump, Impeller, Radiator hoses, Heater hoses, Radiator, Downflow, Crossflow, Transmission oil cooler, Radiator cap, Pressure valve, Vacuum valve, Cap pressure rating, Closed system, Open system, Flex fan, Fluid coupling fan clutch, Thermostatic fan clutch, Electric engine fan, Shroud, Thermostat rating, Bypass valve, Antifreeze, Block heater.

REVIEW QUESTIONS

1. List and explain the five major parts of a cooling system.
2. What are the four functions of a cooling system?
3. Typically, an engine's operating temperature is between _____ and _____°F (_____ and _____°C).
4. Not using a thermostat in hot weather is acceptable because the engine would run cooler. True or False?
5. Why has the liquid cooling system replaced the air types?
6. List and explain the six major parts of a water pump.
7. Which of the following does NOT relate to radiator construction?
   a. Core.
   b. Petcock.
   c. Filler neck.
   d. Tanks.
   e. Impeller.
8. Explain the differences between downflow and crossflow radiators.
9. How does an automatic transmission oil cooler work?
10. Describe the four functions of a radiator cap.
11. Typical radiator cap pressure is _____ to _____ psi (_____ kPa), which raises the boiling point of the coolant to about _____ to _____°F (_____°C).
12. How do closed and open cooling systems differ?
13. A _____ _____ is commonly used to turn an electric engine cooling fan on and off.
14. Why is a radiator shroud used?
15. Summarize the operation of a cooling system thermostat.
16. A temperature _____ _____ (switch) on the engine is used to operate the temperature warning light.
17. List and explain four reasons why antifreeze should be used in the cooling system.
18. For ideal cooling, this mixture of water and antifreeze is typical.
   a. 30 percent water, 70 percent antifreeze.
   b. 50 percent water, 50 percent antifreeze.
   c. 80 percent antifreeze, 20 percent water.
   d. 70 percent water, 30 percent antifreeze.
19. Why could a block heater be helpful with a diesel engine?
20. Should plain water (no antifreeze) be used in a cooling system during warm weather? Why?

ACTIVITIES FOR CHAPTER 35

1. Using the information contained in the chart on most antifreeze containers, construct a line graph to show the relationship between water/antifreeze mixture and the low-temperature protection provided. (For example, the usual 50/50 mixture protects against freezing to temperatures as low as −34°F.)
2. Develop sketches to show how the expansion tank (coolant reservoir) functions in a closed cooling system. Make overhead transparencies from your sketches and use them to describe the expansion tank function to the class.

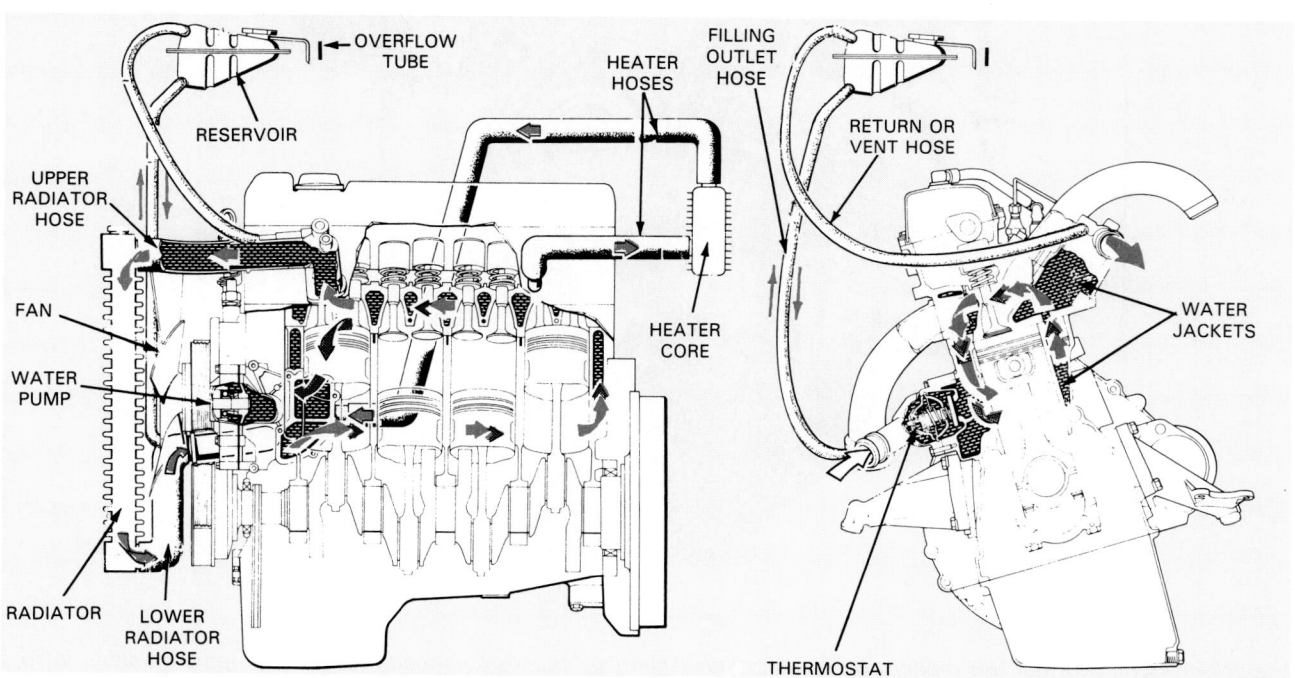

Can you explain the purpose of the major parts of a cooling system? If not, review the chapter! (Mercedes Benz)

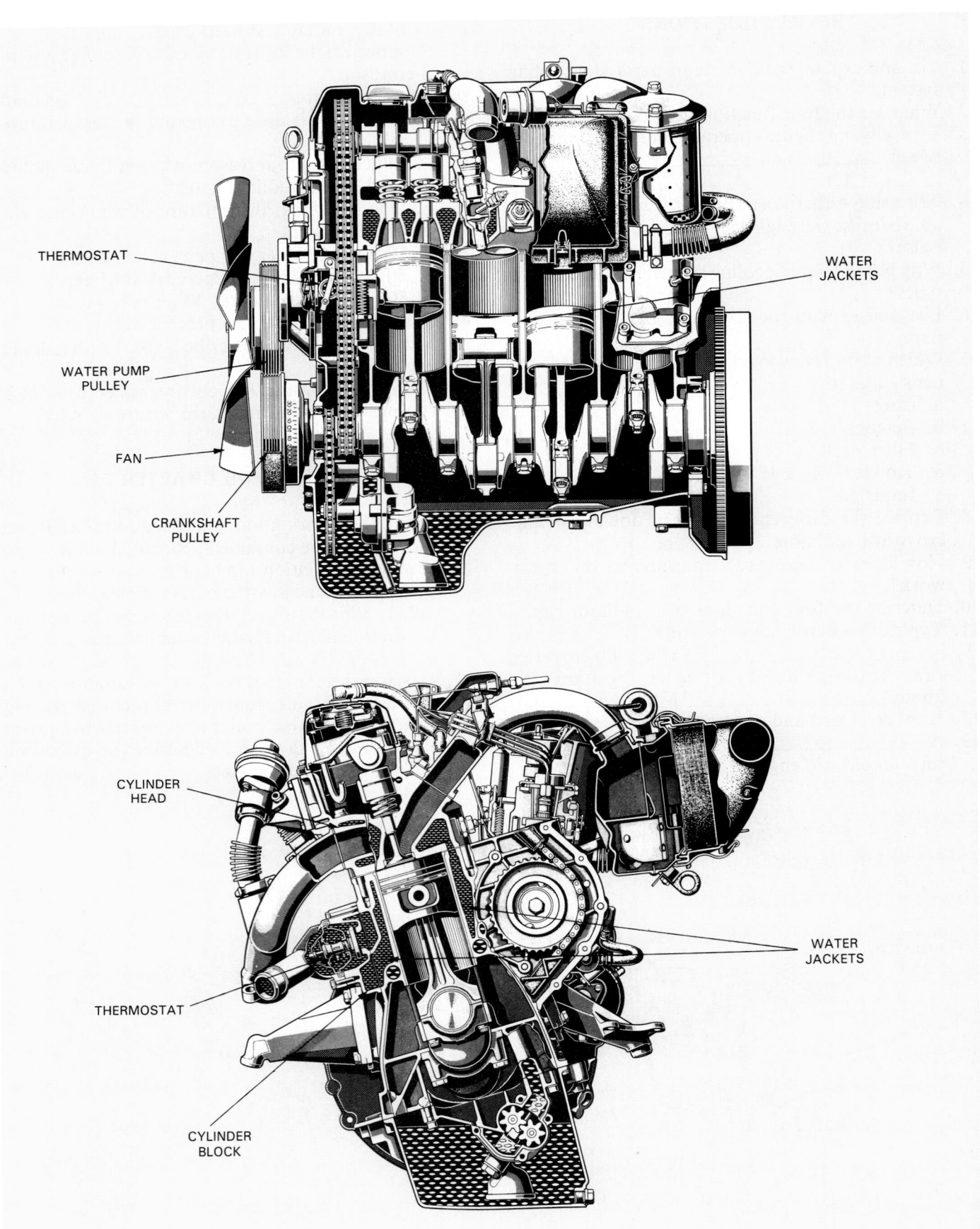

THERMOSTAT

WATER PUMP
PULLEY

FAN

CRANKSHAFT
PULLEY

WATER
JACKETS

CYLINDER
HEAD

THERMOSTAT

CYLINDER
BLOCK

WATER
JACKETS

Study side and front views of this modern four-cylinder diesel engine. It uses overhead camshaft to operate valves. Also, note cooling system water jackets in cylinder head and cylinder block. Thermostat is located at front, center of engine. Can you find it? (Mercedes Benz)

36

Cooling System Testing, Maintenance, Repair

After studying this chapter, you will be able to:
- □ List common cooling system problems and their symptoms.
- □ Describe the most common causes of system leakage, overheating, and overcooling.
- □ Perform a combustion leak test and a system pressure test.
- □ Check the major parts of a cooling system for proper operation.
- □ Replace faulty cooling system components.
- □ Drain, flush, and refill a cooling system with antifreeze.
- □ Describe safe working practices to use when testing, maintaining, or repairing a cooling system.

A cooling system is extremely important to the performance and service life of an engine. Major engine damage could occur in minutes without proper cooling.

Combustion heat could collect in the metal engine parts. The heat could melt pistons, crack or warp the cylinder head or block, cause valves to burn, or the head gasket to "blow." To prevent these costly problems, the cooling system must be kept in good condition.

As an auto service technician, you must be able to locate and correct cooling system problems quickly and accurately. It is equally important that you know how to maintain a cooling system. This chapter will help you develop these skills.

COOLING SYSTEM PROBLEM DIAGNOSIS

The first step toward diagnosing and locating cooling system problems involves gathering information. Talk to the car owner or service writer to find out as much as possible about the symptoms of the problem. For example, you might ask these questions:
1. Can you describe the cooling system problem (temperature light ON, overheating, coolant loss)?
2. When does the problem seem to occur (all the time, at highway speeds, when idling only)?
3. How long have you had the problem?
4. When was the last time the coolant was replaced (year, two years, never)?
5. Have any other repairs been performed (new thermostat, hoses, or engine repairs)?
6. Have you noticed any coolant leaks (puddles on ground, wetness around engine), or have you added coolant?
7. Are there any unusual noises that might relate to the cooling system (grinding at front of engine, hissing)?

The answers to these kinds of questions will be very useful. It will help you eliminate the least likely sources so that you can concentrate on the MOST PROBABLE CAUSES of the malfunction.

After gathering information, verify the complaint. Test drive the car. Inspect the engine compartment. Listen to engine noises. Do what is needed to make sure the symptoms have been properly described.

Inspecting cooling system

A visual inspection will frequently be enough to find the source of the cooling system problem. As shown in Fig. 36-1, look for obvious troubles:
1. Coolant leaks.
2. Loose or missing fan belts.
3. Low coolant level.
4. Abnormal water pump noises.
5. Leaves and debris covering outside of radiator.
6. Coolant in oil (oil looks milky).
7. Combustion leakage into coolant (air bubbles in coolant).

CAUTION! Keep your hands and tools away from a spinning engine fan. Wear eye protection and stand behind, not over, the spinning fan blade. Then, if tools are dropped into the fan or a fan blade breaks off, you are not likely to be hit and injured by flying parts.

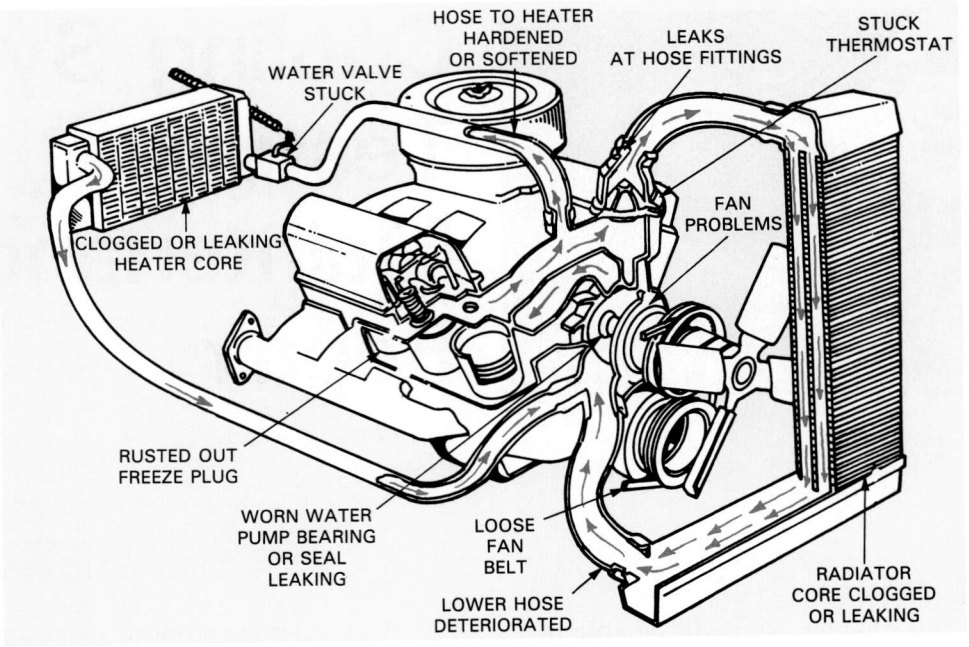

Fig. 36-1. These are common problem areas in a cooling system. Note leakage points.
(Florida Dept. of Voc. Ed.)

COOLING SYSTEM PROBLEMS

Cooling system problems can be grouped into three general categories:
1. COOLANT LEAKS (crack or rupture, allowing pressure cap action to push coolant out of system).
2. OVERHEATING (engine operating temperature too high, warning light on, temperature gauge shows hot, or coolant and steam blowing out overflow).
3. OVERCOOLING (engine fails to reach full operating temperature, engine performance poor or sluggish).

COOLANT LEAKS

Coolant leaks show up as a wet, discolored (darkened or rust colored) areas in the engine compartment or on the ground. The leaking fluid will smell like anti-freeze and have the same general color. Leaks can occur almost anywhere in the system, Fig. 36-1.

A low coolant level may indicate a leak. If not visible, the leak may be internal (cracked engine part, blown head gasket), as illustrated in Fig. 36-2.

Remember to check the coolant level in modern systems at the overflow or reservoir tank. Do NOT remove the radiator cap. Only on older, open systems (no reservoir), do you need to remove the pressure cap to check coolant level.

DANGER! Never remove a radiator cap when the engine is hot. The pressure release can make the coolant begin to boil and expand. Boiling coolant could spurt out of the filler neck — causing SEVERE BURNS!

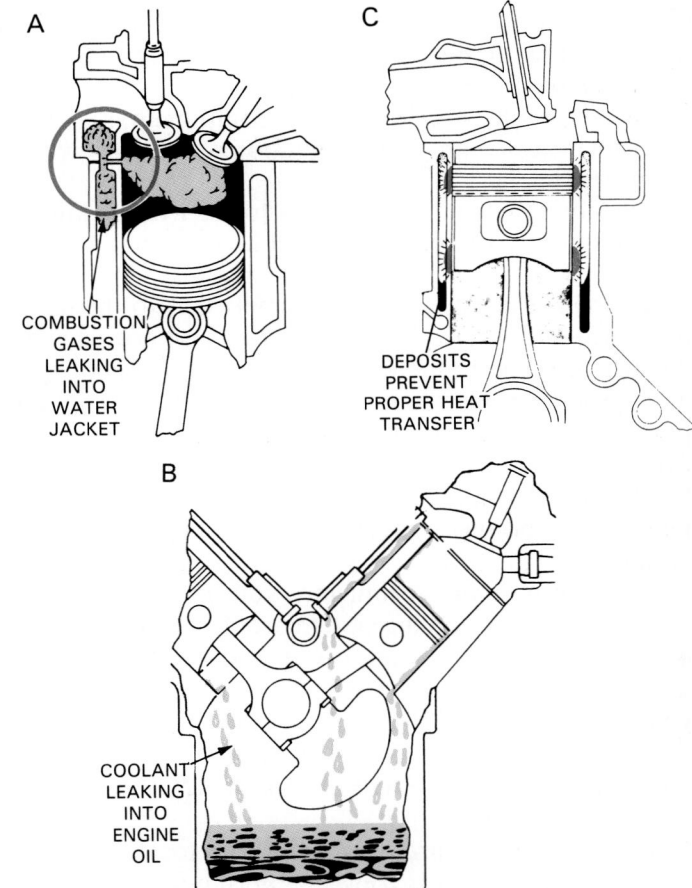

Fig. 36-2. Engine problems can affect cooling system. A — Blown head gasket allowing combustion gases to enter coolant. B — Cracked part or blown head gasket allowing coolant to leak into engine oil. C — Mineral deposits prevent proper heat transfer. Overheating can result. (Deere & Co.)

Engine overheating

Engine overheating is a serious problem that can cause major engine damage. The driver may notice the engine temperature light glowing, temperature gauge reading high, or the coolant boiling. Boiling coolant will expand and blow out through the overflow as steam.

Common causes of engine overheating are:
1. LOW COOLANT LEVEL (leak or lack of maintenance has allowed coolant level in engine and radiator to drop too low).
2. RUST OR SCALE (mineral accumulations in system have clogged radiator core or built up in water jackets, Fig. 36-2).
3. STUCK THERMOSTAT (thermostat fails to open normally, restricts coolant flow).
4. RETARDED IGNITION TIMING (late ignition timing allows combustion flame to blow out open exhaust valve, transferring too much heat into exhaust valves, ports, and manifold).
5. LOOSE FAN BELT (water pump drive belt slips under load and reduces coolant circulation).
6. BAD WATER PUMP (broken pump shaft or damaged impeller blades prevent normal pumping action).
7. COLLAPSED LOWER HOSE (suction from water pump may flatten hose if spring is missing or hose is badly deteriorated).
8. MISSING FAN SHROUD (air circulates between fan and back of radiator, reducing airflow through radiator).
9. ICE IN COOLANT (coolant frozen from lack of antifreeze can block circulation and cause overheating).
10. ENGINE FAN PROBLEMS (fan clutch or electric fan troubles can prevent adequate airflow through radiator).

Any of these, or other troubles, can make the engine overheat. You must use your knowledge of system operation and basic testing methods to find the problem's source. Methods for locating specific troubles will be covered later in this chapter.

Note! Some scanners (computer testers) will give temperature sensor readings. This might be helpful when trying to solve engine overheating and other related problems.

Overcooling

Overcooling may be indicated by slow engine warm up, insufficient warmth from the heater, low fuel economy, and sluggish engine performance.

Overcooling can cause increased part wear. Because parts are not at full operating temperature, their clearances will be too great. The parts will not expand enough to produce the correct fit.

Overcooling also reduces fuel economy because more combustion heat transfers into the metal parts of the engine. Less heat remains to produce expansion of gases and pressure on the pistons.

Overcooling may be caused by:
1. STUCK THERMOSTAT (thermostat stuck open, allowing too much circulation).
2. LOCKED FAN CLUTCH (fan operates all the time to cause excess airflow through radiator).
3. SHORTED FAN SWITCH (electric fan runs all the time, increasing warmup time).

COOLING SYSTEM PRESSURE TEST

A *cooling system pressure test* is used to quickly locate leaks. Low air pressure is forced into the system. This will cause coolant to pour or drip from any leak in the system.

A **pressure tester** is a hand-operated air pump used to pressurize the cooling system for leak detection. It is one of the most commonly used and important cooling system testing devices. Look at Fig. 36-3.

Install the pressure tester on the radiator filler neck. Then pump the tester until the pressure gauge reads radiator cap pressure (around 14 psi or 96 kPa).

CAUTION! Do not pump too much pressure into the cooling system or part (radiator, hose, or gasket) damage may result. Only equal radiator cap pressure when testing.

With pressure in the system, inspect all parts for coolant leakage. Check at all hose fittings, at gaskets, under the water pump, around the radiator, and at engine freeze (core) plugs. If a leak is found, tighten, repair, or replace parts as needed.

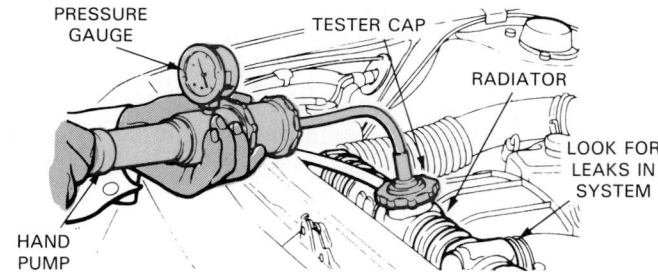

Fig. 36-3. Use pressure tester to pump cap-rated pressure into system. This will cause coolant to drip from any leak. (Toyota)

COMBUSTION LEAK TEST

A *combustion leak test* checks for the presence of combustion gases in the engine coolant. It should be performed when signs (overheating, bubbles in coolant, rise in coolant level upon starting) point to a blown head gasket, cracked block, or cracked cylinder head. Refer back to Fig. 36-2.

A block tester, sometimes called a combustion leak tester, is placed in the radiator filler neck. The engine is started and the tester bulb is squeezed and then

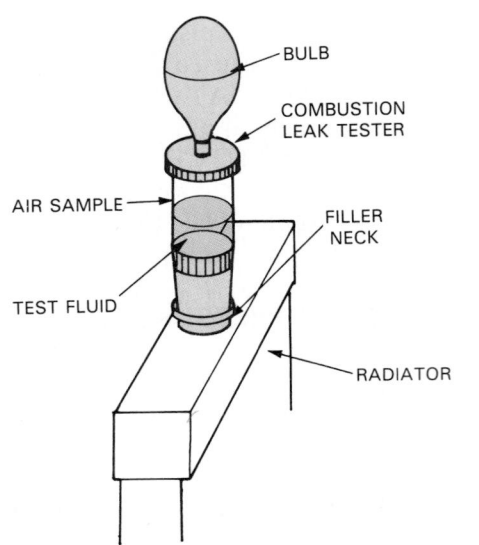

Fig. 36-4. Use bulb to draw radiator air sample into combustion leak tester. If test fluid turns yellow, engine problems are allowing combustion gas leakage into cooling system. Combustion leakage can make engine overheat.

released. This will pull air from the radiator through the test fluid, as in Fig. 36-4.

The fluid in the block tester is normally blue. The chemicals in exhaust gases cause a reaction in the test fluid, changing its color.

A combustion leak will turn the fluid YELLOW. If the fluid REMAINS BLUE, there is no combustion leakage.

If combustion leakage is indicated, short out spark plugs one at a time. Test the cooling system with each plug shorted. When the fluid does not change color, the cylinder being checked (shorted) has a combustion leak.

Combustion leakage into the cooling system is very damaging. Exhaust gases mix with the coolant and

form very corrosive acids. The acids can eat holes in the radiator and etch or corrode other components.

Fig. 36-5 shows how an exhaust gas analyzer will also check for combustion gases in the cooling system. Exhaust gas analyzer use is detailed in Chapter 40.

COOLANT IN OIL

When water, antifreeze, and oil mix, the solution turns milky white in color. See Fig. 36-2. If found in the engine oil or in valve covers, it is an indication of a coolant leak. The cause may be one of the same problems that create combustion leakage (blown head gasket, cracked head or block, or leaking intake manifold gasket on V-type engines).

It is possible to have both combustion leakage into the coolant and coolant leakage into the engine oil. Always correct an engine problem causing internal leakage.

Antifreeze, when mixed with engine oil, can cause engine damage. The antifreeze can collect on the cylinder walls where it burns, causing piston and cylinder gumming or scoring.

DIAGNOSIS CHARTS

A *cooling system diagnosis chart* should be used when problems are difficult to locate and correct. A service manual will give a chart for the particular type engine and cooling system. It will be very accurate and will help you decide what tests and repairs are needed.

WATER PUMP SERVICE

A *bad water pump* may leak coolant (worn seal), fail to circulate coolant (broken shaft or damaged impeller), or it may produce a grinding sound (faulty pump bearings).

Rust in the cooling system or lack of antifreeze are

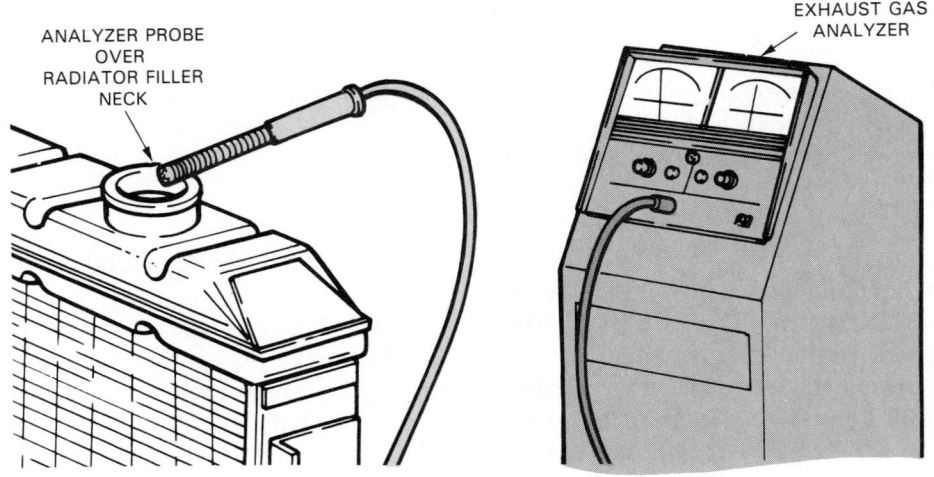

Fig. 36-5. An exhaust gas analyzer will also detect combustion pressure leakage into coolant. Place probe over filler neck and accelerate engine. HC or hydrocarbon reading indicates leakage. (Chrysler)

common reasons for pump failure. These conditions could speed seal, shaft, and bearing wear. An overtightened fan belt is another common cause for premature water pump failure.

Checking water pump

To check for a *bad water pump seal,* pressure test the system and watch for leakage at the pump. Coolant will leak out of the small drain hole at the bottom of the pump or at the end of the pump shaft. Replace or rebuild a leaking pump.

To check for *worn water pump bearings,* try to wiggle the fan or pump pulley up and down. Look at Fig. 36-6. If the pump shaft is loose in its housing, the pump bearings are badly worn. Pump replacement would usually be necessary. A stethoscope can also be used to listen for worn, noisy water pump bearings.

To check *water pump action,* warm the engine. Squeeze the top radiator hose while someone starts the engine. You should feel a pressure surge (hose swelling) if the pump is working. If not, pump shaft or impeller problems are indicated. You can also watch for coolant circulation in the radiator with the engine at operating temperature.

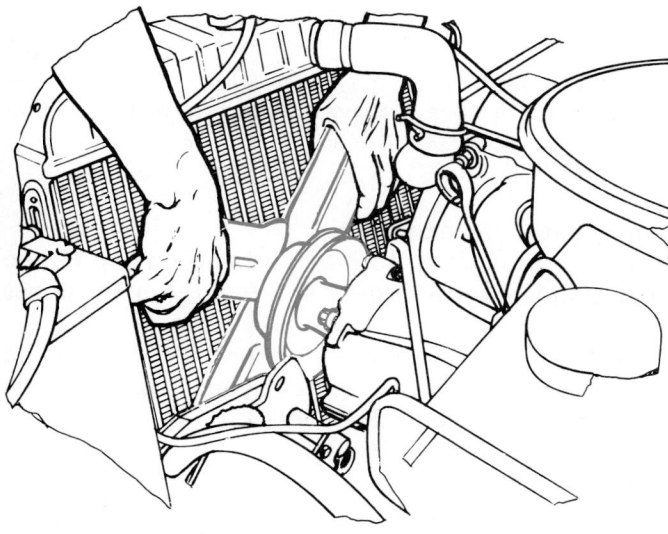

Fig. 36-6. Wiggle engine fan up and down to check for water pump bearing wear. Pump shaft should not wiggle. (Chrysler)

Removing a water pump

To remove the water pump, unbolt all brackets and other components (air conditioning compressor, power steering pump, alternator) preventing pump removal. Then, unscrew the bolts holding the pump to the engine. Keep all bolts organized to aid reassembly.

Scrape off old gasket or sealer material. The engine-to-pump mating surfaces must be perfectly clean to prevent coolant leakage. On soft aluminum parts, be careful not to gouge or scratch the sealing surfaces.

Installing water pump

To install a water pump gasket, use approved sealer to stick the new gasket to the pump. This will keep the gasket in alignment over the bolt holes during pump installation. Look at Fig. 36-7.

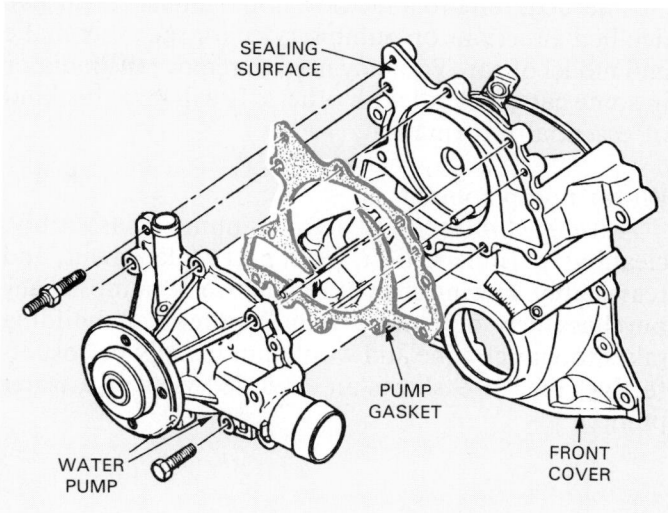

Fig. 36-7. Gasket is used to seal water pump-to-engine sealing surfaces. Make sure gasket is correct one and aligned. (Buick)

To use a chemical gasket (sealer used in place of fiber gasket), squeeze out a bead of approved (usually anaerobic) sealer around the pump sealing surface. Form a continuous bead of consistent width (about 1/8 in. or 3 mm). This is illustrated in Fig. 36-8.

Fit the pump onto the engine. Move it straight into place. Do not shift the gasket or break the sealant bead. Start all of the bolts BY HAND. Screw them in about

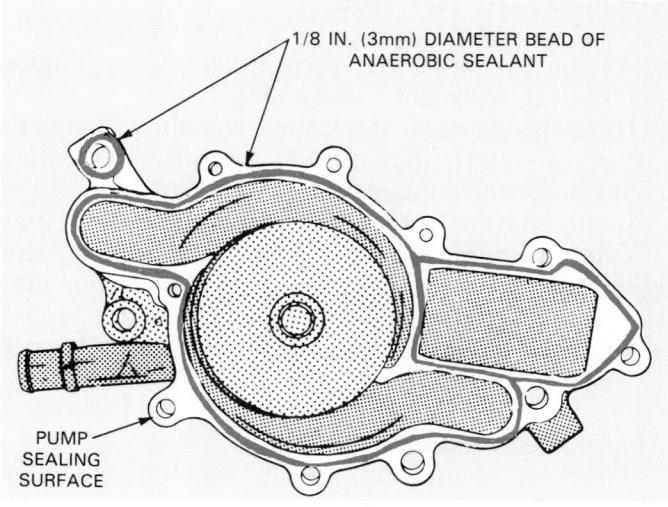

Fig. 36-8. Using sealer instead of water pump gasket. Form continuous bead and do not break bead when installing pump. (Buick)

two turns. Check that all bolt lengths are correct. Each bolt should be sticking out the same amount.

Torque all of the fasteners a little at a time in a crisscross pattern. Go over the bolts several times to assure correct tightening. Install the other components and tighten the belt properly.

If needed, refer to a factory shop manual. It will give detailed directions on pump service for the exact make and model of car. You may need to remove the radiator in some cars, but not with others. It will give this kind of essential information.

Water pump rebuild

A *water pump rebuild* involves pump disassembly, cleaning, part inspection, worn part replacement, and reassembly. Few mechanics rebuild water pumps. They purchase new or factory rebuilt pumps. Rebuilding takes too much time and would not usually be cost effective. Fig. 36-9 shows an exploded view of a water pump.

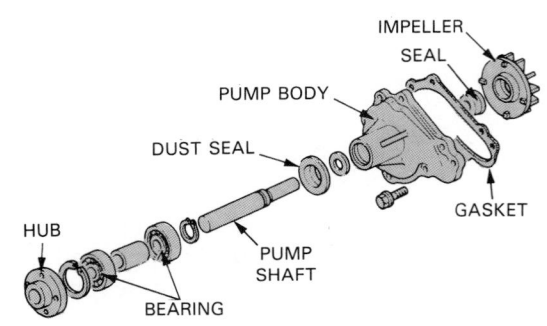

Fig. 36-9. Exploded view shows major parts of water pump. Pump rebuild typically involves replacing pump bearings, seals, shaft, and sometimes impeller. (Mazda)

THERMOSTAT SERVICE

A *stuck thermostat* can either cause engine overheating or engine overcooling.

If the thermostat is stuck shut, coolant will not circulate through the radiator. As a result, overheating could make the coolant boil.

If a thermostat is stuck open, too much coolant may circulate through the radiator. The engine may not reach proper operating temperature. The engine may run poorly for extended periods in cold weather. Engine efficiency (power, gas mileage, and driveability) will be reduced.

Thermostat testing

To check thermostat action, watch the coolant through the radiator neck. When the engine is cold, coolant should NOT flow through the radiator. When the engine warms, the thermostat should open. Coolant should then begin to circulate through the radiator. If

this action does not occur, the thermostat may be defective.

In some instances, the thermostat may have to be removed from the engine for testing on a hot plate in a container of water. The thermostat should open when heated to its operating temperature. Note that a digital thermometer can also be used to check the operating temperature of an engine and thermostat. Simply touch the tester probe on the engine next to the thermostat housing and note its reading. If the thermostat does NOT open at the correct temperature, it is defective and should be replaced, Fig. 36-10.

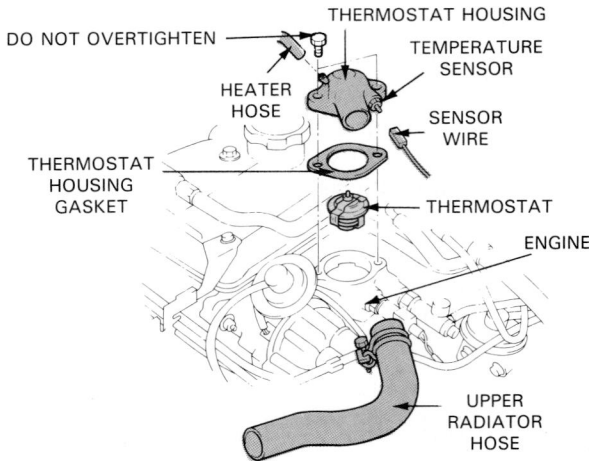

Fig. 36-10. Thermostat is normally in housing at engine end of upper radiator hose. Remove housing bolts and pop out the old thermostat. (Toyota)

Thermostat replacement

The thermostat is normally located on top of the engine under the *thermostat housing* (fitting for upper radiator hose).

To remove the thermostat, unscrew the bolts holding the thermostat housing to the engine. Tap the housing free with a rubber hammer. Lift off the housing and thermostat, Fig. 36-11A.

Scrape all of the old gasket material off the thermostat housing and the sealing surface on the engine. See Fig. 36-11B.

Make sure the thermostat housing is not warped. Place it on a flat surface and check for gaps between the housing and surface. If warped, file the surface flat. This will prevent coolant leakage.

Make sure the temperature rating is correct. Then place the new thermostat into the engine, Fig. 36-11C. Normally, the rod (pointed end) on the thermostat should face the radiator hose. The pellet chamber should face the inside of the engine.

Position the new gasket with approved sealer. Start the fasteners by hand. Then torque them to specs in a crisscross pattern. Do NOT overtighten the thermostat housing bolts or warpage may result. Most housings are made of soft aluminum or "pot metal."

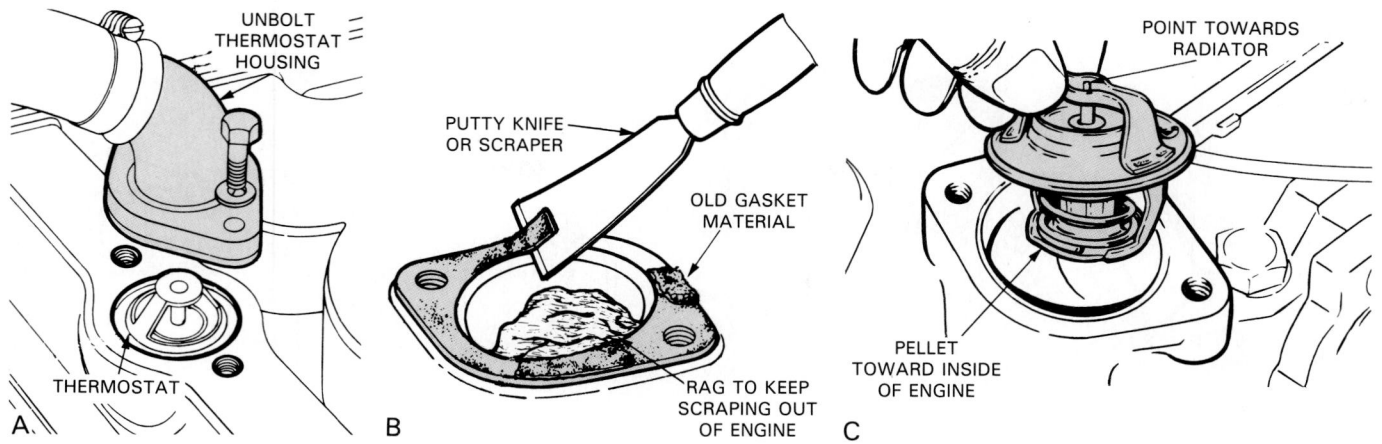

Fig. 36-11. A — Thermostat is removed by unbolting thermostat housing. B — Scrape off all old gasket or sealer from engine and thermostat housing. C — Install thermostat with pellet towards inside of engine. (Mopar and Ford)

COOLING SYSTEM HOSE SERVICE

Old radiator hoses and *heater hoses* are frequent causes of cooling system problems. After a few years of use, hoses deteriorate. They may become soft and mushy, or hard and brittle. Cooling system pressure can rupture the hoses and result in coolant loss.

A softened lower radiator hose can be collapsed by the suction of the water pump. The collapsed hose will restrict coolant circulation and cause overheating. The spring inside the lower radiator hose normally prevents hose collapse and it should never be removed.

Checking cooling system hoses

Inspect the radiator and heater hoses for cracks, bulges, cuts, or any other sign of deterioration or damage. Look at Fig. 36-12.

SQUEEZE the hoses to check whether they are hardened or softened and faulty. Flex or bend the heater hoses and watch for surface cracks. If any problem is detected, the affected hoses should be replaced.

Hose replacement

To remove a hose, loosen the hose clamps. Twist the hose while pulling it, Fig. 36-13A. If a new hose is to be installed, you may cut a slit in the end of the old hose to aid removal.

Clean the metal hose fittings. Coat them with a nonhardening sealer, Fig. 36-13B. Install the new hose.

Position the hose clamps so that they are fully over the metal hose fitting, Fig. 36-13C. Then, tighten the clamps.

Install coolant and pressure test the system. Check all fittings for leaks.

RADIATOR AND PRESSURE CAP SERVICE

When overheating problems occur and the system is NOT leaking, check the radiator and the pressure

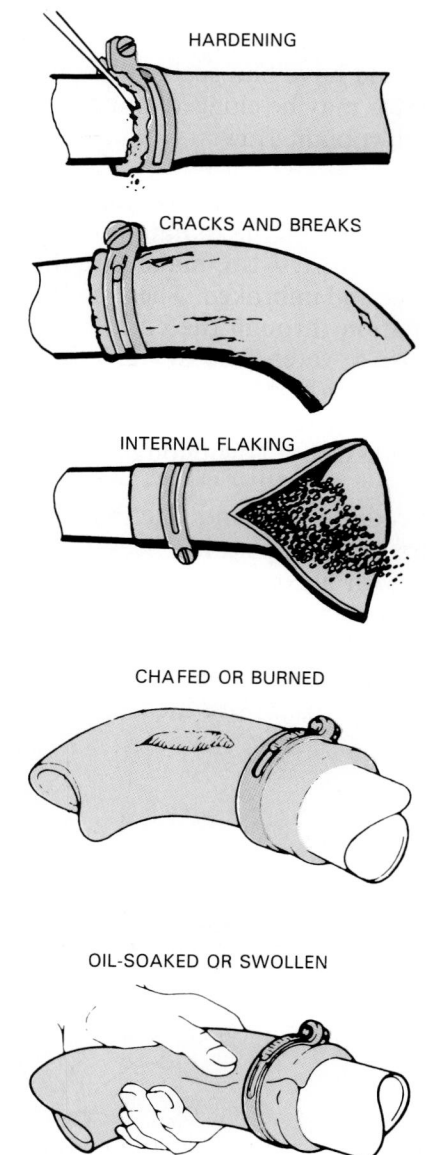

Fig. 36-12. Check cooling system hoses for these kinds of problems. (Gates Rubber Co. and Ford)

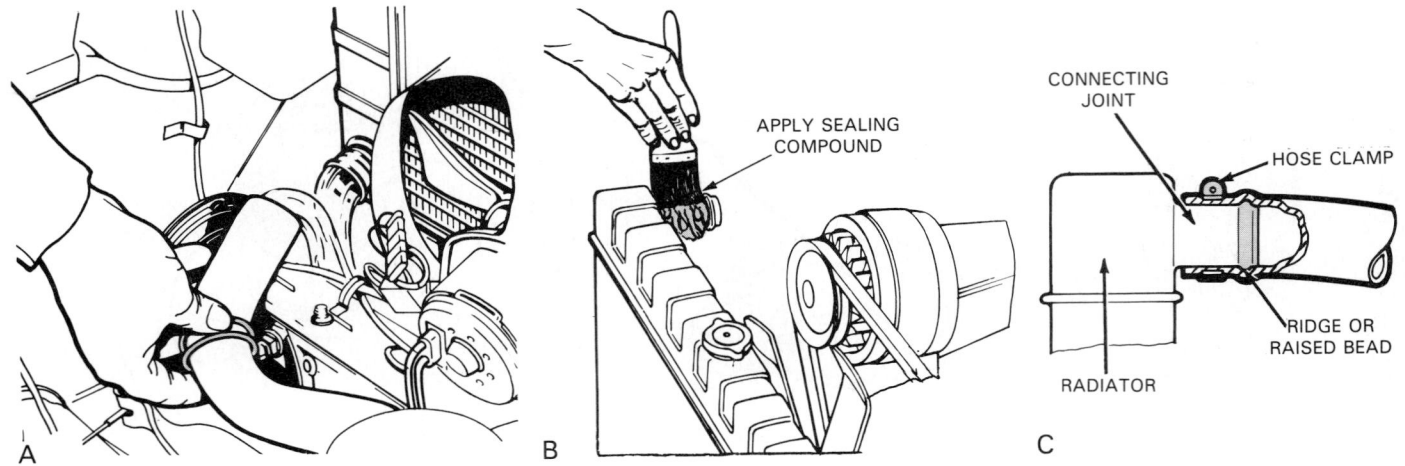

Fig. 36-13. Hose replacement. A — Loosen hose clamp. Twist and pull hose off fitting. B — Clean fitting and coat with nonhardening sealer. C — Slide on new hose and clamp. Make sure clamp is positioned inside bead on fitting. Tighten clamp. (Ford and Mopar)

cap. They are common sources of overheating. The pressure cap could have bad seals, allowing pressure loss. The radiator may be clogged and not permitting adequate air or coolant flow.

Inspecting radiator and pressure cap

Inspect the outside of the radiator for debris such as leaves and road dirt. Also, make sure the radiator shroud is in place and unbroken. These problems could limit air circulation through the core.

If needed, use a water hose to wash debris out of the core. Spray water from the back to push debris out of the front of the radiator. You may also use compressed air if pressure is low enough not to damage the core.

Inspect the radiator cap and filler neck. Check for cracks or tears in the cap seal. Check the filler neck sealing surfaces for nicks or dents. Replace the cap or have the neck repaired as needed.

Pressure testing radiator cap

A *radiator cap pressure test* measures cap opening

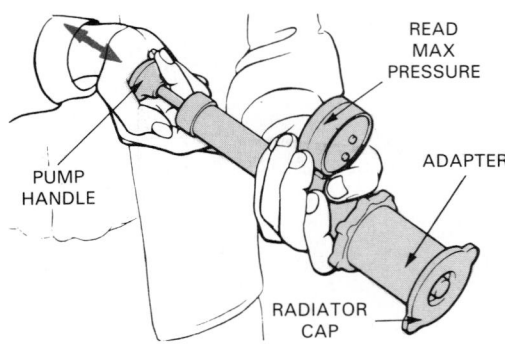

Fig. 36-14. A pressure tester can be used to check opening value of radiator cap. It should open within specs and hold pressure without leaking. (Toyota)

pressure and checks the condition of the sealing washer. The cap is installed on a cooling system pressure tester, as pictured in Fig. 36-14.

Pump the tester to pressurize the cap. Watch the pressure gauge. The cap should release air at its rated pressure (pressure stamped on cap). It should also hold that pressure for at least one minute. If not, install a new cap.

Radiator repair

A *radiator shop* specializes in radiator repair. It has the facilities to properly disassemble, rod out (clean), solder (reassemble or repair), and pressure test a radiator. Few mechanics try to fix a radiator in-shop.

A radiator shop can solder pinhole leaks. It has special cleaning tanks for loosening and removing scale built up inside the radiator. A radiator shop can also remove the tanks and solder in a new core, if needed.

FAN BELT SERVICE

A *loose fan belt* will slip and may rotate the water pump and fan too slowly. The engine may overheat. Always inspect the condition and tension (tightness) of fan belts when servicing a cooling system. If a fan belt is cracked, frayed, glazed (hard, shiny surface), or oil soaked, it should be replaced.

Note! Belt service was covered in Chapter 31, Charging System Diagnosis, Testing, and Repair.

DANGER! Keep your hands away from a moving engine belt. The belt can pull your fingers into the pulleys, causing severe hand injuries.

ENGINE FAN SERVICE

A *faulty engine fan* can cause overheating, overcooling, vibration, and water pump wear, or damage. Always check the fan for bent blades, cracks, and other problems. Flexible fans are especially prone to these problems. If any troubles are found, replace the fan.

DANGER! A fan with cracked or bent blades is extremely dangerous. Broken blades can be thrown out with great force, causing severe lacerations or death!

Testing a fan clutch

To test a thermostatic fan clutch, start the engine. The fan should slip when cold. When the engine warms, the clutch should engage. Air should begin to flow through the radiator and over the engine. You will be able to hear and feel the air movement when the fan clutch locks up.

If the fan clutch is locked all the time (cold and hot), it is defective and must be replaced. Excessive play or oil leakage also indicates fan clutch failure.

Electric cooling fan service

Most electric cooling fans are controlled by a heat sensitive switch located somewhere in the cooling system (radiator, engine block, thermostat housing). When the engine is cold, the switch keeps the electric fan motor OFF to speed engine warmup. Then, when a predetermined temperature is reached, the switch closes and the fan begins to cool the engine.

Testing an electric cooling fan

To test an electric cooling fan, observe whether the fan turns ON when the engine is warm. Make sure the fan motor is spinning at a NORMAL SPEED and is forcing enough air through the radiator.

If the fan does NOT function, check the fuse, electrical connections, and supply voltage to the motor. Refer to Fig. 36-15.

If the fan motor fails to operate with voltage applied, the motor should be replaced.

If the engine is warm and no voltage is supplied to the fan motor, check the action of the fan switch. Use either a voltmeter or test light. The switch should have almost zero resistance (pass current and voltage) when engine is warm. Resistance should be infinite (stop current and voltage) when the engine is cold.

If these tests do not locate the trouble, refer to a factory service manual for instructions. There may be a defective relay, connection, or other problem.

FREEZE PLUG SERVICE

A *leaking engine freeze plug* (core plug) is a frequent cause of coolant loss and overheating. Since the engine plugs are thinner than the metal in the engine block or head, they will RUST through before the other parts of the engine.

Replacing freeze plugs

To replace a freeze plug, drive a drift or large screwdriver (full shank type) through the plug, Fig. 36-16A. Pry sideways, without scraping the engine

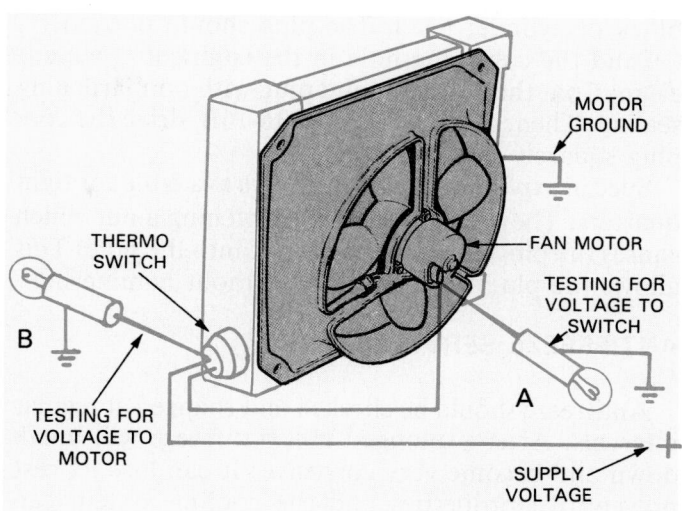

Fig. 36-15. Testing electric fan circuit. A — Check for power to fan with engine warm. Light should glow. B — With no power to fan, check action of fan switch. Switch should be open when cold and closed when hot. (Honda)

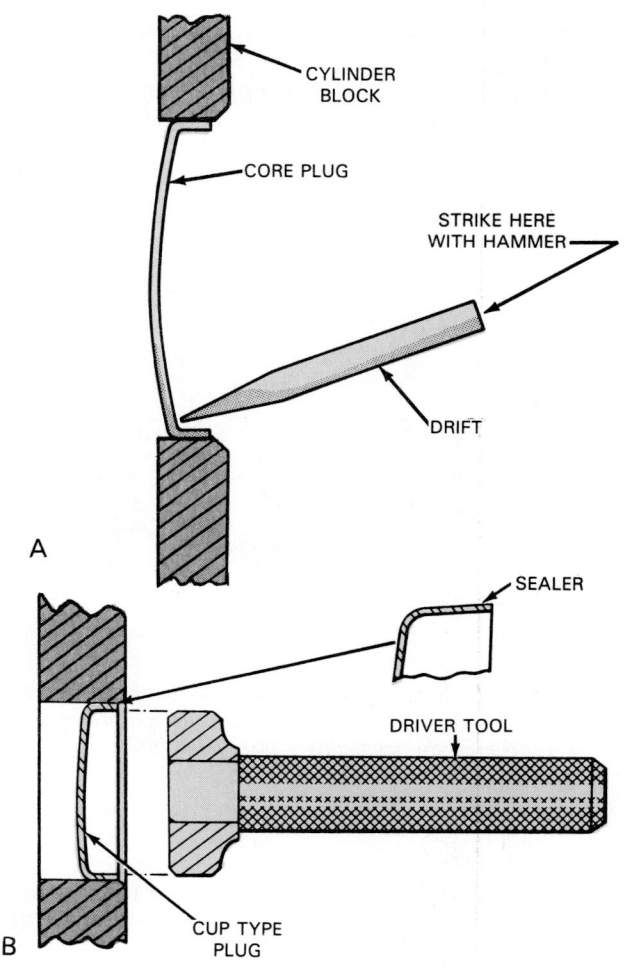

Fig. 36-16. Freeze or core plug replacement. A — Drive drift or full shank screwdriver through old plug. Pry out. B — After cleaning and coating hole with sealer, drive new freeze plug into place. Drive plug in squarely and to proper depth. (Ford Motor Co.)

block or cylinder head. The plug should pop out.

Sand the core plug hole in the engine and wipe it clean. Coat the plug hole and plug with nonhardening sealing. Then, as shown in Fig. 36-16B, drive the core plug squarely into position.

Special *expansion freeze plugs* are available for tight quarters. They are installed by tightening a nut which causes the plug to expand and lock into the hole. This allows the plug to be installed without hammering.

ANTIFREEZE SERVICE

Antifreeze should be checked and changed at regular intervals. After prolonged use, antifreeze will break down and become very corrosive. It can lose its rust preventitive properties and the cooling system can rapidly fill with rust.

Inspecting antifreeze

A visual inspection of the antifreeze will help determine its condition. Rub your finger inside the radiator filler neck, as in Fig. 36-17. Check for rust, oil (internal engine leak), scale, or transmission fluid (leaking oil cooler). Also, find out how long the antifreeze solution has been in service.

If contaminated or too old, replace the antifreeze. If badly rusted, you may also need to flush (clean) the system, as described shortly.

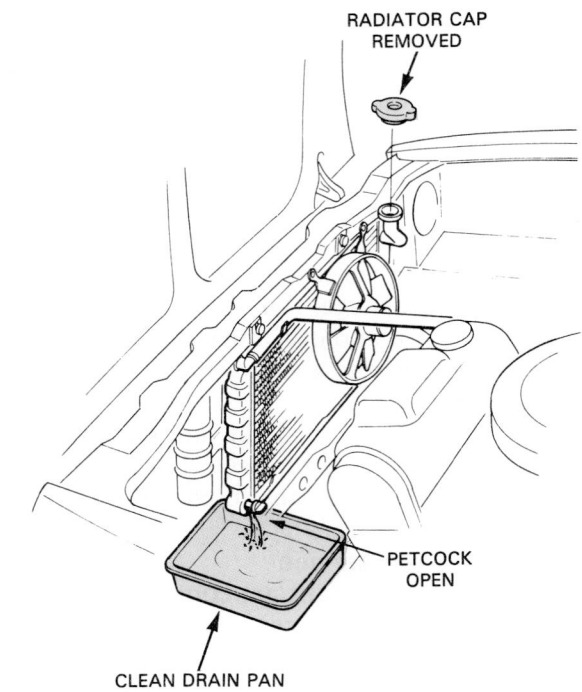

Fig. 36-18. To drain coolant, remove radiator cap. Place pan under drain fitting. Then, turn petcock correct direction. Many have left-hand threads and must be turned clockwise for opening. (Honda)

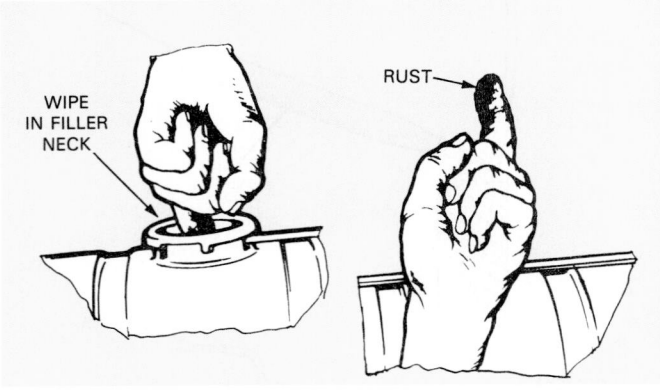

Fig. 36-17. To check for antifreeze contamination, wipe finger inside filler neck. Badly rusted coolant would require replacement of antifreeze and possibly system flushing. (Chrysler)

Changing antifreeze

Antifreeze should be changed when contaminated or when two years old. Check in a service manual for exact change schedules.

With the pressure cap removed, loosen the petcock on the bottom of the radiator. Allow the old coolant to drain into a pan, Fig. 36-18.

If the antifreeze is not contaminated with rust, you may then refill the system. Tighten the petcock. Pour in the needed amount (about two gallons or 7.6 liters) of antifreeze.

Start and warm the engine. The coolant level may drop when the thermostat opens. Add more coolant, if needed. Then install the radiator cap.

Fig. 36-19 shows how to tell when the cooling system is full. Note the difference between checking closed and open cooling systems.

Testing antifreeze strength

Antifreeze strength is a measurement of the concentration of antifreeze compared to water. It determines the freeze up protection of the solution.

A *cooling system hydrometer* can be used to measure the freezing point of the cooling system antifreeze solution. One type is shown in Fig. 36-20.

A *refractometer* is another type of antifreeze strength measuring device. Draw coolant into the tester, as in Fig. 36-21. Place a few drops of coolant on the measuring window (surface). Aim the tester at light and view through the tester. The scale in the refractometer will show freeze protection.

Minimum antifreeze strength

Minimum antifreeze strength should be several degrees lower than the lowest normal temperature for the climate of the area. For example, if the lowest normal temperature for the area is 10°F (-23°C), the antifreeze should test to -20°F (-29°C).

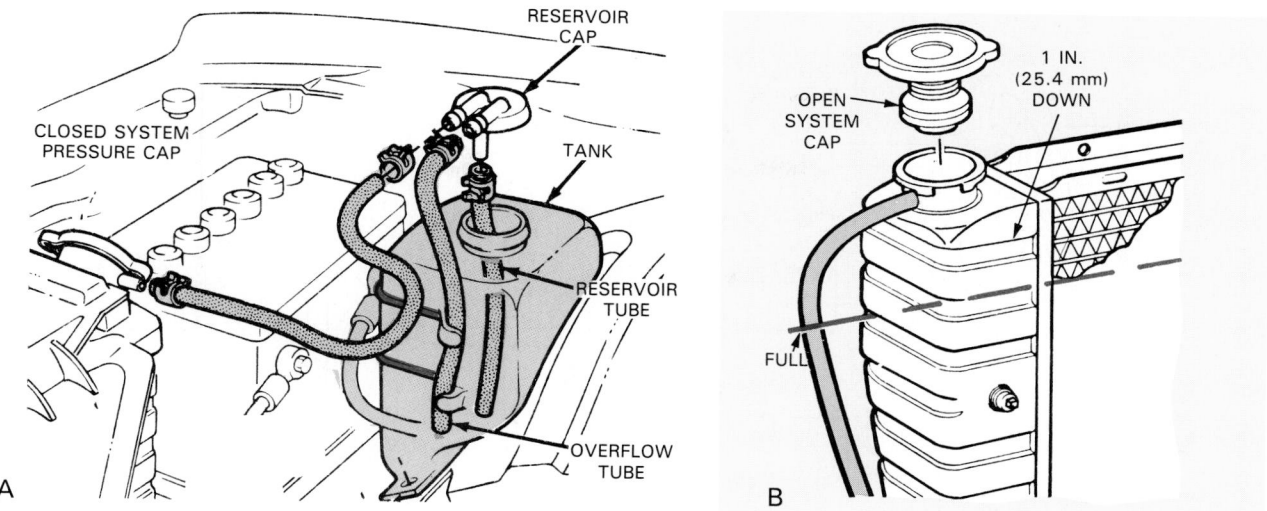

Fig. 36-19. Checking coolant level. A — With closed system, coolant should be even with correct marking on reservoir with coolant at operating temperature. B — With open system, coolant should be about 1 inch or 25 mm down from top of tank. (GMC and Ford)

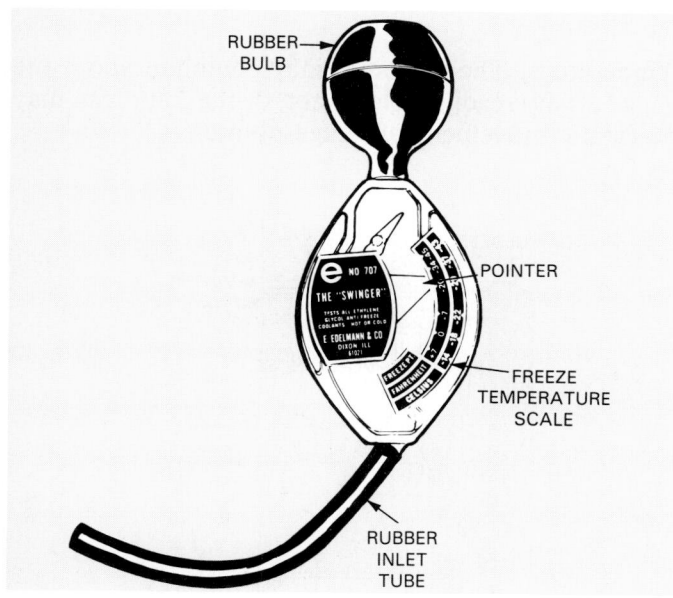

Fig. 36-20. Cooling system hydrometer. Squeeze and release bulb to draw coolant into tester. Needle will float and show freeze protection. Many testers must be corrected for coolant temperature differences. (Edelmann)

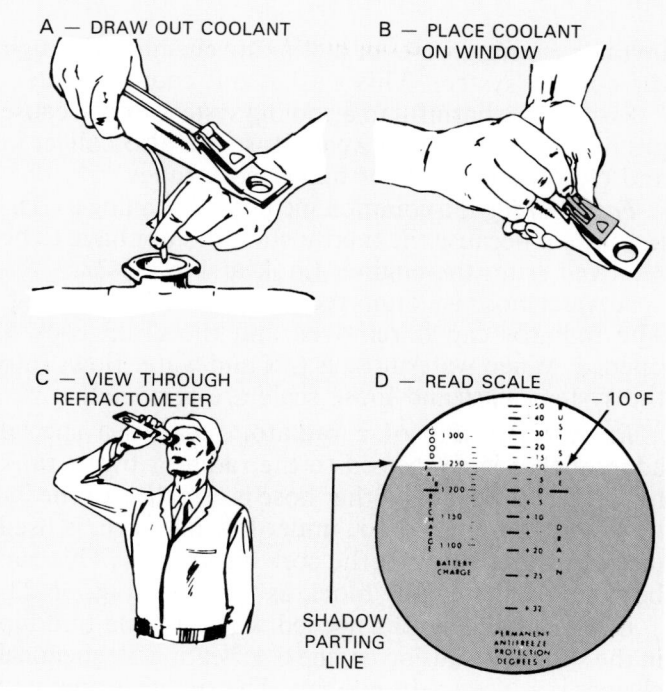

Fig. 36-21. Using refractometer to measure antifreeze protection. Parting line of shadow on scale equals reading. (Oldsmobile)

A 50/50 mix of antifreeze and water is commonly used to provide protection for most weather conditions. Generally, two gallons (7.6 L) of antifreeze is mixed with enough water to fill the cooling system.

Corrosion of aluminum

Note! Many late model cars use aluminum cooling system and engine parts. Radiators, water pumps, cylinder heads, blocks, and intake manifolds can be made of aluminum. Only use antifreeze designed for aluminum components.

Aluminum can be corroded by some types of antifreeze. Check the car's service manual or the antifreeze label for details.

FLUSHING A COOLING SYSTEM

Flushing (cleaning) of a cooling system should be done when rust or scale is found in the system. Flushing

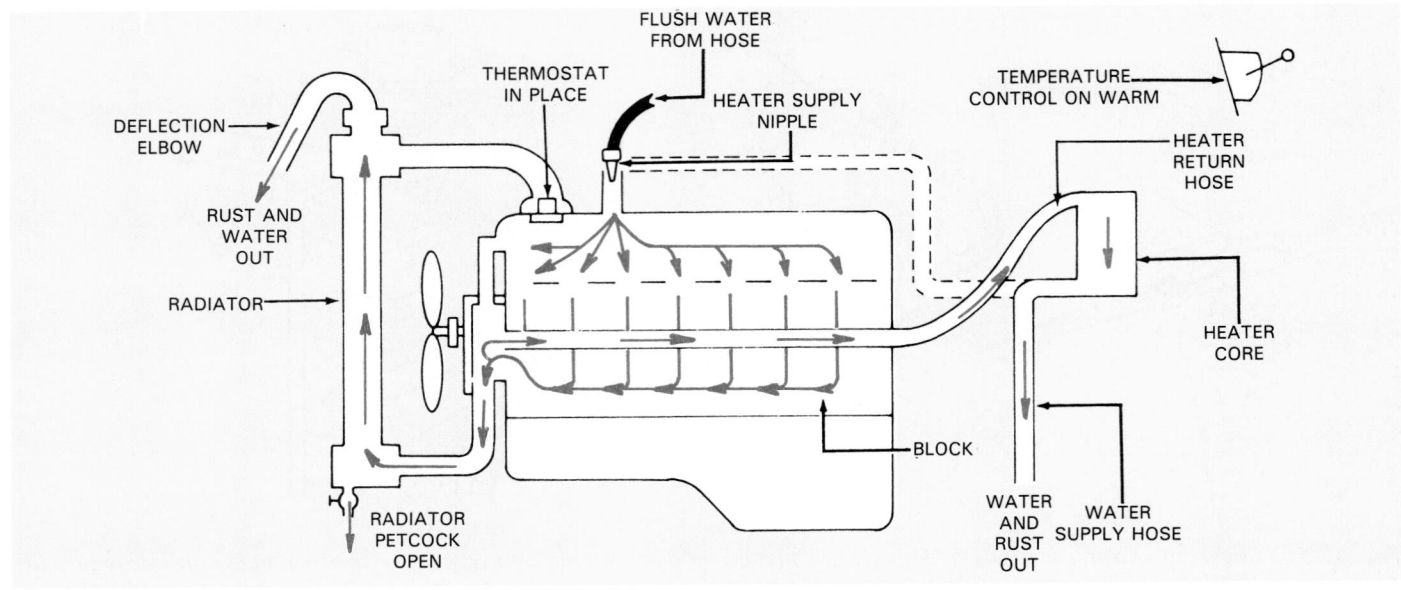

Fig. 36-22. Fast flushing cooling system. Water hose is connected to heater hose fitting. This will force water and rust out heater hose and top of radiator. (Union Carbide Corp.)

involves running water or a cleaning chemical through the cooling system. This washes out contaminants.

Rust is very harmful to a cooling system. It can cause premature water pump wear. Rust can also collect in and clog the radiator or heater core tubes.

Fast flushing is a common method of cleaning a cooling system because the thermostat does not have to be removed from the engine. Look at Fig. 36-22.

A water hose is connected to a heater hose fitting. The radiator cap is removed and the drain cock is opened. When water hose is ON and water flows into the system, rust and loose scale are removed.

Reverse flushing of a radiator requires a special adapter that is connected to the radiator outlet tank by a piece of hose. Another hose is attached to the inlet tank. Compressed air, under low pressure, is used to force water through the core backwards. This can be done on the engine block as well. See Fig. 36-23.

Chemical flushing is needed when a scale buildup in the system is causing engine overheating. A chemical cleaner is added to the coolant. The engine is operated for a specific amount of time to allow the chemical to act on the scale. Then the system is flushed with water.

DANGER! Always follow manufacturer's instructions when using a cooling system cleaning agent. The chemical may cause eye and skin burns.

After flushing, always add the recommended type and amount of antifreeze. Antifreeze has rust inhibitors and lubricants for the water pump. Never leave plain water in the system.

TEMPERATURE GAUGE SERVICE

A *defective temperature gauge* may read hot or cold when the engine is actually at its proper operating temperature. The customer may complain about the gauge always reading cold or hot, or the complaint may be erratic movement of gauge pointer.

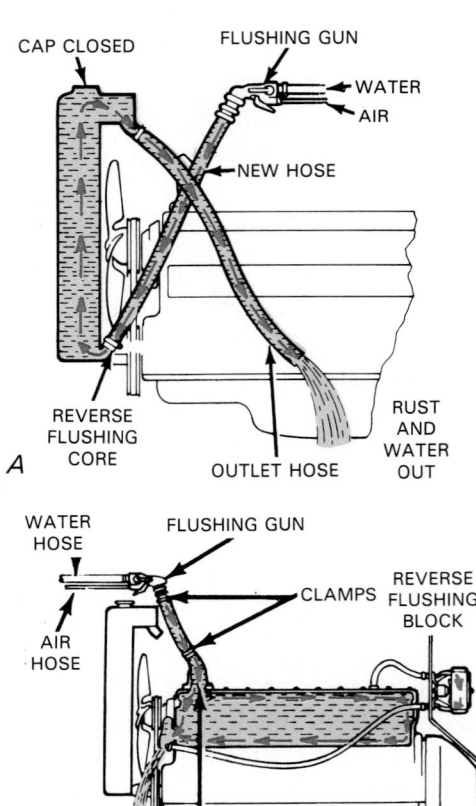

Fig. 36-23. A — Reverse flushing radiator. B — Reverse flushing engine block. (Chrysler)

484   Modern Automotive Technology

To quick-test a temperature gauge, disconnect the wire going to the temperature gauge sending unit. Shown in Fig. 36-24, the sending unit is normally located on the engine.

Using a jumper wire, ground the gauge wire to the engine block. Then, turn the ignition key switch ON and watch the temperature gauge. It will normally swing to hot when the wire is grounded. It should return to cold when the wire is ungrounded.

A *gauge tester* may also be used to check gauge and sending unit operation. It is a special testing device with a variable resistor. Set the tester to a specified ohms value and the temperature gauge should read as specified.

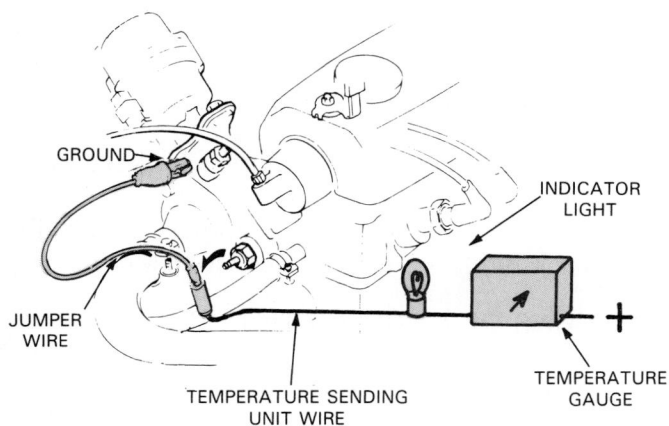

Fig. 36-24. To check action of temperature gauge or indicator light, ground wire to temperature sending unit. This should cause gauge to read hot or light to glow. If not, circuit before sending unit is faulty. If gauge or light function, sending unit may be bad. (Honda)

If available, use a gauge tester. Some temperature gauges could be damaged by grounding the sending unit wire.

If the gauge begins to function when grounded, the sending unit is defective and should be replaced. If the gauge does NOT function when grounded, either the gauge circuit or the gauge is faulty.

To test a temperature indicating light, perform the same basic operation. The light should glow when the sending unit wire is grounded. It should go out when the wire is ungrounded.

KNOW THESE TERMS

Cooling system pressure test, Combustion leak test, Milky or white oil, Water pump rebuild, Pressure cap test, Radiator shop, Expansion plug, Antifreeze strength, Cooling system hydrometer, Refractometer, Fast flushing, Reverse flushing, Chemical flushing, Temperature gauge tester.

REVIEW QUESTIONS

1. An engine can still operate for an extended period without a cooling system. True or False?
2. List seven checks that should be done when inspecting a cooling system.
3. Why should you stand to one side of a spinning engine fan?
4. What can happen if you remove a radiator cap with the coolant at operating temperature?
5. List and explain ten common causes of engine overheating.
6. Which of the following is NOT a typical cause of engine overcooling?
   a. Stuck thermostat.
   b. Locked fan clutch.
   c. Ice in cooling system.
   d. Shorted electric fan switch.
7. A cooling system _____ _____ is used to quickly find leaks in the system.
8. A _____ _____ test checks for the presence of combustion gases in the engine coolant, indicating an engine problem.
9. When water, antifreeze, and oil mix, the solution turns _____ _____ in color.
10. A customer complains of sluggish engine performance and a lack of adequate warmth from the heater.
    Technician A says that this could not be caused by the cooling system. There may be separate problems with the engine and heating system.
    Technician B says that a missing or stuck open thermostat might cause these symptoms. The thermostat should be checked first before checking other possible components.
    Who is correct?
    a. Technician A
    b. Technician B
    c. Both A and B
    d. Neither A nor B
11. How do you replace an engine freeze or core plug?
12. How can you quickly determine if a dash temperature gauge is functioning?

ACTIVITIES FOR CHAPTER 36

1. Obtain a cooling system thermostat and test it for proper opening at its rated temperature, using a pan of water and stove or hot plate.
2. Demonstrate the use of a hydrometer to test antifreeze strength. If a refractometer is available, demonstrate its use, as well.

37

Lubrication System Fundamentals

After studying this chapter, you will be able to:
- □ List the basic parts of a lubrication system.
- □ Summarize the operation of a lubrication system.
- □ Describe the construction of lubrication system parts.
- □ Compare different lubrication system designs.
- □ Explain the characteristics and ratings of motor oil.
- □ Discuss safety procedures to follow when working with the lubrication system.

The lubrication system is extremely important to engine service life because it forces oil to high friction points in the engine. Without a lubrication system, friction between parts would destroy an engine very quickly. Many of the engine parts would rapidly overheat and score from this friction. Engine bearings, piston rings, cylinder walls, and other components could be ruined.

If needed, review the material in Chapters 1 and 10 on lubrication systems.

BASIC LUBRICATION SYSTEM PARTS

A *lubrication system,* as shown in Fig. 37-1, basically consists of:
1. MOTOR OIL (lubricant of moving parts in engine).
2. OIL PAN (reservoir or storage area for motor oil).
3. OIL PUMP (forces oil throughout inside of engine).
4. OIL FILTER (strains out impurities in oil).
5. OIL GALLERIES (oil passages through engine).

Lubrication system operation

With the engine running, the oil pump pulls motor oil out of the oil pan. A screen on the pickup tube removes large particles from the oil before oil enters the pump. The pump then pushes the oil through the oil filter and oil galleries.

The oil filter cleans the oil, removing very small particles. The filtered oil then flows to the camshaft,

crankshaft, lifters, rocker arms, and other moving parts.

When oil leaks out of the engine bearings, it sprays on the outside of internal engine parts. For example, when oil leaks out of the connecting rod bearings, it sprays on the cylinder walls. This lubricates the piston rings, pistons, wrist pins, and cylinders. Oil finally drains back into the oil pan for recirculation.

FUNCTIONS OF A LUBRICATION SYSTEM

An engine lubrication system has several important functions. The system:
1. Reduces friction and wear between moving parts.
2. Helps transfer heat and cool engine parts.
3. Cleans the inside of the engine by removing contaminants (metal, dirt, plastic, rubber, and other particles).
4. Cuts power loss and increases fuel economy.
5. Absorbs shocks between moving parts to quiet engine operation and increase engine life.

The properties of engine oil and the design of modern automotive engines allows the lubrication system to accomplish these functions.

ENGINE OIL

Engine oil, also called *motor oil,* is used to produce a lubricating film on the moving parts in an engine. It is commonly refined from crude oil or petroleum which is extracted from deep within the earth!

Synthetic oils (manufactured oils) are also available. They can be made from substances other than crude oil.

An *oil film* (thin layer of oil) separates engine parts to prevent metal-on-metal contact. This is shown in Fig. 37-2. Without the oil film, the parts would rub together and wear rapidly.

Oil clearance

Oil clearance is the small space between moving engine parts for the lubricating oil film. See Fig. 37-3.

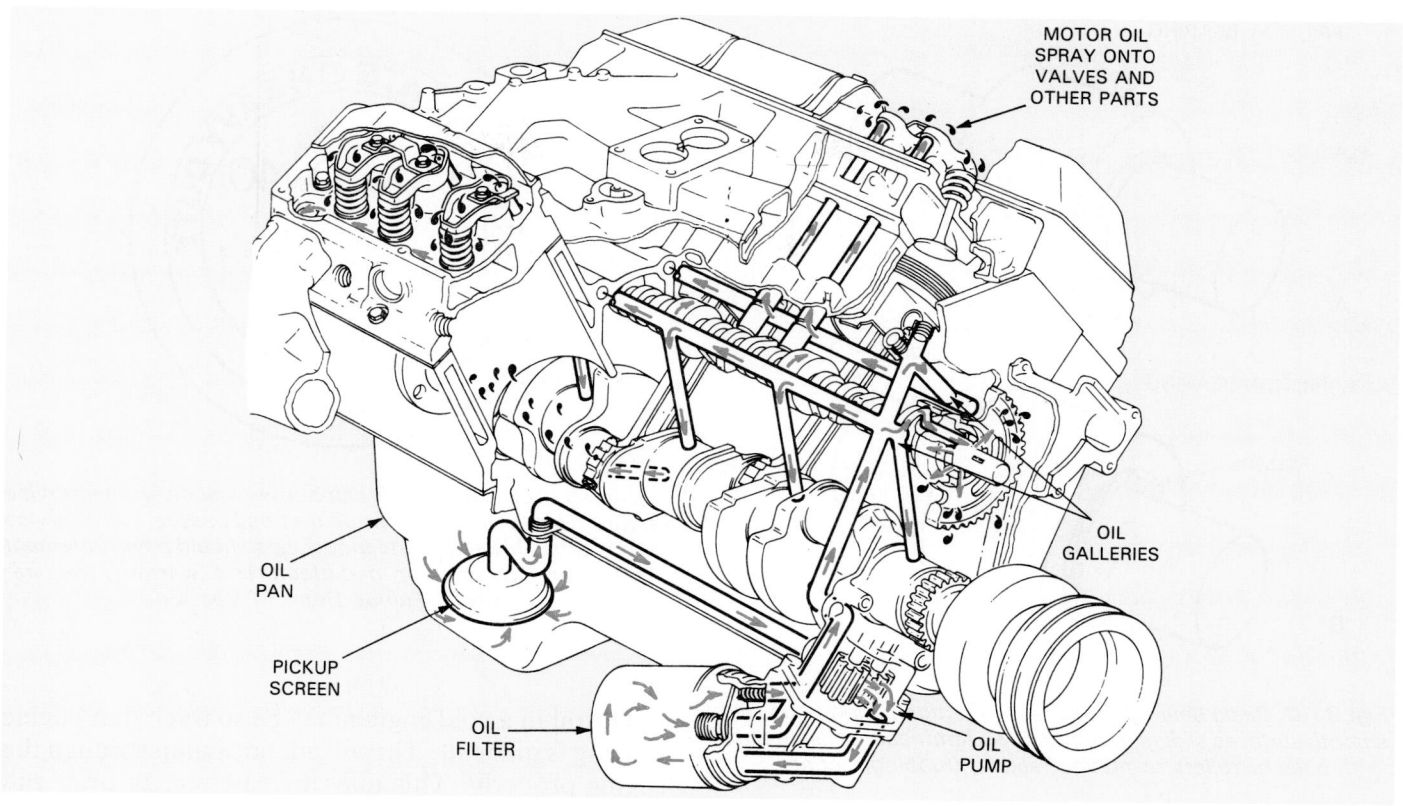

Fig. 37-1. *Study the basic parts of a typical lubrication system. Also, trace flow of oil from pan through engine.* (Chrysler)

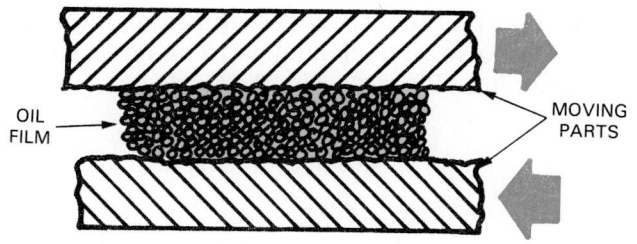

Fig. 37-2. *Close-up view of clearance between moving parts shows how oil film keeps parts from touching and rubbing together.*

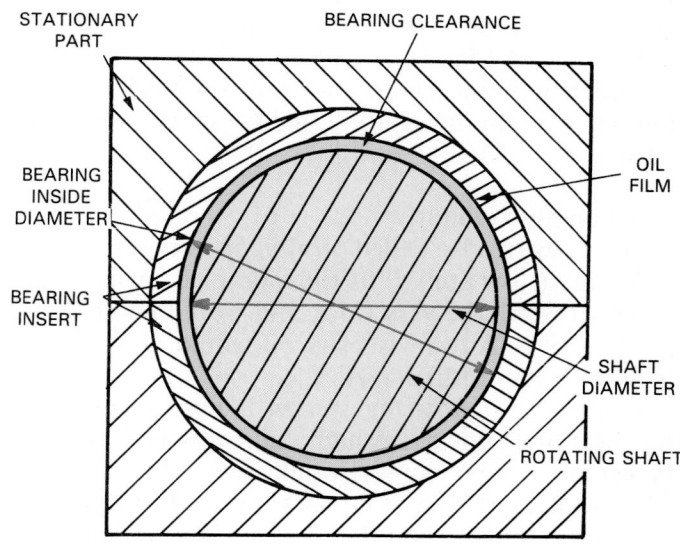

Fig. 37-3. *Bearing clearance, also called oil clearance, allows oil film to hold spinning shaft away from stationary part.*

The clearance allows oil to enter the bearing to prevent part contact.

One example, a connecting rod bearing typically has a bearing or oil clearance of about .002 in. (0.05 mm). This clearance is large enough to allow oil entry. However, it is also small enough to keep the parts from hammering together during engine operation (reciprocating action).

Bearing types

There are two basic types of engine bearings: friction and antifriction types.

A *friction bearing,* also called *plain bearing,* has two smooth surfaces sliding on each other. Look at Fig. 37-4A. It is the most common type of bearing used in an engine.

Crankshaft main bearings, connecting rod bearings, cam bearings are normally friction bearings. They require a constant supply of oil under pressure for proper service life.

An *antifriction bearing* uses balls or rollers to avoid a sliding action between the bearing surfaces. See Fig. 37-4B. They are only used in a few places in an engine.

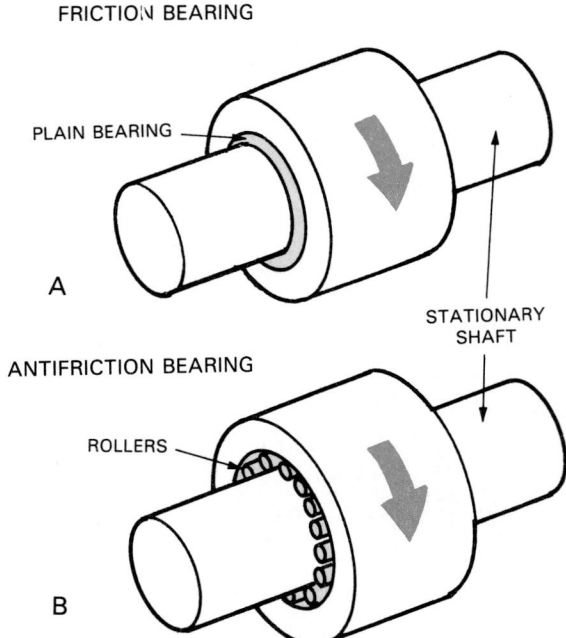

Fig. 37-4. Basic bearing types. A — Friction bearing has two smooth surfaces sliding together. B — Antifriction bearings use balls or rollers to prevent sliding (rubbing) action.

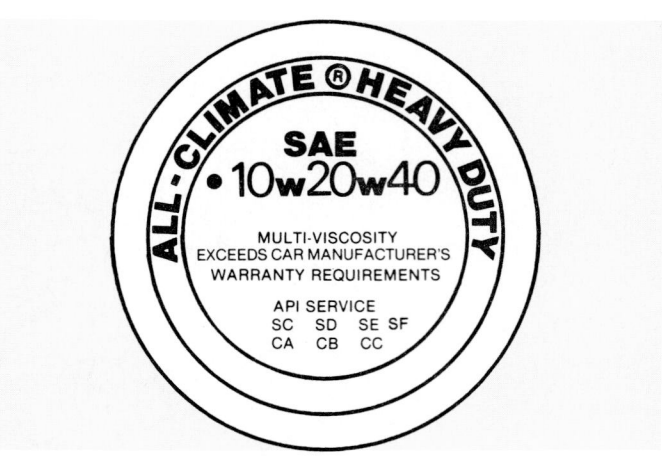

Fig. 37-5. Top view of oil can shows viscosity and service ratings. This is multi-weight oil that has passed strict service rating tests. Oil used in late model cars should have statement "meets or exceeds car manufacturer's warranty requirements." (Florida Dept. of Voc. Ed.)

A good example of an engine antifriction bearing is a roller lifter in a diesel engine. The roller cuts high friction and wear between the camshaft lobe and the bottom of the lifter.

Antifriction bearings do not require as much lubrication as a plain bearing. Usually, splash oiling is sufficient.

Oil viscosity (weight)

Oil viscosity, also called *oil weight,* is the thickness or fluidity (flow ability) of the motor oil. A high viscosity oil would be very thick and would resist flow, like HONEY. A low viscosity oil would be thin and flow easily, more like WATER.

A *viscosity numbering system* is used to rate the thickness of engine oil. A high number would indicate thicker oil. A lower number would denote a thinner oil.

Look at Fig. 37-5. The oil's viscosity number is printed on top of the oil can. The SAE (Society of Automotive Engineers) standardized this numbering system. For this reason, oil viscosity is written SAE 10, SAE 20, SAE 30, etc.

Engine oil viscosities commonly range from a thin SAE 10 weight to a thick SAE 50 weight. Auto manufacturers specify an SAE number for their engines.

Temperature effects on oil

When cold, oil thickens and resists flow. When heated, oil thins and becomes runny. This can pose a problem.

The oil in a cold engine may be so thick that engine starting is difficult. The oil will not pump through the engine properly. This may increase starter drag and result in poor lubrication.

When the engine warms up, the oil thins out. If it becomes too hot and thin, the oil film can break down and part contact can result.

It is important that the oil be thin enough for starting. It must also be thick enough to maintain lubrication when hot. Refer to Fig. 37-6.

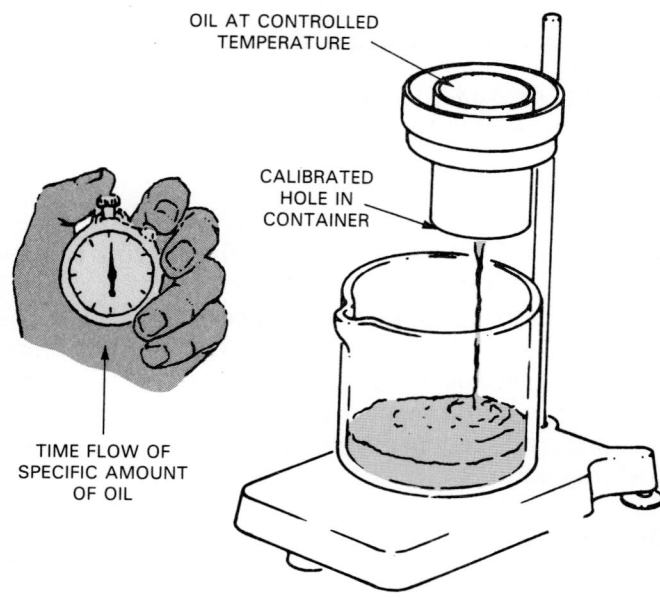

Fig. 37-6. Viscosity rating is determined by measuring how long oil takes to flow through specific opening at a specific temperature. If oil takes longer to flow into container, it would be a thicker, higher viscosity oil. (Binks)

Multi-viscosity oil

Multi-viscosity oil or *multi-weight oil* will exhibit operating characteristics of a thin, light oil when cold and a thicker, heavy oil when hot. A multi-weight oil can be numbered SAE 10W-30, 10W-40, 20W-50, 10W-20W-50, etc.

For example, a 10W-30 weight oil will flow easily (like a 10W oil) when starting a cold engine. It will then act as a thicker oil (like 30 weight) when the engine warms to operating temperature. This will make the engine start more easily in cold weather. It will also provide adequate film strength (thickness) when the engine is at full operating temperature.

Selecting oil viscosity

Normally, you should use the oil viscosity recommended by the auto maker. However, in a very old, high mileage, worn engine, higher viscosity oil may be beneficial. Thicker oil will tend to seal the rings and provide better bearing protection. It may also help cut engine oil consumption and smoking.

Fig. 37-7 is one auto maker's chart showing recommended SAE viscosity numbers for different temperatures.

Oil service rating

An *oil service rating* is a set of letters printed on the

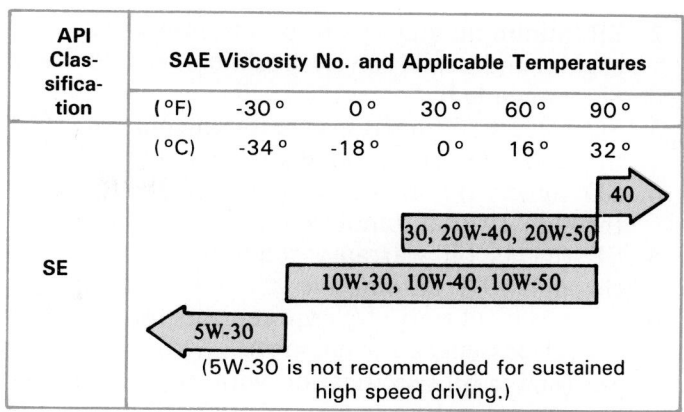

API Classification	SAE Viscosity No. and Applicable Temperatures				
	(°F) -30°	0°	30°	60°	90°
	(°C) -34°	-18°	0°	16°	32°
SE					

Fig. 37-7. Recommended SAE viscosity oil rating from one auto maker. Note how thicker oil is specified for higher outside temperatures. This maker also warns against mixing different brands of oil since different additives may be used in each. (Subaru)

oil can to denote how well the oil will perform under operating conditions. This is a performance standard set by the American Petroleum Institute, abbreviated API. The service rating categories are:

1. SA (lowest quality oil that should NOT be used in automotive engines).

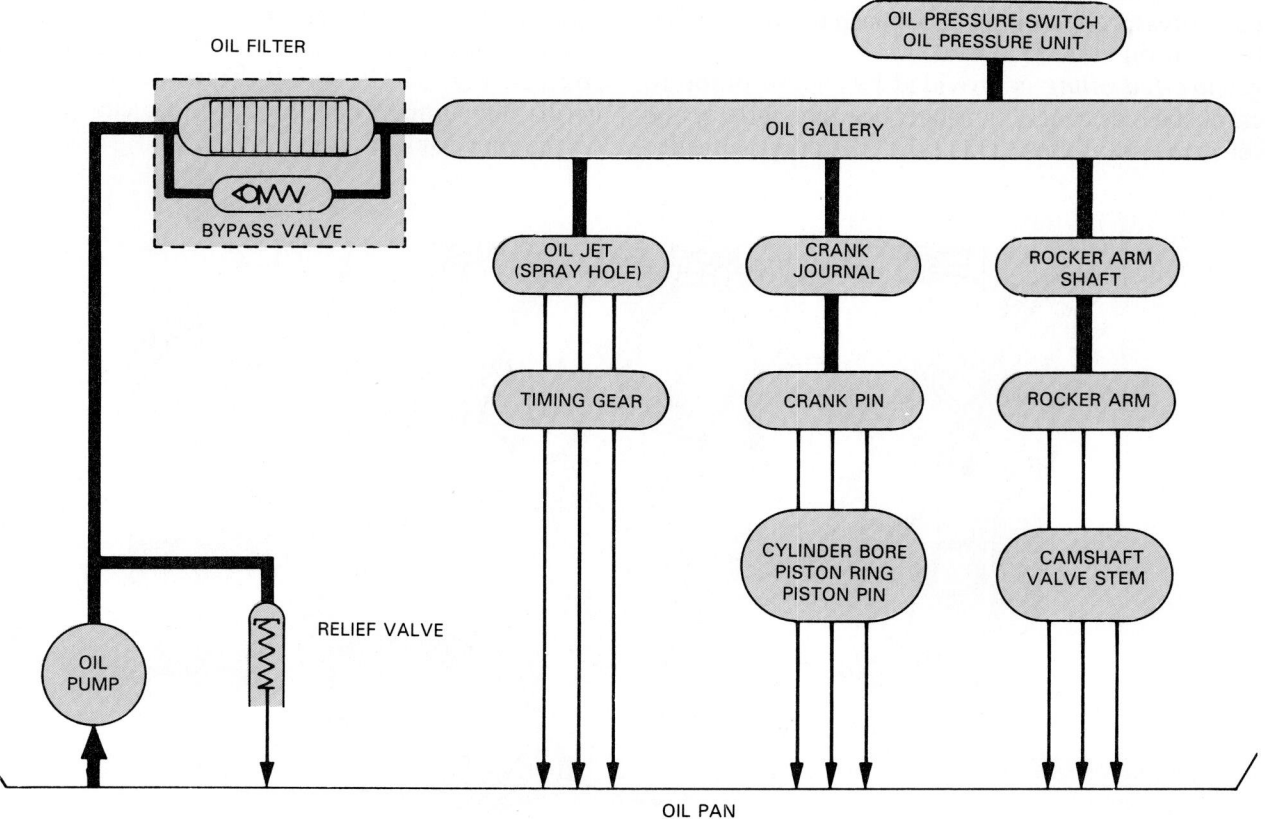

Fig. 37-8. Engine oil flow diagram. This full-flow system requires all oil to pass through filter before entering gallery. Thicker lines represent oil under pressure. Thinner lines stand for oil draining and splashing on parts. Note how filter bypass valve and pressure valve are in system. (GMC)

2. SB (minimum quality oil for automotive gasoline engines under mild service conditions, not normally recommended).
3. SC (meets oil warranty requirements for 1964 through 1967 automotive gasoline engines).
4. SD (meets oil warranty requirements for 1968 through 1970 automotive gasoline engines).
5. SE (meets oil warranty requirements for 1972 through 1979 automotive gasoline engines).
6. SF (meets oil warranty requirements for most late model passenger car engines).
7. SG (newer oil specification with more additivies than SF oils; also can be used as CC or diesel type oils).
8. CA through CD (oil recommended for diesel engines).

A car owner's manual will give the service rating recommended for a specific vehicle. You can use a better service rating than recommended, but NEVER a lower service rating! A high service rating (SG for example) can withstand higher temperatures and loads while still maintaining a lubricating film. It will have more *oil additives* (extra chemicals) to prevent oil oxidation (gumming), engine deposits (sludging), breakdown (oil changes chemically), foaming (air bubbles form in oil), and other problems.

ENGINE OILING SYSTEMS

There are two methods for lubricating engine components: pressure-fed oiling and splash oiling. See Fig. 37-8 for an oil flow diagram.

Pressure-fed oiling is provided by the oil pump to the crankshaft bearings, camshaft bearings, lifters, and rocker arm assemblies. This type of oiling is needed where load and friction are very high.

Splash oiling occurs when oil sprays out and on moving parts to provide lubrication. This type oiling is used between parts with moderate load. For instance, splash oiling is used on the piston rings, cylinders, camshaft lobes, timing chain, and many other parts.

There are two types of full pressure lubrication systems: full flow and bypass types.

Full flow lubrication system

The *full flow lubrication system* forces all of the oil through the oil filter before the oil reaches the parts of the engine. Refer to Fig. 37-8. It is the most common type of lubrication system for automotive engines.

Bypass lubrication system

The *bypass lubrication system* does NOT filter all of the oil that enters the engine bearings. It filters some of the extra oil not needed by the bearings. The bypass lubrication system is not very common. It is not as efficient as the full flow type.

OIL PAN AND SUMP

The *oil pan,* normally made of thin sheet metal or aluminum, bolts to the bottom of the engine block. It holds an extra supply of oil for the lubrication system. Refer to Fig. 37-9.

The oil pan is fitted with a screw-in drain plug for oil changes. Baffles may be used to keep the oil from splashing around in the pan.

The *sump* is the lowest area in the oil pan where oil collects, Fig. 37-10. As oil drains out of the engine, it fills the sump. Then the oil pump can pull oil out of the pan for recirculation.

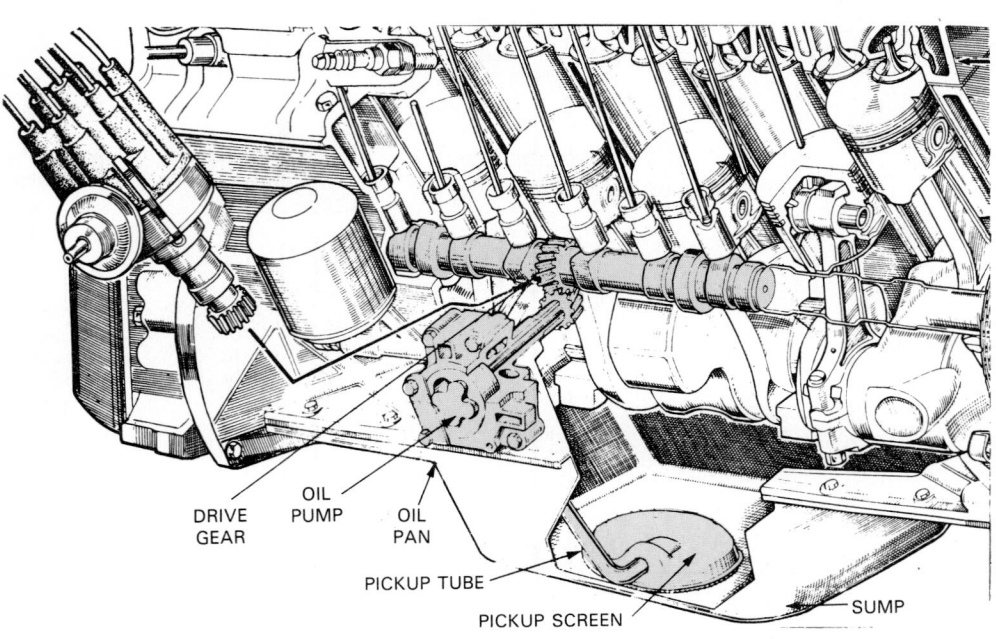

DRIVE GEAR   OIL PUMP   OIL PAN

PICKUP TUBE

PICKUP SCREEN

SUMP

Fig. 37-9. Oil pump is commonly driven by gear on camshaft. Also note how pickup tube extends into pan. (Chrysler)

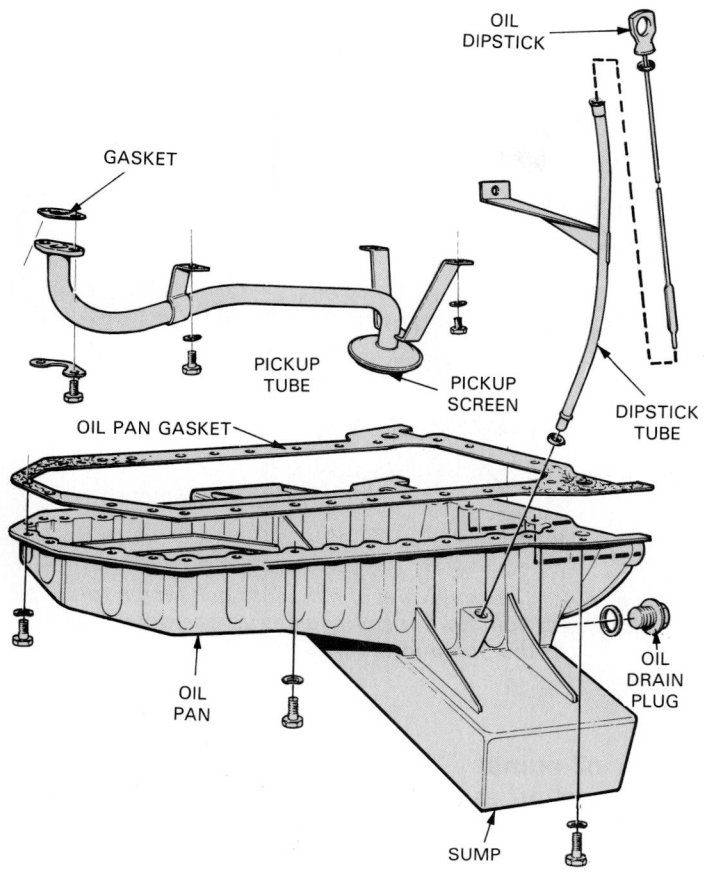

Fig. 37-10. Oil pan forms lower crankcase and sump. Gasket seals mating surface between block and pan. Also note drain plug, pickup tube and screen, and dipstick assembly. (Volvo)

OIL PICKUP AND SCREEN

The *oil pickup* is a tube extending from the oil pump to the bottom of the oil pan. One end of the pickup bolts or screws into the oil pump or to the engine block. The other end holds the pickup screen.

The **pickup screen** prevents large particles from entering the pickup tube and oil pump. See Figs. 37-9 and 10. The screen is usually part of the pickup tube. Without the screen, the oil pump could be damaged by bits of valve stem seals and other debris flushed out of the engine.

OIL PUMPS

The *oil pump* is the "heart" of the engine lubrication system; it forces oil out of the pan, through the engine filter, galleries, and to the engine bearings. The oil pump is frequently driven by a gear on the engine camshaft, Fig. 37-11. It may also be driven by a cogged belt or by a direct connection with the end of the camshaft or crankshaft.

Fig. 37-9 shows a cutaway view of an engine. Note how the oil pump is driven.

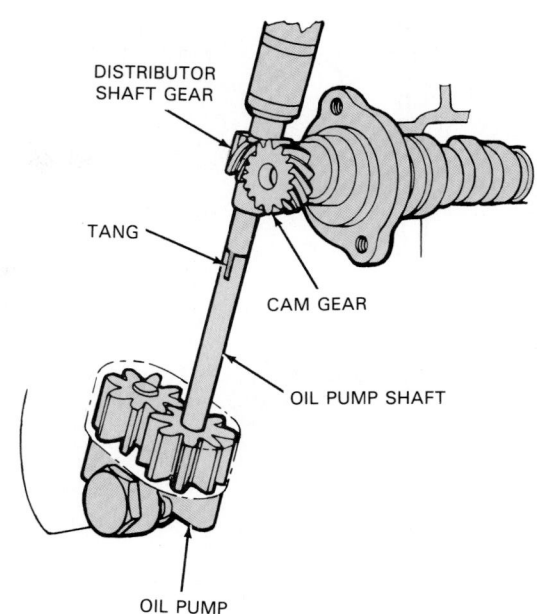

Fig. 37-11. Gear on bottom of distributor meshes with gear on camshaft. Oil pump shaft extends from distributor shaft to oil pump. With engine running, shaft turns at one-half engine speed. (Chrysler Corp.)

There are two basic types of engine oil pumps: rotary and gear. These are illustrated in Fig. 37-12.

Rotary oil pumps

A *rotary oil pump* uses a set of star shaped rotors in a housing to pressurize the motor oil. Look at Fig. 37-13. Study it carefully.

As the oil pump shaft turns, the inner rotor causes the outer rotor to spin. The eccentric action of the two rotors form pockets that change in size.

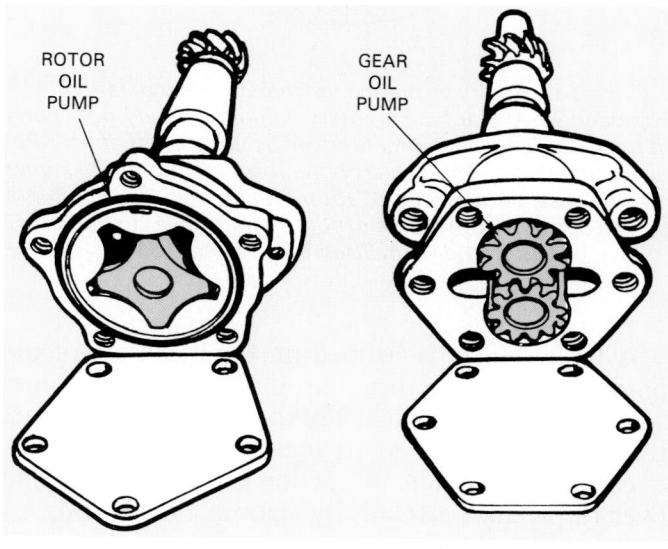

Fig. 37-12. Compare two basic types of oil pumps: rotor pump and gear pump. (Mopar)

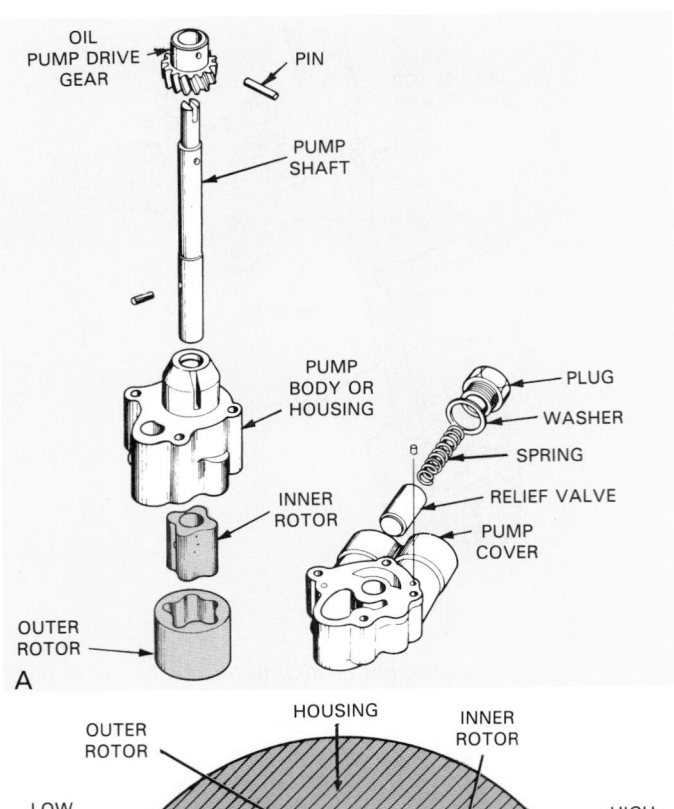

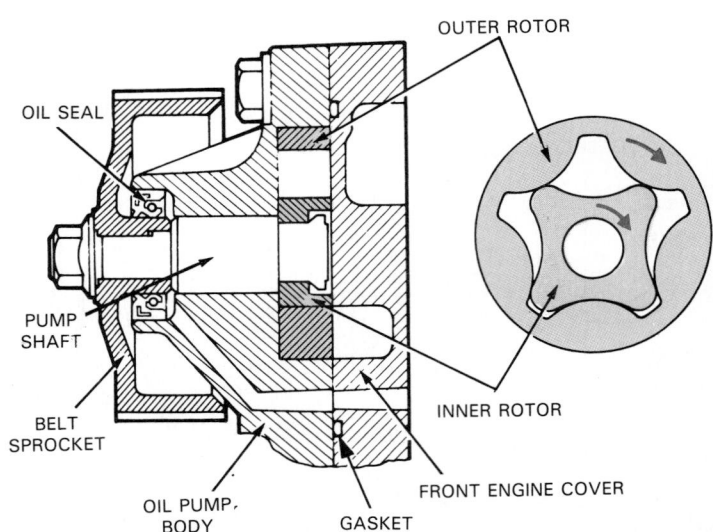

Fig. 37-14. Cutaway view of a modern belt driven rotary oil pump. Pump bolts to front of engine. Its operation is similar to the pump in the previous illustration.

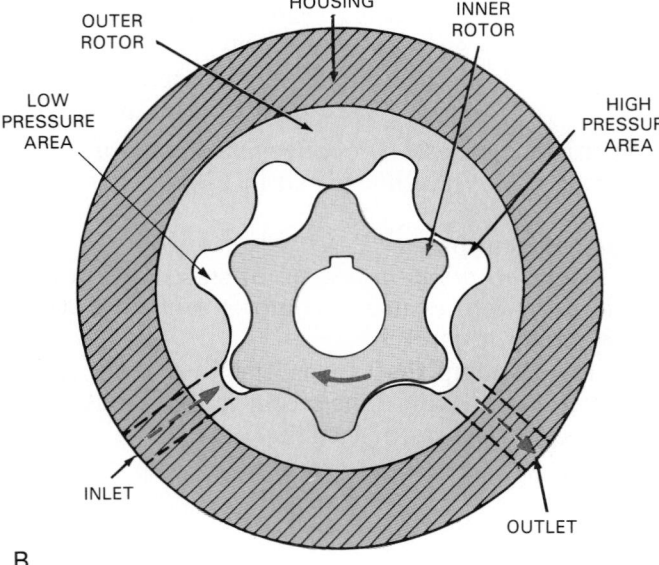

Fig. 37-13. Rotary oil pump construction and operation. A — Exploded view of a typical rotary oil pump. Study how parts fit together. B — Inner rotor is driven by pump shaft. Inner rotor turns outer rotor. This causes outer rotor to walk around inner rotor. Space on one side of rotor enlarges and pulls oil into pump. Space on other side of rotor gets smaller to compress and force oil out. (Deere & Co. and GMC)

A large pocket is formed on the inlet side of the pump. As the rotors turn, the oil filled pocket becomes smaller as it nears the outlet of the pump. This squeezes the oil and makes it spurt out under pressure.

As the pump spins, this action is repeated over and over to produce a relatively smooth flow of oil.

A rotary oil pump mounted on the front of the engine and driven by the timing belt is shown in Fig. 37-14. Compare it to Fig. 37-13.

Gear oil pumps

A *gear oil pump* uses a set of gears to produce lubrication system pressure, Figs. 37-11 and 37-12.

A shaft, usually turned by the distributor, crankshaft, or accessory shaft, rotates one of the pump gears. This gear turns the other pump gear which is supported on a very short shaft inside the pump housing.

Oil on the inlet side of the pump is caught in the gear teeth and carried around the outer wall inside the pump housing. Look at Fig. 37-15. When the oil reaches the outlet side of the pump, the gear teeth mesh and seal.

Oil caught in each gear tooth is forced into the pocket at the pump outlet and pressure is formed. Oil squirts out of the pump and to the engine bearings.

An internal gear oil pump is pictured in Fig. 37-16. It uses the same general principles just discussed.

PRESSURE RELIEF VALVE

A *pressure relief valve* limits maximum oil pressure. It is a spring-loaded bypass valve in the oil pump, engine block, or oil filter housing. Refer to Figs. 37-16 and 37-17.

The pressure relief valve consists of a small piston, spring, and cylinder. Look at Fig. 37-18. Under normal pressure conditions, the spring holds the relief valve closed. All of the oil from the pump flows into the oil galleries and to the bearings.

However, under abnormally high oil pressure conditions (cold, thick oil for example), the pressure relief valve opens. Oil pressure pushes the small piston back in its cylinder by overcoming spring tension. This allows some oil to bypass the main oil galleries and pour back into the oil pan. Most of the oil still flows to the bear-

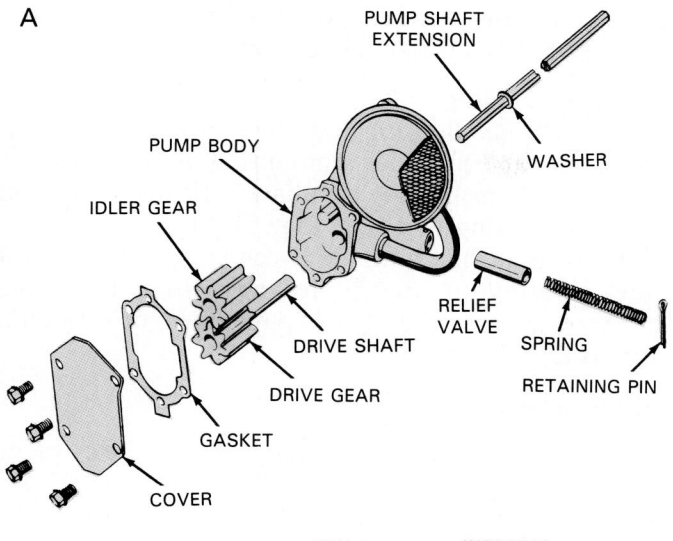

A

PUMP SHAFT EXTENSION

PUMP BODY

IDLER GEAR

DRIVE SHAFT

DRIVE GEAR

GASKET

COVER

WASHER

RELIEF VALVE

SPRING

RETAINING PIN

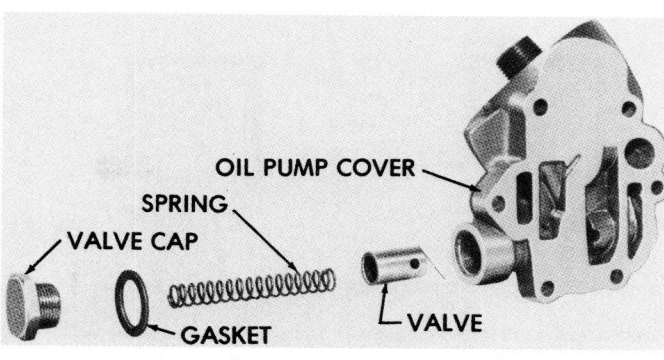

OIL PUMP COVER

SPRING

VALVE CAP

GASKET

VALVE

Fig. 37-17. Exploded view of pressure relief valve. Small piston or valve fits in small cylinder. Spring holds valve in normally closed position. (Oldsmobile)

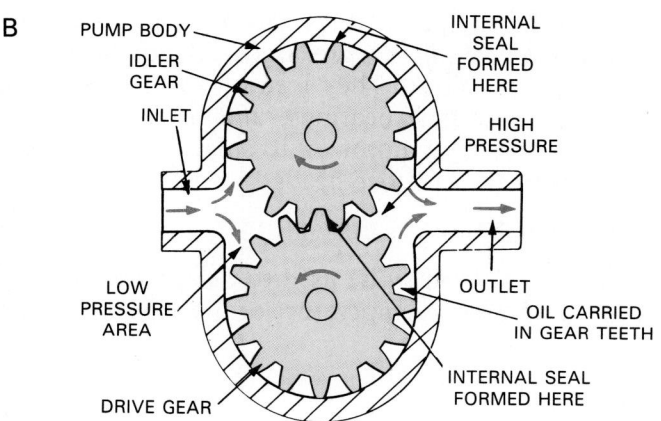

B

PUMP BODY

IDLER GEAR

INLET

LOW PRESSURE AREA

DRIVE GEAR

INTERNAL SEAL FORMED HERE

HIGH PRESSURE

OUTLET

OIL CARRIED IN GEAR TEETH

INTERNAL SEAL FORMED HERE

Fig. 37-15. Gear oil pump construction and operation. A — Exploded view of gear pump shows how it is like and unlike a rotor pump. Compare parts and how they fit together. B — Oil pump shaft turns one gear. That gear drives other gear. Oil is trapped in teeth of gears and carried around housing wall. When on outlet side, oil is trapped and pressurized. (Deere & Co. and GMC)

ings and a preset pressure is maintained.

Some pressure relief valves are adjustable. By turning a bolt or screw or by changing spring shim thickness, the pressure setting can be altered.

OIL FILTERS

An *oil filter* removes small metal, carbon, rust, and dirt particles from the motor oil. It protects the moving engine parts from abrasive wear. Fig. 37-19 shows a cutaway of a modern oil filter.

An **element** is a paper or cotton filtering substance mounted inside the filter housing. It will allow oil flow but will block and trap small debris.

A *filter bypass valve* is commonly used to protect the engine from oil starvation if the filter element becomes clogged. The valve will open if too much pressure is formed in the filter. This allows unfiltered oil to flow to the engine bearings, preventing major part damage.

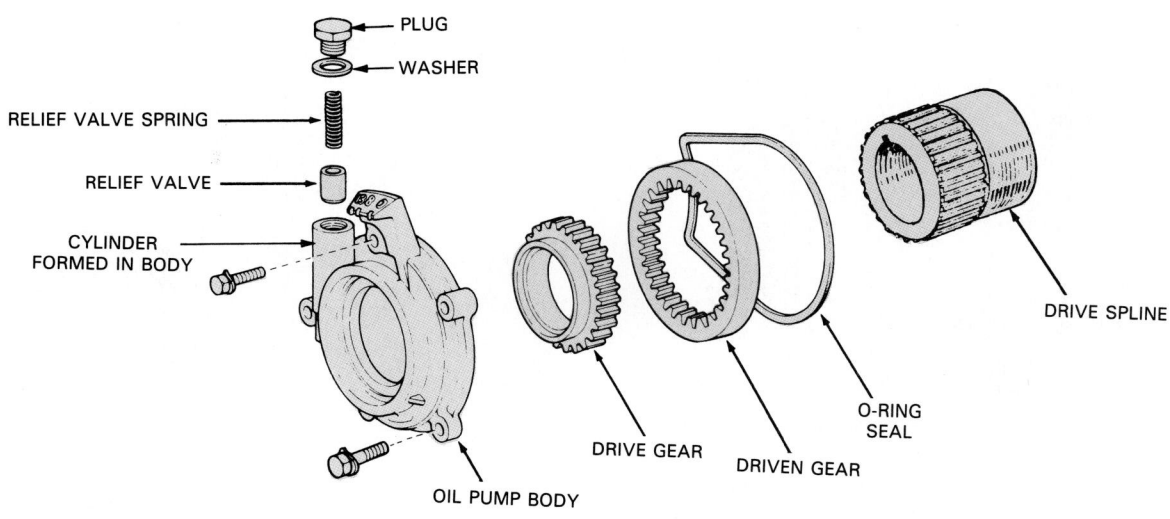

PLUG

WASHER

RELIEF VALVE SPRING

RELIEF VALVE

CYLINDER FORMED IN BODY

OIL PUMP BODY

DRIVE GEAR

DRIVEN GEAR

O-RING SEAL

DRIVE SPLINE

Fig. 37-16. Modern gear pump that mounts on front of engine. Drive spline on crank turns inner gear. Outer gear walks around to pump oil into block. Note pressure relief valve in pump body. (Toyota)

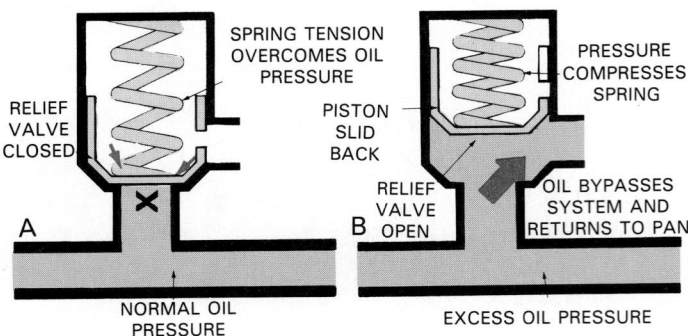

Fig. 37-18. Pressure relief valve action. A — Oil pressure normal. Spring holds relief valve closed to maintain sufficient pressure. B — Oil pressure too high, pressure compresses spring and opens valve. Excess oil bypasses system and drains into pan.

Oil filter types

The two classifications of engine oil filters are: spin-on filter and cartridge filter.

The **spin-on oil filter** is a sealed unit having the element permanently enclosed in the filter body. When it must be serviced, a new filter is simply screwed into place. This is the most common type of modern oil filter.

The **cartridge oil filter** has a separate element and housing. To service this type oil filter, the housing is removed. Then, a new element is installed inside the existing housing. A cartridge type oil filter is sometimes used on heavy duty or diesel applications.

Oil filter housing

The *oil filter housing* is a metal part that bolts to the engine and provides a mounting place for the oil filter. The housing may also have a fitting for the oil pressure sending unit. See Fig. 37-20.

A gasket normally fits between the engine and oil filter housing to prevent leakage. Sometimes, the pressure relief valve, filter bypass valve, or oil pump are inside this housing.

OIL GALLERIES

Oil galleries are small passages through the cylinder block and head for lubricating oil. Refer to Fig. 37-21. They are cast or machined passages that allow oil to flow to the engine bearings and other moving parts.

The **main oil galleries** are large passages through the center of the block. They feed oil to the crankshaft bearings, camshaft bearings, and lifters. The main galleries also feed motor oil to smaller passages running up to the cylinder heads.

OIL COOLER

An *oil cooler* may be used to help lower and control the operating temperature of the engine oil. Look

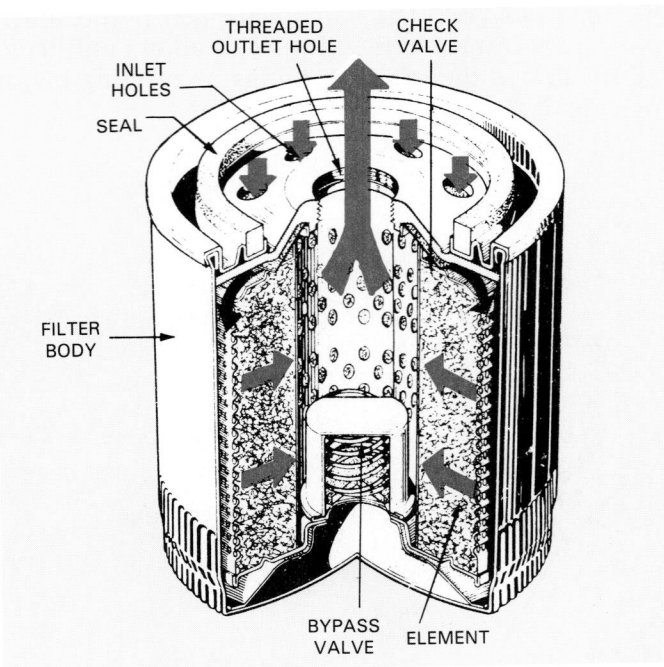

Fig. 37-19. Cutaway of modern spin-on oil filter. Oil enters small holes, passes through element, and then flows out center hole to engine. Rubber O-ring prevents leakage between engine and filter housing. (Saab)

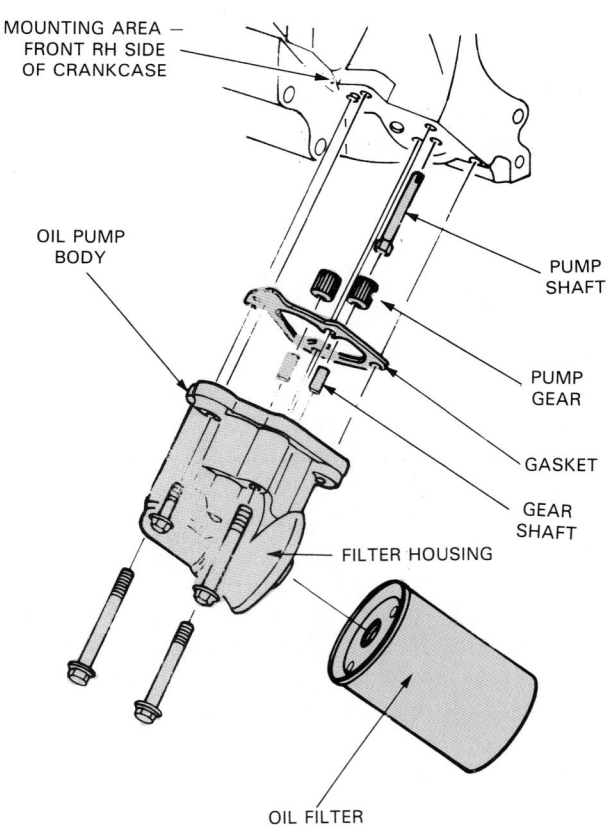

Fig. 37-20. This oil filter housing is also the oil pump housing. Gasket fits between cylinder block and housing. Filter screws on. (Cadillac)

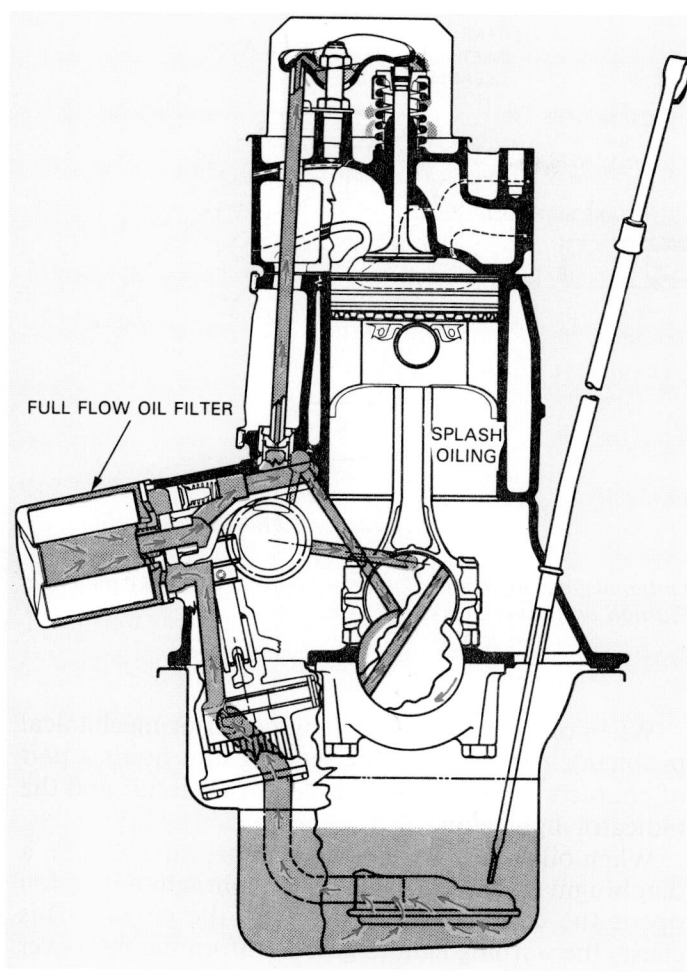

Fig. 37-21. Oil galleries allow oil to pass through engine. Main galleries are larger passages in block. Note how oil flows through hollow push rods to rockers. (Chevrolet)

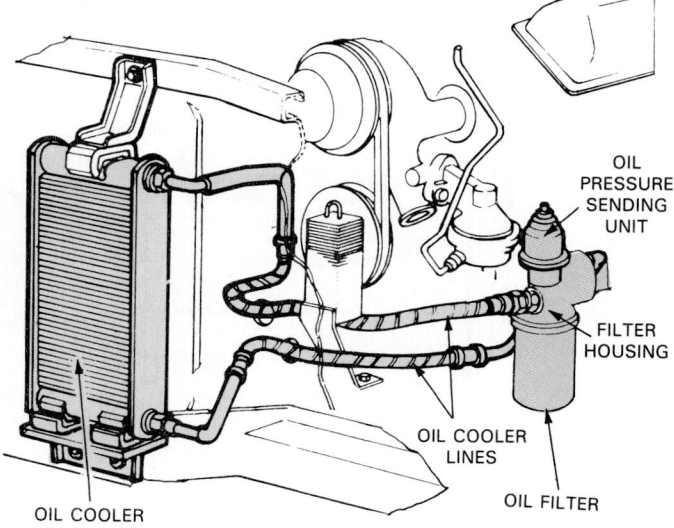

Fig. 37-22. Oil coolers allow transfer of heat out of oil and into surrounding air, like a cooling system radiator. They are used on high performance or heavy duty applications. High pressure lines carry oil to and from cooler. (Mopar)

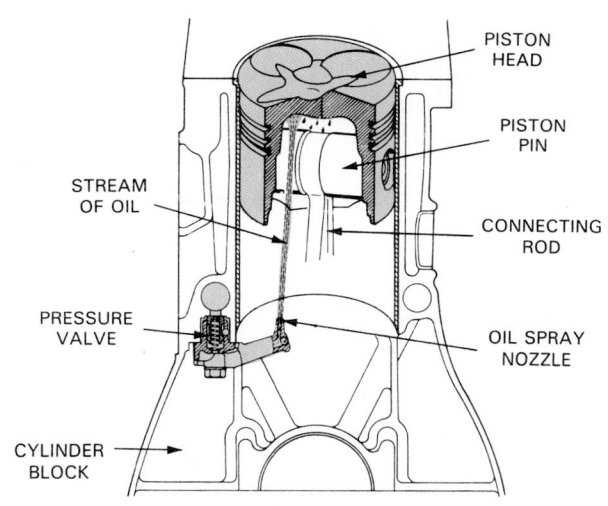

Fig. 37-23. Oil spray nozzles squirt motor oil onto bottoms of pistons for cooling and lubrication. Pressure valve in this type nozzle only opens after specific engine oil pressure is reached. (Mercedes Benz)

at Fig. 37-22. It is a radiator-like device connected to the lubrication system. Oil is pumped through the cooler and back to the engine.

Airflow through the cooler removes heat and lowers the temperature of the oil.

Oil coolers are frequently used on turbocharged engines or heavy duty applications (trailer towing package for instance).

OIL SPRAY NOZZLES

Oil spray nozzles can be used to direct a stream of motor oil onto the bottoms of the engine pistons. This is used to lubricate moving parts and to also cool the heads of the pistons. See Fig. 37-23.

POSITIVE CRANKCASE VENTILATION

The *positive crankcase ventilation system,* abbreviated PCV system, draws fumes out of the engine crankcase and burns them inside the engine. This system helps prevent engine *sludging* (chocolate-pudding-like oil formation) which could restrict oil circulation. It also prevents toxic vapors from entering and polluting the atmosphere. See Fig. 37-24.

For details of a PCV system, refer to Chapter 39, Emission Control Systems.

OIL PRESSURE INDICATOR

An *oil pressure indicator* warns the driver of a low oil pressure problem. The circuit activates a warning light in the vehicle's dash. A basic oil pressure light circuit is shown in Fig. 37-25.

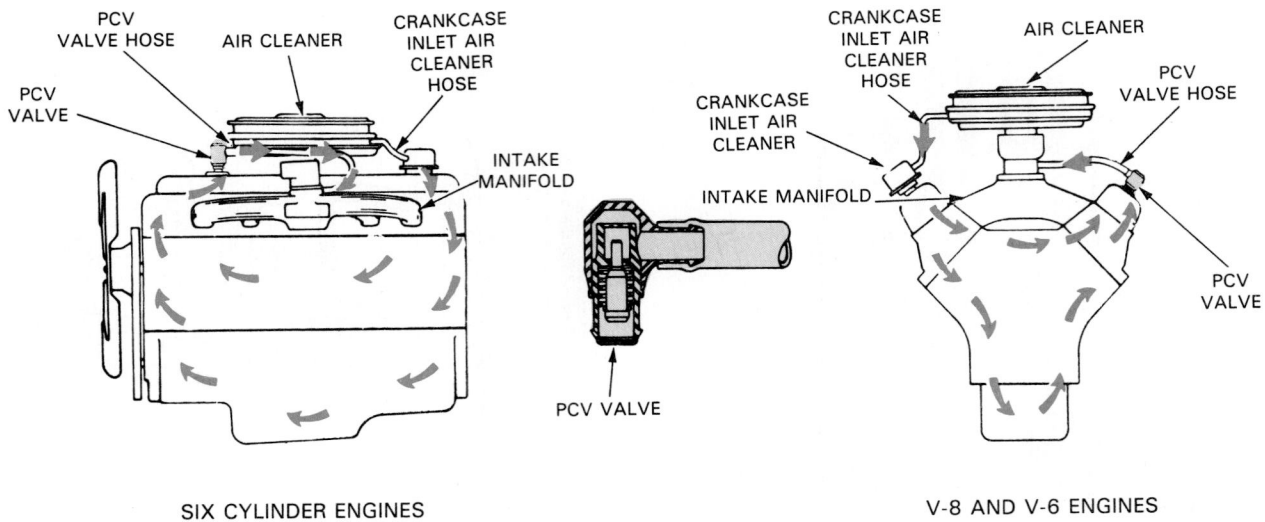

SIX CYLINDER ENGINES

PCV VALVE

V-8 AND V-6 ENGINES

Fig. 37-24. PCV system draws toxic fumes out of oil pan and other internal areas in engine. Fumes are pulled into intake manifold and combustion chambers. Fumes are then burned on power strokes. (Chrysler)

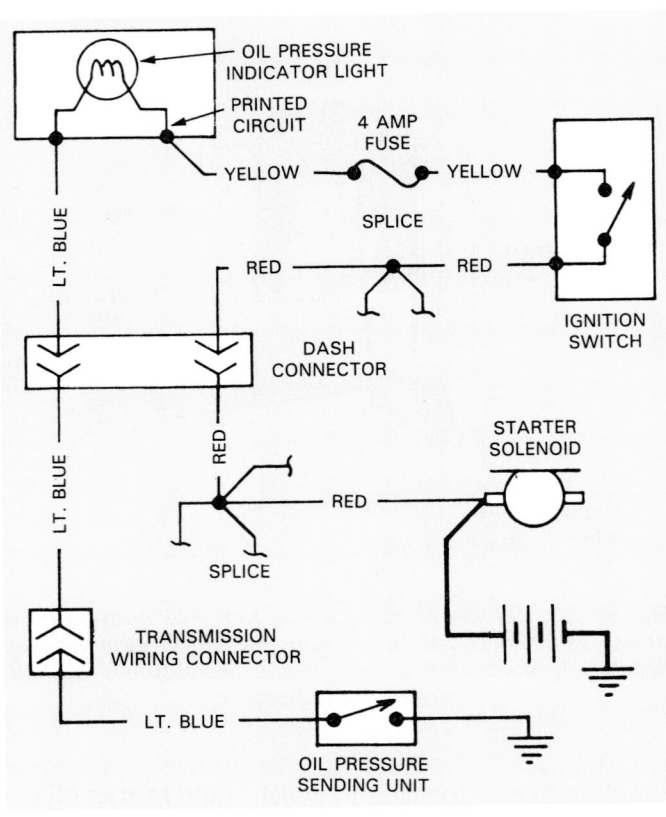

Fig. 37-25. Actual service manual wiring diagram for one make of car. Study how sending unit controls current flow through dash indicator light. Also note wire color coding for tracing wires.

An *oil pressure sending unit* is a pressure sensitive switch that operates the dash indicator light. It screws into the engine and is exposed to one of the oil galleries.

When oil pressure is low (engine off or mechanical problem), the spring in the sending unit holds a pair of contacts closed. This completes the circuit and the indicator light glows.

When oil pressure is normal, oil pressure acts on a diaphragm in the sending unit. Diaphragm deflection opens the contact points to break the circuit. This causes the warning light to go out, informing the driver of good oil pressure.

OIL PRESSURE GAUGE CIRCUIT

Some cars are equipped with an *oil pressure gauge* that registers the actual oil pressure in the engine. See Fig. 37-26. It is similar in operation to the oil pressure indicating light. However, the sending unit uses a VARIABLE RESISTANCE UNIT instead of contact points.

As more oil pressure is developed, the sending unit diaphragm is deflected a proportional amount. This causes an equal amount of sending unit resistance change.

Low pressure causes low sending unit resistance, high current flow, and low oil pressure gauge readings. High engine oil pressure causes high resistance in the sending unit to allow low current flow for deflecting the pressure gauge needle to the right.

LOW OIL PRESSURE SAFETY CIRCUIT

A *low oil pressure safety circuit* can be used to shut the engine off if oil pressure drops too low. This will protect the engine from major damage in case of a lubrication system failure or loss of oil pressure. The circuit usually disables the ignition system to keep the engine from starting.

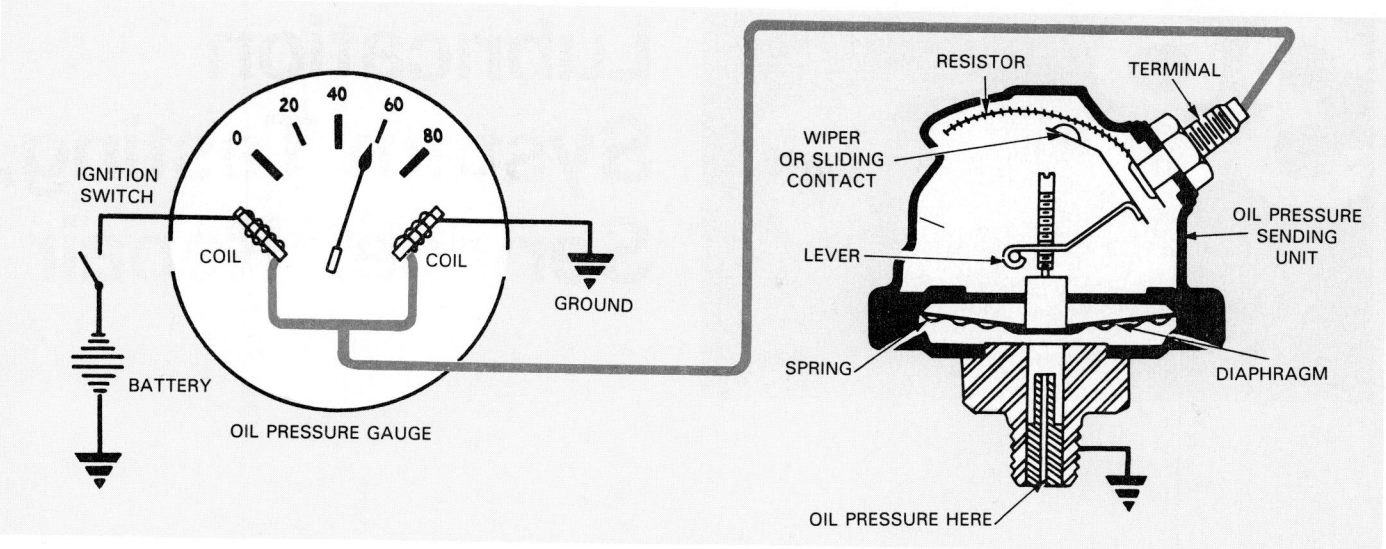

Fig. 37-26. Oil pressure gauge circuit uses variable resistance type sending unit. Changes in oil pressure cause different amounts of diaphragm deflection. This moves sliding contact on resistor. Changes in resistance and current make gauge show engine oil pressure. (Deere & Co.)

KNOW THESE TERMS

Oil film, Bearing clearance, Friction bearing, Antifriction bearing, Viscosity, Multi-weight, Oil service rating, Pressure fed oiling, Splash oiling, Full flow lubrication system, Bypass lubrication system, Oil pan, Sump, Oil pickup, Pickup screen, Oil pump, Rotary pump, Gear pump, Pressure relief valve, Spin-on oil filter, Cartridge oil filter, Oil filter housing, Oil gallery, Oil cooler, PCV, Oil pressure indicator, Oil pressure gauge.

REVIEW QUESTIONS

1. List and describe the five major parts of an engine lubrication system.
2. What are five functions of a lubrication system?
3. How does engine motor oil protect parts from excess wear?
4. _____ _____ is the small space between moving engine parts for the lubricating oil film.
5. Explain the difference between a friction and antifriction bearing.
6. Oil _____, also called oil _____, is the thickness or fluidity of the motor oil.
7. SAE 30 weight oil is thicker and less fluid than SAE 40 weight oil. True or False?
8. What is a multi-weight oil?
9. Pressure-fed oiling is NOT used with:
   a. Crankshaft bearings.
   b. Camshaft bearings.
   c. Hydraulic lifters.
   d. Cylinder walls.
10. There are two basic types of engine oil pumps: _____ and _____ types.
11. How does a pressure relief valve work?
12. Why is an oil filter very important to engine service life?
13. _____ _____ are small passages through the cylinder head and block for lubricating oil.
14. Why is an oil cooler sometimes used?
15. Summarize the operation of an oil pressure gauge circuit.

ACTIVITIES FOR CHAPTER 37

1. Visit a large auto supply store or other store that offers a number of different brands of engine oil. Check the top of the can for the 10W-30 oil for each brand and list the API service ratings (SA, SE, and so on) shown. Do the brands differ, or do they all have the same ratings? List the price per quart for each brand that has an SF or SG rating. Which brand represents the best buy?
2. Using either a CAD program on a computer or conventional drafting equipment, draw a cross-sectional view of a typical spin-on oil filter. Label the parts and use arrows to show oil movement through the filter.
3. Interview the manager or owner of a business that performs "while you wait" oil changes. Has he or she noticed any changes in customer habits (waiting longer between oil changes or changing more frequently, changing brands of oil, or purchasing additional services such as an air conditioning recharge or transmission fluid change)? Does he or she expect the business to be larger, smaller, or about the same in five years? Would she or he suggest the oil change business as an opportunity for a young entrepreneur? Report to the class on your interview.

38 Lubrication System Testing, Service, Repair

After studying this chapter, you will be able to:
- List common lubrication system problems and symptoms.
- Diagnose lubrication system troubles.
- Measure engine oil pressure.
- Change engine oil and filter.
- Remove and install an engine oil pan.
- Service an engine oil pump.
- Test and repair an oil pressure indicating light or gauge.
- Describe safe working practices to use when testing, servicing, or repairing a lubrication system.

This chapter summarizes the most common service and repair operations performed on an engine lubrication system. It prepares you for typical repair tasks. Almost all technicians, at one time or another, are required to work on an engine lubrication system. Study this chapter thoroughly!

LUBRICATION SYSTEM PROBLEM DIAGNOSIS

To troubleshoot an engine lubrication system, begin by gathering information on the trouble. Ask the vehicle owner or service writer questions. Analyze the symptoms using your understanding of system operation. You should be able to arrive at a logical deduction about the cause of the problem.

The problems found in a lubrication system are limited in number. They include:

1. High oil consumption (oil must be added to engine frequently).
2. Low oil pressure (gauge reads low, indicator light glows, or abnormal engine noises).
3. High oil pressure (gauge reads high, oil filter swelled).
4. Defective indicator or gauge circuit (inaccurate operation or readings).

When diagnosing these troubles, make a visual inspection of the engine for obvious problems. Check for oil leakage, disconnected sending unit wire, low oil level, damaged oil pan, or other trouble that would relate to the symptoms.

Fig. 38-1 shows several possible problem areas relating to an engine's lubrication system.

High oil consumption

High oil consumption is caused by external oil leakage out of the engine or by internal leakage of oil into the combustion chambers. If the vehicle owner must frequently add oil to the engine, this is a symptom of high oil consumption.

External oil leakage is easily detected as darkened, oil-wet areas on or around the engine. Oil may also be found in small puddles under the vehicle. Leaking gaskets or seals are usually the source of external engine oil leakage.

To locate oil leakage, you may need to raise the vehicle on a lift and visually look for leaks under the engine. Trace the oil leakage to its highest point. The parts around the point of leakage may be WASHED CLEAN by the constant dripping or flow of oil.

After locating the point of leakage, you must service the gasket, seal, or component at fault.

Internal oil leakage shows up as BLUE SMOKE coming out of the exhaust. For example, if the engine piston rings and cylinders are badly worn, oil can enter the combustion chambers and be burned during combustion.

Do not confuse black smoke (excess fuel in cylinder) and white smoke (water leakage into gasoline engine cylinder) with the blue smoke caused by motor oil.

NOTE! Oil consumption and smoking is covered in the chapter on engine mechanical problems.

Low oil pressure

Low oil pressure is indicated when the oil indicator light glows, oil gauge reads low, or when the engine lifters or bearings rattle. You must make sure of the actual problem.

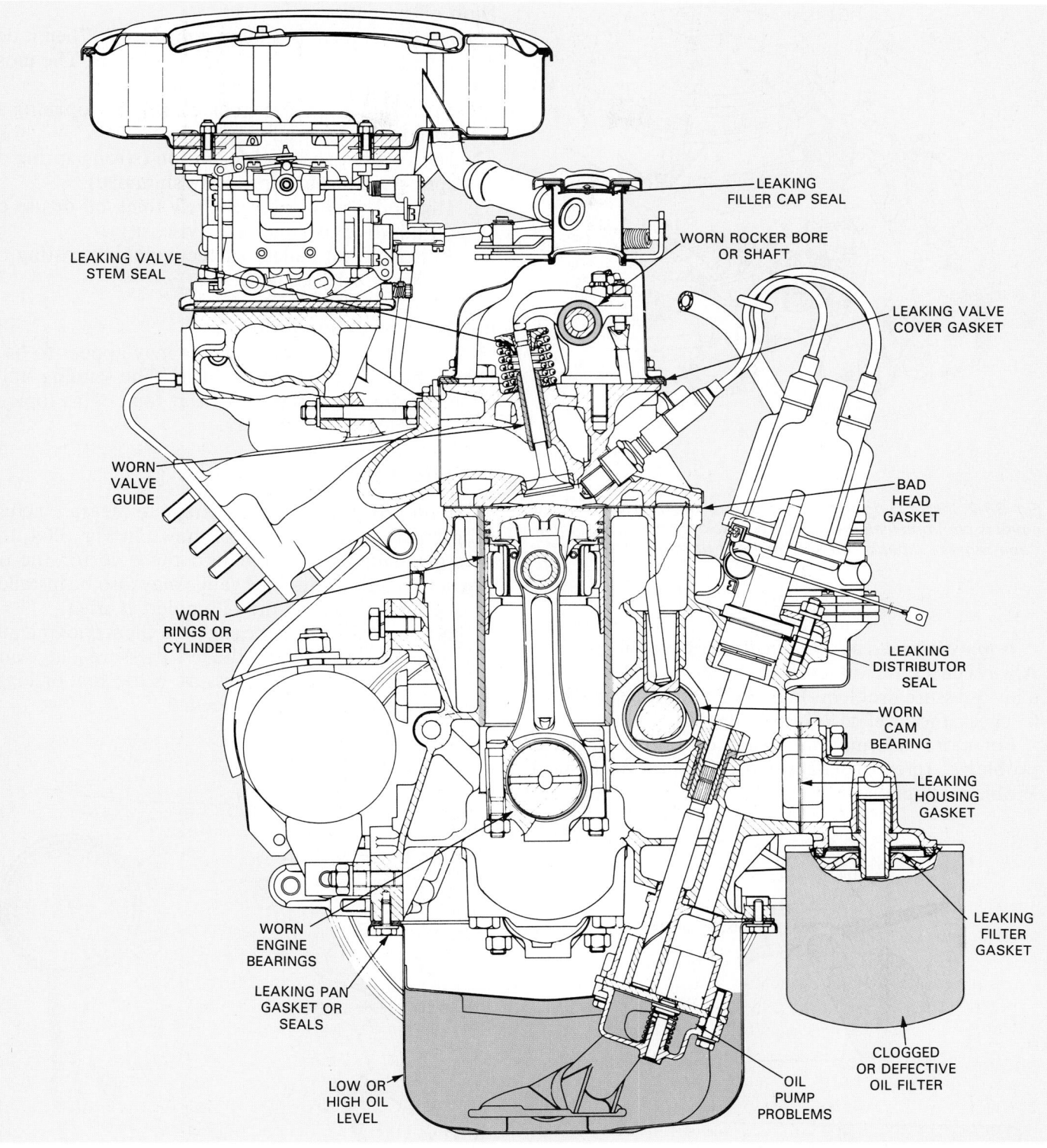

Fig. 38-1. Note typical problem areas relating to engine lubrication system. (Fiat)

The most common causes of low oil pressure are:
1. Low oil level (oil not high enough in pan to cover oil pickup).
2. Worn connecting rod or main bearings (pump cannot provide enough oil volume).
3. Thin or diluted oil (low viscosity or gasoline in oil)
4. Weak or broken pressure relief valve spring (valve opening too easily).
5. Cracked or loose oil pump pickup tube (air being pulled into oil pump).
6. Worn oil pump (excess clearance between rotor or gears and housing).
7. Clogged oil pickup screen (reduced amount of oil entering pump).

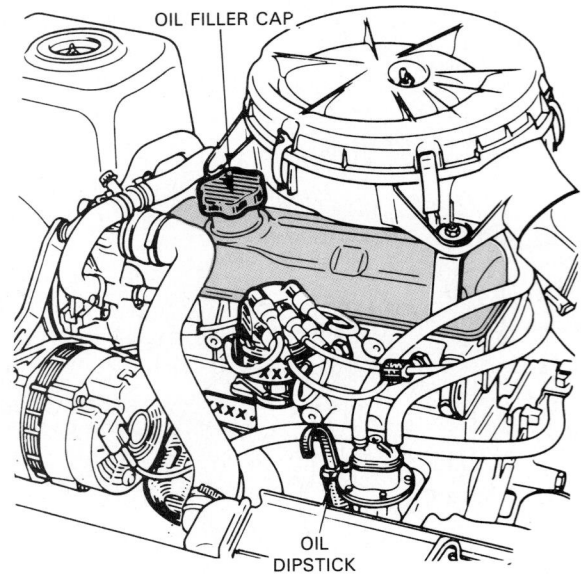

Fig. 38-2. Inspect engine compartment to locate oil leaks. Valve cover is common leakage point. To check for low oil level, find and remove dipstick on side or front of engine. (Renault)

A *low oil level* is a common cause of low oil pressure. Always check the oil level first when troubleshooting a low pressure problem. Figs. 38-2 and 38-3 show how to check the level of oil in an engine.

For more information on low oil pressure related problems, refer to Chapter 45, Engine Mechanical Problem Diagnosis.

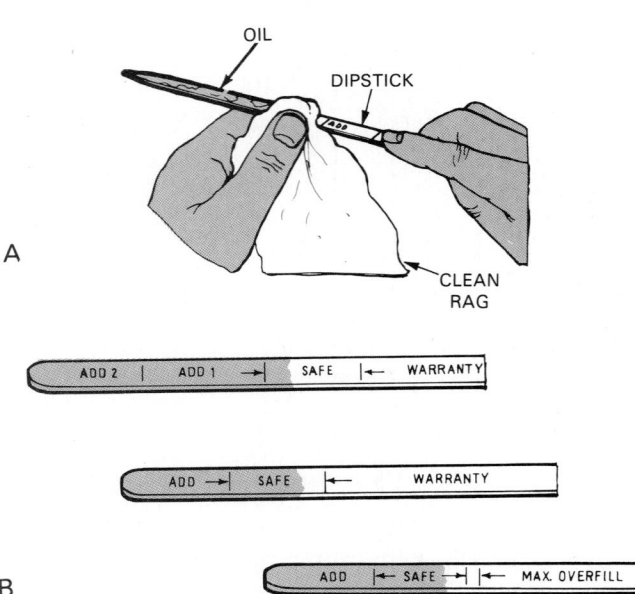

Fig. 38-3. Checking engine oil level. A — Pull out and wipe off dipstick. Then, reinsert fully and pull stick back out. B — Hold stick away from car and note height of oil on stick. Compare oil to markings on dipstick. (Chrysler)

High oil pressure

High oil pressure is seldom a problem. When it occurs, the oil pressure gauge will read high. The most frequent causes of high oil pressure are:

1. Pressure relief valve stuck closed (not opening at specified pressure).
2. High relief valve spring tension (strong spring or spring has been improperly shimmed).
3. High oil viscosity (excessively thick oil or use of oil additive that increases viscosity).
4. Restricted oil gallery (defective block casting or debris in oil passage).

Indicator or gauge problems

A *defective indicator* or *gauge* may appear to be a low or high oil pressure problem. The sending unit, circuit wiring, or gauge may be at fault. This topic is covered later in the chapter.

OIL PRESSURE TEST

An *oil pressure test* uses a gauge to measure actual oil pressure in the engine. As shown in Fig. 38-4, the pressure gauge is screwed into the hole for the oil pressure sending unit. The gauge may also be installed in one of the lines to the oil cooler, if used.

Start the engine. Run the engine at the service manual recommended rpm. Read the test pressure gauge and compare to specs. If oil pressure is too low or high, you must make repairs as needed.

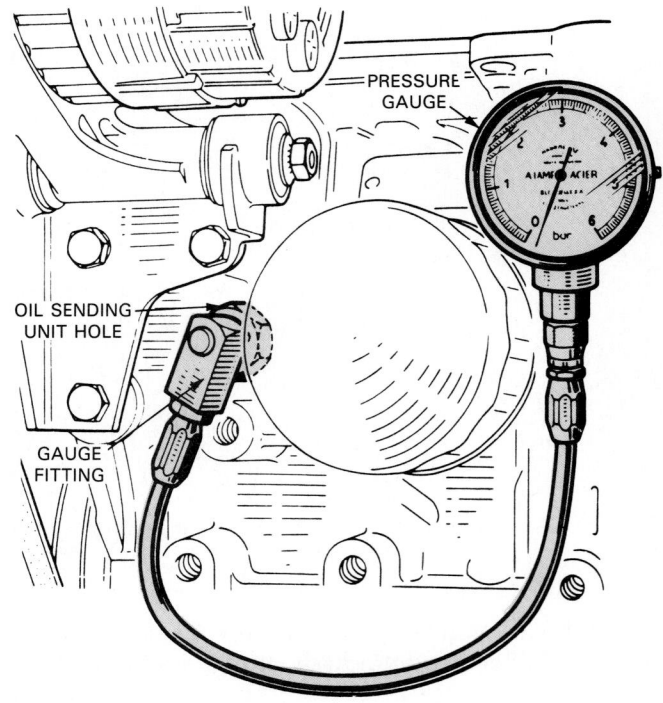

Fig. 38-4. A test gauge can be used to measure actual engine oil pressure. Gauge is normally screwed into hole for oil sending unit. Measure pressure with engine warm and at specified rpm. (Renault)

Depending upon the type of engine and number of miles of use, oil pressure should be at least 20 to 30 psi (138-207 kPa) at idle and 40 to 60 psi (276-413 kPa) at cruising speeds. Check service manual specs when testing.

PRELUBRICATOR

A *prelubricator* can be used to help pinpoint worn engine bearings or other worn parts that lower oil pressure. Look at Fig. 38-5.

A prelubricator is a metal pressure tank with special gauges and fittings. It can be used to force oil through the lubrication system without running the engine.

To check for worn bearings, remove the engine oil pan (covered later). Partially fill the prelubricator tank with oil. Then, connect the tank line to the engine, following equipment instructions. Charge the tank with the recommended amount of air pressure. Place a large catch pan under the engine.

Open the valve on the prelubricator while watching the engine bearings. If an excess amount of oil pours out of any bearing, that bearing is bad. If oil flow out

of all bearings is normal, remove and check the condition of the oil pump.

A prelubricator can also be used to prime the oil galleries with oil after an overhaul. It will assure instant oil pressure when first starting a rebuilt engine.

ENGINE OIL AND FILTER SERVICE

It is extremely critical that the engine's oil and oil filter are serviced regularly. Lack of oil and filter maintenance can greatly shorten engine service life.

Used oil will be contaminated with dirt, metal particles, carbon, gasoline, ash, acids, and other harmful substances. Some of the smallest particles and corrosive chemicals are not trapped in the oil filter. They will circulate through the engine, increasing part wear and corrosion.

Oil and filter change intervals
Auto makers give a maximum number of miles (kilometers) a car can be driven between oil changes. If the oil is not changed at this interval, the car's warranty will become void.

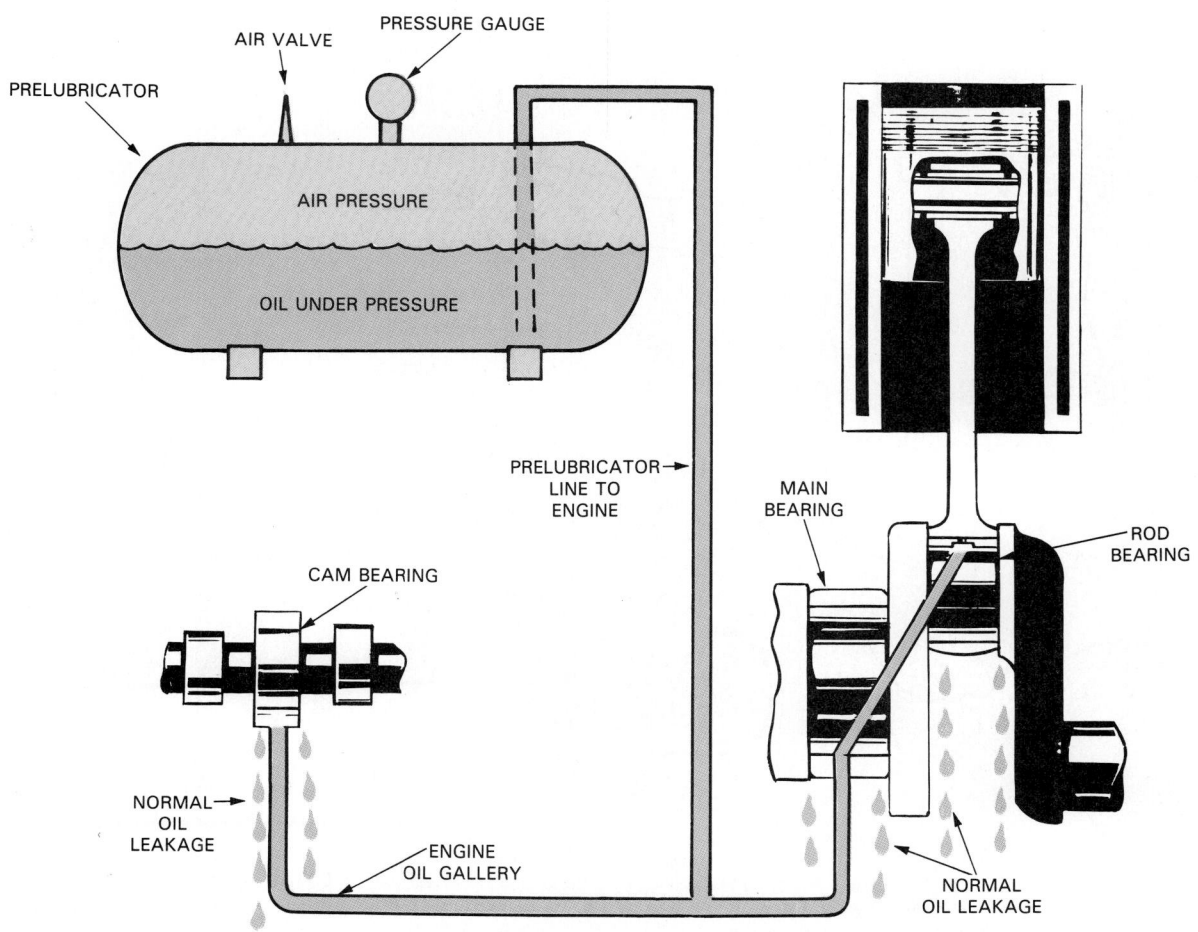

Fig. 38-5. Prelubricator can be used to check for worn bearings. Air pressure pushes oil through system. With oil pan off, you can watch for too much oil (wear) at engine bearings. (Dana Corp.)

New vehicles can go 3000-7500 miles (4800-12 000 km) between oil changes. Older vehicles should have oil changed more often. Refer to a manual for exact values.

An older, worn engine will contaminate the oil more quickly than a new engine. More combustion byproducts will blow past the rings and enter the oil. Also, engine bearing clearance will be larger, requiring more of the oil and lubrication system.

Also, if a car is only driven for short periods and then parked, its oil should be changed more often. Since the engine may not be reaching full operating temperature, the oil can be contaminated with fuel, moisture, and other substances more quickly.

Diesel engines and turbocharged engines usually require more frequent oil and filter service than naturally aspirated (non-supercharged) engines.

Changing engine oil and filter

To change the engine oil, warm the engine to full operating temperature. This will help suspend debris in the oil and make the oil drain more thoroughly. Then, follow the basic steps given in Fig. 38-6.

A few rules to remember when changing engine oil and the oil filter are:

1. Keep the car level so all oil drains from the pan.
2. Do NOT let hot oil pour out on your hand or arm!
3. Check the condition of the drain plug threads and the o-ring washer. Replace them if needed.
4. Do NOT overtighten the oil pan drain plug. It will strip very easily, possibly causing pan damage.
5. Wipe clean oil on the filter o-ring before installation.
6. Hand tighten the oil filter. Do NOT use the filter wrench because the filter canister could distort and leak.
7. Fill the engine with the correct amount and type of oil. Remember that diesel engines usually hold more oil than gasoline engines. Check manufacturer recommendations.
8. Check for oil leaks with the engine running before releasing the car to the customer.

Oil dye

Oil dye is special coloring sometimes added to the motor oil in new cars or for testing purposes. The dye

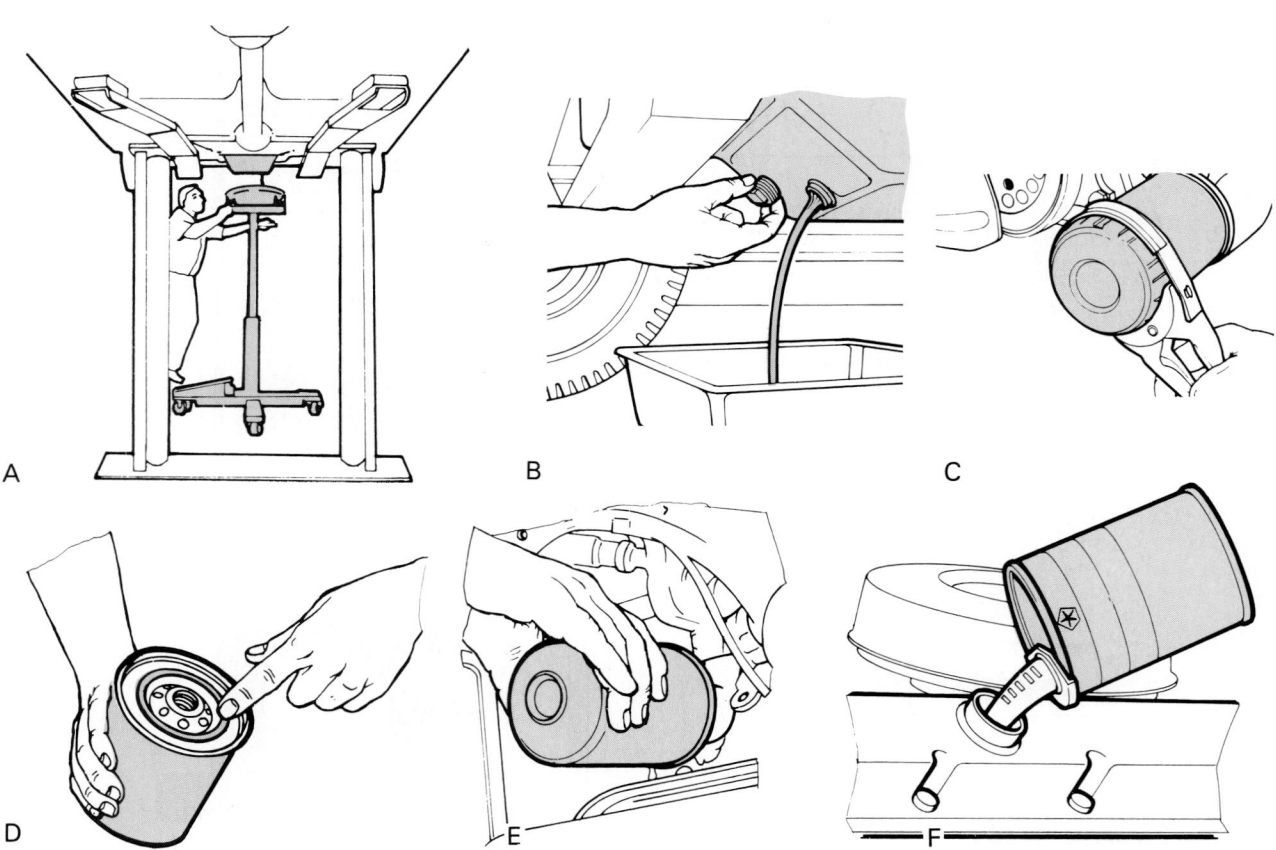

Fig. 38-6. Steps for changing engine oil and filter. A — Use lift or floor jack and jack stands to raise car in level position. Place catch pan under drain plug. B — Unscrew drain plug and allow oil to pour into pan. Be careful of hot oil. It can cause painful burns. C — Use filter wrench to remove old filter. Turn counterclockwise. D — Wipe clean oil on new filter O-ring. This will assure proper tightening. E — Install and tighten oil filter by hand. Hands and filter should be clean and dry. Use a rag if needed. F — Install correct type and quantity of oil. Pour oil into filler or breather opening in valve cover or intake manifold. (Mopar)

may be a rust color on the dipstick. It is used for oil leak detection.

Since the dye is fluorescent, an ultraviolet light can be used to make it glow. When the light is aimed on an oil leak, the dye may appear, for example, a light yellowish-orange color. Any engine oil leak can then be easily traced to its source.

OIL PAN SERVICE

An engine oil pan may need to be removed for various reasons: to service engine bearings or an oil pump, repair a damaged pan or a stripped pan drain plug, or during an engine overhaul.

Some engine oil pans can be removed with the engine in the car, as shown in Fig. 38-7. After removing any bolt-on crossmembers and other obstructions, you must commonly raise the engine off its motor mounts. This may be needed to give enough clearance to unbolt and slide off the oil pan.

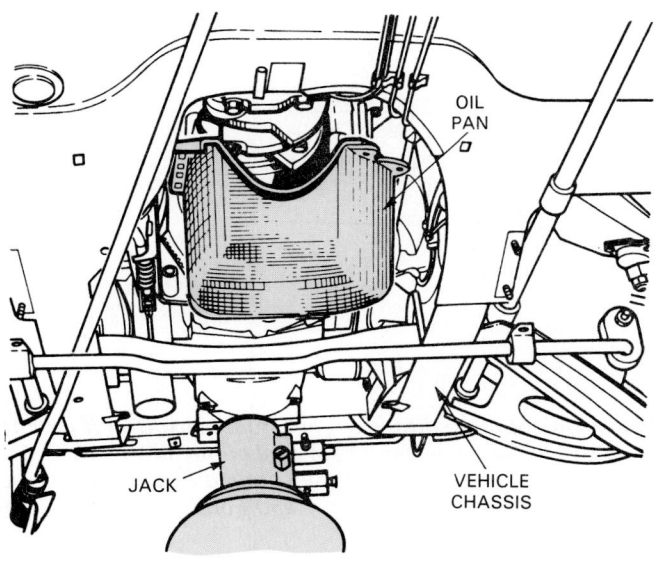

Fig. 38-7. With some cars, oil pan can be removed with engine in car. Use a jack to raise engine off motor mount. Then, slide pan down and out. (Renault)

Other vehicle designs do NOT allow in-car oil pan removal. The engine must be lifted from the frame before the pan will come off. Check the service manual for details.

Removing an engine oil pan

To remove an engine oil pan, first drain out the motor oil. Reinstall the drain plug. Unscrew the bolts around the outside of the pan flange.

To free the pan from the cylinder block, tap on it lightly with a rubber hammer. If stuck tight, carefully pry between the pan flange and the block. Do NOT

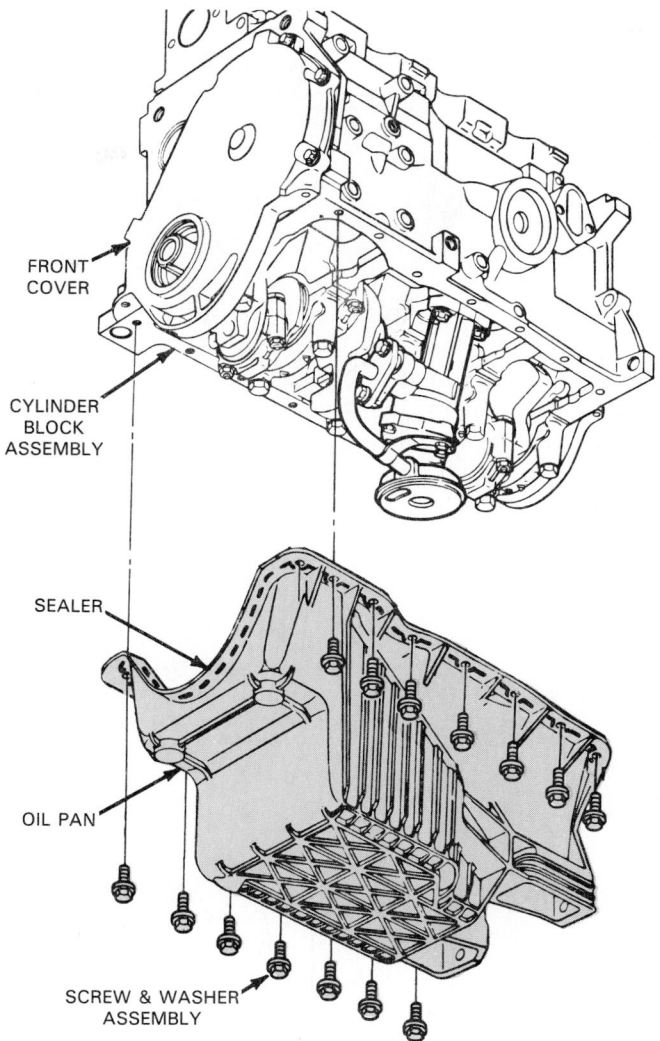

Fig. 38-8. Oil pan is secured by a number of bolts around pan flange. Be careful not to bend flange during removal. (Ford)

bend the oil pan flange or leakage may result upon assembly. Refer to Fig. 38-8.

Using a gasket scraper, remove all old gasket or silicone material from the pan and engine block. Look at Fig. 38-9A. With an aluminum pan, be careful not to nick or dig into the sealing surface.

Check the inside of the pan for debris. Metal bits (bearing particles), plastic pieces (timing gear teeth), rubber particles (valve stem seals) indicate engine mechanical proglems.

Installing an engine oil pan

To install an engine oil pan, wash the pan thoroughly in cold soak cleaner. Check the drain plug hole for stripped threads. Also, lay the pan upside down on a flat workbench. Make sure that the pan flange is NOT bent. Straighten the flange, if needed, with light hammer blows.

Either a gasket or chemical sealer may be recommended for the oil pan. Use approved gasket adhesive

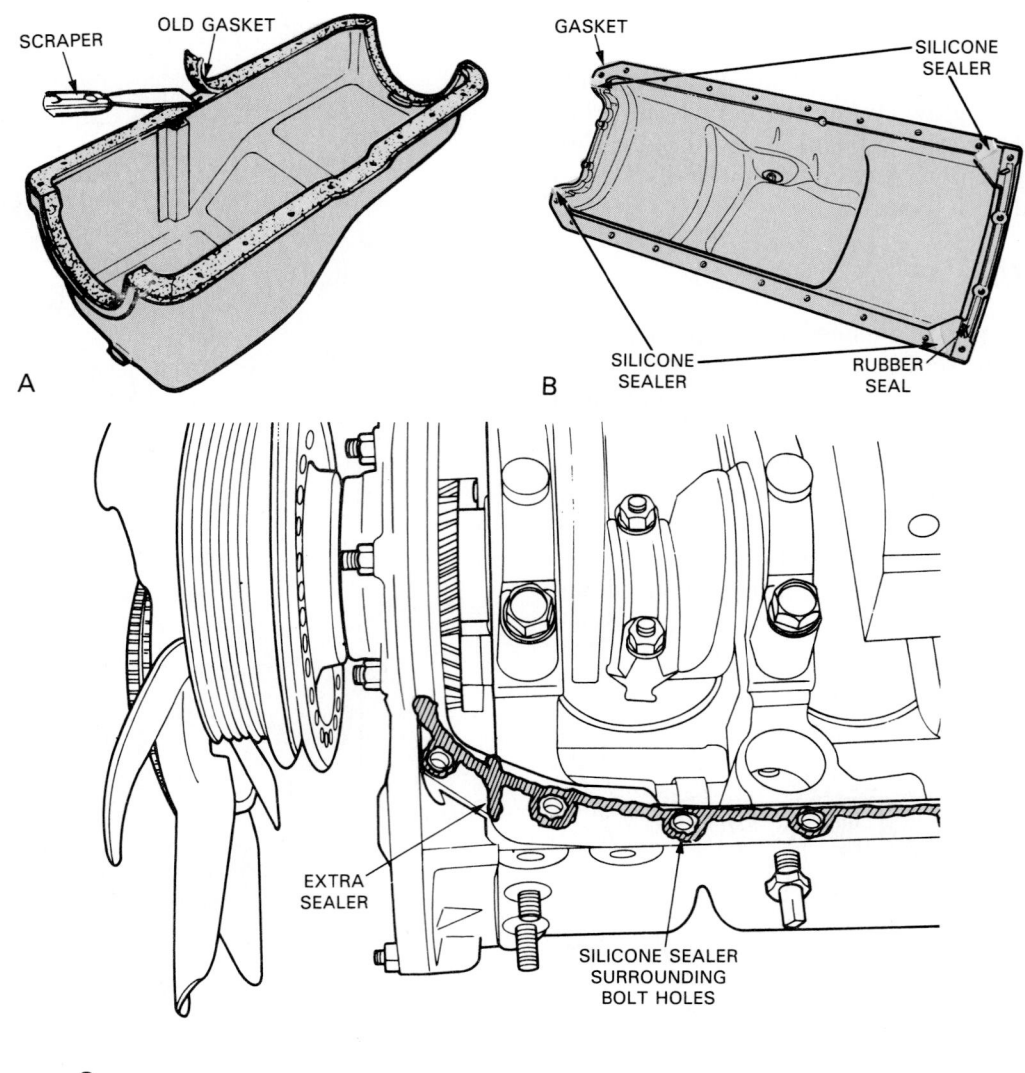

Fig. 38-9. A — Scrape all old gasket or silicone sealer off pan and block. Do not nick surface of aluminum pans. B — If gasket is used, adhere it to flange and align all bolt holes. Fit any seals into place and squirt sealer where gasket meets seal. C — To use silicone sealer only, clean flange with recommended solvent. Then carefully run a bead of sealer around flange and all bolt holes. Use extra sealer where parts or gasket and seals butt together. (Chrysler and Ford)

to position a new gasket. If rubber seals are used on each end, press them into their grooves. Place silicone sealer where the gaskets meet the rubber seals. This is shown in Fig. 38-9B.

To use a chemical or silicone gasket, clean the pan and mating block surfaces with a suitable solvent. Then, run a uniform bead (about 1/8 in. or 3 mm) of sealer around the pan or block flange as recommended. See Fig. 38-9C. Form a continuous bead and place extra sealer at part or gasket-seal joints.

Fit the pan carefully into place on the block, Fig. 38-10. Start all of the pan bolts by hand. Check that the gasket or sealer has not been shifted or smeared. Then, tighten each bolt a little at a time in a crisscross pattern. Torque the bolts to specs.

Double-check drain plug torque. Fill the engine with oil. Inspect for oil leaks with the engine running.

OIL PUMP SERVICE

A *bad oil pump* will cause low or no oil pressure and possibly severe engine damage. When inner parts wear, the pump may leak and have reduced output. The pump drive shaft can also strip in the pump or distributor, preventing pump operation.

If pressure and prelubricator tests point to a faulty oil pump, remove and replace or rebuild the pump.

Oil pump removal

Some oil pumps are located inside the engine oil pan, Fig. 38-10. Others are on the front of the engine under a front cover or on the side of the engine. Since removal procedures vary, refer to a shop manual for direction.

Oil pump rebuild

Most mechanics install a new or factory rebuilt pump

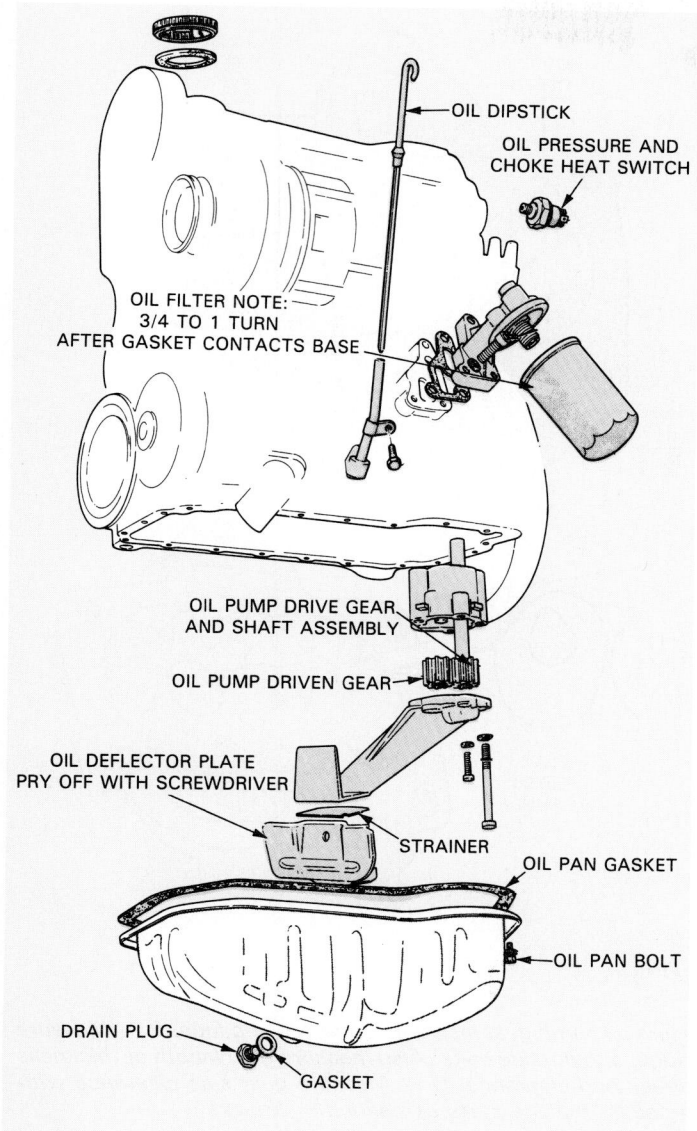

Fig. 38-10. When servicing oil pans, make sure drain plug hole threads are good. Note other parts relating to lubrication system. (Dodge)

when needed. It is usually too costly to completely rebuild an oil pump in-shop. However, you should have a general understanding of how to overhaul oil pumps.

Fig. 38-11 gives the basic steps for servicing a modern rotor type oil pump. Fig. 38-12 summarizes the rebuilding procedures for a gear oil pump. A manual will give full instructions and specs for the exact type of oil pump.

Oil pump installation

Before installation, *prime (fill) the pump* with motor oil. This will assure proper initial operation upon engine starting.

Install the pump in reverse order of removal, Fig. 38-13 and 38-14. Double-check gasket position. Torque all bolts to exact specs. If an oil pickup is used, make sure it is installed properly and tightened.

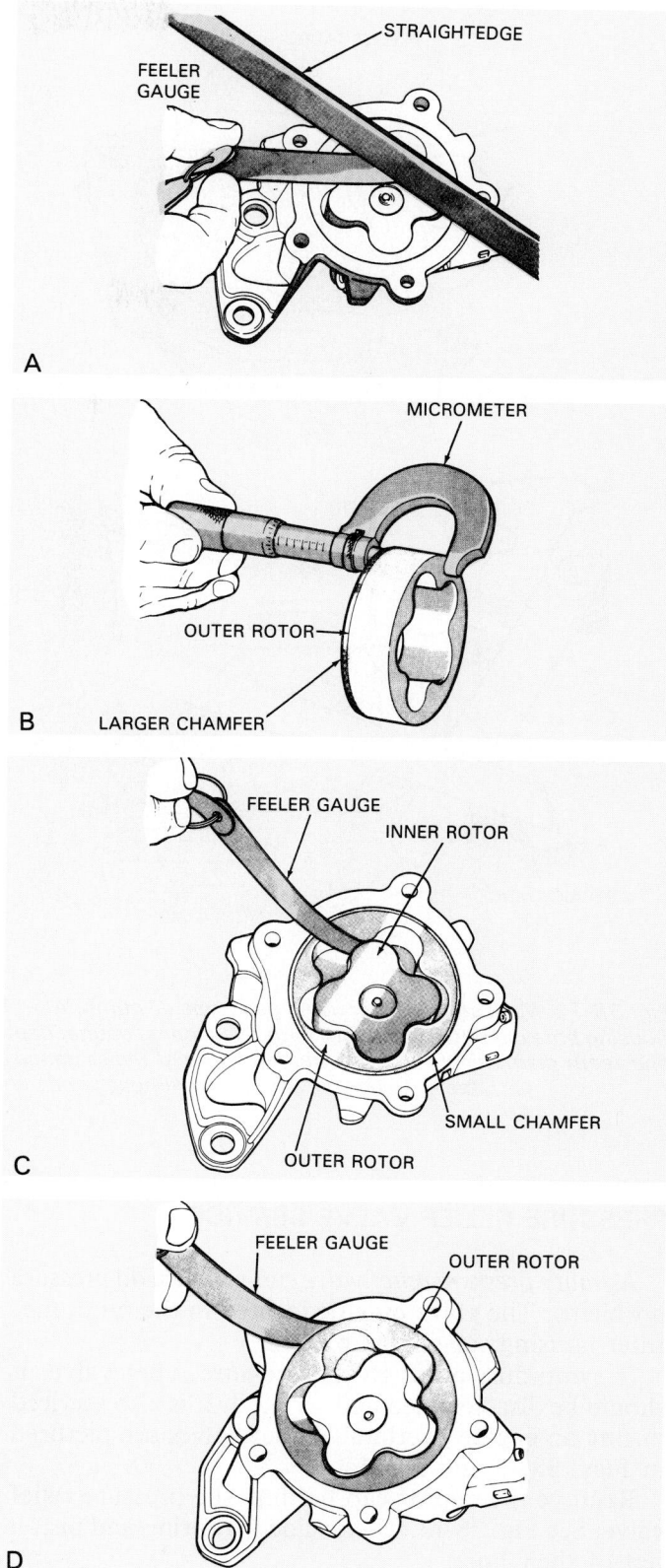

Fig. 38-11. Servicing rotor oil pump. A — Use straightedge and feeler gauge to check rotor end play. B — Measure outer rotor thickness and wear with outside mike. C — Measure clearance between inner and outer rotor with flat feeler gauge. D — Check outer rotor-to-housing clearance with feeler gauge. Also check pump cover for wear or warpage and inspect relief valve components. (Plymouth)

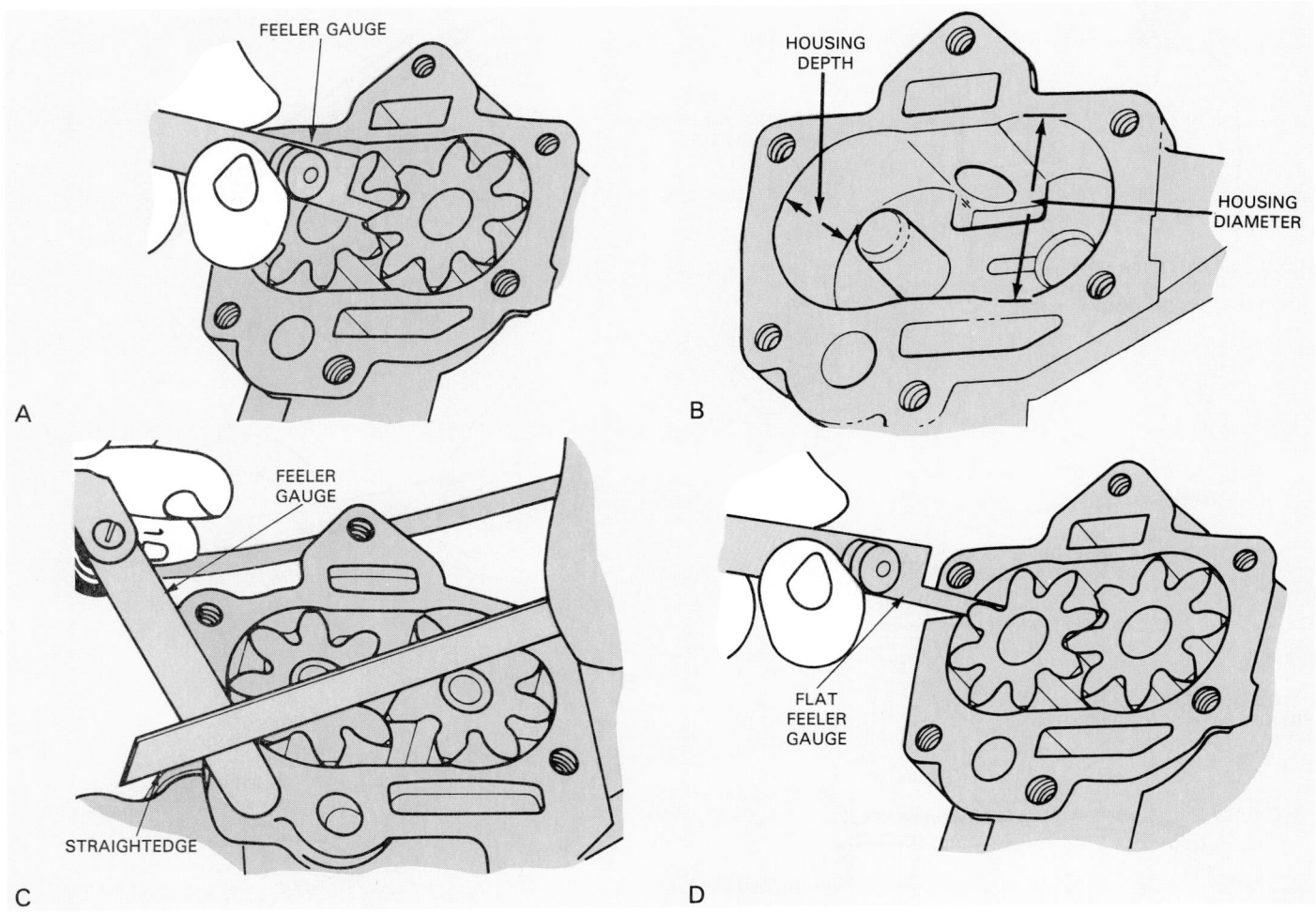

Fig. 38-12. Main steps for servicing gear type oil pump. A — Measure oil pump gear lash with small feeler gauge. B — Measure housing bore diameter and depth with telescoping gauge, depth gauge, and outside mike. Also measure gear length or thickness and teeth diameter. C — Use straightedge and feeler gauge to check end clearance. D — Measure gear side clearance with feeler gauge. If any measurement is not within specs, replace parts as needed.   (Buick)

PRESSURE RELIEF VALVE SERVICE

A *faulty pressure relief valve* can produce oil pressure problems. The valve may be located in the oil pump, filter housing, or engine block.

If symptoms point to the pressure relief valve, it should be disassembled and serviced. It is also serviced during an engine overhaul. Relief valves are pictured in Figs. 38-13 and 38-14.

Remove the cup or cap holding the pressure relief valve. See Fig. 38-13. Then, slide the spring and piston out of their bore.

Measure *spring free length* (length of extended spring) and compare to specs. If the spring is too short or long, install a new spring. One auto maker recommends checking spring tension on a spring tester. Another provides shims for increasing spring tension or an adjustment for changing opening pressure.

Use a micrometer and small hole gauge to check valve and valve bore wear. Also, check the sides of the

valve for scratches or scoring. Replace parts if any problems are found.

Assemble the pressure relief valve. Make sure the valve is facing correctly in its bore. Slide the spring into place. Install any shims and the cover plug or cap. Refer to a manual for details.

OIL PRESSURE INDICATOR AND GAUGE SERVICE

A *bad oil pressure indicator* or *gauge* may scare the customer into thinking there are major engine problems. The indicator light may flicker or stay on, pointing to a low pressure problem. The gauge can read low or high, also indicating a lubrication system problem.

Inspect the indicator or gauge circuit for problems. The wire going to the sending unit may have fallen off (no light, flickering light, improper gauge readings). The sending unit wire may also be shorted to ground (light stays on or gauge always reads high).

To check the action of the indicator or gauge, remove

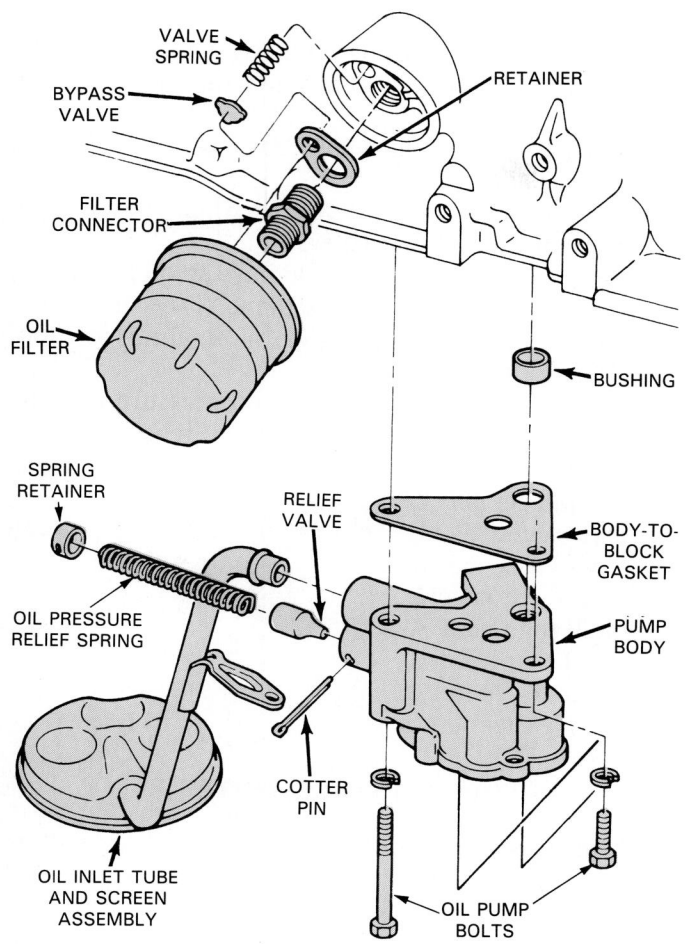

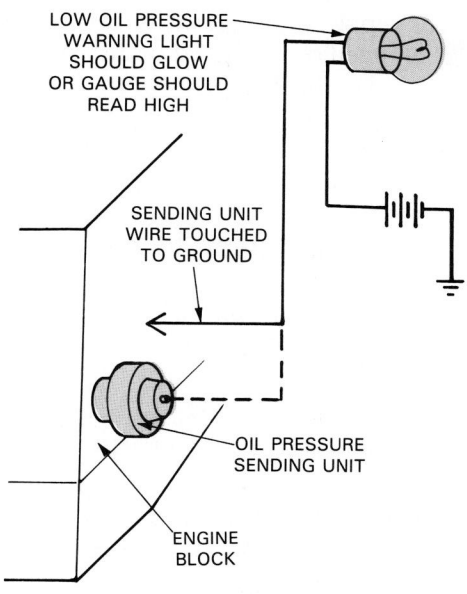

the wire from the sending unit. Touch it on a metal part of the engine. This should make the indicator light glow or the oil pressure gauge read maximum. If it does, the sending unit may be bad. If it does not, then the circuit, indicator, or gauge may be faulty. Look at Fig. 38-15.

Always check the service manual before testing an indicator or gauge circuit. Some auto makers recom-

Fig. 38-13. When servicing oil pump, also service in-housing pressure relief valve. Torque pump mounting to specs. Make sure body-to-block gasket holes are aligned.

Fig. 38-15. Checking action of oil pressure indicator circuit. When sending unit wire is grounded, indicator light should glow or gauge should read maximum. When wire is disconnected, light should go out or gauge should read zero.

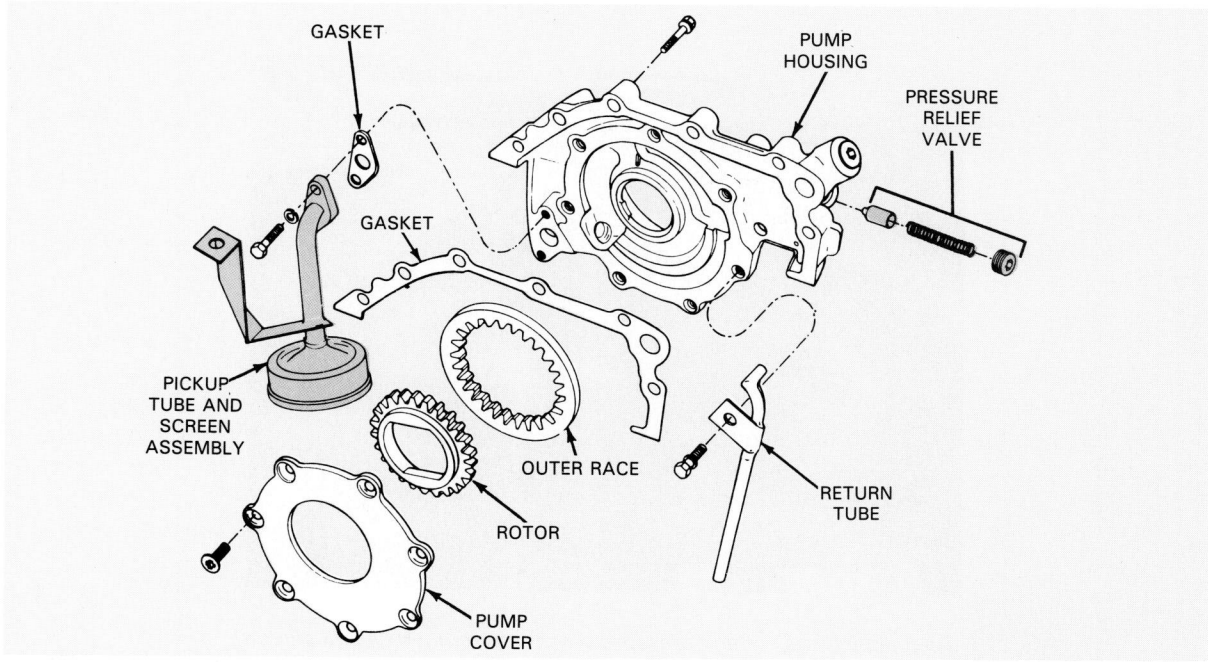

Fig. 38-14. Exploded view shows parts of modern oil pump that mounts on front of engine. Note pressure relief valve, oil pickup, and other parts. Refer to a shop manual for instructions on servicing. (Ford)

mend a special gauge tester. This is especially important with some computer controlled systems. The tester will place a specific resistance in the circuit to avoid circuit damage. Refer to a manual for instructions.

Normally, a low oil pressure light will glow when oil pressure is below 5-10 psi (34-69 kPa).

PCV VALVE SERVICE

A PCV (positive crankcase ventilation) valve should be cleaned or replaced at regular intervals. The valve can become clogged or restricted with dirt and sludge. The valve is usually in the valve cover. It may also be in a breather opening in the intake manifold.

For details of PCV service, look in Chapter 40, Emission Control System Diagnosis, Service, Repair.

KNOW THESE TERMS

Oil consumption, External oil leakage, Internal oil leakage, Oil pressure test, Prelubricator, Oil change interval, Oil dye.

REVIEW QUESTIONS

1. List four common lubrication system problems.
2. High engine oil consumption CANNOT be caused by:
   a. Oil leakage into combustion chambers.
   b. Leaking valve cover gaskets.
   c. Leaking exhaust manifold gaskets.
   d. Worn piston rings or cylinders.
3. List seven common causes of low engine oil pressure.

4. How do you measure actual engine oil pressure?
5. A _____ can be used to help find worn engine bearings or other parts that lower engine oil pressure.
6. How often should a new car's oil and filter be changed?
7. Explain eight rules to follow when changing an engine's oil and oil filter.
8. Some engine oil pans should have an oil pan gasket while others may use a sealant. True or False?
9. Most technicians rebuild worn oil pumps in-shop. True or False?
10. A driver complains that her oil pressure warning light flickers on and off at stop lights.
    Technician A says that the oil level in the engine should be checked.
    Technician B says that the indicator light circuit could also be at fault.
    Who is correct?
    a. Technician A
    b. Technician B
    c. Both A and B
    d. Neither A nor B

ACTIVITIES FOR CHAPTER 38

1. Use the school's video equipment to develop a short videotaped demonstration on how to properly check a vehicle's oil level.
2. Observe an oil change being done at a dealership service department or other facility. Take notes of the steps involved, from moving the car into the bay to completion of the job. Use your notes to write a set of step-by-step instructions for a person doing an oil change for the first time.

Technician is using high pressure washer to remove oil and sludge from outside of engine before repairs. This is a wise practice because it will make work cleaner, more professional, and more enjoyable. (The Eastwood Company)

39 Emission Control Systems

After studying this chapter, you should be able to:
☐ Define the fundamental terms relating to automotive emission control systems.
☐ Explain the sources of air pollution.
☐ Describe the operating principles of emission control systems.
☐ Compare design differences in emission control systems.
☐ Explain how a computer can be used to operate emission control systems.

Emission control systems are used on cars to reduce the amount of harmful chemicals released into the atmosphere. See Fig. 39-1. These systems help keep our air clean and healthy to breathe.

This chapter introduces the terminology, parts, and systems that control automobile emissions. This is an important chapter that prepares you for later textbook chapters. Study it carefully!

AIR POLLUTION

Air pollution is caused by a number of factors. A few natural causes of air pollution are volcanos, forest fires, wind-blown dust, pollen, and decay of vegetation. Factories, home furnaces, fireplaces, and automobiles also pollute our air. All of these factors dirty the air that supports life on earth. Look at Fig. 39-2 on the next page.

The federal government passed strict laws to reduce

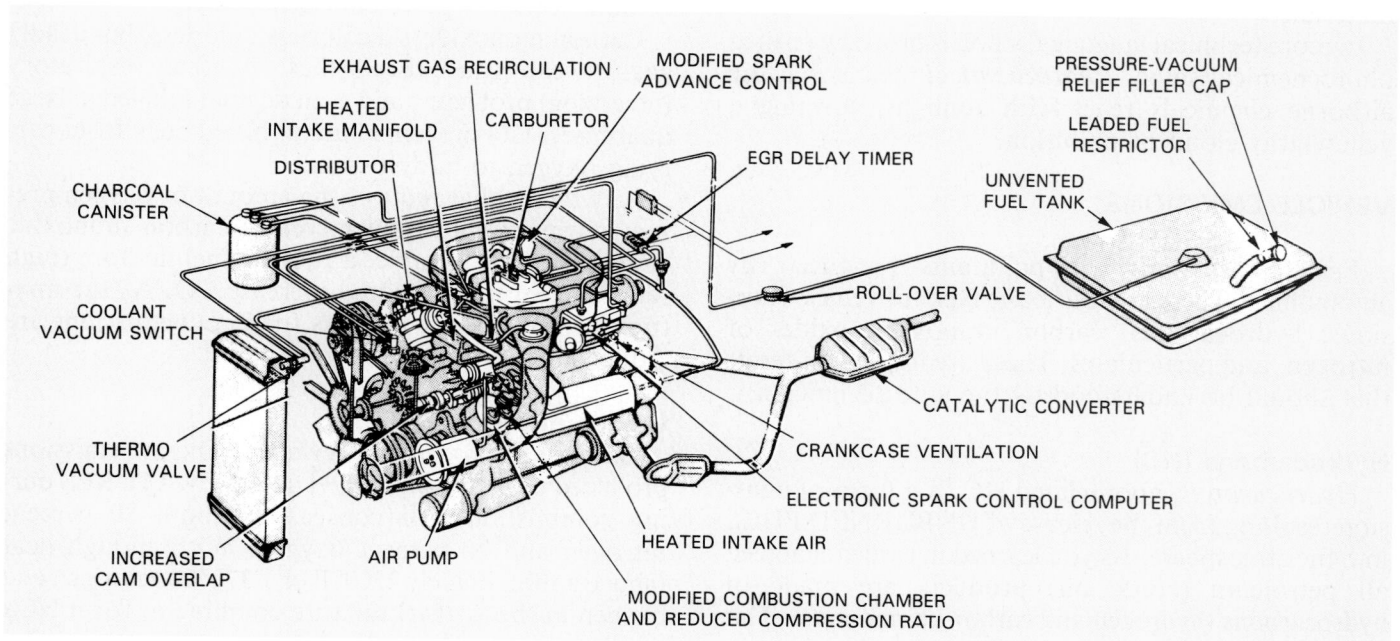

Fig. 39-1. Numerous emission control systems are used on modern autos. All work together to reduce air pollution. (Chrysler)

Fig. 39-2. Smog is common in large cities where there is a concentration of factories, homes, and cars. (American Petroleum Institute)

air pollution. These laws, which are enforced by the EPA (Environmental Protection Agency), limit the amount of emissions that can be emitted. Auto manufacturers have added a number of systems to reduce emissions and meet EPA standards.

Smog

Smog is a nickname given to a visible cloud of airborne pollutants. It is a word derived from the words "smoke" and "fog." Smog is common in large cities. If dense enough, smog can be harmful to humans, animals, vegetation, even paint, rubber, and other materials.

In more technical language, smog is properly termed photochemical smog. *Photochemical* means that the airborne chemicals react with sunlight, forming a yellow-gray cloud of pollution.

VEHICLE EMISSIONS

Vehicle emissions are pollutants produced by automobiles. There are four basic types of vehicle emissions: hydrocarbons, carbon monoxide, oxides of nitrogen, and particulates. These are important terms that should be understood by the auto technician.

Hydrocarbons (HC)

Hydrocarbons, abbreviated HC, is a form of emission resulting from the release of UNBURNED FUEL into the atmosphere. As you learned in earlier chapters, all petroleum (crude oil) products are made of hydrocarbons (hydrogen and carbon compounds). This includes gasoline, diesel fuel, LP-gas, and motor oil.

Hydrocarbon emission can be caused by incomplete combustion or by fuel evaporization. For example, HC is produced when unburned fuel blows out an untuned engine's exhaust system. It can also be caused by fuel vapors escaping from a car's fuel system.

Hydrocarbon emissions are a hazardous form of air pollution. They can contribute to eye, throat, and lung irritation, other illnesses, and possibly cancer.

Carbon monoxide (CO)

Carbon monoxide, abbreviated CO, is an extremely toxic emission resulting from the release of PARTIALLY BURNED FUEL. It is due to the incomplete combustion of a petroleum-based fuel.

Carbon monoxide is a colorless, odorless, but deadly gas. It can cause headaches, nausea, respiratory (breathing) problems, and even death if inhaled in large quantities. CO prevents human blood cells from carrying oxygen to body tissues.

Any factor that reduces the amount of oxygen present during combustion increases carbon monoxide emissions. For example, a rich air-fuel mixture (high ratio of fuel to air) would increase CO. As the mixture is leaned (more air, less fuel), CO emissions are reduced. See Fig. 39-3.

Oxides of nitrogen (NOx)

Oxides of nitrogen, abbreviated NOx, are emissions produced by extremely HIGH TEMPERATURES during combustion. Air consists of about 80 percent nitrogen and 20 percent oxygen. With enough heat (above approximately 2500°F or 1 370°C), nitrogen and oxygen in the air-fuel mixture combine to form NOx emissions.

Oxides of nitrogen produce the dirty brown color

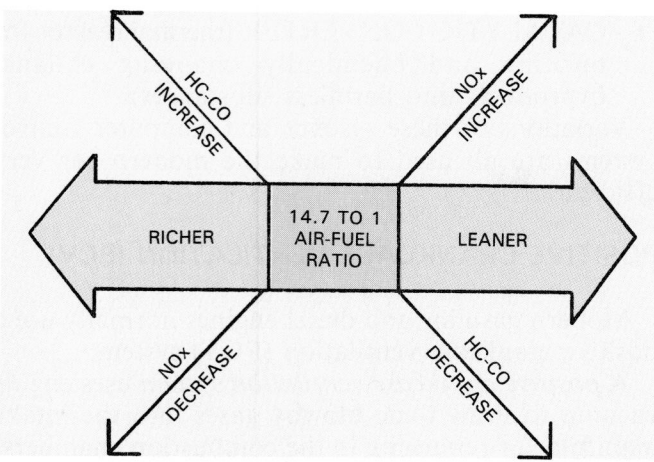

Fig. 39-3. Study relationship between air-fuel ratio and emissions. Close control of the fuel mixture helps keep emissions at a minimum. (Fiat)

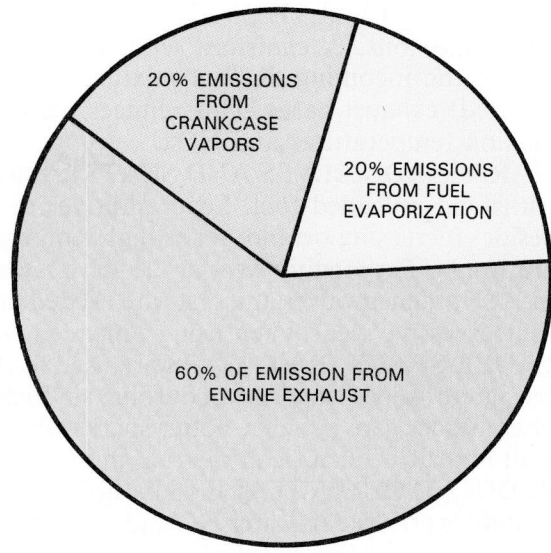

Fig. 39-4. Note three general sources of auto air pollution.

in smog. They also produce ozone in smog which causes an unpleasant smell and an irritant to your eyes and lungs. NOx is also harmful to many types of plants and rubber products.

Basically, an engine with a high compression ratio, lean fuel mixture, high temperature thermostat, and resulting high combustion heat emits high levels of NOx. This poses a problem. These same factors tend to improve gas mileage and reduce HC and CO exhaust emissions. As a result, emission control systems must interact to lower each form of pollution.

Particulates

Particulates are the solid particles of carbon soot and fuel additives that blow out a car's tailpipe. Carbon particles make up the largest percentage of these emissions. The rest of the particulates consist of lead and other additives sometimes used to make gasoline and diesel fuel.

Particulate emissions are a serious problem with diesel engines. You have probably seen a diesel truck or car blowing BLACK SMOKE (particulates) out it's exhaust. Diesel particulates are normally caused by an extremely rich, high powered fuel mixture or a mechanical problem in the injection system.

About 30 percent of all particulate emissions are heavy enough to settle out of the air. The other 70 percent, however, can float in the air for extended periods, causing possible health hazards.

Sources of vehicle emissions

Vehicle emissions, as shown in Fig. 39-4, come from three basic sources:
1. ENGINE CRANKCASE BLOWBY FUMES (20 percent of emissions).
2. FUEL VAPORS (20 percent of emissions).
3. ENGINE EXHAUST GASES (60 percent of emissions).

Various engine modifications and emission control system are used to reduce air pollution from these sources.

ENGINE MODIFICATIONS FOR EMISSION CONTROL

Generally, auto makers agree that the best way to reduce exhaust emissions is to burn all of the fuel inside the engine. For this reason, several engine modifications have been introduced to improve combustion efficiency.

Today's engines generally have the following modifications to lower emissions:
1. LOWER COMPRESSION RATIOS are used to allow the use of unleaded gasoline. Unleaded fuel burns quickly to lower HC emissions. It also does not contain lead additives which cause particulate emissions. Lower compression stroke pressure also reduces combustion temperatures and NOx emissions.
2. LEANER AIR-FUEL MIXTURES are used to lower HC and CO emissions. Leaner mixtures have more air to help all of the fuel burn.
3. HEATED INTAKE MANIFOLDS are used to speed warm-up and permit the use of leaner mixtures during initial start-up.
4. SMALLER COMBUSTION CHAMBER SURFACE VOLUMES are used to reduce HC emissions. A smaller surface area in the combustion chamber increases combustion efficiency by lowering the amount of heat dissipated out of the fuel mixture. Less combustion heat enters the cylinder head and more heat is left to burn the fuel. A hemispherical (hemi) type of combustion chamber typically has the smallest surface volume (abbreviated SV).

5. INCREASED VALVE OVERLAP is used to cut NOx emissions. A camshaft with more overlap dilutes the incoming air-fuel mixture with inert (burned) exhaust gases. This reduces peak combustion temperatures and NOx.

6. HARDENED VALVES AND SEATS are used to withstand unleaded fuel. Lead additives in fuel, besides increasing octane, act as high temperature lubricants. They reduce wear at the valve faces and seats. Hardened valves and seats are needed to prevent excessive wear when using unleaded fuels.

7. WIDER SPARK PLUG GAPS are used to properly ignite "super-lean", clean burning air-fuel mixtures. Wider gaps produce hotter sparks which can ignite hard to burn, lean air-fuel mixtures.

8. REDUCED QUENCH AREAS in the combustion chambers are used to lower HC and CO emissions. A *quench area* is produced when the engine pistons move too close to the cylinder head. When the distance between these metal parts is too close, it tends to quench (put out) combustion and increase emissions due to unburned fuel. Modern engines have redesigned cylinder heads and pistons which prevent high quench areas.

9. HIGHER OPERATING TEMPERATURES are used to improve HC and CO emissions. Today's engines have thermostats with higher temperature ratings. If the metal parts in an engine are hotter, less combustion heat will transfer out of the burning fuel. More heat will remain in the burning mixture to produce gas expansion, piston movement, and more complete combustion.

Various other methods are used to reduce engine emissions. Many of these are covered later in this chapter.

VEHICLE EMISSION CONTROL SYSTEMS

Several different systems are used to reduce the amount of air pollution produced by the automobile. The major ones include:

1. PCV SYSTEM (positive crankcase ventilation system to keep engine crankcase fumes out of atmosphere).

2. HEATED AIR INLET SYSTEM (thermostatic controlled air cleaner maintains constant air temperature entering engine for improved combustion).

3. FUEL EVAPORATION CONTROL SYSTEM (closed vent system prevents fuel vapors from entering atmosphere).

4. EGR SYSTEM (exhaust gas recirculation system injects burned exhaust gases into engine to lower combustion temperature and prevent NOx pollution).

5. AIR INJECTION SYSTEM (air pump forces outside air into exhaust system to help burn unburned fuel).

6. CATALYTIC CONVERTER (thermal reactor for burning and chemically changing exhaust byproducts into harmless substances).

Variations of these systems and computer control systems are all used to make the modern car very efficient.

POSITIVE CRANKCASE VENTILATION (PCV)

Modern gasoline and diesel engines normally use a positive crankcase ventilation (PCV) system.

A *positive crankcase ventilation system* uses engine vacuum to draw toxic blowby gases into the intake manifold for reburning in the combustion chambers. Look at Fig. 39-5.

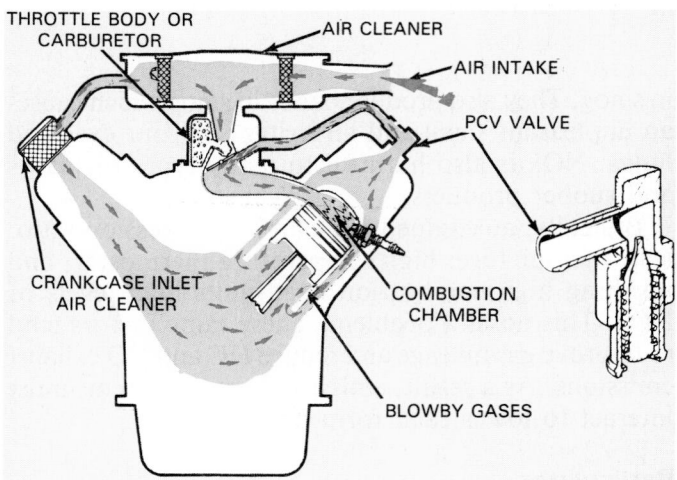

Fig. 39-5. PCV system draws toxic vapors out of crankcase and allows them to be burned in engine. (Chrysler)

Detailed in earlier chapters, engine blowby is caused by pressure leakage past the piston rings on the power strokes. A small percentage of combustion gases can flow through the ring end gaps, back of the piston ring grooves, and into the crankcase.

Engine blowby gases contain unburned fuel (HC), partially burned fuel (CO), particulates, small amounts of water, sulfur, and acid. For this reason, blowby gases must be removed from the engine crankcase. Blowby gases can cause:

1. Air pollution, if released into the atmosphere (HC and CO).

2. Corrosion of engine parts (sulfur and acid).

3. Dilution of engine oil (HC, water, sulfur, and acid).

4. Formation of sludge (chocolate pudding like substance that can clog oil passages).

A PCV system is designed to prevent these problems. It helps keep the inside of the engine clean and also reduces air pollution.

Note! A number of years ago, cars allowed crankcase fumes to enter the atmosphere. A *road draft tube* vented crankcase fumes out the back of the engine. This caused air pollution.

Another engine ventilation system, called an **open PCV system,** was NOT sealed and fumes could leak out when the engine was shut off. These systems have been totally replaced by the closed PCV system.

A *closed PCV system* uses a sealed oil filler cap, sealed oil dipstick, ventilation hoses, and either a PCV valve or flow restrictor. The fumes are drawn into the engine and burned. The system stores the fumes when the engine is not running.

PCV system operation

Although designs vary, the operation of PCV systems are basically the same. Look at Fig. 39-5.

A hose usually connects the intake manifold to the PCV valve in one of the engine valve covers. With the engine running, vacuum acts on the crankcase area of the engine. Air is drawn in through the engine air cleaner, through a vent hose into the other valve cover, and down into the crankcase.

After the fresh air mixes with the crankcase fumes, the mixture is pulled up past the PCV valve, through the hose, and into the engine intake manifold. The crankcase gases are then drawn into the combustion chambers for burning.

Fig. 39-6 shows a cutaway of an air cleaner assembly for a fuel injected engine. Notice the location of parts.

PCV valve

A *PCV valve* is commonly used to control the flow of air through the crankcase ventilation system. It may be located in a rubber grommet in a valve cover or in a breather opening in the intake manifold. The PCV valve changes airflow for idle, cruise, acceleration, wide open throttle, and engine-off conditions.

Refer to Fig. 39-7. It shows the action of a PCV valve under various operating conditions.

At idle, the PCV valve is pulled toward the intake manifold by high vacuum. This restricts flow and prevents a lean air-fuel mixture.

When cruising, lower intake manifold vacuum allows the spring to open the PCV valve. More air can flow through the system to clean out crankcase fumes.

At wide open throttle or with the engine off (low or no intake manifold vacuum), the PCV valve closes completely.

In case of an *engine backfire* (air-fuel mixture in intake manifold ignites), the PCV valve plunger is seated against the body of the valve. This keeps the backfire (burning) from entering and igniting the fumes in the engine crankcase.

Diesel engine PCV system variations

A PCV system for a diesel engine is illustrated in Fig. 39-8. Note how outside air is drawn in through the oil filter cap. The breather cap contains a check valve that keeps crankcase fumes from leaking out of the engine. This maintains a closed PCV system.

HEATED AIR INLET SYSTEM

The *heated air inlet system* speeds engine warmup and keeps the temperature of the air entering the engine

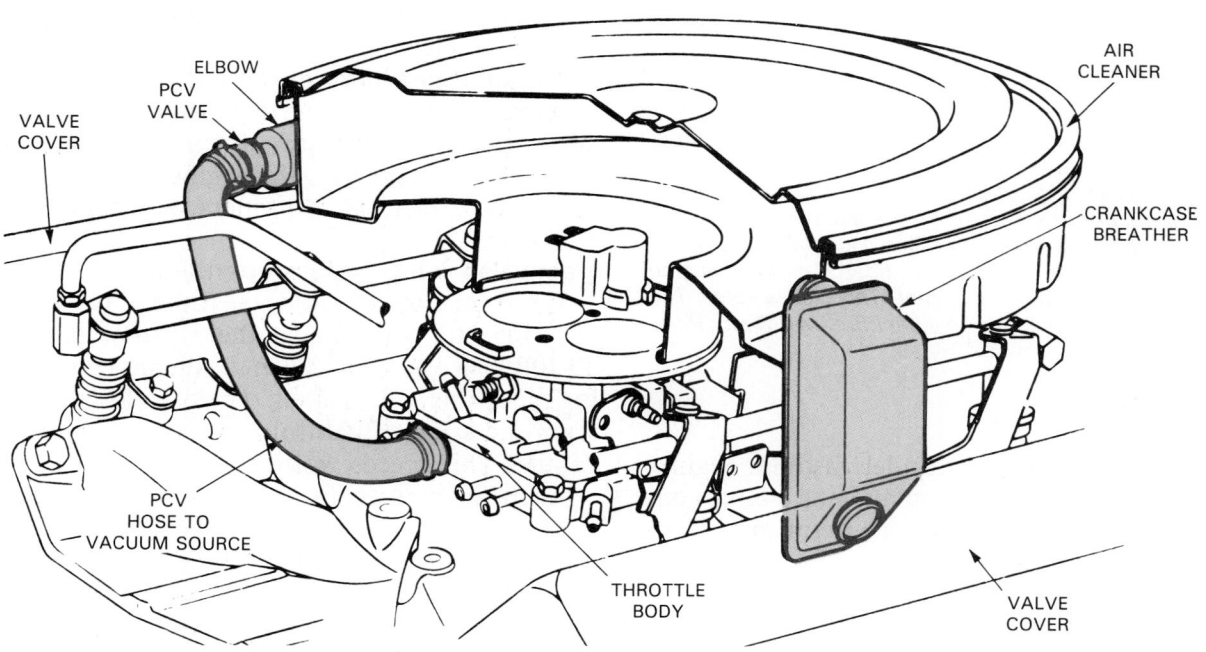

Fig. 39-6. PCV valve is usually located in valve cover. Hose connects valve to source of engine vacuum. Breather allows fresh air to enter other valve cover. (Cadillac)

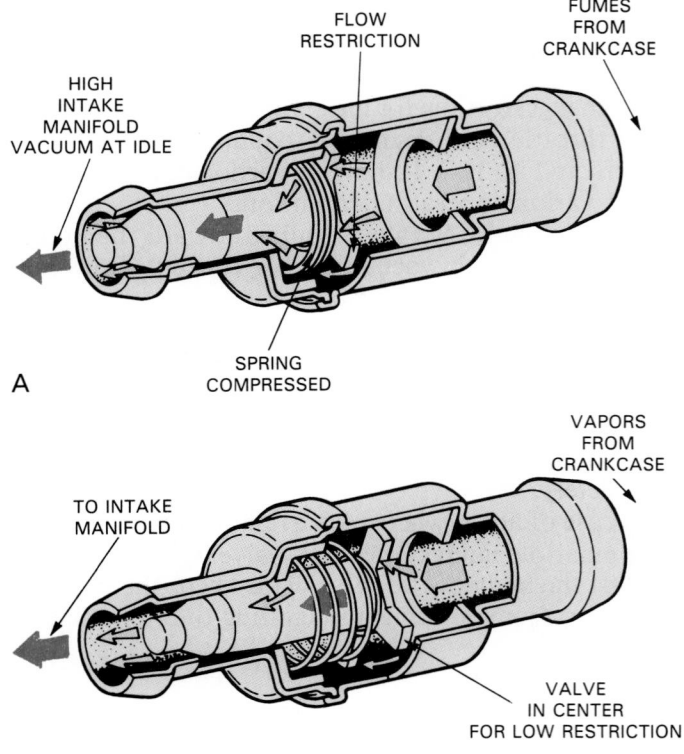

A

B

C

Fig. 39-7. PCV operation under various operating conditions. A — At idle, high manifold vacuum pulls plunger for minimum flow. Only a small amount of air is drawn through valve. Idle air-fuel mixture is not upset. B — During acceleration, intake manifold vacuum drops very low. This allows PCV valve to move to a center position for maximum flow. C — With engine off, spring pushes valve against its seat. This closes valve. The valve is also in this position during a backfire. (AC Spark Plug)

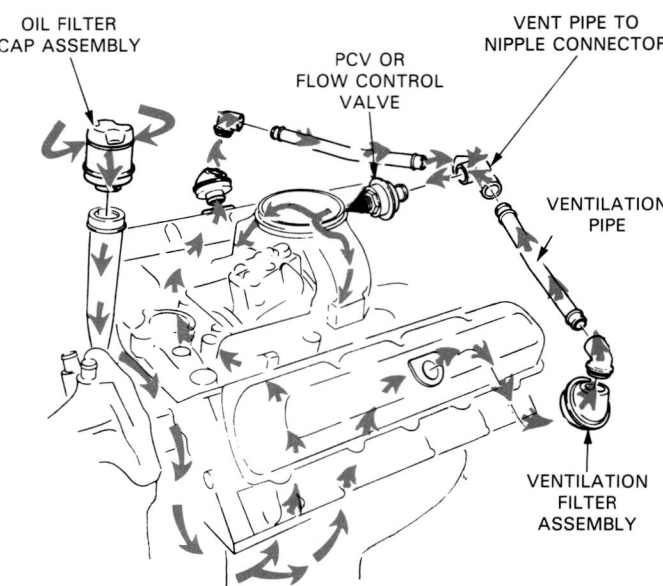

Fig. 39-8. Trace PCV system flow in this diesel engine. (Cadillac)

A *thermal valve* is normally located in the air cleaner to control the vacuum motor and heat control door. Refer to Fig. 39-10A. A vacuum supply is connected to the thermal valve from the engine. Another hose runs from the thermal valve to the vacuum motor (diaphragm).

The *vacuum motor,* also called *vacuum diaphragm,* operates the air control door or flap in the air cleaner inlet. Look at Fig. 39-10B. The vacuum motor consists of a flexible diaphragm, spring, rod, and diaphragm chamber. When vacuum is applied to the unit, the diaphragm and rod are pulled upward, moving the air cleaner door.

The *air cleaner door* or *flap* can be opened or closed to route either cool or heated air into the air cleaner. When the door is closed, hot air from the exhaust manifold shroud enters the engine. When the door is open, cooler, outside air enters the engine.

Heated air inlet system operation

When the engine is cold, the thermal valve is closed, allowing full vacuum to the vacuum motor, Fig. 39-10B. The vacuum acts on the diaphragm, compressing the spring, and pulling the door closed. Warm air from the exhaust manifold shroud is drawn into the engine. This speeds warmup.

As the inlet air temperature rises, the thermal valve starts to close. Spring tension can then begin to open the inlet door, Fig. 39-10C. As a result, both heated air and cool air mix and flow into the engine. In this way, a constant inlet air temperature is maintained.

When the engine and outside air are hot (above inlet system operating temperature), the thermal valve closes. Without vacuum, spring tension in the

at about 70°F (21°C). Late model gasoline engines commonly use this system. By maintaining a more constant inlet air temperature, the carburetor or fuel injection system can be calibrated leaner to reduce emissions.

The heated air inlet system, also called *thermostatic air cleaner system,* also helps prevent carburetor icing during warm-up. This system typically consists of the parts shown in Fig. 39-9.

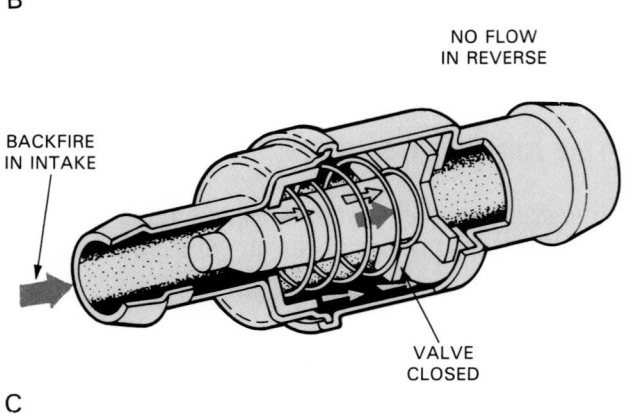

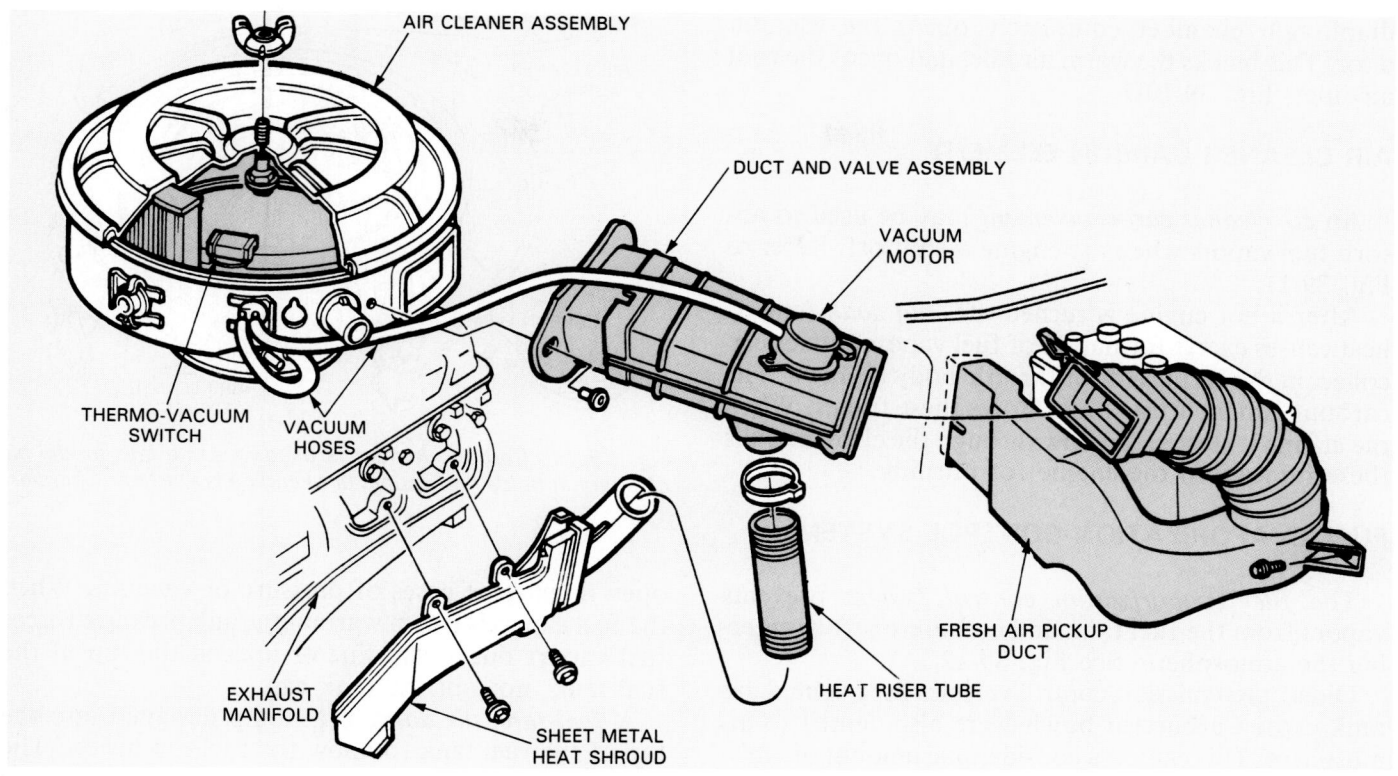

Fig. 39-9. Basic parts of modern thermostatic air cleaner assembly. Note how heat shroud fits around exhaust manifold for warming air charge. (Ford)

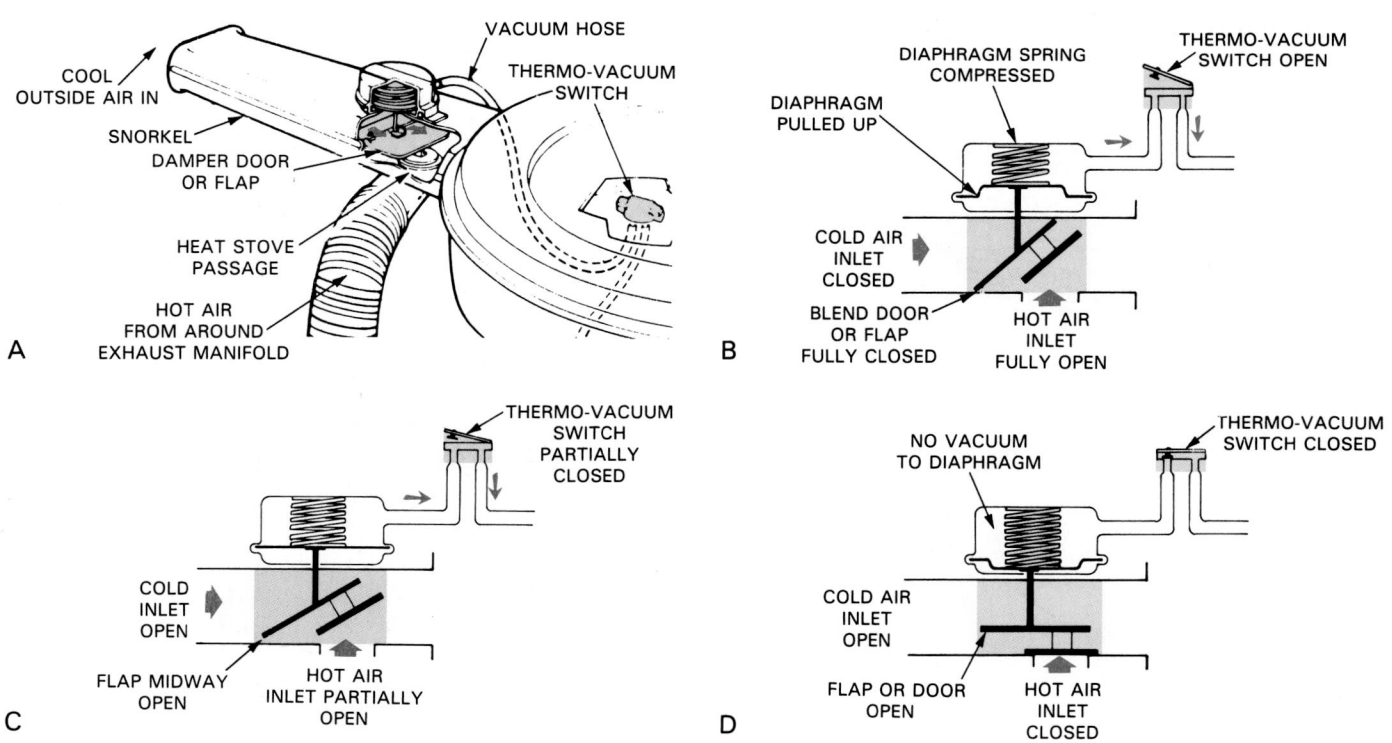

Fig. 39-10. Study thermostatic air cleaner construction and operation carefully. A — Damper or flap is hinged inside snorkel. Thermo-vacuum switch and vacuum motor operate flap. B — Engine cold. Thermo-vacuum switch is open. Vacuum deflects diaphragm to pull flap closed. Warm air from around exhaust manifold shroud then enters air cleaner. C — Engine at operating temperature. Thermo-vacuum switch partially open. Diaphragm or vacuum motor partially closes to mix hot and cool air. D — Engine and outside air hot. Thermo-vacuum switch closed. No vacuum applied to motor. Spring pushes diaphragm down to block warm air entry. (Buick and Fiat)

diaphragm chamber completely opens the vacuum door. This blocks the warm air inlet and opens the cool air inlet, Fig. 39-10D.

AIR CLEANER CARBON ELEMENT

An *air cleaner carbon element* may be used to absorb fuel vapors when the engine is shut off. Refer to Fig. 39-11.

After a hot engine is turned off, **hot soak** (engine heat causes excess formation of fuel vapors) fumes can collect in the carburetor or throttle body air horn. The carbon element attracts and stores these fumes. When the engine is started, airflow through the element pulls these fumes into the engine for burning.

FUEL EVAPORIZATION CONTROL SYSTEM

The *fuel evaporization control system* prevents vapors from the fuel tank and carburetor from entering the atmosphere. See Fig. 39-12.

Older, pre-emission-control vehicles used vented gas tank caps. Carburetor bowls were also vented to atmosphere. This caused a considerable amount of emissions. Modern vehicles commonly use a fuel evaporization control system to prevent this source of air pollution.

A *sealed fuel tank cap* is used to keep fuel vapors from entering the atmosphere through the tank filler neck. It may contain pressure and vacuum valves that

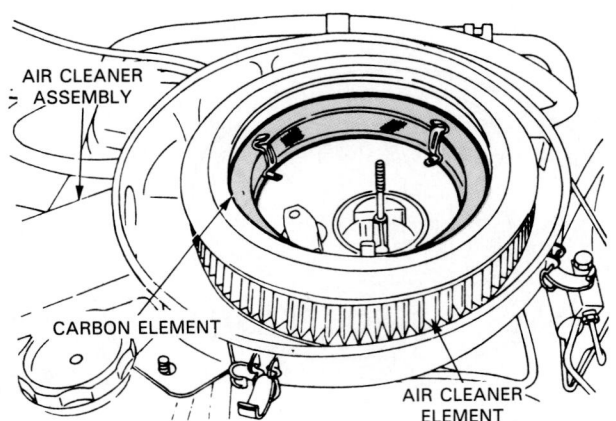

Fig. 39-11. Carbon element is used in some late model air cleaners. It holds fuel vapors until engine is started. (Chrysler)

open in extreme cases of pressure or vacuum. When the fuel expands (from warming), tank pressure forces fuel vapors out a vent line or lines at the top of the fuel tank, not out the tank cap.

A *fuel tank air dome* is a hump designed into the top of the fuel tank to allow for fuel expansion. The dome normally provides about 10 percent air space to allow for fuel heating and the resulting volume increase. Refer to Fig. 39-12.

A *liquid-vapor separator* is frequently used to keep liquid fuel from entering the evaporation control system. It is simply a metal tank located above the main

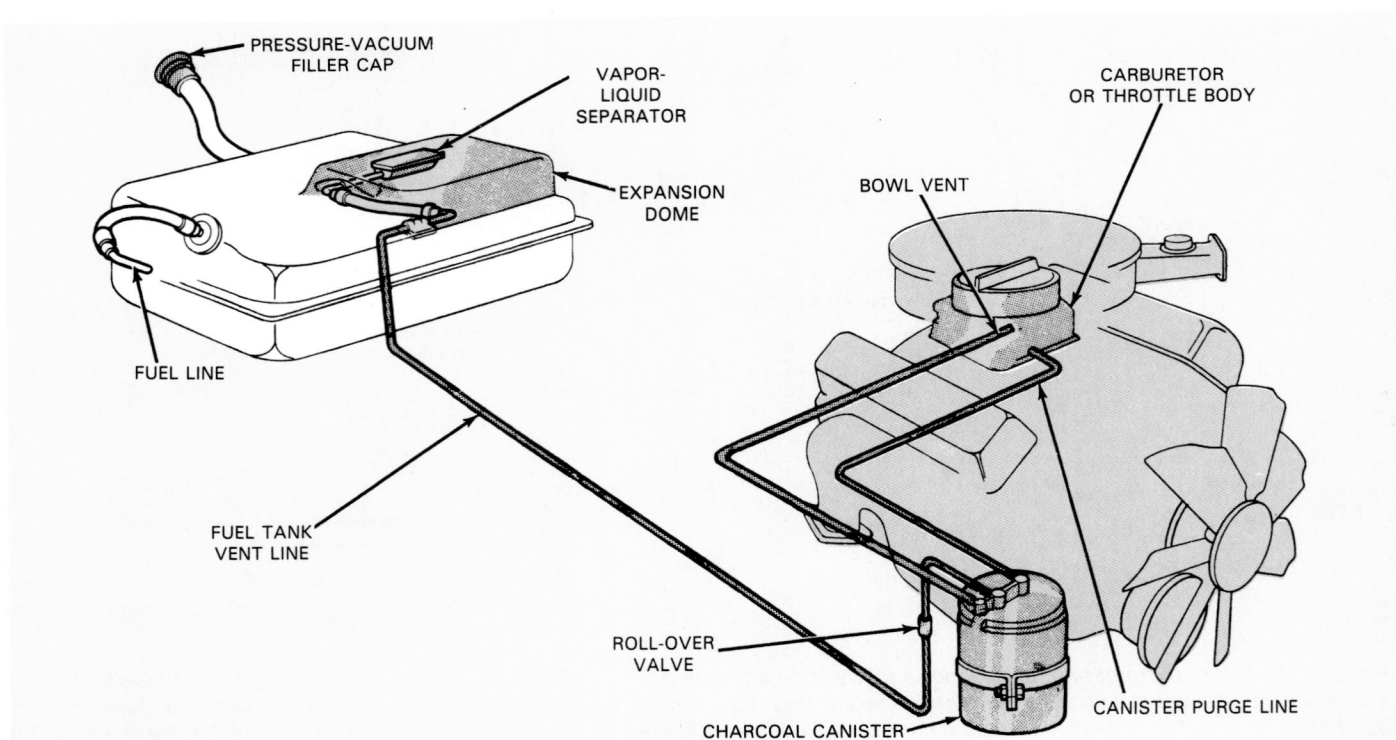

Fig. 39-12. Evaporation control system. Study parts and part locations. System draws fuel vapors into engine for burning. (Plymouth)

fuel tank, Fig. 39-12. Liquid fuel condenses on the walls of the liquid-vapor separator. The liquid fuel then flows back into the fuel tank.

A *roll-over valve* is sometimes used in the vent line from the fuel tank. It keeps liquid fuel from entering the vent line after an auto accident where the vehicle rolls. Refer to Fig. 39-12. The valve contains a metal ball or plunger valve that blocks the vent line when the valve is turned over.

A *fuel tank vent line* carries fuel tank vapors up to a charcoal canister in the engine compartment.

The *charcoal canister* stores fuel vapors when the engine is NOT running. See Fig. 39-12. The metal or plastic canister is filled with activated charcoal granules. The charcoal is capable of absorbing fuel vapors.

The top of the canister has fittings for the fuel tank vent line, carburetor vent line, and the purge (cleaning) line. The bottom of the canister has an air filter that cleans outside air entering the canister.

Fig. 39-13 shows a cutaway view of a charcoal canister. Note that this canister uses a vapor vent valve. This valve is open to allow carburetor bowl venting when the engine is off. It is pulled closed by vacuum when the engine is running to seal the bowl vent line.

A *carburetor vent line* connects the carburetor fuel bowl with the charcoal canister. Bowl vapors flow through this line and into the canister.

A *purge line* is used for removing or cleaning the stored vapors out of the charcoal canister. It connects

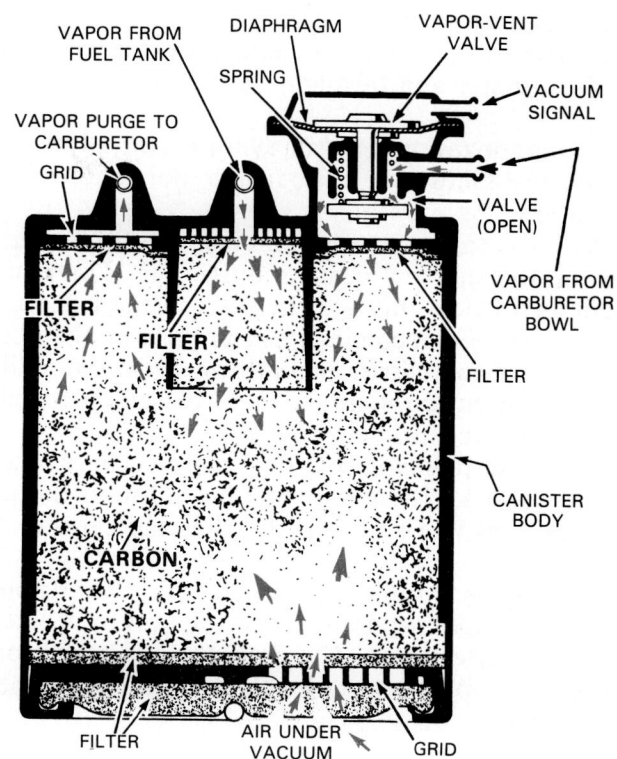

Fig. 39-13. Cutaway view of charcoal canister. Carbon granules store gasoline vapors when engine is off. Then, when engine starts, vacuum draws air through bottom of canister. This pulls vapors into engine. Valve on top of canister closes purge line when engine is not running. (Oldsmobile)

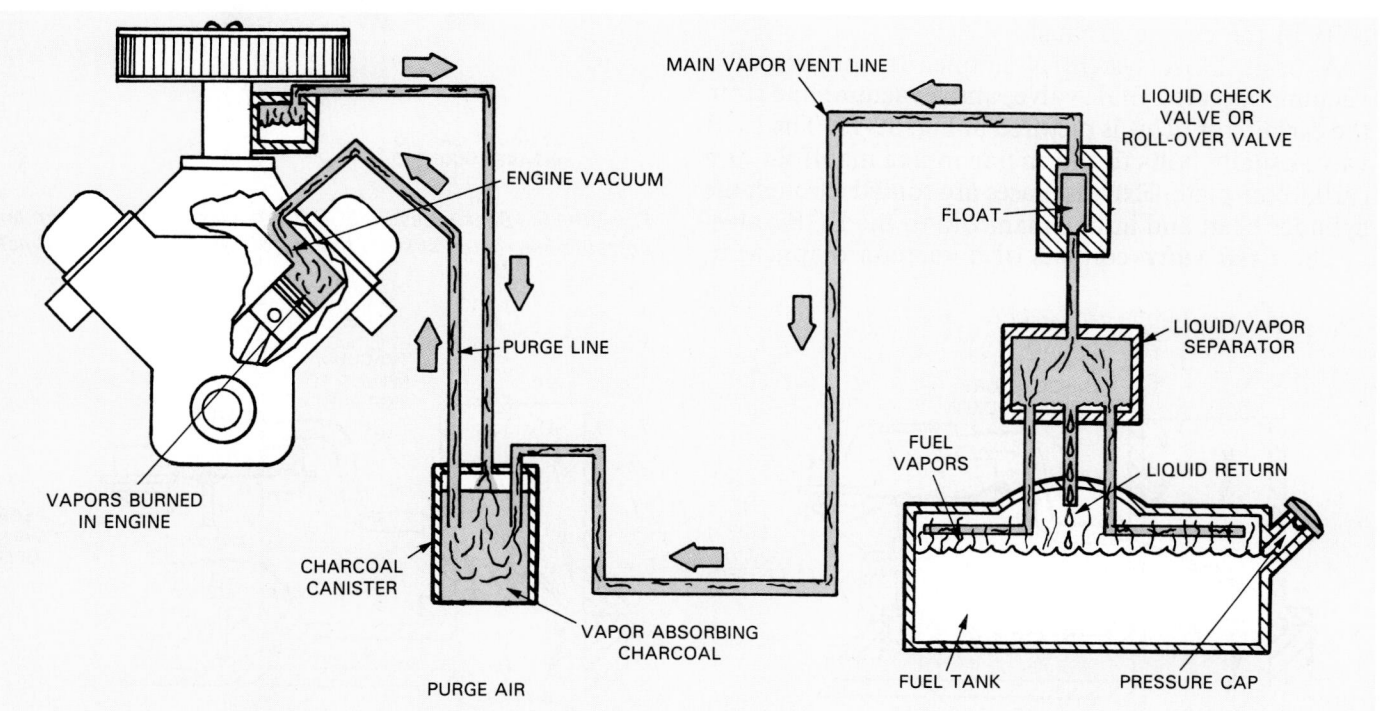

Fig. 39-14. Operation of evaporization control system and related components. Fuel tank and carburetor vapors flow to canister with engine off. When engine starts, vacuum pulls vapors out of charcoal in canister for burning in cylinders. Liquid-vapor separator prevents liquid fuel from entering vent line. Roll-over valve closes during auto accident where car rolls upside-down. This prevents possible fire.

the canister and the engine intake manifold. When the engine is running, engine vacuum draws the vapors out of the canister and through the purge line.

Fuel evaporization control system operation

Fig. 39-14 illustrates basic fuel evaporization system operation.

With the engine running, intake manifold vacuum acts on the charcoal canister purge line. This causes fresh air to flow through the filter in the bottom of the canister. The incoming fresh air picks up the stored fuel vapors and carries them through the purge line. The vapors enter the intake manifold and are pulled into the combustion chambers for burning.

When the engine is shut off, engine heat produces excess vapors. These vapors flow through the carburetor vent line and into the charcoal canister for storage.

Any vapors forming in the fuel tank, flow through the liquid-vapor separator, into the tank vent line to the charcoal canister. The charcoal canister absorbs these fuel vapors and holds them until the engine is started again.

EXHAUST GAS RECIRCULATION SYSTEM

The *exhaust gas recirculation (EGR) system* allows burned exhaust gases to enter the engine intake manifold to help reduce NOx emissions. When exhaust gases are added to the air-fuel mixture, they decrease peak combustion temperatures. For this reason, an exhaust gas recirculation system lowers the amount of NOx in the engine exhaust.

A basic EGR system is simple. It consists of a vacuum operated EGR valve, and a vacuum line from the carburetor. This is pictured in Fig. 39-15. The EGR valve usually bolts to the engine intake manifold or a carburetor plate. Exhaust gases are routed through the cylinder head and intake manifold to the EGR valve.

The *EGR valve* consists of a vacuum diaphragm, spring, plunger, exhaust gas valve, and a diaphragm housing. It is designed to control exhaust flow into the intake manifold. See Fig. 39-16.

Basic EGR system operation

At idle, the throttle plate in the carburetor or fuel injection throttle body is closed, Fig. 39-15. This blocks off engine vacuum so it cannot act on the EGR valve. The EGR spring holds the valve shut and exhaust gases do NOT enter the intake manifold.

If the EGR valve were to open at idle, it could upset the air-fuel mixture and the engine could stall.

When the throttle plate is swung open to increase

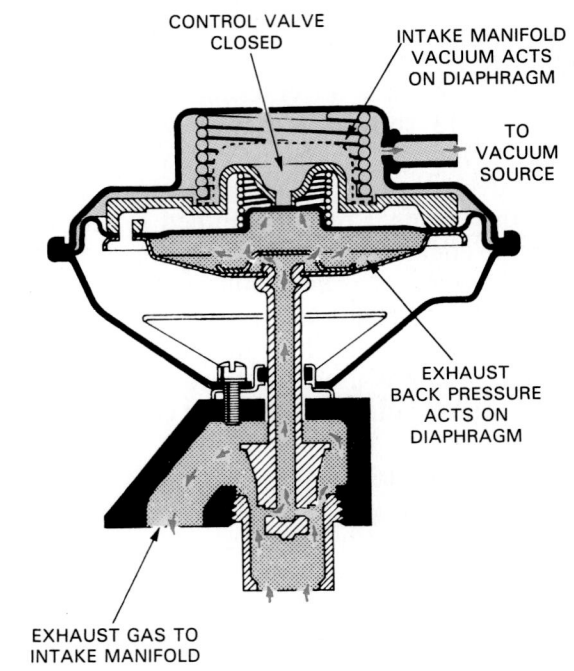

Fig. 39-16. Back pressure EGR valve uses engine vacuum and pressure in exhaust system to control valve opening. (Buick)

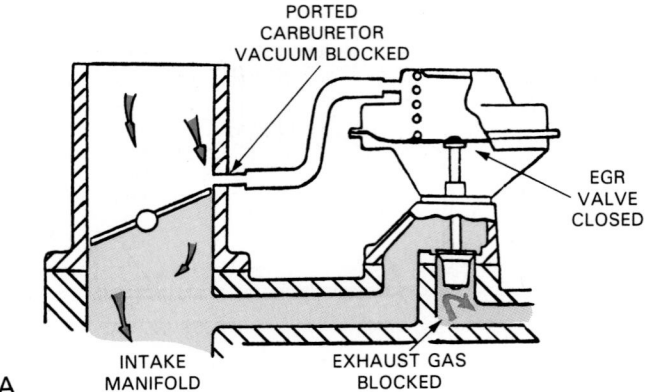

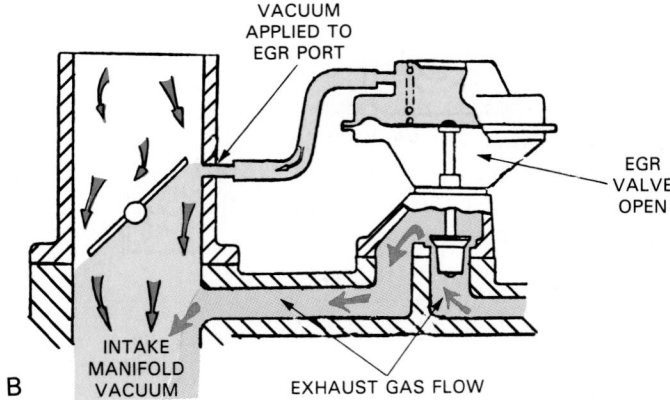

Fig. 39-15. EGR valve operation. A — Throttle is closed for engine idle speed. Vacuum to EGR valve blocked and valve remains closed. B — Throttle opens for more engine speed. This opens vacuum port to EGR valve. Diaphragm is pulled up and exhaust gases enter engine intake manifold.

speed, engine vacuum is applied to the EGR hose. Vacuum pulls the EGR diaphragm up. In turn, the diaphragm pulls the valve open.

Engine exhaust can then enter the intake manifold and combustion chambers. At higher engine speeds, there is enough air flowing into the engine that the air-fuel mixture is not upset by the open EGR valve.

Electronic EGR valve

An *electronic EGR valve* uses electric solenoids to open and close its exhaust passages. It works WITHOUT engine vacuum, as do conventional EGR valves. The EGR solenoids are operated by the vehicle's computer system.

To open one of the exhaust passages in the EGR valve, the ECU energizes a solenoid. The solenoid then lifts up its pintle (valve) to open an exhaust recirculation passage. Exhaust gases flow through *orifices* (metered openings) to limit engine combustion temperatures and prevent NOx pollution. By using several solenoids and valves, more precise control of exhaust gas metering is provided.

The computer or ECU uses input data from the engine temperature sensor, airflow sensor, throttle position sensor, and sometimes other sensors. The sensor signals allow the computer to determine when to open and close each pintle valve for maximum efficiency and minimum exhaust emissions.

EGR system variations

There are several variations of our basic EGR system. The basic function, however, is fundamentally the same for all.

Look at Fig. 39-16. It illustrates a **back pressure EGR valve.** This type valve uses both engine vacuum and exhaust back pressure to control valve action. This provides more accurate control of EGR valve opening.

An **engine coolant temperature switch** may be used to prevent exhaust gas recirculation when the engine is cold. A cold engine does not have extremely high combustion temperatures and does not produce very much NOx. By blocking vacuum to the EGR valve below 100 °F (38 °C), the drivability and performance of the cold engine is improved.

A **wide open throttle valve** (WOT valve) is sometimes connected into the vacuum line to the EGR valve. It opens under full acceleration to provide venturi vacuum to the EGR valve. At wide open throttle, intake manifold vacuum is very low, but venturi vacuum is high.

Figs. 39-17 and 39-18 show two other EGR valve designs. Study them!

Fig. 39-19 shows an EGR system with small jets in the bottom of the intake manifold. The small **EGR jets** meter a small amount of exhaust gases into the air-fuel mixture. The jets are small enough that they do not upset the idle air-fuel mixture.

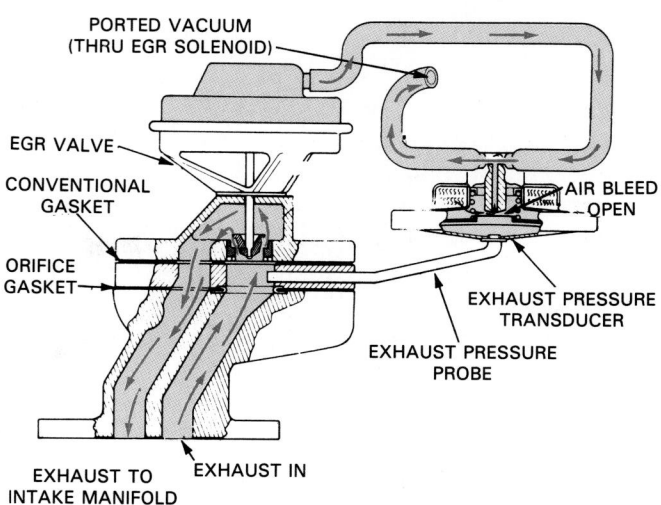

Fig. 39-17. This EGR valve uses a back pressure transducer to control vacuum to EGR diaphragm. Exhaust back pressure acts on the transducer diaphragm. An increase in engine load, for example, increases back pressure. The transducer can then increase vacuum to the EGR valve, maintaining the right amount of exhaust flow into engine for varying operating conditions. (Cadillac)

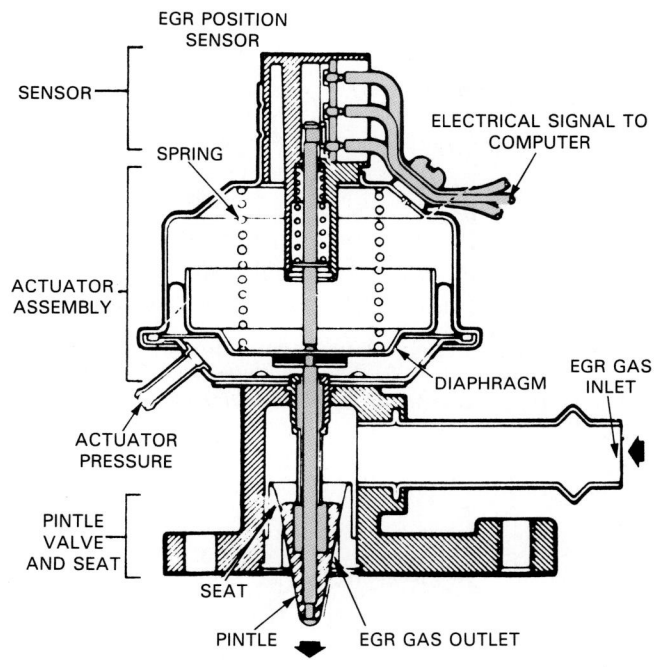

Fig. 39-18. An EGR valve with a sensor connected to car's on-board computer. Movement of EGR plunger changes current flow through sensor, allowing computer to alter operation of engine and other systems. (Ford)

AIR INJECTION SYSTEM

An *air injection system* forces fresh air into the exhaust ports of the engine to reduce HC and CO emissions. See Fig. 39-20.

The exhaust gases leaving an engine can contain unburned and partially burned fuel. Oxygen from the air injection system causes this fuel to continue to burn.

Fig. 39-21 shows the major parts of an air injection system.

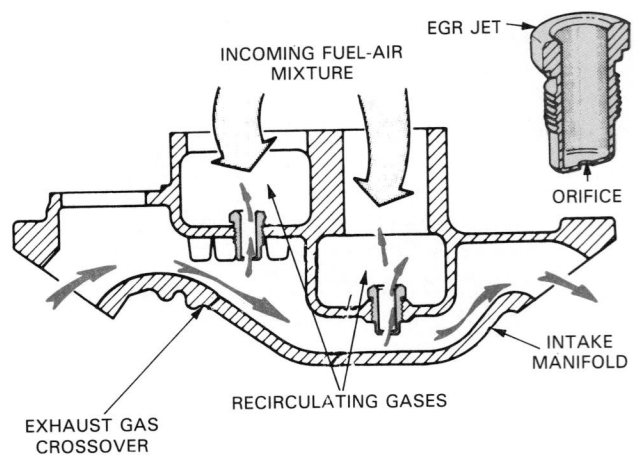

Fig. 39-19. EGR jets are small fittings in base of engine intake manifold. Jet openings are calibrated to allow metered amounts of exhaust gas to mix with air-fuel mixture. (Chevrolet)

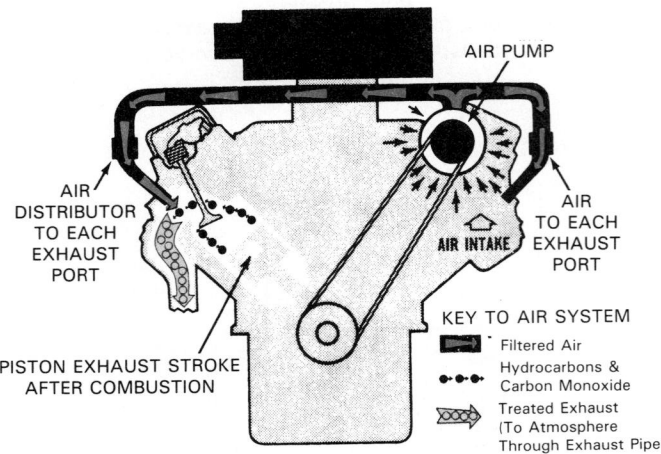

Fig. 39-20. Air injection system operation. Air pump forces outside air into exhaust manifolds. Air helps hot exhaust gases burn as they blow out of open exhaust valves. (GMC)

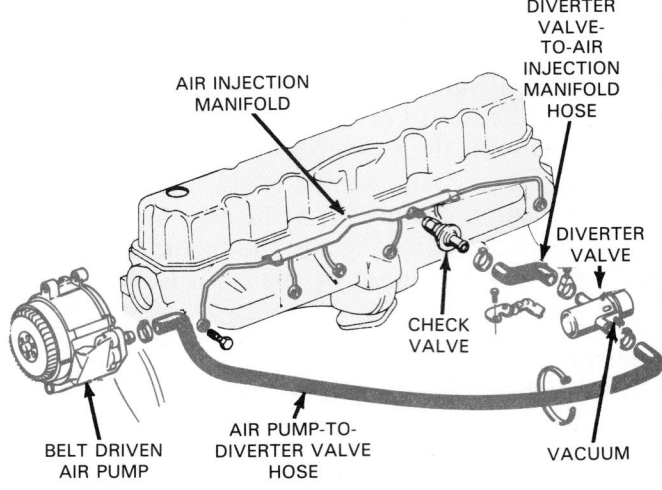

Fig. 39-21. Basic parts of air injection system. Air pump normally bolts to front of engine. Hose carries air to diverter valve. Air then enters exhaust manifold through check valve and distribution manifold. (Chrysler)

The *air pump* is belt driven and forces air at low pressure into the system. As pictured in Fig. 39-21, a rubber hose connects the output of the pump to a diverter valve.

Fig. 39-22 shows a cutaway view of an air injection pump. Note how the spinning vanes or blades pull air in one side of the pump. The air is then trapped and compressed as the vanes rotate. As rotation continues, air is forced out a second opening in the pump.

The *diverter valve* keeps air from entering the exhaust system during deceleration. This prevents backfiring in the exhaust system. Refer to Figs. 39-21 and 39-23. The diverter valve also limits maximum system air pressure when needed. It releases excessive pressure through a silencer or muffler.

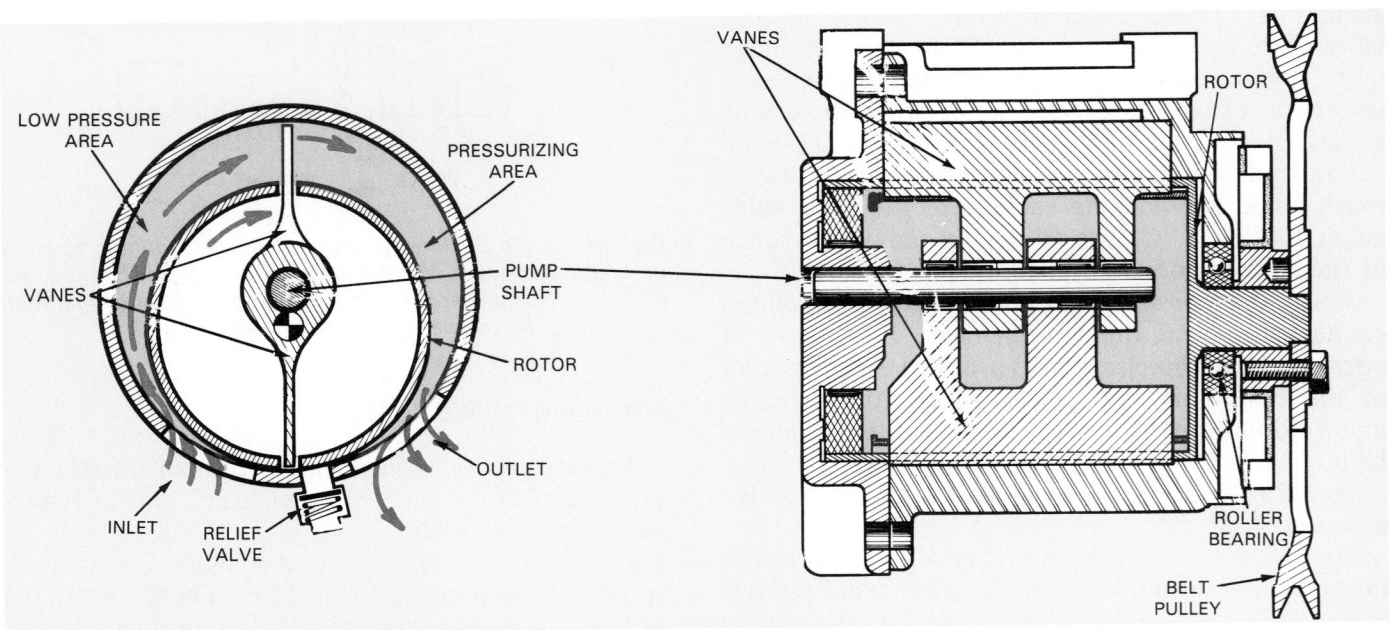

Fig. 39-22. Cutaway show action inside air pump for air injection system. Belt turns pump pulley, shaft, and rotor. Vanes trap and pressurize air. (Peugeot)

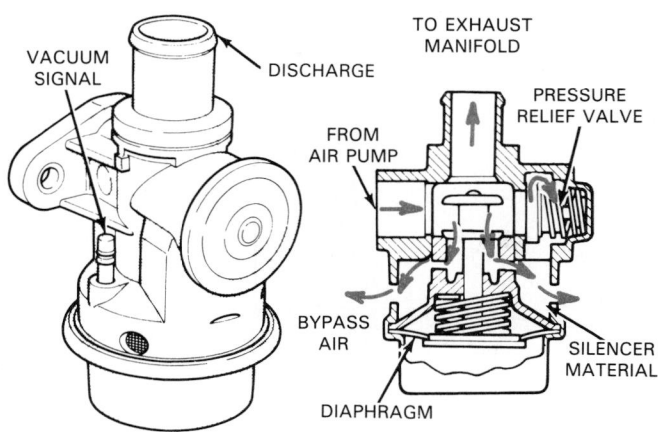

Fig. 39-23. Diverter valve prevents backfire upon sudden engine deceleration. It senses a sudden increase in intake manifold vacuum and opens, allowing air to bypass system. This prevents air from mixing with and igniting rich mixture caused by deceleration. (Chrysler)

An *air distribution manifold* directs a stream of air toward each engine exhaust valve. Fittings on the air distribution manifold screw into threaded holes in the exhaust manifold or cylinder head. Fig. 39-21 pictures a typical air distribution manifold.

An *air check valve* is usually located in the line between the diverter valve and the air distribution manifold. It keeps exhaust gases from entering the air injection system.

Air injection system operation

When the engine is running, the spinning vanes in the air pump force air into the diverter valve. Look at Fig. 39-24. If not decelerating, the air is forced through the diverter valve, check valve, air injection manifold, and into the engine. The fresh air blows on the engine exhaust valves.

During periods of deceleration, the diverter valve blocks airflow into the engine exhaust manifold. This prevents a possible backfire that could damage the car's exhaust system. When needed, the diverter valve's relief valve releases excess pressure.

PULSE AIR SYSTEM

A *pulse air system* performs the same function as an air injection system. However, instead of an air pump, it uses natural pressure pulses in the exhaust system which operate check valves.

Fig. 39-25 shows one type pulse air system. Note how the pulse air system lines and aspirator valves are positioned on the engine.

The *aspirator valves,* also called check valves, gulp valves, or reed valves, block airflow in one direction and allow airflow in the other direction. This is illustrated in Fig. 39-25B and 39-25C.

Pulse air system operation

Pressure in the exhaust manifold fluctuates as the

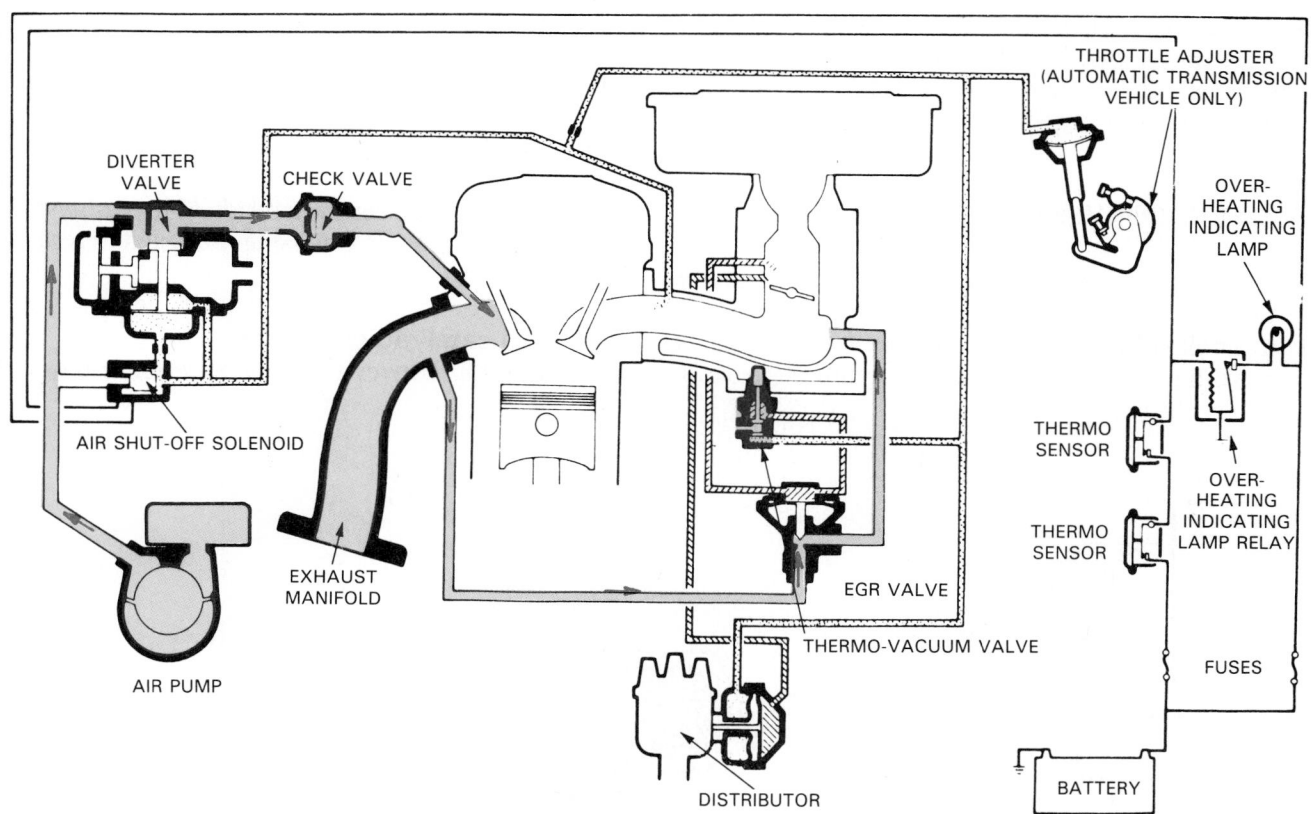

Fig. 39-24. Note relationship of components in air injection and EGR systems. Also note thermo-vacuum valve that alters action of ignition vacuum advance. (Chrysler)

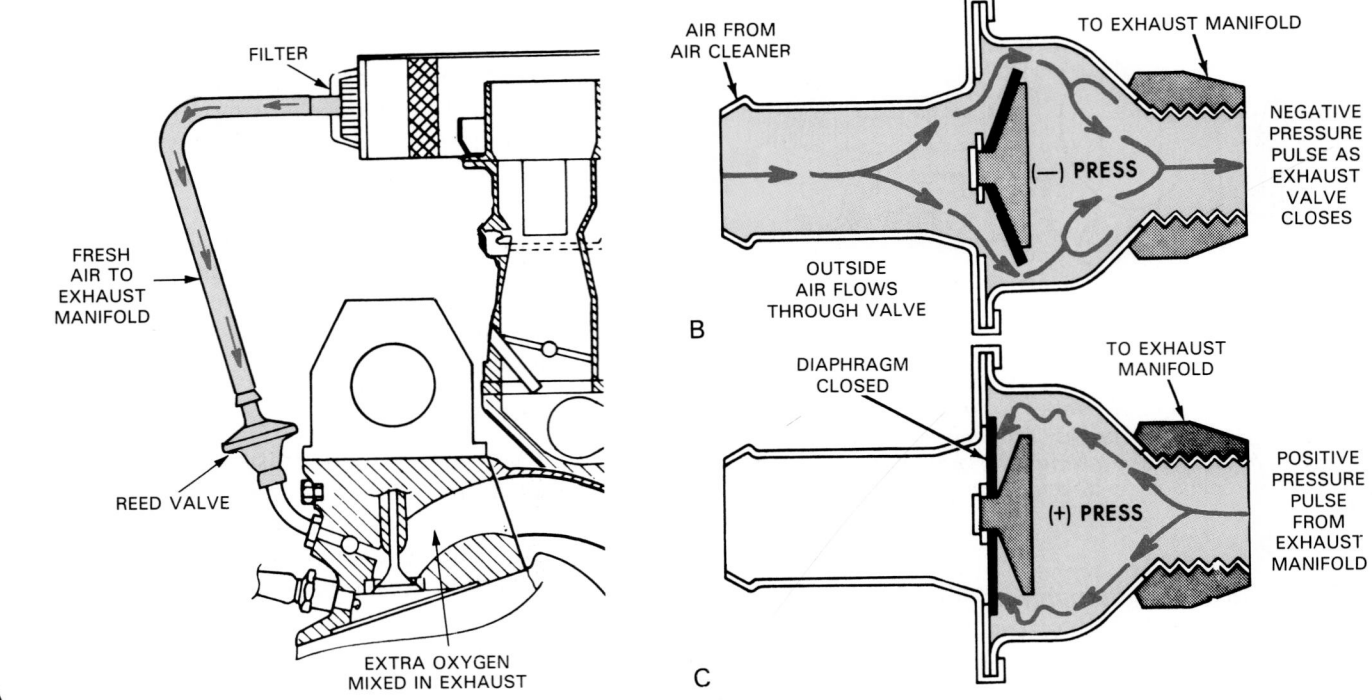

Fig. 39-25. A — Pulse type air injection system does not use an air pump. Instead, aspirator valves act as check valves. B — They allow air to enter engine exhaust manifold when exhaust valves first close, and produce vacuum pulse. C — Aspirators block airflow when exhaust valves open and produce pressure pulse.

engine valves open and close. The aspirator valves allow fresh air to enter the exhaust manifold on the low pressure pulses (when exhaust valve first closes). However, they block backflow on the high pressure pulses (as exhaust valve opens). This causes fresh air to flow through the system and into the engine exhaust manifold.

CATALYTIC CONVERTER

A *catalytic converter* oxidizes (burns) the remaining HC and CO emissions that pass into the exhaust system. Look at Fig. 39-26. Extreme heat (temperatures of approximately 1400°F or 760°C), ignite these emis-

sions and change them into harmless carbon dioxide (CO_2) and water (H_2O).

A catalytic converter contains a catalyst substance, usually platinum, palladium, rhodium, or a mixture of two of these substances.

A *catalyst* is any substance that speeds a chemical reaction without itself being changed. The catalyst agent is coated on either a ceramic honeycomb-shaped block or on small ceramic beads. The catalyst is encased in a stainless steel housing, designed to resist heat. See Fig. 39-27.

Types of catalytic converters

A catalytic converter using a ceramic block type

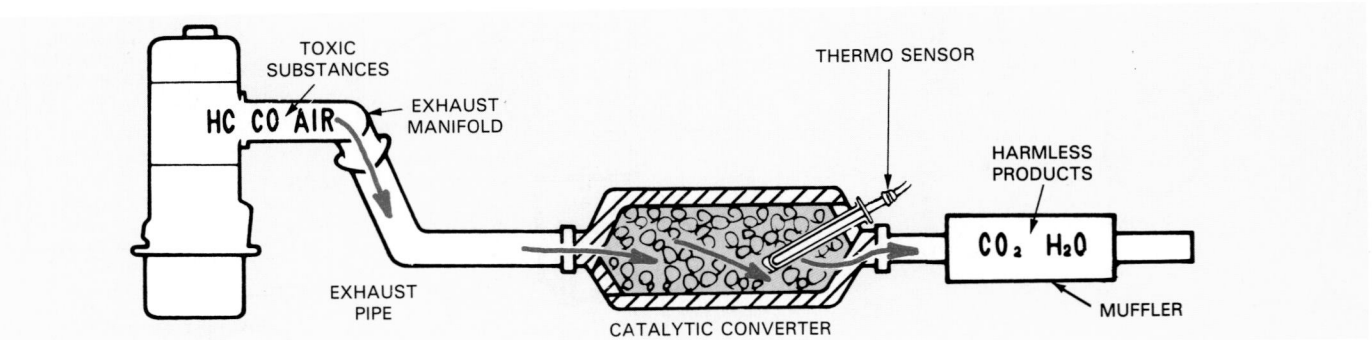

Fig. 39-26. Catalytic converter burns and treats exhaust emissions and changes them into harmless carbon dioxide and water. (Toyota)

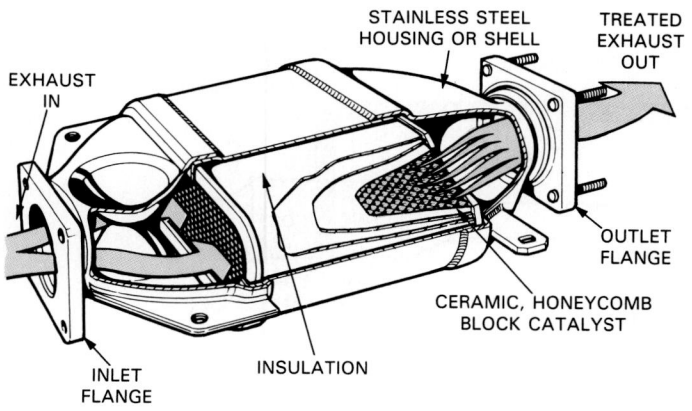

Fig. 39-27. Monolithic catalytic converter uses honeycomb shaped block of ceramic material covered with special substances to treat exhaust gases. Catalyst is enclosed in stainless steel housing. (Lancia)

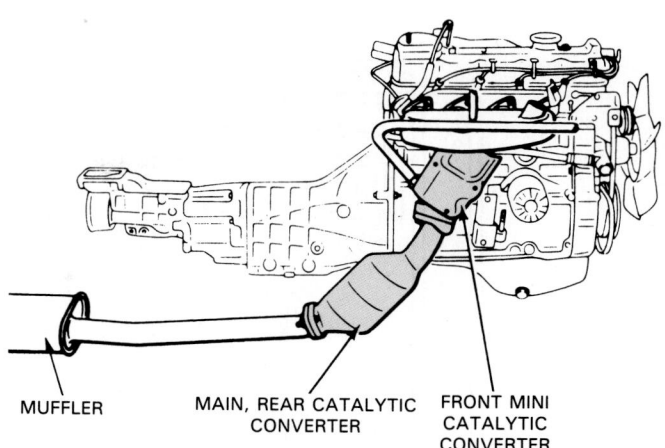

Fig. 39-29. This engine uses a mini catalytic converter and a main converter. Mini converter functions right after engine startup. It heats up quickly to reduce emission when engine and main converter are cold. (Chrysler)

catalyst is often termed a *monolithic* type converter.

When small ceramic beads are used, it is called a *pellet* type catalytic converter.

Figs. 39-27 and 39-28 show cutaway views of each type. Compare them!

A *mini catalytic converter* is a very small converter placed close to the engine. It heats up quickly to reduce emissions during engine warmup. A mini catalytic converter is used in conjunction with a larger, main converter. See Fig. 39-29.

A *two-way catalytic converter,* sometimes called an OXIDATION type converter, can only reduce two types of exhaust emissions (HC and CO). A two-way catalyst is normally coated with platinum.

A *three-way catalytic converter,* also termed a REDUCTION type converter, is capable of reducing all three types of exhaust emissions (HC, CO, and NO_x). A three-way catalyst is usually coated with rhodium and platinum.

A *dual-bed catalytic converter* contains two separate catalyst units enclosed in a single housing. Look at Fig. 39-30. A dual-bed converter normally has both a three-way (reduction) catalyst and a two-way (oxidation) catalyst. A mixing chamber is provided between the two. Air is forced into the mixing chamber to help burn the HC and CO emissions.

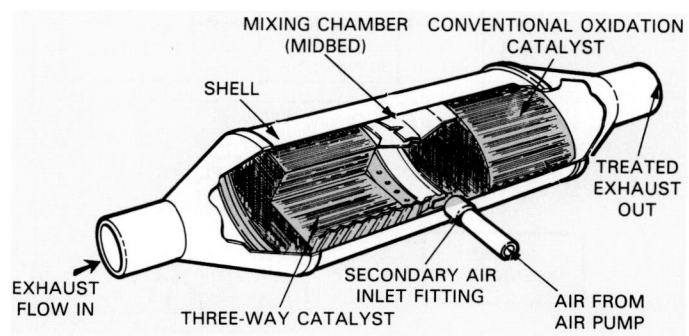

Fig. 39-30. Dual-bed catalytic converter has two ceramic elements. One is a three-way catalyst. Air from air pump is forced into center of converter to aid burning and reaction. (Ford Motor Co.)

Dual-bed catalytic converter operation

When the engine is cold (below approximately 128°F or 52°C), the system routes air into the exhaust manifold, Fig. 39-31. Exhaust heat and the injected air are used to burn exhaust emissions. When the engine warms, the system forces air into the catalytic converter.

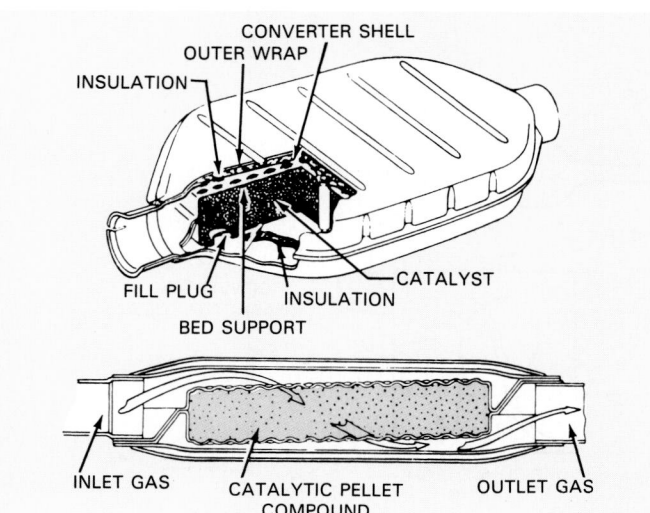

Fig. 39-28. Pellet type catalytic converter uses beads coated with catalyst agent. Study construction and compare to monolithic type in previous illustration. (GMC)

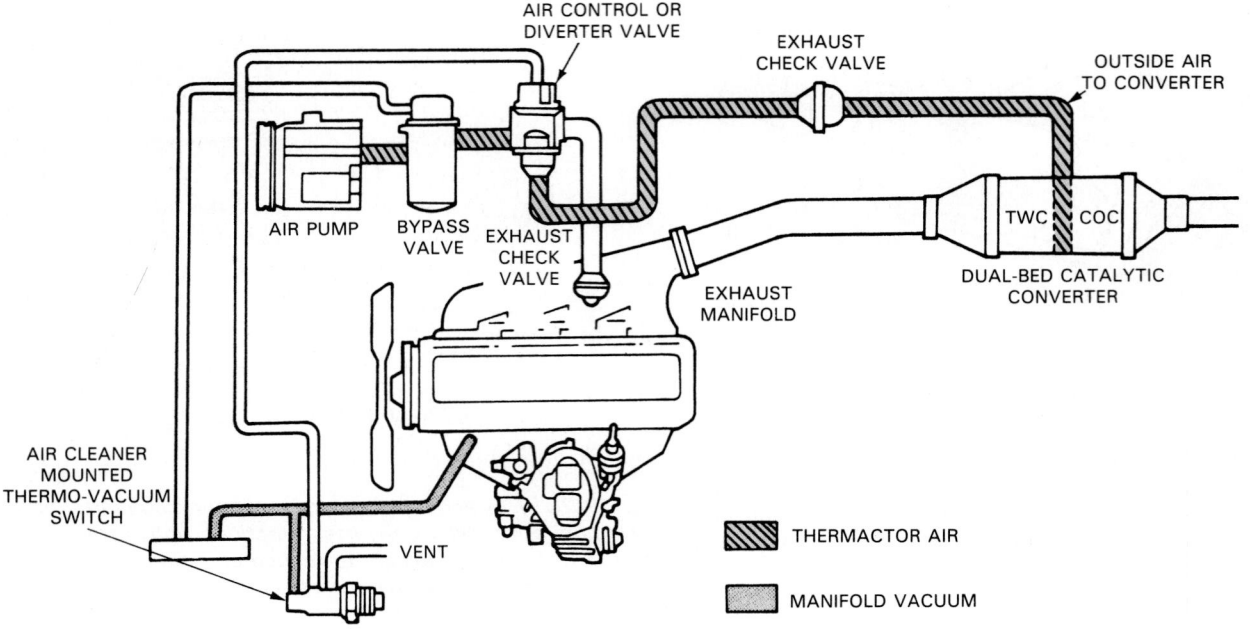

Fig. 39-31. Diagram shows how air pump forces oxygen into dual-bed catalytic converter. Thermal-vacuum switch operates air control valve. It only lets air flow to converter when engine coolant is above set temperature. (Ford)

First, the exhaust gases pass through the front three-way catalyst that removes HC, CO, and NOx. Then, the exhaust gas flows into the area between the two catalysts. The oxygen in the air flowing into the chamber causes the gases to continue to burn. The exhaust flows into the rear two-way catalyst which removes even more HC and CO. Refer again to Fig. 39-31 and study system operation.

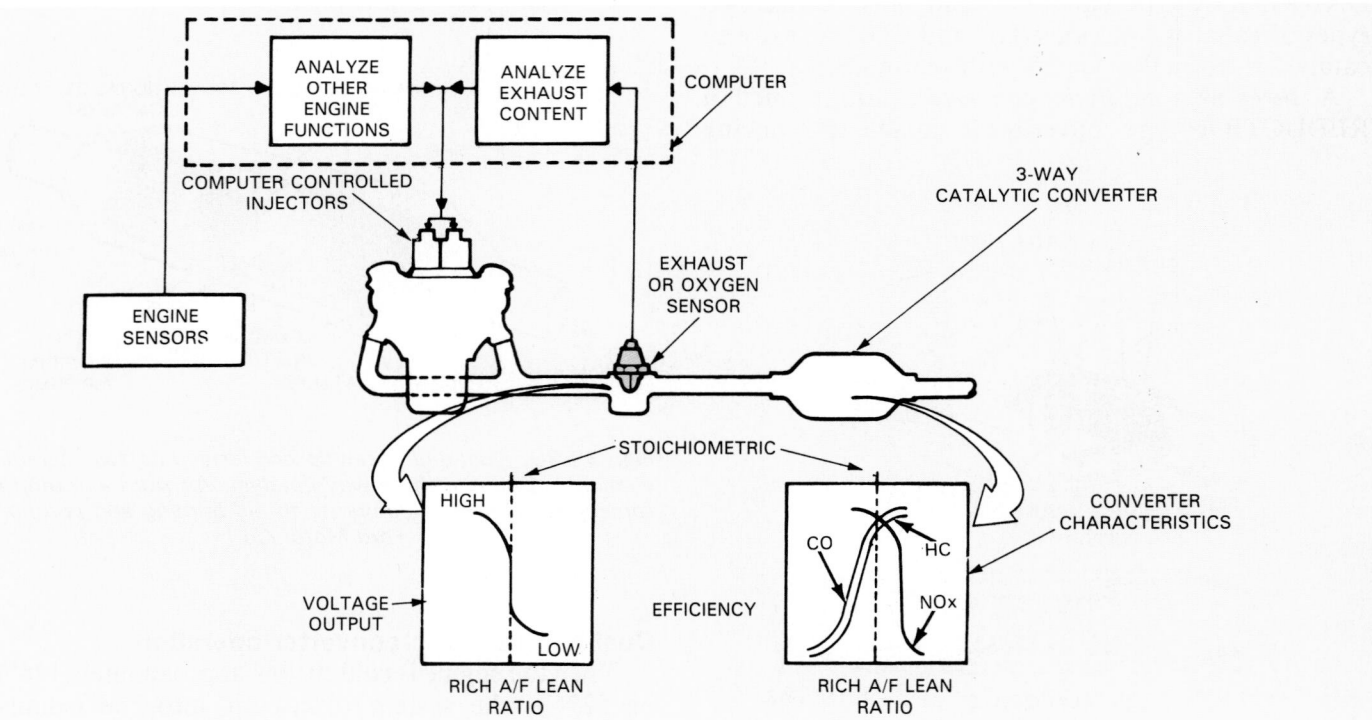

Fig. 39-32. Exhaust gas sensor, also called oxygen sensor, monitors amount of oxygen in exhaust system. Basically, high oxygen content indicates fuel is being completely burned. If oxygen content is too low, computer can lean fuel injection mixture to reduce exhaust emissions. (Oldsmobile)

COMPUTERIZED EMISSION CONTROL SYSTEMS

A *computerized emission control system* commonly uses engine sensors, a three-way catalytic converter, an on-board computer, and either a computer controlled carburetor or fuel injection system.

Fig. 39-32 illustrates the operation of a digital fuel injection system using a dual-bed catalytic converter and an exhaust gas sensor. Study how the engine sensors and exhaust sensor feed electrical information to the computer. The computer analyzes this information and adjusts the throttle body air-fuel mixture for maximum efficiency. Also, note how HC, CO, and NOx are lowest at a *stoichiometric* (theoretically perfect) fuel mixture.

Fig. 39-33 shows a diagram of a computer which controls the fuel and emission control systems. The computer receives data from the engine sensors and the exhaust (oxygen) sensor. It can then control the carburetor air-fuel mixture, ignition timing, EGR valve, air injection system, and charcoal canister purge.

For complete details of computer control systems, refer to the text chapters on carburetion and fuel injection. These chapters explain engine sensor, exhaust gas sensor, computer, and other related components.

KNOW THESE TERMS

Emission control system, Air pollution, Smog, HC, CO, NOx, Particulates, PCV system, Engine blowby,

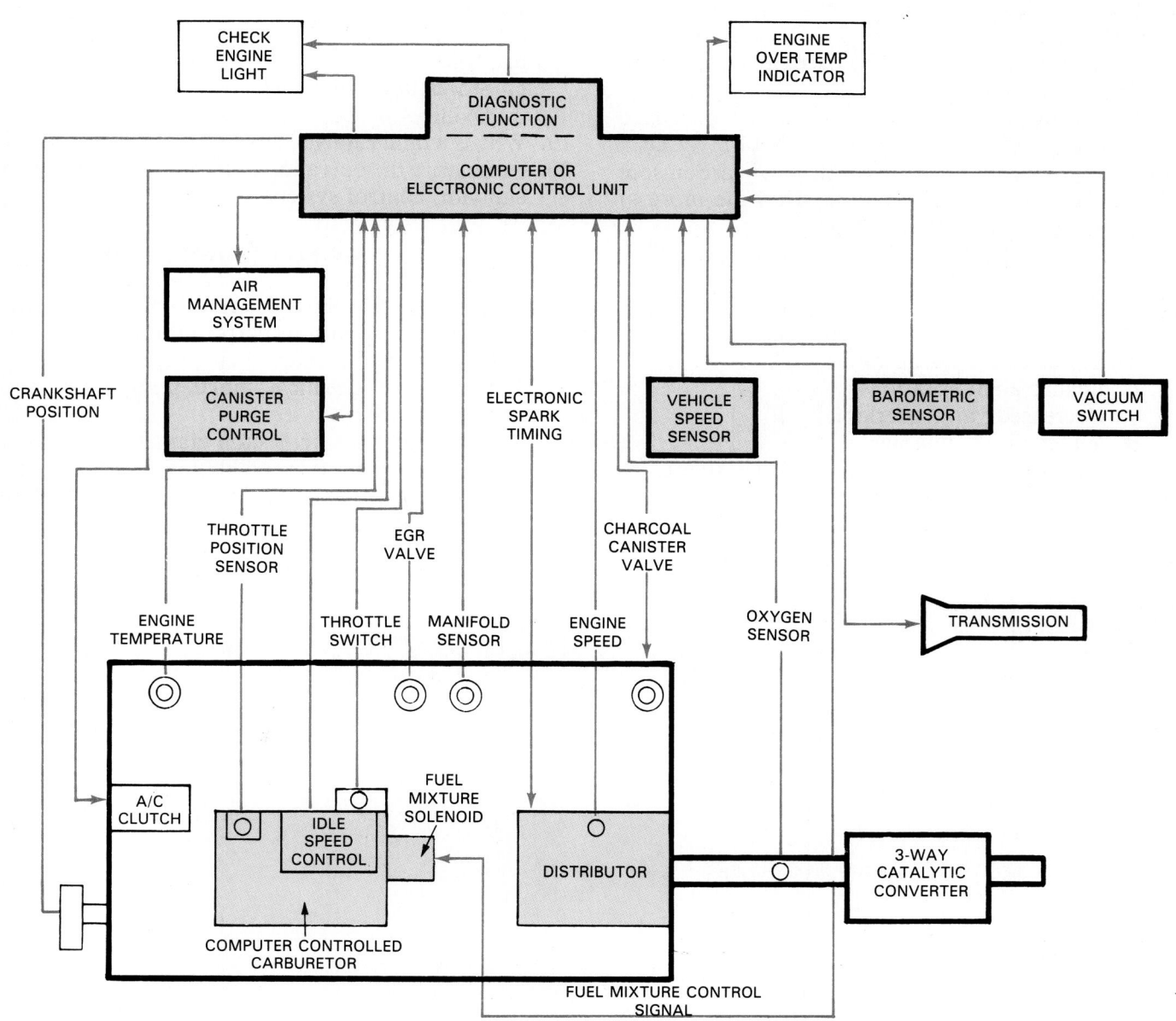

Fig. 39-33. Diagram shows how computer monitors and controls various engine functions. Computer keeps all units operating for maximum efficiency and minimum air pollution. Study parts and connections. (Buick)

Thermostatic air cleaner, Air cleaner carbon element, Fuel evaporization system, Liquid-vapor separator, Roll-over valve, Charcoal canister, Purge line, EGR valve, Air injection system, air pump, Diverter valve, Pulse air system, Catalytic converter, Computerized emission control system.

REVIEW QUESTIONS

1. What are some causes of air pollution?
2. Which of the following agencies enforces air pollution standards?
   a. EGR.
   b. SAE.
   c. ASE.
   d. EPA.
3. Define the term "smog."
4. List and explain the four kinds of vehicle emissions.
5. CO emissions are caused by partially burned fuel. True or False?
6. Increasing peak combustion temperature tends to reduce NOx emissions. True or False?
7. _____ are the solid particles of carbon soot that blow out a car's tailpipe. They are more of a problem with a diesel engine.
8. What are the three basic sources of vehicle emissions?
9. Which of the following is NOT a typical engine modification for reducing emissions?
   a. Lower compression ratios.
   b. Leaner air-fuel ratios.
   c. Decreased valve overlap.
   d. Wider spark plug gaps.
10. Explain six major emission control systems.
11. A _____ _____ _____ or PCV system uses engine vacuum to draw toxic blowby gases into the intake manifold for burning in the combustion chambers.
12. The _____ _____ _____ system speeds engine warmup and keeps the temperature of the air entering the engine at about _____ .
13. Explain the operation of the charcoal canister in a fuel evaporization control system.
14. How does an EGR system work?
15. An air injection system forces fresh air into the _____ _____ of the engine to reduce HC and CO emissions.
16. The diverter valve keeps air from entering the exhaust system during engine deceleration, preventing backfiring. True or False?
17. What is a catalytic converter?
18. Which of the following does NOT relate to catalytic converters?
   a. Monolith.
   b. Pellet.
   c. Stores unburned fuel.
   d. Oxidizes or burns emissions.
19. Why is a mini catalytic converter sometimes used?
20. Summarize the operation of a computer controlled emission control system.

ACTIVITIES FOR CHAPTER 39

1. On a late model vehicle designated by your instructor try to locate various parts of the emission control system and explain their purpose.
2. Research the chemical makeup of smog and prepare a report on it.
3. Study a manufacturer's shop manual and explain where exhaust gases are to be sampled during air-fuel mixture adjustment. Demonstrate or explain the procedure to the class.

40

Emission Control System Testing, Service, Repair

After studying this chapter, you will be able to:
□ Explain the use of two-gas and four-gas exhaust analyzers.
□ Inspect and troubleshoot emission control systems.
□ Perform periodic service operations on emission control systems.
□ Test individual emission control components.
□ Replace or repair major emission control components.
□ Demonstrate and practice safe work procedures.

Emission control systems, like any automotive system, can malfunction. When this happens, emission or air pollution levels increase. It is important that an auto technician be able to diagnose and repair emission control system troubles. By keeping these systems in good working order, the technician is protecting THE AIR WE BREATHE!

EXHAUST ANALYZER

An *exhaust analyzer* is a testing instrument that measures the chemical content of engine exhaust gases. See Fig. 40-1.

The analyzer probe (sensor) is placed in the car's tailpipe, Fig. 40-2. With the engine running, the ex-

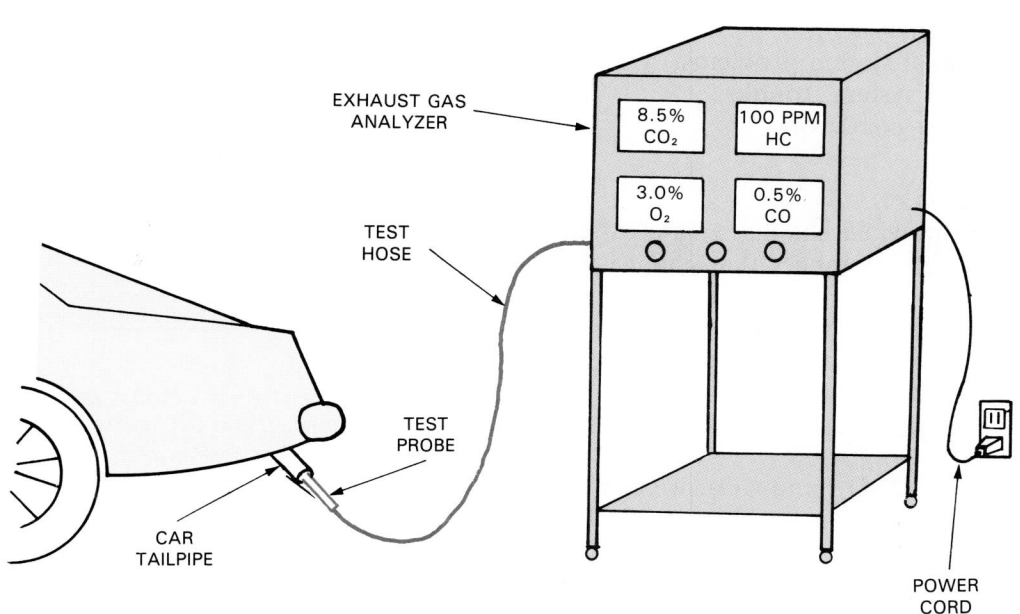

EXHAUST GAS ANALYZER

| 8.5% CO_2 | 100 PPM HC |
| 3.0% O_2 | 0.5% CO |

TEST HOSE

TEST PROBE

CAR TAILPIPE

POWER CORD

Fig. 40-1. Exhaust gas analyzer measures chemical content of engine exhaust. It will tell if car is emitting too much air pollution, indicating system problems. (Sun Electric)

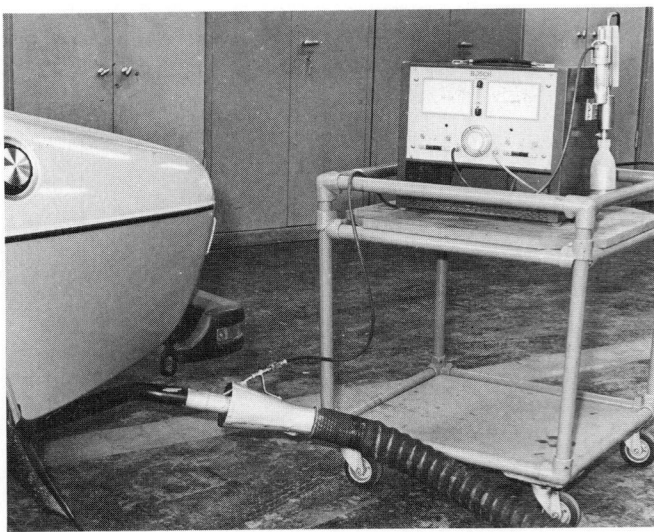

Fig. 40-2. Note how exhaust analyzer is installed in vehicle tailpipe. Adapter on vent hose prevents toxic vapors from entering shop. Warm and calibrate meters before placing test probe in tailpipe. Following equipment instructions, read meters and compare to specs. (Saab)

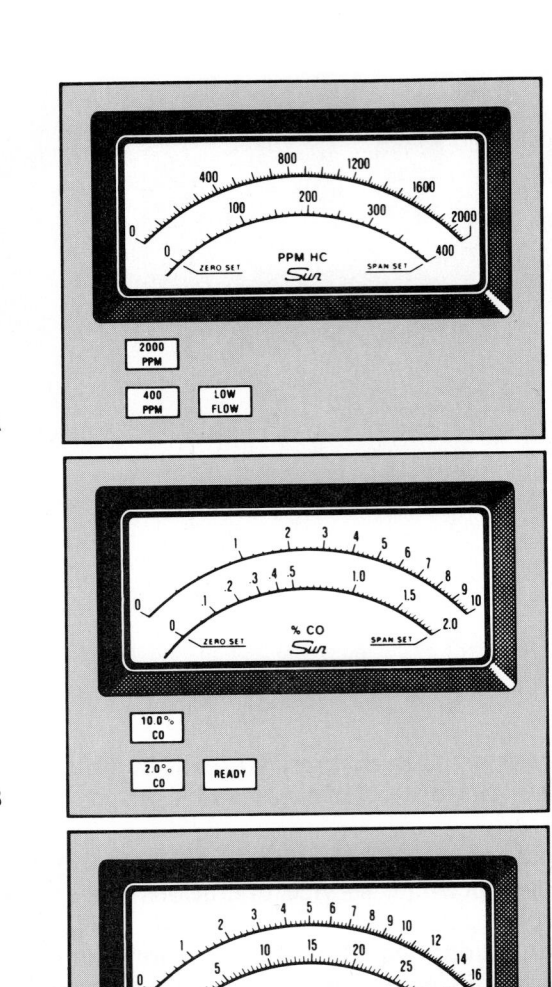

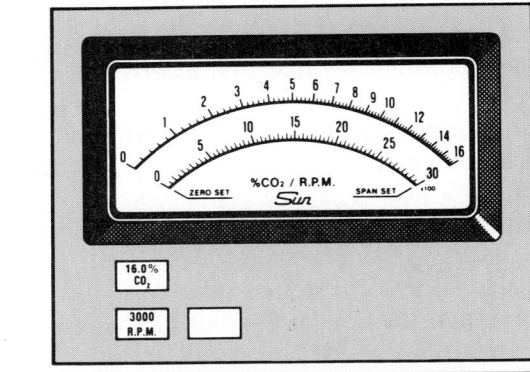

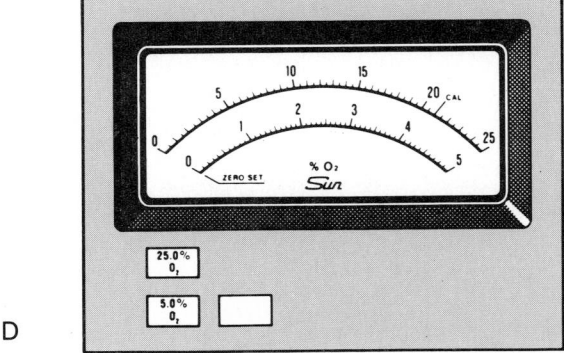

haust analyzer will indicate the amount of pollutants and other gases in the exhaust. The mechanic can use this information to determine the condition of the engine and other systems affecting emissions.

An exhaust gas analyzer is an excellent diagnostic tool that will indicate:

1. Carburetor or fuel injection problems.
2. Engine mechanical problems.
3. Vacuum leaks.
4. Ignition system problems.
5. PCV troubles.
6. Clogged air filter.
7. Faulty air injection system.
8. Evaporative control system problems.
9. Computer control system troubles.
10. Catalytic converter condition.

Engine exhaust gases

As discussed in the previous chapter, engine exhaust gases contain chemical substances that change with combustion (engine) efficiency. Some of these substances, such as hydrocarbons (HC), carbon monoxide (CO), and oxides of nitrogen (NOx), are harmful. Other by-products of combustion such as carbon dioxide (CO_2), oxygen (O_2), and water (H_2O) are not harmful.

By measuring HC, CO, O_2, and CO_2, we can find out if the engine and emission systems are working properly.

Two- and four-gas exhaust analyzers

Two different kinds of exhaust gas analyzers are used in modern garages: the two-gas exhaust analyzer and

Fig. 40-3. Scales for an exhaust gas analyzer. A two-gas analyzer has only HC and CO scales. A four-gas analyzer will measure HC, CO, CO_2, and O_2. A — HC meter shows unburned fuel (hydrocarbons) in parts per million (ppm). Button allows change to different scales. B — CO meter reads partially burned fuel (carbon monoxide) by percent. It also has buttons for changing scales. C — CO_2 meter shows harmless carbon dioxide gas by percent. Note zero and span set lines for calibrating meter. D — O_2 meter reads oxygen by percent. Oxygen content indicates whether all of the fuel is being burned. Generally, it gives more data for making conclusions about engine operation. (Sun Electric)

the four-gas exhaust analyzer.

The *two-gas exhaust analyzer* measures the amount of hydrocarbons (HC) and carbon monoxide (CO) in a car's exhaust system. A common type of analyzer, it has been used for a number of years. However, the two-gas analyzer is being replaced by the more informative four-gas analyzer.

The *four-gas exhaust analyzer* measures the quantity of hydrocarbons (HC), carbon monoxide (CO), carbon dioxide (CO_2), and oxygen (O_2), in an engine's exhaust. Look at Fig. 40-3.

Although CO_2 and O_2 are not toxic emissions, they provide useful data about combustion efficiency. Late model engines are so clean burning, a four-gas exhaust analyzer is needed to accurately evaluate the makeup of the exhaust gases. It provides extra information for diagnosing problems and making adjustments.

HC readings

An exhaust gas analyzer measures *hydrocarbons* (HC) in parts per million (ppm) by volume, Fig. 40-3A. For example, an analyzer reading of 100 ppm means there are 100 parts of HC for every million parts of exhaust gas.

A car that is a few years old, for instance, might have an HC specification of 400 ppm. A newer car, having stricter emission requirements, could have a 100 ppm HC specification. If HC is higher, the car's HC emissions (unburned fuel) are too high. An adjustment or repair is needed.

NOTE! Always refer to the emission control sticker in the engine compartment or a service manual for emission level specs. Values vary year by year.

Higher-than-normal HC readings can be caused by one or more of the following conditions:
1. Rich or lean air-fuel mixture (carburetor or fuel injection system problem).
2. Improper ignition timing (distributor, computer, or adjustment problem).
3. Engine problems (blow-by, worn rings, burned valve, blown head gasket).
4. Faulty emission control system (bad PCV, catalytic converter, evaporative control system).
5. Ignition system troubles (fouled spark plug, cracked distributor cap, open spark plug wire).

CO readings

An exhaust analyzer measures *carbon monoxide* (CO) in percentage by volume, Fig. 40-3B. For instance, a 1 percent analyzer reading would mean that 1 percent of the engine exhaust is made up of CO. The other 99 percent consists of other substances. High CO is basically caused by incomplete burning and a lack of air (oxygen) during the combustion process.

If the exhaust analyzer reading is higher than specs, the engine is producing too much CO air pollution. You would need to locate and correct the cause of the problem.

The exhaust analyzer's CO reading is related to the air-fuel ratio. A HIGH CO reading would indicate an over-rich mixture (too much fuel compared to air). A LOW CO reading would indicate a lean air-fuel mixture (not enough air compared to fuel).

Typical causes of high CO readings are:
1. Fuel system problems (bad injector, high float setting, clogged carburetor air bleed, restricted air cleaner, choke out of adjustment, bad engine sensor, computer troubles).
2. Emission control system troubles (almost any emission control system problem can upset CO).
3. Incorrect ignition timing (timing too far advanced or improper vacuum going to vacuum advance unit).
4. Low idle speed (carburetor or injection system setting wrong).

O_2 readings

Four-gas exhaust analyzers measure *oxygen* (O_2) in percentage by volume, Fig. 40-3D. Typically, O_2 readings should be between .1 and 7 percent. Oxygen is needed for the catalytic converter to burn HC and CO emissions. Without O_2 in the engine exhaust, exhaust emissions can pass through the converter and out the car's tailpipe.

Remember from the previous chapter, there are two systems that add O_2 to the engine exhaust: the air injection system and air pulse system. As air is added to the exhaust, CO and HC emissions decrease. As a result, O_2 readings can be used to check the operation of the carburetor, fuel injection system, air injection system, catalytic converter, and control computer.

Oxygen in the engine exhaust is an accurate indicator of a LEAN air-fuel mixture. When an engine is running lean, O_2 increases proportionately with the air-fuel ratio.

As the air-fuel mixture becomes lean enough to cause a LEAN MISFIRE (engine miss), O_2 readings rise dramatically. This provides a very accurate method of measuring lean and efficient air-fuel ratios.

New car fuel systems must be adjusted almost to the lean misfire point to reduce exhaust emissions and increase fuel economy.

CO_2 readings

The four-gas exhaust analyzer also measures carbon dioxide (CO_2) in percent by volume, Fig. 40-3C. Typically, CO_2 readings should be above 8 percent. CO_2 readings provide more data for checking and adjusting the air-fuel ratio.

Carbon dioxide is a by-product of combustion. It is produced when one carbon molecule combines with two oxygen molecules in the combustion chamber. CO_2 is not toxic at low levels. When you breathe, for example, you exhale carbon dioxide.

Normally, oxygen and carbon dioxide levels are compared when evluating the content of the engine exhaust. For example, if the percent of CO_2 exceeds the percent of O_2, the air-fuel ratio is on the rich side of *stoichiometric* (theoretically perfect) mixture.

Using an exhaust gas analyzer

To use an exhaust gas analyzer, plug in and warm it up as described by the manufacturer. Refer to Fig. 40-3. After warm-up, zero and calibrate the meters. Typically, you must adjust the needles to zero while sampling clean air (no exhaust gases present in room).

CAUTION! When using an exhaust analyzer, do NOT let engine exhaust fumes escape into an enclosed shop area. Engine exhaust can kill! Use a shop exhaust-vent system to trap and remove the toxic fumes.

Since exact procedures vary, always follow the operating instructions for the particular exhaust analyzer. This will assure accurate measurements.

Generally speaking, you must measure HC and CO at idle and approximately 2500 rpm. If you have a four-gas analyzer, also measure O_2 and CO_2. Compare the analyzer readings with specifications.

When testing some electronic (computer) fuel injection systems without a load, only idle readings on the exhaust analyzer will be accurate. A dynomometer must be used to load the engine, simulating actual driving conditions.

Several other textbook chapters discuss how exhaust analyzer readings can be used. Refer to the text index for more information.

INSPECTING EMISSION CONTROL SYSTEMS

After studying your exhaust analyzer readings, you must find the source of any indicated problems. Generally, start out by inspecting all engine vacuum hoses and wires, Fig. 40-4. A leaking vacuum hose or

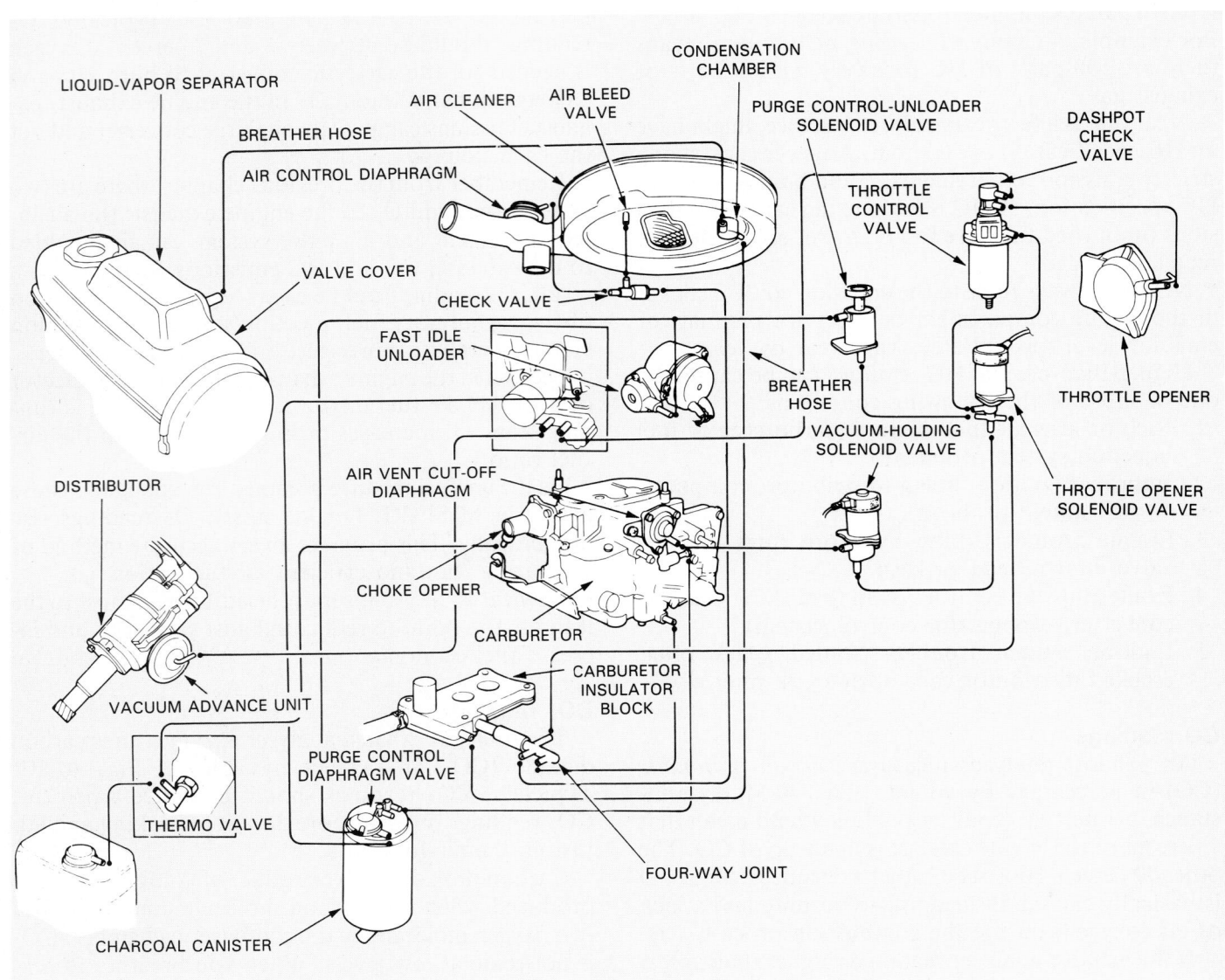

Fig. 40-4. Even one leaking vacuum hose or disconnected wire can increase vehicle emissions. Note great number of parts that must be checked. (Honda)

disconnected wire could upset the operation of the engine and emission control systems.

A section of vacuum hose can be used as a stethoscope (listening device). As in Fig. 40-5, place one end of the hose next to your ear. Move the other end of the hose around the engine compartment, along vacuum hoses and connections. When the hose nears a vacuum leak, you will be able to hear a loud HISS-ING SOUND.

Also, inspect the air cleaner for clogging. Check that the air pump belt is properly adjusted. Try to locate any visual and obvious problems. If nothing is found during your inspection, each system should be checked and tested.

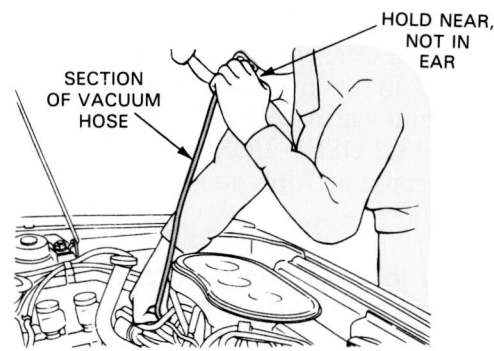

Fig. 40-5. A section of small hose can be used as listening device to find vacuum leaks. Move hose around engine compartment. When you hear a loud hiss, you are near source of vacuum leak. (Subaru)

PCV SYSTEM SERVICE

An *inoperative PCV system* can increase exhaust emissions, cause engine sludging, engine wear, a rough engine idle, and other problems. A leaking PCV system can cause a vacuum leak and produce a lean air-fuel mixture at idle. A restricted PCV system can enrich the fuel mixture, also affecting engine idle.

PCV system maintenance

Most auto makers recommend periodic maintenance of the PCV system. Inspect the condition of the PCV hoses, grommets, fittings, and breather hoses. Replace any hose that shows signs of deterioration. Clean or replace the breather filter if needed. Also, check or replace the PCV valve. Since replacement intervals vary, always refer to the vehicle's service manual.

PCV system testing

To test a PCV system, pull the PCV valve out of the engine. With the engine idling, place your finger over the end of the valve, Fig. 40-6. With airflow stopped, you should feel suction on your finger and the engine idle speed should drop about 40-80 rpm.

If you cannot feel vacuum, the PCV valve or hose

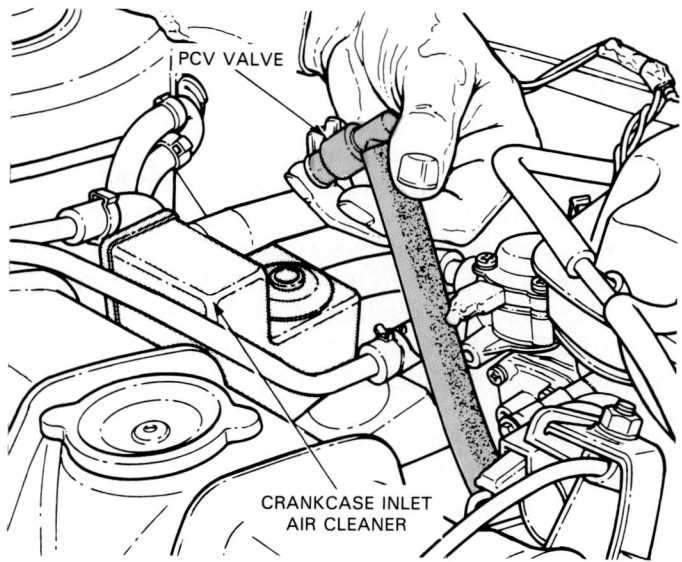

Fig. 40-6. With engine running, place finger over PCV valve. You should feel suction. If not, hose may be plugged. (Chrysler Corp.)

might be plugged with sludge. If engine rpm drops more than 40-80 rpm and the engine begins to idle smoothly, the PCV valve could be stuck open.

PCV valve testers are also available. Look at Fig. 40-7. To use this tester, make sure engine intake manifold vacuum is correct. Then, connect the tester to the PCV valve as described in the operating instructions. Start and idle the engine. Observe the airflow rate on the tester. Replace the PCV valve if airflow is not within specified limits.

Some auto manufacturers suggest placing a piece of

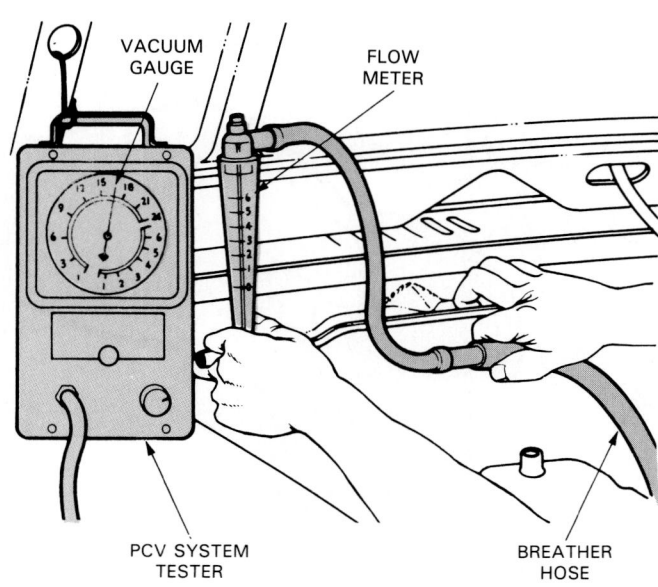

Fig. 40-7. PCV valve tester measures airflow through valve. Follow instructions and compare to specs to determine valve condition. (Chrysler Corp.)

paper over the PCV breather opening to test the PCV system. After sealing the dipstick tube with tape, start and idle the engine. After a few minutes of operation, the piece of paper should be pulled down against the breather opening by crankcase vacuum. If suction does not develop, there is a leak in the system (ruptured gasket, cracked hose) or the system may be plugged.

A four-gas exhaust analyzer can also be used to check the general condition of a PCV system. Measure and note the analyzers readings with the engine idling. Then, pull the PCV valve out of the engine, but not off the hose. Compare the readings after the PCV valve is removed.

A *plugged PCV system* will show up on the exhaust analyzer when O_2 and CO do NOT CHANGE. *Crankcase dilution* (excessive blow-by or fuel in oil) will usually show up as an excessive (1 percent or more) increase in O_2 or a 1 percent or more decrease in CO.

EVAPORIZATION CONTROL SYSTEM SERVICE

A *faulty evaporation control system* can cause fuel odors, fuel leakage, fuel tank collapse (vacuum buildup), excess pressure in the fuel tank, or a rough engine idle. These problems usually stem from a defective fuel tank pressure-vacuum cap, leaking charcoal canister valves, deteriorated hoses, or incorrect hose routing.

Evaporation control system maintenance and repair

Maintenance on an evaporation control system typically involves cleaning or replacing the filter in the charcoal canister. Look at Fig. 40-8. Service intervals for the canister filter vary. However, if the car is operated on dusty roads, clean or replace the filter more often.

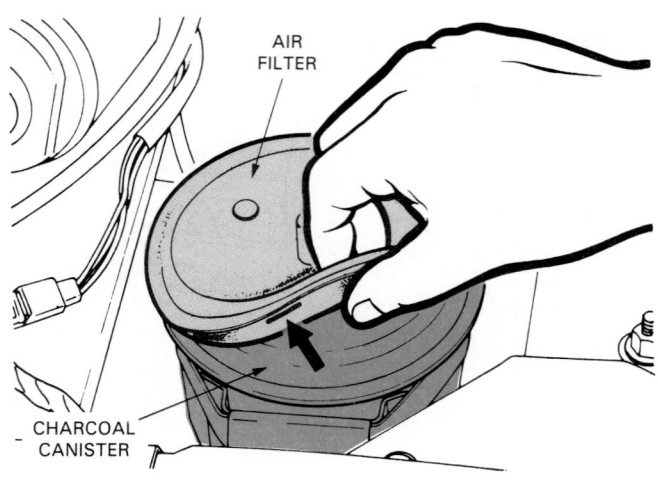

Fig. 40-8. Many charcoal canisters have air filters. Filter should be removed and cleaned or replaced at periodic intervals. (Plymouth)

Also inspect the condition of the fuel tank filler cap. Make sure the cap seals are in good condition. Special testers are available for checking the opening of the pressure and vacuum valves in the cap. The cap should be tested when excessive pressure or vacuum problems are noticed.

All hoses in the evaporization system should also be inspected for signs of deterioration (hardening, softening, cracking). When replacing a hose, make sure you use special fuel resistant type hose. Vacuum hose can be quickly ruined by fuel vapors.

HEATED AIR INLET SYSTEM SERVICE

An inoperative heated air inlet system (thermostatic air cleaner) can cause several engine performance problems. If the air cleaner flap remains in the OPEN POSITION (cold air position), the engine could miss, stumble, stall, and warm up slowly. If the air cleaner flap stays in the CLOSED POSITION (hot air position), the engine could perform poorly when at full operating temperature.

Heated air inlet system maintenance

The heated air inlet system requires very little maintenance. Generally, you should inspect the condition of the vacuum hoses and hot air hose from the exhaust manifold heat shroud. The hot air tube is frequently made of heat resistant paper and metal foil. It will tear very easily, Fig. 40-9A.

If torn or damaged, replace the hot air tube.

Testing heated air inlet system

For a quick test of the heated air inlet system, watch the action of the air flap in the air cleaner snorkel. Start and idle the engine, as shown in Fig. 40-9A. When the air cleaner temperature sensor is cold, the air flap should be closed. Place an ice cube on the sensor if needed. Then, when the engine and sensor warm to operating temperature, the flap should swing open.

If the air cleaner flap does not function, test the vacuum motor and the temperature sensor.

To test the vacuum motor, apply vacuum to the motor diaphragm with a hand vacuum pump or your mouth, Fig. 40-9B. With the prescribed amount of suction, the motor should pull the air flap open. If it leaks or does not open the flap, replace the vacuum motor. Recheck heated air inlet system operation to make sure the air temperature sensor is working properly.

To test the thermo-vacuum switch in the air cleaner, place a thermometer next to the unit. With the sensor cooled below its closing temperature, apply vacuum to the thermo-vacuum switch. It should pass vacuum to the vacuum motor.

Then, warm the thermo-vacuum switch to its closing temperature. A heat gun (hair dryer) can be used to heat the unit. When warm, the switch should block vacuum and the vacuum motor should open. Replace

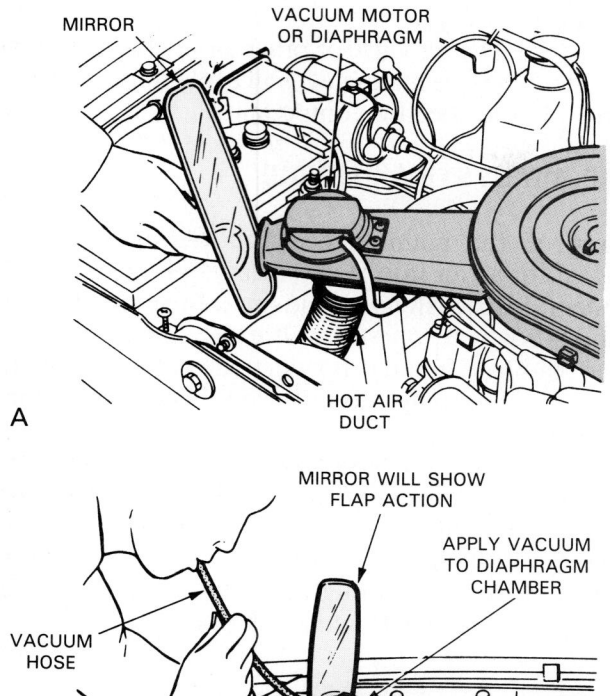

Fig. 40-9. Checking operation of thermostatic air cleaner. A — Mirror can be used to watch action of blend door or flap in snorkel. Flap should block outside air during engine warmup. It should open as engine warms. B — When you apply vacuum to vacuum motor, flap should function. (Subaru)

the thermo-vacuum switch if it fails to open and close properly.

EGR SYSTEM SERVICE

EGR system malfunctions can cause engine stalling at idle, rough engine idling, detonation (knock), and poor fuel economy. If the EGR valve sticks open, it will act as a large vacuum leak, causing a lean air-fuel mixture. The engine will run rough at idle or stall. If the EGR fails to open or the exhaust passage is clogged, higher combustion temperatures can cause abnormal combustion (detonation) and knocking.

EGR system maintenance

Maintenance intervals for the EGR system vary with vehicle manufacturer. Refer to a service manual for exact mileage intervals. Some cars have a reminder light in the dash. The light will glow when EGR maintenance is needed.

Also, check that the vacuum hoses in the EGR

system are in good condition. They can become hardened, which can cause leakage.

EGR system testing

To test an EGR system, start, idle, and warm the engine. Operating the carburetor or throttle body accelerator linkage by hand, increase engine speed to 2000-3000 rpm very quickly. If visible, observe the movement of the EGR valve stem. The stem should move as the engine is accelerated. If it does not move, the EGR system is not functioning.

Sometimes the EGR valve stem is not visible. You then need to test each EGR system component separately. Follow the procedures described in a service manual.

To test the EGR VALVE, idle the engine. Connect a hand vacuum pump to the EGR valve, Fig. 40-10. Plug the supply vacuum line to the EGR valve. When vacuum is applied to the EGR valve with the pump, the engine should begin to MISS or STALL. This lets you know that the EGR valve is opening and that exhaust gases are entering the intake manifold.

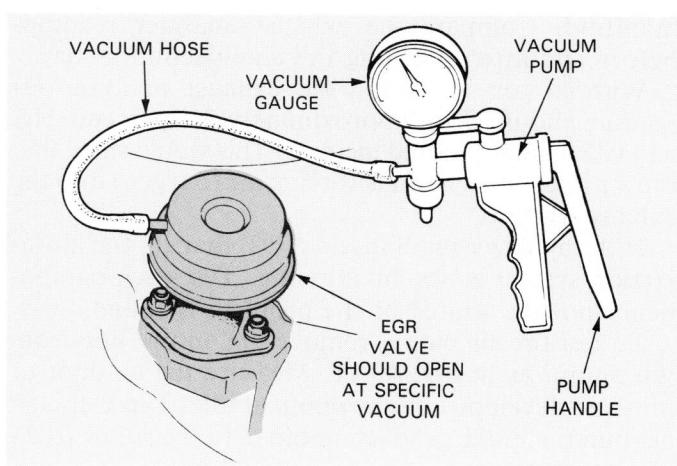

Fig. 40-10. With engine idling, apply vacuum to EGR valve. If EGR valve is working, engine should miss or stall. (Honda)

If EGR valve does NOT affect engine idling, remove the valve. The valve or the exhaust manifold passage could be clogged with carbon. If needed, clean the EGR valve and exhaust passage. When the EGR valve does not open and close properly, replace the valve.

EGR valves that provide electrical data to a computer control system require special testing procedures. Refer to a shop manual covering the specific system. Component damage could result from an incorrect testing method.

AIR INJECTION SYSTEM SERVICE

Air injection system problems can cause engine backfiring (loud popping sound), other noises, and increased HC and CO emissions. Remember, air injection is used to help burn any fuel that enters the exhaust manifolds and exhaust system. Without this system, the fuel could ignite all at once (backfire) with a loud bang. Inadequate air from the air injection system could also prevent the catalytic converter from functioning properly.

Air injection system maintenance

Maintenance of an air injection system typically includes replacing the pump inlet filter (if used), adjusting pump belt tension, and inspecting the condition of the hoses and lines.

If the pump belt or any hoses show signs of deterioration, they should be replaced. Refer to shop manual specs for maintenance intervals.

Testing air injection system

A four-gas exhaust analyzer provides a quick and easy method of testing an air injection system. Run the engine at idle and record the readings. Then, disable the air injection system. Remove the air pump belt or use pliers to pinch the hoses to the air distribution manifold. Compare the exhaust analyzer readings before and after disabling the air injection system.

Without air injection, the exhaust analyzer O_2 reading should drop approximately 2-5 percent. HC and CO readings should increase. This would show that the air injection system is forcing air (oxygen) into the exhaust system.

If the analyzer readings do NOT change, the air injection system is not functioning. Test each component until the source of the problem is found.

To test the air pump, remove the output line from the pump, as in Fig. 40-11. Measure the amount of pressure developed by the pump at idle. Typically, an air pump should produce about 2 to 3 psi (14 to 21 kPa) of pressure.

If a low pressure gauge is not available, place your finger over the line and check for pressure. Replace the pump if faulty.

To test the diverter valve or other air injection system valves, use a service manual. It will explain testing procedures for the specific components.

PULSE AIR SYSTEM SERVICE

Many of the maintenance and testing methods discussed for an air injection system apply to the pulse air system. Inspect all hoses and lines. Measure O_2 with a four-gas analyzer to test the system. Exhaust analyzer oxygen readings should drop when the pulse air system is disabled. If readings do not drop, check the action of the aspirator (Reed) valves.

Fig. 40-12 shows a mechanic testing the operation of the aspirator valves. With the engine running, you should be able to feel vacuum pulses on your fingers. However, you should NOT feel exhaust pressure pulses trying to blow back through the valves. Replace the valves if they do not function as designed.

Fig. 40-12. Aspirator valves can be checked by hand. Place thumbs over valves with engine running. You should feel suction pulses, but not pressure pulses. (Saab)

CATALYTIC CONVERTER SERVICE

Catalytic converter problems are commonly caused by lead contamination, overheating, and extended service. A damaged catalytic converter is pictured in Fig. 40-13. It would block exhaust flow.

A *clogged catalytic converter,* resulting from lead deposits or overheating can increase exhaust system

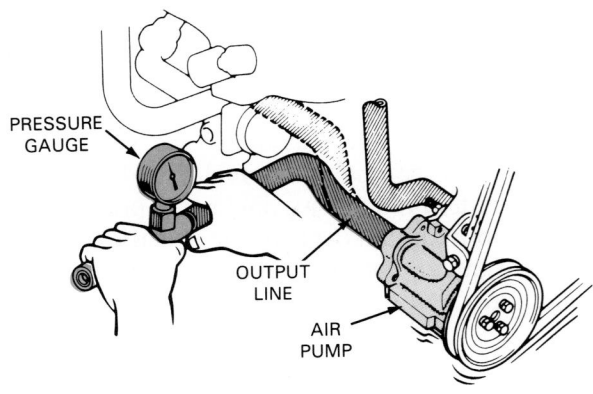

Fig. 40-11. Pressure gauge is used to check air pump output. If pressure is not within specs, replace pump. (Toyota)

Fig. 40-13. Note badly damaged catalytic converter. This would block flow through exhaust system and prevent normal engine operation. (Champion Spark Plug Co.)

back pressure. High back pressure decreases engine performance because gases cannot flow freely through the converter.

After extended service, the catalyst in the converter can become coated with deposits. These deposits can keep the catalyst from acting on the HC, CO, and NOx emissions. Increased air pollution can result.

The inner baffles and shell can also deteriorate. With a pellet type catalytic converter, this can allow BB-size particles to blow out the tailpipe.

Monolithic (honeycomb) catalytic converters must be replaced when the catalyst becomes damaged (overheated) or contaminated (use of leaded fuel or extended service).

Pellet catalytic converters normally have a plug that allows replacement of the catalyst agent. The old pellets can be removed and new ones installed. If the converter housing is damaged or corroded, replace the converter.

Testing catalytic converter

A four-gas exhaust analyzer can be used to check the general condition of the catalytic converter. Follow the specific directions provided with the analyzer. Warm and idle the engine. With some systems, you may need to disable the air injection or pulse air system. Measure the oxygen and carbon monoxide at the tailpipe.

Basically, if O_2 readings are above approximately 5 percent, you know there is enough oxygen for the catalyst to burn the emissions. However, if the CO readings are still above about .5 percent (other systems

operating properly), then the catalytic converter is not oxidizing (burning) the emissions from the engine. The converter or catalyst could require replacement.

NOTE! Before condemning a catalytic converter, refer to a factory service manual. It will give added information on checking other systems before converter replacement.

Catalyst replacement

To install new pellets in a catalytic converter, follow service manual instructions. Generally, do what is illustrated in Fig. 40-14.

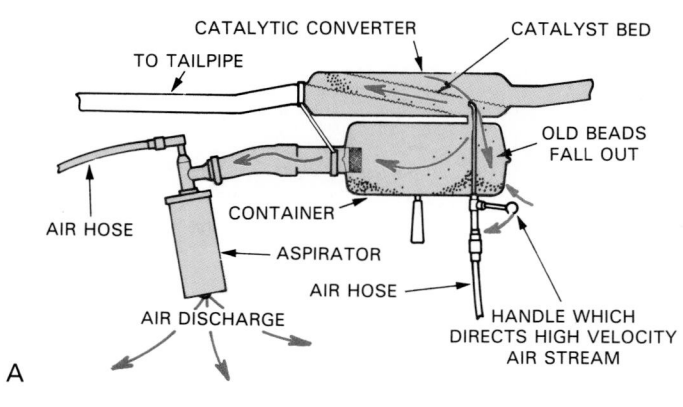

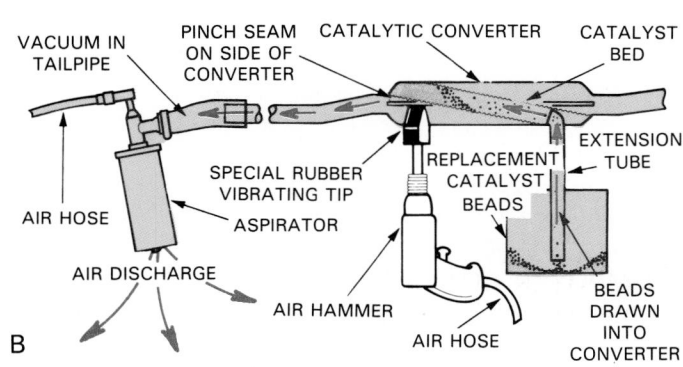

Fig. 40-14. Removing and replacing catalyst from pellet type catalytic converter. A — Use air pressure to blow on and agitate pellets. Old pellets will fall out and enter container. Aspirator forms vacuum to also pull pellets out. B — To install new pellets, place aspirator over tailpipe. This will pull pellets out of container and into converter. Rubber end over air hammer helps shake and fill converter with pellets. (Kent-Moore)

Catalytic converter replacement

Sometimes the catalytic converter is made as an integral part of the exhaust pipe. With this design, the converter and pipe may have to be replaced together. However, with many cars, the converter can be unbolted separately, as in Fig. 40-15. When installing the new converter, use new gaskets and re-install all heat shields.

CAUTION! Remember that the operating temperature of a catalytic converter can be over 1400°F

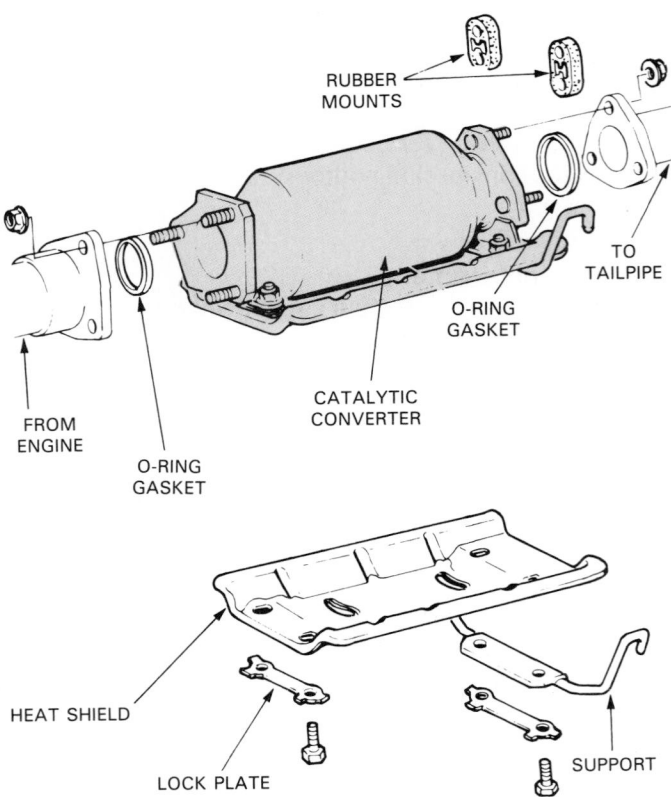

Fig. 40-15. When installing new catalytic converter, replace all gaskets, rubber mounts, and make sure heat shield is in place. (Honda)

Fig. 40-16. Special analyzer can be used to check computer control systems. Auto manufacturers usually recommend specific testers for their cars. (OTC Tools)

(760°C). This is enough heat to cause serious burns. Do NOT touch a catalytic converter until you are sure it has cooled.

COMPUTER CONTROLLED EMISSION SYSTEM SERVICE

Computer controlled engine and emission systems can cause a wide range of problems. The computer may control the carburetor, fuel injection system, EGR valve, evaporative control system, and other components. Any of these parts affect the operation of the total computer system and can increase emissions.

Testing computer controlled emission systems

Since computer systems are so complex, special system analyzers are commonly used to pinpoint specific problems. Fig. 40-16 shows one type of analyzer for checking the operation of a computerized fuel injection system. Following manufacturer operating instructions, the analyzer is plugged into the wiring to the electronic control unit (computer). Then, the analyzer can be used to determine the cause for most system troubles.

Many computerized emission control systems have a built-in diagnostic system. If a problem develops, a dash warning light will glow, indicating a problem. To pinpoint the trouble, follow service manual test procedures.

For example, one computer system is checked by grounding a special "test terminal." This will cause the computer to flash a special Morse-style code at a dash indicating light. The shop manual will tell how to read the code (on-off flashes). This provides a quick and easy way of locating problems in a very complex computer system.

WARNING! Do not connect a VOM (volt-ohm-milliammeter) to a computer system unless told to do so by a service manual. There are several components, including the computer, that can be damaged by incorrect testing procedures.

Chapters 20 and 22 give more information on computer system testing. Refer to these chapters if needed.

Replacing parts in computerized emission system

Depending upon what problem the system tester or self-test mode indicated, you would need to replace faulty components. High emission levels could be due to a faulty oxygen sensor, coolant temperature sensor, throttle position sensor, vehicle speed sensor, intake manifold pressure sensor, fuel injector solenoid, a wiring problem, or by the computer itself.

Before replacing any computer system part, make sure all electrical connections are clean and tight. A corroded connection could be affecting system operation.

When replacing the computer, you may need to remove and reuse the PROM. The **PROM** (programmable read only memory) is a computerized chip (miniaturized electronic circuit) designed for use with the specific vehicle. Usually, it is not faulty and can be used over. Only the control section of the computer usually fails.

Fig. 40-17 shows a wiring diagram for a modern computer-controlled emission control system. Study the location and relationship between the parts. This type of diagram is useful when tracing or troubleshooting circuit problems.

EMISSION CONTROL INFORMATION STICKER

The *emission control information sticker* gives important instructions, diagrams, and specs for complying with EPA regulations. One is shown in Fig. 40-18. Study the information given on the sticker. The emission control sticker is normally located in the engine compartment, on the radiator support, or valve cover.

EMISSION MAINTENANCE REMINDER

The *emission maintenance reminder* is a circuit that automatically turns on a dash light to indicate the need for emission control system service. The system is designed to automatically illuminate an indicator light so the car can be returned to the shop for service.

After the prescribed repairs are done, you must turn off the emission maintenance light. There are numerous methods to turn this light off. You might have to move a small lever hidden in the dash, remove the speedometer cluster, jump across a specific connector, etc. Since there are so many variations, refer to the service manual for instructions. It will give the exact location and methods for deactivating the emission maintenance reminder light.

KNOW THESE TERMS

Exhaust analyzer, Two-gas analyzer, Four-gas analyzer, HC readings, CO readings, O_2 readings, CO_2 readings, Stoichiometric.

REVIEW QUESTIONS

1. An _____ _____ is a testing instrument that measures the chemical content of the engine exhaust gases.
2. What is the difference between a two and a four-gas exhaust analyzer?
3. Name five reasons that HC readings can be higher than normal.
4. High CO readings can be caused by fuel system

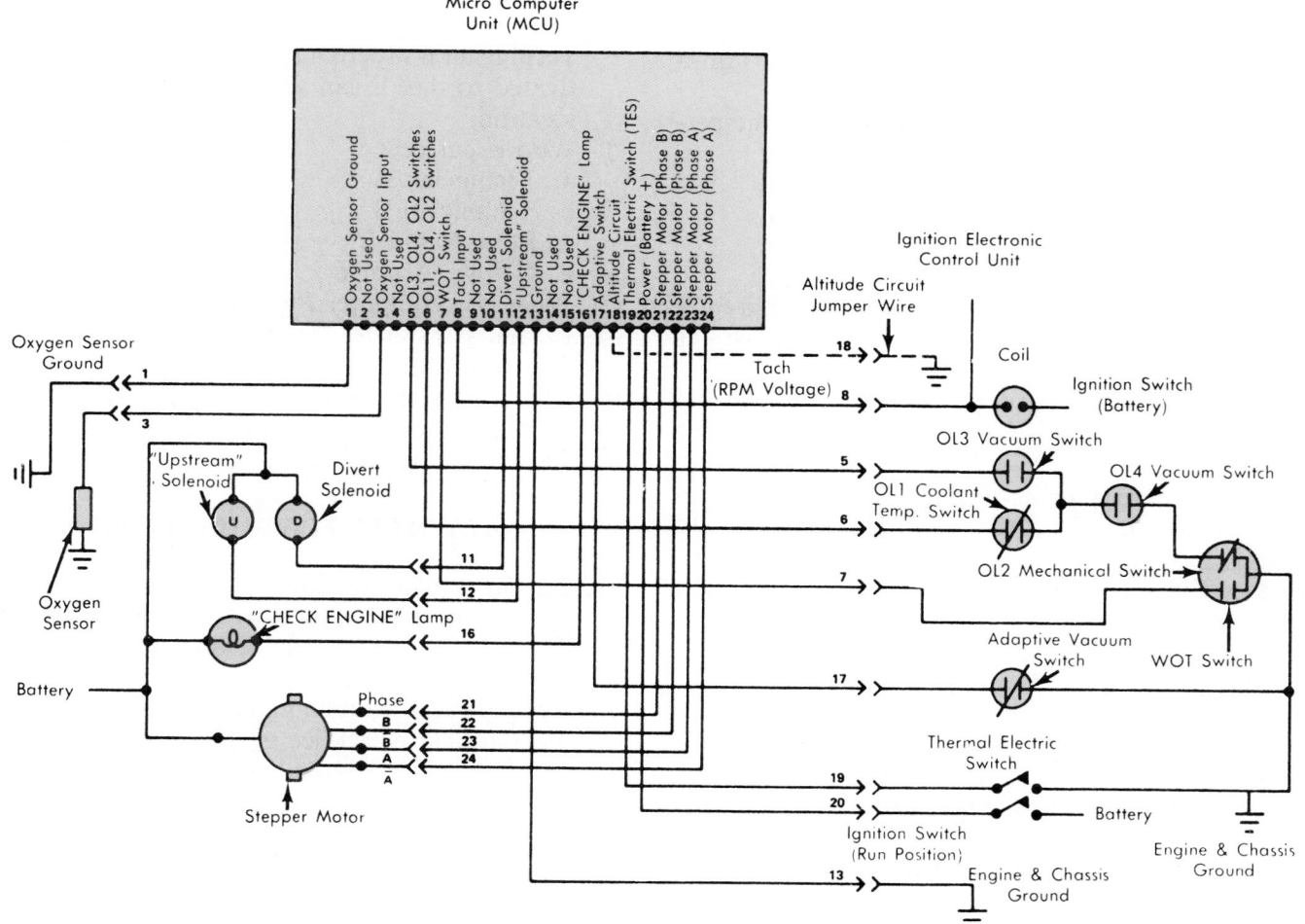

Fig. 40-17. *Wiring diagram of modern computerized emission control system. Note many sensors and other components.* (Chrysler Corp.)

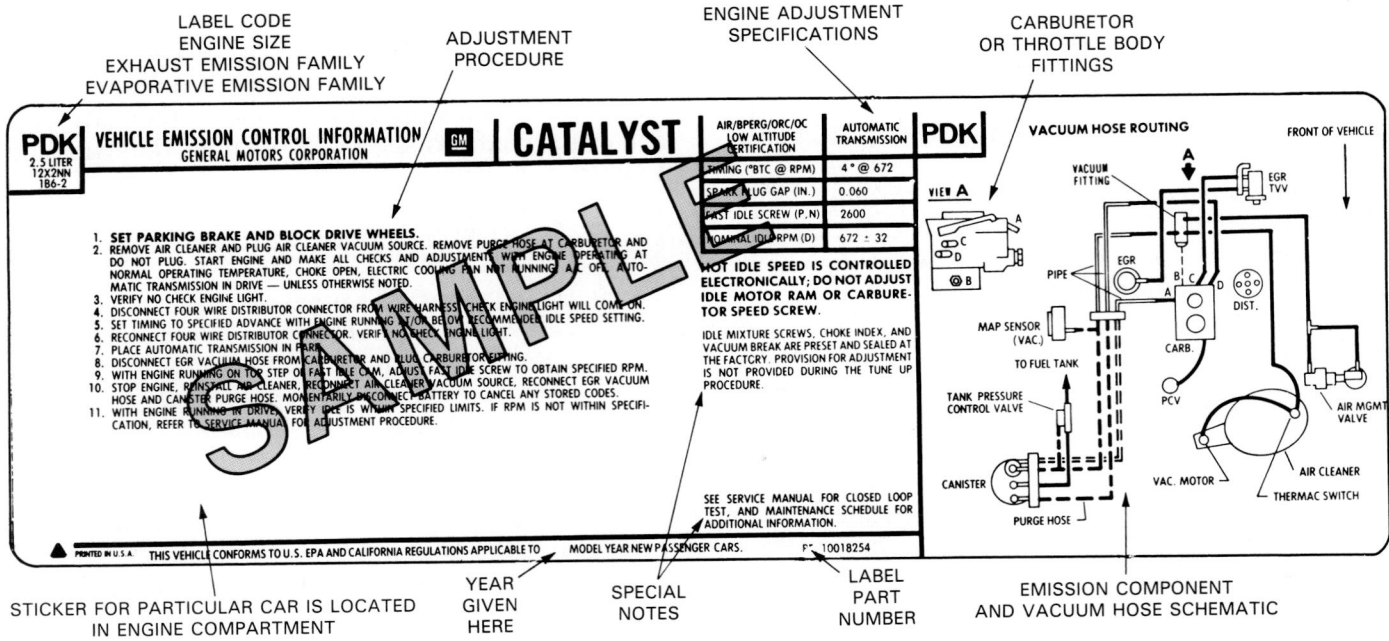

Fig. 40-18. Typical emission control information sticker found in engine compartment. Use it to comply with EPA standards during a tune-up. (Oldsmobile)

problems. True or False?

5. With a four-gas exhaust analyzer, oxygen in the engine exhaust is an accurate indicator of a _____ air-fuel mixture.

6. Typically, if the percent of CO exceeds the percent of O_2, the air-fuel mixture is on the:
   a. Lean side of stoichiometric.
   b. Rich side of stoichiometric.
   c. Stoichiometric.
   d. None of the above are correct.

7. How do you check the general operation of a PCV valve with your finger and with an exhaust gas analyzer?

8. If a vacuum pump is used to activate an EGR valve at idle, the engine should NOT be effected. True or False?

9. An air pump in an air injection system should produce about _____ to _____ psi or _____ to _____ kPa.

10. Describe the results of a clogged catalytic converter.

11. The operating temperature of a catalytic converter may be over _____ or _____ .

12. A driver complains that a check engine (emission trouble) light glows in the dash. The car's periodic service switch has not been activated. The car also has a self-diagnostic computer that controls many emission system components.
    Technician A says that, first, an ohmmeter should be used to measure the resistance of the computer system oxygen sensor. It is a common problem with this make and model.
    Technician B says that the computer should be activated so that it can show the possible problem location.
    Who is correct?
    a. Technician A
    b. Technician B
    c. Both A and B
    d. Neither A nor B

13. What is a computer PROM?

14. In many instances, why should the PROM be reused in a new computer?

15. The emission control _____ _____ gives important instructions, diagrams, and specs for complying with EPA regulations.

ACTIVITIES FOR CHAPTER 40

1. Set up a two- or four-gas analyzer correctly, following the manufacturer's instructions. Demonstrate to your instructor and to the class the proper procedure for checking emission levels. If there are high emission levels, write your recommendations for service of any problems.

2. If a flat rate manual and parts catalog are available, prepare a bill for the service and repair in Activity 1. Use a labor rate suggested by your instructor.

41

Engine Performance Problems

After studying this chapter, you will be able to:
☐ List the most common engine performance problems.
☐ Describe the symptoms for common engine performance problems.
☐ Explain typical causes of engine performance problems.
☐ Use a systematic approach when diagnosing engine performance problems.

An *engine performance problem* is any trouble that affects the power, fuel economy, emission output levels, and dependability of the engine. Performance problems can be caused by the ignition system, fuel system, emission control systems, or the engine itself. This makes diagnosis very challenging. You must be able to narrow down the causes until the faulty system and part are found.

This chapter reviews typical performance problems that are fully explained in other textbook chapters. This summary is needed to prepare you for the next chapters on test equipment and engine tune-up.

LOCATING ENGINE PERFORMANCE PROBLEMS

Use a systematic approach when trying to locate performance problems. Do NOT use hit and miss repairs.

A *systematic approach* involves using your knowledge of automotive service and a logical process of elimination. Think of all of the possible systems and components that could upset engine operation. Then, one by one, mentally throw out the parts that could NOT produce the symptoms.

To troubleshoot properly, ask yourself these kinds of questions:
1. What are the symptoms (noise, miss, smoke)?
2. What system could be producing the symptoms (ignition, fuel, engine)?
3. Where is the most logical place to start testing?

For example, suppose a carburetor-equipped engine misses and emits heavy black smoke shortly after cold starting. The heavy black smoke would tell you that too much fuel is entering the engine. Since the engine only runs poorly when cold, engine temperature relates to the problem.

Through simple deduction, you should think of the carburetor. It controls the fuel mixture and its choke is affected by temperature. Possibly, the choke is sticking shut, allowing an excessively rich air-fuel mixture to enter the engine.

As you can see, logical thought will help you check the most likely problems. If your first idea is incorrect, rethink the problem and check the next most likely trouble source.

Performance problem diagnosis charts

If you have trouble locating an engine performance problem, refer to a service manual diagnosis chart. It will list problem causes and corrections. A service manual chart is written for the particular make and model of car, making it very accurate.

TYPICAL PERFORMANCE PROBLEMS

It is important that you understand the most common engine performance problems. The following will help you use test equipment, troubleshooting charts, and a service manual during diagnosis.

No-start problem

A *no-start problem* occurs when the engine "cranks" (is turned over by starting motor) but fails to "fire" (run on its own power). This is the most obvious and severe performance problem. There is a complete failure of either the fuel system, ignition system, an engine component, or another related system.

With a no-start problem, CHECK FOR SPARK, first. Pull one spark plug wire (gasoline engine). Insert a screwdriver into the wire end. Hold it next to ground (about 1/4 in. or 6.5 mm away, maximum).

A bright spark should jump to ground when the engine is cranked. If not, the problem is in the ignition system.

If you have spark, CHECK FOR FUEL. With a carburetor fuel system, operate the throttle lever. Watch for fuel squirting out the accelerator pump discharge. With throttle body fuel injection, watch the injector outlet. With multi-point injection, pull one injector to check for fuel. If you do not have fuel, then something is wrong with the fuel system.

By checking for fuel and spark, you have narrowed down the possible problem sources to either system. If you have both fuel and spark, then check engine compression. A jumped timing chain or belt could be keeping the engine from starting. With a diesel, a slow cranking speed can prevent starting.

Hard starting

Hard starting is due to partial failure of a system.

The carburetor choke may be inoperative. The fuel injection coolant temperature sensor may be bad. Check components that aid engine starting.

Stalling (dying)

During a *stall*, the engine stops running. This may occur at an idle, after cold starting, or after warm up.

There are many causes of stalling: low idle speed, carburetor or injection system problem, ignition system trouble, severe vacuum leak, or inoperative thermostatic air cleaner.

Misfiring

Engine *misfiring* is a performance problem resulting from one or more cylinders failing to fire (produce normal combustion). The engine may miss at idle, under acceleration, or at cruising speeds.

If an engine only misses at idle, for example, check the components that affect idle. If the engine has a carburetor, the idle circuit may be clogged with debris. With fuel injection, possibly an injector is not

This 4-cylinder engine uses four valves per cylinder, a turbocharger, intercooler, electronic ignition, port fuel injection, and dual overhead camshafts. It takes a knowledgeable service technician to troubleshoot performance problems on an engine like this one. (Saab)

opening. A fouled spark plug, open plug wire, cracked distributor cap, corroded terminals, and vacuum leak are a few other possible causes for a miss.

Vacuum leak

A *vacuum leak* is a common cause of rough idling. If a vacuum hose hardens and cracks, it will allow outside air to enter the engine intake manifold, bypassing the carburetor or throttle body. This will cause a lean air-fuel mixture, preventing normal combustion.

Usually, a vacuum leak will produce a HISSING SOUND. The engine roughness will smooth out when rpm is increased.

A section of vacuum hose can be used to locate vacuum leaks. Place one end of the hose next to your ear. Move the other end around the engine. When the hiss becomes very loud, you have found the leak.

Hesitation (stumble)

A *hesitation,* also called *stumble,* is a condition where the engine does not accelerate normally when the gas pedal is pressed. The engine may almost stall before developing power.

A hesitation is usually caused by a temporary lean air-fuel mixture. With a carburetor, the accelerator pump may not be functioning. With fuel injection, the throttle position switch may be bad. Check the parts that aid engine acceleration.

Surging

Surging is a condition where engine power fluctuates up and down. When driving at a steady speed, the engine seems to speed up and slow down, without movement of the gas pedal.

Surging is sometimes caused by an extremely lean carburetor or fuel injection setting. Lean settings are used to increase fuel economy and reduce emissions. Surging can also be caused by ignition or computer control system problems.

Backfiring

Backfiring is caused by the air-fuel mixture igniting in the intake manifold or exhaust system. A loud BANG or POP sound can be heard when the mixture ignites and burns.

Backfiring can be caused by incorrect ignition timing, crossed spark plug wires, cracked distributor cap, bad carburetor accelerator pump, exhaust system leakage, faulty air injection system, computer system malfunction, or other system faults.

A mild backfire in the throttle body or carburetor is sometimes referred to as a COUGH.

Dieseling (after-running, run-on)

Dieseling, also called *after-running* or *run-on,* occurs when the engine fails to shut off. The engine keeps firing, coughing, and producing power. The air-fuel mixture is igniting spontaneously, forcing the pistons

down without the spark plugs firing.

Dieseling is usually caused by a high idle speed, carbon buildup in the combustion chambers, low octane rating of fuel, or overheated engine.

Pinging (spark knock)

Pinging or *spark knock* is a metallic tapping or light knocking sound, usually when the engine accelerates under load. Pinging is caused by abnormal combustion (preignition or detonation). Preignition and detonation are discussed in Chapter 17.

Pinging is normally caused by low octane fuel, advanced ignition timing, carbon buildup in combustion chambers, or engine overheating.

Vapor lock

Vapor lock occurs when the fuel is overheated, forming air bubbles that upset the air-fuel mixture. Vapor lock can cause engine stalling, lack of power, hard starting, and no starting.

Vapor lock is caused by too much engine heat transferring into the fuel. A gas line may be touching a hot engine part. The fuel return system may be plugged. You would need to locate any condition that could overheat the fuel.

Gas line freeze

Gas line freeze results when moisture in the fuel turns to ice. The ice will block fuel filters and prevent engine operation. With diesel fuel, the overcooled fuel can form wax that blocks the filters.

To correct gas line freeze, replace clogged fuel filters. You may need to place the car in a warm garage until fuel is thawed.

Poor fuel economy

Poor fuel economy is a condition causing the car to use too much fuel for the miles driven. Fuel economy can be measured by comparing the miles that can be driven on one gallon (3.79 L) of fuel.

Poor fuel economy can be caused by a wide range of problems. Some of these include: rich air-fuel mixture, engine miss, incorrect ignition timing, or leakage in a fuel line or the tank.

Lack of engine power

Lack of engine power, also termed a *sluggish engine,* causes the vehicle to accelerate slowly. When the gas pedal is pressed, the car does not gain speed properly.

As with poor fuel economy, there are many troubles that can reduce engine power: fuel system problems, ignition system problems, emission control system problems, engine mechanical problems.

OTHER PERFORMANCE PROBLEMS

There are many other more specific engine performance problems. Many of these are covered in other chapters of this book. Use the index to locate more information if needed.

KNOW THESE TERMS

Systematic approach, Diagnosis chart, No start problem, Hard to start problem, Stalling, Missing, Vacuum leak, Hesitation, Stumble, Surging, Backfiring, Dieseling, Pinging, Vapor lock, Gas line freeze, Poor fuel economy.

REVIEW QUESTIONS

1. How do you use a systematic approach to troubleshooting?
2. If you have difficulty locating an engine performance problem, refer to a service manual _____ _____ .
3. A car is towed into a garage with a no-start problem. The engine cranks but will not "fire" and run on its own power. The car has a carburetor-equipped gasoline engine.
Technician A says to check for spark and fuel. Pull one plug wire and make sure high voltage is arcing to ground. Also, check for fuel by activating the throttle lever while watching for fuel at the accelerator pump nozzle. This will help isolate the problem.
Technician B says that the spark plugs should be removed first. The engine could have a bad timing chain that is lowering compression in all of the cylinders.

Who is correct?
   a. Technician A
   b. Technician B
   c. Both A and B
   d. Neither A nor B
4. Define the term "misfiring."
5. A vacuum leak is a common cause of rough idling. True or False?
6. A _____ , also called a _____ , is a condition where the engine does not accelerate normally when the gas pedal is pressed.
7. What causes "backfiring?"
8. Define the term "dieseling."
9. A _____ or _____ _____ is a metallic tapping or light knocking sound, usually when accelerating under load. It is caused by abnormal _____ .
10. Vapor lock occurs when the gasoline is cooled and forms a gel, preventing fuel flow and engine operation. True or False?

ACTIVITIES FOR CHAPTER 41

1. Check shop manuals for a "no-start" diagnosis chart and demonstrate how you would troubleshoot a "no-start" problem on a vehicle engine.
2. Invite an experienced auto service technician to speak to your class about troubleshooting procedures. Prepare a list of questions that you might ask the technician. Discuss the questions with your instructor beforehand.

Engine Test Instruments

42

After studying this chapter, you will be able to:
□ Identify the most common engine test instruments.
□ Describe typical uses for test instruments.
□ Follow test instrument instructions to make actual engine performance tests.
□ Compare different testing methods.
□ Cite and observe appropriate safety rules.

This chapter summarizes the types and uses of modern test instruments. Other textbook chapters have already covered test instruments. However, a brief review of each type is needed to prepare you for the following chapters on tune-up and engine repair.

TESTING SAFETY RULES

When using test equipment, there are several general rules to remember.

1. Read the operating instructions for the test equipment. Failure to follow directions could cause bodily injury and severe damage to the part or instrument.
2. If the engine is to be running during your tests, set the parking brake. Block the wheels. Place an automatic transmission in park or manual transmission in neutral. Connect an exhaust vent hose to the tailpipe if you are working in an enclosed shop.
3. Keep test equipment leads (wires) or hoses away from engine belts, the fan, and hot engine parts. They can be damaged easily.
4. Wear eye protection when working around an engine fan. Remove jewelry and tie up long hair.
5. Never look into a carburetor or throttle body when cranking or running the engine. Do not cover the air inlet with your hand. If the engine were to backfire, it could cause serious burns.
6. Refer to the auto manufacturer's service manual for specific testing procedures.

SPARK TESTER

A *spark tester* is used to check the basic operation of the engine ignition system. One is shown in Fig. 42-1. The spark tester is connected between the end of a spark plug wire and ground. When the engine is cranked or started, a "hot" spark should jump across the tester gap.

A spark tester has a very wide gap. The gap makes sure the ignition system can produce sufficient voltage. It also protects the ignition system from possible damage from an open circuit when testing.

COMPRESSION GAUGE

A *compression gauge* is used to measure the amount of pressure during the engine compression stroke. See Fig. 42-2. It provides a means of testing the mechanical condition of the engine. If the compression gauge readings are not within specs, something is mechanically wrong in the engine.

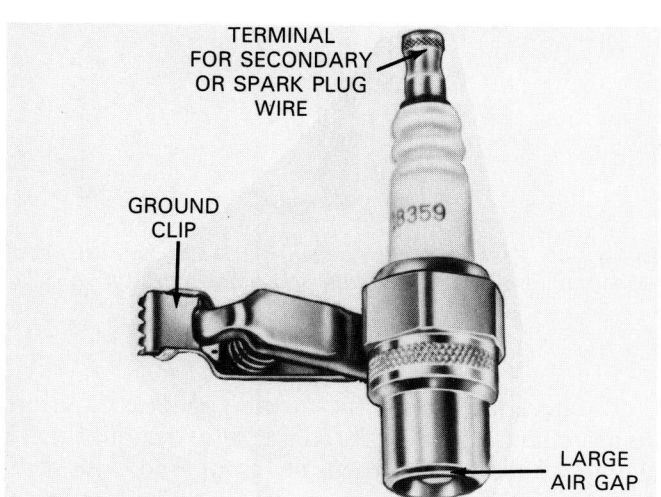

Fig. 42-1. Spark tester will quickly check high voltage output from ignition system. If spark jumps large air gap, there should be enough voltage to fire spark plugs. (OTC Tools)

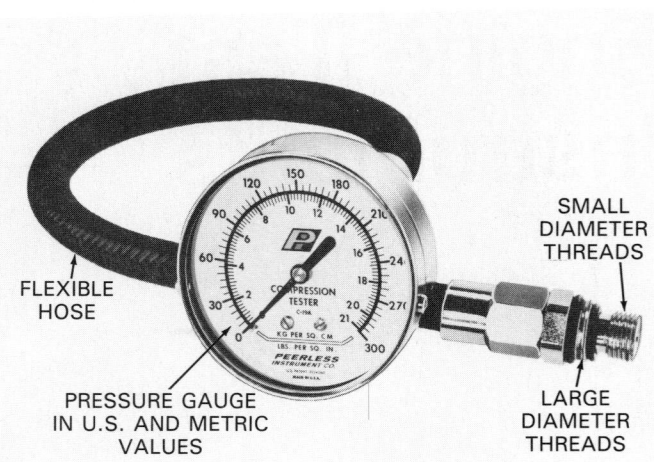

Fig. 42-2. Compression tester is pressure gauge with special fitting for spark plug or glow plug hole. This gauge reads in both conventional and metric values. (Peerless)

A compression test should be performed when symptoms (engine miss, rough idle, puffing noise in induction [intake] system or exhaust) point to major engine problems. Refer to Fig. 42-3.

Compression testing

To do a compression test, remove all of the spark plugs (gasoline engine) or glow plugs (diesel engine). Disable the ignition or injection system. Block open the throttle valve (gasoline engine).

Screw the compression tester into a spark plug or glow plug hole. Crank the engine at least four compression strokes while reading the gauge. Measure and record the pressure for each cylinder. Repeat on other cylinders.

A normal compression reading will make the gauge increase evenly to specs. The pressure in each cylinder should not vary more than about 10 percent.

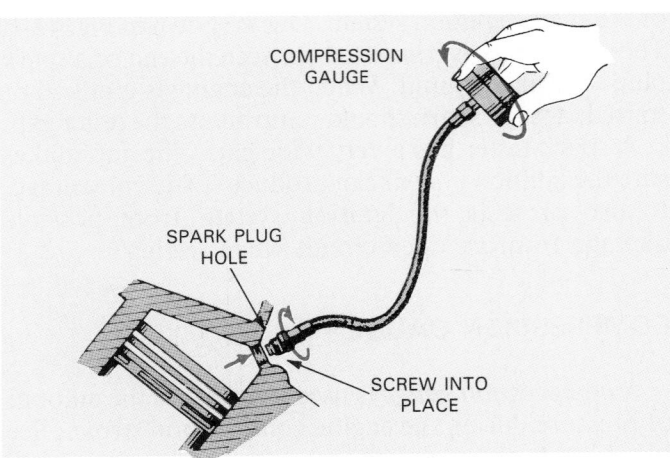

Fig. 42-3. Modern compression testers screw into spark plug or glow plug hole. Older compression testers were hand-held in hole and were not very handy. (Sears)

For more information on compression testing, refer to Chapter 45, Engine Mechanical Problems.

CYLINDER LEAKAGE TESTER

A *cylinder leakage tester* performs about the same function as a compression gauge; it measures the amount of air leakage out of the engine combustion chambers. External air pressure is forced into the cylinder with the piston at TDC. Then, a pressure gauge can be used to determine the percent of air leakage out of the cylinder.

If leakage is severe enough, you will be able to hear and feel air blowing out of the engine. Air may blow out the intake manifold (bad intake valve), exhaust system (burned exhaust valve), breather (bad rings, piston, or cylinder), or into an adjacent cylinder (blown head gasket).

VACUUM GAUGE

A *vacuum gauge* measures negative pressure (suction) produced by the engine, fuel pump, vacuum pump, or other component. It can be used to determine engine condition and to check vacuum devices. Look at Fig. 42-4.

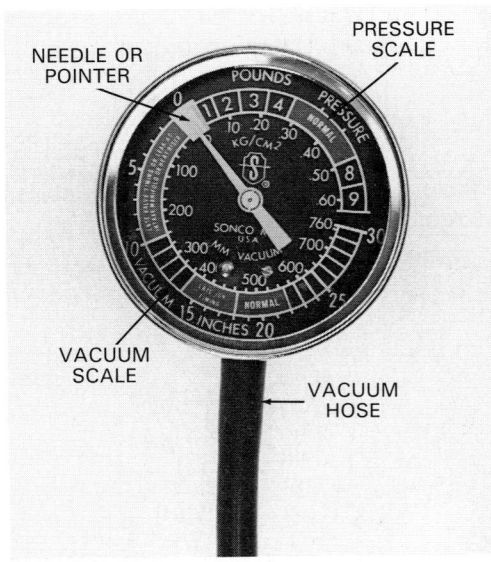

Fig. 42-4. Vacuum-pressure gauge is useful because needle reads vacuum in one direction and pressure in other. Study scales. (Sonco)

To check the engine, the vacuum gauge is connected to a vacuum fitting on the engine intake manifold. The gauge readings can then be compared to normal readings. Fig. 42-5 shows typical vacuum gauge readings and what they mean. Study these closely.

Fig. 42-6 shows a hand-operated vacuum pump and gauge. Fig. 42-7 pictures a vacuum analyzer.

NORMAL ENGINE READING. Vacuum gauge should have reading of 18-22 inches of vacuum. The needle should remain steady.

BURNED OR LEAKY VALVES. Burned valve will cause pointer to drop every time burned valve opens.

WEAK VALVE SPRINGS. Vacuum will be normal at idle but pointer will fluctuate excessively at higher speeds.

WORN VALVE GUIDES. If pointer fluctuates excessively at idle but steadies at higher speeds, valves may be worn allowing air to upset fuel mixture.

CHOKED MUFFLER. Vacuum will slowly drop to zero when engine speed is high.

INTAKE MANIFOLD AIR LEAK. If pointer is down 3 to 9 inches from normal at idle throttle valve is not closing or intake gaskets are leaking.

CARBURETOR OR FUEL INJECTION PROBLEM. A poor air-fuel mixture at idle can cause needle to slowly drift back and forth.

STICKING VALVES. A sticking valve will cause pointer to drop intermittently.

Fig. 42-5. Typical vacuum gauge readings and problem causes.   (Sonco)

PRESSURE GAUGE

A *pressure gauge* measures psi (pounds per square inch) and/or kPa (kilopascals). It is used to check various pressures in a car, such as:
1. Fuel pressure, Fig. 42-8.
2. Power steering pump pressure.
3. Automatic transmission pressures.
4. Tire pressure.
5. Air shock pressure.
6. Air conditioning system pressure.
7. Turbocharger boost pressure, Fig. 42-9.

A mechanic will usually have several pressure gauges. Each will be designed for a specific job.

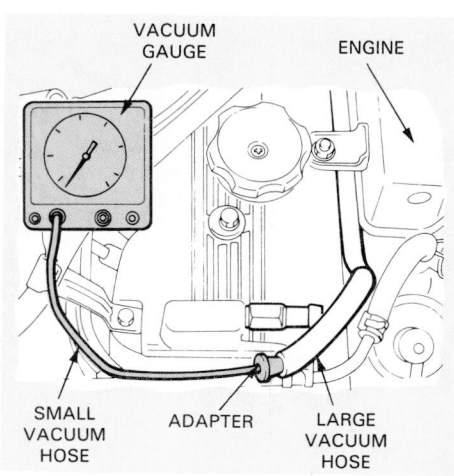

A   B

Fig. 42-6. A — Hand-operated vacuum pump is handy for testing vacuum-operated devices. Pump forms suction without engine running. Gauge reads vacuum applied. B — Conventional vacuum gauge.   (Peerless and Toyota)

Fig. 42-7. Vacuum system analyzer contains electric vacuum pump, gauge, and ohmmeter. Since vacuum and electrical systems often interact, meter is useful. (Peerless)

TIMING LIGHT

A *timing light* is a strobe (flashing) light used to check and adjust ignition timing. See Fig. 42-10.

Normally, the two small timing light leads are connected to the car battery. The larger lead is connected to the NUMBER ONE spark plug wire. The timing light is then shone on the engine timing marks. The marks are usually located on the chain case cover of the engine or on the flywheel.

The timing light, by flashing ON and OFF, makes the spinning crankshaft pulley, balancer, or flywheel appear to stand still. This makes the spinning timing

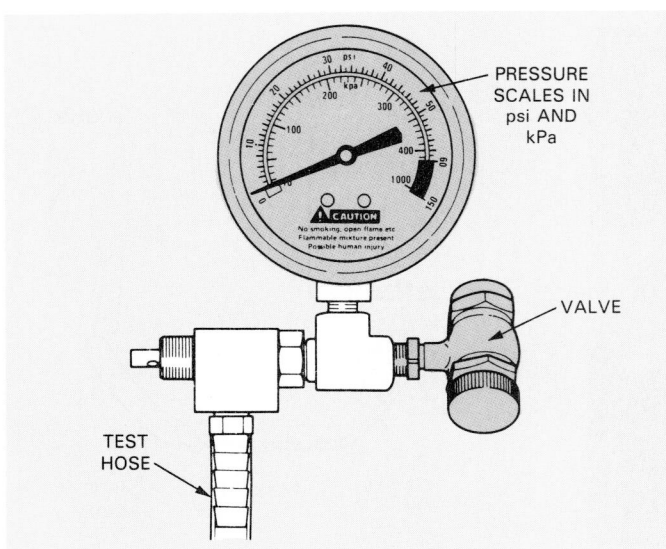

Fig. 42-8. Pressure gauge is commonly used to check fuel pressure and other pressures. This one has shut-off valve in fitting. (Ford Motor Co.)

Fig. 42-9. Small pressure gauge with long section of hose is needed for on-road testing. For example, gauge will read turbocharger boost pressures while vehicle is driven. (Saab)

Fig. 42-10. Timing light flashes whenever spark is delivered to the No. 1 cylinder. It checks ignition timing. (Peerless Instrument Co.)

mark visible. You can then adjust the ignition timing by turning the distributor housing. Other adjustment procedures must be used on vehicles having a distributorless ignition system.

TACH-DWELL METER

A *tach-dwell meter* is a tachometer and a dwell meter combined into one instrument. The tach is for measuring engine rpm (speed). The dwell meter measures in degrees for contact point adjustment or computer controlled carburetor calibration. A tach-dwell is commonly used during tune-ups, Fig. 42-11.

Follow operating instructions when connecting a tach-dwell meter. Procedures vary. To measure rpm for an idle speed adjustment, you must typically connect the red lead to the negative coil terminal or tach terminal. The black tester lead connects to ground.

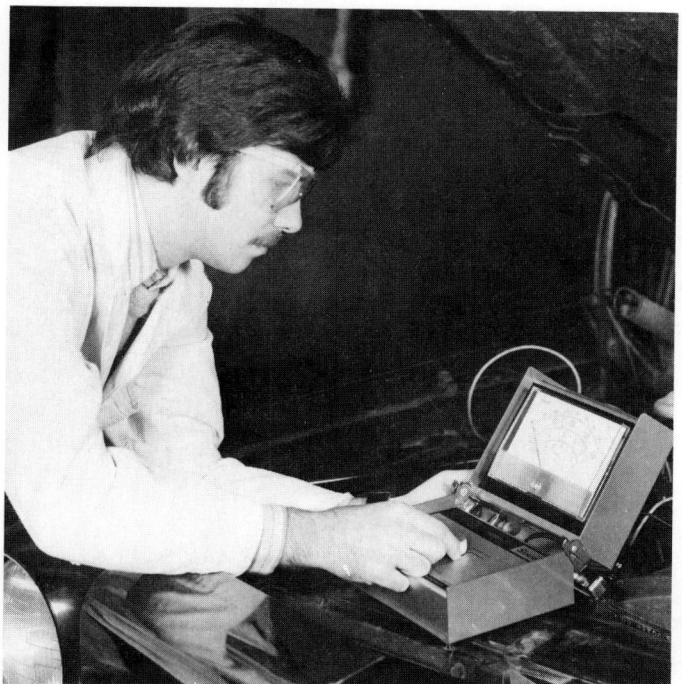

Fig. 42-11. Tach-dwell is commonly used during ignition and fuel system adjustment. Tach shows engine speed. Dwell meter will measure distributor point adjustment or computer output to some late model carburetors. (Snap-On Tools)

MAG-TACH

A *mag-tach* is a magnetically triggered tachometer for measuring engine rpm. It is used on both diesel and gasoline engines. A diesel engine does not have an electrically operated ignition system to power a conventional tachometer.

The mag-tach is operated by a magnet that senses a notch in the engine flywheel or damper. In this way, engine speed can be measured without a connection to the ignition system. Refer to Fig. 42-12.

ELECTRONIC IGNITION SYSTEM TESTER

An *electronic ignition system tester* will accurately check the operation of many ignition system components. A tester is illustrated in Fig. 42-13. Connect it to the ignition system following manufacturer instructions. Indicator lights will tell you whether the parts of the system are functioning properly.

Electronic ignition system testers vary. Some have more testing capabilities than others. Also, different ignition systems require different testing methods. Always refer to a service manual and the tester instructions. This will help assure correct test results.

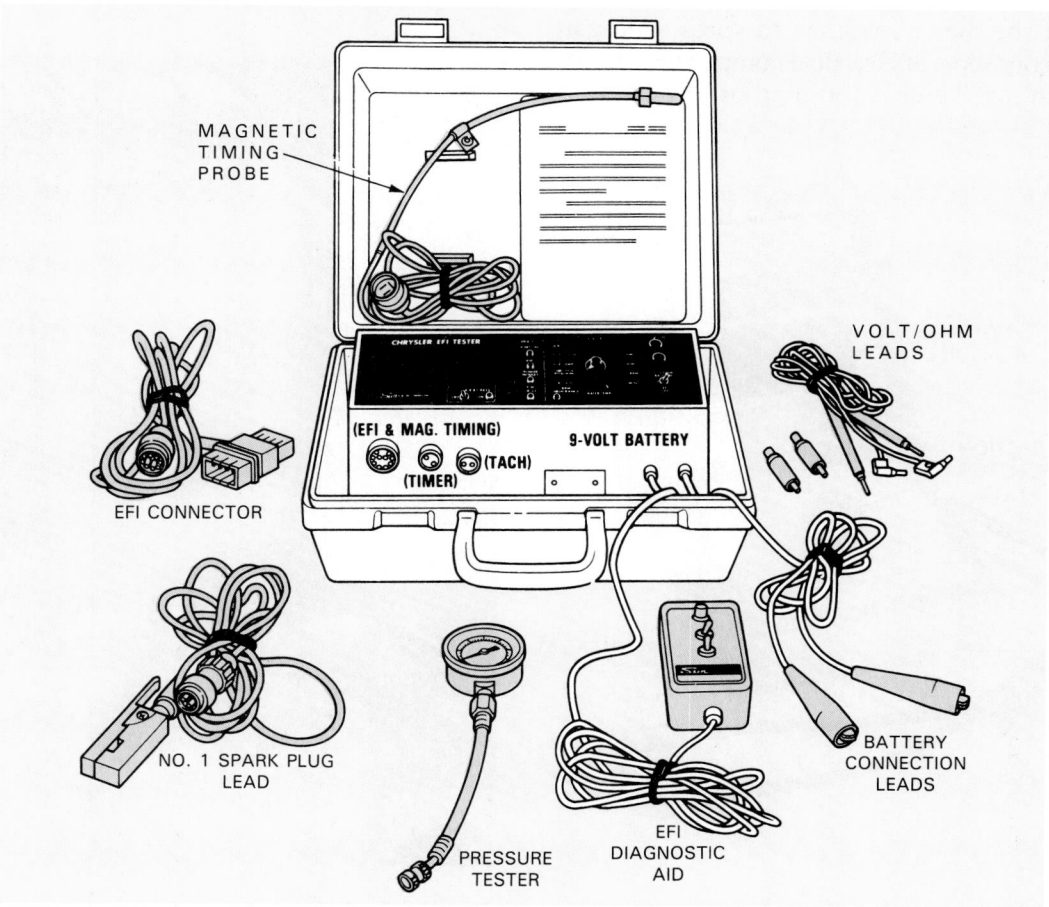

Fig. 42-12. This tester is capable of checking timing magnetically. It will also do several other tests. Readings are given by numbers on face of tester. (Chrysler Corp.)

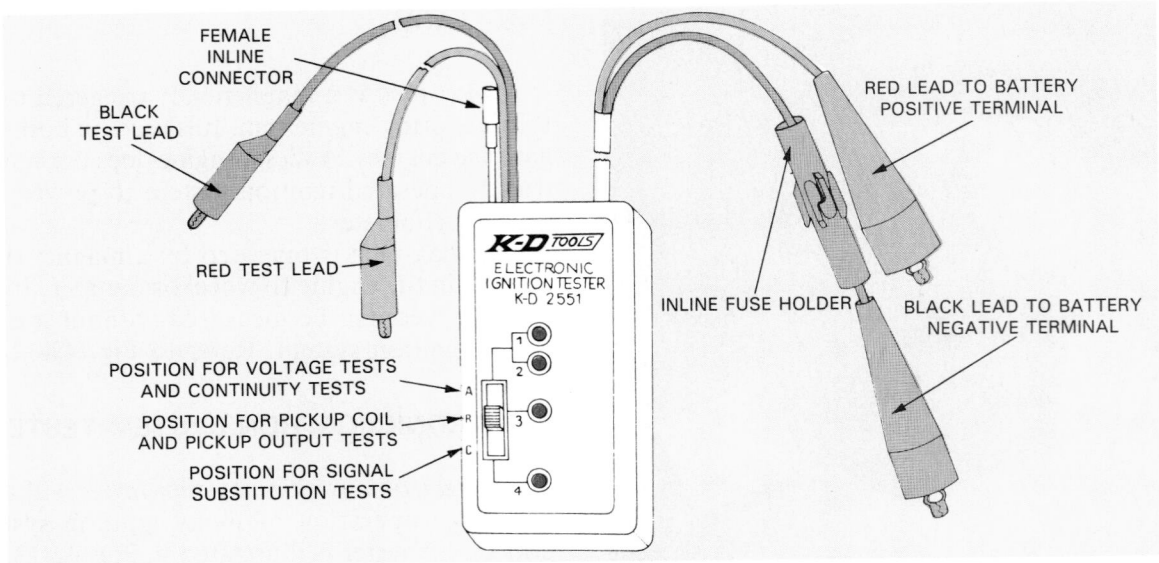

Fig. 42-13. Electronic ignition system tester performs various checks of system. Indicator lights show test results. (K-D Tools)

VOM

A *vom* (volt-ohm-milliammeter), also called a multimeter, is commonly used to check the condition of numerous electrical, engine related components. It will measure voltage current, and resistance, Fig. 42-14. By comparing the meter readings to specs, you can determine the condition of electrical components or circuits. If a resistance value is too high or low, there is a problem.

Look at Fig. 42-15. When using a VOM, make sure all selector settings are correct. Calibrate the meter if need be. Place the meter in a safe location, where it cannot fall or be damaged by moving or hot parts.

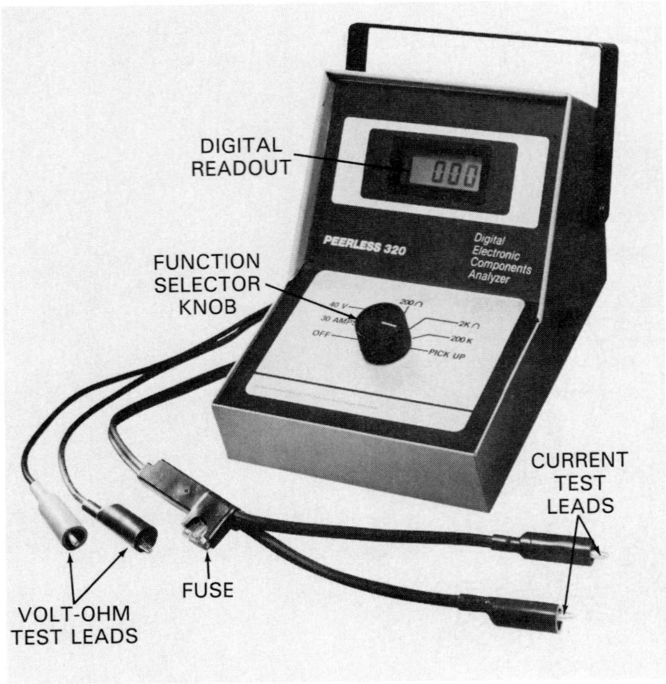

Fig. 42-14. This is a modern digital meter for measuring amps, volts, and ohms. It is an essential instrument when working on today's vehicles. (Peerless)

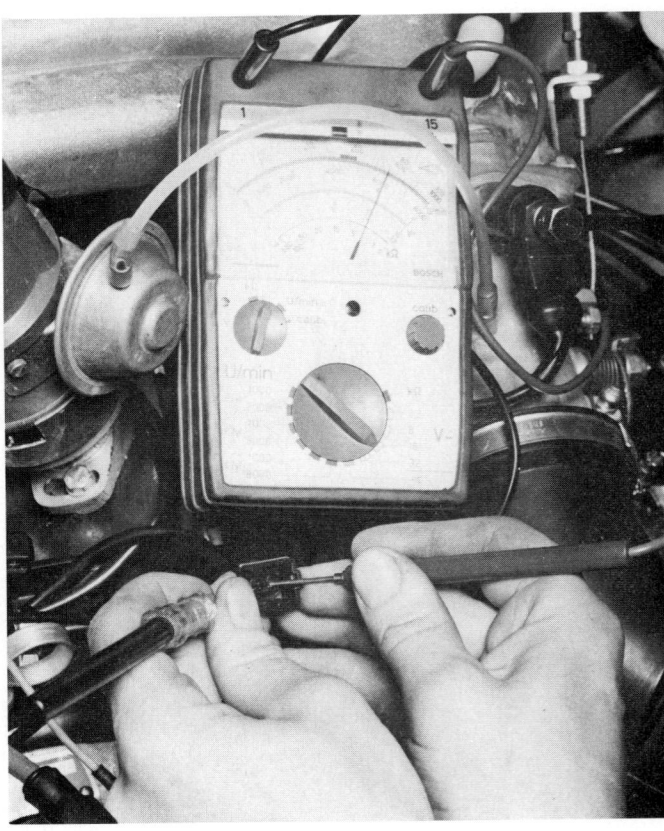

Fig. 42-15. When using any type of meter, make sure it is supported safely. It can be ruined if hit by engine fan, dropped, or in contact with hot engine parts. (Saab)

EFI TESTER

An *EFI tester* will check the operation of modern electronic fuel injection systems. Most EFI testers come with numerous accessory devices, as shown in Fig. 42-16. The tester will usually test all of the system sensors, circuit wiring, and the computer. A pressure gauge is provided for measuring fuel pump and pressure regulator outputs.

EFI test equipment varies. Make sure you follow the operation instructions carefully. Frequently, auto makers recommend a particular brand of tester for their vehicles. The service manual will explain the use of the particular tester.

DIESEL INJECTION TESTER

A *diesel injection tester* is a set of pressure gauges and valves for measuring system pressure. Refer to Fig. 42-17. This tester will check feed pump pressure, fuel volume, injector operation (out of engine), lubrication system pressure, and other functions.

If diesel injection pressures are not within specs, repairs or adjustments are needed. Again, specific

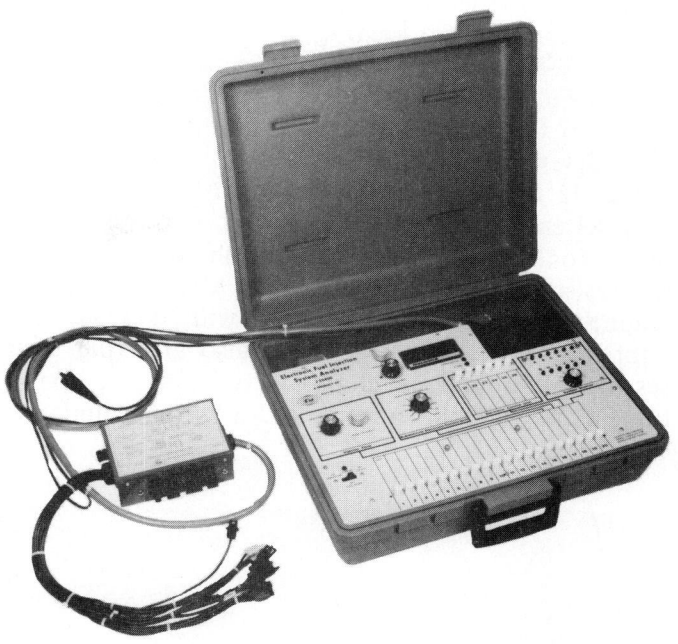

Fig. 42-16. Electronic fuel injection tester plugs into computer circuit. It will then check operation of sensors and the EFI computer. (Kent-Moore)

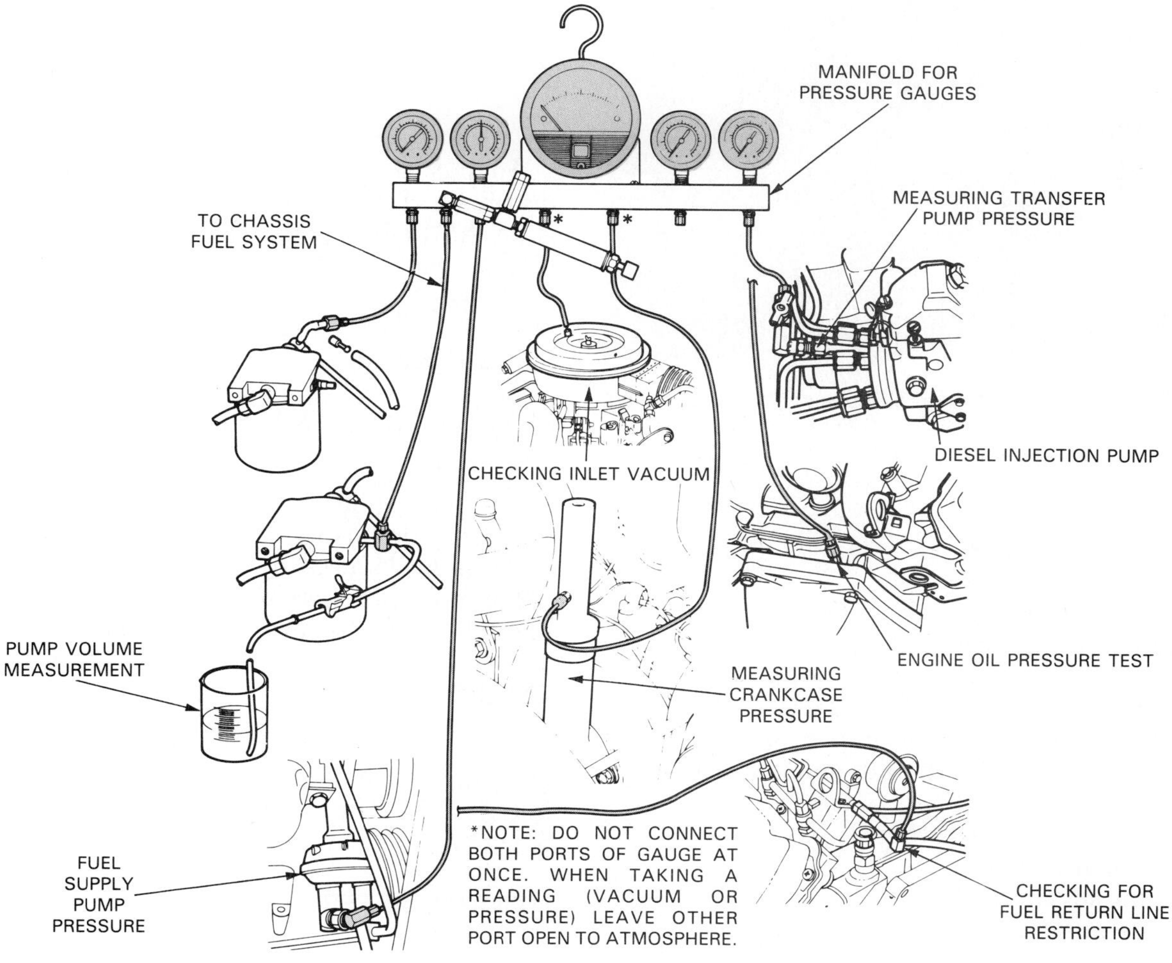

MANIFOLD FOR PRESSURE GAUGES

MEASURING TRANSFER PUMP PRESSURE

TO CHASSIS FUEL SYSTEM

DIESEL INJECTION PUMP

CHECKING INLET VACUUM

PUMP VOLUME MEASUREMENT

MEASURING CRANKCASE PRESSURE

ENGINE OIL PRESSURE TEST

FUEL SUPPLY PUMP PRESSURE

*NOTE: DO NOT CONNECT BOTH PORTS OF GAUGE AT ONCE. WHEN TAKING A READING (VACUUM OR PRESSURE) LEAVE OTHER PORT OPEN TO ATMOSPHERE.

CHECKING FOR FUEL RETURN LINE RESTRICTION

Fig. 42-17. Diesel injection system tester. Note various test connections. (Ford)

operating instructions vary.

DANGER! The operating pressures in a diesel injection system are high enough to cause serious injury. A fitting leak could allow fuel to spray out and puncture your skin or eyes. Follow all safety rules covered in Chapters 23 and 24.

Fig. 42-18 shows a special test harness for checking a diesel engine rough idle problem. Harness is connected to the glow plugs. Then, the ohmmeter will read the resistance of the glow plugs. After a period of engine operation, combustion will increase the temperature of the glow plugs, also affecting their resistance. An unequal change in resistance (temperature) allows a technician to find a "dead cylinder."

Fig. 42-18. Diesel rough idle test harness can be used to find an engine cylinder that is not firing. Glow plug resistance will vary in bad cylinder. (OTC)

DISTRIBUTOR TESTER

A *distributor tester,* also called *distributor machine,* is used to check the operation of an ignition system distributor. See Fig. 42-19. The distributor is removed from the engine and mounted in the tester. After connecting the electrical and vacuum connections, the tester spins the distributor shaft to monitor distributor performance.

A distributor tester will check:
1. Centrifugal advance.
2. Vacuum advance.
3. Contact point or pickup coil operation.
4. Distributor shaft and cam lobe wear.
5. Condenser condition.

Fig. 42-19. Distributor tester is for out-of-car testing of ignition distributor. (Sun Electric Corp.)

Adapter devices are sometimes needed to check distributors for electronic ignition systems. The adapter is an AMPLIFIER that increases the output of the pickup coil.

Fig. 42-20 shows the degree ring for a distributor tester. Note how it uses arrows to show distributor action and accuracy.

EXHAUST GAS ANALYZER

An *exhaust gas analyzer* measures the chemical content of the engine's exhaust. This allows the mechanic to check combustion efficiency and the amount of pollutants produced by the engine.

For more information on exhaust gas analyzers, refer to Chapter 40. It covers emission control system service.

ENGINE ANALYZER

An *engine analyzer* is a group of different testing instruments mounted in one assembly. One is pictured in Fig. 42-21. The next textbook chapter covers the use of an engine analyzer.

DYNAMOMETER

A *dynamometer,* also called *dyno,* is used to measure the power output and performance of an engine. There

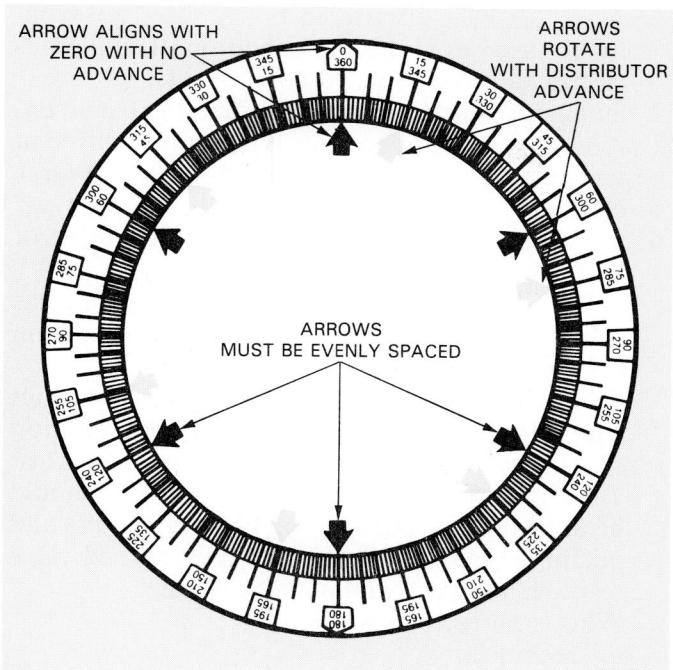

ARROW ALIGNS WITH ZERO WITH NO ADVANCE

ARROWS ROTATE WITH DISTRIBUTOR ADVANCE

ARROWS MUST BE EVENLY SPACED

Fig. 42-20. Degree ring on distributor tester shows operation of contact points or pickup unit. Arrows should be evenly spaced and advance within specs as speed increases. If not, distributor repairs are needed. (Florida Dept. of Voc. Ed.)

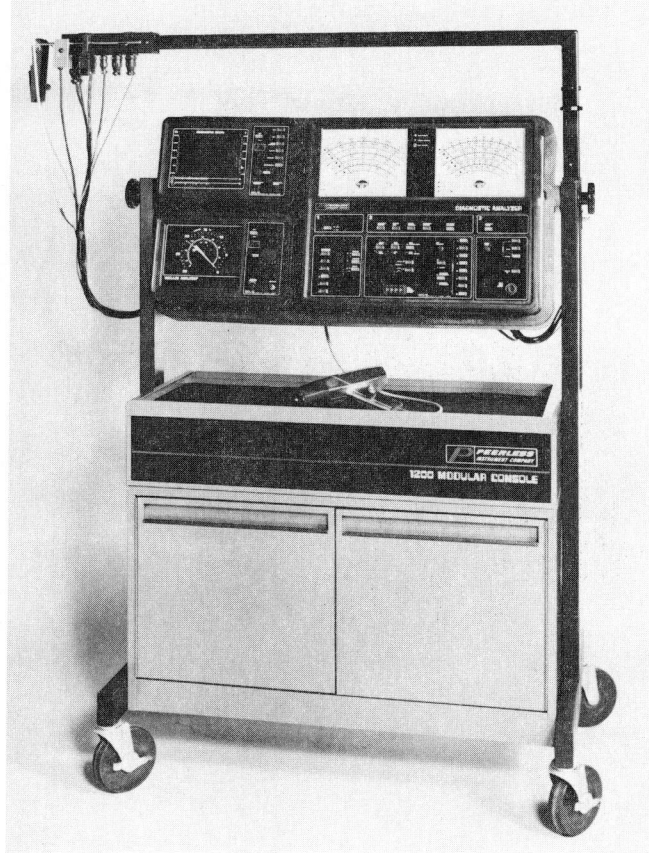

Fig. 42-21. Engine analyzer contains several test instruments in one housing. (Peerless)

are two basic types of dynamometers: the engine dynamometer (engine removed and mounted on dyno) and the chassis dynamometer (car wheels drive it).

By loading the engine, the dynamometer can be used to check engine acceleration, maximum power output, and on-the-road performance characteristics. Fig. 42-22 show a chassis dynamometer.

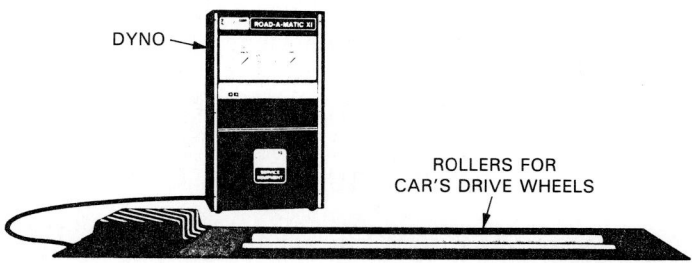

DYNO

ROLLERS FOR CAR'S DRIVE WHEELS

Fig. 42-22. Chassis dynamometer will measure engine power output under road conditions. It will also load engine while doing other tests. (Sun Electric Corp.)

COMPUTER CONTROL SYSTEM TESTER

A *computer control system tester* will help locate specific problems with engine sensors, control devices, and the on-board computer. Pictured in Fig. 42-23, the tester plugs into the computer's wiring harness or a designated test point.

The tester commonly shows a number that indicates system condition. By comparing the meter number to a number listing in the service manual, the mechanic can more quickly locate and correct computer control system troubles.

SCANNERS

Discussed in other chapters, a *scanner* can be used to read computer trouble codes and other electrical

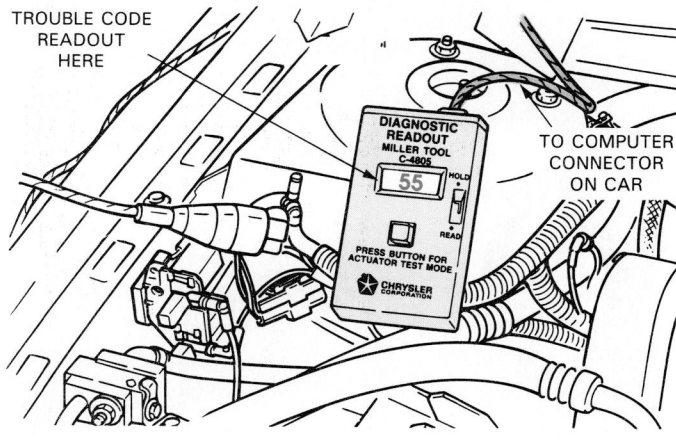

TROUBLE CODE READOUT HERE

TO COMPUTER CONNECTOR ON CAR

Fig. 42-23. This computer system tester has number reading. Reading can be checked against service manual listing to find specific faults. It will help locate troubles in ignition, fuel injection, emission control, and other systems. (Chrysler Corp.)

Engine Test Instruments 551

values produced by the on-board computer. It provides a quick way to check the operating condition of a computer system.

For more information on scanners, refer to the index. Chapter 75 details scanner use.

KNOW THESE TERMS

Spark tester, Compression gauge, Cylinder leakage tester, Vacuum gauge, Pressure gauge, Timing light, Tach-dwell, Mag-tach, Electronic ignition tester, VOM, EFI tester, Diesel injection system tester, Distributor tester, Engine analyzer, Dynamometer.

REVIEW QUESTIONS

1. List six safety rules to follow when using test equipment.
2. A _____ _____ is used to check the basic operation of the ignition system by being connected to a secondary wire.
3. A compression gauge is used to measure the suction inside the engine intake manifold. True or False?
4. When should a compression test be performed?
5. How do you do a cylinder leakage test?
6. This testing device is connected to a fitting on the engine intake manifold.
   a. Compression gauge.
   b. Cylinder leakage tester.
   c. Feeler gauge.
   d. Vacuum gauge.
7. Typically, how do the three leads on a timing light connect to the vehicle?
8. What is a "tach" used for?
9. Explain the use of a dwell meter.
10. Define the term "mag-tach."
11. A _____, also called a _____, is commonly used to check the condition of numerous electrical, engine related components.
12. Summarize the function of an exhaust gas analyzer.
13. A _____ _____ is a group of different testing devices mounted in one assembly or large cabinet.
14. A dynamometer is used to measure the output of an engine alternator. True or False?
15. A car is being tuned up. However, the engine has a "dead miss" and is making a popping or puffing noise at its exhaust.
Technician A says that simply changing spark plugs and adjusting the fuel injection and ignition systems will normally correct all of the symptoms. Technician B says that a compression test should be done during the tune-up. The engine miss and puffing noise could be caused by a burned valve or other mechanical engine problem.
Who is correct?
   a. Technician A
   b. Technician B
   c. Both A and B
   d. Neither A nor B

ACTIVITIES FOR CHAPTER 42

1. Read the manufacturer's instruction manual for an automotive test instrument assigned to you by your instructor. Then, demonstrate its use on "live work."
2. Perform a vacuum test on a vehicle assigned to you by your instructor. Report your findings to the shop class.
3. Take the findings from the test in Activity 2 and prepare a service/repair estimate if trouble was found. Work from a flat rate manual, parts catalog, and an hourly rate set by your instructor.

New cars are becoming more and more "electronic!" The use of an engine analyzer is therefore becoming very important to today's technicians. (Oldsmobile)

Using an Engine Analyzer

After studying this chapter, you will be able to:
□ List the test instruments commonly used in an engine analyzer.
□ Describe how engine analyzer leads are connected to the vehicle.
□ Explain the principles of an oscilloscope.
□ Summarize how to use an engine analyzer.
□ Describe engine analyzer differences.
□ Explain the advantages of a computer print out.

This chapter introduces the operating principles of engine analyzers, concentrating on the use of the oscilloscope (scope). Other textbook chapters have covered more common and smaller test instruments.

ENGINE ANALYZER

An *engine analyzer* consists of a group of test instruments including a scope, tach-dwell, VOM, exhaust

Fig. 43-1. Engine analyzer can do a number of different tests and measurements. It is like having a VOM, tach-dwell, exhaust analyzer, timing light, and other testers connected at once for problem isolation. (Sun Electric Corp.)

gas analyzer. These units are mounted in a large, roll-around cabinet. See Fig. 43-1. When connected to a car, the analyzer will indicate the condition of the engine and engine systems.

Today's professional auto technicians frequently use engine analyzers to help locate problems. It is possible to troubleshoot numerous faults with great accuracy.

Just one example: if an engine is being tuned, the analyzer will help find which parts should be replaced, repaired, or adjusted. It will pinpoint fouled spark plugs, open plug wires, a rich fuel mixture, inoperative fuel injector, or other troubles, even before removing and inspecting parts.

Engine analyzer differences

There are a number of different makes of engine analyzers. The controls and meter faces may be organized differently, but the basic test equipment and operation of each is almost the same.

Some analyzers use rotary knobs to select *test functions* (volts, amps, tach, etc.). Others use push-button controls, Fig. 43-1. One analyzer might have a digital display (screen showing test values in printed or number form) while another uses more conventional meters. Keep these differences in mind.

Most engine analyzers will check the:
1. Battery, charging, and starting systems.
2. Ignition system.
3. Condition of the engine.
4. Fuel system.
5. Emission control systems.

Analyzer test equipment

Typically, an electronic engine analyzer will have several of the following types of test equipment:
1. OSCILLOSCOPE (high speed voltmeter using a television type picture tube).
2. VOLTMETER, AMMETER, AND OHM-METER (meters used to measure electrical values during numerous tests).
3. TACHOMETER (meter measuring engine speed

in rpm. It is commonly used for carburetor, fuel injection, ignition timing, and other adjustments).

4. DWELL METER (instrument that measures contact point or electronic control unit conduction time in degrees of distributor rotation. It will detect point misadjustment and other problems).

5. TIMING LIGHT (strobe light for adjustment of ignition timing. Most analyzer timing lights have a degree meter for measuring distributor vacuum and centrifugal advance).

6. VACUUM GAUGE (gauge measuring vacuum when checking engine operation and action of vacuum-operated devices).

7. VACUUM PUMP (pump capable of producing a supply vacuum for operating and testing vacuum devices).

8. CYLINDER BALANCE TESTER (unit for electrically shorting out one or more cylinders or spark plugs. It will determine if a cylinder is firing properly and producing power).

9. EXHAUST GAS ANALYZER (measures the chemical content and amount of pollution in car's exhaust).

10. DIGITAL DISPLAY (scope screen showing various system values in number form. It often replaces several meters).

11. PRINTER (it types out ignition timing, dwell, engine speed, emission levels, and other values on paper).

OSCILLOSCOPE

An *oscilloscope,* often called a *scope,* is a cathode ray tube that displays a line pattern representing voltages in relation to time. See Fig. 43-2.

When connected to the ignition system, the scope produces a white line on a screen. The line illustrates the various voltages as the spark plugs fire.

By comparing the *scope pattern* (line shape) to a known good pattern, the technician can determine whether something is wrong in any section of the ignition system.

An oscilloscope is usually a major component of an engine analyzer. However, it may be mounted by itself on a small, roll-around cart.

Reading the scope screen

Voltage is shown on the scope screen along the vertical (up and down) axis or scale. Look at Fig. 43-3. Voltage values (0 to 50,000 volts) are given on the right and left borders of the screen.

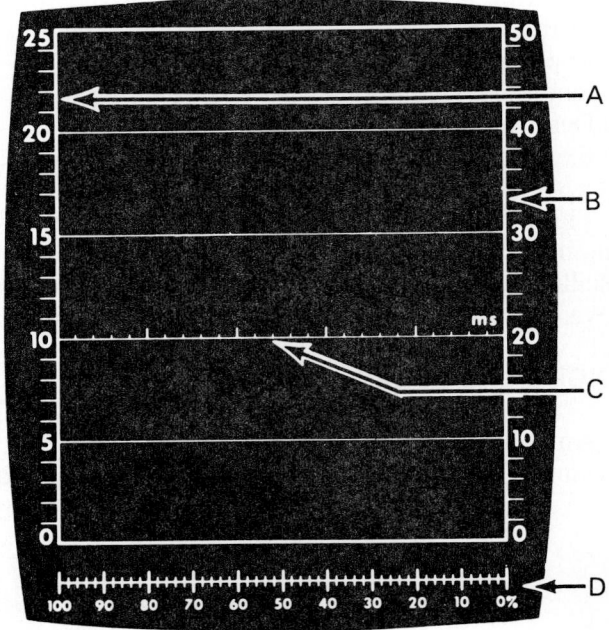

Fig. 43-3. Scales on scope screen allow you to measure voltage and time accurately. A — 0-25 volt or 0—25,000 volt scale. B — 0-5 volt or 0 — 50,000 volt scale. C — Scale for measuring time in milliseconds. D — Scale for measuring in degrees. (Sun Electric Corporation)

With the controls set on kV, volts are in kilovolts. One kV equals 1000 volts. Thus, 5 kV equal 5000 volts. If a line on the scope screen extends from zero to 7 kV, for example, the scope would read 7000 volts.

Voltage is the most commonly used value on a scope screen. As voltage increases, the white, trace line on the scope moves up. As voltage drops, the trace line moves down a proportionate amount.

Time may be given on the scope screen in degrees or milliseconds on horizontal scales. Refer to Fig. 43-2

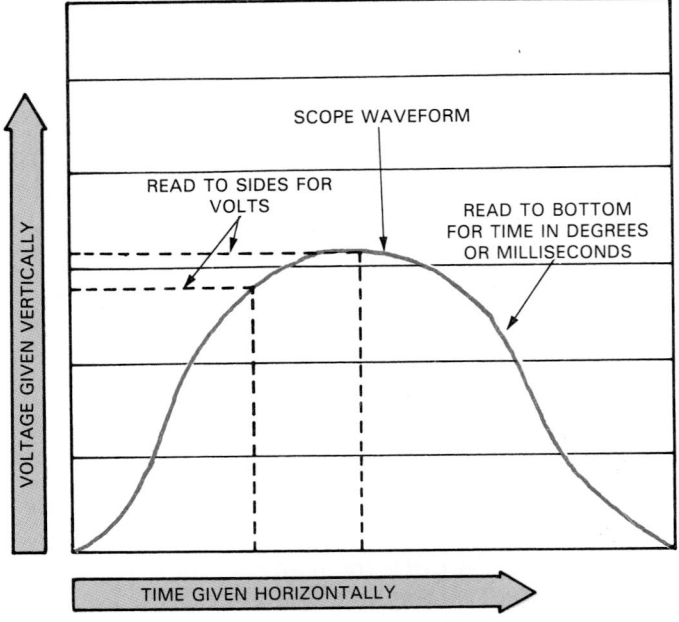

Fig. 43-2. Scope screen shows voltage vertically and time horizontally. Waveform, pattern, or trace is line formed on screen from ignition system voltage.

and 43-3. Different scales may be given on the bottom of the screen for 4, 6, or 8-cylinder engines in degrees of distributor rotation. Degrees may also be given as a percent, for quick reference for any number of cylinders.

The scope screen may also have a *milliseconds scale* for measuring actual time. This makes it possible to measure how long each spark plug fires in milliseconds. A certain amount of time is needed to properly ignite and burn the air-fuel mixture.

The oscilloscope's ability to draw a picture (trace or pattern) of ignition system voltages for very short time spans makes it very useful for testing ignition system performance.

A vehicle's ignition system is designed to produce wide fluctuations in voltage. When an ignition system is functioning properly, these voltages are within certain limits.

A bad component, with a higher-than-normal resistance (open spark plug wire for instance), would show up on the scope as a higher than normal voltage. The higher resistance would produce a higher voltage drop. A shorted component (fouled spark plug) would have a lower resistance and would produce a lower-than-normal voltage.

You should learn to recognize a good scope pattern. Then, you can easily detect a bad scope pattern, indicating problems.

OSCILLOSCOPE PATTERNS

An oscilloscope's controls allow it to display either the primary (low voltage) or secondary (high voltage)

of the ignition system. The scope patterns are similar, but important differences should be understood.

To introduce the basic sections or parts of a scope pattern, both a primary and secondary pattern for ONE CYLINDER will be explained. Then, the more complex patterns for specialized tests will be covered.

Primary scope pattern

A *primary pattern* shows the low voltage or primary voltage changes in an ignition system. A basic primary scope pattern for a contact point type ignition is given in Fig. 43-4.

Note that there are three main sections: firing section, intermediate section, and dwell section. Study how the voltages change in each part of the pattern.

The ignition secondary circuit cannot work properly unless the primary circuit is in good condition. Any problem in the primary circuit will usually show up in and affect the secondary circuit. For this reason, the secondary circuit waveform is used more often than the primary.

SECONDARY SCOPE PATTERN

The *secondary scope patterns* show the actual high voltages needed to fire the spark plugs. Fig. 43-5 illustrates the secondary pattern for one cylinder.

Secondary firing section

The secondary pattern starts on the left with the firing section, Fig. 43-5. The *firing section* will pinpoint problems with spark plugs, plug wires, distributor

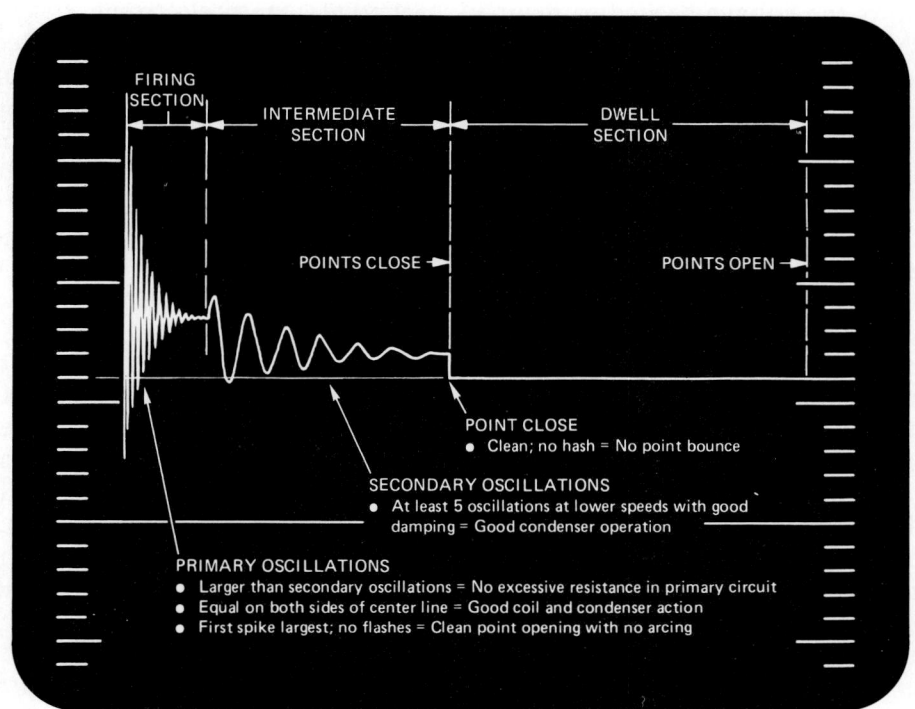

Fig. 43-4. Typical primary waveform for point type ignition. Study parts or sections of trace. (FMC)

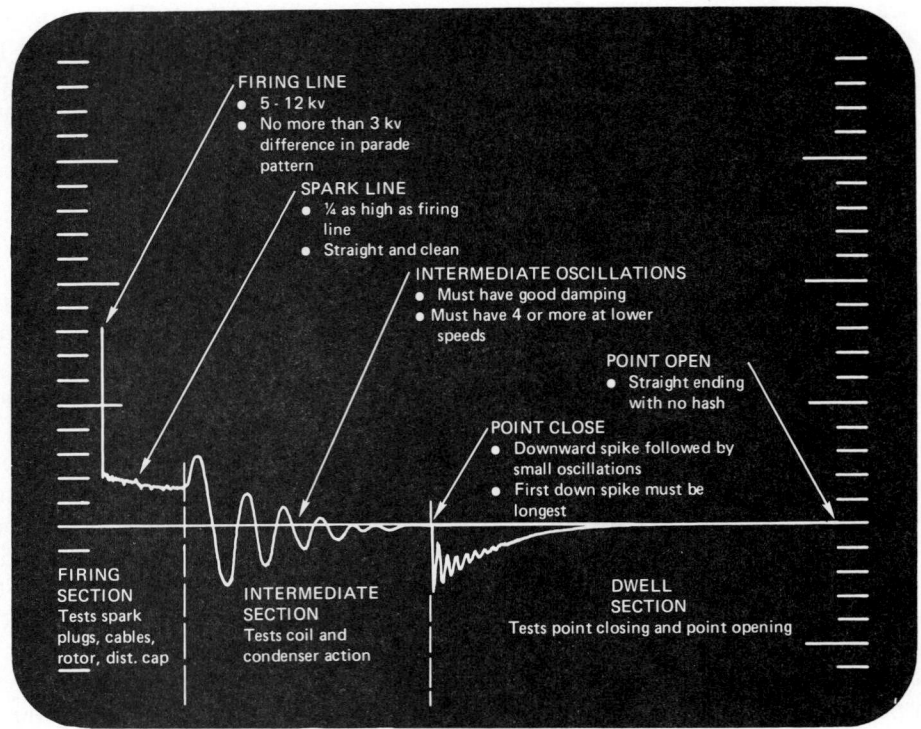

FIRING LINE
● 5 - 12 kv
● No more than 3 kv difference in parade pattern

SPARK LINE
● ¼ as high as firing line
● Straight and clean

INTERMEDIATE OSCILLATIONS
● Must have good damping
● Must have 4 or more at lower speeds

POINT OPEN
● Straight ending with no hash

POINT CLOSE
● Downward spike followed by small oscillations
● First down spike must be longest

FIRING SECTION
Tests spark plugs, cables, rotor, dist. cap

INTERMEDIATE SECTION
Tests coil and condenser action

DWELL SECTION
Tests point closing and point opening

Fig. 43-5. Secondary waveform for one cylinder in point type ignition. Firing line is voltage needed to fire spark plug. Spark line is voltage needed to maintain arc at plug. Intermediate oscillations shows coil and condenser action. Dwell is amount of time primary current flows through ignition coil to build magnetic field. (FMC)

rotor, and the distributor cap.

The *firing line* is the tall spike or line representing the amount of voltage needed to make the electric arc first jump across the spark plug gap. It is normally the highest voltage in the ignition system, Fig. 43-5.

The *spark line* shows the voltage needed to maintain an arc or spark across the spark plug electrodes, Fig. 43·5. Once the spark is started, less voltage is needed to keep it arcing. The spark line should be almost straight (no steep slope), clean (no extra lines feeding off), and about one-fourth as high as the firing line.

Secondary intermediate section

The *intermediate* or *coil oscillations section* of the scope pattern shows the voltage fluctuations after the spark plug stops firing. See Fig. 43-5. Typically, the voltage should swing up and down four times (four waves) at low engine speeds. This section of the pattern will show problems with the ignition coil or condenser.

The voltage oscillations will disappear at the end of the intermediate section because the breaker points close or the electronic control unit begins to conduct.

Secondary dwell section

The *dwell section* of the secondary pattern starts when the points close and ends when the points open. In an electronic ignition system, it is the time that the

electronic control unit conducts primary current through the ignition coil. The ignition coil is building up a magnetic field during the dwell section.

The dwell section of the pattern will indicate problems, such as: burned contact points, misadjusted contact points, faulty electronic control unit, leaking condenser. Contact point dwell (related to point gap) can be read by measuring the length of the dwell section along the bottom scale of the scope screen.

Note! An electronic ignition can have different dwell periods from cylinder to cylinder. However, if the dwell varies in an older, contact point type ignition, it indicates distributor wear or damage.

SCOPE TEST PATTERNS

Now that you understand the basic sections of a scope pattern, you must learn to recognize other scope test patterns. There are five of them commonly used by the mechanic: primary superimposed, secondary superimposed, parade (display), raster (stacked), and expanded display (cylinder select).

As you will learn, each of these patterns is capable of showing certain types of problems.

Primary superimposed pattern

The *primary superimposed pattern* shows the low voltages in the primary parts of the ignition system — condenser, coil primary windings, points or electronic control unit. Look at Fig. 43-6A.

The term *superimposed* means that all of the cylinders are placed one on top of the other. This makes the trace line thicker than the single cylinder pattern discussed earlier.

Sometimes, the mechanic will glance at the primary superimposed pattern before going to the more informative secondary pattern.

Secondary superimposed pattern

The *secondary superimposed pattern* also places all of the cylinder waveforms on top of each other, but it shows the high voltages produced by ignition coil out-

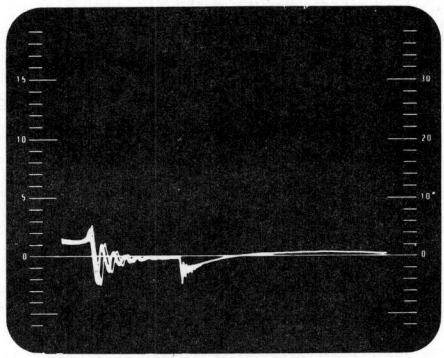

A — Superimposed display has all patterns on top of each other. It checks that all patterns are uniform.

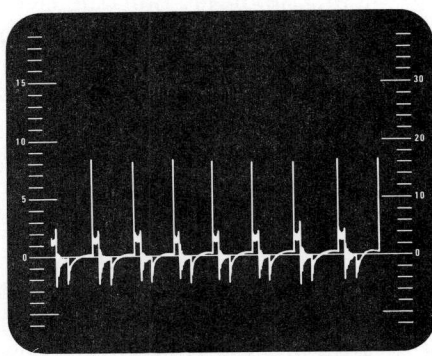

B — Parade display has cylinder's patterns side by side in firing order. It is useful for comparing firing voltages. Number one cylinder is on left, with its firing line on the right.

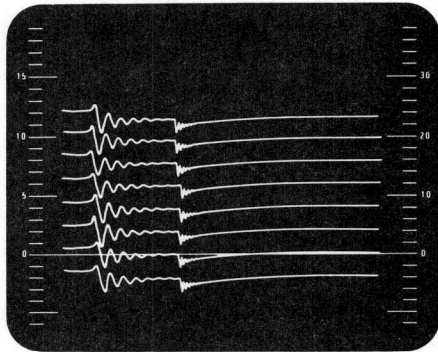

C — Stacked or raster has all cylinders one above other. It is useful for comparing duration of events. Number one is on bottom. Others are in firing order.

Fig. 43-6. Three common scope test patterns. (FMC)

put. Look at Fig. 43-6A. It is one of the most commonly used scope patterns. The superimposed secondary waveform provides a very quick check of the operating condition of ALL cylinders.

For example, if one of the spark plugs is not firing properly, the waveform for that cylinder (spark plug) will not align with the others. The trace will stick out because the firing voltage is higher or lower than normal.

The secondary superimposed pattern will check for GENERAL PROBLEMS in the ignition system. If one of the waveforms is out of place, then other scope patterns may be used to find exactly which component is causing the trouble.

Parade pattern

The *parade pattern,* also called the *display pattern,* lines up the waveform for each cylinder side by side across the screen. Number one cylinder is on the LEFT. The other cylinders are in firing order going to the right, Fig. 43-6B.

The parade pattern has taken the superimposed pattern (all waveforms on top of each other) and spread each pattern out along the horizontal axis. This makes the parade pattern useful for COMPARING FIRING VOLTAGES of each spark plug. If one or more of the firing lines are too tall or too short, there is a problem in that cylinder.

Typically, secondary voltages, during normal operating conditions, will vary from 5-12 kV for contact point type ignitions and 7-20 kV for more modern electronic ignitions. The electronic ignition normally produces higher voltages because of the wider spark plug gaps needed to ignite lean fuel mixtures.

A *tall firing line* on the parade pattern points to a high resistance in the ignition secondary — open spark plug wire, wide spark plug gap, or burned distributor cap side terminal. A high resistance requires a higher voltage output from the ignition coil.

A *short firing line* or spike would indicate low resistance in the ignition secondary — leaking spark plug wire insulation, oil fouled spark plug, or other similar problems. Not as much voltage would be needed.

Raster pattern

The *raster pattern,* also called a *stacked pattern,* has the voltage waveforms one above the other, as in Fig. 43-6C. The BOTTOM waveform is the number one cylinder. The other cylinders are in firing order from the bottom up.

The raster pattern is normally used to check time or dwell variations between cylinders. For example, in a point type ignition, if the point closing signal locations are not aligned vertically, a problem exists. There may be a bent distributor shaft, worn distributor cam, or other trouble upsetting point opening.

Expanded display

Some oscilloscopes have a control that allows one cylinder waveform to be displayed above the parade pattern. This arrangement is called an *expanded display* or *cylinder select*. If it appears that a problem is located in one trace, that trace can be expanded (enlarged and moved up on screen) for closer inspection.

ELECTRONIC IGNITION SCOPE PATTERNS

The scope pattern for an electronic ignition will vary from the pattern of a contact point type ignition. Fig. 43-7 illustrates the general differences. Note that the firing and intermediate sections are similar but the dwell sections differ. An electronic control unit operates the ignition coil, instead of mechanical breaker points.

If you are not familiar with electronic ignition waveforms, you could easily misinterpret them. The dwell section can vary. The design of the circuit inside the electronic control unit determines the shape of the dwell section.

When reading the pattern of an electronic ignition, you can still use much of the information already given. Just remember the differences in the dwell section and that an electronic ignition will often produce much higher voltages.

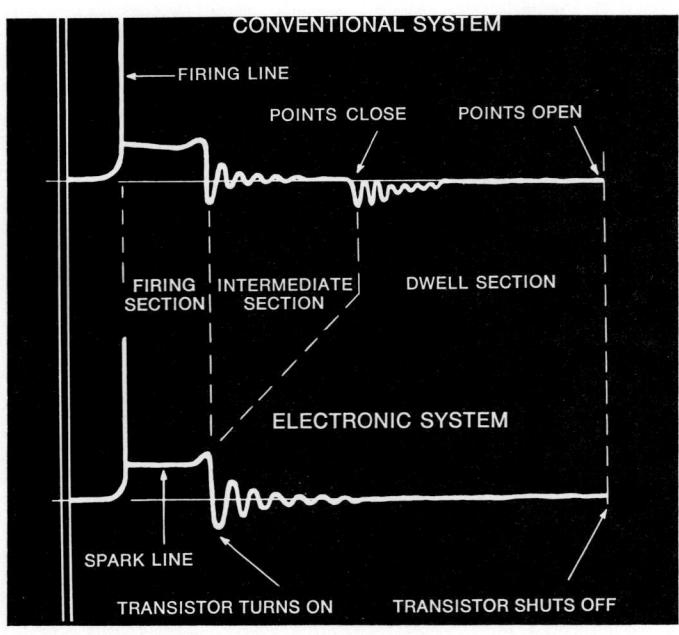

Fig. 43-7. Contact point and electronic ignitions produce different waveforms. Note variations. There are even differences between makes of electronic ignitions because circuit designs in electronic control units vary. (Champion Spark Plug Co.)

READING OSCILLOSCOPE PATTERNS

To *read a scope pattern,* inspect the waveform for abnormal shapes (high or low voltages, incorrect dwell or time periods). Visualize a good pattern as you look over each section of the oscilloscope test pattern.

Since there are so many variations of electronic ignition waveforms, refer to the scope operating manual or another reference. Locate an illustration of a good scope pattern for the particular ignition. Compare it to the one you are testing.

Fig. 43-8 gives several faulty scope patterns. Study each pattern carefully.

ENGINE ANALYZER CONNECTIONS

The connections for engine analyzers differ with the type and model of the unit. However, most have the same general types of test connections. Fig. 43-9 shows how to connect an engine analyzer to conventional and unitized ignition systems.

Analyzer leads should be connected as described in the analyzer operating manual. Special leads and hoses may be provided for measuring starting current, charging voltage, engine vacuum, fuel pump pressure, and exhaust gas content. These tests are generally the same as those covered in other textbook chapters.

USING AN ENGINE ANALYZER

The reason for using an engine analyzer is to check engine performance quickly, yet thoroughly.

To use an engine analyzer, plug the electrical cord into a wall outlet. Set the controls and connect the test leads to the vehicle. If needed, read the operating manual for the analyzer.

CAUTION! Before starting the engine, make sure all leads are well away from hot or moving parts. The analyzer leads are very expensive and can be easily ruined by a hot exhaust manifold or a spinning fan blade or pulley.

Set the parking brake and start the engine. Many analyzer manufacturers recommend increasing engine idle speed to around 1500 rpm during scope tests.

Closely inspect each pattern. Check each section of each waveform carefully. Look for any sign of variation from normal. Voltages should be within specs. Spark lines should be clean and almost straight. Dwell times must be correct.

Ignition coil output test

A scope *ignition coil output test* measures the maximum available voltage produced by the ignition coil. A spark plug only requires about 5 to 20 kV for operation. However, the ignition coil should have a higher reserve voltage. Without extra voltage, the spark plugs could misfire under load or at high engine speeds when voltage requirements are higher.

To perform the coil output test, set the engine analyzer controls to the highest kV range and to display. Run the engine at 1000 to 1500 rpm. Using insulated pliers, disconnect a spark plug wire. Hold it

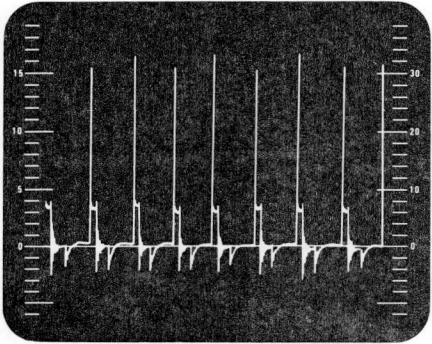

All firing lines fairly even but too high. Look for problems common to all cylinders such as: worn spark plug electrodes, excessive rotor gap, coil high-tension wire broken or not seated fully, late timing, excessively lean air/fuel mixture, or air leaks in intake manifold.

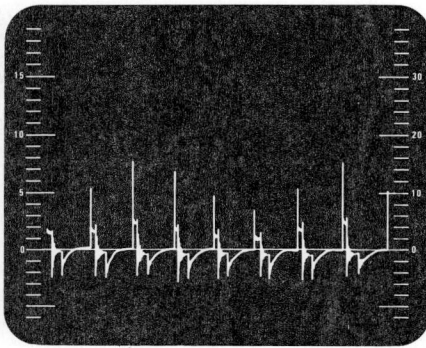

Uneven firing lines. Can be caused by worn electrodes, a cocked or worn distributor cap, fuel mixture variations, vacuum leaks, or uneven compression.

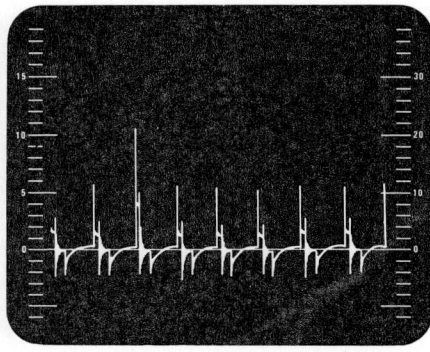

Consistently high firing line in one or more cylinders. Caused by a broken spark plug wire, a wide spark plug gap, or a vacuum leak.

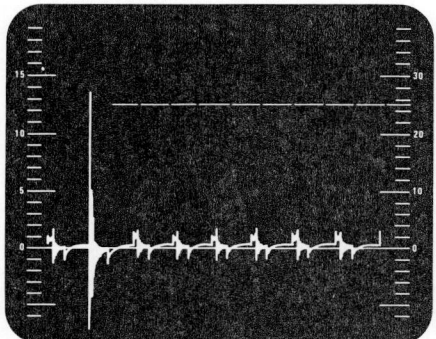

Maximum available voltage during coil test should be within the manufacturer's specifications. Disconnect plug wire to check maximum coil output.

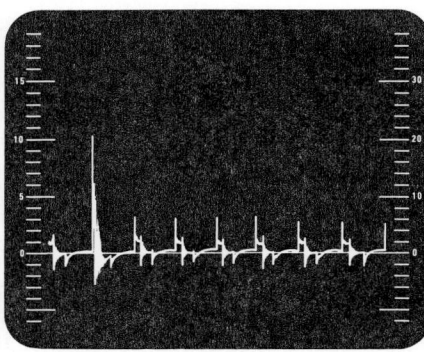

With plug wire removed for coil output test, a short intermittent, or missing lower spike indicates faulty insulation. This is usually caused by a defective spark plug wire, distributor cap, rotor, coil wire, or coil tower.

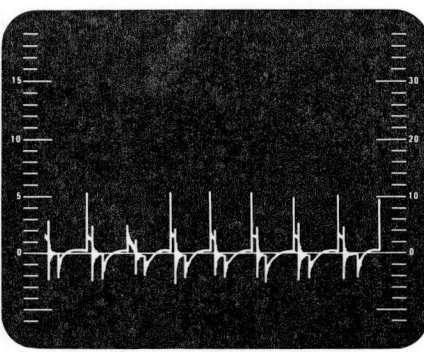

Consistently low firing line in one or more cylinders. Caused by fouled plug, shorted wire, low compression (valve not closing), or rich mixture.

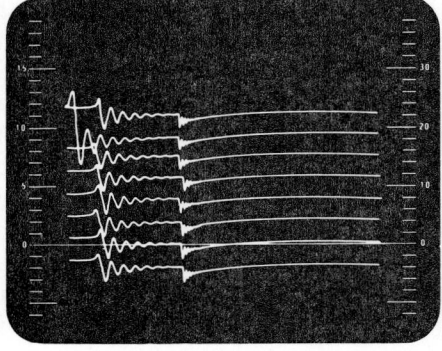

No spark line. Caused by complete open in cable or connector.

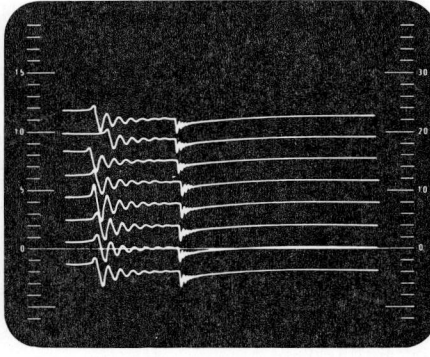

Long spark line. Caused by a shorted spark plug or partially grounded plug wire.

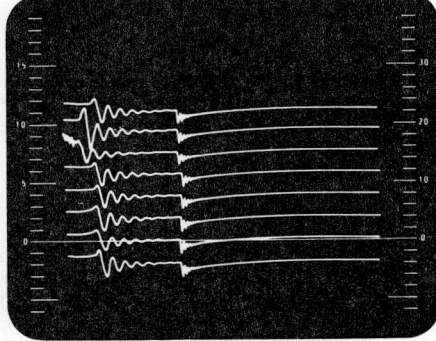

Sloped spark line, usually with hash. Caused by fouled spark plug.

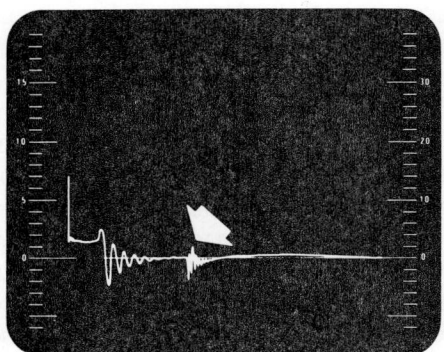

Oscillations above zero line. Caused by bouncing points.

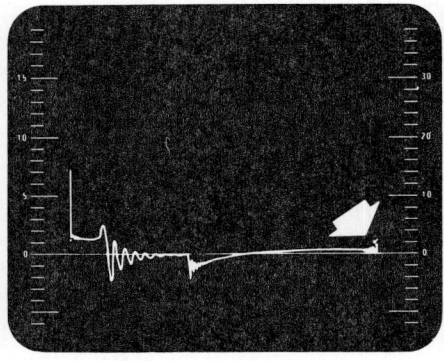

Hash or flashing at point-open spike. Caused by defective condenser or bad points.

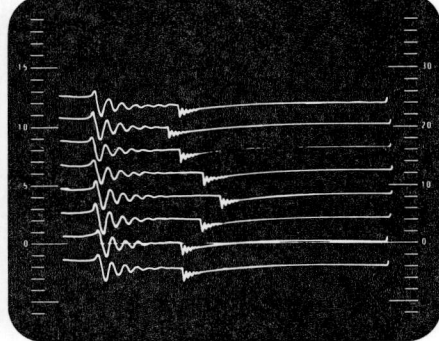

Poor vertical alignment of point-open spikes. Caused by worn or defective distributor shaft, bushings, cam lobes or breaker plate.

Fig. 43-8. Examples of bad scope patterns. Study shape of trace and problem for each. (FMC)

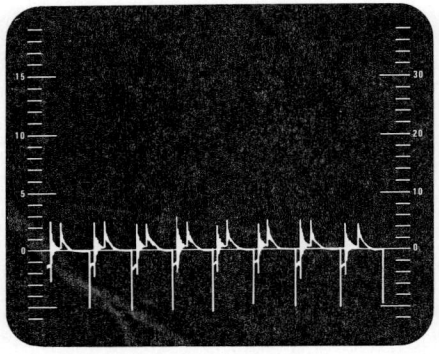

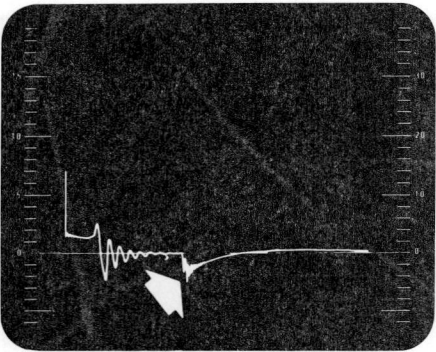

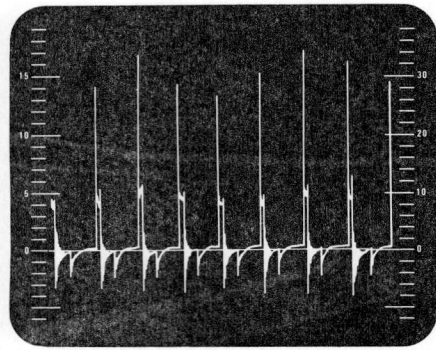

Reversed coil polarity. The pattern is upside down. This problem is usually caused by someone accidentally connecting the primary leads to the coil backwards. The ignition will still work, but not as well.

Misaligned points. The first downward spike is not longest.

Run the engine at about 1000 rpm. While watching firing lines on scope, snap throttle fully open, then quickly release it. Highest firing line peaks should not be more than 75% of coil output.

Fig. 43-8 continued.

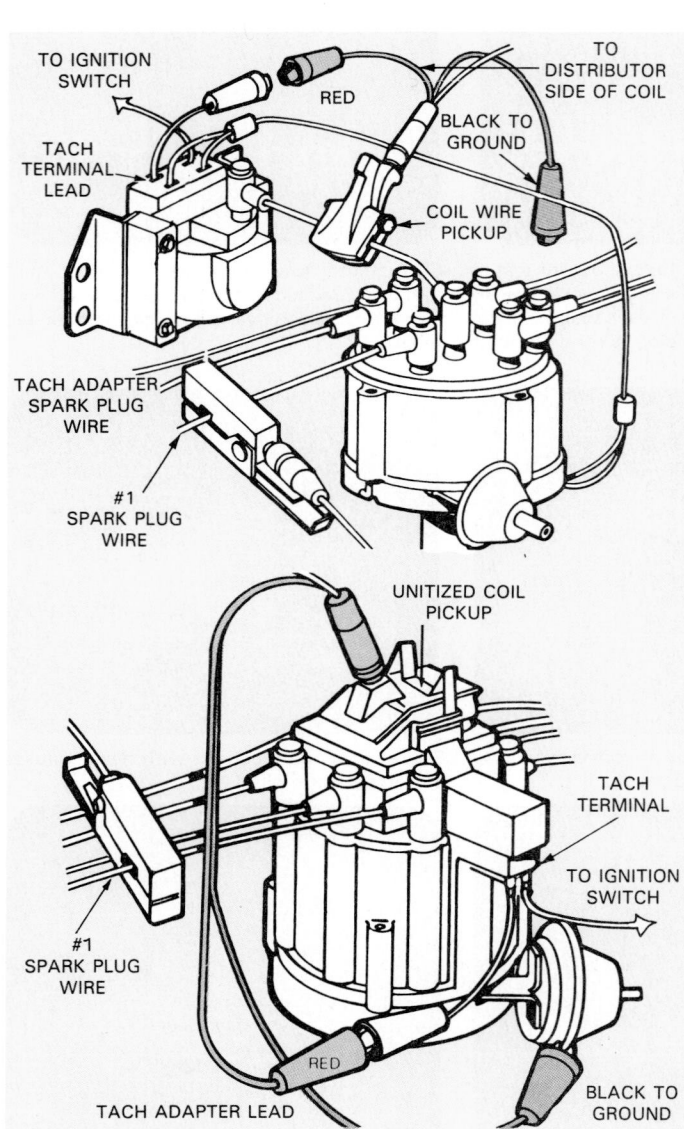

Fig. 43-9. Connecting engine analyzer to ignition systems. Top. System in which coil is separate from distributor. Bottom. System with unitized coil.

away from ground while watching the scope screen.

CAUTION! A few electronic ignitions may be damaged by disconnecting certain spark plug wires with the engine running. Be sure to check manufacturer's directions.

With the spark plug wire removed, a tall firing line should stick up above the others. Look over to the scope scale on the side of the screen. Read the voltage even with the top of the spike. This value will equal the capacity of the ignition coil.

With contact point and early-style electronic ignitions, coil output voltage should range between 20,000 and 25,000 volts. However, some electronic ignition coils are able to produce up to 35,000 volts.

If ignition coil voltage is below specs, do not condemn the coil until completing further tests. Low coil output could be due to low primary supply voltage (partially open ballast resistor or resistance wire), leaking secondary wires (electricity passing through insulation to ground), or other similar types of problems. Eliminate these sources of trouble before replacing the ignition coil.

Load or acceleration test

A *load* or *acceleration test* measures the firing voltage of the spark plugs when engine speed is rapidly increased. When an engine is accelerated, higher voltage is needed to fire the plugs. A defective component may NOT produce an abnormal scope pattern at idle. However, this same component may break down (not operate properly) under load.

To perform a load test, set the scope on parade and idle the engine between 1000 and 1200 rpm. While watching the firing lines on the scope, quickly snap the carburetor or injection throttle valve open. Then release it. The firing voltage should increase, but within certain limits.

The highest firing line should not be more than 75

percent of coil output (value obtained in previous test). Typically, voltage should NOT exceed 15 kV (point type ignition) or 20 kV (electronic type ignition).

Also, the upward movement of the firing lines during the load test should be the same. If any of the firing lines are too high or too low, there could be a defective part.

Alternator diode test

Some engine analyzers are capable of using the scope to check alternator diode condition. By pressing a special test button, the scope will display the voltage output of the alternator, as in Fig. 43-10. If the alternator diodes are good, the pattern should be wavy but almost even.

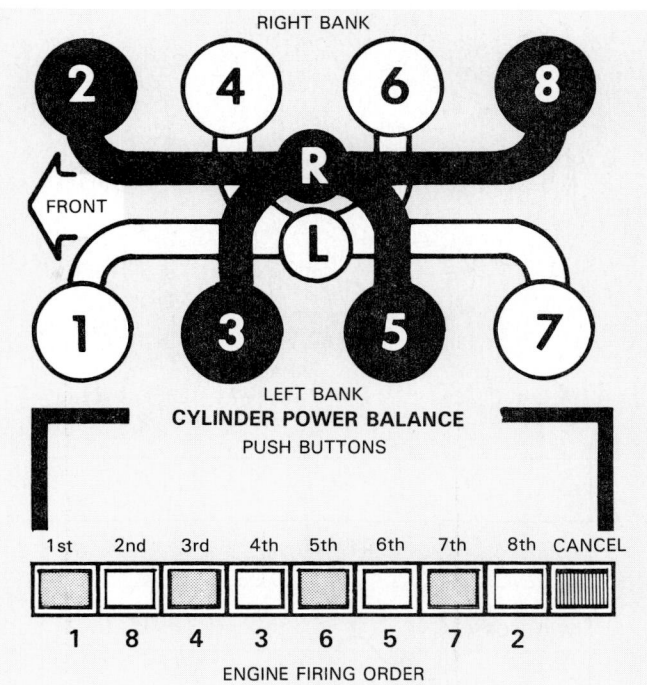

Fig. 43-11. Cylinder balance test is done by pressing buttons on engine analyzer control panel. Each button will short and disable one cylinder. If rpm does not drop sufficiently, that cylinder is not producing enough power. Note how buttons correspond to sample firing order. (Sun)

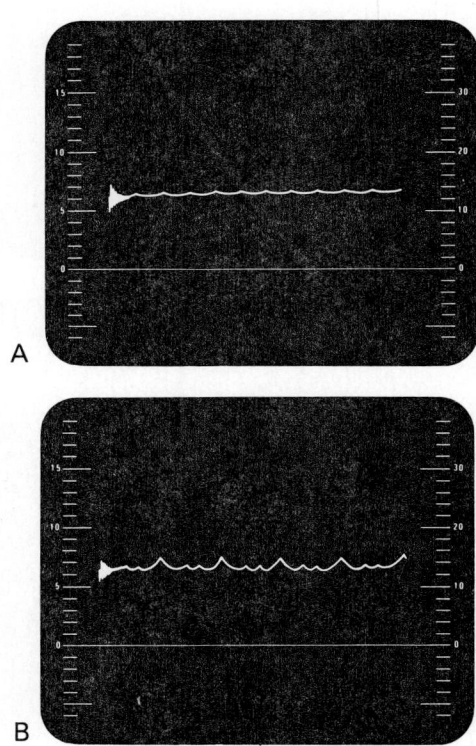

Fig. 43-10. Waveforms showing alternator output. A — Good alternator diodes produce even, wavy voltage. B — Open or shorted alternator diodes show up as uneven trace. (FMC)

Cylinder balance test

A *cylinder balance test,* also called a *power test,* measures the power output from each of the engine's cylinders. As each cylinder is shorted, engine rpm should drop on the tachometer. If a shorted cylinder does NOT produce an adequate amount of rpm drop, then that cylinder is NOT firing properly. Look at and study Fig. 43-11.

NOTE! Never short a cylinder in a car with a catalytic converter for more than 15 seconds; converter damage could result.

During a cylinder balance test, all cylinders should have the same percentage of speed drop (within a 5 percent range of each other). If the drop in one or more cylinders is below normal, then a problem common to that cylinder is indicated. The cylinder could have low compression (burned engine valve, blown head gasket, worn piston rings), lean mixture (vacuum leak, poorly adjusted carburetor, faulty fuel injector, computer malfunction), or other problems.

Distributor pickup coil test

An oscilloscope may also be used to check the output signal of a distributor pickup coil. Connect the scope primary leads to the pickup coil, as in Fig. 43-12A. Set the selector to primary and the primary height control to 40 V. Adjust the pattern length to minimum.

With the engine cranking, an AC (alternating current) signal within specs (about 1.5 V peak to peak) should be generated, Fig. 43-12B.

EFI injector test

Many scopes will also check the operation of the injectors in an electronic fuel injection system. Refer to equipment and service manual instructions for details. Fig. 43-13 shows typical waveforms for good and bad fuel injectors.

DIGITAL DISPLAY

Some very modern engine analyzers have a scope screen that displays a digital (number) reading of

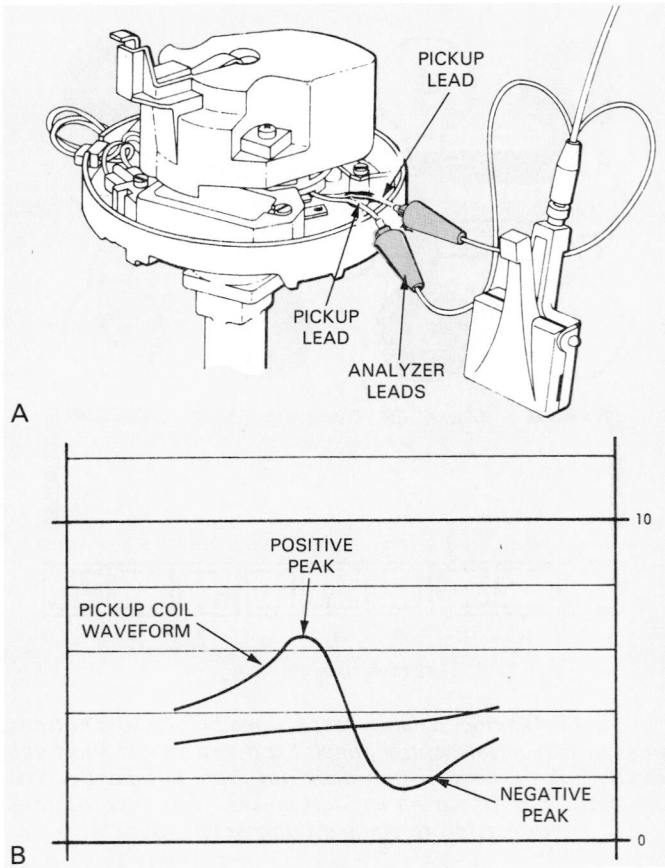

Fig. 43-12. Most scopes can be used to check pickup coil in electronic ignition distributor. A — Connect analyzer leads to pickup coil leads. B — With scope set on lowest voltage range, crank engine and check for voltage output. (Sun Electric)

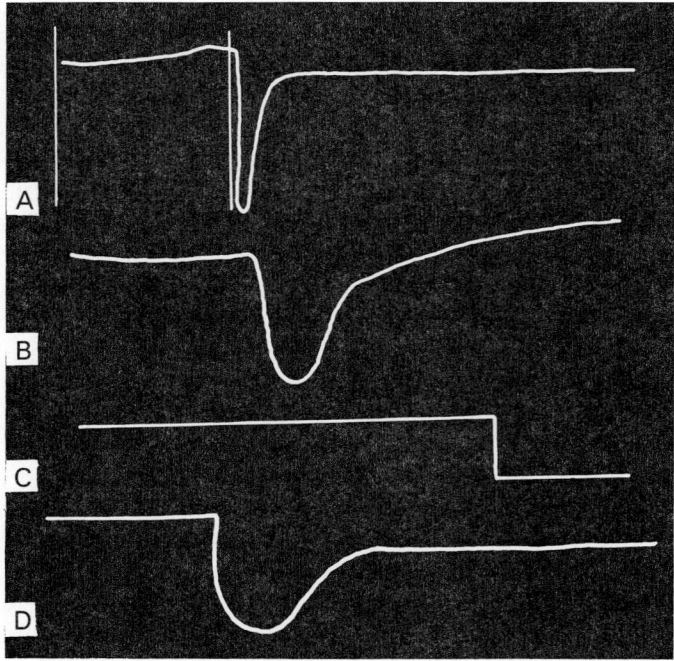

Fig. 43-13. Waveforms for electronic injectors. A — Normal injector pattern. B — Stuck injector. C — Open injector. D — Partially shorted injector. (Snap-On Tools)

various test values. The digital display replaces the conventional meters and gauges which use a needle and meter face.

The *digital display* prints these values (engine rpm, charging system voltage, exhaust gas content) on the scope screen in a list form. This makes it much easier for the technician to analyze the condition of vehicle systems. See Fig. 43-14.

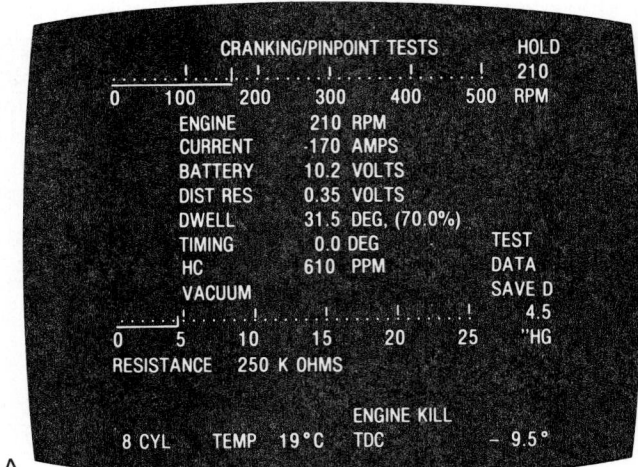

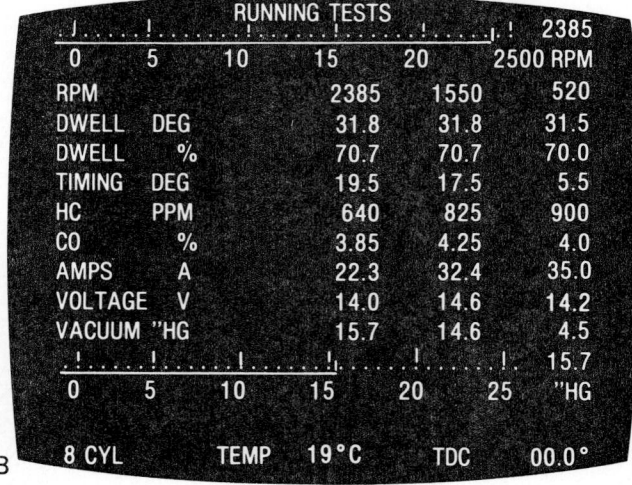

Fig. 43-14. Many modern engine analyzers are capable of producing a digital or number display on extra screen. A — Digital display for cranking tests. B — Digital display for running tests. Study readout capabilities. (Sun Electric Corp.)

PRINTER

A *printer* is sometimes added to an engine analyzer so that the customer can have a written (printed) record of the test values. This lets the customer actually see the condition of the vehicle. Look at Fig. 43-15.

If repairs are needed, the technician can show the customer the improper readings on the print out. If the vehicle is in good condition, the print out will be a record for later repairs, Fig. 43-16.

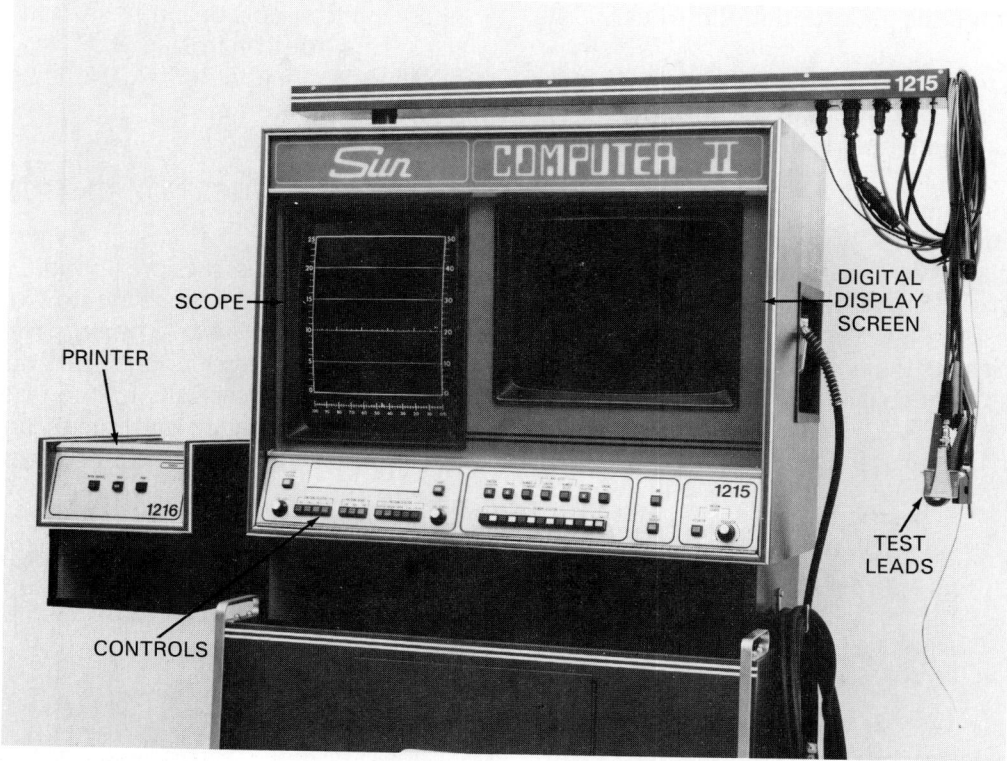

Fig. 43-15. Printer on side of engine analyzer will type or print test results on paper tape. (Sun Electric Corp.)

OTHER ENGINE ANALYZER FUNCTIONS

An engine analyzer is usually capable of performing other tests besides those discussed in this chapter. These include starter cranking amps, charging voltage, and exhaust gas analysis. Such tests are almost identical to those done with small, hand-held instruments.

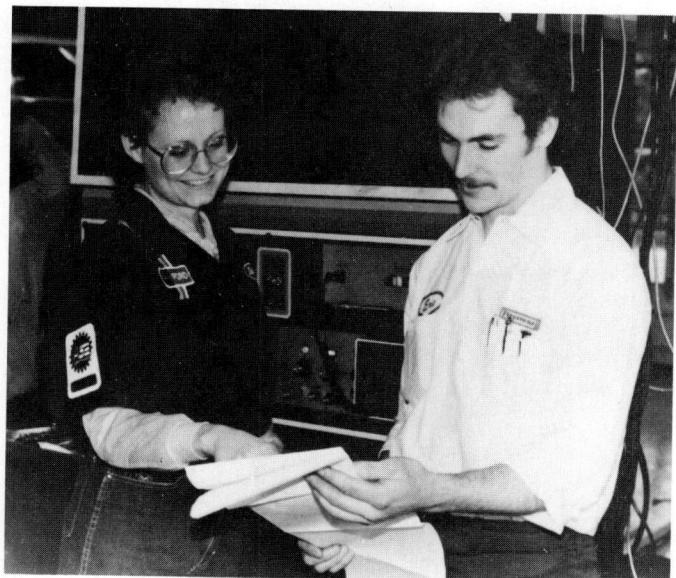

Fig. 43-16. Analyzer print out. This will show customer repairs were needed or give records for later service.

KNOW THESE TERMS

Engine analyzer, Oscilloscope, kV, Millisecond, Primary pattern, Secondary pattern, Firing line, Spark line, Coil oscillations, Dwell section, Superimposed pattern, Parade pattern, Raster pattern, Load or acceleration test, Cylinder balance test, Digital display, Printer.

REVIEW QUESTIONS

1. Which of the following is NOT commonly used as part of an engine analyzer?
   a. Tach-dwell.
   b. Oscilloscope.
   c. VOM.
   d. All of the above are correct.
   e. None of the above are correct.
2. On the scope screen, _____ is given on the vertical scale and _____ is given on the horizontal scale.
3. One kV equals 100 volts. True or False?
4. If a scope waveform is higher or taller than normal, this indicates a higher-than-normal resistance. True or False?
5. The _____ scope pattern shows the actual voltages needed to fire the spark plugs.
6. Sketch and explain the three major parts of a scope secondary waveform.
7. Electronic ignition system waveforms will vary

depending upon the make and model of car. True or False?

8. As it relates to a scope, define the term "superimposed."

9. What is the advantage of using the parade pattern of a scope?

10. Explain a common use for the raster pattern.

11. How do you read a scope pattern?

12. Most engine analyzers recommend that engine idle speed be increased to about _____ rpm during scope tests.

13. This test measures the power output from each of the engine's cylinders.
    a. Load test.
    b. Cylinder balance test.
    c. Ignition coil output test.
    d. EFI injector test.

14. What is a scope digital display?

15. Why is a printer sometimes used on an engine analyzer?

ACTIVITIES FOR CHAPTER 43

1. Study the instruction manual for an engine analyzer and demonstrate how to hook it up for a test designated by your instructor.

2. With the analyzer hooked up and working, point out the three sections of the trace.

3. Interpret the trace patterns of an analyzer scope set up to test the ignition system.

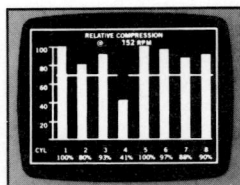

Problem: Manual compression testing eats up time.
Solution: In 6 seconds, HTS750 gives you visual comparisons of all cylinders.

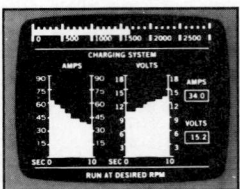

Problem: Getting accurate, useable alternator output data.
Solution: A 10-second test gives you separate volt and amp graphs for trend comparison.

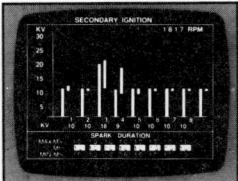

Problem: Locating high/low resistance in secondary ignition circuit by oscilloscope.
Solution: Easy-to-read KV graphs and digital spark duration readings. Memory Bar® displays freeze highs/lows to detect intermittent problems.

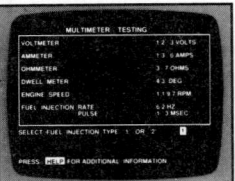

Problem: Determining whether the ECM is properly controlling the fuel injectors.
Solution: Quick isolation of problem with multimeter test showing injector on-time and frequency measurements.

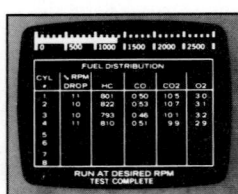

Problem: Diagnosing clogged fuel injectors.
*Solution: The HTS750 automatically measures the amount of fuel reaching each cylinder with the fuel distribution test option.

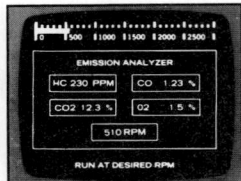

Problem: Diagnosing engine condition from after-converter exhaust reading.
*Solution: HTS750, a 4-gas emissions tester, measures gasses not affected by converters, assuring true diagnosis.

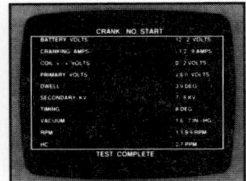

Problem: Quickly isolating the problem in a crank/no start situation.
*Solution: In 10 seconds, HTS750 reports vital fuel/ignition/engine data.

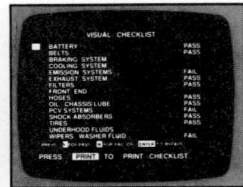

Problem: Showing customers that you have done a thorough, professional inspection.
Solution: Enter your pass/fail ratings on the HTS750 visual checklist—and give your customer a print-out. It builds goodwill—and sales!

Note problems and tests that can be done with this vehicle analyzer. It can save time and help you isolate hard-to-find troubles.
(Hamilton Test Systems)

Engine Tune-up

After studying this chapter, you will be able to:
□ Describe the typical difference between a minor tune-up and major tune-up.
□ List the basic steps for an engine tune-up.
□ Explain service operations commonly done during a tune-up.
□ List the safety precautions that should be remembered during a tune-up.
□ Observe appropriate safety rules during tune-up.

This chapter summarizes details given in several other textbook chapters. Use the index to find added tune-up information.

ENGINE TUNE-UP

An *engine tune-up* returns the engine to a condition of peak performance. It involves the replacement of worn parts, performance of basic service tasks, making adjustments, and, sometimes, minor repairs.

A tune-up assures that the engine, ignition system, fuel system, and emission control systems are within factory specs. Auto manufacturers normally recommend a tune-up after a specific engine operating period.

The exact procedures for a tune-up will vary from shop to shop. In one shop, a tune-up may only include the most routine operations. In another shop, it may involve a long list of tests, adjustments, and repairs.

Minor tune-up

A *minor tune-up* is a basic tune-up done when the engine is in good operating condition. For example, a new vehicle only driven 20,000-30,000 miles (32 187-48 280 km) may only require a minor tune-up. Most of the engine systems would be in satisfactory condition with little or no wear.

A minor tune-up typically involves these tasks:
1. Replacing spark plugs.
2. Distributor service (points and condenser replacement or electronic distributor maintenance).
3. Check and adjustment of ignition timing.

4. Replacement of air and fuel filters.
5. Fuel system adjustments (idle speed, for example).
6. Emission control system tests and service.
7. General inspection for obvious problems.
8. Road test.

Major tune-up

A *major tune-up* is more thorough and is done when the engine systems (ignition, fuel, emission) are in worn condition. After prolonged use, these systems can deteriorate, requiring more attention.

Besides the steps listed for a minor tune-up, a major tune-up typically includes more diagnostic tests (scope, compression gauge, VOM, vacuum gauge) to determine system condition. It may also include carburetor or injection system repairs, distributor rebuild, and other more time-consuming tasks.

Importance of a tune-up

A tune-up is very important to the operation of an engine. It can affect:
1. Engine power and acceleration.
2. Fuel consumption.
3. Exhaust pollution.
4. Smoothness of engine operation.
5. Ease of starting.
6. Engine service life.

You must make sure you return every engine related system to peak operating condition during a tune-up. If you overlook just one problem, the engine will NOT perform properly, and the car owner will NOT be happy with your work.

TUNE-UP SAFETY RULES

During a tune-up, there are several safety rules you must remember:
1. Engage the emergency brake and block the wheels when the engine is to be running.
2. Place an exhaust hose over the tailpipe when running the engine in an enclosed shop.

3. Keep clothing, your hands, tools, and equipment away from a running engine fan.
4. Disconnect the battery when recommended in the service manual. This will help avoid accidental engine cranking or an electrical fire.
5. Be careful not to touch the hot exhaust manifold when removing old spark plugs. Keep test equipment leads away from the engine exhaust manifolds.
6. Wear eye protection when blowing debris away from spark plugs or when working close to the engine fan when the engine is running.
7. Keep a fire extinguisher handy when performing fuel system tests and repairs.
8. With a diesel engine, disable the injection pump when removing an injection line. System pressure is high enough to puncture your skin and eyes.

TYPICAL TUNE-UP PROCEDURES

The following is a summary of the most common procedures for an engine tune-up. They are typical and apply to most makes and models of cars.

Preliminary tests and inspection

To begin a tune-up, most mechanics inspect the engine compartment. They try to find signs of trouble:
1. BATTERY PROBLEMS (dirty case top, corroded terminals, physical damage).
2. AIR CLEANER PROBLEMS (clogged filter, inoperative air flap, disconnected vacuum hoses).
3. BELT TROUBLES (looseness, fraying, slippage).
4. LOW FLUID LEVELS (engine oil, brake fluid, power steering fluid, etc.).
5. DETERIORATED HOSES (hardened or softened cooling system, fuel system, and vacuum hoses).
6. POOR ELECTRICAL CONNECTIONS (loose or corroded connections, frayed or burned wiring).

If any problems are found, correct them before beginning the tune-up. Many of these problems could affect the performance of the engine.

Evaluating engine systems

During a tune-up, it is very important that you test and evaluate the condition of the engine and engine systems. Various test instruments are used for this purpose.

Chapter 42 covers engine test instruments. An ignition scope, electronic ignition tester, vacuum gauge, exhaust analyzer, timing light, and VOM are a few of the test instruments used during a tune-up.

A *compression test* is frequently made during a tune-up to check engine condition. It is impossible to tune an engine that is not in good mechanical condition. If the engine fails the compression test, mechanical repairs must be made BEFORE the tune-up.

Valve adjustment

When mechanical (solid) lifters are used, the valves require periodic adjustment. Proper valve adjustment is important to the performance of the engine.

If a valve opens too much or not enough, it will upset the amount of air-fuel mixture pulled into the cylinder. It also affects valve lift and duration. This will affect combustion and reduce engine efficiency.

Chapter 48, Engine Top End Service, covers valve adjustment.

Tune-up parts replacement

Depending upon the age and condition of the car, any number of parts may need replacement during a tune-up. With a new, late-model car, you may only need to replace the spark plugs and filters.

With an older, high mileage car, you may have to replace the spark plugs, injectors, distributor components, spark plug wires, or any other parts reducing engine efficiency.

Tune-up adjustments

Again, the adjustments needed during a tune-up will vary with the make, model, and condition of the car. A few of the most common tune-up adjustments include:
1. Spark plug gap.
2. Pickup coil air gap (electronic ignition), or breaker point gap (contact point ignition).
3. Ignition timing (gasoline engine) or injection timing (diesel engine).
4. Idle speed.

Other adjustments may also be needed. Follow the specific directions and specs in a service manual. This will assure a thorough and long-lasting tune-up.

GENERAL TUNE-UP RULES

There are several general rules you should remember when doing a tune-up.
1. Gather information about the performance of the engine. Ask the customer about the car. This may give you clues about what components should be tested and replaced.
2. Make sure the engine has warmed to full operating temperature. Usually, you cannot evaluate engine operation and make tune-up adjustments with a cold engine.
3. Use professional, high quality tools and equipment. Make sure the equipment is accurate and will give precise readings.
4. Refer to the car service manual or emission sticker for specs and procedures. Today's cars are so complex, the slightest mistake could ruin the tune-up.
5. Use quality parts. Quality parts will assure that your tune-up lasts for a long time. Cheap, bargain parts are usually inferior and can fail quickly.
6. Keep service records. You should write down all of the operations performed on the car. This will give you and the customer a record for future reference. If a problem develops, you can check

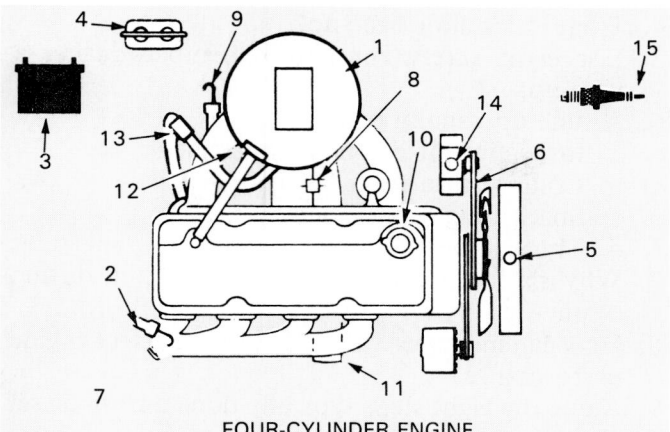

FOUR-CYLINDER ENGINE

Footnotes

a. For normal use, no automatic transmission maintenance is required except regular fluid checks. For heavy-duty operation, change fluid and filter and adjust bands at the interval shown.

b. Change coolant initially at 25 months or 25,000 miles (40 000 km), whichever occurs first, then at the start of each winter season.

c. Perform service initially at 5,000 miles (8 000 km), then at 15,000 miles (24 000 km) and every 15,000 miles (24 000 km) thereafter.

d. Four-cylinder engines are not equipped with exhaust heat valves.

e. Clean filter with kerosene. See Positive Crankcase Ventilation in the Owner's Manual for details.

f. California cars equipped with automatic transmissions only.

g. Eight-cylinder cars only. (Eight-cylinder equipped cars in California do not require this service.)

Legend of Symbols

- ✔ CHECK OR INSPECTION
- DRAIN AND REPLACE FLUID
- ENGINE TUNE-UP
- HEAVY-DUTY OPERATION
- LUBRICATION
- SERVICE COMPONENT REPLACEMENT

COMPONENT	SERVICE	INTERVAL FOUR-CYLINDER	SIX- AND EIGHT-CYLINDER
1. AIR CLEANER		30.000 mi (48 000 km)	30.000 mi (48 000 km)
		15 mo/15.000 mi (24 000 km)	15 mo/15.000 mi (24 000 km)
2. AUTOMATIC TRANSMISSION	✔ a.	5 mo/5.000 mi (8 000 km)	7 mo/7.500 mi (12 000 km)
		15 mo/15.000 mi (24 000 km)	15 mo/15.000 mi (24 000 km)
3. BATTERY	✔	15 mo/15.000 mi (24 000 km) and start of each winter season	15 mo/15,000 mi (24 000 km) and start of each winter season
4. BRAKE MASTER CYLINDER	✔	5 mo/5.000 mi (8 000 km)	7 mo/7 500 mi (12 000 km)
5. COOLANT (RADIATOR)	✔ / b.	5 mo/5.000 mi (8 000 km)	7 mo/7.500 mi (12 000 km)
		25 mo/25.000 mi (40 000 km)	25 mo/25.000 mi (40 000 km)
6. DRIVE BELTS	✔	5.000 mi (8 000 km)	5.000 mi (8 000 km) c.
7. EXHAUST HEAT VALVE		— d.	30.000 mi (48 000 km)
8. FUEL FILTER		15 000 mi (24 000 km)	15.000 mi (24 000 km)
9. OIL DIPSTICK (OIL LEVEL)	✔	At Each Fuel Fill	At Each Fuel Fill
10. OIL (FILLER CAP)		5 mo/5.000 mi (8 000 km)	7 mo/7.500 mi (12 000 km)
		2 5 mo/2.500 mi (4 000 km)	3.5 mo/3.700 mi (6 000 km)
11. OIL FILTER		5 mo/5.000 mi (8 000 km)	7 mo/7.500 mi (12 000 km)
12. PCV FILTER	✔ e.	30.000 mi (48 000 km)	30.000 mi (48 000 km)
13. PCV VALVE		30.000 mi (48 000 km) f.	30.000 mi (48 000 km)
14. POWER STEERING PUMP	✔	5 mo/5.000 mi (8 000 km)	7 mo/7.500 mi (12 000 km)

COMPONENT	SERVICE	INTERVAL FOUR-CYLINDER	SIX- AND EIGHT-CYLINDER
15. TUNE-UP	✔ c.	5,000 mi (8 000 km) Retorque cylinder head bolts, adjust engine valves check and adjust curb and high idle speeds	5.000 mi (8 000 km) Check and adjust curb and high idle speeds.
	✔	15,000 mi (24 000 km) Check and reset ignition timing as required Replace ignition points and condenser.	15.000 mi (24 000 km) g. Check the following and correct as required : Choke system. idle mixture. ignition timing. and vacuum fittings hoses and connections
		30,000 mi (48 000 km) Complete Engine tune-up	30.000 mi (48 000 km) Complete engine tune-up
		Engine Mechanical Systems Inspect: Air Guard system hoses vacuum lines and fittings Exhaust Gas Recirculation lines hoses and connections Also: Retorque cylinder head bolts Adjust engine valves Ignition System Inspect: coil and spark plug wires distributor—cap and rotor vacuum and centrifugal advance mechanisms distributor shaft and cam lobes transmission controlled spark system (TCS) if equipped Replace ignition points. condenser and spark plugs. Fuel System Inspect: fuel tank. cap. lines and connections air cleaner thermostatic control sytem (TAC) choke linkage for free movement PCV system hoses Clean PCV filter in air cleaner. Replace PCV valve f. Replace charcoal canister air inlet filter Final Adjustment Ignition timing. Idle mixture Curb and high idle speeds.	Engine Mechanical Systems inspect Air Guard system hoses vacuum lines and fittings. Exhaust Gas Recirculation lines. hoses and connections Ignition System Inspect: coil and spark plug wires distributor—cap and rotor vacuum and centrifugal advance mechanisms transmission controlled spark system (TCS). if equipped Replace spark plugs Fuel System Inspect: fuel tank. cap. lines and connections air cleaner thermostatic control system (TAC) choke linkage for free movement PCV system hoses Clean PCV filter (6-cyl in air cleaner. 8-cyl in oil filler cap) Replace PCV valve and charcoal canister air inlet filter Final Adjustment Ignition timing Idle mixture Curb and high idle speeds.

Fig. 44-1. Specific tune-up intervals and special recommendations will be in service manual. Always use service manual for particular vehicle being tuned. Read through this example and note recommendations, symbols, and footnotes. (Chrysler)

your records to help correct the trouble.

7. Complete basic maintenance service. Most good garages will lubricate door, hood, and trunk latches and hinges during a tune-up. They will also check all fluid levels, belts, and hoses. This will build good customer relations and assure vehicle safety and dependability.

DIESEL ENGINE TUNE-UP (MAINTENANCE)

Diesel engines do NOT require tune-ups like gasoline engines. A diesel does NOT have spark plugs to replace or an ignition system to fail. The diesel injection system is very dependable and only requires major service when problems develop.

A *diesel engine tune-up,* more accurately called *diesel maintenance,* typically involves:
1. Replacing air filter element.
2. Cleaning, draining, or replacing fuel filters.
3. Adjusting engine idle speed.
4. Adjustment of throttle cable.
5. Inspecting engine and related systems.
6. Check of injection timing.
7. Changing engine oil and oil filter.
8. Periodic service of emission control systems.

Refer to the text index for more information on diesel engine maintenance.

ENGINE TUNE-UP (MAINTENANCE) INTERVALS

Engine tune-up intervals, also called *maintenance intervals,* are specific periods (in miles or months) for component service. They are given in the car's service manual. A typical example is shown in Fig. 44-1.

When doing an actual tune-up, it is very important to check in a manual for interval information. Recommended service intervals vary.

KNOW THESE TERMS

Engine tune-up, Minor tune-up, Major tune-up, Compression test, Valve adjustment, Tune-up parts, Diesel engine maintenance, Maintenance interval.

REVIEW QUESTIONS

1. What is an engine tune-up?
2. A tune-up assures that the _____, _____ system, _____ system, and _____ systems are operating within factory specifications.
3. List eight tasks commonly done during a minor tune-up.
4. What is a major tune-up?
5. List eight safety rules to remember during a tune-up.
6. A tune-up usually begins with:
   a. Inspection of engine compartment.
   b. Compression test.
   c. Spark plug replacement.
   d. Throttle body injector service.
7. Why is a compression test frequently done during a tune-up?
8. How can improper valve adjustment affect engine performance?
9. Name the eight steps typically done during diesel engine maintenance.
10. Engine tune-up or maintenance _____ are specific periods (in miles or months) for component service.

ACTIVITIES FOR CHAPTER 44

1. Visit the service manager of a local auto repair shop or auto dealer and determine what the shop would include in:
   a. A minor tune-up.
   b. A major tune-up.
2. Taking the information gathered in Activity 1, using a flat rate manual, and a parts catalog, determine the cost of (a) a minor tune-up and (b) a major tune-up at a labor rate of $48 per hour.

Engines using distributorless ignition, such as this 3.4 liter V-6, permit longer intervals between tuneups than older engines with distributor-type ignition systems. (Pontiac)

45

Engine Mechanical Problems

After studying this chapter, you will be able to:

☐ Explain why proper diagnosis methods are important to engine repair.

☐ List common symptoms of engine mechanical problems.

☐ Discuss how to find abnormal engine noises.

☐ Summarize procedures for gasoline and diesel engine compression testing.

☐ Explain when and how to do a wet compression test.

☐ Summarize common causes of engine mechanical problems.

☐ Discuss safety practices to follow while performing engine inspections.

In earlier chapters, you learned about engine part construction and operation. To further your understanding of automotive engines, this chapter will explain the most common types of engine mechanical problems. It will introduce symptoms and describe the basic inspections and tests needed to find the source of these problems. As a result, you should be well prepared for the next chapters on engine removal and engine overhaul.

Note! This chapter discusses only problems that relate to mechanical part wear and damage, Fig. 45-1. It does NOT cover engine performance problems, and problems caused by other engine systems. Use the index to find information on these topics.

WHY IS DIAGNOSIS IMPORTANT?

If a technician does not know how to properly diagnose (locate) engine problems, a great deal of time, effort, and money will be wasted. In fact, an untrained technician may unknowingly rebuild an engine when a minor repair might have corrected the fault.

For example, a worn or stretched timing chain can cause the engine valves to open and close at the wrong times in relation to piston movement. This could cause low compression stroke pressure in all cylinders. The engine would have low power output and low compression readings.

The technician could incorrectly diagnose the trouble (worn timing chain) as more major problems (worn piston rings, scored cylinders, etc.). The engine could be overhauled when a new timing chain would have corrected the problem. Unfortunately, the customer would have to pay for the technician's lack of training.

SYMPTOMS OF ENGINE MECHANICAL PROBLEMS

A few common engine mechanical problems include: leaking gaskets, worn piston rings, burned and leaking valves, loose or worn engine bearings, worn timing chains, and damaged (cracked, broken, scored) engine parts. See Fig. 45-1.

These problems can occur after extended service (high mileage), engine overheating, lack of periodic maintenance, and other types of abuse. The symptoms (signs) that result from these types of problems include:

1. Excessive oil consumption (engine oil must be added too often).
2. Crankcase blowby (combustion pressure blows past piston rings into crankcase, and out breather).
3. Abnormal engine noises (knocking, tapping, hissing, rumbling).
4. Engine smoking (blue-grey, black, or white smoke blows out tailpipe).
5. Poor engine performance (rough idle, vehicle accelerates slowly, engine vibrates).
6. Coolant in engine oil (oil has white, milky appearance).
7. Engine locked up (crankshaft will not rotate).

With any of these troubles, inspect and test the engine to determine the exact problem source. You must find out what repair is needed. Then, determine whether the engine can be repaired in the car or if it must be removed for more major repairs.

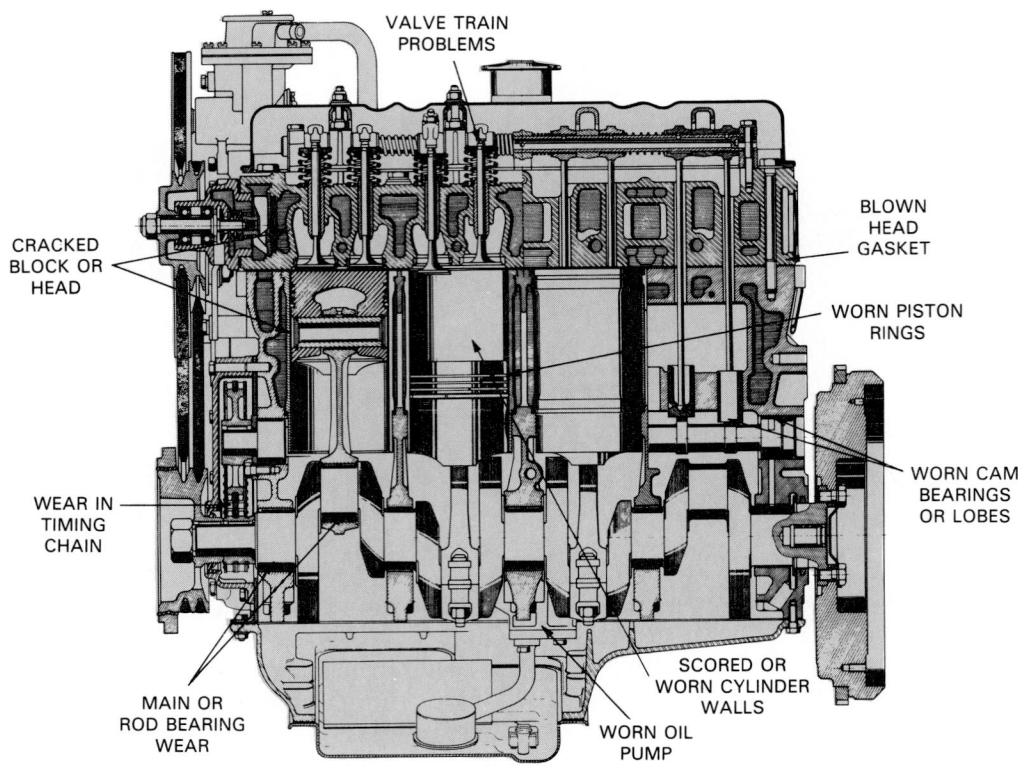

Fig. 45-1. Many mechanical problems can occur in an engine.

ENGINE PRE-TEARDOWN INSPECTION

After gathering information from the customer or service writer, inspect the engine using all of your senses (sight, smell, hearing, touch). Look for external problems (oil leaks, vacuum leaks, part damage, contaminated oil).

If a leak is found, smell the fluid to determine if it is oil, coolant, or other type of fluid. Listen for unusual noises that indicate part wear or damage.

Increase engine speed while listening and watching for problems. The engine may run fine at idle but act up at higher speeds.

A few engine problems that may be located through inspection are:

Coolant in oil will show up as white or milky looking oil. Look at Fig. 45-2. It is caused by a mechanical problem that allows engine coolant to leak into the engine crankcase. There may be a cracked block or head, leaking head gasket, leaking intake manifold gasket (V-type engine), or similar troubles.

Oil fouled spark plugs point to internal oil leakage into the engine combustion chambers. They are an indication that the engine has worn rings, worn or scored cylinder walls, or bad valve seals. You will need to perform additional tests to find the source of the problem.

Oil in the coolant is usually NOT an engine problem. It is commonly caused by a leak in the radiator (transmission) oil cooler.

Engine oil leaks occur when gaskets harden and crack, when seals wear, when fasteners work loose, or

when there is part damage (warped surfaces, cracked parts). To find oil leaks, clean the affected area on the outside of the engine. Then, trace the leak upward to

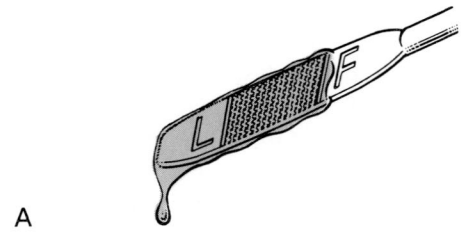

Fig. 45-2. During engine inspection, check condition of oil and spark plugs. A — Check dipstick for coolant, gasoline, or other contaminants in oil. B — Check spark plugs for oil fouling. This would point to bad rings, cylinder walls, or valve seals causing oil leakage into combustion chambers. (Toyota and Champion Spark Plugs)

its source. Oil will usually flow down and to the rear of the engine because of cooling fan action.

External coolant leaks will show up as a puddle of coolant under the engine. Leaks can be caused by hose problems, rusted-out freeze (core) plugs, or warped, worn, or damaged parts. Use a pressure tester (see Chapter 35) to locate external coolant leaks.

Engine blowby occurs when combustion pressure blows past the piston rings into the lower block and oil pan area of the engine. See Fig. 45-3. Pressure then flows up to the valve covers and out the breather. Excessive blowby will show up as an oil wet area around the breather. With the valve cover breather removed, oil vapors may blow out when the engine speed is increased.

Engine vacuum leaks show up during inspection as a hissing sound, like air leaking out of a tire. Vacuum leaks are loudest at idle and temporarily quiet down as the engine is accelerated (manifold vacuum drops with engine acceleration). Very ROUGH ENGINE IDLING usually accompanies a vacuum leak.

Engine smoking is normally noticed at the tailpipe when the engine is accelerated or decelerated. The color of the smoke can be used to help diagnose the source of the problem.

With a GASOLINE ENGINE, the exhaust smoke may be:
1. BLUE-GREY SMOKE (indicates motor oil is entering combustion chambers. May be due to worn rings, worn cylinders, leaking valve stem seals, or other troubles).
2. BLACK SMOKE (caused by extremely rich air-fuel mixture, not an engine mechanical problem).
3. WHITE SMOKE (if not water condensation on cool day, may be due to internal coolant leak into cylinders).

With a DIESEL ENGINE, exhaust smoke may be:
1. BLUE SMOKE (oil entering combustion chambers and being burned because of ring, cylinder, or valve seal problems).
2. BLACK SMOKE (injection system problem or low compression keeping fuel from burning).

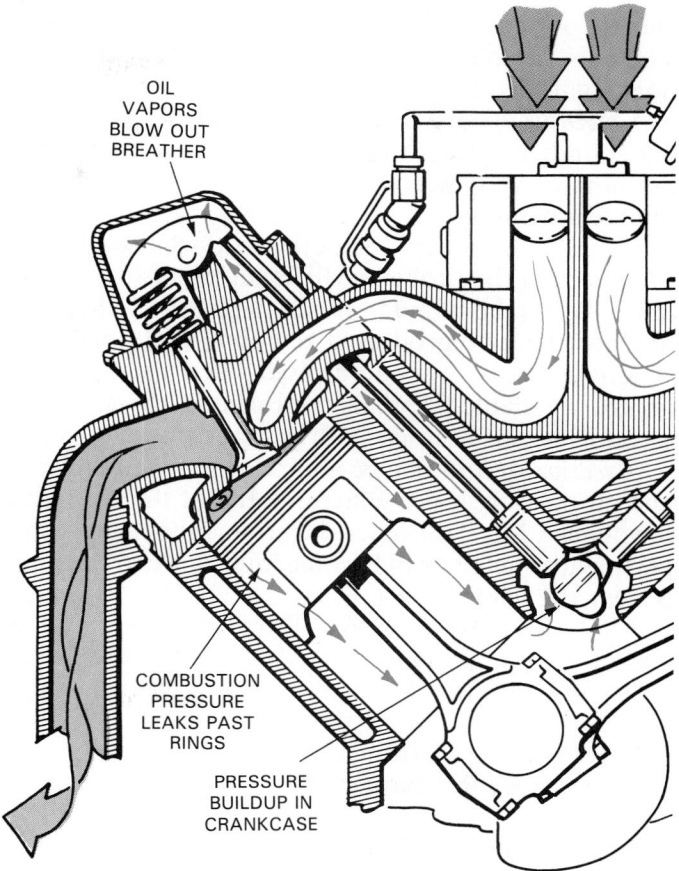

Fig. 45-3. Blowby allows combustion pressure to enter engine crankcase past piston rings. Pressure buildup in lower end of engine can cause oil mist to blow out breather openings. (Cadillac)

3. WHITE SMOKE (unburned fuel, cold engine, or coolant leaking into combustion chambers).

Fig. 45-4 shows engine exhaust smoke problems for a gasoline engine. Refer to Chapter 24 for more information on diesel exhaust smoke.

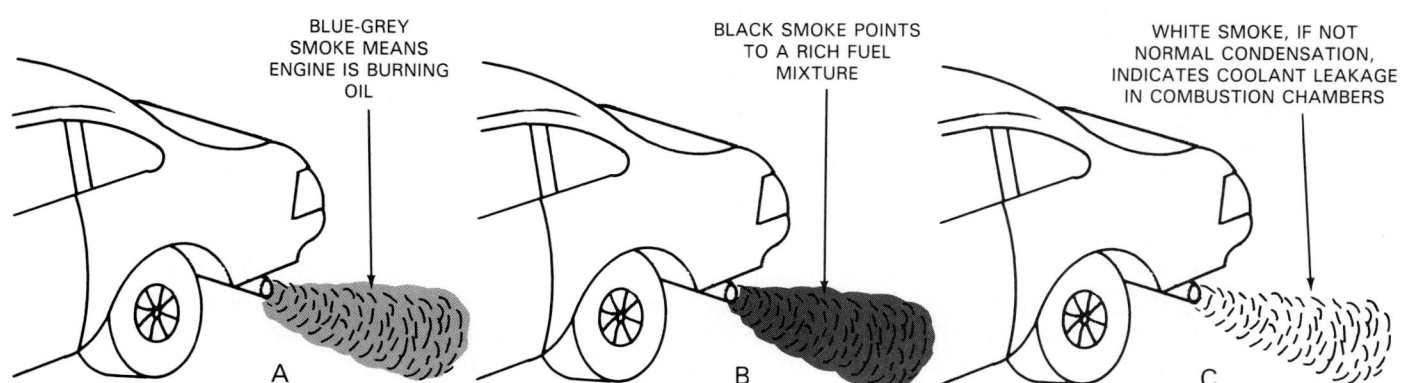

Fig. 45-4. Engine smoke may indicate major problems. A — Blue smoke points to oil entering combustion chambers. B — Black smoke suggests rich fuel mixture. C — White smoke, if not condensation, may indicate coolant leakage into cylinders.

ABNORMAL ENGINE NOISES

Abnormal engine noises (hisses, knocks, rattles, clunks, popping) may indicate part wear or damage. You must be able to quickly locate and interpret engine noises and decide what repairs are needed.

A *stethoscope* is a listening device for finding internal sounds in parts. Like a doctor's stethoscope for listening to your heart, it will amplify (increase) the loudness of noises.

To use a stethoscope, place the head set in your ears. Then, touch the probe on different parts around the noise. When the sound becomes the loudest, you have touched the part producing the abnormal noise.

A *long screwdriver* can be used when a stethoscope is not available. Sounds will travel through the screwdriver, as they do with a stethoscope.

A *section of hose* can be used to locate vacuum leaks and air pressure leaks. Place one end of the hose next to your ear. Move the other end around the engine compartment. The hiss will become loudest when the hose is near the leaking part.

CAUTION! When using a listening device, keep it away from the spinning engine fan or belts. Severe injury could result if the stethoscope, screwdriver, or hose were hit or pulled into the fan or belts!

Note! For more information on sound detection and location, refer to Chapter 10.

COMPRESSION TEST

A *compression test* is one of the most common methods of determining ENGINE MECHANICAL CONDITION. It should be done anytime symptoms point to cylinder pressure leakage. An extremely rough idle, popping noise from air inlet or exhaust, excessive blue smoke, or blowby are all reasons to consider a compression test.

Fig. 45-5 shows several mechanical problems that could cause compresison leakage, requiring a compression test.

A *compression gauge* is used to measure compression stroke pressure during this test. If gauge pressure is lower than normal, pressure is leaking out of the engine combustion chamber.

Low engine compression can be caused by:
1. BURNED VALVE (valve face damaged by combustion heat).
2. BURNED VALVE SEAT (cylinder head seat damaged by combustion).
3. PHYSICAL ENGINE DAMAGE (hole in piston, broken valve, etc.).
4. BLOWN HEAD GASKET (head gasket ruptured).
5. WORN RINGS OR CYLINDERS (part wear prevents ring-to-cylinder seal).
6. VALVE TRAIN TROUBLES (valves adjusted with insufficient clearance, which keeps them from fully closing, broken valve spring, etc.).
7. JUMPED TIMING CHAIN OR BELT (loose or worn chain or belt has jumped over teeth, upsetting valve timing).

For other less common sources of low compression, refer to a service manual troubleshooting chart.

Gasoline engine compression testing

To perform a compression test on a gasoline engine, remove all of the spark plugs so that the engine will rotate easily. Block open the carburetor or fuel injection throttle plate. This will prevent a restriction of airflow into the engine.

Disable the ignition system to prevent sparks from arcing out of the disconnected spark plug wires. Usually, the feed wire going to the ignition coil can be removed to disable the system.

If electronic fuel injection is used, it should also be disabled so that fuel will not spray into the engine. Check your service manual for specific directions.

Screw the compression gauge into one of the spark plug holes, Fig. 45-6A. Crank the engine and let the engine rotate for about four to six compression strokes (compression gauge needle moves four to six times). Write down the gauge readings. Repeat for each cylinder and compare to specs.

Diesel engine compression test

A diesel engine compression test is similar to a compression test for a gasoline engine. However, DO NOT use a compression gauge intended for a gasoline engine. It can be damaged by the high compression stroke pressure. A diesel compression gauge must read up to approximately 600 psi (4 134 kPa).

To perform a diesel compression test, remove either the injectors or the glow plugs. Refer to a service

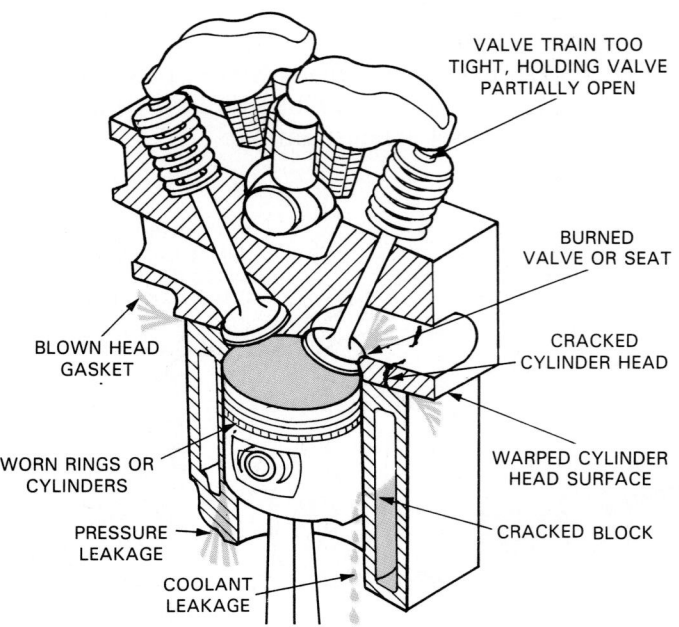

VALVE TRAIN TOO TIGHT, HOLDING VALVE PARTIALLY OPEN

BURNED VALVE OR SEAT

CRACKED CYLINDER HEAD

WARPED CYLINDER HEAD SURFACE

CRACKED BLOCK

BLOWN HEAD GASKET

WORN RINGS OR CYLINDERS

PRESSURE LEAKAGE

COOLANT LEAKAGE

Fig. 45-5. Typical reasons for combustion pressure leakage.

manual for instructions. Install the compression gauge in the recommended hole. A heat shield must be used to seal the gauge when installed in place of an injector. Disconnect the fuel shut-off solenoid to disable the injection pump. Crank the engine and note the highest reading on the gauge.

Wet compression testing

A *wet compression test* should be completed if cylinder pressure reads below specs. It will help you determine what engine parts are causing the problem.

Squirt a tablespoon of 30-weight motor oil into the cylinder with the low pressure reading, Fig. 45-6B. Install the compression gauge and recheck cylinder pressure.

If the compression gauge reading GOES UP with oil in the cylinder, the piston rings and cylinders may be worn and leaking pressure, Fig. 45-6C. The oil will temporarily coat and seal bad compression rings to increase pressure.

If the pressure reading STAYS ABOUT THE SAME, then the engine valves or head gasket may be leaking. The engine oil will seal the rings but will NOT seal a burned valve or blown head gasket. In this way,

a wet compression test will help diagnose low compression problems.

Do NOT squirt too much oil into the cylinder during a wet compression test or a false reading will result. With excessive oil in the cylinder, compression readings will go up even if the piston rings and cylinders are in good condition. Oil, like any liquid, WILL NOT COMPRESS. It will take up space in the cylinder, raising the compression ratio and gauge readings.

NOTE! Some auto makers warn against performing a wet compression test on a diesel. If too much oil is squirted into the cylinder, hydraulic lock and part damage could result because the oil will NOT compress in the small cylinder volume.

Compression test results

Gasoline engine compression readings should run around 125 to 175 psi (861 to 1 206 kPa). Generally, the compression pressure should not vary more than 15 to 20 psi (103 to 138 kPa) from the highest to the lowest cylinder. Readings must be within 10 to 15 percent of each other.

Diesel engine compression readings will average approximately 275 to 400 psi (1 895 to 2 756 kPa),

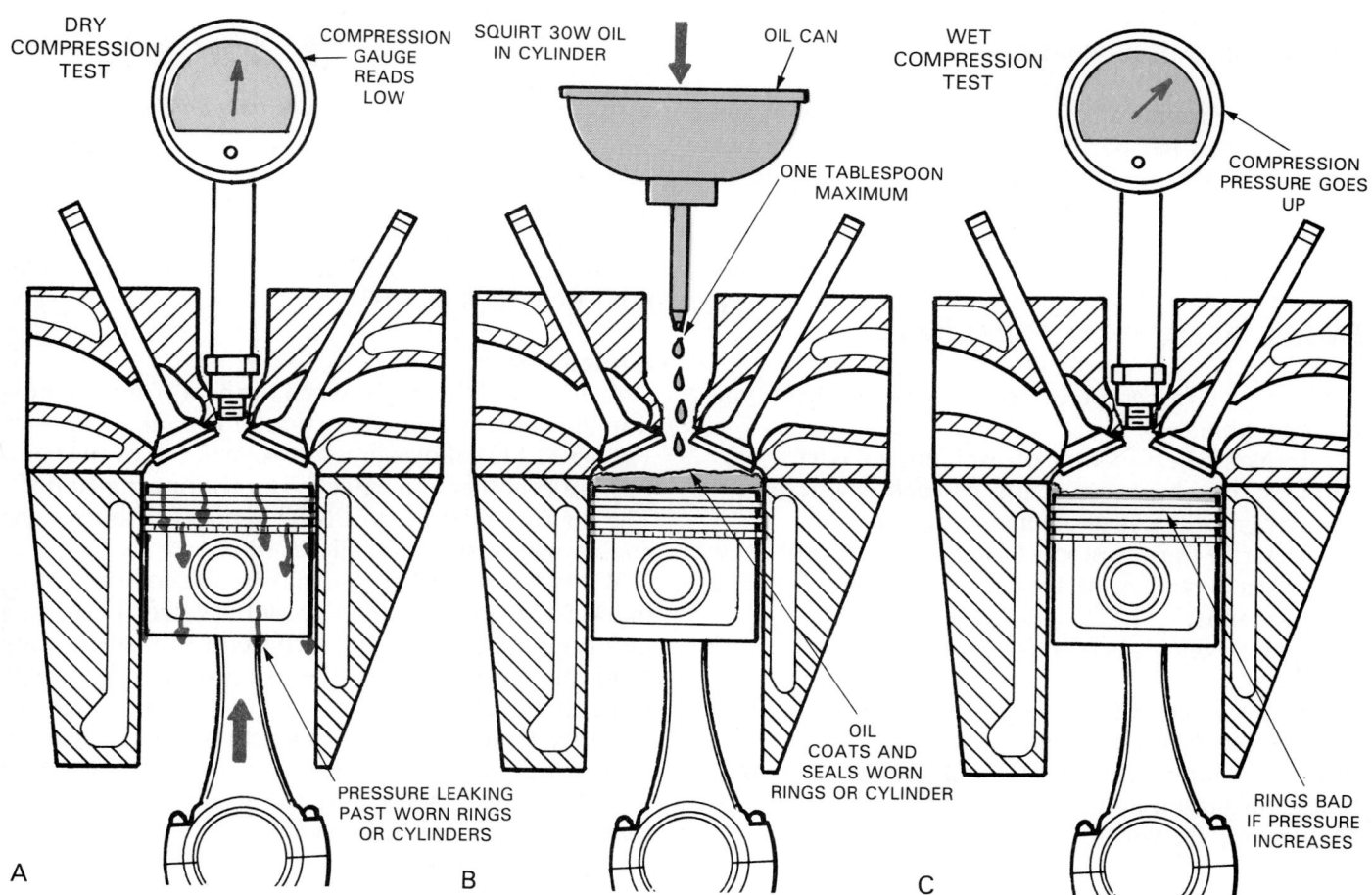

Fig. 45-6. Basic method of making dry and wet compression test. A — Complete conventional, dry compression test with pressure gauge. Record all readings and compare to specs. B — If compression is low, squirt a tablespoon of oil into cylinder. This will temporarily seal rings. C — Measure compression pressure again. If pressure reading goes up, that cylinder may have bad rings or worn cylinder. Same pressure reading might point to burned valve or blown head gasket.

depending upon engine design and compression ratio. Compression levels must not vary more than about 10 to 15 percent (30 to 50 psi or 206 to 344 kPa).

Look for cylinder PRESSURE VARIATION during an engine compression check. If some cylinders have normal pressure and one or two have low readings, engine performance will be reduced. The engine will have a rough idle and lack power.

If ALL of the cylinders are low (worn timing chain for example), the engine may run smoothly but lack power and get poor gas mileage.

If TWO ADJACENT CYLINDERS read low, it might point to a blown head gasket between the two cylinders. A blown head gasket will sometimes produce a louder than normal puffing noise from the spark plug, injector, or glow plug holes with the gauge removed.

OTHER TESTS

There are several other, less common tests that can be used to diagnose mechanical problems in an engine. These tests include a cylinder leakage test, vacuum gauge test, or exhaust gas analysis. Use the textbook index to locate these topics.

DECIDE WHAT TYPE OF ENGINE REPAIR IS NEEDED

After performing all of the necessary inspections and tests, decide what part or parts must be repaired or replaced to correct the engine problem. Evaluate all data from your pre-teardown diagnosis. If you still cannot determine the exact problem, the engine may have to be partially disassembled for further inspection.

ENGINE MECHANICAL PROBLEMS

Before you can properly repair engine problems, you must be able to:
1. Explain the function of each engine part.
2. Describe the construction of each engine part.
3. Explain the cause of engine problems.
4. Describe the symptoms of major engine problems.
5. Select specific methods to pinpoint specific problems.
6. Know which parts must be removed for certain repairs.
7. Know whether the engine must be removed from the car during the repair.

This section of the chapter will summarize important information about major engine problems. This should prepare you for following chapters.

Valve train problems

Valve train problems can cause engine missing, oil consumption, blue-grey exhaust smoke, light tapping sounds from the upper area of the engine, rough idling, overall performance problems, and even cylinder and

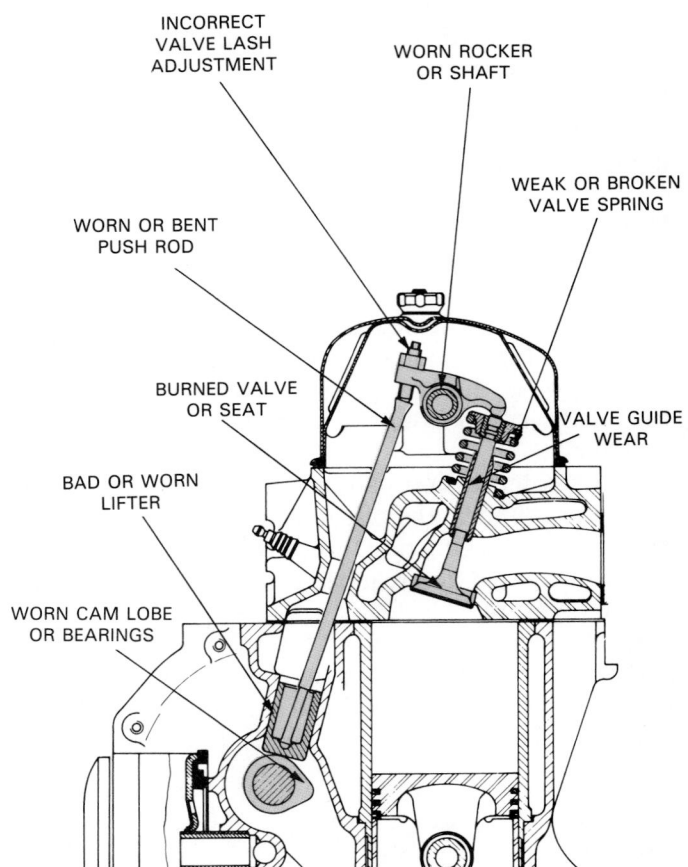

Fig. 45-7. Typical valve train problems.

piston damage. A worn or damaged camshaft, timing chain, gear or belt, valves, valve guides, push rods, cam bearings, or rocker arms can all upset engine operation. Refer to Fig. 45-7.

Burned valve

A *burned valve* results when the heat from combustion blows away a small portion of the valve face. See Fig. 45-8. This allows pressure to leak out of the combustion chamber and enter the intake or exhaust port. The air-fuel mixture will NOT ignite and burn. The engine will miss, especially at idle.

With a burned valve, you may be able to hear a puffing sound as pressure blows past the valve. There may be a popping sound at the carburetor or throttle body (bad intake valve) or at the exhaust system tailpipe (burned exhaust valve).

To fix a burned valve, you must remove the cylinder head from the engine. Then, as described in Chapter 47, all of the valves and seats should be ground (machined). A new valve would normally be needed to replace any that are burned.

Worn valve guides and stems

A *worn valve guide* or *stem* will allow the valve to rock or tip sideways in the cylinder head. Excess clearance between the stem and guide will result, as

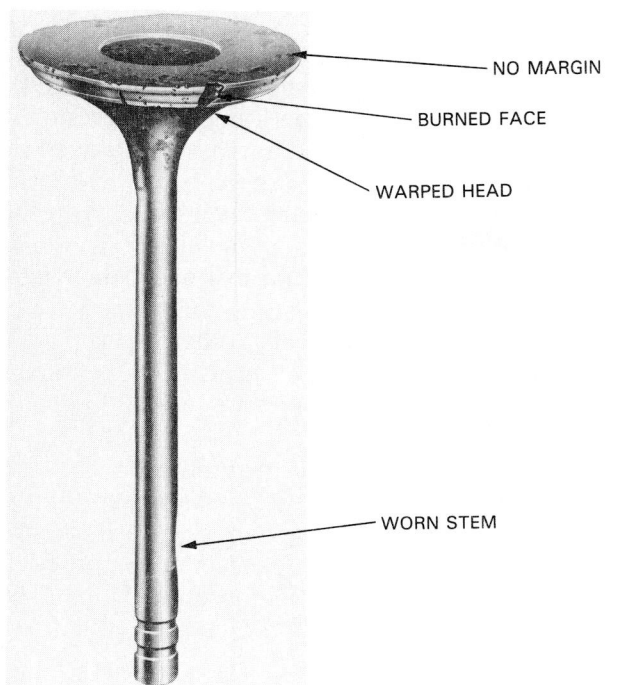

Fig. 45-8. Common problems that can develop with an engine valve. (Sioux Tools)

shown in Fig. 45-9. This can cause a tapping noise, oil consumption, spark plug fouling, or valve stem breakage.

To check for worn valve guides, remove the valve cover. Use a large screwdriver to pry sideways on the valve stem. If the valve wiggles in its guide, remove the cylinder head for guide repairs.

Leaking valve stem seals

Leaking valve stem seals will let oil drain into the clearance between the valve stem and guide. Look at Fig. 45-9. Oil will be pulled into the intake or exhaust

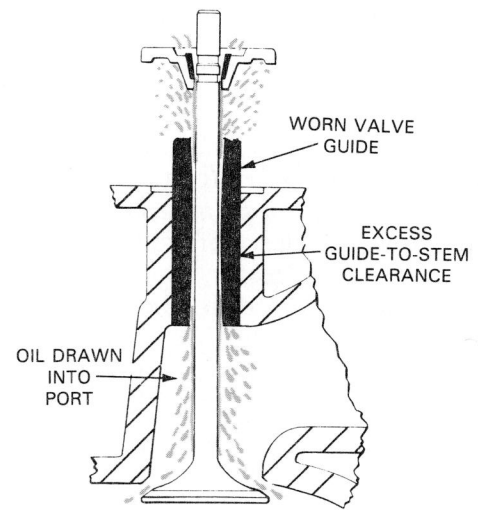

Fig. 45-9. Worn valve guide can let valve wiggle sideways in head, causing oil to be drawn into port. Bad valve seals can also cause oil consumption. (Dana Corp.)

port, and burned. The engine will emit blue smoke, especially after initial starting or upon deceleration.

Valve seals can usually be replaced WITHOUT removing the cylinder head. As described in Chapter 47, air pressure is used to hold the valve up in the head. Then, a special tool is used to compress the valve spring. The keepers, springs, and seals can then be removed for service.

Valve breakage

Valve breakage may be caused by valve stem fatigue or a broken or weak valve spring allowing the piston to hit the valve head. When the head of a valve breaks off, it usually causes severe damage to the piston, cylinder wall, and combustion chamber. Major engine repairs are normally needed.

Stuck valve

A *stuck valve* results when the valve stem rusts or corrodes and locks in the valve guide. This can happen when the engine sits in storage for an extended period.

A stuck or frozen valve can sometimes be fixed by squirting rust penetrant around the top of the valve guide. If this fails to correct the problem, remove the cylinder head for service.

Valve float

Valve float is a condition in which weakened valve springs, hydraulic lifter problems, or excess engine rpm causes the valves to remain partially open. This problem usually occurs at higher engine speeds. The engine may begin to miss, pop, or backfire as the valves float.

Weak valve springs are the result of prolonged use. The springs lose some of their tension. The springs may become too weak to close the valves properly.

A *broken valve spring* will frequently let the valve hang partially open. Excess valve-to-rocker clearance may cause valve train clatter (light tapping noise). Popping or backfiring can also result.

Valve springs can be replaced WITHOUT cylinder head removal. As with valve seal replacement, air pressure and a special tool will permit spring replacement.

Worn timing chain

A *worn timing chain* will upset valve timing, reducing compression stroke pressure and engine power. Wear can cause slack between the crankshaft sprocket and camshaft sprocket. Refer to Fig. 45-10. The cam and valves will no longer be kept in time with the pistons.

To check for a worn timing chain, rotate the crankshaft back and forth while watching the distributor rotor or rocker arms. If you can turn the crank several degrees without rotor or valve movement, the timing chain is worn. The timing chain would need to be replaced.

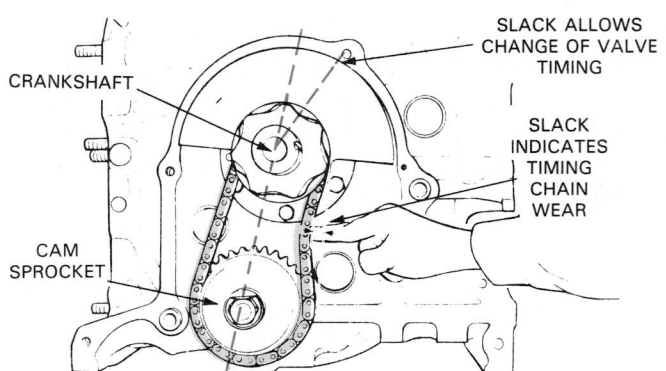

Fig. 45-10. Timing chain wear can let camshaft rotate out of time with crankshaft. Valves do not open when they should, reducing engine power and efficiency. (Mazda)

Worn timing gears

Worn timing gears will cause symptoms similar to those caused by a worn timing chain. However, problems will not be as common nor as severe. Timing gears are very dependable and resistant to wear.

If a tooth breaks on one of the gears, a growling noise may be produced. When worn or broken, timing gears must be replaced as a set.

Worn timing belt

A *worn timing belt* will usually break, jump off its sprockets, or skip over a few sprocket teeth. Severe performance problems or valve damage can result. The pistons can move up and slam into the open valves, bending or breaking them.

Camshaft problems

Camshaft problems typically include lobe wear, cam journal wear, cam breakage, distributor drive gear wear, and wear or loosening of the fuel pump drive eccentric.

Cam lobe wear will reduce valve lift (distance valve slides open), as shown in Fig. 45-11. This reduces engine power and can cause a rough idle.

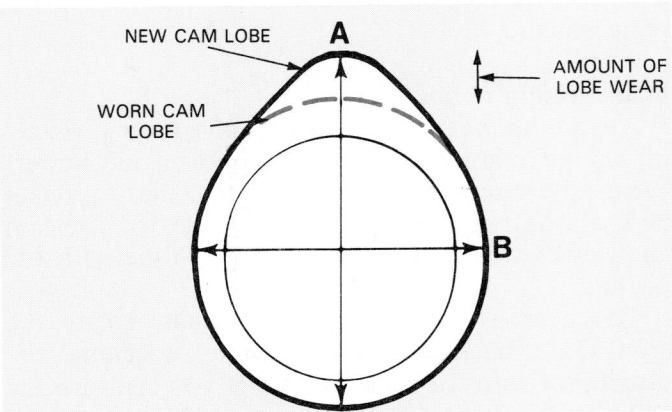

Fig. 45-11. Cam lobe wear will reduce valve lift. Note difference in lift between new and worn lobe. (Ford)

Camshaft breakage, though not common, will keep some of the valves from operating. The lobes on one end of the broken cam will not rotate and open their valves. Severe performance problems or valve damage can result. Removal of a valve cover will let you check valve train and camshaft action.

Worn cam bearings or *journals* will reduce engine oil pressure. Generally, this only happens after prolonged engine service. Normally, other engine parts will fail before journal or cam bearing wear becomes critical.

Rocker arm and push rod problems

Worn rocker arms can cause valve clatter (light tapping noise) by upsetting valve clearance, Fig. 45-12. Worn rocker arms have little effect on engine performance. Rocker arm wear usually results from lubrication system problems (dirty oil, clogged oil passages) that increase friction.

A rocker arm will wear at the points of contact between the valve, push rod, and rocker shaft or ball socket. After removal, the rockers should be inspected closely for identations or roughness indicating wear.

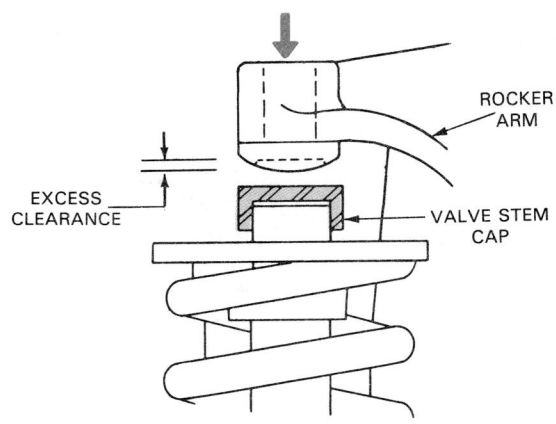

Fig. 45-12. Excess clearance in valve train can produce clattering sound from under valve cover. Rocker will clack as it strikes valve stem tip or cap. (Deere & Co.)

Worn or *bent push rods* can also cause valve clatter. To check wear, measure push rod length and compare to specs. To check for bent push rods, roll them on a flat work surface.

When a push rod is bent, check the opening action of that push rod's valve. The valve may be stuck and could bend a new push rod if not repaired. Replace bent push rods. Do not try to straighten them.

Hydraulic lifter problems

A *worn* or *defective hydraulic lifter* may produce valve clatter identical to that produced by a maladjusted, worn, or loose rocker arm, worn valve guide, or bent push rod. It will sound like a small ball pein hammer tapping on the cylinder head.

After removing the valve cover to check the valve noise, try adjusting the valves. If adjustment will not quiet the valve noise, check for valve train wear. If other valve train parts are good, the valve lifter is probably bad.

Low engine oil pressure can cause hydraulic lifter clatter. Check the oil level and oil pressure before condemning the lifter or lifters. Contaminated or dirty oil can also cause lifter noise.

ENGINE GASKET PROBLEMS

A *blown head gasket* can cause a wide range of problems: overheating, missing, coolant or oil leakage, engine smoking, even head or block damage (burned mating surfaces). Quite often, a blown head gasket will show up during a compression test. Two adjacent cylinders, usually the two center ones, will have low pressure.

A *leaking intake manifold gasket* can cause a vacuum leak, with resulting rough idle. To check for an intake gasket leak, squirt oil along the edge of the gasket. The oil may temporarily seal the leak, showing an intake gasket rupture. A low vacuum gauge reading can also indicate an intake leak.

A *leaking exhaust manifold gasket* will show up as a clicking type sound. As combustion gases blow into the manifold and out the bad gasket, an almost metallic-like rap is produced.

Part warpage (sealing surface on part not flat) is a common cause of gasket failure. Always check for warpage when servicing a bad gasket.

PISTON AND CYLINDER PROBLEMS

Piston and *cylinder problems* are major and usually require engine removal. It is important for you to be able to detect and diagnose the source of piston and cylinder-related troubles.

Piston knock (slap)

Piston knock or *slap* is a loud metallic knocking sound produced when the piston flops back and forth inside its cylinder. Refer to Fig. 45-13. It is caused by excess piston skirt or cylinder wear, clearance, and possibly damage.

Piston slap is normally LOUDER when the engine is COLD and tends to quiet down as the engine reaches operating temperature. Heat expansion of the aluminum piston takes up some of the clearance.

Piston pin knock

Piston pin knock occurs when too much clearance exists between the piston pin and piston pin bore or connecting rod bushing. Excessive clearance allows the pin to hammer against the rod or piston as the piston changes direction in the cylinder.

Piston pin knock will usually make a DOUBLE

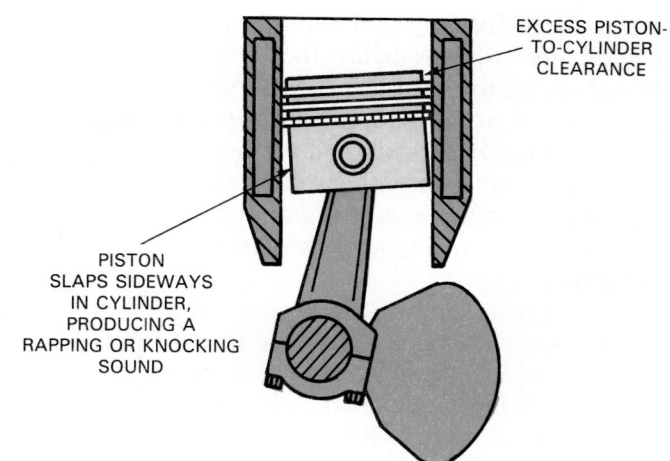

Fig. 45-13. Worn cylinder wall or piston skirt can let piston flop back and forth. This can produce a knocking sound and oil consumption. Piston knock or slap is loudest when engine is cold. It tends to quiet down as engine warms and piston expands.

KNOCK (two rapid knocks and then a short pause). It does NOT change much with engine load.

Worn piston rings and cylinder

Worn piston rings or *cylinders* result in blowby, blue-grey engine smoke, low engine power, spark plug fouling, and other problems caused by poor ring sealing. See Fig. 45-14.

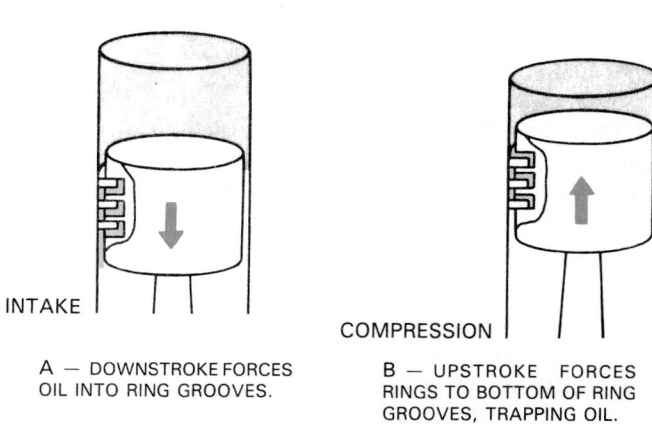

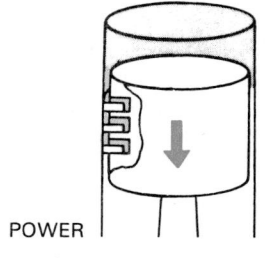

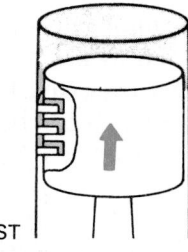

Fig. 45-14. Study how oil is trapped in worn rings and then burned on power stroke. (Deere & Co.)

To check for ring and cylinder problems, increase engine speed while watching the tailpipe and valve cover breather opening. If blue-grey smoke pours out of the car's exhaust under load, the oil rings and cylinders may need service. If excsssive oil vapors and air blow out the valve cover breather, blowby is entering the crankcase. Compression ring or cylinder problems are indicated. Worn ring grooves can also cause oil consumption, Fig. 45-15.

If after disassembly, the engine cylinders are found to be worn, the engine must be removed from the vehicle. The block must be sent to a machine shop for *boring* (cylinders machined oversize) or *sleeving* (liners installed to restore cylinders).

If just the rings are found to be worn, NOT the cylinders, the engine may be rebuilt while still installed in the car. Check a manual for details.

Burned piston

A *burned piston,* discussed in the chapter on combustion, is often a result of preignition or detonation damage. Abnormal combustion, excessive pressure, and heat actually melt and blow a hole in the piston crown or area around the ring lands, Fig. 45-16. The engine may smoke, knock, have excessive blowby, or other symptoms.

A compression test or cylinder leakage test (discussed in chapter on engine test equipment) may indicate a burned piston, but engine disassembly is usually needed to verify the problem. If the cylinder wall is not damaged, the repair can be an in-vehicle operation.

CRANKSHAFT PROBLEMS

Crankshaft problems include journal wear, main bearing wear, rod bearing wear, and resulting low oil pressure.

Rod bearing knock

Connecting rod bearing knock is caused by wear and excessive rod bearing-to-crankshaft clearance. It will produce a light, regular, rapping noise with the engine floating (point at which throttle is held constant and engine is not accelerating). It is loudest after engine warmup. In a cold engine, thickened oil tends to cushion and quiet rod knock, Fig. 45-17.

To locate a bad rod bearing, short out or disconnect each spark plug wire one at a time. The loose, knocking rod bearing may quiet down or change pitch when its spark plug is disabled.

Main bearing knock

Main bearing knock is similar to rod bearing knock but is slightly deeper or duller in pitch. It is usually more pronounced when the engine is pulling or lugging under a load. Bearing and possibly journal wear are letting the crankshaft move up and down inside the cylinder block.

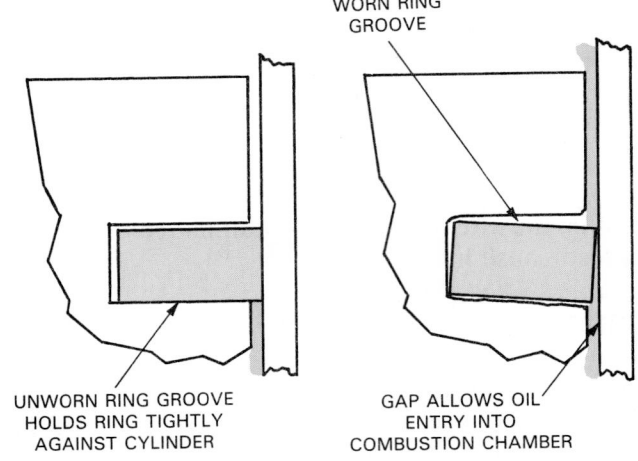

Fig. 45-15. If ring grooves are worn, they can allow rings to tip on cylinder wall, causing oil consumption.

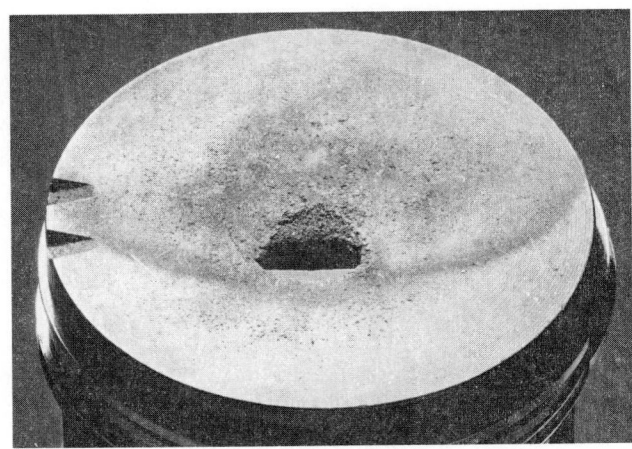

Fig. 45-16. Burned piston usually results from prolonged preignition or detonation. Symptoms would be low compression, blowby, smoking, rough idle, etc.
(Champion Spark Plugs)

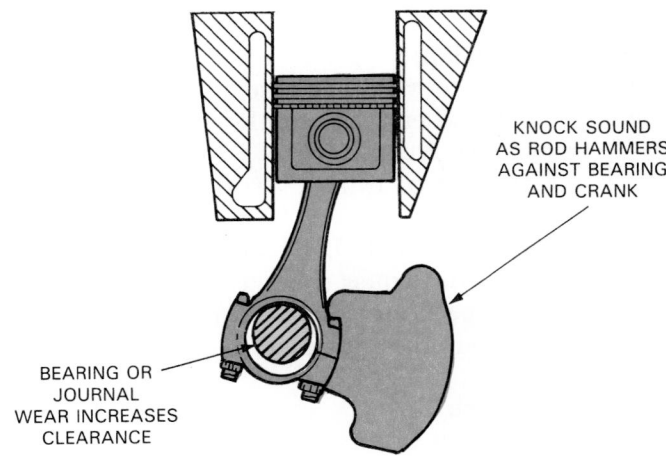

Fig. 45-17. Worn engine bearing will produce loud, deep, knocking sound as parts hammer together. This shows worn rod bearing. Rod and bearing would slam into crank journal as combustion pressure acts on piston. Bearing knock gets louder as engine warms and oil thins out.

Main bearing wear will usually reduce oil pressure significantly. To verify main bearing noise, remove the oil pan and pressure test the lubrication system. Excessive oil flow out of one or more of the main bearings implies too much bearing clearance. If a pressure tester is not available, remove and inspect each of the main bearings. If the crankshaft is not worn, bearing insert replacement should correct the problem.

Excess crankshaft end play

Excess crankshaft end play is caused by a worn main thrust bearing. Thrust bearing wear can produce a deep knock, usually when applying and releasing the clutch (manual transmission). With an automatic transmission, the end play problem may only show up as a single thud or knock upon acceleration or deceleration.

Note! A knock occurring with clutch or torque converter action could also be caused by loose flywheel bolts or other drive train problems. Check out all possible causes before beginning repairs.

SERVICE MANUAL TROUBLESHOOTING CHARTS

Service manual troubleshooting charts give lists of possible problems and needed repairs. Refer to these charts when you have difficulty locating or correcting an engine mechanical problem. A service manual chart will be written for the specific make and model of engine, making it very accurate.

The information in this chapter has prepared you to use service manual diagnosis charts.

KNOW THESE TERMS

Blowby, Vacuum leak, Engine smoke, Stethoscope, Compression test, Wet compression test, Burned valve, Worn valve guide, Leaking valve seal, Stuck valve, Valve float, Worn timing chain, Cam lobe wear, Worn cam bearings, Worn rocker arms, Bad hydraulic lifter, Bent push rod, Blown head gasket, Leaking intake manifold gasket, Leaking exhaust manifold gasket, Part warpage, Piston slap or knock. Piston pin knock, Worn piston rings, Cylinder wear, Burned piston, Rod bearing knock, Main bearing knock.

REVIEW QUESTIONS

1. List seven symptoms of engine mechanical problems.
2. Oil fouled spark plugs are an indication of worn _____, worn or scored _____ _____ or bad _____ _____.

3. With a gasoline engine, blue-grey smoke indicates:
   a. Rich fuel mixture.
   b. Coolant leakage into combustion chambers.
   c. Oil leakage into combustion chambers.
   d. Lean fuel mixture.
4. A section of vacuum hose can be used to find engine vacuum leaks. True or False?
5. Low cylinder compression CANNOT be caused by:
   a. Worn camshaft bearings.
   b. Blown head gasket.
   c. Burned valve.
   d. Worn piston rings.
6. Why is a wet compression test helpful?
7. What are typical gasoline engine and diesel engine compression readings?
8. Valve breakage can be caused by valve _____ _____ or by a broken or weak _____ _____.
9. Define the term "valve float."
10. How can you tell if an engine has a worn timing chain?
11. What are the problems resulting from camshaft lobe wear?
12. A leaking intake manifold gasket can cause a _____ leak, with resulting _____ idle.
13. Explain the symptoms of piston pin knock.
14. Why is piston slap loudest with the engine cold?
15. What are the symptoms of worn piston rings and cylinders?
16. Why is connecting rod bearing knock loudest with the engine warm?
17. A car enters the shop and the driver complains of a deep knock that seems to occur as the clutch is engaged or released.
    Technician A says that the problem could be a worn crankshaft thrust bearing. Clutch action could be allowing the crankshaft to slide to the front and rear of the block.
    Technician B says that the problem could also be loose flywheel bolts or drive train problems.
    Who is correct?
    a. Technician A
    b. Technician B
    c. Both A and B
    d. Neither A nor B

ACTIVITIES FOR CHAPTER 45

1. Demonstrate the steps for making a dry compression test on a gasoline engine. Compare your readings to specs.
2. Make a poster listing the probable causes of blue-grey, black, and white exhaust emissions.

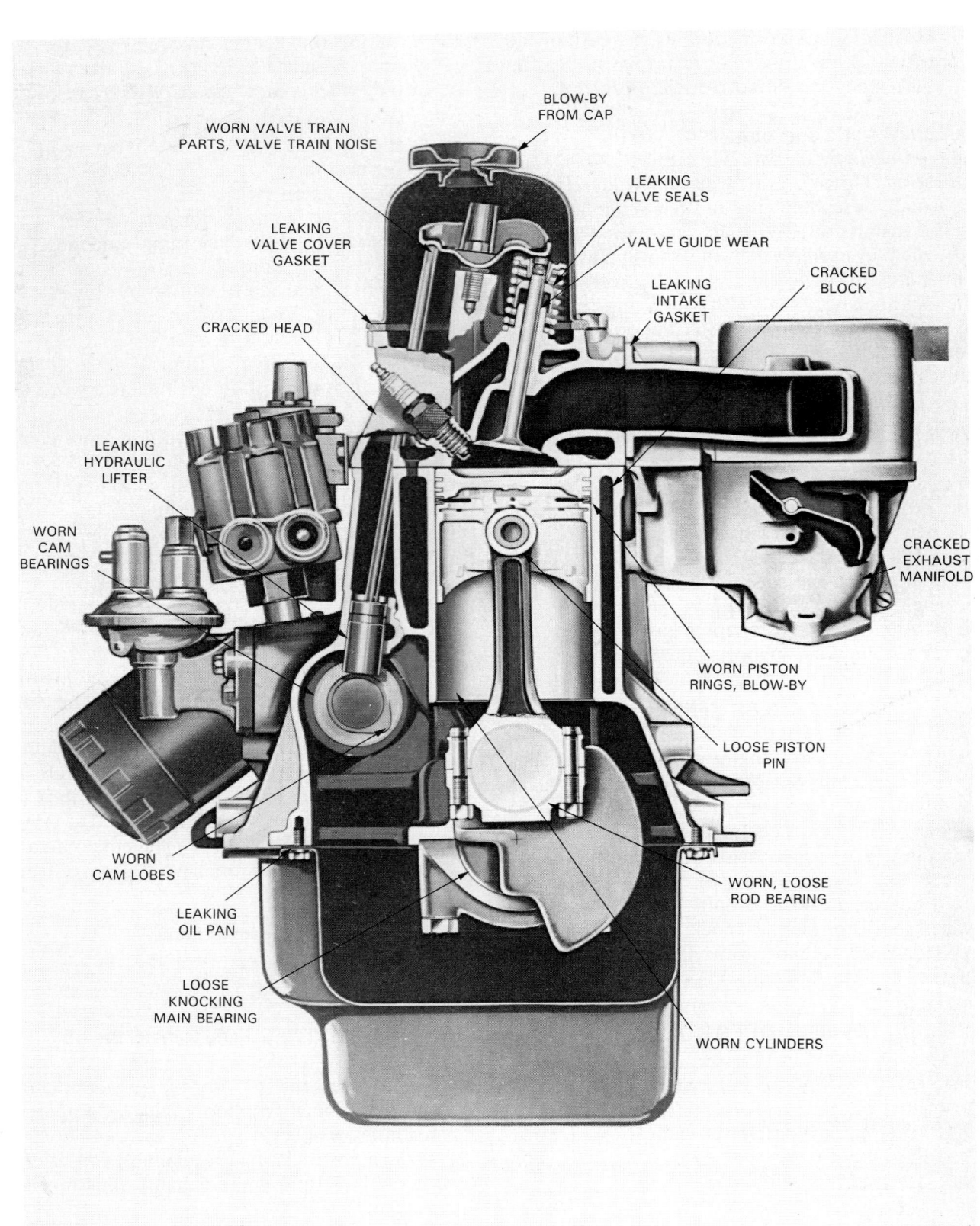

WORN VALVE TRAIN
PARTS, VALVE TRAIN NOISE

BLOW-BY
FROM CAP

LEAKING
VALVE SEALS

VALVE GUIDE WEAR

LEAKING
VALVE COVER
GASKET

LEAKING
INTAKE
GASKET

CRACKED
BLOCK

CRACKED HEAD

LEAKING
HYDRAULIC
LIFTER

WORN
CAM
BEARINGS

CRACKED
EXHAUST
MANIFOLD

WORN PISTON
RINGS, BLOW-BY

LOOSE PISTON
PIN

WORN
CAM LOBES

LEAKING
OIL PAN

WORN, LOOSE
ROD BEARING

LOOSE
KNOCKING
MAIN BEARING

WORN CYLINDERS

Proper methods must be used when removing, disassembling, and cleaning engine parts. One mistake could ruin a part or cause part failure after engine operation.   (Chrysler)

46

Engine Removal, Disassembly, Parts Cleaning

After studying this chapter, you will be able to:
- ☐ Determine if engine removal is needed to make specific engine repairs.
- ☐ List the preparations for engine removal.
- ☐ Describe the general safety rules pertaining to engine removal, disassembly, and parts cleaning.
- ☐ Explain the use of an engine lifting fixture or chain, and an engine crane.
- ☐ Summarize how to properly disassemble an engine.
- ☐ Describe typical inspections that should be made during engine disassembly and cleaning.
- ☐ List various methods for cleaning engine parts.
- ☐ Describe safety practices to follow when cleaning parts.

Engine removal and disassembly procedures vary from vehicle to vehicle. However, there are many general rules and methods that apply to all cars and small trucks. This chapter will outline the most important steps for engine removal, teardown, and cleaning. This should make an engine R&R (remove and repair) job much easier.

IS ENGINE REMOVAL NECESSARY?

Many engine repairs can be made with the engine block still mounted in the chassis. Repairs limited to the cylinder head, valve train, and other external parts are commonly in-vehicle operations.

Engines are removed when the cylinder block or crankshaft is badly damaged. Depending upon the year, make, and model of the vehicle, engine removal may be required for other repairs.

For example, one vehicle might need engine removal simply to replace a damaged oil pan. Another may allow quick and easy oil pan removal, permitting in-vehicle replacement of piston rings, bearings, and other major components.

When in doubt, always refer to a manufacturer's service manual. It will give directions for the exact vehicle and engine.

PREPARING FOR ENGINE REMOVAL

To prepare for engine removal, use the following general steps and a shop manual:
1. Park the car so there is plenty of work space on both sides and in front of the engine compartment.
2. Use fender covers to protect the paint.
3. Scribe the hood hinges to aid realignment, Fig. 46-1. Then have someone help you remove the hood. Store the hood in a safe place.
4. Disconnect the battery to prevent electrical shorts. Remove the battery if in the way.
5. Drain the engine oil and coolant.
6. Unplug all electrical wires between the engine and chassis. If needed, use masking tape to label or identify the wires. This will simplify reconnection.
7. Remove all coolant and vacuum hoses that prevent engine removal. Label vacuum hoses if necessary for proper reconnection.
8. When disconnecting fuel lines, be careful not to let fuel spray out. Wrap a shop rag around the hose or fitting.
9. Do NOT disconnect any power steering or air conditioning lines or hoses unless absolutely necessary. Usually, the power steering pump or air conditioning compressor can be unbolted and placed on one side of the engine compartment, Fig. 46-2.
10. Remove the radiator, fan, and other accessory units in front of the engine. Be careful not to hit or drop the radiator.
11. Keep fasteners organized in several different containers. For instance, keep all of the bolts and nuts from the front of the engine in one container. Keep engine top end and bottom end fasteners separate

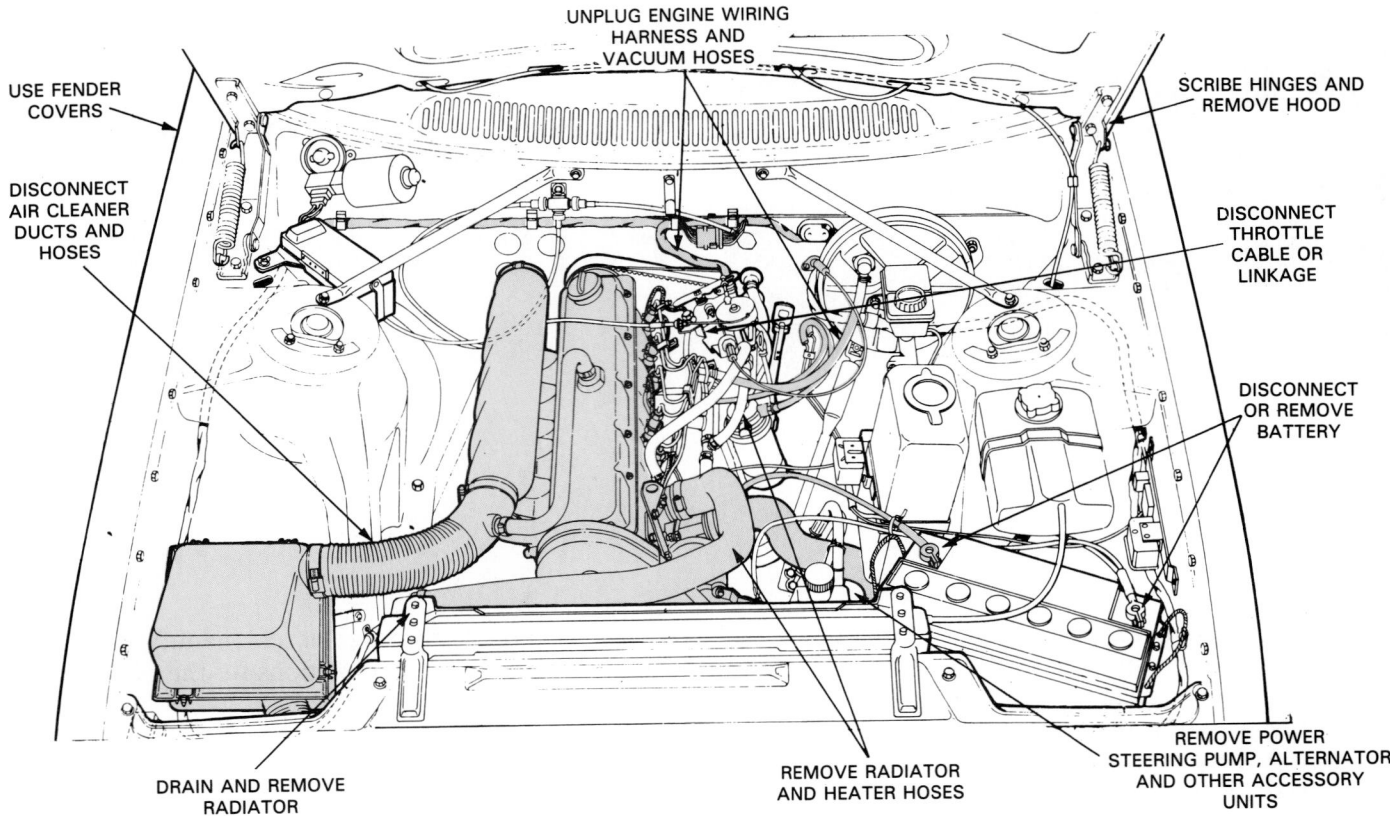

USE FENDER COVERS

DISCONNECT AIR CLEANER DUCTS AND HOSES

UNPLUG ENGINE WIRING HARNESS AND VACUUM HOSES

SCRIBE HINGES AND REMOVE HOOD

DISCONNECT THROTTLE CABLE OR LINKAGE

DISCONNECT OR REMOVE BATTERY

REMOVE POWER STEERING PUMP, ALTERNATOR AND OTHER ACCESSORY UNITS

REMOVE RADIATOR AND HEATER HOSES

DRAIN AND REMOVE RADIATOR

Fig. 46-1. These are many of the components that must be disconnected in upper area of engine compartment before engine removal. (Volvo)

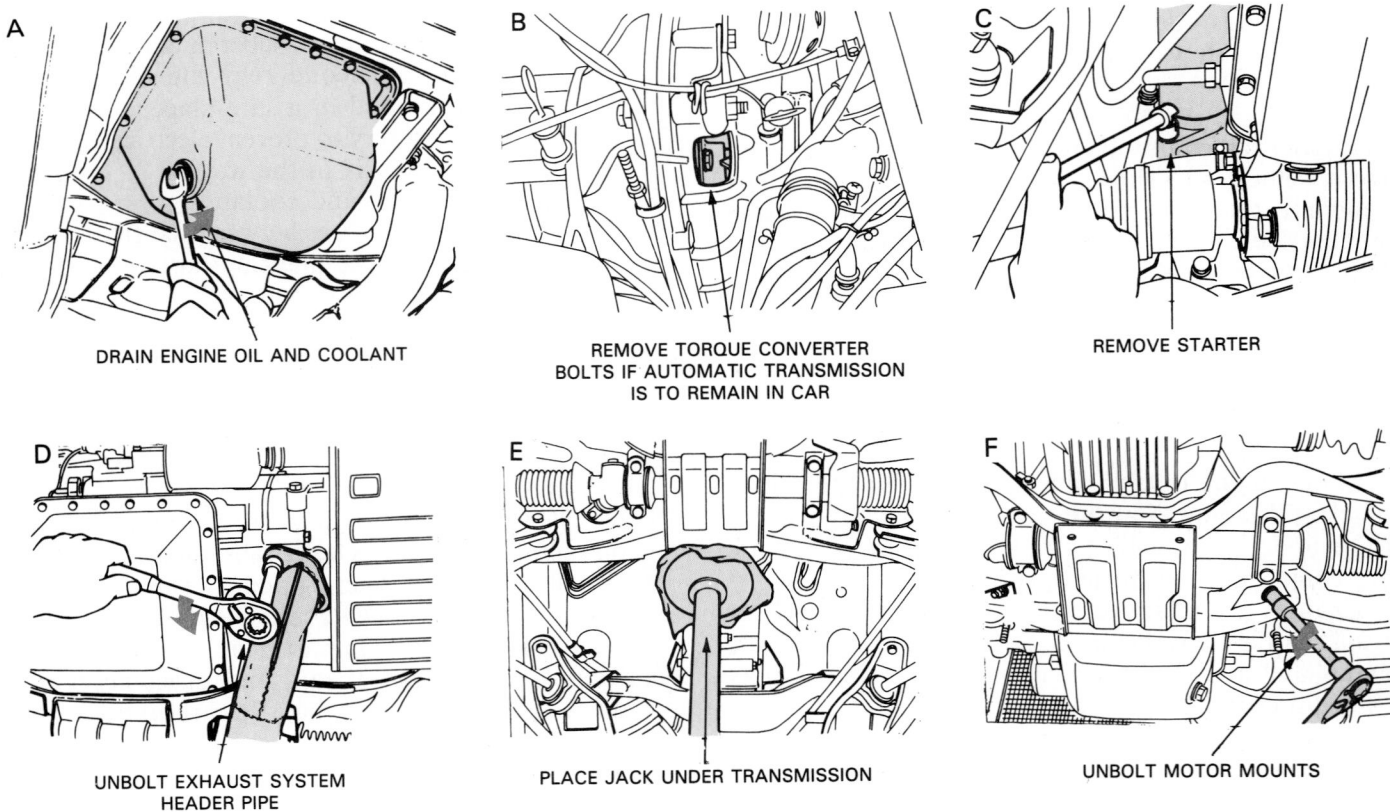

A — DRAIN ENGINE OIL AND COOLANT

B — REMOVE TORQUE CONVERTER BOLTS IF AUTOMATIC TRANSMISSION IS TO REMAIN IN CAR

C — REMOVE STARTER

D — UNBOLT EXHAUST SYSTEM HEADER PIPE

E — PLACE JACK UNDER TRANSMISSION

F — UNBOLT MOTOR MOUNTS

Fig. 46-2. When under car, these are some of the parts that must be disconnected before engine removal. Check a service manual for details. (Subaru)

in two more containers. This will speed reassembly.

12. Remove any other part that prevents engine removal: air cleaner, automatic transmission flywheel fasteners, and bell housing bolts. Refer to Fig. 46-2.

REMOVING TRANSMISSION WITH ENGINE

It is sometimes necessary or desirable to remove the engine and transmission together. Some front-wheel drive vehicles that use a transaxle, require that the two be removed as a unit. Check in a service manual for details.

You may want to drain the fluid from the transmission or transaxle if it is to be removed.

With rear-wheel drive, the drive shaft, transmission and clutch linkage, speedometer cable, rear motor mount, and other parts must also be removed. With a transaxle, the axle shafts must be disconnected.

ENGINE REMOVAL

Before engine removal, double-check that everything is disconnected or removed. For example, check:

1. Behind and under engine for hidden wires or ground straps.
2. That all bell housing bolts are out.
3. To see that you have removed the torque converter bolts (automatic transmission to stay in car).
4. That all fuel lines are disconnected and plugged.
5. That motor mounts are unbolted.
6. That a floor jack is supporting the transmission.

Installing lifting fixture or chain

Connect the lifting fixture or chain to the engine. Position the fixture at recommended lifting points. Sometimes brackets are provided on the engine.

If a lifting chain is to be used, fasten it to the engine as shown in Fig. 46-3. Install a bolt, nut, and washers on the chain to keep it from slipping and dropping the engine.

If bolts are used to secure the chain to the engine, make sure they are large enough in diameter and that they are fully installed. The bolts must not be too long (stick out from chain) or too short (they must thread into hole a distance that is equal to one and one-half times thread diameter).

Generally, position the fixture or chain so that it will raise the engine in a level manner. If one lifting point is at the right-front of the cylinder head, the other should be on the left-rear of the head. Use common sense and follow manufacturer's instructions.

Lifting engine out of car

Attach the lifting device (crane or hoist) to the fixture or chain on the engine. Fig. 46-4 shows the use of a portable crane. Make sure the crane boom or hoist is centered directly over the engine. Place a floor jack under the transmission.

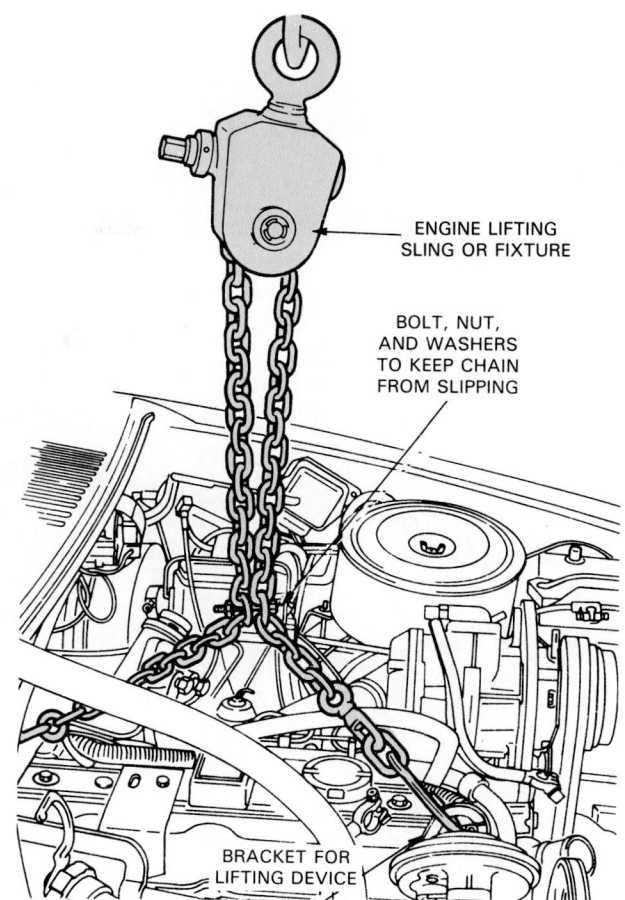

Fig. 46-3. Make sure lifting chain or fixture is attached properly. Note how this engine has factory eye type brackets for engine removal. If chain is attached with bolts, make sure bolts are strong enough and fully threaded into holes. (Ford)

Raise the engine slowly about an inch or two. Then check that everything is out of the way and disconnected.

DANGER! Never place any part of your body under an engine held in the air. A heavy engine can chop off fingers, cripple, or even kill you if dropped!

Continue raising the engine while pulling forward. This will separate the engine from the transmission or slide the transmission out from under the firewall. Do not let the engine bind or damage parts.

When the engine is high enough to clear the radiator support, roll the crane and engine straight out and away from the car. With a stationary hoist, roll the car out from under the engine.

Do NOT let a transmission hang unsupported after engine removal. This could damage the rear, rubber mount or the drive shaft (rear-wheel drive car). See Fig. 46-5 for one method of holding transmission.

Note! With some front-wheel drive cars, the engine and transaxle are removed from below the vehicle. With some vans, the engine must be removed through the large door in the side of the body. Again, check a service manual for details.

As soon as you can, lower the engine to the ground or mount it on an engine stand. See Fig. 46-6.

DANGER! NEVER work on an engine that is held

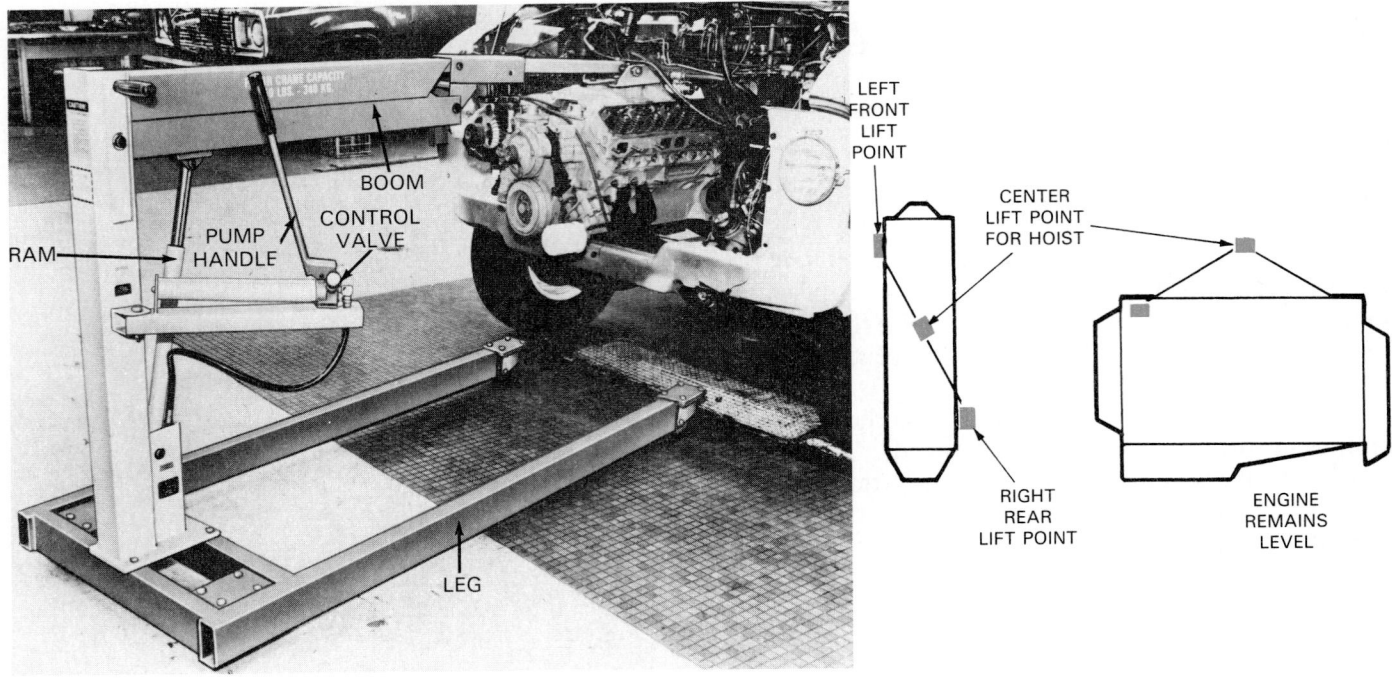

Fig. 46-4. A — Crane is handiest method for lifting engine out of vehicle. Pump handle to operate hydraulic ram that raises boom. Small valve should be slowly opened to lower boom and engine after removal. B — Typical lift points. (Owatonna Tool Co.)

by a crane or hoist. The engine could shift and fall, damaging the engine or causing serious injury!

Keep your work area clean

Coolant and engine oil will usually drip onto the shop floor during engine removal. To prevent an accident, wipe up spills as soon as they occur. There is nothing professional about trying to work in a "grease pit."

ENGINE DISASSEMBLY

With the engine bolted to an engine stand or sitting on blocks, you are ready to begin teardown. During engine teardown, go slowly and inspect each part for signs of trouble. Look for wear, cracks, damage, seal leakage, or gasket leakage.

Remember! If you overlook one problem, your engine repair may fail in service. All of your work could be for nothing.

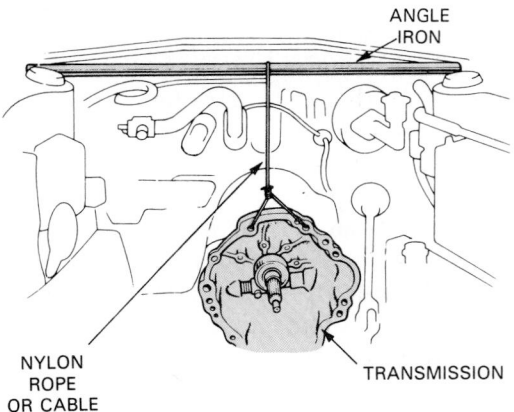

Fig. 46-5. If transmission is not removed, it must be supported. Note use of angle iron and rope to hold up on transmission, protecting rear mount and drive line. (Toyota)

Fig. 46-6. Engine stand makes engine repair much easier. Engine can be rotated into different positions. Also note catch pan for dripping oil and coolant. (OTC Division of SPX Corp.)

Teardown methods vary somewhat from engine to engine. However, general procedures are similar and apply to all engines. The following will serve as a guide:

Engine top end disassembly

The engine top end generally includes the valve train and cylinder head related components. These are normally the first parts of the engine to be serviced.

1. Remove external engine parts (carburetor, fuel rail or throttle body unit, spark plug wires, distributor, etc.). Take off all parts that could be damaged or that would prevent the later removal of the cylinder head.
2. Figs. 46-7 and 46-8 show exploded views of a modern engine. These types of service manual illustrations can be helpful during teardown and reassembly.
3. Unbolt the valve cover(s), exhaust manifold(s), and intake manifold. If light prying is needed, be careful not to damage the mating surfaces.
4. Keep groups of fasteners organized in different containers. Note odd bolt lengths. Inspect the gaskets and mating surfaces for signs of leakage. If leaking, use a straightedge to check for warpage. If not true or flat, the manifolds must be milled (machined).
5. With V-type push rod engines, you may need to remove the valve train components before the intake manifold. The push rods can pass through the bottom of the intake.
6. If the lifters, push rods, and rocker arms are to be reused, keep them in exact order. Use an ORGANIZING TRAY (tray or board with holes in it for push rods and lifters) or label these parts with masking tape. Wear patterns and select-fit parts require that most components be installed

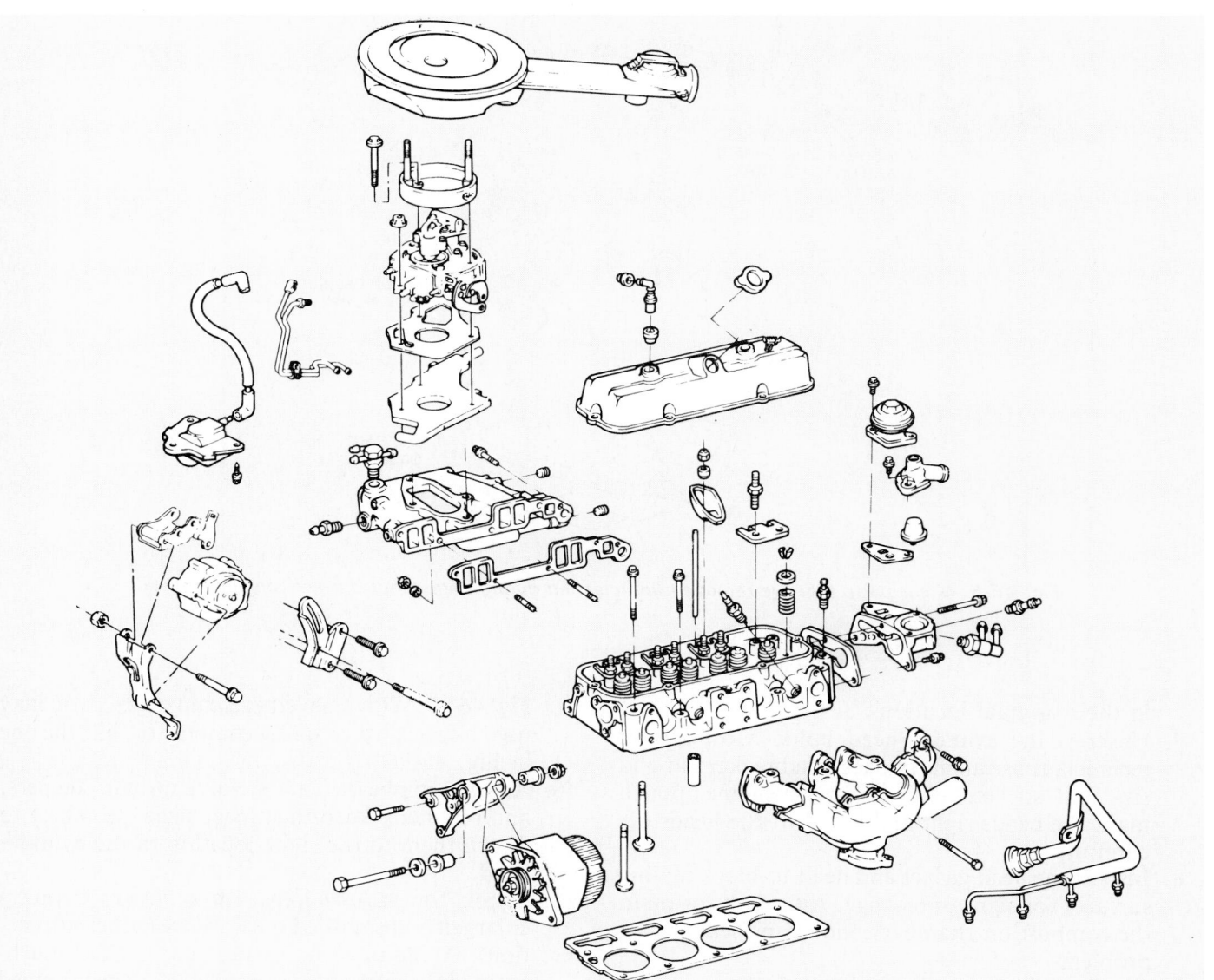

Fig. 46-7. Exploded view of engine may be helpful during disassembly and reassembly. Find one for your engine in service manual. Can you identify every part? If you cannot, refer to earlier chapters for a quick review.

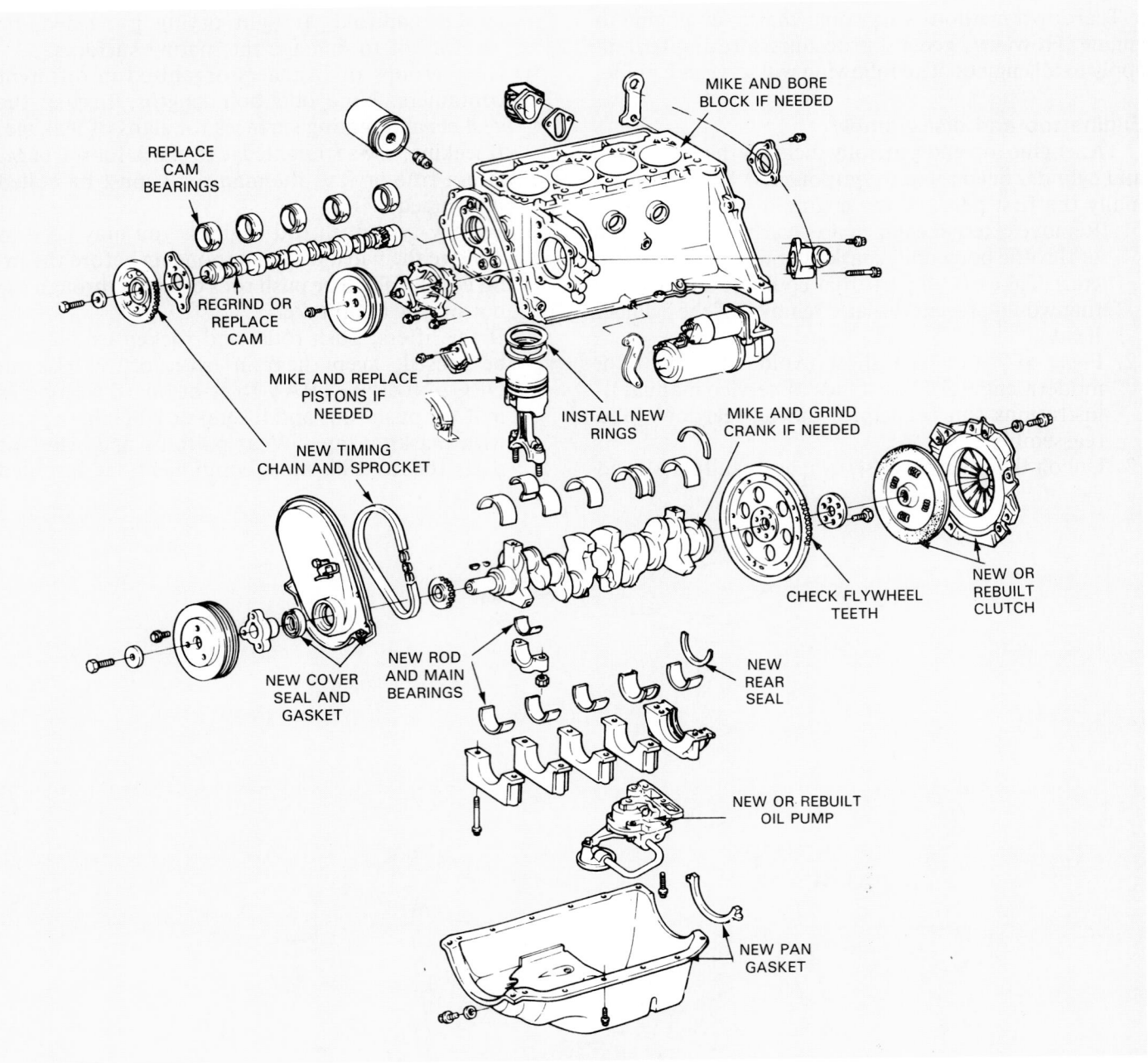

Fig. 46-8. Major parts that are removed and cleaned during engine bottom end service. (Buick)

in their original locations.

7. Unscrew the cylinder head bolts. Most service technicians use an air impact or a breaker bar and six-point socket. With a V-type engine, punch mark the heads right and left. Lift the heads off carefully.

8. Inspect the head gasket and head-to-block mating surfaces for signs of leakage. Also look for oil in the combustion chambers, indicating seal or ring problems.

9. Disassemble the cylinder head(s). Use a *valve spring compressor* to compress the valve springs, as in Fig. 46-9. This will let you lift off the keepers,

Fig. 46-10. With an overhead cam engine, you may need a special valve spring compressor, like the one in Fig. 46-11.

10. As you remove the valves, valve springs, keepers, and retainers, keep them organized. It is best to return them to the same location in the cylinder head.

11. Check for *mushroomed valve stems* (stem tip enlarged and smashed outward by rocker arm action). A file must be used to cut off the mushroomed tip before valve removal. If a mushroomed valve stem is forced out, it can SCORE and CRACK the valve guide and head.

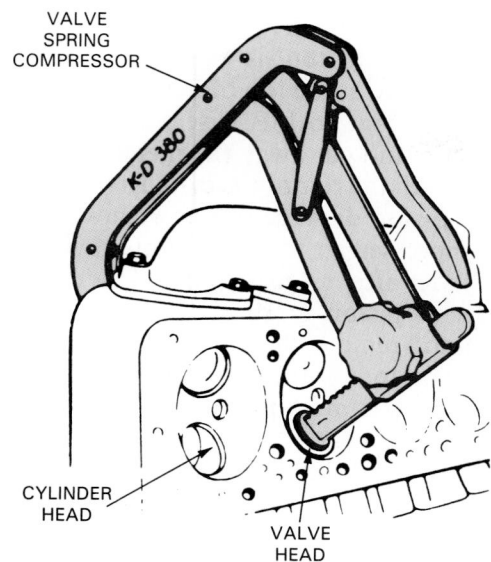

A

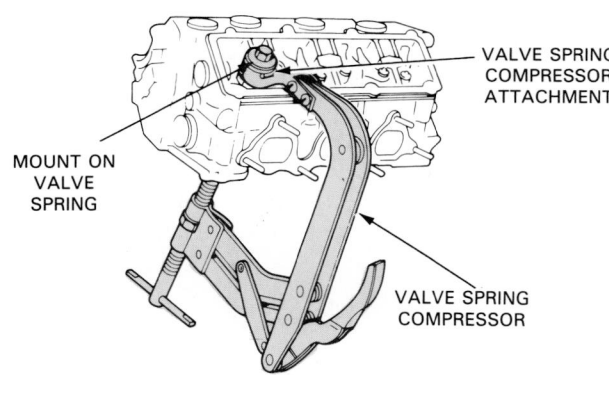

B

Fig. 46-9. To disassemble cylinder head, use valve spring compressor. One end of tool fits on valve head. Other end fits over valve spring retainer. A — Chamber view. B — Spring view.   (K-D Tools and Honda)

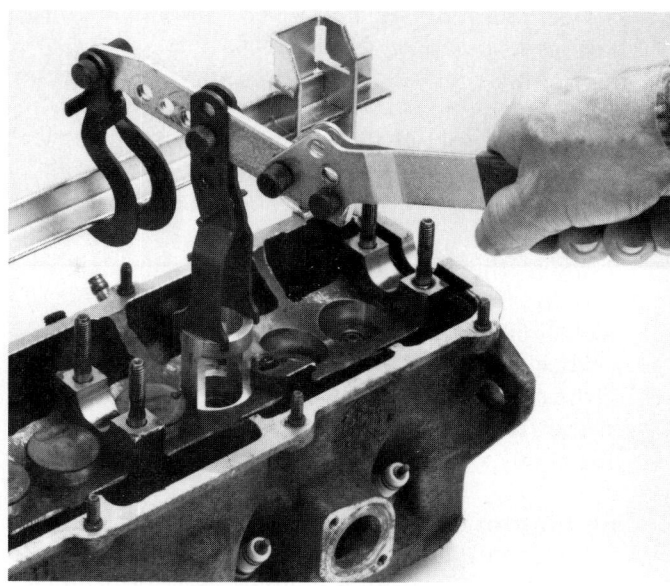

Fig. 46-11. A special valve spring compressor may be needed on modern OHC engine cylinder heads. Note how this one will operate in pocket formed around valve spring. (K-D Tools)

Engine front end disassembly

Engine front end disassembly is simple if a few basic rules and service manual instructions are followed.

1. Remove the water pump and any other parts bolted in front of the engine timing cover. If a timing belt is used, remove the belt cover. Loosen the tensioner and slip off the belt (this would have to be done before cylinder head removal).

2. NOTE! Do not attempt to rotate the crankshaft of an OHC engine with the timing belt off (cylinder head still in place). The pistons could slide up and bend the valves.

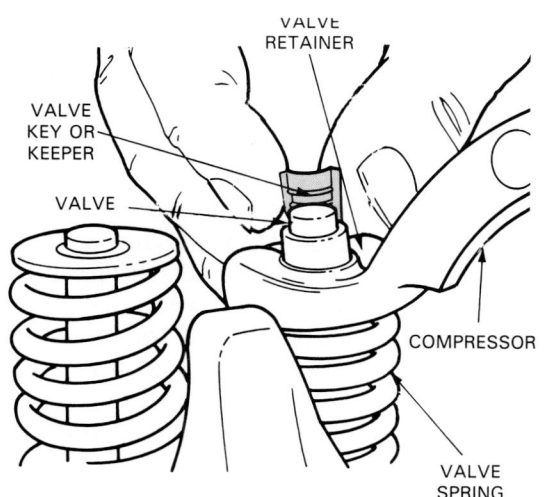

Fig. 46-10. With spring compressed, keepers can be lifted from their grooves. Release compressor and valve assemblies can be removed from head. (General Motors Corp.)

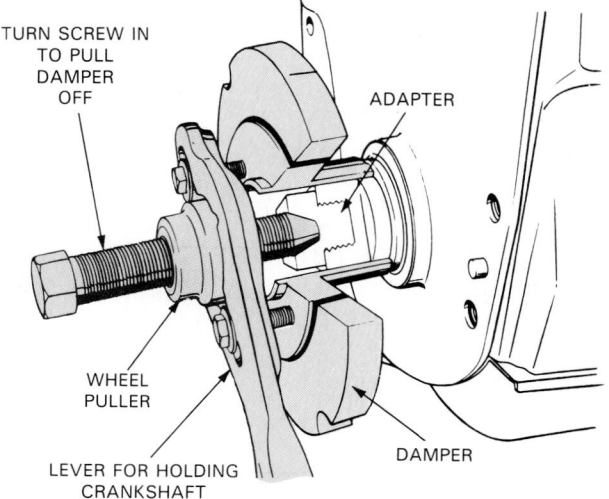

Fig. 46-12. Wheel puller is normally needed to force damper off of crankshaft snout. Use wrench to turn screw inward. This will force damper outward. (Buick)

3. A *wheel puller* is normally needed to remove the harmonic balancer or damper. The balancer is commonly press-fitted onto the crankshaft. Fig. 46-12 shows how to use a wheel puller.

4. Unbolt and remove the timing chain or gear cover. If prying is necessary, do it lightly while tapping with a rubber hammer. Do not bend or scar mating surfaces.

5. Remove the oil slinger and timing mechanism. Usually, the timing gears or sprockets will slide off after light taps with a brass hammer. If not, use a wheel puller.

6. If the oil pump or other components are mounted in the front cover, refer to a service manual for directions.

Engine bottom end disassembly

After top end and front end disassembly, you are ready to take the bottom end apart. The bottom end typically includes the pistons, rods, crankshaft, and related bearings.

1. Inspect the cylinders for signs of excess wear. Use your finger nail to feel for a lip or ridge at the top of the cylinder wall. See Fig. 46-13A.

   A *cylinder* or *ring ridge* may be formed at the top of the cylinder walls, where ring friction does not wear the cylinder.

2. A *ridge reaming tool* is needed to cut out and remove a ridge at the top of a worn cylinder. One is shown in Fig. 46-13B. Use a wrench to rotate the reamer and cut away the metal lip. Cut until FLUSH with the rest of the cylinder wall. This will prevent piston damage during removal.

3. Use compressed air to blow metal shavings out of the cylinder after ridge reaming. This will prevent cylinder or piston scoring.

4. Unbolt and remove the oil pan and oil pump. Inspect the bottom of the pan for debris. Metal chips and plastic bits may help you diagnose and find engine problems.

5. Unbolt one of the connecting rod caps. Then, use a wooden hammer handle to tap the piston and rod out of the cylinder. Refer to Fig. 46-14.

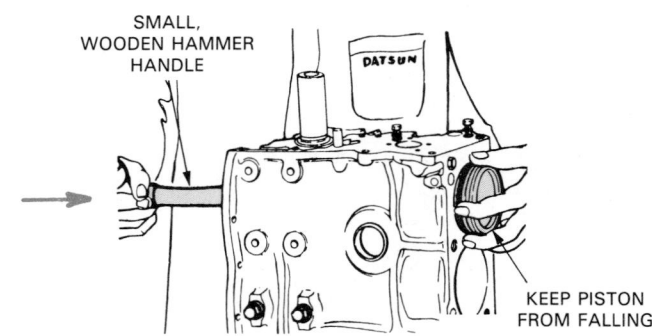

Fig. 46-14. To remove pistons, unbolt rod cap. Use a wooden hammer handle to carefully tap assembly out of block. (Nissan)

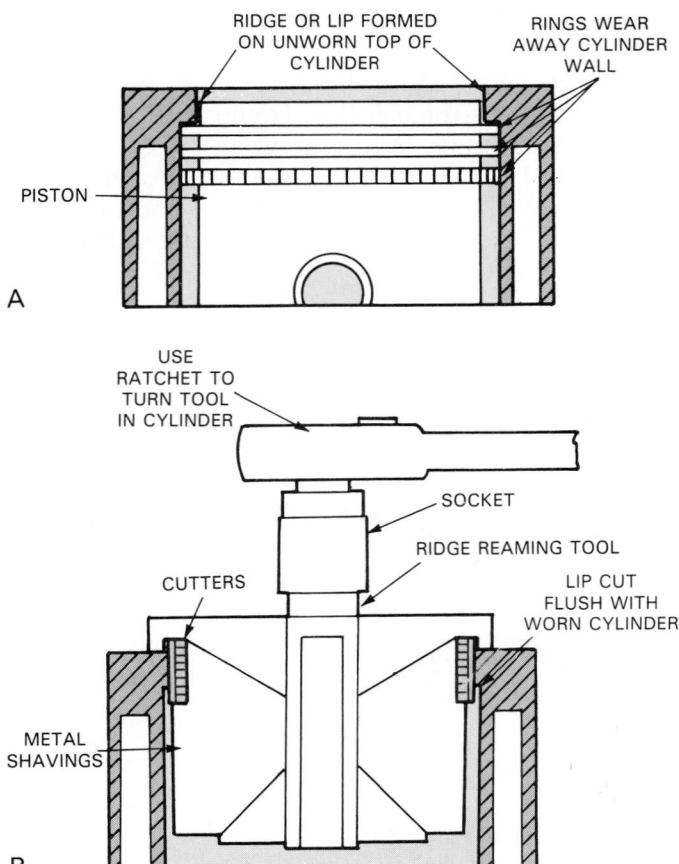

Fig. 46-13. A — If cylinder is badly worn, ridge forms at top of cylinder wall. B — Ridge reamer cuts off this lip so rings will not catch and damage piston during removal.

6. As soon as the piston is out, replace the rod cap. Also, check the piston head and connecting rod for identification markings. The piston will usually have an arrow pointing to the front of the engine. The connecting rod and rod cap should have numbers matching the cylinder number. This is shown in Fig. 46-15.

7. If needed, mark the piston heads with arrows or numbers. Also, if needed, number the connecting rods. If you mix up the pistons or rod caps, severe problems can develop when trying to reassemble the engine. This topic is discussed further in Chapter 48.

8. Remove the other piston and rod assemblies one at a time. Reinstall each cap on its rod. Mark them if needed.

9. Remove all of the old rings from their pistons. Spiral the rings off with your fingers or use a ring expander, Fig. 46-16.

10. If the car has a manual transmission, check for flywheel warpage. Use a dial indicator setup, as illustrated in Fig. 46-17.

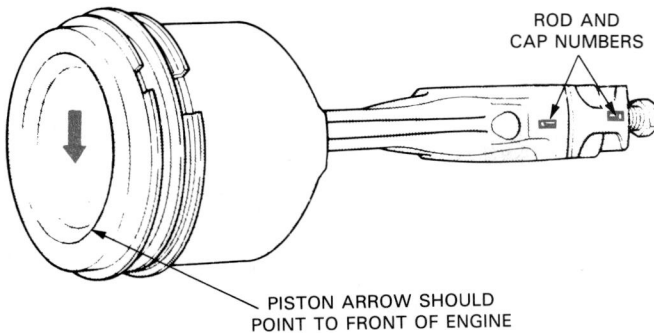

Fig. 46-15. As soon as piston and rod assembly is removed, check it for markings. Numbers on cap and rod are same to make sure caps are not mixed up. Arrow on piston is needed when pistons are removed from rod. They show how pistons go back on rod and in block. Number or mark parts if needed. (Chrysler)

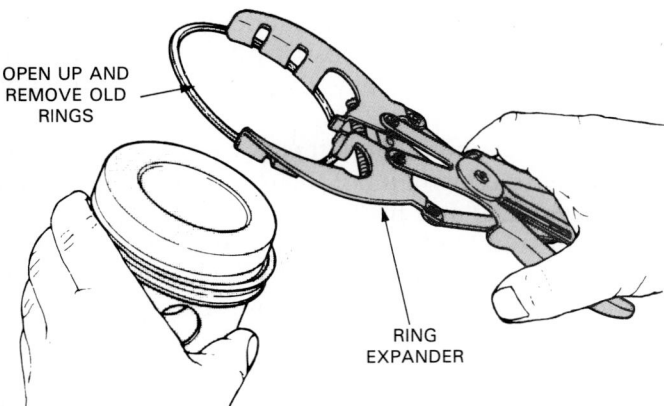

Fig. 46-16. You can remove old rings by hand or with ring expander, as shown. Inspect for groove wear or damage as you work. (Chrysler Corp.)

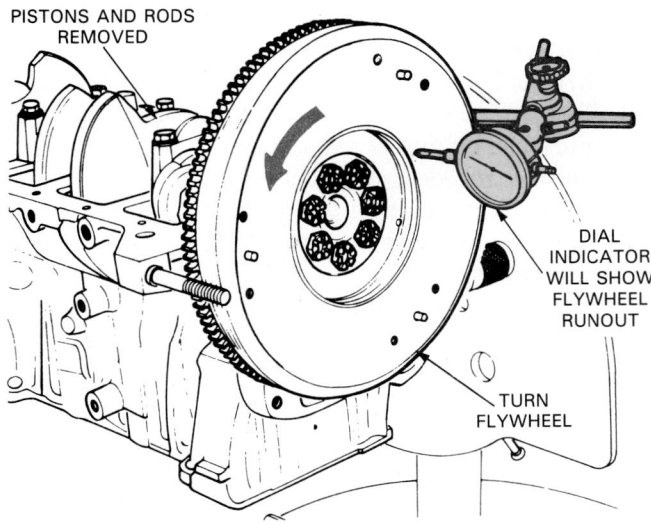

Fig. 46-17. With pistons out of block, check for flywheel warpage. Mount dial indicator on block. Position pointer parallel with surface of flywheel. Rotate flywheel. Indicator will show runout or warpage. If beyond specs, send flywheel to machine shop. (Renault)

Turn the crankshaft while noting the indicator reading. The crank will turn easily with all of the piston out of the block. If runout is beyond specs, send flywheel to a machine shop for resurfacing.

11. Before removing the main bearing caps, check that they are numbered. Normally, numbers and arrows are cast on each cap. Number one cap is at the front of the engine. See Fig. 46-18.

12. If needed, use a *number set* (punch set for indenting numbers in metal parts) or a center punch to mark the main caps. If the caps are mixed up, the crank bore may be misaligned and the crank can lock in the bore and main bearings during reassembly.

13. Unbolt the main caps. To remove the caps, wiggle them back and forth while pulling. Then, lift the crankshaft carefully out of the block. Do NOT hit and nick the journals.

14. If the engine is old, pry out the block and head core or freeze plugs. They rust out and will leak after prolonged service. This also must be done if the block is going to be *boiled* (cleaned in strong chemicals at machine shop to remove mineral deposits in water jackets).

15. If the cylinders have deep ridges, the block must be sent to a machine shop for boring and hot tank cleaning. Make sure all external hardware (motor mount brackets, oil and coolant temperature sending units) are removed.

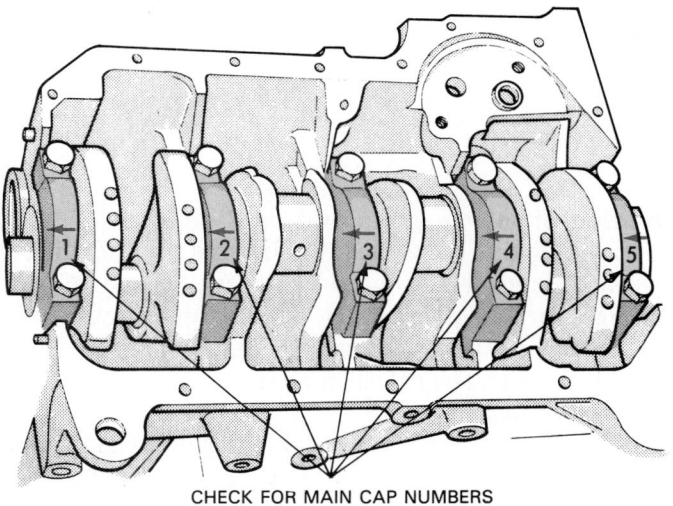

Fig. 46-18. Before removing block main caps, make sure they are identified with arrows and numbers. Number them if needed. Main caps must be reinstalled in same location or block bore will be misaligned. (Chrysler)

CLEANING ENGINE PARTS

After you have removed all of the parts from the engine block and cylinder head, everything should be cleaned. Different cleaning techniques are needed depending upon part construction and type of material.

Closer part inspection can be done during and after part cleaning. Problems can be hard to see when a part is covered with oil, grease, or carbon deposits, as in Fig. 46-19.

A

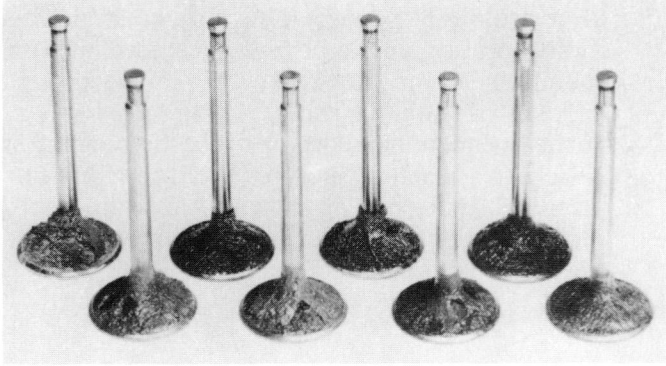

B

Fig. 46-19. Thorough cleaning of engine parts is very important. Note two major types of engine deposits: A — Sludge and oil film. B — Hard carbon deposits. Different cleaning methods are used on each. (Texaco)

Scrape off old gaskets and hard deposits

Begin engine parts cleaning by scraping off all old gasket material and hard deposits. Scrape off the gaskets for the valve covers, head, front cover, intake manifold, oil pan, and other components. See Fig. 46-20. Also scrape off as much hardened oil and carbon as you can.

Use a dull scraper and work carefully when cleaning soft aluminum parts. The slightest nick, in a cylinder head for instance, could cause head gasket leakage when returned to service.

WARNING! When using a gasket scraper, push the scraper away from your body, NOT toward your body. A scraper can inflict serious cuts.

Use cleaning solvent

After scraping off the gaskets, use cleaning solvent to remove hard-to-reach deposits.

A *hot tank* is a large cleaning machine filled with strong, corrosive chemicals. One is pictured in Fig.

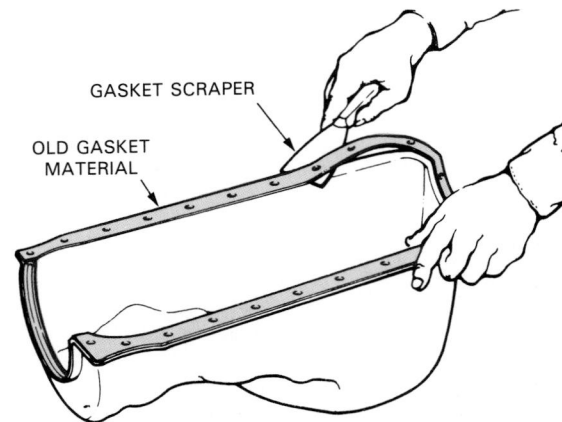

GASKET SCRAPER

OLD GASKET MATERIAL

Fig. 46-20. Use a scraper to remove old, thick gaskets from mating surfaces on parts. A dull scraper should be used on soft aluminum parts to avoid nicks. (Ford Motor Co.)

46-21A. It will remove mineral deposits in the water jackets, hard carbon deposits, oil, grease, and even paint. Automotive machine shops normally have a hot tank.

Note! Aluminum components can be corroded or etched by soaking in a hot tank. Clean only cast iron and steel parts in a hot tank.

A *cold soak tank* is a cleaning machine for removing oil and grease from parts. It will NOT remove hard carbon or mineral deposits. Most auto shops have a cold cleaning tank or machine, Fig. 46-21B. It has a pump and filter that circulates clean solvent out of a spout. To wash off parts, direct the stream of solvent on the part while rubbing with a soft bristle brush. Refer to Fig. 46-22.

DANGER! Never use gasoline to clean parts. The slightest spark or flame could ignite the fumes, causing a deadly fire!

Use power cleaning tools

There are several power cleaning tools used by the professional mechanic. If used properly, they can speed up and ease engine repairs.

A *power brush* is driven by an air or electric drill to remove hard carbon. Look at Fig. 46-23. It is especially handy inside hard-to-reach areas — combustion chambers, for example. Fig. 46-24 shows two more types of power cleaning tools.

DANGER! Always wear eye protection when cleaning parts with power tools. Metal bristles, bits of carbon, or metal chunks from tool or part breakage can fly into your face.

A *wire wheel* on a grinder is another common method of cleaning engine parts. Frequently it is used to clean carbon off valves. Keep the safety shield and tool rest in place.

Special cleaning tools

Other special cleaning tools may also be needed for

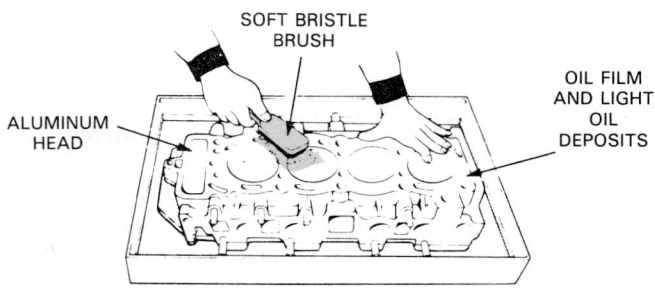

Fig. 46-22. Rub soft bristle brush on parts while washing with cold soak solvent. This will clean off oil film and grease. This aluminum head must be cleaned carefully to avoid major damage. (Toyota)

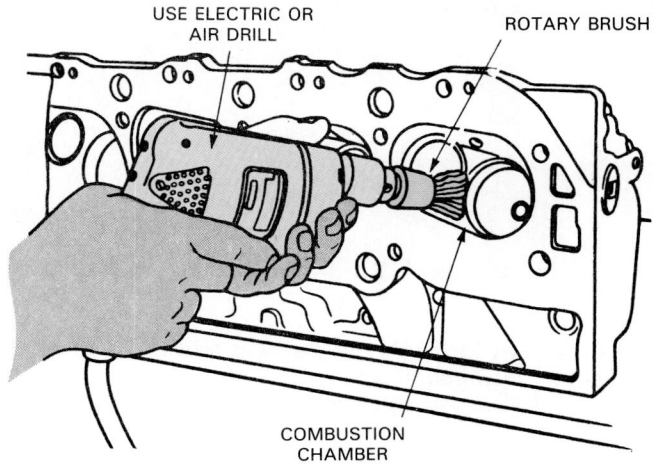

Fig. 46-23. Power brush is normally used to remove hard carbon in cylinder head combustion chambers. Do not use too much pressure or metal can be rubbed off. Do not let tool nick valve seats. (GMC)

engine components.

A *ring groove cleaner* is used to scrape carbon from inside piston ring grooves. It is a special cleaning tool commonly used during piston service. The groove cleaner is rotated around the piston. A scraper bit, the same size as the groove, removes the carbon, Fig. 46-25.

A *valve guide cleaner* is another special tool for use on engine cylinder heads. One is pictured in Fig. 46-26. It is inserted into each valve guide. An electric or air drill spins the tool to remove deposits.

Air blow gun

An *air blow gun* is normally the last method of cleaning parts. It uses pressure from the shop's air compressor to blow off small bits of dirt, solvent, water, and other debris.

When using a blow gun, direct the blast of air into all pockets and holes in parts. This will prepare the parts for reassembly.

WARNING! Use extreme care when using an air

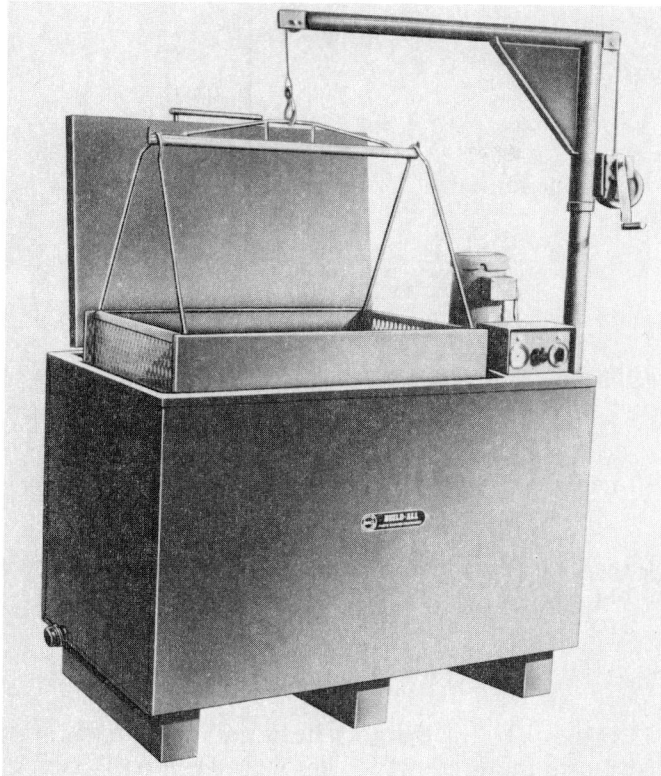

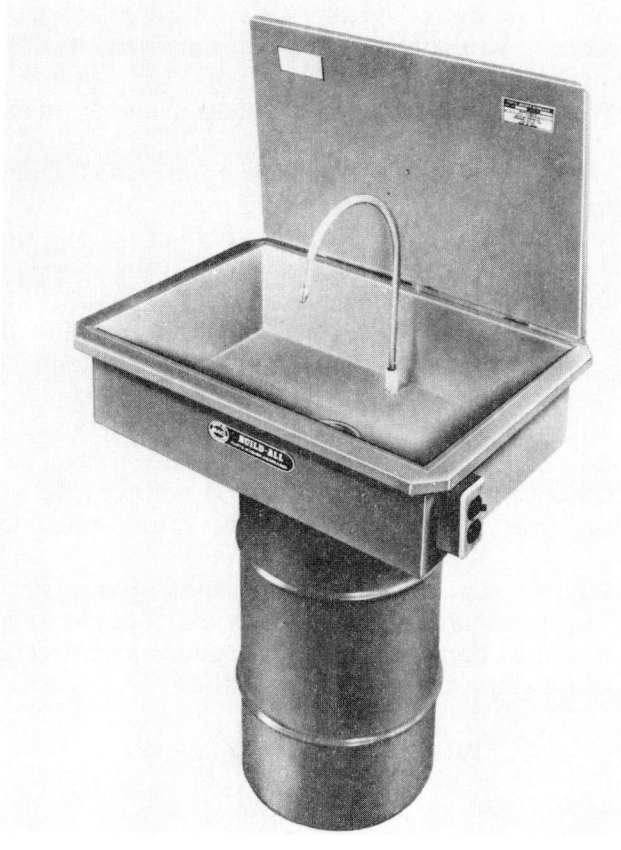

B

Fig. 46-21. Two types of cleaning machines. A — Large, hot tank cleaner is commonly found in automotive machine shops. Complete block can be lowered and cleaned, removing even hard carbon and mineral deposits. B — Smaller, cold soak cleaning machine is common in most auto shops. It will remove oil and grease, but not carbon deposits. (BAC)

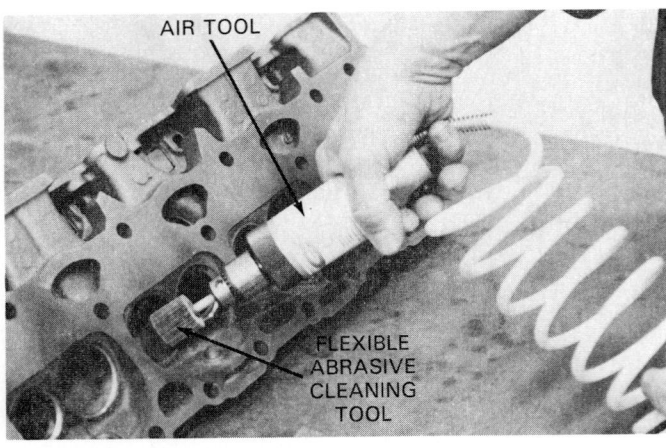

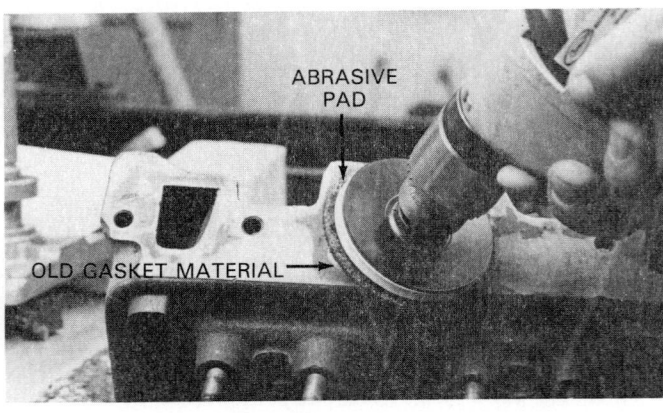

Fig. 46-24. Two other power cleaning tools: A — Flexible abrasive tool mounted in air tool. B — Disc abrasive tool in electric drill. (Goodson Auto Machine Shop Supplies)

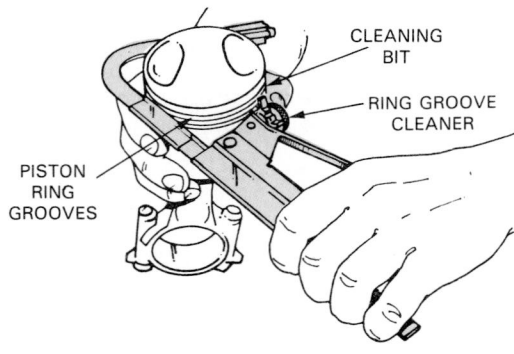

Fig. 46-25. Always use a ring groove cleaner to scrape carbon from piston grooves. If grooves are not cleaned, new rings can be forced out against cylinder wall, scoring rings and cylinder walls as soon as engine starts.   (Lisle Tools)

gun. Wear goggles and avoid aiming the gun at your body. If air bubbles enter your bloodstream, the result could be death!

KNOW THESE TERMS

Lifting fixture or chain, Engine crane, Organizing tray, Valve spring compressor, Mushroomed valve stem, Wheel puller, Ridge reamer, Number set, Boiling a block, Gasket scraper, Hot tank, Cold soak

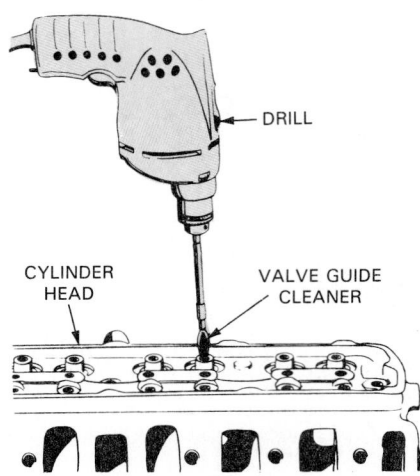

Fig. 46-26. Valve guide cleaner is needed to remove carbon. Use electric drill to spin tool while pulling up and down. Do not let tool come completely out of valve guide. (Oldsmobile)

cleaner, Power brush, Wire wheel, Ring groove cleaner, Valve guide cleaner, Air blow gun.

REVIEW QUESTIONS

1. Repairs to the cylinder head and valve train normally require engine removal. True or False?
2. List six things to double-check right before lifting an engine out of its chassis.
3. How do you keep a chain from slipping in its lifting hook?
4. Why should you support the transmission or transaxle after engine removal?
5. Which of the following statements does NOT apply to proper engine disassembly methods?
   a. Note bolt lengths and organize bolts in containers.
   b. Inspect gasket mating surfaces.
   c. Keep critical parts (lifter, valves, etc.) organized so they can be installed in same location.
   d. All of the above are true.
   e. None of the above are true.
6. A _____ _____ tool is used when the cylinders are badly worn. It will remove a lip at the top of the cylinders, preventing possible _____ damage.
7. Explain methods of cleaning automotive parts.
8. Do not use an air gun to blow off your clothing or hands because air entering your bloodstream could cause death. True or False?

ACTIVITIES FOR CHAPTER 46

1. Review the safety tips (printed in red) in this chapter. Use the information to create a small brochure or flyer that could be distributed to automotive technology students.
2. Show classmates how to remove piston rings with a ring expander, or by spiraling them off manually.

47 Engine Bottom End Service

After studying this chapter, you will be able to:
- Explain how to measure cylinder bore wear.
- Hone cylinder walls.
- Check block main bore straightness.
- Measure block, head, and manifold warpage.
- Measure piston wear and piston-to-cylinder clearance.
- Explain how to assemble a rod and piston.
- Describe how to check piston ring end gap, ring side clearance, and installation of piston rings.
- Measure crank journal wear and crankshaft straightness.
- Install a rear main oil seal.
- Use Plastigage to measure rod and main bearing clearance.
- Measure rod and crank side clearance.
- Properly assemble an engine bottom end.
- Describe safety practices to be followed while performing engine bottom end service.

In previous chapters, you learned how to diagnose engine problems, remove an engine from a vehicle, and disassemble, clean, and inspect the parts of an engine. This chapter will continue your study of engine service by detailing bottom end overhaul.

Engine *short block* (bottom end) service is needed after extended engine operation. Ring and cylinder wear can cause engine smoking and oil consumption. Bearing wear can also cause low oil pressure, bearing knock, or complete part failure. Fig. 47-1.

An *engine overhaul* involves the service of the engine bottom end, top end, and front end. All of the internal parts are serviced.

This chapter, Chapters 48 and 49, along with earlier chapters, will complete your study of engines. You should then be able to use a service manual to rebuild or overhaul a complete engine.

DO YOU NEED REVIEW?

You may want to refer to Chapter 41. It covers engine disassembly and several specialized tools (cylinder ridge reamer, piston ring groove cleaner, etc.) that are needed to properly service engine bottom end parts.

CYLINDER BLOCK SERVICE

Cylinder block service commonly includes measuring cylinders for wear, inspecting for cylinder wall damage, installing core plugs, honing or deglazing cylinders, and cleaning after honing. All of these operations are very important and essential to satisfactory engine operation.

Some cylinder block repairs, cylinder boring (machining), or crack repair, may require the special equipment found in a machine shop. This will be detailed later.

Servicing cylinder walls

Using a drop light, closely inspect the surface of each cylinder wall. Look for vertical scratches, scoring, or cracks. Rub your fingernail around in the cylinder. This will help you feel and locate problems.

If you had to remove a large ring ridge, the cylinder is badly worn. Cylinder boring and oversize pistons may be required.

Cylinder boring is done by machining the cylinders larger in diameter to make the cylinder walls perfectly smooth and straight. It is needed to remove scratches, scoring, or excess wear.

The block is sent to a machine shop for boring. The machine shop will have a large *boring bar* (machine tool) that can cut a thin layer of metal off the cylinder wall. Normally, a cylinder block is bored in increments of .010 in. or .025 mm (.030 or .060 in.) until the desired diameter is achieved.

The *overbore limit* (.030 to .060 in. typical) is the largest possible diameter increase a cylinder can be bored. It is a spec given by the engine manufacturer and can vary with block design. If the overbore limit is exceeded, the cylinder wall can become too thin. The wall can distort or crack in service from combustion heat and pressure.

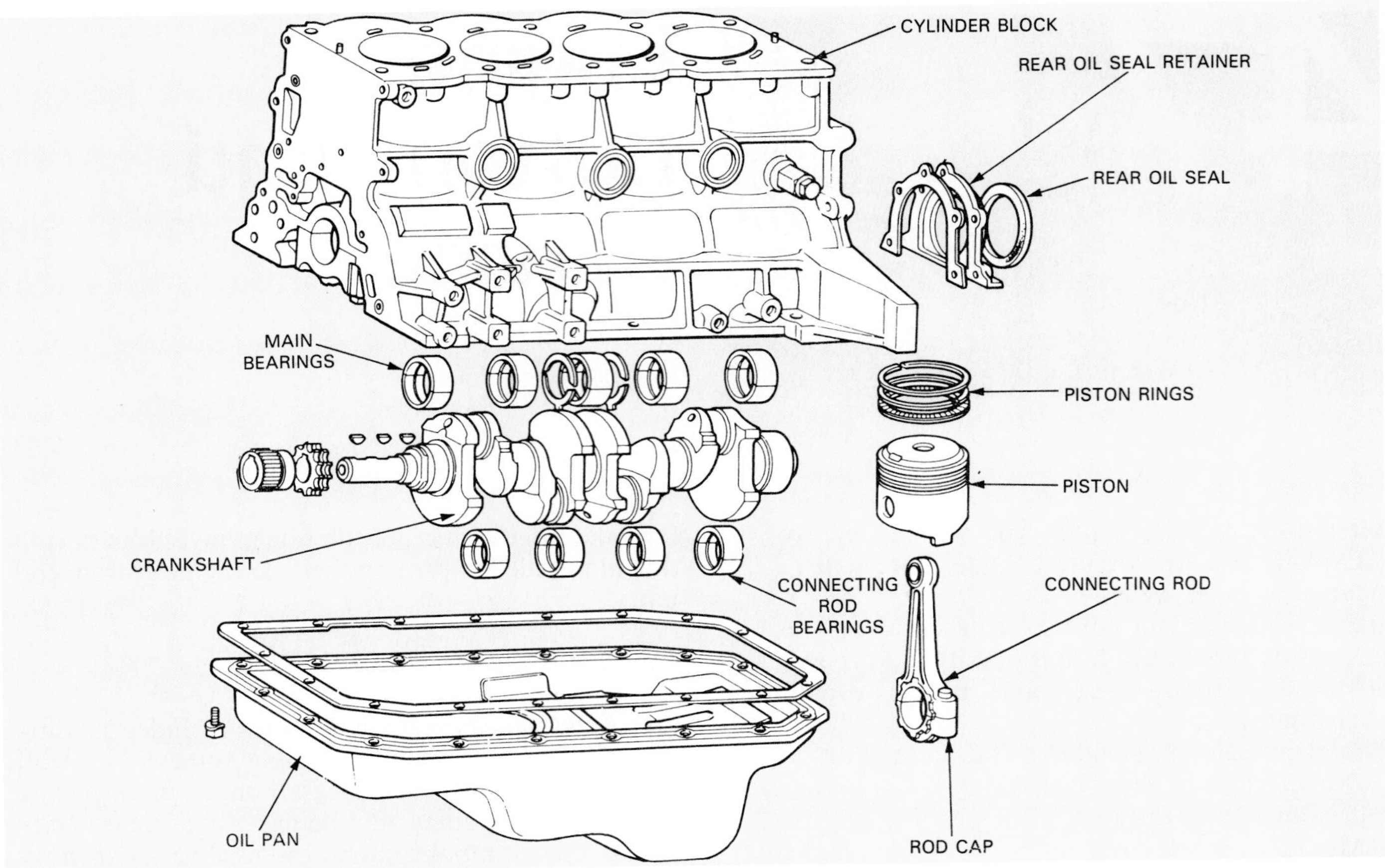

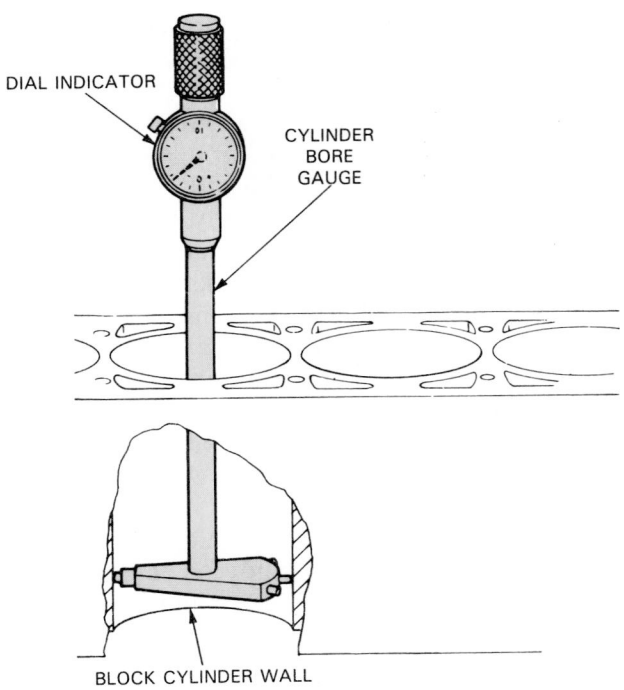

Fig. 47-1. These are major engine bottom end parts requiring service. Do you remember function and construction of each? If not, review earlier chapters. (Toyota)

Oversize pistons and *rings* are required to fit a cylinder block that has had its cylinders bored out. The pistons must be purchased to match the oversize of the cylinders.

Boring and oversize pistons will make the engine like new. New pistons and rings will operate on a freshly machined cylinder surface, providing excellent ring sealing and service life.

Cylinder sleeving involves machining one or more of the cylinders oversize and pressing in a cylinder liner. Sleeving is needed, for example, after part breakage has severely damaged (gouged, nicked, chipped, or cracked) the cylinder wall. The damage is too deep to clean up with boring.

Sleeving also allows the bad cylinder to be restored to its original diameter. The same size pistons can be reused. If only one piston is damaged, for instance, all of the other pistons and cylinders may be good and useable. This would save the customer money on the repair.

Measuring cylinder wear

If the cylinder is not badly scratched or scored, you must measure cylinder wear to assure that the new rings will seal properly. Obviously, new, round rings cannot seal in a worn, out-of-round, or tapered cylinder.

Fig. 47-2. Cylinder bore gauge is quick and easy way to check for wear in cylinder. Slide gauge up and down. Indicator movement indicates difference in diameter. (Chrysler)

Also, cylinder measurement will let you determine piston-to-cylinder clearance.

Cylinder taper is a difference in the diameter at the top and bottom of the cylinder. It is caused by less lubricating oil at the top of the cylinder. More oil splashes on the lower area of the cylinder. As a result, the top of the cylinder wears faster (larger) than the bottom, producing a taper.

Cylinder out-of-roundness is a difference in cylinder diameter when measured front-to-rear and side-to-side in the block. Piston thrust action normally makes the cylinders wear more at right angles to the centerline of the crankshaft or piston pins.

Cylinder taper should not exceed approximately .005 in. (0.13 mm). Some manufacturers do not permit even this much wear. Refer to a service manual for exact specs. If worn beyond limits, replace the block or bore the block and install oversize pistons.

A *dial bore gauge* is a quick and accurate tool for measuring cylinder taper. As shown in Fig. 47-2, slide the bore gauge up and down in the cylinder. Check both parallel and perpendicular to the crank bore centerline, as shown in Fig. 47-3.

An *inside micrometer* can also be used to measure cylinder wear. This is much more time-consuming, however. If needed, refer to Chapter 6, Automotive Measurement, for a review of measuring tools.

Cylinder honing

Cylinder honing, also called *deglazing,* is used to break the *glaze* (polished surface) on a used cylinder. It must also be used to smooth a very rough cylinder after boring. Most ring manufacturers recommend deglazing; some do not. Check the instructions provided with the new piston rings for details.

A *cylinder hone* produces a precisely textured, cross-hatched pattern on the cylinder to aid ring seating and sealing. Tiny scratches from the hone cause initial ring and cylinder wall break-in wear. This makes the ring fit in the cylinder perfectly after only a few minutes of engine operation.

There are several types of engine cylinder hones:
1. A BRUSH HONE has small balls of abrasive material formed on the ends of round metal brush bristles, Fig. 47-4. It is desirable when the cylinder is in good condition and requires very little honing.

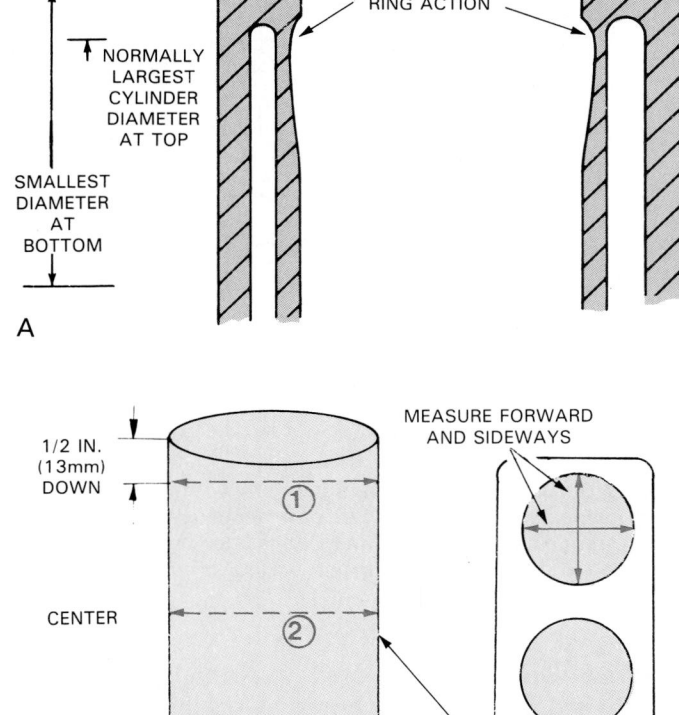

Fig. 47-4. When honing or deglazing cylinder, pull drill up and down, but do not let hone come out of cylinder. Check manual and equipment instructions for how long to hone each cylinder. Hone more at bottom than top to help remove taper. (Goodson Auto Machine Shop Supplies)

2. A FLEX HONE has hard, flat, abrasive stones attached to spring-loaded, movable arms. It is used when the cylinder wear is slight and a moderate amount of honing is needed.
3. A RIDGED or SIZING HONE has stationary, but adjustable, stones that lock into a preset position.

Fig. 47-3. A — Cylinder will wear more at top than bottom. There is more lubricating oil splashing on bottom of cylinder. B — Measure at top, center, and bottom as well as sideways and forward in block. This will let you detect taper and out-of-round.

It will remove a small amount of cylinder taper or out-of-roundness. A ridged hone can be used like a boring bar to true a cylinder when wear is within specs. Do NOT hone more than tool manufacturer recommendations, however.

To hone a cylinder, follow equipment manufacturers instructions. Install the hone in a large, low-speed electric drill. Compress the stones (squeeze inward) and slide them into the cylinder. Be careful not to scratch the cylinder. Turn on the electric drill and move the spinning hone up and down in the cylinder.

WARNING! Make sure you do NOT pull the hone completely out of the cylinder while honing. The hone could break and bits of stone fly out.

Move the hone up and down in the cylinder fast enough to produce a 50 to 60 degree CROSS-HATCH PATTERN. This is illustrated in Fig. 47-5. Moving the hone up and down faster or slower will change the pattern.

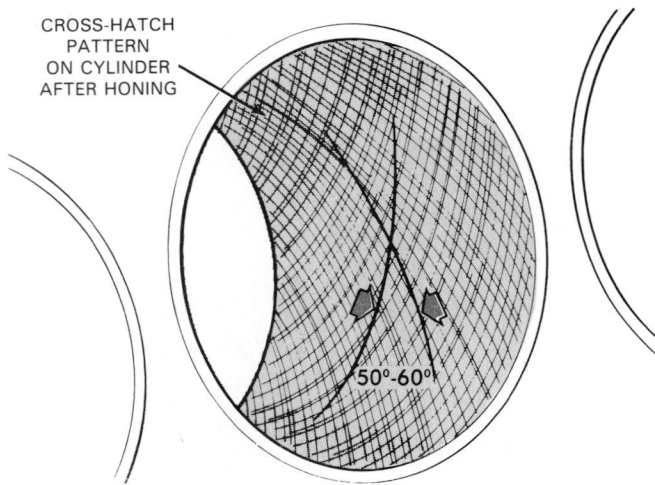

Fig. 47-5. When honing cylinder, try to produce a 50 to 60 degree cross-hatch pattern. Moving drill up and down faster or slower alters angle. (Chrysler)

Cleaning cylinder walls

After honing, it is very important to clean and remove all *honing grit* (bits of stone and metal) from inside the engine. This grit, if not removed, will act like grinding compound on bearings, rings, and other vital engine parts.

First, wash out the cylinders with warm WATER and SOAP (detergent). A soft bristle brush, NOT a wire brush, will quickly loosen and remove particles inside the hone marks. Blow the engine cylinders dry with compressed air.

Next, place motor oil on a clean shop rag. Wipe the cylinder down thoroughly with the OIL-SOAKED RAG. The heavy oil will pick up any remaining stone grit embedded in the cylinder honing marks. Wipe the cylinders down until the rag comes out perfectly clean.

After cleaning, recheck the cylinder for scoring or scratches. If honing did NOT clean up all of the vertical scratches in the cylinder, cylinder boring or sleeving may be needed.

New rings will NOT seal deep, vertical marks in the cylinder. Engine oil consumption and compression leakage may result.

Checking main bores

After repeated heating and cooling or overheating, the main bearing bores in the cylinder block can warp or twist. This will affect main bearing insert alignment and crankshaft fit in the block. Under severe cases of main bearing bore misalignment, the crankshaft can lock up when the main caps are torqued.

To measure main bearing bore alignment, lay a straightedge on the bores. See Fig. 47-6. Insert the thickest possible feeler gauge under the straightedge. The thickest blade that will fit indicates main bearing bore misalignment. ALWAYS check bore misalignment after main bearing failure.

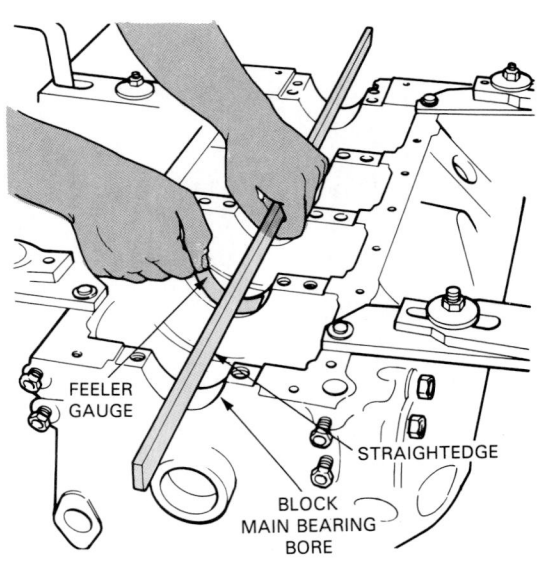

Fig. 47-6. After block overheating or physical damage, check main bearing bore alignment. Size of feeler gauge that fits under straightedge equals misalignment. If greater than specs, send block to machine shop for line boring. (Federal Mogul)

Block line boring is used to straighten or true misaligned main bearing bores. A machine shop will have a boring bar for machining the bore back into alignment. Line boring is becoming more common with today's thin-wall, lightly constructed blocks.

Measuring deck warpage

Deck warpage is measured with a straightedge and feeler gauge on the head gasket sealing surface of the block. It should be checked when the old head gasket was blown and leaking. It should also be done on late model aluminum blocks since they distort easily.

To check for block deck warpage, lay a straightedge on the clean block surface. Try to slip different thickness feeler gauge blades between the block and straightedge. The thickest blade that fits indicates warpage. Check in different locations and the block. See Fig. 47-7.

If beyond specs (about .003 to .005 in. or 0.08 to 0.13 mm), replace the block or send it to a machine shop for surface milling.

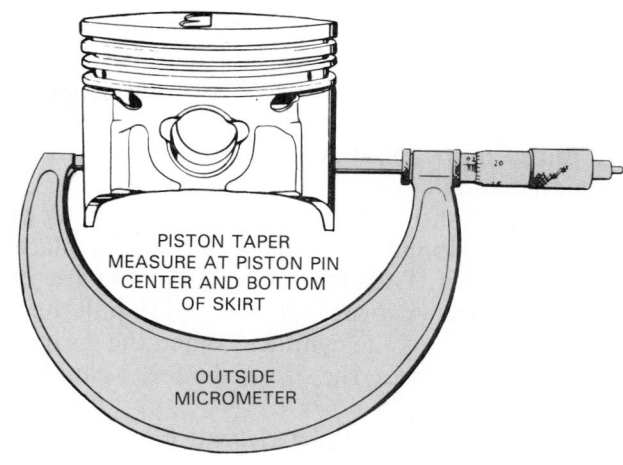

Fig. 47-8. Outside micrometer is used to measure piston diameter and wear. To measure taper, measure on skirt bottom and on skirt even with pin hole. To measure piston size, measure about 3/4 in. (19 mm) down from pin hole on skirt. (Pontiac)

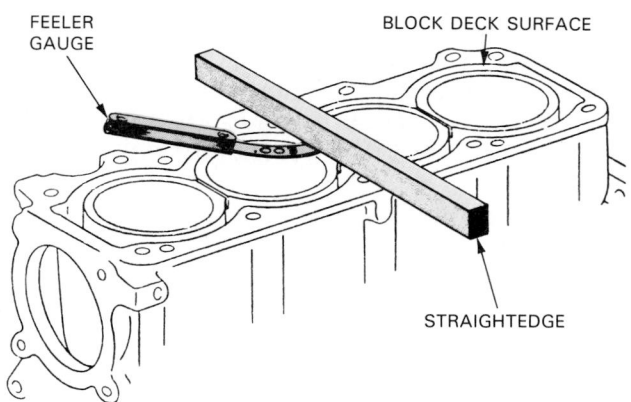

Fig. 47-7. Block warpage should be checked after overheating or at any overhaul of today's, thin-wall aluminum blocks. Use straightedge and feeler gauge. Warpage is usually greatest between two center cylinders. (Sealed Power)

PISTON SERVICE

Pistons are made of aluminum, which is very prone to wear and damage. It is very critical that each piston be checked thoroughly. Look for cracked skirts, worn ring grooves, cracked ring lands, pin bore wear, or other problems. You must find any trouble that could affect piston performance and engine service life.

Cleaning piston ring grooves (using a ring groove cleaner) was covered in Chapter 46. Review this material if needed.

Measuring piston wear

A large outside micrometer is used to measure piston wear. Mike readings are compared to specs to find wear.

Piston size is measured on the skirts, just below the piston pin hole, as in Fig. 47-8. Adjust the micrometer for a slight drag as it is pulled over the piston. If worn more than specs, replace or knurl (denting operation that raises surface) the piston(s).

Piston taper is measured by comparing piston diameter at the top (even with pin hole) and bottom of the skirt. The difference in the two measurements equals piston taper. If not within service manual limits, replace or knurl the pistons.

Knurling a piston

Piston knurling can be used to increase the diameter of the skirt a few thousandths of an inch (hundredths of a mm). A machine shop can usually knurl pistons using the operation shown in Fig. 47-9. Knurling makes dents in the skirts, pushing up metal next to the dents. This increases piston diameter.

Fig. 47-9. Piston knurling increases piston skirt diameter. It can be used to correct small amount of wear and restore proper piston dimensions. (Deere & Co.)

Measuring piston clearance

To find *piston clearance,* subtract piston diameter from cylinder diameter. The difference between the cylinder bore measurement and the piston diameter measurement will equal piston clearance.

Average piston-to-cylinder clearance is about .001 in. (0.025 mm). Since specs vary, always refer to the service manual.

Fig. 47-10 shows another way of measuring piston clearance. A long, flat feeler gauge strip is placed on the piston skirt. Then the gauge and piston are pushed into a cylinder. A spring scale is used to pull the feeler gauge strip out of the cylinder. When the spring scale reading equals specs, the size of the feeler gauge equals piston clearance.

When piston-to-cylinder clearance is excessive, you must either:

1. Knurl the pistons.
2. Install new standard size pistons (providing cylinders are not worn beyond specs).
3. Bore the cylinders and purchase oversize pistons.
4. Sleeve the cylinders.

Measuring piston ring side clearance

Piston ring side clearance is the space between the side of a compression ring and the inside of the piston groove. Ring groove wear tends to increase this clearance. If worn too much, the ring will not be held square against the cylinder wall. Oil consumption and smoking can result.

To measure ring side clearance, obtain the new piston rings to be used during the overhaul. As in Fig. 47-11, insert the new ring into its groove. Then slide a feeler gauge between the ring and groove.

The largest feeler gauge that fits between the ring and groove indicates ring side clearance. The top ring groove is usually checked because it suffers from more combustion heat and wear than the second groove.

If ring side clearance is beyond specs, either replace the pistons or have a machine shop fit ring spacers in the grooves.

Ring spacers are thin steel rings that fit next to the compression rings. The piston groove is machined wider to accept the spacer. This will restore ring side clearance to desired limits.

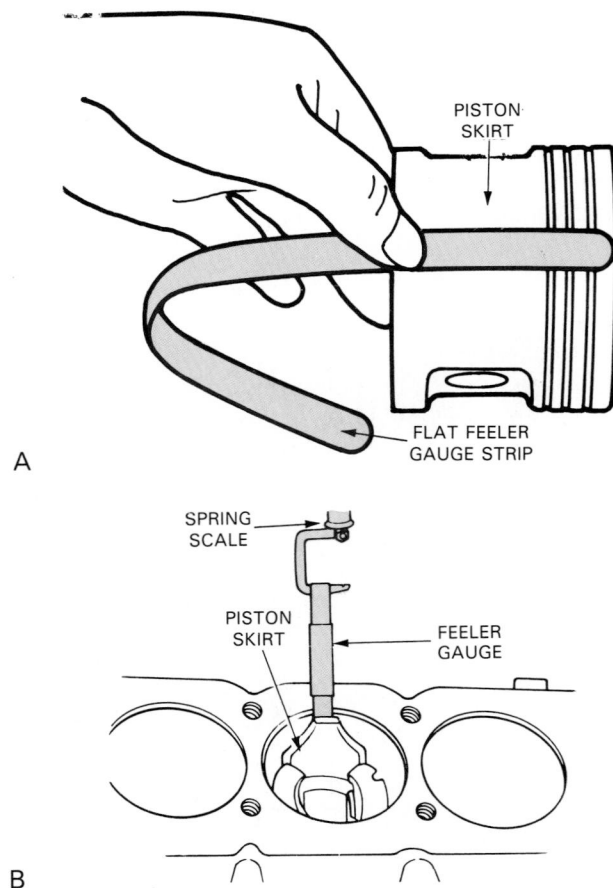

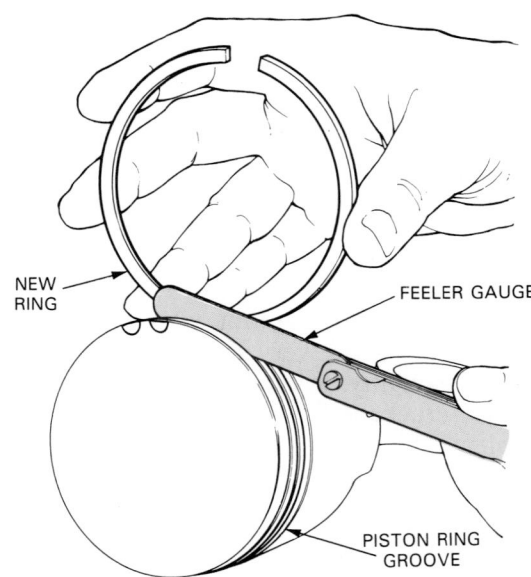

Fig. 47-11. To measure ring side clearance, fit ring into its groove. Then, find feeler gauge that will fit snugly into groove next to piston ring. Feeler gauge size equals ring side clearance. If greater than specs, ring groove is worn or you have wrong piston ring set for engine. (Chrysler)

Fig. 47-10. Measuring piston clearance can be done with feeler gauge and spring scale. A — Place long, strip feeler gauge on piston skirt. Insert piston and gauge into cylinder. B — Use spring scale to pull piston out of cylinder. When spring scale reads within specs, feeler gauge size equals piston clearance. Refer to the service manual for details. (Chevrolet)

Measuring piston ring gap

Discussed in earlier chapters, *piston ring gap* (clearance between ends of ring when installed in cylinder) is very important. If the gap is too small, the ring could lock up or score the cylinder upon heating and expanding. If the ring gap is too large, ring tension against the cylinder wall may be low, causing blowby.

To check ring gap, compress and place a compression ring in its cylinder. Then, push the ring to the bottom of normal ring travel with the head of a piston. This will square the ring in the cylinder and locate it at the smallest cylinder diameter.

Illustrated in Fig. 47-12, measure ring gap with a flat feeler gauge. Compare to specs. If not correct, you may have the wrong piston ring set or cylinder dimensions may be off.

Some manufacturers allow *ring filing* (using a special, thin grinding wheel to remove metal) to increase piston ring gap. Others do not!

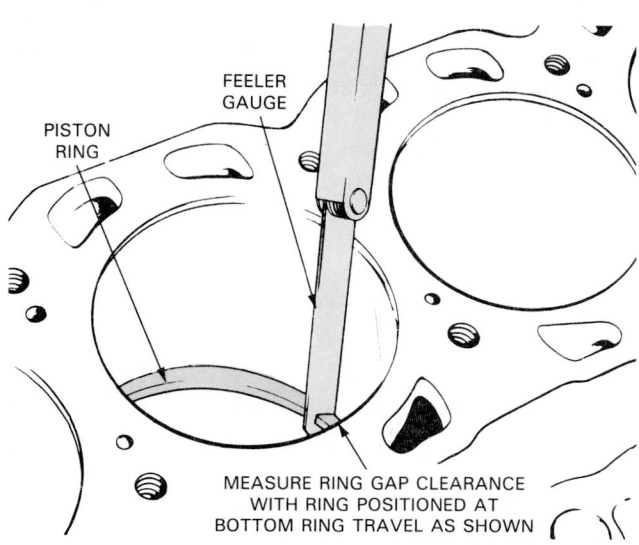

Fig. 47-12. To measure piston ring end gap, install and push ring to bottom of ring travel with head of piston. Use feeler gauge to measure gap. If too small, check ring size or file ends. If too large, double-check cylinder dimensions and rings. (Cadillac)

PISTON PIN SERVICE

Depending upon the type and make of engine, the piston pin may either be *free-floating* (pin will turn in both rod and piston) or *press-fit* (pin force-fitted in rod but turns in piston). Other setups have been manufactured but are not common.

During piston and rod service, check the pin clearance on both floating and pressed-in pins. Check pin-to-connecting rod fit on floating type piston pins. With pressed-in pins, the piston pin should be locked tightly in the connecting rod.

To check for excessive piston pin clearance, clamp the connecting rod I-beam lightly in a vise. Holding the piston in one position, rock the piston against normal pin movement. If play can be detected, the pin, rod bushing, or piston bore is worn. A small telescoping gauge and outside micrometer should be used to measure exact part wear after pin removal.

Free-floating pin service

To remove a free-floating pin from the piston, use snap ring pliers to compress and lift out the snap rings on each end of the pin. Then, push the pin out of the piston with your thumb. A brass drift and light hammer blows may be needed. Refer to Fig. 47-13.

When the pin is worn, it should be replaced. If the pin bore in the pistons measures larger than specs, replace the pistons. The pin bore may also be reamed larger. Oversize piston pins can then be used. Pin bore reaming is usually done by a machine shop.

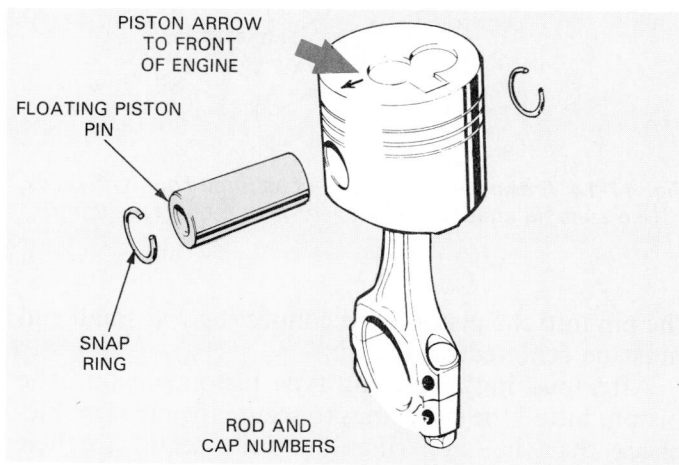

Fig. 47-13. Floating piston pin is held by snap rings. Pin should slide in and out of piston and rod with fingers or with light taps with brass drift and hammer. Make sure piston notch or arrow and rod numbers are facing properly. Most pistons can only be installed on rod in one direction. Piston pin offset or valve reliefs must face correctly. (Volvo)

Pressed-in pin service

To remove a pressed-in piston pin, you will need to use a press and a driver setup similar to the one shown in Fig. 47-14. Wear eye protection and make sure the piston is mounted properly.

Measure pin and pin bore wear. Compare to specs and replace or repair parts as needed. Many shops send new pistons and pins to a machine shop for fitting (honing piston pin bores to correct clearance).

Piston pin installation

Before installing a piston pin, make sure the piston is facing in the right direction in relation to the connecting rod. Normally, a piston will have some form of marking on its head which should point towards the front of the engine. See Fig. 47-13.

The connecting rod may have one edge of the big end bore chamfered (faces outside of journal on V-type engines). The rod may also have an oil spray hole or rod numbers that must face in only one direction. Check the vehicle's shop manual for directions.

To start a pressed-in type piston pin, tap it into the bore with a brass hammer. Then, use a press to force

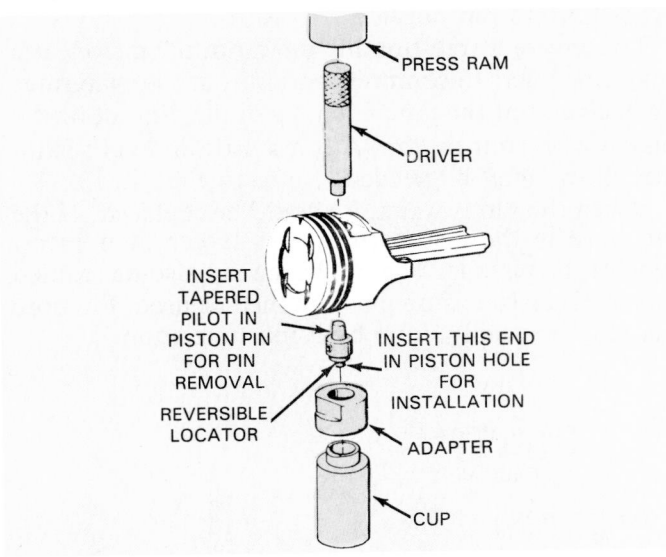

Fig. 47-14. Press-fit piston pin must be forced out with press. Use suitable adapters to prevent piston damage. (Ford)

the pin into the piston. The connecting rod small end must be centered on the pin.

After pushing a floating type piston pin into the piston, install the snap rings to secure the pin. Double-check that the snap rings are fully seated in their grooves.

CONNECTING ROD SERVICE

Connecting rods are subjected to tons of force during engine operation. As a result, they can wear, bend, or even break. The old piston and the bearing inserts will indicate the condition of the connecting rod. If any piston or bearing wear abnormalities are found, there may be a problem with the connecting rod!

For example, if one side of the bearing is worn, the connecting rod may be bent. If the back of the bearing insert has marks on it, the rod big end may be distorted, allowing the insert to shift inside the rod.

Rod small end service

Measure the rod small end with a telescoping gauge and a micrometer. If worn beyond specs, have a machine shop replace the rod bushing. The pin will have to be FITTED (bushings reamed for proper clearance) in the rod.

Rod big end service

To check the connecting rod big end for problems, remove the bearing insert and bolt the rod cap to the rod. Torque to specs. Then, measure the rod bore diameter on both edges and in both directions.

Any difference in edge diameter equals rod big end taper. Any difference in the cross diameters equals rod big end out-of-roundness. If taper or out-of-round are greater than specs, have a machine shop rebuild the rod or purchase a new rod.

Checking rod straightness

To determine if a rod is bent, a special *rod alignment fixture* is needed. It will check whether the rod small end and big end are perfectly parallel. Use the operating instructions provided with the particular fixture.

PISTON RING SERVICE

With the cylinders, pistons, and connecting rods all checked, you are ready to install the new piston rings on the pistons.

Installing oil ring

Before installing the compression rings, install the oil ring into its bottom groove. Wrap the expander-spacer around the groove and BUTT the ends together.

Spiral the bottom rail next to the bottom of the expander-spacer. Look at Fig. 47-15.

Then, spiral in the top oil ring rail. Double-check

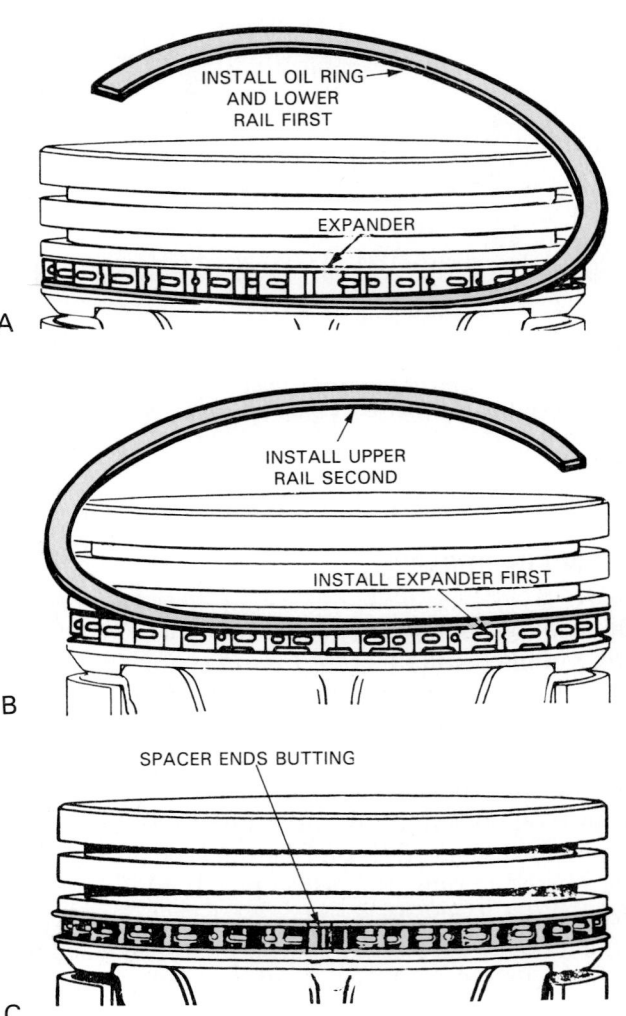

Fig. 47-15. A—Install oil ring first. Fit expander-spacer into its groove. Then spiral bottom oil rail around bottom of expander-spacer. B—Spiral rail in groove. C—Double-check that expander-spacer ends are butted. They must not overlap.

that the expander-spacer is NOT overlapped. Its ends must butt together.

Make sure the oil ring assembly will rotate on the piston. There will be a moderate drag as the oil ring is turned. One ring gap should be almost aligned with the end of the piston pin. The other gap should be at the opposite end of the pin.

Installing compression rings

Note the instructions with the new piston ring set. There will usually be hints on proper ring installation. Usually, compression rings have a top and a bottom. If installed up-side down, ring failure or leakage may result.

Ring markings are usually provided to show how compression rings should be installed. For instance, look at Fig. 47-16. The markings show the top of each ring and which ring goes into the top or second piston groove.

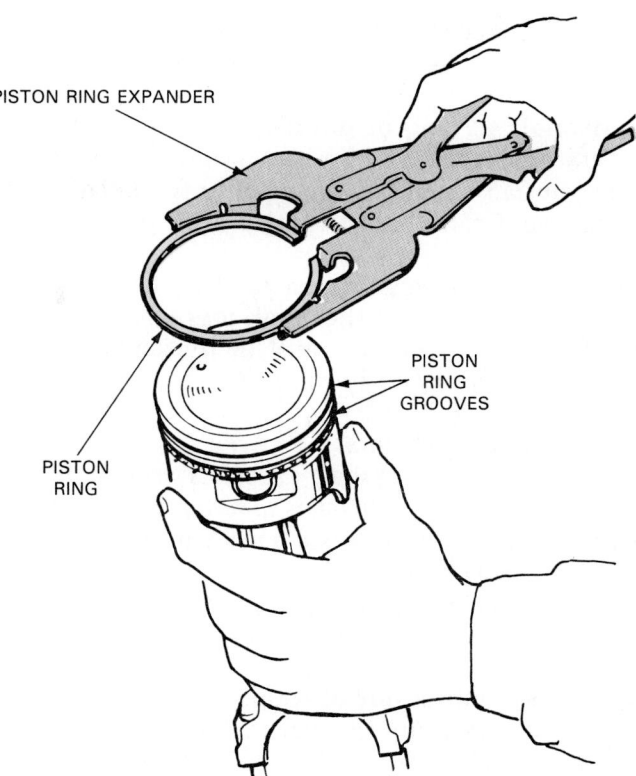

Fig. 47-17. Be careful not to open compression rings too much when installing them on piston. They are brittle and can break easily. (Honda)

  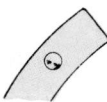 

Fig. 47-16. Compression ring markings and instructions with ring set will tell you how and in which groove each ring should be installed. (American Motors Corp.)

CAUTION! Compression rings, unlike steel oil rings, are made of very brittle cast iron. They will BREAK EASILY if expanded or twisted too much.

Using a *piston ring expander* (special tool for spreading and installing rings), slip the compression rings into their grooves. See Fig. 47-17. If a ring expander is not available, use your fingers to carefully spiral the compression rings onto the piston.

Piston ring gap spacing

A specific *piston ring gap spacing* is normally recommended to reduce blowby and ring wear. Fig. 47-18 shows a typical method.

Note that each gap is directly opposite the one next to it. The gaps are also in line with the piston pin hole. This provides maximum distance between each gap for minimum pressure leakage. Being next to the pin hole reduces ring wear because the gap is not on a major thrust surface.

CRANKSHAFT SERVICE

Before final inspection, make sure the crankshaft is perfectly clean. Use compressed air to blow out all of the oil passages. Look at each connecting rod and main journal surface closely. Look for scratching, scoring, and any signs of wear. The slightest nick or groove is very serious.

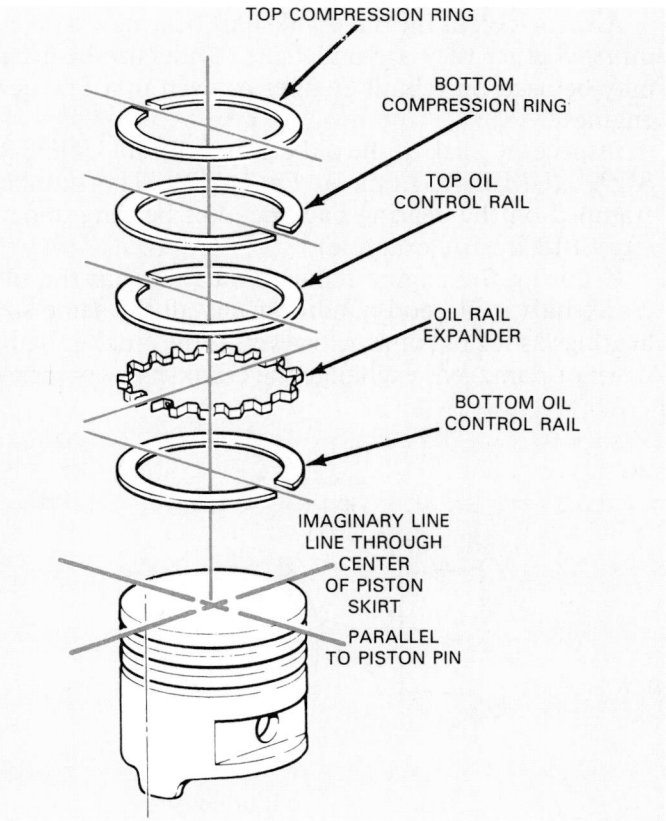

Fig. 47-18. Align piston ring end gaps as shown. They should be staggered and face ends of piston pin. (Chrysler)

Very fine crocus cloth may be used to clean up minor burrs or marks.

Crankshaft turning or grinding

Turning a crankshaft involves grinding the rod and main journals smaller in diameter to fix journal wear or damage. Crankshaft turning is done by a machine shop.

Undersize bearings are needed after the crankshaft has been turned. Since the crank journals are smaller in diameter, the bearings must be thicker to provide the correct bearing-to-journal fit.

Measuring journal taper

If one side of a crankshaft journal is worn more than the other, the crank journal is *tapered,* Fig. 47-19. To measure journal taper, use an outside micrometer, Fig. 47-20. Measure both ends of each journal. Any difference indicates taper. Taper beyond recommended limits requires crankshaft turning.

Measuring journal out-of-round

When you measure for journal taper, also measure *journal out-of-roundness* (journal worn more on top than bottom). As shown in Fig. 47-19, measure across the journal from side to side and then from top to bottom. If not within spec limits, send the crankshaft to a machine shop for turning.

Undersize bearing markings

Always look at the old crankshaft bearings to determine whether they are undersize. Undersize bearings may be used on rebuilt engines or even in a few new engines.

Inspect the back of the old bearings for an UNDERSIZE NUMBER. Look at Fig. 47-21. The number stamped on the bearing back denotes bearing undersize (.010 in. for example).

If during the engine repair, you find that the old crankshaft is in good condition, install the same size bearings as the old ones. However, if the crank is badly worn or damaged, exchange the crankshaft for a new

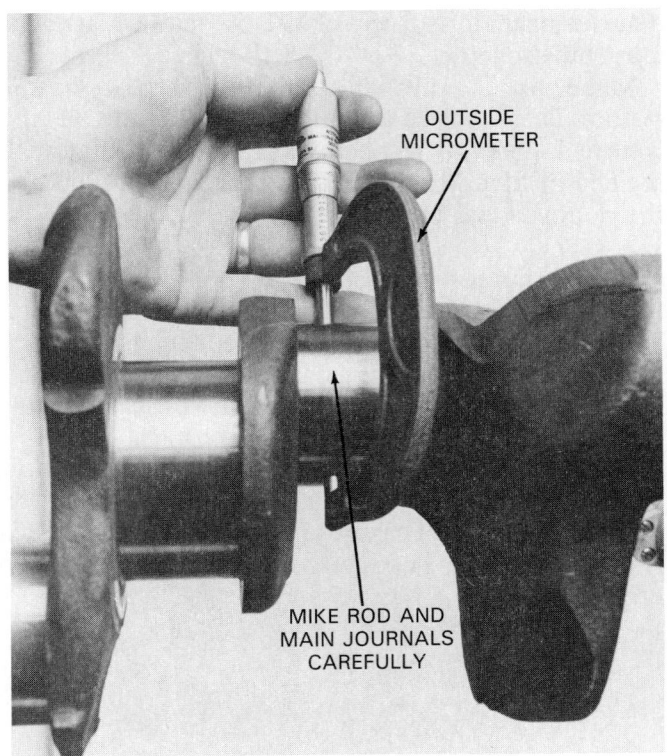

Fig. 47-20. Outside micrometer is used to measure crankshaft journal wear. If not within specs, crank must be replaced or turned for undersize bearings. (Goodson)

or reconditioned (ground undersize) crank. Then, install the appropriate size bearings.

Checking crankshaft straightness

A *bent crankshaft* can ruin new main bearings or cause the engine to lock up when the main caps are tightened.

To measure crankshaft straightness, mount a dial

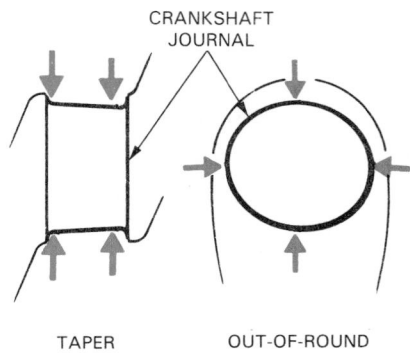

Fig. 47-19. When measuring crankshaft journal wear, check as shown to detect taper and out-of-round. (Volvo)

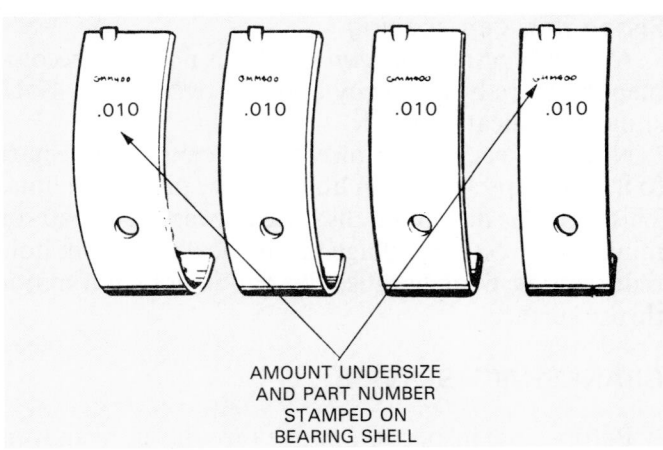

Fig. 47-21. Inspect old crankshaft bearings for undersize markings. A .010 on back of bearing shell would indicate crank journals have been machined .010 in. smaller in diameter. If crank is in good condition, same undersize bearings should be purchased. (Oldsmobile)

indicator against the center main journal. The crank can be mounted on V-blocks, as in Fig. 47-22. The crank can also be placed in the block main bearings.

Slowly turn the crank while watching the indicator. Indicator movement equals crankshaft bend. If not within limits, replace the crank or have it straightened and turned by a machine shop.

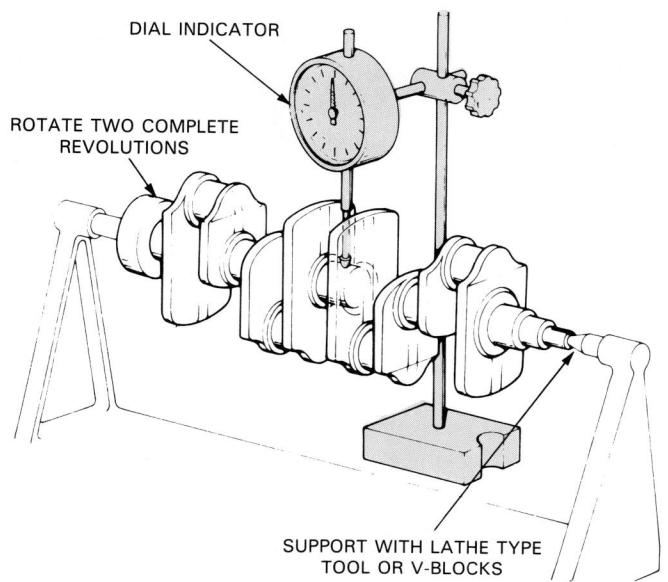

Fig. 47-22. Crankshaft straightness can be measured as shown. If special holding tool or V-blocks are not available, lay crank in block main bearings, leaving center main cap off. (Honda)

Installing crankshaft bearings

Purchase the correct (standard or undersize) main bearings. With the main bearing bore and back of each bearing CLEAN and DRY, fit each bearing half into place. One bearing insert goes into the block and the other matching insert goes into the corresponding main cap. Also install the main thrust bearing into the correct position in the block and cap. Make sure block and bearing oil holes align!

Fig. 47-23 shows how a crankshaft can be replaced without cylinder head, piston, and connecting rod removal.

Installing rear main oil seal

There are three basic types of rear main oil seals: two-piece synthetic rubber seal, two-piece rope (wick) seal, and one-piece synthetic rubber seal. Each requires a different installation technique.

The two-piece *synthetic rubber rear seal* is very easy to install. Look at Fig. 47-24. Simply press it into place in the block and rear main cap.

The sealing lip on the rear main seal must point towards the INSIDE of the engine. If installed backwards, oil will pour out of the back of the seal upon engine starting. Lubricate the sealing lip with

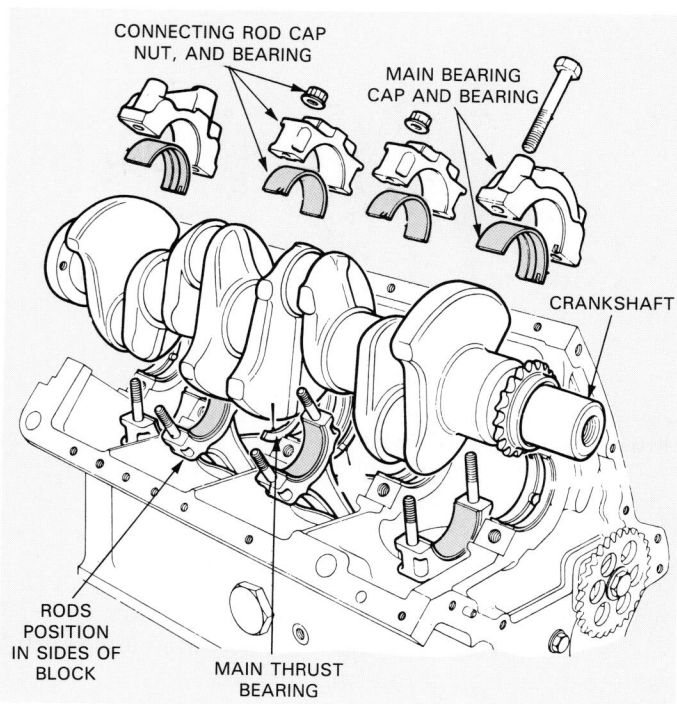

Fig. 47-23. Crankshaft and engine bearings can be replaced without removing heads, pistons, and rods. Unbolt rod caps and main caps. Carefully lift crankshaft out of block.

motor oil, Fig. 47-24.

A *two-piece rope* or *wick* rear main oil seal must be worked down into its cap and block groove carefully. Use a special seal installing tool and light hammer blows or hand pressure and a smooth steel bar, as in Fig. 47-25. Use a single-edge razor blade to cut the rope seal flush with the cap and block parting line.

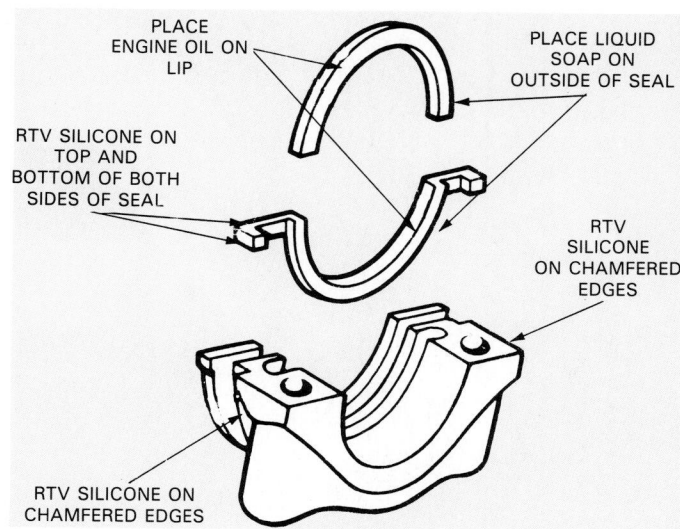

Fig. 47-24. Common synthetic rubber rear main bearing oil seal. Note seal installation recommendations by this auto manufacturer. Oil seal lip must face inside of engine.

Engine Bottom End Service 603

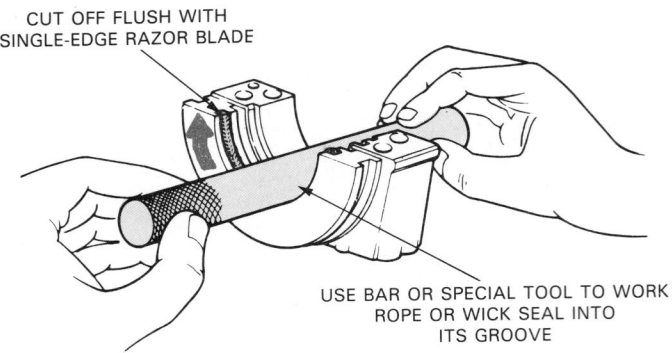

Fig. 47-25. With rope or wick rear main oil seal, work seal down into groove. Use single-edge razor blade to cut excess seal off flush with cap and block. (GM)

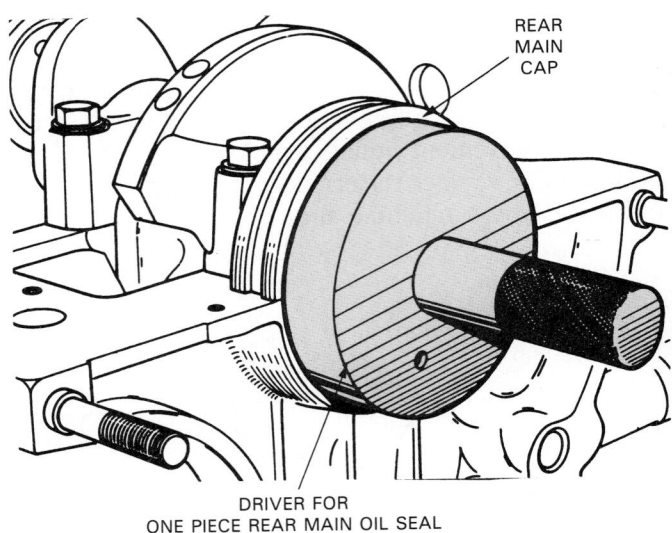

Fig. 47-27. One piece, synthetic rubber rear main oil seal being installed with special driver. Make sure seal is perfectly square and fully seated. (Renault)

Frequently, *silicone sealer* is recommended on the rear main cap to prevent oil leakage. Refer to Fig. 47-26. The sealer keeps oil from seeping between the main cap and block mating surfaces.

If additional side seals are provided for the cap, follow the instructions with the gasket set. Sealer is commonly recommended on main cap side seals.

A *one-piece synthetic rubber seal* is usually installed after the rear main cap has been bolted to the block. It is driven into position from the rear of the engine using a seal driver. Look at Fig. 47-27. After installation, make sure the seal is square and undamaged.

Installing crankshaft

After main bearing installation, coat the bearings in the block with motor oil. Carefully lay the crankshaft into place, Fig. 47-28. Do not rotate the crankshaft

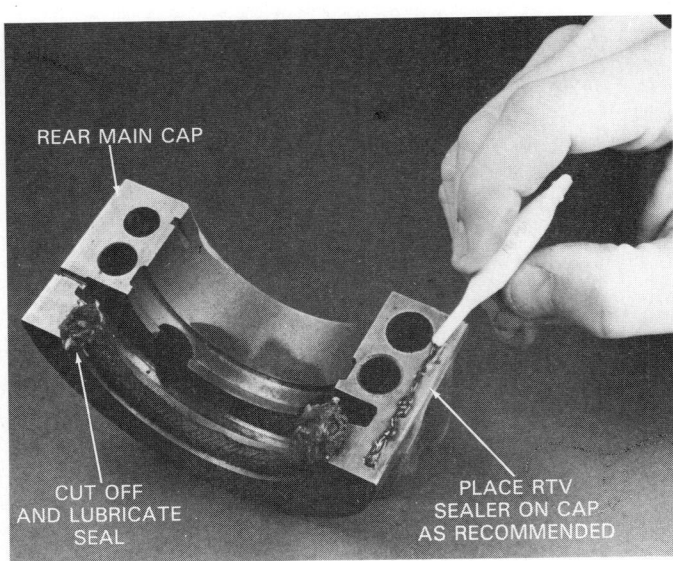

Fig. 47-26. Most auto makers recommend sealer at cap-to-block parting line. This will keep oil from leaking out of back of engine. (Fel-Pro)

without the main caps bolted to the block or the inserts may spin and be damaged.

Checking main bearing clearance

To check the oil clearance between the crank journal and main bearing, place a small bead of PLASTIGAGE (clearance measuring material) on the unoiled crankshaft. See Fig. 47-29. Install and torque the main cap.

Remove the main bearing cap and compare the smashed Plastigage to the provided paper scale. If clearance is not correct, check bearing sizes and crankshaft journal measurements.

An average main bearing clearance would be .002 in. (0.05 mm). The use of Plastigage will be illustrated shortly, when checking rod bearing clearance.

Torquing main bearing caps

Oil the crank journals and bearing faces. Place each main bearing cap into place in the block. Double-check bearing installation. Also check that the arrows and numbers on each cap are correct, as in Fig. 47-28. They should usually read 1, 2, 3 going from the front to the rear of the block.

Run each cap bolt down a little at a time. This will pull the cap squarely down into the block. Then, use a torque wrench to tighten the main cap bolts to factory specs, Fig. 47-29.

Checking crankshaft endplay

Crankshaft endplay is the amount of front-to-rear movement of the crankshaft in the block. It is controlled by the clearance between the main thrust bearing and the crankshaft thrust surface or journal.

To measure crankshaft endplay, mount a dial indicator on the block. Position the dial indicator against

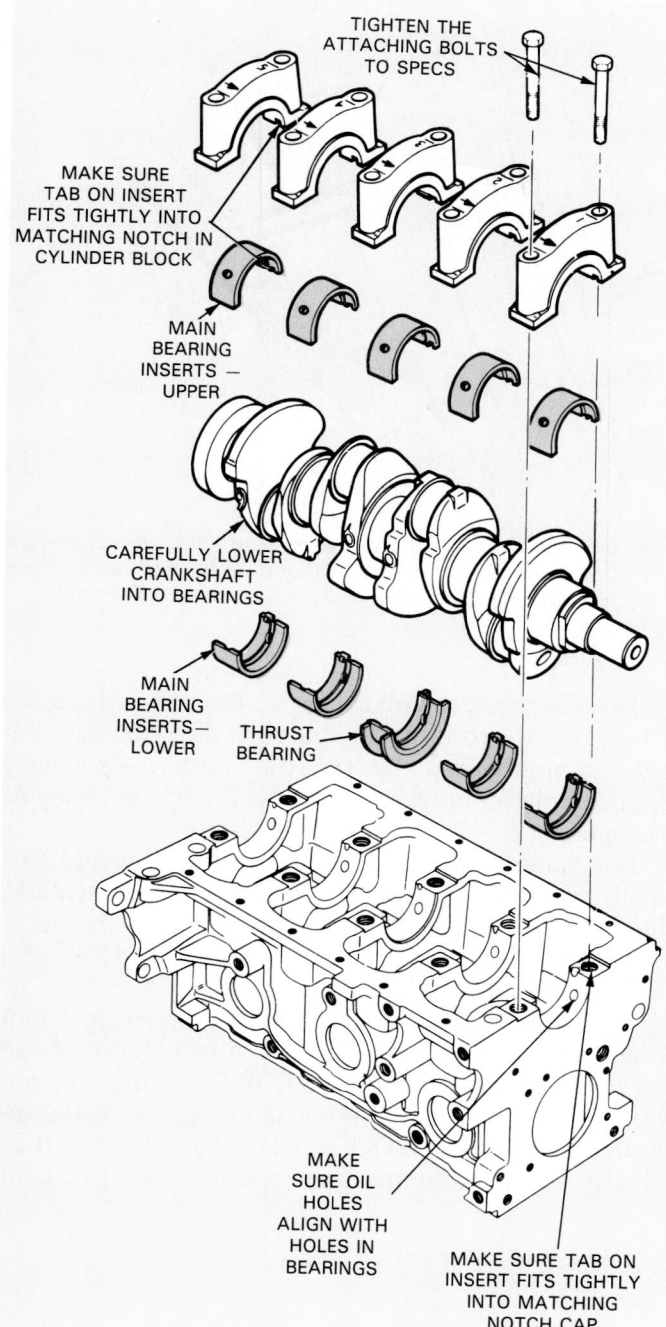

Fig. 47-28. Fit each main bearing insert into its bore. Make sure bearing tab fits fully into notch in block or cap. Back of bearings should be clean and dry. Oil front or face of bearing with motor oil. Carefully lower crank into block without bumping bearings or journals. Double-check that rear seal is installed correctly. (Ford)

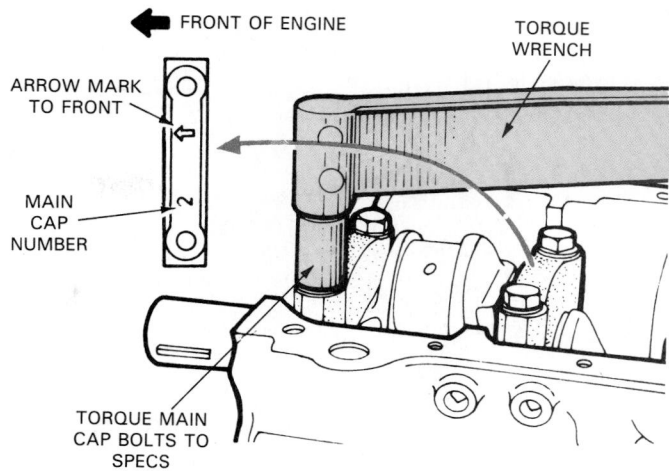

Fig. 47-29. Torque main bearing caps to specifications using a torque wrench. Bolts must be clean and oiled. Also, check cap numbers and arrows. (Chrysler)

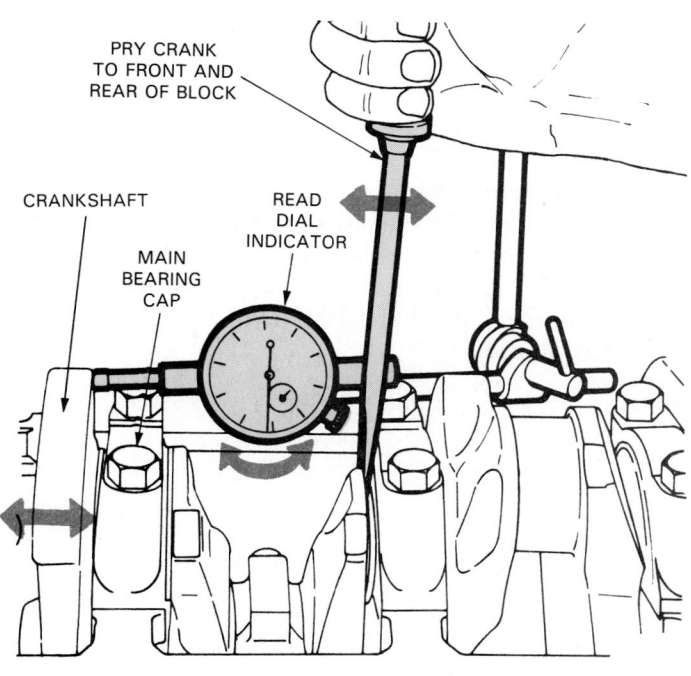

Fig. 47-30. Use dial indicator to measure crankshaft end play. Pry back and forth on crank while reading indicator. If not within specs, check thrust bearing and thrust surfaces on crankshaft. (Chrysler)

the crankshaft with the stem parallel to the crank centerline. See Fig. 47-30. Pry the crank back and forth in the block.

Indicator movement equals crankshaft endplay. Compare your measurements to specs. If incorrect, check the thrust bearing insert size and the crankshaft thrust journal width.

INSTALLING PISTON AND ROD ASSEMBLY

To install a piston assembly in the block, dip the head of the piston and new rings into clean engine oil. Double-check that the ring gaps are still spaced properly.

Clamp a ring compressor around the rings, as in Fig. 47-31. While tightening the compressor, hold the compressor square on the piston. The small dents or indentations around the edge of the compressor should face

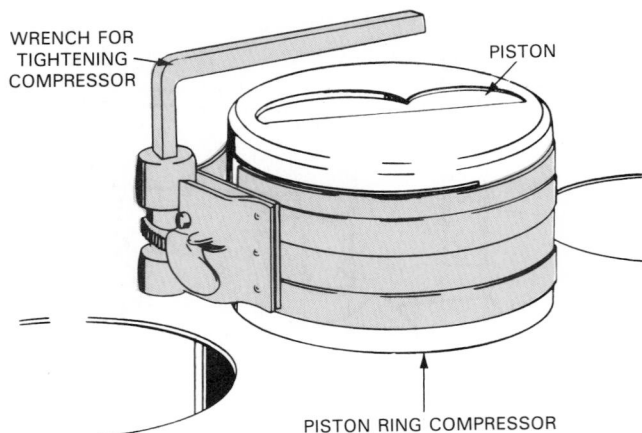

Fig. 47-31. After checking ring gap spacing and placing oil on rings and piston, install ring compressor. Tighten compressor handle firmly. (Cadillac)

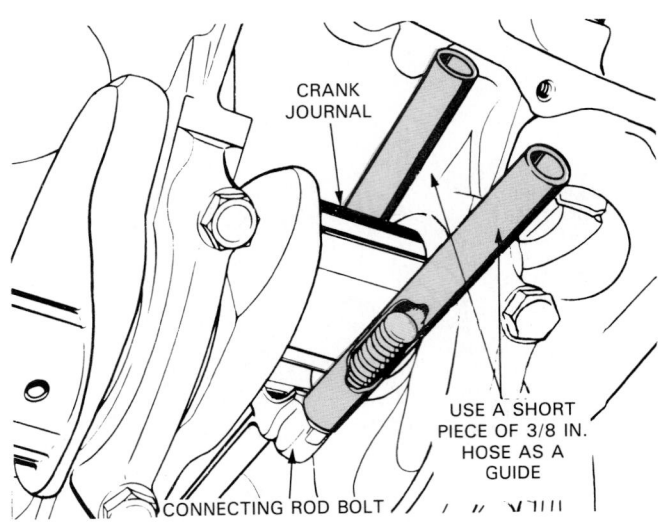

Fig. 47-33. Be careful not to let rod bolts hit and nick crankshaft journals during installation. Sections of rubber hose or soft plastic tubing will protect crank. (Buick)

the bottom of the piston.

Fit the unoiled rod bearing insert into the connecting rod and the matching insert into the correct cap. Refer to Fig. 47-32. Then, wipe a generous layer of oil on the face of the bearings.

Protect the crankshaft

Slide *plastic* or *rubber hoses* or *rod bolt covers* over the connecting rod bolts. This will prevent the rod bolts from possibly scratching the crankshaft journal, Fig. 47-33. Turn the crankshaft until the corresponding rod journal is at BDC.

Double-check the markings on the rod and piston. Make sure the rod is facing the right direction and that the cap number matches the rod number. Also check that the piston notch or arrow is facing the front of the engine.

For example, if the rod is number one, it would normally go in the very front cylinder with the piston marking to the front. Check the service manual if in doubt.

Installing piston and rod in block

To install the piston and rod in its cylinder, turn that crank journal to BDC. Place the piston and rod into its cylinder. Look at Fig. 47-34. While guiding the rod bolts over the crank with one hand, tap the piston into the engine with a WOODEN HAMMER HANDLE. A soft wooden hammer handle will not mar or dent

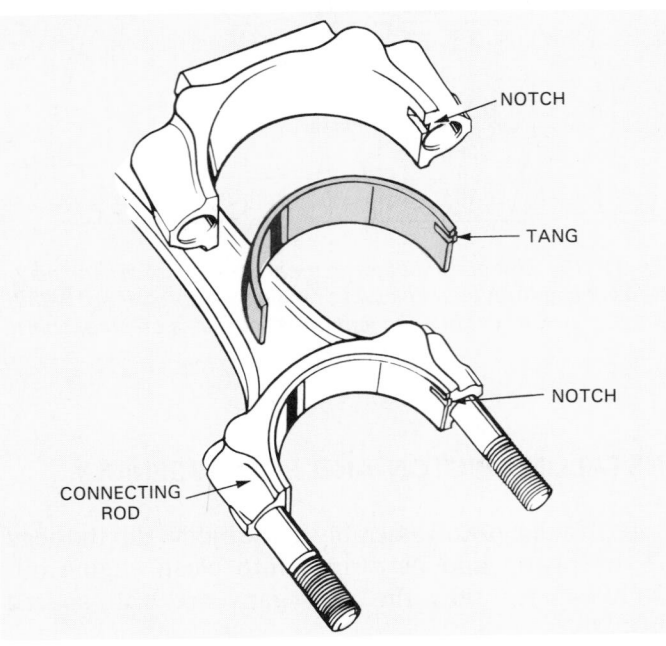

Fig. 47-32. Install clean, dry, unoiled bearings into connecting rod and cap. Keep your fingers off bearing face. Fit bearing tangs into rod notches. After installing, coat bearing faces with motor oil. (Oldsmobile)

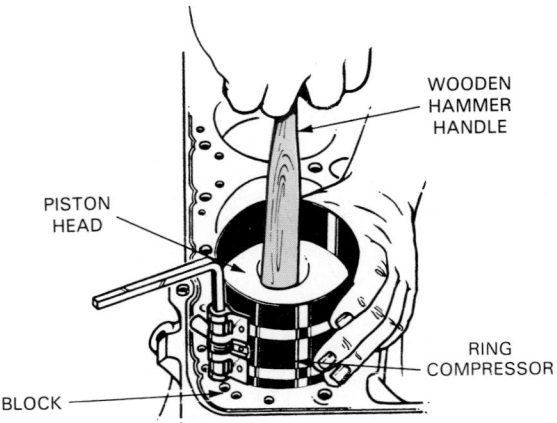

Fig. 47-34. Use wooden hammer handle to tap piston and rod assembly into cylinder block. Rod journal for that piston should be at BDC. Carefully guide rod over crank as you tap piston into cylinder. (Lisle Tools)

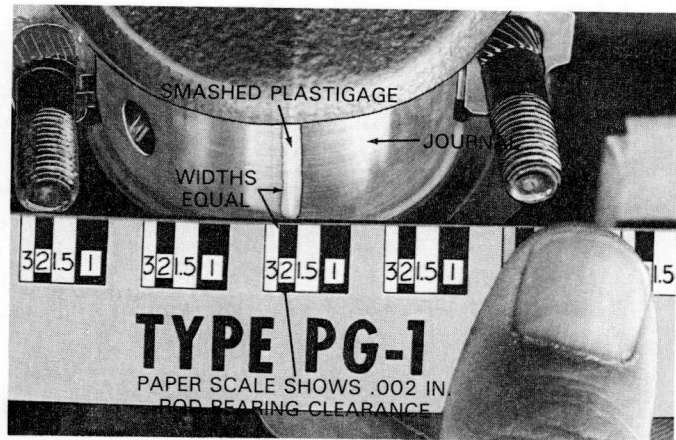

Fig. 47-35. Plastigage may be used to check rod or main bearing clearance. Place small piece of Plastigage across clean, dry journal. Then, install and torque cap. Remove cap and compare paper scale with smashed Plastigage. Match Plastigage width with width on scale. Clearance must be within specs. (Chevrolet)

the head of the piston. Hold the ring compressor squarely against the block deck. Keep tapping until the rod bearing bottoms around the crank journal.

If a piston ring pops out of the compressor, do NOT try to force the piston down into the cylinder. This would break or damage the piston rings or piston. Instead, loosen the ring compressor and start over.

Check rod bearing clearance

To measure connecting rod bearing clearance, use Plastigage. Place a bead of Plastigage across the crank journal. Bolt and torque the rod cap. Then, remove the cap and compare the smashed Plastigage to the paper scale. See Fig. 47-35. The width of the smashed Plastigage will let you determine bearing clearance.

When installing a connecting rod cap, make sure the rod and cap NUMBERS ARE THE SAME. If the rod is numbered with a five, then the cap should also have five stamped on it. Mixing up rod caps will damage the bearings or crankshaft.

Torque connecting rods

It is very important for you to properly torque each rod nut or bolt to specifications.

If a rod is over-tightened, the rod bolt could break during engine operation. Severe block, crank, piston, and cylinder head damage could result as parts fly around inside the engine.

If a rod is under-tightened, the bolts could stretch under load allowing the bearing to spin or hammer against the crank. Again, serious engine damage could result.

Using a TORQUE WRENCH, tighten each rod fastener a little at a time. This will pull the rod cap down squarely. Keep increasing torque until full specs are reached. Double-check each rod bolt or nut several times.

Checking rod side clearance

Connecting rod side clearance is the distance between the side of the connecting rod and the side of the crankshaft journal or other rod. To measure rod side clearance, insert different size feeler gauge blades into the gap between the rod and crank. See Fig. 47-36.

The largest feeler blade that slides between the rod indicates side clearance. Compare your measurements to specs. If not within specs, crankshaft journal or connecting rod width is incorrect.

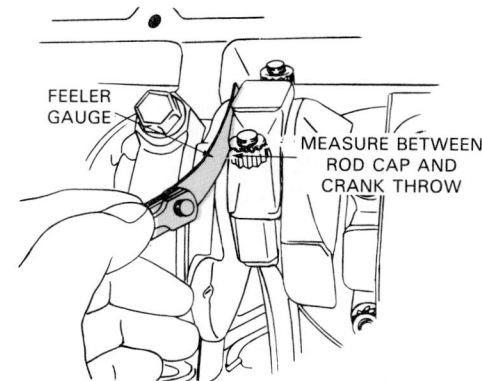

Fig. 47-36. Feeler gauge is used to measure rod side play. If incorrect, measure rod width and journal width. (Buick)

TORQUE-TO-YIELD BOLTS

Torque-to-yield bolts have been tightened at the factory to a preset yield or stretch point. Usually, the auto maker recommends that you install new bolts and/or use a torque angle meter to tighten these bolts properly. See Fig. 47-37.

A *torque angle meter* is a numbered wheel for measuring rotation in degrees. It can be mounted on a ratchet or torque wrench to measure how far a bolt has been turned while tightening.

To use a torque angle meter, you must normally tighten the bolt to a given specification. The service manual spec will also give an additional number of degrees you must turn the bolt tighter. After torquing

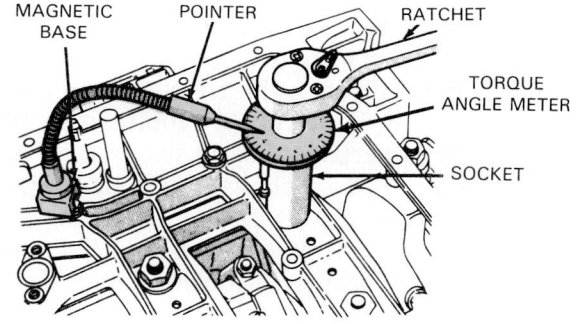

Fig. 47-37. To use a torque angle meter, first tighten the bolt to specs. Then, zero the pointer and tighten the bolt additional number of degrees given in specs. (Chrysler)

to specs, zero the pointer on the torque angle meter. Then tighten the bolt the extra number of degrees.

Various engine parts can require you to use a torque angle meter. A few of these include cylinder head bolts, main cap bolts, etc.

ENGINE BALANCING

Engine balancing may be needed when the weight of the pistons, connecting rods, or crankshaft is altered. Engine balancing is done to prevent engine vibration.

For example, if new, oversize pistons are installed and they weigh more than the old, standard pistons, engine (crankshaft) balancing may be required.

Most large automotive machine shops have engine balancing equipment. Basically, the pistons, rings, piston pins, connecting rods, and rod bearings are weighed on an accurate scale. Material is machined or ground off the pistons and rods until each weighs the same. All rod big ends and small end should also be equal in weight.

Then, bob weights comparable to the weight of each piston and rod assembly are bolted to the crankshaft rod journals. The crankshaft, front damper, and flywheel are bolted together and rotated on the engine balancing machine. It will show where weight should be added (metal welded on) or removed (metal drilled out) from the crankshaft counterweights, damper, and flywheel.

Proper engine balance is very critical with today's small, high rpm, economy car engines. Keep engine balancing in mind when major engine modifications are made.

FINAL ASSEMBLY OF ENGINE

With all of the pistons and rods installed and torqued, you can now install all of the other parts on the block: oil pump, oil pan, cylinder heads, camshaft drive, manifolds.

NOTE! The procedures for installing these engine parts are described in following and earlier chapters. Use the index to find this information if needed.

KNOW THESE TERMS

Short block, Engine overhaul, Cylinder boring, Overbore limit, Oversize pistons and rings, Cylinder sleeving, Cylinder taper, Cylinder out-of-roundness, Dial bore gauge, Cylinder hone, Honing grit, Block line boring, Deck warpage, Piston size, Piston taper, Piston knurling, Piston clearance, Ring-to-groove clearance, Ring spacers, Piston ring gap, Ring markings, Ring expander, Ring gap spacing, Crankshaft turning, Undersize bearings, Journal taper, Journal out-of-roundness, Plastigage, Main bearing cap torque, Crankshaft end play, Piston and rod markings, Rod bolt covers, Rod bolt torque, Connecting rod side clearance.

REVIEW QUESTIONS

1. What is an "engine overhaul?"
2. _____ _____ is done by machining the cylinders larger in diameter to make the cylinder walls perfectly smooth and straight.
3. Normally, a cylinder is bored in increments of:
   a. .050 in. (1.27 mm).   c. .005 in. (0.127 mm).
   b. .010 in. (0.254 mm). d. .001 in. (0.025 mm).
4. _____ pistons and rings are needed in a cylinder block that has had its cylinders bored out.
5. Why is cylinder sleeving frequently used?
6. Define the term "cylinder taper."
7. A dial bore gauge is a quick and accurate tool for measuring cylinder taper. True or False?
8. Explain the purpose of honing a cylinder.
9. Describe three types of cylinder hones.
10. How do you measure main bearing bore alignment?
11. Measure piston size on the piston _____, just below the _____ _____.
12. How do you find piston clearance?
13. What can happen if the piston ring gap is too large or too small?
14. To measure piston ring end gap, you would use:
    a. Feeler gauge.   c. Dial bore gauge.
    b. Micrometer.   d. Telescoping gauge.
15. A specific piston ring gap spacing is recommended to reduce _____ and _____ _____.
16. What are undersize main and rod bearings?
17. How do you check crankshaft straightness?
18. When installing a rear main seal, the sealing lip should point towards the inside of the engine. True or False?
19. Explain how Plastigage is used to measure rod and main bearing clearance.
20. Which of the following is NOT a recommended practice when installing a piston and rod assembly?
    a. Cover rod bolts with rubber hose or plastic tubing.
    b. Use ring compressor to squeeze rings into grooves.
    c. Drive pistons into block with blows from hammer head.
    d. Check that rod cap numbers align and are correct.

ACTIVITIES FOR CHAPTER 47

1. Use a cylinder bore gauge to measure wear in a cylinder, making and recording at least five measurements. Then, use Computer-Aided Drafting (or manual drafting) to draw a precise, full size cross section of the cylinder. Note the bore dimensions on your drawing.
2. If a video camera is available, arrange to visit a machine shop and videotape the process of boring cylinders. Play the tape for the class and explain what they see happening.

Engine Top End Service

After studying this chapter, you will be able to:
□ Check for cylinder head damage, valve guide wear, and other engine top end related problems.
□ Describe how to correct worn valve guides, head warpage, valve seat damage, and other troubles.
□ Grind valve seats and valves.
□ Remove and install diesel engine precombustion chambers.
□ Test and shim valve springs.
□ Assemble a cylinder head.
□ Inspect, test, and service valve lifters, push rods, and rocker assemblies.
□ Reassemble the top end of an engine.
□ Adjust engine valves.
□ Describe safety practices to be followed while performing engine top end service.

A *valve job* typically involves servicing the cylinder head and valve train. Fig. 48-1 shows the basic components involved and lists typical part failures. A specialized engine technician must be capable of quickly and accurately servicing any of these parts. This chapter discusses engine top end service and repair.

CYLINDER HEAD SERVICE

Cylinder head and valve service are very critical to engine performance and service life. The valves, head gasket, and cylinder head work together to contain the tremendous heat and pressure of combustion. If the technician makes the slightest mistake when working on the head or valve train, the repair can fail in a very short period of time.

Inspecting cylinder head

A *cylinder head stand* is used to hold the head off the workbench surface. After cleaning the head, mount it on a stand. Then, inspect the head closely for problems. Look for cracks, burning, and erosion between combustion chambers. Also, check the valve guides and seats for wear or damage.

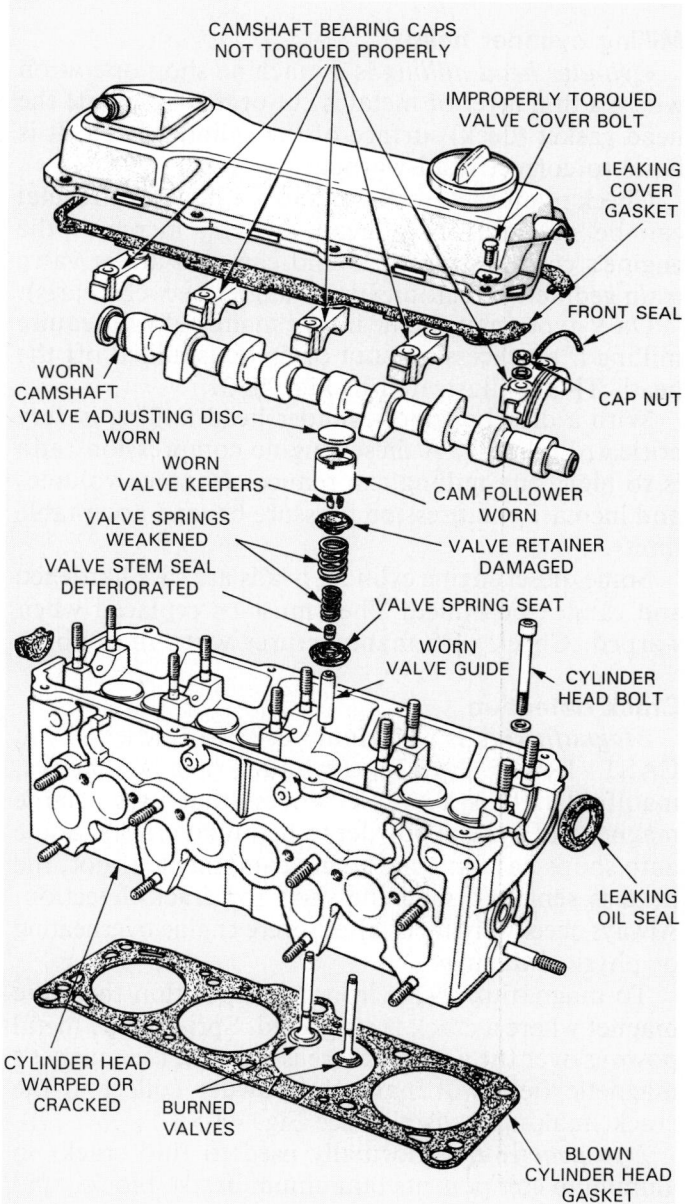

Fig. 48-1. These are typical parts of modern engine top end assembly. (Chrysler)

Measuring cylinder head warpage

A *warped cylinder head* has a bent or curved deck surface, usually from engine overheating. This is a common and serious problem with today's aluminum heads.

A straightedge and feeler gauge are used to measure cylinder head warpage. Illustrated in Fig. 47-2, lay the straightedge on the head. Try to slip different feeler gauge blade thicknesses under the straightedge. The thickest gauge that fits equals head warpage.

Check warpage in different positions across the head surface, Fig. 48-2. The most common place warpage shows up is between the two center combustion chambers.

A straightedge and feeler gauge can also be used to check the cam bore in an OHC engine for misalignment.

Milling cylinder head

Cylinder head milling is a machine shop operation where a thin layer of metal is cut or machined off the head gasket (deck) surface of the cylinder head. It is done to correct head warpage.

Check manufacturer's specs to see how much metal can be milled from a head. Milling increases the engine's compression ratio and can also affect valve train geometry (relationship or angles between parts).

On V-type engines, the intake manifold will require milling if an excess amount of metal is milled off the head. This is illustrated in Fig. 48-3.

With a diesel engine, cylinder head milling is very critical, Fig. 48-4. A diesel engine compression ratio is so high, any milling can reduce clearance volumes and increase compression pressure beyond acceptable limits.

Some diesel engine cylinder heads are case hardened and cannot be milled. They must be replaced when warped. Check with manufacturer when in doubt.

Crack detection

Magnafluxing is commonly used to find cracks in CAST IRON PARTS (cylinder heads, blocks, manifolds). It is a simple process that uses a large magnet and a metal powder to highlight cracks. Some auto shops have magnafluxing equipment. If not, the head is sent to a machine shop for crack detection. Always check for cracks after severe engine overheating or physical damage.

To magnaflux a cast iron head, position the large magnet where a crack is suspected. Sprinkle the metal powder over the area. If there is a crack, the magnet's magnetic field will make the powder collect in the crack, making it visible. See Fig. 48-5.

Dye penetrant is normally used to find cracks in aluminum components (aluminum heads, blocks, and manifolds). It can also be used on cast iron when magnafluxing is not possible (crack area inside hole or pocket).

Fig. 48-2. Position straightedge on cylinder head. Feeler gauge that fits under straightedge equals head warpage. If more than specs, mill or replace head. (Fel-Pro Incorporated)

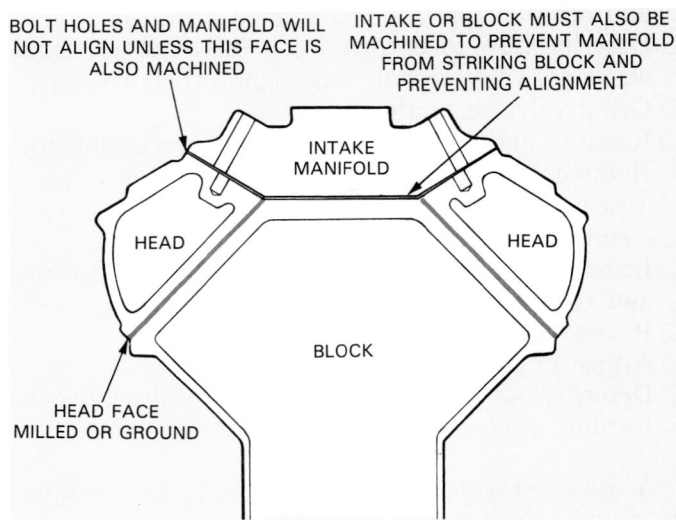

Fig. 48-3. With excessive milling of heads with V-type engine, you may also need to mill intake manifold or block. Check service manual for details. (Sealed Power)

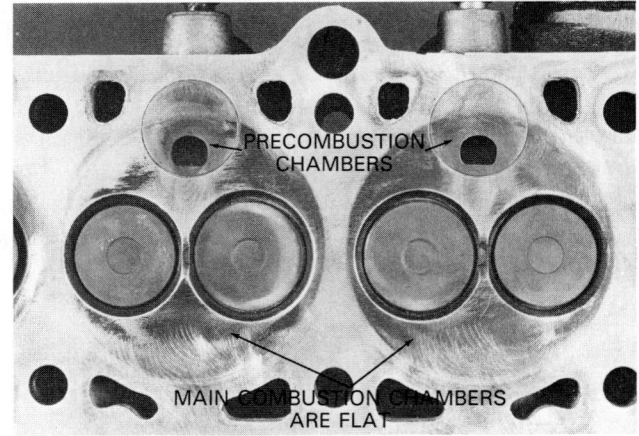

Fig. 48-4. Bottom view of diesel engine cylinder head shows flat surface forming combustion chamber top. Milling of head is very critical with diesel. (Fel-Pro Incorporated)

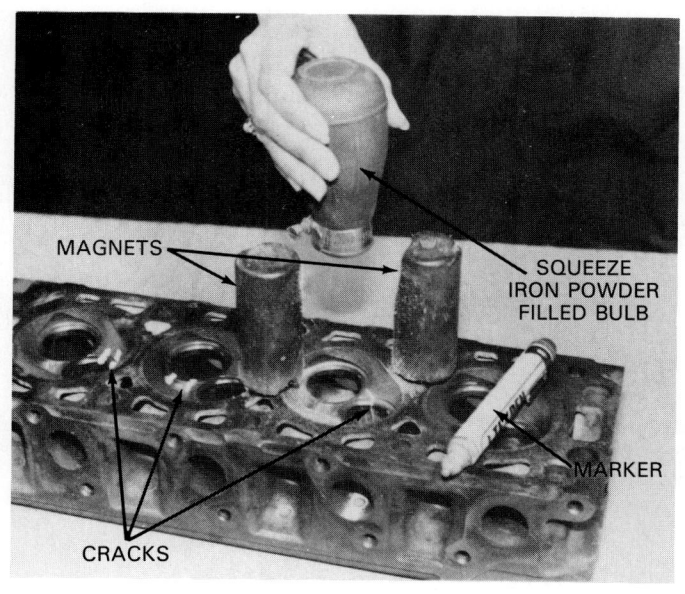

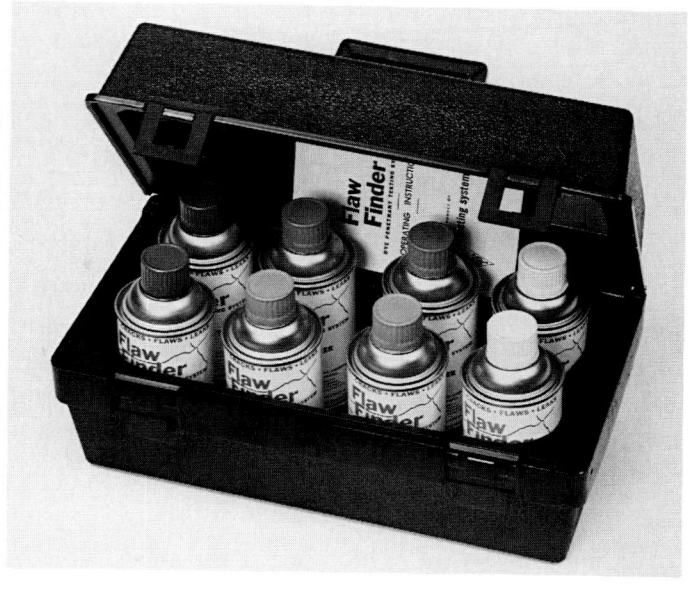

Fig. 48-5. A — Magnafluxing will make metal powder collect in crack, making crack detection easy. B — Dye penetrant for finding cracks in aluminum parts. (Magnaflux Corp.)

The special dye penetrant is sprayed on the part. Then, a chemical developer is sprayed over the penetrant. The powder-like developer will turn the penetrant inside a crack RED. This makes any crack show up.

Repairing cracked cylinder heads

When a cylinder head is cracked, it can either be welded, plugged (series of holes and metal plugs used to fix crack), or replaced. With most heads, replacement is more cost effective. With more exotic or expensive heads, welding may be desirable.

The welding of cast iron heads normally requires a specialty shop. The head should be heated in a furnace. Then, a NI (high nickel content) welding rod is used to repair the crack.

Aluminum heads can be welded using a heli-arc welder. Preheating in a furnace is usually NOT needed.

Note! Crack repair in heads and blocks should be done by an expert. Special welding skills are essential.

DIESEL PRECOMBUSTION CHAMBER SERVICE

Auto diesel engines use precombustion chambers, Fig. 48-4. They are small chambers pressed into the cylinder head. The tips of the diesel injectors and glow plugs extend into the precombustion chambers. Look at Fig. 48-6.

After prolonged use, the precombustion chambers may require removal for cleaning or replacement because of damage.

Precombustion chamber removal and installation

A *brass drift* and *hammer* are commonly used to remove a diesel engine precombustion chamber. The

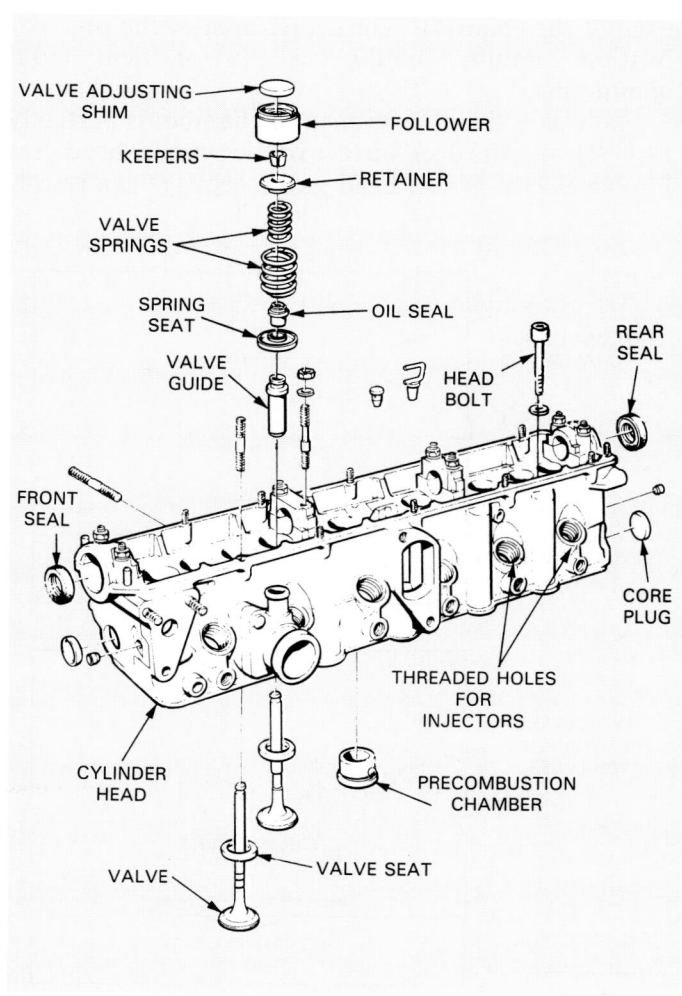

Fig. 48-6. Exploded view of cylinder head assembly. Note relationship of parts. (Volvo)

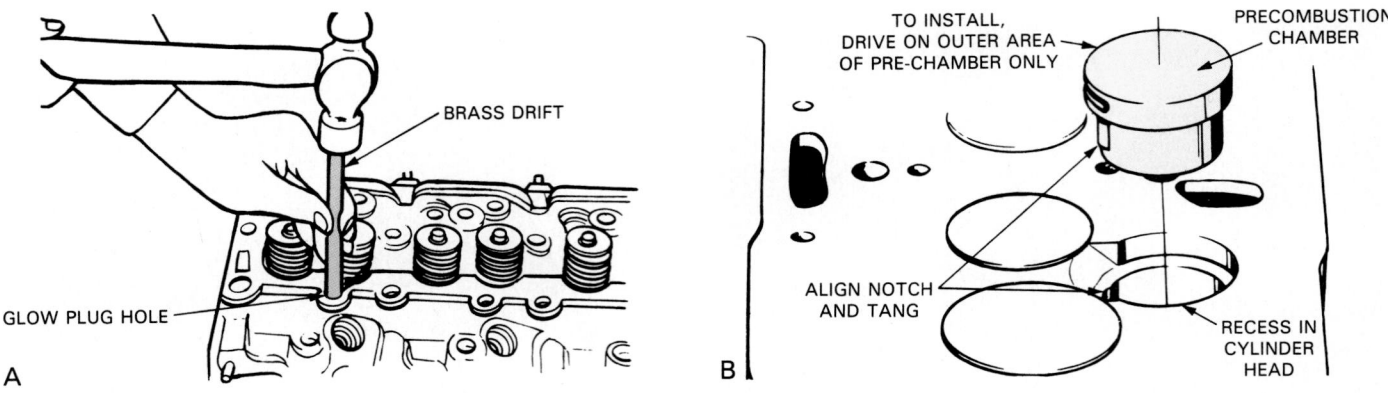

Fig. 48-7. A — If damaged or filled with carbon, you may need to drive out precombustion chambers. Use brass, not steel, drift. B — When installing diesel precombustion chamber, use special driver, if available. Do not hammer on inner portion of chamber. (Ford and Oldsmobile)

drift, Fig. 48-7A, may be inserted through a hole in the head. Light blows with the hammer will drive out the chamber.

When installing a precombustion chamber, be careful not to damage the chamber, Fig. 48-7B. Use a special driver or brass hammer to tap the unit back into the head, Fig. 48-7B. Hammer only on the outer edge of the chamber. The center area of the precombustion chamber could cave in or dent from hammering.

Make sure the precombustion chamber is perfectly FLUSH with the deck surface of the cylinder head. See Fig. 48-8. If it is not, head gasket leakage can result.

VALVE GUIDE SERVICE

Valve guide wear is a common problem; it allows the valve to move sideways in its guide during operation. This can cause oil consumption (oil leaks past valve seal and through guide), burned valves (poor seat-to-valve face seal), or valve breakage. Refer to Fig. 48-9 for example.

Measuring valve guide and stem wear

To check for valve guide wear, slide the valve into its guide. Pull it open about 1/2 in. (12.7 mm). Then, try to wiggle the valve sideways. If the valve moves sideways in any direction, the guide or stem is worn.

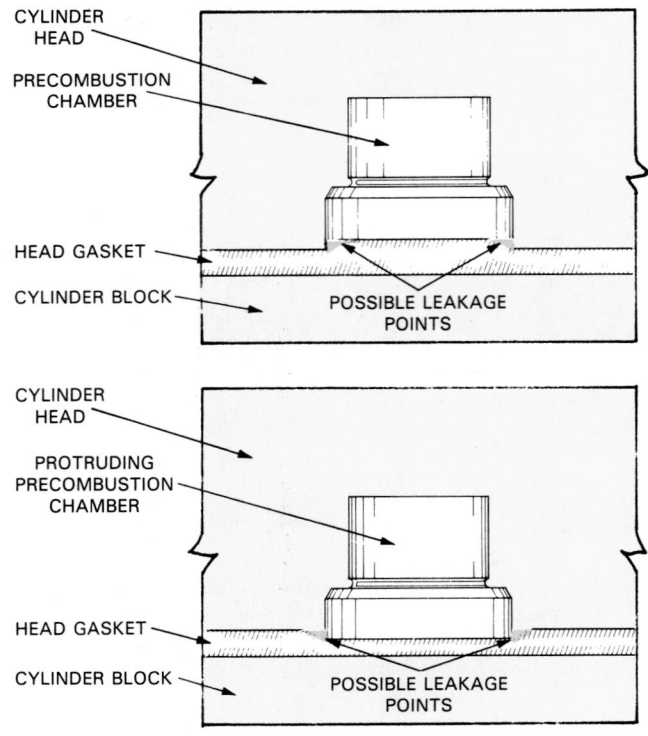

Fig. 48-8. After installation, precombustion chamber must be perfectly flush with cylinder head gasket surface. If not, head gasket could leak. (Fel-Pro Incorporated)

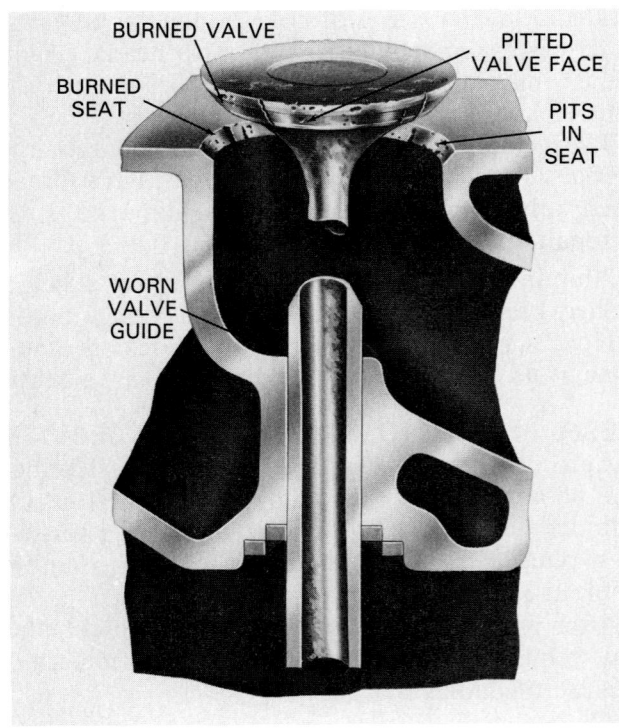

Fig. 48-9. Valve job is mainly needed to recondition valve faces and valve seats. However, other repairs may also be needed, such as valve guide replacement. (Sioux Tools)

Fig. 48-10 shows how a small hole gauge and outside micrometer are used to measure guide and valve stem wear. Fig. 48-11 pictures how a dial indicator is used to measure valve stem clearance. If not within specs, part replacement or repair is needed.

Repairing valve guide wear

There are three common methods used to repair worn valve guides. These include:

1. KNURLING VALVE GUIDE (machine shop tool used to press indentations in guide to reduce its inside diameter), Fig. 48-12.
2. REAMING VALVE GUIDE (guide reamed to larger diameter and new valves with oversize stems installed), Fig. 48-13.
3. INSTALLING VALVE GUIDE INSERT (old guide pressed or machined out and new guide pressed into head), Fig. 48-14.

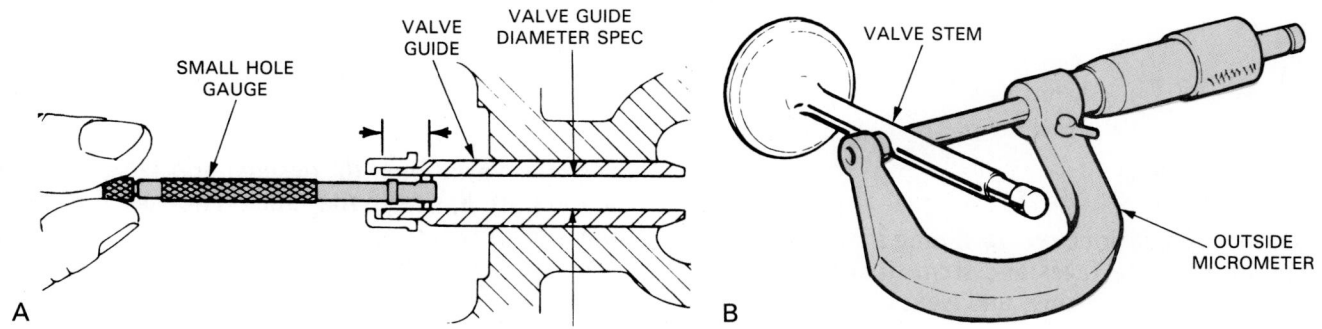

Fig. 48-10. A — Hole gauge measuring inside diameter of valve guide. B — Outside mike measuring diameter of valve stem. If not within specs, repairs to guide or replacement of guide and valves are required.   (Chrysler and Honda)

Fig. 48-11. Dial indicator can also be used to measure valve guide wear. Mount indicator stem against side of valve head. Wiggle valve sideways and read indicator. Check in different positions and compare to specs. (Chrysler)

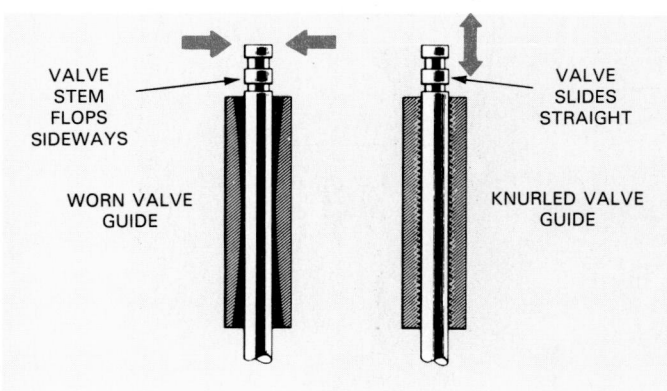

Fig. 48-12. Knurling can be used to decrease inside diameter of valve guide thus restoring proper stem-to-guide clearance. (TRW)

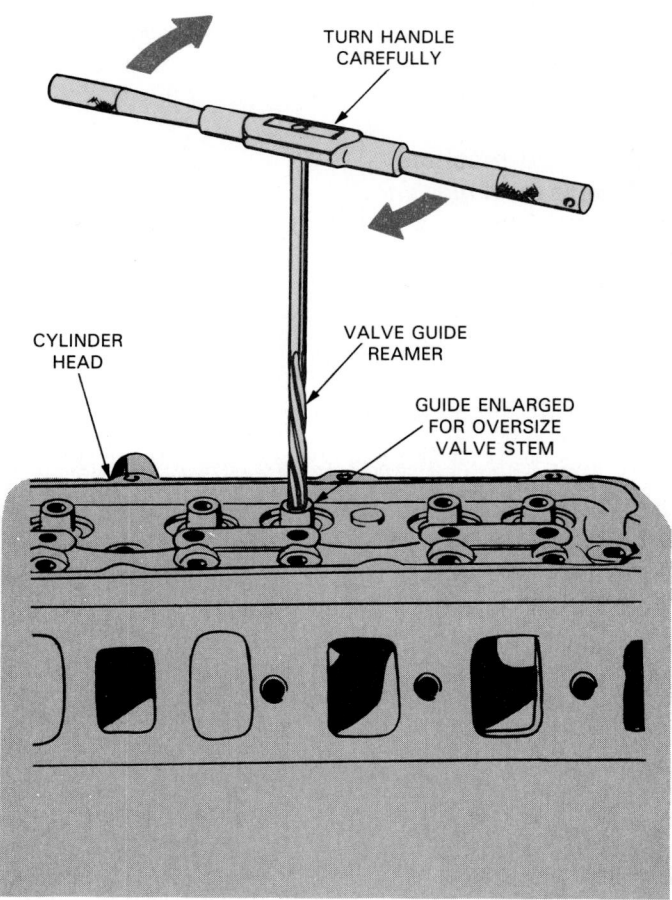

Fig. 48-13. Reamer can be used to enlarge valve guide diameter. Then new valves with oversize stems can be installed. (Oldsmobile)

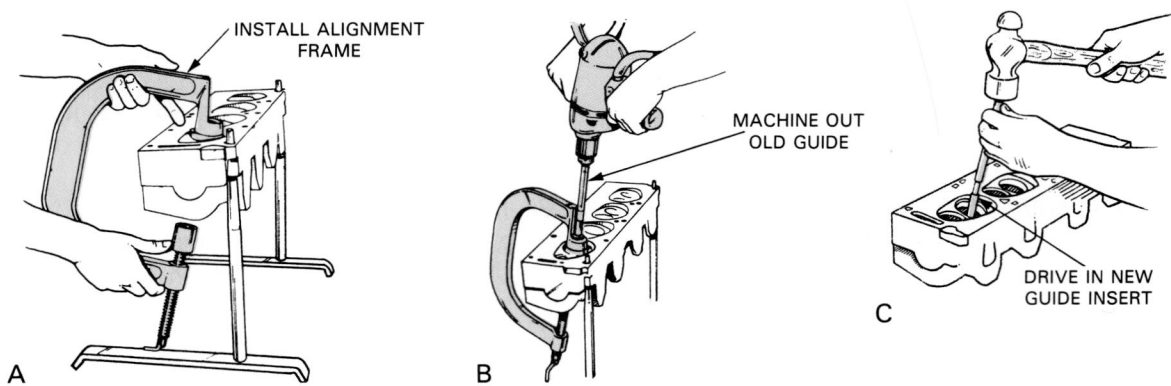

Fig. 48-14. Installing valve guide insert. (Lisle Tools)

VALVE GRINDING

Valve grinding is done by machining a fresh, smooth surface on the valve faces and stem tips. Valve faces suffer from burning, pitting, and wear caused by opening and closing millions of times during the service life of an engine. Valve stem tips wear because of friction from the rocker arms.

Before grinding, inspect each valve face for burning and each stem tip for wear. Refer back to Fig. 48-9. Replace any that are badly burned or worn. Grind a new valve along with the old, used valves.

DANGER! Wear a face shield when grinding valves. The stone could shatter, throwing debris into your face.

Valve grind machine

A *valve grind machine* is used to resurface valve faces and stems. One is pictured in Fig. 48-15. Although there are some variations in design, most valve grind machines are basically the same. They use a grinding stone and precision chuck to remove a thin layer of metal from the valve face and stem tip.

Dress the stone by using a diamond cutter to true stone surface. Do this before grinding the valves. A diamond tipped cutting attachment will be provided with the valve grind machine for truing the stone. Follow equipment manufacturer's instructions.

CAUTION! Be very careful when using a diamond tool to dress a stone. Wear eye protection and feed the diamond into the stone SLOWLY. If fed in too fast, tool or stone breakage may result.

Set the chuck angle by rotating the valve grinding machine chuck assembly. A degree scale is provided so that the cutting angle can be set precisely. Normally, you must loosen a locknut and swivel the chuck assembly into the desired angle.

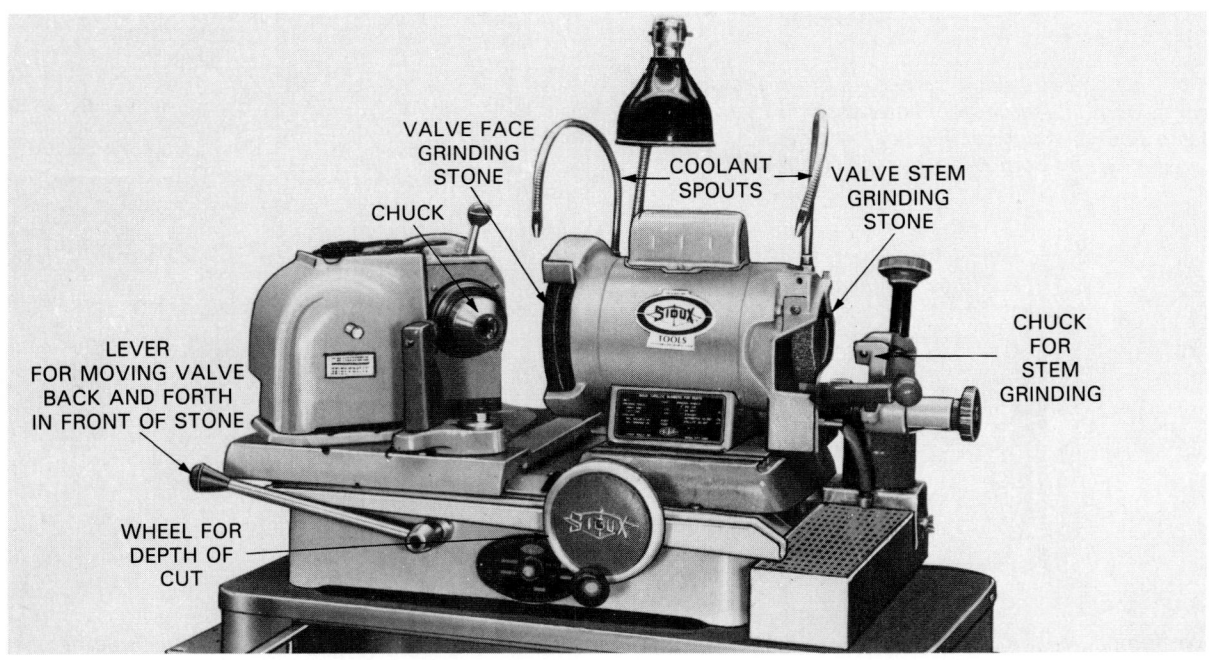

Fig. 48-15. Valve grind machine. Study various parts. (Sioux Tools)

An *interference angle* (normally one degree difference in valve face angle and valve seat angle) is set on the valve grind machine. If the valve seat angle is 45 degrees, the chuck is set to 44 degrees. As shown in Fig. 48-16, this produces an interference angle between the valve face and seat. The break in and sealing time of the valve is reduced.

Chuck the valve in the valve grind machine by inserting the valve stem into the chuck. Look at Fig. 48-17. Make sure the stem is inserted so that the chuck grasps the machined surface nearest the valve head. The chuck must NOT clamp onto an unmachined surface or runout will result.

Grinding valve face

Turn on the valve grind machine and the cooling fluid. SLOWLY feed the valve face into the stone, Fig. 48-17 and 48-18. While feeding, slowly move the valve back and forth in front of the stone. Use the full face of the stone but do NOT let the valve face move out of contact with the stone while cutting.

Note! Grind the valve only long enough to *"clean up"* its face. When the full face looks shiny, with no darkened pits, shut off the machine and inspect the face. Look carefully for pits or grooves.

Grinding, by removing metal from the face, will make the valve stem extend through the head more. This will affect spring tension and rocker arm geometry. Grind the face of each valve as little as possible.

If the valve head wobbles as it turns on the valve grind machine, the valve is either bent or chucked improperly. Shut off the machine and find the cause.

A *sharp valve margin* indicates excess valve face removal and requires valve replacement. Manufacturers give a spec for minimum valve margin thickness. Refer to Fig. 48-19.

If the margin is too thin, the valve can burn when returned to service. It may not be thick enough to dissipate heat fast enough. The head of the valve can actually begin to melt, burn, and blow out the exhaust port.

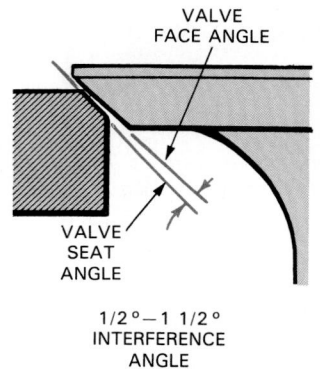

Fig. 48-16. Valve grind chuck is commonly set for one degree interference angle. Valve is ground one degree less than valve seat. This aids valve seating and sealing. (Sioux Tools)

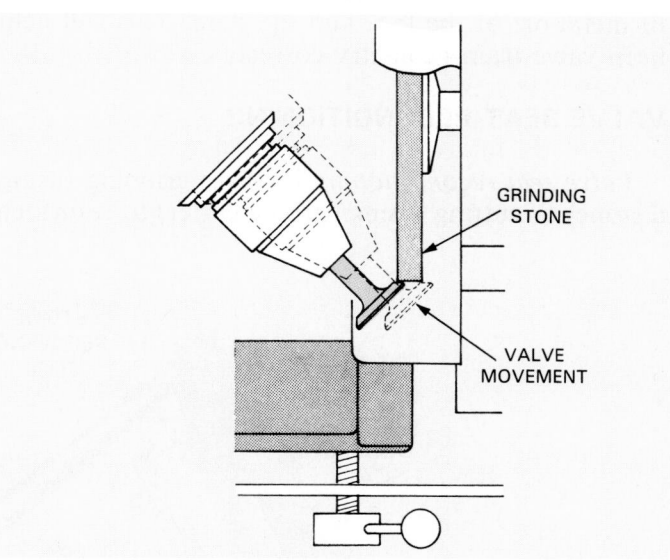

Fig. 48-18. Use lever to move valve back and forth on stone but do not let valve lose contact with stone. (TRW)

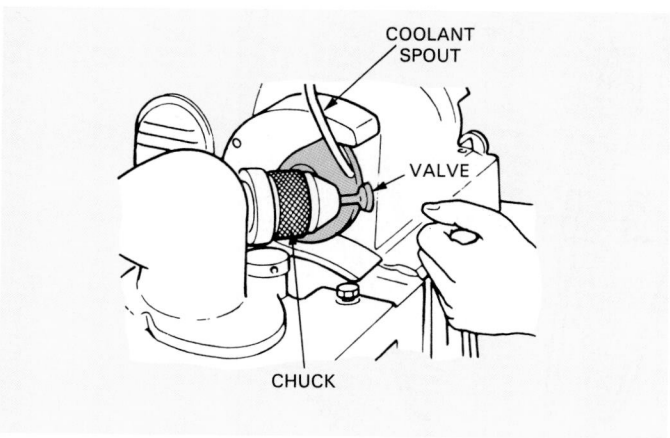

Fig. 48-17. Direct coolant on valve head while grinding. Move valve into stone slowly to avoid valve or stone damage. (Subaru)

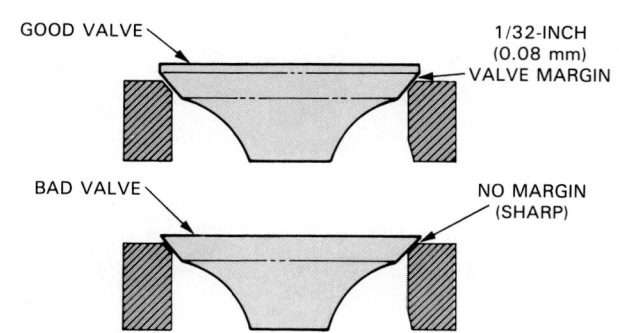

Fig. 48-19. Valve must have margin to be used in engine. Too much grinding can remove margin and sharpen valve head. Without margin, valve could overheat and burn. (AMC)

A *burned valve,* if not noticed during initial inspection, will show up when excess grinding is needed to clean up the valve face. A normal amount of grinding will not remove a deep pit or groove. Replace the valve if burned.

Repeat the grinding and inspecting operation on the other valves. Return each ground valve to its place in an organizing tray. Used valves should be returned to the same valve guide in the cylinder head. The stems may have been select fit at the factory.

Grinding valve stem tip

Another stone on the valve grind machine is normally provided for truing the valve stem tips. This is pictured in Fig. 48-20. Note how the valve is chucked in the machine.

Grind as little off the stem as possible. Many stems are hardened. Too much grinding will cut through the hardened layer and result in rapid wear when the valve is returned to service.

An indicator is provided on the valve grind machine to show the depth of cut for both the valve face and valve stem tip. Generally, CUT THE SAME amount of metal off of the face and the stem. This will help keep valve train geometry correct.

VALVE SEAT RECONDITIONING

Valve seat reconditioning involves grinding (using a stone) or cutting (using carbide cutter) to resurface

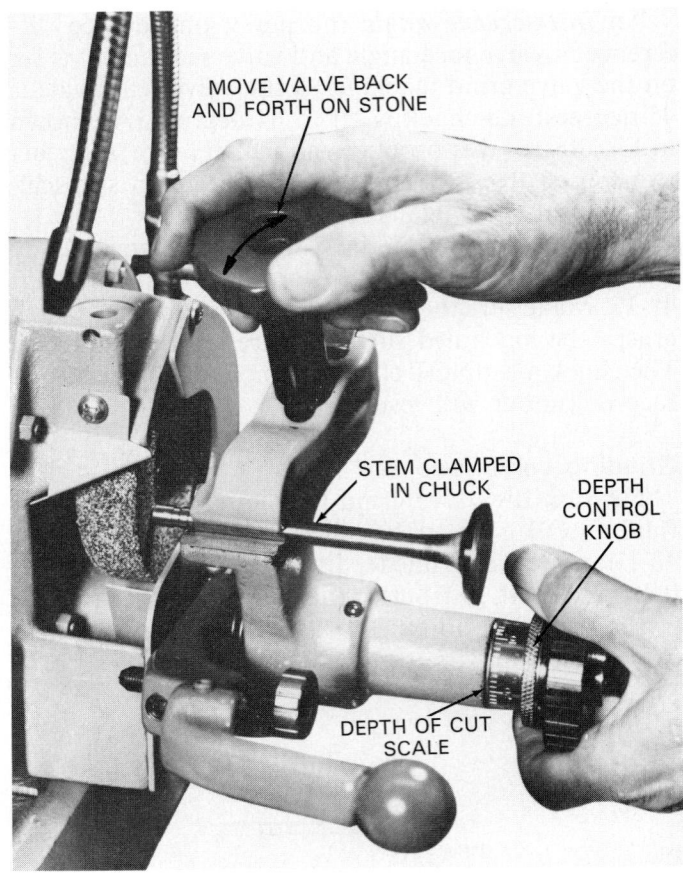

Fig. 48-20. Grind valve stem as little as possible. Wear eye protection. (Sioux Tools)

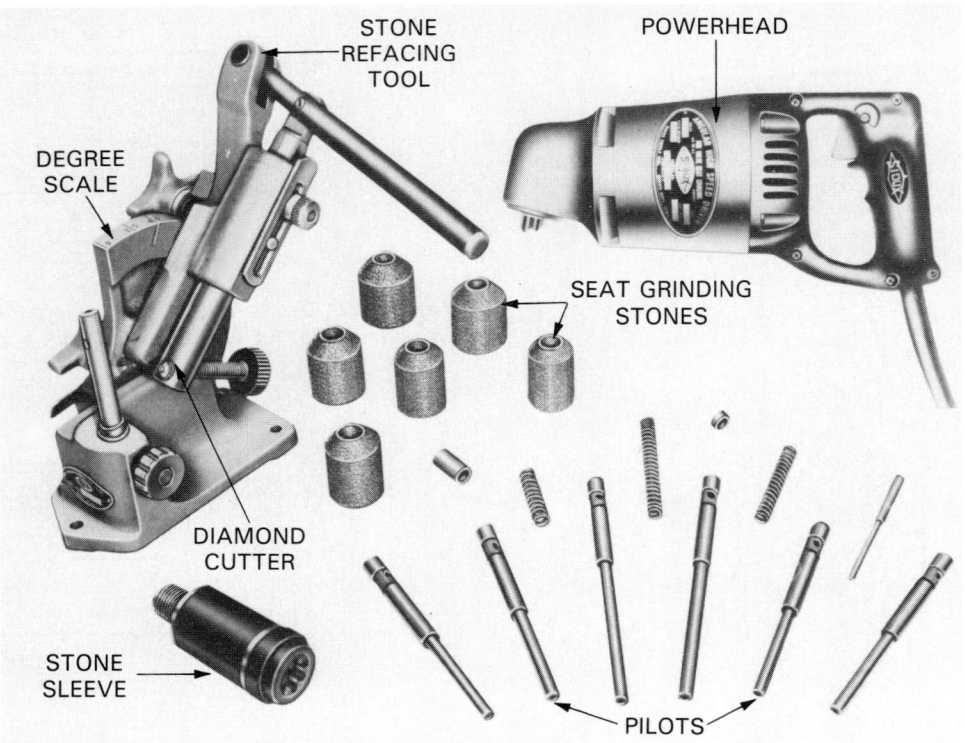

Fig. 48-21. One make of valve seat grinding equipment. Note different tool names. (Sioux Tools)

the cylinder head valve seats. Like a valve, the seats are exposed to tremendous heat, pressure, and wear.

Valve seat replacement

Valve seat replacement is needed when a valve seat is cracked, burned and pitted, or recessed (sunk) in the cylinder head. Replacement is only needed when seat wear or damage is severe. Normally, valve seats can be machined and returned to service.

Most technicians send the cylinder head to an automotive machine shop for seat replacement. Most repair shops do NOT have the specialized tools required for seat removal and installation.

To remove a pressed-in seat, split the old seat with a sharp chisel. Then, pry out the seat. Use a seat cutting tool to machine out an integral valve seat. Extreme care must be taken not to damage the cylinder head.

To install a seat, some machinists chill the seat in dry ice to shrink it. The seat will expand when returned to room temperature. This helps lock the seat in the head.

Use a driving tool to force the seat into the recess in the head. Seat installation tools vary. Follow equipment directions.

Staking the seat involves placing small dents in the cylinder head next to the seat. The stakes will swell the head metal over the seat and keep the seat from falling out. Top cutting may be needed to make the top of the seat flush with the surface of the combustion chamber.

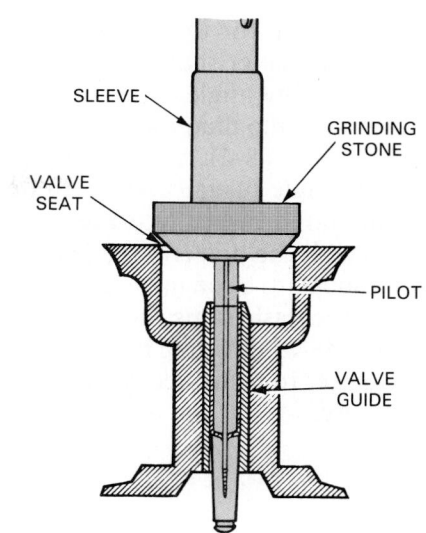

Fig. 48-22. Cutaway view shows how pilot, stone, and sleeve fit on cylinder head for seat grinding.

Grinding valve seats

After new seat installation, or when the old valve seats are in servicable condition, grind or cut the face of the valve seats. The equipment needed to grind valve seats is shown in Fig. 48-21.

To grind valve seats, select and install the correct size *pilot* (metal shaft that fits into guide and supports cutting stone or carbide cutter). The pilot should fit snugly in the valve guide and not wiggle, Fig. 48-22.

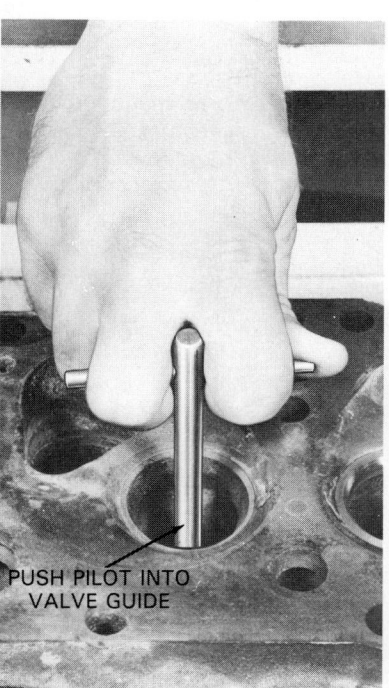

A

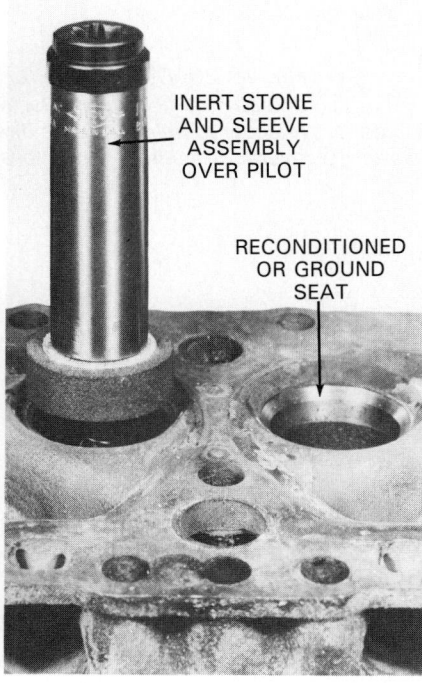

B

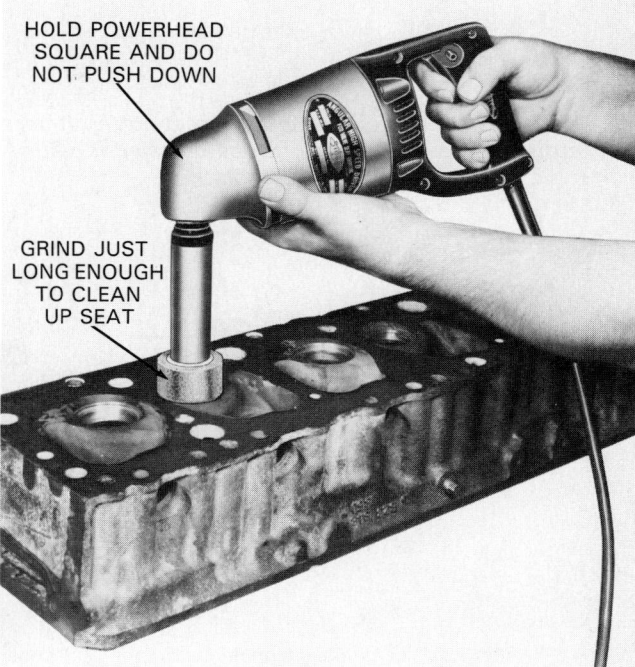

C

Fig. 48-23. Grinding valve seat. A — Push pilot securely into valve guide. Pilot must be tight in guide. B — Slip stone and sleeve assembly over pilot. Make sure stone has right angle and is slightly larger than seat. C — Use power head to spin stone. Support weight of power head. Grind only long enough to clean up pits in seat.

Select the correct stone for the valve seat. It must be slightly larger in diameter than the seat and must also have the correct face angle.

Dress the stone using the diamond cutter provided with the equipment, Fig. 48-21. Set the cutter attachment to the correct angle (usually 45 or 30 degrees). Slowly feed the diamond cutter into the stone while spinning the stone with the power head (electric drive motor). Cut only enough to clean up and true the stone.

Fig. 48-23 shows the basic steps for grinding a valve seat. Figs. 48-24 and 48-25 illustrate how to use a hand-operated carbide cutter to resurface valve seats. Study both methods closely.

Narrowing or positioning valve seat

Narrowing or *positioning a valve seat* is needed to center or locate the valve-to-seat contact point. Fig. 48-26 illustrates seat contact patterns. If the seat does not touch near the center of the valve face, with the correct contact width, valve service life can be reduced.

Typically, an intake valve should have a valve-to-seat CONTACT WIDTH of about 1/16 in. (1.6 mm). An exhaust valve should have a valve-to-seat contact width of approximatley 3/32 in. (2.4 mm). Check manual specs for exact values.

When the valve seat does NOT touch the valve face properly (wrong width or location on valve), regrind

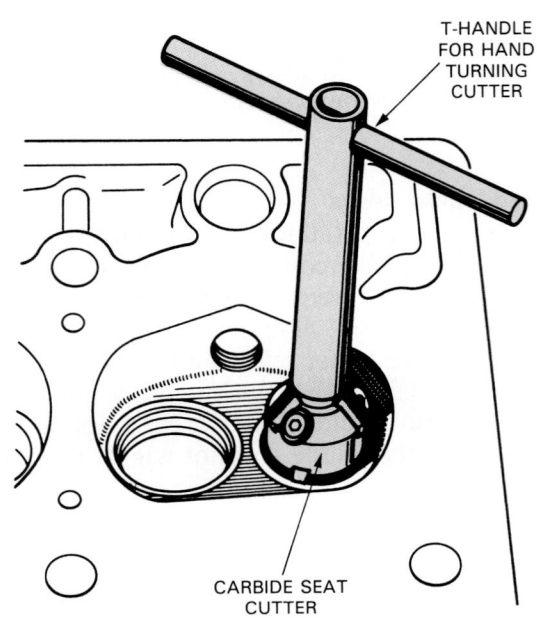

Fig. 48-24. Hand-operated valve seat cutter. It uses carbide cutters instead of stones. Stone dressing is not necessary. (Renault)

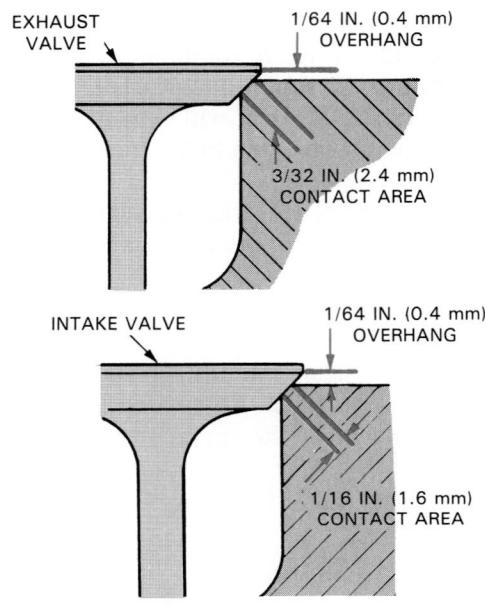

Fig. 48-26. General rule for positioning valve-to-seat contact on both intake and exhaust valves. Exhaust seat must be slightly wider to help dissipate heat. Note typical contact width and overhang values. Refer to a service manual for exact specs. (TRW)

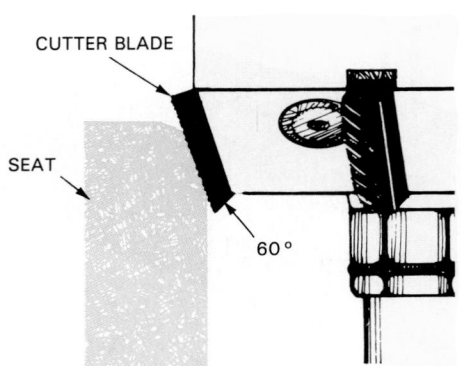

First cut cleans and reconditions area below seat.

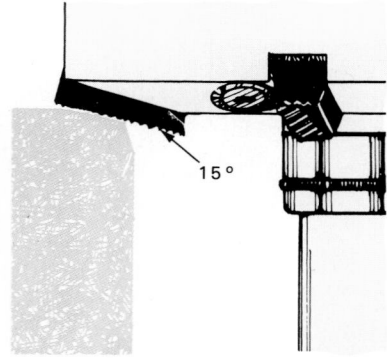

Second cut cleans and reconditions area above seat.

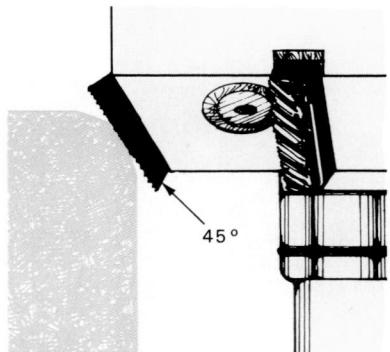

Three or four revolutions of cutter produce a precision seat.

Fig. 48-25. Basic steps for using a carbide cutter to produce three-angle valve job. This will produce very accurate valve seat. (Neway)

the seat using different stone angles, usually 15 and 60 degree stones.

To MOVE THE SEAT IN and narrow it, grind the valve seat with a 15 degree stone. Shown in Fig. 48-27, this will remove metal from around the top of the seat. The seat face (valve contact surface) will move closer to the valve stem.

To MOVE THE SEAT OUT and narrow it, machine the valve seat with a 60 degree stone or cutter. This will cut metal away from the inner edge of the seat. See Fig. 48-27. The seat contact point will move toward the margin or outer edge of the valve.

Checking seat runout

Valve seat runout occurs when the seat is not centered around the valve guide. Some auto makers suggest checking seat runout after seat grinding. If special dial indicator setup, Fig. 48-28, shows runout, regrind the seat or check guide installation.

Lapping valves

Lapping valves is done to check the location of the valve-to-seat contact point and to smooth the mating surfaces.

Grinding compound (abrasive paste) is dabbed on the valve face. The valve is then installed in the cylinder head and rotated with a *lapping stick* (wooden stick with rubber plunger for holding valve head).

Rub your hands back and forth on the lapping stick to spin the valve on its seat. This will rub the grinding compound between the valve face and seat.

Remove the valve and check the contact point. A DULL GREY STRIPE around the seat and face indicates the valve-to-seat contact point. This will help you narrow or move the valve seat as needed.

A few manufacturers do NOT recommend valve lapping. Refer to a service manual for details.

WARNING! Make sure you clean all of the valve grinding compound off of the valve and cylinder head. The compound can cause rapid part wear.

TESTING VALVE SPRINGS

After prolonged use, valves springs tend to weaken, lose tension, or even break. During engine service, always test valve springs to make sure they are usable.

Valve spring squareness is easily checked with a combination square. Look at Fig. 48-29A. Place each spring

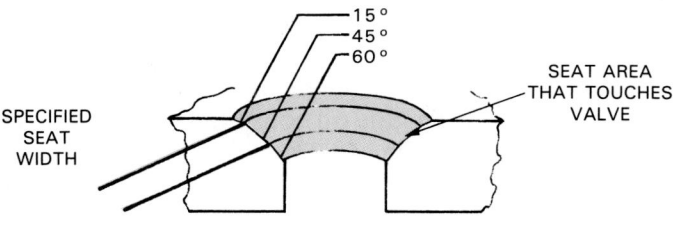

Fig. 48-27. Study how different stone or cutter angles can be used to move or narrow seat. A 60° cut would narrow and move seat up on valve face. A 15° cut would narrow and move seat down on valve face.

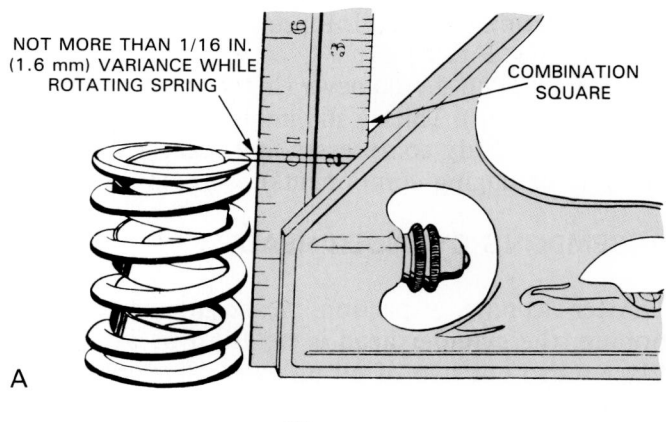

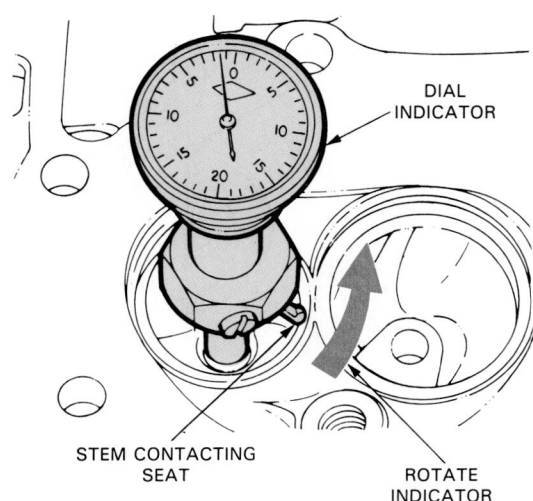

Fig. 48-28. Some auto makers suggest a check of valve seat runout. Indicator reading equals runout.

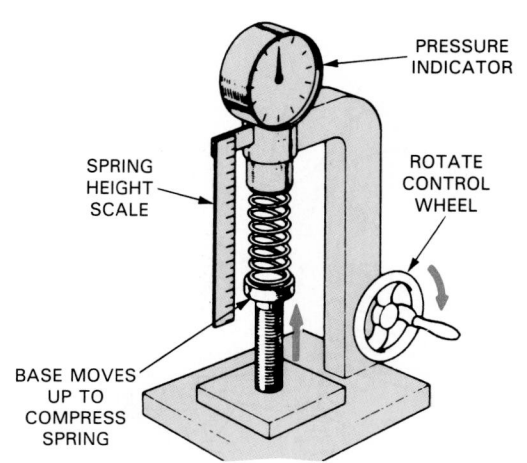

Fig. 48-29. A — Combination square can be used to check valve spring squareness. If not square, replace spring. B — Valve spring tester will measure spring pressure or tension at specific spring height or length. If weakened, shim or replace springs. (Cadillac and Toyota)

next to the square on a flat work surface. Rotate the spring while checking for a gap between the side of the spring and the square. Replace the spring(s) if not square.

Valve spring free height can also be measured with the combination square or with a valve spring tester. Simply measure the length of each spring in a normal, uncompressed condition. If too long or too short, replace the spring.

Valve spring tension or pressure is measured on a spring tester. See Fig. 48-29B. Compress the spring to specification height and read the scale. Spring pressure must be within specs. If too low, the spring has weakened and needs replacement or shimming.

Valve spring shimming

Valve spring shimming is used to keep correct tension when the springs are installed on the cylinder heads. When valves and seats are ground, the valve stem sticks through the head farther. This increases installed height and reduces spring pressure.

Valve spring installed height is the distance from the top to the bottom of the valve spring with the spring installed on the cylinder head. It can be measured with a sliding caliper, as in Fig. 48-30. If greater than specs, add enough shims to reduce installed height and return spring pressure to normal. Place the shim(s) under the valve spring, Fig. 48-31.

Generally, you should never shim a valve spring over .060 in. (1.5 mm). Thicker shimming could cause *spring bind* (spring fully compresses and locks valve train, possibly damaging components).

ASSEMBLING CYLINDER HEAD

After cleaning, inspection, measuring, and reconditioning, the cylinder head is ready to be assembled. Place a drop or two of oil on each valve stem. Slide the valves into their valve guides.

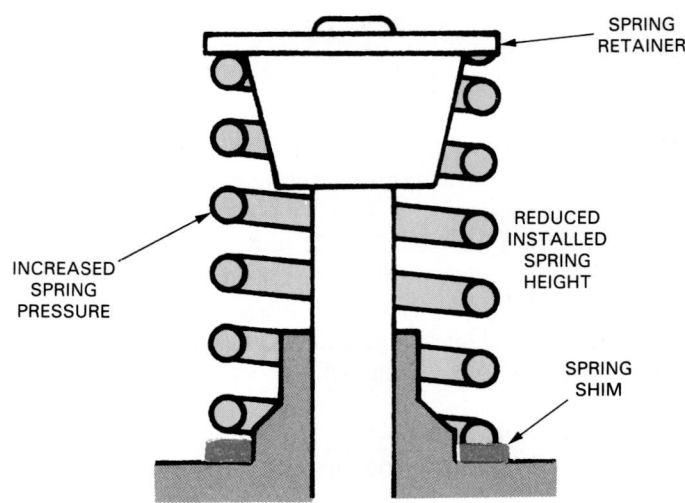

Fig. 48-31. Valve spring shim installed under valve spring. This will restore spring pressure, preventing possible valve float. (TRW)

Installing valve seals and spring assemblies

With UMBRELLA type valve seals, simply slide the seals over the valve stems. Some locking type seals require a special installation tool to force the seal around the upper end of the valve guide. Look at Fig. 48-32.

NOTE! With O-RING type valve seals, compress the valve spring BEFORE fitting the seal on the valve stem. If you install the seal first, it will be cut, split, or pushed out of its groove. Engine oil consumption and smoking will result. See Fig. 48-33.

With the spring compressed, fit the retainer and keepers into place on the valve. Install all of the valve

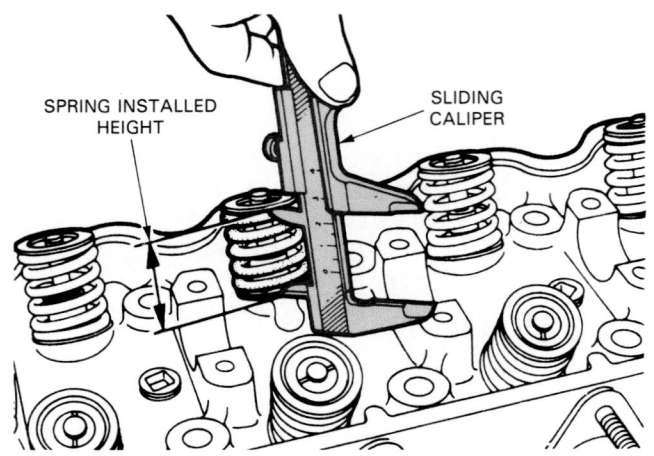

Fig. 48-30. Measuring valve spring installed height. Grinding valves and seats tend to increase installed height. Shims are needed to restore correct spring pressure. (Chrysler)

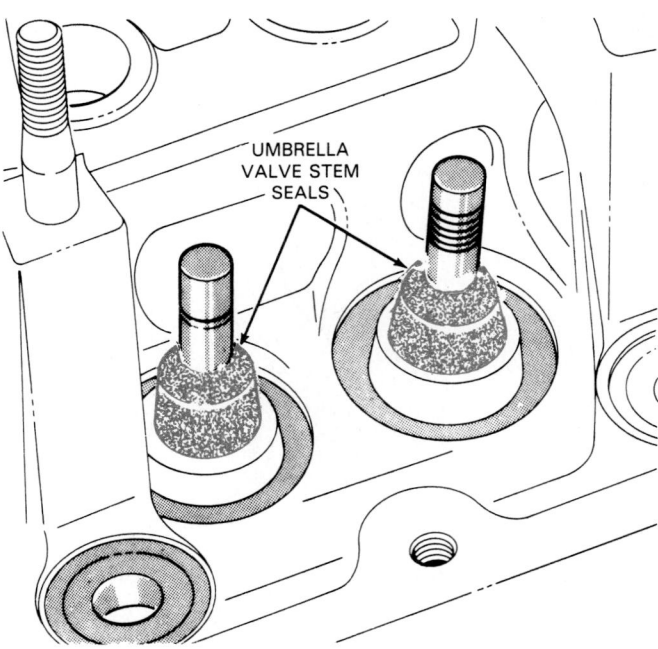

Fig. 48-32. To install umbrella valve seals, oil valve stems and slide seals into place. Then compress and install springs. (Chrysler)

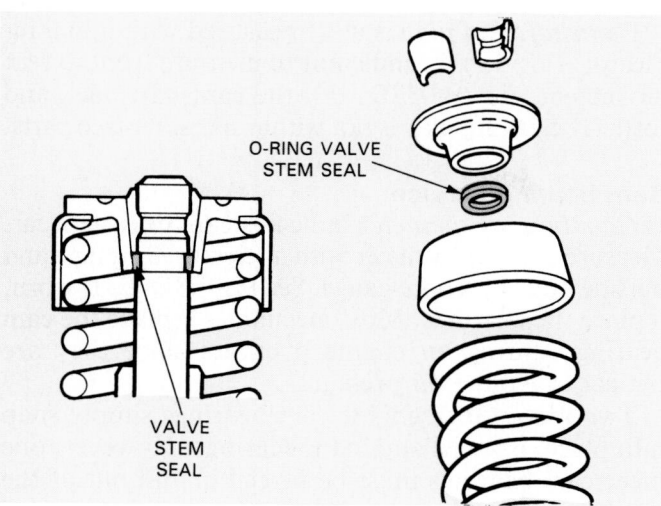

Fig. 48-33. Note! With O-ring type valve seals, compress the spring and retainer first. Then, fit valve seal into its groove, install keepers, and release spring. If seal is installed first, it can be ruined. Engine smoking or oil consumption can result. (Buick)

assemblies. Tap on the valve stems with a brass hammer to seat the keepers in their grooves.

Fig. 48-34 shows how a special valve spring compressor is used to install the springs on an OHC engine. A conventional valve spring compressor was shown in Chapter 46.

Checking for valve leakage

To check for valve leakage after head reconditioning and assembly, lay the cylinder head on its side. Pour clean cold soak solvent or water into the intake and exhaust ports. With the fluid in the ports, watch for leakage around the valve heads. If solvent or water drips from around a valve, that valve is leaking. Remove the valve from the head and check for problems.

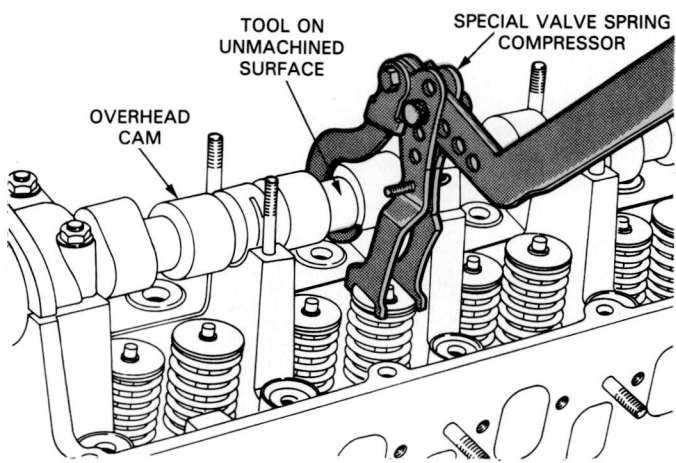

Fig. 48-34. Special valve spring compressor may be needed on some OHC engines. Tap valve stems lightly with brass hammer to seat keepers. (Chrysler)

IN-CAR VALVE SEAL SERVICE

Valve seals and springs can be serviced without cylinder head removal, as shown in Fig. 48-35. Use a shop air hose and a special fitting to inject air into one of the cylinders. The air will hold the valves in that cylinder up against their seats. Then, use a special pry bar type compressor to remove the keepers and springs for that cylinder. This will allow in-vehicle seal or spring replacement.

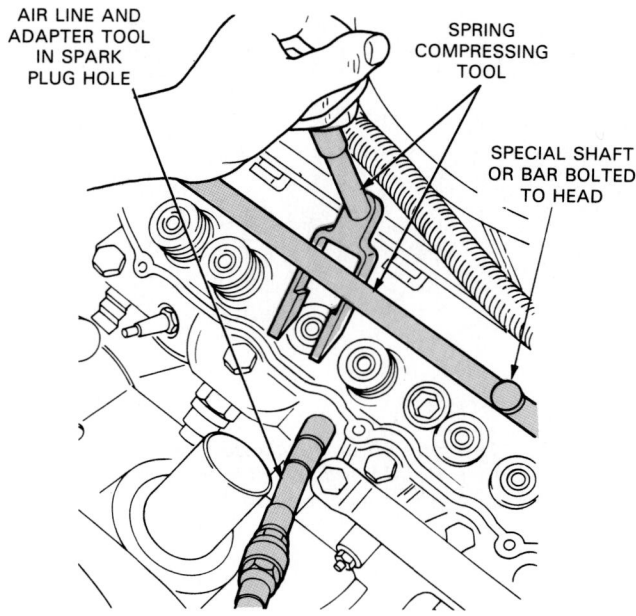

Fig. 48-35. Valve seals can be replaced without cylinder head removal. Inject shop air pressure into cylinder to hold valves up in head. Use special pry bar tool to compress valve springs for seal replacement. (Ford)

CAMSHAFT SERVICE

Camshaft service involves measuring cam lobe and journal wear. It also includes distributor-oil pump gear inspection and cam bearing measurement or replacement.

Measuring camshaft wear

Cam lobe wear can be measured with a dial indicator with the camshaft installed in the engine. Refer to Fig. 48-36. When the camshaft is out of the engine, an outside micrometer is used, Fig. 48-37A. If lobe lift or dimensions are too small, the cam is worn and should be reground or replaced.

Cam journal wear is measured with an outside micrometer, as in Fig. 48-37B. A worn cam is usually replaced. Journal wear lowers engine oil pressure.

Camshaft straightness is checked with V-blocks and a dial indicator. This is illustrated in Fig. 48-37C. If the dial indicator reads more than specs, the cam is bent and must be replaced.

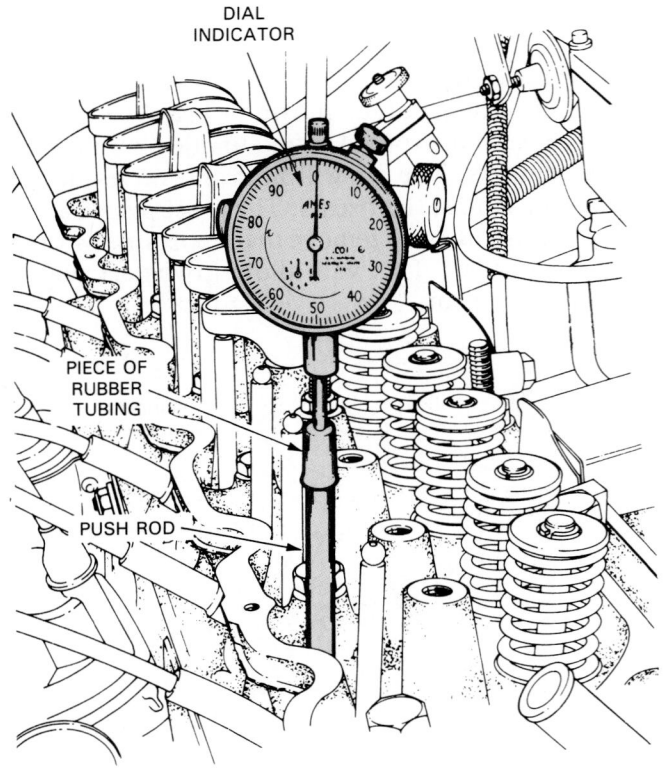

Camshaft end play is also measured with a dial indicator. Position the indicator to measure front to rear movement, Fig. 48-37D. Pry the camshaft back and forth. If cam end play is not within specs, replace parts.

Cam bearing service

Cam bearing diameter indicates cam bearing wear. Measure bearing diameter with a telescoping gauge and outside mike or a bore gauge. See Fig. 48-37E. If worn, replace the bearings. Most mechanics replace the cam bearings during an engine overhaul since they are critical to engine oil pressure.

Two-piece OHC engine cam bearings simply snap into place, like rod and main bearings. However, one piece cam bearings must be forced in and out of the block or head with a special tool. Many mechanics send the head or block to a machine shop for cam bearing replacement.

When installing cam bearings, be careful not to dent or mar the bearing surfaces. Also, make sure you align the oil holes in the engine with the holes in the cam bearings. Since exact procedures vary, refer to a shop manual for details.

LIFTER (TAPPET) SERVICE

The contact surface between a lifter and cam lobe is one of the highest friction and wear points in an

Fig. 48-36. Cam lobe lift and wear can be measured before engine teardown. Rotate engine while reading dial indicator. If lift is less than specs, camshaft is worn.

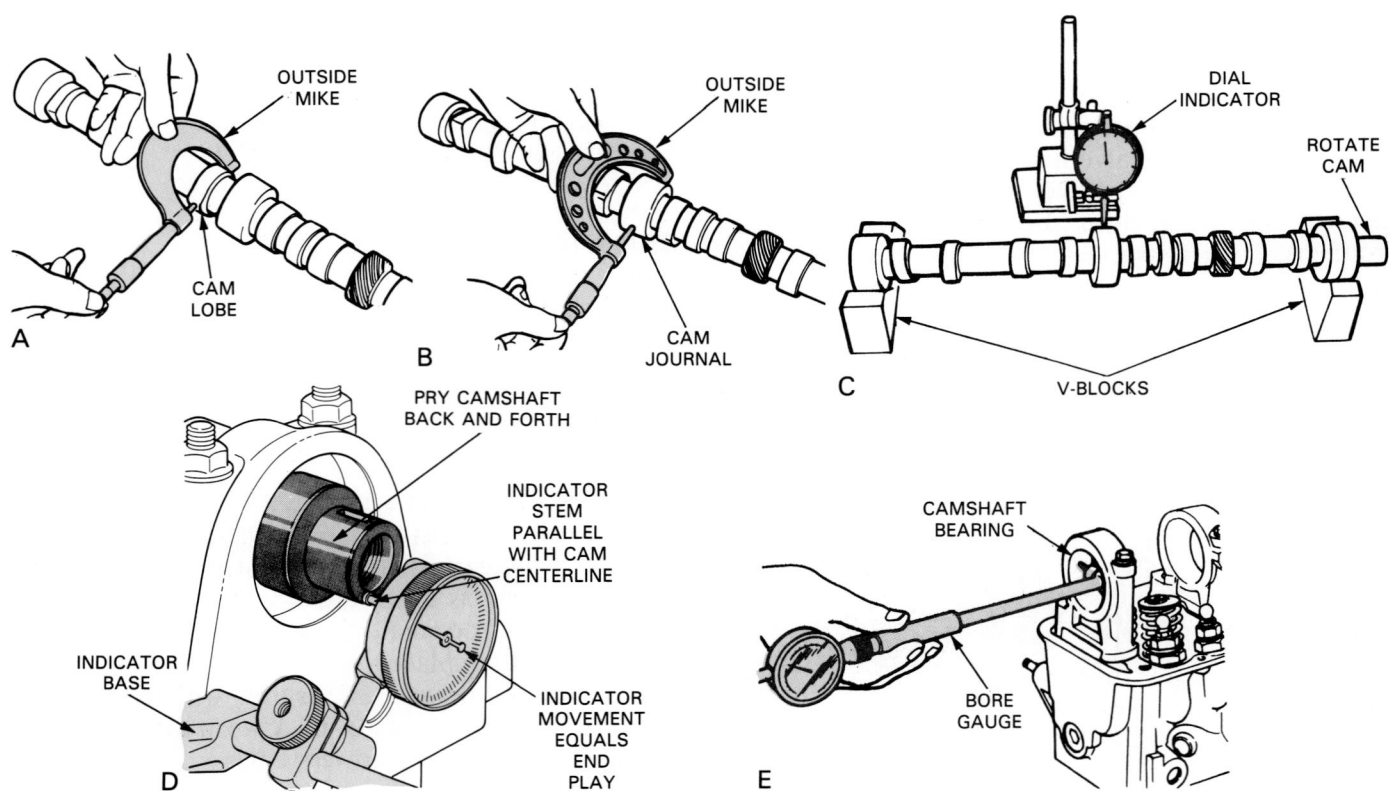

Fig. 48-37. Measuring camshaft wear. A — Mike cam lobe and compare to specs. B — Measure cam journal diameter and compare to specs. C — Mount camshaft in V-blocks. Position dial indicator on center journal. Turn cam and read indicator. If not straight, replace camshaft. D — To check camshaft end play, install cam in engine. Position dial indicator. Pry back and forth on camshaft while reading indicator. E — Dial bore gauge can be used to check cam bearing or cam bore diameter. (Ford, Chrysler, and Nissan)

engine. Hydraulic lifters can also wear internally, causing valve train clatter (tapping noise).

Inspecting lifters

Inspect the bottoms of the lifters for wear. A good, unworn lifter will have a slight hump or convex shape on the bottom. See Fig. 48-38. Worn lifters will be flat or concave on the bottom. Replace the lifters if the bottoms are worn.

NEVER install used, worn lifters on a new camshaft. Worn lifters will cause rapid cam lobe wear and additional lifter wear. Install new lifters when a camshaft is replaced.

Testing lifter leak down rate

Lifter leak down rate is measured by timing how long it takes to push the lifter plunger to the bottom of its stroke under controlled conditions. A lifter tester is pictured in Fig. 48-39.

Generally, fill the tester with a special test fluid. Place the lifter in the tester. Then, follow specific instructions to determine lifter leak down rate. If leak down is too fast or slow, replace or rebuild the lifter.

Rebuilding hydraulic lifters

Rebuilding hydraulic lifters typically involves complete disassembly, cleaning, and measurement of lifter components. All worn or scored parts must be replaced following manufacturer instructions.

Many shops do NOT rebuild hydraulic lifters. If the lifters are defective, new ones are installed. This can save time and money under most circumstances.

PUSH ROD SERVICE

Check each push rod tip for wear. The center of a worn push rod tip may be pointed where it fits into the oil hole in the rocker arm. Also, make sure that none of the push rods is bent. Check by rolling them on a flat surface. If the push rods are hollow, look down through each one to make sure it is clean (not clogged).

ROCKER ARM ASSEMBLY SERVICE

Inspect the rocker arms for wear, clogged oil holes, or other problems. If wear is indicated inside the rocker

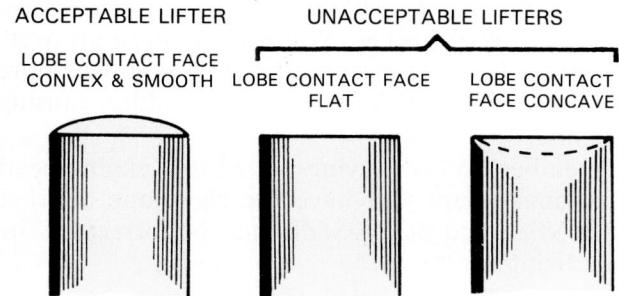

Fig. 48-38. Bottoms of lifter should be checked for wear as shown. (Ford Motor Co.)

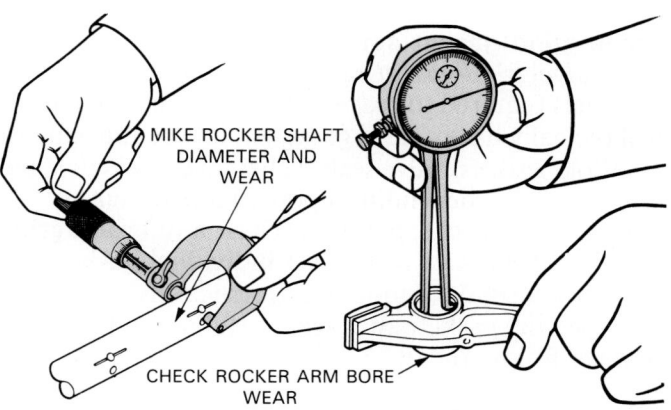

Fig. 48-40. Measure wear on rocker arm shaft and inside rocker arm bore. If out of specs, replace it. (Toyota)

bore, measure it with a telescoping gauge and micrometer or bore gauge. See Fig. 48-40. Replace any rocker arm showing wear.

Also inspect the rocker arm shaft for wear. A *worn rocker shaft* will have indentations where the rocker arms swivel on the shaft. Wear will usually be greater on the bottom of the shaft. Mike the shaft to determine if wear is within specs, Fig. 48-40.

When reassembling a rocker shaft, make sure the oil holes are facing in the proper direction. The oil holes normally face down to lubricate the loaded side of the shaft.

With a ball or stand type valve train, inspect the ball or stand for wear. If the rocker stand is made of aluminum, check it closely for grooves, which indicate wear. Replace any part worn beyond safe limits.

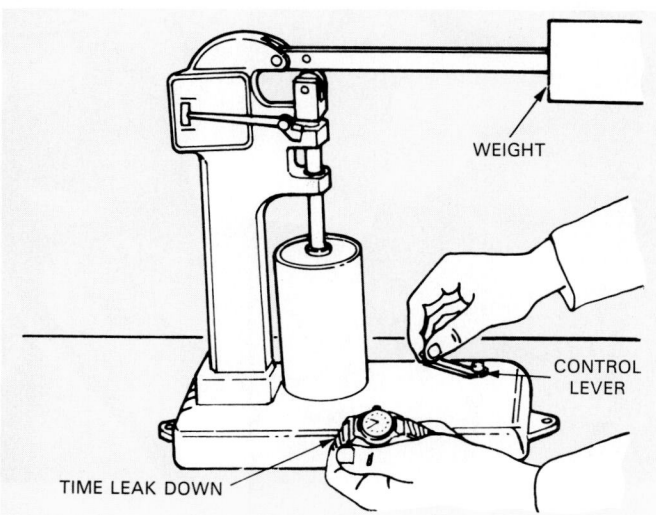

Fig. 48-39. Special equipment for measuring hydraulic lifter leak down rate. Follow directions provided with tester. Replace or rebuild lifter if it fails leak down test. (Buick)

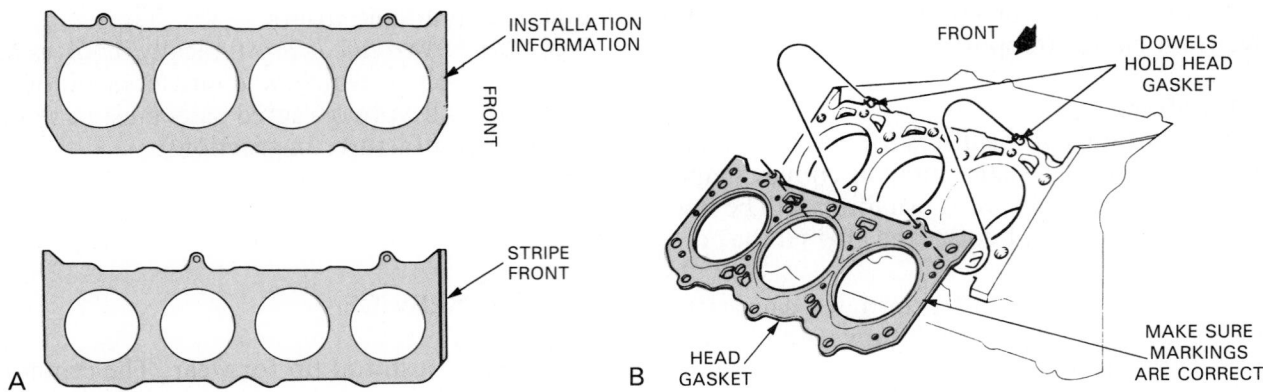

Fig. 48-41. A — Cylinder head gaskets are normally marked front. This assures proper coolant flow through block and heads. B — Fit new head gasket over dowels. Sealer is not required with many modern head gasket designs. Double-check that gasket is installed properly. (Oldsmobile and Buick)

ENGINE TOP END REASSEMBLY

Proper engine assembly procedures are very critical to good engine operation. The slightest mistake can result in major engine problems. The next section will outline the most important facts to remember when reassembling an engine top end.

Valve grind gasket set

A *valve grind gasket set* includes all of the gaskets and seals required to reassemble an engine top end. It will typically have a head gasket(s), intake and exhaust manifold gaskets, valve seals, valve cover gasket(s), and other gaskets, depending upon engine design.

It is normally cheaper to purchase a full valve grind set of gaskets than to request individual gaskets.

A gasket set commonly has instructions summarizing specific gasket and seal installation methods. Always follow them!

Installing cylinder head gasket

Cylinder head gasket markings are normally provided to show the front or top of the gasket. Usually, a head gasket can only be installed one way. If installed backwards, coolant or oil passages may be blocked, causing serious problems.

The head gasket may be marked "TOP," "FRONT," or it may have a LINE to show installation direction. See Fig. 48-41A. Metal dowels are frequently provided to align the head gasket on the block. See Fig. 48-41B.

Most modern teflon-coated, permanent torque (retorquing is not needed after engine operation) cylinder head gaskets should be installed clean and dry. Sealer is NOT recommended. However, some head gaskets may require retorquing and sealer. Refer to manufaturer's instructions when in doubt.

Diesel engine head gaskets

With diesel engines, head gasket thickness and bore size are very critical. Head gaskets are provided in different thicknesses to allow for cylinder head milling or varying block deck heights. Gasket thickness may be denoted with a color code, series of notches, holes, or other marking method.

Fig. 48-42 pictures how one manufacturer recommends checking TDC piston height in the block. This measurement will let you use service manual information to determine the required head gasket thickness.

When a diesel engine block is bored oversize, it also requires a special gasket. You must request an overbore gasket from the parts supplier. A standard bore gasket will usually stick out into the cylinder, causing problems.

Remember! When buying a DIESEL engine head gasket, make sure you have the right one. Gasket THICKNESS and BORE SIZE must be correct for the engine being repaired.

Fig. 48-42. One manufacturer suggests checking piston height in block with diesel engine. Service manual data can then be used to calculate correct head gasket thickness. (Fel-Pro Incorporated)

Installing cylinder head

Gently place the cylinder head over the head gasket and block. You must do this without bumping and damaging the gasket. See Fig. 48-43.

Make sure the head is over its dowels. If dowels are NOT provided, stud bolts should be screwed into the block to serve as guide dowels for gasket and head alignment.

Start all of the head bolts and spin them in by hand. Sealer is needed on any bolt that enters a water jacket. Refer to Fig. 48-44.

Use a TORQUE WRENCH to tighten the head bolts to SPECS. Tighten in a factory recommended crisscross pattern. A service manual will give the exact sequence. One example is given in Fig. 48-45.

Generally, tighten the bolts starting in the middle. Then, work your way outward, tightening each bolt a little at a time (1/2, 3/4, then full torque).

For example, if the head bolt torque is 100 ft.-lb. (130 N·m), tighten all of the bolts to 50 ft.-lb. (68 N·m), then 75 ft.-lb. (101 N·m), then 100 ft.-lb. (130 N·m). Tighten each bolt to full torque several times to assure an accurate torque.

Installing intake manifold

Position the intake manifold gasket. Silicone sealer may be recommended, especially where the front and rear seals on a V-type engine meet the side gaskets. Look at Fig. 48-46.

Fig. 48-44. Any head bolt that protrudes into a water jacket should be sealed. Use a nonhardening sealer and a service manual to find out which bolts should be sealed. If not coated with sealer, coolant could leak out around the bolt threads and bolt head. (Fel-Pro Incorporated)

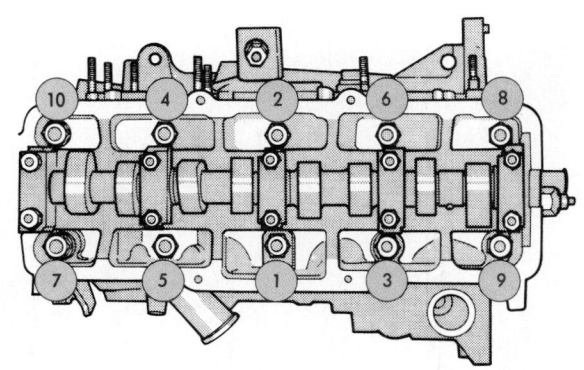

Fig. 48-45. Torque a cylinder head in exact torque pattern recommended by manufacturer. Generally, use a crisscross pattern. Start in the middle and work your way to outer bolts. Tighten in steps: half torque, three-quarter torque, and full torque several times. (Chrysler)

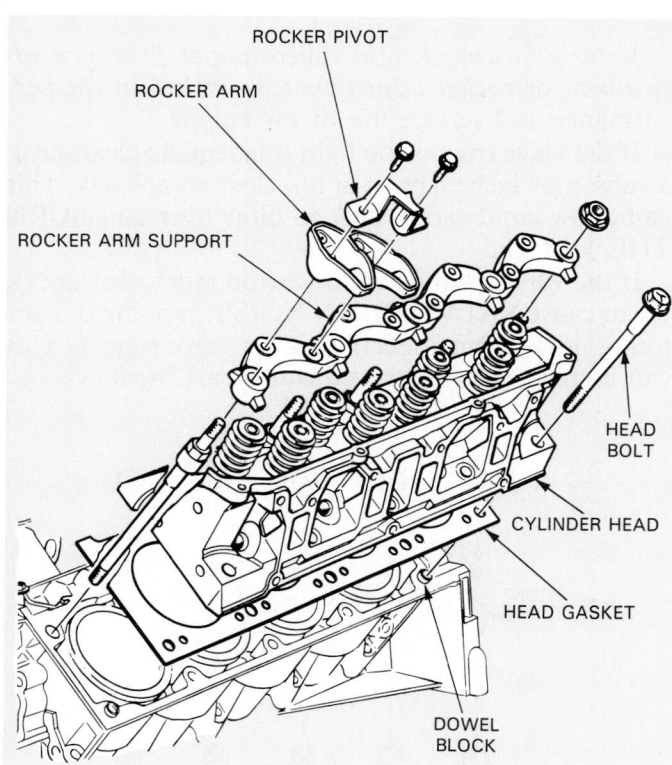

Fig. 48-43. When installing a cylinder head, do not bump the head gasket or the gasket could be damaged. Slowly lower head onto dowels. (Cadillac)

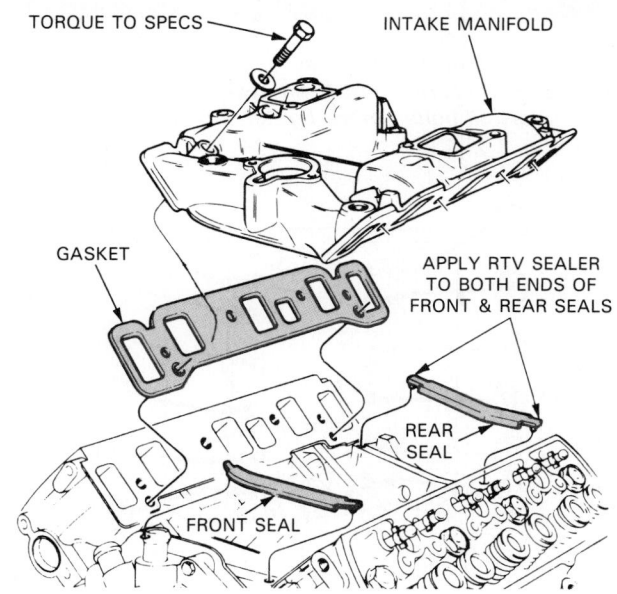

Fig. 48-46. When rubber end seals butt against a fiber gasket in corners of V-type engines, use silicone sealer. Place a dab of sealer where two join. (Oldsmobile)

With some in-line engines, sealer is not needed on the intake gasket. Dowels may be provided to hold the gasket in place during manifold installation. See Fig. 48-47 for an example.

Start ALL of the fasteners before tightening. This will aid bolt hole alignment.

Torque the intake manifold to specifications. Use the specific torque pattern given in the shop manual. Basically, the pattern will be a crisscross pattern, like the one in Fig. 48-48.

Installing exhaust manifolds

Most used exhaust manifolds require a gasket. Sealer is NOT commonly recommended because of the extreme heat at the exhaust manifold. Hold the gasket in place by hand as you start the bolts, Fig. 48-49. Torque the bolts to specs in a crisscross sequence.

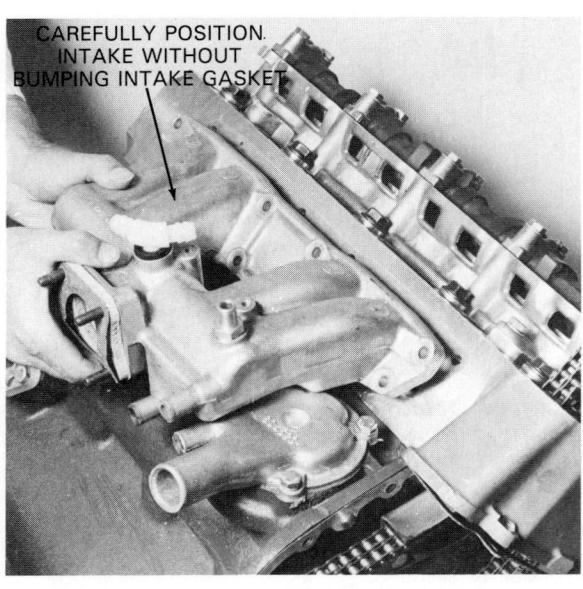

Fig. 48-47. As with cylinder head, slowly lower intake manifold into position. Be careful not to hit gasket or gasket may leak. Start all bolts before tightening any. (Saab)

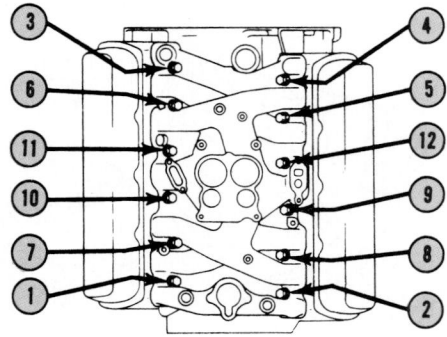

Fig. 48-48. Torque intake manifold in crisscross pattern. Sequence for one particular engine is shown. Lubricate bolt threads in motor oil. (Oldsmobile)

Fig. 48-49. Often, you must hold exhaust gasket on head while starting bolts. To simplify installation, some manufacturers now provide exhaust manifold gaskets with slots, as shown at bottom. This allows you to start the bolts before slipping the gasket into place. (Fel-Pro Incorporated)

Rocker assembly installation

With a rocker shaft, fit the shaft and rocker assembly on the cylinder head. Start the bolts by hand.

Next, torque to specs. Use the sequence given for the particular engine. Fig. 48-50 shows a rocker shaft tightening sequence for a modern OHC engine.

If nonadjustable individual rocker stands or studs are used, torque the bolts or nuts to specs. With adjustable rockers, simply start the nuts but do NOT tighten them. You will have to adjust the valves. This is also true with solid lifters.

VALVE ADJUSTMENT (TAPPET CLEARANCE)

Valve adjustment, also called *tappet clearance adjustment* or *rocker adjustment,* is critical to the performance and service life of the engine.

If the valve train is too tight (inadequate clearance), a valve may be held open or not close completely. This can allow combustion heat to blow over and BURN THE VALVE.

If the valve train is too loose (too much clearance), it can cause VALVE TRAIN NOISE (tapping or clattering noise from rockers striking valve stems). This can increase part wear and cause part breakage.

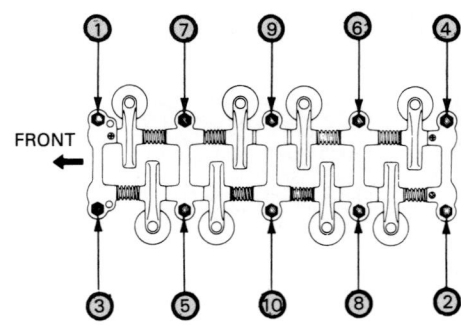

Fig. 48-50. Tighten rocker arm shaft assembly as described in service manual. Tighten each bolt a little at a time to prevent bending of shaft(s). (Toyota)

Nonadjustable rocker arms

Nonadjustable rocker arms are used on many push rod engines with hydraulic (self-adjusting) lifters. The hydraulic lifter automatically compensates for changes in valve train clearance, maintaining *zero valve lash* (no clearance in valve train for quiet operation).

The hydraulic lifter can adjust valve train clearance as parts wear, with changes in temperature (part contraction or expansion), and with changes in oil thickness.

If adjustment is needed because of valve grinding, head milling, or other conditions, different PUSH ROD LENGTHS can be used with nonadjustable rocker arms. Refer to the service manual for details.

Adjusting hydraulic lifters

Hydraulic lifter adjustment is done to center the lifter plunger in its bore. This will let the lifter automatically adjust itself to take up or allow more valve train clearance. Some manuals recommend adjustment with the engine off. However, many technicians adjust hydraulic lifters with the engine running.

To adjust hydraulic lifters with the **engine off,** turn the crankshaft until the lifter is on the camshaft base circle (not on lobe). As illustrated in Fig. 48-51, the valve must be fully closed.

Loosen the adjusting nut until you can wiggle the push rod up and down. See Fig. 48-52. Then, slowly tighten the rocker until all play is out of the valve train (cannot wiggle push rod).

To center the lifter plunger, tighten the adjusting nut about ONE MORE TURN. Refer to a manual for details because this can vary with engine design. Repeat the adjusting procedure on the other rockers.

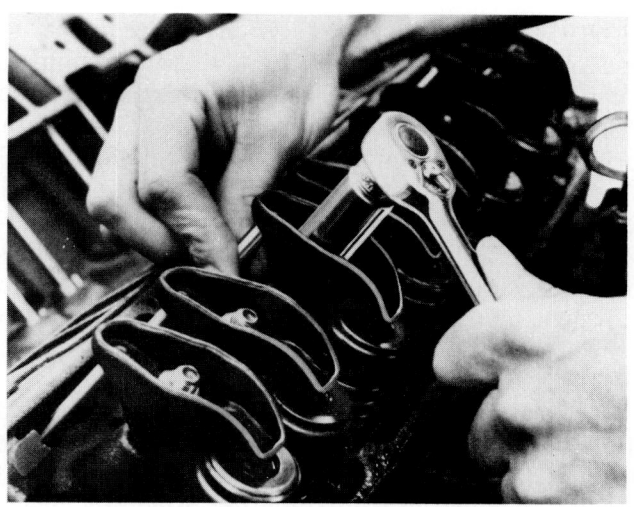

Fig. 48-52. Adjust hydraulic lifters to specs by following detailed directions in service manual. Generally, loosen rocker until push rod shows clearance. Tighten until no clearance. Then, tighten rocker about one more turn to center lifter plunger in its bore. (Oldsmobile)

To adjust hydraulic lifters with the **engine running,** install special oil shrouds, clothes pins, or other devices for catching oil spray off the rockers. Start and warm the engine to operating temperature.

Tighten all of the rockers until they are quiet. One at a time, loosen a rocker until it CLATTERS. Then, tighten the rocker slowly until it QUIETS DOWN. This will be zero valve lash.

To set the lifter plunger halfway down in its bore, tighten the rocker about one-half to ONE MORE TURN. Tighten the rocker slowly to give the lifter time to leak down and prevent engine missing or stalling. Repeat the adjustment on the other rockers.

Other adjustment methods may also be recommended. Check the manual for more detailed information.

Adjusting mechanical lifters

Mechanical lifters, also called *solid lifters,* are adjusted to assure proper valve train clearance. Since hydraulic lifters are NOT used to maintain zero valve lash, you must adjust mechanical lifters periodically. Check the car's service manual for adjustment intervals and clearance specs.

Typical valve clearance is approximately .014 in. (0.35 mm) for the intake valves and .016 in. (0.40 mm) for the exhaust valves.

Mechanical lifters make a clattering or pecking sound during engine operation. Unlike hydraulic lifters, this is normal. Mechanical lifters are used on heavy-duty engines (taxi cabs, pickup trucks, diesel engines) and high performance engines (early model, high horsepower engines for example).

To adjust mechanical lifters, position the lifter on its base circle (valve fully closed). This can easily be done by cranking the engine until the piston is at TDC

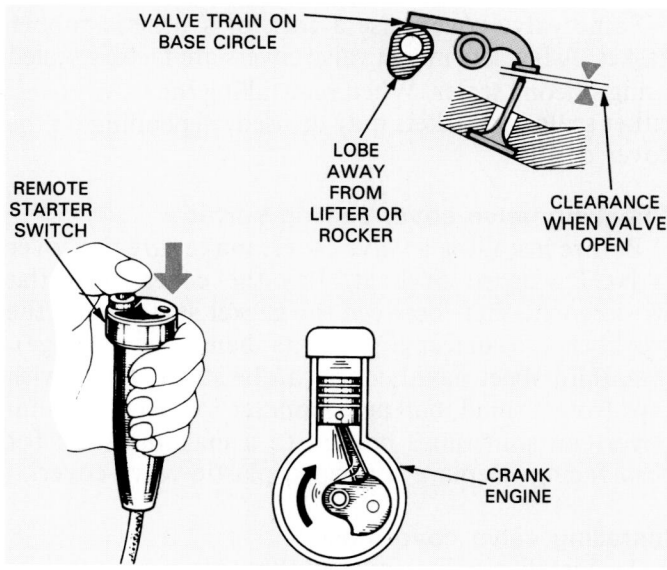

Fig. 48-51. When adjusting valves, crank engine until valve to be adjusted has cam lobe on base circle. This will assure that valve is fully closed and proper clearance adjustment will be made. (Renault)

on its COMPRESSION STROKE (you can feel air blow out of spark plug hole). At TDC on the compression stroke, both valves in that cylinder can be adjusted.

Slide the correct size flat feeler gauge between the rocker arm and the valve stem, as shown in Fig. 48-53. When properly adjusted, the feeler gauge should slide between the valve and rocker with a slight drag.

If needed, adjust the rocker to obtain specified valve clearance. You will normally have to loosen a locknut and turn an adjusting screw. Tighten the locknut and recheck adjustment. Repeat the procedure on the other valves.

Note! Some engines must have valves (mechanical lifters) adjusted with the ENGINE COLD. Others require a HOT ENGINE (at operating temperature). Check in a manual for information because a change in engine temperature will cause part expansion or contraction. This, in turn, causes a change in valve train clearance.

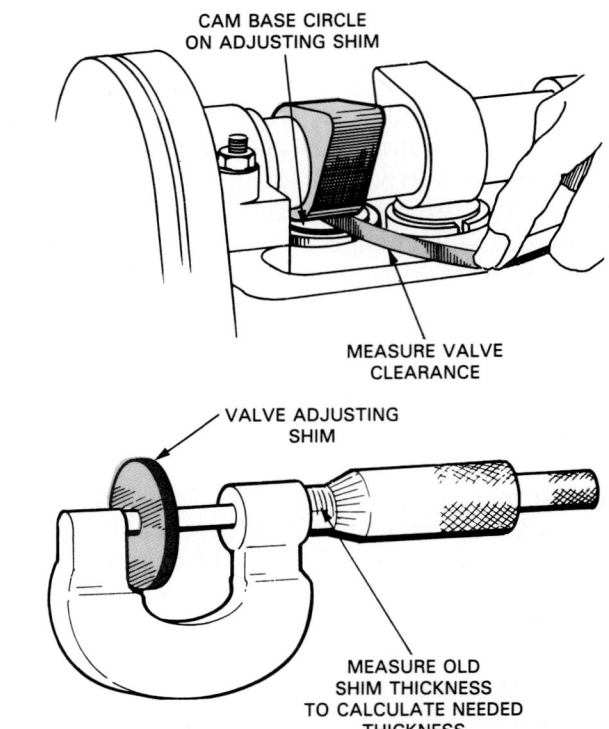

Fig. 48-54. When valve adjusting shims are used, measure clearance with feeler gauge. If incorrect, remove and measure shim thickness. Calculate required thickness of new shim and install. (Volvo)

Fig. 48-53. To adjust mechanical lifters, bump engine until cam lobe is away from lifter or rocker. Insert specified thickness feeler gauge between rocker and valve stem. If needed, loosen locknut and turn adjusting screw to obtain correct clearance. Feeler gauge should have light drag when pulled back and forth. (Chrysler)

OHC engine valve adjustment

There are several different methods of adjusting the valves on an overhead cam engine. Many are adjusted like mechanical lifters in a push rod engine. The rocker arm adjuster is turned until the correct size feeler gauge fits between the rocker or cam lobe and valve stem.

Valve adjusting shims may also be used on modern OHC engines to allow the adjustment of cam-to-valve clearance. Look at Fig. 48-54. Measure valve clearance with a feeler gauge. Then, if needed, remove and change shim thickness as needed.

Other OHC engines have an Allen adjusting screw in the cam followers. Turning the screw changes valve clearance. Always refer to a shop manual for detailed directions.

INSTALLING VALVE (ROCKER) COVERS

If not installed properly, valve or rocker covers can leak oil very easily. It is important for you to realize how easily a valve cover will leak. This may help prevent an incorrect installation technique and "comeback" (customer returns to shop after failure of repair).

Some valve covers use a cork or synthetic rubber gasket. A few late model valve covers are factory sealed using silicone sealer. When reinstalling the valve cover, either sealer or gaskets may be used, depending on the cover design.

Checking valve cover sealing surface

Before installing a valve cover, make sure the cover is NOT warped or bent. Lay the cover on a flat workbench. View between the gasket surface and the workbench to detect gaps (dents, bends, or warpage).

A thin, sheet metal cover can be straightened with taps from a small, ball pein hammer. A cast aluminum cover can sometimes be sent to a machine shop for resurfacing. Replace a warped plastic valve cover.

Installing valve cover gasket

To install a valve cover gasket, place a very light coating of approved sealer or adhesive around the edge of the valve cover. This is mainly needed to hold the gasket in place during assembly. Fit the gasket on the cover and align the bolt holes. Refer to Fig. 48-55.

After letting the sealer cure slightly, place the cover and gasket on the cylinder head and hand start ALL of the bolts. Tighten the valve cover bolts to specs using a crisscross pattern.

NOTE! A very common mistake is to OVER-TIGHTEN valve cover bolts. Overtightening can smash and split the gasket. It can also bend the valve cover, causing oil leakage. Torque the bolts to specs, generally just enough to lightly compress the gasket.

Installing valve cover with silicone sealer

To use silicone or RTV sealer on the valve cover, double-check that the cover and cylinder head gasket surfaces are PERFECTLY CLEAN. Sealer will NOT bond and seal on a dirty, oily surface.

Apply a continuous bead of sealer all the way around the valve cover sealing surface. Typically, the bead should be about 3/16 in. (1.6 mm) wide. Look at Fig. 48-56 for a typical example.

Fig. 48-55. Apply a bead of quick-drying, pliable sealer to valve cover. This will hold the gasket in place during assembly. (Fel-Pro Incorporated)

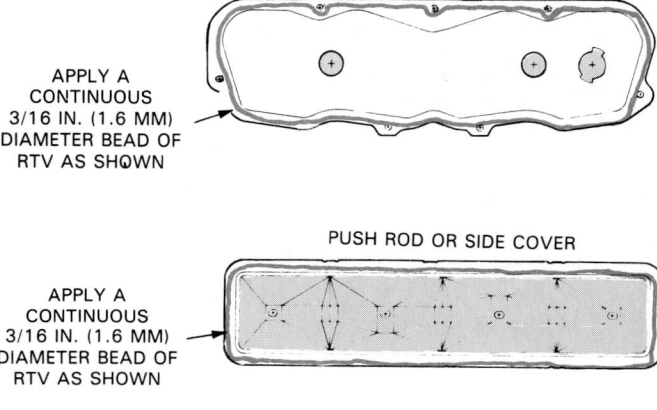

ROCKER ARM OR VALVE COVER

APPLY A CONTINUOUS 3/16 IN. (1.6 MM) DIAMETER BEAD OF RTV AS SHOWN

PUSH ROD OR SIDE COVER

APPLY A CONTINUOUS 3/16 IN. (1.6 MM) DIAMETER BEAD OF RTV AS SHOWN

Fig. 48-56. To use silicone sealer, instead of gaskets, on engine covers, make sure sealing surface is perfectly clean. Run a uniform bead of specified thickness all the way around cover. Install without bumping and breaking bead. (Chevrolet)

KNOW THESE TERMS

Valve job, Cylinder head stand, Warped cylinder head, Straightedge, Milling, Magnafluxing, Dye penetrant, Valve guide knurling, Reaming, Valve guide insert, Valve grinding, Interference angle, Sharp valve margin, Valve seat reconditioning, Staking, Seat width, Valve seat runout, Lapping valves, Valve spring tester, Valve spring shims, Valve spring installed height, Spring bind, Lifter leak down rate, Valve grind gasket set, Head gasket markings, Head gasket torque sequence, Crisscross pattern, Nonadjustable rocker arms, Tappet clearance, Valve adjusting shims.

REVIEW QUESTIONS

1. How can you tell if a cylinder head is warped?
2. _____ is commonly used to find cracks in cast iron engine parts.
3. _____ _____ is normally used to find cracks in aluminum engine components.
4. Typically, how do you remove and install a precombustion chamber in an automotive diesel engine?
5. Which of the following is NOT a common method of repairing worn valve guides?
   a. Shimming existing guide.
   b. Reaming old guide for oversize stem.
   c. Knurling guide to reduce inside diameter.
   d. Installing new guide insert.
6. Valve grinding is done by machining a fresh, smooth surface on the valve faces and stem tips. True or False?
7. How do you "dress the stone" on a valve grind machine?
8. What is an interference angle?
9. Explain what can happen if a valve margin is too thin.
10. The two most common valve and seat angles are _____ and _____ degrees.
11. Typically, an intake valve should have a valve-to-seat contact width of _____ . An exhaust valve valve-to-seat contact width should be about _____ .
12. How do you move the valve-to-seat contact point in and out on the valve face?
13. Which of the following is NOT a normal check done on valve springs?
    a. Squareness.
    b. Free height.
    c. Horizontal dimension.
    d. Tension.
14. Valve spring _____ is used to maintain correct tension when the springs are installed on the engine.
15. Install an O-ring type valve seal before compressing the valve spring over the stem. True or False?
16. Valve springs and valve seals can be replaced

without cylinder head removal. True or False?

17. Lifter _____ _____ _____ is measured by timing how long it takes to push the plunger to the bottom of its stroke during controlled conditions.
18. What is included in a valve grind gasket set?
19. Why are cylinder head gasket markings provided?
20. Explain why head gasket selection on a diesel engine is extremely critical.
21. Generally, tighten cylinder head bolts starting on each end and work your way to the middle. True or False?
22. If engine valves are adjusted too tight, it can _____ the valves.
23. How can you adjust engine valves with hydraulic lifters while the engine is running?
24. How do you adjust engine valves with mechanical lifters?
25. When using RTV sealer on a valve cover gasket, typically run a bead of sealer about _____

wide all the way around the cover. All sealing surfaces must be perfectly _____ and dry.

ACTIVITIES FOR CHAPTER 48

1. Use a dial indicator to measure valve guide wear on all the valves of an engine. Make a chart showing your readings, and compare them to specs. If one or more guides is out of spec, determine which technique should be used to correct the problem.
2. Demonstrate the steps required to set up and operate a valve grinding machine. Grind the face of an actual valve, if one is available.
3. Micrometers are used to make many measurements while servicing engine top ends. For practice in reading a standard outside micrometer, use it to check a variety of known thicknesses, such as the blades of a feeler gauge set. Further practice can be done by checking such components as valve stems, cam journals, rocker shafts, or gaskets.

This modern six-cylinder engine has four valves per cylinder, dual overhead cams, and fuel injection.   (Subaru)

49

Engine Front End Service, Engine Installation

After studying this chapter, you will be able to:
□ Inspect for timing chain and sprocket wear.
□ Service a chain tensioner and timing chain assembly.
□ Properly align timing marks.
□ Check timing gears for wear or damage.
□ Remove and install timing gears.
□ Measure timing gear runout and backlash.
□ Install a timing chain or timing gear cover.
□ Remove and install a front cover oil seal.
□ Service a timing belt.
□ Summarize engine installation procedures.
□ Describe safety practices to be followed while servicing engine front ends and installing engines.

Modern cars and trucks use several types of engine front end designs. Many late model engines use a rubber timing belt to drive the overhead camshaft. Others use a timing chain to transfer turning force to the camshaft. Some heavy duty gasoline engines and diesel engines use timing gears to operate the camshaft and valve train.

It is very important that you know how to service and repair all types of camshaft drive mechanisms. This chapter summarizes the most essential information on this subject, preparing you to use a service manual for actual repairs.

Earlier textbook chapters covered subjects relating to engine front end service. Review these chapters if needed. For example, Chapter 46 explained engine front end teardown (crankshaft damper, front cover, and camshaft drive mechanism removal) and part cleaning methods.

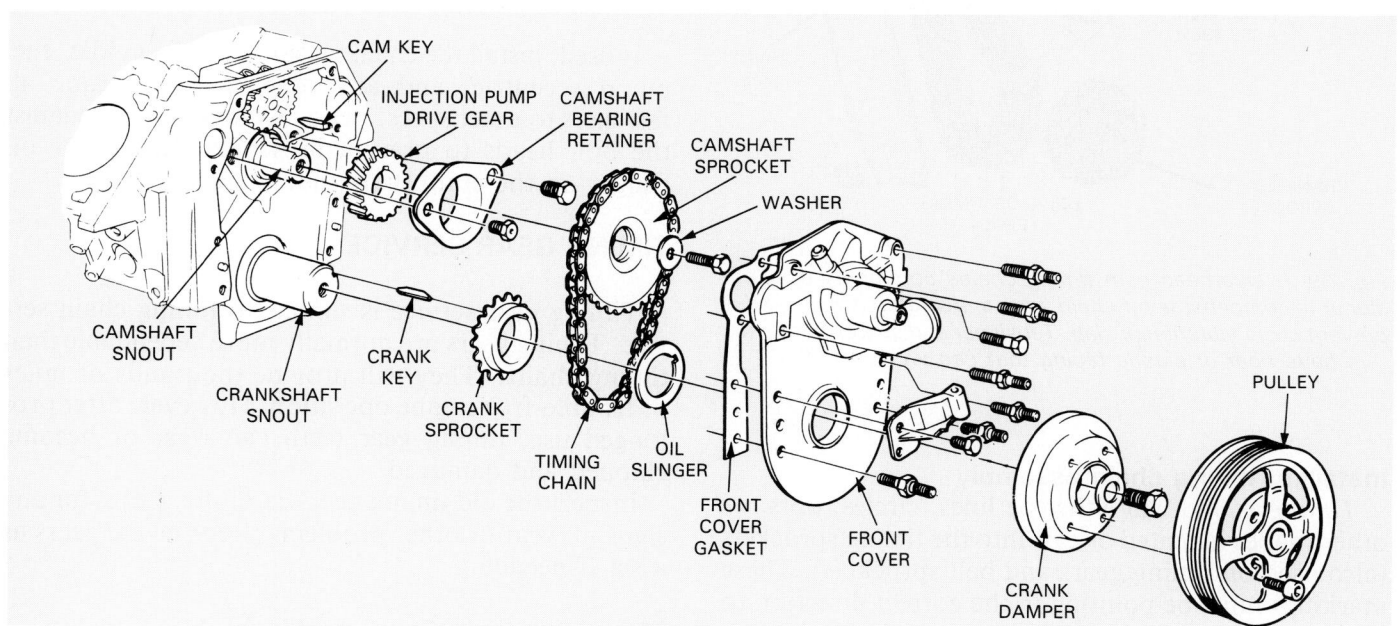

Fig. 49-1. Review parts of engine front end assembly. This is a V-type, diesel engine with timing chain. Note extra gear for driving fuel injection pump. (Buick)

TIMING CHAIN SERVICE

Timing chains can be used on both push rod and OHC engines. Fig. 49-1 is an exploded view of a timing chain and front end assembly for a cam-in-block (push rod) engine. Fig. 49-2 pictures a timing chain setup for an overhead cam engine. Study the parts and part relationships.

Inspecting timing chain and sprockets

You should inspect the timing chain for looseness during engine disassembly. Excess SLACK or PLAY in the chain normally requires replacement of the chain and sprockets.

If used, check the chain tensioner and chain guides for wear, Fig. 49-2. Also check the crankshaft key or camshaft dowel, if used. Replace any component showing wear or damage.

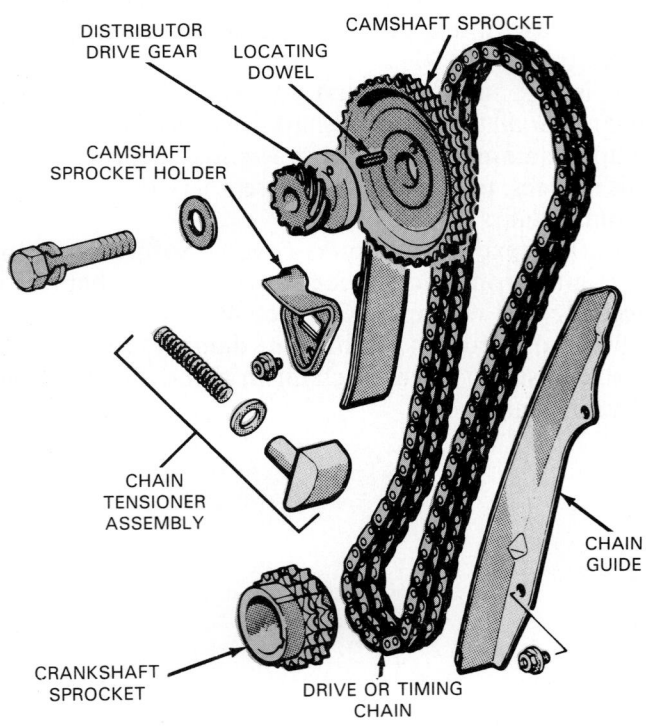

Fig. 49-2. Overhead cam timing chains commonly use tensioner to compensate for chain wear and stretch. Chain guides prevent chain vibration or slap. Tensioner and guides frequently have fiber or plastic facing that can wear. (Dodge)

Installing timing chain assembly

Timing marks will either be lines, circles, dots, or other shapes indented or cast into the timing sprockets (also used on timing gears and belt sprockets). These markings must be pointing in the correct direction to time the camshaft (valves) with the crankshaft (pistons).

To align the timing marks, fit the sprockets on the camshaft and crankshaft. Do not install the timing chain. Rotate the cam and crank by hand until the TIMING MARKS ALIGN. Refer to a service manual if needed.

Without turning the cam or crank, remove the sprockets. Then, fit the chain over the sprockets so that the timing marks face correctly. Install the chain and sprockets on the engine as a unit. Double-check the alignment of the timing marks, as in Fig. 49-3.

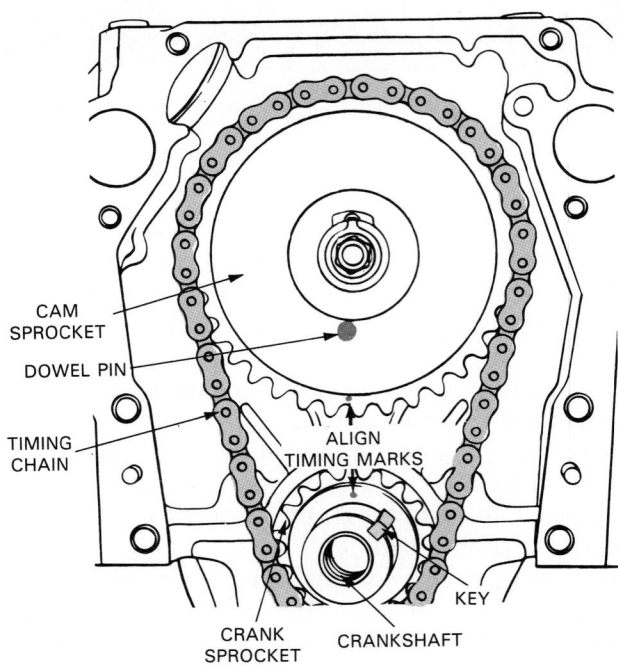

Fig. 49-3. Key aligns crankshaft sprocket. Dowel aligns camshaft sprocket. You must align marks on sprockets to time crankshaft with camshaft. (General Motors Corp.)

If used, install the chain tensioner, chain guides, fuel pump eccentric, and any other parts. Torque all fasteners to exact specs. Bend any locking tabs against the bolt heads to prevent loosening. Install the oil slinger on the crankshaft snout. See Fig. 49-4.

TIMING GEAR SERVICE

Timing gear service is similar to timing chain service. Timing gears are normally more dependable than timing chains. They will provide thousands of miles of trouble-free engine operation. However, after prolonged use, timing gear teeth can wear or become chipped and damaged.

Inspect the old timing gears carefully. Look for any signs of wear or other problems. Replace the gears as a set if needed.

Measuring timing gear backlash

Timing gear backlash is the amount of clearance between the timing gear teeth. Backlash can be measured

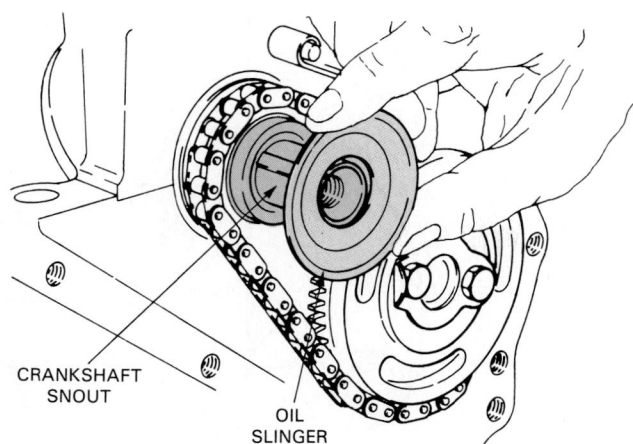

Fig. 49-4. Oil slinger fits next to crankshaft sprocket. It helps keep oil from leaking out front seal and it also sprays oil on chain and sprockets to aid their lubrication. (Ford Motor Co.)

to determine timing gear wear.

A dial indicator is an accurate tool for measuring timing gear backlash. Set the indicator stand on the engine. Locate the indicator stem on one of the cam gear teeth. The stem must be parallel with gear tooth travel. Look at Fig. 49-5.

Rotate the cam gear one way and then the other, without turning the crankshaft. Read the indicator at the end of tooth travel in each direction.

If timing gear backlash is greater than specs, the gears are worn. They should be replaced. Refer to the service manual for backlash specs.

Installing timing gears

Timing gears are usually press-fitted on the crankshaft and camshaft. A wheel puller is normally needed to remove the crankshaft gear.

Fig. 49-6 shows how a press is used to remove the cam gear from the camshaft. With this design, the cam-

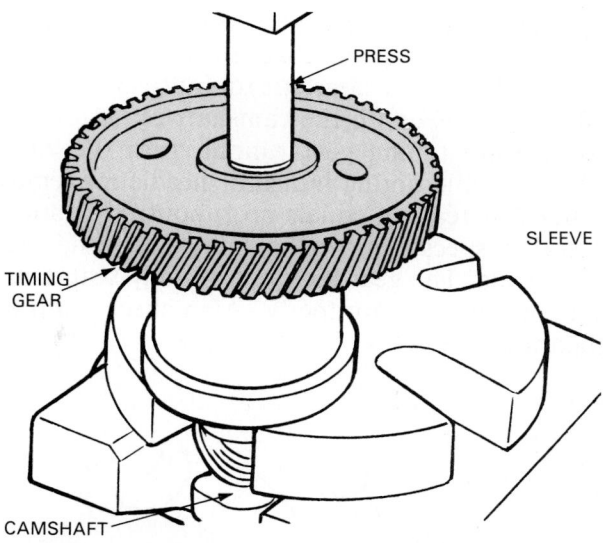

Fig. 49-6. Some camshaft timing gears must be pressed on and off. Camshaft must be removed from engine. Other engine designs allow gear to slide off installed cam with light taps from brass hammer. (Buick)

shaft must be out for timing gear replacement.

Timing gears can usually be installed with light blows from a brass hammer. Make sure the key and keyways are aligned. Tap in a circular motion to force the gears squarely into position. A press may also be needed to install the cam gear on the camshaft.

As with a timing chain and sprockets, double-check the alignment of the timing marks. The timing marks must be positioned properly to time the camshaft with the crankshaft.

Fig. 49-7 pictures how one auto maker recommends timing gear alignment on a small truck diesel engine.

Measuring timing gear runout.

Timing gear runout or wobble is measured with a

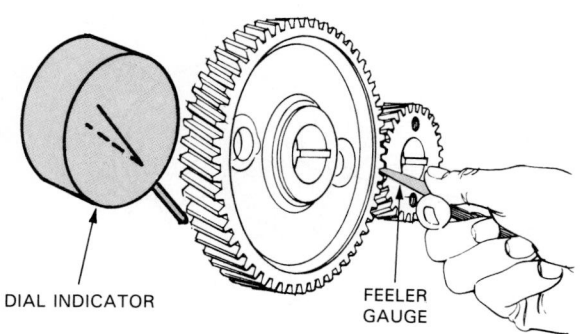

Fig. 49-5. Either dial indicator or feeler gauge can be used to measure timing gear backlash or clearance. Position indicator as shown. Rotate cam gear back and forth while reading indicator to find clearance. Largest feeler gauge that fits properly in gear teeth also indicates clearance. If backlash is too great, gears are worn. (Deere & Co.)

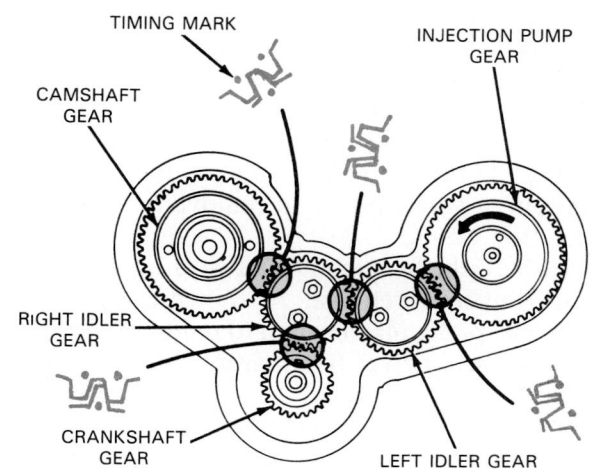

Fig. 49-7. Study timing marks on timing gears in this diesel engine. (Ford)

dial indicator, as in Fig. 49-8. Position the indicator stand on the engine block. Place the indicator stem on the outer edge of the camshaft timing gear. The stem should be parallel with the camshaft centerline.

To measure timing gear runout, turn the engine crankshaft while noting indicator needle movement. No indicator reading equals no runout. If runout is greater than specs, remove the timing gears and check for problems. The gear may not be fully seated or it may be machined improperly. Also check camshaft straightness.

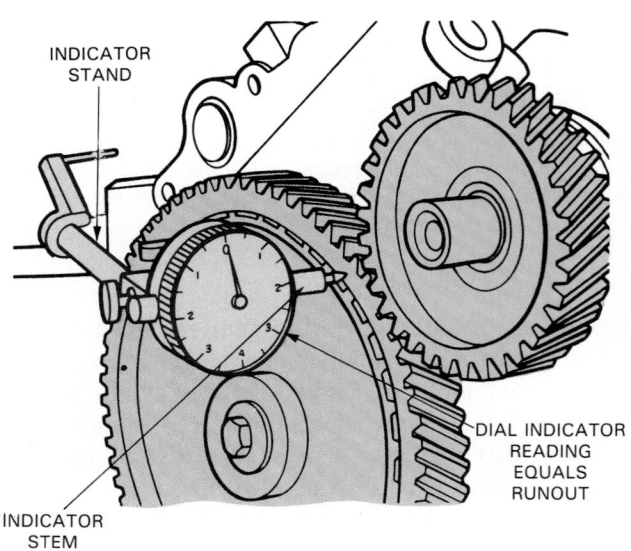

Fig. 49-8. After installing timing gears, check gear runout or wobble as shown. Turn crankshaft and read indicator. Correct problem if runout is beyond specs. (Ford Motor Co.)

CRANKSHAFT FRONT SEAL SERVICE

The *crankshaft front seal* keeps engine oil from leaking out from between the crankshaft snout and the engine front cover. Replace the front seal whenever it is leaking or any time the front cover is removed.

Seal replacement in the car requires only partial engine disassembly. Typically, you must remove the radiator and other accessory units on the front of the engine. Use a wheel puller to remove the crankshaft damper, Fig. 49-9.

Sometimes, the front crankshaft seal can be replaced without front cover removal. As shown in Fig. 49-10A, a special seal puller may be used to remove the old seal. Then, use a seal driver to squarely seat the new seal into its bore, Fig. 49-10B.

Before installing a front seal, coat the outside diameter of the seal with nonhardening sealer. This will prevent oil seepage between the seal body and the front cover. Coat the rubber sealing lip with engine oil. This will lubricate the seal during initial engine startup.

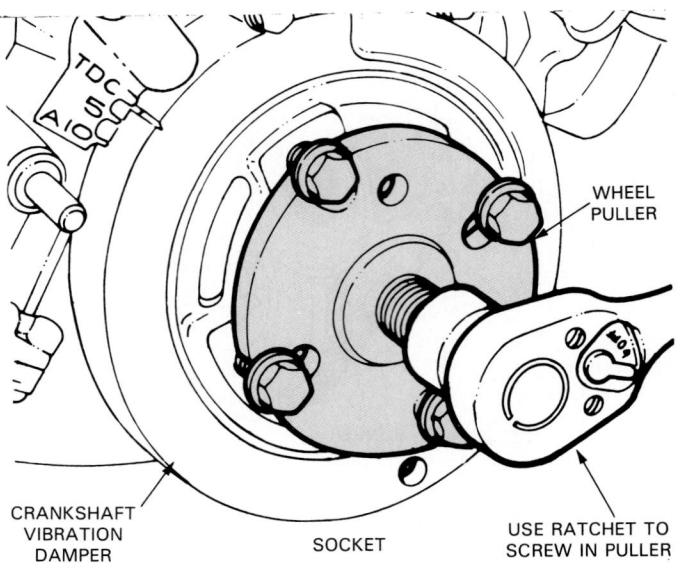

Fig. 49-9. To service a front cover seal, crankshaft damper must be removed with wheel puller. Threaded holes are normally provided in damper for puller bolts. Do not hammer or pry on outer edge of damper or rubber ring in damper will be damaged. (Chrysler)

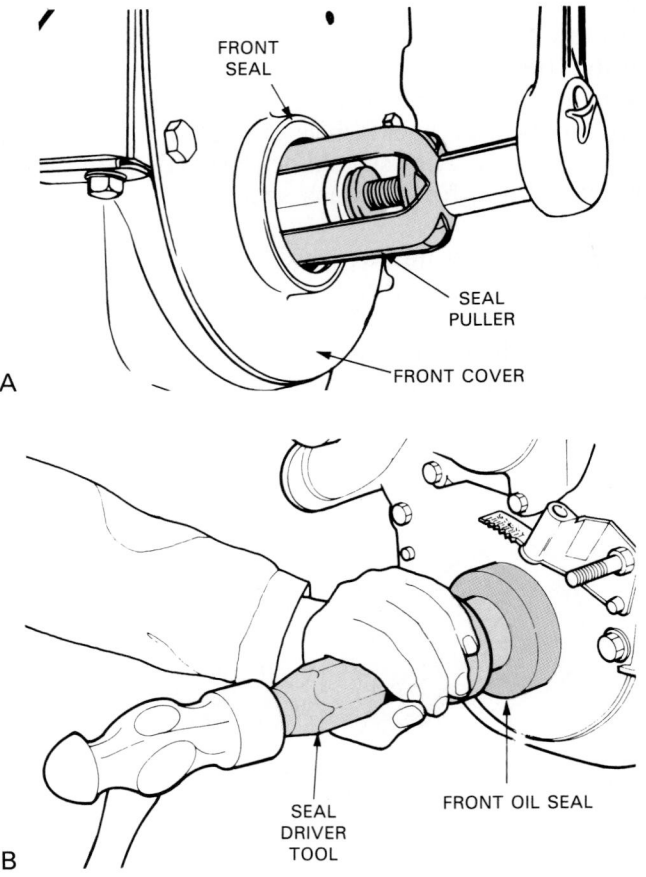

Fig. 49-10. When seal is pressed in from front, it can be replaced without front cover removal. A — Special seal puller will pull out old seal. B — Use seal driver to force new seal squarely into bore in front cover. Coat outside diameter of seal with non-hardening sealer. (GMC)

Note! When the crankshaft front seal drives in from the rear, cover removal is necessary. You must remove the cover to drive the old seal out and the new seal in. When in doubt, check the service manual for detailed instructions.

ENGINE FRONT COVER SERVICE

The *engine front cover,* also called *timing cover,* encloses the timing chain or the timing gears. It is usually made of thin sheet metal or cast aluminum. Make sure a sheet metal cover is not warped.

Installing front cover gasket or silicone sealer

To install an engine front cover gasket, coat the flange on the cover with approved gasket adhesive. This will hold the gasket in place while you fit the cover on the engine. Align all bolt holes in the gasket and cover. Allow the adhesive to become tacky (partially dried, but still sticky and moist).

To use silicone sealer instead of a gasket, apply an even bead of sealer, Fig. 49-11. The bead should be of specified thickness and should surround all bolt holes and coolant passages.

When the engine front cover butts against the oil

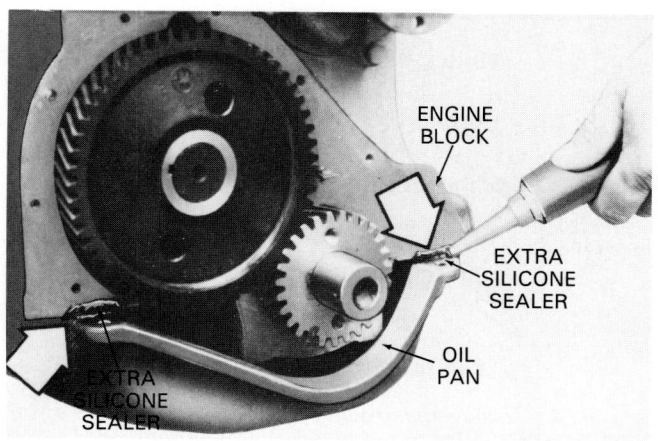

Fig. 49-12. Extra silicone sealer is normally recommended where front cover meets oil pan. Without sealer, gap could form and allow oil leakage. (Chevrolet)

disturbing the gasket or silicone sealer. With some engine designs, you may need to loosen the oil pan bolts and partially drop (lower) the pan. Also, you may need to center the seal around the crankshaft using a *seal alignment tool,* Fig. 49-13.

Start all of the engine front cover fasteners by hand. Do NOT tighten any fastener until all are started. Double-check that the gasket is properly aligned and that bolt lengths are correct. Start the oil pan bolts into the bottom of the cover, if needed.

Torque all fasteners to specs in a crisscross pattern. Remove seal alignment tool (if used) and reinstall all of the components on the front of the engine.

Fig. 49-14 shows a front cover for an engine using a timing belt. The cover simply houses the crankshaft oil seal. Note how sealer is needed on one of the bolts that extends into a water jacket. A service manual is needed to obtain this kind of detailed information.

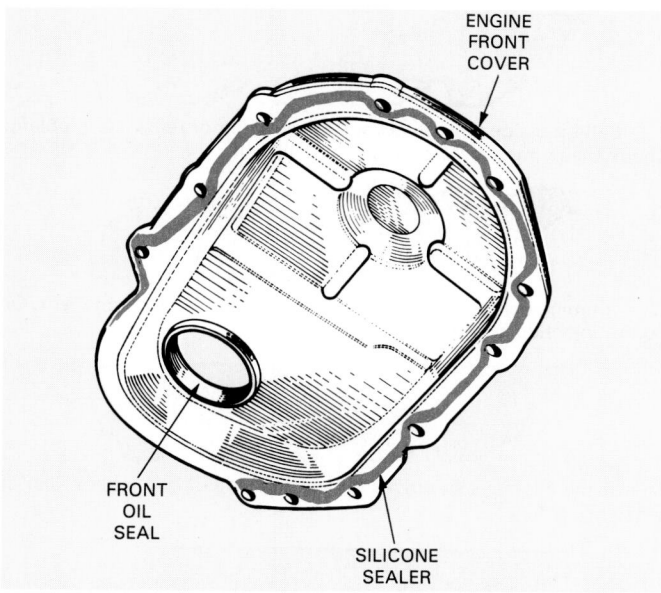

Fig. 49-11. To use silicone sealer on front cover, make sure cover is perfectly clean and dry. Coat flange with approved sealer. Use correct diameter bead and surround all bolt holes and water passages. (Renault)

pan, use silicone sealer as in Fig. 49-12. The sealer will keep oil from leaking between any gap between the cover and pan.

Installing engine front cover

Carefully fit the engine front cover into place without

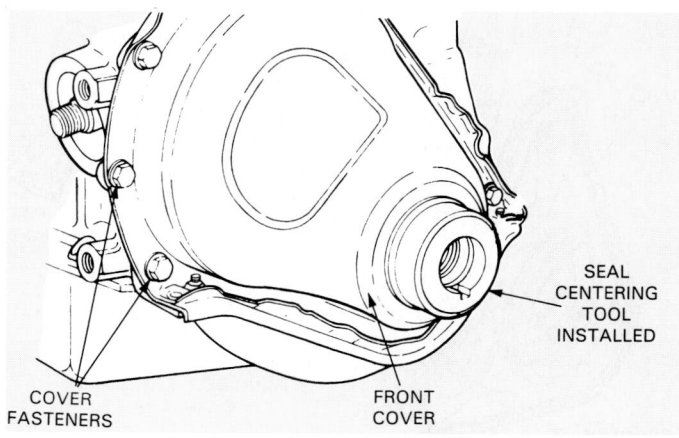

Fig. 49-13. Sometimes an alignment sleeve is needed to center seal around crankshaft. Fit sleeve over crankshaft snout during front cover installation. Remove sleeve after tightening cover fasteners. (Buick)

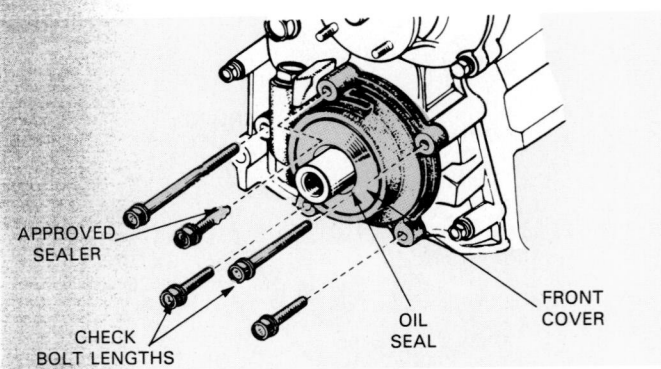

Fig. 49-14. This overhead cam engine has a small front cover, since an external timing belt is used. Cover does not have to enclose a timing chain or gears. Note specific bolt lengths and how one bolt requires sealer because it enters water jacket. Check service manual for details of engine being repaired. (Toyota)

TIMING BELT SERVICE

Many late model OHC engines use a synthetic rubber belt to operate the engine camshaft. The cogged (toothed) belt provides an accurate, quiet, light, and

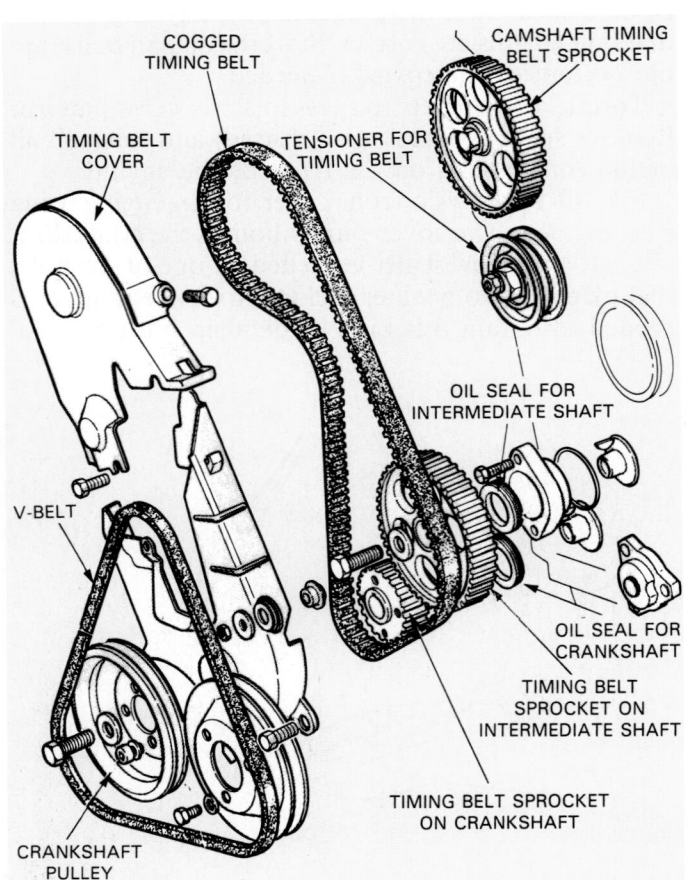

Fig. 49-15. Study front end components of this OHC engine using a timing belt. (Plymouth)

dependable means of turning the camshaft, Fig. 49-15.

Timing belt service is very important. If the timing belt were to break or be timed improperly, engine valves, pistons, and other parts could be damaged. If the cam is out of time with the crankshaft, the pistons could slide up and hit the open valves.

CAUTION! Never use the starting motor to crank an engine when the timing belt, chain, or gears are removed. Valves could be bent or broken.

Inspecting timing belt

Inspect the engine timing belt for signs of deterioration (cracks, hardening, softening, fraying). Look for the kind of problems illustrated in Fig. 49-16. Most

A — Do not bend, twist, or turn belt excessively. Oil and water will deteriorate belt. Fix all engine leaks.

B — Belt breakage may be caused by sprocket or tensioner problem. Check these parts before installing new belt.

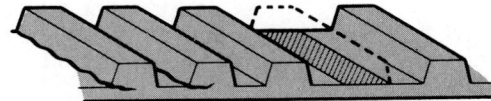

C — If timing belt teeth are missing, check for locked component. Oil pump, injection pump, etc., could be frozen.

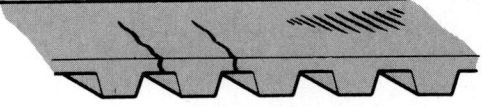

D — If there is wear or cracks on smooth side of belt, check idler or tensioner pulley.

E — With damage or wear on one side of belt, check belt guide and pulley alignment.

F — Wear on timing belt teeth may be caused by timing sprocket problem. Inspect sprockets carefully. Oil contamination will also cause this trouble.

Fig. 49-16. Always inspect timing belt very closely. Timing belt failure can cause major engine damage. (Toyota)

manufacturers recommend timing belt replacement at intervals of about 50,000 miles (80 450 km).

When severe timing belt damage is found, inspect for mechanical problems. Check sprocket condition and installation. Make sure no leaking oil can reach and ruin the belt. Turn the tensioner wheel, to make sure its bearing spins freely. Correct any trouble that could reduce timing belt life.

Timing belt sprocket installation

The camshaft timing belt sprocket is normally secured to the camshaft with a hex bolt. Hold the camshaft by fitting a wrench on a flat formed on the camshaft. A special tool may be needed. Use another wrench to loosen the bolt holding the sprocket. This is shown in Fig. 49-17.

When holding camshaft stationary, be careful not to damage the cam lobes. Place your wrench or holding tool on the flat or other unmachined surface.

When installing a timing belt sprocket, align any key or dowel that positions the sprocket. Make sure you have the right washer and bolt for the sprocket. Install and torque the bolts to specs.

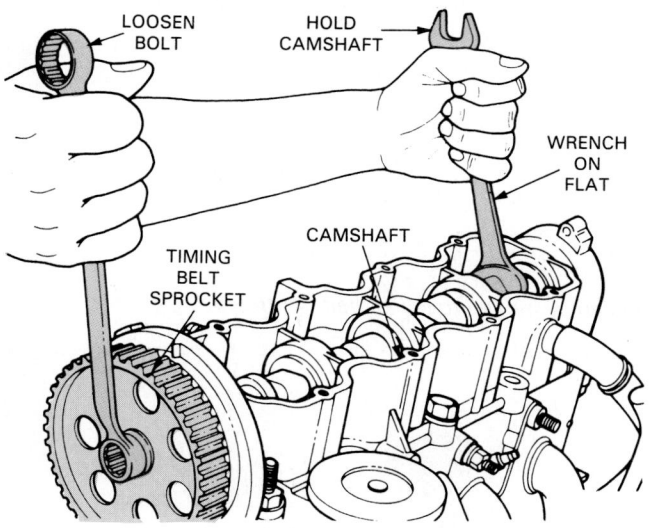

Fig. 49-17. To remove belt sprocket, hold camshaft stationary while loosening sprocket bolt. Special holding tool may also be needed. (Buick)

Installing timing belt

To install a timing belt, line up the timing marks on the camshaft and crankshaft sprockets. Find service manual illustrations similar to the ones in Fig. 49-18. They will give you details of how the marks on the sprockets align with marks on the engine.

When the distributor is driven by an accessory sprocket, it will also have timing marks that must be aligned properly. See Fig. 49-18.

With the sprocket marks positioned correctly, slip

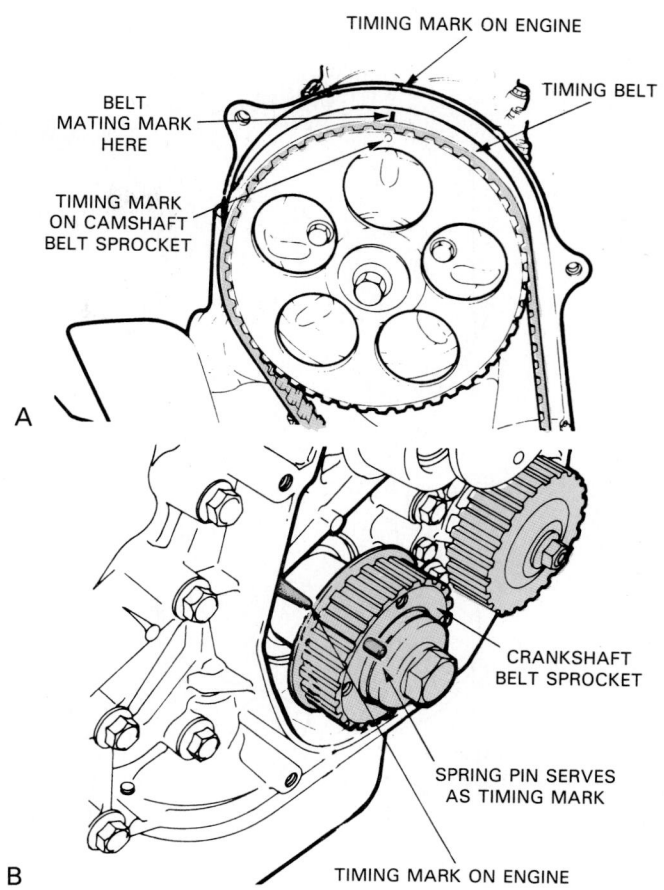

Fig. 49-18. When installing new timing belt, align timing marks properly. Sometimes belt is also marked. Do not crank engine with belt OFF or valves may be bent. Turn sprockets by hand. A — Camshaft belt sprocket mark is aligned with belt marking and timing mark on engine. B — This crankshaft sprocket uses dowel as timing reference. Align dowel with timing pointer on engine. Types of markings vary. Check the service manual. (Chrysler)

the belt over the sprockets. Move the tensioner into the belt to hold the belt on its sprockets, Fig. 49-19.

Adjusting timing belt tension

Proper timing belt tension (tightness) is very important to belt service life. If the belt is too tight, it can wear out quickly or break. If too loose, the belt can flap or vibrate, or fly off.

Generally, a pry bar is used to adjust the belt tensioner into the timing belt. See Fig. 49-20. Sometimes however, a special tool is needed to measure tension.

Fig. 49-21 shows a simple way to check timing belt tension for many OHC engines. Adjust the belt until moderate finger and thumb pressure is needed to twist the belt about one-quarter turn.

After you are sure belt tension is adjusted to specs, install the timing belt cover. Pictured in Fig. 49-22, the *timing belt cover* is a sheet metal or plastic cover that surrounds the belt and sprockets. It does NOT contain an oil seal nor require a gasket.

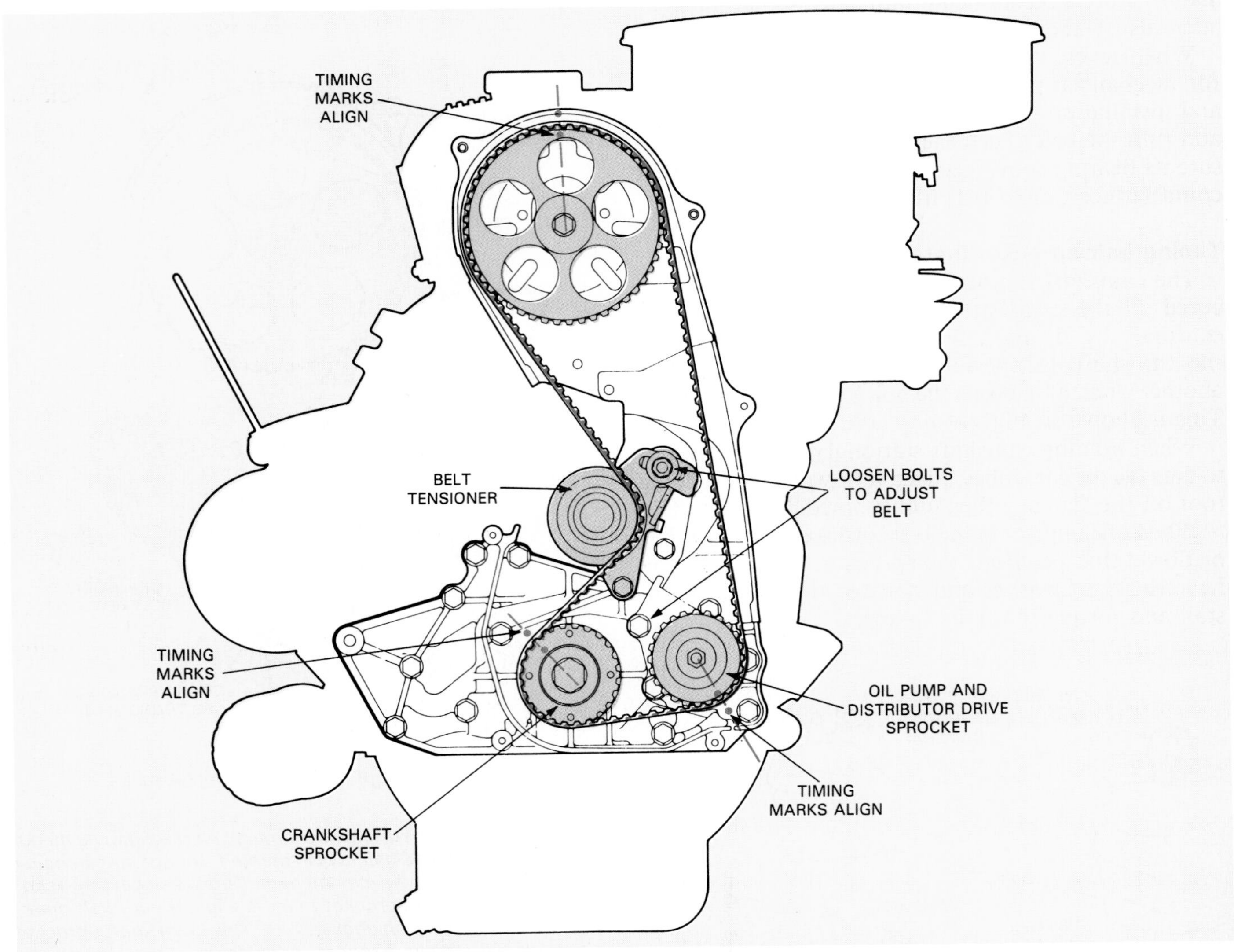

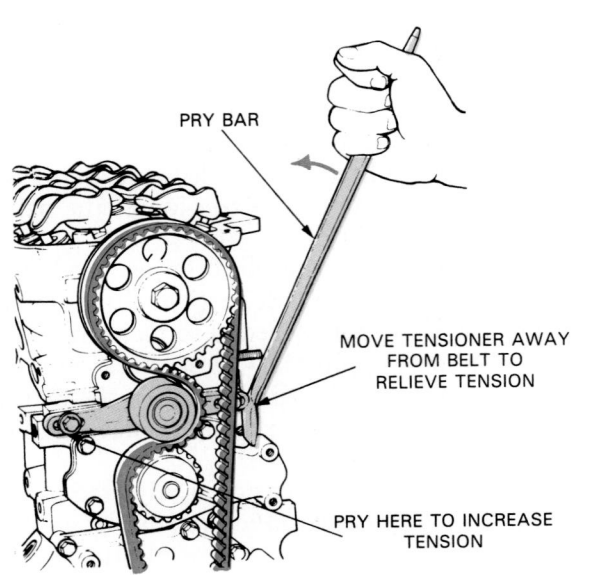

TIMING
MARKS
ALIGN

BELT
TENSIONER

LOOSEN BOLTS
TO ADJUST
BELT

TIMING
MARKS
ALIGN

OIL PUMP AND
DISTRIBUTOR DRIVE
SPROCKET

CRANKSHAFT
SPROCKET

TIMING
MARKS ALIGN

Fig. 49-19. Study timing marks and how tensioner can be moved to adjust belt tightness.
(Dodge)

PRY BAR

MOVE TENSIONER AWAY
FROM BELT TO
RELIEVE TENSION

PRY HERE TO INCREASE
TENSION

Fig. 49-20. Pry bar is commonly used to shift tensioner and
adjust timing belt. (Ford)

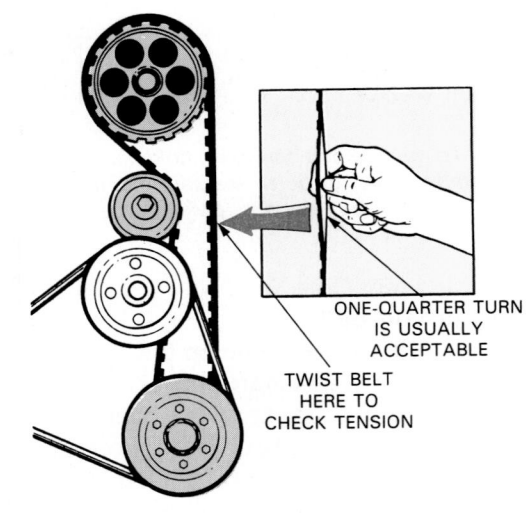

ONE-QUARTER TURN
IS USUALLY
ACCEPTABLE

TWIST BELT
HERE TO
CHECK TENSION

Fig. 49-21. General rule for checking belt tension. One-quarter
turn with moderate finger pressure normally will indicate correct tension. However, refer to service manual for exact
method. (Chrysler)

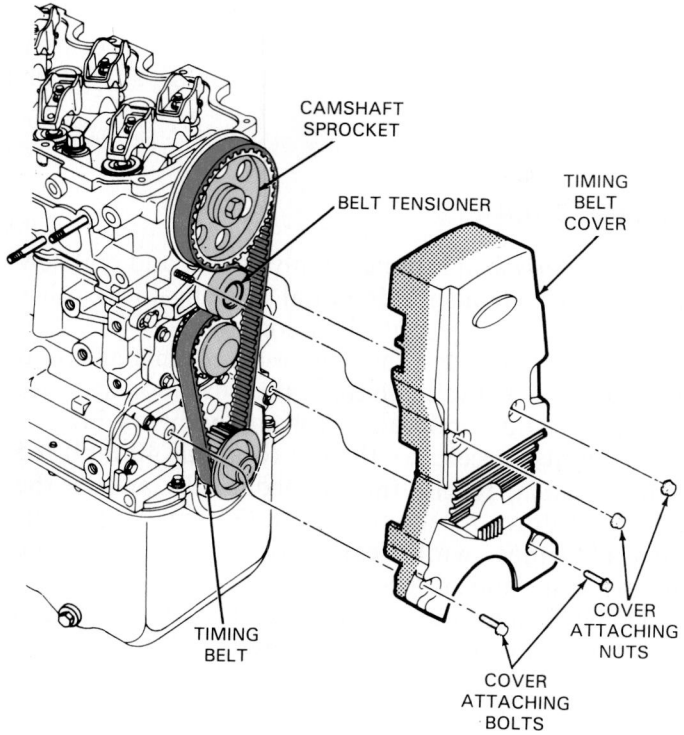

Fig. 49-22. *Double-check timing marks and belt tension. Then install belt cover. Tighten fasteners to specs. (Ford Motor Co.)*

COMPLETE ENGINE ASSEMBLY

Information summarizing complete engine assembly has been given in the previous chapters. Look at Fig. 49-23.

Chapter 46 outlined engine removal and disassembly. Chapter 47 explained how to service and assemble an engine bottom end (short block). Chapter 49 discussed engine top end service (valve job). This chapter completed your study of engine service by summarizing final assembly of the engine front end.

Quickly scan through these chapters. Look at the illustrations and read the captions. This will strengthen your background for using a service manual when doing an engine repair or complete engine rebuild.

INSTALLING ENGINE IN THE CAR

Installing an engine in a car is about the opposite as removing the engine. Engine removal was covered in Chapter 46. It explains the use of an engine hoist, lifting chain or fixture, and other equipment. Refer to this chapter as needed.

A few rules to remember when installing an engine include:

1. Keep your hands and feet out from under the engine.

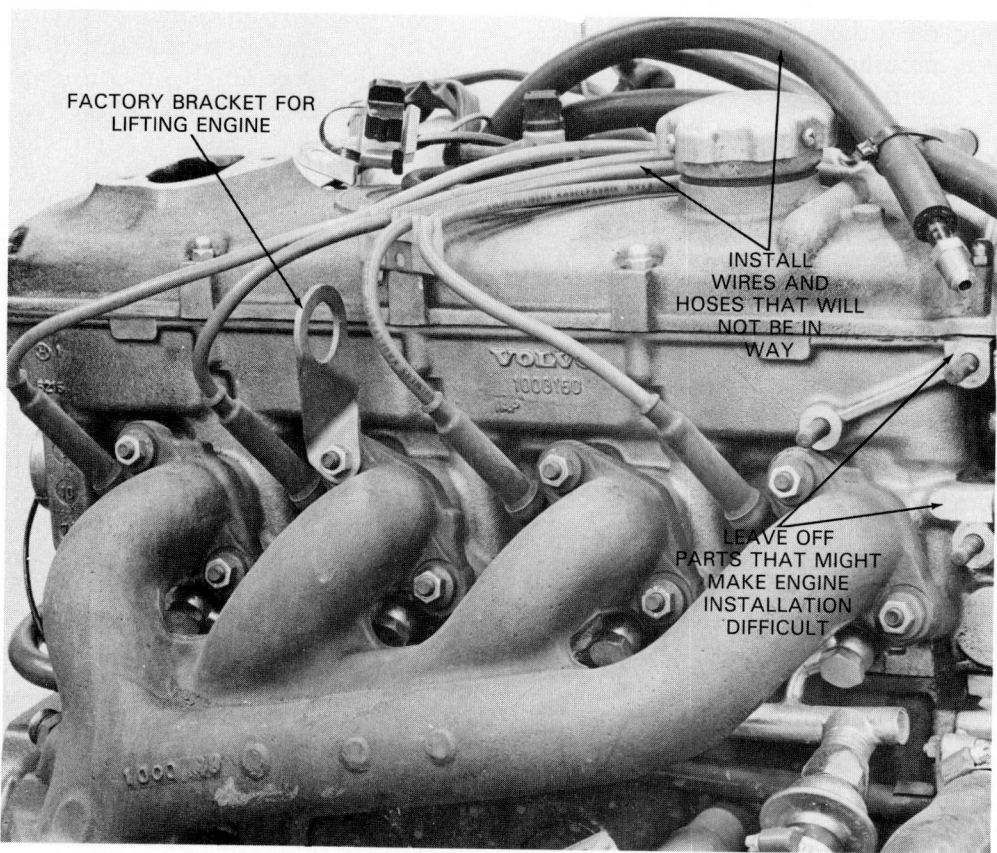

Fig. 49-23. *Before installing engine in car, install all parts that will not obstruct engine installation. Spark plug wires, some hoses, sending units, lifting brackets are a few examples. (Volvo)*

2. Raise the engine on the hoist ONLY while it is being placed in the vehicle. Never work on an engine raised in the air on a hoist or lift.

3. With many automatic transmission equipped cars, turn the engine flywheel so that the large hole in the flywheel faces straight down. Rotate the transmission torque converter until its drain plug is also facing down. This will make it easier to align the engine and transmission.

4. With a manual transmission, check the condition of the pilot bearing (bushing in end of crankshaft). Replace it if worn (see chapter on clutches).

5. Position the lifting chain or fixture on the engine so that the engine is raised LEVEL. If NOT level, it will be difficult to slide engine onto transmission.

6. Slowly lower engine into vehicle while watching for clearance all around the engine compartment. Position the engine so that its crankshaft centerline aligns with the transmission input shaft centerline.

7. Push the engine back and align the engine dowel pins with the holes in the transmission. Use a large bar to shift the engine.

8. As soon as the dowel pins slide FULLY into their holes, install an engine-to-transmission bolt, but do NOT tighten it. Start another bolt on the other side of the engine.

9. Check that the torque converter is properly lined up with the holes in the flywheel. Turn the converter if needed. Tighten the bell housing bolts.

10. Finish installing the other components on the engine — motor mounts, oil filter, fuel lines, coolant hoses, throttle linkage, battery ground cable, and fan belts. Refer to Fig. 49-24.

11. Fill engine with oil and radiator with coolant.

12. Start and fast idle the engine until warm while watching for adequate oil pressure.

13. Shut the engine off and recheck carburetor or fuel injection adjustments, ignition timing, and other related adjustments.

14. Look for fluid leaks or any other signs of trouble.

ENGINE BREAK-IN

Engine break-in is done mainly to seat and seal new piston rings. It also aids initial wearing in of other components under controlled conditions.

After warm-up at a fast idle, most technicians road test the car. At the same time, they use moderate acceleration and deceleration for engine break-in.

Generally, accelerate the car to about 40 mph (65 km/h). Then, release the gas pedal fully and let the car coast down to about 20 mph (32 km/h). Do this several times while carefully watching engine temperature and oil pressure.

Do NOT allow the engine to overheat during break-in; ring and cylinder scoring may result.

Warning! When road testing and breaking in an engine, drive the car on a road that is free of traffic. Do NOT exceed posted speed limits nor normal safe driving standards.

Inform the car owner of the following rules concerning the operation of a freshly overhauled engine:

1. Avoid prolonged highway driving during the first 100 to 200 miles (161 to 322 km). This will prevent ring friction from overheating the rings and cylinders, possibly causing damage.

2. Do not worry about oil consumption until after about 2000 miles (3 220 km) of engine operation. It will take this long for full ring seating.

3. Check engine oil and other fluid levels frequently.

4. Change the engine oil and filter after approximatley 2000 miles (3 220 km) of driving. This will help remove any particles in oil.

5. Inform the customer of any problems not corrected by the engine repair or overhaul.

For example, if the radiator is in poor condition (has been previously repaired or was filled with rust), tell the customer about the consequences of NOT correcting the problem. The problem may upset engine performance or reduce engine service life. Having the customer sign a release form will protect you if the unserviced part fails.

KNOW THESE TERMS

Sprocket timing marks, Timing gear backlash, Timing gear runout, Crankshaft front oil seal, Engine front cover, Front cover gasket, Seal alignment tool, Cogged belt, Timing belt tension, Engine break-in.

REVIEW QUESTIONS

1. Timing chains can be used on both push rod and OHC engines. True or False?

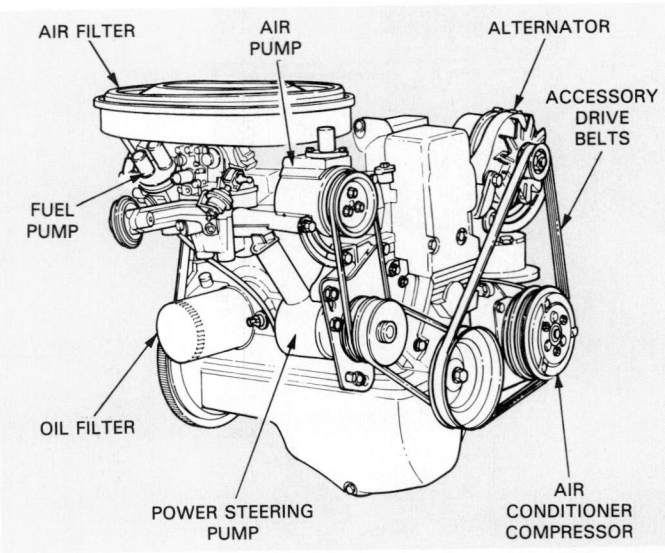

Fig. 49-24. After engine installation in car, install all other accessory units, wires, and hoses. Fill engine with oil and radiator with coolant. Double-check everything before starting engine.

2. Excess slack or play in a timing chain requires chain adjustment. True or False?
3. Timing marks on the timing chain sprockets are given as:
    a. Lines.
    b. Circles.
    c. Dots.
    d. All of the above are correct.
4. Explain how you align timing chain marks.
5. Timing gear _____ is the amount of clearance between the timing gear teeth.
6. Summarize the basic procedure for replacing a front crankshaft seal.
7. What is a seal alignment tool?
8. Most auto makers recommend timing belt replacement every _____ miles or _____ km.
9. List fourteen rules to remember when installing an engine in a car.

10. Engine _____ is done mainly to seat and seal the new piston rings.
11. Explain a general method of engine break-in.
12. Why should the customer avoid prolonged highway driving right after an engine overhaul?

ACTIVITIES FOR CHAPTER 49

1. Examine service manuals for as many different makes of cars or light trucks as you can find. Determine whether the engine uses timing gears, a timing chain, or a timing belt. Are certain sizes or types of engines more likely to use a particular timing device?
2. Demonstrate the proper use of a wheel puller in removing a pulley or a crankshaft damper (harmonic balancer).

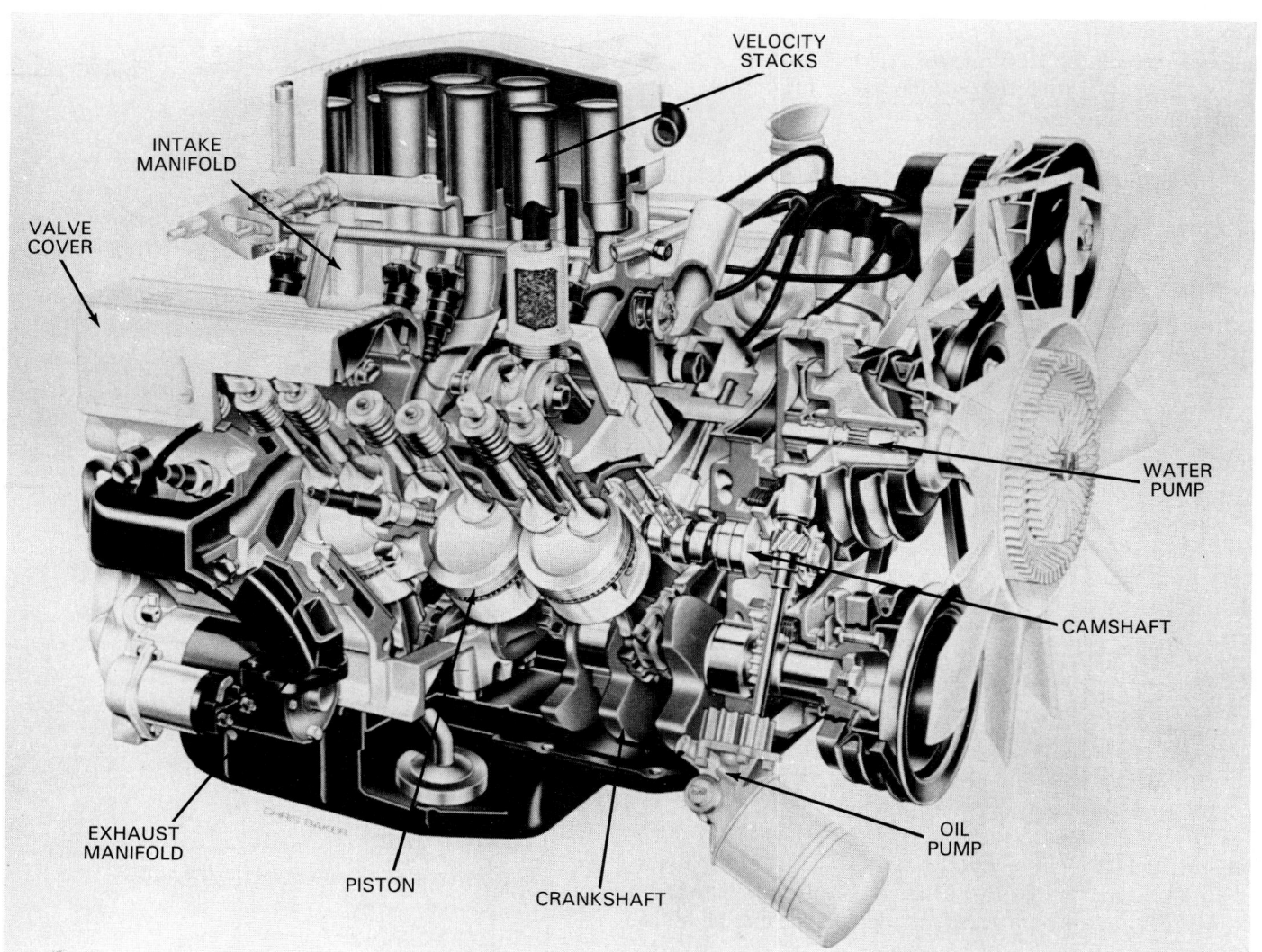

Note large velocity stacks on this late model, high performance engine. Engine has electronic fuel injection and an aluminum block, and displaces 241 cubic inches. (Range Rover)

Clutch Fundamentals

After studying this chapter, you will be able to:
- [ ] List the basic parts of an automotive clutch.
- [ ] Explain the operation of a clutch.
- [ ] Describe the construction of major clutch components.
- [ ] Compare clutch design differences.
- [ ] Explain the different types of clutch release mechanisms.

This chapter begins your study of a vehicle's drivetrain. The clutch is the first drivetrain component powered by the engine crankshaft. The clutch lets the driver control power flow between the engine and transmission or transaxle (transmission-differential unit).

Fig. 50-1 shows the basic parts of drivetrains for both rear and front-wheel drive vehicles. Review the relationship of the parts.

The next chapters cover transmissions, drive shafts, transfer cases, differentials, transaxles, and other drivetrain units. To fully understand these later chapters, you must first understand clutches.

Each succeeding chapter builds upon the knowledge gained in the previous chapter. For this reason, it is very important that you learn everything about to be discussed. Study carefully!

PURPOSE OF THE CLUTCH

An *automotive clutch* is used to connect and disconnect the engine and manual (hand-shifted) transmission or transaxle. The clutch is located between the engine and the transmission.

Only vehicles with manual transmissions require a clutch. Vehicles with automatic transmissions do NOT need a clutch. They have a fluid coupling or torque converter that automatically disengages the engine and transmission at low engine rpm.

CLUTCH PRINCIPLES

Power flow from one unit to another can be controlled with a drive disc and a driven disc. Look at Fig.

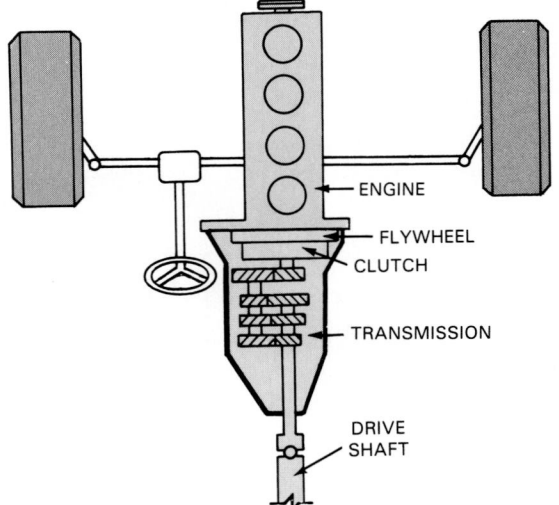

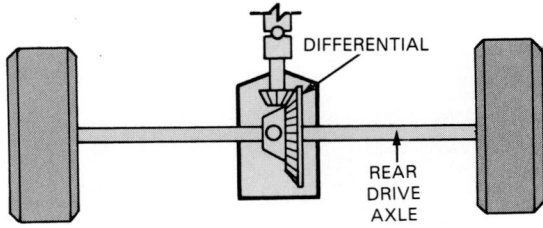

REAR WHEEL DRIVE

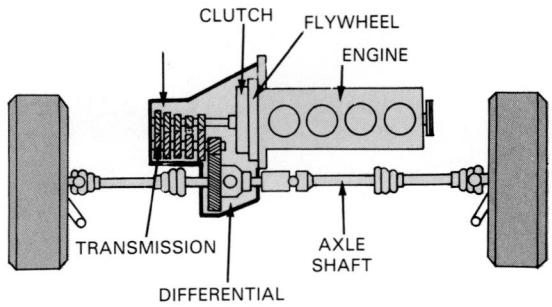

FRONT-WHEEL DRIVE

Fig. 50-1. Compare drivetrains for front- and rear-wheel drives. Clutch mounts on engine flywheel.

50-2. Relating to an automotive clutch, one disc is fastened to the rear of the engine crankshaft. The other disc is attached to the input shaft of the transmission.

When the discs do NOT touch, the crankshaft can rotate while the transmission input shaft remains stationary. However, when the transmission disc is forced into the spinning disc on the crankshaft, both spin together. Power flow is then transferred out of the engine and into the transmission. This principle is used in a car's clutch.

BASIC CLUTCH PARTS

Fig. 50-3 shows the major parts of an automotive clutch. Study the names, locations, and relationship of the components.

1. CLUTCH RELEASE MECHANISM (cable, linkage, or hydraulic system allows driver to disengage clutch with foot pedal).
2. CLUTCH FORK (lever that forces release bearing into pressure plate).
3. RELEASE BEARING (bearing that reduces friction between clutch fork and pressure plate).

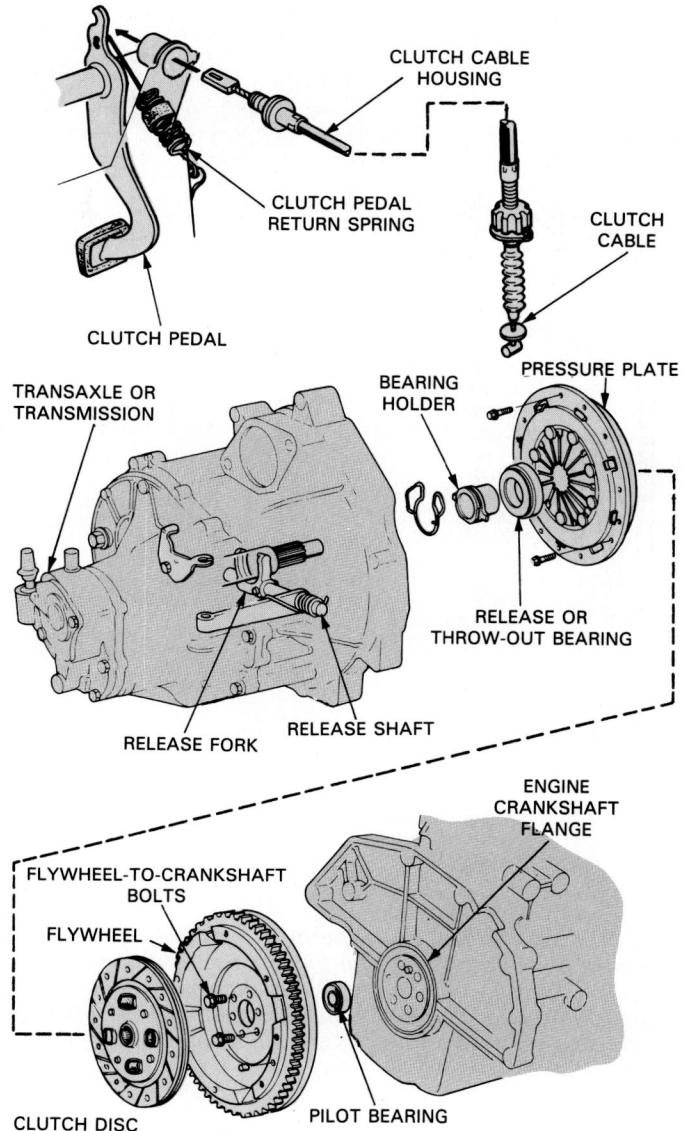

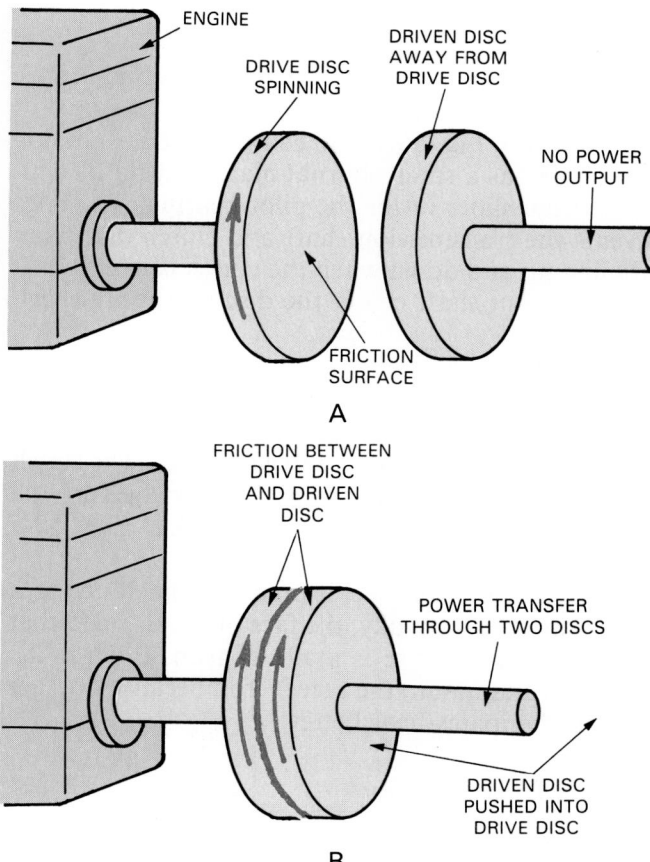

Fig. 50-2. Rotating discs demonstrate action of automotive clutch. A — Crankshaft spins drive disc on left. Other disc is not in contact with drive disc. No power transfers. B — Two discs are pushed together. Friction causes crankshaft disc to turn other disc connected to transmission input shaft. Power is transferred through clutch.

Fig. 50-3. Fundamental components of a clutch. Note how parts are located in relation to each other and with rear of engine. (Honda)

4. PRESSURE PLATE (spring-loaded device that presses clutch disc against flywheel).
5. CLUTCH DISC (friction disc splined [fastened] to transmission input shaft and pressed against face of flywheel).
6. FLYWHEEL (provides mounting place for clutch and friction surface for clutch disc).
7. PILOT BEARING (bushing or bearing that supports forward end of transmission input shaft).

Clutch action

When the driver presses the clutch pedal, the clutch release mechanism pulls or pushes on the clutch release lever or fork. See Fig. 50-4.

The fork moves the release bearing into the center of the pressure plate. This causes the pressure plate face to pull away from the clutch disc, releasing the disc

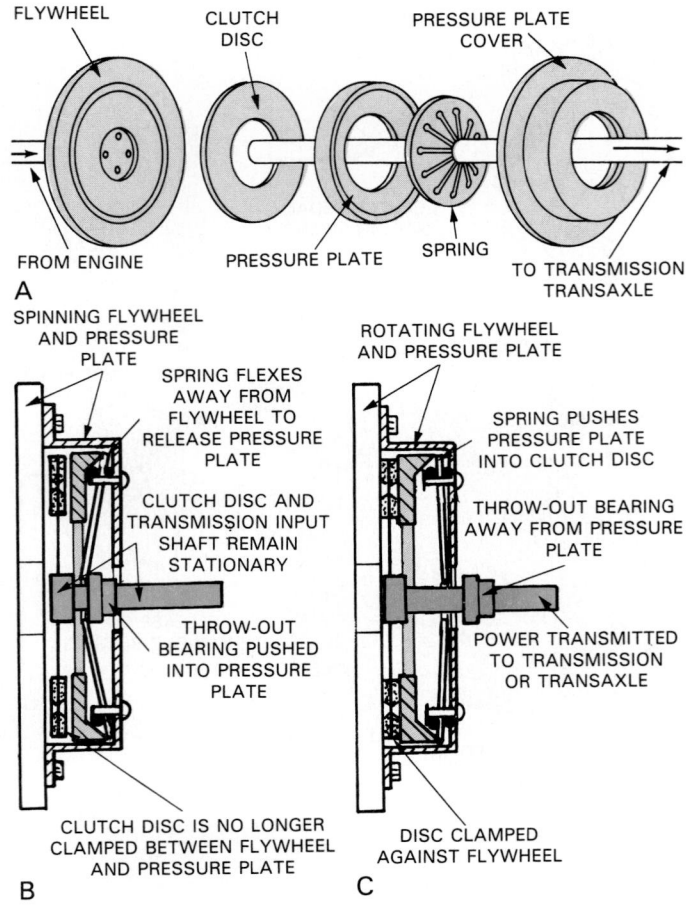

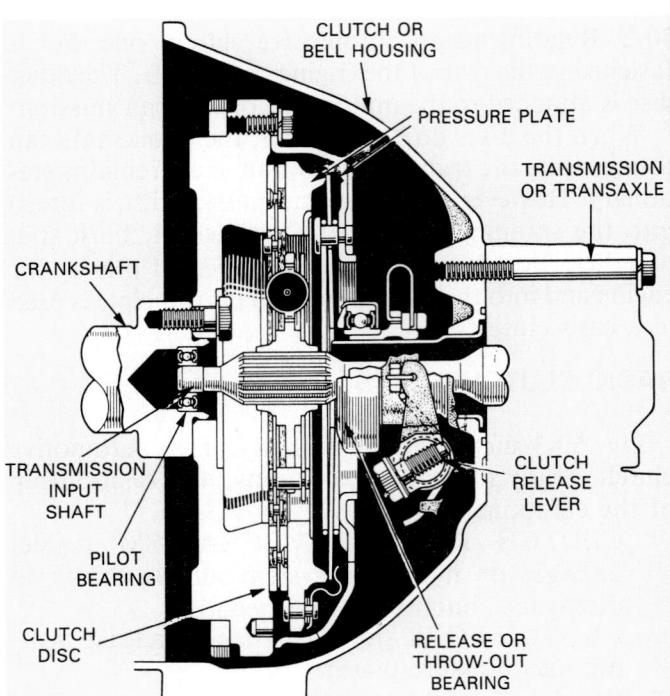

Fig. 50-4. A — Basic clutch parts. B — Clutch disengaged. Pressure plate does not clamp friction disc against flywheel. No power flow through clutch. C — Clutch engaged. Pressure plate spring action clamps friction disc and flywheel together. Clutch disc then turns transmission input shaft. (Deere & Co.)

Fig. 50-5. Cutaway view shows how clutch looks when assembled. Note how transmission input shaft extends through clutch and into pilot bearing in crankshaft. (Toyota)

from the flywheel. The engine crankshaft can then turn without turning the clutch disc and transmission input shaft.

When the clutch pedal is released by the driver, spring pressure inside the pressure plate pushes forward on the clutch disc. It locks the flywheel, disc, pressure plate, and transmission input together. The engine again rotates the transmission input shaft, transmission gears, drivetrain, and vehicle's wheels.

CLUTCH CONSTRUCTION

Now that you understand the basic action of a clutch, we will discuss, in more detail, how each part is made. This information will be useful when learning to diagnose and repair a clutch.

Refer to Fig. 50-5. It shows a side view of an assembled clutch.

PILOT BEARING

A *pilot bearing* or *pilot bushing* is pressed into the end of the crankshaft to support the end of the trans-

mission input shaft. Usually, the pilot is a solid bronze bushing. It may also be a roller or ball bearing.

As shown in Fig. 50-5, the end of the transmission input shaft has a small journal machined on its end. This journal slides inside the pilot bearing. The pilot prevents the transmission shaft and clutch disc from wobbling up and down when the clutch is released. It helps the input shaft center the disc on the flywheel.

FLYWHEEL

The *flywheel* is the mounting place for the clutch. The pressure plate bolts to the flywheel face. The clutch disc is pinched and held against the flywheel by the spring action of the pressure plate. Look at Figs. 50-5 and 50-6.

The face of the flywheel is precision machined to a smooth surface. Normally, the face of the flywheel that touches the clutch disc is made of iron. Even if the flywheel is aluminum, the face is iron because it wears well and dissipates heat better.

CLUTCH DISC

The *clutch disc,* also called *friction disc,* consists of a splined hub and a round metal plate covered with friction material (lining). One is pictured in Fig. 50-7.

The splines (grooves) in the center of the clutch disc mesh with splines on the transmission input shaft. This makes the input shaft and disc turn together. However, the disc is free to slide back and forth on the shaft.

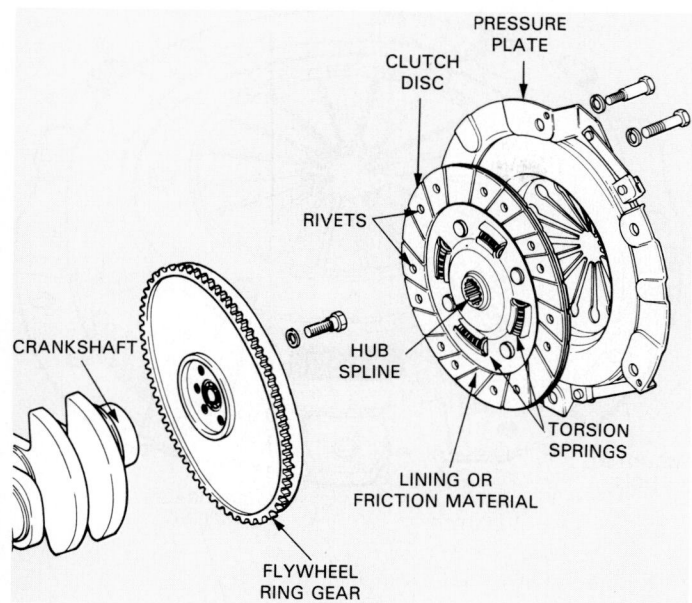

Fig. 50-6. Flywheel bolts to crankshaft flange. Pressure plate bolts to flywheel. Clutch disc is clamped between flywheel and pressure plate. (Mazda)

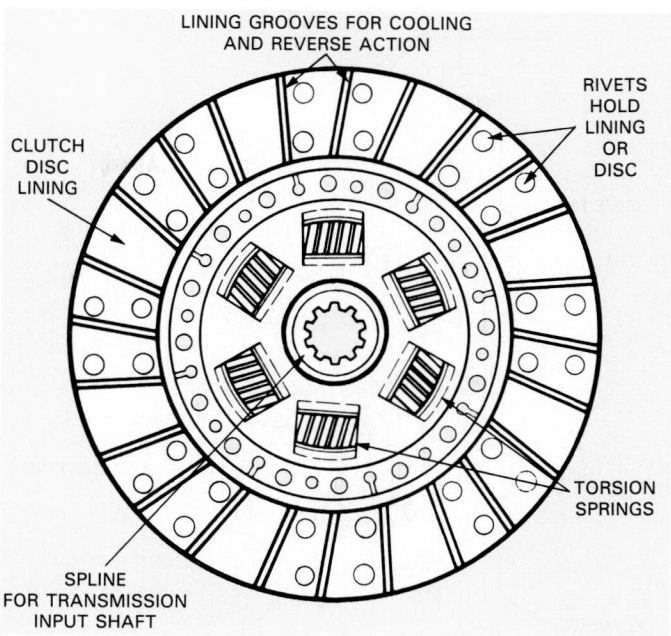

Fig. 50-7. Clutch disc construction. Asbestos lining or friction material is held on metal disc by rivets. Splines in center of disc fit over splines on transmission input shaft. (Chrysler Corp.)

Clutch disc torsion springs

Clutch disc *torsion springs,* also termed *damping springs,* help absorb some of the vibration and shock produced by clutch engagement. They are small coil springs located between the clutch disc splined hub and the friction disc assembly.

When the clutch is engaged, the pressure plate jams the stationary disc against the spinning flywheel. The torsion springs compress and soften the shock as the disc first begins to turn with the flywheel, Fig. 50-7.

Clutch disc facing springs

Clutch disc *facing springs,* also called *cushioning springs,* are flat, metal springs located under the disc's friction material. These springs have a slight wave or curve. They allow the friction material to flex inward slightly during initial clutch engagement. This also smooths engagement.

Clutch disc friction material

The clutch disc *friction material,* also called *disc lining* or *facing,* is usually made of heat resistant asbestos, cotton fibers, and copper wires woven or molded together. Refer to Fig. 50-7.

Grooves are cut in the friction material to aid cooling and release of the clutch disc. Rivets are used to bond the friction material to both sides of the metal body of the disc.

PRESSURE PLATE

The *pressure plate* is a spring-loaded device that can either lock or unlock the clutch disc and the flywheel. It bolts to the flywheel. The clutch disc fits between the flywheel and pressure plate, as in Fig. 50-6.

There are two basic types of pressure plates: the coil spring type, Fig. 50-8, and the diaphragm spring type, Fig. 50-9.

Coil spring pressure plate

A *coil spring pressure plate* uses small, coil springs, similar to valve springs. Study Fig. 50-8.

The *pressure plate face* is a large ring that contacts the friction disc during clutch engagement. It is normally made of iron. Refer to Fig. 50-8. The backside of the pressure plate face has pockets for the coil springs and brackets for hinging the release levers. During clutch action, the pressure plate face moves back and forth inside the clutch cover.

Pressure plate release levers are hinged inside the pressure plate to pry on and move the pressure plate face away from the disc and flywheel. Small clip-type springs fit around the release levers to keep them from rattling and in the fully retracted (released) position.

The *pressure plate cover* fits over the springs, release levers, and pressure plate face. Its main purpose is to hold the parts of the pressure plate assembly together. Holes around the outer edge of the cover are for bolting the pressure plate to the flywheel.

Coil spring pressure plate action

When the clutch is disengaged, the release levers are pushed forward or toward the flywheel. This pries the pressure plate face away from the flywheel, compressing the coil springs. The clutch disc slides back and power is NOT transferred into the transmission.

When the clutch is engaged, the release bearing moves away from the release levers. Then, the pressure

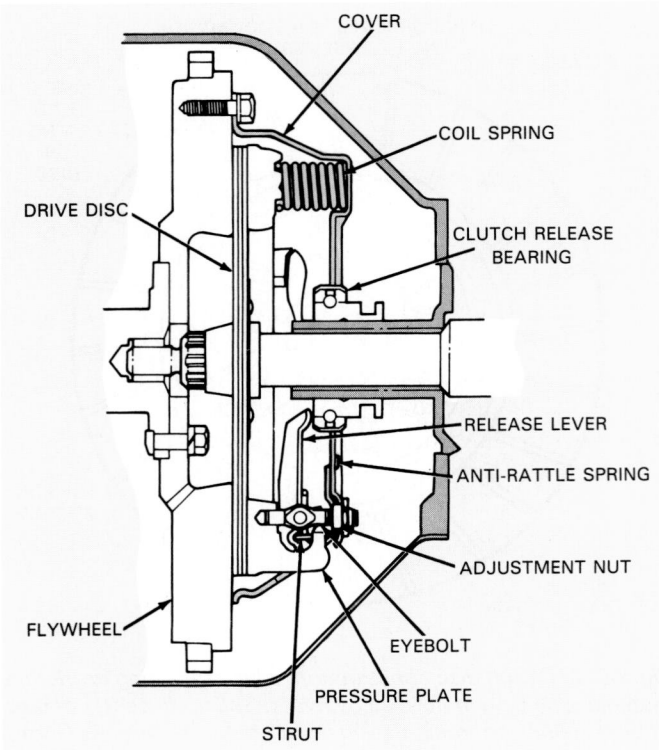

Fig. 50-8. Cutaway view of coil spring type pressure plate. Study parts. (GMC)

Labels in figure: COVER, COIL SPRING, DRIVE DISC, CLUTCH RELEASE BEARING, RELEASE LEVER, ANTI-RATTLE SPRING, ADJUSTMENT NUT, FLYWHEEL, EYEBOLT, PRESSURE PLATE, STRUT

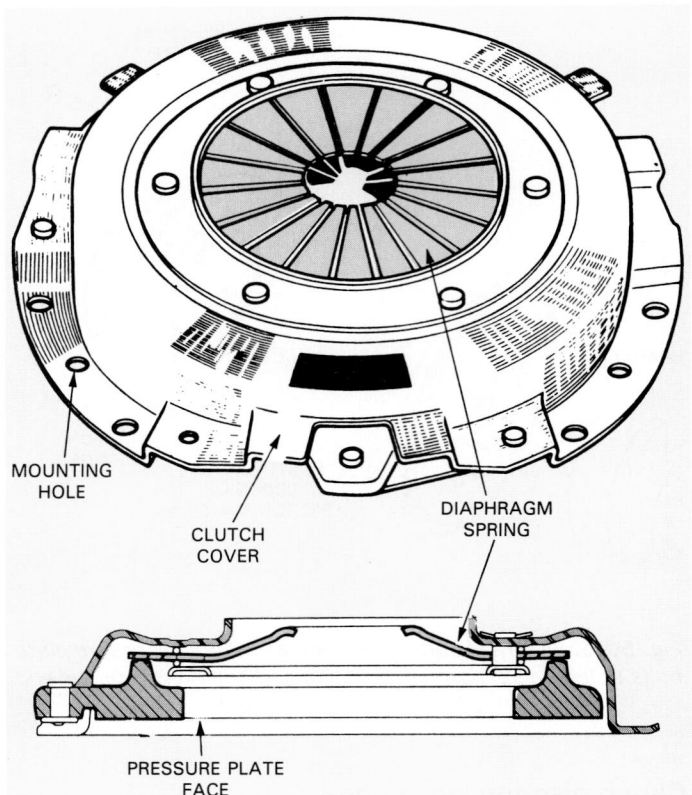

Fig. 50-9. Diaphragm type pressure plate uses single spring instead of several small, coil springs. Pushing in on center of spring bends outer edge of spring away from drive disc. This releases clutch disc. (Renault and Chrysler)

Labels in figure: MOUNTING HOLE, CLUTCH COVER, DIAPHRAGM SPRING, PRESSURE PLATE FACE

plate springs force the face and disc forward, into the rotating flywheel. The disc and transmission input shaft begin to spin and transmit power.

Centrifugal action of pressure plate

A *semi-centrifugal pressure plate* uses weighted release levers or rollers, and the resulting centrifugal force, to increase clamping pressure on the clutch disc. The weights on the release levers or the rollers are positioned so that, as engine speed increases, their outward thrust acts on the release levers. The extra force helps keep the clutch from SLIPPING. It also permits the use of slightly weaker coil springs to reduce the amount of foot pedal pressure required to disengage the clutch.

Diaphragm pressure plate

A *diaphragm pressure plate* uses a single diaphragm spring instead of several coil springs. One is pictured in Fig. 50-9. This type pressure plate functions almost like a coil spring pressure plate.

The *diaphragm spring* is a large, round disc of spring steel. The spring is bent or dished and has pie-shaped segments (pieces) running from the outer edge to the center opening. The diaphragm spring is mounted in the pressure plate with the outer edge touching the back of the pressure plate face.

A *pivot ring* mounts behind the diaphragm spring. It is located partway in from the outer edge of the diaphragm spring.

Diaphragm pressure plate action

When the center of the diaphragm spring is pushed toward the engine, its outer edge bends back away from the engine. This lets the pressure plate face and clutch disc slide away from the spinning flywheel.

When the center of the diaphragm spring is released, the spring tries to return to its normal dished shape. As a result, the outer edge of the spring pushes the pressure plate face into the clutch disc.

RELEASE BEARING (THROW-OUT BEARING)

The *release bearing,* also called a *throw-out bearing,* is usually a ball bearing and collar assembly. It reduces friction between the pressure plate levers and the clutch fork. The release bearing is a sealed unit packed with grease. It slides on a hub or sleeve extending out from the front of the manual transmission or transaxle. Refer to Fig. 50-10.

A few vehicles, especially foreign, use a graphite type throw-out bearing. The ring-shaped block of friction resistant graphite presses on a smooth flat plate on the clutch release levers.

The throw-out bearing usually snaps over the end of the clutch fork. Small spring clips hold the bearing on the fork (throw-out lever). Then, fork movement in either direction slides the throw-out bearing along the transmission hub sleeve.

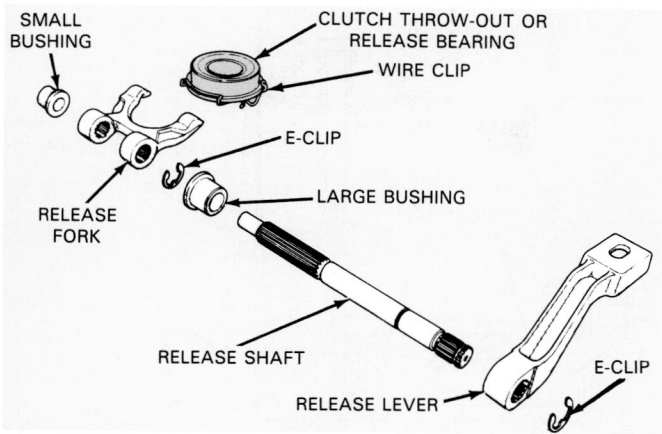

Fig. 50-10. Throw-out or release bearing acts on center of pressure plate. It is an antifriction bearing that cuts down rubbing contact between clutch fork and pressure plate. Note other parts that operate this throw-out bearing. (Chrysler)

CLUTCH HOUSING (BELL HOUSING)

The *clutch housing,* sometimes called a *bell housing,* bolts to the rear of the engine, enclosing the clutch assembly. It can be made of aluminum, magnesium, or cast iron. Look at Fig. 50-11. The manual transmission bolts to the back of the clutch housing.

A hole is provided in the side of the clutch housing for the clutch fork. The fork or fork shaft sticks through the housing. A bracket or ball is needed to hold an arm type fork, Fig. 50-11.

The lower front of the clutch housing usually has a thin, sheet metal cover, Fig. 50-11. It can be removed for flywheel ring gear inspection or when the engine must be separated from the clutch assembly.

CLUTCH FORK (CLUTCH ARM)

The *clutch fork,* also called a *clutch arm, throw-out lever,* or *release arm,* transfers motion from the clutch release mechanism to the throw-out bearing and pressure plate. There are two basic types of clutch forks.

A lever type clutch fork sticks through a square hole in the bell housing and mounts on a pivot. Refer to Fig. 50-11. When moved by the release mechanism, the clutch fork PRIES on the throw-out bearing to disengage the clutch.

A rubber dust boot fits over the pivot type clutch fork. The boot keeps road dirt, rocks, oil, water, and other debris from entering the clutch housing.

The second type of clutch fork has a ROUND SHAFT. Look at Fig. 50-10. When the lever on the outer end of the assembly is moved, the shaft rotates. This swings the fork to push on the throw-out bearing. This action releases the pressure plate.

CLUTCH RELEASE MECHANISMS

A *clutch release mechanism* allows the driver to operate the clutch. Generally, it consists of clutch pedal assembly, either mechanical linkage, a cable, or

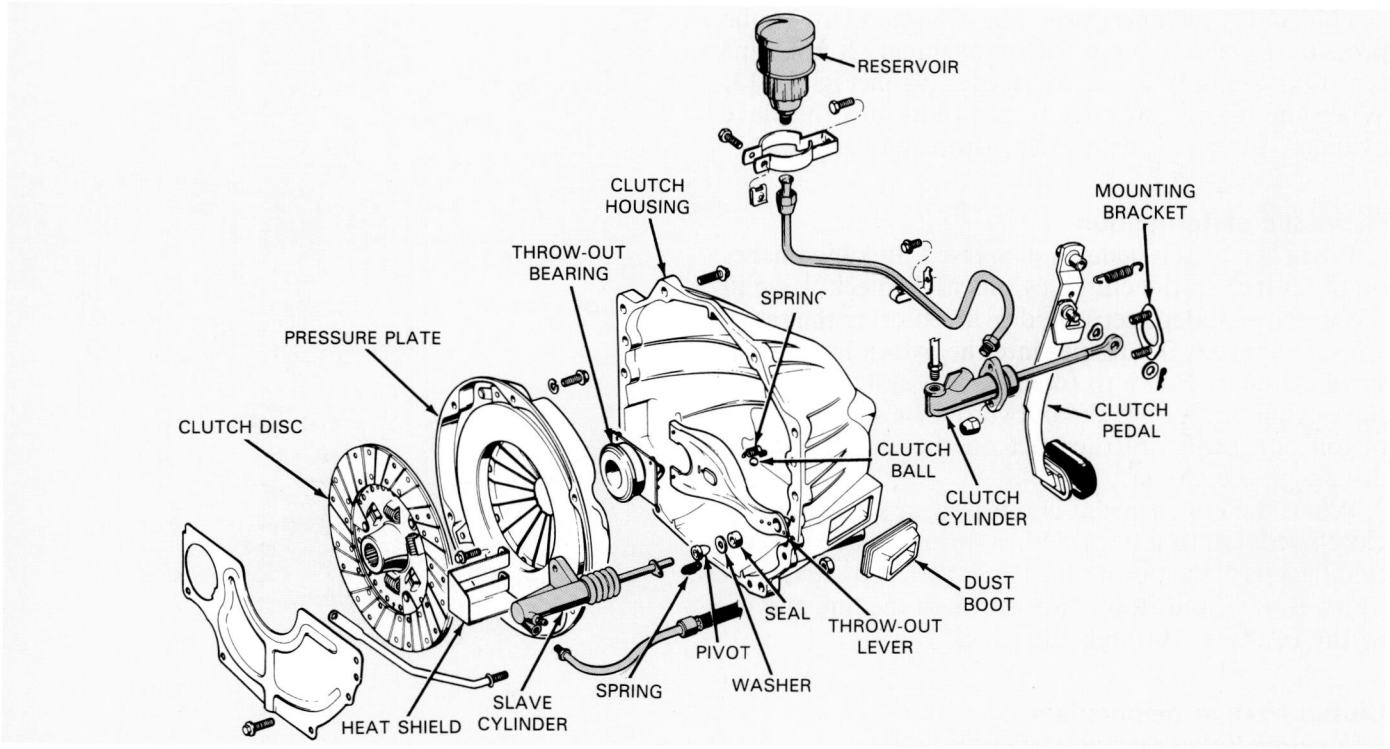

Fig. 50-11. This diaphragm type clutch is operated by a hydraulic release mechanism (slave cylinder). When driver presses clutch pedal, clutch master cylinder develops pressure in system. Pressure actuates slave cylinder piston and operates clutch fork to release clutch. (Chrysler)

hydraulic circuit, and the clutch fork. Many manufacturers include the throw-out bearing as part of the clutch release mechanism.

Hydraulic clutch release mechanism

A *hydraulic clutch release mechanism* uses a simple hydraulic circuit to transfer clutch pedal action to the clutch fork. It has three basic parts: clutch cylinder, hydraulic line, and slave cylinder. Refer to Fig. 50-11.

The **clutch cylinder,** sometimes called the *clutch master cylinder,* produces the hydraulic pressure for the system. Look at Fig. 50-12. It contains a piston mounted in a cylinder. The piston has *rubber cups* that produce a leakproof seal between the piston and cylinder wall.

A *fluid reservoir* is mounted above or on top of the clutch cylinder to hold extra fluid. See Figs. 50-11 and 50-12. Most hydraulic clutch systems use BRAKE FLUID as the medium for pressure transfer.

A cap and seal are threaded onto the reservoir to keep fluid from leaking out and to keep road dirt, and water, from entering the system.

The clutch cylinder usually mounts on the firewall. A push rod links the clutch pedal and the cylinder piston. When the clutch pedal is pressed, the push rod moves the piston to produce pressure in the cylinder.

The *hydraulic line* is a high pressure, rubber hose— metal line assembly that moves fluid from the clutch cylinder to the slave cylinder. When pressure is produced in the clutch cylinder, fluid flows through the hydraulic line, Fig. 50-11.

The *slave cylinder* uses the system's hydraulic pressure to cause clutch fork movement. It contains a piston assembly inside a cylinder, as in Fig. 50-13. When the master cylinder forces fluid into the slave cylinder, pressure pushes the piston outward.

Hydraulic clutch action

When the clutch pedal is depressed, linkage pushes on the piston in the clutch cylinder. A check valve in the clutch cylinder keeps fluid from entering the reservoir. As a result, fluid flows into the hydraulic line and slave cylinder. Pressure forms in the system and the slave cylinder piston is slid outward. The slave cylinder piston and push rod then act on the clutch fork to disengage the clutch.

When the clutch pedal is released, a spring on the clutch pedal pulls it back. Other springs inside the two cylinders push the pistons back into their retracted positions. Brake fluid flows back through the line and into the reservoir through the check valve.

Clutch linkage mechanism

A *clutch linkage mechanism* uses levers and rods to transfer motion from the clutch pedal to the clutch fork. One arrangement is shown in Fig. 50-14. When the pedal is pressed, a push rod shoves on the bellcrank.

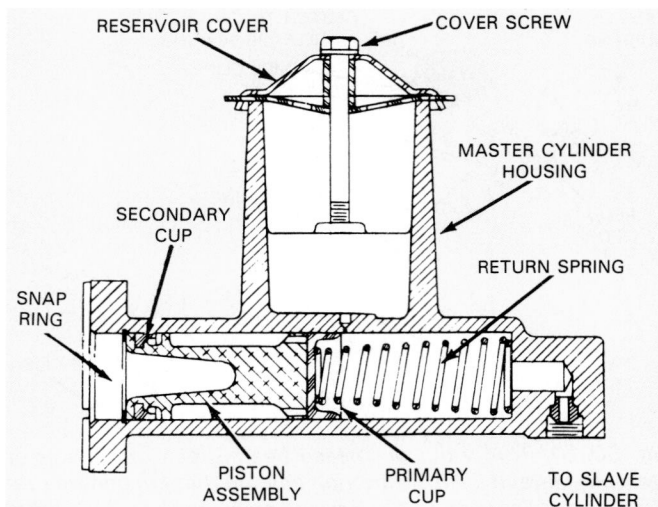

Fig. 50-12. Cutaway view shows inside of clutch master cylinder. Clutch pedal and linkage push piston and cup into cylinder, producing hydraulic pressure.

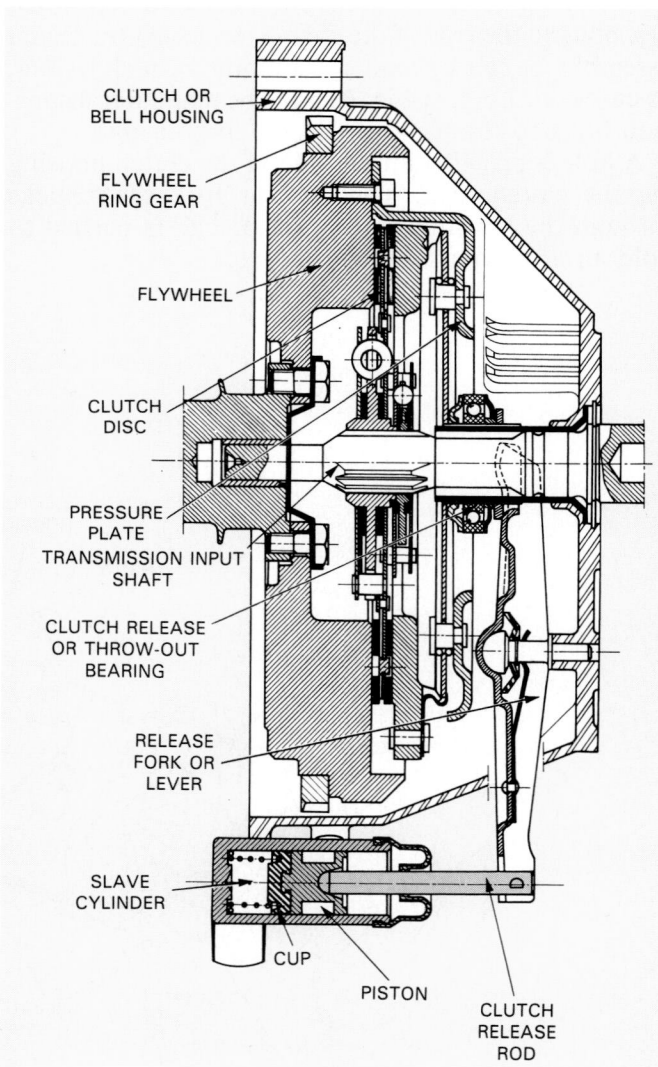

Fig. 50-13. Slave cylinder releases this clutch. Pressure from master cylinder enters cylinder, moving small piston towards clutch fork. Study other components. (Peugeot)

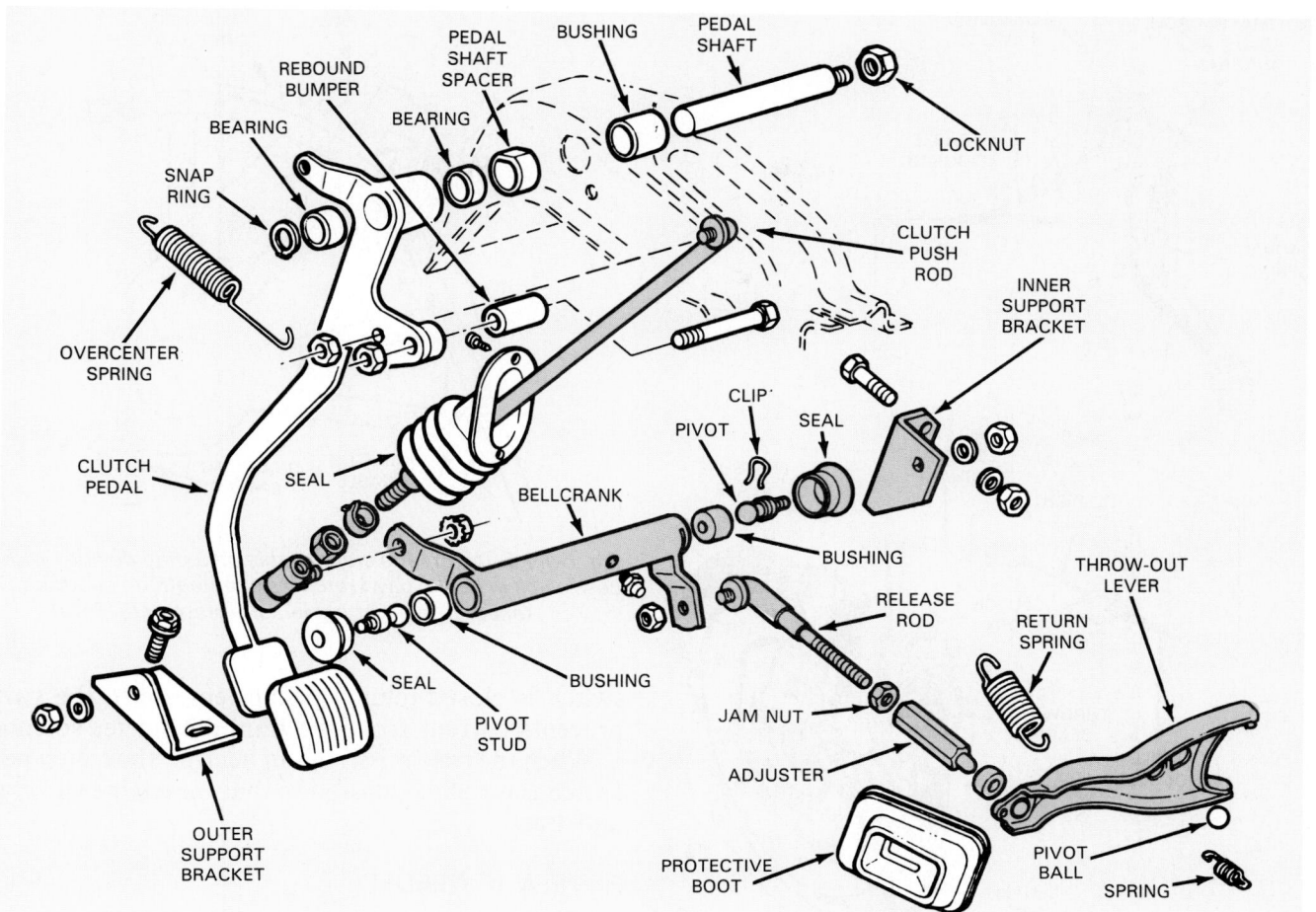

Fig. 50-14. Clutch linkage release mechanism. Arms and rods transfer clutch pedal action to clutch fork.   (Chrysler)

The **bellcrank** reverses the forward movement of the clutch pedal. The other end of the bellcrank is connected to a release rod.

The **release rod** transfers bellcrank movement to the fork and usually provides a method of adjustment.

Study the clutch linkage parts and their locations in Fig. 50-14 very carefully. This is a typical arrangement.

Clutch cable mechanism

A *clutch cable mechanism* uses a steel cable inside a flexible housing to transfer pedal movement to the clutch fork. This is a simple mechanism.

Shown in Fig. 50-15, the cable is usually fastened to the upper end of the clutch pedal. The other end of the cable connects to the clutch fork. The cable housing is mounted in a stationary position. This causes the cable to slide inside the housing whenever the clutch pedal is moved.

When the clutch pedal is depressed, the cable pulls on the clutch fork to disengage the clutch. When the clutch pedal is released, a strong spring pulls back on the pedal, cable, and fork to engage the clutch.

One end of the clutch cable housing usually has a threaded sleeve for CLUTCH ADJUSTMENT.

Automatic clutch adjuster

An *automatic clutch adjuster* removes play from the clutch cable as components wear, Fig. 50-15. The clutch pedal has a quadrant and pawl device, Fig. 50-16. A spring inside the quadrant applies light tension on the cable to take up extra slack.

When the clutch is applied, the pawl locks into one of the quadrant teeth and the clutch cable is activated. Then, if there is too much play in the cable, the pawl will ratchet over the quadrant teeth when the clutch pedal is released. This positions the pawl in another quadrant tooth and takes up any slack in the clutch cable, Fig. 50-16.

CLUTCH START SWITCH

The *clutch start switch* prevents the engine from cranking (starting motor operation) unless the clutch pedal is depressed. It serves as a safety device that keeps the engine from possibly starting while in gear. The clutch start switch is usually mounted on the clutch pedal assembly.

Wires from the ignition switch feed starter solenoid current through the clutch start switch. Unless the

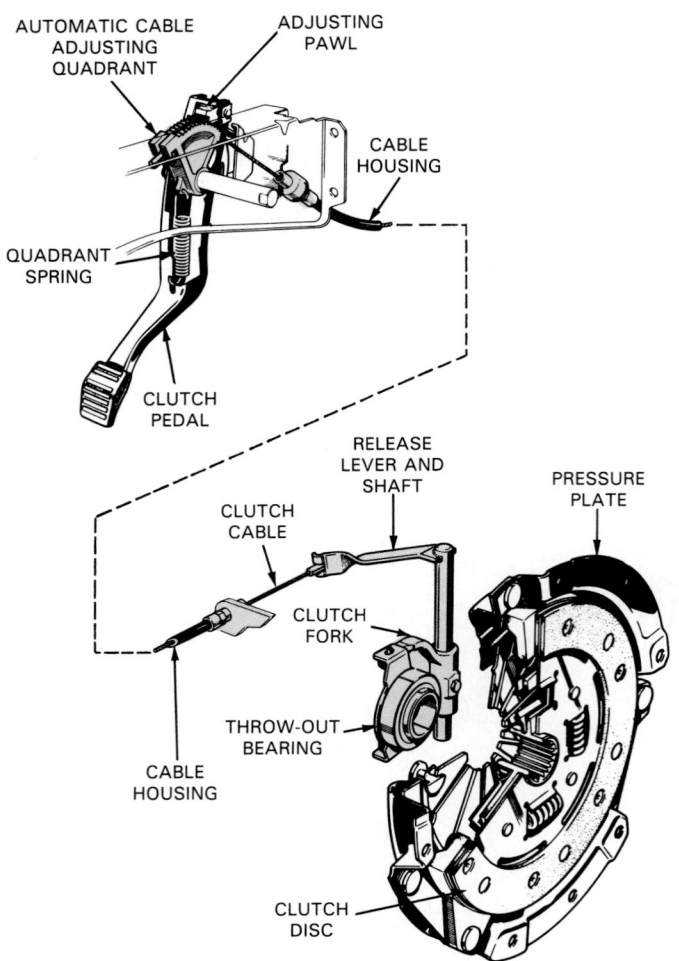

Fig. 50-15. Clutch cable mechanism. Steel cable runs through stationary housing. When clutch pedal is pressed, cable slides in housing to operate release lever and throw-out bearing. Also note automatic cable adjuster on foot pedal assembly. (Ford)

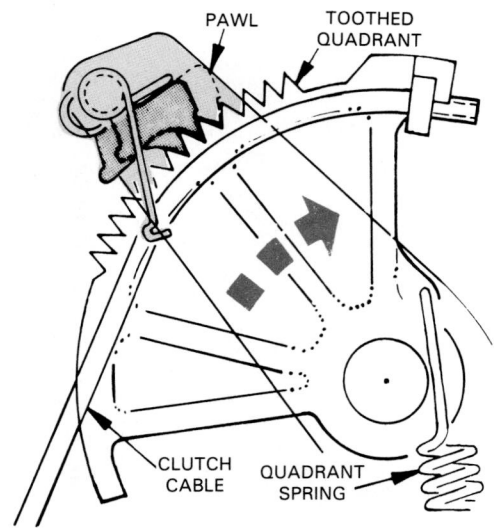

Fig. 50-16. Automatic clutch cable adjusting device. With excess slack in cable, pawl ratchets over teeth on quadrant. This takes up play in cable as parts wear. (Ford)

switch is closed (clutch pedal depressed), the switch prevents current from reaching the starter solenoid.

When the transmission is in neutral, the clutch pedal switch is usually bypassed so that the engine will crank and start.

REVIEW IF NEEDED

The information you just covered on clutches will be useful when studying many of the following chapters on drivetrain components.

Look at Figs. 50-17 and 50-18. They show the location of clutches for transmission (rear-wheel drive) and

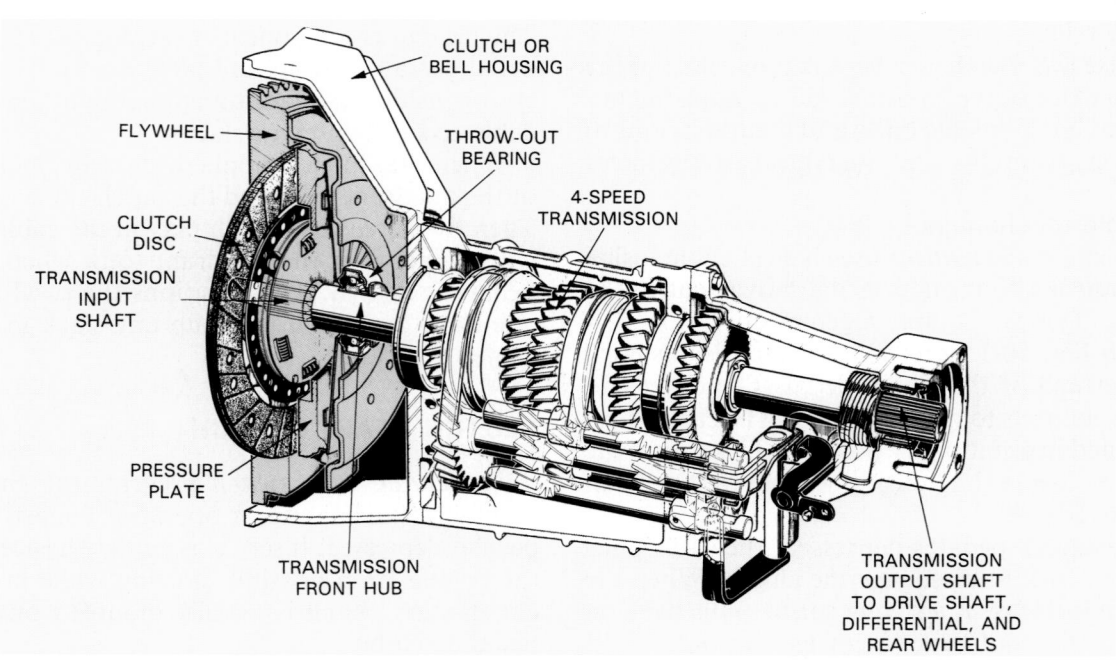

Fig. 50-17. Note how clutch installs in bell housing. Transmission bolts to rear of bell housing. Manual transmissions are covered in Chapters 52 and 53. (Peugeot)

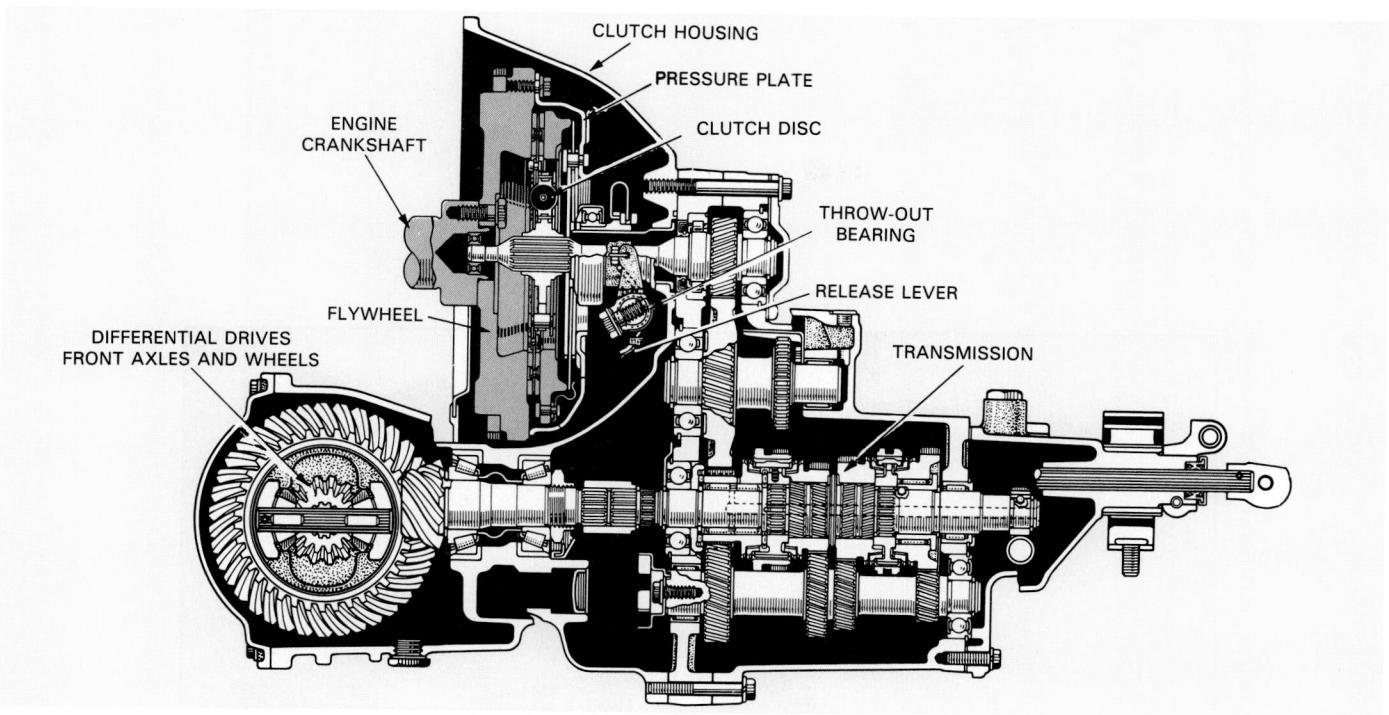

Fig. 50-18. See how clutch is located in relation to manual transaxle for this front-wheel drive vehicle. Transaxles are covered in Chapters 60 and 61.

transaxle (front-wheel drive) equipped cars. Locate the clutch components. If you cannot describe the functions of each part, quickly review the chapter.

KNOW THESE TERMS

Automotive clutch, Clutch release mechanism, Clutch fork, Throw-out bearing, Pressure plate, Clutch disc, Pilot bearing, Clutch lining, Torsion springs, Cushioning springs, Pressure plate face, Pressure plate release levers, Pressure plate cover, Semi-centrifugal clutch, Diaphragm spring clutch, Bell housing, Clutch master cylinder, Slave cylinder, Clutch linkage, Clutch cable, Automatic clutch adjuster, Clutch start switch.

REVIEW QUESTIONS

1. An automotive _____ connects and disconnects the engine and manual transmission or transaxle.
2. List and explain the seven basic parts of an automotive clutch.
3. What is the purpose of the pilot bearing or bushing?
4. The _____ is the mounting place for the clutch.
5. The clutch _____ , also called _____ _____ , consists of a splined hub and round metal plate covered with friction material (lining).
6. Clutch disc torsion springs help absorb some of the vibration and shock produced by clutch engagement. True or False?
7. What part of a clutch is commonly made of asbestos.
8. The _____ _____ is a spring-loaded device that can either lock or unlock the clutch disc and flywheel.
9. This is NOT a common type of pressure plate.
   a. Coil spring pressure plate.
   b. Diaphragm spring pressure plate.
   c. Both of the above are correct.
   d. None of the above are correct.
10. How does the release or throw-out bearing work?
11. What is the clutch or bell housing?
12. Explain clutch fork action.
13. A _____ clutch release mechanism uses a clutch cylinder to operate a slave cylinder.
14. Clutch linkage and clutch cable release mechanisms are both common. True or False?
15. What is a clutch start circuit?

ACTIVITIES FOR CHAPTER 50

1. Identify principles of fluids that underlie the operation of a hydraulic clutch; explain its operation to the class.
2. Sketch out a simple clutch, label its parts and explain its operation.

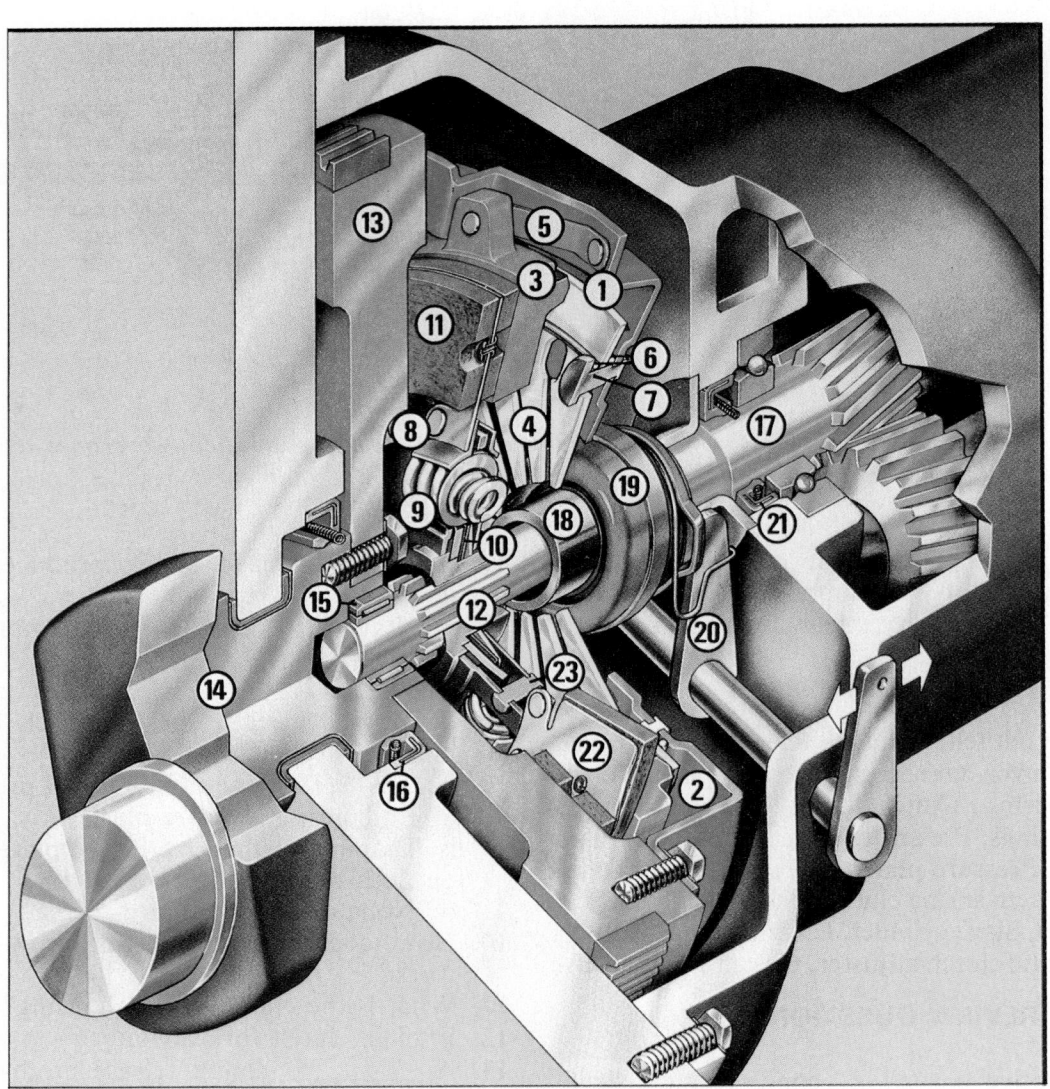

Parts of a manual clutch. 1. Clutch pressure plate. 2. Clutch cover. 3. Pressure plate. 4. Diaphragm spring. 5. Leaf springs/straps. 6. Pivot ring. 7. Diaphragm rivet. 8. Disc plate. 9. Torsion damper. 10. Friction device. 11. Clutch facing. 12. Hub. 13. Flywheel. 14. Crankshaft. 15. Pilot bearing. 16. Main seal (crank). 17. Transmission shaft. 18. Quill. 19. Throw-out bearing. 20. Release fork. 21. Shaft seal. 22. Cushion segment. 23. Stop pin. (LUK)

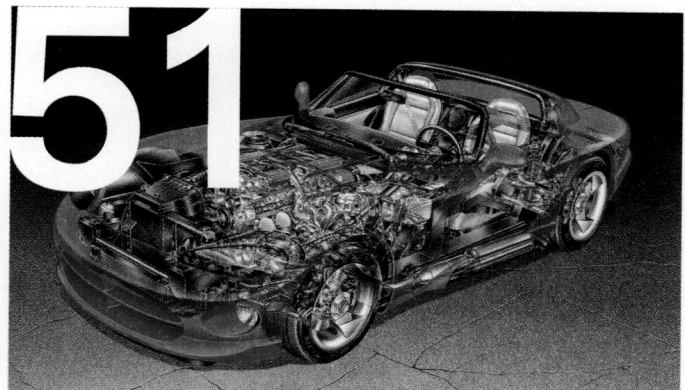

Clutch Diagnosis and Repair

After studying this chapter, you will be able to:
- ☐ Troubleshoot common clutch problems.
- ☐ Describe symptoms of typical clutch troubles.
- ☐ Adjust a clutch.
- ☐ Remove, repair, and install a clutch.
- ☐ Inspect clutch parts for wear and damage.
- ☐ Cite safety rules and demonstrate safe work procedures.

An auto technician must be able to quickly and accurately diagnose and repair clutch problems. Simply replacing parts is not sufficient. A technician must know why the old clutch failed. If she or he installs new parts without properly diagnosing the cause of the failure, the new parts could also fail.

This chapter will help develop the skills needed to service automotive clutches. It will provide the background to use a service manual properly.

ASBESTOS DANGER

Automotive clutch disc lining or friction material sometimes contains asbestos. Asbestos is a known CANCER-CAUSING SUBSTANCE. Do NOT breathe asbestos dust. Avoid using an air hose to blow asbestos dust off clutch parts. Wear a respirator or use an enclosed vacuum system.

DIAGNOSING CLUTCH PROBLEMS

An automobile clutch normally provides dependable service for thousands of miles. However, one vehicle's clutch might last 100,000 miles, while another's could fail in only 50,000 miles.

Stop-and-go city traffic will wear out a clutch quicker than highway driving. Everytime a clutch is engaged, the clutch disc and other components are subjected to considerable friction, heat, and wear.

Driver abuse commonly causes premature clutch troubles. For instance, "riding the clutch" (overslipping clutch and resting a foot on the clutch pedal while driving) can cause early clutch failure.

Verify clutch problem

After talking to the service writer or customer about the problem, verify the complaint. Test drive the vehicle and make your own decisions about the clutch troubles. Gather as much information as you can. Check the action of the clutch pedal. Listen for unusual noises. Feel for clutch pedal vibrations.

Use this information, your knowledge of clutch principles, and a service manual troubleshooting chart (if needed) to decide which components are at fault. You must determine whether the clutch failure was due to normal wear, improper driving techniques, incorrect clutch adjustment, or other problems.

There are several types of clutch problems: slipping, grabbing, dragging, abnormal noises, and vibration. It is important to know the symptoms produced by these problems and the parts that might be the cause. Then, you will have a good idea of the repairs needed to permanently correct the clutch problem, Fig. 51-1.

Clutch slips under load

Typically, *clutch slippage* is noticed when the engine *races* (engine rpm increases quickly) without an increase in the vehicle's road speed. This is caused by the clutch friction disc sliding between the flywheel and pressure plate. Clutch slippage usually occurs as the vehicle is accelerated from a standstill, when shifting, or when under a heavy load (climbing a hill, or pulling a trailer for example).

To test the clutch for slippage, set the emergency brake and start the engine. Place the transmission or transaxle in high gear. Then, try to drive the vehicle forward by slowly releasing the clutch brake.

A clutch in good condition should lock up and *kill* (stall or stop) the engine immediately. A badly slipping clutch may allow the engine to run, even with the clutch pedal fully released. Partial clutch slippage could let the engine run momentarily before stalling.

Never let a clutch slip for more than a second or two. The extreme heat generated by slippage could damage the flywheel or pressure plate faces.

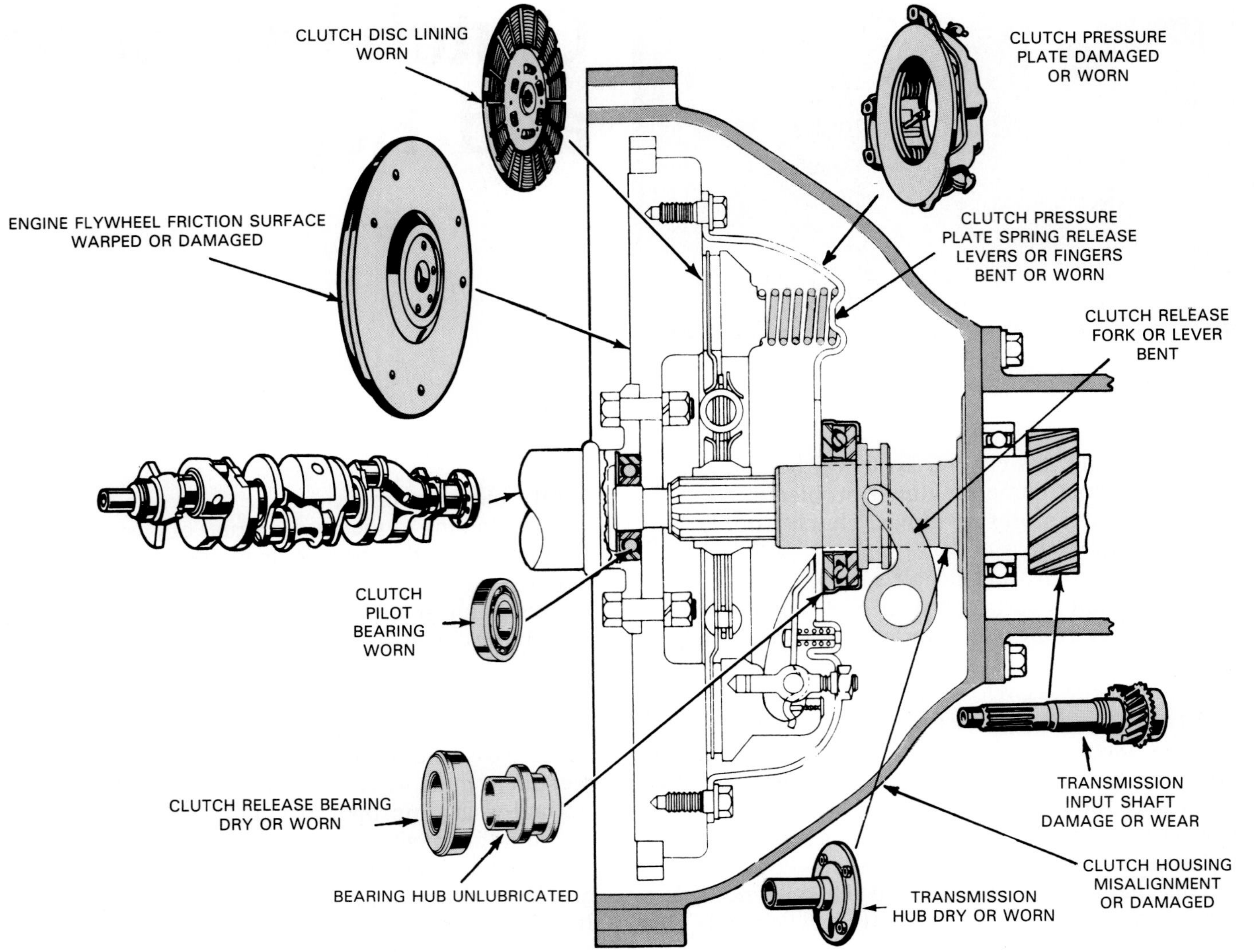

CLUTCH DISC LINING
WORN

CLUTCH PRESSURE
PLATE DAMAGED
OR WORN

ENGINE FLYWHEEL FRICTION SURFACE
WARPED OR DAMAGED

CLUTCH PRESSURE
PLATE SPRING RELEASE
LEVERS OR FINGERS
BENT OR WORN

CLUTCH RELEASE
FORK OR LEVER
BENT

CLUTCH
PILOT
BEARING
WORN

TRANSMISSION
INPUT SHAFT
DAMAGE OR WEAR

CLUTCH RELEASE BEARING
DRY OR WORN

CLUTCH HOUSING
MISALIGNMENT
OR DAMAGED

BEARING HUB UNLUBRICATED

TRANSMISSION
HUB DRY OR WORN

Fig. 51-1. Study types of problems that can develop in a clutch. Keep these problems in mind during clutch diagnosis and repair.

Some common causes of clutch slippage include: a maladjusted clutch, binding clutch linkage or cable, clutch disc wear, broken motor mount, oil or grease on clutch disc (leaking oil seal).

Improper clutch adjustment can cause slippage by keeping the throw-out bearing in contact with the pressure plate in the released position. Even with your foot off the pedal, the release mechanism will act on the clutch fork and throw-out bearing. This can make the clutch slip under load.

Free travel (free play) is the distance the clutch pedal or clutch fork moves before the throw-out bearing acts on the pressure plate. Free travel is needed to assure complete clutch engagement. Some auto makers recommend checking clutch free play at the clutch fork, Fig. 51-2. Others recommend checking pedal free play, Fig. 51-3.

A *binding clutch release mechanism* can also cause clutch slippage. Inspect release mechanism parts. Check for rusted, bent, misaligned, sticking, or damaged components. Wiggle the throw-out fork to check for free

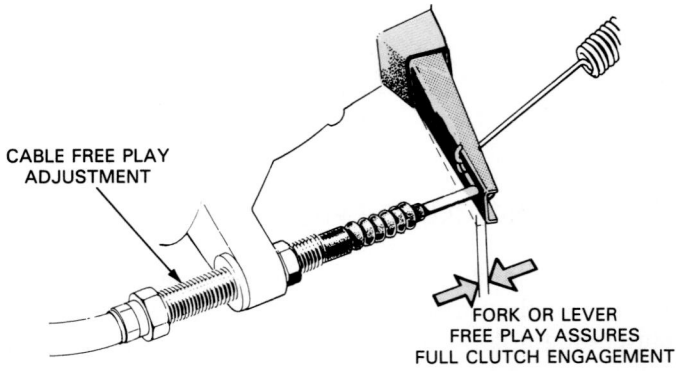

CABLE FREE PLAY
ADJUSTMENT

FORK OR LEVER
FREE PLAY ASSURES
FULL CLUTCH ENGAGEMENT

Fig. 51-2. Without free play in clutch release mechanism, fork could push throw-out bearing into pressure plate, even with clutch pedal fully released. Clutch slippage could result. (Volvo)

play. See Fig. 51-4.

A *broken motor mount* (engine mount) can cause clutch slippage by allowing engine movement to bind

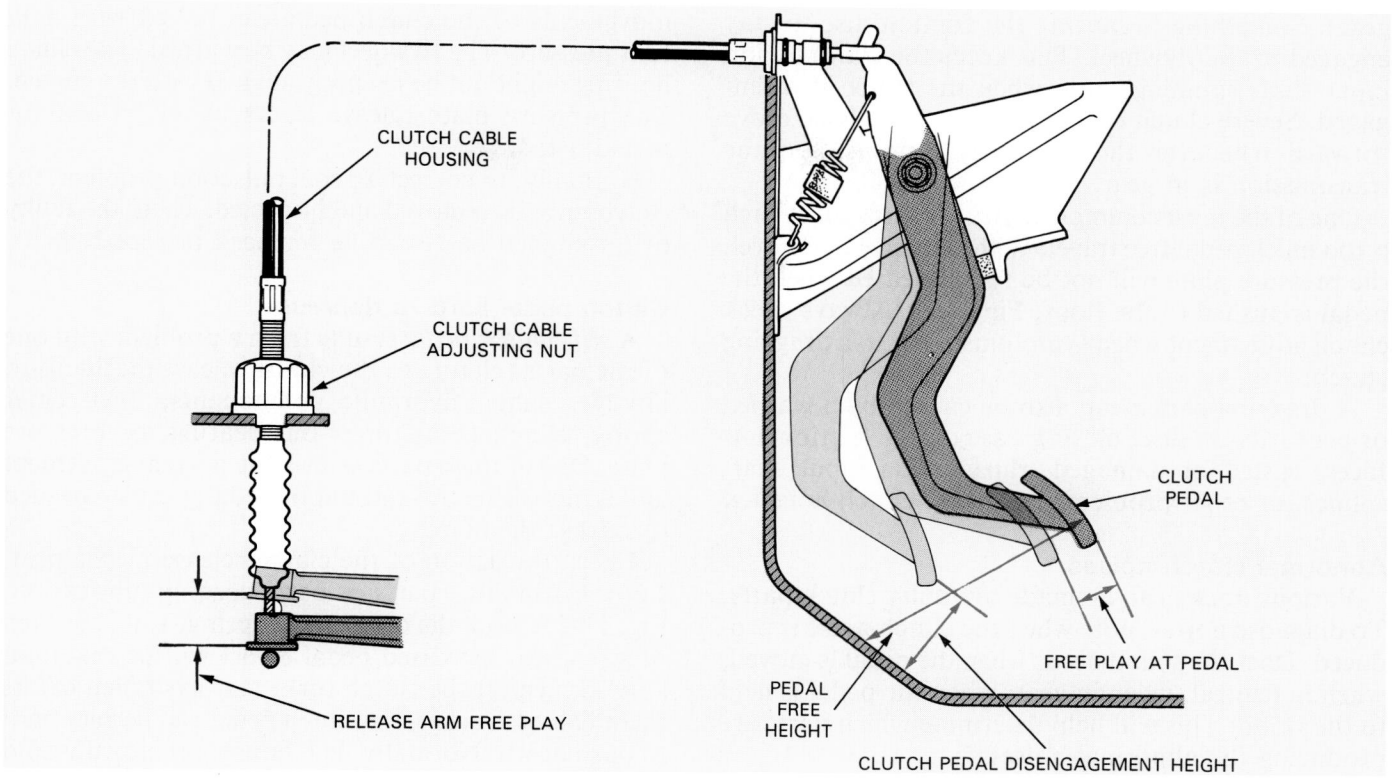

Fig. 51-3. Clutch pedal free play is distance pedal moves until throw-out bearing touches pressure plate. Release arm or fork free play is distance end of arm moves back and forth with clutch released. Note adjuster nut for changing cable free play. (Honda)

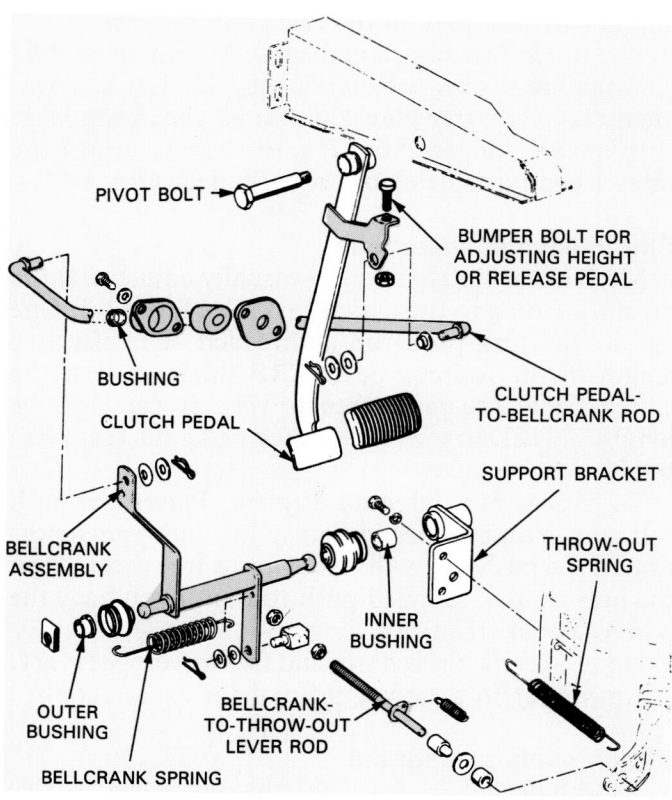

Fig. 51-4. Always check clutch linkage when clutch pedal action is faulty. Look for bent rods, worn bushings, missing springs, unlubricated bearings, damaged bellcrank, and other troubles. (Chrysler Corp.)

the clutch linkage. Under load, the engine can lift up in the engine compartment. This can shift the clutch linkage and push on the clutch fork.

If clutch slippage is NOT caused by a problem with the clutch release mechanism, then the trouble is normally inside the clutch housing. You would need to remove the transmission and clutch components for further inspection.

Grabbing (chattering) clutch

A *grabbing* or *chattering clutch* will produce a very severe vibration or jerking motion when the vehicle is accelerated from a standstill. Even though the driver is slowly releasing the clutch pedal, it will feel as if the clutch pedal is being rapidly pumped up and down. A loud banging or chattering sound may be heard as the car body vibrates.

Normally, clutch grabbing or chatter is caused by problems with components inside the clutch housing (friction disc, flywheel, or pressure plate). The clutch will usually require disassembly.

Note, however, a broken motor mount, as noted earlier, can also cause erratic clutch linkage operation. Check the engine mounts before removing the clutch.

Dragging clutch

A *dragging clutch* will normally make the transmission or transaxle grind when trying to engage or shift gears. Something is causing the friction disc to stay engaged to the flywheel. This keeps the transmission input shaft spinning, even when the clutch is disengaged. Severe clutch drag will make the vehicle move forward whenever the engine is running and the transmission is in gear.

One of the most common causes of a dragging clutch is too much pedal free travel. With excessive free travel, the pressure plate will not be fully released when the pedal is pushed to the floor, Fig. 53-3. Always check clutch adjustment when symptoms point to a dragging clutch.

A dragging clutch can also be caused by a warped or bent friction disc, oil or grease on the friction surfaces, rusted or damaged transmission input shaft splines, or other problems inside the clutch housing.

Abnormal clutch noises

Various noises can be made by faulty clutch parts. To diagnose noises, note when the clutch noise is produced. Does the sound occur when the pedal is moved, when in neutral, when in gear, when the pedal is held to the floor? This will help determine which parts are producing the abnormal noises.

A worn or unlubricated clutch release mechanism will produce odd sounds (squeaks, clunks, scrapes) whenever the clutch pedal is moved up or down. With the engine shut off, pump the clutch pedal while listening for the sound.

If needed, have a helper work the pedal while you locate the source of the noise. Use a stethoscope or section of vacuum hose as a listening device. Clean, lubricate, or replace parts as required.

Sounds from the clutch, when the clutch is initially ENGAGED, are normally due to friction disc problems. The lining could be worn, causing an abrasive, metal-on-metal grinding sound. If the friction disc damper springs are weak or broken, a knocking or rattling sound may be produced.

Abnormal sounds from the clutch that occur when the clutch is DISENGAGED, may be from a bad throw-out bearing. It may be dry and badly worn.

A worn pilot bearing in the crankshaft may also produce noises during clutch disengagement. The worn pilot can let the transmission input shaft and clutch disc vibrate up and down.

Abnormal sounds, heard only in NEUTRAL, that disappear when the clutch pedal is pressed, are usually caused by problems inside the transmission. The manual transmission input shaft is still spinning whenever the clutch is engaged. However, the input shaft stops turning when the clutch is disengaged. The front input shaft bearing could be worn, for example.

Pulsating clutch pedal

A *pulsating clutch pedal* is normally caused by the runout (wobble or vibration) of one of the rotating components of the clutch assembly. Slight up and down movements of the clutch pedal can be felt with light foot pressure. The flywheel may be warped. The clutch housing might not be properly aligned with the engine. The pressure plate release levers could be bent or maladjusted.

Normally, to correct a pedal pulsation problem, the clutch must be removed and inspected. Then, the faulty or misaligned parts can be replaced or repaired.

Clutch pedal hard to depress

A *stiff clutch pedal* results from a problem with one of the parts relating to the clutch release mechanism: linkage, cable, hydraulic components, over-center spring, clutch fork, throw-out bearing, or pressure plate. One of these parts is resisting normal movement and is increasing the amount of pedal pressure needed to release the clutch.

Check the action of the clutch release mechanism. Look for binding parts or parts needing lubrication, Fig. 51-4. Check the over-center spring. If it is broken or stretched, increased pedal effort will be required.

Also, inspect the clutch fork. If it has fallen off its pivot ball or bracket, the clutch pedal can be very hard to push down. Normally, bell housing removal would be needed to reinstall the clutch fork or repair the pivot.

ADJUSTING THE CLUTCH

Clutch adjustment involves setting the correct amount of free play in the release mechanism.

Too much free play could cause the clutch to *drag* (continue to propel vehicle) during clutch disengagement. Too little free play could cause clutch *slippage*.

It is important for you to know how to adjust the three basic types of clutch release mechanisms.

Clutch linkage adjustment

Mechanical clutch linkage is usually adjusted at the push rod going to the clutch fork. See Fig. 51-4. One end of the fork push rod is threaded. The effective length of the rod can be INCREASED to raise the clutch pedal (decrease free travel). It can also be SHORTENED to lower the clutch pedal (increase free travel).

To change the clutch adjustment, loosen the push rod nuts. You may need to grasp the unthreaded portion of the push rod with vise grips to free them. Turn the nuts on the threaded push rod until you have the correct pedal free travel.

Note! Specific procedures and free travel specs vary. Always refer to a service manual for exact details.

Clutch cable adjustment

As with the linkage release mechanism, a clutch cable may require periodic adjustment to maintain the correct pedal height and free travel. Look at Fig. 51-3. Typically, the clutch cable housing will have an adjusting nut. When the nut is turned, the length of the cable housing increases or decreases.

In most cases, to INCREASE clutch pedal free travel, turn the cable housing nut to shorten the housing. To DECREASE clutch pedal free travel, lengthen the clutch cable housing.

Some cable release mechanisms have an automatic adjusting mechanism. If the clutch requires adjustment, the automatic clutch adjuster may be faulty or the clutch may be badly worn.

Hydraulic clutch release mechanism adjustment

A hydraulic clutch release mechanism may need adjustment after prolonged clutch operation. Normal wear of the friction disc, throw-out bearing, and other parts can cause the pedal free travel to increase. The adjustment of a hydraulic type clutch may be located on the fork push rod or the push rod going to the clutch master cylinder. See Fig. 51-5 and 51-6.

To adjust a hydraulic clutch, simply turn the nut or nuts on the push rod as needed. Generally, lengthening the rod decreases pedal free travel. Shortening the rod increases free travel. Check a service manual for specs and procedures.

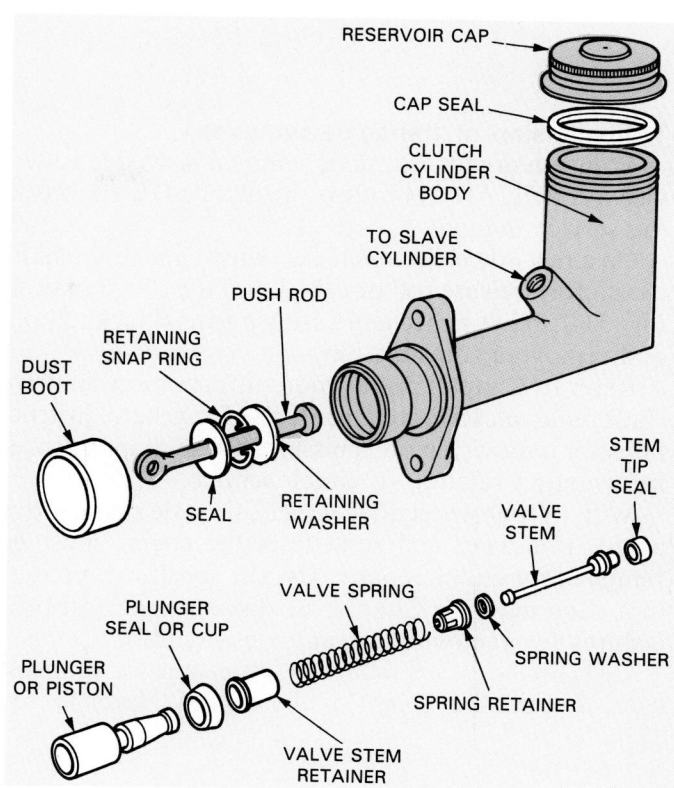

Fig. 51-6. Clutch master cylinder is serviced much like a brake system master cylinder. When leaking, either rebuild or replace unit. Study part names. (Chrysler Corp.)

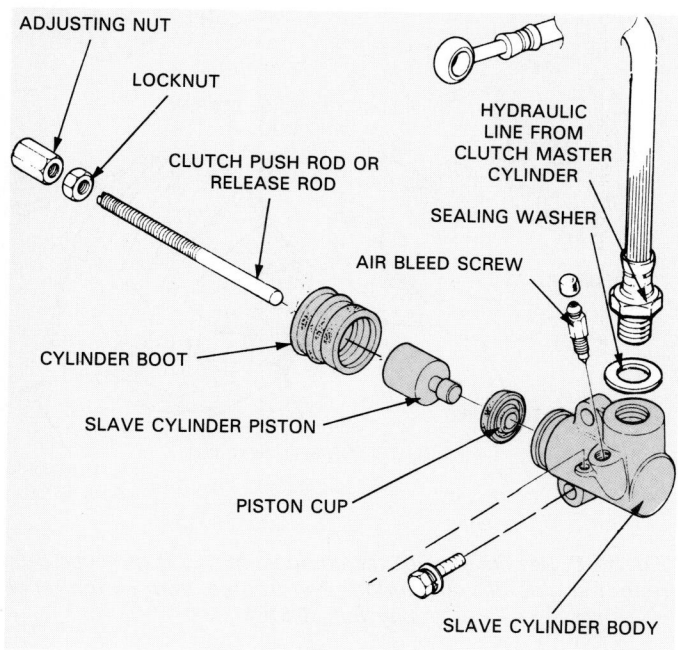

Fig. 51-5. Exploded view of clutch slave cylinder. To rebuild unit, hone cylinder and replace cup and boot. Also note adjustable push rod for setting free play. (Honda)

Servicing hydraulic clutch release mechanism

Hydraulic type clutch release mechanism problems are usually caused by FLUID LEAKAGE. The rubber cups inside the master cylinder or slave cylinder can wear and begin to leak. After enough fluid loss, the reservoir can empty and the clutch will not release.

If leakage is indicated, inspect the system closely. Look behind the master cylinder and at the end of the slave cylinder. If leaks are found, replace or repair the components as needed. Refer to Figs. 51-5 and 51-6.

After reassembly, the hydraulic clutch will require *bleeding* (removal of air from inside hydraulic system). Air is compressible and will cause the clutch pedal to be very soft and spongy.

CAUTION! Install only the recommended type of fluid in a hydraulic clutch system. Also, oil, kerosene, or grease must NEVER enter the hydraulic system. These substances can swell and deteriorate the rubber cups. Keep your hands clean!

Hydraulic clutch service (bleeding, honing cylinders, cup replacement) is very similar to servicing a hydraulic brake system. For more information on how to work on hydraulic components, refer to Chapter 69, Brake System Diagnosis and Repair.

SERVICING A CLUTCH

Clutch removal procedures vary from one vehicle to another. However, general procedures and safety warnings should be understood.

DANGER! Always disconnect the battery ground when removing a clutch assembly. This will prevent accidental cranking of the engine and possible injury.

It can also prevent electric shorts that could damage the vehicle's wiring.

Transmission or transaxle removal

Transmission or transaxle removal is needed to service a clutch. Always follow the detailed directions in the service manual.

On a rear-wheel drive vehicle, remove the drive shaft, clutch fork release rod or cable, and the transmission. Fig. 51-7 shows a mechanic using a special jack to hold and remove a transmission.

Refer to Chapter 56 for more information on drive shaft removal. Refer to Chapter 53 for general instructions for removing a transmission. These chapters cover information relating to clutch service.

With a front-wheel drive vehicle, the axle shafts (drive axles), transaxle, and sometimes the engine must be removed for clutch repairs. Use the specific directions in a shop manual. Chapter 61 discusses general procedures for removing a transaxle assembly.

CAUTION! When removing a transmission or transaxle, support the weight of the engine. Never let the engine, transmission, or transaxle hang unsupported. The transmission input shaft, clutch fork, motor mounts, and other parts could be damaged.

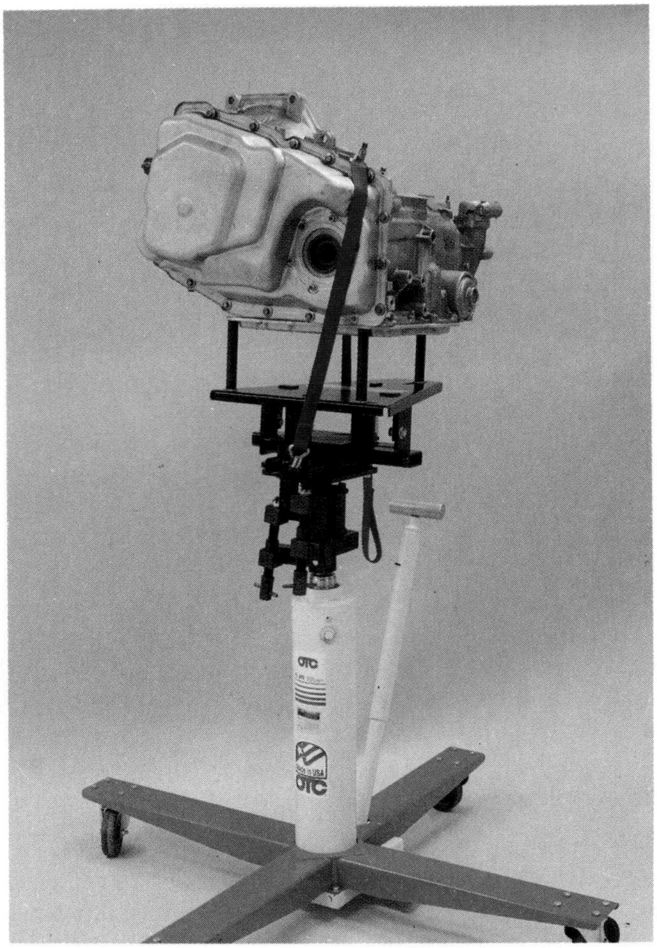

Clutch removal

After removing the transmission or transaxle, unbolt the bell housing from the rear of the engine. See Fig. 51-8. Hold the housing as the last bolt is removed. Be careful not to drop the bell housing as you pull it off its dowel pins.

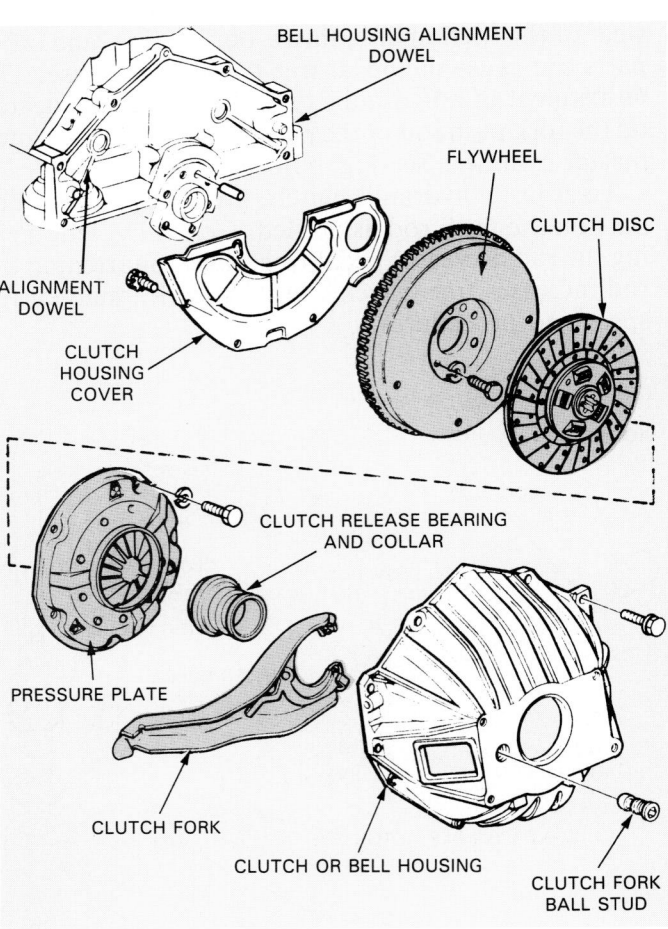

Fig. 51-8. Inspect each clutch component as it is removed from rear of engine. If you overlook any trouble, your clutch repair may fail. (GMC)

Use a hammer and center punch to mark the pressure plate and flywheel. These marks may be needed to reinstall the same pressure plate and assure correct balancing of the clutch.

Slide a *pilot shaft* (clutch alignment tool or old transmission input shaft) into the clutch. This will keep the clutch disc from falling as you unbolt the pressure plate. Loosen each pressure plate bolt a little at a time to avoid placing too much stress on any one bolt. Hold the pressure plate against the flywheel as the last bolt is removed. Look at Fig. 51-9.

Fig. 51-7. This transmission jack is designed to be used when car is raised with lift. Transmissions are very heavy; be careful. (OTC Div. of SPX Corp.)

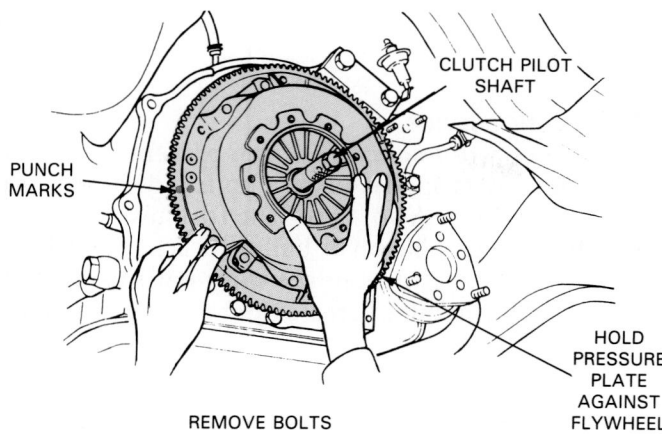

Fig. 51-9. Punch mark pressure plate and flywheel before disassembly. You will need to align these marks to reuse old pressure plate. Pilot shaft will keep disc from falling as pressure plate bolts are removed. (Mazda)

Lift the pilot shaft, pressure plate, and clutch disc off the back of the engine without dropping them. They are fairly heavy. Be prepared to support their weight.

Inspecting and cleaning clutch parts

With the clutch removed, each component must be carefully inspected for wear and damage.

NOTE! Be careful how you clean the parts of a clutch. Avoid using compressed air to blow clutch dust off the parts. A clutch disc often contains asbestos — a powerful cancer-causing substance.

DO NOT wash the throw-out bearing in cleaning solvent. This could wash the grease out of the bearing and ruin it.

Preferably, wipe the clutch parts down with a clean rag. Use sandpaper to deglaze and polish the surface of the flywheel and face of pressure plate. Keep cleaning solvent, which might contain traces of oil, off the friction surfaces (clutch disc, flywheel, and pressure plate faces).

Pilot bearing service

A *worn pilot bearing* will allow the transmission input shaft and clutch disc to wobble up and down. This can cause clutch vibration, abnormal noises, and damage to the transmission.

Closely inspect the pilot bearing or bushing. Using a telescoping gauge and micrometer, measure the amount of wear in the bushing. If a roller bearing is used, turn the bearing with your finger. Feel for roughness and wear. If needed, replace the bearing.

The pilot bearing can be removed from the crankshaft with a slide hammer puller. A few light blows will drive the bearing out of the crank.

If a puller is NOT available, fill the inside of the bearing with heavy grease. Then, insert the metal pilot shaft in the bearing. Tap on the shaft with a mallet and the grease will force the pilot bearing out of the crankshaft.

Check the fit of the new pilot bearing by sliding it over the input shaft of the transmission. Then, drive the new pilot bearing into the end of the engine crankshaft, as in Fig. 51-10. Place a small amount of grease in the pilot bearing if needed.

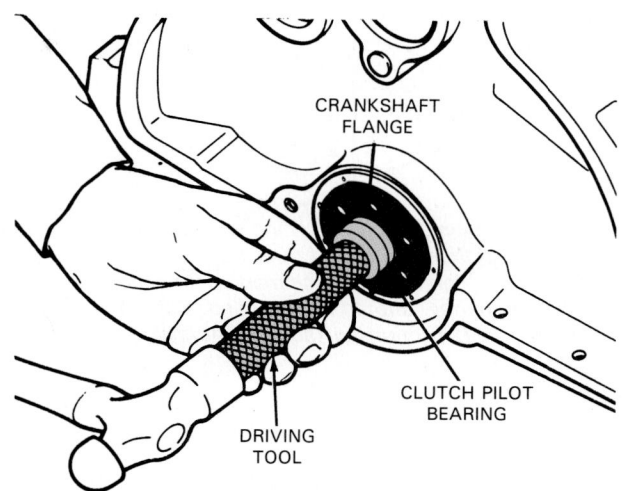

Fig. 51-10. Always check pilot bearing for wear during clutch service. If worn, remove old bearing with puller or with packed-in grease and driver. Install new pilot bearing as shown. (Ford)

Flywheel service

An *overheated flywheel* can have surface cracks and hardened or warped areas that upset clutch operation. Cracks in the surface of a flywheel can cause rapid clutch disc wear. If the flywheel is warped, the clutch may grab or vibrate upon acceleration.

Closely inspect the surface of the flywheel. Look for overheated, discolored areas, and cracks. Measure flywheel runout with a dial indicator. If warped or damaged, either replace the flywheel or have it resurfaced by a machine shop.

Also, check the ring gear teeth on the flywheel. If they are worn or chipped, a new ring gear should be installed on the flywheel. Heat the old ring gear with an acetylene torch. This will expand the gear and allow it to be easily knocked off the flywheel with a hammer and punch. To install the new ring gear, heat the ring gear with your torch. Then, carefully position the ring gear and drive it on with light hammer blows.

Clutch disc service

A *worn clutch disc* will cause clutch slippage and, sometimes, damage to the flywheel and pressure plate. To check disc wear, inspect the depth of the rivet holes. The closer the rivets are to the surface of the friction material, the more worn the disc. Look at Fig. 51-11.

Normally, the friction disc is replaced anytime the clutch is torn down for repairs. The disc is reasonably inexpensive and highly prone to wear.

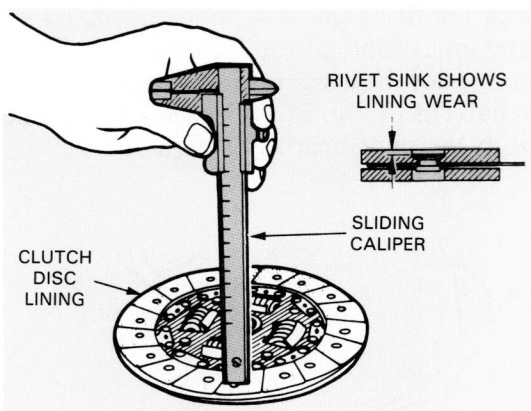

Fig. 51-11. Measure clutch disc lining wear at rivets. If distance from surface of lining to top of rivet head is too small, install new clutch disc. Refer to a service manual for specs. Only when disc is relatively new should it be reused. Keep grease and oil off friction surfaces. (Chrysler)

Pressure plate service

A *bad pressure plate* can also cause clutch slippage as well as clutch release problems (stiff clutch pedal, clutch grabbing, abnormal noises, clutch dragging). The springs inside the clutch could lose tension or break. The release levers could be bent or out of adjustment. The face of the pressure plate could also be scored.

Inspect the pressure plate closely using the information in a service manual. The manual will describe various measurements to determine its condition.

Modern practice is to replace the pressure plate. Most mechanics no longer rebuild or repair them. Considering the cost of labor, it is normally cheaper to purchase and install a new or rebuilt unit.

Throw-out bearing service

A *bad throw-out bearing* will produce a grinding noise whenever the clutch pedal is pushed down. The roller bearings may be dry (out of grease).

To check the action of the throw-out bearing, insert your fingers into the bearing. Then, turn the bearing while pushing in on it. Try to detect any roughness. The throw-out bearing should rotate smoothly.

Also, if used, inspect the spring clips on the throw-out bearing or fork. They hold the bearing on the end of the clutch fork. If bent, worn, or fatigued, the bearing collar or fork must be replaced.

To replace the throw-out bearing, the bearing must usually be driven off of its collar. Use a vise and hammer or a hydraulic press. Follow the detailed procedures in a service manual to avoid damage to the collar and new bearing.

Most mechanics replace the throw-out bearing anytime the clutch is disassembled for repairs. The throw-out bearing is subjected to considerable wear and is a frequent cause of clutch problems.

Lubricate the throw-out bearing collar as shown in Fig. 51-12.

Clutch fork service

A *bent* or *worn clutch fork* can prevent the clutch from releasing properly. Inspect both ends of the fork closely, Fig. 51-8. Also, check the fork pivot point in the bell housing. The pivot ball or bracket should be undamaged and tight. Replace worn parts as needed. Place a small amount of grease on the fork pivot point.

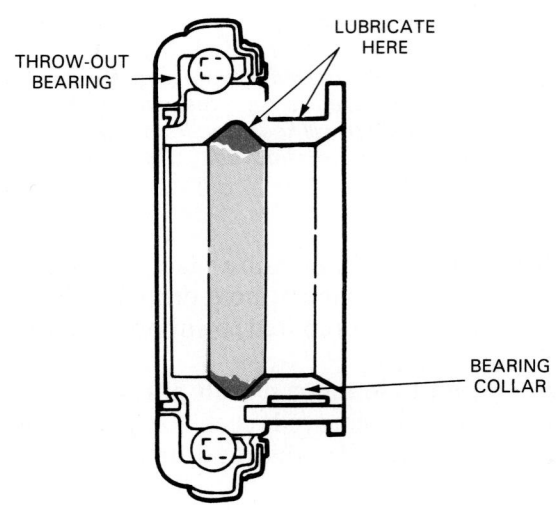

Fig. 51-12. When installing new throw-out bearing, place high temperature grease on areas shown. This will let bearing collar slide freely on transmission hub. Do not use too much grease; it could contaminate and ruin clutch disc. (Oldsmobile)

Look for oil leaks

With the clutch removed, check the rear of the engine and the front of the transmission for oil leaks. If oil were to leak on the new clutch, it would be ruined. Refer to the appropriate text chapters on procedures for replacing a crankshaft rear main seal and transmission front seal.

Clutch installation

Assemble the clutch in the reverse order of disassembly. Mount the clutch disc and pressure plate on the flywheel. Use a clutch alignment tool (pilot shaft) to center the disc. Align any punch marks.

Make sure the friction disc is facing the right direction. Usually, the disc's offset center section (hub and torsion springs) fits into the pressure plate. Start all of the pressure plate bolts by hand.

WARNING! Never let oil or grease come in contact with the friction surfaces of a clutch. The slightest amount of oil or grease could cause clutch slippage or grabbing. KEEP YOUR HANDS AND TOOLS CLEAN!

Tighten each pressure plate bolt a little at a time in a CRISSCROSS PATTERN, Fig. 51-13. This will apply equal stress on each bolt as the pressure plate spring(s) are compressed. When all of the bolts are snug, torque them to specs.

Never replace a clutch pressure plate bolt with a weaker bolt. Always install the special case hardened bolt recommended by the manufacturer. A weaker aftermarket bolt could break, causing severe part damage.

With the pressure plate bolts properly torqued, slide the pilot out of the clutch. The pilot assures that the clutch friction disc is centered on the flywheel. If a pilot is NOT used, the transmission input shaft will NOT slide into the crankshaft pilot bearing. It would be impossible to install the transmission or transaxle.

Next, install the clutch fork and throw-out bearing in the bell housing. Refer to Fig. 51-14.

Fit the bell housing over the rear of the engine. Large dowels are provided to align the housing on the engine. Install and tighten the bell housing bolts in a crisscross pattern.

Finally, install the transmission and drive shaft or the transaxle assembly and axle shafts. Connect the transmission linkage, cables, any wires, battery, and other parts. Adjust clutch pedal free travel as described earlier. Test drive the vehicle.

KNOW THESE TERMS

Asbestos, Clutch slippage, Clutch pedal free travel, Clutch chatter, Dragging clutch, Stiff clutch pedal, Clutch adjustment, Bleeding, Transmission jack, Clutch pilot shaft.

REVIEW QUESTIONS

1. Clutch disc lining is commonly made of asbestos which is a known _____ causing substance.

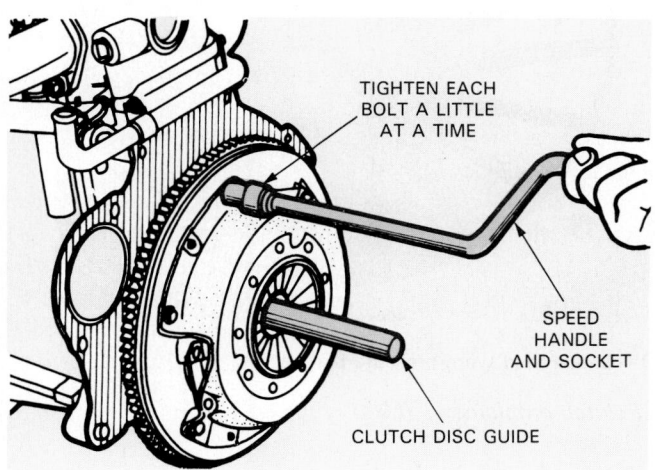

Fig. 51-13. Tighten each pressure plate bolt a little at a time. Then torque them to specs. Remove pilot after bolts are fully torqued. Slide shaft in and out of pilot bearing to double-check disc alignment. (Dodge)

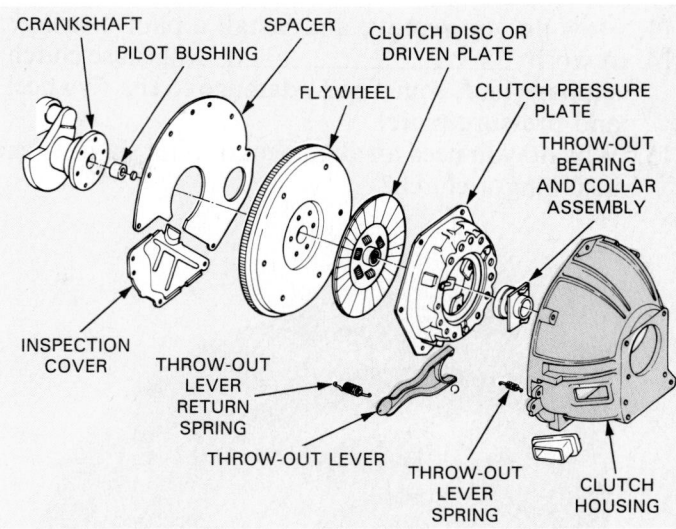

Fig. 51-14. Make sure fork is properly installed inside clutch housing. If it falls off during transmission installation, housing removal may be needed. Torque bell housing bolts to specs before installing transmission.

2. What are the symptoms of clutch slippage?
3. How do you check for clutch slippage?
4. Which of the following could NOT cause clutch slippage?
   a. Improper clutch adjustment.
   b. Binding release mechanism.
   c. Broken motor mount.
   d. Worn disc lining.
   e. All of the above are correct.
5. Describe some causes of a dragging clutch.
6. A dragging clutch make the transmission or transaxle gears grind. True or False?
7. A driver complains of a grinding sound when the clutch pedal is pressed to release the clutch. Otherwise, clutch operation is normal.
   Technician A says that the clutch lining is worn, resulting in metal-on-metal contact. The transmission and clutch will require removal for disc replacement.
   Technician B says that the problem could be a worn, dry throw-out bearing. The bearing is grinding when the clutch fork pushes the bearing into the spinning pressure plate.
   Who is correct?
   a. Technician A
   b. Technician B
   c. Both A and B
   d. Neither A nor B
8. What commonly causes a pulsating clutch pedal?
9. Define the term clutch pedal "free play."
10. A hydraulic clutch release mechanism requires bleeding after major repairs. True or False?
11. Why should you disconnect the car battery when servicing a clutch?
12. What precautions should you take when cleaning clutch parts prior to reinstalling them?

13. How do you remove and install a pilot bearing?
14. A worn _____ _____ will cause clutch slippage and, sometimes, damage to the flywheel and pressure plate.
15. Why do you need an alignment or pilot shaft when installing a clutch?

ACTIVITIES FOR CHAPTER 51

1. Study damaged and worn clutch parts and try to determine why they failed.
2. Study a shop manual for manual clutch service; demonstrate to your instructor the proper procedure for removal and disassembly.

A—Severely damaged clutch disc friction material.

B—Dry, worn, clutch throw-out bearing.

C—Heat checked surface on pressure plate.

D—Broken and worn pressure plate spring.

Learn to recognize various types of clutch problems.   (LUK)

52

Manual Transmission Fundamentals

After studying this chapter, you will be able to:
☐ Describe gear operating principles.
☐ Identify and define all of the major parts of a transmission.
☐ Explain the fundamental operation of a manual transmission.
☐ Trace the power flow through transmission gears.
☐ Compare the construction of different types of manual transmissions.
☐ Explain the purpose and operation of a transmission overdrive ratio.

A *manual transmission* must be shifted by hand. It is normally bolted to the clutch housing at the rear of the engine. See Fig. 52-1. The clutch disc rotates the transmission input shaft. Gears inside the transmission transfer engine power to the drive shaft and rear wheels. A column or floor shift lever allows the driver to select which set of transmission gears to engage.

A manual transmission should not be confused with an automatic transmission or automatic transaxle. It is normally used in a front engine, rear-wheel or front-wheel drive vehicle. A foot-operated friction clutch is

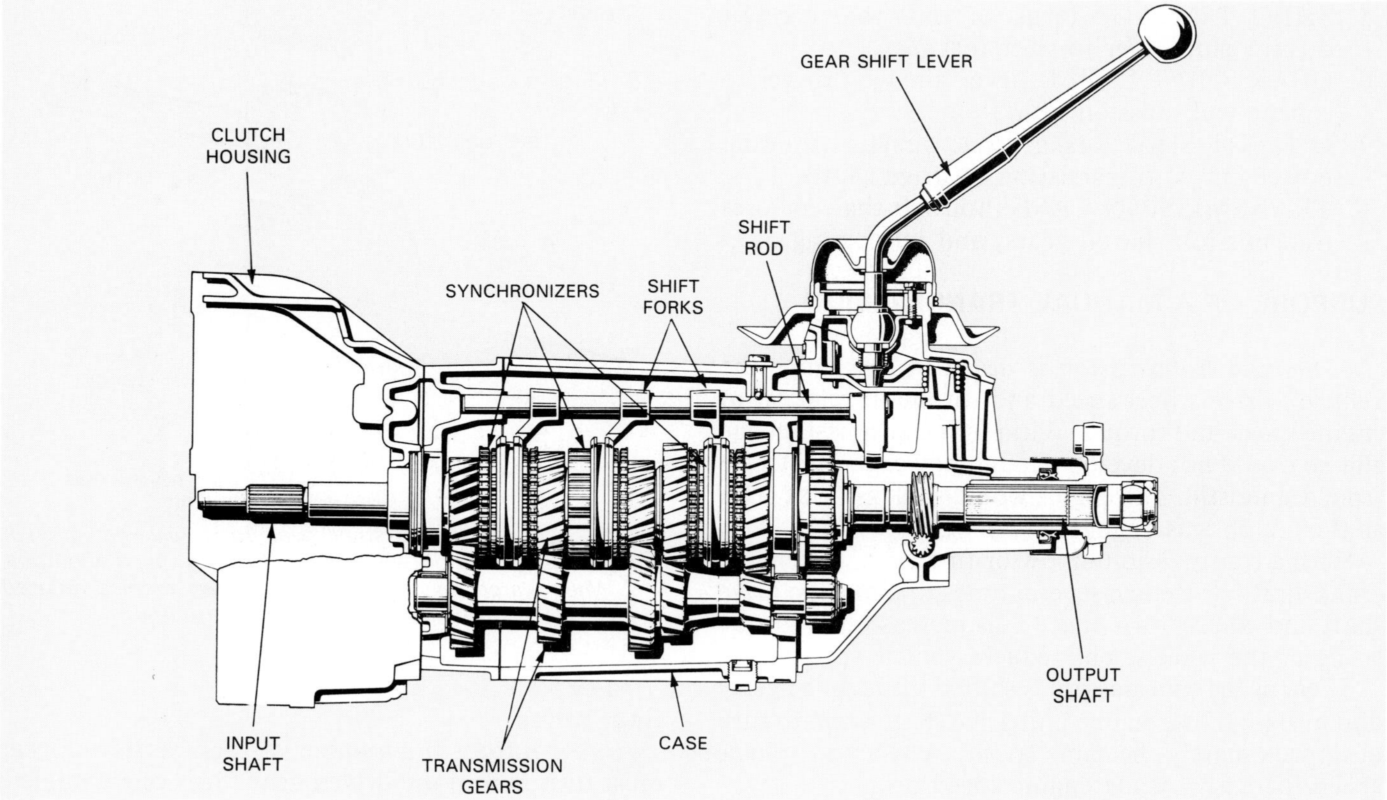

Fig. 52-1. Study basic names and locations of manual transmission parts. This will help you as you learn about each part in more detail. (Fiat)

needed to disengage the engine.

An automatic transmission, covered in Chapters 54 and 55, uses hydraulic pressure and sensing devices to shift gears. It detects engine speed and load to determine shift points. An automatic transmission also uses a fluid coupling instead of a dry friction clutch.

A transaxle combines both the transmission and the differential into a single housing. It is commonly used with front-wheel drive vehicles. A transaxle can contain either a manual or automatic transmission. Transaxles are covered in Chapters 60 and 61.

BASIC TRANSMISSION PARTS

To understand later sections of the chapter, study the parts of the transmission in Fig. 52-1. Learn to identify and locate the fundamental components. This knowledge will prepare you for more specific details of transmission construction and operation.
1. TRANSMISSION INPUT SHAFT (shaft, operated by clutch, that turns gears inside transmission).
2. TRANSMISSION GEARS (provide a means of changing output torque and speed leaving transmission).
3. SYNCHRONIZERS (devices for meshing or locking gears into engagement).
4. SHIFT FORKS (pronged units for moving gears or synchronizers on their shaft for gear engagement).
5. SHIFT LINKAGE (arms or rods that connect driver's shift lever to shift forks).
6. GEAR SHIFT LEVER (lever allowing driver to change transmission gears).
7. OUTPUT SHAFT (shaft that transfers rotating power out of transmission to drive shaft).
8. TRANSMISSION CASE (housing that encloses transmission shafts, gears, and lubricating oil).

PURPOSE OF A MANUAL TRANSMISSION

A *manual transmission* is designed to change the vehicle's drive wheel speed and torque in relation to engine speed and torque. Without a transmission, the engine would not develop enough power to accelerate from a standstill. The engine would stall or lug as soon as the clutch was engaged.

With a transmission in low or first gear, the engine crankshaft has to turn several times to make the drive shaft and wheels turn once. This increases the torque going to the wheels, but reduces vehicle speed.

Then, as the transmission is shifted through the gears and into high, the engine and drive shaft begin to turn at approximately the same speed. Wheel and vehicle speed increases, while engine speed drops.

A manual transmission in proper operating condition should:
1. Be able to increase torque going to the drive wheels

for quick acceleration.
2. Supply different gear ratios to match different engine load conditions.
3. Have a reverse gear for moving backwards.
4. Provide the driver with an easy means of shifting transmission gears.
5. Operate quietly, with minimum power loss.

GEAR FUNDAMENTALS

Gears are round wheels with teeth machined on their perimeter (rim). They are commonly used to transmit turning effort from one shaft to another. Basically, one size gear is used to turn another size gear to change output speed and torque (turning power). This is illustrated in Fig. 52-2.

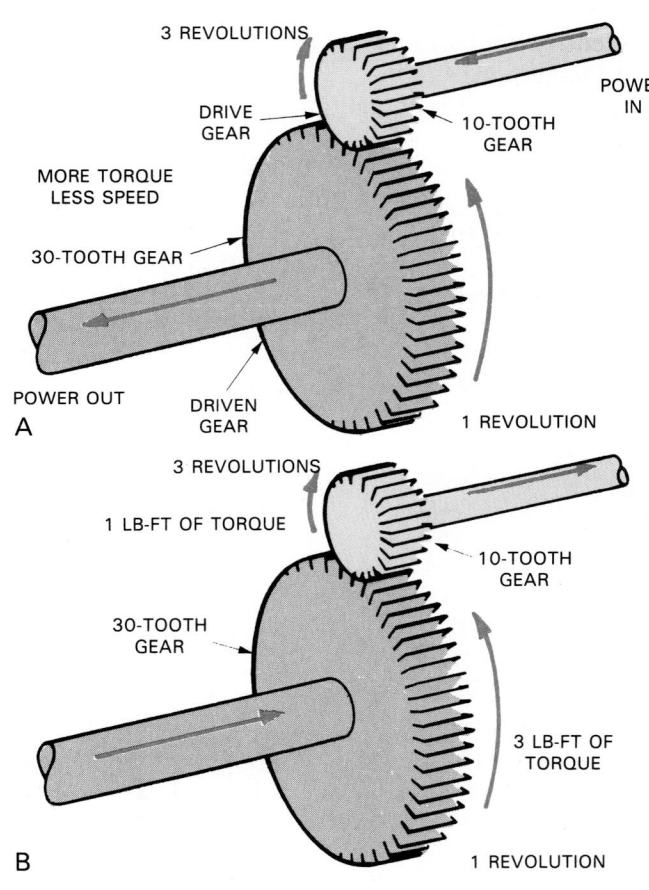

Fig. 52-2. A — When a small gear drives a larger gear, it increases torque output but reduces rotating speed of output. B — When a larger gear drives a smaller gear, torque is reduced but rotating speed increases at output.

Gear ratios

A *gear ratio* is the number of turns a driving gear must turn before the driven gear turns one complete revolution. Gear ratio is calculated by dividing the number teeth on the driven gear by the number of teeth on the driving gear.

For example, look at Fig. 52-3. If the drive gear has 12 teeth and the driven gear 24 teeth (24 divided by 12), the gear ratio would be TWO TO ONE, written 2:1.

In this example, the drive gear would have to revolve two times to turn the other gear once. As a result, the speed of the larger, driven gear would be half as fast as the drive gear. However, the torque on the shaft of the larger gear would be twice that of the input shaft.

Various sizes of drive and driven gears can be used to produce any number of gear ratios. As the number of teeth on the driven gear increase in relation to the number of teeth on the drive gear, the gear ratio increases. A gear ratio of 10:1 would be larger than a ratio of 5:1, for example.

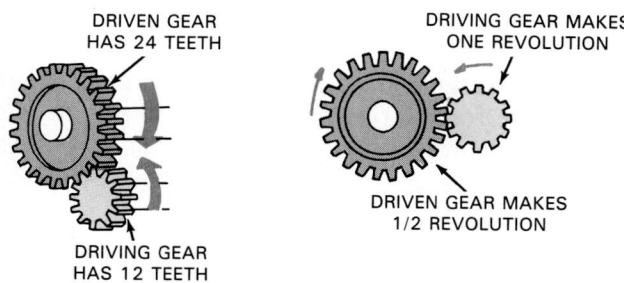

Fig. 52-3. Gear ratio is determined by number of teeth on drive and driven gears. If drive gear has half as many teeth as driven gear, a two to one ratio would be produced. (Deere & Co.)

Transmission gear ratios

Transmission gear ratios vary with the manufacturer. However, approximate gear ratios average 3:1 for first gear, 2:1 for second gear, 1:1 for third or high gear, and 3:1 for reverse gear.

In first or low gear, there would be a high gear ratio. A small gear would drive a larger gear This would reduce output speed but increase output torque. The car would accelerate easily, even with low engine rpm and low power conditions.

In high gear, the transmission frequently has a 1:1 ratio. The transmission output shaft would spin at the same speed as the engine crankshaft. There would be NO torque *multiplication* (increase), but the vehicle would travel faster. Very little torque is needed to propel a vehicle at a constant speed on level ground.

Gear reduction and overdrive

Gear reduction occurs when a small gear drives a larger gear to increase turning force. Gear reduction is used in the lower transmission gears, Fig. 52-2.

An *overdrive ratio* results when a larger gear drives a smaller gear. As shown in Fig. 52-2, the speed of the output gear increases, but torque drops.

Gear types

Manual transmissions commonly use two types of gears: spur gears and helical gears.

Spur gears have their teeth cut parallel to the centerline of the gear shaft. As shown in Fig. 52-4A, they are sometimes called straight-cut gears.

Spur gears are somewhat noisy and are no longer used as the main drive gears in a transmission. They may be used for the sliding reverse gear, however.

Helical gears have their teeth machined at an angle to the centerline of gear rotation. Modern transmissions commonly use helical gears as the main drive gears. See Fig. 52-4B. Helical gears are quieter and stronger than spur gears.

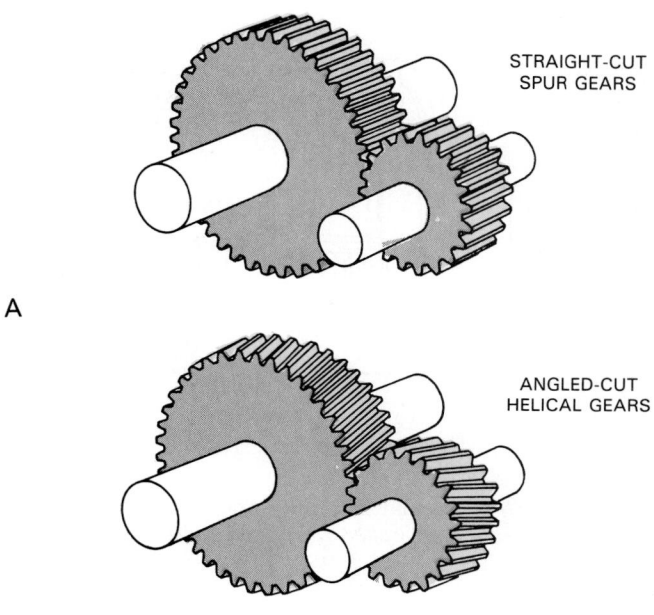

Fig. 52-4. Two basic types of gears used in manual transmissions are straight-cut spur gears and angled-cut helical gears. (Deere & Co.)

Gear backlash

Gear backlash is the small clearance between the meshing gear teeth. Clearance allows lubricating oil to enter the high friction area between the gear teeth. This reduces friction and wear. Backlash also allows the gears to heat up and expand during operation without binding or being damaged.

MANUAL TRANSMISSION LUBRICATION

The bearings, shafts, gears, and other moving parts in a transmission are lubricated by oil throw-off or *splash*. As the gears rotate, they sling oil around inside the transmission case.

Typically, 80 or 90W *gear oil* is recommended for use in a manual transmission. However, follow manufacturer's recommendations.

TRANSMISSION BEARINGS

Manual transmissions normally use three basic types of bearings: ball bearings, roller bearings, and needle bearings. These three types are shown in Fig. 52-5. Bearings are used to reduce the friction between the surfaces of rotating parts in the transmission.

The bearings are lubricated by oil spray from the spinning transmission gears. Typically, *antifriction bearings* (bearing using a rolling action) fit between the transmission shafts and housing or between some of the gears and shafts. These are high friction points that must be capable of withstanding the engine's power.

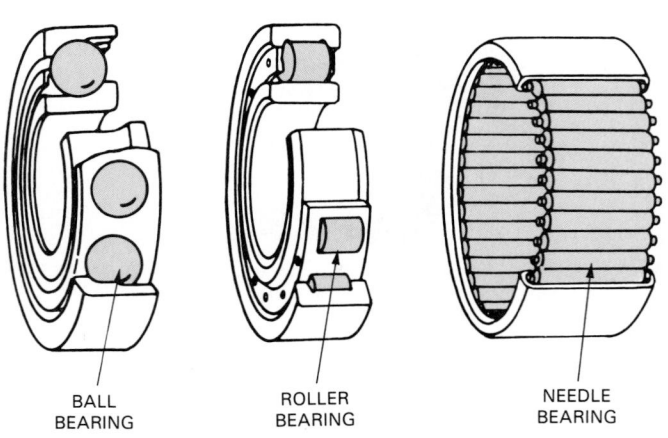

BALL BEARING   ROLLER BEARING   NEEDLE BEARING

Fig. 52-5. Three types of antifriction bearings found in transmissions: ball, roller, and needle. (Deere & Co.)

MANUAL TRANSMISSION CONSTRUCTION

Now that you have a general grasp of gear and transmission principles, we will assemble each part of a working transmission. We will start out with the case, then install the shafts, gears, bearings, and other parts.

Transmission case

The *transmission case* must support the transmission bearings and shafts and provide an enclosure for gear oil. Refer to Fig. 52-6. A manual transmission case is usually cast of either iron or aluminum. Aluminum is becoming more common because of its lightness.

A drain plug and a fill plug are usually provided in the transmission case. The drain plug is on the bottom of the case. The fill plug is on the side of the case.

The fill plug also serves as a means of checking the oil level in the transmission. Typically, the oil should be level with the fill plug when the transmission is at operating temperature.

Extension housing and front bearing hub

The *extension housing,* also called the *tailshaft housing,* bolts to the rear of the transmission case. It encloses the transmission output shaft and holds the rear oil seal. See Fig. 52-6.

A flange on the bottom of the extension housing provides a base for the rubber transmission mount, also called rear motor mount. A gasket usually seals the mating surfaces between the transmission case and extension housing.

A *front bearing hub,* sometimes called *front bearing cap,* covers the front transmission bearing and acts as a sleeve for the clutch throw-out bearing. It bolts to the transmission case. A gasket fits between the front hub and case to prevent oil leakage.

Transmission shafts

Basically, a manual transmission has four steel shafts mounted inside its case. It normally has an input shaft, countershaft, reverse idler shaft, and an output shaft. Figs. 52-7 and 52-8 show the general location and shape of these shafts.

The **input shaft,** often termed *clutch shaft,* transfers rotation from the clutch disc to the countershaft gears in the transmission. The outer end of the shaft is

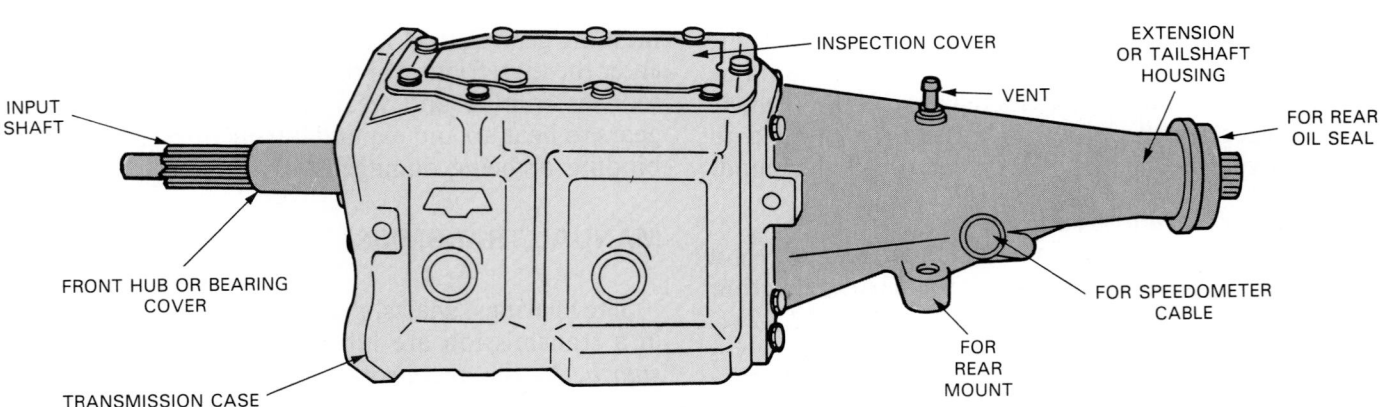

INSPECTION COVER

EXTENSION OR TAILSHAFT HOUSING

VENT

FOR REAR OIL SEAL

INPUT SHAFT

FRONT HUB OR BEARING COVER

TRANSMISSION CASE

FOR REAR MOUNT

FOR SPEEDOMETER CABLE

Fig. 52-6. Case is center section of transmission. Extension housing bolts to rear of case. Front bearing cover bolts to front of case. It encloses front output shaft bearing and supports clutch throw-out bearing. This transmission also has a sheet metal inspection cover bolted to top of case. (GMC)

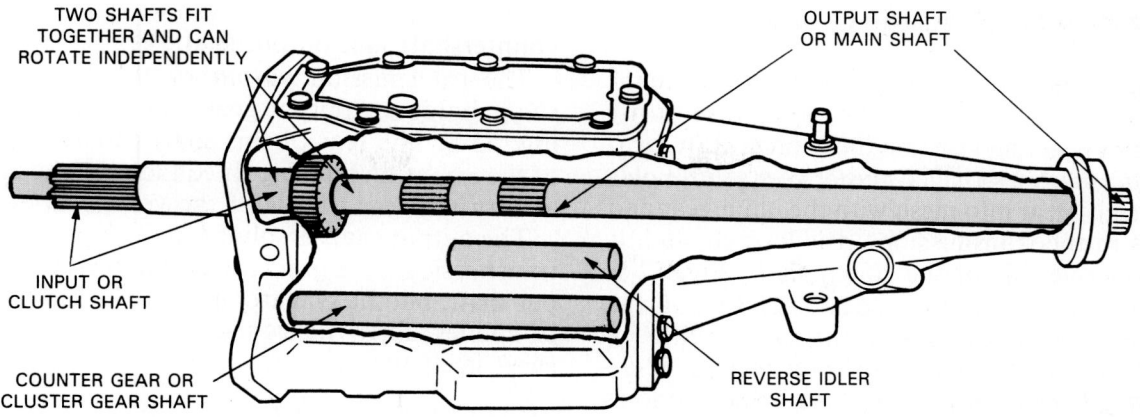

Fig. 52-7. Note how transmission shafts are located in transmission case. Input shaft is driven by clutch. Output shaft is on same centerline as input shaft. Countershaft and reverse idler shafts mount below and to one side in case.

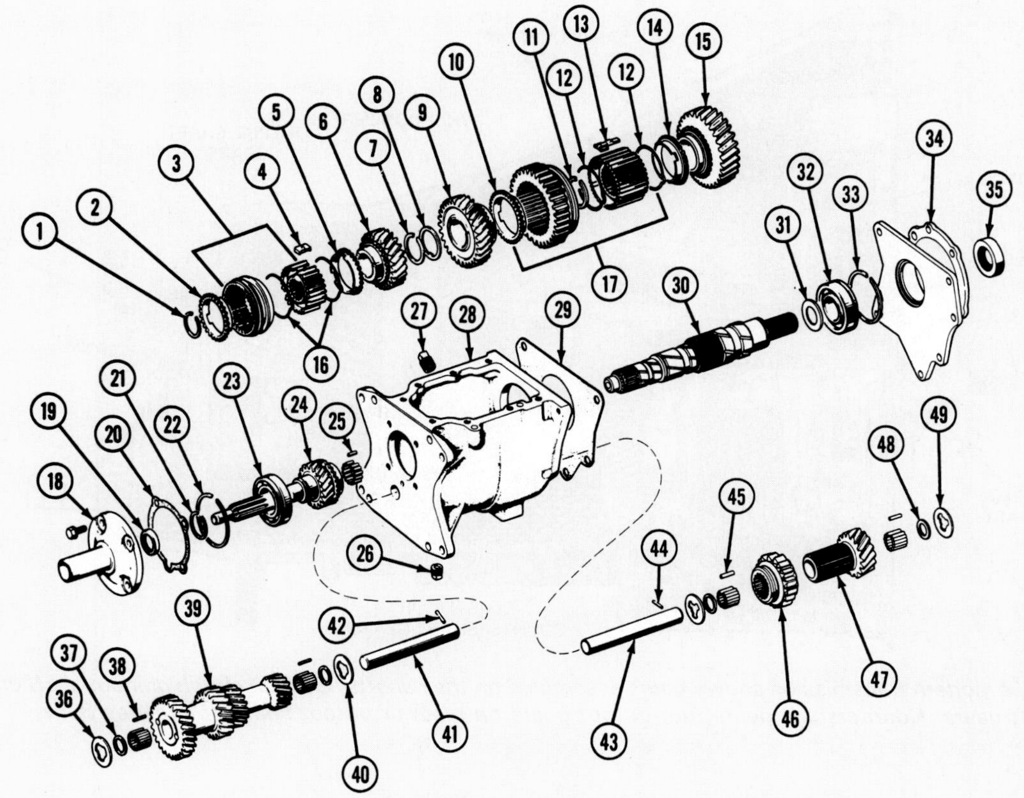

Fig. 52-8. Exploded view shows major parts of typical transmission. Note four shafts and components. (Chrysler)

1. 3rd-4th GEAR SNAP RING	18. FRONT BEARING CAP	35. ADAPTER SEAL
2. 4th GEAR SYNCHRONIZER RING	19. OIL SEAL	36. FRONT COUNTERSHAFT GEAR THRUST WASHER
3. 3rd-4th GEAR CLUTCH ASSEMBLY	20. GASKET	37. ROLLER WASHER
4. 3rd-4th GEAR PLATE	21. SNAP RING	38. REAR ROLLER BEARING
5. 3rd GEAR SYNCHRONIZER RING	22. LOCK RING	39. COUNTERSHAFT GEAR
6. 3rd SPEED GEAR	23. FRONT BALL BEARING	40. REAR COUNTERSHAFT THRUST WASHER
7. 2nd GEAR SNAP RING	24. CLUTCH SHAFT	41. COUNTERSHAFT
8. 2nd GEAR THRUST WASHER	25. ROLLER BEARING	42. PIN
9. 2nd SPEED GEAR	26. DRAIN PLUG	43. IDLER GEAR SHAFT
10. 2nd GEAR SYNCHRONIZER RING	27. FILL PLUG	44. PIN
11. MAIN SHAFT SNAP RING	28. CASE	45. IDLER GEAR ROLLER BEARING
12. 1st-2nd SYNCHRONIZER SPRING	29. GASKET	46. REVERSE IDLER SLIDING GEAR
13. LOW-2nd PLATE	30. SPLINE SHAFT	47. REVERSE IDLER GEAR
14. 1st GEAR SYNCHRONIZER RING	31. 1st GEAR THRUST WASHER	48. IDLER GEAR WASHER
15. 1st GEAR	32. REAR BALL BEARING	49. IDLER GEAR THRUST WASHER
16. 3rd-4th SYNCHRONIZER SPRING	33. SNAP RING	
17. 1st-2nd GEAR CLUTCH ASSEMBLY	34. ADAPTER PLATE	

splined. The inner end of the shaft has a gear machined on it. See Fig. 52-8.

A bearing in the transmission case supports the input shaft in the case. Anytime the clutch disc turns, the input shaft gear and gears on the countershaft turn.

The *countershaft,* also called *cluster gear shaft,* holds the countershaft gear into mesh with the input gear and other gears in the transmission. It is located slightly below and to one side of the clutch shaft, Fig. 52-9.

Normally, the countershaft does NOT turn in the transmission case. It is locked in the case by either a steel pin, force fit, or locknuts. Refer to Fig. 52-8.

The *reverse idler shaft* is a short shaft that supports the reverse idler gear, Fig. 52-8. It normally mounts stationary in the case about midway between the countershaft and output shaft. See Fig. 52-7. Then,

the reverse idler gear can mesh with gears on both the countershaft and output shaft.

The transmission *output shaft,* also called *main shaft,* holds the output gears and synchronizers. See Fig. 52-8. The rear of this shaft extends to the back of the extension housing. It connects to the drive shaft to turn the rear wheels of the vehicle.

The output shaft is splined in the center. In modern transmissions, the gears are free to revolve on the output shaft, but the synchronizers are locked on the shaft by splines. The synchronizers will only turn when the shaft itself turns.

TRANSMISSION GEARS

Transmission gears can be typically classified into four groups: input shaft gear, countershaft gears, out-

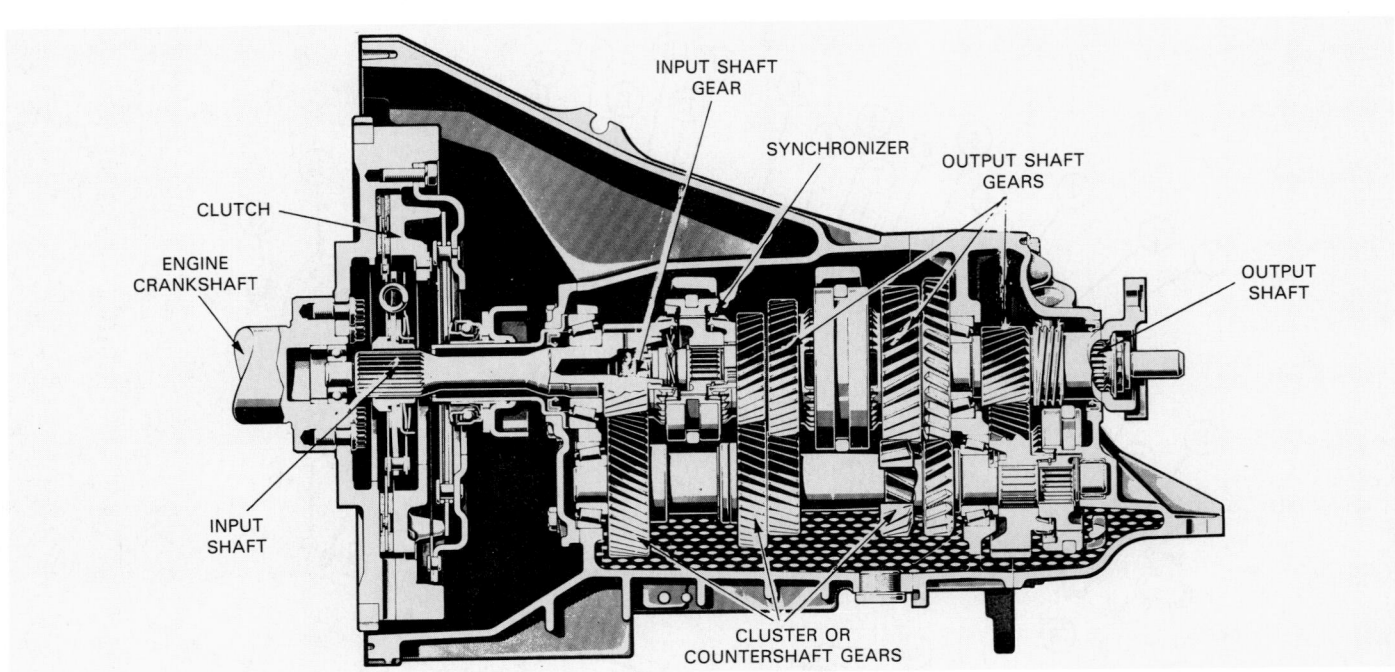

Fig. 52-9. Cutaway of modern transmission shows gears assembled on their shafts. Gear on clutch or input shaft drives countershaft gears. Countershaft gears turn output gears on main or output shaft. (Mercedes Benz)

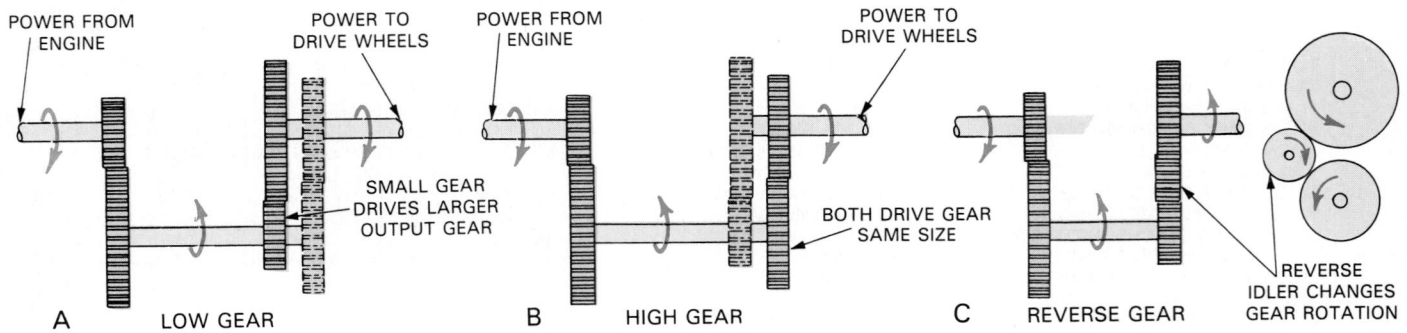

Fig. 52-10. Simplified transmission action. A — Low gear. Input shaft gear turns gears on countershaft. Small countershaft gear drives larger output shaft gear to produce gear reduction. B — High gear. Engaged gears are same size. Output shaft turns faster than when in low gear. Less torque increase is needed. C — Reverse. Reverse idler gear is used between countershaft gear and output shaft gear. This reverses direction of rotation at output shaft. (Deere & Co.)

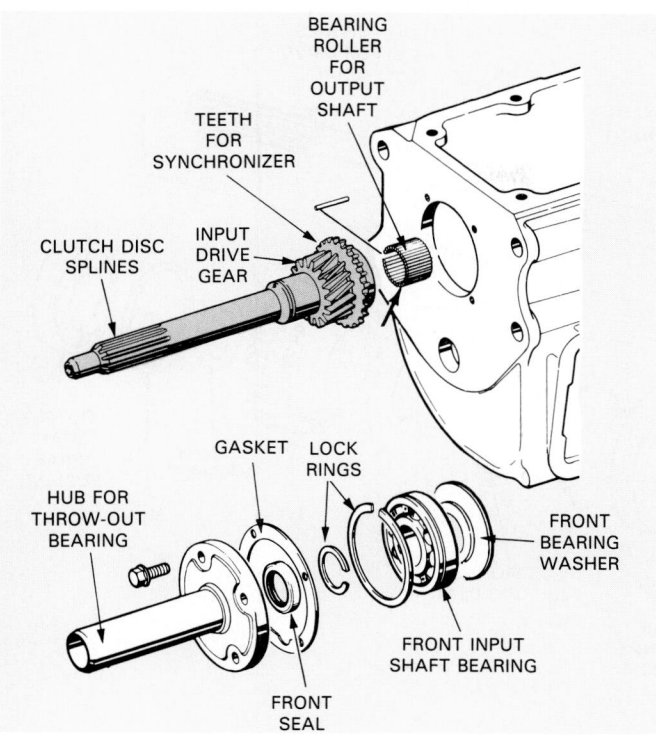

Fig. 52-11. Exploded view of input shaft and gear. Gear is normally machined part of shaft. Large bearing supports shaft in front of transmission case. Individual roller bearings support rear of shaft. Snap rings secure assembly in case. (Chrysler)

put shaft gears, and reverse idle gear. Illustrated in Fig. 52-9, the input shaft gear turns the countershaft gears. The countershaft gears turn the output shaft gears and reverse idle gear.

In low gear, a small gear on the countershaft drives a larger gear on the output shaft, Fig. 52-10A. This provides a high gear ratio for accelerating. Then, in high gear, a larger countershaft gear drives an equal or smaller size output shaft gear, Fig. 52-10B. This reduces the gear ratio and the vehicle moves faster.

When in reverse, power flows from the countershaft gear, to the reverse idler gear, and to the engaged gear on the output shaft. This reverses output shaft rotation as shown in Fig. 52-10C.

Input gear assembly

Mentioned briefly, the *transmission input gear* is a machined part of the steel input shaft. Fig. 52-11 shows an input gear with its related parts. Study the shape and relationship of each component carefully.

The input gear drives the forward gear on the countershaft gear. A small set of spur gear teeth are usually located next to the main, helical drive gear. This small gear is for engagement of the synchronizer.

Countershaft gear assembly

The *countershaft gear,* also called *countergear,* turns the gears on the output shaft. This gear is actually

several gears machined out of a single piece of steel. Hence, it is often called the *cluster gear,* Fig. 52-12.

When the input gear drives the matching countershaft gear, all of the countershaft gears turn as a single unit. However, since each forward gear is a different size, the countershaft gear unit is capable of providing several gear ratios.

Note in Fig. 52-12 how the countershaft gear rides on roller bearings. Thrust washers fit on each end of the gear to set end play or case-to-gear clearance.

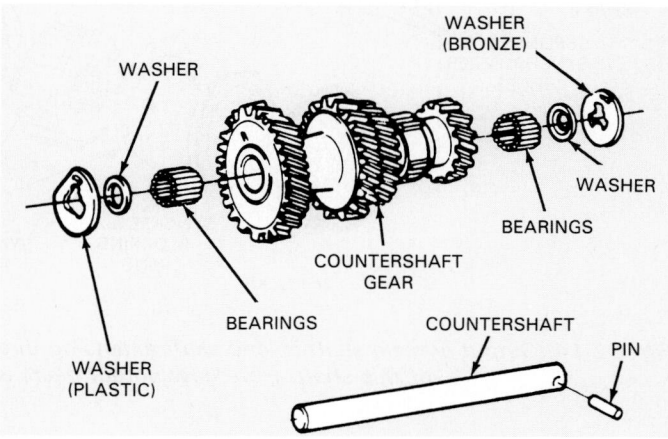

Fig. 52-12. Countershaft assembly. Countershaft gear has several gears formed as a single unit. They mount on roller bearings and countershaft. Washers control end play of unit in case. (Ford Motor Co.)

Reverse idler gear assembly

A *reverse idler gear assembly* is shown in Fig. 52-13. Note how it is constructed like the other transmission shaft-gear assemblies just discussed.

Output shaft gears

The *output shaft gears* or *main shaft gears* transfer

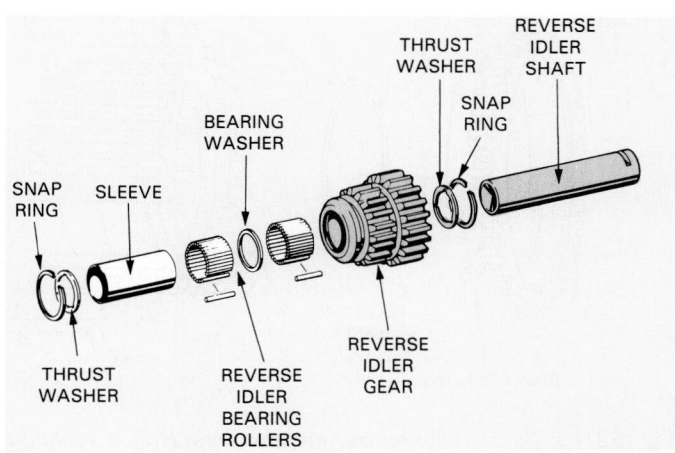

Fig. 52-13. Reverse idler gear and shaft assembly. (Chrysler)

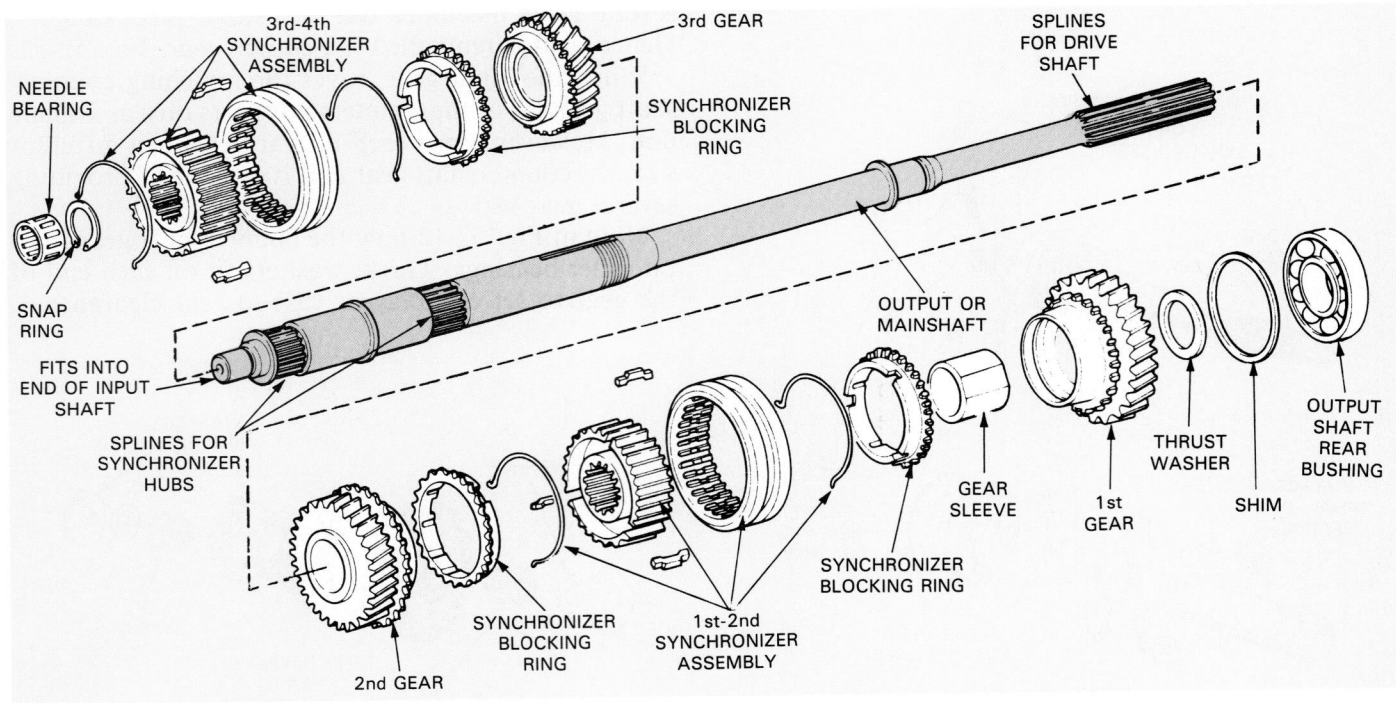

Fig. 52-14. Output or main shaft is long shaft extending through transmission tailshaft housing. Drive shaft is splined to rear of this shaft. Note how output gears and synchronizers install on shaft. (Mazda)

rotation from the countershaft gears to the output shaft. Only one of the output shaft gears is normally engaged and locked to the shaft at a time.

Fig. 52-14 pictures a set of output shaft gears. Notice how it has a main drive gear (helical gear) and a smaller synchronizer gear (spur gear).

The inside bore of each output shaft gear is smooth so that it can spin freely on its shaft when not engaged. Normally, one output shaft gear will be provided for each transmission speed, including reverse.

TRANSMISSION SYNCHRONIZERS

A *transmission synchronizer*, Fig. 52-14, has two functions. It must:

1. Prevent the gears from grinding or clashing during engagement.
2. Lock the output gear to the output shaft.

When the synchronizer is away from an output gear, the output gear freewheels or spins on the output shaft. No power is transmitted to the output shaft. When the

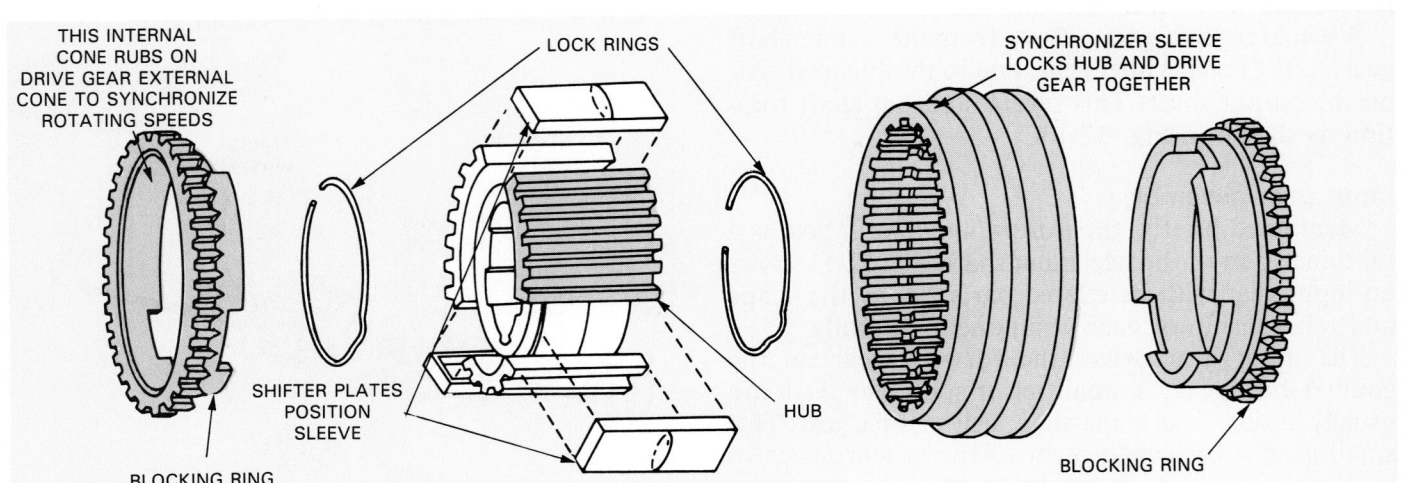

Fig. 52-15. Basic synchronizer components. Hub is splined to output shaft. It will slide but not turn on shaft. Sleeve fits over hub. Shifter plates position sleeve. Blocking rings allow sleeve to slide into and mesh with output gear without clashing or grinding. (Deere & Co.)

synchronizer is slid against a gear, the gear is locked to the synchronizer and to the output shaft. Power is then sent out the transmission and to the rear wheels.

Synchronizer construction

The most popular type synchronizer consists of an inner splined hub, inserts, insert springs, an outer sleeve, and blocking rings. See Fig. 52-15.

The synchronizer hub is splined on the output shaft. It is held in a stationary position between the transmission gears. Inserts fit between the hub and sleeve. The springs push the inserts into the sleeve. This helps hold and center the sleeve on its hub. The blocking rings fit on the outer ends of the hub and sleeve.

Synchronizer operation

When the driver shifts gears, the synchronizer sleeve slides on its splined hub toward the main drive gear.

First, the *blocking ring* cone rubs on the side of the gear cone, setting up friction between the two, Fig. 52-16. This causes the gear, synchronizer, and output shaft to begin to spin at the SAME SPEED.

As soon as the speed is equalized or synchronized, the sleeve can slide completely over the blocking ring and over the small, spur gear teeth on the drive gear. This locks the output gear to the synchronizer hub and to the shaft. Power then flows through that gear and to the rear wheels.

FULLY SYNCHRONIZED TRANSMISSION

Fully synchronized means that all of the forward output gears use a synchronizer. This allows the driver to downshift into any lower gear (except reverse) with the car moving. Most modern manual transmissions are fully synchronized.

Many older three-speed transmissions did NOT have first gear synchronized. The driver had to wait until the vehicle came to a complete stop before downshifting into first. Trying to shift into first with the vehicle in motion would cause first gear to clash.

SHIFT FORKS

The *shift forks* fit around the synchronizer sleeves to transfer movement to the sleeves from the gear shift linkage. This is illustrated in Fig. 52-17.

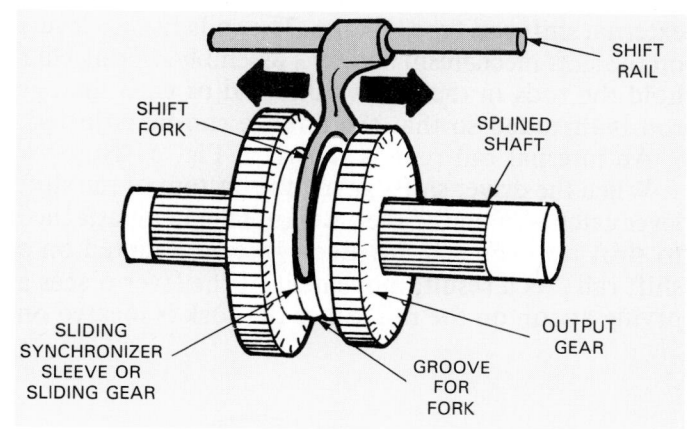

Fig. 52-17. Shift fork is used to move synchronizer sleeve or sliding gear on splined shaft. Shift linkage or rail operates shift fork.

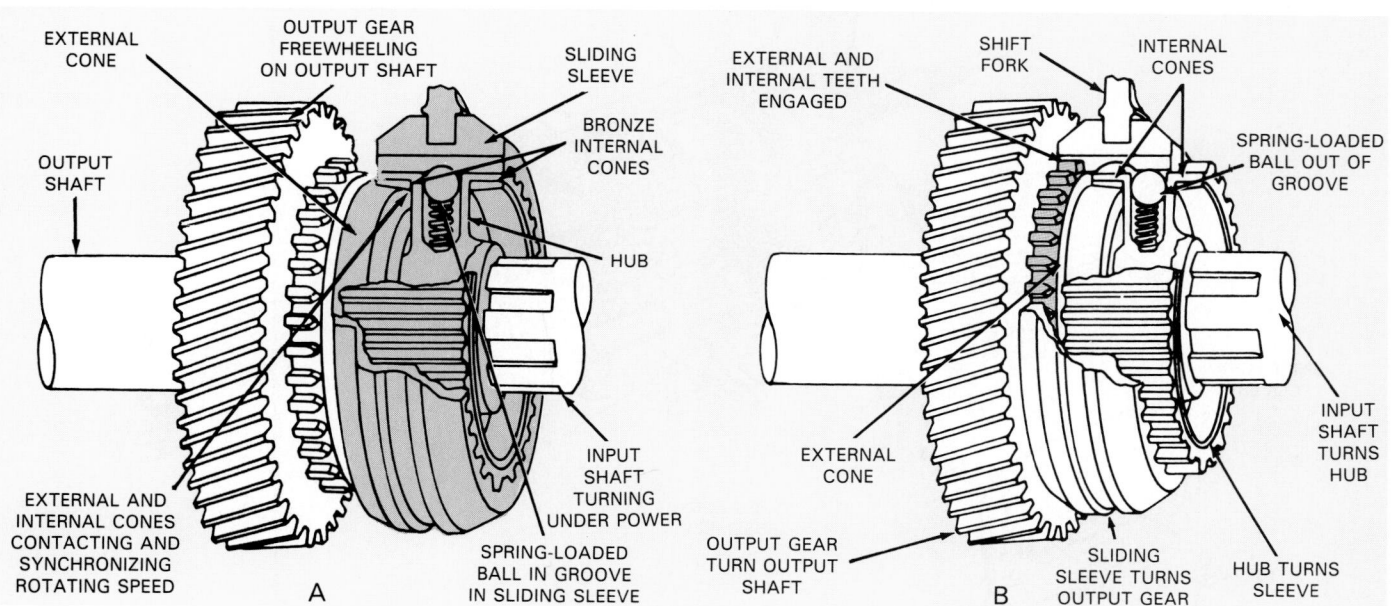

Fig. 52-16. Synchronizer operation. A — As synchronizer sleeve moves into output gear, cone on sleeve rubs against cone on gear. Friction makes gear and sleeve begin to turn at same speed. B — When at same speed, sleeve can slide over and mesh with small, spur teeth on side of output gear. This locks output gear, sleeve, hub, and input shaft together. Output gear is then engaged to output shaft.

The shift fork fits into a groove cut into the synchronizer sleeve. A linkage rod or shift rail connects the fork to the driver's shift lever. When the lever moves, the linkage or rail moves the shift fork and sleeve to engage the correct transmission gear.

Fig. 52-18 pictures a typical, complete shift fork assembly. Study the parts and how they fit together.

TRANSMISSION SHIFT LINKAGE AND SHIFT LEVER

There are two general types of transmission linkage: EXTERNAL ROD type and INTERNAL SHIFT RAIL type. Both perform the same function. They connect the shift lever with the shift fork mechanism.

Look at Fig. 52-19. It shows the components of an external shift rod type linkage. The rods fit into levers on the shift mechanism and fork assembly. Spring clips hold the rods in the levers. One end of each linkage rod is threaded so that the linkage can be adjusted.

An internal rail type is shown in Fig. 52-20.

When the driver shifts gears, the bottom of the shift lever catches in one of the gates (notched unit attached to shift rail), Fig. 52-21. Each gate is mounted on a shift rail. As a result, movement of the lever places a prying action on the rail. Since the fork is located on

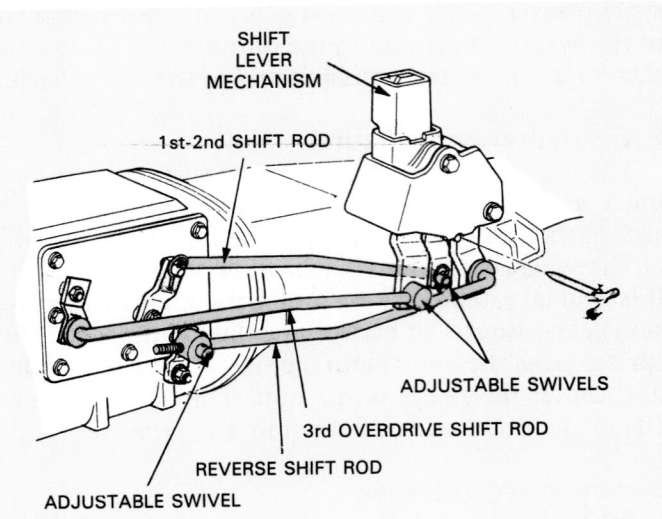

Fig. 52-19. Side view of transmission showing shift linkage and lower part of shift lever. Study parts. (Chrysler)

the rail, it is also moved to change transmission gears. Spring-loaded balls are sometimes used to lock the shift rail(s) into position when in neutral or in gear.

Variations in shift rail linkages are also available. However, their basic construction and operation are

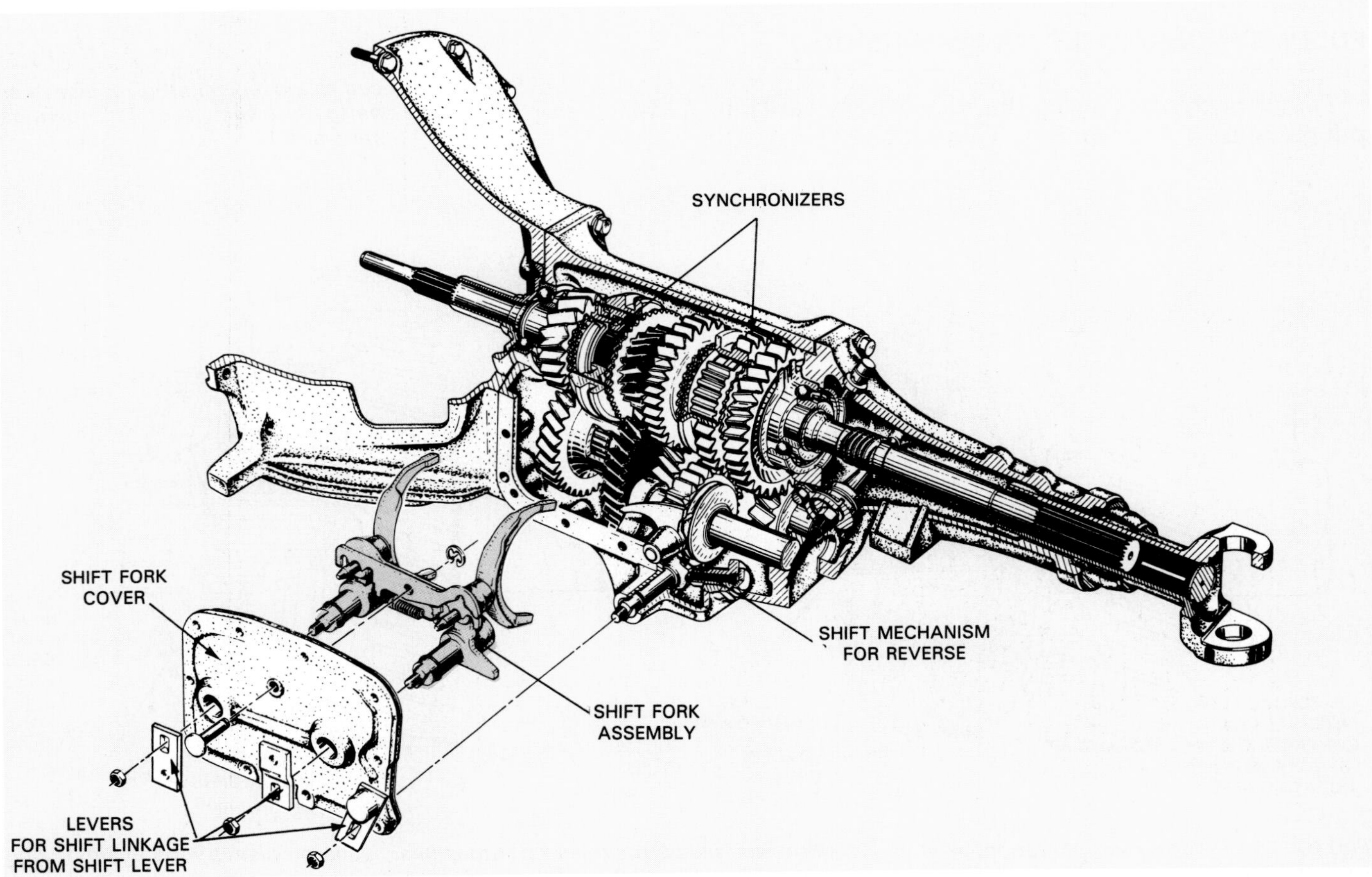

Fig. 52-18. Shift fork fits over groove machined in center of synchronizer sleeve. Movement of shift linkage to transmission moves shift fork forward or rearward in transmission to engage different output gear. (Plymouth)

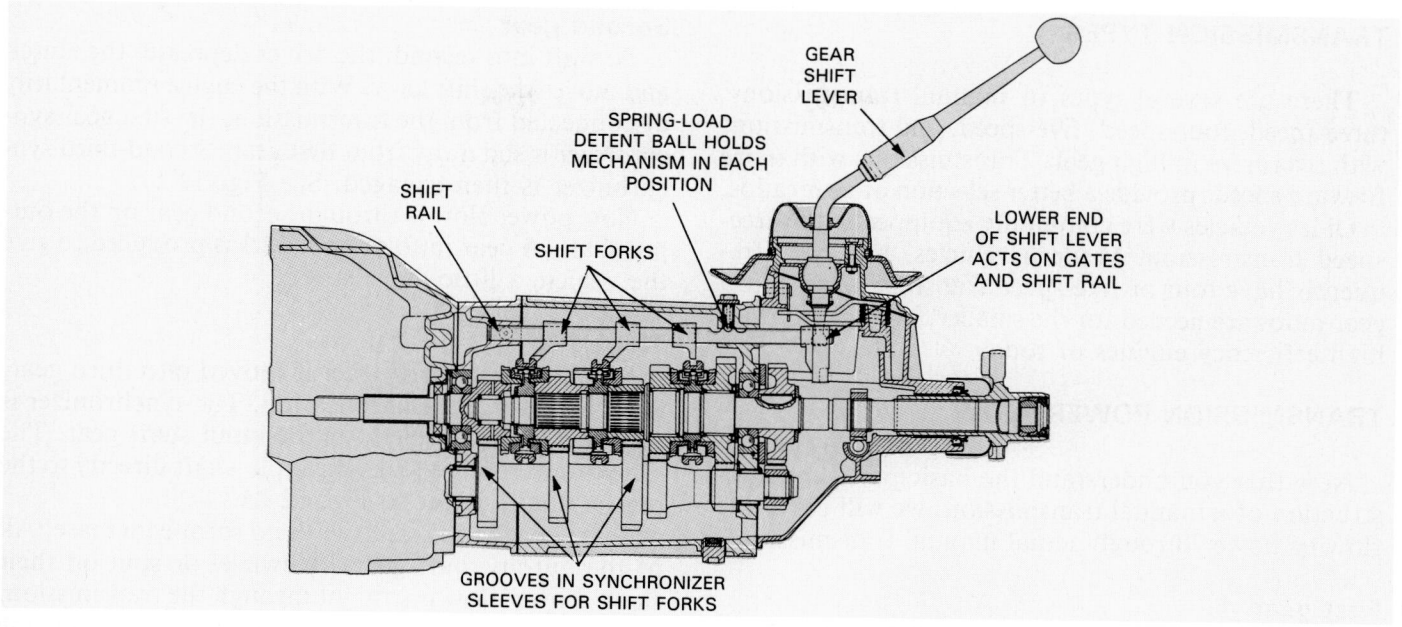

Fig. 52-20. This transmission uses an internal shift rail mechanism instead of external shift rods. Shift lever acts on rail. Rail then operates shift forks and synchronizer sleeves. (Fiat)

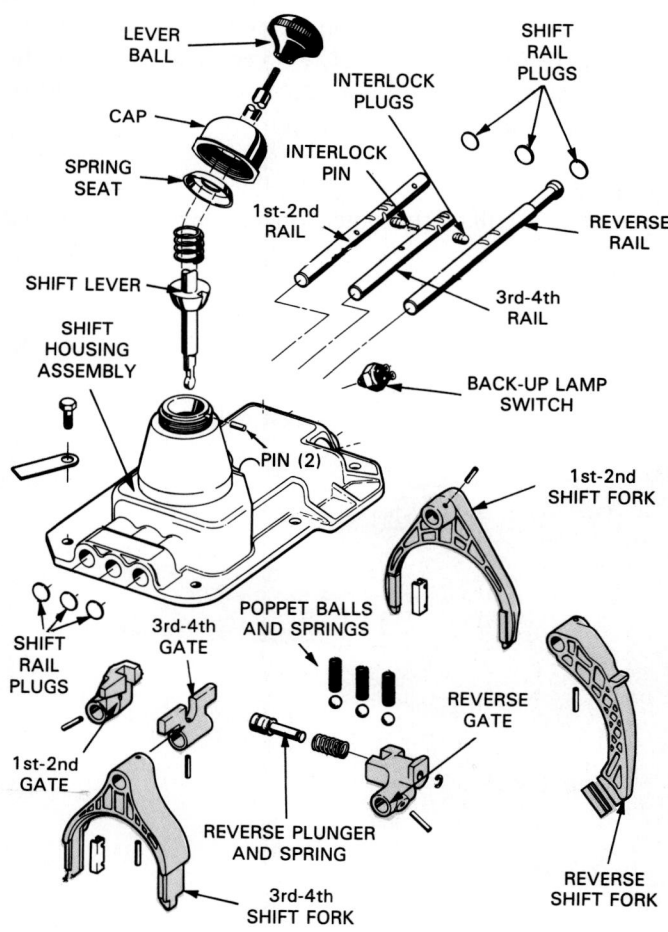

Fig. 52-21. Exploded view of shift mechanism for late model transmission. Shift lever acts on shift gates. Shift gates are attached to shift rails. Rails move forks for gear changes. Spring-loaded balls and plunger help position shift forks during each gear change. Note back-up lamp switch. (Chrysler)

almost the same.

The transmission shift lever assembly can be moved to cause movement of the shift linkage or rail, shift forks, and synchronizers.

The parts of a floor mounted shift lever assembly are shown in Figs. 52-19, 20, and 21. One has external shift rods and the others internal rails. Fig. 52-22 pictures a steering column mounted shift lever. Study the parts and how they function.

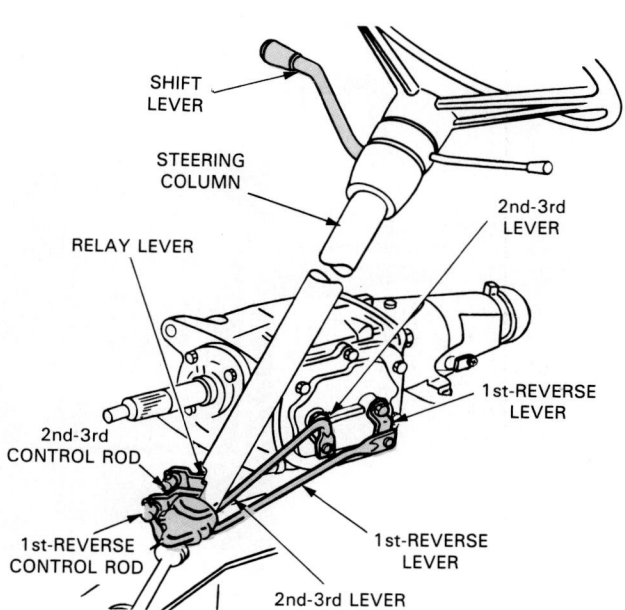

Fig. 52-22. Column type shift mechanism. Gear shift lever operates levers on bottom of column. Rods then transfer movement to transmission. (GMC)

Manual Transmission Fundamentals 673

TRANSMISSION TYPES

There are several types of manual transmissions: three-speed, four-speed, five-speed, and transmissions with overdrive in high gear. Transmissions with more forward speeds provide a better selection of gear ratios.

Older vehicles were commonly equipped with three-speed transmission. Modern vehicles, however, frequently have four or five-speed transmissiosns. Extra gear ratios are needed for the smaller, low horsepower, high efficiency engines of today.

TRANSMISSION POWER FLOW

Now that you understand the basic parts and construction of a manual transmission, we will cover the flow of power through actual manual transmissions.

First gear

To get the vehicle moving from a standstill, the driver moves the gear shift lever into first. The clutch pedal must be pressed to stop power flow into the transmission. The linkage rods move the shift forks so that first gear synchronizer is engaged to first output gear. The other output gears are in neutral. Look at Fig. 52-23.

As the driver releases the clutch pedal, the clutch shaft gear begins to spin the countershaft gears. Since only first gear is locked to the output shaft, a small gear on the countershaft drives a larger gear on the output shaft. The gear ratio is approximately 3:1 and the vehicle accelerates easily.

Second gear

To shift into second, the driver depresses the clutch and moves the shift lever. With the engine momentarily disconnected from the transmission, the first gear synchronizer is slid away from first gear. Second-third synchronizer is then engaged. See Fig. 52-24.

Now power flow is through second gear on the output shaft. A gear ratio of about 2:1 is produced to give the vehicle a little more speed.

Third gear

When the gear shift lever is moved into third gear, there is no torque multiplication. The synchronizer is slid over the small teeth on the input shaft gear. The synchronizer sleeve locks the input shaft directly to the output shaft. Refer to Fig. 52-25.

A 1:1 gear ratio results with no torque increase. All of the output shaft gears freewheel or spin on their shaft. Power flow is straight through the transmission. The vehicle travels at highway speeds while the engine rpm is relatively low.

Reverse

When shifted into reverse, a synchronizer is moved into the reverse gear on the output shaft. This locks the gear to the output shaft. Power flows through the countershaft, reverse idler gear, reverse gear, and to the drive shaft, as in Fig. 52-26.

Neutral

In neutral, all of the synchronizer sleeves are located

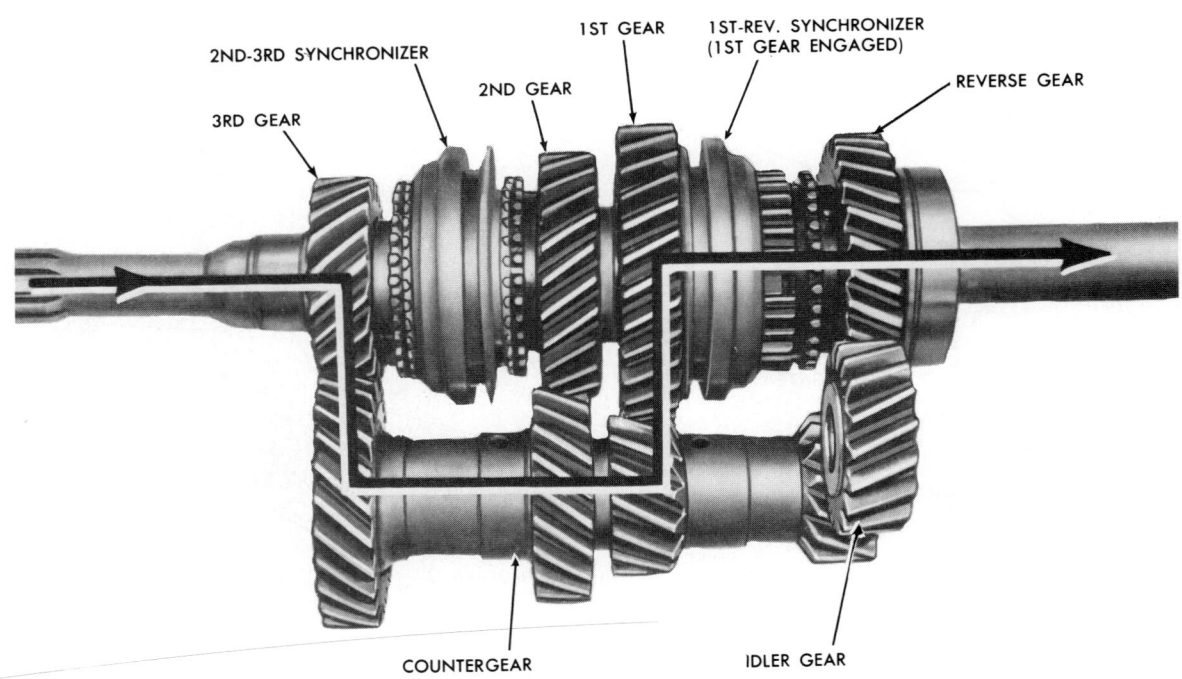

Fig. 52-23. Transmission in first gear. First-reverse synchronizer engaged with first output gear. Other synchronizer is in neutral position. First output gear is locked to output shaft and transfers high torque to drive shaft. (Chevrolet)

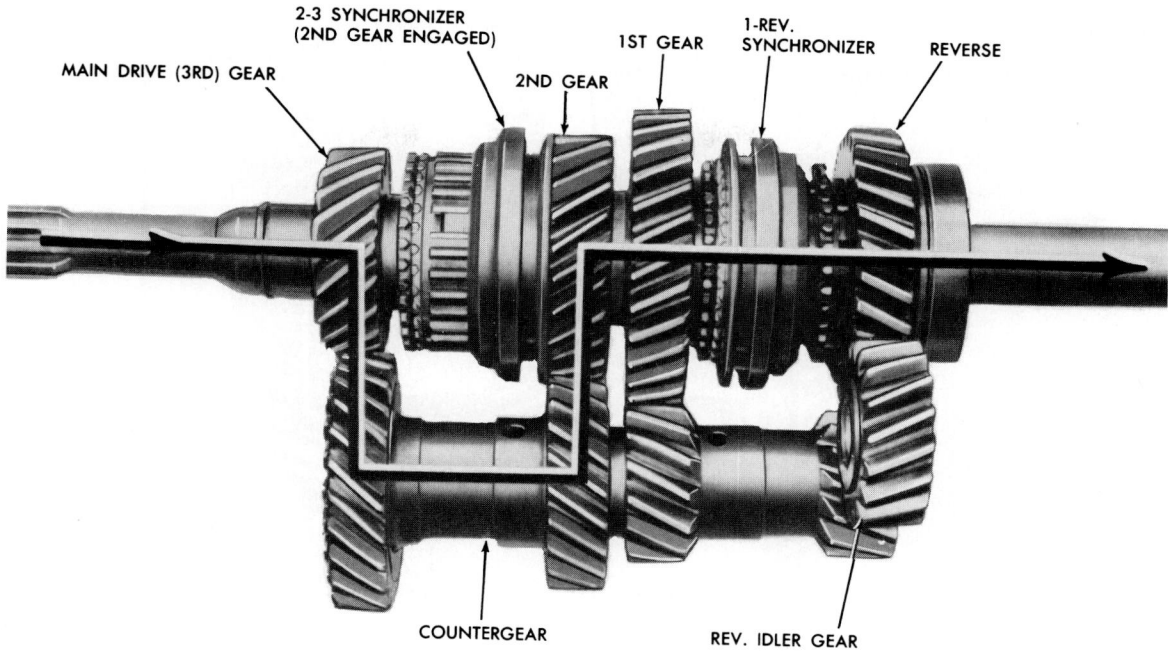

Fig. 52-24. Transmission in second gear. First-reverse synchronizer is moved into neutral. Second-third synchronizer is engaged with second output gear, locking it to its shaft. (Chevrolet)

in the center of their hubs, Fig. 52-27. This allows all of the output shaft gears to freewheel on the output shaft. No power is transmitted to the output shaft.

Overdrive gear

When in high gear, many modern transmissions have overdrive. Either fourth (4-speed) or fifth (5-speed) has a ratio of less than 1:1 (0.87:1 for example) to increase fuel economy.

Fig. 52-28 shows the power flow through a late model, 5-speed, overdrive transmission. It is designed for a low horsepower, diesel engine. Trace flow through the transmission in each gear. The first four forward speeds allow the diesel to accelerate quickly. The overdrive high gear keeps engine rpm down at highway speeds to increase fuel economy and engine service life.

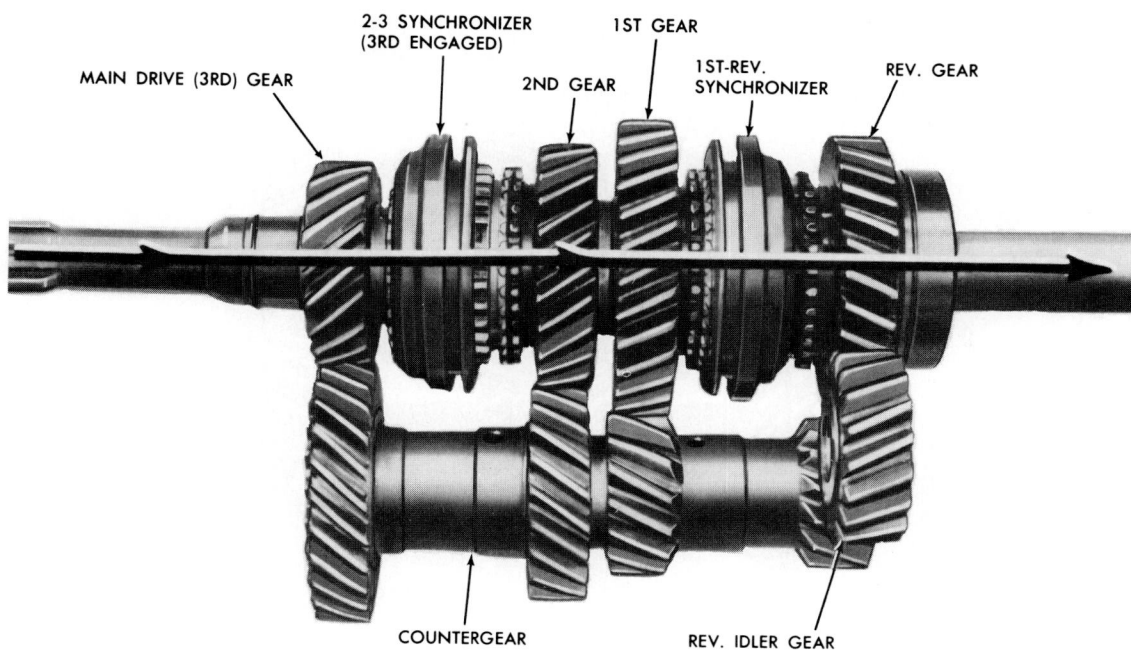

Fig. 52-25. Transmission in third gear. Second-third gear synchronizer is slid to engage gear on input shaft. This locks input shaft directly to output shaft. Both shafts turn at same speed for no gear reduction. (Chevrolet)

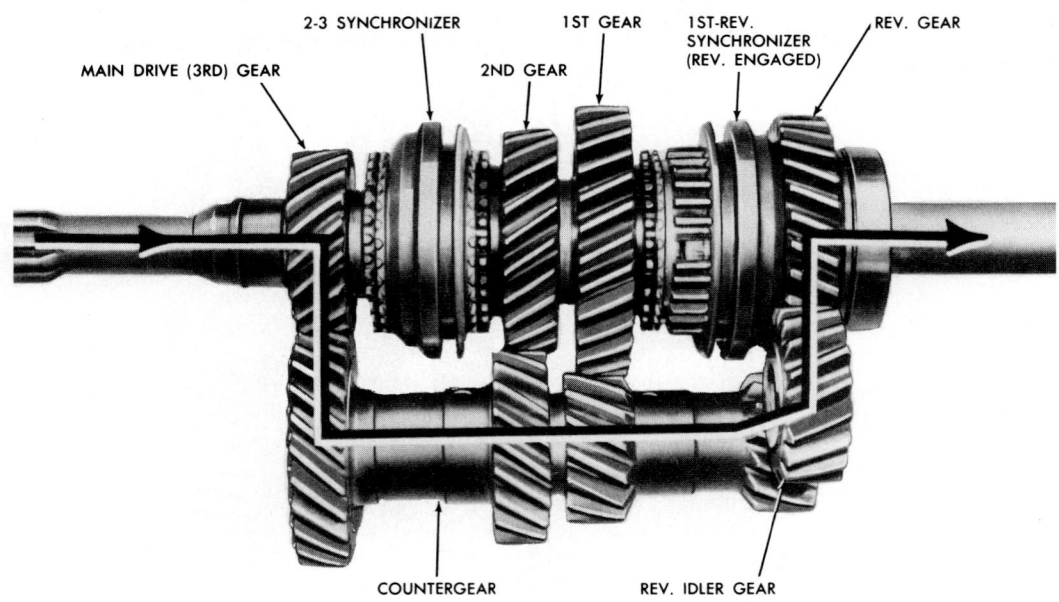

Fig. 52-26. Transmission in reverse. Second-third synchronizer moved into neutral. First-reverse synchronizer slid into mesh with reverse output gear. Countershaft gear drives reverse idler. Idler drives output shaft backwards. (Chevrolet)

OTHER TRANSMISSION DESIGNS

Many transmission design variations are used by the numerous auto manufacturers. However, all transmissions use the basic operation and construction principles just explained.

Review the transmission parts in Figs. 52-29 and 52-30. Can you explain the basic function of each part?

SPEEDOMETER DRIVE

Normally, a manual transmission has a worm gear on the output shaft that drives the speedometer gear and cable. See Fig. 52-29. The gear on the output shaft turns a plastic gear on the end of the speedometer cable. The cable runs through a housing up to the speedometer head (speed indicator assembly) in the dash.

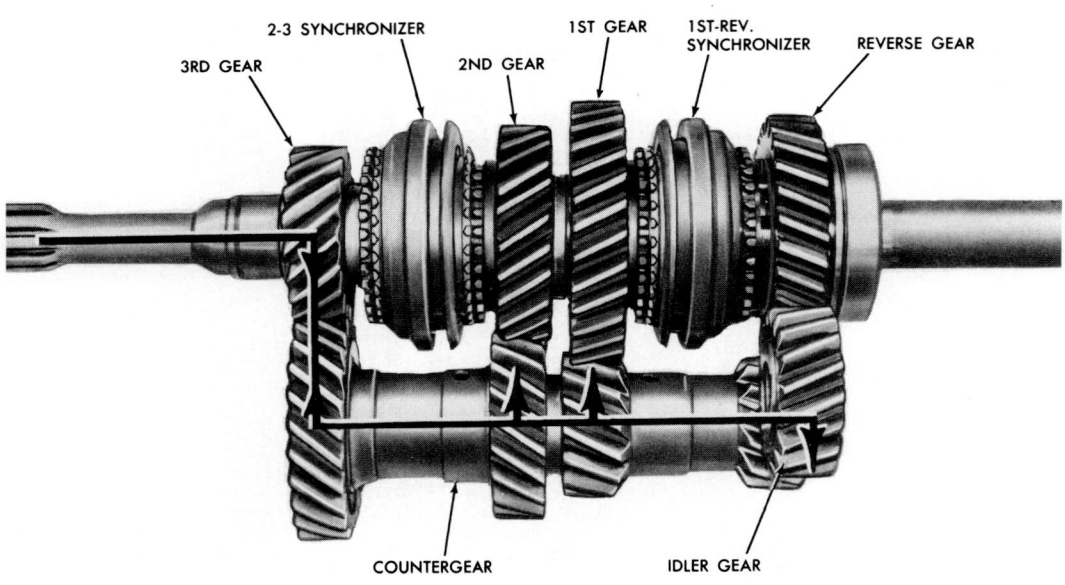

Fig. 52-27. In neutral, both synchronizers are in center positions. No output gears are locked to output shaft. Gears freewheel and do not transfer power to drive shaft. (Chevrolet)

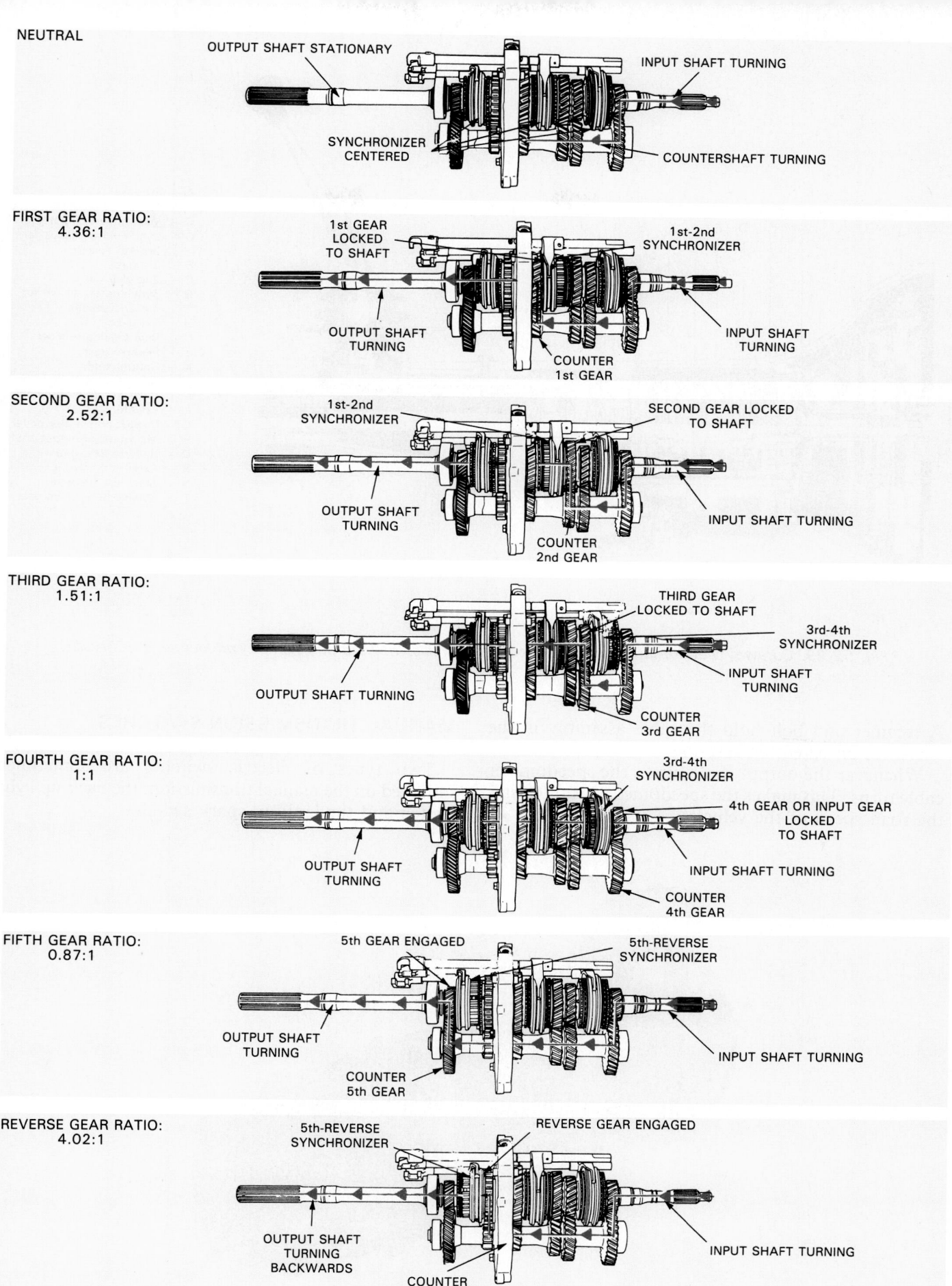

NEUTRAL

OUTPUT SHAFT STATIONARY

INPUT SHAFT TURNING

SYNCHRONIZER CENTERED

COUNTERSHAFT TURNING

FIRST GEAR RATIO: 4.36:1

1st GEAR LOCKED TO SHAFT

1st-2nd SYNCHRONIZER

OUTPUT SHAFT TURNING

INPUT SHAFT TURNING

COUNTER 1st GEAR

SECOND GEAR RATIO: 2.52:1

1st-2nd SYNCHRONIZER

SECOND GEAR LOCKED TO SHAFT

OUTPUT SHAFT TURNING

INPUT SHAFT TURNING

COUNTER 2nd GEAR

THIRD GEAR RATIO: 1.51:1

THIRD GEAR LOCKED TO SHAFT

3rd-4th SYNCHRONIZER

OUTPUT SHAFT TURNING

INPUT SHAFT TURNING

COUNTER 3rd GEAR

FOURTH GEAR RATIO: 1:1

3rd-4th SYNCHRONIZER

4th GEAR OR INPUT GEAR LOCKED TO SHAFT

OUTPUT SHAFT TURNING

INPUT SHAFT TURNING

COUNTER 4th GEAR

FIFTH GEAR RATIO: 0.87:1

5th GEAR ENGAGED

5th-REVERSE SYNCHRONIZER

OUTPUT SHAFT TURNING

INPUT SHAFT TURNING

COUNTER 5th GEAR

REVERSE GEAR RATIO: 4.02:1

5th-REVERSE SYNCHRONIZER

REVERSE GEAR ENGAGED

OUTPUT SHAFT TURNING BACKWARDS

INPUT SHAFT TURNING

COUNTER REVERSE GEAR

Fig. 52-28. Power flow through a five speed transmission with overdrive in high gear. Study each illustration carefully.

Manual Transmission Fundamentals 677

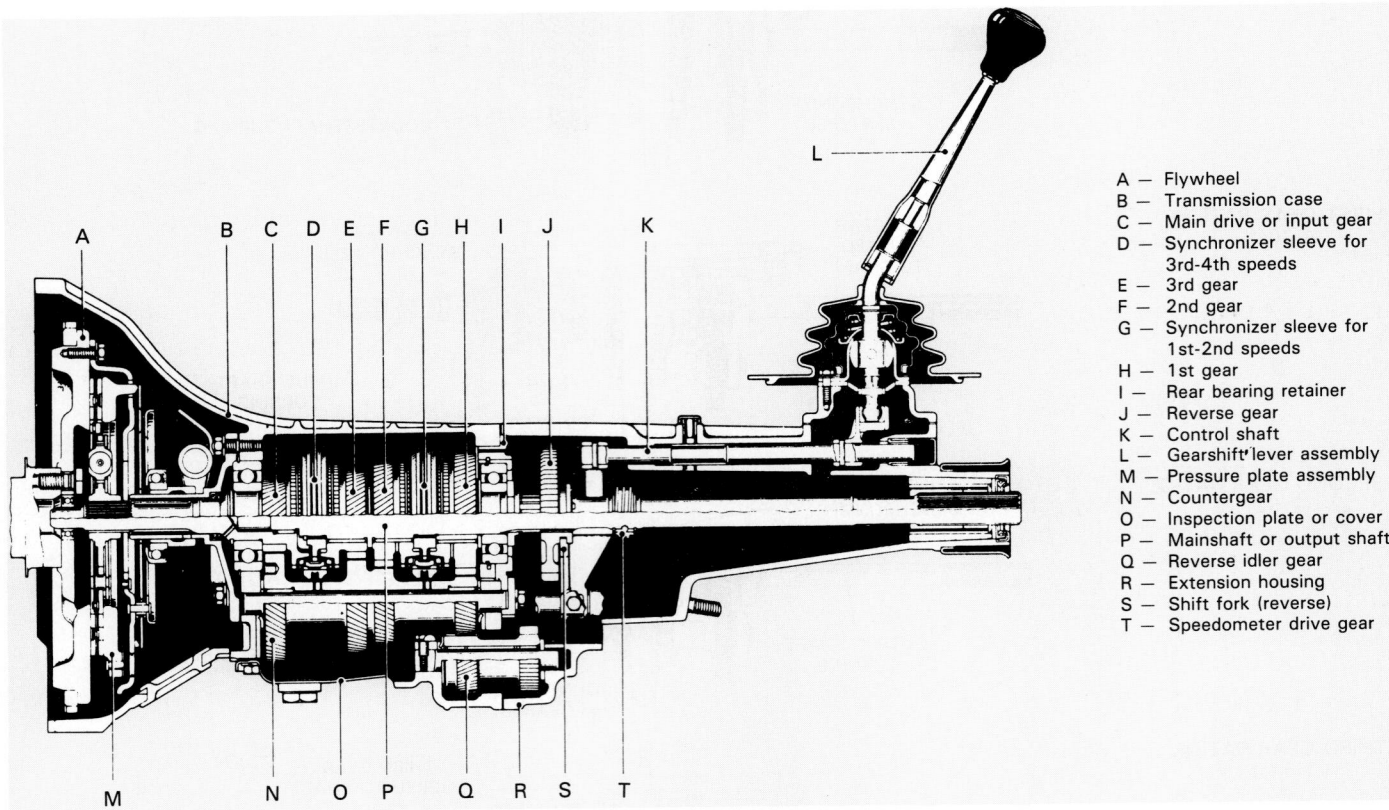

Fig. 52-29. Cutaway view of late model four speed transmission. Note part names and locations. (Chrysler)

A — Flywheel
B — Transmission case
C — Main drive or input gear
D — Synchronizer sleeve for 3rd-4th speeds
E — 3rd gear
F — 2nd gear
G — Synchronizer sleeve for 1st-2nd speeds
H — 1st gear
I — Rear bearing retainer
J — Reverse gear
K — Control shaft
L — Gearshift lever assembly
M — Pressure plate assembly
N — Countergear
O — Inspection plate or cover
P — Mainshaft or output shaft
Q — Reverse idler gear
R — Extension housing
S — Shift fork (reverse)
T — Speedometer drive gear

A retainer and bolt hold the cable assembly in the transmission extension housing.

Whenever the output shaft turns, the speedometer cable turns. This makes the speedometer head register the road speed of the vehicle.

MANUAL TRANSMISSION SWITCHES

Two types of electric switches are sometimes mounted on the manual transmission: the back-up light switch and the ignition spark switch.

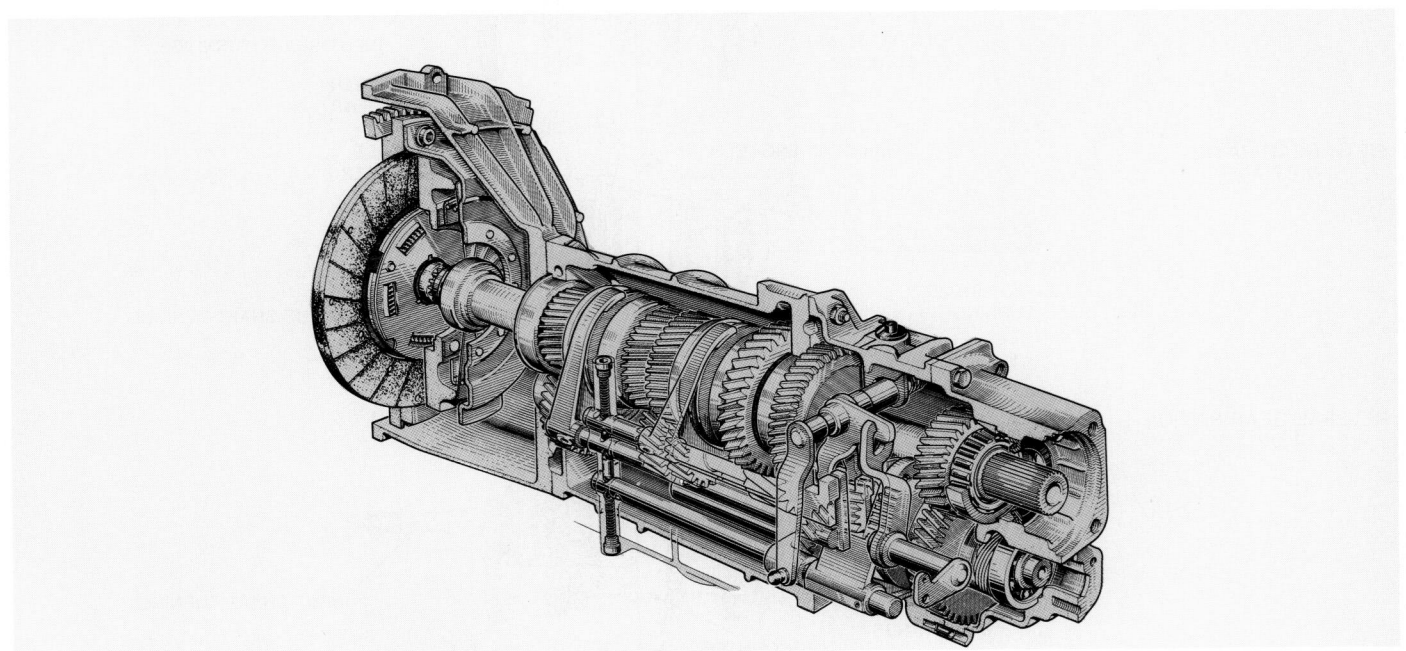

Fig. 52-30. Five speed, manual transmission with clutch installed on input shaft. Can you describe function of major parts? (Peugeot)

The *back-up light switch* is an electric switch closed by the action of the reverse gear shift linkage. Refer to Fig. 52-21. When shifted into reverse, the linkage closes the switch to connect the back-up lamps to battery.

A few manual transmissions have an *ignition spark switch* which only allows distributor vacuum advance in high gear. The switch usually mounts in the side of the transmission. It is normally closed until activated in high gear. This retards the ignition timing in lower gears to reduce exhaust pollution.

KNOW THESE TERMS

Manual transmission, Gear ratio, Gear reduction, Overdrive ratio, Spur gears, Helical gears, Gear backlash, Gear oil, Transmission case, Extension housing, Input shaft, Countershaft, Reverse idler shaft, Output shaft, Countershaft gear, Output shaft gears, Synchronizer, Fully synchronized transmission, Shift fork, Transmission linkage, Shift rail, Shift lever, Back-up light switch, Ignition spark switch.

REVIEW QUESTIONS

1. List and explain the eight major parts of a manual transmission.
2. Define the term "gear ratio."
3. How do you find the gear ratio of two gears?
4. Approximate manual transmission gear ratios are _____ for first, _____ for second, _____ for high, and _____ for reverse.
5. A gear reduction results when a small gear drives a larger gear to increase turning force. True or False?
6. This would be an overdrive ratio.
   a. 1:1.
   b. 0.87:1.
   c. 1:0.87.
   d. 3:1.
7. _____ _____ is the small clearance between the meshing gear teeth for lubrication and heat expansion.
8. Typically, _____ or _____ gear oil is used in a manual transmission.
9. What is the transmission extension housing?
10. Name and describe the four shafts in a manual transmission.
11. List and explain the general gear classifications found in a manual transmission.
12. A manual transmission synchronizer is used to:
    a. Prevent gear clashing or grinding.
    b. Lock output gear to output shaft.
    c. Both of the above are correct.
    d. None of the above are correct.
13. What is a fully synchronized transmission?
14. Describe the two major types of transmission shift linkages.
15. Why is an overdrive ratio used?

ACTIVITIES FOR CHAPTER 52

1. Locate a drive gear and a driven gear on a manual transmission and determine the gear ratio when the two gears are meshed. Show your calculations.
2. Locate the transmission section in a shop manual and study the names of the gears. Locate these same gears on an actual transmission.
3. Demonstrate the adjustment procedures for a manual transmission linkage.

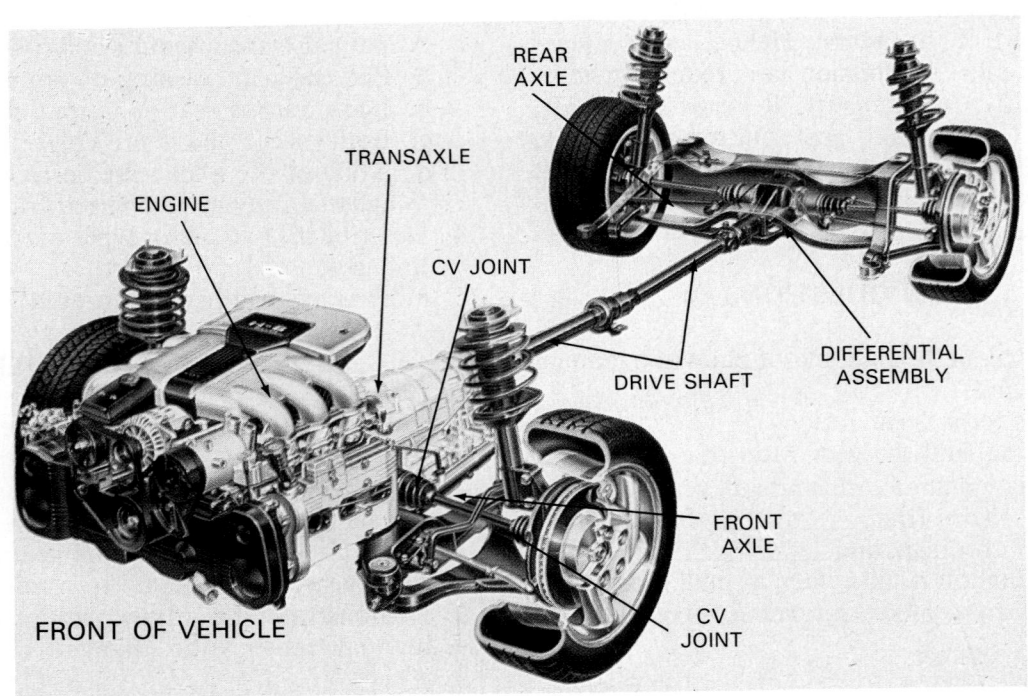

REAR AXLE

TRANSAXLE

ENGINE

CV JOINT

DIFFERENTIAL ASSEMBLY

DRIVE SHAFT

FRONT AXLE

CV JOINT

FRONT OF VEHICLE

Note parts of this four-wheel drive system. Engine and transaxle are at front; a drive shaft transmits power to rear differential assembly.   (Subaru)

53

Manual Transmission Diagnosis and Repair

After studying this chapter, you will be able to:
- ☐ Diagnose common manual transmission problems.
- ☐ Remove a standard transmission from a car.
- ☐ Disassemble and inspect a manual transmission.
- ☐ Assemble a manual transmission.
- ☐ Install a manual transmission.
- ☐ Adjust manual transmission linkage.
- ☐ Cite and observe safety rules for transmission service.

Since manual transmission construction varies with the manufacturer, a service manual should be used for exact specifications and procedures. This chapter discusses typical methods and rules that apply to most makes and models. As a result, you will be much better prepared to use a shop manual and perform actual transmission repairs.

MANUAL TRANSMISSION PROBLEM DIAGNOSIS

Normally, a manual transmission will provide thousands of miles of trouble-free service. Quite often, it will last the life of the vehicle without major repairs. However, driver abuse and normal wear after prolonged service can cause transmission failure.

A technician's first step toward fixing a transmission is to determine why the problem developed. Was it because of driver abuse (speed shifting, drag racing,

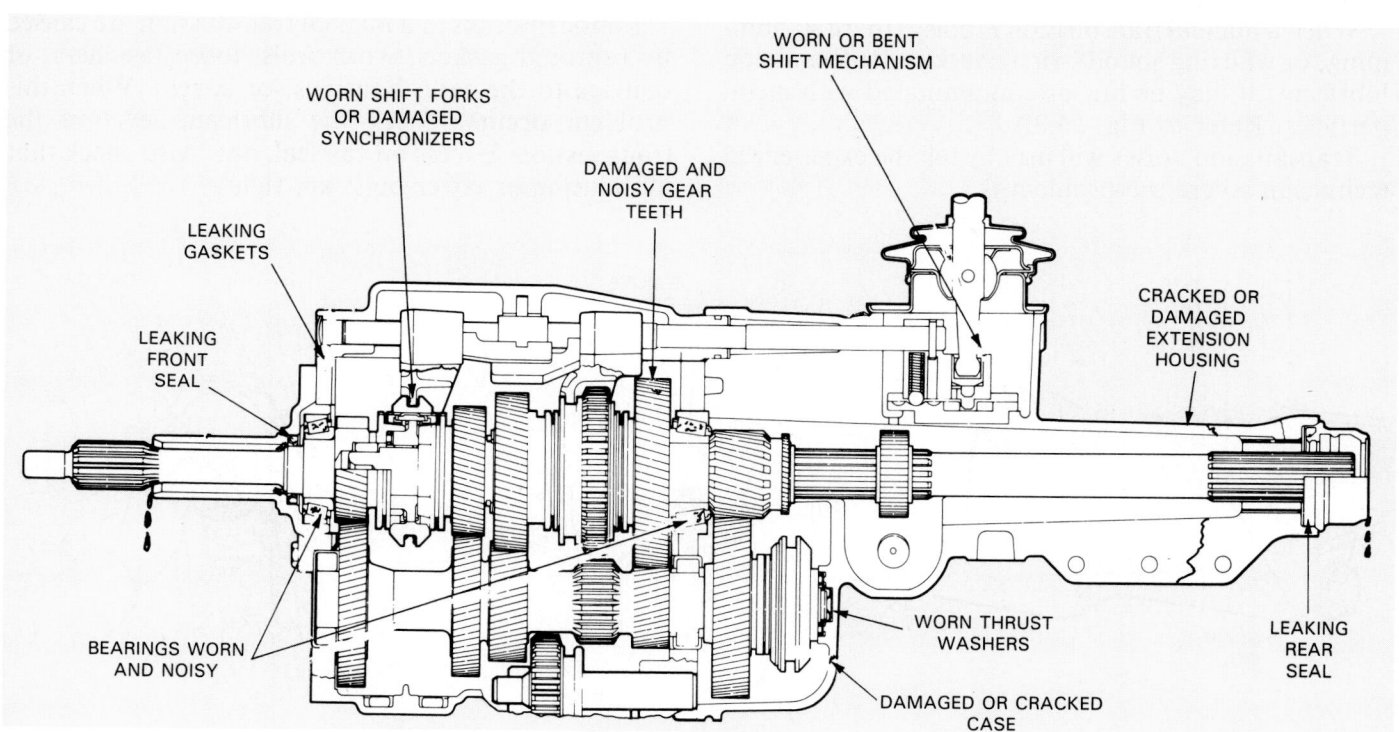

WORN OR BENT SHIFT MECHANISM

WORN SHIFT FORKS OR DAMAGED SYNCHRONIZERS

DAMAGED AND NOISY GEAR TEETH

LEAKING GASKETS

LEAKING FRONT SEAL

CRACKED OR DAMAGED EXTENSION HOUSING

BEARINGS WORN AND NOISY

WORN THRUST WASHERS

LEAKING REAR SEAL

DAMAGED OR CRACKED CASE

Fig. 53-1. Study types of problems found in manual transmissions.

lack of maintenance), normal wear (extremely high mileage), or another cause?

After proper diagnosis, the service technician can decide whether the transmission must be removed for major repairs. On the other hand a simple linkage or clutch adjustment may correct the problem.

Gather information on problem

To begin diagnosis, gather information on the transmission trouble. Then, test drive the car to verify the complaint.

Find out which gears in the transmission act up: first, second, high, all forward gears. Does it happen at specific speeds? This information will help determine which parts are at fault.

Fig. 53-1 shows typical transmission troubles. Study them carefully.

Gears grind when shifting

A grinding sound or gear clashing when shifting is frequently caused by incorrect transmission linkage adjustment. If the transmission linkage is badly worn, the gears inside the transmission may not engage properly. If the clutch is dragging, the synchronizer teeth may grind trying to equalize gear and output shaft speed, especially when shifting out of neutral.

Problems inside the transmission may also cause gear grinding during shifts. Worn or damaged synchronizers, shift forks or rails, and excessive wear in bearings and shafts may all prevent the gears from engaging smoothly.

Manual transmission noise

When a manual transmission is noisy (roaring, humming, or whirring sound), first check the transmission lubricant. It may be low or contaminated with metal particles. Refer to Fig. 53-2A.

Transmission noises will usually tell the experienced technician where the problem is.

For example, if the transmission is NOISY IN ALL GEARS, something common to all of the gears is at fault. Transmission bearings or shaft end play spacers may be worn, or a shaft may be damaged.

On the other hand, if there is only a NOISE IN ONE GEAR (first, second, third), the problem is due to components related to that gear. Look at Fig. 53-1.

Transmission hard to shift

When a manual transmission is hard to shift into gear, first check the linkage, Fig. 53-1. Make sure the linkage is lubricated and moving freely. A bent or misaligned shift rod will cause hard shifting. Also, inspect the operation of the clutch linkage. If the clutch is not releasing completely, the transmission can be hard to shift.

Transmission jumps out of gear

When a transmission jumps out of gear, the driver's shift lever "pops" into neutral while driving.

First, check the transmission linkage and shift lever arms. If the shifter assembly is badly worn, it should be rebuilt or replaced.

A worn clutch pilot bearing may also cause the transmission to jump out of gear. Severe vibration, set up by the wobbling transmission input shaft, can wiggle and move the shift forks and synchronizers.

Other problems inside the transmission can cause jumping out of gear. They include: worn synchronizer inserts and springs, worn shift fork assembly or shift rails, wear and excessive play in the countershaft and mainshaft assembly.

Manual transmission leaks lubricant

Lubricant leaks in a manual transmission are caused by ruptured gaskets, worn seals, loose fasteners, or damage to the case, housings, or covers. When this problem occurs, check the lubricant level in the transmission. Excess oil can leak out. Also check that all housing or cover bolts are tight.

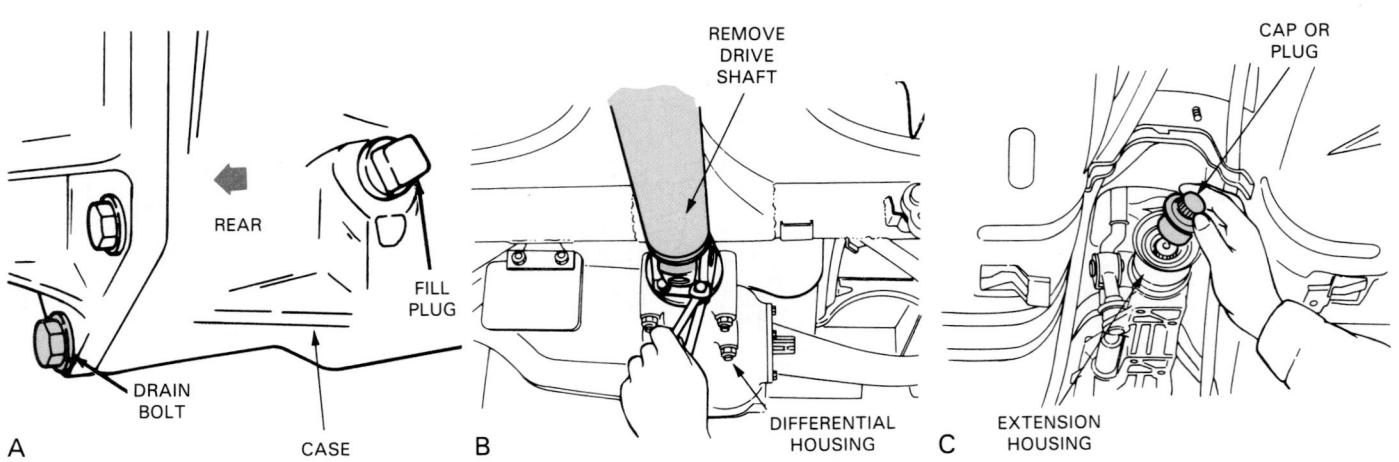

Fig. 53-2. Preparing for transmission removal. A — Drain gear oil. B — Remove drive shaft. C — If you do not or cannot drain transmission, install plastic cap to prevent oil leakage during removal. (GMC and Subaru)

When a seal leaks, always check the shaft bearing or bushing. A worn bearing or bushing and the wobbling action of the shaft can make a NEW SEAL LEAK.

Some of the gaskets and seals in a transmission can be replaced without removing the transmission from the vehicle. For example, the rear housing seal and gasket can normally be installed in-vehicle.

Manual transmission locked in gear

When the shifter is locked in one gear, check the transmission shifter assembly and linkage. Look for bent shift rods, worn linkage, bushings, or shifter arms. Also check linkage adjustment. With a shift rail type mechanism, worn or damaged rails, detents, or forks could be the cause.

A transmission can also become locked in gear when drive gear teeth are broken. The teeth can jam together and be locked by bits of metal from chipped gear teeth.

Manual transmission diagnosis chart

Refer to a diagnosis chart in a service manual when a problem is difficult to locate. It will be written for the exact type of transmission.

TRANSMISSION IDENTIFICATION

When repairing a manual transmission, you must be able to identify the exact type of transmission. Usually, there will be an ID TAG (identification label) or stamped set of numbers on the transmission. These numbers can be given to the parts counterperson when you are ordering new parts.

MANUAL TRANSMISSION SERVICE

Many problems which seem to be caused by the transmission are caused by clutch, linkage, or drive line problems. Keep this in mind before removing and disassembling a transmission.

Manual transmisison removal

To remove a manual transmission, first secure the car on a hoist or set of jack stands. A hoist is better because it allows you to stand while working.

Remove the transmission drain plug and drain the oil into a catch pan, Fig. 53-2A. Remove the drive shaft, Fig. 53-2B. Install a plastic cap over the end of the transmission shaft, Fig. 53-2C. This will help keep oil from dripping out.

Disconnect the transmission linkage at the transmission. Unbolt and pull the speedometer cable out of the extension housing. Also, remove all electrical wires going to switches on the transmission.

Often, the crossmember (transmission support bolted to frame) must first be removed. Support the transmission with a jack and use another jack under the rear of the engine. Operate the jack on the engine to take

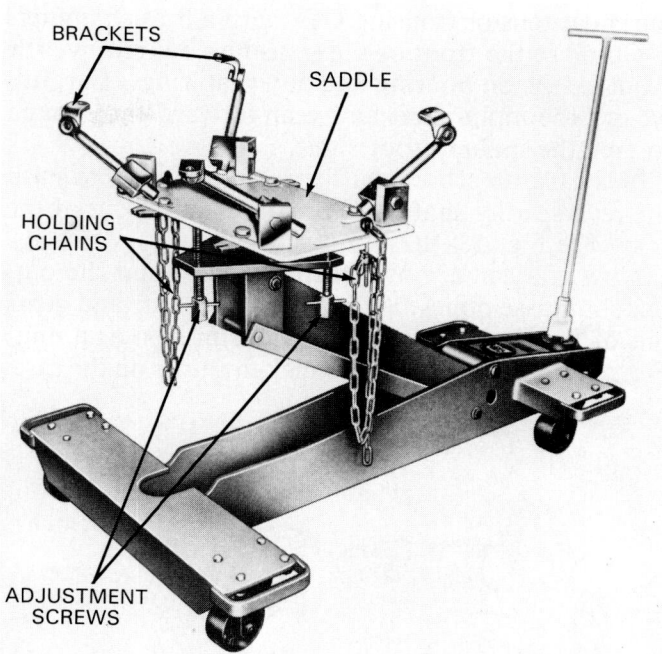

Fig. 53-3. Transmission jack should be used to avoid back injuries when transmissions are removed or installed by hand. Note arms and chains for securing transmission to jack saddle. (Owatonna Tool Co.)

the weight off the transmission. Be careful not to crush the oil pan. Never let the engine hang suspended by only the front motor mounts.

Depending upon what is recommended in the service manual, remove either the transmission-to-clutch cover bolts or the bolts going into the engine from the clutch cover.

CAUTION! A manual transmission is heavy and clumsy. If you are NOT using a transmission jack, Fig. 53-3, ask another technician to help you lift the transmission out of the vehicle.

Slide the transmission straight back, holding it in alignment with the engine. You may have to wiggle the transmission slightly to free it from the engine. Clean the outside of the transmission and take it to a workbench.

Manual transmission disassembly

Teardown procedures will vary from one transmission to another. Always consult a service manual. Improper disassembly methods could cause major part damage.

Basically, remove the shift fork assembly and cover. With a shift rail type, remove the shift lever assembly.

If the transmission has an inspection cover, observe transmission action with the cover removed. Shift the transmission into each gear by moving the small levers on the shift forks. At the same time, rotate the input shaft while inspecting the condition of the gears and synchronizers.

Unbolt the rear extension housing. As in Fig. 53-4A, tap the extension housing OFF with a brass hammer.

Going to the front of the transmission, remove the front extension housing and any snap rings. Carefully, pry the input shaft and gear forward far enough to free the main output shaft.

Next, use an arbor (shaft type driving tool) to push the reverse idler shaft and/or countershaft out of the case. See Fig. 53-4B.

Now you can remove the input shaft and the output shaft assemblies. Slide the output shaft and gears out of the back or top of the transmission as a unit, Fig. 53-4C. Be careful not to nick the gears on the case.

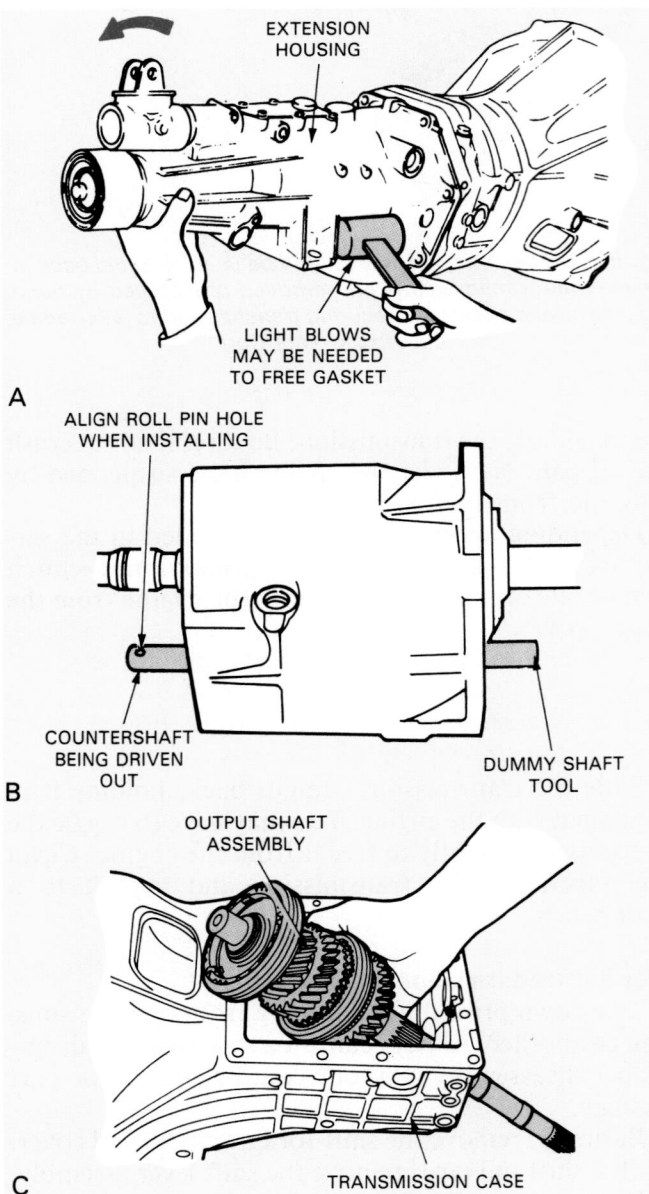

Fig. 53-4. Follow manual directions during transmission disassembly. A — A soft mallet may be needed to free rear extension housing from case. B — Dummy shaft is used to drive out countershaft and reverse idler shaft. C — After removing snap rings, front bearing cover, and other parts, lift output shaft and other components out of case. (Nissan, GMC, Chrysler)

Cleaning and inspecting parts

With all of the parts removed from the case, inspect everything closely. First check the inside of the case for metal shavings. If brass colored particles are found, one or more of the synchronizers or thrust washers are damaged. These are normally the only parts in the transmission made of this material. If iron chips are found, main drive gears are probably damaged. After checking the case, clean the inside with solvent. Then, blow it dry with compressed air while wearing eye protection. Also, clean the transmission bearings and blow them dry.

DANGER! When blowing bearings dry with compressed air, do NOT allow the bearing to spin. Air pressure can make the bearing whirl at tremendously high rpm. The bearing can explode and fly apart with lethal force.

Next, inspect all of the main drive gears, Fig. 53-5. Look for wear patterns or chips on the gear teeth. The gears are usually casehardened. If wear is more than a few thousandths of an inch, the casehardening will be worn through and the gear must be replaced.

If gear tooth wear is uneven, check the shaft bearings and shafts. They may be worn or bent. A dial indicator can be used to check the transmission shafts for straightness. Look at Fig. 53-6. Refer to specifications for the amount of allowable runout.

Inspect the synchronizer assemblies, especially if the transmission had gear shifting related problems. Check the teeth, splines, and grooves on the synchronizers, Fig. 53-7. Replace parts as needed.

When removing the gears from the output shaft, keep everything organized on your workbench. All snap rings, spacers, and other parts should be installed

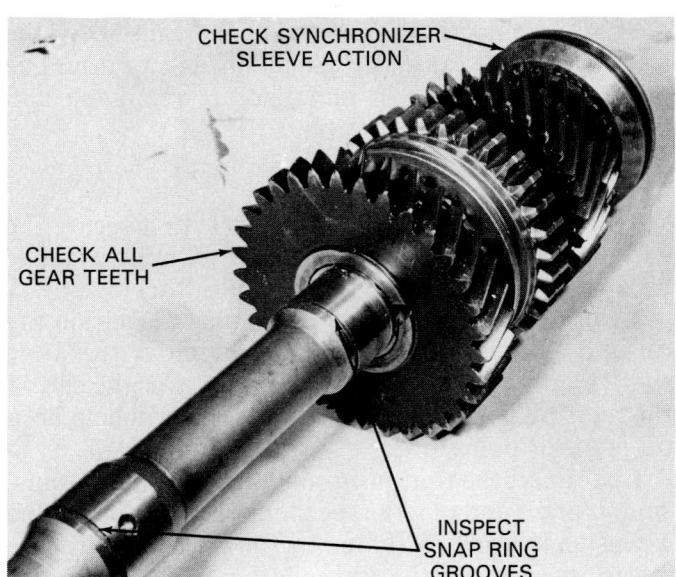

Fig. 53-5. Clean and inspect parts closely after removal. Check shaft snap ring grooves for wear or damage. Inspect gear teeth closely for signs of wear, chipped teeth, or other troubles. Also check synchronizers. (Chrysler Corp.)

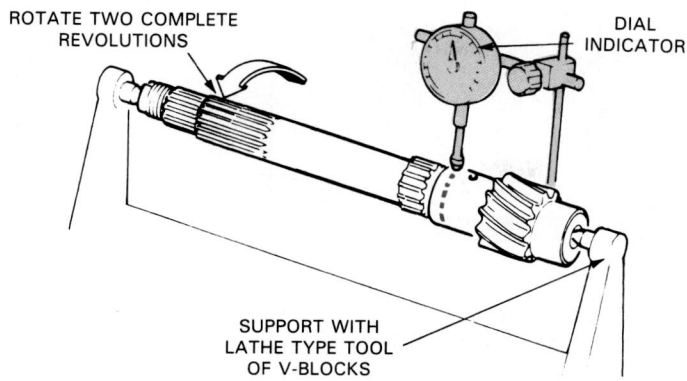

Fig. 53-6. If gear wear is irregular, check shafts for runout. Lathe type support or V-blocks will hold shaft. Use dial indicator to measure runout. Reading indicates a worn or bent shaft. (Honda)

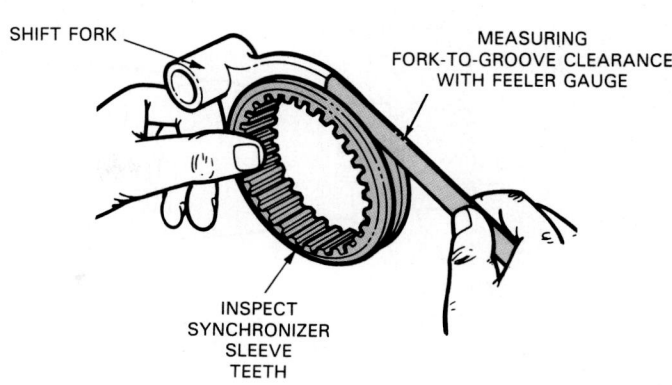

Fig. 53-7. Check shift forks and synchronizers for wear. Install feeler gauge between fork and groove. If more than specs, replace parts as needed.

1. MAINSHAFT PILOT BEARING ROLLER SPACER
2. THIRD-FOURTH BLOCKING RING
3. THIRD-FOURTH RETAINING RING
4. THIRD-FOURTH SYNCHRONIZER SNAP RING
5. THIRD-FOURTH SHIFTING PLATE (C)
6. THIRD-FOURTH CLUTCH HUB
7. THIRD-FOURTH CLUTCH SLEEVE
8. THIRD GEAR
9. MAINSHAFT SNAP RING
10. SECOND GEAR THRUST WASHER
11. SECOND GEAR
12. SECOND GEAR BLOCKING RING
13. MAINSHAFT
14. FIRST-SECOND CLUTCH HUB
15. FIRST-SECOND SHIFTING PLATE (C)
16. POPPET BALL
17. POPPET SPRING
18. FIRST-SECOND INSERT RING
19. FIRST-SECOND CLUTCH SLEEVE
20. COUNTERSHAFT GEAR THRUST WASHER
    (STEEL, REAR)
21. COUNTER SHAFT GEAR THRUST WASHER
    (STEEL BACKED BRONZE, REAR)
22. COUNTERSHAFT GEAR BEARING WASHER
23. COUNTERSHAFT GEAR BEARING ROLLERS (88)
24. COUNTERSHAFT GEAR BEARING SPACER
25. COUNTERSHAFT GEAR BEARING SPACER
26. COUNTERSHAFT GEAR THRUST WASHER (FRONT)
27. REAR BEARING
28. REAR BEARING LOCATING SNAP RING
29. REAR BEARING SPACER RING
30. REAR BEARING SNAP RING
31. ADAPTER PLATE SEAL
32. ADAPTER PLATE-TO-TRANSMISSION GASKET
33. ADAPTER TO TRANSMISSION
34. COUNTERSHAFT-REVERSE IDLER SHAFT LOCKPLATE
35. REVERSE IDLER GEAR SHAFT
36. REVERSE IDLER GEAR SNAP RING
37. REVERSE IDLER GEAR THRUST WASHER
38. REVERSE IDLER GEAR
39. REVERSE IDLER GEAR BEARING ROLLERS (74)
40. REVERSE IDLER GEAR BEARING WASHER
41. REVERSE IDLER SHAFT SLEEVE
42. COUNTERSHAFT
43. FRONT BEARING RETAINER WASHER
44. FRONT BEARING
45. FRONT BEARING LOCATING SNAP RING
46. FRONT BEARING LOCK RING
47. FRONT BEARING CAP GASKET
48. FRONT BEARING CUP SEAL
49. FRONT BEARING CAP
50. MAINSHAFT PILOT BEARING ROLLERS (22)
51. CLUTCH SHAFT
52. DRAIN PLUG
53. FILLER PLUG
54. TRANSMISSION CASE

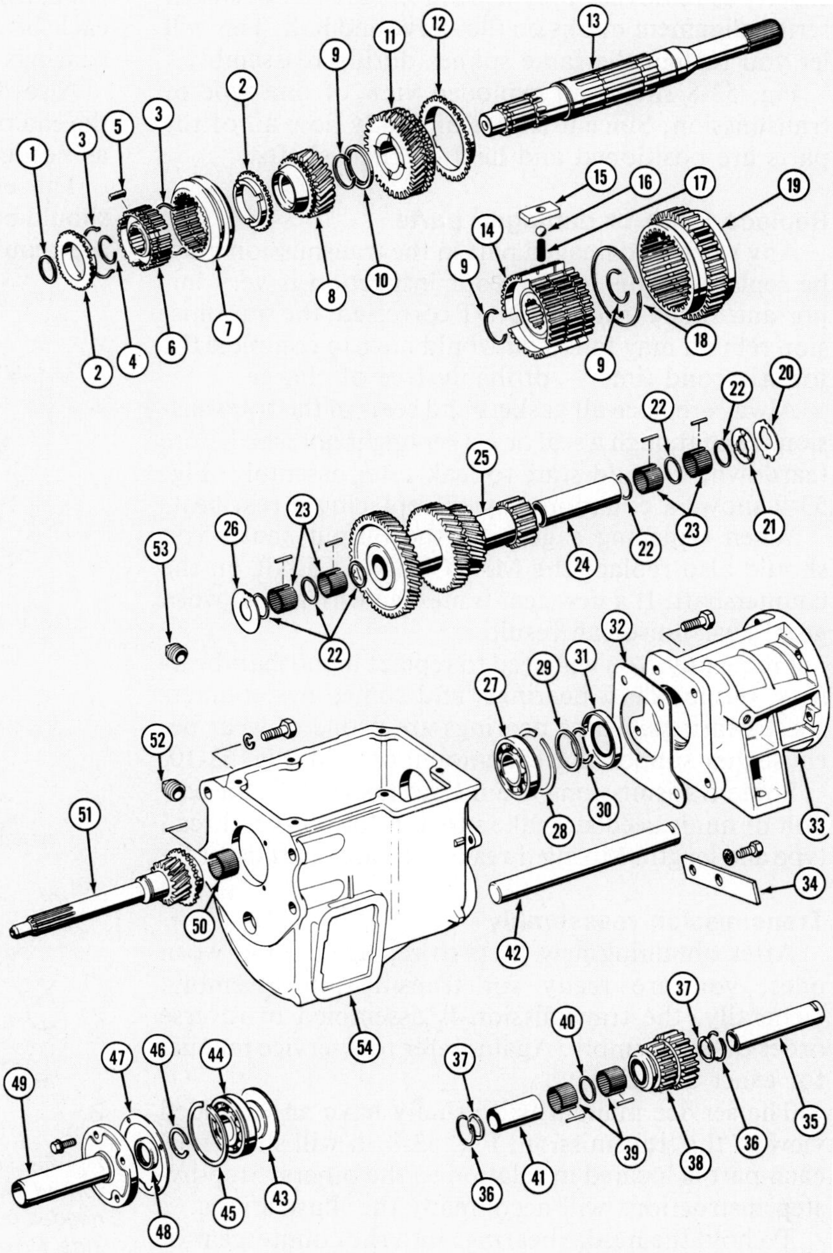

Fig. 53-8. Check every part closely for wear or damage. A service manual will normally provide an illustration like this one for exact transmission being repaired. This can be helpful during teardown and reassembly. (Chrysler Corp.)

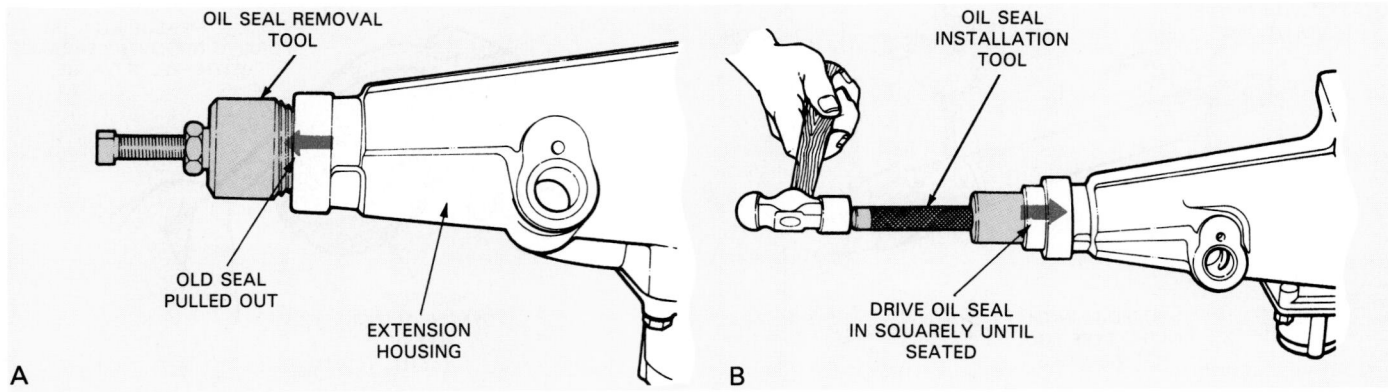

A

OIL SEAL REMOVAL
TOOL

OLD SEAL
PULLED OUT

EXTENSION
HOUSING

B

OIL SEAL
INSTALLATION
TOOL

DRIVE OIL SEAL
IN SQUARELY UNTIL
SEATED

Fig. 53-9. All seals should be replaced during a transmission rebuild. Rear seal can be removed and installed with transmission in car. A — Removing oil seal. B — Driving in new seal. Coat outside diameter of new seal with nonhardening sealer before installing. (Ford)

exactly as removed. If synchronizers are to be reused, scribe alignment marks on the sleeve and hub. This will let you realign the same splines during reassembly.

Fig. 53-8 shows an exploded view of one type of transmission. Since it is typical, study how all of the parts are positioned and held on their shafts.

Replace worn or damaged parts

Any worn or damaged part in the transmission must be replaced. This is why your inspection is very important. If any trouble is NOT corrected, the transmission rebuild may fail. You would have to complete the job a second time — probably free of charge.

Always replace all gaskets and seals in the transmission. Even though a seal or gasket might not leak before teardown, it could start to leak after assembly. Fig. 53-9 shows a common way of replacing a rear seal.

When replacing a gear on the output shaft, you should also replace the MATCHING GEAR on the countershaft. If a new gear is meshed with an old worn gear, gear noise can result.

Frequently, you will need to replace input shaft bearings, output shaft bearings, and sometimes countershaft bearings. These bearings are prone to wear because they support a great amount of load, Fig. 53-10.

Some transmissions use metric fasteners. If a new bolt or nut is needed, make sure it is the correct thread type and length. Mixing threads will cause part damage.

Transmission reassembly

After obtaining new parts to replace the old worn ones, you are ready for transmission assembly. Generally, the transmission is assembled in reverse order of disassembly. Again, refer to a service manual for exact directions.

The service manual will usually have an exploded view of the transmission, Fig. 53-8. It will show how each part is located in relation to the others. Step-by-step instructions will accompany the illustrations.

To hold the needle bearings into the countergear or other component, coat the bearings with HEAVY

GREASE. This is illustrated in Fig. 53-11. Then, fit each bearing into position. The grease will hold the bearings as you slide the countershaft into the gear.

Also, following manufacturer instructions, measure the end play or clearance of the gears and synchronizers as needed. Look at Fig. 53-12.

The end play between the countergear and case should be checked. If excessive, thicker thrust washers are required.

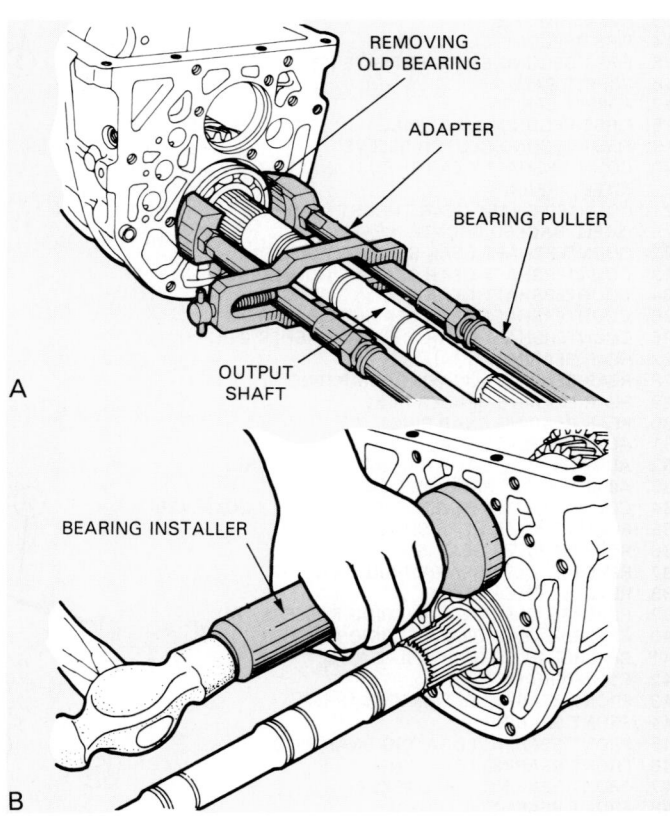

A

REMOVING
OLD BEARING

ADAPTER

BEARING PULLER

OUTPUT
SHAFT

B

BEARING INSTALLER

Fig. 53-10. If bearings show signs of wear or feel rough when turned by hand, replace them. A — Special puller may be needed on some bearings. B — Use driver to install new bearings. Do not hammer on the inner portion of bearing or damage will result. (Chrysler)

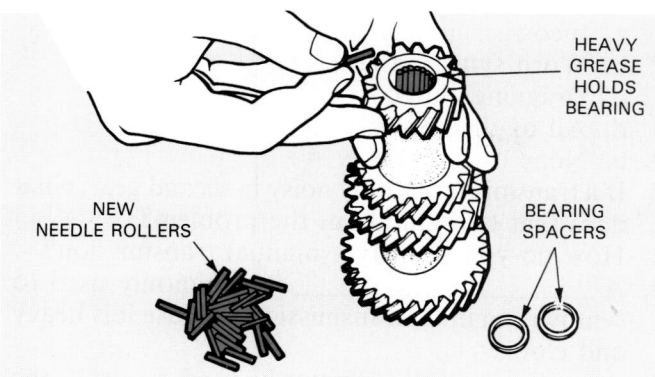

Fig. 53-11. Heavy wheel bearing grease is commonly used to hold small needle roller bearings during reassembly. Grease will hold bearings in countershaft gear as shaft is slid into place. (Dodge)

NEW NEEDLE ROLLERS

HEAVY GREASE HOLDS BEARING

BEARING SPACERS

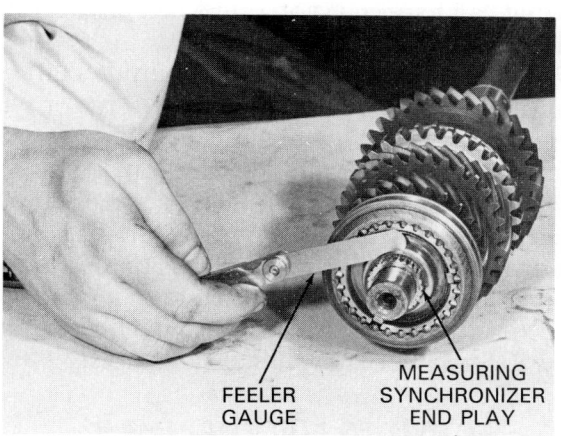

Fig. 53-12. After installing gears and synchronizers on output shaft, check clearances as described in service manual. This mechanic is checking clearance between snap ring and synchronizer hub. If greater than specs, snap ring or other parts are worn. (Chrysler Corp.)

FEELER GAUGE

MEASURING SYNCHRONIZER END PLAY

After the transmission shafts and gears are in place, pour the recommended quantity of oil into the case.

Assemble the shift fork mechanism. Look at Fig. 53-13. Then, with the synchronizers and shift forks in neutral, fit the shift fork assembly on or in the case. Check the action of the shift forks.

Make sure the transmission shifts properly before installing it. This could save you from having to remove the transmission if there are still problems.

Note! With the transmission out of the vehicle, it is wise to inspect the condition of the clutch.

Transmission installation

Before transmission installation, place a small amount of grease in the pilot bearing and on the throw-out bearing inner surface. Do NOT, however, place lubricant on the end of the clutch shaft, input shaft splines, or pressure plate release levers. Grease in these locations can spray onto the clutch friction disc, causing clutch slippage and failure.

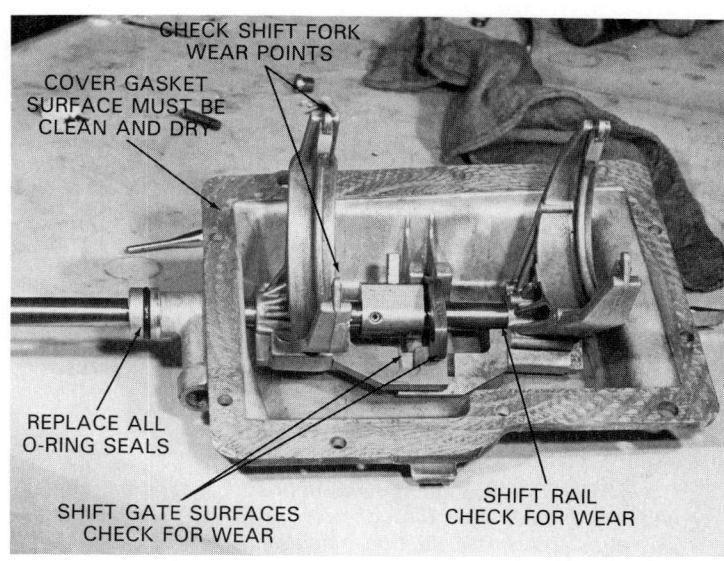

CHECK SHIFT FORK WEAR POINTS

COVER GASKET SURFACE MUST BE CLEAN AND DRY

REPLACE ALL O-RING SEALS

SHIFT GATE SURFACES CHECK FOR WEAR

SHIFT RAIL CHECK FOR WEAR

Fig. 53-13. Make sure nothing in the shift mechanism is worn or damaged. Check shift rail, fork-to-synchronizer contact points, shift gates, and other components. Use approved method of sealing shift cover on case. Refer to a service manual for details. (Chrysler)

Place the transmission on the transmission jack. Position it behind the engine. Double-check that the throw-out bearing is in place on the clutch fork. Carefully align the transmission with the engine.

The input and output shaft must line up perfectly with the centerline of the engine crankshaft. If the transmission is tilted, even slightly, it will NOT fit into place.

With the transmission in high gear to hamper input shaft rotation, slowly push the transmission into the clutch housing. You may need to raise or lower the transmission slightly to keep it in alignment. When the transmission is almost in place, wiggle the extension housing in a circular pattern while pushing toward the engine. This should help start the input shaft in the crankshaft pilot bearing.

WARNING! Do NOT use the transmission bolts to draw the transmission into the clutch housing. The transmission input shaft could be smashed into the crankshaft pilot bearing. Serious part damage may result. If the clutch and pilot bearing are installed correctly, the transmission should slide fully into place BY HAND.

With the transmission bolted to the clutch cover, install the rear crossmember and motor mount. Reinstall the clutch linkage, transmission linkage, and other parts. Adjust the clutch linkage.

ADJUSTING TRANSMISSION LINKAGE

To adjust many types of transmission linkage, place the gear shift lever and transmission levers in neutral. Then, as in Fig. 53-14, insert a steel pin in the hole in the shifter levers.

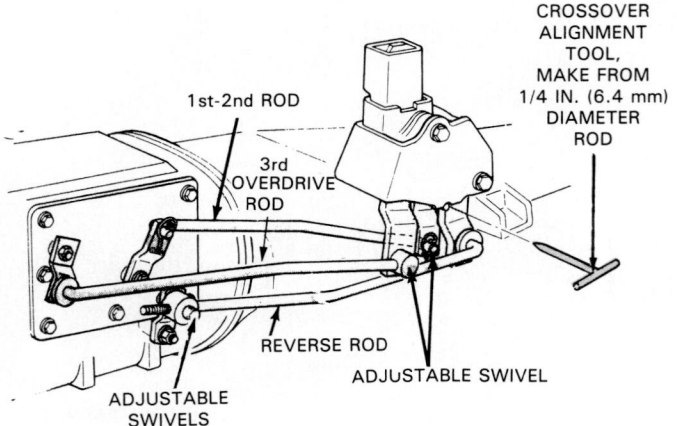

1st-2nd ROD

3rd OVERDRIVE ROD

CROSSOVER ALIGNMENT TOOL, MAKE FROM 1/4 IN. (6.4 mm) DIAMETER ROD

REVERSE ROD

ADJUSTABLE SWIVEL

ADJUSTABLE SWIVELS

Fig. 53-14. External linkage and floor shifter is commonly adjusted by installing pin through holes in shifter arms. Transmission arms and shifter must be in neutral. Adjust rod length until rod passes easily through holes in each shift lever arm.

If the pin will NOT fit through the hole, lengthen or shorten the linkage rods. Adjust the rods so that the alignment pin fits easily through the hole in the shifter assembly.

This basic procedure will vary with different types of gear shift mechanisms. When in doubt, refer to the specific directions in a manual.

After adjustment, lower the vehicle to the ground. Road test the vehicle and check for leaks.

KNOW THESE TERMS

Gear clash, Hard to shift, Jumps out of gear, Locked in gear, Transmission diagnosis chart, Transmission ID tag, Transmission jack, Dummy shaft, Shaft runout, Shift linkage alignment pin.

REVIEW QUESTIONS

1. A grinding or gear clashing noise when shifting out of neutral could be caused by:

a. Incorrect linkage adjustment.
b. Worn synchronizers.
c. Dragging clutch.
d. All of the above.
e. None of the above.

2. If a transmission is only noisy in second gear, what does that tell you about the problem?

3. How do you identify a manual transmission?

4. A _____ _____ is commonly used to remove a manual transmission because it is heavy and clumsy.

5. An _____ is commonly used to drive the reverse idler shaft out of the case during transmission disassembly.

6. If you find bronze- or brass-like metal shavings in the case, synchronizers or thrust washers may be damaged. True of False?

7. What can happen if you spin a ball or roller bearing with compressed air?

8. When replacing a gear on the output shaft, you must also replace the output shaft. True or False?

9. Heavy _____ will hold needle bearings in place during transmission assembly.

10. Which of the following is NOT a normal procedure during transmission linkage adjustment?
a. Measure linkage-to-transmission clearance.
b. Place all shift rods in neutral.
c. Insert an alignment pin through linkage arms.
d. Refer to service manual directions.

ACTIVITIES FOR CHAPTER 53

1. Disassemble a defective transmission assigned by your instructor. Clean and examine parts, listing those that are defective.

2. Remove a transmission from a vehicle.

3. Reassemble a transmission and reinstall it in the vehicle.

4. Operate a transmission selected by your instructor; identify noise and possible causes.

Automatic Transmission Fundamentals

After studying this chapter, you will be able to:
☐ Identify the basic components of an automatic transmission.
☐ Describe the function and operation of the major parts of an automatic transmission.
☐ Trace the flow of power through automatic transmissions.
☐ Explain how an automatic transmission shifts gears.
☐ Compare different types of automatic transmissions.

An *automatic transmission* performs the same functions as a standard transmission. However, it "shifts gears" and "releases the clutch" automatically. A majority of modern cars use an automatic transmission (or transaxle) because it saves the driver from having to move a shift lever and depress a clutch pedal.

As you will learn, an automatic transmission normally senses engine rpm (speed) and engine load (engine vacuum or throttle position) to determine gear shift points. It then uses internal oil pressure to shift gears. Computers can also be used to sense or control automatic transmission shift points.

BASIC AUTOMATIC TRANSMISSION

Before detailing the construction and operation of each individual part, it is important for you to have a general idea of how an automatic transmission works. Then, you will be able to relate the details of each part to the complete transmission assembly.

Refer to Fig. 54-1 as the following parts of an automatic transmission are introduced.
1. TORQUE CONVERTER (fluid coupling that connects and disconnects engine and transmission).
2. INPUT SHAFT (transfers power from torque converter to internal drive members and gearsets).
3. OIL PUMP (produces pressure to operate

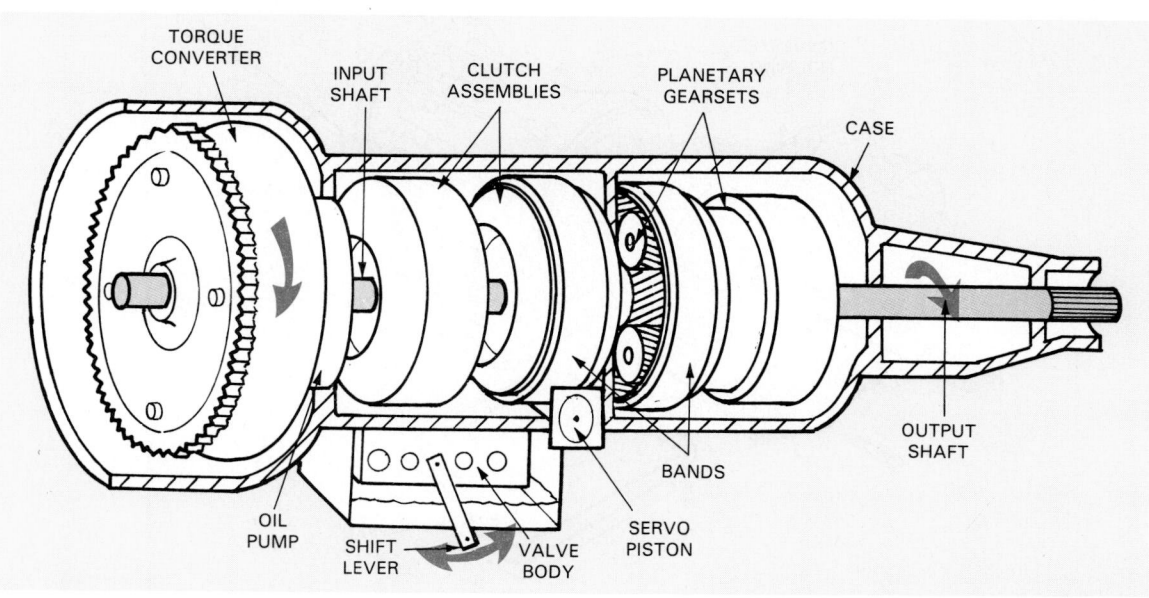

Fig. 54-1. Study basic parts of simplified automatic transmission. Note general shape and location of components. This will help prepare you to learn details of each part.

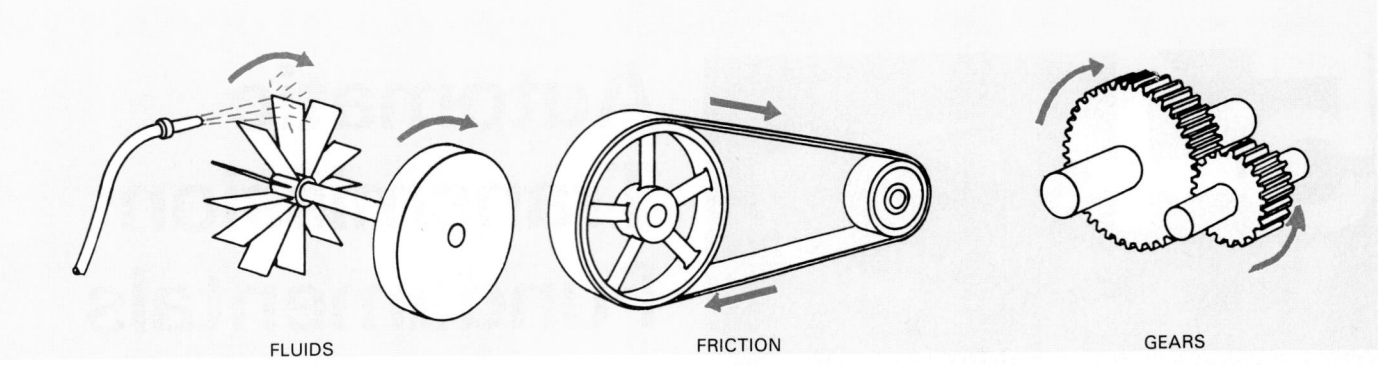

Fig. 54-2. An automatic transmission uses these methods of transmitting power. (Deere & Co.)

FLUIDS   FRICTION   GEARS

hydraulic components in transmission).

4. VALVE BODY (operated by shift lever and sensors, controls oil flow to pistons and servos).
5. PISTONS and SERVOS (actuate bands and clutches).
6. BANDS and CLUTCHES (apply clamping or driving pressure on different parts of gearsets to operate them).
7. PLANETARY GEARSETS (provide different gear ratios and reverse gear).
8. OUTPUT SHAFT (transfers engine torque from gearsets to drive shaft, and rear wheels).

TRANSMITTING POWER

As you will see, an automatic transmission uses three methods to transmit power: fluids, friction, and gears. This is illustrated in Fig. 54-2.

The torque converter uses FLUID to transfer power. The bands and clutches use FRICTION. The transmission GEARS, not only transmit power, they can increase or decrease speed and torque.

TRANSMISSION HOUSINGS AND CASE

An automatic transmission is normally constructed with four main components: converter housing, case, pan, and rear extension housing. These parts support and enclose all of the other components in the transmission. Refer to Fig. 54-3.

The *converter housing* or *bell housing* surrounds the converter and holds the transmission against the engine. It is usually made of aluminum.

Bolts fit through holes in the converter housing and attach to the engine block. The converter housing also keeps road dirt, rocks, and other debris off the spinning torque converter and flywheel, Fig. 54-3.

The *transmission case* encloses the clutches, bands, gearsets, and inner ends of the transmission shafts. The converter housing bolts to the front of the case. The

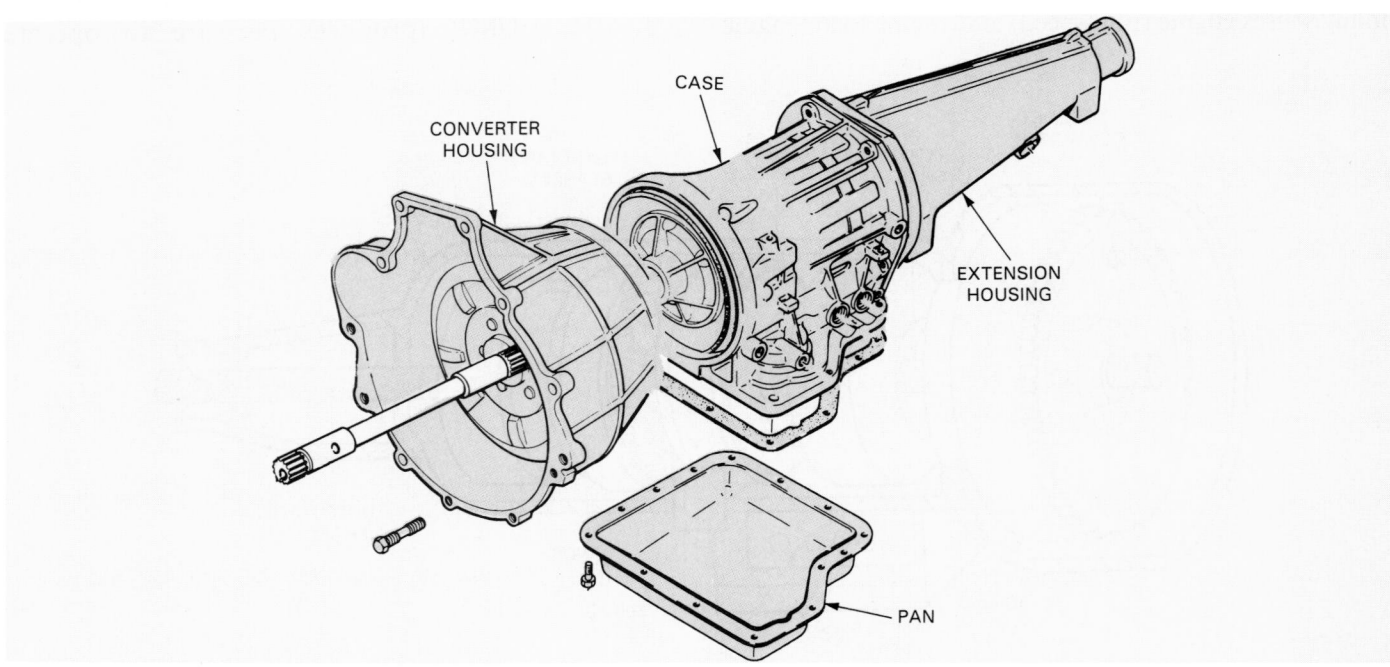

Fig. 54-3. Most automatic transmissions are constructed with front converter housing, central case, rear extension housing, and lower pan. Most parts fit inside case.

extension housing bolts to the rear of the case. The valve body and pan bolt to the bottom of the case. It may be made of aluminum or cast iron, Fig. 54-3.

The *oil pan,* also called *transmission pan,* collects and stores a supply of transmission fluid. It is usually made of thin, stamped steel or cast aluminum. The pan fits over the valve body. A gasket or sealant prevents leakage between the case and oil pan, Fig. 54-3.

The *extension housing* slides over and supports the output shaft. The housing uses a gasket on the front and a seal on the rear to prevent oil leakage. It is often made of aluminum, or sometimes cast iron, Fig. 54-3.

TORQUE CONVERTER

The *torque converter* is a fluid clutch that performs the same basic function as a manual transmission's dry friction clutch. It provides a means of uncoupling the engine for stopping the car in gear. It also provides a means of coupling the engine for acceleration.

Torque converter principles

Two house fans can be used to demonstrate the basic action inside a torque converter. Look at Fig. 54-4. One fan is plugged in and is spinning. The other fan is NOT plugged into electrical power.

Since the whirling fan is facing the other, it can be used to spin the unplugged fan, transferring power through a fluid (air). This same principle applies inside a torque converter, but oil is used instead of air.

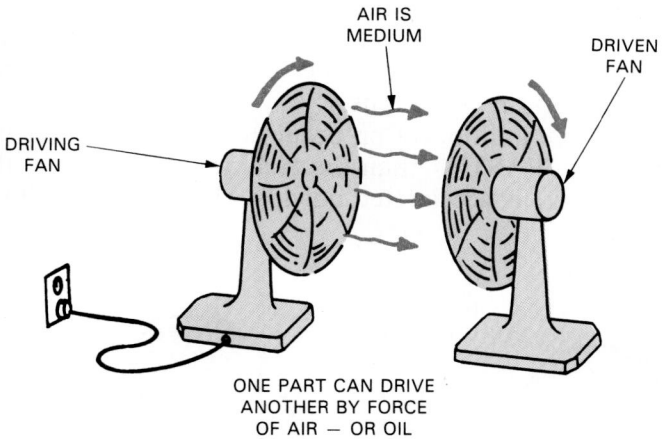

Fig. 54-4. Two fans demonstrate principle of fluid coupling or torque converter. (Deere & Co.)

Torque converter construction

A torque converter consists of four basic parts: the outer housing, an impeller or pump, a turbine, and a stator. These parts are shown in Fig. 54-5.

The impeller, stator, and turbine have curved or curled fan blades, as shown in Fig. 54-6. They work like our simple example of one fan driving another. The impeller drives the turbine.

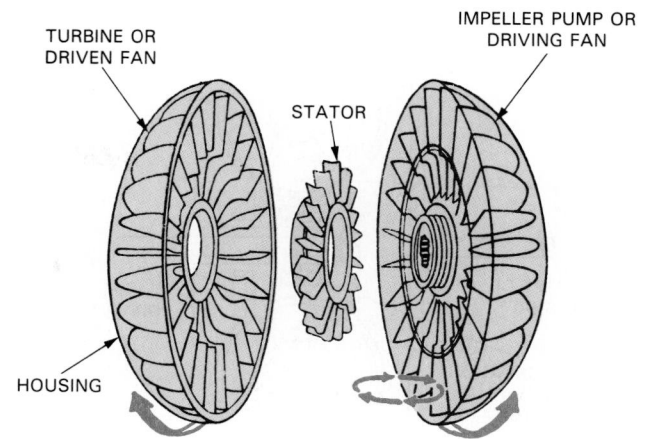

Fig. 54-5. Four major parts of torque converter: housing, impeller or pump, stator, and turbine. (Texaco)

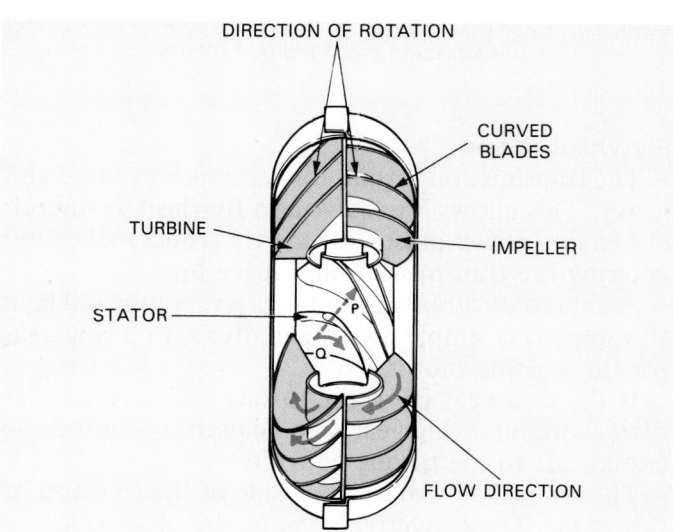

Fig. 54-6. Blades on impeller and stator direct oil circulation onto blades of turbine. Impeller is driven by engine. Turbine is driven by impeller. (Subaru)

Converter housing

The impeller, stator, and turbine are housed inside a doughnut-shaped housing. The converter housing is normally made of two pieces of steel welded together. The housing is filled with transmission fluid (oil).

The *impeller* is the driving fan that produces oil movement inside the converter whenever the engine is running. It is sometimes called the *converter pump,* Figs. 54-6 and 54-7.

The *turbine* is a driven fan splined to the input shaft of the automatic transmission. It fits in front of the stator and impeller in the housing. The turbine is NOT fastened to the impeller, but is free to turn independently. Oil is the only connection between the two.

The *stator* is designed to improve oil circulation inside the torque converter. It increases efficiency and torque by causing the oil to swirl around inside the converter housing. This makes use of all of the force produced by the moving oil.

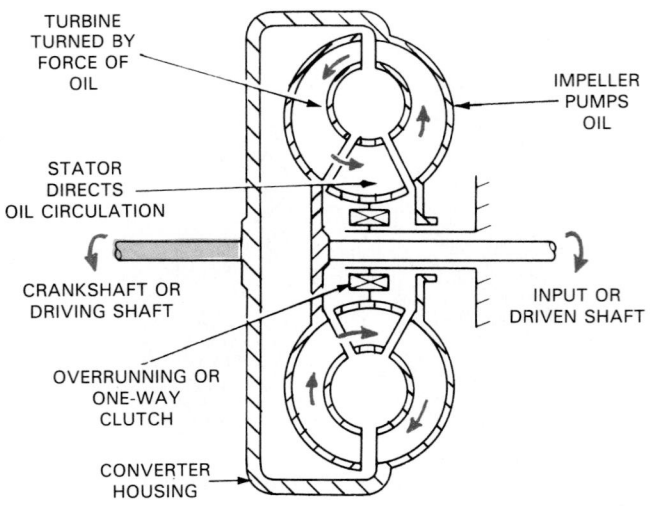

Fig. 54-7. Crankshaft is fastened to converter housing and impeller. Stator is mounted on one-way clutch. When engine crankshaft spins fast enough, oil movement rotates turbine and transmission input shaft. (Subaru)

Flywheel action

The transmission torque converter is very large and heavy. This allows it to serve as a flywheel to smooth out engine power pulses. Its inertia reduces vibration entering the transmission and drive line.

An automatic transmission uses a very thin and light flywheel. It is simply a stamped disc with a ring gear for the starting motor.

If the ring gear is on the torque converter, a *flex plate,* without a ring gear, can be used to connect the crankshaft to the torque converter.

The crankshaft bolts to one side of the flywheel or flex plate. The converter bolts to the other side.

Torque converter operation

With the ENGINE IDLING, the impeller spins slowly. Only a small amount of oil is thrown into the stator

and turbine. Not enough force is developed inside the torque converter to spin the turbine. The car would remain stationary with the transmission in gear.

During ENGINE ACCELERATION, the engine crankshaft, converter housing, and impeller begin to spin faster. More oil is thrown out by centrifugal force. This makes the turbine begin to turn. As a result, the transmission input shaft and vehicle start to move, but with some slippage, Fig. 54-7.

At CRUISING SPEEDS, the impeller and turbine spin at almost the same speed, with very little slippage. When the impeller is spun fast enough, centrifugal force throws the oil out hard enough to almost lock the impeller and turbine. See Fig. 54-7.

Converter one-way clutch

A *one-way clutch* allows the stator to turn in one direction but not the other. See Fig. 54-8. The stator mounts on the clutch mechanism. Stator action is only needed when the impeller and turbine are turning at different speeds.

The one-way clutch locks the stator when the impeller is turning faster than the turbine. This causes the stator to route oil flow over the impeller vanes properly. Then, when turbine speed almost equals impeller speed, the stator can freewheel on its shaft, so not to obstruct oil flow.

Torque multiplication

Torque multiplication refers to the ability of a torque converter to increase the amount of engine torque applied to the transmission input shaft. Just as a small gear driving a large gear increases torque, a torque converter can act as several different gear ratios to alter torque output. Torque can be doubled by the converter under certain conditions.

Torque multiplication occurs when the impeller is spinning FASTER than the turbine. For instance, if the engine is accelerated quickly, the engine and im-

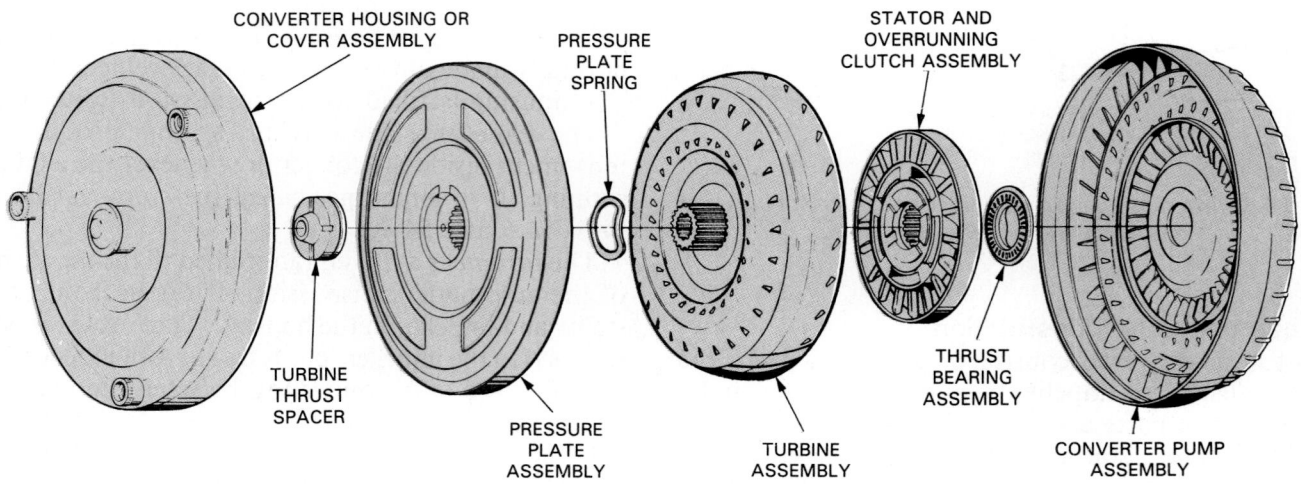

Fig. 54-8. Lock-up torque converter is conventional converter with a friction pressure plate added. The pressure plate can be used to lock turbine to converter housing, eliminating slippage and increasing fuel economy. (Oldsmobile)

peller rpm might increase rapidly while the turbine is almost stationary. At this time, torque multiplication would be maximum. When the turbine speed nears impeller speed, torque multiplication drops off.

Torque is increased in the converter by sacrificing motion. The turbine spins slower than the impeller during torque multiplication.

Torque converter stall speed

The *stall speed* of a torque converter basically occurs when the impeller is at maximum speed without rotation of the turbine. This causes the oil to be thrown off the stator vanes at tremendous speeds. The greatest torque multiplication occurs at stall speed.

Lock-up torque converters

A *lock-up torque converter* has an internal friction clutch mechanism for locking the impeller to the turbine in high gear. In a conventional converter, there is always some slippage between the impeller and turbine. By locking these components with a friction clutch, the torque converter does not slip. This improves fuel economy.

Typically, a lock-up mechanism in a torque converter consists of a hydraulic piston, torsion springs, and clutch friction material. See Figs. 54-8 and 54-9.

In lower transmission gears, the converter clutch is released. The torque converter operates normally, allowing slippage and torque multiplication.

Then, when shifted into high or direct drive, oil is channeled to the converter piston. The piston pushes the friction discs together to lock the converter. The torsion springs help dampen engine power pulses entering the drivetrain. Refer to Fig. 54-9.

AUTOMATIC TRANSMISSION SHAFTS

Typically, an automatic transmission has two main shafts: the input shaft and output shaft.

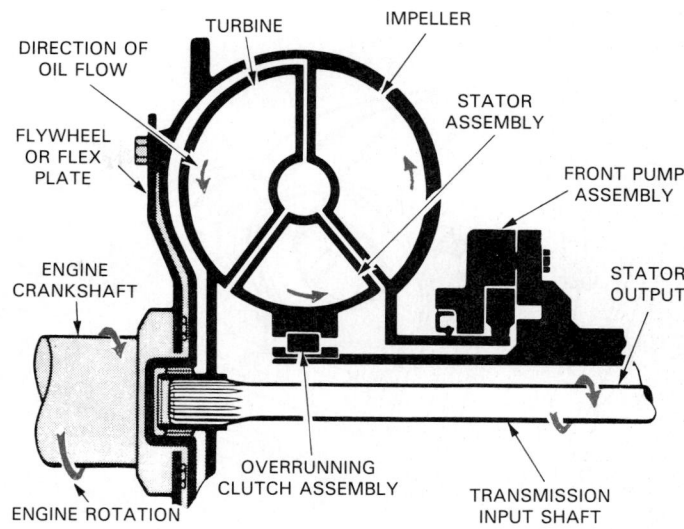

Fig. 54-10. Transmission input shaft extends through stator support. Shaft is splined to turbine. Also note how stator mounts on one-way clutch. (Ford)

An automatic transmission **input shaft** or *turbine shaft* connects the torque converter with the driving components in the transmission. Look at Fig. 54-10.

Each end of the input shaft has male (external) splines. These splines fit into splines in the torque converter turbine and a driving unit in the transmission. The input shaft rides on bushings. Transmission fluid lubricates the shaft and bushings.

The **output shaft** connects the driving components in the transmission with the drive shaft. Refer to Fig. 54-11. This shaft runs in the same centerline as the input shaft. Its front end almost touches the input shaft.

STATOR SUPPORT

The **stator support,** also called *stator shaft,* is usually a stationary shaft splined to the torque converter stator

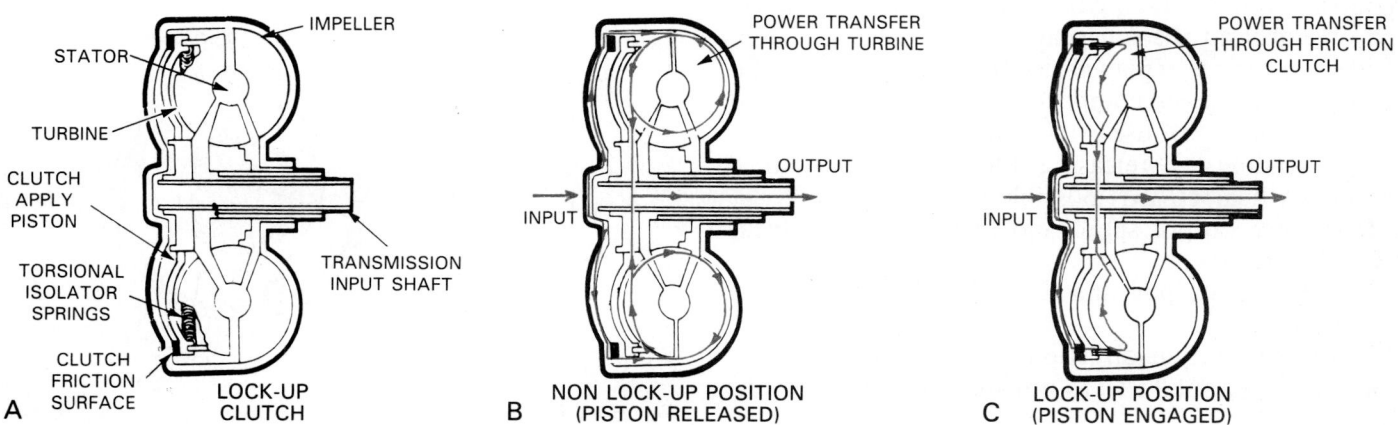

Fig. 54-9. Lock-up torque converter operation. A — Parts of lock-up converter. B — In lower gears, no oil pressure acts on clutch apply piston. Torque converter operates like conventional unit, impeller drives turbine. C — In high gear, oil is transferred into piston chamber. Clutch apply piston forces friction surfaces together. Turbine is mechanically locked to converter housing and impeller. Crankshaft drives transmission input shaft directly, without slippage.

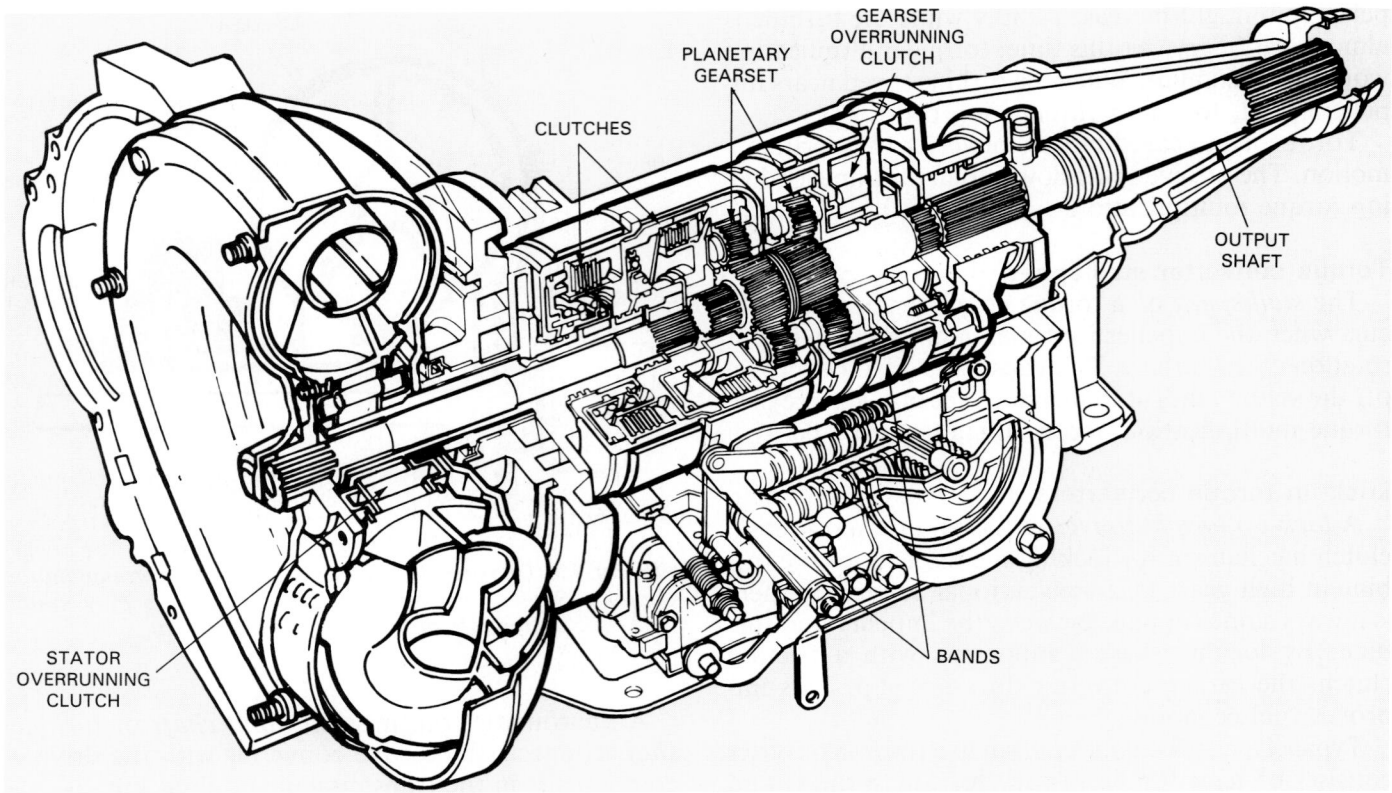

Fig. 54-11. Study location of gearsets and holding devices. Clutches, bands, and rear one-way clutch operate gearsets. Other one-way clutch operates torque converter stator. (Ford Motor Co.)

assembly. As pictured in Fig. 54-10, it is a tube that extends forward from the front of the transmission. It surrounds the input shaft.

PLANETARY GEARS

A *planetary gearset* consists of a sun gear, several planet gears, a planet gear carrier, and a ring gear. A simple planetary gearset is shown in Fig. 54-12.

The name planetary gearset is easy to remember because it refers to our solar system. Just as our planets (Earth, Jupiter, Mars) circle the sun, the planet gears revolve around the sun gear.

As you can see, a planetary gearset is always in mesh. It is very strong and compact. An automatic transmission will commonly use two or more planetary gearsets.

By holding or releasing the components of a planetary gearset, it is possible to:

1. Reduce output speed and increase torque (gear reduction).
2. Increase output speed while lowering torque (overdrive).
3. Reverse output direction (reverse gear).
4. Serve as a solid unit to transfer power (one-to-one ratio).
5. Freewheel to stop power flow (park or neutral).

Planetary reduction

One method of obtaining a gear reduction and torque

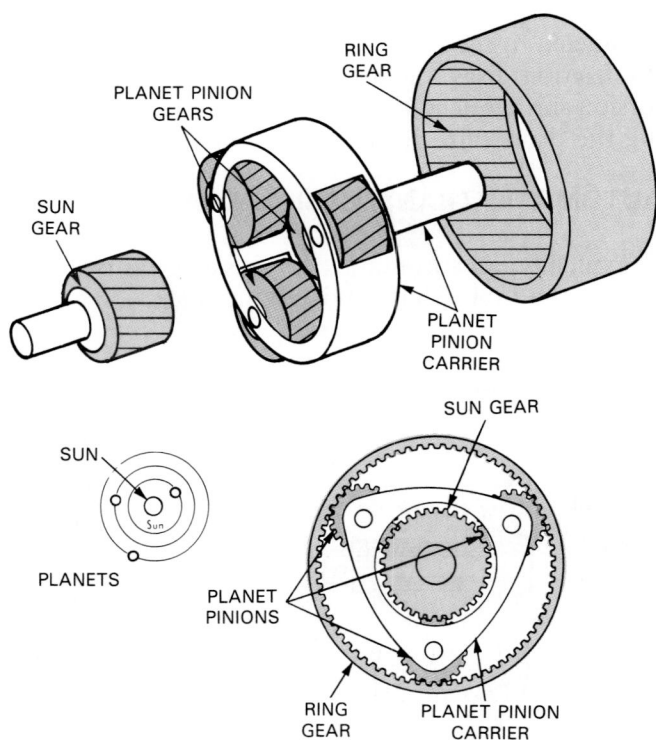

Fig. 54-12. Simplified planetary gearset. Planet gears fit between ring gear and sun gear. Planet gears are mounted on planet carrier. Gears are always in mesh, making a compact, strong, and dependable assembly. Name (planetary gears) is derived from how planet gears revolve around sun gear, like solar system planets.

increase is to hold the sun gear (stop it from turning) while driving the ring gear. This makes the planet carrier the output member. Refer to Fig. 54-13A.

When power turns the ring gear, the planet pinion gears "walk" (rotate) around the locked sun gear. The planet gears move in the same direction as the ring gear, but NOT as fast. As a result, more torque is applied to the output member (planet carrier) and output shaft.

Gear reduction can also be produced in the planetary gearset by turning the sun gear and holding the ring gear.

Planetary overdrive

Driving the carrier while holding the ring gear achieves an overdrive ratio in a planetary gearset. Look at Fig. 54-13B.

The input shaft powers the planet carrier. The sun gear is the output member driving the output shaft. The planet gears "walk" in the ring gear and power the sun gear. The sun gear spins faster than the carrier. Torque is lost but speed is increased.

Planetary reverse

A planetary gearset can also reverse output direction. The input shaft drives the sun gear, as in Fig. 54-13C. The carrier is held and the ring gear turns the output shaft. The planet pinion gears simply act as idler gears. They reverse the direction of rotation between the sun gear and ring gear.

Planetary direct drive

A planetary gearset will act as a solid unit when TWO of its members are held. This causes the input and output members to turn at the same speed, Fig. 54-13D.

Planetary neutral

When none of the planetary members are held, the unit will NOT transfer power. This freewheeling condition is used when an automatic transmission is placed in neutral or park.

Compound planetary gearset

A *compound planetary gearset* combines two

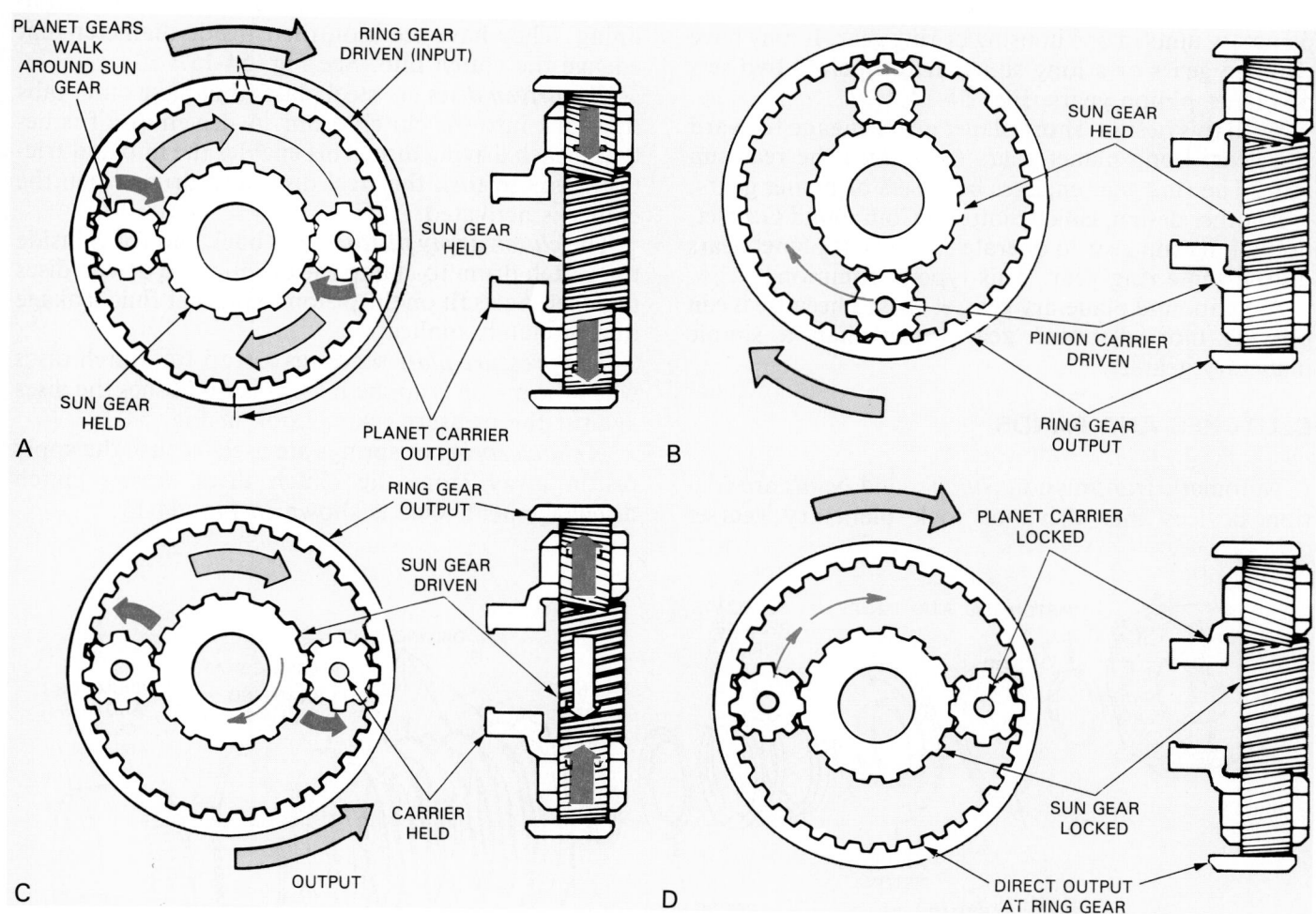

Fig. 54-13. Study how different planetary gearset members can be held to provide different gear ratios and reverse. A — Simple gear reduction. Sun gear is stationary. Ring gear is driven. Planet carrier is output. Input torque increases and speed decreases. B — Overdrive. Sun gear is held stationary. Pinion carrier is driven. Ring gear is output and turns faster than input. C — Simple reverse gear. Pinion carrier is held. Sun gear is driven. Ring gear turns backwards as output. D — Direct drive results when any two members of planetary gearset are held, or by driving any two members from same input.

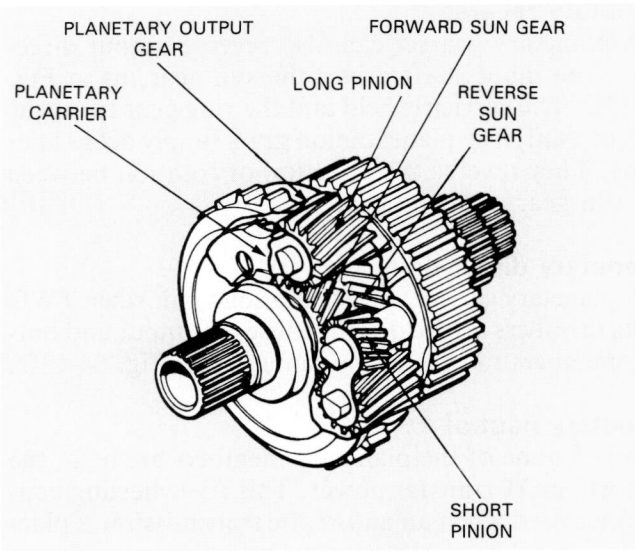

Fig. 54-14. Compound planetary gearset acts like two gearset assemblies mounted together. Normally, a common ring gear is used for two separate sets of planet gears. (Subaru)

planetary units in one housing or ring gear. It may have two sun gears or a long sun gear to operate two sets of planet pinion gears, Fig. 54-14.

With this design, short planet gears engage forward sun gear. Long planet gears mesh with the rear sun gear. The ring gear engages both sets of planet gears.

Another design, called Simpson Compound Gearset, uses a long sun gear to operate two sets of planet gears on the same ring gear. This type is common.

A compound planetary gearset is used because it can provide more forward gear ratios than a simple planetary gearset.

CLUTCHES AND BANDS

Automatic transmission *clutches* and *bands* are friction devices that drive or lock planetary gearset members. They are used to cause the gearsets to transfer power. Refer again to Figs. 54-1 and 54-11.

Multiple disc clutches

A *multiple disc clutch* has several clutch discs that can be used to couple or hold planetary gearset members. As shown in Fig. 54-15, the front clutch assembly usually drives a planetary sun gear. The next clutch transmits power to the planetary ring gear when engaged. This can vary, however.

A clutch assembly generally consists of a drum, hub, apply piston, spring(s), driving discs, driven discs, pressure plate, and snap rings.

Clutch construction

The **clutch drum,** also called a *clutch cylinder,* encloses the apply piston, discs, pressure plate, seals, and other parts of the clutch assembly, Fig. 54-15.

The **clutch hub** fits inside the clutch discs and clutch drum. It has teeth on its outer surface that engage the teeth on the driving discs. The front clutch hub is also splined to the transmission input shaft.

The **driving discs** are usually covered with friction lining. They have teeth on their inside diameter that engage the clutch hub. See Fig. 54-15.

The **driven discs** are steel plates that have outer tabs that lock into the clutch drum. A driven disc fits between each driving disc. This enables the hub and friction discs to turn the steel discs and drum when the clutch is activated.

The **clutch apply piston** slides back and forth inside the clutch drum to clamp the driving and driven discs together. Seals fit on the piston to prevent fluid leakage during clutch application.

The **pressure plate** serves as a stop for clutch discs when the piston is applied. The piston pushes the discs against the pressure plate. Look at Fig. 54-15.

A **clutch spring** or springs are used to push the apply piston away from the clutch discs during clutch disengagement. One is shown in Fig. 54-15.

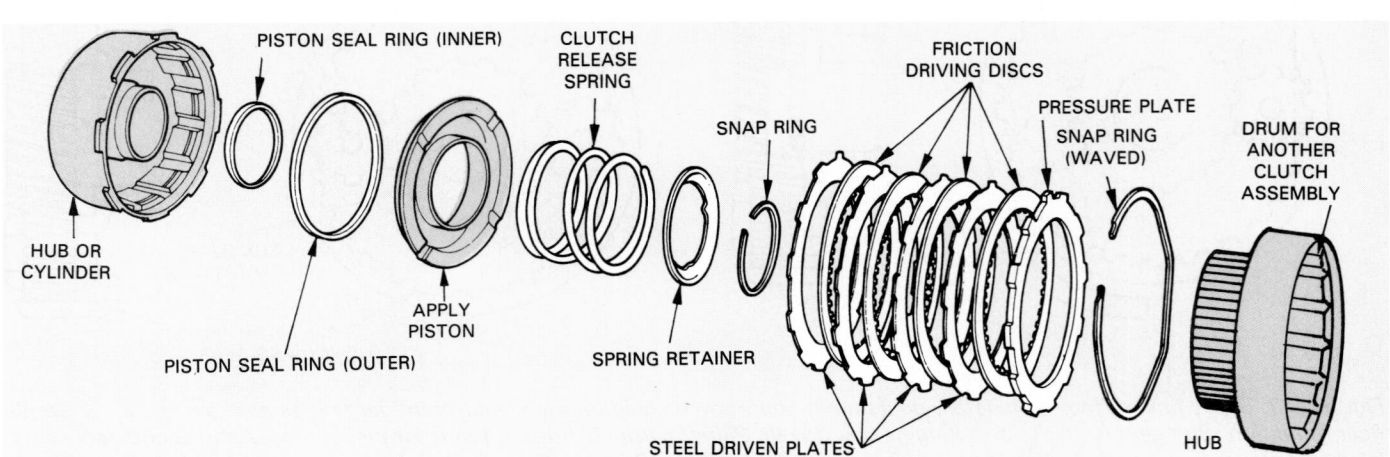

Fig. 54-15. Study construction of clutch assembly from automatic transmission. Clutch parts and hub fit inside clutch drum. Also note difference in clutch discs. Driving discs are splined to hub. Driven discs are locked in drum by tabs. (Chrysler)

Clutch operation

When oil pressure is blocked from the piston, the return spring pushes the clutch discs apart, Fig. 54-16A. Power is no longer transferred through the clutch. The driving and driven discs are free to turn independently.

During clutch engagement, oil pressure is routed into the clutch drum. Shown in Fig. 54-16B, oil pressure acts on the large piston. The piston is then forced into the clutch discs. Friction locks the driving and driven discs together to transfer power through the clutch assembly.

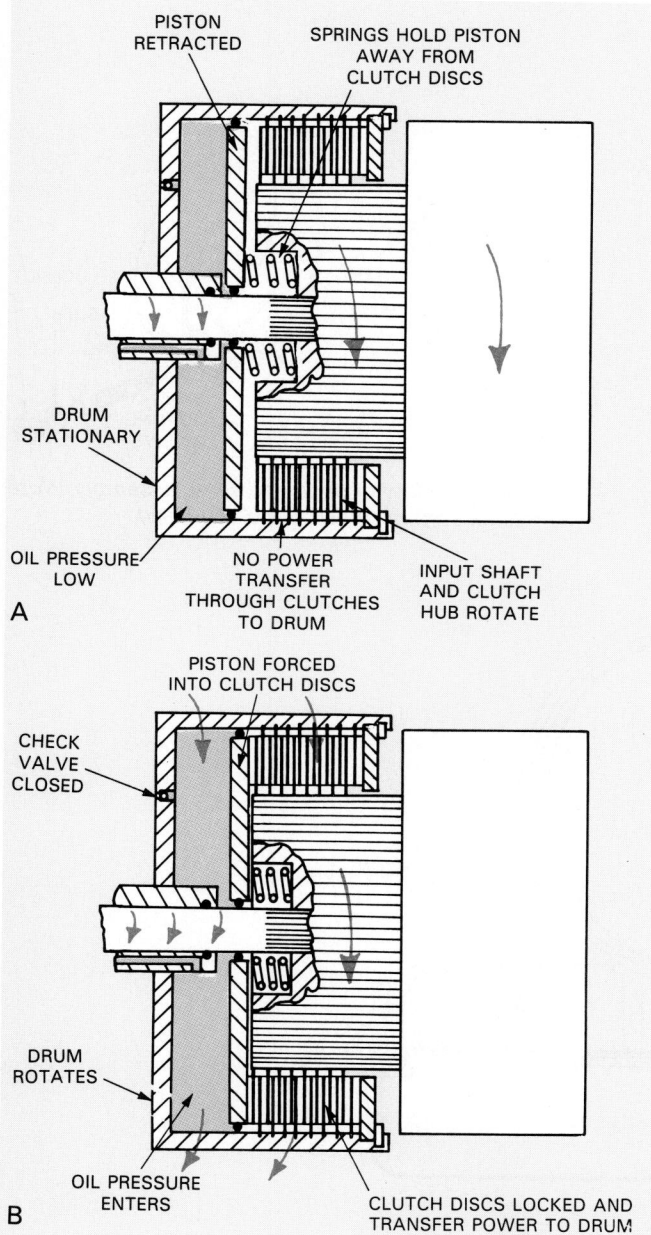

Fig. 54-16. Basic clutch operation. A — No oil pressure enters drum. Springs hold piston away from clutch discs. Input shaft turns clutch hub and driving discs but driven discs and drum remain stationary. B — Oil is routed into clutch drum. Oil pressure pushes piston into clutch discs, forcing discs into pressure plate. This locks discs, hub, and drum together. Power is then transferred from input to drum.

Driving shell

A *driving shell* or *clutch shell* is commonly used to transfer power to one of the planetary sun gears, Fig. 54-17. It is a thin, metal cylinder-shaped part that frequently connects the front clutch drum and sun gear.

The shell may surround the second clutch assembly and forward planetary gearset. Tabs on the shell fit into notches on the front clutch drum. This makes the shell, drum, and sun gear turn together.

Bands and servos

Automatic transmission *bands* are also friction devices for holding members of the planetary gearsets. Two or three bands are commonly used in modern transmissions. Bands are shown in Figs. 54-1, 54-11, 54-17, and 54-18.

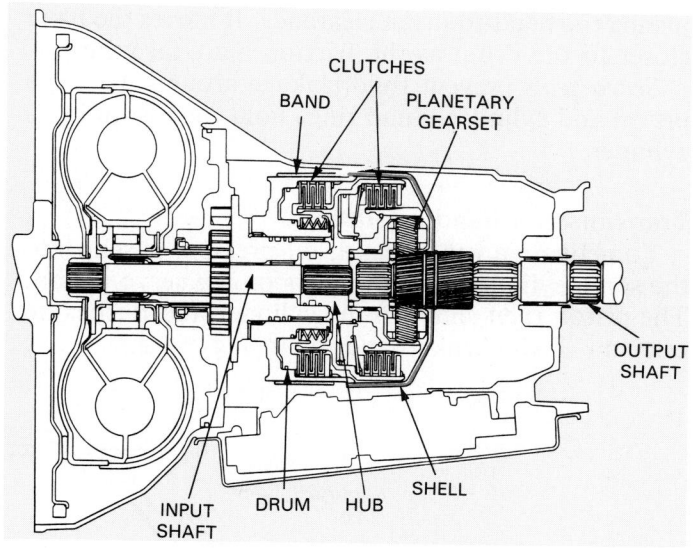

Fig. 54-17. Drive shell connects front drum to sun gear. Note how it surrounds second clutch assembly and front planetary gearset. When front clutch is locked, shell turns sun gear. Also note band used to hold front drum and sun gear stationary. (Ford)

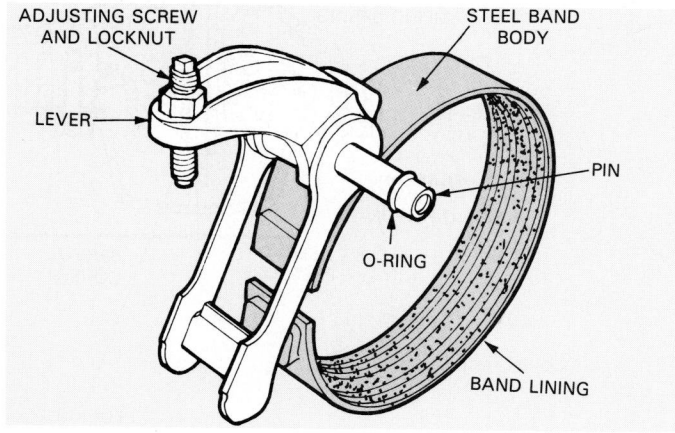

Fig. 54-18. Band is steel strap with friction lining on its inner surface. One end of band is anchored in case. (Dodge)

Servos are apply pistons that operate the bands. Fig. 54-19 shows the parts of a band and servo assembly.

Band and servo construction

A band is a steel strap with *lining* (friction material) on its inner surface. The band's lining can be clamped around clutch drum to stop drum rotation.

The friction material on the inside of the band is designed to operate in automatic transmission fluid. It resists the lubricating qualities of the fluid.

The *servo piston* is a metal plunger that operates in a cylinder machined in the transmission case. Rubber seals fit around the outside of the piston to prevent fluid leakage. See Fig. 54-20.

A rod on the servo piston attaches to one end of the brake band. The other end of the brake band is anchored to the transmission case.

A *band adjustment screw* provides a means of adjusting the band-to-drum clearance. It moves the band closer to the drum as the friction material wears.

Servo seals prevent fluid leakage around the servo piston and cylinder. Snap rings hold the piston in its cylinder.

Transmission band operation

To activate a brake band, oil pressure is sent into the servo cylinder. Pressure acts on the servo piston. The piston then slides in the cylinder and pushes on one end of the brake band, as in Fig. 54-20.

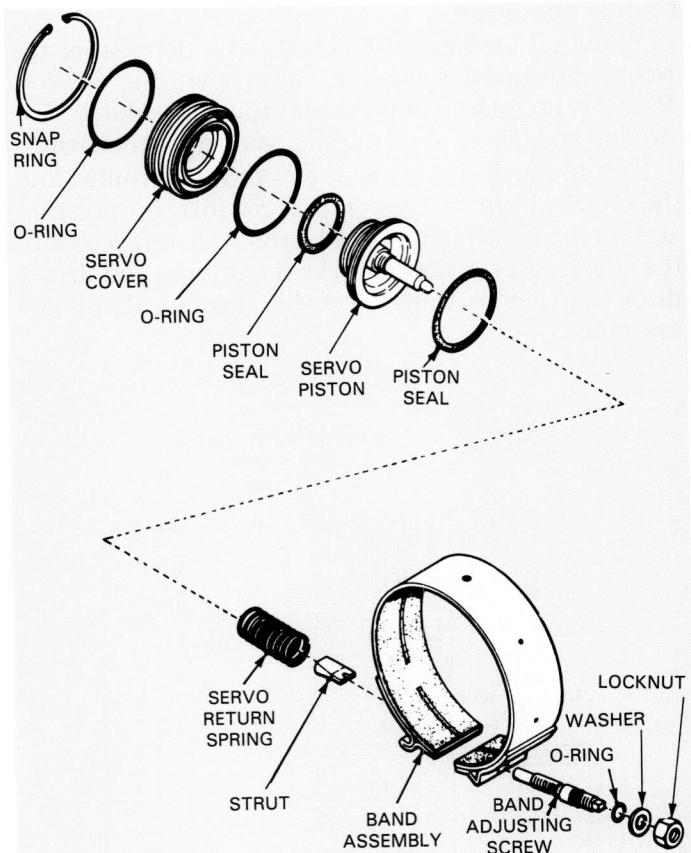

Fig. 54-19. Exploded view of band and servo assembly. Note relationship between parts. (Subaru)

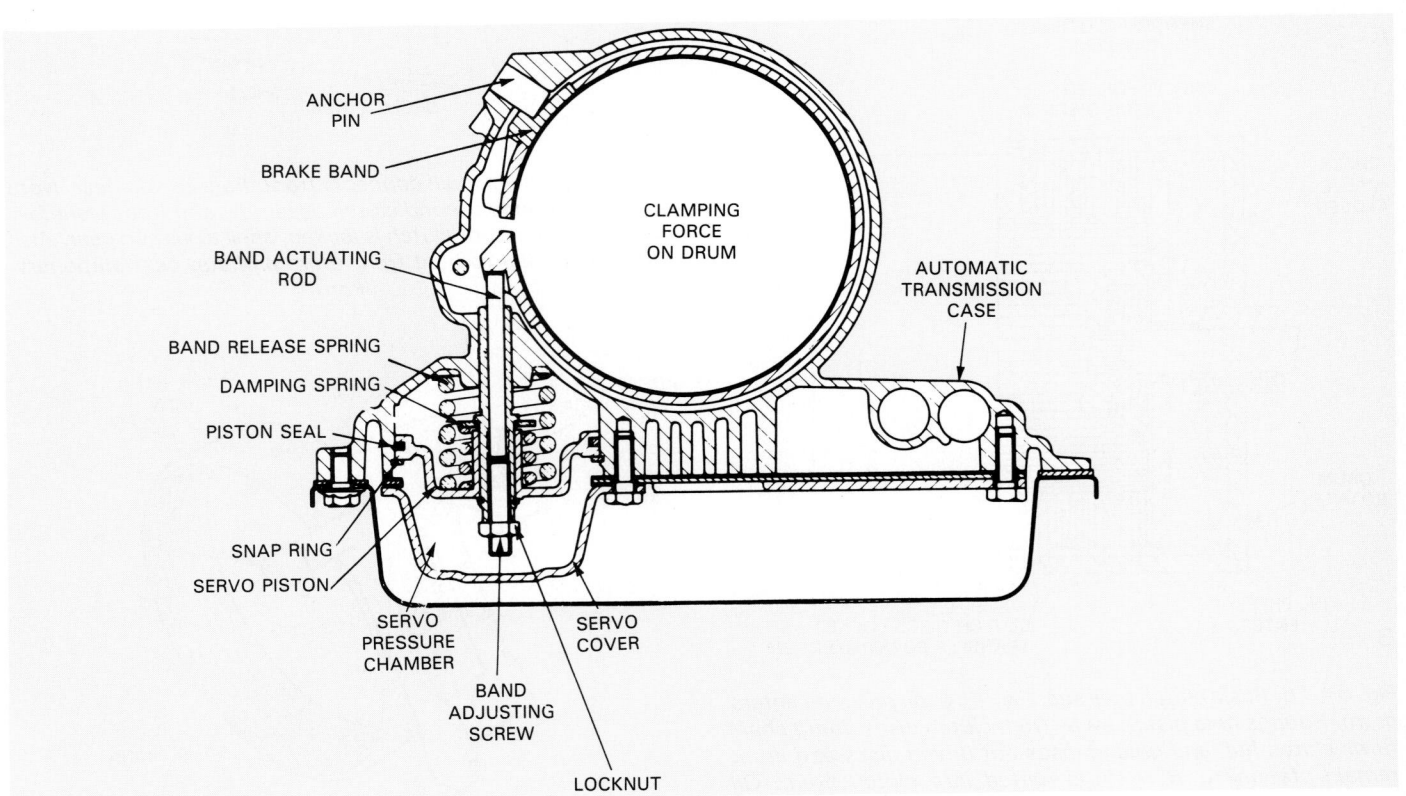

Fig. 54-20. Servo piston and band action. When oil pressure enters servo pressure chamber, servo piston slides up in cylinder. Actuating rod then pushes on band to squeeze band inward on drum. (Fiat)

Since the other end of the band is anchored, the band tightens or squeezes around the drum. The friction material rubs on the drum and stops it from turning. This keeps one of the planetary components from revolving.

When the oil flow to the piston servo is blocked, the servo spring pushes on the piston. This slides the piston rod away from the band. The band then releases the drum and planetary gearset member.

Accumulator

An *accumulator* is used in the apply circuit of a band or clutch to cushion initial application. It temporarily absorbs some of the oil pressure to cause slower movement of the apply piston.

OVERRUNNING CLUTCHES

Besides the bands and clutches, an *overrunning clutch* can be used to hold a planetary gearset member. It is a one-way, roller clutch that locks in one direction and freewheels in the other.

An overrunning clutch for the planetary gears is similar to the ones in a torque converter stator or an electric starting motor drive gear. The typical locations of automatic transmission overrunning clutches (stator clutch and gearset clutch) are illustrated in Fig. 54-11.

A planetary gearset overrunning clutch consists of an inner race, set of springs, rollers, and an outer race. Fig. 54-21 shows overrunning clutch operation.

HYDRAULIC VALVE ACTION

The basic action of a hydraulic valve and a piston are illustrated in Fig. 54-22. Oil pump pressure causes

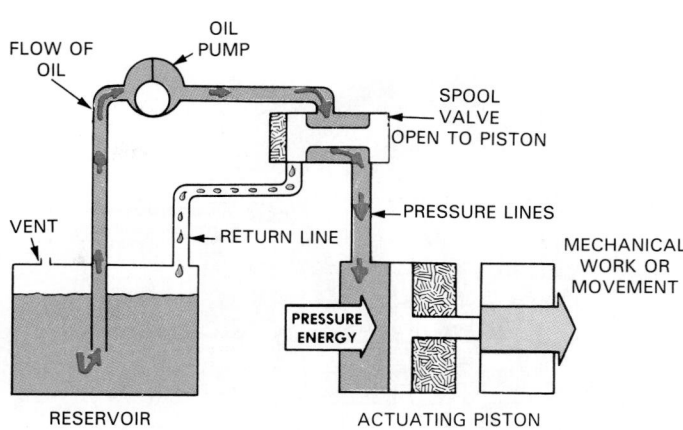

Fig. 54-22. Basic hydraulic circuit. Pump draws oil out of reservoir and forces it through spool valve. In this position, spool valve routes oil to piston. Piston uses oil pressure to produce movement or clamping pressure. (Chrysler)

oil to flow through the spool valve pressure lines to the left end of the piston cylinder. This pushes the piston to the right.

When the spool valve is moved the other way, pump pressure is not sent to the piston. The piston is then forced back into its cylinder.

Valves like this are used to operate the band servos and clutch pistons.

HYDRAULIC SYSTEM

The *hydraulic system* for an automatic transmission typically consists of a pump, pressure regulator valve, manual valve, vacuum modulator valve, governor valve, shift valves, servos, pistons, and valve body.

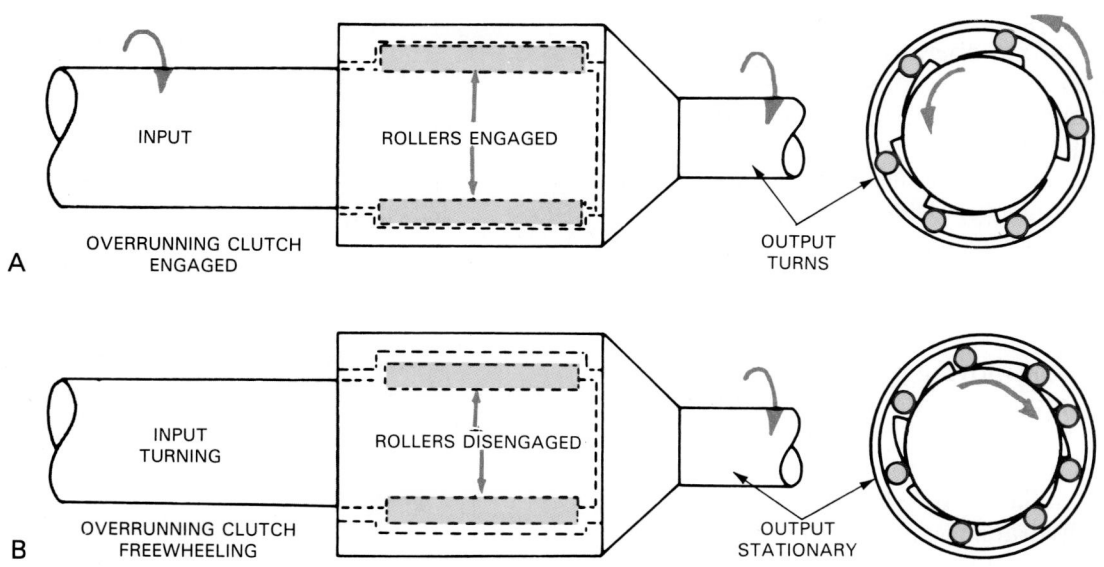

Fig. 54-21. Overrunning or one-way clutch action A — When driven in one direction, rollers lock between ramps on inner race and on outer race. Both races turn together. This action can also be used to stop movement of planetary member, for example. B — When turned in other direction, rollers walk off ramps. Two races are free to turn independently. (Deere & Co.)

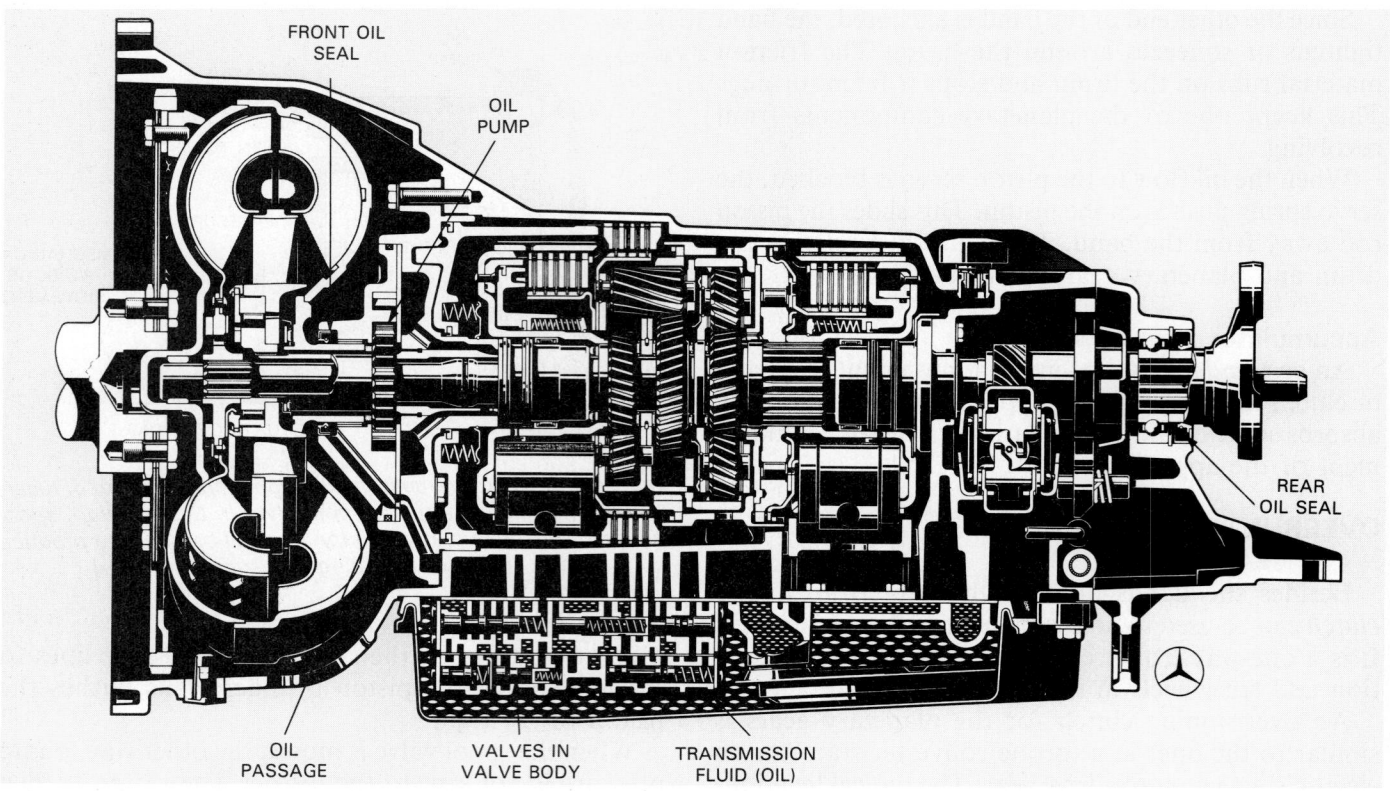

Fig. 54-23. Oil pump is normally located in front of case. Oil is drawn out of pan, circulated through passages to hydraulic components. Also note location of oil seals.   (Mercedes Benz)

These parts work together to form the "brain" (sensing) and "muscles" (control) of an automatic transmission. See Fig. 54-23.

The hydraulic system also forces oil to high friction points in the transmission. This prevents wear and overheating by lubricating the moving parts.

Hydraulic pump (oil pump)

The *hydraulic pump,* also called the *oil pump,* produces the pressure to operate an automatic transmission. Automatic transmissions can have one or two pumps. They are often located behind the torque converter or in the valve body.

Look at Fig. 54-23. The sleeve or collar on the rear of the torque converter drives the pump.

The automatic transmission oil pump has several basic functions:

1. Produces pressure to operate the clutches, bands, and gearsets.
2. Lubricates the moving parts in the transmission.
3. Keeps the torque converter filled with oil for proper operation.
4. Circulates oil through the transmission and cooling tank (radiator) to transfer heat.
5. Operates hydraulic valves in the transmission.

There are two commonly used oil pumps: the gear type and the rotor type, Fig. 54-24.

When the torque converter spins the oil pump, transmission fluid is drawn into the pump from the

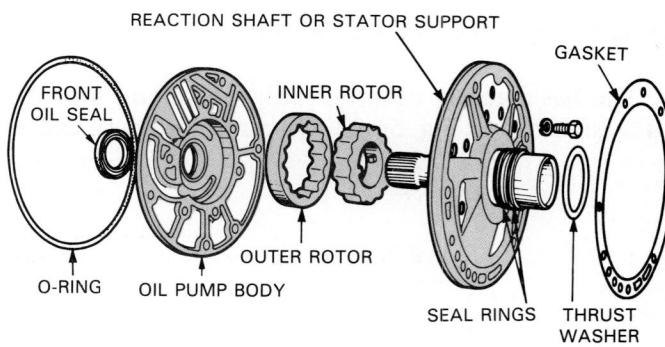

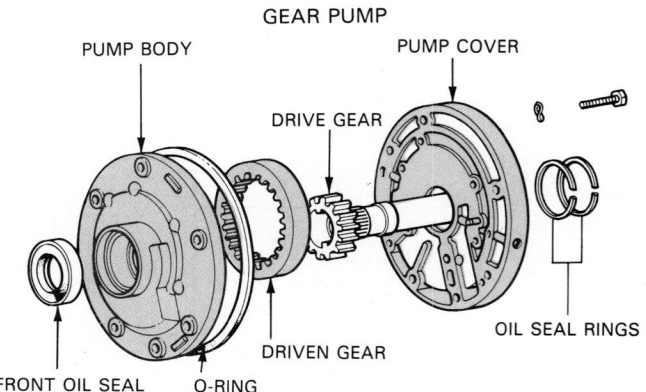

Fig. 54-24. Two basic types of automatic transmission pumps: rotor and gear. Study similarities and differences. Torque converter normally drives pump. (Chrysler and Toyota)

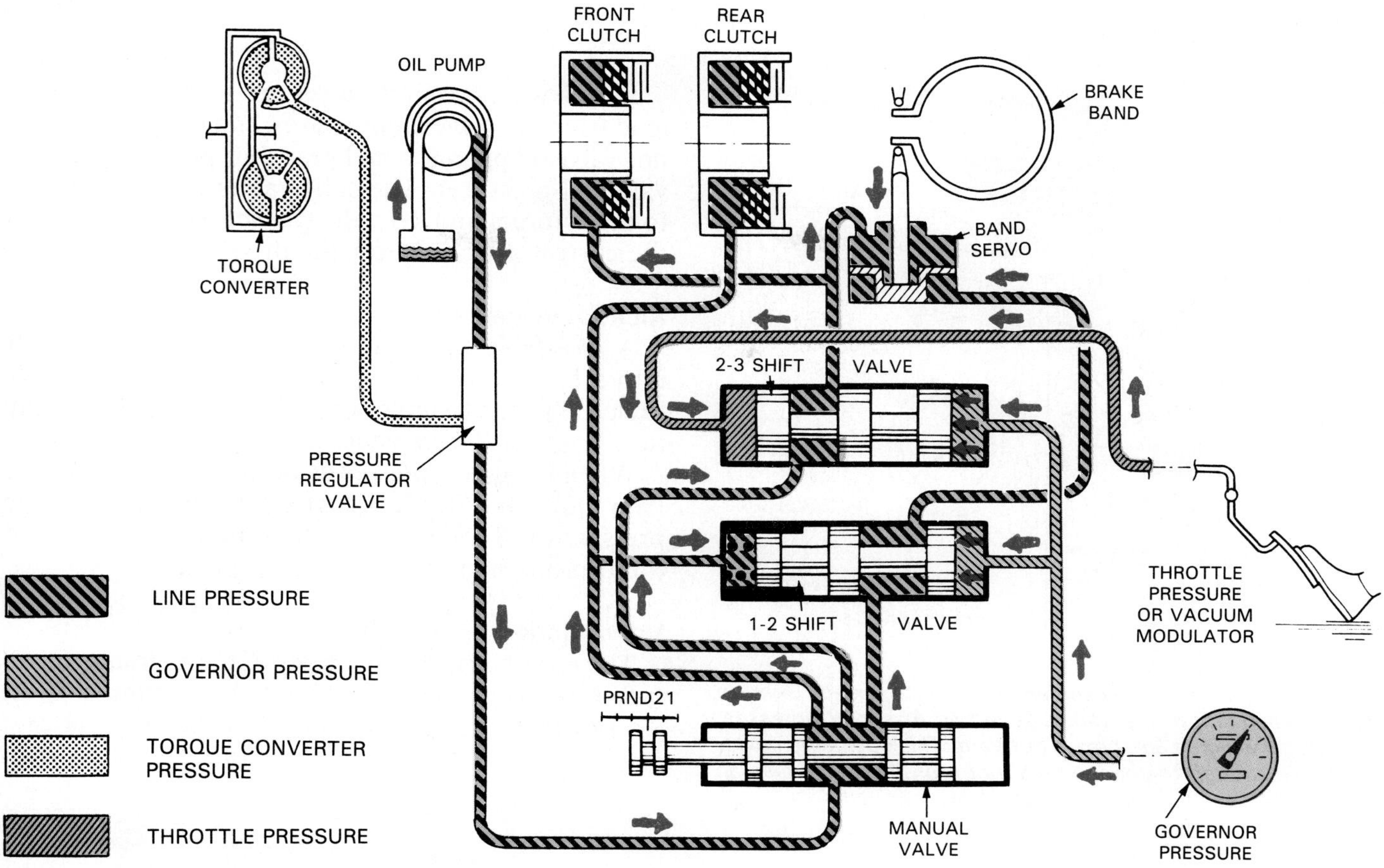

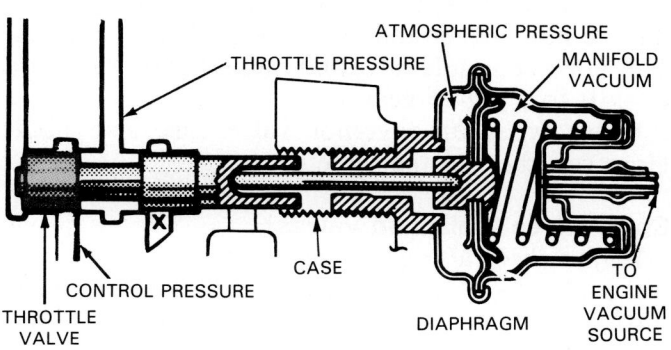

Fig. 54-25. Simplified circuit showing hydraulic action in automatic transmission. Manual valve pressure, throttle valve pressure, and governor valve pressure operate balance or shift valves. Shift valves then direct oil pressure to correct clutch or band pistons. Study this diagram carefully. (Nissan)

Legend:
- LINE PRESSURE
- GOVERNOR PRESSURE
- TORQUE CONVERTER PRESSURE
- THROTTLE PRESSURE

Diagram labels: TORQUE CONVERTER, OIL PUMP, FRONT CLUTCH, REAR CLUTCH, BRAKE BAND, BAND SERVO, PRESSURE REGULATOR VALVE, 2-3 SHIFT VALVE, 1-2 SHIFT VALVE, THROTTLE PRESSURE OR VACUUM MODULATOR, PRND21, MANUAL VALVE, GOVERNOR PRESSURE

pan. The pump compresses the oil and forces it to the pressure regulator. This is illustrated in Fig. 54-25.

Pressure regulator

The *pressure regulator* limits the maximum amount of oil pressure developed by the oil pump, Fig. 54-25. It is a spring-loaded valve that routes excess pump pressure out of the hydraulic system. This assures proper transmission operation.

Manual valve

A *manual valve,* operated by the shift mechanism, allows the driver to select park, neutral, reverse, or different drive ranges. When the gear shift lever is moved, the shift linkage moves the manual valve. As a result, the valve routes oil pressure to the correct components in the transmission. Look at Fig. 54-25.

Vacuum modulator valve

The *vacuum modulator valve,* also termed *throttle valve,* senses engine load (vacuum) and determines when the transmission should shift to a higher gear. Refer to Figs. 54-25 and 54-26. A vacuum line runs from the engine intake manifold to this valve.

As engine vacuum (load) rises and falls, it moves the diaphragm inside the vacuum modulator. This, in turn, moves the rod and hydraulic valve to change throttle control pressure in the transmission. In this way, the

vacuum modulator can match transmission shift points to engine loading.

For example, if a vehicle is climbing a steep hill (under a heavy pull), engine vacuum will be very low. This will allow the spring in the modulator to slide the modulator valve further into the transmission. The valve then directs oil pressure to delay the upshift. The transmission stays in a lower gear longer to allow the car to accelerate up the hill. Look at Fig. 54-26.

Fig. 54-26. Vacuum modulator operates throttle valve. Engine vacuum allows modulator to sense engine load. For example, with engine acceleration and high load, vacuum drops. The vacuum modulator spring could then overcome vacuum pull on the diaphragm. The spring would push the valve to the left. This would alter throttle oil pressure, keeping the transmission in a lower gear. (Ford)

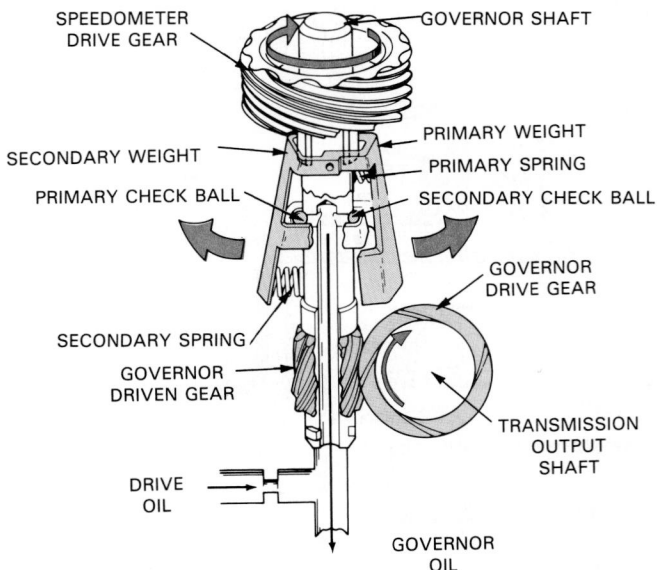

Fig. 54-27. Governor senses engine vehicle speed. Gear on transmission output shaft spins governor. As speed increases, centrifugal weights are thrown outward. This opens the governor valve enough to change governor pressure and cause an upshift. (Cadillac)

Governor valve

The *governor valve* senses vehicle speed to help control gear shifting. The vacuum modulator and governor work together to determine shift points. See Fig. 54-25.

Illustrated in Fig. 54-27 is one type of governor assembly. It consists of a drive gear, centrifugal weights, springs, hydraulic valve, and shaft. The governor gear is usually meshed with a gear on the transmission output shaft. Whenever the car and output shaft are moving, the centrifugal weights rotate.

When the output shaft and weights are spinning slowly, the weights are held IN by the governor springs. This causes a low pressure output and the transmission remains in a low gear ratio.

As engine and shaft speed increase, the weights are thrown out further and governor pressure increases. This moves the shift valve and causes the transmission to shift to a higher gear.

Other types of governor valves are also used. However, they do the same job.

Shift valves (balanced valves)

Shift valves, also called *balanced valves,* use control pressure (oil pressure from regulator, governor, throttle, and manual valves) to operate the bands, servos, and gearsets. Fig. 54-25 shows how the shift valves are connected to the other transmission components.

Oil pressure from the other transmission valves act on each end of the shift valves. For example, if the pressure from the governor is high and the pressure from the throttle and manual valves are low, the shift valves will be moved sideways in their cylinder.

In this way, the shift valves are sensitive to engine load (throttle valve oil pressure), engine speed (governor valve oil pressure) and gear shift position (manual valve oil pressure). The shift valves move according to these forces and keep the transmission shifted into the correct gear ratio for the driving conditions.

Kickdown valve

A *kickdown valve* causes the transmission to shift into a lower gear during fast acceleration. A rod or cable links the carburetor or fuel injection throttle body to a lever on the transmission.

When the driver presses down on the gas pedal, the lever moves the kickdown valve. This causes hydraulic pressure to overide normal shift control pressure and the transmission downshifts, Fig. 54-28.

Valve body

The *valve body* contains many of the hydraulic valves (pressure regulating valve, shift valves, manual valve, etc.) of an automatic transmission. See Fig. 54-28.

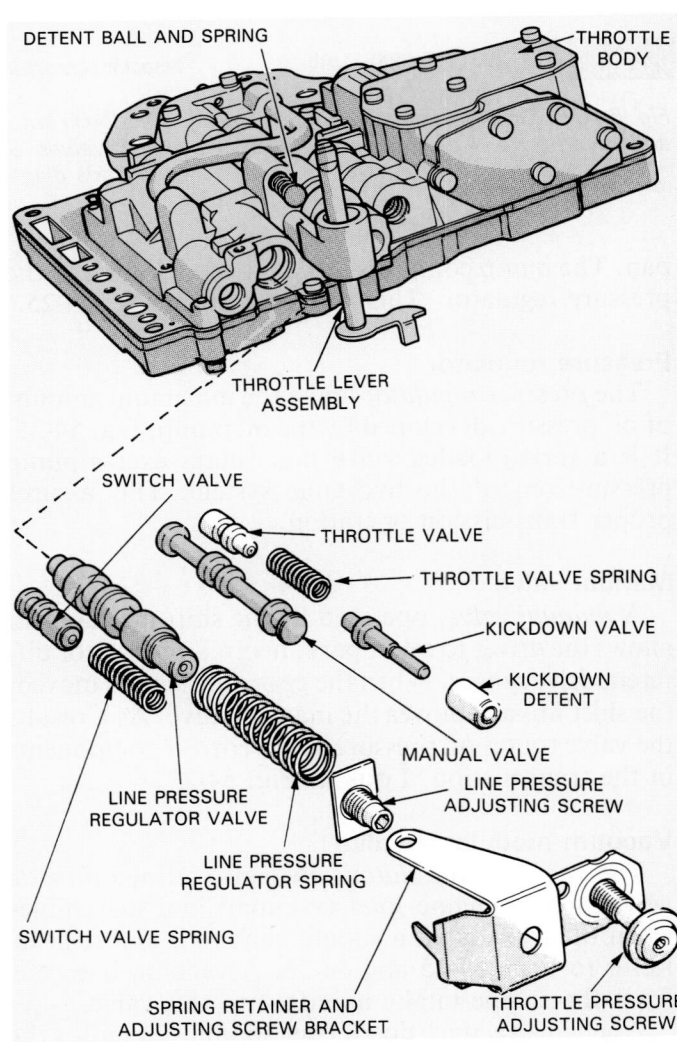

Fig. 54-28. Valve body bolts to bottom of transmission case. It houses manual valve, pressure regulator valve, kickdown valve, and other valves. (Plymouth)

The valve body bolts to the bottom of the transmission case. It is housed in the transmission pan. A filter or screen is usually attached to the bottom of the valve body, Fig. 54-29.

Passages in the valve body route fluid from the pump to the valves and then into the transmission case. Passages in the case carry fluid to the other hydraulic components.

Automatic transmission fluid

Automatic transmission fluid is a special type oil having several additives that make it compatible with the friction clutches and bands in the transmission. Different types of automatic transmission fluids are available for different transmissions.

Transmission oil cooling

A tremendous amount of heat is developed inside an automatic transmission. When the torque converter slips, friction heats the fluid. This heat must be removed or transmission failure could result.

Many transmissions have an oil cooling system which includes external oil lines and a cooling tank inside the engine radiator. Look at Fig. 54-30.

When the engine is running, the transmission pump forces oil through the cooling lines and into the radiator tank. Since transmission oil is hotter than the engine coolant, oil temperature drops. The cooled oil returns to the transmission through the other line.

Some cars, especially those designed to pull a heavy load (trailers, boats) have an auxiliary *transmission oil cooler*. It is a small radiator, separate from the engine radiator. Air passes over the radiator to cool the transmission fluid.

PARKING PAWL

A *parking pawl* is used to lock the transmission output shaft and keep the car from rolling when not in use. Fig. 54-31 shows its basic action.

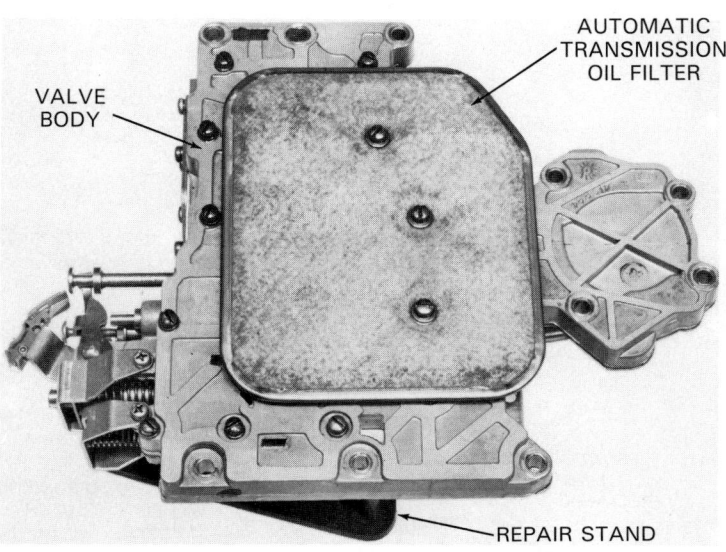

Fig. 54-29. Oil filter is fastened to bottom of valve body. It removes particles of dirt before they can enter hydraulic circuit. (Chrysler Corp.)

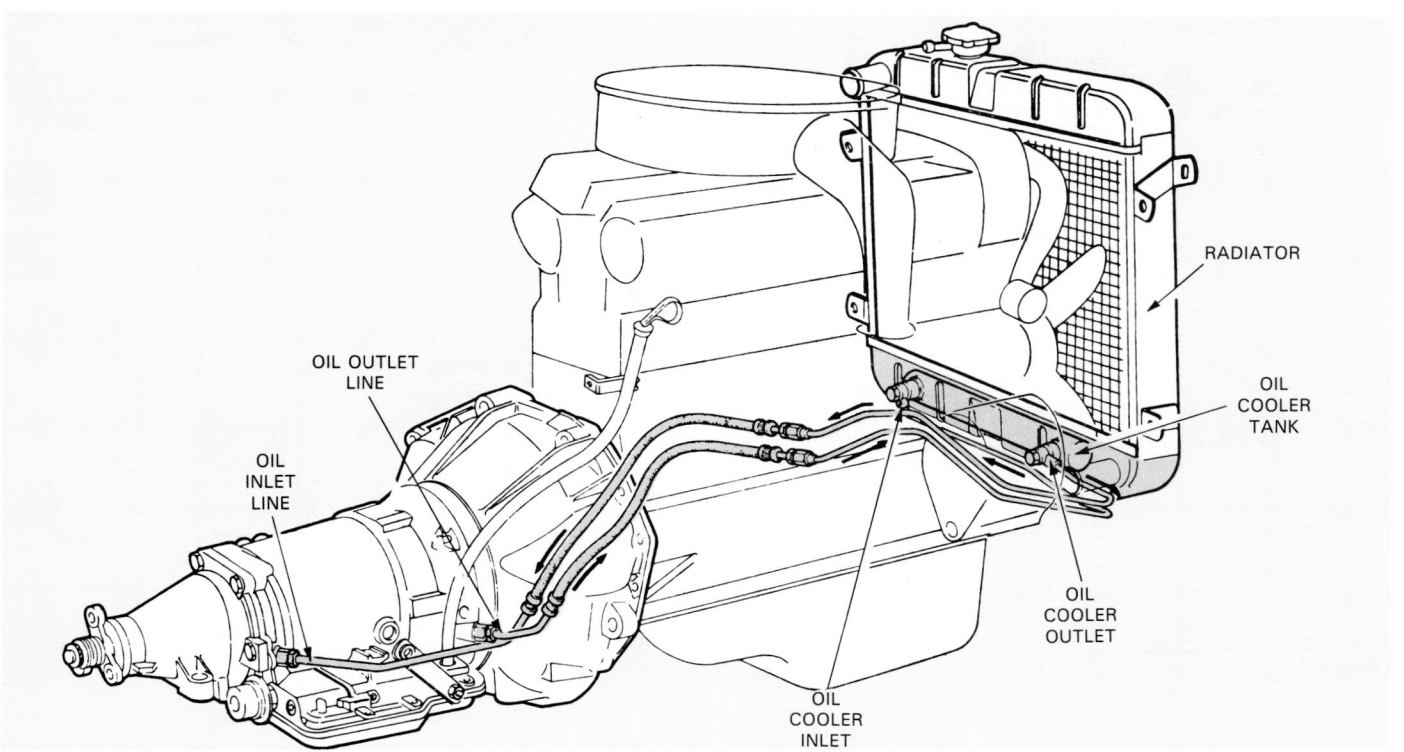

Fig. 54-30. Oil cooler tank is commonly used in transmission. Oil pump pushes oil through lines and cooler tank to maintain acceptable oil temperature. (Fiat)

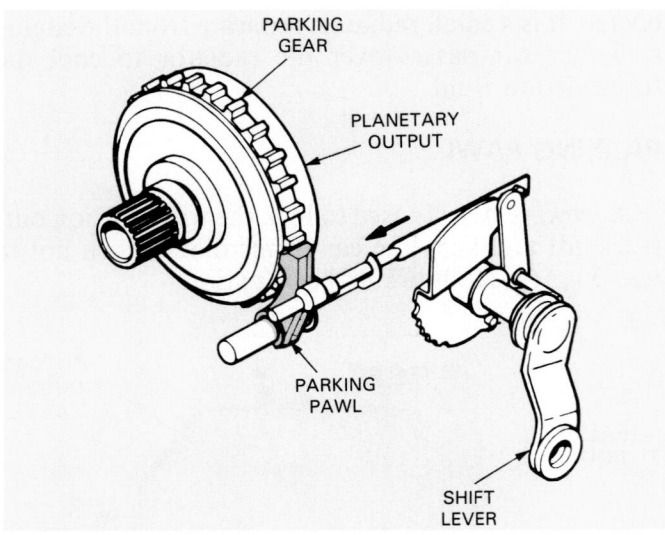

Fig. 54-31. Parking pawl is simply a latch that locks into large teeth on parking gear. Since pawl is mounted on case, this locks parking gear and output shaft. (Subaru)

AUTOMATIC TRANSMISSION POWER FLOW

The flow of power through an automatic transmission depends on its specific design. However, you should have a GENERAL understanding of how power is transmitted through the major parts of modern transmissions.

Fig. 54-32 shows how torque moves from the input shaft to the output shaft. This is a typical three-speed transmission. Study each illustration carefully, noting which clutches, bands, and gearset members are activated.

Overdrive power flow

Fig. 54-33 shows the power flow through a late model, four-speed, overdrive automatic transmission in high gear. This is a new design that uses two input shafts (turbine shaft and direct input shaft). Trace the power flow and compare it to the other more conventional transmissions covered earlier.

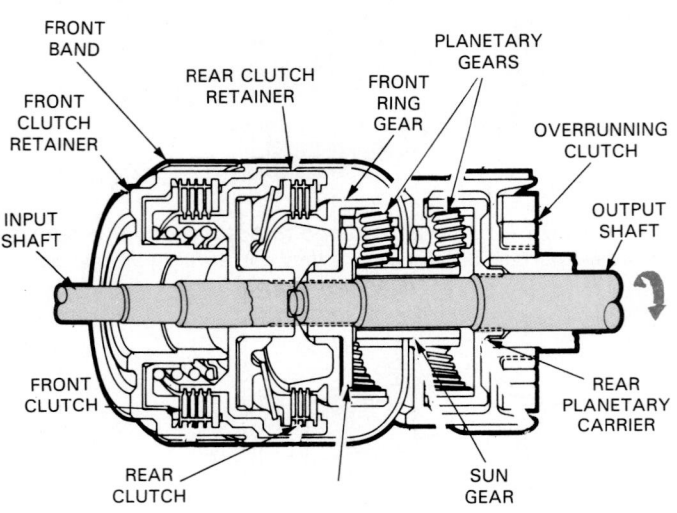

A — Study parts relating to power flow.

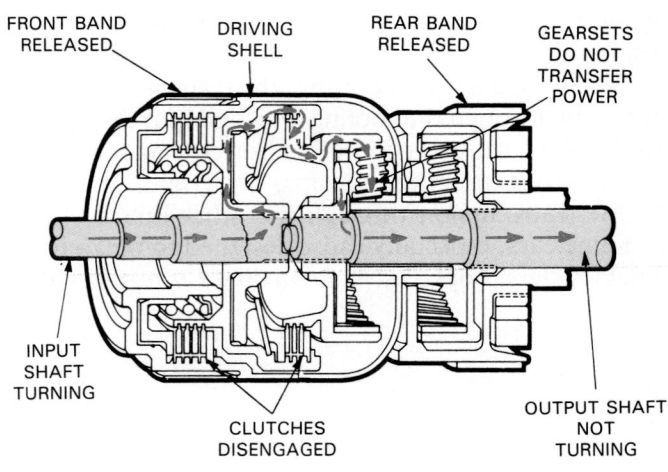

B — Neutral. Clutches and bands disengaged. Input shaft and hub turn but power does not flow through clutches or drum. Output stationary.

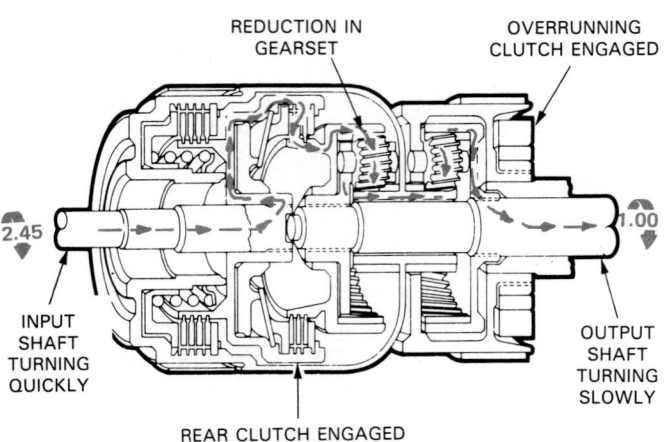

C — First gear. Rear clutch and overrunning clutch engaged. Gear reduction through planetary gearsets results in high ratio, high torque output to driveline.

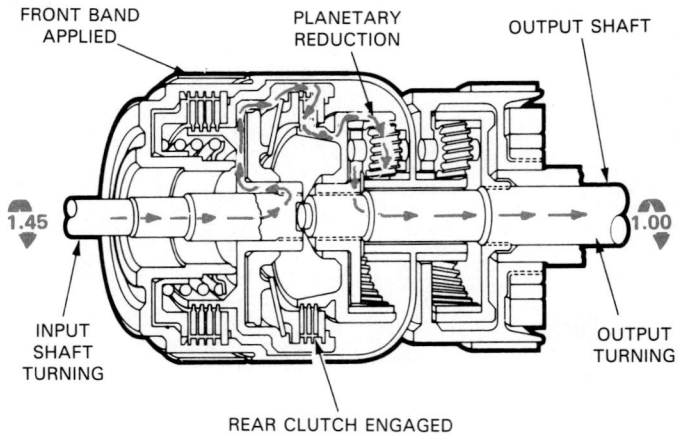

D — Second gear. Front band applied. Rear clutch engaged. Power flows through input, hub, clutch, drum, and front gearset to output. Less reduction results.

Fig. 54-32. Power flow through a typical automatic transmission. (Chrysler)

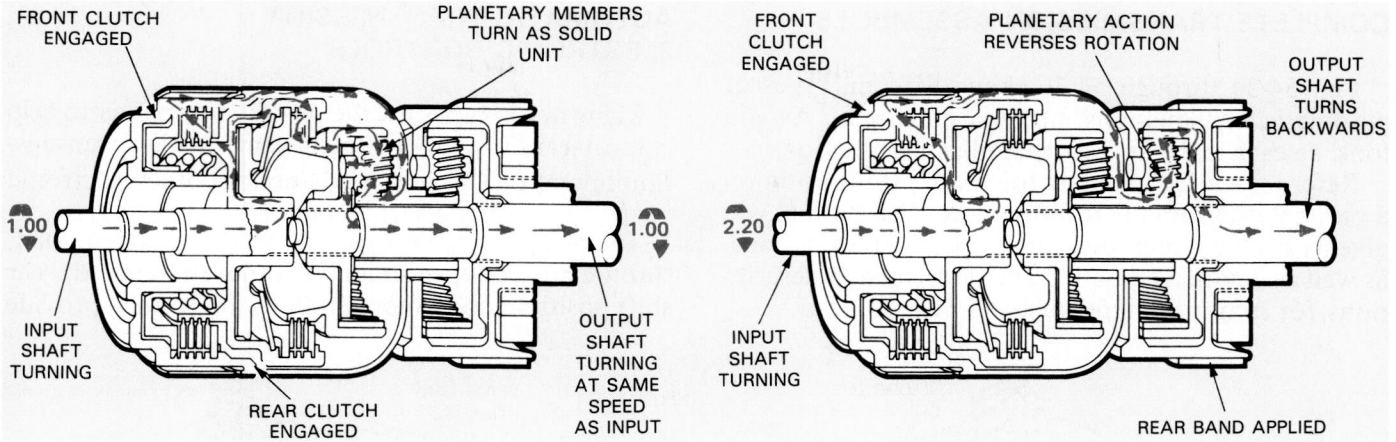

E — Third gear. Front and rear clutches engaged. Planetary members locked for direct drive. One-to-one ratio for higher vehicle speeds results.

F — Reverse. Front clutch and rear band applied. Power flows through clutch, shell, and sun gear to rear planetary gearset which reverses rotation.

(Fig. 54-32 continued)

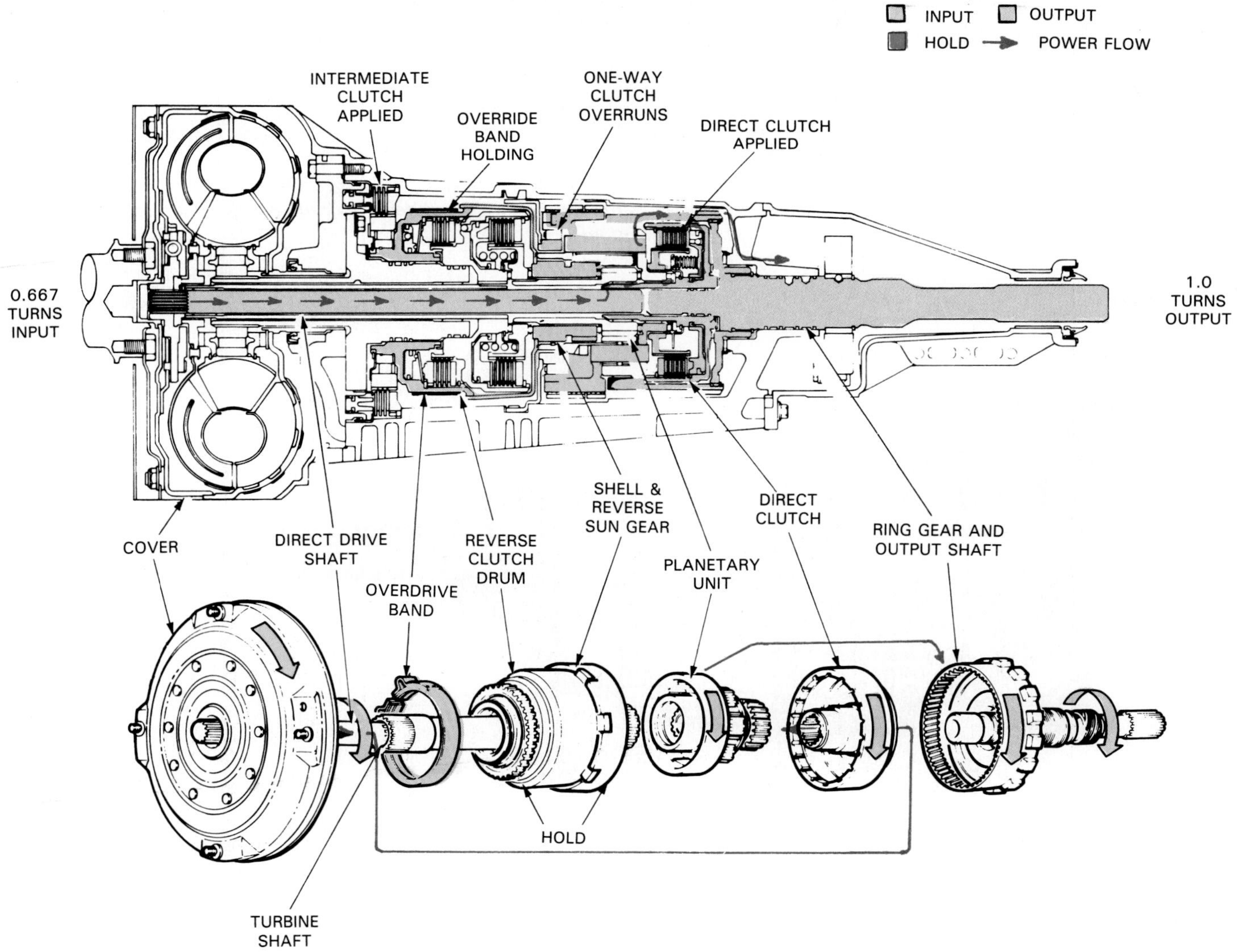

INPUT OUTPUT
HOLD → POWER FLOW

INTERMEDIATE CLUTCH APPLIED

OVERRIDE BAND HOLDING

ONE-WAY CLUTCH OVERRUNS

DIRECT CLUTCH APPLIED

0.667 TURNS INPUT

1.0 TURNS OUTPUT

COVER

DIRECT DRIVE SHAFT

OVERDRIVE BAND

REVERSE CLUTCH DRUM

SHELL & REVERSE SUN GEAR

DIRECT CLUTCH

PLANETARY UNIT

DIRECT CLUTCH

RING GEAR AND OUTPUT SHAFT

HOLD

TURBINE SHAFT

Fig. 54-33. Power flow in high gear of modern four-speed automatic with overdrive. Study differences with transmissions already covered in chapter. (Ford)

Automatic Transmission Fundamentals 705

COMPLETE TRANSMISSION ASSEMBLIES

Fig. 54-34 through 54-36 show different types of automatic transmissions. Study each closely. As you look at each part, try to remember its function.

Refer to service manuals for more information on a particular automatic transmission. The manual will give hydraulic circuit diagrams, specific illustrations, as well as detailed operating and construction descriptions for major components.

AUTOMATIC TRANSMISSION ELECTRONIC CONTROLS

Many new vehicles use the on-board computer to help control transmission shift points and monitor transmission operation. A simplified diagram of an electronic control system is given in Fig. 54-37.

The computer typically monitors engine speed, load, throttle position, transmission output shaft speed, gear shift position, and other variables. It can then provide

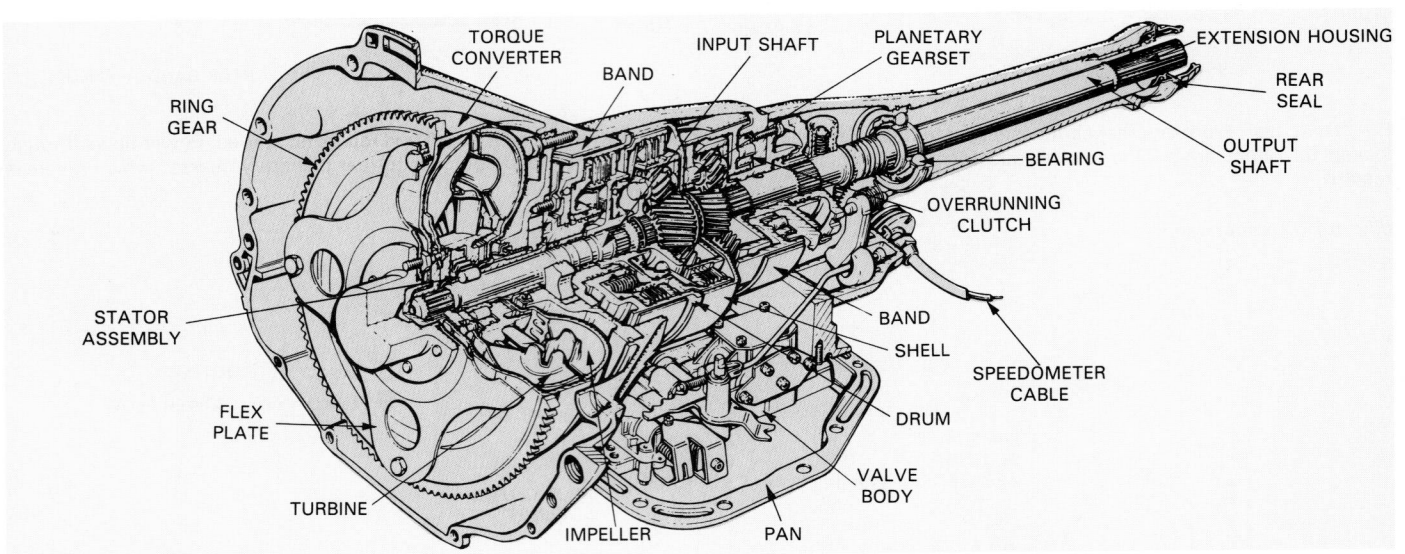

Fig. 54-34. This is a three-speed automatic transmission. Study part locations. Can you recall their function? (Dodge)

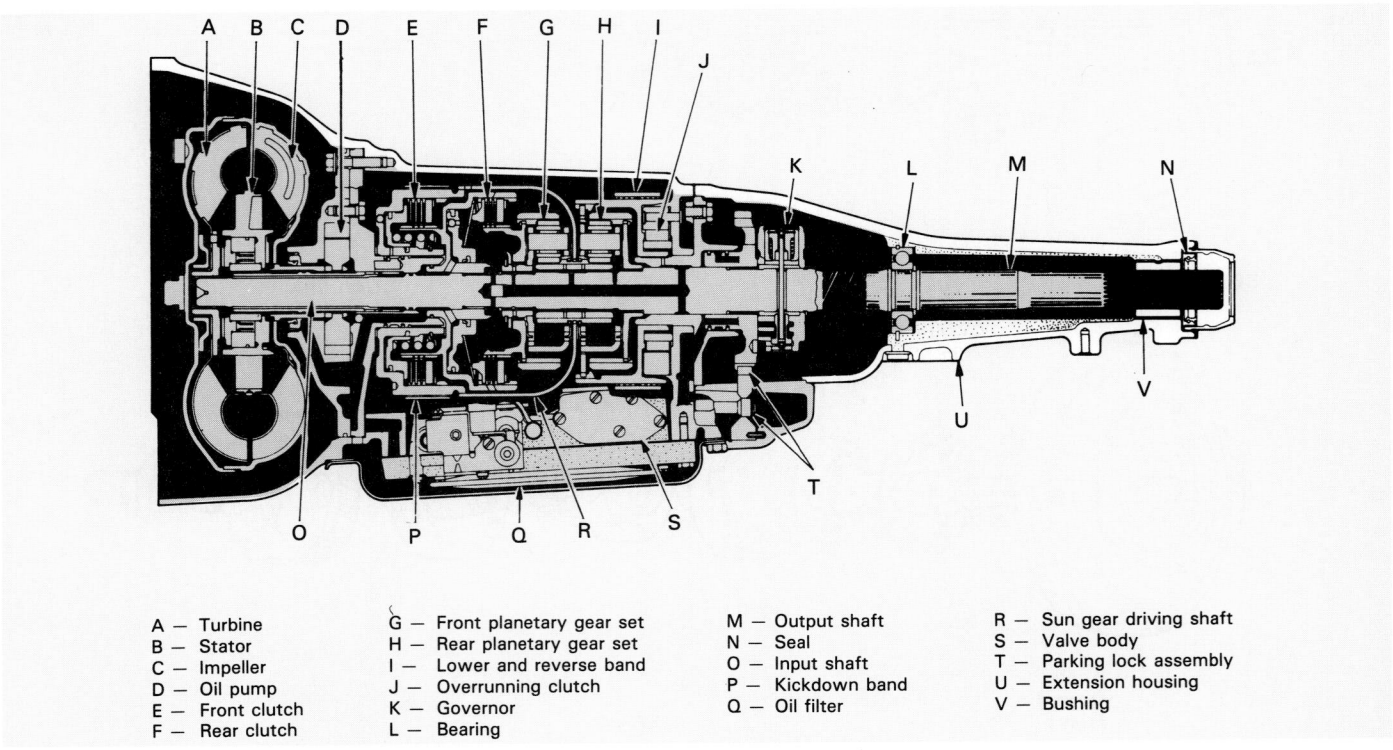

A — Turbine	G — Front planetary gear set
B — Stator	H — Rear planetary gear set
C — Impeller	I — Lower and reverse band
D — Oil pump	J — Overrunning clutch
E — Front clutch	K — Governor
F — Rear clutch	L — Bearing

M — Output shaft	R — Sun gear driving shaft
N — Seal	S — Valve body
O — Input shaft	T — Parking lock assembly
P — Kickdown band	U — Extension housing
Q — Oil filter	V — Bushing

Fig. 54-35. Cutaway of Chrysler Torqueflite transmission. Compare it to the transmission in previous illustration. (Chrysler Corporation)

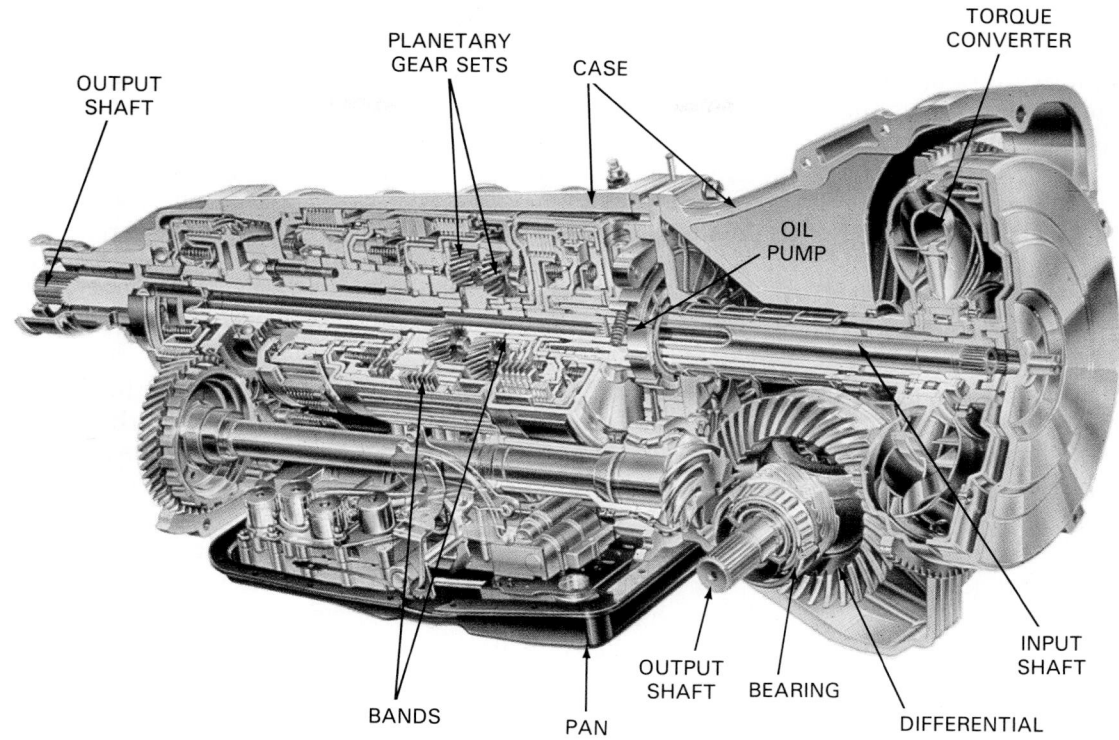

Fig. 54-36. Cutaway view shows internal parts of an all-wheel automatic transmission. (Subaru)

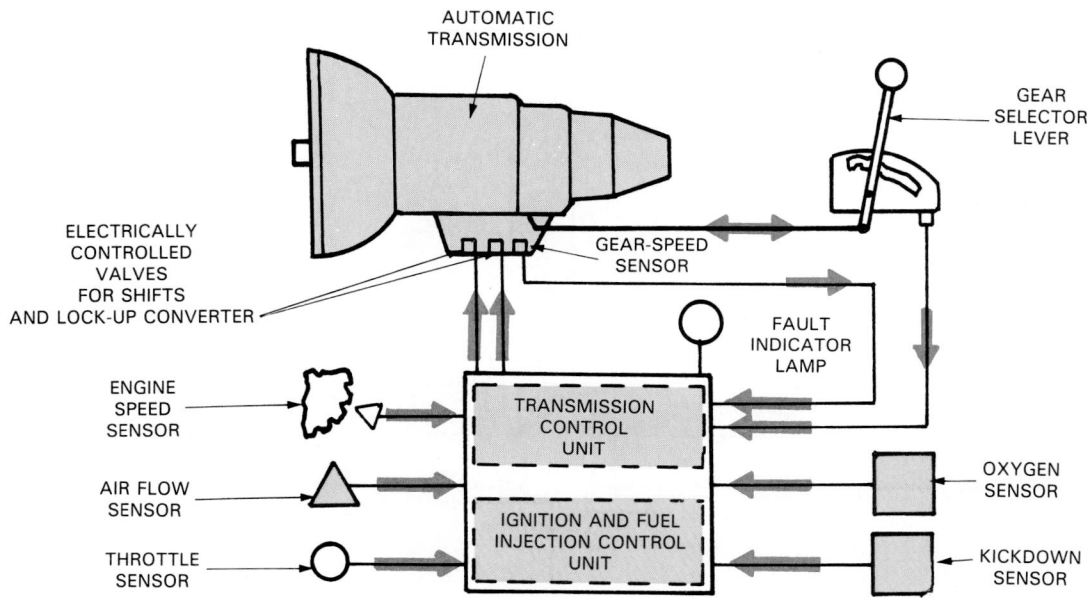

Fig. 54-37. Some late model automatic transmissions use a computer to help control shift points. Note flow of data to and from computer and transmission.

control for transmission shift points, torque converter lockup, ignition timing, fuel injection timing, emission control system operation, and other functions. This keeps the transmission and other engine systems functioning at maximum efficiency.

ELECTRONIC TRANSMISSION CONTROL

Electronic transmission control involves using sensors, actuators, and a computer to controls shift points, torque converter lockup, etc. Basically, solenoids on the transmission can be used to move hydraulic valves. This allows the computer to help control automatic transmission operation.

Note! For more information on computers, sensors, actuators, and electronic control of automotive transmissions, refer to Chapters 74, 75, and 76 in the back of the book.

CONTINUOUSLY VARIABLE TRANSMISSION

A *continuously variable transmission,* abbreviated CVT, has an infinite number of driving ratios, NOT three, four, or five forward speeds, as with conventional transmissions. It uses centrifugally operated two-piece pulleys whose diameters are variable. V-belts—usually two of them—run between the pulley sets. This arrangement takes the place of the planetary gearsets.

Fig. 54-38 shows a simplified drawing of a CVT. During initial acceleration, a small drive pulley turns a larger pulley, drive reduction results.

As speed increases, centrifugal force pushes the halves of the drive pulley together. The belt rides out in the pulley, increasing the pulley's effective diameter. As a result, a larger pulley drives a smaller pulley for more vehicle speed.

A CVT transmission is used in some foreign makes and is being experimented with by many U.S. manufacturers. It is capable of increasing fuel economy approximately 25 percent because it keeps the engine at its most efficient operating speed. Engine rpm can be kept relatively constant. The engine does NOT have to accelerate through each gear. The result is an almost perfectly smooth increase in vehicle speed.

KNOW THESE TERMS

Converter housing, Case, Extension housing, Torque converter, Impeller, Stator, Turbine, Lock-up converter, Overrunning clutch, Torque multiplication, Stall speed, Stator support, Planetary gearset, Multiple disc clutch, Clutch piston, Drum, Hub, Shell, Band, Servo, Oil pump, Pressure regulator, Manual valve, Kickdown valve, Valve body, Accumulator, Automatic transmission fluid, Transmission cooler, Parking pawl, Automatic transmission electronic controls, Continuously variable transmission.

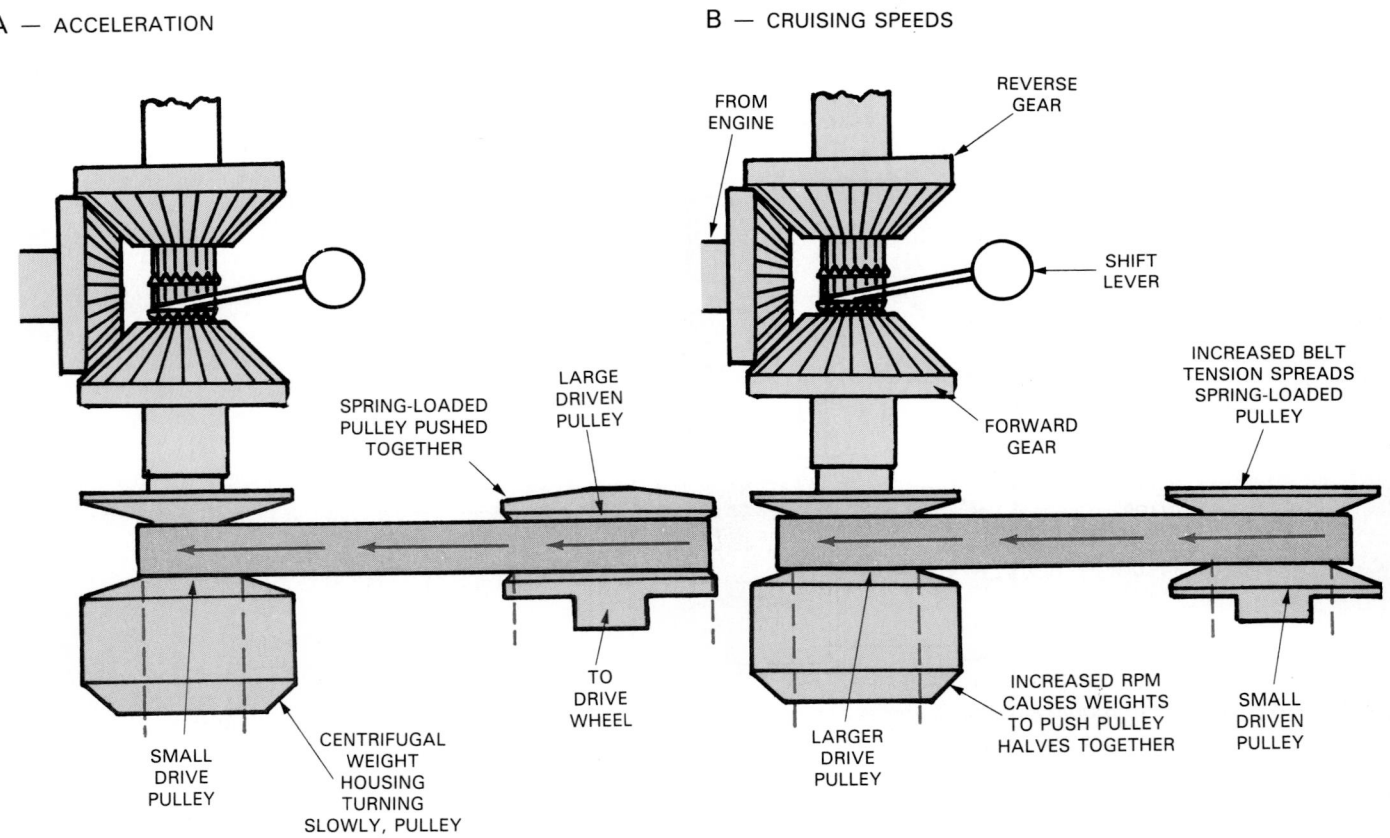

A — ACCELERATION

B — CRUISING SPEEDS

Fig. 54-38. Basic action of continuously variable transmission. Centrifugal weights in housing cause pulley diameters to change with vehicle speed. Two drive belt mechanisms are commonly used on automobiles. A — Upon initial acceleration, drive pulley has small diameter and driven pulley has larger diameter. This provides gear reduction for rapid acceleration. B — As car and pulley speed increase, centrifugal weights push one pulley together, increasing its diameter. This increases belt tension, pulling other pulley apart. As a result, ratio constantly decreases with increase in speed.

REVIEW QUESTIONS

1. List and explain the eight major parts of an automatic transmission.
2. An automatic transmission uses the following methods of transferring power.
   a. Friction.
   b. Fluids.
   c. Gears.
   d. All of the above.
   e. None of the above.
3. Describe the four major housings or components of an automatic transmission.
4. A _____ _____ is a fluid clutch that provides a means of coupling and uncoupling the engine and transmission.
5. Which of the following is NOT part of a torque converter?
   a. Band.
   b. Stator.
   c. Impeller.
   d. Turbine.
6. _____ _____ refers to the ability of a torque converter to increase the amount of engine torque applied to the transmission's input shaft.
7. Define the term "stall speed."
8. Why do many late model vehicles use a lock-up torque converter?
9. A planetary gearset consists of a _____ gear, several _____ gears, _____ gear _____, and a _____ gear.
10. List five functions of a planetary gearset.
11. Automatic transmission _____ and _____ are friction devices that drive and lock planetary gearset members.
12. Explain the operation of a clutch apply piston.
13. What is a servo?
14. An _____ is used in the apply circuit of a band or clutch to cushion initial application.
15. An overrunning clutch locks in one direction and freewheels in the other. True or False?
16. List and describe the major parts of the hydraulic system in an automatic transmission.
17. List five functions of the oil pump in an automatic transmission.
18. This valve senses engine speed (transmission output shaft rpm) to help control gear shifting.
   a. Vacuum modulator valve.
   b. Governor valve.
   c. Regulator valve.
   d. Manual valve.
19. How do the shift or balanced valves work?
20. Engine oil is compatible with the friction material in an automatic transmission. True or False?

ACTIVITIES FOR CHAPTER 54

1. Disassemble an automatic transmission and identify the parts.
2. Demonstrate to the class how an automatic transmission works.
3. Design and set up a demonstration that will help explain the operating principle of an automatic transmission.

55

Automatic Transmission Service

After studying this chapter, you will be able to:
- ☐ Troubleshoot an automatic transmission.
- ☐ Explain the types of problems common to an automatic transmission.
- ☐ Describe the tests needed to locate automatic transmission problems.
- ☐ Change automatic transmission fluid and filter.
- ☐ Make basic external adjustments on an automatic transmission.
- ☐ Locate and repair automatic transmission leaks.
- ☐ Cite and observe safety rules while working on transmissions.

Though transmission service is usually done by specialists, it is very important that EVERY technician have some knowledge of transmission service. Problems with an automatic transmission can affect, or appear to affect, the operation of other vehicle systems.

For example, a torque converter malfunction (inoperative stator or frozen lock-up clutch) could seem like an engine performance problem. The faulty converter could consume a tremendous amount of engine power or not allow engine rpm to increase normally.

A technician WITHOUT some training in automatic transmissions might think the engine lacked sufficient

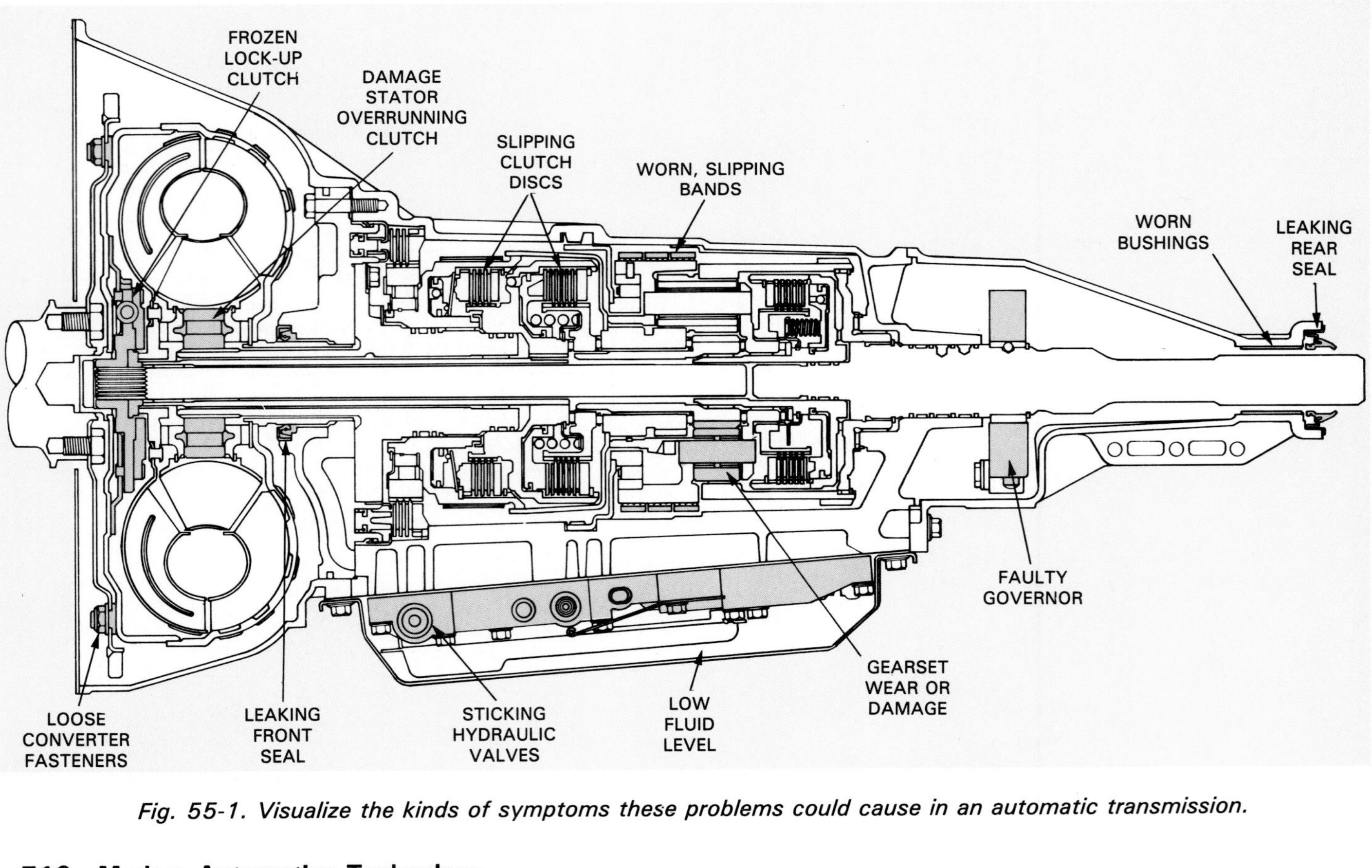

FROZEN LOCK-UP CLUTCH
DAMAGE STATOR OVERRUNNING CLUTCH
SLIPPING CLUTCH DISCS
WORN, SLIPPING BANDS
WORN BUSHINGS
LEAKING REAR SEAL
LOOSE CONVERTER FASTENERS
LEAKING FRONT SEAL
STICKING HYDRAULIC VALVES
LOW FLUID LEVEL
GEARSET WEAR OR DAMAGE
FAULTY GOVERNOR

Fig. 55-1. Visualize the kinds of symptoms these problems could cause in an automatic transmission.

power. The untrained technician could be led to think the vehicle had a clogged fuel filter, worn engine timing chain, or other engine performance trouble.

AUTOMATIC TRANSMISSION DIAGNOSIS

Several problems are common to an automatic transmission. A few of these are illustrated in Fig. 55-1.

Automatic transmission slippage is often caused by low fluid level, misadjusted linkage, worn clutches or bands, or valve body problems. With partial slippage, the engine may briefly *race* (engine speed increase) as the transmission shifts to a higher gear. With severe slippage, the vehicle may NOT move.

Incorrect shift points are sometimes caused by a low fluid level, faulty vacuum modulator circuit, engine performance problem, damaged governor, or trouble with hydraulic valves, servos, or pistons. The transmission could shift too soon (engine lugs in higher gear), shift too late (engine races in lower gear), or not shift at all (locked in one gear or fails to upshift).

Mushy or *harsh shifts* are normally due to the same types of problems mentioned for slippage or incorrect shifts. A *mushy shift* is noticed when the transmission takes too much time changing gears. A *harsh shift* is just the opposite; the vehicle will jerk during shifts.

A *noisy transmission* (whining, whirring, grinding) may result from an improper fluid level, planetary gear troubles, damaged bearings, faulty torque converter, loose components, or other troubles. Refer to Fig. 55-1.

If the abnormal sound occurs in every gear, then the problem might be in the torque converter, oil pump, or other part common to all gears. If the transmission only makes the noise in one gear, then only parts operating in that gear could be at fault.

Remember! When trying to find the source of transmission noises, make sure the problem is inside the transmission before making transmission repairs. Worn wheel bearings, dry universal joints, and engine problems can all produce noises that seem like they are coming from near the transmission.

Other transmission problems also relate to the types of symptoms and causes just mentioned. You should refer to a service manual troubleshooting chart when more specific troubles cannot be located.

CAUTION: Servicing transmissions often requires the vehicle to be raised and supported. Make sure to use proper jacks and supporting tools.

Let vehicle cool; hot fluids can cause serious burns. Wear safety glasses or a face shield to protect eyes. Remove rings and jewelry when working on electrical parts. Disconnect the battery.

Stay clear of drivelines when testing a transmission.

PRELIMINARY CHECKS

Before road testing the car, there are several checks you should make: fluid level, fluid condition, linkage operation, and engine condition. You may find a problem and quickly fix the transmission. Refer to Fig. 55-2.

Check fluid level

A *low fluid level,* normally caused by a leak, may cause the oil pump to take in air. Air is compressible and can prevent the fluid from acting like a solid when pressurized in the hydraulic system. Pressure may build up too slowly, causing various engagement and shifting problems.

A *high fluid level* can produce symptoms similar to those produced by a low fluid level. The transmission can churn the fluid into a foam. The air bubbles in the foam will make the fluid compressible, upsetting normal operation.

Check fluid condition

Transmission *fluid condition* can tell you a great deal about the condition of the transmission. Whenever you pull out the transmission dipstick, wipe the fluid off on your finger or a white paper towel. See Fig. 55-3.

Inspect the fluid closely for signs of foreign matter or an unusual smell.

Burned transmission fluid will be dark or black, and have a burned odor. The darkness is normally caused by band and clutch friction material failure. The friction material has been slipping and overheating.

Usually, when you find burned transmission fluid, accompanied by slipping or shifting problems, serious damage has ocurred. Typically, the transmission would need major repairs.

GENERAL DIAGNOSIS SEQUENCE

1. CHECK FLUID LEVEL AND CONDITION.

2. CHECK ALL EXTERNAL LINKAGES AND CABLES FOR WEAR, STICKING, AND INCORRECT ADJUSTMENT. CHECK MODULATOR VALVE AND MODULATOR VACUUM HOSE.

3. CHECK WIRES TO SENSORS AND SOLENOIDS ON TRANSMISSION.

4. ROAD TEST VEHICLE TO CHECK TRANSMISSION AND ENGINE PERFORMANCE.

5. STALL TEST

6. LINE PRESSURE TEST

7. CASE AIR PRESSURE TESTS

Fig. 55-2. Note major steps for diagnosing automatic transmission troubles.

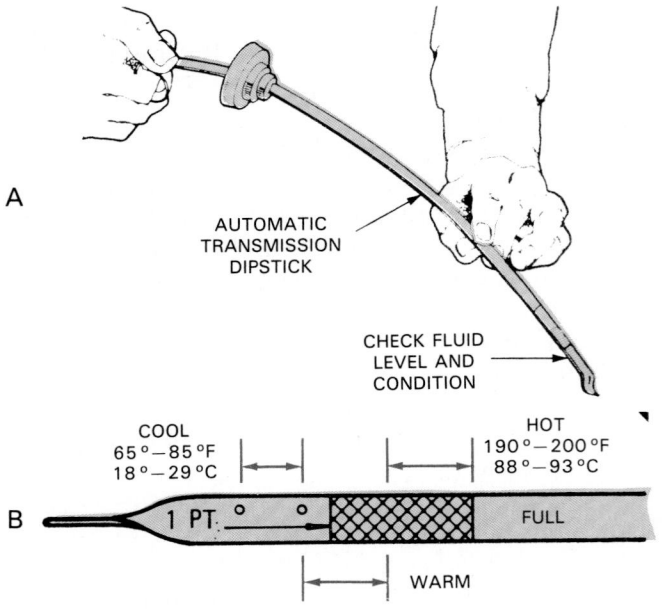

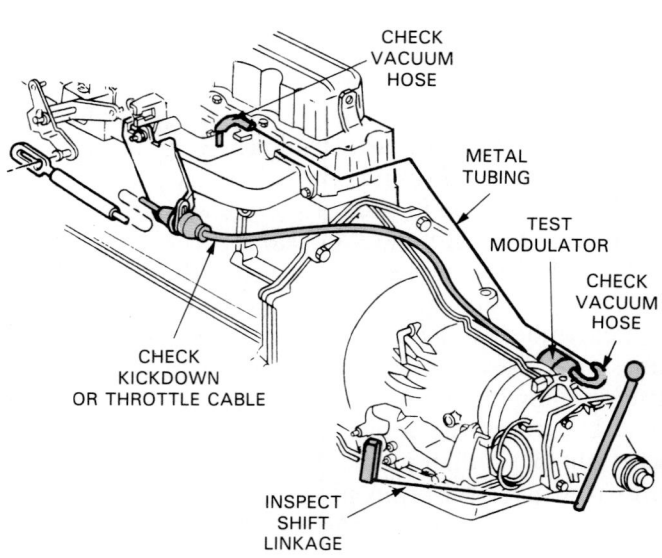

COOL
65°–85°F
18°–29°C

HOT
190°–200°F
88°–93°C

B

1 PT.

FULL

WARM

NOTE: DO NOT OVERFILL. IT TAKES ONLY ONE PINT TO RAISE LEVEL FROM ADD TO FULL WITH A HOT TRANSMISSION.

Fig. 55-3. Always check fluid level with automatic transmission problems. A — Feel, inspect, and smell fluid. If burned or contaminated, problems are indicated. B — Make sure fluid is to proper level on stick. Follow directions for each transmission. (AC-Delco and GMC)

Milky transmission fluid (white appearance) is normally due to engine coolant mixing with the transmission fluid. The oil or heat exchange tank in the engine radiator is leaking and allowing antifreeze to enter the transmission lines. Coolant in the transmission fluid can sometimes cause oil seals and friction material (clutches and bands) to deteriorate. The seals can swell and leak. The clutch and band material can soften and wear quickly.

Transmission fluid varnish is evident when a light brown coating is found on the dipstick. The transmission fluid has broken down, coating the internal parts of the transmission with a sticky, glue-like substance.

The fluid varnish can cause a wide range of transmission problems. It can cause hydraulic valves to stick open or close. Servos and pistons can also stick. With an extreme case of varnish build up, the transmission filter can clog.

Check engine condition

During your preliminary checks, always inspect the operating condition of the engine. The engine should start properly, idle smoothly without missing, and perform normally under acceleration.

Check for vacuum leaks

Check for vacuum leaks on the engine or vacuum modulator circuit when shift problems occur. If a hose, fitting, or gasket is leaking, it can upset vacuum modulator operation. See Fig. 55-4.

The modulator, used on many transmissions, senses engine vacuum (load) and helps to determine shift points. If not receiving the correct amount of vacuum, the transmission will not shift gears properly.

Check shift linkage and cables

Inspect the operation of the shift linkage, Fig. 55-4. Move the shift lever through the gears while feeling the transmission click into each gear. Make sure the shift linkage is not worn. Also, check the kickdown rod or cable, Fig. 55-4, if used. Make sure it is free to move. Move the throttle lever while watching the kickdown rod. If the kickdown rod is locked in the full throttle position, the transmission will be slow to upshift.

Check electrical connections

Inspect any electrical connections on the transmission. Many late model automatic transmissions have sensors and actuators on them. A poor connection could upset the operation of the transmission and also other systems. Look for disconnected wires, frayed wires, corroded connectors, and other basic problems.

Fig. 55-4. Check kickdown cable or rod, shift linkage, and vacuum line to modulator for problems. They frequently are source of automatic transmission troubles. (Chevrolet)

ROAD TESTING

If you do not find the source of the transmission problem through your preliminary checks, road test the vehicle. Drive the vehicle while checking transmission shift points, noises, and the general operation of the transmission. The test route should be a smooth road with little traffic. This will help reduce outside noise and distractions.

With the transmission in drive, accelerate normally. Make sure the transmission upshifts correctly. Listen for noises in each gear and try to detect any slippage.

Then, manual shift the transmission through the gears. For example, if you think you heard a noise in second gear, manual shift into second. This will give you more time to evaluate performance in second gear.

SHOP TESTING

Various shop tests are used when the preliminary checks and the road test fail to locate the transmission problem. These tests can be divided into three classifications: stall test, pressure test, and air test.

Stall test

A *stall test* can be used to detect transmission slippage or a malfunctioning torque converter.

To perform a stall test, connect a tachometer to measure engine speed. Apply the emergency brake and press down firmly on the brake pedal. Start the engine and place the transmission in low. Refer to Fig. 55-5.

STALL SPEED MARKED

TACHOMETER

Fig. 55-5. To do stall test, connect tachometer to engine. Apply emergency brake and foot brake. Place transmission in appropriate gear and accelerate engine. The maximum rpm or stall speed should meet specs. It not, problem is indicated. (Ford)

When the gas pedal is slowly pressed to the floor, the engine should "stall" (speed stop increasing) at a recommended rpm. If the tachometer reads above or below specs, a problem exists. The transmission should be tested in every gear position.

If engine rpm is HIGH, let off the gas immediately to prevent further transmission damage. The transmission is slipping and could quickly overheat, burning friction material.

The problem may be low hydraulic control pressure

so that pistons and servos are not applying enough clamping force to bands. Friction material could be worn. If the stall speed is TOO LOW, the engine might have a performance problem or the torque converter stator could be inoperative.

CAUTION! Some auto makers do NOT recommend a stall test. It could damage motor mounts, clutches, and bands.

The service manual will give more details on performing a stall test. You might have to disconnect the kickdown lever or other components to keep the transmission in each gear.

Fig. 55-6 shows a clutch and band application chart for one type transmission. It can be used to determine which parts are faulty when a transmission slips.

CLUTCH AND BAND APPLICATION CHART

LOW(D) (Breakaway) 2.74 RWD 2.69 FWD	LOW(1) (Manual) 2.74 RWD 2.69 FWD	SECOND 1.54 RWD 1.55 FWD	DIRECT 1.0:1	REVERSE 2.22 RWD 2.10 FWD
REAR CLUTCH Drives Front Ring Gear	REAR CLUTCH Drives Front Ring Gear	REAR CLUTCH Drives Front Ring Gear	REAR CLUTCH Drives Front Ring Gear	FRONT CLUTCH Drives Sun Gear
OVER-RUNNING CLUTCH Holds Rear Planet Carrier	LOW AND REVERSE BAND Holds Rear Planet Carrier	KICK-DOWN BAND Holds Sun Gear	FRONT CLUTCH Drives Sun Planet	LOW AND REVERSE BAND Holds Rear Carrier

Fig. 55-6. Clutch and band application chart will show which components are slipping in each gear during stall test. It is also useful during road and pressure tests. Service manual will give chart for exact transmission being diagnosed.

Pressure tests

Pressure tests are used to determine whether oil pressures in the various transmission circuits are normal. As in Fig. 55-7, plugs are provided on the outside of the transmission case for pressure tests.

To measure control pressure, for example, connect a 300 psi (2 067 kPa) gauge to the line pressure port on the transmission. See Fig. 55-8.

Run the engine until it is at operating temperature. Typically, the engine should be at curb idle.

While holding your foot on the brake, shift through all of the gears while noting the pressure gauge. Compare your pressure readings to those in a service manual The service manual will tell you which components might be leaking or frozen when pressure is low or high in any gear.

The pressure gauge may be installed in the other plug

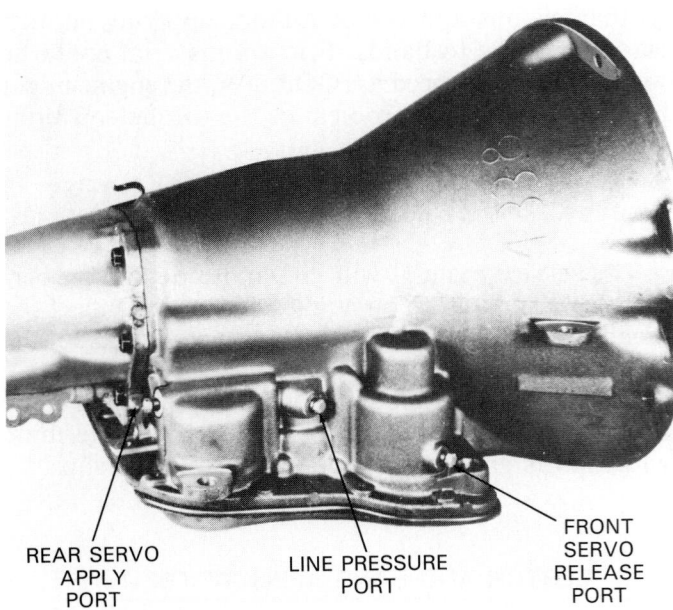

Fig. 55-7. Plugs on side of automatic transmission cover ports or passages to hydraulic components. To pressure test, install pressure gauge in ports. Compare pressure to specs to determine condition of various components. (Chrysler)

REAR SERVO APPLY PORT

LINE PRESSURE PORT

FRONT SERVO RELEASE PORT

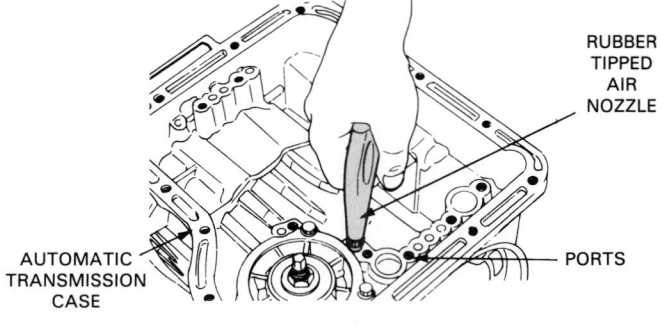

RUBBER TIPPED AIR NOZZLE

AUTOMATIC TRANSMISSION CASE

PORTS

Fig. 55-9. Air pressure tests involve injecting shop air pressure into transmission passages. Air pressure should activate pistons and servos, making a clunking or thudding sound. Other sounds can be made when air is injected into ports to other parts. Refer to a service manual for details. (Nissan)

To perform an air test, look up the exact procedure in a shop manual. The manual will show which case passages lead to particular components. An example is shown in Fig. 55-10. Quite often, a rubber tipped air nozzle and about 25-35 psi (172-241 kPa) air pressure is recommended.

When air pressure is blown into the piston or servo

holes to check more specific hydraulic pressures. Refer to Fig. 55-7.

Air test

An *air test* is used to further isolate problems in automatic transmission circuits. After removing the oil pan and valve body, air pressure is blown into the passages in the transmission. Look at Fig. 55-9.

The air pressure should activate the pistons, servos and other components. This will let you detect leaks, stuck components, bad check valves, or blockage of passages.

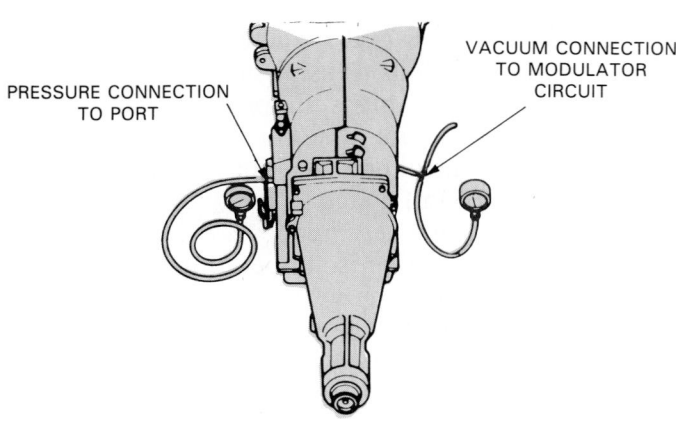

PRESSURE CONNECTION TO PORT

VACUUM CONNECTION TO MODULATOR CIRCUIT

Fig. 55-8. Pressure and vacuum gauges have been connected to automatic transmission. Gauges can be run into passenger compartment for watching pressures during road test. (Ford)

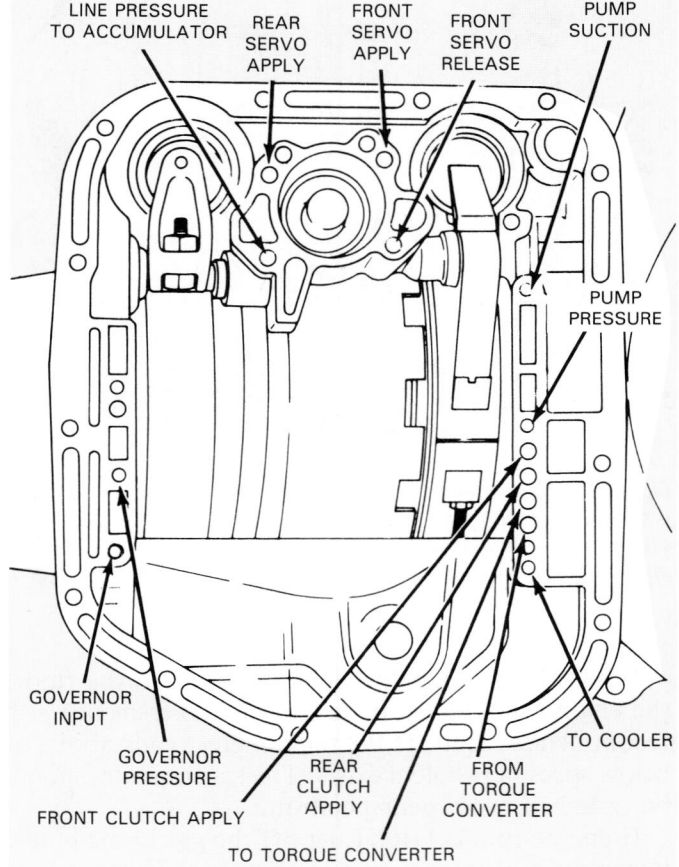

LINE PRESSURE TO ACCUMULATOR

REAR SERVO APPLY

FRONT SERVO APPLY

FRONT SERVO RELEASE

PUMP SUCTION

PUMP PRESSURE

GOVERNOR INPUT

GOVERNOR PRESSURE

FRONT CLUTCH APPLY

REAR CLUTCH APPLY

FROM TORQUE CONVERTER

TO COOLER

TO TORQUE CONVERTER

Fig. 55-10. Service manual illustration shows function of each port in bottom of specific transmission case. Look up this type illustration in manual when needed. (Chrysler)

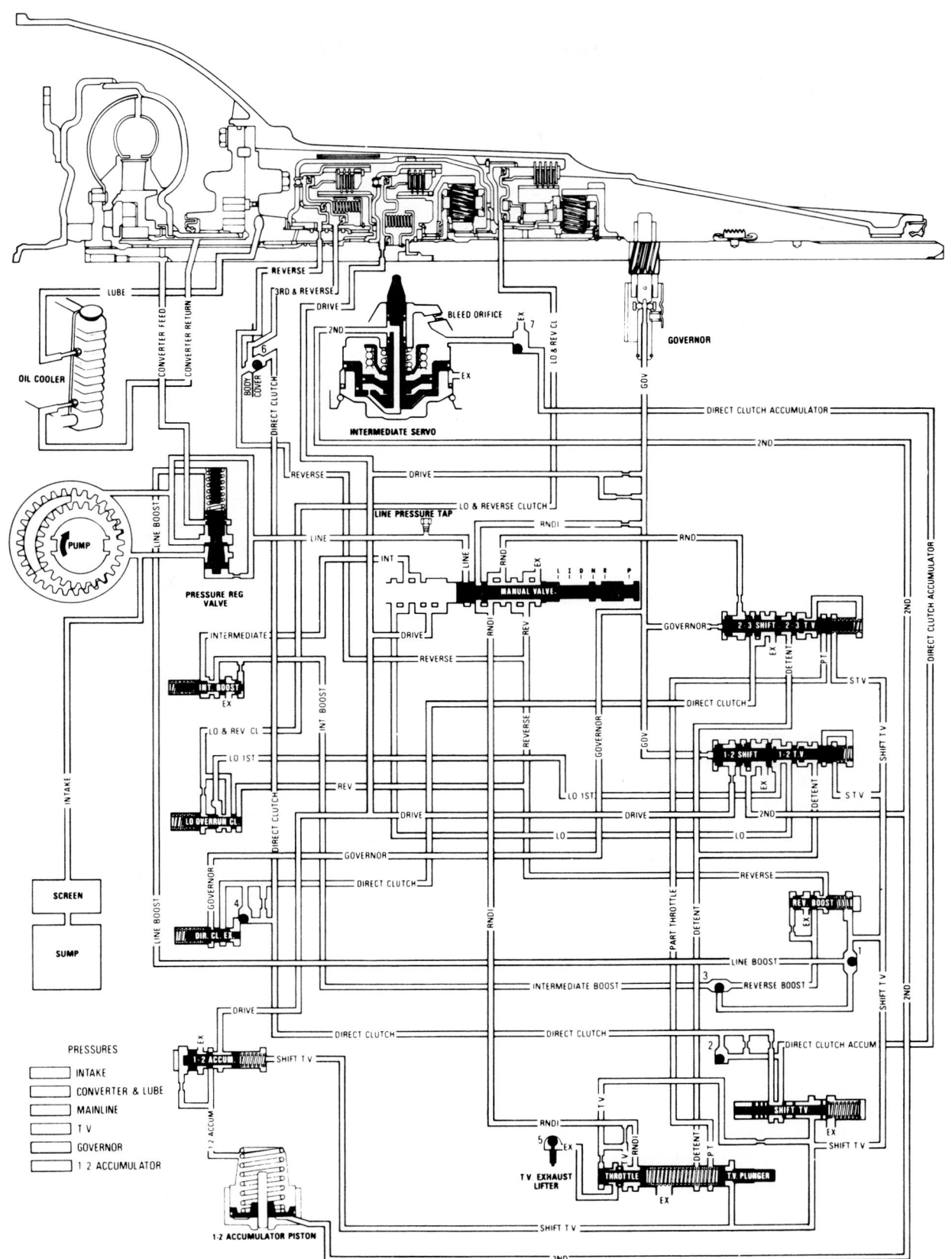

Fig. 55-11. Service manual will also have hydraulic circuit diagrams, similar to this one. Diagram will show how each part and passage interconnect. This is very useful during diagnosis. (Cadillac)

passages, a dull thud should be heard. This sound is made as the piston slides in its cylinder and bottoms. A hissing sound would indicate a leak. No sound at all would point to blockage or a frozen piston.

Air forced into the governor passage may (some types of governors) produce a whistling sound. No sound might mean the governor is stuck or damaged.

Electrical tests

Electrical tests on an automatic transmission involve checking sensors, actuators, and wiring for basic troubles. For example, if an automatic transmission has a solenoid on it, you could simply use an ohmmeter to check the windings in the solenoid. If a transmission has a vehicle speed sensor, you could also test it with a multimeter. Compare your test values to service manual specs.

Note! For more information on working with electronic components, refer to the last three chapters in this textbook.

HYDRAULIC CIRCUIT DIAGRAMS

Hydraulic circuit diagrams show how the oil passages inside an automatic transmission are connected to each component. Look at Fig. 55-11. The circuit diagram is frequently used by the technician when tracing hard-to-find problems or when doing pressure or air tests.

Vacuum test

A *vacuum test* is sometimes used to check the operation of the vacuum modulator valve. It measures the amount of supply vacuum reaching the valve. If the valve is inoperative or is not receiving a correct vacuum signal (broken, leaking, or kinked vacuum line), the transmission cannot shift properly.

A vacuum gauge is connected to the modulator valve line with a T-fitting. Refer to Fig. 55-8. Then, the engine is started. The vacuum gauge should read within specs, usually full engine vacuum.

If modulator supply vacuum is LOW, there may be a vacuum leak, blockage in the supply line, or a hole in the modulator diaphragm. If vacuum is normal, you may need to adjust or replace the valve.

AUTOMATIC TRANSMISSION MAINTENANCE

Maintenance is very important to the life of an automatic transmission. Automatic transmission fluid, just like engine oil, can become filled with foreign matter after prolonged operation. Bits of metal, friction material, water condensation, dust, and other substances can circulate through the hydraulic system, causing premature wear.

Note! Refer to Chapter 10 for a review of automatic transmission fluid service.

A few of the most important steps to remember when servicing the fluid and filter of an automatic transmission are:

1. Make sure fluid is between add and full on dipstick with fluid at full operating temperature and with engine running in park. Apply the parking brake and block the wheels.
2. Do NOT overfill transmission, only add a partial quart if needed. Add a little and recheck dipstick.
3. Use the right kind of automatic transmission fluid (Type-F, Dexron, etc.). Refer to a service manual for recommendations.
4. To add fluid, use a long funnel inserted in dipstick tube. Make sure funnel is perfectly clean.
5. Refer to service manual on how often to change

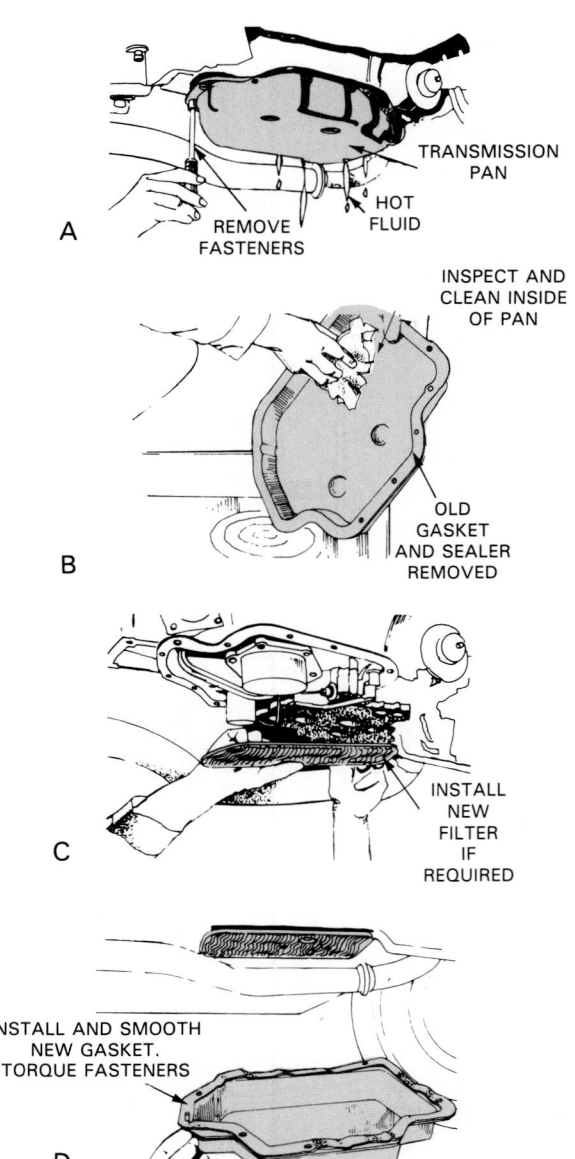

Fig. 55-12. If recommended, replace automatic transmission filter. A — Be careful not to be burned by hot fluid when removing pan. B — Inspect pan for debris before cleaning. C — Install new filter. D — Install new gasket or sealer and torque pan fasteners. (AC-Delco)

automatic transmission fluid. A typical fluid change interval might be 15 to 20,000 miles (24 100 to 32 200 km).

6. When draining an automatic transmission, be careful not to be burned by HOT fluid, Fig. 55-12.
7. Find out from a service manual if you must drain both pan and torque converter and change filter.
8. When removing pan, keep it level and lower it slowly to prevent spilling.
9. Inspect pan for debris. Bits of metal or friction material may indicate transmission problems. Then, clean pan thoroughly.
10. If sealer is used on pan, make sure you do NOT use too much. If sealer is squeezed into the pan during pan installation, sealer may block oil passages and upset transmission operation.
11. Torque pan bolts to specs in a crisscross pattern.
12. Look up transmission capacity. Fill transmission with correct amount and type of fluid. Capacity will vary depending upon whether torque converter was drained.
13. Start engine. Shift transmission through its gears. Check for leaks.

FLUID LEAKS

Automatic transmission *fluid leaks* commonly occur at the rear seal, front seal, oil pan gasket, extension housing gasket, and shift lever shaft seal. Whenever the fluid level is excessively low, always inspect the transmission for leaks. Raise the car on a hoist and check for automatic transmission fluid, Fig. 55-13.

Normally, the source of the leak will have the cleanest looking transmission fluid. When touched with your finger, the fluid will be fairly clean and usually RED. The leaking fluid tends to wash road dirt OFF the outside of the transmission.

If the leak is found at the rear seal, pan gasket, or extension housing, you can normally repair the leak without removing the transmission.

Seal replacement

To replace a rear transmission seal, use a seal removing tool. This is covered in Chapter 53 on manual transmission service.

To install the seal, force the new seal into place with a seal driving tool. Drive the seal into the housing squarely, until seated. The front transmission seal is usually replaced in a similar manner. However, the transmission must be removed from the vehicle.

AUTOMATIC TRANSMISSION ADJUSTMENTS

There are several adjustments that can be made with the transmission installed in the vehicle. The most common of these are: band adjustment, linkage adjustment, throttle or kickdown lever adjustment, and neutral safety switch adjustment.

Transmission band adjustment

Transmission band adjustment is needed to set the correct amount of clearance between the band's friction material and its drum. If the clearance is too large, the band could slip. If it is too tight, the band could drag and burn up.

To adjust a transmission band, loosen the locknut on the side of the transmission case. Turning the screw IN (clockwise) normally tightens the band.

Typically, a service manual will require that you tighten the adjustment screw to a specific torque value. See Fig. 55-14. After torquing, the screw is backed off (one turn typical) to provide band-to-drum clearance. The nut is then tightened to lock the setting.

Many modern automatic transmissions do not need band adjustment. They have improved friction material that is very resistant to wear. If a band slips in a late model transmission, major repairs are usually needed.

Shift linkage adjustment

Exact procedures for adjusting the shift linkage on an automatic transmission vary. Generally, make sure the lever going into the valve body is synchronized with the shift selector in the driver's compartment. If the selector is set to drive, the lever on the transmission must also be centered in the drive mode.

To adjust most shift linkages, a locknut is loosened on the shift rod, Fig. 55-15. Then, the rod can be shortened or lengthened as needed.

Neutral safety switch adjustment

Neutral safety switch adjustment is needed when the

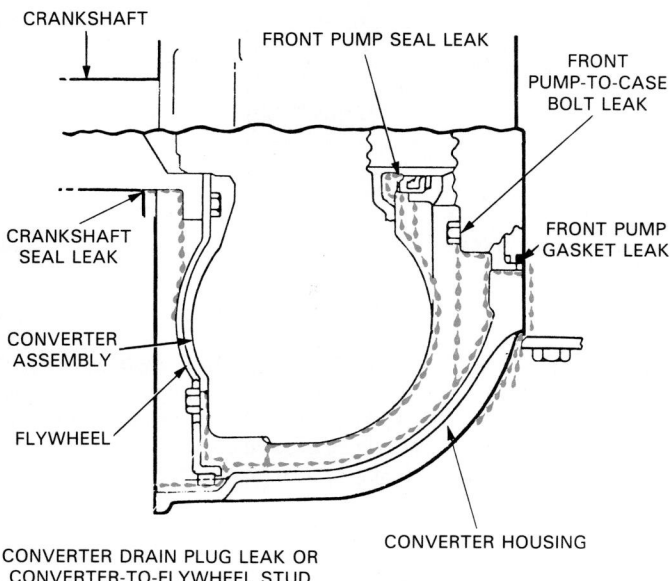

CRANKSHAFT
FRONT PUMP SEAL LEAK
FRONT PUMP-TO-CASE BOLT LEAK
CRANKSHAFT SEAL LEAK
CONVERTER ASSEMBLY
FLYWHEEL
FRONT PUMP GASKET LEAK
CONVERTER HOUSING
CONVERTER DRAIN PLUG LEAK OR CONVERTER-TO-FLYWHEEL STUD WELD LEAK

Fig. 55-13. Diagnose automatic transmission leaks properly. Note how engine rear main seal leak and transmission front seal leak will drip out of same location. (Ford)

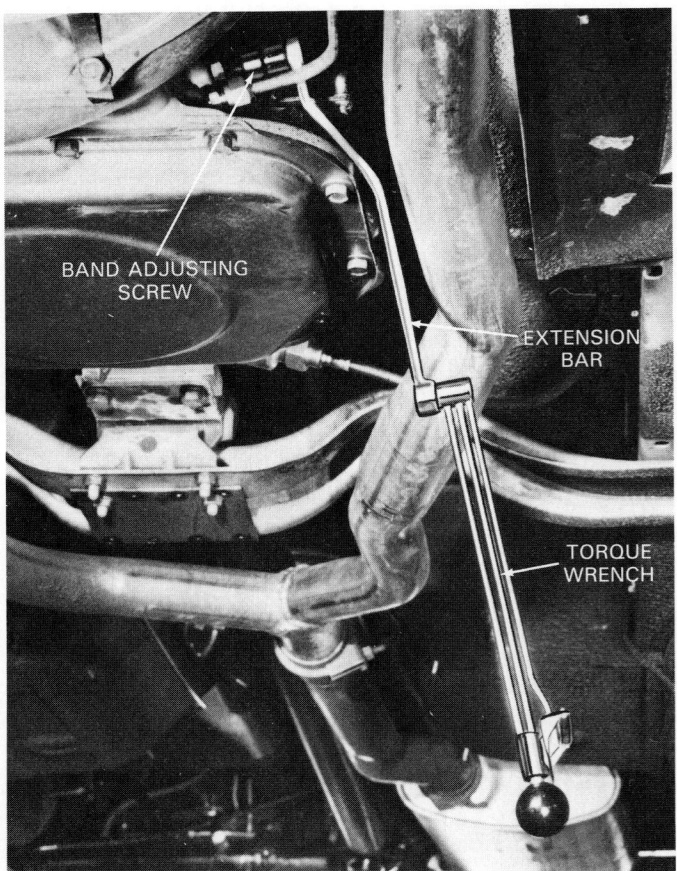

Fig. 55-14. *Use service manual directions when adjusting transmission bands. Generally, loosen locknut. Torque band adjusting screw to specs. Then, loosen screw specific number of turns before tightening locknut. Extension bar is needed to reach adjustment. You would need to calculate new torque wrench reading with use of extension bar.* (Chrysler Corp.)

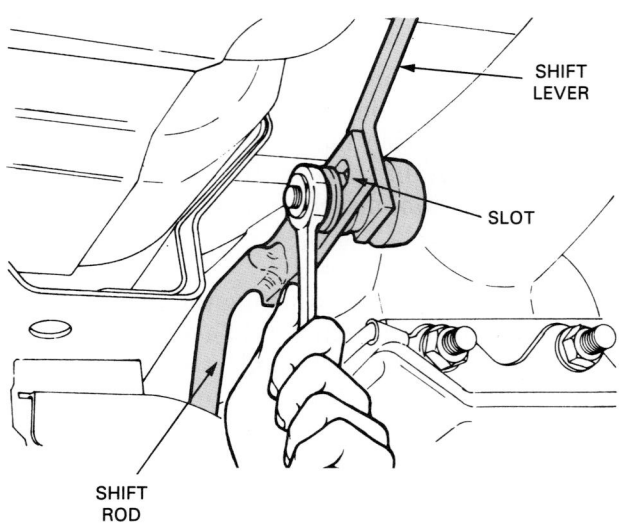

Fig. 55-15. *To adjust automatic transmission linkage, loosen nut on linkage rod. Position driver's shift lever and lever on transmission in same gear, usually park. Then tighten nut and check action.* (Chrysler)

engine does not start (crank) with the shift selector in park. You might have to wiggle the shifter or hold it forward before the engine cranks. Either the linkage has worn, upsetting the neutral switch setting, or the switch itself is faulty.

To adjust a neutral safety switch, loosen the bolts that hold it in place. Refer to Fig. 55-16. Position the shift selector in park.

While holding the ignition key to START, slide the switch toward the park position. As soon as the engine begins to crank, release the key and tighten the switch bolts. Be careful not to move the switch while tightening.

Double-check your adjustment by starting the engine with the selector in park and neutral.

Testing neutral safety switch

To check for a bad (open or shorted) neutral safety switch, connect an ohmmeter across the switch, as shown in Fig. 55-16.

The ohmmeter should read zero ohms (closed) with the switch in park and neutral. It should read infinite resistance (open) in all other gear positions.

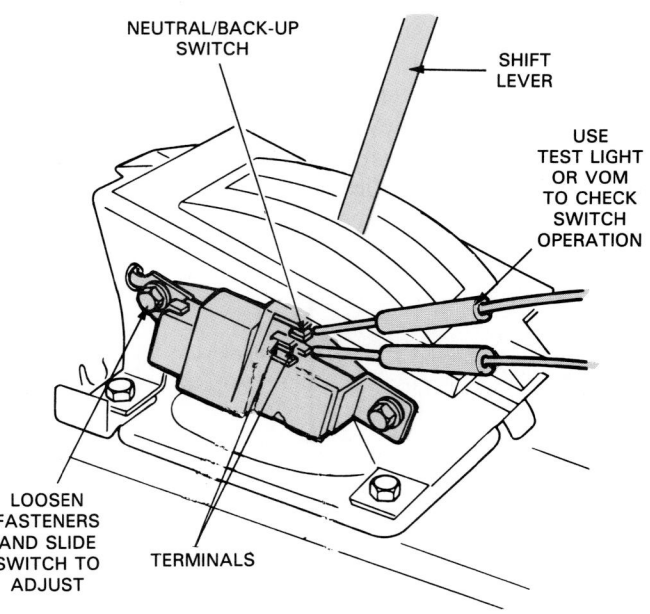

Fig. 55-16. *To adjust neutral/back-up light switch, loosen fasteners. Hold key to start with transmission in park while sliding switch forward. As soon as engine cranks, lock down switch. Test light or VOM can be used to check action of switch while moving shifter.* (Honda)

Back-up light switch

Sometimes, the neutral safety switch also operates the back-up lights. This side of the switch may also be checked with your ohmmeter or with a test light. The back-up light circuit should only have continuity

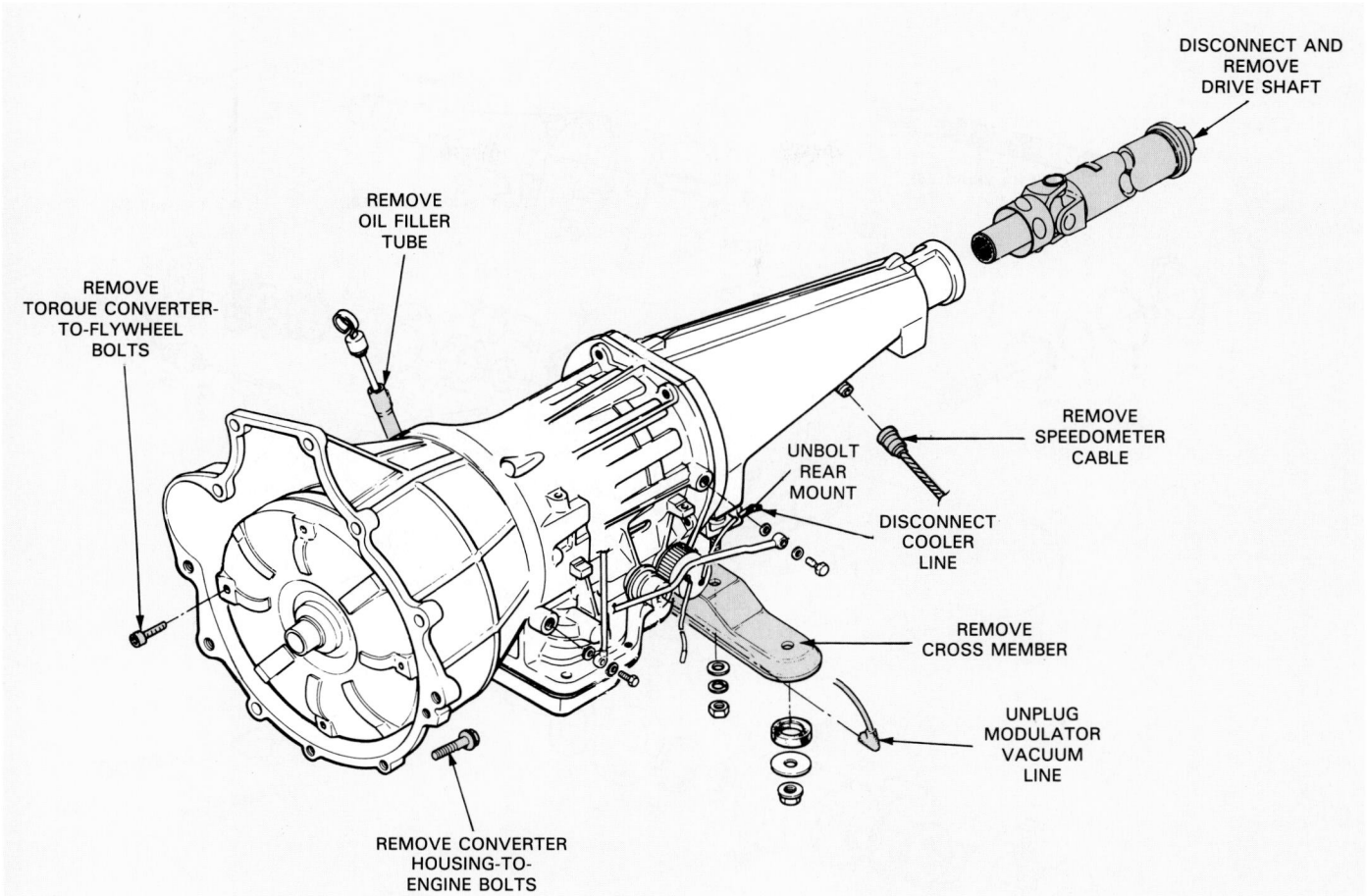

Fig. 55-17. Note parts that must be disconnected for removal of automatic transmission. Procedure is similar as that described for manual transmission in earlier chapter. (Mazda)

(zero ohms or test light glow) when the shift lever is in reverse.

MAJOR TRANSMISSION SERVICE

When your tests find major internal problems, the automatic transmission must be removed from the car. The manufacturer's service manual will give accurate instructions on how to remove, disassemble, inspect, rebuild, and install the transmission. Special training is needed to become competent with major internal repairs on automatic transmissions.

Fig. 55-17 shows most of the parts that must be disconnected for automatic transmission removal. Described in the chapter on manual transmission service, use a transmission jack and proper safety rules.

Fig. 55-18 is an exploded view of an automatic transmission. The service manual will frequently have an illustration like this for your particular transmission. Use it during reassembly.

Fig. 55-19 shows the manufacturer's special tools for an automatic transmission and automatic transaxle. Some of them are essential. Others simply make service easier.

KNOW THESE TERMS

Automatic transmission slippage, Incorrect shift points, Harsh shifts, Mushy shifts, Fluid contamination, Burned fluid, Milky fluid, Fluid varnish, Modulator vacuum leakage, Stall test, Pressure tests, Air tests, Hydraulic circuit diagrams, Band adjustment, Shift linkage adjustment, Neutral safety switch adjustment.

REVIEW QUESTIONS

1. Which of the following can cause automatic transmission slippage?
   a. Low fluid level.
   b. Misadjusted linkage.
   c. Worn clutches or bands.
   d. Valve body problems.
   e. All of the above.
2. What is burned transmission fluid and what does it tell you?
3. Engine vacuum leaks can affect automatic transmission operation. True or False?
4. What is a stall test?

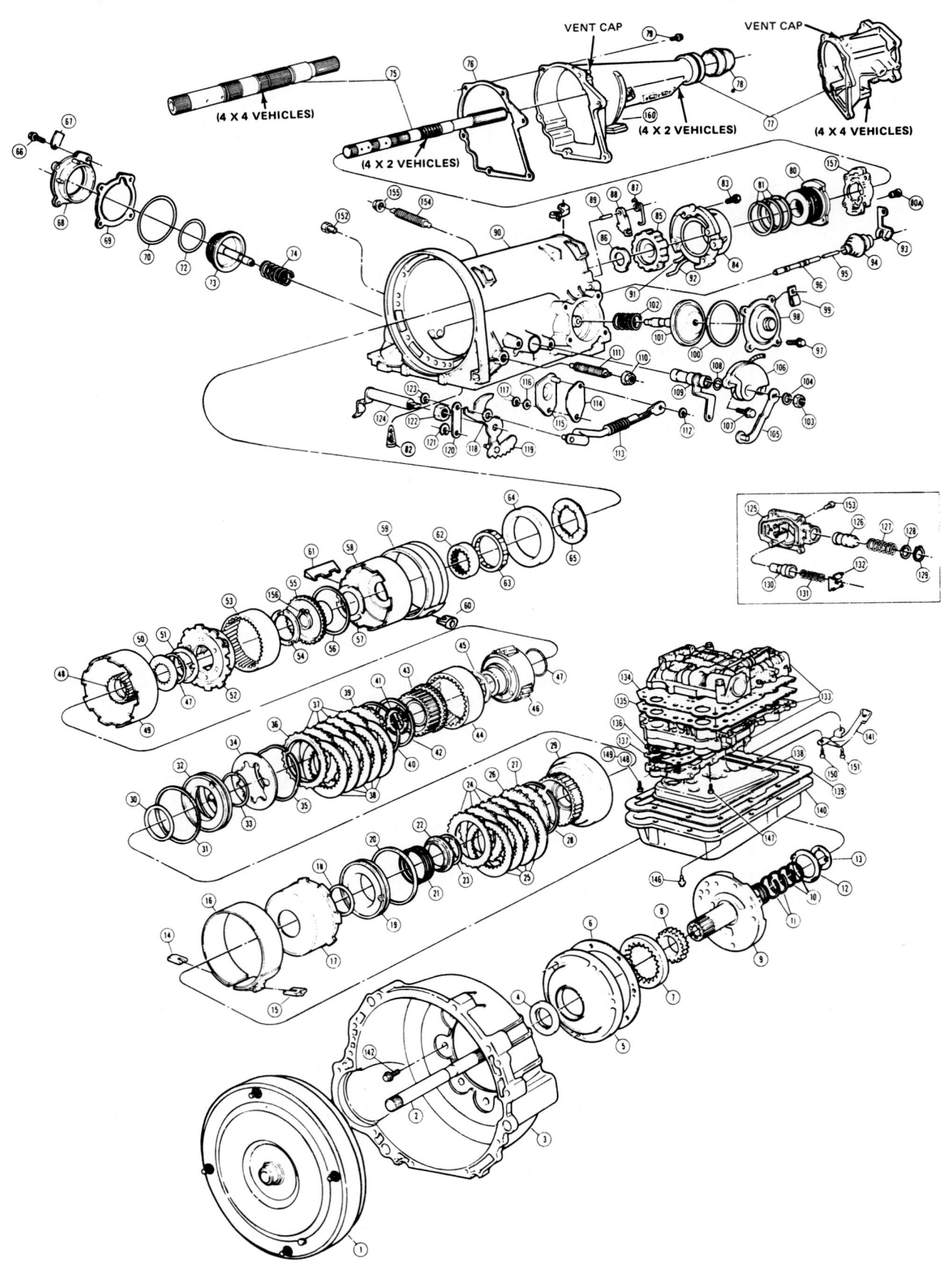

Fig. 55-18. Exploded view is helpful during transmission disassembly and reassembly. (Mercury)

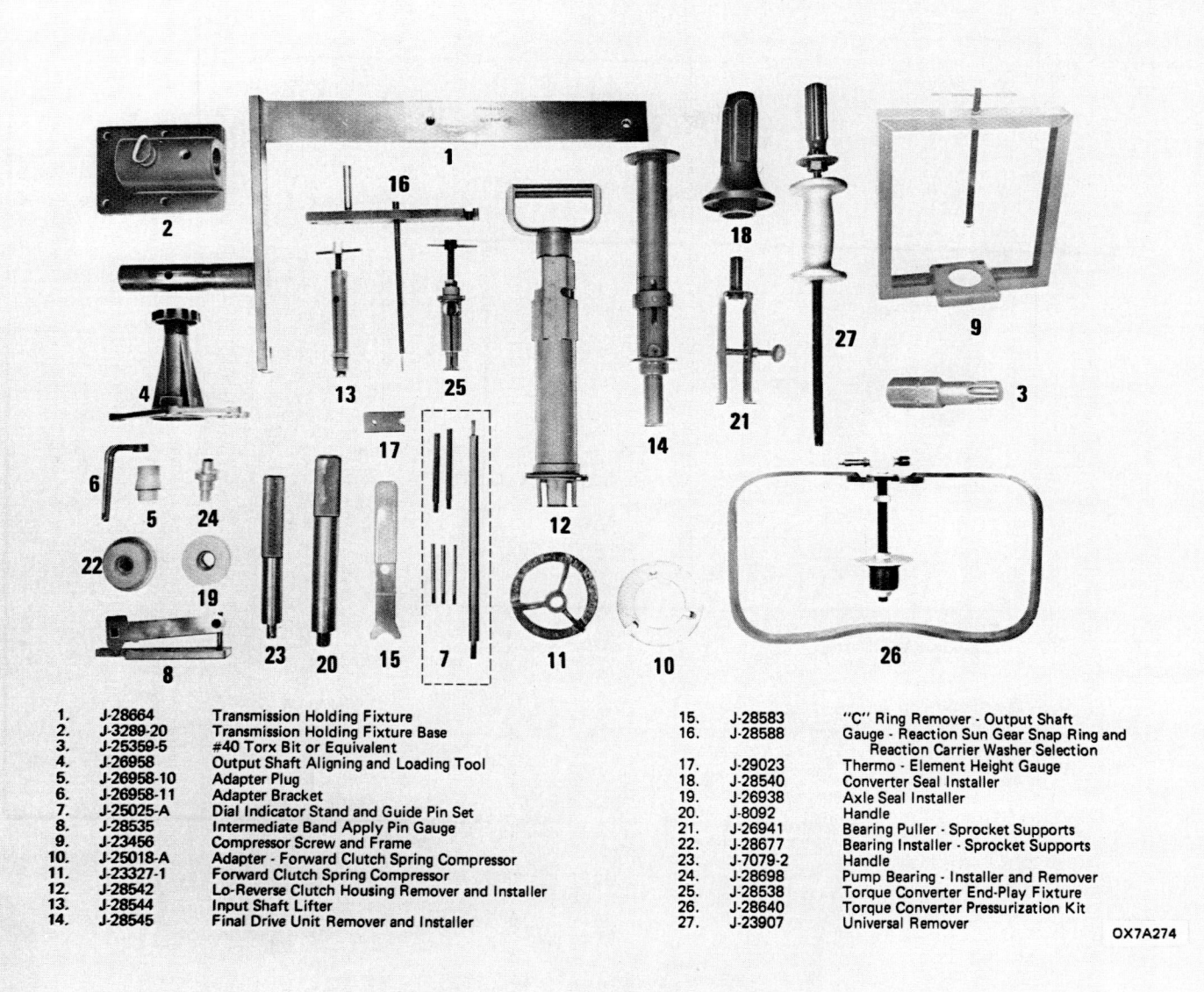

1.	J-28664	Transmission Holding Fixture
2.	J-3289-20	Transmission Holding Fixture Base
3.	J-25359-5	#40 Torx Bit or Equivalent
4.	J-26958	Output Shaft Aligning and Loading Tool
5.	J-26958-10	Adapter Plug
6.	J-26958-11	Adapter Bracket
7.	J-25025-A	Dial Indicator Stand and Guide Pin Set
8.	J-28535	Intermediate Band Apply Pin Gauge
9.	J-23456	Compressor Screw and Frame
10.	J-25018-A	Adapter - Forward Clutch Spring Compressor
11.	J-23327-1	Forward Clutch Spring Compressor
12.	J-28542	Lo-Reverse Clutch Housing Remover and Installer
13.	J-28544	Input Shaft Lifter
14.	J-28545	Final Drive Unit Remover and Installer
15.	J-28583	"C" Ring Remover - Output Shaft
16.	J-28588	Gauge - Reaction Sun Gear Snap Ring and Reaction Carrier Washer Selection
17.	J-29023	Thermo - Element Height Gauge
18.	J-28540	Converter Seal Installer
19.	J-26938	Axle Seal Installer
20.	J-8092	Handle
21.	J-26941	Bearing Puller - Sprocket Supports
22.	J-28677	Bearing Installer - Sprocket Supports
23.	J-7079-2	Handle
24.	J-28698	Pump Bearing - Installer and Remover
25.	J-28538	Torque Converter End-Play Fixture
26.	J-28640	Torque Converter Pressurization Kit
27.	J-23907	Universal Remover

OX7A274

Fig. 55-19. Study special tools needed to service one make of automatic transmission. Many are also needed with front-wheel drive transaxle. (Chevrolet)

5. _____ tests are used to determine whether oil pressure in the various circuits is normal.

6. _____ _____ _____ show how the oil passages inside the automatic transmission are connected to each component.

7. List thirteen steps you should carefully follow when servicing the fluid and filter for an automatic transmission.

8. Where do automatic transmission fluid leaks commonly occur?

9. Summarize the general adjustment of an automatic transmission band.

10. A car fails to crank (starting motor operation) when in park. It will only crank when the shift lever is in neutral.
Technician A says that the neutral safety switch must be bad and should be replaced.
Technician B says that the neutral safety switch could require adjustment.
Who is correct?
a. Technician A
b. Technician B
c. Both A and B
d. Neither A nor B

ACTIVITIES FOR CHAPTER 55

1. Demonstrate proper method of checking transmission fluid level.

2. Check and diagnose the condition of the transmission fluid for a vehicle in the shop for service.

3. Demonstrate the procedure for band adjustment.

Now that you have studied automatic transmission operation and repair, you should be able to identify and explain the major parts of this transmission. Can you? (General Motors Corp.)

Drive Shafts and Transfer Cases

After studying this chapter, you will be able to:
☐ Identify the parts of a modern drive shaft assembly.
☐ Explain the functions of a drive shaft.
☐ Define the major drive shaft parts.
☐ List the different types of drive lines.
☐ Describe the different types of universal joints.
☐ Identify the major parts of four-wheel drive type drive line.
☐ Explain the basic operation of a transfer case.

The term *driveline* generally refers to the parts that transfer power from the transmission to the drive wheels. Vehicles with the engine in the front and drive axle assembly in the rear have a driveline with a long drive shaft. Fig. 56-1 shows these basic parts.

Front-wheel drive and rear or mid-engine cars do NOT use a driveline with a single, long drive shaft.

Instead, they use a transaxle (transmission-differential assembly) and two drive axle shafts or swing axles. The short axle shafts extend directly out of the transaxle to power the drive wheels.

Chapters 60 and 61 cover front-drive axles and transaxles. Refer to these chapters for more information.

DRIVE SHAFT ASSEMBLY

A *drive shaft assembly* typically consists of a front slip yoke, two universal joints, drive or propeller shaft, and rear yoke. This is illustrated in Fig. 56-1.

1. SLIP YOKE (connects transmission output shaft to front universal joint).
2. FRONT UNIVERSAL JOINT (swivel connection that fastens slip yoke to drive shaft).
3. DRIVE SHAFT (hollow metal tube that transfers

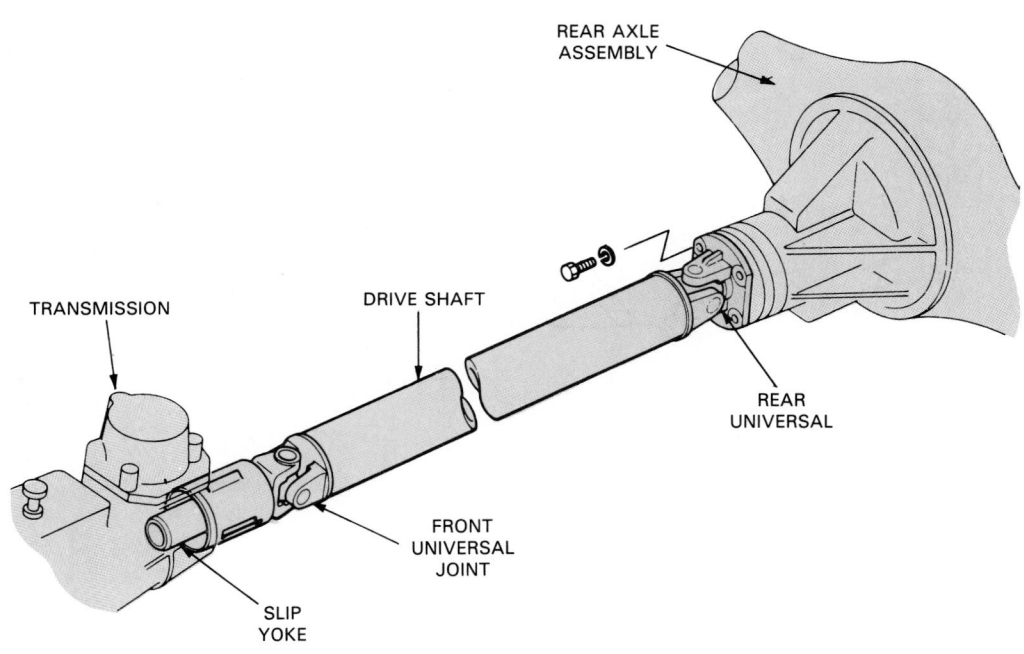

Fig. 56-1. Drive shaft assembly connects transmission output shaft with rear axle assembly. Note major parts. (Mazda)

turning power from front universal joint to rear universal joint).

4. REAR UNIVERSAL JOINT (another flex joint connecting drive shaft to differential yoke).
5. REAR YOKE (it holds rear universal and transfers torque to gears in rear axle assembly).

This drive shaft, Fig. 56-1, is the most common type used on front engine, rear-wheel drive automobiles. Discussed shortly, a few variations are sometimes used to satisfy special applications or to improve the smoothness of power transfer.

FUNCTIONS OF DRIVE SHAFT

The drive shaft assembly has several important functions. It must:

1. Send turning power from the transmission to the rear axle assembly.
2. Flex and allow up and down movement of the rear axle assembly.
3. Provide a sliding action to adjust for changes in drive line length.
4. Provide smooth power transfer.

DRIVE SHAFT OPERATION

With the car moving, the transmission output shaft turns the slip yoke. Refer to Fig. 56-2. The slip yoke then turns the front universal, drive shaft, rear universal, and rear yoke on the differential. The differential contains gears that transfer power to the rear drive axles. The axles rotate the wheels.

Driveline flex

When the tires strike a bump in the road, the rear suspension and springs are compressed. This pushes the rear axle upward in relation to the body. Suspension movement smooths the ride.

The universal joints let the driveline flex without damaging the drive shaft. This is illustrated in Fig. 56-2.

Changes in driveline length

The movement of the rear axle assembly also causes the distance between the rear axle and transmission to change. The slip yoke allows for this change of length. Look at Fig. 56-2.

SLIP YOKE (SLIP JOINT) CONSTRUCTION

The *slip yoke* or *slip joint,* splined to the transmission output shaft, allows for any changes in driveline length by sliding in and out of the transmission. Cutaway views of a slip joint are shown in Fig. 56-3.

Note how the inside of the slip joint has splines that fit over the transmission output shaft splines. This causes the two to rotate together. However, it also permits the yoke to slide on the splines.

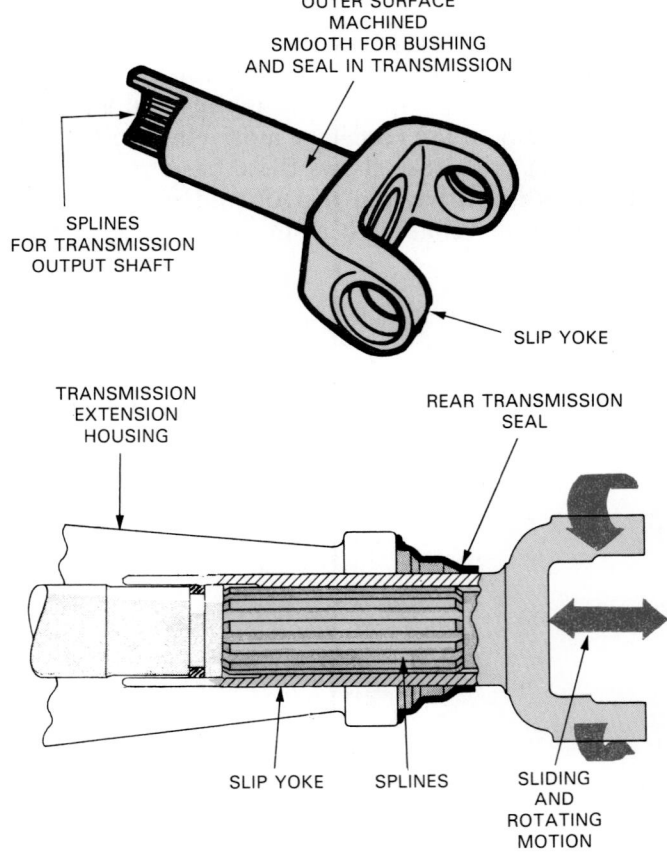

Fig. 56-3. Slip yoke is splined to transmission output shaft and fits inside transmission extension housing. Transmission seal contacts slip yoke. Yoke rides on bushing in extension housing. Slip yoke rotates with output shaft but is free to slide in and out of transmission. (Ford Motor Co.)

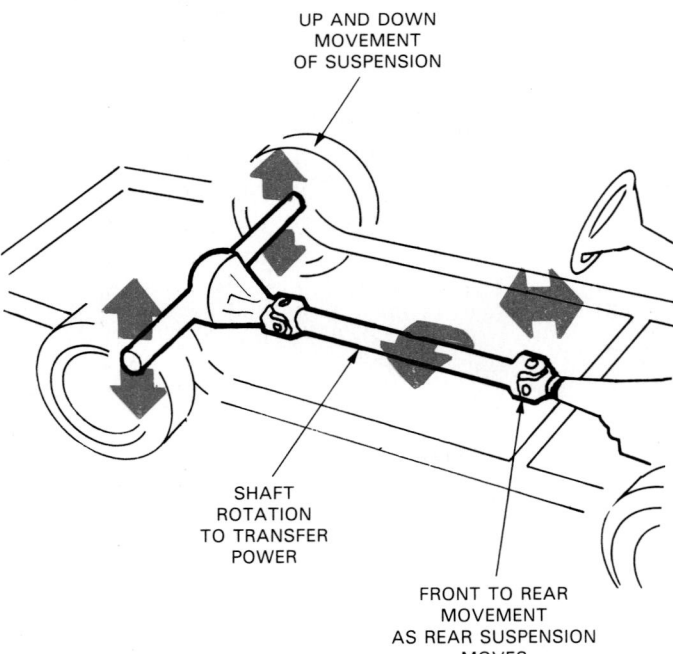

Fig. 56-2. Drive shaft universal joints let driveline bend or flex as rear axle moves up and down over bumps in road. Most types also allow for length changes to allow suspension action.

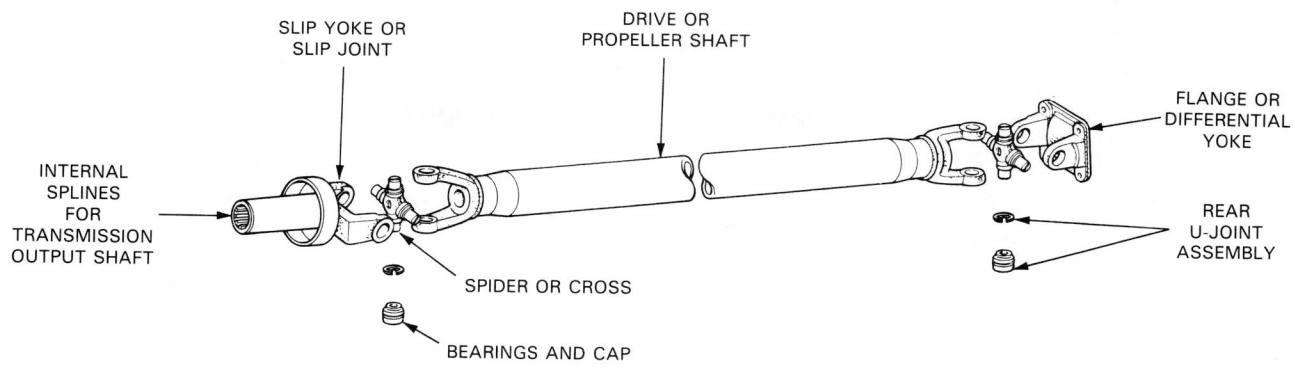

Fig. 56-4. Typical drive or propeller shaft assembly. Note basic components. (Toyota)

The outer diameter of the yoke is machined smooth. This smooth surface provides a bearing surface for the bushing and oil seal in the transmission.

The *extension housing bushing* supports the slip yoke as it spins in the transmission. Refer to Fig. 56-3.

The *transmission rear seal* rides on the slip yoke and prevents fluid leakage out of the rear of the transmission. The seal also keeps road dirt out of the transmission and off the slip yoke.

Normally the outside of the slip joint is lubricated by the transmission fluid. Transmission lubricant prevents bushing, yoke, and seal wear.

Some types of yokes, however, require special heavy grease on their splines. The splines are sealed from the transmission lubricant. This keeps the oil or fluid from washing the grease off the splines.

DIFFERENTIAL YOKE CONSTRUCTION

The *differential yoke* is the yoke bolted to the outer end of the pinion (drive) gear on the rear axle assembly. The rear universal is held by this yoke, Fig. 56-4.

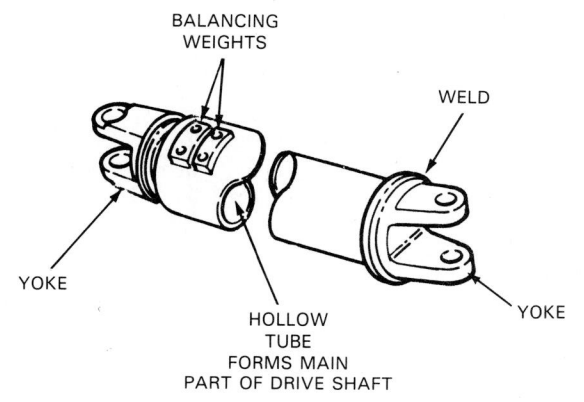

Fig. 56-5. Drive shaft is normally hollow tube with yokes welded to each end. Note balancing weights welded to shaft to prevent vibration. (Ford)

DRIVE SHAFT (PROPELLER SHAFT)

The *drive shaft,* also called a *propeller shaft,* is commonly a hollow steel tube with permanent yokes welded on each end. See Figs. 56-4 and 56-5. A tubular design makes the drive shaft very strong and light. Since the drive shaft spins much faster than the wheels and tires, it must be straight and perfectly balanced.

Most cars use a single, one-piece drive shaft. However, a few large passenger cars and some pickup trucks have a two-piece drive shaft. This cuts down the length of each shaft to avoid driveline vibration.

Drive shaft balance

Since a drive shaft can spin at full engine rpm in high gear, it must be perfectly *balanced* (weight evenly distributed around centerline of shaft). If NOT balanced, the shaft could vibrate violently.

Drive shaft balancing weights are frequently welded to the shaft, as in Fig. 56-5. The drive shaft is spun on a balancing machine at the factory. If needed, small, metal weights are attached to the shaft on the light side. This counteracts the heavy side to smooth operation.

Sometimes, the drive shaft has a large ring-shaped weight mounted on rubber. This ring, called a *drive shaft vibration damper,* also helps keep the shaft spinning smoothly by absorbing torsional (twisting) vibrations.

UNIVERSAL JOINTS

A *universal joint,* also called *U-joint,* is a swivel connection capable of transferring power or turning force through an angle. A simple universal joint is made of two Y-shaped yokes or knuckles connected by a cross or spider. See Fig. 56-6. Bearings on each end of the cross allow the two yokes to swing into various angles while turning.

Today's drive shafts use two or more U-joints. A majority only use two. Extra universals are sometimes needed in very long drive shafts.

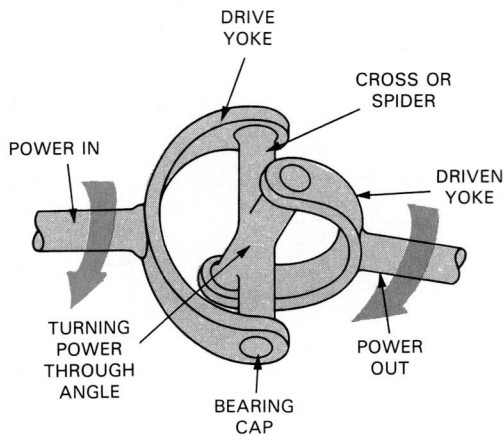

Fig. 56-6. Universal joint or U-joint will swivel to allow for changes in transmission-to-differential alignment. Two yokes are connected to central spider. Needle bearings fit between yokes and spider. Each yoke can be swiveled in relation to the other.

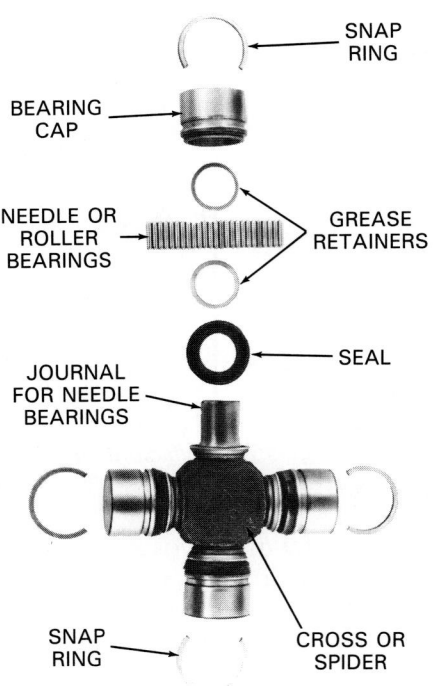

Fig. 56-8. Partially disassembled view of cross and roller type U-joint. Needle bearings are packed with grease. Snap rings hold bearing caps in their yokes. Rubber cup or boot keeps grease inside joint. (Oldsmobile)

There are three common types of automotive drive shaft universal joints used on rear-wheel drive vehicles: cross and roller, ball and trunnion, and double-cardan (constant velocity). These are pictured in Fig. 56-7.

Cross and roller universal joint

The *cross and roller,* also called a *cardan universal joint,* is the most common type of drive shaft U-joint. Pictured in Fig. 56-8, it consists of four bearing caps, four needle roller bearings, a spider or cross, grease seals, grease retainers, and snap rings.

The bearing caps are held stationary in the drive shaft yokes. Roller bearings fit between the caps and cross to reduce friction. The cross is free to rotate inside the caps and yokes.

Snap rings usually fit into grooves cut in the caps or the yoke bores. There are several other methods of securing the bearing caps in the yokes. These are pictured in Fig. 56-9. Sometimes, bearing covers, U-bolts, or injected plastic rings keep the caps and rollers from flying out of the spinning drive shaft assembly.

Fig. 56-10 shows an exploded view of a cross and roller drive shaft assembly. Note how the universal joint components fit together.

Hotchkiss and torque tube drives

A *hotchkiss driveline* has an open drive shaft which operates a rear axle assembly mounted on springs. This is the most common rear-wheel drive type. It usually has cross and roller U-joints.

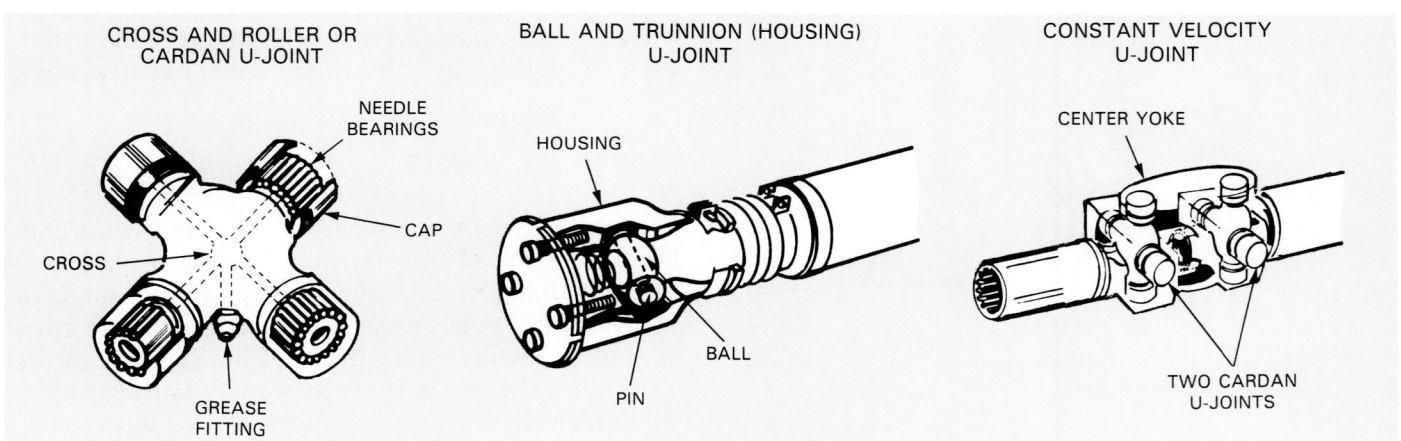

Fig. 56-7. Three basic types of universal joints are used in drive shaft going to rear axle assembly. Other types are used in front drive axles.

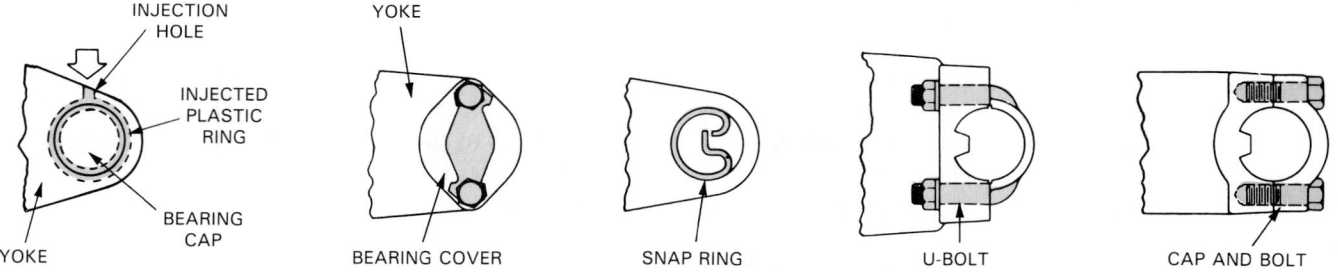

Fig. 56-9. Several methods can be used to hold U-joint caps in yoke. Study each. (Dana Corp.)

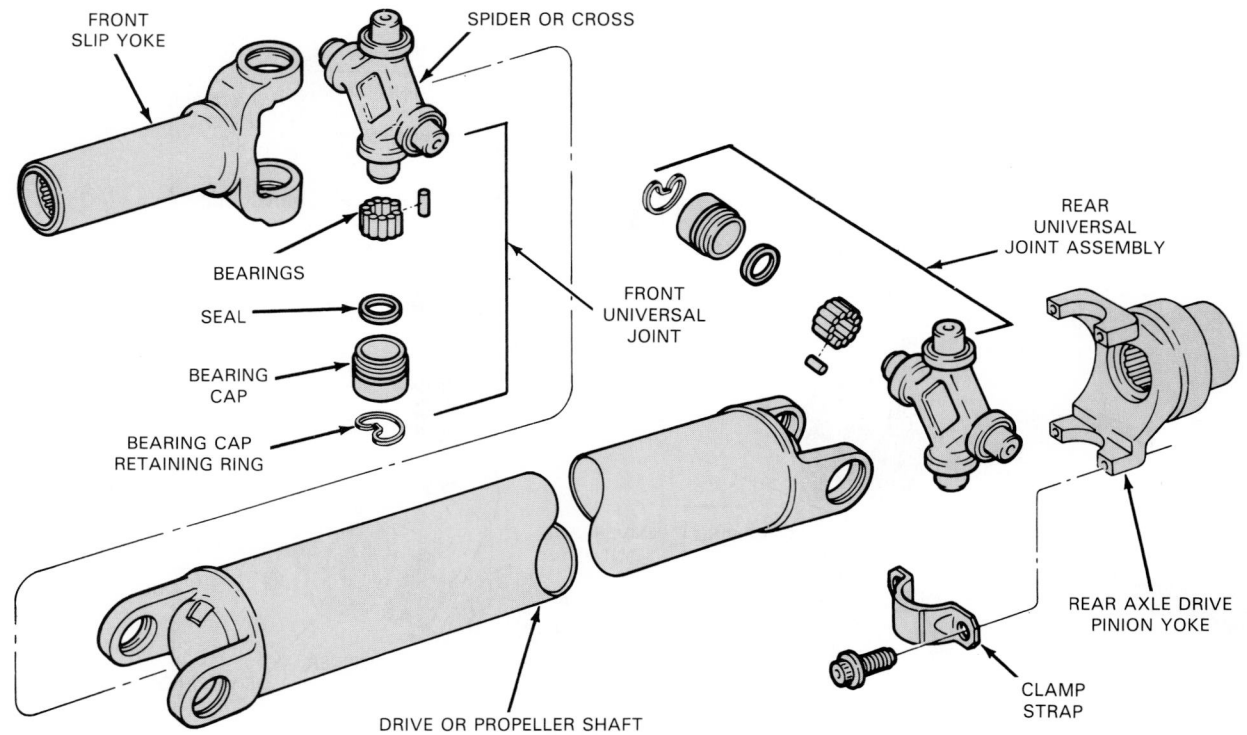

Fig. 56-10. Exploded view of drive shaft using cross and roller universals. Note how parts fit together. (Chrysler Corp.)

A hotchkiss type driveline is pictured in Fig. 56-10. It has almost totally replaced the torque tube setup.

The **torque tube** driveline uses a solid steel drive shaft enclosed in a large hollow tube. Only one swivel joint is used at the front. The rear of the torque tube is formed as a rigid part of the rear axle housing.

Constant velocity U-joints

When a cross and roller universal joint is driven at a sharp angle, its output speed tends to accelerate and decelerate during each revolution. This can set up tiny torque fluctuations and torsional vibrations. One-piece drive shaft vibration problems can be reduced by using one or more constant velocity U-joints.

A *cardan constant velocity joint* normally has TWO cross and roller joints connected by a centering socket and center yoke. See Fig. 56-11. Another name for this type of joint is the *double-cardan joint*.

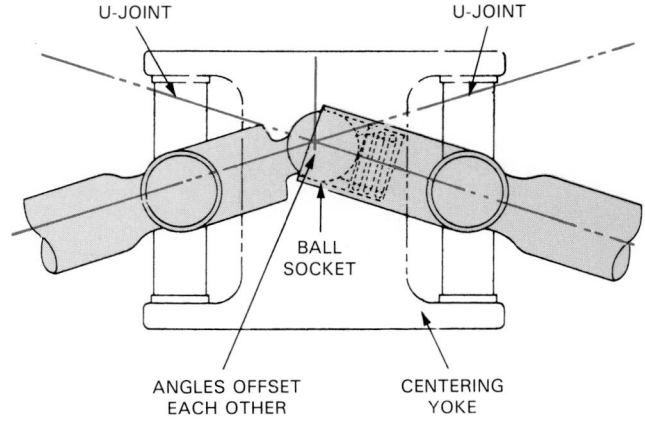

Fig. 56-11. Simplified illustration of constant velocity universal joint. With two cross and roller joints connected to same center yoke, rpm variations are counteracted. Speed changes at output of first joint are offset by speed changes of other joint. (GMC)

Drive Shafts and Transfer Cases 727

With two U-joints operating together on one end of the drive shaft, output shaft speed fluctuations are counteracted. The action of the second universal cancels the shaft speed changes produced by the first joint. Some drive shafts use only one constant velocity U-joint. Others can use more than one, Fig. 56-12.

The *ball and trunnion joint,* Fig. 56-7, is another type designed for constant velocity. It not only eliminates shaft speed fluctuations, but can also allow slight length change in the driveline. It is seldom used, however.

NOTE! Refer to the chapters on transaxles and independent rear suspensions for more information on constant velocity universal joints.

CENTER SUPPORT BEARING

A *center support bearing* is needed to hold the middle of a two-piece drive shaft. See Fig. 56-13. The center bearing bolts to the vehicle frame or underbody. It supports the center of the drive shaft, where the two shafts come together.

Pickup trucks commonly use a center support bearing. A two-piece drive shaft is required because of the great distance between the transmission and rear axle.

A cutaway view of a center support bearing is shown in Fig. 56-14. A sealed ball bearing allows the drive shaft to spin freely. The outside of the ball bearing is

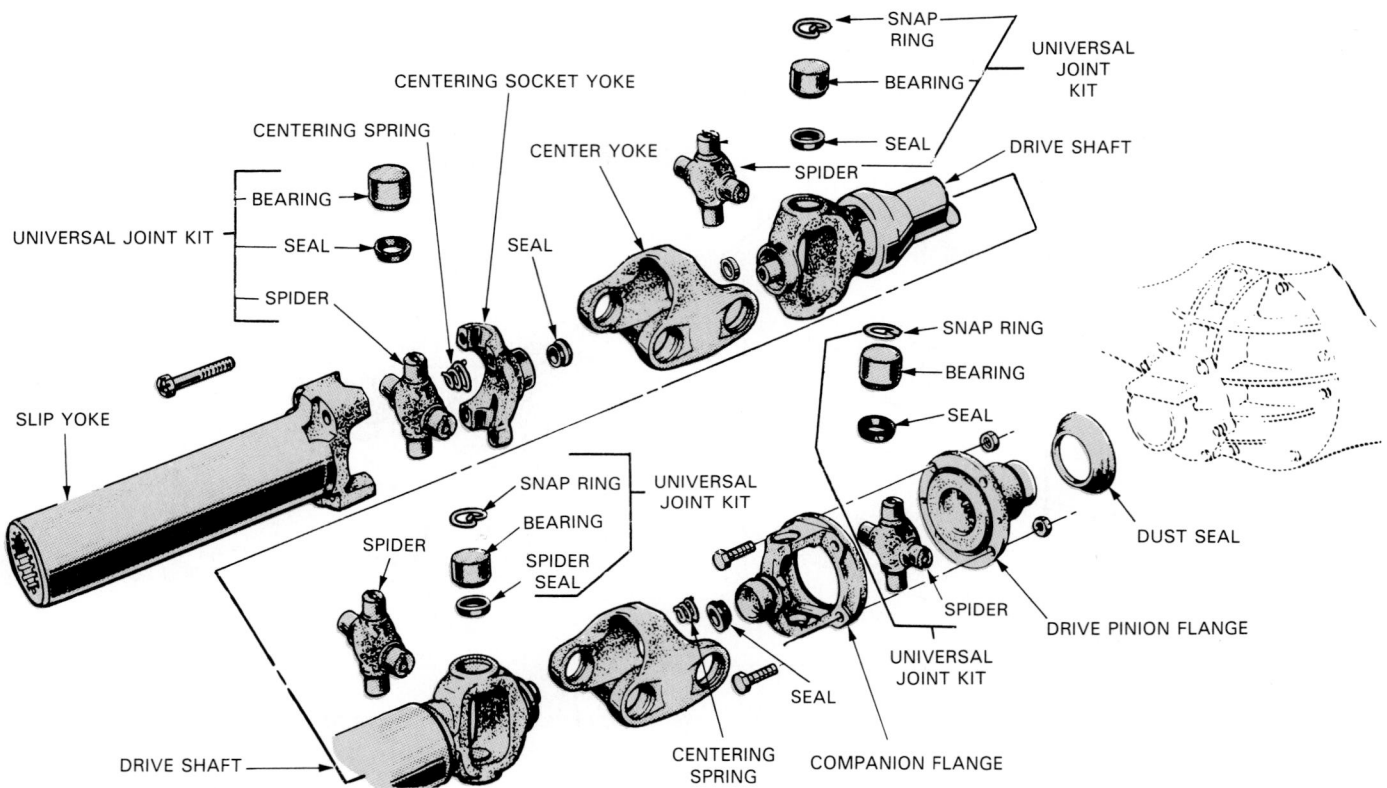

Fig. 56-12. Note construction of drive shaft using two constant velocity U-joints. Two center yokes and four cross and roller joints are needed. (Ford)

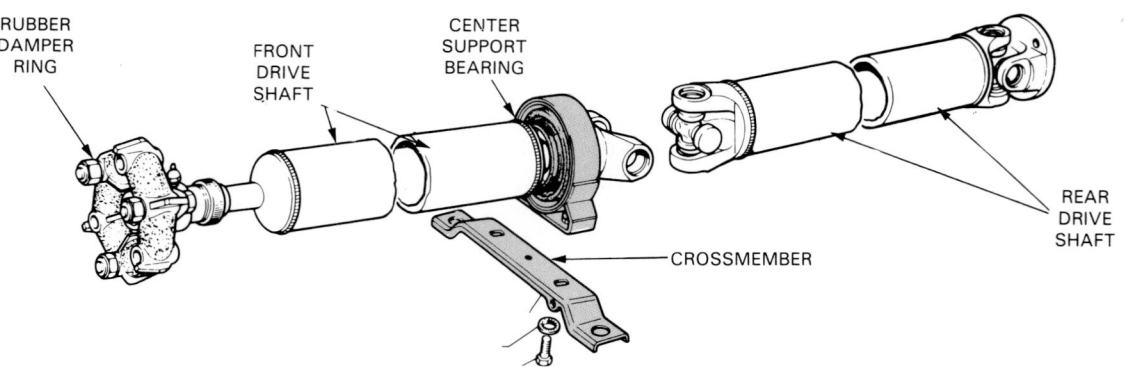

Fig. 56-13. Center support bearing holds center of two-piece drive shaft. It is roller bearing mounted in rubber. Also note rubber torsion damping ring. (Fiat)

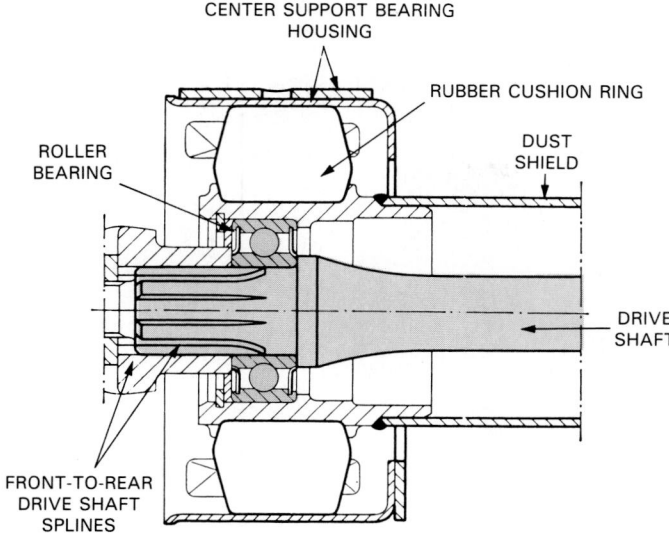

Fig. 56-14. Cutaway view of center support bearing. Study parts. (Fiat)

held by a thick, rubber, doughnut-shaped mount. The rubber mount prevents noise and vibration from transferring into the driver's compartment.

TRANSFER CASES

A *transfer case* sends power to both the front and rear axle assemblies in a four-wheel drive vehicle. Look at Fig. 56-15. The transfer case usually mounts behind and is driven by the transmission. Two drive shafts normally run from the transfer case, one to each drive axle.

Most modern transfer cases provide a 2H (two-wheel drive, high range), a 4H(four-wheel drive, high range), and a 4L(four-wheel drive, low range). High range normally has a gear ratio of 1:1. Low range typically has a gear ratio of 2:1 for climbing steep hills or pulling heavy loads. A 2H is provided for highway driving, when four-wheel drive traction is not needed.

Transfer case operation

Fig. 56-16 shows the major parts of a transfer case. Fig. 56-17 shows how power flows through a transfer case in different shifter positions. Study and compare the parts in both illustrations.

Notice that this unit uses a planetary gearset to produce the two gear ratios. A hand-shifted sliding clutch regulates power transfer for two and four-wheel drive.

Two-wheel drive, high range (2H)

In 2H, torque flows from the input gear, through the locked planetary gearset, and annulus gear which rotate as a single unit. Torque is transferred to the mainshaft through the planetary carrier splined to the mainshaft. Power finally flows out the rear yoke, through the rear drive shaft, and to the rear differential. Refer to Fig. 56-17.

In 2H, the sliding clutch remains in the neutral position. As a result, torque is NOT transferred to the front axle assembly.

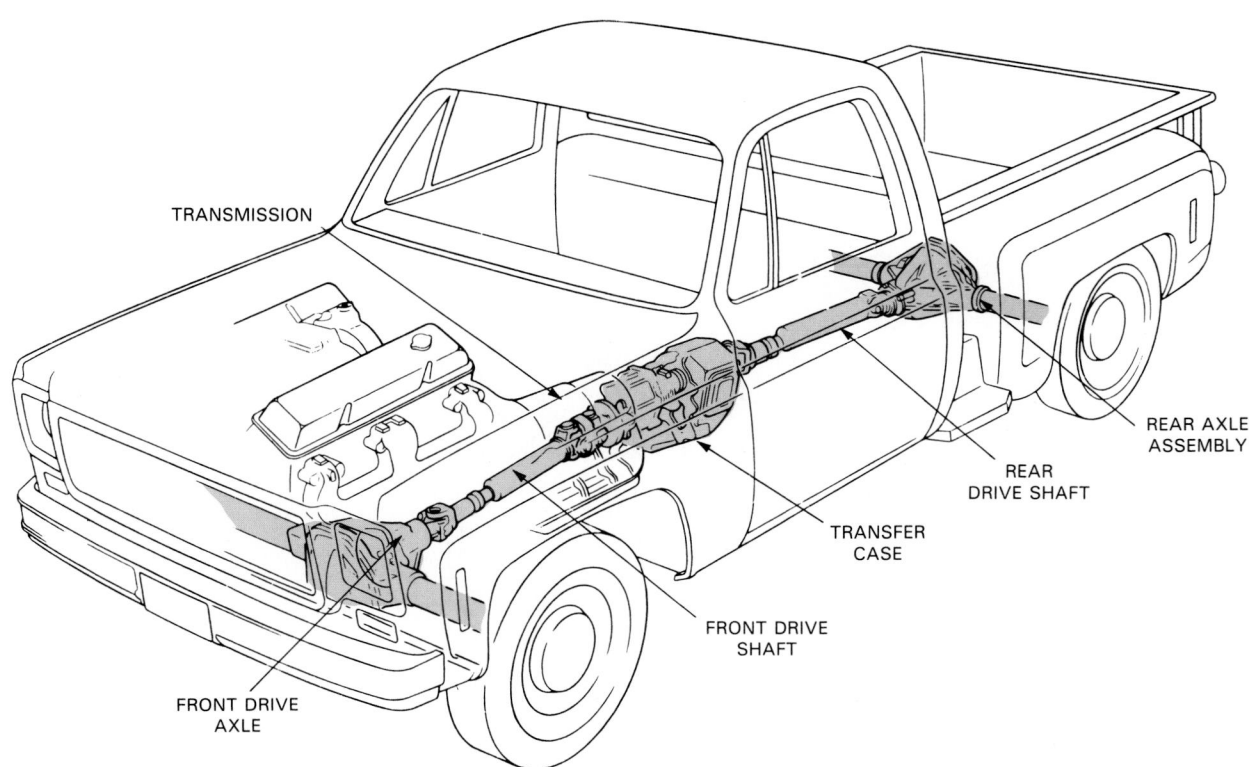

Fig. 56-15. Small trucks and passenger cars commonly use four-wheel drive. Transfer case is power takeoff unit that sends power to both front and rear drive axle assemblies. Drive shafts extend out of front and rear of transfer case. (GMC)

Drive Shafts and Transfer Cases 729

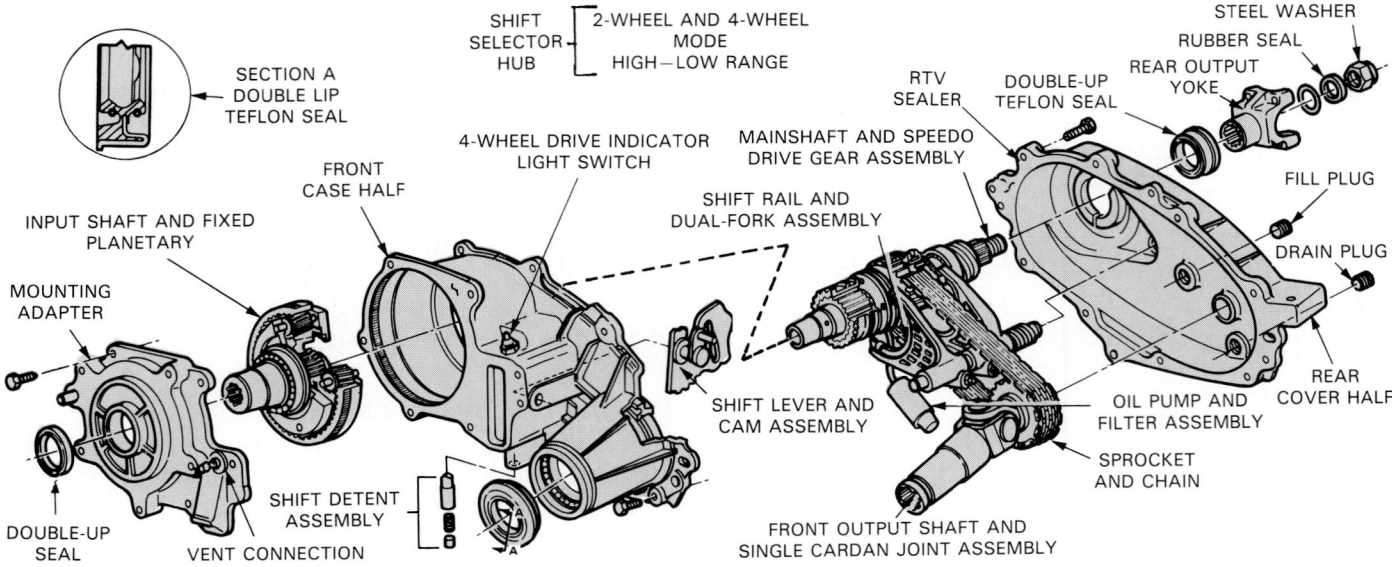

Fig. 56-16. Major parts of modern transfer case. Planetary gearset provides high and low ranges. Large chain sends power to front output shaft. Shift rail and fork assembly is activated to control two-wheel or four-wheel drive mode. (Ford)

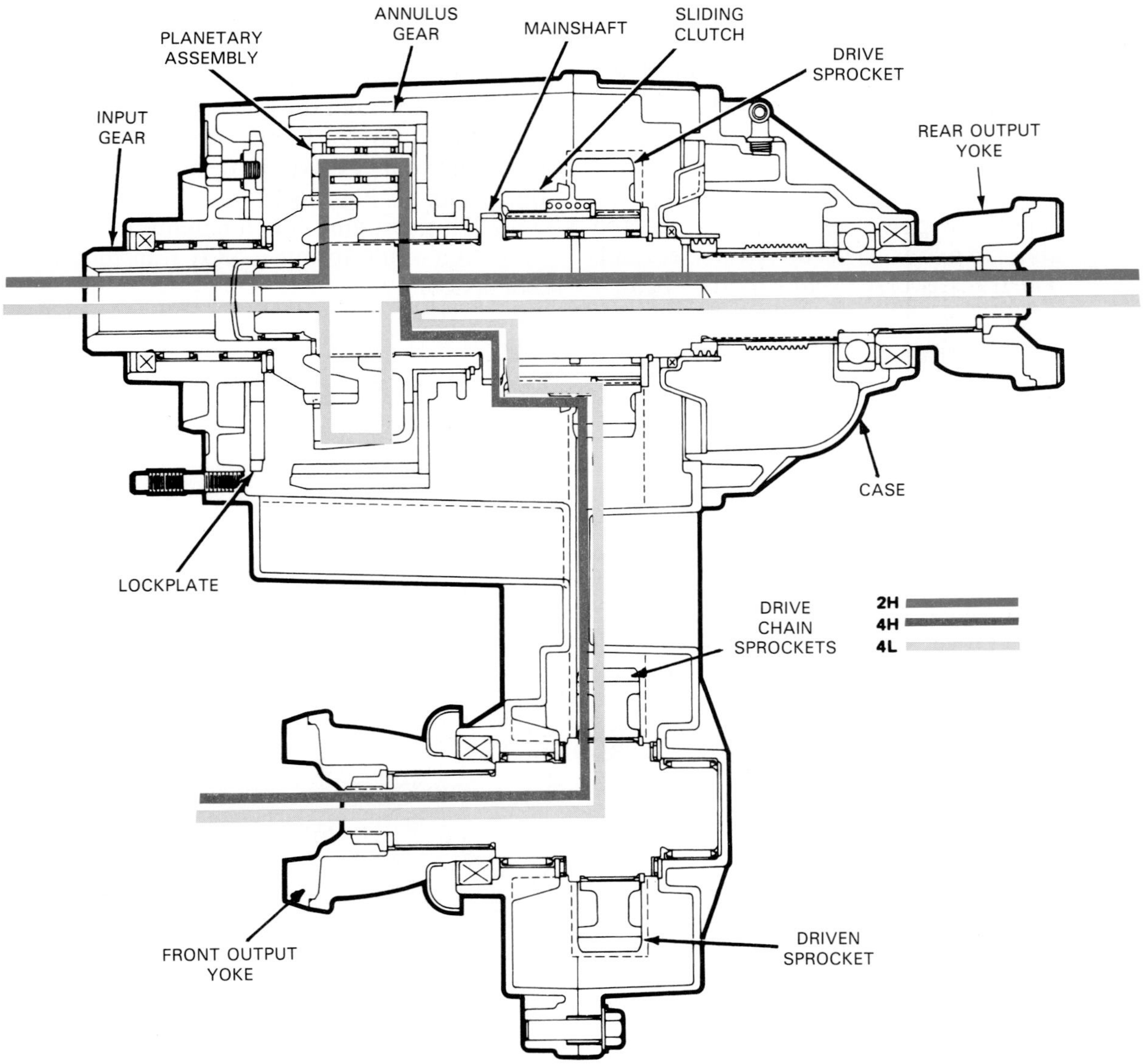

Fig. 56-17. Trace power flow through transfer case in 2H, 4H, and 4L modes. Note parts transferring power in each mode. (Chrysler Corp.)

730   Modern Automotive Technology

Four-wheel drive, high range (4H)

In 4H, torque flows from the input gear, through the planetary gear and annulus (ring) gear in the same fashion as in 2H. However, the sliding clutch is shifted into the mainshaft clutch gear. Torque then flows through the drive chain, front output yoke, and to the front drive axle assembly, Fig. 56-17. Both the front and rear axles drive the vehicle.

Four-wheel drive, low range (4L)

In 4L, torque transfer is almost the same as in 4H. However, the annulus gear is shifted forward into the lock plate. This holds the annulus gear stationary. As a result, the planetary pinions walk inside the annulus gear, producing a gear reduction.

Transfer case construction

A transfer case is constructed something like a transmission. It uses shift forks, splines, gears, shims, bearings, and other components found in manual and automatic transmissions. Look at Fig. 56-16.

A transfer case has an outer case made of cast iron or aluminum. It is filled with lubricant (oil) that cuts friction on all moving parts. Seals hold the lubricant in the case and prevent leakage around shafts and yokes. Shims set up the proper clearances between the internal components and the case.

If needed, review chapters 52 through 55. They cover principles relating to transfer cases. Also, refer to a service manual for details of the particular unit.

All-wheel drive

All-wheel drive refers to a four-wheel drivetrain that does not use a conventional transfer case. It is a relatively new system designed from a front-wheel drive transaxle. Shown in Fig. 56-18, it is a simple system using the principles covered earlier.

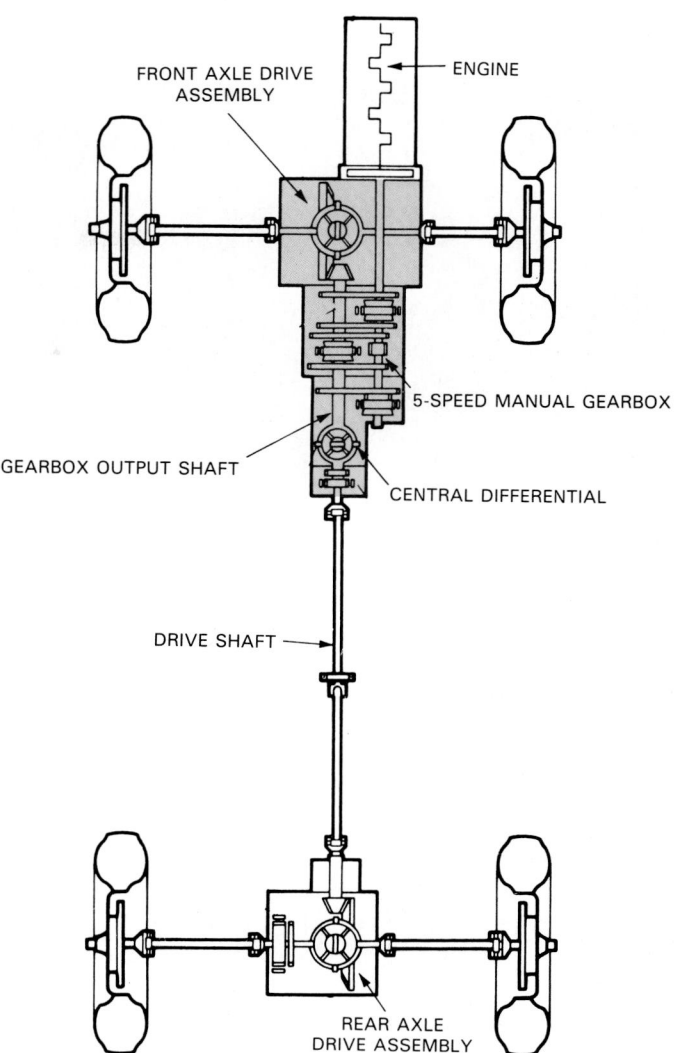

Fig. 56-18. All-wheel drive uses design variation of transmission and transaxle. Main gearbox shaft drives front differential directly. Rear of same gearbox shaft turns drive shaft going to rear axle assembly. A conventional transfer case is not needed. (Porsche-Audi)

KNOW THESE TERMS

Drive line, Drive shaft assembly, Slip yoke, Differential yoke, Drive shaft, Universal joint, Hotchkiss drive, Torque tube, Constant velocity U-joint, Ball and Trunnion U-joint, Center support bearing, Transfer case.

REVIEW QUESTIONS

1. The term _____ _____ generally refers to the parts that transfer power from the transmission to the drive wheels.
2. List and explain the five major parts of a drive shaft.
3. What are four functions of a drive shaft?
4. The movement of the rear axle assembly also causes the distance between the rear axle and transmission to change. True or False?
5. The _____ _____ or _____ _____ is splined to the transmission output shaft.
6. Describe the construction of a typical drive shaft, not including the universal joints or other parts.
7. Which of the following does NOT attach to or touch an assembled drive shaft?
   a. Balance weights.
   b. Yokes.
   c. Universal joints.
   d. All of the above are correct.
   e. None of the above are correct.
8. How does a constant velocity U-joint work?
9. When is a center support bearing needed and why?
10. Explain the basic operation of a transfer case.

ACTIVITIES FOR CHAPTER 56

1. Identify the components of a drivetrain on a vehicle in the automotive shop for service.
2. Sketch the parts of a universal joint or constant velocity joint and label all the parts.
3. Prepare an overhead transparency from the sketches made in Activity 2; use it to teach the parts of the universal joint or constant velocity joint.

Drive Shaft, Transfer Case Diagnosis, Service, Repair

After studying this chapter, you will be able to:
- ☐ Troubleshoot common drive shaft problems.
- ☐ Check U-joint wear.
- ☐ Measure drive shaft runout.
- ☐ Remove and replace a drive shaft assembly.
- ☐ Replace universal joints.
- ☐ Perform basic service operations on a transfer case.
- ☐ Cite and practice good safety procedures.

A drive shaft is subjected to very high loads and rotating speeds. When a vehicle is cruising down the highway, the drive shaft and universals may be spinning at full engine rpm. They are also sending engine power to the rear axle assembly.

To function properly, the drive shaft must be perfectly straight and its universals must be unworn. If any component allows the drive shaft to wobble, severe vibration, abnormal noises, or even major damage may result. See Fig. 57-1.

DRIVE SHAFT PROBLEM DIAGNOSIS

When driving the vehicle to verify a complaint, keep in mind that other components could be at fault. A worn wheel bearing, squeaking spring, defective tire, transmission or differential troubles could be at fault. You must use your knowledge of each system to detect which component is causing the trouble.

Drive shaft problems can normally be divided into two categories: drive shaft noise and drive shaft vibration.

Drive shaft noise

Drive shaft noises are usually caused by worn U-joints, slip joint wear, or a faulty center support bearing. Refer to Fig. 57-1.

Grinding and *squeaking* from the drive shaft is frequently caused by worn universal joints. The joints may become dry, causing the rollers to wear. The un-

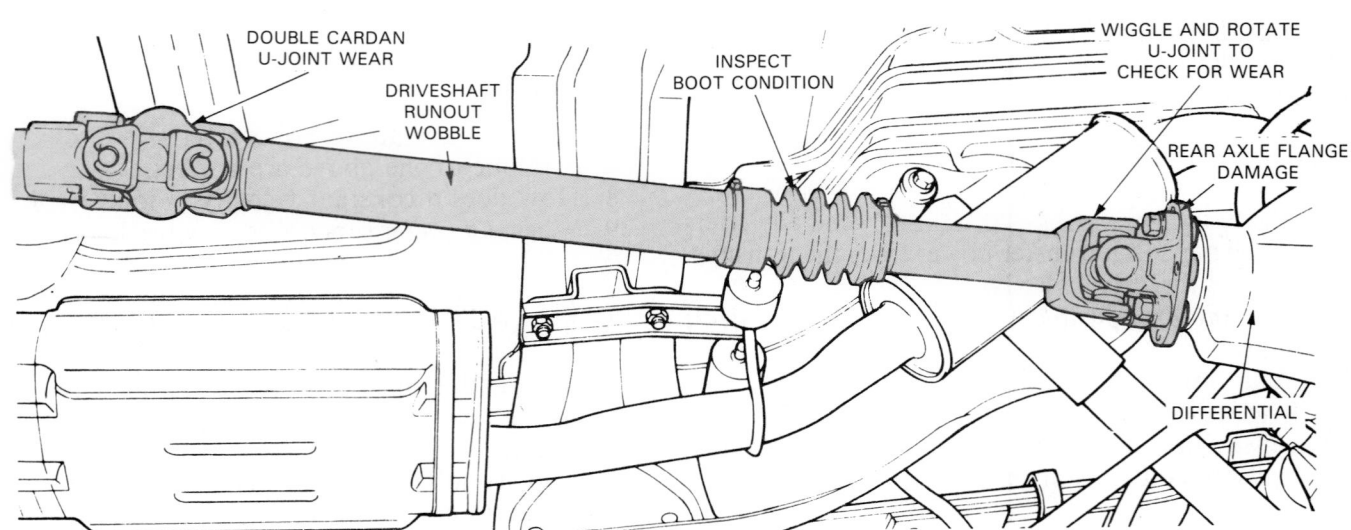

Fig. 57-1. Drive shaft inspection will frequently detect troubles. Wiggle joints to check for wear and looseness. (Ford)

lubricated, damaged rollers then produce a grinding or squeaking sound as they operate on the scored cap and cross surfaces. NOTE: Use special care in diagnosing squeaking noises that seem to come from the universal joints. Wheel covers can make similar noises, as tires flex against them. Remove covers if uncertain of the noise.

A *clunking sound*, when going from acceleration to deceleration or deceleration to acceleration, may be caused by slip yoke problems. The splines may be worn. The yoke's transmission extension housing bushing may also be worn. This will let the yoke flop up and down with changes in driveline torque.

An excessively worn U-joint or differential problems can also cause similar symptoms.

A *whining noise* from the drive shaft is sometimes caused by a dry, worn center support bearing. Since this bearing makes complete revolutions, it will make a different sound than a bad universal joint. A high pitched, MORE CONSTANT whine will usually come out of a faulty center support bearing.

Other abnormal sounds should be traced using your knowledge of mechanical principles, a stethoscope, and a service manual troubleshooting chart.

Drive shaft vibration

Drive shaft vibration can be caused by any problem that affects drive shaft balance, runout (straightness), and angle. Driveline vibration is usually more rapid than vibration caused by wheels and tires.

Drive shaft vibration may be similar to the vibration produced by an unbalanced clutch, flywheel, or engine crankshaft.

When test driving, drive in high gear at the engine rpm that causes the most vibration. Then shift into different transmission gears or neutral while maintaining vehicle speed. If there is NOT a change, the vibration may be in the drive shaft. A vibration change indicates the engine, clutch, torque converter, or transmission is at fault. When vehicle speed remains the same, drive shaft rpm remains the same.

Drive shaft inspection

To inspect the drive shaft, raise the vehicle on a hoist. Look for undercoating or mud on the drive shaft. Check for a sharp driveline angle, missing balance weights, cracked welds, and other drive shaft problems.

Check also for worn U-joints, WIGGLE and ROTATE each U-joint back and forth. Watch the universal joint carefully. Try to detect any play between the cross and yoke. If the cross moves inside the yoke, the U-joint is worn and should be replaced.

Also, wiggle the slip yoke up and down. If it moves in the transmission bushing excessively, either the yoke itself or the bushing is worn. Also inspect the rear yoke bolts for tightness. Make sure the rear motor mount is NOT broken. Look for any condition that could upset the operation of the drive shaft.

If you fail to find a problem, you may need to measure drive shaft runout (wobble) and check balance.

Measuring drive shaft runout

Drive shaft runout is caused by a bent drive shaft, damaged yokes, or worn U-joints. A dial indicator is normally used to measure drive shaft runout.

First, sand and clean around the front, center, and rear of the drive shaft. This will give the dial indicator a smooth surface for accurate measurements. Mount the dial indicator perpendicular to the shaft. See Fig. 57-2. The indicator base must be placed on a rigid surface (differential, floor pan, transmission, or special post stand).

The drive shaft must NOT be in a sharp angle during runout measurement. See Fig. 57-3.

With the transmission in neutral, turn the drive shaft. Measure runout at the front, center, and rear of the shaft, Fig. 57-2. Compare your measurements to specs. Generally, drive shaft runout should NOT exceed .010 to .030 in. (0.25 to 0.76 mm).

If drive shaft runout is beyond specs, try removing and rotating the shaft 180 degrees in the rear yoke. Make sure the universal joints are in good condition and that the yokes are not damaged.

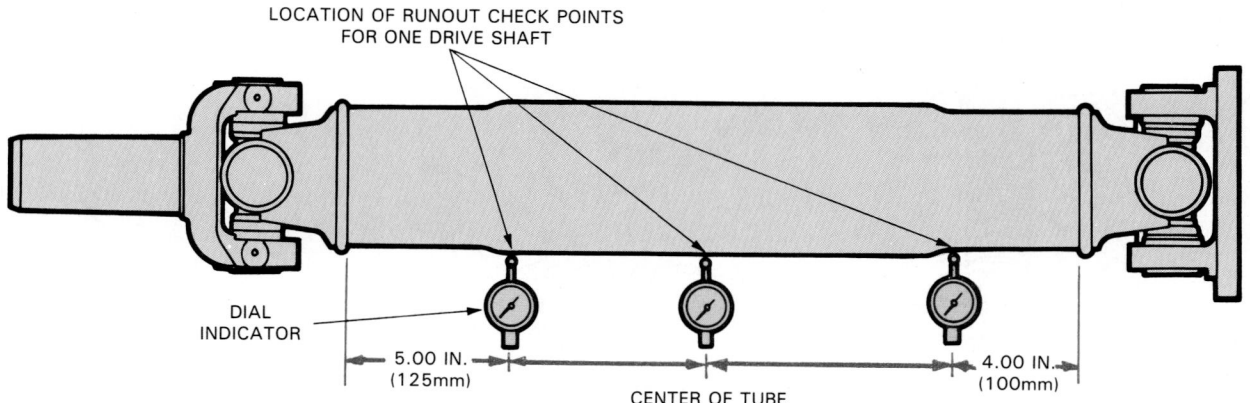

LOCATION OF RUNOUT CHECK POINTS
FOR ONE DRIVE SHAFT

DIAL INDICATOR

5.00 IN. (125mm)

CENTER OF TUBE

4.00 IN. (100mm)

Fig. 57-2. Dial indicator can be used to measure drive shaft runout. Check in middle and on each end. If runout is more than specs, shaft is bent or yokes are damaged. (Cadillac)

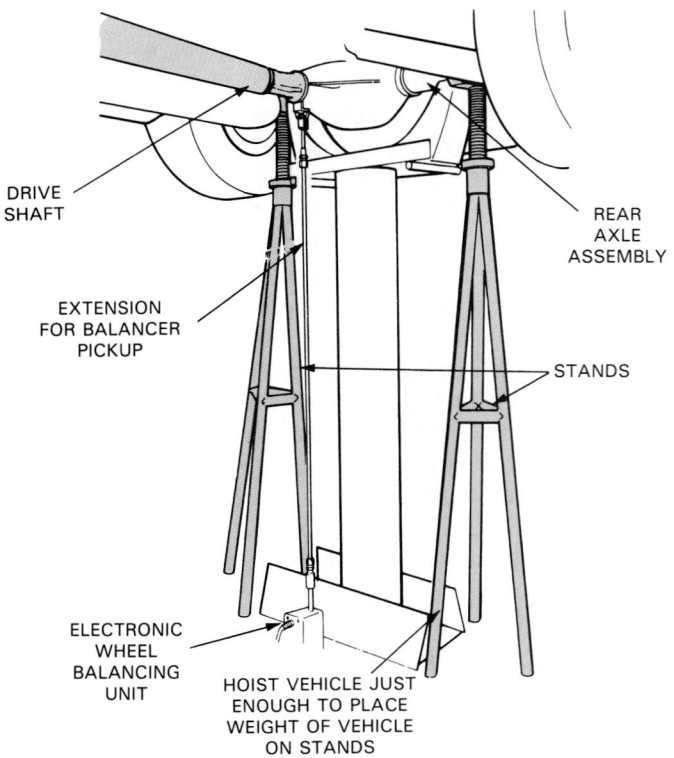

Fig. 57-3. When checking drive shaft, support rear axle assembly. This will keep transmission and rear axle in normal alignment. Also note use of electronic wheel balancing unit for checking shaft vibration. (Buick)

ported on the rear axle housing. The rear axle must be held up in its normal position with the wheels free to rotate. If needed, use long hoist type jack stands, as in Fig. 57-3.

Ask another worker to start the engine and engage the transmission in high gear. With the drive shaft rotating at a speedometer reading of 40 to 50 mph (64 to 81 km/h), carefully bring a crayon or pencil up to the drive shaft a few inches away from the rear universal.

As soon as the marker touches the spinning drive shaft, pull the marker back from the shaft. As shown in Fig. 57-4A, a mark on only one side of the drive shaft indicates the HEAVY SIDE of the shaft.

CAUTION! Be extremely careful not to let any part of your body come in contact with the spinning drive shaft or rear wheels. If your hair, for example, touches a spinning U-joint, scalp and head injuries can result.

If needed, install two screw or worm type hose clamps on the drive shaft, as in Fig. 57-4B. The screw heads on the clamps should be located opposite the crayon or pencil marks. The weight of the screws will offset the heavy side of the drive shaft. Tighten the clamps securely.

Run the speedometer back up to the vibration speed. If the vibration is gone, lower and take a test drive. If an imbalance still exists, rotate the clamps 45 degrees away from each other and recheck vibration. Continue rotating the clamps apart or together, in smaller increments until the vibration is gone.

If required, repeat this balancing operation on the front of the drive shaft. If you cannot balance the shaft, send it to a machine shop that has specialized shaft balancing equipment.

If runout is still excessive, replace the drive shaft or send it to a machine shop for repairs. Some specialized shops can replace center section or tube of drive shaft.

Balancing a drive shaft

If the drive shaft is within recommended runout limits, the drive shaft may need to be balanced. Place the vehicle on a twin post lift so that the rear is sup-

Measuring drive shaft angle

When your runout and balance checks fail to find a problem, you may need to check drive shaft or drive

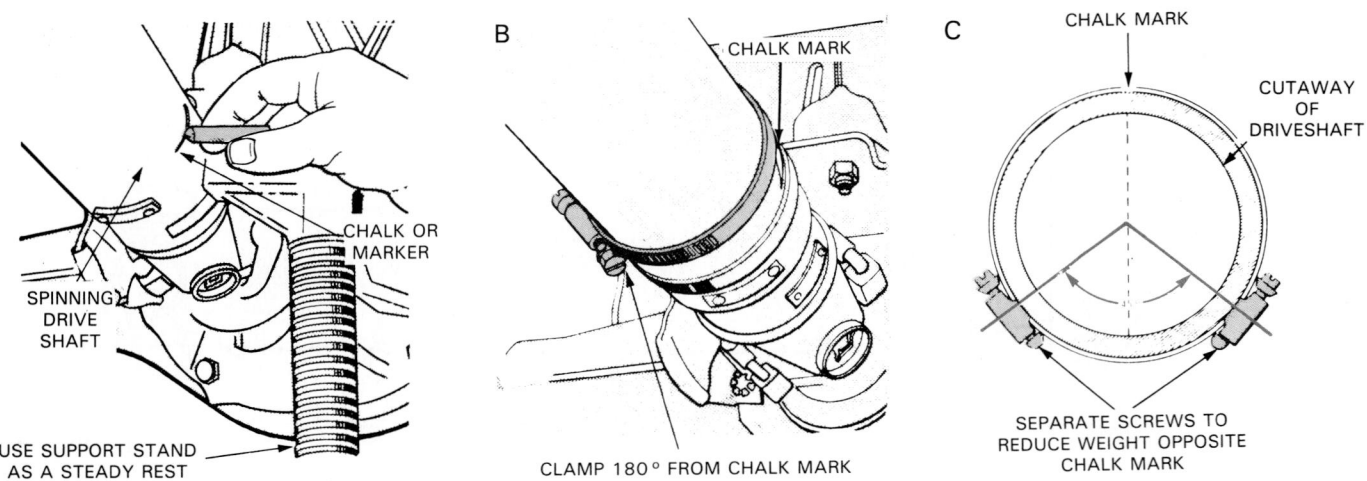

Fig. 57-4. Checking for drive shaft imbalance. A — Idle engine in gear while bringing marker up to drive shaft slowly. Move marker away as soon as it touches shaft. B — Place hose clamps around shaft. Screw heads should be opposite mark. C — Move screw heads away from each other as needed to attain correct balance. (Ford)

line angle. If the angle is too sharp, the universal joints can cause speed fluctuations and vibration.

There are various methods used to check drive shaft angle. Some auto makers recommend a bubble gauge that reads in degrees. One is shown in Fig. 57-5.

By placing the gauge on the drive shaft (car in level position with rear axle supporting vehicle weight), read exact drive line angle. If the angle is incorrect, you can adjust drive shaft angle by placing shims under the rear axle housing or transmission mount. Refer to a service manual for exact procedures.

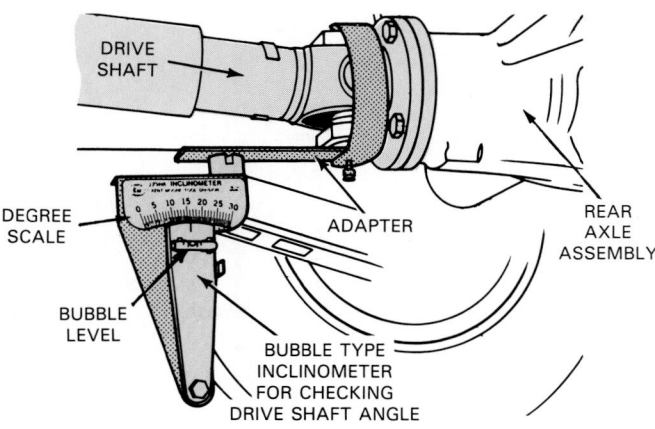

Fig. 57-5. Special angle gauge or inclinometer may be used to check drive line alignment. Shim rear axle or transmission, or replace springs and other parts to correct misalignment problem. Misalignment can cause vibration and U-joint wear. (Cadillac)

DRIVE SHAFT MAINTENANCE

Normally, very little maintenance is required on modern drive shafts. The universals are usually sealed units that are filled with grease at the factory. However, some U-joints, especially aftermarket types, have grease fittings that allow lubrication.

A grease gun can be used to lubricate universal joints that have fittings, Fig. 57-6.

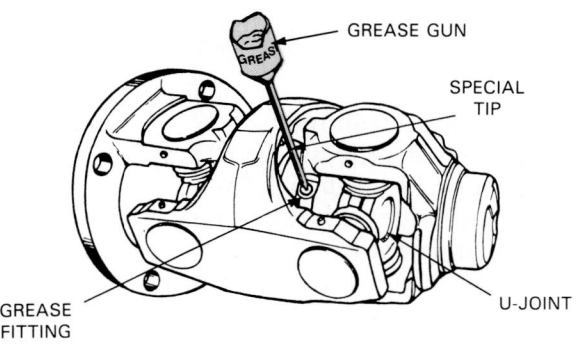

Fig. 57-6. Some U-joints have grease fittings. Use grease gun and special, long stem, if needed, to keep universal joint bearings lubricated. (GMC)

DRIVE SHAFT SERVICE

Drive shaft service requires that the drive shaft be removed for repairs. The universal joints may be worn and require replacement or possibly the drive shaft itself is damaged. Although some design variations are used, general procedures are the same for most rear-wheel drive vehicles.

Drive shaft removal

To remove the drive shaft, raise the car on a hoist. Scribe marks on the differential yokes and the universal joints. See Fig. 57-7. This will help assure proper drive shaft balance upon reassembly.

Unbolt the rear joint from the differential. Pry the shaft forward and lower the shaft slightly.

Do NOT allow the full weight of the drive shaft to hang on the front slip yoke. Support the drive shaft to prevent damage to the extension housing, rear bushing, and front U-joint.

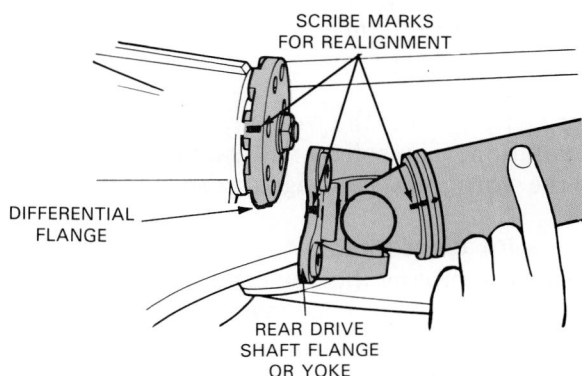

Fig. 57-7. Scribe mark drive shaft, rear yoke, and U-joints before disassembly. This will help maintain shaft balance when reassembling. (Ford)

Wrap tape around the two caps on the rear universal joint if needed. This will keep the caps from falling off and spilling the small roller bearings. If used, also unbolt the center support bearing, Fig. 57-8.

Slide the drive shaft out of the transmission. If transmission lubricant begins to leak out, install a plastic plug or old slip yoke in the extension housing.

UNIVERSAL JOINT SERVICE

A *worn universal joint,* the most common drive shaft problem, can cause squeaking, grinding, klunking, or clicking sounds. The grease inside the joint can dry out. The roller bearings can then wear small indentations (dents) in the cross. When the bearings try to roll over these imperfections, a loud metal-on-metal grinding or chirp sound can result.

Quite often, a worn U-joint will show up in REVERSE. When the car is backed up, it will force

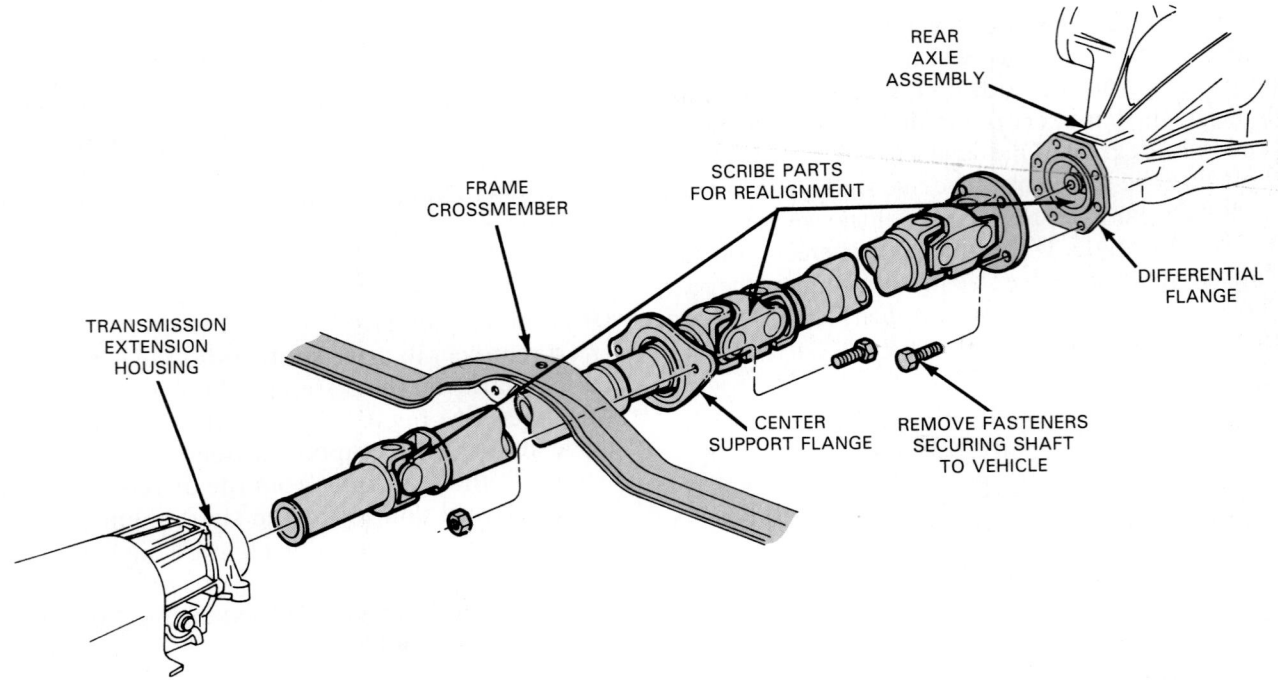

Fig. 57-8. To remove drive shaft, unbolt rear yoke from differential. You may also have to remove center support bearing or flange. Slide shaft out of transmission. If applicable, wrap tape around U-joints to keep caps from falling off. (Cadillac)

the roller bearings over the wear indentations against normal rotation. The rollers will catch on the sharp edges in the worn joint, causing an even louder sound.

Universal joint disassembly

Before disassembling the universal joint, especially a constant velocity type, scribe mark each component. The marks will show you how to reassemble the joint.

Clamp the drive shaft yoke in a vise. Do NOT clamp the weaker center section of the drive shaft or it may be bent.

CAUTION! Avoid excessive force when holding a drive shaft in a vise. If the shaft or yokes are bent, the drive shaft may vibrate when returned to service.

If used, remove the snap rings from the universal joint caps or yokes. Look at Fig. 57-9. Use screwdrivers, snap-ring pliers, or needle nose pliers.

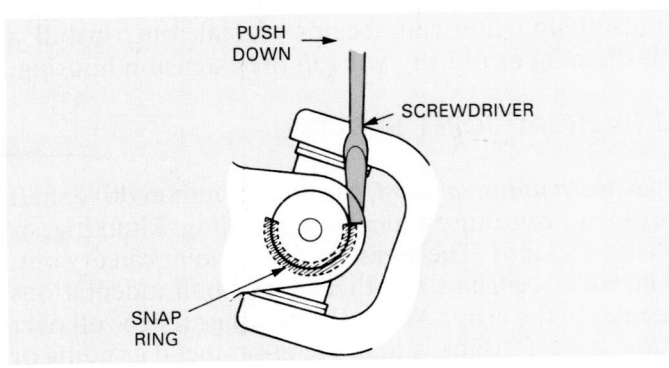

Fig. 57-9. To disassemble cross and roller universal joint, remove snap rings using screwdriver or snap ring pliers. (Toyota)

DANGER! Wear safety glasses to protect your eyes in case the snap-rings fly out of the joint during removal.

To remove the universal from the yokes, use a vise and two sockets, Fig. 57-10. Place a socket SMALLER than the bearing cap on one end of the universal joint. Place a socket with an inside diameter LARGER than the bearing cap on the opposite side of the joint.

Fit both sockets and the universal inside a vise. Slowly tighten the vise to force the bearing caps out of the yoke. Repeat this operation on the other yoke if needed.

Universal joint replacement

Normally, a universal joint is replaced anytime it is disassembled. However, if the joint is relatively new, you can inspect, lubricate, and reassemble it.

During inspection, clean the roller bearings and other parts in solvent. Then, check the cross and rollers for signs of wear. If the slightest sign of roughness or wear is found on any part, REPLACE the U-joint.

Universal joint assembly

To assemble a universal joint, make sure the roller bearings are packed with high temperature grease. Position the cross inside one of the yokes. Align your punch marks. Then, fit the bearing caps into each end of the yoke. Center the cross partially into each cap to keep the roller bearings from falling out. Place the assembly in a vise. Tighten the vise so that the bearing caps are forced into the yoke.

To press the caps fully into position, place a small socket on one bearing cap. See Fig. 57-11. Tighten the

Fig. 57-10. With snap rings removed, press spider and bearing caps out of yokes. Use small socket as driver. Use large socket to accept bearing cap on other side. (Chrysler)

Fig. 57-11. To install universal, use one small socket and vise to press caps into yoke. Make sure small needle bearings are in place or part damage can result. Press in until you can install one snap ring. Then, press other cap in and install other snap ring. (Chrysler Corp.)

vise until the cap is pushed in far enough for snap ring installation. With one snap ring in place, use the socket to force the other cap into place. Install its snap ring. Repeat this procedure on the other universal and yoke, if needed. Look at Fig. 57-12.

WARNING! If the bearing cap fails to press into place with normal pressure, disassemble the joint and check the roller bearings. It is easy for a roller bearing to fall down and block cap installation. If you try to force the cap with excess pressure, the universal and drive shaft could be RUINED.

After assembly, check the action of the universal joint. Swing it back and forth into various positions. The joint should move freely, without binding.

Double-check that all of the snap rings have been installed properly. Refer to Fig. 57-13.

Some universal joint caps are secured by a special PLASTIC RESIN injected into the universal. Refer to a service manual for exact procedures. Generally, a tube of glue-like plastic is used to force the plastic into holes in joint. When dry, the plastic forms a ring to hold joint together. Allow adequate drying time before installing and using drive shaft.

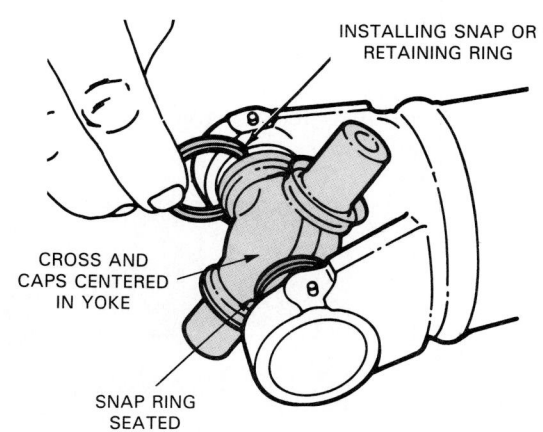

Fig. 57-13. Make sure snap rings are fully installed in their grooves. Start them by hand. Then use small hammer and drift to seat them, if needed. (Cadillac)

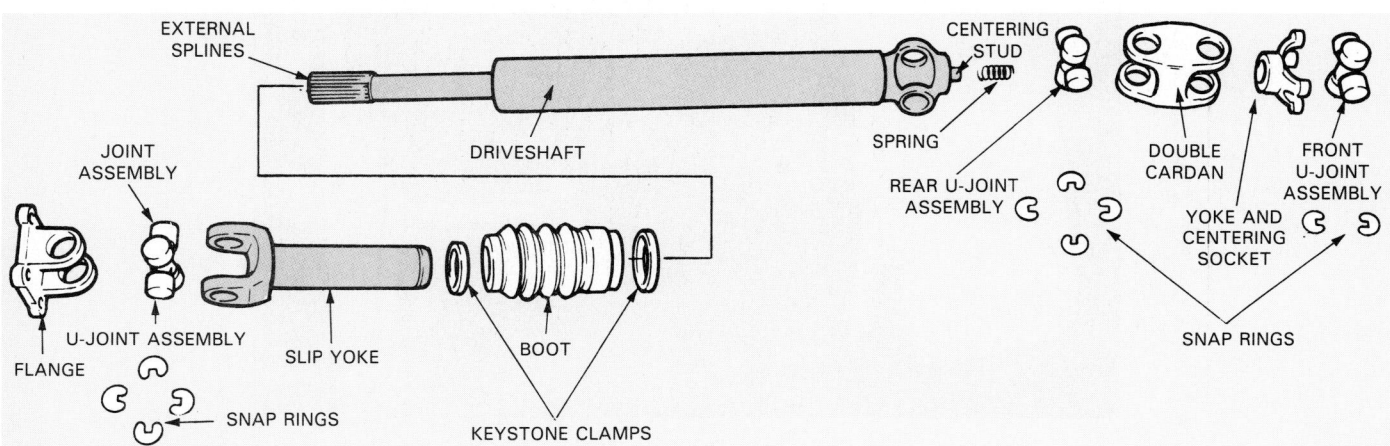

Fig. 57-12. Inspect all drive shaft assembly components carefully. In particular, check snap ring grooves, yokes, and universals. Replace any part not in good condition. Also, make sure you mark position of all parts. They must be installed in same position to prevent possible shaft vibrations. (Ford Motor Co.)

INSTALLING DRIVE SHAFT

To install the drive shaft, wipe the slip joint clean. Place a small amount of grease on its internal splines if recommended. Align your marks and slide the yoke into the rear of the transmission.

Push the shaft all the way into the extension housing and position the rear joint in the differential. Pull the shaft back and center the rear universal properly. Check your rear alignment marks.

Install the U-bolts, bearing caps, or yoke bolts to secure the rear universal to the differential. Lower the car to the ground.

TRANSFER CASE SERVICE

Transfer case service is required when the unit makes abnormal noises (grinding, whining), fails to engage properly, or is locked in gear.

When removing a transfer case, use a transmission jack, Fig. 57-14. A transfer case is heavy and can cause injury or part damage if dropped.

To repair a transfer case, follow the procedures outlined in a service manual. It will give directions for repairing the particular make and model. Fig. 57-15 shows the parts of a modern transfer case.

To service the drive shafts on a four-wheel drive vehicle, use the general instructions given for a cross and roller universal joint. A four-wheel drive simply uses two drive shafts instead of one.

Transfer case maintenance

The fluid level in a transfer case should be checked at recommended intervals. To check the lubricant level, remove the transfer case fill plug. It is normally located on the side or rear of the transfer case, Fig. 57-16.

Lubricant should be almost even with the fill hole. If required, add the recommended type and amount.

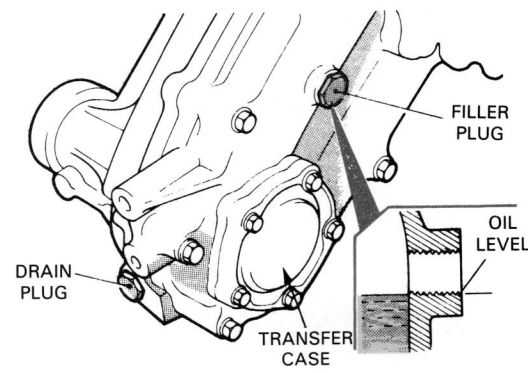

Fig. 57-16. Remove the filler plug to check the amount of lubricant in a transfer case. Fluid should be about even with hole. (Chrysler)

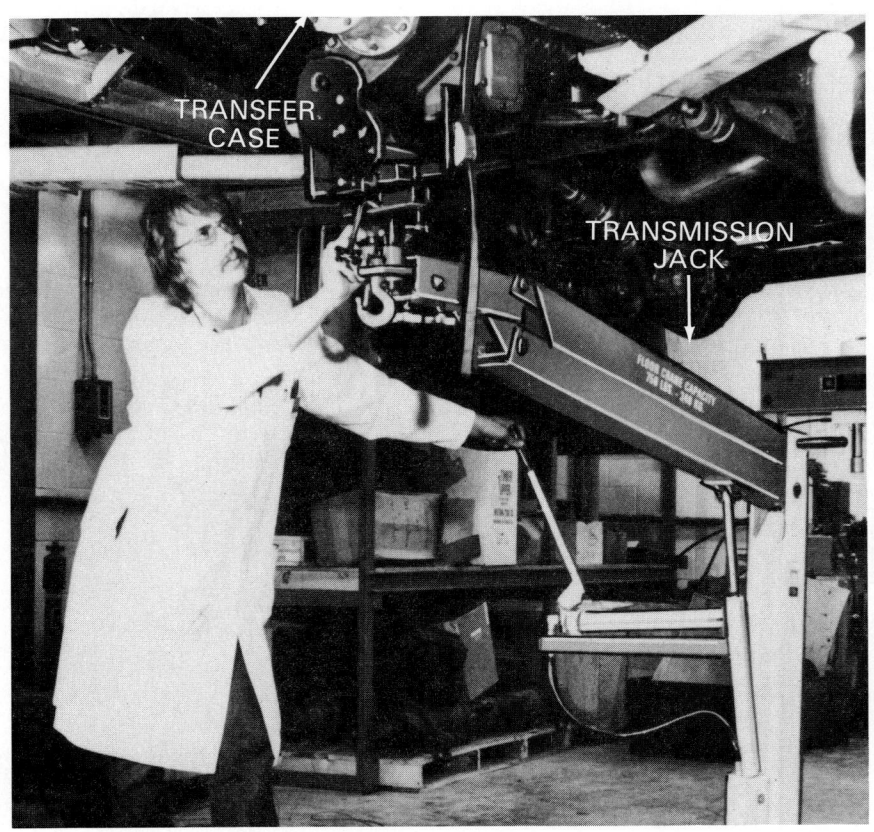

Fig. 57-14. A transfer case is heavy. Use a transmission jack to lower unit from vehicle. Removal typically involves disconnecting shift linkage, drive shafts, and transfer case mounts. (OTC, Div. of SPX Corp.)

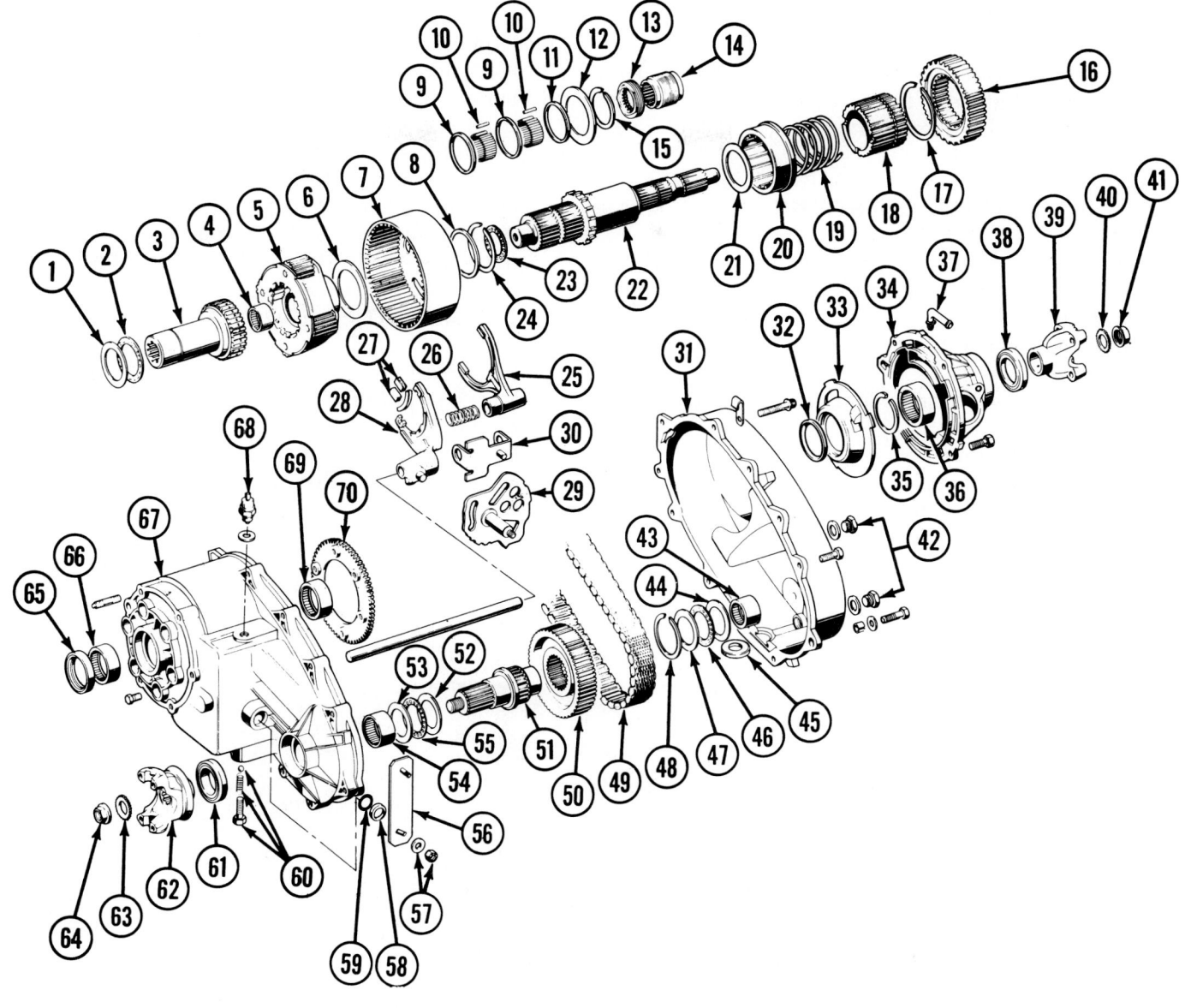

1. Input gear thrust washer
2. Input gear thrust bearing
3. Input gear
4. Mainshaft pilot bearing
5. Planetary assembly
6. Planetary thrust washer
7. Annulus gear
8. Annulus gear thrust washer
9. Needle bearing spacers
10. Mainshaft needle bearings (120)
11. Needle bearing spacer
12. Thrust washer
13. Oil pump
14. Speedometer gear
15. Drive sprocket retaining ring
16. Drive sprocket
17. Sprocket carrier stop ring
18. Sprocket carrier
19. Clutch spring
20. Sliding clutch
21. Thrust washer
22. Mainshaft
23. Mainshaft thrust bearing
24. Annulus gear retaining ring
25. Mode fork
26. Mode fork spring

27. Range fork inserts
28. Range fork
29. Range sector
30. Mode fork bracket
31. Rear case
32. Seal
33. Pump housing
34. Rear retainer
35. Rear output bearing
36. Bearing snap ring
37. Vent tube
38. Rear seal
39. Rear yoke
40. Yoke seal washer
41. Yoke nut
42. Drain and fill plugs
43. Front output shaft rear bearing
44. Front output shaft rear thrust bearing race (thick)
45. Case magnet
46. Front output shaft rear thrust bearing
47. Front output shaft rear thrust bearing race (thin)
48. Driven sprocket retaining ring
49. Drive chain

50. Driven sprocket
51. Front output shaft
52. Front output shaft front thrust bearing race (thin)
53. Front output shaft front thrust bearing race (thick)
54. Front output shaft front thrust bearing
55. Front output shaft front bearing
56. Operating lever
57. Washer and locknut
58. Range sector shaft seal retainer
59. Range sector shaft seal
60. Detent ball, spring, and retainer bolt
61. Front seal
62. Front yoke
63. Yoke seal washer
64. Yoke nut
65. Input gear oil seal
66. Input gear front bearing
67. Front case
68. Lock mode indicator switch and washer
69. Input gear rear bearing
70. Lockplate

Fig. 57-15. *During transfer case repairs, refer to instructions and illustrations in factory service manual. It will give details of particular unit being serviced. Study construction of this transfer case.* (Chrysler Corp.)

KNOW THESE TERMS

Drive shaft noise, Drive shaft vibration, Worn U-joint, Drive shaft runout, Drive shaft balance, Drive shaft angle, U-joint alignment marks, Transfer case fill plug.

REVIEW QUESTIONS

1. Drive shaft problems can normally be classified into two categories: drive shaft _____ and drive shaft _____ .
2. What are some common causes of drive shaft noise?
3. Grinding or squeaking from the drive shaft is frequently caused by:
   a. Worn slip joint.
   b. Bent drive shaft.
   c. Worn, dry universals.
   d. None of the above.
   e. All of the above.
4. List three common causes of drive shaft vibration.
5. How do you check for worn U-joints?
6. How do you check drive shaft runout?
7. How do you balance a drive shaft in-shop?
8. Summarize the procedure for disassembly of a cross and roller U-joint.
9. If a universal joint fails to press together with normal force, it is possible that one of the needle bearings has fallen out of place. True or False?
10. A transmission jack is commonly used when removing a transfer case. True or False?

ACTIVITIES FOR CHAPTER 57

1. Inspect a universal joint on a vehicle in the shop. State its condition and indicate if replacement is required.
2. Explain and desmonstrate a procedure for checking runout on a drive shaft.
3. Replace a universal joint using appropriate procedure.
4. Demonstrate proper technique for removing and replacing a drive shaft.

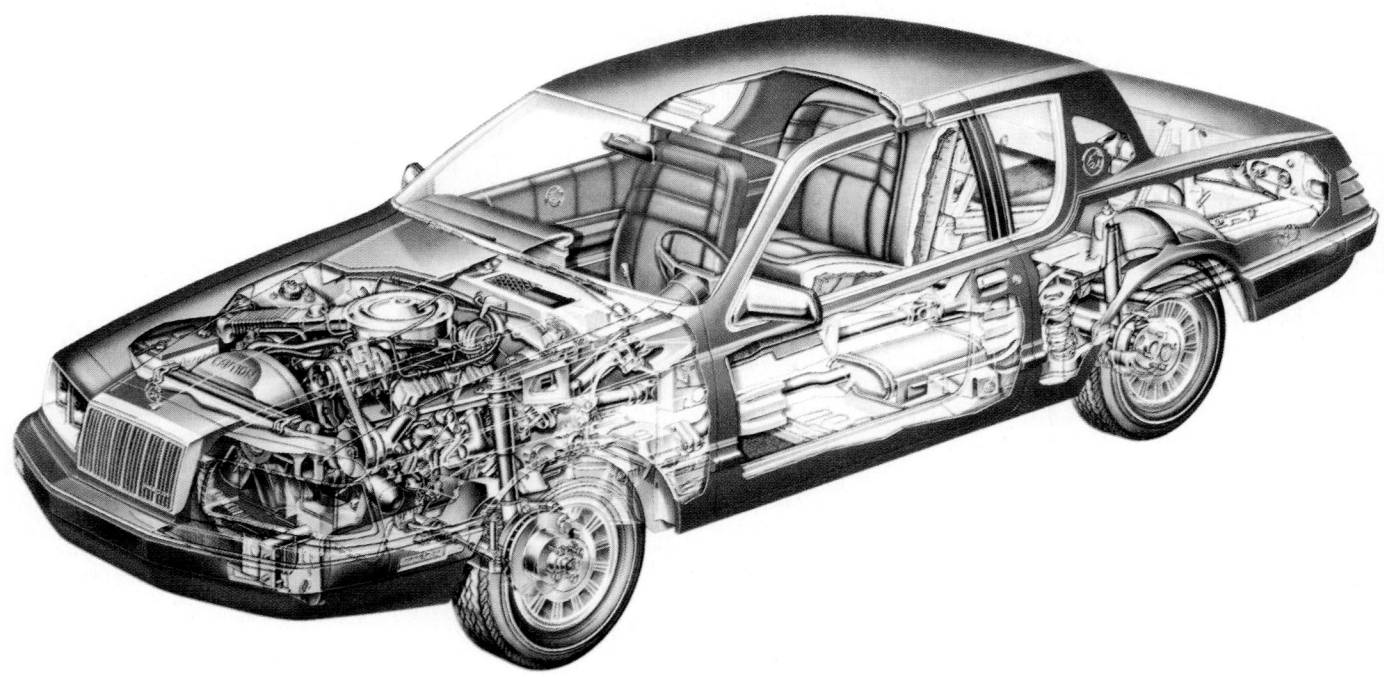

Phantom view of modern automobile shows clearly the drive shaft for a rear-wheel drive arrangement. (Ford Motor Co.)

Differential and Rear-Drive Axle Fundamentals

After studying this chapter, you will be able to:
□ Identify the major parts of a rear drive axle assembly.
□ List the functions of a rear axle assembly.
□ Describe the operation of a differential.
□ Explain differential design variations.
□ Compare different types of axles.
□ Describe the principles of a limited-slip differential.
□ Relate rear axle ratios to vehicle performance.

After engine power flows through the transmission and drive shaft, it enters the rear axle assembly. The rear axles transfer torque to the rear wheels.

When the engine is in the front and drive wheels are at the rear, a rear drive axle and differential assembly is needed. Today's high performance cars and older vehicles commonly use this setup.

Many new vehicles are front engine, front-wheel drive and they use a transaxle (rear axle drive not needed). However, many of the operating principles in a transaxle and a differential are the same. This chapter, as a result, will prepare you for later chapters covering front-wheel drive vehicles.

BASIC REAR DRIVE AXLE ASSEMBLY

A simple *rear drive axle assembly,* Fig. 58-1, consists of:
1. PINION DRIVE GEAR (transfers power from drive shaft to ring gear).

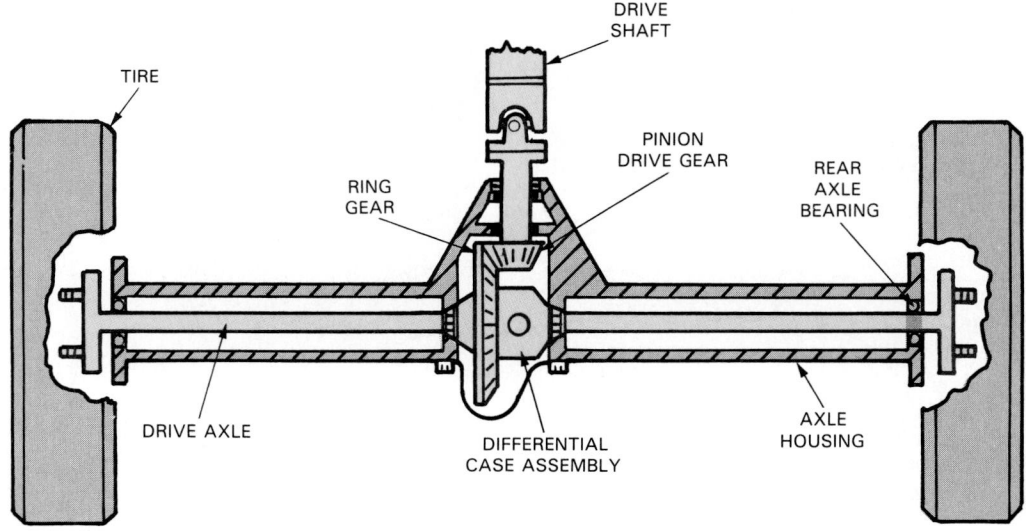

Fig. 58-1. Study fundamental components of rear drive axle. Drive shaft turns pinion gear. Pinion gear turns ring gear and differential case assembly. Differential transfers power to drive axles and wheels.

2. RING GEAR (transfers turning power to differential case assembly).
3. DIFFERENTIAL CASE ASSEMBLY (holds ring gear and other components that drive rear axles).
4. REAR DRIVE AXLES (steel shafts that transfer torque from differential assembly to drive wheels).
5. REAR AXLE BEARINGS (ball or roller bearings that fit between axles and inside of axle housing).
6. AXLE HOUSING (metal body that encloses and supports parts of rear axle assembly).

Rear axle power flow

Power enters the rear axle assembly from the drive shaft, Fig. 58-1. The drive shaft spins the pinion drive gear. The pinion drive gear turns the larger ring gear to produce a gear reduction.

Since the ring gear is bolted to the differential case, the case rotates with the ring gear. Small gears, inside the differential case, send torque to each axle.

The axles extend beyond the axle housing. The axles normally hold and turn the rear wheels and tires to propel the vehicle.

FUNCTIONS OF A REAR-WHEEL DRIVE AXLE

A rear-wheel drive axle assembly has several functions. These include:
1. Send power from the drive shaft to the rear wheels.
2. Provide a final gear reduction.
3. Transfer torque through a 90° angle.
4. Split the amount of torque going to each wheel.
5. Allow for different wheel rotating speeds in turns.
6. Support the rear axles, brake assemblies, suspension components, and chassis.

DIFFERENTIAL CONSTRUCTION

A *differential assembly* uses drive shaft rotation to transfer power to the axle shafts. The term "differential" can be remembered by thinking of the words "different" and "axle." The differential must be capable of providing torque to both AXLES, even when they are turning at DIFFERENT speeds (vehicle turning corner, for example).

Look at Fig. 58-2. It shows the major parts of a rear drive axle.

Pinion gear

The *pinion gear* turns the ring gear when the drive shaft is rotating. One is shown in Fig. 58-2.

The outer end of the pinion drive gear is splined to the rear U-joint companion flange or yoke. The inner end of the pinion gear meshes with the teeth on the ring gear. The pinion gear is normally mounted on tapered roller bearings. They allow the pinion gear to revolve freely in the carrier. Either a crushable sleeve or shims are used to preload the pinion gear bearings.

With some differentials, the extreme inner end of the pinion gear is supported by a *pinion pilot bearing*. It is a straight roller bearing. The pinion pilot bearing

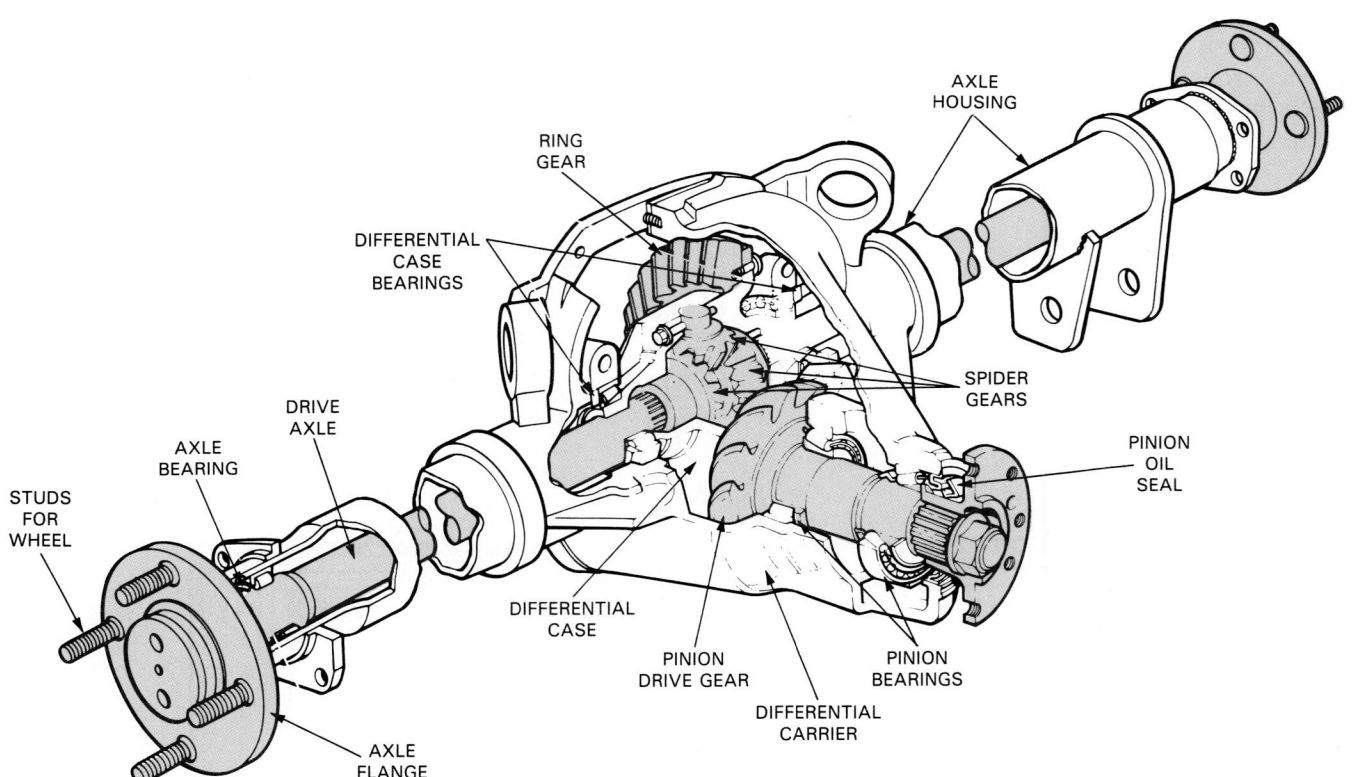

Fig. 58-2. Cutaway shows detailed view inside axle housing. Note relationship of parts. Axle housing fastens to suspension components. (Ford)

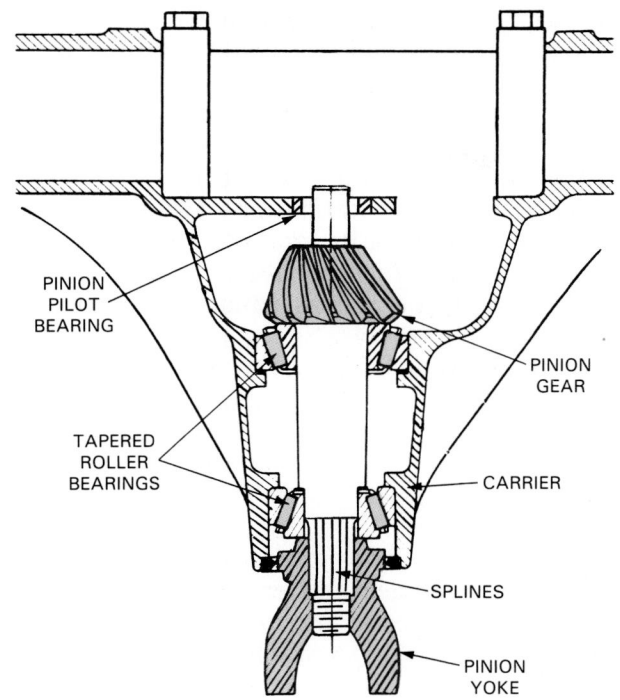

Fig. 58-3. Pinion gear is mounted on tapered roller bearings and sometimes pinion pilot bearing. Drive shaft yoke is splined to pinion drive gear. (Ford)

helps the two tapered roller bearings support the pinion gear during periods of heavy load. See Fig. 58-3.

Ring gear

The *ring gear* is driven by the pinion gear; it transfers rotating power through an angle change of 90 degrees.

The ring gear has more teeth than the pinion gear.

Bolts hold the ring gear securely to the differential case. Refer to Fig. 58-4.

The ring and pinion drive gears are commonly a matched set. They are *lapped* (meshed and spun together with abrasive compound on teeth) at the factory. Then, one tooth on each gear is marked to show correct teeth engagement. Lapping produces quieter operation and assures longer gear life.

Hunting and nonhunting gears

A *hunting gearset* does NOT mesh the same gear teeth during operation. The number of teeth on the pinion compared to the ring gear causes different teeth to mesh.

A *nonhunting gearset* meshes the same gear teeth over and over during gear operation. Most ring and pinion gears are nonhunting types. They will have markings that must be aligned during assembly.

Hypoid and spiral bevel gears

Hypoid gears have the driving pinion centerline offset or lowered from the centerline of the ring gear. Modern differential ring and pinion gears are hypoid type. Refer to Fig. 58-5.

Spiral bevel gears have curved gear teeth with the pinion and ring gears on the same centerline. This type gear setup is no longer used.

Hypoid gears have replaced spiral bevel gears because they lower the hump in the vehicle floor and improve gear meshing action. With more than one gear tooth in contact, a hypoid design increases gear life and reduces gear noise.

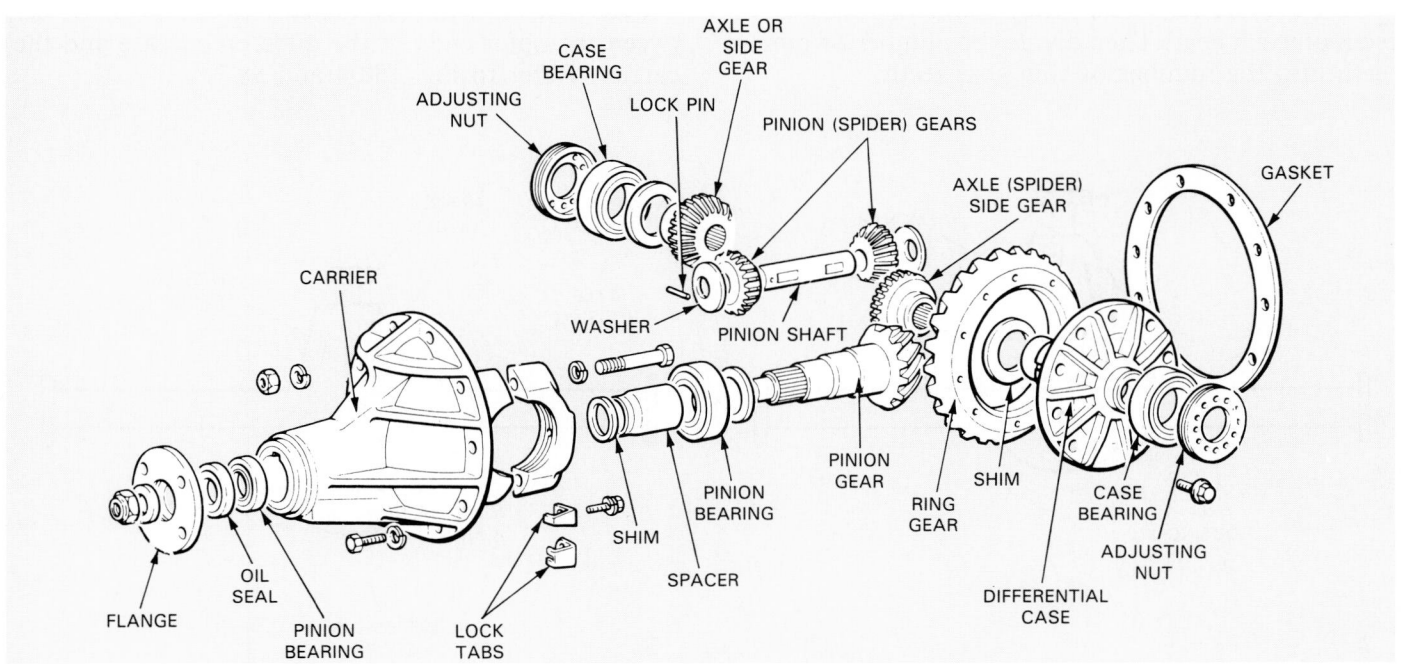

Fig. 58-4. Exploded view shows all of major parts of differential assembly. Ring gear bolts to differential case. Case mounts in bearings which are adjusted using large nuts. Study part names and how they fit together. (Chrysler)

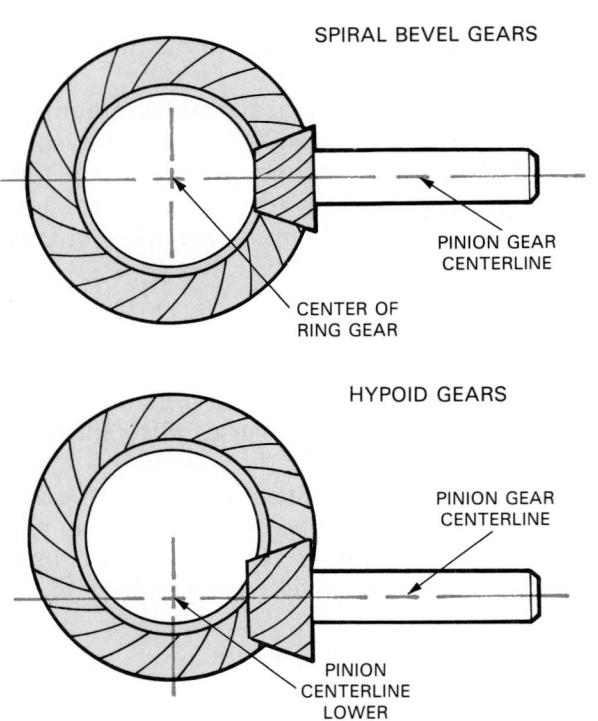

Fig. 58-5. Modern ring and pinion gears are hypoid type. Note how hypoid lowers centerline of drive pinion gear. This improves gear tooth contact and lowers drive shaft hump in floor of vehicle.

Rear axle ratio

Rear axle ratio, also termed *differential ratio,* is determined by comparing the number of teeth on the pinion drive gear and on the ring gear.

To calculate rear axle ratio, count the number of teeth on each gear. Then divide the number of pinion teeth into the number of ring gear teeth.

For example, if the drive pinion gear has 10 teeth and the ring gear 30 teeth (30 divided by 10), the rear axle ratio would be 3:1.

Generally, auto makers install a rear axle ratio that provides a compromise between performance and economy. An average ratio is 3.50:1.

A higher axle (numerical) ratio, 4.11:1 for instance, could increase acceleration and pulling power but it would also decrease fuel economy. The engine would have to run at a higher rpm to maintain an equal cruising speed.

A lower axle (numerical) ratio, 3:1, would reduce acceleration and pulling power but it could increase fuel mileage. The engine would run at a lower rpm while maintaining the same speed.

Differential carrier

The *differential carrier* provides a mounting place for the drive pinion gear, differential case, and other differential components. There are two basic types of differential carriers: the removable type and the integral (unitized) type.

A *removable carrier* bolts to the front of the axle housing, as in Fig. 58-6A. Stud bolts are installed in the housing to provide proper carrier alignment.

A gasket fits between the carrier and housing to prevent oil leakage.

An *integral carrier* is constructed as part of axle housing, Fig. 58-6B. A stamped metal or cast aluminum cover bolts to the rear of the integral carrier.

Differential case

The differential case holds the ring gear, spider gears, and inner ends of the axles. It mounts and rotates in the carrier, Fig. 58-7.

Case bearings, also called *carrier bearings,* fit between the outer ends of the differential case and the carrier. Refer to Figs. 58-4 and 58-7.

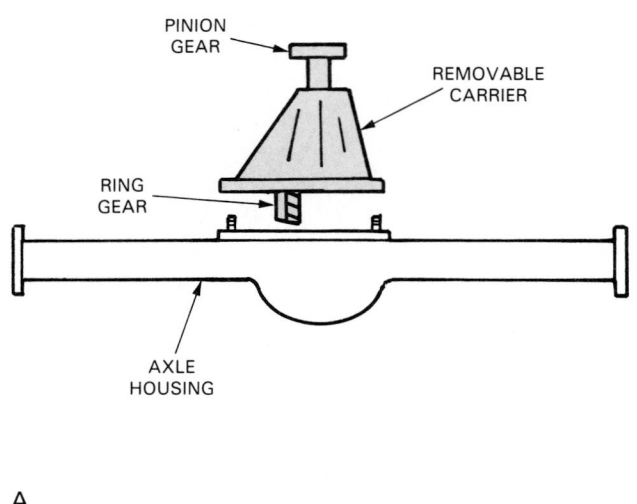

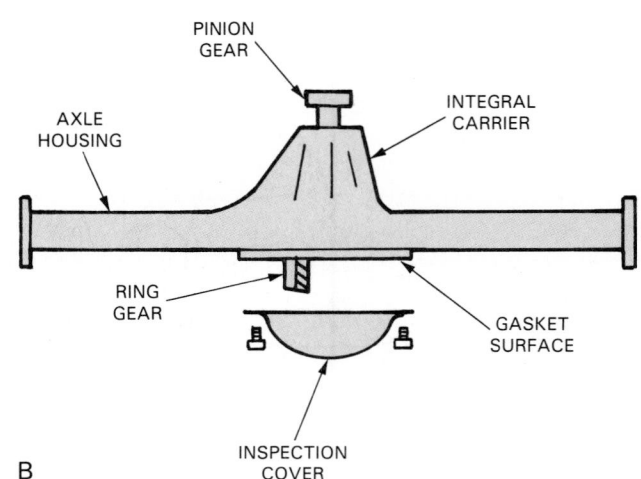

Fig. 58-6. Two basic types of rear axle carriers: A — Removable carrier is handy because it can be serviced at workbench. B — Integral or unitized carrier is formed as part of axle housing. It must be serviced in-vehicle or in housing.

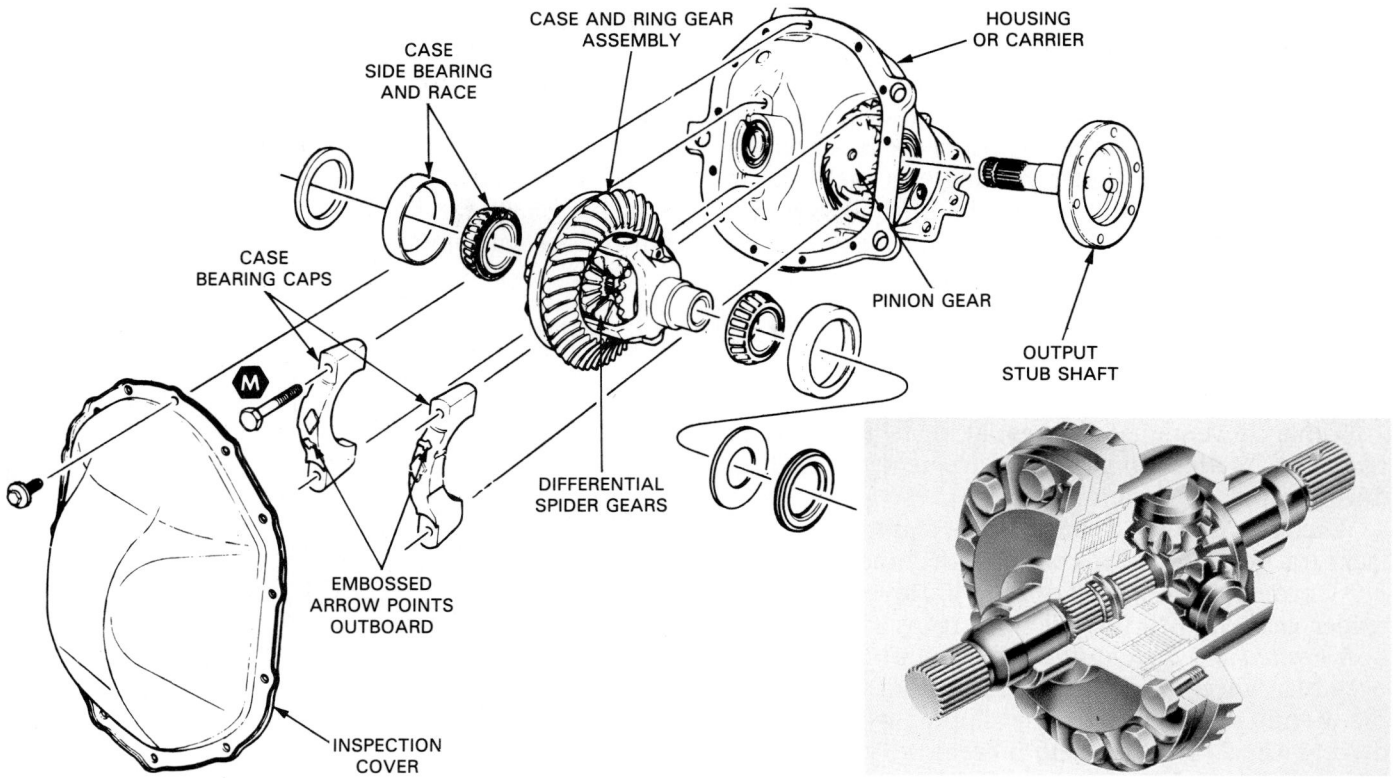

Fig. 58-7. Left. Differential case mounts in carrier on tapered roller bearings. Races fit between bearings and carrier. Large caps secure bearing assemblies. (Cadillac) Inset. Cutaway of rear differential. (Subaru)

Spider or differential gears

The *spider gears* or *differential gears* basically include two *axle gears* (differential side gears) and two *pinion gears* (differential idler gears). Refer to Figs. 58-4 and 58-7. The spider gears mount inside the differential case. They are small bevel gears.

A *pinion shaft* passes through the two pinion gears and case. The two side gears are splined to the inner ends of the axles. This is shown in Fig. 58-8A.

DIFFERENTIAL ACTION

The rear wheels of a car do not always turn at exactly the same speed. When the car is turning, or when tire diameters differ slightly, the rear wheels must rotate at different speeds.

If there were a solid connection between each rear axle and the differential case, the tires would tend to slide, squeal, and wear whenever the driver turned the steering wheel. A differential is designed to prevent this problem.

Driving straight ahead

Look at view A, Fig. 58-8. Both rear wheels are turning at the same speed. The spinning case and pinion shaft rotate the differential pinion gears. The teeth on pinion gears apply torque to the axle side gears and axles. Balanced forces make the differential seem to be locked.

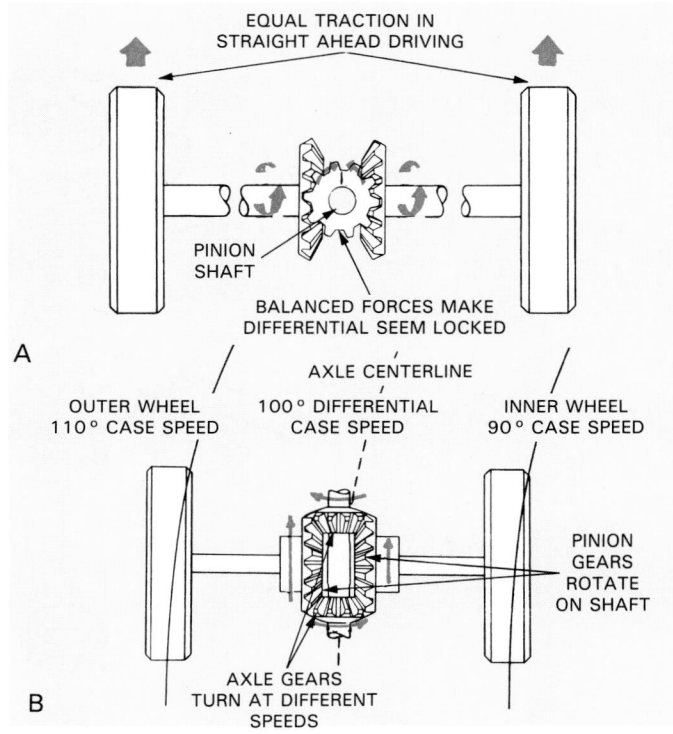

Fig. 58-8. Differential action allows wheels to turn at different speeds. A — Car traveling straight ahead. Differential spider gears inactive. Spider gears seem locked. B — With car turning corner, outer wheel must travel farther and turn faster than inner wheel. Pinion spider gears can rotate on their shaft, allowing axle side gears to turn at different speeds. (General Motors)

Turning corners

Fig. 58-8, view B, illustrates the action of a differential when the car is rounding a corner. Note how the outer wheel is turning faster than the inside wheel. The outer wheel must travel farther than the inner wheel.

The action of the spider gears allows each axle to change speed while still transferring torque to propel the car. Without a differential (solid case holding axles), you could break an axle or wear out tires because of the different turning speeds of the rear wheels.

LIMITED SLIP DIFFERENTIALS

With a conventional differential, there may NOT be adequate traction on slippery pavement, in mud, or during rapid acceleration.

When one wheel of a conventional rear axle assembly lacks traction (on ice for example), the other wheel will NOT propel the vehicle. Torque will flow through the spider gears and to the axle that turns easiest.

A *limited slip differential* provides driving force to both rear wheels at all times. It transfers a portion of the driving torque to both the slipping wheel and the driving wheel. This will help prevent the vehicle from becoming stuck in mud or snow.

Other names for a limited slip differential are *positraction, sure-grip, equal-lock,* or *no-spin*.

Clutch pack differential

The most popular type of limited-slip differential uses a *clutch pack* (set of friction discs and steel plates). Look at Fig. 58-9. The friction discs are sandwiched between the steel plates inside the differential case.

The friction discs are usually splined to the differential side gears, Fig. 58-10. The steel plates have tabs which lock into notches in the differential case. The

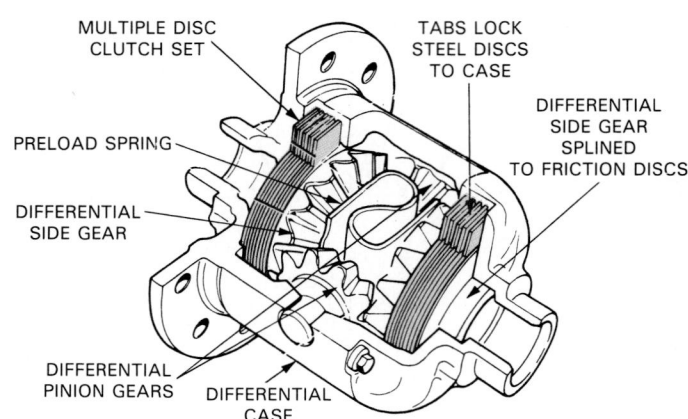

Fig. 58-9. Section view of limited slip differential shows how clutch discs and spider gears fit in case. Spring pushes side gears and clutch discs together. This sets up predetermined amount of friction that makes both axles drive car. (Ford)

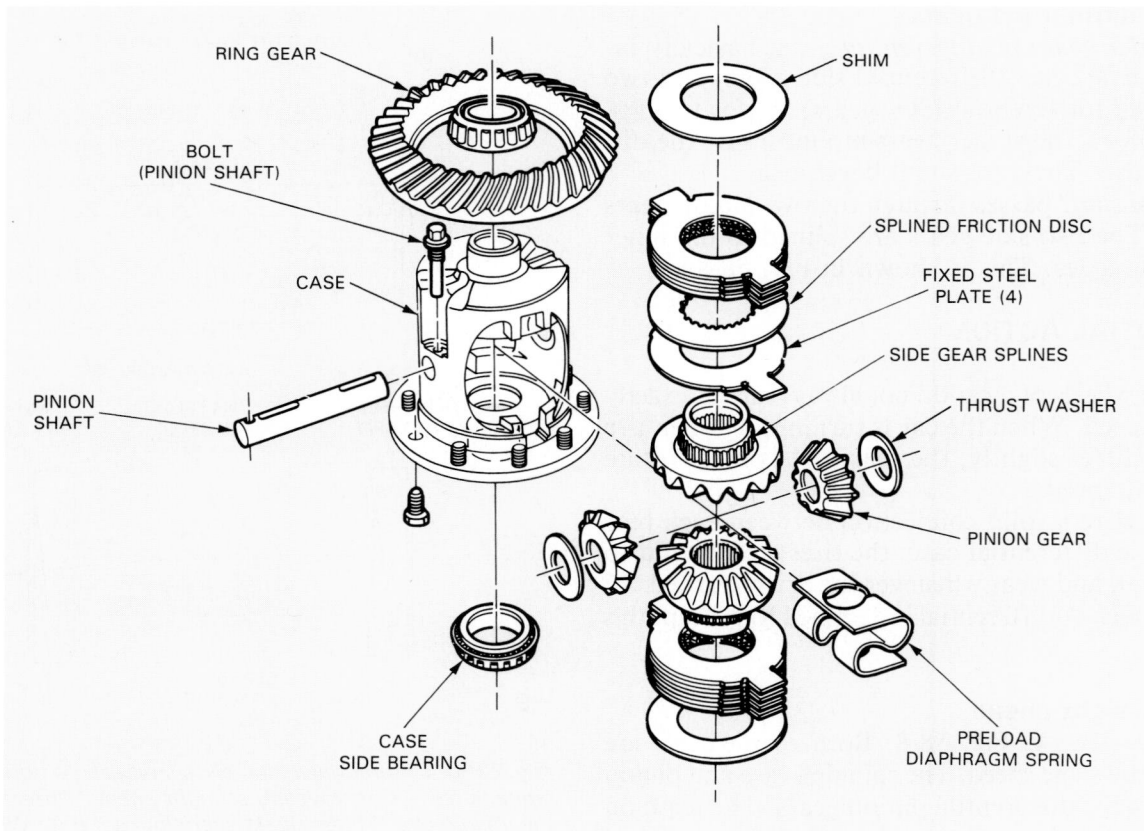

Fig. 58-10. This limited slip differential uses belleville or diaphragm springs to preload clutch discs. Friction discs are splined to axle side gears. Steel discs are locked to case by large tabs. (Chrysler Corp.)

friction discs turn with the axle side gears. The plates turn with the case.

Springs (belleville springs, coil springs, or leaf spring) force the friction discs and steel plates together. As a result, both rear axles try to turn with the differential case. Look at Figs. 58-10 and 58-11.

The thrust action of the spider gears normally helps the clutch spring(s) apply the clutch pack. Under high torque conditions, the rotation of the differential pinion gears PUSHES OUT on the axle side gears. The axle side gears then push on the clutch discs. This action helps lock the discs and keep both rear wheels turning.

However, when driving normally, the vehicle can turn a corner without both wheels rotating at the same speed. The clutch pack will slip in turns, Fig. 58-11.

Cone clutch differential

A *cone clutch limited slip differential* uses the friction produced by cone shaped axle gears to provide improved traction. See Fig. 58-12.

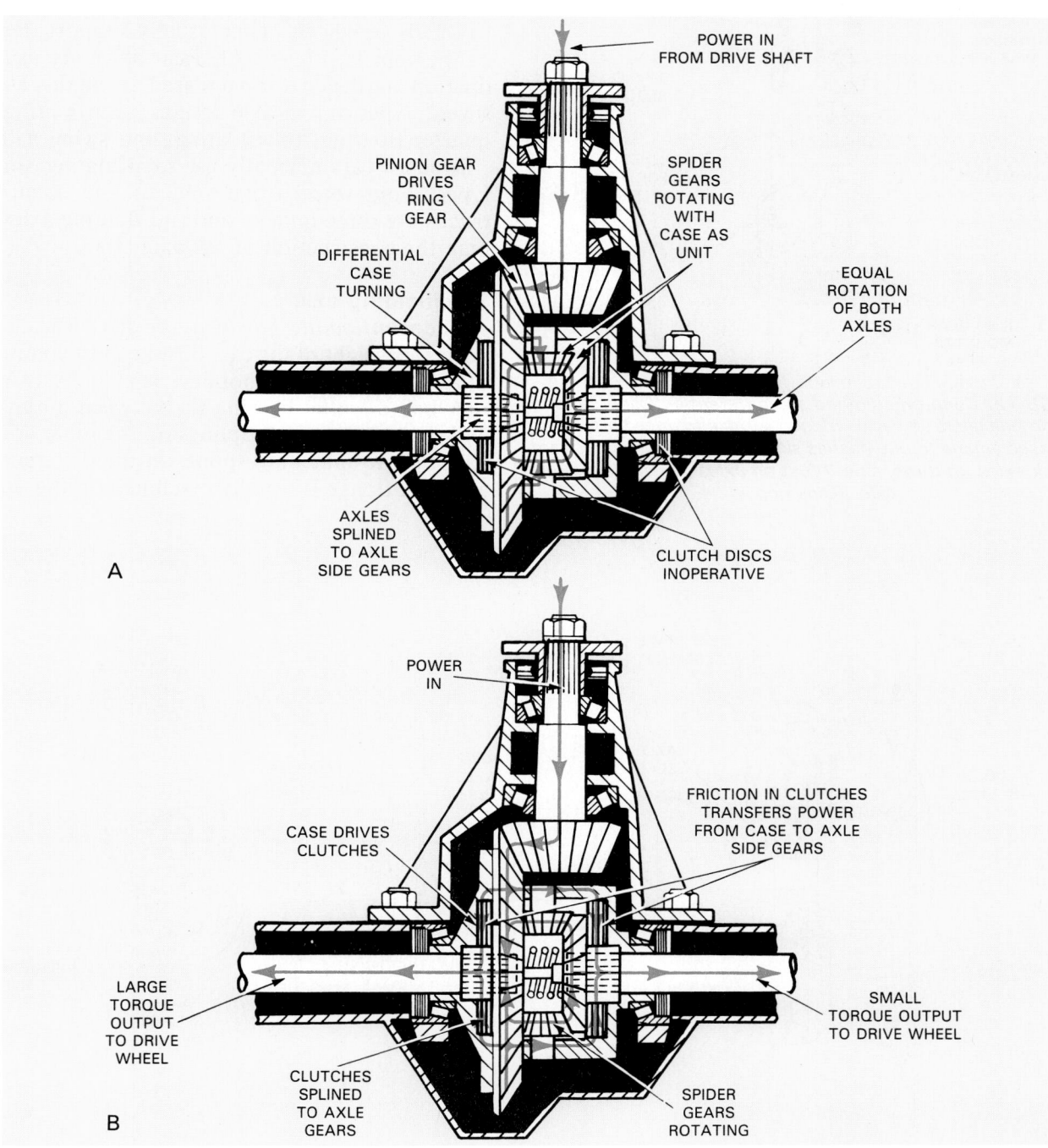

Fig. 58-11. Power flow through limited slip or positive traction differential. A — Car is traveling straight ahead or on dry pavement. Spider gears transfer power normally. Clutch discs turn together and do not slip. B — One wheel is on slippery pavement and it spins, friction between clutches still transfers torque to other axle. This gives vehicle more traction than with conventional differential.

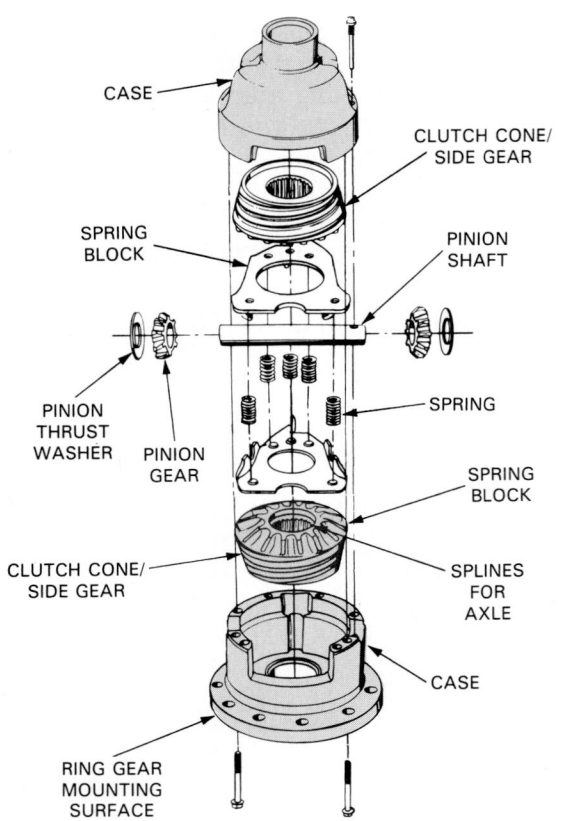

Fig. 58-12. Cone type limited slip differential. Cone surface on axle side gears serves as friction surface to drive both axles. Increased engine torque pushes side gears and cones outward to lock axles. In turns, side thrust on axles helps release one axle. (Oldsmobile)

Springs are used to force the cones against the ends of the differential case. With the axles splined to cone gears, the axles tend to rotate with the case.

Under rapid acceleration, the differential pinion gears, as they drive the cone gears, push outward on the cone gears. This increases friction between the cones and case even more and the drive wheels are turned with even greater torque.

REAR DRIVE AXLES

The *rear drive axles* connect the differential side gears to the drive wheels. They usually support the weight of the vehicle, Fig. 58-13. Rear axles are usually induction hardened for increased strength. There are several types of rear axle designs: semifloating, three-quarter floating, full floating, and swing axles.

Modern cars normally use semifloating and swing types. Four-wheel drive vehicles and some pickup trucks use three-quarter and full floating axles. Compare the construction of the axle types in Fig. 58-14.

Semifloating axle

The *semifloating axle* turns the drive wheel and supports the weight of the car. It is the most common type of axle found on automobiles. See Fig. 58-14A and B.

A ball or roller bearing fits between the axle shaft and the axle housing. Splines on the inner end of the axle fit into matching splines in the differential side gears. A flange is usually machined on the outer end

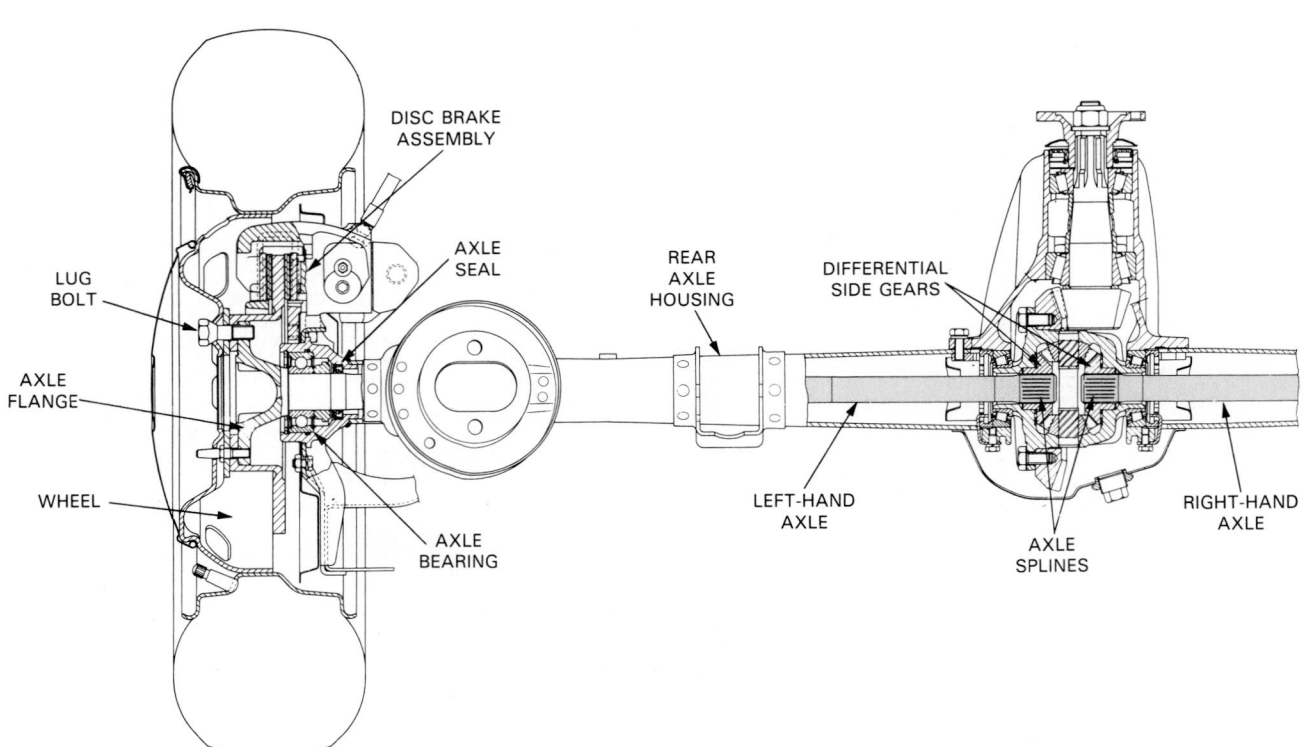

Fig. 58-13. Solid steel, case hardened rear drive axle extends beyond differential to outside of axle housing. Case and side gear supports inner end of axle. Rear wheel bearing supports outer end of axle. Also note flange on axle for wheel.

of the axle shaft. A collar may be used to hold the axle bearing on the axle.

A variation of the semifloating axle is shown in Fig. 58-14B. It has a tapered end that accepts a wheel hub. A key and large nut lock the hub to the axle. Fig. 58-14C shows a full floating axle.

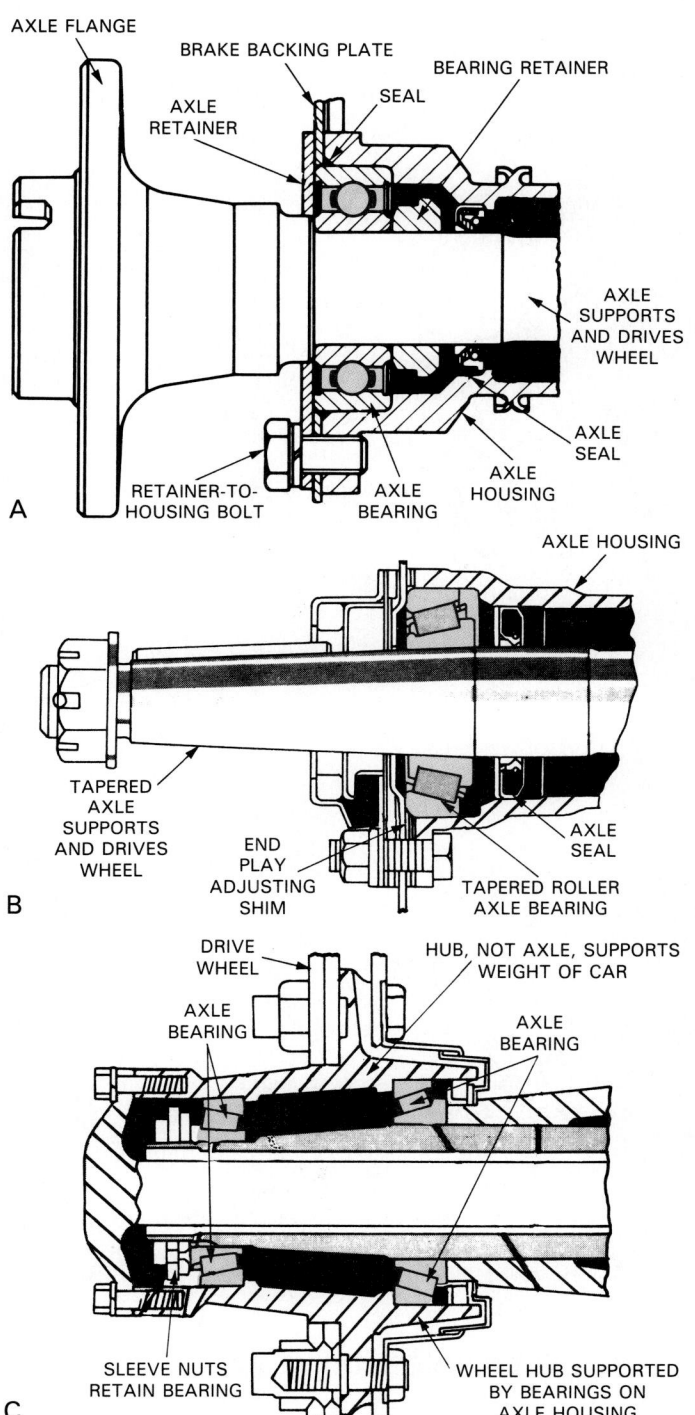

A

B

C

Fig. 58-14. Three common rear wheel bearing variations: A — Semifloating, ball bearing type. B — Semifloating, roller bearing type. C — Full floating axle, used on heavy duty, pickup and large truck applications. Other types of wheel bearings for swing axle or front-wheel drive cars are also used. These are covered in later chapters. (Fiat and Deere & Co.)

The *rear wheel bearings* reduce friction between the axle and axle housing. They allow the axle to turn freely. The inner bearing race fits against the axle. The outer bearing race fits into the machined end of the axle housing. Ball or roller bearings can be used.

The *rear axle seals* usually press into the axle housing, as shown in Fig. 58-14A. The seal lips contact the axles or axle collars to prevent lubricant leakage from the housing.

Axle shaft retainers can bolt to the outside of the axle housing to keep the axles from sliding out. They are normally used with a removable carrier type differential. See Fig. 58-15.

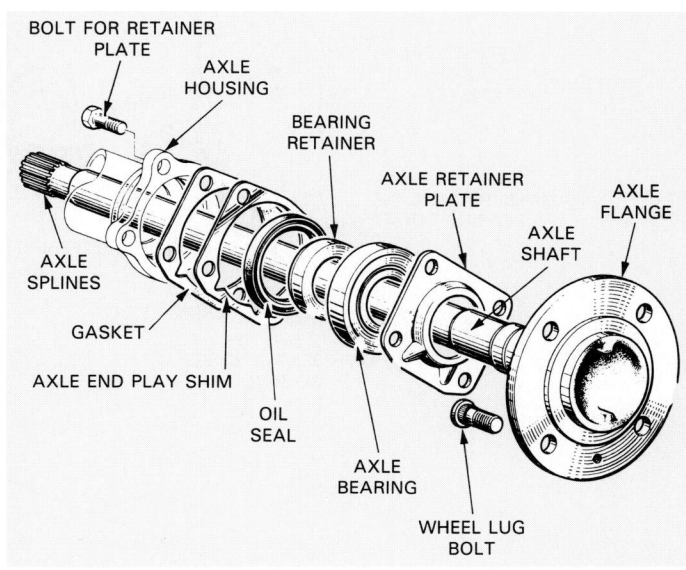

Fig. 58-15. Most rear axles with removable carriers have an axle retainer plate that bolts to axle housing. Shims are used to adjust axle end play. Gasket and oil seal prevent leakage of differential fluid. (Toyota)

Special bolts usually fit through holes in the housing flange and retainer. Nuts screw on these bolts to secure the axle into the housing.

Axle shims are frequently used between the axle shaft retainer and the housing to limit axle end play (in and out movement). A thicker shim can be used to reduce end play. A thinner shim will increase axle end play. Refer to Figs. 58-15 and 58-16.

DIFFERENTIAL LUBRICANT

Differential lubricant, usually SAE 80W-90 gear oil, is used to reduce friction between the moving parts in the rear axle assembly. Ring gear rotation splashes the oil on all moving parts to prevent wear.

A limited-slip differential usually requires use of a SPECIAL GEAR LUBRICANT. It is needed for the clutch pack. The friction discs will NOT function properly with regular gear oil.

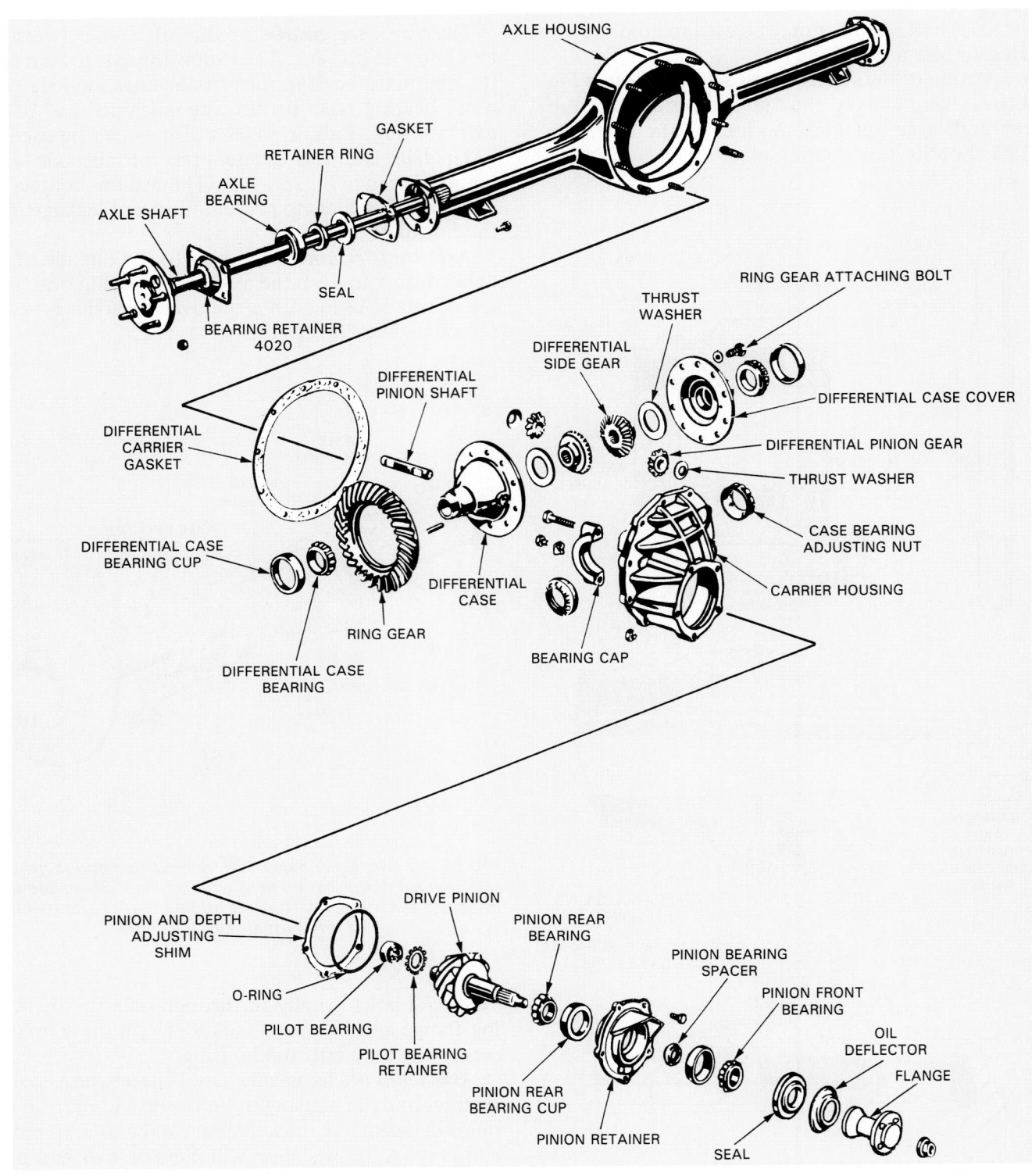

Fig. 58-16. This rear axle assembly has removable carrier, semifloating axles, and conventional differential. (Ford)

Differential breather tube

A *differential breather tube* vents pressure or vacuum in or out of the rear axle housing with changes in temperature. Look at Fig. 58-17.

Without a breather tube, pressure could build as the diffrential lubricant warmed to operating temperature. Lubricant could blow out the axle seals or pinion drive gear seal.

FRONT, FOUR-WHEEL DRIVE AXLE

A *front, four-wheel drive axle* assembly is similar to a rear drive axle, however, provisions must be made for steering the front wheels. Look at Fig. 58-18. Note how the outer ends of the axles have universal joints. The U-joints let the front wheels and hubs swivel while still transferring driving power to the hubs and wheels.

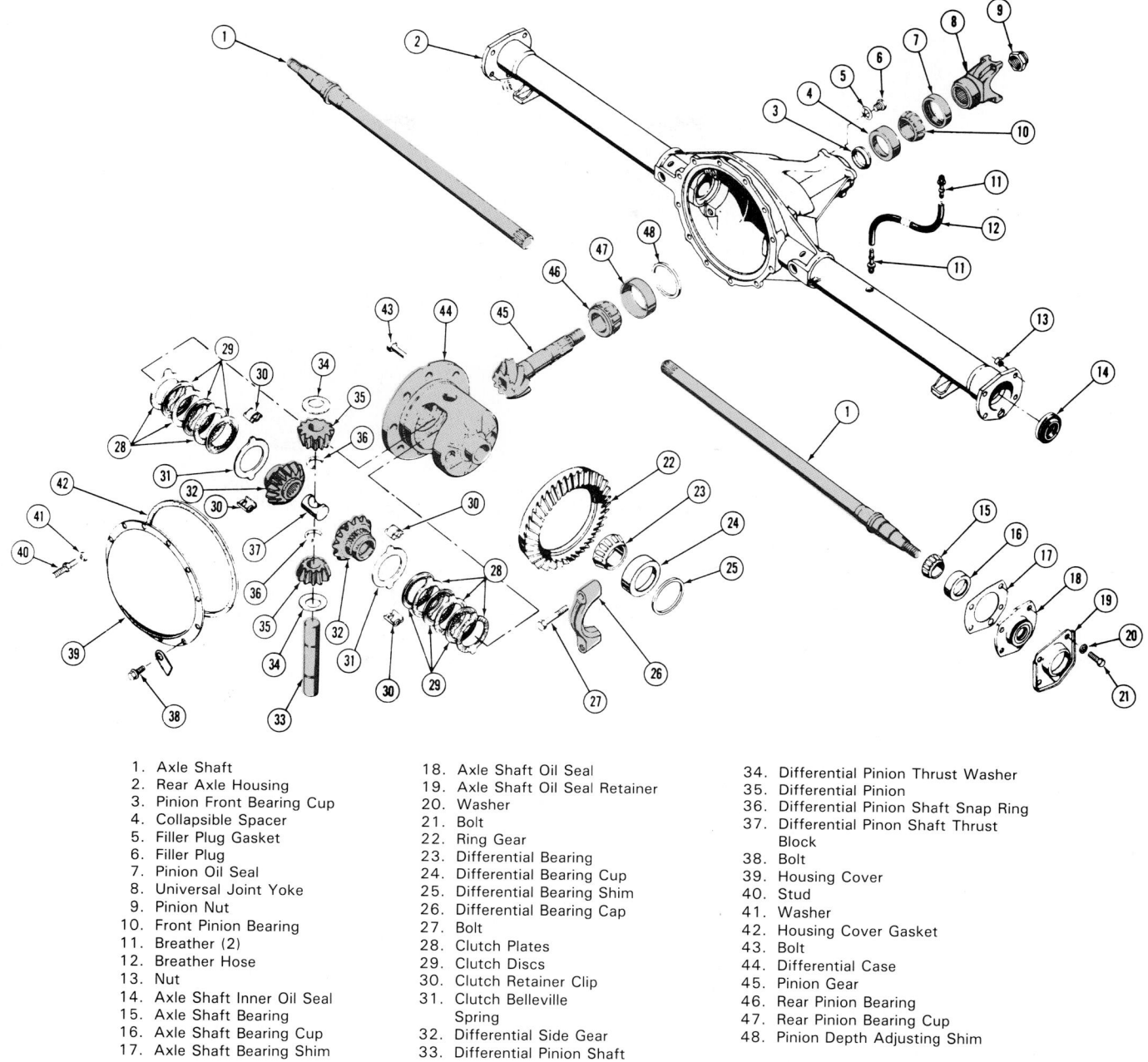

Fig. 58-17. *Disassembled view of complete rear axle assembly. Study parts carefully. Note that axles use tapered roller bearings that ride on separate races. Differential is limited slip. Carrier is integral (one piece) with axle housing.* (Chrysler)

1. Axle Shaft
2. Rear Axle Housing
3. Pinion Front Bearing Cup
4. Collapsible Spacer
5. Filler Plug Gasket
6. Filler Plug
7. Pinion Oil Seal
8. Universal Joint Yoke
9. Pinion Nut
10. Front Pinion Bearing
11. Breather (2)
12. Breather Hose
13. Nut
14. Axle Shaft Inner Oil Seal
15. Axle Shaft Bearing
16. Axle Shaft Bearing Cup
17. Axle Shaft Bearing Shim

18. Axle Shaft Oil Seal
19. Axle Shaft Oil Seal Retainer
20. Washer
21. Bolt
22. Ring Gear
23. Differential Bearing
24. Differential Bearing Cup
25. Differential Bearing Shim
26. Differential Bearing Cap
27. Bolt
28. Clutch Plates
29. Clutch Discs
30. Clutch Retainer Clip
31. Clutch Belleville
    Spring
32. Differential Side Gear
33. Differential Pinion Shaft

34. Differential Pinion Thrust Washer
35. Differential Pinion
36. Differential Pinion Shaft Snap Ring
37. Differential Pinon Shaft Thrust
    Block
38. Bolt
39. Housing Cover
40. Stud
41. Washer
42. Housing Cover Gasket
43. Bolt
44. Differential Case
45. Pinion Gear
46. Rear Pinion Bearing
47. Rear Pinion Bearing Cup
48. Pinion Depth Adjusting Shim

Fig. 58-19 shows a modern front-drive axle for a four-wheel drive pickup truck. Study the construction of the axle housing and locking hubs.

Locking hubs transfer power from the driving axles to the driving wheels on a four-wheel drive vehicle. There are three basic types of locking hubs:
1. Manual locking hub (driver must turn latch on hub to lock hub for four-wheel drive action).
2. Automatic locking hub (hub locks front wheels to axles when driver shifts into four-wheel drive).
3. Full time hub (front hubs are always locked and drive front wheels).

Manual and automatic locking hubs are common.

Used with part-time, four-wheel drive, they enable the driveline to be in two-wheel drive for vehicle use on dry pavement. The front wheels can turn without turning the front axles. This increases fuel economy and reduces driveline wear. Fig. 58-19 shows the basic parts of automatic and locking hubs.

Note! For more information on four-wheel drive operation and service, refer to Chapters 56 and 57.

SWING AXLES (REAR-WHEEL DRIVE)

Swing axles are used when the differential is mounted solidly on the car's frame. Universal joints in the axles

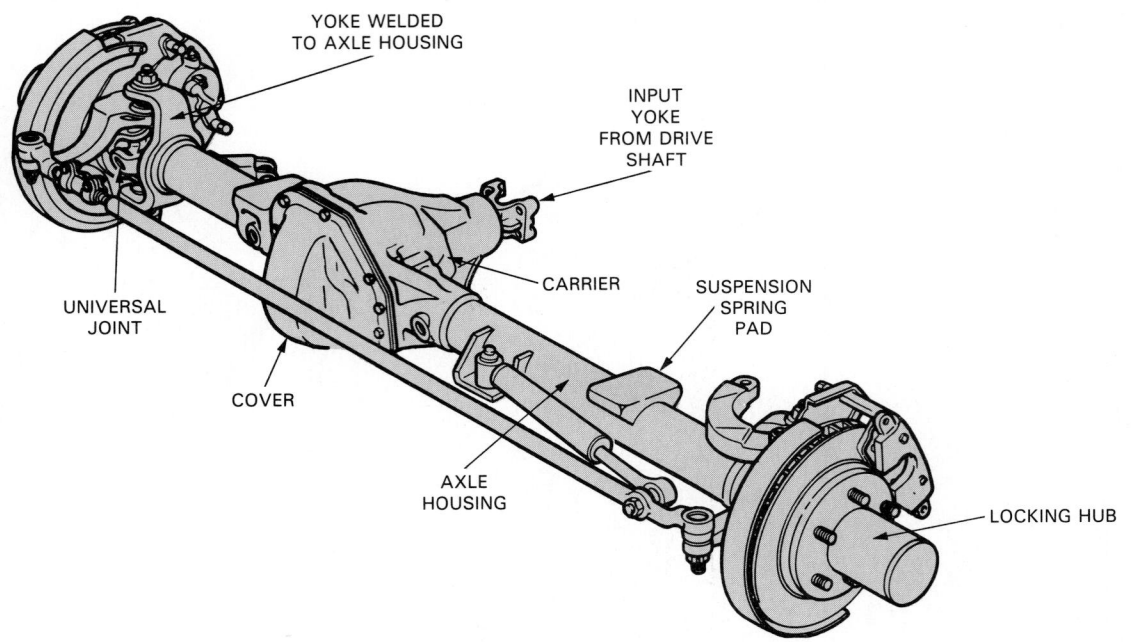

YOKE WELDED TO AXLE HOUSING

INPUT YOKE FROM DRIVE SHAFT

CARRIER

SUSPENSION SPRING PAD

UNIVERSAL JOINT

COVER

AXLE HOUSING

LOCKING HUB

Fig. 58-18. Front drive axle for four-wheel drive vehicle. It is conventional differential with U-joints on outer end of axles to allow for steering action. Special hubs lock drive axle to hub and wheel when in four-wheel drive. (GM Trucks)

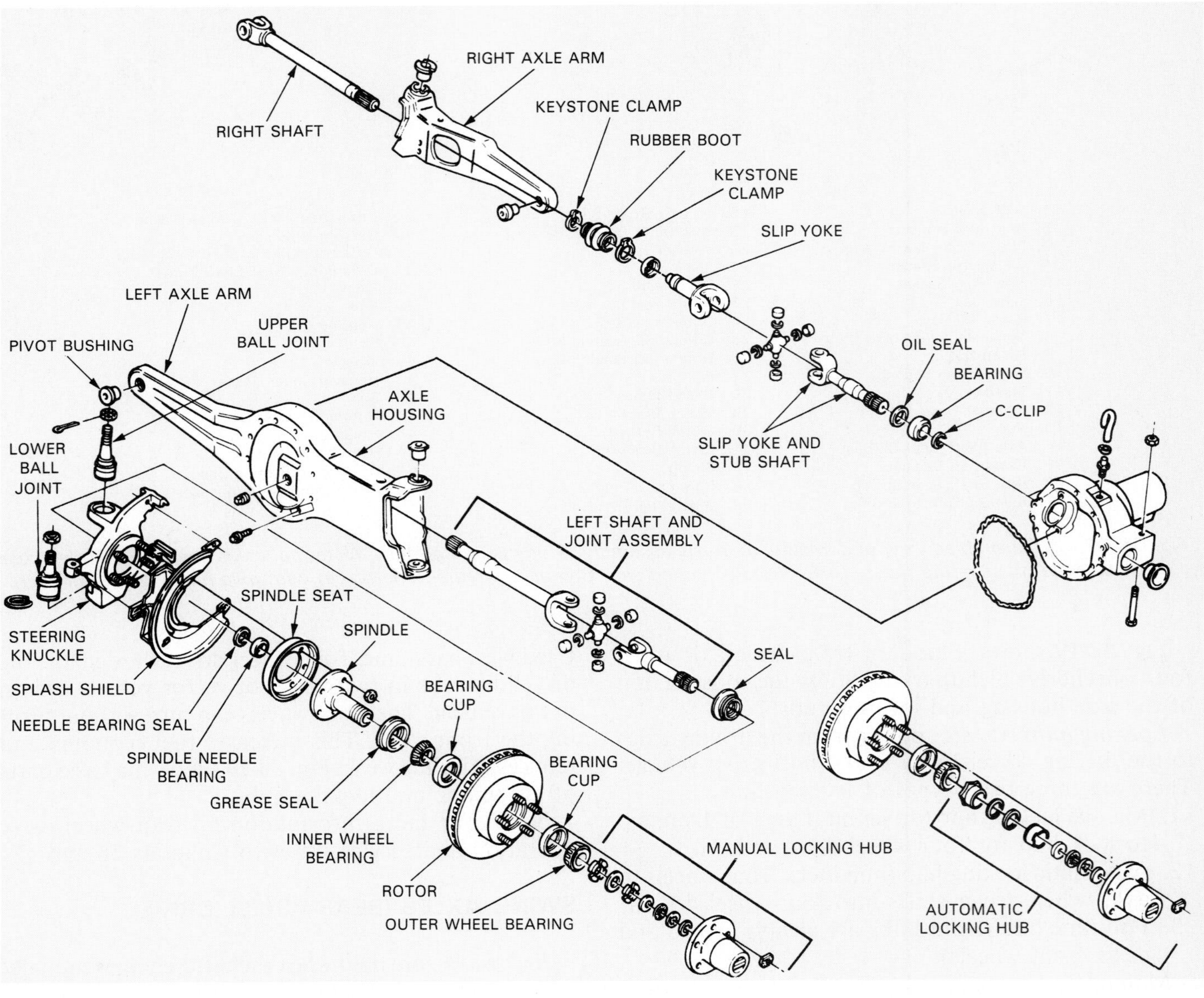

RIGHT AXLE ARM

RIGHT SHAFT

KEYSTONE CLAMP

RUBBER BOOT

KEYSTONE CLAMP

SLIP YOKE

LEFT AXLE ARM

UPPER BALL JOINT

PIVOT BUSHING

OIL SEAL

BEARING

C-CLIP

AXLE HOUSING

LOWER BALL JOINT

SLIP YOKE AND STUB SHAFT

LEFT SHAFT AND JOINT ASSEMBLY

STEERING KNUCKLE

SPINDLE SEAT

SPINDLE

SEAL

SPLASH SHIELD

NEEDLE BEARING SEAL

BEARING CUP

SPINDLE NEEDLE BEARING

GREASE SEAL

BEARING CUP

INNER WHEEL BEARING

MANUAL LOCKING HUB

ROTOR

OUTER WHEEL BEARING

AUTOMATIC LOCKING HUB

Fig. 58-19. Exploded view shows components of another front drive axle for four-wheel drive. Note how manual or automatic locking hubs are available. Differential carrier seals on housing. Axles are exposed on rear of housing.

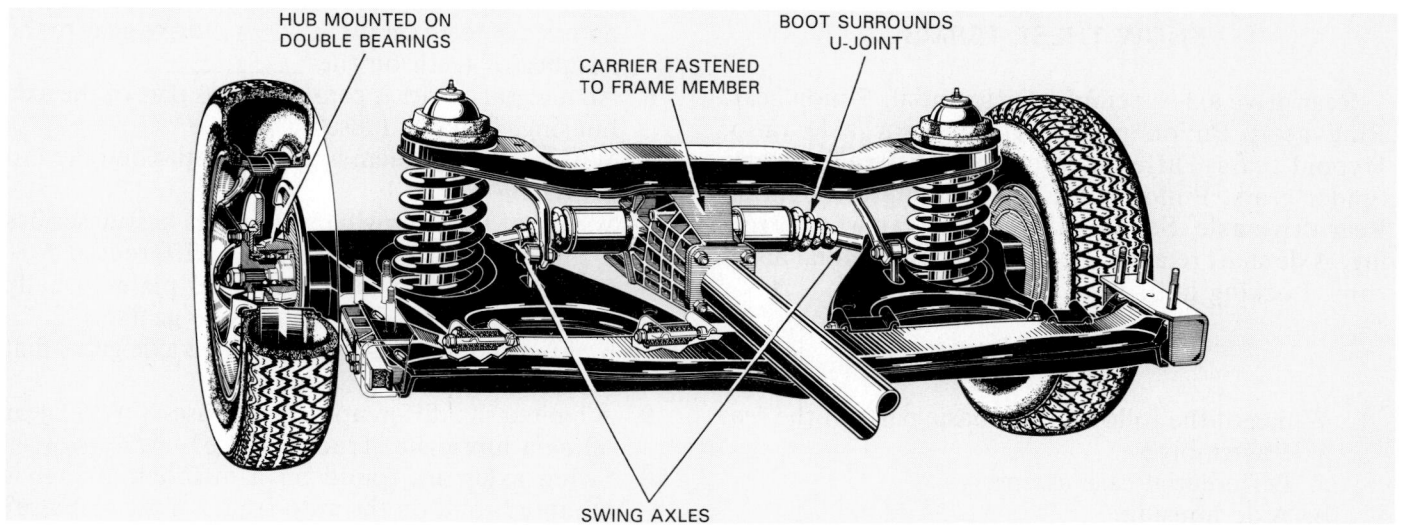

Fig. 58-20. Swing axle has differential assembly mounted on frame member. Universal joints let axles and wheels move up and down with suspension action. (Peugeot)

are needed to allow for up and down suspension action. Fig. 58-20 illustrates a rear drive axle assembly using swing axles.

The differential works like a conventional unit. However, the drive axles are not solid, steel shafts. They are flexible. Each has two U-joints, one of them mounted on each end.

For more information on swing axles, refer to Chapter 60. It covers front-wheel drive transaxles which use similar drive axles.

Fig. 58-21 is a cutaway of a unique automatic transaxle for an all-wheel drive vehicle. Note the location of the differential with auxiliary shaft going to the rear drive wheels.

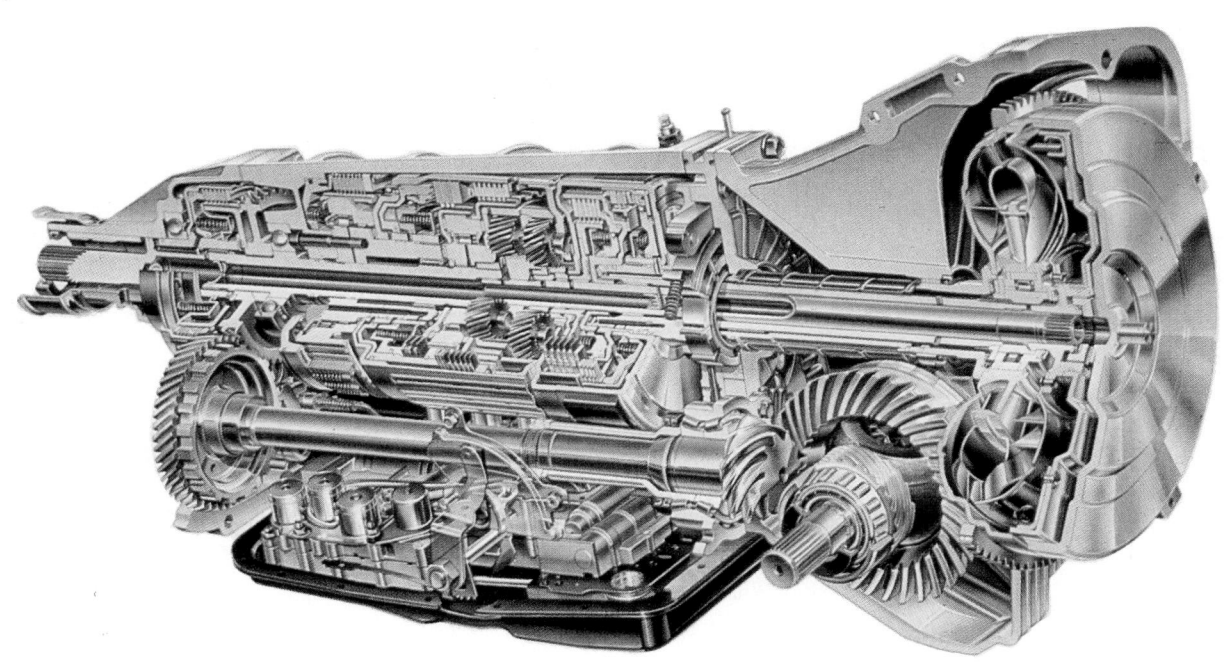

Fig. 58-21. This transaxle is designed for an all-wheel drive vehicle. (Subaru)

KNOW THESE TERMS

Rear drive axle assembly, Differential, Pinion gear, Ring gear, Pinion pilot bearing, Rear axle ratio, Hypoid gears, Differential carrier, Differential case, Spider gears, Pinion shaft, Limited slip differential, Rear drive axle, Semifloating axle, Rear wheel bearing, Axle shaft retainer, Axle shims, Differential lubricant, Locking hub, Swing axle.

REVIEW QUESTIONS

1. Which of the following are basic parts of the rear axle assembly?
   a. Differential case assembly.
   b. Axle housing.
   c. Pinion drive gear.
   d. Rear axle bearings.
   e. Rear drive axles.
   f. Ring gear.
   g. All of the above.
2. The _____ must be capable of providing torque to both axles when turning corners.
3. The purpose of the pinion gear is to transfer power from the ring gear to the axle. True or False?
4. Explain the difference between a hunting gearset and a nonhunting gearset.
5. Rear axle ratio is determined by comparing the number of teeth on the _____ drive gear to the number of teeth on the _____ _____ .
6. An integral carrier is constructed as part of the axle housing. True or False?
7. What major problem is a differential designed to prevent?
8. Which of the following statements best describes a clutch pack for a limited-slip differential?
   a. Set of friction discs and steel plates usually splined to the differential side gears.
   b. Friction-producing cone shaped axle gears that are splined to the axles.
9. A limited slip differential usually uses 80W-90 gear oil as a lubricant. True or False?
10. Swing axles are found on a differential that is mounted solid on the auto frame. True or False?

ACTIVITIES FOR CHAPTER 58

1. Using a mock-up of a differential provided by your instructor, identify its various parts.
2. Count the number of teeth on a ring gear and on its mating pinion gear. Write down these numbers and then determine the gear ratio.
3. Demonstrate to the rest of the class how power is transmitted from the drive pinion through the rest of the differential to the drive wheels.

59

Differential, Rear-Drive Axle Diagnosis and Repair

After studying this chapter, you will be able to:
☐ Diagnose and locate common differential and rear drive axle problems.
☐ Explain the basic service and repair of a differential assembly.
☐ Remove and replace axles, axle bearings, and seals.
☐ Describe limited-slip differential testing and service.
☐ Adjust ring and pinion gears.
☐ Check and replace rear axle lubricant.
☐ Cite safety rules and practice safe work habits.

In the previous chapter, you studied the operating principles of a rear drive axle assembly. In this chapter, you will utilize this information.

Much of the information in this chapter will help you when studying about late model, front-drive transaxles in Chapters 60 and 61. A transaxle also contains a differential.

DIFFERENTIAL, REAR AXLE PROBLEM DIAGNOSIS

"Rear end" (rear axle assembly) problems usually show up as abnormal noises. It is critical that correct procedures be used when trying to find the source of these noises. Other problems (worn wheel bearings, universals, or transmission gears for example) can produce symptoms similar to those caused by faulty rear drive axle components.

To begin diagnosis, gather information. Ask when the noise or condition occurs — when accelerating, coasting at certain speed, when rounding a corner. Use common sense and your understanding of operating principles to narrow down the possible sources.

Road test the vehicle on a smooth road surface. Listen for changes in the noise under different driving conditions. Fig. 59-1 lists some of the kinds of problems you may find.

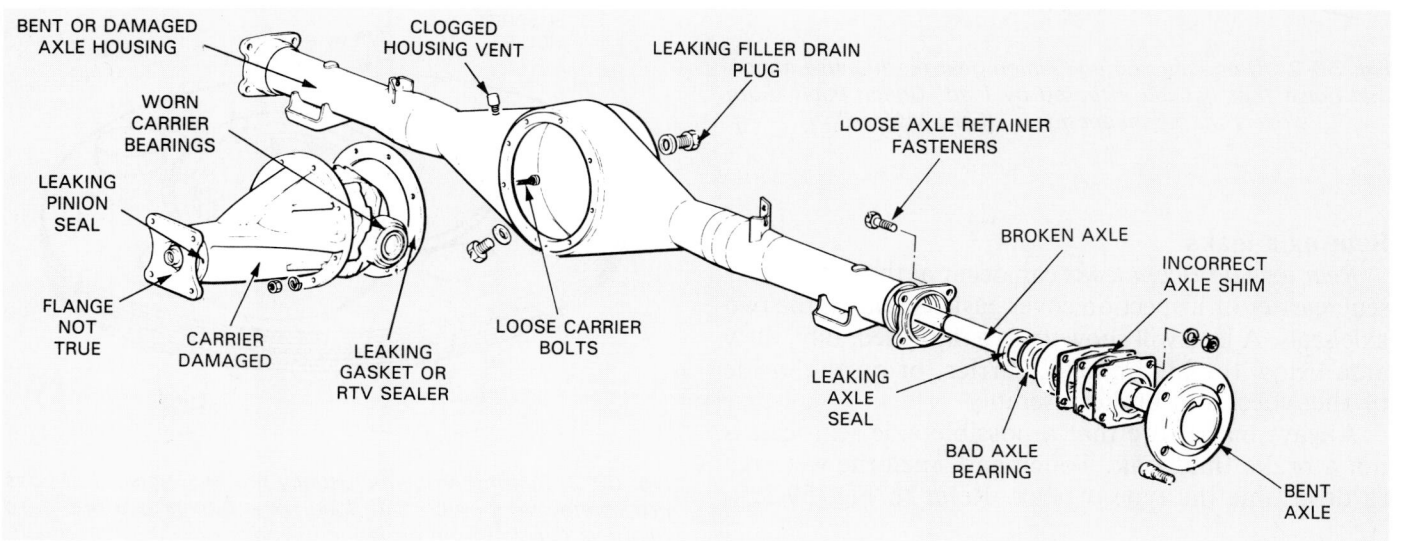

Fig. 59-1. These are typical problems that can develop in a rear axle assembly.

Ring and pinion problems

Ring and pinion problems usually show up as a howl or whining noise that CHANGES when going from acceleration to deceleration. Since the ring gear and pinion gear transfer engine power through a 90 degree angle, they are very sensitive to load. The sound of bad ring and pinion gears will usually CHANGE PITCH (noise frequency or tone) as you press and release the gas pedal while driving.

The ring and pinion gears can become worn, scored, out of adjustment, or damaged. These problems can result from prolonged service, fatigue, and lack of lubricant. You would need to inspect the differential to determine whether adjustment or part replacement is required. See Fig. 59-2.

If the backlash (clearance) between the ring and pinion is too great, a CLUNKING SOUND can be produced by the gears. For example, when an automatic transmission is shifted into drive, the abrupt rotation of the drive shaft could bring the gears together with a loud thump.

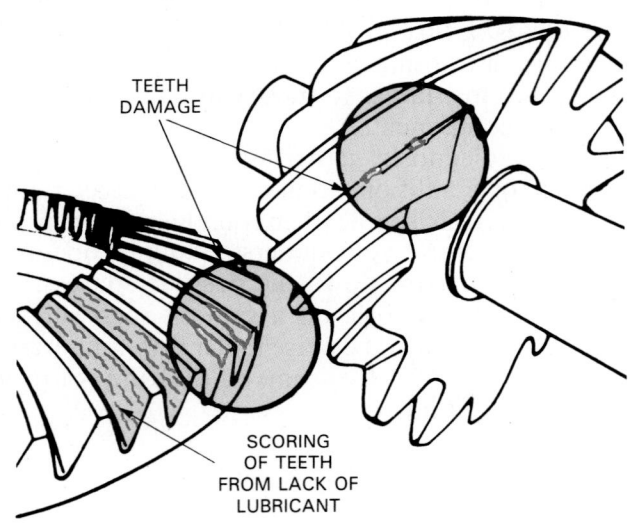

Fig. 59-2. Damaged ring and pinion gear teeth cause abnormal noise that can be affected by load. Check each tooth closely during inspection. (Ford Motor Co.)

Rear axle leaks

Rear axle lubricant leaks can occur at the pinion gear seal, carrier or inspection cover gaskets, and at the two axle seals. A leak will show up as a darkened, oily, dirty area below the pinion gear, carrier, or on the inside of the wheel and brake assembly.

Always make sure that a possible axle seal leak is not a brake fluid leak. Touch and smell the wet area to determine the type of leak. Refer to Fig. 59-1.

Axle and carrier bearing problems

Worn or *damaged bearings* in the carrier or on the axles often produce a CONSTANT whirring or humming sound. These bearings, when bad, make about the same sound whether accelerating, decelerating, or coasting.

Fig. 59-3 shows some typical bearing failures. These apply to both differential and axle bearings.

When diagnosing and repairing bearing failures, do the following:

1. Check general condition of all parts during disassembly, not just the most badly worn or damaged parts.
2. Compare the failure to any added information in a service manual and your knowledge of component operation.
3. Determine the cause of the part failure. This helps assure that the problem does NOT reoccur.
4. Make all repairs following manufacturer's recommendations and specifications.

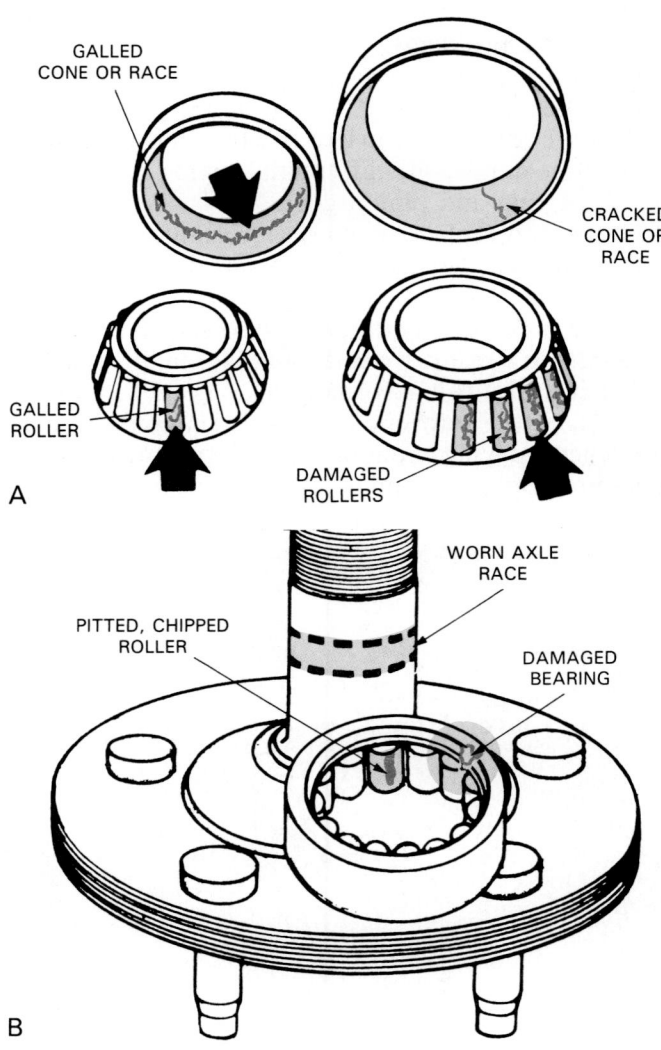

Fig. 59-3. Bearing problems usually produce noise that does not change very much with load. A — Pinion gear and case bearings can fail from prolonged service or lack of lubricant. B — Axle bearings are common source of trouble. They are not as well lubricated as bearings in carrier. (Ford)

Differential case problems

Differential case troubles frequently show up when rounding a corner. With the rear wheels turning at different speeds, any problem (damaged spider gears, grabbing limited slip clutch pack for example) will usually show up as an abnormal sound (clunking or clattering) from the rear of the vehicle.

A limited-slip differential (clutch type) can sometimes make a chattering sound when turning a corner. The clutches are sticking to each other and then releasing. Many auto makers recommend that the differential fluid be drained and replaced.

Problem isolation

A *stethoscope* (listening device) can often be used to isolate the source of a differential or rear axle bearing problem. Raise the vehicle on a lift. Ask another technician to start engine, place transmission in gear, and take speedometer up to about 30 mph (48 km/h).

Touch your stethoscope on the ends of the axle housing and on the housing near the carrier bearings. The area producing the LOUDEST NOISE contains the faulty parts.

WARNING! When using a stethoscope to listen for rear axle noise, be careful to stay away from the spinning tires and driveline. Serious injury could result if you touch these parts.

Eliminate other problem sources

After your road test to verify the complaint, use your knowledge of noise diagnosis to determine which components should be checked further.

If the noise could possibly be tire related, increase inflation pressure in the tires as described in a service manual. If the abnormal noise changes, then the tires may be at fault.

If the sound came near the middle or front of the car, listen for noises in the transmission or transaxle. Also, check for bad front wheel bearings.

DIFFERENTIAL MAINTENANCE

Many automobile manufacturers recommend that the differential fluid be checked or replaced at specific intervals. See Fig. 59-4.

Refer to Chapter 10 for more information on checking differential lubricant.

NOTE! Always install the correct type of differential lubricant. Limited-slip differentials often require a special type of lubricant intended for the friction clutches.

REAR AXLE SERVICE

Rear axle service is needed when an axle bearing is noisy, when an axle is broken, bent, damaged, or when an axle seal is leaking. As you will learn later, the rear axles must also be removed to allow removal and repair of the differential assembly.

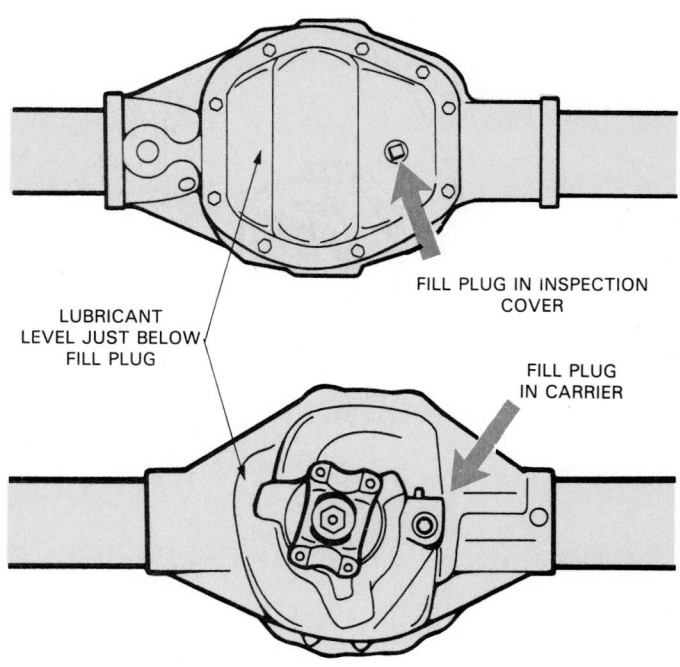

Fig. 59-4. Check lubricant level first when you detect problems in rear drive axle assembly. Lubricant should be almost even with fill hole with lubricant warm. If drain plug is not provided, you must remove cover or carrier or use suction gun to remove old lubricant. (Chrysler Corp.)

Axle removal

Generally, two methods are used to hold axles in their housing: retainer plate on the outside of the housing or C-clips on the inner ends of the axles.

A *retainer plate type axle* is commonly used with a removable carrier. A *C-clip type axle* is frequently used with an integral carrier.

To remove an axle with a RETAINER PLATE, secure the car on jack stands. Unbolt the rear wheel and slide off the brake drum, Fig. 59-5.

Unscrew the nuts on the ends of the axle housing. A socket, extension, and ratchet can normally be used to reach through a hole in the axle flange.

As in Fig. 59-6, you may need to install a slide hammer puller on the axle studs. Tap the axle out of the housing. Repeat on the other axle if needed.

CAUTION! While pulling an axle, be careful not to pull the brake backing plate off with the axle. You could bend and damage the brake line.

To remove an axle with a C-CLIP, drain the axle lubricant. Unbolt the cover on the rear of the axle housing. On most differentials, remove the pinion shaft bolt, pinion shaft, and slide the axle inward. This will allow you to remove the C-clip from a groove in the axle end, Fig. 59-7. The axle can then be slid out.

With the axle removed, inspect the bearings and splines for damage. Rotate the bearings by hand while feeling for roughness.

A few vehicles use axles with tapered ends. This type

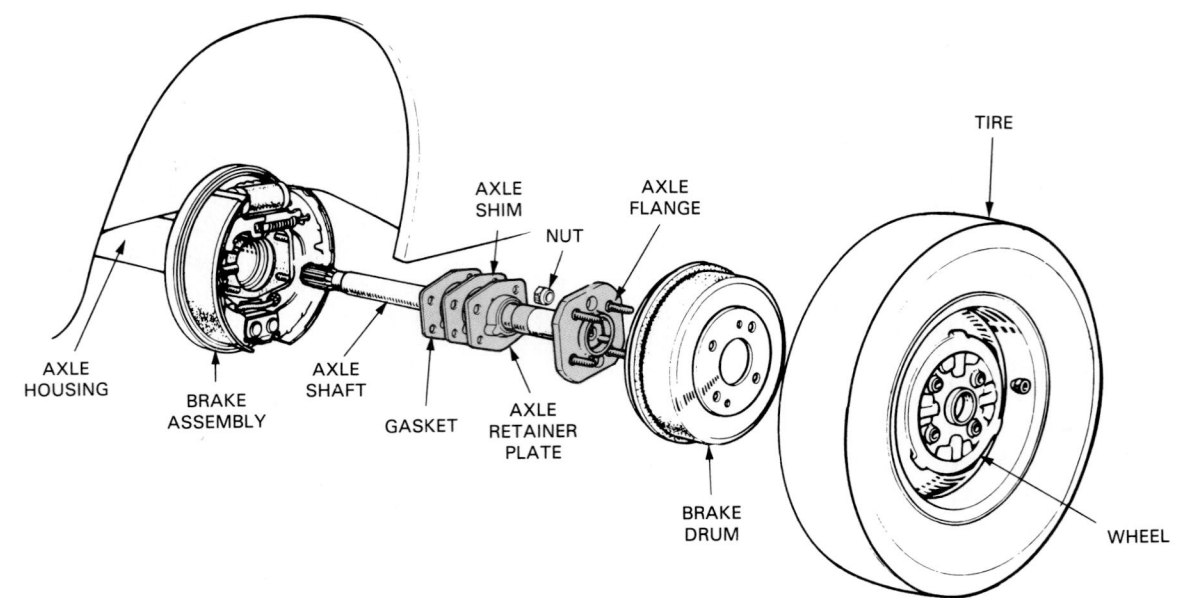

Fig. 59-5. To remove an axle with a retainer plate, remove four nuts on plate and end of housing. Reach through axle flange with socket and extension to loosen fasteners. Pull axle out without moving brake backing plate assembly. (Toyota)

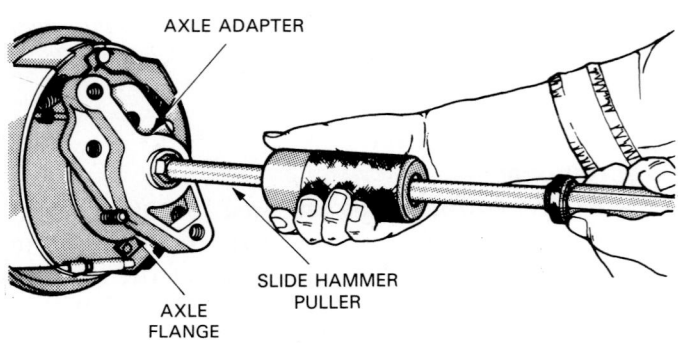

Fig. 59-6. If axle is stuck in housing, use a slide hammer puller as shown. (Plymouth)

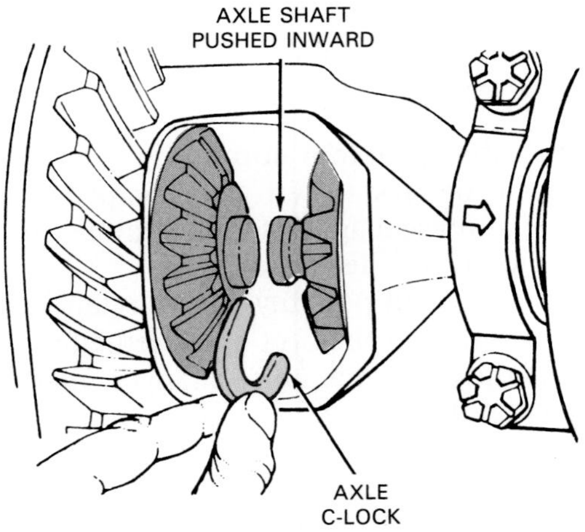

Fig. 59-7. With many integral carriers, you must remove pinion shaft bolt and pinion shaft. Slide axle inward and remove C-clip. This will let you pull axle out of housing. (Ford)

of axle may require a puller for removal of the hub. Refer to a service manual for details.

Axle bearing service

When an axle bearing is faulty, it must be removed from the axle or housing carefully and a new one installed. Most axle bearings are press fitted on the axle. A collar may also be pressed on the axle to help secure the bearing.

To remove this type axle bearing, carefully cut the collar off with a grinder and sharp chisel. See Fig. 59-8.

Note! Do NOT use a cutting torch to remove an old collar and axle bearing. The heat can weaken and ruin the axle.

With the collar cut off, place the axle in an hydraulic press, as shown in Fig. 59-9A. The driving tool should be positioned so that it contacts the INNER bearing race. NEVER press a bearing off using the outer race

surface or bearing damage or explosion will result.

CAUTION! Wear eye and face protection when pressing a bearing on or off an axle. The tremendous pressure could cause the bearing to shatter and fly into your face with deadly force.

To install the new bearing, slide the retainer and bearing onto the axle. Make sure the bearing is facing in the right direction. Sometimes, a chamfer on the inner bearing race must face the axle flange.

Applying force on the inner bearing race, press the bearing fully into place. Look at Fig. 59-9B. Then, if needed, press the bearing collar or retaining ring onto the axle.

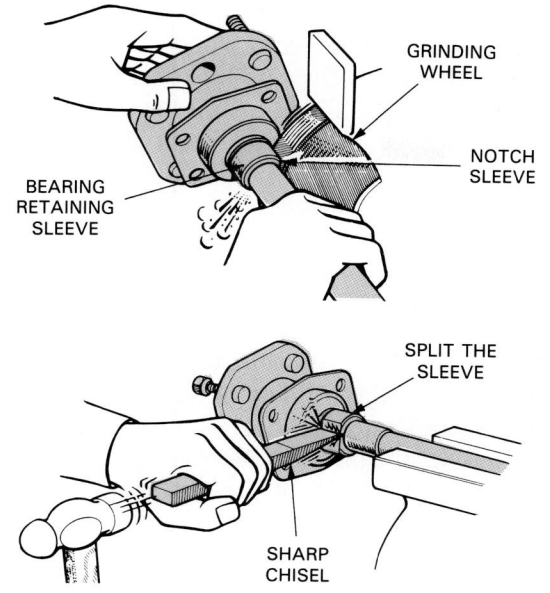

BEARING RETAINING SLEEVE

GRINDING WHEEL

NOTCH SLEEVE

SPLIT THE SLEEVE

SHARP CHISEL

Fig. 59-8. To prepare for axle bearing removal, grind notch in bearing retainer. Then, split retainer with sharp chisel. Wear safety glasses. (Toyota)

Do NOT attempt to press the bearing and collar on at the same time. Bearing or collar damage could result.

Rear axle seal service

Anytime the axle is removed for service, it is wise to install a new axle seal. The axle seal is normally force fitted in the end of the axle housing.

To remove a housing-mounted seal, use a slide hammer puller equipped with a hook nose. As pictured in Fig. 59-10A, place the hook on the metal part of the seal. Jerk outward on the puller slide to pop out the seal. A large screwdriver will also work. Be careful not to scratch the bearing bore in the axle housing.

Make sure that you have the correct new seal. Its outside and inside diameters must be the same as the old seal. A *seal part number* is normally stamped on the side of a seal. This number and the seal manufacturers name may help when ordering the replacement.

Before installing the new seal, coat its outer diameter with nonhardening sealer. Coat the inside of the seal with lubricant. With the seal facing in the right direction (sealing lip towards inside of housing), drive the

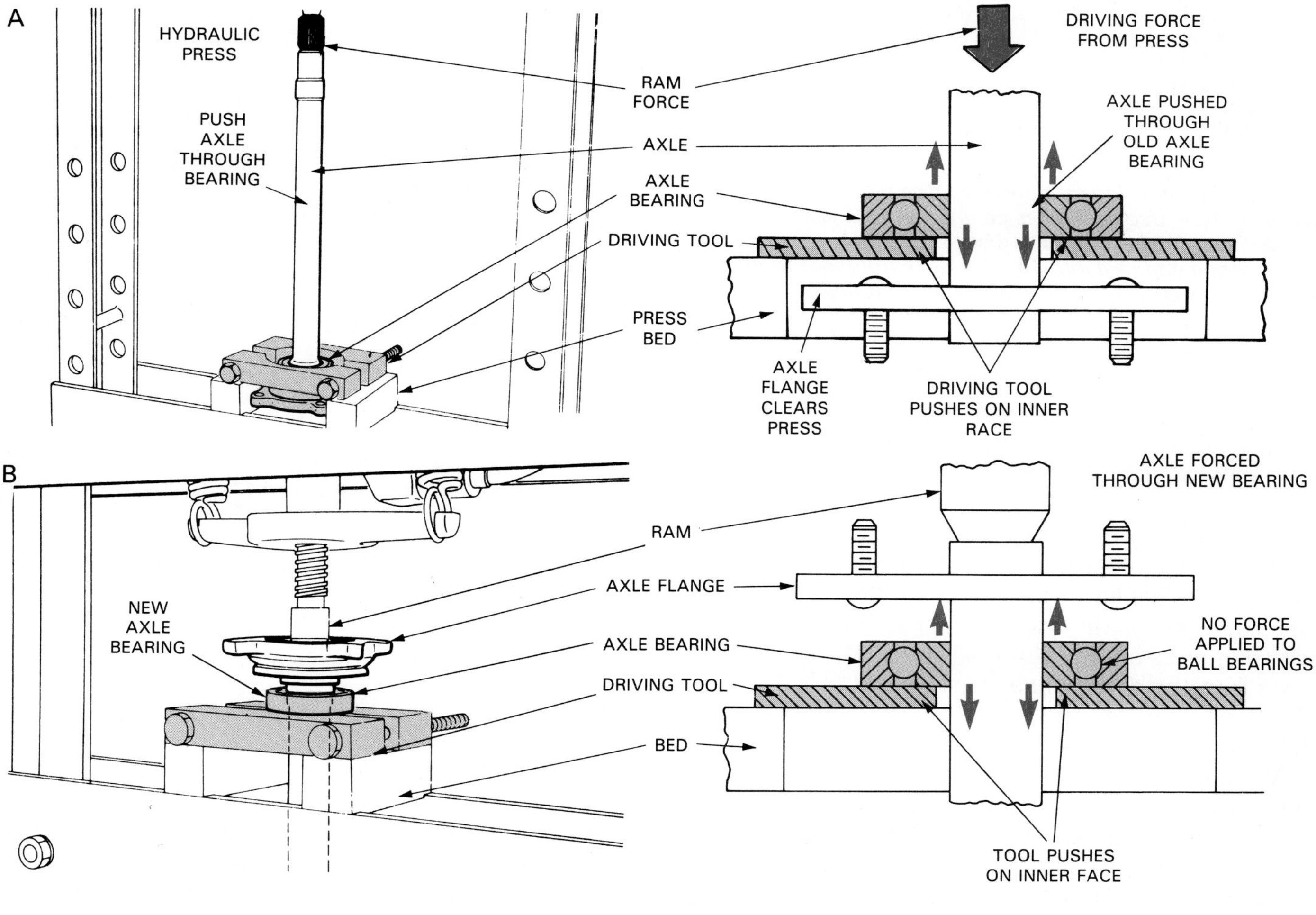

A

HYDRAULIC PRESS

PUSH AXLE THROUGH BEARING

RAM FORCE

AXLE

AXLE BEARING

DRIVING TOOL

PRESS BED

DRIVING FORCE FROM PRESS

AXLE PUSHED THROUGH OLD AXLE BEARING

AXLE FLANGE CLEARS PRESS

DRIVING TOOL PUSHES ON INNER RACE

B

NEW AXLE BEARING

RAM

AXLE FLANGE

AXLE BEARING

DRIVING TOOL

BED

AXLE FORCED THROUGH NEW BEARING

NO FORCE APPLIED TO BALL BEARINGS

TOOL PUSHES ON INNER FACE

Fig. 59-9. Axle bearing removal and installation. A — Position special tool so it contacts inner bearing race. Use press to push axle through bearing for removal. B — Again, position tool to contact inner race. Press axle back through bearing for installation. Wear a face shield and do NOT exceed recommended ram pressure. (Dodge)

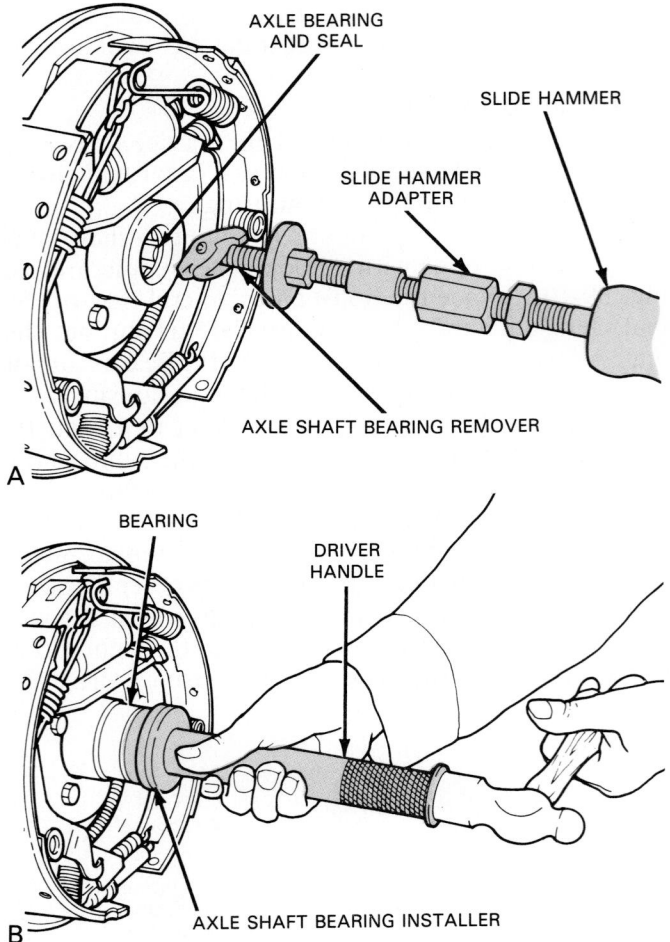

Fig. 59-10. Servicing axle bearing and seal pressed into axle housing. A — Use hook-nose adapter on slide hammer to pull out old seal and bearing. B — Use special driver to force new axle bearing and seal into housing. Be careful not to damage housing bore, bearing, or seal. (Cadillac)

seal squarely into place. Use a seal driving tool, Fig. 59-10B. Be careful not to bend the metal seal housing or a leak could result. Make sure the seal is fully seated.

Axle stud service

Before installing the axle, make sure that the lug studs on the flange are in good condition. If the threads are damaged or the lugs are loose, install new lugs. Drive or press out the damaged studs. Then, force new ones into the axle flange.

Rear axle installation

Wipe the axle clean. Then, carefully slide the axle into the housing.

To prevent seal damage, support the weight of the axle as it slides over the seal. Do NOT allow the axle to rub on the new seal or the seal could be ruined.

Wiggle the axle up and down and around until its splines fit into the splines in the differential side gear. Align axle bearing and push axle fully into place.

If the axle has a retainer, tighten the retainer nuts. Install the brake drum and wheel.

If the axle has C-clips (C-locks), fit the clips over the inner axle ends. Then, install the pinion shaft and differential cover. Fill the differential with lubricant.

Measuring axle end play

Excessive axle end play can cause a clunking sound as the car rounds a corner. The axle can slide one way and then the other with an audible clunk or knock.

Insufficient axle end play can result in axle bearing, retainer, or differential side gear failure.

To measure axle end play, mount the dial indicator so that the indicator plunger is parallel with the axle centerline. Set the indicator needle on zero, Fig. 59-11. Pull the axle in and out while watching the indicator. Compare the readings to factory specs.

If there is too much end play, you may need to add shims next to the axle retainer plate. If the axle end play is too small, install thinner shims. With a C-clip type axle, you would have to replace parts or install shims behind the side gears in the differential. Check a service manual for details.

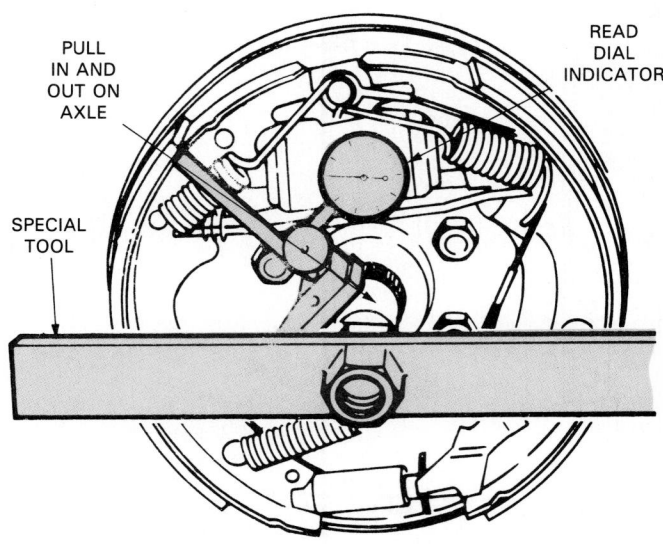

Fig. 59-11. Many auto makers recommend measurement of axle end play. Mount adapter over axle. Then use dial indicator to measure in and out movement of axle. Compare to specs. Add or remove shims or replace parts as needed to correct end play. (Chrysler Corp.)

DIFFERENTIAL SERVICE

When symptoms point to differential troubles, remove the differential carrier or rear inspection cover. Inspect the ring gear, pinion drive gear, bearings, and spider gears.

A *differential ID* (identification) *number* is provided to show the exact type of differential for ordering parts and looking up specs. The number may be on a tag under one of the carrier or inspection cover fasteners. It may also be stamped on the axle housing or carrier. Use the ID number to find the axle type, axle ratio, make of unit, and other information.

Differential removal

To remove a separate carrier differential, remove the drive shaft. Unbolt the nuts around the outside of the carrier. Place a drain pan under the differential. Force the differential away from the housing, Fig. 59-1. Drain the lubricant into the pan.

CAUTION! A differential carrier can be surprisingly heavy. Grasp it securely during removal. A carrier can cause painful injuries if dropped.

To remove an integral differential, remove the cover on the rear of the axle housing. Drain the lubricant. With the cover off, inspect and MARK the individual components as they are removed. Look at Fig. 59-12.

Differential disassembly and reassembly

Procedures for repairing a differential will vary with the particular unit. However, there are several service procedures that relate to almost any type of differential.

Differential service rules

When using a service manual to repair a differential, remember to:
1. Check for markings before disassembly. Carrier caps, adjustment nuts, shims, ring and pinion, spider gears, and pinion yoke or flange should be reinstalled exactly as they are removed. If needed, punch mark, label, or scribe these components so

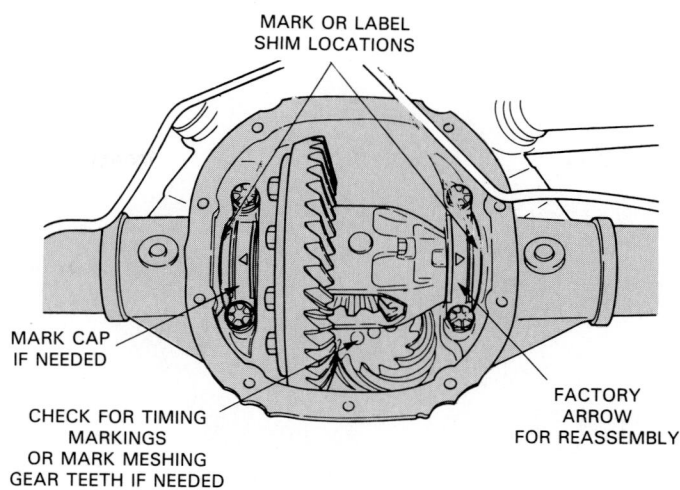

Fig. 59-12. As you disassemble differential, make sure you check markings or mark critical components. Most parts must be installed in same location during reassembly. Note markings on this unit. (Ford)

they can be reassembled properly, Fig. 59-12.
2. Clean all parts carefully. Then, inspect them closely for wear or damage. Fig. 59-13 shows the most important parts needing inspection.
3. Use a holding fixture for the differential, if available. One is shown in Fig. 59-14. It will make your work easier.
4. Rotate the pinion and case bearings by hand while checking for roughness. Inspect each roller and race. To install new bearings, use a press, Fig.

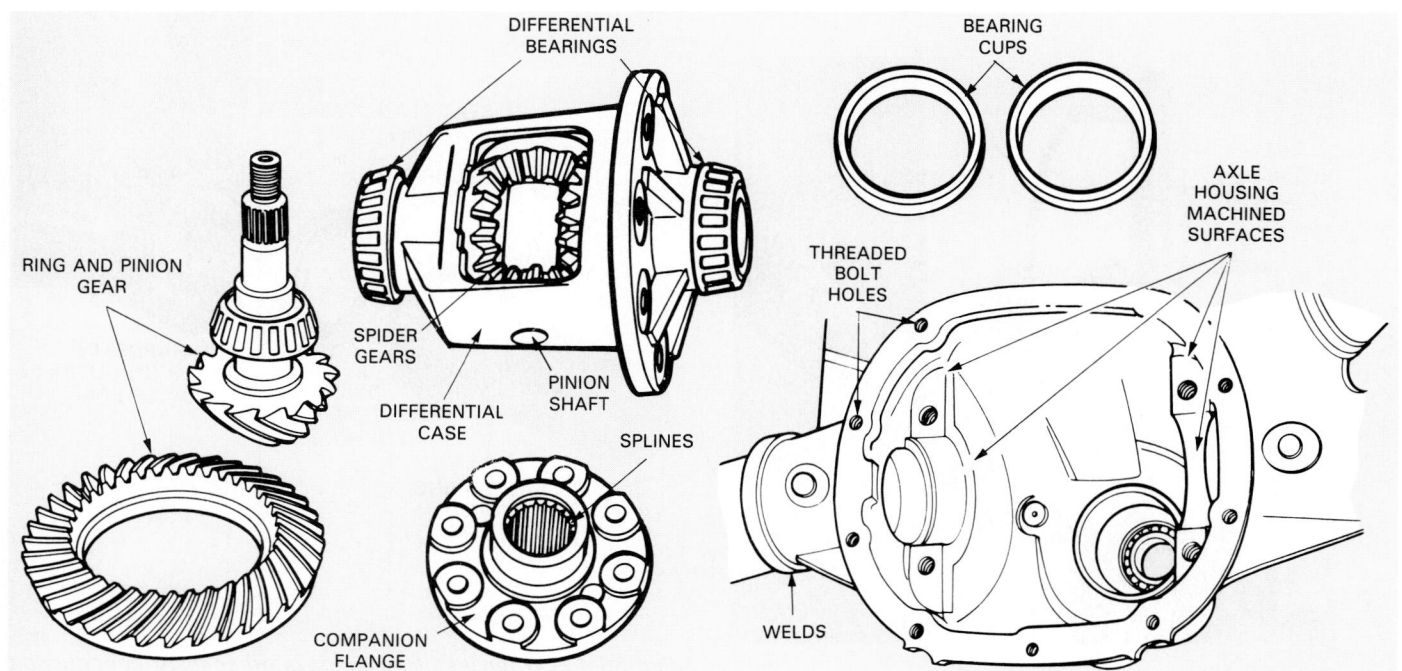

Fig. 59-13. Inspect all differential components carefully. If you overlook even one bad part, your repair could fail. (Ford)

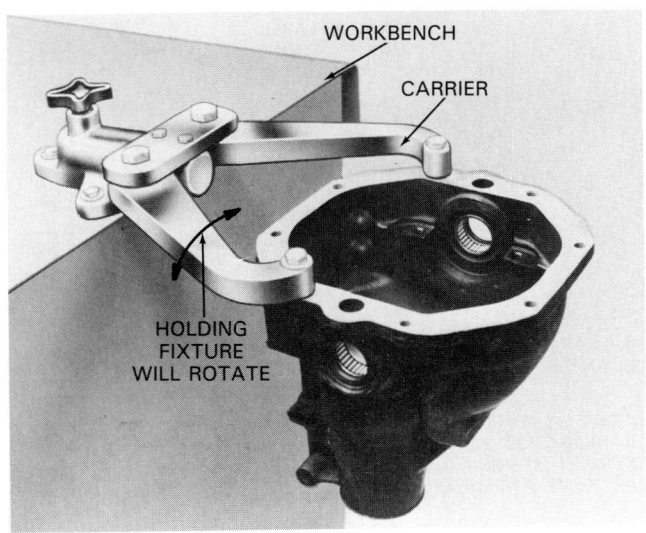

Fig. 59-14. Holding fixture is handy. It will let you swivel heavy differential carrier into different positions while working. (Owatonna Tools Co.)

59-15, or a puller, if required. Replace the bearing and race as a set if faulty.

5. If the pinion gear has a collapsible spacer (device for preloading pinion bearings), always replace it. One is pictured in Fig. 59-16.

6. To avoid seal damage, use a seal driver, Fig. 59-17. Coat the outside of all seals with nonhardening sealer. Lubricate the seal ID. Make sure the sealing lip faces the inside of the differential.

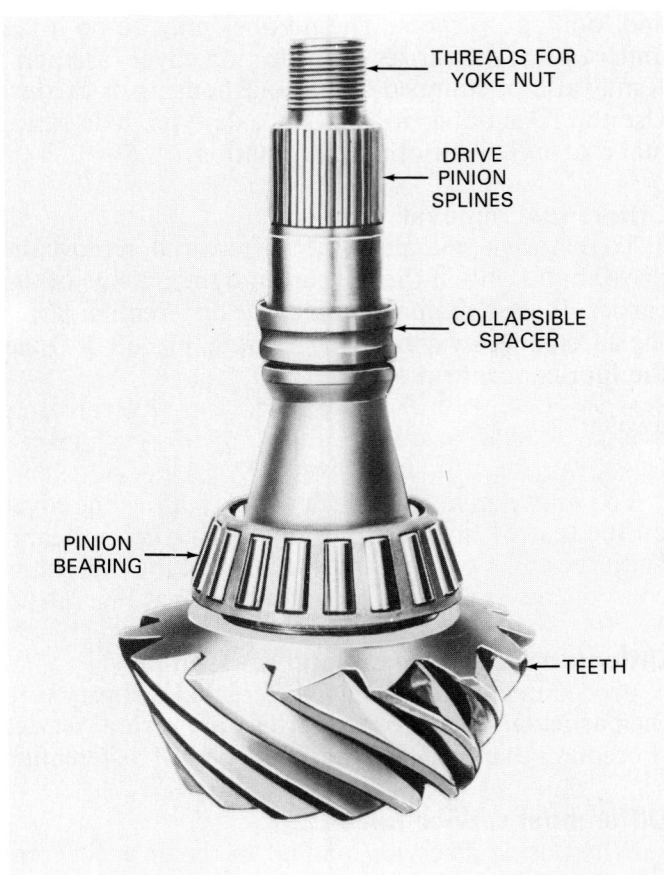

Fig. 59-16. If pinion gear uses a collapsible spacer, install a new one anytime bearings are disassembled. If old spacer is used, bearing preload cannot be accurately obtained. (Oldsmobile)

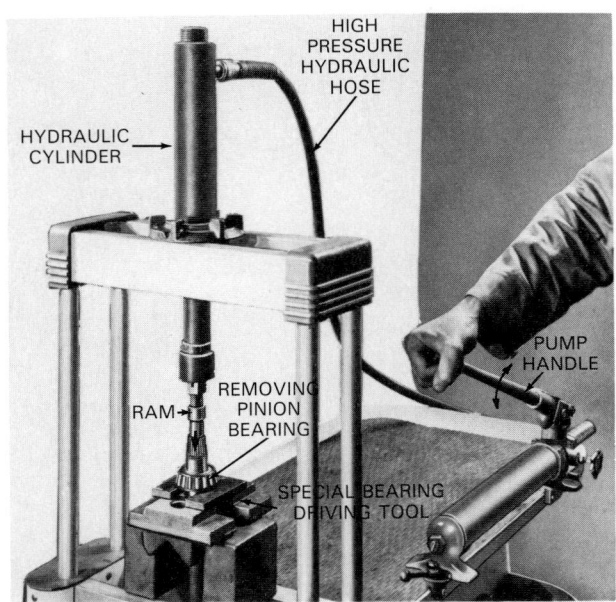

Fig. 59-15. Use a press to remove pinion bearing. Stand back and use recommended driving tools. (Chrysler Corp.)

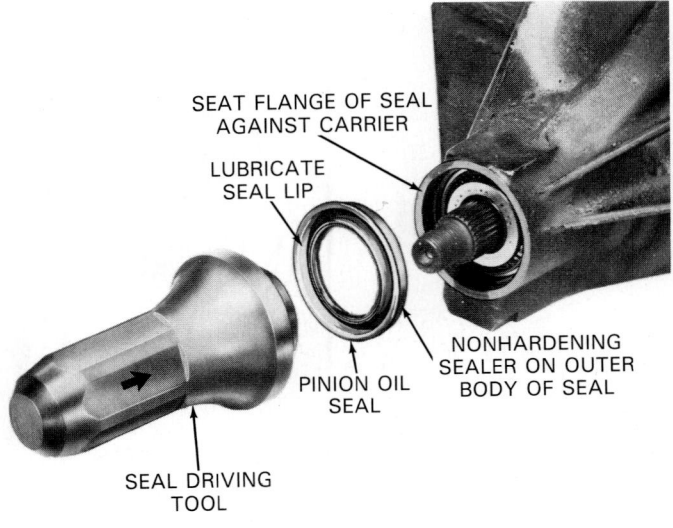

Fig. 59-17. When installing pinion or other seals, coat outside diameter with nonhardening sealer. Coat inside lip with lubricant. Use seal driver to squarely install seal. (Oldsmobile)

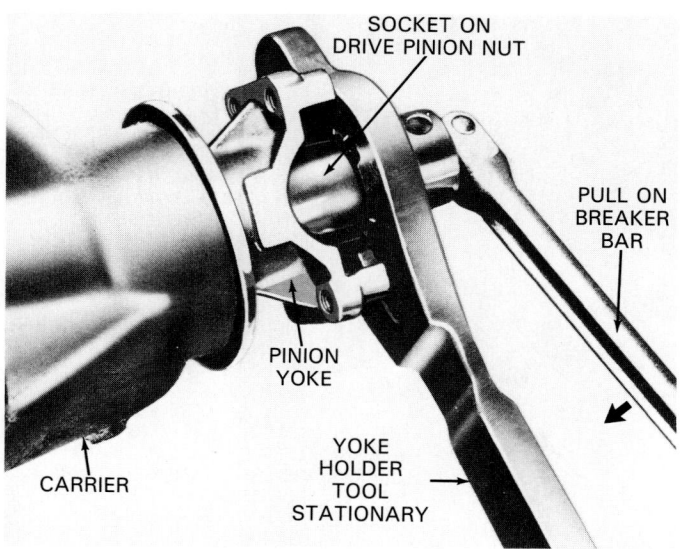

Fig. 59-18. Large holding bar is best way to keep yoke from turning when tightening drive pinion nut. With collapsible spacer, tighten in small increments and measure preload. Without collapsible spacer, you must normally torque nut to specific spec. (Oldsmobile)

7. When tightening the pinion yoke nut, clamp the yoke in a vise or use a special holding bar, as shown in Fig. 59-18.
8. Replace the ring and pinion gears as a set, Fig. 59-19. Mesh or align the *gear timing markings* (painted lines or other markings) on the ring and pinion gears if used. This will match the proper teeth that have been lapped together at the factory.
9. Torque all fasteners to specs. Refer to the service manual for torque values.
10. Use new gaskets and/or approved sealer.
11. Align all markings during reassembly, Fig. 59-20.

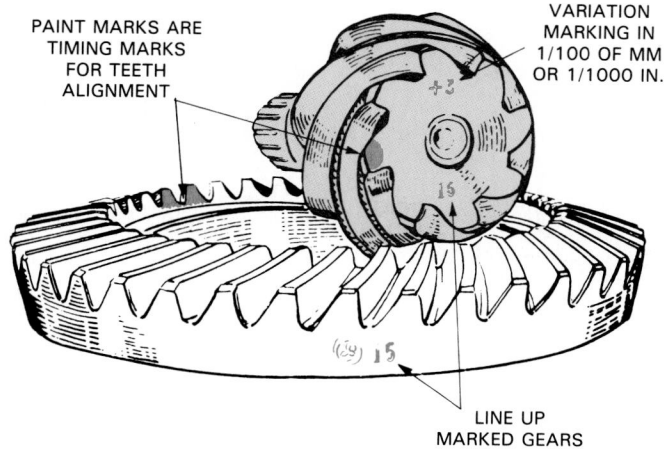

Fig. 59-19. Replace ring and pinion together. They are a matched set. Note markings. Some give information for adjustment. Others show which teeth must be meshed together during installation. (Chrysler)

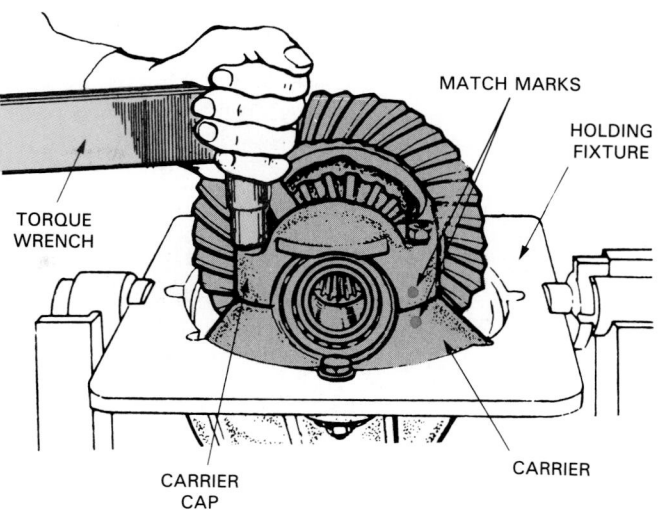

Fig. 59-20. Torque all fasteners to specs. Make sure you align markings during assembly. (Plymouth)

If you install the carrier caps backwards, for example, the caps could crush and damage the bearings and races. The differential could fail as soon as it is returned to service.
12. Use a shop manual for detailed directions, Figs. 59-21 and 59-22. Differential designs and repair procedures vary. Special tools and methods are frequently needed.

LIMITED-SLIP DIFFERENTIAL SERVICE

Limited-slip differential repair may be required after prolonged service or after part damage from abuse or lack of maintenance. The clutch discs can wear, losing much of their frictional qualities. This can make the differential act like a conventional unit.

Break-away torque is the amount of torque needed to make one axle or differential side gear rotate the limited slip differential clutches. Fig. 59-23 shows the procedure recommended by one auto maker for testing a limited-slip differential.

Bolt a special tool to the wheel. Then, raise that tire off the shop floor. Place the transmission in neutral.

Turn the wheel and axle with a torque wrench, Fig. 59-23. Note the torque reading when the wheel begins to turn. This is the clutch pack break-away torque.

If break-away torque is too low (worn clutches, weakened clutch springs, or part damage) or too high (shimmed improperly, part damage), repairs are needed. Fig. 59-24 shows a typical limited-slip differential.

DIFFERENTIAL MEASUREMENTS AND ADJUSTMENTS

There are several measurements and adjustments that must be made when assembling a differential. When "setting up" (measuring and adjusting) a differential,

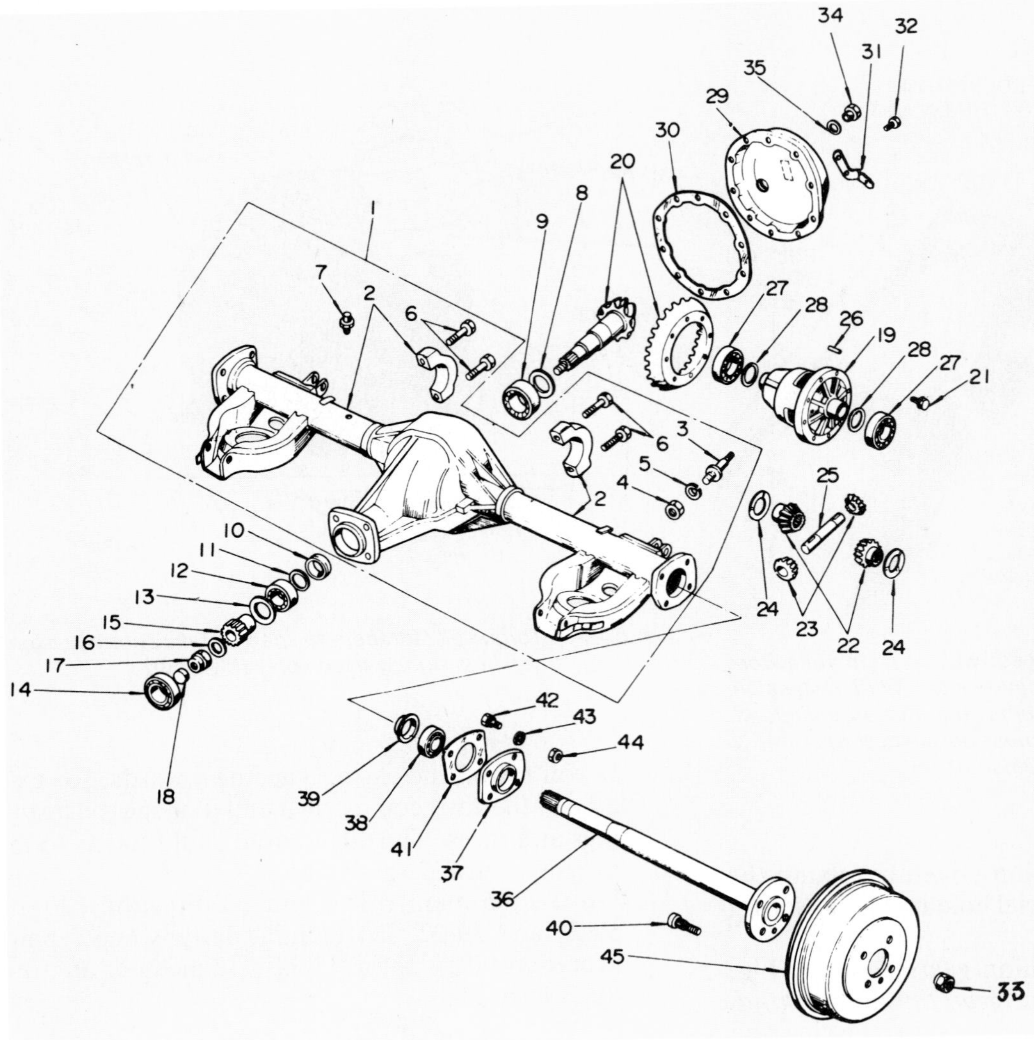

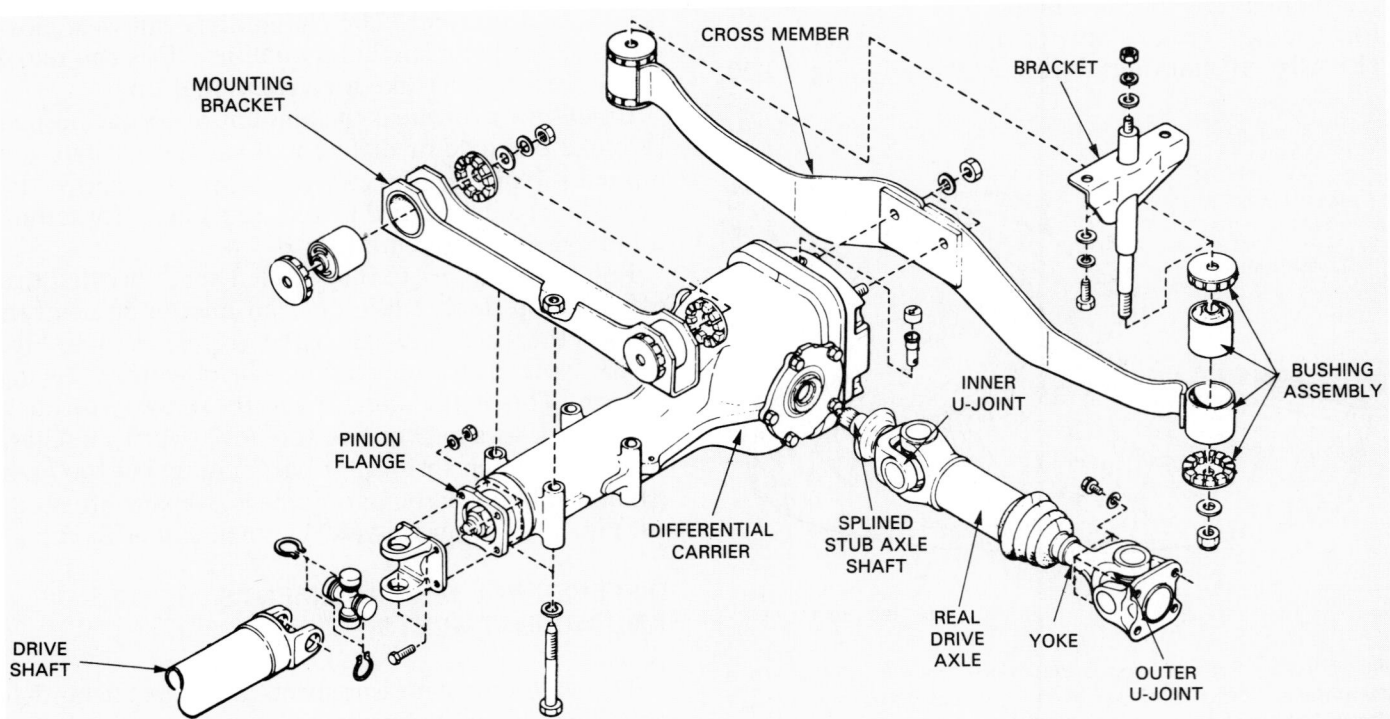

1. REAR AXLE HOUSING ASSEMBLY
2. REAR AXLE CASE
3. BOLT — AXLE HOUSING TO LATERAL ROD
4. NUT
5. WASHER
6. BOLT — BEARING CAP TO AXLE HOUSING
7. REAR AXLE BREATHER ASSEMBLY
8. PINION BEARING SHIM
9. PINION BEARING (INNER)
10. COLLAPSIBLE DISTANCE SPACER
11. SHIM — DISTANCE PIECE
12. PINION BEARING (OUTER)
13. OIL THROWER
14. SLIDING SLEEVE OIL SEAL
15. BARREL SPLINE SLEEVE
16. FINAL PINION WASHER
17. PINION NUT
18. PRESSURE CAP
19. DIFFERENTIAL CASE
20. RING GEAR AND PINION
21. RING GEAR SETTING BOLT
22. DIFFERENTIAL SIDE GEARS
23. DIFFERENTIAL PINION GEARS
24. SIDE GEAR THRUST WASHER
25. DIFFERENTIAL PINION PIN
26. LOCK PIN
27. SIDE BEARING
28. SIDE GEAR SHIM
29. REAR AXLE HOUSING REAR COVER
30. REAR AXLE HOUSING GASKET
31. BRAKE PIPE UNION BRACKET
32. UNION BRACKET BOLT
33. WHEEL NUT
34. OIL FILLER PLUG
35. OIL FILLER GASKET
36. REAR AXLE SHAFT
37. AXLE SHAFT BEARING RETAINER
38. AXLE SHAFT BEARING
39. AXLE SHAFT SLEEVE
40. WHEEL PIN
41. AXLE SHAFT SHIM
42. BOLT — BRAKE-TO-AXLE CASE
43. SPRING WASHER
44. NUT
45. REAR BRAKE DRUM

Fig. 59-21. Use service manual illustration like this one to help you with reassembly. (GMC)

Fig. 59-22. If car has swing axles, service is similar to repairs made on drive shaft. Refer to Chapter 57 for details. (Subaru)

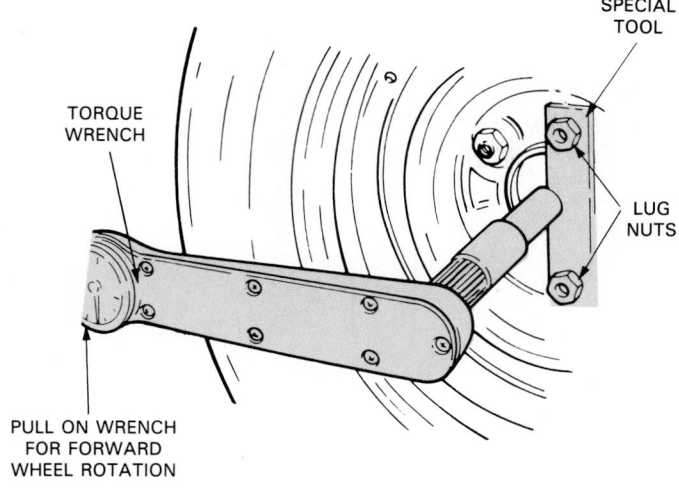

Fig. 59-23. To check operation of most clutch type limited slip differentials, measure break-away torque. With test wheel off ground and other on ground, mount tool on wheel. Then measure how much torque is needed to turn wheel and slip clutches. Compare to specs and repair if too high or low. (Ford)

correct bearing preloads and gear clearances are extremely critical.

The most important differential measurements and adjustments include:

1. Pinion gear depth.
2. Pinion bearing preload.

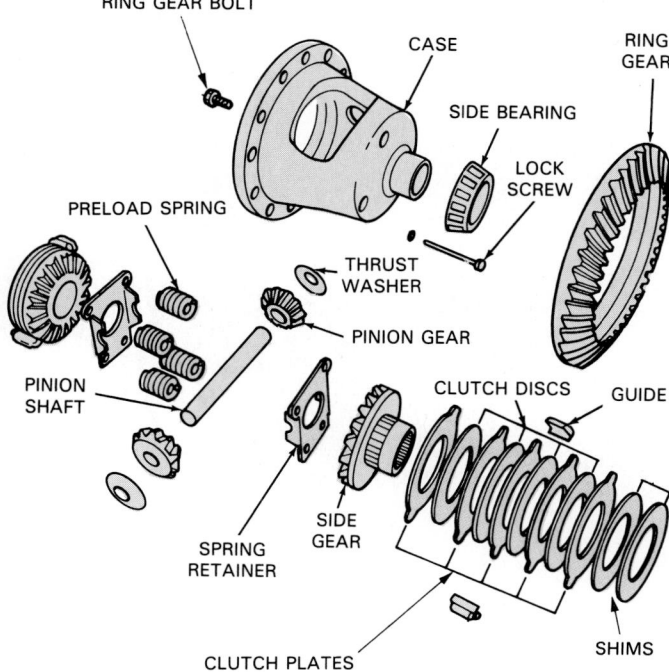

Fig. 59-24. If limited slip unit needs service, you must usually replace clutches and springs. Refer to service manual for detailed instructions. (Cadillac)

3. Case bearing preload.
4. Ring gear runout.
5. Ring and pinion backlash.
6. Ring and pinion contact pattern.

Pinion gear depth refers to the distance the pinion gear extends into the carrier. Pinion depth affects where the pinion gear teeth mesh with the ring gear teeth.

Pinion gear depth is commonly adjusted by varying shim thickness on the pinion gear and bearing assembly. Fig. 59-25 illustrates how shims affect pinion depth in both removable and integral type carriers.

Pinion gear preload is frequently adjusted by torquing the pinion nut to compress a collapsible spacer. The more the pinion nut is torqued, the more the spacer will compress to increase the preload or tightness of the bearings.

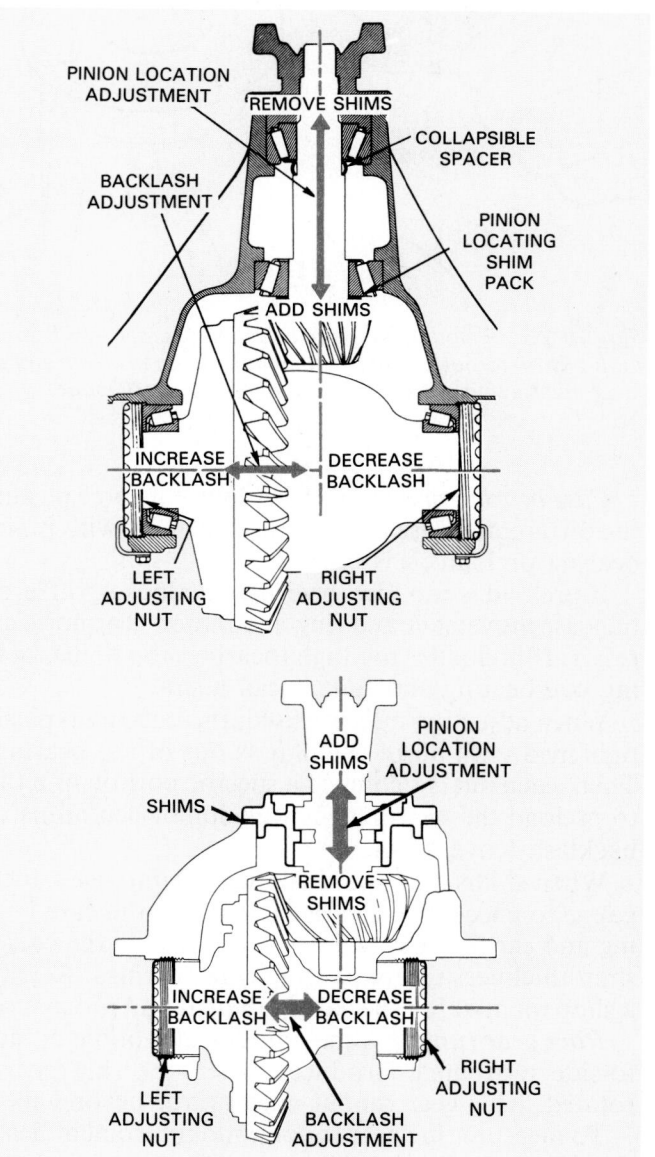

Fig. 59-25. Study how movement of pinion or ring gears adjusts two differentials. Shim thickness change affects each differently. (Ford)

When a solid spacer and pinion nut torque is used, shims commonly control pinion bearing preload. The pinion nut is usually torqued to a specific value.

To set pinion gear preload, a holding tool is used to keep the pinion gear stationary. Then, a breaker bar or torque wrench can be used to tighten the pinion nut. Refer to Fig. 59-18.

With a collapsible spacer, only tighten the nut in small increments. Then measure pinion preload by turning the pinion nut with an inch-pound (N·m) torque wrench. See Fig. 59-26.

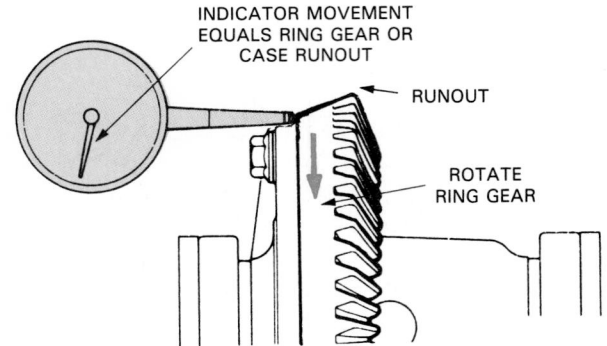

Fig. 59-27. If gears seem to tighten up and loosen when turned, measure ring gear runout. Indicator needle movement equals runout. (Plymouth)

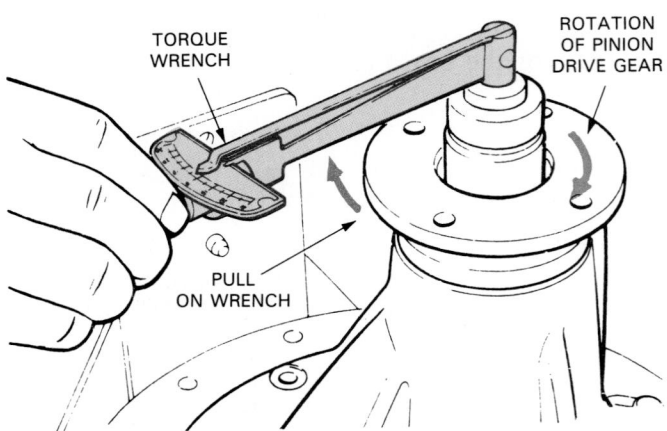

Fig. 59-26. Pinion bearing preload measurement with small, in.-lb. (N·m) torque wrench. Compare reading to specs and adjust using service manual directions. (Dodge)

Case bearing preload is the amount of force pushing the differential case bearings together. As with pinion bearing preload, it is critical.

If preload is too low (bearings too loose), differential case movement and ring and pinion gear noise can result. If preload is too high (bearings too tight), bearing overheating and failure can result.

When adjusting nuts are used, the nuts are typically tightened until all of the play is out of the bearings. Then, each nut is tightened a specific portion of a turn to preload the bearings. This is done when adjusting backlash (covered shortly).

When shims are used, you may need to use a feeler gauge to check side clearance between the case bearing and carrier. This will let you calculate the correct shim thickness to preload the case bearings. Refer to a shop manual for special equipment and procedures.

Ring gear runout is the amount of wobble or side-to-side movement produced when the ring gear is rotated. Ring gear runout must not be beyond specs.

To measure ring gear runout, mount a dial indicator against the back of the ring gear. See Fig. 59-27. The indicator stem should be perpendicular to the ring gear surface. Then turn the ring gear and note the indicator reading.

If ring gear runout is excessive, check ring gear mounting and differential case runout. If not a mounting problem, replace either the ring gear (and pinion) or the case as needed.

Ring and pinion backlash refers to the amount of space between the meshing teeth of the gears. Backlash is needed to allow for heat expansion.

As the gears operate, they produce friction and heat. This makes the gears expand, reducing the clearance between meshing teeth. Without backlash, the ring and pinion teeth could jam into each other. The gears could fail in a short time.

Too much ring and pinion backlash could cause gear noise (whirring, roaring, or clunking).

To measure ring and pinion backlash, mount a dial indicator as shown in Fig. 59-28. Position the indicator stem on one of the ring gear teeth. Then, while holding

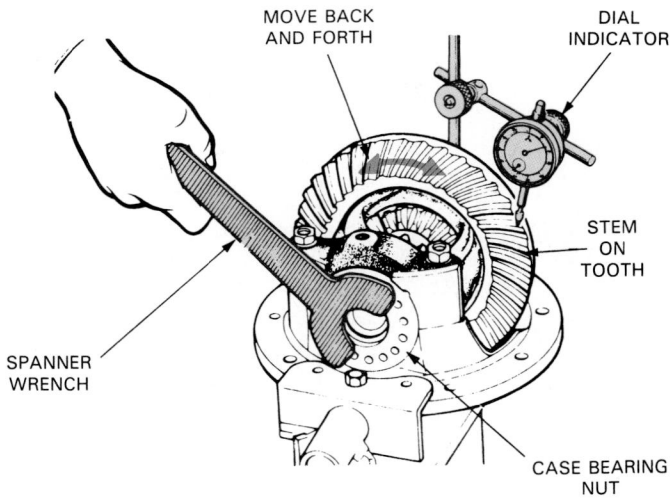

Fig. 59-28. After setting pinion bearing preload and depth, adjust backlash and case bearing preload. This unit is adjusted by turning nuts. Indicator is mounted with direction of gear rotation. Indicator is touching outer end of tooth. To get reading, hold pinion stationary and move ring gear back and forth while watching indicator.

the pinion gear STATIONARY, move the ring gear back and forth. Indicator needle movement will reveal gear backlash. Compare your measurement to specs and adjust backlash as needed.

To increase backlash, move the ring gear away from the pinion gear. To decrease backlash, move the ring gear toward the pinion gear. Refer to Fig. 59-25.

With some differentials, ring gear position is controlled by the case bearing nuts. In others, shims are used to move the ring gear.

Differential gear tooth contact pattern

A check of the *gear tooth contact pattern* in a differential is used to double-check ring and pinion adjustment.

Wipe white grease, red lead, or hydrated ferric oxide (yellow oxide of iron) on the teeth of the ring gear. This is illustrated in Fig. 59-29. Spin the ring gear one way and then the other.

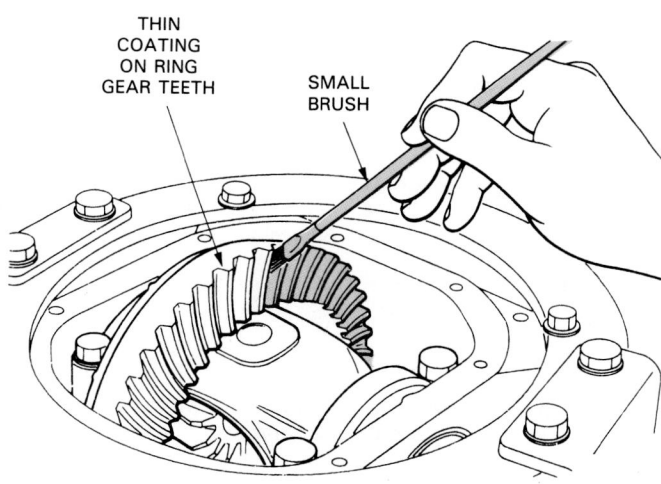

Fig. 59-29. To check contact between drive pinion gear and ring gear, coat ring gear teeth with approved substance: white grease, red lead, etc. Turn ring gear one way and then the other to rub teeth together, producing contact pattern on teeth. (Chrysler)

Carefully note the contact pattern which shows up on the teeth where the grease or red lead has been WIPED OFF.

A good contact pattern is one located in the center of the gear teeth, Fig. 59-30. Fig. 59-31 shows several ring and pinion gear contact patterns. Study each and note the suggested correction for the faulty contact. Also, note the names of the areas on the ring gear teeth. These include the:
1. TOE (narrow part of gear tooth).
2. HEEL (wide part of gear tooth).
3. PITCH LINE (imaginary line along center of tooth).
4. FACE (area on tooth above pitch line).

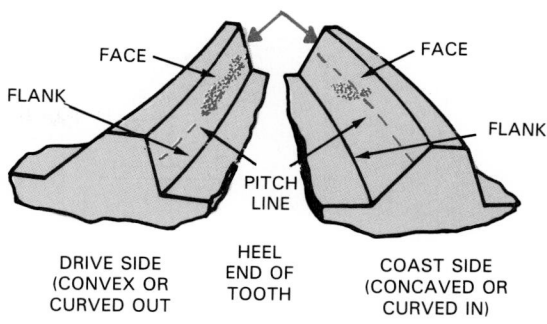

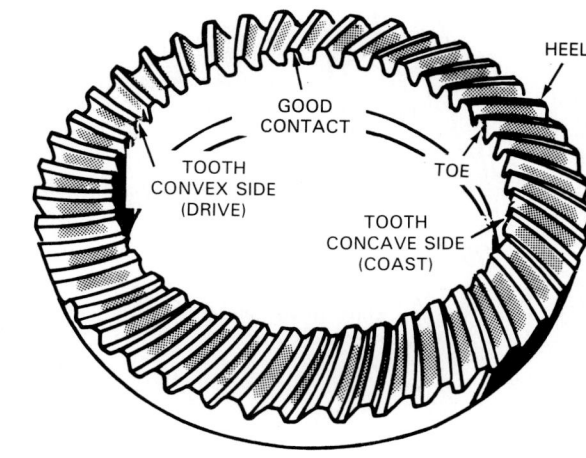

Fig. 59-30. Ring gear teeth nomenclature. Study names. They are needed when reading or interpreting gear contact patterns. (Oldsmobile)

5. FLANK (area on tooth below pitch line).
6. DRIVE SIDE (convex side of tooth).
7. COAST SIDE (concave side of tooth).

KNOW THESE TERMS

Ring and pinion noise, Bearing noise, Limited-slip differential chatter, Stethoscope, Axle retainer plate, Axle C-clip, Slide hammer puller, Seal part number, Axle end play, Part alignment marks, Break-away torque, Timing gear marks, Pinion gear depth, Pinion gear bearing preload, Case bearing preload, Ring gear runout, Ring and pinion backlash, Toe, Heel, Pitch line, Face, Flank, Drive side, Coast side, Contact pattern.

REVIEW QUESTIONS

1. Describe ring and pinion noise.
2. Excess ring and pinion backlash can cause a "clunk" sound when the transmission is placed in drive. True or False?
3. Worn or damaged bearings in the carrier or on the axles produce a humming sound that changes with

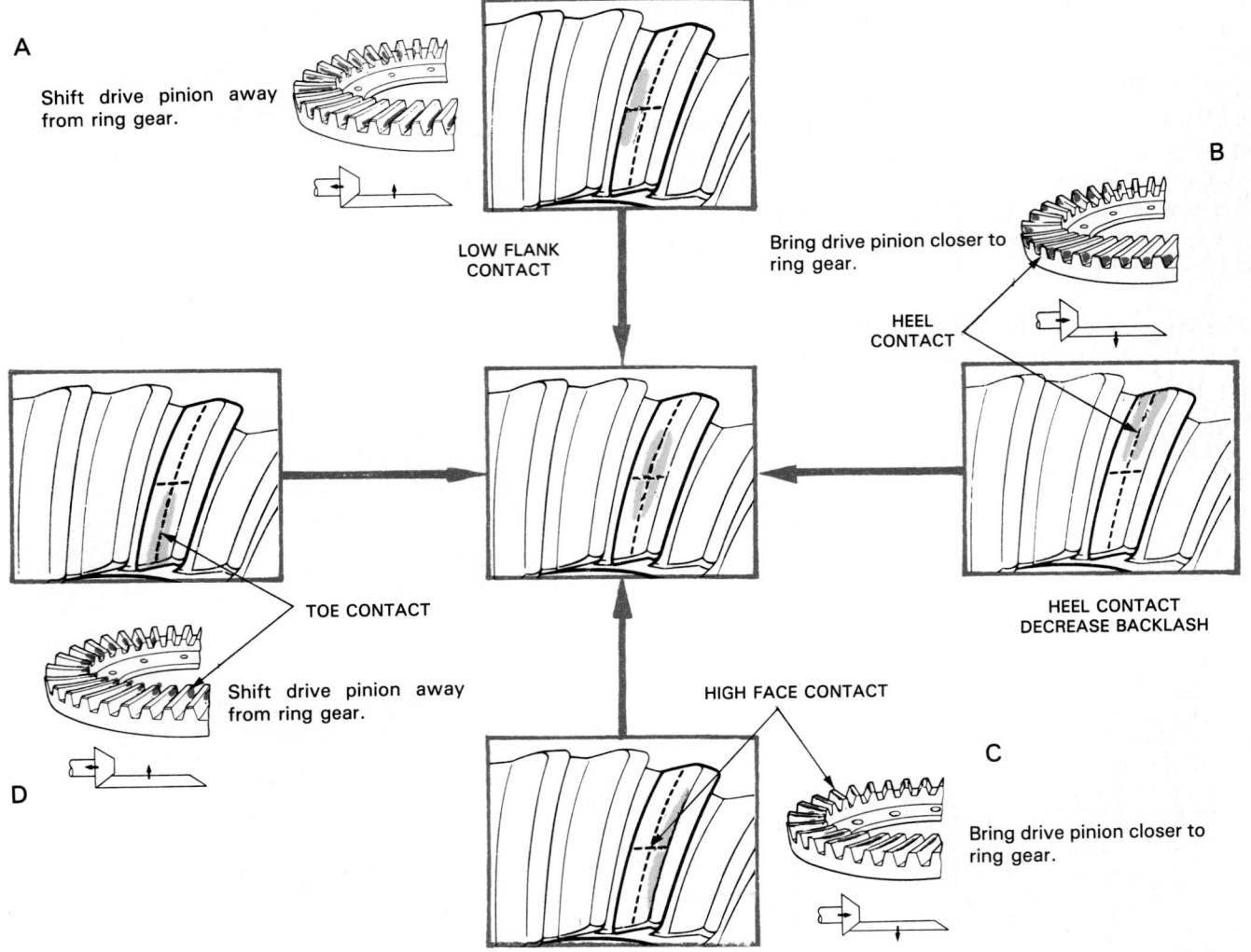

A Shift drive pinion away from ring gear.

LOW FLANK CONTACT

B Bring drive pinion closer to ring gear.

HEEL CONTACT

HEEL CONTACT DECREASE BACKLASH

TOE CONTACT

Shift drive pinion away from ring gear.

D

HIGH FACE CONTACT

C Bring drive pinion closer to ring gear.

Fig. 59-31. *Area where grease, red lead, or ferric oxide is rubbed off ring gear indicates contact point. It must be centrally located on teeth. Note typical methods of correcting patterns.* (General Motors Corporation and Toyota)

load. True or False?
4. List four points to consider when diagnosing bearing failures.
5. A _____ is a listening device that can be used to isolate differential and axle noises.
6. _____ _____ often require a lubricant that is compatible with friction clutches.
7. Explain the two methods commonly used to hold a rear drive axle in its housing.
8. How do you measure axle end play?
9. List twelve service rules for differentials.
10. Which of the following is NOT a common differential adjustment?

a. Pinion gear depth.
b. Pinion gear preload.
c. Case bearing preload.
d. Ring and pinion backlash.
e. Ring and pinion preload.

ACTIVITIES FOR CHAPTER 59

1. Check out a rear axle assembly on a shop vehicle and report on its condition.
2. Remove an axle of the retainer plate type.
3. Remove an axle of the C-clip type.
4. Clean a differential and replace the fluid.

60

Transaxle, Front-Drive Axle Fundamentals

After studying this chapter, you should be able to:
- ☐ Identify the major parts of a transaxle assembly.
- ☐ Explain the operation of a manual transaxle.
- ☐ Explain the operation of an automatic transaxle.
- ☐ Trace the flow of power through manual and automatic transaxles.
- ☐ Describe design differences in transaxles.
- ☐ Identify the parts of front-wheel drive axles.
- ☐ Compare design differences in front-wheel drive axle CV-joints.

This chapter describes the construction and operating principles of both manual and automatic transaxles. It relies and builds upon the information given in previous text chapters on clutches, manual transmissions, automatic transmissions, and differentials.

TRANSAXLE

A *transaxle* is a transmission and a differential combined in a single assembly. See Fig. 60-1. A transaxle is commonly used in late model, front-wheel drive cars. However, a few rear or mid-engine sports cars and some older, rear engine economy cars also use a transaxle.

A transaxle allows the wheels next to the engine to propel the vehicle. Short drive axles can be used to connect the transaxle output to the hubs and drive wheels.

Auto makers claim that a vehicle having a transaxle and front-wheel drive has several advantages over a front engine vehicle with rear-wheel drive. A few of these advantages are:

1. Reduced drive train weight and improved efficiency.
2. Improved traction on slippery pavement because of more weight on the drive wheels.
3. Increased passenger compartment space (no hump in floor for drive shaft to rear axle).
4. Smoother ride because of less unsprung weight

(weight that must move with suspension action).
5. Quieter operation, since engine and drivetrain noise are centrally located in engine compartment (no transmission, drive shaft, and rear axle under passenger compartment).
6. Improved safety because of increased mass in front of passengers.

Both manual and automatic transaxles are available. A manual transaxle uses a friction clutch and standard transmission type gearbox. An automatic transaxle uses

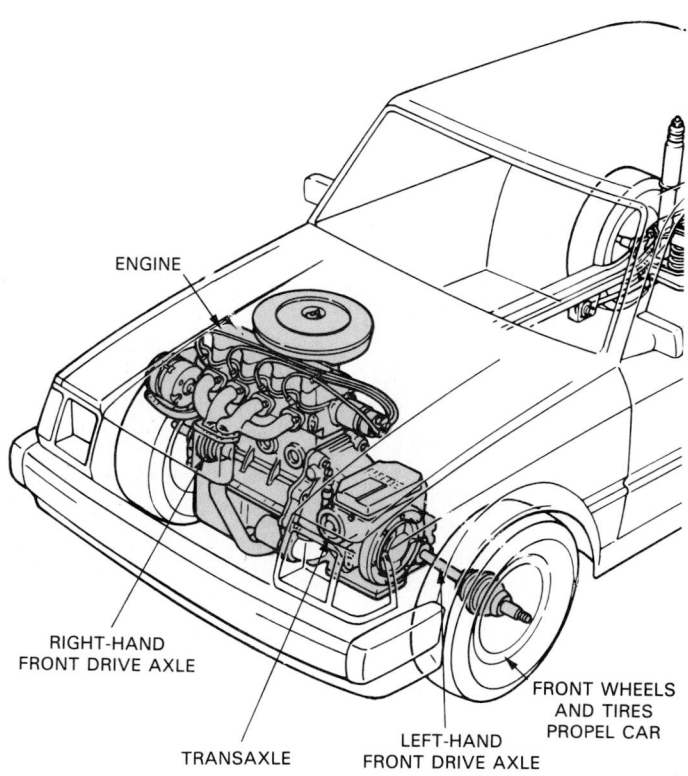

ENGINE

RIGHT-HAND
FRONT DRIVE AXLE

TRANSAXLE

LEFT-HAND
FRONT DRIVE AXLE

FRONT WHEELS
AND TIRES
PROPEL CAR

Fig. 60-1. *Transaxle is used in modern front-wheel drive car. It combines a transmission and differential that drive front axles. (Ford)*

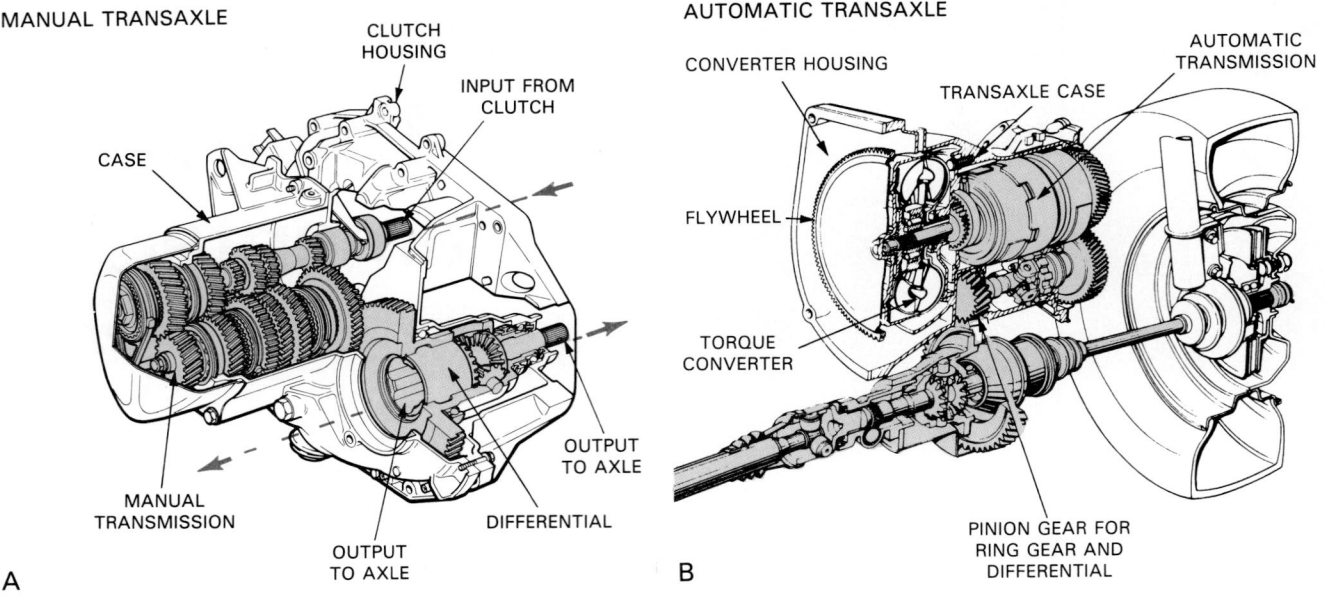

Fig. 60-2. A — Manual transaxle is a manual transmission and a differential in single assembly. B — Automatic transaxle is automatic transmission and differential combined. (Renault and Chrysler)

a torque converter and a hydraulic system to control gear engagement. Compare the manual and automatic transaxles in Fig. 60-2.

Transaxle for transverse engine

Most transaxles are designed so that the engine can be *transverse* (sideways) mounted in the engine compartment. Look at Fig. 60-3A. Study the basic arrangement of this drive system. The engine crankshaft centerline points at both drive wheels. The transaxle bolts to the rear of the engine. This produces a very compact unit.

Engine torque enters the clutch and transaxle's transmission. The transmission transfers power into the differential. Then, the differential turns the drive axles which rotate the front wheels, Fig. 60-4A.

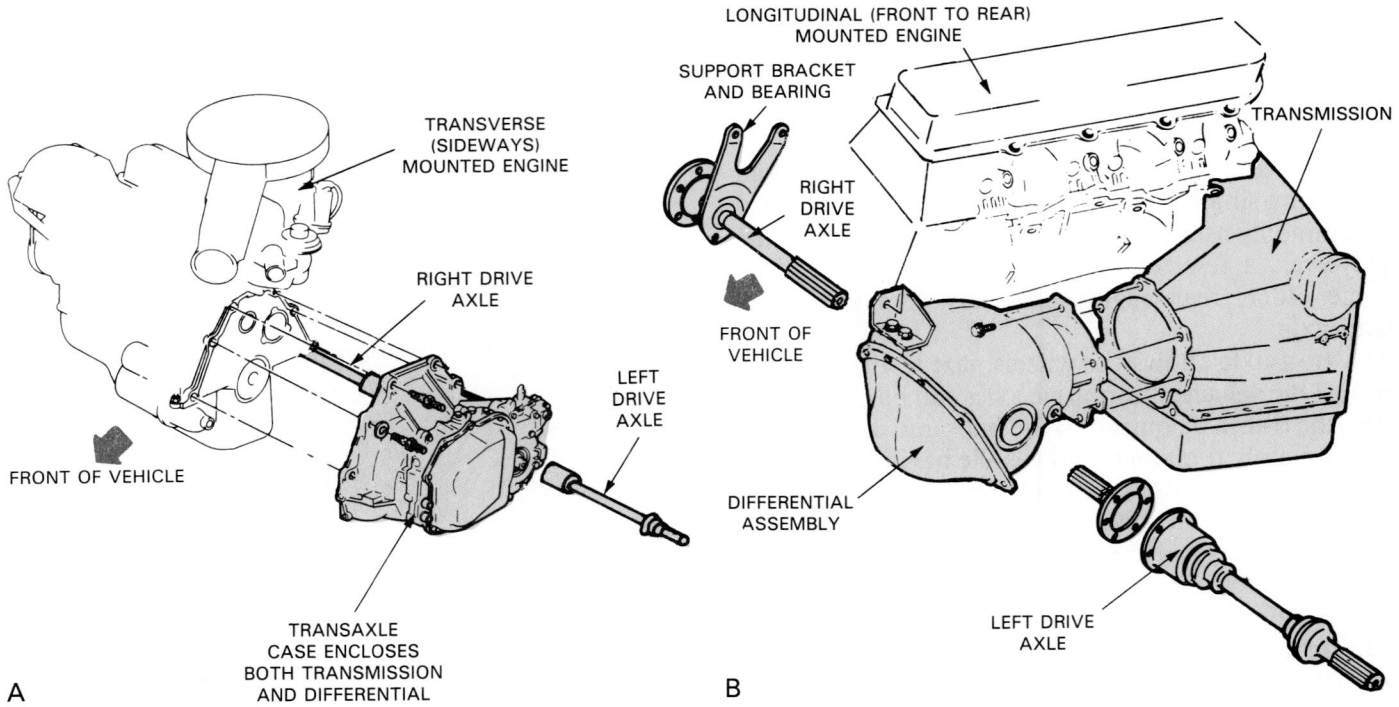

Fig. 60-3. There are two basic transaxle differential design variations: A — With transverse mounted engine, engine crankshaft centerline and axle centerline are on same plane. B — With longitudinal mounted engine, differential must change power flow 90 degrees, as with rear-wheel drive. (Ford and Cadillac)

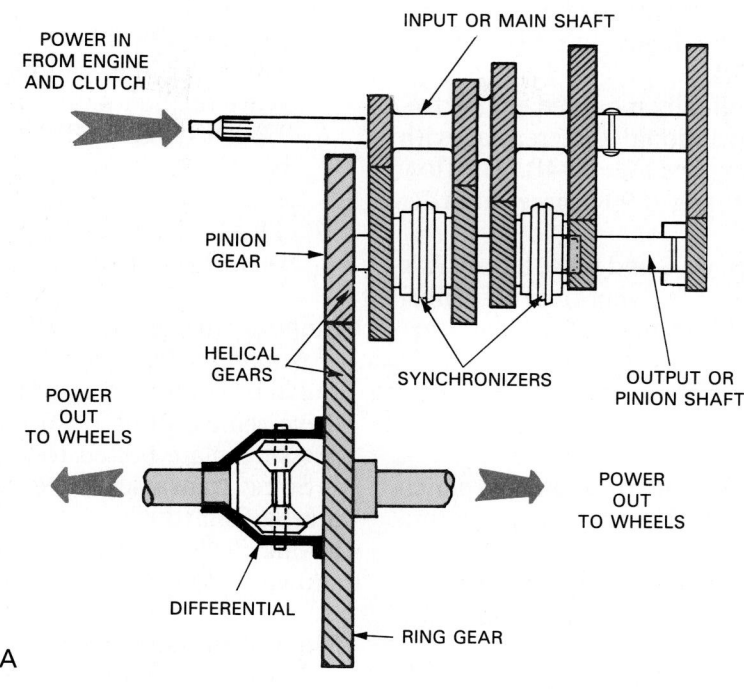

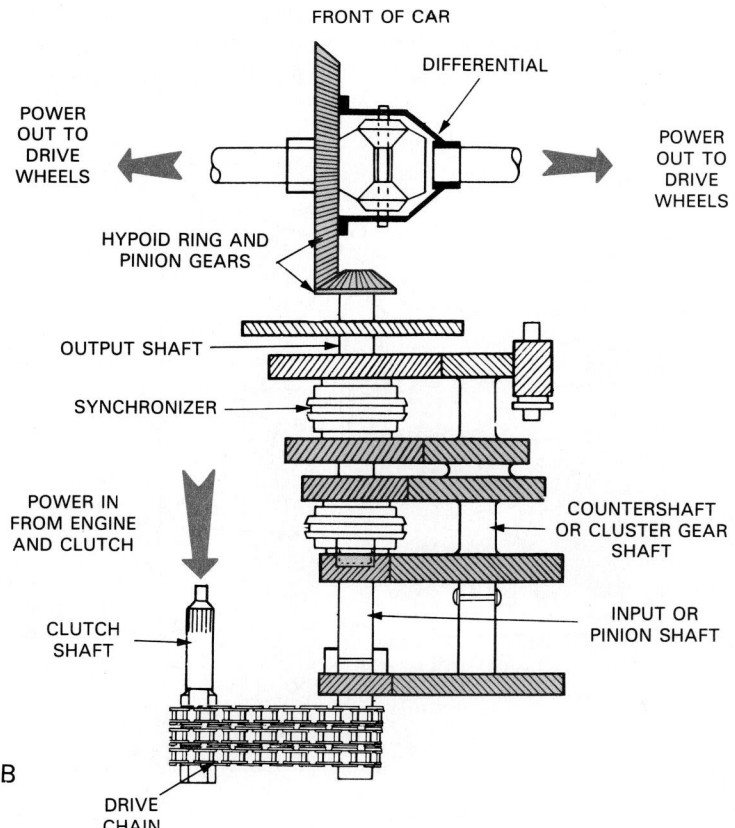

Fig. 60-4. Study transmission-to-differential locations. A — With transverse mounted engine, pinion and ring gears are helical gears. They are positioned in same direction as transmission gears. B — With longitudinal engine, differential uses hypoid gears to change direction of output. Also note drive link or chain that transfers power from crankshaft and clutch to input shaft. (Saab)

Transaxle for longitudinal engine

A few transaxles are made so that the engine is mounted *longitudinally* (lengthwise). The crankshaft centerline points toward the front and rear of the vehicle. Look at Fig. 60-3B.

A transaxle for a longitudinally mounted engine frequently uses a more conventional differential with helical ring and pinion gears. See Fig. 60-4B. The flow of engine torque must be changed 90 degrees in order to turn the drive axles.

As you can see from Figs. 60-3 and 60-4, a transaxle uses the same principles as a conventional transmission and rear axle assembly. However, the parts are arranged differently.

MANUAL TRANSAXLE

A *manual transaxle* uses a standard or manual clutch and transmission. A foot-operated clutch engages and disengages the engine and transaxle. A hand-operated shift lever allows the driver to change gear ratios.

As the basic parts relating to a manual transaxle are introduced, refer to Fig. 60-5.

1. TRANSAXLE INPUT SHAFT (main shaft splined to clutch disc; turns gears in transaxle).
2. TRANSAXLE INPUT GEARS (either freewheeling or fixed gears on input shaft; mesh with output gears).
3. TRANSAXLE OUTPUT GEARS (either freewheeling or fixed gears driven by input gears).
4. TRANSAXLE OUTPUT SHAFT (pinion shaft that transfers torque to ring and pinion gears and differential).
5. TRANSAXLE SYNCHRONIZERS (splined hub assemblies that can be used to lock freewheeling gears to their shafts for engagement).
6. TRANSAXLE DIFFERENTIAL (transfers gearbox torque to driving axles and allows axles to turn at different speeds).
7. TRANSAXLE CASE (aluminum housing that encloses and supports parts of transaxle).

Manual transaxle clutch

A *manual transaxle clutch* is almost identical to a clutch used with a manual transmission for a rear-wheel drive vehicle. It uses a friction disc and spring-loaded pressure plate bolted to a heavy flywheel, Fig. 60-6.

Some transaxles use a conventional clutch release mechanism (throw-out bearing and fork). Others use a long push rod passing through the input shaft, as shown in Fig. 60-6.

Manual transaxle transmission

A *manual transaxle transmission* provides several (usually four or five) forward gear ratios and reverse. Sometimes, high gear can provide an overdrive ratio for increased fuel economy.

As you read service manuals, you will find that the names of the shafts, gears, and other parts in a transaxle will vary. This will depend upon the location and

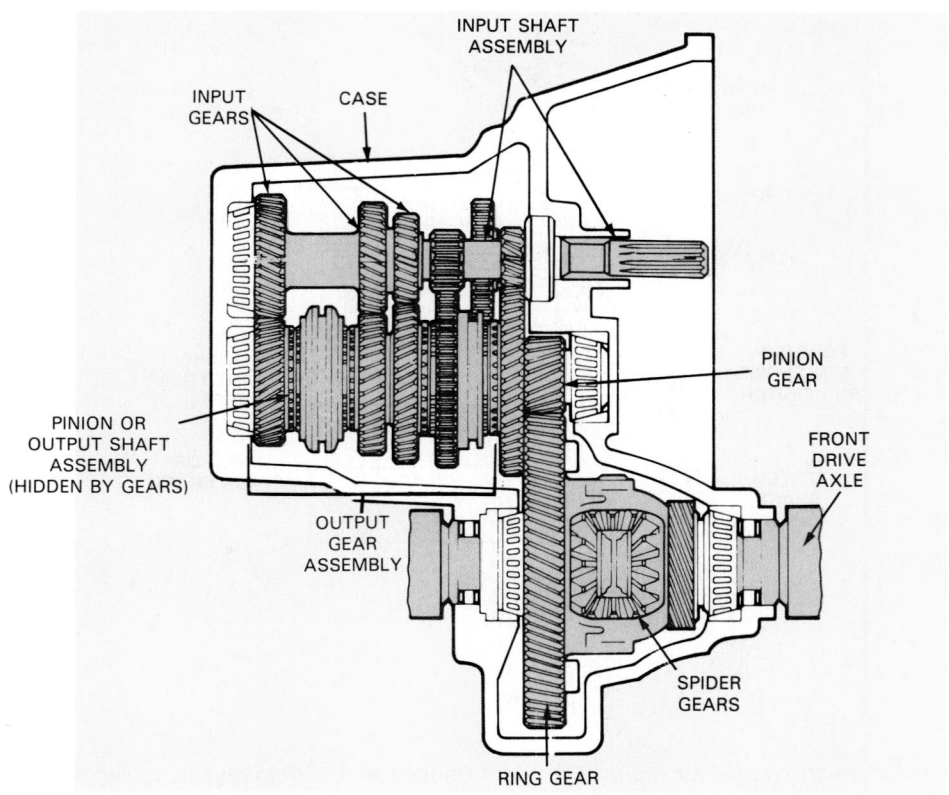

Fig. 60-5. Note basic parts of typical transaxle assembly. (Ford)

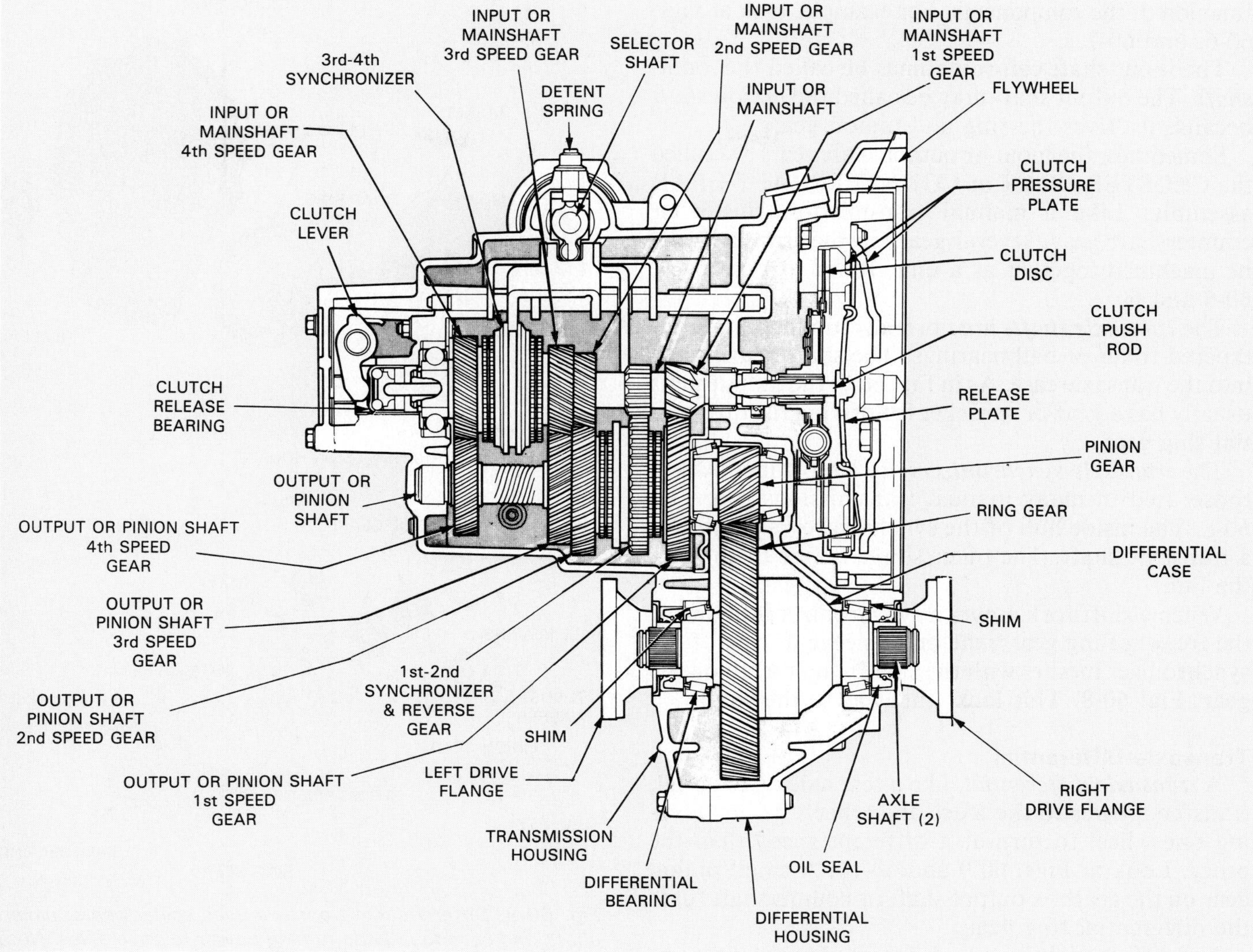

Fig. 60-6. Detailed view shows all major parts of manual transaxle. Study names and locations carefully. In this unit, long push rod extends through center of input shaft to actuate clutch. (Plymouth)

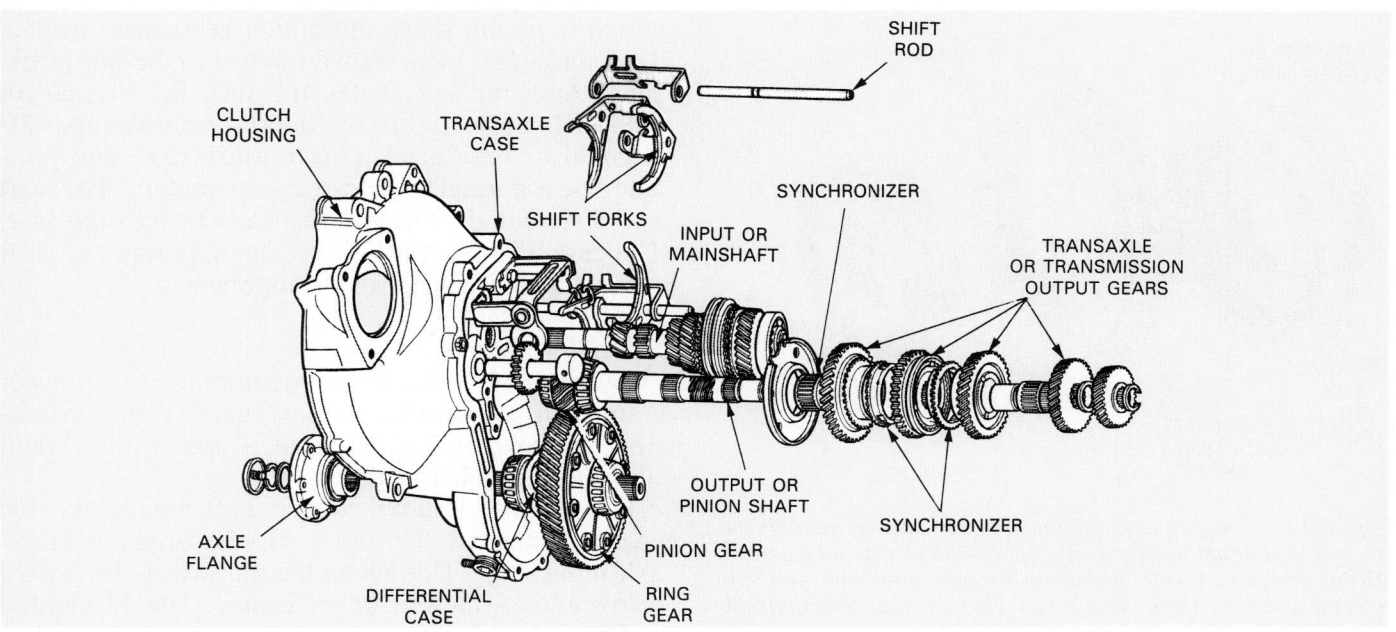

Fig. 60-7. As you can see, the inside of manual transaxle is very similar to manual transmission. However, this transaxle has freewheeling gears and synchronizers on both the input and output shafts. Shift rods and forks operate synchronizers. (Dodge)

function of the components. For example, look at Figs. 60-6, and 60-7.

The input shaft can sometimes be called the *main-shaft*. The output shaft may be called the *pinion shaft* because it drives the ring and pinion gears.

Sometimes, the input or output shaft gears are called the CLUSTER GEAR or COUNTERSHAFT GEAR assembly. Like a manual transmission cluster or countershaft gear, several gears in the transaxle can be machined together as a unit. Refer to Figs. 60-5, 60-6 and 60-7.

The *transaxle shafts* are normally mounted in either tapered roller or ball bearings. The shaft bearings fit into the transaxle case. As in Fig. 60-7, the output shaft usually has a gear or sprocket for driving the differential ring gear.

The *transaxle synchronizers* are almost identical to those used in many manual transmissions. See Fig. 60-8. The inside hub of the synchronizer is splined to a transaxle shaft. The outer sleeve is free to slide on the hub.

When a shift fork moves a synchronizer into one of the freewheeling gears, the outer sleeve or ring of the synchronizer meshes with the small, outer teeth on the gear, Fig. 60-8. This locks the gear to the shaft.

Transaxle differential

A *transaxle differential,* like a rear axle differential, transfers power to the axles and wheels while allowing one wheel to turn at a different speed than the other. Look at Figs. 60-9 and 60-10. A small pinion gear on the gearbox output shaft or countershaft turns the differential ring gear.

The differential ring gear is fastened to the differential case. The case holds the spider gears (pinion gears and axle side gears) and a pinion shaft. The axle shafts are splined to the differential side gears.

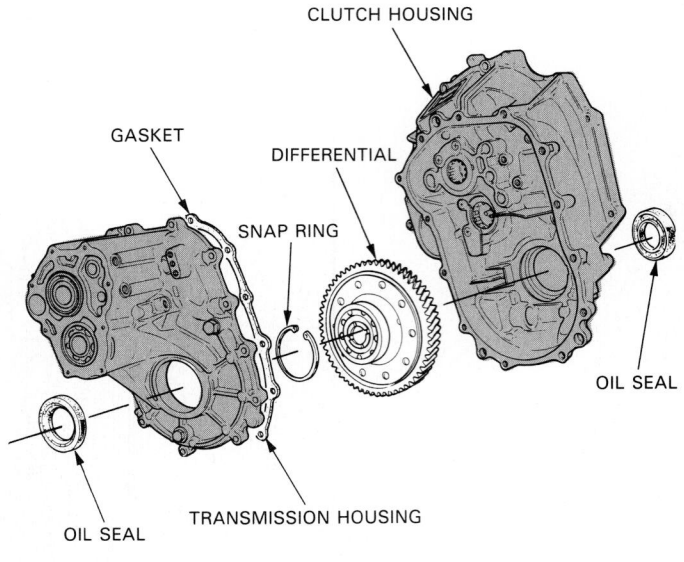

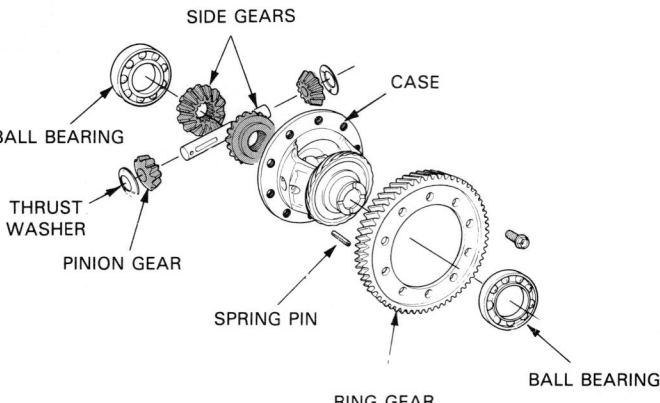

Fig. 60-9. Differential in transaxle uses spider gears, pinion shaft, and case to provide turning power to drive axles. Note that this unit for transverse engine uses helical ring and pinion gears instead of hypoid gears. (Plymouth)

When the gearbox spins the differential ring gear and case, the pinion shaft and pinion gears also revolve. The pinion gear teeth transfer power to the side gears. This causes the axle shafts to rotate. See Fig. 60-10.

Fig. 60-9 illustrates how the transmission and differential are positioned in the transaxle case. The transaxle case is normally made of cast aluminum. The shaft and differential bearing races press fit into the case. The case also has provisions for mounting the shift forks and other accessory components.

Drive link (chain)

A *drive link* or *chain* is sometimes used to transfer crankshaft power to the transaxle gearbox or transmission. Pictured in Fig. 60-11, it is used with a longitudinally mounted engine.

One sprocket is mounted on a shaft connected to the engine crankshaft. The other sprocket drives the transaxle input shaft. This allows the transaxle to be located below and to one side of the engine. The differential and drive axles are under about the center of the engine.

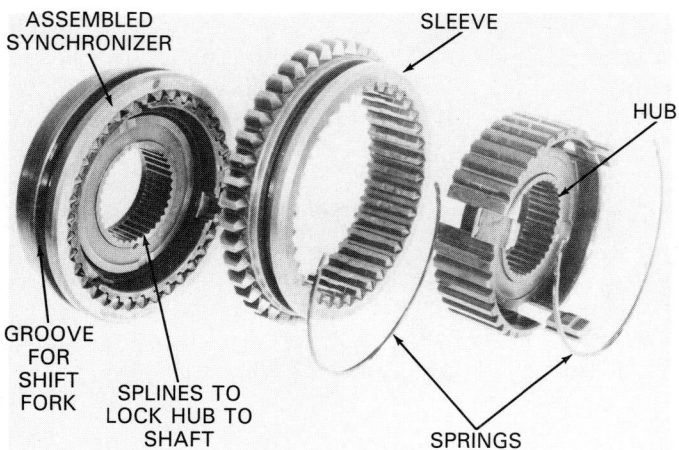

Fig. 60-8. Synchronizer for manual transaxle is also similar to one in manual transmission. Inner hub is splined to shaft. Outer sleeve can slide on hub to engage small teeth on side of freewheeling gear. This locks gear to hub and shaft for engagement. (Chevrolet)

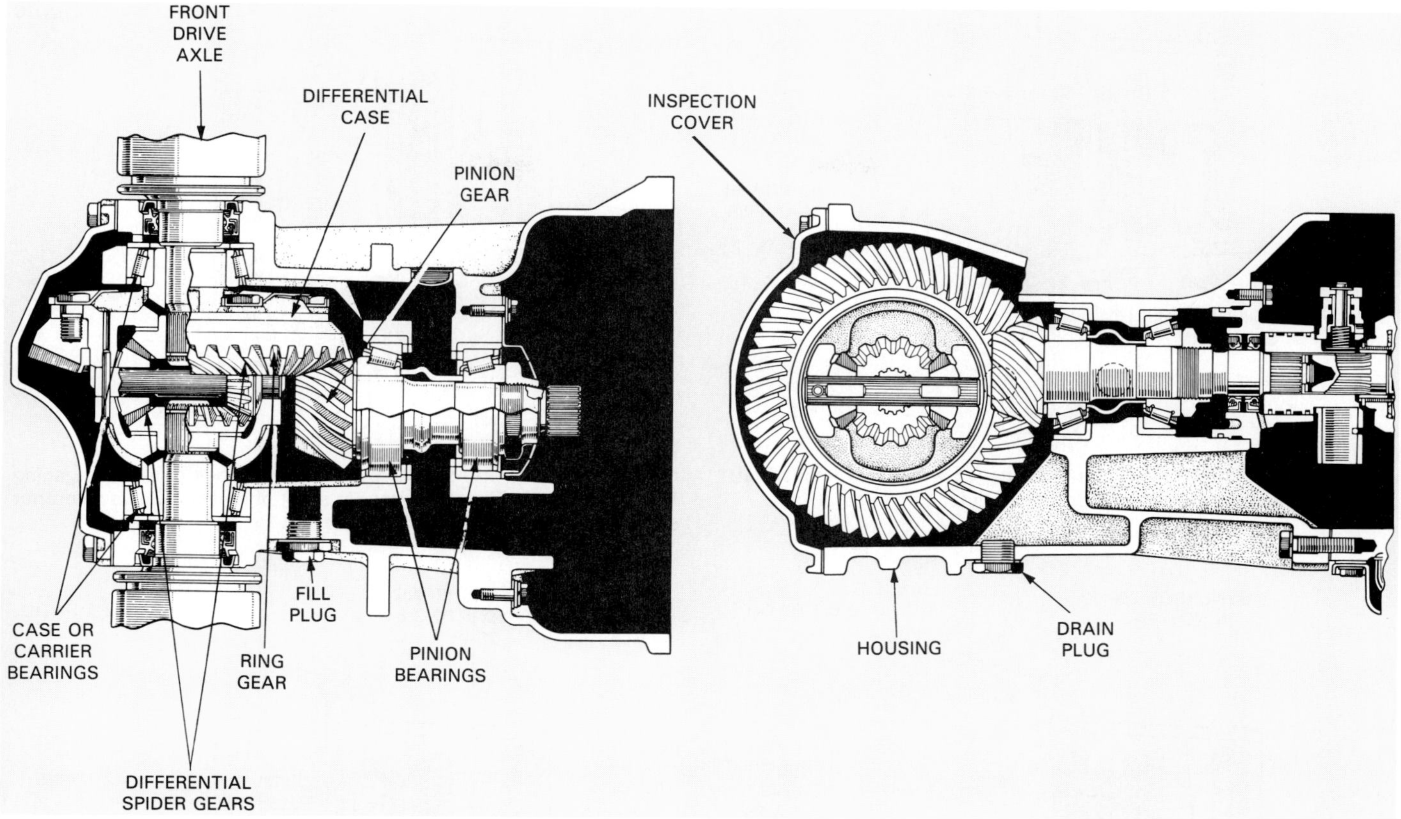

Fig. 60-10. Transaxle for longitudinal engine is almost identical to differential in rear-wheel drive axle. Hypoid gears transfer driving power. (Toyota)

MANUAL TRANSAXLE POWER FLOW

As the operation of a manual transaxle is explained, refer to Fig. 60-12. This illustration shows how power flows through a modern four-speed transaxle.

Transaxle in neutral

With the transaxle in neutral, the engine spins the input shaft. However, since the synchronizers are centered away from any freewheeling gears, power is NOT transferred to the output shaft and differential. See Fig. 60-12A.

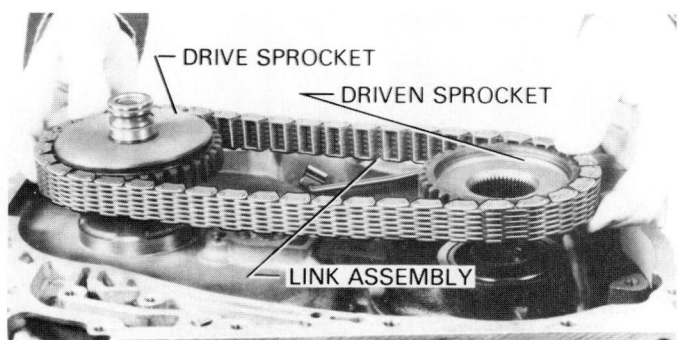

Fig. 60-11. Drive link or chain transfers power from crankshaft input shaft to main shaft in transaxle. This allows transaxle to be mounted to one side and below engine. (Buick)

Transaxle in first gear

When the driver shifts the transaxle into first gear, a shift fork slides the first-second synchronizer into mesh with first gear. This locks the synchronizer teeth with the small teeth on the side of first gear. The first gear is now locked to its shaft.

Power flows through the input shaft first gear, output shaft first gear, pinion gear, ring rear, and to the drive axles through the differential spider gears, Fig. 60-12B.

Since the input shaft first gear is much smaller than the first gear on the output, a gear reduction is produced. Torque is increased since the engine must rotate several times to produce one axle shaft rotation.

Transaxle in second gear

When the transaxle is shifted into second, the first-second synchronizer is moved into mesh with second gear on the input shaft. The second gear can no longer freewheel on its shaft. Power then flows through the second gears and into the differential. From the differential, power flows to the axle shafts and drive wheels. Refer to Fig. 60-12C.

Transaxle in third gear

With the transaxle in third gear, the first-second synchronizer is shifted into neutral so that the first and second gears freewheel. At the same time, the third-fourth synchronizer is slid into mesh with third gear.

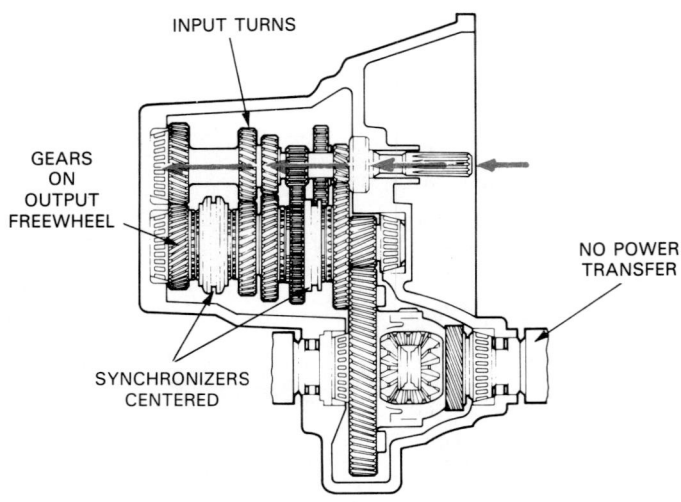

A — In neutral, no synchronizers are engaged with gears. Input shaft spins but gears freewheel and do not transfer power to output.

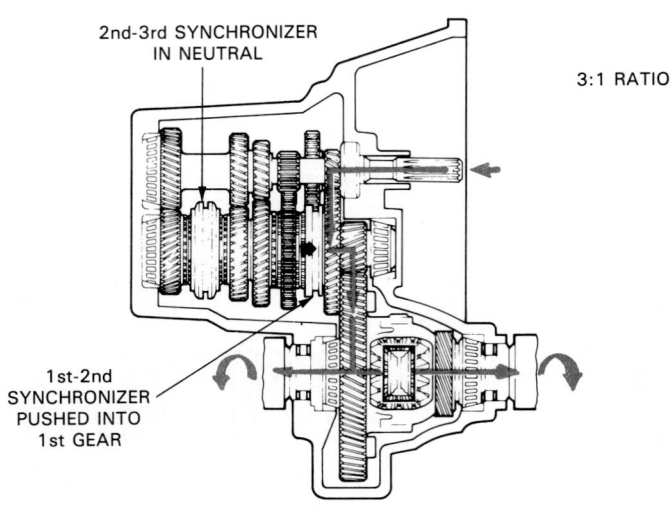

B — In first gear, first-second synchronizer slides to right, engaging first output gear. This locks gear to shaft and power flows to output shaft and differential.

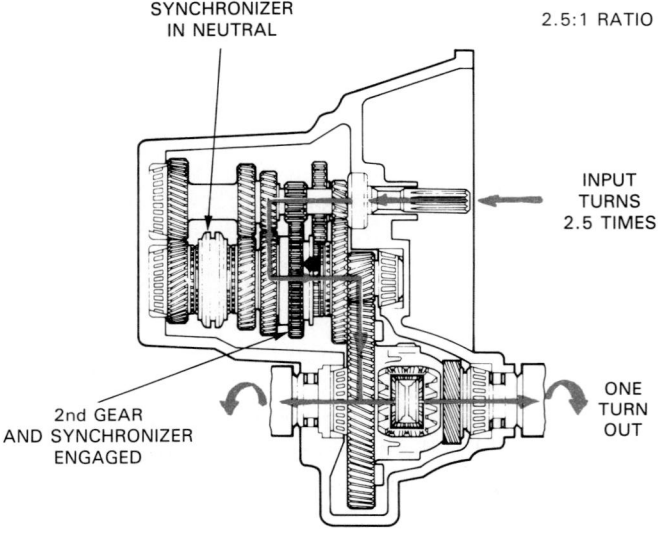

C — In second gear, same synchronizer slides to left. This locks output second gear to shaft. Power flows through second gears and to differential.

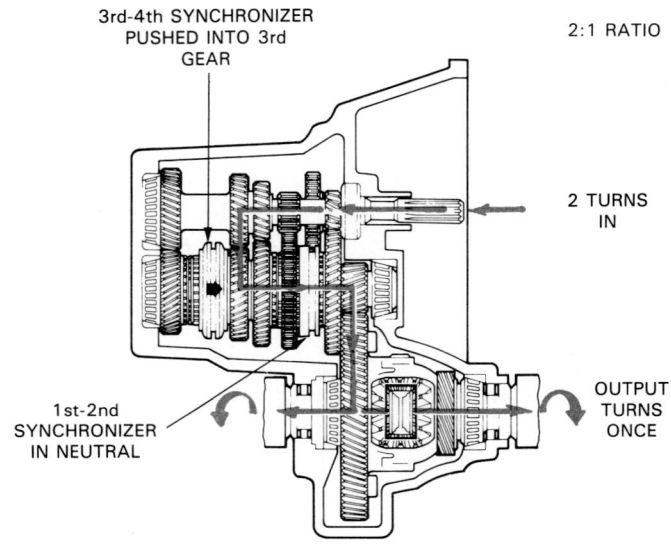

D — In third gear, first-second synchronizer is centered. Third-fourth synchronizer moves to right, engaging third output gear to its shaft.

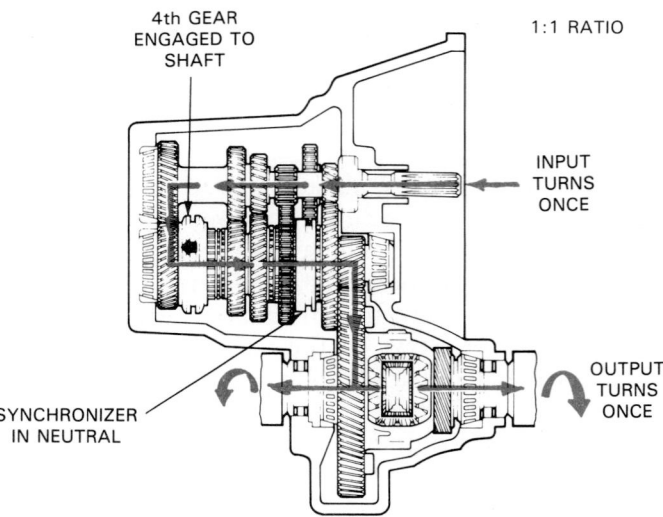

E — When shifted into fourth, the same synchronizer is slid the other way. Fourth output gear is locked to shaft and transmits power.

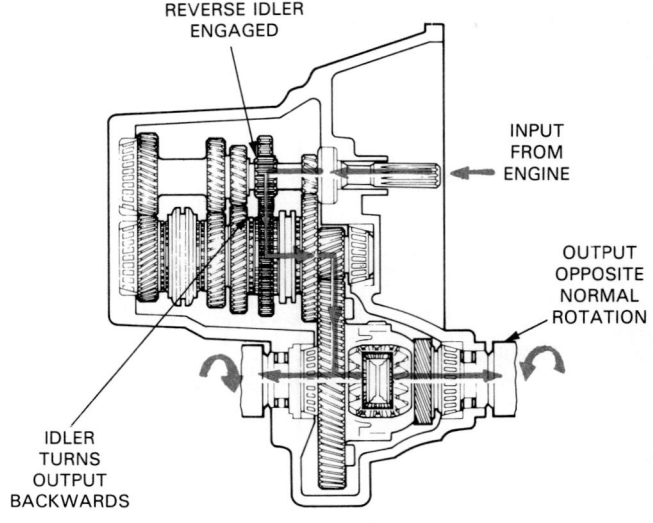

F — In reverse, the reverse idler gear is engaged. It causes the output shaft and differential to turn backwards.

Fig. 60-12. Tracing power flow through typical manual transaxle. (Ford)

Third gear is then locked to its shaft. Power flows through the transaxle, Fig. 60-12D.

Transaxle in fourth gear

When the transaxle is in fourth gear, the three-four synchronizer is moved into contact with fourth gear. Power flows through the two fourth gears, into the differential, and to the front wheels. Fig. 60-12E.

Since the fourth gear on the input shaft and the fourth gear on the countershaft are almost the same size, the gear ratio is reduced. Compared to its rotation in the other gears, the engine turns slowly while the differential case and axles spin at a relatively high speed. This allows the vehicle to cruise at highway speeds with the engine running at low rpm.

Transaxle in reverse

When the transaxle is shifted into reverse, the reverse sliding gear is moved into mesh with the reverse gears on the input shaft and output shaft. The sliding gear reverses the direction of rotation. As a result, the differential and axle shafts are turned backwards and the car moves in reverse. Look at Fig. 60-12F.

Figs. 60-13 and 60-14 show two more manual transaxles. Compare these to the ones shown earlier.

AUTOMATIC TRANSAXLE

An *automatic transaxle* is a combination automatic transmission and differential combined into a single assembly. One type of automatic transaxle is pictured in Fig. 60-15. Study this illustration as the following basic parts are introduced.

1. TRANSAXLE TORQUE CONVERTER (fluid type clutch that slips at low speed but locks up and transfers full engine power at a predetermined speed; it couples or uncouples engine crankshaft to transaxle input shaft and gear train).
2. TRANSAXLE OIL PUMP (produces hydraulic pressure to operate, lubricate, and cool automatic transaxle; its pressure activates the pistons and servos).
3. TRANSAXLE VALVE BODY (controls oil flow to pistons and servos in transaxle; it contains hydraulic valves operated by driver's shift linkage and by engine speed and load-sensing devices).
4. TRANSAXLE PISTONS and SERVOS (operate clutches and bands when activated by oil pressure from valve body).
5. TRANSAXLE BANDS and CLUTCHES (apply planetary gears in transaxle; different bands and

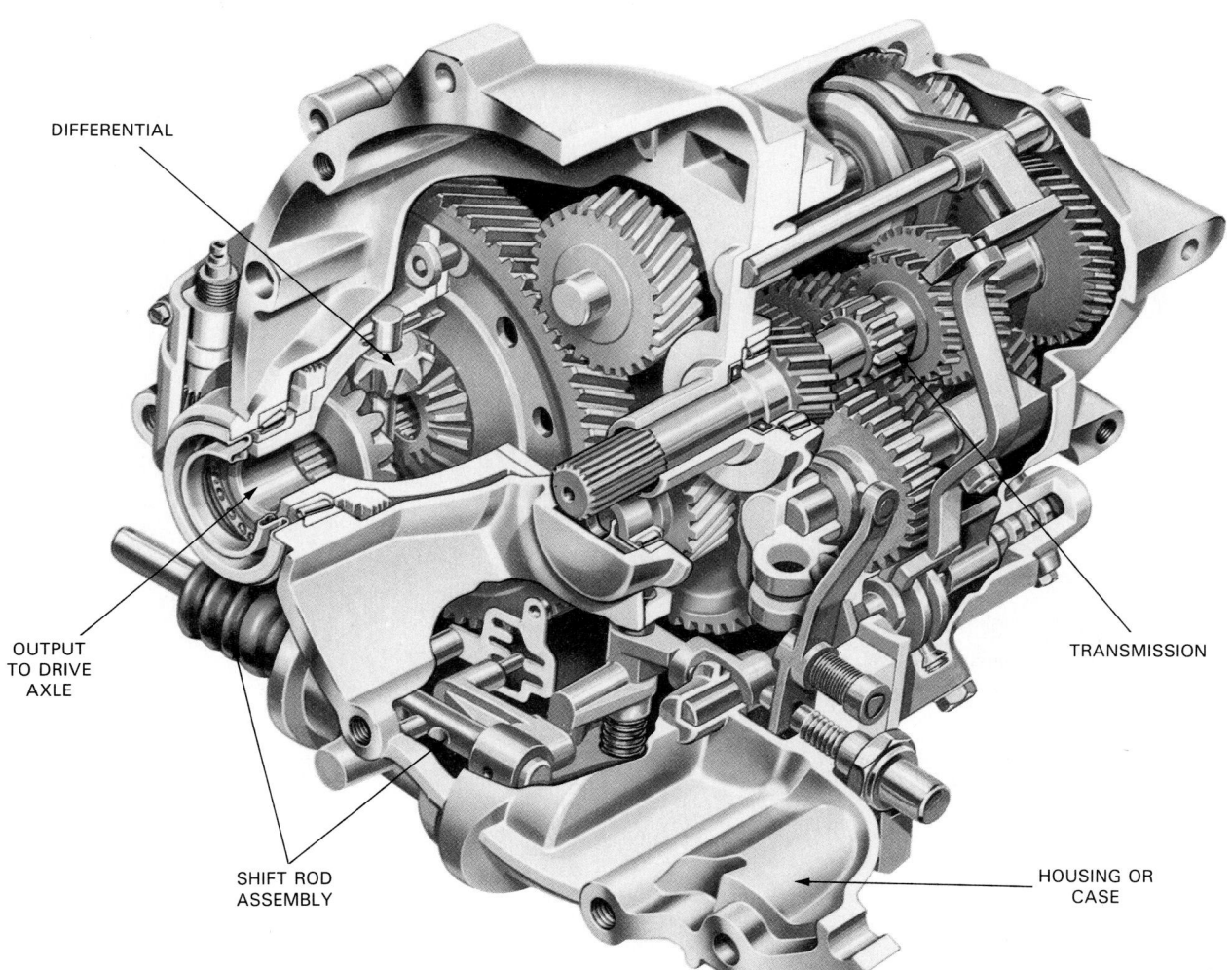

DIFFERENTIAL

OUTPUT
TO DRIVE
AXLE

SHIFT ROD
ASSEMBLY

TRANSMISSION

HOUSING OR
CASE

Fig. 60-13. Cutaway view shows inside of modern 5-speed manual transaxle with overdrive in high gear. Study how shift levers and rods connect to shift forks. (Ford Motor Co.)

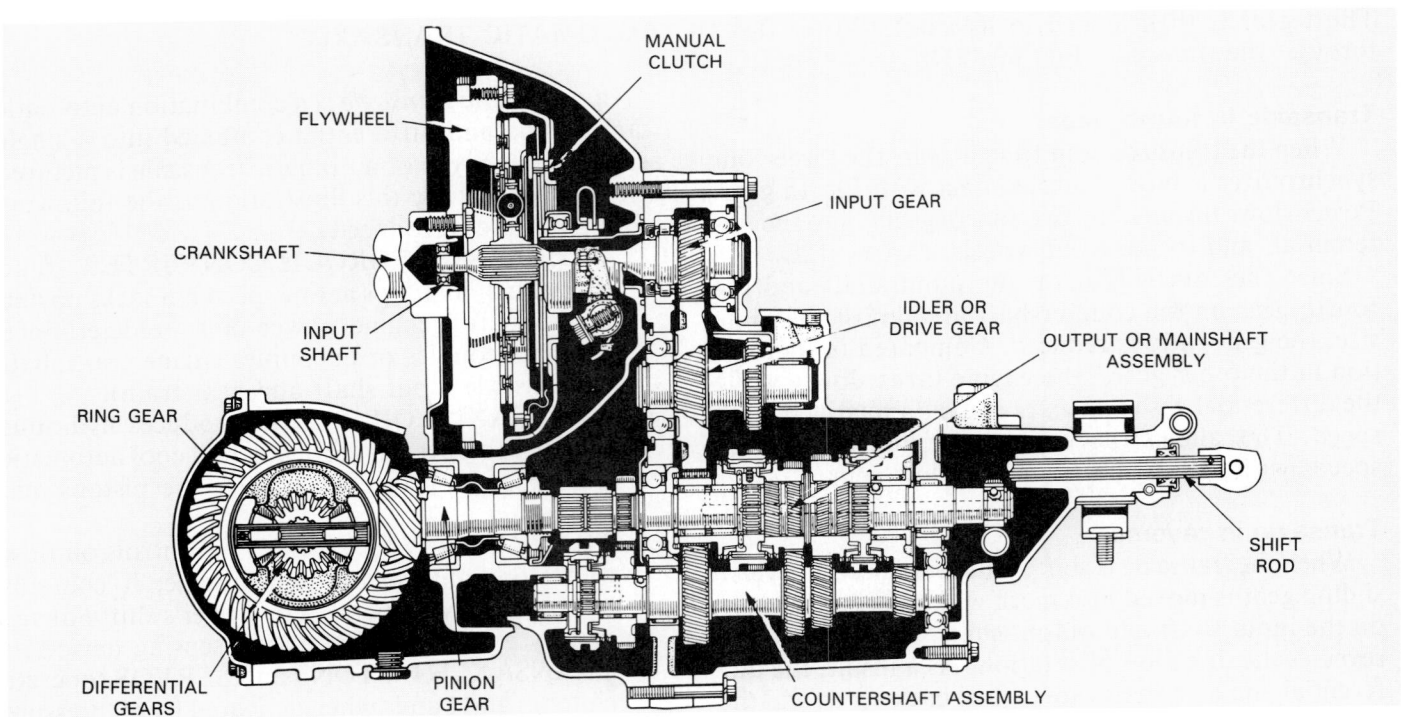

Fig. 60-14. Late model manual transaxle for longitudinally mounted engine. Note how gears, instead of drive chain, transfer power to transaxle gearbox.

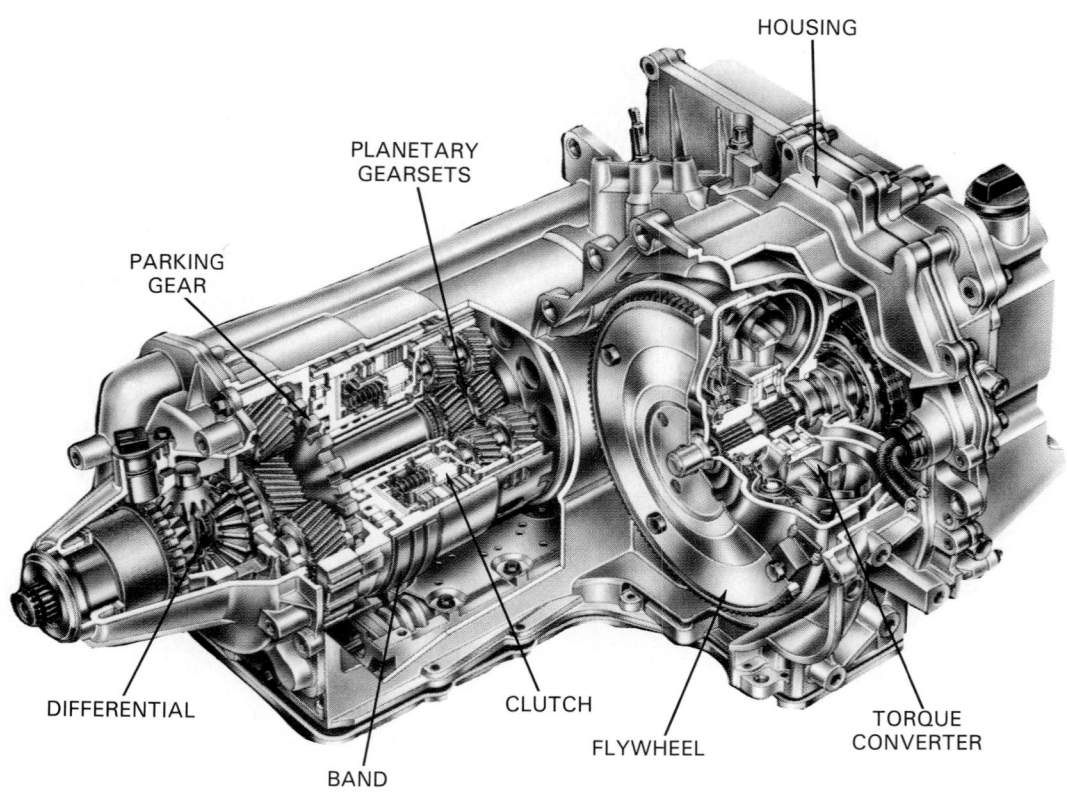

Fig. 60-15. Study basic parts of automatic transaxle. It uses same parts covered in chapter on automatic transmissions. (GM)

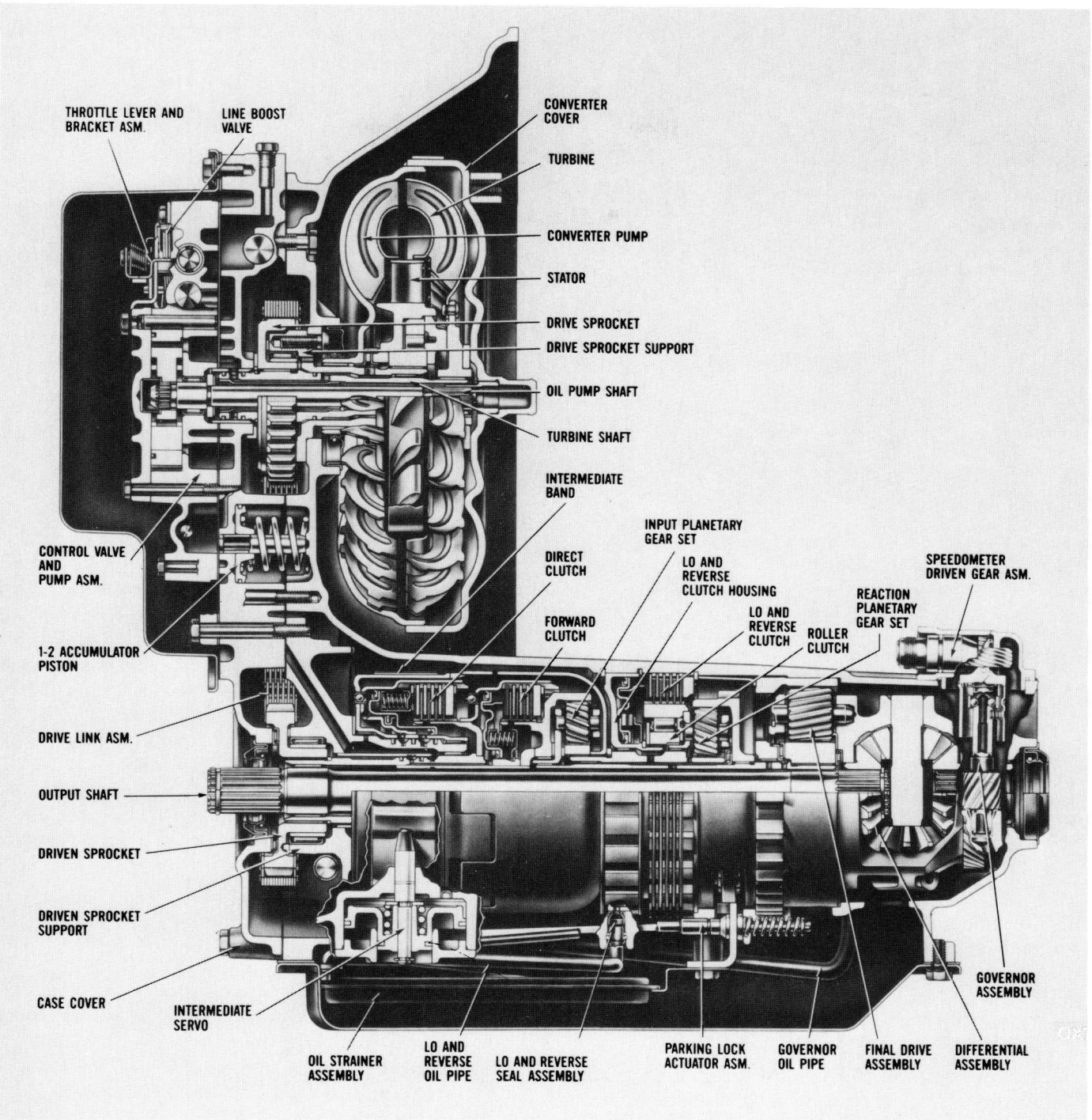

Fig. 60-16. This automatic transaxle uses drive link or chain between torque converter input and transmission proper. Output shaft connects to pinion gear in conventional type differential. (Buick)

clutches can be activated to operate different units in gearsets).

6. TRANSAXLE PLANETARY GEARSETS (provide different gear ratios and reverse gear in automatic transaxle).

7. TRANSAXLE DIFFERENTIAL (transfers power from transmission components to axle shafts).

As you can see, an automatic transaxle uses many of the same parts found in an automatic transmission.

For a review of the operating principles of these components, turn back to Chapter 54, Automatic Transmission Fundamentals.

Fig. 60-16 shows another variation of an automatic transaxle. Study how the major parts are located differently than in the transaxle given in Fig. 60-15.

Fig. 60-17 shows some of the parts of a transaxle hydraulic system. Note that the valve body on this particular unit bolts to the top of the transaxle case. The

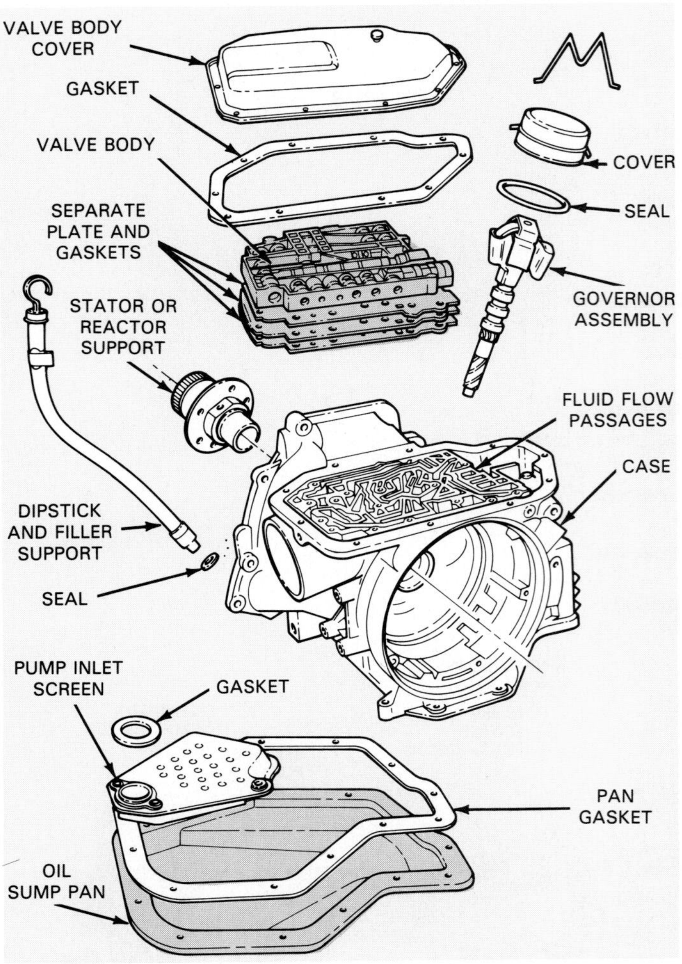
VALVE BODY COVER
GASKET
VALVE BODY
SEPARATE PLATE AND GASKETS
STATOR OR REACTOR SUPPORT
COVER
SEAL
GOVERNOR ASSEMBLY
FLUID FLOW PASSAGES
CASE
DIPSTICK AND FILLER SUPPORT
SEAL
PUMP INLET SCREEN
GASKET
PAN GASKET
OIL SUMP PAN

Fig. 60-17. General arrangement of major hydraulic components in automatic transaxle. With this particular unit, valve body is on top and sump and pan are on bottom. Case construction is similar to automatic transmission. (Ford)

oil filter and sump are located on the bottom of the case. Gaskets seal the valve body cover and oil pan to the case.

AUTOMATIC TRANSAXLE POWER FLOW

The flow of power through an automatic transaxle is similar to power flow through an automatic transmission. Engine torque enters the torque converter. The torque converter then turns the input shaft and planetary gearsets.

Depending upon which bands and clutches hold the gearset members, power flows through the planetary gearsets to the ring and pinion gears. The differential powers the axle shafts and front wheels.

Fig. 60-18 shows the power flow through one make of automatic transaxle.

In A, the transaxle is in first gear. The band holds the forward sun gear. The one-way clutch sends turbine shaft torque to the low-reverse sun gear. This produces a gear reduction in the planetary gearset for initial acceleration.

In B, the transaxle is in second gear. The band remains applied and holds the forward sun gear. The intermediate clutch is applied, locking the intermediate shaft to the ring gear. This causes a slightly less gear reduction in the planetary gearset.

In C, the transaxle is in third gear. Both clutches are applied. This locks both members of the planetary gearset and the unit turns as a single member for direct drive to the differential.

In D, the transaxle is in reverse. The reverse clutch holds the planetary ring gear stationary. The direct clutch locks the turbine shaft to the low-reverse sun gear. The one-way clutch allows the turbine shaft to turn low-reverse sun gear clockwise. Then, the output from the planetary gearset is reversed.

Figs. 60-19 and 60-20 illustrate other automatic transaxle design variations. Compare these transaxles. Make sure you can identify all of the major components.

FRONT DRIVE AXLES (AXLE SHAFTS)

Front drive axles, also called *axle shafts* or *front drive shafts,* transfer power from the differential to the hubs and wheels of the car, Fig. 60-21.

Most modern front drive axles consist of two or three separate shafts and two universal joints. This enables the drive axle to transfer power smoothly as the front wheels move up and down over bumps and to the left or right for steering.

Front drive axles turn much SLOWER than a drive shaft for a rear-wheel drive vehicle. They turn about one-third slower than a rear drive shaft. They are connected directly to the drive wheels and do NOT have to act through the reduction of rear axle ring and pinion gears.

Axle shafts (front-wheel drive)

The *axle shafts* of a front drive axle typically consist of:

1. INNER STUB SHAFT (short shaft splined to side gears in differential and connected to inner universal joint), Fig. 60-22.
2. OUTER STUB SHAFT (short shaft connected to outer universal joint and front wheel hub).
3. INTERCONNECTING SHAFT (center shaft that fits between two universal joints), Fig. 60-22.

The outer ends of each shaft are machined. They may have splines for meshing with splines on mating parts. They may also have a portion of a universal joint machined as an integral part. Grooves are also cut in the shafts for snap rings, boots, and other components.

Universal joints (front-wheel drive)

Universal joints in the front drive axle assemblies allow the shafts to operate through an angle without damage. They are normally the CONSTANT VELOCITY (abbreviated CV) type. Normally, either Rzeppa (ball and cage) or tripod (ball and housing) type

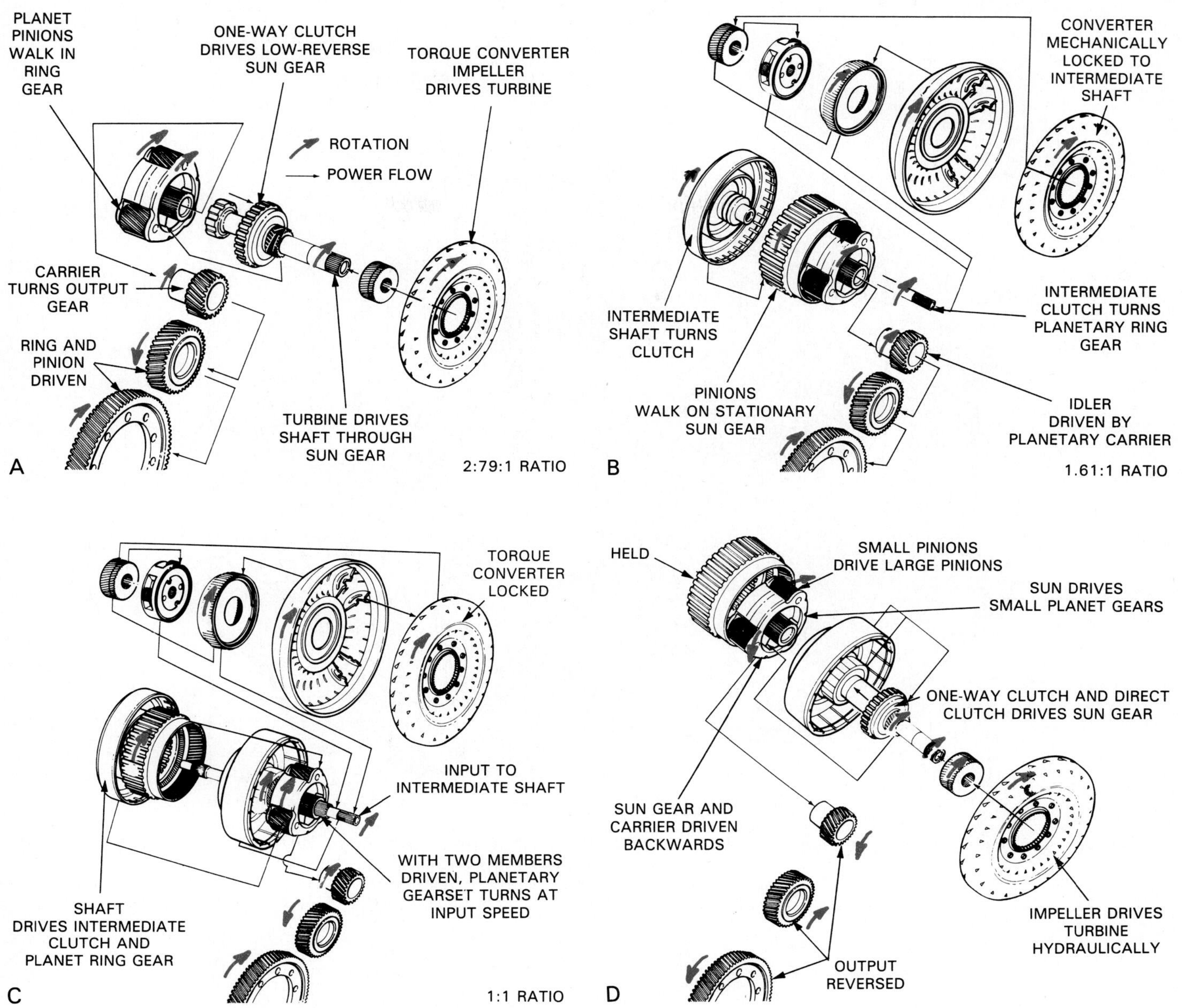

A

PLANET PINIONS WALK IN RING GEAR

ONE-WAY CLUTCH DRIVES LOW-REVERSE SUN GEAR

TORQUE CONVERTER IMPELLER DRIVES TURBINE

→ ROTATION
→ POWER FLOW

CARRIER TURNS OUTPUT GEAR

RING AND PINION DRIVEN

TURBINE DRIVES SHAFT THROUGH SUN GEAR

2:79:1 RATIO

B

CONVERTER MECHANICALLY LOCKED TO INTERMEDIATE SHAFT

INTERMEDIATE SHAFT TURNS CLUTCH

PINIONS WALK ON STATIONARY SUN GEAR

INTERMEDIATE CLUTCH TURNS PLANETARY RING GEAR

IDLER DRIVEN BY PLANETARY CARRIER

1.61:1 RATIO

C

TORQUE CONVERTER LOCKED

INPUT TO INTERMEDIATE SHAFT

WITH TWO MEMBERS DRIVEN, PLANETARY GEARSET TURNS AT INPUT SPEED

SHAFT DRIVES INTERMEDIATE CLUTCH AND PLANET RING GEAR

1:1 RATIO

D

HELD

SMALL PINIONS DRIVE LARGE PINIONS

SUN DRIVES SMALL PLANET GEARS

ONE-WAY CLUTCH AND DIRECT CLUTCH DRIVES SUN GEAR

SUN GEAR AND CARRIER DRIVEN BACKWARDS

IMPELLER DRIVES TURBINE HYDRAULICALLY

OUTPUT REVERSED

Fig. 60-18. Basic power flow through modern automatic transaxle. (Ford)

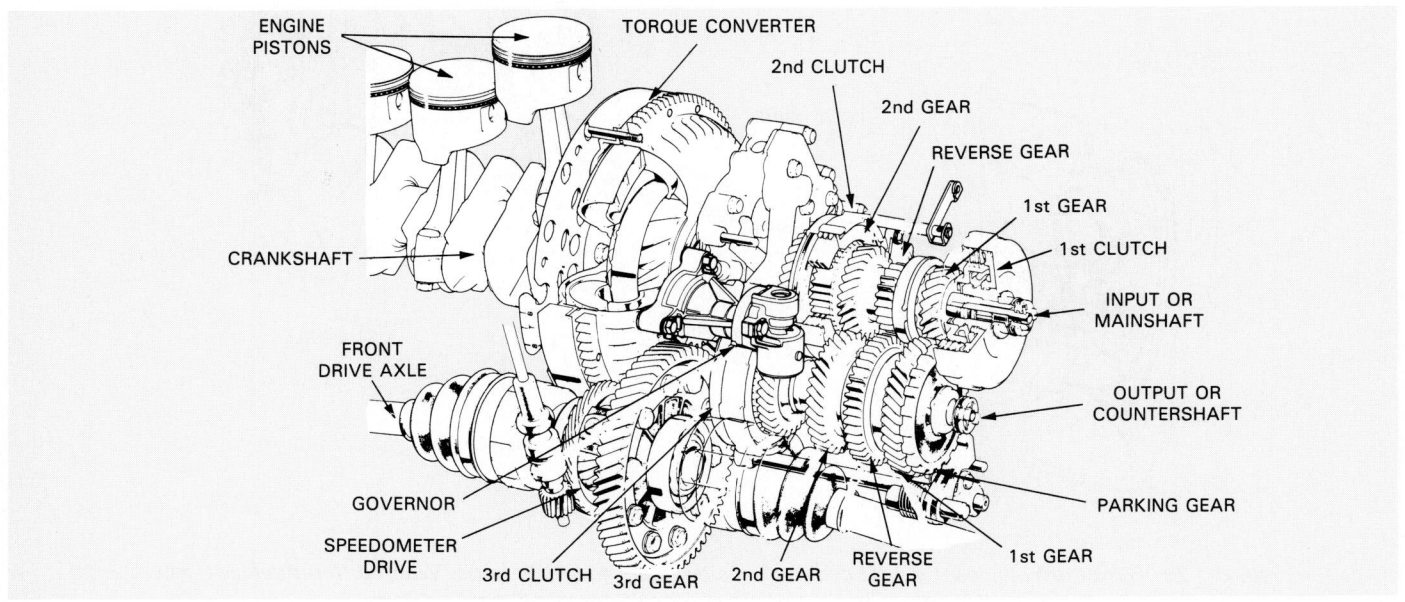

ENGINE PISTONS

TORQUE CONVERTER

2nd CLUTCH

2nd GEAR

REVERSE GEAR

1st GEAR

1st CLUTCH

CRANKSHAFT

INPUT OR MAINSHAFT

FRONT DRIVE AXLE

OUTPUT OR COUNTERSHAFT

PARKING GEAR

GOVERNOR

SPEEDOMETER DRIVE

3rd CLUTCH   3rd GEAR   2nd GEAR   REVERSE GEAR   1st GEAR

Fig. 60-19. This automatic transaxle does not use planetary gears. It uses hydraulically operated clutches to activate helical gears. Study its construction. (Honda)

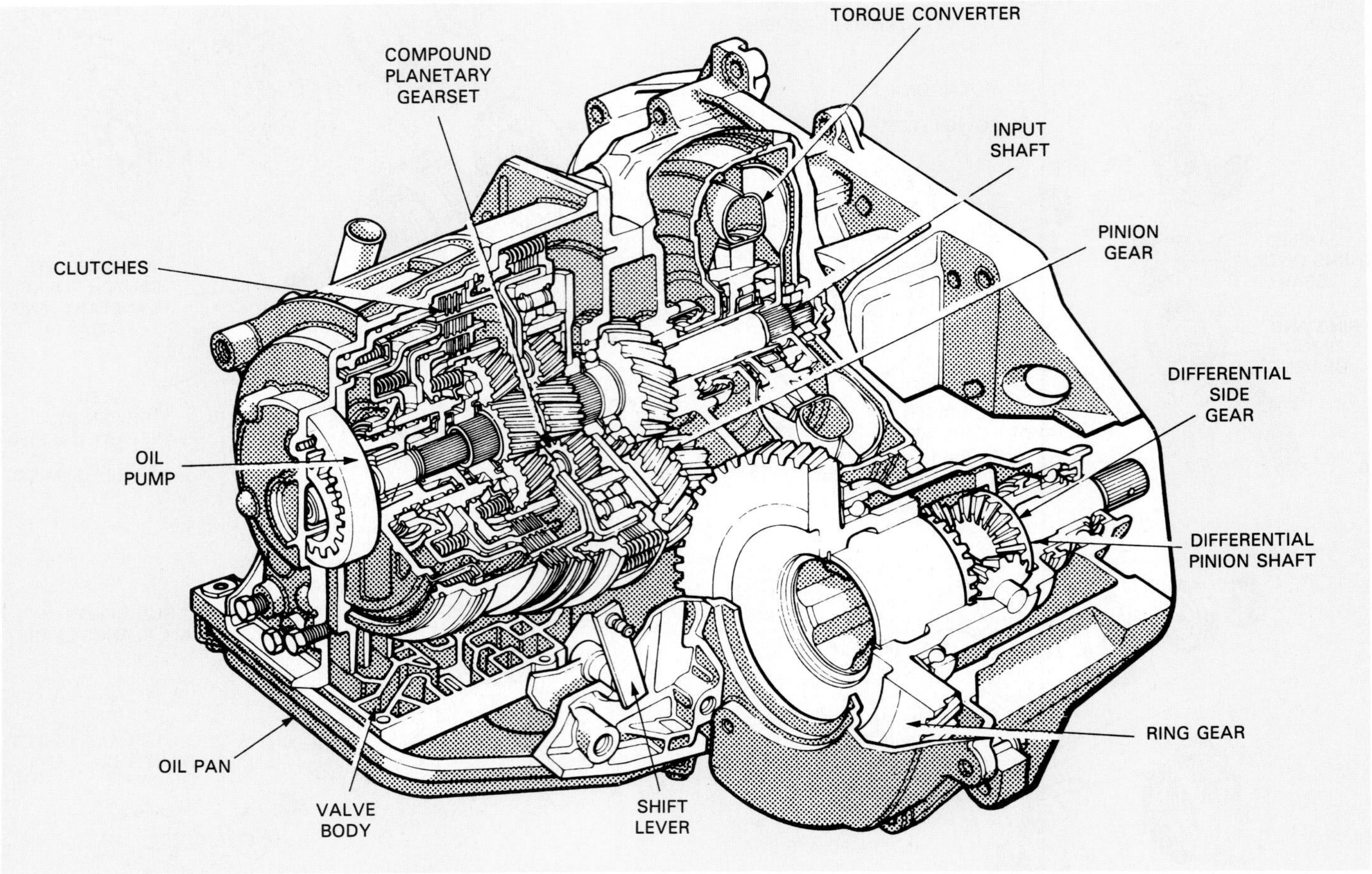

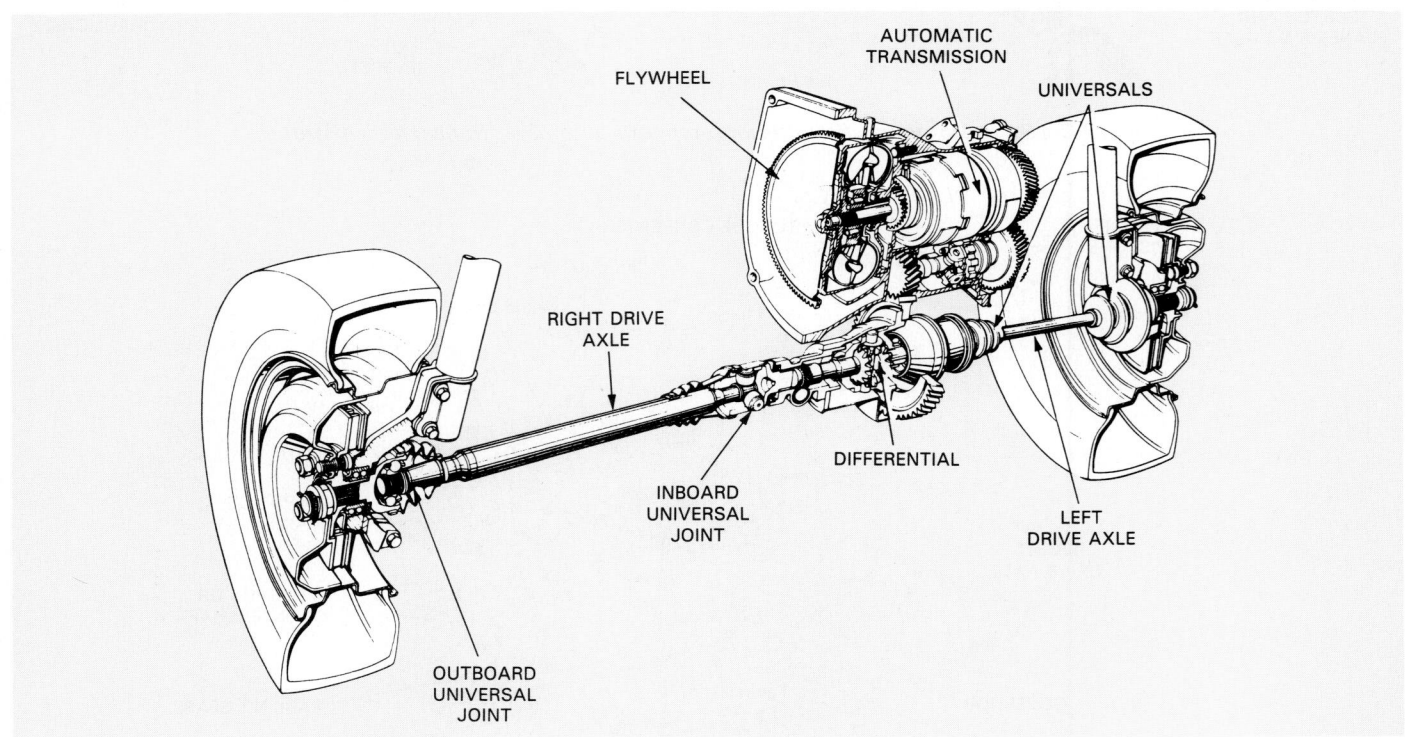

Fig. 60-20. Another automatic transaxle. This is a typical unit that uses compound planetary gearset, bands, and clutches.   (Chrysler Corp.)

Fig. 60-21. Front drive axles connect differential side gears to wheel hubs. When differential side gears turn, axles rotate hubs and front wheels to propel car.   (Dodge)

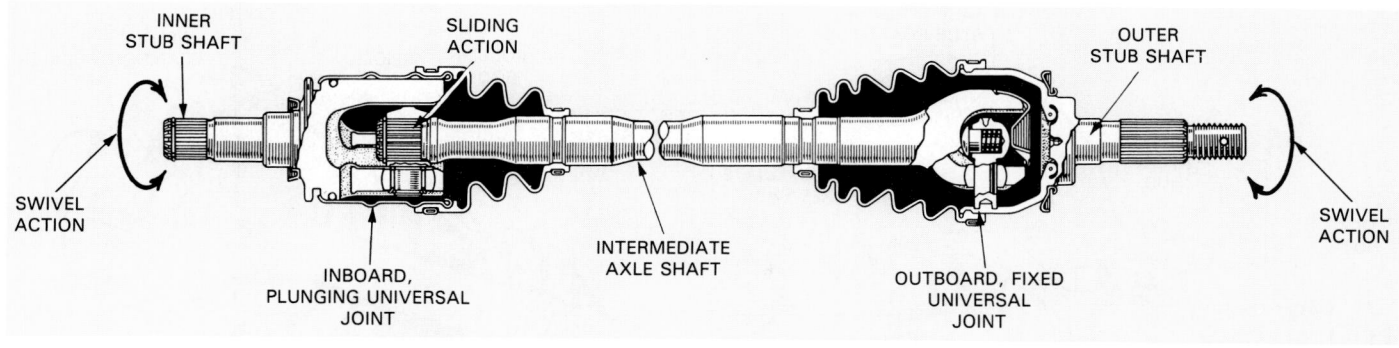

Fig. 60-22. Constant velocity universal joints, commonly called CV-joints, allow drive axle to swivel into various angles. This is a three-piece drive axle: inner stub shaft, intermediate shaft, and outer stub shaft. Inboard CV-joint is normally a sliding joint to allow for length changes with suspension and steering action. (Toyota)

CV-joints are used in front drive axles. A Cardan (cross and roller) joint, however, may sometimes be used.

The *outboard CV-joint* (outer universal) is normally a FIXED (nonsliding) ball and cage or Rzeppa type joint, Fig. 60-23. Sometimes, it is a fixed tripod type, Fig. 60-22. The outboard CV-joint transfers rotating power from the axle shaft to the hub assembly.

The *inboard CV-joint* (inner universal) is commonly a PLUNGING (sliding) ball and housing or tripod joint. It acts like a slip joint in a drive shaft for a rear-wheel drive vehicle.

The plunging action of the inner CV-joint allows for a change in distance between the transaxle and wheel hub. As the front wheels move up and down over bumps in the road, the length of the drive axle (inner joint) must change. Look at Figs. 60-22 and 60-23.

CV-joint construction (front-wheel drive)

A *Rzeppa* or *ball and cage* CV-joint consists of a star-shaped inner race, several ball bearings, bearing cage, outer race or housing, and a rubber boot. Refer to Fig. 60-24A.

The inner race of this type joint is normally splined to the axle shaft. The outer race can be made as part of the axle or it may be splined and held on the axle with snap rings.

The ball bearings fit between the inner and outer races, Fig. 60-24B. When the axle turns, power is

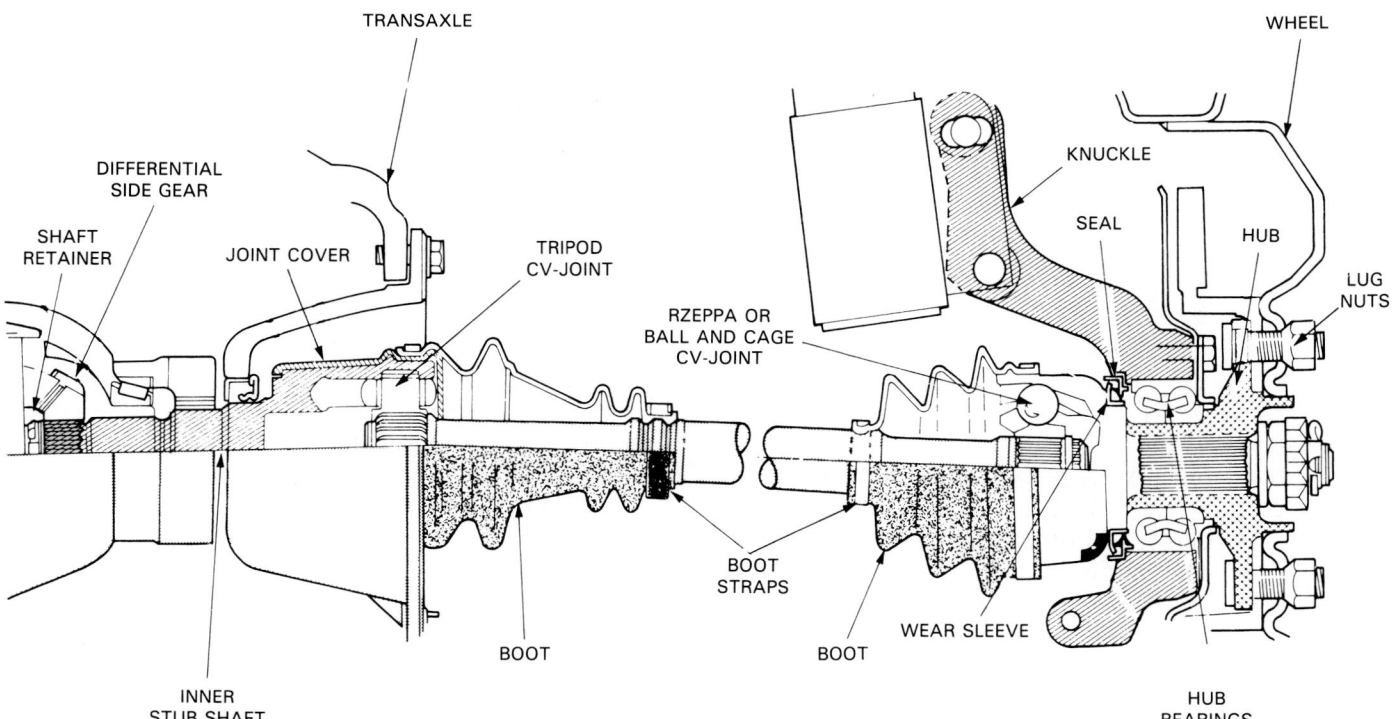

Fig. 60-23. Study how inner end of front drive axle is splined to axle side gear in transaxle differential. Outer end of drive axle extends through and is splined to front wheel hub. Outer CV-joint is fixed Rzeppa or ball and cage type. Inboard CV-joint is plunging tripod type. (Chrysler)

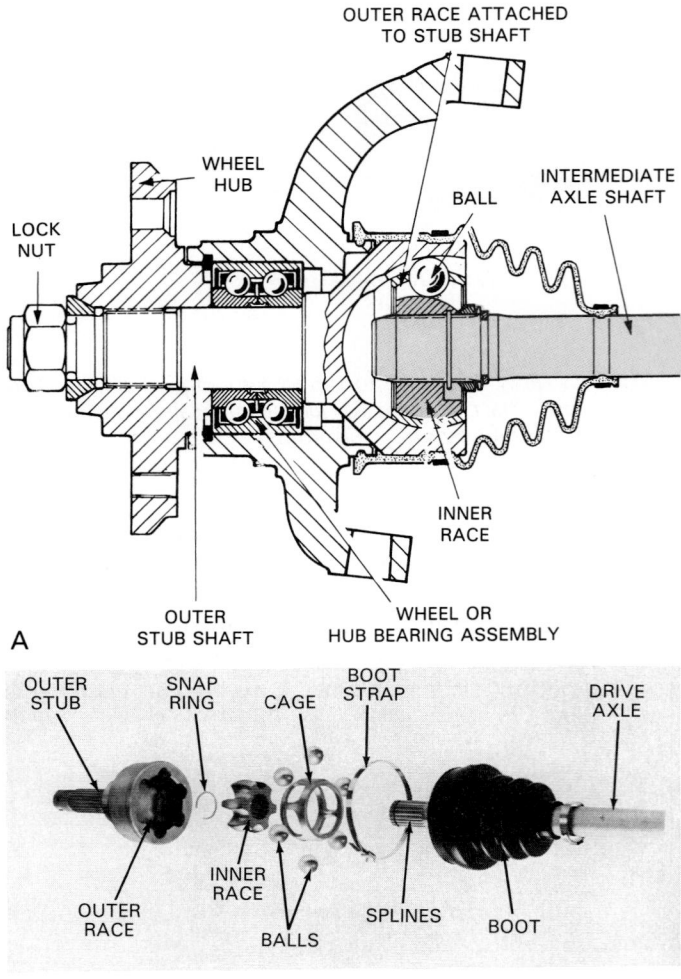

Fig. 60-24. Study construction of Rzeppa or ball and cage CV-joint. A — Drive axle turns inner race. Inner race turns balls. Balls transfer turning force to outer race and hub, rotating wheels to propel vehicle. B — Exploded view of ball and cage joint. Study how parts fit together. When inner joint, this type of joint is plunging type. When outer joint, it is fixed type. (Saab and Dana Corp.)

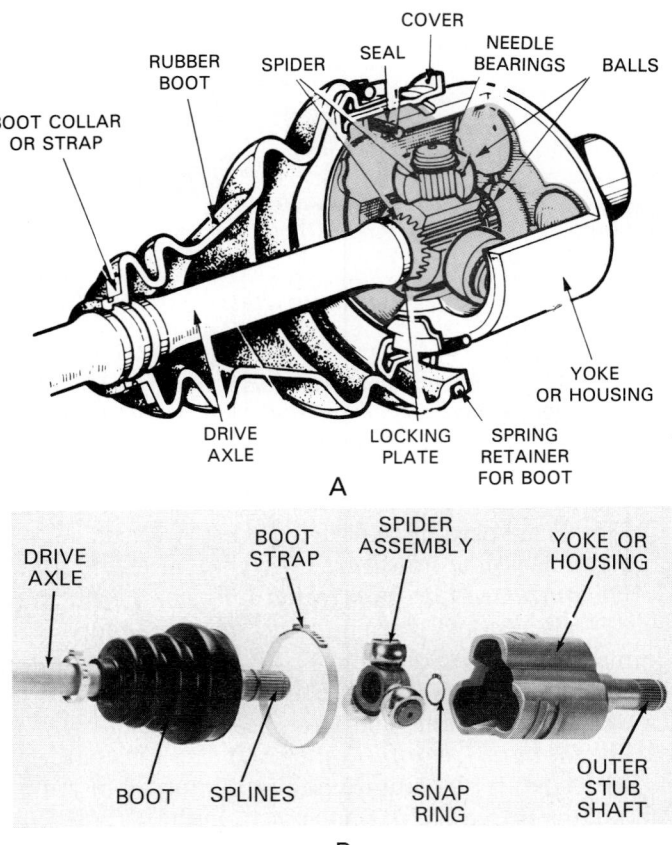

Fig. 60-25. Tripod type CV-joint construction. A — Cutaway view shows how tripod fits together. Axle is splined to spider. Spider rotates balls and housing. Balls turn on needle bearing to allow swiveling action. B. — Exploded view of tripod joint. When inboard CV-joint, it serves as sliding or plunging joint. When used as outboard joint, tripod joint is fixed and does not slide in and out. Tripod is commonly inboard plunging joint. (Renault and Dana Corp.)

transferred through inner race, balls, outer race, and to the wheel hub.

A *tripod* or *ball and housing* CV-joint consists of a spider, usually three balls, needle bearings, outer yoke, and boot. A cutaway view of a modern tripod joint is shown in Fig. 60-25A.

The inner spider is normally splined to the axle shaft. The needle bearings and three balls fit around the spider. The yoke or housing then slides over the balls. Slots in the yoke allow the balls to slide in and out and swivel.

During operation, the axle shaft turns the spider and ball assembly. The balls transfer power to the outer housing. Since the housing is connected to the axle stub shaft or hub, power is sent through the joint to propel the car.

In Fig. 60-25B, study how the balls would allow the axle shaft to swivel and slide in the yoke.

CV-joint boots

Boots are used to keep road dirt out of the CV-joints on a front drive axle. They also prevent the loss of lubricant (grease). Shown in Figs. 60-24 and 60-25, they are accordion-shaped or pleated to flex with movement of the CV-joint.

Retaining collars or *straps* secure the boots to the drive axle. They are usually plastic straps or metal spring clamps that hold or squeeze in on the ends of the boot, providing a tight seal.

Fig. 60-26 is a phantom (see-through) view of a complete engine and front-wheel drive assembly.

KNOW THESE TERMS

Transaxle, Transverse, Longitudinal, Manual transaxle, Transaxle input shaft, Transaxle output shaft, Transaxle differential, Transaxle gearbox, Drive chain, Front drive axles, Inner stub shaft, Interconnecting shaft, Outer stub shaft, CV, Outboard CV-joint, Inboard CV-joint, Rzeppa CV-joint, Tripod CV-joint, Boot.

Fig. 60-26. Cutaway view of engine and front-wheel drive assembly. Can you explain basic function of major components? If not, review text material as needed. (Chevrolet)

REVIEW QUESTIONS

1. Define the term "transaxle."
2. List six possible advantages of front-wheel drive.
3. Both manual and automatic transaxles are available. True or False?
4. Summarize the differences between transaxles for transverse and longitudinally mounted engines.
5. Name and explain the seven major parts of a manual transaxle.
6. Which of these parts is NOT found in a manual transaxle?
   a. Synchronizers.
   b. Differential.
   c. Transmission.
   d. Fluid coupling.
   e. All of the above.
   f. None of the above.
7. A drive _____ or _____ is sometimes used to send crankshaft power to the transaxle with a longitudinally mounted engine.

8. List and explain the seven major components of an automatic transaxle.
9. Describe the two common types of CV-joints used on front-drive axles.
10. Which of the following is NOT part of a front-drive axle assembly?
    a. Boots.
    b. CV-joints.
    c. Stub shafts.
    d. Interconnecting shaft.
    e. Pivot shaft.

ACTIVITIES FOR CHAPTER 60

1. Identify the major parts of a transaxle chosen by your instructor.
2. Identify the various parts of front-wheel drive axles.
3. Compare two different designs of front-wheel drive axle CV-joints.

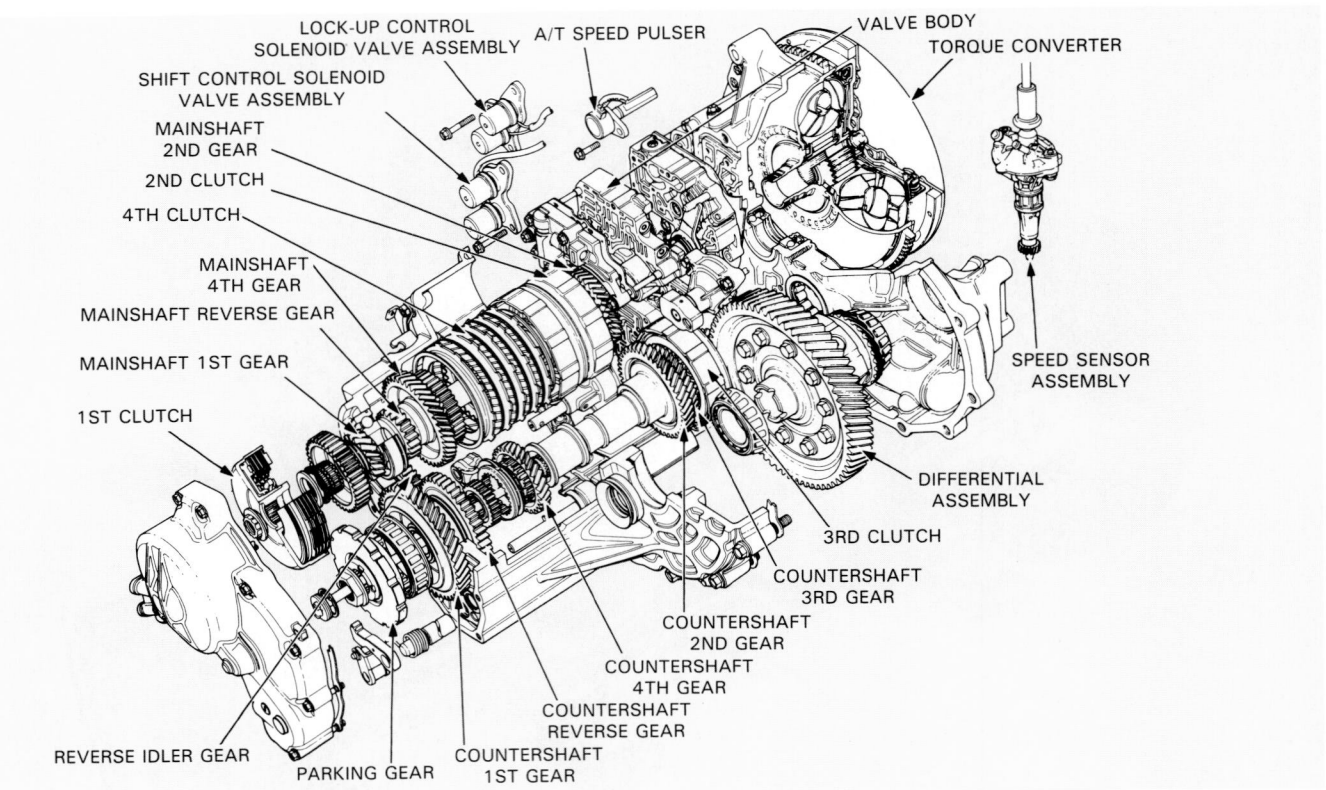

LOCK-UP CONTROL
SOLENOID VALVE ASSEMBLY

A/T SPEED PULSER

VALVE BODY
TORQUE CONVERTER

SHIFT CONTROL SOLENOID
VALVE ASSEMBLY

MAINSHAFT
2ND GEAR

2ND CLUTCH

4TH CLUTCH

MAINSHAFT
4TH GEAR

MAINSHAFT REVERSE GEAR

MAINSHAFT 1ST GEAR

1ST CLUTCH

SPEED SENSOR
ASSEMBLY

DIFFERENTIAL
ASSEMBLY

3RD CLUTCH

COUNTERSHAFT
3RD GEAR

COUNTERSHAFT
2ND GEAR

COUNTERSHAFT
4TH GEAR

COUNTERSHAFT
REVERSE GEAR

COUNTERSHAFT
1ST GEAR

REVERSE IDLER GEAR

PARKING GEAR

Note unique construction of this automatic transaxle. It uses solenoids to shift gears and lock the torque converter. Conventional clutches are also used. (Honda)

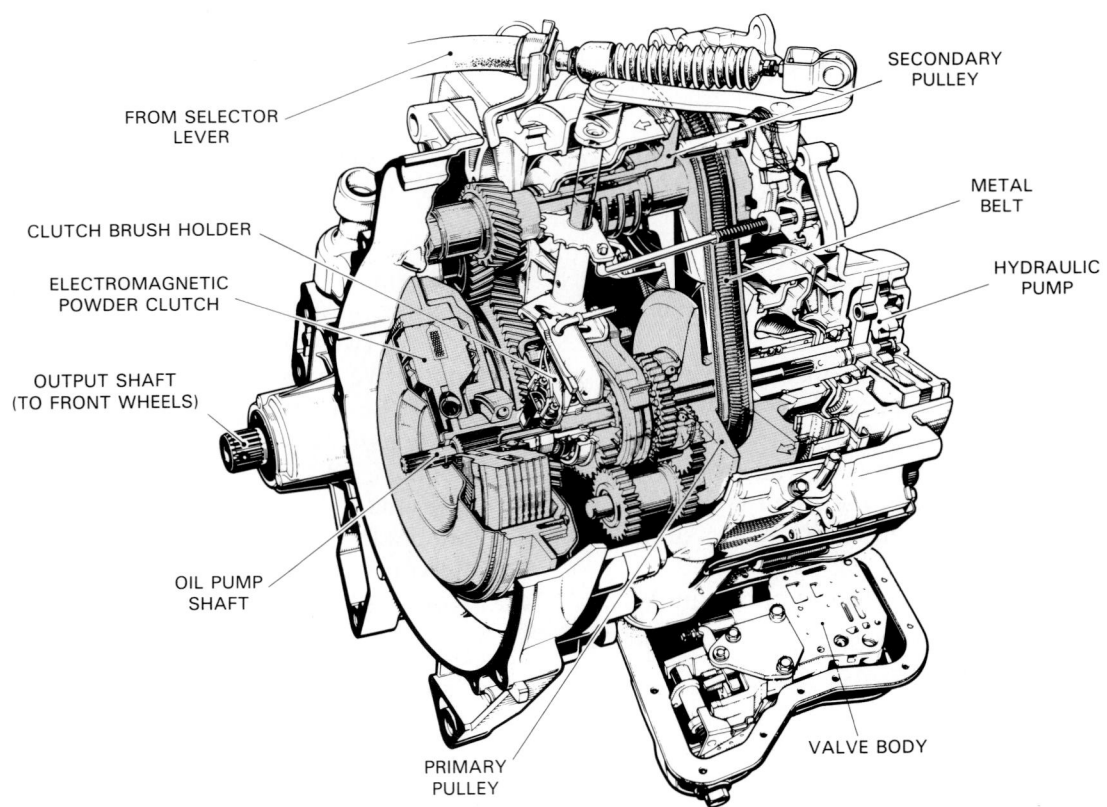

FROM SELECTOR
LEVER

SECONDARY
PULLEY

CLUTCH BRUSH HOLDER

METAL
BELT

ELECTROMAGNETIC
POWDER CLUTCH

HYDRAULIC
PUMP

OUTPUT SHAFT
(TO FRONT WHEELS)

OIL PUMP
SHAFT

PRIMARY
PULLEY

VALVE BODY

Study the construction of this CVT or continuously variable transmission. It does not shift gears. Instead, a metal belt rides in two variable split pulleys. As engine and vehicle speed changes, the pulleys open and close to alter their effective diameters. This constantly changes the gear ratio of the transmission. The car keeps gaining speed while the engine runs at a constant, efficient rpm. An electromagnetic clutch engages and disengages the engine and transmission like an air conditioning compressor. (Subaru)

61 Transaxle, Front-Drive Axle Diagnosis and Repair

After studying this chapter, you will be able to:
☐ Diagnose common transaxle and drive axle problems.
☐ Adjust transaxle shift linkage.
☐ Complete maintenance operations on a transaxle.
☐ Remove and install a transaxle assembly.
☐ Remove and install a front-drive axle.
☐ Replace constant velocity (CV) drive axle universal joints.

Transaxles suffer from the same kinds of problems as transmissions and differentials. The gears, shafts, bearings, seals, and other parts can wear and fail. The drive axles, as they follow the movement of the steering and suspension systems, can also cause problems after prolonged service.

Since new vehicles commonly use front-wheel drive, it is very important for you to understand the basic service and repair of transaxles and front-drive axles.

This chapter will explain the service procedures which are UNIQUE to transaxle equipped vehicles. You may want to review earlier chapters on transmission, drive shaft, and differential repair.

TRANSAXLE PROBLEM DIAGNOSIS

Correct diagnosis of transaxle and drive axle problems can require a great deal of care. With the engine,

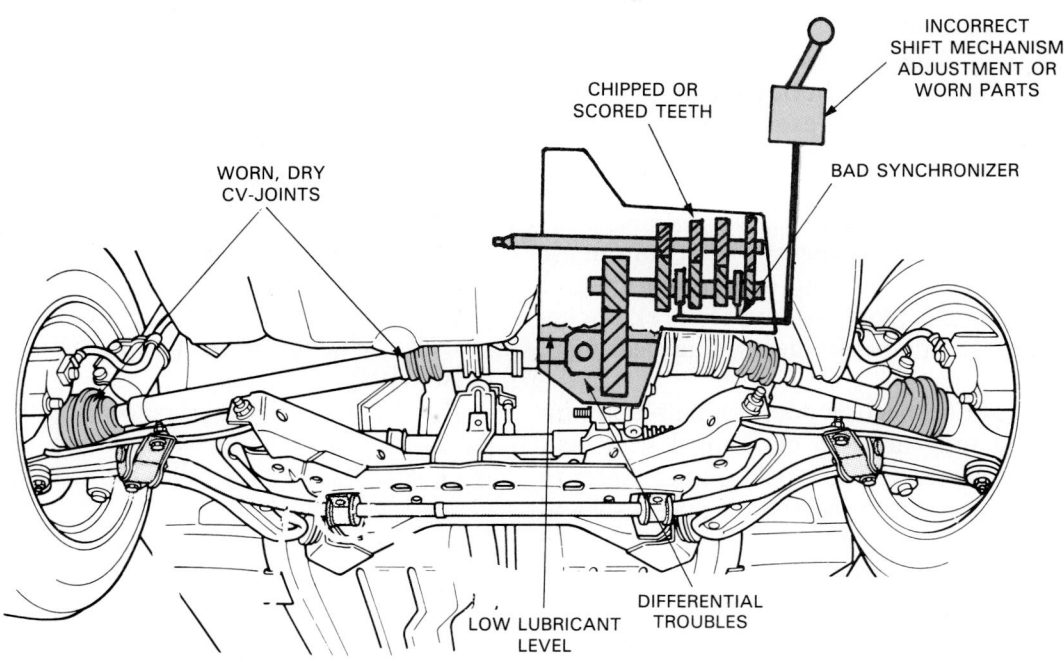

Fig. 61-1. When diagnosing transaxle and drive axle problems, visualize the operation of all components. Compare this information to symptoms. (Chrysler)

clutch, transmission, differential, and drive axles close together in the engine compartment, noises and other symptoms can be difficult to pinpoint. However, if you use your knowledge of component operation and basic troubleshooting techniques, transaxle problems can be isolated without too much trouble.

Test drive the vehicle to check out the customer complaint. Shift the transmission into each gear under DRIVE (cruising at constant speed), ACCELERATION (increasing speed moderately), DECELERATION (reducing speed with transaxle in gear), and COAST (partially closed throttle with transaxle in gear) conditions. Check for abnormal noises and vibration under each driving condition.

Use your understanding of CV-joints, gears, bearings, shafts, synchronizers, and shift mechanisms to decide what might be the trouble. Approach diagnosis of a transaxle as you would problems in a transmission or a differential. See Fig. 61-1.

Manual transaxle problems

Manual transaxle problems include abnormal bearing and gear noises (whirring, howling, whining), shifting problems (hard to shift into gear, grinds when shifted, will not shift, pops out of gear), and fluid leaks (ruptured gasket or RTV sealer, damaged seal, etc.).

If the transaxle is noisy, find out when the abnormal sounds are the loudest.

For example, when the transaxle is only noisy in second gear, the input second gear and output second gear might be at fault.

If a transaxle noise occurs in ALL gears, under all driving conditions, a common problem exists (bad shaft bearings or scored ring and pinion, for example). Use this kind of elimination technique to narrow down the possible sources of trouble.

A manufacturer's *diagnosis chart* may also be helpful in determining what parts might be causing the symptoms. It will be written for the exact year, make, and model of unit.

Automatic transaxle problems

Automatic transaxle problems, like automatic transmission problems, show up as slipping in gear (worn bands or clutches, low system pressure), abnormal noises (damaged planetary gears, bad bearings), and fluid leaks.

If a test drive and inspection does not help pinpoint the trouble, you may need to perform a stall test, pressure tests, or air tests. Look at Fig. 61-2. Refer to the chapter on automatic transmission diagnosis and repair for instructions on completing these tests. A shop manual will provide even more detailed procedures and specs for testing an automatic transaxle. It will give pressure values, passage locations for air tests, rpm values for a stall test, and hydraulic circuit diagrams.

Fig. 61-3 shows a hydraulic circuit for one type of automatic transaxle. It is handy when you need to trace

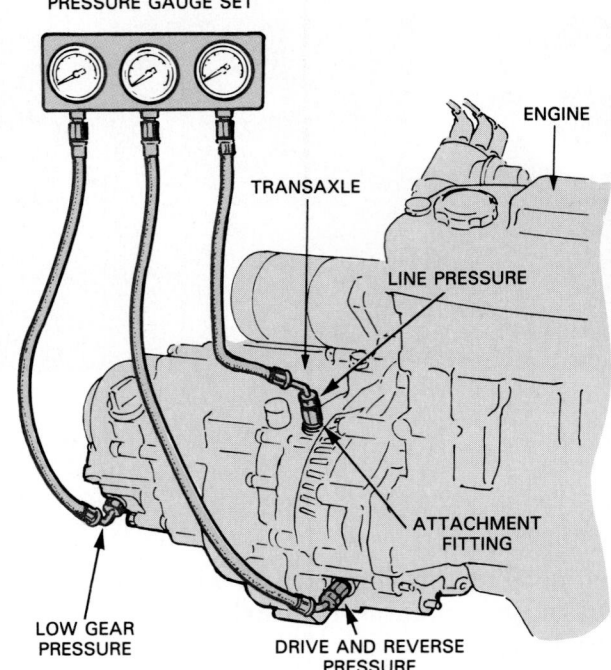

Fig. 61-2. As with automatic transmission, pressure gauges are used for measuring oil pressure to determine condition of automatic transaxle components. (Honda)

the passages in the transaxle to find out how each component is connected to oil pressure.

FRONT-DRIVE AXLE PROBLEMS

Front-drive axle problems are usually noticed as abnormal noises (clicking, grinding, clunking, humming), vibration, or excessive play in the universals. Drive axles are under stress from engine torque while operating at various angles. This can cause the CV-joints to fail after prolonged service.

If a rubber boot around a CV-joint is ruptured, road dirt and water can enter and cause joint failure in a very short time.

When symptoms point to possible drive axle troubles, raise the vehicle on a lift. Inspect the axle shafts, Fig. 61-1. Make sure the rubber boots are not torn or cracked. Wiggle and rotate the joints to check for excessive play and wear.

DANGER! Do NOT operate the engine and transaxle with the suspension system hanging unsupported on a lift. The drive axle CV-joints may be bent at a sharp angle. When spun, the joints could BIND and fly apart with lethal force.

TRANSAXLE MAINTENANCE

Proper maintenance is very important to the service life of a transaxle. If the transaxle lubricant is not changed at recommended intervals, abnormal part wear

PARK

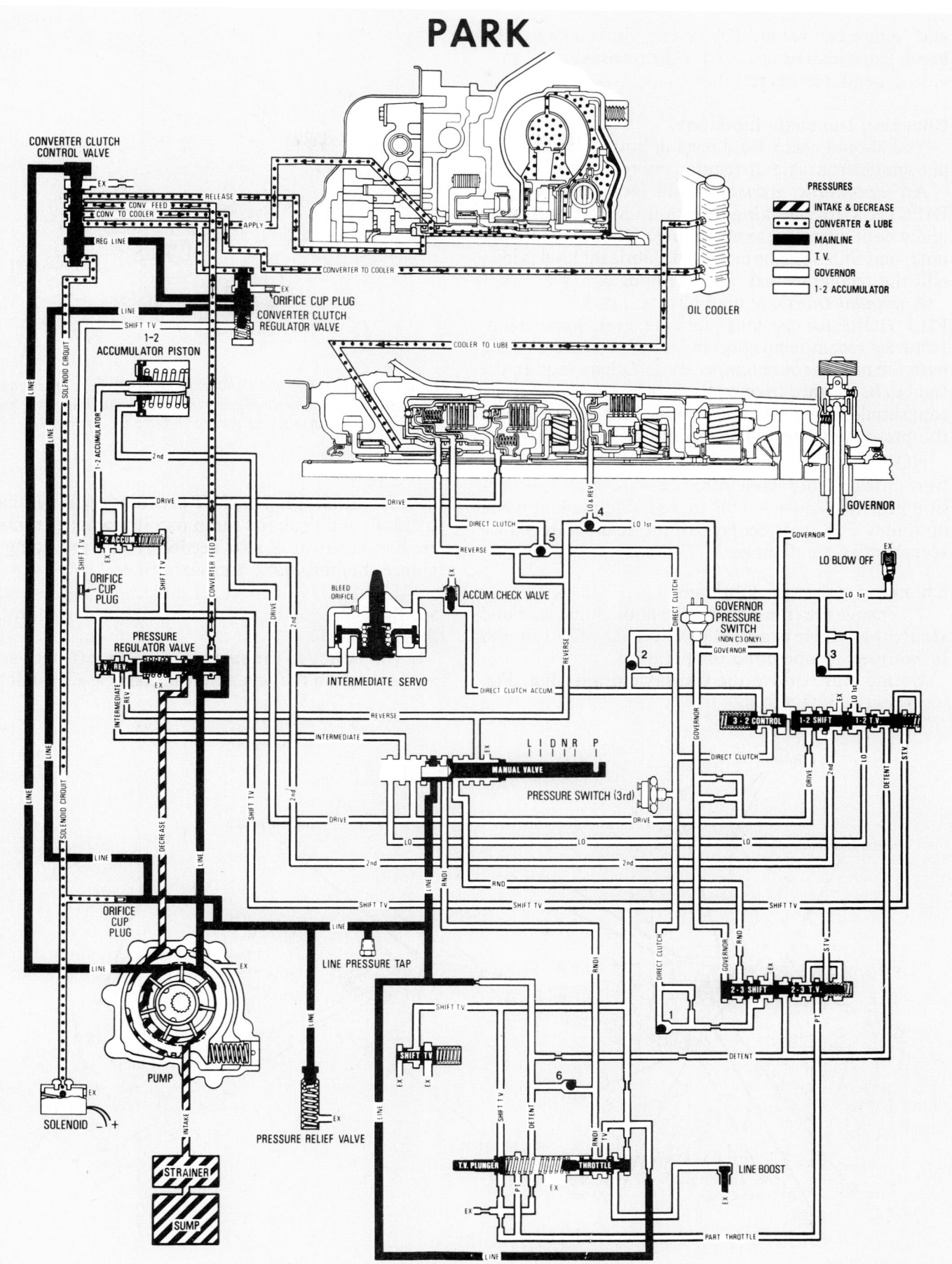

Fig. 61-3. Hydraulic oil circuit in service manual will help trace passages to each component for diagnosis. (Oldsmobile)

and failure can result. The clutch, shift linkage, and bands must also be adjusted if the transaxle is to provide dependable operation.

Checking transaxle lubricant

You should check fluid level in both a manual and automatic transaxle at regular intervals, Fig. 61-4.

An *automatic transaxle* will normally have a DIPSTICK for checking lubricant level. It must normally be at operating temperature, with the engine running, and shift selector in park. If lubricant level is low, add the recommended type of fluid.

A *manual transaxle* may have a dipstick or just a FILL HOLE for checking lubricant level. Some manufacturers recommend checking manual transaxle fluid with the unit at room temperature. Others require the fluid to be warmed to operating temperature. The lubricant should be almost even with the fill hole or between the prescribed lines on the dipstick.

NOTE! Some manual transaxles use automatic transmission fluid while others use manual transmission gear oil. Always refer to a service manual when in doubt. The incorrect type of lubricant could cause severe transaxle damage.

Changing transaxle lubricant

To change the transaxle lubricant or fluid, raise and secure the vehicle in a level position. The fluid should be warmed to operating temperature.

Locate and remove the transaxle drain plug, Fig.

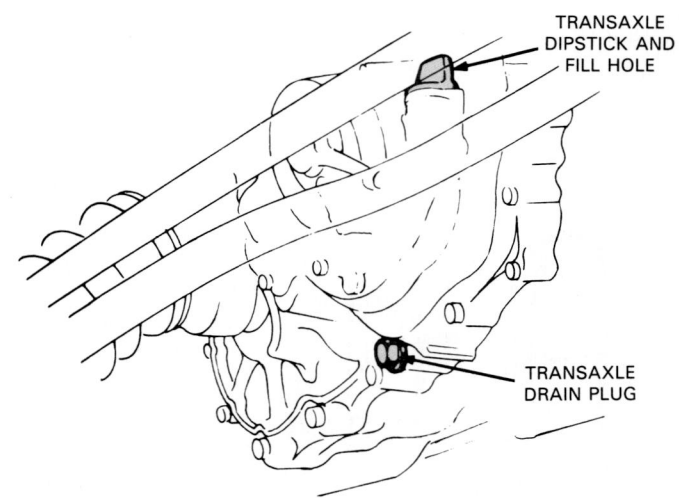

Fig. 61-4. Transaxle drain and fill plugs or dipstick are normally provided. Use manufacturer's recommended checking and changing procedures and type of lubricant. (Honda)

61-4. If a drain plug is NOT provided, you will have to unbolt and drop the sump pan (automatic transaxle). Pan removal is also needed if you are going to replace the automatic transaxle filter.

WARNING! When at operating temperature, transaxle fluid can cause painful burns. Do NOT allow hot fluid to run down your arm when draining.

If you removed the sump pan, clean off both sealing surfaces on the pan and transaxle case. Install the

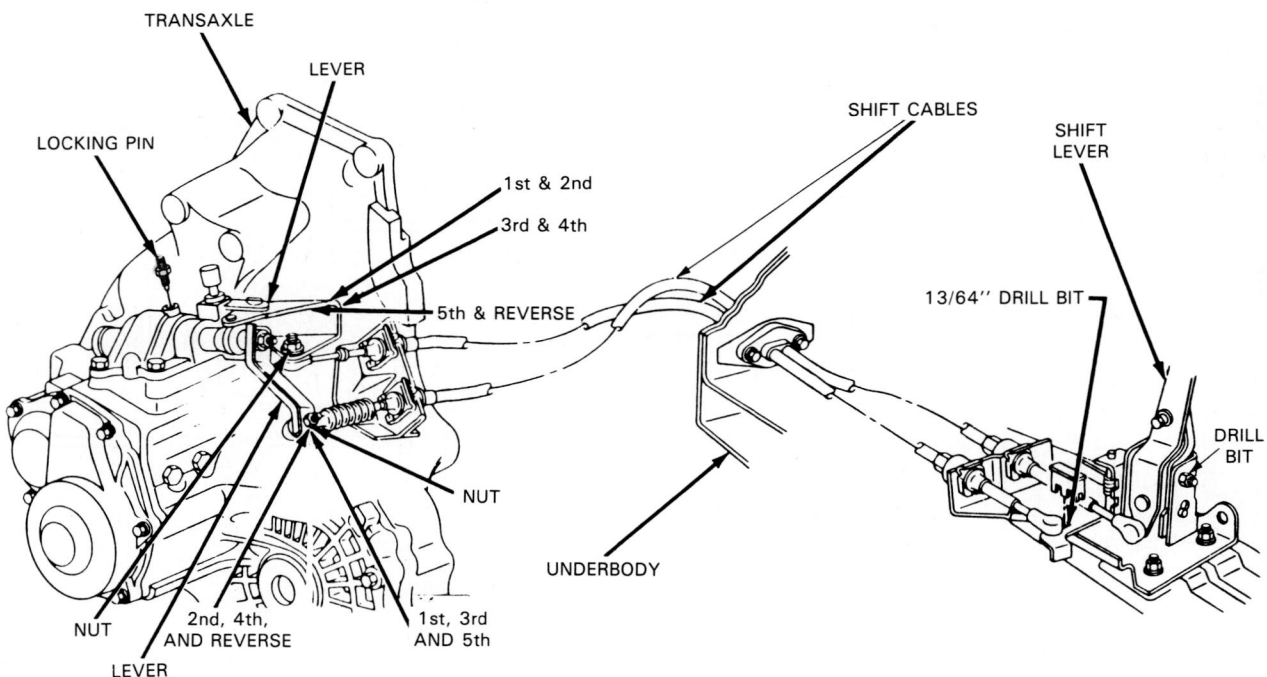

Fig. 61-5. Shift cable adjustment is similar to procedures for manual transmission. With this particular unit, lock pin is used to hold transaxle in third gear. Two drill bits are then installed in shifter to align levers. Then, cable lengths are adjusted to position levers on transaxle properly. (Buick)

new filter, if needed. Install a new gasket or RTV sealer on the pan and bolt the pan to the transaxle. Tighten the pan bolts to specs in a crisscross pattern.

Using a long funnel, fill the transaxle with the correct type and amount of lubricant. A shop manual will indicate how much fluid the transaxle will hold. Lower the vehicle and start the engine. Shift the transaxle through each gear. Then, check under the vehicle for lubricant leaks.

Transaxle external adjustments

Some auto makers recommend clutch, shift linkage, and other adjustments at regular intervals.

A manual transaxle clutch is adjusted something like the linkage on a manual transmission. You must make sure the clutch pedal has the correct free play and applied height. Transaxle shift linkage or cables are also adjusted using procedures similar to those for transmissions. See Fig. 61-5. Check that the shift arm or arms on the transaxle are in the right position in relation to the driver's shift lever. Some transaxles require a special linkage holding fixture for adjustment.

A few automatic transaxle bands have an adjusting screw inside the pan. By loosening the locknut, the screw can be turned to set the band-to-drum clearance. Normally, the screw is turned in until it bottoms at a specific torque. Then, the screw is turned out a specified number of turns and the locknut is tightened.

FRONT-DRIVE AXLE SERVICE

When you find problems with a front-wheel drive axle shaft, the axle shaft must normally be removed for service. The most common problem is worn universal or CV-joints.

Axle shaft removal

To remove a front-wheel drive axle, you must usually remove the hub nut. As shown in Fig. 61-6, either leave the vehicle on the ground or hold the brake disc with a large screwdriver. This will let you turn the nut without the hub and disc turning.

Some cars require a puller to free the axle stub shaft from the hub. See Fig. 61-7A. The puller grasps the hub lug studs and pushes in on the axle shaft. With other vehicles, the stub shaft may slide easily out of the hub.

Frequently, before the drive axle will slide out of the transaxle, you must remove the lower ball joint, Fig. 61-7B. The stub axle shaft will not slide out far enough unless the steering knuckle is free to swing away from the transaxle.

With some transaxles, the inner end of the axle shafts are held in place by snap rings, Fig. 61-8A. With this design, the transaxle differential cover must be removed. The snap rings or circlips must be removed from the grooves in the axle shafts. Then the axles can be pulled out of the transaxle.

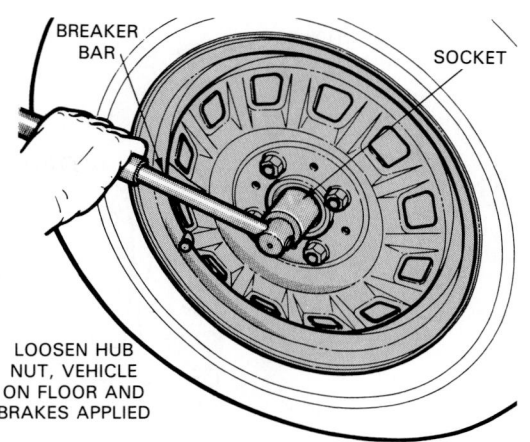

Fig. 61-6. To begin removal of a front-drive axle, loosen hub nut. Leave vehicle on ground with emergency brake applied. Turn nut with breaker bar and socket. (Plymouth)

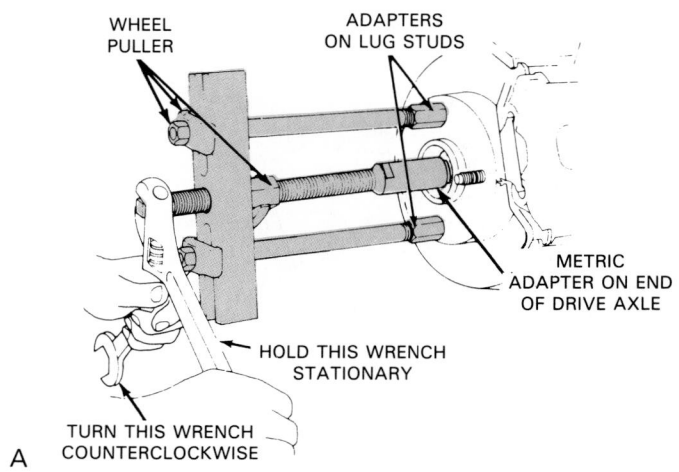

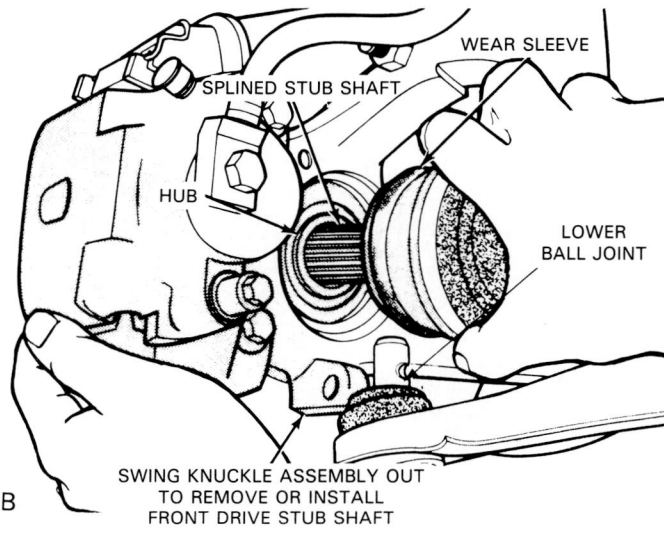

Fig. 61-7. Disconnecting outer stub axle shaft from hub. A — A puller is sometimes needed to force outer stub axle splines from hub. If needed, make sure you have removed ball joint, lower control arm fastener, sway bar, etc. Refer to service manual to avoid part damage. B — With lower ball joint removed, swing steering knuckle outward so axle splines will slide out. Support axle. (Ford and Dodge)

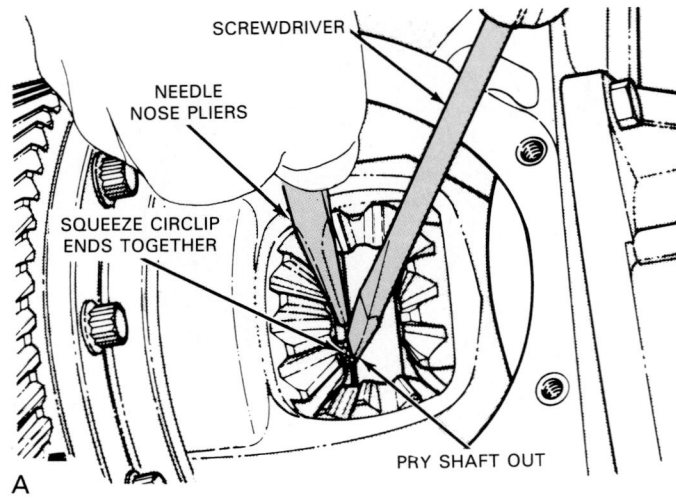

A

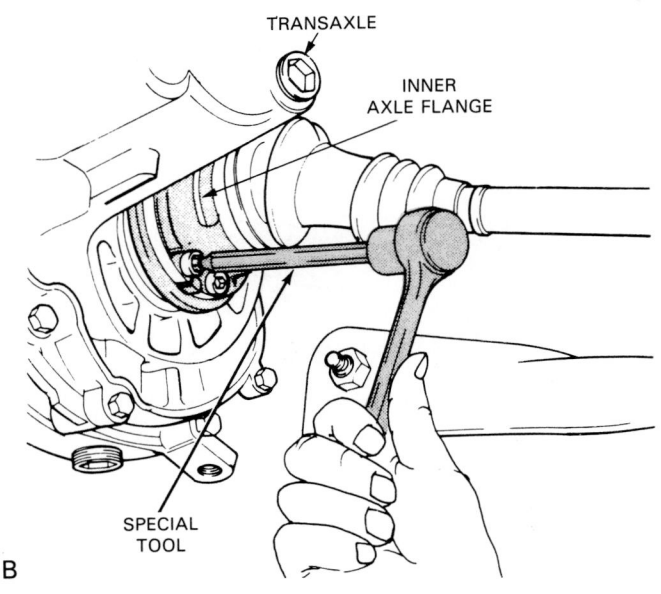

B

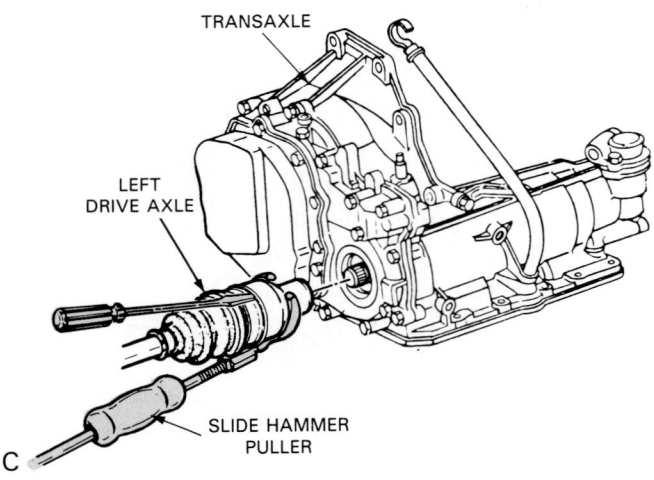

C

Fig. 61-8. Inner ends of front-drive axles are commonly held in or on transaxle in two ways: Snap rings or bolts. A — Snap ring or spring clip locks axle in differential. It must be removed from groove for axle removal. B — Inner drive axle flange bolted to drive flange. Remove fasteners and axle can be removed. C — Prying or slide hammer may be needed to free snap ring and axle from differential. Check your manual.

With other designs, unbolt the inner axle flange for axle removal from the transaxle. This is shown in Fig. 61-8B. If required, use a slide hammer to pull the inner stub axle from the transaxle. See Fig. 61-8C.

While holding the axle assembly together, pull it out or off the transaxle, as illustrated in Fig. 61-9.

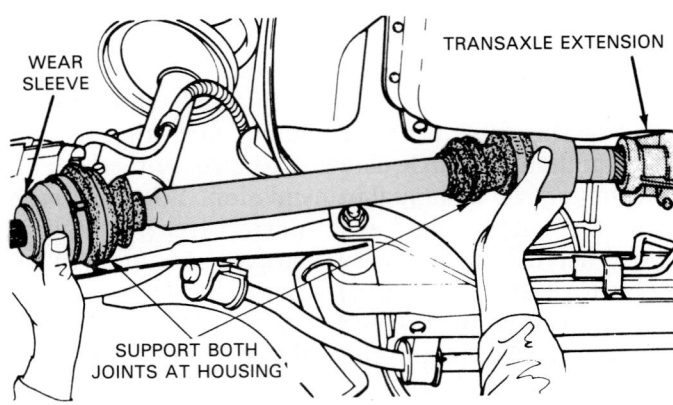

Fig. 61-9. When lifting front-drive axle, support both ends of axle and hold plunging joint together. Never let axle hang unsupported or joint or boot damage can result.   (Dodge)

Transaxle CV-joint replacement

To replace axle shaft CV-joints, mount the shaft in a vise, Fig. 61-10. If you have a tubular or hollow type axle shaft, be careful not to bend or dent the shaft. The slightest dent could cause vibration.

To service a ***tripod CV-joint,*** cut (plastic type) or pry off (reusable spring type) the old boot straps. See Fig. 61-11A. Separate the tripod from the housing, view B. If any parts are to be reused, scribe mark the housing, spider, and axle shaft, view C. To remove the spider from the axle splines, remove the snap ring in the end of the axle shaft. Then, drive off the old spider, as in Fig. 61-11D.

Obtain a *CV-joint repair kit* (usually includes new joint components, grease, boot, and boot straps). Look

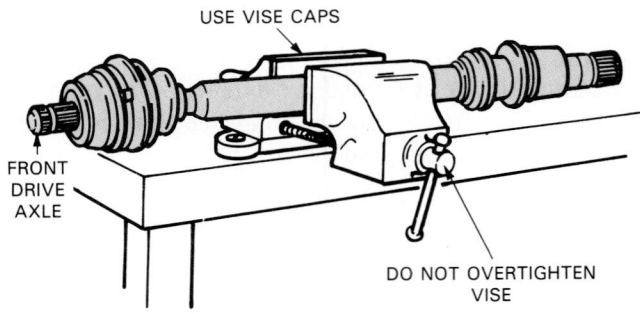

Fig. 61-10. To service CV-joints, mount drive axle in vise. With hollow drive axles, be extremely careful not to bend or dent shaft. This could cause shaft vibration. (Dana Corp.)

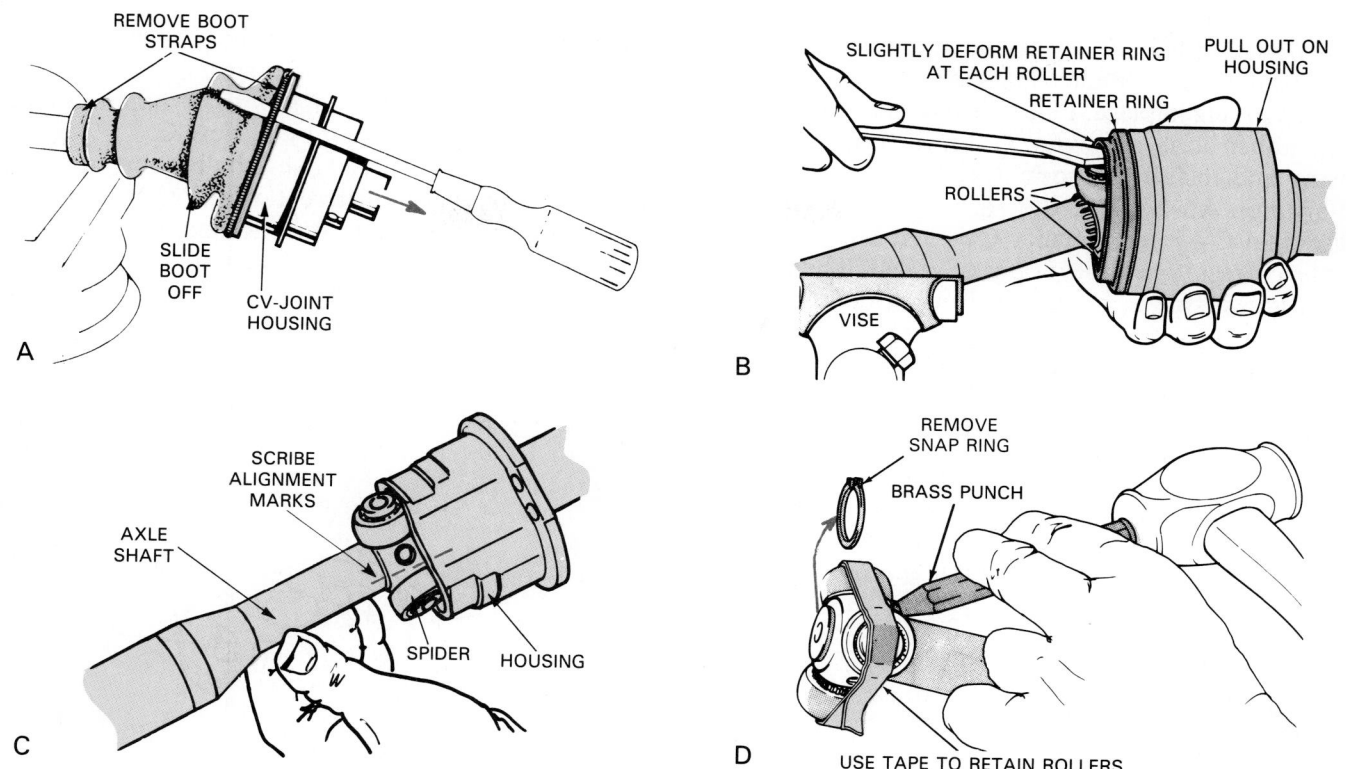

Fig. 61-11. Basic steps for disassembling front-wheel drive tripod type CV-joint. A — Remove straps or clamps holding boot around joint. If plastic straps, pry or cut them off. If spring straps, pry them off carefully because they can be reused. Slide boot OFF joint. B — Slide spider out of housing. If needed, flex retainer ring out of way. C — If any joint components are to be reused, mark their alignment during disassembly. This will let you reassemble parts in same position. D — Remove snap ring holding spider on axle splines. Then use brass drift or punch to push spider off axle. Tape is used to keep rollers and needles from falling off. (Renault, Chrysler, Dana Corp.)

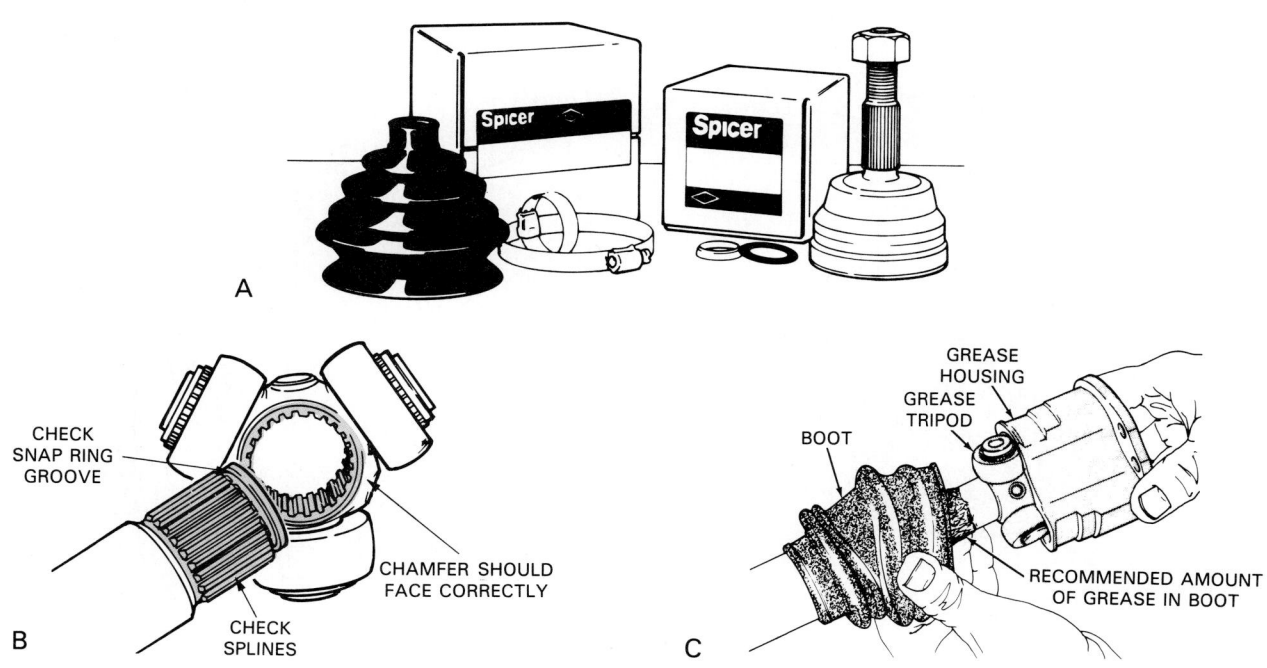

Fig. 61-12. Fundamental steps for rebuilding tripod type CV-joint. A — Purchase CV-joint kit. It will normally contain new joint spider, rollers, needle bearings, snap rings, boot, and boot straps. This will assure quality repair. B — Inspect axle shaft splines and snap ring grooves. They should be in good condition. Make sure spider is fitted on splines correctly. Chamfer may have to face certain direction. Install new snap ring holding spider on axle. C — Grease spider and housing. Place recommended amount of grease in boot. Then fit parts together. Install boot and boot straps. (Dana Corp. and Chrysler)

at Fig. 61-12A. Slide the new rubber boot onto the axle. Then install the new spider on its axle splines, view B. Fit the snap ring in place. Place the remaining kit grease in the rubber boot, as in view C. Fit the boot over the housing and install the boot straps.

Warning! Always use the recommended type of grease on a CV-joint. Quality CV-joint kits will provide the correct type and amount of grease. The wrong type of grease can cause boot deterioration and joint failure.

To service a **ball and cage** or **Rzeppa CV-joint,** remove the boot straps. Slide the boot back and remove the retaining ring, as in Fig. 61-13A. You may need

to use light taps with a brass hammer to free the joint from its shaft. Tilt the cage and inner race using thumb pressure, view B. Light taps with a hammer and wooden dowel may be required, view C.

With the cage tilted, remove a ball from the cage, view D. Tilt the cage in different directions to free each ball. Swivel the inner cage and race and remove them from the housing, view E. Then, rotate the inner race and remove it from the cage, view F. Clean and inspect the parts to be reused.

Obtain the correct CV-joint repair kit or parts as needed. Grease the inner race and fit it into the cage. Refer to Fig. 61-14A. Install the cage and inner race

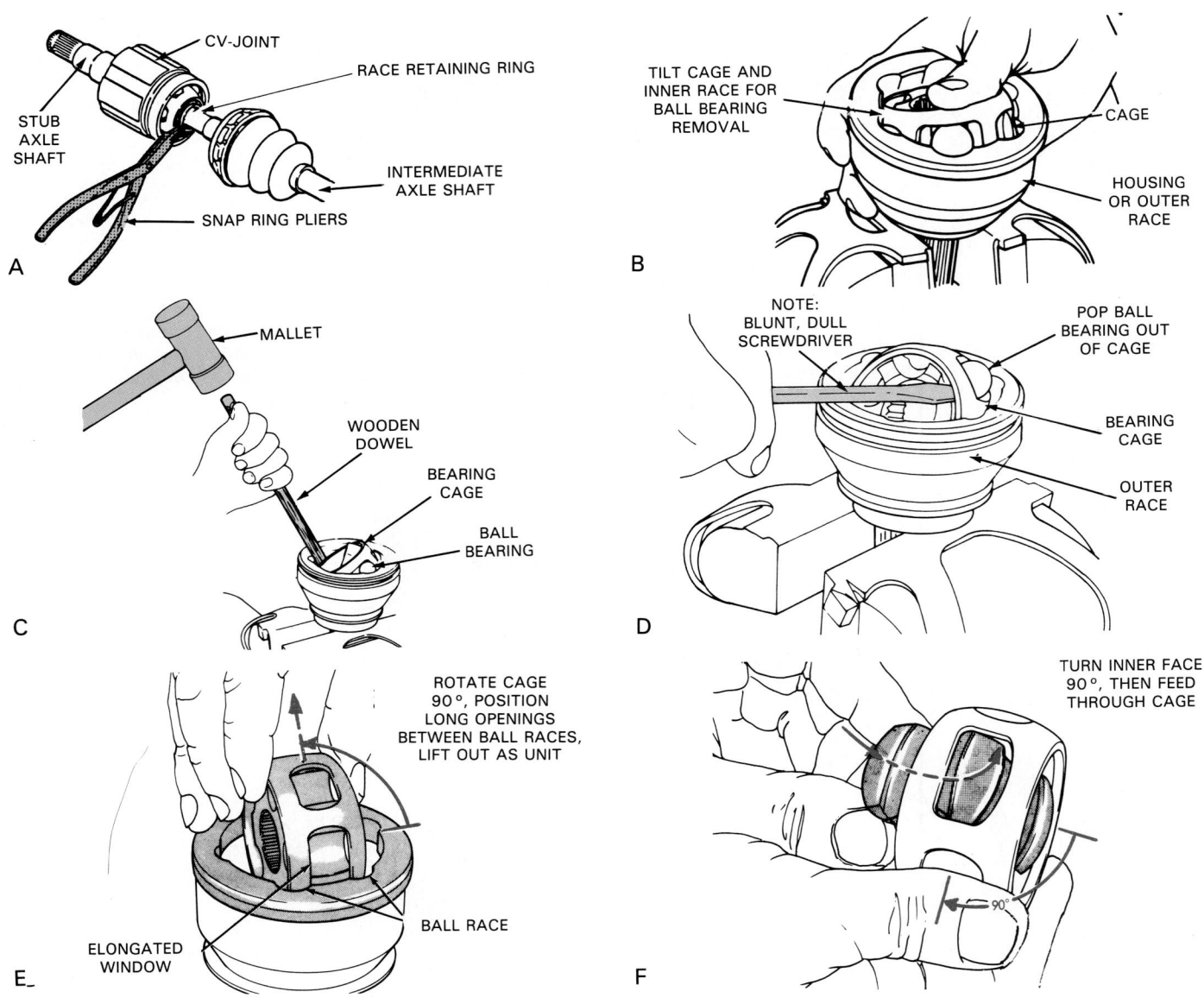

Fig. 61-13. General procedures for disassembling Rzeppa or ball and cage type CV-joint. A — Remove boot straps and pull back boot. Use snap ring pliers to spread retaining ring and pull axle shafts apart. B — Use thumb pressure to tilt cage so ball can be removed. Tilt in different directions to free each ball. C — To tilt cage, you may need to use hammer and wooden dowel. Do not use metal rod or housing damage will result. D — Remove each ball until they are all out of cage. Do not damage cage with screwdriver. Screwdriver should have dull tip edges to prevent scratches. E — Swivel cage and inner race 90 degrees in housing. This will let you pull cage and inner race out of housing. F — Rotate inner race in cage for removal. Clean and inspect parts. If slightest sign of wear or damage is noticed, replace parts. (GMC, Ford, and Chrysler)

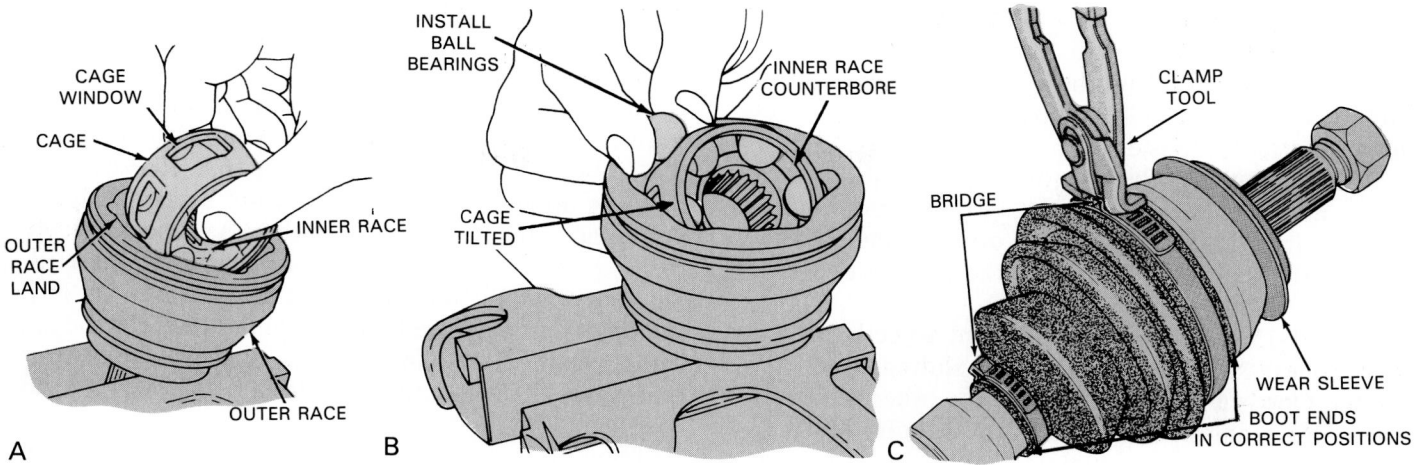

Fig. 61-14. Reassembly steps for Rzeppa or ball and cage CV-joint. A — Lubricate parts as recommended by manufacturer. Assemble inner race in cage. Then fit them inside housing. B — Tilt cage and install balls one at a time. With a sliding Rzeppa joint, balls, cage, and inner race will slide into housing as a unit. This is a fixed CV-joint that requires individual installation of balls. C — Install snap rings, wear sleeve, stop ring, and other parts. Fit boot over joint and install boot straps. Note use of special pliers designed for boot installation. (Ford and Chrysler)

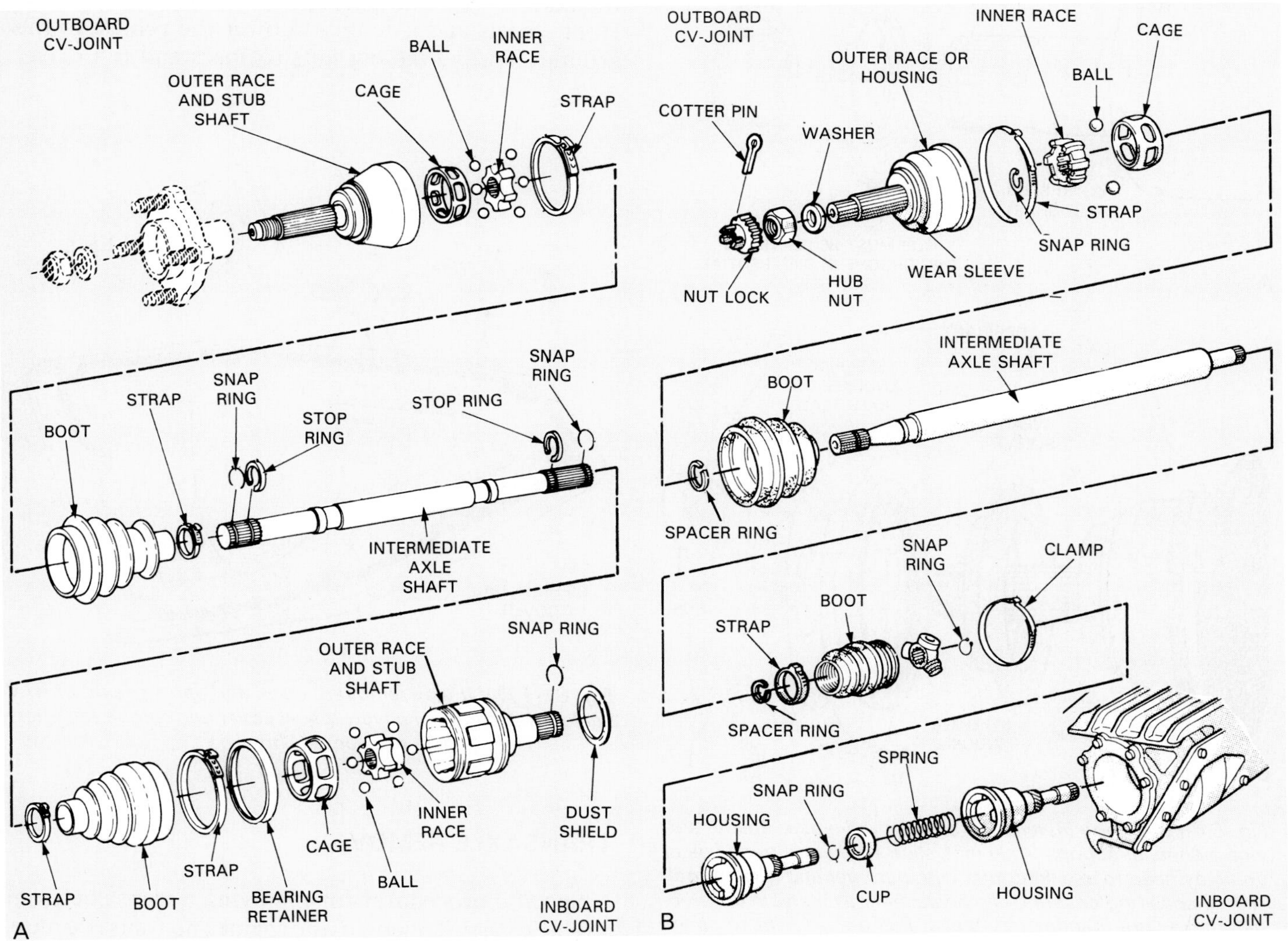

Fig. 61-15. Exploded view of two typical front-wheel drive axles. A — This axle has two Rzeppa or ball and cage joints. Outer CV-joint is fixed. Inner Rzeppa joint is sliding. B — This axle has a fixed, outer Rzeppa and inner, sliding tripod joints. Study construction and location of parts.

into the joint housing, view B. Tilt the cage so that you can position each ball.

Assemble the joint on the axle shaft. Make sure all snap rings are in good condition. Sometimes, a press is needed to force the joint over its splines.

After assembling the CV-joint, fit the boot over the joint, as in Fig. 61-14C. Make sure the boot ends fit into their grooves. Install the boot straps. Do not tighten the straps. You may cut the boot or break the strap.

Fig. 61-15 shows two typical front-wheel drive axle assemblies. Note how both have sliding inner CV-joints. One is a Rzeppa joint and the other is a tripod joint. Both axles have fixed outer Rzeppa joints.

Refer to a service manual when servicing either type of CV-joint. The manual will give special, detailed directions that are very important.

Installing front-drive axle

To install a front-drive axle, basically, reverse the directions for removal.

Fit or slide the inner end of the axle on or in the transaxle. If used, make sure the snap ring or spring clip locks in the differential, Fig. 61-16A. Reinstall any bolts or other parts removed during disassembly.

Replace and lubricate the hub seal. Also lubricate the *wear sleeve* (bushing between axle and seal) if used. See Fig. 61-16B. Slide the outer end of the axle into the hub. You may need to use a puller to force the axle through the hub splines. If needed, reinstall the lower ball joint. Screw on the spindle nut and torque it to specs.

If you had to remove the differential cover and snap rings on the inner ends of the axle shafts, make sure the snap rings are installed. Clean the differential cover. If recommended, adhere the new gasket to the cover. If RTV sealer is to be used, coat the cover with an even bead of sealer as illustrated in Fig. 61-17.

Bolt the cover to the transaxle and torque the bolts to specs in a crisscross pattern. Fill the transaxle with the correct type and amount of lubricant. Install the front wheels and axle nuts. Lower the vehicle to the ground. Torque the lug nuts to specs and test drive.

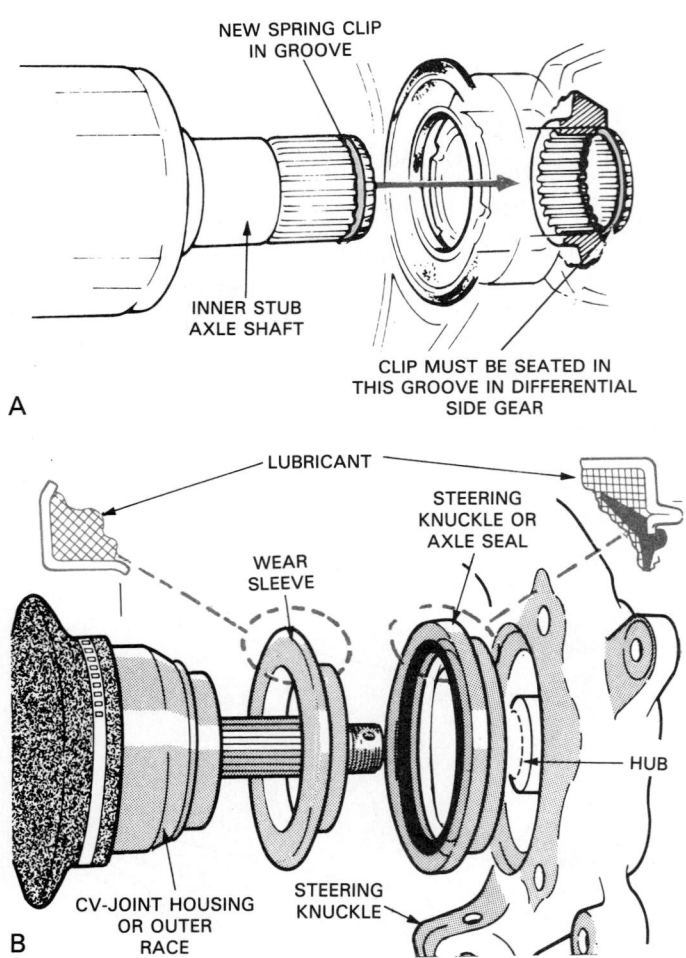

Fig. 61-16. During installation of front-drive axle, follow service manual directions. Axle may slide easily into transaxle or you may need to use light taps with hammer and driving tool. A — If snap ring or spring clip holds inner axle end in differential, make sure it snaps into place. Pull out on joint to check that it is locked in side gear. B — Lubricate parts as recommended. Note how this axle design requires grease on wear sleeve and seal. Replacement of grease seal is normally recommended during front-drive axle service.

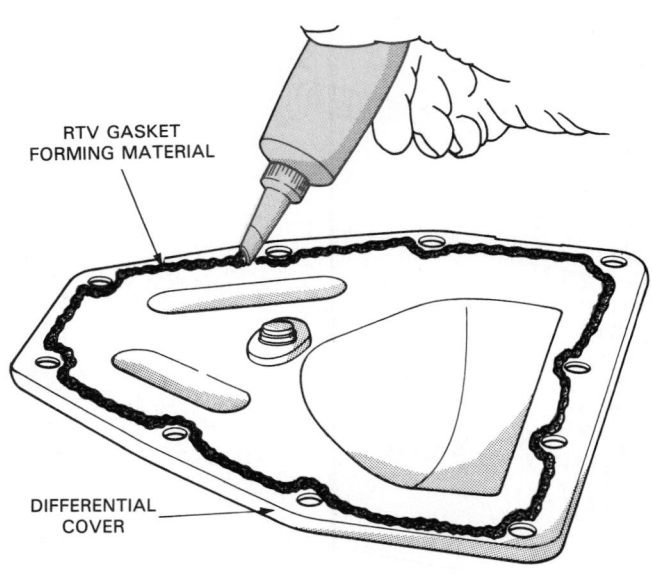

Fig. 61-17. If it was removed, clean and apply gasket or RTV sealer to differential cover. Install cover and torque fasteners to specs. (Chrysler)

TRANSAXLE REMOVAL

Specific procedures for removing a transaxle from a vehicle vary. Sometimes the engine and transaxle must be removed together out the top of the engine compartment. However, with most front-wheel drive vehicles, the transaxle can be separated from the engine

Fig. 61-18. When removing transaxle assembly, make sure you support weight of engine. It must not hang from motor mounts. Note holding fixture on this vehicle.   (OTC Div. of SPX Corp.)

and removed from below or the BOTTOM of the engine compartment.

Generally, remove the battery negative cable, engine mounts, clutch cable or torque converter bolts, shift cables or rods, speedometer cable, crossmember, drive axles, starting motor, and engine-to-transaxle bolts. If a *cradle* (engine supporting subframe) is used, it will have to be removed first.

CAUTION! Before removing all of the bolts securing the transaxle to the engine, mount an engine holding fixture on the vehicle, Fig. 61-18. It is needed to keep the engine from dropping as you remove the transaxle.

Place a transmission jack under the transaxle, Fig. 61-19. Remove the last engine-to-transaxle bolts. Force the transaxle away from the engine. Then, slowly lower the jack while watching for components still connected.

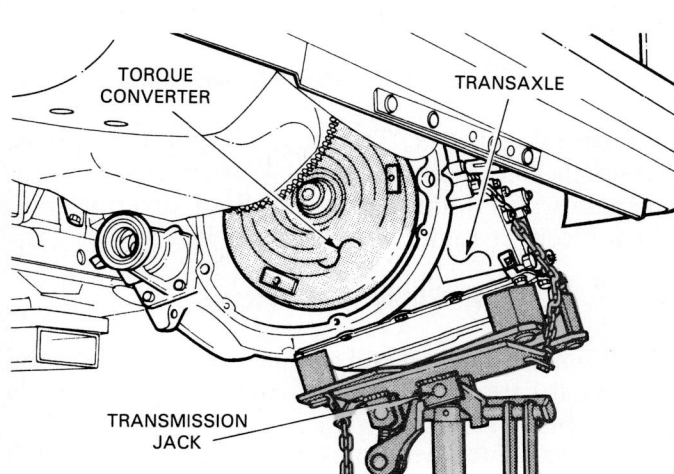

Fig. 61-19. Use a transmission jack to remove transaxle. It is heavy and can cause injuries or serious part damage if dropped. Most transaxles can be separated and removed with engine in vehicle. A few require engine removal. Check service manual.

TRANSAXLE SERVICE

When repairing or rebuilding a transaxle, follow the detailed procedures given in a service manual.

A few general rules to remember are:

1. Do NOT dent or nick gasket sealing surfaces during disassembly or when cleaning.
2. Keep all parts organized so that used parts can be returned to their original positions, Fig. 61-20.
3. Clean and inspect all parts closely for damage. Replace any part showing wear. See Fig. 61-21.
4. Replace all gaskets and seals.
5. Use special tools when needed, Fig. 61-22.
6. During reassembly, measure all gear, shaft, bearing, and other critical components as described in a shop manual, Fig. 61-23.

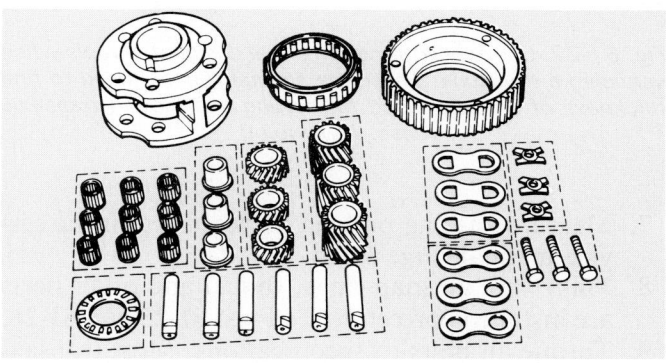

Fig. 61-20. Always keep all parts organized during major repairs. This can avoid confusion and will help you return all parts to correct locations. (Subaru)

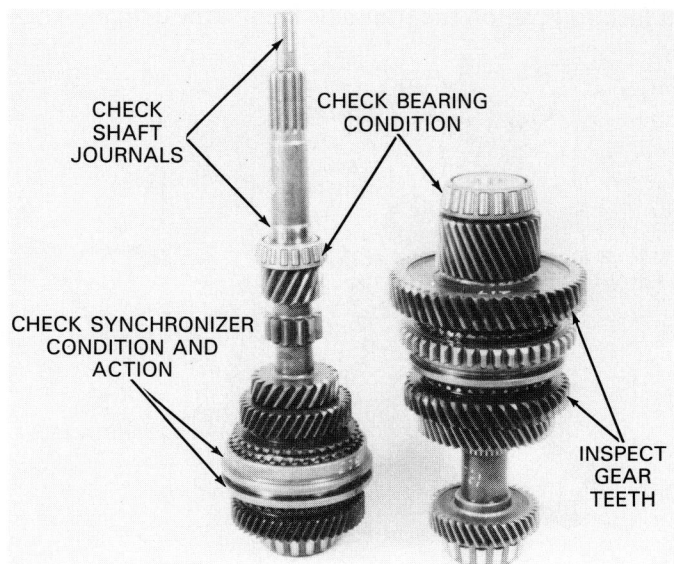

Fig. 61-21. Clean and inspect all components very carefully. If you overlook just one problem, your repair may fail. (Chevrolet)

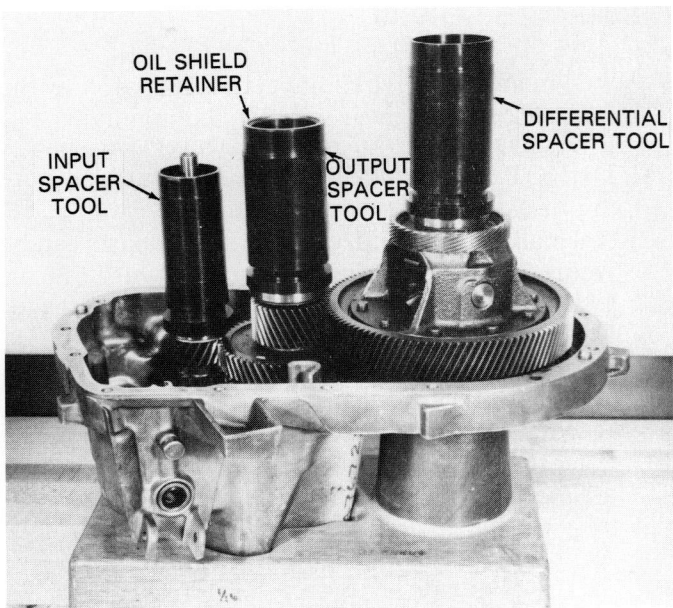

Fig. 61-22. Use special service manual designated tools when servicing a transaxle. These are special spacers used to find thickness of shims needed for setting end play in transaxle case. (Chevrolet)

7. Measure bearing preload as described in the service manual, Fig. 61-24.
8. Make sure all snap rings, shims, and other parts are installed correctly. See Figs. 61-25 and 61-26.
9. Torque all bolts to specifications. Most transaxles have aluminum cases which are very sensitive to bolt torque.

TRANSAXLE INSTALLATION

Install a transaxle in the reverse order of removal. Use a jack to position the transaxle behind the engine. Align

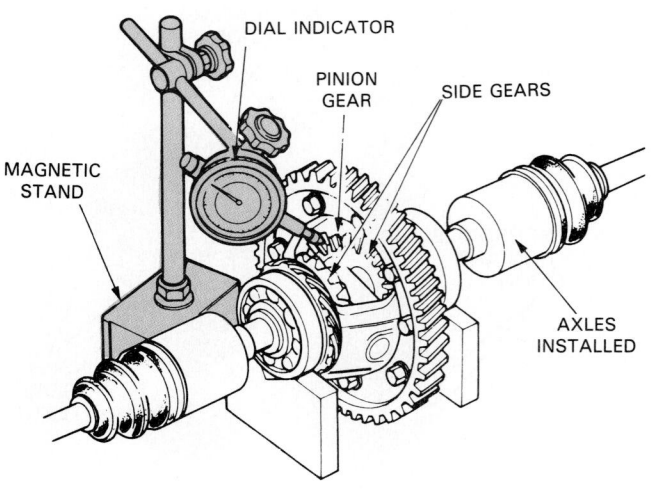

Fig. 61-23. Measure all clearances as described in manual. This shows how you should measure differential pinion gear backlash. Many other measurements are also essential. (Honda)

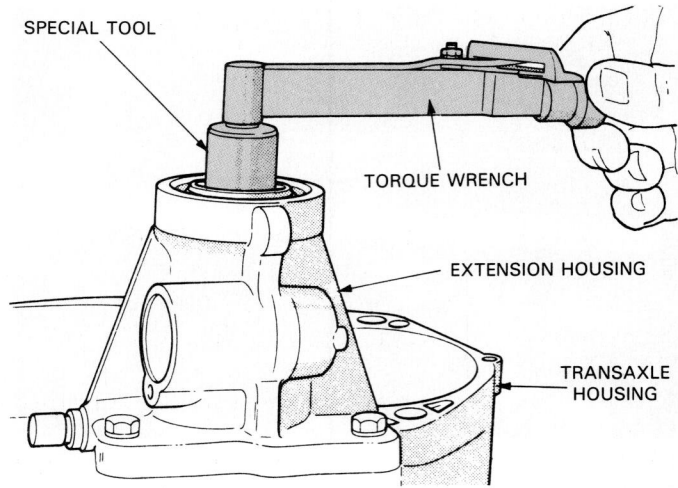

Fig. 61-24. As with a rear axle differential, torque wrench may be used to measure transaxle differential case bearing preload. Reading must be within specs. (Dodge)

the engine crankshaft centerline with the transaxle input shaft centerline.

If you have a manual transaxle, make sure the throwout bearing is new or in good condition. Make sure it is installed correctly.

Slowly push the transaxle against the engine. Watch that the studs on the engine fit into the holes in the transaxle bell housing. With an automatic transaxle, you may also have to align the torque converter bolts with the flywheel while fitting the transaxle.

WARNING! As with a transmission, double-check that the torque converter is correctly installed. If the converter is NOT fully into position, serious part damage could result when you tighten the bolts holding the transaxle to the engine.

Start and torque the engine-to-transaxle bolts. Then, install the other components (cradle, starter, mounts, etc.). Fill transaxle with lubricant and test drive car.

KNOW THESE TERMS

Transaxle dipstick, Transaxle fill and drain plugs, Transaxle pan, Transaxle filter, Transaxle external adjustments, CV-joint repair kit, Boot deterioration, Wear sleeve, Cradle, Transmission jack.

REVIEW QUESTIONS

1. What are three general manual transaxle problems?
2. What are three general automatic transaxle problems?
3. Explain three symptoms or problems noticed with front-drive axle troubles?
4. Some manual transaxles use _____ _____ _____ while others use _____ _____ _____ oil.
5. How do you check the oil or lubricant level in

automatic and manual transaxles?

6. This is NOT an adjustment relating to an automatic transaxle.
   a. Clutch fork.
   b. Bands.
   c. Shift cable.
   d. All of the above.
   e. None of the above.
7. The most common problem with a front-drive axle is worn CV-joints. True or False?
8. What components are normally included in a CV-joint repair kit?
9. Reuse the old hub seal when replacing a front-drive axle. True or False?
10. Besides following the directions in a service manual, name nine general rules for servicing a transaxle.

ACTIVITIES FOR CHAPTER 61

1. Given a transaxle by your instructor, be prepared to show proper diagnosis procedure for that transaxle.
2. Remove, disassemble, and replace a CV drive axle universal joint.
3. Change the transaxle lubricant in a transaxle assigned by your instructor.
4. Given a flat rate manual, a list of parts to be replaced, and a parts catalog, prepare a repair estimate for replacing CV-joints on a transaxle. Use an hourly rate suggested by your instructor.

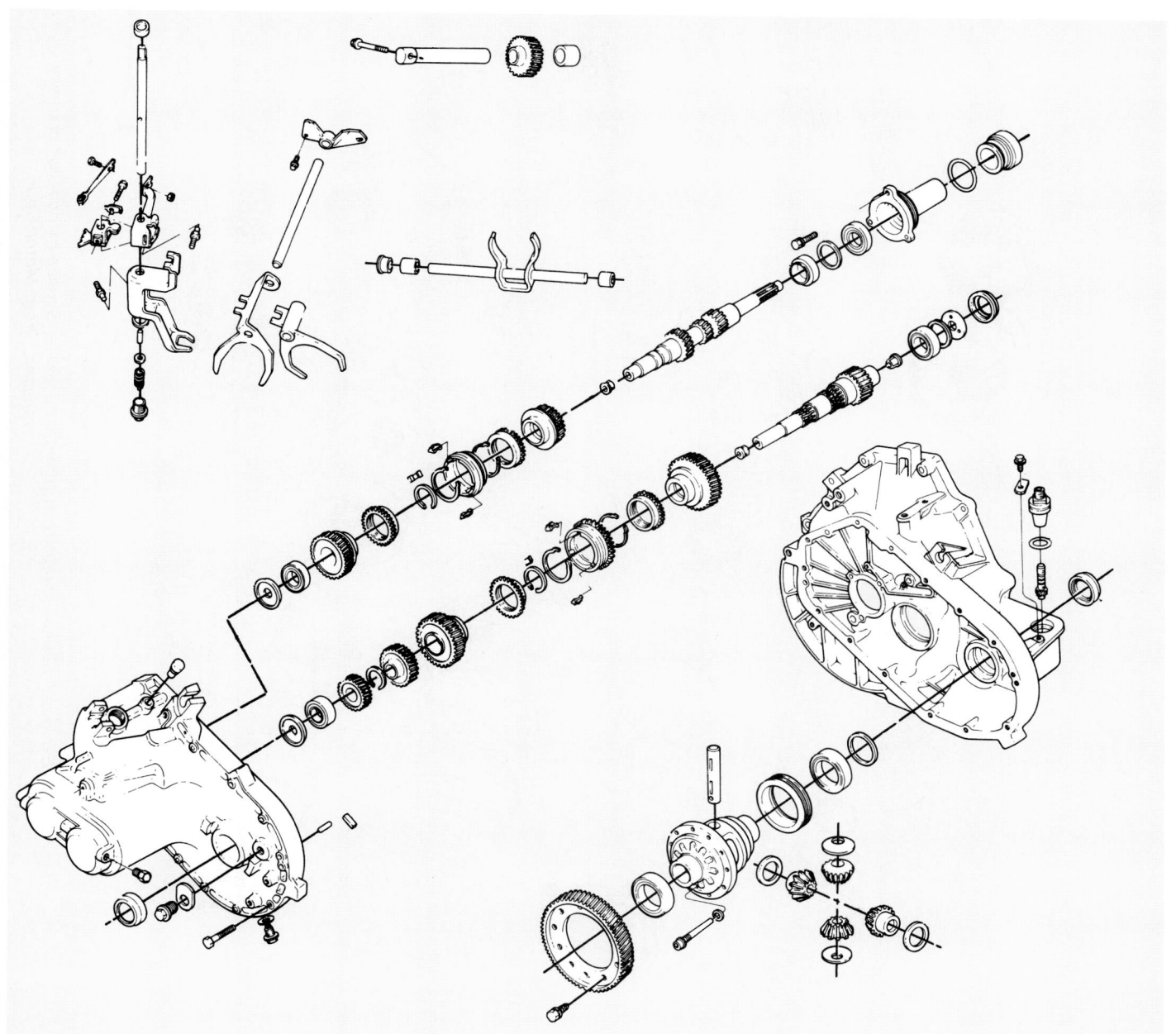

Fig. 61-25. Exploded view of manual transaxle. Study location of parts and visualize their reassembly. (General Motors)

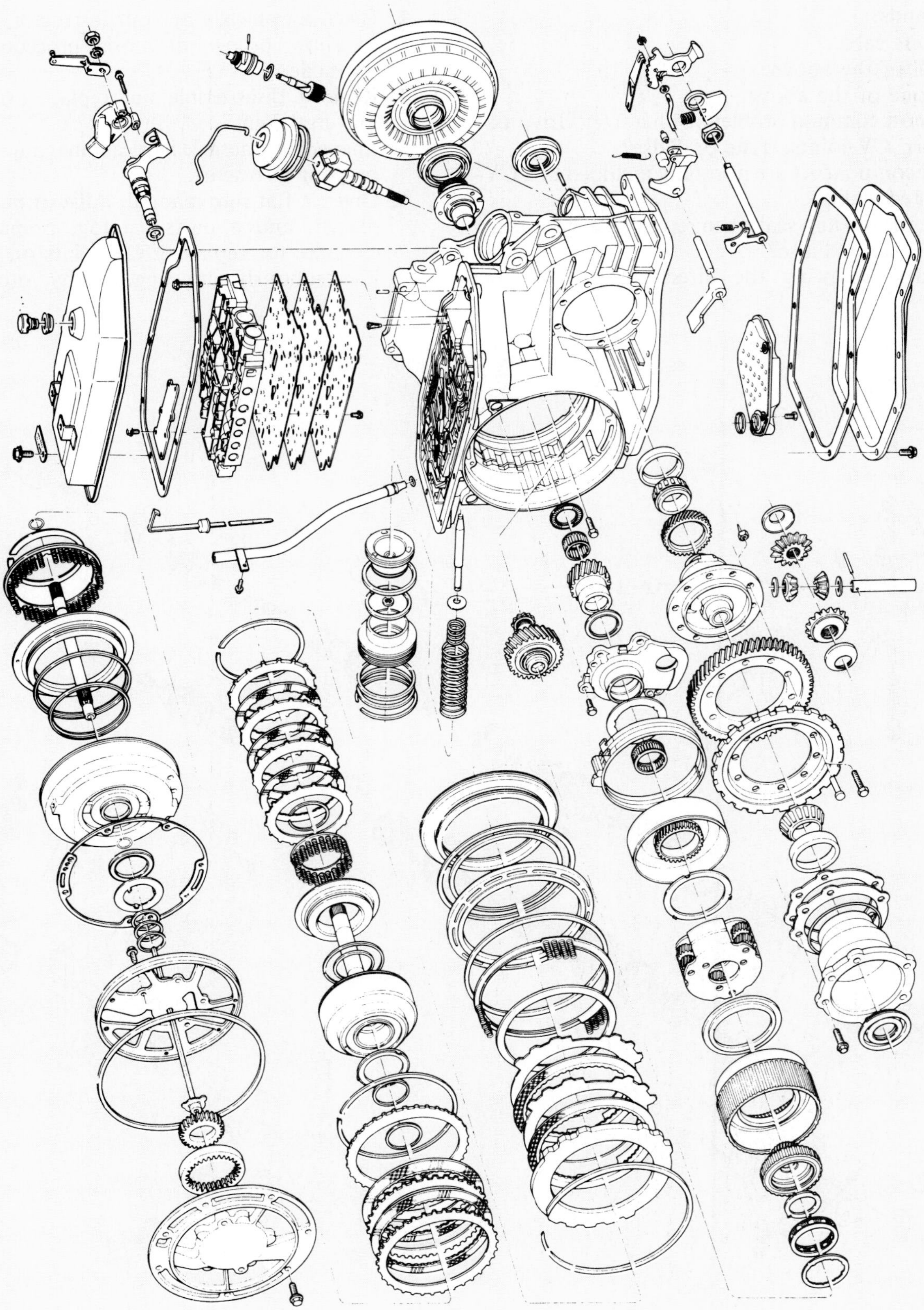

Fig. 61-26. Exploded view of complete automatic transaxle. Service manual will normally give similar illustration of unit being repaired. (Ford Motor Co.)

62

Tire, Wheel, Hub, Wheel Bearing Fundamentals

After studying this chapter, you will be able to:
□ Identify the parts of a tire and wheel.
□ Describe different methods of tire construction.
□ Explain tire and wheel sizes.
□ Describe tire ratings.
□ Identify the parts of driving and nondriving hub and wheel bearing assemblies.

This chapter introduces the various tire designs used on modern cars. It explains how tires and wheels are constructed to give safe and dependable service. The chapter also covers hub and wheel bearing construction for both rear-wheel and front-wheel drive vehicles. As a result, you should be prepared to study later chapters on brakes, suspension systems, and wheel alignment.

TIRES

Automobile *tires* perform two basic functions: they act as a soft CUSHION between the road and the metal wheel. Tires must also provide adequate TRACTION (friction) with the road surface.

Tires must transmit driving, braking, and cornering forces to the road in good weather, when raining, and in snow. At the same time, they should resist punctures and wear.

Parts of a tire

Although there are several tire designs, the basic parts of a tire are the same. See Fig. 62-1. Refer to this illustration as each part is introduced.

1. TIRE BEADS (two rings made of steel wires encased in rubber that hold tire sidewalls snugly against wheel rim).
2. BODY PLIES (rubberized fabric and cords

wrapped around beads; they form the *carcass* or body of the tire).
3. TREAD (outer surface of tire that contacts road).
4. SIDEWALL (outer part of tire extending from bead to tread; it contains information about tire).
5. BELTS (sometimes used to strengthen plies and stiffen tread; they lie between tread and inner plies).
6. LINER (thin layer of rubber bonded to inside of plies; provides leakproof membrane for modern tubeless tire).

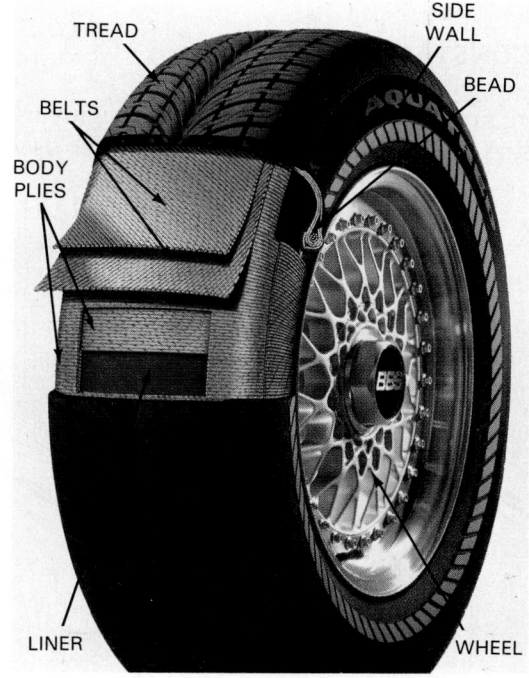

Fig. 62-1. Study basic parts of a tire.   (Goodyear)

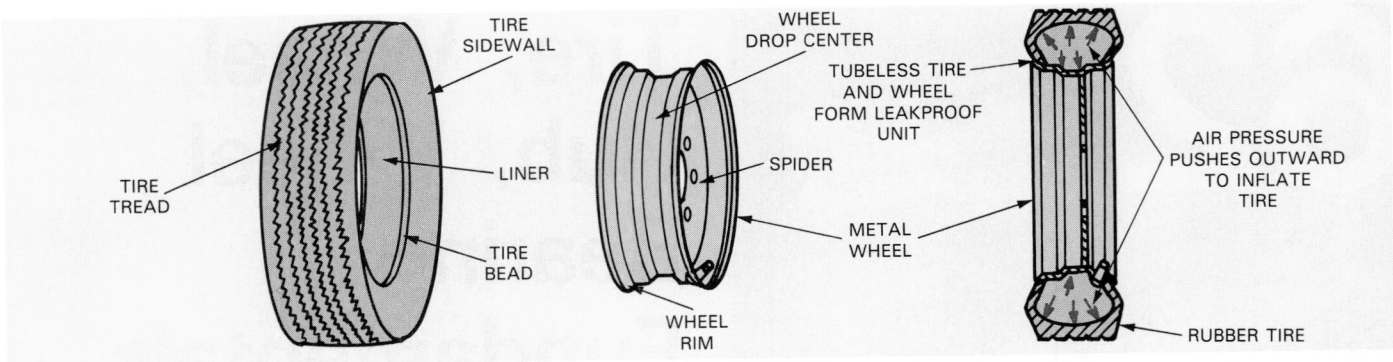

Fig. 62-2. Tire fits over wheel. With tubeless tire, tire and wheel form leakproof unit. Air pressure pushes outward on inside of tire for inflation.

Pneumatic tires

Car tires are *pneumatic* which means they are filled with air. As pictured in Fig. 62-2, internal air pressure pushes out on the inside of the tire to support the weight of the vehicle.

Tubeless tires

Today's vehicles use *tubeless tires* that do NOT have a separate inner tube. The tire and wheel form an airtight unit.

Older vehicles used *inner tubes* (soft, thin, leakproof rubber liner) that fit inside the tire and wheel assemblies.

Rolling resistance

Tire rolling resistance is a measurement of the amount of friction produced as the tire operates on the road surface. A high rolling resistance would increase fuel consumption and wear. Typically, tire rolling resistance is reduced by higher inflation pressure, proper tire design, and a lighter vehicle.

TIRE CONSTRUCTION

There are many construction and design variations in tires. A different number of plies may be used. The plies may run at different angles. Also, different materials may be utilized.

Three types of tires are found on late model vehicles: bias ply, belted bias, and radial.

Bias ply tire

A *bias ply tire* has plies running at an angle from bead to bead. See Fig. 62-3A. The cord angle is also reversed from ply to ply. The tread is bonded directly to the top ply.

A bias ply tire is one of the oldest designs and it does NOT use belts. The position of the cords in a bias ply tire allows the body of the tire to flex easily. This tends to improve cushioning action. A bias ply tire provides a very smooth ride on rough roads.

One disadvantage is that the weakness of the plies and tread reduce traction at high speeds and increase rolling resistance.

Belted bias tire

A *belted bias tire* is a bias tire with belts added to increase tread stiffness. Look at Fig. 62-3B. The plies and belts normally run at different angles. The belts do NOT run around to the sidewalls but only lie under the tread area.

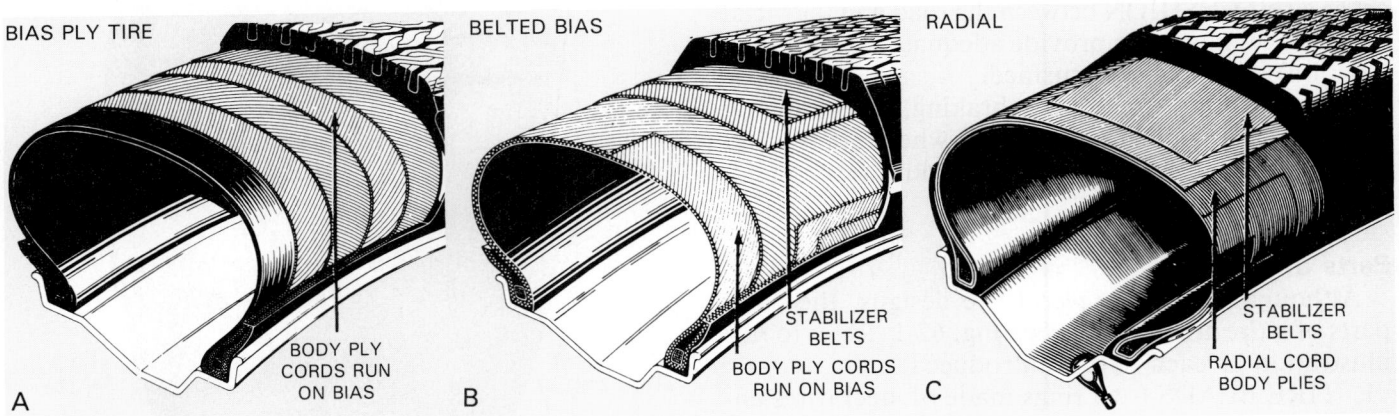

Fig. 62-3. Three tire types: bias ply, belted bias, and radial. (Firestone)

Usually, two stabilizer belts and two or more plies are used to increase tire performance.

A belted bias tire provides a smooth ride, good traction, and offers some reduction in rolling resistance over a bias ply tire.

Radial ply tire

A *radial ply tire* has plies running straight across from bead to bead with stabilizer belts directly beneath the tread. This is illustrated in Fig. 62-3C.

A radial tire has a very flexible sidewall, but a stiff tread. The belts can be made of steel, flexten, fiberglass, or other materials.

Radial tires have a very stable *footprint* (shape and amount of tread touching road surface). This improves safety, cornering, braking, and wear.

One possible disadvantage of a radial tire is that it may produce a harder ride at low speeds. The stiff tread area does NOT give or flex as much on rough roads.

TIRE MARKINGS

Tire markings on the sidewall of a tire give information about tire size, load carrying ability, inflation pressure, number of plies, identification numbers, quality ratings, and manufacturer. It is important that you understand these tire markings. Refer to Fig. 62-4.

Tire size

Tire size is given on the sidewall as a letter-number sequence. There are two common size designations: alpha-numeric (conventional measuring system) and P-metric (metric measuring system).

The *alpha-numeric* (alphabetical-numerical) tire size rating system uses letters and numbers to denote tire

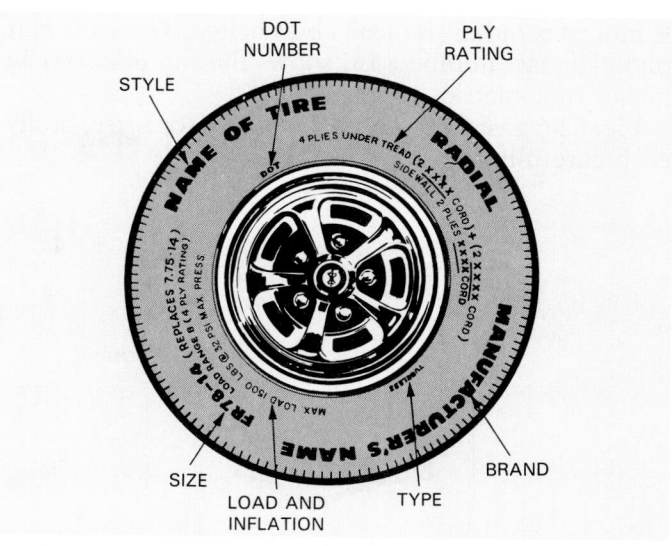

Fig. 62-4. Sidewall will give information about tire. Study what is given on this tire.

size in inches and load-carrying capacity in pounds. An example is given in Fig. 62-5A.

The first letter, G, indicates the load and size relationship. The higher the letter, the larger the size and load-carrying ability. G is smaller than H, for example. An R in the designation means radial. The first number, 78, is the height-to-width radio. The last number, 15, is the rim diameter in inches.

The *P-metric* tire is the newest tire identification system using metric values and international standards. Look at Fig. 62-5B.

The letter P indicates passenger car tire. The first number, 155, gives section width in millimeters. The second number, 80, is the height-to-width radio. The

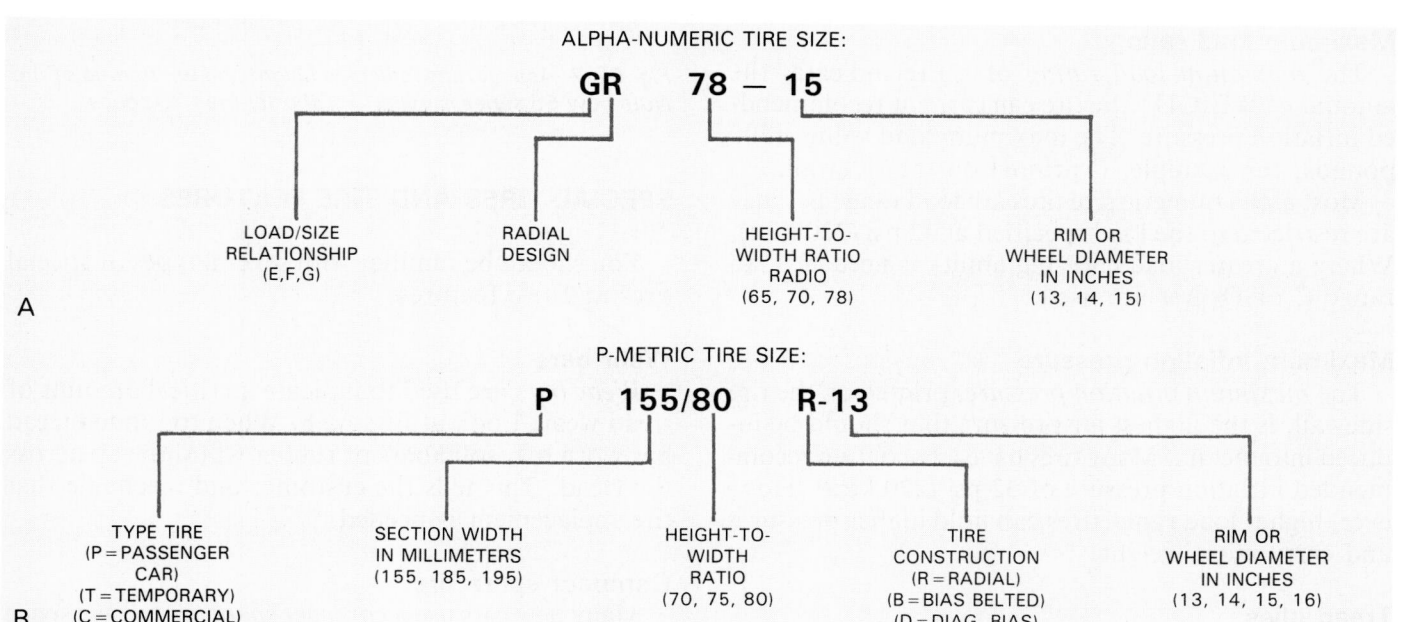

Fig. 62-5. Two modern tire size designation numbering systems.

R indicates radial (B means bias belted, D means bias ply). The last number, 13, shows the rim diameter in inches (not metric values).

Fig. 62-6 gives the points of measure for a tire. Study each carefully.

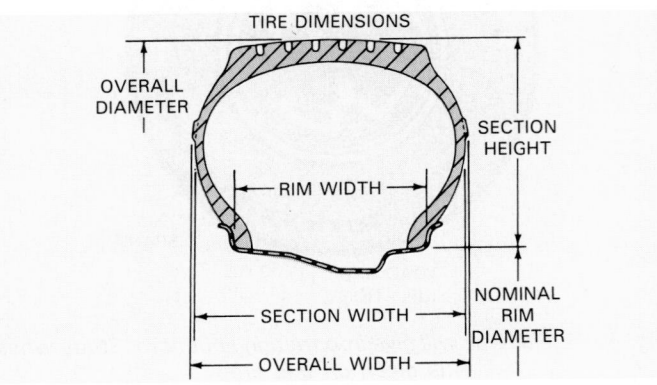

Fig. 62-6. Points of measurement on a tire. These dimensions are important when ordering new tires or wheels. (BF Goodrich)

Aspect ratio

The *aspect ratio* or height-to-width ratio in the tire size designation is the most difficult value to understand. Fig. 62-7 illustrates different aspect ratios.

Note that, as the number becomes smaller, the tire becomes more squat (wider and shorter). The aspect ratio is the comparison of the tire's height (bead-to-tread) and width (sidewall-to-sidewall).

A 70-series tire, for example, has a profile ratio of 70; the height of the tire is 70 percent of the width. A 60 series tire would be "short" and "fat." A 78 tire would be "narrower" and "taller."

Maximum load rating

The *maximum load rating* of a tire indicates the amount of WEIGHT the tire can carry at recommended inflation pressure. The maximum load value, 1500 pounds, for example, is printed on the sidewall.

Most alpha numeric size tires are load range B. They are restricted to the load specified at 32 psi (220 kPa). Where a greater load carrying ability is needed, load range C or D tires are used.

Maximum inflation pressure

The *maximum inflation pressure,* printed on the tire sidewall, is the highest air pressure that should be induced into the tire. Many tires have a maximum recommended inflation pressure of 32 psi (220 kPa). However, higher load range tires can hold higher pressures and carry more weight.

Tread plies

The tire sidewall also states the number of plies and ply rating. The tire may be a 2-ply, 2-ply with 4-ply rating (plies are made stronger than normal), or 4-ply, for example. A greater number of plies or higher ply rating generally increases load-carrying ability.

DOT number

DOT stands for DEPARTMENT OF TRANSPORTATION. When you see "DOT" on the tire sidewall, the tire has passed prescribed safety tests.

Following the letters DOT is the *DOT number* that identifies the particular tire (manufacturer, plant location, type tire construction, and date of manufacture). The DOT number is stamped into the tire sidewall.

Tire grades

Tread wear, traction, and temperature grades are normally shown on the tire sidewall according to the Uniform Tire Quality Grading System.

Tread wear is given as a number: 100, 120, or 130 for instance. The higher the number, the more resistant the tire is to wear.

Tire traction is classified as A, B, or C. The letter A would provide the most traction while C would provide the least traction.

Tire temperature resistance is also given as A, B, or C. A grade A tire resists a temperature buildup better than B or C.

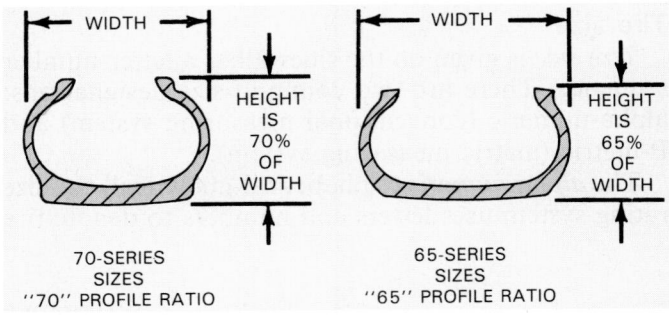

Fig. 62-7. Aspect ratio indicates height and width ratio of tire. Note how 65 series is wider and shorter than 70 series.

SPECIAL TIRES AND TIRE FEATURES

You should be familiar with several types of special tires and tire features.

Wear bars

Wear bars are used to indicate a critical amount of tread wear. Look at Fig. 62-8. When too much tread has worn off, solid bars of rubber will show up across the tread. This tells the customer and mechanic that tire replacement is needed.

Compact spare tire

Many new cars use a *compact spare tire* to save space in the trunk. One is shown in Fig. 62-9. Some types of compact tires are very small in diameter. Others are

Fig. 62-8. When wear bars show up, tire is worn enough to be unsafe. It should be replaced. (Goodyear)

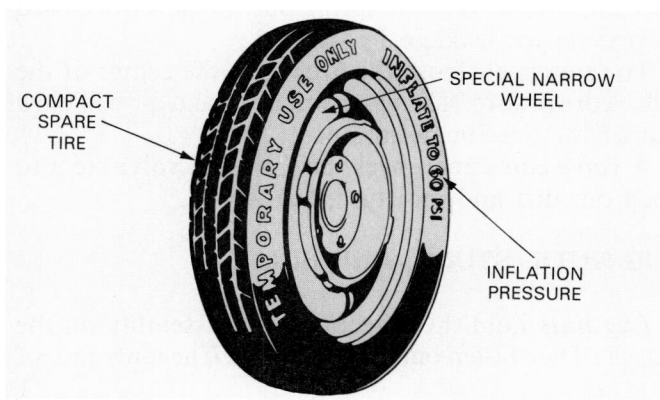

Fig. 62-9. Compact spare tire is for temporary use only. This one should be inflated to 60 psi or 415 kPa. It requires a special narrow wheel. (Oldsmobile)

NOT inflated when in storage. A small bottle of compressed air may be used to inflate the tire when needed.

WARNING! Most compact spare tires are designed only for TEMPORARY USE. Refer to manufacturer's specifications on inflation pressure, maximum driving speed, and number of miles it can be driven.

Self-sealing tires

Some tires are *self-sealing* (seal small punctures) because of a coating of sealing compound applied to the tire liner. Refer to Fig. 62-10. If a nail punctures the tire, air pressure pushes the soft compound into the hole to stop air leakage.

Retreads

Retreads are old, used tires that have had a new tread vulcanized (applied using heat and pressure) to the old carcass or body. Retreads, also called *recaps,* are seldom used on passenger cars. However, large truck tires are frequently recapped because of the high cost of new truck tires.

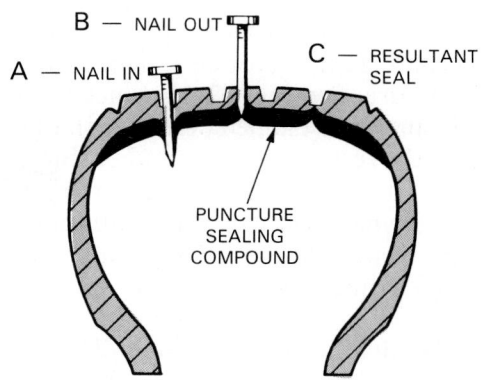

Fig. 62-10. Puncture sealing tire action. A — Nail punctures tire. B — Nail is pulled out. C — Sealing compound flows in and plugs hole in tire to prevent flat. (GMC)

Run-flat tires

Run-flat tires have an extremely stiff sidewall construction so that they are still usable with a loss of air pressure. If the tire leaks its air, you can drive the vehicle to a repair shop without tire and wheel damage. The tire will retain most of its shape because the sidewall is strong enough to support vehicle weight.

WHEELS

Wheels must be designed to support the tire while withstanding loads from acceleration, braking, and cornering. Most wheels are made of steel. A few optional types are cast in aluminum or magnesium. Refer to Fig. 62-11.

"Mag wheels" or *"mags"* is a nickname for aluminum or magnesium wheels. They do not need wheel covers as do conventional steel wheels. One is pictured in Fig. 62-12.

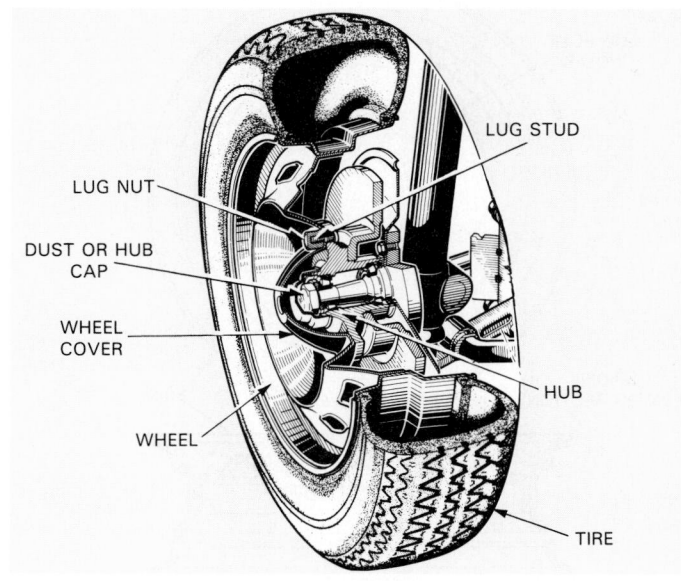

Fig. 62-11. Cutaway view shows many components relating to wheel and tire assembly. (Peugeot)

A *drop center wheel* is commonly used on passenger vehicles because it allows for easier installation and removal of the tire. See Fig. 62-13. Since the center of the wheel is smaller in diameter (dropped), the tire bead can fall into the recess. Then, the other side of the tire bead can be forced over the rim for removal.

A standard wheel consists of the *rim* (outer lip that contacts tire bead) and the *spider* (center section that bolts to vehicle hub). Normally, the spider is welded to the rim.

Fig. 62-14 illustrates the various dimensions of a wheel. Compare this illustration with Fig. 62-13.

Fig. 62-12. Aluminum or magnesium wheel is often called a "mag." It does not need a wheel cover. (Plymouth)

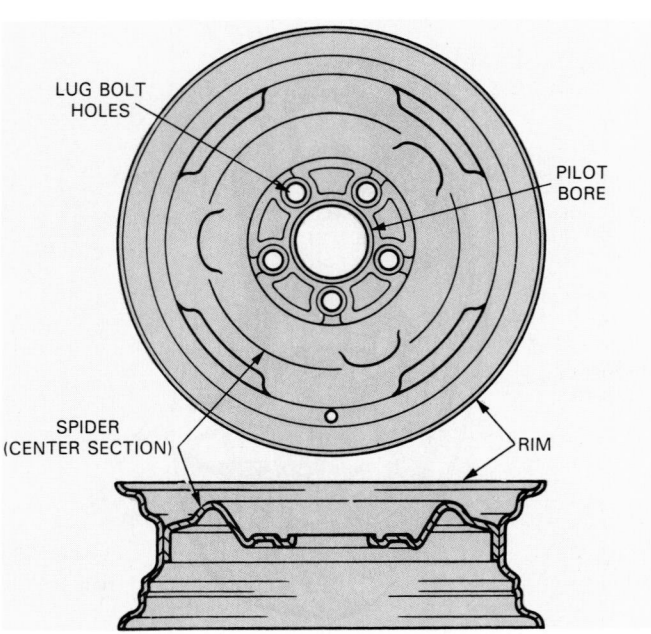

Fig. 62-13. Two views show parts of a conventional drop center wheel. Study part names.

Safety rim

A *safety rim* has small ridges that hold the tire beads on the wheel during a tire *blow-out* (instant rupture and air loss) or *flat* (slow leak reduces inflation pressure). Look at Fig. 62-15. Small raised lips around the rim keep the tire beads from sliding into the drop center section. This improves safety by keeping the tire from coming off the wheel.

VALVE STEM AND CORE

A *valve stem* snaps into a hole in the wheel of a tubeless tire to allow inflation and deflation, Fig. 62-15.

The stem is made of rubber. A threaded metal tube is formed in the end of the stem.

The *valve core* is an air valve inside the valve stem. It is a spring-loaded valve, Fig. 62-15.

The valve core allows air to be added to inflate the tire. However, when the *air chuck* (tool for filling tire with air) is removed, the spring pushes the valve closed to prevent air leakage.

To remove air from the tire, push the center of the valve core inward. The valve will open and air will blow out of the tire for deflation.

A *valve cap* screws over the threaded valve stem to keep out dirt and moisture, Fig. 62-15.

LUG NUTS, STUDS, AND BOLTS

Lug nuts hold the wheel and tire assembly on the vehicle. They fasten onto special studs. The inner face of

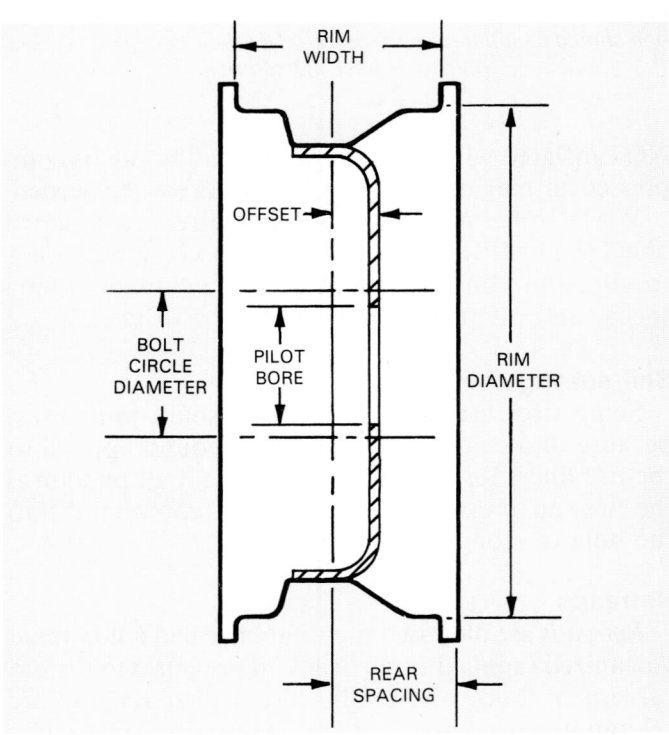

Fig. 62-14. Study basic points of measurement for a wheel. (Goodyear)

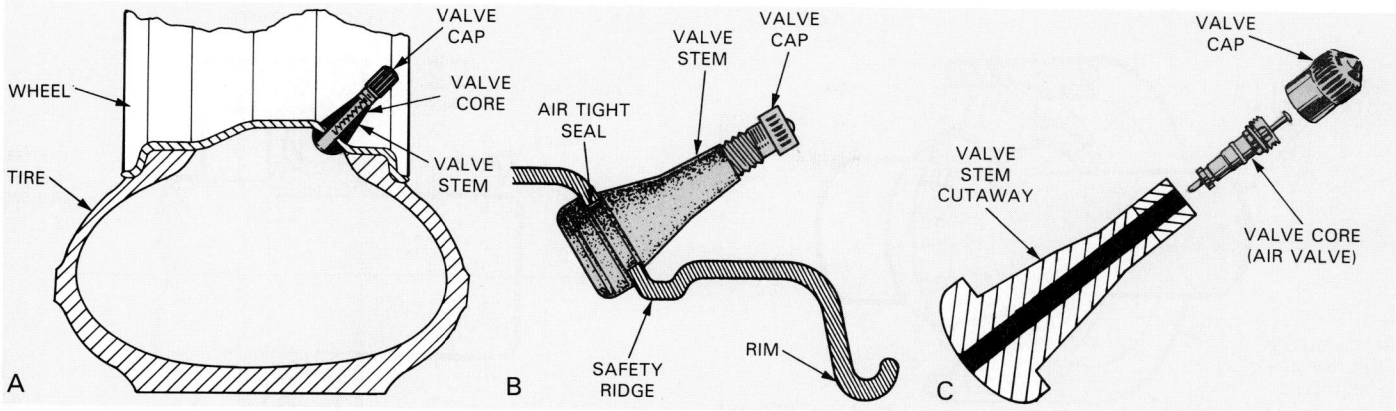

Fig. 62-15. A — Valve stem snaps into hole in wheel. B — Press fit between stem and wheel forms airtight seal. C — Valve core is air valve screwed into valve stem. Valve cap screws over end of stem. (Toyota)

the lug nut is tapered to help center the wheel on the hub. Refer to Fig. 62-16.

Lug studs are the special studs that accept the lug nuts. The studs are pressed through the back of the hub or axle flange. See Fig. 62-16.

Normally, the lug nuts and studs have right-hand threads (turn clockwise to tighten). When left-hand threads are used, the nut or stud will be marked with an "L." Metric threads will be identified with an "M" or the word "Metric."

A few cars use *lug bolts* instead of lug nuts. The bolts screw into threaded holes in the hub or axle flange.

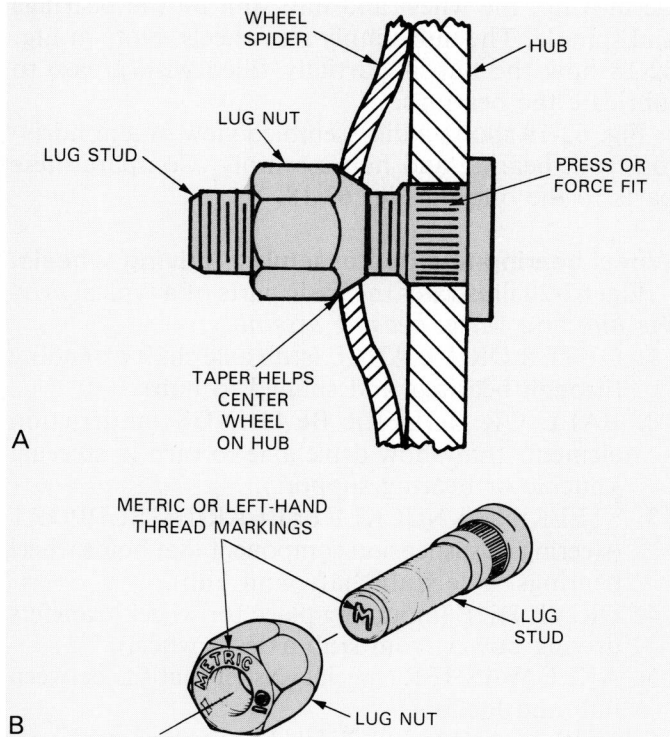

Fig. 62-16. A — Lug nut screws onto lug stud to secure wheel to hub. Tapered end of nut must contact and center the wheel. Stud presses into hub. B — If metric or if threads are left-hand, markings will normally be given on nut or stud. (Cadillac)

Wheel weights

Wheel weights are small lead weights attached to the wheel rim to balance the wheel-tire assembly and prevent vibration. The weights are used to offset a heavy area of the wheel and tire.

WHEEL BEARING AND HUB ASSEMBLY

Wheel bearings allow the wheel and tire to turn freely around the spindle, in the steering knuckle, or in the bearing support. Most wheel bearings are either tapered roller or ball bearing types, Fig. 62-17.

The wheel bearings are lubricated with heavy, high-temperature grease. This lets the elements (rollers or balls) operate with very little friction and wear.

The basic parts of a wheel bearing are:
1. OUTER RACE (cup or cone pressed into hub, steering knuckle, or bearing support).
2. BALLS OR ROLLERS (antifriction elements that fit between inner and outer races).
3. INNER RACE (cup or cone that rests on spindle or drive axle shaft).

There are two basic wheel bearing and hub designs: those for the nondriving wheels and those for driving wheels. For example, the front wheels on a rear-wheel drive car would be nondriving. However, the front wheels on a front-wheel drive car are the driving wheels (hubs transfer power to wheels and tires).

Wheel bearing and hub assembly (nondriving wheels)

A *wheel bearing and hub assembly* for a vehicle's NONDRIVING WHEELS would, typically, include the following, Fig. 62-18.
1. SPINDLE (stationary shaft extending outward from steering knuckle or suspension system).
2. WHEEL BEARINGS (usually tapered roller bearings mounted on spindle and in wheel hub).
3. HUB (outer housing that holds brake disc or drum, front wheel, grease, and wheel bearings).
4. GREASE SEAL (seal that prevents loss of lubri-

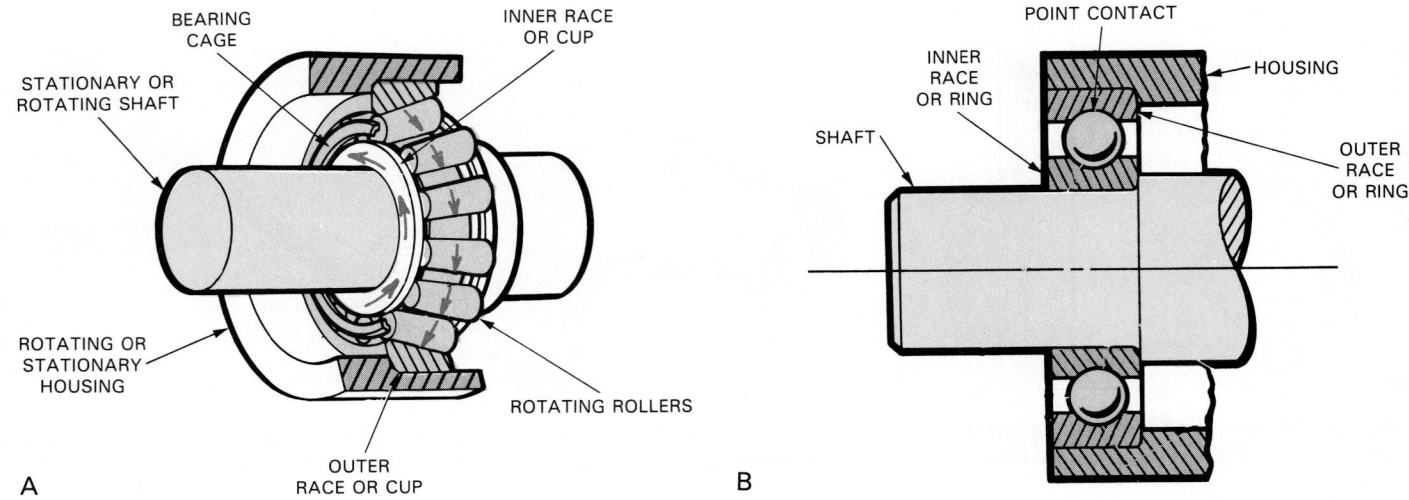

Fig. 62-17. Two basic wheel bearing configurations. A — Tapered roller bearing has cylinder shaped roller operating between inner and outer races. If shaft is stationary, bearing will allow outer housing or hub to turn. If outer bearing mount is stationary, shaft or axle can turn in bearing. B — Ball bearings are also used as wheel bearings, especially on front-wheel drive, front bearings or driving hub and bearing assemblies. Balls allow parts to rotate with a minimum amount of friction and wear. (Federal Mogul)

cant from inner end of spindle and hub).

5. SAFETY WASHER (flat washer that keeps outer wheel bearing from rubbing on and possibly turning adjusting nut).

6. SPINDLE ADJUSTING NUT (nut threaded on end of spindle for adjusting wheel bearing).

7. NUT LOCK (thin, slotted nut that fits over main spindle nut).

8. COTTER PIN (soft metal pin that fits through

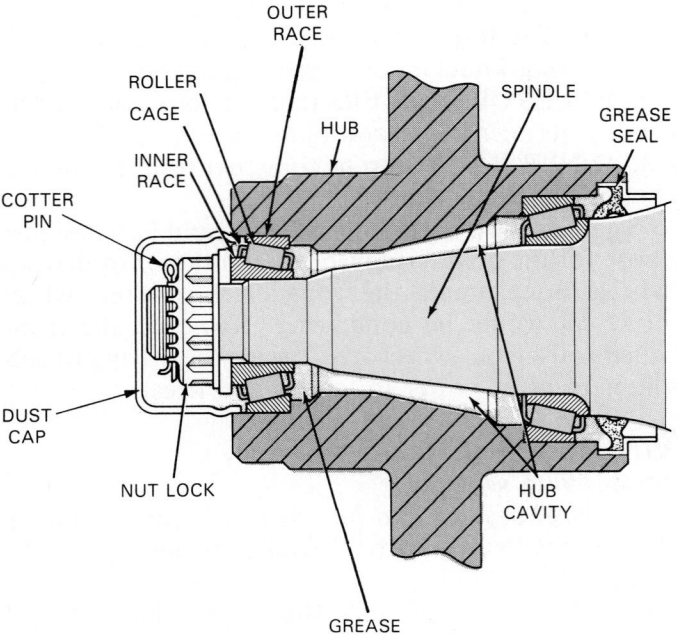

Fig. 62-18. Typical freewheeling or nondriving wheel bearing assembly for front or rear of car. Two tapered roller bearings allow hub and wheel to revolve around stationary spindle. Grease partially fills hub to lubricate bearings. Inner seal prevents loss of grease. Nut on end of spindle allows adjustment of bearing preload. (Chrysler)

hole in spindle, adjusting nut, and nut lock to keep adjusting nut from turning in service).

9. DUST CAP (metal cap that fits over outer end of hub to keep grease in and road dirt out of bearings).

Since this wheel bearing and hub assembly does NOT transfer driving power, the spindle is stationary. It simply extends outward and provides a mounting place for the wheel bearings, hub, and wheel. With the vehicle moving, the wheel and hub spin on the bearings and spindle. The hub simply freewheels. Note in Fig. 62-18 how the hub is partially filled with grease to lubricate the bearings.

Fig. 62-19 shows a disassembled view of a nondriving front bearing and hub assembly. Compare these parts to the ones in Fig. 62-18.

Wheel bearing and hub assembly (driving wheels)

Fig. 62-20 illustrates the basic parts of a typical *driving hub* and *wheel bearing assembly*:

1. OUTER DRIVE AXLE (stub axle shaft extending through bearings and splined to hub).

2. BALL OR ROLLER BEARINGS (antifriction elements that allow drive axle to turn in steering knuckle or bearing support).

3. STEERING KNUCKLE or BEARING SUPPORT (steering or suspension component that holds wheel bearings, axle stub shaft, and hub).

4. DRIVE HUB (mounting place for wheel, transfers driving power from stub axle to wheel).

5. AXLE WASHER (special washer that fits between hub and locknut).

6. HUB or AXLE LOCKNUT (nut that screws on end of drive axle stub shaft to secure hub and other parts of assembly).

7. GREASE SEAL (prevents lubricant loss between inside of axle and knuckle or bearing support).

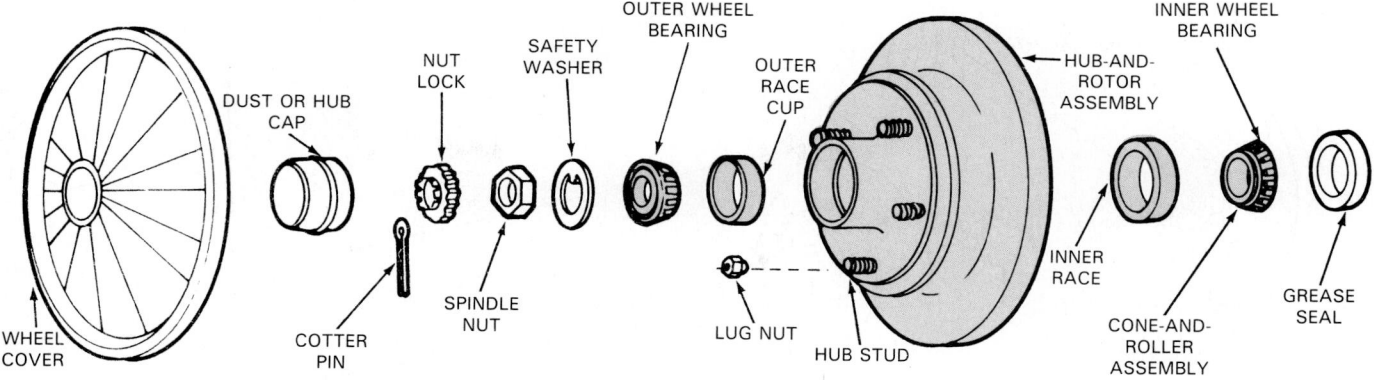

Fig. 62-19. Disassembled view of nondriving wheel bearing and hub assembly. Note names and relationship between parts. This type assembly can be used on front of rear-wheel drive car or rear of front-wheel drive car. (Florida Dept. of Voc. Ed.)

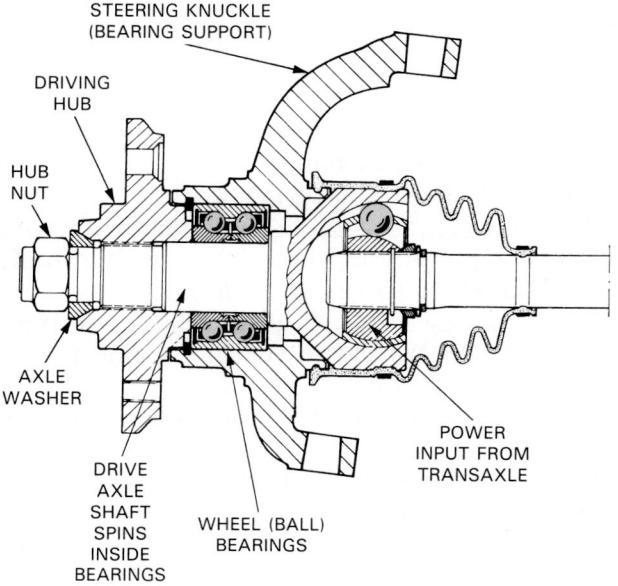

Fig. 62-20. Driving hub and wheel bearing assembly has bearings mounted in stationary steering knuckle or bearing support. Drive axle shaft fits through center of bearings. Hub is splined to axle shaft. Ball bearings are lubricated by thick, high temperature grease.

As you can see in Fig. 62-20, a wheel bearing and hub assembly for a driving axle is very different from a nondriving unit. Instead of a stationary spindle, the axle shaft spins inside a stationary support.

Fig. 62-21 shows an exploded view of a driving hub and bearing assembly. Compare them to Fig. 62-20.

Other hub and wheel bearing assemblies

A four-wheel drive hub and wheel bearing assembly is given in Fig. 62-22. Note that it has a driving axle extending through a stationary spindle. A special freewheel or locking hub transfers power from the axle to the hub-disc assembly.

A rear wheel bearing assembly for a front-wheel drive vehicle is almost identical to a front wheel bearing for a rear-wheel drive vehicle.

Modern vehicles use a wide variation of hub and wheel bearing assemblies. This is due to the increased use of front-wheel drive. When you want more information on a specific vehicle, always refer to the factory service manual. It will explain and illustrate the hub and wheel bearing assembly clearly. Most designs, however, will be similar.

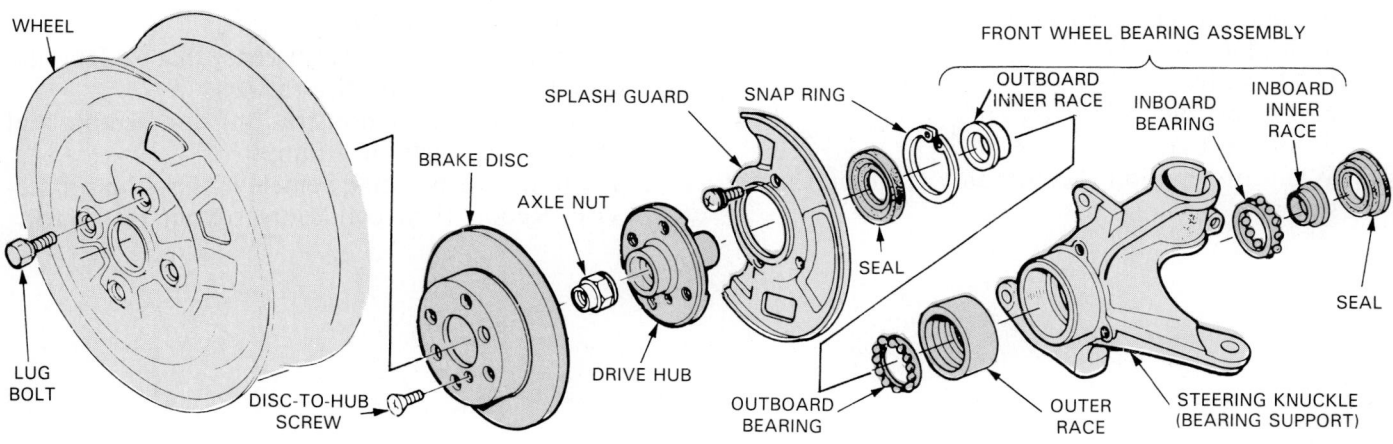

Fig. 62-21. Disassembled view of driving hub and wheel bearing assembly. Study names of parts. This type assembly is commonly used on front of front-wheel drive car. However, it can also be found on rear engine, rear-wheel drive sports cars. (Honda)

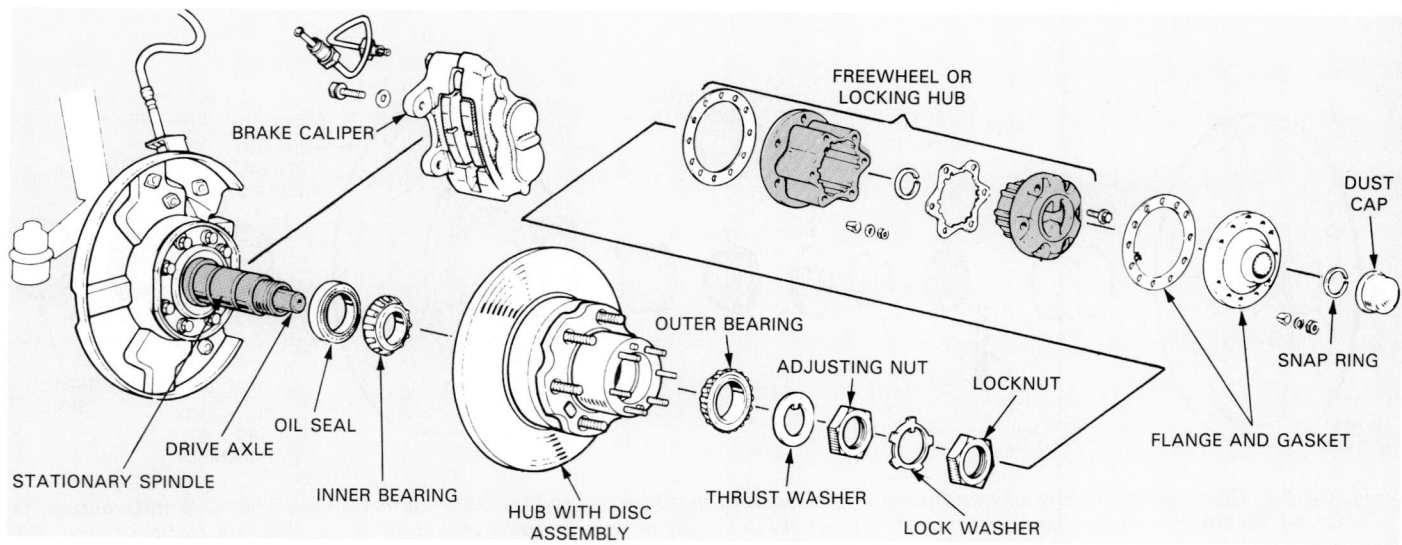

Fig. 62-22. Front hub and wheel bearing assembly for a four-wheel drive vehicle. Compare this unit to ones shown earlier. Note how drive axle sticks through stationary spindle. Freewheel or adjustable hub allows drive axle to be connected and disconnected from hub and wheel assembly for two- and four-wheel drive. (Toyota)

KNOW THESE TERMS

Tire bead, Tire ply, Tread, Sidewall, Belts, Liner, Pneumatic, Tubeless, Rolling resistance, Bias ply tire, Belted bias tire, Radial tire, Tire markings, Aspect ratio, Load rating, Inflation pressure, DOT number, Wear bar, Compact spare, Self-sealing tire, Retreads, Safety rim, Valve stem, Valve core, Lug nut, Lug stud, Wheel weight, Wheel bearing, Driving hub, Nondriving hub, Spindle, Hub, Grease seal, Safety washer, Spindle adjusting nut, Nut lock, Cotter pin, Dust cap.

REVIEW QUESTIONS

1. What are the two basic functions of a tire?
2. List and explain the six major parts of a tire.
3. Car tires are _____ which means that they are filled with air.
4. Tire _____ _____ is a measurement of the amount of friction produced as the tire operates on the road surface.
5. This is NOT a type of tire commonly used on modern passenger cars.
   a. Radial.
   b. Bias ply.
   c. Lateral ply.
   d. Belted bias.
6. What information is commonly given on the tire sidewall?
7. A typical tire inflation pressure would be 22 psi (152 kPa). True or False?
8. How does a self-sealing tire work?
9. A _____ _____ has small ridges that hold the tire on the wheel during a "blow-out."
10. Explain why a valve core is needed.
11. _____ _____ are attached to the rim to balance the wheel-tire assembly and prevent vibration.
12. Name and describe the basic parts of a wheel bearing.
13. List and explain the nine basic parts of a nondriving hub assembly.
14. List and explain the seven basic parts of a driving hub assembly.
15. A driving hub and a nondriving hub are almost identical. True or False?

ACTIVITIES FOR CHAPTER 62

1. Using a section of an old, worn tire, prepare a cutaway teaching aid showing the different parts and layers of the tire.
2. Prepare an overhead transparency that explains tire and wheel sizes and tire ratings.
3. As a classroom demonstration, disassemble and identify the parts of a hub.
4. Examine the tires on a vehicle in the shop for service. Report their condition to your instructor.

63

Tire, Wheel, and Wheel Bearing Service

After studying this chapter, you will be able to:
□ Diagnose common tire, wheel, and wheel bearing problems.
□ Describe tire inflation and rotation procedures.
□ Measure tire and wheel runout.
□ Explain static and dynamic wheel balance.
□ Summarize different methods of balancing wheels and tires.
□ Explain service procedures for wheel bearings.
□ Use safe practices while servicing tires and wheels.

The information in this chapter will prepare you for the material given in later textbook chapters. For instance, you may need to remove the front wheels or adjust wheel bearings when servicing brake, steering, or suspension systems. Knowledge of wheels and tires is also needed when doing a front end alignment.

TIRE, WHEEL, WHEEL BEARING DIAGNOSIS

Tire problems usually show up as vibration, abnormal tread wear patterns, steering wheel pull, abnormal noises, and other similar symptoms. In some cases, you may need to test drive the car to verify the customer complaint. Make sure the symptoms are NOT being caused by steering, suspension, or front wheel alignment problems.

Closely inspect the tires, Fig. 63-1. Check for bulges, splits, cracks, chunking, cupping of the tread, and other signs of abnormal wear or damage. Look closely at the outer sidewall, tread area, and inner sidewall. If problems are found, determine what caused the failure before replacement or repair.

Tire impact damage

Tire impact damage, also termed *road damage,* includes punctures, cuts, tears, and other physical tire injuries. Some are illustrated in Fig. 63-2. Depending upon the severity of the damage, you must either repair or replace the tire.

Fig. 63-1. Tire service normally begins with thorough inspection. Look for damage and wear all around surfaces of tire. Rotate and wiggle tire to check for dry, rough, or loose wheel bearings. (Moog)

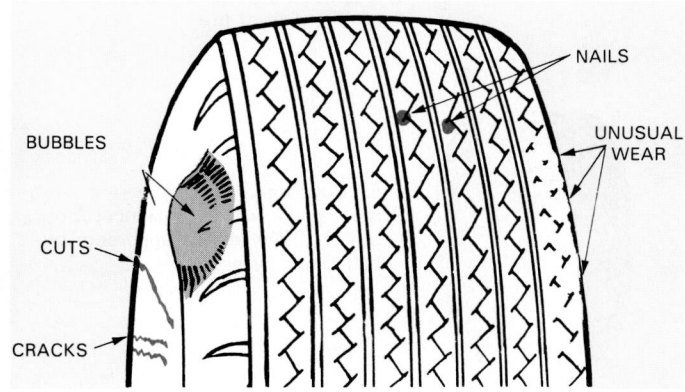

Fig. 63-2. These are some typical types of damage found on used tires. (Florida Dept. of Voc. Ed.)

Tire wear patterns

A *tire wear pattern* (area of tread worn OFF) can usually be studied to determine the cause of the abnormal wear. Look at Fig. 63-3. Improper tire inflation, ply separation, incorrect front wheel alignment, lack of periodic tire rotation, and an out-of-balance condition can cause excessive tire wear. By carefully inspecting the tire tread, a technician can determine what parts should be serviced or repaired.

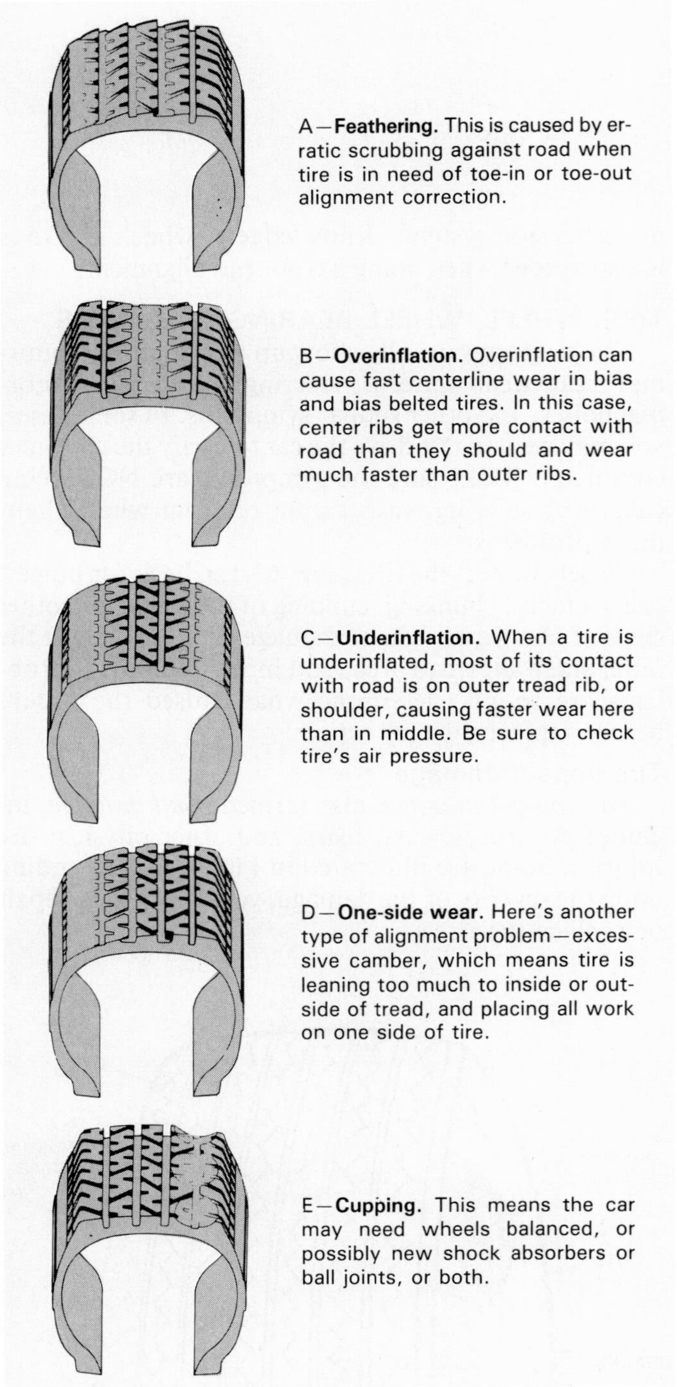

A—**Feathering**. This is caused by erratic scrubbing against road when tire is in need of toe-in or toe-out alignment correction.

B—**Overinflation**. Overinflation can cause fast centerline wear in bias and bias belted tires. In this case, center ribs get more contact with road than they should and wear much faster than outer ribs.

C—**Underinflation**. When a tire is underinflated, most of its contact with road is on outer tread rib, or shoulder, causing faster wear here than in middle. Be sure to check tire's air pressure.

D—**One-side wear**. Here's another type of alignment problem—excessive camber, which means tire is leaning too much to inside or outside of tread, and placing all work on one side of tire.

E—**Cupping**. This means the car may need wheels balanced, or possibly new shock absorbers or ball joints, or both.

Fig. 63-3. Tire tread wear patterns will tell you about cause of rapid or abnormal wear. Study patterns and causes. (Goodyear)

Note! Chapter 70, Front Wheel Alignment, has more information on tire wear patterns.

Tire inflation problems

Correct tire inflation pressure is very important to the service life of a tire. Proper inflation is needed so the full tire tread contacts the road, Fig. 63-4.

Tire underinflation (low air pressure) is a very common and destructive problem that wears the outer corners of the tread. The low pressure allows the tire sidewalls to flex, building up heat during operation. The center of the tread flexes upward and does NOT wear, Fig. 63-4A.

Underinflation can cause rapid tread wear, loss of fuel economy and possibly, ply separation (plies tear away from each other). It will cause the tire sidewalls to bulge outward near the road surface.

Tire overinflation (too much air pressure) causes the center area of the tread to wear. Illustrated in Fig. 63-4B, the high pressure causes the body of the tire to stretch outward. This pushes the center of the tread against the road surface, but lifts the outer edges of the tread OFF the road.

An overinflated tire will produce a very rough or hard ride. It will also be more prone to impact damage. With practice, you can usually detect overinflation by pressing in on the tire sidewall with your thumb. It will feel too hard.

Proper tire inflation makes the full tread area of the tire touch the road, Fig. 63-4C. The tire will wear evenly across the tread. This increases tire life and improves handling and safety.

Steering wheel pull can be caused by uneven tire in-

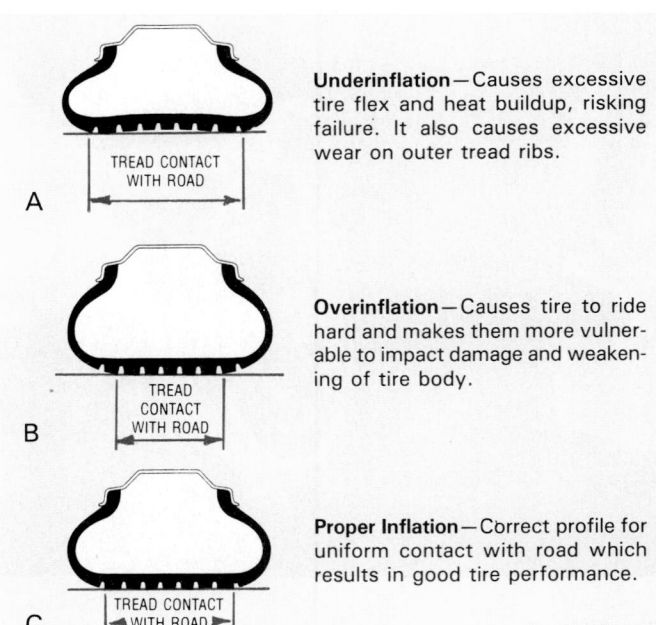

Underinflation—Causes excessive tire flex and heat buildup, risking failure. It also causes excessive wear on outer tread ribs.

Overinflation—Causes tire to ride hard and makes them more vulnerable to impact damage and weakening of tire body.

Proper Inflation—Correct profile for uniform contact with road which results in good tire performance.

Fig. 63-4. Tire inflation pressure is critical to tire life, vehicle handling, and ride.

flation. For example, if the left front tire (driver's side) is underinflated and the right tire is properly inflated, the car may pull to the left. The tire with low air pressure will have more rolling resistance. It will tend to pull the steering wheel away from the normally inflated tire.

Tire vibration problems

Tire vibration is commonly caused by an out-of-balance condition, ply separation, tire runout, a bent wheel, or tire cupping wear. Refer to Fig. 63-5.

When one of the FRONT tires is vibrating, it can usually be felt in the STEERING WHEEL. When one of the REAR tires is vibrating, the vibration will be felt more in the CENTER and REAR of the car.

Tire and wheel bearing noise

Tire noise usually shows up as a thumping sound caused by ply separation or as a whine due to abnormal tread wear (cupping for example). Inspect the tire for an out-of-round condition or tread cupping. Tire replacement is needed to correct these problems.

Wheel bearing noise is normally produced by a dry, worn wheel bearing. The bearing will make a steady humming type sound. The balls or rollers are damaged from lack of lubrication and are no longer smooth. The weight of the car pressing down on the chipped, pitted bearings emits a noticable hum or growl.

To check for a worn or loose wheel bearing, raise and secure the vehicle. As shown in Fig. 63-1, rotate the tire by hand. Feel and listen carefully for bearing roughness. Also, wiggle the tire back and forth to check for bearing looseness. You may have to disassemble the wheel bearing to verify the problem.

WHEEL COVER REMOVAL AND INSTALLATION

A *wheel cover* is the large metal or plastic decorative cover for the wheel. It press fits over the wheel rim to hide the lug nuts, dust cap, and other less attractive parts. To remove the cover, use the pointed end of lug wrench or a large screwdriver. Working carefully, pry at four alternating points between the wheel and cover as shown in Fig. 63-6A.

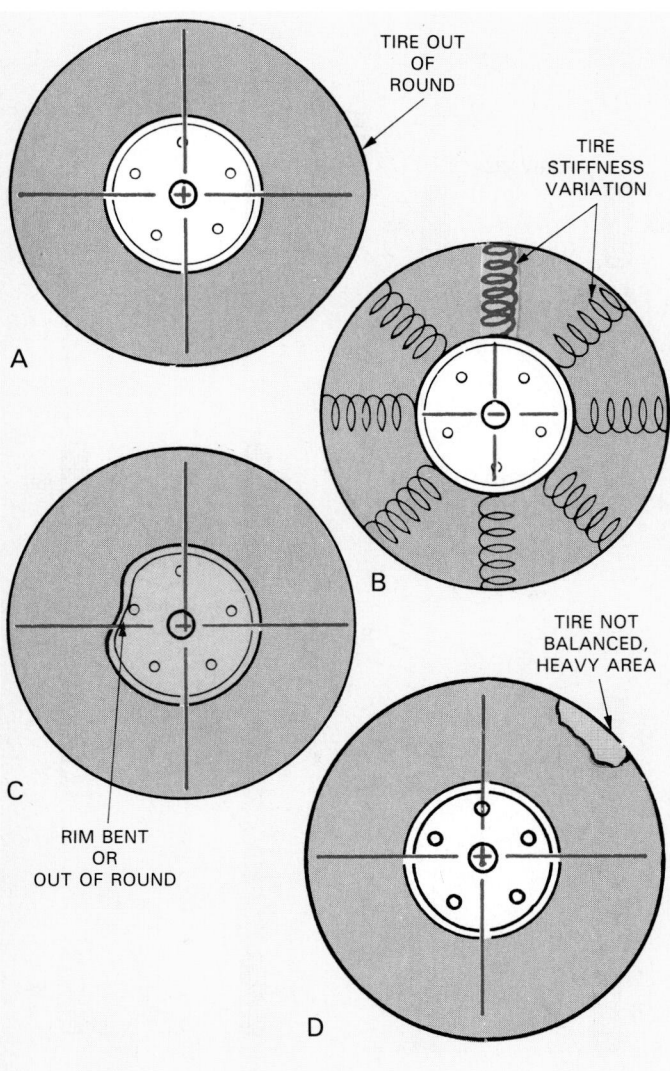

Fig. 63-5. Four common causes of tire-related vibration: A— Tire runout. B—Stiffness variation in rubber. C—Bent rim or rim runout. D—Wheel-tire assembly not balanced. (Buick)

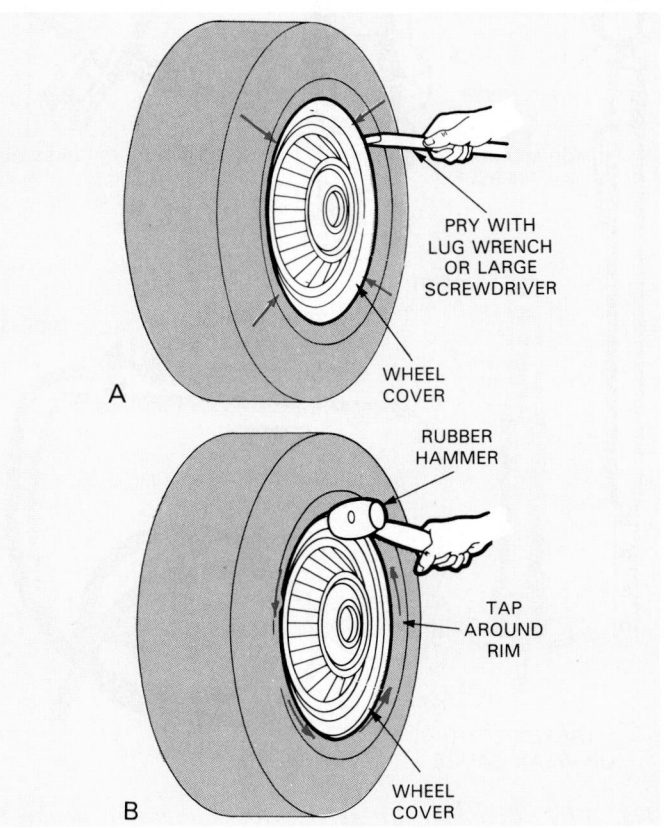

Fig. 63-6. A—Pry off wheel cover carefully, working from side to side as shown by colored arrows. B—Use rubber hammer and an alternating or circular tapping motion to reinstall. (Florida Dept. of Voc. Ed.)

Tire, Wheel, Bearing Service 813

To install a wheel cover, use a rubber hammer. Hold the wheel cover snugly in place with the valve stem aligned and sticking through the cover. Tap in a circular or alternating pattern, as in Fig. 63-6B.

Be careful not to drop, bend, or dent wheel covers during removal or installation. They are very thin and can be easily damaged.

TIRE MAINTENANCE

Tire maintenance involves periodic inspection, checking of inflation pressure, and rotation. These preventive maintenance steps will help assure vehicle safety and longer tire life.

Checking tire inflation pressure

A *tire pressure gauge* is used to measure tire inflation pressure, Fig. 63-7. With the valve stem cap removed, press the tire gauge squarely over the stem. Then, read the air pressure given on the gauge. Compare your reading to the recommended maximum tire pressure printed on the sidewall. If tire is low, add air. If high, press in on the valve core stem to release air pressure. Inflate the tire to manufacturer's recommendations.

Note! Most tire manufactures recommend COLD INFLATION PRESSURE 1 to 3 psi (21 kPa) below the maximum listed air pressure. This allows for tire heating, air expansion, and pressure increase without exceeding maximum pressure limits.

Rotating tires

Tire rotation is also needed to assure maximum tire service life. Normally, the front or rear tires may wear differently. Rotation is used to EVEN OUT tire wear and to prevent premature failure of any one tire. Generally, tires should be rotated at intervals suggested by the tire manufacturer (typically every 3000 miles or 4 827 km) or sooner if irregular wear develops.

Fig. 63-8 shows the tire rotation patterns for bias

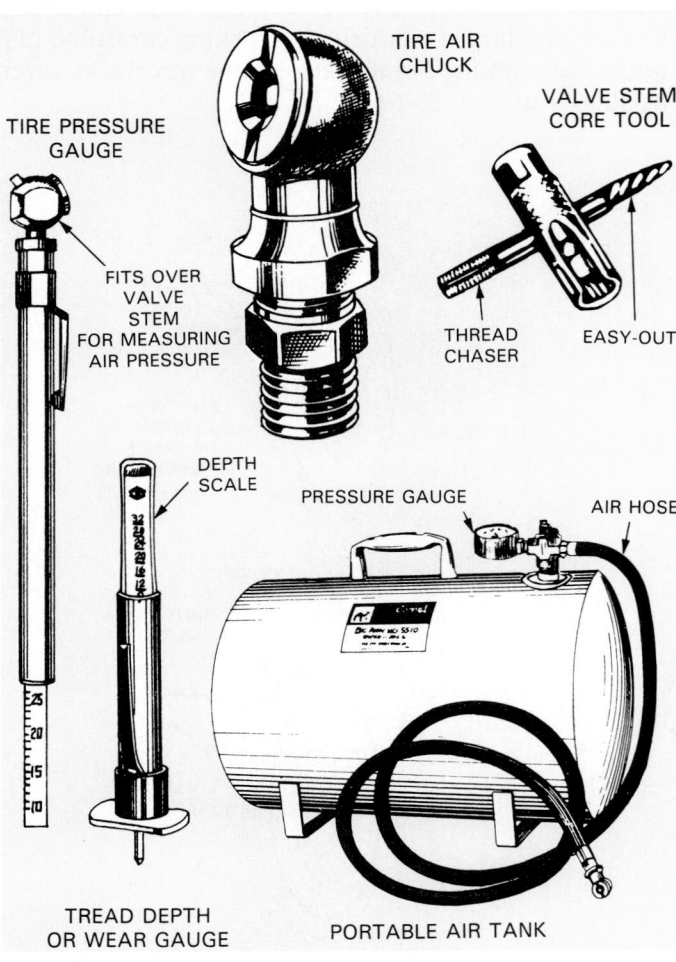

Fig. 63-7. Common tire service tools: Pressure gauge to measure tire inflation. Depth gauge will accurately check tread depth and wear. Tire air chuck for filling tire with air. Portable air tank for filling car tire in remote areas. Core tool for removing and installing core in valve stem.
(Camel and Snap-On)

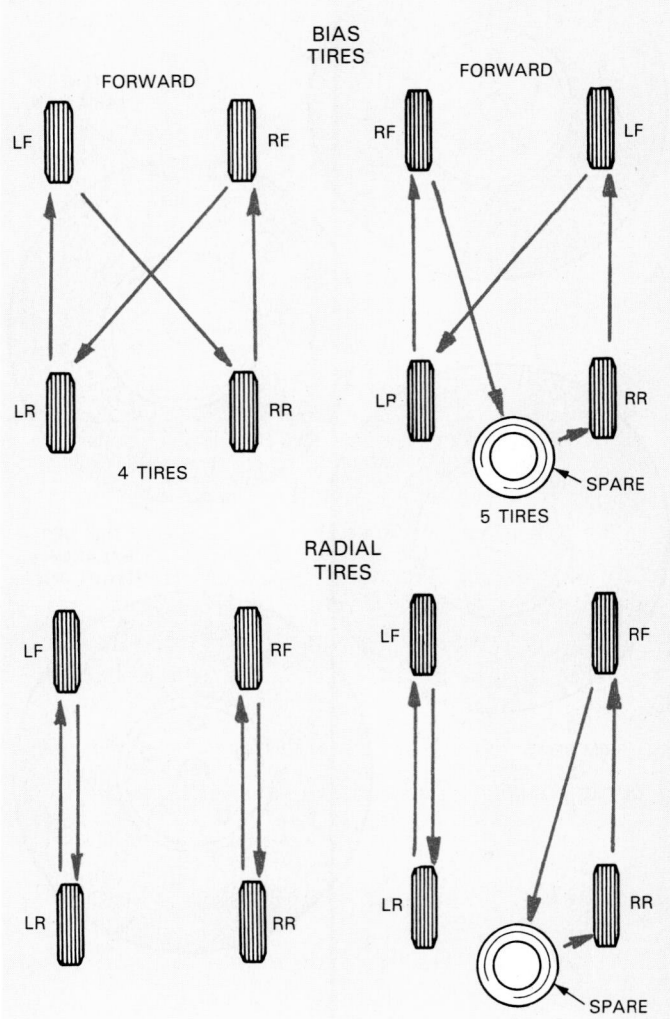

Fig. 63-8. Study typical recommendations for rotating both radial and bias tires. Do not change sides with radials! (Dodge)

and radial tires. Note that bias and radial tires have different patterns. BIAS TIRES USE AN X-TYPE (cross rotation) pattern. RADIAL TIRES often require a front-to-rear and rear-to-front rotation pattern.

Torquing lug nuts

Lug nut torque is very important, especially with many new cars using mag wheels and lightweight hubs. Overtorquing can cause wheel or hub distortion, runout, and vibration. Undertorquing might allow the lug nuts to loosen, with loss of a wheel.

Auto makers suggest that lug nuts are tightened to specs with a torque wrench. Tighten the nuts in a crisscross pattern, as in Fig. 63-9.

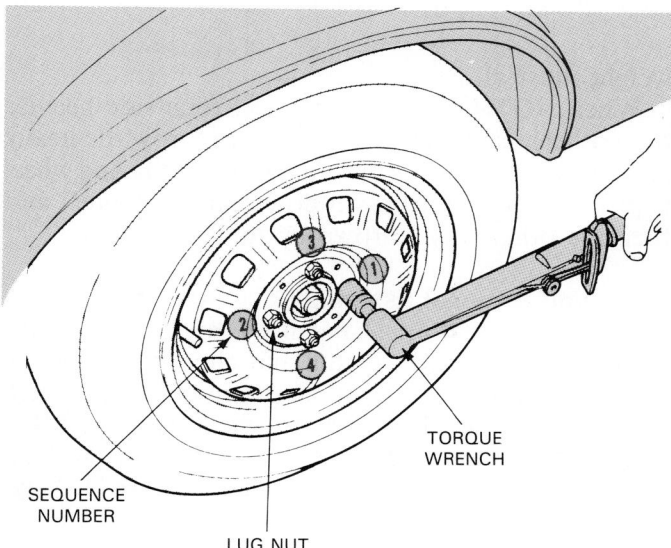

Fig. 63-9. Use a torque wrench to tighten lug nuts to specs in crisscross pattern. Modern lightweight wheels and hubs require exact lug nut torque. (Dodge)

Replacing lug studs

Lug studs can become stripped or damaged. To replace them, drive out the old stud with a special pressing tool or a hydraulic press, Fig. 63-10. Do not hammer the studs out because it could damage the wheel bearing.

To install the new stud, use flat washers and a lug nut. You can usually draw the new stud into place by tightening the nut on the washers. Double-check that the stud is fully seated before installing the wheel.

MEASURING TIRE AND WHEEL RUNOUT

Tire runout or wobble is caused by a faulty tire (ply separation or manufacturing defect).

Wheel runout or wobble is caused by impact damage or incorrect welding of the spider and rim.

When you suspect a minor runout problem, use a

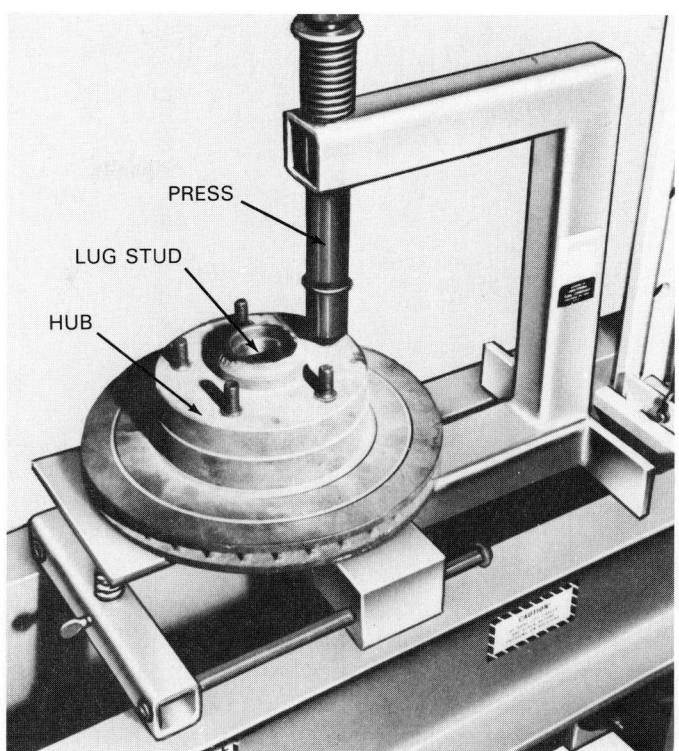

Fig. 63-10. If lugs are damaged, press them out and press in new ones. C-clamp type on-car pressing tools are also available. (Owatonna Tool Co.)

dial indicator to measure tire and wheel runout.

Lateral runout is side-to-side movement. It is measured by placing a dial indicator against the side of the rim or on the tire sidewall. See Fig. 63-11A. A special indicator with a small wheel or roller is commonly used. The tire is turned by hand while the technician notes the indicator reading.

Radial runout is caused by a difference in diameter from the center axis of rotation. It is measured by placing the dial indicator on the tire tread and on the inner part of the rim. This is illustrated in Fig. 63-11B. Again, the tire is turned by hand while noting the indicator reading.

Compare your dial indicator readings to specs. If either lateral or radial runout is beyond specs, replace the wheel or tire.

Note! Sometimes, it is possible to reduce tire runout by rotating the tire 180 deg. on the wheel.

Typically, tire radial runout should NOT exceed .060 in. (1.5 mm). Tire lateral runout should be under .090 in. (2.0 mm). Wheel radial runout should NOT be over .035 in. (0.9 mm). Wheel lateral runout should NOT exceed .045 in. (1.0 mm). However, always refer to exact specs before condemning a wheel or tire.

WHEEL BALANCE

Improper wheel balance is one of the most common causes of tire vibration. When one side of the tire is

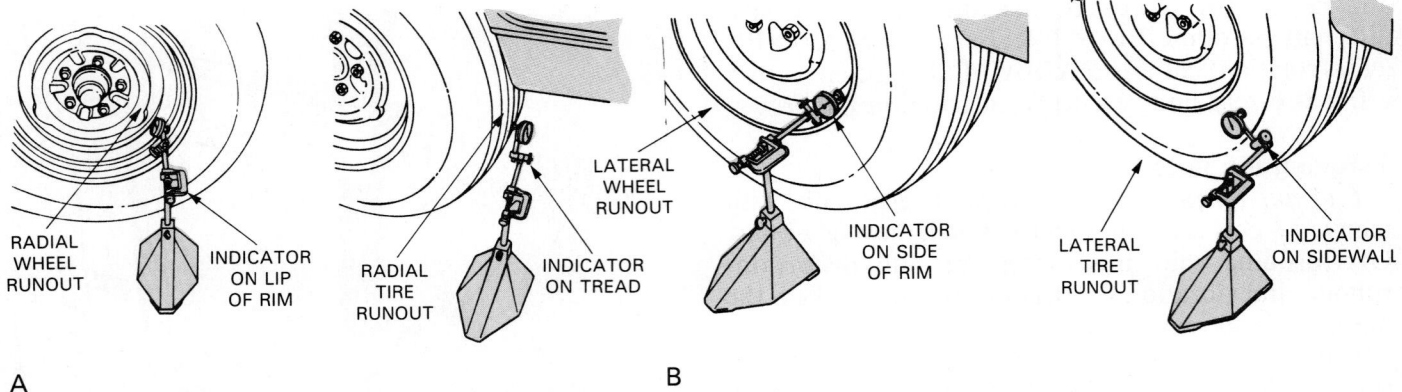

Fig. 63-11. Using dial indicator and large base to measure tire and wheel runout (wobble). A — To measure radial runout or out-of-round, mount indicator on tread and wheel inner lip as shown. Turn tire by hand and read indicator. B — To measure lateral or side-to-side runout, mount indicator on tire sidewall and side of rim. Rotate tire and make reading. (Chrysler)

heavier than the other, centrifugal force tries to throw the heavy area outward during operation. There are two types of tire imbalance: static imbalance and dynamic imbalance.

Static imbalance, called WHEEL TRAMP or HOP, causes the tire to vibrate up and down. See Fig. 63-12A. For a wheel and tire assembly to be in static balance, the weight must be evenly distributed around the axis of rotation.

Dynamic imbalance makes the tire vibrate up and down and from side to side. It causes WHEEL HOP (up and down movement) and WHEEL SHIMMY (side to side movement), Fig. 63-12B. To be in dynamic balance, the top-to-bottom weight and side to side weight must all be equal.

When NOT in dynamic balance (one side heavier than other), centrifugal force tries to throw the heavy area outward and inward. As a result, the tire and wheel is pushed one way (thrown down and to center) and then the other way (thrown up and to center).

Balancing a wheel assembly

A wheel assembly is balanced by adding *wheel weights* (special lead weights that clip on rim) to the side opposite the heavy area. Shown in Fig. 63-13, there are various types and sizes of wheel weights. Most press-fit onto the wheel. Weights for some mag wheels, however, stick onto the wheel with an adhesive backing.

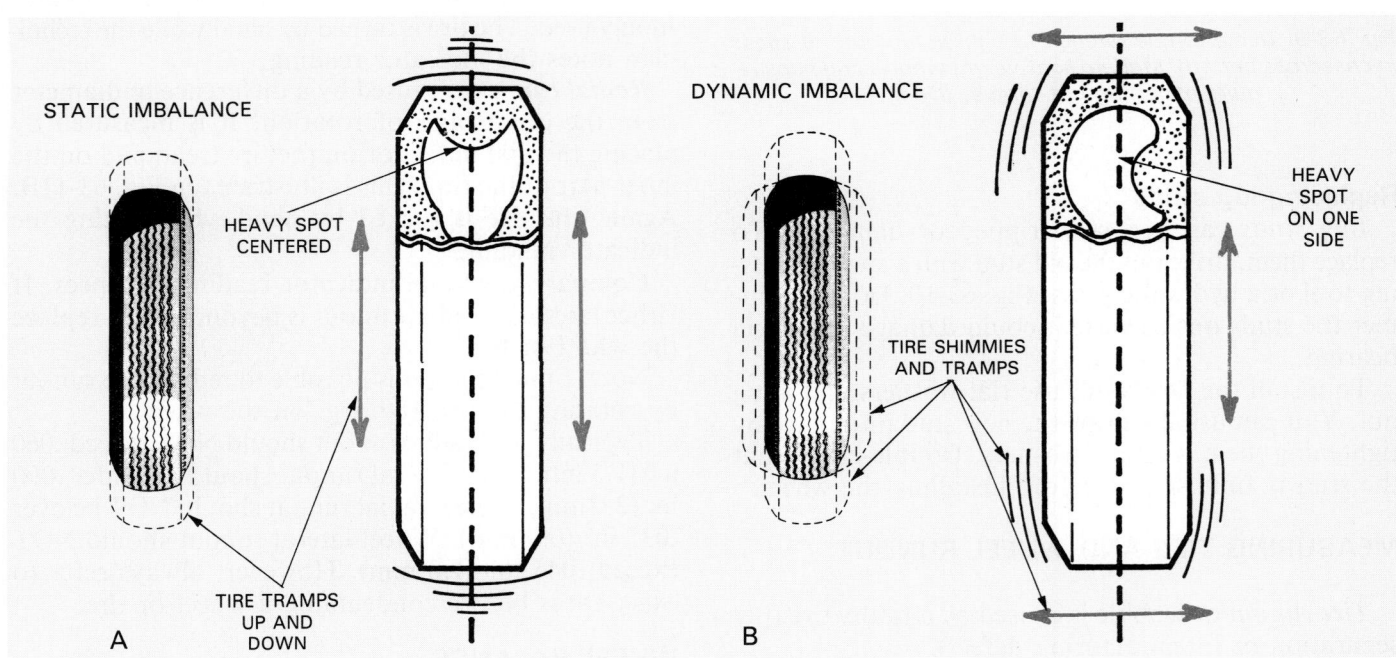

Fig. 63-12. Static and dynamic imbalance are common causes of vibration. A — Static imbalance will cause tire to vibrate up and down. A heavy spot is located in center of tire tread. B — Dynamic imbalance will make tire vibrate from side to side and up and down. Heavy spot on tire is to one side or on sidewall.

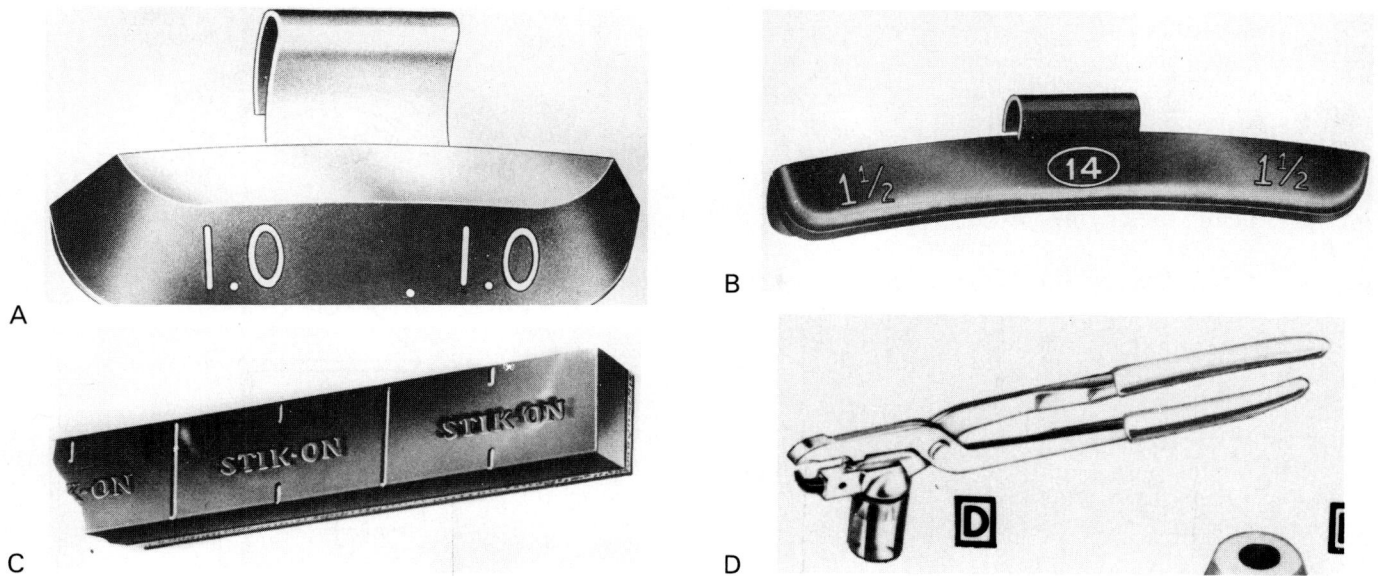

Fig. 63-13. Wheel weights are used to counteract heavy area on wheel-tire assembly. A — One ounce wheel weight. B — One and one-half ounce wheel weight. C — Stick-on wheel weight for mag wheels. D — Wheel weight tool for removing and installing wheel weights. (Speed clip and Snap-On)

To static balance a wheel and tire, add wheel weights opposite the heavy area of the wheel. Look at Fig. 63-14A. If a large amount of weight is needed, add half to the inside and the other half to the outside of the wheel. This helps keep dynamic balance correct.

To dynamically balance a wheel and tire, you must add weights exactly where needed, Fig. 63-14B.

DANGER! When balancing a wheel assembly,

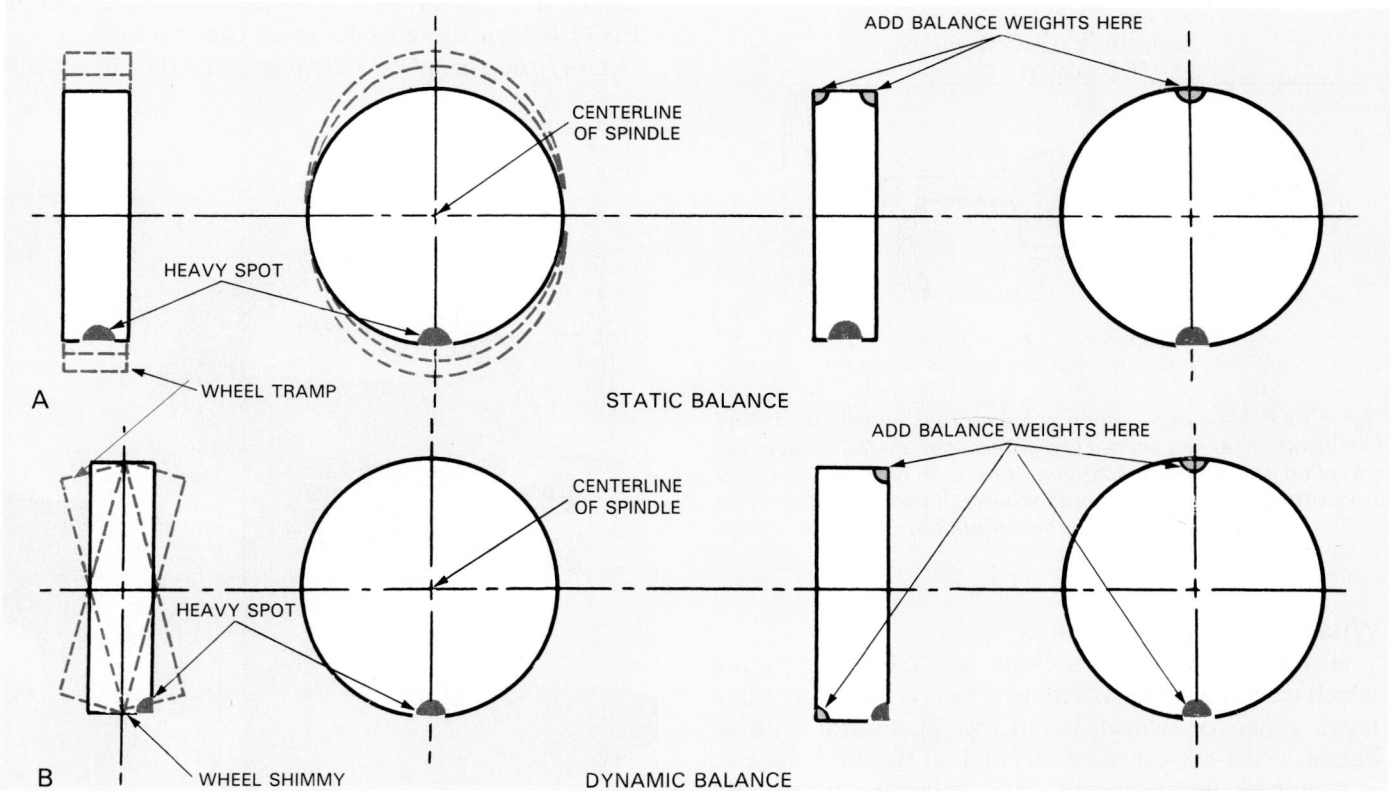

Fig. 63-14. Basic procedure for correcting static and dynamic balance problems. A — Static balance will cause wheel tramp. Add weight opposite heavy area on both sides of wheel. Each weight should be half as heavy as heavy spot on tire. B — Dynamic imbalance will cause wheel shimmy. Add weight in two locations as shown to counteract heavy area. (Buick)

follow these safety rules:

1. Wear eye protection when spinning the wheel and tire assembly.
2. Pick rocks and other debris from tire tread.
3. Place a jack stand under the vehicle when balancing.
4. When using the engine to spin the rear wheels, do NOT exceed 25 to 35 mph (40 to 56 km/h) on the speedometer. When one wheel is on the ground, the free wheel will spin at TWICE NORMAL SPEED. If the speedometer reads 60 mph, the tire will be spinning at a VERY DANGEROUS 120 mph (193 km/h).
4. With a limited slip differential, raise both rear wheels off of the ground when balancing. Refer to Fig. 63-15.
5. Follow the operating instructions provided with the wheel balancing equipment. Machine designs vary and so do operating procedures.

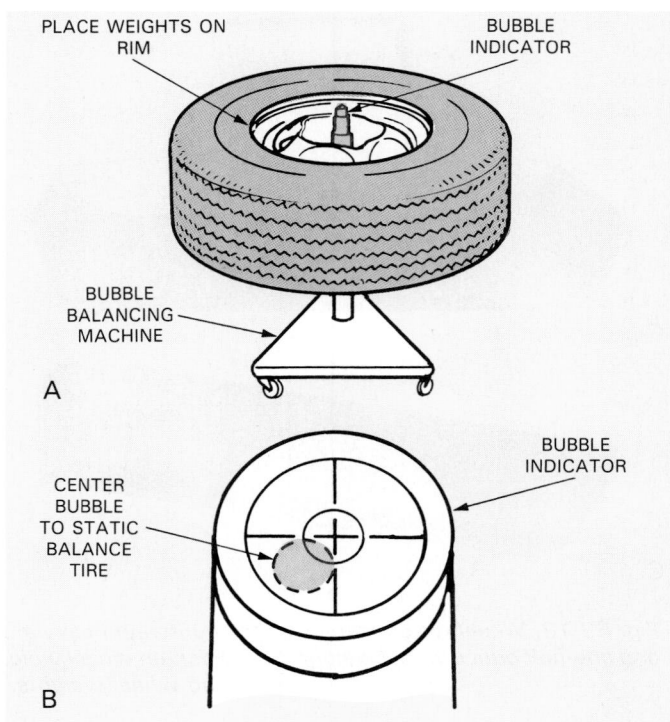

Fig. 63-16. Bubble balancer will correct static imbalance only. A — Tire is mounted on bubble balancer as shown. B — Use balancer instructions to place weights on wheel until bubble centers in circle on balancer head. (Ammco)

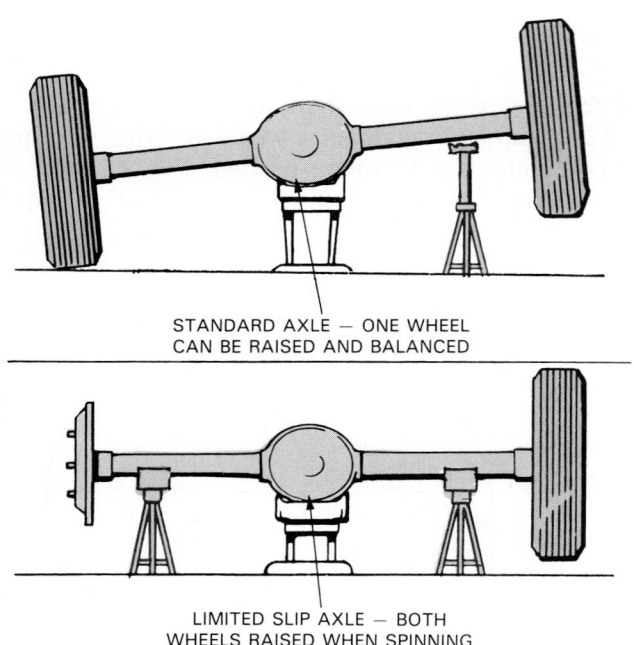

Fig. 63-15. Be careful when spinning rear wheels for wheel balancing. If car has limited slip differential, do NOT leave one wheel on ground while spinning other with engine. Car could drive off jack stands. Raise both wheels. Remove one tire while balancing other. (Pontiac)

Wheel balancing machines

A *wheel balancing machine* is used to determine which part of a wheel assembly is heavy. There are three basic types of wheel balancing machines: bubble balancer, off-the-car balancer, and on-the-car balancer.

A *bubble balancer* will static balance a wheel and tire. One is illustrated in Fig. 63-16. The wheel and tire must be removed from the car and placed on the balancer. An indicating bubble on the machine is then used to locate the heavy area of the assembly. Wheel weights are added to the wheel until the bubble CENTERS on the crosshairs of the machine.

An *off-the-car wheel balancer* can either be a static

Fig. 63-17. Off-car wheel balancer is very common. This unit will correct both static and dynamic imbalance. Always use safety guard when spinning tire. (Hunter)

or dynamic type machine. Look at Fig. 63-17. The wheel and tire assembly is mounted on the balancer and spun. The machine will detect vibration of the assembly and indicate where wheel weights should be added. After adding weights, spin the tire again to check for vibration.

An *on-the-car wheel balancer* may also be a static or dynamic type. An electric motor is used to spin the wheel and tire assembly. Either an electronic pick-up unit or a hand-operated device is used to determine where wheel weights are needed, Fig. 63-18.

An on-the-car balancer is sometimes desirable because it can balance the wheel cover, brake disc, and lug nuts along with the tire and wheel. Everything is rotated and balanced as a unit.

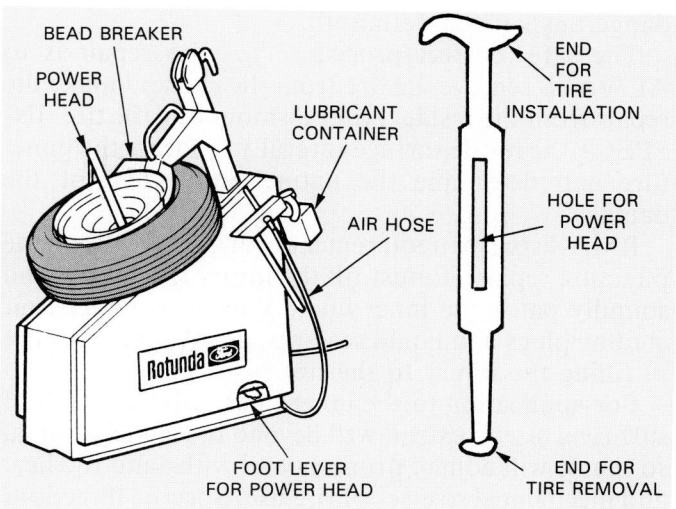

Fig. 63-19. Modern tire changers use air pressure to force tire on and off wheel. Again, follow all safety rules provided with equipment instructions. Bar is mounted on power head. Head turns bar to force beads over rim. (Ford)

Fig. 63-18. This on-car balancer is good because it will balance wheel, tire, hub, and even wheel cover. Some heavy wheel covers can cause vibration if not balanced. Note large power unit for spinning front tires. Always use specific operation instructions provided with equipment. Procedures vary. (Hunter)

MOUNTING AND DISMOUNTING TIRES

When mounting or dismounting a tire on its wheel, a *tire changing machine* is used to force the tire on and off the wheel. One make of tire changer is illustrated in Fig. 63-19. Note the basic parts of the machine.

The bead breaker is used first to force the tire bead away from the wheel rim. Then, a special bar is attached to the drive head. The head turns the bar and pries the bead over and off the rim. The other end of the bar is used when installing the tire on the wheel.

A few rules to follow when mounting or dismounting tires are:
1. Wear eye protection and remove the valve core before breaking the bead away from the wheel.
2. Keep your fingers out of the way.

3. Never mount a tire on a rim that is NOT smooth and clean.
4. Always lubricate the tire beads and wheel flange with proper lubricant (vegetable oil-soap solution) before mounting. NEVER use antifreeze, motor oil, or other nondrying petroleum-based substances or tire deterioration or movement on the wheel may result.
5. Do NOT inflate a tire when it is lying on the floor. When the beads seat, the tire could fly dangerously into the air.
6. Stand away from the tire when adding air after mounting. Usually, a loud "pop" sound will be made when the beads seat.
7. Do NOT exceed over 40 to 50 psi (276 to 345 kPa) when inflating.
8. After initial inflation, install the core and reduce tire pressure to recommended limits.

TIRE PUNCTURE REPAIR

To find the leak, fill the tire with air. Then, place the tire in a drum full of water or wet the tire down with a hose. Look for air bubbles forming on the tire. The air bubbles indicate a leak. Mark the puncture with a crayon or chalk.

Practice in past years was to attempt repair of some punctures without dismounting the tire, through the use of a rubber plug. This is NO LONGER RECOMMENDED, because of serious safety concerns.

According to the Rubber Manufacturer's Association (RMA), using a plug to attempt tire repair without dismounting is effective only 80 percent of the time. The remaining 20 percent of such repairs will result in TIRE FAILURE, which may take the form of a dangerous sudden deflation.

The safe, correct procedure for tire repair is to ALWAYS remove the tire from the rim and make the repair from the inside. After dismounting the tire, INSPECT the inside surface carefully to locate the puncture and determine the nature and extent of the damage.

RMA lists two requirements for a correctly made puncture repair: it must fill the injury to the tire, and soundly patch the inner liner. Various products, including plugs and liquid sealants, are available for use in filling the injury to the tire.

For application to the inner liner, select a patch of sufficient size to extend well beyond the damaged area, so that it will adhere properly and withstand the heat and mechanical stresses of tire use. Specific directions for patch application are supplied with the patching kit. The general procedure is to scuff (roughen) the area that the patch will cover, so that it will adhere tightly. Next, apply the proper cement (adhesive), following kit directions. Remove the covering from the adhesive side of the patch and carefully place it on the inner liner. As shown in Fig. 63-20, a tool called a stitcher is used to tightly bond the patch to the inner liner.

A few basic rules for tubeless tire repair are:

1. Do NOT attempt to repair a puncture by plugging it from the outside. Always dismount the tire and patch the inner liner.
2. Do NOT attempt to repair sidewalls or tires with punctures larger than 1/2 in. (13 mm).
3. When removing an object from the tire, reduce air pressure to at least 15 psi (103 kPa).
4. Broken strands in steel belted tires may indicate more serious damage than might be suspected. Also, the broken strands could possibly repuncture the patch or plug causing a serious tire failure.

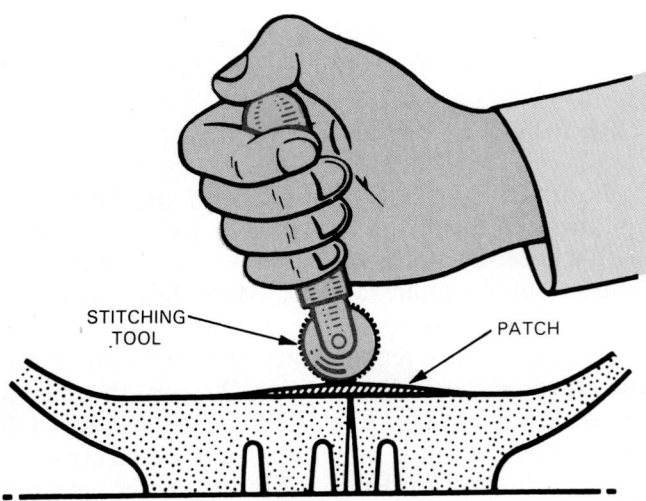

Fig. 63-20. Patch on inside of tire is needed for larger cuts. Basically, scuff area around cut. Apply coat of approved cement. Remove cover from patch and apply over cut. Use stitcher to adhere patch to tire liner. (Renault)

5. Follow the exact procedures given with the tire repair kit.

WHEEL BEARING SERVICE

Wheel bearings are normally filled with grease. If this grease dries out, the bearing will fail. It is wise to check wheel bearings for wear when performing wheel and tire-related service. Some wheel bearings can be disassembled and packed (filled) with grease. Others are sealed units that require replacement when worn.

As you will learn, service methods for cars with rear-wheel drive are quite different from vehicles with front-wheel drive.

Servicing wheel bearings (nondriving wheels)

Fig. 63-21 shows an exploded view of a typical non-driving wheel bearing assembly. Note the names and locations of each part.

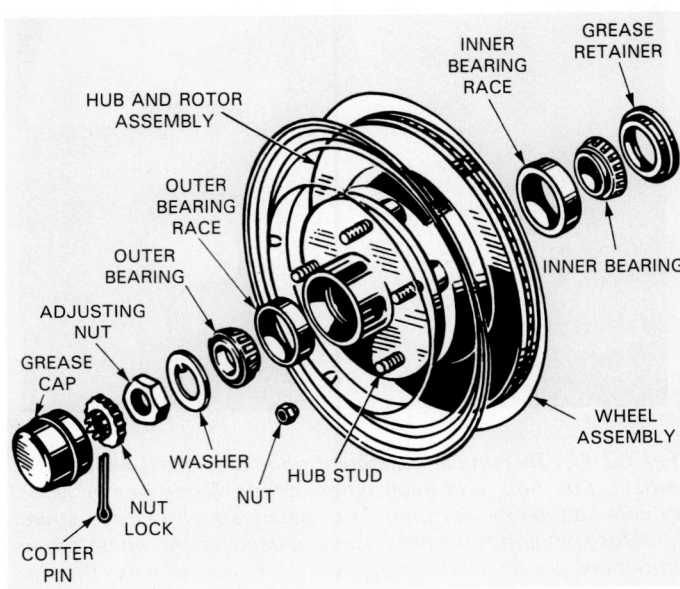

Fig. 63-21. Service of nondriving hub and wheel bearing assembly involves cleaning, inspection, lubrication, and adjustment of bearings. Study how parts fit together. (Ford)

To disassemble the bearings, partially loosen the lug nuts. Then, raise the car and secure it on jack stands. Remove the wheel, grease cap, cotter pin, adjusting nut, and safety washer. Wiggle the hub and pull out the outer wheel bearing.

Screw the adjusting nut back onto the spindle. Unbolt and secure the brake caliper to one side if needed. Slide the hub outward on the spindle. When the inner bearing catches on the nut, the grease seal and inner wheel bearing will pop out.

Wipe the bearings and races clean. Keep the bearings in ORDER because they must be installed in the

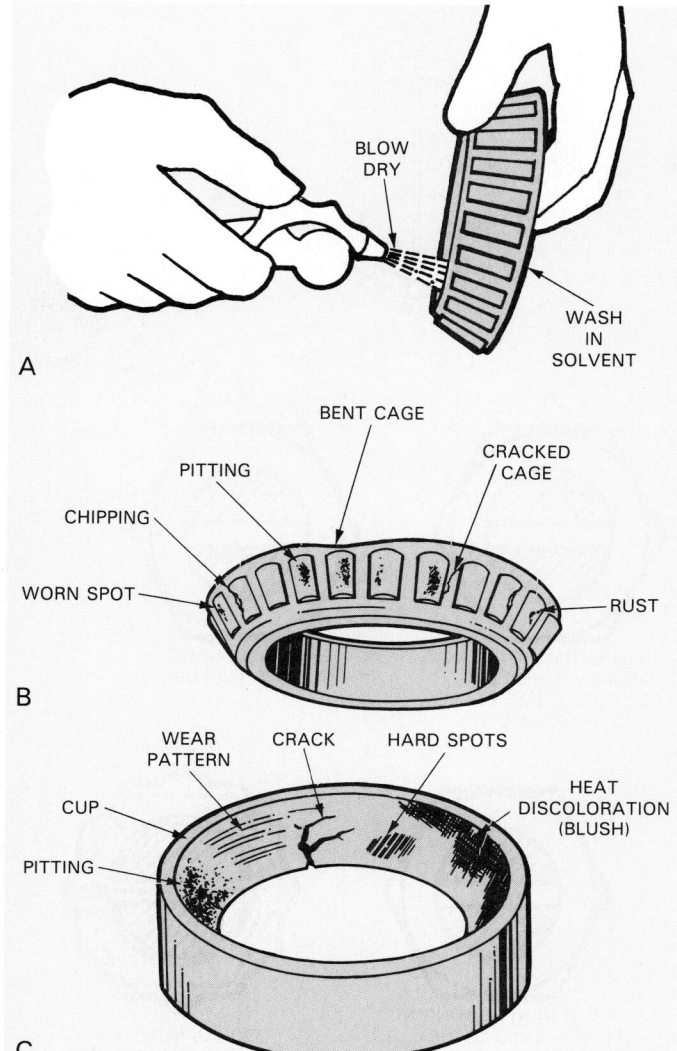

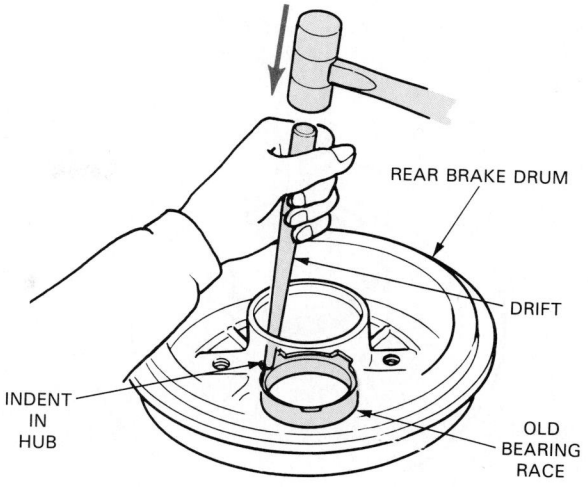

Fig. 63-23. If bearing is bad, also replace race. Use flat-nose drift to force old race out of hub.   (Honda)

Fig. 63-22. A — Wash and dry bearings. Do NOT let bearings spin while blowing dry. B and C — Inspect bearing and race for these kinds of troubles.   (Florida Dept. of Voc. Ed.)

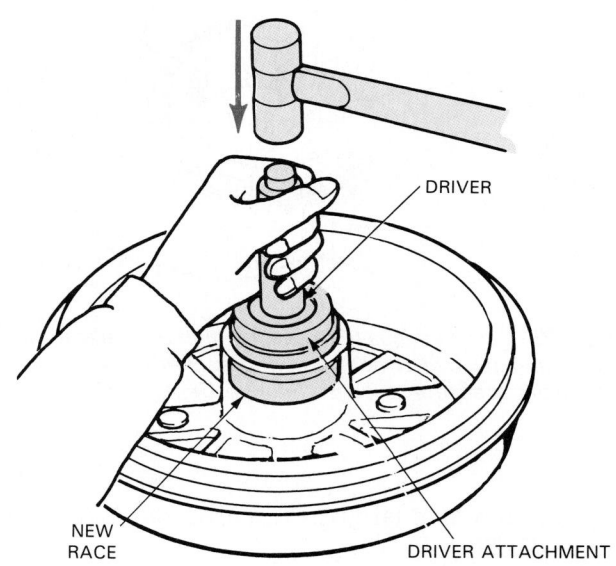

Fig. 63-24. Use driver to squarely seat new bearing race. Be careful not to damage bearing contact surface.   (Honda)

same races. Closely inspect the bearings and races for damage. See Fig. 63-22. If problems are found, you will have to replace both the bearing and race as a SET.

To replace a bearing race, drive out the old race with a large drift punch and hammer, Fig. 63-23. Be careful not to damage the hub. To install the new race, use a driving tool, as shown in Fig. 63-24.

Wipe out all of the old grease from inside of the hub. Partially fill the cavity with new wheel bearing grease. Use the recommended type grease, normally HIGH TEMPERATURE WHEEL BEARING GREASE.

WARNING! Do NOT use all purpose wheel bearing grease on cars with disc brakes. The heat generated by the brakes can liquify the grease and cause leakage out of the grease seals.

To **pack the bearings,** use your hands or a *bearing packer* (device for filling bearing cage with grease) to properly lubricate the bearing assemblies. This is shown

in Fig. 63-25. Make sure grease is worked completely through each bearing cage and around every ball or roller.

Place the inner bearing into its race. Tap the NEW GREASE SEAL into the hub with light taps from a hammer. Tap in a circular pattern around the seal or use a seal driver. Make sure you do not dent the seal.

CAUTION! Keep grease off the brake disc or drum when servicing the wheel bearings. The slightest amount of grease could ruin or cause squeaking of the brake pads or shoes.

Wipe the spindle clean. Slide the hub into position and install the outer bearing. Fit the safety washer against the bearing. Then, screw on the adjusting nut.

Adjust the wheel bearing nut as described in a service

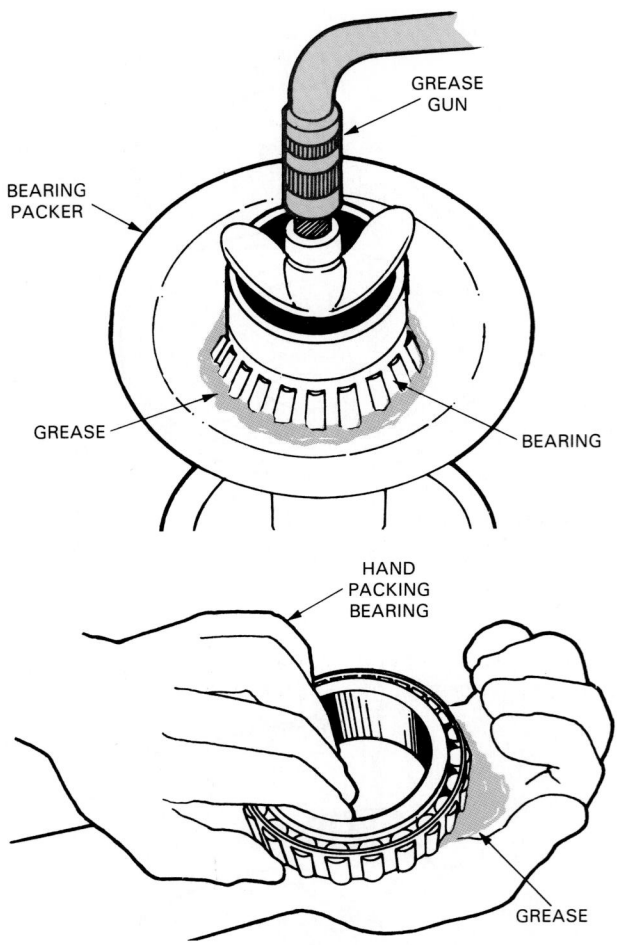

Fig. 63-25. Pack bearings with quality, high temperature wheel bearing grease. Use either a bearing packer or palm of hand to work grease into cage. (Florida Dept. of Voc. Ed.)

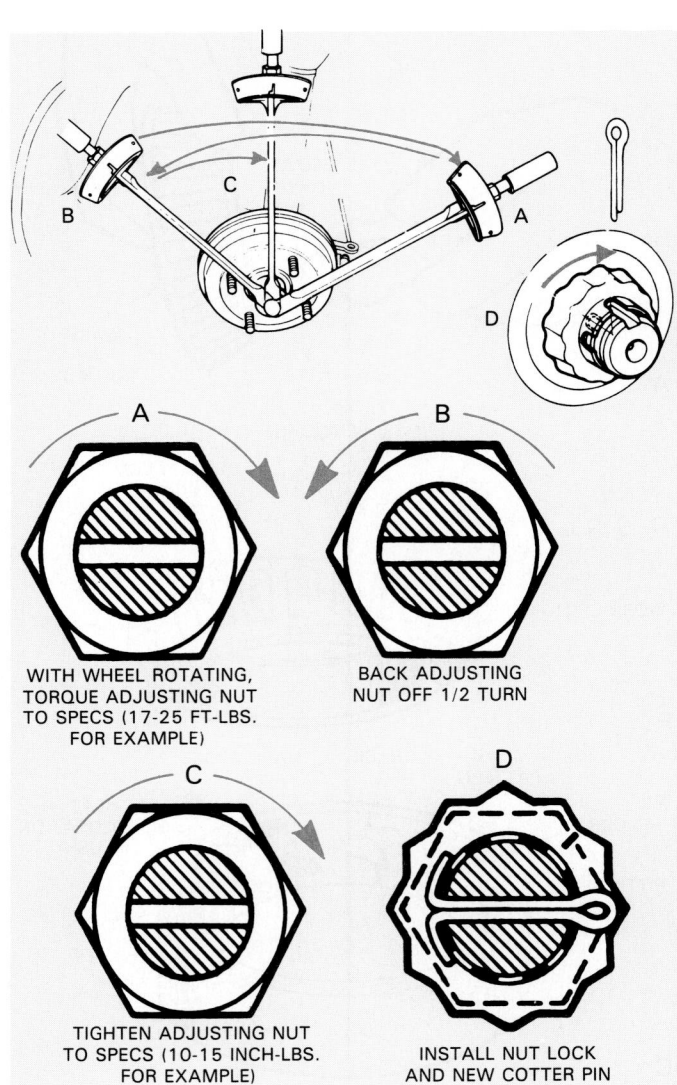

Fig. 63-26. Typical procedure for adjusting nondriving wheel bearing assembly. A — Torque nut to specs to seat bearings. Rotate hub. B — Back off adjusting nut one-half turn. C — Tighten adjusting nut to specs, about one foot-pound or less. D — Install new cotter pin. (Honda and Ford)

manual. One manual gives the procedures presented in Fig. 63-26.

Install and bend the NEW cotter pin. This is very important because it keeps the adjusting nut, bearings, hub, and front wheel from falling off.

Servicing wheel bearings (driving wheels)

Front wheel bearings on a driving hub and wheel bearing assembly are normally not serviced unless specified or when major repairs are needed. Fig. 63-27 shows an exploded view of a typical driving type hub and wheel bearing assembly.

NOTE! For more information on front-wheel drive bearing service, refer to Chapter 61. It explains front-drive axle shaft removal.

Generally, to disassemble a front-drive wheel bearing, loosen the wheel lug nuts and spindle nut. Raise the car and secure it on jack stands. Remove the lug nut or bolts, wheel, and axle nut.

Remove the caliper and hang it to one side. Unbolt the brake disc from the hub if needed. Remove the steering knuckle and hub assembly from the car.

Depending upon the design of the driving hub, you may need to remove the hub either before or after the steering knuckle. Refer to a service manual for detailed procedures.

Fig. 63-28A shows one type of puller removing the hub with the steering knuckle held in a vise. After hub and bearing removal, new bearings and a new seal must be installed.

To install new front-wheel drive bearings, pack the new bearings with grease, if not sealed units. Using a press or driving tool, as in Fig. 63-28B, force the new bearings into place. Follow service manual procedures.

DANGER! When pressing new front-wheel drive bearings into position, do NOT exceed manufacture press load limits. If excessive pressure is used, parts can be shattered. Wear eye protection!

After pressing or driving the bearings into the steering

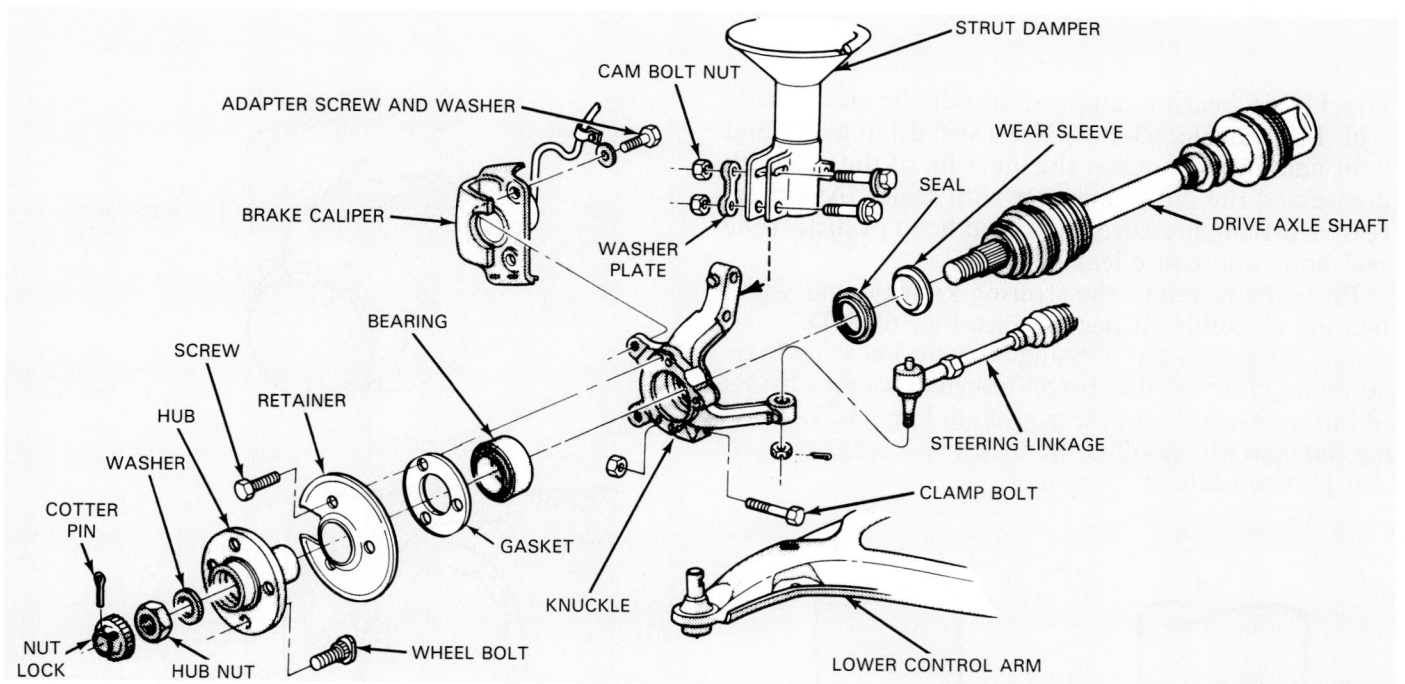

Fig. 63-27. Driving hub assembly, like this one, requires different service procedures than nondrive unit. Steering knuckle or bearing support must frequently be removed from car to service bearings. (Plymouth)

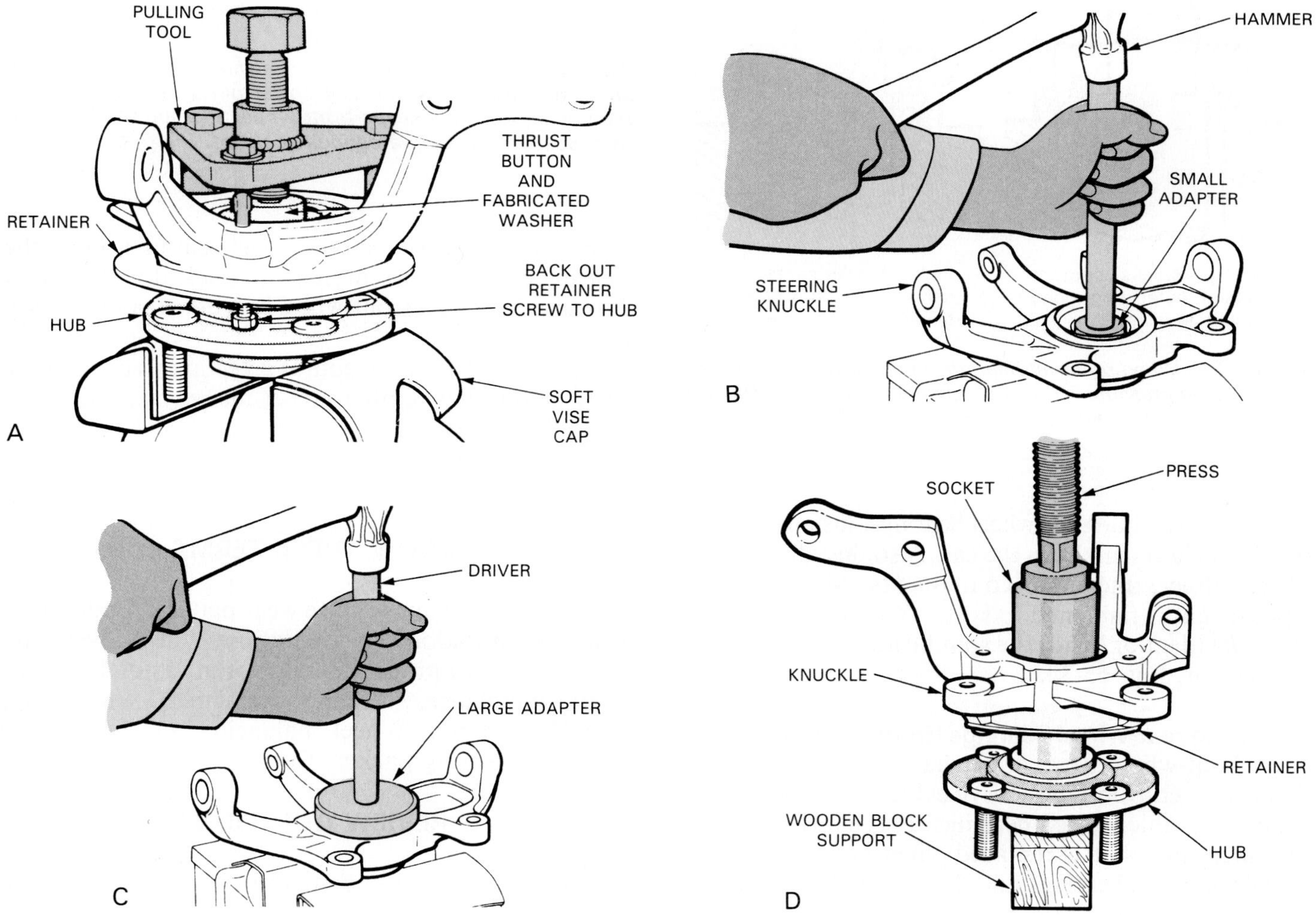

Fig. 63-28. Basic steps for replacing wheel bearings in driving hub assembly. A — After knuckle or support removal, use special puller to remove hub if needed. B — Remove old bearings using a driver or hydraulic press. Wear safety glasses! C — Install new bearings. Drive in squarely as described in service manual. D — Use press to reinstall hub if needed. Install new grease seals.

Tire, Wheel, Bearing Service   823

knuckle or bearing support, install the new grease seal. Look at Fig. 63-28C. Use a seal driving tool and light hammer taps. Coat the inner lip of the seal with grease and the outer diameter with sealer. Avoid excessive driving pressure that could bend or distort the seal body and cause leakage.

Press the hub into the steering knuckle and wheel bearing assembly, if needed. See Fig. 63-28D.

CAUTION! When pressing the wheel bearing in or out, apply force to the correct bearing race (one press-fit into part). An example is given in Fig. 63-29. Bearing damage will result if the incorrect race is pressed and jammed into the bearings.

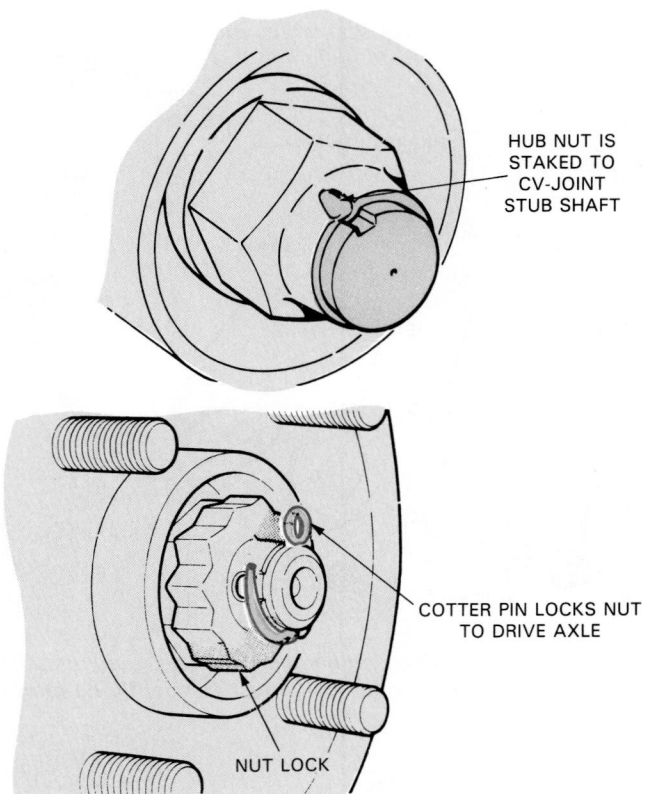

Fig. 63-30. After reassembling driving hub and bearings, make sure you torque and stake or cotter pin axle or hub nut as recommended. This keeps front wheel and hub from coming off, possibly causing a serious accident. (Ford and Dodge)

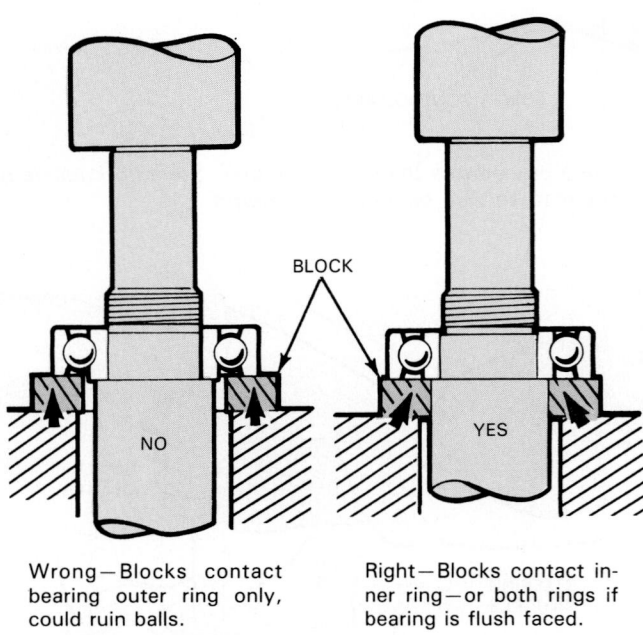

Wrong—Blocks contact bearing outer ring only, could ruin balls.

Right—Blocks contact inner ring—or both rings if bearing is flush faced.

Fig. 63-29. When pressing bearings in and out, apply driving force so that pressure is not applied to balls or rollers. This will prevent bearing damage. (Federal Mogul)

After assembling the wheel bearings, install the steering knuckle assembly on the car. Also, install the brake disc, caliper, and other components. Make sure the spindle nut is tightened to specs. You will either need to *stake* (dent or bend) the spindle nut or install a new cotter pin, Fig. 63-30.

Servicing rear-wheel bearings (front-wheel drive car)

A front-wheel drive car can have two types of wheel bearings: conventional serviceable type bearings or nonserviceable, sealed bearings. Fig. 63-31 illustrates a sealed unit that is replaced when bad.

When sealed bearings fail, the bolts holding the bearing and hub to the axle or control arm must be removed. When installing the new bearing assembly, torque bolts to specs. Some manufacturers require new fasteners when rear bearings and hubs are replaced.

When a conventional type wheel bearing is used, the bearing can be disassembled and packed with grease. It is serviced like a front-wheel bearing on a rear-wheel drive car.

Remember! The procedures given in this chapter are general and they apply to most makes of cars. When in doubt, always use service manual procedures written for the specific year, make, and model car you are working on.

KNOW THESE TERMS

Tire impact damage, Tire wear pattern, Underinflation, Overinflation, Ply separation, Wheel cover, Tire gauge, Tire rotation, Lateral runout, Radial runout, Static imbalance, Dynamic imbalance, Wheel hop, Wheel shimmy, Wheel balancing machine, Tire changer, Bearing packer, Cotter pin.

REVIEW QUESTIONS

1. What are four common symptoms of tire problems?
2. How is a tire wear pattern useful?
3. A customer complains of right-front tire wear. The outer edges of both treads are worn. The center

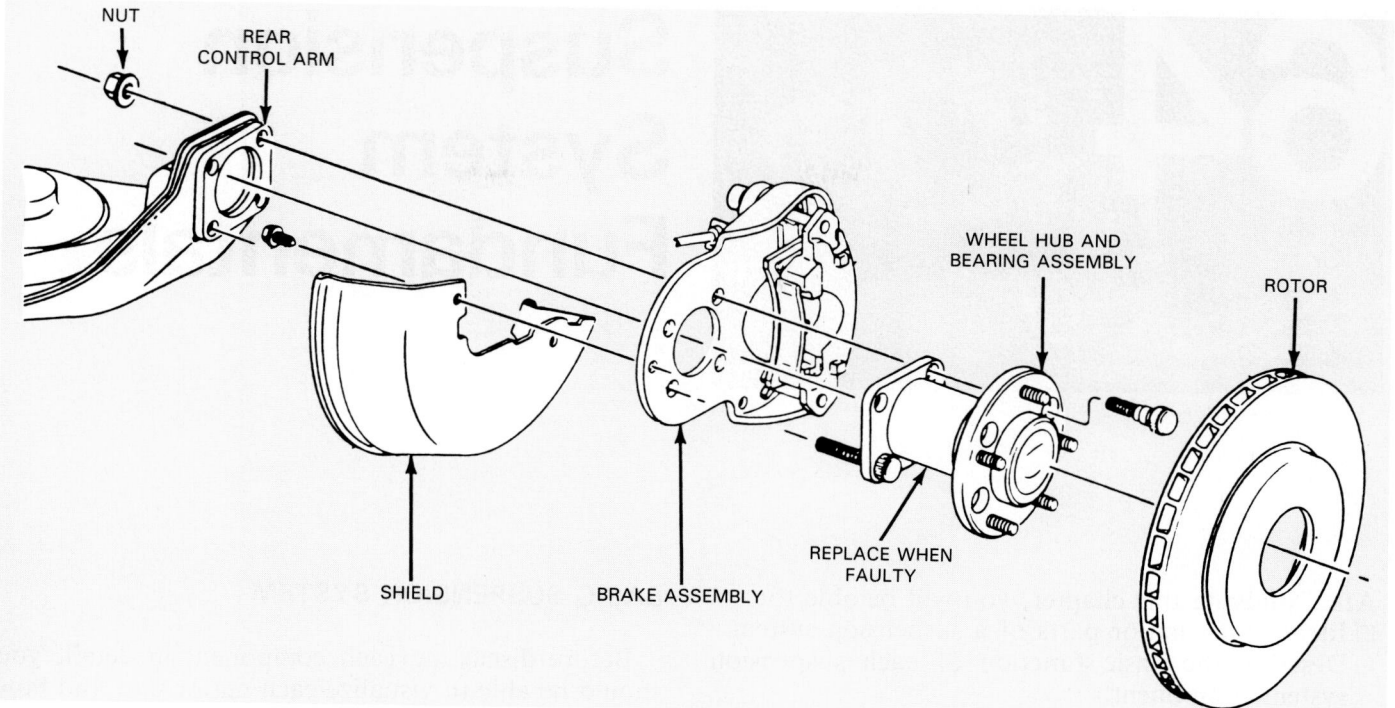

Fig. 63-31. This rear wheel bearing and hub assembly is NOT serviceable. If bearings are dry and noisy when turned by hand, remove and replace entire assembly. Torque all fasteners to specs and follow shop manual instructions. (Cadillac)

of the tread shows little wear.

Technician A says that the car needs a wheel alignment. Incorrect alignment is causing the wear. Technician B says that underinflation could be the problem. Tire pressure should be checked. Who is correct?

a. Technician A
b. Technician B
c. Both A and B
d. Neither A nor B

4. What is ply separation?
5. A metal, ball peen hammer should be used to install wheel covers. True or False?
6. Why is periodic tire rotation important?
7. Lug nut _____ is important because _____ can cause wheel or hub distortion and runout.
8. Explain the difference between lateral and radial tire runout.
9. Describe the major differences between static and dynamic tire imbalance.
10. This is NOT a type of wheel balancer.
    a. Bob-weight balancer. c. On-the-car balancer.
    b. Bubble balancer.   d. Off-the-car balancer.

11. How can you repair a hole in a tire without dismounting the tire?
12. All purpose grease can be used to pack wheel bearings on a car with disc brakes. True or False?
13. Define the term "pack the bearings."
14. Why should a new cotter pin be used when assembling a wheel bearing?
15. When pressing a front-wheel drive bearing in or out, what part of the bearing should contact the driving tool?

ACTIVITIES FOR CHAPTER 63

1. On a vehicle assigned by your instructor, test a wheel bearing complaint and diagnose the problem.
2. Perform a tire rotation on a vehicle assigned by your instructor.
3. Demonstrate the procedure for balancing a wheel and tire. Explain each step of the procedure and why it is done.
4. Prepare a bill for a tire rotation using a flat hourly rate suggested by your instructor.

64 Suspension System Fundamentals

After studying this chapter, you will be able to:
□ Identify the major parts of a suspension system.
□ Describe the basic function of each suspension system component.
□ Explain the operation of the four common types of springs.
□ Compare the various types of suspension systems.
□ Explain automatic suspension leveling systems.

The suspension system works with the tires, frame or unit body, wheels, wheel bearings, brake system, and steering system. All of the parts in these systems work together to provide a safe and comfortable means of transportation. For this reason, make sure you learn all of the material in this chapter. You will then be prepared to study later chapters.

FUNCTIONS OF A SUSPENSION SYSTEM

A *suspension system* has several important functions:
1. Support the weight of the frame, body, engine, transmission, drivetrain, and passengers.
2. Provide a smooth, comfortable ride by allowing the wheels and tires to move up and down with minimum movement of the vehicle body.
3. Allow rapid cornering without extreme *body roll* (vehicle leans to one side).
4. Keep the tires in firm contact with the road, even after striking bumps or holes in the road.
5. Prevent excessive *body squat* (body tilts down in rear) when accelerating or heavily loaded.
6. Prevent excessive *body dive* (body tilts down in front) when braking.
7. Allow the front wheels to turn from side-to-side for steering.
8. Work with the steering system to help keep the wheels in correct alignment.
As you will learn, a suspension system uses springs, swivel joints, damping devices, movable arms, and other components to accomplish these functions.

BASIC SUSPENSION SYSTEM

Before discussing each component in detail, you should be able to visualize each major part and how it functions in relation to the other parts. Look at Fig. 64-1 as each component is introduced.
1. CONTROL ARM (movable lever that fastens steering knuckle to the vehicle frame or body).
2. STEERING KNUCKLE (provide spindle or bearing support for mounting wheel hub, bearings, and wheel assembly).
3. BALL JOINT (swivel joint that allows control arm and steering knuckle to move up or down and from side to side).
4. SPRING (supports weight of vehicle; permits control arm and wheel to move up and down).
5. SHOCK ABSORBER or DAMPER (keeps suspension from continuing to bounce after spring compression and extension).
6. CONTROL ARM BUSHING (sleeve allowing control arm to swing up and down on frame).

INDEPENDENT AND NONINDEPENDENT SUSPENSION

Suspension systems may be grouped into two broad categories: independent and nonindependent.

Independent suspension
Independent suspension allows one wheel to move up and down with a minimum effect on the other wheels. Look at Fig. 64-2A.

Since each wheel is attached to its own suspension unit, movement of one wheel does NOT cause direct movement of the wheel on the other side of the car.

Detailed later in this chapter, there are many types of independent suspension. This type of suspension is the most widely used for modern vehicles, especially passenger cars.

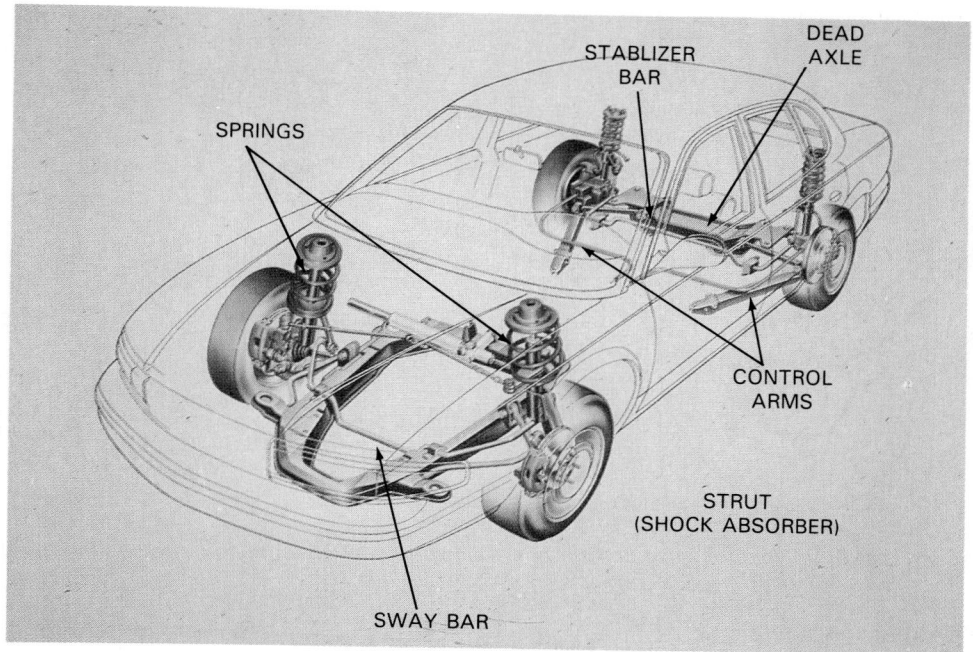

Fig. 64-1. Elementary parts of suspension system. Study basic motion of components. (Chrysler)

Nonindependent suspension

Nonindependent suspension has both the right and left wheels attached to the same, solid axle, Fig. 64-2B. When one tire hits a bump in the road, its upward movement causes a slight upward TILT of the other

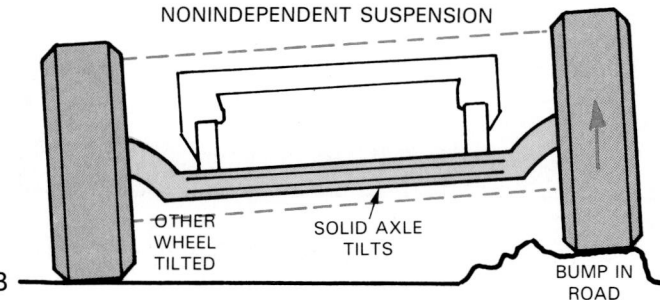

Fig. 64-2. Comparison of independent and nonindependent suspensions. A—Independent suspension allows one wheel to roll over bump with minimum effect on other wheel. B—Nonindependent suspension causes action of one wheel to tilt and affect other wheel.

wheel. Hence, neither wheel is independent of the other.

SUSPENSION SYSTEM SPRINGS

Suspension system springs must *jounce* (compress) and *rebound* (extend) with bumps and holes in the road surface. They support the weight of the car while still allowing suspension *travel* (movement).

The most common types of springs are the coil spring, leaf spring, air spring, and torsion bar.

Coil spring

A *coil spring* is a length of spring steel rod wound into a spiral, Fig. 64-3A. This is the most common type

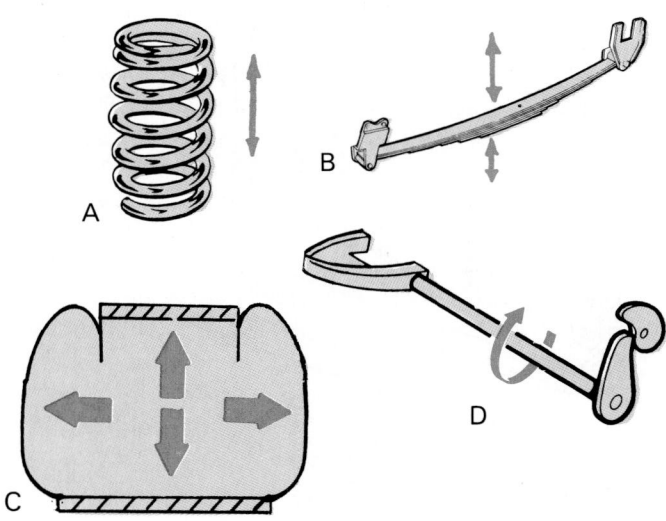

Fig. 64-3. Suspension system springs. A—Coil spring. B—Leaf spring. C—Air spring. D—Torsion bar.

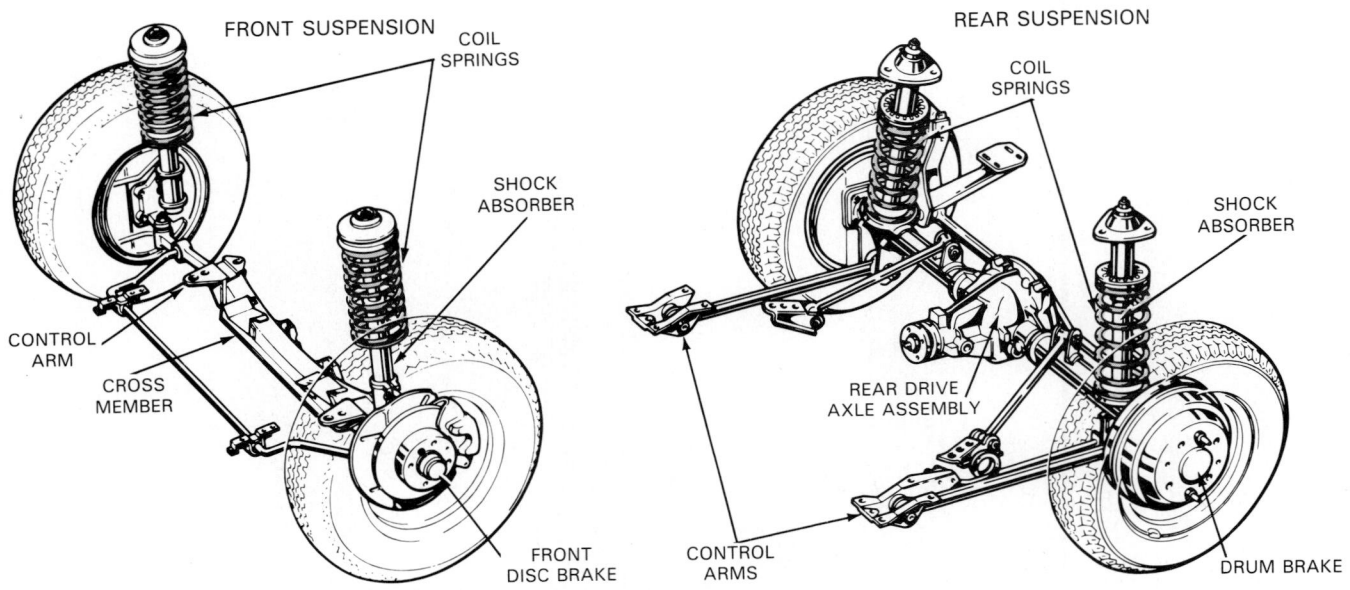

Fig. 64-4. Both front and rear of vehicle may use coil springs. Coil springs are becoming more common with today's suspension system designs. (Fiat)

of spring found on modern suspension systems. Coil springs may be used on either the front or rear of the car, as shown in Fig. 64-4.

Leaf spring

A *leaf spring* is commonly made of flat plates or strips of spring steel bolted together. A few are made of fiberglass. Although leaf springs were once used on front suspension systems, they are now limited to the rear of some older cars. Fig. 63-3B illustrates a simple leaf spring rear suspension.

Fig. 63-5 illustrates an exploded view of a leaf spring assembly.

Insulators are placed between the springs to prevent squeaks and rattles.

Each end of the leaf spring has an *eye* (cylinder-shaped hole) which holds a bushing.

A *shackle* fastens the rear leaf spring eye to the car frame. It allows the spring to change length when bent.

The front spring eye normally bolts directly to the frame structure. Two large U-bolts secure the axle or axle housing to the leaf springs.

Leaf spring windup is a condition causing the rear leaf springs to flex when driving or braking force is applied to the suspension system. Fig. 64-6 illustrates spring windup. The twisting and distortion of the spring can cause body squat and dive.

Air spring

An *air spring* is typically a two-ply rubber cylinder filled with air. End caps are formed on the air spring for mounting. Air pressure in the rubber cylinder makes the unit have a spring action, like a coil spring. Refer to Fig. 64-7.

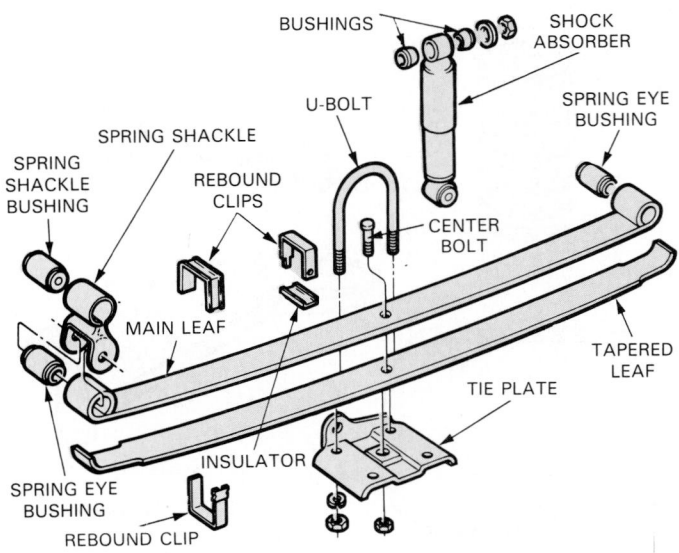

Fig. 64-5. Exploded view of simple leaf spring assembly. (Chrysler)

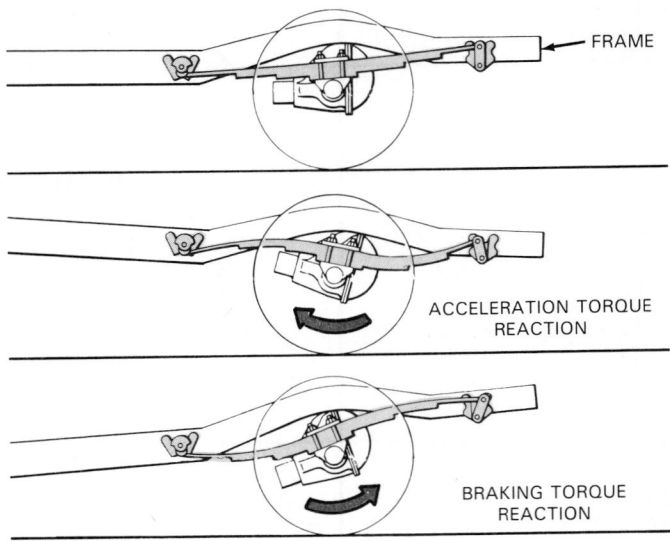

Fig. 64-6. Leaf spring windup is problem when leaves support driving axle. Torque tends to twist spring. (Ford)

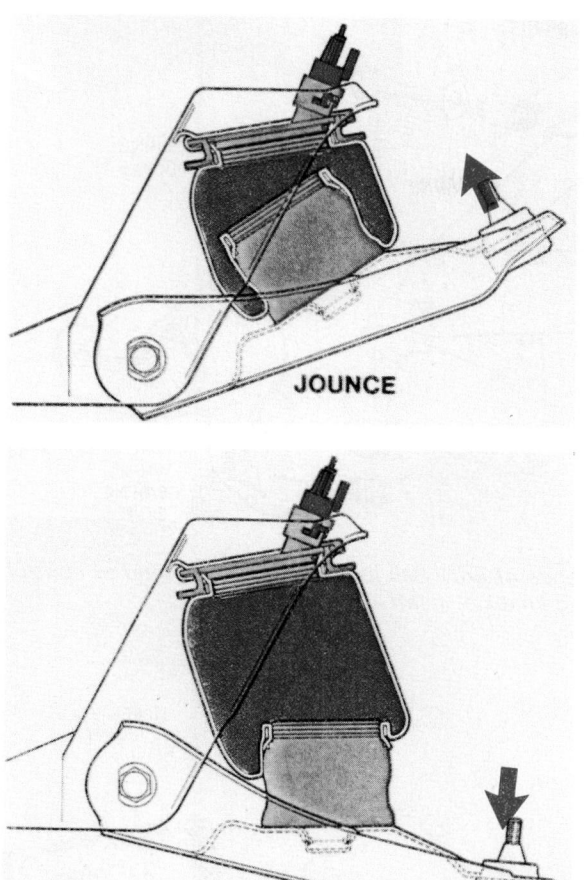

Fig. 64-7. Air springs are used on some late model cars. They are especially adaptable to automatic leveling systems.

An air spring is lighter than a coil spring. This gives it the potential to produce a smoother ride than a coil spring. Special synthetic rubber compounds must be used so the air spring can operate properly in cold weather. Low temperatures tend to harden or stiffen rubber.

Torsion bar (spring)

A *torsion bar* is another type of spring made of a large, spring steel rod. See Fig. 64-8. One end of the torsion bar is attached to the frame. The other end is fastened to the suspension system control arm.

Up and down movement of the suspension system twists the steel bar. It will then try to return to its original shape, moving the suspension arm back into place.

Spring terminology

Spring rate refers to the stiffness or tension of a spring. The rate of a spring is determined by the weight needed to bend it.

Sprung weight refers to the weight of the parts that are supported by the springs and suspension system.

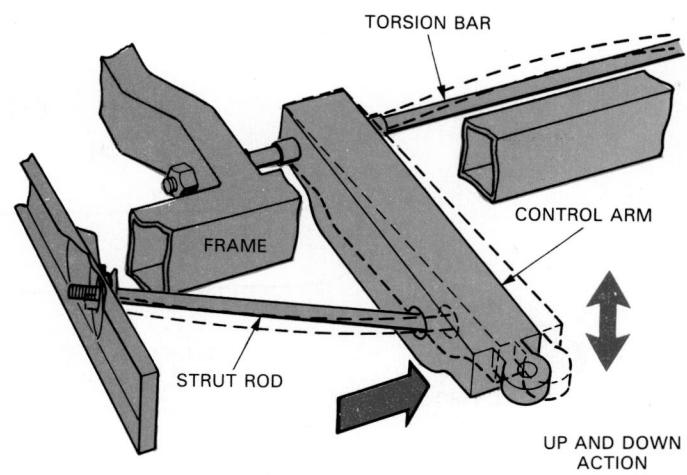

Fig. 64-8. Torsion bar is twisted with control arm movement. Bar resists twisting action and acts like conventional spring. (Moog)

Sprung weight should be kept HIGH in proportion to unsprung weight.

The *unsprung weight* of a car is the weight of the parts that are NOT supported by the springs. The tires, wheels, wheel bearings, steering knuckles, or axle housing would be considered unsprung weight.

Unsprung weight should be kept LOW to improve ride smoothness. Movement of a high unsprung weight (heavy wheel and suspension components) would tend to transfer movement into the passenger compartment.

SUSPENSION SYSTEM CONSTRUCTION

Now that you have been introduced to suspension system basics, we will cover the construction of each part in detail.

Control arms

A *control arm* holds the steering knuckle, bearing support, or axle housing in position as the wheel moves up and down. Look at Fig. 64-8.

The outer end of a control arm has a ball joint. The inner end has bushings. A rear suspension control arm may have bushings on both ends.

Control arm bushings act as bearings, allowing the arm to swing up and down on a shaft bolted to the frame or suspension unit. Refer to Fig. 64-9. These bushings may either be pressed or screwed into the holes in the control arm.

Strut rod

A *strut rod* fastens to the outer end of the lower control arm and to the frame. See Fig. 64-8. It keeps the control arm from swinging toward the rear or front of the car.

The front of the strut rod has rubber bushings that

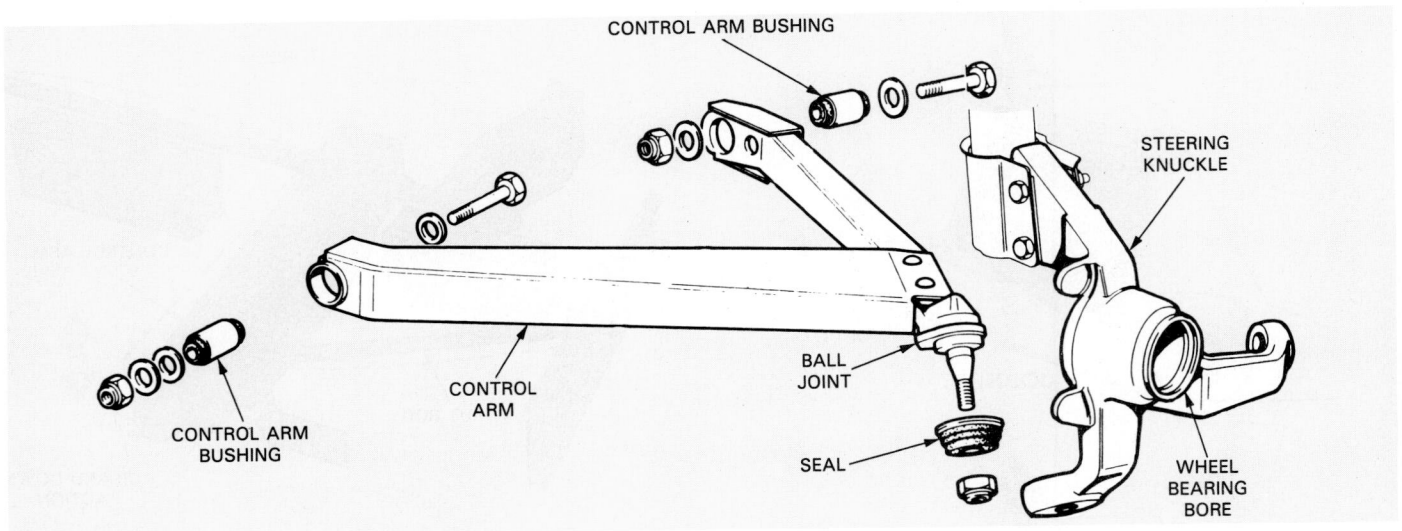

Fig. 64-9. Study basic parts of control arm. Bushings fit into inner ends of arm. Ball joint fits into outer end of control arm. Ball joint connects to steering knuckle. (Fiat)

soften the action of the strut rod. They allow a controlled amount of lower control arm movement while allowing full suspension travel.

Ball joints

Ball joints (short for ball-and-socket joints) are connections that allow limited rotation in every direction. They are used at the outer ends of control arms where the arms attach to the steering knuckle. See Fig. 64-9. Fig. 64-10 shows typical upper and lower ball-joint connections.

Since the ball joint must be filled with grease, a grease fitting and grease seal are normally placed on the joint, Fig. 64-11. The end of the stud on the ball joint is threaded for a large nut. When the nut is tightened, it force fits the tapered stud in the steering knuckle or bearing support.

SHOCK ABSORBERS

Shock absorbers limit spring oscillations (compression-extension movements) to smooth the vehicle's ride. Without shock absorbers, the car would continue to bounce up and down after striking a dip or hump in the road. This would make the ride uncomfortable and unsafe.

Fig. 64-12 shows the basic parts of a shock absorber. They include a piston rod, rod seal, piston, reservoir, compression cylinder, extension cylinder, and flow control valves. Most shocks are filled with oil. Some are air or gas and oil filled.

Whether the shock is compressed or extended, the oil causes resistance to movement. The rod tends to drag slowly in or out. This dampens spring and suspension system action.

One end of the shock absorber connects to a suspension component, usually a control arm. The other end

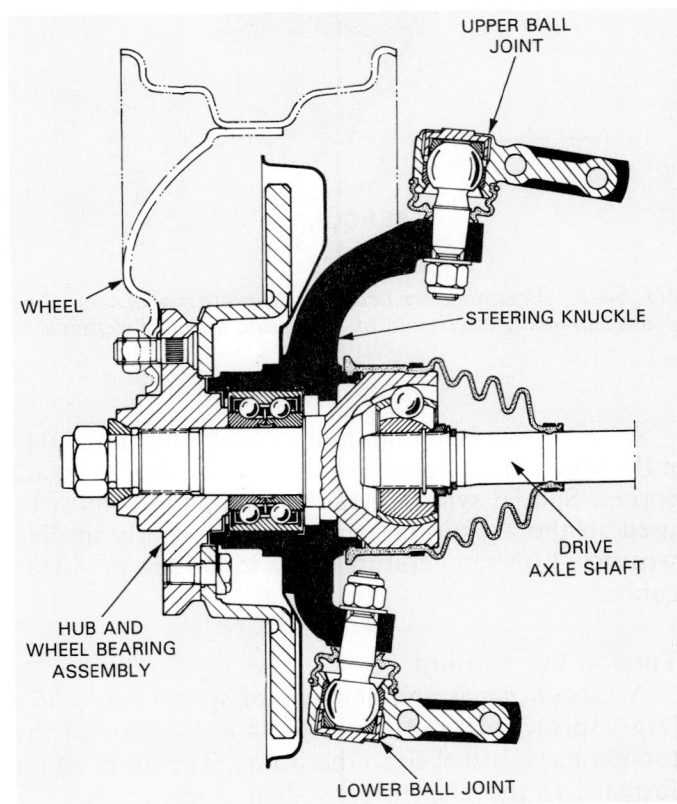

Fig. 64-10. Cutaway view shows ball joints, steering knuckle, and driving hub for front-wheel drive vehicle. Study construction of parts. (Chrysler)

of the shock fastens to the frame. In this way, the shock rod is pulled in and out and resists these movements. Fig. 64-13 shows shock absorber operation.

Shock absorber compression occurs when the vehicle's tire is forced upward upon hitting a bump. *Shock absorber extension* is the outward movement of the

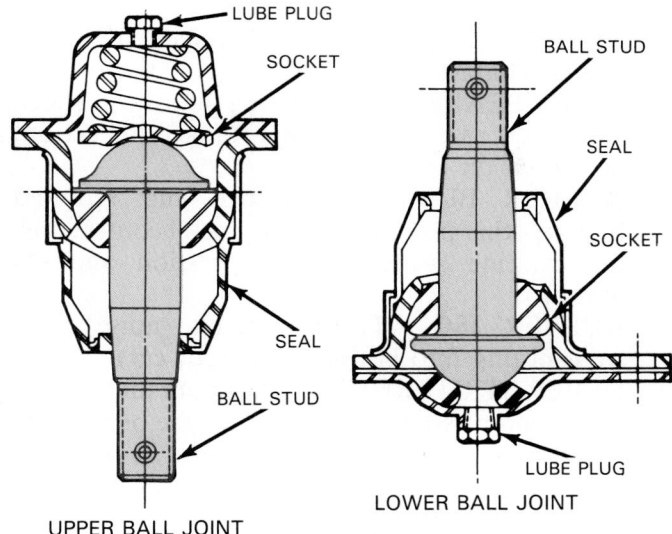

Fig. 64-11. Ball joint is simply a ball in a socket. Ball stud is free to move in all directions. This allows control arm and steering knuckle to move up and down freely. (Buick)

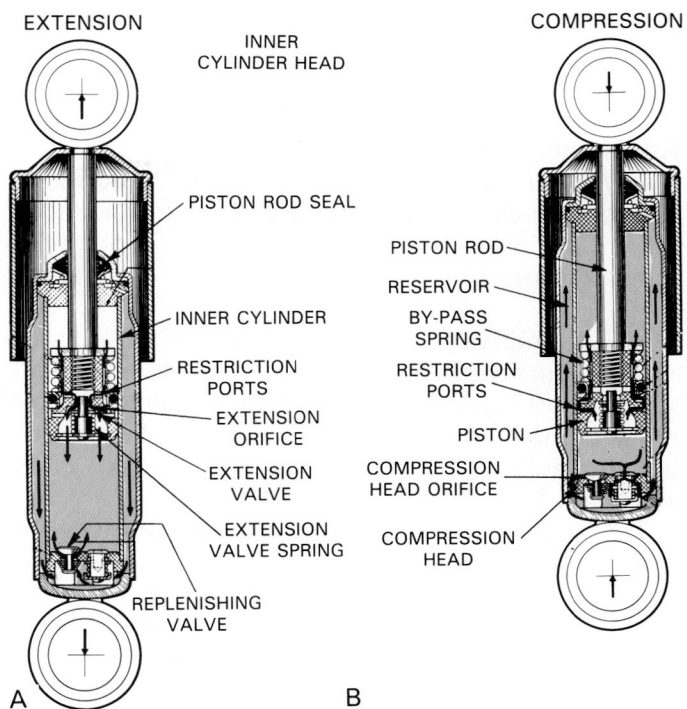

Fig. 64-13. Cutaway view of shock absorber in action. A—Extension stroke causes oil to be pulled back into lower area. Note valve action. B—Compression stroke forces piston down in cylinder. Oil is forced into upper area of shock. (Gabriel)

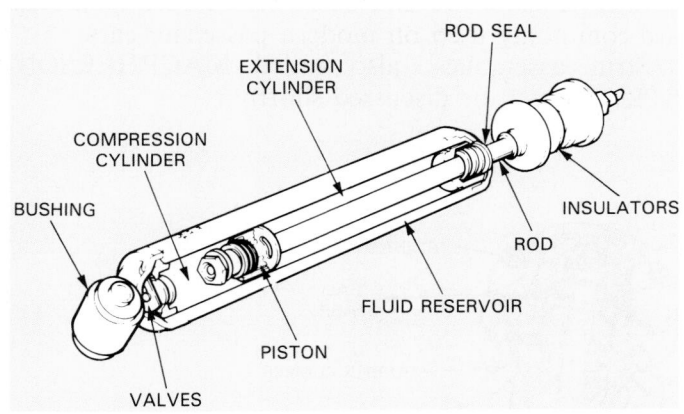

Fig. 64-12. Basically, shock absorber is a piston operating inside an oil-filled cylinder. Small oil passages cause oil to resist flow between each side of piston. This produces damping action that restricts spring bounce. (Ford)

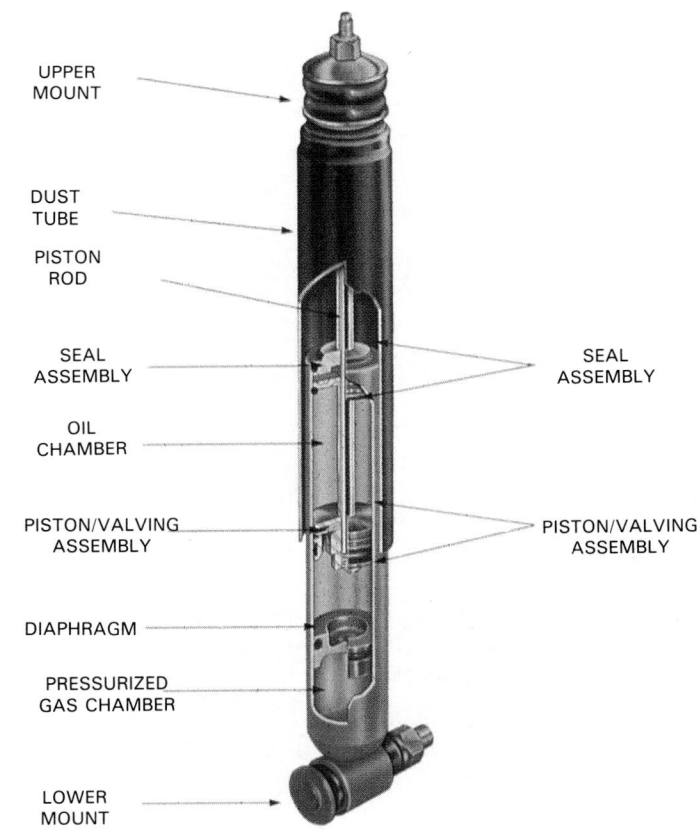

piston and rod as the control arm moves down. This occurs right after a compression stroke or when the tire encounters a hole in the road.

Gas-charged shock absorbers

Gas-charged shock absorbers use a low-pressure gas to help keep the oil in the shock from foaming. See Fig. 64-14. Usually, hydrogen gas is enclosed in a chamber separate from the main oil cylinder. The shock piston operates in the oil. The gas maintains constant pressure on the oil to stop air bubbles from forming. This increases shock performance during continuous, rapid up and down motion.

Self-leveling shock absorbers

A *self-leveling shock absorber* uses a special design

Fig. 64-14. Gas-pressure damped shocks operate like conventional oil-filled shocks. Gas is used to keep oil pressurized, which reduces oil foaming and increases efficiency on rough roads. (Pontiac)

that causes a hydraulic lock action to help maintain normal vehicle curb height. One is shown in Fig. 64-14C. Study its construction and operation.

Adjustable shocks

Adjustable shock absorbers provide a means of changing shock stiffness. Usually, by turning the shock outer body or an adjustment knob, you can set the shock soft for a smooth ride or stiff for better handling.

Strut assembly

A *strut assembly* consists of a shock absorber, coil spring (most types), and upper damper unit. The strut replaces the upper control arm. Only the lower control arm and strut are needed to support the front wheel assembly. Look at Fig. 64-15.

The basic parts of a typical strut assembly are shown in Fig. 64-16. They include:
1. STRUT SHOCK ABSORBER (piston operating in oil-filled cylinder to prevent coil spring oscillations).
2. DUST SHIELD (metal shroud or rubber boot that keeps road dirt off shock absorber rod).
3. LOWER SPRING SEAT (lower mount formed around shock body for coil spring).
4. COIL SPRING (supports weight of car and allows

suspension action).
5. UPPER SPRING SEAT (holds upper end of coil spring, contacts strut bearing).
6. STRUT BEARING (ball bearing that allows shock and spring assembly to rotate for steering action; only used on front of car).
7. RUBBER BUMPERS (jounce and rebound bumpers that prevent metal-on-metal contact during extreme suspension compression and extension).
8. RUBBER ISOLATORS (prevent noise from transmitting into body structure of car).
9. UPPER STRUT RETAINER (mount that secures upper end of strut assembly to frame or unitized body).
10. STRUT ROD NUT (hex nut that holds shock absorber rod in upper strut retainer).

A strut shock absorber is similar to a conventional shock absorber. However, it is longer and has provisions (brackets or connections) for mounting and holding the steering knuckle (front of vehicle) or bearing support (rear of vehicle) and spring.

Study Figs. 64-15 and 64-16 very carefully. Struts are commonly used on modern passenger cars.

Strut assemblies, also called MACPHERSON STRUTS, will be discussed shortly.

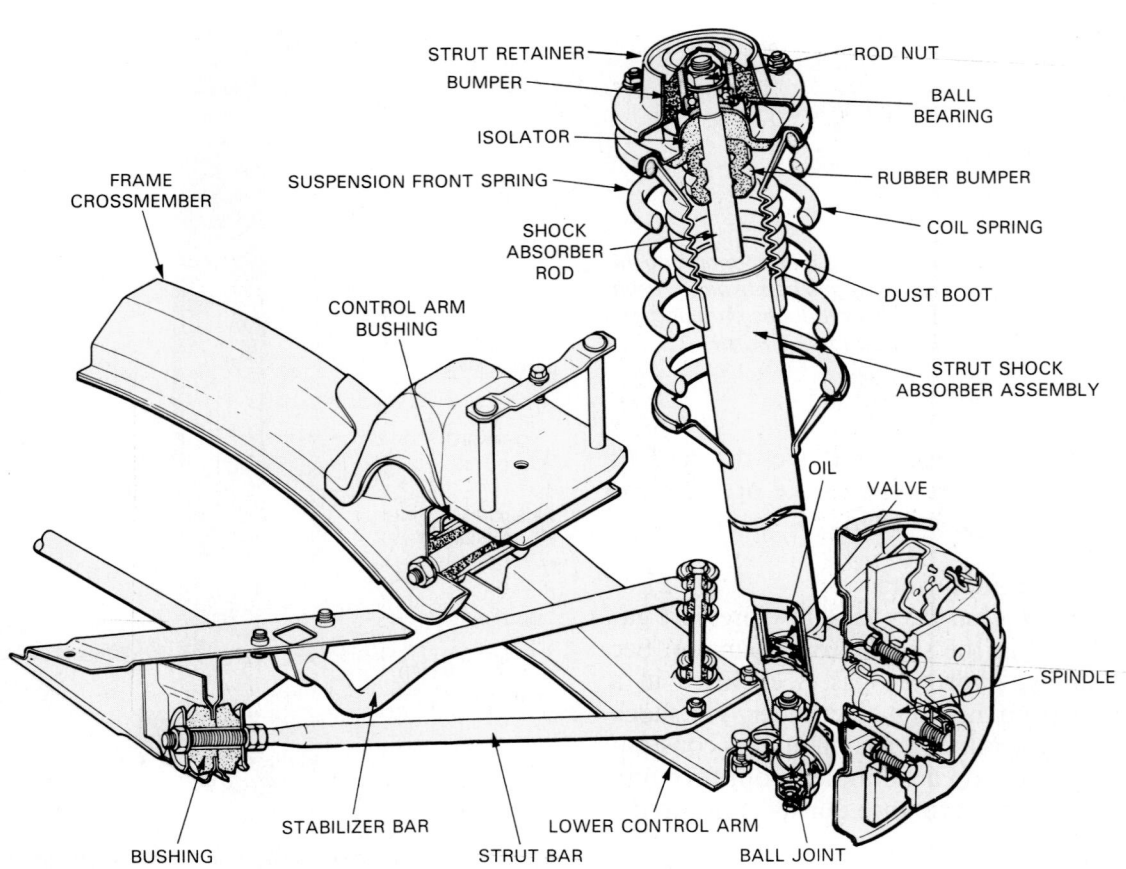

Fig. 64-15. Study parts of strut assembly very closely. This is one of the most modern suspension systems and is commonly used on today's vehicles.   (Chrysler Corp.)

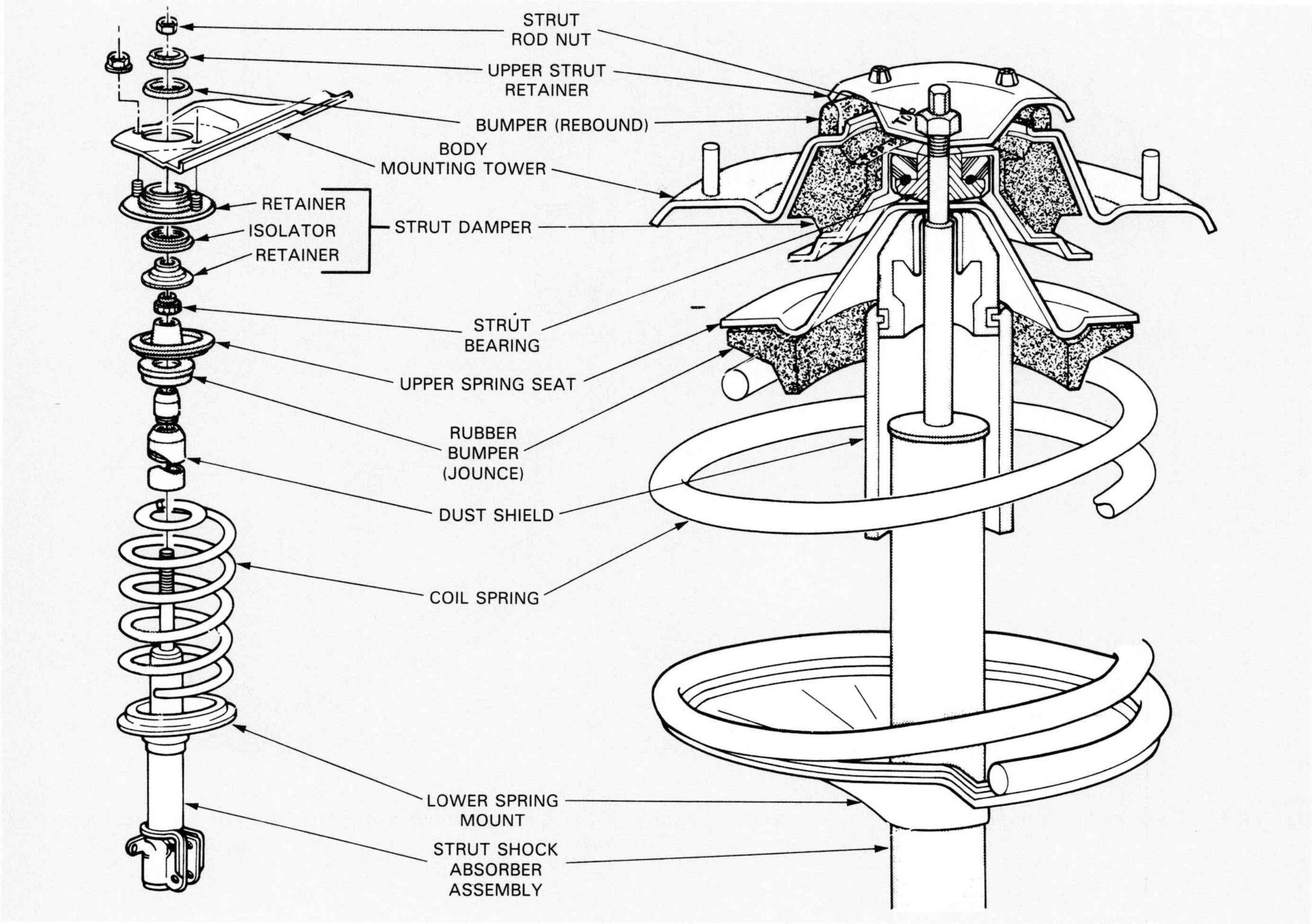

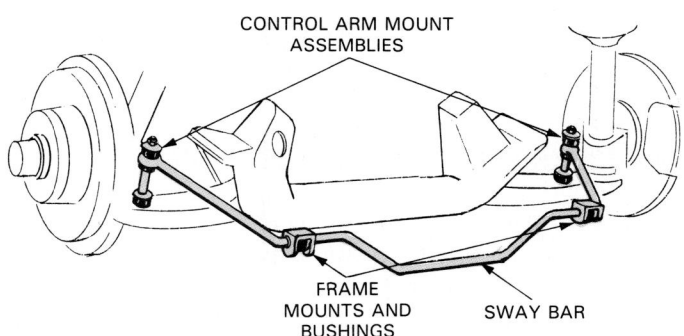

Fig. 64-16. Exploded and cutaway views of strut. Note strut bearing that allows front wheel, steering knuckle, and strut to revolve for steering action. (Chrysler)

Labels (exploded view):
- STRUT ROD NUT
- UPPER STRUT RETAINER
- BUMPER (REBOUND)
- BODY MOUNTING TOWER
- RETAINER
- ISOLATOR
- RETAINER
- STRUT DAMPER
- STRUT BEARING
- UPPER SPRING SEAT
- RUBBER BUMPER (JOUNCE)
- DUST SHIELD
- COIL SPRING
- LOWER SPRING MOUNT
- STRUT SHOCK ABSORBER ASSEMBLY

Sway bar (stabilizer bar)

A *sway bar,* also called *stabilizer bar,* is used to keep the body from leaning excessively in sharp turns. Pictured in Fig. 64-17, the sway bar is made of spring steel. It fastens to both lower control arms and to the frame. Rubber bushings fit between the bar, control arms, and frame.

Fig. 64-17. Sway bar attaches to both control arms. When car rounds a corner, car body tends to lean to one side. This bends bar. As a result, bar lessens sway or body lean in turns. (Moog)

CONTROL ARM MOUNT ASSEMBLIES

FRAME MOUNTS AND BUSHINGS

SWAY BAR

When the vehicles round a corner, centrifugal force makes the outside of the body drop and the inside of the body rise. This twists the sway bar. The bar's resistance to this twist limits body lean in corners.

Track rod (lateral control rod)

A *track rod,* also known as a *lateral control rod,* is sometimes used on rear suspension systems to prevent side-to-side axle movement during cornering, Fig. 64-18. The track rod is almost parallel to the rear axle. It fastens to the axle and to the frame or body structure.

Jounce bumpers

Jounce bumpers are blocks of hard rubber that keep the suspension system parts from hitting the frame when the car hits large bumps or holes, Fig. 64-19.

LONG-SHORT ARM SUSPENSION

A *long-short arm suspension* uses control arms of different lengths to keep the tires from tilting with suspension action. The upper control arms are made

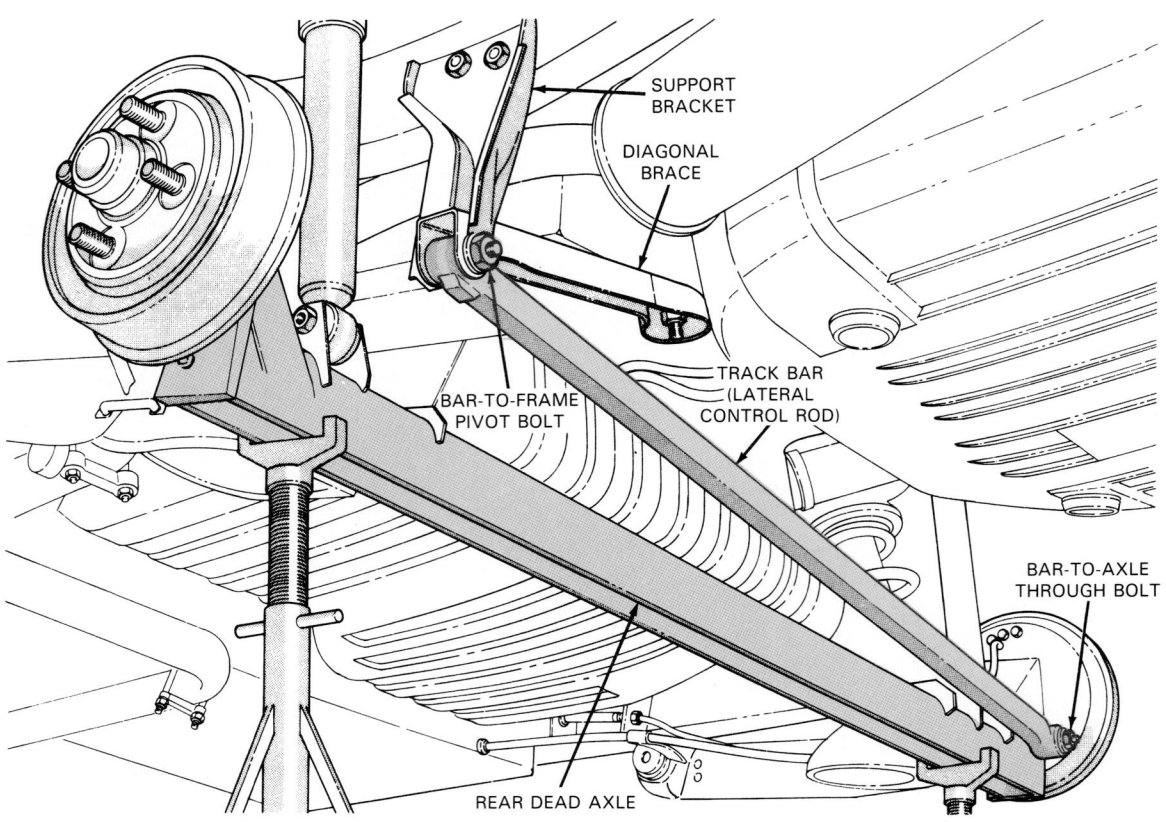

Fig. 64-18. Track rod is commonly used on rear axle to prevent side-to-side movement. Note how rod connects to frame and axle. (Chrysler)

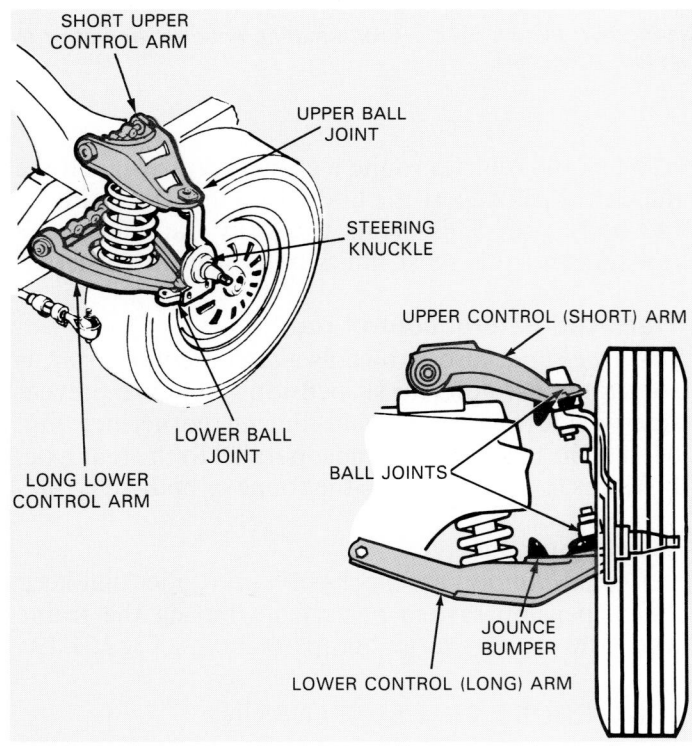

Fig. 64-19. Long-short arm suspension has different control arm lengths. This helps keep steering knuckle in alignment with suspension travel. (Ford)

shorter than the lower, as in Fig. 64-19.

If the control arms were the same length, the front tires would pivot outward at the top when the car hit a bump. This would cause undue tire scuffing and wear. See Fig. 64-19.

TORSION BAR SUSPENSION

A *torsion bar suspension* is a long-short arm suspension with torsion bar springs replacing the coil springs. Fig. 64-20 illustrates two types.

Most torsion bar suspensions allow easy adjustment of curb height (distance from road up to specific point on car). By turning an adjustment bolt, you can increase or decrease the tension on the torsion bar. This will either raise or lower the body and frame of the car.

MACPHERSON STRUT SUSPENSION

A *MacPherson strut suspension* uses only ONE control arm and a *strut* (spring, damper, and shock absorber unit) to support each wheel assembly, Fig. 64-21.

A conventional lower control arm attaches to the frame and to the lower ball joint. The ball joint holds the control arm to the steering knuckle or bearing support. The top of the steering knuckle or bearing sup-

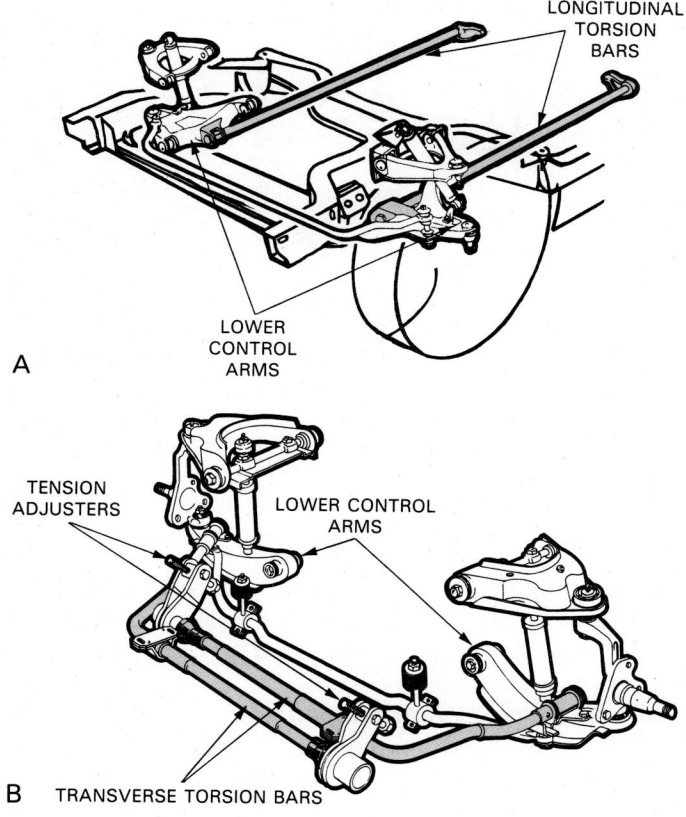

Fig. 64-20. A — Torsion bar suspension using bars mounted parallel with frame. B — Torsion bars on this modern suspension mount crosswise in vehicle. Both can be adjusted to raise or lower vehicle height. (Moog)

port is bolted to the strut. The top of the strut is fastened to the reinforced body structure.

A MacPherson strut is the most common type of suspension found on late model cars, Fig. 64-22. It may be used on both the front or rear wheels. It reduces the number of parts in the suspension system, lowering unsprung weight, and smoothing the ride.

A *modified strut suspension* has the coil spring mounted on top of the lower control arm, not around the strut. This type is illustrated in Fig. 64-23.

PICK-UP TRUCK SUSPENSION SYSTEMS

Pick-up trucks use numerous suspension system designs: long-short control arm, MacPherson strut, solid axle, and twin axle or twin I-beam suspension. The control arm and strut type are basically the same as those used on passenger cars.

Fig. 64-24 shows a twin-axle or TWIN I-BEAM suspension.

A four-wheel drive car or truck can have a solid axle housing and differential in the front. The steering knuckles are mounted on the axle housing so that they will swivel left or right for cornering.

REAR SUSPENSION SYSTEMS

Rear suspension systems are similar to front suspension systems but normally they do NOT have to provide for steering. With a rear-wheel drive vehicle, the rear

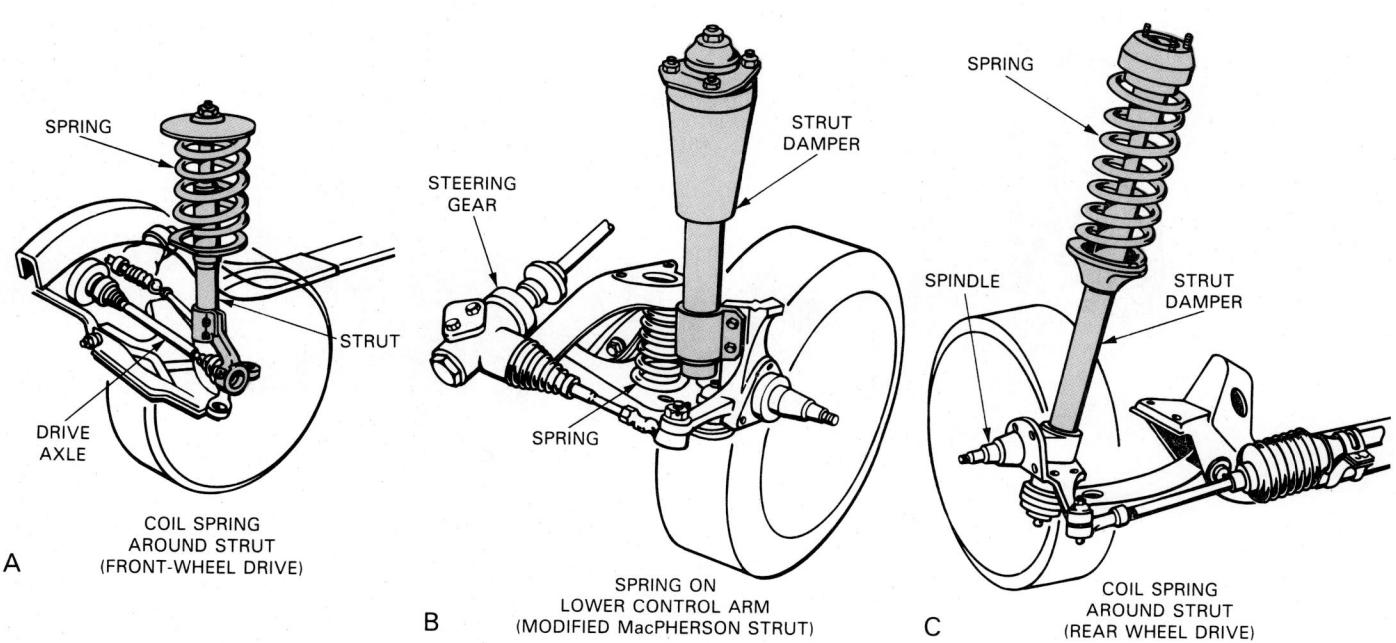

Fig. 64-21. MacPherson strut suspensions. A — Coil spring around strut, front-wheel drive. B — Modified strut has coil spring mounted on control arms. C — Same as A, but without front-wheel drive. (Moog)

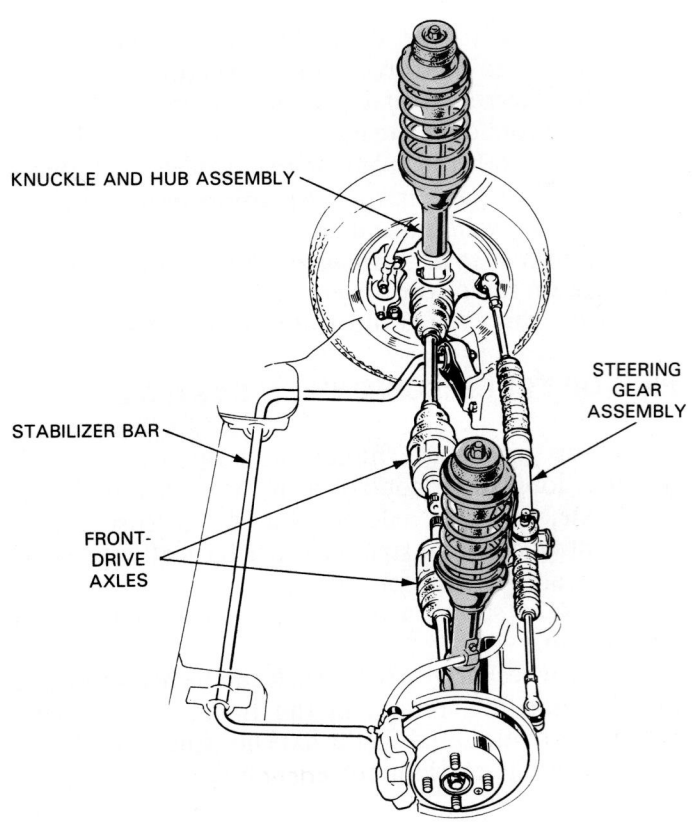

Fig. 64-22. Another view of MacPherson strut suspension. (Honda)

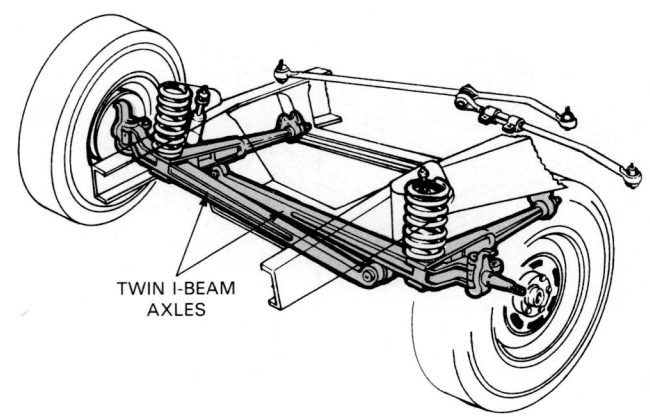

Fig. 64-24. Twin I-beam suspension is used on a few pickup trucks. (Ford)

axle housing may be solid, resulting in nonindependent suspension. However, rear swing axles and independent suspension can also be used.

Nonindependent rear suspension

Fig. 64-25 shows a typical rear suspension setup for a rear-wheel drive car. It has a solid axle housing and vertically mounted shock absorbers. Note how the coil springs are mounted between the control arms and frame of the vehicle.

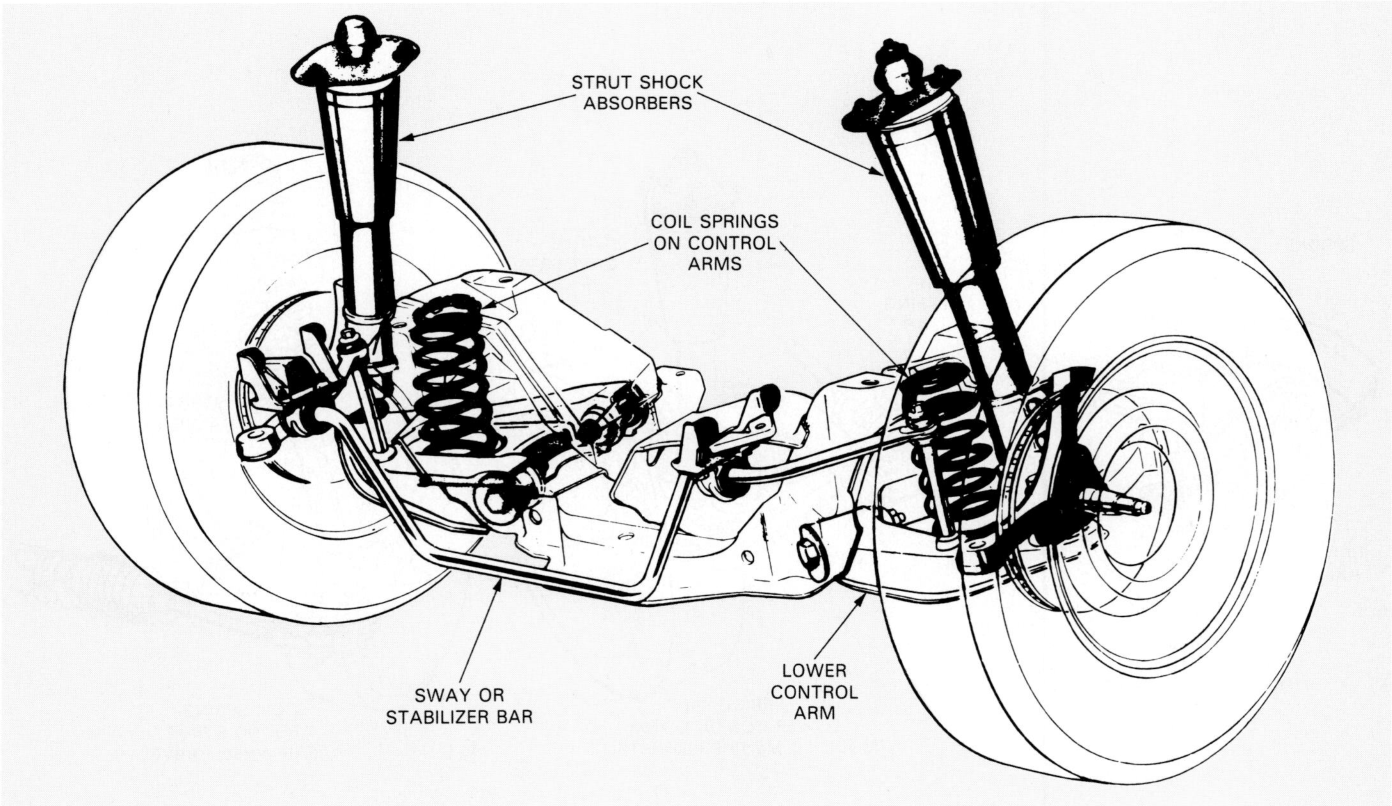

Fig. 64-23. Modified strut for front of rear-wheel drive vehicle.   (Ford)

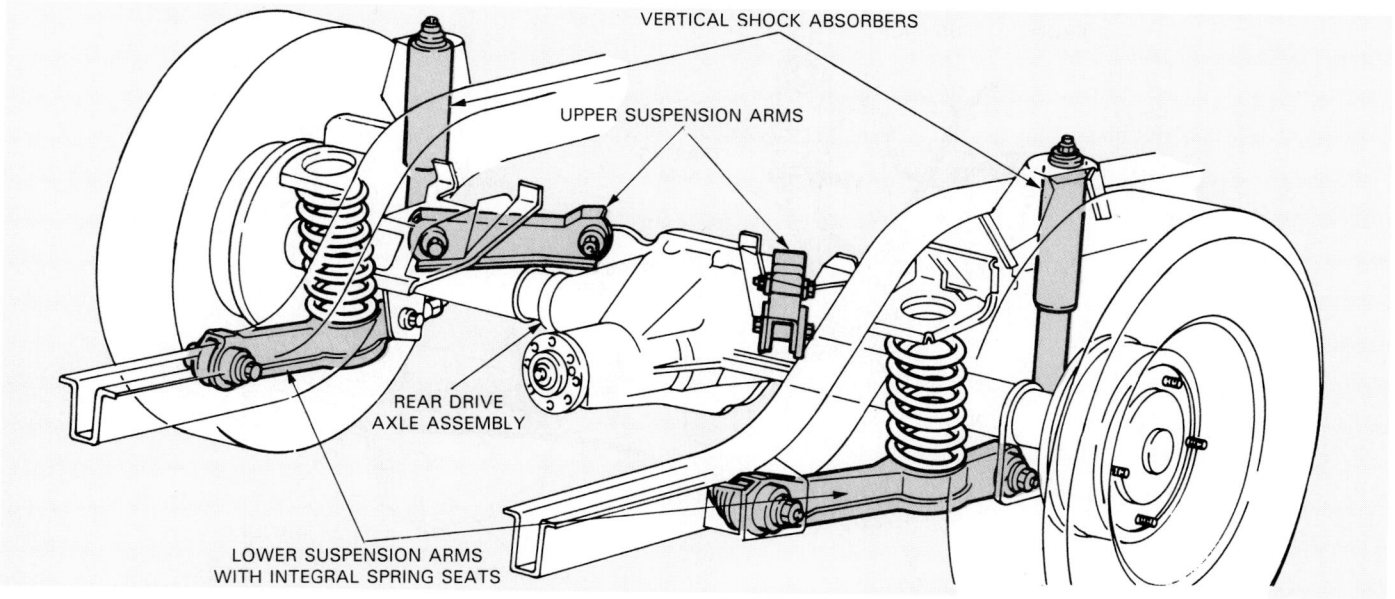

Fig. 64-25. Solid axle housing, rear suspension for rear-wheel drive vehicle. Study parts. (Ford)

VERTICAL SHOCK ABSORBERS

UPPER SUSPENSION ARMS

REAR DRIVE
AXLE ASSEMBLY

LOWER SUSPENSION ARMS
WITH INTEGRAL SPRING SEATS

Dead axle

A *dead axle* is a term used to describe a solid rear axle on a front-wheel drive vehicle, Fig. 64-26. Since the front wheels transfer driving power to the road, the rear axle is simply a straight or solid type axle.

Semi-independent suspension

Semi-independent suspension means that the right and left wheel are partially independent of each other. This type suspension uses a flexing axle, like the one in Fig. 64-26. When one tire hits a bump, its control arm moves up. Since the axle can flex or twist, the other tire is not affected or tilted as much.

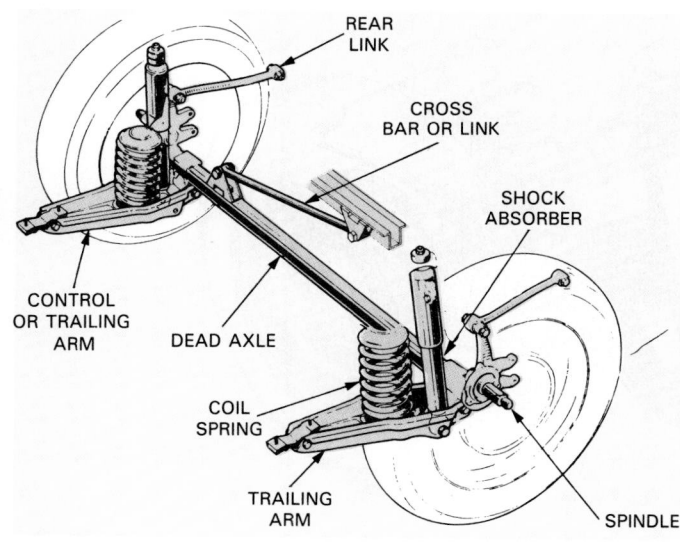

REAR
LINK

CROSS
BAR OR LINK

SHOCK
ABSORBER

CONTROL
OR TRAILING
ARM

DEAD AXLE

COIL
SPRING

TRAILING
ARM

SPINDLE

Fig. 64-26. Dead axle generally refers to solid axle that does not drive wheels. (Saab)

Independent rear suspension

Many new cars use independent rear suspension. As with front suspension, independent suspension increases ride smoothness. This type suspension can be used with either a front or rear-wheel drive car. Refer to Figs. 64-27 and 64-28.

SUSPENSION LEVELING SYSTEMS

A *suspension leveling system* is used to maintain the same vehicle *attitude* (body height) with changes in the amount of weight in the car. For example, if weight is added in the trunk, the suspension leveling system keeps the springs from compressing and lowering the body height.

There are two classifications of suspension leveling systems: manual and automatic.

Manual suspension leveling system

A *manual suspension leveling system* uses air shocks and an electric compressor to counteract changes in passenger and luggage weight. A manual switch can be used to activate the compressor to alter air shock pressure and body height.

Automatic suspension leveling system

Automatic suspension leveling systems use air shocks or air springs, height sensors, and a compressor to maintain curb height. System designs vary.

Fig. 64-29 shows an automatic suspension leveling system that uses air-filled shock absorbers. A height sensor is connected to the frame and to the axle housing. If load changes, the sensor can turn the compressor on to counteract increased load. It can also bleed air out to counteract decreased load.

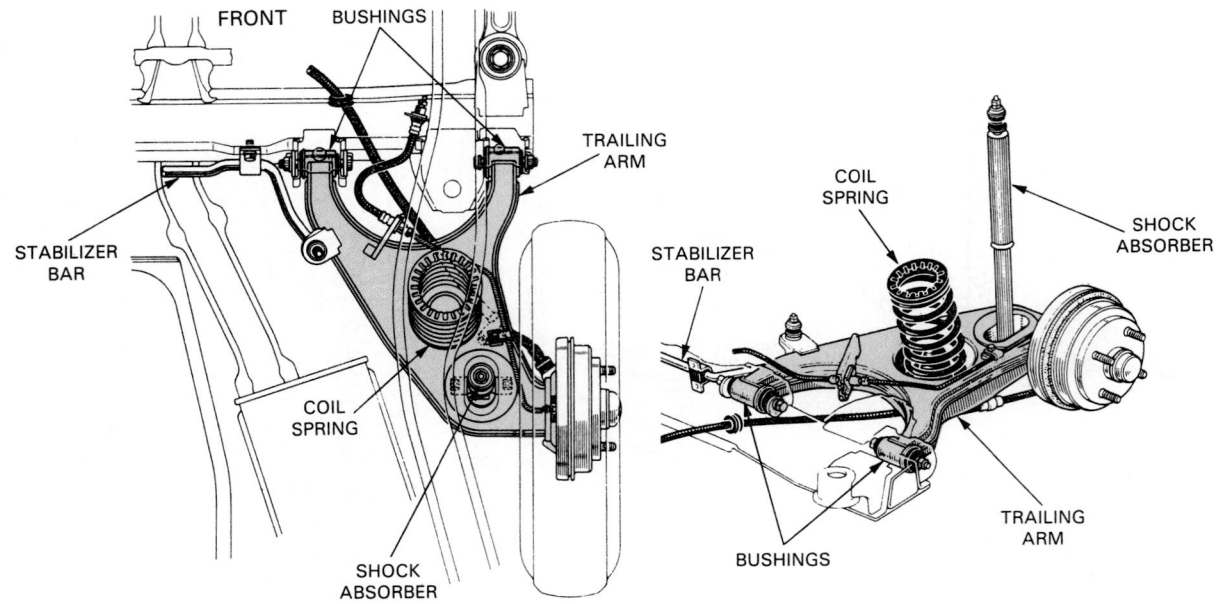

Fig. 64-27. Top and side views of trailing arm, independent rear suspension. Note location of bushings, spring, and shock absorber. (Toyota)

Fig. 64-30 shows a very modern automatic air suspension system. It uses AIR SPRINGS and height sensors on all four wheels. A microcomputer uses information (electric signals) from the sensors to operate the air compressor.

ACTIVE SUSPENSION SYSTEM

An *active suspension system*, Fig. 64-31, uses hydraulic rams instead of conventional suspension system springs and shock absorbers. The hydraulic

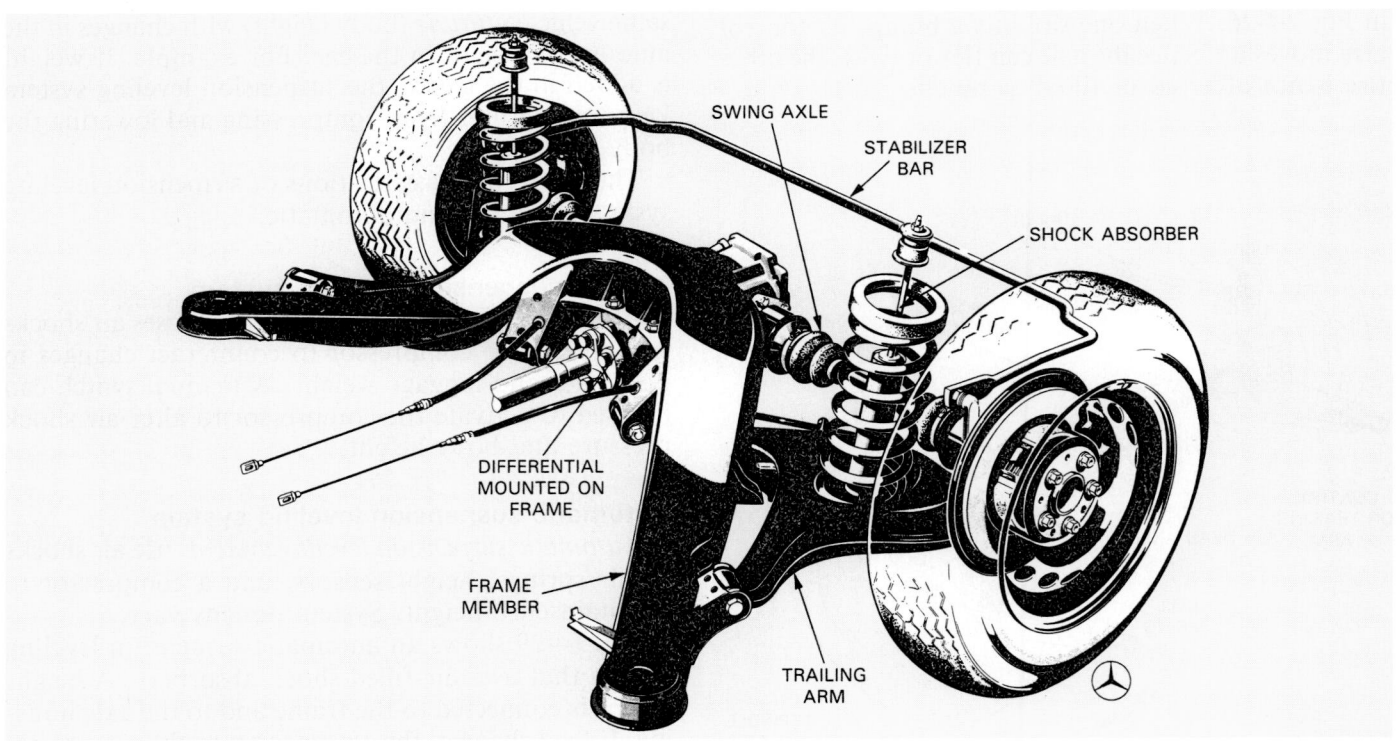

Fig. 64-28. This rear drive axle uses a differential that is mounted solid on frame. Swing axles extend out to drive wheels. Note trailing arms and other components. (Mercedes Benz)

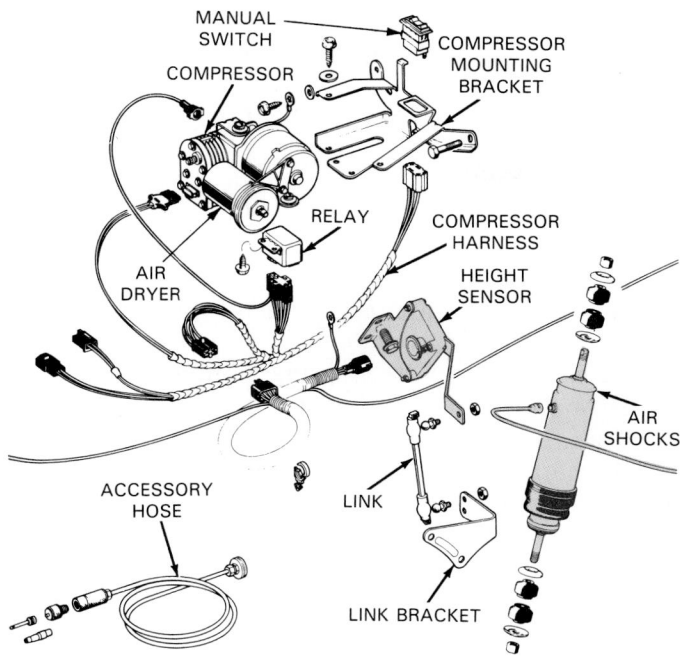

Fig. 64-29. Major parts of suspension leveling system. Basically, height sensor operates air pump. Air pump operates air shocks to maintain correct vehicle height. (American Motors)

The active suspension system can eliminate most body movement as the vehicle travels over small dips and bumps in the road. It can prevent body roll or even tilt the vehicle body against a turn to improve handling. It can also prevent nose dive on braking and body squat on acceleration.

Basically, pressure sensors on each hydraulic ram are used as the main control for the system. They react to suspension system movement and send signals to the computer. The computer can then extend or retract each ram to match the road surface.

For example, if one side of the vehicle travels over a bump in the road, the pressure sensors can instantly detect a rise in pressure inside the ram as the tire and wheel push up on the suspension and hydraulic ram. Instead of making the vehicle body rise with spring action, the computer can release enough ram pressure to allow the suspension to move up over the bump without chassis or body movement.

Then, as the tire travels back down over the bump, the sensor detects a pressure drop in the ram and the computer can increase ram pressure so the tire follows the road surface. A hydraulic pump provides pressure to operate the suspension system rams.

KNOW THESE TERMS

Control arms, Steering knuckle, Ball joint, Shock absorber, Control arm bushing, Independent suspension, Nonindependent suspension, Coil spring, Leaf spring, Air spring, Torsion bar, Spring rate, Unsprung

rams help support the weight of the vehicle and also react to the road surface and different driving conditions. An active suspension system is similar to an electronic shock absorber system but is more complex.

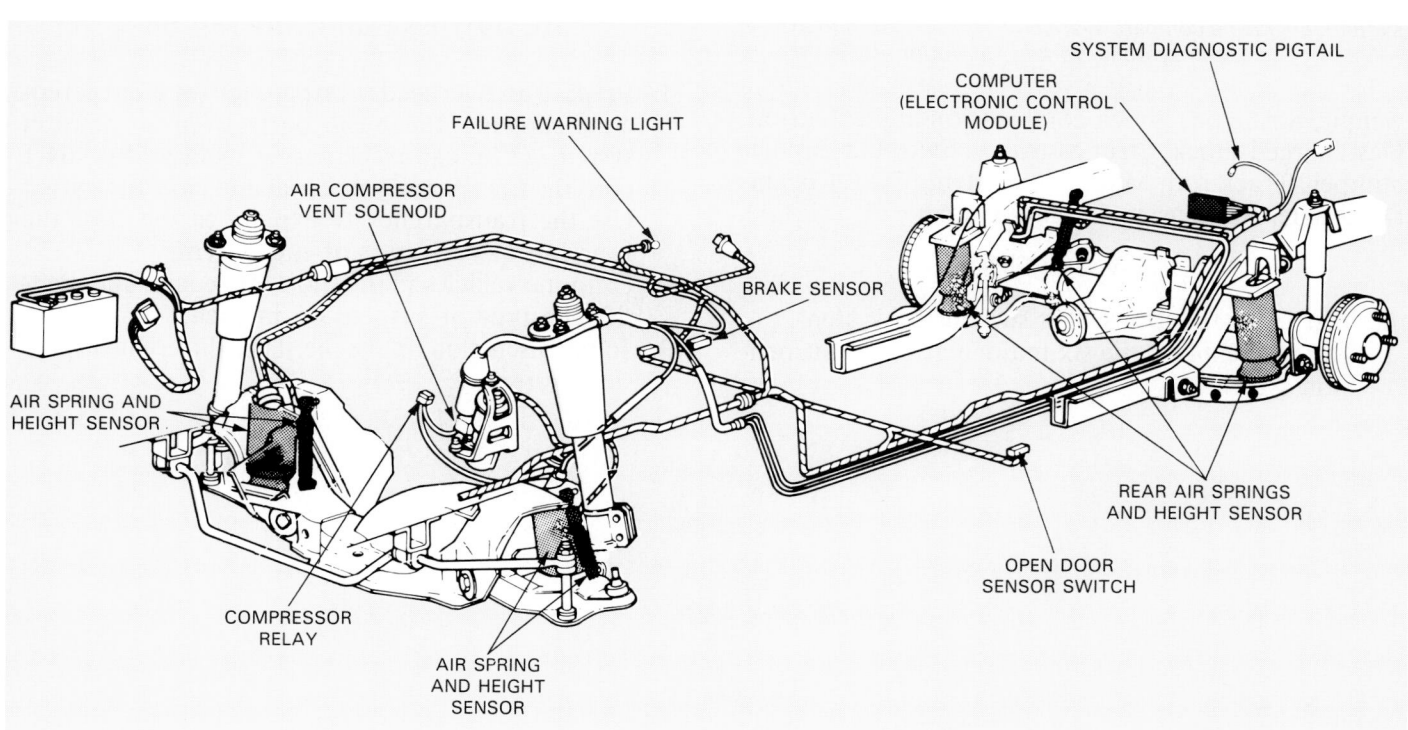

Fig. 64-30. Suspension leveling system using air springs. Study parts. (Ford Motor Co.)

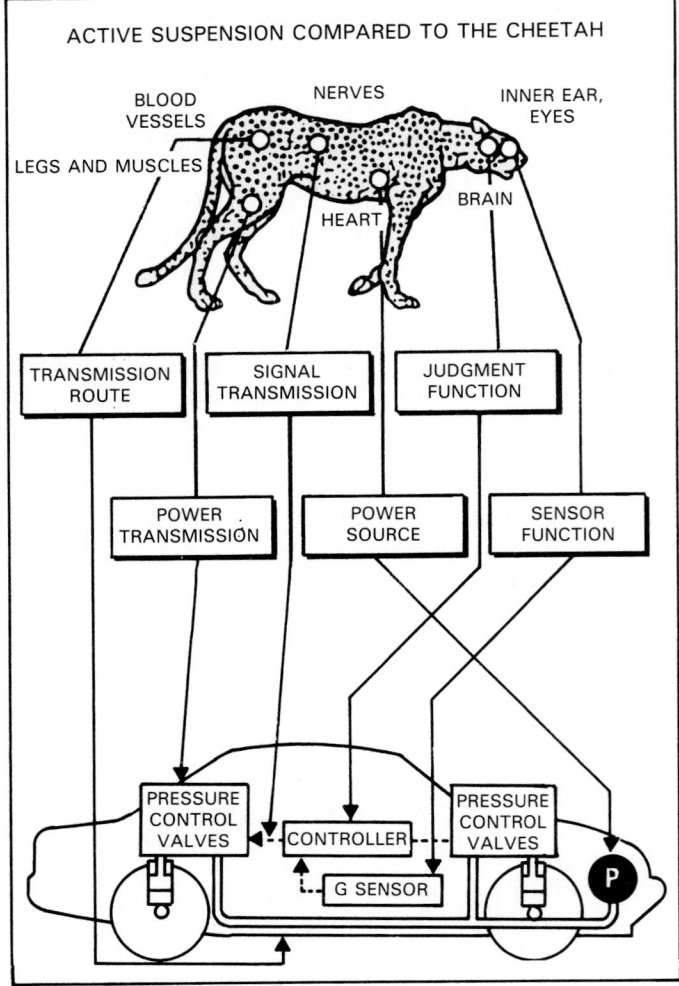

ACTIVE SUSPENSION COMPARED TO THE CHEETAH

Fig. 64-31. Full-Active Suspension is called an "intelligent" suspension because computer is used to control hydraulic system. Engineers compare system with the cheetah to explain how system works. (Infiniti)

weight, Strut rod, Shock compression and extension, Gas-charged shock, Strut assembly, Sway bar, Jounce bumper, Track rod, MacPherson strut, Twin I-beam, Dead axle, Suspension leveling system.

REVIEW QUESTIONS

1. List eight functions of a suspension system.
2. List and explain the six major parts of a suspension system.
3. _____ _____ allows one wheel to move up and down with a minimum effect on the other wheels.
4. This is the most common type of suspension system spring:
   a. Leaf.
   b. Coil.
   c. Air.
   d. Torsion bar.
5. A _____ fastens the rear of a leaf spring to the car frame.
6. Define the term "leaf spring windup."
7. How does a torsion bar work?
8. The _____ weight of a car is the weight of the parts NOT supported by the springs.
9. A strut rod is used to keep the steering knuckle from swiveling. True or False?
10. Why are ball joints needed?
11. Summarize the basic operation of a conventional shock absorber.
12. What is the advantage or purpose of gas-charged shocks?
13. List and explain the ten major parts of a strut assembly.
14. This part is used to keep the car body from rolling or leaning excessively in turns or corners.
    a. Strut rod.
    b. Jounce bumper.
    c. Track rod.
    d. Sway bar.
15. In your own words, describe a MacPherson strut suspension.

ACTIVITIES FOR CHAPTER 64

1. Prepare an overhead transparency (or transparencies) showing the basic parts of a suspension system. (You can trace and/or enlarge Fig. 64-1 onto the transparency material and label the parts.) Use the transparency to explain to the class the function of each part of the system.
2. Examine vehicles in the shop for repairs and identify the type of suspension in each.
3. Join a discussion on the merits of different suspension systems.

65

Suspension System Diagnosis and Repair

After studying this chapter, you will be able to:
- ☐ Diagnose problems relating to a suspension system.
- ☐ Replace shock absorbers and ball joints.
- ☐ Describe the removal and replacement of springs.
- ☐ Service a strut assembly.
- ☐ Replace control arm bushings.
- ☐ Use safe work procedures while repairing suspension systems.

A suspension system takes a tremendous "pounding" during normmal vehicle operation. Bumps and potholes in the road cause constant movement, fatigue, and wear of shock absorbers, ball joints, bushings, springs, and other parts. This chapter covers the most common procedures for diagnosing and repairing the problems of modern vehicular suspension systems. Study carefully before attempting repair work.

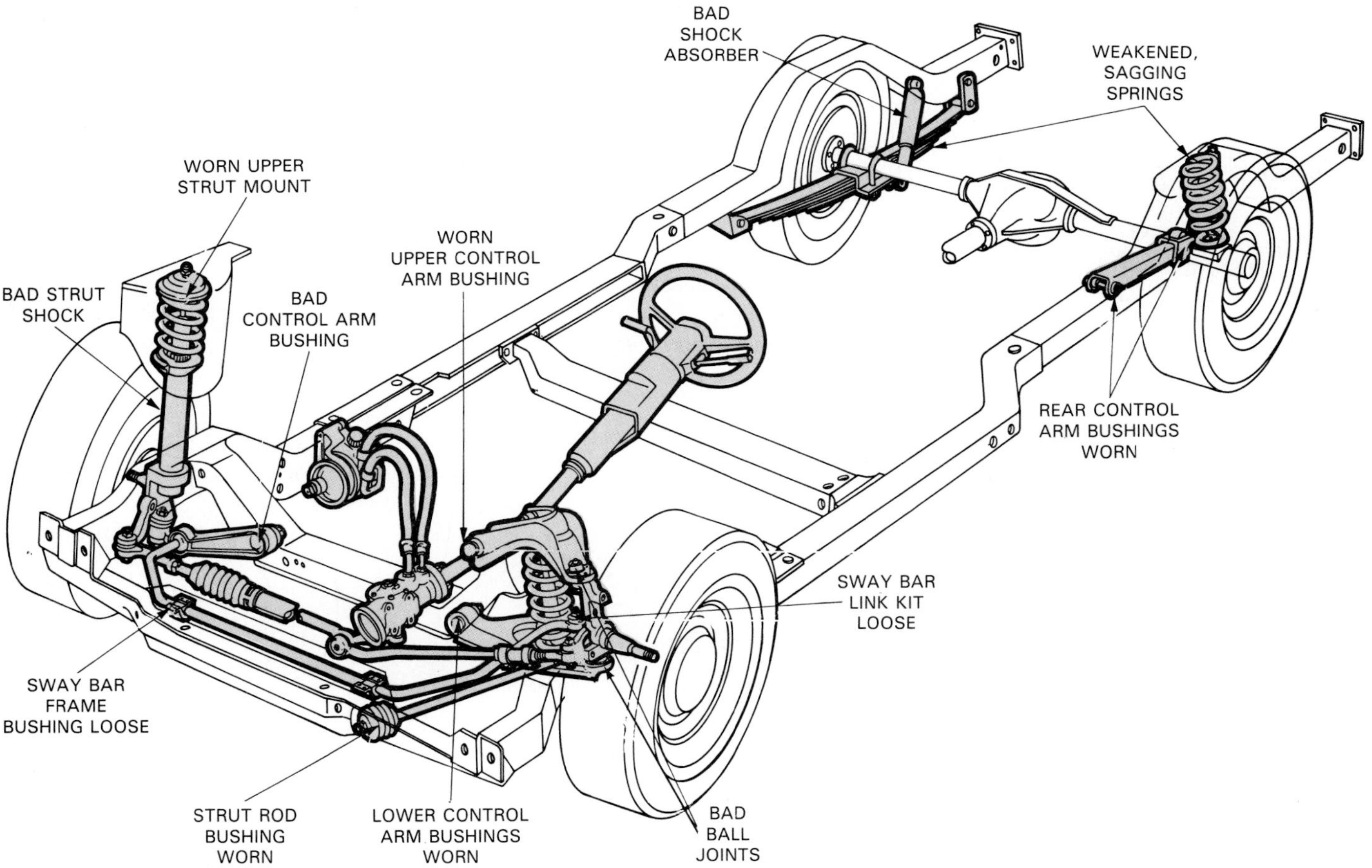

BAD SHOCK ABSORBER

WEAKENED, SAGGING SPRINGS

WORN UPPER STRUT MOUNT

WORN UPPER CONTROL ARM BUSHING

BAD STRUT SHOCK

BAD CONTROL ARM BUSHING

REAR CONTROL ARM BUSHINGS WORN

SWAY BAR LINK KIT LOOSE

SWAY BAR FRAME BUSHING LOOSE

STRUT ROD BUSHING WORN

LOWER CONTROL ARM BUSHINGS WORN

BAD BALL JOINTS

Fig. 65-1. Study types of problems that can develop in suspension system. (Moog)

SUSPENSION SYSTEM DIAGNOSIS

Suspension system problems usually show up as abnormal noises (pops, squeaks, clunks), tire wear, steering wheel pull, or *front end shimmy* (side to side vibration). You must make sure that the trouble is in the suspension system, and NOT in the steering, wheel bearings, tires, or other related parts.

Suspension system wear can upset the operation of the steering system and change wheel alignment angles. Worn ball joints may let the steering knuckles tilt sideways on their control arms. This, in turn, allows the wheels and tires to cock or lean.

To begin diagnosis of a suspension system, talk to the customer or service writer. Then, either inspect the parts that could cause the problem or test drive the car. Fig. 65-1 shows typical problem areas.

Fig. 65-2 is an exploded view of the parts of a common front-wheel suspension assembly. Study the relationship between the parts.

SHOCK ABSORBER SERVICE

Worn shock absorbers will cause a car to ride poorly on rough roads, Fig. 65-2. When the tire strikes a bump, the bad shock does not dampen spring oscillations. The suspension system will continue to jounce and rebound. This movement is transferred to the frame, body, and passenger compartment.

A *loose* or *damaged shock absorber* may produce a loud clanking or banging sound. The rapid up and down suspension movement can hammer the loose shock absorber against the body, shock tower, or control arm.

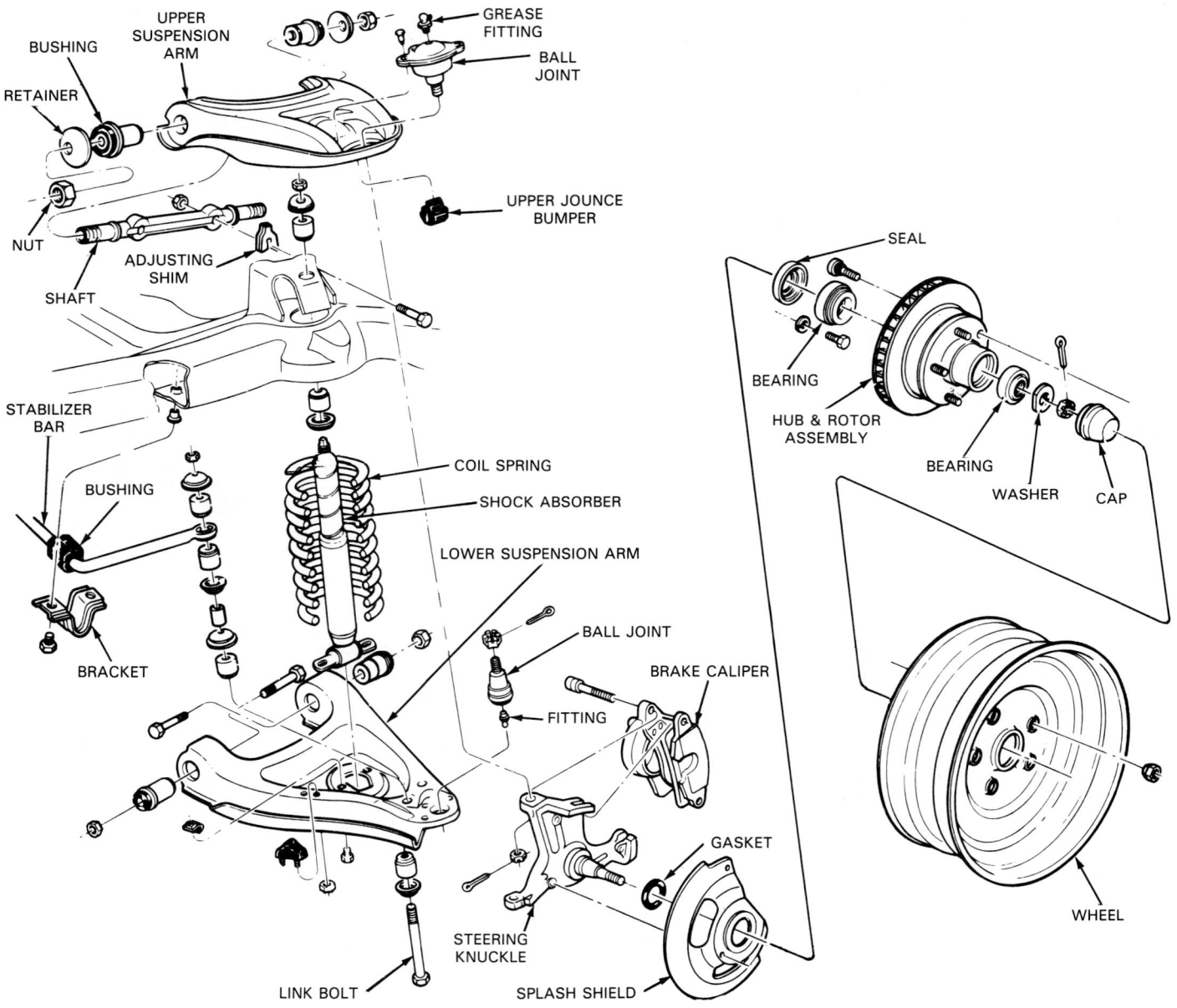

Fig. 65-2. Note parts of this long-short arm suspension. (Cadillac)

Checking shock absorber condition

A shock bounce test and visual inspection will normally locate shock absorber problems.

To perform a **shock bounce test,** simply push up and down on each corner of the car body. Then release the body and count the number of times the car moves up and down.

Generally, GOOD shock absorbers should stop body movement in two or three rebounds. BAD shock absorbers will let the body bounce over three times.

Also, inspect the shock absorbers for signs of leakage (oily wetness) and damage. If the shock is leaking oil, new shocks are needed.

Check the rubber bushings on each end of the shock. They should NOT be smashed or split. Make sure the shock absorber fasteners are tight.

Replacing shock absorbers

When shock absorber replacement is needed, the wheels and tires must usually be removed. Place the car on jack stands or on a lift.

WARNING! With many suspension systems, you must place the jack stands or lift devices under the control arms or axle. This will keep the control arms or axle from flying downward when the shock is unbolted.

Remove the old shock absorbers, Fig. 65-3. If the fasteners are rusted, spray rust penetrant on the threads. When a threaded stud and nut are used, you may need to hold the stud while turning the nut. Install the new shock in reverse order of removal.

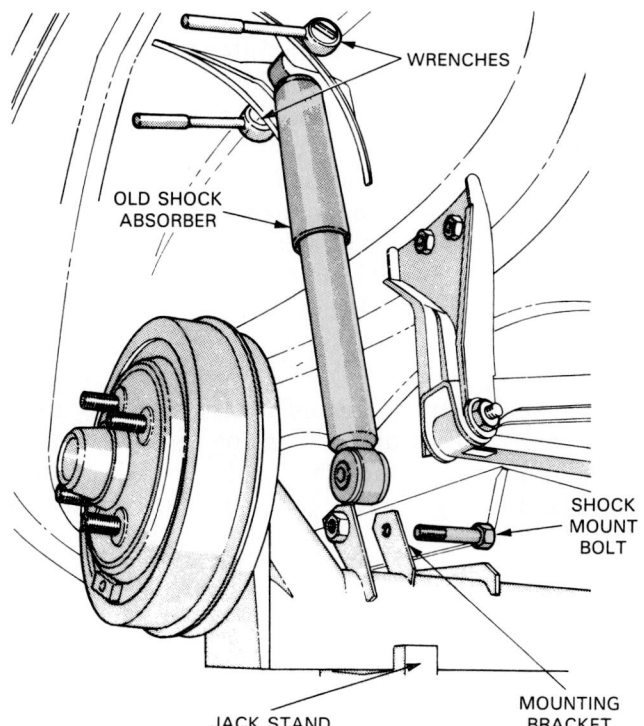

Fig. 65-3. Conventional shock absorber removal simply involves unbolting top and bottom of shock. Support weight of suspension if needed.   (Chrysler Corp.)

Air- and gas-charged shock service

Air- and *gas-charged shocks* are replaced using the same general procedures described for conventional shocks. Gas-filled shocks must be replaced when faulty. Air shocks may be repairable.

The most common problem with air shocks is AIR LEAKAGE. The air lines, air valve, or shocks can develop pinhole leaks that let air pressure bleed off.

To find air leaks, wipe on a soap and water solution at possible leakage points (air line fittings, around shock boots, and air valve). Bubbles are signs of leakage. If a line, fitting, or shock leaks, it should be tightened or replaced.

CAUTION! NEVER exceed the recommended maximum air pressure given for air shocks. If excess pressure is forced into the system, the shocks can be ruptured (blown apart) and ruined.

SUSPENSION SPRING SERVICE

Spring fatigue (weakening) lowers the height of the vehicle, allowing the body to settle toward the axles. Fatigue can occur after prolonged service. This settling or sagging changes the position of the control arms, resulting in misalignment of the wheels. This condition also affects the ride and appearance of the vehicle.

Curb height and curb weight

To check spring condition or torsion bar adjustment, measure **curb height** (distance from point on car to ground). Place the car on a level surface. Then, measure from a service manual specified point on the frame, body, or suspension down to the shop floor. Compare your measurements to specs.

If the curb height is too low (measurement too small), replace the fatigued springs or adjust torsion bar tension.

Curb weight is generally the total weight of the car with a full tank of fuel and no passengers or luggage. It is given in pounds or kilograms. The car should be at curb weight when checking spring condition and curb height. Remove everything from the trunk except the spare tire and jack. Also make sure nothing is in the back or front seats that could increase curb weight.

Coil spring replacement

A *coil spring compressor* may be needed when removing and installing a coil spring. Pictured in Fig. 65-4, it is a special tool for squeezing the spring coils to reduce their height. This will give you enough room to slide the spring out of the control arm.

DANGER! A compressed coil spring has a tremendous amount of stored energy. NEVER unbolt the ball joint without FIRST compressing the coil spring. If the spring is NOT compressed, the lower control arm and spring could move downward with DEADLY FORCE.

To remove a coil spring from most front suspensions, place the car on jack stands. Remove the shock ab-

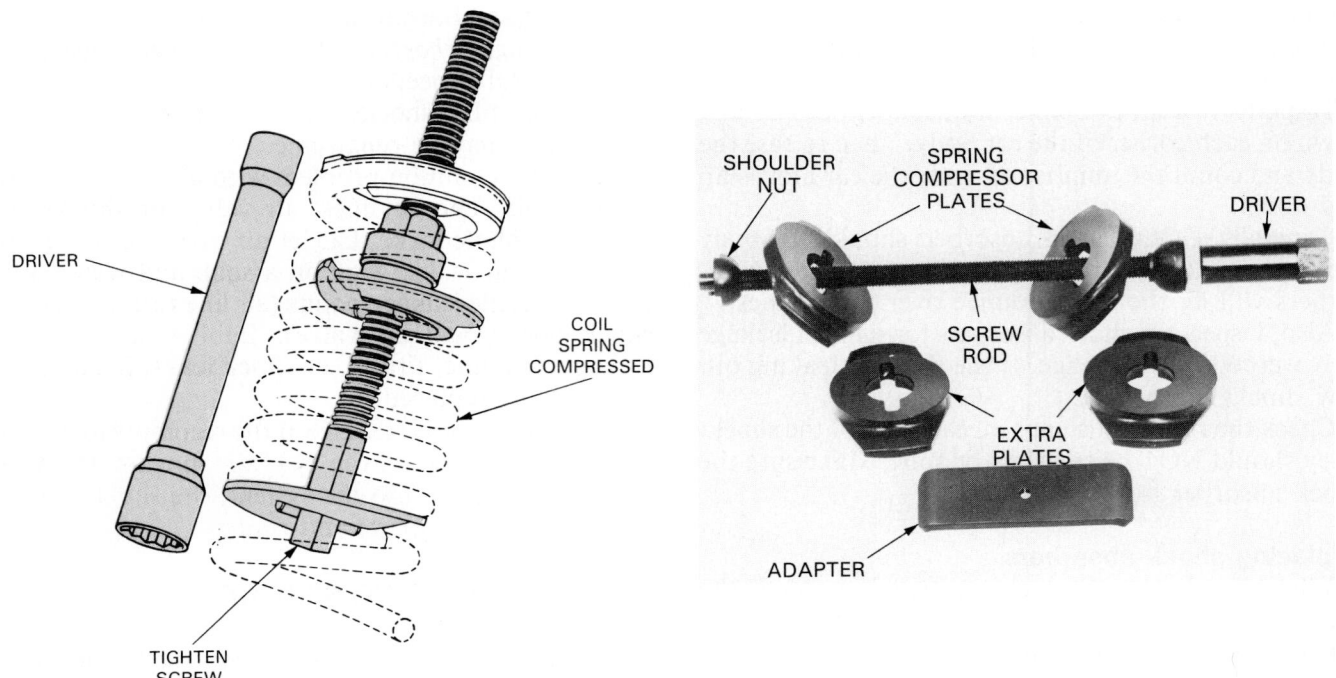

Fig. 65-4. Coil spring compressor must be used to squeeze coils together before unbolting ball joints. This will keep the spring from flying out with deadly force. (OTC Div. of SPX Corp.)

sorber. Install the spring compressor. Then, unbolt the lower ball joint.

Use a *fork tool* or *ball joint separator,* Fig. 65-5, and hammer blows to remove the lower ball joint from the steering knuckle. Special pullers and drivers are also available for ball joint separation.

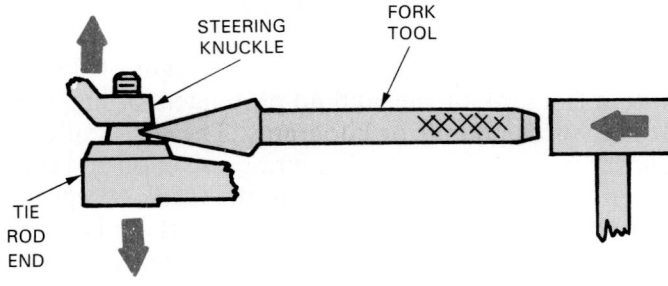

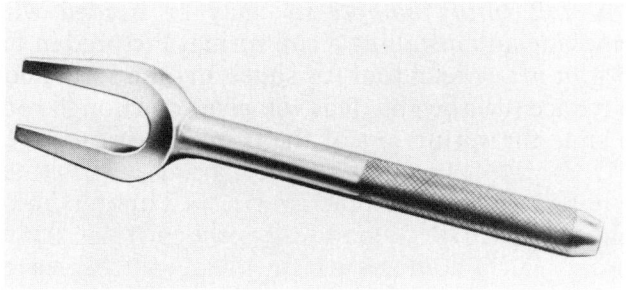

Fig. 65-5. Fork or separator is used to force ball joint stud out of steering knuckle. (OTC Div. of SPX Corp.)

Make sure you also remove any other component (brake line, strut rod, steering linkage) that could be damaged when the control arm is lowered. Pull the spring and compressor out as a unit.

Install the compressor on the new spring. Slip the spring into place and position the coil ends in the same location as the old spring. Reassemble the ball joint and other components. Then, unscrew the spring compressor while guiding the coil into its seats. Keep your fingers out from under the spring!

When replacing a rear coil spring, a spring compressor may NOT be needed. As shown in Fig. 65-6, the axle should drop far enough to free the coil spring. Support the weight of the axle on jack stands or a floor jack. Always reinstall isolators or the new spring could squeak or rattle. Check a manual for exact procedures.

Leaf spring service

Leaf spring service usually involves spring or bushing replacement. Basically, for spring replacement, place jack stands under the frame. Then, use a floor jack to raise the weight of the rear axle off the leaf spring.

WARNING! Never drive out the leaf spring eye or shackle bolts unless all force is released from the spring. The eye bolts should pull out or drive out easily. If removed with weight on the spring, the spring could FLY UPWARD OR DOWNWARD with LETHAL FORCE.

Install the new leaf spring in the opposite order. Make sure you position the axle assembly on the leaf spring correctly. A small guide pin may be provided to assure proper rear axle alignment.

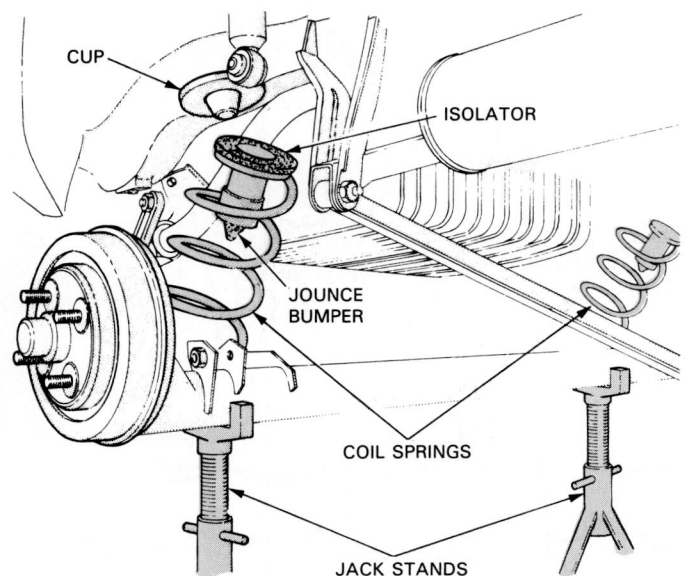

Fig. 65-6. Rear coil spring can usually be removed by simply dropping axle slowly after unbolting shock. (Chrysler)

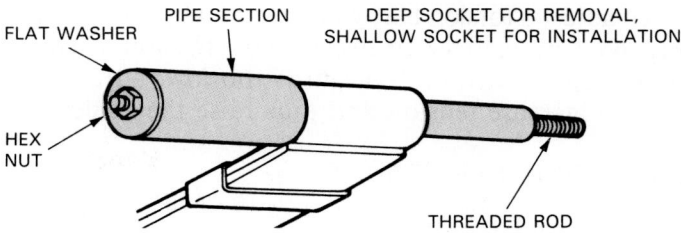

Fig. 65-7. Driving tool makes worn bushing removal easy. When hex nut is tightened, tool pushes bushing out of spring. (Chrysler)

When just the leaf spring bushings are worn, they can be replaced without spring removal. Use a special pulling-driving tool, like the one in Fig. 65-7.

Torsion bar service

Most torsion bars are adjustable. Thus, torsion bar replacement is NOT frequently needed. Fig. 65-8 illustrates a torsion bar and its related components.

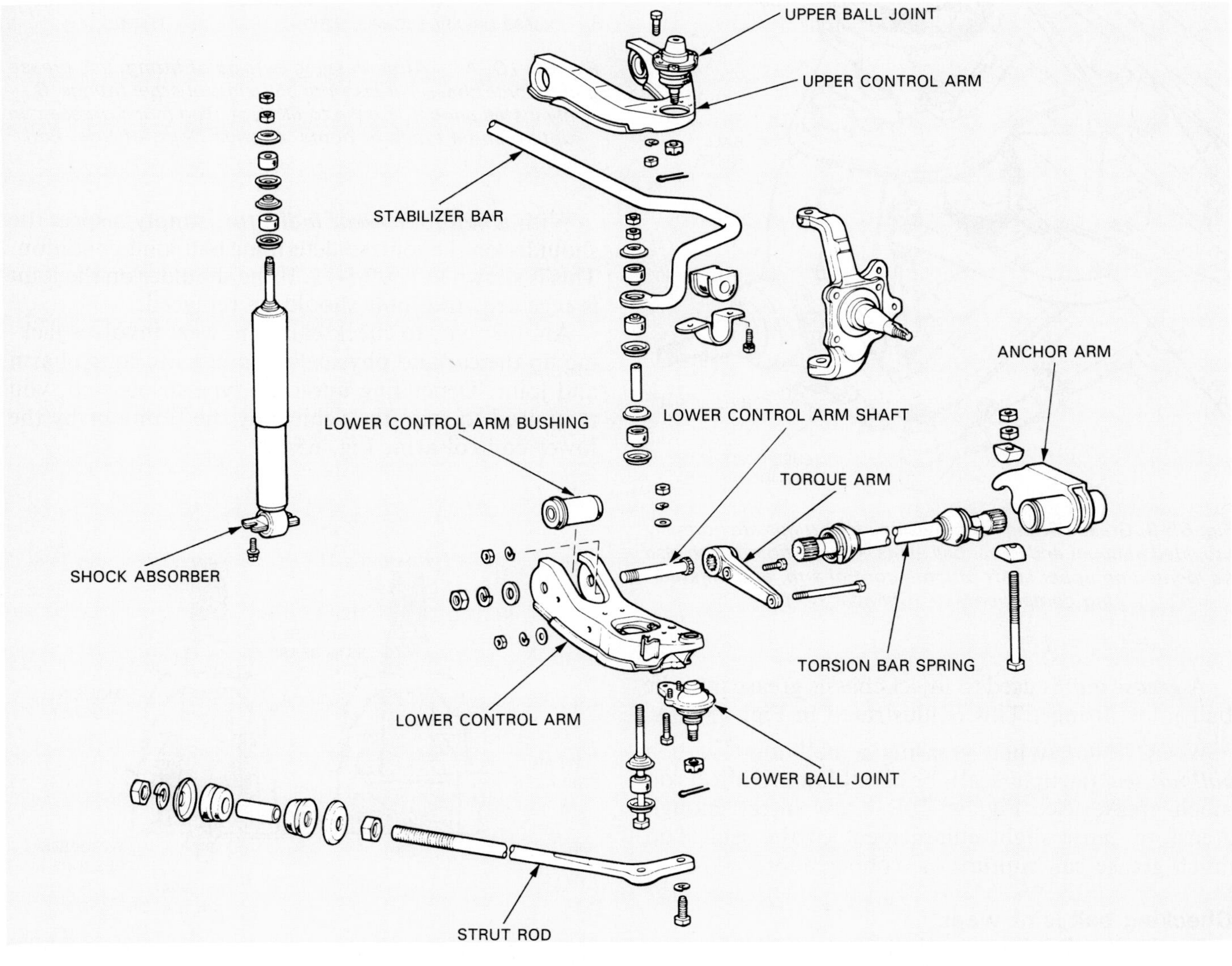

Fig. 65-8. Exploded view of torsion bar suspension. Study part relationships (Toyota)

To adjust a torsion bar, you must usually turn a bolt, Fig. 65-8, to increase or decrease the tension or twist on the bar. When curb height is too low, adjust the bolt to increase tension and thus raise the vehicle.

BALL JOINT SERVICE

Worn ball joints cause the steering knuckle and wheel assembly to be loose on the control arms. A worn ball joint might make a clunking or popping sound when turning or when driving over a bump.

Ball joint lubrication

Ball joint wear is usually a result of improper lubrication or prolonged use. The load-carrying ball joints support the weight of the vehicle while swiveling into various angles. If dry, the joints can wear out quickly.

Look at Fig. 65-9. Grease fittings or lube plugs are provided for ball joint lubrication. The plugs must be removed. Then, grease fittings can be installed.

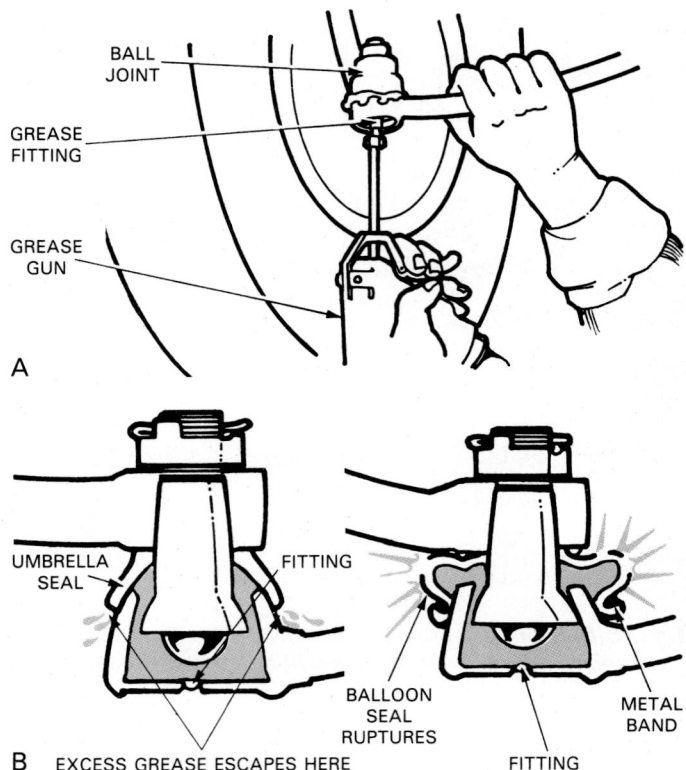

Fig. 65-10. A — After cleaning outside of fitting, use grease gun to force chassis grease into ball joints or other fittings. B — Only install enough grease to fill boot. Too much grease can rupture some types of boots. (Florida Dept. of Voc. Ed.)

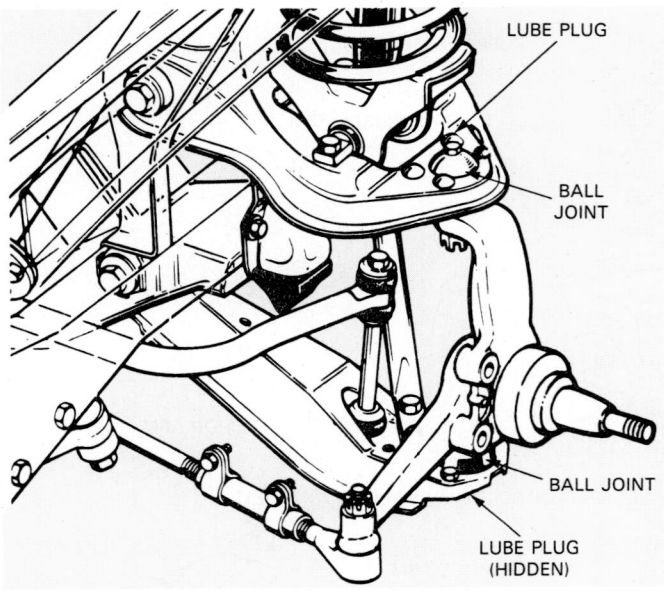

Fig. 65-9. Grease fittings or provisions for fittings are normally provided at upper and lower ball joints. Grease fittings can also be located on upper shaft of inner control arm, and on steering components. (Chrysler Corp.)

A *grease gun* is used to inject chassis grease into the ball joint fittings. This is illustrated in Fig. 65-10A.

WARNING! When greasing a ball joint with a *balloon seal* (airtight seal), be careful not to inject too much grease. See Fig. 65-10B. Only inject enough grease to cause slight enlargement of the seal. Too much grease can rupture the rubber boot.

Checking ball joint wear

To check ball joint wear, inspect the ball joint wear indicator or measure the play in the joint.

With a *ball joint wear indicator,* simply inspect the shoulder on the joint to determine ball joint condition. This is shown in Fig. 65-11. If the shoulder on the joint is recessed, the joint should be replaced.

Another way to check ball joint wear involves jacking up the car and physically moving the control arm and joint. Depending upon the type suspension, you may need to raise the vehicle by the frame or by the lower control arm, Fig. 65-12.

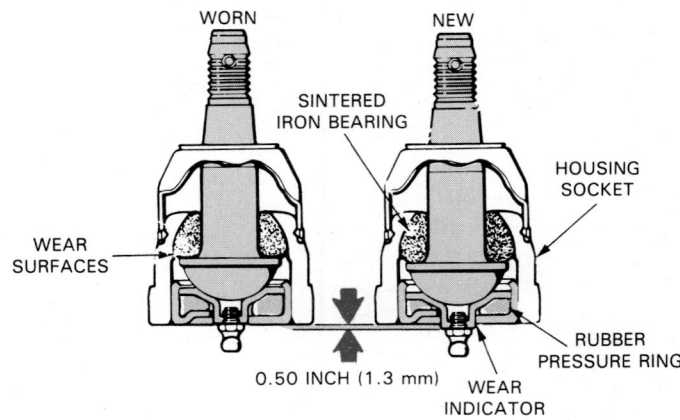

Fig. 65-11. This ball joint has wear indicator. When shoulder recedes into socket, new joint is needed. (Moog)

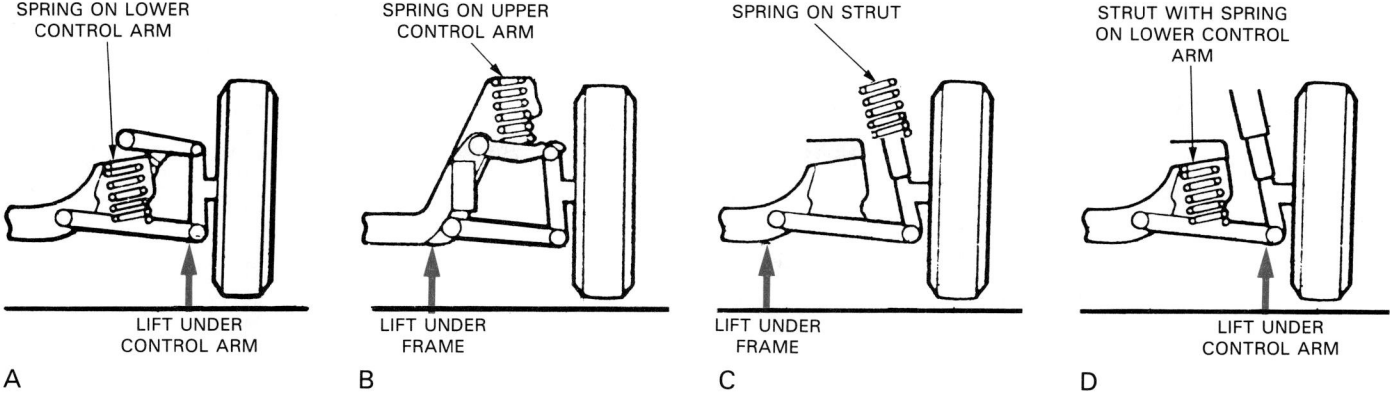

Fig. 65-12. Study lift points for different suspension systems. Specific lift point is needed when checking for ball joint and bushing wear. (Ford)

With the suspension properly raised, use a long steel pry bar to wiggle the tire up and down and sideways. See Fig. 65-13. While wiggling, note the amount of movement in the ball joints. Refer to service manual specs and replace any ball joint worn too much.

Ball joint replacement

Ball joint replacement can usually be done without removing the control arm. Generally, place the vehicle on jack stands. Remove the shock absorber and install a spring compressor on the coil spring. Unbolt the steering knuckle and separate the knuckle and joint.

Fig. 65-13. With car jacked up properly, use long pry bar to wiggle up and down on tire. This will help detect part wear. (Moog)

The ball joint may be pressed, riveted, bolted, or screwed into the control arm. Fig. 65-14 shows how to remove and install a press-in ball joint. Fig. 65-15 illustrates service of a riveted ball joint. Bolts are commonly used to replace the rivets, Fig. 65-16.

A service manual will give the details.

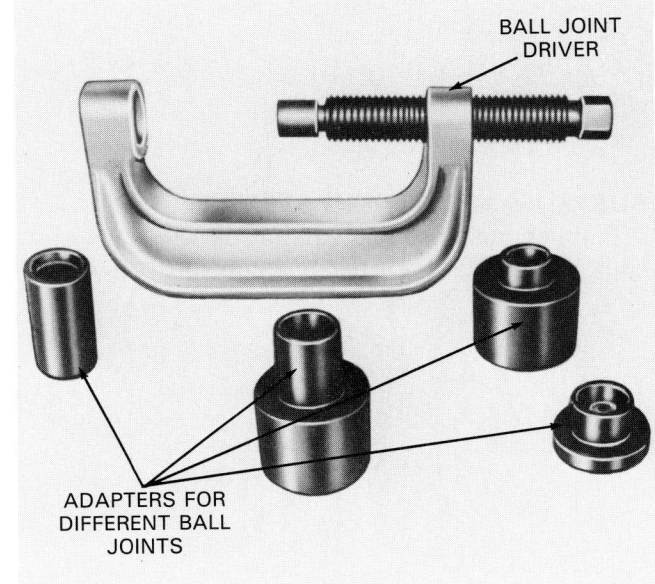

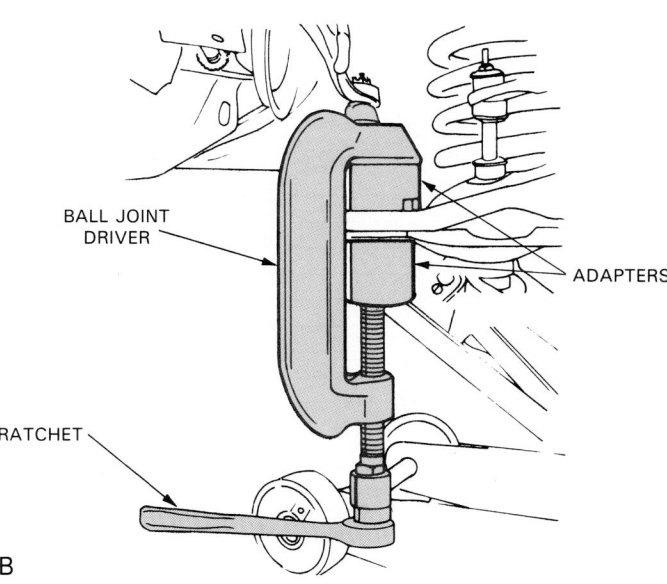

Fig. 65-14. A — Special driving tool. B — Driver is being used to force ball joint out of control arm. Wear eye protection. (Buick)

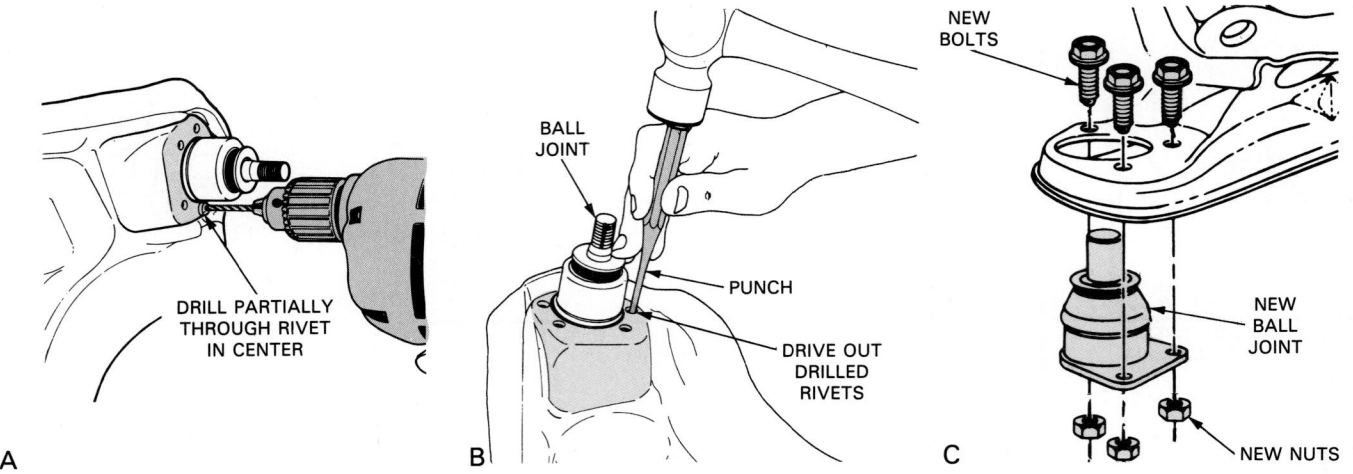

Fig. 65-15. Replacement of riveted ball joint. A — Drill out rivet heads. B — Use punch to drive out rivets. C — Bolt on new ball joint. (Oldsmobile)

CAUTION! Always install a NEW COTTER PIN when a ball joint nut is removed. An old cotter pin could break, causing a serious auto accident.

SUSPENSION BUSHING SERVICE

Rubber bushings are commonly used in the inner ends of front control arms, rear control arms, and other parts. These bushings are wear prone and should be inspected periodically.

Worn control arm bushings can let the control arms move sideways, causing tire wear and steering problems. Look at Fig. 65-16. It shows the various bushings used on a front suspension. Fig. 65-17 pictures the bushings used on a rear suspension system.

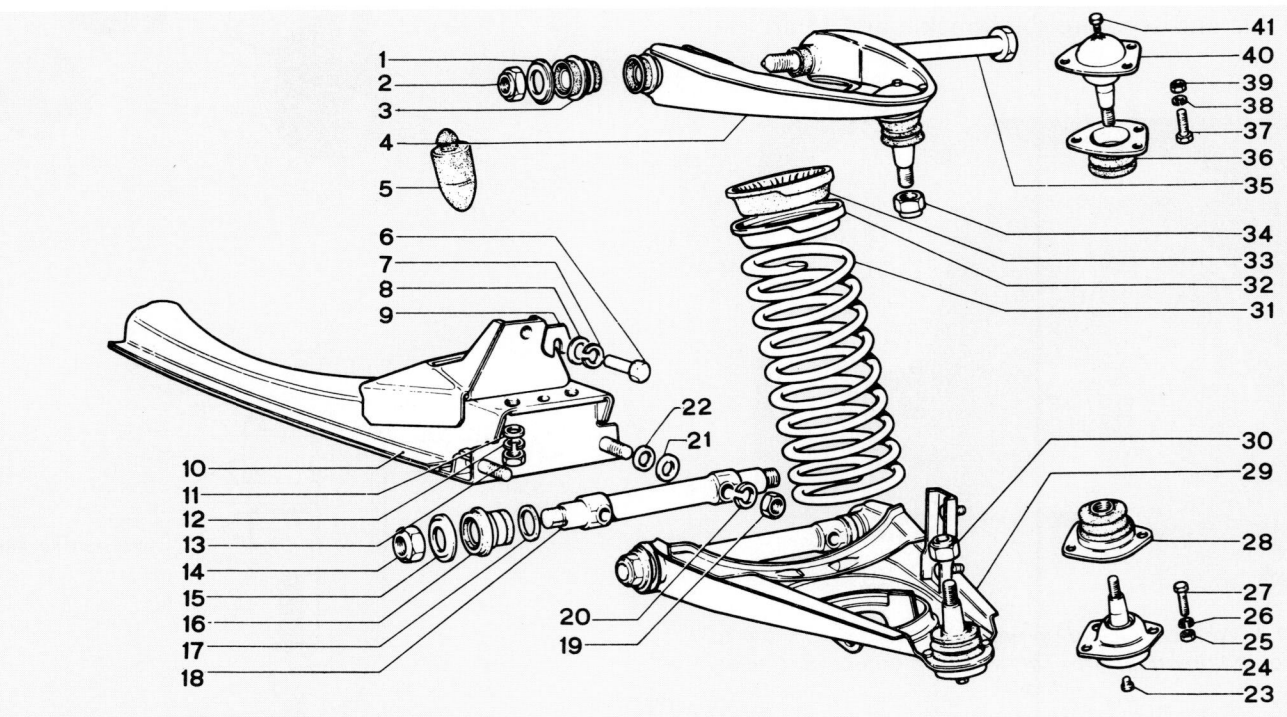

1. Cup. - 2. Nut fixing upper control arm to body. - 3. Resilient bushing. - 4. Upper control arm. - 5. Buffer. - 6. Bolt. - 7. Spring washer. - 8. Flat washer. - 9. Tab strip. - 10. Crossmember. - 11. Flat washer. - 12. Spring washer. - 13. Nut. - 14. Nut fixing pivot bar 18 to lower control arm. - 15. Cup. - 16. Resilient bushing. - 17. Flat washer. - 18. Pivot bar. - 19. Nut fixing lower control arm to crossmember 10. - 20. Spring washer. - 21. Flat washer. - 22. Tab strip. - 23. Plug. - 24. Lower ball joint. - 25. Nut. - 26. Spring washer. - 27. Bolt. - 28. Seal. - 29. Lower control arm. - 30. Self-locking nut fixing steering knuckle to lower control arm. - 31. Spring. - 32. Spring seat. - 33. Rubber pad. - 34. Self-locking nut fixing steering knuckle to upper control arm. - 35. Bolt. - 36. Seal. - 37. Bolt. - 38. Spring washer. - 39. Nut. - 40. Upper ball joint. - 41. Plug.

Fig. 65-16. Study how ball joints fit into upper and lower control arms. Bolts secure joints. Also note location of control arm bushings.

Checking bushing wear

To check for bushing wear, try to move the control arm against normal movement. For example, pry the control arm back and forth while watching the bushings. If the arm moves in relation to its shaft, the bushings are worn and must be replaced.

Bushing replacement

Exact procedures for installing new suspension system bushings vary. Refer to a service manual for exact directions.

Generally, to replace the bushings in a front suspension, remove the control arm, Fig. 65-18. This usually

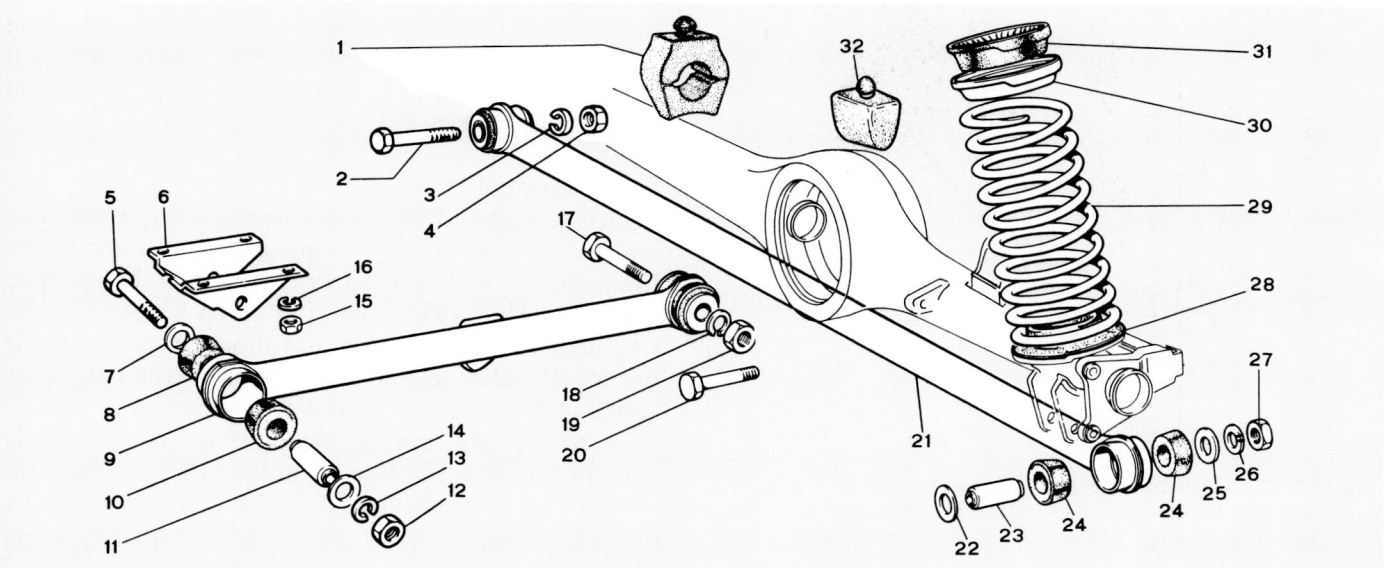

1. Rubber pad. - 2. Bolt anchoring cross rod to body. - 3. Lock washer. - 4. Nut. - 5. Bolt anchoring lower side rod to bracket 6. - 6. Bracket. - 7. Flat washer. - 8. Rubber bushing. - 9. Lower side rod. - 10. Rubber bushing. - 11. Spacer. - 12. Nut. - 13. Lock washer. - 14. Flat washer. - 15. Nut. - 16. Lock washer. - 17. Bolt anchoring lower side rod to axle housing. - 18. Lock washer. - 19. Nut. - 20. Bolt anchoring cross rod to axle housing. - 21. Cross rod. - 22. Flat washer. - 23. Spacer. - 24. Rubber bushings. - 25. Flat washer. - 26. Lock washer. - 27. Nut. - 28. Lower ring-pad. - 29. Coil spring. - 30. Upper seating ring. - 31. Upper rubber ring-pad. - 32. Rubber buffer.

Fig. 65-17. Exploded view shows bushings on one type of rear suspension. (Fiat)

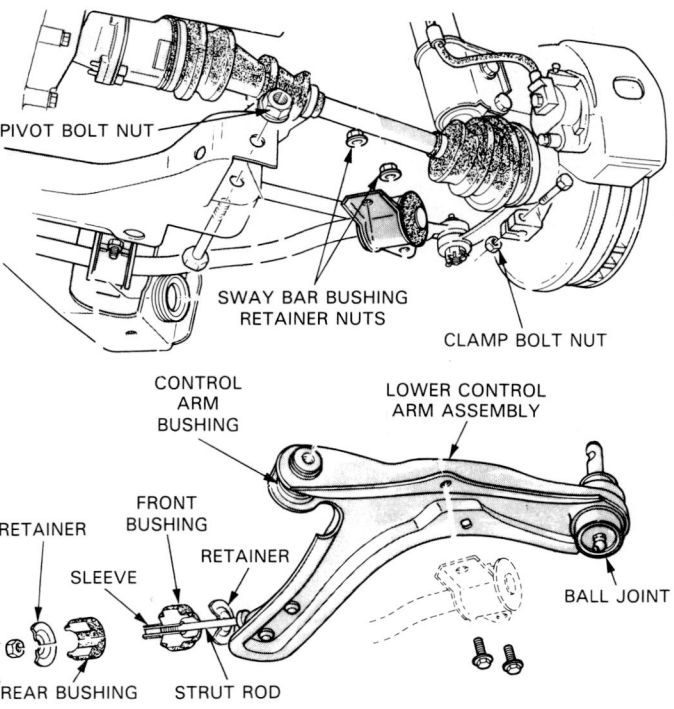

Fig. 65-18. Control arm bushing replacement requires control arm removal. Note parts that must be disconnected on front-wheel drive vehicle. (Chrysler)

requires ball joint separation and compression of the coil spring. The stabilizer bar and strut rod are also unbolted from the control arm. The bolts passing through the bushings are then removed.

With the control arm mounted in a vise, the new bushings may be installed. Either press or screw out the old bushings. Fig. 65-19 shows a tool for pressing a bushing in and out of a control arm. Always refer to a service manual for exact directions and specifications. This will assure a safe, quality repair.

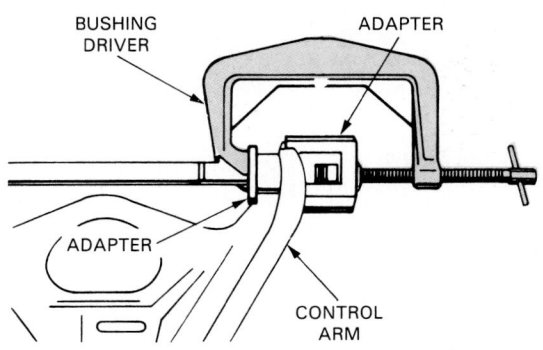

Fig. 65-19. Driving tool is helpful when removing control arm bushings. (Buick)

Assemble and install the control arm in reverse order, Fig. 65-20. Torque all bolts properly. Install the ball joint cotter pin and other components. Check the service manual for information on preloading control arm bushings.

Strut rod bushings and stabilizer (sway) bar bushings also require replacement when worn. See Fig. 65-18.

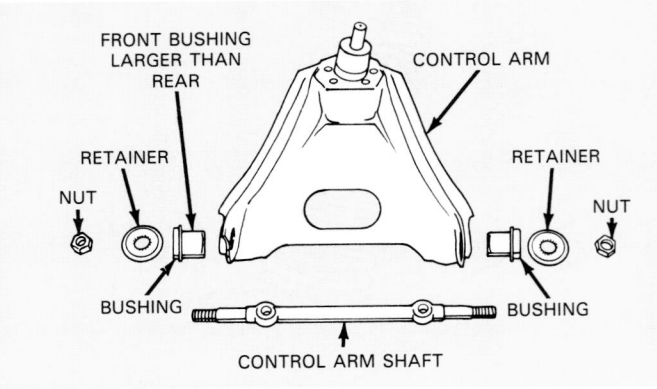

Fig. 65-20. With this design, nuts are used to force new bushings into control arm. Follow service manual directions as specific preload is normally needed. (Oldsmobile)

MACPHERSON STRUT SERVICE

The MacPherson strut suspension can wear and cause problems similar to those covered for other types of suspension systems. The major difference in service procedures relates to how the strut assembly is disassembled and reassembled.

The most common trouble with a strut type suspension is worn shock absorbers. Just like conventional shocks, the pistons and cylinders inside the struts can begin to leak. This reduces the dampening action and the vehicle rides poorly.

Strut removal

Basically, strut removal involves unbolting the steering knuckle (front), or bearing support (rear), any brake lines, and the upper strut assembly-to-body fasteners. This is illustrated in Fig. 65-21. Remove the strut assembly (coil spring and shock) as a single unit, Fig. 65-22. Do not remove the nut on the end of the shock rod or the unit could fly apart.

A *strut spring compressor* is needed to remove the coil spring from the strut. Look at Fig. 65-23. After the coil spring has been squeezed together, remove the upper damper assembly. Then, release spring tension

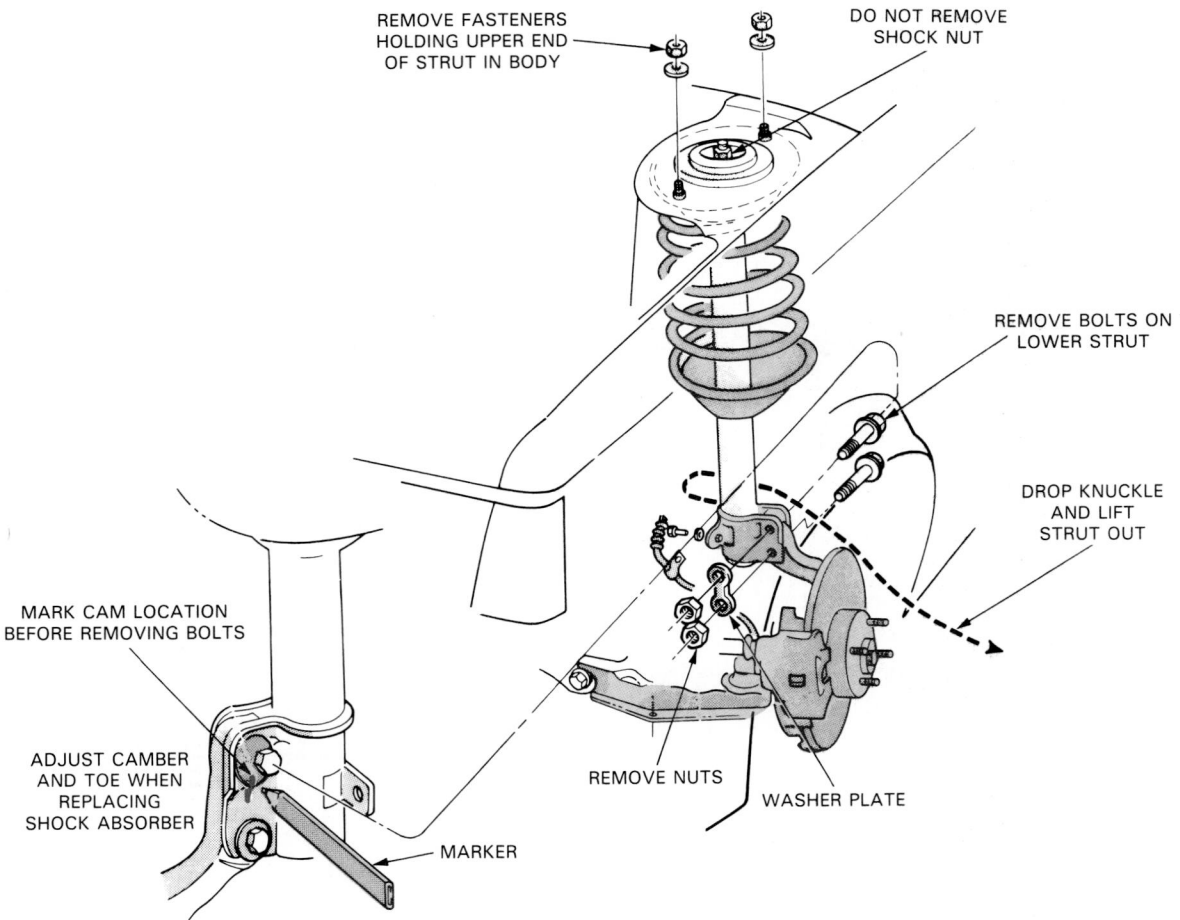

Fig. 65-21. To remove a strut assembly, mark cam type bolt, if used. Unbolt steering knuckle and upper fasteners from strut. (Dodge)

STRUT ASSEMBLY
SUPPORT WEIGHT OF STRUT WHILE REMOVING
HUB AND DISC ASSEMBLY
BALL JOINT AND CONTROL ARM DISCONNECTED

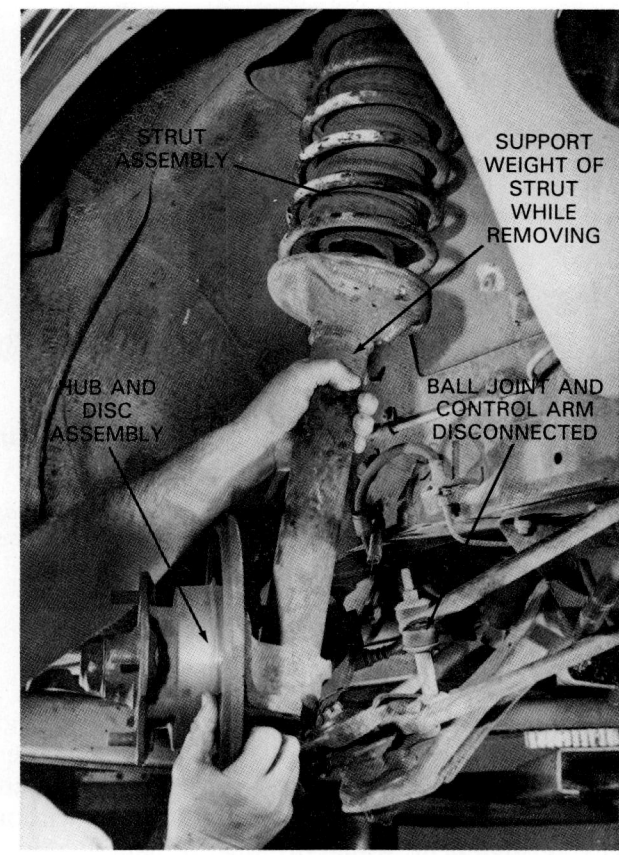

Fig. 65-22. Lift strut out of vehicle carefully. Be ready to support its weight. (Moog)

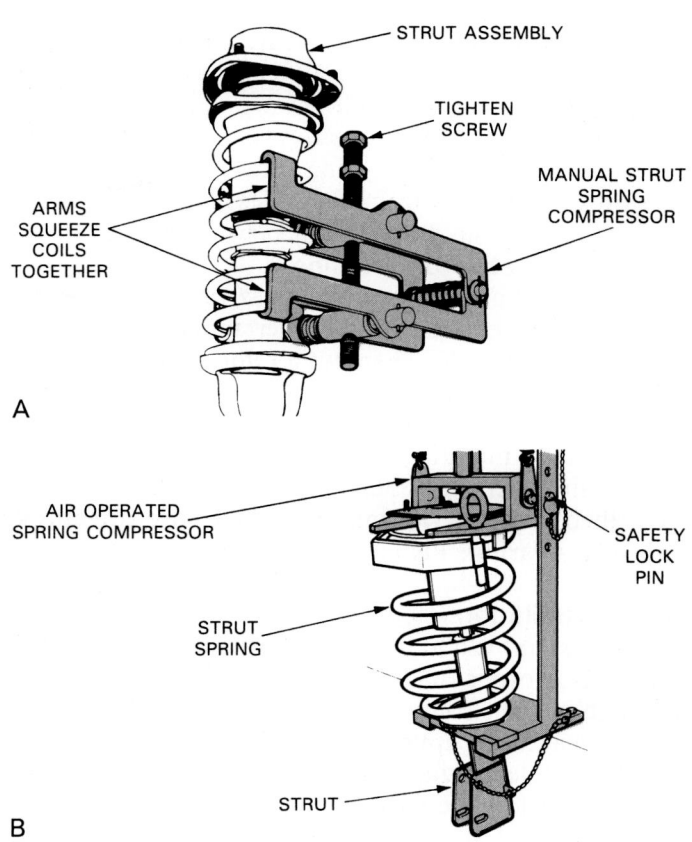

STRUT ASSEMBLY
TIGHTEN SCREW
MANUAL STRUT SPRING COMPRESSOR
ARMS SQUEEZE COILS TOGETHER
A
AIR OPERATED SPRING COMPRESSOR
SAFETY LOCK PIN
STRUT SPRING
STRUT
B

Fig. 65-23. Spring compressor is needed to remove spring from shock. A — Small portable strut spring compressor. B — Larger, bench-mounted strut spring compressor. (Moog)

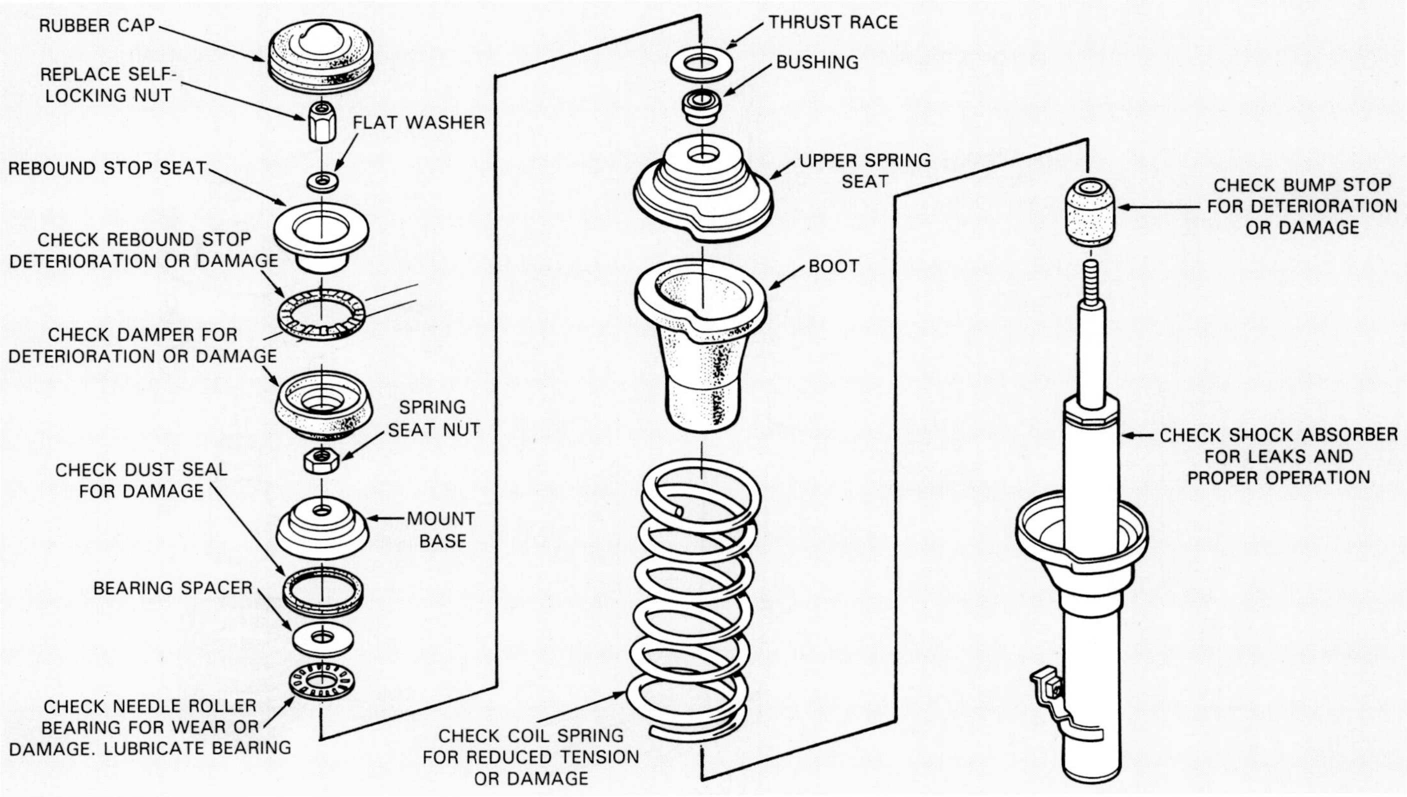

RUBBER CAP
REPLACE SELF-LOCKING NUT
FLAT WASHER
REBOUND STOP SEAT
CHECK REBOUND STOP DETERIORATION OR DAMAGE
CHECK DAMPER FOR DETERIORATION OR DAMAGE
SPRING SEAT NUT
CHECK DUST SEAL FOR DAMAGE
MOUNT BASE
BEARING SPACER
CHECK NEEDLE ROLLER BEARING FOR WEAR OR DAMAGE. LUBRICATE BEARING
THRUST RACE
BUSHING
UPPER SPRING SEAT
BOOT
CHECK COIL SPRING FOR REDUCED TENSION OR DAMAGE
CHECK BUMP STOP FOR DETERIORATION OR DAMAGE
CHECK SHOCK ABSORBER FOR LEAKS AND PROPER OPERATION

Fig. 65-24. Exploded view shows parts of strut assembly. Note strut bearing that should be in good condition. Inspect all parts carefully. (Honda)

and lift the spring off the strut. Inspect all parts closely, Fig. 65-24.

DANGER! When compressing any suspension system spring, be extremely careful to position the compressor properly. If the spring were to pop out of the compressor, serious injuries or death could result.

Strut shock absorber service

Most auto makers recommend *strut* or *shock cartridge* (removable shock absorber unit) replacement when faulty. Fig. 65-25 shows a removable strut cartridge. It can simply be installed in the strut outer housing to restore the strut to perfect condition.

Other auto manufacturers recommend that the strut shock absorber be rebuilt. A strut rebuild will be described in the service manual. Make sure you check the strut bearing, Fig. 65-26.

Strut installation

To reassemble and install the strut assembly, follow the reverse order of disassembly. See Fig. 65-27. Fit the strut into the compressor. Compress the coil spring. Then, install the upper spring seat and related components. Release the spring compressor and you are ready to install the strut in the car.

Lift the strut into position in the upper body mount. Attach the lower end of the strut to the steering knuckle or bearing support. Align your reference marks. Install and torque the fasteners to specs. Install any other parts as needed and double-check your work.

Fig. 65-26. After replacing or rebuilding shock, compress spring and install spring seat. Make sure strut bearing is in good condition. (Moog)

WHEEL ALIGNMENT IS NEEDED

After servicing ball joints, control arm bushings, strut rods, springs, strut assemblies, and other suspension parts, wheel alignment must be checked and adjusted. NEVER let a car leave the shop without checking alignment. Rapid tire wear or handling problems could occur.

Wheel alignment is covered in Chapter 70. You should, however, study steering systems first.

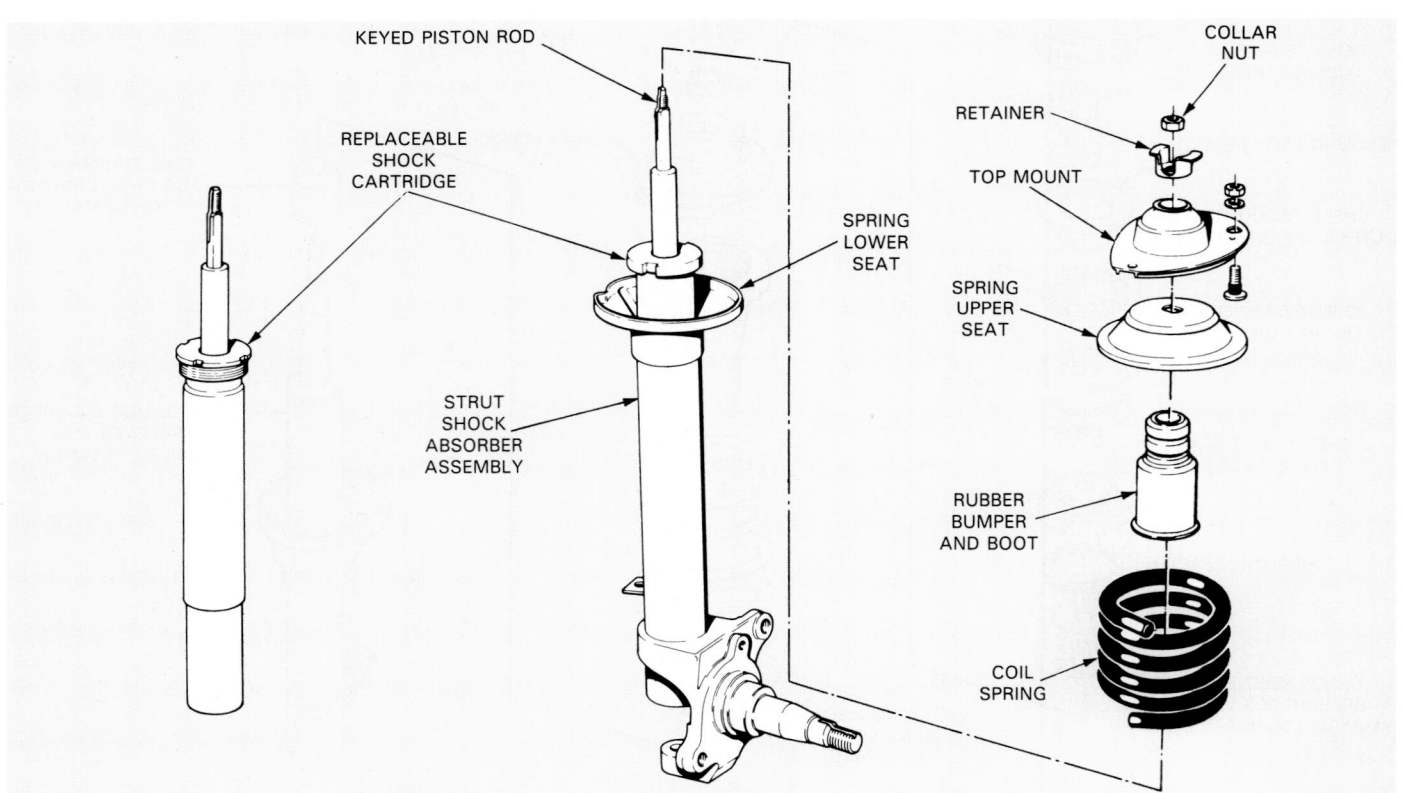

Fig. 65-25. New strut cartridge simply screws into shock housing with this design. (Mercury)

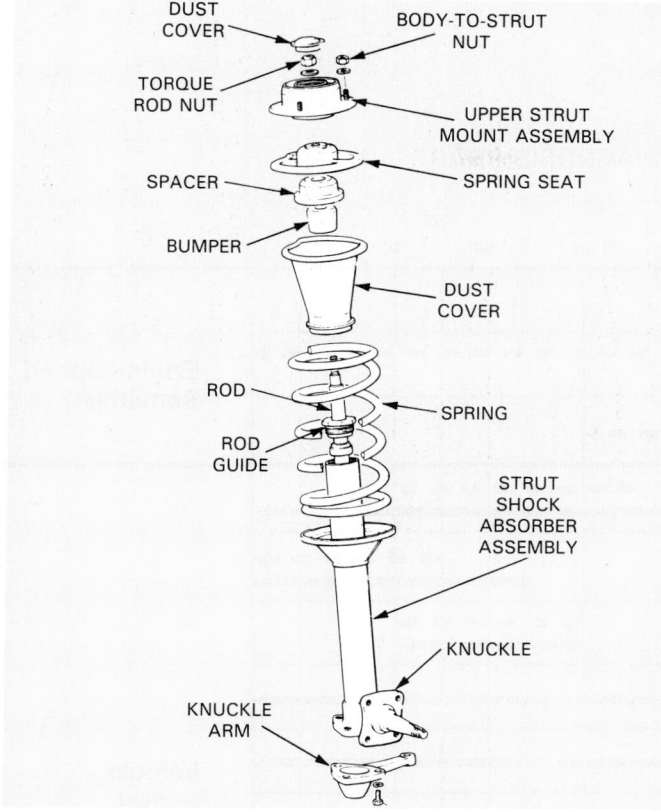

Fig. 65-27. Exploded view shows how strut parts fit together.

COMPUTERIZED SUSPENSION DIAGNOSIS

Most computer-controlled suspension systems provide a means of self-diagnosis. The computer will output a code that shows where problems might be located in the system.

A scanning tester can be connected to many systems to read the trouble codes. Then you can refer to a service manual trouble code chart to find out what the number code indicates.

For more information on computers, refer to Chapters 74, 75, and 76 in this textbook.

KNOW THESE TERMS

Shock bounce test, Spring fatigue, Curb height, Curb weight, Coil spring compressor, Ball joint balloon seal, Grease gun, Ball joint wear indicator, Strut cartridge.

REVIEW QUESTIONS

1. What are some common symptoms that indicate suspension system problems?
2. A customer complains that his or her car rides very rough and continues to rebound after going over humps in the road.
   Technician A says that a bounce test is needed to check the shocks.
   Technician B says that a general inspection for worn suspension parts is also needed.
   Who is correct?
   a. Technician A
   b. Technician B
   c. Both A and B
   d. Neither A nor B
3. What happens with spring fatigue?
4. Define the terms "curb height" and "curb weight."
5. A _____ _____ _____ is needed to remove a suspension system coil spring.
6. A _____ tool or _____ _____ _____ is needed to force the ball joint stud from the steering knuckle.
7. Why is suspension spring removal dangerous?
8. How do you check ball joint wear?
9. Generally, how do you remove a strut assembly?
10. Which of the following is NOT normally needed during strut service?
    a. Shock or strut cartridge.
    b. Floor jack.
    c. Spring compressor.
    d. Air chisel.

ACTIVITIES FOR CHAPTER 65

1. Measure a vehicle for proper curb height after checking curb weight.
2. Inspect ball joints for wear and report their condition to your instructor.
3. Inspect and test drive a vehicle with suspension problems. Diagnose the problem and suggest what service is needed.
4. Prepare a bill for a customer for replacement of front struts. Base your bill on an hourly charge rate established by your instructor. Find cost of parts from a parts catalog or by contacting an automotive parts store. Use a flat rate manual or a time suggested by your instructor.

NOISE AND VIBRATION DIAGNOSIS CHART

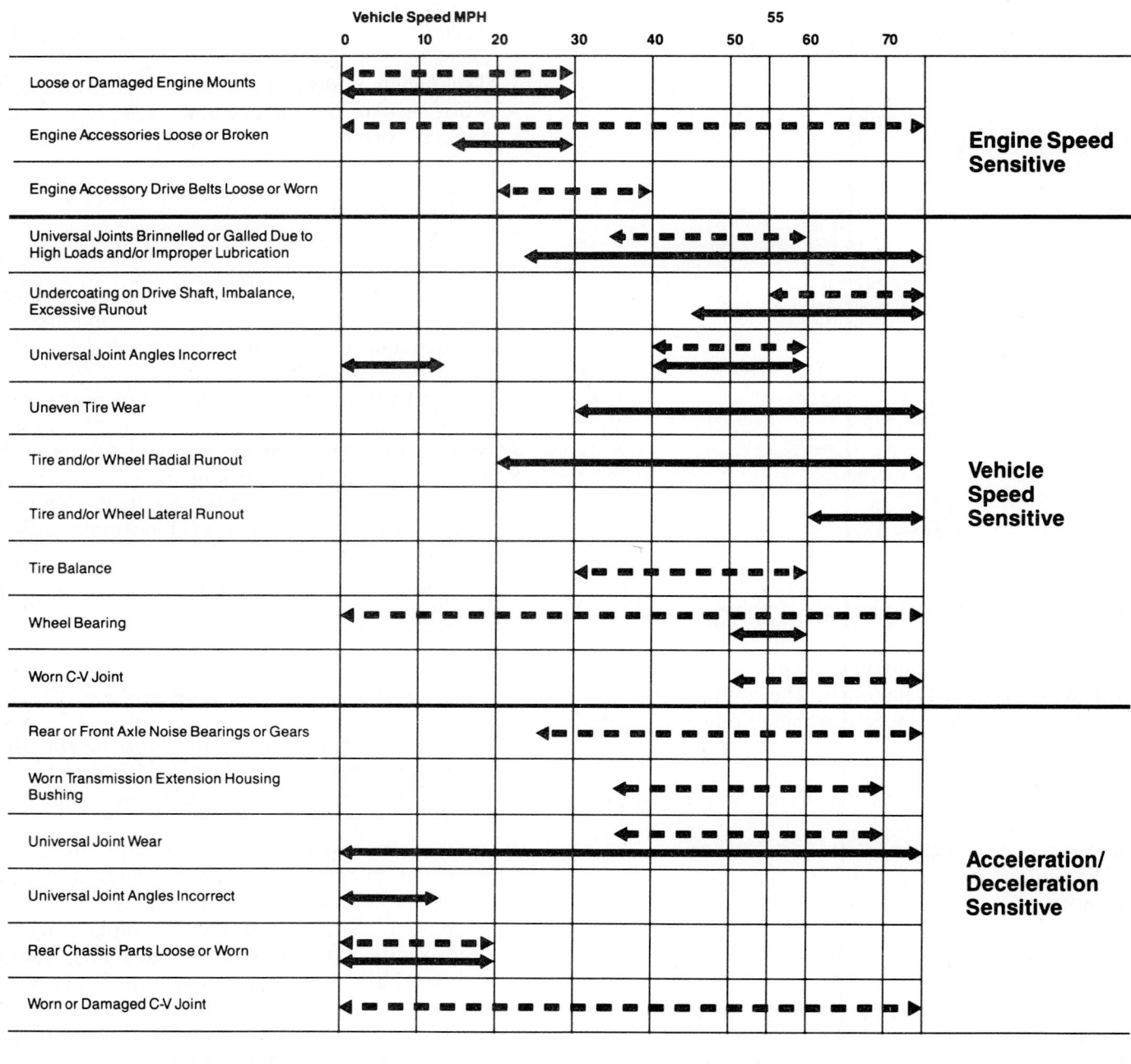

Study this vibration and noise diagnosis chart. Note how various components tend to emit noise and/or vibrate at specific speeds. This will help you find the source of problems. (Dana-Perfect Circle)

Steering System Fundamentals

After studying this chapter, you will be able to:
□ Identify the major parts of a steering system.
□ Explain the operating principles of steering systems.
□ Compare the differences between linkage and rack and pinion type steering.
□ Describe the operation of power steering systems.

This chapter will build upon your knowledge of auto mechanics by introducing modern steering systems. The steering mechanism works with the suspension system to provide a safe-handling vehicle.

There are two basic kinds of steering systems in wide use today: linkage (worm gear) steering and rack and pinion steering. See Fig. 66-1. They may be operated manually or with power assist.

FUNCTIONS OF A STEERING SYSTEM

The steering system must perform several important functions.
1. Provide precise control of front wheel direction.
2. Maintain correct amount of effort needed to turn the front wheels.
3. Transmit *road feel* (slight steering wheel pull caused by road surface) to the driver's hands.
4. Absorb most of the shock going to the steering wheel as the tires hit bumps and holes in road.
5. Allow for suspension action.

BASIC STEERING SYSTEM PARTS

Before studying each part, you should have a basic understanding of both linkage and rack and pinion type steering systems. This will allow you to develop a better "picture" of how each component operates.

Basic linkage steering system

A linkage steering system, Fig. 66-1A, consists of the following parts:
1. STEERING WHEEL (used by driver to rotate steering shaft that passes through steering column).

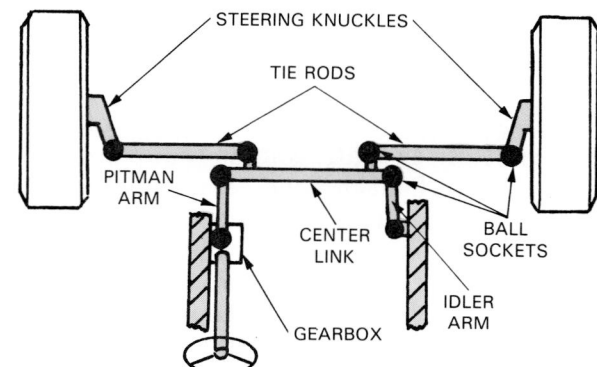

A   PARALLELOGRAM OR LINKAGE STEERING

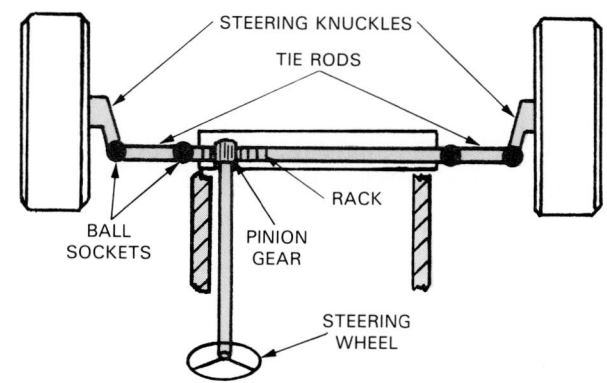

B   RACK AND PINION STEERING

Fig. 66-1. *There are two types of steering systems. Both are found on today's vehicles.*

2. STEERING SHAFT (transfers turning motion from steering wheel to steering gearbox).
3. STEERING COLUMN (supports steering wheel and steering shaft).
4. STEERING GEARBOX (changes turning motion into straight-line motion to the left or right).
5. STEERING LINKAGE (connects steering gearbox to steering knuckles and wheels).

6. BALL SOCKETS (allow linkage arms to swivel up and down for suspension action and from left to right for turning).

Basic rack and pinion steering system

A rack and pinion steering system also uses a steering wheel, steering column, and steering shaft. See Fig. 66-1B. These components transfer the driver's turning effort to gears in the steering gear assembly.

Other than the parts just covered, the major components of a rack and pinion steering system are:
1. PINION GEAR (rotated by steering wheel and steering shaft; its teeth mesh with teeth on rack).
2. RACK (long steel bar with teeth along one section; slides sideways as pinion gear turns).
3. GEAR HOUSING (holds pinion gear and rack).
4. TIE-RODS (connect rack with steering knuckles).

STEERING COLUMN ASSEMBLY

The *steering column assembly* consists of the steering wheel, steering shaft, column (outer housing), ignition key mechanism, and, sometimes a flexible coupling and universal joint. Look at Fig. 66-2.

The steering column normally bolts to the underside of the dash. The column sticks through the firewall and fastens to the steering gear assembly.

Bearings fit between the steering shaft and column. They let the shaft rotate freely. The steering wheel is locked to the shaft by splines. A large nut holds the steering wheel on the shaft splines.

Air bags are part of the steering column assembly. Refer to Chapter 74, page 999 for information.

Ignition lock and switch

Most modern cars have the ignition lock and switch mechanism mounted on the steering column. The *key mechanism* is normally on the top, right-hand side of the column. The *ignition switch* is usually bolted to the steering column. For more information on ignition switches, see Chapters 28 and 32.

Locking steering wheel

To help prevent theft, late model cars also have a *locking steering wheel*. When the ignition key is off, the steering wheel cannot be turned. Fig. 66-3 shows a common method of locking the steering wheel.

A rack and a sector are used to slide a steel pin into mesh with a slotted disc. Since the disc is splined to the steering shaft, the steering wheel will NOT turn.

Collapsible steering column

Today's cars use a *collapsible steering column* to help prevent driver injury during an auto accident. The column is designed to crumple or slide together when forced forward. Look at Fig. 66-4.

When a car hits a stationary object, the engine and front body structure can be pushed rearward, into the steering column. At the same time, the driver could be thrown forward into the steering wheel. With a rigid steering column, the driver's chest could be injured.

There are several types of collapsible steering columns: steel mesh (crushing) type, tube and ball (sliding) type, and the shear capsule (break and slide) type. In all types, the column is two-piece.

STEERING GEAR PRINCIPLES

As was mentioned briefly, some steering systems use a worm type steering gear assembly. Others use a pinion gear and a rack. These two gear principles are illustrated in Figs. 66-5 and 66-6.

Recirculating ball gearbox

The *recirculating ball gearbox* is the most common type used with a linkage steering system. Pictured in

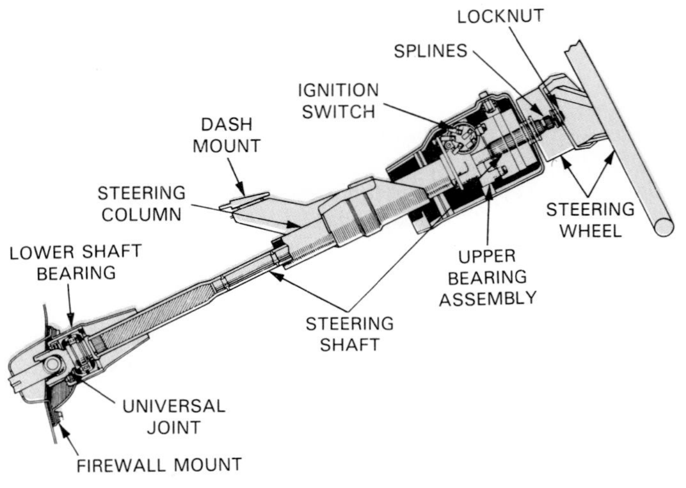

Fig. 66-2. Note steering column components. Steering wheel is splined to shaft that extends through column and down to steering gearbox. (Toyota)

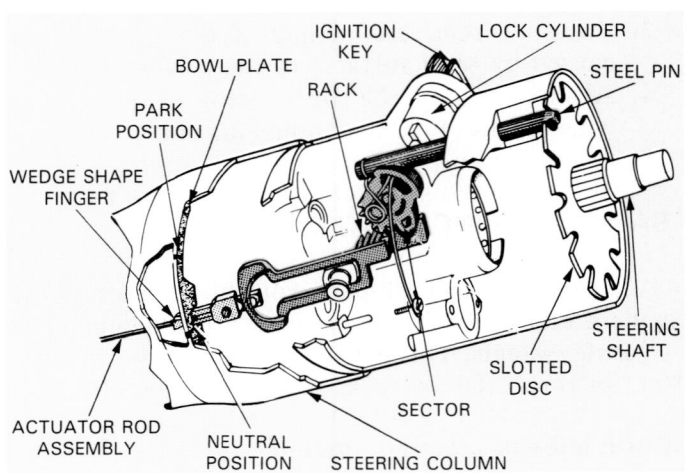

Fig. 66-3. Cutaway view shows how locking steering column functions. Steel pin slides into slot in disc to keep wheel from turning with key removed. Also note small rod that extends down to ignition switch. (Buick)

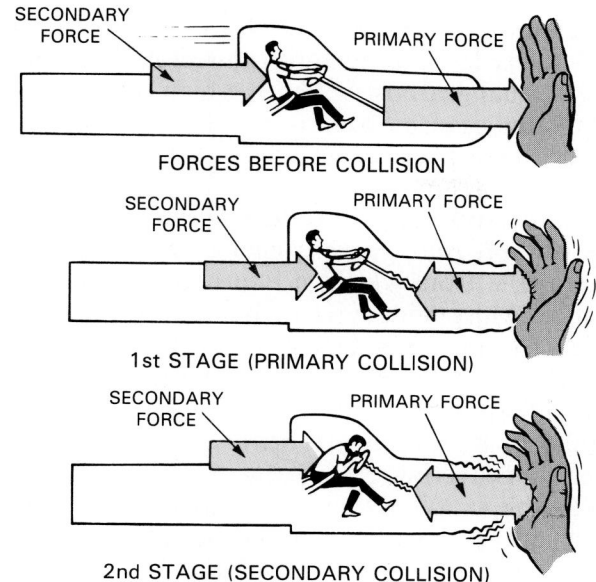

Fig. 66-4. Collapsible steering column crushes and protects driver. (GMC)

SECONDARY FORCE — PRIMARY FORCE
FORCES BEFORE COLLISION

SECONDARY FORCE — PRIMARY FORCE
1st STAGE (PRIMARY COLLISION)

SECONDARY FORCE — PRIMARY FORCE
2nd STAGE (SECONDARY COLLISION)

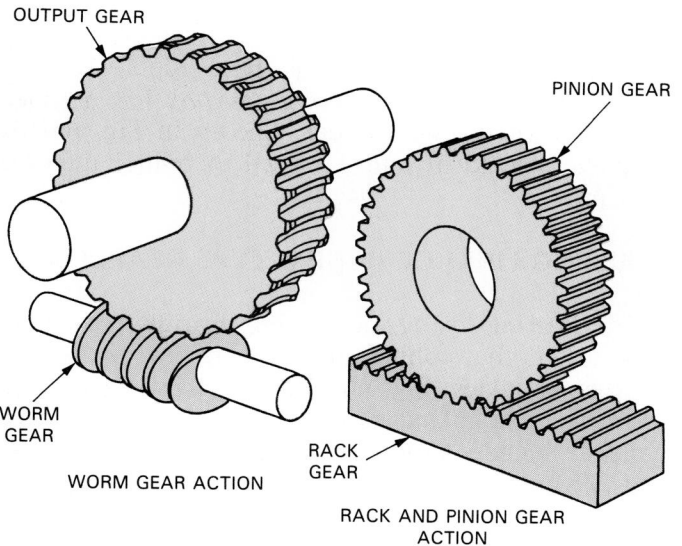

OUTPUT GEAR

PINION GEAR

WORM GEAR

WORM GEAR ACTION

RACK GEAR

RACK AND PINION GEAR ACTION

Fig. 66-5. Two basic types of gear mechanisms found in steering gearboxes: worm gear and rack and pinion gearset. (Deere & Co.)

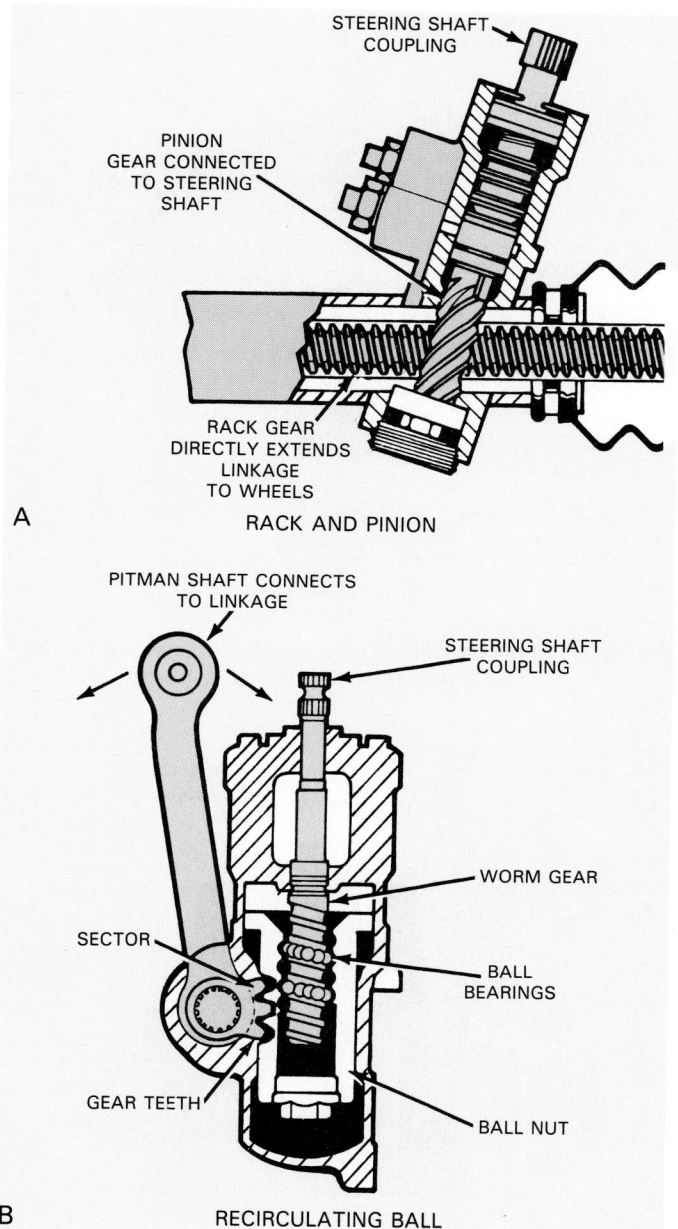

STEERING SHAFT COUPLING

PINION GEAR CONNECTED TO STEERING SHAFT

RACK GEAR DIRECTLY EXTENDS LINKAGE TO WHEELS

A   RACK AND PINION

PITMAN SHAFT CONNECTS TO LINKAGE

STEERING SHAFT COUPLING

SECTOR

GEAR TEETH

WORM GEAR

BALL BEARINGS

BALL NUT

B   RECIRCULATING BALL

Fig. 66-6. Another view of two types of steering gears. A—Rack and pinion steering gear. B—Worm steering gearbox. (Chrysler Corp.)

Fig. 66-7, it has small steel balls that circulate between the gear members.

A *worm shaft* is the input gear connected to the steering column shaft. The balls fit and ride in the grooves in the worm gear.

The *sector shaft* is the output gear from the steering gearbox. It transfers motion to the steering linkage, Fig. 66-7. A sector gear is machined on the inner end of the sector shaft.

A *ball nut* rides on the ball bearings and worm gear. See Fig. 66-8. Grooves are cut in the ball nut to match the shape of the worm gear. Since the ball nut cannot rotate, it slides up and down as the worm gear rotates.

Ball guides route extra balls in and out from between the worm and ball nut.

The worm shaft is mounted in either ball or roller bearings. The sector shaft is also mounted on antifriction bearings.

A bearing *adjuster nut* is usually provided to set worm shaft bearing preload.

An *adjusting screw* is used to set the sector shaft clearance.

The *gearbox housing* provides an enclosure for the other components, Fig. 66-8. Seals press into the housing to prevent lubricant leakage at the worm and sector shafts. The shaft bearings also press into the gearbox housing.

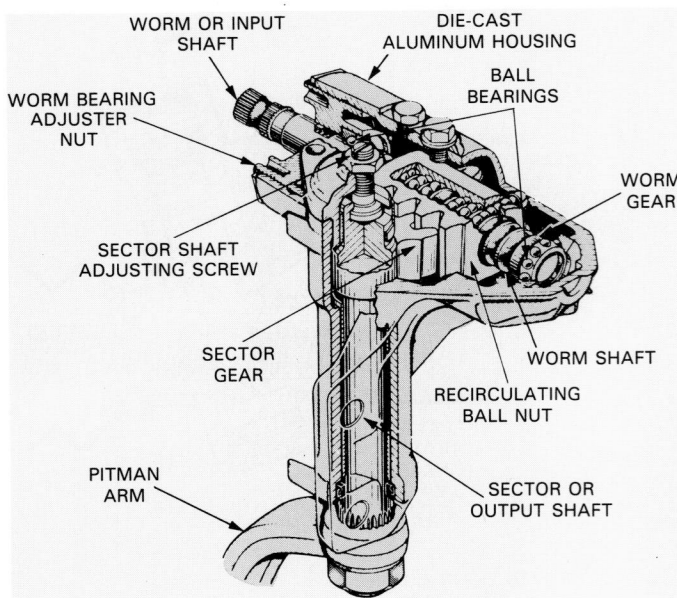

Fig. 66-7. Cutaway view of recirculating ball steering gearbox. Study part relationships. (Chrysler)

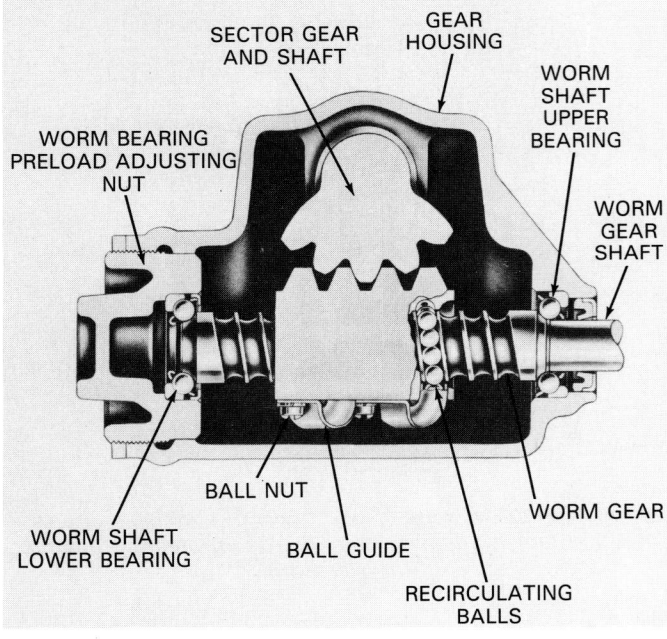

Fig. 66-8. When steering wheel is turned, shaft and worm gear rotate. This causes balls and ball nut to walk on worm. As a result, ball nut turns sector gear and shaft. (Chrysler Corp.)

The housing bolts to the vehicle frame or reinforced area on the unitized body. An **end cover** normally bolts on the housing to cover the end of the sector gear. It can be removed for gearbox service.

Gearbox ratio (steering gear reduction)

Gearbox ratio, also termed *steering gear reduction,* is basically a comparison between steering wheel rotation and sector shaft rotation. Steering gearbox ratios

range from 15:1 up to 24:1. With a 15:1 ratio, the worm shaft turns 15 times to turn the sector shaft once.

A manual gearbox will have a high ratio to reduce the amount of effort needed to turn the steering wheel. Power steering gearboxes have a lower ratio.

Constant and variable ratio steering

A *variable ratio gearbox* changes the internal gear ratio as the front wheels are turned from the center position. Most modern recirculating ball gearboxes are variable ratio. Refer to Fig. 66-9.

Variable ratio steering is faster when cornering, requiring fewer turns of the steering wheel from full right to full left. It also provides better control and response when maneuvering.

Variable ratio steering is accomplished by changing the length of the gear teeth on the sector shaft gear. This changes the effective LEVER ARM action between the gears. Many manual steering gearboxes and most power steering gearboxes are variable ratio.

A *constant ratio gearbox* has the same gear reduction from full left to full right. The sector gear teeth are the same length.

Worm and roller steering gearbox

A *worm and roller steering gearbox* has a roller meshed with the worm gear. Shown in Fig. 66-10, a roller, instead of balls, is used to reduce internal friction.

STEERING LINKAGE (WORM TYPE GEARBOX)

The *steering linkage* is a series of arms, rods, and ball sockets that connect the steering gearbox to the steering knuckles. Fig. 66-11 shows these parts.

The steering linkage used with a worm type gearbox typically includes a pitman arm, center link, idler arm, and two tie-rod assemblies.

Pitman arm

The *pitman arm* transfers gearbox motion to the steering linkage. The pitman arm is splined to the gear-

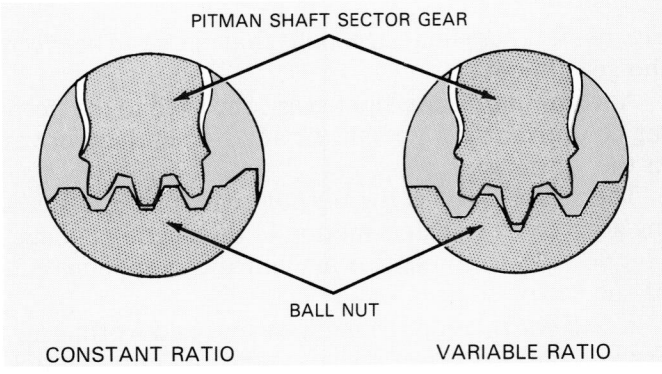

Fig. 66-9. Note difference in teeth with constant and variable ratio gearboxes. (General Motors Corp.)

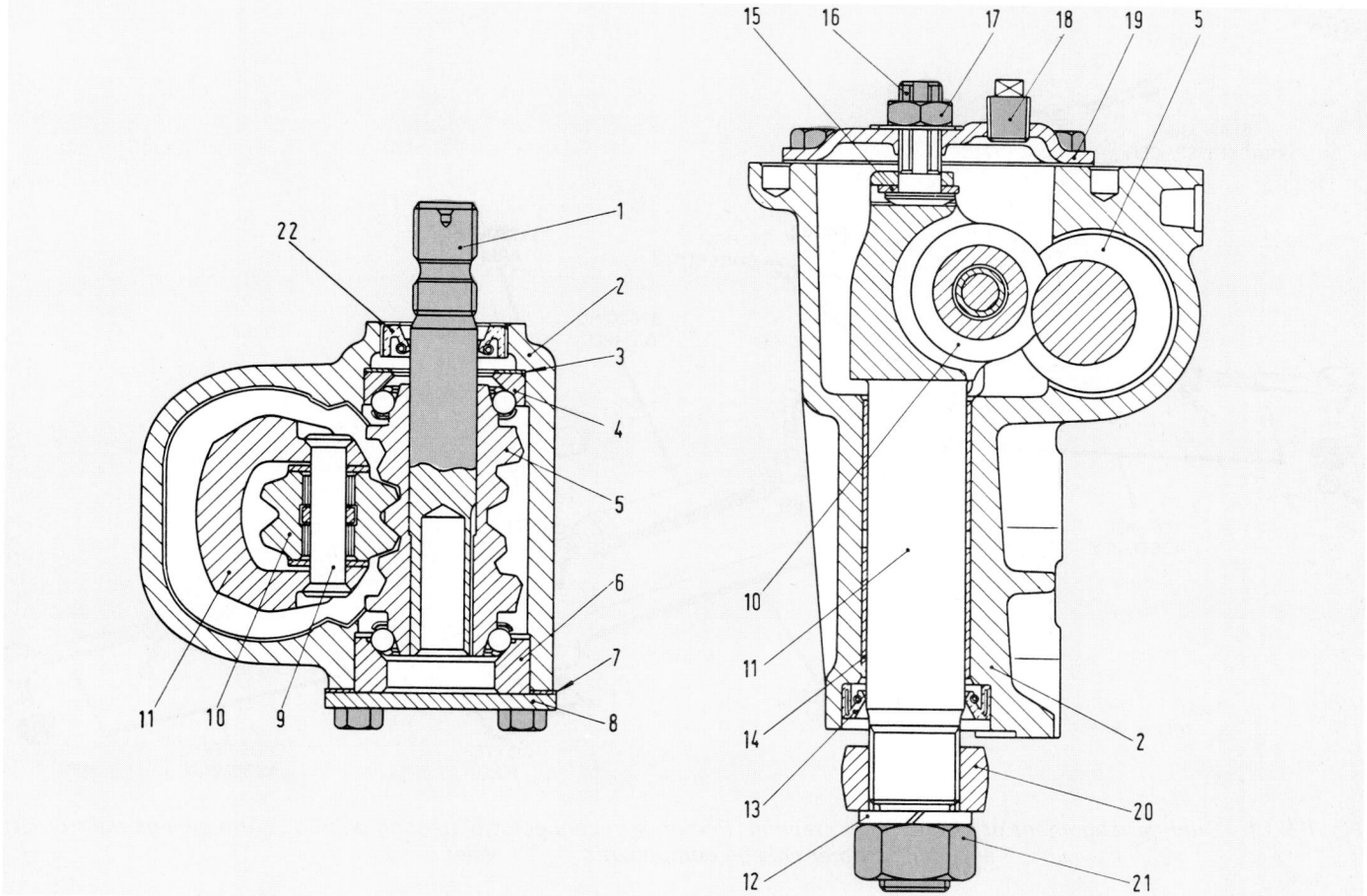

1. Steering shaft. - 2. Steering box. - 3. Worm upper bearing shims. - 4. Rear ball bearing. - 5. Worm. - 6. Front ball bearing. - 7. Worm lower bearing shims. - 8. Worm thrust cover. - 9. Roller pin. - 10. Roller. - 11. Roller shaft. - 12. Spring washer under pitman arm nut. - 13. Roller shaft oil seal. - 14. Roller shaft bushing. - 15. Roller shaft adjusting disc. - 16. Roller shaft adjusting screw. - 17. Locknut. - 18. Plug. - 19. Steering box cover. - 20. Pitman arm. - 21. Pitman arm nut. - 22. Steering shaft oil seal.

Fig. 66-10. Worm and roller gearbox is similar to recirculating ball type. Single roller replaces balls and ball nut. (Fiat)

box sector (output) shaft. A large nut and lock washer secure the arm to its shaft. Refer to Fig. 66-7.

The outer end of the pitman arm normally uses a ball and socket joint, Fig. 66-11.

Center link (relay rod)

The *center link,* also called a *relay rod,* is simply a steel bar that connects the right and left sides of the steering linkage. As shown in Fig. 66-11, it has holes that accept the pitman arm, tie rod ends, and idler arm.

Idler arm

The *idler arm* supports the end of the center link on the passenger side of the car. As pictured in Fig. 66-11, the idler arm bolts to the car frame or subframe.

Ball sockets

Ball sockets are like small ball joints; they provide for motion in all directions between two connected parts. See Fig. 66-11. Ball sockets are needed so the steering linkage is NOT bent and damaged when the wheels turn or move up and down over rough pavement.

Cutaway views for various ball sockets are given in Fig. 66-12. Note how a ball stud fits into a socket.

Ball sockets are filled with grease to reduce friction

and wear. Some ball sockets are sealed. Others have a grease fitting that allows chassis grease to be inserted with a grease gun.

Tie rod assemblies

Two *tie-rod assemblies* are used to fasten the center link to the steering knuckles. Ball sockets are normally used on both ends of both tie-rods. Look at Figs. 66-11 and 66-12. An adjustment sleeve is provided for changing the length of the tie-rod during wheel alignment.

MANUAL RACK AND PINION STEERING

Rack and pinion steering is the most popular type of steering system on today's vehicles. For this reason, it is important that you understand its parts and operating principles.

Fig. 66-13 pictures the external parts of a manual rack and pinion steering mechanism. Note that the steering gear bolts to the frame crossmember.

Steering shaft, flexible coupling, and U-joint

Many steering systems have a flexible coupling or a universal joint in the steering shaft. Look at Figs. 66-13 and 66-14.

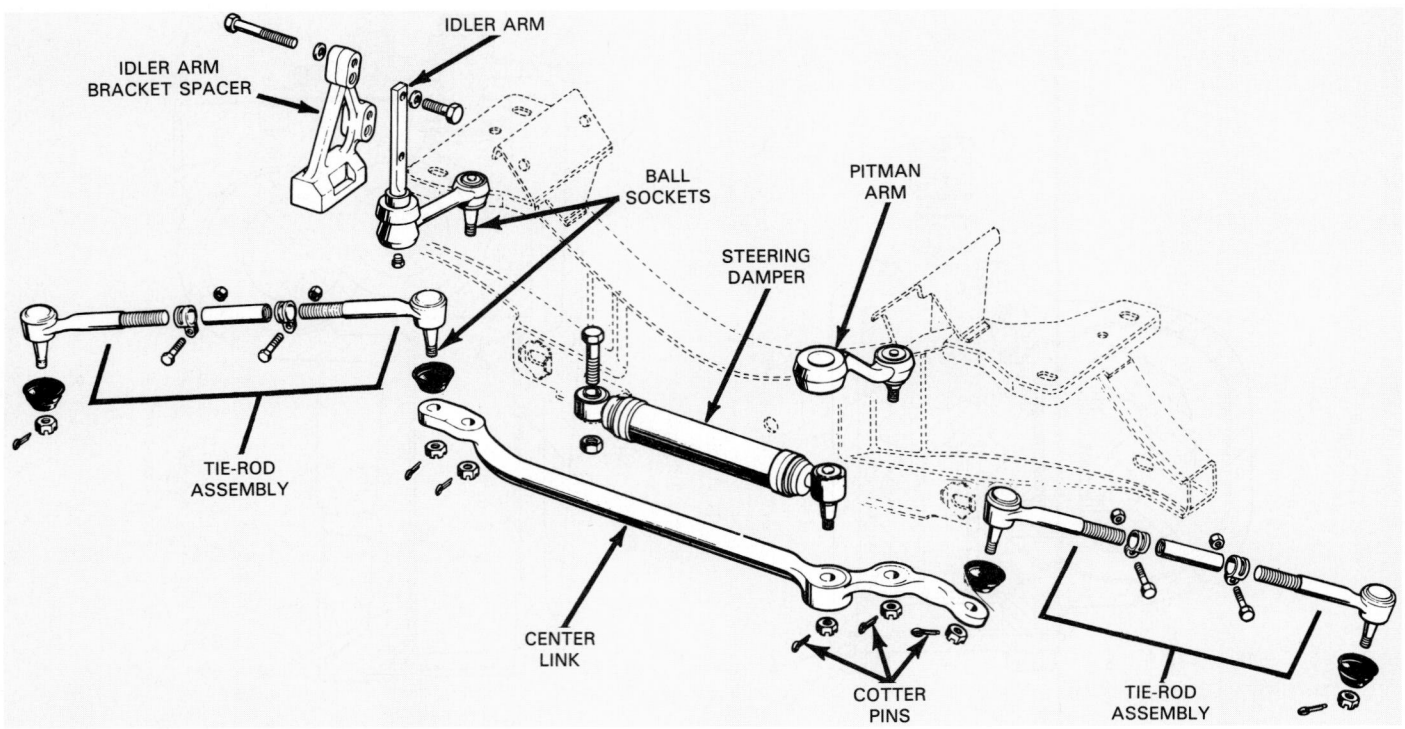

Fig. 66-11. Study arrangement of linkage type steering. Pitman arm connects to steering gearbox. Arm swings right or left and moves other linkage components. (Chrysler Corp.)

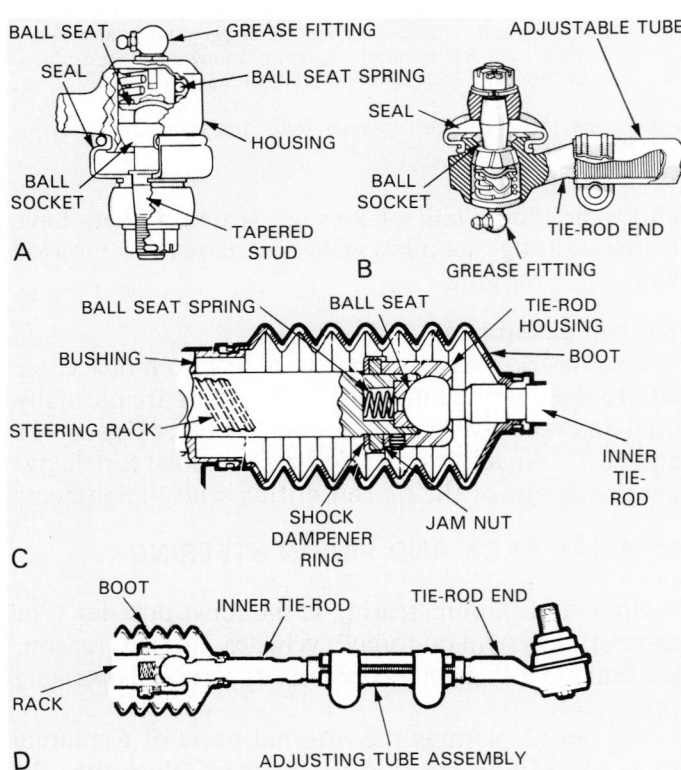

Fig. 66-12. Ball sockets allow linkage components to swivel freely when steering car. They are commonly used on end of pitman arm, idler arm, and tie-rods. A — Ball socket for idler arm. B — Ball-socket for tie-rod end. C — Ball socket for inner end of tie-rod on rack and pinion setup. D — Ball sockets on both ends of tie-rod for rack and pinion steering. (Ford and Chrysler)

The *flexible coupling* helps keep road shock from transmitting to the steering wheel. It also allows for slight misalignment of the steering shaft and steering gear input shaft.

A *universal joint* allows for a change in angle between the steering column and steering gear input shaft. One is shown in Fig. 66-13.

Rack and pinion steering gear

A manual *rack and pinion steering gear* basically consists of a pinion shaft, rack, thrust spring, bearings, seals, and gear housing. A cutaway view of one is shown in Fig. 66-14.

When the steering shaft turns the pinion shaft, the pinion gear acts on the rack gear. The rack then slides sideways inside the gear housing, Fig. 66-15.

The *thrust spring* preloads the rack and pinion gear teeth to prevent excessive gear backlash (play), Fig. 66-15. Adjustment screws or shims may be used for setting thrust spring tension.

Either bushings or roller bearings may be used on the pinion shaft and rack. Frequently, the pinion shaft uses roller bearings and the rack uses plain bushings. This is pictured in Figs. 66-15 and 66-16.

Rack and pinion tie-rods

Tie-rod assemblies for rack and pinion steering connect the ends of the rack with the steering knuckles. Look at Fig. 66-16.

Note the unique construction of the inner ends of the tie-rods used on rack and pinion steering, Fig.

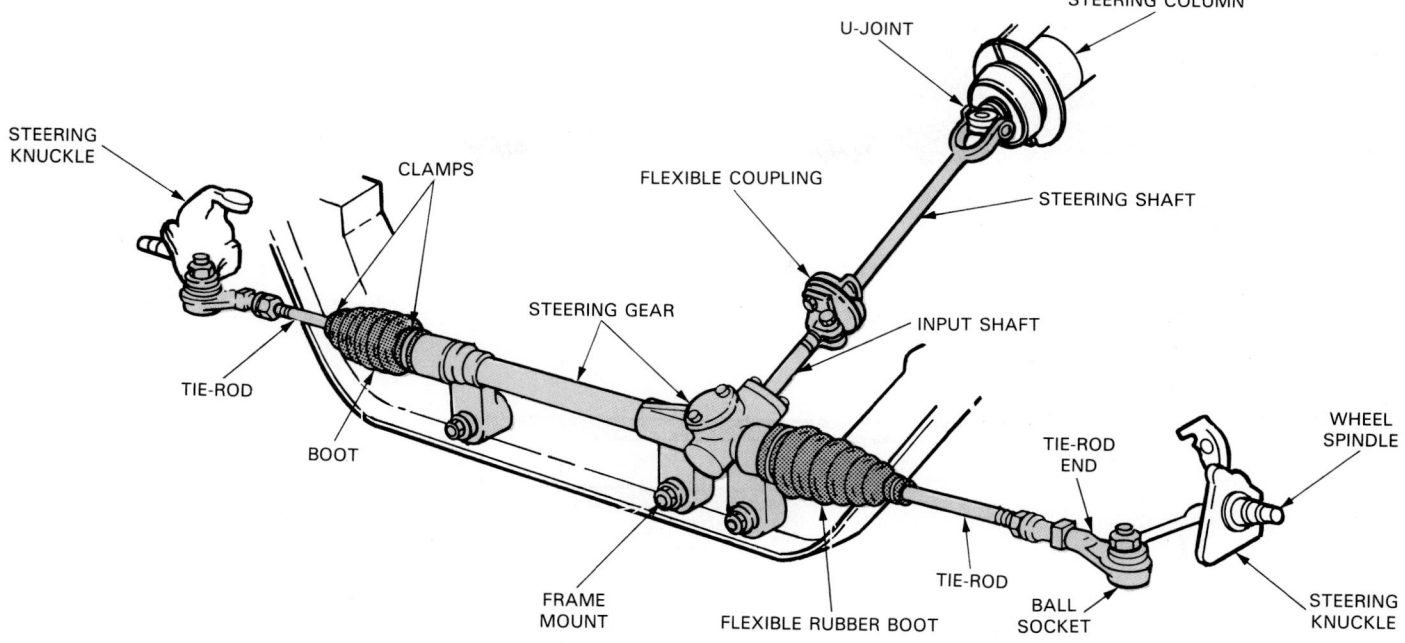

Fig. 66-13. Study components of manual rack and pinion steering gear. It uses fewer parts than linkage system. (Ford)

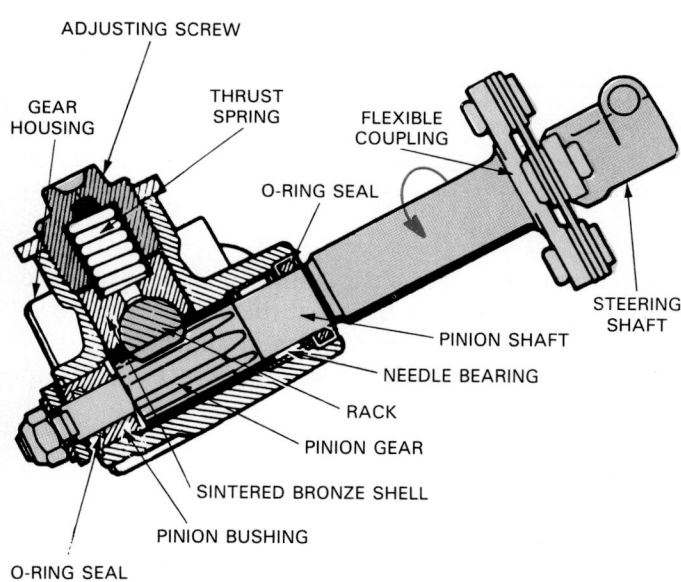

Fig. 66-14. Cutaway shows how pinion shaft gear rotates in housing. Pinion gear teeth mesh and act on rack gear teeth to slide rack left or right for steering action. Thrust spring holds rack and pinion gears in contact. (Ford)

66-17. They have very large ball sockets formed on the end of the tie-rod. These balls fit into a separate socket that normally screws onto the end of the rack. Conventional ball sockets are used on the outer ends of the tie-rods.

Rubber dust boots fit over the inner ball sockets to keep out road dirt, water, and to hold in lubricating grease. Clamps secure each end of the dust boots.

POWER STEERING SYSTEMS

Power steering systems normally use an engine driven pump and hydraulic system to assist steering action. The schematic in Fig. 66-17 illustrates a power steering system.

Pressure from an oil pump is used to operate a piston and cylinder assembly. When the control valve routes oil pressure into one end of the piston, the piston slides in its cylinders. Piston movement can then be used to help move the steering system components and front wheels of the car.

There are three major types of power steering systems used on modern autos: integral piston-linkage

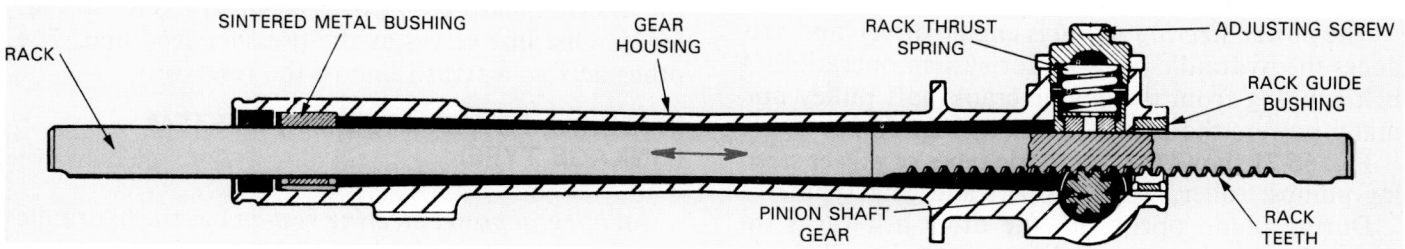

Fig. 66-15. Rack slides sideways and pushes or pulls on tie-rods. This rotates steering knuckles and front wheels. (Buick)

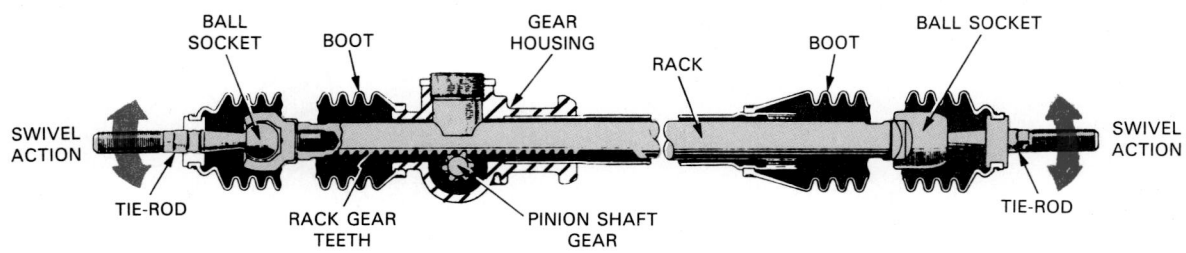

Fig. 66-16. Note how tie-rods attach to rack with ball-and-socket joint. (Toyota)

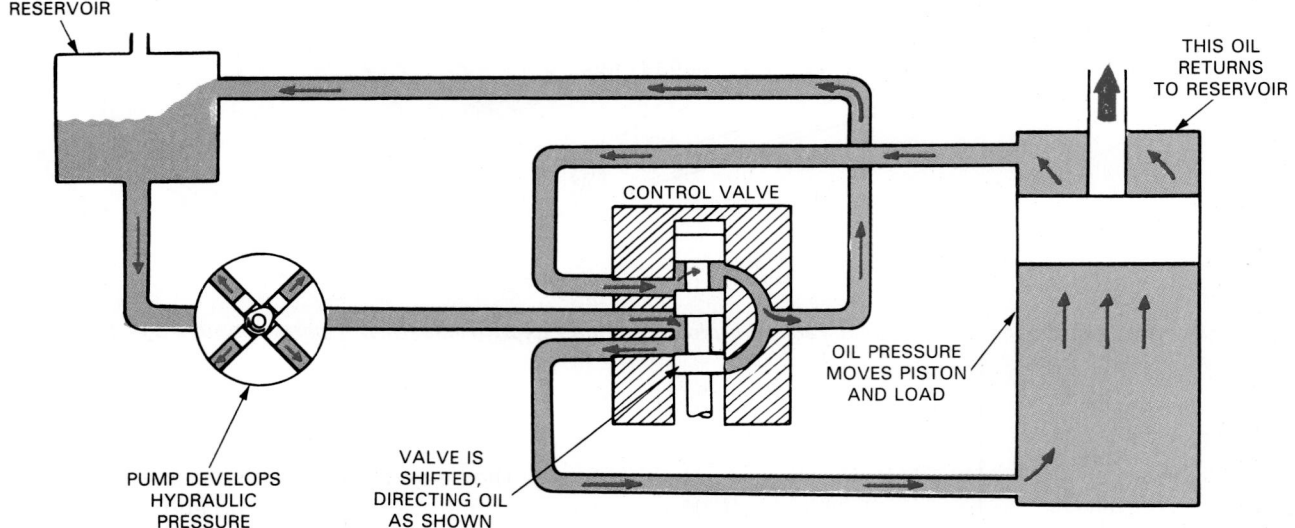

Fig. 66-17. Basic components of power steering system. Hydraulic or oil pump pressurizes system. Control valve routes oil into either side of piston. Piston action can then be used to aid steering of front wheels. (Deere & Co.)

type, external piston-linkage type, and rack and pinion type. The rack and pinion system is further divided into the integral and the external power piston. The integral rack and pinion power steering system is the most common. Fig. 66-18 shows the three main types.

Speed-sensitive steering unit

Some modern vehicles have a power steering system that senses speed of the vehicle and varies power to the system. The system has an electronically-operated solenoid that controls fluid flow into the steering gear valve chamber. As vehicle speed increases, the system provides increased effort. Variation in the powered effort begins at 20 mph (32 km/h). Refer to Fig. 66-19.

Power steering pumps

The *power steering pump* is engine driven and produces the hydraulic pressure for system operation. A belt running from the engine crankshaft pulley normally powers the pump. Refer to Fig. 66-20.

Fig. 66-21 shows the four basic types of power steering pumps: roller, vane, slipper, and gear types.

During pump operation, the drive belt turns the pump shaft and pumping elements. Oil is pulled into one side of the pump by vacuum. The oil is then

trapped and squeezed into a smaller area inside the pump. This pressurizes the oil at the output as it flows to the rest of the power steering system.

A cutaway view of a modern power steering pump is in Fig. 66-22.

Pressure relief valve

A *pressure relief valve* is used in a power steering system to control maximum oil pressure. It prevents system damage by limiting pressure when needed. Fig. 66-23 shows the fundamental operation of a pressure relief valve in a modern power steering pump.

Power steering hoses

Power steering hoses are high pressure, hydraulic, rubber hoses that connect the power steering pump and the integral gearbox or power cylinder. Refer to Fig. 66-20. One line serves as the pressure feed line. The other acts as a return line to the reservoir.

INTEGRAL POWER STEERING SYSTEM (LINKAGE TYPE)

An *integral power steering system* has the hydraulic piston mounted inside the steering gearbox housing. It is a very common type of linkage power steering

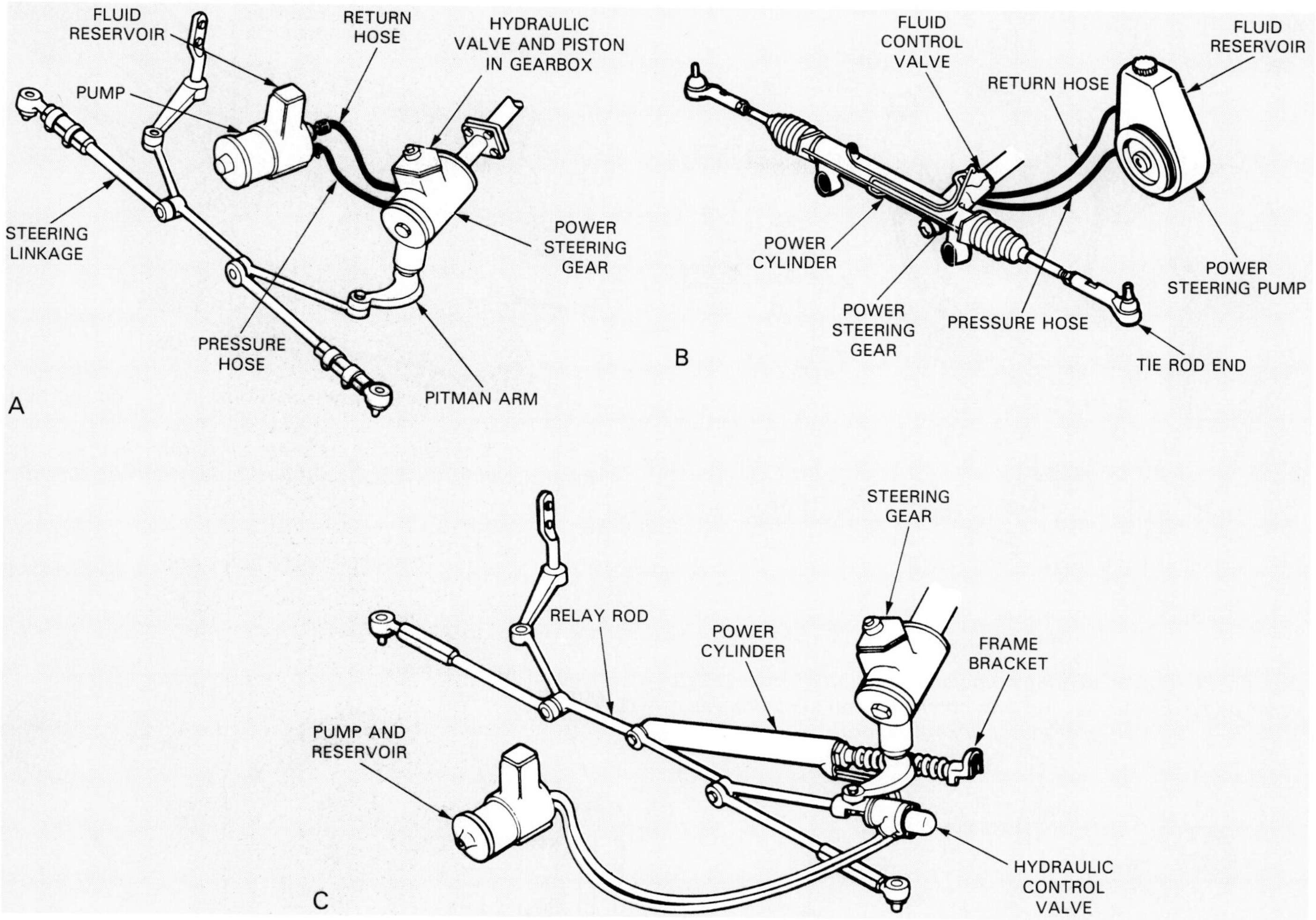

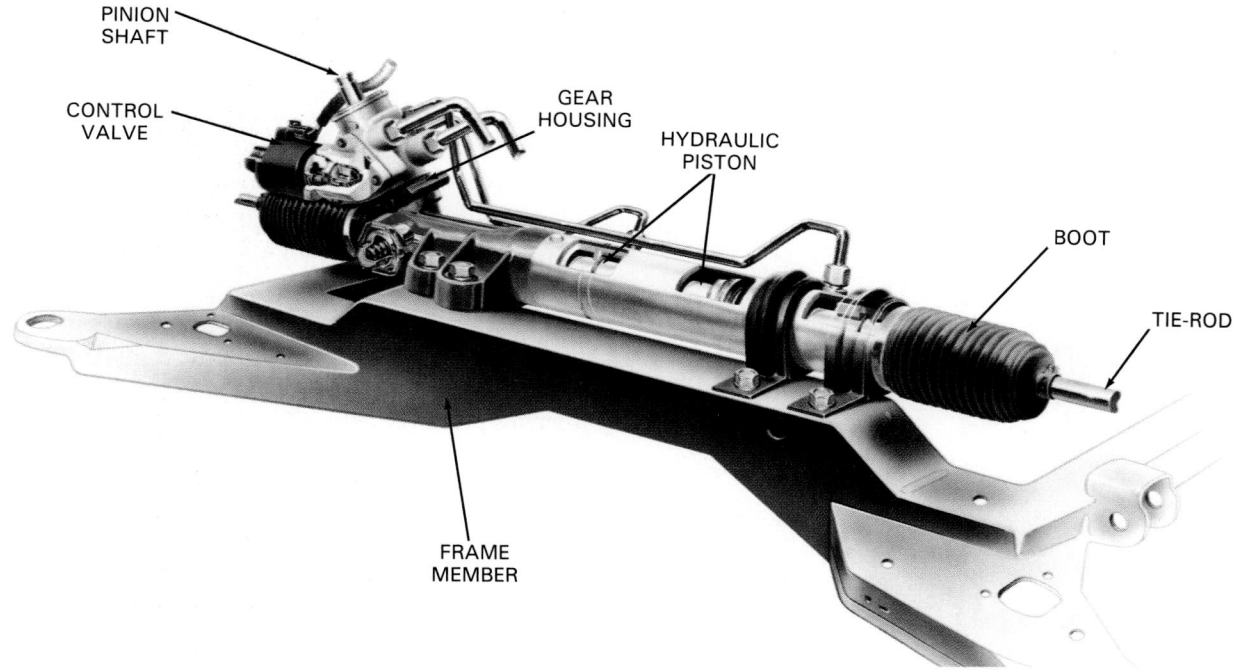

Fig. 66-18. The three major power steering systems. A — Integral piston-linkage type. B — Rack and pinion type. C — External piston-linkage type. (Florida Dept. of Voc. Ed.)

Fig. 66-19. Cutaway of speed-sensitive steering unit. Study its parts carefully. (Ford)

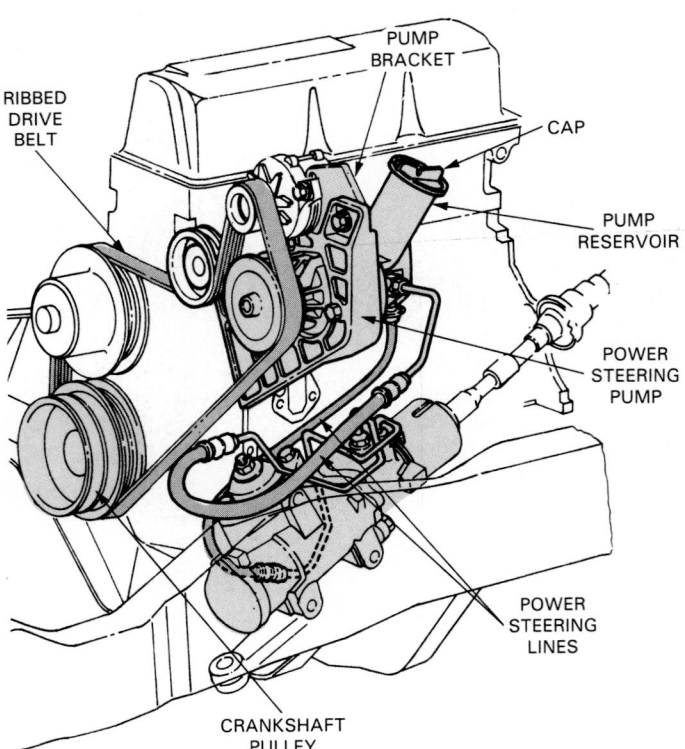

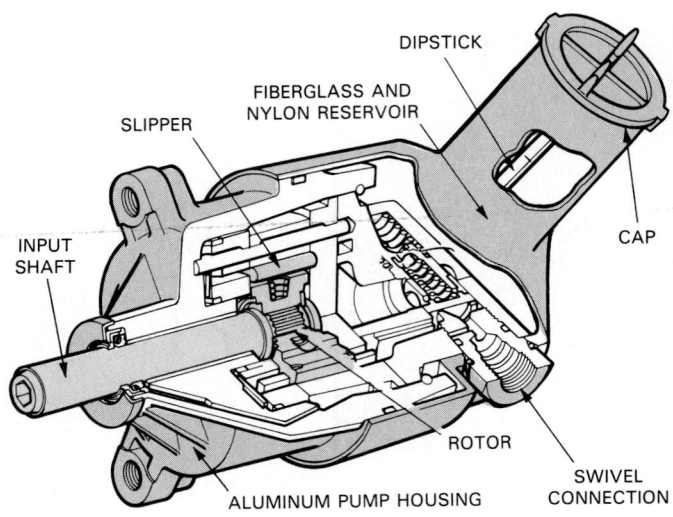

Fig. 66-20. Power steering pump bolts to front of engine. Belt spins pump. Power steering lines connect pump to control valve on gearbox or linkage. (Ford)

Fig. 66-22. Rotation of input shaft turns rotor and slippers. Power steering fluid is forced out under pressure. (Ford)

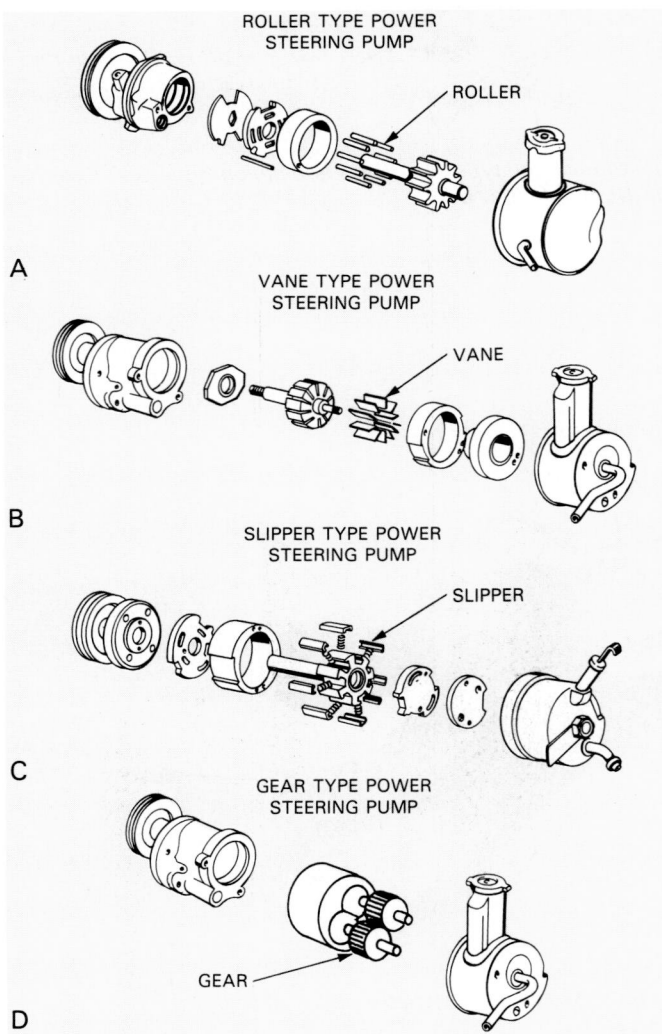

Fig. 66-21. Four basic types of power steering pumps. (Moog)

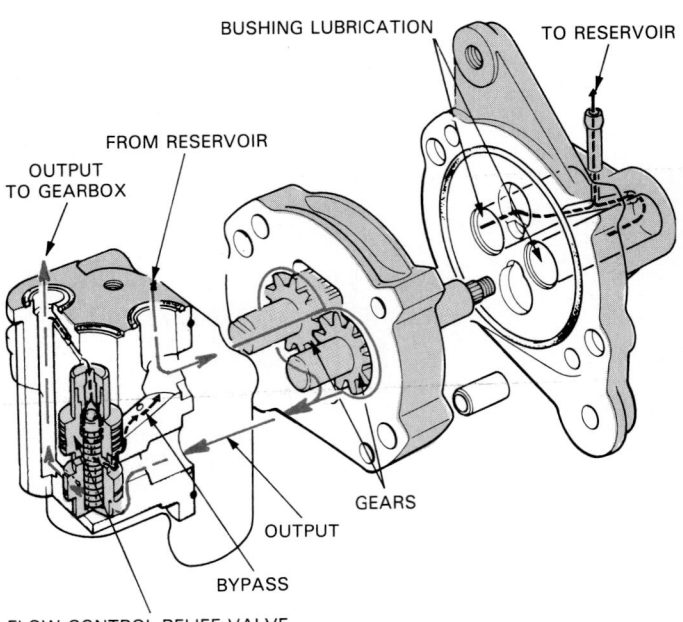

Fig. 66-23. Note action inside this gear type power steering pump. Flow control-relief valve is built into body of pump.

system. Basically, it consists of a power steering pump, hydraulic lines, and a special integral power-assist gearbox.

The *integral power steering gearbox* contains a conventional worm and sector gear, a hydraulic piston, and a flow direction valve. One type of integral power steering gearbox uses a spool valve. Another popular type has a rotary valve.

Fig. 66-24 shows a **spool valve** type power steering gearbox. Note that it uses a small spool valve to control pressure entering the two power chambers on each side of the piston.

When the steering wheel is turned to the right, the pivot lever moves the spool valve so that pressure enters the right turn chamber. This forces the power piston to the left and helps turn the sector shaft for a right turn. Pressure enters the opposite chamber when the steering wheel is turned to the left.

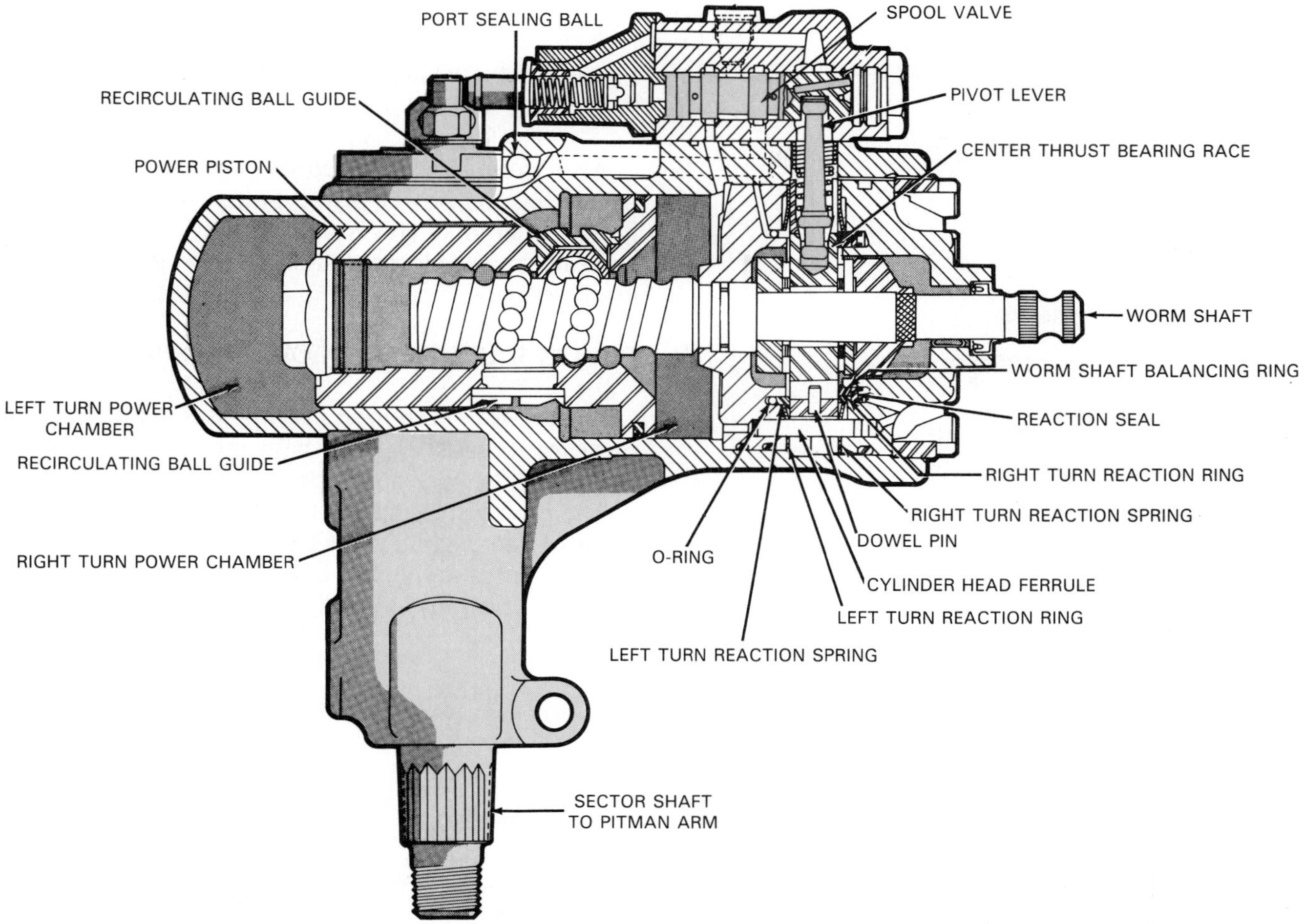

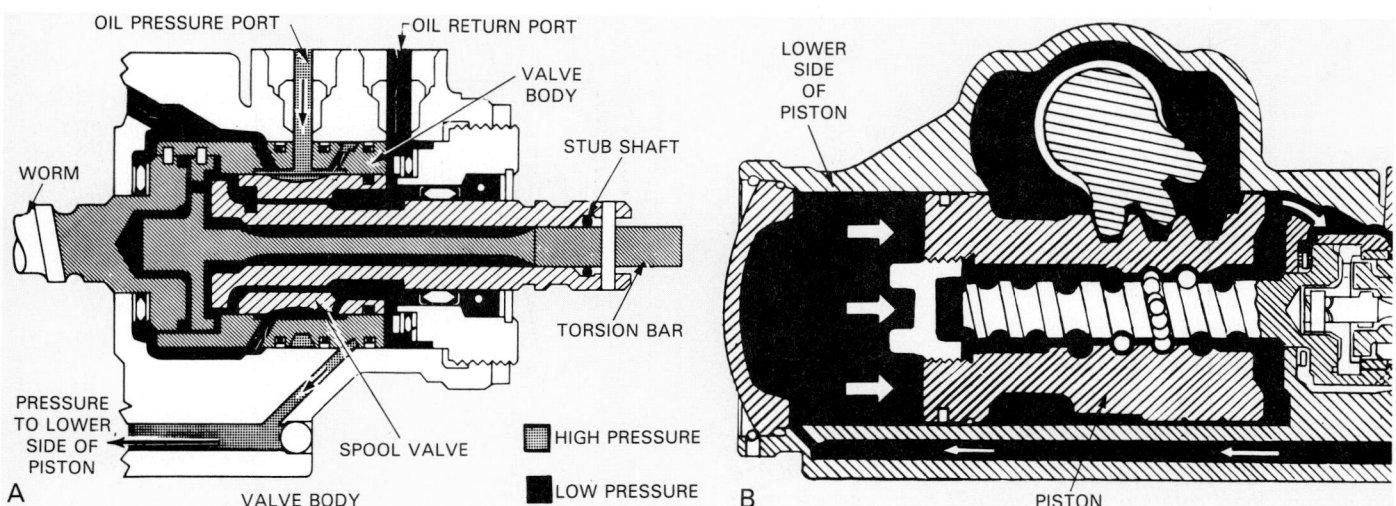

Fig. 66-24. Cutaway of power steering gearbox for linkage steering system. Spool valve controls pressure on each side of power piston. (Chrysler)

A *rotary valve* type power steering gearbox has a small torsion bar to detect steering wheel turning direction and turning effort. See Fig. 66-25.

When the steering wheel is turned, the torsion bar twists and turns the rotary valve. The rotary valve then directs hydraulic pressure to the correct side of the power piston.

Rotary valve action will be covered later when discussing power rack and pinion steering.

Study the flow of oil in Fig. 66-26. Notice how the pressure is used to slide the power piston. The piston pushes on and turns the sector shaft and pitman arm.

Fig. 66-25. This power steering gearbox uses a rotary valve and torsion bar to control pressure to power piston. Twist of torsion bar causes rotary valve to open port to right or left piston chamber. (Chrysler Corp.)

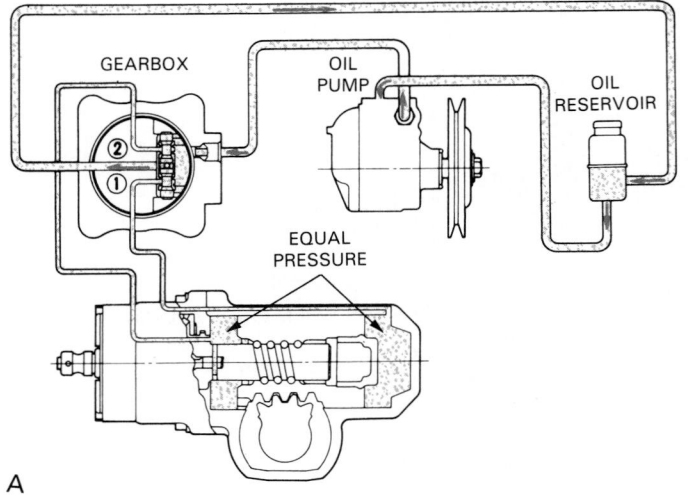

A

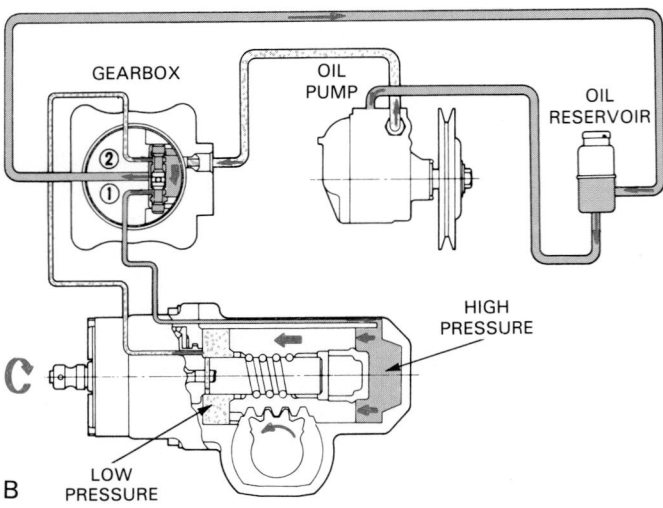

B

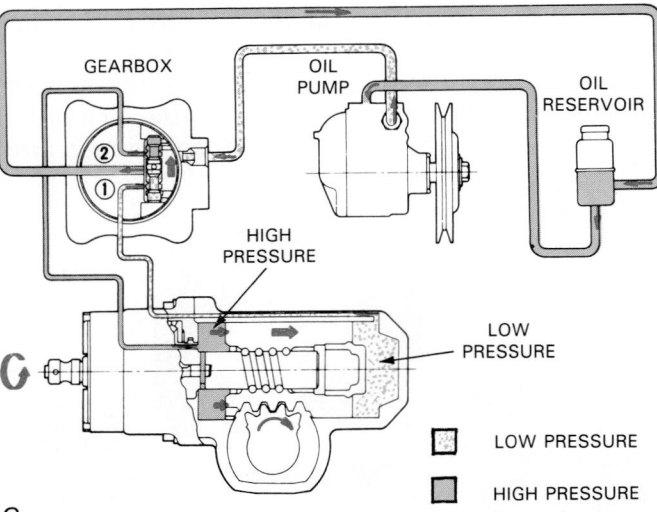

C

Fig. 66-26. Integral power steering gear operation. A — Steering wheel held straight ahead or neutral. Control valve balances pressure on both sides of power piston. Oil returns to pump reservoir from valve. B — With right turn, control valve routes oil to one side of power piston. Piston is pushed in cylinder to aid pitman shaft rotation. C — With left turn, control valve routes oil to other side of power piston. Piston movement forces oil on nonpressure side of piston back through control valve and to pump. (Plymouth)

EXTERNAL CYLINDER POWER STEERING (LINKAGE TYPE)

An *external cylinder power steering system* commonly has the power piston bolted to the frame and to the center link. This is shown in Fig. 66-27. The control valve may be located in the gearbox or on the steering linkage.

POWER RACK AND PINION STEERING

Power rack and pinion steering uses hydraulic pump pressure to assist the driver in moving the rack and front wheels. Fig. 66-28 shows this type of system.

The power steering pump normally mounts on the front of the engine. A belt powers the pump. Power steering hoses and metal lines connect the pump with the rack and pinion gear.

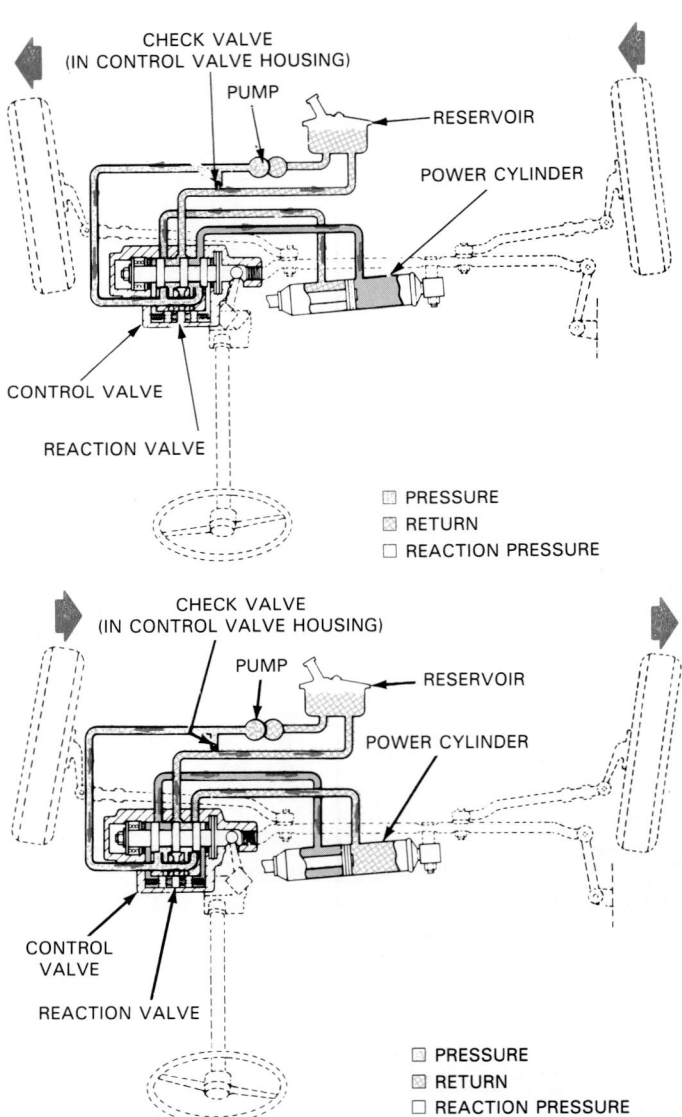

Fig. 66-27. Power steering system using power cylinder mounted on steering linkage. Note system pressures for right and left turns. (Ford)

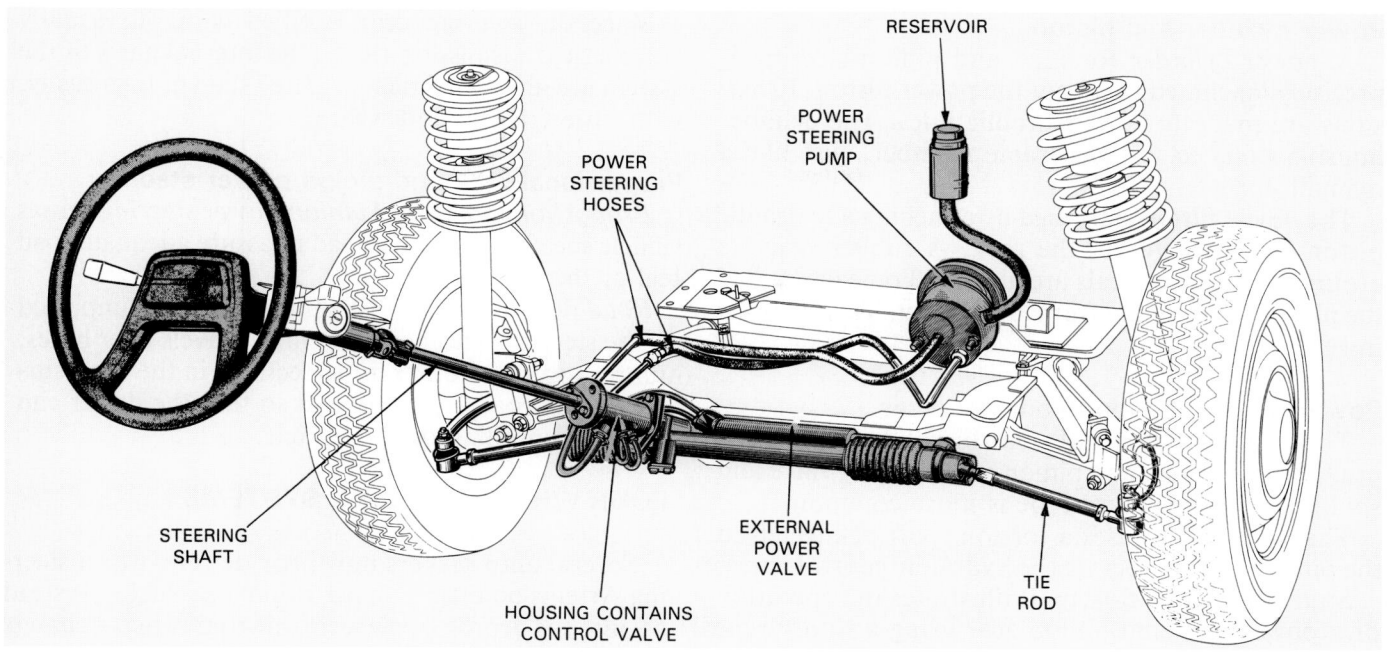

Fig. 66-28. External view of power rack and pinion setup. (Peugeot)

A power rack and pinion assembly basically consists of:
1. POWER CYLINDER (hydraulic cylinder machined inside rack or gear housing). See Fig. 66-29.
2. POWER PISTON (hydraulic, double-acting piston formed on rack).
3. HYDRAULIC LINES (steel tubing connecting control valve and power cylinder).

4. CONTROL VALVE (either a rotary or spool type hydraulic valve that regulates pressure entry into each end of power piston).

The other parts of the assembly are similar to those that are found on a manual rack and pinion steering system. Note in Fig. 66-29 how routing oil pressure into either end of the power cylinder causes piston operation.

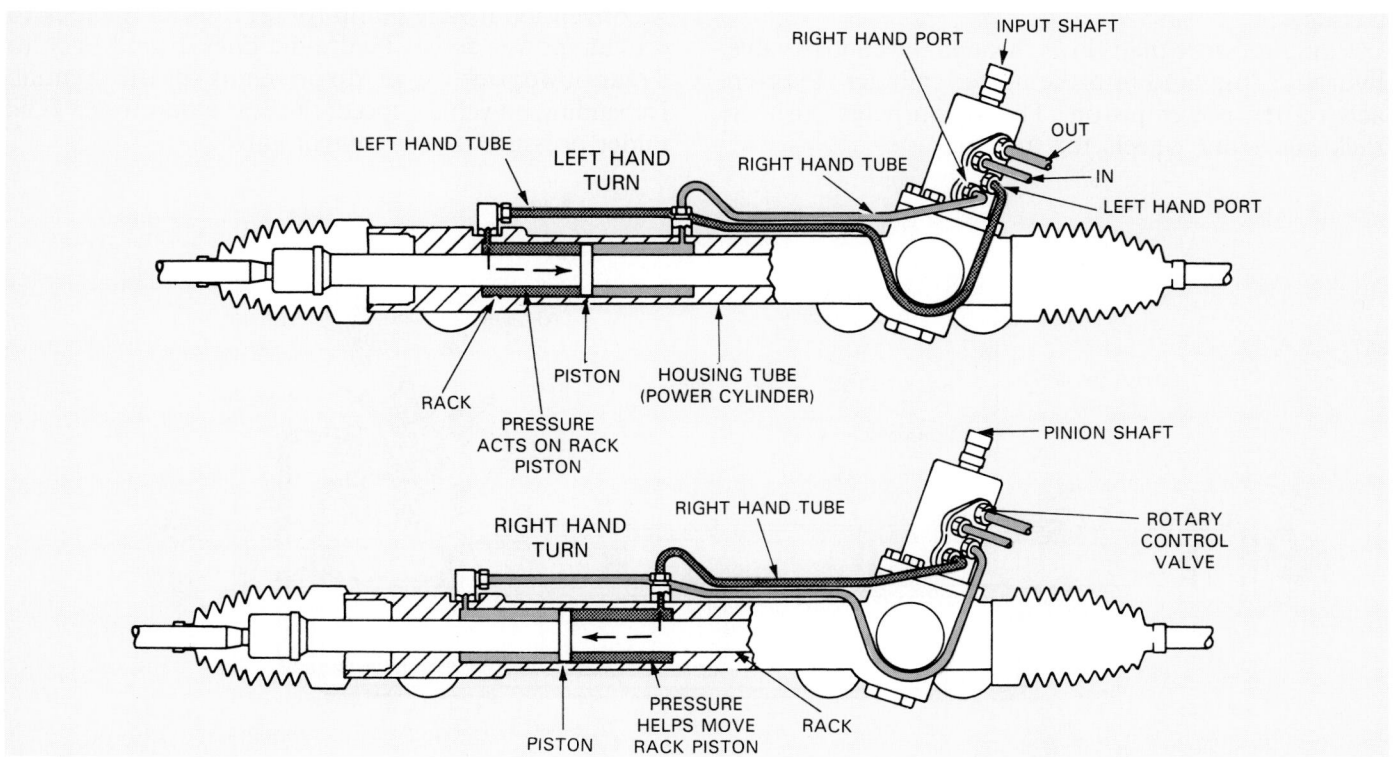

Fig. 66-29. Power cylinder is formed around rack. Pressure acts on rack piston to help slide rack in its housing. (Ford Motor Co.)

Power cylinder and piston

A *power cylinder* for rack and pinion steering is precisely machined to accept the power piston. Provisions are made for the hydraulic lines. The cylinder housing bolts to the car frame member, just like a manual unit.

The *power piston* is formed by attaching a hydraulic piston to the center of the rack. A rubber seal fits around this piston. Seals are also used on each end of the piston to keep fluid from leaking out. This is shown in Fig. 66-30.

Power rack and pinion control valves

There are two types of control valve mechanisms used on power rack and pinion gears: rotary valve and spool valve. The rotary type is more common.

The *rotary valve* uses a torsion shaft connected to the pinion gear to operate the hydraulic control valve.

Study Fig. 66-30 closely. It illustrates the operation of a power rack and pinion gear using a rotary type control valve. Today's cars frequently use this design.

A *spool valve* uses the thrust action of the pinion shaft to shift the control valve. The control valve can then route oil to the power cylinder.

Fig. 66-31 shows a simplified view of a power rack and pinion gear with a spool type control valve.

Power rack and pinion operation

When the steering wheel is turned, the weight of the vehicle causes the front tires to resist turning. This twists a torsion bar (rotary valve mechanism) or thrusts the pinion shaft (spool valve mechanism) slightly. This makes the control valve move and align specific oil passages.

Pump pressure than flows through the control valve, hydraulic line, and into the power cylinder. Pressure acts on the power piston. The piston helps push the rack and front wheels for turning.

Since the steering gear is filled with oil (usually automatic transmission fluid), the internal parts of the system are always lubricated. They slide or turn easily, with little friction and wear.

Proportional rack and pinion power steering

Proportional rack and pinion power steering senses vehicle speed and steering load to assure adequate road feel at the steering wheel.

Road feel is the pull or slight turning force imparted on the steering wheel as the vehicle travels over holes, humps, dips, and other imperfections in the road surface. Some road feel is needed so that the driver can sense the handling of the vehicle.

FOUR-WHEEL STEERING SYSTEMS

Several auto makers now provide four-wheel steering systems on their high performance vehicles. Instead of just the front two wheels, all four wheels change direction to improve handling, stability, feel, and maneuverability.

There are three types of four-wheel steering systems: mechanical, hydraulic, and electronic.

The *mechanical four-wheel steering system* uses a special front rack and pinion gearbox with an extra transfer box. The transfer box operates a long shaft that extends back to the rear rack. When the front wheels are turned, the shaft rotates to steer the rear wheels. This was the first four-wheel steering system on the market.

A *hydraulic four-wheel steering system* uses a conventional power rack and pinion steering system up front. A conventional vane pump forces fluid to the rack to provide power assist. Hydraulic lines extend back to a rear power steering pump driven by the differential. Depending on vehicle speed, the rear pump forces fluid under pressure into a control valve.

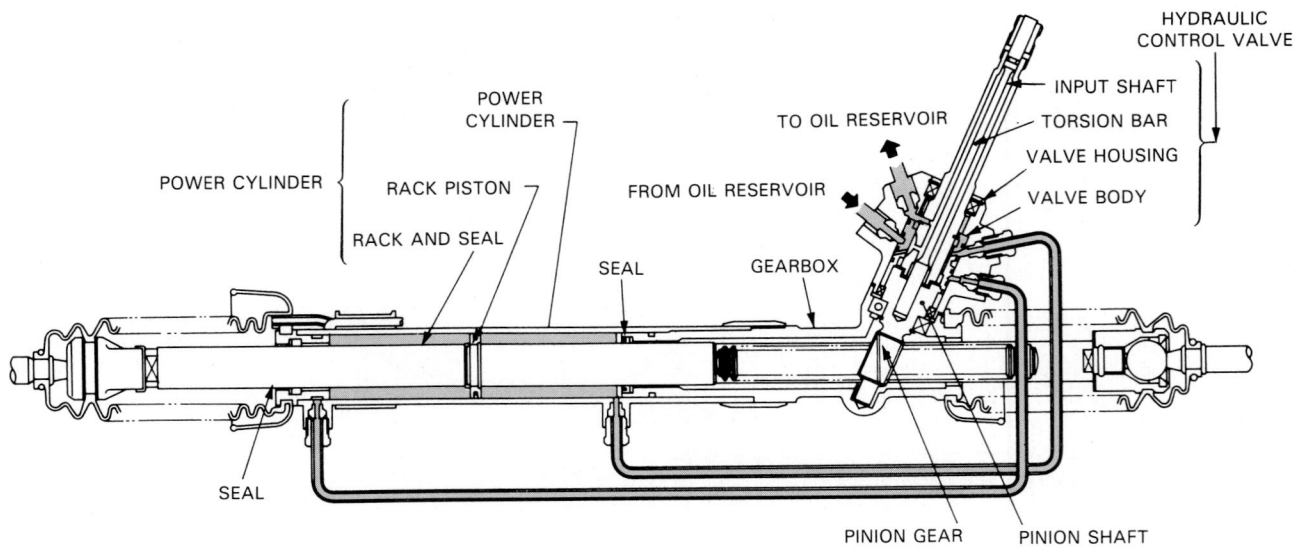

Fig. 66-30. Study parts of modern power steering system. (Subaru)

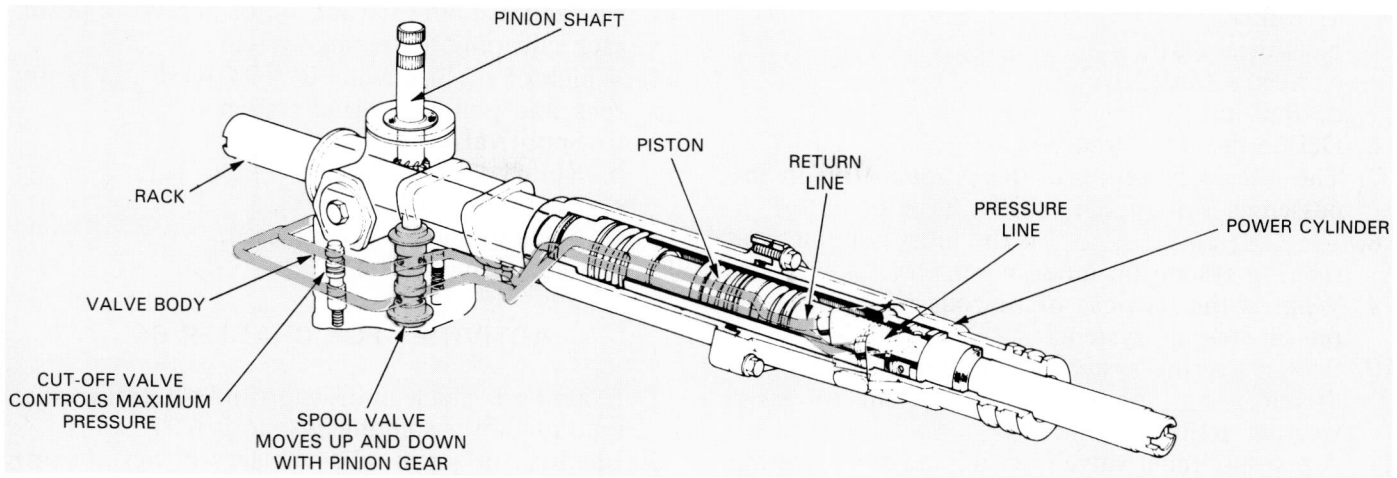

Fig. 66-31. This power rack and pinion steering assembly uses a spool valve that detects thrust action of helical pinion gear. It can then control oil pressure to rack piston. (Honda)

When a specific road speed is reached, the control valve can then operate the rear steering system. With this design, the rear rack tie-rod ends attach to the suspension system trailing arm. When activated, the rack shifts the control arm to steer the rear wheels.

Modern *electronic four-wheel steering systems* have an electric-motor-driven power rack that acts upon the rear wheels via its own recirculating ball drive and mechanical links. A computer controls rear wheel steering angles. The computer analyzes signals from angle sensors in the front steering and from speed signals from the anti-lock brake system wheel speed sensors. The motor-controlled power rack is then energized by the computer to steer the rear wheels as needed. The computer energizes a dc electric motor inside the power rack. The motor powers a recirculating ball drive to slide the rack right or left to respond to computer signals.

With a slight turn of the steering wheel, mechanical four-wheel steering systems turn the rear wheels in the same direction as the front. However, during a sharp turn, the special gear box straightens out the wheels and turns them in the opposite direction of the front. Electronic systems operate in a similar fashion, but they also react to changes in vehicle speed. Generally, at high speeds, the wheels steer in the same direction to improve maneuverability, as when changing lanes on the highway. At low vehicle speeds, the wheels steer in opposite directions to reduce turning radius, as when parking a vehicle. See Fig. 66-32.

KNOW THESE TERMS

Steering shaft, Steering gearbox, Steering linkage, Ball sockets, Pinion gear, Rack, Tie rod, Steering column, Recirculating ball, Worm shaft, Sector shaft, Ball nut, Gearbox ratio, Pitman arm, Center link, Idler arm, Power steering pump, Relief valve, Integral power steering.

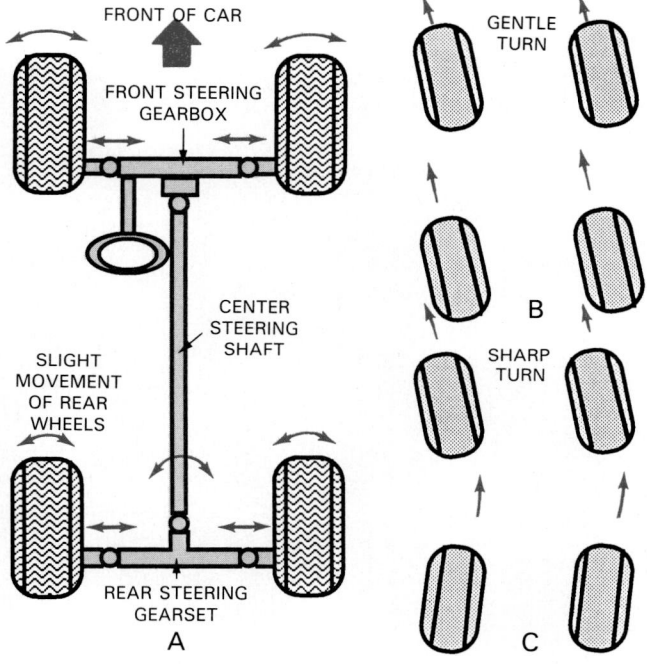

Fig. 66-32. A—Note basic parts of four-wheel steering system. B—When steering wheel is turned gently, wheels pivot in same direction. C—When steering wheel is turned more sharply, wheels pivot back and then turn in opposite directions.

REVIEW QUESTIONS

1. Name five functions of a steering system.
2. List and explain the six major parts of a linkage type steering system.
3. List and explain the four major parts of a manual rack and pinion steering system.
4. Today's vehicles commonly use a _____ steering column to help prevent driver injury during an accident.
5. Which of the following is NOT a part in a recirculating ball steering gearbox?

a. Roller.
b. Worm shaft.
c. Sector shaft.
d. Ball nut.
6. Define the term "gearbox ratio."
7. The idler arm supports the pitman arm on the passenger side of the vehicle. True or False?
8. _____ and _____ is the most popular type steering system on modern vehicles.
9. What is the purpose of tie-rods on a rack and pinion steering system?
10. Power steering systems normally use an engine driven _____ and _____ system to assist steering action.
11. A pressure relief valve is used in a power steering system to control maximum system pressure. True or False?
12. Describe an integral, linkage power steering system.

13. List and explain the four major parts of a power rack and pinion steering system.
14. Which of the following is NOT used in a power rack and pinion steering system?
a. Spool valve.
b. Rotary valve.
c. Poppet valve.
d. None of the above are used.
15. Define the term "road feel."

ACTIVITIES FOR CHAPTER 66

1. Examine a vehicle in the shop and determine what type of power steering system it has.
2. Identify the parts of a vehicle's power steering system.
3. On an overhead transparency, trace the flow of hydraulic fluid through a power steering system.

Power steering is standard equipment today on full-size passenger cars and on station wagons like this one.   *(Buick)*

67

Steering System Diagnosis and Repair

After studying this chapter, you will be able to:
- □ Describe common steering system problems.
- □ Properly inspect and determine the condition of a steering system.
- □ Explain basic steering column repair operations.
- □ Adjust both worm and rack and pinion gears.
- □ Describe service and repair procedures for a rack and pinion steering gear.
- □ Service power steering belts, hoses, and fluid.

- □ Explain how to complete basic power steering tests.
- □ Use safe work procedures.

After prolonged use, ball sockets, idler arm, gearbox, belts, hoses, and other system parts can fail.

It is important that the steering system be kept in perfect working condition for obvious safety reasons. As a technician, it is your job to find and correct steering system troubles quickly and properly.

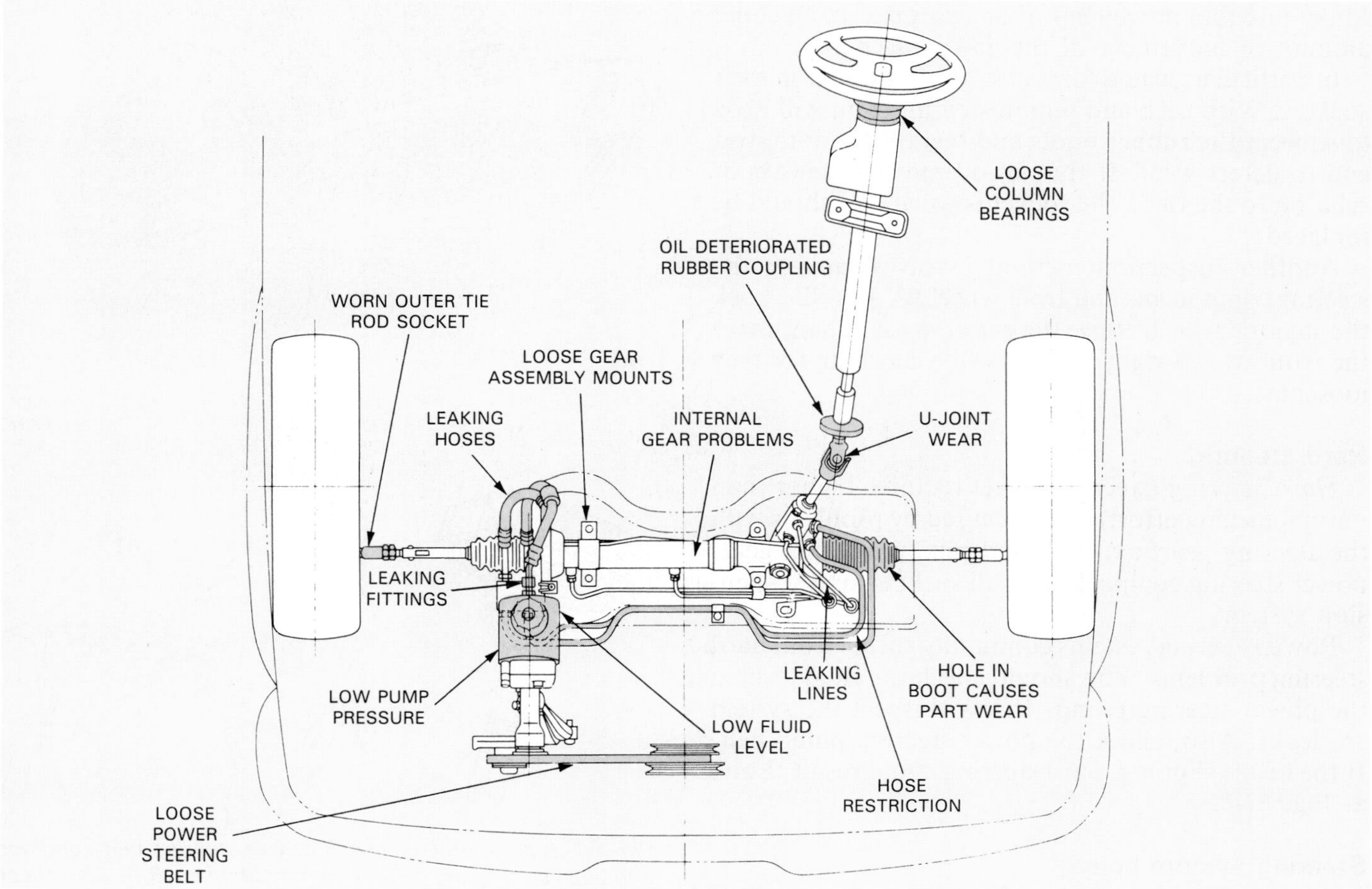

LOOSE COLUMN BEARINGS

OIL DETERIORATED RUBBER COUPLING

WORN OUTER TIE ROD SOCKET

LOOSE GEAR ASSEMBLY MOUNTS

LEAKING HOSES

INTERNAL GEAR PROBLEMS

U-JOINT WEAR

LEAKING FITTINGS

LOW PUMP PRESSURE

LEAKING LINES

HOLE IN BOOT CAUSES PART WEAR

LOW FLUID LEVEL

HOSE RESTRICTION

LOOSE POWER STEERING BELT

Fig. 67-1. Study types of problems that can develop in modern steering system.

STEERING SYSTEM PROBLEM DIAGNOSIS

The most common steering system problems are play in the steering wheel, hard steering, and abnormal noises when turning the steering wheel. These problems normally point to part wear, lack of lubrication, or an incorrect adjustment. You must inspect and test the steering system to find the source of the trouble. Refer to Fig. 67-1.

Steering wheel play

The most frequent of all steering system problems is excessive play in the steering wheel.

Steering wheel play is normally caused by worn ball sockets, worn idler arm, or too much clearance in the steering gearbox (worm or rack and pinion types).

Typically, you should NOT be able to turn the steering wheel more than about 1 1/2 in. (33 mm) without causing movement of the front wheels. If the steering wheel rotates excessively, a serious steering problem exists.

The *dry park test* is an effective way to check play in the steering linkage or rack and pinion mechanism. With the full weight of the vehicle on the front wheels, ask someone to rock the steering wheel while you look for looseness in the steering system.

Start your inspection at the steering column shaft and work your way out to the tie-rod ends, Fig. 67-2. Make sure that movement of one part causes an equal amount of movement of the adjoining part.

In particular, watch for ball studs that wiggle in their sockets. With rack and pinion steering, you will need to squeeze the rubber boots and feel the inner tie-rod end to detect wear. If the tie-rod moves sideways in relation to the rack, the socket is worn and should be replaced.

Another inspection method involves moving the steering components and front wheel BY HAND. Lock the steering wheel. Raise the car on a lift. Then, force the front wheels right and left while checking for part looseness.

Hard steering

Hard steering (steering wheel requires higher than normal turning effort) can be caused by problems with the steering gearbox, rack and pinion steering gear, power steering components, ball sockets, and suspension system.

Power steering systems commonly suffer from hard steering problems. You should check the fluid level in the power steering pump. If low, inspect the system for leaks. Also, check the power steering pump belt. If the belt is slipping, hard steering could result. Look at Fig. 67-3.

Steering system noise

Steering systems, when problems exist, can produce abnormal noises. *Noises* can be signs of worn parts,

Fig. 67-2. Check steering ball sockets closely for wear. Move steering wheel back and forth or wiggle components to detect looseness in joints. (Moog)

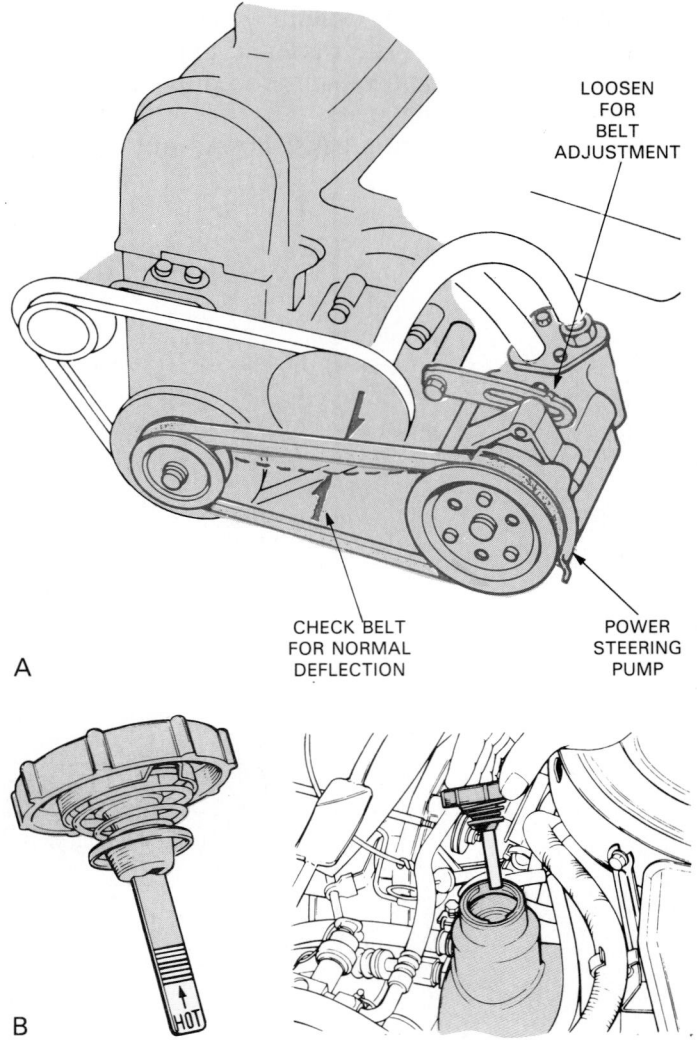

Fig. 67-3. A — Always check power steering belt condition and tension. Slipping belt is common problem. B — Also check power steering fluid level. If low, check for leaks and add correct type and amount of fluid. (Honda and Subaru)

unlubricated bearings or ball sockets, loose, rattling parts, slipping belts, low power steering fluid, or other system troubles.

Belt squeal is a loud screeching sound produced by belt slippage. A slipping power steering belt will usually show up when turning. Turning the steering wheel to the full right or left will increase system pressure and belt squeal.

STEERING SYSTEM MAINTENANCE

Steering system maintenance typically involves checking for low fluid level, incorrect belt adjustment, system leaks, and other troubles. It may also include lubricating (greasing) ball sockets.

Remember! The safety of the automobile and its passengers are dependent upon the condition of the steering system.

Checking power steering fluid

To check the level of fluid in the power steering system, the engine should NOT be running. Set the parking brake and place the transmission in park or in neutral.

As shown in Fig. 67-3, unscrew and remove the cap from the power steering reservoir. The cap will normally have a dipstick. Wipe off the dipstick and reinstall the cap. Remove the cap and inspect the level of fluid on the stick.

Most power steering dipsticks will have markings for checking the fluid when HOT and COLD. Make sure you read the correct marking on the dipstick. The fluid level will rise on the stick as the system warms.

If needed, only add enough fluid to reach the correct mark on the dipstick. Do NOT overfill the system. Overfilling could cause fluid to spray out the top of the reservoir onto the engine and other components.

Automatic transmission fluid is commonly used in a power steering system. Since there are several types of transmission fluid, obtain and install the right kind.

WARNING! Some power steering systems do NOT use automatic transmission fluid. They require special power steering fluid. Check manufacturer recommendations when in doubt.

Servicing power steering hoses

Always inspect the condition of power steering hoses when checking a power steering system. The high pressure hose can be exposed to tremendous pressures. If this hose ruptures, a sudden and dangerous loss of power assist can occur.

DANGER! Power steering pump pressure can exceed 1000 psi (6 895 kPa). This is enough pressure to cause serious eye injury. Wear eye protection when working on a power steering system.

When installing a new hose, use a flare nut or tubing wrench. Start the new hose fitting by hand to avoid crossthreading. Tighten the hose fittings properly.

Make sure the hose does NOT rub on moving or hot parts. This could cause hose failure.

Servicing power steering belts

A loose power steering belt can slip, cause belt squeal, and erratic or high steering effort. A worn or cracked belt may snap. This could cause a loss of power assist. Always inspect the belt very closely.

CAUTION! When tightening a power steering belt, do NOT pry on the side of the pump. If the thin housing of the pump is dented, the pump can be ruined. Only pry on a reinforced flange or recommended point.

To install a new power steering belt, loosen the bolts holding the power steering pump to its brackets, Fig. 67-3. Push inward on the pump to release tension.

Obtain the correct belt and install it in reverse order. Pry on a recommended point when adjusting belt tension to specs.

STEERING COLUMN SERVICE

Steering column service is needed after a collision (crushing of collapsible steering column) or when internal parts of the column fail. Most steering column repairs can be done with the column mounted in the car. However, some repairs require steering column removal. Refer to Fig. 67-4.

Steering wheel removal and replacement

A *wheel puller* is used to remove a steering wheel from its shaft. After removing the horn button and steering shaft nut, scribe alignment marks on the steering wheel and steering shaft. This may help you position the steering wheel correctly during assembly.

Mount the wheel puller as shown in Fig. 67-5. Screw the bolts into the threaded holes in the wheel. Make sure the bolts have the correct thread type. Using a wrench or ratchet, tighten the puller down against the steering shaft.

WARNING! Wear eye protection when tightening a wheel puller. If one of the bolts were to break, bits of metal could fly into your face.

After following service manual directions to replace the worn or damaged parts in the steering column, assemble everything in reverse order.

Steering column joint replacement

Many steering column assemblies use a flexible coupling or a universal joint on the lower part of the steering shaft. The flexible coupling is normally made of reinforced rubber. The rubber coupling can deteriorate after being exposed to prolonged service, engine heat, or oil leakage. The metal universal joint can wear and develop play.

Note! Refer to the index of this book to locate additional information relating to steering column service. Modern steering columns house the ignition switch, turn signal mechanism, horn button, and sometimes other accessory items.

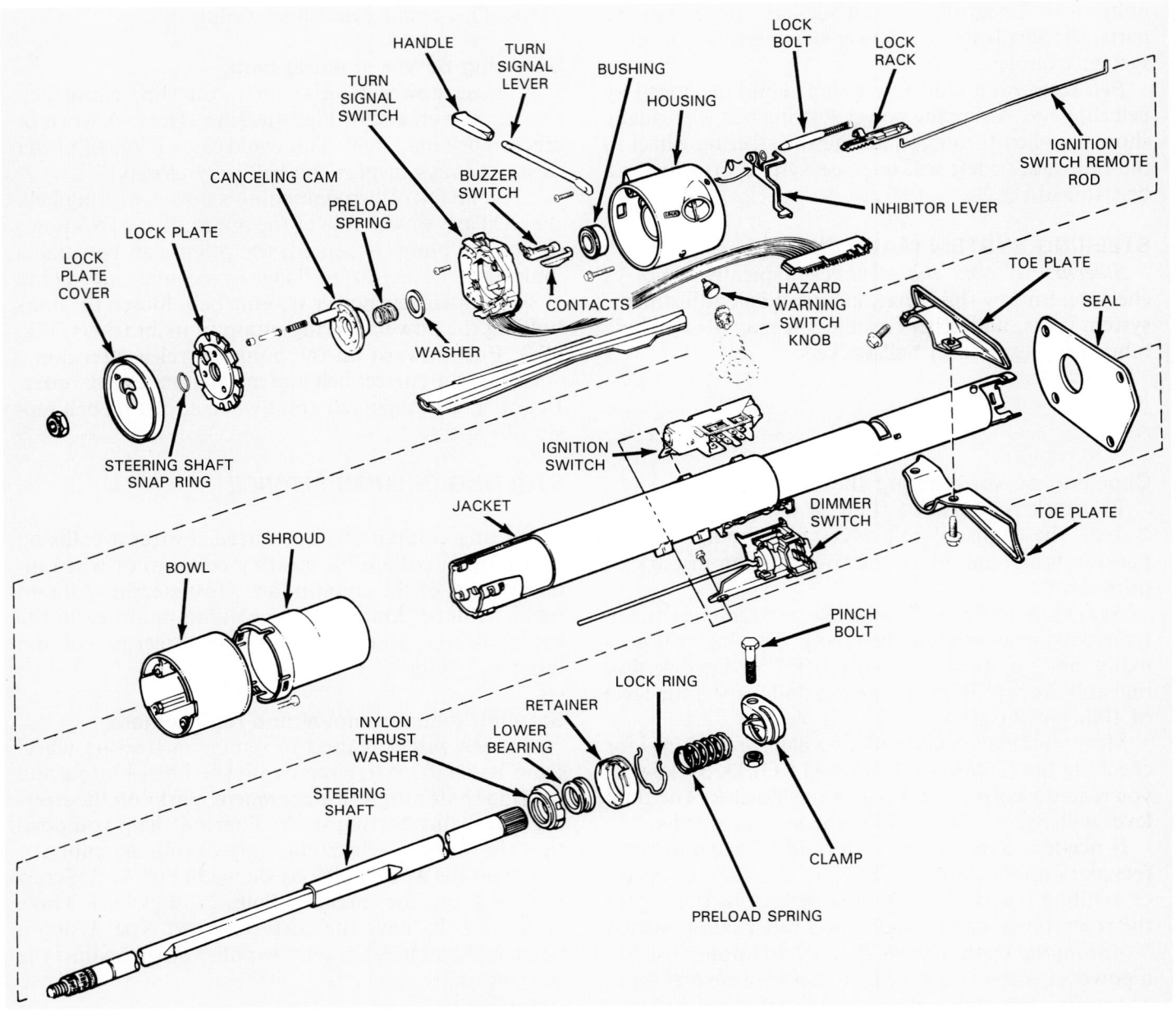

Fig. 67-4. Exploded view shows relationship between parts of steering column. Partial or complete disassembly may be needed depending upon problem. (Chrysler Corp.)

MANUAL STEERING GEARBOX SERVICE (RECIRCULATING BALL TYPE)

Steering gearbox service usually involves the adjustment or the replacement of worn parts (bearings, seals, bushings). Service is frequently needed when the worm shaft rotates back and forth WITHOUT normal pitman shaft movement. This points to play inside the gearbox. If adjustment does not correct the excess clearance, the unit must be rebuilt or replaced.

Manual steering gearbox adjustment

There are two basic adjustments on manual, recirculating ball steering gearboxes: worm bearing preload and over-center clearance. You should set the worm

bearing preload first and the over-center clearance second. Refer to Fig. 67-6.

A *worm bearing preload adjustment* assures that the worm shaft is held snugly inside the gearbox housing. If the worm shaft bearings are too loose, the worm shaft could move sideways and up and down during operation.

To make a worm bearing preload adjustment, disconnect the pitman arm (if gearbox installed in car). Loosen the pitman shaft over-center adjusting locknut and screw a couple of turns. Then, turn the steering wheel or worm shaft (gearbox out of car) from side to side slowly.

Using a torque wrench or spring scale, measure the amount of force needed to turn the steering wheel

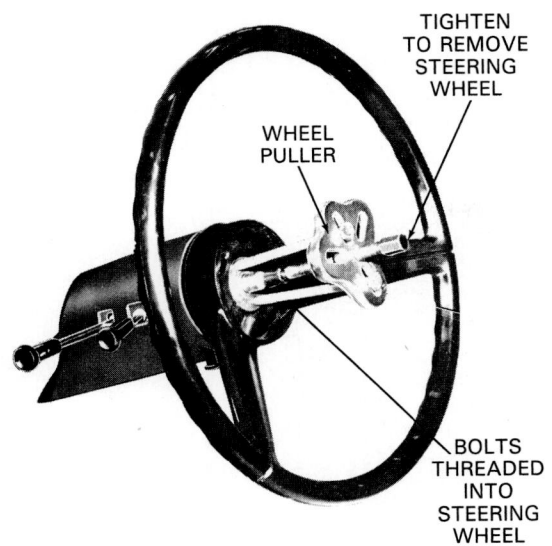

Fig. 67-5. Wheel puller is normally needed to force steering wheel off of its shaft. Tighten center puller bolt while wearing safety glasses. (Ford)

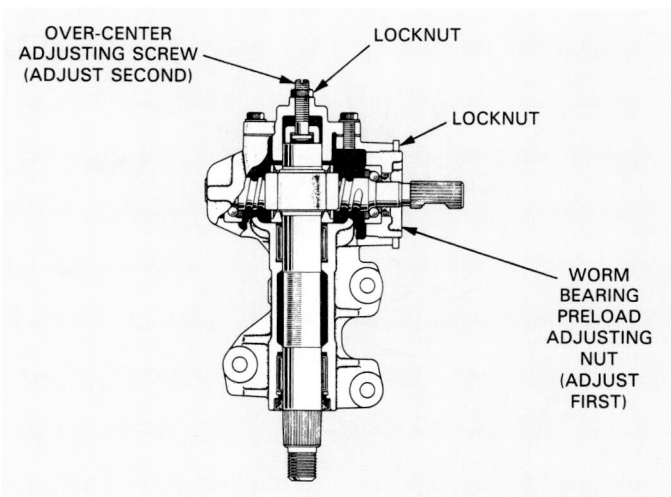

Fig. 67-6. Worm bearing preload controls play in worm shaft bearings. Over-center adjustment controls play between pitman shaft sector gear and ball nut. Both are critical. (Toyota)

worm shaft to the center position. See Fig. 67-7A. Note the reading on the torque wrench or spring scale. Compare your measurement to specs.

If needed, loosen the worm adjuster locknut, as in Fig. 67-7B. Then, tighten the the worm bearing adjuster to increase preload. Loosen it to decrease preload and turning effort.

Tighten the locknut and make sure the steering wheel or shaft turns freely from stop to stop. If it binds or feels rough, then the gearbox has damaged parts and should be rebuilt or replaced.

After setting worm bearing preload, adjust the pitman shaft over-center clearance.

Pitman shaft over-center clearance controls the amount of play between the pitman shaft (sector) gear and the teeth on the ballnut. It is the most critical adjustment affecting steering wheel play, Fig. 67-6.

To make the over-center gearbox adjustment, find the center position of the steering wheel. Turn the steering wheel or worm shaft from full right to full left while counting the number of turns. Divide the number of turns by two to find the middle. This will let you turn the steering wheel from full stop to the center.

The steering wheel or shaft must be centered during over-center adjustment. Most gearboxes are designed to have more gear tooth backlash (clearance) when turned to the right or left. A slight preload is produced in the center position to avoid steering wheel play during straight ahead driving.

Generally, loosen the screw locknut, Fig. 67-8A. Turn the over-center screw in until it bottoms lightly. This will remove the backlash. Using the specific instructions in a service manual, measure the amount of force needed to turn the steering wheel or gearbox

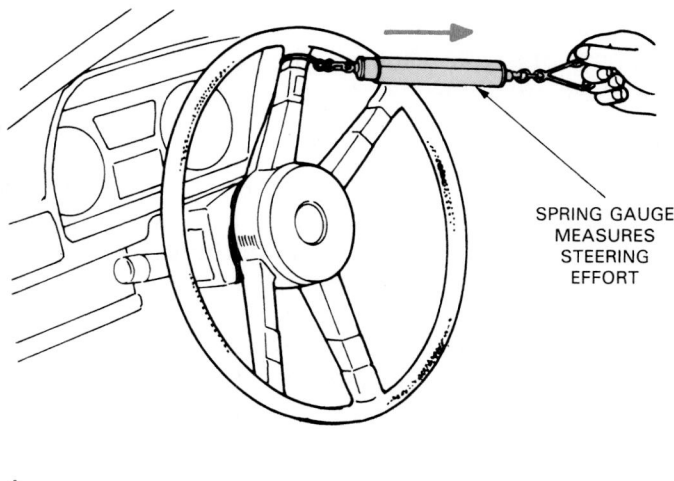

A

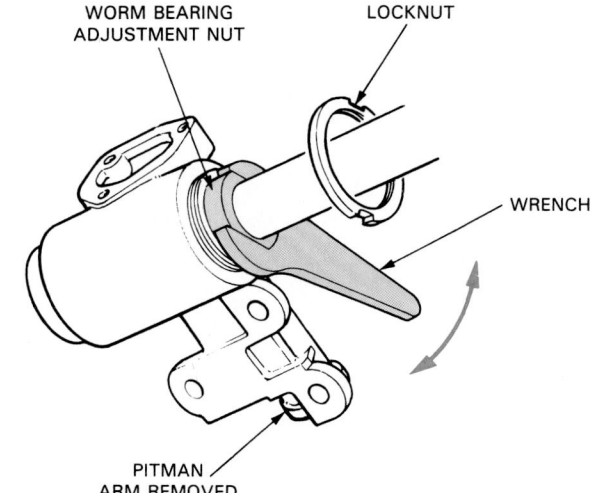

B

Fig. 67-7. Worm bearing preload adjustment. A — Measure pull required to turn steering wheel with spring scale. Compare to specs. B — If needed, tighten or loosen large adjustment nut until spring scale reading is correct. (Mazda)

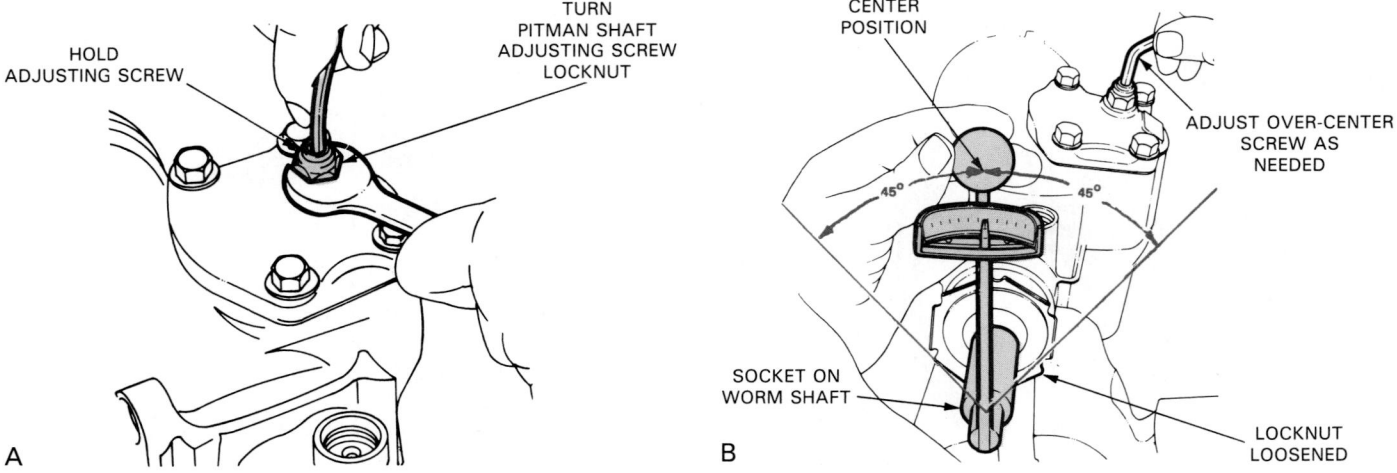

A — HOLD ADJUSTING SCREW / TURN PITMAN SHAFT ADJUSTING SCREW LOCKNUT

B — CENTER POSITION / 45° / 45° / ADJUST OVER-CENTER SCREW AS NEEDED / SOCKET ON WORM SHAFT / LOCKNUT LOOSENED

Fig. 67-8. Pitman shaft over-center adjustment. A — Center worm shaft or steering wheel. Loosen locknut and bottom adjustment lightly. B — Use a torque wrench or spring scale to measure amount of pull needed to turn shaft back and forth through center position. Tighten or loosen adjustment until within specs. Secure locknut and recheck. (Chrysler Corp.)

worm shaft, Fig. 67-8B. Loosen or tighten the pitman shaft screw as needed to meet specs. Tighten the locknut and recheck gearbox action.

Power steering gearboxes sometimes require the adjustment of rack-piston preload. Since procedures differ, refer to a shop manual for directions.

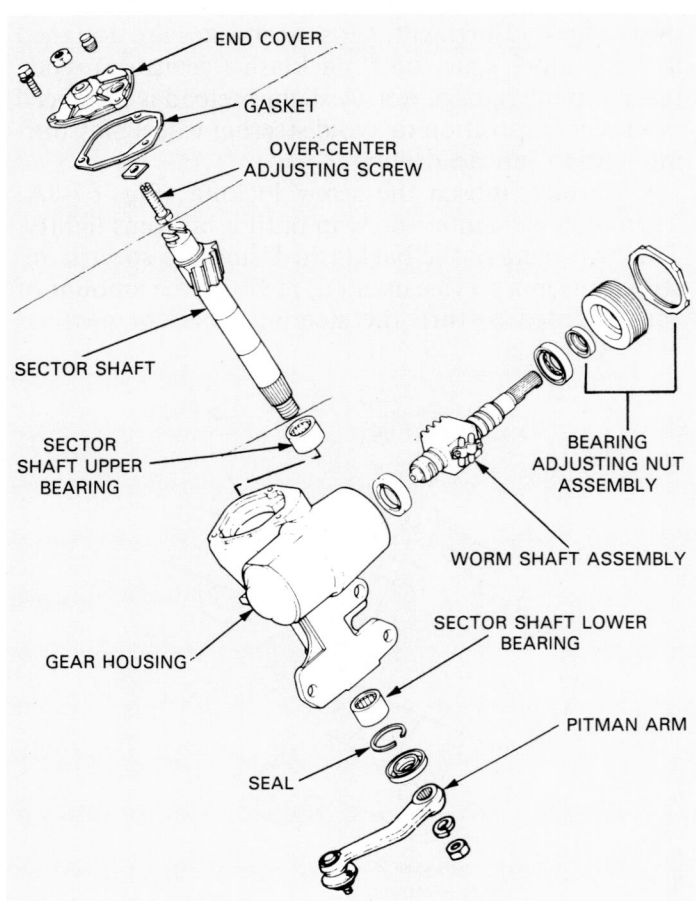

Fig. 67-9. Service manual illustration like this one, would be helpful during gearbox overhaul. (Toyota)

END COVER / GASKET / OVER-CENTER ADJUSTING SCREW / SECTOR SHAFT / SECTOR SHAFT UPPER BEARING / GEAR HOUSING / SEAL / BEARING ADJUSTING NUT ASSEMBLY / WORM SHAFT ASSEMBLY / SECTOR SHAFT LOWER BEARING / PITMAN ARM

Manual steering gearbox overhaul

When adjustment fails to correct a gearbox problem, the gearbox needs to be overhauled or replaced. Basically, *gearbox overhaul* is done by disassembling, cleaning, inspecting, and replacing parts as needed. All worn parts and used rubber seals are replaced. Refer to a service manual for the particular gearbox since procedures and specs vary.

Fig. 67-9 shows an exploded view of a typical manual steering gearbox.

After replacing worn parts, assembling, and installing the gearbox, fill the housing with the correct type lubricant. Most manual steering gearboxes use SAE 90 GEAR OIL. Make sure you do NOT overfill the gearbox. A shop manual will give information on filling and correct oil type.

STEERING LINKAGE SERVICE

When your inspection finds worn steering linkage parts, new parts must be installed. Fig. 67-10 illustrates the parts of a typical linkage type steering system. Study the types of problems you might find.

Idler arm service

A *worn idler arm* will cause play in the steering wheel. The front wheels, mainly the right wheel, can turn without causing movement of the steering wheel. An idler arm is a very COMMON WEAR POINT in a linkage steering system. Check it carefully, Fig. 67-10.

To check an idler arm for wear, grasp the outer end of the arm (end opposite frame). Force the idler arm up and down by hand. Note the amount of movement at the end of the arm. Compare this movement to specs.

Typically, an idler arm should NOT wiggle up and down more than about 1/4 in. (6.5 mm).

A worn idler arm is replaced by separating the outer end of the arm and the center link. A fork or puller,

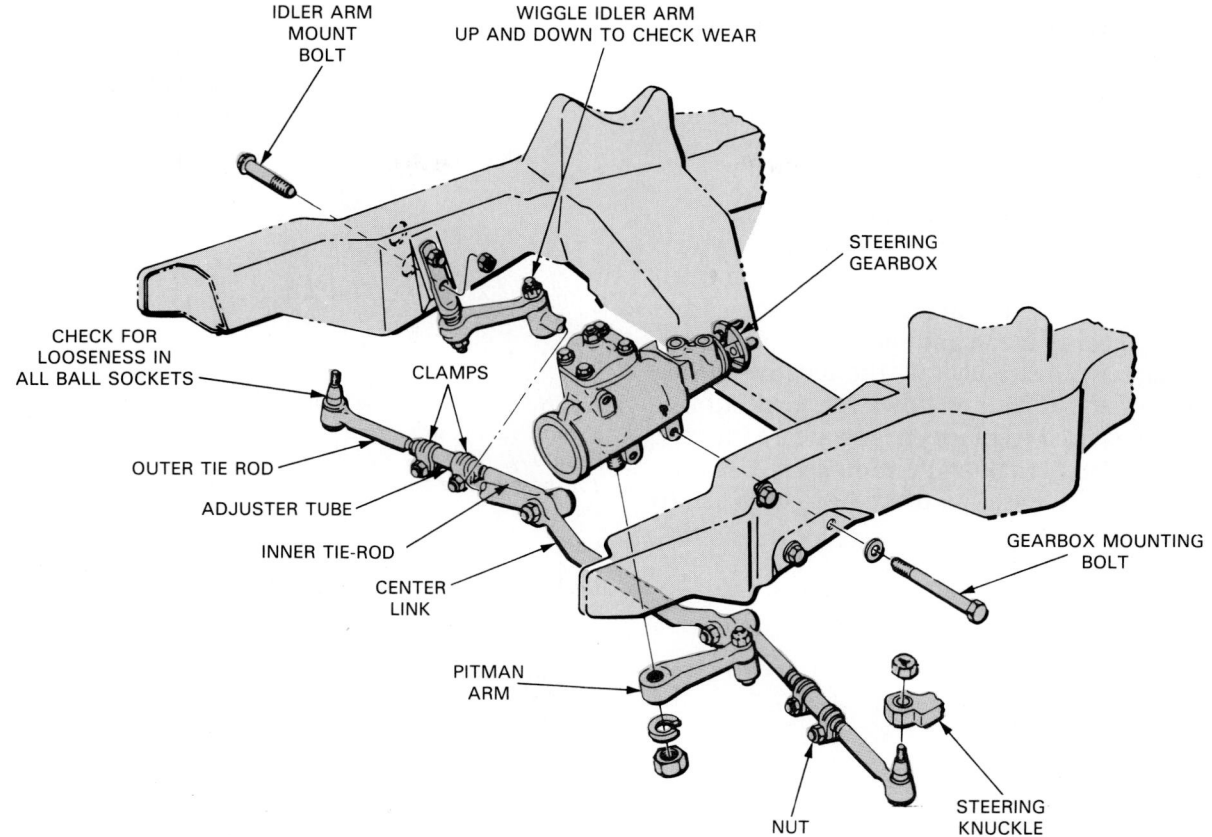

Fig. 67-10. Every part of the linkage system must be checked carefully to find worn components. (Buick)

like the one in Fig. 67-11, can be used to force the idler arm's ball stud out of the hole in the center link. Then, unbolt the idler arm from the frame, Fig. 67-10.

Install the new idler arm in reverse order of removal. Make sure you torque the idler arm fasteners properly. Install the new cotter pin and bend it properly.

Tie rod end service

A *worn tie-rod end* will also cause steering play. When you detect movement between the ball stud and its socket, install a new tie-rod end.

To remove a tie-rod end, separate the tie-rod from the steering knuckle or center link. Use a fork or a puller as shown in Fig. 67-11. Be careful NOT to damage any components.

Before loosening the adjustment sleeve, measure or mark tie-rod length. This will allow you to set the new tie-rod at about the same length as the old one. The alignment of the front wheels is altered when the length of a tie-rod is changed.

Loosen and unscrew the tie-rod adjustment sleeve. Look at Fig. 67-10. Turn the new tie-rod into the sleeve until it is the exact length of the old tie-rod.

Install the tie-rod ball stud in the center link or steering knuckle. Tighten the fasteners to specifications. Double-check that all new cotter pins are installed and bent correctly. Tighten the adjustment sleeve and check steering action.

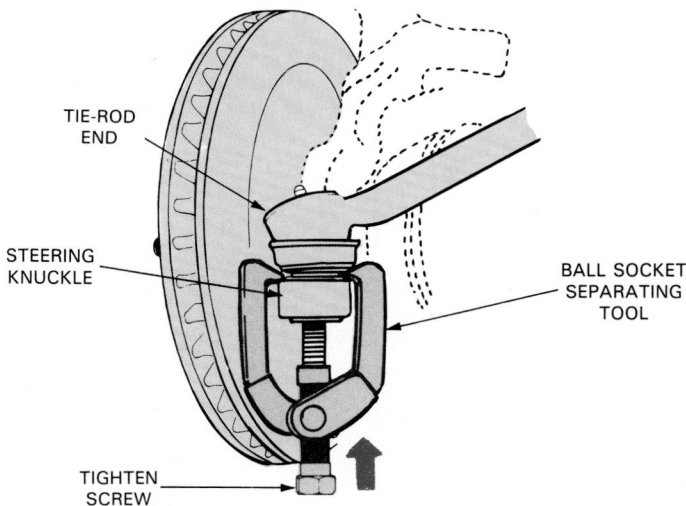

Fig. 67-11. Special puller, as shown, or fork tool can be used to separate tie-rod end from steering knuckle. This tool can also be used on other ball sockets. (Cadillac)

MANUAL RACK AND PINION SERVICE

A manual rack and pinion steering system can develop problems similar to those described for a linkage type system. However, a rack and pinion system has few parts to fail. When problems do develop, they are frequently in the tie-rod ends. When NOT properly lubricated, the rack and pinion gear may also wear, causing problems.

Since so many new cars use rack and pinion steering, it is important that you learn common service and repair procedures for this type system.

Manual rack and pinion lubrication

Some manual rack and pinion steering gears require periodic lubrication. Others only need lubrication when the unit is torn down for repairs. Fig. 67-12 shows one type of steering gear that can and should be lubricated. Note the grease fittings and how the technician has removed one of the rubber bellows for inspection.

A grease gun is used to place chassis grease into the fittings on the manual rack and pinion gear. Use only a small amount of grease, as described by the auto manufacturer.

Manual rack and pinion gear adjustment

Most manual rack and pinion steering gears have a

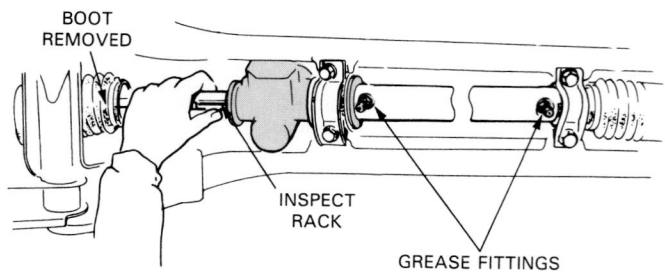

Fig. 67-12. Many steering system components have grease fittings that require lubrication. This technician has removed boot to inspect inner tie-rod socket. (Honda)

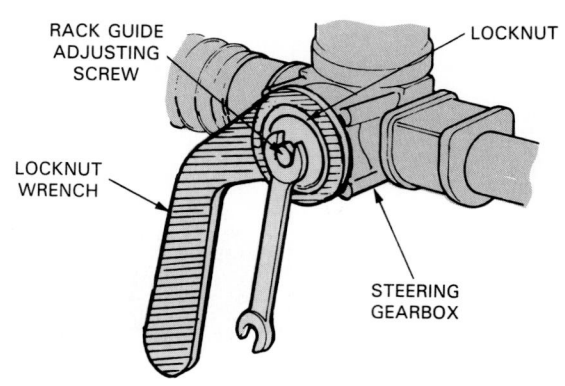

Fig. 67-13. Many rack and pinion steering mechanisms have a rack guide adjustment. Follow manufacturer directions. Basically, hold the locknut while turning adjustment. Bottom the screw and then back it off prescribed amount. (Honda)

rack guide adjustment screw. When there is play in the steering, try adjusting the steering gear, Fig. 67-13.

Typically, to adjust the rack guide screw, loosen the locknut on the screw. Then, turn the rack guide screw in until it bottoms lightly. Back off the screw the recommended amount (approximately 45° or until a prescribed turning effort is obtained). Tighten the locknut. Check for tight or loose steering and measure steering effort. If not within specs, the steering gear may require major repairs.

Rack and pinion gear removal

To remove a rack and pinion steering gear, separate the outer tie-rod ends from the steering knuckles. Then, unbolt the steering gear mounting brackets from the frame or crossmember, Fig. 67-14. Also, disconnect

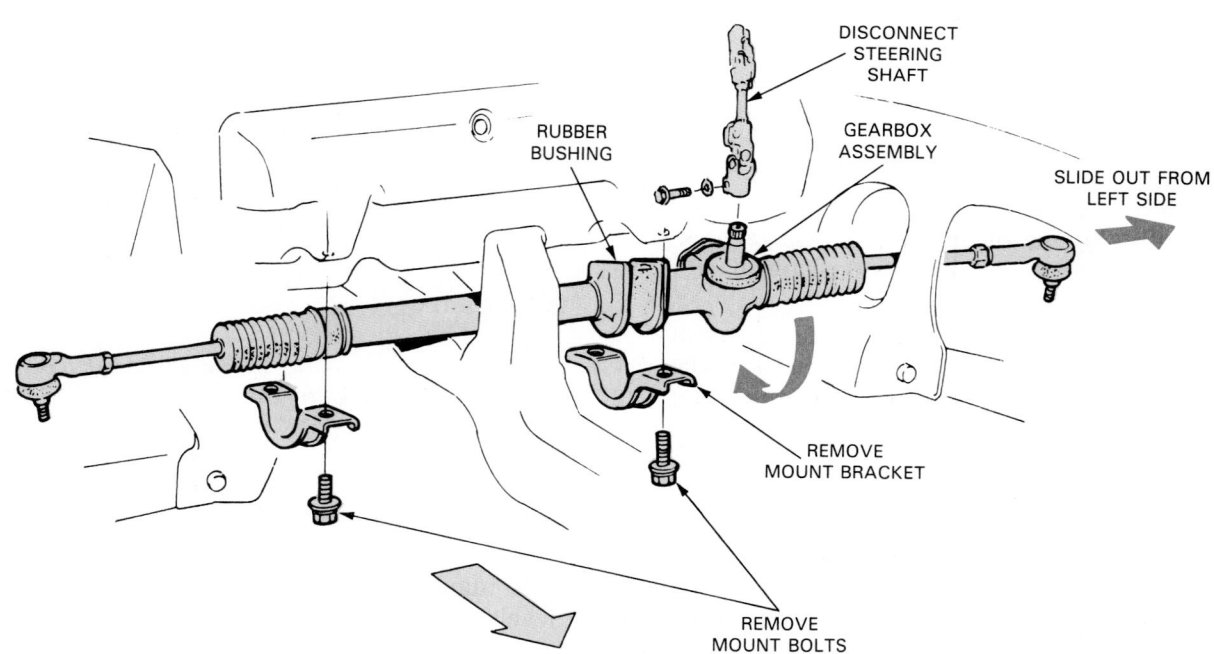

Fig. 67-14. Removal of rack and pinion gear mechanism usually involves disconnecting these parts. Slide unit out one side of car. (Honda)

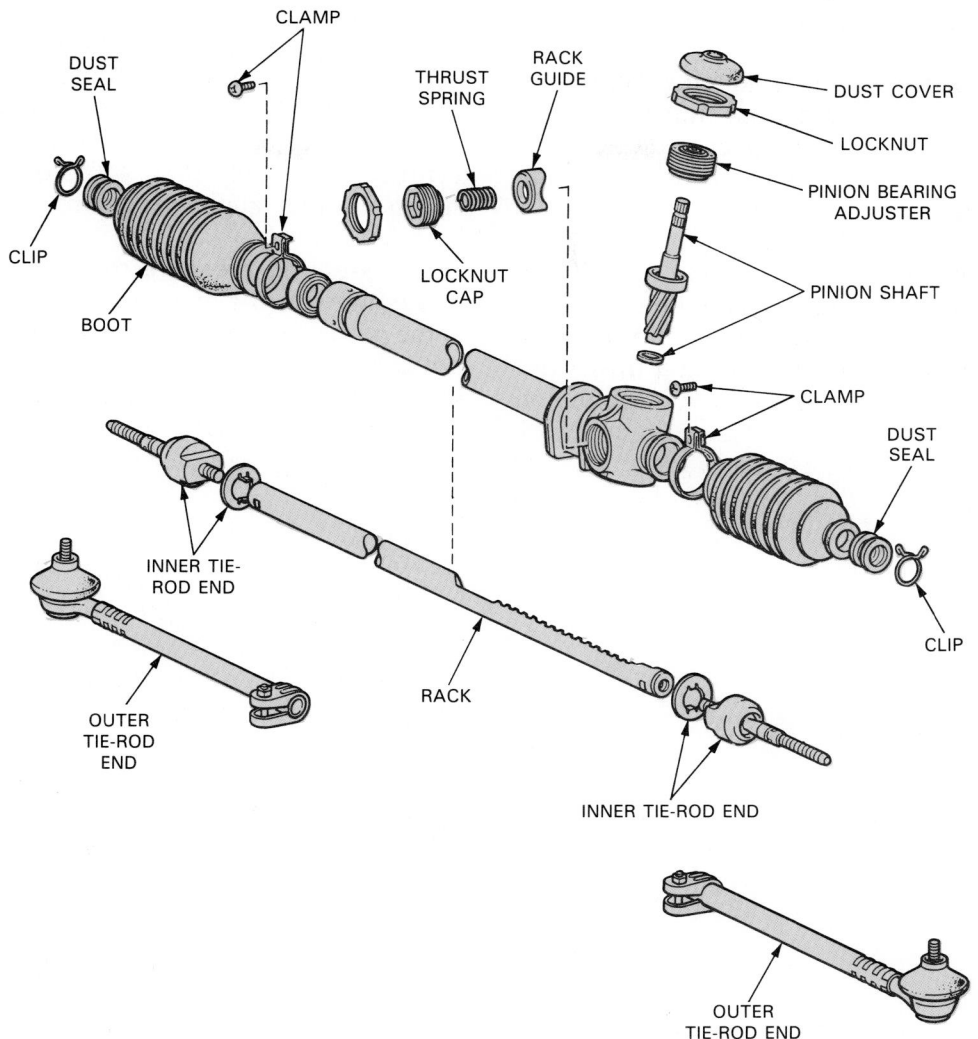

Fig. 67-15. Disassembled view of typical rack and pinion steering mechanism. During service, inspect each component and measure wear. Any part worn beyond specs must be replaced. All seals and other rubber or plastic parts must also be replaced. (Toyota)

the steering column coupler or universal joint. Rotate the steering gear and slide it out of the chassis.

Refer to a service manual for additional information. You may have to remove the front wheels or slide the gear out one particular side of the car.

Rack and pinion gear overhaul

Exact procedures for overhauling a rack and pinion steering gear will vary with car make and model. Generally, however, you must disassemble the unit and check each part closely. Replace any part that shows signs of wear.

Fig. 67-15 shows a disassembled manual rack and pinion steering gear. Study how all of the parts fit together. Use a service manual to obtain exact procedures for rebuilding the particular unit.

An example of a critical repair method is pictured in Fig. 67-16. A special guide fixture is being used to drill a lock pin out of the gear assembly. The manual gives correct drill size, and replacement pin number.

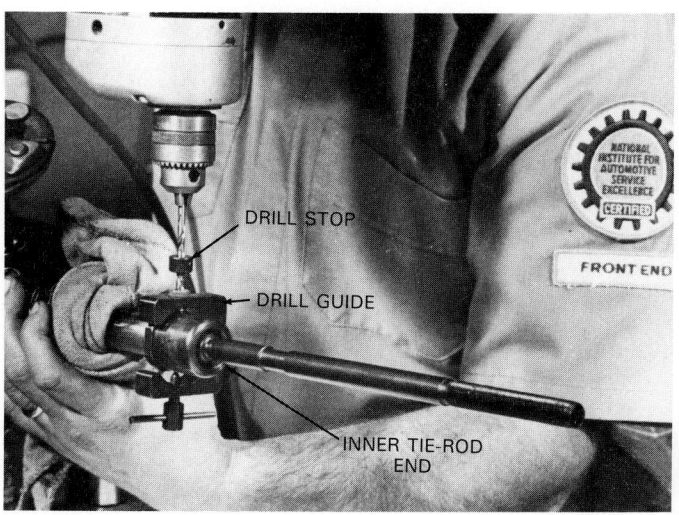

Fig. 67-16. A service manual is very important when doing major steering system repairs. For example, it will give information about correct drill bit size for drilling out pin in this tie-rod ball socket. (Moog)

POWER STEERING SYSTEM SERVICE

Many of the parts of a power steering system are the same as those used on a manual steering system. However, a pump, hoses, power piston, and control valve are added. These parts can also fail, requiring repair or replacement.

Power steering leaks

Power steering fluid leakage is a common problem. With the extremely high pressure (over 1000 psi or 6 895 kPa), leaks can easily develop around fittings, in hoses, at the gearbox seals, or at the rack and pinion assembly.

Fig. 67-17 shows the common leakage points for two common types of power steering systems.

To check for leaks, wipe fluid soaked areas clean. Then, have a friend start and idle the engine. You should watch for leaks as the steering wheel is turned to the right and left. This will pressurize all parts of the system that might be leaking.

Power steering pressure test

A *power steering pressure test* checks the operation of the power steering pump, pressure relief valve, control valve, hoses, and power piston. As shown in Fig. 67-18, connect a pressure gauge and shut-off valve into the high pressure hose.

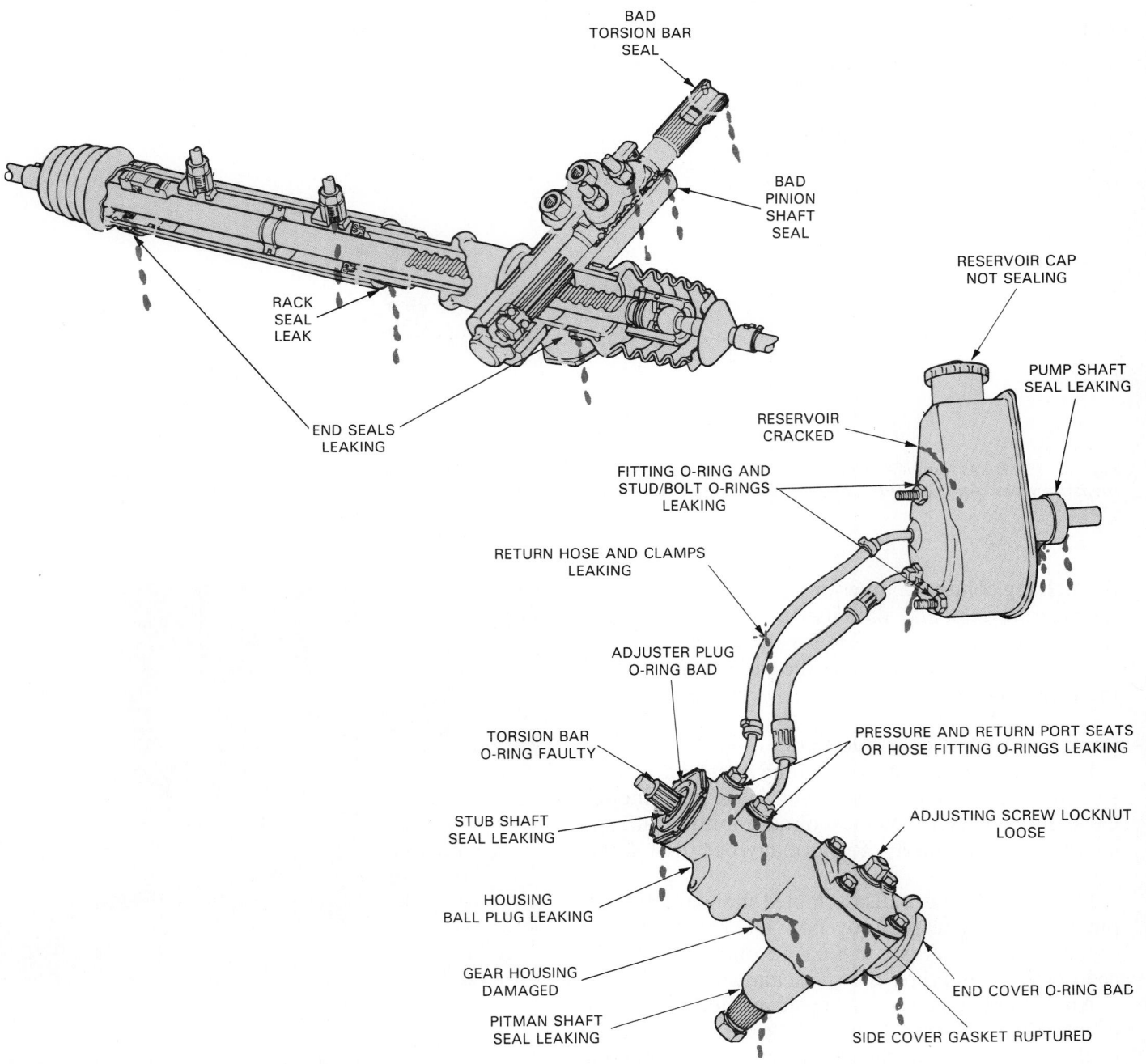

Fig. 67-17. Note possible leakage points on power steering systems.

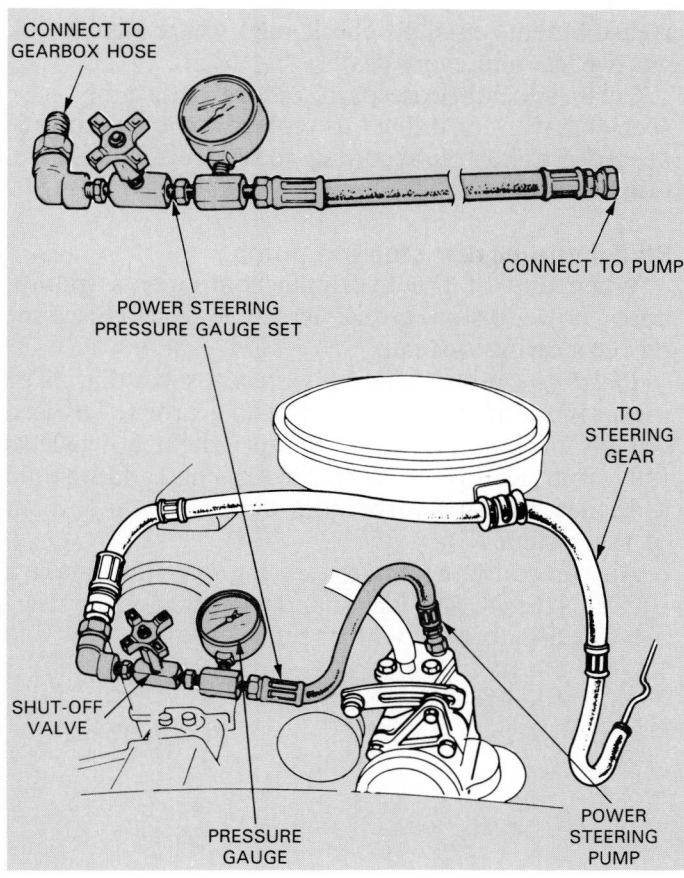

CONNECT TO GEARBOX HOSE

CONNECT TO PUMP

POWER STEERING PRESSURE GAUGE SET

TO STEERING GEAR

SHUT-OFF VALVE

PRESSURE GAUGE

POWER STEERING PUMP

Fig. 67-18. Pressure test gauge is connected to high pressure hose or line from pump. This will let you follow manual directions when testing power steering system. (Honda)

When using the steering system pressure tester, follow manufacturer recommended procedures. Torque the hose fittings properly. Make sure the system is full of fluid. Start and idle the engine (test valve open) while turning the steering wheel back and forth. This will bring the fluid up to operating temperature.

To check system pressure, close the test valve, Fig. 67-18. Compare your pressure reading with specifications. When the pressure is NOT within specs, check the pressure relief valve and pump condition.

CAUTION! Do NOT close the test valve for more than approximatley FIVE SECONDS. If closed longer, power steering pump overheating damage could result.

To check the action of the power piston, control valve, and hoses, measure system pressure as you turn the steering wheel to full lock (right and left) with the test valve open. Note the gauge readings and compare them to specs. Use the information in a service manual to determine the source of any trouble.

Power steering pump service

When your tests indicate a bad power steering pump, the pump must be removed for repair or replacement. Most shops simply replace a bad power steering pump with a NEW or factory REBUILT UNIT. A few shops disassemble and rebuild the pump.

Before attempting to rebuild a power steering pump, check in a service manual and with the parts department to make sure a rebuild kit is available for the particular unit.

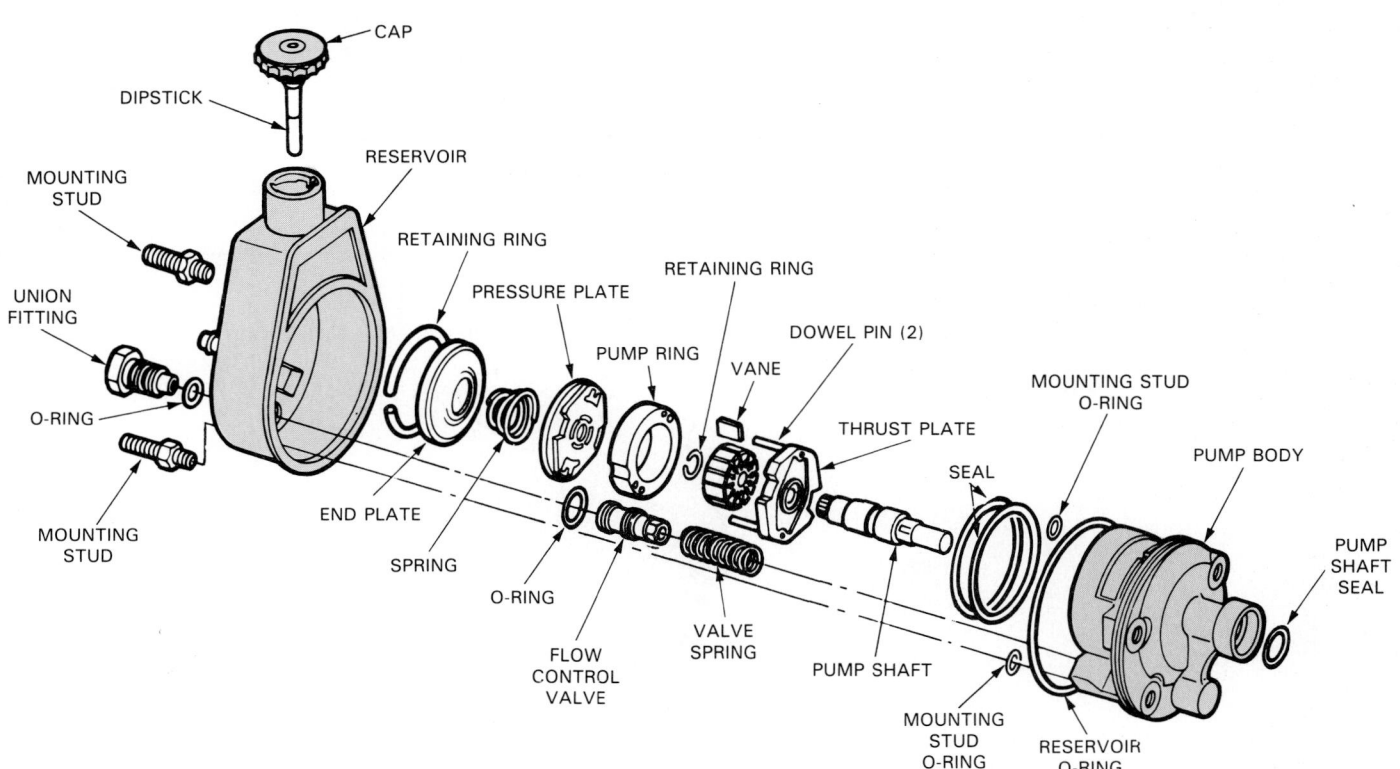

CAP

DIPSTICK

RESERVOIR

MOUNTING STUD

RETAINING RING

RETAINING RING

PRESSURE PLATE

MOUNTING STUD O-RING

UNION FITTING

PUMP RING

DOWEL PIN (2)

VANE

O-RING

THRUST PLATE

PUMP BODY

MOUNTING STUD

SEAL

PUMP SHAFT SEAL

END PLATE

SPRING

O-RING

FLOW CONTROL VALVE

VALVE SPRING

PUMP SHAFT

MOUNTING STUD O-RING

RESERVOIR O-RING

Fig. 67-19. Study parts of this power steering pump. (Chrysler Corp.)

Fig. 67-19 illustrates the internal parts of a typical power steering pump. During a rebuild, clean and inspect all of these parts. In particular, check and, possibly, replace the pump vanes, thrust plate, and pump ring. Replace all O-rings, gaskets, seals, and any other parts showing signs of wear or damage. Lubricate the parts before assembly with system fluid.

Power steering gear service

The procedures for servicing power steering gears also vary with the make and model of the car and type of gear assembly. Follow manual directions.

Fig. 67-20 shows an exploded view of one type of worm power steering gearbox. A service manual will have this type illustration for the particular type unit you are overhauling.

Fig. 67-21 shows a power rack and pinion gear assembly. Note how the parts are positioned.

The major steps for servicing a rack and pinion gear assembly are illustrated in Fig. 67-22. Note the measurements used to check part wear. Replace all worn parts and every seal.

Clean and lubricate parts before reassembly. Use special drivers or pullers to replace worn bushings if needed. Reassemble according to service manual directions and specs.

Bleeding a power steering pump

When any of the hydraulic components (pump, hoses, power piston) are serviced, you should bleed the power steering system.

Bleeding a power steering system assures that all of the air is out of the lines, pump, and gearbox. To bleed out any air, start the engine and turn the steering wheel fully from side to side. Keep checking and adding fluid as needed. This will force air into the reservoir and out of the system.

Air can cause the power steering system to make a BUZZING SOUND. The sound will occur as the steering wheel is turned right or left.

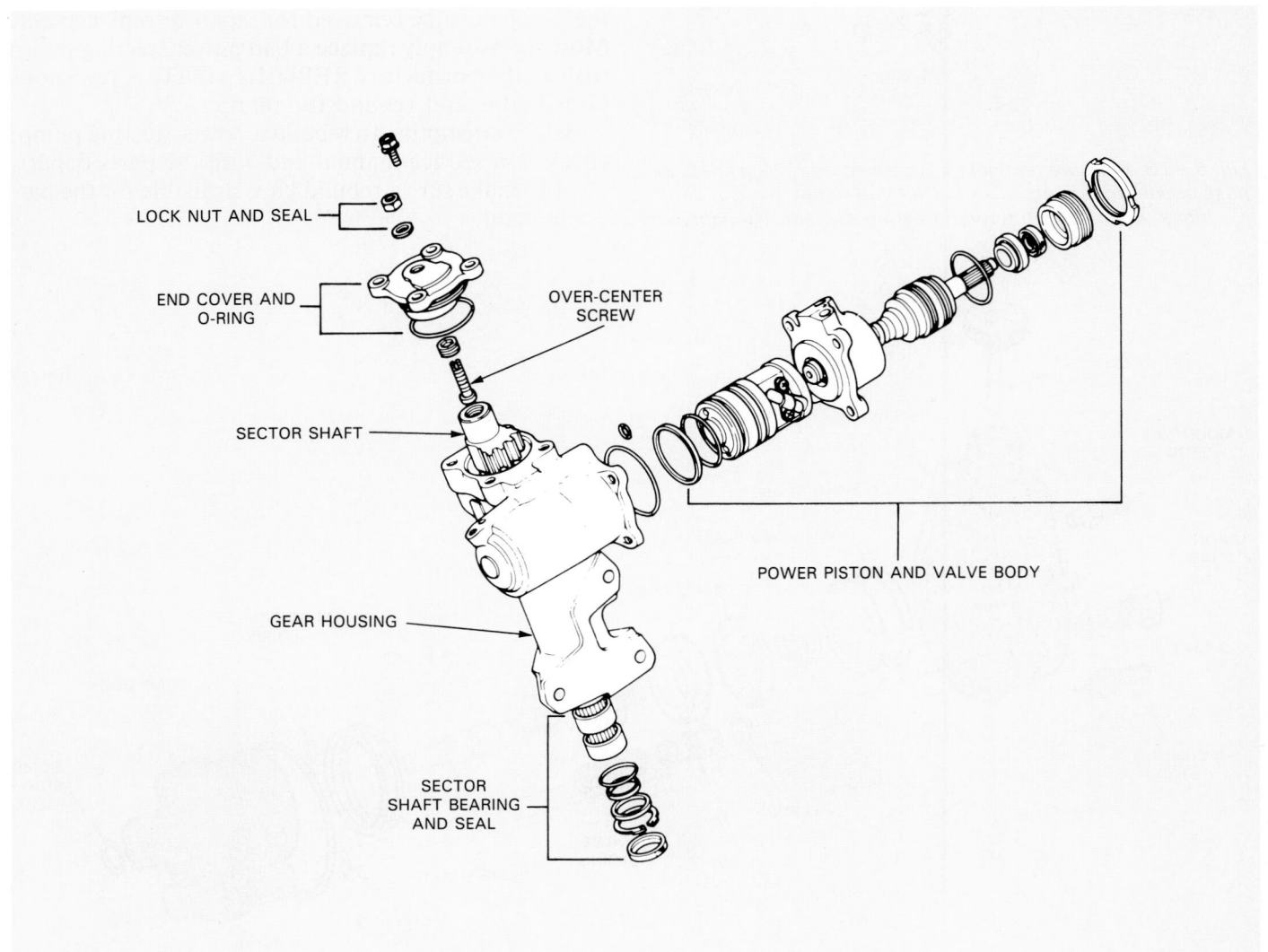

LOCK NUT AND SEAL

END COVER AND O-RING

OVER-CENTER SCREW

SECTOR SHAFT

GEAR HOUSING

SECTOR SHAFT BEARING AND SEAL

POWER PISTON AND VALVE BODY

Fig. 67-20. Exploded view of integral power steering gearbox. Note relationship of parts. (Toyota)

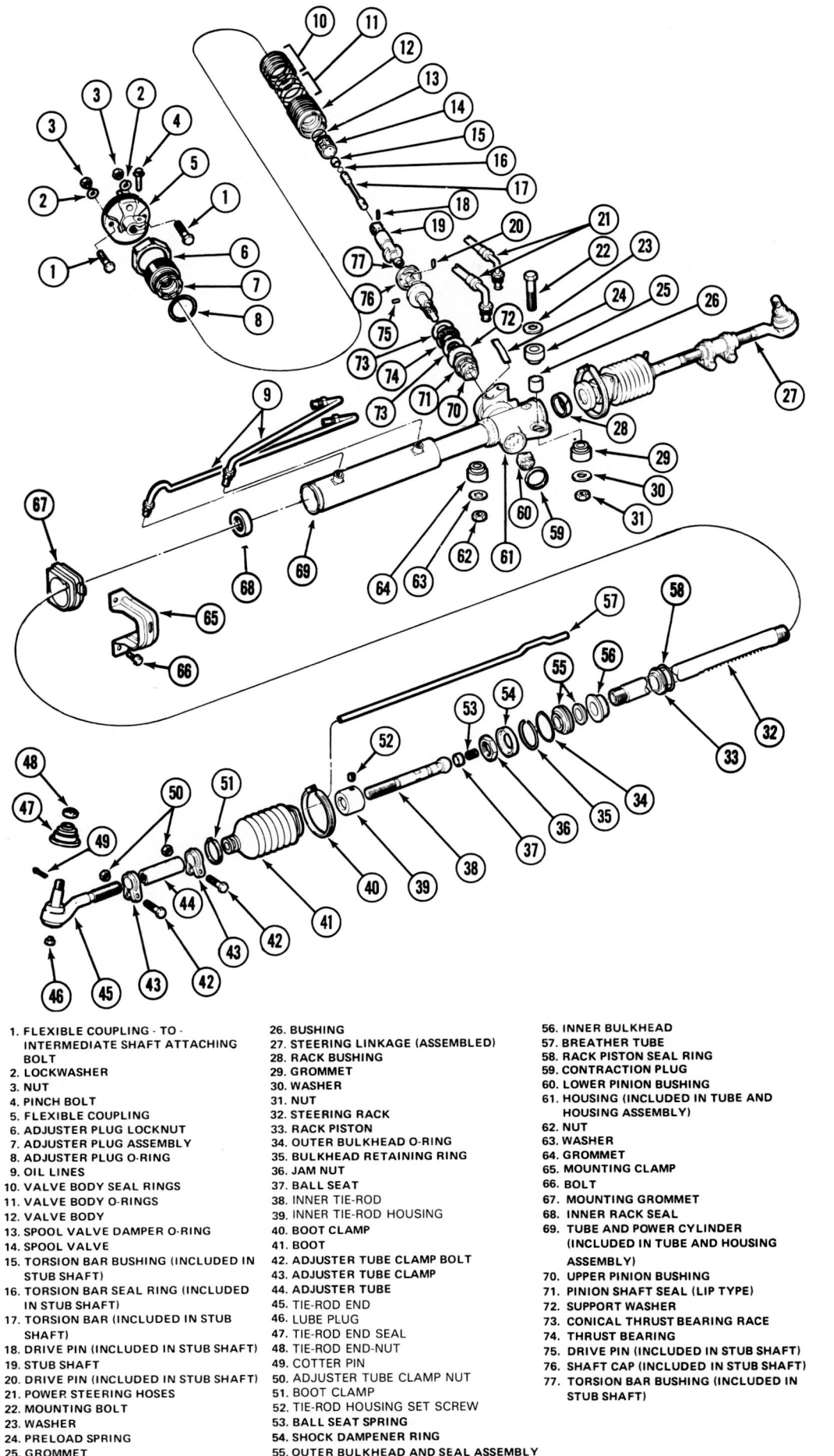

Fig. 67-21. Disassembled view of complete power rack and pinion steering gear. Study location of all components. (Ford)

1. FLEXIBLE COUPLING - TO - INTERMEDIATE SHAFT ATTACHING BOLT
2. LOCKWASHER
3. NUT
4. PINCH BOLT
5. FLEXIBLE COUPLING
6. ADJUSTER PLUG LOCKNUT
7. ADJUSTER PLUG ASSEMBLY
8. ADJUSTER PLUG O-RING
9. OIL LINES
10. VALVE BODY SEAL RINGS
11. VALVE BODY O-RINGS
12. VALVE BODY
13. SPOOL VALVE DAMPER O-RING
14. SPOOL VALVE
15. TORSION BAR BUSHING (INCLUDED IN STUB SHAFT)
16. TORSION BAR SEAL RING (INCLUDED IN STUB SHAFT)
17. TORSION BAR (INCLUDED IN STUB SHAFT)
18. DRIVE PIN (INCLUDED IN STUB SHAFT)
19. STUB SHAFT
20. DRIVE PIN (INCLUDED IN STUB SHAFT)
21. POWER STEERING HOSES
22. MOUNTING BOLT
23. WASHER
24. PRELOAD SPRING
25. GROMMET

26. BUSHING
27. STEERING LINKAGE (ASSEMBLED)
28. RACK BUSHING
29. GROMMET
30. WASHER
31. NUT
32. STEERING RACK
33. RACK PISTON
34. OUTER BULKHEAD O-RING
35. BULKHEAD RETAINING RING
36. JAM NUT
37. BALL SEAT
38. INNER TIE-ROD
39. INNER TIE-ROD HOUSING
40. BOOT CLAMP
41. BOOT
42. ADJUSTER TUBE CLAMP BOLT
43. ADJUSTER TUBE CLAMP
44. ADJUSTER TUBE
45. TIE-ROD END
46. LUBE PLUG
47. TIE-ROD END SEAL
48. TIE-ROD END-NUT
49. COTTER PIN
50. ADJUSTER TUBE CLAMP NUT
51. BOOT CLAMP
52. TIE-ROD HOUSING SET SCREW
53. BALL SEAT SPRING
54. SHOCK DAMPENER RING
55. OUTER BULKHEAD AND SEAL ASSEMBLY

56. INNER BULKHEAD
57. BREATHER TUBE
58. RACK PISTON SEAL RING
59. CONTRACTION PLUG
60. LOWER PINION BUSHING
61. HOUSING (INCLUDED IN TUBE AND HOUSING ASSEMBLY)
62. NUT
63. WASHER
64. GROMMET
65. MOUNTING CLAMP
66. BOLT
67. MOUNTING GROMMET
68. INNER RACK SEAL
69. TUBE AND POWER CYLINDER (INCLUDED IN TUBE AND HOUSING ASSEMBLY)
70. UPPER PINION BUSHING
71. PINION SHAFT SEAL (LIP TYPE)
72. SUPPORT WASHER
73. CONICAL THRUST BEARING RACE
74. THRUST BEARING
75. DRIVE PIN (INCLUDED IN STUB SHAFT)
76. SHAFT CAP (INCLUDED IN STUB SHAFT)
77. TORSION BAR BUSHING (INCLUDED IN STUB SHAFT)

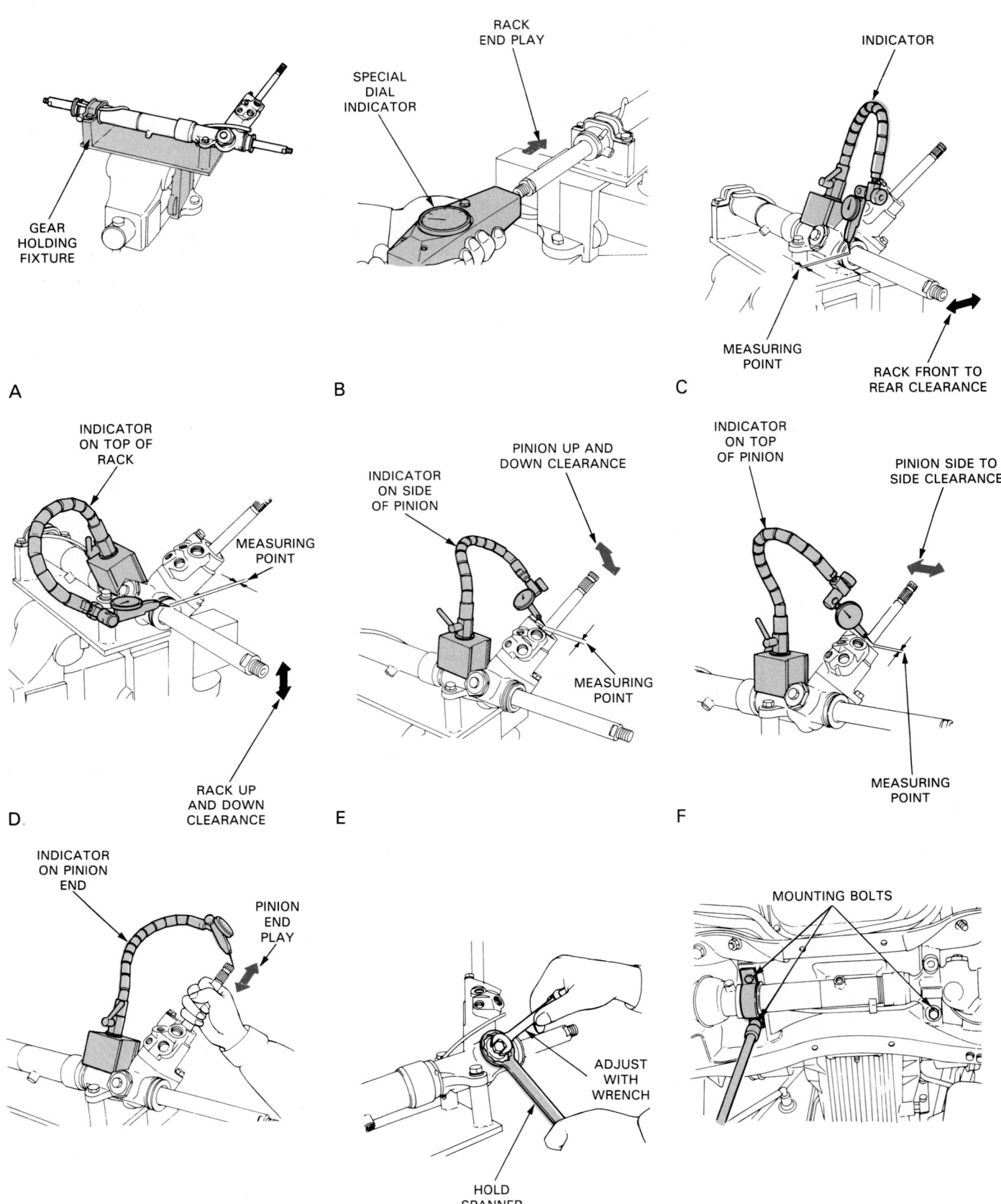

Fig. 67-22. Fundamental measurements and servicing steps for a rack and pinion steering gear. A — Mounting unit in holding fixture. B — Using special indicator to measure rack end play. C — Using indicator to check front-to-rear clearance at rack. D — Measuring rack up and down movement. E — Measuring pinion shaft up and down clearance. F — Measuring pinion shaft side to side clearance. G — Measuring pinion end play. H — Adjusting rack guide screw. I — Installing rack and pinion assembly in car. (Fiat)

KNOW THESE TERMS

Steering wheel play, Dry park test, Hard steering, Belt squeal, Power steering fluid, Worm bearing preload, Pitman shaft over-center adjustment, Gearbox overhaul, Worn idler arm, Worn tie-rod end, Rack and pinion steering gear adjustment, Power steering pressure test, Bleeding.

REVIEW QUESTIONS

1. What normally causes play in the steering wheel?
2. How do you do a "dry park test" of a steering system?
3. _____ _____ fluid is commonly used as power steering fluid.
4. Power steering pump pressure can exceed:
   a. 10,000 psi (68 900 kPa).
   b. 5,000 psi (34 450 kPa).
   c. 100 psi (689 kPa).
   d. 1000 psi (6 895 kPa).
5. A _____ _____ is commonly needed to force a steering wheel off its shaft.
6. Summarize the two major adjustments for a manual recirculating ball type steering gearbox.
7. Which of these components can wear and cause play in the steering system?
   a. Tie-rod end.
   b. Idler arm.
   c. Ball socket.
   d. All of the above.
   e. None of the above.
8. What adjustment(s) is (are) commonly done on a manual rack and pinion steering system?
9. A power steering pressure test checks the operation of the pump, relief valve, control valve, hoses, and power piston. True or False?
10. Most mechanics install rebuilt or new power steering pumps, rather than doing an in-shop overhaul of the unit. True or False?

ACTIVITIES FOR CHAPTER 67

1. Check the power steering lubricant level of a vehicle in the shop for service.
2. Check a shop manual for lube points and then lubricate a steering system.
3. Test a steering system and diagnose any problems detected.
4. Prepare a repair bill for a repair to the steering system. (Use a flat rate manual to determine time on the job or use an hourly rate set by your instructor. Check a parts catalog for cost of parts. Your instructor will suggest a flat rate charge for the labor.)

68

Brake System Fundamentals

After studying this chapter, you will be able to:
- ☐ Explain the hydraulic and mechanical principles of a brake system.
- ☐ Identify the major parts of an automotive brake system.
- ☐ Define the basic function of the major parts of a brake system.
- ☐ Compare drum and disc type brakes.
- ☐ Describe the operation of an emergency brake.
- ☐ Explain the operation of power brakes.
- ☐ Summarize the operation of anti-skid systems.

Automotive brakes provide a means of using friction to either slow down, stop, or hold the wheels of the car. When a car is moving down the highway, it has a tremendous amount of stored energy in the form of inertia (tendency to keep moving). To stop the car, the brakes convert kinetic (moving) energy into heat.

As you will learn, a modern automobile uses numerous devices to improve braking ability. For example, dual hydraulic brake systems, hydraulic valves to equalize braking pressure, and computer controlled anti-skid systems are all found on today's vehicles.

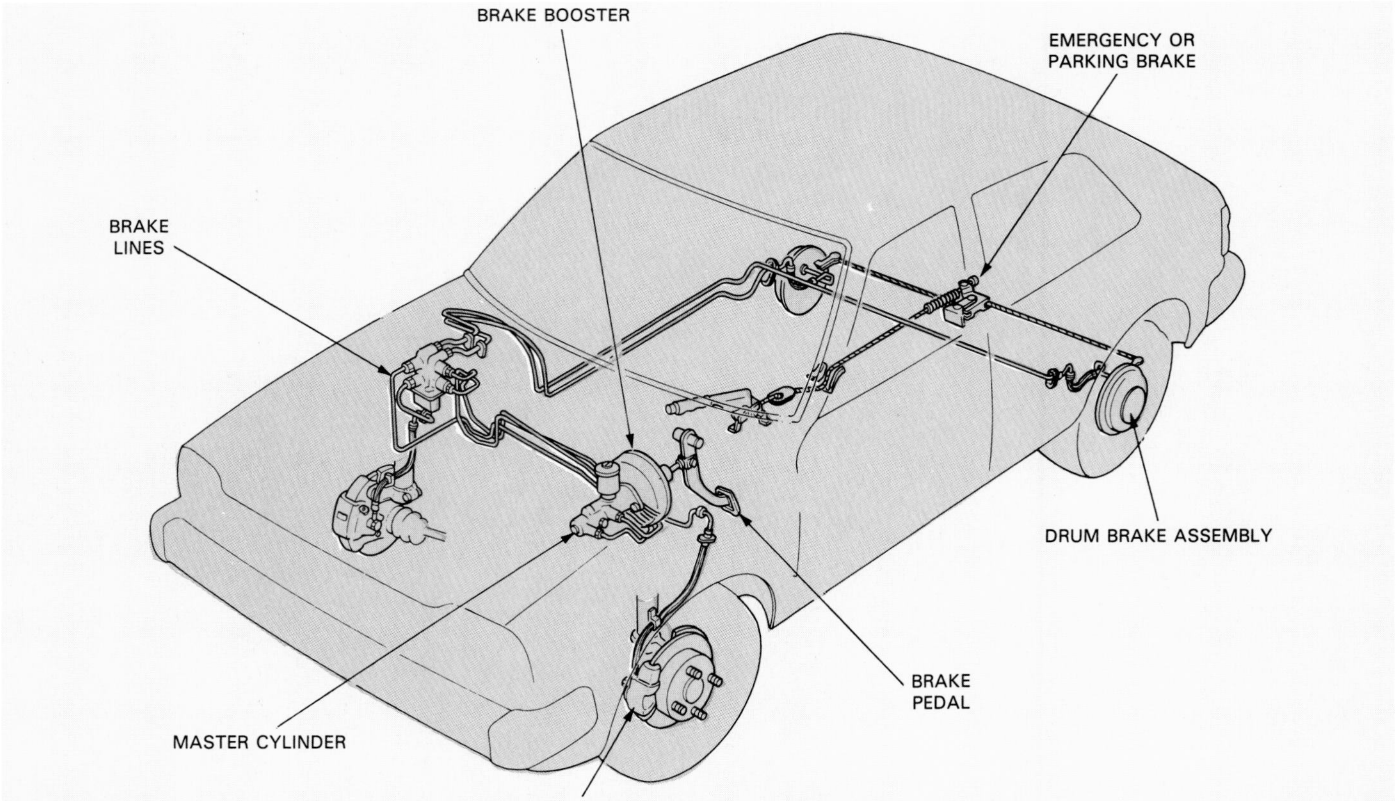

Fig. 68-1. These are the basic parts of an automotive brake system. Study them! (Honda)

BASIC BRAKE SYSTEM

Before studying the construction and operation of each part, you should have a basic understanding of a brake system. Look at Fig. 68-1. It shows the major components of a simple system. Study the location of the parts as they are introduced:

1. BRAKE PEDAL ASSEMBLY (foot lever for operating master cylinder and power booster).
2. MASTER CYLINDER (hydraulic piston type pump that develops pressure for brake system).
3. BRAKE BOOSTER (vacuum or power steering-operated device for assisting brake pedal application).
4. BRAKE LINES (metal tubing and rubber hose for transmitting pressure to wheel brake assemblies).
5. WHEEL BRAKE ASSEMBLIES (devices that use system pressure to produce friction for slowing or stopping wheel rotation).
6. EMERGENCY OR PARKING BRAKE (mechanical system for applying rear wheel brake assemblies).

When the driver pushes on the brake pedal, lever action pushes a rod into the brake booster and master cylinder. This produces hydraulic pressure in the master cylinder. Fluid flows through the brake lines to the wheel brake assemblies. The brake assemblies use this pressure to cause friction for braking.

An emergency or parking brake system uses cables or rods to mechanically apply the rear brakes. This provides a system for holding the wheels on hills or during complete hydraulic brake system failure.

Drum and disc type brakes

There are two common types of brake assemblies used on modern automobiles: disc and drum brakes. Refer to Fig. 68-2.

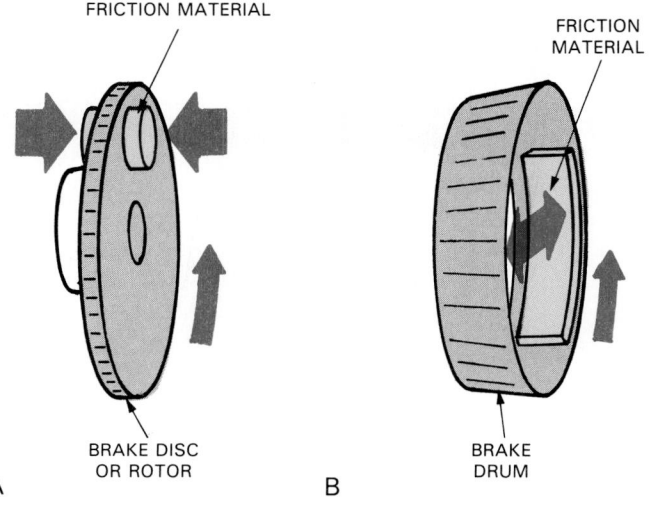

Fig. 68-2. Compare disc and drum brakes. A — Disc brakes are commonly used on front of car and sometimes on rear. B — Drum brakes are normally used on rear of cars.

Disc brakes are frequently used on the two front wheels of a car. Drum brakes are commonly used on the rear wheels. However, disc or drum brakes may be used on all four wheels.

A *disc brake assembly* basically includes:
1. CALIPER (holds wheel cylinder piston and brake pads).
2. CALIPER CYLINDER (machined hole in caliper, piston fits into this cylinder).
3. BRAKE PADS (friction members pushed against rotor by action of the master cylinder, wheel cylinder, and piston).
4. ROTOR (metal disc that uses friction from brake pads to stop or slow wheel rotation).

A *drum brake assembly* basically includes:
1. WHEEL CYLINDER ASSEMBLY (hydraulic piston forced outward by fluid pressure).
2. BRAKE SHOES (friction units pushed against the rotating brake drum by action of the wheel cylinder assembly).
3. BRAKE DRUM (rubs against brake shoes to stop wheel rotation and vehicle movement).

BRAKE SYSTEM HYDRAULICS

A *hydraulic system* is basically a system that uses a liquid to transmit motion or pressure from one point to another. Modern brake systems are hydraulic. They use a confined brake fluid to transfer brake pedal pressure and motion to each of the wheel brake assemblies.

Several principles apply to the operation of a hydraulic system. These include:
1. Liquids in a confined area will NOT compress. However, air in a confined area does compress.
2. When pressure is applied to a closed system, pressure is exerted equally in all directions.
3. A hydraulic system can be used to increase or decrease force or motion.

Hydraulic system action

Suppose two cylinders of equal diameter are placed side by side with a tube connecting them. The system is filled with liquid. Pistons are in each of the cylinders. If you push down on one of the pistons, the other piston will move an equal distance and with equal force.

Since the liquid will not compress and the cylinders are the same diameter, the same amount of liquid is moved from one cylinder to the other.

When pistons of different sizes are used, motion and force can be increased or decreased.

Suppose a small piston acts on a larger piston. The larger piston will move with more force. However, it will move a shorter distance.

When a large diameter piston acts on a smaller piston, the opposite is true. The smaller piston slides farther in its cylinder, but with less force.

A simple hydraulic jack demonstrates the principles

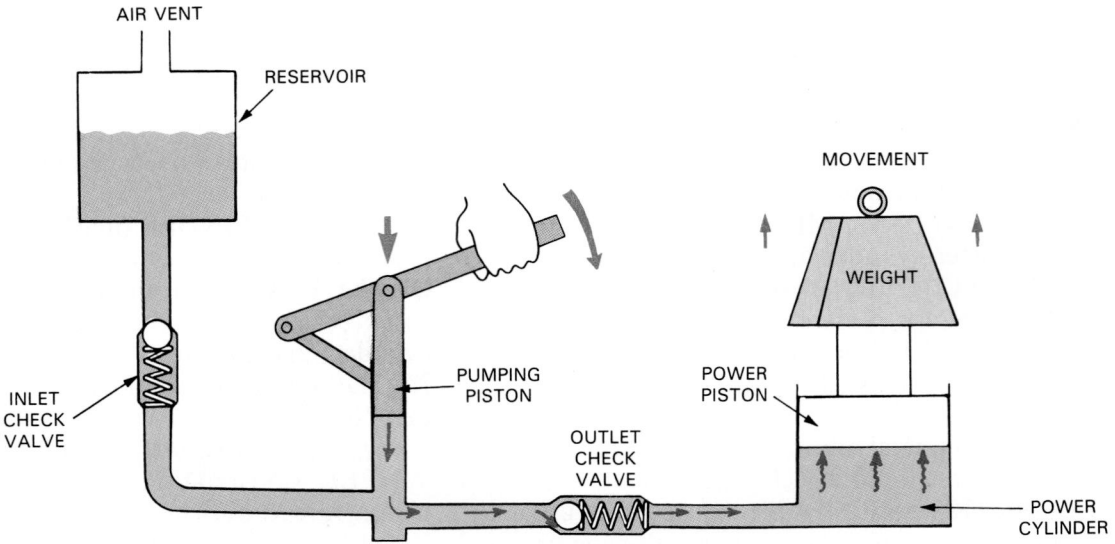

Fig. 68-3. Drawing of hydraulic jack demonstrates how small piston, acting on large piston, can increase force tremendously. Study how check valves only allow oil flow in one direction. (Deere & Co.)

just discussed. Look at Fig. 68-3.

Applying these hydraulic principles to a brake system, you can see how stopping force is transmitted from the master cylinder to each wheel brake assembly.

The master cylinder, Fig. 68-4, acts as the pumping piston that supplies system pressure. The wheel cylinders act as the power piston to move the friction linings into contact with the rotating drums or discs.

BRAKE PEDAL ASSEMBLY

The *brake pedal assembly* acts as a lever arm to increase the force applied to the master cylinder piston. A manual master cylinder bolts directly to the engine

firewall. The brake pedal assembly bolts under the dash, Fig. 68-5.

The pedal swings on a hinge in the pedal support bracket. A push rod connects the brake pedal to the master cylinder piston.

MASTER CYLINDER

A *master cylinder* is a foot-operated pump that forces fluid into the brake lines and wheel cylinders. Refer to Fig. 68-6. A master cylinder can have four basic functions:

1. It develops pressure, causing the wheel cylinder pistons to move towards the rotors or drums.

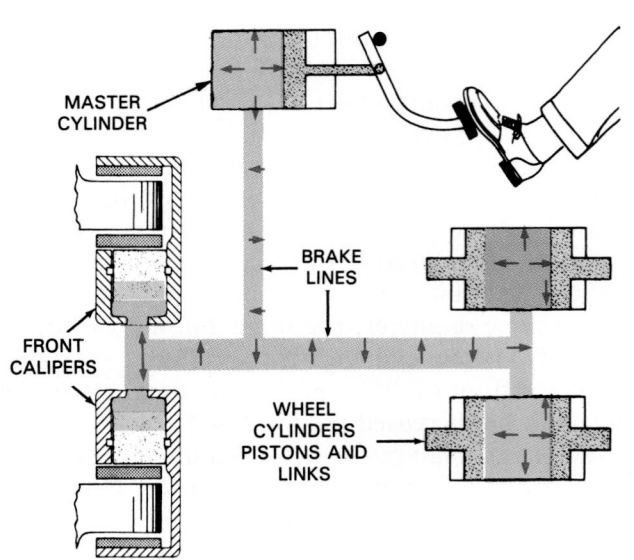

Fig. 68-4. Like basic hydraulic jack, master cylinder acts as pumping piston to move pistons at wheel brake assemblies. (GM Trucks)

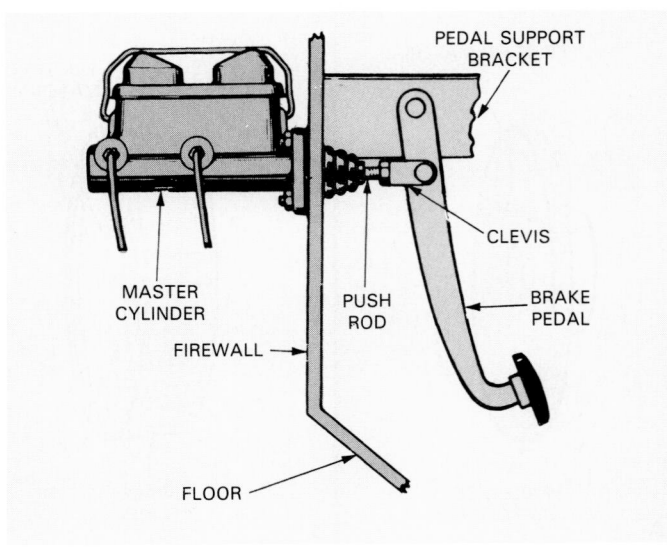

Fig. 68-5. Brake pedal assembly bolts under dash. Push rod transfers pedal movement into master cylinder and operates piston in master cylinder. (Bendix)

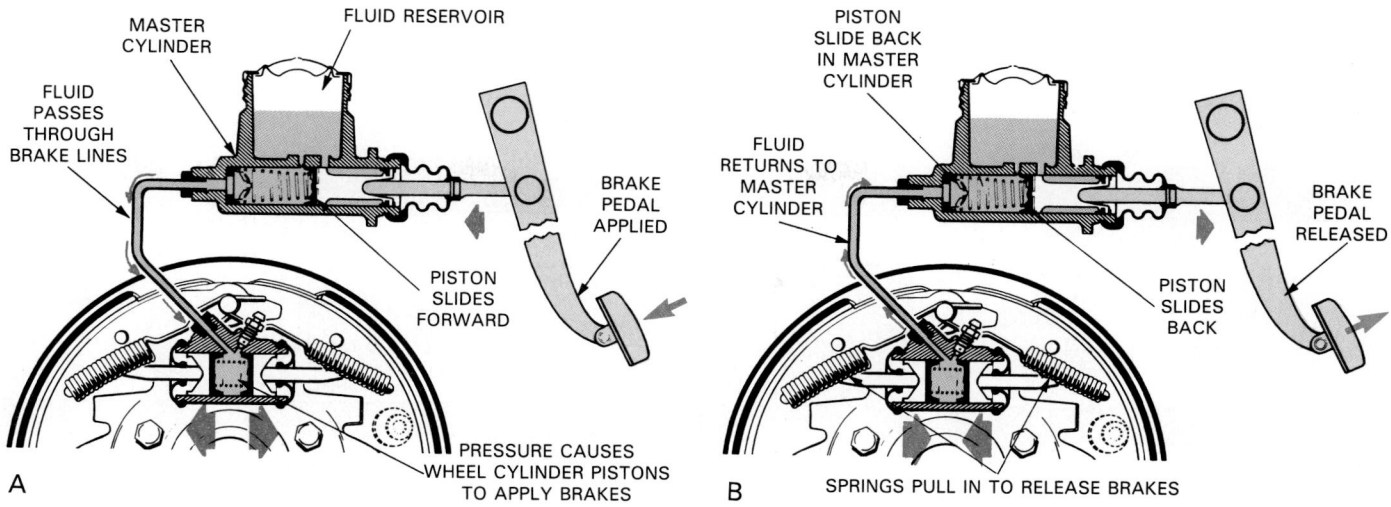

Fig. 68-6. Older, single piston master cylinder demonstrates action in system. A — Application of pedal moves push rod into piston. Master cylinder piston pressurizes fluid in cylinder and line. Pressure pushes wheel cylinder pistons apart and brakes are applied. B — Release of brake pedal allows retracting springs to pull brake shoes away from brake drum. Fluid flows back through line and into master cylinder. (FMC)

2. After all of the shoes or pads produce sufficient friction, the master cylinder helps equalize the pressure required for braking.
3. It keeps the system full of fluid as the brake linings wear.
4. It can maintain a slight pressure to keep contaminants (air and water) from entering the system.

Master cylinder components

In its simplest form, a master cylinder consists of a housing, reservoir, piston, rubber cup, return spring, and a rubber boot. Look at Fig. 68-7.

A cylinder is machined in the housing of the master cylinder. The spring, cup, and metal piston slide in this cylinder. Two ports are drilled between the reservoir and cylinder.

The *cup* and *piston* in the master cylinder are used to pressurize the brake system. When they are pushed forward, they trap the fluid, building pressure.

The master cylinder *intake port* or vent allows fluid to enter the rear of the cylinder as the piston slides forward. Refer to Figs. 68-8A and 68-8B. Fluid flows out of the reservoir, through the intake port, and into the area behind the piston and cup.

Then, when the brake pedal is released, the spring forces the piston and cup back in the cylinder. If needed, the rubber cup flexes forward allowing fluid to enter the area in front of the piston and cup. Usually, small

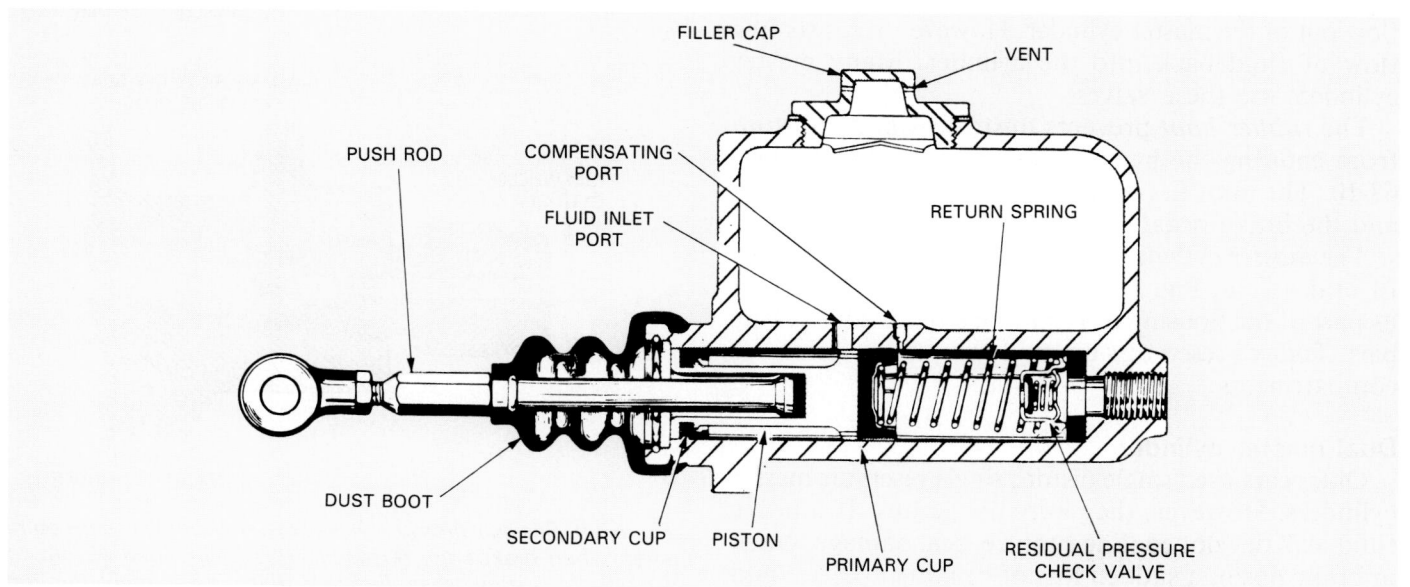

Fig. 68-7. Study the basic parts of a master cylinder. (Bendix)

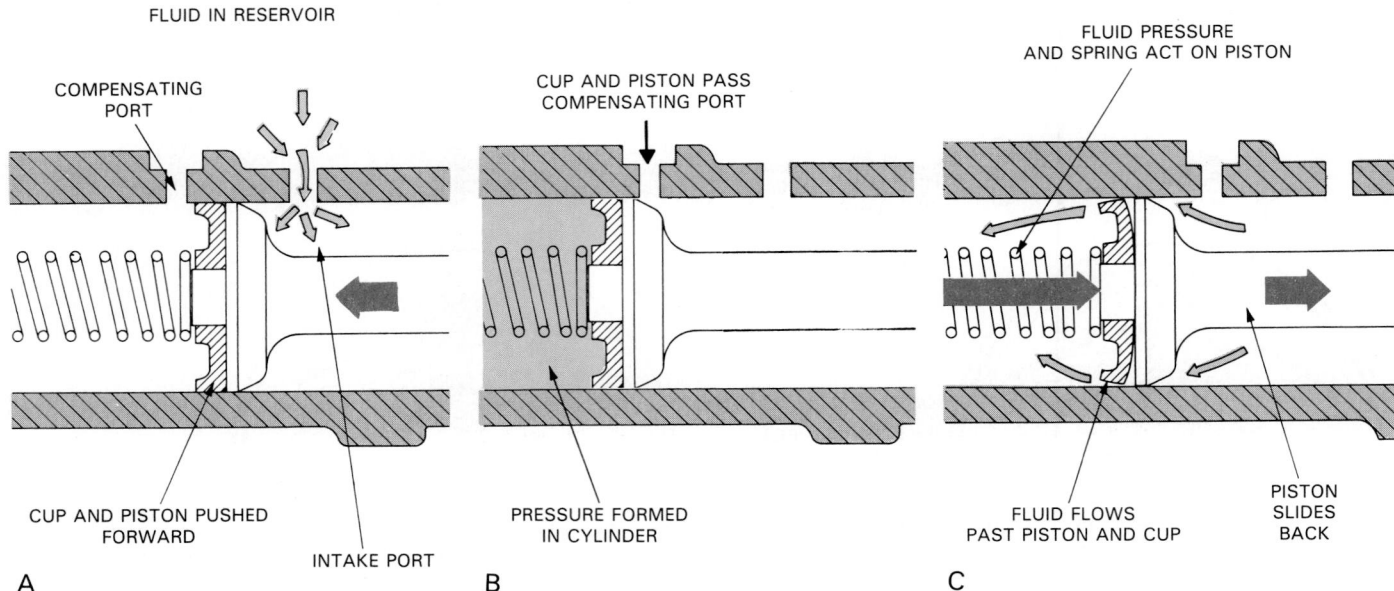

Fig. 68-8. Piston and cup action inside master cylinder. A — Piston slides forward. Fluid flows into area behind piston. Excess fluid flows into reservoir through compensating port. B — Piston and cup move past compensating port and pressure forms in front section of cylinder to apply brakes. C — When brake pedal is released, cup flexes forward so that fluid can flow to front of piston for release of brakes. (EIS)

holes are drilled in the edge of the piston so that fluid can flow past the cup. See Fig. 68-8B.

The **compensating port** releases extra pressure when the piston returns to the released position. Fluid can flow back into the reservoir through the compensating port. The action of the intake port and the compensating port keep the system full of fluid, Fig. 68-8C.

Residual pressure valves maintain residual fluid pressure of approximately 10 psi (69 kPa) to help keep contaminants out of the system.

Fig. 68-9 gives a cutaway view of a typical residual valve. One is in each outlet fitting to the brake lines.

Note how the residual pressure valve allows fluid flow out of the master cylinder. However, it resists free flow of fluid back into the cylinder. Many master cylinders use these valves.

The **rubber boot** prevents dust, dirt, and moisture from entering the back of the master cylinder, Fig. 68-10. The boot fits over the master cylinder housing and the brake pedal push rod.

The **master cylinder reservoir** stores an extra supply of brake fluid, Fig. 68-10. The reservoir may be cast as part of the housing or it may be a removable plastic part. Today's reservoirs normally have two sections or compartments.

Dual master cylinder

Older cars used single piston, single reservoir master cylinders. However, they were dangerous. If a brake fluid leak developed (line rupture, seal damage, crack in brake hose), a sudden loss of braking ability could occur. Modern cars use a dual master cylinder for added safety, Fig. 68-10.

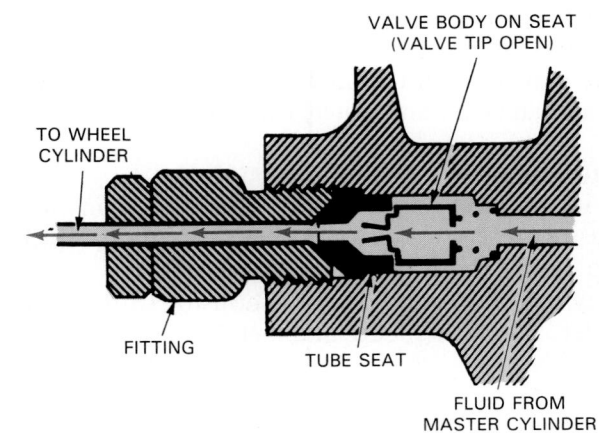

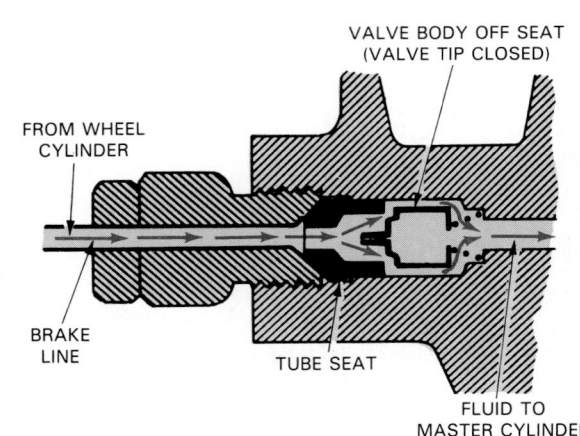

Fig. 68-9. Residual pressure valves maintain some line pressure even when brakes are released. This helps keep air out of system. A — Brakes applied and fluid flows freely through valve. B — After brake release, valve closes to restrict return of fluid to master cylinder. (FMC)

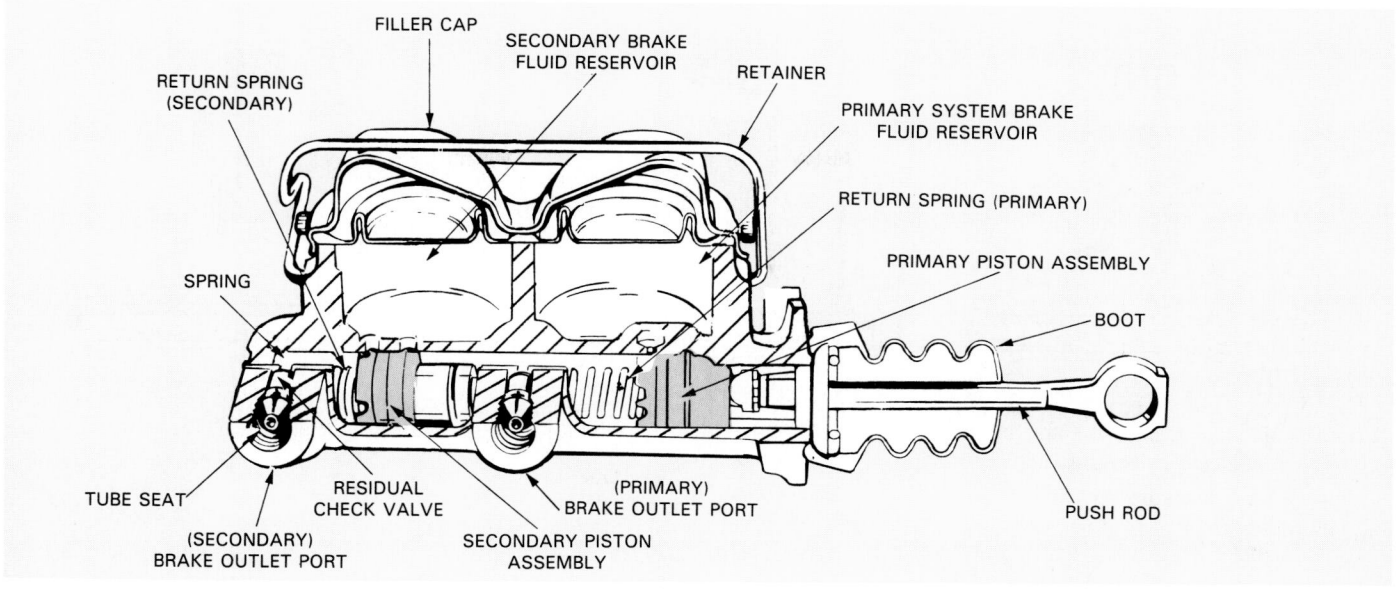

FILLER CAP

RETURN SPRING (SECONDARY)

SECONDARY BRAKE FLUID RESERVOIR

RETAINER

PRIMARY SYSTEM BRAKE FLUID RESERVOIR

RETURN SPRING (PRIMARY)

PRIMARY PISTON ASSEMBLY

BOOT

SPRING

TUBE SEAT

(SECONDARY) BRAKE OUTLET PORT

RESIDUAL CHECK VALVE

SECONDARY PISTON ASSEMBLY

(PRIMARY) BRAKE OUTLET PORT

PUSH ROD

Fig. 68-10. Dual master cylinders are now used because they will still provide braking action when a major hydraulic leak develops. With single-piston master cylinder, a leak could cause sudden and complete loss of brakes. (Delco)

The **dual master cylinder,** also called a *tandem master cylinder,* has two separate hydraulic pistons and two fluid reservoirs. See Fig. 68-11. One piston normally operates two of the wheel cylinders. The other piston operates the two other wheel cylinders. Then,

if there is a system leak, the other master cylinder piston can still provide braking action on two wheels.

In the dual master cylinder, the rear piston assembly is called the *primary piston.* The front piston is termed the *secondary piston.*

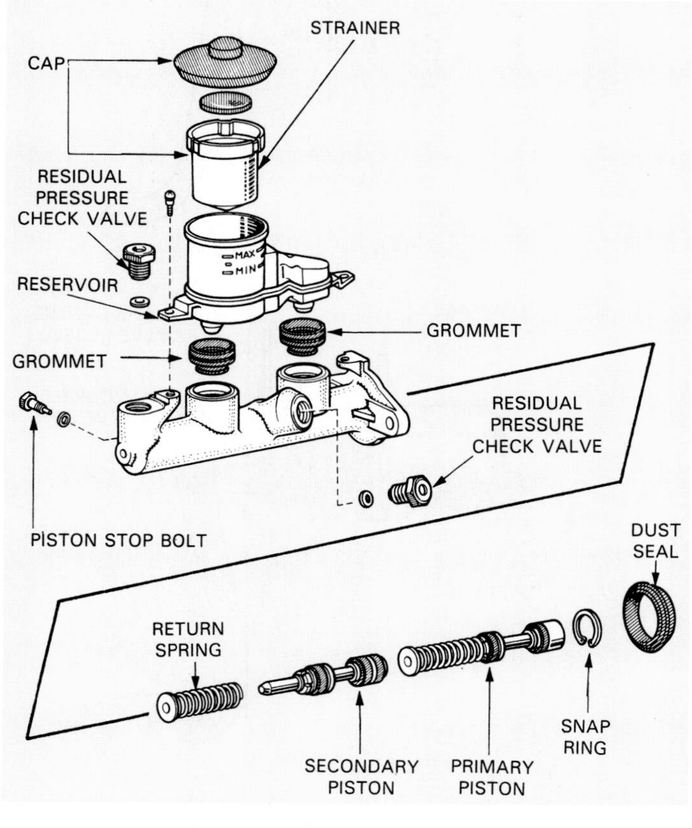

Dual master cylinder operation

The action of the pistons, cups, and ports in the dual master cylinder is similar to a single piston unit.

Look at Fig. 68-12A. When both systems are intact (no fluid leaks), both pistons produce and supply pressure to all four of the wheel cylinders.

If there is a pressure loss in the primary section of the brake system (rear section of master cylinder), the primary piston slides forward and pushes on the secondary piston. As shown in Fig. 68-12B, this forces the secondary piston forward mechanically, building pressure in two of the wheel brake assemblies.

When a brake line, wheel cylinder, or other component leaks in the secondary circuit (parts fed by secondary piston), the secondary piston slides completely forward in the cylinder. See Fig. 68-12C. Then, the rear, primary piston provides hydraulic pressure for the other two brake assemblies.

It is very unlikely that both systems should fail at the same time.

POWER BRAKES

Power brakes use engine vacuum, a vacuum pump, or power steering pump pressure to assist brake pedal application. The booster (assisting mechanism) is located between the brake pedal linkage and the master cylinder. When the driver presses the brake pedal, the brake booster helps push on the piston.

STRAINER

CAP

RESIDUAL PRESSURE CHECK VALVE

RESERVOIR

GROMMET

GROMMET

PISTON STOP BOLT

RESIDUAL PRESSURE CHECK VALVE

DUST SEAL

RETURN SPRING

SECONDARY PISTON

PRIMARY PISTON

SNAP RING

Fig. 68-11. Note major parts of modern dual master cylinder. (Toyota)

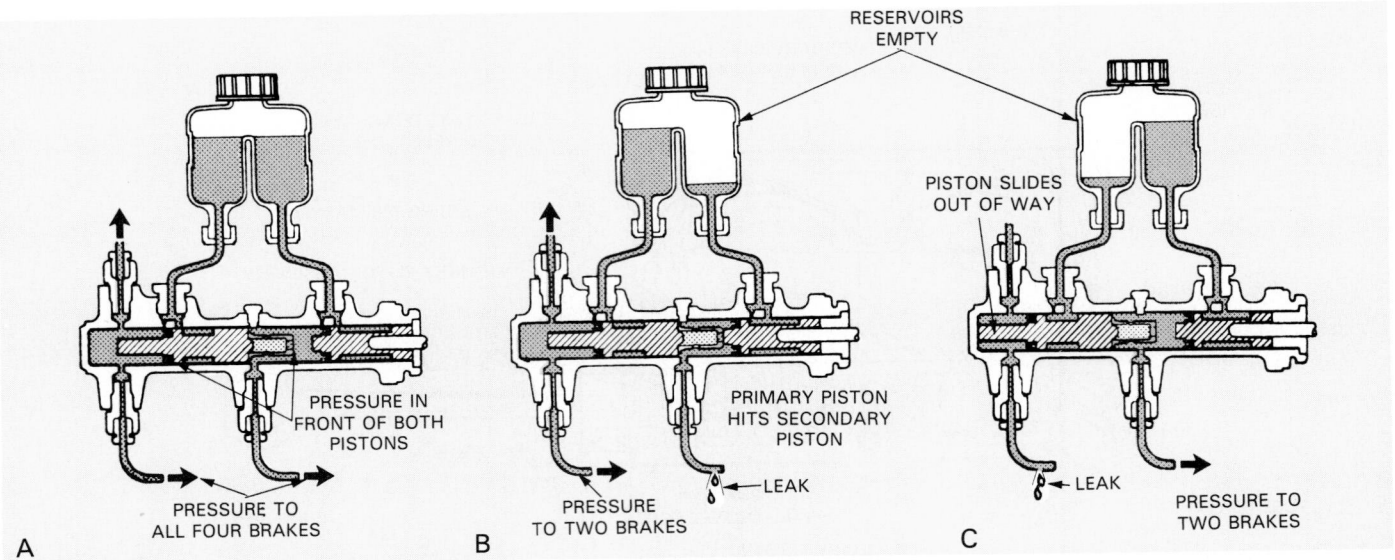

Fig. 68-12. Operation of dual master cylinder. A — No problem in brake system. Both pistons produce pressure for all four brake assemblies. B — Rear brake circuit leaking. Primary piston pushes on secondary piston and two brake assemblies still work to stop car. C — With front brake line leak, secondary piston is slid forward in cylinder. Primary piston then operates normally to apply two brake assemblies. (Delco)

Power brake vacuum boosters

A power brake *vacuum booster* uses engine vacuum (or vacuum pump action on diesel engine) to apply the hydraulic brake system. The principles of a vacuum booster are shown in Fig. 68-13.

A vacuum booster basically consists of a round housing that encloses a diaphragm or a piston. When vacuum is applied to one side of the booster, the piston or diaphragm moves towards the low vacuum area. This movement is used to help force the piston into the master cylinder.

Vacuum booster types

There are two general types of vacuum brake boosters: atmospheric suspended type and vacuum suspended type.

An *atmospheric suspended brake booster* has normal air pressure on both sides of the diaphragm or piston when the brake pedal is released. As the brakes are applied, a vacuum is formed in one side of the booster. Atmospheric pressure then pushes on and moves the piston or diaphragm.

A *vacuum suspended brake booster* has vacuum on both sides of the piston or diaphragm when the brake pedal is released. Pushing down on the brake pedal releases vacuum on one side of the booster. The difference in pressure pushes the piston or diaphragm for braking action.

Figs. 68-14 and 68-15 show views of two vacuum brake boosters.

Power brake hydraulic boosters

A power brake *hydraulic booster* uses power steering pump pressure to help the driver apply the brake pedal. Sometimes called *hydro-boost* or *hydra-booster,*

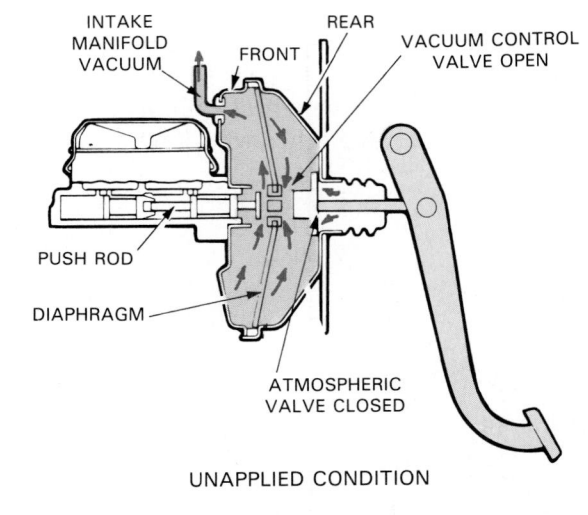

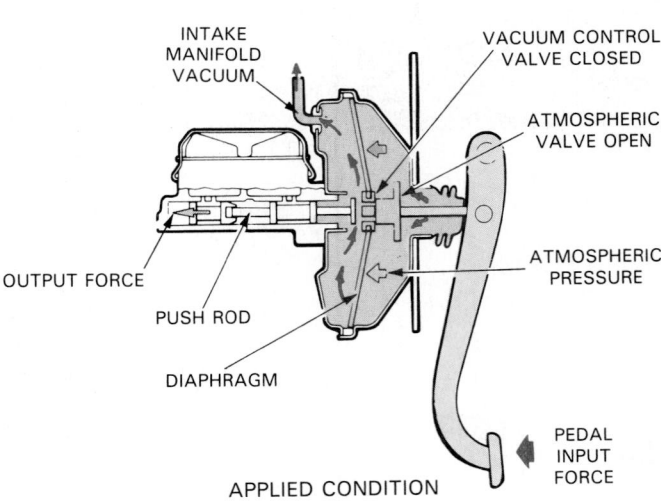

Fig. 68-13. Vacuum booster helps apply brake pedal. It uses engine vacuum or vacuum pump to act on diaphragm which pushes on push rod. (Mopar)

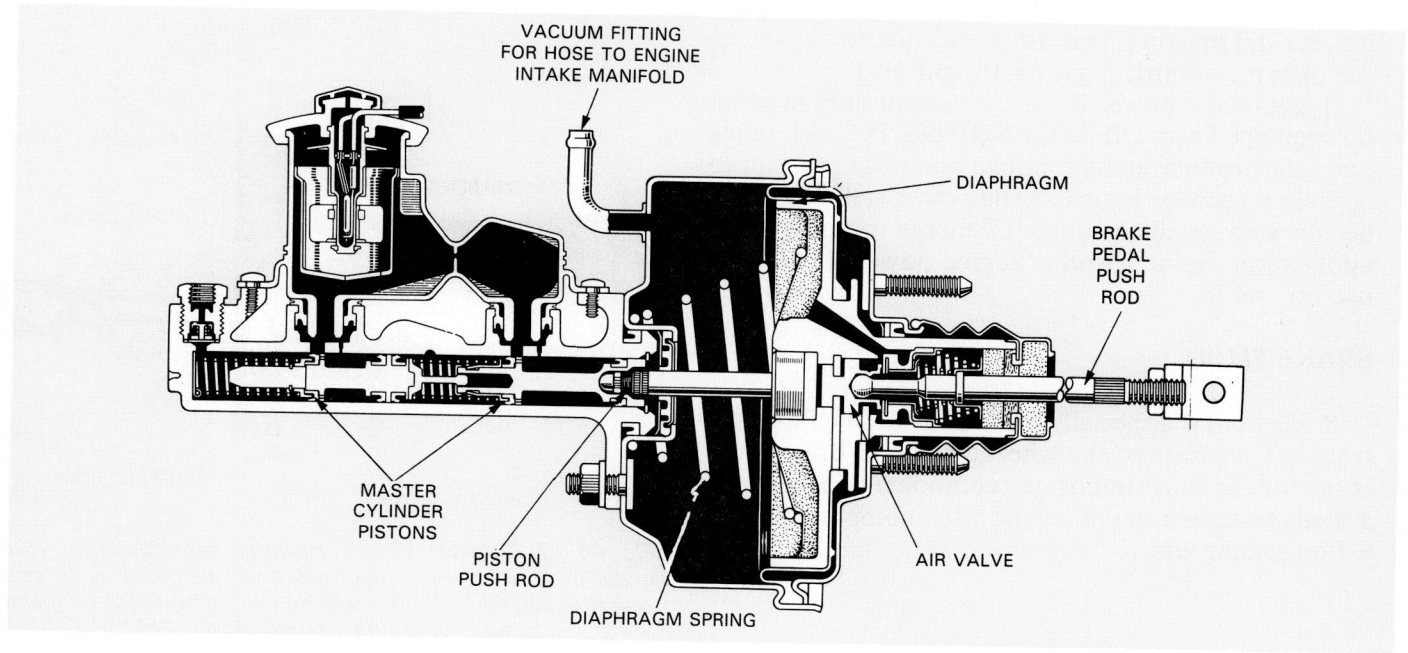

Fig. 68-14. Study internal parts of brake booster and master cylinder. (Toyota)

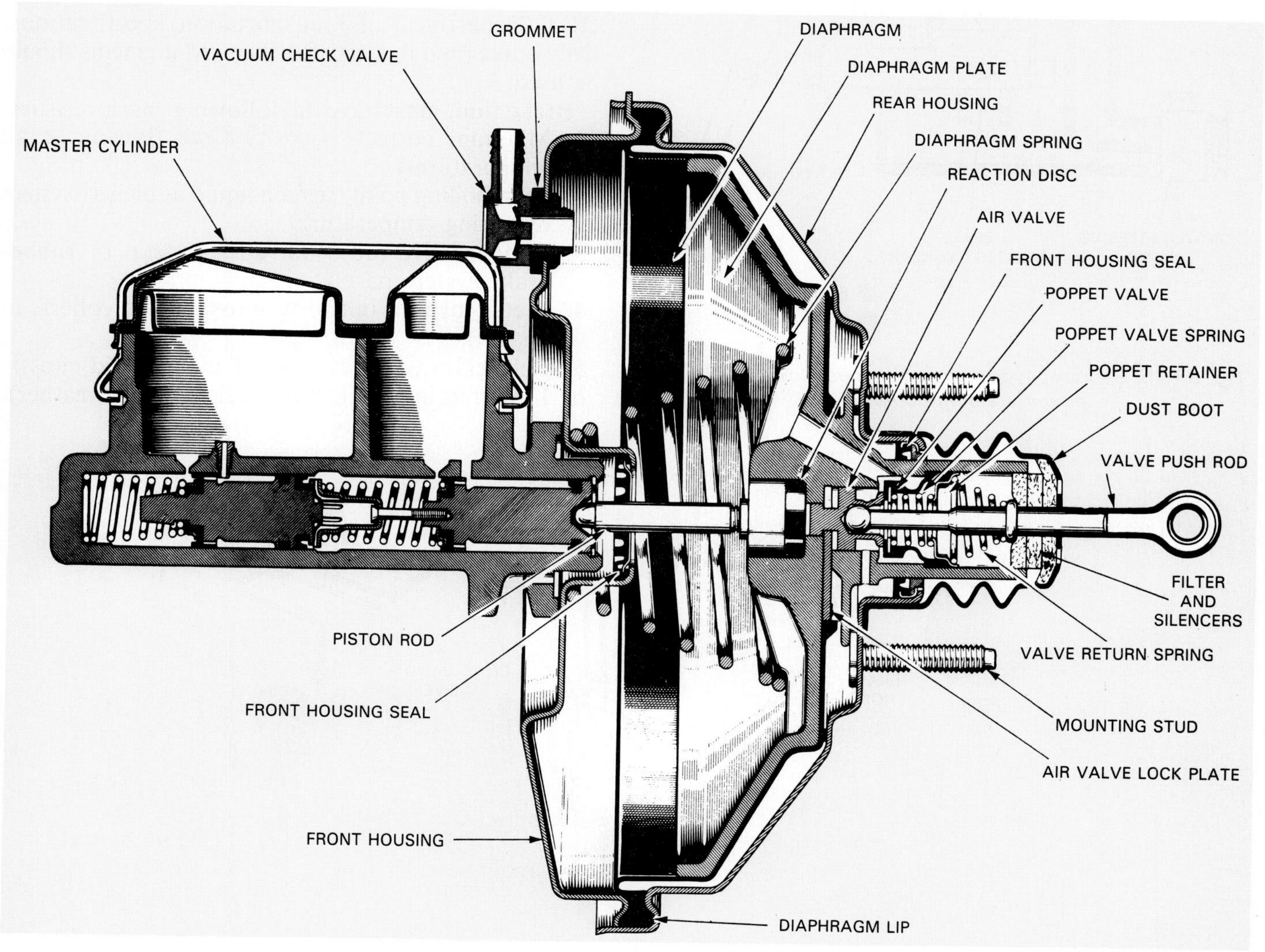

Fig. 68-15. Another type of vacuum brake booster. (Bendix)

it uses fluid pressure, instead of vacuum, to help force the piston forward, Figs. 68-16 and 68-17.

Hydro-boost power brakes are commonly used on cars equipped with DIESEL ENGINES. A diesel engine does not produce enough intake manifold vacuum to operate a vacuum booster. The power steering pump becomes an excellent source of energy to assist brake application. Some gasoline engine powered cars also use this setup.

BRAKE FLUID

Brake fluid is a specially blended hydraulic fluid that transfers pressure to the wheel cylinders. Brake fluid is one of the most important components of a brake system because it ties all of the other components into a functioning unit.

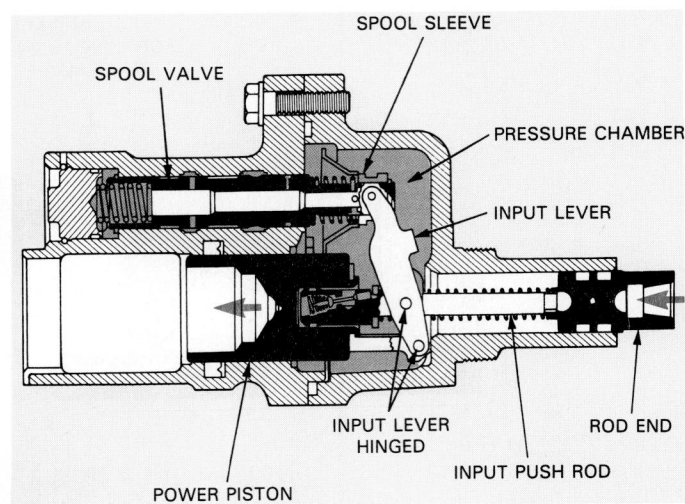

Fig. 68-17. Cutaway view of hydraulic brake booster. When pedal pushes on unit, spool valve allows more oil to enter pressure chamber. This causes power piston to act on master cylinder to provide power assist. (FMC)

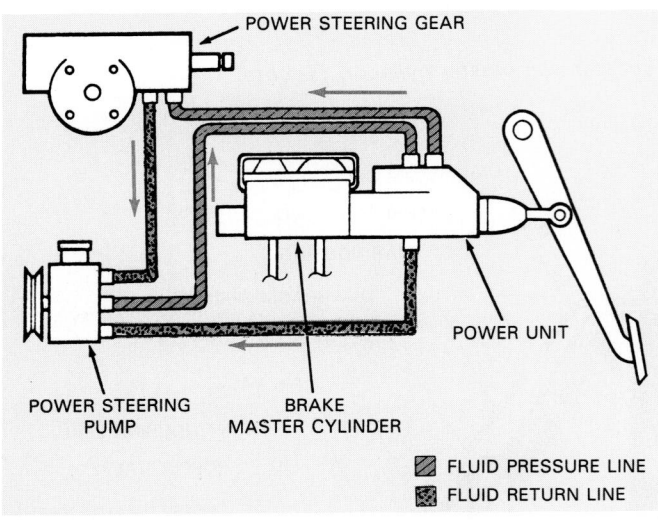

Fig. 68-16. Hydraulic type brake booster uses oil pressure from power steering pump. (FMC)

Auto makers recommend brake fluid that meets or exceeds SAE (Society of Automotive Engineers) and DOT (Department of Transportation) specifications. Only brake fluid that satisfies their requirements should be used.

Brake fluid must have the following characteristics:
1. Maintain correct viscosity (free flowing at all temperatures).
2. High boiling point (remain liquid at highest system operating temperature).
3. Noncorrosive (does not attack metal or rubber brake system parts).
4. Water tolerant (absorbs moisture that collects in system).
5. Lubricates (reduces wear of pistons and cups).
6. Low freezing point (not freeze in cold weather).

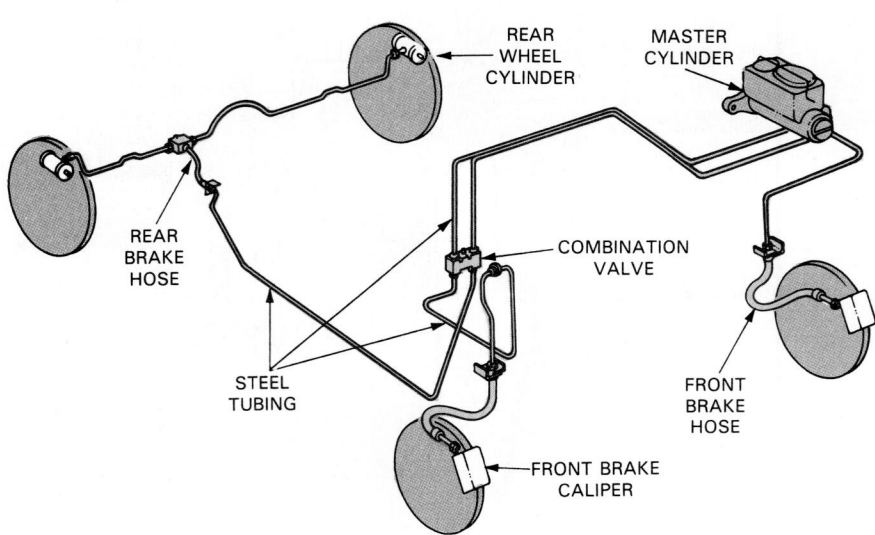

Fig. 68-18. Note routing and location of metal brake lines and flexible hoses. Hoses are needed because suspension movement would break steel tubing. (Chrysler Corp.)

BRAKE LINES AND HOSES

Brake lines and *hoses* transfer fluid pressure from the master cylinder to the wheel cylinders, Fig. 68-18. The brake lines are made of double-wall steel tubing and usually have double-lap flares on their ends.

Rubber brake hoses are used where a flexing action is needed. For instance, brake hose is used between the frame and front wheel cylinders. This allows the wheels to move up and down or from side to side without brake line damage.

Fig. 68-19 shows the details of how brake lines and brake hoses fit together.

A *junction block* is used where a single brake line must feed two wheel cylinders. It is simply a hollow fitting with one inlet and two or more outlets.

A *longitudinally* (front to rear) *split* brake system has one master cylinder piston operating the front wheel brake assemblies and the other operates the rear brakes. This is shown in Fig. 68-20A.

A *diagonally* (corner to corner) *split* brake system has each master cylinder piston operating a brake assembly on opposite corners of the car, Fig. 68-20B.

DISC BRAKES

Disc brakes are basically like the brakes on a ten-speed bicycle. The friction elements are shaped like

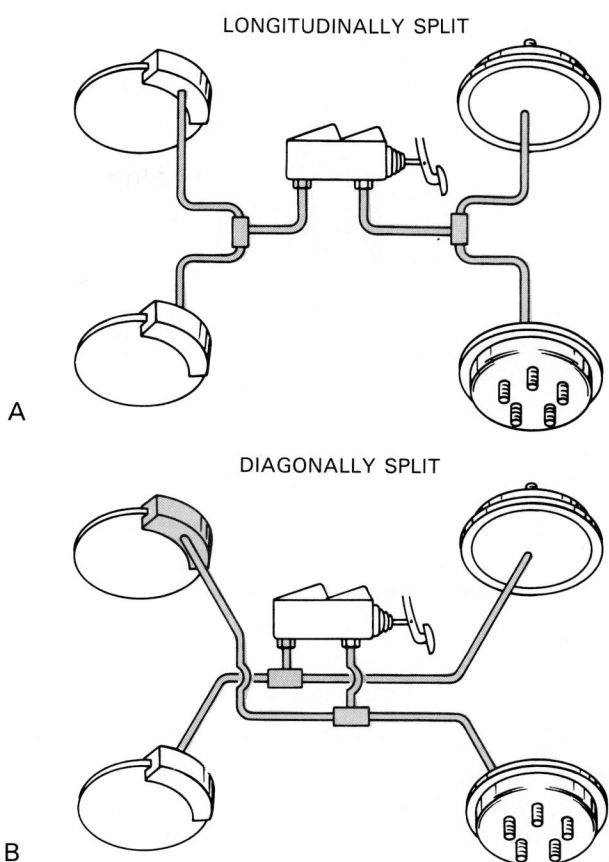

A

B

Fig. 68-20. Study how each master cylinder piston operates different wheel brake assemblies. (EIS)

pads and are squeezed inward to clamp against a rotating disc or wheel.

A *disc brake assembly* consists of a caliper, brake pads, rotor, and related hardware (bolts, clips, springs). See Fig. 68-21.

Fig. 68-22 shows sectioned views of typical disc brake assemblies. Note how the caliper pistons move inward to clamp the brake pads against the rotor. The single piston type caliper is much more common.

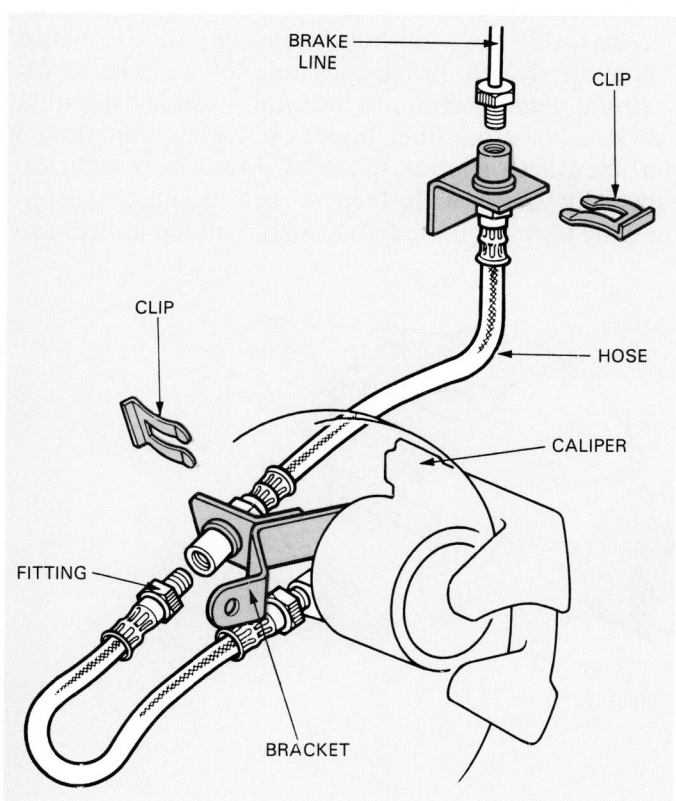

Fig. 68-19. Brackets and clips are used to secure brake hoses and lines to frame or unibody. Lines must not be allowed to vibrate or they can fatigue and break. (Toyota)

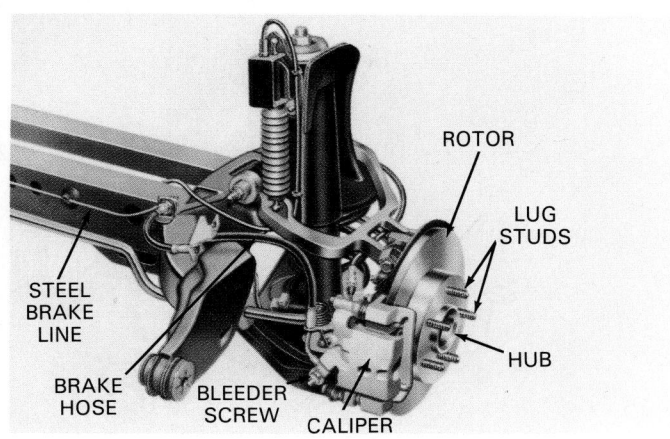

Fig. 68-21. Note externally visible parts of disc brake unit. (Cadillac Motor Div.)

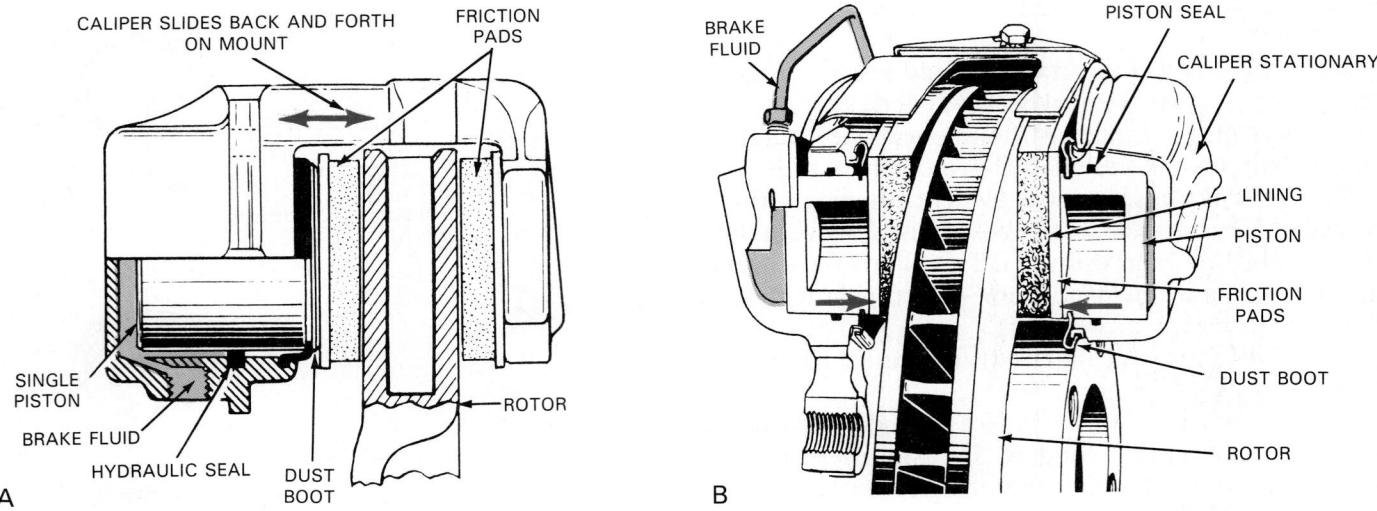

Fig. 68-22. Caliper piston pushes brake pad into revolving disc to slow or stop car. A — Single piston caliper is very common. Caliper floats or slides on mount so both pads contact disc. B — Fixed caliper uses pistons on both sides of disc. Caliper remains stationary on its mounting.

Brake caliper

The *brake caliper* assembly includes the caliper housing, piston, piston seal, dust boot, brake pads or shoes, special hardware (clips, springs), and a bleeder screw. These parts are pictured in Fig. 68-23.

Fig. 68-24 shows how a brake caliper piston operates. When the brake pedal is applied, brake fluid flows into the caliper cylinder. The piston is then pushed outward by fluid pressure to jam the brake pads into the rotor.

The **piston seal** in the caliper prevents pressure leakage between the piston and cylinder. The piston seal also helps pull the piston back into the cylinder when the brakes are NOT applied. The elastic action of the seal acts as a spring to retract the piston.

The **piston boot** keeps road dirt and water off the caliper piston and wall of the cylinder. Pictured in Fig.

68-24, the boot and seal usually fit into grooves cut in the caliper cylinder and piston.

A **bleeder screw** allows air to be removed from the hydraulic brake system. It is threaded into the side or top of the caliper housing, Fig. 68-23. When loosened, system pressure can be used to force fluid and air out the bleeder screw.

Disc brake pads

Disc brake pads or shoes are steel plates to which linings are riveted. Brake pads are shown in Fig. 68-23.

Brake pad linings are normally made of either asbestos (asbestos fiber filled) or semimetallic (metal particle filled) friction material. Many new vehicles, especially those with front-wheel drive, use semimetallic linings on the front. Semimetallic linings can

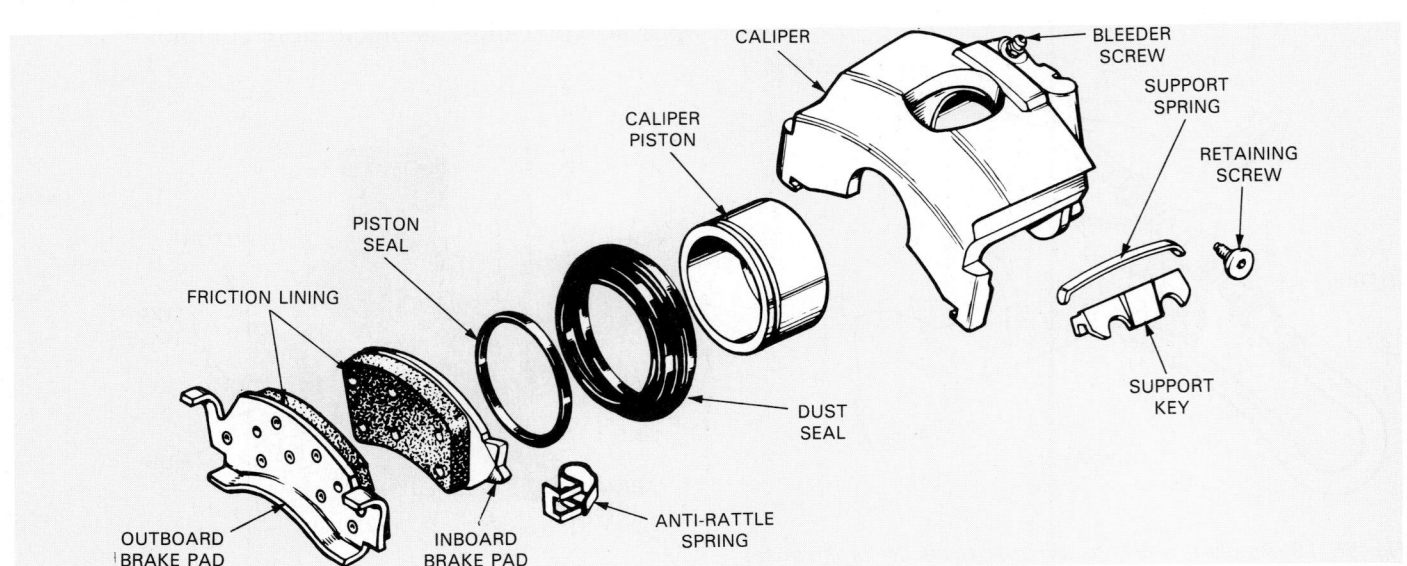

Fig. 68-23. Disassembled view of caliper shows parts. Note how they fit together.   (Chrysler Corp.)

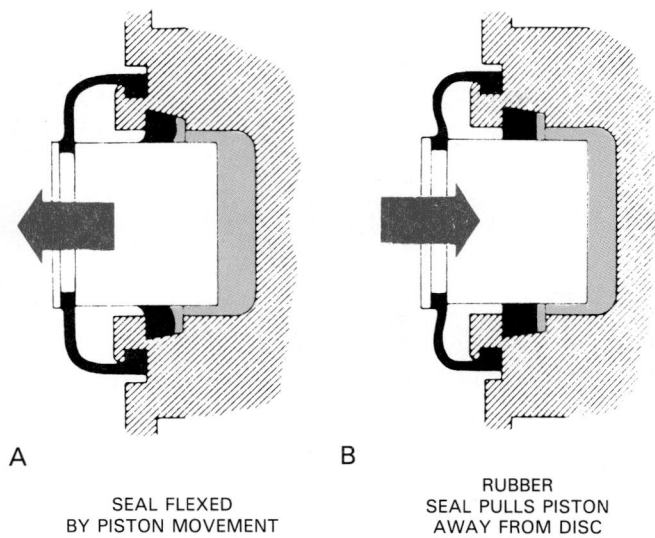

A

B

SEAL FLEXED
BY PISTON MOVEMENT

RUBBER
SEAL PULLS PISTON
AWAY FROM DISC

Fig. 68-24. Operation of caliper piston. A — Brakes applied and piston is pushed partially out of cylinder. B — Stretched piston seal pulls piston back after brake release. This keeps pads from rubbing on disc. (EIS)

withstand higher operating temperatures without losing their frictional properties.

Anti-rattle clips are frequently used to keep the brake pads from vibrating and rattling, Fig. 68-25A. The clip snaps onto the brake pad to produce a force fit in the caliper. Sometimes, an anti-rattle spring is used instead of a clip.

A *pad wear sensor* is a metal tab on the brake pad that informs driver of worn brake pad linings. The wear sensor tab will emit a loud squeal or squeak when it scrapes against the brake disc. The sensor only touches the disc when the brake lining has worn too thin.

Brake disc or rotor

The *brake disc,* also called *brake rotor,* uses friction from the brake pads to slow or stop wheel rotation. The brake disc is normally made of cast iron. It may be an integral part of the wheel hub. However, many front-wheel drive cars have the disc and the hub as separate units. Refer to Figs. 68-21 and 68-25A.

The brake disc may be solid or ventilated rib type.

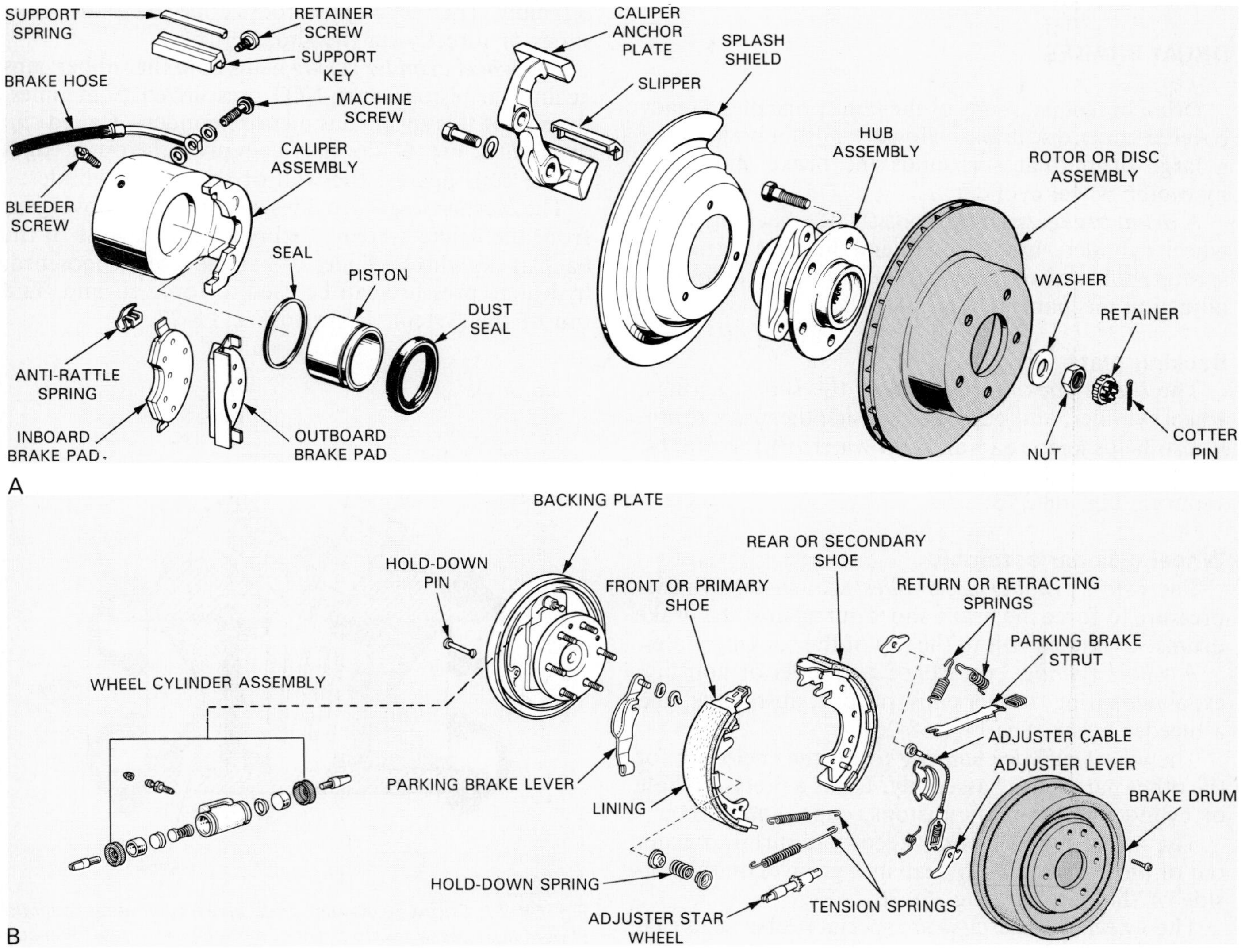

SUPPORT SPRING

RETAINER SCREW

SUPPORT KEY

BRAKE HOSE

MACHINE SCREW

CALIPER ASSEMBLY

BLEEDER SCREW

SEAL

PISTON

DUST SEAL

ANTI-RATTLE SPRING

INBOARD BRAKE PAD

OUTBOARD BRAKE PAD

CALIPER ANCHOR PLATE

SPLASH SHIELD

SLIPPER

HUB ASSEMBLY

ROTOR OR DISC ASSEMBLY

WASHER

RETAINER

NUT

COTTER PIN

A

BACKING PLATE

HOLD-DOWN PIN

FRONT OR PRIMARY SHOE

REAR OR SECONDARY SHOE

RETURN OR RETRACTING SPRINGS

PARKING BRAKE STRUT

WHEEL CYLINDER ASSEMBLY

PARKING BRAKE LEVER

LINING

HOLD-DOWN SPRING

ADJUSTER STAR WHEEL

TENSION SPRINGS

ADJUSTER CABLE

ADJUSTER LEVER

BRAKE DRUM

B

Fig. 68-25. Compare complete disc and drum brake assemblies. A — Disc brake. B — Drum brake. (Chrysler and Toyota)

Brake System Fundamentals 897

The ventilated rib disc is hollow which allows cooling air to circulate inside the disc.

Disc brake types

Disc brakes can be classified as floating, sliding, and fixed caliper types. Floating and sliding calipers are common. The fixed caliper was used on some older passenger cars.

The *floating caliper* disc brake is mounted on two bolts supported by rubber bushings. The one-piston caliper is free to shift or float in the rubber bushings.

The *sliding caliper* type disc brake is mounted in slots machined in the caliper adapter. The one-piston caliper is free to slide sideways in the slots or grooves as the linings wear. Look at Fig. 68-25A.

The *fixed caliper* type disc brake normally uses more than one piston and cylinder. The caliper is bolted directly to the steering knuckle. It is NOT free to move in relation to the disc. Pistons on both sides of the disc push against the brake pads, Fig. 68-22B.

Floating and sliding calipers are used to avoid vibration problems. With a fixed caliper, severe vibrations can occur with a slight runout (wobble) of the disc.

DRUM BRAKES

Drum brakes use many of the same principles already covered under disc brakes. However, drum brakes have a large drum that surrounds the brake shoes and hydraulic wheel cylinder.

A *drum brake assembly* consists of a backing plate, wheel cylinder, brake shoes and linings, retracting springs, hold-down springs, brake drum, and automatic adjusting mechanism, Fig. 68-25B.

Backing plate

The *brake backing plate* holds the shoes, springs, wheel cylinder, and other parts inside the brake drum. It also helps keep road dirt and water off the brakes. The backing plate bolts to the axle housing or spindle support, Fig. 68-25B.

Wheel cylinder assembly

The *wheel cylinder assemblies* use master cylinder pressure to force the brake shoes out against the brake drums. Cylinders bolt to the top of the backing plates.

A *wheel cylinder* consists of a cylinder or housing, expander spring, rubber cups, pistons, dust boots, and a bleeder screw. See Fig. 68-26.

The *wheel cylinder housing* forms the enclosure for the other parts of the assembly. It has a precision hole or cylinder in it for the pistons, cups, and spring.

The *wheel cylinder boots* keep road dirt and water out of the cylinder. They snap into grooves on the outside of the housing, Fig. 68-26.

The *wheel cylinder cups* are special rubber seals that keep fluid from leaking past the pistons. They fit in the cylinder and against the pistons, as in Fig. 68-27.

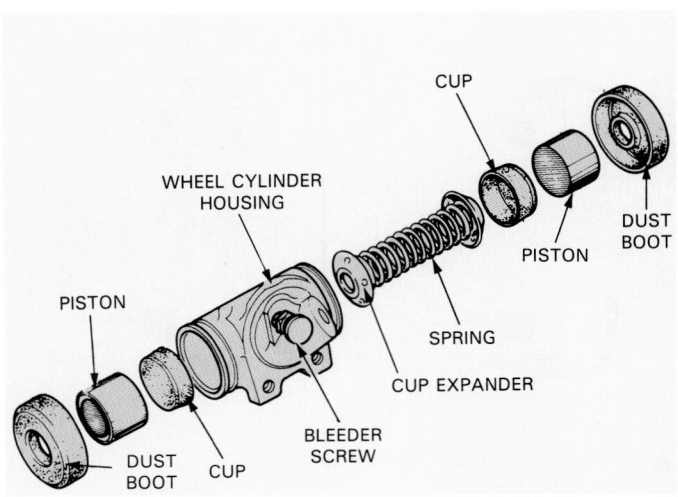

Fig. 68-26. Disassembled view of wheel cylinder for drum brake. Cups prevent fluid leakage out of cylinder. Boots keep debris out of cylinder. (Renault)

The *wheel cylinder pistons* are metal or plastic plungers that transfer force out of the wheel cylinder assembly. They act on push rods connected to the brake shoes or directly on the shoes.

The *wheel cylinder spring* helps hold the rubber cups against the pistons when NOT pressurized. Sometimes, the end of this spring has metal expanders. Called *cup expanders,* Fig. 68-26, they help press the outer edges of the cups against the wall of the wheel cylinder.

The *bleeder screw* provides a means of removing air from the brake system. It threads into a hole in the back of the wheel cylinder. When the screw is loosened, hydraulic pressure can be used to force air and fluid out of the system. Refer to Fig. 68-27.

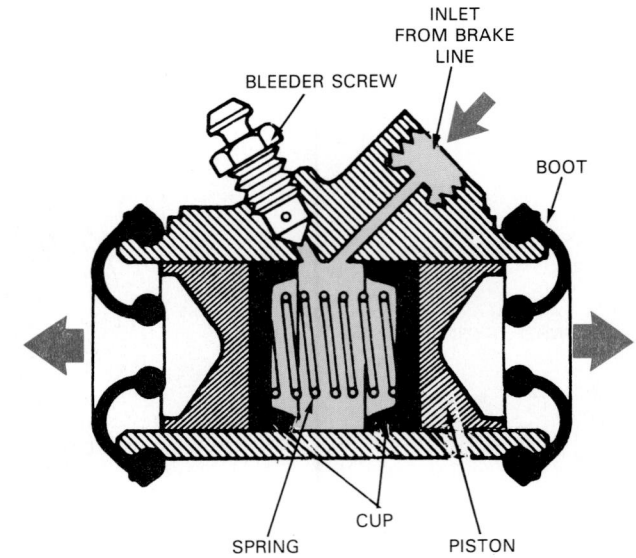

Fig. 68-27. Cutaway view of drum brake type wheel cylinder shows fluid passage into cylinder and bleeder screw. Pressure inside pushes cups and pistons outward to force linings into drum. (EIS)

Drum brake shoes

The *drum brake shoes* rub against the revolving brake drum to produce braking action, Fig. 68-25B. Drum brake shoe assemblies are made by fastening ASBESTOS LINING, a friction material, onto the METAL SHOES.

The linings may be held on the shoes by either rivets or a bonding agent (glue). Like disc brake pads, the asbestos lining serves as a heat resistant surface that contacts the brake drum. The metal shoe supports and holds the soft lining material.

The *primary brake shoe* is the front shoe, Fig. 68-28. It normally has a slightly SHORTER LINING than the secondary shoe.

The *secondary brake shoe* is the rear shoe, Fig. 68-28. It has the LARGEST LINING surface area.

Retracting and hold-down springs

Retracting springs pull the brake shoes away from the brake drums when the brake pedal is released. They also push the wheel cylinder pistons inward. Usually, the retracting springs fit in holes in the shoes and around an anchor pin at the top of the backing plate. Refer to Fig. 68-28.

Hold-down springs hold the brake shoes against the backing plate when the brakes are in the released position. A hold-down pin fits through the back of the backing plate, Fig. 68-28. A metal cup locks onto these pins to secure the hold-down springs to the shoes.

As shown in Fig. 68-29, other springs are used on the automatic adjusting mechanism. Brake springs are high quality steel, capable of withstanding the high temperatures encountered inside the brake drum.

Brake shoe adjusters

Brake shoe adjusters maintain correct drum-to-lining clearance as the brake linings wear. Look at Fig. 68-29.

Many cars use a star wheel (screw) type brake shoe adjusting mechanism. This type includes a *star wheel* (adjusting screw assembly), adjuster lever, adjuster spring, and either an adjuster cable, lever arm, or link (rods). See 68-29A through D.

Automatic brake shoe adjusters normally function when the brakes are applied with the car moving in

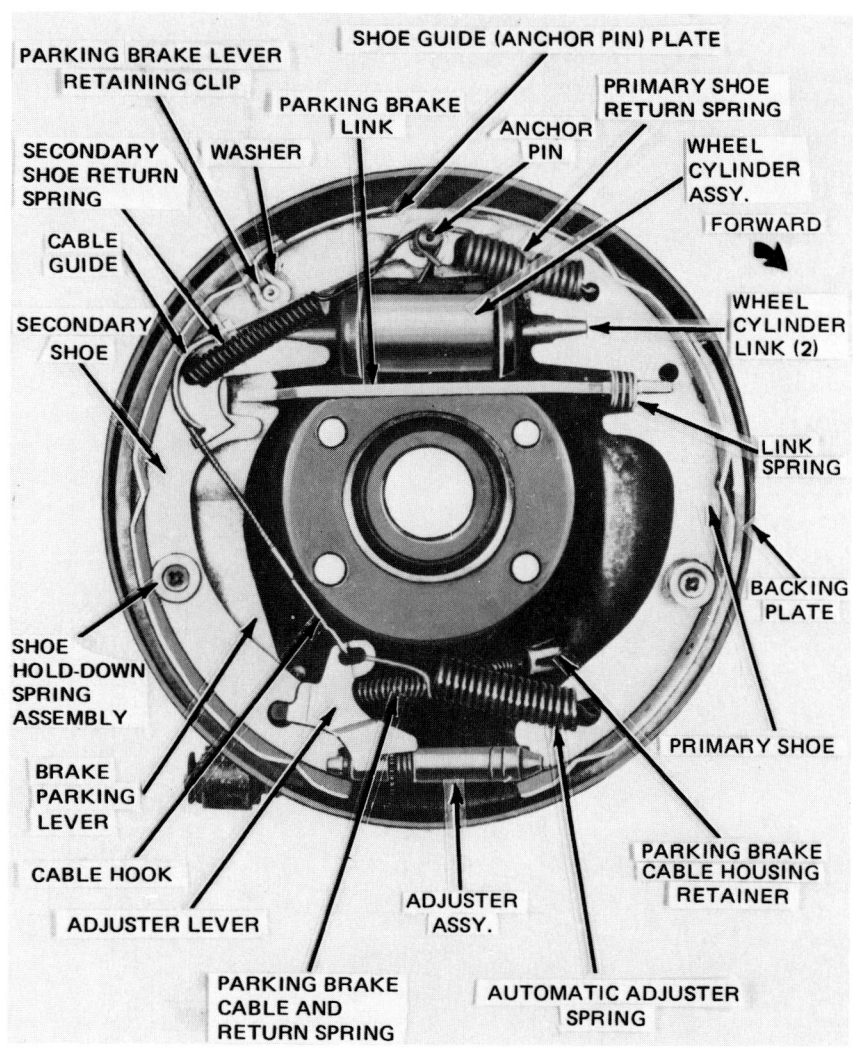

Fig. 68-28. Study parts of common brake assembly mounted on backing plate. (Ford)

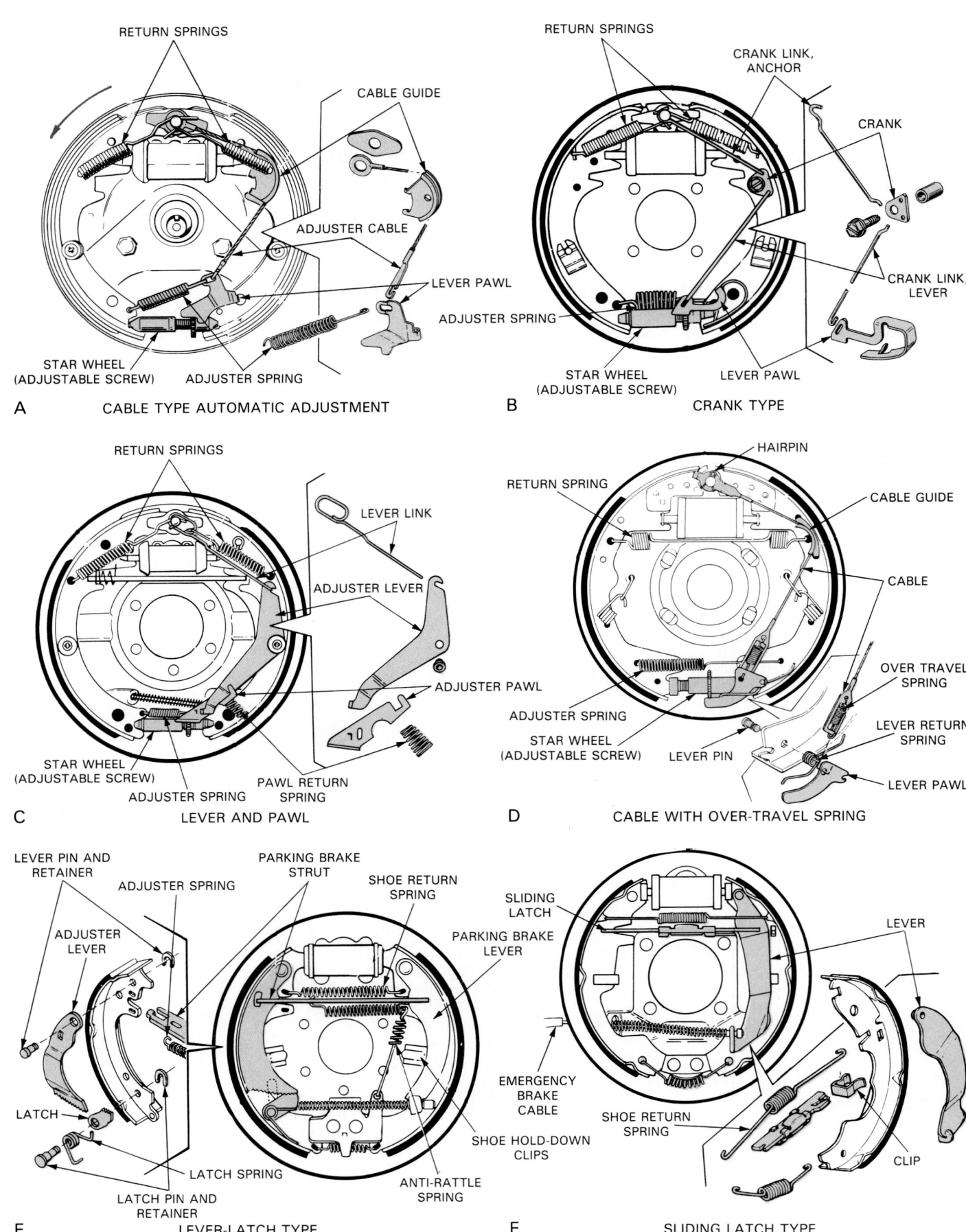

Fig. 68-29. Major variation in drum brake design is in automatic adjusting mechanism. A — Cable type. B — Crank type. C — Lever and pawl type. D — Cable with over-travel spring type. E — Lever-latch type. F — Ratcheting type. (FMC)

reverse. If there is too much lining clearance, the brake shoes move outward and rotate with the drum enough to operate the adjusting lever. This lengthens the star wheel assembly. The linings are moved closer to the brake drum, maintaining the correct lining-to-drum clearance.

Fig. 68-29 E and 68-29F picture brake assemblies that use modern latch type adjusters.

Brake drums

Brake drums provide a rubbing surface for the brake shoe linings, Fig. 68-30. The drum usually fits over the wheel lug studs. A large hole in the middle of the drum centers the drum on the front hub or rear axle flange. The wheel and drum turn together as a unit.

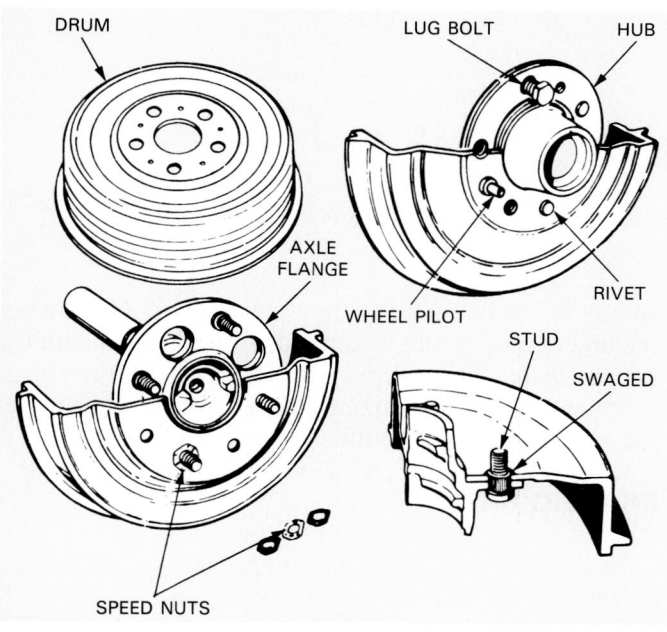

Fig. 68-30. Brake drum provides friction surface for brake shoe linings. Note construction of drum. (Ford)

Brake shoe energization

When the brake shoes are forced against the rotating drum, they are pulled away from their pivot point by friction. This movement, called *self-energizing action,* draws the shoes tighter against the drum, Fig. 68-31.

With most drum brake designs, shoe energization is supplemented by servo action. *Servo action* results when the primary (front) shoe helps apply the secondary (rear) shoe. Look at Fig. 68-31B.

The backing plate anchor pin holds the secondary shoe during brake application. However, the primary shoe is free to float out and push against the end of the secondary shoe through the star wheel assembly. This action presses the secondary shoe into the drum with extra force.

Less wheel cylinder hydraulic pressure is needed to apply the brakes because of servo action.

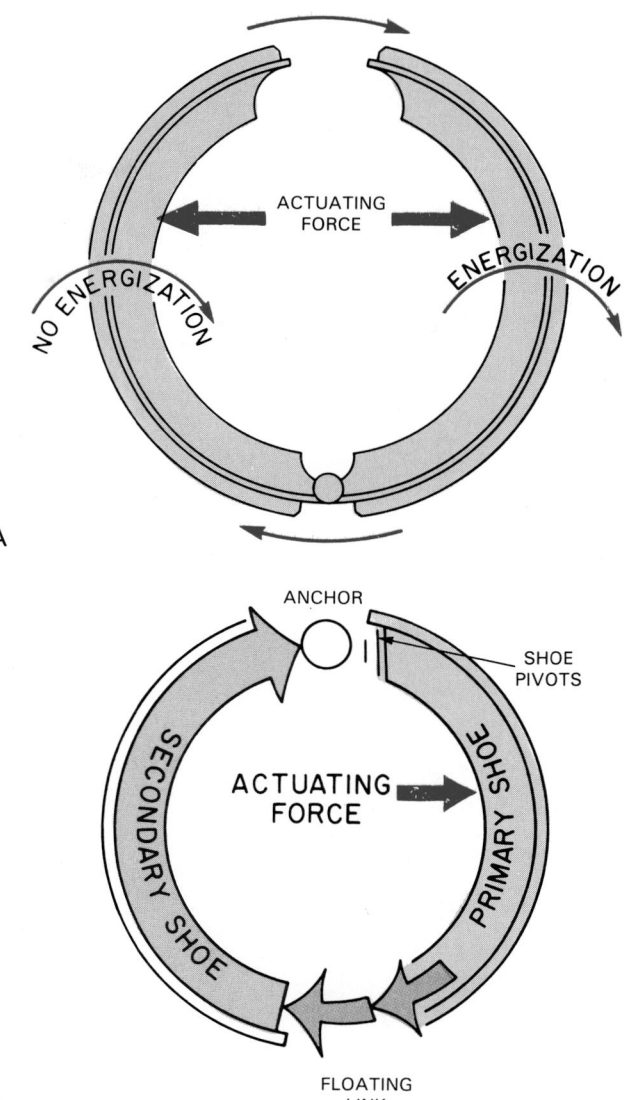

Fig. 68-31. A — Self-energizing brakes use friction to force one brake shoe tighter against drum. B — Servo action results when both shoes are free to swing into drum and primary shoe helps apply secondary shoe. (EIS)

Fig. 68-31A shows a non-servo type brake assembly. Fig. 68-31B shows the more common servo or floating type brakes.

EMERGENCY (PARKING) BRAKES

Emergency brakes, also called *parking brakes,* provide a mechanical means (cable and levers) of applying the brakes. Fig. 68-32 pictures one type.

When the parking brake hand or foot lever is activated, it pulls a steel cable that runs through a housing. The movement of the cable pulls on a lever inside the drum or disc brake assembly. The lever action forces the brake linings against the rear drums or discs to resist vehicle movement. Fig. 68-33 shows a foot operated emergency brake unit.

When disc brakes are used on the rear, a thrust screw

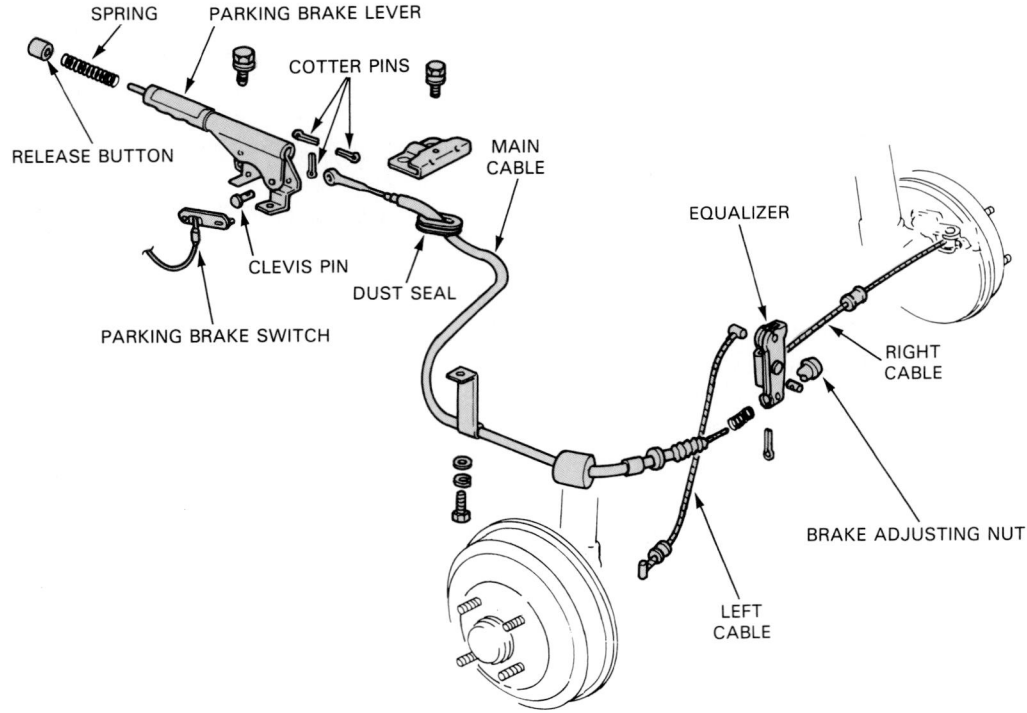

Fig. 68-32. Study parts of typical emergency or parking brake mechanism. (Toyota)

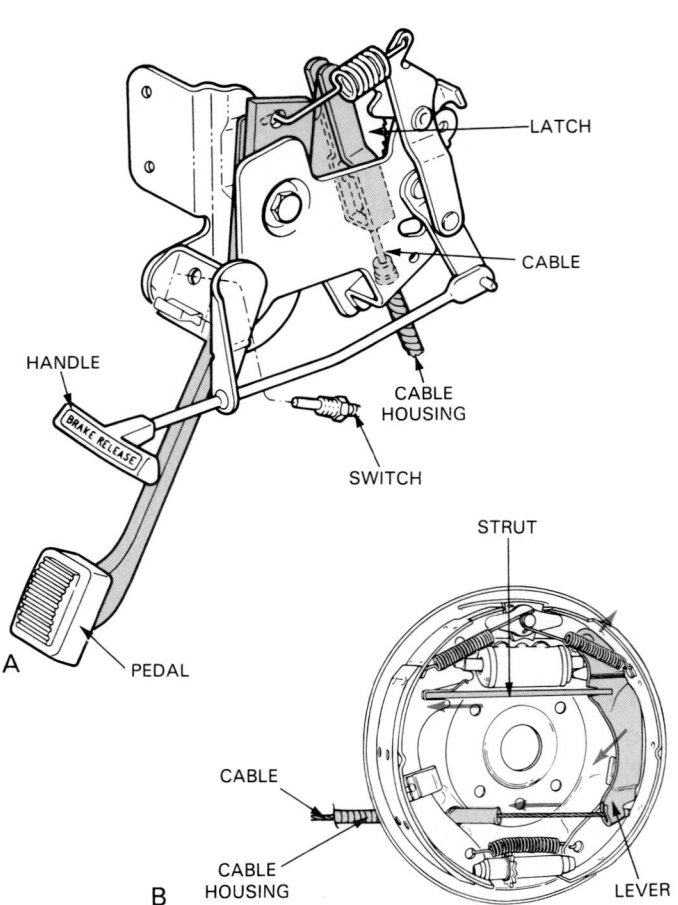

Fig. 68-33. Parts of an emergency brake system. A — Foot-operated emergency brake pedal. Note latch and release handle. B — Cable activates lever in brake assembly that pries shoes out against drum. (Chrysler and Ford)

and lever can be added to the brake caliper. Then, when the emergency brake is applied, the cable pulls on the caliper lever. The caliper lever turns the large thrust screw which pushes on the caliper piston and applies the brake pads to the disc. See Fig. 68-34.

BRAKING RATIO

Braking ratio refers to the comparison of front wheel to rear wheel braking effort. When a car stops, its weight tends to transfer onto the front wheels. The front tires are pressed against the road with greater force. The rear tires lose some of their grip on the road. As a result, the front wheels do more of the braking than the rear.

For this reason, many cars have disc brakes on the front and drum brakes on the rear. Disc brakes are capable of producing more stopping effort than drum brakes. If drum brakes are used on both the front and rear wheels, the front shoe linings and drums normally have a larger surface area.

Typically, front wheel brakes handle 60 to 70 percent of the braking power. Rear wheels handle 30 to 40 percent of the braking. Front-wheel drive cars, having even more weight on the front wheels, can have even a higher braking ratio at the front wheels.

BRAKE SYSTEM SWITCHES

There are two types of switches commonly used in a brake system: the stop light switch and the brake warning light switch.

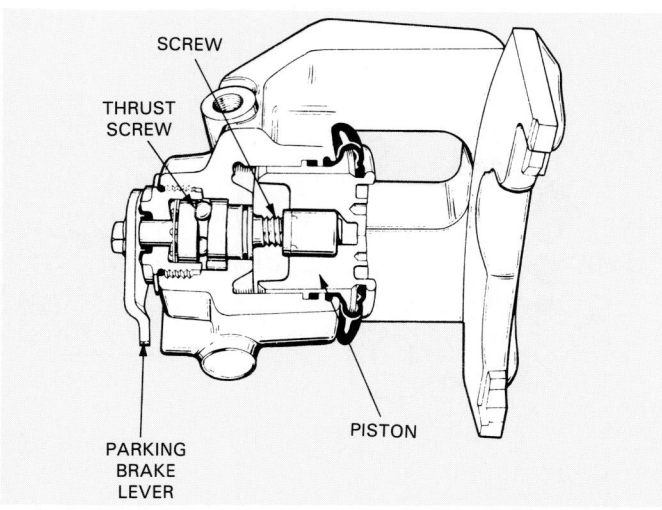

Fig. 68-34. Cross sectional view of caliper that has emergency brake mechanism. Cable pulls on and rotates lever. Lever turns screw that pushes piston outward to apply brake. (Bendix)

Stop light switch

The *stop light switch* is a spring-loaded electrical switch that operates the rear stop lights of the car. Most modern cars use a mechanical switch on the brake pedal mechanism. The switch is normally open. When the brake pedal is pressed, it closes the switch and turns on the brake lights.

Hydraulically operated stop light switches are used on some older cars. Brake system pressure pushed on a switch diaphragm and closed the switch to operate the brake lights.

Note! Brake light circuits are covered in Chapter 34, Lights, Wipers, Horn Fundamentals.

Brake warning light switch (Pressure differential valve)

The *brake warning light switch,* also called a *pressure differential valve,* warns the driver of a pressure loss on one side of a dual brake system. Look at Fig. 68-35.

If a leak develops in either the primary or secondary brake system, unequal pressure acts on each side of the warning light switch piston. This pushes the piston to one side, grounding the indicator, Fig. 68-36.

BRAKE SYSTEM CONTROL VALVES

Many brake systems use control valves to regulate the pressure going to each wheel cylinder. The three types of valves are the metering valve, proportioning valve, and the combination valve. Fig. 68-35 shows the general locations of these valves.

Metering valve

A *metering valve* is designed to equalize braking action at each wheel during light brake applications. A metering valve is used on cars with front wheel disc brakes and rear wheel drum brakes. The metering valve is in the line to the disc brakes, Fig. 68-35.

The metering valve functions by preventing the front disc brakes from applying until approximately 75 to 135 psi (517 to 930 kPa) has built up in the system. This overcomes the rear drum brake return springs.

Proportioning valve

A *proportioning valve* is also used to equalize braking action with front disc and rear drum brakes. It is commonly located in the brake line to the rear drum brakes. Look at Fig. 68-35.

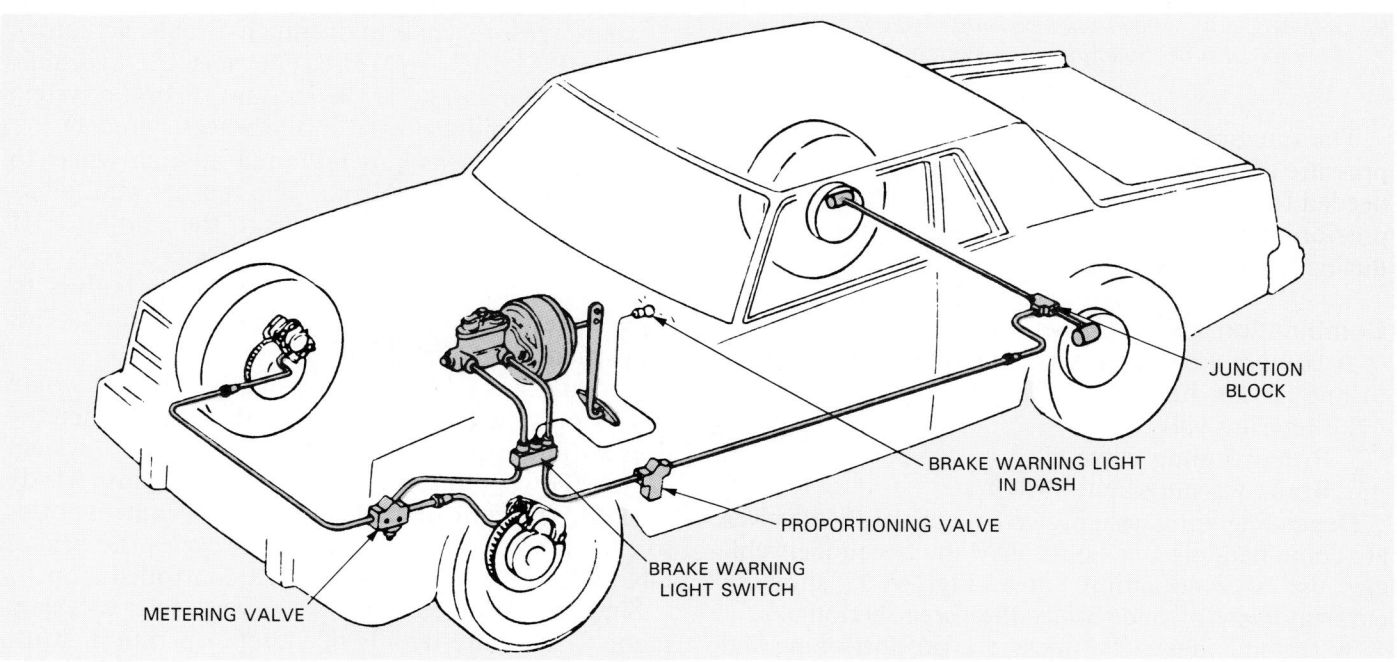

Fig. 68-35. Note location of various valves used in brake system. (EIS)

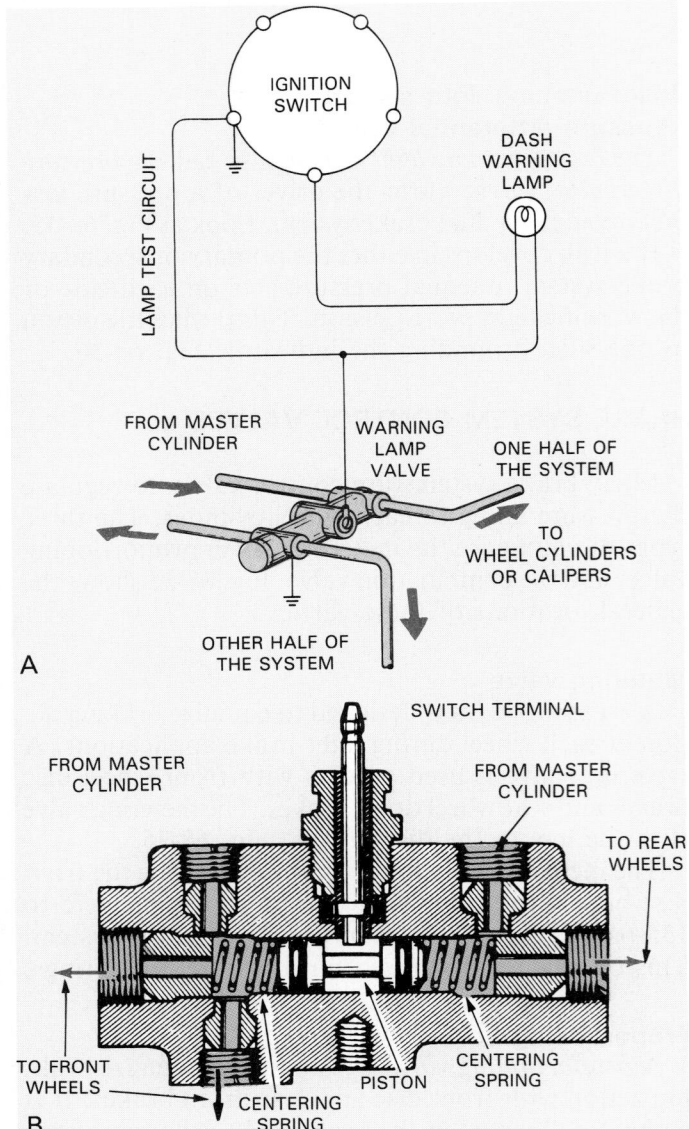

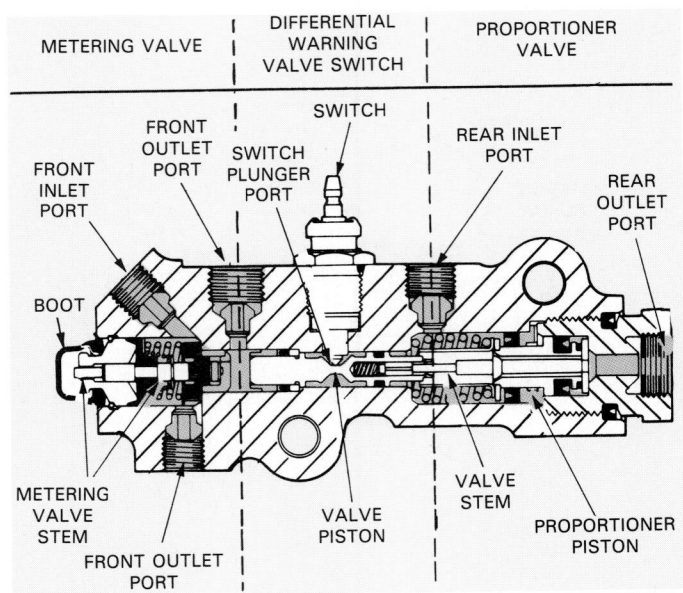

Fig. 68-37. Study the sections of combination valve. (Chrysler Corp.)

Fig. 68-36. Brake warning light switch is activated by difference in pressures in primary and secondary systems. Pressure difference pushes small piston in valve to close warning lamp circuit. A — Brake warning lamp circuit. B — Cutaway view of brake warning lamp switch. (Bendix)

The function of the proportioning valve is to limit pressure at the rear drum brake when high pressure is needed to apply the front disc brakes. Thus, the proportioning valve prevents rear wheel lockup and skid during heavy brake applications.

Combination valve

A *combination valve* serves as two or three valves in one. It can function as a:

1. Metering valve.
2. Proportioning valve.
3. Brake warning light switch.

Depending upon design, two or more of these valves are combined into one housing. Many late model vehicles use a combination valve. Fig. 68-37 shows a cutaway view of one. Study the three sections.

With some master cylinders, the proportioning and warning lamp valves are mounted inside the master cylinder housing. This design uses the same operating principles, Fig. 68-38.

SKID CONTROL BRAKE SYSTEM

A *skid control brake system,* also termed *anti-lock brake system,* uses wheel speed sensors, hydraulic valves, and the on-board computer to prevent or limit tire lockup. One system is given in Fig. 68-39.

Pictured in Fig. 68-40, the basic parts of a computerized brake system are:

1. TRIGGER WHEELS (toothed rings mounted on each wheel spindle or hub).
2. WHEEL SPEED SENSORS (magnetic sensors that use trigger wheel rotation to produce a weak alternating current signal).
3. ABS COMPUTER (small processor that uses wheel speed sensor signals to operate hydraulic actuator).
4. HYDRAULIC ACTUATOR (electric-hydraulic device that can cycle the amount of brake system pressure going to each brake wheel cylinder).

An electrical sensor is mounted at each wheel to measure wheel and tire rpm. The sensors send alternating or pulsing current signals to the computer. If one wheel slows, the sensor signal reduced frequency and the computer activates the hydraulic valves to reduce pressure to that wheel's brake assembly. This keeps that tire from skidding.

If a car's tires were to lock up and slide, the car would NOT stop efficiently. A car stops the fastest when the tires are almost ready to skid. The skid control system can detect when the wheel speed drops rapidly (ready to skid). The control unit can then send control pulses to the actuator. The actuator then cycles the brakes ON and OFF very quickly, for a controlled stop.

Since exact skid control systems vary, refer to a shop manual for more details of system operation. Most systems, however, use the principles just discussed.

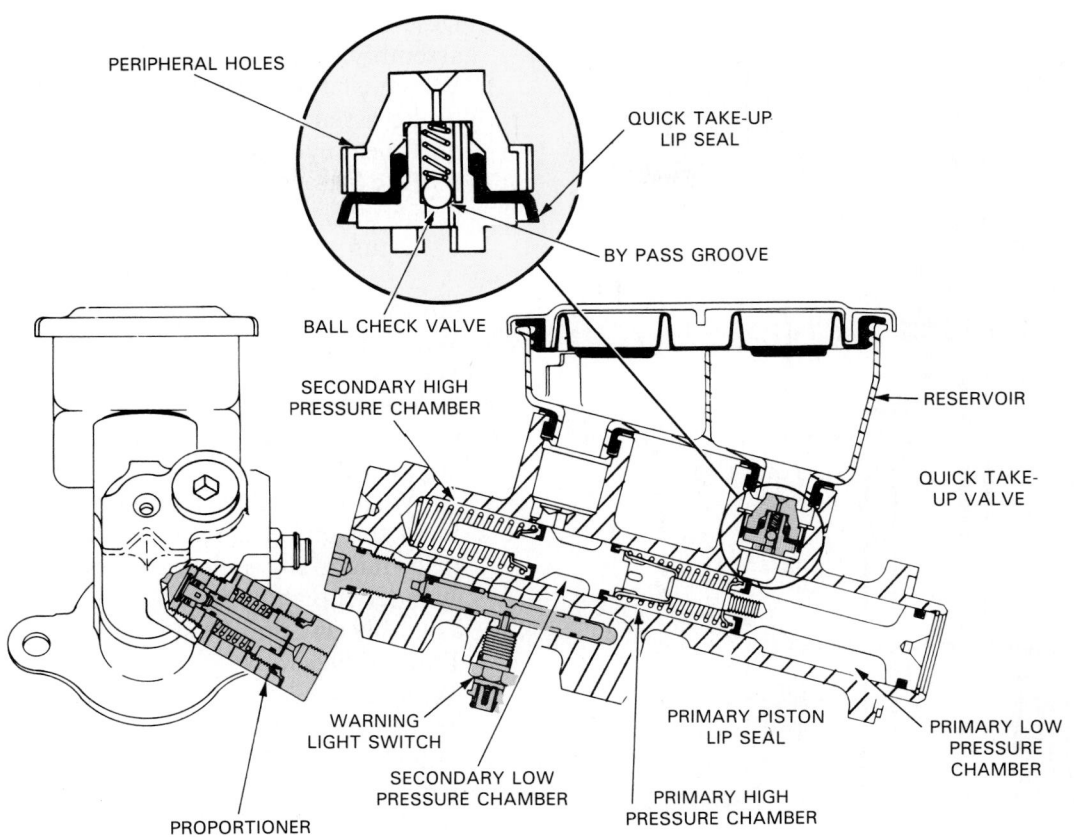

Fig. 68-38. This master cylinder has proportioning and warning lamp valves mounted internally (Delco)

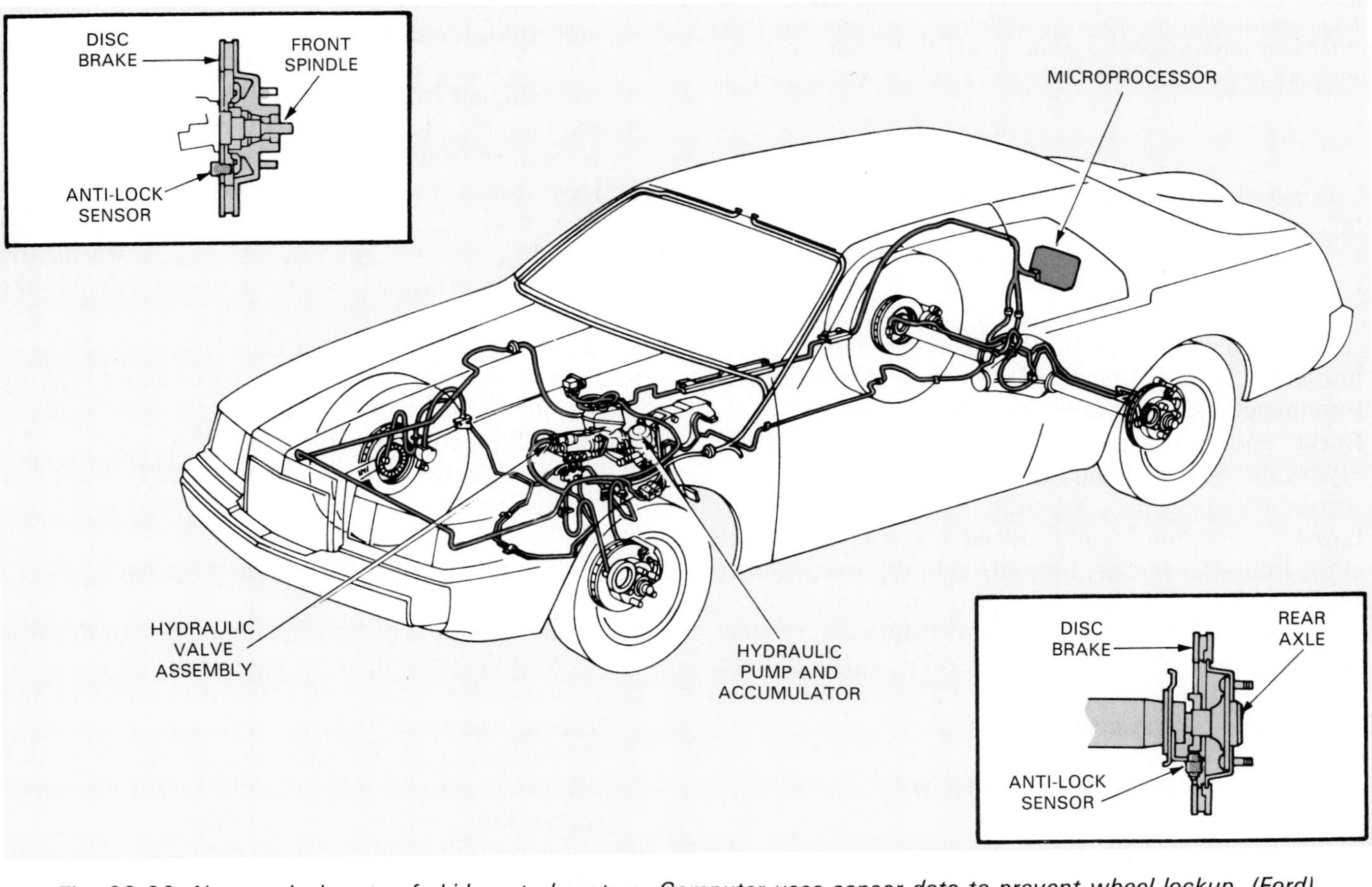

Fig. 68-39. Note typical parts of skid control system. Computer uses sensor data to prevent wheel lockup. (Ford)

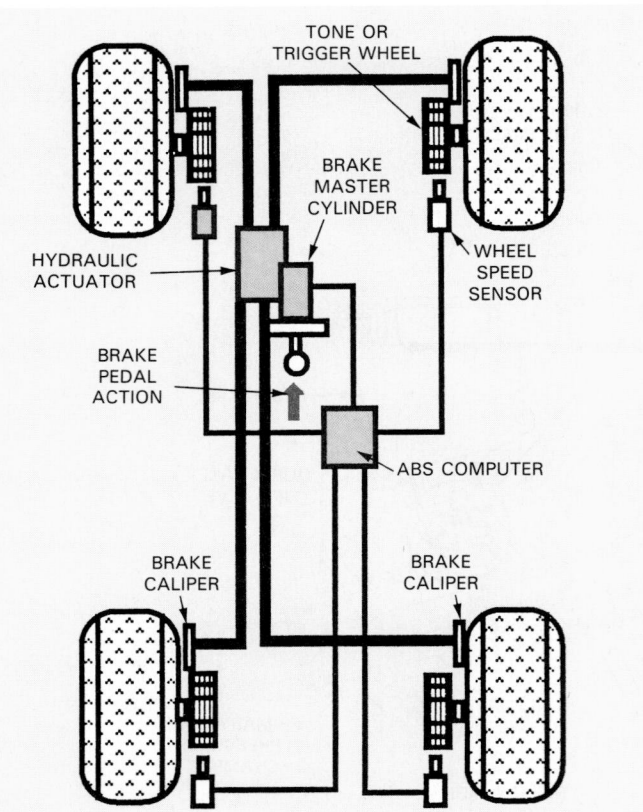

Fig. 68-40. *Note basic parts of anti-lock or computerized braking system. Trigger wheels are mounted on each spindle. Magnetic sensors produce an AC signal that equals wheel speed. Computer can detect if one or more wheels are skidding because the sensor signal will decrease in frequency. Computer can then trigger hydraulic actuator to cycle hydraulic pressure to keep the tires from skidding and losing traction.*

For additional information on ABS systems, refer to Chapter 74, page 992.

KNOW THESE TERMS

Brake pedal assembly, Master cylinder, Brake booster, Brake lines, Wheel brake assemblies, Emergency brake, Disc brakes, Drum brakes, Caliper, Brake pads, Rotor, Wheel cylinder, Brake shoes, Hydraulic system, Dual master cylinder, Primary and secondary pistons, Vacuum booster, Hydraulic booster, Diagonally split, Bleeder screw, Anti-rattle clips, Pad wear sensor, Floating caliper, Fixed caliper, Backing plate, Asbestos lining, Primary and secondary shoes, Retracting and hold-down springs, Star wheel, Servo action, Braking ratio, Brake warning light, Metering valve, Proportioning valve, Combination valve, Anti-skid system.

REVIEW QUESTIONS

1. List and explain the six major parts of a brake system.
2. Describe the four major parts of a disc brake assembly.
3. Which of the following is NOT part of a drum brake assembly?
   a. Wheel cylinder.
   b. Booster.
   c. Shoes.
   d. Drum.
4. A _____ system uses a liquid to transmit motion or pressure from one part to another.
5. What are four functions of a master cylinder?
6. Why is a dual master cylinder used?
7. A power brake _____ _____ uses pedal pressure and engine vacuum to assist brake application.
8. A hydro-boost power brake system uses pressure from the power steering pump. True or False?
9. In a diagonally split brake system, each master cylinder cup and piston assembly operates a brake assembly on opposite sides and corners of the car. True or False?
10. What causes a brake caliper piston to retract away from the rotor after brake application?
11. Which of the following is NOT part of a brake caliper?
    a. Piston seal.
    b. Bleeder screw.
    c. Piston boot.
    d. All of the above are correct.
12. Why are floating and sliding calipers more common than fixed calipers?
13. The _____ _____ provides a means of removing air from the wheel cylinder after repairs.
14. Explain the difference between a primary and secondary brake shoe.
15. How does the emergency brake work?
16. The brake _____ _____ _____ , also called _____ _____ _____ , warns the driver of a pressure loss on one side of a dual brake system.
17. Why is a metering valve used?
18. How does a proportioning valve equalize braking action?
19. Describe a combination valve.
20. Summarize the operation of a typical skid control or ABS system.

ACTIVITIES FOR CHAPTER 68

1. Identify the type of brake system — disc or drum — on a vehicle assigned by your instructor.
2. Examine the calipers of a disc brake system and identify the type: floating or fixed.
3. Prepare an overhead transparency from Fig. 68-1 and use it to explain to your class the function of the various parts of a brake system.
4. Using a small hydraulic jack, explain and demonstrate the principle of the hydraulic brake.

Brake System Diagnosis and Repair

After studying this chapter, you will be able to:
- ☐ Diagnose common brake system problems.
- ☐ Inspect and maintain a brake system.
- ☐ Describe basic procedures for servicing a master cylinder and brake booster.
- ☐ Explain how to service a disc brake assembly.
- ☐ Explain how to service a drum brake assembly.
- ☐ Describe procedures for both manual and pressure bleeding of a brake system.
- ☐ Cite safety rules for brake service and work safely.

Remember! The brake system is the most important system on a car from a safety standpoint. The customer trusts the mechanic to do every service and repair operation correctly.

When working on a brake system, always keep in mind that a brake system failure could result in a deadly auto accident. It is up to you to make sure the car's brake system is in perfect operating condition before leaving the shop.

BRAKE SYSTEM PROBLEM DIAGNOSIS

Use *symptoms* (noises, smells, abnormal brake pedal movements, improper braking action) when diagnosing brake system problems. Listen to the customer's complaints or service writer's explanation. Then inspect the brake system or test drive the vehicle.

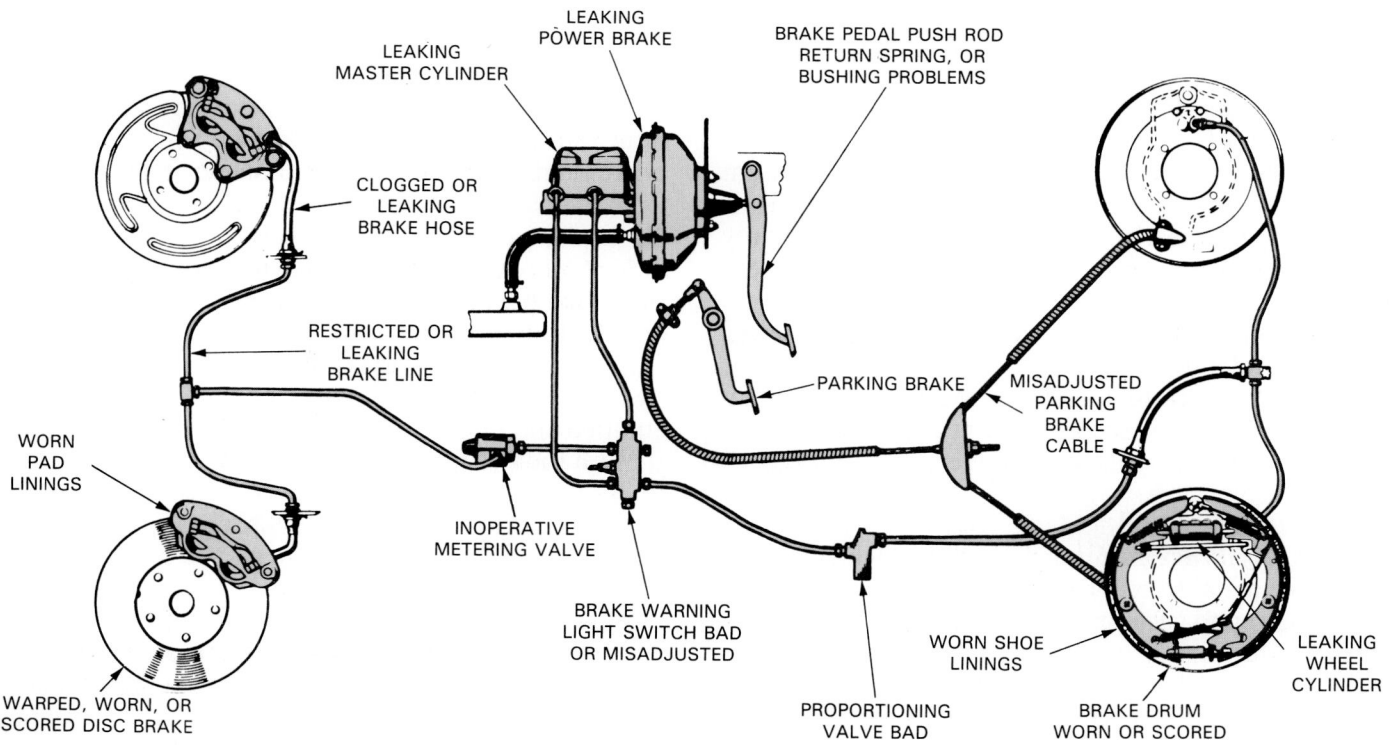

Fig. 69-1. Note some common problems that can develop in brake system. (Bendix)

It is important for you to be able to interpret the symptoms. You will then be prepared to decide what adjustments or repairs are needed. Refer to Fig. 69-1.

Almost all brake system problems can be sorted into the following basic symptom categories:

Brake pedal vibrates

Brake pedal vibration shows up as a chatter, pulsing, or shake. It happens only when the brake pedal is applied. The vibration may be felt mostly in the steering wheel (front brake assembly problems) or the brake pedal itself (could be problems at any wheel). When severe, the whole chassis and body of the car may vibrate when braking.

Brake pedal vibration is usually caused by an OUT-OF-ROUND brake drum or warped disc. Hard spots on the disc or drum can also cause this.

Grabbing brakes

Grabbing is a condition in which the brakes apply too quickly, with only light brake pedal application. It will be very difficult to stop slowly.

Grabbing is usually caused by a brake booster malfunction, brake fluid or grease on the linings, worn brake linings, faulty metering valve, or mechanical problem in the wheel brake assembly.

Excessive brake pedal effort

Excessive brake pedal effort is a noticeable increase in the amount of foot pressure needed to apply the brakes and stop the car. It can come from a variety of causes. The problem could be a frozen wheel cylinder or caliper piston, clogged brake hose or line, faulty master cylinder, contaminated linings, disconnected brake booster vacuum line, or defective brake booster.

Pulling brakes

Pulling brakes is a symptom in which the car veers to the right or left when braking. When the symptom is in the front brakes, a strong pulling force will be noticed on the steering wheel. Rear brake pull is only noticeable during very hard braking. One of the rear brakes may lock up, causing tire skid and squeal.

Brake pull is usually caused by a frozen caliper or wheel cylinder piston, grease- or fluid-coated lining, leaking cylinder, faulty automatic adjuster, or buildup of brake lining dust. Incorrect front end alignment can also make the car pull to one side when braking.

Spongy brake pedal

A *spongy brake pedal* is a condition which causes the brake pedal to feel like it is connected to a spring or rubber band. The brakes will apply but the pedal does not feel solid. It will travel farther towards the floor before full braking action occurs.

This condition is usually caused by AIR in the brake system. The air is compressing so it takes up less space. A spongy pedal can also result from faulty residual

pressure check valves in the master cylinder or unadjusted brake shoes.

Dropping brake pedal

A *dropping brake pedal* is a symptom where the brake pedal slowly moves all the way to the floor when steady pressure is applied to it.

For example, the condition usually shows up when the driver is stopped at a stop light. The brake may apply normally at first. However, while holding the brakes, the pedal steadily creeps downward. Pumping usually restores pedal height momentarily.

A dropping brake pedal is usually caused by an internal leak in the master cylinder. Pressure is slowly leaking past the piston cups. Since fluid returns to the reservoir, the fluid level will not drop.

A fluid leak anywhere else in the system can also cause the same symptom. With fluid leaking out, however, the fluid level in the master cylinder will drop.

Low brake pedal

A *low brake pedal* is a condition causing the pedal to travel too far toward the floor before braking. The pedal is NOT spongy and braking is normal once the pedal applies the brakes.

A low brake pedal can be caused by inoperative brake adjusters, maladjusted master cylinder push rod, or mechanical problem in the wheel brake assemblies.

Dragging brakes

Dragging brakes are brakes that remain partially applied even though the brake pedal is released. The brakes will overheat if the car is driven very far. To detect dragging brakes, feel each wheel assembly. The dragging brake or brakes will be abnormally HOT.

Dragging brakes can be caused by frozen wheel cylinder pistons, an overadjusted parking brake, weak return springs, overadjusted master cylinder push rod, brake fluid contamination, or master cylinder problem.

No brake pedal

No brake pedal is a very dangerous situation in which the brake pedal moves to the floor, with no braking action. Pumping the brakes does NOT help.

Lack of braking action is usually caused by a hydraulic problem. A system leak or leaks may have emptied the master cylinder reservoir.

With today's dual master cylinders, a complete loss of braking is unlikely. However, it can occur from driver neglect.

Brake warning light on

When the *brake warning light is on,* it indicates either an internal (master cylinder) or external (brake line, hose, wheel cylinder) leak. Unequal pressure in the dual master cylinder system has caused the differential pressure valve (usually part of combination valve) to shift to one side. Inspect the system for leaks and check the action of the master cylinder.

Braking noise

Braking noise can be a grinding sound, squeaks, rattles, and other abnormal sounds. Use your understanding of system operation to determine the cause.

A *metal-on-metal grinding* sound occurring only when braking, may be due to worn brake linings. The shoe may be rubbing on the metal drum or disc.

A *squeak* when braking may be caused by glazed (hardened) brake linings, unlubricated brake drum backing plate, foreign material embedded in the linings, or a wear indicator rubbing on a rotor.

A *rattle* may be due to a missing anti-rattle clip or spring on the brake pads. Loose or disconnected parts in the drum brake assembly can also cause a rattle from inside the brake assembly.

COMPUTER SELF-DIAGNOSIS

Many computerized or anti-lock brake systems provide self-diagnosis. The computer will detect an abnormal operating condition and illuminate a dash light. You can then energize self-diagnosis so the computer can register a trouble code number to show the brake system problem. Refer to the last three chapters in this book for more information on computer systems.

BRAKE SYSTEM INSPECTION

Most auto manufacturers recommend a periodic inspection of the brake system. This involves checking brake pedal action, fluid level in the master cylinder, and condition of the brake lines, hoses, and wheel brake assemblies, Fig. 69-1. The inspection is a form of preventive maintenance that helps assure safety.

Checking brake pedal action

A fast and accurate way of checking many components of the brake system is the *brake pedal check*. This is done by applying the brake pedal and comparing its movement to specs. The three brake pedal application specs (distances) are: pedal height, pedal free play, and pedal reserve distance.

Brake pedal height is the distance from the pedal to the floor with the pedal at rest. Fig. 69-2 illustrates how to check brake pedal height.

If height is incorrect, it usually points to problems in the pedal mechanism. There may be worn pedal bushings, weak return spring, or maladjusted master cylinder push rod.

Brake pedal free play is the amount of pedal movement before the beginning of brake application, Fig. 69-2. It is the difference between the "at rest" and initially applied positions.

Brake pedal free play is needed to prevent brake drag and overheating. If pedal free play is NOT correct, check the adjustment of the master cylinder push rod.

A worn pedal bushing or a bad return spring can also increase pedal free play.

Brake pedal reserve distance is measured from the car floor to the brake pedal with the brakes applied. See Fig. 69-2. Typically, brake pedal reserve distance should be 2 in. (51 mm) for manual brakes and 1 in. (25 mm) for power brakes.

If brake pedal reserve distance is incorrect, check push rod adjustment. Also, there may be air in the system or the brake adjusters may not be working. Numerous other problems can cause incorrect pedal reserve distance.

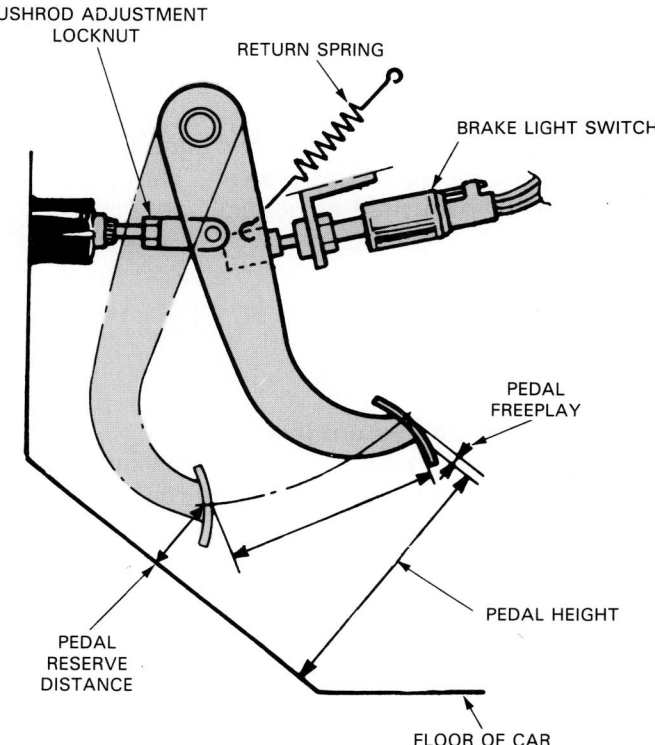

Fig. 69-2. Brake pedal height, reserve distance, and free play are important. Some cars have adjustable push rod. Also note brake light switch location. (Honda)

When checking brake pedal action, apply and hold the brake pedal firmly for about 15 seconds. The engine should be running if the car has power brakes. Try to detect any system leakage which would cause the pedal to slowly move towards the floor. Also, make sure the pedal is firm and returns properly.

While checking the brake pedal, you should also make sure the brake lights are operating. If they do not work, check the bulbs, fuses, or switch.

Checking brake fluid

An important part of a brake system inspection involves checking the level and condition of the brake fluid. To check the fluid, remove the master cylinder cover. Pry off the spring clip or unbolt the cover.

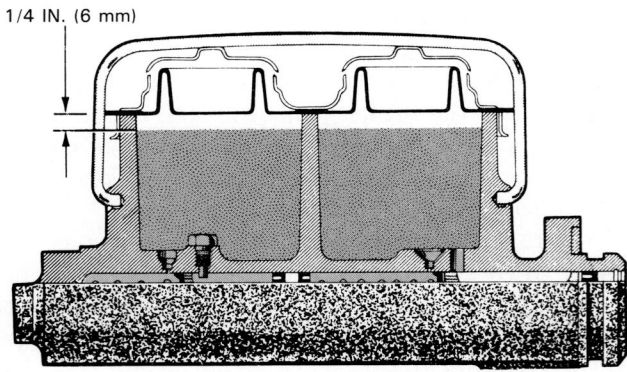

1/4 IN. (6 mm)

Fig. 69-3. Master cylinder reservoir should be kept full and checked periodically. Refer to service manual for specifications on filling reservoir. One-fourth inch down is average. (GM Trucks)

Typically, the **brake fluid level** should be 1/4 in. (6 mm) from the top of the reservoir. This is illustrated in Fig. 69-3. Add fluid as needed.

CAUTION! Only use the manufacturer's recommended type of brake fluid. Also, keep oil, grease, and other substances out of the brake fluid. Contamination can cause rapid deterioration of the master cylinder cups. A sudden loss of braking ability could result.

Check for brake system leaks

When the fluid level in the master cylinder is low, you should inspect the brake system for leaks. Check all brake lines, hoses, and wheel cylinders.

Brake fluid leakage will show up as a darkened, damp area around one of the components. Verify brake system leakage by checking that the leaking fluid smells like brake fluid.

Check parking brake

Apply the parking brake. The pedal or lever should NOT move more than 2/3 of full travel. The parking brake should keep the car from moving with the engine idling in drive.

The cables and linkage should also be inspected. The cables should NOT be frayed. The linkage should be tight, undamaged, and well lubricated.

Checking brake assemblies

When inspecting a brake system, remove one of the front and rear wheels. This will let you inspect the condition of the brake linings and other components.

When *inspecting disc brakes,* check the thickness of the brake pad linings. Pads should be replaced when the thinnest (most worn) part of the lining is no thicker than the metal shoe (approximately 1/8 in. or 3 mm).

Fig. 69-4 shows common disc brake problems. Study them closely.

Check the caliper piston for fluid leakage and the disc for damage. The disc should not be scored, cracked, or *heat checked* (overheating causes small hardened and cracked areas). The wheel bearings should be adjusted properly. To check for rattles, strike the caliper with a rubber mallet. Repair any of these problems while following a service manual.

When *inspecting drum brakes,* you must remove the brake drum. This will expose the brake shoe linings, wheel cylinder, braking surface of the drum, adjuster mechanism, and other parts. See Fig. 69-5.

The brake shoe linings must never be allowed to wear thinner than approximately 1/16 in. (1.5 mm). The shoes should NOT be glazed or coated with brake fluid, grease, or differential fluid. Any of these problems require lining replacement.

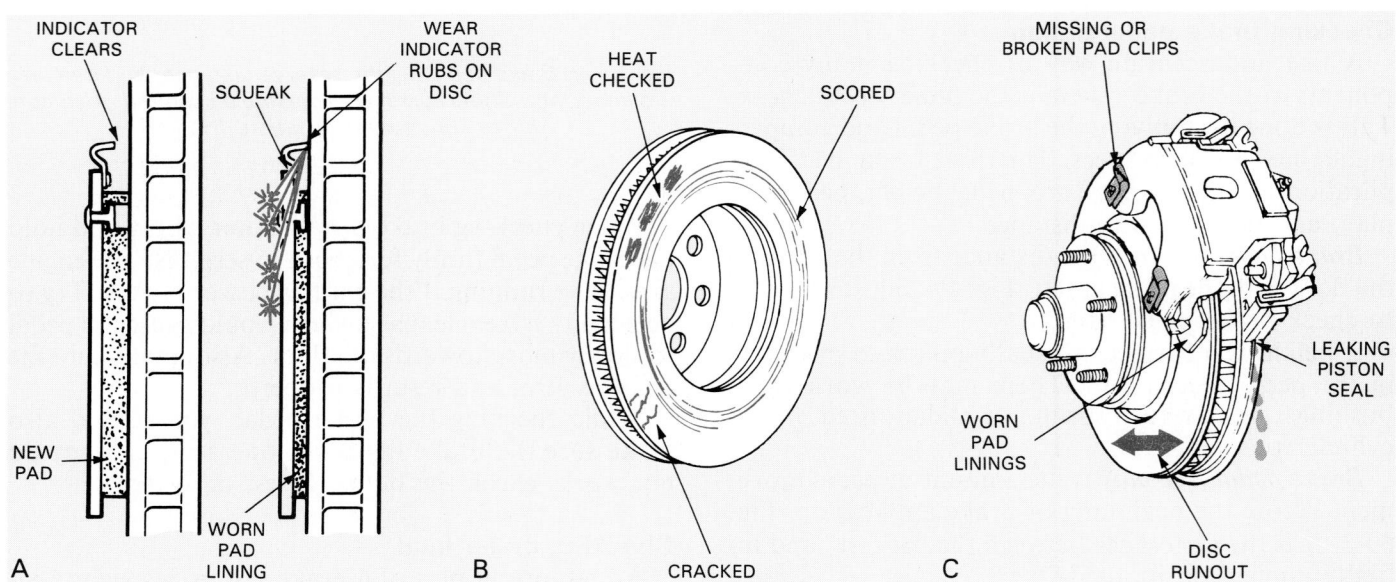

Fig. 69-4. Disc brake problems. A — Wear indicator clip will produce loud squeal when lining wears enough to let clip touch rotor. B — Check rotor for heat checking, cracks, and deep scoring. C — Also check for leaking piston seal, worn pad linings, and missing clips. (Cadillac and FMC)

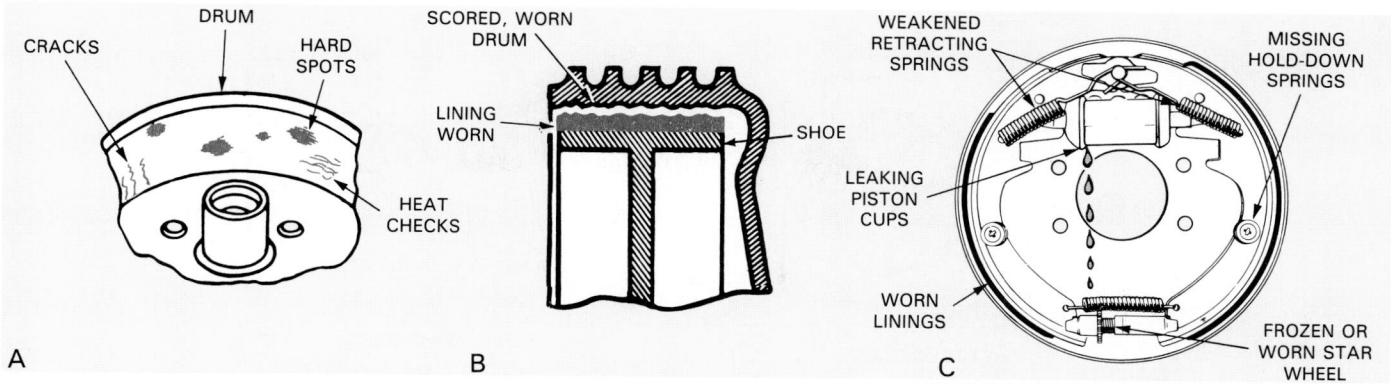

Fig. 69-5. Drum brake problems. A — Check drum for cracks, heat checks, and hard spots. B — Badly scored drum must be machined. If worn too much, it must be replaced. C — Check for leaking wheel cylinder, worn linings, and missing or damaged parts. (Bendix and FMC)

Pull back the wheel cylinder boots and check for leakage. If the boot is full of fluid, the wheel cylinder should be rebuilt or replaced. Also, check the automatic adjuster, return springs, and brake drum. The brake drum should NOT be scored, cracked, heat checked, or worn beyond specs.

DANGER! Do NOT use compressed air to blow brake dust off a wheel brake assembly. Most brake linings are made of ASBESTOS, a known CANCER-causing substance. Use a special brake vacuum machine and a clean rag to remove the dust. Take every precaution not to breathe brake lining dust. If needed, wear an approved filter mask over your nose and mouth.

VACUUM BOOSTER SERVICE

When a car has vacuum type power brakes, you should inspect the brake booster and vacuum hose. Make sure the vacuum hose from the engine is in good condition. It should NOT be hardened, cracked, or swollen. Also, check the hose fitting in the booster.

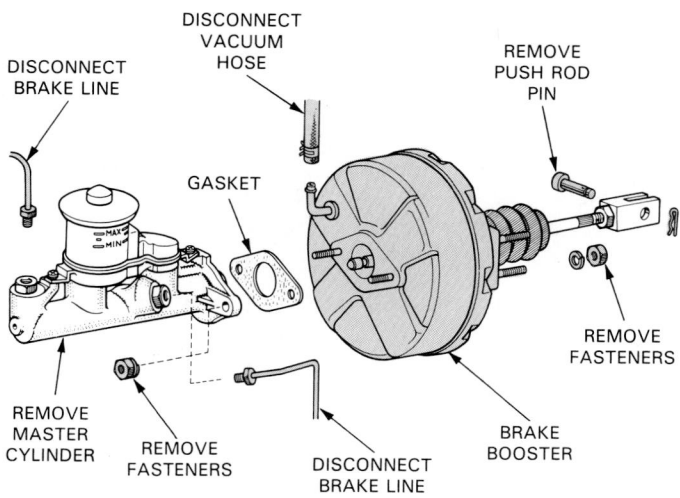

Fig. 69-6. These components may need to be removed for service of master cylinder and brake booster. (Toyota)

To **test the vacuum booster,** pump the brake pedal several times to remove any vacuum from the booster. Then, press and hold down lightly on the brake pedal as you start the engine. If the vacuum booster is functioning, the brake pedal will MOVE DOWNWARD SLIGHTLY as soon as the engine starts.

Many shops do NOT rebuild vacuum brake boosters. Instead, they install a new or factory rebuilt unit. Some boosters are sealed and cannot be disassembled.

Fig. 69-6 shows the parts that must be removed when replacing a vacuum booster.

Fig. 69-7 gives an exploded view of a vacuum booster. This particular unit is NOT sealed and can be rebuilt. A rebuild normally involves replacing the diaphragm, valves, and other plastic or rubber parts. Refer to a service manual for exact procedures on the particular booster.

HYDRAULIC BOOSTER SERVICE

A hydraulic type brake booster should be checked when inspecting a brake system. Check all of the hydraulic lines for signs of leakage. Tighten connections or replace any line that leaks.

If the booster is inoperative, check the fluid level in the power steering pump. A low fluid level can prevent hydro-boost operation. When the hydraulic booster is found to be faulty, it should be replaced. Most types are NOT repairable.

Refer to a shop manual when testing or servicing a hydraulic brake booster. System designs and repair procedures vary.

MASTER CYLINDER SERVICE

A *faulty master cylinder* usually leaks fluid past the rear piston or leaks internally. When leaking out the back, you should find brake fluid in the rear boot or on the firewall. When the leak is internal, the brake pedal will slowly sink to the floor. Inoperative valves in the master cylinder are also a reason for service.

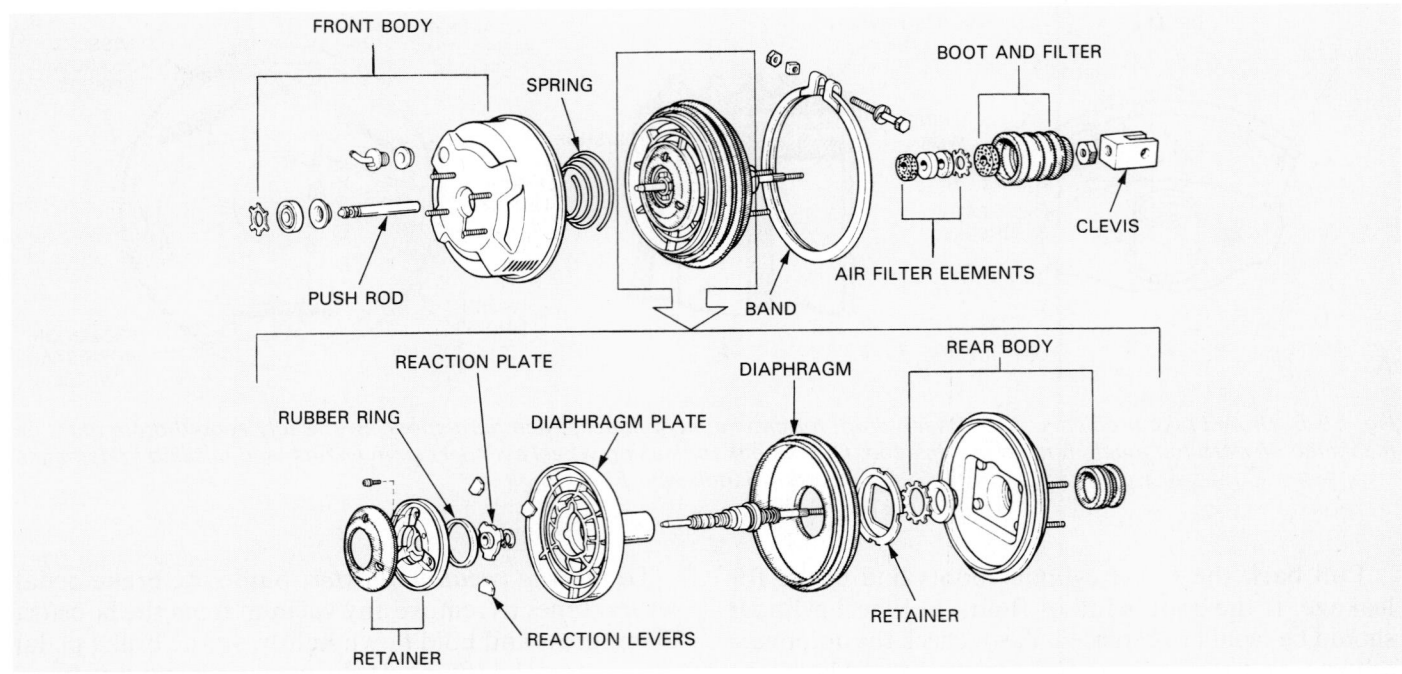

Fig. 69-7. Exploded view of modern vacuum brake booster. Most technicians replace unit when it is bad. (Toyota)

Master cylinder removal

To remove a master cylinder, disconnect the brake lines from the master cylinder using tubing wrenches. Then, unbolt the master cylinder from the brake booster or firewall. Sometimes, the push rod must be disconnected from the brake pedal assembly.

Master cylinder rebuild

Many shops simply replace a bad master cylinder with a new or factory rebuilt unit. A replacement cylinder may be cheaper than the cost of labor and parts for an in-shop rebuild. Further, the new or factory rebuilt master cylinder will have a remachined cylinder and a guarantee.

To rebuild a master cylinder, drain the fluid from the reservoir. Then, completely disassemble the unit, following the instructions in a service manual, Fig. 69-8. Basically, you must hone the cylinder and replace the piston cups and valves. Clean the parts in brake fluid or a recommended cleaner.

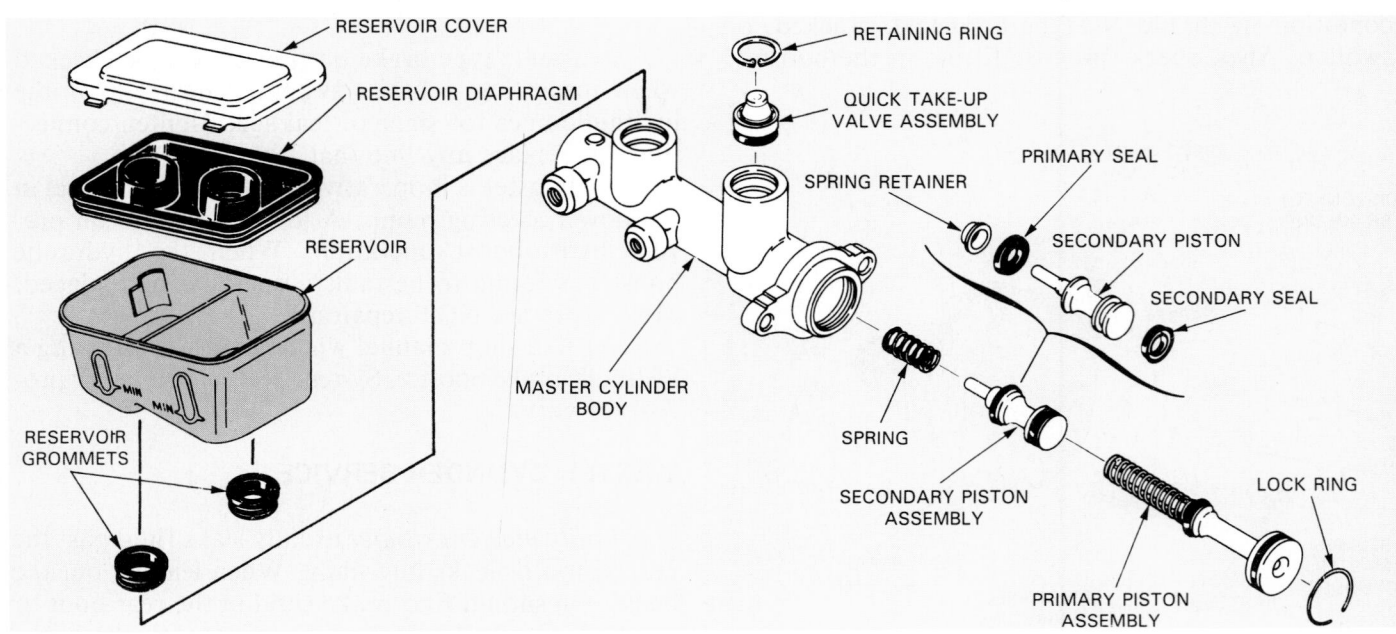

Fig. 69-8. Exploded view of dual master cylinder with removable reservoir. Note how parts fit into cylinder. (Oldsmobile)

WARNING! Do NOT clean the hydraulic parts of a brake system with conventional parts cleaners. They can destroy the special rubber cups in the brake system. Use only brake fluid or a manufacturer-suggested cleaner (denatured alcohol for example).

After cleaning, measure the piston-to-cylinder clearance. Use a telescoping gauge and an outside micrometer or a strip type feeler gauge. The cylinder must NOT be tapered or worn beyond specifications. Also, make sure the cylinder is not corroded, pitted, or scored.

REPLACE the master cylinder if the cylinder is not in perfect condition after honing.

Blow all parts dry with compressed air. Blow out ports and check that they are unobstructed. Lubricate the parts with brake fluid and assemble the unit using manufacturer's instructions. Fig. 69-8 shows an exploded view of a typical dual master cylinder.

Bench bleeding a master cylinder

A master cylinder is *bench bled* to remove air from inside the cylinder. This must be done before installing the unit on the car.

Mount the master cylinder in a vise, as shown in Fig. 69-9. Install short sections of brake line and bend them into each reservoir. Fill the reservoirs with approved brake fluid. Then, pump the piston in and out by hand until air bubbles no longer form in the fluid.

Installing a master cylinder

To install a master cylinder, replace the reservoir cover after bench bleeding. Bolt the master cylinder to the firewall or booster. Check the adjustment of the push rod if a means of adjustment is provided.

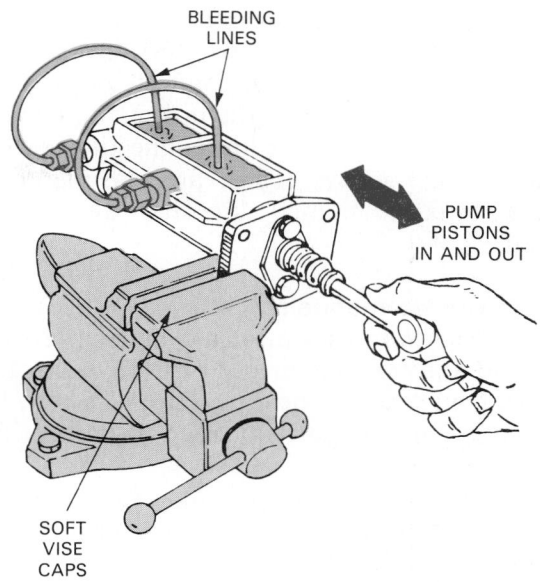

Fig. 69-9. Before installing new or rebuilt master cylinder, bench bleed unit. Fill with brake fluid. Install bleeding lines. Then pump piston in and out until no air bubbles are visible in reservoir (EIS)

Without crossthreading the fittings, screw the brake lines into the master cylinder. Lightly snug the fittings. Then, *bleed* (remove air from) the system.

Tighten the brake line fittings. Fill the reservoir with fluid and check brake pedal feel. Test drive the car.

BRAKE SYSTEM BLEEDING

The brake system must be free of air to function properly. Air in the system will compress, causing a

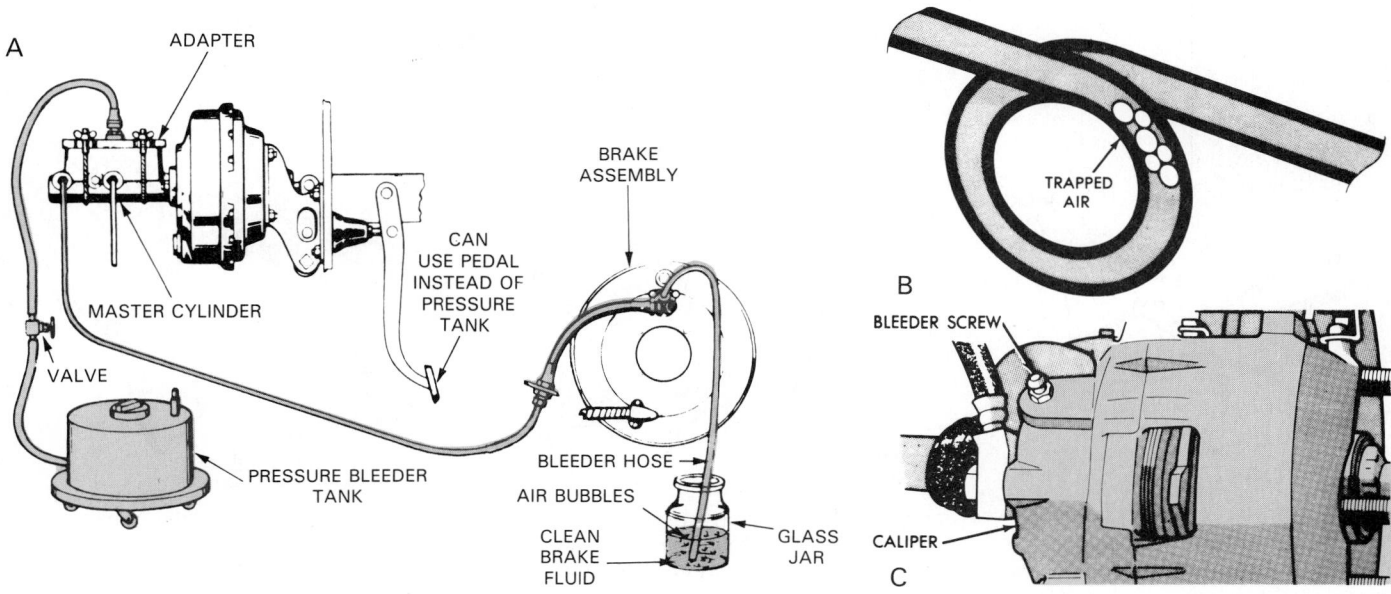

Fig. 69-10. Bleeding brake system involves forcing brake fluid through lines and wheel cylinders. This forces air out of system. Note how pressure bleeder is connected to master cylinder. With pressure in system, open each bleeder screw until air is purged out. A—Complete setup. B—Trapped air. C—Bleed screw location. (Bendix and Chrysler)

spongy brake pedal. Air can enter the system anytime a hydraulic component (brake line, hose, master cylinder, wheel cylinder) is disconnected or removed.

Brake system bleeding is the use of fluid pressure to force air out of the brake line connections or wheel cylinder bleeder screws. There are two methods of bleeding brakes: manual bleeding and pressure bleeding.

Bleeding brakes manually

Manual bleeding uses master cylinder pressure to force fluid and trapped air out of the system. Basically, attach one end of a hose to a bleeder screw. Place the other end in a jar partially filled with brake fluid. See Fig. 69-10.

Have another mechanic apply light foot pressure on the brake pedal. Open the bleeder screw or fitting while watching for air bubbles at the hose.

Close the bleeder screw or fitting and tell your helper to release the pedal. Repeat this procedure until no air bubbles come out the hose.

Perform this operation on the other wheel cylinders or at brake line connections, if needed.

Typically, start bleeding at the wheel cylinder farthest from the master cylinder. Work your way closer to the master cylinder. Some brake systems require special procedures when bleeding. When in doubt, refer to the vehicle's service manual.

Pressure bleeding a brake system

Pressure bleeding a brake system is done using air pressure trapped inside a metal air tank. Pressure bleeding is quick and easy because you do not need a helper to work the brake pedal.

As shown in Fig. 69-10, a special adapter is installed over the master cylinder reservoir. A pressure hose connects the master cylinder and pressure tank. A valve in the hose controls flow.

Note! Check manufacturer's instructions. You may need to push or pull out the metering valve stem before bleeding the brake system.

Pour enough brake fluid in the bleeder tank to reach the prescribed level. Charge the tank with 10 to 15 psi (69 to 103 kPa) of air pressure. Fill the master cylinder with brake fluid. Install the adapter and hose on the master cylinder. Open the valve in the hose. You are now ready to bleed the brakes.

Open each bleeder screw or fitting until all air bubbles are removed, Fig. 69-10. As soon as fluid becomes clear, close the screw or fitting. Repeat bleeding operation on the other wheel cylinders in proper order.

NOTE! A special pressure bleeding adapter is needed on master cylinders using a PLASTIC RESERVOIR. Use an adapter that seals over the ports in the bottom of the master cylinder. This will avoid possible reservoir damage. A special vacuum or suction bleeder, mounted at each wheel bleeder screw, will also work.

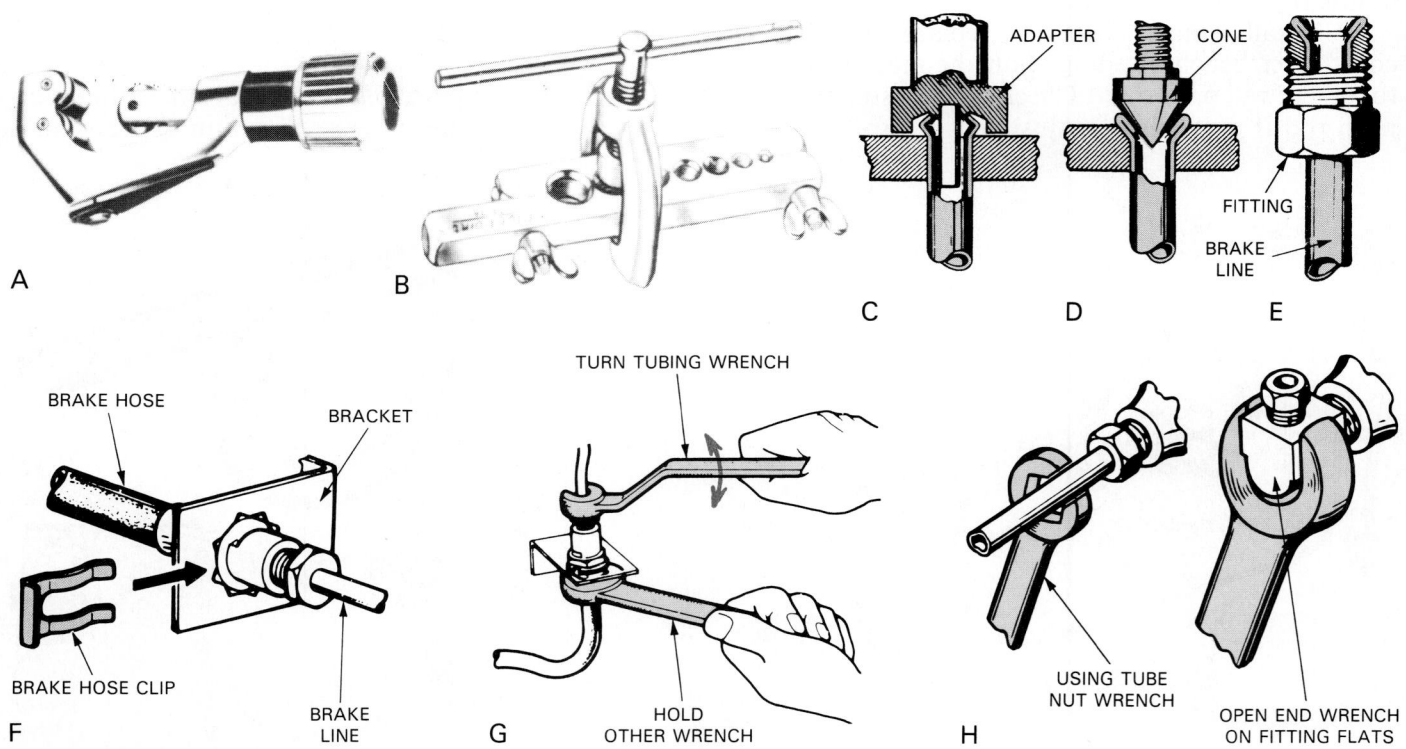

Fig. 69-11. Proper service of brake lines and hoses is critical to vehicle safety. A — Tubing cutter. B — Flaring tool for forming ends on tubing. C — Using adapter to fold tubing inward. D — Using cone on flaring bar to form double-lap. E — Fitting slid over double-lap flare. F — Clips are commonly used to secure end of brake hose. G — Two wrenches are normally needed to loosen or tighten this type tube-to-hose connection. H — Use tubing or line wrench on fitting nuts. An open end wrench will hold flats on some fittings. (Bendix and Snap-On)

Flushing a brake system

Brake system flushing is done by pressure bleeding ALL of the old fluid out of the system. Flushing is needed when the brake fluid is contaminated (filled with dirt, rust, corrosion, oil, or water). Bleed each wheel cylinder until there is new, clean fluid at each bleeder screw.

BRAKE LINE AND HOSE SERVICE

Brake lines and hoses can become damaged or deteriorated after prolonged service. When replacing a brake line, only use approved double-wall steel tubing. Brake lines normally use double-lap type flares.

Fig. 69-11 shows common service methods and tools used when servicing brake lines and hoses.

DISC BRAKE SERVICE

Complete *disc brake service* typically involves four major operations:
1. Replacing worn brake pads.
2. Rebuilding caliper assembly.
3. Turning (machining) brake discs.
4. Bleeding the system.

Depending upon the condition of these parts, the mechanic may need to do one or more of these operations. Service manual and shop policies vary. In any case, you must make sure the brake assembly is in sound operating condition.

Replacing brake pads

To replace worn brake pads on a floating caliper,

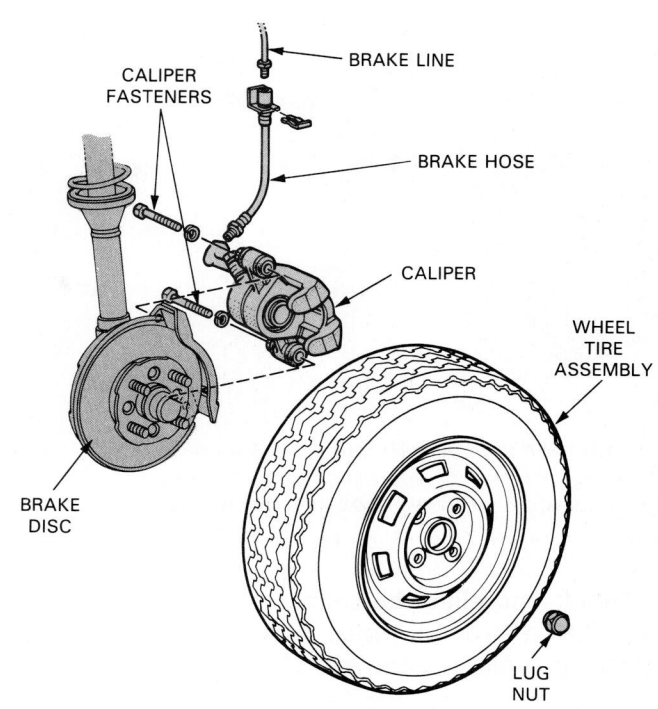

Fig. 69-12. On modern cars, two bolts commonly hold caliper on steering knuckle. Brake hose connects caliper to metal brake line. (Toyota)

first loosen the lug bolts. Place the vehicle on jack stands and remove the wheels and tires, Fig. 69-12.

Before caliper removal, use a large C-clamp to push the piston back into its cylinder. Then, the piston will be retracted and out of the way, allowing the new, thicker pads to fit into the caliper. Refer to Fig. 69-13A.

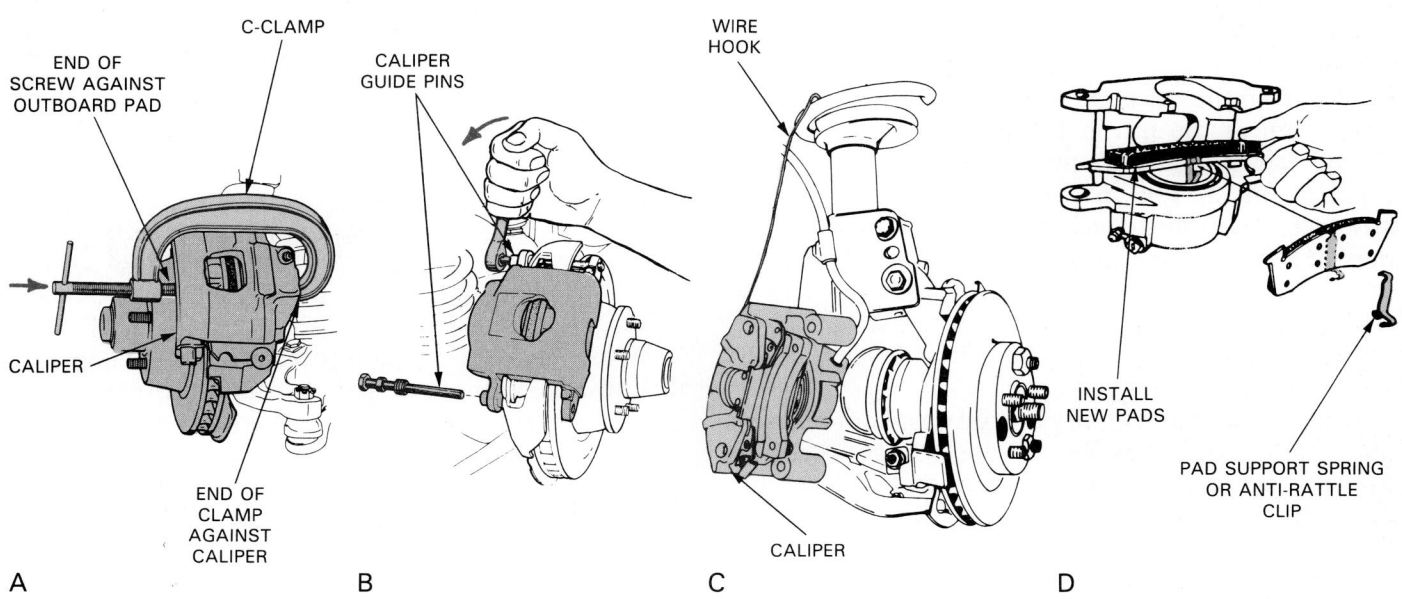

Fig. 69-13. Basic steps for floating caliper pad service. A — Use C-clamp or large screwdriver to force piston back into caliper. This will open caliper wide enough for new, thicker pad linings. B — Use six-point or Allen socket to unscrew bolts holding caliper. C — Lift caliper off knuckle and support it on piece of wire. Do not let unit hang by hose or hose could be damaged. D — Remove old pads. Note position of anti-rattle clips since they are reused if in good condition. New pads can be installed without caliper service if vehicle has low mileage and if boot and seals are in good condition. (Bendix, Buick, EIS)

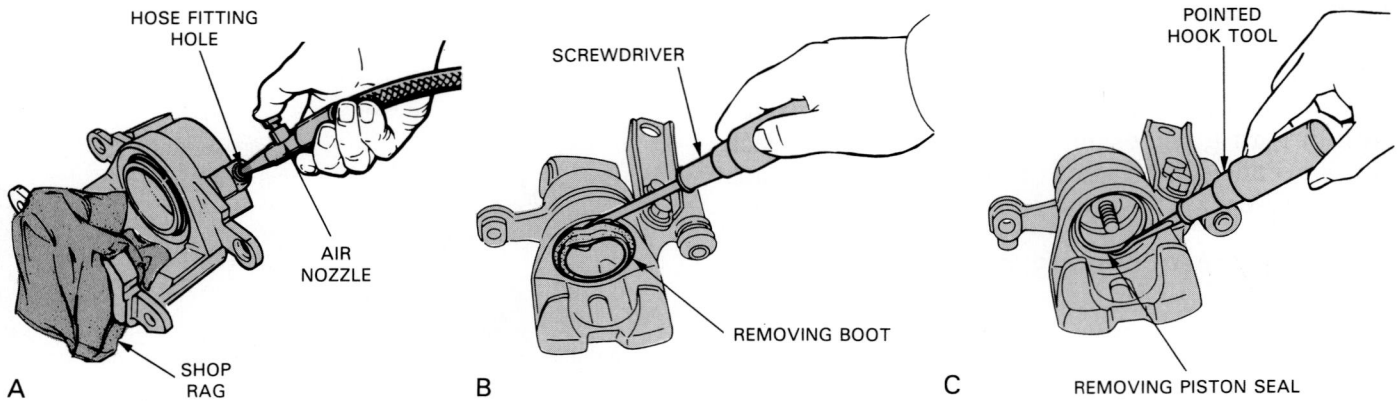

Fig. 69-14. Fundamental steps for caliper disassembly. A—Use air or brake system pressure to push piston out of caliper. Place thick rag or block of wood in caliper and keep your hands out of the way. B—Use screwdriver or similar tool to pry old boot out of caliper. C—Pointed hook type tool will make removal of old seal easy. It is positioned inside groove in cylinder. (Buick, Subaru)

Unbolt and slide the caliper off of the disc, Fig. 69-13B. To prevent brake hose damage, hang the caliper by a piece of mechanic's wire, if the caliper is not to be removed, Fig. 69-13C.

Remove old pads. Install anti-rattle clips on new pads. Fit pads back into caliper, Fig. 69-13D. Slide the caliper assembly over the disc. Assemble the caliper mounting hardware in reverse order of disassembly. Make sure all bolts are torqued properly. Install wheels and tighten wheel lug nuts to specs. Repeat these operations on the other disc brake assemblies as needed.

NOTE! It is acceptable to service just the front or just the rear brakes. However, NEVER service only the right or left brake assemblies. This could cause dangerous brake pull.

Rebuilding a caliper assembly

When a caliper piston is frozen, leaking, or has extremely high mileage, it must be rebuilt. Remove the caliper from the car and take it to a clean work area.

To remove the piston from the caliper, use just enough air pressure to push the piston out of its cylinder, as in Fig. 69-14A. Some auto makers, however, recommend using brake system hydraulic pressure to force the pistons out of the calipers.

DANGER! Keep your fingers out of the way when using compressed air to remove caliper pistons. A stuck piston could fly out with tremendous force. Serious hand injuries could result.

After piston removal, pry the old dust boot and seal out of the caliper, Fig. 69-14B and 69-14C. Keep all of the parts organized on your workbench. Do not mix up right- and left-hand side or front and rear parts. See Fig. 69-15.

Check caliper cylinder wall for wear, scoring, or pitting. Light surface imperfections can usually be cleaned up with a cylinder hone. Fig. 69-16A shows a technician honing a caliper cylinder. When honing, use brake fluid to lubricate the hone. If excessive honing is needed, replace the caliper.

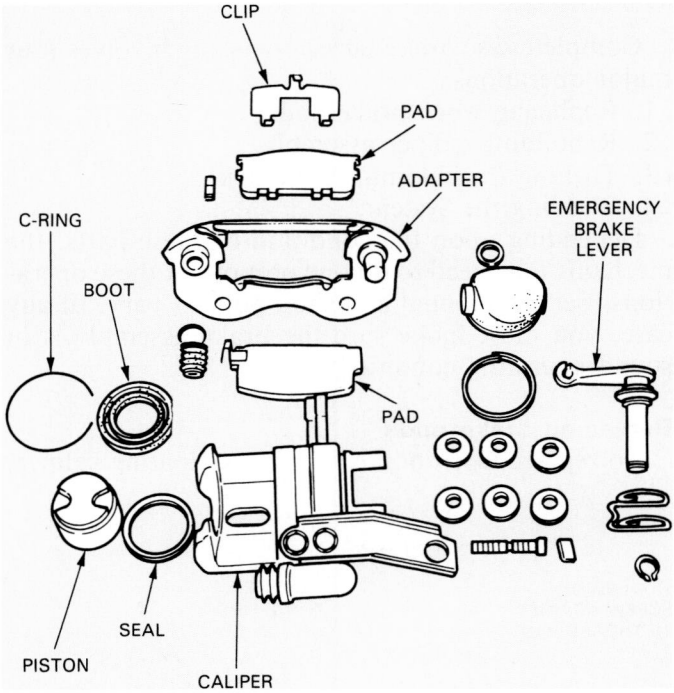

Fig. 69-15. When servicing calipers, keep all parts organized on workbench. Do not mix right and left side parts. Inspect all parts closely for signs of wear or damage. (Subaru)

Also, check the caliper piston for wear or damage. Install a new piston if you find any problems. The piston and the cylinder are very critical and must be in perfect condition.

Clean all of the parts with an approved cleaner. Wipe the parts clean with a clean shop rag. Then coat them with brake fluid.

Assemble the caliper in reverse order of disassembly. Typically, fit the new seal in the cylinder bore groove. Work it in with your fingers, Fig. 69-16B. Then, install the new boot in its groove. Coat the piston with more brake fluid. Spread the boot with your fingers and slide the piston into the cylinder, Fig. 69-16C.

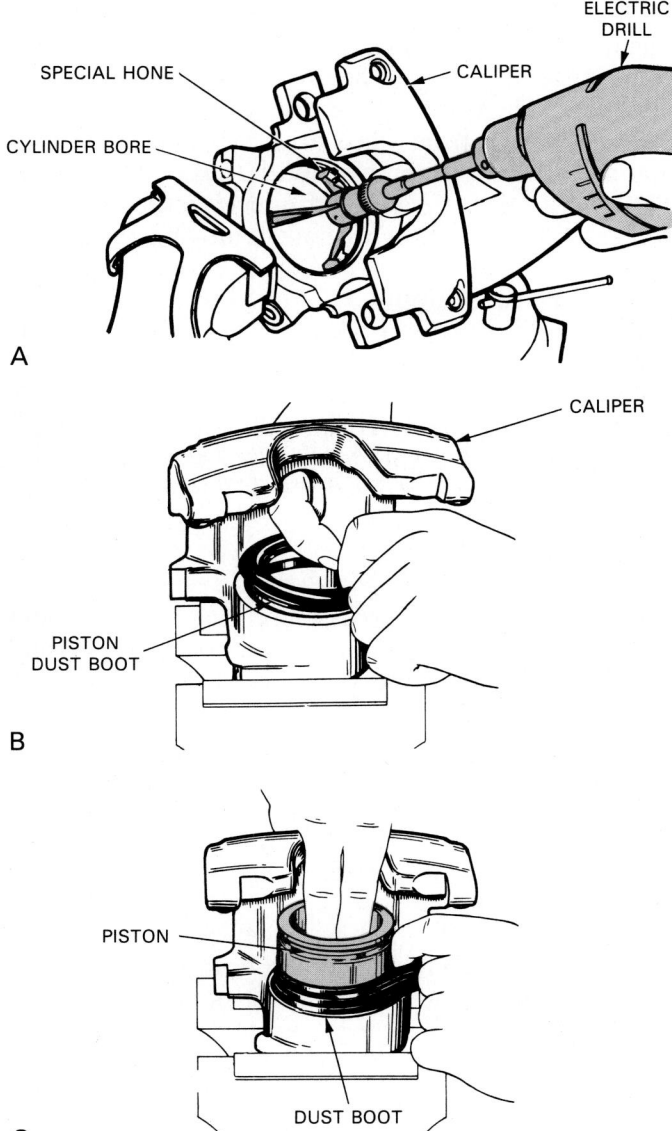

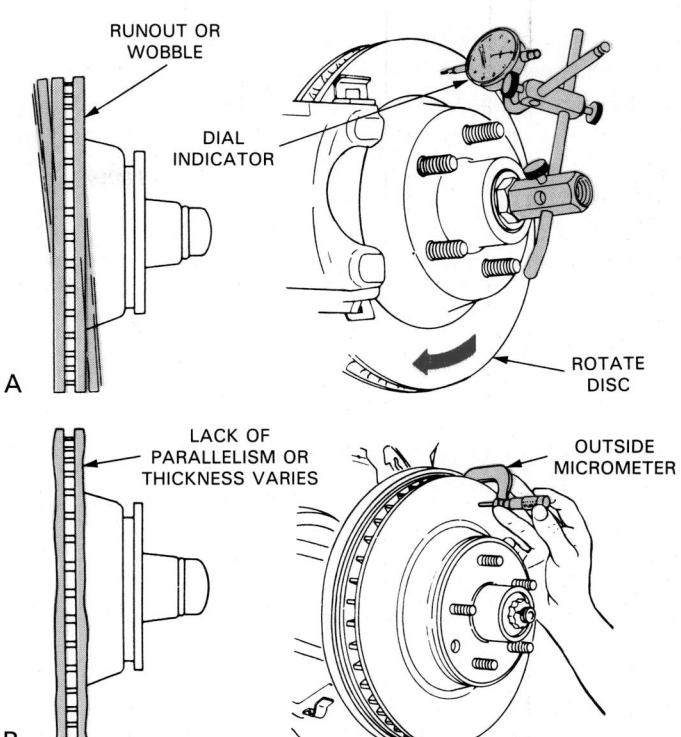

Fig. 69-17. Checking for rotor runout and thickness variations. A — Mount a dial indicator as shown to measure disc runout or wobble. Rotate disc by hand and read indicator. If more than specs, rotor should be turned or replaced. B — An outside micrometer will detect any thickness variations. If readings are not same or within specs at different locations around disc, turn or replace it. (EIS)

Fig. 69-16. Honing and reassembling caliper. A — Electric drill is used to spin special hone inside caliper cylinder. This will remove minor surface flaws. B — Fit new seal and boot into position. Seal must be down in its groove. Sometimes, it is easier to install boot after piston. C — Slide piston into cylinder squarely. Make sure seal does not come out of its groove. Fit boot into groove on outside of piston. (Chrysler and Bendix)

BRAKE DISC (ROTOR) SERVICE

When servicing a brake system, it is important to check the condition of the brake disc. Auto makers provide specifications for minimum disc thickness and maximum disc runout (wobble). Also, the disc must NOT be scored, cracked, or heat checked.

Measuring disc runout

Brake disc runout is the amount of side-to-side movement measured near the outer friction surface of the rotor. Shown in Fig. 69-17A, a dial indicator is used to measure disc runout.

Compare your indicator reading to factory specs. Typically, disc runout should not exceed .004 in. (0.10 mm). If runout is beyond specs, turn (machine) the rotor on a brake lathe to true its friction surface.

Measuring disc thickness

Brake disc thickness is measured across the two friction surfaces in several locations. Variation in disc thickness indicates wear.

To measure disc thickness, use an outside micrometer, as in Fig. 69-17B. Measure in several places. Compare your measurements to specifications.

Minimum disc thickness will sometimes be printed on the side of the disc. If not, refer to a manual or brake spec chart. If disc thickness is under specs, replace the disc. A thin disc cannot dissipate heat properly and may warp or fail in service.

Resurfacing a brake disc

Brake disc resurfacing involves machining the friction surfaces on a brake lathe, Fig. 69-18. Disc resurfacing is needed to correct runout, thickness variation, or scoring.

When a disc is in good condition, most manufacturers do NOT recommend disc resurfacing. Only machine a disc when it is absolutely necessary.

To resurface a brake disc, mount the disc on the brake lathe. See Fig. 69-19. Use the appropriate spacers and cones to position the disc on the machine's arbor. Follow the directions provided with the brake lathe. Wrap a spring or rubber damper around the disc to prevent vibration, Fig. 69-20.

While wearing eye protection, adjust the cutting tools until they contact the friction surface on the disc. Then, with the machine feeds and controls set properly, machine smooth surfaces on the disc.

DANGER! Do not attempt to operate a brake lathe without first obtaining proper training. The machine could be damaged or you could be injured by incorrect operating procedures.

Only machine off enough metal to true the disc. Then, without touching the machined surfaces with your fingers, remove the disc. Double-check disc thickness. Then, install the disc on the vehicle.

Some foreign, front-wheel drive cars have brake discs that are difficult to remove. With these cars, an ON-THE-CAR DISC LATHE (grinder) is a time saver. It will resurface the discs without removing them.

Disc brake reassembly

Reassemble the disc brake in the opposite order of disassembly. After installing the brake disc, fit the caliper assembly into place. Make sure the new pads are properly installed. Torque all fasteners to specs.

Fig. 69-21 is an exploded view of a complete disc brake assembly.

DRUM BRAKE SERVICE

Although specific procedures vary, you should understand the most important methods for servicing a drum brake. Brake service is needed anytime your diagnosis finds faulty brake components. A leaking wheel cylinder, worn or contaminated linings, scored drum, or other troubles require immediate repairs.

Complete *drum brake service* typically involves:
1. Removing parts from backing plate.
2. Cleaning and inspecting parts.
3. Replacing brake shoes.
4. Replacing or rebuilding wheel cylinders.
5. Turning (resurfacing) brake drums.
6. Lubricating and reassembling brake parts.
7. Preadjusting, bleeding, and testing brakes.

Fig. 69-22 shows some special brake service tools.

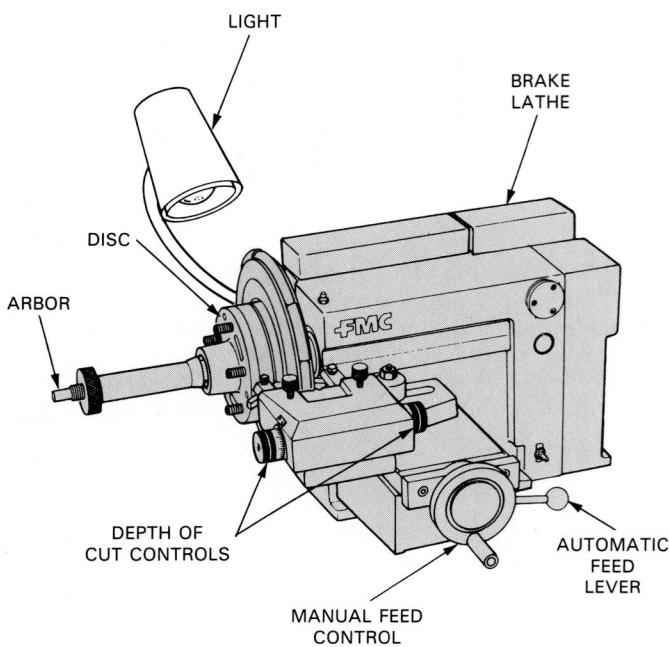

Fig. 69-18. Disc or rotor being turned on brake lathe. Note controls. (FMC)

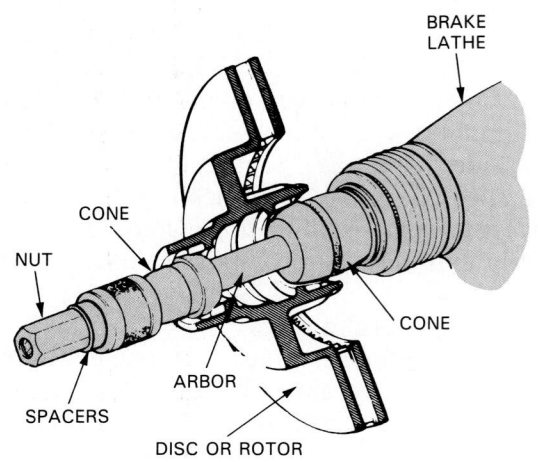

Fig. 69-19. Special cones are used to mount rotor on brake lathe. Cones must contact bearing races. Spacers and nut then lock assembly on arbor. (EIS)

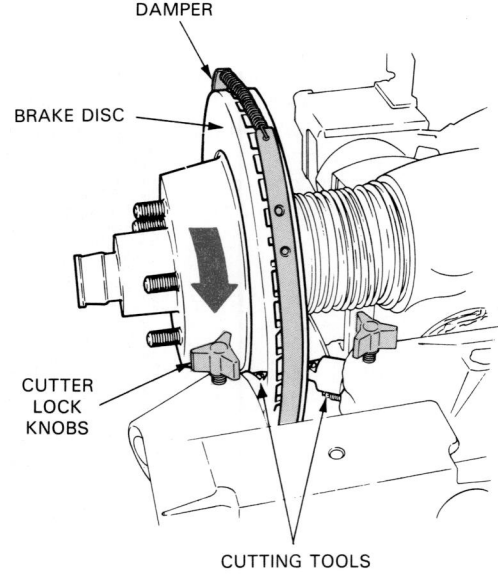

Fig. 69-20. After installing damper to prevent vibration, small cutters are fed into rotor a prescribed depth. Then, controls are set so cutters advance over rotor surface automatically. (Chrysler)

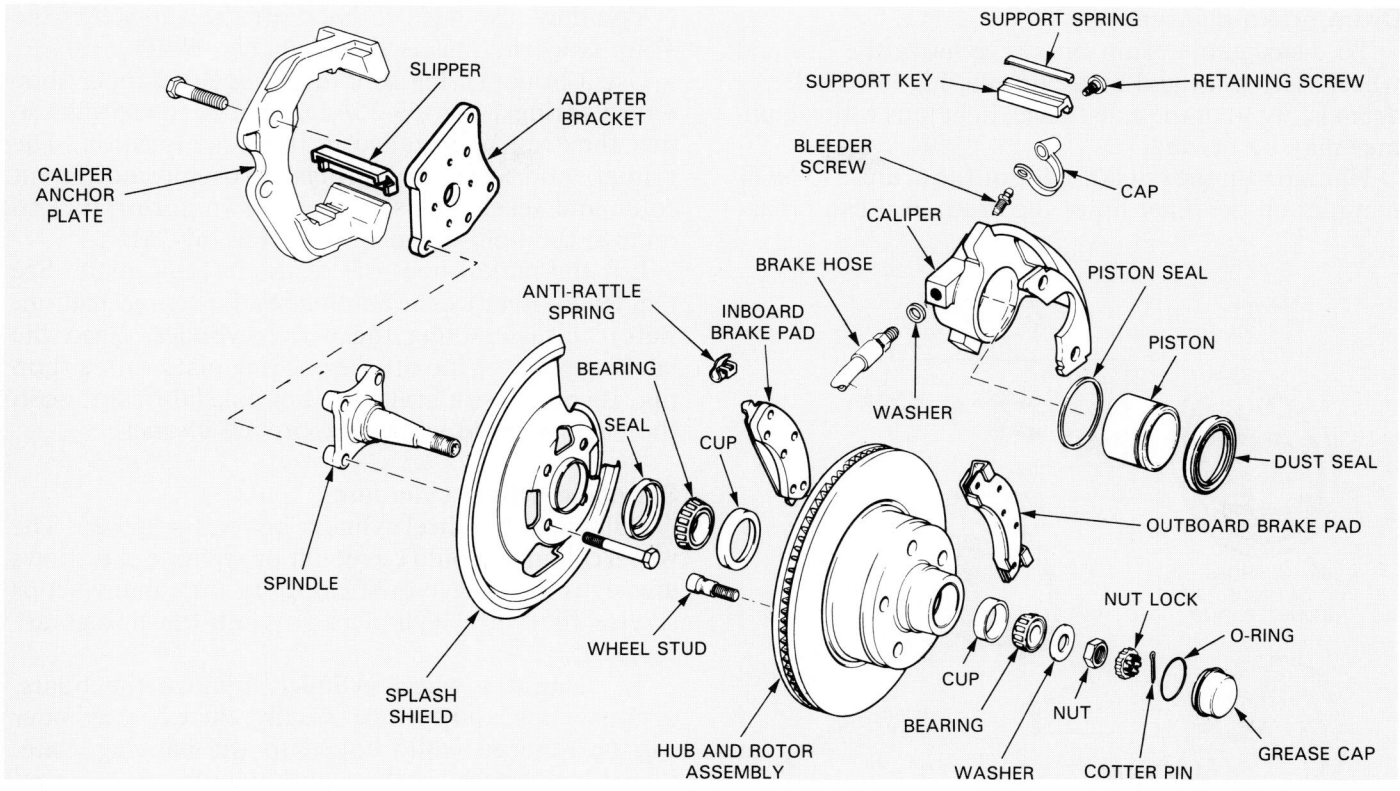

Fig. 69-21. Disassembled view of disc brake. Study how parts fit together. (Chrysler Corp.)

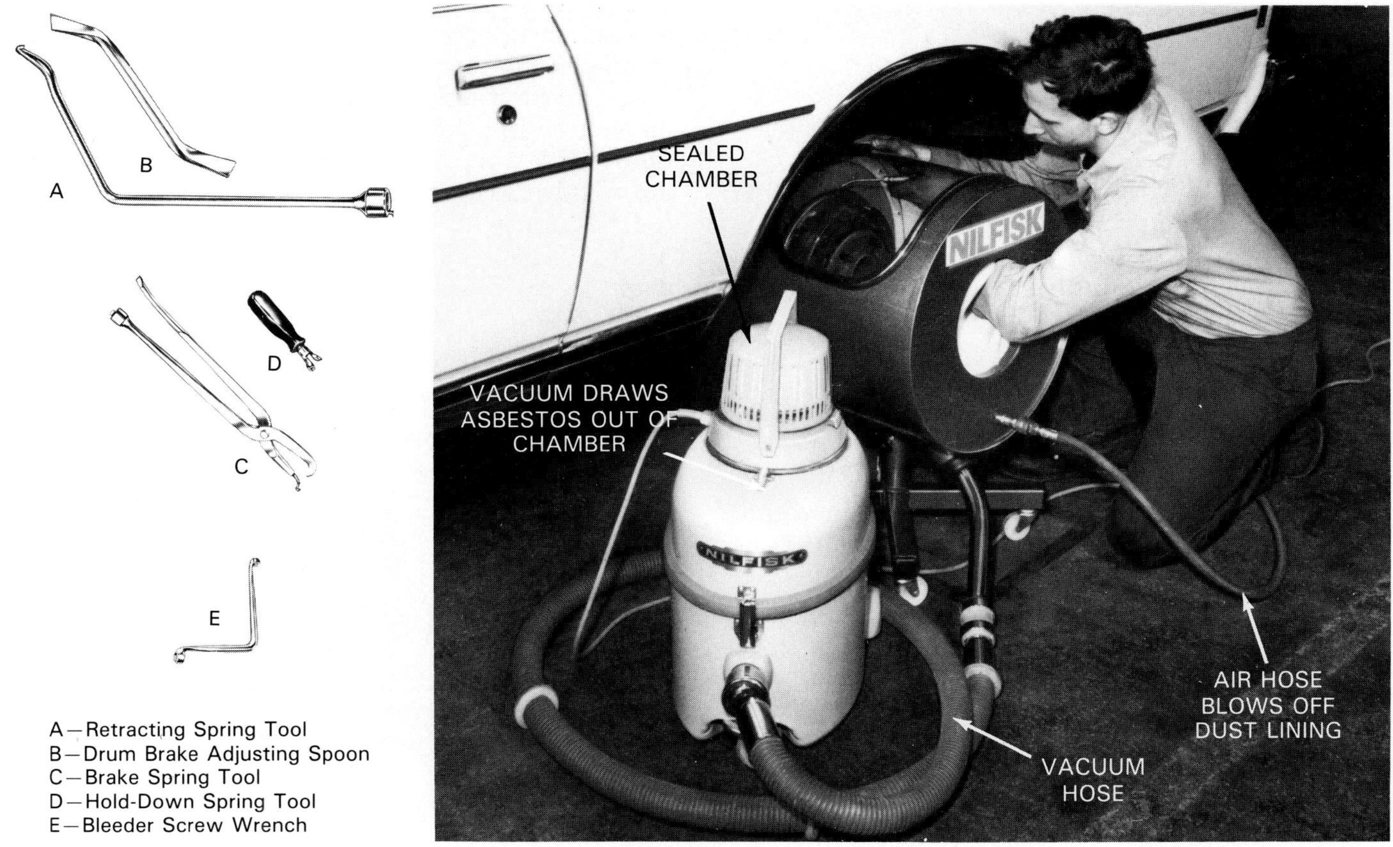

A—Retracting Spring Tool
B—Drum Brake Adjusting Spoon
C—Brake Spring Tool
D—Hold-Down Spring Tool
E—Bleeder Screw Wrench

SEALED CHAMBER

VACUUM DRAWS ASBESTOS OUT OF CHAMBER

AIR HOSE BLOWS OFF DUST LINING

VACUUM HOSE

Fig. 69-22. Special tools and equipment for servicing drum brakes. Small brake tools make work fast and easy. Brake vacuum, for cleaning off brakes, helps prevent you from breathing brake lining dust which can contain asbestos—a cancer causing agent. (Snap-On and Nilfisk)

Drum brake disassembly

To disassemble drum brakes, remove the tire and wheel assemblies and brake drums, Fig. 69-23. If the drum is rusted to the axle flange, light taps with a hammer may be needed.

Hammer on the outside edge of the drum. Do NOT hammer on the inner lip of the drum or it can break.

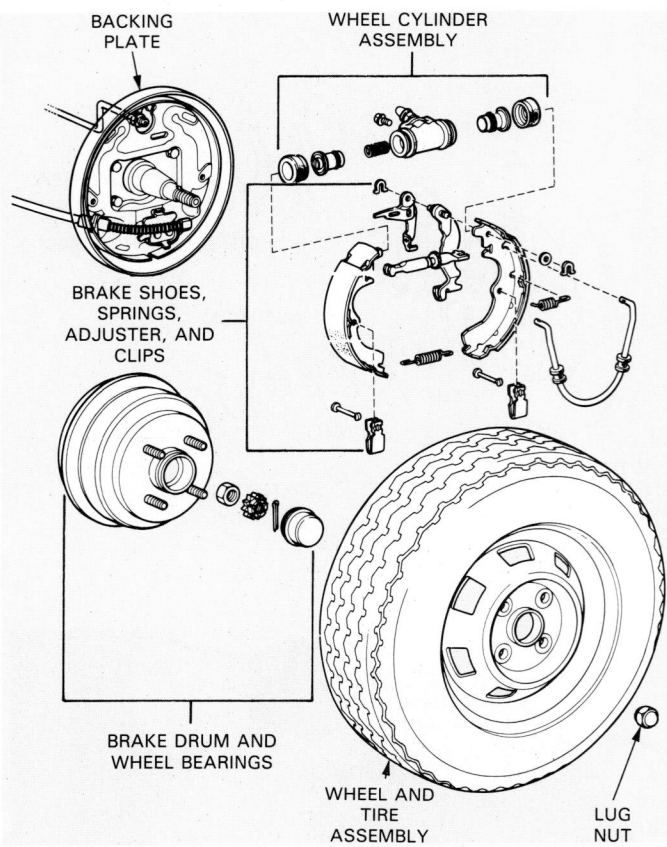

Fig. 69-23. Disassembled view of drum brakes. Note part relationships. (Toyota)

You may also need to back off the adjuster if the drum is worn. This is shown in Fig. 69-24.

Use a brake spring tool to remove the upper shoe return springs, Fig. 69-25A. Organize the springs so that they can be installed in the same location. The primary and secondary springs are usually a different color and tension. Use a hold-down spring tool to remove the hold-down springs, Fig. 69-25B.

Lift the brake shoes off of the backing plate. See Fig. 69-26. Remove the automatic adjuster mechanism. Before disassembling the wheel cylinder, clean the backing plate. Wipe off the backing plate with a shop rag. If coated with brake fluid or axle lubricant, wash the backing plate with an approved cleaner.

Servicing wheel cylinders

Pull back the wheel cylinder boots, Fig. 69-26. The wheel cylinder should be rebuilt or replaced if it shows any signs of leakage or sticking. In fact, many shops service the wheel cylinders anytime the linings are replaced.

To rebuild a wheel cylinder, remove the boots, pistons, cups, and spring. Usually, the wheel cylinder can be serviced while bolted to the backing plate. Sometimes however, the wheel cylinder must be removed before disassembly.

A *wheel cylinder rebuild* normally involves honing the cylinder and replacing the rubber cups and boots, Fig. 69-26. It is very important that the inside of the cylinder be in good condition. Any sign of scratches, scoring, or pitting requires cylinder replacement.

To hone a wheel cylinder, mount the small hone in an electric drill. Insert the hone in the cylinder. Turn on the drill while moving the hone back and forth in the cylinder. Keep the hone lubricated with brake fluid.

CAUTION! When honing a wheel cylinder, do not let the hone pull out of the cylinder. The spinning hone could fly apart. Wear eye protection!

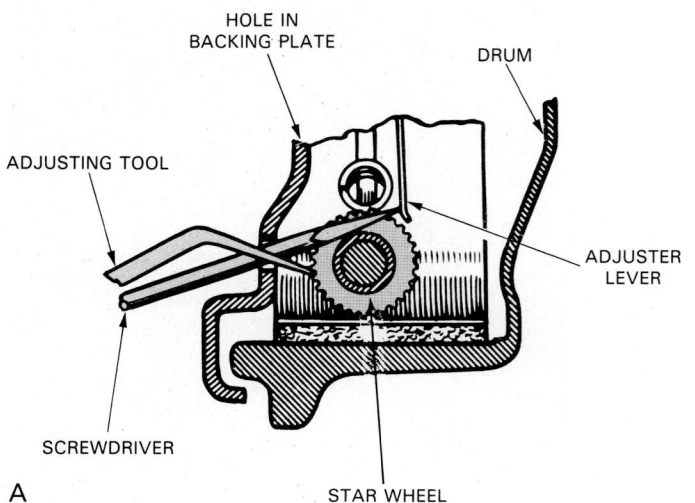

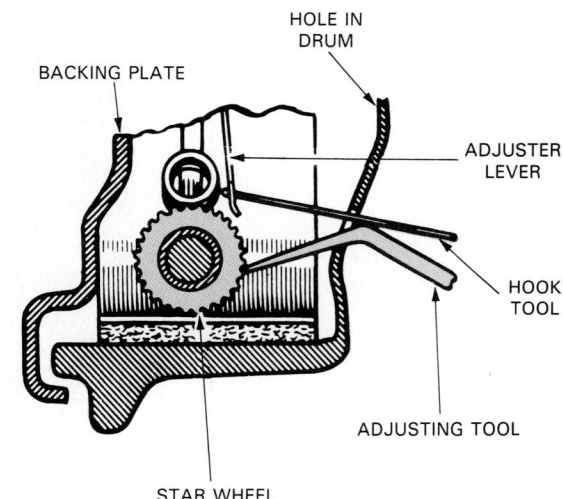

Fig. 69-24. Backing off star wheel to allow drum removal. A — With hole in backing plate, hold lever and turn star wheel as shown. B — Turning star wheel when access hole is in drum. (Bendix)

Fig. 69-25. A — Brake retracting spring tool can be turned to pry springs off anchor pin. B — Hold-down spring tools can be pushed in and turned to free spring from pin. Use finger to hold pin from rear of backing plate. (Bendix and Mopar)

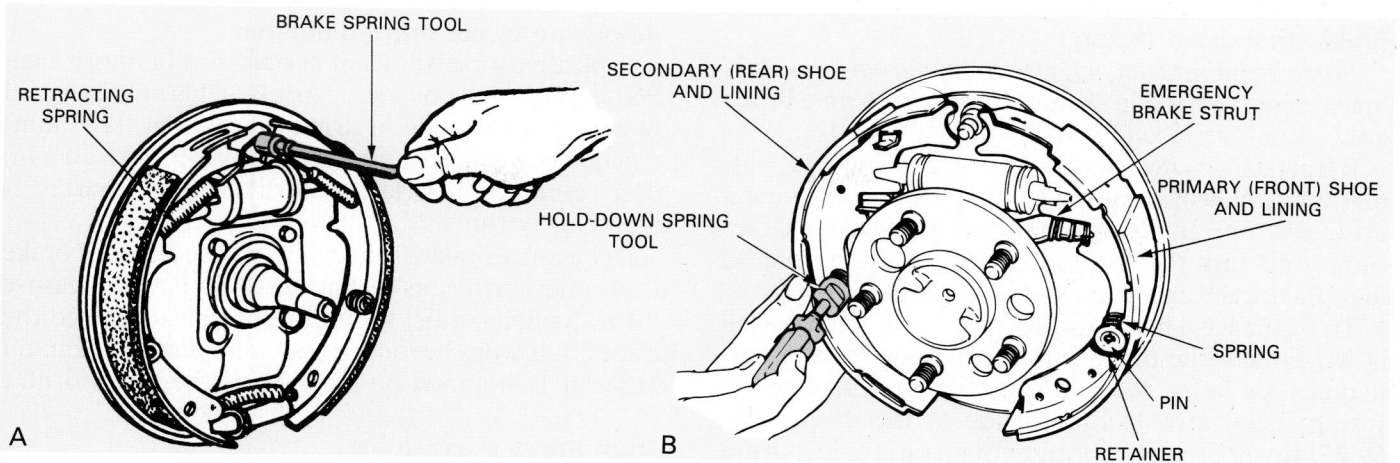

After honing, clean the wheel cylinder thoroughly with clean shop rags and brake fluid or an approved cleaning solvent. Make sure the cylinder is CLEAN and in perfect condition before reassembly. The slightest bit of grit or roughness could cause cup leakage.

Make sure the new wheel cylinder cups are the same size as the old ones. *Cup size* is normally printed on the face of the cup.

Coat the parts with brake fluid and fit them into the cylinder, Fig. 69-26.

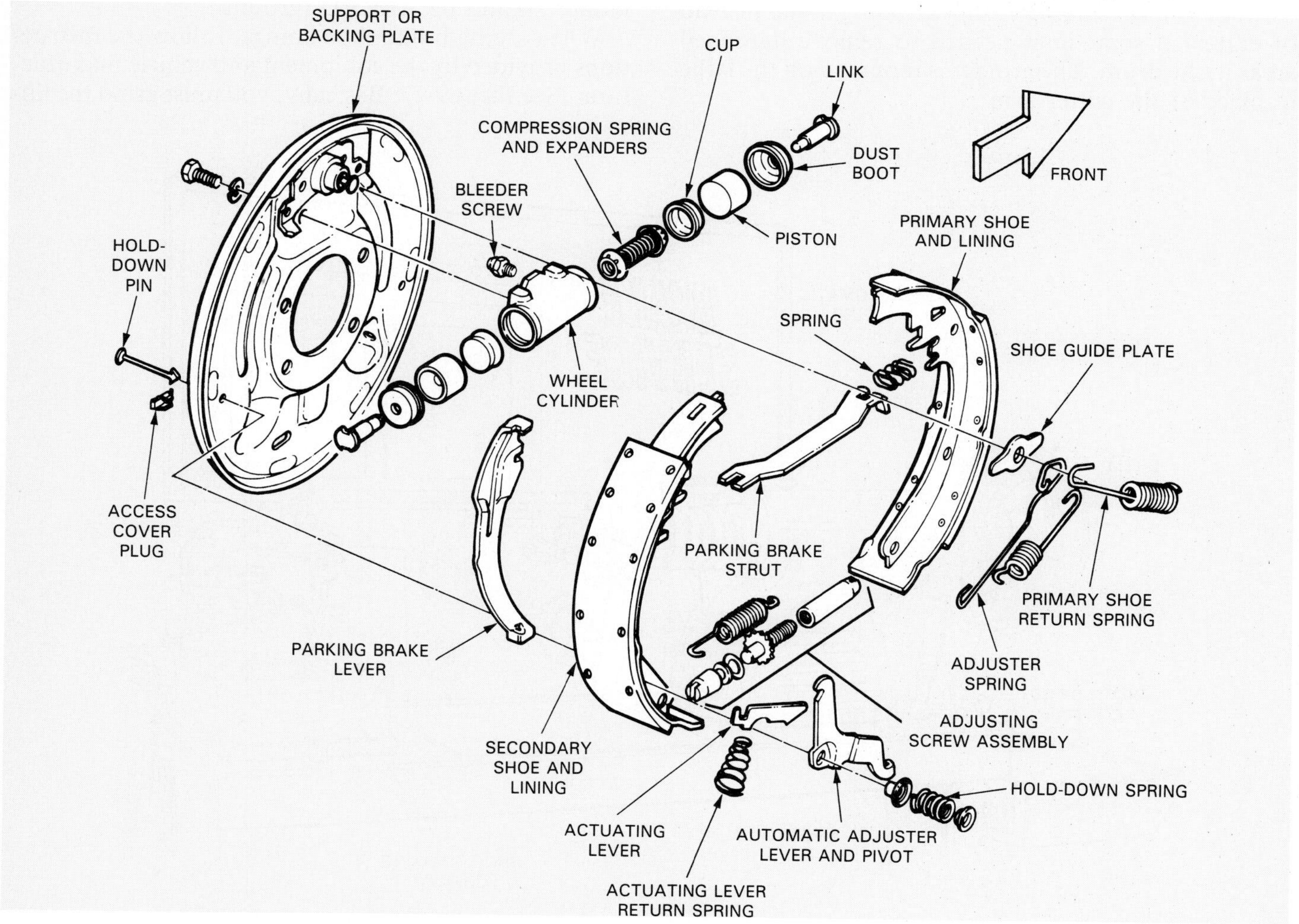

Fig. 69-26. Disassembled view of typical drum brake unit. Study part names and locations. (Chrysler Corp.)

Brake drum resurfacing

Brake drum resurfacing, also called *turning*, involves machining the friction surface of the drum on a brake lathe. Look at Fig. 69-27.

Resurfacing is needed when the drum is scored, out-of-round, or worn unevenly. Some shops machine a drum anytime the brake linings are replaced. Other shops only turn the drum when needed. Refer to auto manufacturer suggestions when in doubt.

To resurface a brake drum, mount the drum on the lathe. Follow the operating instructions for the particular type lathe. Wrap a silencing band (rubber or spring strap) around the outside of the drum, Fig. 69-27. It will prevent vibration that could affect drum surface smoothness. Wearing eye protection, feed the cutting tool against the inner surface of the drum. Adjust the depth of cut to lathe specs and activate the automatic feed.

When resurfacing a drum, machine as little material off as possible. Resurfacing thins the metal around the friction surface. As a result, the drum is more prone to overheating and warping.

Machine the right- and left-hand drums to the SAME DIAMETER. This will help assure even, straight-line braking.

Brake drum grinding (using grinding stone instead of cutter) is sometimes needed to remove hardened areas in the drum. The grinder is mounted on the lathe in place of the cutter arm.

Measuring brake drum diameter

Typically, a brake drum should not be more than .060 in. (1.5 mm) oversize. Look at Fig. 69-28A and 69-28B. For example, a drum that is 9 in. (229 mm) in diameter when new, must not be over 9.060 (230 mm) after resurfacing. If larger in diameter, the drum is dangerously thin.

To measure brake drum diameter, use a special brake drum micrometer, as in Fig. 69-28C. It will measure drum diameter quickly and accurately. Replace the drum if it is worn beyond specs. Sometimes, maximum diameter is stamped on the side of the brake drum.

Drum brake reassembly

To reassemble drum brakes, lubricate the small pads or bumps on the backing plate, Fig. 69-29. This will keep the shoes from squeaking. Avoid using too much lubricant or the linings could become contaminated and ruined. Also, lubricate the threads on the star wheel screw if there is one.

Before installing the new shoes, check their fit inside the brake drum. There should be a small clearance between the ends of the lining and the drums. The shoes should rock slightly when moved in the drum. If the center of the linings are not touching the drum, the linings should be ARCED (ground).

When arcing brake shoe linings, follow the instructions provided by the equipment and vehicle manufacturer. See Fig. 69-27. Basically, you must grind the lin-

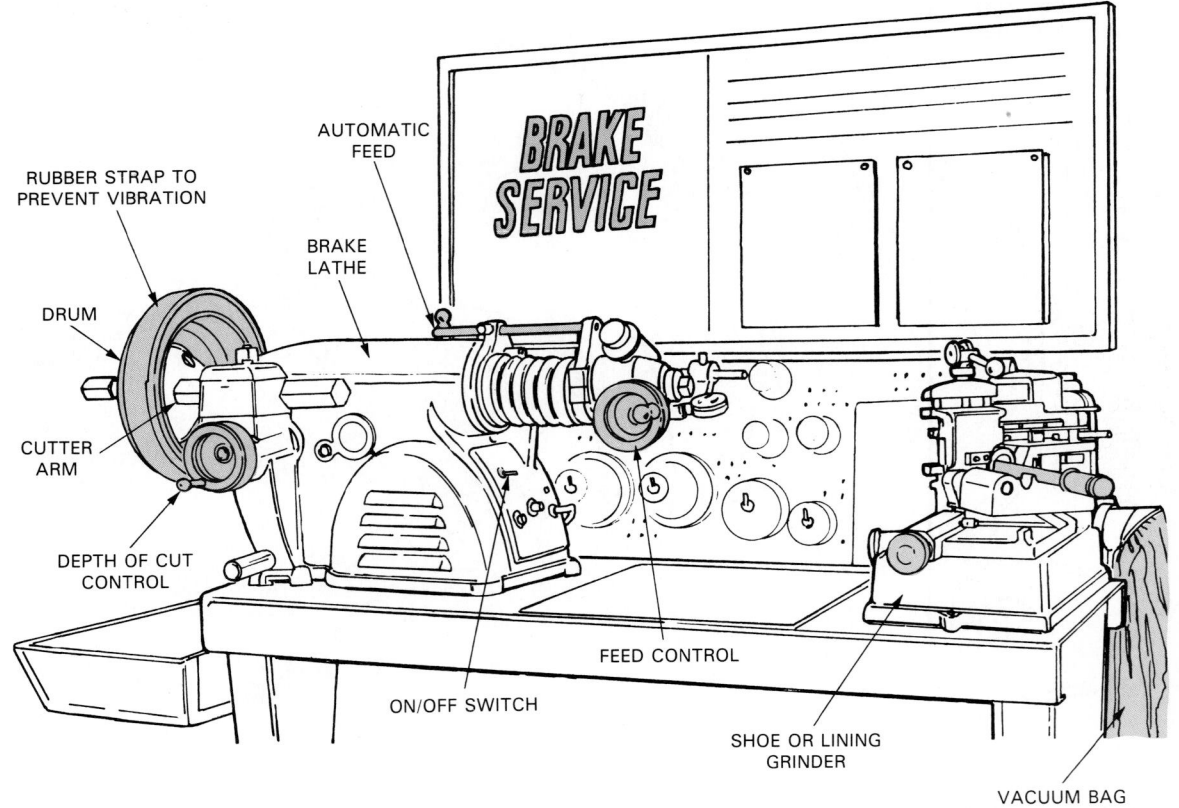

Fig. 69-27. Note parts and how drum is mounted on brake lathe. Shoe grinder is also shown. (EIS)

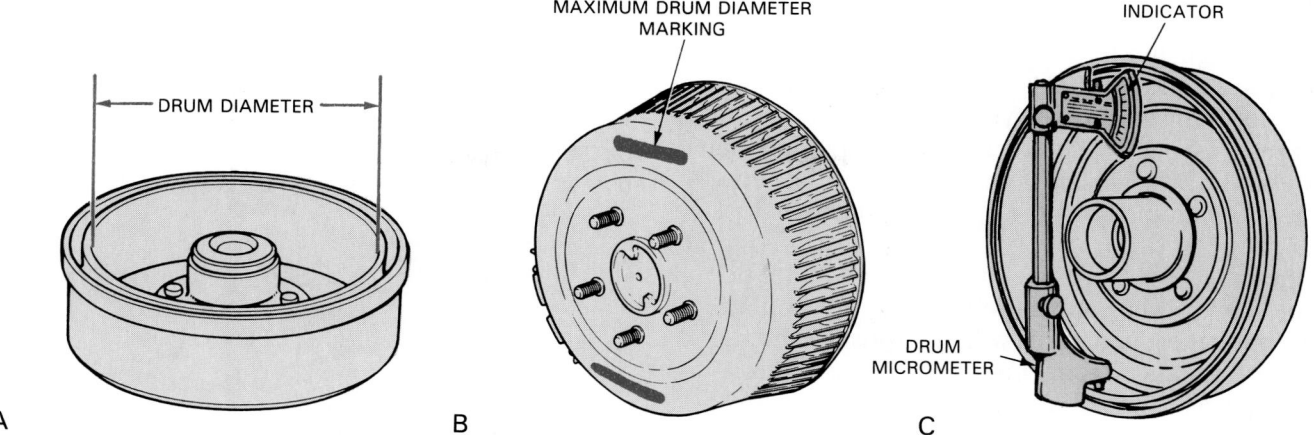

Fig. 69-28. Checking brake drum wear. A — Drum diameter is distance across inside friction surface. B — Drum diameter is normally stamped on outside of drum. Oversize limits may also be given. C — Special drum micrometer will quickly and accurately measure drum diameter and wear. Generally, drums should not be more than .060 in. (1.5 mm) oversize. (Toyota, Chrysler, FMC)

ing so that they are 0.35 in. or 0.89 mm smaller in diameter than the drum. Without clearance, the linings could chatter and vibrate when returned to service.

CAUTION! Make sure the vacuum system on the lining grinder is working properly. Remember! Asbestos brake lining dust can cause CANCER.

Install the new shoes and the adjuster mechanism on the backing plate. Make sure all of the parts are positioned correctly, Fig. 69-30. Ask yourself these kinds of questions:

1. Are the wheel cylinders in perfect condition and assembled properly?
2. Did I lubricate the backing plate and star wheel?

3. Is the primary (smaller) lining facing the front of the vehicle and the secondary (larger) lining facing the rear?
4. Are the shoes centered on the backing plate and contacting the anchor correctly?
5. Are all springs installed properly?
6. Does the automatic adjuster work?
7. Are the lining surfaces perfectly clean (sand if needed)?
8. Do I need to bleed the brakes?

Your service manual will have assembly illustrations for the particular brake design being serviced. Use them to help position the parts on the backing plate correctly.

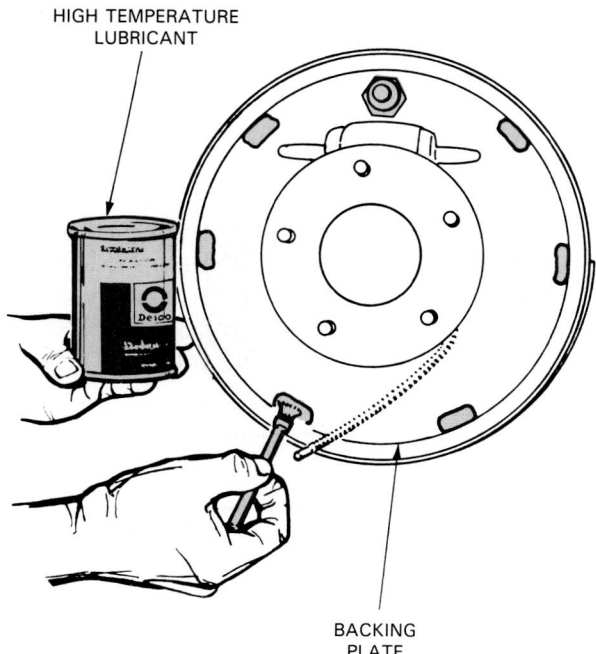

Fig. 69-29. Wipe high temperature grease on raised pads on backing plate and on star wheel threads. (Bendix)

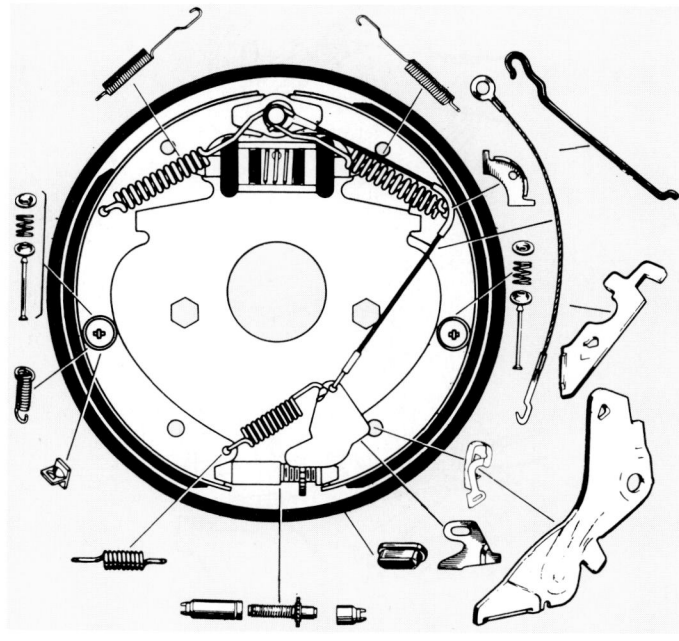

Fig. 69-30. When assembling brakes, make sure every part is in proper location. This illustration shows locations for one type unit.

Preadjusting drum brakes

Even though modern brakes have automatic adjusters, you should preadjust the brake shoes. This will assure proper initial brake system operation.

To preadjust the brake shoes, fit a brake adjusting gauge into the brake drum, Fig. 69-31A. Set the gauge for the inside diameter of the drum. Tighten the lock on the gauge.

Fit the gauge over the brake shoes, Fig. 69-31B. Then turn the star wheel or move the adjuster arm until the linings touch the gauge. This will preadjust the linings the correct distance from the inside of the drum.

Another way to preadjust drum brakes involves use of a brake spoon (star wheel tool) to turn the adjuster or star wheel. Turn the star wheel until the brake drums drag lightly when turned by hand.

PARKING BRAKE ADJUSTMENT

To adjust the parking brake, you must normally tighten an adjustment nut on the cable mechanism. Refer to Fig. 69-32.

During adjustment, release the parking brake lever or pedal. Lubricate cables and linkages. To prevent overadjustment, engage the parking brake one notch. Then, turn the cable adjuster to remove excess slack. Operate the emergency brake and make sure the brakes are not dragging when released.

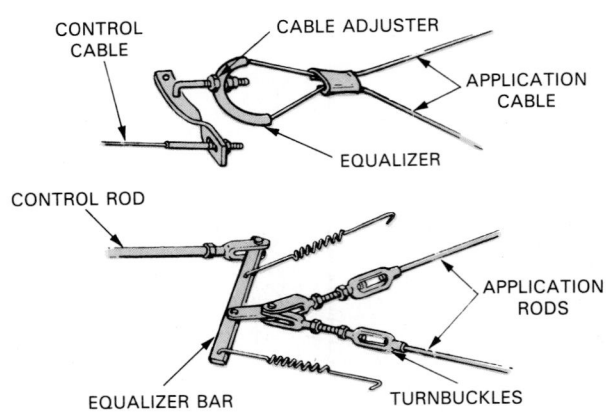

Fig. 69-32. Emergency or parking brake adjustment. Simply turn threaded fastener or turnbuckle until excess slack is out of cable. Do not overtighten or brakes can drag and overheat. (FMC)

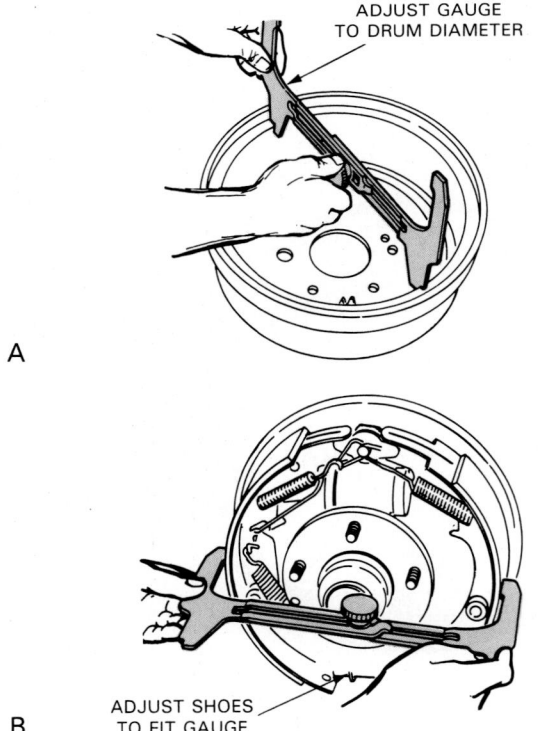

Fig. 69-31. Drum brake preadjustment. A — Fit gauge into brake drum and adjust out against drum. Lock unit into position. B — Fit gauge around outside of brake shoes. Adjust shoes outward until they just touch gauge. (Pontiac)

KNOW THESE TERMS

Brake pedal vibration, Grabbing brakes, Pulling brakes, Spongy brakes, Dropping brake pedal, Low brake pedal, Dragging brakes, Pedal height, Pedal free play, Reserve distance, Bench bleed, System bleeding, Manual bleeding, Pressure bleeding, Brake system flushing, Disc brake service, Disc runout, Minimum disc thickness, Disc resurfacing, Drum brake service, Wheel cylinder rebuild, Drum resurfacing, Turning, Drum grinding, Drum maximum diameter.

REVIEW QUESTIONS

1. What usually causes brake pedal vibration?
2. _____ _____ is a condition where the brakes apply too quickly, with only light pedal application.
3. _____ _____ is a symptom where the car tries to steer to the right or left when braking.
4. A spongy brake pedal is normally caused by air in the system. True or False?
5. A driver complains that the brake pedal slowly moves toward the floor when stopped at street lights. Pumping the pedal temporarily returns the pedal height. Also, the brake fluid has been checked and is at a normal height in the reservoir.

   Technician A says that a bad master cylinder is a common cause of the problem. Fluid could be leaking internally in the cylinder.

   Technician B says that a leaking wheel cylinder could also be allowing pressure to drop.

   Who is correct?
   a. Technician A
   b. Technician B
   c. Both A and B
   d. Neither A nor B
6. List and explain three types of brake noise.

7. Which of the following is NOT a brake pedal measurement.
   a. Brake pedal free play.
   b. Brake pedal pressure.
   c. Brake pedal height.
   d. Brake pedal reserve distance.
8. How much fluid should typically be in a master cylinder?
9. How do you check brake pad lining and brake shoe lining wear?
10. How do you quickly test the basic operation of a vacuum brake booster?
11. Most mechanics install a new or factory rebuilt master cylinder when one is needed. True or False?
12. Cleaning brake system parts in cold soak solvent is recommended. True or False?
13. A master cylinder should be _____ _____ before installation to remove air from the unit.
14. How do you pressure bleed a brake system?
15. List the four major operations done during disc brake service.

16. _____ _____ _____ is the amount of side to side movement measured near the outer friction surface of a rotor.
17. What can happen if a brake disc is too thin?
18. List the seven major steps for drum brake service.
19. Typically, a brake drum should NOT be _____ oversize or it can warp or break.
20. Summarize the preadjustment procedure for drum brakes.

ACTIVITIES FOR CHAPTER 69

1. Demonstrate the safe method of removing asbestos-laden dust from a brake assembly.
2. Bleed a set of brakes and explain your procedure.
3. Using a flat rate manual and a parts catalog prepare a bill for a brake job.
4. Using a labor rate set by your instructor and a price list for parts, add up the cost of the brake job. Fill in the price on the bill prepared in Activity 3.

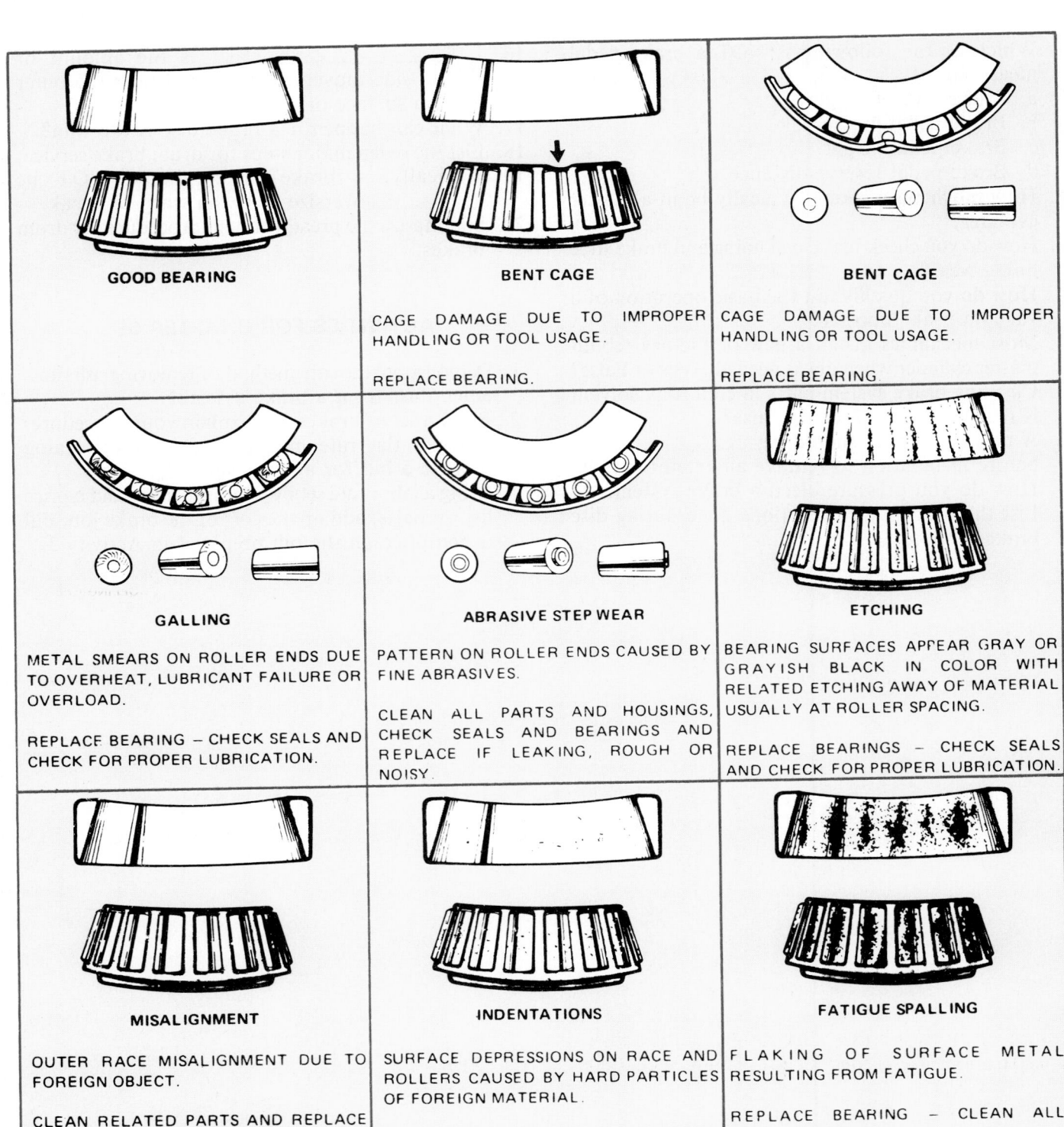

GOOD BEARING

BENT CAGE

CAGE DAMAGE DUE TO IMPROPER HANDLING OR TOOL USAGE.

REPLACE BEARING.

BENT CAGE

CAGE DAMAGE DUE TO IMPROPER HANDLING OR TOOL USAGE.

REPLACE BEARING.

GALLING

METAL SMEARS ON ROLLER ENDS DUE TO OVERHEAT, LUBRICANT FAILURE OR OVERLOAD.

REPLACE BEARING – CHECK SEALS AND CHECK FOR PROPER LUBRICATION.

ABRASIVE STEP WEAR

PATTERN ON ROLLER ENDS CAUSED BY FINE ABRASIVES.

CLEAN ALL PARTS AND HOUSINGS, CHECK SEALS AND BEARINGS AND REPLACE IF LEAKING, ROUGH OR NOISY.

ETCHING

BEARING SURFACES APPEAR GRAY OR GRAYISH BLACK IN COLOR WITH RELATED ETCHING AWAY OF MATERIAL USUALLY AT ROLLER SPACING.

REPLACE BEARINGS – CHECK SEALS AND CHECK FOR PROPER LUBRICATION.

MISALIGNMENT

OUTER RACE MISALIGNMENT DUE TO FOREIGN OBJECT.

CLEAN RELATED PARTS AND REPLACE BEARING. MAKE SURE RACES ARE PROPERLY SEATED.

INDENTATIONS

SURFACE DEPRESSIONS ON RACE AND ROLLERS CAUSED BY HARD PARTICLES OF FOREIGN MATERIAL.

CLEAN ALL PARTS AND HOUSINGS, CHECK SEALS AND REPLACE BEARINGS IF ROUGH OR NOISY.

FATIGUE SPALLING

FLAKING OF SURFACE METAL RESULTING FROM FATIGUE.

REPLACE BEARING – CLEAN ALL RELATED PARTS.

Study types of problems to look for with wheel bearings. These conditions apply to both front-wheel drive and rear-wheel drive bearings. (Cadillac)

70

Wheel Alignment

After studying this chapter, you will be able to:
☐ Explain the principles of wheel alignment.
☐ List the purpose of each wheel alignment setting.
☐ Perform a prealignment inspection of tires, steering, and suspension systems.
☐ Describe how to adjust caster, camber, and toe.
☐ Explain toe-out on turns, steering axis inclination, and tracking.
☐ Describe the different types of equipment used during wheel alignment service.

The term *alignment* means "to position in a straight line." Relating to vehicles, alignment means to position the four tires so that they roll freely and evenly over the road surface.

Correct wheel alignment is essential to automobile safety, sure handling, maximum fuel economy, and long tire life. This chapter introduces both the principles and the basic procedures for wheel alignment.

WHEEL ALIGNMENT PRINCIPLES

The main purpose of *wheel alignment* is to make the tires roll without scuffing, slipping, or dragging under all operating conditions. Six fundamental angles or specifications are needed for proper wheel alignment:
1. CASTER.
2. CAMBER.
3. TOE.
4. STEERING AXIS INCLINATION.
5. TOE-OUT ON TURNS.
6. TRACKING.

CASTER

Caster is basically the forward or rearward tilt of the steering knuckle (spindle support) when viewed from the side of the car. You are probably familiar with the term caster from furniture casters, Fig. 70-1.

Caster controls where the tire touches the road in relation to an imaginary centerline drawn through the

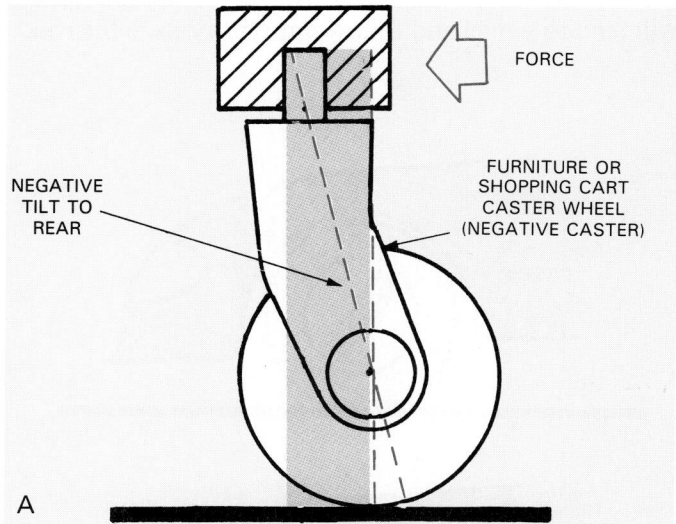

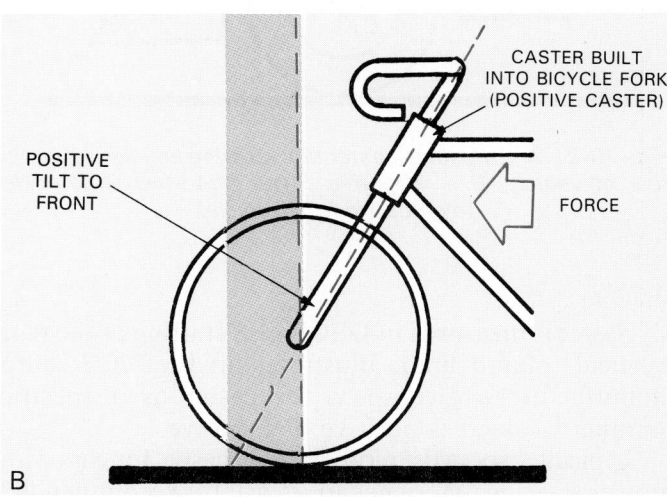

Fig. 70-1. Caster is determined by contact point of tire and imaginary centerline through spindle support. A—Negative caster of ball joints is illustrated by shopping cart. Wheel follows irregular surfaces in floor. B—Positive caster, like on bike, makes front wheel travel straight ahead.

spindle support. Is it NOT a tire wearing angle.

The basic purposes of caster are:

1. To aid directional control of the vehicle.
2. To cause the wheels to return to the straight-ahead position.
3. To offset *road crown pull* (that is, steering wheel pull caused by hump in center of road).

Positive caster tilts the top of the steering knuckle toward the rear of the car. See Fig. 70-2A. Positive caster helps to keep the car's wheels traveling in a straight line. When you turn the wheels, it lifts the car. Since this takes extra turning force, the wheels resist turning and try to return to the straight-ahead position.

Negative caster tilts the top of the steering knuckle toward the front of the car. Look at Fig. 70-2B. It is the opposite of positive caster. With negative caster, the wheels will be easier to turn. However, the wheels will tend to swivel and follow imperfections in the road.

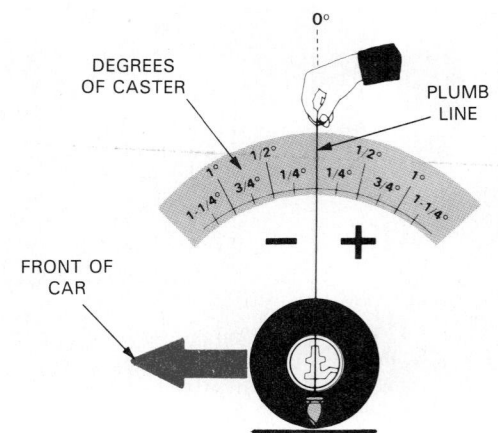

Fig. 70-3. Caster is measured in degrees, as shown. (Bear)

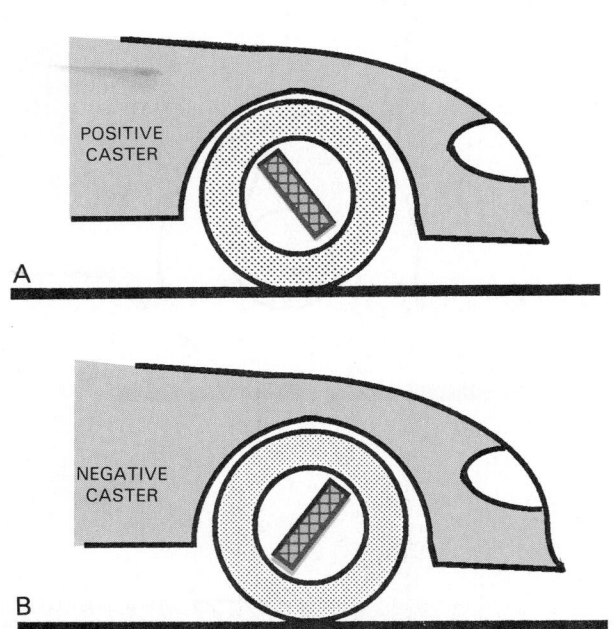

Fig. 70-2. A — Positive caster tilts steering knuckle towards rear of vehicle. B — Negative caster tilts steering knuckle towards front of vehicle.

Caster is measured in DEGREES starting at the true vertical (plumb line). Illustrated in Fig. 70-3, auto manufacturer's give specs for caster as a specific number of degrees positive or negative.

Typically, specs list more positive caster for cars with power steering. More negative caster is recommended for cars with manual steering to ease steering effort.

Caster-road crown effect

Caster is a DIRECTIONAL CONTROL angle. It determines whether the car travels straight or pulls

(steering wheel tries to turn) to the right or left.

Road crown is the normal slope of the road surface, Fig. 70-4. Most road surfaces angle downward from the center. This helps keep rain water from collecting on the pavement. If the caster of both front wheels were the same, the road crown could make the car pull to the right. The car would want to steer off the outside (lower) edge of the road.

Since caster is a directional control angle, it is commonly used to offset the effect of road crown. The right front wheel may be set with slightly more positive caster than the left. This counteracts the forces caused by the road crown and the car will travel straight ahead.

Note! Always refer to the service manual for exact caster specs. They vary with vehicle design.

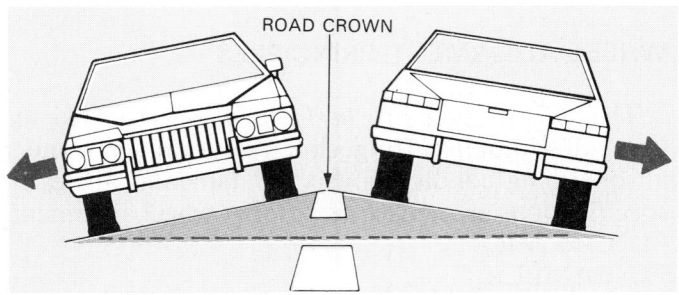

Fig. 70-4. Most roads are crowned in center to help water flow off surface. Unequal caster can be used to offset road crown and keep car from trying to steer off road. (Bear)

CAMBER

Camber is the inward or outward tilt of the wheel and tire assembly when viewed from the front of the car. It controls whether the tire tread touches the road surface evenly. This is pictured in Fig. 70-5. Camber is a tire-wearing angle measured in degrees.

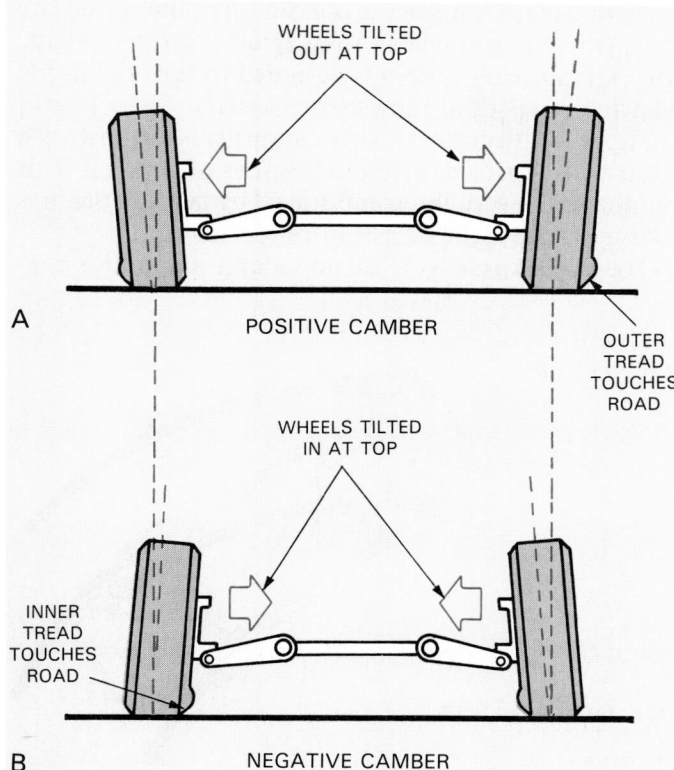

Fig. 70-5. Camber is determined by inward or outward tilt of wheels when viewed from front of car. Positive camber has wheels tilted out at top. Negative camber has wheels tilted out at bottom.

There are three reasons for camber:
1. To prevent tire wear on the outer or inner tread.
2. To load the larger inner wheel bearing.
3. To aid steering by placing vehicle weight on the inner end of the spindle.

With *positive camber,* the tops of the wheels tilt outward when viewed from the front, Fig. 70-5A.

With *negative camber,* the tops of the wheels tilt inward when viewed from the front. Refer to Fig. 70-5B.

Negative and positive camber are measured from the true vertical (plumb line). As in Fig. 70-6, if the wheel is aligned with the plumb line, camber is zero.

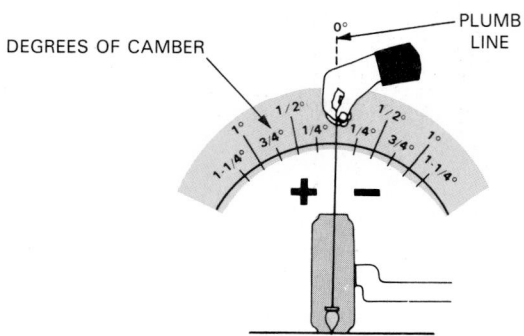

Fig. 70-6. Camber is measured in degrees as shown. (Bear)

Camber settings

Most vehicle manufacturers suggest a slight positive camber setting (about 1/4 to 1/2 deg.). Suspension wear and above-normal curb weight caused by several passengers or extra luggage tends to increase negative camber. Positive camber counteracts this.

TOE

Toe is determined by the difference in distance between the front and rear of the left and right-hand wheels. Look at Fig. 70-7. Measured in inches or millimeters, toe controls whether the wheels roll in the direction of travel. Toe is very critical to TIRE WEAR. If the wheels do NOT have the correct toe setting, the tires will scuff or skid sideways.

Toe-in is produced when the front of the wheels are closer than the rear. As shown in Fig. 70-7A, toe-in causes the wheels to point inward at the front.

Toe-out results when the front of the wheels are farther apart than the rear. See Fig. 70-7B. Toe-out causes the front of the wheels to point away from each other.

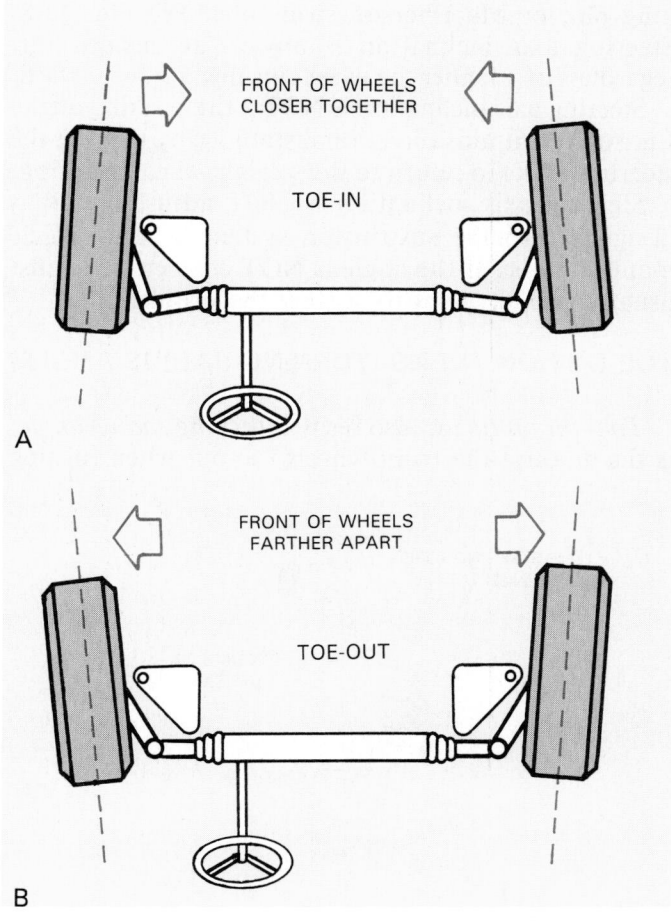

Fig. 70-7. Toe is inward or outward angle of wheels. Toe-in is produced when front of wheels are closer together than the rear. Toe-out results when front of wheels are farther apart than the rear.

Toe settings

Rear-wheel drive cars are usually set to have TOE-IN at the front wheels. This is because the front wheels tend to toe-out while driving. Toe-in is needed to compensate for the action of tire rolling resistance, play in the steering system, and suspension system action.

As the tires roll over the road, they are pushed rearward. This turns the tires outward at the front, causing toe-out. By adjusting the wheels for a slight toe-in (approximately 1/16 to 1/4 in. or 1.6 to 6 mm), the wheels and tires roll straight ahead when driving.

Front-wheel drive cars require different adjustment for toe. Since the front wheels propel the car, they are pushed forward by engine torque. This makes the wheels toe in or point inward while driving.

To compensate for this action, front-wheel drive vehicles normally have front wheels adjusted for a slight toe-out (approximately 1/16 in. or 1.5 mm). Theoretically, this will give the front end a zero toe setting when the car moves down the road.

STEERING AXIS INCLINATION

Steering axis inclination is the angle, away from the vertical, formed by the inward tilt of the ball joints, king pin, or MacPherson strut tube. See Fig. 70-8. Steering axis inclination is always an inward tilt, regardless of whether the wheel tilts inward or outward.

Steering axis inclination is NOT a tire wearing angle. Like caster, it aids directional stability by helping the steering wheel to return to the straight-ahead position.

Steering axis inclination is NOT adjustable. It is designed into the suspension system by the vehicle manufacturer. If the angle is NOT correct, you must usually replace parts to correct the problem.

TOE-OUT ON TURNS (TURNING RADIUS ANGLE)

Toe-out on turns, also termed *turning radius angle,* is the amount the front wheels toe-out when turning

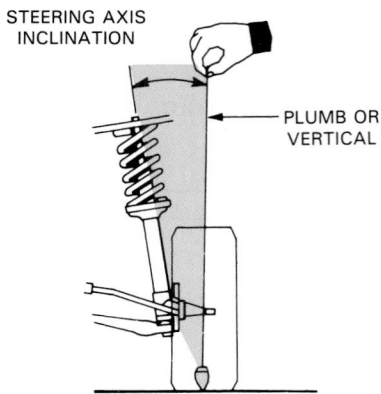

Fig. 70-8. Steering axis inclination is determined by vertical line and projected line through upper ball joint, king pin, or MacPherson strut tube. (Bear)

corners. As the car goes around a turn, the inside tire must travel in a smaller radius circle than the outside tire. The steering system is designed to turn the inside wheel sharper than the outside wheel.

Fig. 70-9 illustrates toe-out on turns. Note how each front wheel turns a different number of degrees. This eliminates tire scrubbing and squeal by keeping the tires rolling in the right direction on corners.

Toe-out turns is NOT an adjustable angle. It is con-

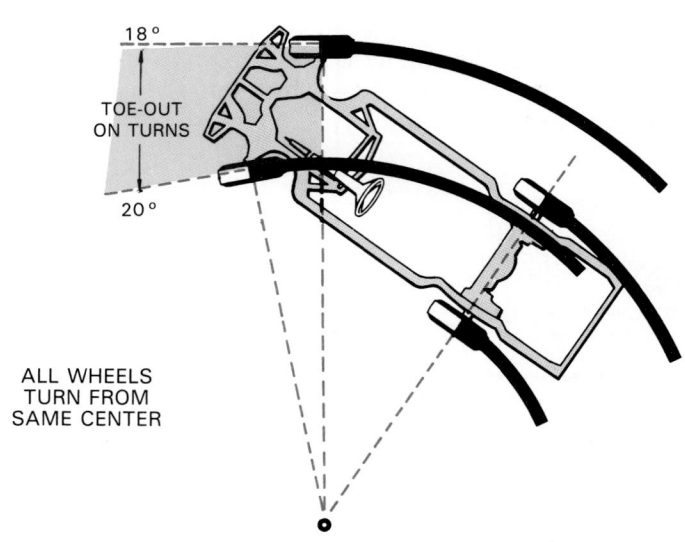

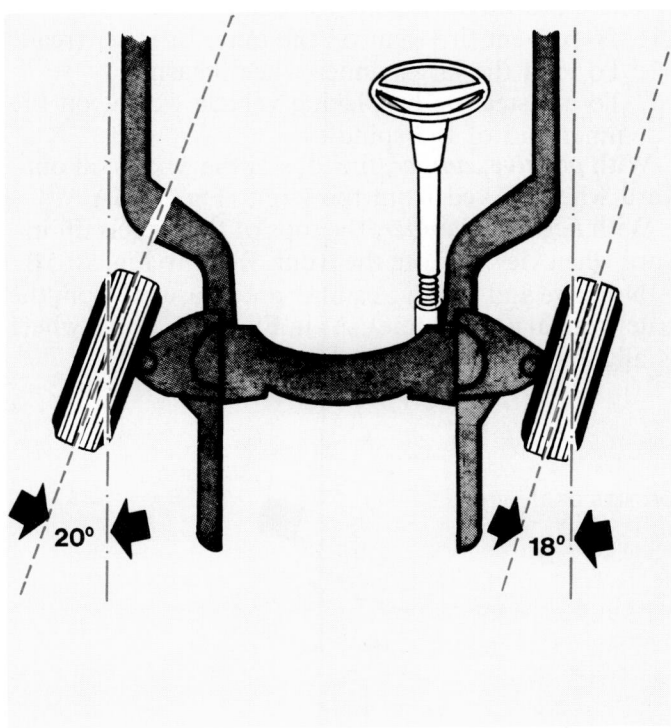

Fig. 70-9. When rounding corners, inside tire must turn more sharply. Angles built into steering system produces proper toe-out on turns. (Hunter)

trolled by the built-in angle of the steering arms. If incorrect, it indicates bent or damaged steering parts.

TRACKING

Tracking refers to the position or direction of the two front wheels in relation to the two rear wheels. With proper tracking, the rear tires follow in the tracks of the front tires, with the car moving straight ahead. Look at Fig. 70-10.

With improper tracking, the rear tires do NOT follow the tracks of the front tires. This causes the car body or frame to actually shift partially sideways when moving down the road. Poor tracking will increase tire wear, lower fuel economy, and upset handling.

4. Adjust toe.
5. Check toe-out in turns (needed if there is damage).
6. Check caster, camber, and toe on rear wheels (if needed).
7. Check tracking (if needed).

Caster adjustment methods

Caster is adjusted by moving the control arm so that the ball joint moves to the front or rear of the car. Depending on suspension system type, a control arm can be moved by adding or removing SHIMS, adjusting the STRUT ROD, turning an ECCENTRIC BOLT, or by shifting the control arm shaft bolts in SLOTTED HOLES. See Fig. 70-11.

If the upper control arm ball joint is moved forward,

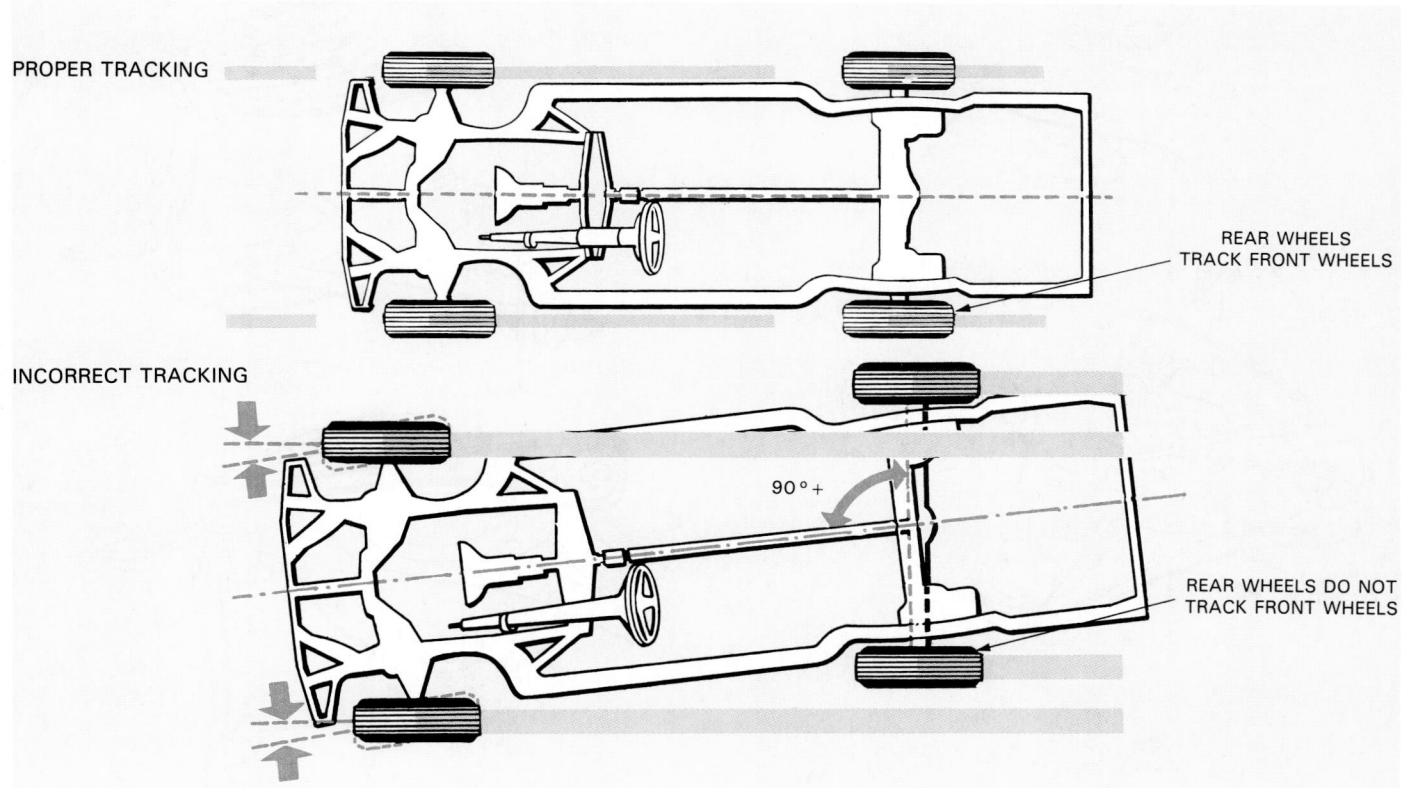

PROPER TRACKING

REAR WHEELS TRACK FRONT WHEELS

INCORRECT TRACKING

90° +

REAR WHEELS DO NOT TRACK FRONT WHEELS

Fig. 70-10. Proper tracking causes the rear wheels to follow directly behind front wheels. (Hunter)

ADJUSTING WHEEL ALIGNMENT

Caster, camber, and toe are the three commonly adjustable wheel alignment angles.

Before studying wheel alignment equipment, you should have a basic understanding of how alignment angles are changed. Then, you can relate this knowledge to the use of specific alignment equipment.

The basic sequence for wheel alignment is:
1. Inspect and correct tire, steering, and suspension problems.
2. Adjust caster.
3. Adjust camber and recheck caster.

it increases negative caster, Fig. 70-12. If the upper control arm is adjusted to move its ball joint rearward, it would increase positive caster. The opposite is true for the lower control arm, Fig. 70-12.

Figs. 70-11 and 70-12 show various means for caster adjustment.

Camber adjustment methods

Camber is usually adjusted right after setting caster. Camber is changed by moving the control arm in or out so that the ball joint does NOT move forward or rearward. Again, refer to Fig. 70-12. SHIMS or SLOTS in the control arm mount and ECCENTRIC BOLTS

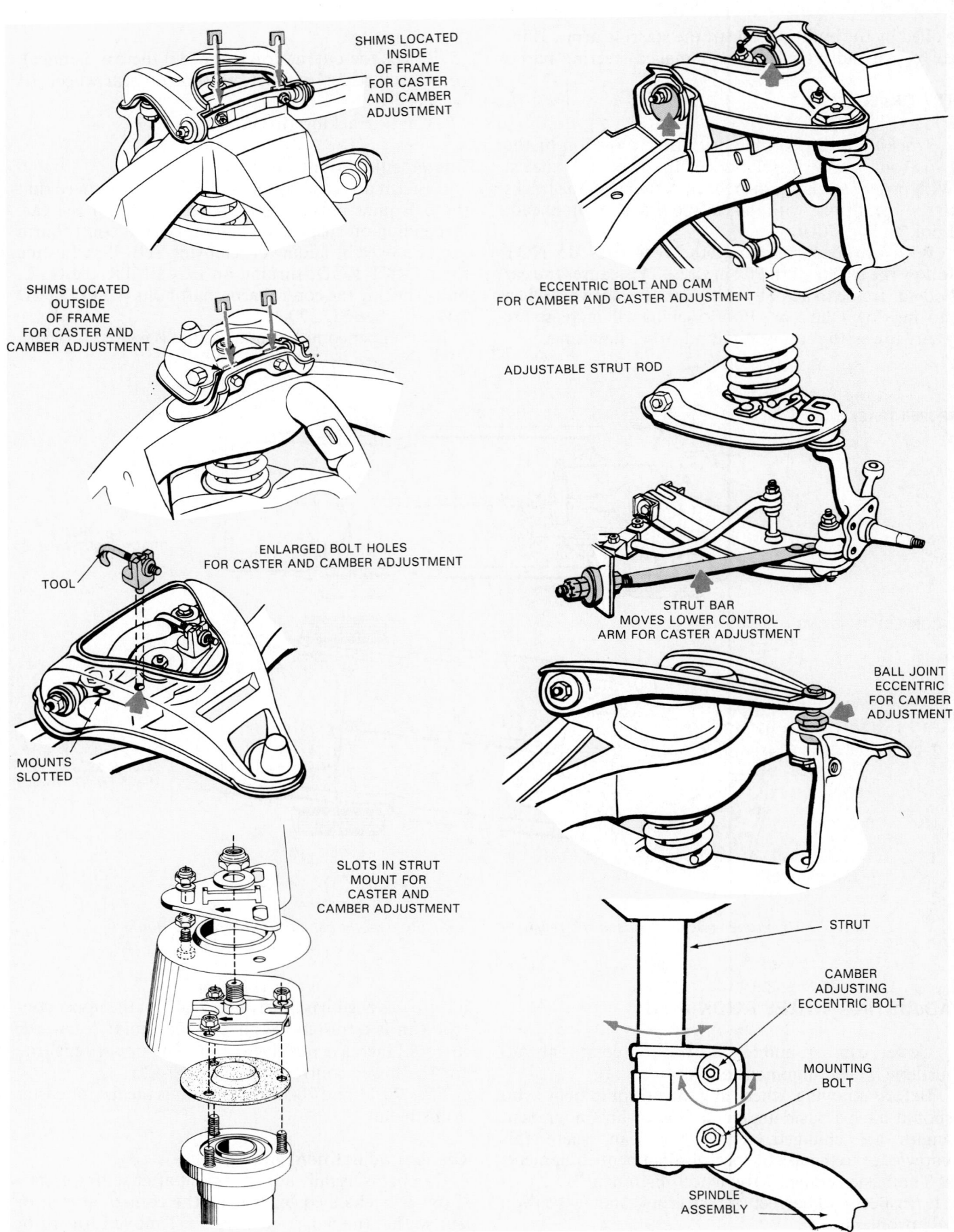

SHIMS LOCATED INSIDE OF FRAME FOR CASTER AND CAMBER ADJUSTMENT

SHIMS LOCATED OUTSIDE OF FRAME FOR CASTER AND CAMBER ADJUSTMENT

TOOL

ENLARGED BOLT HOLES FOR CASTER AND CAMBER ADJUSTMENT

MOUNTS SLOTTED

SLOTS IN STRUT MOUNT FOR CASTER AND CAMBER ADJUSTMENT

ECCENTRIC BOLT AND CAM FOR CAMBER AND CASTER ADJUSTMENT

ADJUSTABLE STRUT ROD

STRUT BAR MOVES LOWER CONTROL ARM FOR CASTER ADJUSTMENT

BALL JOINT ECCENTRIC FOR CAMBER ADJUSTMENT

STRUT

CAMBER ADJUSTING ECCENTRIC BOLT

MOUNTING BOLT

SPINDLE ASSEMBLY

Fig. 70-11. Study various methods used to change caster and camber settings. (Hunter, Moog, Florida Dept. of Voc. Ed.)

932   Modern Automotive Technology

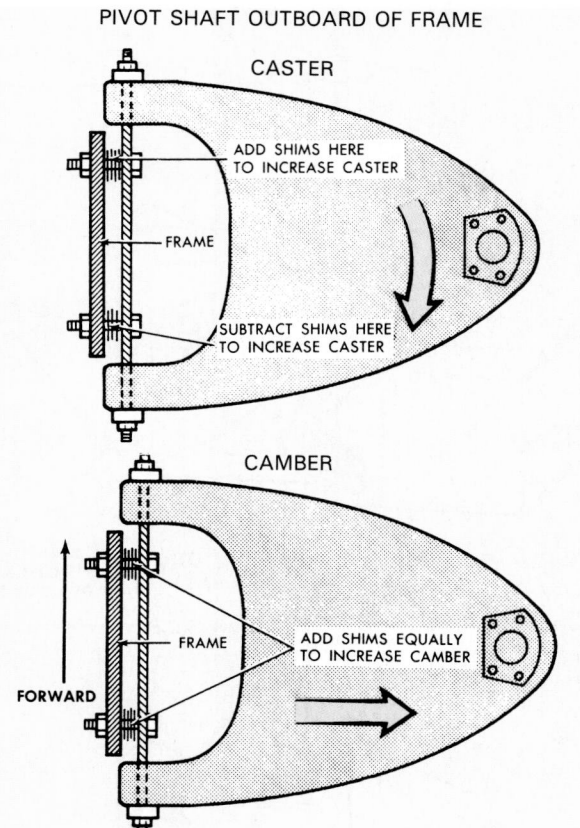

Fig. 70-12. Caster is adjusted by moving either upper or lower control arm to front or rear of car.

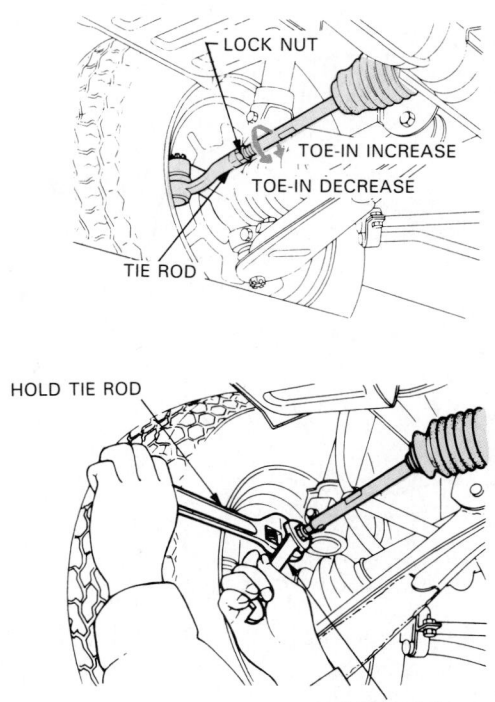

Fig. 70-13. Toe is adjusted by lengthening or shortening tie rods. (Subaru)

are the most common methods for adjustment.

Some MacPherson strut suspensions do not have provisions for caster and camber adjustments. However, other strut type suspension systems have a camber adjustment at the connection between the steering knuckle and strut. See Fig. 70-11.

The top of the steering knuckle and bottom of the strut can be pivoted in or out. The upper bolt on the steering knuckle may have an eccentric that moves the knuckle when turned.

Toe adjustment

Toe is adjusted by lengthening or shortening the TIE-RODS. On most rack and pinion steering systems, the tie rod is threaded into the outer ball socket, Fig. 70-13. Linkage type steering systems normally have a sleeve threaded on a two-piece tie rod, Fig. 70-14.

When the steering arms point to the rear of the vehicle, lengthen each tie-rod to increase toe-in and shorten them to increase toe-out. The opposite is true when the steering knuckle arms are pointed forward.

Centering a steering wheel

To keep the steering wheel spokes centered, shorten or lengthen each tie-rod the same amount. Changing one more than the other will rotate the steering wheel spokes. When the vehicle is traveling straight ahead, the

wheel spokes should be positioned correctly. Fig. 70-15 shows a service manual illustration for centering a steering wheel.

Adjusting rear wheel alignment

Depending upon vehicle make and model, a car may or may NOT have provisions for adjusting rear wheel alignment. If the wheels fail to track properly, it may point to frame, unibody, or rear suspension damage. The vehicle might have been in an accident that shifted

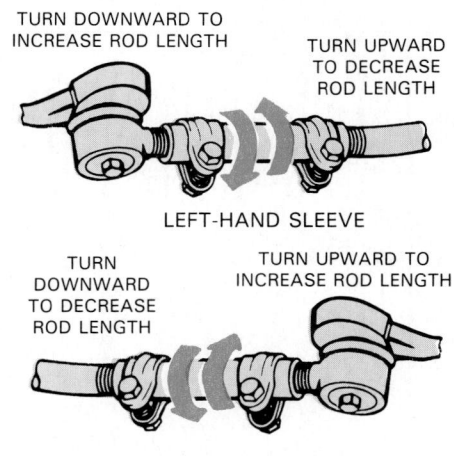

Fig. 70-14. Linkage type steering system uses a sleeve to lengthen or shorten tie-rod. Note adjustment method. (Ford)

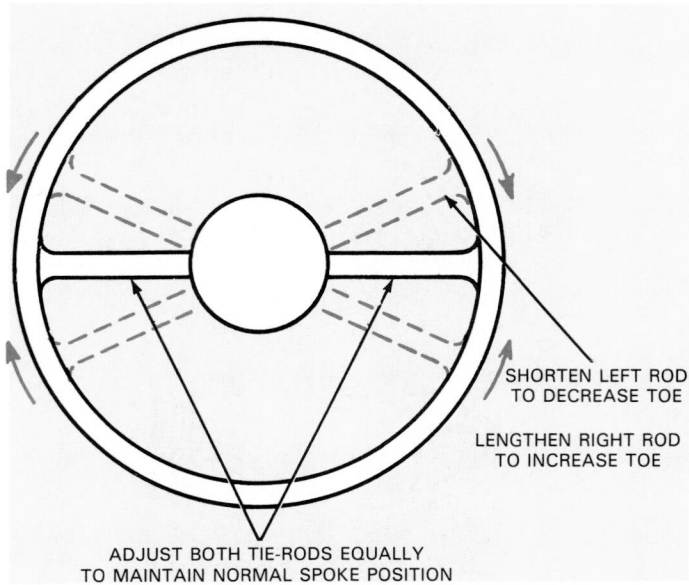

SHORTEN LEFT ROD
TO DECREASE TOE

LENGTHEN RIGHT ROD
TO INCREASE TOE

ADJUST BOTH TIE-RODS EQUALLY
TO MAINTAIN NORMAL SPOKE POSITION

Fig. 70-15. When adjusting toe, steering wheel must be kept in center position. Study how turning each tie-rod end affects position of steering wheel spokes. (Ford)

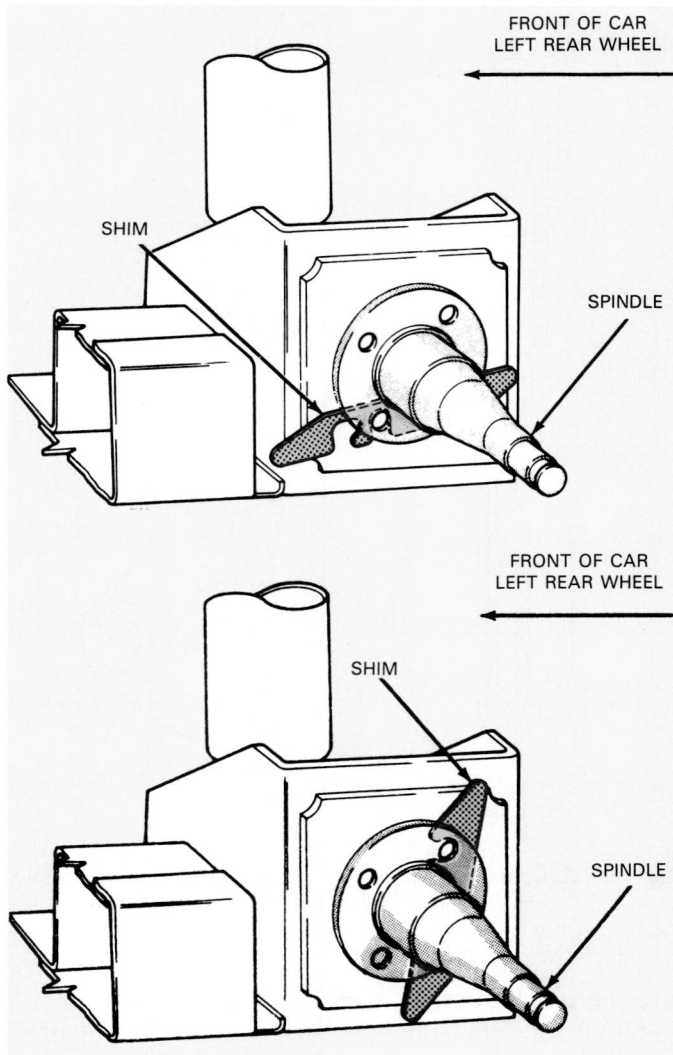

Fig. 70-16. Note how shim can be used to adjust alignment angles on rear axle of this front-wheel drive vehicle. Shim can be placed at bottom, top, front, or rear to change any alignment angle. (Dodge)

the rear wheels out of place. Worn suspension system bushings can also upset tracking, Fig. 70-16. It shows how shims can be used to align the rear wheels of one type of front-wheel drive vehicle. A shim of the correct thickness can be added to adjust camber and toe.

Other methods are sometimes used for aligning the rear wheels of a vehicle. They normally use the principles already covered for aligning the front wheels.

PREALIGNMENT INSPECTION

Now that you understand alignment principles and basic adjustment methods, you are ready to learn how

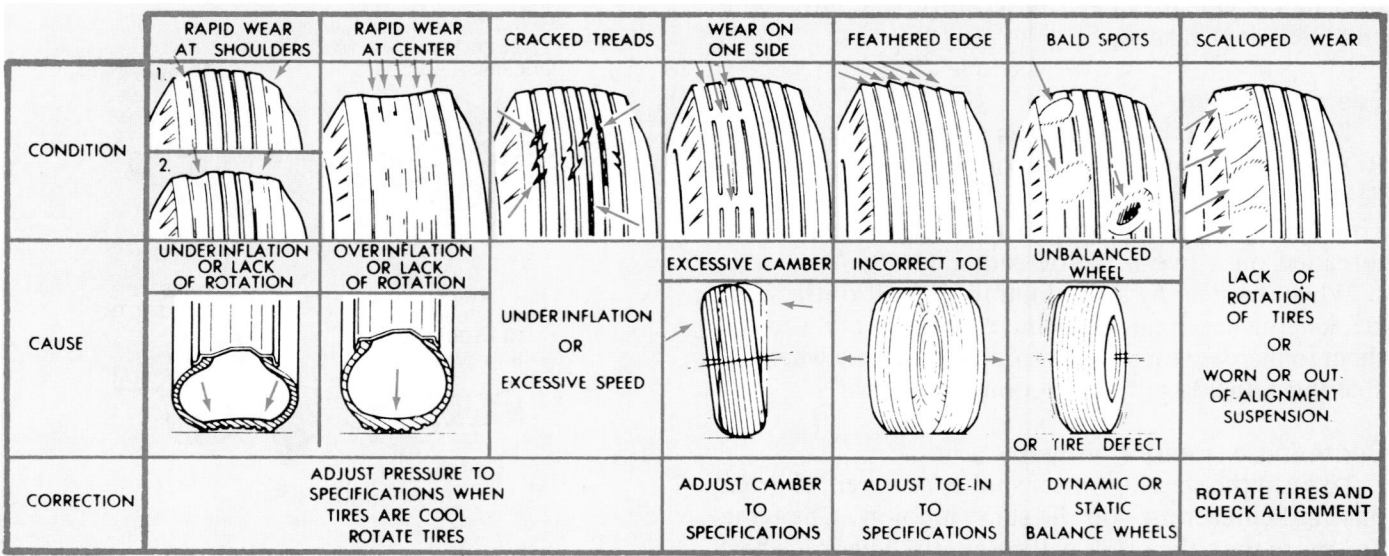

Fig. 70-17. Tire wear patterns should be read to help determine which steering or suspension parts are worn and to help with alignment checks. (Chrysler Corp.)

to inspect a vehicle before measuring and setting wheel alignment. Inspection of the tires, wheels, suspension, and steering systems is essential. If any front end part is worn, you must adjust or replace that part before doing a wheel alignment.

Reading tire wear

Reading tires is done by inspecting tire tread wear and diagnosing the cause for any abnormal wear. Fig. 70-17 shows a chart for reading tire wear patterns. Note that incorrect camber and toe show up as specific tread wear patterns.

Incorrect camber produces wear on one side of the tire tread, Fig. 70-17. Too much negative camber would wear the INSIDE of the tire tread. Too much positive camber would wear the OUTER tread only. Correct camber will wear the FULL tread area evenly.

Incorrect toe will cause a feathered edge to form on the tire tread. A *feather edge* is a tire wear pattern with one side of each tread rib worn sharp and raised and the other side worn rounded or recessed. See Fig. 70-17.

With too much toe-in, the sharp feathered edge

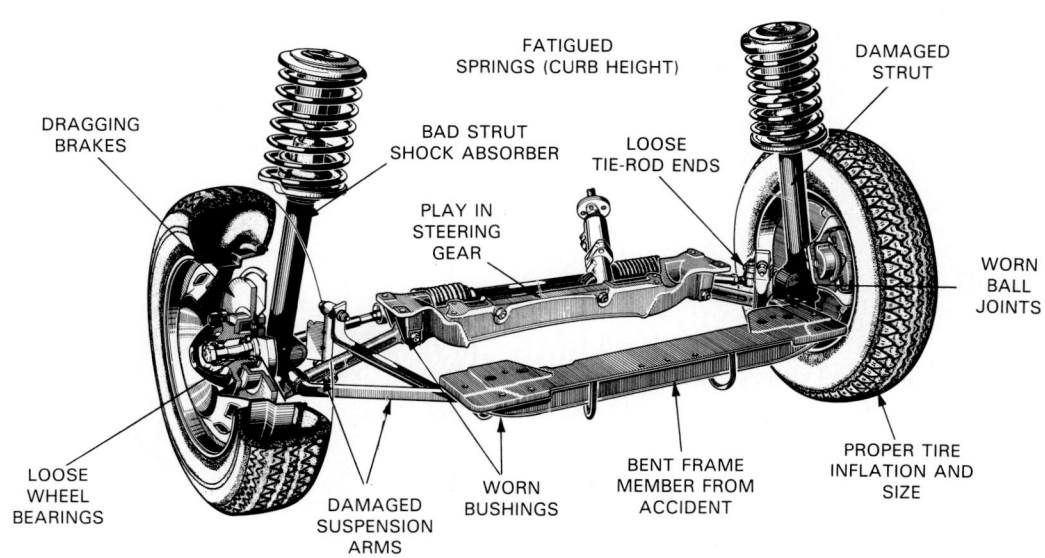

ALIGNMENT INSPECTION REPORT FORM

Name_____ Date_____, 19____

Address _____ Phone: Bus._____ Home_____

Make _____ Yr. and Model_____ License _____ Odometer _____

TIRE AND WHEEL CHECKS

Tire Condition-	Inspection	OK: LF__ RF__ LR__ RR__	**Comments:**
Tire Pressure		OK: LF__ RF__ LR__ RR__	
Wheel Bearings-	Adjustment	OK: LF__ RF__ LR__ RR__	
	Roughness	OK: LF__ RF__ LR__ RR__	
Runout-Lateral		OK: LF__ RF__ LR__ RR__	
	Radial	OK: LF__ RF__ LR__ RR__	
Wheel Balance		OK: LF__ RF__ LR__ RR__	
Shock Absorbers-Operational		OK: LF__ RF__ LR__ RR__	
	Leakage and		
	Bushings	OK: LF__ RF__ LR__ RR__	
Riding Height		OK: LF__ RF__ LR__ RR__	

SUSPENSION CHECKS

Tracking	OK:__	**Comments:**
MacPherson-type Struts	OK: LF__ RF__	
Ball Joints	OK: LU__ LL__ RU__ RL__	
Front Control Arm Assembly	OK: LU__ LL__ RU__ RL__	
Strut Rod and Bushing Assembly	OK: L__ R__	
Stabilizer (or Sway) Bar,		
Mounting Brackets, and	Front: OK____	
Links	Rear: OK____	
Leaf Spring Assembly	OK: L__ R__	
Rear Coil Spring Assembly	OK: L__ R__	
Rear Control Arm Assembly	OK: LU__ RU__ LL__ RL__	
Track Bar and Bushings	OK: ____	

STEERING LINKAGE CHECKS

Tie-Rod End	OK: L__ R__	**Comments:**
Tie-Rods and Inner Ball/Stud		
Sockets	OK: L__ R__	
Steering Arms	OK: L__ R__	
Tie-Rod Adjusting Sleeves	OK: L__ R__	**Comments:**
Relay Rod	OK: ____	
Pitman Arm	OK: ____	
Idler Arm and Bracket	OK: ____	
Steering Shock Absorber and		
Bushings	OK: ____	
Steering Gear Mountings	OK: ____	

MANUAL STEERING GEAR—INSPECTION

Lubricant Leakage	OK: ____	**Comments:**
Operation	OK: ____	
Sector Shaft and Bearings	OK: ____	
Adjustment of Gear	OK: ____	
Lubricant Level	OK: ____	

POWER STEERING GEAR—INSPECTION

Fluid Leakage	OK: ____	**Comments:**
Power Steering Hoses	OK: ____	
Power Steering Pump	OK: ____	
Fluid Level	OK: ____	
Pump Belt	OK: ____	
Power Steering Operation	OK: ____	
Steering Gear Adjustment	OK: ____	
Sector Shaft and Bushings	OK: ____	
Pinion Shaft and Bearings	OK: ____	
Control Valve	OK: ____	

FRONT ALIGNMENT CHECK	Reading	Manufacturer's Standard	OK
Caster	L__° R__°	L__° R__°	
Camber	L__° R__°	L__° R__°	
Steering Axis Inclination	L__° R__°	L__° R__°	
Turning Radius	L__° R__°	L__° R__°	
Toe	In__ Out__	In__ Out__	

Fig. 70-18. Study types of problems that can affect front wheel alignment. All of these must be corrected first.

points inward. With too much toe-out, the sharp edge on the thread ribs point away from the center of the car.

Covered in earlier chapters, tire wear patterns can also indicate incorrect wheel balance, incorrect tire inflation pressure, tire construction defects, and tire damage.

Common front end problems

Before adjusting alignment, always check the vehicle for problems that could affect wheel alignment. You should check for:

1. Loose wheel bearings.
2. Wheel or tire runout.
3. Worn tires or tires of different sizes and types.
4. Incorrect tire inflation.
5. Worn steering components.
6. Worn suspension components.
7. Incorrect curb height and weight.

Fig. 70-18 shows several components that frequently cause problems during alignment.

WHEEL ALIGNMENT TOOLS AND EQUIPMENT

Various special tools and equipment are needed to adjust wheel alignment. Fig. 70-19 shows several special tools. Fig. 70-20 shows two other commonly used tools. Note the name and basic function of each.

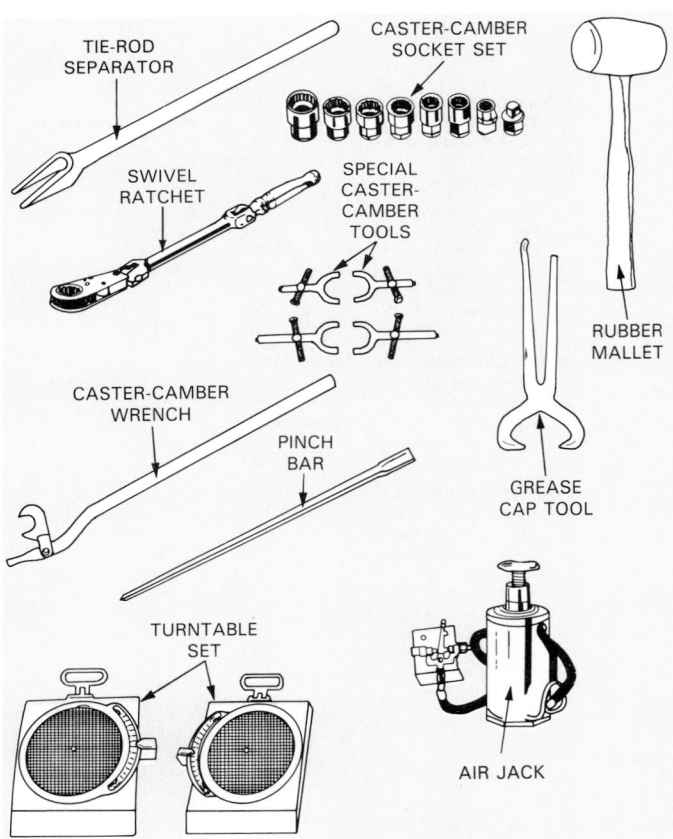

Fig. 70-19. These are common front end alignment tools. (Snap-On)

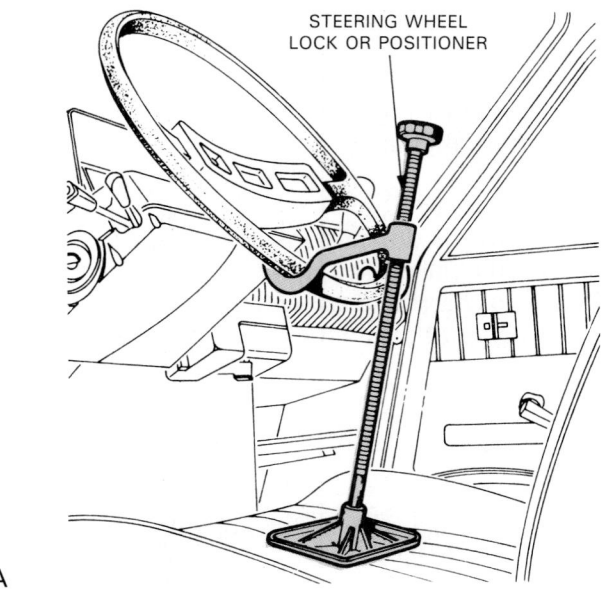

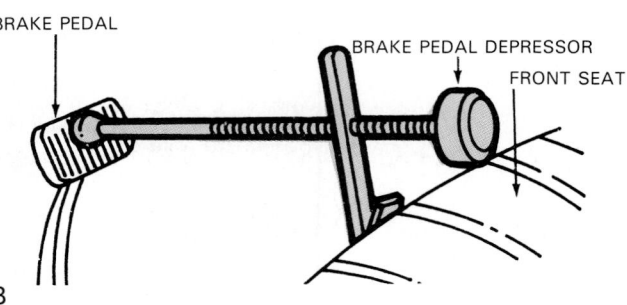

Fig. 70-20. A — Steering wheel lock will hold front wheels straight ahead. B — Brake pedal lock will keep vehicle from rolling. (Florida Dept. of Voc. Ed. and Renault)

The most basic equipment for wheel alignment is the turning radius gauge, caster-camber gauge, and the tram gauge. These are the least complicated of all alignment equipment and illustrate the fundamentals for wheel alignment easily.

Covered shortly, these basic types of equipment are normally replaced with a large alignment rack. The rack will have special measuring instruments.

TURNING RADIUS GAUGES

Turning radius gauges measure how many degrees the front wheels are turned right or left. Look at Fig. 70-21. They are commonly used when measuring caster, camber, and toe-out on turns.

Turning radius gauges may be portable units. However, they are commonly mounted in an alignment rack as integral units.

The front wheels of the vehicle are centered on the turning radius gauges. Then, when the locking pins are pulled out, the gauge and tire turn together. The pointer on the gauge will indicate how many degrees the wheels have been turned.

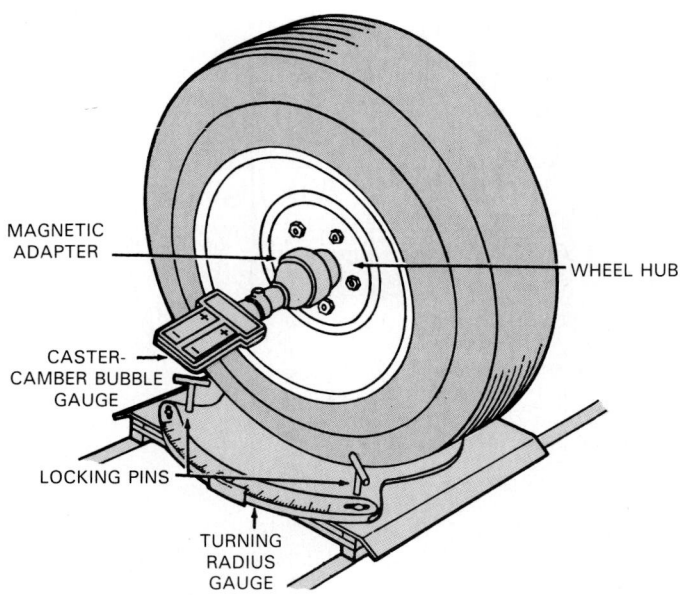

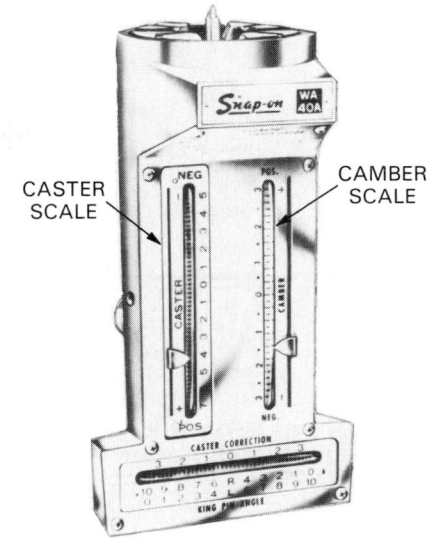

A

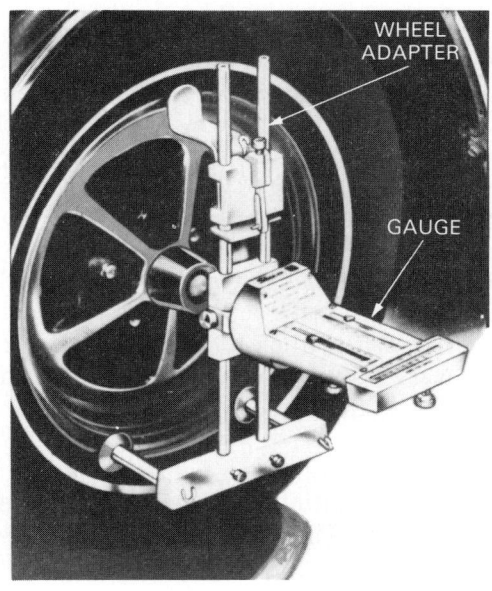

B

Fig. 70-21. Turning radius gauge will measure number of degrees wheels are turned. Also note caster-camber gauge mounted on hub. (Florida Dept. of Voc. Ed.)

Fig. 70-22. Caster-camber gauge. A — Gauge has bubbles that read tilt of hub in degrees. Note scales for caster and camber. B — Gauge may mount on wheel with adapter or may have magnet that sticks to hub. (Snap-On)

Checking toe-out on turns

To check toe-out on turns, center the front tires of the car on the turning radius gauges. Turn one of the front wheels until the gauge reads 20 deg. Then, read the number of degrees showing on the other gauge. Check toe-out on turns on both the right and left sides. If not within specs, check for bent or damaged parts.

CASTER-CAMBER GAUGE

A *caster-camber gauge* is used with the turning radius gauge to measure caster and camber in degrees. The gauge either fits on the wheel hub magnetically, Fig. 70-21, or may fasten on the wheel rim, Fig. 70-22. Normally, caster and camber are adjusted together since one affects the other.

Measuring caster

To measure caster with a bubble type caster-camber gauge, turn one of the front wheels inward until the radius gauge reads 20 deg. Turn the adjustment knob on the caster-camber gauge until the bubble is centered on zero. Then, turn the wheel out 20 deg.

The degree marking next to the bubble will equal the caster of that front wheel. Compare your reading to specifications and adjust as needed. Repeat this operation on the other side of the car.

Measuring camber

To measure camber with a bubble type caster-camber gauge, turn the front wheels straight ahead (radius gauges on zero). The car must be on a perfectly level surface (alignment rack).

Read the number of degrees next to the bubble on the camber scale of the gauge. It will show camber for that wheel. If not within specs, adjust camber.

If shims are used, add or remove the same amount of shims from the front and rear of the control arm. This will keep the caster set correctly. Double-check caster, especially when an excessive amount of camber adjustment is needed.

TRAM GAUGE

A *tram gauge* is used to compare the distance between the front and rear of a car's tires for toe adjustment. Look at Fig. 70-23.

A tram gauge is a metal rod or shaft with two

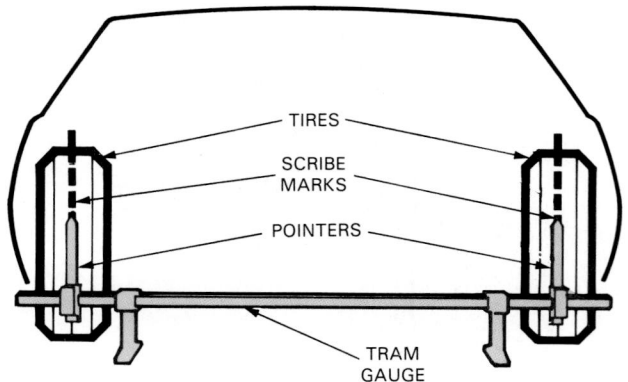

Fig. 70-23. Tram gauge provides simple method of adjusting toe. Lines are scribed on chalked tire tread. Then tram is used to measure distance between lines at front and rear of tires. Difference equals toe. (Blackhawk)

Fig. 70-24. Alignment rack contains all equipment needed to set alignment angles. Note turning radius gauges, ramps, and other equipment on wall board. (Bear)

pointers. The pointers slide on the gauge so that they can be set to the distance between the tires. The tram gauge will indicate toe-out or toe-in in inches or millimeters.

Measuring toe

To measure toe with a tram gauge, raise the wheels and rub a chalk line all the way around the center rib on each tire. Then, using a scribing tool, rotate each tire and scribe a fine line on the chalk line. This will give you a very thin reference line for measuring the distance between the tires. Lower the car back on the radius gauges.

First, position the tram gauge at the back of the tires. Move the pointers until they line up with the lines you scribed on the tires. Then, without bumping the gauge, position the gauge at the front of the tires.

The difference in the distance between the lines on the front and rear of the tires shows toe.

For example, if the lines on the front of the tires are closer together than on the rear, the wheels are toed-in. If the lines are the same distance apart at the front and rear, toe is zero.

Using service manual instructions, adjust the tie rods until the tram gauge reads within specs.

ALIGNMENT RACKS

Most medium to large size garages have an alignment rack. The *alignment rack* consists of ramps, turning radius gauges, and one of several kinds of equipment for measuring alignment angles. Refer to Fig. 70-24. The ramps are adjusted perfectly level so that all equipment readings are accurate.

To use an alignment rack, the car is driven up on the ramps. The front tires must be carefully centered on the turning radius gauges, Fig. 70-25. Once on the rack, the rear wheels are blocked to keep the car from

accidentally rolling off the rack.

CAUTION! Use extreme care when positioning a car on an alignment rack. Ask a friend to guide you up the ramps and onto the turning radius gauges. Block the rear wheels!

Since there are so many types of alignment equip-

Fig. 70-25. This modern alignment rack is electronic and reads caster and camber on meter face. (Bear)

ment designs, always follow the operating instructions provided by the manufacturer. Remember that alignment principles are the same. Apply your knowledge of wheel alignment to the specific type of equipment.

Fig. 70-25 pictures a computerized alignment machine. Instead of a bubble type caster-camber gauge, it uses electronic sensing devices to measure the tilt of the steering knuckle and wheel. Note how the instrument mounts on the wheel.

Look at Fig. 70-26. It shows modern alignment equipment being used to measure toe. A light beam shines across from the front wheels. When the light beam shines directly into the sensor on the opposite wheel, toe is zero. This is an easy-to-use type machine since you can adjust toe without crawling out from under the car.

Fig. 70-27. Mechanic is using alignment equipment to reflect light up to scale on board for toe adjustment. (Hunter)

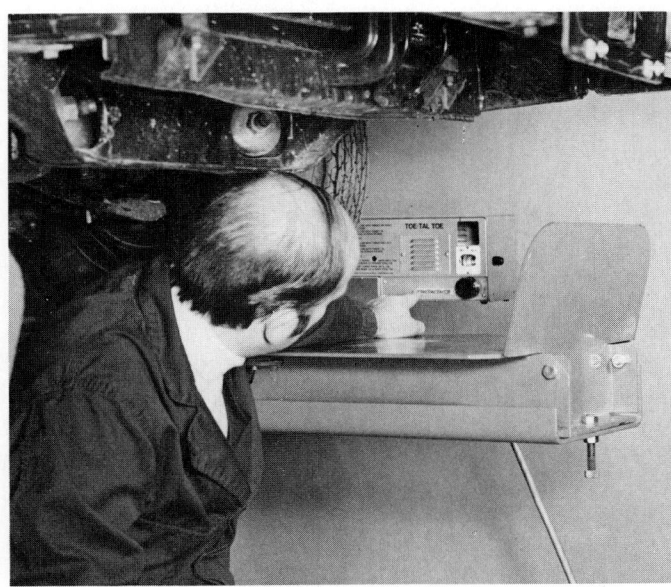

Fig. 70-26. This alignment rack uses light beams shining between wheels to set toe. (Bear)

Fig. 70-27 shows another type of alignment machine. It projects a light beam (line) onto a large scale mounted next to the wall at the end of the rack. Caster, camber, toe, and other alignment angles are read off the wall-mounted scale.

A computerized wheel alignment machine is being used to measure tracking in Fig. 70-28. Note how both the alignment of the front and rear wheels is being compared. A light beam projects back to mirrors mounted on the rear wheels. With proper tracking, the light beam will reflect off of the mirrors and back into the sensor on the front wheels.

WARNING! Always remember to use the operating manual provided with the specific alignment equipment. Procedures vary and the slightest mistake could upset proper wheel alignment.

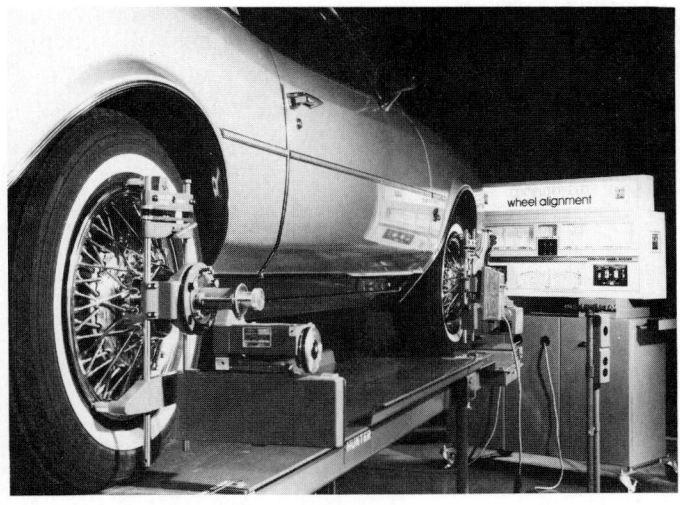

Fig. 70-28. State of the art electronic alignment rack is being used to check track of front and rear wheels. (Hunter)

KNOW THESE TERMS

Wheel alignment, Caster, Camber, Toe, Steering axis inclination, Toe-out on turns, Tracking, Reading tires, Incorrect camber, Incorrect toe, Feathered edge, Turning radius gauge, Caster-camber bubble gauge, Tram gauge, Alignment rack.

REVIEW QUESTIONS

1. Define the term "alignment."
2. What is the main purpose of wheel alignment?
3. _____ is the inward or outward tilt of the wheel and tire assembly when viewed from the front of the vehicle.
4. List the three basic functions of caster.
5. Explain the difference between positive and negative caster.
6. Which of the following pertains to caster?
   a. Measured in inches or millimeters.
   b. A directional control angle.
   c. Can be used to offset road crown.
   d. All of the above are correct.
   e. All of the above are incorrect.
7. _____ is the forward or rearward tilt of the steering knuckle or steering support when viewed from the side of the vehicle.
8. List three functions of camber.
9. Explain the difference between positive and negative camber.
10. Most vehicle manufacturer's suggest a slight negative camber setting. True or False?
11. _____ is determined by the distance between the front and rear of the left and right-hand wheels.
12. Explain the difference between toe-in and toe-out.
13. Rear-wheel drive cars commonly use toe-in and front-wheel drive cars commonly use toe-out. True or False?
14. Define the term "tracking."
15. List the seven basic steps for wheel alignment.
16. How do you change caster?
17. How do you change camber?
18. How do you adjust toe?
19. _____ _____ is done by inspecting tread wear and diagnosing the cause of abnormal wear.
20. Name seven possible problems you should check before attempting to align a vehicle's front end.
21. Turning radius gauges measure how many degrees the front wheels are turned right or left. True or False?
22. Summarize the use of a caster-camber gauge.
23. A _____ gauge is used to compare the distance between the front and rear of a vehicle's tires for toe adjustment.
24. A customer complains of excess tire wear. When checked, the tires show a feather edge wear pattern.
    Technician A says that the toe is improperly adjusted.
    Technician B says that a thorough front end alignment is needed.
    Who is correct?
    a. Technician A
    b. Technician B
    c. Both A and B
    d. Neither A nor B
25. What is an alignment rack?

ACTIVITIES FOR CHAPTER 70

1. Demonstrate for your instructor a prealignment inspection of tires, steering, and suspension of a vehicle in the shop for a front-end alignment.
2. Check and adjust the caster, camber, or toe-in of a front suspension.
3. Prepare a bill for a front end alignment. Use a flat labor rate established by your instructor and a $25/hour charge. Include the cost of any parts used. Add up all costs.

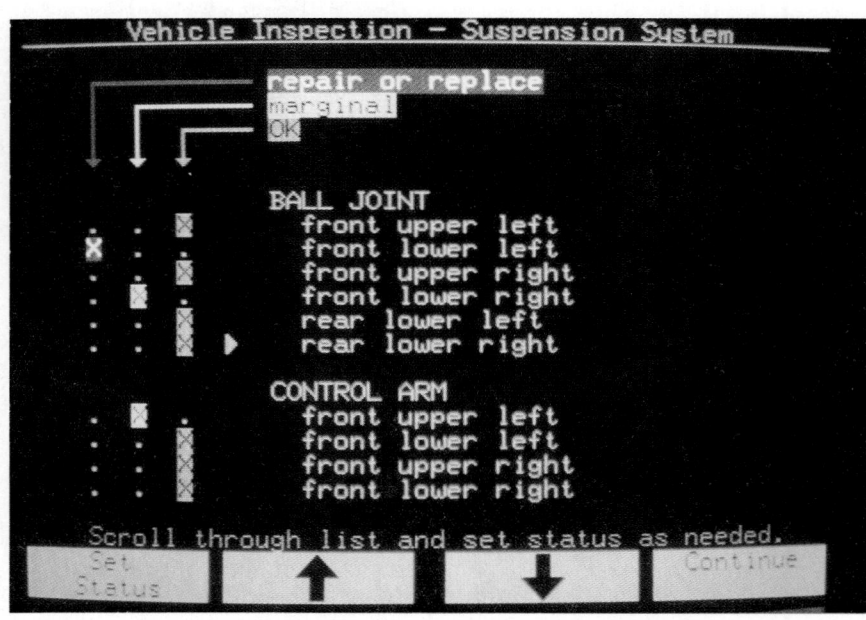

Study tests shown on display screen of this electronic or computerized front end rack. Note how it has checked that the front, lower, left control arm should be repaired or replaced.

Heating and
Air Conditioning
Fundamentals

After studying this chapter, you will be able to:
□ Explain the principles of refrigeration.
□ Describe the four cycles of refrigeration.
□ Describe the high and low pressure sides of an air conditioning system.
□ Explain the basic function and construction of the major parts of heating and air conditioning systems.
□ Summarize the operation and interaction of heating, ventilation, and air conditioning systems.
□ Describe safety precautions to be observed when working on heating and air conditioning systems.

An air conditioning system normally works with the heating and ventilation systems, as in Fig. 71-1. The *air conditioning system* provides cool, dehumidified (dried) air. The *heating system* supplies warm air, using heat from the engine cooling system. The *ventilation system* carries fresh outside air into the vehicle.

PRINCIPLES OF REFRIGERATION

An automotive air conditioning system uses the same principles found in a home refrigerator. For this reason,

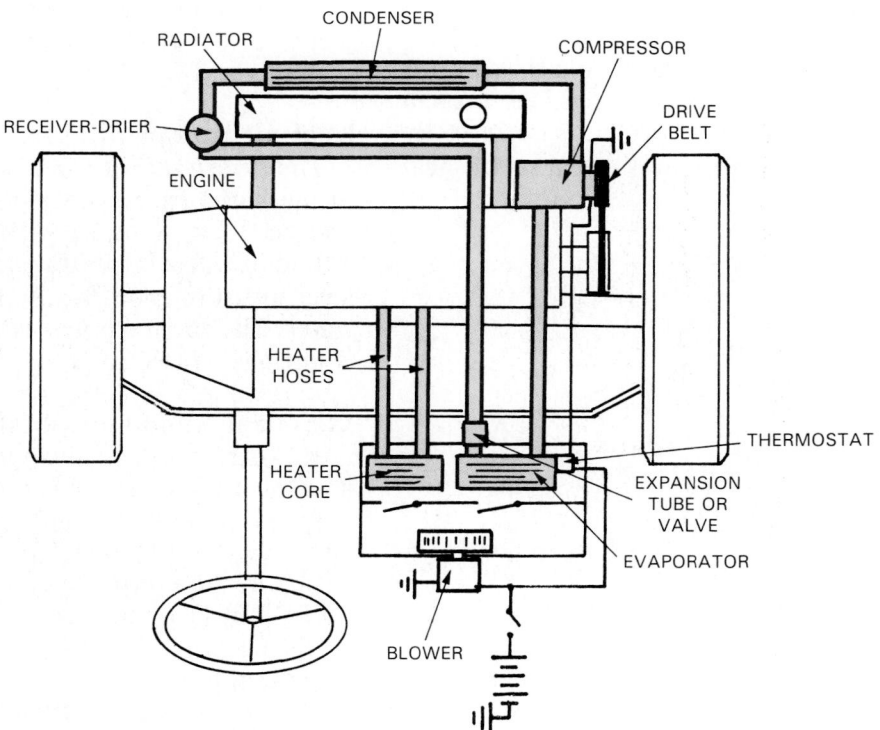

Fig. 71-1. Heating, ventilation, and air conditioning systems work together to provide passenger comfort. Study basic parts.

you should understand a few rules that apply to refrigeration before studying an automotive air conditioning system.

States of matter

There are three basic *states of matter:* vapor, liquid, and solid. For example, look at Fig. 71-2. It shows the three states of water. Water can exist as a vapor (steam), a liquid (tap water), or as a solid (ice). The temperature of the water controls its state.

Heat and matter

As you can see with the three states of water, heat is a controlling factor in the state of matter. *Heat* is caused by molecular motion inside a substance. The hotter an object, the faster its molecules move. The colder an object, the slower its molecules move.

When water is hot enough, its molecules move fast enough to separate, forming water vapor. When water is cold enough, the molecules move slowly enough to join and form a solid chunk of ice.

Methods of heat transfer

There are three methods of heat transfer: conduction, convection, and radiation.

Conduction is heat transfer through objects that are touching each other, Fig. 71-3A. An example, engine combustion heat is conducted into the water jackets through the block and cylinder head. The metal parts of the engine would carry or CONDUCT heat.

Convection is heat transfer caused by the air surrounding objects, Fig. 71-3B. For instance, when air blows through a radiator, heat is convected into the air. Air would be the medium of heat transfer.

Radiation, the third method of heat transfer, is commonly caused by infrared rays (rays from the sun, for example). See Fig. 71-3C. When the sun shines through the windows of a vehicle, the interior parts (seats, steering wheel) can become very hot because of heat radiation.

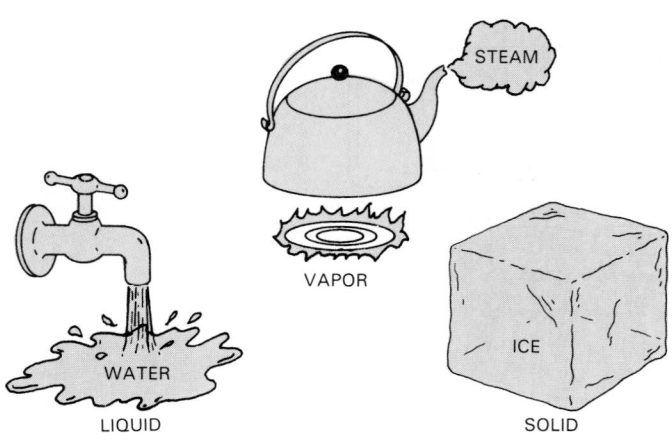

Fig. 71-2. These are the three fundamental states of matter. (Deere & Co.)

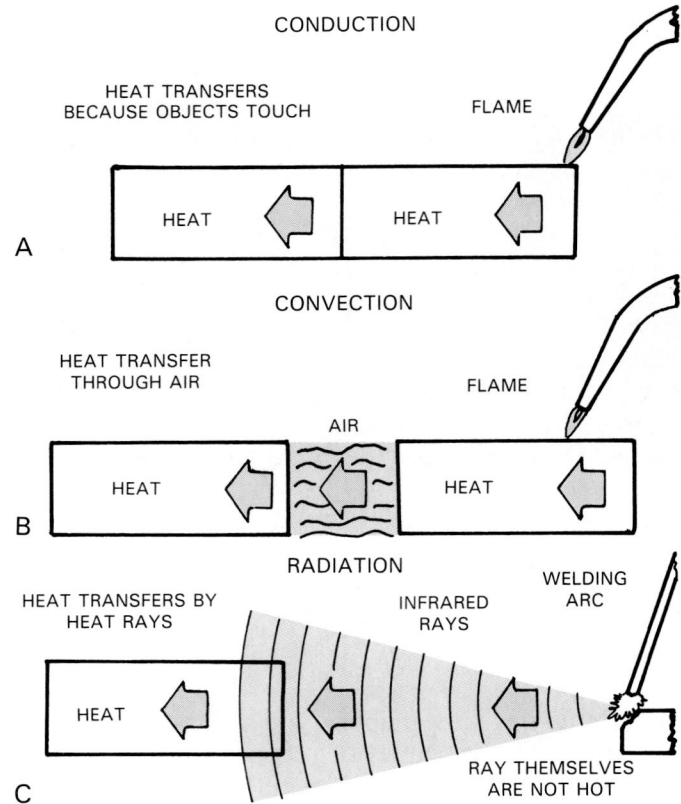

Fig. 71-3. Note three means of heat transfer.

Heat movement

Heat always transfers from a hotter object to a colder object. Technically, when you hold a piece of ice, the ice does not really cool your hand, it removes heat from your hand. This makes your hand feel cold.

Cold is actually an absence of heat. Hot and cold are relative (dependent on each other). When one object is colder than another, the colder object simply contains less heat.

Heat measurement

The *British thermal unit,* abbreviated Btu, is the unit of measurement for heat transfer from one object to another. For example, when the temperature of one pound of water increases one degree Fahrenheit at sea level pressure, one Btu of heat has moved into the water. The cooling potential of home air conditioning is normally rated in Btus.

Vaporization and evaporation

Vaporization and *evaporation* generally refer to a liquid changing into a vapor (gas) state. For instance, boiling water changing into steam (vapor) demonstrates vaporization. Water slowly changing to a vapor while sitting in the hot sun would be evaporation. Heat is ABSORBED when a liquid changes into a vapor.

Condensation

Condensation, the opposite of vaporization, occurs when a vapor changes back into a liquid. For example, when water collects on the outside of a soft drink bottle on a warm day, moisture has condensed out of the air. Heat is GIVEN OFF when a vapor changes into a liquid.

Pressure and temperature

When pressure is placed on a substance, the temperature of the substance increases. The substance gives off heat. Look at Fig. 71-4. When pressure is removed from a substance, the temperature of the substance drops. The substance absorbs heat (cools).

Pressure also affects change of state. When a liquid is placed in a closed container and pressurized, its boiling (vaporizing) point increases.

For example, the boiling point of water at sea level pressure (14.7 psi or 101 kPa) is 212 °F or 100 °C. However, when this pressure is increased, water's boiling point increases. If pressure is decreased, the boiling point decreases. This principle is true for other substances.

Refrigerant

A *refrigerant* is a substance with a very low boiling point. It is circulated through a refrigeration or air conditioning system. Refrigerant-12, called R-12 or Freon, has been the most stable, safest, and easiest-to-handle refrigerant. It has a boiling point of −22 °F (−30 °C) and vaporizes at room temperature and pressure. However, it has been found that R-12 is dangerous to the environment, because of a chemical reaction with the atmosphere. Production will cease in 1995. A new refrigerant, R-134a, is currently being phased in. Certain A/C system seals, controls, sensors, receiver-driers, leak-detection tools, and safety procedures may have to be changed with this new environmentally safe refrigerant.

Fig. 71-5 illustrates how a refrigerant can be used to reduce the temperature in an enclosed area.

BASIC REFRIGERATION CYCLE

In the *basic refrigeration cycle,* the refrigerant goes through four phases: compression, condensation, expansion, and vaporization. As shown in Fig. 71-6, when the refrigerant condenses, heat transfers out of it and

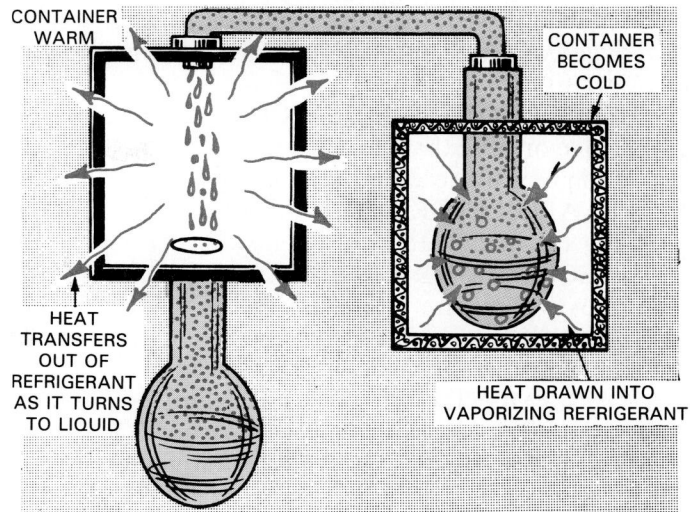

Fig. 71-5. Refrigerant can be used to cool object when it vaporizes. It releases gathered heat when it condenses. (General Motors)

into the surrounding air. Then, when the refrigerant evaporates, heat is absorbed by it to cool the air in that area.

Fig. 71-7 illustrates the operation of a refrigeration system. Eight basic parts are used:
1. REFRIGERANT (R-12 that carries heat through system to lower air temperature in vehicle).
2. COMPRESSOR (pump that pressurizes refrigerant and forces it through system).

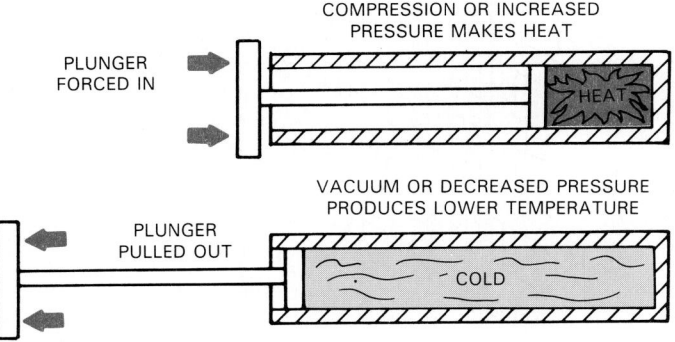

Fig. 71-4. Study pressure and temperature relationship.

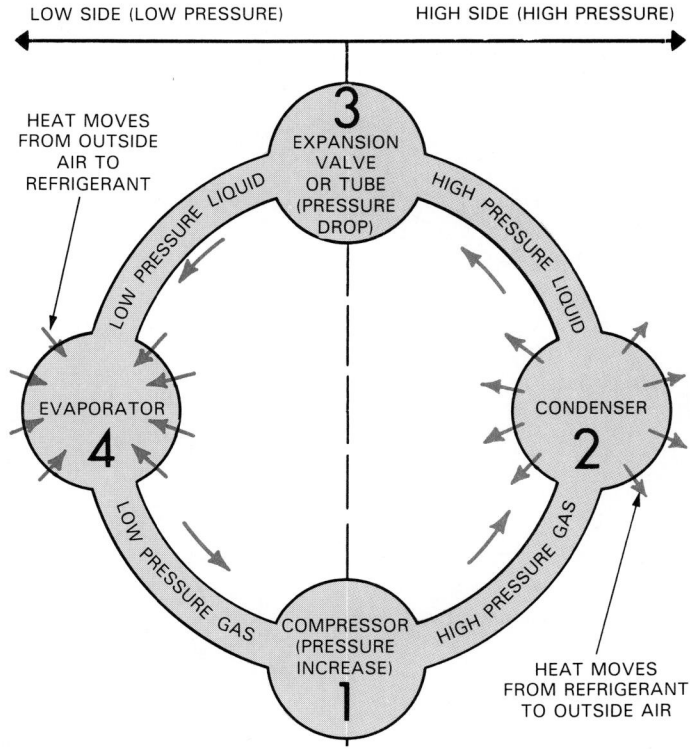

Fig. 71-6. Study diagram showing basic refrigeration cycle. (Deere & Co.)

3. CONDENSER (causes refrigerant to change from a gaseous state into a liquid state, causing it to give off its stored heat).
4. FLOW CONTROL DEVICE (usually expansion valve or tube that causes refrigerant pressure and temperature to drop, cooling the evaporator).
5. EVAPORATOR (uses cooling action of vaporizing refrigerant to cool air inside car).
6. RECEIVER-DRIER or ACCUMULATOR (removes moisture from and stores refrigerant).
7. BLOWER (fan that forces air through evaporator and into passenger compartment).
8. THERMOSTATIC SWITCH (shuts compressor off when evaporator temperature nears freezing).

As shown in Fig. 71-7, refrigerant circulates around inside the system. The compressor pressurizes the refrigerant and forces it into the condenser, where it condenses into a liquid. Heat is transferred into the condenser and then into the outside air.

Liquified refrigerant then flows to a restriction (orifice tube or expansion valve). As it passes through the restriction, pressure suddenly drops. This makes the refrigerant turn into a vapor as it enters the evaporator. There, it absorbs heat from the evaporator and the evaporator becomes very cold.

Since the blower is forcing air through the evaporator, cold air blows into the area to be cooled. The refrigerant vapor is then pulled back into the compressor for another cycle.

AUTOMOTIVE AIR CONDITIONING SYSTEM

An *automotive air conditioning system,* abbreviated A/C system, performs four basic functions. It cools, dehumidifies (dries), cleans, and circulates the air in the car.

All automotive air conditioning systems contain the same basic components shown in Fig. 71-7. Additional components (valves and switches) are utilized to increase system efficiency and dependability.

Fig. 71-8 illustrates a diagram of a basic automotive air conditioning system. Compare it to the basic refrigeration system shown in Fig. 71-7.

High and low sides

There are two major divisions of an air conditioning system: high and low pressure sides, Fig. 71-9.

The **high side** or *discharge side* of an A/C system consists of the parts between the output of the compressor and the flow control restriction. All of the lines

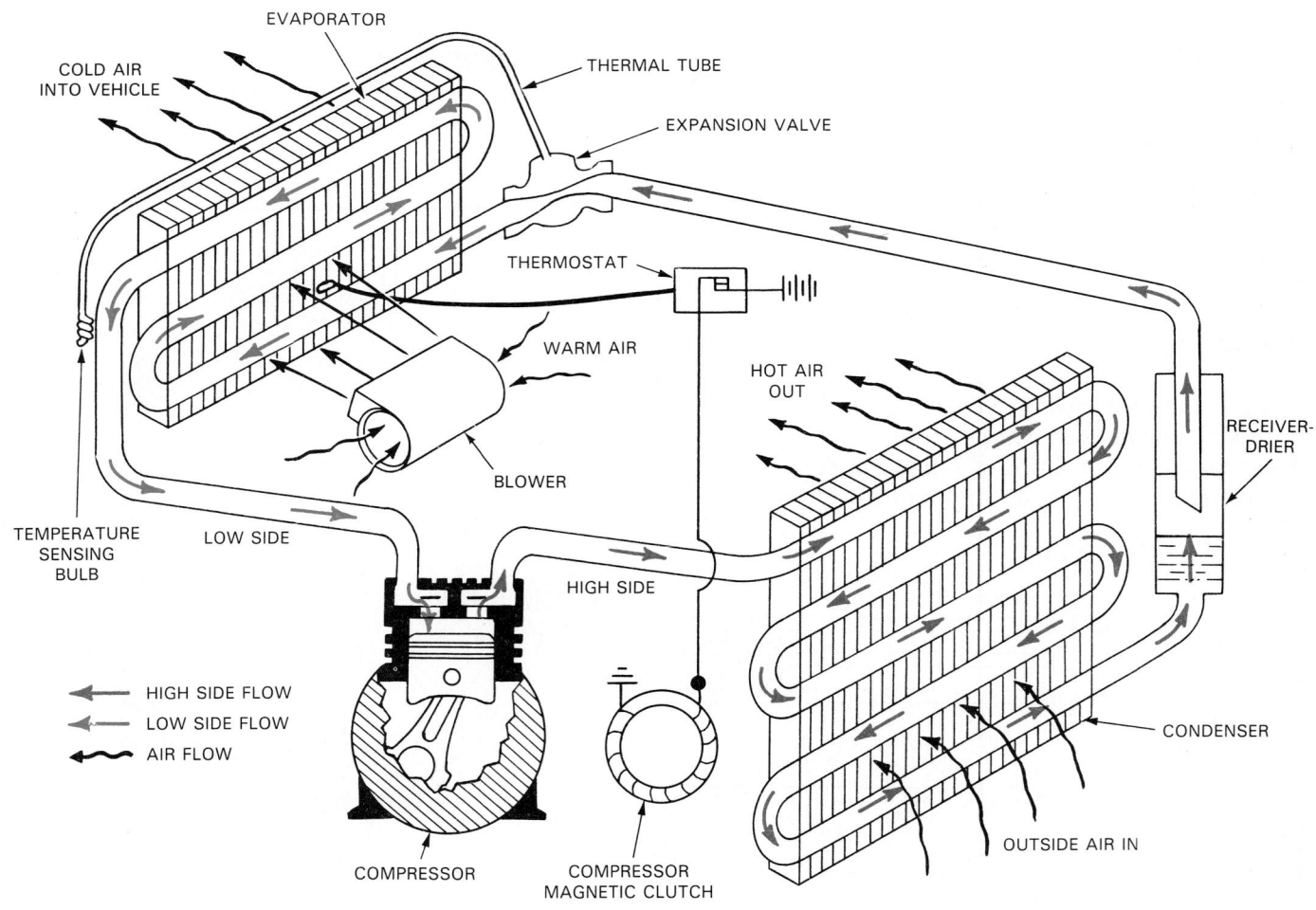

Fig. 71-7. Fundamental parts and action of an auto air conditioning system. (Deere & Co.)

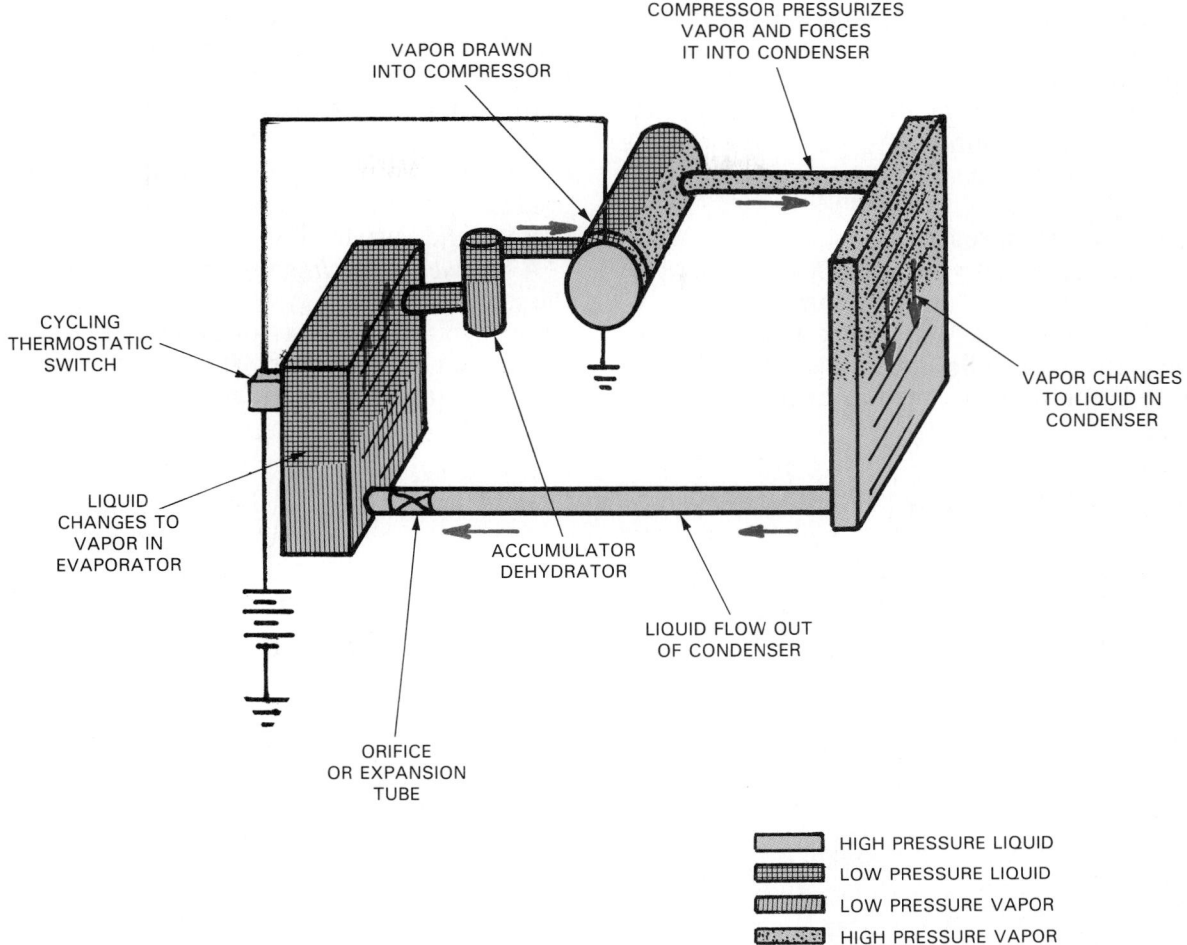

VAPOR DRAWN INTO COMPRESSOR

COMPRESSOR PRESSURIZES VAPOR AND FORCES IT INTO CONDENSER

CYCLING THERMOSTATIC SWITCH

VAPOR CHANGES TO LIQUID IN CONDENSER

LIQUID CHANGES TO VAPOR IN EVAPORATOR

ACCUMULATOR DEHYDRATOR

LIQUID FLOW OUT OF CONDENSER

ORIFICE OR EXPANSION TUBE

HIGH PRESSURE LIQUID
LOW PRESSURE LIQUID
LOW PRESSURE VAPOR
HIGH PRESSURE VAPOR

Fig. 71-8. Trace flow of refrigerant liquid and vapor through system.

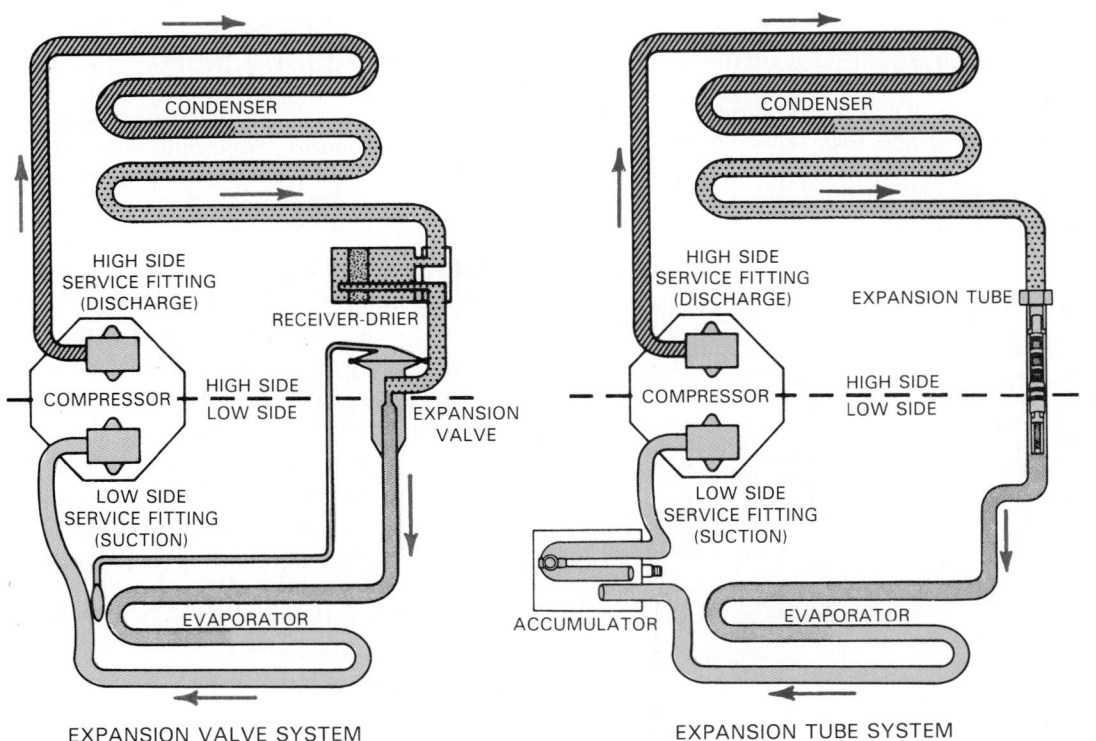

CONDENSER

HIGH SIDE SERVICE FITTING (DISCHARGE)

RECEIVER-DRIER

COMPRESSOR

HIGH SIDE
LOW SIDE

EXPANSION VALVE

LOW SIDE SERVICE FITTING (SUCTION)

EVAPORATOR

EXPANSION VALVE SYSTEM

CONDENSER

HIGH SIDE SERVICE FITTING (DISCHARGE)

EXPANSION TUBE

COMPRESSOR

HIGH SIDE
LOW SIDE

LOW SIDE SERVICE FITTING (SUCTION)

ACCUMULATOR

EVAPORATOR

EXPANSION TUBE SYSTEM

Fig. 71-9. Note parts in high and low sides of typical air conditioning system. (Mitchell Manuals)

Heating and Air Conditioning 945

and other parts operating on high pressure would be considered in the high side of the system.

The *low side* or *suction side* of an A/C system consists of the parts between the flow control restriction and the inlet of the compressor. All of these parts would have low pressure.

Air conditioning compressor

An *air conditioning compressor* is a piston or vane type pump bolted to the front of the engine, Fig. 71-10. It is normally driven by a V or ribbed-type belt from the engine crankshaft pulley. Although exact designs vary, an A/C compressor operates as in Fig. 71-11.

In a piston type compressor, a piston is forced to slide up and down in a cylinder. This produces an intake (suction) stroke when the piston moves down. An output (pressure) stroke occurs when it moves up.

A *reed valve* is simply a thin piece of metal that bends to open and close an opening. Reed valves are normally used as check valves to produce flow through the compressor and system, Fig. 71-12.

A *magnetic clutch* is used to engage and disengage the air conditioning system compressor. A magnetic clutch typically consists of an electric coil, a pulley, and a front clutch plate. These parts bolt around or on the shaft going into the compressor. See Fig. 71-13.

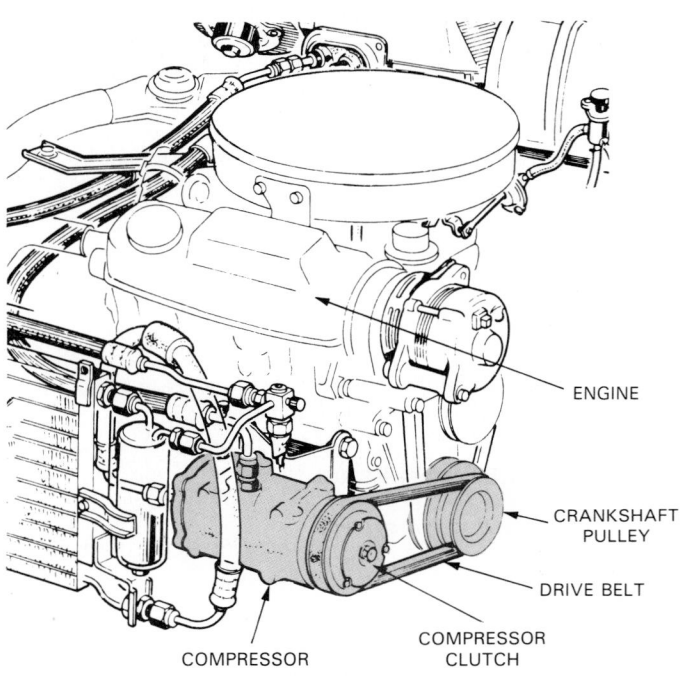

Fig. 71-10. Air conditioning compressor is normally belt driven off front of engine. This engine is transverse mounted in car. (Honda)

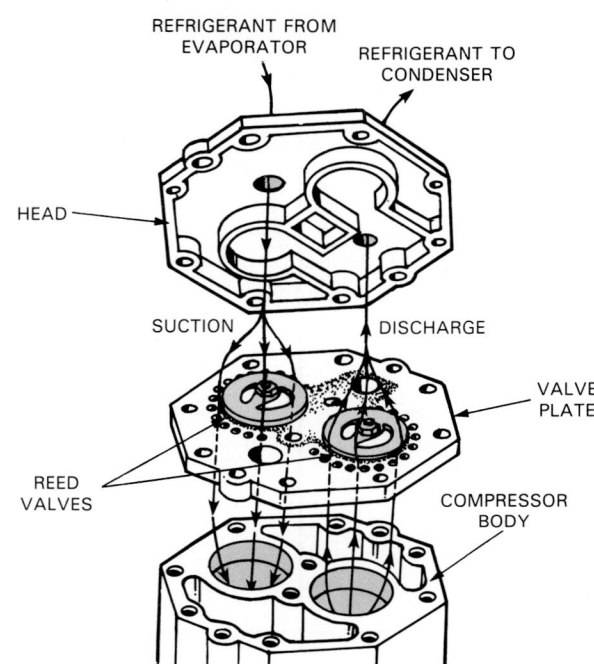

Fig. 71-12. Compressor reed valves control flow in and out of compressor. Note how they mount in unit. (Florida Dept. of Voc. Ed.)

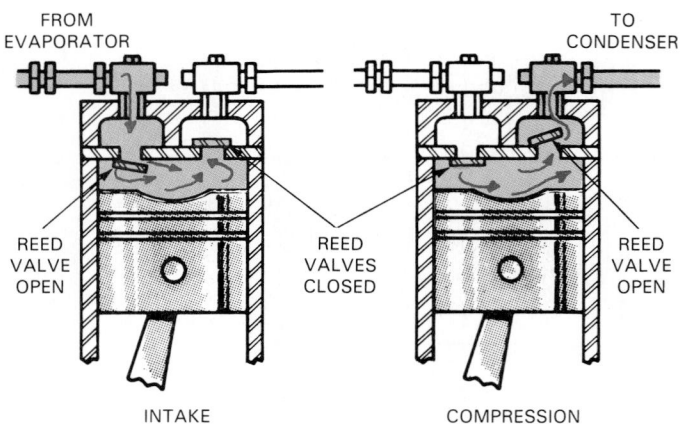

Fig. 71-11. Study basic operation of air conditioning compressor. During intake stroke, piston slides down and pulls vapor into cylinder. On compression stroke, piston slides up and forces vapor through system. (Ford Motor Co.)

When current is passed through the compressor coil, a strong magnetic field develops. The magnetic field pulls the front clutch plate into contact with the compressor pulley, Fig. 71-14. This locks the clutch plate and pulley together. The compressor shaft then rotates to operate the internal parts of the compressor.

When current to the compressor coil is shut off, it releases the clutch plate. This lets the compressor pulley free-wheel, so the compressor doesn't function.

There are five types of automotive air conditioning compressors:
1. Crank (in-line or V-type), 2-cylinder type compressor, Fig. 71-15.
2. Axial, 4-cylinder type compressor, Fig. 71-16.
3. Radial, 6-cylinder type compressor, Fig. 71-17.
4. Rotary vane compressor, Fig. 71-18.
5. Scroll compressor, Fig. 71-19.

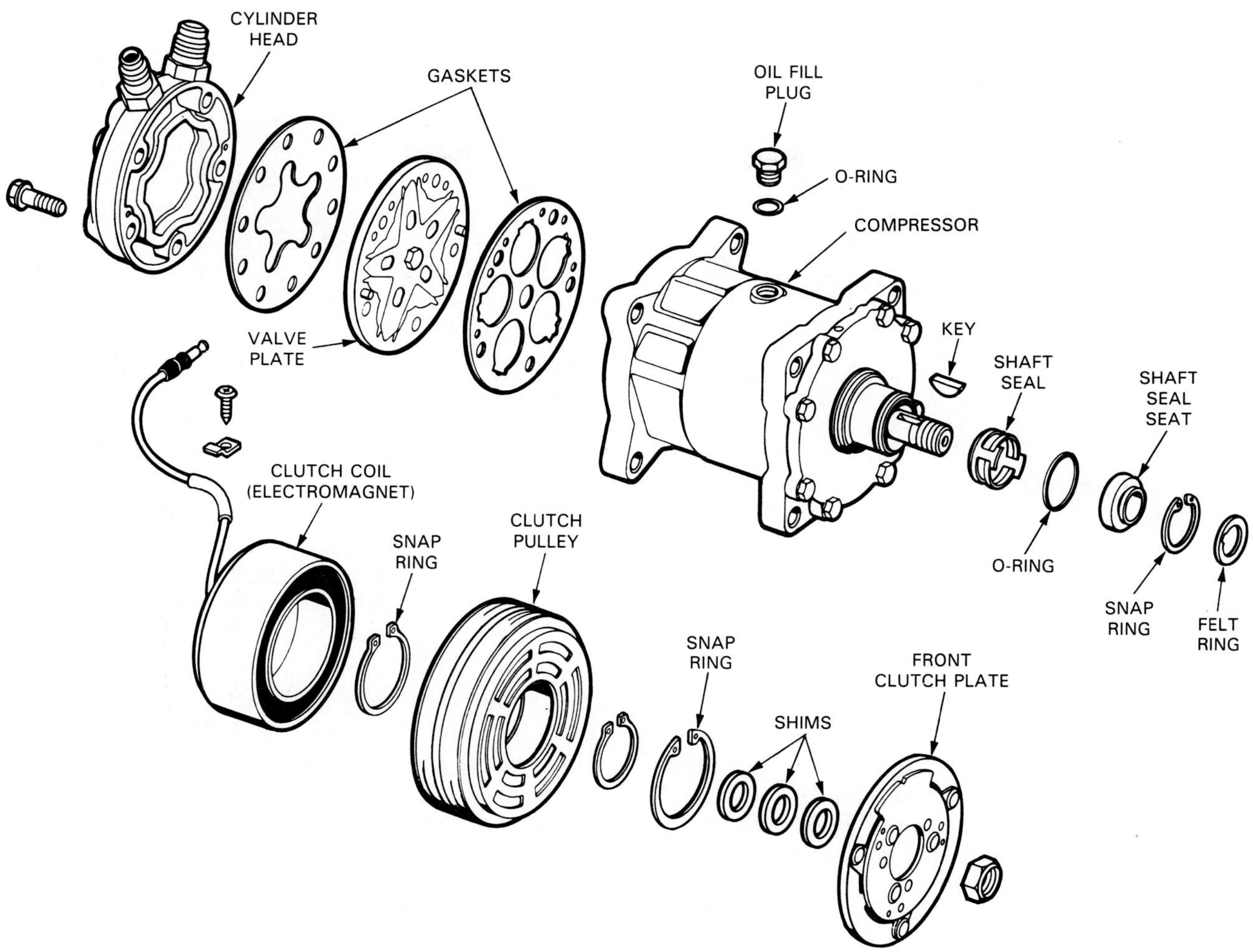

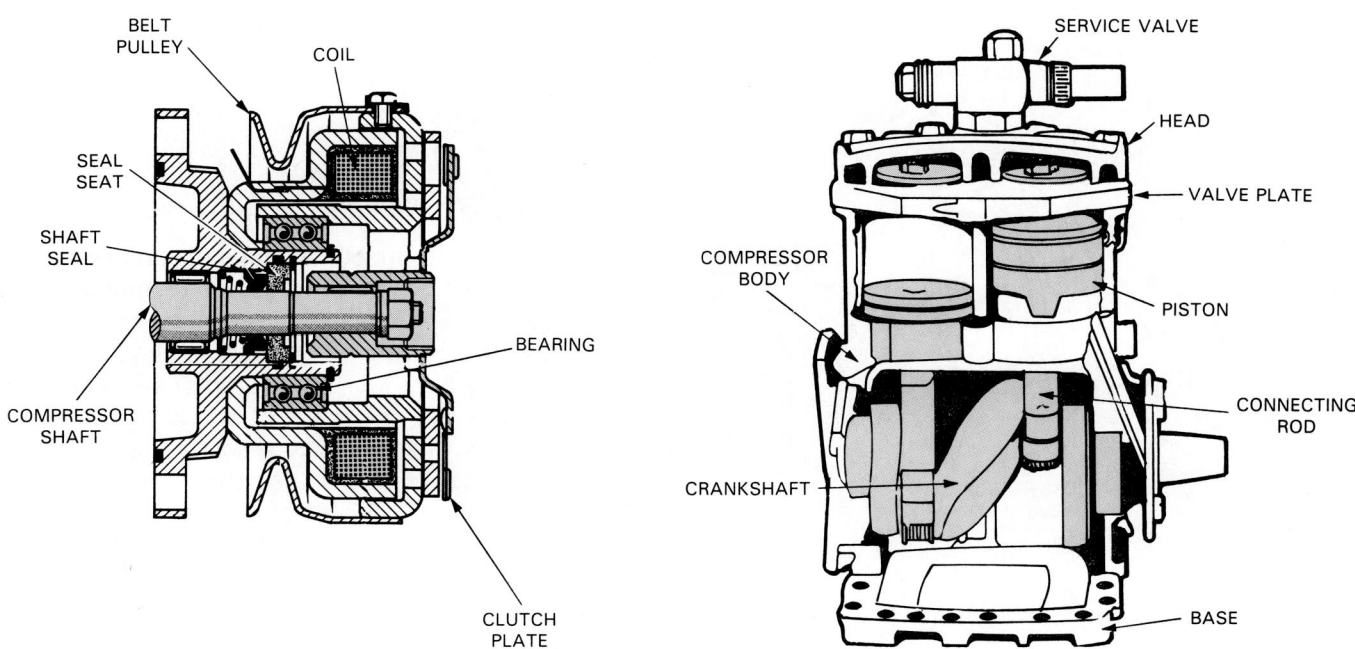

Fig. 71-13. Exploded view of modern compressor shows how valve plate and clutch mount on main body of compressor. (Chrysler)

Fig. 71-14. Cutaway of compressor clutch shows electromagnetic coil that pulls clutch plate into hub, locking assembly together to rotate drive or input shaft. (Mercedes Benz)

Fig. 71-15. Crank type compressor is similar to small gasoline engine. Crankshaft, connecting rods, and pistons make up reciprocating assembly. Note other parts. (Florida Dept. of Voc. Ed.)

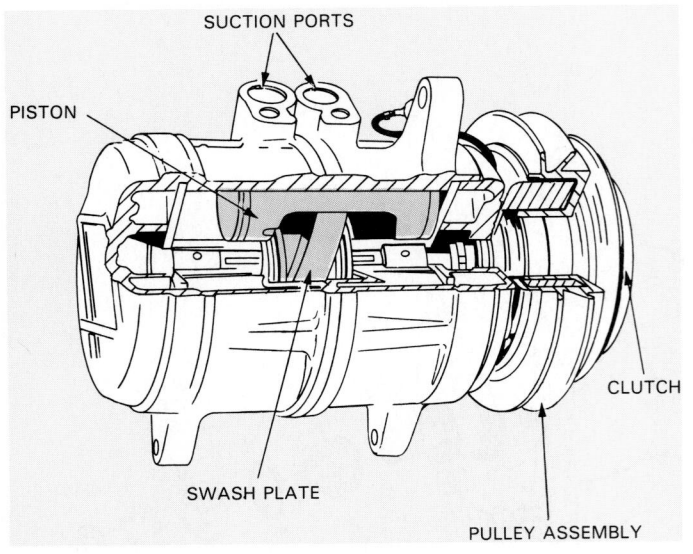

Fig. 71-16. Axial compressor has pistons moving lengthwise in body. Swash plate moves pistons. (Mitchell Manuals)

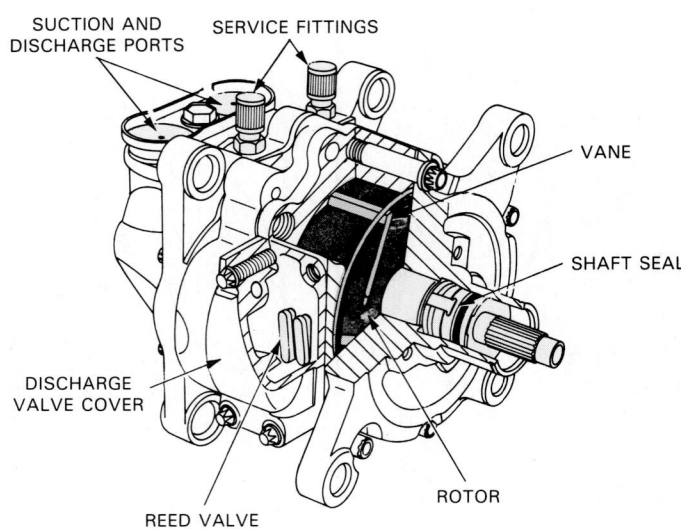

Fig. 71-18. Modern rotary vane compressor works something like oil or air injection pump. Blades spin inside housing to pressurize refrigerant. (Mitchell Manuals)

Compare the shape and construction of each type. Note that three of the five types use pistons, cylinders, and reed valves to produce system pressure. The main difference is the position of these parts.

The crank type compressor uses a CRANKSHAFT similar to the crankshaft used in a vehicle engine. The axial compressor uses a SWASH PLATE to produce piston motion. A SHAFT ECCENTRIC (egg-shaped component) causes piston movement in a radial type compressor. Vanes (blades), as in oil or power steering pumps, pressurize the refrigerant in a rotary vane compressor.

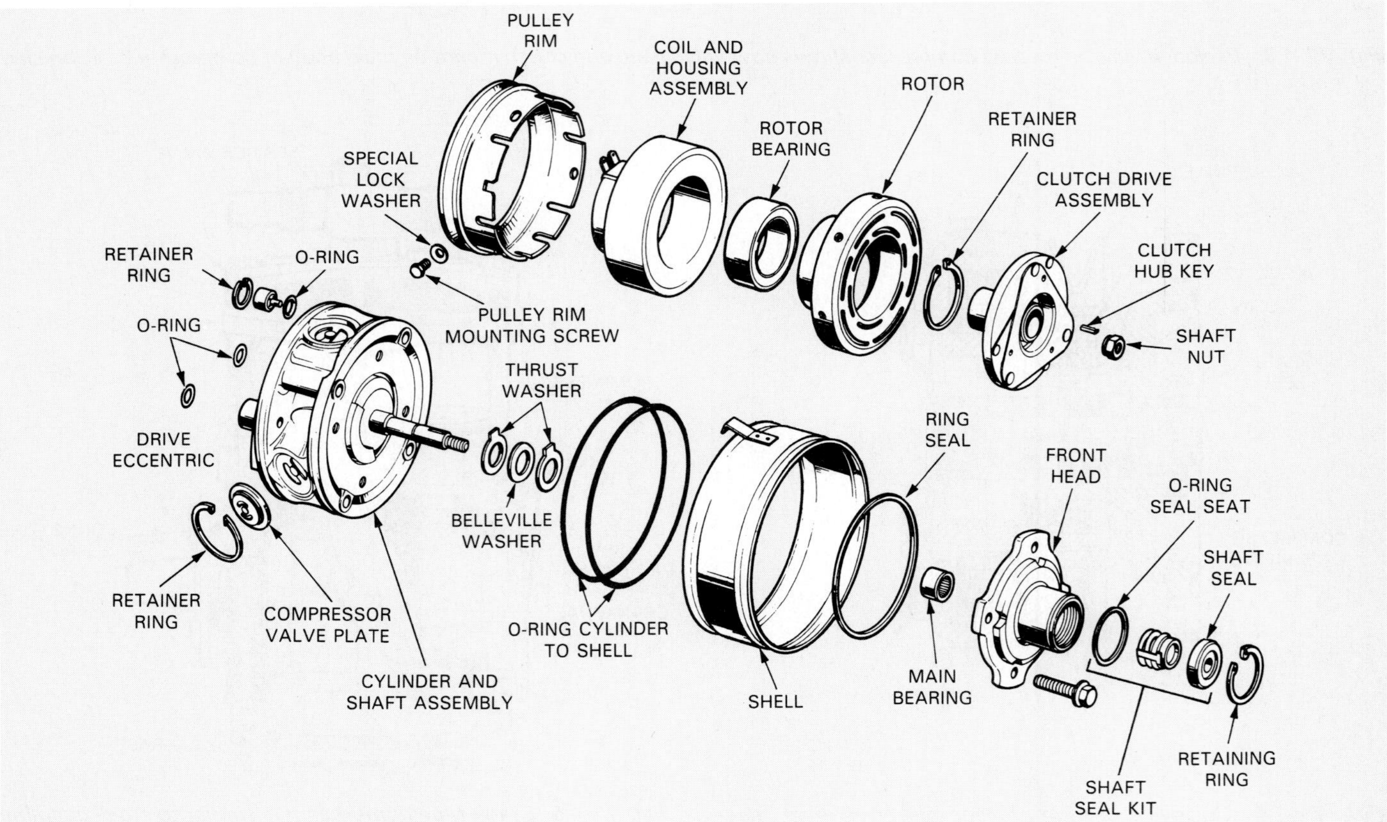

Fig. 71-17. Radial compressor has shaft-mounted eccentric that moves pistons in and out. Pistons are arranged in circle around shaft. Study parts. (Chrysler)

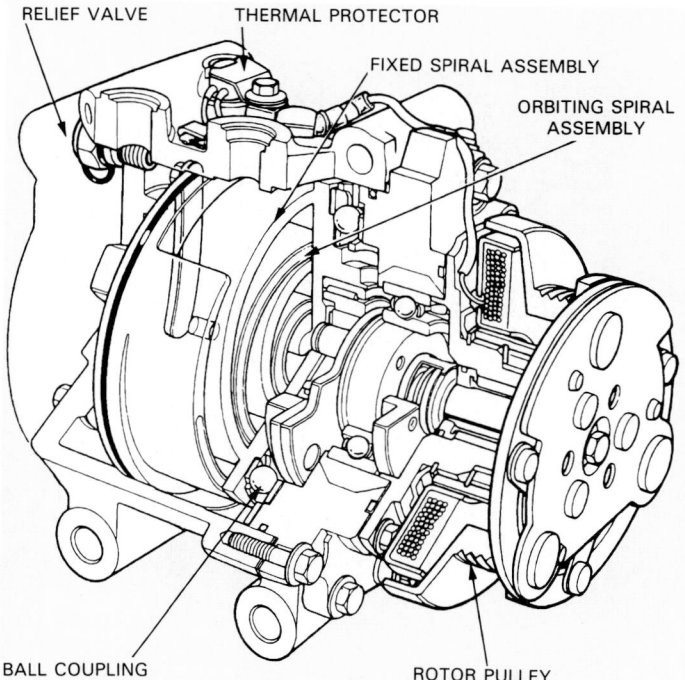

Fig. 71-19. A cutaway view of the scroll compressor. (Honda)

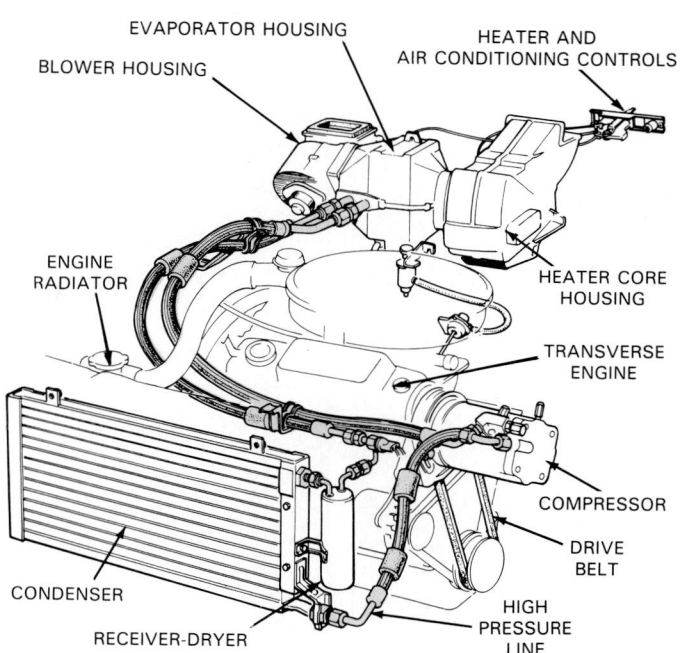

Fig. 71-20. High pressure refrigerant hoses and lines carry refrigerant through system. (Honda)

Refrigerant oil

Refrigerant oil is high viscosity, highly refined (pure) oil used to keep the parts of the air conditioning system lubricated, especially the compressor. Since the refrigerant oil and the refrigerant mix, oil droplets are carried throughout the system. The refrigerant oil also splashes around inside the compressor to reduce friction and wear.

Refrigerant hoses

Refrigerant hoses carry refrigerant to each air conditioning system component and back to the compressor. They are special high pressure hoses designed to withstand compressor pressure as high as 250 psi (1 725 kPa), Fig. 71-20.

Special fittings are used on the ends of refrigerant hoses. O-ring seals, hose clamps, or flared tube ends are used on the fittings to prevent leakage. Fig. 71-21 shows the most common types of fittings.

Air conditioning condenser

An *air conditioning condenser* is a radiator-like device for transferring heat from the refrigerant to the outside air. Shown in Fig. 71-20, it normally bolts in front of the cooling system radiator.

The condenser is simply a long metal tube wound back and forth inside hundreds of metal fins. The fins increase the amount of surface area for heat transfer.

Receiver-drier

A *receiver-drier* is used to remove moisture from the system and store extra refrigerant. It is normally located

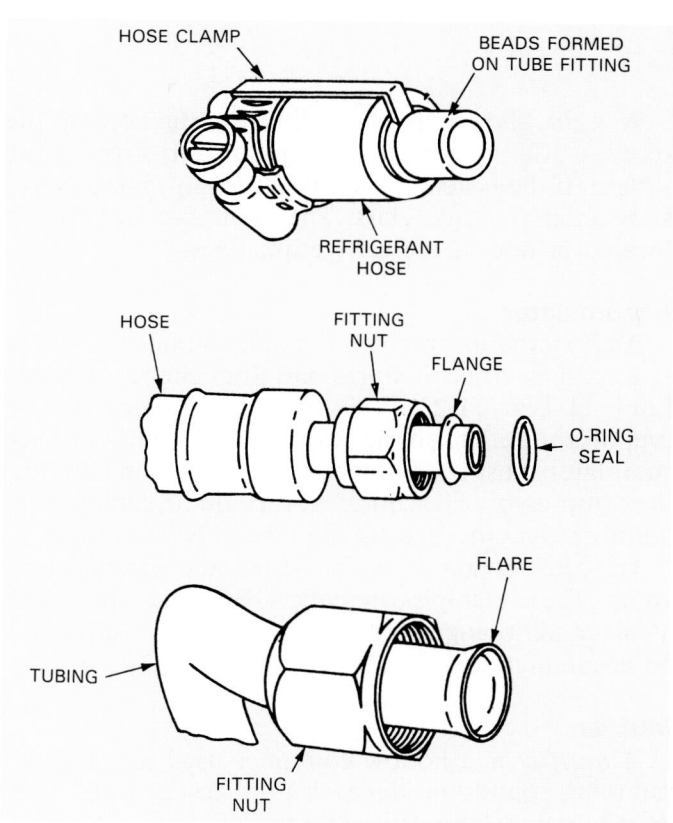

Fig. 71-21. Note common types of fittings found in vehicle air conditioning systems. (GMC)

in the system HIGH SIDE. A cutaway view of a typical receiver-drier is given in Fig. 71-22. Note that the inside of the unit contains a DESICCANT (drying agent or silica gel) to remove water from the refrigerant.

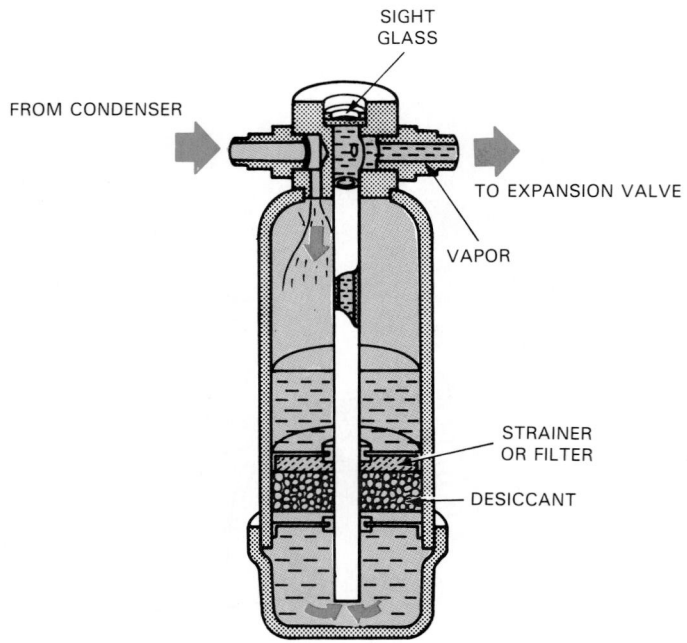

Fig. 71-22. Receiver-drier or dehydrator filters and removes moisture from air conditioning system. Desiccant is substance that absorbs and stores moisture. This unit has sight glass in top of housing. (Nissan)

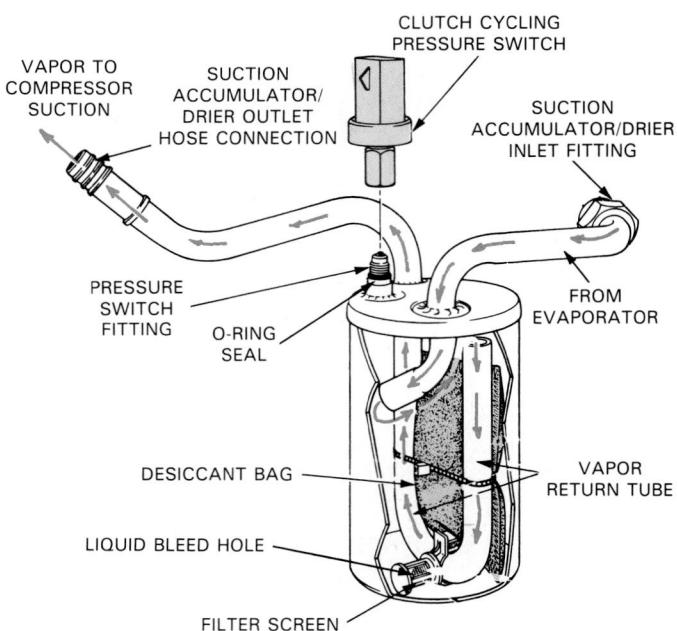

Fig. 71-23. Accumulator serves same basic function as a receiver-drier. It serves as a reservoir and moisture trap. Note how clutch cycling switch mounts on accumulator. (Ford)

A *sight glass* may be located in the top of the receiver-drier to show the amount of refrigerant in the system. If the system is low on refrigerant, bubbles will show up in the sight glass. The sight glass can also be located in one of the refrigerant lines.

Accumulator

An *accumulator* performs almost the same function as a receiver-drier: it stores and dries the refrigerant. Look at Fig. 71-23. It is normally located at the evaporator outlet, on the system LOW SIDE. The accumulator must keep liquid refrigerant from entering the compressor. The compressor could be damaged by liquid refrigerant, because liquids do NOT compress.

The construction of receiver-driers and accumulators varies. These examples are typical. Fig. 71-24 illustrates an air conditioning system that uses both a receiver and an accumulator.

Muffler

A *muffler* is a hollow container used to quiet the pumping sounds produced by the compressor. It is usually a metal can formed into the high pressure or compressor discharge refrigerant line.

Evaporator

The *evaporator,* like the condenser, is a refrigerant coil mounted in cooling fins, Fig. 71-24. The evaporator is usually mounted on the right side of the vehicle. It fits inside the blower housing, either on the outside or inside of the firewall, Fig. 71-20.

AIR CONDITIONING SYSTEM CONTROLS

All A/C systems use a compressor, condenser, evaporator, drier, or accumulator. However, many different devices are used to control the flow of refrigerant and the operation of the compressor.

For example, the two most common types of air conditioning systems are:
1. Cycling clutch or expansion (orifice) tube A/C system.
2. Thermostatic expansion valve A/C system.

Over the years, other systems have been used. However, these two represent the most typical and easiest to understand A/C systems found on today's vehicles. They will provide typical examples.

Expansion tube system

An *expansion tube A/C system* controls refrigerant flow and the temperature of the evaporator by cycling the compressor on and off. Look at Fig. 71-25. This type system is one of the simplest.

The **expansion tube,** also termed *orifice tube,* has a fixed opening that meters into the evaporator. The expansion tube usually fits near or in the evaporator inlet. It is usually a straight tube made of plastic or sintered metal, Fig. 71-26.

Cycling switches

Two types of *compressor cycling switches* can be used in an orifice tube type A/C system: thermostatic cycling switch and pressure cycling switch.

A **thermostatic cycling switch** turns the compressor on and off to maintain the correct evaporator

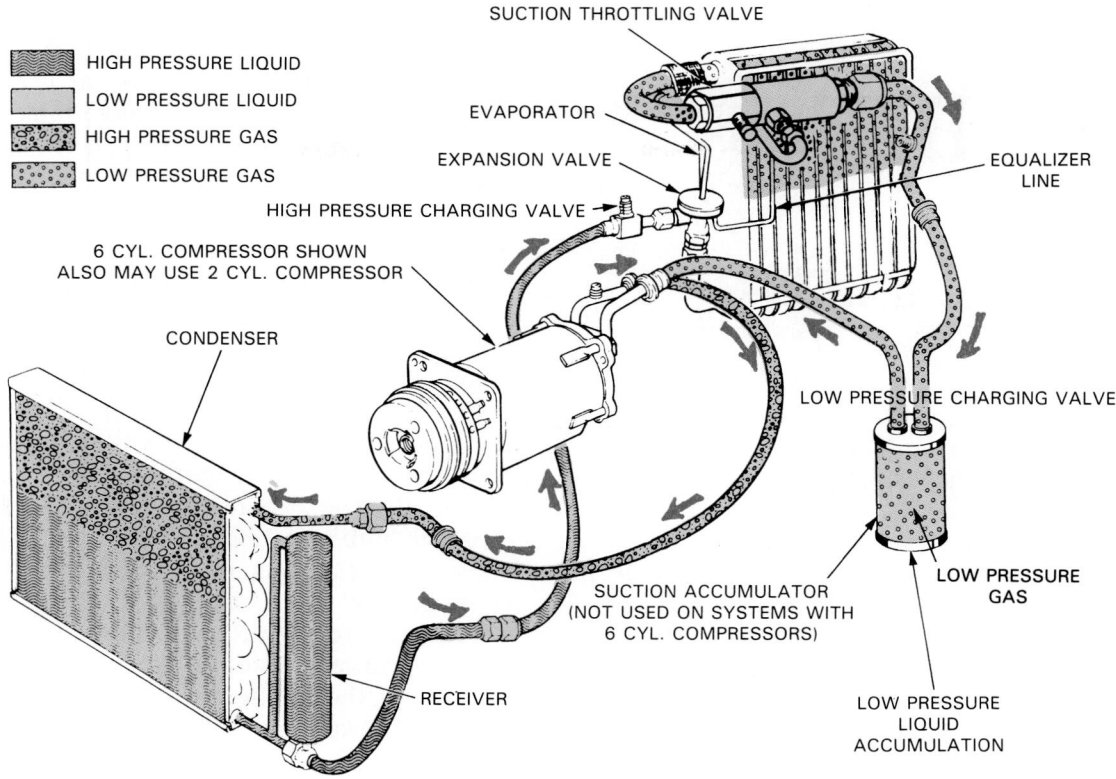

HIGH PRESSURE LIQUID
LOW PRESSURE LIQUID
HIGH PRESSURE GAS
LOW PRESSURE GAS

SUCTION THROTTLING VALVE

EVAPORATOR

EXPANSION VALVE

HIGH PRESSURE CHARGING VALVE

6 CYL. COMPRESSOR SHOWN
ALSO MAY USE 2 CYL. COMPRESSOR

CONDENSER

EQUALIZER
LINE

LOW PRESSURE CHARGING VALVE

LOW PRESSURE
GAS

SUCTION ACCUMULATOR
(NOT USED ON SYSTEMS WITH
6 CYL. COMPRESSORS)

LOW PRESSURE
LIQUID
ACCUMULATION

RECEIVER

Fig. 71-24. *Trace flow of liquid and vapor refrigerant through system. Note location of accumulator.* (Ford Motor Co.)

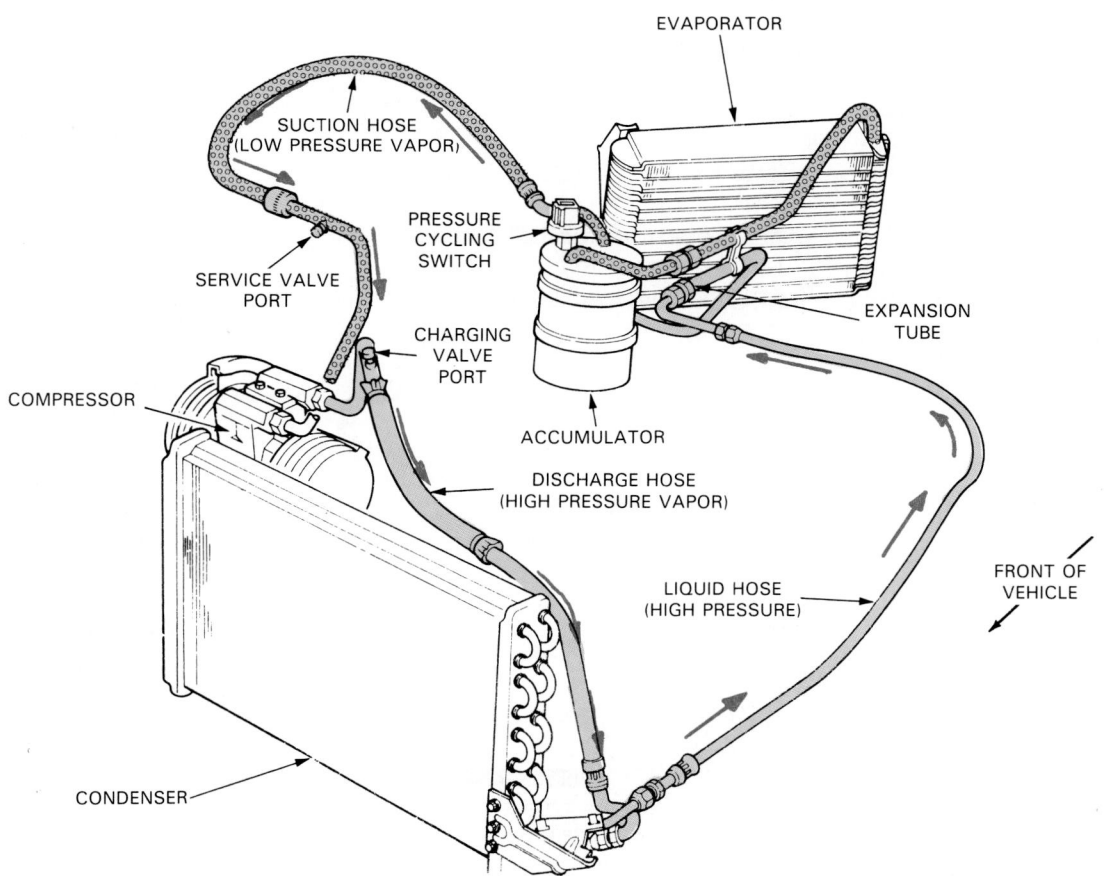

EVAPORATOR

SUCTION HOSE
(LOW PRESSURE VAPOR)

PRESSURE
CYCLING
SWITCH

SERVICE VALVE
PORT

CHARGING
VALVE
PORT

EXPANSION
TUBE

COMPRESSOR

ACCUMULATOR

DISCHARGE HOSE
(HIGH PRESSURE VAPOR)

FRONT
OF
VEHICLE

LIQUID HOSE
(HIGH PRESSURE)

CONDENSER

Fig. 71-25. *Orifice tube or clutch cycling system turns compressor on and off to control amount of refrigerant flowing through evaporator. This provides simple method of maintaining temperature.*

Heating and Air Conditioning 951

Fig. 71-26. Expansion tube has metering orifice or hole that allows specific amount of refrigerant to enter evaporator. It is used in clutch cycling type systems. (Mitchell Manuals)

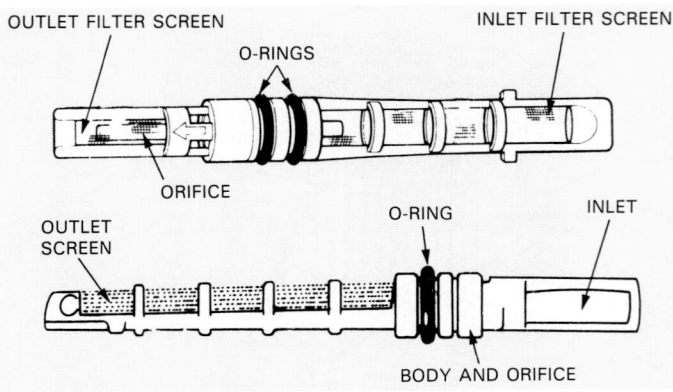

temperature (approximately 32 °F or 0 °C) at the evaporator. See Fig. 71-25.

When the evaporator is warm, the switch is closed and current flows to the compressor clutch coil. This causes the compressor to function and cool the evaporator. Then, when the evaporator becomes cold enough (near freezing point), the cycling switch opens the circuit to the compressor clutch. This lets the evaporator temperature increase as needed.

Since evaporator pressure determines evaporator temperature, a ***pressure cycling switch*** can be used in place of a thermostatic switch to maintain the correct evaporator temperature.

Thermostat expansion valve

An *expansion valve* is a temperature-sensitive valve that controls refrigerant flow and the evaporator temperature. See Fig. 71-27. Instead of constantly cycling the compressor on and off, the expansion valve can open and close to meter the right amount of refrigerant into the evaporator.

Basically, an expansion valve consists of a thermostatic bulb and tube, a diaphragm, actuating pins, valve and seat, metering orifice, and a spring. A cutaway view of an expansion valve is in Fig. 71-28.

When the temperature of the evaporator and bulb is too warm, expansion in the thermostat bulb places pressure on the diaphragm. This flexes the diaphragm, pushing the expansion valve open. More refrigerant can

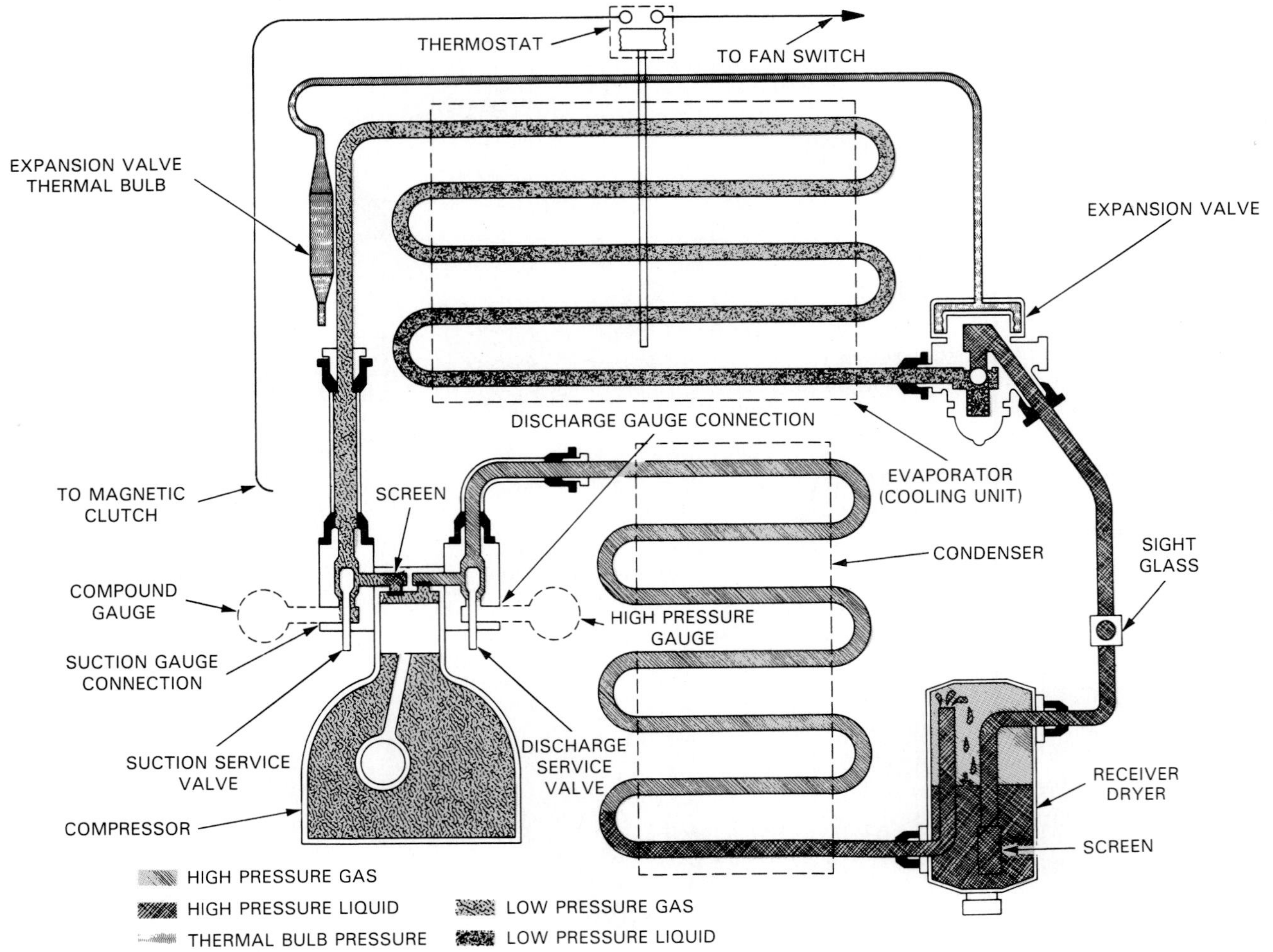

Fig. 71-27. A/C system using a thermostatic expansion valve. Thermal bulb senses evaporator outlet temperature. It can then open or close expansion valve to maintain temperature. (Chrysler)

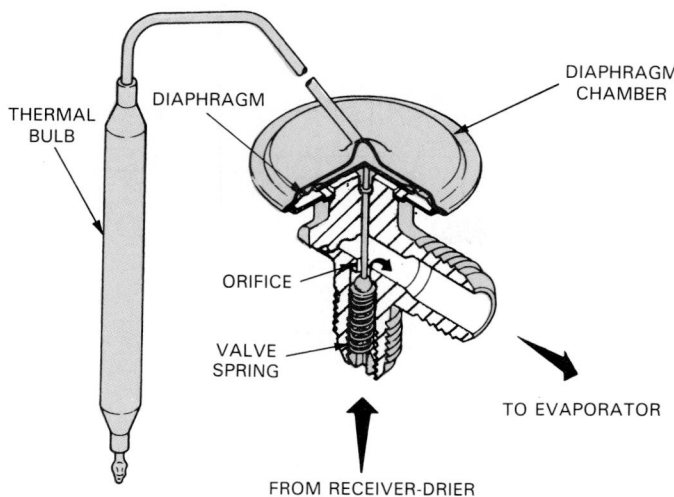

Fig. 71-28. Expansion valve opens and closes with temperature change to regulate amount of refrigerant entering evaporator. Compressor is not cycled on and off to control evaporator temperature. It runs all the time. (Nissan)

then flow into the evaporator to provide more cooling. When the system becomes too cold, bulb pressure drops. Then the spring in the expansion valve closes off the metering orifice to reduce refrigerant flow and cooling action, Fig. 71-28.

Other A/C system controls

Besides the thermostatic cycling switch, pressure cycling switch, and expansion valve, other controls are needed to increase system efficiency and protection.

Either a *POA* (pilot operated absolute) *valve* or *STV* (suction throttling) *valve* can be used with the expansion valve to control evaporator temperature. They sense and control EVAPORATOR PRESSURE to provide added protection against evaporator freeze-up. Look at Figs. 71-24 and 71-29.

A *combination valve* combines both the expansion valve and suction throttling valve into one assembly. Its operation is similar to the individual valves just introduced.

Valves in receiver (VIR) means that the expansion valve and POA valve are both enclosed in the receiver-drier. This is shown in Fig. 71-30.

An *ambient temperature switch* can be used to keep the compressor from operating with very cold outside (ambient) air temperatures. This prevents possible seal, gasket, and reed valve damage.

A *low pressure cutout switch* prevents compressor overheating damage when system pressure drops too low. Low system pressure can result from a refrigerant leak. The low pressure cutout is needed to interrupt the circuit to the compressor clutch. If the compressor continued to operate without refrigerant circulation, it could overheat and lock up.

A *high pressure cutout switch* can be used to shut the compressor off if discharge pressure is too high.

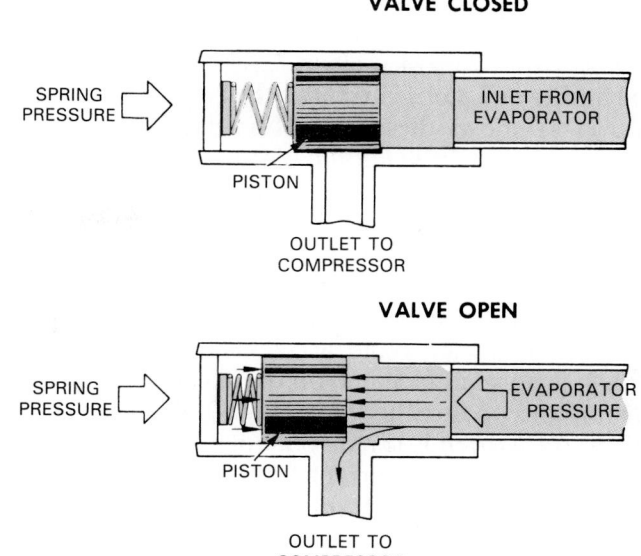

Fig. 71-29. Suction throttling valve, like thermostatic expansion valve, allows compressor to run constantly. Located in evaporator outlet, it senses evaporator pressure to control refrigerant flow and temperature. (AC-Delco)

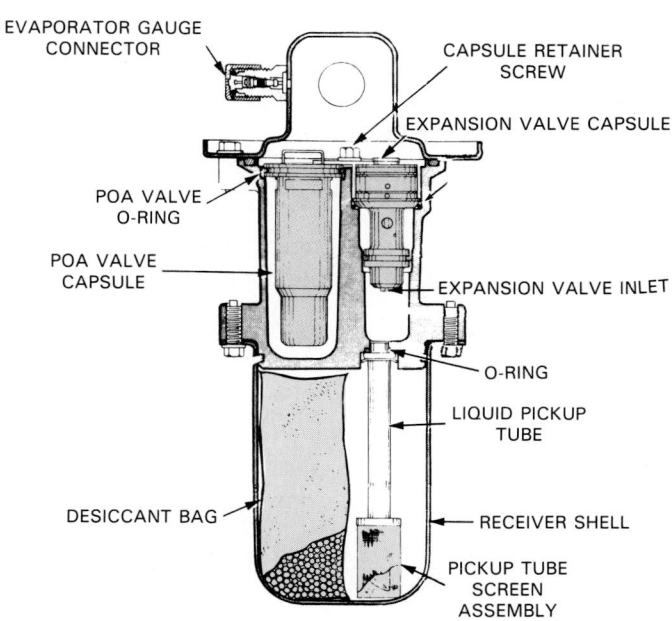

Fig. 71-30. VIR or valves in receiver has air conditioning flow control valves located inside receiver-drier. Note location of all components. (GMC)

Like the low pressure cutout switch, it prevents compressor damage from abnormal operating conditions.

The high pressure cutout switch is normally located in the service fitting of the discharge muffler. It opens the compressor coil circuit when pressure reaches approximately 375 psi (2 584 kPa).

A *thermal limiter* and *superheat switch* can be used to prevent compressor damage when the refrigerant level or OIL level is too low. The superheat switch senses low system pressure and high compressor temperature. It can then send current to the thermal limiter. Current flow melts a fusible link in the thermal limiter and stops current to the compressor clutch. Fig. 71-31 shows these protection devices.

A *pressure relief valve* will bleed off excess pressure to prevent compressor damage. It is a pop-off or spring-loaded type valve located on the receiver-drier, compressor, or other component in the high side.

The *wide open throttle (WOT) switch* is used on cars with small gasoline or diesel engines to shut off the compressor during rapid acceleration to save power loss. It is normally located on the accelerator linkage, carburetor, or throttle body, Fig. 71-31.

The *A/C switch* is the driver-operated switch in the car's dash that feeds current to the compressor clutch and other electric components. Shown in Fig. 71-31, the A/C switch provides a manual means of controlling system operation.

SERVICE VALVES

Service valves are basically provided to allow refrigerant installation, refrigerant removal, and pressure gauge tests of the A/C system, Fig. 71-27.

The *discharge service valve* is located at the output from the compressor, in the system high side.

The *suction service valve* is located at the inlet to the compressor, in the system low side.

HEATING SYSTEM

The *heating system* uses engine cooling system heat to warm the passenger compartment in cold weather.

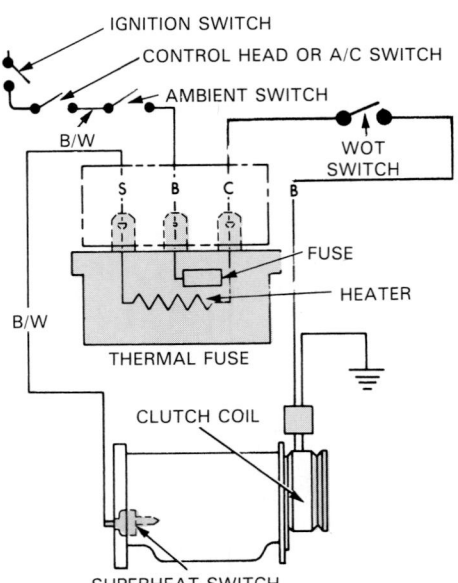

Fig. 71-31. Study how switches are wired in A/C system circuit. (AC-Delco)

A heating system typically consists of two heater hoses, a heater core, a blower (fan), and a control mechanism.

The *heater hoses* are small diameter hoses that carry engine coolant to the heater core, Fig. 71-32. Hot engine coolant flows through one heater hose, through the heater core, and back into the engine.

A vacuum-operated valve may be used in one of the heater hoses to control coolant flow to the heater core.

The *heater core* is a small radiator-like unit that provides a large surface area for heat dissipation into the

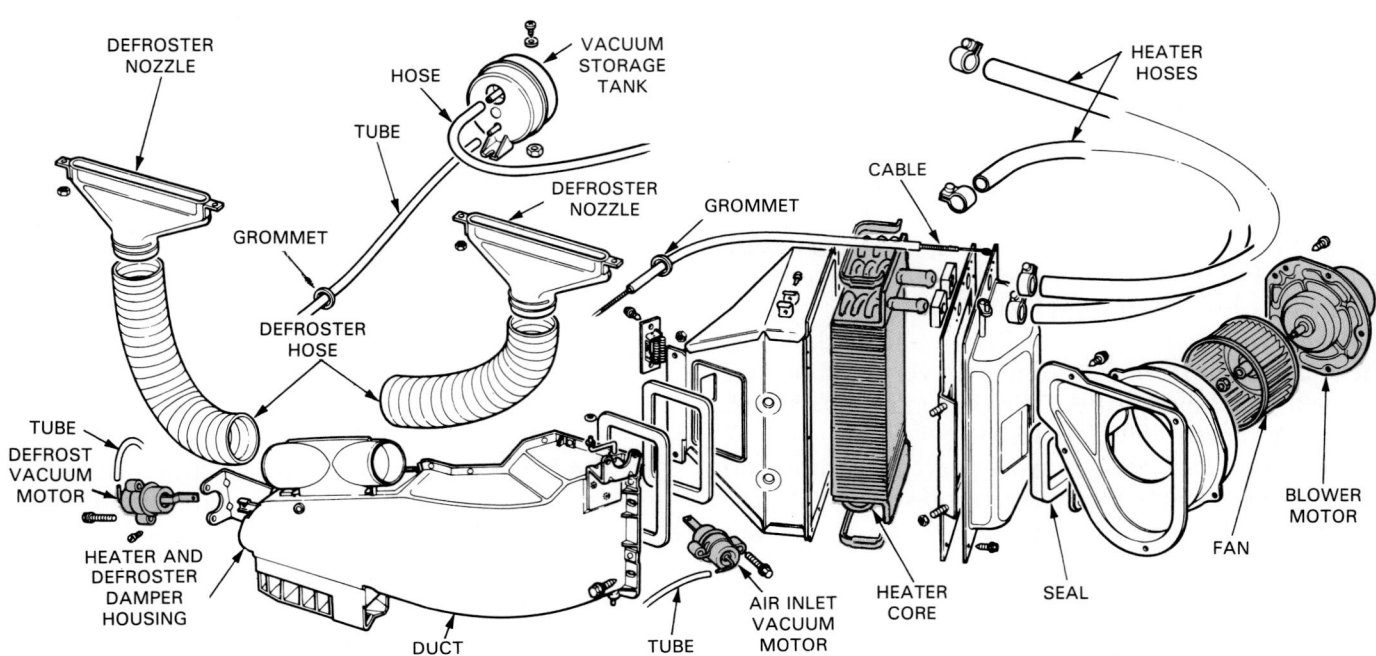

Fig. 71-32. Exploded view of vent and heat components that mount under dash of car. Note vacuum motors, heater core, and blower. (Chrysler)

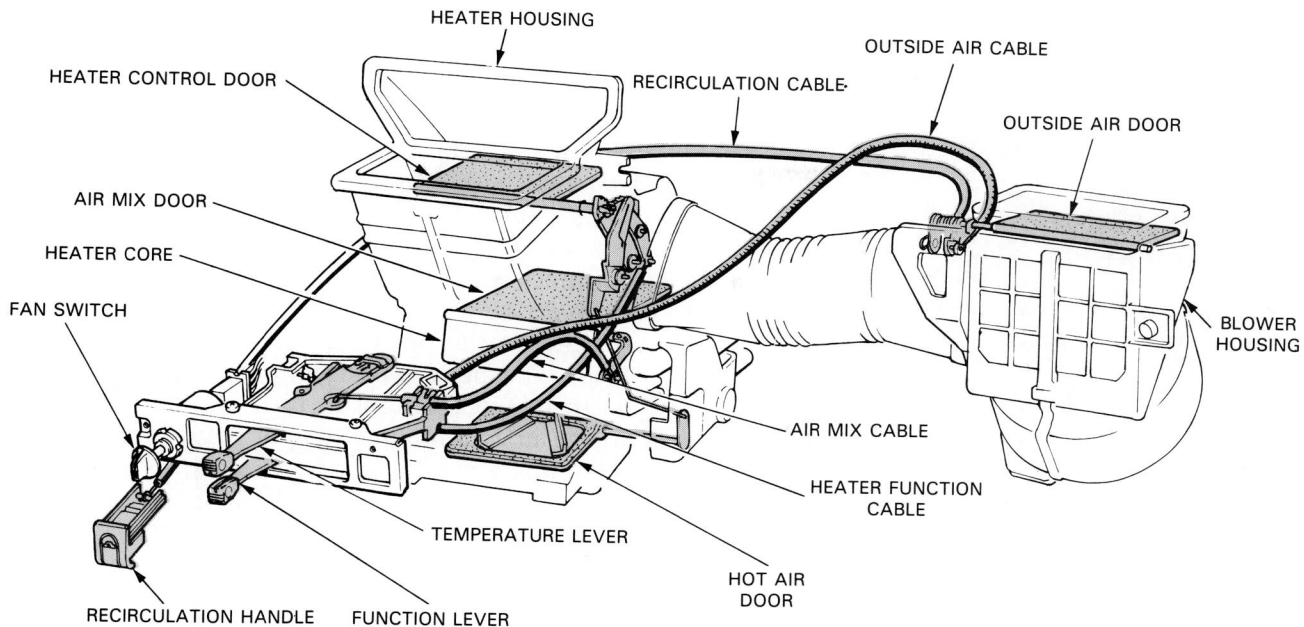

Fig. 71-33. *Driver's dash levers can be moved to operate cables to air control doors. Doors then open or close ducts to regulate whether warmed or cooled air enters passenger compartment.* (Honda)

passenger compartment. It is made of a series of tubes surrounded by fins. As air passes through the tubes and fins, heat transfers into the air. Look at Fig. 71-32.

The **blower** consists of an electric motor and fan assembly. When current is fed to the electric motor, the fan spins to force air through the heater core or air conditioning evaporator. The blower mounts in a housing that surrounds the heater core, evaporator (if used), and air doors. See Fig. 71-32.

Heater controls can be set to move the duct flaps so that cool outside air is mixed with hot heater core air, as in Fig. 71-33. This permits control of the passenger compartment temperature.

HEATING AND AIR CONDITIONING CONTROLS

The driver controls the operation of the heating and air conditioning systems using levers, buttons, or switches in the instrument panel. When the driver activates one of the instrument panel controls, one of four methods may be used to operate the system components:

1. An ELECTRIC SWITCH may operate, usually through relay(s), the blower motor, compressor clutch, and other electric components.
2. MECHANICAL LEVERS and CABLES can operate air doors (air flaps) over the heater core, evaporator, and ducts.
3. A VACUUM SWITCH can operate VACUUM MOTORS (vacuum diaphragms) that open and close the vacuum doors.
4. AN ELECTRONIC CONTROL UNIT (computer) and SENSORS can operate the heating and air conditioning systems automatically.

Manual temperature control

Manual controls for the heating and air conditioning systems are driver controlled. The driver must select the blower speed and air door positions to control the heating or cooling temperature.

Look at Fig. 71-33. It shows a typical **cable type** manual control for a heater.

A manual control system can also use *vacuum motors* to operate the air doors, Fig. 71-34. The control panel will also contain a *vacuum switch* that routes engine vacuum to the correct vacuum motor. The vacuum motors then move the air doors.

Fig. 71-35 shows how air can be mixed to control the temperature of the air entering the passenger compartment.

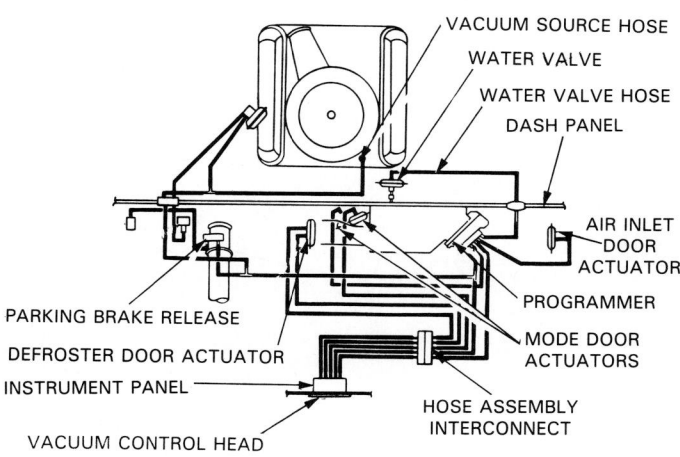

Fig. 71-34. *Vacuum diagram for typical heating and air conditioning system.* (Cadillac)

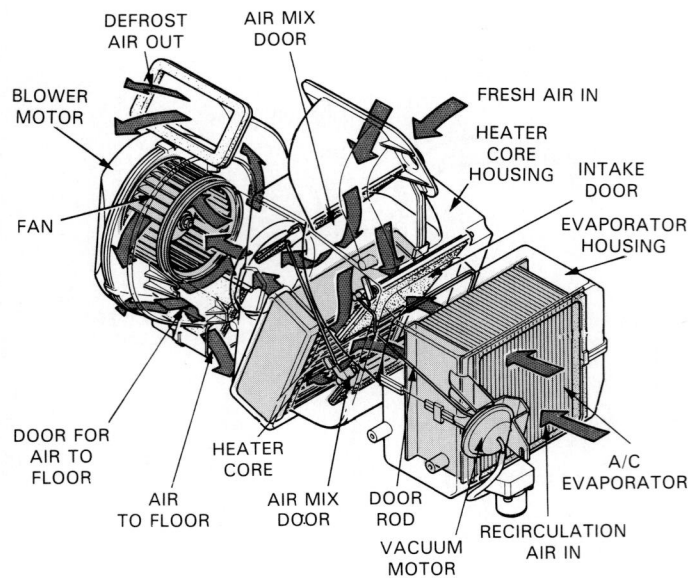

Fig. 71-35. *Trace airflow through heater core and air conditioning evaporator. Hot and cold air blend when needed to maintain comfortable temperature output. (Nissan)*

Automatic temperature control

Automatic temperature control systems use temperature sensors and an electronic control unit (computer) to maintain a preset passenger compartment temperature. The driver sets the instrument panel controls to a specified temperature, then the heating and air conditioning system automatically keep the inside of the car at this temperature.

An automatic temperature control system can use three temperature sensors: an in-car sensor, a duct sensor, and an ambient (outside) air sensor. These temperature sensors may be thermistors.

A *thermistor* is an electrical device that changes resistance with a change in temperature. For example, the in-car sensor's (thermistor's) internal resistance may drop when the passenger compartment temperature drops. The increased current flow could be used by the electronic control unit to turn on the heater or turn off the air conditioning system. In this way, the system maintains a preset temperature.

Fig. 71-36 illustrates a layout for one type of automatic temperature control system.

Fig. 71-37 shows a wiring diagram for an automatic temperature control system. Study how the *control head* (driver operated unit), the *programmer* (electronic control unit), in-car sensor, outside (ambient) temperature sensors, and other components are connected. Also, note the *dropping resistors* which produce different blower motor speeds.

KNOW THESE TERMS

States of matter, Conduction, Convection, Radiation, Btu, Vaporization, Condensation, Refrigerant,

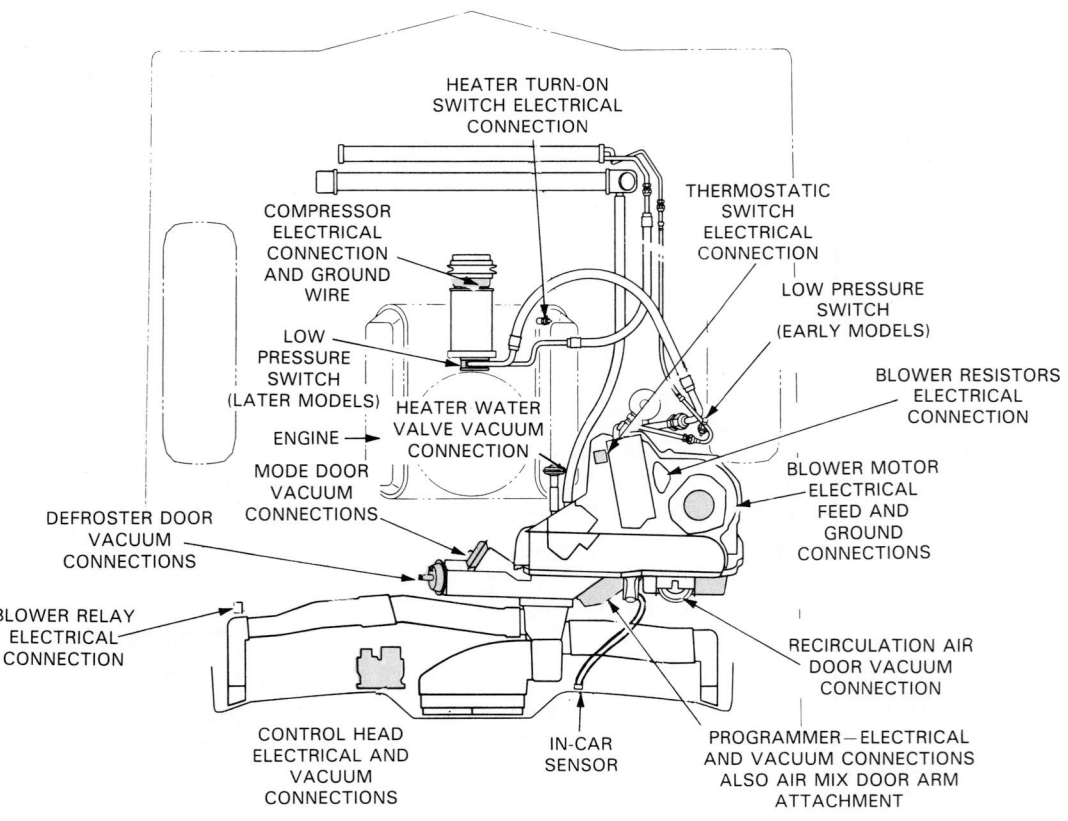

Fig. 71-36. *Study general layout and parts of automatic temperature control system. In-car temperature sensor is primary controller of system.* (Oldsmobile)

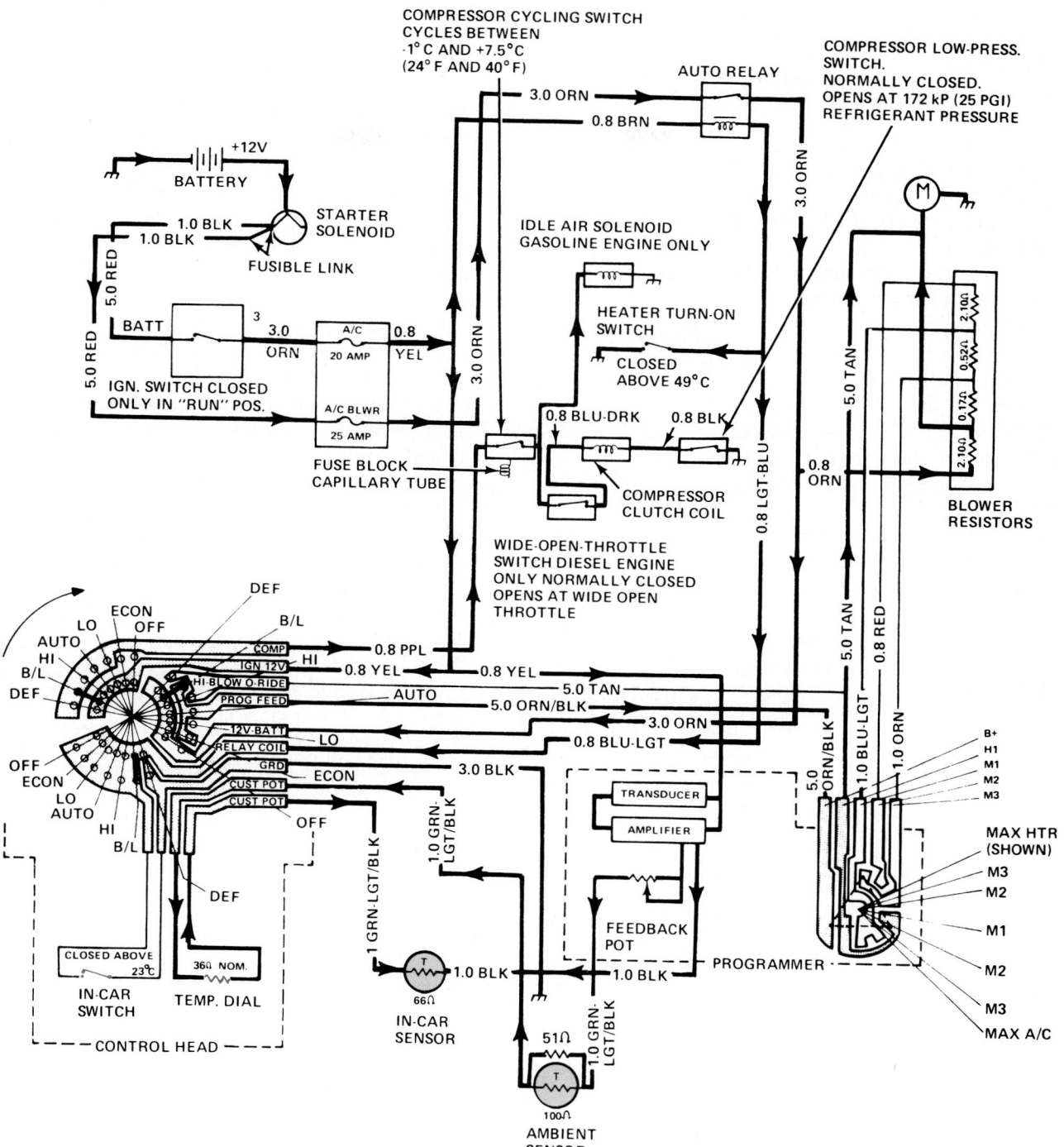

Fig. 71-37. Study this wiring diagram for a typical automatic temperature control system. Note how in-car switch, temperature dial, in-car sensor, and ambient temperature sensor are connected in circuit. (Buick)

Compressor, Condenser, Evaporator, Blower, Thermostatic switch, High side, Low side, Magnetic clutch, Refrigerant oil, Receiver-drier, Accumulator, Muffler, Expansion tube, Expansion valve, POA, STV, Combination valve, Valves in receiver, Ambient temperature switch, Low pressure cutout switch, Superheat switch, Pressure relief valve, WOT switch, Service valves, Heating system, Heater core, Automatic temperature control system.

REVIEW QUESTIONS

1. The three basic states of matter are _____, _____, and _____.
2. Explain the three methods of heat transfer.
3. Heat always moves from the colder object to the warmer object. True or False?
4. What is a Btu?
5. _____, the opposite of _____, occurs

when a vapor changes back into a liquid.

6. This substance circulates inside an air conditioning system.
   a. Refrigerant.
   b. R-12.
   c. Freon.
   d. All of the above are correct.
   e. None of the above are correct.
7. List and explain the eight basic parts of a refrigeration system.
8. Which of the following is NOT a function of an air conditioning system?
   a. Cools air.
   b. Circulates air.
   c. Dehumidifies air.
   d. Cleans air.
   e. All of the above are correct.
   f. None of the above are correct.
9. Describe the high and low side of an air conditioning system.
10. How does an air conditioning compressor turn on and off?
11. Name the five types of air conditioning compressors.
12. _____ _____ is used in the A/C system to keep the compressor lubricated.
13. How does the expansion tube A/C system control output temperature?
14. How does the thermostatic expansion valve A/C system control outlet temperature?
15. Why are service valves provided?
16. Most car heaters get heat from the engine exhaust. True or False?
17. The _____ _____ is a small radiator-like device that provides a large surface area for heat dissipation into the passenger compartment.
18. Explain four methods used to operate heater components.
19. Define the term "thermistor."

ACTIVITIES FOR CHAPTER 71

1. Make a sketch (or use a Computer-Aided Drafting program, if one is available) of a basic refrigeration system. Create an overhead transparency from your sketch and use it to explain to the class the refrigeration cycle.
2. Obtain a junked automotive air conditioning compressor and disassemble it. Identify the type of compressor and the basic parts, then reassemble the components.
3. Visit the library and do research to find out why R-12 and other CFC refrigerants are dangerous to the environment. Write a short (1- to 2-page) report on the problem and what is being done to solve it.

72

Heating and Air Conditioning Service

After studying this chapter, you will be able to:

□ Visually inspect a heating and air conditioning system and locate obvious troubles.

□ Diagnose common heating and air conditioning problems.

□ Describe the functions and uses of air conditioning test equipment.

□ Locate air conditioning and heating system leaks.

□ Explain how to replace major heating and air conditioning components.

□ Describe the general procedures for evacuating and charging an air conditioning system.

□ Demonstrate safe working practices when servicing heating and air conditioning equipment.

Most technicians who work on heating and air conditioning systems are specialists. They are experts in this area of repair. All auto technicians, however, should have basic skills in heating and air conditioning service. Also, some knowledge of A/C will help you decide if you would like to specialize in this field of service.

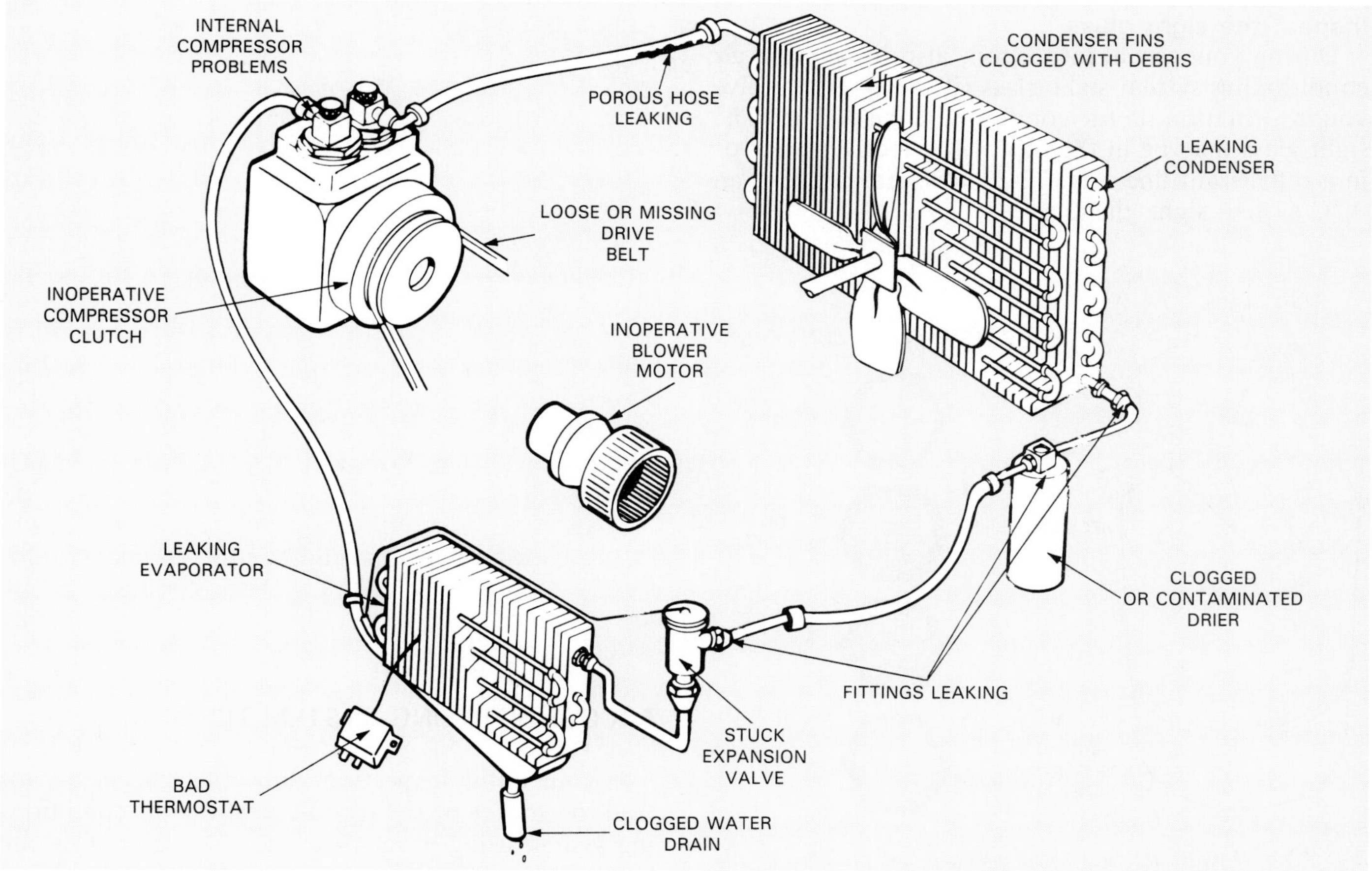

INTERNAL COMPRESSOR PROBLEMS

POROUS HOSE LEAKING

CONDENSER FINS CLOGGED WITH DEBRIS

LEAKING CONDENSER

INOPERATIVE COMPRESSOR CLUTCH

LOOSE OR MISSING DRIVE BELT

INOPERATIVE BLOWER MOTOR

LEAKING EVAPORATOR

CLOGGED OR CONTAMINATED DRIER

FITTINGS LEAKING

BAD THERMOSTAT

STUCK EXPANSION VALVE

CLOGGED WATER DRAIN

Fig. 72-1. Note types of problems that develop in air conditioning system. (Florida Dept. of Voc. Ed.)

AIR CONDITIONING SYSTEM INSPECTION

When an air conditioning system does not cool properly, inspect the system. Look for obvious signs of trouble, Fig. 72-1. Generally, check for:
1. Loose or missing compressor drive belt.
2. Inoperative compressor clutch.
3. Disconnected or damaged wiring or vacuum hoses.
4. Leaks (wetness) around lines or fittings.
5. Blockage (leaves, mud) in the condenser fins.
6. Inoperative air control doors.

Check line temperatures

To check the basic action of the A/C system, start the engine. Turn the air conditioning system on high and allow it to run for about ten minutes. Feel the refrigerant lines.

The HIGH-SIDE (discharge) line should be warm or hot. The LOW-SIDE (suction) line should be cool. This would let you know that the refrigerant is moving through the system.

When the low-side line is cold but the system does NOT cool, there might be a problem with the air control doors or instrument panel controls.

If the high-side line is NOT warm and the low-side is NOT cold, you know that a problem exists inside the refrigeration section of the system. You need to perform other tests to pinpoint the problem source.

Inspect the sight glass

During your visual inspection, also inspect the air conditioning system sight glass (if used). It can give you information on the condition of the system. The sight glass may be in the top of the receiver-drier or in a refrigerant line. Fig. 72-2 shows how to read an A/C system sight glass.

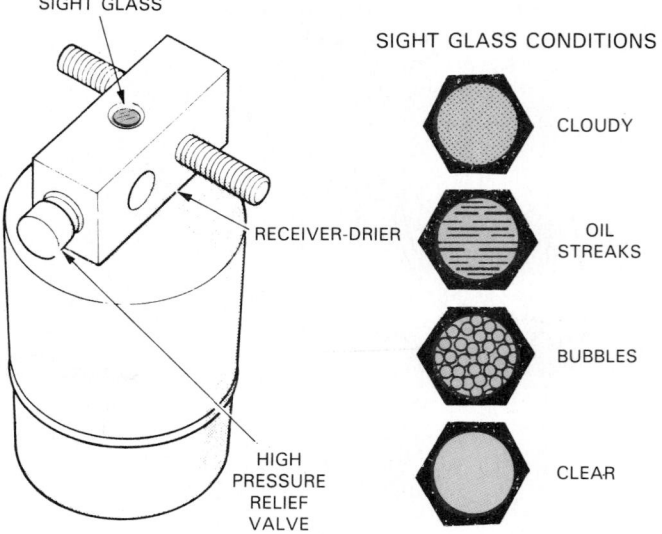

SIGHT GLASS

SIGHT GLASS CONDITIONS

CLOUDY

OIL STREAKS

BUBBLES

CLEAR

RECEIVER-DRIER

HIGH PRESSURE RELIEF VALVE

Fig. 72-2. If used, inspect sight glass. It will indicate condition of A/C system. Sight glass may be in top of receiver-dryer or in line. (Chrysler)

A *clear sight glass* usually indicates the A/C system has the correct charge of refrigerant; however, it can also indicate an empty system. If the low-side line is cool, there is refrigerant in the system. If the sight glass is clear and the low-side line is warm, then the system could have a refrigerant leak.

A *foamy* or *bubbling sight glass* indicates the A/C system is low on refrigerant and that air is in the system. However, an occasional bubble during clutch cycling or system start-up may be normal.

An *oil streaked sight glass* denotes a low refrigerant level which is allowing excessive compressor oil to circulate through the system.

A *cloudy sight glass* may indicate that the desiccant (drying) agent in the receiver-drier or accumulator has broken down and is circulating through the system. You would probably need to replace the unit or the dessicant bag.

These sight glass readings can be used only as indicators of system problems. They are not totally accurate. You need to perform other tests.

REFRIGERANT SAFETY PRECAUTIONS

To avoid injury, observe the following safety precautions when working with refrigerant:

DANGER! Refrigerant can cause severe FROST-BITE if it comes into contact with your skin. Be careful when opening an air conditioning system line. Place a rag around the fitting.

WARNING! Always wear safety glasses when working with refrigerant. It can cause BLINDNESS if it sprays into your face and eyes. If refrigerant sprays into your eyes, flush them with water, without rubbing. Always consult a doctor.

CAUTION! Keep refrigerants away from excessive heat. Pressure in a refrigerant container will increase with an increase in temperature. Expansion could RUPTURE the can.

DANGER! Keep refrigerant away from an open flame. When burned, it turns into *phosgene gas,* a well-known fumigator (bug killer) and highly TOXIC POISON. When using a torch-type leak detector, carefully follow directions and make sure the work area is well ventilated.

WARNING! Never discharge refrigerant into the air. To prevent environmental damage, all refrigerant must now be reclaimed or recycled. Also, discharging any vapor in a confined space, where it could displace air, could cause SUFFOCATION.

AIR CONDITIONING SYSTEM TESTING

If your initial inspections and other checks do not find the source of the trouble, test the air conditioning system using pressure gauges. By comparing the high and low-side pressures to specifications, you can determine the possible causes of the problem.

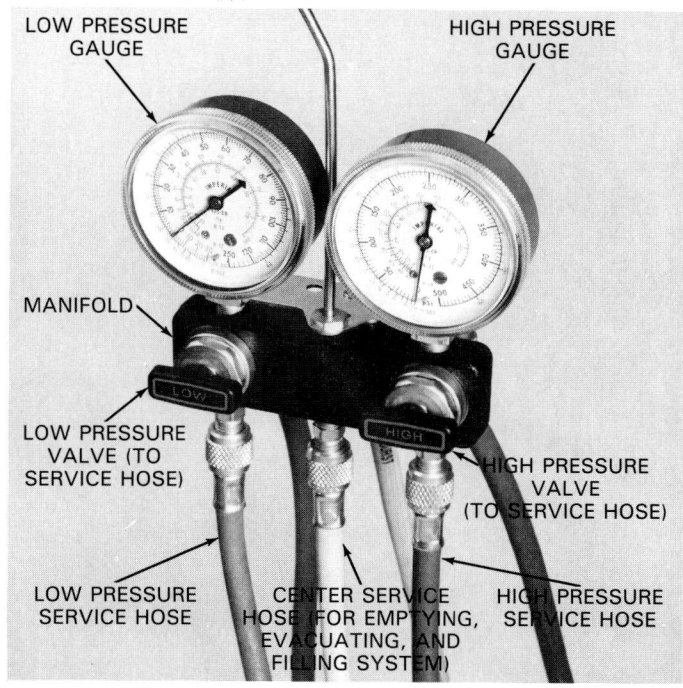

Fig. 72-3. Study parts of pressure gauge or manifold assembly. It is commonly used when servicing air conditioning system. (Imperial)

Pressure gauge (manifold) assembly

A *pressure gauge* or *manifold* assembly typically consists of two pressure gauges, a manifold, two on-off valves, and three service hoses, Fig. 72-3.

The high pressure gauge is used to measure compressor discharge pressure. The low pressure gauge measures suction or low-side pressure.

The two outer service hoses connect to fittings on the air conditioning system. The center service hose is commonly connected to a recovery or recycling unit for cleaning or evacuating or to a refrigerant container for charging (filling) the system.

Service valves

Service valves provide a means of connecting the pressure gauge assembly for testing, discharging, evacuating, and charging (filling) the air conditioning system. Most systems have two service valves. A few have three. The service valves may be located on the compressor fittings or in the refrigerant lines.

There are two basic types of service valves: Schrader and stem types.

A *Schrader service valve* is a spring-loaded valve, similar to the air valve in a tire. See Fig. 72-4. The service hoses on the pressure gauge set have depressors that open these valves when installed.

A *stem type service valve* is a manual valve that is opened and closed by screwing the valve stem in or out. Refer to Fig. 72-5. Normally, when the valve stem is

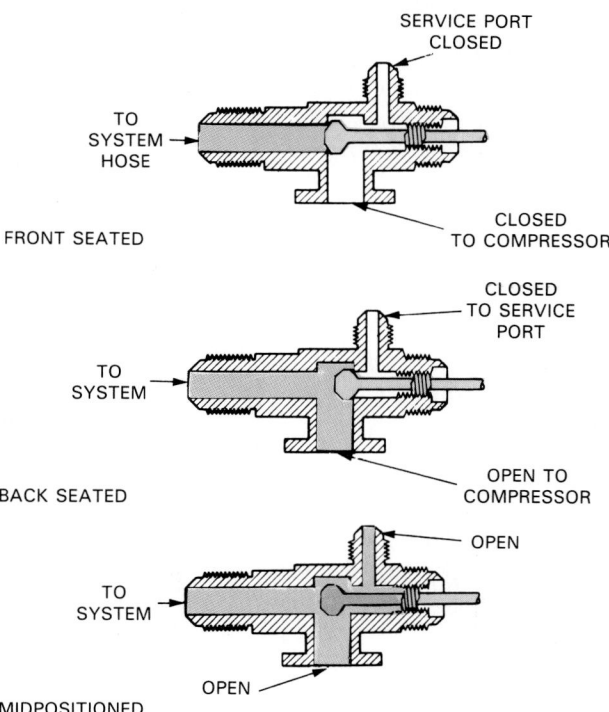

Fig. 72-5. Stem type service valve has hand valve that must be turned to open valve. Note how position of stem opens different passages in valve. (Chrysler)

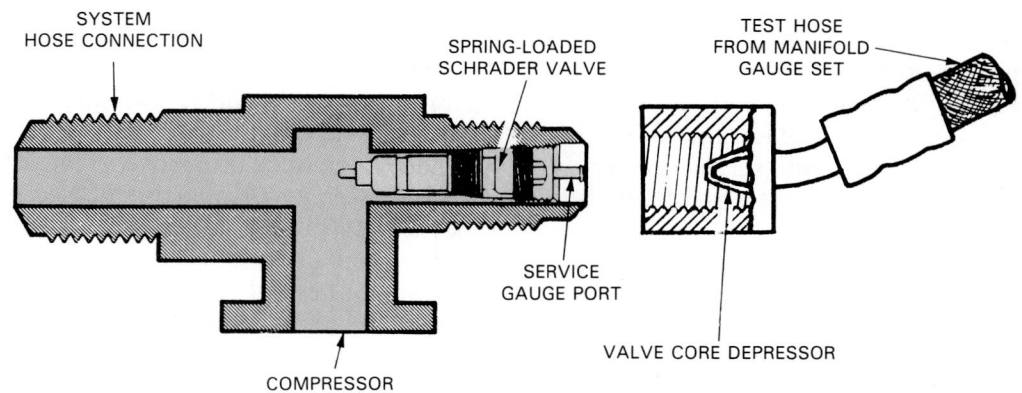

Fig. 72-4. Schrader type service valve has valve core, similar to one used in car tire. When pressure gauge hose is connected to valve, valve is pushed open. (Sun Electric)

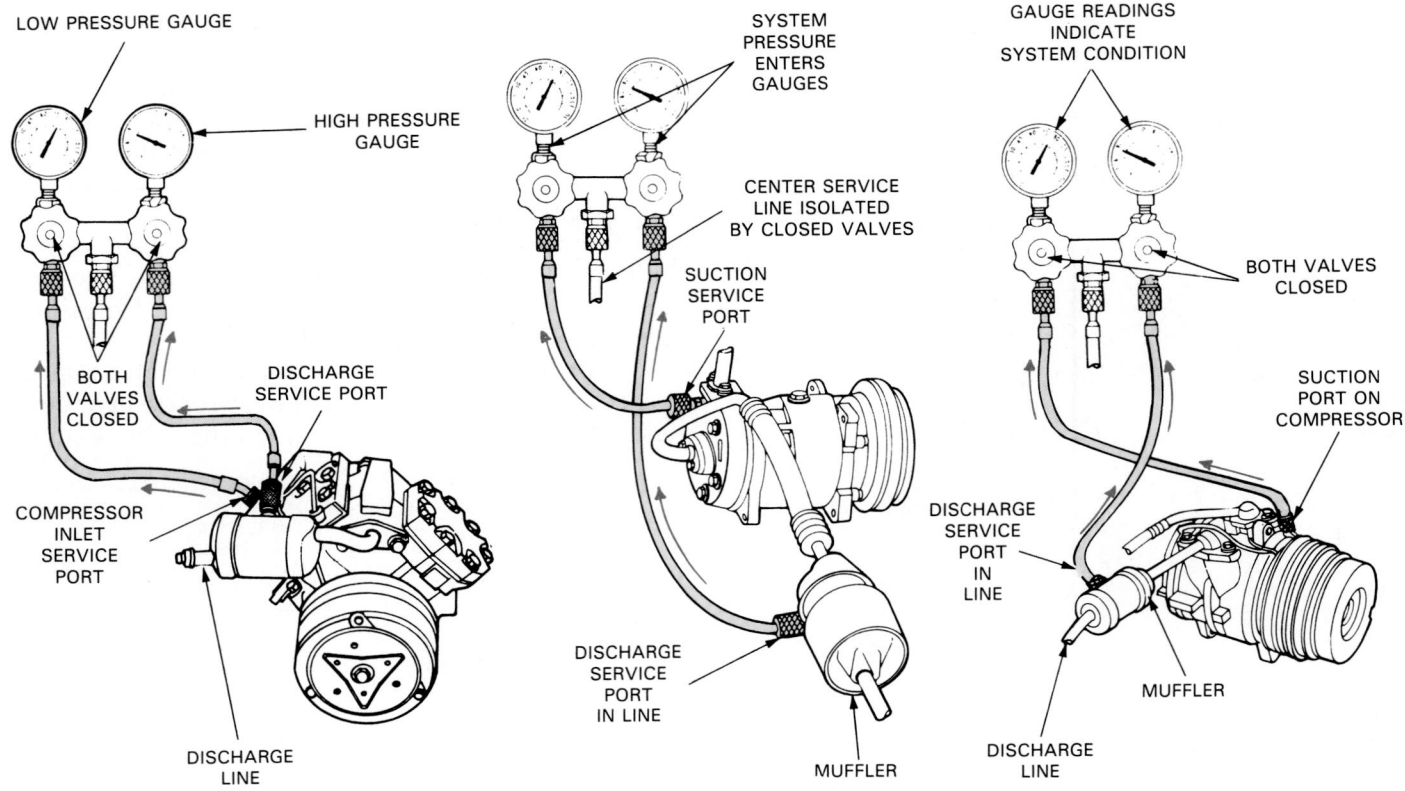

Fig. 72-6. *Study how pressure gauge connects. Manifold valves are kept closed so that refrigerant cannot flow out center hose on manifold.* (Florida Dept. of Voc. Ed.)

backseated (fully counterclockwise), the service port is blocked.

When the valve is turned midway, the service port is open to the pressure gauges. When the valve is frontseated (fully clockwise), the service port is only open to the compressor. The compressor is isolated from the rest of the system. This makes it possible to remove the compressor without losing the refrigerant in the other parts of the system.

CAUTION! Never operate an air conditioning system with stem type valves in the frontseated position. Excessive pressure could build in the compressor, causing part overheating and damage.

Connecting A/C pressure gauges

With the engine stopped and safety glasses on, remove the dust caps from the service valves. Make sure the pressure gauge valves are both closed.

Connect the high side line first. Screw the RED (highside) hose fitting on the high side service valve.

Then screw the BLUE (low-side) hose fitting over the low side service valve, Fig. 72-6.

Note! With a few systems, a third pressure gauge is needed to check the action of the suction throttle valve. Refer to a service manual for details.

If you have stem type service valves, open them 1 1/2 turns clockwise. You can now measure air conditioning system pressures as a means of testing the system. This will also let you discharge or charge the system.

Static A/C pressure reading

A *static A/C pressure reading* will indicate how much refrigerant is in the system. With the engine OFF, read the high-side pressure gauge.

If the high pressure gauge shows approximately 50 psi (345 kPa), then the system should have an adequate charge. If the pressure gauge reads below 50 psi (345 kPa), some of the refrigerant charge has leaked out and the system should have NOT be operated. Correct any leak. Add refrigerant before making other tests.

Performance testing A/C system

A *performance test* indicates air conditioning system condition by measuring system pressures with the engine running. Start and fast idle the engine at approximatley 1500 rpm. Set the system for maximum cooling for about 10 minutes to allow pressures to stabilize. Close the car's doors and windows. Leave the hood fully open.

Place a temperature gauge in one of the air outlets in the passenger compartment. See Fig. 72-7. Place another temperature gauge at the condenser to measure ambient (outside) air temperature. Both temperatures are usually needed to analyze system performance.

Read the pressure gauges and compare them to factory specs. Fig. 72-8 gives a chart showing typical readings for several types of systems. Note that pressure gauge readings vary with *ambient air temperature, humidity,* and *system design.*

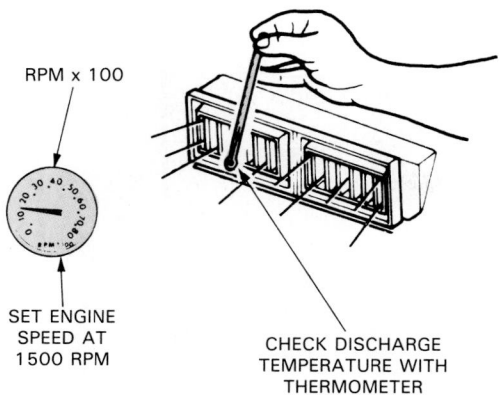

RPM x 100

SET ENGINE
SPEED AT
1500 RPM

CHECK DISCHARGE
TEMPERATURE WITH
THERMOMETER

Fig. 72-7. During performance test of A/C system, check air temperature at duct outlets and next to condenser. Service manual specs will then let you evaluate system operation. (Chrysler)

APPROXIMATE TEST PRESSURE RANGES FOR NORMAL FUNCTIONING SYSTEMS

OUTSIDE TEMPERA-TURES	HIGH SIDE PRESSURES	LOW SIDE PRESSURES		
Ambient Temperature In Front Of Condenser	Psi At At High Pressure Test Fitting	Psi With STV, POA or VIR Systems	Psi With Expansion Valve Systems	Psi With Orifice Tube Systems
60 °F	120-170	28-31	7-15	—
70 °F	150-250	28-31	7-15	24-31
80 °F	180-275	28-31	7-15	24-31
90 °F	200-310	28-31	7-15	24-32
100 °F	230-330	28-35	10-30	24-32
110 °F	270-360	28-38	10-35	24-32

Fig. 72-8. Chart shows typical pressures for common types of A/C systems. Service manual values should be used during actual tests. (GMC)

With an outside temperature of 70 °F, for example, an orifice tube system with a cycling switch should have approximately 150-250 psi high-side pressure and 24-31 psi low-side pressure.

If your pressure gauge readings are not within factory specs, there is a problem in the system. You need to use these readings, other symptoms, service manual diagnosis charts, and your knowledge of system operation to find the trouble.

A few examples of improper gauge readings are pictured in Fig. 72-9.

Locating A/C system leaks

An air conditioning system should be considered leaking (needing repairs) when more than one-half pound of refrigerant must be added per year. There are several methods used to locate leaks.

An *internally charged detector* is a colored agent that can be charged into the system. Any leak will show up as a bright color (usually orange-red) spot at the point of leakage.

A *bubble detector* is a solution applied on the outside of possible leak points. A refrigerant leak will make bubbles or foam in the leak detecting agent.

A *torch detector* uses a gas flame to indicate A/C leaks, Fig. 72-10. Any leaking refrigerant is drawn into and changes the color of the flame. If the flame does not change color, refrigerant is not present.

CAUTION! When refrigerant is burned it turns into very toxic phosgene gas. Use a flame type leak detector only in a ventilated area. Keep your face away from the detector to avoid inhaling fumes.

An *electronic leak detector* uses a special sensor and an electronic amplifier to locate A/C leaks by producing a sound or light signal. One is shown in Fig. 72-11.

An electronic leak detector is the fastest, safest, and most modern method of locating system leaks. Move the tester probe around *possible leakage points* (line

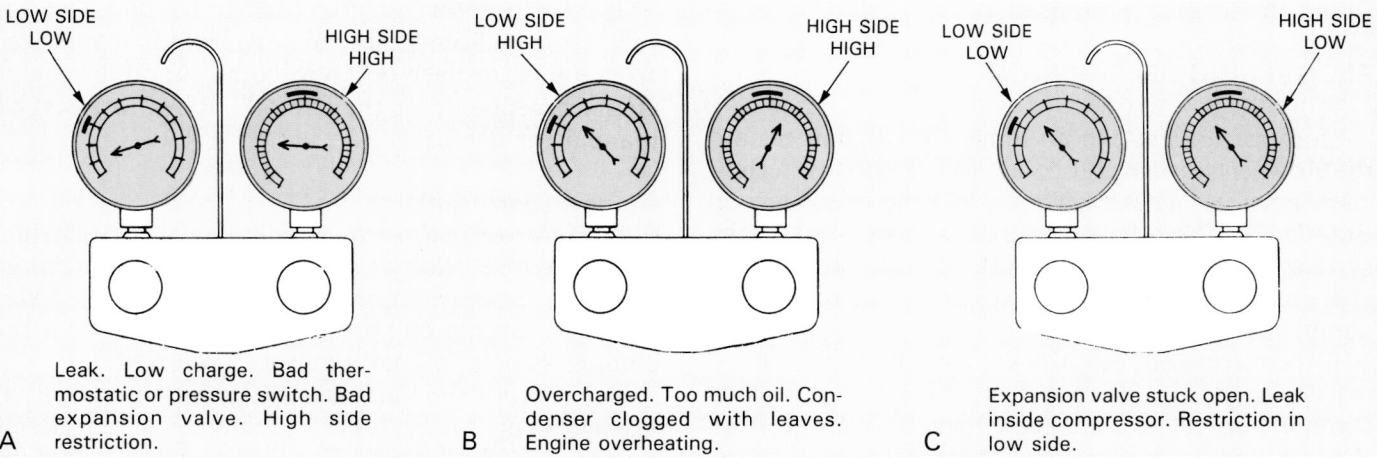

LOW SIDE LOW   HIGH SIDE HIGH

LOW SIDE HIGH   HIGH SIDE HIGH

LOW SIDE LOW   HIGH SIDE LOW

A Leak. Low charge. Bad thermostatic or pressure switch. Bad expansion valve. High side restriction.

B Overcharged. Too much oil. Condenser clogged with leaves. Engine overheating.

C Expansion valve stuck open. Leak inside compressor. Restriction in low side.

Fig. 72-9. Note how basic gauge readings, whether too high or too low, can be used to troubleshoot possible problems. Gauge readings are only indicators. You must also use information on system design and your knowledge of air conditioning to find trouble. (Nissan)

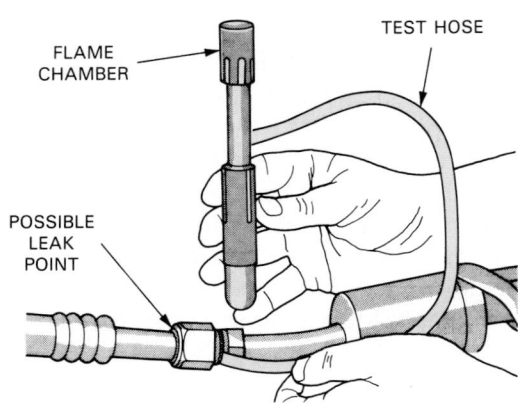

Fig. 72-10. Flame type leak detector will change color when it burns refrigerant. This indicates a leak. Only use in well ventilated area, since burned refrigerant becomes poisonous phosgene gas. (Dodge)

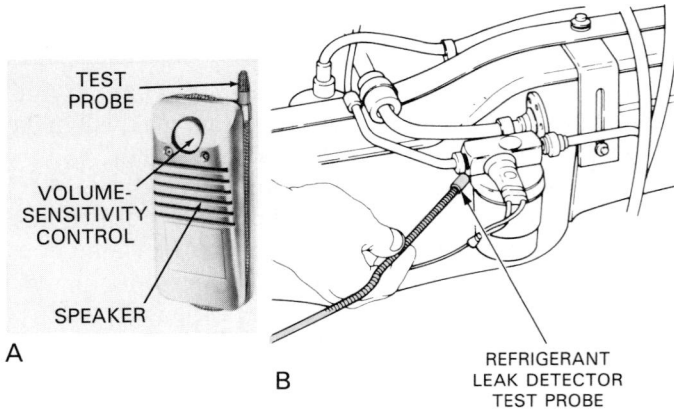

Fig. 72-11. Electronic A/C system leak detector. A — Note parts of detector. B — Turn on detector and move probe around leak points on system. Buzzing sound indicates leakage. (Ford and Snap-On)

fittings, condenser, compressor seals, valves, evaporator). When the tester buzzes or lights up, you have found the leaking component.

RECOVERING REFRIGERANT

Since refrigerant can no longer be discharged into the air when servicing air conditioning systems, technicians must use a *recovery unit,* like the one shown in Fig. 72-12. The refrigerant that is drawn out of the system is stored in a refillable container, and can be charged back into the same system when repairs are completed.

If the refrigerant has become contaminated, or if it is to be used in another system, it must be processed through a *recycling unit.* These units separate oil from the refrigerant, then use filter-driers to remove acids, moisture, and other contaminants.

Recycling will become increasingly important in coming years as production of R-12 and other CFC

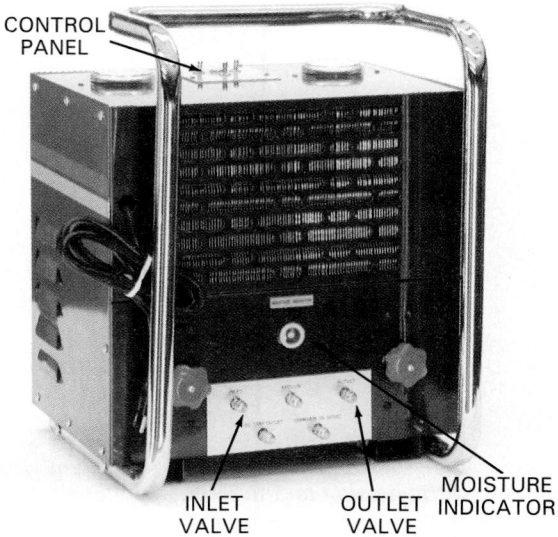

Fig. 72-12. A typical refrigerant recovery unit, which allows refrigerant to be withdrawn from an air conditioning system and stored in a refillable container for reuse or recycling. (Thermal Engineering)

refrigerants is phased out. Environmentally safer refrigerants will be used in new vehicles, but systems in many older cars and trucks will still require use of R-12.

COMMON A/C COMPONENT PROBLEMS

When your performance (pressure) tests indicate faulty components, remove and replace or repair the inoperative parts. The next section of the chapter outlines typical symptoms and problems.

Refer to a service manual for details. It will outline special procedures and tools.

Evaporator problems

With a *bad evaporator,* the trouble will normally show up as inadequate cooling. An evaporator can develop leaks that show up when testing with a leak detector around the evaporator case.

The evaporator would need to be removed for replacement. Sometimes, the evaporator is removed from under the dash or it may come out on the engine compartment side of the firewall. Refer to a service manual for details.

Compressor problems

Compressor malfunctions will appear as abnormal noises, seizure, leakage, or high inlet or low discharge pressures. Some pumping noise is normal. However, if a loud rattling or knocking noise comes from the compressor, faulty parts may be indicated.

The *compressor shaft seal* is a common refrigerant leakage point. Always check the compressor seal closely during your leak tests. The seal can sometimes be replaced without compressor removal.

To check the *compressor clutch,* connect battery voltage directly to the clutch, as in Fig. 72-13. This

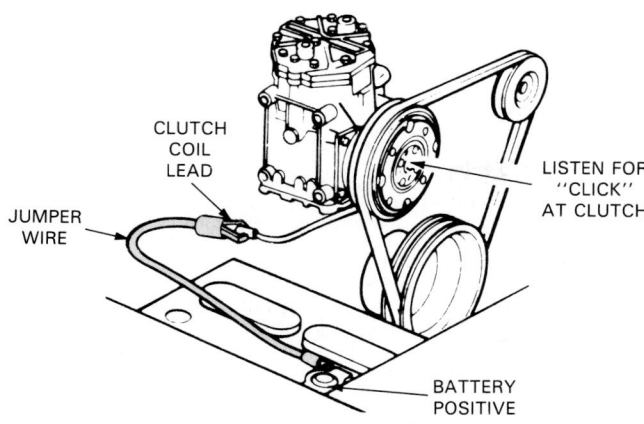

Fig. 72-13. If compressor fails to turn on, check clutch by applying battery voltage to clutch coil. This should make clutch kick in. (Chrysler)

should produce a click sound and the compressor plate and pulley should lock together.

If the clutch does not engage, the compressor coil may be opened or shorted and need replacement. If the clutch engages, then there may be a problem in the circuit supplying voltage to the compressor clutch. Trace the circuit and locate the problem (bad switch, wire connection, broken wire).

During *compressor service,* follow the directions in a service manual. The manual will outline the procedures for removal, disassembly, overhaul, and reassembly. Special tools are needed, Fig. 72-14.

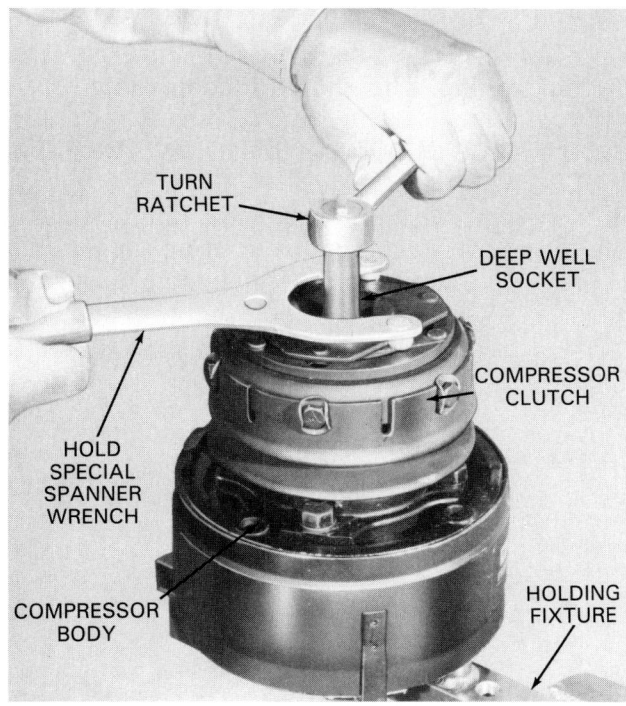

Fig. 72-14. Special tools are commonly needed to work on A/C system compressor. Note spanner wrench used to hold clutch while removing shaft nut. (Chrysler)

Air conditioning compressors are complicated to the inexperienced technician, Fig. 72-15. Do not attempt to overhaul a compressor without proper specialized training and supervision. Most technicians replace bad compressors with NEW or REBUILT units.

Condenser problems

A *bad condenser* can leak refrigerant or it can become restricted internally. A restricted condenser will cause a high pressure reading in the discharge (high) side of the system. A partial condenser restriction can make ice or frost form on the outside of the condenser. During normal condenser operation, the outlet tube will be slightly cooler than the inlet tube.

Receiver-dehydrator problems

Receiver-dehydrator problems are very common; it is one of the most frequently replaced air conditioning components. The dessicant (drying) agent can become contaminated or the unit may become internally restricted. A restricted receiver-drier will alter system pressures and the outlet fitting on the unit may be abnormally cold.

Typically, replace the receiver-drier when:
1. The sight glass is cloudy.
2. System fittings have been left open for more than an hour.
3. The system has been leaking and operated on a partial charge.
4. The system has been opened and serviced for the third time.
5. Moisture is found in the system.
6. A restriction is indicated in the unit.

Expansion valve or tube problems

A *faulty expansion valve* will usually show up as low suction (low-side) and low discharge (high-side) pressure readings. Usually, the failure is due to the power element (bulb) not operating the valve properly. A less common failure of the expansion valve is due to a clogged inlet screen (corrosion particles, loose desiccant beads).

A *clogged orifice tube* will produce symptoms similar to those caused by a restricted expansion valve. Contaminants can fill and clog the orifice tube or tube screen, blocking refrigerant flow.

Refer to a service manual for detailed procedures for diagnosing and replacing these and other types of flow control valves. Fig. 72-16 shows the special extractor tool needed to replace one type of orifice (expansion) tube.

Thermostat problems

A *bad thermostat* will usually keep the compressor clutch from engaging and the system will not cool. When the compressor coil operates when connected to voltage, you may need to test the thermostat. It may not be sending current to the clutch coil when needed.

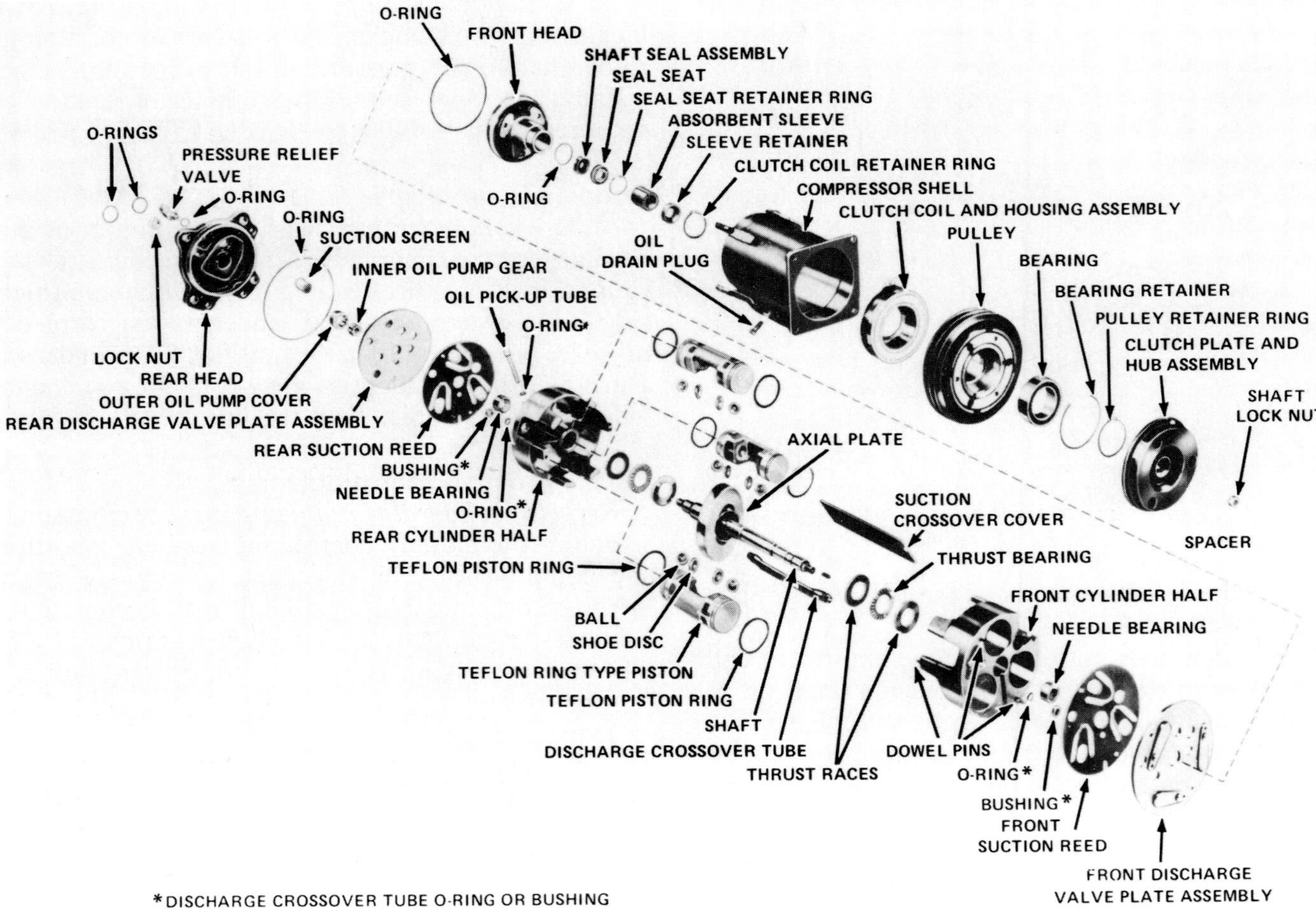

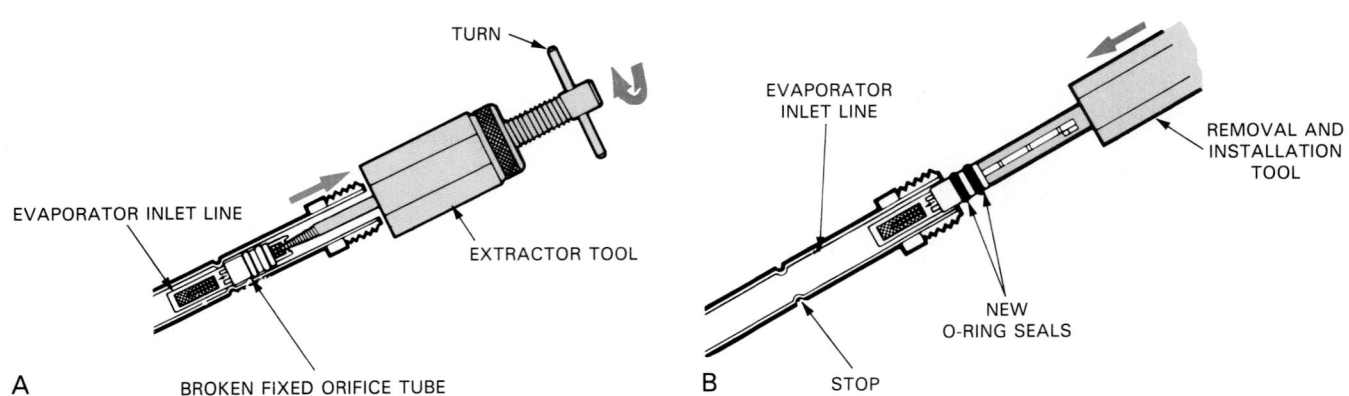

O-RING
FRONT HEAD
SHAFT SEAL ASSEMBLY
SEAL SEAT
SEAL SEAT RETAINER RING
ABSORBENT SLEEVE
SLEEVE RETAINER
CLUTCH COIL RETAINER RING
COMPRESSOR SHELL
CLUTCH COIL AND HOUSING ASSEMBLY
PULLEY
BEARING
BEARING RETAINER
PULLEY RETAINER RING
CLUTCH PLATE AND HUB ASSEMBLY
SHAFT LOCK NUT

O-RINGS
PRESSURE RELIEF VALVE
O-RING
O-RING
O-RING
SUCTION SCREEN
INNER OIL PUMP GEAR
OIL PICK-UP TUBE
O-RING*
OIL DRAIN PLUG
LOCK NUT
REAR HEAD
OUTER OIL PUMP COVER
REAR DISCHARGE VALVE PLATE ASSEMBLY
REAR SUCTION REED
BUSHING*
NEEDLE BEARING
O-RING*
REAR CYLINDER HALF
TEFLON PISTON RING
BALL
SHOE DISC
TEFLON RING TYPE PISTON
TEFLON PISTON RING
SHAFT
DISCHARGE CROSSOVER TUBE
THRUST RACES

AXIAL PLATE
SUCTION CROSSOVER COVER
THRUST BEARING
FRONT CYLINDER HALF
NEEDLE BEARING
DOWEL PINS
O-RING*
BUSHING*
FRONT SUCTION REED
FRONT DISCHARGE VALVE PLATE ASSEMBLY
SPACER

*DISCHARGE CROSSOVER TUBE O-RING OR BUSHING

Fig. 72-15. Exploded view of compressor for air conditioning system. Most technicians install a new or factory rebuilt unit when needed. It is frequently too time-consuming to overhaul unit in-shop. (Oldsmobile)

Fig. 72-17 shows how to test one type of thermostat. Replace the thermostat if faulty.

Refrigerant line problems

Defective refrigerant lines may leak, harden and crack, or restrict refrigerant flow.

Replace any refrigerant lines that are faulty. When installing a line using an O-ring seal, coat the seal with compressor oil, Fig. 72-18. This will help prevent the seal from leaking. This should be done on all seals.

EVACUATING AN AIR CONDITIONING SYSTEM

A/C system evacuation involves using a vacuum pump to remove air and moisture from the inside of the system. Evacuation is needed anytime the air con-

TURN
EVAPORATOR INLET LINE
EXTRACTOR TOOL
A
BROKEN FIXED ORIFICE TUBE

EVAPORATOR INLET LINE
REMOVAL AND INSTALLATION TOOL
NEW O-RING SEALS
B
STOP

Fig. 72-16. Another special tool is being used to service broken orifice tube. A — Thread screw into broken tube. Then tighten to pull out unit. B — Forcing new orifice tube into place. (Ford)

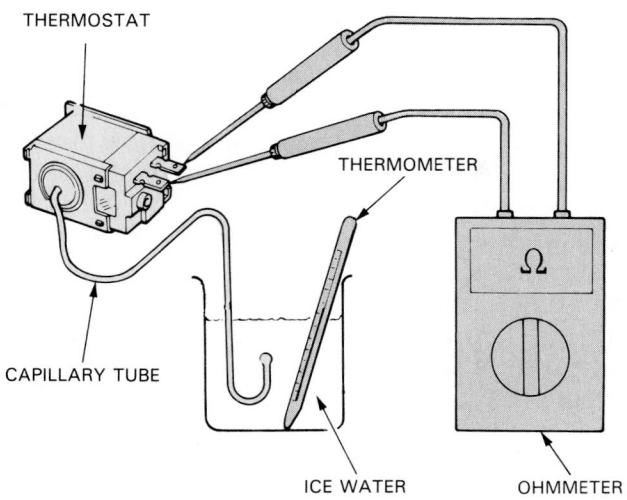

Fig. 72-17. Thermostat should change resistance when specific temperature is reached. This should make ohmmeter reading change accordingly. Refer to manual for temperature and resistance specs. (Honda)

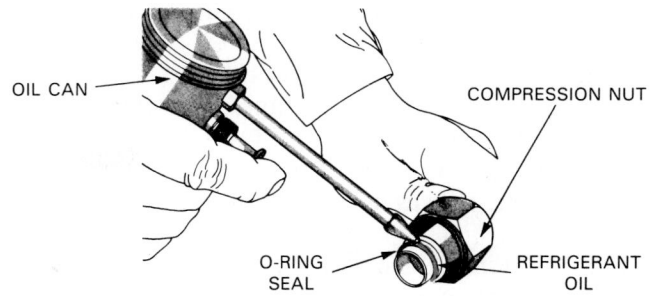

Fig. 72-18. Lubricate all A/C system O-rings and seals with refrigerant oil. This will help seal them and prevent leaks. (Plymouth)

ditioning system has been discharged or opened to the atmosphere.

To evacuate an A/C system, connect the pressure gauges to the system, Fig. 72-19. Connect the vacuum pump to the center service hose on the gauge set. Open the compressor valves (stem type). Open the valves on the pressure gauge set.

Plug in and turn on the vacuum pump. Operate the vacuum pump until the pressure gauges read approximately 26 to 28 in/hg at sea level. After reaching this vacuum, run the pump another 5 or 10 minutes to assure complete removal of air and moisture.

If you cannot draw the service-manual-recommended vacuum, check the operation of the pump and examine the system for leaks. This is an easy way to detect major leaks before installing refrigerant.

After evacuating, shut off the vacuum pump and close both gauge valves. The system vacuum should not drop more than about 2 to 3 in/hg in a five-minute period. If it does, then a small system leak is indicated. You need to leak-test the system as described earlier.

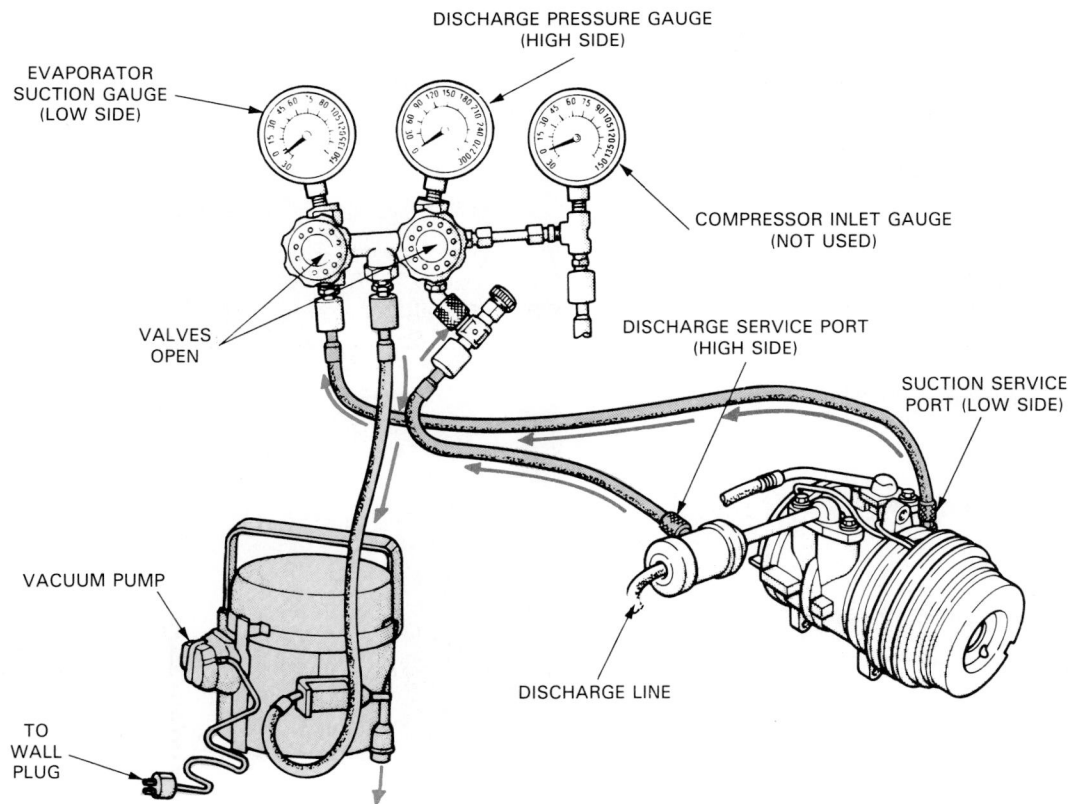

Fig. 72-19. Evacuating system. Connect vacuum pump as shown. Pump will draw moisture out. Operate pump until gauge reads 26 to 28 in/hg, then run pump about five minutes more to assure complete evacuation. (Chrysler)

CHARGING AN AIR CONDITIONING SYSTEM

A/C *system charging* involves filling the system with the correct amount of refrigerant. The system should be charged only after it has been leak-tested and evacuated. Most shops use 10- to 30-pound containers of refrigerant. However, larger bulk containers are also used.

Fig. 72-20 shows the basic connections for charging an air conditioning system. The pressure gauge set is left on the system service valves after evacuation. However, the center service hose is connected to the refrigerant container.

With the gauge valves closed, connect the center hose to the refrigerant container. Open the center valve of the manifold gauge set, and the service valve on the refrigerant container. This will transfer control of refrigerant flow to the gauge valves.

To charge the system, leave the gauge discharge (high pressure) valve closed. Open the suction (low pressure) gauge valve. Start the engine and turn on the air conditioning system.

Compressor suction will then draw refrigerant into the system, as in Fig. 72-20. Adjust the suction line valve so that gauge pressure does NOT exceed about 50 psi (345 kPa). This will assure that liquid refrigerant does not enter and damage the compressor. You may want to place the refrigerant container in warm water (not hotter than 125 °F or 52 °C). This will expand the refrigerant, helping it to flow into the system.

Note! Keep the refrigerant container right-side up when charging. This will assure that refrigerant vapor, not liquid refrigerant, enters the system.

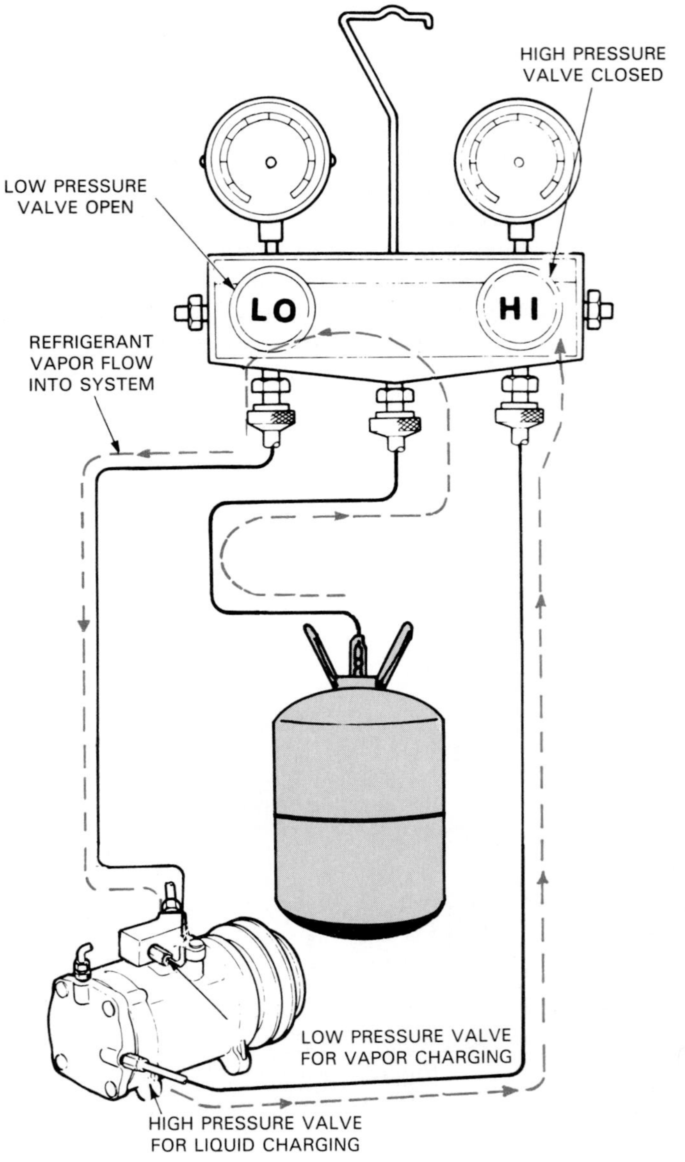

Charging station

A *charging station* usually contains a vacuum pump, pressure gauge set, oil injection cylinder, and a charging tank of refrigerant. See Fig. 72-21.

A charging station can be used to evacuate and charge the system without disconnecting the service hose. The same general procedures covered for a separate vacuum pump and test gauges apply. Remember to follow the directions for the specific type of equipment.

After charging the A/C system, double-check system pressures and temperatures. Make sure the high and low-side pressures are satisfactory. Also, use a thermometer to measure the temperature of the air blowing out of the passenger compartment vents.

HIGH PRESSURE VALVE CLOSED

LOW PRESSURE VALVE OPEN

LO **HI**

REFRIGERANT VAPOR FLOW INTO SYSTEM

LOW PRESSURE VALVE FOR VAPOR CHARGING

HIGH PRESSURE VALVE FOR LIQUID CHARGING

Fig. 72-20. Adding refrigerant with gauges attached to service valves. Attach container to center hose. Open lower pressure valve and allow refrigerant to flow into low side of system with engine running.   (Honda)

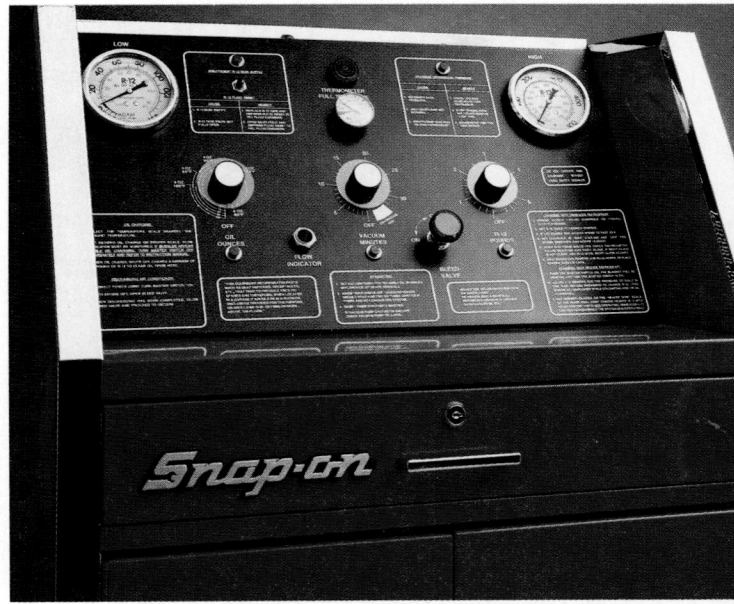

Fig. 72-21. Charging station contains vacuum pump, refrigerant tank, and gauge set that makes AC system service easy.   (Snap-on Tools)

If these checks are within specs, the air conditioning system is ready to be returned to service.

ADDING REFRIGERANT OIL

The refrigerant oil should be checked anytime you add or replace the refrigerant. Before checking, the system should be operated for 10 or 15 minutes. Then, isolate the compressor by closing the stem type service valves. If Schrader valves are used, you must discharge the system to check the oil level.

Refer to a service manual for detailed procedures for checking the refrigerant oil level. Follow directions for the type of compressor you are servicing.

If low, add the specified amount and type of refrigerant oil. Do not overfill the compressor or system efficiency will be reduced.

A/C SYSTEM SERVICE RULES

When servicing an air conditioning system, remember to follow these basic rules:
1. Inspect for obvious problems first (loose or missing belt, clogged condenser fins, disconnected wires, inoperative compressor clutch).
2. Check sight glass to see if system has refrigerant charge.
3. Feel hose temperatures to determine general condition of system.
4. Leak test system.
5. Wear safety glasses when servicing refrigerant system.
6. Discharge system only into recovery unit; never into air.
7. Make sure system is fully discharged before attempting to remove and replace any pressurized component.
8. Cap fittings when disconnected to prevent moisture entry that will ruin drying agent.
9. Replace receiver-drier or dessicant if needed.
10. Coat all O-rings with refrigerant oil before installing. Add oil to system if needed.
11. Torque all fittings to specs.
12. Evacuate system and check for leakage (vacuum drop) before charging.
13. Charge system with correct amount of refrigerant.
14. Add refrigerant to suction side of system with engine running. Do not let liquid refrigerant enter and damage compressor.
15. Use service manual directions and specifications.
16. Recheck system operation after service.

HEATER SERVICE

Heater problems typically show up as coolant leaks or as insufficient warming of the passenger compartment. The heater hoses, where they are near the hot engine, can harden, break, or leak. The heater core can rust and develop leaks that drip coolant on the car's floor or carpet.

When the system does not produce heat, the heater core may be clogged, a heater hose valve may be inoperative, or the air control doors may not be functioning.

Checking heater coolant flow

To check heater coolant flow, let the engine and hoses cool. Then, start and fast idle the engine. Turn the heater on high.

As the engine coolant warms, feel both the inlet and outlet heater hoses. If used, feel on both sides of the coolant flow control valve.

If both heater hoses are about the same temperature, coolant is passing through the heater core and valve. If one hose is hot and the other is cool, there is BLOCKAGE in the system. The heater core could be clogged or the flow valve stuck closed.

To check the operation of a heater flow valve, use a hand vacuum pump to apply suction to the diaphragm. When vacuum is applied, the valve should activate. If the valve does not move or the diaphragm does not hold vacuum, replace it. If the valve and diaphragm are good, check that vacuum is reaching the unit through the supply line, using a vacuum gauge or your finger. See Fig. 72-22.

Flushing heater core

A clogged heater core is a common problem that can reduce system heating. The inside of the core can become filled with rust from the engine cooling system.

To flush the heater core, remove both heater hoses. Connect a garden hose to the outlet heater hose, as in Fig. 72-23. Turn the hose on and let water force rust out of the core for about five minutes.

Other heater problems

When there are other heater problems, refer to a service manual. It will explain how to check the operation of each component.

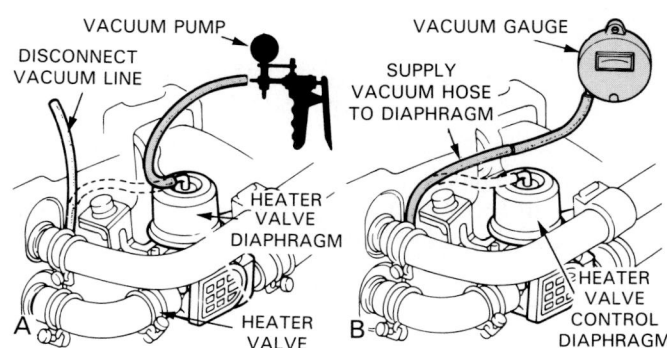

Fig. 72-22. Heater valve can stick opened or closed and vacuum diaphragm can rupture. A—Use vacuum pump to check its operation. B—Also check that vacuum is being fed to diaphragm from vacuum line. (Honda)

Heating and Air Conditioning Service 969

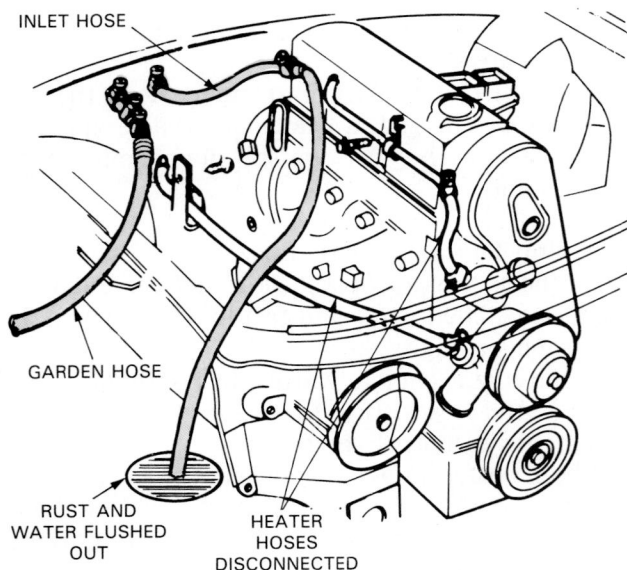

Fig. 72-23. Clogged heater core is common. Remove heater hoses and use garden hose to force water through core backwards. This may remove rust and fix heater. (Ford)

SCANNING CLIMATE CONTROL SYSTEMS

Discussed in later chapters, a scanner (computer system tester) can be used to help find problems in many late model climate control systems. Since the heater and air conditioning are controlled by a computer, the scanner can "talk" with the car's computer and output a message giving the possible location of problems. Some climate control systems will output trouble codes on the dash, eliminating the need for a scanner or other testing method.

KNOW THESE TERMS

Clear sight glass, Bubbling sight glass, Oil streaked sight glass, Cloudy sight glass, R-12 frostbite, Pressure gauge or manifold assembly, Service valves, Schrader valve, Stem type valve, Static pressure reading, Performance test, Leak detector, Compressor shaft seal, Evacuation, Charging, Charging station, Leaking heater core, Clogged heater core.

REVIEW QUESTIONS

1. List six check points when inspecting an air conditioning system.
2. How can feeling line temperatures help you when inspecting an air conditioning system?
3. Which of the following sight glass conditions could indicate system troubles?
   a. Clear sight glass.
   b. Bubbling sight glass.
   c. Cloudy sight glass.
   d. All of the above.
   e. None of the above.
4. Explain five important safety precautions for air conditioning system service.
5. What is a pressure gauge or manifold assembly?
6. _____ valves provide a means of connecting the pressure gauge assembly for testing, discharging, evacuating, and charging the system.
7. Describe the difference between Schrader valves and stem type service valves.
8. A static A/C pressure reading will indicate if the compressor is in good condition. True or False?
9. Why is an electronic leak detector safer than a torch type detector?
10. Give a reason why you should not discharge (empty) an A/C system into the air.
11. The compressor shaft seal is a common point of refrigerant leakage. True or False?
12. List six reasons for replacing the receiver-drier.
13. A customer complains that the heater does not warm the passenger compartment properly. The heater never blows hot air.
   Technician A says to feel both heater hoses to check for coolant circulation through the heater core. The core could be clogged.
   Technician B says to also check the heater controls. One of the lever-cable mechanisms may not be operating an air control door properly.
   Who is correct?
   a. Technician A
   b. Technician B
   c. Both A and B
   d. Neither A nor B

ACTIVITIES FOR CHAPTER 72

1. Talk to the owners of several shops that service auto air conditioners. Ask if they have had to raise the price of servicing systems to cover the cost of adding recovery or recycling equipment. How have their customers reacted? Report to the class on your findings.
2. Demonstrate the proper connections and use of a gauge manifold set for making a static pressure reading on an A/C system.
3. Use a video camera to show proper use of an electronic refrigerant leak detector.

Radios, Power Options

After studying this chapter, you will be able to:
- ☐ Describe the operating principles of a radio.
- ☐ Explain the basic difference between an AM and FM radio.
- ☐ Diagnose basic radio problems.
- ☐ Explain the operation of power windows.
- ☐ Sketch a rear window defogger circuit.
- ☐ Describe a power door lock system.
- ☐ Summarize the operation of a speed control system.
- ☐ Describe safety practices to use when working with electrical accessory circuits.

Most new cars are ordered from the dealer with a radio and other optional devices. Since these devices are very common, understanding their operating principles and service methods is important, even to the general technician. After studying this chapter, you should be prepared to use a service manual when troubleshooting and repairing optional systems.

RADIO SYSTEMS

A basic *radio system* consists of an antenna, radio (receiver-amplifier), speaker, and power supply circuit. This is illustrated in Fig. 73-1.

The broadcasting or radio station sends out an electromagnetic signal from a large tower. When this signal moves past the vehicle antenna, tiny electrical modulations (fluctuations) are induced into the antenna.

The radio amplifies these small electrical signals into stronger current pulses that operate the speaker. The speaker diaphragm moves back and forth, producing

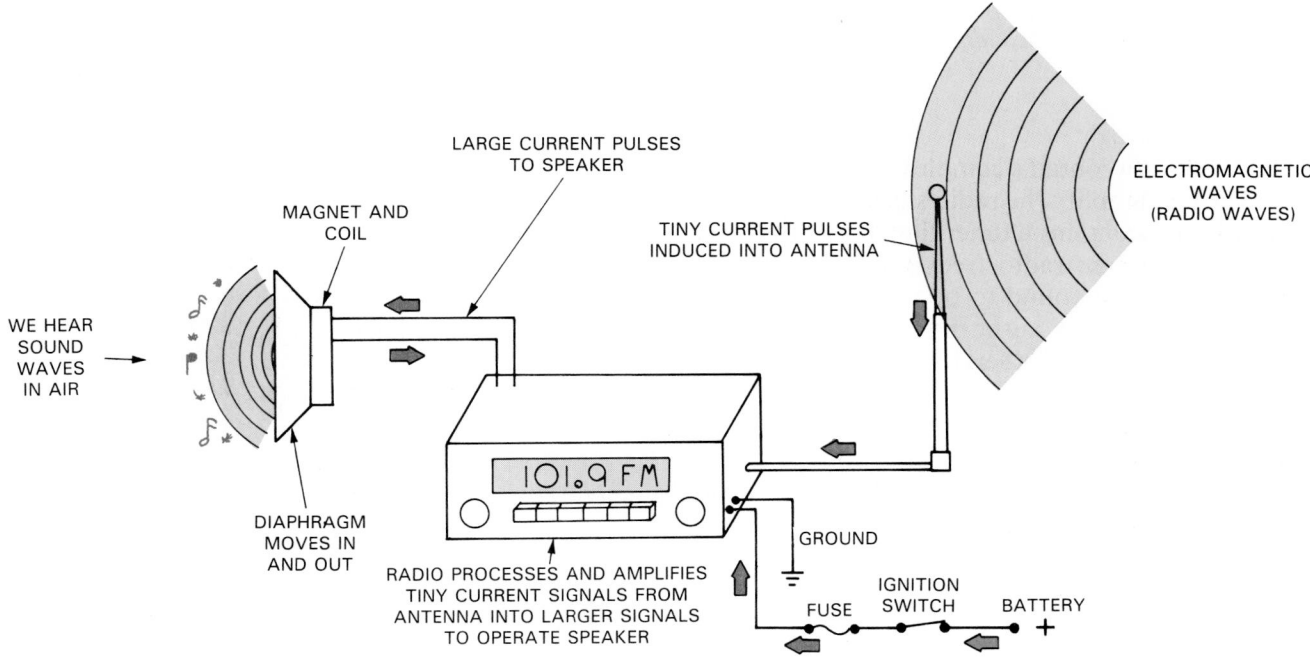

Fig. 73-1. Study basic principle of car radio. Radio waves are tiny electrical pulses picked up by antenna. Radio amplifies these waves into strong current signals for speaker. Physical movement of speaker diaphragm causes air pressure pulses that we hear as sound.

air pressure waves. We hear these air pressure waves as sounds (voices or music).

AM and FM radio

There are two types of radio signals: AM (amplitude modulating) and FM (frequency modulating).

An *AM radio* is designed to pick up a radio signal that varies in amplitude (strength). It operates on a frequency of 530 to 1 610 kilohertz (kHz) which gives it a longer broadcasting range than FM.

Fig. 73-2 illustrates the differences between AM and FM radio signals.

An *FM radio* is designed to receive a radio signal that varies in frequency (fluctuating speed). The FM band is from 88 to 108 megahertz (MHz). Since the FM radio wave is not reflected off the ionosphere (upper atmosphere), it has a short broadcasting range (approximately 35 miles or 56 kilometers). FM radio is capable of producing stereo (stereophonic or multidimensional) sound. A *stereo* uses at least two speakers and has different sounds coming from each speaker.

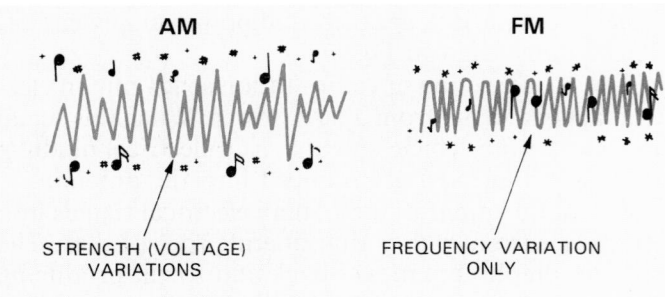

Fig. 73-2. Note difference between AM and FM signals. Radio must have circuitry that can ''read'' these different radiowaves. (Chrysler)

Radios

A modern *radio* contains complex electronic circuits that receive and amplify the radio signal to operate the speakers. It also contains a tuner that allows the driver to adjust to different radio frequencies (stations).

When the radio is found to be faulty, it should be removed and sent to an authorized repair technician.

Use the information in a service manual to diagnose radio problems. You may have external problems: blown fuse, open antenna lead, bad speakers, or other problems keeping the radio from functioning properly. Do NOT condemn the radio until all other problem sources have been eliminated.

An *antenna trimmer screw* should be adjusted when the radio has been removed for repairs or after antenna replacement. After reconnecting the radio to the antenna, speakers, and power supply in the vehicle, set the tuner to a weak station. Then, as shown in Fig. 73-3, turn the trimmer screw until the weak station comes in as loud and clear as possible.

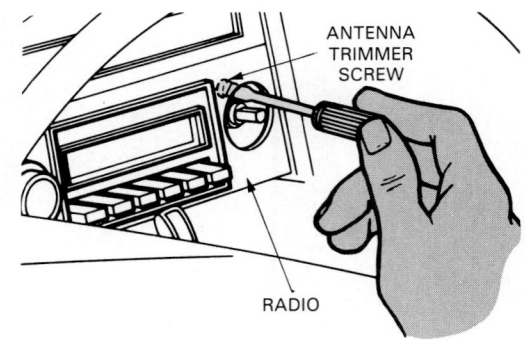

Fig. 73-3. Antenna trim screw provides one of the few in-car adjustments that can be done on a radio. Radio is set on weak station. Then screw is turned for best reception. (Buick)

Antennas

An *antenna* picks up the broadcast signal and feeds it through the antenna lead to the radio. Some antennas are a very fine piece of wire mounted in the windshield glass. Other antennas are a metal mast (rod) mounted on the body.

A *power antenna* is a telescoping type antenna, extended and retracted by an electric motor. Look at Fig. 73-4. The electric motor turns a gear. The gear then

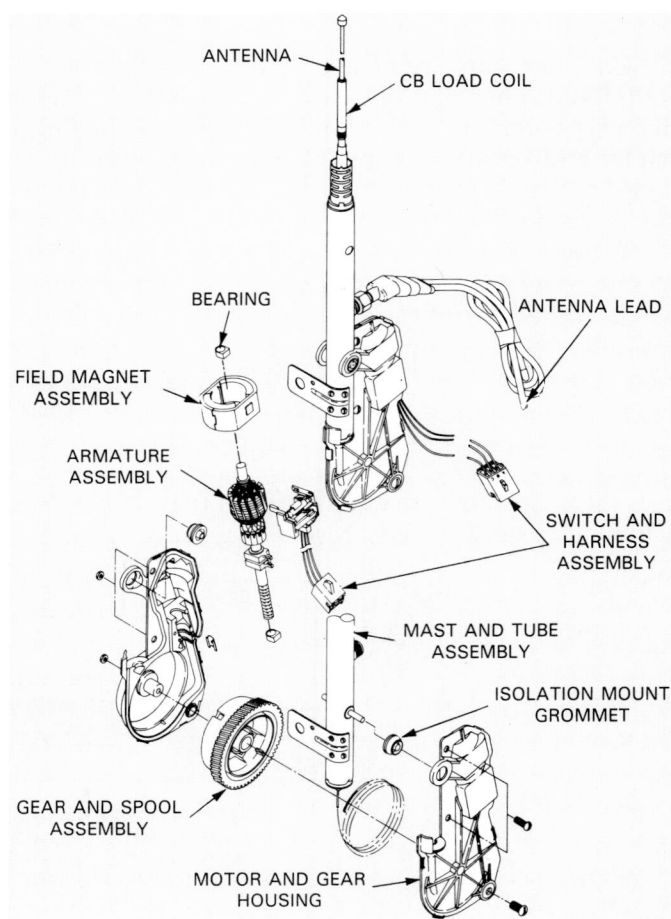

Fig. 73-4. Most power or retractable antennas use these basic parts. (Oldsmobile)

operates a cable or slide mechanism on the antenna mast. A dash switch actuates the electric motor to move the antenna up or down.

Refer to a service manual for service procedures for power antennas.

Speakers

A *speaker* uses a permanent magnet and a coil of wire mounted on a flexible diaphragm to convert electricity into motion and sound. When current passes through the coil of wire, the resulting magnetic field pulls the coil and diaphragm toward the permanent magnet. Rapid movement of the speaker diaphragm causes pressure waves in the air. We hear these pressure waves as sound. Look at Fig. 73-5.

The speakers may be mounted in the doors, dash, or behind the rear seat. AM radios normally have only one speaker in the top of the dash. FM stereo radios have two, or four speakers.

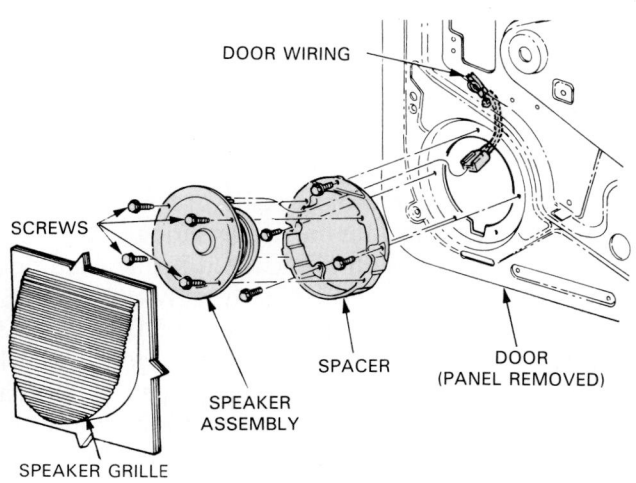

Fig. 73-5. Speakers can be mounted in doors, upper dash, interior side panels, or behind rear seat. Mounting is similar to this door mounted speaker. (Ford)

A *faulty speaker* will usually distort the sound of the radio. The speaker may rattle, especially when the volume is adjusted to a higher output level. A broken coil winding or terminal-to-coil wire can make the speaker totally inoperable.

Speakers are not usually repairable and should be replaced when defective. Terminal-to-coil wires can sometimes be soldered when broken.

Tape player

A cassette *tape player* is often incorporated into the radio in newer vehicles, Fig. 73-6.

As with radios, internal problems with a tape player require a specialized electronic technician. However, an auto technician can perform external repairs: removing broken recording tape or cleaning the tape head.

Refer to the details in a service manual for diagnosis, cleaning, removal, and replacement procedures.

COMPACT DISC PLAYER

A *compact disc player*, also called a *CD player*, uses a laser disc instead of a conventional magnetic tape. It provides higher quality sound reproduction than a tape player. Many CD players mount the disc changer in the trunk and have the controls on the dash. Refer to the service manual for specifics since designs vary.

Fig. 73-6. This vehicle radio incorporates AM/FM receiver, audio cassette player, and a controller for a compact disc changer located in the vehicle's trunk. (Denon America)

Radio noise

Radio noise is undesired interference or static (popping, clicking, or crackling) obstructing the normal sound of the radio station. Radio noise is commonly caused by a bad antenna, open or shorted noise suppressor (capacitor), bad spark plug wire, radio troubles, or other problems. If the stations are too far away, noise will interfere with the signal.

Generally, study the sound of the radio noise to determine its source. For example, a low pitch clicking, that changes with engine speed, may be from the ignition system (open spark plug wire). A higher pitched, whirring sound that also changes with engine speed could be from the electrical system (bad capacitor), Fig. 73-7.

One of the first parts to check with radio noise is the antenna. Plug a known good antenna into the radio. Ground the antenna base and note any changes in radio output. If the noise is eliminated, the old antenna is faulty. If the noise remains the same, then check the noise suppressors.

Noise suppressors are capacitors that absorb voltage fluctuations in the car's electrical system. They result in smoother DC current entering the radio, which reduces radio noise.

Noise suppressors can be located at the alternator, voltage regulator, ignition coil, distributor, and heater blower motor. All of these components can produce voltage fluctuations and noise. Refer to a service manual for exact suppressor locations.

A clip-on capacitor can be used to test noise suppressors, Fig. 73-8. Connect the test capacitor across

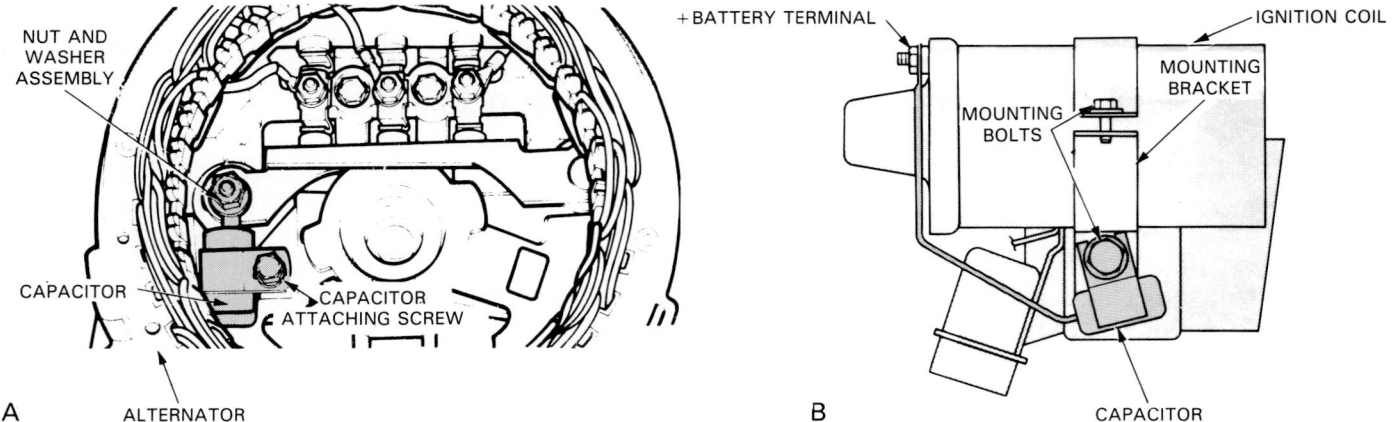

Fig. 73-7. Two common locations for radio noise suppressors. They are simply capacitors or condensors connected to car electrical system. A — Noise suppressor mounted inside alternator. B — Noise suppressor mounted on ignition coil. (Chrysler)

or in place of the suppressor. If the radio static is reduced, install a new suppressing capacitor.

POWER SEATS

Power seats typically use switches in the driver's door and electric motors under the seats to change the front seat position, Fig. 73-9.

The reversible DC motors, when activated by a switch, operate a gear mechanism. The gear mechanism changes the rotating motion of the motor armature into linear motion that positions the seat. Most power seats have more than one seat motor.

If both front power seats fail to function, check the common section of the circuit. Inspect the fuse, circuit breaker, wire connections, or any other component affecting both seats.

If only one of the seats is inoperative, test its control switch and wiring between the switch and motors. When the seat only fails in one mode (up and down, for example), check the motor and transmission (gear

mechanism) providing that action.

If you have difficulty repairing a power seat, read the information in a service manual. It will give directions for servicing the particular type unit.

POWER WINDOWS

A *power window* basically uses a control switch, reversible electric motor, circuit breaker, fuse, and related wiring to operate the door windows, Fig. 73-10.

A small electric motor is located inside each door. The motors have a transmission (usually worm and ring gear) that changes rotating motion of the motor armature into a partial rotation of a larger gear. This action is used to push the window open or closed.

A circuit breaker protects the window motor from overheating damage. The points can open if the switch is held in one position too long. A basic power window circuit is shown in Fig. 73-11.

When none of the power windows work, first check the fuse or circuit breaker for the system. If only some of the windows are inoperative, use a test light to check for power to those switches and motors.

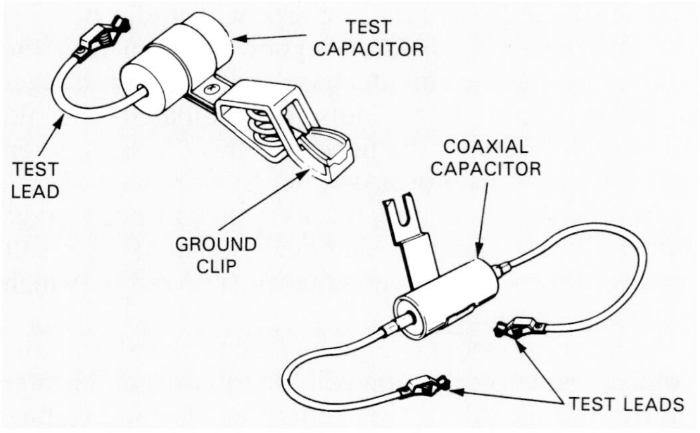

Fig. 73-8. Test capacitors can be used to check existing noise suppressors. If radio static quiets when test unit is connected to circuit, old capacitor is bad or there may be other electrical problems. (Pontiac)

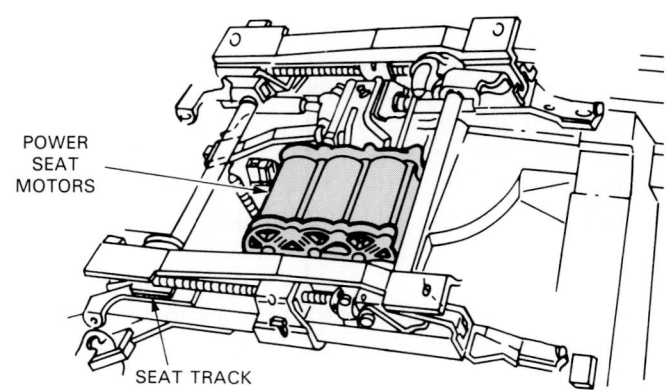

Fig. 73-9. Note location of power seat motors. Each motor provides specific function: front-to-rear movement, up-and-down movement, and tilting action. (Ford)

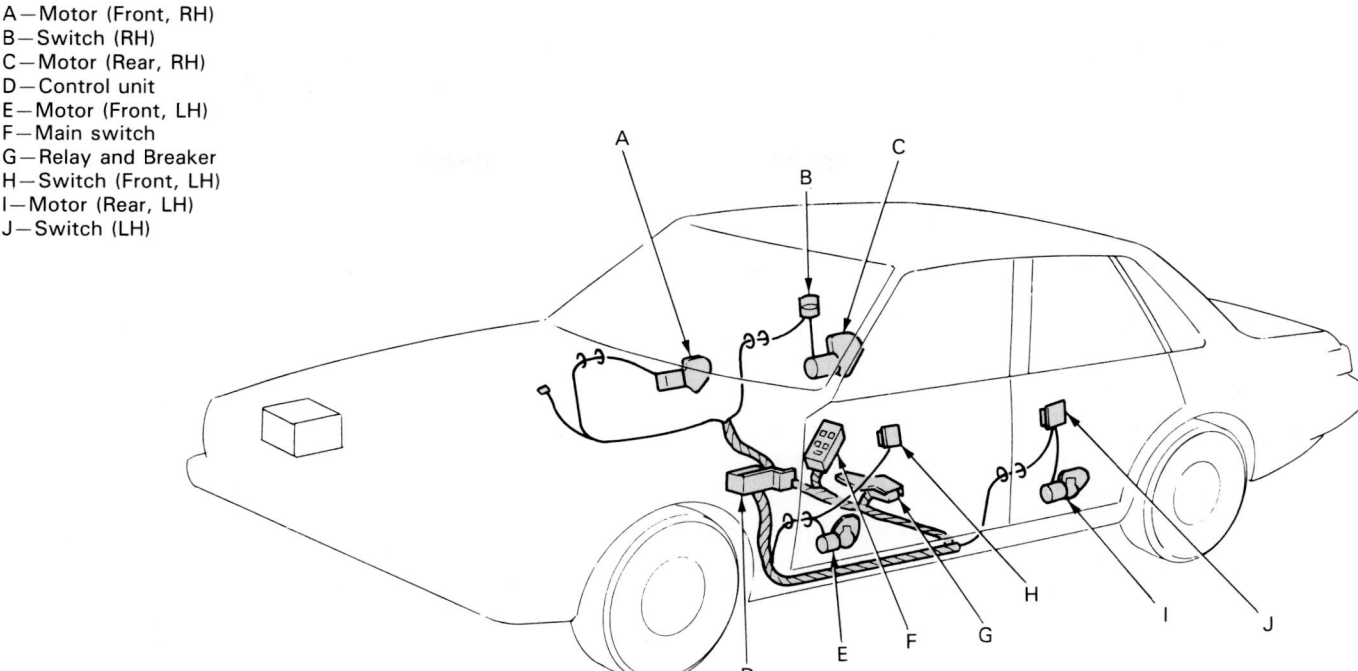

A—Motor (Front, RH)
B—Switch (RH)
C—Motor (Rear, RH)
D—Control unit
E—Motor (Front, LH)
F—Main switch
G—Relay and Breaker
H—Switch (Front, LH)
I—Motor (Rear, LH)
J—Switch (LH)

Fig. 73-10. Study basic layout of complete power window system. Switches operate electric motors inside each door. With inoperative power windows, check fuses and switches first. (Subaru)

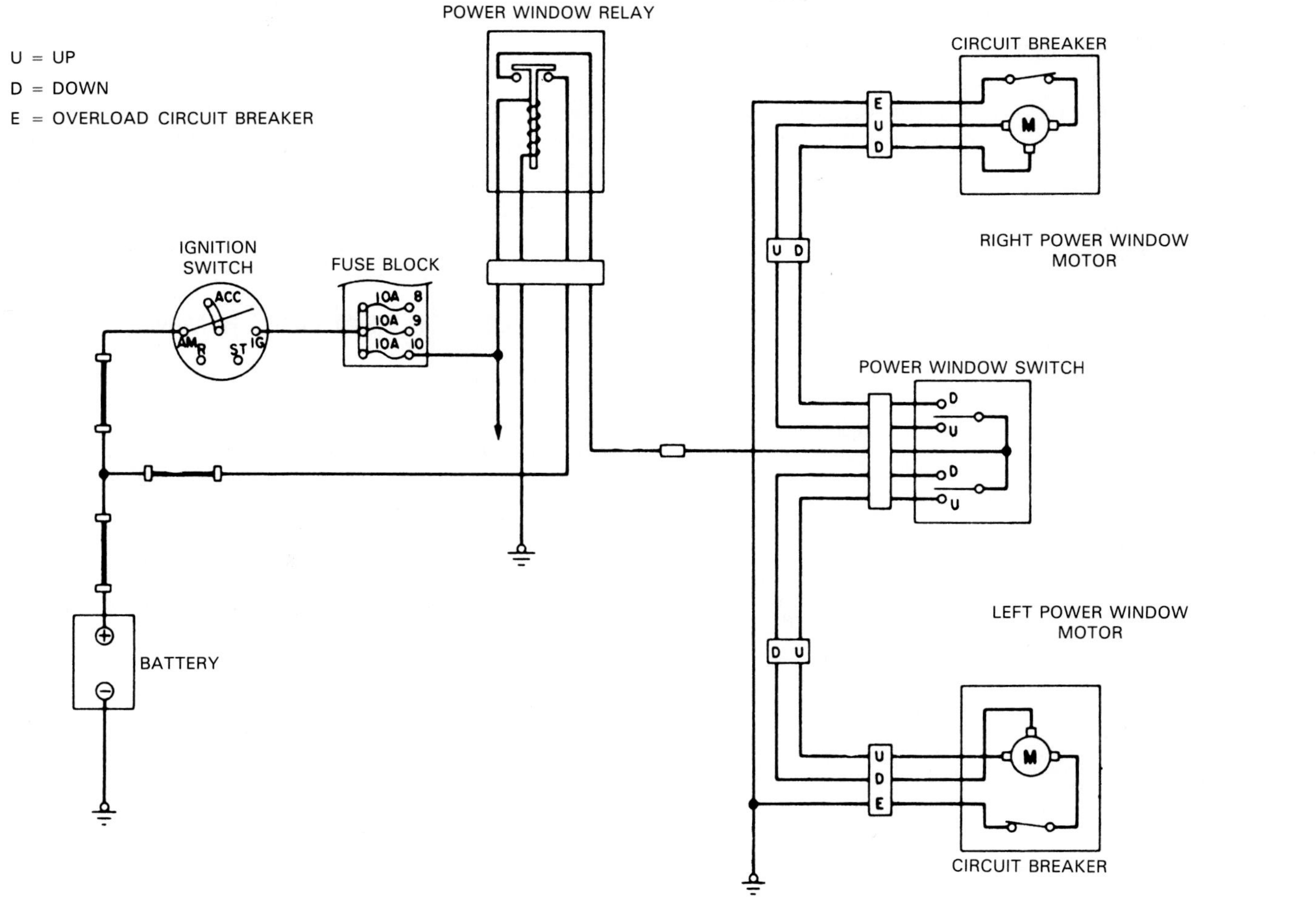

U = UP
D = DOWN
E = OVERLOAD CIRCUIT BREAKER

POWER WINDOW RELAY

CIRCUIT BREAKER

RIGHT POWER WINDOW MOTOR

IGNITION SWITCH

FUSE BLOCK

POWER WINDOW SWITCH

LEFT POWER WINDOW MOTOR

BATTERY

CIRCUIT BREAKER

Fig. 73-11. Service manual electric diagram, like this one, can be used when tracing faults in circuit. Study how switch operates each motor and how relay and circuit breakers are connected in circuit. (Subaru)

Listen for a humming sound that indicates motor operation. The plastic gears in the window motor transmission can strip. The motor will spin but movement will not be transferred to the window.

If the switches or motor itself are found to be bad, they should be replaced.

POWER DOOR LOCKS

Power door locks typically use an electric switch and a solenoid or motor to operate the door lock mechanism. Illustrated in Fig. 73-12, when the door key is turned, it closes a switch. The motor or solenoid then moves an arm on the door latch to lock or unlock the door. An additional switch is normally provided on the driver's door panel.

If all of the power door locks fail to function, check the fuse, electrical connections, and other components common to the whole circuit. If only one door lock is bad, check its switch and solenoid or motor. A manufacturer's manual will give details for testing the particular system.

REAR WINDOW DEFOGGER

A *rear window defogger,* also called a rear window defroster, commonly uses a switch, relay, indicating light, and a window heating grid. See Fig. 73-13.

When the switch is turned on, it allows current to flow to the indicator light and to the heating grid. The heating grid is resistance wire, usually mounted on or in the window glass.

Current flowing through the grid causes the wire to heat up and defog or deice the vehicle's window. A typical circuit for such a system is given in Fig. 73-13.

A few vehicles use a more conventional blower or fan to defog and deice the rear window. Its operation is similar to a heater blower.

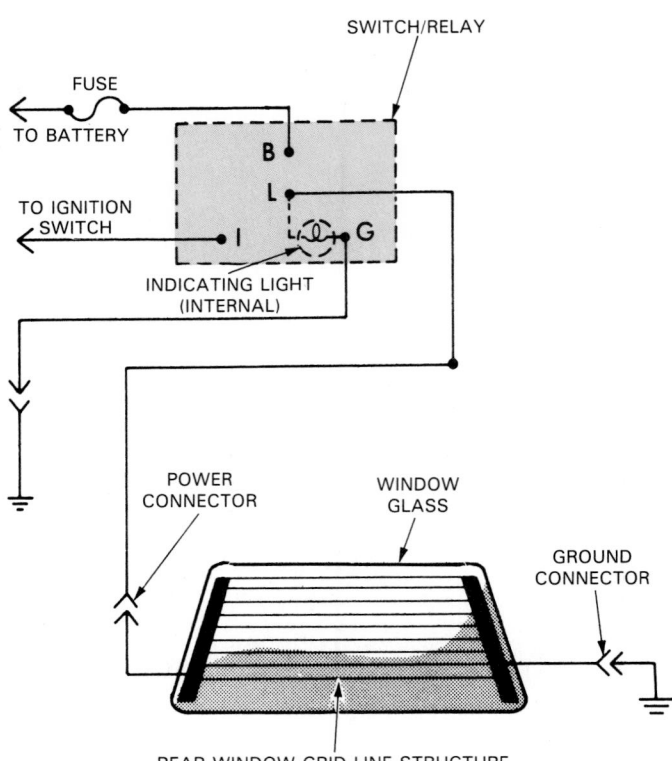

Fig. 73-13. This is a circuit for a rear window defog or defrost system. When fed current from switch and relay, resistance wire on glass heats up. (Chrysler)

When the grid type rear window defogger does not work, check the fuse first. Then, check for adequate voltage going to the grid with the power switch closed.

If voltage is low at the grid input, test the circuit for opens. If power is being fed to the grid, the grid may be bad. Test the grid as described by the manufacturer.

SEAT BELT, KEY, HEADLAMP REMINDER SYSTEM

A *seat belt, key, headlamp reminder system,* called several other names (warning system, chime system), makes an audible signal (buzz, chime, voice) if:
1. Seat belts are NOT fastened when engine is started.
2. Keys are left in the ignition with engine off.
3. The headlamps are left on with engine off and door is open.

An illustration of a three chime reminder or warning system is shown in Fig. 73-14. Note how the tone generator can be activated by the seat belts, ignition key, and headlamp switch.

Refer to a service manual when troubleshooting and repairing a reminder system. Numerous design variations are used by different vehicle makers.

SPEED CONTROL (CRUISE CONTROL)

Speed control, also termed *cruise control,* senses engine speed and controls the throttle opening of the carburetor or fuel injection system. In this way, the

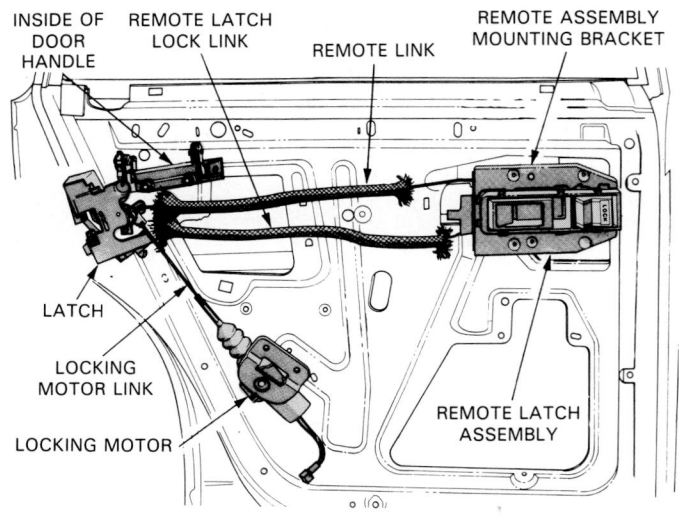

Fig. 73-12. Most power door lock systems use large solenoid to activate latch. Study construction of system. (Chrysler)

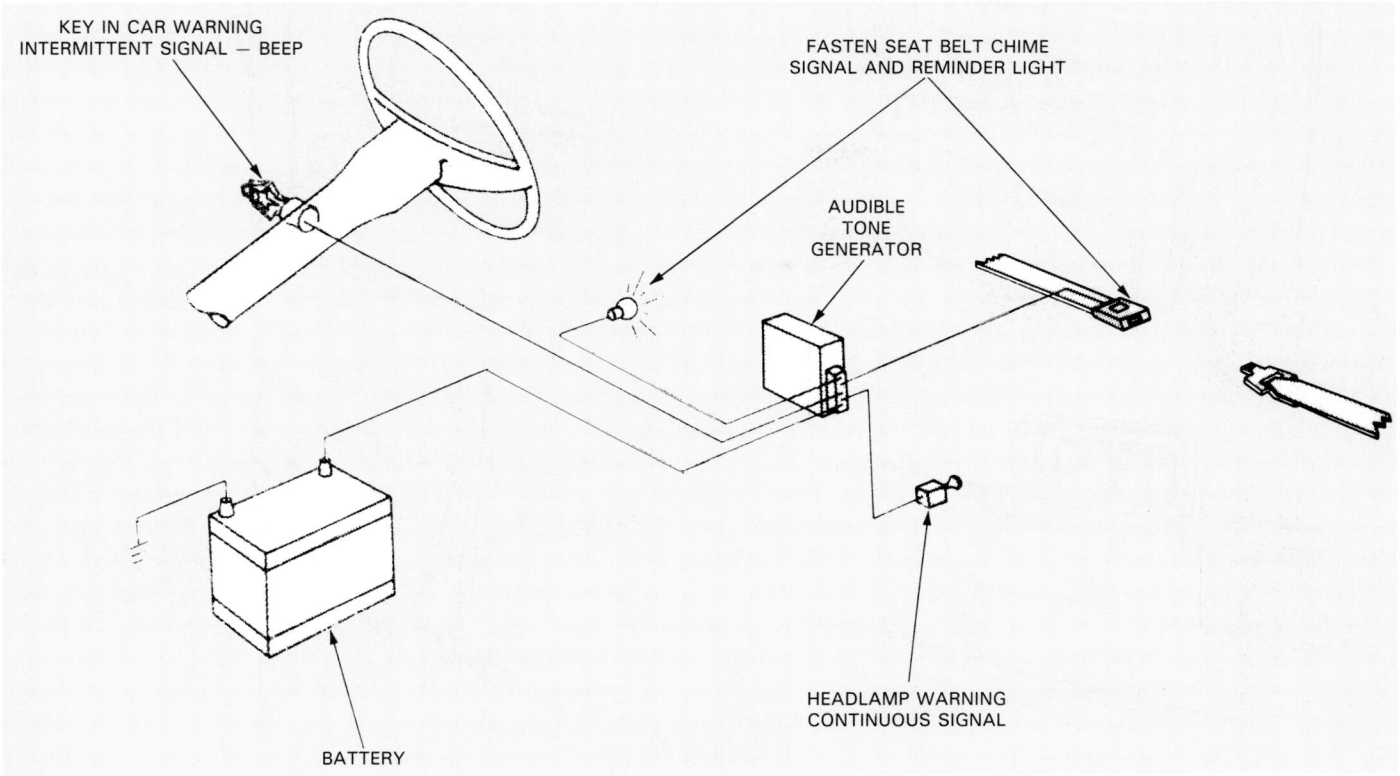

Fig. 73-14. Warning or reminder system makes sound when key is left in ignition, when seat belts are not fastened, and when lights are left on. Circuit in tone generator is ''heart'' and ''brain'' of system. (Plymouth)

driver can set the driving speed of the vehicle and the cruise control system will maintain that road speed.

Although systems vary, a typical late model speed control system consists of a speed control amplifier, speed control servo, speed control switch, speed sensor, and brake switch. See Fig. 73-15.

When the driver activates the speed control, power is fed to the *speed control amplifier*. The amplifier then activates the speed control servo.

The *servo* pulls on the throttle linkage to maintain engine power and vehicle speed.

The *speed sensor* sends electrical pulses (speed information) to the amplifier.

If the vehicle starts to slow down when climbing a hill, the slower speed pulses cause the amplifier to make the servo open the throttle wider. This keeps the vehicle cruising at the correct speed. The opposite is true if speed increases (moving down a hill).

When the driver presses on the brakes, the *brake switch* deactivates the speed control amplifier and the system. The *resume switch* allows the driver to reset the same cruising speed when desired.

Since cruise control systems vary from vehicle to vehicle, refer to a service manual for details.

DOOR PANEL REMOVAL

Door panel removal may be necessary to service power windows, seat control switches, door latches,

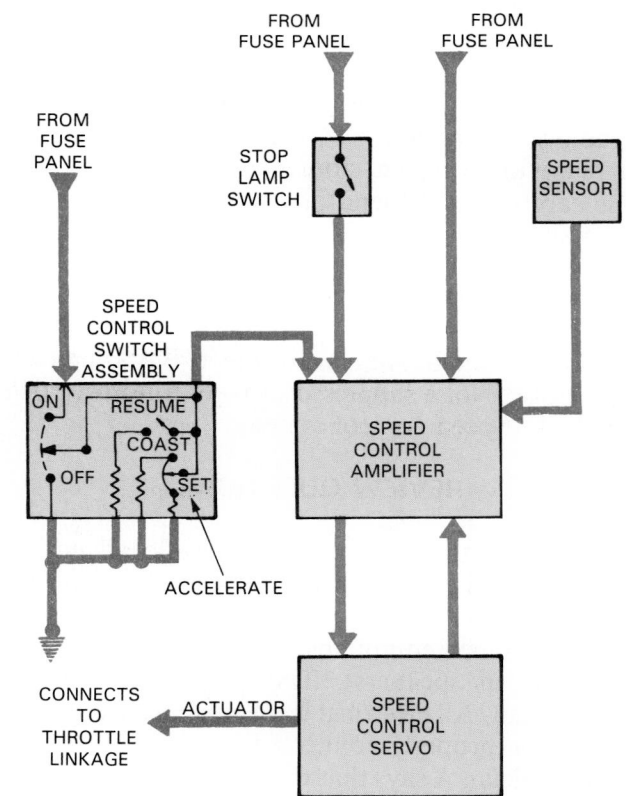

Fig. 73-15. Layout of modern electronic speed control system. Speed sensors sends electrical information to control unit. Control unit can then operate servo that connects to throttle linkage on engine. Also note circuit in speed control switch. (Ford)

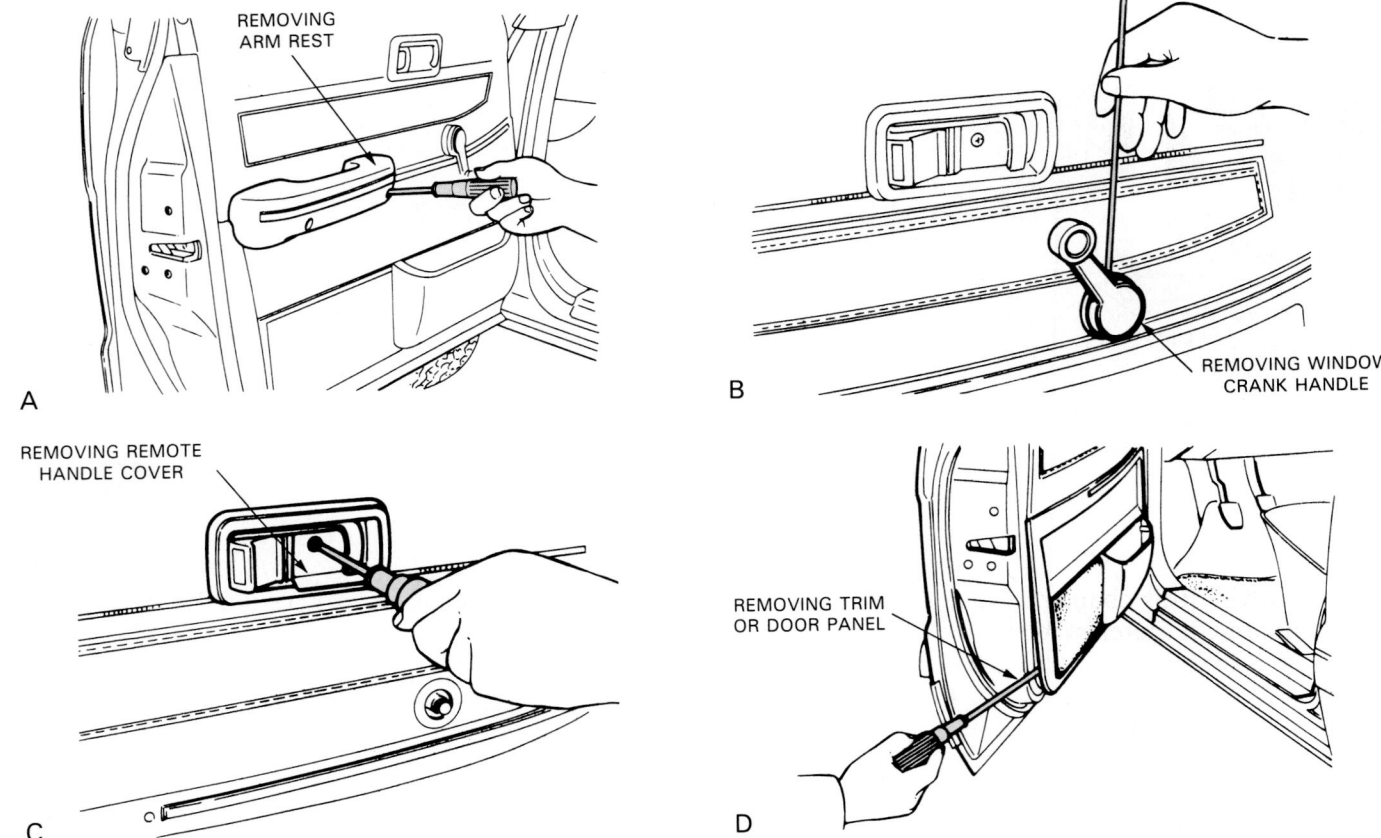

Fig. 73-16. Basic procedure for removing door panel. A — Remove screws from panel and arm rest, if used. Screws may be under pop-off cover or plugs. B — Remove window crank handles. They may be held with screws or you may need to release special clip from behind handle as shown. C — Remove other hardware that is screwed into body of door: lock mechanism, lock knob, speaker cover, etc. D — Use standard screwdriver or special tool to pop clips out of door and free panel. Be careful to pry directly under each clip or door panel will tear. (Subaru)

or radio speakers. Fig. 73-16 illustrates the basic steps for removing a typical door panel.

Be careful not to bend or tear the panel. Refer to a manual if you have difficulty.

KNOW THESE TERMS

AM, FM, Radio, Antenna trimmer, Power antenna, Radio noise, Noise suppressor, Power window, Power door lock, Speed control system.

REVIEW QUESTIONS

1. What are the basic parts of a radio system?
2. Explain the difference between AM and FM signals.
3. A customer complains of poor radio reception (static in speakers). The radio has just been replaced. All electrical leads, including the antenna, are properly connected.
   Technician A says that the antenna trimmer screw may need adjustment.
   Technician B says that the new radio must be defective.
   Who is correct?

a. Technician A
b. Technician B
c. Both A and B
d. Neither A nor B

4. A _____ uses a permanent magnet and coil of wire mounted on a flexible diaphragm.
5. What are some of the symptoms of a faulty speaker?
6. Why are noise suppressors used?
7. If one power window fails to go up and down, check the circuit fuse first. True or False?

ACTIVITIES FOR CHAPTER 73

1. Use a car radio to "hunt" for radio stations broadcasting from other communities, on both the AM and FM bands. Note the call letters and towns, then mark them on a map. Check the distance the farthest signal traveled. Was it AM or FM?
2. Take a survey among students at your school to determine which vehicle music system options are most popular. Determine how many student cars have just radios, radios with cassette players, radios with CD changer/players, etc. Make a bar graph to show your results.

Computer System Networking

After studying this chapter, you will be able to:

☐ Compare computer systems to the human body's nervous system.

☐ Describe the input, processing, and output sections of a basic computer system.

☐ Explain sensor classifications.

☐ Explain actuator classifications.

☐ Sketch a block diagram for a computer network.

☐ Summarize where computers, control modules, sensors, and actuators are typically located.

☐ Explain the basic parts of a computer.

☐ Summarize the flow of data through a computer.

☐ Explain how a computer uses sensor inputs to determine correct outputs for actuators.

☐ Describe the operation of vehicle sensors.

☐ Explain the operation of vehicle actuators

☐ Describe how automotive computer systems contribute to safe vehicle operation.

In many previous chapters, you learned how computers are used to monitor and control major systems of a vehicle. In the Fuel System Section, you learned how sensors and a computer could open and close the injectors to meter fuel into the engine. In the Electrical Section of the book, you learned how computers could more precisely control the ignition system. In the Emission Control Section, you studied how the computer was used to reduce air pollution. In the Drive Train Section, computer control of the transmission was introduced. In the Chassis Section, electronic suspensions, anti-lock brakes, and other topics relating to the computer were summarized.

To give you the "bigger picture" of computers, this chapter will overview this information so you can more fully understand an on-board computer system. Even though many previous chapters discussed computer components, a review of the COMPLETE NETWORK is needed.

In the past, systems (ignition and fuel for example), worked independently of each other. Now almost all major systems use common sensors. This makes it important for you to fully understand how the complete computer network on a vehicle operates and interacts with other systems.

Computers can be a "blessing" to the vehicle owner because of the conveniences they provide. However, computers can also be a "curse" to the poorly trained technician. Study carefully!

CYBERNETICS

The term *cybernetics* refers to the study of how electrical-mechanical devices can duplicate the action of the human body. Comparing the human body to a computer is an easy way to explain this subject. Just as your brain can communicate with and control the parts of your body, an automotive computer can communicate with and control parts of a vehicle. See Fig. 74-1.

Nervous system (input)

Your *nervous system* uses chemical-electrical signals to control body functions. If you touch a sharp needle, nerve cells in your finger "fire" and send a signal through a strand of nerve cells up your arm and into your brain. The strand of nerve cells form a "wire" that connects your finger and brain.

The nerve cells in the tip of your finger would be comparable to an *input* of a VEHICLE SENSOR. They convert the pain of a pin prick into a signal or data.

The brain (processing)

Our brain is a complex network of billions of cells interconnected by linking cells called neurons. Each linking neuron can chemically-electrically connect tens of thousands of neighboring cells. When our brain "thinks," minute electrical impulses travel from neuron to neuron. One simple thought might involve electrical impulses between thousands of cells in a specific pattern. This is very similar to the electrical action inside the circuits of a computer.

Your brain is comparable to a "super powerful" computer. It can *process* the inputs from the nervous system

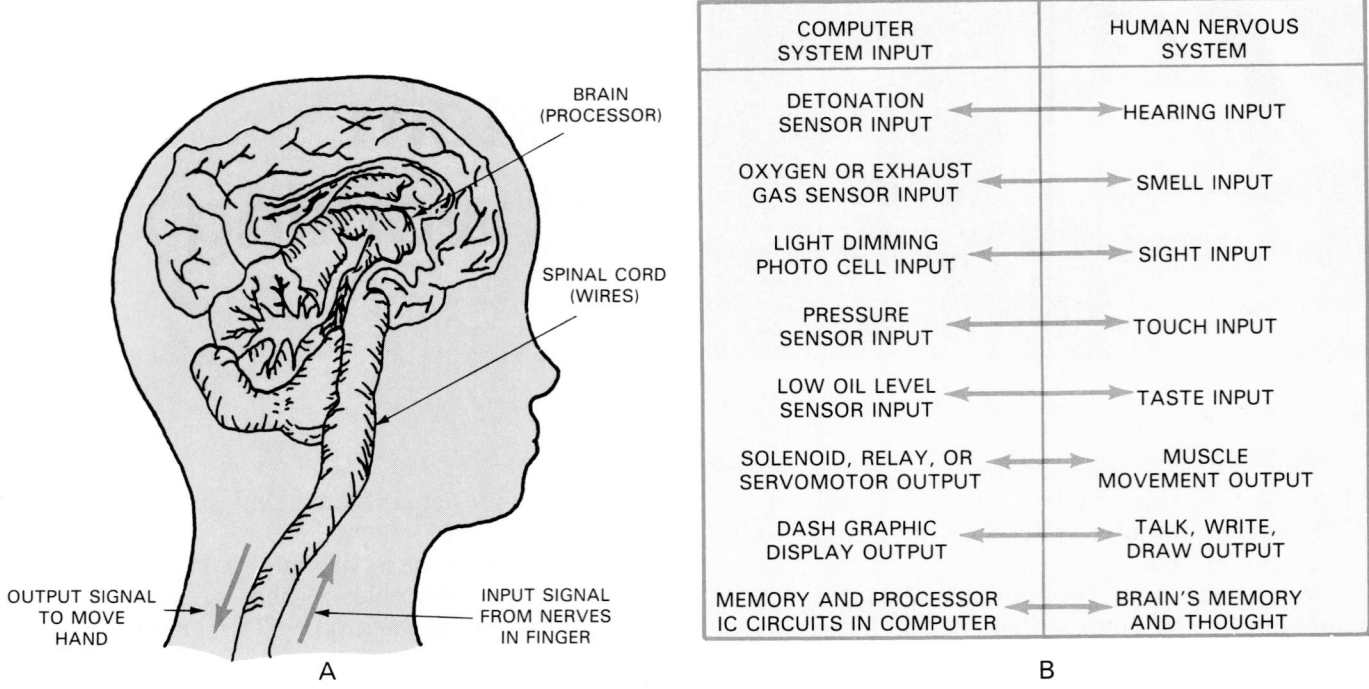

COMPUTER SYSTEM INPUT	HUMAN NERVOUS SYSTEM
DETONATION SENSOR INPUT	HEARING INPUT
OXYGEN OR EXHAUST GAS SENSOR INPUT	SMELL INPUT
LIGHT DIMMING PHOTO CELL INPUT	SIGHT INPUT
PRESSURE SENSOR INPUT	TOUCH INPUT
LOW OIL LEVEL SENSOR INPUT	TASTE INPUT
SOLENOID, RELAY, OR SERVOMOTOR OUTPUT	MUSCLE MOVEMENT OUTPUT
DASH GRAPHIC DISPLAY OUTPUT	TALK, WRITE, DRAW OUTPUT
MEMORY AND PROCESSOR IC CIRCUITS IN COMPUTER	BRAIN'S MEMORY AND THOUGHT

A ... B

Fig. 74-1. A—Input comes from our nerves. Brain is computer that processes these input signals. Brain then outputs signals to control our muscles. B—Study chart comparing human body and a computer system.

and determine what actions should be taken. Its billions of cells are comparable to billions of *computer gates* (switching circuits).

In our example, the chemical-electrical signal of a sharp needle would be sent into a specific area in the brain. The brain cells in that area are organized or *programmed* to analyze the inputs from your finger. Since the signal would tell the brain "my finger is being injured," the brain would take corrective action to protect your finger.

The brain makes decisions much like computer chips or integrated circuits (introduced in Chapter 8) produce logical outputs depending upon inputs. The billions of cells in the brain can be either chemically-electrically CHARGED (on or one) or they may NOT be charged (off or zero). By connecting all of the brain cells into logic circuits, the brain can decide what to do with each situation.

The reflex action (output)

The finger prick signal would activate specific brain cells and a reflex output would be produced by the brain. The brain would send a signal back into the arm. This chemical-electrical output would stimulate the muscles in the arm to pull back and protect the finger from the sharp object.

The reflex action of your muscles would be like an actuator or *output* in a car's computer system. Depending upon sensor inputs, the computer will produce logical outputs to make the actuators (solenoids, motors, etc.) make corrective actions.

DIGITAL ELECTRONICS

Digital electronics is a field of study dealing with how a computer has "artificial intelligence." A computer analyzes inputs or signals from sensors. It has memory. It can make logical choices on how to control specific outputs using the inputs. Digital electronics explains how a computer can have this ability or "intelligence."

Binary numbering system

The *binary numbering system* only uses two numbers, zero and one, and is the key to digital electronics and computers. Zero (0) and one (1) can be arranged into different sequences to represent other numbers, letters, words, a computer input, a computer output, or a condition. Since electronic devices, like a light switch, can be either on or off, the binary system is ideal.

To use the binary system, a computer can turn switches (transistors, for example) either on or off. OFF would represent a zero (0) and ON would represent one (1) in the binary system, Fig. 74-2. Note that a 0011 in binary would equal a three (3) in our decimal system. A 0110 in binary would equal a six (6) in decimal. Binary code numbers could also be used to represent letters, words, etc., Fig. 74-3.

In binary or computer language, a zero or a one is called a *bit*. A pattern of four bits is a *nibble*. A pattern of eight bits (zeros or ones) is called a *byte*, pronounced "bite." You are quite likely to hear this terminology used when you work with home or personal computers.

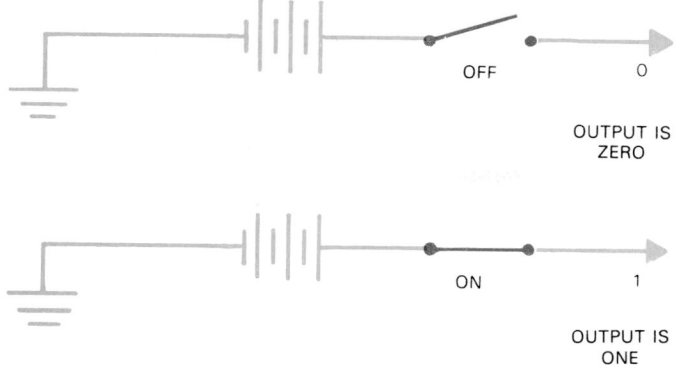

Fig. 74-2. *Since electronic components can be on or off, binary numbering system is ideal for digital logic or computer circuits. Binary system only has two numbers, zero and one, which represent ON and OFF conditions.*

DECIMAL NUMBER	BINARY NUMBER CODE 8 4 2 1	BINARY TO DECIMAL CONVERSION
0	0000	= 0 + 0 = 0
1	0001	= 0 + 1 = 1
2	0010	= 2 + 0 = 2
3	0011	= 2 + 1 = 3
4	0100	= 4 + 0 = 4
5	0101	= 4 + 1 = 5
6	0110	= 4 + 2 = 6
7	0111	= 4 + 2 + 1 = 7
8	1000	= 8 + 0 = 8

Fig. 74-3. *Chart shows how binary numbers can be converted into decimal (base ten) numbers. Note how right-hand binary number equals one and left-hand number equals eight. Study this chart.*

Gating circuits

A *gate* is an electronic circuit that produces a specific output voltage for a given input voltage. Just as a diode will pass current when forward biased (output lead would have voltage representing one) or stop current when reverse biased (output would be zero or no voltage), gates have programmed (known) outputs.

Shown in Fig. 74-4, the most common computer gates are:

1. **Inverter.** An *inverter gate,* also called a NOT GATE, will reverse its input. If the input has voltage applied (input one), the output terminals will NOT have voltage (output zero) or vice versa. An inverter can be used to make other gates.
2. **AND gate.** An *AND gate* requires voltage (1) at BOTH INPUTS to produce a voltage (1) at the output. If pins A and B are BOTH ONE (voltage applied or on), then the output will be ONE (on). If only A and NOT B has voltage, the output will be ZERO (off).
3. **NAND gate.** A *NAND gate* is an inverted AND gate. Note the small circle or dot on the output lead of the gate. The small circle represents an inverter. It will reverse the normal output of the AND gate, producing a NAND gate.
4. **OR gate.** An *OR gate* will produce an output (one or on) if EITHER input gate is energized (1). A or B input voltage (1) will result in voltage (1) at the output lead.
5. **NOR gate.** A *NOR gate* is an inverted OR gate. Again, the output is inverted to produce an output opposite that of an OR gate.

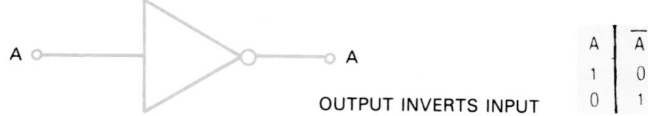

A—Inverter simply reverses its input.

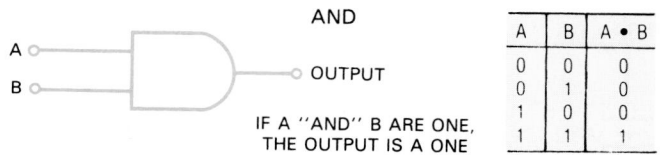

B—AND gate requires both inputs to be on for an output.

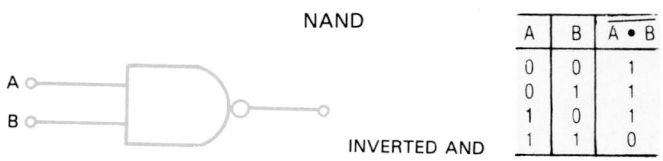

C—NAND gate is inverted AND gate; both inputs must be off for an output.

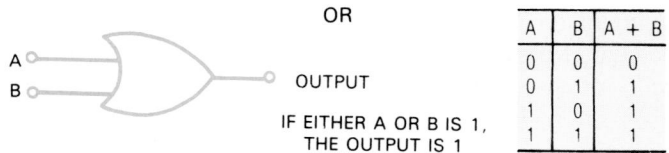

D—OR gate only needs input voltage on either terminal to get an output voltage.

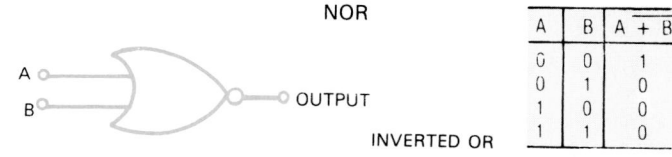

E—NOR gate is inverted OR gate; no input voltage will produce an output voltage.

Fig. 74-4. *Study basic types of computer gates.*

Truth tables

A *truth table* is a chart that shows what the output of a gate will be with different inputs. Look at the truth table for an OR gate, Fig. 74-5. The output will be ON (one) with A or B or both energized. Only when neither input is ON will the output be OFF (zero). A truth table graphically shows how a gate functions.

Gates are called logic devices because they make logical decisions (outputs) for specific inputs (facts). It will require you to have several inputs (learning experiences) to develop good outputs (skills) as an automotive technician.

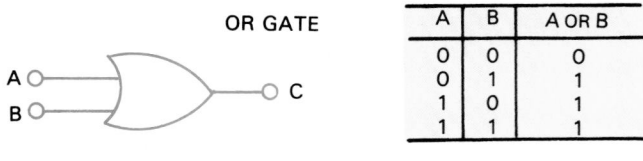

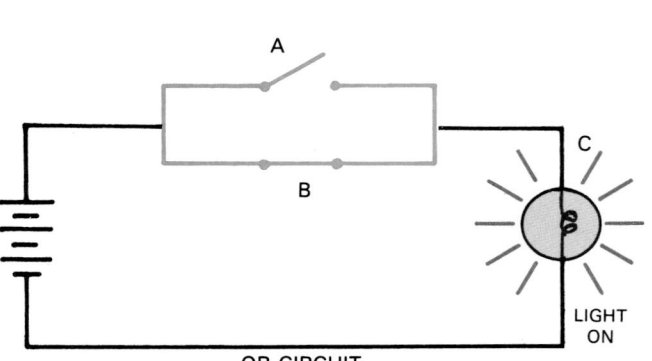

Fig. 74-5. Compare OR gate and this simple circuit. Either A or B will turn on the light and produce an output.

Note that if two light switches are wired in parallel, either switch A or switch B (OR gate) will turn the light ON (output one). However, if the two light switches are wired in series, both switch A and switch B (AND gate) must be ON to activate the light bulb, Fig. 74-6. Compare these circuits to the action of the gates and the truth tables.

Using gates

Since one gate will produce a logical output from certain inputs, several gates can be wired together to make more complex outputs. This is how a computer operates. Thousands of gates can be wired together to make a complex circuit that can produce hundreds of outputs (decisions) from hundreds of inputs (facts).

INTEGRATED CIRCUITS

Discussed briefly in Chapter 8, an *integrated circuit* is an electronic circuit that has been reduced in size and placed on the surface of a tiny semiconductor chip. Abbreviated IC, it is an electronic device containing microscopic components. In fact, a microscope is needed to see the components on an IC, Fig. 74-7.

Fig. 74-8 shows the basic construction of an integrated circuit. Note how different semiconductor substances are deposited in the silicone chip to produce resistors, diodes, and transistors. Metal conductors on the top of the chip connect these various electronic components to form the circuit. Wire leads allow for input and output connections to the IC chip.

COMPUTER ADVANTAGES

There are several reasons that computers are being used in modern vehicles. Computers provide several advantages. A few of these are:

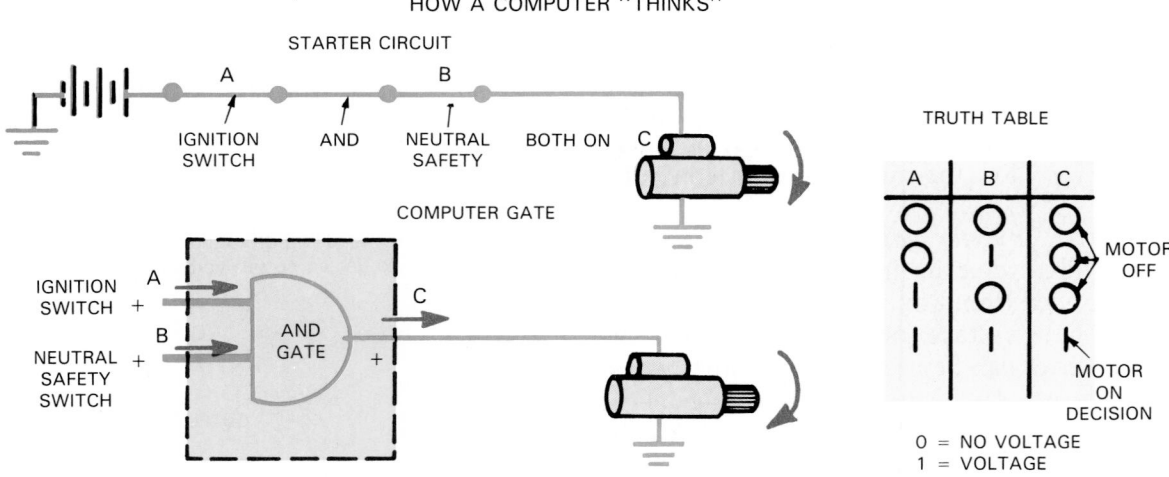

Fig. 74-6. Compare this starting circuit with the computer gate circuit and truth table. It shows how a computer gate can make a decision. Two input conditions (A and B on or one) must be satisfied in both circuits for there to be an output to the starting motor. This same principle, only with thousands of gates and dozens of inputs and outputs, is used inside an automotive computer.

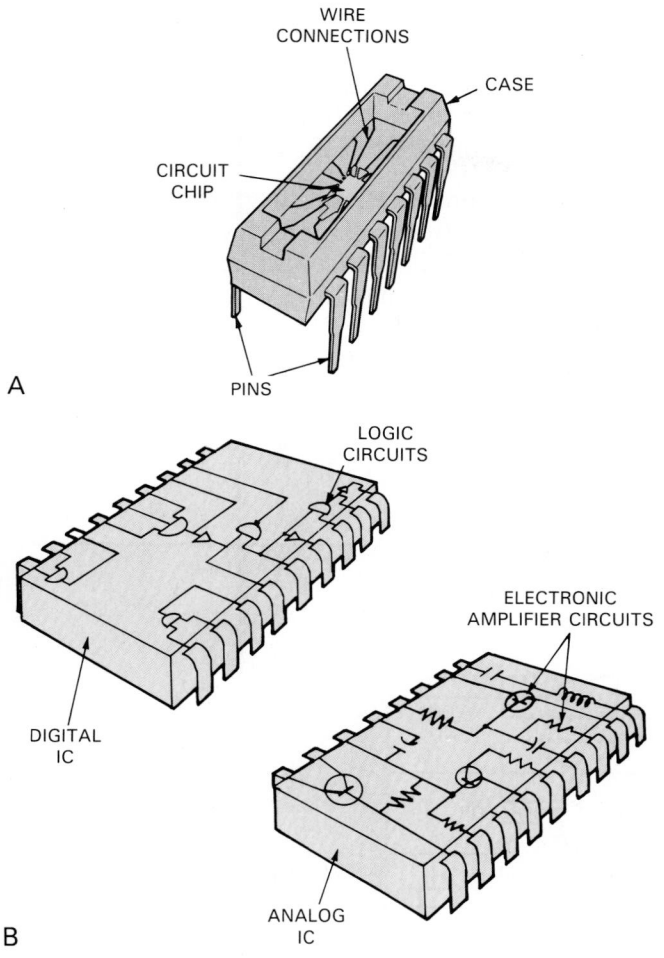

Fig. 74-7. *A—Note how tiny chip installs inside plastic case. Tiny wires connect chip to metal pins. Pins then plug in or solder to other parts of circuit. B—These are two broad classifications of integrated circuits. Digital circuit uses gates to produce logic circuits for computers. Analog IC is small amplifier circuit for increasing output strength or altering output.*

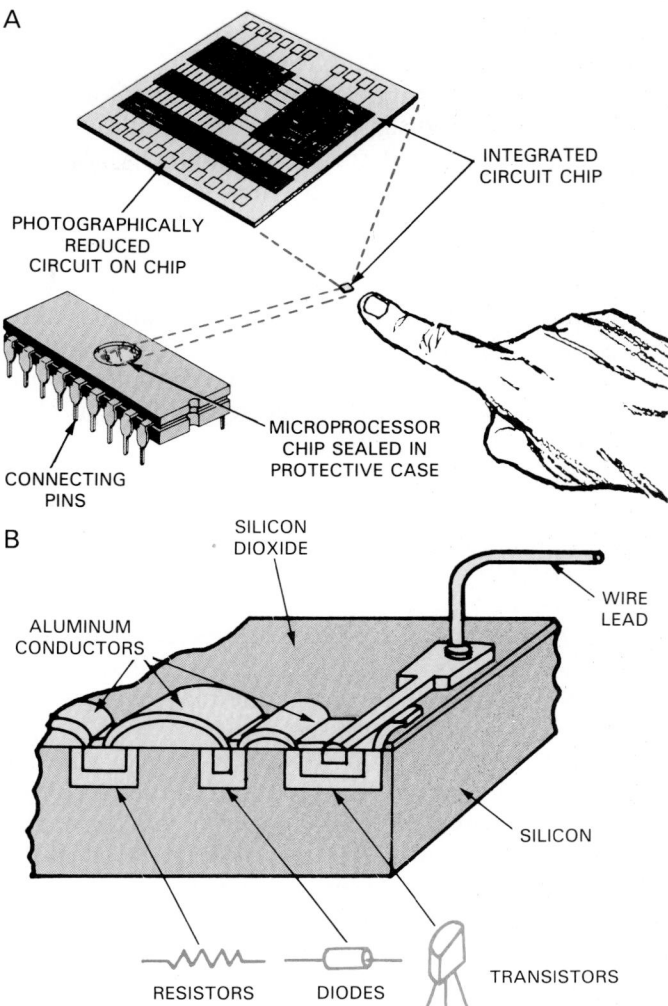

Fig. 74-8. *A—An integrated circuit has been photographically reduced in size and placed inside a protective case. B—Not how components are deposited on doped silicone in an IC.   (Ford)*

1. Computer systems can compensate for mechanical wear of parts. Also, they do NOT have as many mechanical parts to wear and go out of calibration.
2. Computers are very fast and can alter outputs in *milliseconds* (thousandths of a second). This lets a computer alter outputs almost instantly as input conditions change.
3. Computers reduce fuel consumption by more precise control of fuel metering into the engine. Today's systems actually "sniff" the exhaust gases to find out if too much or too little fuel is entering the engine.
4. Computers can increase engine power by more accurate control of ignition timing, fuel injection, emission control system operation, etc.
5. Computers can reduce vehicle weight because they are much lighter than mechanical control mechanisms.
6. Computers can help find system problems. Most computers have a self-test or self-diagnosis capability. They can produce an output code that tells the mechanic where a fault might be located.
7. Computers can increase driver convenience by better control of the passenger compartment environment and dash displays.
8. Computers can improve passenger safety by controlling the brake and suspension systems.
9. Computers can compensate and correct for component wear and failure to keep the car driveable.

The main disadvantage of a computer system is complexity. An untrained technician will have a very difficult time trying to fix a faulty computer system. However, as automakers standardize systems by using the same number and types of components and similar self-diagnosis, computer systems will hopefully become less confusing in the future.

COMPUTER OPERATION

There are three stages of computer operation:
1. INPUT (vehicle sensors convert a condition into an electrical signal for the computer).
2. PROCESSING (computer uses sensor signals or inputs to determine what action should be taken to control vehicle).
3. OUTPUT (computer produces electrical output so actuators can perform physical actions to alter component operation).

Fig. 74-9 shows the three stages of computer operation. You must be able to visualize this flow of electrical data.

Input classification (sensor categories)

An automobile uses several types of sensors to provide electrical data to the computer. The major sensor types are:
1. VARIABLE RESISTOR SENSOR—This type sensor changes its internal resistance with a change in a condition; its ohms value may change with temperature, pressure, etc.
2. POTENTIOMETER SENSOR—Like a variable resistor, it also varies resistance (and the resulting voltage signal) with a change in a condition; this type is commonly used to sense part movement.
3. SWITCHING SENSOR—It opens or closes the sensor circuit to provide an electrical signal for the computer; it can sense almost any condition.
4. VOLTAGE GENERATING SENSOR—Instead of changing resistance, this type sensor produces its own voltage output internally.
5. MAGNETIC SENSOR—It uses part movement and induced current to produce a signal for the computer; this type is commonly used to sense speed or part rotation.

There are dozens of specific names for vehicle sensors. However, they can all be classified into one of these five categories. See Fig. 74-10.

Output classification (actuator categories)

A computer system also uses several types of actuators or output devices to control part operation. The major actuator types include:
1. SOLENOID OUTPUT (current through solenoid winding forms magnetic field that can move metal core and act upon other components).
2. RELAY OUTPUT (current flow from computer

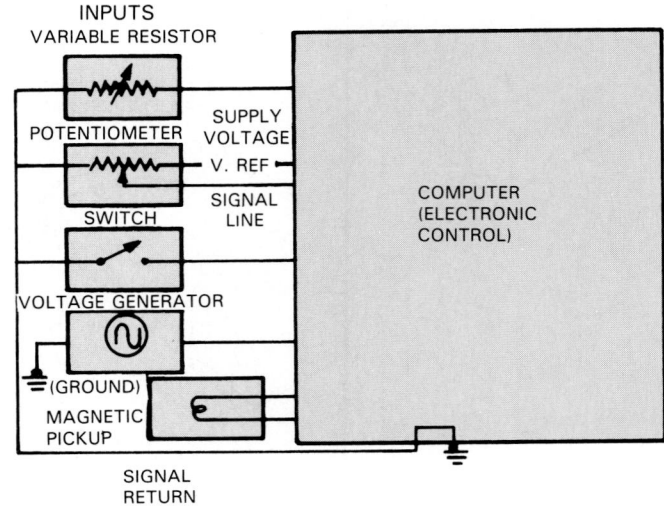

Fig. 74-10. These are the basic input classifications of sensors. They feed different types of signals to computer.

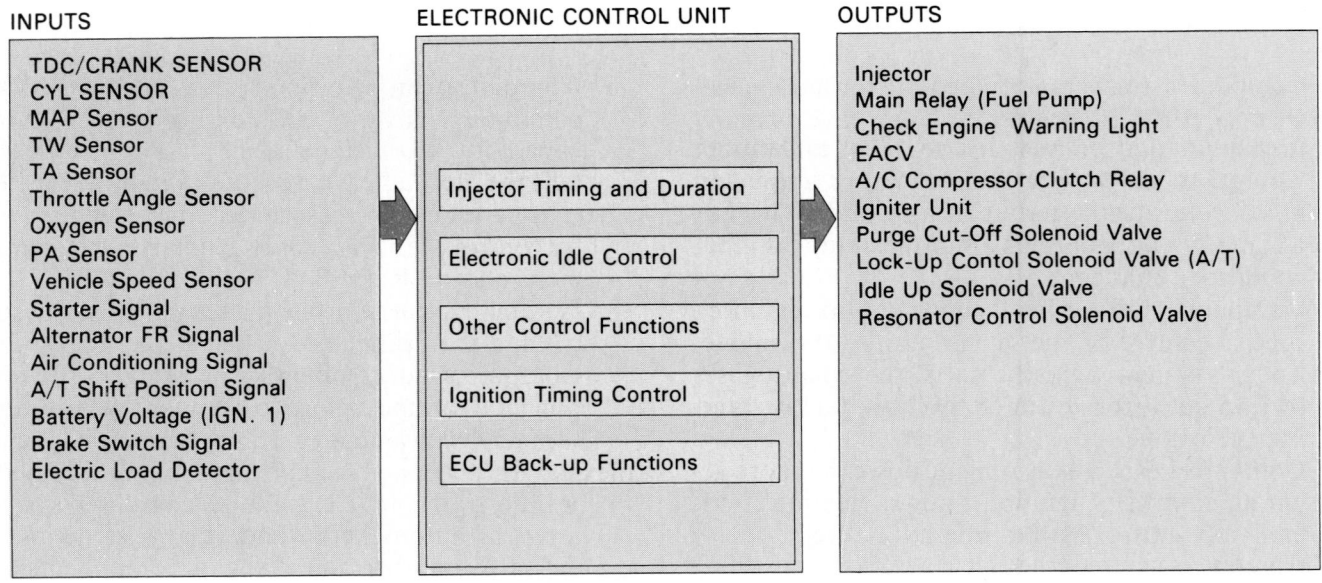

Fig. 74-9. Modern computer systems can have numerous inputs and outputs.　(Honda)

energizes relay to control larger current flow to another electrical component).

3. SERVO MOTOR OUTPUT (current is sent to small DC motor that can produce an output by turning and moving parts).

4. DISPLAY OUTPUT (current is sent to vacuum fluorescent or liquid crystal display to provide output data in car dash).

5. CONTROL MODULE OUTPUT (computer sends electrical signal to electronic control module; control module then amplifies or modifies signal to operate one of the previous four output devices).

Look at Fig. 74-11. Imagine how these devices could be used to control engine functions: idle speed, EGR valve action, etc.

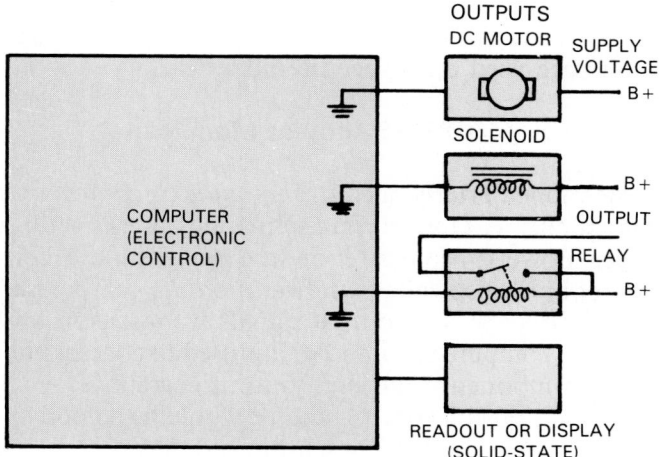

Fig. 74-11. These are the basic output classifications for actuators. They serve as the "hands and arms" of a computer network.

Computer block diagram

A *computer block diagram* is a simple drawing that shows how the sensors, actuators, and computer interact. It uses basic squares or rectangles to show components and lines to show wires. A computer block diagram is handy when trying to find out what types of sensors are used and what conditions are controlled by a specific computer system.

A block diagram for one computer control system is in Fig. 74-12. Study the various inputs and outputs.

COMPUTER LOCATIONS

Automotive computers are commonly located under the car's dash, Fig. 74-13. This protects the delicate circuits and components in the computer from engine heat, vibration, and moisture. However, computers can

also be located in the engine compartment, trunk, under seats, etc.

When in the engine compartment, the computer is

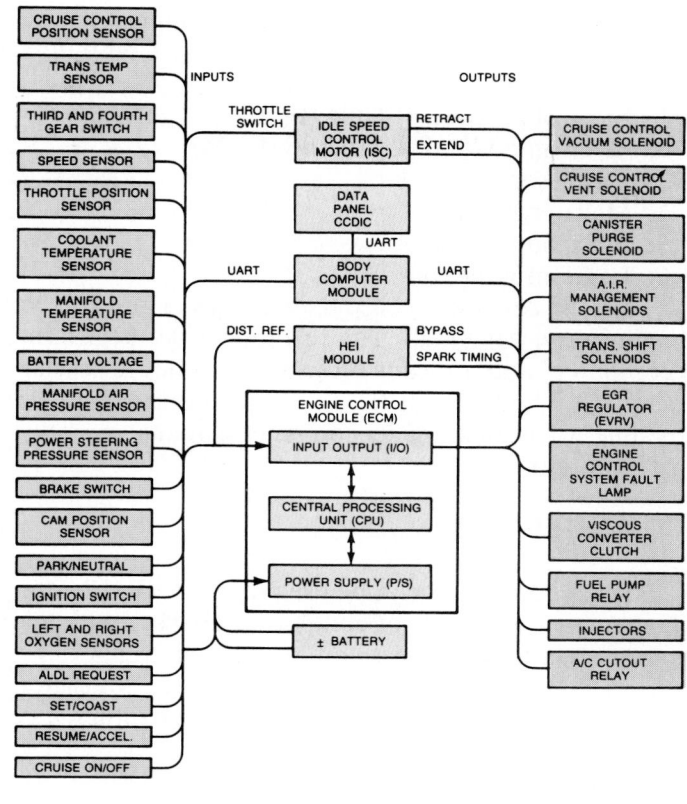

Fig. 74-12. Study block diagram for this computer system. Note different electronic control units or computers. (Cadillac)

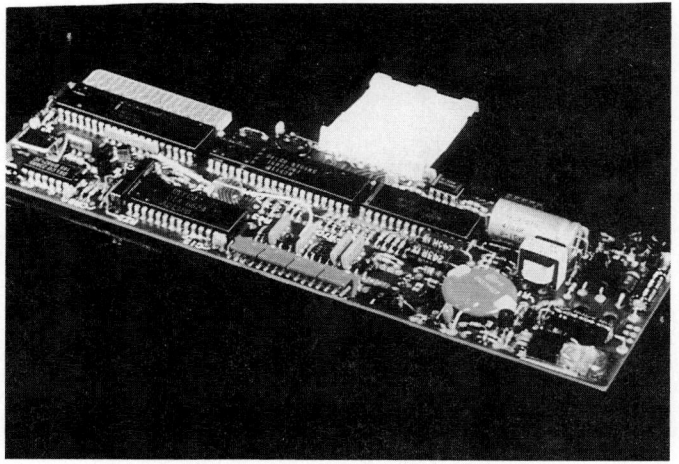

Fig. 74-13. Microprocessor or computer is very complex. They are not serviced in the field but replaced. (General Motors Corporation)

closer to most sensors and actuators. Less wiring and connectors are needed to tie the system together.

Computer names

The term *computer* is a general term that refers to any electronic circuit configuration that can use multiple inputs to find outputs. Service manuals will use many other names other than computer. Computers can also be called:

1. Electronic Control Unit (ECU).
2. Electronic Control Module (ECM).
3. Processor.
4. Microprocessor.
5. Electronic Control Assembly (ECA).
6. Logic module.

To avoid confusion, keep these names in mind when reading service manuals. This textbook will use the term "computer" and it means these other names in service manuals. The text will use the term "control unit or module" to mean a smaller computer that analyzes only a few inputs.

COMPUTER TYPES

Several computers can be used in a car, Fig. 74-14. The number and types of computers will vary with the manufacturer. The most common types are:

1. MAIN COMPUTER (large, powerful computer that processes data from sensors and other less powerful control units).
2. INSTRUMENTATION COMPUTER (control module that uses sensor inputs to operate dash displays).
3. ANTI-LOCK BRAKE COMPUTER (small control module that uses wheel sensor inputs and other inputs to control brake application).
4. IGNITION COMPUTER (small control module that uses sensor inputs to control ignition timing or spark plug firing).
5. ENGINE COMPUTER (computer that concentrates on using sensors to control engine operating conditions: idle speed, fuel injection, ignition timing, emission control devices, etc.).
6. SUSPENSION SYSTEM COMPUTER (small control module that uses suspension system, speed, and possibly steering sensors to control ride stiffness or shock absorber action).
7. CLIMATE CONTROL COMPUTER (small module used to control operation of heating, ventilation, and air conditioning systems).

Again, the number and types of computers will vary with the year, make, and model of car. The trend is to use a main computer to process most of the input data and control most outputs. In conjunction with the main computer, *smaller computers* (electronic modules) are used for the brake system, suspension system, instrumentation, etc. Refer to the car's service manual to find out how many and what types of computers are used on a specific model car.

CONTROL MODULES (Power Modules)

Mentioned briefly, a *control module* or *control unit* is a smaller computer that sometimes works with a larger, powerful computer on late model cars. A control module, also called a *power module*, can be used to amplify or process output signals from sensors and the main computer. Primarily, it is used to control only a few components and high output currents.

An ignition coil control module would be a good example. It uses inputs from sensors and the main engine computer to fire the ignition coils and spark plugs at the right time in the power stroke.

VEHICLE SENSOR OPERATION

A *vehicle sensor* is a transducer that changes a condition into an electrical signal. *Transduce* means to change from one medium or means of transmission to another. Just as our eyes, ears, nose, fingers, etc. can sense conditions, vehicle sensors can detect the operating conditions of a car. The computers use these "senses" (voltage signals) to control the actuators.

Sensor types

The most common vehicle sensors, Fig. 74-15, are:

1. AIR TEMPERATURE SENSOR (measures temperature of air entering engine intake manifold).
2. ENGINE TEMPERATURE SENSOR (measures temperature of engine coolant).
3. OXYGEN SENSOR (measures amount of oxygen in engine exhaust gases).
4. MANIFOLD PRESSURE SENSOR (measures pressure or vacuum inside engine intake manifold).
5. BAROMETRIC PRESSURE SENSOR (measures atmospheric pressure around engine).

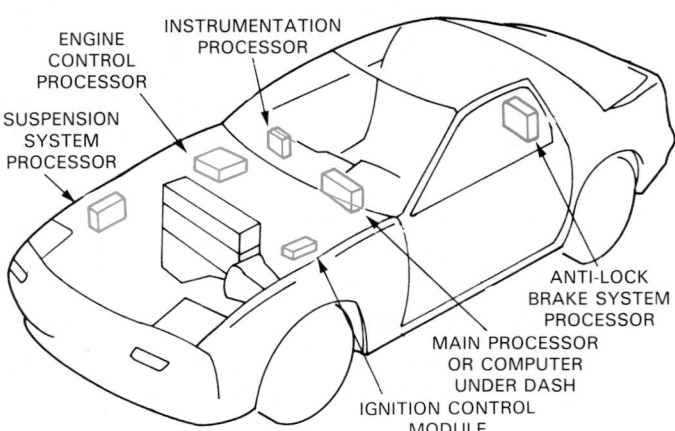

ENGINE CONTROL PROCESSOR

INSTRUMENTATION PROCESSOR

SUSPENSION SYSTEM PROCESSOR

ANTI-LOCK BRAKE SYSTEM PROCESSOR

MAIN PROCESSOR OR COMPUTER UNDER DASH

IGNITION CONTROL MODULE

Fig. 74-14. One or more computers or control modules can be used on the same car. Note potential locations.

6. THROTTLE POSITION SENSOR (measures opening angle of throttle valves on engine).
7. ENGINE SPEED SENSOR (measures engine rpm or ignition system operation).
8. CRANK POSITION SENSOR (measures rotation or location of crankshaft and rpm).
9. AIRFLOW SENSOR (measures amount of air flowing into engine).
10. KNOCK SENSOR (detects engine pinging, preignition, or detonation).
11. TRANSAXLE/TRANSMISSION SENSOR (checks transaxle or transmission gear selection).
12. BRAKE SENSOR (detects brake pedal application).
13. CRANKSHAFT SENSOR (checks rotation or position of engine camshaft).
14. OIL LEVEL SENSOR (measures amount of oil in engine oil pan).
15. EGR SENSOR (measures position of exhaust gas recirculation valve).
16. IMPACT SENSOR (detects a collision to shut OFF fuel pump and engine).
17. KNOCK SENSOR (microphone type sensor that listens for engine pinging or abnormal combustion so computer can retard ignition timing or reduce turbocharger boost pressure).
18. VEHICLE SPEED SENSOR (transmission mounted sensor to measure road speed of car so computer can adjust fuel, ignition, transmission, and other system operation).

Older cars use none or just a few of these sensors. Newer cars might use these and many other sensors.

Ionization knock sensing uses a low voltage ignition system discharge to detect abnormal combustion and knocking. The computer triggers the ignition coil to send a low voltage discharge across the spark plug right after combustion. The quality of combustion affects the resistance across the plug gap because of varying degrees of *ionization* (the process by which atoms lose or gain electrons). This affects current flow. Feedback to the computer allows it to determine if the turbo boost or spark advance should be lowered to reduce knocking. A conventional knock sensor is NOT needed.

Sensor locations

Sensors can be found almost anywhere on a vehicle. Many are mounted on the engine, Fig. 74-16. Others can be on the transmission or transaxle, on the wheel hubs, on the suspension, or even in the trunk (impact sensor). If in doubt, refer to the service manual for the specific vehicle to find sensor types and locations.

Active and passive sensors

An *active sensor,* also called *active transducer,* is one that generates its own voltage signal. Examples would be the oxygen sensor, knock sensor, and a magnetic pickup type sensor. See Fig. 74-17.

A *passive sensor,* also termed a *passive transducer,*

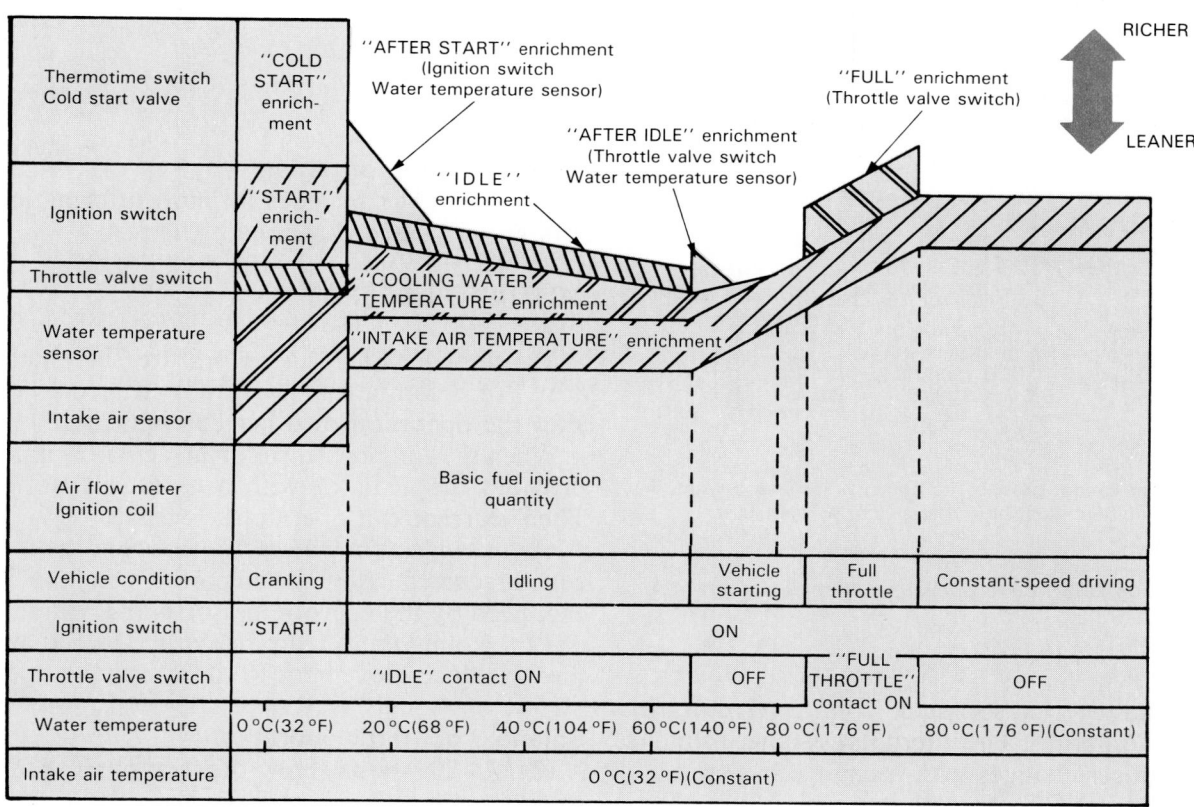

Fig. 74-15. Graph shows conditions or sensors and how they affect air-fuel ratio. Top line represents air-fuel ratio. (Nissan)

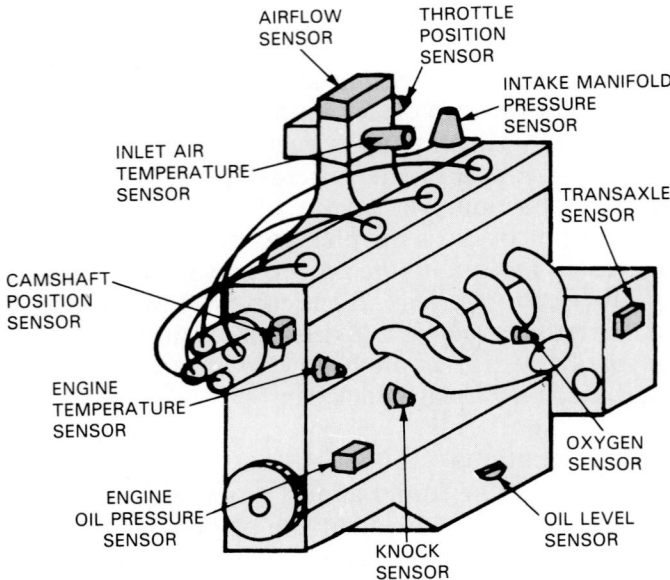

Fig. 74-16. *Here are some of the many sensors that can be found on the engine and transaxle assemblies. Others can also be used elsewhere on car.*

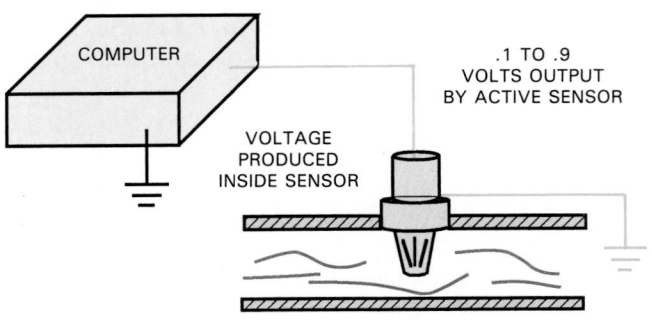

A—Active sensor produces its own voltage and current. The weak signal is sent to the computer.

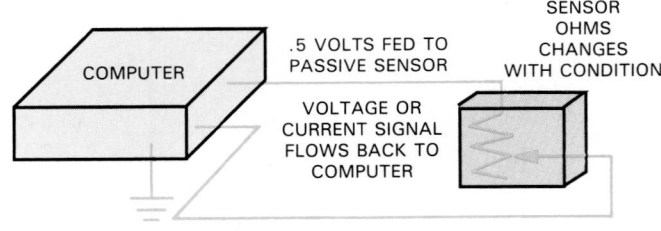

B—Passive sensor cannot produce its own voltage and current. A reference voltage must be fed to sensor by computer.

Fig. 74-17. *Compare active and passive sensor operation.*

depends on an external source of voltage to return a signal to the computer. The internal resistance (ohms) of the transducer changes with a change in a condition, but it does NOT generate its own voltage. Examples of passive sensors include temperature sensors, throttle position sensors, switching type sensors, etc.

Sensor reference voltage

Sensor reference voltage is fed to passive sensors by the computer. A supply voltage is needed so that a change in sensor resistance can be read by the computer as a change in current and voltage. Fig. 74-18 shows this principle.

The *reference voltage,* abbreviated Vref, is typically around 5 volts. The computer steps-down battery voltage so that a smooth, constant supply of DC voltage is fed to the passive sensors.

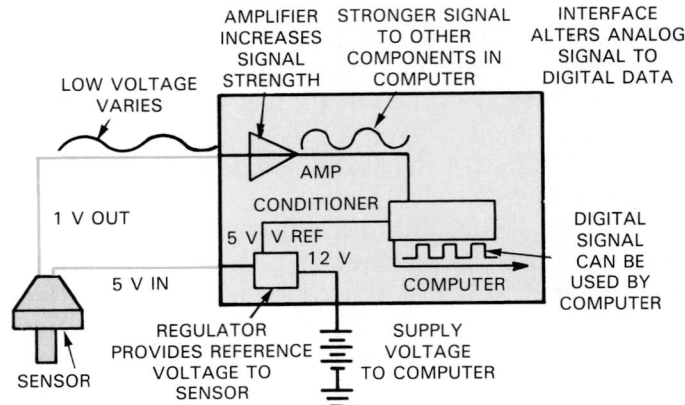

Fig. 74-18. *A computer power supply or voltage regulator must send current to passive type sensors. Most sensors produce an analog signal. If weak, the analog signal is first amplified or increased in strength. A conditioner or interface converts the analog signal into a digital or binary signal. The digital signal can then be sent to the microprocessor chip in the computer.*

More sensor information

Note! Refer to the index for more information. Sensors are discussed throughout the text.

ACTUATOR OPERATION

Mentioned earlier, *actuators* are the "hands and arms" of a computer. They allow it to do work and alter the operation of other components.

When the computer turns on an actuator, it normally provides the actuator with a GROUND CIRCUIT. Then, current can operate the actuator, Fig. 74-19.

Output drivers or *power transistors* in the computer control current flow through the actuators. When energized by the microprocessor in the computer, the drivers ground the actuator circuits. The actuators can then produce movement to affect vehicle operation.

Solenoid actuator operation

Fig. 74-20 shows how the computer can use a solenoid actuator. Input from the vehicle speed sensor enters the computer. When the computer detects vehicle travel or forward motion, it can use solenoid

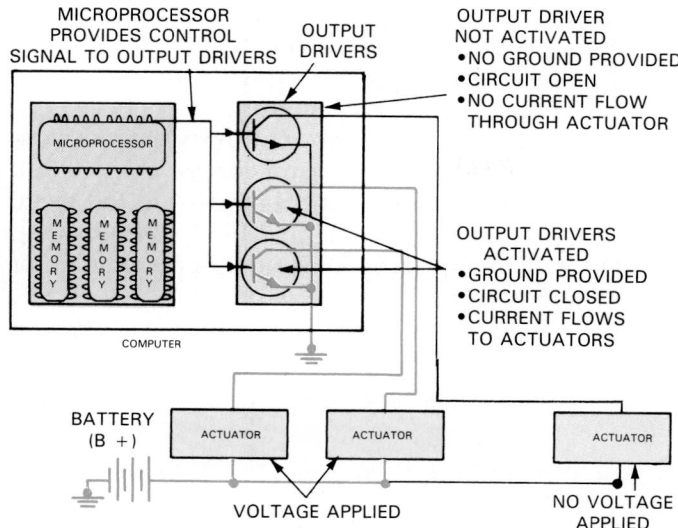

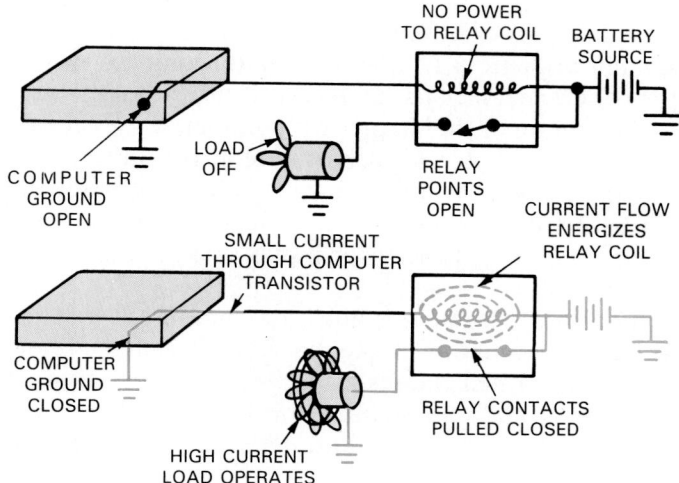

Fig. 74-19. A computer will normally activate outputs to actuators by grounding their circuits. Power is present at actuator at all times but there is not a complete circuit path. When drivers or power transistors are turned on, they will conduct current through ground to energize actuators. (Ford)

computer will simply ground the relay coil windings. Then, the relay coil field will pull the mechanical contacts closed and a large current will flow to the load. See Fig. 74-21.

Fig. 74-21. A relay can also serve as an actuator to control a high current load. Small computer control current will close relay points. Then higher current will flow to load.

Motor actuator operation

A *small DC motor* provides another way that a computer can act or produce an output. The computer can ground the motor circuit and turn the motor on or off or reverse motor rotation as needed.

Sometimes, the motor actuator is simply a reversible DC motor. The motor will turn a thread mechanism to produce a controlled movement of a part. A good example would be an idle speed motor. Look at Fig. 74-22.

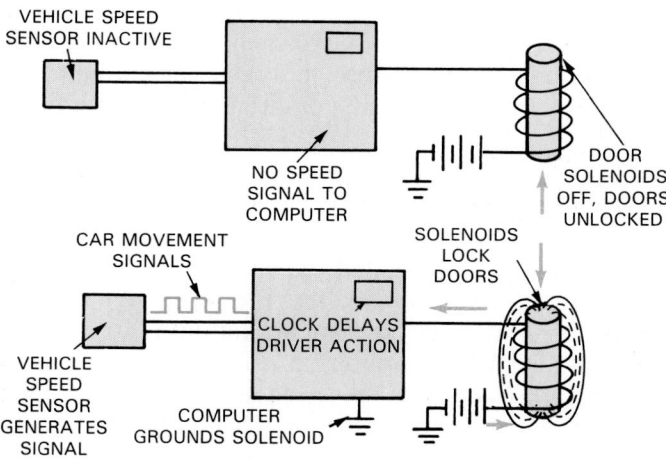

Fig. 74-20. Simple illustration of how sensor input can be used by computer to operate solenoid type actuator. When speed sensor produces a signal, computer can ground solenoid. The solenoid movement might be used to lock the doors of the car automatically.

actuators to lock all of the car's doors.

The computer grounds the solenoid circuits and current flows through the solenoid windings. This produces a magnetic field in the windings. The magnetic field pulls on and moves the plunger mounted in the solenoid windings. This plunger movement locks the doors.

Relay actuator operation

A *relay* can serve as a good actuator when a high current load must be controlled by the computer. The

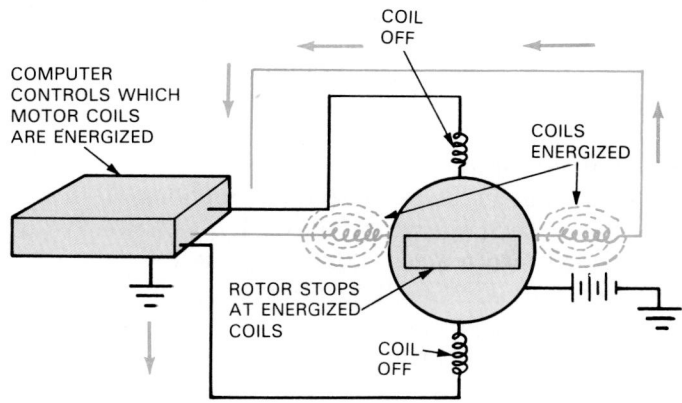

Fig. 74-22. Servo or stepper motor can be stopped in an exact position. Computer can energize specific coils so armature is attracted to and stopped next to coils.

Note that some actuator motors also serve as sensors for the computer. They can inform the computer as to their position.

COMPUTER OPERATION

A computer is often nicknamed a "black box." This is because it is enclosed in a box-shaped housing and contains mysterious circuits that can do complex operations. Few technicians have seen inside a computer.

This section of the chapter will summarize the operation of a computer or electronic control unit. Even though you will probably never repair a computer, it will be helpful to you as a technician to understand how a computer uses sensor inputs and produces actuator outputs.

Fig. 74-23 shows a photo of the inside of an automotive computer. Note that it uses printed circuit boards, integrated circuits, capacitors, resistors, power transistors, and many other basic electronic components. You learned about these components in Chapter 8 of this text.

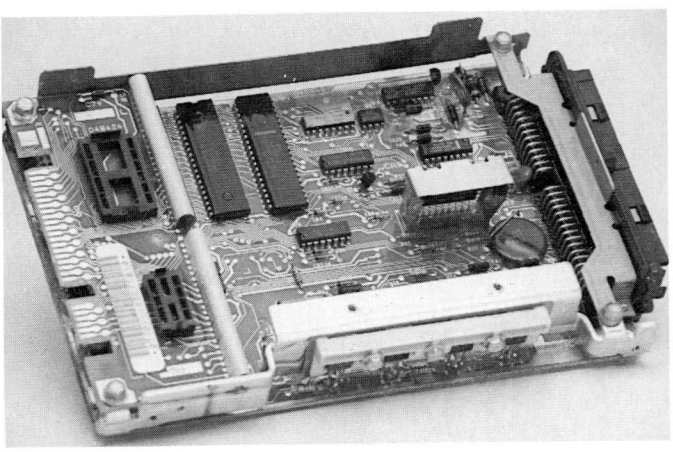

Fig. 74-23. Photo shows inside of computer or "black box." Note that it uses integrated circuits attached to printed circuit board. (Sun Electric Corp.)

Parts of a computer

All computers can be divided into sections. Each section has a specific function. Basically, a computer can be divided into ten parts. These include:
1. VOLTAGE REGULATOR (supply lower voltage for computer and sensors).
2. AMPLIFIERS (increase voltage and current for other computer devices), Fig. 74-24.
3. CONDITIONERS (interface units that alter signals for use by computer and actuators).
4. MICROPROCESSOR (IC chip that makes decisions or calculations for computer).

5. MEMORY (IC chips that store data for microprocessor), Fig. 74-24.
6. CLOCK (IC that produces constant pulse rate to coordinate events in computer).
7. OUTPUT DRIVERS (power transistors that step-up current to operate actuators or power modules).
8. CIRCUIT BOARDS (fiber boards with flat metal conductors that connect and hold components).
9. HARNESS CONNECTOR (multi-pin terminal for attaching to wiring harness of car).
10. COMPUTER HOUSING (metal enclosure that protects electronic components from induced currents and physical damage).

Computer voltage regulator operation

A *computer voltage regulator* is needed to provide a reduced voltage for the electronic components in the computer and for some passive sensors. This voltage must be very *smooth DC voltage* that does NOT vary and that does NOT have small *spikes* (abrupt changes in voltage).

Computer amplifier operation

A *computer amplifier* simply strengthens various signals when inside the computer. One might increase the voltage signal from the oxygen sensor which is less than one volt. Then, the signal is strong enough to be used by other components or circuits in the computer.

Computer conditioner (interface) operation

There are two basic types of conditioners in a computer: input conditioners and output conditioners. A conditioner can be called *converter* or *interface*.

An *input conditioner* alters the input signals from some sensors. They treat incoming data (voltage and current) for the computer so it can be utilized.

An *output conditioner* is needed to change the digital signals back into analog signals. The output of the computer must usually be analog to operate the actuators and control modules.

Buffer

A *buffer* is a computer device that can serve as a temporary storage area for the data. A buffer can also protect internal computer chips from improper data. For example, if data comes into the computer too quickly, the buffer can hold the data and then slowly feed it into other devices as needed.

Computer microprocessor operation

Microprocessor means SMALL (micro) COMPUTER (processor). A microprocessor is a small computer chip or integrated circuit capable of analyzing data and calculating what should be done. It is the "brain" of a computer, Fig. 74-25.

A microprocessor chip uses the binary number system to make decisions, comparisons, or calculations.

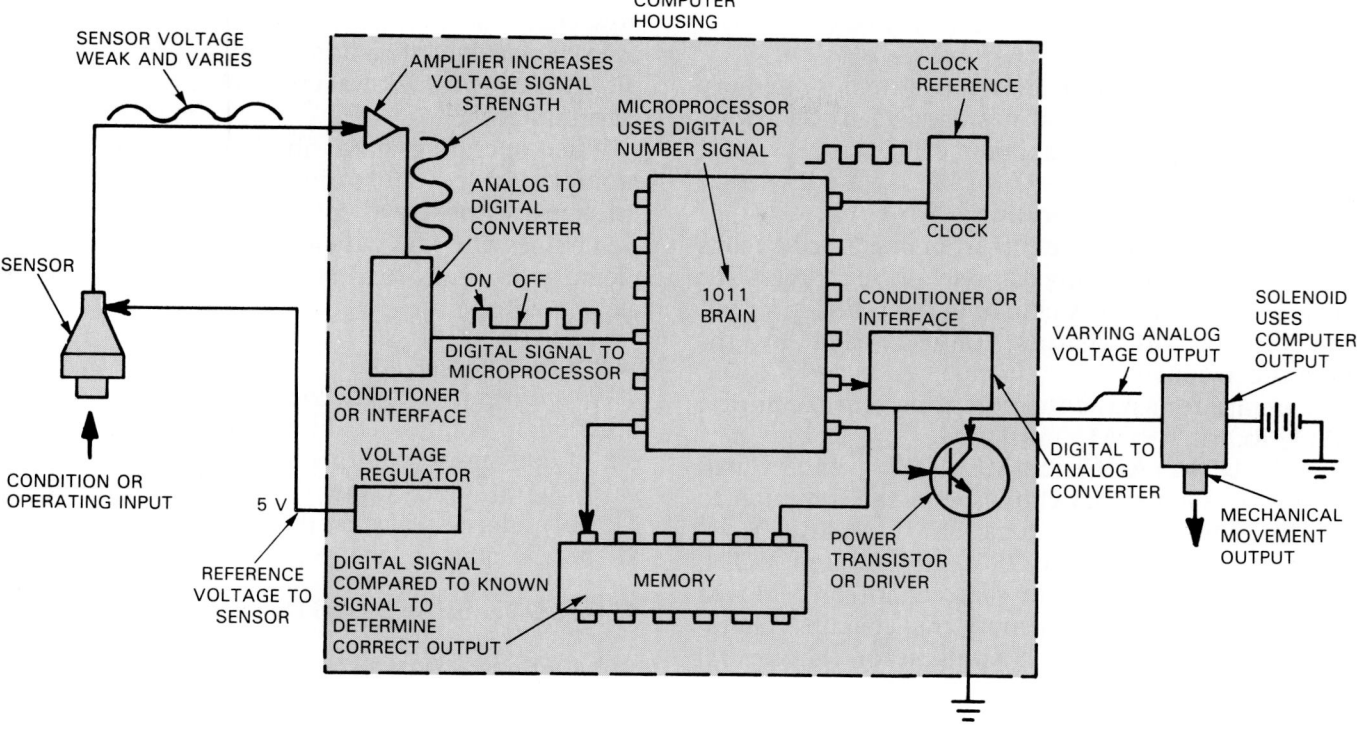

Fig. 74-24. Trace flow of data through this simplified computer system. Can you explain the purpose of each component?

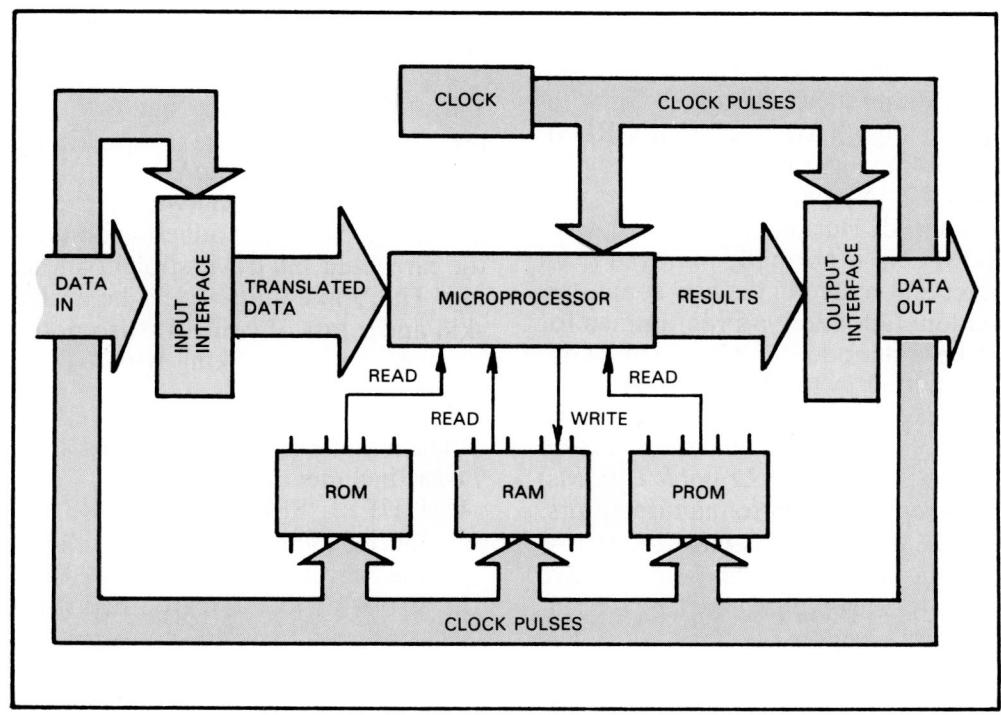

Fig. 74-25. Note flow of data in this flow or block diagram. Data comes in from sensors. Interface or conditioner changes input data into digital signal. Clock times when data moves from one place to another. Microprocessor can read from memory or write into memory. Microprocessor decides on outputs using logic gates. Results are sent from microprocessor to output interface or conditioner that changes binary data back into analog for actuators.   (General Motors)

Computer System Networking   991

Digital pulses from the conditioners or interfaces are fed into the microprocessor. Since these inputs are zero (off) or one (on) voltages, they can be used by the logic gates in the processor.

A microprocessor also uses data stored in memory chips. It compares input and memory data to decide what outputs should be for maximum efficiency.

Computer memory operation

A *computer memory* results from integrated circuits that are capable of storing data as voltage charges. The gates inside the memory chips will hold their information (on or off charges) until needed by the microprocessor.

There are four basic types of computer memories: RAM, ROM, PROM, and KAM.

1. RANDOM ACCESS MEMORY, abbreviated RAM, is a memory chip used by the computer to store information or data TEMPORARILY.

2. READ ONLY MEMORY, abbreviated ROM, stores permanent data that cannot be removed from memory. This memory chip contains calibration tables and look-up tables for the general make and model car.

3. PROGRAMMABLE READ ONLY MEMORY, abbreviated PROM, is a memory chip containing permanent data like ROM, but the data is more specific. The microprocessor can read from PROM but it cannot write to PROM.

   The PROM contains memory about the specific engine (number of cylinders, valve sizes, compression ratio, fuel system type), transaxle (shift points, gear ratios, etc.), vehicle weight, optional accessories, and other unique concerns. A car with a manual transaxle might have a different PROM than one with an automatic transaxle, for example.

   The PROM is the only part of a computer that is commonly serviced. During computer replacement, the PROM chip is normally removed from the old computer and reused in the new computer. The PROM seldom fails and it is programmed for the specific make and model car with all of its options. Data is retained in the PROM even when removed from the computer. PROMs that can be reprogrammed for equipment or specification changes (known as EPROMs or *Erasable* PROMs) are now being introduced by auto manufacturers.

4. KEEP ALIVE MEMORY, abbreviated KAM, is a memory chip that allows the computer to have an adaptive strategy. An *adaptive strategy* is needed as parts wear and components deteriorate. The adaptive memory in KAM allows the computer to maintain normal vehicle performance with abnormal inputs from sensors. It can also ignore false inputs to maintain driveability.

Note! Different computer designs will use different memory chips. Also, the names of these chips can vary. The ones discussed are basic and typical.

Processor-memory bus

The term PROCESSOR-MEMORY bus refers to how the two sections of a computer communicate or exchange data. Just as a school bus transports people, a *data bus* allows the exchange of computer information.

When operating, data rapidly shuffles between the memory chips and microprocessor chip. The microprocessor chip controls this flow of data. Sometimes, it writes data about vehicle operation into memory or it may read out data about how the vehicle should operate.

Memory address

An *address* is a specific location in memory. One address might contain a calibration for the correct output of one sensor. Another address might temporarily store the present output value of the same sensor. Memory address will store this data as a binary number at specific pins or locations in memory chips.

ANTI-LOCK BRAKE SYSTEMS (ABS)

An *anti-lock brake system,* abbreviated ABS, uses wheel speed sensors, a computer, and an electro-hydraulic unit to prevent tire skid during hard braking. If a tire locks up and skids on the road surface, braking distance can increase and steering control can be lost.

The anti-lock brake system improves driver and passenger safety by reducing stopping distances and increasing directional stability under panic stop conditions. Look at Fig. 74-26.

Fig. 74-27 shows the advantages of having ABS. With this example, one side of the road is very slippery and the other side is dry. This poses a problem if a panic stop is required.

Without ABS, the car would tend to skid to the right because of higher tire adhesion on the right. With ABS, the car would still travel straight ahead with hard braking. The brake units would be cycled to prevent tire skid and a loss of control. Also note how the car can be steered while braking with ABS.

ABS components

The major parts of an anti-lock braking system, Fig. 74-28, include:

1. WHEEL SPEED SENSORS (magnetic pickups for detecting rolling or rotating speed of each tire and wheel assembly).

2. SENSOR ROTOR (toothed wheel that rotates at same rpm as wheel and tire).

3. ELECTRONIC CONTROL UNIT (small computer or processor that uses sensor inputs to control hydraulic actuator).

4. HYDRAULIC ACTUATOR (solenoid-operated valve and electric pump mechanism for controlling how much hydraulic pressure is applied to each wheel brake cylinder).

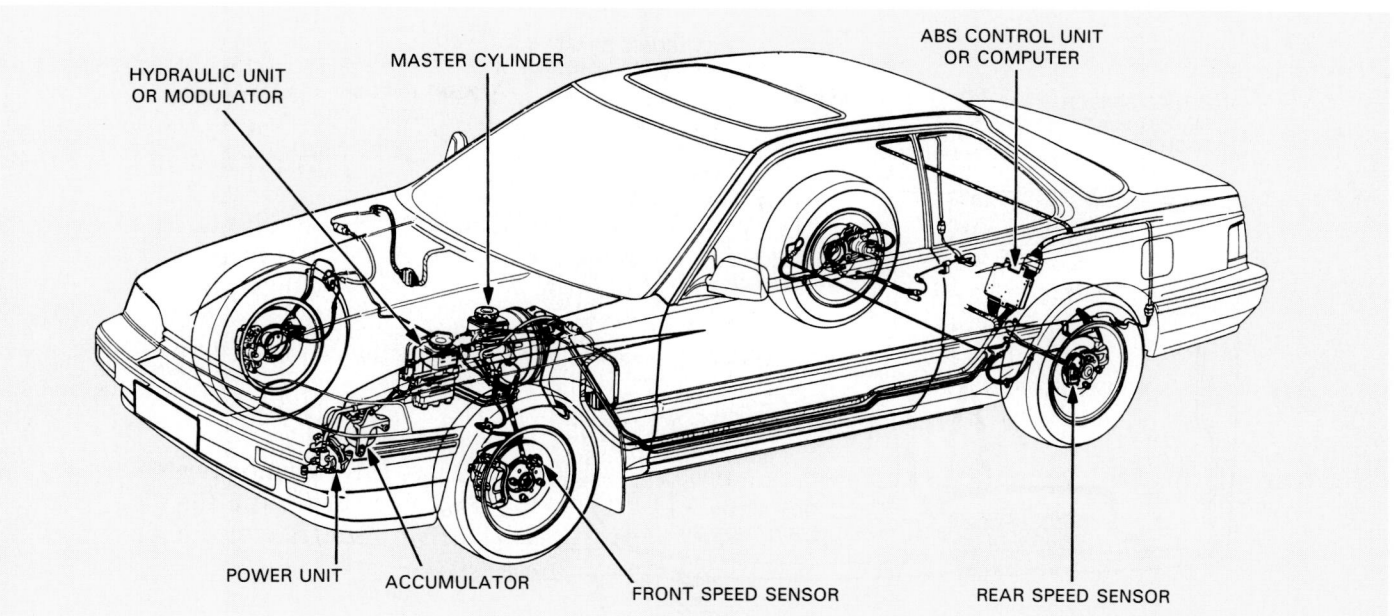

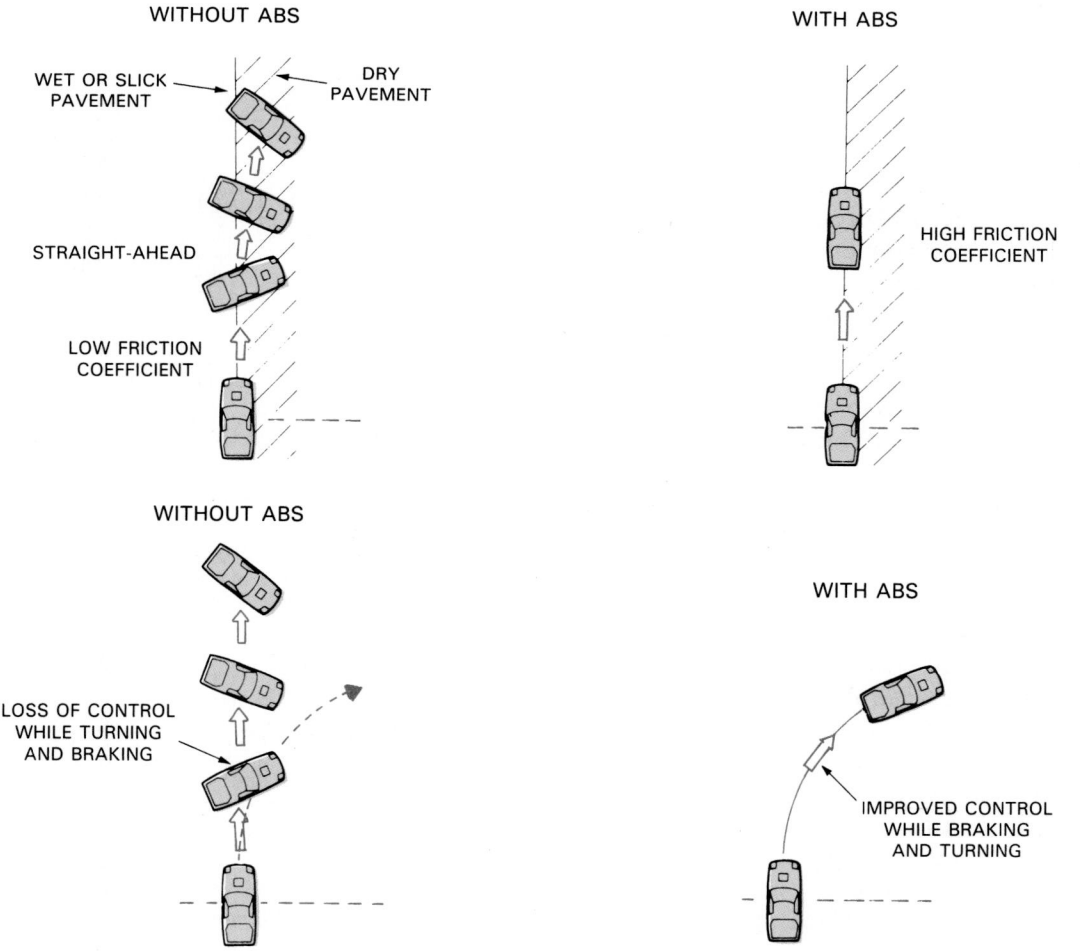

Fig. 74-26. ABS or anti-lock brake system has wheel sensors mounted next to trigger wheels. If one wheel begins to skid, the sensor at that wheel will produce a progressively lower frequency signal. Computer can then operate modulator or hydraulic unit to cycle brake pressure to that wheel cylinder to prevent tire skid. (Honda)

Fig. 74-27. Without ABS, tires can lock up and lose adhesion with road. This can cause a loss of control during hard braking or when braking and trying to steer. Even if one side of road is slick, brakes will be cycled so that none of the tires skid. Maximum braking results when tires are just about ready to skid; traction is reduced if tires lock up.

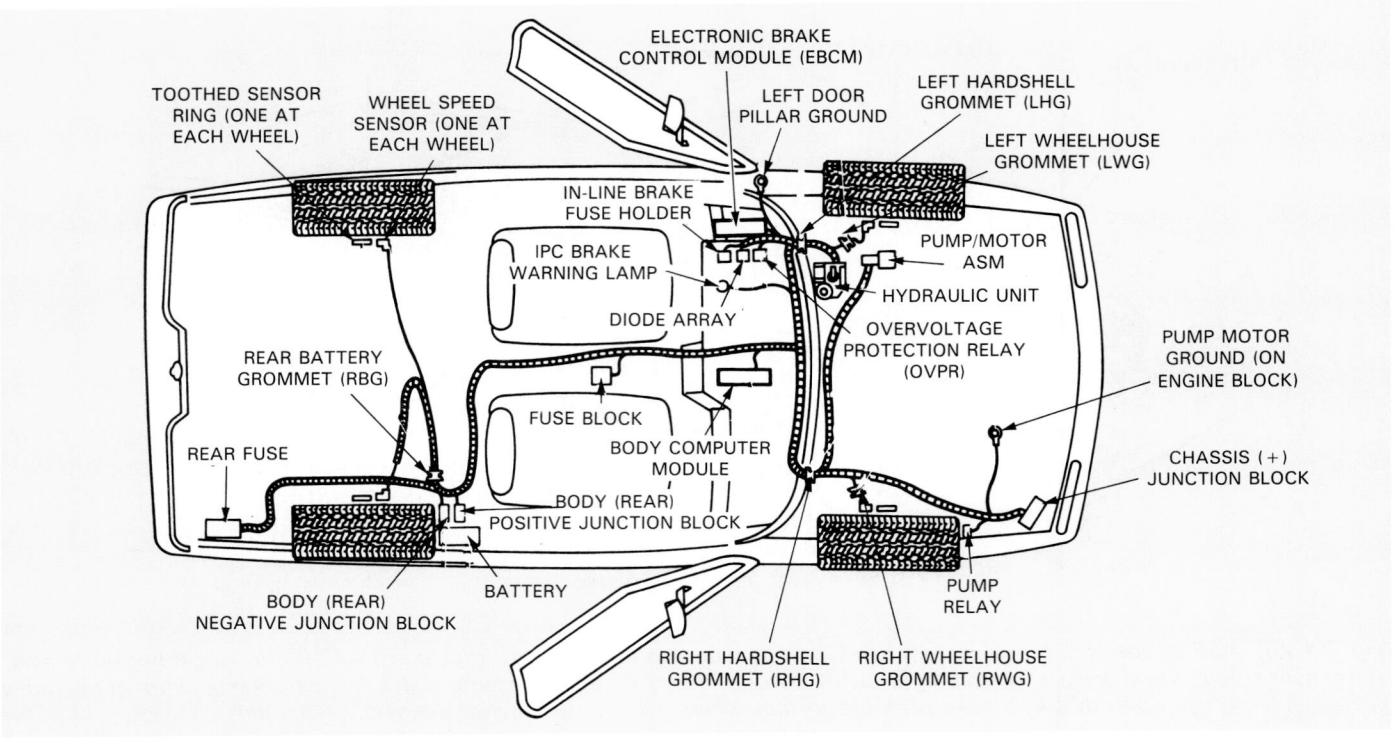

Fig. 74-28. Study parts of a typical ABS.   (General Motors)

5. INDICATOR LIGHT (dash light that informs driver of problem in ABS system).

Wheel speed sensors

The *wheel speed sensors* produce an AC type signal that corresponds to wheel and tire speed. These signals are fed into the anti-lock brake system computer.

Fig. 74-29 shows how one wheel speed sensor mounts in the car's steering knuckle assembly. The sensor tip is located next to the sensor rotor. Only a small air gap separates the sensor tip from the teeth on the sensor rotor. In this example, the sensor rotor is mounted on the back of the brake disc. A hex bolt and O-rings secure the sensor in the steering knuckle.

Wheel speed sensors can also mount on the axle shaft and drive shaft. However, their function and operation are very similar.

As the tire and wheel rotates, the sensor rotor spins next to the wheel speed sensor. As each tooth passes the sensor, the magnetic field around the sensor is affected. This induces a weak AC or alternating current signal in the wheel sensor coil. The frequency of this AC signal is dependent upon tire and wheel speed. The AC signal is used by the anti-lock brake system computer to check for tire skid. A rapid decrease in sensor AC signal frequency would indicate that a tire is starting to lock up and skid.

Note! The operation of a wheel speed sensor is similar to a crankshaft sensor and a magnetic pickup coil in an ignition system. Refer to the discussion of these sensors for more information on coil and trigger wheel operation.

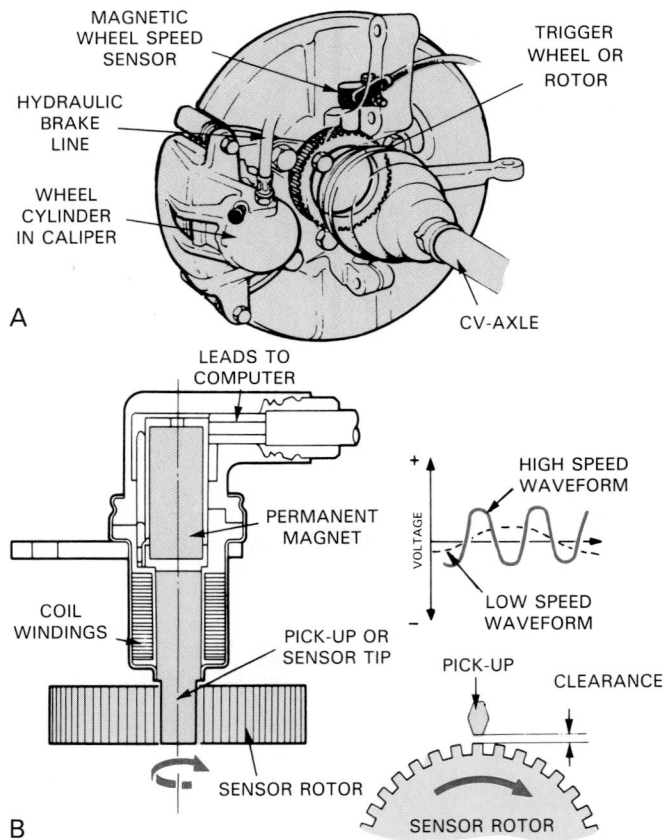

Fig. 74-29. A—Wheel speed sensor is mounted next to trigger wheel. As tire rotates, teeth on trigger wheel make magnetic sensor produce weak AC signal for computer. B—Current is induced in sensor windings as teeth pass sensor. Note waveform. Specific clearance is needed between sensor and teeth for proper operation.   (Saab)

ABS computer

The *ABS computer* uses wheel speed sensor inputs to control the operation of the hydraulic actuator. It is constructed and operates like the other computers discussed in this book, Fig. 74-30.

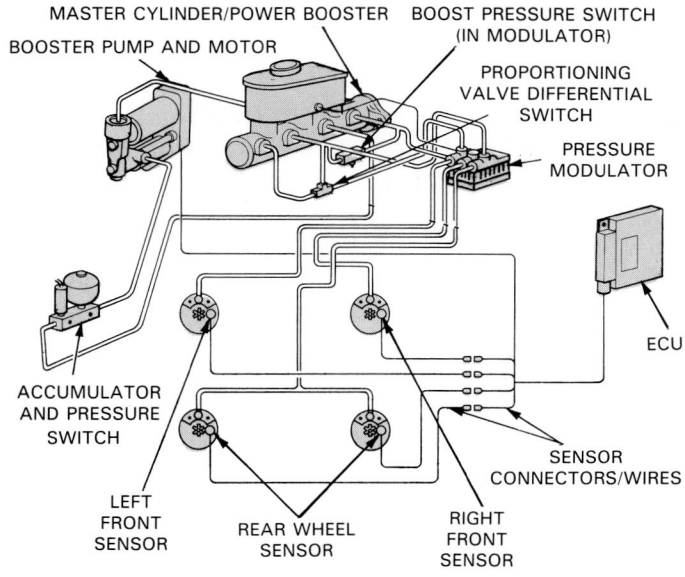

Fig. 74-30. Accumulator is used to store small amount of pressure to reduce pressure cycling. Electric motor driven pump produces pressure assist for this ABS system. (Chrysler)

ABS hydraulic actuator

The *ABS hydraulic actuator* regulates the amount of fluid pressure applied to each wheel brake assembly during hard braking. It is controlled by the ABS computer. The hydraulic actuator normally mounts on the firewall in the engine compartment, Fig. 74-31.

1. FLUID RESERVOIR (container for holding extra supply of brake fluid).
2. SOLENOID VALVE BLOCK (coil-operated valves that control brake fluid flow to wheel brake cylinders; they are contained in valve block).
3. ACCUMULATOR (chamber for storing fluid under high pressure).
4. HYDRAULIC PUMP AND MOTOR (high pressure pump operated by small electric motor; they provide brake fluid pressure for system).
5. PRESSURE SWITCH (monitors system pressure and controls operation of electric motor for hydraulic pump).
6. MASTER CYLINDER-BOOSTER ASSEMBLY (conventional master cylinder with power assist for operating brakes under normal conditions).

ABS systems and hydraulic actuators vary with the specific make and model car.

ABS operation

Under normal braking, the ABS system is not used. The master cylinder reacts to brake pedal movement. It sends fluid pressure out to each wheel cylinder normally. A proportioning valve is commonly used to

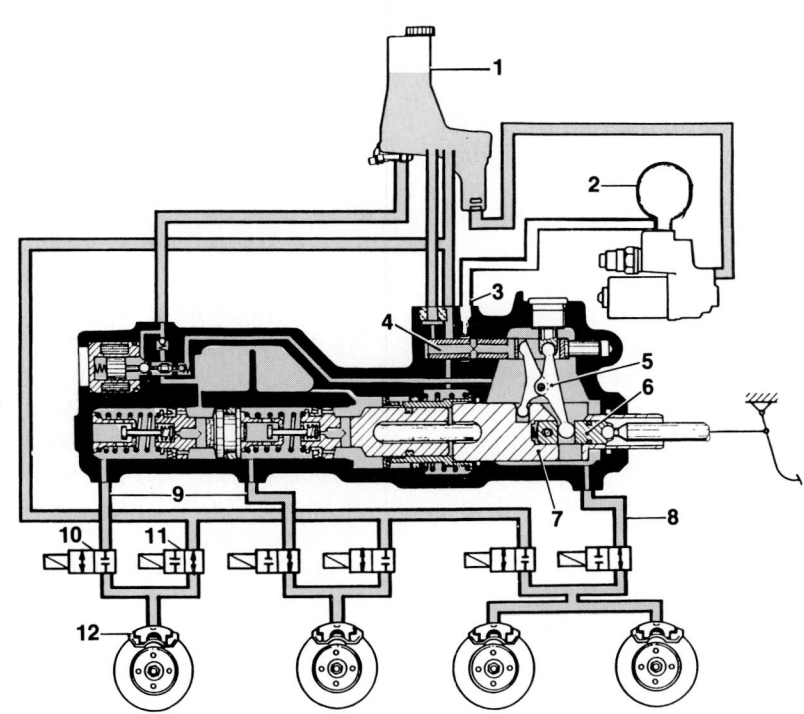

Fig. 74-31. Study this variation of an ABS system. Note how system is blocking pressure to one of the wheel cylinders to keep the brakes from locking and skidding the tire. (Saab)

reduce pressure to the rear brakes.

If the brakes are applied in a panic stop and one wheel begins to stop rotating, the ABS system activates. The wheel sensor on the slowing wheel would instantly send a slower AC pulsing signal to the computer. The computer would detect that this wheel is slowing down more than the others and is getting ready to slide or skid. The computer would then send an electrical current output to the correct solenoid on the hydraulic actuator assembly.

When current is sent to the solenoid, the solenoid closes a valve to limit the pressure to the brake unit with the slowing wheel. The computer will quickly cycle the current to the solenoid on and off to artificially "pump the brakes" to keep the tire from skidding and losing traction. It does this several times a second.

When ABS takes over, the brake pedal will usually rise and vibrate slightly. This is due to the pressure entering the system from the accumulator and from the cycling of the solenoid valves. This is normal and will stop when ABS system is no longer functioning.

If hydraulic pressure in the system drops below a specific point, the pressure switch closes and energizes the electric motor. This drives the pump to build pressure back up. Once pressure is normal, the pressure switch opens and the motor and pump shut off.

If an ABS component malfunctions, the computer will detect an abnormal condition. It will then light an ABS warning light in the dash and deactivate the ABS. The brake system will still function normally, but without the anti-lock feature.

ELECTRONIC HEIGHT CONTROL

An *electronic height control system* uses a height sensor to control the operation of a small electric air compressor. This type system is used on the rear of the car to compensate for loads placed in the trunk or when passengers fill the back seat. These parts include:

1. HEIGHT SENSOR (lever-operated switch that reacts to changes in car body height and suspension movement).
2. COMPRESSOR ASSEMBLY (motor-powered air pump that produces pressure for system).
3. PRESSURE LINES (air hoses that connect compressor with air shock absorbers).
4. AIR SHOCKS (air-filled shock absorbers that act on suspension system to alter ride height).
5. SENSOR LINK (linkage rods that connect height sensor to suspension).
6. SOLENOID VALVE (solenoid-operated air valve that can release air pressure from the system).

When the car body is at a normal riding height, the electronic height control system is off. Air pressure in the shocks is adequate to keep the car body the correct distance from the road surface. The height sensor does not feed current to the compressor or solenoid.

If the trunk is loaded with heavy luggage, for example, it will compress the rear air shocks. This makes the ride height too low. When the car is started, the height sensor will be activated by the action of the sensor link, and the sensor switch will close to energize the compressor. The compressor motor turns on and pumps more air pressure into the rear shock absorbers. This extends the shocks, raising the car body.

When the specific ride height is reached, the height sensor switch opens to turn off the compressor. This restores the previous ride height, even with extra weight in the trunk.

When the weight is removed from the trunk, the car body would tend to rise. The height sensor switch is then moved in the other direction by the link. This closes another set of contacts in the switch. This energizes a pressure release solenoid valve. Air pressure is then expelled from the rear shocks until the body drops down the correct ride height.

ELECTRONIC SHOCK ABSORBER SYSTEM

An *electronic shock absorber system* uses various vehicle sensors, a computer, and shock absorber actuators to control ride stiffness. It is designed to increase comfort and safety by matching suspension system action to driving conditions, Fig. 74-32.

Although exact designs vary, the major components of a typical electronic shock absorber system are:

1. STEERING SENSOR (detects steering wheel rotational direction and speed to feed data about vehicle direction to computer).
2. BRAKE SENSOR (usually brake light switch is used to report when brakes are applied).
3. ACCELERATION SENSOR (usually throttle position sensor is used to detect when car is accelerating rapidly).
4. MODE SWITCH (dash switch that allows driver to input desired shock action or ride stiffness).
5. ELECTRONIC CONTROL UNIT (small computer that uses sensor inputs to control shock actuators).
6. SHOCK ACTUATORS (solenoid-operated valves for controlling fluid flow inside shock absorbers.

If the car is being driven on curving country roads, the driver might switch to a stiff setting with the mode switch. The computer would then energize the shock actuators to close or restrict the shock valves to increase dampening action. This would make the car ride more stiffly but corner better.

If driving on rough highways, the mode switch might be set to soft. The computer would then energize the shock actuators to open the valves more. This would soften the ride by allowing easier shock movement.

Under hard braking, the brake sensor would send a signal to the computer. The computer could then stiffen shocks to prevent front of car from diving.

With rapid turning or cornering, the steering sensor could also signal the computer. The computer could

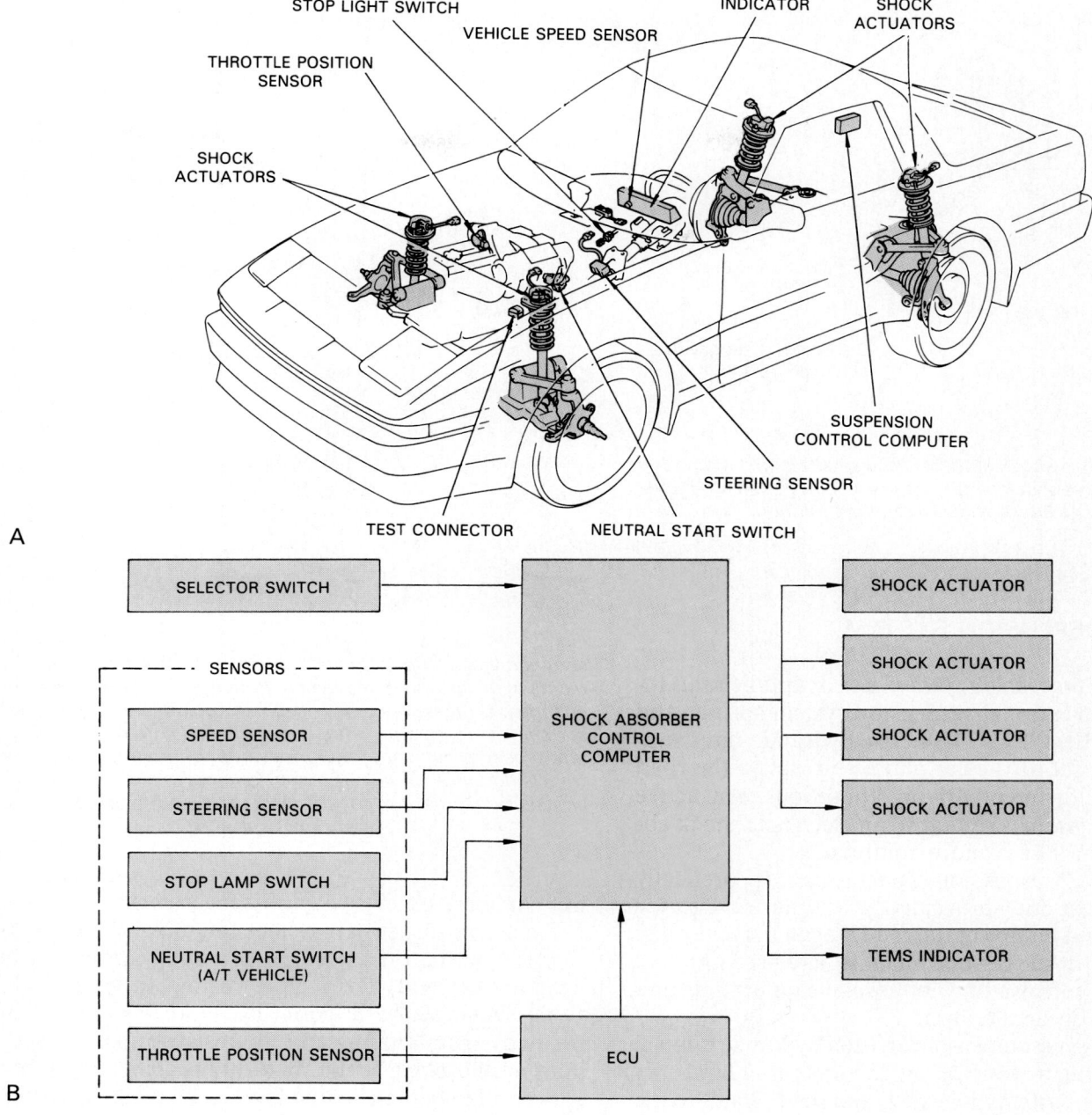

Fig. 74-32. A—This computer controlled suspension system can automatically adjust shock stiffness depending upon driving and road conditions. For instance, it will produce a soft, smooth ride when traveling down a straight highway. However, it will stiffen shock damping when cornering on a country road. B—Block diagram shows how various sensors feed electrical data to computer. Computer can then energize shock actuators to control ride stiffness and shock action. (Toyota)

then stiffen the shocks to prevent excess body roll or lean in turns.

Fig. 74-33 shows one type of shock actuator. Note how it uses a solenoid and small DC motor to act upon the shock absorber piston rod. The shock piston rod can be moved up or down to control fluid flow resistance and shock stiffness or dampening.

Some cars use air type shocks or air bags instead of hydraulic shock absorbers. The operation of this type system is similar.

One type of electronic shock absorber system uses a *sonar* (sound wave) type sensor to detect actual road conditions. The sensor mounts at the front of the car.

The *sonar sensor* produces sound waves that bounce off the road and are deflected back into the sensor. The sensor action detects the time needed for the waves to bounce back into the sensor. If there is a dip in the road, the sensor can signal a different distance. The computer can then adjust shock action for the road surface.

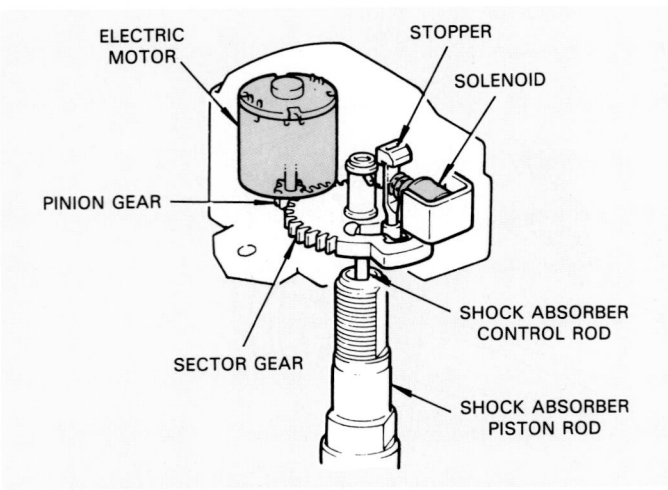

Fig. 74-33. This shock actuator uses small electric motor and solenoid to move shock piston rod in and out. Piston rod movement alters shock dampening action.

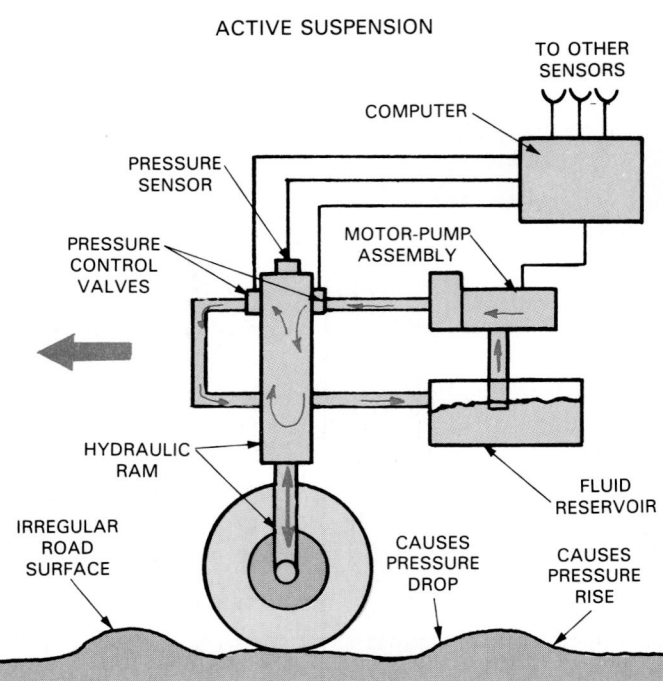

Fig. 74-34. Simplified illustration of active suspension system shows major components. Pressure sensor on hydraulic ram reacts to up and down movement of ram and resulting pressure changes. If pressure in ram rises from going over bump, sensor signals computer. Computer can quickly react to release ram pressure so suspension moves up with bump. As wheel travels down other side of bump, sensors make computer increase ram pressure so suspension travels back down to original road surface.

ACTIVE SUSPENSION SYSTEM

An *active suspension system* uses hydraulic rams instead of conventional suspension system springs and shock absorbers, Fig. 74-34. The hydraulic rams support the weight of the car and also react to the road surface and different driving conditions. An active suspension system is similar to an electronic shock absorber system but is more complex.

The active suspension system can theoretically eliminate most body movement as the car travels over small dips and bumps in the road. It can prevent body roll or even tilt the car body against a turn to improve handling. It can also prevent nosedive on braking and body squat on acceleration.

Basically, pressure sensors on each hydraulic ram are used as the main control for the system. They react to suspension system movement and send signals to the computer. The computer can then extend or retract each ram to match the road surface.

For example, if one side of the car travels over a bump in the road, the pressure sensors can instantly detect a rise in pressure inside the ram as the tire and wheel push up on the suspension and hydraulic ram. Instead of car body rising with spring action, the computer can release enough ram pressure to allow suspension to move up over the bump without body movement.

Then, as the tire travels back down over the bump, the sensor detects a pressure drop in the ram and the computer can increase ram pressure so the tire follows the road surface.

A hydraulic pump provides pressure to operate the suspension system rams.

Many auto manufacturers are experimenting with active suspension systems of this type. We may well see them in the future, at first on more exotic sports cars,

but someday on everyday passenger cars.

An active suspension system can make a car feel as if it is floating on a cushion of air. It can also help keep the car body level under various driving conditions. During hard braking, it can keep the front of the body from dipping and the rear from rising, thus improving braking action. In turns, its ability to prevent lean can make the car stay level to increase cornering ability. It could also be used to lower the car body for highway driving aerodynamics and raise the car for ground clearance during city driving.

ELECTRONIC CRUISE CONTROL SYSTEM

A modern *electronic cruise control system* uses a computer, sensors, and a throttle actuator to maintain vehicle speed when highway driving. The major parts of a modern cruise control system include:
1. POWER SWITCHES (feed current to computer to activate and ready system for operation).
2. CONTROL SWITCH (signals computer to maintain present vehicle speed when activated).
3. VEHICLE SPEED SENSOR (feeds pulsing signal into computer that represents velocity of car in mph or km/h).
4. CRUISE COMPUTER (uses input signals to con-

trol outputs to throttle actuator).

5. THROTTLE ACTUATOR (physically moves engine throttle lever to control engine power and resulting vehicle speed).

6. BRAKE LIGHT SWITCH (stop light switch that signals computer to shut off cruise control when brakes are applied).

7. CLUTCH SWITCH (signals computer to deactivate cruise control when clutch pedal is depressed).

8. NEUTRAL SAFETY SWITCH (signals computer to shut off cruise when shift lever is moved out of drive to prevent engine overreving).

When set on cruise using the power and control switches, the vehicle speed sensor feeds an AC type signal into the computer. The computer circuits use this signal to move the throttle actuator back and forth to maintain the same speed or vehicle sensor frequency.

For example, if the car starts to go up a hill, the vehicle speed will start to drop. The computer will detect a slower frequency signal from the speed sensor. It can then move the throttle actuator for more engine power to keep the car traveling at the preset speed. The opposite occurs if the car starts down a hill.

ELECTRONIC AIRBAG SYSTEM

An *electronic airbag system* uses an inflatable balloon to help protect the driver during a head-on collision. It uses several impact sensors to detect a severe collision. The sensors feed their signals to the airbag electronic module. When at least two impact sensors are energized, the module activates a gas-filled cartridge. See Fig. 74-35.

The gas-filled cartridge inflates the airbag in about 1/20 of a second before the driver's body flies forward from the collision. The tough nylon airbag can easily absorb the forward inertia of the driver's body. This helps protect the driver from injury. Passenger-side airbags are also coming into use.

ELECTRONIC TRANSMISSION/TRANSAXLE CONTROL

An *electronic transmission/transaxle control system* uses a computer, sensors, and solenoids to control shift points and torque converter (fluid clutch) lockup. This provides more accurate shift points and converter lockup for increasing fuel economy.

A diagram of a modern electronic system for operating an automatic transaxle is shown in Fig. 74-36. Note how various vehicle sensors feed data to the electronic control unit. The control unit can then use preprogrammed information to know when to activate the shift solenoids and torque converter lockup solenoid. The solenoids open and close fluid pressure passages to operate the transmission or transaxle.

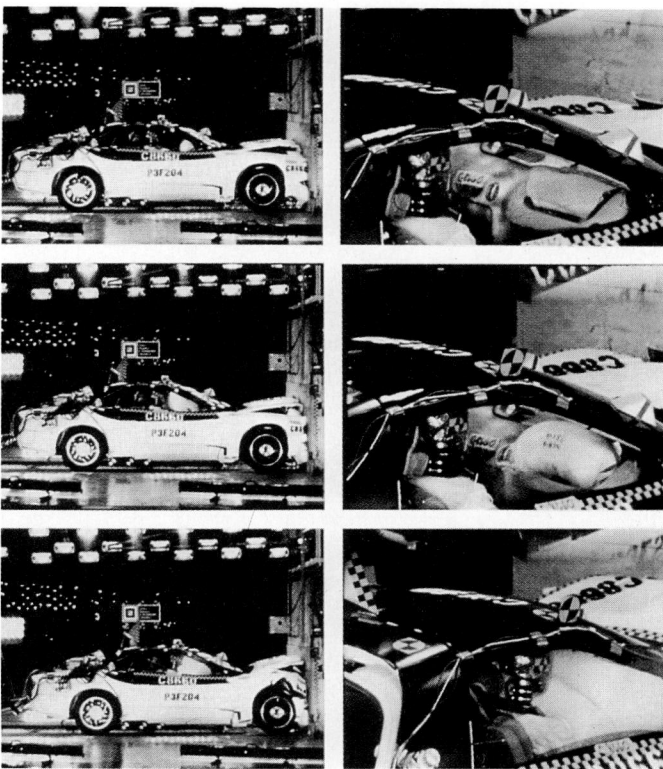

Fig. 74-35. Deployment of a passenger-side airbag in a test with crash dummies. (Pontiac)

ELECTRONIC STEERING ASSIST

Electronic steering assist uses a small electric motor to help move the rack and pinion steering gearbox. The motor is mounted inside the rack housing. The motor acts upon the steering rack.

A *steering control unit* electrically reacts to steering pressure. It operates the electric motor to help the driver steer the wheels of the car. The unit can be used to reverse motor rotation and alter motor speed as needed.

An electronic steering mechanism eliminates the need for hydraulic steering assist and the bulky power steering pump, hoses, and hydraulic cylinder, Fig. 74-37.

VOICE ALERT SYSTEM

A *voice alert system* uses numerous sensors, a computer, and a small speaker to inform the driver of various conditions. The computer is programmed to output spoken words when a specific sensor detects a bad condition. This might include saying—"Your washer fluid is low; Check your brake fluid; Your door is ajar;" and similar types of messages.

Fig. 74-38 shows the major parts of one type of voice alert system. Note the numerous sensors and imagine what the computer might drive the speaker to say.

KNOW THESE TERMS

Cybernetics, Input, Process, Output, Variable resistor sensor, Potentiometer sensor, Switching sen-

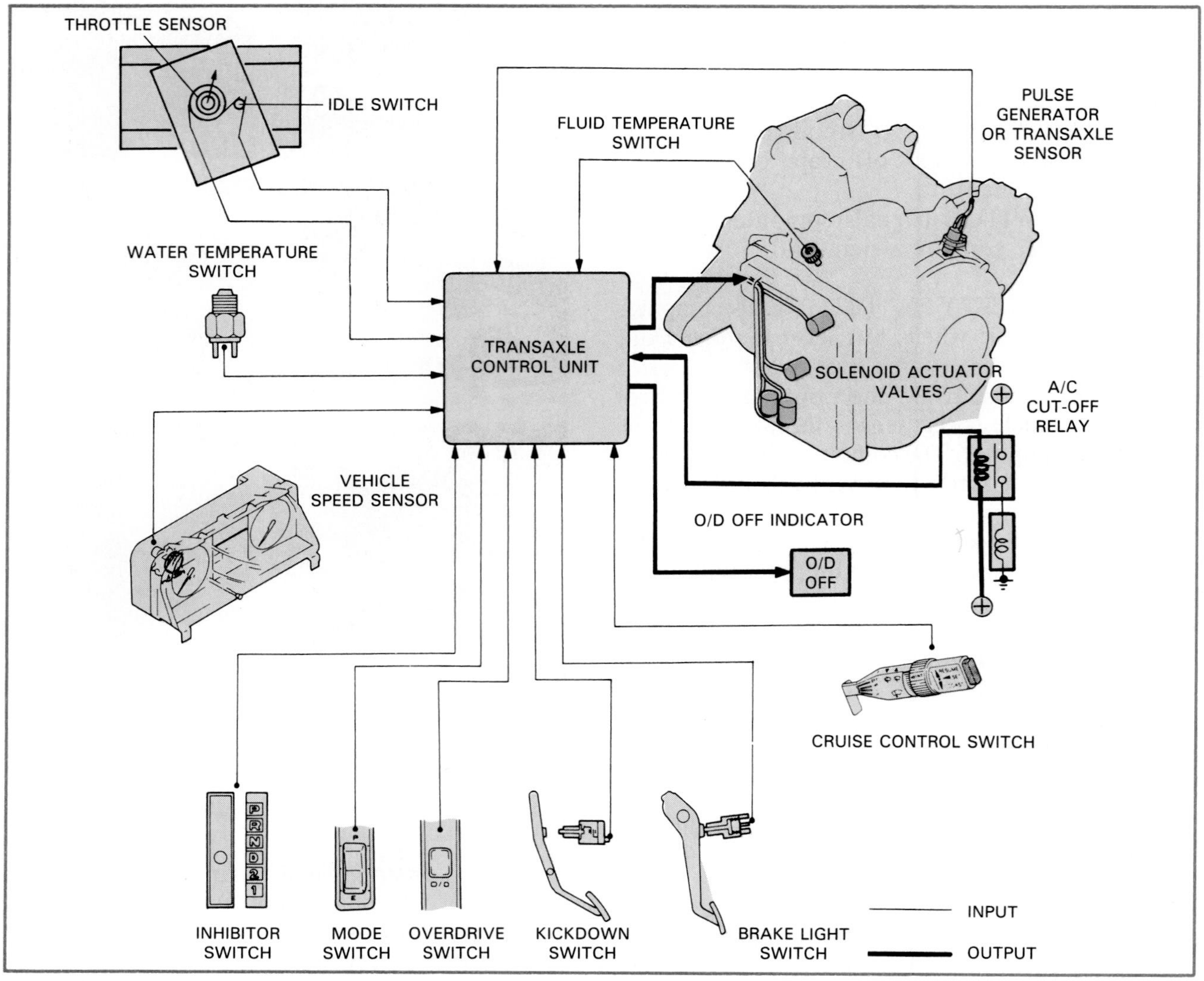

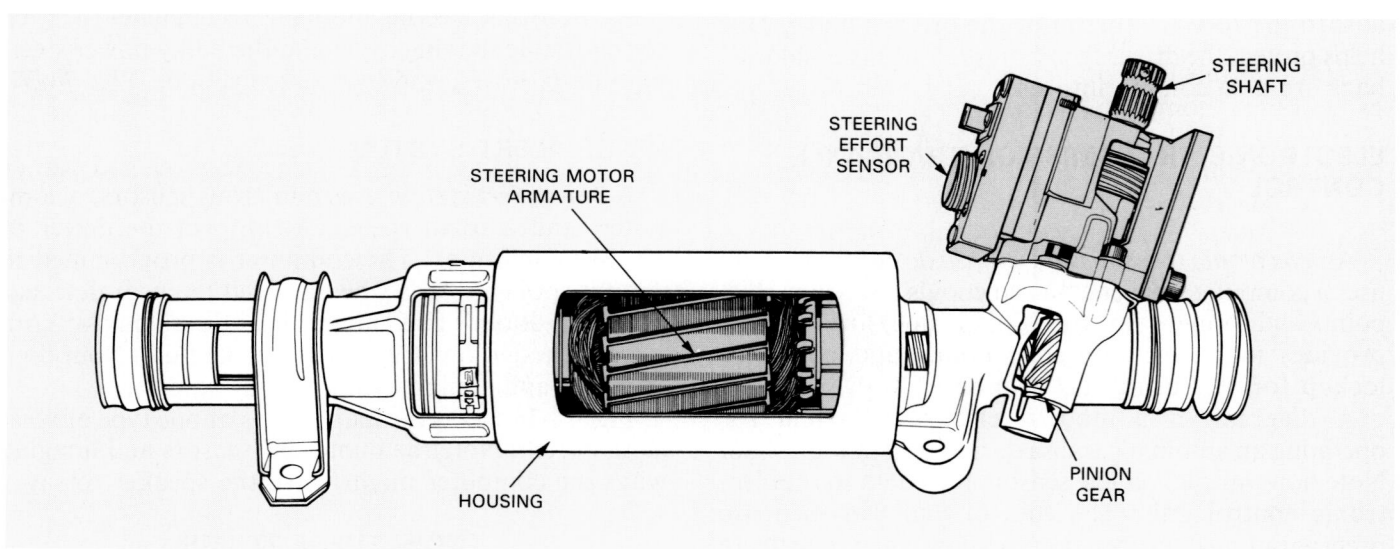

THROTTLE SENSOR

IDLE SWITCH

FLUID TEMPERATURE SWITCH

PULSE GENERATOR OR TRANSAXLE SENSOR

WATER TEMPERATURE SWITCH

TRANSAXLE CONTROL UNIT

SOLENOID ACTUATOR VALVES

A/C CUT-OFF RELAY

VEHICLE SPEED SENSOR

O/D OFF INDICATOR

O/D OFF

CRUISE CONTROL SWITCH

INHIBITOR SWITCH

MODE SWITCH

OVERDRIVE SWITCH

KICKDOWN SWITCH

BRAKE LIGHT SWITCH

—— INPUT

—— OUTPUT

Fig. 74-36. Computer is used to control operation of this automatic transaxle.

STEERING SHAFT

STEERING EFFORT SENSOR

STEERING MOTOR ARMATURE

HOUSING

PINION GEAR

Fig. 74-37. Electronic assist rack and pinion steering gear has small electric motor inside housing and steering effort sensor on steering shaft. Motor is used to supplement manual effort and provide power assist. This system is much lighter and more compact than conventional hydraulic power steering system. (Moog)

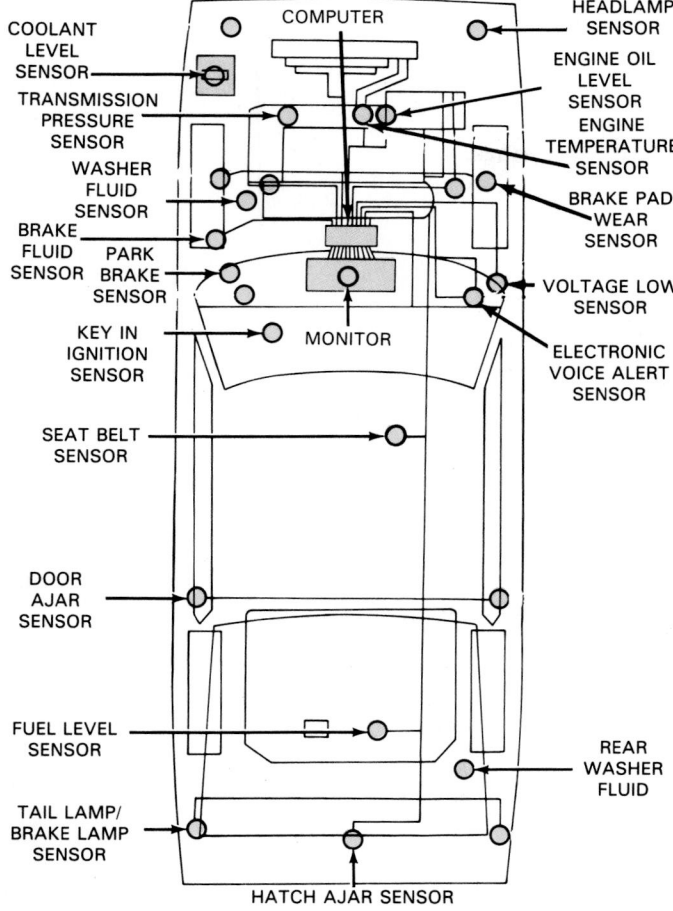

COOLANT LEVEL SENSOR

TRANSMISSION PRESSURE SENSOR

WASHER FLUID SENSOR

BRAKE FLUID SENSOR

PARK BRAKE SENSOR

KEY IN IGNITION SENSOR

SEAT BELT SENSOR

DOOR AJAR SENSOR

FUEL LEVEL SENSOR

TAIL LAMP/ BRAKE LAMP SENSOR

COMPUTER

MONITOR

HATCH AJAR SENSOR

HEADLAMP SENSOR

ENGINE OIL LEVEL SENSOR

ENGINE TEMPERATURE SENSOR

BRAKE PAD WEAR SENSOR

VOLTAGE LOW SENSOR

ELECTRONIC VOICE ALERT SENSOR

REAR WASHER FLUID

Fig. 74-38. Top view of vehicle shows general location of the many sensors used in this voice alert system. It will inform driver of numerous conditions.

sor, Voltage generating sensor, Magnetic sensor, Solenoid actuator, Relay actuator, Servo motor actuator, Display output, Block diagram, Computer, ECU, ECM, ECA, Main computer, Instrumentation computer, Anti-lock brake computer, Ignition computer. Engine computer, Suspension system computer, Climate control computer, Electronic modules, Amplify, Vehicle sensor, Transducer, Active sensor, Passive sensor, Reference voltage, Digital, Analog, Actuator, Drivers, Vacuum switch, Servo motor, Computer voltage regulator, Computer amplifier, Computer conditioner, Interface, Microprocessor, Computer memory, Computer clock, Circuit board, Computer

harness connector, Smooth DC, Programmed, RAM, ROM, PROM, EPROM, KAM, Bus, Anti-lock brakes, Wheel speed sensors, Hydraulic actuator, Sensor rotor, ABS, ABS pressure switch, Height sensor, Compressor assembly, Air shocks, Height sensor link, Electronic shock absorber system, Steering sensor, Brake sensor, Acceleration sensor, Shock mode switch, Shock actuators, Sonar sensor, Active suspension system. Electronic climate control, Power supply, Vacuum actuator, Vacuum diaphragms, Electronic airbag system, Electronic transmission/transaxle control system, Electronic steering assist, Voice alert system.

REVIEW QUESTIONS

1. Define the term "cybernetics."
2. The binary numbering system only uses _____ and _____ and is the key to _____ _____.
3. How do a bit, a nibble, and a byte differ?
4. Describe the five basic types of computer gates.
5. Name the five sensor classifications.
6. Explain seven types of computers used on a car.
7. An active sensor requires a reference voltage. True or False?
8. Typically, a reference voltage is about _____ _____.
9. _____ are the "hand and arms" of a computer network.
10. Describe the five major parts of an anti-lock brake system.
11. Explain the operation of an ABS.
12. Explain the six major parts of an electronic shock absorber system.
13. In your own words, how does an active suspension system work?

ACTIVITIES FOR CHAPTER 74

1. Convert your ZIP Code or your telephone number into binary number form. Make a chart that shows how the decimal numbers were converted to binary.
2. Visit several automobile dealerships and gather literature on the anti-lock brake system offered on their cars. If possible, compare the number of models that offer ABS as standard. Also compare the cost of ABS as an option from different manufacturers.

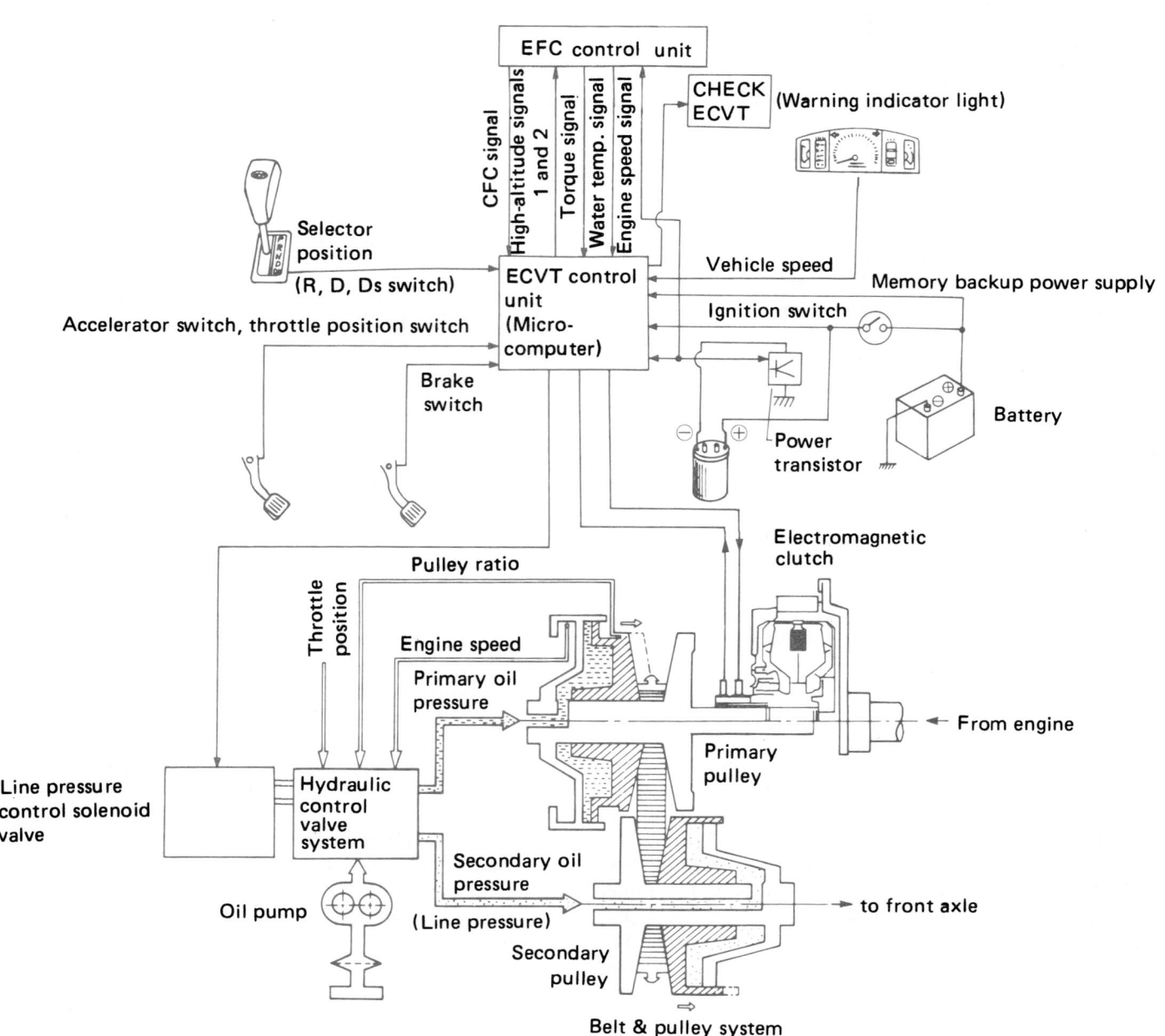

Study components in computer-controlled, constantly-variable transmission system. It consists of five basic sections: electromagnetic clutch, forward-reverse changeover, belt and pulleys, hydraulic control, and final reduction systems. Electromagnetic clutch replaces conventional torque converter. Variable pulley and steel V-belt replace gearsets. Sensors feed data to computer. Then computer can control hydraulics, pulley ratios, clutch, and other components.   (Subaru)

Computer System Troubleshooting

After studying this chapter, you will be able to:
- [ ] Locate the diagnostic connector on most makes and models of cars.
- [ ] Activate the computer self-diagnosis.
- [ ] Explain the many procedures to energize self-diagnosis.
- [ ] Read trouble codes.
- [ ] Use a trouble code chart in a service manual.
- [ ] Perform wiggle and switch tests.
- [ ] Energize a computer to operate the actuators.
- [ ] Erase trouble codes.
- [ ] Explain the use of scanners to simplify reading of trouble codes.
- [ ] Describe the operation of analyzers as an aid to troubleshooting computer systems.
- [ ] Describe safety precautions to observe while working with computer systems.

This chapter will build upon the information given throughout this book. It will explain the most important steps for using a computer's ability to find its own circuit problems. There are several ways to activate self-diagnosis, read trouble codes, energize the system actuators, etc. Various makes and models of cars require different procedures. The chapter will review the most common self-test procedures for both domestic and foreign vehicles. This will give you the background to use a manufacturer's manual and equipment operating instructions when working on any computer network. The chapter will also explain the use of scanners to simplify the reading of trouble codes.

Note! Refer to the text index for more basic information on subjects discussed in this chapter.

COMPUTER SELF-DIAGNOSIS (SELF-TEST)

Computer self-diagnosis, sometimes called *computer self-test,* refers to a vehicle computer's ability to analyze the operation of its circuits and output a code showing problems. Most new cars come equipped with one or more computers and most have this self-diagnosis

feature. It is critical that you know how to use this vital troubleshooting aid.

Thankfully, automotive computer systems are now designed to detect problems and indicate where these problems might be located. The computer is programmed to detect an abnormal operating condition. It actually scans it input and output circuits to detect an incorrect voltage, resistance, or current.

Warning light

If an unusual condition or electrical value is detected, the computer will turn on a DASH WARNING LIGHT. The computer system warning or indicator light can be called "service engine," "check engine," "service engine soon," or similar type of name.

The dash light will tell the driver to take the vehicle in for service or repairs. The electronic technician can then energize the computer self-diagnosis. The computer will produce a number code that represents the area or circuit with the abnormal condition. A trouble code chart in the manual will state what each number code represents. The technician then knows where to start his or her tests to further isolate the problem.

Since some vehicles have five or six computers, self-diagnosis can save time when trying to narrow down possible trouble causes. The computers can interact with dozens of sensors and actuators, and can even interact with each other. No longer can the untrained "shade tree mechanic" hope to repair modern vehicles. It takes the skill of a well-trained technician.

Computer system problems

Fig. 75-1 shows problems that can affect performance and the computer system:
1. LOOSE ELECTRICAL CONNECTION (input signal from sensor not reaching computer properly or computer output not energizing actuator).
2. CORRODED ELECTRICAL CONNECTION (high resistance in wiring connector upsets sensor inputs or actuator outputs).
3. FAILED SENSOR (opened or shorted sensor or other sensor malfunction prevents normal com-

puter system operation).

4. FAILED ACTUATOR (solenoid, servo motor, relay, or display shorts or opens and does not react to computer signals).

5. LEAKING VACUUM HOSE (vacuum leak upsets operation of engine or vacuum-operated actuator to reduce engine or system performance).

6. ELECTRICAL SHORT (wires touching ground or each other to cause increased current or incorrect current path).

7. IGNITION SYSTEM PROBLEMS (one example, spark plug misfire can cause unburned fuel to enter exhaust and cause oxygen sensor to try to lean mixture; this upsets computer system operation).

8. FUEL SYSTEM PROBLEMS (leaking or clogged injectors, bad pressure regulator, faulty electric fuel pump etc., can make computer system try to compensate for lean or rich condition).

9. EMISSION SYSTEM PROBLEMS (troubles with catalytic converter, EGR valve, vapor storage system, etc., can also make computer system try to compensate).

10. ENGINE PROBLEMS (mechanical problem tricks sensor into modifying computer system operation).

11. COMPUTER MALFUNCTION (incorrect PROM, internal failure of integrated circuit, or other component can disable computer and alter the operation of related systems).

Remember! There are many things that can upset a computer system. Most systems interact through the computer. A problem in one system (ignition, for instance) can cause symptoms that appear to be in another system (computerized fuel system, for example).

Remember the basics!

Most problems that affect a computer system are conventional: loose wire, corroded electrical connection, leaking vacuum hose, fouled spark plug, bad plug wire, burned engine valve, etc. For this reason, always check for the most common types of problems before condemning and testing more complex computer-controlled components.

A GENERAL RULE: Only about 20 percent of all performance problems are caused by the computer and its sensors. Most problems are NOT in the computer and its sensors.

Computer trouble codes

Computer trouble codes are pulsing signals (number codes) produced by the computer when an operating parameter is exceeded. An *operating parameter* is an acceptable minimum and maximum electrical value. It might be an acceptable voltage range from the oxygen sensor, a resistance range for a temperature sensor, or an acceptable current draw from an injector coil. In any case, the computer "knows" the limits for most inputs and output levels. If an electrical value is too weak or too strong for known parameters, the computer is programmed to store a trouble code and turn on a dash warning light.

Diagnostic connector

The *diagnostic connector,* also called *assembly line diagnostic link* (ALDL) or *self-test connector,* is a multi-pin terminal for triggering computer trouble codes or scanning problems. See Fig. 75-2. Most vehicles today have a diagnostic connector. The most com-

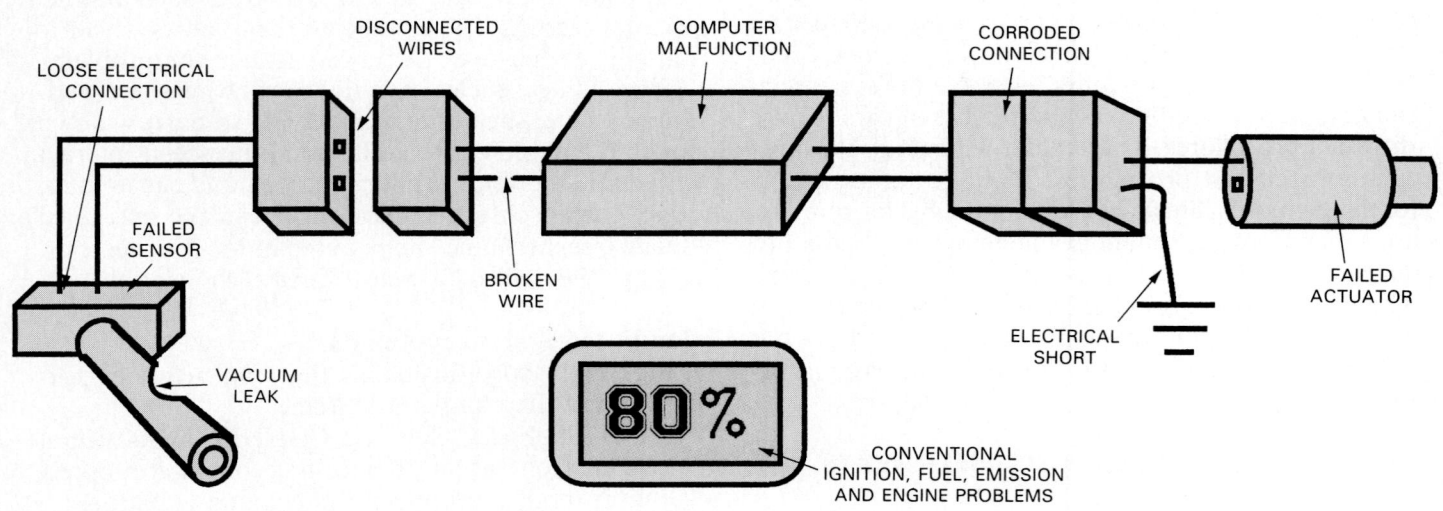

Fig. 75-1. Always remember that about 80% of all performance problems are NOT caused by the computer, its sensor, and its actuators. Most problems are conventional, like loose wires, broken wires, vacuum leaks, mechanical problems, etc.

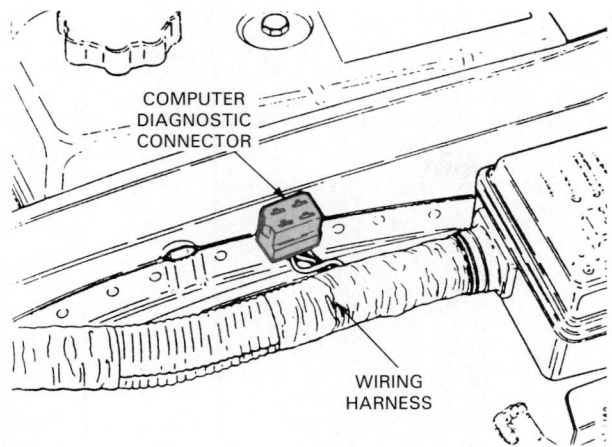

COMPUTER
DIAGNOSTIC
CONNECTOR

WIRING
HARNESS

Fig. 75-2. Most vehicles today have a computer diagnostic connector. Depending upon the make of vehicle, you might be able to use a voltmeter, test light, jumper wire, or scanner to trigger self-diagnosis at this connector. When in self-diagnosis, computer will output a code indicating the problem circuit.

mon locations for the diagnostic connector, Fig. 75-3, include:

1. Near firewall in engine compartment.
2. Near fuse box under dash.
3. Under glove box and dash.
4. Near inner fender panel in engine compartment.
5. On side of fuse box.
6. Under center console.
7. Sometimes in other locations.

Energizing self-diagnosis

Depending upon the make and model of the vehicle, there are several ways to activate or energize computer self-diagnosis to pull out trouble codes. The most common methods are:

1. Connect jumper wire or paper clip across two terminals in computer self-test connector, Fig. 75-3.
2. Connect jumper wire to ground one of the diagnostic connector terminals.
3. Connect an analog voltmeter to the battery positive

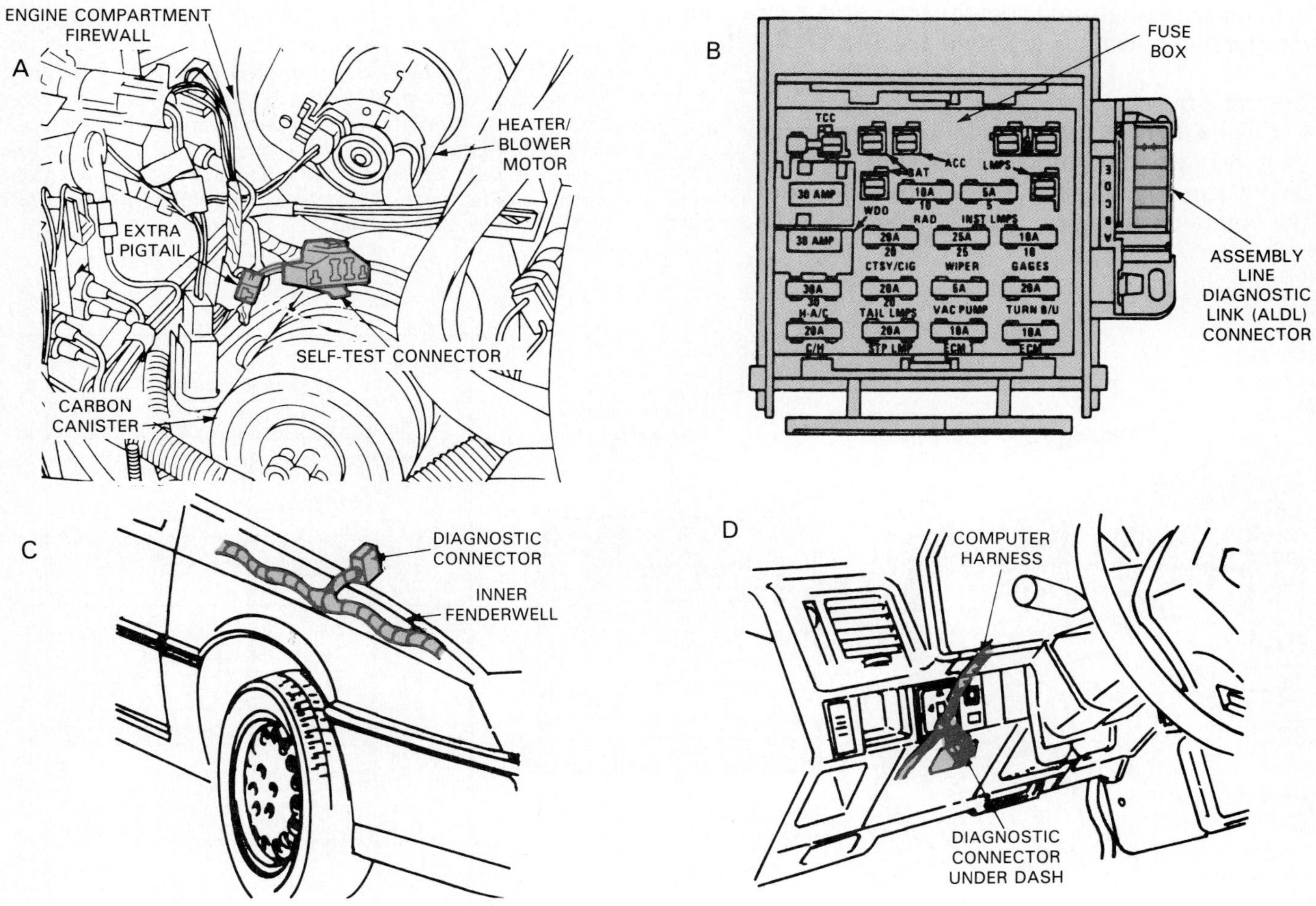

ENGINE COMPARTMENT
FIREWALL

A

HEATER/
BLOWER
MOTOR

EXTRA
PIGTAIL

SELF-TEST CONNECTOR

CARBON
CANISTER

B

FUSE
BOX

TCC

BAT
ACC   LMPS
30 AMP   10A   5A
10   5
WDO
RAD   INST LMPS
30 AMP   20A   25A   10A
20   25   10
CTSY/CIG   WIPER   GAGES
30A   20A   5A   20A
30   20
H-A/C   TAIL LMPS   VAC PUMP   TURN B/U
20A   20A   10A   10A
C/H   STP LMP   ECM   ECM

ASSEMBLY
LINE
DIAGNOSTIC
LINK (ALDL)
CONNECTOR

C

DIAGNOSTIC
CONNECTOR

INNER
FENDERWELL

D

COMPUTER
HARNESS

DIAGNOSTIC
CONNECTOR
UNDER DASH

Fig. 75-3. Diagnostic connector locations vary. A—Ford diagnostic connectors are usually on firewall, near back of engine. B—General Motors connectors are usually under dash. C—Chrysler diagnostic connectors are usually on inner fenderwell in engine compartment. D—Other cars may have connectors under dash, in or behind glove box, under center console, etc.   (GM and Ford)

terminal and to one terminal on the diagnostic connector while jumping from pigtail (extra wire) to diagnostic connector terminal, Fig. 75-4.

4. Pushing two dash climate control buttons at the same time, Fig. 75-5.
5. Turn small mode selector on the side of the computer with a screwdriver.
6. Activate wide open throttle switch on engine and have idle actuator closed while having someone turn on ignition.
7. Turn ignition key on and off several times within a few seconds. See Fig. 75-6.
8. Plug scanner into diagnostic connector while jumping from special pigtail to connector.

These are very general ways that the self-test mode can be energized. Always refer to the service manual for detailed instructions. Procedures vary for each model as well as from year to year. Look at Fig. 75-7.

Note that some older vehicles with on-board computers do NOT have a self-diagnosis feature. You would have to use conventional testing methods.

CAUTION! Connecting a jumper wire or voltmeter to the wrong terminal on a diagnostic connector could ruin delicate electronic components. Make sure your electrical connections are right the FIRST TIME!

Engine off self-test

Engine off self-test is done by triggering self-diagnosis with the ignition key ON but WITHOUT the engine running. This pulls stored trouble codes out of the computer memory chips. The engine off/key on

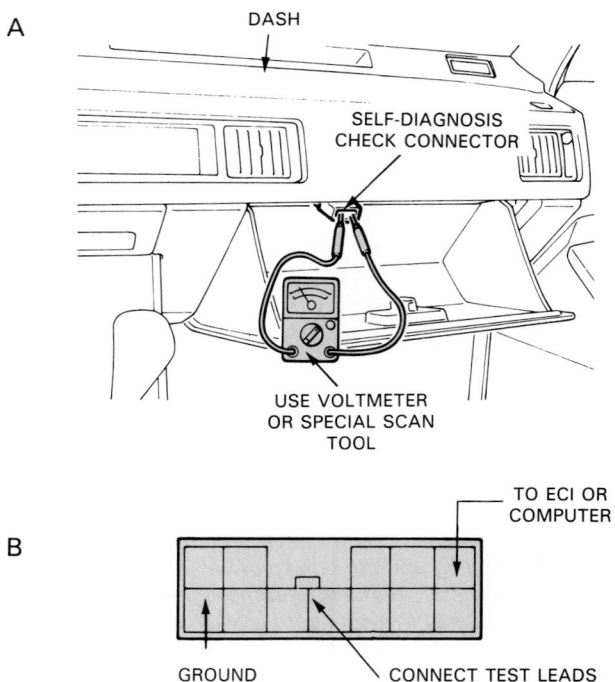

Fig. 75-4. Some automakers recommend that you use a voltmeter to read trouble codes. Meter must be connected across specific terminals in computer diagnostic connector. Other manufacturers recommend using a test light or special scanner. Always follow service manual directions. A—Meter connected to terminals. B—Service manual illustration of which pins must be touched with test leads.

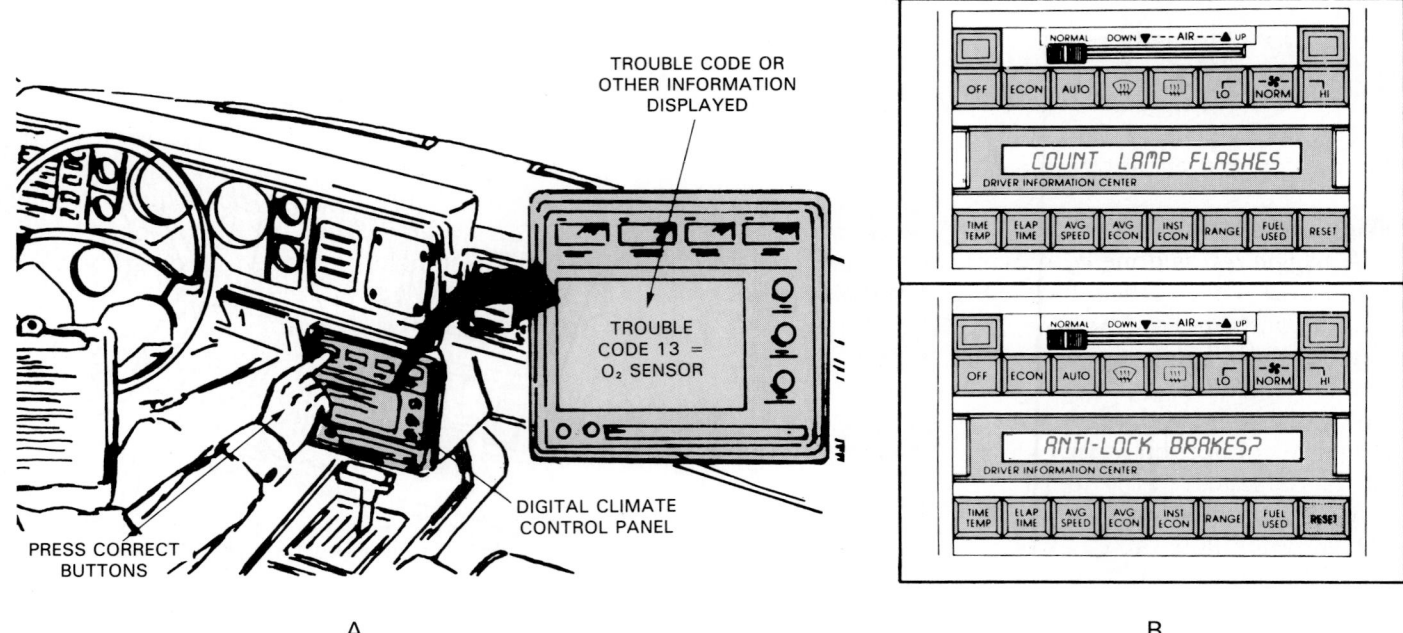

Fig. 75-5. A few vehicles have you read trouble codes in the dash climate control digital readout panel. A—By pressing two buttons at same time, readout will give trouble code number. B—Some systems actually show words explaining trouble codes and procedures. (Ford and General Motors)

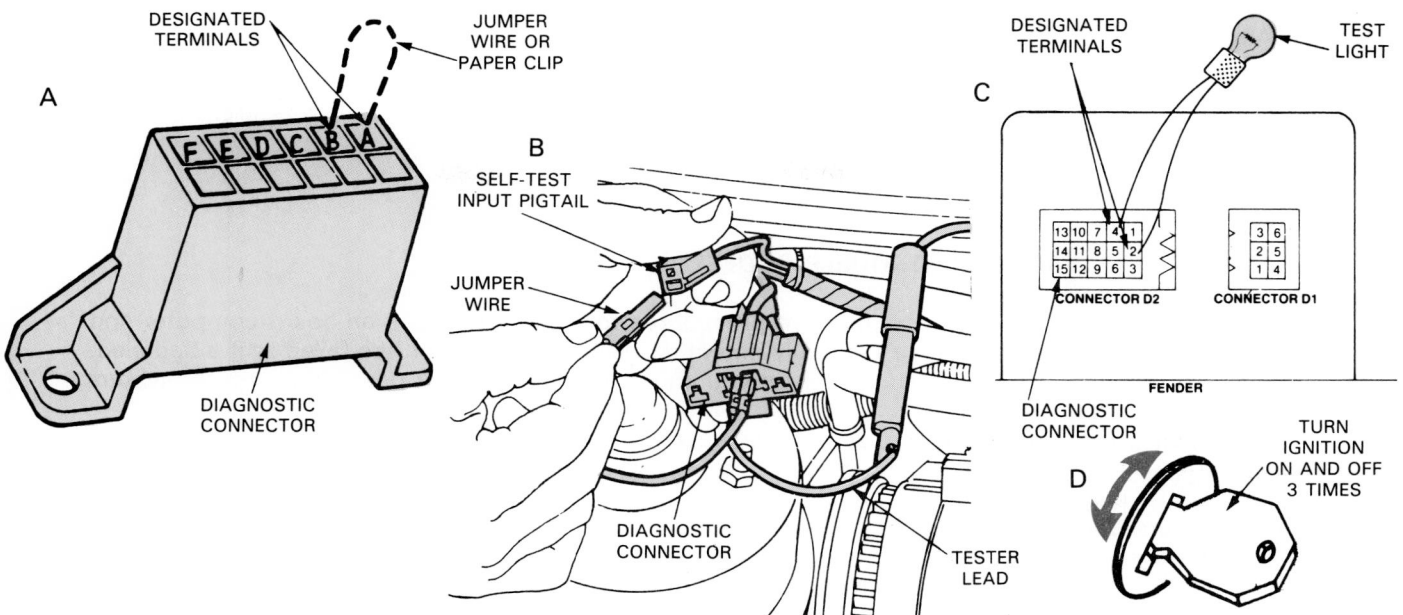

Fig. 75-6. Note typical ways to energize computer self-diagnosis or trouble codes. A—Use jumper wire or paper clip to go across specified terminals in most GM connectors. B—Jump from extra pigtail to specified terminal in many Ford connectors. C—Connect test light across specified terminals in this AMC connector. D—Turning ignition key on, off, on, off, and then on within five seconds will energize self-diagnosis with most Chrysler cars. (Chrysler, GM, and Ford)

self-test is usually performed BEFORE the engine running self-test.

If you are in the engine off/key on diagnosis mode for over 30 minutes, connect a battery charger to the car. This will prevent extended current draw from draining the battery and upsetting the operation of the computer when in self-diagnosis. False trouble codes could result from a partially "dead" battery.

Engine running self-test

Engine running self-test has the engine warmed to full operating temperature and operating to check electrical values. It checks the condition of the sensors, actuators, computer, and wiring.

Wiggle test

A *wiggle test* is done by moving wires and harness connectors while in the self-diagnosis mode. It is commonly completed with the engine OFF and the ignition key ON. This will help locate any *soft codes* (intermittent troubles) that are NOT always present. If wiggling a wire produces a new trouble code, check at electrical connection of wire. It may be loose, corroded, or damaged.

You might also want to use a heat gun to moderately heat potentially faulty components during a wiggle test. For example, electronic amplifiers tend to act up when hot. This could help find an intermittent problem.

A *hard failure* is a problem that is always present in a computer system. An example of a hard failure would be a disconnected wire. It does not come and go.

A *soft failure* is a computer term meaning an intermittent problem that only happens under some conditions. It might be present one minute and gone the next. Soft or intermittent failures will usually be stored in memory for 30 to 50 engine starts. An example of a soft failure could be a loose terminal that connects and disconnects over bumps in the road.

Reading trouble codes

Reading trouble codes involves noting the output after the self-test connector has been energized. There are several different ways that trouble codes can be read. The most typical methods include:

1. Observing Morse or on-off type code when engine or dash light flashes on and off.
2. Noting Morse or on-off type code as analog voltmeter needle deflects back and forth.
3. Watching test light connected to diagnostic terminals flash on and off.
4. Reading digital number on scanner.
5. Reading digital display in climate control panel.
6. Observing LED display on side of computer.
7. Using analyzer to display or print number code.

Dash light code

The *dash light code* is produced as the check engine light blinks on and off with long and short pauses between each flash. Some codes are single digit and others are two digit numbers. Number of flashes between pauses are added for each number, Fig. 75-8.

With a single digit code, count the number of pulses and this equals the code number. After a pause, the next code number would be given.

ENERGIZING SELF-DIAGNOSIS (TROUBLE CODES)

The three major auto makers use different procedures to make their car's on-board computer spit out trouble codes. The computer can actually detect if a sensor or actuator has failed or if a bad electrical connection has developed. This will help you know where to test for possible computer system problems.

The following is a summary of typical methods used to make an on-board computer produce these codes:

General Motors Corporation Trouble Codes
1. Locate diagnostic connector. It is usually under dash near fuse panel or steering column.
2. Use a jumper wire or paper clip to short across designated terminals in connector.
3. Watch engine light flash on and off in a Morse type code. Count number of flashes between each pause and note them. Three flashes, a pause, and two flashes would equal code 32.
4. Refer to trouble code chart in service manual for an explanation of code number.
5. Test suspected component or circuit with a digital VOM. Compare your test readings to factory specs.
6. Note that some GM cars require you to press two climate control buttons on dash at same time to enter self-diagnosis. Then, trouble code number will appear in dash. You would then need to find the same number in service manual trouble code chart.

Ford Motor Co. Trouble Codes
1. Locate diagnostic connector. It is usually in engine compartment on firewall, fenderwall, or near engine intake manifold.
2. Connect an analog or needle type VOM to designated terminals in diagnostic connector.
3. Use a jumper wire to connect extra pigtail near connector to service-manual-designated terminal in connector.
4. Observe needle fluctuations on voltmeter as you did when watching engine light for a GM car. Count needle movements between each pause. Two needle movements, a pause and then six needle movements would equal code 26.
5. Refer to service manual trouble code chart to find out what number code means.
6. Use conventional testing methods and your VOM to pinpoint cause for problem.

Chrysler Corporation Trouble Codes
1. Chrysler provides a diagnostic connector in engine compartment on late model cars. However, connector is NOT needed to energize self-diagnosis. It is provided so a scanner-tester can be connected to system.
2. To trip trouble codes, simply turn ignition key on and off three times within five seconds. Turn key on, off, on, off, and then leave it ON.
3. Observe engine light flashing on and off. Count number of flashes between each pause. Three flashes, a pause, and then one flash would equal a trouble code of 31.
4. Refer to the service manual trouble code chart to find out which component or circuit is indicated by the trouble code.
5. Use conventional VOM tests to find the source of the trouble. Test the sensor or actuator and the wiring between the device and the computer.

Note! Computer self-diagnosis systems and procedures can vary from the methods just described. Always refer to a factory service manual when in doubt!

Fig. 75-7. Study basic methods for reading computer trouble codes without a scanner or computer printer. (TIF Instruments)

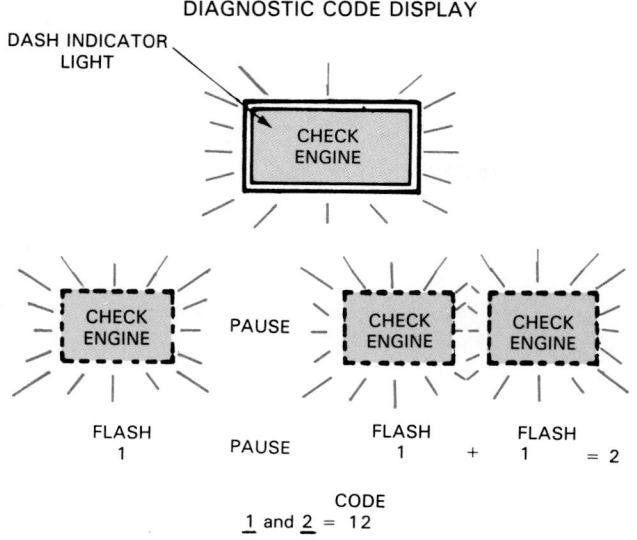

DIAGNOSTIC CODE DISPLAY

Fig. 75-8. An engine light will normally glow if computer detects a potential fault. This tells driver and technician something is wrong. After entering diagnosis mode, dash light may flash on and off to produce number code. Note how code is read. (General Motors)

With a two digit code, if the check engine light blinks twice, pauses, and then blinks two more times, the trouble code would be 22 (2 pause 2). If the light would flash once, pause, and flash three more times, the trouble code would be 13 (1 pause 3).

Analog voltmeter code

An *analog voltmeter code* is also read by counting the number of needle deflections between each pause. This is similar to the dash light flashes. However, computer usually produces 5 V pulses for the test meter.

An example of a two digit code would be if the voltmeter deflected once, paused, and then deflected four more times. The first digit would be one and the second four. This would be a trouble code 14. Look at Fig. 75-9.

Note! A few digital test meters have a bar graph that will show trouble code pulses. However, most digital meters do NOT and cannot read trouble codes.

Test light code

A *test light code* is read by noting the flashes of the tester bulb. The square wave is sometimes used to represent the on-off signals from the computer.

LED code

An *LED trouble code* is produced by indicator lights on the side of the computer or ECU. This is another less common method to produce a computer trouble code. Fig. 75-10 summarizes how to use the LED trouble code.

Digital code

A *digital trouble code* is a number code displayed directly in the car's dash or with the use of an electronic scanner. This is the easiest way to read a trouble code since you do not have to convert flashes or voltmeter deflections into numbers.

Dash digital codes are read like scanner codes after pressing two dash buttons, usually climate control buttons, at the same time. The climate control or temperature readout will then show any trouble codes.

Trouble code charts

A *trouble code chart* in the service manual will ex-

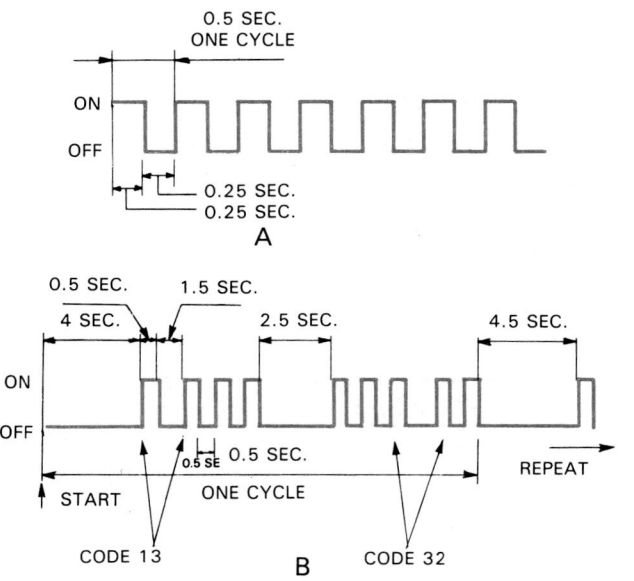

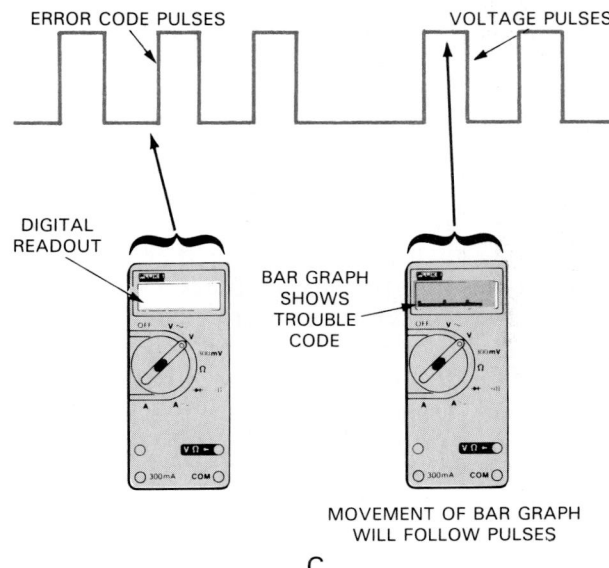

Fig. 75-9. Another variation of a computer code read by noting light flashes or pulses. A—If the computer system is normal, pulses or flashes will occur two times per second. B—With malfunction, flashes and pauses denote trouble code. C—This digital VOM has bar graph for reading coded voltage pulses. (Fluke)

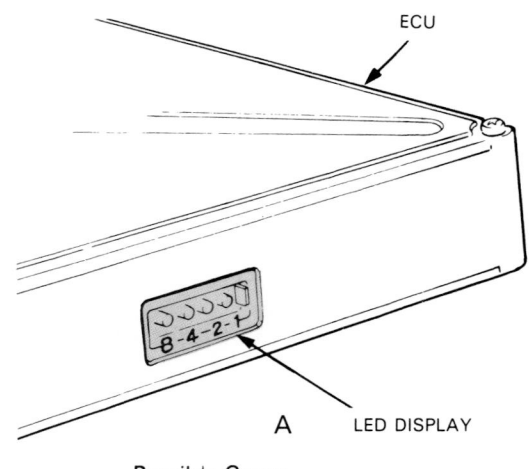

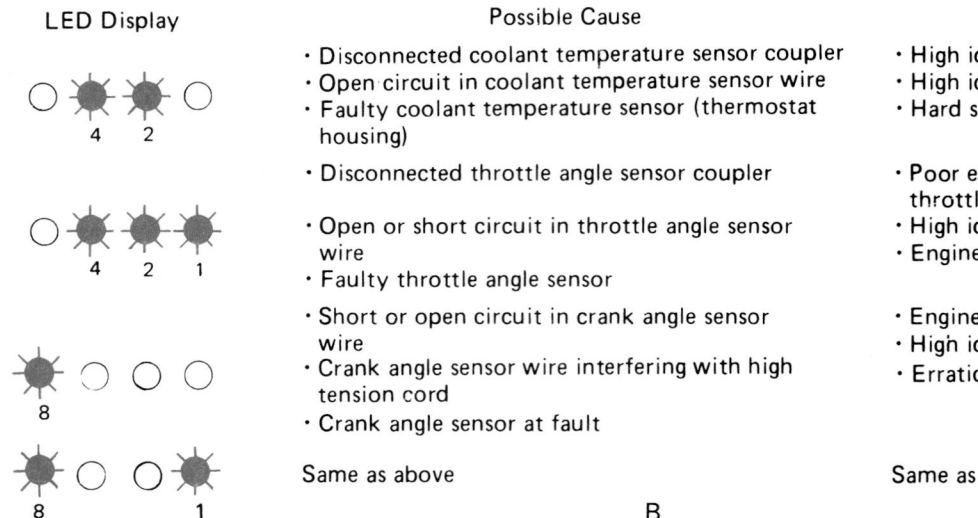

LED Display	Possible Cause	Symptom

4 2
- Disconnected coolant temperature sensor coupler
- Open circuit in coolant temperature sensor wire
- Faulty coolant temperature sensor (thermostat housing)

- High idle speed during warm-up
- High idle speed
- Hard starting at low temp

4 2 1
- Disconnected throttle angle sensor coupler
- Open or short circuit in throttle angle sensor wire
- Faulty throttle angle sensor

- Poor engine response to opening throttle rapidly
- High idle speed
- Engine does not rev up when cold

8
- Short or open circuit in crank angle sensor wire
- Crank angle sensor wire interfering with high tension cord
- Crank angle sensor at fault

- Engine does not rev up
- High idle speed
- Erratic idling

8 1
Same as above

Same as above

B

Fig. 75-10. *This car has light emitting diodes on side of computer. They can be read to obtain trouble code. Note how LED codes are read. A—LED flashes. B—Code chart.* (Honda)

plain what each trouble code number means, Fig. 75-11. It will indicate which section of the computer system might have faults. This will help you know where to start further tests on specific components. Quality scanners will also display or print the meaning of the code number in plain English.

When using a trouble code chart, always remember that the circuit indicated might NOT have a fault. For example, even dirty engine oil can trigger an oxygen sensor or rich mixture trouble code. The PCV system can pull fumes into the engine intake manifold. The sensor would be producing an overly rich signal because of the fumes in the exhaust.

A trouble code does NOT always mean that a component is bad. It simply indicates possible problems.

A general rule is to correct the cause of the LOWEST NUMBER CODE FIRST. Sometimes fixing the lowest code will clear other codes because of component interaction.

Scanners

A *scanner,* discussed earlier, is an electronic test instrument designed to convert computer pulses or signals directly into a digital or number display. Also called a *diagnostic readout tool,* this type tester makes it easier to read trouble codes.

Fig. 75-12 shows a scanner connected to a diagnostic connector. Some auto manufacturers recommend a specific scanner for their vehicles. Each will also have a specialized name for the scanner: STAR (self-test auto readout) tester, diagnostic readout unit, etc.

Fig. 75-13 shows how to use a typical scanner. It is connected to the battery and plugged into the computer system diagnostic connector. Look at Fig. 75-14.

Computer scan values

Computer scan values output by the vehicle's ECU give electrical operating values. These can be read on a scanner digital readout or a printout. Fig. 75-15 gives an example.

The scan values can be compared to known good specs to help find problems. This feature allows you to check several sensors and other conditions quickly.

Switch self-test

A *switch self-test* involves activating various switches

A ## CODE IDENTIFICATION

The "Service Engine Soon" light will only be "ON" if the malfunction exists under the conditions listed below. If the malfunction clears, the light will go out and the code will be stored in the ECM. Any codes stored will be erased if no problem reoccurs within 50 engine starts.

CODE AND CIRCUIT	PROBABLE CAUSE	CODE AND CIRCUIT	PROBABLE CAUSE
Code 13 - O_2 Sensor Open Oxygen Sensor Circuit	Indicates that the oxygen sensor circuit or sensor was open for one minute while off idle.	Code 33 - MAP Sensor Low Vacuum	MAP sensor output to high for 5 seconds or an open signal circuit.
Code 14 - Coolant Sensor High Temperature Indication	Sets if the sensor or signal line becomes grounded for 3 seconds.	Code 34 - MAP Sensor High Vacuum	Low or no output from sensor with engine running.
Code 15 - Coolant Sensor Low Temperature Indication	Sets if the sensor, connections, or wires open for 3 seconds.	Code 35 - IAC	IAC error
		Code 42 - EST	ECM has seen an open or grounded EST or Bypass circuit.

B ## DIAGNOSIS CHART (FAULT TREE)

Output preference order	Diagnosis item	Malfunction code			Check item (Remedy)
		Output signal pattern	No.	Memory	
1	Engine control unit	 H ⎍⎓⎓⎓⎓⎓ L	–	–	(Replace engine control unit)
2	Oxygen sensor	 H ⎍⎍ L	11	Retained	• Harness and connector • Oxygen sensor • Fuel pressure • Injectors (Replace if defective) • Intake air leaks
3	Air flow sensor	 H ⎍⎍⎍ L	12	Retained	• Harness and connector (If harness and connector are normal, replace air flow sensor assembly.)
4	Intake air temperature sensor	 H ⎍⎍⎍⎍ L	13	Retained	• Harness and connector • Intake air temperature sensor

Fig. 75-11. A—This is a trouble code chart for one type of General Motors vehicle. Study how different code numbers show possible problems and causes. B—This is a trouble code chart for a foreign vehicle. Note that code is given as pulses read by needle type voltmeter. (GM and Toyota)

while using a scanner. As each switch is activated, the scanner will quickly indicate if the switch is working.

For example, you might be told to shift the transmission shift lever through the gears, press on the brake pedal, and turn the air conditioning on and off. As each is done, the scanner will illuminate an indicator light. This will show that the brake switch, neutral safety switch, and A/C switch are functioning. See Fig.

75-16A and B.

Refer to the service manual for details of the switch self-test. Chrysler vehicles have the ability but other makes do NOT have this feature.

Actuator self-test

An *actuator self-test* uses the scanner or analyzer and computer to energize specific output devices with the

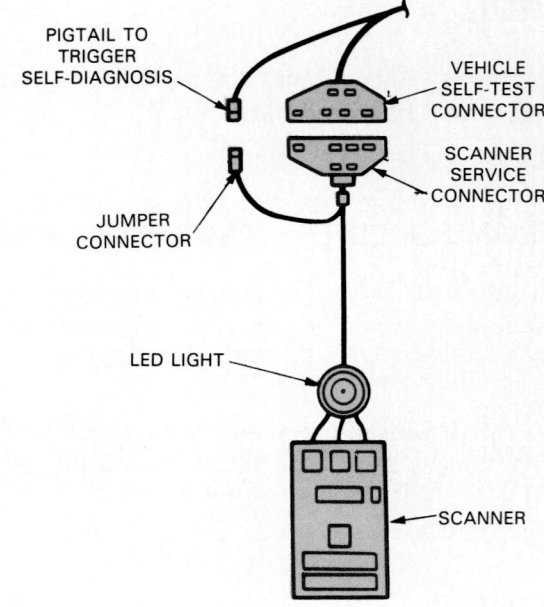

A

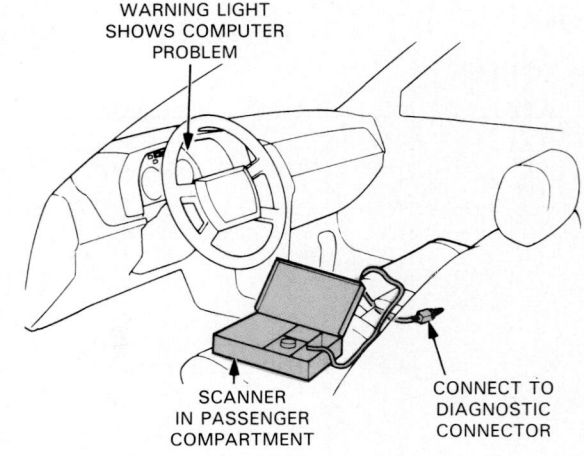

B

Fig. 75-12. A—With this system, scanner is plugged into connector while trigger wire is jumped to connector. Number code can be quickly noted on scanner display. B—To road test car while scanning, use long test lead and place scanner on seat. (Ford and Honda)

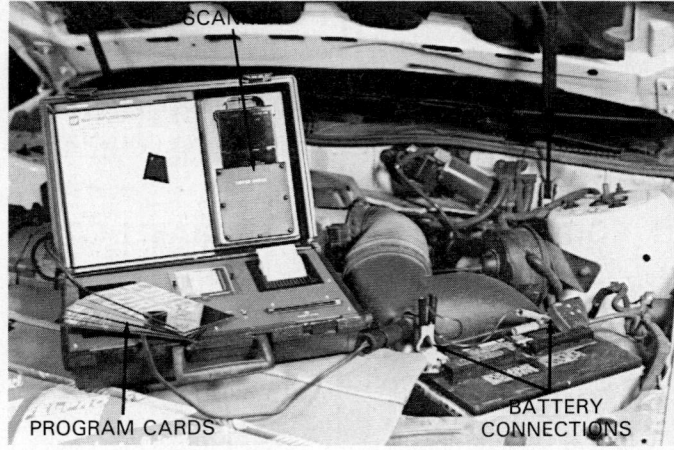

Fig. 75-13. This scanner is connected to a source of battery voltage and plugged into the computer diagnostic connector. It can then "talk" to on-board computer and print out trouble codes and an explanation of what trouble code means. (TIF Instruments)

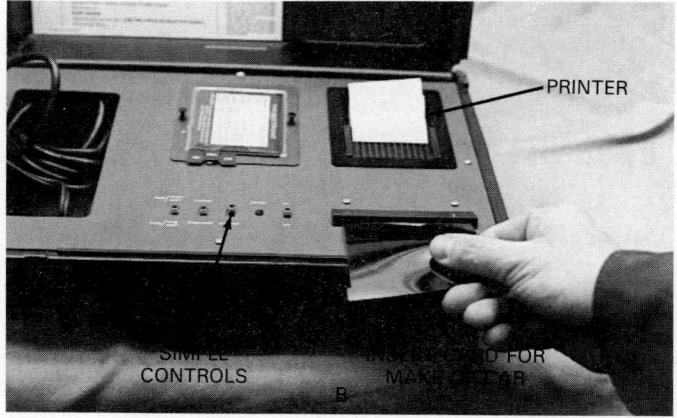

Fig. 75-14. A—Easy to use computer printer plugs into diagnostic connector. It will convert code numbers into names of failed components. B—It will print circuit values and do actuator and switch tests. Scanner will work on GM, Ford, and Chrysler vehicles. (TIF Instruments)

engine off. This will let you find out if the actuators are working. See Fig. 75-16.

The computer is sometimes placed into the actuator self-test mode by the scanner or an analyzer right after the end of trouble code outputs. This will make the computer trigger some actuators. It might:

1. Fire the ignition coil.
2. Open and close the injectors.
3. Cycle the idle speed motor or solenoid.
4. Operate other actuators.

You can then watch or listen to make sure these actuators are working.

Pinpoint tests

Pinpoint tests are more specific tests of individual components. They are completed after doing the self-diagnosis test. The service manual will normally have

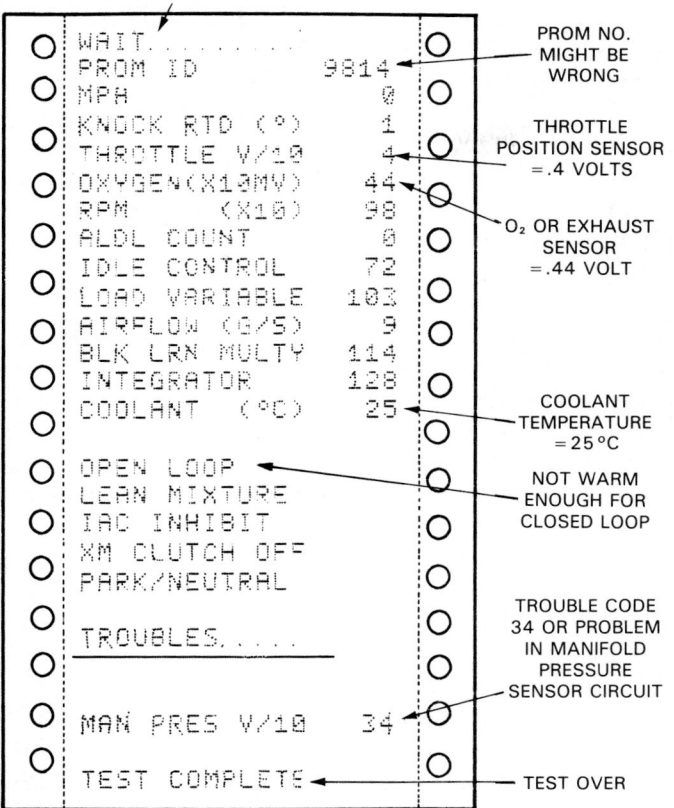

WAIT.........		
PROM ID	9814	PROM NO. MIGHT BE WRONG
MPH	0	
KNOCK RTD (°)	1	
THROTTLE V/10	4	THROTTLE POSITION SENSOR = .4 VOLTS
OXYGEN(X10MV)	44	
RPM (X10)	98	O₂ OR EXHAUST SENSOR = .44 VOLT
ALDL COUNT	0	
IDLE CONTROL	72	
LOAD VARIABLE	103	
AIRFLOW (G/S)	9	
BLK LRN MULTY	114	
INTEGRATOR	128	
COOLANT (°C)	25	COOLANT TEMPERATURE = 25°C
OPEN LOOP		NOT WARM ENOUGH FOR CLOSED LOOP
LEAN MIXTURE		
IAC INHIBIT		
XM CLUTCH OFF		
PARK/NEUTRAL		
TROUBLES....		
MAN PRES V/10	34	TROUBLE CODE 34 OR PROBLEM IN MANIFOLD PRESSURE SENSOR CIRCUIT
TEST COMPLETE		TEST OVER

Fig. 75-15. *Study scanner printout from tester in Fig. 75-13. Printout shows actual values produced by the on-board computer. A few are explained. Values can be compared to manual specs to quickly find problems. Note how printer explains trouble code so you do not have to look up chart in manual.* (TIF Instruments)

charts that explain how to do each pinpoint test. It will give meter hookups, component electrical values, and other critical instructions.

Note! Chapter 76 explains tests and service procedures for sensors, actuators, and computers. This will give you more information on pinpoint tests.

Computer terminal values

Computer terminal values are tested at the metal pins of the ECU or computer connector. A digital VOM can be used to read actual terminal voltage and resistance values and compare them to known good voltages. This saves you from having to unplug connectors to make electrical measurements.

CAUTION! Never connect a low impedance (resistance) analog meter or test light to a computer system unless instructed to do so by the service manual. A low impedance meter or tester could draw enough current to damage delicate electronic devices.

Erasing trouble codes

Erasing trouble codes removes the number codes from computer memory. There are various methods

A — PRINTOUT SHOWS PROBLEM RELATING TO TPS

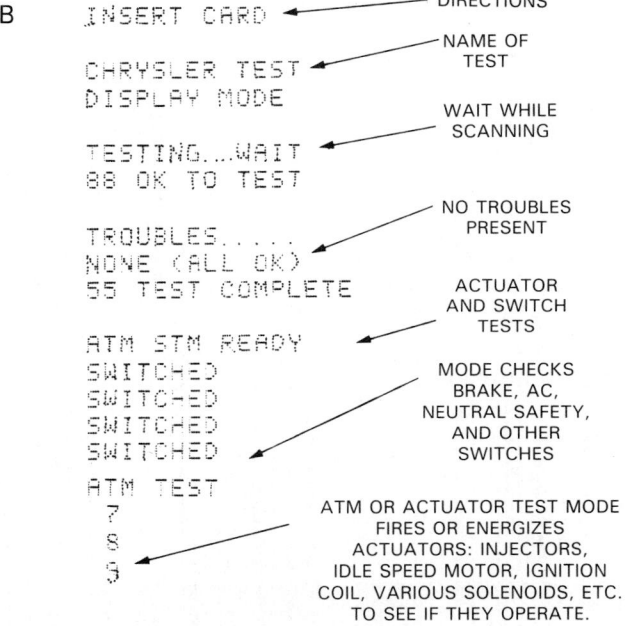

B

INSERT CARD	DIRECTIONS
CHRYSLER TEST	NAME OF TEST
DISPLAY MODE	
TESTING....WAIT	WAIT WHILE SCANNING
88 OK TO TEST	
TROUBLES.....	NO TROUBLES PRESENT
NONE (ALL OK)	
55 TEST COMPLETE	
ATM STM READY	ACTUATOR AND SWITCH TESTS
SWITCHED	
SWITCHED	MODE CHECKS BRAKE, AC, NEUTRAL SAFETY, AND OTHER SWITCHES
SWITCHED	
SWITCHED	
ATM TEST	
7	ATM OR ACTUATOR TEST MODE FIRES OR ENERGIZES ACTUATORS: INJECTORS, IDLE SPEED MOTOR, IGNITION COIL, VARIOUS SOLENOIDS, ETC. TO SEE IF THEY OPERATE.
8	
9	

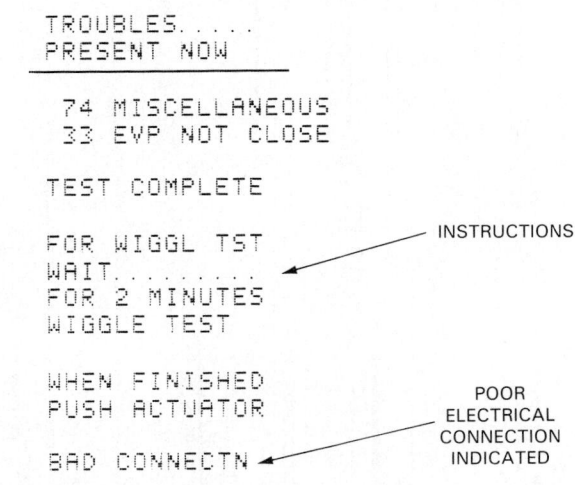

C

TROUBLES.....	
PRESENT NOW	
74 MISCELLANEOUS	
33 EVP NOT CLOSE	
TEST COMPLETE	
FOR WIGGL TST	INSTRUCTIONS
WAIT.........	
FOR 2 MINUTES	
WIGGLE TEST	
WHEN FINISHED	
PUSH ACTUATOR	
BAD CONNECTN	POOR ELECTRICAL CONNECTION INDICATED

Fig. 75-16. *This scanner printer will save time when trying to find problems in computer system. A—After connecting to diagnostic connector and inserting program card, printer will output circuit values and any trouble codes with explanation of code number. B—Example of printout for one model vehicle. C—Wiggle test shows bad connection.* (TIF Instruments)

used to erase trouble codes from the computer:
1. Unplug fuse to computer or ECU.
2. Disconnect battery ground strap or cable. This will also erase digital clock memory, however.
3. Leave engine off for several days.
4. Use scanner or analyzer to disconnect power to computer or ECU.
5. Codes will erase automatically after 30-50 engine starts.
6. Unplug computer harness.

WARNING! Some automakers warn against unplugging or plugging in the harness connector with the ignition key on or the engine running. This could cause a voltage spike that could damage the computer.

After erasing trouble codes, you might want to again energize self-diagnosis. If no trouble codes are then displayed, you have corrected the problem.

COMPUTER ANALYZERS

A *computer analyzer* is a more complex testing instrument than a scanner. Fig. 75-17 shows a computer analyzer connected to a computer code storage unit. The two can be connected to the computer diagnostic connector and used while the vehicle is being driven. This is helpful in finding *soft* (intermittent) problems.

The test setup will read fast codes and store operating parameters occurring in very short time spans. This will help the technician find any small "glitches" that upset computer system operation.

Once back at the shop, the computer-stored data can be further analyzed or sent over phone lines to a mainframe computer.

Modem analyzer systems

A *modem analyzer system* allows a shop-owned analyzer to communicate over telephone lines with a larger mainframe computer. This lets the technician tie into large amounts of stored information that could be needed to troubleshoot difficult problems.

Many large dealerships are installing modem analyzer systems like the one in Fig. 75-18. The analyzer is plugged into the vehicle's diagnostic connector and sometimes into a modem.

A *modem* is an electronic device that allows computer data or signals to be sent over telephone lines. A modem must be on both ends of the phone line. One sends data while the other receives the sent data. Data can be sent back and forth between modems.

A *mainframe computer* is a very large computer that can store tremendous amounts of data. It can also do multiple tasks or *"talk"* (transfer information) to several computer analyzers at the same time.

The modem allows the electronic technician to have access to a large mainframe computer. The auto manufacturer or equipment manufacturer can have frequent or common problems, both hard and soft codes, stored in mainframe memory for each car. Common faults for a particular model can be stored. Steps for finding problems, specific voltages and other electrical values for each model can also be in mainframe memory. The technician can use the analyzer and modem to pull this data out of the mainframe.

Fig. 75-19A shows a *computer menu* that allows the technician to quickly select different kinds of information from computer network. Note different areas.

Fig. 75-19B shows how the analyzers can display actual circuits and give instructions when trying to find the cause of complex electronic problems. It is like having the service manual on a computer disk or having an "electronic service manual."

Fig. 75-17. This technician has test driven car with a hand-held scanner connected to a "flight recorder" type tester. When back at the shop, data collected on testers can be fed into a computer for further evaluation. This might be useful on difficult-to-find problems. (OTC Div. of SPX Corp.)

Fig. 75-18. Electronic technician is using analyzer tied to mainframe computer through modem. (General Motors)

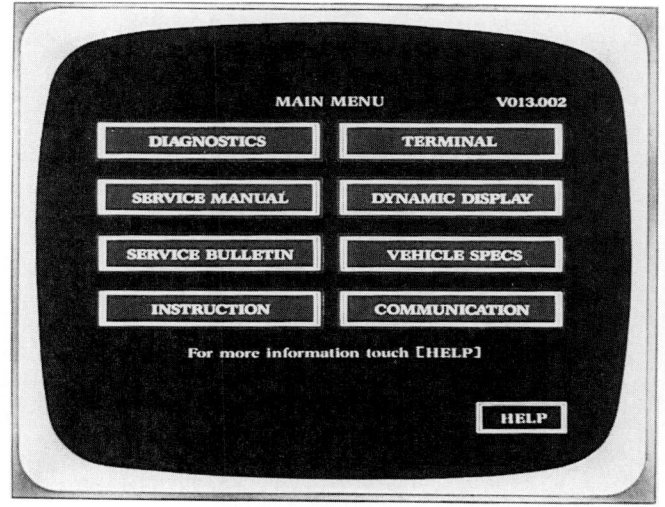

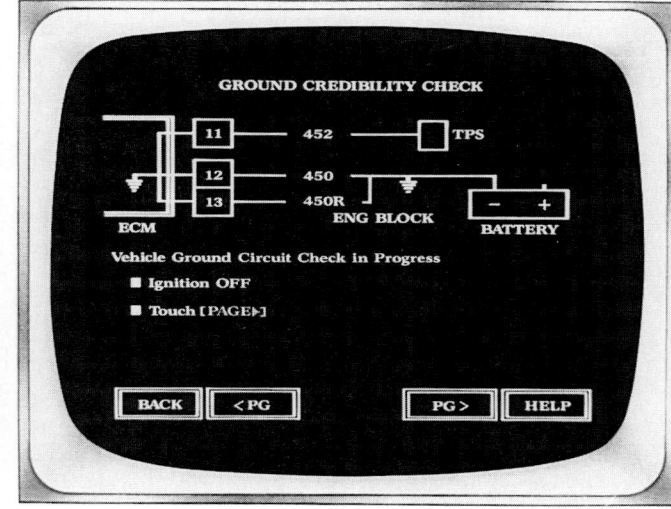

Fig. 75-19. A—This analyzer display screen menu allows technician to quickly select area or subject by touching CRT screen. B—Display screen of analyzer is now showing circuit drawing and is giving specific instructions for testing. (GM)

KNOW THESE TERMS

Self-diagnosis, Dash warning light, Computer trouble codes, Operating parameter, Diagnostic connector, ALDL, Engine off self-test, Engine on self-test, Wiggle test, Hard failure, Soft failure, Reading trouble code, Dash light code, Analog voltmeter code, Test light code, LED code, Digital code, Trouble code chart, Scanner, Computer scan values, Switch self-test, Actuator self-test, Pinpoint tests, Computer terminal values. Erasing trouble codes, Computer analyzer, Modem analyzer system, Modem, Mainframe computer, Computer menu.

REVIEW QUESTIONS

1. What is computer self-diagnosis?
2. If an unusual condition or electrical value is detected, most computer systems will turn on a _____ _____ _____.
3. List and summarize 11 types of computer system problems.
4. Only about _____ of all performance problems are caused by the computer, sensors, and actuators.
5. A Chrysler car enters the shop with the computer warning light on.
   Technician A says to trigger self-diagnosis by jumping across specified terminals in the diagnostic connector.
   Technician B says to trigger self-diagnosis by turning the ignition key on and off three times.
   Who is correct?
   a. Technician A
   b. Technician B
   c. Both A and B
   d. Neither A nor B
6. Describe eight ways that you can energize self-diagnosis on modern automobiles.
7. Why do most technicians do the engine OFF self-test first?
8. What is a wiggle test?
9. A _____ _____ is always present and a _____ _____ is intermittent.
10. Explain seven ways to read trouble codes.
11. How do you use trouble code charts?
12. When a trouble code number is looked up in a trouble code chart, the chart says "oxygen sensor." Technician A says to test the sensor and its circuit. Technician B says to replace the oxygen sensor. Who is correct?
    a. Technician A
    b. Technician B
    c. Both A and B
    d. Neither A nor B

ACTIVITIES FOR CHAPTER 75

1. Demonstrate, on at least one vehicle, the proper method for activating the self-diagnosis feature on the computer. Also show how to read a trouble code on that vehicle, and how to locate the trouble code in a service manual.
2. Videotape a service technician using a computer analyzer to "check out" an engine. Ask the technician to explain each step as he or she performs it. Show the completed tape to the class.

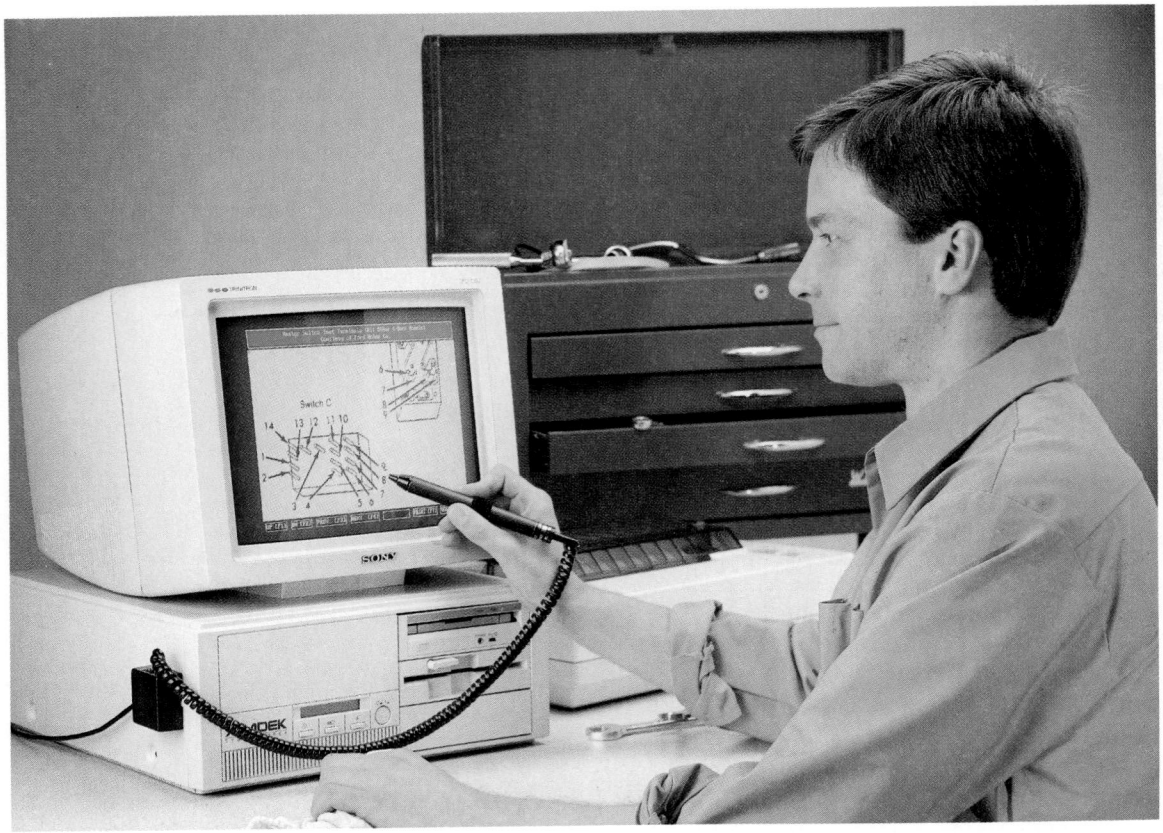

A— Technician is using light pen to touch screen and scan for tune-up specs.

B— Computer screen shows exploded view of starting motor for specific make and model of vehicle.

This computer system can hold thousands of pages of information on the service and repair of vehicles. Instead of thumbing through pages in service manuals, technician can quickly touch computer screen to find data. (Mitchell International)

Computer System Service

After studying this chapter, you will be able to:
- ☐ Describe why remembering basic tests and problems is important to working on vehicles with computers.
- ☐ Test sensors.
- ☐ Service an oxygen sensor.
- ☐ Properly remove and replace various sensors.
- ☐ Test actuators.
- ☐ Remove and replace a computer PROM.
- ☐ Measure computer reference voltage output to sensors with a VOM.
- ☐ Remove and replace a computer.
- ☐ Demonstrate safe working practices when servicing automotive computers.

In previous chapters, you learned how sensors, actuators, computers, and other electronic components operate. You also learned how to use computer self-diagnosis, scanners, and analyzers to help find electronic problems. This chapter will concentrate on how to do specific tests on computer system components. Most sensors and actuators can be checked with a digital VOM. The wiring leading from the computer to these devices can also be checked for opens and shorts.

This chapter will help you develop the skills needed to verify WHERE PROBLEMS ARE after reading trouble codes and using scanners or analyzers. Remember that trouble codes indicate only the area of trouble, NOT what part is at fault. It is therefore imperative that you know how to do pinpoint tests on individual components.

PRELIMINARY INSPECTION

A *preliminary inspection* involves looking for signs of obvious trouble: loose wires, leaking vacuum hoses, part damage, etc. For example, if the trouble code says that there is something wrong in the coolant sensor circuit, you could check the sensor resistance and the wiring going to that sensor.

When there is a malfunction in a system, always remember that the cause is usually SOMETHING SIMPLE. It is easy for the untrained person to instantly

think "computer problems," when an engine misses, runs rough, fails to start properly, or exhibits some other performance problem.

Studies have shown that 80% of all performance problems are caused by something other than the computer system electronics. Only 20% of all performance problems are due to the computer, sensors, or actuators.

For example, DIRTY ENGINE OIL can trigger a computer trouble code, Fig. 76-1. Contaminated oil fumes can be drawn into the engine intake manifold from the crankcase. The PCV system is designed to remove these fumes from the lower engine area and burn them in the engine. If these fumes are excessively strong, the oxygen sensor could be fooled into signaling a rich fuel mixture. The computer would then lean the fuel mixture to compensate for the crankcase fumes. An oxygen sensor trouble code could be produced and engine performance problems could result.

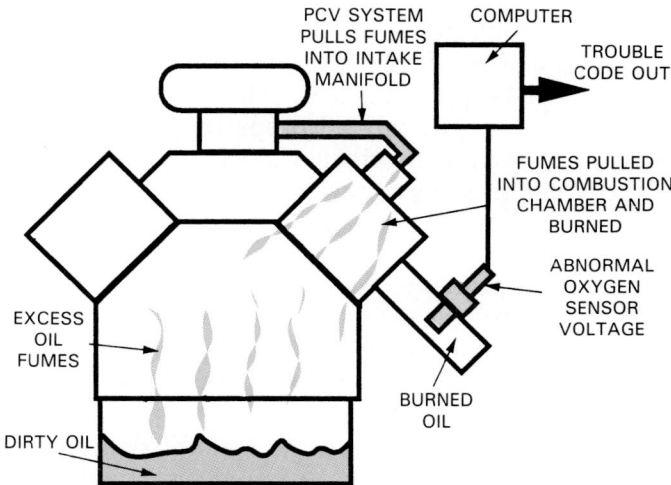

Fig. 76-1. This example shows that a trouble code can be tripped without a problem in computer system. One example, very contaminated engine oil could cause excess fumes to be pulled in by the PCV system. When burned in the combustion chambers, it could fool the computer into thinking there was something wrong with the oxygen sensor circuit.

As this points out, it's critical that you check or troubleshoot conventional or BASIC PROBLEMS FIRST. Start checking for computer problems only after all basic system troubles have been eliminated.

Kiss principle

Kiss is an abbreviation that could help you find the source of performance problems on a computer-controlled car. *Kiss* stands for "keep it simple, stupid!" This means that you should start your troubleshooting with the simple checks and tests. Then, as the simpler, more common problems are eliminated, move to more complex tests of sensors and actuators. The "kiss principle" will help you become a more competent auto electronic technician.

COMPUTER CIRCUIT PROBLEMS

Almost all electrical-electronic problems are actually basic circuit problems. A *basic circuit problem* is caused by something in the circuit that increases or decreases current, resistance, or voltage. For example, a broken wire could stop or decrease current flow or a charging system problem could increase output voltage and current flow.

Unfortunately, when a basic circuit problem occurs in a complex circuit, like a computer control system, it may NOT seem like a simple circuit problem. For example, a poor electrical connection in a feed wire to a sensor can cause a false signal returning to the computer. The computer, "fooled" by low sensor voltage, might alter operation of the fuel injection system, emission control systems, or ignition system.

A technician could think that any of these systems or the computer itself is at fault. Several systems could appear to have a problem. In reality, it is simply a poor electrical connection in one wire that is causing all of the problems.

As you can see, it is important for an automotive technician to keep a "level head" when diagnosing electrical problems. If analyzed properly, problems can usually be found and corrected easily. If analyzed improperly, electrical-electronic problems can "drive you crazy."

What is the problem?

The most difficult aspect of making electrical repairs is finding the source of the problem. To find the source of electrical problems, you must ask yourself these kinds of questions:
1. What could be causing the specific symptoms? Mentally picture the parts in the circuit and how they function. Trace through the circuit or use a wiring diagram to find out which wires, connections, and components are in the circuit leading to potential trouble source.
2. How many components are affected? If several components are NOT working, you would know

that something close to the power source should be at fault. If only one or two sections of the circuit are faulty, you would know to begin your tests at that section of the circuit.
3. Is the problem always present or is it intermittent (only occurs under some conditions)? If trouble is intermittent, you would know that the conditions causing the problem would have to be simulated. For example, a loose electrical connection could open and close with vibration or movement. By wiggling wires in the circuit, you might simulate the driving conditions and make the problem occur.
4. Is the problem affected by heat or cold? If it occurs only on a hot day or with engine warmed to full operating temperature, you can arrive at a few conclusions. Heat may be activating the problem. For example, electronic circuits (transistors in particular) are greatly affected by heat. In fact, too much heat can ruin an electronic component. This might tell you which component is at fault. It might also help you decide to use a heat gun to simulate the heat in an engine compartment.
5. Is the problem affected by moisture? If the trouble occurs only on wet days, you again have more information to use when analyzing the source of a problem. Obviously, moisture cannot enter a sealed electronic circuit, but it can enter and affect wire connections and components exposed to the environment. This type of thinking might help you.

SENSOR SERVICE

Sensor service involves testing and sometimes replacing computer system sensors. Since sensor designs vary and some can be damaged by incorrect testing methods, it is important for you to know the most common ways of checking sensor values.

Basically, a VOM is used to measure the actual sensor output. Then, this output (voltage, resistance, or current) can be compared to factory specs. If the test value is too high or too low, you would know that the sensor is faulty and must be replaced.

The number and types of sensors will vary with the specific make and model of vehicle. Refer to the service manual for exact sensor types and locations. Sometimes, the manual will show what sensors are used and where they are located.

The shop manual will also have a wiring diagram for the computer system. The diagram will show the color codes of wires and number of connectors that are used to feed data from the sensor back to the computer. This can be very helpful when servicing a computer system that you have never worked on before.

Poor electrical connections

Poor electrical connections are the most common cause of electrical-related problems in a computer system. Discussed in previous chapters, a wiggle test will help find bad connections and intermittent problems. Always check electrical connections when diagnosing sensors and other electronic components. Fig. 76-2 shows how to test a wiring harness for opens or poor connections.

Vacuum leaks

Vacuum leaks are frequently caused by deteriorated, broken, or loose vacuum hoses. Some vacuum leaks can upset the operation of a computer system and cause a wide range of symptoms. Also, several engine sensors and vacuum actuators (vacuum switches) rely on engine vacuum for operation.

Always check for vacuum leaks when they could be causing a performance problem. For example, if the trouble code indicates a problem with the MAP (manifold absolute pressure) sensor, always check vacuum lines leading to the sensor. If lines are leaking, the sensor cannot function normally.

Air leaks after an airflow sensor can also cause problems. The sensor cannot measure the air being drawn into the engine through the leak and an incorrect air-fuel mixture will result.

SENSOR PROBLEMS, TESTING, REPLACEMENT

Sensors and their circuits can sometimes cause computer system malfunctions. As with other electronic components, sensors and sensor circuits can develop opens, shorts, or abnormal resistance or voltage values. When your tests find a problem, the sensor should be replaced or the circuit repaired.

Detailed in earlier chapters, sensors can produce signals for the computer in several ways:

1. Voltage generating sensor (oxygen sensor and some speed sensors produce an internal voltage).
2. Switching-type sensors (sensor simply acts as either a conductor or an insulator to switch on and off with condition changes; a brake switch and neutral safety switch would be examples).
3. Variable resistance sensors (sensor ohms change with condition to signal computer by altering current flow back to computer).

Each type of sensor needs a slightly different testing method. A voltage generating sensor requires a digital meter to read the small or weak voltage output. An ohmmeter and voltmeter are used to check switching and variable resistance type sensors. Voltage drop specs can also be given for resistance type sensors.

Sensor categories for testing

For testing purposes, you can also classify sensors into either passive or active categories. This will help you select a testing method.

Passive sensors typically include the following:
1. Temperature sensors (air temperature, engine temperature, etc.).
2. Position sensors (throttle position, transmission linkage position, EGR sensors, etc.)
3. Pressure sensors (manifold pressure sensor, brake system pressure sensors, etc.).
4. Flow sensors (airflow, fuel flow, etc.)
5. Level sensors (oil level sensors, brake fluid level sensors, suspension height sensors, etc.)
6. Other similar types.

Active sensors include these types:
1. Oxygen sensors.
2. Magnetic sensors (engine speed sensors, camshaft sensors, vehicle speed sensors, etc.).
3. Knock sensors.
4. Solar sensors.
5. Other similar types.

Testing passive sensors

Discussed earlier, *passive sensors* do NOT generate their own voltage. The computer must feed them voltage and current for them to report back to the computer. A passive sensor can change its internal resistance with a change in a condition. This resistance change can be interpreted and used by the computer to control the system.

To test a passive sensor, either measure its internal resistance with an ohmmeter or measure the voltage drop across the sensor with its reference voltage applied.

To test a passive sensor with an ohmmeter, disconnect the sensor wires and connect the meter test leads, Fig. 76-3A. The sensor ohms must be within factory specifications.

For example, if you are testing a temperature sensor, you could connect an ohmmeter to the sensor terminals and then measure temperature with a digital thermometer. By comparing your two measurements

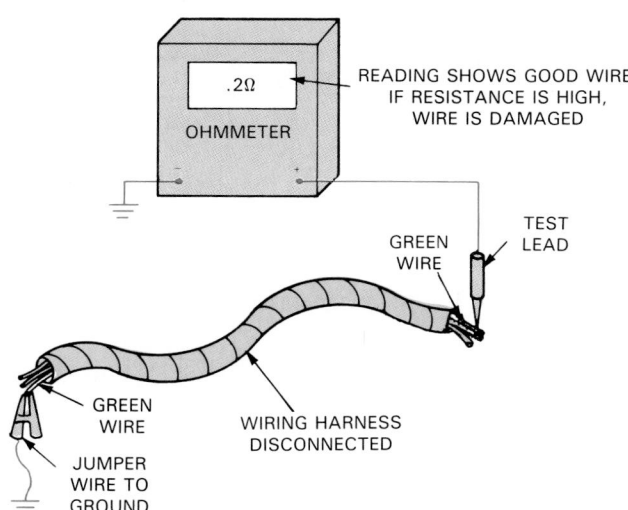

Fig. 76-2. If you suspect a wire is broken inside harness, this is an easy way to test wire. Disconnect harness at both ends, ground suspected wire on one end. Then use ohmmeter to check resistance of wire. If high, wire would have to be by-passed or replaced.

to specs, you can find out if the sensor is faulty.

With a switching type passive sensor, you can simply check that the switch is opening and closing. As in Fig. 76-3B, connect your ohmmeter and move the switch opened and closed. Your meter should then register infinite and zero ohms. Replace the sensor if it tests bad. You could also use a high impedance (resistance) test light to quickly check the operation of a switching type sensor.

To check a passive sensor with a voltmeter, you must leave the sensor wired into its circuit. Measure the voltage drop across the passive sensor with the computer reference voltage applied. Pictured in Fig. 76-3C, you must connect a voltmeter in parallel with the sen-sor, leaving the computer wires connected to the sen-sor. Compare your measurements to specifications.

Note that some automakers do not give resistance specs for passive sensors; they only give voltage drops. You may have to use a specially fabricated test harness to connect the meter in parallel with the sensor. You can make or purchase this type test harness.

Testing reference voltage

A *reference voltage* (typically FIVE VOLTS) is fed to switching and variable resistance type sensors. Then, when conditions and sensor resistance change, the amount of current flowing back to the computer also changes. The reference voltage is needed so that a signal returns to the computer.

To measure reference voltage to a passive sensor, disconnect the wires leading to the sensor. Turn the ignition key on. Connect a digital voltmeter to the wires and note your reading. Typically, the open circuit

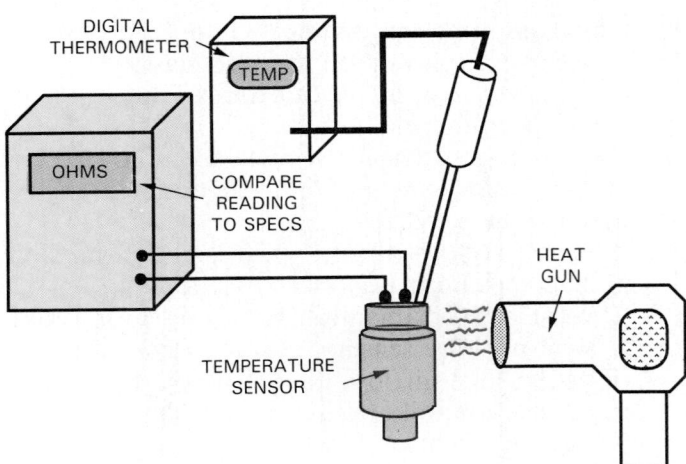

A—This is how you might test a passive temperature sensor. An ohmmeter is used to measure internal resistance. You can heat the sensor with a heat gun while measuring temperature with a digital ther-mometer. Your readings must be within specs.

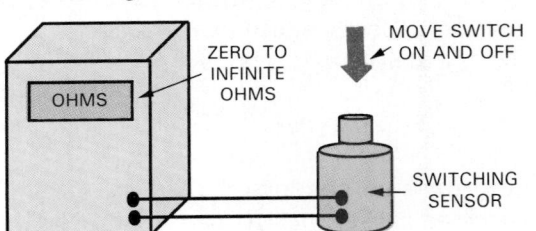

B—Switching type sensor can be tested with an ohmmeter or a high impedance test light. When switch is turned on and off, the meter or test light should show change in condition.

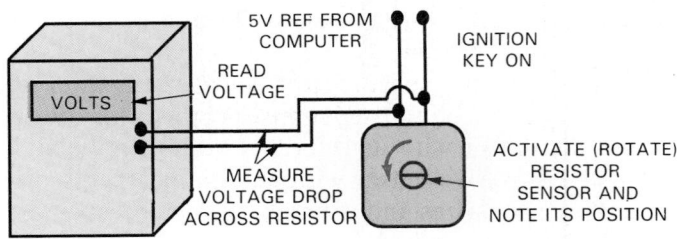

C—A voltmeter may have to be wired into circuit if specs are only given as a voltage drop. The reference voltage must still be con-nected to the sensor while testing. If not within specs, test the harness and sensor more thoroughly.

Fig. 76-3. Study three ways to test a passive type sensor.

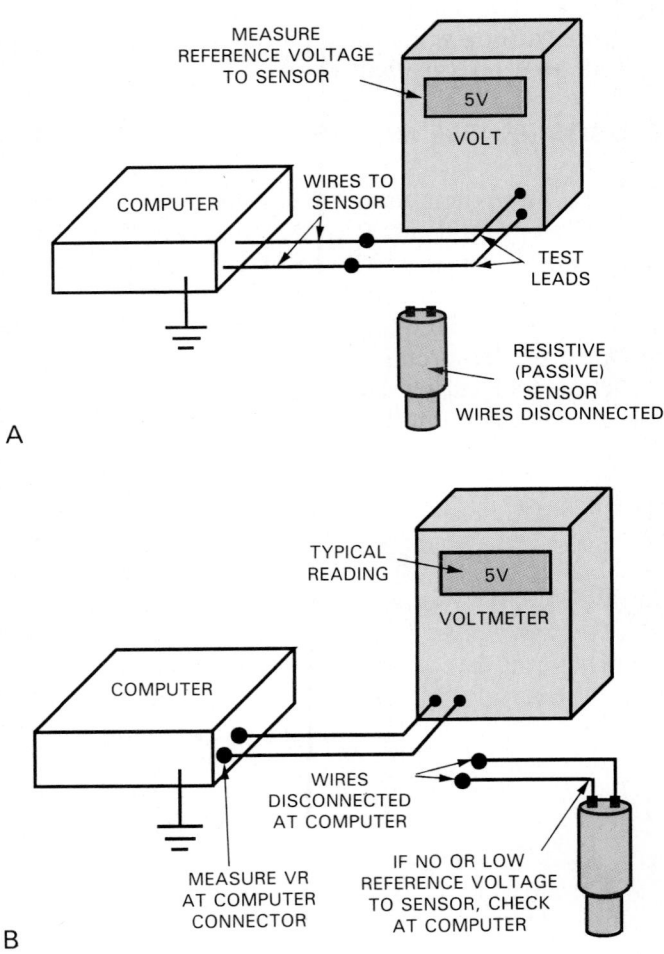

Fig. 76-4. Passive sensors rely on a computer reference voltage for proper operation. Always measure this voltage when needed. A—Use digital voltmeter to measure how much voltage is being fed to sensor. Typical reading might be 5 volts, but refer to specifications. B—If reference voltage is not cor-rect, test at the computer. If ok at computer, then a problem with wiring harness is indicated.

voltage should be about five volts. Refer to Fig. 76-4.

If the reference voltage going to the sensor is low, check the wiring harness for high resistance. Something is preventing the full reference voltage from reaching the sensor. A low reference voltage would trick the sensor and computer into analyzing false data. It is possible for the reference voltage to be too high (if a current carrying wire is shorted into the circuit or a computer malfunctions), but this is rare.

Testing active sensors

As mentioned, active sensors make their own voltage and send it back to the computer. The voltage produced by an active sensor is very low, often under one volt. This makes sensor output and wiring harness continuity very critical. One poor electrical connection can keep the low voltage from returning to the computer and a system malfunction will result.

Fig. 76-5 shows several ways to test an active sensor.

In A, an ohmmeter is connected to a common magnetic or coil type sensor. The ohmmeter will measure the resistance of the coil winding. If high or low, replace the sensor.

In B, an AC voltmeter is connected to a magnetic sensor. The trigger wheel must be rotated (engine cranked over, wheel in ABS system turned, etc.) to make the sensor generate voltage. A magnetic sensor should typically produce about 1.5 to 3 volts AC. A magnet can also be passed by a coil to make it produce a voltage.

In C, a digital voltmeter is connected to another type of active sensor (an oxygen sensor in this example). With the system running (engine running to produce exhaust), the voltmeter should show spec values. If the output voltage from the sensor is low or high, the sensor may require replacement.

Note! Whenever a sensor tests good, check the wiring leading to the sensor. Bad wiring may be blocking current flow back to the computer.

Engine speed sensor service

A *bad engine speed sensor* will usually keep an engine from running by disabling the ignition system. The engine speed sensor can be mounted in the distributor (pickup coil) or on the engine (crank position sensor) so that it can detect crankshaft rotation.

Most speed sensors are magnetic and produce a weak voltage signal. Use a VOM or scope to check the speed sensor. An ohmmeter can also be used to measure internal resistance of sensor coil windings.

An ohmmeter will produce a static (nonrunning) test of a speed sensor. Disconnect the sensor wires and measure the internal resistance of the sensor coil. Resistance specs will vary from about 250 to 1500 ohms so refer to the manual for an accurate value.

To use a digital VOM, set the meter on AC volts and connect the test leads to the sensor wires. Crank the engine and read the meter. Typically, a good speed

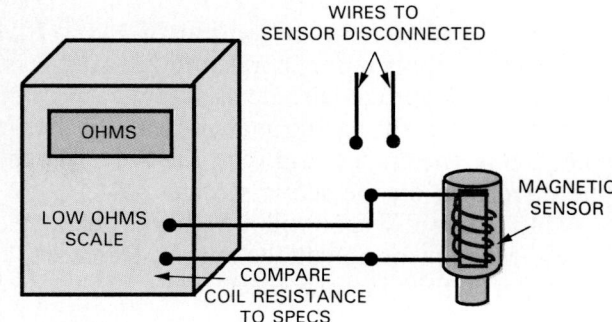

A—Ohmmeter may be recommended for measuring internal coil resistance of magnetic type sensor. Coil can be opened or shorted to ground.

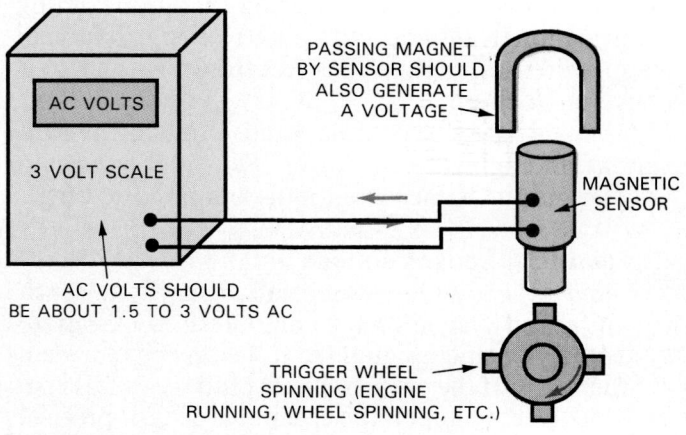

B—An AC voltmeter can also be used to check magnetic sensor while it is operating. With trigger device moving, a 1.5 to 3 volt AC signal should be generated. A permanent magnet can also be passed next to the coil to generate voltage surges and check the sensor.

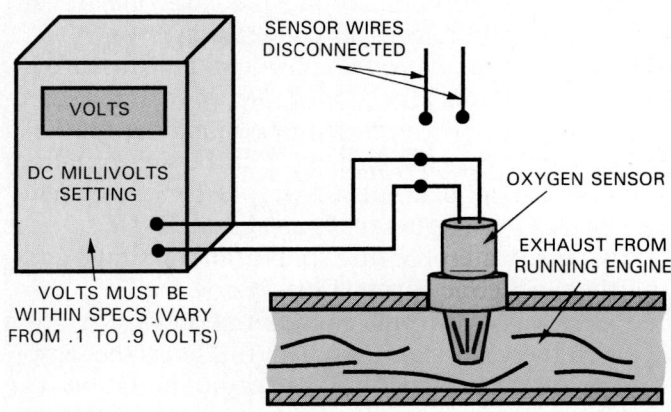

C—With some active sensors, it is best to connect a high impedance voltmeter to the sensor. With the sensor operating, you can compare its output with specs. Also make sure you test the harness leading to an active sensor since voltages are so low.

Fig. 76-5. Since an active sensor makes its own output signal, testing methods are slightly different than for passive sensors.

sensor will produce an AC output of 1.5 to 3 volts. Again, check specs before condemning a speed sensor.

An oscilloscope can also be used to measure voltage output. Connect the engine analyzer leads to the pickup coil. Crank the engine and read the AC voltage output waveform on the scope screen.

A faulty speed sensor will have high resistance, low resistance, a low or no voltage output. Replace the sensor if not within factory specs.

Vehicle speed sensor service

A *bad vehicle speed sensor* will usually reduce engine performance and fuel economy but will not normally keep the engine from running. It provides data for precise control of fuel metering, ignition timing, transmission/transaxle shift points, etc. A bad vehicle speed sensor might also affect transmission torque converter lock-up.

A vehicle speed sensor is tested in much the same way as an engine speed sensor. Sensor resistance or voltage output is measured and compared to specs.

Oxygen (O₂) sensor service

A *bad oxygen or O₂ sensor* will primarily upset the fuel injection system or the computerized carburetor system. The voltage signal from the sensor represents air-fuel ratio. If the oxygen sensor produces a false output (incorrect voltage), the computer cannot precisely control how much fuel is metered into the engine. A rich mixture or lean misfire condition could result.

Note! Some systems use TWO oxygen sensors—one before and one after the catalytic converter.

O₂ sensor contamination

Normally, an oxygen sensor is designed to last about 50,000 miles (81 000 km). However, its life can be shortened by contamination, blocked outside air, shorts, and poor electrical connections.

Oxygen sensor contamination can be caused by:
1. LEADED FUEL. Leaded fuel is the most common cause of oxygen sensor contamination. Lead coats the ceramic element and the sensor cannot produce enough voltage output for computer.
2. SILICONE. Sources are antifreeze, RTV silicone sealers, waterproofing sprays, and gasoline additives. Silicone forms a glassy coating.
3. CARBON. Carbon contamination results from rich fuel mixtures. Carbon in fuel coats the sensor.

Carbon and moderate lead contamination can sometimes be reversed. Run the engine at high speeds with a large vacuum hose (PCV hose, for example) removed and with only unleaded fuel in the tank. This will sometimes burn off light lead and most carbon deposits. The sensor may start working normally again.

O₂ sensor inspection

Also, check that the outside of the sensor and its electrical connection are free of oil, dirt, undercoating, and other deposits. If outside air cannot circulate through the oxygen sensor, the sensor will not function.

An oxygen sensor generates only a tiny voltage (an average of about .5 volts). A poor electrical connection can prevent this small voltage from reaching the computer. Always check the sensor's electrical connections.

O₂ sensor testing

Discussed earlier, most computer systems will now produce a trouble code indicating when the output from the oxygen sensor is NOT within normal parameters. This would tell you to do further tests on the oxygen sensor and its circuit.

Many computer systems have a limp-in mode. If the oxygen sensor or some other sensor fails and produces an incorrect output, the system will go into this emergency limp-in mode. A predetermined oxygen sensor voltage (.5 volts for example) will be simulated by the computer and used to keep the engine running well enough to drive in for repairs.

A digital voltmeter can also be used to test the output of an oxygen sensor. Warm the engine to full operating temperature to shift the computer system into closed loop. The sensor must be hot (about 600°F or 315°C) to operate properly. You may have to warm the engine at fast idle for up to 15 minutes with some cars. Note that a few systems can drop out of closed loop at idle.

WARNING! Only use a high impedance digital meter to measure oxygen sensor voltage. A conventional analog or low-resistance meter can draw too much current and damage the O₂ sensor.

Unplug the sensor leads and connect a digital voltmeter to the oxygen sensor.

O₂ sensor output voltage

Oxygen sensor output voltage should cycle up and down from about .4 volts (400 mV) to .7 volts (700 mV). A .4 volt or low reading would show a lean air-fuel ratio and a .7 volt or high reading would show a richer condition. A high or low reading does not always mean the O₂ sensor is bad. Another problem (leaking or clogged fuel injector, for example) could make the sensor read high or low.

A quick test to see if the oxygen sensor reacts to a change in air-fuel mixture is to pull off a large vacuum hose, like to the PCV valve. This extra air should make the oxygen sensor try to richen the fuel mixture and compensate for the air leak (lean condition). The output voltage should then go DOWN (to about .3 or .4 volts), to signal a need for more fuel to adjust for the vacuum leak or extra air.

When the engine throttle is snapped open and closed, O₂ sensor output should also cycle up and down to show the change in air-fuel mixture.

If you block the air inlet at the air cleaner or inject propane gas into the air inlet (creating a rich mixture), the oxygen sensor voltage should INCREASE (go up to about .8 to .9 volts). It should try to signal the computer that too much fuel, or not enough air, is entering the combustion chambers.

If the oxygen sensor voltage does not change properly as you simulate rich and lean air-fuel ratios, the oxygen sensor is faulty. You might try running the engine at high speed, with a large vacuum hose removed, to clean off light lead or carbon contamination.

A faulty oxygen sensor will usually be locked at one voltage level and will not cycle voltage up and down. It also may not produce enough voltage.

Testing O₂ sensor circuit

If the oxygen sensor has normal voltage, you should check the circuit leading to the sensor. Measure the resistance of the wires leading to the oxygen sensor. You can use long test leads. You can also ground one end of the sensor wire and check it for continuity at the other end.

Oxygen sensor replacement

Disconnect the negative battery cable. Then, separate the sensor from the wiring harness by unplugging the connector. Never pull on the wires themselves, as damage may result.

The oxygen sensor may have a permanently attached pigtail. Never attempt to remove it. Use a wrench to unscrew the sensor. Inspect its condition. Some sensors may be difficult to remove at temperatures below 120°F. Use care to avoid thread damage.

Follow these rules when replacing an oxygen sensor:
1. Do NOT touch the sensor element with anything (water, solvents, etc.)
2. Coat oxygen sensor threads before installation with anti-seize compound to prevent seizure and thread damage.
3. Do NOT use silicone-based sealers on or around exhaust system components. Use only low volatile silicone sealers sparingly on engine components. The PCV system can draw silicone fumes into engine intake manifold and over O₂ sensor.
4. Hand start sensor to prevent cross threading.
5. Do NOT overtighten the O₂ sensor. It could be damaged.
6. Make sure outside vents are clear so that air can circulate through the sensor.
7. Make sure wiring is reconnected securely to sensor.
8. If sensor checks out good, check continuity of wiring between sensor and computer.
9. Check oxygen sensor output and fuel system operation after installing sensor.
10. Repair any engine oil leaks that might contaminate new oxygen sensor right away.

Reading oxygen sensor

To *read an oxygen sensor,* inspect the color of the sensor's tip.

1. A LIGHT GREY TIP is normal for an oxygen sensor.
2. A WHITE SENSOR TIP might indicate a lean mixture or silicone contamination. Sensor must usually be replaced.
3. A TAN SENSOR TIP could be lead contamination. It can sometimes be cleaned away but a new sensor is usually needed.
4. A BLACK SENSOR TIP normally indicates a rich mixture and carbon contamination which can sometimes be cleaned after correcting the cause.

Note that some manufacturers recommend OXYGEN SENSOR REPLACEMENT after only 12,000 miles (19 308 km) when the sensor is removed. Therefore, the O₂ sensor is normally replaced with a new one when unscrewed from the exhaust system. Reading an oxygen sensor can indicate fuel system problems, silicone contamination, leaded fuel in the tank, and other troubles.

Manifold pressure sensor service

A *bad manifold pressure sensor* can affect the air-fuel ratio when the engine accelerates and decelerates. It serves the same basic function as a power valve in a carburetor. It senses engine vacuum to signal when more fuel is needed under a load or when gaining speed. It might also have some effect on ignition timing and a few other computer outputs.

To test a manifold pressure sensor, measure sensor circuit voltage or sensor resistance while applying vacuum to the unit. Use a vacuum pump on the vacuum fitting of the sensor. Apply spec vacuum levels while measuring the output of the MAP sensor.

Some manuals instruct you to measure sensor voltage at a specified test terminal. Others might have you disconnect the wires from the sensor and compare ohmmeter readings to specs.

In any case, sensor values must be within limits at the various vacuum levels. If testing at the test terminal, check the wiring harness before condemning the sensor. A poor connection or short could upset a reference voltage flowing to the sensor.

Throttle position sensor service

A *bad throttle position sensor* (TPS) can affect fuel metering, ignition timing, and other computer outputs. It can also trip several trouble codes on some systems and can be a frequent cause of problems. Many throttle position switches uses contact points or variable resistors that can wear and fail.

A throttle position sensor is comparable to a carburetor accelerator pump and metering rod. It signals the computer when the gas pedal is depressed to different positions for acceleration, deceleration, idle, cruise, and full power. It can cause a wide range of performance problems. If shorted, it might make the fuel mixture too rich or, if open, too lean.

The throttle position sensor can sometimes be tested

at a special tester terminal in the wiring harness. Some manuals say you should measure voltage drops across the sensor at specified throttle positions. A reference voltage is fed to the sensor by the computer.

Many manuals also recommend checking the resistance of the throttle position sensor at different throttle openings. The manual might have you measure ohms at idle, half throttle, and full throttle. If resistance is within specs, check the wiring leading to the TPS.

Throttle position sensor removal

To remove many throttle position sensors, you must file or grind off stakes (small welds) on the sensor screws. You might also have to drill into the screws from the bottom of the throttle body assembly. This will let you turn and remove the screws and TPS. Refer to the service manual for details.

Throttle position sensor adjustment

Some throttle position sensors must be adjusted; some cannot be adjusted. Many are mounted so that they can be rotated on the carburetor or throttle body. Either a special tester or an ohmmeter is commonly used to adjust a throttle position sensor.

Basically, you must measure sensor resistance or note tester output with the throttle at specific positions. You may have to insert a feeler gauge under the throttle lever, or have the throttle plates at curb idle, for example. With the throttle plates at the correct angle, the TPS should trigger the tester or show a specified ohms value. If an adjustment is needed and possible, loosen the sensor mounting screws. Rotate the TPS until the correct ohms reading is obtained. Then, tighten the mounting screws and recheck the meter reading.

Idle switch service

A *bad idle switch* can fail to signal the computer when the engine is at curb idle. It can affect idle fuel mixture and ignition timing slightly.

An ohmmeter is commonly recommended to test the idle switch. Generally, the switch should open and close as the throttle lever is opened and closed. If not, the switch has failed and must be replaced.

Coolant sensor service

A *bad coolant sensor* can also affect air-fuel ratio and ignition timing by not accurately informing the computer of the engine operating temperature. The coolant sensor serves a similar function to a carburetor choke; it richens the mixture when cold and leans the mixture when hot. If open, the coolant sensor might affect cold engine driveability. If shorted, it might affect warm engine driveability.

An ohmmeter is commonly used to measure coolant sensor resistance when cold and when hot. The service manual will give a chart giving ohms readings for specific temperatures.

You can test the sensor while still in the engine by checking ohms when the engine is cold and after is warms. However, a more precise method is to touch a digital pyrometer (thermometer) to the sensor to get a reading of its operating temperature. This will let you compare sensor temperature and resistance readings with exact specs. Different ohms specs are given for different temperatures.

Note that temperature sensor operation and ratings can vary. When purchasing a new temperature sensor, or any sensor, make sure you have the RIGHT ONE. If you install the wrong sensor, it will upset the operation of the computer system.

When replacing a coolant sensor, use a deep socket or six-point wrench to unscrew the old unit. You might want to coat the sensor threads with approved sealer. Then, hand start and tighten the sensor in the engine. Do not overtighten the coolant sensor or it could bottom out in the engine and be ruined.

Thermal-vacuum switch service

A *bad thermal-vacuum switch* will fail to control vacuum to another device and can cause a wide range of symptoms depending upon its function. The unit should pass or block vacuum with a change in temperature. The service manual will explain specific temperatures and switch points.

Air temperature sensor service

A *bad air temperature sensor* will usually not have a pronounced effect on vehicle operation. It normally allows the computer system to make fine adjustments of air-fuel ratio and timing with changes in outside air temperature. If the sensor fails, it will normally trigger a self-diagnosis code and you would know to test the sensor and its circuit.

An ohmmeter is commonly recommended for checking an air temperature sensor. As with a coolant sensor, the unit is frequently a thermistor that changes internal resistance with temperature. The sensor should have spec ohms for certain temperatures.

Airflow sensor service

A *bad airflow sensor* will normally cause the system to go into limp-in mode, as will several other sensors. If shorted or opened, the computer will begin to operate on preprogrammed values. The car will perform poorly and get lower fuel economy.

Since there are various types of airflow sensors, you must refer to the shop manual for exact procedures. Many manufacturers have you use an ohmmeter to check the airflow sensor when it is a variable resistance type. Others have integrated circuits. Special testing methods are required to prevent sensor damage.

If faulty, you must remove and replace the airflow sensor. During replacement, make sure that you have the correct unit. Also, tighten all fittings carefully. An AIR LEAK after the airflow sensor will upset its operation, and can trigger trouble codes.

Knock sensor service

A *bad knock sensor* can upset ignition timing and affect turbocharger boost pressure. It is used to detect abnormal combustion or ping. When it "hears" pinging or knocking, it will retard ignition timing or lower turbo boost with the turbo wastegate. Many computers will store a trouble code if there is a potential problem with the knock sensor.

To check a knock sensor, tap on the running engine, possibly on a bracket, with a wrench or small hammer. This will simulate pinging or knocking and should make the computer retard the ignition timing. The light taps should make the engine speed drop slightly. You might need to prop open the throttle to increase engine speed slightly so timing is advanced and will retard.

If tapping on the engine has no effect on timing and engine speed, you can check it with a VOM. Refer to the manual for recommendations. Remember to check the wiring leading to the knock sensor before removing or replacing the sensor!

ACTUATOR SERVICE

Actuator service involves testing solenoids, servo motors, displays, and other output devices for possible electrical and mechanical problems. Like sensors, if an actuator fails to function properly, the computer cannot control the vehicle system.

Testing actuators

Since actuators are simply relays, solenoids, and motors, they are fairly easy to test. Fig. 76-6 shows several ways to test actuators.

In A, a source of voltage has been connected to a servo motor. The wiring harness to the motor has been disconnected. Jumper wires feed current directly to the motor. This is a simple way to check the operation of a servo motor. If the motor begins to function with an external voltage source, you would know to test the wire harness leading to the motor.

In B, a power supply is being used to check a solenoid. When jumper wires are connected to the car battery and to the solenoid, the solenoid should operate. If the solenoid tests good, you should check the voltage coming to the solenoid through its harness.

In C, you can see how to test a relay type actuator. Check for power entering the relay and for output voltage leaving the relay. It is possible that voltage is applied to the relay but the relay points are not sending voltage out to the controlled device.

An ohmmeter can also be used to test actuators. You can use the meter to measure the internal resistance of the unit. By comparing ohms readings to specs, you can find out if the actuator must be replaced.

Idle speed motor service

A *bad idle speed motor* may not be able to maintain the correct engine idle speed. Engine idle speed

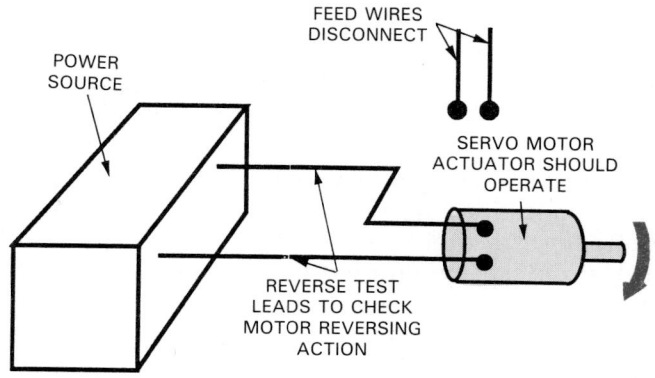

A—Voltage can be jumped to a motor type actuator. The actuator should function when energized by the jumper wires. Motor direction should reverse when test leads are reversed.

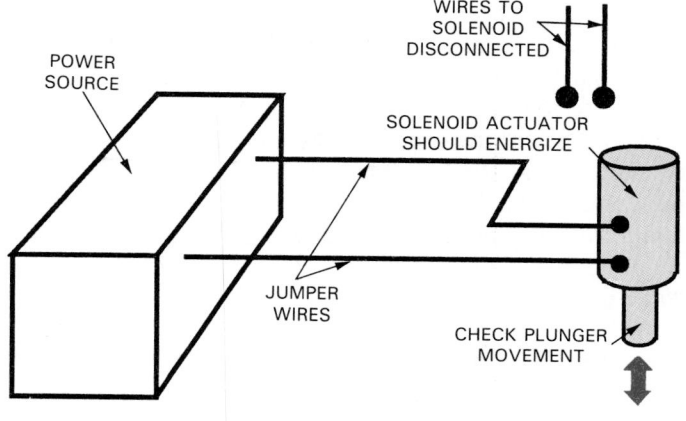

B—A similar testing method can be used for a solenoid type actuator. The solenoid should activate when the jumpers are connected to its terminals.

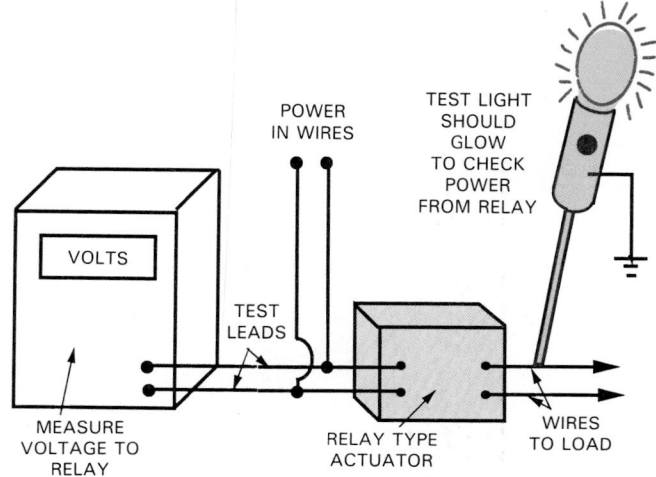

C—A relay is slightly more complex to test. You must make sure that there is an output when voltage is supplied to its input terminals. You can use a voltmeter or a high impedance test light.

Fig. 76-6. Actuator testing is straight forward; it is like testing a conventional motor, relay, or solenoid.

may be too low or too high for conditions. The servo motor could have shorted windings, open windings, bad internal parts, or other problems.

To check an idle speed motor, jump battery voltage to specific terminals on the servo motor. This should make the idle speed motor plunger retract and extend as the connections are reversed. A faulty motor will usually not function.

If the idle speed motor works when jumped to battery voltage, check wiring leading to motor. Wiring harness could have an open or short. A computer or relay problem could also prevent motor operation.

Idle air control valve service

A *bad idle air control valve* will upset engine idle speed like a bad idle speed motor. It uses solenoid action to open and close an air passage bypassing the throttle plates. In this way, it can increase or decrease engine idle rpm. If it fails, engine rpm will be constant and may not increase with a cold engine or decrease as the engine warms to operating temperature.

To check the idle air control valve, jump battery voltage to the windings. This should trigger the solenoid and change engine speed. If the engine speed does not change, check for blockage in the passage at the idle air control valve before replacing the unit. An ohmmeter may also be recommended to check the windings.

MORE INFORMATION

NOTE! For information on testing other actuators, refer to the index in this textbook. You can find instructions on testing fuel injectors, glow plugs, and more specialized actuators.

The service of other actuators is similar to those just discussed. A solenoid for a door latch is constructed like a solenoid in a fuel injector or other solenoid type actuator. Servo motor actuators are also similar to

other motors, as in fuel pumps. Remember to refer to the service manual for testing and replacement details.

COMPUTER SERVICE

Computer service usually involves a few tests, and computer replacement if needed. The computer is usually one of the last components to be tested and suspected. Only after all other potential sources of trouble have been eliminated, is the computer suspected of being the problem source. It is sometimes possible for an integrated circuit, transistor, or other electronic part in the computer to fail and upset system operation.

Radiation interference

Radiation interference can cause a computer to malfunction. For example, induced voltage from a loose spark plug wire could enter a sensor wire. This unwanted voltage can then enter the computer as false data. Numerous computer malfunctions or false outputs can then be caused, Fig. 76-7.

A small, inexpensive transistor radio can be used to find induced or radiated voltage sources. Turn the radio on but do not tune it to a station. Then move the radio around the engine compartment and under the dash with the engine running. If the noise (static) is induced into the radio, a popping or cracking noise will be produced by the transistor radio. You can also use a car antenna cable and the car radio as a "noise sniffer."

To correct a radiation problem affecting the computer, you must stop the source of the radiation (fix bad spark plug wire, use suppressing condensor, etc.) or shield the computer wiring from the radiation (wrap sensor wire with foil-type tape, for example).

Measuring computer output

A *computer output* can be a reference voltage to a sensor, current flow or supply voltage to operate an

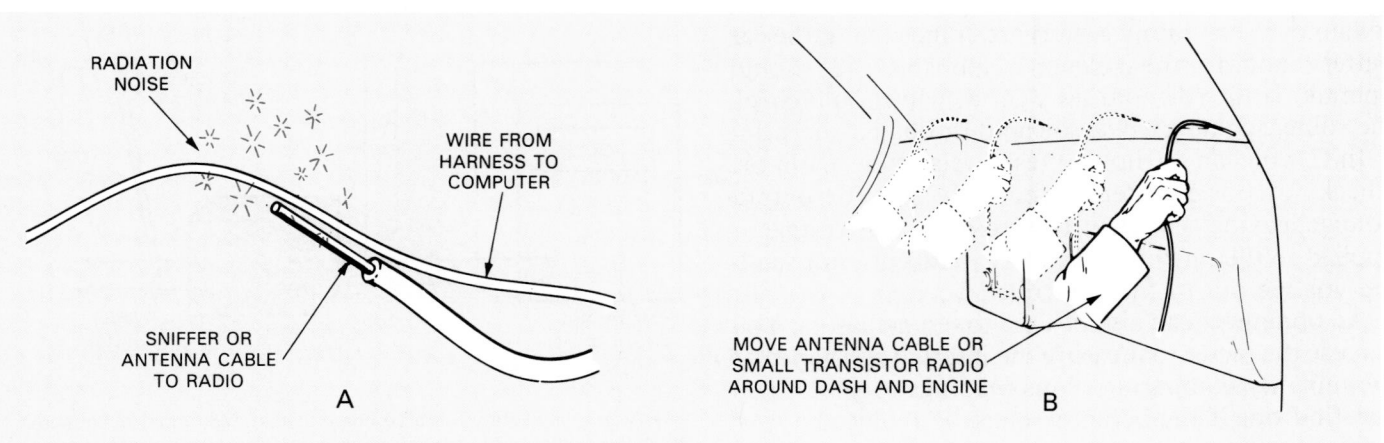

Fig. 76-7. A—Radiation interference can be caused by ignition secondary voltage, leaking diode in alternator, and other sources of voltage spikes or magnetic field. B—A cheap transistor radio or an extra antenna cable connected to car's radio will "listen" or "sniff" for source of interference. Radiation can upset operation of computer and car radio.   (GM)

actuator, or an electronic control module, or a dwell signal to open and close a mixture solenoid or injector.

Use a voltmeter to make sure the correct reference voltage is being sent to a sensor. Most computers produce a reference voltage of about five volts. If not correct, check the wiring before condemning the computer. You can also measure voltage to make sure the correct voltage output is being fed to the actuators.

Again, always refer to service manual for exact procedures for testing a computer system. One wrong electrical connection can "fry" electronic components.

Saving memory

Saving memory can be done by connecting a small battery (such as a 9V transistor radio battery) across the two battery cables BEFORE the car battery is disconnected. This will provide enough voltage to keep the computer memories alive. You are still disconnecting the large car battery for safety. The smaller battery cannot produce enough current to cause an electrical fire or operate the starting system.

Computer replacement

When removing a computer, the ignition key should be off and car battery disconnected. This will prevent any voltage spike from possibly damaging components when the harness connectors are pulled apart. Unplug the computer connectors and unbolt the brackets holding the computer in place.

Identification information is usually stamped or printed on the computer. Use this data and the year, make, and model of car to order the correct replacement computer. The VIN (vehicle identification number) may be helpful, as well.

PROM service

Most computers use the old *PROM* (memory chip) during computer replacement, since it stores data for the specific make and model car. You must commonly remove the old PROM and install it in the new computer.

Remove the cover over the PROM. Then, use a PROM tool to grasp and pull the chip out of its socket. Avoid touching the PROM with your fingers because the body oils on your hand could affect operation.

Before installing the old PROM in the new computer, check that the pins (terminals) are straight. Check the reference mark on the PROM (an indentation or other marking to show how to reinstall the unit). Make sure that the PROM has the correct part number for the car.

To install the PROM, place the pins into the socket with the reference mark correctly positioned. Then, use a blunt tool, like a wooden dowel, to carefully press the PROM down into the computer. Press on each corner to make sure the pins are fully seated in their sockets.

Most PROMs use a *carrier,* which is a plastic part that surrounds the outside of the integrated circuit chip.

You must use a blunt tool to push the PROM so that its top is flush with the top of the carrier. This will ready the PROM for installation into the computer. Install the carrier and PROM in the computer with the reference mark pointing properly. First press down on the carrier only. Then, press down on the center of the PROM with a blunt tool. Press on the corners until the PROM is fully seated.

Install the access cover and then install computer into its mounts. Connect the connectors to the computer. Reconnect the car battery, turn on the ignition, and activate self-diagnostics. Make sure no trouble codes are set as a check of the computer and PROM. A code might be set if the PROM is not fully seated or a pin is bent over, for example.

NOTE! If you install a PROM backwards, it will usually require replacement because of physical damage.

Up-date PROMs

An *up-date PROM* is a modified integrated circuit

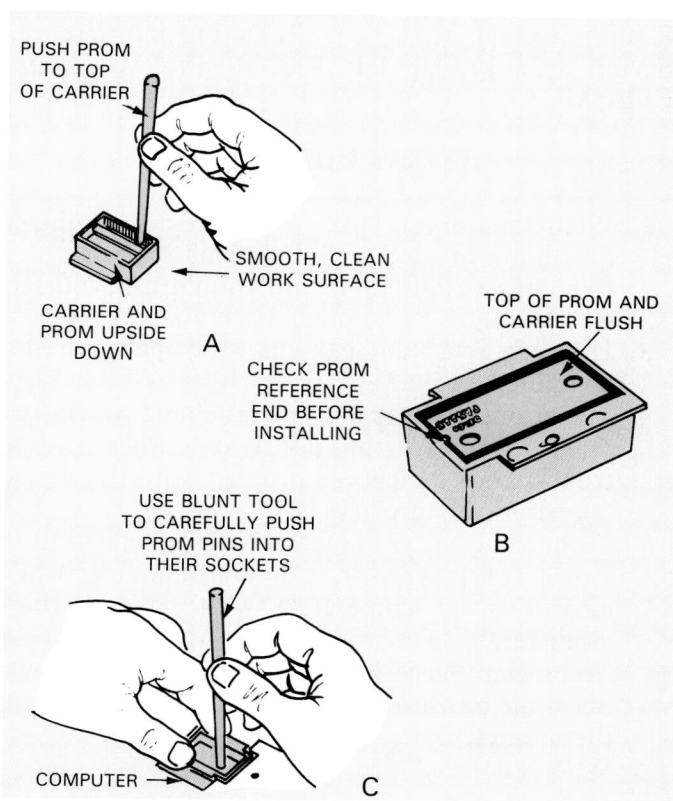

Fig. 76-8. *Most PROMs use a carrier, which is a plastic case around IC chip. A—Before installing chip in new computer, use a blunt tool to push top of chip flush with top of carrier. Pins should be sticking up and straight. B—Make sure reference mark is positioned correctly before installation. If you install PROM backwards, it will normally be ruined. PROM and carrier are flush on top. C—Touching only carrier, position PROM pins into socket in computer. Use blunt tool or small wooden dowel to carefully push PROM into its socket. Push lightly on each corner until fully seated. Do not press too hard.* (General Motors)

used to improve a car's driveability. They are produced by the auto manufacturer to correct problems or improve the performance of the engine and its related systems. The old PROM is simply popped out of the computer and replaced with the up-date PROM, Fig. 76-8.

Check with the auto dealership to find out if up-date PROMs are available for specific makes and models of cars. PROMs can prevent problems like surging, long cranking periods, hot start troubles, etc.

In the near future, up-date PROMs will probably give way to EPROMs, which can be reprogrammed to correct problems or improve performance.

NOTE! *Aftermarket PROMs* can increase engine power by richening the fuel mixture and advancing ignition timing. However, they also increase exhaust emissions and can make a car fail an emissions test or inspection. Avoid installing aftermarket PROMs in cars to be operated on city streets.

KNOW THESE TERMS

Kiss, Basic circuit problem, Intermittent problem, Passive sensor, Active sensor, Reference voltage, Reading oxygen sensor tip, Radiation interference, Saving memory, Up-date PROM, PROM carrier, EPROM.

REVIEW QUESTIONS

1. What should you look for during a preliminary inspection of a computer system?
2. Explain five questions you should ask yourself when analyzing computer system problems.
3. How can a vacuum leak upset the operation of a computer system?
4. Symptoms indicate a problem related to temperature. The engine runs poorly only when cold. A trouble code indicates a problem with the engine temperature sensor.
   Technician A says to measure engine temperature sensor resistance with a digital ohmmeter while measuring its temperature with a digital thermometer.
   Technician B says to measure its AC voltage output while measuring its temperature with a digital thermometer.
   Who is correct?
   a. Technician A
   b. Technician B
   c. Both A and B
   d. Neither A nor B
5. How do you check sensor reference voltage?
6. Explain three ways to test an active sensor.
7. Oxygen sensors are normally designed to last about _____ miles or _____ km.
8. A faulty oxygen sensor will usually be locked at _____ _____ _____ _____ and will NOT _____.
9. How do you adjust a throttle position sensor?
10. An engine coolant temperature sensor serves the same purpose as a carburetor choke; it _____ the fuel mixture when cold.
11. How can you check a knock sensor?
12. Describe three ways to test an actuator.
13. Induced voltage from a bad spark plug wire will often cause:
    a. Computer PROM failure.
    b. Computer RAM failure.
    c. Radiation interference.
    d. None of the above.
    e. All of the above.
14. How do you save computer memory?
15. A car engine is performing poorly. No trouble codes could be retrieved. A visual inspection found nothing wrong.
    Technician A says to check with the dealer or manufacturer because an up-date prom may be available to correct the problem.
    Technician B says to use a scanner to check all electrical parameters and compare them to specs.
    Who is correct?
    a. Technician A
    b. Technician B
    c. Both A and B
    d. Neither A nor B

ACTIVITIES FOR CHAPTER 76

1. Describe and sketch the procedure you would use to test a temperature sensor for proper operation.
2. Demonstrate two methods of checking a knock sensor—with a VOM, and by manual tapping.
3. Obtain an unserviceable vehicle computer from a junkyard or other source, and use it to practice removing and replacing the PROM.

Appendix A

Recycling/Disposal of Auto Shop Fluids and Chemicals

Automotive maintenance may generate hazardous wastes that come under the requirements of the Resource Conservation and Recovery Act. This federal Act covers businesses that generate, transport, and manage hazardous wastes. Any business that maintains or repairs vehicles, heavy equipment, or farm equipment comes under the classification of vehicle maintenance.

Vehicle maintenance fluid and solid wastes would include:
- Used motor oil (combustible and may contain toxic chemicals).
- Other discarded lubricants such as transmission and differential fluids (like motor oil, may contain toxic chemicals).
- Used parts cleaners and degreasers that are contaminated from parts cleaning operations.
- Carburetor cleaners (contain flammable or combustible liquids).
- Rust removers (may contain strong acid or alkaline solutions).
- Paint thinners or reducers (may be ignitable or contain toxic additives).
- Worn out batteries (lead and toxic chemicals).
- Tires and catalytic converters.

(See chart: Hazardous Wastes Developed from Typical Vehicle Maintenance Operations, next page.)

Repair or maintenance facilities (such as service stations, automotive dealerships, or independent auto repair garages) that generate 220 lb. (100 kg) of hazardous waste monthly must fill out a Uniform Hazardous Waste Manifest before shipping the wastes off the property. The Manifest must list the proper Department of Transportation (DOT) shipping descriptions for a number of wastes. Tables listing these descriptions are available from each state's hazardous waste management agency or a Regional EPA office.

However, EPA regulations also say that no Manifest is needed for used oil or acid batteries if they are sent off for recycling. In such cases, the material is not regarded as hazardous. Your state might have its own requirements; check with your state hazardous waste management agency.

Unless recycled for scrap metal, used oil filters are considered hazardous waste. If not recycled they must be listed on the monthly Manifest as hazardous. Before disposal, filters should be gravity drained so that they do not contain free-flowing oil. Store them uncrushed in a closed, labeled container for pickup by a recycler.

Automotive coolants and refrigerants

Antifreeze has been reclassified as a hazardous waste due to heavy metal and chlorinated solvents that it picks up circulating through cooling systems. It should never be mixed with used oil. The entire mixture would then be classified as a hazardous waste, even though the used oil may not be, under federal regulations. (Some states classify used oil as a hazardous waste).

Regulations require that spent antifreeze solutions be collected by a registered hazardous waste hauler. Several major companies offer pick-up and recycling services.

Refrigerants, such as R-12, removed from automotive air conditioning systems during servicing, should not be vented to the atmosphere. State regulations are beginning to require that they be recovered and recycled. See Fig. A-1. Recovery systems are available for a cost of about $3500.

Other automotive recyclables

Other recyclable materials that have been removed from service during maintenance and repair of vehicles include:
- Catalytic converters, which contain platinum.
- Worn tires which can be sold to a retreader (if the carcass is sound) or to a shredder. Shredded rubber is an ingredient in road resurfacing materials and other products that give the rubber a second use.

**Table
Hazardous Wastes
Developed From Typical
Vehicle Maintenance Operations**

Process/Operation	Materials Used	Typical Material Ingredient	General Types of Waste Generated
Degreasing	Degreasers (gunk), carburetor cleaners, engine cleaners, solvents, acids/alkalies, cleaning fluids	Petroleum distillates, aromatic hydrocarbons, mineral spirits, benzene, toluene, petroleum naphtha	Acid/alkaline wastes Spent Solvents Ignitable wastes Toxic wastes
Rust Removal	Naval jelly, strong acids, strong alkalies	Phosphoric acid, hydrochloric acid, hydrofluoric acid, sodium hydroxide	Acid/alkaline wastes
Paint Preparation	Paint thinners, enamel reducers, white spirits	Alcohols, petroleum distillates, oxygenated solvents, mineral spirits, ketones	Paint wastes Spent solvents Ignitable wastes Toxic wastes
Painting	Enamels, lacquers, epoxies, alkyds, acrylics, primers, solvents	Acetone, toluene, benzene, petroleum distillates, epoxy ester resins, methylene chloride, xylene, VM&P naphtha, aromatic hydrocarbons, methyl isobutyl, ketones	Paint wastes Spent solvents Ignitable wastes Toxic wastes
Spray Booth, Spray Guns, and Brush Cleaning	Paint thinners, enamel reducers, solvents, white spirits	Ketones, alcohols, toluene, acetone, isopropyl alcohol, petroleum distillates, mineral spirits	Paint wastes Spent solvents Toxic wastes
Paint Removal	Solvents, paint thinners, enamel reducers, white spirits	Acetone, toluene, petroleum distillates, methanol, methylene chloride, isopropyl alcohol, mineral spirits, alcohols, ketones, other oxygenated solvents	Paint wastes Spent solvents Toxic wastes
Tank Cleanout	Solvents or cleaners to wash out tanks, residues	Solvents, petroleum products in tanks	Tank draws containing toxic residues
Installing Lead-Acid Batteries	Used batteries of cars, trucks, boats, motorcycles, and other vehicles	Lead dross	Acid/alkaline wastes Batteries (lead-acid)

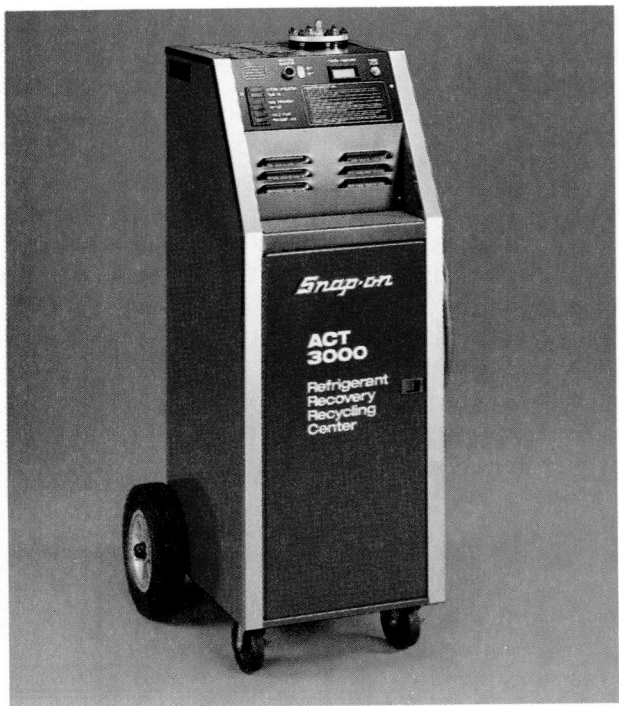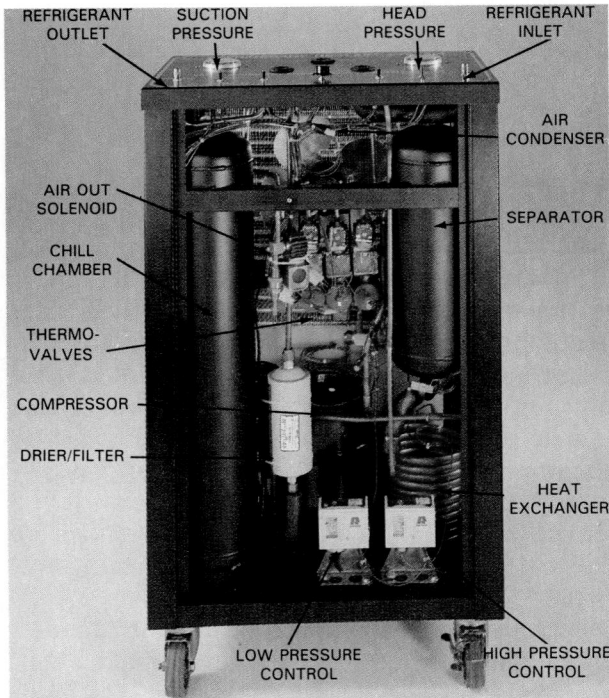

Fig. A-1. Systems are now available for recovery, cleaning, and recycling of air conditioning refrigerants which can no more be exhausted to the atmosphere. Left. Front view of a refrigerant recovery system. It will remove, filter, and ready used refrigerant for installation in another vehicle. (Snap-On Tools) Right. "Back-of-the-cabinet" view of another "refrigerant reclaim system."
(Van Steenburgh Engineering Laboratories, Inc.)

Appendix B

Using Basic Mathematics

Automotive technicians use mathematics during servicing and repair of vehicles. They must be familiar with conventional measurement systems. In addition, they must understand the metric system of measurement since metric sizes and measurements are often used in the automotive field. There are four basic math operations: addition, subtraction, multiplication, and division.

Addition

Addition is the combining of two or more numbers to find the total quantity or number of anything. The result of the addition process is called the *sum* or the *total*. A plus (+) sign is sometimes used to indicate that the numbers are to be added. Numbers to be added may be written two ways:

In a string: $5 + 3 + 4 = 12$ (total)

In a column:
$$\begin{array}{r} 5 \\ 3 \\ +4 \\ \hline 12 \text{ (total)} \end{array}$$

When there are large numbers or a long series of numbers, it is best to write them in columns so sums of 10 and over can be carried to the next column. Always start adding from the right-hand column so that sums exceeding 9 can be carried from that column to the next column to the left:

122	First, add the	- - 2	Since the total is 19,
804	right-hand column	- - 4	place the "9" under-
644		- - 4	neath the right-
+829		- - 9	hand column and
		9	add the "1" to the
			next column

		1		
Add up the 2nd	- 22	Now, add up the	122
column including	- 04	next column to the	804
the number carried	- 44	left and place the	644
over	- 29	sum below the	829
	99	column (Answer is	2399
		2399.)	

Addition is used, for example, in adding up the cost of parts or the items in a customer's bill.

Subtraction

Subtraction is taking away a certain quantity from another number. The amount that is left after subtracting is called the *remainder* or *difference*. The minus (−) sign indicates that the number to the right of it is to be subtracted. Subtraction problems might be written in two ways. For example:

In a string: $495 - 125 = 370$

In a column:
$$\begin{array}{r} 495 \\ -125 \\ \hline 370 \text{ (remainder)} \end{array}$$

Subtraction might be used in determining a customer's bill, but it might also be used by the technician, for example, to check the deductions made on a paycheck for taxes and social security. Suppose that a customer's bill totaled $253, but there had been a $25 deposit before the work was done. To determine the amount due, you would subtract ($253 − $25).

Or: $\begin{array}{r} \$253 \\ -25 \\ \hline \$228 \end{array}$ (Notice that we had to borrow 10 from the second column, since 5 cannot be subtracted from 3.)

Division and multiplication

To find out how many times one number is contained in another, we use *division*. The divide (÷) sign indicates that one number is to be divided by another. The number being divided is called the *dividend*. The number a dividend is divided by is called the *divisor*. The answer is called the *quotient*. A division problem can be written one of three ways. For example:

In a string: $860 \div 10 = 86$ (quotient)

Or: $10\overline{)860}$ 86 (quotient)

Or: $\frac{860}{10} = 86$ (quotient)

Division problems occur frequently in an automotive repair facility. For example, suppose that 10 fuel pumps had been ordered and placed in stock and the total bill came to $860. What is the cost of each to the shop?

This is found by dividing ($860 ÷ 10 = $86). This information plus a percentage for profit would determine what the customer would be charged for the pump. When dividing, not all answers come out to full numbers. In such cases, the decimal point is placed to the right of the last number of the dividend and a decimal point is also placed in the answer when the zero to the right of the decimal point is brought down. One or more zeros may be added to the dividend, depending on how many places the decimal number is carried out. For example: suppose that the cost of the fuel pumps in the previous example came to $865 instead of $860.

$$\begin{array}{r} 86.50 \text{ (quotient—each pump cost \$86.50)} \\ 10\overline{)865.00} \\ \underline{80} \\ 65 \\ \underline{60} \\ 50 \\ \underline{50} \\ 0 \end{array}$$

Multiplication is a shortcut for adding the same number over and over. Suppose that the number 15 were to be added 12 times: One could set up the problem as $15 + 15 + 15 + 15 + 15$, and so on, until there were 12 additions. It is faster, however, to multiply 15 once by 12. The multiplication ($\times$) sign indicates numbers are to be multiplied. The result is called the *product*. Multiplication problems can be written two ways.

In a string: $15 \times 12 = 180$ (product)

In a column:
$$\begin{array}{r} 15 \\ \times 12 \\ \hline 180 \text{ (product)} \end{array}$$

Multiplication is often useful in the automotive field. For example, suppose that a customer purchased four new tires. The tires cost $104 each. Rather than adding each tire individually it is easier to multiply

$$\$104 \times 4 = \$416 \text{ or } \begin{array}{r} 104 \\ \times 4 \\ \hline 416 \end{array}$$

Numbers of more than one digit used as multipliers are multiplied one digit at a time. The products for each multiplication are stacked and then added together. Suppose that the customer in the previous example purchased 41 tires:

$$\begin{array}{r} 104 \\ \times 41 \\ \hline 104 \\ 416 \\ \hline 4264 \text{ (product)} \end{array}$$

Note that the second product (416) is shifted one column to the left. This is done because the multiplier is actually 40, not 4. To help make this clear, mentally place a 0 after the 6 in the second product (104 $\times$ 40 = 4160).

Decimal fractions and fractions

Decimal fractions and fractions are less than whole numbers. Decimal fractions are tenths, hundredths, thousandths, etc., of a whole number or combinations of these values.

Fractions are written as two numbers, one over the other, or beside the other:

$\dfrac{4}{5}$ or 4/5 (The fraction is read as "four-fifths.")

The number below the line or after the slash is called the *denominator*. This number tells how many parts the whole is divided into; the number above the line or ahead of the slash tells how many parts are present in the fraction. This number is called the *numerator*. When reading a fraction, the top or first number is always read first; thus, read 12/32 as "twelve thirty-secondths."

Decimal fractions also have a numerator and denominator. The denominator is always a multiple of 10. However, it is never written. A dot or period, called a decimal point, is used in its place. For example, 9/10 is written as .9 in decimal notation. The number of digits to the right of the decimal point tell what multiple of 10 the denominator is. Thus:

.9 or 9/10 is nine-tenths.

.09 or 9/100 is nine-hundredths.

.009 or 9/1000 is nine-thousandths, and

.0009 or 9/10,000 is nine ten-thousandths.

Since decimal fractions are easier to work with than fractions, it is common to convert fractions to decimal fractions. This is especially true in the automotive service field. Very small measurements are given in thousandths of an inch. However, wrenches are still sized in fractions for many tasks.

Decimal fractions are used for fine measurements such as the exact size of machined engine parts. Often, the technician must use a micrometer to check a dimension such as a crankshaft journal or the runout on a brake rotor.

Decimal fractions can be added, subtracted, multiplied, and divided the same as whole numbers.

There are rules that must be remembered when working with decimal numbers. The first set of rules has to do with placement of zeros.
- A zero placed to the right of a decimal does not change its value (.60 is the same as .6).
- A zero placed to the left of the decimal point does not change its value (0.6 is the same as .6).

Addition and subtraction of decimals

The rules for addition and subtraction of decimal fractions are:
- Line up the decimal points in a column.
- The decimal point in the answer must be in the same position as the decimal point in the column.
- Since some decimal fractions will have more numbers to the right of the decimal point, you may fill in with zeros on the shorter numbers. This is optional.

Example:	1.5	(could also be	1.500
	9.356	written with	9.356
	3.62	zeros in	3.620
	.96	the blanks)	0.960
	15.436		15.436

Multiplication and division of decimals

Multiplying decimal numbers is not much different from multiplying whole numbers. The rules explain how to deal with the decimal point.
- In setting up the problem, the decimal points do not need to be aligned.
- Multiply the two numbers, ignoring the decimal points.
- Count the total number of digits (places) to the right of the decimal points of both numbers. Starting from the right-hand digit, count to the left the same number of digits in the answer. Place the decimal point to the left of the last digit counted.

Dividing decimals is also similar to dividing whole numbers. Several steps are involved.
- If neither the dividend nor divisor contain decimal points, but the division does not come out even:

   Place a decimal point to the right of the last number of the dividend. Add one or more zeros after the decimal and continue dividing to the number of decimal places necessary.

$$
\begin{array}{r}
\text{(Division carried out} \\
\text{2 decimal places)}
\end{array}
$$

For example:
$$
\begin{array}{r}
7.71 \\
7\overline{)54.00} \\
\underline{49} \\
50 \\
\underline{49} \\
10 \\
\underline{7} \\
3
\end{array}
$$

- When the dividend has a decimal and the divisor does not:

   Divide as usual.

   Place a decimal point in the answer directly above the decimal point in the dividend. It will occur at the time that the division process moves past (to the right) of the decimal point.

For example:
$$
\begin{array}{r}
2.01 \\
25\overline{)50.25} \\
\underline{50} \\
02 \\
\underline{0} \\
25 \\
\underline{25} \\
0
\end{array}
$$

- When the divisor has a decimal point:

   If the dividend does not have a decimal point, add one at the far right.

   If the dividend has a decimal point, move it one place to the right for each decimal place in the divisor. Move the decimal point in the divisor accordingly to the right. Use zeros as place holders, if necessary.

   Divide as usual.

   Place a decimal point in the answer directly above the relocated decimal point in the dividend. It will occur when the division process moves to the right past the decimal point.

For example: $2.5\overline{)50.25}$
$$
\begin{array}{r}
20.1 \\
25.\overline{)502.5} \\
\underline{50} \\
02 \\
\underline{0} \\
25 \\
\underline{25} \\
0
\end{array}
$$

Appendix C

Useful Charts

DECIMAL CHART

inches fractional	decimal	inches fractional	decimal
1/64	.0156	33/64	.5156
1/32	.0312	17/32	.5312
3/64	.0469	35/64	.5469
1/16	.0625	9/16	.5625
5/64	.0781	37/64	.5781
3/32	.0938	19/32	.5938
7/64	.1094	39/64	.6094
1/8	.1250	5/8	.6250
9/64	.1406	41/64	.6406
5/32	.1562	21/32	.6562
11/64	.1719	43/64	.6719
3/16	.1875	11/16	.6875
13/64	.2031	45/64	.7031
7/32	.2188	23/32	.7188
15/64	.2344	47/64	.7344
1/4	.2500	3/4	.7500
17/64	.2656	49/64	.7656
9/32	.2812	25/32	.7812
19/64	.2969	51/64	.7969
5/16	.3125	13/16	.8125
21/64	.3281	53/64	.8281
11/32	.3438	27/32	.8438
23/64	.3594	55/64	.8594
3/8	.3750	7/8	.8750
25/64	.3906	57/64	.8906
13/32	.4062	29/32	.9062
27/64	.4219	59/64	.9219
7/16	.4375	15/16	.9375
29/64	.4531	61/64	.9531
15/32	.4688	31/32	.9688
31/64	.4844	63/64	.9844
1/2	.5000	1	1.0000

m/m	inches	m/m	inches	m/m	inches	m/m	inches	m/m	inches	m/m	inches
1	0.0394	51	2.0079	101	3.9764	151	5.9449	201	7.9134	251	9.8819
2	0.0787	52	2.0472	102	4.0157	152	5.9843	202	7.9527	252	9.9212
3	0.1181	53	2.0866	103	4.0551	153	6.0236	203	7.9921	253	9.9606
4	0.1575	54	2.1260	104	4.0945	154	6.0630	204	8.0315	254	10.0000
5	0.1969	55	2.1654	105	4.1339	155	6.1024	205	8.0709	255	10.0394
6	0.2362	56	2.2047	106	4.1732	156	6.1417	206	8.1102	256	10.0787
7	0.2756	57	2.2441	107	4.2126	157	6.1811	207	8.1496	257	10.1181
8	0.3150	58	2.2835	108	4.2520	158	6.2205	208	8.1890	258	10.1575
9	0.3543	59	2.3228	109	4.2913	159	6.2598	209	8.2283	259	10.1968
10	0.3937	60	2.3622	110	4.3307	160	6.2992	210	8.2677	260	10.2362
11	0.4331	61	2.4016	111	4.3701	161	6.3386	211	8.3071	261	10.2756
12	0.4724	62	2.4409	112	4.4094	162	6.3780	212	8.3464	262	10.3149
13	0.5118	63	2.4803	113	4.4488	163	6.4173	213	8.3858	263	10.3543
14	0.5512	64	2.5197	114	4.4882	164	6.4567	214	8.4252	264	10.3937
15	0.5906	65	2.5591	115	4.5276	165	6.4961	215	8.4646	265	10.4331
16	0.6299	66	2.5984	116	4.5669	166	6.5354	216	8.5039	266	10.4724
17	0.6693	67	2.6378	117	4.6063	167	6.5748	217	8.5433	267	10.5118
18	0.7087	68	2.6772	118	4.6457	168	6.6142	218	8.5827	268	10.5512
19	0.7480	69	2.7165	119	4.6850	169	6.6535	219	8.6220	269	10.5905
20	0.7874	70	2.7559	120	4.7244	170	6.6929	220	8.6614	270	10.6299
21	0.8268	71	2.7953	121	4.7638	171	6.7323	221	8.7008	271	10.6693
22	0.8661	72	2.8346	122	4.8031	172	6.7717	222	8.7401	272	10.7086
23	0.9055	73	2.8740	123	4.8425	173	6.8110	223	8.7795	273	10.7480
24	0.9449	74	2.9134	124	4.8819	174	6.8504	224	8.8189	274	10.7874
25	0.9843	75	2.9528	125	4.9213	175	6.8898	225	8.8583	275	10.8268
26	1.0236	76	2.9921	126	4.9606	176	6.9291	226	8.8976	276	10.8661
27	1.0630	77	3.0315	127	5.0000	177	6.9685	227	8.9370	277	10.9055
28	1.1024	78	3.0709	128	5.0394	178	7.0079	228	8.9764	278	10.9449
29	1.1417	79	3.1102	129	5.0787	179	7.0472	229	9.0157	279	10.9842
30	1.1811	80	3.1496	130	5.1181	180	7.0866	230	9.0551	280	11.0236
31	1.2205	81	3.1890	131	5.1575	181	7.1260	231	9.0945	281	11.0630
32	1.2598	82	3.2283	132	5.1969	182	7.1654	232	9.1338	282	11.1023
33	1.2992	83	3.2677	133	5.2362	183	7.2047	233	9.1732	283	11.1417
34	1.3386	84	3.3071	134	5.2756	184	7.2441	234	9.2126	284	11.1811
35	1.3780	85	3.3465	135	5.3150	185	7.2835	235	9.2520	285	11.2205
36	1.4173	86	3.3858	136	5.3543	186	7.3228	236	9.2913	286	11.2598
37	1.4567	87	3.4252	137	5.3937	187	7.3622	237	9.3307	287	11.2992
38	1.4961	88	3.4646	138	5.4331	188	7.4016	238	9.3701	288	11.3386
39	1.5354	89	3.5039	139	5.4724	189	7.4409	239	9.4094	289	11.3779
40	1.5748	90	3.5433	140	5.5118	190	7.4803	240	9.4488	290	11.4173
41	1.6142	91	3.5827	141	5.5512	191	7.5197	241	9.4882	291	11.4567
42	1.6535	92	3.6220	142	5.5906	192	7.5591	242	9.5275	292	11.4960
43	1.6929	93	3.6614	143	5.6299	193	7.5984	243	9.5669	293	11.5354
44	1.7323	94	3.7008	144	5.6693	194	7.6378	244	9.6063	294	11.5748
45	1.7717	95	3.7402	145	5.7087	195	7.6772	245	9.6457	295	11.6142
46	1.8110	96	3.7795	146	5.7480	196	7.7165	246	9.6850	296	11.6535
47	1.8504	97	3.8189	147	5.7874	197	7.7559	247	9.7244	297	11.6929
48	1.8898	98	3.8583	148	5.8268	198	7.7953	248	9.7638	298	11.7323
49	1.9291	99	3.8976	149	5.8661	199	7.8346	249	9.8031	299	11.7716
50	1.9685	100	3.9370	150	5.9055	200	7.8740	250	9.8425	300	11.8110

CONVERSION CHART

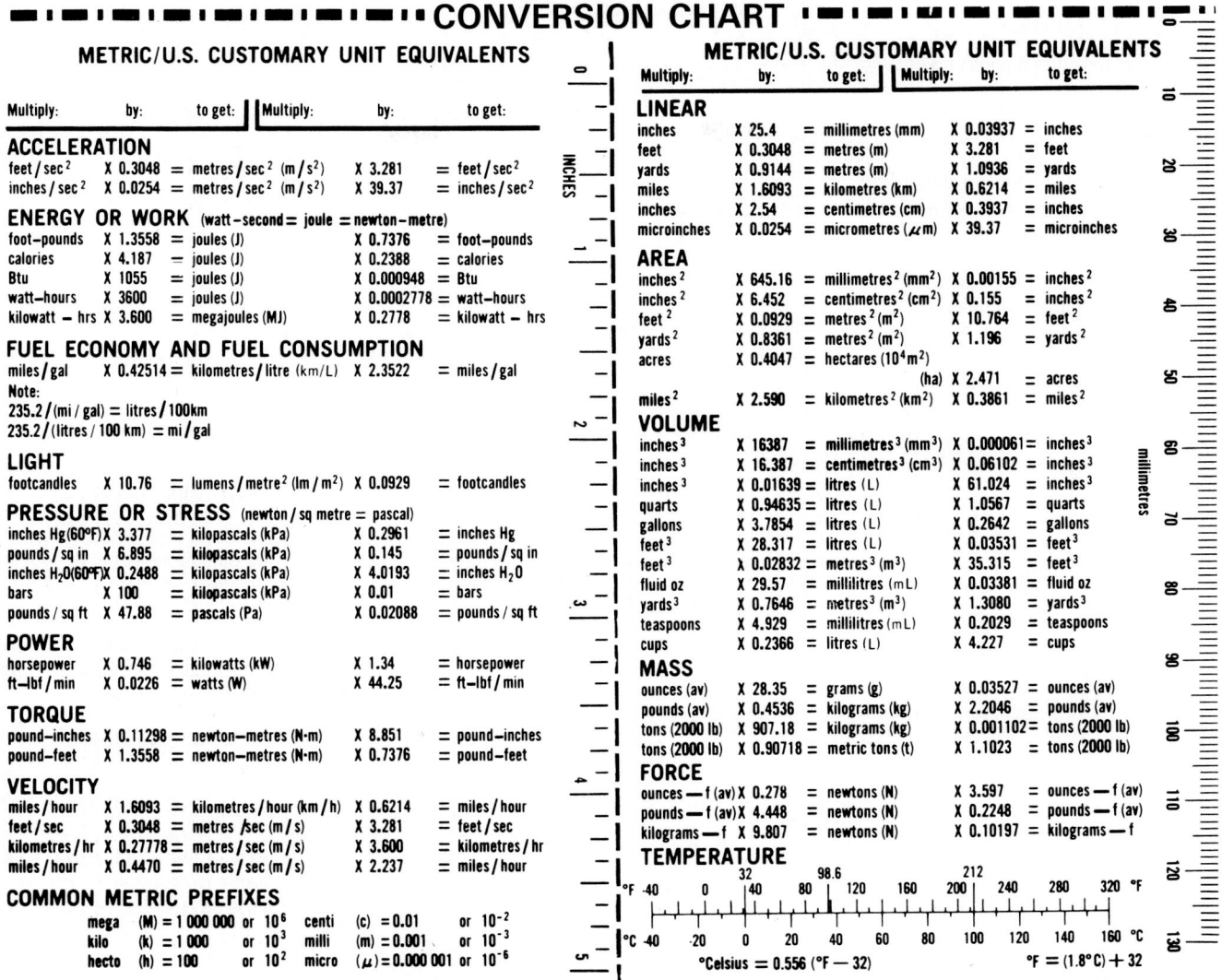

METRIC/U.S. CUSTOMARY UNIT EQUIVALENTS

Multiply:	by:	to get:		Multiply:	by:	to get:
ACCELERATION						
feet/sec²	X 0.3048	= metres/sec² (m/s²)		X 3.281	= feet/sec²
inches/sec²	X 0.0254	= metres/sec² (m/s²)		X 39.37	= inches/sec²
ENERGY OR WORK (watt−second = joule = newton−metre)						
foot−pounds	X 1.3558	= joules (J)		X 0.7376	= foot−pounds
calories	X 4.187	= joules (J)		X 0.2388	= calories
Btu	X 1055	= joules (J)		X 0.000948	= Btu
watt−hours	X 3600	= joules (J)		X 0.0002778	= watt−hours
kilowatt − hrs	X 3.600	= megajoules (MJ)		X 0.2778	= kilowatt − hrs

FUEL ECONOMY AND FUEL CONSUMPTION

miles/gal   X 0.42514   = kilometres/litre (km/L)   X 2.3522   = miles/gal

Note:
235.2/(mi/gal) = litres/100km
235.2/(litres/100 km) = mi/gal

LIGHT

footcandles   X 10.76   = lumens/metre² (lm/m²)   X 0.0929   = footcandles

PRESSURE OR STRESS (newton/sq metre = pascal)						
inches Hg(60°F)	X 3.377	= kilopascals (kPa)		X 0.2961	= inches Hg
pounds/sq in	X 6.895	= kilopascals (kPa)		X 0.145	= pounds/sq in
inches H₂0(60°F)	X 0.2488	= kilopascals (kPa)		X 4.0193	= inches H₂0
bars	X 100	= kilopascals (kPa)		X 0.01	= bars
pounds/sq ft	X 47.88	= pascals (Pa)		X 0.02088	= pounds/sq ft

POWER						
horsepower	X 0.746	= kilowatts (kW)		X 1.34	= horsepower
ft−lbf/min	X 0.0226	= watts (W)		X 44.25	= ft−lbf/min

TORQUE						
pound−inches	X 0.11298	= newton−metres (N·m)		X 8.851	= pound−inches
pound−feet	X 1.3558	= newton−metres (N·m)		X 0.7376	= pound−feet

VELOCITY						
miles/hour	X 1.6093	= kilometres/hour (km/h)		X 0.6214	= miles/hour
feet/sec	X 0.3048	= metres/sec (m/s)		X 3.281	= feet/sec
kilometres/hr	X 0.27778	= metres/sec (m/s)		X 3.600	= kilometres/hr
miles/hour	X 0.4470	= metres/sec (m/s)		X 2.237	= miles/hour

COMMON METRIC PREFIXES

mega	(M) = 1 000 000 or 10⁶	centi	(c) = 0.01	or	10⁻²
kilo	(k) = 1 000 or 10³	milli	(m) = 0.001	or	10⁻³
hecto	(h) = 100 or 10²	micro	(μ) = 0.000 001	or	10⁻⁶

METRIC/U.S. CUSTOMARY UNIT EQUIVALENTS

Multiply:	by:	to get:		Multiply:	by:	to get:
LINEAR						
inches	X 25.4	= millimetres (mm)		X 0.03937	= inches
feet	X 0.3048	= metres (m)		X 3.281	= feet
yards	X 0.9144	= metres (m)		X 1.0936	= yards
miles	X 1.6093	= kilometres (km)		X 0.6214	= miles
inches	X 2.54	= centimetres (cm)		X 0.3937	= inches
microinches	X 0.0254	= micrometres (μm)		X 39.37	= microinches
AREA						
inches²	X 645.16	= millimetres² (mm²)		X 0.00155	= inches²
inches²	X 6.452	= centimetres² (cm²)		X 0.155	= inches²
feet²	X 0.0929	= metres² (m²)		X 10.764	= feet²
yards²	X 0.8361	= metres² (m²)		X 1.196	= yards²
acres	X 0.4047	= hectares (10⁴ m²)			
		(ha)		X 2.471	= acres
miles²	X 2.590	= kilometres² (km²)		X 0.3861	= miles²
VOLUME						
inches³	X 16387	= millimetres³ (mm³)		X 0.000061	= inches³
inches³	X 16.387	= centimetres³ (cm³)		X 0.06102	= inches³
inches³	X 0.01639	= litres (L)		X 61.024	= inches³
quarts	X 0.94635	= litres (L)		X 1.0567	= quarts
gallons	X 3.7854	= litres (L)		X 0.2642	= gallons
feet³	X 28.317	= litres (L)		X 0.03531	= feet³
feet³	X 0.02832	= metres³ (m³)		X 35.315	= feet³
fluid oz	X 29.57	= millilitres (mL)		X 0.03381	= fluid oz
yards³	X 0.7646	= metres³ (m³)		X 1.3080	= yards³
teaspoons	X 4.929	= millilitres (mL)		X 0.2029	= teaspoons
cups	X 0.2366	= litres (L)		X 4.227	= cups
MASS						
ounces (av)	X 28.35	= grams (g)		X 0.03527	= ounces (av)
pounds (av)	X 0.4536	= kilograms (kg)		X 2.2046	= pounds (av)
tons (2000 lb)	X 907.18	= kilograms (kg)		X 0.001102	= tons (2000 lb)
tons (2000 lb)	X 0.90718	= metric tons (t)		X 1.1023	= tons (2000 lb)
FORCE						
ounces−f (av)	X 0.278	= newtons (N)		X 3.597	= ounces−f (av)
pounds−f (av)	X 4.448	= newtons (N)		X 0.2248	= pounds−f (av)
kilograms−f	X 9.807	= newtons (N)		X 0.10197	= kilograms−f

TEMPERATURE

°F -40   0   32   40   80   98.6   120   160   200   212   240   280   320 °F

°C -40   -20   0   20   40   60   80   100   120   140   160 °C

°Celsius = 0.556 (°F — 32)   °F = (1.8°C) + 32

BOLT TORQUING CHART

METRIC STANDARD

GRADE OF BOLT	5D	8G	10K	12K	SIZE OF SOCKET OR WRENCH OPENING
MIN. TENSILE STRENGTH	71,160 P.S.I	113,800 P.S.I.	142,200 P.S.I.	170,679 P.S.I.	
GRADE MARKINGS ON HEAD	5D	8G	10K	12K	
METRIC					METRIC

BOLT DIA.	U.S. DEC EQUIV.	FOOT POUNDS				BOLT HEAD
6mm	.2362	5	6	8	10	10mm
8mm	.3150	10	16	22	27	14mm
10mm	.3937	19	31	40	49	17mm
12mm	.4720	34	54	70	86	19mm
14mm	.5512	55	89	117	137	22mm
16mm	.6299	83	132	175	208	24mm
18mm	.709	111	182	236	283	27mm
22mm	.8661	182	284	394	464	32mm

SAE STANDARD / FOOT POUNDS

GRADE OF BOLT	SAE 1 & 2	SAE 5	SAE 6	SAE 8	SIZE OF SOCKET OR WRENCH OPENING	
MIN. TEN STRENGTH	64,000 P.S.I.	105,000 P.S.I.	133,000 P.S.I.	150,000 P.S.I.		
MARKINGS ON HEAD	⬡	⬡	⬡	⬡		
U.S. STANDARD					U.S. REGULAR	

BOLT DIA.	FOOT POUNDS				BOLT HEAD	NUT
1/4	5	7	10	10.5	3/8	7/16
5/16	9	14	19	22	1/2	9/16
3/8	15	25	34	37	9/16	5/8
7/16	24	40	55	60	5/8	3/4
1/2	37	60	85	92	3/4	13/16
9/16	53	88	120	132	7/8	7/8
5/8	74	120	167	180	15/16	1.
3/4	120	200	280	296	1-1/8	1-1/8

WIRE SIZE CHART

The selection of the correct gage primary wire of a heavy enough gage is very important for automotive and other low-voltage wiring to assure safe and reliable performance.

When too small a gage primary wire is used a voltage drop occurs due to electrical resistance and on lighting equipment there is also a loss of candlepower (visible light measurement).

The two factors that should always be considered in selecting an adequate gage primary wire and (1) the total amperages the circuit will carry and (2) the total length of wire used in each circuit, including the return.

Select the correct gage Belden wire for either 6 or 12 volt systems from the wiring diagram below and primary wiring guide below. Allowance for the return circuits, including grounded returns, has been computed on the recommendations below. The length cable should be determined by totaling both wires in a two-wire circuit.

Total Approx. Circuit Amperes	Total Circuit Watts	Total Candle Power	Wire Gauge (For Length in Feet)											
12V	12V	12V	3'	5'	7'	10'	15'	20'	25'	30'	40'	50'	75'	100'
1.0	12	6	18	18	18	18	18	18	18	18	18	18	18	18
1.5		10	18	18	18	18	18	18	18	18	18	18	18	18
2	24	16	18	18	18	18	18	18	18	18	18	18	16	16
3		24	18	18	18	18	18	18	18	18	18	18	14	14
4	48	30	18	18	18	18	18	18	18	18	16	16	12	12
5		40	18	18	18	18	18	18	18	18	16	14	12	12
6	72	50	18	18	18	18	18	18	18	16	16	14	12	10
7		60	18	18	18	18	18	18	16	16	14	14	10	10
8	96	70	18	18	18	18	18	16	16	16	14	12	10	10
10	120	80	18	18	18	18	16	16	16	14	12	12	10	10
11		90	18	18	18	18	16	16	14	14	12	12	10	8
12	144	100	18	18	18	18	16	16	14	14	12	12	10	8
15		120	18	18	18	18	14	14	12	12	12	10	8	8
18	216	140	18	18	16	16	14	14	12	12	10	10	8	8
20	240	160	18	18	16	16	14	12	10	10	10	10	8	6
22	264	180	18	18	16	16	12	12	10	10	10	8	6	6
24	288	200	*18	18	16	16	12	12	10	10	10	8	6	6
30			18	16	16	14	10	10	10	10	10	6	4	4
40			18	16	14	12	10	10	8	8	6	6	4	2
50			16	14	12	12	10	10	8	8	6	6	2	2
100			12	12	10	10	6	6	4	4	4	2	1	1/0
150			10	10	8	8	4	4	2	2	2	1	2/0	2/0
200			10	8	8	6	4	4	2	2	1	1/0	4/0	4/0

HOW TO USE CHART

1
Measure Length of Wire in Circuit—chart applies to ground return. Two-wire circuits will be total of both wire lengths. Be sure to indicate both vehicles on auto and trailer applications.

2
Find the total amperes, watts or candlepower and choose nearest value in proper column.

3
Move horizontally to proper footage column and find nearest wire gage.

4
For 6 volt applications use two wire sizes larger. Example: If chart shows 16 ga. for 12 volt system use 14 ga. on 6 volt system.

Based on maximum of 10% voltage drop

*18 AWG indicated above this line could be 20 AWG electrically—18AWG is recommended for mechanical strength.

PRIMARY WIRING AMPERAGE GUIDE

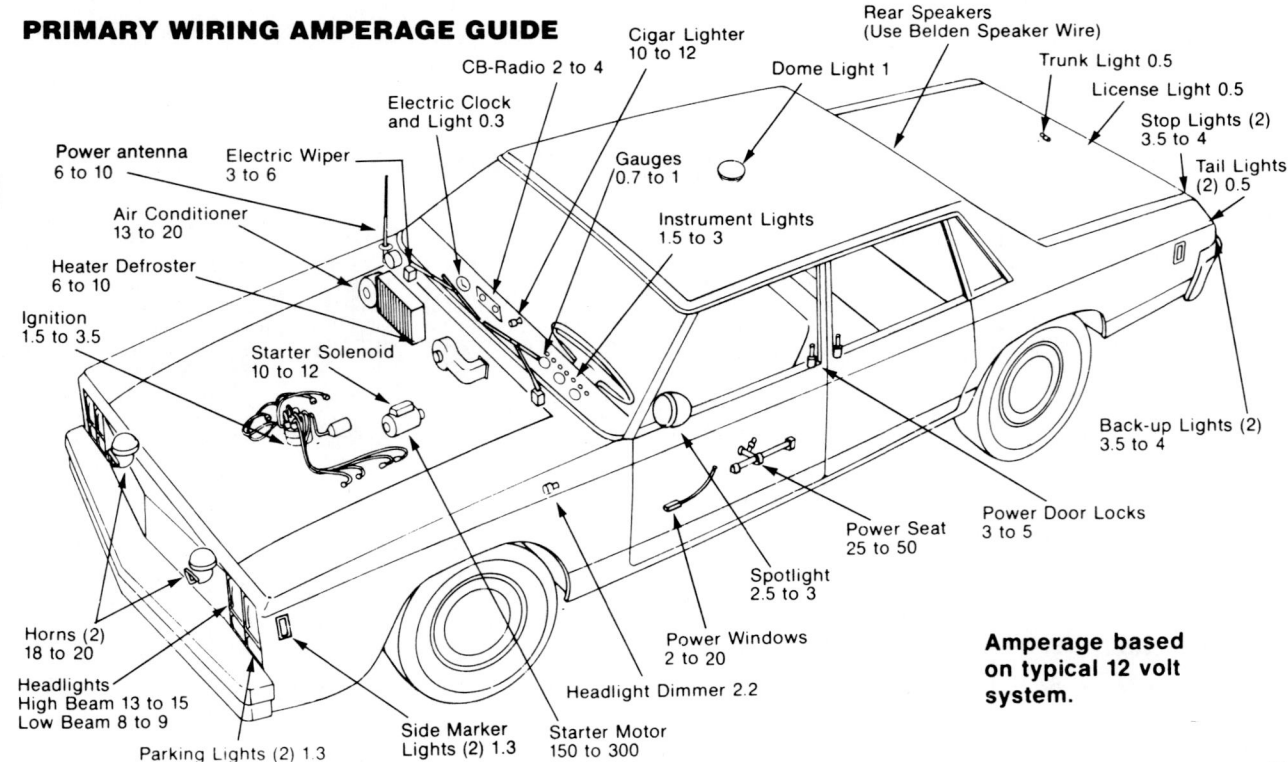

Power antenna 6 to 10
Electric Wiper 3 to 6
Air Conditioner 13 to 20
Heater Defroster 6 to 10
Ignition 1.5 to 3.5
Starter Solenoid 10 to 12
Horns (2) 18 to 20
Headlights High Beam 13 to 15 Low Beam 8 to 9
Parking Lights (2) 1.3
Side Marker Lights (2) 1.3
Starter Motor 150 to 300
Headlight Dimmer 2.2
Power Windows 2 to 20
Spotlight 2.5 to 3
Power Seat 25 to 50
Power Door Locks 3 to 5
Back-up Lights (2) 3.5 to 4
CB-Radio 2 to 4
Electric Clock and Light 0.3
Gauges 0.7 to 1
Instrument Lights 1.5 to 3
Cigar Lighter 10 to 12
Dome Light 1
Rear Speakers (Use Belden Speaker Wire)
Trunk Light 0.5
License Light 0.5
Stop Lights (2) 3.5 to 4
Tail Lights (2) 0.5

Amperage based on typical 12 volt system.

(Belden)

SERVICE MANUAL ABBREVIATIONS

Acc.	— Accessory	EPR-DV	— Exhaust Pressure Regulator Delay Valve	NO	— Normally open
A/C	— Air Conditioning	ESC	— Electronic Spark Control	NOx	— Nitrogen, Oxides of
ADJ	— Adjust	ESC	— Electrostatic Discharge		
ADL	— Automatic Doorlock	EST	— Electronic Spark Timing	OD	— Outside Diameter
ADRC	— Adaptive Ride Control	ETR	— Electronically Tuned Receiver	OHC	— Overhead Camshaft
A/F	— Air Fuel Ratio	EVRV	— Electronic Vacuum Regulator Valve	OL	— Open Loop
AIR	— Air Injection Reaction System			O^2	— Oxygen
ALCL	— Assembly Line Communication Link	EXH	— Exhaust		
				PAIR	— Pulse Air Injection System
Alt.	— Altitude	°F	— Degrees Fahrenheit	P/B	— Power Brakes
AM	— Amplitude Modulation	FED	— Federal (All States Except Calif)	PCB	— Printed Circuit Board
AMP	— Ampere(s)	FL	— Fusible Link	POS	— Positive
ANT	— Antenna	FM	— Frequency Modulation	Pri	— Primary
APS	— Absolute Pressure Sensor	ft. lb.	— foot pounds	PROM	— Programmable Read Only Memory
AT	— Automatic Transmission/Teansaxle	FWD	— Front Wheel Drive	P/S	— Power Steering
ATDC	— After Top Dead Center	FWL	— Forward Lamps	PSI	— Pounds per Square Inch
Auth	— Authority			Pt.	— Pint
		g	— grams	PWM	— Pulse Width Modulated
BARO	— Barometric Pressure Sensor	GND	— Ground		
Bat.	— Battery			Qt.	— Quart
Bat+	— Battery Positive Terminal	Harn	— Harness	QTU	— Quick Take Up
B+	— Battery Voltage	HC	— Hydrocarbons	QVR	— Quick Vacuum Response
Bbl	— Barrel	HD	— Heavy Duty		
BCM	— Body Computer Module	HEI	— High Energy Ignition	R-12	— Refrigerant -12
BP	— Back Pressure	HG	— Mercury	RAP	— Retained Accessory Power
Brk	— Brake	HiAlt	— High Altitude	REF	— Reference
BTDC	— Before Top Dead Center	HP	— Horsepower	RF	— Right Front
		HPAA	— Housing Pressure Altitude Advance	RH	— Right Hand
°C	— Degrees Celsius			Rly	— Relay
Calif	— California	HPCS	— Housing Pressure Cold Advance	RPM	— Revolutions per minute
CALPAK	— Prom (Engine Calibrator)			RPO	— Regular Production Option
Cat. Conv.	— Catalytic Converter	Htd	— Heated	RR	— Right rear
CCC	— Computer Command Control	HTR	— Heater	RS	— Right side
CCOT	— Cycling Clutch Orifice Tube	HVAC	— Heating Ventilation Air Conditioning	RTV	— Room Temperature Vulcanizing
CCP	— Controlled Canister Purge		Conditioning	RVB	— Rear Vacuum Break
CDVR	— Crankcase Depression Regulator Valve			RVR	— Response Vacuum Reducer
CID	— Cubic Inch Displacement	IAC	— Idle Air Control	RWD	— Rear Wheel Drive
CKT	— Circuit	IC	— Integrated Circuit		
CL	— Closed Loop	ID	— Identification	SAE	— Society of Automotive Engineers
CLCC	— Closed Loop Carburetor Control		— Inside Diameter	Sec	— Secondary
CNS	— Console	IGN	— Ignition	SFI	— Sequential Fuel Injection
CO	— Carbon Monoxide	ILC	— Idle Load Compensator	SI	— System International
Conn.	— Connector	in. lbs.	— inch pounds	Sol	— Solenoid
Conv.	— Converter	INJ	— Injection	Spkr	— Speaker
CP	— Canister Purge	IP	— Instrument Control Panel	Spl	— Splice
CPS	— Central Power Supply	IPC	— Instrument Panel Cluster	Stg	— Steering
CRT	— Cathode Ray Tube	ISC	— Idle Speed Control	Sync	— Synchronization
CRTC	— Cathode Ray Tube Controller	ISS	— Idle Speed Solenoid	Sw	— Switch
CTR	— Center				
CTS	— Coolant Temperature Signal	KAM	— Keep Alive Memory	TAC	— Thermostatic Air Cleaner
	— Coolant Temperature Sensor	km	— kilometer	Tach	— Tachometer
CTSY	— Courtesy	km/h	— kilometer per hour	TBI	— Throttle Body Injection
CV	— Constant Velocity	kPa	— Kilopascals	TCC	— Transmission/Transaxle Converter Clutch
Cyl	— Cylinder(s)	KV	— Kilovolts (thousands of volts)		
				TDC	— Top Dead Center
Da	— Dash	L	— Liter	Temp	— Temperature
DBM	— Dual Bed Monolith	LED	— Light Emitting Diode	Term	— Terminal
DECS	— Diesel Electronic Control System	LF	— Left Front	Thermo	— Thermostatic Air Cleaner
Diff	— Differential	LH	— Left Hand	TPS	— Throttle Position Sensor
Dist	— Distributor	LR	— Left Rear	TT	— Telltail
DVM	— Digital Voltmeter (10 meg)	LS	— Left Side	TV	— Throttle Valve
DVDV	— Differential Vacuum Delay Valve	Ltr	— Lighter	TVRS	— Television & Radio Suppression
		L4	— In-Line four cylinder	TVS	— Thermal Vacuum Switch
				Twi	— Twilight
		MAF	— Mass Air Flow		
EAC	— Electric Air Control	MAP	— Manifold Absolute Pressure	U-Joint	— Universal Joint
EAS	— Electric Air Switching	Max	— Maximum		
ECM	— Electronic Control Module	M/C	— Mixture Control	V	— Volt(s)
ECU	— Engine Calibration Unit (PROM)	Mm	— Minimum	VAC	— Vacuum
EE	— Electronically Eraseable	ml	— Millilitres	VF	— Vacuum Fluorescent
EECS	— Evaporative Emission Control System	mm	— millimeter	VIN	— Vehicle Identification Number
		MFI	— Multi-Port Fuel Injection	V-ref	— Reference Voltage
EFE	— Early Fuel Evaporation	MPG	— Miles Per Gallon	VSS	— Vehicle Speed Sensor
EFI	— Electronic Fuel Injection	MPH	— Miles Per Hour	V6	— Six Cylinder "V" Engine
EGR	— Exhaust Gas Recirculation	MT	— Manual Transaxle/Transmission	V8	— Eight Cylinder "V" Engine
EGR/TVS	— Exhaust Gas Recirculation/ Thermostatic Vacuum Switch	Mtr	— Motor		
		MUX	— Multiplexing	w/	— With
EL	— Electroluminescent	MVS	— Metering Valve Sensor	w/b	— Wheel Base
ELC	— Electronic Level Control	NC	— Normally closed	wdo	— Window
ENG	— Engine	NEG	— Negative	w/o	— without
EPR	— Exhaust Pressure Regulator	N·m	— Newton Meters	wot	— Wide Open Throttle

Cover photos courtesy of Chrysler Corp.

ACKNOWLEDGEMENTS

The author would like to thank all of the companies and individuals that helped make this book possible:

AMERICAN AUTO MANUFACTURERS

Buick Motor Car Division; Cadillac Motor Car Division; Chevrolet Motor Division; Chrysler Motor Corp.; Ford Motor Company; GMC Truck & Coach Division; Oldsmobile Division; Pontiac Motor Division.

FOREIGN AUTO MANUFACTURERS

Alfa Romeo, Inc.; American Honda Motor Co.; Aston Martin Lagonda, Inc.; BMW of North America, Inc.; British Leyland Motors, Inc. (Triumph and MG); Fiat Motors of North America, Inc.; Infinity; Isuzu; Jaguar; Lexus; Maserati Automobiles, Inc.; Mazda Motors of America, Inc.; Mercedes-Benz of North America, Inc.; Mitsubishi Motor Sales of America; Nissan Motor Corp.; Peugeot, Inc.; Renault USA, Inc.; Rolls-Royce, Inc.; Saab-Scandia of America, Inc.; Subaru of America, Inc.; S.A. Automobiles Citroen; Toyota Motor Sales, USA, Inc.; Volkswagen of America, Inc.-Porsche; Volvo of America.

DIESEL AND TRUCK RELATED COMPANIES

Airesearch Industrial Div.; Caterpillar Tractor Co.; Cummins Engine Co., Inc.; Detroit Diesel Allison Div.; GMC Truck and Coach Div.; International Harvester; Motor Vehicle Manufacturer's Assn.; White Diesel Div.

AUTOMOTIVE RELATED COMPANIES

AC—Delco; Airtex Automotive Division; Alloy; American Bosch; American Hammered Automotive Replacement Division; Ammco Tools, Inc.; AP Parts Co.; Armstrong Bros. Tool Co.; AP Parts Co.; Applied Power, Inc.; Automotive Control System Group; Beam Products Mfg. Co.; Bear Automotive; Belden Corp.; Bendix; Binks Mfg. Co.; Black & Decker, Inc.; Blackhawk Mfg. Co.; Bonney Tools; Borg-Warner Corp,; Bosch Power Tools; Carter Div. of AFC Inc., Brodhead Garrett; Champion Spark Plug Co.; C.A. Laboratories, Inc.; Clayton Manufacturing Co.; Cleveland Motive Products; Clevite Corp.; Colt Industries; Chicago Rawhide Mfg. Co.; CRC Chemicals; Cy-lent Timing Gears Corp.; D.A.B. Industries, Inc.; Dana Corp.; Dake; Dayco Corp.; Debcor, Inc.; Deere & Co.; Delco-Remy Div. of GMC; Detroit Art Services, Inc.; The DeVilbiss Co.; Duro-Chrome Hand Tools;

The Echlin Mfg. Co.; Edu-Tech-A Division of Commercial Service Co.; E & L Instruments; H.B. Egan Manufacturing Co.; Ethyl Corp,; Exxon Co. USA; Fairgate Fuel Co., Inc.; Federal Mogul; Fel-Pro Inc.; Firestone Tire and Rubber Co.; Ford Parts and Service Division; Florida Dept. of Vocational Education; FMC Corporation; Fram Corp.; Gates Rubber Co.; General Tire & Rubber Co.; Goodall Manufacturing Co.; The B.F. Goodrich Co.; The Goodyear Tire & Rubber Co.; Gould Inc.; Gunk Chemical Div.; Hartridge Equipment Corp.; Hastings Mfg. Co.; Heli-Coil Products; Helm Inc.; Hennessy Industries; Holley Carburetor Div.; Hunter Engineering Co.; Ingersoll-Rand Co.; International Harvester Co.; Kansas Jack, Inc.; K-D Tool Manufacturing Co.; Keller Crescent Co.; Kem Manufacturing Co., Inc.; Kent-Moore; Killian Corp.; Kline Diesel Acc.; Kwick-Way Mfg. Co.; Lincoln St. Louis, Div. of McNeil Corp.; Lisle Corp.; Lister Diesels, Inc.; Lufkin Instrument Div.-Cooper Industries Inc.; Lyons, Marquette Corp.; McCord Replacement Products Division; Mac Tools Inc.; Maremont Corp.; Minnesota Curriculum Services Center; Mobile Oil Corp.; Moog Automotive Inc.; Motorola; National Institute for Automotive Service Excellence; NAPA: OTC Tools & Equipment; Owatonna Tool Co.; Parker Hannifin Corp.; Precision Brand Products; Proto Tool Co.; Purolator Filter Division; Quaker State Corp.; Rochester Div. of GM; Roto-Master; Sealed Power Corp-Replacement Products Group; SATCO: Schwitzer Cooling Systems; Sears, Roebuck and Co.; Sellstrom Mfg. Co.; Sem Products, Inc.; Shell Oil Co.; Simpson Electric Co.; Sioux Tools, Inc.; Snap-on Tools Corp.; Speed Clip Sales Co.; Stanadyne, Inc.; The L.S. Starrett Co.; Stewart-Warner; Sun Electric Corp.; Sunnen Product Co.; Test Products Divison-The Allen Group, Inc.; Texaco Inc.; 3-M Company; Tomco (TI) Inc.; TRW Inc.; TWECO Products, Inc.; Uniroyal, Inc.; American Bosch Diesel Products; Vaco Products Co.; Valvoline Oil Co.; Victor Gasket Co.; Waukesha Engine Division, Dresser Industries, Inc.; Weatherhead Co.; a special thanks goes to the Eastwood Co. (1-800-345-1178); TIF Instruments (1-800-327-5060) and to my wife (Jeanette) and children (Danielle, Jimmy, and DJ).

Glossary of Terms

A

Abbreviations: Letters or letter combinations that stand for words. They are used extensively in service manuals.

ABS: Abbreviation for "anti-lock braking system."

ABS pressure switch: Sensor that monitors hydraulic system pressure and controls pump motor in an ABS application.

AC: Alternating current.

Acceleration sensor: Provides acceleration data to computer in electronic shock absorber system.

Accelerator pump: Device to force a fuel stream into air horn as needed.

Accessory systems: Those that increase comfort or are a convenience for vehicle occupants, such as air conditioning or power windows, and a window defogger.

Accumulator: Air conditioning system component that removes moisture and stores extra refrigerant.

AC generator: Device that produces alternating current; an alternator.

Active sensor: One that generates its own voltage signal in response to a change in a condition.

Active suspension system: A method of ride control using hydraulic rams, rather than conventional shock absorbers and springs.

Actuator: Device that performs an action or outputs a signal in response to a signal from a computer.

Adhesive: Substance used to chemically and mechanically bond two materials together.

Adjustable rocker arm: Used with mechanical lifters; permits changing valve train clearance.

Air blow gun: Tool used to blow off bits of dirt, solvent, or other debris from parts.

Air chisel: Cutting tool, powered by compressed air, that is used to remove faulty exhaust system parts.

Air cleaner carbon element: Canister of carbon granules that absorbs fuel vapors when engine is shut off.

Air compressor: A pump that forces air, under pressure, into a storage tank.

Air cooling system: The use of cooling fins and air movement to dissipate heat from the engine.

Airflow sensor: Device to monitor flow of outside air into engine.

Air horn: Part of the carburetor that channels air into the intake manifold.

Air injection system: A method of reducing HC and CO emissions by forcing fresh air into the exhaust ports of the engine.

Air jet chamber: One that uses an injected stream of air for improved fuel mixing and combustion.

Air pollution: Release of harmful substances into the air due to engine operation and similar causes.

Air pump: Belt-driven pump that provides input for the air injection system.

Air shocks: Shock absorbers that use air pressure, rather than springs, to maintain vehicle height.

Air spring: Air-filled rubber cylinder that is lighter than the equivalent coil spring.

Air tests: The use of air pressure to diagnose automatic transmission problems.

Air tool: A power tool that is supplied with energy by compressed air.

ALDL: Assembly line diagnostic link, also called the diagnostic connector.

Alignment rack: Fixture onto which the vehicle is driven for alignment measurement and adjustment activities.

Alternate engine: Engine types other than traditional internal combustion, four-stoke-cycle, piston engine.

Alternate fuel: Fuels other than gasoline and diesel fuel.

Alternator: An AC generator.

Alternator bearings: Needle or ball-type bearings used to provide a low-friction surface for a rotor.

Altitude compensator: A system that changes the air-fuel ratio as vehicle moves to higher or lower elevations.

AM: Amplitude modulation (type of radio broadcasting).

Ambient temperature switch: One that prevents air conditioner operation when outdoor temperatures are below a set point.

Amplifier: Electronic circuit that uses a small current to control a much larger current.

Amplify: To increase in strength or volume.

Anaerobic sealer: A sealer that cures in the *absence* of air.

Analog: A signal that can vary continuously in value.

Analog signal: One that continually changes strength.

Analog voltmeter code: Trouble code read by counting the number of needle deflections on a meter.

Antenna trimmer: Adjustment screw on a radio, used to obtain best reception.

Antifreeze: Liquid used in a cooling system that is mixed with water and prevents the water from freezing. The solution serves as the engine coolant.

Antifreeze strength: Measurement of concentration of coolant solution.

Antifriction bearing: Bearing that uses balls or rollers to decrease friction.

Anti-lock brake computer: ECM that accepts wheel sensor inputs and controls braking of the vehicle.

Anti-lock brakes: Computer-controlled brakes that will not "lock" and permit wheels to skid.

Anti-rattle clips: Metal components designed to keep brake pads from vibrating and rattling.

Anti-skid system: Another name for anti-lock braking system.

Apprentice mechanic: A beginner who is learning under direction of an experienced auto technician.

Armature: Rotating support for multiple windings in a motor.

Asbestos: A mineral material once widely used on clutches and brake linings. Asbestos dust is a known cancer-causing agent.

Asbestos lining: Anti-friction material once widely used for brake linings.

ASE: Abbreviation for National Institute for Automotive Service Excellence, which certifies auto technicians.

Aspect ratio: The relationship of tire height to width, or profile.

Asphyxiation: Death resulting from lack of oxygen to breathe.

Atmospheric pressure: The pressure exerted by the Earth's atmosphere (14.7 psi at sea level).

Automatic clutch adjuster: A mechanism designed to automatically remove any play from a clutch cable system.

Automatic temperature control system: A method of climate control using sensors and a computer to maintain a preset temperature in the vehicle's passenger compartment.

Automatic transmission: One that does not have to be shifted manually.

Automatic transmission electronic controls: Computerized selection of shift points, based on input from sensors.

Automatic transmission fluid: Oil with special additives to make it compatible with friction clutches and bands.

Automatic transmission slippage: Condition in which engine races as transmission shifts (in severe cases, car may not move at all).

Automotive clutch: A mechanical device used to connect and disconnect a manual transmission from engine power.

Auto technician's certification: A program in which technicians take written tests to become certified by the National Institute for Automotive Service Excellence (ASE).

Auxiliary chain: A chain and sprocket combination used to drive engine auxiliaries, such as the oil pump.

Axle C-clip: Spring steel retainer that fits in a groove on the axle end.

Axle end play: In-and-out movement of the axle, adjusted to specification by using shims.

Axle retainer plate: See axle shaft retainer.

Axle shaft retainer: Devices that attach to the outside of an axle housing to prevent axles from sliding out.

Axle shims: Used between axle housing and retainer to limit end play of the axle.

B

Backfiring: Condition caused by air-fuel mixture igniting in the intake manifold or exhaust system.

Backing plate: Component that holds the shoes, wheel cylinder, and other parts inside a drum brake.

Back pressure: Pressure developed in the exhaust system when the engine is running.

Backup light switch: An electrical switch on a manual transmission that completes a circuit to the backup lights whenever the reverse gear is engaged.

Bad hydraulic lifter: A cause of valve clatter.

Balancer shaft: Rotating component used in some engines to cancel vibrations produced by rotating crankshaft and other components.

Ball and trunnion U-joint: A seldom-used type of constant velocity U-joint.

Ball joint: Swivel joint that provides free movement for steering knuckle and control arm.

Ball joint balloon seal: Airtight seal used for protection of a ball joint.

Ball joint wear indicator: An indicator on the shoulder of the ball joint that shows amount of wear.

Ball nut: Component that rides up and down a worm gear as the worm rotates in a recirculating ball gearbox.

Ball sockets: Components that allow motion in up-and-down and side-to-side directions.

Band: Metal strap with frictional material lining that can clamp a clutch drum in an automatic transmission to stop its rotation.

Band adjustment: Checking and altering tightness of automatic transmission bands as necessary for proper operation.

Bare cylinder head: A head with all parts removed.

Barrel: Cylinder that holds a pumping plunger.

Basic circuit problem: One caused by something in the circuit itself that increases or decreases an electrical value.

Battery activation: Filling and charging a dry charged battery prior to installation.

Battery cables: The heavy wires connecting the batter to the vehicle's electrical system.

Battery charge condition: The state of its plates and electrolyte.

Battery charger: Device for restoring battery to a proper electrical charge.

Battery drain test: A method of checking for unusual current draw with ignition key off.

Battery leakage test: Check to determine if current is discharging across top of battery case.

Battery load test: A test for battery capacity, made under full electrical load.

Battery terminal test: A test for good contact between cables and terminals.

Battery voltage: For batteries used in modern cars, 12.6V; older cars, 6.3V.

Battery voltage test: Check of battery charge with a voltmeter.

BDC: Bottom Dead Center.

Bearing clearance: Small space between moving parts, permitting oil to enter for lubrication.

Bearing crush: Slight oversize of bearings to jam them in place when cap is tightened on connecting rod.

Bearing housing: Section of the turbocharger housing containing the shaft bearings and oil seals.

Bearing noise: Constant whir or humming sound due to damage or wear of bearings in the carrier or axle assemblies.

Bearing packer: Tool used to simplify packing of grease into wheel bearings.

Bearing spread: Practice of making bearing halves slightly wider than necessary to hold them in place during installation.

Bell housing: The metal shell surrounding the clutch assembly that bolts to the rear of the engine.

Belted bias tire: A bias-ply tire with extra belts added beneath the tread area.

Belts: Fabric made of steel or other material that is placed between body plies and tread.

Belt squeal: Noise resulting from a slipping drive belt.

Bench bleed: Method of filling and hand-pumping a master cylinder before installation to remove trapped air.

Bent push rod: A cause of valve clatter. Bent rods usually must be replaced.

bhp: Abbreviation for brake horsepower, a measurement of usable horsepower of an engine.

Bias ply tire: One with plies running at an angle from bead to bead.

Bleeder screw: Fitting on top of brake caliper that allows air to be bled from system.

Bleeding: Process of removing any trapped air from a hydraulic system.

Block diagram: A simple drawing, using rectangles and lines, that shows how sensors, computers, and actuators are interconnected.

Block heater: A heating device used to warm the block of a diesel engine in cold weather.

Block line boring: A technique used to "true" misaligned main bearing bores.

Blowby: Oil vapors and other emissions that leak past piston rings into the crankcase.

Blower: A fan that forces air to move though the evaporator of an air conditioning system.

Blow gun: An air-powered device used for cleaning and drying parts washed in solvent, or blowing away accumulations of dust and dirt.

Blown head gasket: Leak of compression from one or more cylinders results from failure of the gasket.

Blow-through turbo: A turbocharger located ahead of the compressor or throttle body. It compresses only air.

Body lubrication: Applying oil and grease to such friction points as hinges and latches.

Boiling a block: Cleaning technique in which strong solvents and heat are used to remove mineral deposits from the water jacket.

Bolt size: Measurement of the outside thread diameter.

Boost pressure: A measure of engine power provided by a turbocharger.

Boot: Flexible pleated covers placed over the CV joints of a front-wheel-drive vehicle to keep road dirt out of them.

Boot deterioration: Cracking, tearing, or other damage to a boot which would allow road dirt and moisture to enter the CV-joint.

Bowl vent: Passageway that prevents a pressure buildup in fuel bowl.

Box end: A wrench that has completely closed ends that surround and grip a bolt head.

Brake booster: Component operated by vacuum or power steering system to decrease braking effort needed.

Brake lines: Metal tubing and rubber hoses connecting master cylinder to wheel brake assemblies.

Brake pads: Replaceable friction surfaces mounted on caliper of disc brake system.

Brake pedal assembly: Foot lever for operating brake system.

Brake pedal vibration: Pulsing movement of brake pedal, usually caused by out-of-round brake drum or warped rotor.

Brake sensor: Provides braking data to computer in electronic shock absorber system.

Brake shoes: Curved, replaceable friction surfaces used with drum-type brakes.

Brake system: Components that are used to stop a vehicle.

Brake system flushing: Removal of all old fluid by pressure bleeding, then replacing it with fresh fluid.

Brake warning light: Dashboard indicator that warns of low brake system hydraulic pressure.

Braking ratio: Comparison of front wheel to rear wheel braking effort.

Break-away torque: In a limited-slip differential, the amount of torque needed to make one axle rotate the clutches.

Brushes: Sliding electrical contacts that ride on the slip rings of a generator.

Btu: British thermal units; the units used to measure heat transfer.

Bubbling sight glass: A sign that the air conditioning system is low on refrigerant and that air may be present.

Burned fluid: Condition caused by overheating due to slippage of transmission bands.

Burned piston: Actual melting or breakage of a part of the piston, resulting in a hole.

Burned valve: Valve face damaged by heat, allowing leakage of air-fuel mixture from cylinder during compression.

Bus: A pathway for data inside a computer.

Bypass lubrication system: One that filters only some of the oil going to bearings.

Bypass valve: Method used to permit coolant circulation in engine when thermostat is closed.

C

Calibration fluid: A fluid that is less flammable than diesel fuel, used when testing injectors out of the engine.

Caliper: Disc brake assembly that holds brake pads and wheel cylinder. Also, a two-jaw measuring device that is adjusted to the outside or inside dimension being measured.

Camber: The inward or outward tilt of a wheel assembly.

Cam ground piston: One that is ground slightly out of round to compensate for different rates of expansion.

Cam lobe wear: Reduces valve lift, causing reduced engine power and rough idle.

Camshaft: Rotating shaft with lobes that open valves at the correct times for proper engine operation.

Camshaft drive: Gears, a chain and sprockets, or a belt and sprockets that run the camshaft at half the speed of crankshaft rotation.

Camshaft lift: Amount of valve train movement produced by the cam lobe.

Cam thrust plate: Component that limits front-to-rear movement of camshaft.

Cap pressure rating: Pressure at which the cap valve opens to vent coolant to the overflow tube or recovery tank.

Caps: Covers over cell openings on top of a battery.

Carbon trace: Small line of conductive carbon-like material on a distributor cap or rotor.

Carburetor cleaner: A chemical used to dissolve gums and material from carburetor parts.

Carburetor flooding: Excess fuel flow, preventing starting of engine.

Carburetor fuel system: One that mixes air and fuel and directs it to engine cylinders through an intake manifold.

Carburetor kit: Gaskets, needle valves, and other parts needed to rebuild a carburetor.

Carburetor rebuild: Overhaul, with cleaning and part replacement.

Carburetor system: Network of passages that control the air-fuel ratio under specific engine conditions.

Cartridge oil filter: One with a replaceable filter element.

Case: The outer protective shell of a battery, or any other component or device.

Case bearing preload: Amount of force pushing differential case bearings together.

Caster: Forward or backward tilt of steering knuckle.

Caster-camber bubble gauge: Instrument with bubbles that indicate degree of tilt.

Catalytic converter: Device in the exhaust system that oxidizes most harmful emissions from the engine.

Cell: Electrical energy storage device, consisting of negative and positive plates immersed in a conductive fluid (electrolyte).

Cell voltage test: Check of individual battery cells for correct charge.

Center support bearing: A ball or roller bearing unit that supports the middle of a two-piece drive shaft.

Centrifugal advance: System that uses pivoting weights to advance timing as engine speed increases.

Certified master technician: Auto technician who has passed all eight ASE tests.

Certified technician: Auto technician who has passed at least one ASE test.

Cetane number: An indication of the cold-starting ability of a diesel fuel.

CFM: Cubic feet of air per minute.

Chain slap: Flapping motion of chain if slack is permitted.

Charcoal canister: Unit that traps and stores fuel vapors when engine is not running.

Charge indicators: Dash-mounted warning light, voltmeter, or ammeter used to show charging system status. Also the visual symbol (often a green dot) that shows state of charge in a battery.

Charging: Current flowing into a battery from an alternator. Also, adding new or recycled refrigerant to an air conditioning or refrigeration system.

Charging station: Usually, a wheeled cart containing a tank of refrigerant, vacuum pump, and manifold set for adding refrigerant to an air conditioning system.

Charging system: One that uses an alternator to replace the electrical energy drawn from the battery during starting.

Charging system output test: A measurement of current and voltage output of the charging system under load.

Charging voltage: Alternator output that is higher than battery voltage (usually 13V-15V).

Chassis: The frame and other parts of a vehicle, other than the body.

Check valve: Valve that permits fuel flow in only one direction.

Chemical burns: Injury to the skin from exposure to toxic or corrosive chemical substances.

Chemical flushing: Method of removing scale buildup, using a strong chemical and water flush.

CID: Cubic inch displacement.

Circuit board: A base upon which computer circuits are printed and components are mounted.

Circuit breaker: Device that interrupts current if a circuit is overloaded or a short occurs. Unlike a fuse, it can be reset.

Circuit resistance tests: Measurements of resistance in the insulated and ground circuits of the system.

Clear sight glass: A sign that the air conditioning system is operating properly.

Climate control computer: ECM that controls temperature levels in the vehicle's passenger compartment.

Clogged heater core: One that restricts or blocks flow of coolant, due to an accumulation of rust particles.

Closed loop: Control system that is constantly changing, based on inputs from sensors.

Closed system: Cooling system using a recovery tank for coolant.

Cloud point: Temperature at which wax separates out of the fuel.

Cloudy sight glass: A sign that desiccant from the receiver-drier is circulating through the air conditioning system.

Clutch: Device that allows the driver to engage or disengage the engine and transmission.

Clutch adjustment: Process of setting the correct amount of free play in the release mechanism.

Clutch cable: A simple mechanical arrangement that uses a cable to transmit clutch pedal movement to the clutch fork.

Clutch chatter: A condition in which clutch severely vibrates as car accelerates.

Clutch disc: A disc that is splined to transmission input shaft and pressed against the face of the flywheel.

Clutch fork: Lever that forces the throw-out (release) bearing into pressure plate of clutch.

Clutch lining: Frictional material riveted to the face of the clutch disk.

Clutch linkage: A mechanical arrangement of levers and rods that transmits force from the clutch pedal to the clutch fork.

Clutch master cylinder: The device that produces the hydraulic pressure needed to operate the clutch.

Clutch pedal free travel: Distance the pedal moves before the throw-out bearing acts on the pressure plate.

Clutch pilot shaft: Tool used to keep clutch disc from falling as pressure plate is loosened during clutch disassembly.

Clutch piston: A piston that moves back and forth inside the clutch drum to clamp driving and driven discs together.

Clutch release mechanism: Cable or linkage permitting driver to disengage clutch with foot pedal.

Clutch slippage: Condition in which engine rpm increases without increase in car's road speed.

Clutch start switch: Safety switch that prevents starting motor operation until the clutch is disengaged.

CO: Abbreviation for carbon monoxide, a toxic byproduct of partial burning of fuel.

CO_2 readings: Used to evaluate the air-fuel ratio of the engine; measured in percent by volume.

Coast side: Concave side of gear tooth.

Cogged belt: Rubber belt with built-in cogs (teeth) that engage the teeth of camshaft and crankshaft sprockets to form a positive drive.

Coil oscillations: Voltage fluctuation shown on an oscilloscope after the spark plug stops firing.

Coil spring: Length of spring steel rod wound into a spiral.

Coil spring compressor: Tool used to safely compress a spring for removal or installation on a vehicle.

Coil wire: Conductor carrying high voltage from the coil to the distributor.

Cold cranking rating: The amount of current a battery can deliver for 30 seconds at 0°F.

Cold plug: One with a short insulator tip, used in engines operated at high speed.

Cold soak cleaner: Cleaning method using unheated solvents to remove oil and grease from disassembled engine parts.

Cold start injector: Valve that supplies extra fuel for cold starts.

Combination valve: One that includes both a suction valve and an expansion valve (used in air conditioning systems). Also braking system valve that can function as a metering or proportioning valve and a brake warning light switch.

Combination wrench: One that has an open jaw on one end and a box (closed end) on the other.

Combustion chamber: Area at the top of the cylinder where a spark plug ignites the compressed air-fuel mixture.

Combustion leak test: Test that checks for presence of combustion gases in cooling system.

Commutator: Sliding electrical connection between motor windings and brushes.

Commutator end frame: The end housing on a motor, holding the brushes, brush springs, and shaft bushing.

Compact spare: Small-diameter spare tire for use in emergencies.

Compression gauge: Dial indicator used to measure cylinder compression.

Compression ignition: Ignition of an air-fuel mixture by heat that results from high pressure (compression).

Compression pressure: The amount of pressure produced in the cylinder by the compression stroke.

Compression ratio: The relationship of cylinder volumes with the piston at TDC and at BDC.

Compression ring: Ring that fills the gap between the piston and cylinder wall, preventing blow-by of compression pressure into the crankcase.

Compression stroke: Piston stroke that compresses the air-fuel mixture in the cylinder.

Compression test: Check of the compression developed in each engine cylinder. A means of determining engine condition.

Compressor: Device that pressurizes a refrigerant and forces it through a refrigeration system.

Compressor assembly: Motor-powered air pump that produces pressure for an electronic height-control system.

Compressor housing: Outer case around the compressor wheel section of turbocharger.

Compressor shaft seal: A common point of refrigerant leakage in a system.

Compressor wheel: Fan-like wheel that forces air, under pressure, into the engine's intake manifold.

Computer: Electronic device used to control many systems of modern vehicles.

Computer amplifier: Device that strengthens signals inside the computer.

Computer analyzer: A more complex testing instrument than a scanner.

Computer clock: Pacing device that keeps all input, processing, and output operations "in step."

Computer-coil ignition: A distributorless ignition system using sensors, a control unit, and multiple ignition coils.

Computer conditioner: Interface that converts digital signals to analog and vice versa.

Computer controlled carburetor: One that calculates and sets air-fuel ratio based on input from sensors.

Computer harness connector: Plug at the end of a wiring harness, with one prong for each wire.

Computerized emission control system: A computer-controlled system that uses sensors, a catalytic converter, and fuel injection to minimize emissions of harmful substances.

Computer memory: Storage area where data is held electronically.

Computer menu: The list of tasks or programs initially shown on a computer screen

Computer scan values: Output from the vehicle's computer system that can be read by a diagnostic scanner.

Computer terminal values: Voltage and resistance values at the ECU connector, read by a digital VOM.

Computer trouble codes: Numeric codes, shown on a display or as pulses, that indicate the nature or location of a problem.

Computer voltage regulator: Device that provides a very smooth DC voltage for circuits and devices controlled by the computer.

Condensation: Change from a gas to a liquid state.

Condenser: An electrical component in contact point distributors that prevents arcing as points open and close. Also, a device that allows refrigerant to give off absorbed heat and change from a gas back to a liquid state.

Conduction: Method of heat transfer through direct contact.

Conductor: A material that permits easy flow of electrons.

Connecting rod: Part that fastens the piston to the crankshaft.

Connecting rod side clearance: Distance between side of the connecting rod and the side of the crankshaft journal.

Constant velocity U-joint: One that uses two cross-and-roller joints connected by a centering socket and center yoke.

Contact pattern: The area of a gear tooth where the matching gear's tooth physically contacts it.

Contact point regulator: An older type of voltage regulator that has largely been replaced by the electronic type.

Contact points: In older distributors, the spring-loaded electrical "make/break" switch contacts.

Continuous injection: Fuel injection that is constant.

Continuously variable transmission: One that has an infinite number of driving ratios and uses belts and pulleys, rather than planetary gearsets.

Control arm bushing: Sleeve that allows control arm to swing up and down.

Control arms: Movable lever arm that forms part of a vehicle's suspension system.

Control rod: A toothed shaft that rotates control sleeves to control the output of a diesel injector pump.

Control sleeve: Rotating sleeve around the plunger of a diesel injection pump that helps control pump output.

Convection: Method of heat transfer through the air or other fluid medium.

Conventional measuring system: The system of feet, inches, pounds, etc., traditionally used in the United States.

Converter housing: Case containing the fluid coupling (torque converter) used with an automatic transmission.

Cooling system: Radiator and other components that allow a coolant to circulate and maintain a constant engine operating temperature.

Cooling system hydrometer: Test instrument used to check specific gravity of coolant.

Cooling system pressure test: Method of checking for leaks by placing system under pressure.

Cooperative training: Work release program combining school classes with work experience.

CO readings: When reading CO levels, an exhaust analyzer provides a percentage by volume output.

Cotter pin: Soft metal pin that fits through hole in a nut and is then spread to lock components in place.

Countershaft: Shaft on which cluster gears are mounted. They transmit force from input gears to output gears.

Countershaft gear: Cluster of gears in a manual transmission that transmit force from input gears to output gears.

Cradle: Sub-frame supporting the engine of some vehicles.

Crankcase: Lower portion of the block, containing the crankshaft.

Crank position sensor: Similar to a distributor pickup coil, the sensor is activated by the teeth on a pulse ring in a crankshaft triggered ignition system.

Crankshaft: Component that changes the up-and-down motion of the pistons into rotating motion.

Crankshaft end play: End-to-end movement of crankshaft in block.

Crankshaft front oil seal: Component that keeps oil from leaking between the crankshaft snout and the engine front cover.

Crankshaft position sensor: Device to monitor engine speed.

Crankshaft pulley: Pulley, attached to harmonic balancer, that drives belts for alternator and other units.

Crankshaft triggered ignition: System that places trigger wheel and pickup coil on the crankshaft damper at the front of the engine.

Crankshaft turning: Grinding or otherwise smoothing the surface of crankshaft rod and main journals to repair damage or wear.

Creeper: A low, wheeled cart used to work under a car supported by jackstands.

Crimping pliers: Special tool used to mechanically fasten connectors to wires.

Crisscross pattern: Typical pattern used to tighten cylinder head bolts to provide even pressure.

Crossflow: Type of radiator arrangement with tubes running horizontally.

Crossover pipe: Connector between left and right header pipes in a dual exhaust system, used to equalize back pressure.

Curb height: Distance from a given point on the car to the ground.

Curb weight: Weight of vehicle with full gas tank and no passengers or cargo.

Current: The flow of electrons through a conductor.

Cushioning springs: Flat springs under the friction material on the clutch disc that help smooth the clutch engagement.

CV: Constant velocity.

CV-joint repair kit: Kit containing joint components, replacement boot, grease, and other necessary items for joint repair.

Cybernetics: The study of how electrical-mechanical devices can duplicate actions of the human body.

Cylinder balance test: Oscilloscope test that measures the power output from each of the engines cylinders.

Cylinder block: Another name for the engine block, or main body of the engine.

Cylinder bore: Diameter of the engine cylinder.

Cylinder boring: Machining of cylinder walls to make them perfectly straight and smooth, removing signs of wear and damage.

Cylinder head: Component that bolts to the top of the engine, enclosing the tops of the cylinders.

Cylinder head stand: A fixture used to hold the cylinder head off the workbench surface.

Cylinder hone: A tool used to develop a pattern of fine scratches on cylinder walls to aid in new ring break-in.

Cylinder leakage tester: Instrument used to determine amount of air leakage from combustion chamber.

Cylinder out-of-roundness: Condition in which a cylinder diameter is different when measured front-to-back than when measured side-to-side.

Cylinder sleeving: The practice of inserting a liner into a bored cylinder to restore it to its original diameter.

Cylinder taper: The slight difference in diameter, due to wear, from the top to the bottom of an engine cylinder.

Cylinder wear: Physical erosion of cylinder walls, requiring serious repair work.

D

Dash light code: Morse-type trouble code conveyed by flashing light on dashboard.

Dash warning light: A labeled indicator that lights to show there is a problem of malfunction.

DC: Direct current.

DC generator: Device that produces direct current.

Dead axle: A solid, straight rear axle on a front-wheel-drive vehicle.

Dead battery: One that has become discharged.

Dead cylinder: One in which the spark plug is not firing.

Decimal conversion chart: Table showing equivalent quantities in fractions of an inch, decimal fractions, and millimeters.

Deck warpage: Twisting or distortion of engine block surfaces as a result of overheating.

Delivery valve: Spring-loaded valves in the outlet fittings to diesel injector pump.

Detonation: Explosive, uneven burning of fuel, causing engine knock.

Diagnosis chart: A listing of problem causes and corrections.

Diagnostic connector: A terminal to which a diagnostic scanner can be connected to check vehicle operation.

Diagonally split: Term for a braking system that has each master cylinder piston actuating wheel cylinders that are diagonally opposed.

Diagrams: Drawings that are used to show wiring, vacuum, or hydraulic systems.

Dial bore gauge: A tool used to quickly and accurately measure cylinder taper.

Dial indicator: Device used to measure tiny movements and display the distance on a dial.

Diaphragm spring clutch: One that uses a single

diaphragm spring, rather than several coil springs, to help release the clutch disk.

Die: Tool for cutting threads on the outside of a rod or shaft.

Diesel cylinder balance test: Diagnostic procedure to determine whether cylinders are firing properly.

Diesel engine maintenance: Since diesel engines do not have ignition systems, maintenance (tune-up) work is primarily devoted to making adjustments, changing oil, and replacing filters.

Diesel fuel grade: Viscosity rating of a diesel fuel.

Dieseling: Continued engine operation with the ignition turned off (also called "run-on").

Diesel injection: A mechanical system that forces diesel oil directly into combustion chambers.

Diesel injection system tester: Device used to test a number of diesel components and functions by checking pressures.

Diesel maximum speed adjustment: A limitation that can be set by using an adjusting screw on the injection pump.

Diesel tachometer: Device used to establish the revolutions per minute of a diesel engine.

Differential: An assembly of gears used to provide power to the rear axles and allow them to rotate at different speeds as necessary.

Differential carrier: Component used to mount the differential assembly on the rear axle housing.

Differential case: Case that holds the ring gear, spider gear, and inner ends of the axles.

Differential lubricant: A heavy oil used to reduce friction between differential components.

Differential yoke: Component that connects the rear universal of the drive line to the differential.

Digital code: Trouble code displayed as actual digits (numbers), rather than flashes.

Digital display: An oscilloscope that displays a numerical reading (digital display) on a separate screen.

Digital pyrometer: An electronic device for making accurate temperature measurements.

Digital signal: One made up of strictly on-off (or high-low) pulses.

Dimmer switch: Control for high-beam and low-beam headlamp functions.

Diode: Electronic device that allows current flow in only one direction.

Diode test: Check for open or shorted conditions in a diode, using an ohmmeter or special test equipment.

Dipstick: Strip of stiff metal used to check fluid levels. Markings indicate whether more fluid must be added.

Disc brakes: Brakes using a caliper that clamps against a rotor for stopping.

Disc brake service: Procedure involving worn pad replacement, caliper rebuilding, rotor surfacing, and system bleeding.

Discharging: Flowing out (describing current movement related to a battery).

Disc resurfacing: Machining the rotor surface to remove wear marks or correct runout.

Disc runout: Amount of side-to-side movement of brake disc (rotor).

Displacement: The volume displaced by the pistons in moving from BDC to TDC.

Display output: Actuator that provides readable characters on a small screen or liquid crystal display.

Distilled water: Water that has been purified.

Distributor cap: A plastic, insulating cover that encloses the distributor rotor and other components.

Distributor injection pump: A pump that uses one or two cylinders to handle injection of diesel fuel for an engine, as compared to an inline pump with a plunger for each cylinder.

Distributor point gap: Recommended distance between points when fully open.

Distributor rotor: A slotted shaft on a distributor injector pump that controls fuel flow to each nozzle.

Distributor tester: Test device used to check operation of an ignition system distributor.

Distributor wrench: Specially shaped wrench that allows technician to reach under distributor housing to adjust timing.

Diverter valve: Component that prevents air from entering the exhaust system during deceleration.

DOHC: Dual Overhead Cam engine.

DOT number: The Department of Transportation code that indicates the tire has passed required safety tests. It also identifies manufacturer, construction type, and other data.

Double lap flare: Approved method of preparing steel fuel lines for connection.

Downflow: Type of radiator arrangement with tubes running vertically.

Dragging brakes: Those that remain partially applied, even though pedal is released.

Dragging clutch: Failure of friction disc to fully disengage from flywheel, even though clutch pedal is depressed.

Draw-through turbo: A turbocharger located behind the compressor or throttle body. It compresses the air-fuel mixture.

Drilled rod: Connecting rod with an oil passage drilled through its length to deliver oil to the piston pin.

Drive chain: A chain used with some longitudinally mounted engines to transfer power from the engine crankshaft to the transaxle.

Drive housing: Case surrounding the pinion gear on a starter motor.

Drive line: The parts that transfer power from the transmission to the drive wheels.

Drivers: Power transistors in a computer that control current flow to actuators.

Drive shaft: Steel tube that transfers rotating motion from transmission to rear wheels of a car.

Drive shaft angle: The angle at which the drive line meets the differential or the transmission.

Drive shaft assembly: Components between the transmission and differential, including front and rear yokes, universal joints, and a drive shaft.

Drive shaft balance: Equal weight distribution around the axis of the shaft.

Drive shaft noise: Sounds typically caused by worn U-joints, worn slip joints, or a faulty center support bearing.

Drive shaft runout: Lack of straightness, due to being bent or because of U-joint wear.

Drive shaft vibration: A rapid oscillation caused by a shaft imbalance or excessive shaft runout.

Drive side: Convex side of gear tooth.

Drive size: The size of the square opening for the handle of a socket wrench set.

Driving hub: Mounting for wheel on end of axle.

Driving range: Distance a vehicle can be driven without refueling.

Drop light: An electrical extension cord with a light bulb in a safety cage attached.

Dropping brake pedal: Slow descent of brake pedal to floor when brakes are applied. Usually caused by internal leak in master cylinder.

Drum: The housing that holds the parts of a clutch assembly for an automatic transmission.

Drum brakes: System that forces brake shoes against the inside of a rotating drum to stop vehicle.

Drum brake service: Process that involves dismounting, disassembling, cleaning, and replacing parts as necessary. Usually, shoes are replaced, wheel cylinders replaced or rebuilt, and the drum is turned (resurfaced). System is then reassembled, bled, and tested.

Drum grinding: Sometimes done to remove hard spots on a brake drum.

Drum maximum diameter: Largest inside diameter allowed for safe operation of drum brakes.

Drum resurfacing: Machining of brake drum to remove surface damage.

Dry charged: Battery that is filled with electrolyte just before being installed in a vehicle.

Dry park test: Visual check for looseness of steering components.

Dry sleeve: A thin cylinder liner that is not exposed to coolant.

Dual master cylinder: Brake system pump with two pistons and fluid reservoirs for safety.

Dummy shaft: Tool used to drive out countershaft and reverse idler shaft when disassembling manual transmission.

Dust cap: Metal cover on end of axle or spindle to keep grease in and road dirt out of bearings..

Dwell: The amount of time distributor points remain closed between openings.

Dwell meter: One that measures point setting in degrees of distributor rotation.

Dwell section: Section of oscilloscope pattern used to identify problems in the distributor or electronic control unit.

Dwell signal: Electronic signal output by carburetor that can be read on a special meter for troubleshooting.

Dwell variation: Change in meter readings indicating distributor wear.

Dye penetrant: A testing material that can be sprayed on aluminum or cast iron engine parts to locate cracks.

Dynamic imbalance: Tire imbalance that causes both up-and-down and side-to-side movement while rotating.

Dynamometers: Instrument used to measure power output and performance of an engine.

Dyno: An engine dynamometer, used to measure brake horsepower.

E

ECA: Electronic control assembly; another name for an automotive computer.

ECM: Electronic control module; another name for an automotive computer.

ECU: Electronic control unit; another name for an automotive computer.

Effective plunger stroke: The amount of plunger movement that pressurizes fuel in a diesel injector pump.

EFI: Electronic fuel injection.

EFI self-diagnosis: The ability of an electronic fuel injection system to display trouble codes.

EFI tester: A diagnostic device used with EFI systems that do not feature self-diagnosis.

EFI trouble code: A digital display or on-off sequence that shows a number code for problem identification.;

EGR valve: Valve that allows exhaust gases to re-enter the intake manifold to be burned again, reducing some forms of toxic emissions.

Electrical fire: One that involves, or begins in, electrical wiring.

Electric engine fan: One operated by an electric motor, under control of a thermostatic switch.

Electric fuel pump: Device that uses a rotary motion to move fuel.

Electrolyte: Liquid that surrounds the plates of a battery and allows a free flow of electrons.

Electronic advance: A system that uses sensor input and the vehicle's computer to control spark timing.

Electronic airbag system: System using impact sensors to deploy an airbag that cushions vehicle operator (and in some cases, passengers) in a collision.

Electronic coil module: Grouping of ignition coils and the control unit needed to operate them.

Electronic control unit: Another term for a computer used in a vehicle.

Electronic ignition system: One that uses an electronic control circuit and distributor pickup coil.

Electronic ignition tester: Instrument used to identify source of ignition problems.

Electronic modules: Small computers in a vehicle, used for specific systems (such as anti-lock brakes or climate control).

Electronic regulator: Solid-state regulator separate from the alternator.

Electronic shock absorber system: One that uses a computer, actuators, and adjustable shock absorbers to regulate stiffness of the vehicle's suspension.

Electronic steering assist: Power steering system using an electric motor, rather than hydraulic components.

Electronic transmission/transaxle control system: A computer-based system that controls shift points and torque converter lockup for improved fuel economy.

Element: One of the cells that can be combined to form a battery.

Emergency brake: Mechanical means of applying rear brakes.

Emission control system: Components and adjustments used to reduce the amount of pollutants released by operation of an automobile.

Engine: The propulsion system that provides motive power for a vehicle.

Engine analyzer: Grouping of instruments used to check various engine functions and components.

Engine blowby: Leakage of unburned fuel and other pollutants past piston rings and into the crankcase.

Engine bottom end: The block, crankshaft, connecting rods, pistons, and related components.

Engine break-in: Sequence of acceleration, deceleration, and other operations designed to properly seat and seal new piston rings.

Engine crane: A portable, wheeled hoist used to lift and remove engines from vehicles.

Engine efficiency: Ratio of power produced by the engine to the power supplied to that engine.

Engine firing order: The sequence in which spark plugs are fired.

Engine flooding: Excess fuel in the intake manifold, preventing starting.

Engine front cover: Housing of sheet metal or cast aluminum that covers the timing chain or gears.

Engine front end: A combination of components that operates the camshaft.

Engine miss: Roughness in engine operation, indicating failure of a spark plug to fire.

Engine off self-test: Test conducted with engine off but ignition key on to cause displaying of trouble codes.

Engine on self-test: One conducted with the engine fully warmed up, allowing check of the sensors under normal conditions.

Engine operating temperature: Temperature reached by coolant during normal engine operation.

Engine overhaul: Process of servicing all internal parts of an engine.

Engine sensors: Devices that monitor temperatures, fluid levels, and other engine conditions for computer input.

Engine smoke: Emissions during acceleration or deceleration. Color can indicate engine condition.

Engine surge: Rise and fall of engine speed in cruising operation.

Engine temperature sensor: Component that measures temperature of engine coolant.

Engine top end: The cylinder heads, valves, camshaft, and related parts.

Engine torque: A rating of turning force at the engine crankshaft.

Engine tune-up: A process of parts replacement and adjustment to return an engine to its peak performance.

EPROM: Erasable programmable read-only memory.

Erasing trouble codes: Removing trouble codes from computer memory after they have been read and the problems corrected.

Ethyl alcohol: Grain alcohol or ethanol.

Evacuation: A process of removing air and moisture from an emptied air conditioning system, using a vacuum pump.

Evaporator: A device in which refrigerant changes from a liquid to a gas and absorbs heat from its surroundings.

Exhaust gas analyzer: Testing device to measure the chemical content of exhaust gases.

Exhaust gas sensor: See oxygen sensor.

Exhaust manifold: Component that directs output of the exhaust ports to the exhaust system.

Exhaust manifold heat valve: Component that forces hot exhaust gases to circulate through intake manifold as an aid to cold-weather starting.

Exhaust stroke: Piston stroke that forces byproducts of combustion out of the cylinder.

Exhaust system: Components that quiet engine operation and direct combustion products (exhaust gases) to the rear of the vehicle.

Expander-spacer: Metal ring used with two rails to form oil control ring.

Expansion plug: Freeze plug designed for installation in tight quarters.

Expansion tube: A device with a small orifice that meters refrigerant into the evaporator of an air conditioning system.

Expansion valve: Temperature-sensitive valve that controls refrigerant flow and air conditioner evaporator temperature.

Extension housing: A separate housing bolted to the transmission housing, containing the output shaft and rear oil seal.

External oil leakage: Escape of oil from the engine, usually around gaskets or seals.

F

Face: Area of a gear tooth above the pitch line.

Fast charger: One that provides a high current flow for quickly recharging a battery.

Fastener: Devices that hold parts together.

Fast flushing: Flushing system through a heater hose fitting, without removing the thermostat.

Fast idle cam: A cam that increases idle speed when the choke is closed.

Fast idle solenoid: Device that holds throttle plates open when engine is operating, but lets them almost close when engine is shut off.

Feathered edge: One side of each tread rib is worn sharp and raised; the other side is rounded or recessed.

Feeler gauge: A thin metal strip or wire of identified thickness, used to measure clearance.

Fender cover: Cloth or plastic blankets placed over auto body sections to protect the finish while repairs go on.

fhp: Frictional horsepower.

Field frame: Housing on a motor that holds the field coils.

Field windings: Stationary windings in a motor that creates a magnetic field to keep the armature rotating.

Filler neck restriction: Metal piece preventing introduction of the larger fuel nozzle used for leaded fuel.

Fill ring: Electrolyte level indicator in older style batteries.

Firing line: The tall spike shown on an oscilloscope, representing the voltage needed to make the spark jump the plug gap.

Firing order: Sequence in which the spark plugs fire in cylinders.

Fixed caliper: Brake caliper rigidly mounted to steering knuckle.

Flank: Area on a gear tooth below the pitch line.

Flex fan: One with blades that alter airflow with engine speed.

Float: Device that rises and falls with fuel level in bowl, opening and closing the needle valve.

Floating caliper: Brake caliper mounted on two rubber bushings, allowing some movement.

Fluid contamination: Inclusion of foreign matter in transmission fluid.

Fluid coupling fan clutch: Clutch designed to slip at higher fan speeds.

Fluid varnish: Sticky, glue-like substance resulting from breakdown of automatic transmission fluid.

Flywheel: Large, heavy wheel mounted on the rear end of the crankshaft. Usually includes a ring gear that is engaged by the starter pinion.

FM: Frequency modulation (type of radio broadcasting).

Force: A pushing or pulling action.

Forward bias: Arrangement in which diode acts as a conductor.

Four-gas analyzer: Measuring instrument that provides reading of oxygen and carbon dioxide, as well as HC and CO, levels in exhaust.

Four-stroke cycle: An engine that takes four piston movements (intake, compression, power, exhaust) to complete a cycle.

Frame: The strong steel structure that supports the body of a vehicle.

Friction bearing: Plain bearing, with two smooth surfaces sliding on each other.

Front cover gasket: Thin sealing component that is compressed between the cover and the engine.

Front drive axles: Shafts that transfer power from the transaxle differential to the vehicle's wheels.

Front end rack: Alignment stand.

Fuel accumulator: Diaphragm that dampens pressure pulses in a fuel injection system.

Fuel distributor: Hydraulically operated valve used to control fuel flow in a continuous injector system.

Fuel evaporization system: A combination of technologies and components that prevents fuel vapors from entering the atmosphere.

Fuel heater: A device used to warm diesel fuel and keep it from jelling into a semi-solid during cold weather.

Fuel injection system: General term for systems used with either gasoline or diesel fuel.

Fuel injector: Fuel valve controlled by a coil or solenoid.

Fuel pressure regulator: System that controls pressure of fuel entering injector valves.

Fuel pump pressure: The pressure of a fuel pump's output.

Fuel pump vacuum: The amount of "pull" exerted on fuel by the pump.

Fuel pump volume: The amount of fuel discharged by a pump in a measured period.

Fuel rail: Tubing that connects several injectors to the main fuel line.

Fuel return system: One that keeps cool fuel circulating to prevent vapor lock.

Fuel tank capacity: How much fuel a tank can hold.

Full-floating piston pin: One that is free to rotate. It is secured in place with snap rings.

Full flow lubrication system: One that forces all oil through a filter before it reaches the parts to be lubricated.

Fully synchronized transmission: One in which all forward gears are equipped with synchronizers to allow downshifting while in motion.

Fuse: Device that interrupts current if a circuit is overloaded or a short occurs.

G

Gas-charged shock: Type that contains low-pressure gas to keep the oil from foaming, and thus improve performance.

Gasket: A soft, flexible material placed between two parts to prevent leaks.

Gasket scraper: Metal tool used to remove pieces of gasket and hardened oil or carbon deposits from engine parts.

Gas line freeze: Condition caused by moisture in fuel turning to ice and blocking fuel line.

Gasohol: Gasoline with from 2 to 20 percent alcohol added.

Gasoline injection: System that uses computers, sensors and electrically operated injectors to meter fuel into an engine.

Gas turbine: Engine that uses burning and expanding fuel vapor to spin fan-type blades.

Gear backlash: Small amount of clearance between meshing gear teeth.

Gearbox overhaul: Disassembly, cleaning, adjusting, and replacing parts as necessary.

Gearbox ratio: The relationship (number of turns) between the steering wheel as the sector gear.

Gear clash: Noise that is heard when gears fail to mesh properly in a manual transmission.

Gear oil: A high viscosity (80W or 90W) oil used for transmissions.

Gear pump: Oil pump using meshing gears to provide pressure and oil movement.

Gear ratio: The number of rotations a driving gear must make while the driven gear is completing one revolution.

Gear reduction: The situation in which a small gear is used to drive a larger gear, with an increase in torque as a result.

General repair manual: Service manual covering many makes and models of cars, usually over a several-year span.

Glow plug: A heating element that helps start a diesel in cold weather.

Glow plug resistance-balance test: A diagnostic procedure used to determine whether all cylinders of a glow plug equipped diesel engine are firing.

Governor: A device used to control an engine's speed.

Grabbing brakes: Abrupt, hard application of brakes when pedal is only lightly depressed.

Grade markings: Lines on bolt head, indicating tensile strength.

Grease gun: Tool used to inject lubricating grease, under pressure, into fittings.

Grease job: Process of forcing a thick lubricant, under pressure, into friction points on the chassis, steering system, and drive line.

Grease rack: Lift used to raise car for lubrication or other work.

Grease seal: Component that prevents lubricant leaking from axle assembly into steering knuckle or bearing support.

Gross hp: Horsepower developed with only basic accessories in use.

Group injection: Operation of some (usually half) of the injectors simultaneously.

Growler: Testing device used to check armatures for shorts.

H

Hall effect: A type of pickup used with many electronic ignition systems.

Halogen headlamp: One with a small, high-intensity halogen lamp inside a conventional sealed housing.

Hangers: Rubber and metal fasteners that suspend the exhaust components from the underside of the vehicle.

Hard failure: One that is always present (not intermittent), such as a disconnected wire.

Hard steering: Greater than normal effort needed to turn steering wheel.

Hard to shift: A manual transmission problem often caused by damaged or sticking linkage.

Hard to start problem: Usually caused by a partial system failure, such as a choke refusing to open.

Harmonic vibration: High-frequency vibration caused by the crankshaft.

Harsh shifts: Transmission changes gears in a jerky manner.

HC: Abbreviation for hydrocarbons (unburned fuel).

HC readings: Measurements of hydrocarbon emissions in parts-per-million.

Header pipe: Steel tubing connecting the exhaust manifold to the catalytic converter.

Head gasket markings: Lines or words printed on gasket to indicate proper installation orientation.

Head gasket torque sequence: Tightening head bolts in specified sequence and in several stages of torque.

Headlamp system: Components, such as battery, switches, fuses, and lamps that make up the headlamp lighting circuit.

Headlight aimer: Device used to adjust headlights to specified positions.

Headlight aiming screen: Set of measured lines on a wall, used to adjust headlight aim.

Heater core: A radiator-like unit that circulates heated engine coolant through a series of tubes. A fan blows air past the tubes to heat the passenger compartment of the vehicle.

Heater hoses: Flexible tubes that carry heated coolant between engine and the heater core.

Heating system: Components that use engine cooling system heat to warm an automobile passenger compartment.

Heat shields: Metal plates that keep exhaust heat from transferring to other parts of the vehicle.

Heel: The wide part of a gear tooth.

Height sensor: Lever-operated switch that reacts to changes in car-body height.

Height sensor link: Rods that connect height sensor to suspension system.

Helical gears: Those with teeth cut at an angle to the centerline of the driveshaft.

Helicoil: Spring steel insert used to repair damaged internal threads.

Hemi chamber: A dome-shaped (hemispherical) combustion chamber.

Hesitation: Condition in which engine does not accelerate immediately when gas pedal is pressed.

High side: Section of an air conditioning system in which refrigerant is under high pressure.

Holding tools: Vises, clamps, and fixtures that grip a part while it is being worked on.

Honing grit: Fine bits of stone and metal remaining after a cylinder is honed. This material must be removed from the engine before it is reassembled, or it will cause severe wear.

Horsepower: Measure of an engine's ability to perform work.

Hotchkiss drive: Open drive shaft that operates a rear axle assembly mounted on springs. The most common rear-wheel drive type.

Hot idle compensator: Component that prevents stalling when engine temperature is high.

Hot plug: One with a long insulator tip, often used in older engines.

Hot tank: Cleaning tank with heated chemicals in which parts are immersed.

Hub: Mounting place for vehicle wheel on end of axle or spindle.

Hybrid: A vehicle using two different methods of propulsion, such as a small gasoline engine and an electric motor with batteries.

Hydraulic actuator: Solenoid-operated valve and electric pump mechanism.

Hydraulic booster: Braking system booster actuated by hydraulic pressure from the power steering pump.

Hydraulic circuit diagrams: Schematic showing how transmission parts and passages interconnect.

Hydraulic head: The housing around a diesel injection pump plunger.

Hydraulic lifter: Oil-filled lifter that maintains zero valve clearance.

Hydraulic press: Machine used to exert pressure on parts that are being forced (press-fit) together.

Hydraulic system: Arrangement of pistons and tubing that uses pressure to transmit force from one part to another.

Hydrocarbon: Chemical mixtures (12 percent hydrogen, 82 percent carbon) making up crude oil, or petroleum.

Hydrometer: Tool used to test for specific gravity (and thus, battery charge).

Hypoid gears: Gear arrangement with the pinion centerline well below the centerline of the ring gear.

I

Idle air control valve: Solenoid operated valve in a TBI system that regulates idle speed.

Idle mixture screw: Adjusting device that meters fuel into the air horn.

Ignition coil: Device used to produce the high voltage needed for ignition spark.

Ignition computer: ECM that controls ignition timing, based on sensor input.

Ignition distributor: Component that directs coil voltage to each spark plug at the appropriate time.

Ignition lag: The time required for diesel fuel to vaporize, heat up, and begin to burn.

Ignition spark switch: Used on some manual transmissions, this switch permits distributor vacuum advance in high gear.

Ignition system: Components that produce a spark to ignite the air-fuel mixture in the engine.

Ignition timing: How early or late the spark plug fires in relation to the piston position.

I-head: One with intake and exhaust valves in the cylinder head.

ihp: Indicated horsepower.

Impact socket: An attachment to an air-powered impact wrench.

Impeller: Pump component with fan-like blades that spins inside a housing to move liquid.

Improper injector spray pattern: One that is restricted due to foreign matter in the injector.

Inboard CV-joint: The inner universal joint on a front-wheel drive vehicle.

Incorrect camber: Condition that produces wear on one side of tire tread.

Incorrect shift points: Transmission shifts too soon or too late in relation to engine speed.

Incorrect toe: Condition that produces a feathered edge on tire tread.

Independent suspension: System that permits each wheel to move up and down without seriously affecting any other wheel.

Inflation pressure: The amount of air pressure that a tire can safely handle.

Initial ignition timing: Timing set with ignition idling.

Injection pressure tester: A test device for precisely measuring diesel injection pressure.

Injection pump: A pump that meters fuel in a diesel system.

Injection pump test stand: Specialized testing equipment for use with injector pumps.

Injection pump timing: Adjustment of the pump operation to match the engine's operating cycle.

Injection timing: The relationship between injection of fuel and the positions of the engine's pistons.

Injector: A spring-loaded valve that meters fuel into the precombustion chamber of a diesel engine.

Injector leakage: Dripping or spraying of fuel when the injector nozzle is closed.

Injector opening pressure: Amount of pressure needed to open the injector nozzle.

Injector output volume: The amount of fuel output over a specific time period.

Injector rebuild: A process involving cleaning, disassembly, replacement of worn parts, and reassembly of a nozzle.

Injector spray pattern: Shape of the spray produced by an injector.

Inlet air temperature sensor: The device that checks temperature of air entering the engine.

In-line engine: One with cylinders lined up in a row.

In-line pump: A diesel injection pump with one plunger (piston) for each cylinder.

Inner stub shaft: Section of front-drive axle that is splined to differential gears. It is connected to the interconnecting shaft through a universal joint.

Input: The information provided to a computer by a sensor.

Input shaft: Metal shaft that transfers motion from the engine (via the clutch) to the transmission.

Instrumentation computer: One that uses sensor output to control dashboard displays.

Insulated current resistance test: Check of all parts between the battery positive and the starting motor for excess resistance.

Insulator: A material that resists the flow of electrons.

Intake and exhaust ports: Openings into the combustion chamber. They are controlled by valves.

Intake manifold: Component that directs the air-fuel mixture from the carburetor or throttle body to the cylinders.

Intake stroke: Piston stroke that draws the air-fuel mixture into the cylinder.

Integral power steering: A system in which the hydraulic piston is mounted inside the gearbox.

Integral regulator: A regulator that is mounted in or on an alternator.

Integral valve guide: One machined into the cylinder head.

Integral valve seat: One machined into the cylinder head.

Integrated circuit: A tiny "chip" of silicon containing complete electronic circuits.

Interconnecting shaft: Component of front-drive axle that connects inner and outer universal joints.

Interface: Another name for a computer conditioner.

Interference angle: Slight difference in angle between valve face and valve seat for improved sealing when valve is closed.

Intermittent problem: One that occurs only under some conditions.

Internal cam ring: A collar with lobes that operates diesel injectors.

Internal oil leakage: Loss of oil by burning in the cylinders as a result of piston ring wear.

J

Jounce bumper: Rubber blocks that keep suspension parts from hitting the frame when the vehicle encounters large bumps or holes.

Journal out-of-roundness: Greater wear on the top or bottom section of a crankshaft journal.

Journal taper: Difference in diameter of a crankshaft journal from one side to the other.

Jumper cables: Electrical cables used to start a car with a dead battery.

Jumper wire: A wire used to make temporary electrical connections for testing.

Jumps out of gear: A manual transmission problem in which the transmission will unexpectedly disengage and move into neutral.

Jump starting: Providing current to a car with a dead battery by connecting cables to the battery of an operating car.

K

KAM: Keep-alive memory.

Key: Metal piece that locks into a slot (keyway) to keep a part and a shaft turning together.

Kickdown valve: Component that causes automatic transmission to shift down into a lower gear during fast acceleration.

Knock: Engine noise caused by detonation.

Knock sensor: Engine sensor that detects detonation in the engine.

kV: Kilovolt (1000 volts).

L

Lapping valves: A polishing operation with a fine grinding compound that helps smooth the mating surfaces of valve faces and valve seats.

Lateral runout: Side-to-side movement of a wheel or tire.

Leaded gasoline: Fuel with an antiknock additive.

Leaf spring: Flat pieces of spring steel that are stacked and bound together. Normally used as part of a vehicle's rear suspension.

Leak detector: Device used to locate refrigerant leaks in a system.

Leaking exhaust manifold gasket: Creates metal-like rapping sound.

Leaking heater core: Rusted or cracked tube in core, allowing coolant to escape.

Leaking injector: One that allows extra fuel to drip out, causing a richer mixture.

Leaking intake manifold gasket: Possible case of vacuum leak resulting in rough idle.

Leaking valve seal: A condition that allows oil to be drawn into intake or exhaust port and burned, causing blue smoke.

Lean air-fuel ratio: An air-fuel mixture that contains more air than a stoichiometric mixture.

LED code: Trouble code displayed as a pattern of lighted diodes.

L-head: One with both the intake and exhaust valves in the block.

Lift: See Grease rack.

Lifter leakdown rate: Time required for a hydraulic lifter plunger lobe pushed to the bottom of its stroke under controlled conditions.

Lifting fixture or chain: Device fastened to an engine to allow it to be lifted by a crane or hoist.

Limited slip differential: One that provides driving force to both rear wheels at all times.

Limited slip differential chatter: Sound made when turning a corner, caused by sticking and releasing of clutches in the differential.

Line bore: A machining operation resulting in a carefully aligned series of holes through an engine block for the crankshaft bearings.

Liner: Thin rubber layer bonded to plies and forming the inside surface of the tire.

Line wrench: Special wrench with split jaw that can be slipped over tubing (such as a fuel line) to tighten or loosen compression fittings.

Liquid-vapor separator: Tank that permits liquid fuel to settle out and flow back to fuel tank.

Liquid cooling system: Circulation of a heat-absorbing medium through engine passages, with the accumulated heat dissipated by further circulation through heat exchanger (radiator).

Load or acceleration test: Oscilloscope reading that measures the firing voltages of the spark plugs when the engine is accelerating rapidly.

Load rating: The maximum amount of weight a tire can carry when inflated to the recommended pressure.

Locked in gear: A manual transmission problem often caused by damaged or sticking linkage. Broken gear teeth can also be at fault.

Locking hub: Components that transfer power from driving axles to driving wheels on a four-wheel-drive vehicle.

Lock-up converter: A variation of the fluid coupling, with an internal friction clutch mechanism. It "locks up" in high gear, improving fuel economy.

Longitudinal: Lengthwise; term used to identify an engine mounted with its centerline on or parallel to the centerline of the vehicle.

Low brake pedal: Farther than normal brake pedal travel before braking begins.

Low pressure cutout switch: One that prevents compressor operation and possible damage if air conditioning system pressure drops below a setpoint.

Low side: Section of an air conditioning system in which refrigerant is under high pressure.

LPG: Liquefied petroleum gas, an alternate fuel.

Lubrication service: The process of checking and adjusting the levels of all lubricants in a vehicle.

Lubrication system: Method of distributing lubricant (oil) to moving parts to minimize friction.

Lug nut: Large steel nuts used to hold a wheel into the axle hub.

Lug stud: Special bolts that are press-fit into the axle hub and accept lug nuts to mount the vehicle's wheels.

M

MacPherson strut: Suspension system that uses one control arm and one strut for each wheel assembly.

Magnafluxing: Testing procedure that uses a magnet and metal powder to find cracks in cast iron parts.

Magnetic clutch: Device used to engage and disengage the compressor of an air conditioning system.

Magnetic field: Field of force generated around an electrical conductor.

Magnetic sensor: One that uses part movement (such as rotation) and induced current to produce a signal for a computer.

Mag-tach: A magnetically triggered tachometer usable on both gasoline and diesel engine.

Main bearing bores: Holes machined into the bottom of the block for the crankshaft and its bearings.

Main bearing cap torque: The factory recommended degree of tightness for main cap bolts.

Main bearing knock: Deep, resonant sound caused by wear of bearing and possibly crankshaft journal.

Main body: Central portion of the carburetor, forming the air horn and fuel bowl.

Main caps: Pieces the bolt to the bottom of the block to hold the crankshaft in place.

Main computer: The largest and most powerful microprocessor in a vehicle's system. It can control other computers.

Main discharge tube: Passage between fuel bowl and venturi.

Mainframe computer: A large, centralized computer with a great deal of memory and computing power.

Main jet: Fuel inlet metering device for normal-speed engine operation.

Main journals: Carefully machined surfaces on the ends of the crankshaft that fit into the block main bearings.

Maintenance-free battery: One without removable filler caps that does not require periodic filling with water.

Maintenance interval: The specific number of miles or months that should elapse between tune-ups, as described in the vehicle owner's manual.

Main thrust bearing: Flanged version of main bearing, designed to limit crankshaft endplay.

Major tune-up: A tune-up requiring some degree of repair to systems, in addition to the work done for a minor tune-up.

Manifold pressure sensor: Measures pressure inside intake manifold. Also called MAP sensor.

Manual bleeding: A method of system bleeding using only master cylinder pressure.

Manual transaxle: One with a manual (driver-operated) transmission.

Manual transmission: One that is shifted from gear to gear by the vehicle operator.

Manual valve: In an automatic transmission, a valve actuated by the gear shift lever that routes oil pressure to the components required for the selected gear.

Manufacturer's manual: Service manual produced by an auto maker and restricted to its vehicles.

Master cylinder: Hydraulic piston type pump that develops pressure for the braking system.

Mechanical choke unloader: A linkage that opens the choke plate whenever the throttle swings fully open.

Mechanical efficiency: A comparison of brake horsepower to indicated horsepower, measuring frictional loss.

Mechanical fuel pump: Device that uses a reciprocating motion to move fuel.

Mechanical lifter: Solid lifters that must be adjusted periodically.

Metering rod: Stepped rod that moves in and out of main jet to alter fuel flow.

Metering valve: Valve designed to equalize pressure at

wheel cylinders on vehicles with front disc and rear drum brakes.

Methyl alcohol: Wood alcohol, or methanol.

Metric measuring system: System of measure, based on units of 10, that is used by most of the world.

Mica: Mineral used as an insulator between commutator segments.

Micrometer: A precision measuring device for very small distances.

Microprocessor: A small computer, sometimes called a "chip" or "IC" (integrated circuit).

Milky fluid: Condition caused by contamination of transmission fluid by engine coolant.

Milky or white oil: Lubricant that has become contaminated by the presence of coolant.

Milling: A machining process that removes a thin layer of metal; often used to repair warped engine cylinder heads.

Millisecond: Fraction (1000th) of a second.

Minimum disc thickness: Thinnest rotor dimension allowed for proper and safe operation of disc brakes.

Minor tune-up: A tune-up done on an engine in good condition, involving primarily adjustment and ignition parts replacement or maintenance.

Missing: Failure of one or more cylinders to fire.

Mixture control solenoid: Electromechanical; device that opens and closes air and fuel passages in carburetor.

Modem: A modulator-demodulator; a device that changes analog signals to digital, and vice versa, for communications.

Modem analyzer system: System that allows a shop computer analyzer to communicate via telephone line with a large mainframe that stores information needed for advanced troubleshooting.

Modulated injection: Injection of fuel intermittently, without reference to intake valve timing.

Modulator vacuum leakage: Cause of incorrect shift point operation in an automatic transmission.

Movable pole shoe: Device that uses a yoke lever to move the pinion gear into contact with the flywheel gear.

Muffler: An exhaust-system component that decreases the noise of vehicle operation.

Muffler clamps: U-shaped connectors for fastening parts of the exhaust system together.

Multi-cylinder engine: One that has two or more cylinders.

Multi-point: Fuel injection system that sprays fuel into port for each cylinder.

Multi-weight: Motor oil that exhibits different viscosity characteristics under different conditions.

Multimeter: An electrical test device that can be used to measure voltage, current, or resistance.

Multiple disc clutch: One with several discs that can be used to drive planetary gearsets.

Mushroomed valve stem: Stem end that had been enlarged and spread outward by rocker arm contact.

Mushy shifts: Transmission changes gears too slowly.

N

Needle valve: A precisely machined rod used to control fuel flow from in the injector.

Net hp: Maximum horsepower developed with all accessories in use.

Neutral safety switch: Switch that prevents engaging the starter when the vehicle is in gear.

Neutral safety switch adjustment: Altering position of the switch to permit starting of the engine when gear selector is in the "park" position.

NIASE: National Institute for Automotive Service Excellence.

Noise suppressor: Capacitors that absorb voltage fluctuations in a car's electrical system, reducing radio noise.

Nonadjustable rocker arm: One that does not allow clearance to be changed. Used with hydraulic lifters.

Nondriving hub: One that rotates freely on spindles (axle ends).

Nonindependent suspension: System in which wheels are attached to each end of a solid axle.

Normal aspiration: System that provides air to the engine at normal atmospheric pressure.

No start problem: Engine turns over but refuses to fire.

NOx: Abbreviation for oxides of nitrogen, pollutants resulting from high combustion temperatures.

Number set: Punches used to indent identifying numbers in metal.

Nut lock: Thin, slotted nut that fits over main spindle nut on a nondriving wheel.

O

O_2 readings: Oxygen must be present for proper catalytic converter functioning. Analyzers measure it in percentage by volume.

Octane number: Indicators of the antiknock value of a gasoline.

OHC follower: Component that fits between camshaft and lifter.

Ohm's law: A simple formula for computing unknown electrical values when two values are known.

Oil change interval: Mileage or period of time after which oil should be changed (3000 miles or three months, typically).

Oil consumption: The loss of oil caused by internal or external leakage.

Oil cooler: A radiator-like device used to regulate oil temperature.

Oil dye: Additive used to help locate leaks.

Oil filler cap: Metal or plastic cap used to cover the opening on an engine where oil is added.

Oil film: Thin layer of lubricant between parts, preventing metal-to-metal contact.

Oil filter housing: Part of the engine on which the filter is mounted.

Oil gallery: Passage in the engine block through which oil can flow to point requiring lubrication.

Oil pressure gauge: Instrument that provides a direct reading of engine oil pressure.

Oil pressure indicator: Warning light on control panel to alert driver to low pressure situation.

Oil pressure switch: Safety device that shuts off the fuel pump if engine oil pressure drops.

Oil pressure test: Measurement of actual oil pressure using a special testing device.

Oil pump: Device for forcing oil under pressure to the points where lubrication is needed.

Oil ring: Piston ring that scrapes excess oil off the cylinder wall.

Oil service rating: Identification of type of service for which an oil is suited.

Oil slinger: Washer-shaped part mounted on crankshaft sprocket to throw oil onto timing chain during operation.

Oil spurt hole: Small hole drilled in connecting rod for improved cylinder lubrication.

Oil streaked sight glass: A sign that the air conditioning system is low on refrigerant and allowing excess oil to circulate.

One-wire circuit: One that uses the vehicle frame as a return wire to the power source.

Open circuit: Electrical circuit with a gap or break in continuity so that current cannot flow.

Open end: A type of wrench with an open jaw on both ends.

Open injector coil: A broken wire in the solenoid coil is preventing operation.

Open loop: Control system using preset values in the computer to operate engine.

Open system: Cooling system that does not use a recovery tank.

Operating parameter: An acceptable maximum or minimum electrical value.

Opposed engine: One with cylinders lying flat on either side of the crankshaft.

Organizing tray: Tray or board with holes in it for holding push rods and lifters during engine disassembly.

O-ring seal: A synthetic rubber ring that fits into a groove and is compressed when parts are assembled.

O-ring valve seal: Small round ring, usually of rubber, that fits in a groove on a shaft to prevent oil leakage.

Oscilloscope: Instrument that displays line patterns that relate voltages to time.

Outboard CV-joint: The outer universal joint on a front-wheel drive vehicle.

Outer stub shaft: In a front-wheel drive vehicle, the short shaft connecting outer universal joint and the front wheel hub.

Output: The signal sent by a computer (for example, to an actuator) as a result of processing inputs it has received.

Output shaft: Transmission shaft on which the output gears are mounted.

Output shaft gears: Gears that turn the output shaft of a manual transmission.

Overbore limit: The largest possible diameter to which a cylinder can be bored without weakening its walls.

Overdrive ratio: The situation in which a large gear is used to drive a smaller gear, with an increase in speed as a result.

Overhead valve: One located in the cylinder head, rather than the block.

Overinflation: Operating tire with a higher-than-recommended air pressure.

Overrunning clutch: Device that locks a pinion gear in one direction and releases it in the other.

Oversize piston and rings: Larger components sized to fit a rebored cylinder.

Oxygen sensor: Device that monitors oxygen content in engine exhaust to correct air-fuel ratio.

P

Packing wheel bearings: Filling the bearing shells with grease to prevent excessive wear.

Pad wear sensor: Metal tab on brake pad that makes a squealing noise to signal the need for pad replacement.

Pancake chamber: Combustion chamber that forms a flat pocket over the piston.

Parade pattern: Oscilloscope pattern that shows traces for each cylinder from left to right across the screen.

Parking pawl: A latch that locks the transmission so that the vehicle will not roll when the selection lever is in the "Park" position.

Part alignment marks: Lines or other marks scribed on parts by a technician during disassembly, so that components can be reassembled properly.

Particulates: Solid particles of soot and other substances that result from combustion.

Part warpage: Often causes gasket failure, since parts do not seal together properly.

Passive sensor: One that changes an externally produced signal, but does not generate its own voltage.

PCV system: Positive crankcase ventilation, a system that decreases pollution by drawing toxic gases back through the combustion process.

Pedal free play: The amount of brake pedal movement before braking action begins to take place.

Pedal height: Distance of brake pedal above floor of vehicle.

Performance test: A measurement of air conditioning system performance made with the vehicle engine running.

Petroleum: Oil taken directly out of the ground.

Pickup coil: Component that sends pulses to the control unit of an electronic ignition system as a result of trigger wheel rotation.

Pickup coil air gap: Space between the pickup coil and trigger wheel tooth.

Pilot bearing: The bushing or bearing that supports the forward end of the transmission input shaft.

Ping: A mild knock (light tapping noise) caused by preignition of fuel.

Pinion gear: Differential gear turned by the drive line. It meshes with the ring gear. Also, gearbox component that meshes with rack, or a small gear on a starter motor that engages a larger gear to rotate the engine flywheel.

Pinion gear bearing preload: Degree of tightness of bearings, adjusted by compressing a spacer or using shims.

Pinion gear clearance: Distance between the pinion gear and drive end frame when gear is engaged.

Pinion gear depth: The distance the pinion gear extends into the carrier to mesh with the ring gear.

Pinion pilot bearing: A bearing used to support the pinion gear in the differential.

Pinion shaft: Shaft holding the two differential idler (pinion) gears.

Pinpoint tests: Specific tests of individual components of a vehicle, using the electronic scanner.

Pintle: An inward-opening diesel injector nozzle, with fuel flow controlled by a pintle (needle tip).

Pipe expander: Tool used to slightly enlarge inner diameter of steel exhaust pipes to make assembly easier.

Pipe shaper: Tool used to remove dents from pipe ends.

Piston: Component that rides up and down in the cylinder.

Piston and rod markings: Identifying marks on pistons and connecting rods to aid in proper assembly.

Piston clearance: Difference between cylinder bore and piston diameter.

Piston knurling: Technique in which the piston skirt is grooved, pushing up metal a few thousandths of an inch to slightly increase piston diameter.

Piston pin: Fastening device that holds piston onto the connecting rod.

Piston pin knock: Double knock caused by excessive clearance between pin and connecting rod bushing.

Piston pin offset: Positioning of the piston pin hole slightly off the piston centerline for quieter operation.

Piston ring gap: Clearance between ends of rings when installed on cylinder.

Piston size: Diameter of the piston, measured on the skirt.

Piston slap or knock: Loud metallic sound caused by excessive wear to piston skirt or cylinder.

Piston stroke: Distance the piston moves from BDC to TDC.

Piston taper: A slight top-to-bottom difference in piston diameter to adjust for differences in expansion rates.

Pitch line: Imaginary line along the center of a gear tooth.

Pitman arm: Component that transfers gearbox motion to the steering linkage.

Pitman shaft over-center adjustment: Adjustment of clearance between sector gear and ballnut teeth in recirculating ball gearbox.

Planetary gearset: A set of gears consisting of several "planet" gears rotating around a central "sun" gear.

Plastigage: A clearance measuring tool that is compressed between bearing surfaces, then compared to a scale to find thickness.

Plate: A grid, covered with porous lead, that will store electrical energy.

Pleated paper filter: An in-line fuel filter.

Plug gap: Distance between the center and side electrodes on a spark plug.

Plug heat range: Numeric indicator of how hot a spark the plug will develop.

Plug reach: Length of the threaded portion of a spark plug.

Ply separation: Pulling apart of tire plies as a result of overheating due to underinflation, or other causes.

Pneumatic: Filled with air.

POA: Pilot operated absolute valve.

Pole piece: Magnetic component of motor that keeps the armature rotating.

Poor fuel economy: High fuel usage caused by such conditions as overly rich air-fuel mixture, or incorrect engine timing.

Pop tester: Unit used to test diesel injectors when they are out of the engine.

Port injection: Another name for multi-point injection.

Potentiometer sensor: One that changes resistance in response to external change (such as part movement).

Power: The rate or speed at which work is done.

Power antenna: A radio antenna equipped with a small electric motor for raising and lowering.

Power brush: Cleaning tool used with an electric or air-driven drill.

Power door lock: One that is opened or closed with a solenoid.

Power steering fluid: A hydraulic oil, usually automatic transmission fluid.

Power steering pressure test: Use of a pressure gauge to check pump and associated components for correct pressure.

Power steering pump: Unit that provides the hydraulic pressure needed in a power steering system.

Power stroke: Stroke in which the piston is driven downward by the explosion of the air-fuel mixture in the cylinder.

Power train: Gearing system and other components used to transfer energy from the engine to the vehicle's wheels.

Power valve: Device that performs the same function as a metering rod.

Power window: One that is raised and lowered through use of a small electric motor.

Prechamber cup: Pressed in combustion area equipped with a glow plug for easier winter starting of a diesel engine.

Precombustion chamber: Used in diesel engines with a glow plug for easier winter starting.

Preignition: Ignition of fuel before it is fully compressed in the cylinder.

Prelubricator: Pressure tank used to force oil through a lubrication system without running the engine, as a means of testing for worn engine bearings.

Press-fit piston pin: One forced into the connecting rod end. The piston can move freely, however.

Pressed-in valve guide: One that uses a sleeve pressed into a hole machined in the cylinder head.

Pressure bleeding: A method of system bleeding using additional pressure supplied by an external air tank.

Pressure cap test: Measurement of the opening pressure of a radiator cap.

Pressure chamber: Area around the needle valve of an injector where pressure builds up to open valve.

Pressure fed oiling: Oil provided to high-friction areas by means of a pump.

Pressure gauge: Test instrument used to read positive pressure values.

Pressure gauge or manifold assembly: A combination of pressure gauges, valves, and hoses used to check air conditioning system pressures and remove or add refrigerant.

Pressure plate: Springloaded device that clamps clutch disc against flywheel.

Pressure plate covers: Lid that bolts on the pressure plate to hold various components in place.

Pressure plate face: A large ring that contacts the friction disk as the clutch engages.

Pressure plate release levers: Levers hinged inside the pressure plate that help move the pressure plate face away from the clutch disk and flywheel.

Pressure regulator: A limiting device in an automatic transmission, regulating maximum hydraulic oil pressure.

Pressure relief valve: Springloaded bypass that operates when pressure reaches a preset point.

Pressure tests: Diagnostic test using gauge to check fluid pressures in various transmission hydraulic circuits.

Pressure valve: Springloaded disc inside radiator cap that opens when system pressure increases past its setpoint.

Primary: In a carburetor, the components that operate under normal driving conditions.

Primary and secondary pistons: The two pistons in a brake system dual master cylinder.

Primary and secondary shoes: Front and back shoes in a drum brake system. The secondary shoe has a larger surface area.

Primary circuit: In an ignition system, all components operating on battery (low) voltage.

Primary pattern: Pattern of low-voltage (ignition primary) changes, as shown on an oscilloscope.

Primary wire: Small insulated conductor that carries battery or alternator voltage.

Printed circuit: One that consists of conductors that are flat metallic strips applied to an insulating board base. Other components are mounted on the board, as well.

Printer: A device attached to an engine analyzer that can print out a "hard copy" of test results.

Probe tools: Used to view or retrieve items in hard-to-reach areas. Mirrors and magnetic pickups are examples.

Process: The action taken by a computer program as a result of information from inputs.

Programmed: Provided with a specific set of directions for actions to be taken.

PROM: Programmable read-only memory.

PROM carrier: A plastic case used to protect a PROM and make installation easier.

Proportioning valve: Valve designed to equalize pressure at wheel cylinders on vehicles with front disc and rear drum brakes.

Pulling brakes: Situation in which car veers to one side when brakes are applied.

Pulse air system: System that produces the same results as an air injection system, but uses natural pressure pulses in the exhaust system to provide airflow.

Pulse ring: Trigger wheel placed on the crankshaft damper in a crankshaft triggered ignition system.

Pulse width: An indication of how long an injector is energized and kept open.

Pumping plunger: Small pistons used to pump and pressurize diesel fuel.

Purge line: Line connecting the charcoal canister and engine intake manifold.

Push rod: When camshaft is located in block, the long push-rod transmits motion from lifter to rocker arm.

Q

Quick charge test: A method of determining whether battery plates are sulfated (no longer able to hold a charge).

R

R-12 frostbite: Injury resulting from contact with extremely cold refrigerant.

Rack: Flat toothed bar that is moved left or right by rotation of pinion gear.

Rack and pinion steering gear adjustment: Tightening or loosening rack adjustment screw as necessary for optimum steering.

Radial runout: Uneven rotation caused by differences in diameter.

Radial tire: One that has cord plies running straight across, from bead to bead. Additional stabilizer plies are placed beneath the tread.

Radiation: Method of heat transfer through infrared radiation.

Radiation interference: Unwanted voltage that can cause a computer to malfunction.

Radiator: An arrangement of tubes and cooling fins that serves as a heat exchanger on a vehicle.

Radiator cap: Closure that seals and pressurizes the cooling system of a vehicle.

Radiator hoses: Flexible tubes that carry coolant between the engine and radiator.

Radiator shop: Specialized repair facility for radiators.

Radio: The receiving unit for broadcast AM or FM signals.

Radio noise: Static or interference that interferes with signal reception.

RAM: Random access memory.

Raster pattern: Oscilloscope pattern that shows the traces for the cylinders stacked vertically, bottom to top.

Reading oxygen sensor tip: A visual inspection of tip color, which indicates engine condition.

Reading spark plugs: Determining cause of a problem by examining condition of the spark plug.

Reading tires: Identifying alignment, suspension, and other problems through the wear patterns on tire treads.

Reading trouble code: Identifying the code number for the indicated condition from any of the various display systems.

Reaming: Process of cutting valve guide to slightly larger diameter. Valves with oversize stems can then be installed.

Rear axle assembly: A combination of gears and axles converting rotary motion of the drive shaft to forward or backward motion of the vehicle.

Rear axle ratio: The relationship between the numbers of teeth on the pinion gear and ring gear. Ratio affects acceleration, pulling power, and fuel economy.

Rear drive axle assembly: Differential, axles, and other components transferring power from drive line to rear wheels.

Rear drive axles: The components that transmit power from the differential gears to the wheels.

Rear main oil seal: Seal that fits around the rear of the crankshaft to prevent oil leakage.

Rear wheel bearing: Ball or roller-type bearings that reduce friction between the axle and axle housing.

Receiver-drier: Air conditioning system component that removes moisture and stores extra refrigerant.

Recirculating ball: Most common type of gearbox used with linkage steering system.

Rectified: Term used to describe AC current that has been changed to DC.

Reduction starter: One that uses extra gears to increase the torque applied to the flywheel gear.

Reference voltage: A known voltage (usually 0.5V) fed to passive sensors by a computer. Changes in sensor resistance can then be read by the computer.

Refractometer: Test instrument used to measure antifreeze protection.

Refrigerant: Substance with a very low boiling point that can be used to absorb heat.

Refrigerant oil: Lubricant used in the compressor of an air conditioning system.

Regulator bypass test: Test that connects full battery voltage to the alternator field, leaving the regulator out of the circuit.

Regulator voltage test: Test of the charging system under low output, low load conditions.

Relay: Electrically operated switch.

Relay actuator: One that uses a smaller current flow to operate a switch controlling a larger current flow.

Relief valve: Valve that opens to protect steering or other hydraulic system when pressure becomes too high.

Reserve capacity rating: The amount of time a battery will continue to provide an acceptable current flow when not being recharged by the alternator.

Reserve distance: Amount of travel remaining between pedal and floor when brakes are applied.

Reservoir: A tank or other container to hold a supply of fluid (such as the brake master cylinder reservoir).

Resistance: Opposition to current flow.

Resistance plug wire: Special type of spark plug wire that eliminates most radio interference.

Retracting and hold-down springs: Springs that pull the shoes away from the brake drum surface when the pedal is released.

Retreads: Tire bodies that have had new tread rubber applied to extend useful life.

Reverse bias: Arrangement in which diode acts as an insulator.

Reverse flushing: System cleaning done by forcing water backward through the radiator and block to remove scale and sediments.

Reverse idler shaft: Shaft in a manual transmission on which the reverse idler gear is mounted.

Reverse polarity: Accidental backward connection of primary wires.

Rich air-fuel ratio: An air-fuel mixture that contains more fuel than a stoichiometric mixture.

Ridge reamer: Device used to remove metal ridge formed at top end of cylinder due to metal wear.

Ring and pinion backlash: The amount of space between the meshing gear teeth.

Ring and pinion noise: Whining or howling sounds that change pitch with speed changed, usually caused by wear or damage to differential components.

Ring expander: Tool used to spread a ring sufficiently to slip it over the piston.

Ring gap: Space between the ends of a piston ring.

Ring gap spacing: Staggered alignment of ring gaps to reduce ring wear.

Ring gear: Large gear in differential that is driven by the pinion gear and, in turn, drives the spider gears.

Ring gear runout: Amount of wobble that occurs as the gear rotates.

Ring groove cleaner: Special scraper used to loosen and remove deposits from piston grooves.

Ring markings: Information cast into the ring to show the top side or proper positioning on piston.

Ring spacers: Thin steel rings inserted next to compression rings to restore proper side clearance.

Ring-to-groove clearance: Also called ring side clearance, this is the space between a compression ring and the edges of the groove in the piston.

Rocker arm: Pivoted mechanism that operates valves.

Rod bearing knock: Rapping sound resulting from excessive wear of bearings.

Rod bolt covers: Temporary protective coverings, such as pieces of rubber hose, used when inserting piston and connecting rods in cylinders.

Rod bolt torque: Recommended degree of tightness for connecting rod bolts.

Rod cap numbers: Numbers used to match sets of rods and rod caps.

Rod journals: Machined and polished surfaces on the crankshaft to which the connecting rods are attached.

Roll-over valve: Safety feature that prevents gasoline from leaking out tank vent if car rolls over.

Roller lifter: One with a roller riding on the cam lobe to reduce wear.

Rolling resistance: A measure of the amount of resistance that is generated as a tire rolls on the road surface.

ROM: Read-only memory.

Rosin core solder: Soft metal compound used to join electrical wires. The rosin is a noncorrosive flux to aid bonding.

Rotary brush: A stiff brush, used with an air tool for cleaning parts.

Rotary pump: Oil pump using star-shaped rotors.

Rotor: A rotating contact inside the distributor that routes electrical pulses from the coil to the spark plugs. Also, the metal disc against which brake pads are forced to stop vehicle.

Rotor current test: Method used to check alternator windings for an internal short.

Rotor winding open: An open (broken) winding in an alternator rotor.

Rotor winding short: A short-to-ground fault in an alternator rotor.

RTV: Room temperature vulcanizing — a type of sealant that cures at approximately 72°F.

Rust penetrant: Lubricant that helps loosen rusted joints or fasteners.

Rzeppa CV-joint: Ball-and-cage type constant velocity joint used on front-wheel drive vehicles..

S

Safety rim: Wheel designed with small ridges that hold a tire in place if a blowout or flat occurs.

Safety washer: On a nondriving wheel, flat washer that keeps wheel bearing from rubbing on spindle adjusting nut.

Satellite face: Valve face coated with hard metal to withstand high temperatures.

Saving memory: A method of preventing loss of information in computer memory by connecting a small voltage source to it before disconnecting the vehicle's battery cables.

Scanner: Electronic system used to analyze engine and computer operations.

Schrader valve: A spring-loaded valve, similar to a tire valve, used in air conditioning systems.

Screw extractor: Tool threaded opposite normal direction, so it can be used to unscrew a broken bolt or screw.

Seal: A formed material or paste-like substance used to prevent leaks.

Seal alignment tool: Device used to center seal around the crankshaft snout when mounting some engine front covers.

Sealant: A material applied, in liquid or paste form, to prevent leakage between parts.

Sealing rings: Rings placed around either end of a turbo shaft to keep oil from leaking into the turbocharger housing.

Seal part number: Code number stamped on a seal that is used when ordering a replacement.

Seat width: The area of the valve seat that is actually in contact with the valve face.

Secondary: In a carburetor, the components that operate under high engine output conditions.

Secondary circuit: In an ignition system, all components operating on coil (high) voltage.

Secondary pattern: Pattern of high-voltage (ignition secondary) changes, as shown on an oscilloscope.

Secondary wire: Wire used in a vehicle ignition system. It carries high voltage from coil to spark plugs.

Secondary wire resistance: A type of test performed to check condition of a spark plug wire or coil wire.

Sector shaft: Output gear in a recirculating ball gearbox.

Select fit parts: Parts that have been selected and installed to improve fit or clearance.

Self-diagnosis: The ability of a computer system to check circuits and output a code showing the nature or location of the problem.

Self-sealing tire: One with a sealing compound applied to its liner to stop air leakage in case of puncture.

Semi-centrifugal clutch: One that uses weighted release levers or rollers on the pressure plate, and the effects of centrifugal force, to increase clamping pressure on the clutch disk.

Semiconductor: Substance that acts as an insulator or a conductor, depending upon conditions.

Semi-floating axle: Most common type of rear axle for automobiles.

Sensor: Device that monitors and reports a condition (such as engine temperature) to the vehicle computer.

Sensor rotor: A toothed wheel that operates at the same rpm as the vehicle wheel.

Separator: An insulating material placed between plates of a battery.

Service manager: Person responsible for the complete service and repair operation.

Service manual: Book with detailed information on specific car repairs. Also called a shop manual.

Service publications: In addition to service manuals, there are other publications (such as owner's manuals and technical bulletins) that provide information on vehicle servicing.

Service valves: Points at which pressures in an air conditioning system can be checked, and refrigerant removed or replaced.

Servo: Piston that operates a band in an automatic transmission.

Servo action: Situation in which primary shoe of a drum brake system helps apply the secondary shoe.

Servo motor: One that can be stopped in exact positions (degrees of rotation).

Servo motor actuator: A small DC motor that can turn or move parts.

Set screw: Headless fastener used to secure a part onto a shaft.

Shaft runout: Wear or damage (bending) causing a shaft to not run true around its axis.

Sharp valve margin: A result of excessive grinding of valve face, leaving no margin.

Shell: A component of an automatic transmission clutch that connects the front clutch drum and the sun gear of a planetary gear set.

Shift fork: Device that physically moves synchronizer and gear together as a result of shift lever (gearshift) movement.

Shift lever: The handle operated by the vehicle driver to manually shift from gear to gear.

Shift linkage adjustment: Making sure transmission linkage positions match the gear selector positions.

Shift linkage alignment pin: Tool used to properly align shift linkage rods for proper operation.

Shift rail: A manual transmission linkage that is contained within the transmission case.

Shock absorber: Device that uses air or hydraulic pressure to dampen up-and-down motion of vehicle.

Shock actuators: Solenoid-operated valves that control fluid flow inside shock absorbers in an electronic shock absorber system.

Shock bounce test: Method of quickly checking whether shock absorbers need replacement.

Shock compression and extension: Actions of shock absorbers resulting from the vehicle traveling over road bumps.

Shock mode switch: Dash switch that allows driver to select desired ride stiffness in an electronic shock absorber system.

Shop supervisor: A person in charge of a group of technicians in a large garage.

Short block: The bottom end of the engine, including the cylinders, pistons, and crankshaft.

Short circuit: Excess current flow that occurs when a conductor touches ground.

Shorted condenser: One with a direct electrical connection to ground.

Shorted injector coil: A short-circuited solenoid coil is preventing injector operation.

Shroud: Enclosure around a fan, used to direct airflow through the radiator.

Sidewall: Portion of tire between tread and bead.

Simple circuit: One consisting of a power source, a load, and conductors.

Single-point: Injection system with fuel sprayed from a single location into the intake manifold.

Sintered bronze filter: A porous metal fuel filter.

Six-point: Box end wrench with six indentations, or gripping teeth.

Slant engine: One with a single bank of cylinders, tilted to one side.

Slave cylinder: Hydraulic cylinder that produces the movement of the clutch fork.

Slide hammer puller: Tool used to break loose and remove an axle that is stuck in its housing.

Slipper skirt: Material remaining after part of piston below pin is removed for better crankshaft clearance.

Slip rings: Components mounted on the rotor shaft of a generator to provide current to rotor windings.

Slip yoke: Component that connects transmission to the front universal joint of the drive line.

Slow charger: One that feeds a small current into the battery over a long period of time.

Smog: The cloud of airborne pollutants visible over major population centers.

Smoke meter: Device for testing the amount of smoke (ash or soot) in diesel exhaust.

Smooth DC: Direct current without "ripples" or "spikes" due to fluctuating voltages.

Snap ring: Spring steel ring that snaps into a groove to act as a retainer on a shaft.

Sodium filled valve: Hollow construction accepts sodium filling for more even cooling.

Soft failure: One that is intermittent, such as the make/break connection from a loose terminal.

SOHC: Single overhead cam engine.

Soldering gun: Tool that applies heat to joined wires so that solder can be melted into the joint.

Solenoid actuator: One with a moving metal core that is actuated by an induced magnetic field.

Solvent tank: Container holding a cleaning solution used for removing grease and other dirt from a part.

Sonar sensor: Sound wave sensor used to detect road conditions in some electronic shock absorber systems.

Spark ignition: System that uses an electric arc to ignite fuel.

Spark knock: Noise caused by spark plug firing too early.

Spark line: Oscilloscope line showing voltage needed to maintain an arc across the spark plug gap.

Spark plug: Devices that emit an electrical arc at the tip to ignite the air-fuel mixture in an engine cylinder.

Spark plug gap: See Plug gap.

Spark test: Check of the spark intensity (brightness and length of arc).

Spark tester: Device used to check operation of ignition system.

Specialized manual: Service manual devoted to a specific vehicle area, such as engines or braking systems.

Specialized mechanic: A technician who is an expert on one system of a car.

Special tools: Fixtures or tools needed for certain repairs or adjustments. They are described in service manuals.

Specific gravity: Weight or density of a liquid.

Speed control system: Method of regulating a car's throttle to maintain a preset speed. Also called cruise control.

Spider gears: Idler and axle gears in the differential that drive the rear axles of a vehicle.

Spindle: Stationary shaft used to support rotating wheel assembly on nondriving wheels.

Spindle adjusting nut: Nut threaded on end of wheel spindle to adjust wheel bearing.

Spin-on oil filter: One that is replaced as a unit.

Splash oiling: Oil distributed to needed areas by spraying or splashing.

Splines: A series of slots cut into a shaft and mating part.

Spongy brakes: Braking system that is "soft" feeling, usually as a result of air trapped in the hydraulic system.

Spring bind: Situation that can occur when a valve spring is fully compressed and locks the valve train.

Spring fatigue: Weakening of springs that allows the height of the car (and thus road clearance) to decrease.

Spring free length: The length of a spring when removed from the engine.

Spring rate: The stiffness or tension; amount of weight needed to compress or bend a spring.

Spring tension: The stiffness of a valve spring.

Sprocket timing marks: Lines, circles, or dots on crankshaft and camshaft sprockets, aligned to set engine timing.

Spur gears: Those with teeth cut parallel to the centerline of the driveshaft.

Squish area: Part of a wedge-shaped combustion chamber.

Staking: Making a small dent in cylinder head metal next to a valve seat to hold it in place after replacement.

Stall: Work area of a repair shop.

Stalling: Condition in which the engine merely stops running.

Stall speed: Highest speed of impeller rotation in a torque convertor without rotation of the turbine.

Stall test: Method used to shop-test for transmission slippage.

Starter current draw test: Starting test that establishes the number of amps used by the starting system.

Starter ground circuit resistance test: Check of all parts between the battery negative and the starting motor ground for excess resistance.

Starter mounted solenoid: One with a plunger that moves to engage the pinion gear with the flywheel gear.

Starter relay: Device that uses a small current flow from the ignition switch to control a larger current flow to the starter solenoid.

Starter shims: Thin metal pieces used to adjust the space between the pinion gear and the flywheel gear.

Starter solenoid: A high current relay that energizes the starter motor.

Starting headlight test: Starting test conducted with headlights turned on to provide a load on the battery.

Starting motor rebuild: Process involving disassembly, cleaning, parts replacement, and reassembly of the motor.

Starting system: Electric motor and other components used to rotate the engine until it starts.

Star wheel: Adjusting screw assembly for drum brakes.

States of matter: Forms in which a substance can exist (solid, liquid, gas).

Static imbalance: Lack of balance that causes a wheel to vibrate up and down as it rolls.

Static pressure reading: A reading made with the engine off to determine whether a system has an adequate refrigerant charge.

Stator: The stationary magnetic field in a generator. Also component of torque convertor that improves oil circulation and thus, torque.

Stator support: A stationary tube surrounding the input shaft of a torque convertor and supporting the stator.

Stator test: Ohmmeter check for open or shorted windings in the stator.

Steering axis inclination: Angle formed by the inward tilt of ball joints, king pin, or struts.

Steering column: Assembly consisting of the steering wheel, steering shaft, ignition key mechanism and associated parts.

Steering gearbox: Gear assembly that turns rotary motion into linear (straight line) left-right motion.

Steering knuckle: Component that provides support for wheel spindle or bearings surrounding an axle.

Steering linkage: Components connecting steering gearbox to steering knuckles.

Steering sensor: Provides wheel orientation and speed data to computer in electronic shock absorber system.

Steering shaft: Component that transfers turning motion from steering wheel to steering gearbox.

Steering system: The components that let the driver change direction of a vehicle.

Steering wheel play: Excessive movement of wheel without causing front wheel movement.

Stem type valve: Manual valve that is opened or closed by screwing the valve stem in or out.

Stethoscope: A medical device, also used by auto technicians to better hear internal engine noises.

Stiff clutch pedal: A condition caused by binding or

other restriction in the clutch mechanism, making the pedal hard to depress.

Stoichiometric fuel mixture: A perfect (chemically correct) air-fuel mixture.

Straightedge: A metal ruler or bar, with one edge known to be smooth and straight, used to determine flatness of surfaces.

Strap: Connector between cells of a battery.

Stratified charge: A combustion chamber design that first ignites the air-fuel mixture in a small chamber connected to the main chamber.

Strut assembly: Suspension component combining shock absorber, coil spring, and upper damper unit. It replaces the upper control arm.

Strut cartridge: Replaceable shock absorber unit on a MacPherson strut.

Strut rod: Rod that fastens to the control arm and frame to keep arm properly oriented.

Stuck valve: One that will not move up and down freely in the guide; usually, a condition occurring after long storage.

Stumble: See Hesitation.

STV: Suction throttling valve.

Supercharger: Air pump used to push denser fuel-air charge into combustion chambers for increased power.

Superheat switch: One that shuts down an air conditioning system if refrigerant or oil levels are low.

Superimposed pattern: Oscilloscope pattern in which the traces for all cylinders are placed one on top of the other.

Surging: Condition in which engine power fluctuates up and down.

Suspension leveling system: Suspension system designed to keep vehicle level and at proper height even when carrying a heavy load in the truck.

Suspension system: Components that let the wheels move up and down without body movement.

Suspension system computer: One that accepts sensor input and regulates the stiffness of the vehicle's suspension system.

Sway bar: A stabilizer that keeps the vehicle body from leaning excessively in turns.

Swing axle: Axle provided with U-joints to allow for up-and-down suspension movement. Used on vehicles with differential mounted solidly on frame.

Swirl chamber: Combustion chamber shape that causes the air-fuel mixture to spin as it enters, for better mixing.

Switching sensor: One that opens or closes a switch in response to a change in condition.

Switch self-test: Systematic actuation of various switches while using the scanner, providing a check of switch operation.

Synchronizer: Assembly of hub, sleeve, and other components that locks the selected output gear to the output shaft to transmit power. It permits meshing of gears without grinding.

Synthetic fuels: Liquid fuels made from such solids as coal or tar sand.

System: A group of related parts that perform a specific function.

Systematic approach: Combining knowledge and a logical process of elimination to solve a problem.

System bleeding: Removing any trapped air from the entire braking system.

T

Tach-dwell: Combined meter that measures engine rpm and degrees of breaker cam rotation for distributor point adjustment.

Tailpipe: Tubing that carries exhaust from muffler to point at rear or side of the vehicle, where it can be dispersed.

Tank pickup-sending unit: Component that extends into fuel tank to withdraw fuel and send fuel-level information to the fuel gauge.

Tap: Tool for cutting threads inside a hole.

Tappet clearance: The proper degree of tension (neither too tight nor too loose) for the valve train of an engine.

Taxable hp: General rating of engine size.

TBI: Throttle body (single-point) fuel injection.

TBI rebuild: Similar to a carburetor rebuild.

TDC: Top Dead Center.

Telescoping gauge: Spring-loaded device for measuring inside dimensions (such as a cylinder bore).

Temperature gauge tester: Electronic device for testing accuracy of engine temperature gauge.

Tensile strength: The amount of stretching a material can withstand before breaking.

Terminals: The positive and negative posts or threaded connectors on a battery.

Test light: Device that will light up to show the presence of voltage (electrical potential).

Test light code: Trouble code read by counting the flashes of a test light.

Thermal efficiency: A comparison of fuel burned to horsepower output.

Thermo-time switch: Control circuit that energizes cold start injector when temperature is low enough.

Thermostatic air cleaner: System that heats the air being drawn through the engine air inlet to prevent carburetor icing.

Thermostatic fan clutch: Clutch that locks up for maximum airflow when it reaches operating temperature.

Thermostatic spring: Bimetal coil spring that responds to engine heat and opens or closes the choke.

Thermostatic switch: Electrical component that shuts off an air conditioning compressor when the evaporator temperature approaches the freezing point.

Thermostat rating: Temperature at which the thermostat opens.

Thread pitch: Number of threads per inch or (metric sizes) distance between threads.

Throttle body: Section of the carburetor containing the throttle valves.

Throttle positioner: Device that works with idle air control valve in a TBI system to control idle speed.

Throttle position sensor: Device that senses how much throttle is opening or closing.

Throttle return dashpot: Diaphragm device that prevents engine stalling when returning from high speed to idle operation.

Throttle valve: Disc-shaped valve that controls air flow through the air horn.

Throw-out bearing: Bearing that decreases friction between clutch fork and pressure plate.

Thrust bearing: Special bearings with flanges that limit crankshaft forward and rearward movement.

Thrust washers: Metal pieces that can be slipped between block and crankshaft to limit endplay.

Tie rod: Connectors between rack ends and steering knuckles.

Tightening sequence: Recommended pattern for tightening multiple fasteners to obtain even tension.

Timed injection: System timed to inject fuel as the intake valves open.

Timing advance: Making the spark plug fire sooner in the compression stroke.

Timing belt: Rubber belt performing the same job as timing chain or timing gears.

Timing belt cover: See Engine front cover.

Timing belt sprockets: Toothed wheels driving a cogged timing belt.

Timing belt tension: The proper degree of tightness: one that will transmit power efficiently without causing excessive belt wear.

Timing belt tensioner: Part performing same function as timing chain tensioner.

Timing chain: Sprocket-and-chain combination that performs same function as timing gears.

Timing chain guide: Channel that helps support chain and prevents chain slap.

Timing chain tensioner: Spring-loaded plastic or fiber block that pushes on chain to eliminate slack.

Timing gear backlash: The amount of clearance between timing gear teeth.

Timing gear marks: Markings on differential ring and pinion gear sets that permit proper alignment.

Timing gear runout: The amount of wobble that occurs when gear is rotating.

Timing gears: Meshing gears on crankshaft and camshaft that rotate camshaft at half crankshaft speed.

Timing light: Strobe-like light that makes moving parts appear to stand still, allowing timing marks to be observed.

Timing marks: Calibrating marks on timing gears or other timing devices.

Timing retard: Making the spark plug fire later in the compression stroke.

Timing sprockets: Gear-like toothed wheels used with timing chain.

Tire bead: Wire ring, encased in rubber, that helps hold tire sidewall against the rim.

Tire changer: Air-powered machine that automates many steps of tire changing.

Tire gauge: Small instrument used to check inflation pressure of a tire.

Tire impact damage: Punctures, cuts, or tears caused by running over debris in road.

Tire markings: Information shown on the sidewall to indicate inflation pressure, load carrying ability, size, and other data.

Tire plug: Rubber insert sometimes used to repair punctures. The tire industry discourages the use of plugs under most circumstances.

Tire ply: Layer of fabric or other material that forms the carcass or body of the tire.

Tire rotation: Moving tires to different wheels periodically to even out wear.

Tire wear pattern: Areas of tread that are worn off, which can provide information on causes of the wear.

Toe: Degree to which opposing wheels are on converging or diverging lines (not parallel). Also, the narrow part of a gear tooth.

Toe-out on turns: Steering feature that turns inside wheel more sharply than outside wheel.

Torque converter: Fluid coupling that acts as a clutch on an automatic transmission.

Torque multiplication: Variation in torque achieved by turning the impeller of a torque convertor faster than the turbine.

Torque specifications: Information on the correct amount of force to be applied in tightening a fastener.

Torque tube: A solid steel drive shaft enclosed in a hollow tube, with a single swivel joint at the front.

Torque wrench: A tool that is used to indicate the amount of force being applied to a fastener.

Torsion bar: Spring steel rod that operates by twisting and untwisting.

Torsion springs: Small coil springs that help absorb the shock and vibration that occur when the clutch engages.

Tracking: The position or direction of the front wheels in relation to the rear wheels.

Track rod: Metal rod used to prevent axle side-to-side movement when cornering.

Tram gauge: Instrument used to compare distances between the front and rear of a set of tires for toe adjustment.

Transaxle: A combination of transmission and differential in one case, used on front-wheel-drive vehicles.

Transaxle differential: Transaxle assembly that transfers torque to driving axles and allows them to rotate at different speeds.

Transaxle dipstick: Metal rod used to check level of lubricant in transaxle.

Transaxle external adjustments: Clutch, shift linkage, bands, and other components often can be adjusted from outside the transaxle housing.

Transaxle fill and drain plugs: Removable plugs that can be used to drain and refill lubricant in a transaxle.

Transaxle filter: Replaceable element used to trap metal particles and other debris circulating with the lubricant.

Transaxle gearbox: The transmission section of the transaxle, housing the forward and reverse gears.

Transaxle input shaft: Main shaft that turns the gears in a transaxle.

Transaxle output shaft: Shaft that transfers power to the ring and pinion gears of the differential.

Transaxle pan: Lubricant sump at bottom of a transaxle.

Transducer: A device that changes an action or signal from one medium to another (an electrical pulse into a physical movement, for example).

Transfer case: A power takeoff unit that sends power to both the front and rear axle assemblies on a four-wheel-drive vehicle.

Transfer case fill plug: Removable plug to allow checking and adjusting of fluid level in the transfer case.

Transfer pump: A small pump that supplies fuel to a diesel injector.

Transistor: Tiny electronic component that functions as a switch, but has no moving parts.

Transmission case: Metal housing surrounding and supporting the transmission.

Transmission cooler: A small separate radiator used to cool transmission oil in vehicles pulling heavy loads.

Transmission diagnosis chart: A diagnostic aid listing symptoms and probable causes.

Transmission ID tag: A separate tag or set of stamped numbers identifying the exact type of transmission being serviced.

Transmission jack: A special tool used to support the weight of a transmission as it is being removed from a vehicle.

Transmission linkage: System that connects the shift lever with the transmission shift forks.

Transmission oil cooler: Small tank within the radiator, used to regulate transmission fluid temperature.

Transverse: Crosswise; term used to identify an engine rotated 90° from the traditional longitudinal mounting.

Tread: Outer surface of tire that contacts the road.

Trigger wheel: Rotating component with one tooth for each cylinder.

Tripod CV-joint: Constant velocity joint used on front-wheel drive vehicles, consisting of a spider and ball arrangement inside a housing.

Trouble code chart: Diagnostic aid that lists the trouble for each code.

Troubleshooting chart: A guide that lists methods for finding and correcting vehicle problems.

Tubeless: Tire that does not have a separate inner tube to hold air.

Tumbler: Ignition switch lock mechanism.

Tune-up parts: Spark plugs, filters, and other periodic-replacement items.

Turbine: The driven fan assembly in a torque converter.

Turbine housing: The outer case that routes gases around the turbine wheel.

Turbine wheel: A fan-like wheel driven by the exhaust gases of an engine. It turns a shaft and compressor wheel.

Turbo bearing: Bearings supporting the turbo shaft.

Turbocharger: A form of supercharger that is driven by exhaust gases.

Turbo lag: A short delay before turbocharging becomes effective.

Turbo shaft: Shaft connecting turbine and compressor wheels in a turbocharger.

Turning: Term usually used for machining a brake drum or rotor, since process is carried out on a lathe.

Turning radius gauge: Instruments that measure how many degrees left or right the front wheels are turned.

Turn signal flasher: Bimetallic strip and heater unit that makes and breaks contact to cause on-off operation of the turn signals.

Twelve-point: Box end wrench with twelve indentations, or gripping teeth.

Twin I-beam: Double-axle suspension system used on some pickup truck models.

Two-gas analyzer: Measuring instrument that provides reading of HC and CO levels in exhaust.

Two-stroke cycle engine: One that completes a full power-producing cycle with only one full crankshaft revolution.

U

U-joint alignment marks: Scribed marks made on U-joint components before disassembly, allowing the joint components to be reassembled in the same positions to avoid possible imbalance and vibration.

Umbrella valve seal: Rubber or plastic seats that fit over opening at top of valve guide to keep oil out of them.

Underinflation: Operating tire with a lower-than-recommended air pressure.

Undersize bearing: One designed for use on a crankshaft journal that has been machined to a smaller diameter.

Unibody: A vehicle structure in which body and frame are one unit.

Universal joint: A flex joint allowing limited up-and-down and side-to-side movement.

Unleaded gasoline: Fuel that does not contain lead-based antiknock additives.

Unsprung weight: The weight of vehicle parts that are not supported by springs, such as the wheels.

Up-date PROM: A PROM with new programming that is plugged into the computer in place of the old one.

V

Vacuum: A pressure lower than atmospheric, in an enclosed area.

Vacuum advance: System that provides additional ignition advance when engine load is low at medium throttle positions.

Vacuum booster: Braking system booster actuated by vacuum.

Vacuum choke break: A device that uses vacuum to open and close the choke to prevent engine flooding at startup.

Vacuum delay valve: Mechanism that restricts air flow to slow down action of vacuum on a device.

Vacuum gauge: Test instrument used to read negative pressure values.

Vacuum leak: Loss of negative pressure due to crack or hole in a vacuum hose.

Vacuum pump: A device providing vacuum for operation of engine accessories.

Vacuum switch: One that opens or closes on a change in vacuum.

Vacuum valve: Valve inside radiator cap that allows flow of coolant from recovery tank back into radiator.

Valve: Component that opens or closes a port to permit flow into and out of the combustion chamber.

Valve adjusting shims: Thin metal plates used to alter the cam-to-valve clearance.

Valve adjustment: Correcting any malfunction in the opening and closing of valves actuated by mechanical lifters.

Valve body: Housing containing most of the valves used in operation of an automatic transmission.

Valve core: Threaded air valve that screws into place in a valve stem.

Valve cover: A metal or plastic cover over the top of the cylinder head.

Valve float: A tendency for valves to remain partly open, especially at high speeds. It usually results from a weak or broken valve spring.

Valve grind gasket set: Set of gaskets needed for top end reassembly after valve grinding.

Valve grinding: Process of machining a smooth surface on valve faces and valve stem tips.

Valve guide: Holes machined into the engine block to support the valve stems as they slide up and down.

Valve guide cleaner: Rotating tool use to remove deposits from valve guides.

Valve guide insert: Replacing the worn guide with a new one.

Valve guide knurling: Grooving process that raises metal to restore inside diameter of guide.

Valve job: Servicing of the cylinder head and valve train.

Valve lifter: Component that is moved by the camshaft lobe and in turn moves the push rod or the rocker arm.

Valve overlap: The short period when both valves in a cylinder are open.

Valve reliefs: Indentations in a piston crown to provide valve clearance.

Valve rotator: Device that turns the valve to prevent carbon buildup.

Valve seal: Seals that fit over valve stems to prevent oil leakage.

Valve seat: Machined surfaces on the intake and exhaust ports, against which the valve rests and seals.

Valve seat angle: The angle formed by the finished face of the seat.

Valve seat insert: One that is pressed into a recess cut into the head.

Valve seat reconditioning: Grinding or cutting valve seats to obtain a smooth surface.

Valve seat runout: Improper centering, so that the seat is not centered around the valve guide after grinding or cutting.

Valves in receiver: Expansion and POA valves enclosed within the receiver drier of an air conditioning system.

Valve spring: Assembly that closes the valve when rocker arm pressure is removed.

Valve spring compressor: Tool used to compress valve springs during disassembly.

Valve spring installed height: The distance from top to bottom of the spring as installed in the cylinder head.

Valve spring seat: Cup-shaped washer that holds the bottom of the valve spring.

Valve spring shim: Precisely machined washer used to increase valve spring tension.

Valve spring shims: Thin metal pies used to adjust spring tension after valve grinding.

Valve spring tester: Device for measuring the tension or pressure exerted by the spring.

Valve stem: A rubber inflation tube with a threaded metal core that snaps into a hole on the rim of a wheel designed for use with tubeless tires.

Valve stem cap: Cap placed over end of valve stem to prevent stem wear.

Valve timing: Intervals at which valves open and close, determined by camshaft configuration.

Valve train: The parts that operate the engine valves: camshaft, lifters, push rods, rocker arms, and springs.

Vaporization: A rapid change of state from liquid to gas.

Vapor lock: Condition caused by bubbles in fuel due to overheating. Can cause stalling, hard starting, or failure to start.

Vapor separator-filter: Fuel filter that collects bubbles of vaporized fuel and returns them to the tank.

Variable resistance sensor: One with internal resistance that changes in response to changes in a condition (such as temperature).

Variable venturi carburetor: One in which the venturi size adjusts to maintain a constant air speed in the carburetor.

Vehicle identification number (VIN): Individual number identifying a vehicle and displayed on a plate attached to the body.

Vehicle maintenance: Term for all operations performed to keep a vehicle in good running condition.

Vehicle sensor: Device that changes a condition into

an electrical signal that can be used as an input by a computer.

Venturi: Restriction (narrowed area) in air horn.

Vibration damper: Heavy, rubber-mounted wheel on front of crankshaft to counter harmonic vibrations.

VIN: See Vehicle identification number.

Viscosity: A measure of the thickness, or ability to flow, of a lubricant.

Voice alert system: Computer-based system that provides audible messages, in an electronically generated voice, to warn of safety problems or vehicle malfunctions.

Voltage: Electrical pressure that causes current flow.

Voltage drop: Reduction of the amount of curerent flowing in a circuit.

Voltage drop tests: Starting system tests that identify parts showing high resistance.

Voltage-generating sensor: One that changes voltage in response to external change.

Voltage regulator: Device used to control alternator output.

VOM: Volt-ohm-milliammeter for determining electrical values.

V-type engine: One with two banks of cylinders, arranged in a "V" configuration.

W

Wankel: A rotary engine with few moving parts.

Warped cylinder head: Head with a distorted (twisted or curved) surface as a result of overheating.

Waste gate: A valve that limits the amount of boost developed by the turbocharger by venting excess exhaust gases.

Water corrosion: Injector damage caused by the presence of water in diesel fuel.

Water detector: Warning device that tells the driver there is water in diesel fuel.

Water pump: A pump (usually of the centrifugal type) that circulates coolant through the engine and radiator of a vehicle.

Water pump rebuild: Process of disassembly, cleaning, parts replacement, and reassembling a water pump.

Wear bar: Solid bars of rubber across the tread that appear when a tire has worn to the safe limit.

Wear sleeve: Bushing between the axle and seal on a front-wheel drive vehicle.

Wedge chamber: Combustion chamber with a triangular shape.

Wet charged: Battery that is filled with electrolyte and fully charged at the factory.

Wet compression test: Test made by placing small amount of oil in a cylinder with a low reading, to determine whether worn rings are cause of low compression.

Wet sleeve: A thick cylinder liner exposed to coolant.

Wheel alignment: Adjusting wheels of a vehicle to roll in a straight line.

Wheel balancing machine: Device used to identify locations where weights must be placed to balance a tire.

Wheel bearing: Ball or roller bearing assemblies that reduce friction as wheels or axles rotate.

Wheel brake assemblies: Components that use hydraulic pressure to apply friction for stopping vehicle.

Wheel cover: Metal or plastic disk designed to fit over center section of wheel for better appearance.

Wheel cylinder: Hydraulic piston that actuates braking at each wheel.

Wheel cylinder rebuild: Process that typically involves honing the cylinder and replacing all rubber parts (cups and boots).

Wheel hop: A bouncing or up-and-down movement.

Wheel puller: A device used to remove pressed-on parts, such as gears.

Wheel shimmy: A side-to-side movement caused by dynamic imbalance.

Wheel speed sensors: Magnetic pickups to detect wheel speed (used on anti-lock braking systems).

Wheel weight: Small pieces of lead that are clipped to the wheel rim to balance the wheel and tire combination.

Wiggle test: Physically moving wires and connectors to locate broken wires or other causes of intermittent problems.

Winding: Loop of wire on a motor armature that generates a magnetic field.

Wire wheel: Cleaning tool with wires arranged radially, rotated at moderately high speed to remove carbon deposits from parts.

Wiring diagram: Drawings that show relationships of components in an electrical circuit.

Wiring harness: A group of primary wires enclosed in a protective plastic covering.

Work: The result of force causing movement; measured in foot-pounds, watts, or joules.

Worm shaft: Input gear in a recirculating ball gearbox.

Worn cam bearings: After prolonged engine use, this condition can cause reduced oil pressure.

Worn idler arm: Condition that can cause steering wheel play.

Worn piston rings: Many engine problems are caused by failure of worn rings to properly seal against cylinder walls.

Worn rocker arms: Primarily cause noise (valve clatter).

Worn tie rod end: A cause of excessive play in the steering wheel.

Worn timing chain: Permits slack between camshaft and crankshaft sprockets, so valves no longer keep proper timing with the pistons.

Worn U-joint: Excessive play between the cross and yoke.

Worn valve guide: Enlarged guide that allows valve to move excessively, causing various engine problems.

WOT switch: Device that shuts off air conditioning compressor when a small car is accelerating.

Index

Engine overhaul, 593
Engine performance problems,
    539-542
  backfiring, 541
  diagnosis charts, 539
  dieseling (after-running or run-
    on), 541
  gas line freeze, 541
  hard starting, 540
  hesitation (stumble), 541
  lack of power, 541
  locating, 539
  misfiring, 540
  no-start, 539, 540
  pinging (spark knock), 541
  poor fuel economy, 541
  stalling (dying), 540
  surging, 541
  typical, 539, 540
  vacuum lead, 541
  vapor lock, 541
Engine powered fans, 466
Engine pre-teardown inspection,
    570, 571
Engine removal,
  installing lifting fixture or chain,
    583
  lifting engine out of car, 583
  transmission, 583, 584
Engine removal disassembly, parts
    cleaning, 581-592
Engine removal preparation, 581
Engine sensor, 255
Engine sensor service, 284, 285
  exhaust gas (oxygen), 285
  temperature, 285
  throttle position, 284
Engine sensors, 255-260
  analog and digital signals, 259
  open loop and closed loop, 259,
    260
Engine size, 171
Engine size and performance
    measurements, 171-177
Engine size measurement, 171, 172
  bore and stroke, 171,172
  engine displacement, 172
  piston displacement, 172
Engine smoking, 571
Engine stand, 48
Engine surge, 236
Engine technician, 26
Engine temperature gauge, 470
Engine temperature sensor, 258
Engine test instruments, 543-552
Engine top end, 113-118, 137
  camshaft, 115
  construction, 137-150
  cylinder head, 113
  disassembly, 585-587
  exhaust manifold, 117
  intake manifold, 117
  push rods, 116

  rocker arms, 116
  service, 609-639
  valve cover, 118
  valve lifters, 115, 116
  valve seals, 116
  valve spring assembly, 116
  valve train, 114
  valves, 116
Engine top end reassembly, 624-626
  diesel engine head gaskets, 624
  installing cylinder head, 625
  installing cylinder head gasket,
    624
  installing exhaust manifolds, 626
  installing intake manifold, 625,
    626
  rocker assembly installation, 626
  valve grind gasket set, 624
Engine torque, 174
Engine tune-up, 565-568
  adjustments, 566
  evaluating engine systems, 566
  general rules, 566, 568
  importance, 565
  major, 565
  minor, 565
  parts replacement, 566
  preliminary tests and inspection,
    566
  safety rules, 565, 566
  typical procedures, 566
  valve adjustment, 566
Engine tune-up intervals, 568
Engine vacuum leaks, 571
Entrepreneurship, 29
Erasable PROMs (EPROMs), 992
Ethyl alcohol, (grain alcohol or
    ethanol), 188
Evacuating an air conditioning
    system, 966, 967
Evaporization control system
    maintenance and repair, 532
Evaporization control system ser-
    vice, 532
Excess crankshaft problems, 579
Exhaust analyzer, 527-530
  CO_2 readings, 529, 530
  CO readings, 529
  engine exhaust gases, 528
  HC readings, 529
  O_2 readings, 529
  two- and four-gas, 528, 529
Exhaust camshaft, 142
Exhaust gas analyzer, 233, 245, 550
  using, 530
Exhaust gas (oxygen) sensor ser-
    vice, 285
Exhaust gas recirculation system
    (EGR), 518, 519
Exhaust gas sensor, 257
Exhaust manifold, 117, 149, 320
Exhaust manifold heat valve, 320
Exhaust pipes, 320

Exhaust stroke, 14, 108
Exhaust system, 20, 319
Exhaust system service, 321
  inspection, 321
  repairs, 321-323
Exhaust systems, turbocharging,
    319-334
Exhaust valve, 116
Expanded display, 558
Exploration tests, 178
Explosions, 54, 55
  car batteries, 54, 55
  fuel tanks, 55
Extensions, 35
Exterior lights, 447
External combustion engine, 127
External coolant leaks, 571
External cylinder power steering
    (linkage type), 866

F

Factory horsepower ratings,
    174-176
Fan belt service, 480
Fan motor, 467
Fan switch or thermo switch, 467
Fast flushing, 484
Fast idle cam, 222, 223
Fast idle solenoid, 223, 224
Fast (quick) charger, 348
Fasteners, 85
  removing damaged, 90, 91
Faulty fuel lines and hoses, 202
Faulty fuel tank sending unit, 201
Faulty mixture control solenoid or
    computer control circuit, 236
Feeler gauge, 433
  flat, 63
  use of, 64
  wire, 63
Fender covers, 51
  seat covers, 51
Field coil service, 373
Field winding, 356
File safety, 39
Files, 38, 39
  coarse, 38, 39
  fine, 38, 39
Filler neck restrictor, 192
Filter service, 102
Fine threads, 86
Finger pickup tool, 41
Fires, 54
  electrical, 54
  gasoline, 54
  oily rags, 54
  paints, thinners, 54
Firing line, 556
  short, 557
  tall, 557
Firing order, 122
Flat feeler gauge, 63